OXFO[obscured]
HINDI–EN[obscured]
DICTIONARY

OXFORD HINDI–ENGLISH DICTIONARY

EDITED BY

R. S. McGREGOR

OXFORD DELHI
OXFORD UNIVERSITY PRESS
1993

OXFORD
UNIVERSITY PRESS

Great Clarendon Street, Oxford OX2 6DP

Oxford University Press is a department of the University of Oxford.
It furthers the University's objective of excellence in research, scholarship,
and education by publishing worldwide in

Oxford New York

Auckland Bangkok Buenos Aires Cape Town Chennai
Dar es Salaam Delhi Hong Kong Istanbul Karachi Kolkata
Kuala Lumpur Madrid Melbourne Mexico City Mumbai Nairobi
São Paulo Shanghai Singapore Taipei Tokyo Toronto

Published in the United States
by Oxford University Press Inc., New York

First published 1993
This reprint 2002

British Library Cataloguing in Publication Data
Data available

Library of Congress Cataloging in Publication Data
Data available

ISBN 0-19-864339-X

9 10 8

Printed in China

PREFACE

The tradition of lexicography in Hindi-Urdu goes back some two centuries, but in most of the work undertaken in this field before the present century it was the Urdu aspect of Hindi-Urdu, with its extensive Persian and Arabic vocabulary, that was stressed. The monumental *Hindī śabd-sāgar* (1929) was the first major dictionary in the field of Hindi-Urdu to reflect the new circumstances of use of Hindi in the twentieth century. During this period Hindi has developed dramatically in scope, status, and literary versatility and has become effectively standardised as a language of public life, with corresponding effects upon its lexicon. Several successful monolingual and bilingual dictionaries of the modern language have been based upon the *Hindī śabd-sāgar* during recent decades. Yet the monolingual *Hindī śabd-sāgar* itself drew on its predecessors. One of these, J. T. Platts's *Dictionary of Urdū, Classical Hindī and English* (1884), has continued to be regarded by speakers of English as a valuable complement to it for the study of both modern and early Hindi. The organisation of Platts's work as an Urdu dictionary has limited its accessibility to students of Hindi, however, while the datedness of its lexical record, style of presentation, and treatment of etymology has made production of a new Hindi-English dictionary of comparable scale desirable for some time. The present work is an attempt to meet that need. There was good reason to make an editing of Platts's dictionary (as proposed by Oxford University Press, its publisher) the first stage in producing such a work, but clearly the task would go far beyond this, and would involve not only a complete revision of Platts's material but also collation of the *Hindī śabd-sāgar* and reference to other modern lexicographical materials, together with collection of new material from Hindi literary texts and other printed sources.

The chief requirement in a modern dictionary of Hindi was without doubt a treatment of the spoken and written language of the twentieth century in which the broad standard of urban usage was emphasised. Many words and expressions falling outside that standard which were recorded in the late nineteenth century also deserved inclusion, however, being still current in north India. It seemed desirable to retain, and to supplement, Platts's treatment of the vocabulary of early Hindi literature, and to retain some nineteenth century material illustrating the early development of the modern language. Items belonging to the more literary ranges of Urdu in prose and poetry might, however, in many cases be excluded from a dictionary of Hindi.

The work was planned in 1971 and I began to collect materials in that year. Between 1972 and 1975 Dr S. K. Mathur of Agra read through and commented on the text of Platts's dictionary and a part of the text of the *Mānak hindī koś* (1962) from the viewpoint of a speaker of the modern standardised language. He also compiled a file of words from modern newspapers and journals. During the years 1975–80 and 1984–92 I produced the present text. This involved reconsidering Platts's entire materials, revising and reorganising each entry to be retained, collating other lexicographical materials, reading Hindi sources, and adding in consequence many new entries. I was assisted in the earlier stages of the work by Dr Mathur's comments on standardised usage, and later, in considering regional usage, by those of Dr T. N. Sharma of Ambikapur, Madhya Pradesh (my colleague from 1976 to 1980) and Dr S. M. Pandey of Ballia. Many modern Hindi words and expressions were reconsidered during the years 1987–92 by Dr S. N. Srivastava, of Banaras, and myself. Dr Srivastava, my colleague from 1980 to the present, gave generously of his time to comment on innumerable points of detail that arose during this period. He also read through and commented on the text of the dictionary before its publication and made various suggestions for its improvement. Various of the etymologies proposed have benefited from comments by Professor K. R. Norman.

By the time the work was nearing completion, production by computer combining roman and Devanāgarī scripts had become feasible. Dr K. E. Bryant of the University of British Columbia designed the Devanāgarī font; it was redrawn for typesetting this dictionary by Bruno Maag. The processing and sorting of the materials and their preparation for final production were carried out by Dr J. L. Dawson, Dr D. R. de Lacey, and their colleagues of the Literary and Linguistic Computing Centre of Cambridge University. The Centre's support for the project was indispensable in all these stages of the work, and its members' constant assistance from 1984 onwards is greatly appreciated. Dr J. D. Smith assisted the Centre in adapting the font for use with the Cambridge University computer. I would like to thank the British Academy for an award made in 1985 which covered most of the costs of inputting the materials to the computer. Most of this work was done by E. McGregor and by S. K. Y. Zangmo.

I would like to record my gratitude to my above-mentioned former and present colleagues for the help which I have received in preparing this dictionary, as well as to other persons who have given me assistance in various ways. For the shortcomings that will undoubtedly be found in the work I am of course responsible. My warmest thanks are due to my wife Elaine, for her generous support and help, as well as for her patience and encouragement, without all of which this work might not have reached completion.

R. S. McG.

December 1992

INTRODUCTION

The term 'modern Hindi' denotes a language written in the Devanāgarī script and relatively standardised in its written form (but less so in pronunciation and spoken usage) which is in general use today in most of north and central India. Modern Hindi co-exists in this region with regional forms of speech more or less closely cognate to it and with many local dialects, as well as with Urdu, a complementary style of language: one potentially identical with modern Hindi at the spoken level while expressing a distinctively Persian cultural orientation at more literary levels. Urdu, an earlier specialisation than Hindi of a mixed speech of the Delhi area which had gained currency as a lingua franca, had arisen broadly because of an increasing artificiality in the use of Persian for literary and other formal purposes in Indo-Muslim circles during the later Mughal period. Modern Hindi by contrast arose in the nineteenth century to meet a different need: that for a linguistic vehicle which should allow communication with, and among, a wider section of the north Indian population than had been possible in practice in the case of Urdu. The use of an Indian script, and of a smaller component of Persian and Arabic vocabulary than was often used in the Urdu of the time, were essential prerequisites to this end. There was a correspondingly increased use of words of Indian origin in the new style, and in particular of Sanskritic words.

The modern Hindi style gained currency in the period up to the 1860s above all because it was a medium of education and instruction. The rise of a modern sense of Indian identity in north India from the 1860s onwards became the mainspring of an accelerating increase in the use of Hindi in the later nineteenth century. The new style won increasing official recognition first in parts of north and central India where Urdu was less firmly established and finally, by 1900, in the United Provinces (now Uttar Pradesh). It had by this time become a well established vehicle for journalism and *belles lettres*. The factors responsible for its rise continued to operate during the following decades, and this meant that its further development in terms both of numbers of users and range of functions was assured. By contrast the development of Urdu suffered some retardation in the twentieth century. The potential of Hindi as a favoured form of Hindi-Urdu, and the great geographical range of Hindi-Urdu across the sub-continent and indeed beyond (which makes this language probably the world's third in terms of number of users) brought it about that 'Hindi in the Devanagari script' was recognised in 1947 as the official language of India. The main factors influencing the further development of Hindi were to be, first as before, the rate of spread of education and literacy, and secondly the relationships of competition and contact existing between Hindi and English and between Hindi and the Indian regional languages.

The lexicon of Hindi comprises in historical terms a body of words which has evolved from Old and Middle Indo-Aryan linguistic forms (and from non-Indo-Aryan forms assimilated at an early period into Indo-Aryan) together with a large accretion of words borrowed at later periods from different sources. Of the words which have evolved organically from OIA and MIA, many are everywhere in use today among speakers of the standardised language. Others, however, are restricted in their currency to the regional and local varieties of Hindi which are the mother tongues of a large proportion of Hindi speakers. Regional and local words are always liable to intrude into the standardised language as used locally, and also as used by writers in conveying local atmosphere or for other stylistic purposes. Of the loanwords, many of Persian or Arabic origin, and some of Turkish origin, are fully acclimatised in everyday usage, especially in urban usage. Other readily distinguishable groups of loanwords are those borrowed from Sanskrit, or based on Sanskrit forms, and those borrowed from English and other European languages.

Loanwords of Sanskritic origin have been used in north Indian vernacular speech and also in vernacular poetry over many centuries. Many became acclimatised in early Hindi dialect poetry, and we may presume these to have been widely known. Their currency in dialect poetry provided an important typological precedent for the later Sanskrit loanwords and other Sanskritic formations of modern Hindi and was crucial in aiding the assimilation of many of these, both into literary style and formal usage, and also into more everyday usage. The latter words and formations have tended to be pronounced in ways more conformable to their spellings than had been the case with their predecessors in dialect poetry: a tendency owing something to the desire to express a sense of modern cultural identity lexically, in terms of age-old values. Such words can show changes of meaning as compared to the central meaning or meanings they or their constituent parts originally had as Sanskrit words. The immediate source for a number was not Sanskrit itself, but the Sanskritised Bengali of the late nineteenth and early twentieth centuries; some words borrowed via this route have yielded ground today to alternatives drawn more directly from Sanskrit. Other Sanskrit loanwords and coinages of modern Hindi had limited success from the outset, however, and are today obsolete; while some found in the contemporary written language are clearly experimental, and likely in many cases to prove ephemeral. Various Sanskritic loanwords and expressions are acclimatised chiefly in poetry of more formal style.

Very different in kind from the above loanwords are the neologisms of the modern language. These words are either, again, loanwords from Sanskrit or coinages based on Sanskrit words. Many such coinages can be seen to be lexical calques on English words of Latin or Greek origin. Acclimatisation of words of this kind was impeded from the outset by several facts. First, knowledge of the things or concepts they refer to often spread slowly, and in the more technical fields has so far generally remained restricted to small sections of the Hindi-speaking population. In these quarters, moreover, the English words in question have remained generally more familiar than the new coinages. Components of the coinages were, again, sometimes used in ways which bore little relationship to their main senses or areas of meaning as Sanskrit words; and their Sanskritic origins could seem awkwardly at variance with a modern context of use. The above factors have worked against ready acceptance of the neologisms (especially those in more technical fields) that have been proposed in numbers both by lexicographers and by Indian Government agencies, as well as introduced by writers and journalists on an *ad hoc* basis. A further factor working against wide acceptance of neologisms has been that there has been no agreement on the forms to be used, or on their exact senses, so that competing expressions have sometimes gained a confusing, nominal currency. It was always unlikely given the importance of English in India throughout the years from *c.*1800, and the cultural and linguistic distance at which modern India stands from its Sanskritic past, that the lexical modernisation of Hindi could have proceeded solely via a process of coining Sanskritic neologisms. In the case of most scientific and technical terms it seems that the English words themselves are now being successfully acclimatised; although in other spheres (such as those of law and non-technical journalism) many coinages have established themselves in the written language and appear in various cases to be gaining currency in the spoken.

The different sections of the Hindi vocabulary described in the above paragraphs have been treated in this dictionary as follows. Of the words of Old and Middle Indo-Aryan derivation and the acclimatised loanwords of Persian, Arabic, and Turkish origin, which together form the bedrock of the later language, a relatively comprehensive record has been aimed at, except in the case of words restricted to regional and local varieties of Hindi. These are represented more selectively. Regional words listed by Platts or in the *Hindī śabd-sāgar* and for which some contemporary verification has been found have generally been included, together with a selection of regional usages found in modern literature and some regional items confirmed for earlier periods of the modern language. To avoid ambiguity in a dictionary intended to display both the vocabulary of the modern standardised language and other aspects of the Hindi word-stock, regional words and other words not current in the contemporary standardised language are marked with distinguishing labels. Of the Sanskrit loanwords and Sanskritic formations found in early and modern Hindi literature and in modern usage more generally, a generous representation has been given. Neologisms of the modern language are represented more selectively, for the reasons indicated above.

Many English words are used naturally in everyday contexts by Hindi speakers not educated in English and are indisputably part of the modern Hindi lexicon, e.g. *aspatāl* 'hospital', *akṭūbar* 'October', *reḍiyo* 'radio', *grāmophon* 'gramophone'. The pronunciation of these words is often

Indianised appreciably, especially in the case of words long current in Hindi, such as the first two examples. English loanwords which are substantially Indianised in pronunciation (such as *aspatāl*) have frequently been included in this dictionary as Hindi words in their own right; but while words of the type of *reḍiyo* (everyday words of modern life borrowed more recently, but known to all) are no less acclimatised, their claims to inclusion in a bilingual dictionary of Hindi to English did not seem strong. The same applied to the large class of technical and scientific terms and words dealing with less familiar spheres of modern life, despite the crucial importance of these words in modern usage.

Finally, Hindi contains loanwords from a number of other languages than those referred to above. A few words ultimately of Greek or Latin origin have made their way into the language via Persian and Arabic. Some common Hindi words are derived from Portuguese. There are some isolated borrowings from other European languages than English and Portuguese, and a few from Malay/Indonesian and Chinese. Other words have been acquired by Hindi speakers from contact with particular Indian languages or regions, especially in more modern times.

EXPLANATORY NOTES

Some information about the structure and presentation of the dictionary entries is provided below.

STRUCTURE OF ENTRIES

Entries may contain up to twelve parts, in the following order: 1. Headword. 2. Transliteration. 3. Derivation. 4. Grammatical designation. 5. Phonemic transcription. 6. Subject label. 7. Linguistic label. 8. Stylistic label. 9. Gloss. 10. Examples of use. 11. Compound words containing the headword. 12. Run-on forms.

1. **Headword** (the word to be glossed), in Devanāgarī script. The structure of the language favours use of compound words built up on single base units. Compound words are usually not entered individually as headwords but under the base word on which they are formed, e.g. *jal-kriyā* 'offering of water' is entered under *jal* 'water', and similarly many other compounds formed on this base. This procedure is normally followed in the case of compounds consisting of words borrowed from Sanskrit. Compounds formed on words of other origin have in various cases been entered as headwords, however, rather than under their first members. If the user of

the dictionary fails to find a given word, which appears to be a compound, in the entry for its apparent first member, he or she should therefore look for it as a headword before concluding that it has not been included.

Some items which are not independent lexical units of the language have been entered as headwords, viz. Hindi prefixes, various Hindi suffixes, various Sanskrit, Persian, and Arabic prefixes, compounding forms (such as *du-*, *dvi-* 'two, bi-') and some formative elements (such as *-d* 'giving', *-prad* 'productive of', *-pūrvak* '-ly', *-dār* '-having') which occur only finally in compounds. Citation of these items as headwords should allow identification of the meanings of many compound words of Sanskritic origin which have not been included in the dictionary; as well as the meanings of many Hindi words and some Urdu words.

2. **Transliteration** of the headword, in roman script. The transliteration is an adaptation of that used for Sanskrit (which has been often used, with modifications, for Hindi). Broadly speaking it will serve as a guide to the pronunciation of the headword in educated modern usage. The 'inherent' Sanskritic vowel /ə/ (which is weakened by Hindi speakers in many phonetic contexts, and dropped in others) is represented where weakened by *ă*, and where dropped is unrepresented. Prefixes and a few prefixed elements are identified by the use of hyphens, e.g. *pari-śram*, *vy-avă-hār*, *be-kār*, *lā-javāb*; and *sandhi* junctions by the use of circumflex accents, e.g. *prôtsāhan*.

3. **Derivation,** or **Linguistic connection**, of the headword, in square brackets. Derivational processes are indicated as follows:

(*a*) Hindi *tadbhava* words (words which have evolved organically from OIA or MIA) are referred to OIA source-words or constructs (unlabelled) where possible; MIA forms (labelled Pa. or Pk.) are frequently added to the latter in clarification, e.g. *bāt* [*vārttā-*]; *usīsā* [**ut-śīrṣa-* : Pa. *ussīsaka-*]; *patlā* [*pattrala-*, Pk. *pattala-*].[1] Most of the source-words and constructs cited are to be found in R. L. Turner's *Comparative Dictionary of the Indo-Aryan Languages*.

(*b*) For *tatsama* loanwords (words borrowed from Sanskrit, or formed on Sanskrit structural models, which show minimal phonetic adjustment to Hindi phonological patterns) the source is denoted 'S.', e.g. *mātsaryă* [S.].

(*c*) For loanwords borrowed from OIA which show appreciable adaptation (chiefly phonetic adaptation) as compared to corresponding Sanskrit forms, derivations are prefixed by the abbreviation 'ad.', e.g. *pragaṭ* [ad. *prakaṭa-*]; *jantar* [ad. *yantra-*].

(*d*) For loanwords of Persian or Arabic origin the source form is cited. Where Arabic words show a modified Persian form, that form is indicated;

[1] Attested OIA source-words include 'lexical' items not recorded in published texts, and some items recorded only in the nineteenth century. Some lexical items are back-formations on NIA forms. OIA lexical items cited in derivations precede commas (see third example) in cases where corresponding MIA forms are adduced.

similarly in most cases where Arabic and Persian words acquire suffixes in passing to Hindi, e.g. *namak* [P. *namak*]; *śikāyat* [A. *śikāya*: P. *śikāyat*];[2] *mātamī* [A. *ma'tam* + P. *-ī*]; *nek* [P. *nek*].[3]

(*e*) Where a headword is formed by extension from an Indian word (whether by prefixation, infixation or suffixation)[4] or shows a change of grammatical function, the abbreviation 'cf.' is used with its referend, e.g. *angaṇit* [cf. *gaṇita-*]; *asūjh* [cf. H. *sūjh*]; *sunvānā* [cf. H. *sunnā*]; *laṛakpan* [cf. H. *laṛkā*]; *māt-*, vb. [cf. *matta-*].

(*f*) Where re-formation of a word has taken place (as in folk etymologies) the abbreviation 'f.' is sometimes used, e.g. *bacnāg* [f. *vatsanābha-*]; *kaṛābīn* [f. P. *qarābīn*: ← F].

4. **Grammatical designation.** The usual abbreviations are employed. Gender variation in nouns is marked, e.g. *qalam*, f. m. (primarily feminine); *āśnā*, m., f. (of varying gender according to sex of referend).

5. **Phonemic transcription.** A broad transcription is given in some cases where a common pronunciation of the headword varies unpredictably from what is suggested by its spelling, e.g. *vah* var. /vŏh/; *guṇ* var. /gũṛ/.

6. **Subject label,** denoting a particular field of knowledge, e.g. *hort.*, *bot.*, *gram.*

7. **Linguistic label,** referring the headword to a particular variety of language. Use of a particular label does not mean that another, or others, may not also apply. The following are used:

U. words belonging to Urdu rather than to Hindi usage

reg. regional words not part of normal educated usage in the standardised language.

This abbreviation may be followed by any of the designations

- E. current in or recorded from the eastern Hindi area;
- W. current in or recorded from the western Hindi area;
- Raj. current in or recorded from Rajasthan;
- N., or Panj. current in or recorded from the Haryana-Panjab region

E.H. words recorded in early Hindi literature

Brbh. words recorded in early Hindi (Brajbhāṣā) literature

Av. words recorded in early Hindi (Avadhī) literature

S.H. words recorded in early Hindi poetry of southern (Deccan) origin.[5]

[2] The letters *shīn* and *vau* of Arabic and Persian words have been transliterated as *ś* and *v* respectively.

[3] Where earlier rather than present-day values of Persian vowels are reflected in Hindi pronunciations these values are shown.

[4] But not suffixation by MIA *-ka-*.

[5] A few such words only are listed.

8. **Stylistic label,** referring the headword to a particular stylistic register. The following are used:

arch.	archaic
colloq.	colloquial
euphem.	euphemistic
iron.	ironic
joc.	jocular
obs.	obsolete
pej.	pejorative
pronun. var.	pronunciation variant[6]
sl.	slang
vulg.	vulgar.

9. **Gloss,** or numbered glosses, illustrating the main sense(s) of the headword. A primary gloss may be followed by secondary glosses giving related senses, or translation equivalents, of the headword. Secondary glosses are divided from the primary gloss and from one another by semicolons.

Order of numbered glosses. Prominent meanings of headwords are usually entered before less prominent meanings. In cases where this has not been done, prominent meanings are marked with an asterisk. These cases are most usually loanwords where the order of glosses points to a historical development of meaning. Technical senses of loanwords generally follow non-technical senses.

Some examples of use are introduced to clarify the sense of numbered glosses, but most material illustrating use of a given headword is placed in the separate section of entries concerned with usage.

Glosses are separated from any following section of an entry by the divider —.

10. **Examples of use,** with translation. These illustrate use of headwords (denoted by ~) in both more straightforward, and more idiomatic or figurative contexts. Where a word enters into many idiomatic expressions a wide range of these (sometimes including expressions influenced by regional usage) is given.

Examples of use are separated from any following section of an entry by the divider –.

11. **Compound words containing the headword.** As indicated above compound words have generally been entered under their first members to save space. A wide range of compound words has been included in the dictionary, but many compounds the meanings of which can be inferred

[6] Some of the variants indicated in this way are common, but others are hardly used by educated speakers.

from their members have been excluded. Derivatives of compound words are indicated by citing the suffixes concerned following the words, e.g. the form *paramārthī* is indicated by °*ī* following *paramārtha*.[7] Compound words are hyphenated insofar as the practice of careful users of Hindi appears to allow. Co-ordinative (*dvandva*) compounds are regularly hyphenated; determinative (*tatpuruṣa* and *karmadhāraya*) compounds have sometimes been hyphenated, but not if one member occurs in a phonetically shortened form (e.g. *bhikhmaṁgā*, *ghuṛsavār*, *jalad*); possessive (*bahuvrīhi*) compounds are unhyphenated (e.g. *pragatiśīl*, *dumanzilā*, *haṃsmukh*). Quasi-compounds (e.g. *ās-pās*, *gaṛbaṛ-śaṛbaṛ*) are hyphenated.

Words formed with certain suffixes having clearly defined lexical senses (e.g. *-may* 'consisting of', *-vān* 'possessing', *-pūrvak* 'in the manner of, -ly') are treated as compounds. Words formed with suffixes such as *-tā* (abstract noun formant) are treated as headwords.

Supplementary information about the derivation of compounds is often provided, e.g. *akaṛ-bāī* [*-vāta-*, or *-vāyu-*[1]]; *astarkārī* [P. *-kārī*]; *iktarfā* [cf. A. *taraf*]; *dhūp-snān* [Engl. *sunbathing*].

Compound words are separated from any following section of an entry by the divider –.

12. **Run-on forms.** These comprise grammatical derivatives of headwords, such as participial forms of verbs with their derivatives, and some reduplicative formations not treated as compounds, e.g. *mārā*, adj.; *mārā-mārī*, f.; *dinbadin*, adv.; *raṅgbiraṅgā*, adj.

TYPOGRAPHICAL CONVENTIONS

1. **Brackets** are used

(*a*) to clarify contexts of use, e.g. *mārnā*, to blunt (a blade, an edge); to round off (a corner, &c.); to assail (as hunger, emotion, or perplexity; or as a vice); *apnā karnā*, to make (a person or thing) one's own;

(*b*) to indicate cases where addition or deletion of a term has little bearing on the effective sense of an expression, e.g. (*ṭhīk*) *samay par*, punctually;

(*c*) to indicate the nature of the constructions into which words enter. In many of these cases, the relevant English and Hindi words are bracketed together, e.g. *bolnā*, to speak (to, with, *se*); *milnā*, to accrue (to, *ko*); *kośiś karnā*, to try (to, *kī*).

2. **Hyphens** are used, in headwords,

(*a*) with verb stems, to indicate that a given stem is a regional one not used in the modern standardised language, e.g. *māt-*;

(*b*) with stems of masculine nouns and of adjectives recorded from

[7] Suffixes consisting of vowels or containing an initial vowel are to be understood as conjoined with loss of stem final *-a*: परमार्थ + °ई = परमार्थी; पुनर्वास + °अन = पुनर्वासन.

Brajbhāṣā of which the direct case singular ending is unverified (e.g. *alsaumh-*);

(*c*) in some items of reduplicative form, e.g. *car-car*.

3. **Colons** are used

(*a*) occasionally to mark off an explanatory word or phrase from following numbered glosses, e.g. *a-śeṣ*, without remainder: 1. complete, entire. 2. without end, vast;

(*b*) following a gloss to a headword which occurs only in compound words (examples of which follow after the divider —).

TREATMENT OF VARIANT SPELLINGS, AND CERTAIN REGIONAL FORMS

1. Spellings such as गङ्गा, पञ्जा, पण्डा, हिन्दी and लम्बा (in which nasal consonants preceding plosives are represented explicitly in conjunct characters) are discarded in favour of their commoner equivalents गंगा, पंजा, पंडा, हिंदी and लंबा (in which *anusvāra* is used).

2. In other cases of variant spellings, where more than one spelling has general acceptance in modern Hindi the forms concerned are usually entered separately, e.g. दुकान and दूकान. Where common variant spellings involve use or non-use of conjunct characters, e.g. गर्म and गरम, अंतर्राष्ट्रीय and अंतरराष्ट्रीय, cross-references are made from the variant judged to have lesser standing in the spelling practice of educated users of modern Hindi to the other variant. Where spelling practice varies more at random (as in the use of *virāma*, in certain vowel sequences, in some markings of nasality, in the writing of some conjunct consonants and by metrical licence in poetry) the variations concerned are usually not indicated. This also applies to various spellings which reflect less favoured pronunciations of received forms (e.g. शरीरिक for शारीरिक), or regional pronunciation tendencies (e.g. रसाला for रिसाला, अरझ- for अरुझ-, जलाव- for जलाना, v.t.).

3. Spellings involving the use of subscript dots to denote sounds of Persian and Arabic (sometimes pronounced by Hindi speakers) have been preferred to those in which the dots are dispensed with, despite the fact that the latter type of spelling is today more common.

4. Many spellings found in the older language (and current today chiefly in less careful or less well-educated usage) reflect adaptations of pronunciation undergone by words borrowed from Sanskrit sources (e.g. जंतर alongside यंत्र). Most such spellings are of readily recognisable types, especially

use of ज for य:	जंतर	=	यंत्र
use of ब for व:	प्रबीन	=	प्रवीण

use of न for ण: प्रबीन = प्रवीण
use of स for श: सबद = शब्द
use of ख for ष: तोख = तोष
use of छ (च्छ) for क्ष: अंतरिच्छ = अंतरिक्ष
use of C^1aC^2 for C^1C^2: धरम = धर्म[8]
use of पर- for प्र-: परालब्ध = प्रारब्ध.

Examples of these spelling types have mostly not been entered in the dictionary. Some adaptive spellings more difficult to identify have been included, however, e.g. दुतिया, cross-referenced to द्वितीया.

5. Spellings of the following types, that reflect regional or dialectal pronunciations, are often disregarded:

use of ए for ऐ: पेवंद = पैवंद
use of ओ for औ: ओसाना = औसाना
use of औ for ओ: बरौठा = बरोठा
use of ल for र: परालब्ध = परारब्ध
use of र for ल: टार = टालना
use of र for ड़: थोरौ = थोड़ा
use of व for ब: वरना, v.t. = बरना.

IDENTIFICATION OF CERTAIN DERIVATIVE FORMS

Sanskrit words or coinages containing the *vṛddhi* (increased grade) vowels *ā*, *ai*, *au* have sometimes been omitted from the dictionary where their meanings can be readily inferred from related words containing the non-*vṛddhi* vowels *a*, *i*, *ī*, *e*, *u*. Thus from the word *caritra* 'character' the meaning of *cāritrik* 'having to do with character' can be inferred; from *anugat* 'followed' that of *ānugatya* 'what follows, result'; from *siktā* 'sand, gravel' that of *saikat* 'sandy, gravelly'; from *ekātma* 'of one nature' that of *aikātmya* 'identity'; and from *upanyāsa* 'novel' that of *aupanyāsika* 'having to do with novels'; &c.

THE DEVANĀGARĪ SCRIPT: ORDER OF CHARACTERS

The order of characters of the Devanāgarī script (which reflects the sound values that they represent) is shown, together with the roman transliterations used for the characters, in the table below.

1. The vocalic sounds precede the consonants, starting with अ:[9]

[8] C = 'consonant'.

[9] Vowels to which the superscript signs *anusvāra* (dot) or *candrabindu* ('moon-and-dot') are attached, or which are followed by the sign *visarga* ('colon'), precede the same vowels written without any of these signs. Thus हीं precedes ही, हाँ precedes हा, हिंदी precedes हिदायत and दुःख precedes दुख.

अ *a* आ *ā* इ *i* ई *ī* उ *u* ऊ *ū* ऋ *r̥*
ए *e* ऐ *ai* ओ *o* औ *au.*

2. The consonants (क, ख . . . ह) follow:[10]

क *ka*	ख *kha*	ग *ga*	घ *gha*	ङ *ṅa*
च *ca*	छ *cha*	ज *ja*	झ *jha*	ञ *ña*
ट *ṭa*	ठ *ṭha*	ड *ḍa*[11]	ढ *ḍha*[11]	ण *ṇa*
त *ta*	थ *tha*	द *da*	ध *dha*	न *na*
प *pa*	फ *pha*	ब *ba*	भ *bha*	म *ma*
य *ya*	र *ra*	ल *la*	व *va*	
	श *śa*	ष *ṣa*	स *sa*	
		ह *ha.*[11]		

SIGNS AND ABBREVIATIONS

SIGNS

*	(in square brackets) hypothetical
	(with glosses) marks prominent sense of a headword
>	(has) become
<	(is) derived from
←	(is) borrowed from
→	(is) borrowed into
×	conflated with
+	extended by
~	stands for the headword of an entry
=	is equivalent to
°	(in square brackets) used as a sign of abbreviation of words in *sandhi* junction
	(elsewhere) stands for the preceding word or headword in composition
?	doubtful
??	very doubtful

ABBREVIATIONS

A.	Arabic
abl.	ablative
abs.	absolutive
acc.	accusative
ad.	adapted from, adaptation of
adj.	adjective
adv.	adverb
allus.	allusive
alt.	alternative
anal.	analogical
Ap.	Apabhraṃśa
aphet.	aphetic, or by aphaeresis
appar.	apparently
approx.	approximately
arch.	archaic
attrib.	attributive(ly)

[10] Conjunct consonants are arranged in groups following the full (syllabic) form of their first members. Thus क्क, क्ख and क्त follow क in that order and precede ख.

[11] ड़ and ढ़ take the same positions as ड and ढ.

Austro-as.	Austro-Asiatic
Av.	Avadhī
B.	Bengali
Brbh.	Brajbhāṣā
c.	century
c.	*circa*
caus.	causative
cf.	compare
colloq.	in colloquial use
comp.	composition
compar.	comparative
conj.	conjunction
conn.	(in derivations) to be connected with
corr.	corrupt form
cpd(s).	compound(s)
def.	definite
dem.	demonstrative
dep. auxil.	dependent auxiliary
dimin.	diminutive
dir.	direct
do.	ditto
Drav.	Dravidian
E.	eastern
e.g.	for example
E.H.	Early Hindi
ellipt.	elliptical(ly)
emphat.	emphatic
encl.	enclitic
Engl.	English
esp.	especially
euphem.	euphemism
exc.	except
excl.	excluding
exclam.	exclamation
ext.	extension
f.	(in derivations) formed on (otherwise) feminine
fig.	figurative(ly)
fmn.	formation
foll.	following
Fr.	French
freq.	frequently
G.	Gujarati
gen.	genitive
Germ.	German
Gk.	Greek
H.	Hindi
hon.	honorific
HŚS.	cited by *Hindī śabd-sāgar*[12]
hw(w).	headword(s)
i.	intransitive
id.	the same meaning(s)
i.e.	that is
imp.	imperative
imperf.	imperfective
incl.	including
in comp.	used in composition
incorr.	incorrectly
Ind.	Malay/ Indonesian
indef.	indefinite
inf.	infinitive
infld.	influenced (by)
instr.	instrumental
interj.	interjection
interr.	interrogative
inv.	invariable
Ir.	Iranian
iron.	ironical
joc.	jocular
Kan.	Kannada
KhB.	Khaṛī Bolī
L.	Latin
lit.	literal(ly)
loc.	locative
lw.	loanword
m.	masculine
M.	Marathi
med.	medieval
metath.	metathesis (of)
metr.	metrical, metrical form
MIA	Middle Indo-Aryan
n.	noun
N.	northern
neg.	negative, negatived
neol.	neologism
neut.	neuter
next	next word or entry
NIA	New Indo-Aryan
NW	north-western
obj.	object
obl.	oblique
obs.	obsolete
OIA	Old Indo-Aryan
onom.	onomatopoeic
orig.	origin(ally)
orthogr.	orthographical
P.	Persian
Pa.	Pali
Panj.	Panjabi
part.	participle, participial
partic.	particular
pass.	passive
pej.	pejorative
perf.	perfective
pers.	person
Pk.	Prakrit
pl.	plural
Pl.	cited by J. Platts[13]
poet.	poetic, in poetic style
pop.	popular(ly)
ppn.	postposition
prec.	preceding (entry, item)
predic.	in predicative use
pref.	prefix
prep.	preposition
prob.	probable, probably
pron.	pronoun
pronun.	pronunciation
prop	proper(ly)
prop. n.	proper name
prov.	proverbial
Pt.	Portuguese
q.v.	which see
Raj.	Rājasthānī
redupl.	reduplicative
refl.	reflexive
reg.	regional, or of local currency
rel.	relative
repl.	replaced
rhetor.	(of a question) rhetorical
Ś.	Śaurasenī
S.	(in derivations) Sanskrit (otherwise) southern
sc.	*scilicet*, there is to be understood
sg.	singular
S.H.	southern (Deccan) Hindi
Sk.	Sanskrit
sl.	slang
specif.	specifically
sthg.	something
subj.	subjunctive

[12] Words or senses so marked are not current in the contemporary standardised language. Some are recorded for Sanskrit (in some cases as lexical items, see p. xi, note 1). Others are regional words.

[13] See preceding note, which also applies here.

subj.-pres.	subjunctive-present	tr.	transitive	viz.	*videlicet*, that is to say
s.v(v).	under headword(s)	trad.	traditional(ly)	voc.	vocative
syn.	synonymous, synonym	transf.	in a transferred sense	vulg.	vulgar
T.	Turkish, or Turkic	U.	Urdu	w.	with
Tam.	Tamil	usu.	usually	W.	western
		v.	verb, verbal	w.r.	wrong reading
		var.	variant		

SUBJECT LABELS

admin.	in administration	*econ.*	in economics	*mil.*	in military usage
aeron.	in aeronautics	*electr.*	in electricity	*min.*	in mineralogy
agric.	in agriculture	*engin.*	in engineering	*mus.*	in music
alg.	in algebra	*entom.*	in entomology	*musl.*	in Muslim society
anat.	in anatomy	*fin.*	in finance	*mythol.*	in mythology
anthropol.	in anthropology	*geog.*	in geography	*nat. hist.*	in natural history
arch.	in architecture	*geol.*	in geology	*naut.*	in nautical contexts
archaeol.	in archaeology	*geom.*	in geometry	*ornith.*	in ornithology
arith.	in arithmetic	*govt.*	in government	*pharm.*	in pharmacology
astrol.	in astrology	*gram.*	in grammar	*philos.*	in philosophy
astron.	in astronomy	*hind.*	in Hinduism	*phys.*	in physics
athl.	in athletics and sport	*hist.*	in history, historical	*pol.*	in politics
ayur.	in Āyurvedic medicine	*hort.*	in horticulture	*pros.*	in prosody and metrics
biochem.	in biochemistry	*indol.*	in Indology	*psychol.*	in psychology
biol.	in biology	*isl.*	in Islam	*rhet.*	in poetics and rhetoric
bot.	in botany	*ling.*	in linguistics	*techn.*	in technology
chem.	in chemistry	*lit.*	in literature	*zool.*	in zoology
chronol.	in chronology	*math.*	in mathematics		
comm.	in commerce	*mech.*	in mechanics		
dipl.	in diplomacy	*med.*	in medicine		
		meteorol.	in meteorology		

REFERENCE WORKS

DICTIONARIES

1. *Major sources*

Platts, J. T., *A Dictionary of Urdū, Classical Hindī and English* (London, 1884).

Śyāmsundardās (ed.), *Hindī śabd-sāgar, arthāt hindī bhāṣā kā ek bṛhat koś*. Nāgarīpracāriṇī sabhā. 2nd edn. (Banaras, 1965–75).

Turner, R. L., *A Comparative Dictionary of the Indo-Aryan Languages* (London, 1966).

2. *Other dictionaries and glossaries*

Brajmohan and Badrīnāth Kapūr (eds.), *Mīnākṣī hindī-aṅgrezī koś*. 2nd edn. (Meerut, 1983).

Caturvedī, Paraśurām, *Kabīr koś* (Allahabad, 1972).

Crooke, W., *A Rural and Agricultural Glossary for the N.-W. Provinces and Oudh* (Allahabad, 1879; Calcutta, 1888).

Desāī, Maganbhāī (ed.), *Joḍanī koś*. 3rd edn. (Ahmadabad, 1937).

Fallon, S. W., *A New Hindustani-English Dictionary* (Banaras, 1879).

Gupta, Dīndayālu, and Ṭaṇḍan, Premnārāyaṇ, *Brajbhāṣā sūr-koś* (Lucknow, 1950, 1962).

Kiśorīlāl, *Rītikāvya śabd-koś* (Allahabad, 1976).

Molesworth, J. T., *Marathi-English Dictionary* (repr., Poona, 1975).

Monier-Williams, M., *A Sanskrit-English Dictionary*. 2nd edn. (Oxford, 1899).

Prasād, Viśvanāth, *Kṛṣi-koś*, pt. I (Patna, 1959). Pāṇḍey, Vaidyanāth, and Śāstrī, Śrutidev, pt. II (1966).

Rabinovitch, I. S., and Serebryakov, I. D., *Pandjabsko-russkii Slovar'* (Moscow, 1961).

Seṭh, Hargovinddās Trikamcand, *Pāia-sadda-mahaṇṇavo*. 2nd edn. (Banaras, 1963).

Shackle, C., *A Gurū Nānak Glossary*. School of Oriental and African Studies (London, 1981).

Steingass, F., *A Comprehensive Persian-English Dictionary* (repr., Beirut, 1975).

Sūryakānta, *Index Verborum to Tulasī Dāsa's Rāmāyaṇa* (Lahore, 1937).

Varmā, Rāmcandra (ed.), *Mānak hindī koś* (Allahabad, 1962).

Wehr, H., *A Dictionary of Modern Written Arabic*, ed. J. Milton Cowan. 4th edn. (Wiesbaden, 1979).

Wilson, H. H., *Glossary of Judicial and Revenue Terms* (London, 1855).

OTHER WORKS

Bhayani, Harivallabh Chunilal, and Jinavijaya Muni (eds)., *Sandeśa rāsaka*. Singhi Jain Series 22 (Bombay, 1945).

Chatterji, Suniti Kumar, *The Origin and Development of the Bengali Language* (Calcutta, 1926).

Dāmodara, *Uktivyaktiprakaraṇa*, ed. Jinavijay Muni, with linguistic study by Suniti Kumar Chatterji. Singhi Jain Series 39 (Bombay, 1953).

Grierson, G. A., *Bihar Peasant Life* (Patna, 1885).

Mathur, Ramesh, *Padmāvata: an Etymological Study*. Kansai University Intercultural Research Institute Series no. 1 (Calcutta, 1974).

Saksena, Baburam, *The Evolution of Awadhi*. 2nd edn. (Delhi, 1971).

Tagare, Gajanan Vasudev, *A Historical Grammar of Apabhraṁśa* (Poona, 1948).

Tiwari, Udai Narain, *The Origin and Development of Bhojpuri*. Asiatic Society Monograph Series, vol. 10 (Calcutta, 1960).

Watts, G., *The Commercial Products of India* (London, 1908).

अ

अ *a*, the first vowel of the Devanāgarī syllabary. — **अकार**, m. the sound /ə/; the letter **अ**. **°आदि क्रम**, m. alphabetical order.

अंक *aṅk* [S.], m. **1.** a number, a figure. **2.** a mark, spot, line; stamp; brand; price-mark. **3.** sthg. written: a letter, syllable; marginal annotation. **4.** number, issue (of a publication). **5.** numerical position: place, or mark (as in a class); valuation. **6.** act (of a drama). **7.** point (in a game). **8.** hip (of a mother as when carrying a young child), lap; embrace. **9.** the body. — **~ देना**, or **भरना**, or **लगाना (को)**, to embrace. – **अंक-गणित**, m. arithmetic. **अंकगत**, adj. taken into an embrace; seated close beside. **अंकधारण**, m. bearing a mark, &c.; marking with a stamp, &c. **अंकधारी**, adj. = id., 1.; possessing a body. **अंक-पट्टी**, f. a wooden slate. **अंक-पत्र**, m. a stamp (postage, revenue). **अंक माल**, m. Brbh. embrace. **अंक-शास्त्र**, m. statistics. **°ई**, m. statistician. **अंकेक्षक** [°*ka*+*ī*°], m. auditor. **अंकेक्षण** [°*ka*+*ī*°], f. = next. **अंकेक्षा** [°*ka*+*ī*°], f. auditing, audit.

अंकक *aṅkak* [S.], m. stamp, seal.

अँकड़ना *aṁkaṛnā* [cf. H. *aṁkṛānā*], v.i. to curl or to shrink (as through heat); to become crisp or dry.

अँकड़ा *aṁkṛā* [cf. *aṅka-*], m. **1.** a hook; hooked implement. **2.** an arrowhead. **3.** *Pl.* = **अँकड़ी**, 3.

अँकड़ाना *aṁkṛānā* [? conn. H. *akaṛnā*], v.t. **1.** to cause to curl or shrink (as with heat). **2.** to make crisp; to parch; to dry.

अँकड़ाहट *aṁkṛāhaṭ* [cf. H. *aṁkṛānā*], f. **1.** shrinking. **2.** crispness, dryness. **3.** cramp.

अँकड़ी *aṁkṛī* [H. *aṁkṛā*], f. **1.** a small hook; any implement with a curved or hooked end. **2.** an arrowhead, barb. **3.** *Pl.* tendril.

अंकन *aṅkan* [S.], m. **1.** outlining, drawing. **2.** marking. **3.** noting, registering. **4.** valuing, appraising.

अँकना *aṁknā* [cf. H. *āṁknā*], v.i. & v.t. **1.** v.i. to be valued, appraised, assessed. **2.** to be marked. **3.** v.t. = **आँकना**.

अंकनीय *aṅkănīyă* [S.], adj. requiring noting, or registering.

अँकरी *aṁkrī* [cf. *aṅkura-*], f. **1.** wet grain (liable to sprout). **2.** reg. = **अँकड़ी**. **3.** *Pl.* [? × *aṅkuṭa-*] partic. plants: a vetch, *Vicia sativa*; bramble.

अँकरौरी *aṁkraurī*, f. Av. a small stone, shard.

अँकवाना *aṁkvānā*, v.t. = **अँकाना**.

अँकवार *aṁkvār* [*aṅkapāli-*, Pk. *aṅkavālī-*], f. reg. **1.** the embrace, the bosom; lap. **2.** the breast. **3.** reg. (Bihar) an armful of cut corn. — **~ देना (को)**, to embrace. **~ भरना**, to embrace (one, **को**); to become the mother of a child, or to have children (a woman). **~ में लेना**, to take in one's arms, or lap. **~ लेना (को)**, to embrace.

अँकवैया *aṁkvaiyā* [cf. H. *aṁkvānā*], m. a valuer, appraiser, assessor.

अँकाई *aṁkāī* [cf. H. *aṁkānā*], f. **1.** valuing, appraising; *HŚS.* specif. valuation of crops for division between tenant and landlord. **2.** cost of or payment for valuing, &c.

अँकाना *aṁkānā* [cf. H. *aṁknā*], v.t. to cause to be valued or appraised (by, **से**).

अँकाव *aṁkāv* [cf. H. *aṁkānā*], m. valuation, appraisal.

अंकित *aṅkit* [S.], adj. **1.** numbered; noted. **2.** marked; ruled (with lines); stamped, branded; lettered. **3.** outlined, drawn. **4.** spotted, stained.

अँकुड़ा *aṁkuṛā* [cf. *aṅka-*], m. see **अँकड़ा**.

अंकुर *aṅkur* [S.], m. **1.** sprout, shoot. **2.** bud. **3.** scar (of a healing wound). **4.** fig. offspring. — **~ आना**, or **उगना**, or **निकलना**, or **फूटना**, sprouts or buds to shoot.

अंकुरक *aṅkurak* [S.], m. *HŚS.* nest.

अंकुरण *aṅkuraṇ* [S.], m. sprouting, shooting; germination.

अँकुरना *aṁkurnā* [ad. **aṅkurayati*: w. H. *aṅkur*], v.i. **1.** to sprout, to shoot; to germinate. **2.** to bud.

अंकुरित *aṅkurit* [S.], adj. **1.** sprouted; germinated. **2.** begun (a girl's adolescence).

अंकुश *aṅkuś* [S.], m. var. /əṅkəs/. **1.** a goad. **2.** transf. spur, impetus. **3.** inhibition. — **~ देना**, or **मारना**, or **लगाना (को)**, to goad; to spur; = next. **~ में रखना**, to hold in submission; to curb.

अँकुसी *aṁkusī* [cf. H. *aṅkuś-*]. f. reg. **1.** a hook, hooked implement. **2.** fire-rake, poker. **3.** skeleton key.

अंकेक्षक *aṅkêkṣak* [S.], m. see s.v. अंक.

अंकेक्षण *aṅkêkṣaṇ* [S.], m. see s.v. अंक.

अँकोड़ा *aṁkoṛā*, m. a large hook; grappling iron.

अँकोर *aṁkor* [conn. *aṅkolikā-*], m. Brbh. Av. 1. = अँकवार. **2.** [? × **aṅkapuṭikā-*] a gift. **3.** a bribe. **4.** a light meal (as eaten by farm workers in the fields).

[1]**अँकोरना** *aṁkornā* [cf. *aṅkolikā-*, H. *aṁkvār*], v.t. to take to the bosom, to embrace.

[2]**अँकोरना** *aṁkornā*, v.t. reg. **1.** to make crisp, to dry. **2.** to heat, to warm.

अँकोरी *aṁkorī* [conn.*aṅkolikā-*], f. Brbh. = अँकवार.

अँकौर *aṁkaur*, m. Brbh. = अँकोर.

अँखिया *aṁkhiyā*, f. Brbh. = आँख.

अँखुआ *aṁkhuā* [*akṣa-*[3]], m. sprout, shoot.

अंग *aṅg* [S.], m. **1.** limb, member; organ. **2.** the body. **3.** part, constituent; branch (of knowledge); genre (of literature); section (of a whole). **4.** member (of a society, group). **5.** side, aspect (of a question). **6.** *gram.* base. — ~ ऐंड़ा करना, to twist the body or limbs: to show haughtiness. ~ करना, to take to oneself, to accept (e.g. a deity, as supreme); to incorporate. ~ गोदना (का), to tattoo (one). ~ चुराना, to feel constraint; to feel shame. ~ छूना, Brbh. to touch the body (of, का): to swear devotion (to). ~ ढीले होना, fig. to grow weak; to grow old. ~ तोड़ना, to stretch the body; to flail in distress (with the limbs). ~ देना, to rest briefly, to take a rest. ~ मोड़ना, to turn, or to stretch the body; to yawn; to turn (from, से), to shun; fig. to be humble or unassuming. ~ लगना, to be brought close to the body (of, के): to be embraced, to embrace; to nourish the body (food); to be of use (to); bedsores to form on the body (of, के). ~ लगाना, to bring close to the body; to embrace; to put on (clothes); to take away (with one); to join (to, के: in marriage). – अंग-घाट, m. paralysis, stroke. अंग-छेदन, m. mutilation of the body. अंगज, adj., produced from the body: a son. °आ, f. daughter. अंग-जाई, f. = अंगजाता. अंगजात, m., a son. °आ, f. a daughter. अंगधारी, adj. & m. having a body; a living creature. अंग-भंग, m. & adj. mutilation of the body; mutilated; crippled. अंग-भंगिमा, f. = अंग-भंगी. अंग-भंगी, f. flirtatious movements or gestures (of a woman). अंग-भाव, m. conventional movements and postures (in dancing). अंगभूत, adj. incorporated, assimilated. अंग-मर्दन, m. massage. अंग-मोड़ी, f. *Pl.* stretching; yawning. अंग-रक्षक, m. a protector, bodyguard. अंग-राग, m. application of ointments or cosmetics to the body (esp. after bathing). अंग-वस्त्र, m. a shawl or garment (ceremonial gift). अंग-विन्यास, m. good physical build. अंग-सिहरी, shivering of the body, fit of fever. अंगहीन, adj. & m. bodiless; limbless, mutilated; a title of the god Kāmdev. अंगीकरण, m. assent, agreement; acceptance; acknowledgment. अंगीकार, m. assent, &c. अंगीकार करना, to assent (to); to accept, to admit; to undertake, to promise. अंगीकृत, adj. assented to; accepted; *law.* naturalised; acknowledged. °इ, f. = अंगीकरण.

अंगड़-खंगड़ *aṅgaṛ-khaṅgaṛ*, m. & adj. **1.** m. discarded things, junk, rubbish. **2.** adj. run-down, dilapidated (as buildings, a town).

अँगड़ाई *aṁgṛāī* [cf. H. *aṁgṛānā*], f. twisting or stretching the limbs (as through fatigue). — ~ लेना, to twist, to stretch.

अँगड़ाना *aṁgṛānā*, v.t. to twist, to stretch (body, limbs).

अंगद *aṅgad* [S.], m. **1.** Brbh. a bracelet worn on the upper arm. **2.** *mythol.* name of the son of Bali, king of the monkeys.

अँगनई *aṁgănaī*, f. reg. = आँगन.

अंगना *aṅgănā* [S.], f. a woman.

अँगरखा *aṁgarkhā* [**aṅgarakṣa-*: Pk. *aṁgarakkha-*], m. a long coat worn by men.

अँगरी *aṁgrī* [cf. *aṅga-*[1]], f. Av. protective clothing; armour.

अंगलेट *aṅgleṭ*, f. bodily build, physique.

[1]**अंगा** *aṅgā* [cf. *aṅgikā-*], m. = अँगरखा.

[2]**अंगा** *aṅgā* [S.], f. *Pl.* nurse, nursemaid.

अंगाकड़ी *aṅgākṛī*, f. *Pl. HŚS.* a small bread-cake baked on hot coals.

अँगाकरि *aṁgākri*, f. Brbh. = अंगाकड़ी.

अंगार *aṅgār* [*aṅgāra-*], m. = अंगारा.

अंगारा *aṅgārā* [*aṅgāra-*], m. /ɜgara/. **1.** a glowing coal. **2.** a spark; cinder; burning matter. **3.** adj. fiery red, blood red; raging (with anger). — ~ बनना, to flush with rage. अंगारे उगलना, to belch hot coals: to utter searing or venomous words. अंगारे का कीड़ा, m. salamander. अंगारे (or अंगारों) पर लोटना, to roll on glowing coals (as an ascetic practice); to burn with rage, envy or jealousy; to be very restless or uneasy. अंगारे फाँकना, to toss hot coals about: to play with fire. अंगारे बरसना, to rain hot coals: to be extremely hot (esp. of temperature during the hot season).

[1]**अंगारी** *aṅgārī* [conn. *aṅgāri-*], f. /ə̃garī/. **1.** a small cooking vessel. **2.** small stove, brazier. **3.** reg. bread-cake baked on hot coals.

[2]**अंगारी** *aṅgārī* [cf. H. *aṅgārā*], f. /ə̃garī/. a small spark, scintilla.

अँगिया *aṁgiyā* [cf. *aṅgikā-*], f. bodice; brassiere.

अंगी *aṅgī* [S.], adj. & m. **1.** adj. having a body. **2.** leading, prominent. **3.** m. *HŚS.* leading character (in a drama).

अंगीकरण *aṅgīkaraṇ* [S.], m. see s.v. अंग.

अंगीकार *aṅgīkār* [S.], m. see s.v. अंग.

अंगीकृत *aṅgīkṛt* [S.], m. see s.v. अंग.

अंगीकृति *aṅgīkṛti* [S.], f. = अंगीकरण.

अँगीठा *aṁgīṭhā* [*agniṣṭha-*], m. **1.** a fire-stand. **2.** a goldsmith's furnace.

अँगीठी *aṁgīṭhī* [*agniṣṭha-*], f. **1.** a brazier. **2.** a grate, stove.

अंगुल *aṅgul* [*aṅgula-*], m. **1.** a finger's length. **2.** finger's breadth. **3.** reg. the finger; thumb; big toe.

अंगुलि *aṅguli* [S.], f. = अँगुली. — अंगुलि-छाप, f. or °-प्रतिमुद्रा, f. fingerprint. अंगुलि-मुद्रा, f. signet ring.

अँगुली *aṁgulī* [*aṅguli-*], f. = उँगली.

अंगुश्त *aṅguśt* [P. *anguśt*], f. the finger. — अंगुश्तनुमा [P. *-numā*], adj. inv. pointed out by the finger: famous; notorious; vilified.

अंगुश्ताना *aṅguśtānā* [P. *anguśtāna*], m. **1.** thimble. **2.** a ring (esp. one worn on the thumb).

अंगुष्ठ *aṅguṣṭh* [S.], m. **1.** the thumb. **2.** the big toe. **3.** thumb's breadth (as a measure).

अँगूठा *aṁgūṭhā* [*aṅguṣṭha-*], m. **1.** the thumb. **2.** the big toe. — ~ चूमना, to grovel, to toady (to, का). ~ दिखाना, to gesture with the thumb in derision or defiance; to make an indecent gesture. ~ लगाना, to make a thumb-print (instead of signature). अँगूठे के बल पर चलना, to walk on tiptoe. अँगूठे तले होना, to be under the thumb (of, के). अँगूठे पर मारना, to regard as contemptible.

अँगूठी *aṁgūṭhī* [**aṅguṣṭhiya-*], f. a ring. — ~ कर-, Av. to surround, to lay siege to.

अंगूर *aṅgūr* [P. *angūr*], m. **1.** a grape. **2.** a scar: scab. — ~ की टट्टी, f. a trellis for vines. ~ का मंडवा, m. id.

अँगूर *aṁgūr* [*aṅkūra-*; ? ← Panj.], m. Av. sprout, shoot.

अँगूरी *aṁgūrī* [P. *angūrī*], adj. having to do with grapes. — ~ बाग, m. vineyard.

अँगेट *aṁgeṭ*, f. Brbh. = अँगलेट.

अँगोछना *aṁgochnā* [conn. *aṅgoñcha-*], v.i. to wipe the body with a towel.

अँगोछा *aṁgochā* [*aṅgoñcha-*], m. a cloth, towel (for drying the body).

अँगोछी *aṁgochī* [cf. H *aṁgochā*], f. a small cloth, towel.

अँगोट *aṁgoṭ*, f. E.H. = अँगलेट.

अँगोरा *aṁgorā*, m. a mosquito.

अँगोरना *aṁgornā*, v.t. = अगोरना.

अँगौंगा *aṁgauṁgā*, m. *Pl. HŚS.* part of a crop set aside at threshing as an offering to a village god; money in lieu of this.

अँगौरिया *aṁgauriyā*, m. *HŚS.* one who borrows an employer's plough to plough his own field.

अँग्रेज़ *aṁgrez* [Pt. *inglês*], m. an Englishman.

अँग्रेज़िन *aṁgrezin* [cf. H. *aṁgrez*], f. an Englishwoman.

अँग्रेज़ियत *aṁgreziyat* [cf. H. *aṁgrez*], f. **1.** English (or western) ways; cultivation of the English language in India. **2.** an Anglicism.

अँग्रेज़ी *aṁgrezī* [cf. H. *aṁgrez*], adj. & f. **1.** adj. English; British; western. **2.** f. the English language. — अँग्रेज़ीदाँ [P. *-dān*], adj. & m. knowing English; affecting knowledge of English, or western attitudes; one who knows English, &c. °-दान, id. अँग्रेज़ीपसंद, m. an anglophile, &c.; one affecting the use of English.

अँघड़ा *aṁghṛā*, m. *Pl. HŚS.* metal toe-ring.

अंघ्रि *aṅghri* [S.], f. poet. foot.

अंचकैं *añckaiṁ*, adv. Brbh. = अचानक.

अंचल *añcal* [S.], m. **1.** the border or hem at the end of a sari, or shawl, &c. **2.** transf. edge. **3.** border region. **4.** region, tract; zone.

अँचव- *aṁcav-*, v.t. Brbh. = अचव-.

अँचवा- *aṁcvā-*, v.t. Av. = अचवाना.

अंछर *añchar* [ad. *akṣara-*], m. reg. a mystical or magical word or formula; spell, charm. — ~ पढ़के मारना, to cast a spell (over).

अँज- *aṁj-* [cf. *añjati*], v.t. = आँजना.

[1]**अंजन** *añjan* [S.], m. **1.** lampblack (as applied to the eyes and eyelashes as a cosmetic, or an ointment). **2.** antimony. — ~ करना, or लगाना, to apply a collyrium. – अंजनकेश, adj. black-haired.

°ई, adj. id. अंजनसार, m. painted with collyrium (the eyes). अंजनहारी, f. a stye on the eye; a partic. insect.

[2]**अंजन** *añjan* [Engl. *engine*], m. = इंजन.

[3]**अंजन** *añjan* [? = [1]*añjan*], m. *Pl.* 1. = [1]अंजना. **2.** a species of grass, *Memecylon tinctorum*, used as fodder.

[1]**अंजना** *añjănā*, m. the rice crop in the hills (sown in unirrigated lands in March-April and cut in August-September).

[2]**अंजना** *añjănā*, [S.], f. *mythol.* name of the mother of Hanumān.

[3]**अंजना** *añjănā* [S.], f. a stye on the eye.

[1]**अंजनी** *añjănī* [S.], f. a woman (whose eyes are painted with collyrium, or who is perfumed with sandal, &c).

[2]**अंजनी** *añjănī* [cf. S. *añjana-*], f. *mythol.* a title of the mother of Hanumān. — अंजनी-कुमार, m. *mythol.* a title of Hanumān.

[3]**अंजनी** *añjanī* [*āñjaniya-*], f. a stye on the eye.

[4]**अंजनी** *añjanī* [cf. H. [1]*añjanā*], f. dimin. reg. (W.) a rice crop in the hills, cut in September.

अंजबार *añjbār* [P. *anjabār, injabār*], m. *Pl. HŚS.* a creeper, *Polygonum bistorta*, used medicinally in treating colds and haemorrhages.

अंजर-पंजर *añjar-pañjar* [f. H. *pañjar*], m. **1.** bodily frame, skeleton. **2.** joints, parts (of a body, machine). — ~ ढीले होना, the joints to be loose: to be out of order (an appliance); to have become tired or old (the body, &c).

अंजरा *añjarā* [P. *anjara*], m. *Pl.* a nettle.

अंजल *añjal* [*añjali-*], m. = अंजलि.

अंजलि *añjali* [S.], f. **1.** the hollowed hands placed together and raised to the forehead (in salutation, or entreaty). **2.** a double handful. — अंजलिगत, adj. Av. offered in the hollowed hands (as flowers). अंजलिबद्ध, adj. with hands hollowed (as in salutation).

अंजली *añjălī* [*añjali-*], f. = अंजलि.

अंजाम *añjām* [P. *anjām*], m. **1.** end, completion, conclusion. **2.** result, upshot. — ~ पाना, to be finished, &c. ~ देना (को), to finish, &c.; to manage, to carry out (a task).

अंजीर *añjīr* [P. *anjīr*, S. *añjīra-*], m. the fig-tree, and its fruit.

अंजुमन *añjuman* [P. *anjuman*], m. a society, assembly.

अंजुल *añjul* [*añjali-*], m. = अंजलि.

अंजू *añjū*, m. reg. a tear (= आँसू).

अँजोरा *aṁjorā*, adj. reg. light, bright.

अंझा *añjhā*, m. reg. **1.** interval. **2.** postponement.

अंट *aṇṭ* [H. *āṁṭ*], f. twist, entanglement (see आँट). — ~ की संट, adj. incoherent (words); rambling (argument); inappropriate. – अंट-संट, adj. id. (= अंड-बंड).

अँटना *aṁṭnā* [*aṭṭ-*[1]], v.i. **1.** to be contained (in, में), to fit (into). **2.** to fit (on to, में: as a shoe). **3.** to be filled, or crammed full (of, से). **4.** to suffice (for, को).

अँटवाना *aṁṭvānā* [cf. H. *aṁṭnā*], v.t. **1.** to cause to be contained (in); to make (sthg.) fit (into), to cram (into). **2.** to cause to be filled full (of, से).

अंटा *aṇṭā*, m. **1.** a ball; a marble. **2.** a pill (as of opium). **3.** a large shell or *kauṛī*. **4.** transf. billiards. — अंटा-गुड़गुड़, adj. colloq. dead drunk. अंटा-चित्त, adj. colloq. prostrate (on the back), down and out. अंटाधार, adj. 19c. shot through.

अँटाना *aṁṭānā* [cf. H. *aṁṭnā*], v.t. = अँटवाना.

अँटिया *aṁṭiyā* [cf. H. *āṁṭī*], f. **1.** bundle. **2.** bunch, handful.

अँटियाना *aṁṭiyānā* [cf. H. *aṇṭī*], v.t. = अंटी करना.

अंटी *aṇṭī* [**aṇṭa-*], f. **1.** a reel or frame on which thread, &c. is wound. 2. = आँटी, 2.-4. **3.** [? × *aṭṭ-*[1]], the space between two fingers. **4.** two fingers placed one over the other (to ward off effects of touching a polluting object). — ~ करना, to wind (thread, &c.) on the hand; to gather into a bunch, or sheaf; to hide between the fingers, to pilfer. ~ देना, to throw down (an opponent). ~ मारना, = ~ करना, 3. – अंटीबाज़ [P. *-bāz*], m. a light-fingered person.

अँठई *aṁṭhaī* [*aṣṭapāda-*], f. reg. a tick found on dogs.

[1]**अँठलाना** *aṁṭhlānā*, v.i. *Pl.* = इठलाना.

[2]**अँठलाना** *aṁṭhlānā*, v.i. *Pl.* to stutter.

अँठली *aṁṭhlī*, f. dimin. = आँठी.

[1]**अंड** *aṇḍ* [S.], m. **1.** egg. **2.** testicle. **3.** *mythol.* (world-)egg: the universe. **4.** Brbh. *mythol.* a title of Kāmdev. — अंड-कटाह, m. shell of the world-egg, the world. अंड-कोश (or -कोष), m. scrotum; musk-bag (of the musk deer); transf. rupture, hernia. अंडज, adj. & m. egg-born; egg-born creatures (reptiles, fish, birds). °-राय, m. Av. king of birds: the fabulous bird Garuṛ. अंड-वृत्त, m. an ellipse. अंडाकार [°*ḍa*+*ā*°], m. egg-shaped, oval; elliptical. अंडाकृति [°*ḍa*+*ā*], f. an oval; ellipse. अंडाशय [°*ḍa*+*ā*°], m. the ovaries.

[2]**अंड** *aṇḍ* [*āmaṇḍa-*, Pk. *āmaṁḍa-*], m. the castor-oil tree.

अंड-बंड *aṇḍ-baṇḍ*, adj. entangled, incoherent (as thought or speech: = अंट-संट, see s.v. अंट).

अंडा *aṇḍā* [*aṇḍa-*], m. **1.** egg. **2.** a kind of firework (contained in an eggshell). — ~ खटकना, or फूटना, an egg to hatch. ~ देना, to lay eggs. ~ ढीला हो जाना (का), colloq. to be reduced to dire straits; to become enfeebled; to become bankrupt. ~ सरकना, = ~ ढीला हो जाना. ~ सेना, to sit on eggs, to brood; to be a recluse, a stay-at-home. अंडे का शहज़ादा, m. a greenhorn. – अंडा-सा, adj. egg-like, oval; elliptical. अंडे-बच्चे, m. pl. children, chicks, brood.

अँड़ियाना *aṁṛiyānā* [cf. H. *aṇḍā*], v.t. colloq. to prod an animal in the hindquarters in order to make it move more quickly.

[1]**अंडी** *aṇḍī* [conn. *eraṇḍa-*], f. the oil-bearing fruit of the castor tree. — ~ का तेल, m. castor oil.

[2]**अंडी** *aṇḍī*, f. *Pl. HŚS.* a kind of material (coarse silk).

अँड़ैल *aṁṛail* [cf. *aṇḍa-*], adj. about to lay (a bird).

अंतः- *antaḥ-* [S]. pref. inner, &c. (= अंतर्-). — अंतःकक्ष, m. inner chamber. अंतःकरण, m. the inner faculty: heart, soul, mind; conscience. अंतःकालीन, adj. provisional; temporary (as a measure). अंतःक्रिया, f. inner or hidden process. अंतःक्षेत्रीय, adj. inter-regional. अंतःपटी, f. inner curtain: stage scenery. अंतःपुर, m. inner or women's quarters (in a palace, a house). अंतःप्रकृति, f. inner nature. अंतःप्रत्यय, m. *ling.* infix. अंतःसलिल, adj. subterranean (a stream). °आ, f. the river Sarasvatī. अंतःस्थ, adj. & m. situated in the middle: the semi-vowels and liquid consonants य, र, ल, व (which fall between the *vargīya* and sibilant consonants in the Devanāgarī syllabary). अंतःस्थ राज्य, m. buffer state. अंतःस्थित, adj. internal; medial. अंतःस्वर, m. inner voice, heart's promptings.

अंत *ant* [S.], m. **1.** end. **2.** completion, conclusion. **3.** outcome, result. **4.** limit, boundary; utmost extent; outskirts; frontier region. **5.** death. **6.** destruction. **7.** inner or hidden part, essence; soul, heart, mind. **8.** inner knowledge; secret (of the heart, &c). — ~ करना (का), to complete, &c. ~ को, adv. = ~ में. ~ में, adv. at last, finally. ~ लेना (का), to plumb (a person's) mind; to worry, to harass. ~ समय, adv. at the hour of death. ~ हो जाना, to be completed, &c.; to die out; to die. – अंतकर, adj. = अंतकारी. अंत-कर्म, m. death; destruction; funeral rites. अंतकारी, adj. causing death, or destruction. अंत-काल, m. time of death. अंत-क्रिया, f. = अंत-कर्म, 3. अंत-गति, f. decease, death. अंतज, adj. last born (of brothers); m. *hind.* a śūdra. अंततः, adv. finally; inside. अंतत, adv. Brbh. id. अंतभूत, adj. = अंतर्भूत. अंततोगत्वा, adv. finally, in the last resort. अंताक्षरी [°*a*+*a*°], f. a game of forming words (linked end-wise by the same *akṣara*).

अँतड़ी *aṁtṛī* [cf. *āntra-*], f. usu. pl. **1.** entrails. **2.** the vitals. — अँतड़ियाँ टटोलना (की), to feel the stomach (of a patient); to sound out (a person, about an obscure matter). अँतड़ियाँ जलना, to suffer pangs of hunger. अँतड़ियों का, or के, बल खोलना, to undo twist(s) in the entrails: to eat one's fill after starving. अँतड़ियों में आग लगना, = अँतड़ियाँ जलना. अँतड़ियों में बल आना, or पड़ना, to have a stomach-ache. ~ गले में पड़ना, fig. to suffer distress at some calamity.

अंतर्- *antar-* [S]. pref. **1.** interior, inner; internal. **2.** intermediate. **3.** within, among; inter-. — अंतरंग, adj. & m. internal, inner; close, intimate (friend, or associate); subsidiary (a sub-committee); the heart; relative, intimate friend. अंतरात्मा, f. inner soul, spirit. अंतरायण, m. internment; house arrest. अंतराल, m. & adj. interval; interior; internal, central. अंतरीप [S. *-ap*], m. island; promontory, cape; peninsula. अंतर्कालीन, adj. = अंतःकालीन. अंतर्गत, adj. internal, innermost, hidden; included; ppn. (with के) within, inside. °-गति, f. mental, or emotional, state or process. अंतर्ग्रस्त, adj. involved, concerned (in). अंतर्घट, m. = अंतःकरण. अंतर्जात, adj. innate; endogamous. °ईय, adj. international; inter-caste. अंतर्ज्ञान, m. intuition. अंतर्ज्वाला, f. fire within: grief, remorse. अंतर्दर्शी, adj. of perceptive vision or understanding; introspective. अंतर्दाह, m. inner pangs (as of grief, remorse); heat (of fever). अंतर्दृष्टि, f. perceptive vision, subtle understanding. अंतर्देशीय, adj. inland; internal, domestic (as national affairs). अंतर्द्वंद्व, inner conflict; internal conflict (as in a family, a state). अंतर्द्वार, m. an inner door; private or secret door. अंतर्धान, m. & adj. disappearance; concealment; disappeared, &c.; secret. अंतर्ध्यान, adj. sunk in thought; Brbh. (corr.) = अंतर्धान. अंतर्ध्वंस, m. sabotage; internal damage. अंतर्नाद, m. a mystic sound expressing the longing of the soul. अंतर्निष्ठ, based in or relating to a particular entity: inherent (in), proper (to). अंतर्निविष्ट, adj. permeated. अंतर्निहित, adj. placed within: absorbed, engulfed; hidden. अंतर्पट, m. covering, screen; curtain. अंतर्पत्रण, m. interleaving. अंतर्बोध, m. inner enlightenment; intuition. अंतर्भाव, inclusion; absorption (in, में); inner nature or purport. °ना, f. inner thought; inner emotion. °भावित, adj. brought within, included; assimilated. अंतर्भुक्त, adj. = id., 1. अंतर्भूत, adj. being within, included, internal. अंतर्भेदी, adj. penetrating (as a glance). अंतर्भौम, adj. found or occurring within the earth. अंतर्मन, m. inner heart. °-मनन, m. cogitation. °-मना, adj. inv. preoccupied; dejected. अंतर्मुख, adj. turned or facing inwards; introspective. °ई, adj. id. अंतर्यामी, adj. & m. controlling the mood or heart (the supreme being); knowing the inner thoughts or feelings; the supreme being. अंतर्राज्यिक, adj. = next. °-राज्यीय, adj. inter-state; international. अंतर्राष्ट्रीय, adj. international. अंतर्लापिका, f. a riddle, the answer to which is contained in a sequence of its syllables. अंतर्वर्ती, adj. inner, internal; included; intermediate. °-वर्तीय, adj. temporary, provisional. अंतर्वस्तु, f. contents, substance. अंतर्वासन, m. internment. °-वासित, adj. interned. अंतर्विकास, m. development from within; evolution. अंतर्वेग, m. disturbance of mind or spirit; a type of fever. अंतर्वेद, m. within the sacrificial ground: the Gangetic Doab. °ई, m. one resident in the Doab; f. the speech of the Doab. अंतर्वेदना, f. inward suffering. अंतर्वेशन, m. interpolation. °-वेशित, adj. interpolated. अंतर्व्यापी, adj. diffused within, inner (as a quality). अंतर्हित, adj. disappeared; concealed; secret.

अंतर *antar* [S.], m. **1.** interior, middle, midst. **2.** soul, mind, heart. **3.** mystery, secret. **4.** property, peculiarity. **5.** intervening space or time; distance; separation; gap; period; pause, stop. **6.** difference (between, में); distinction. **7.** (esp. in E.H.) = अंतर्. **8.** in comp. sthg. different. युगांतर [°*ga*+*a*°], m. new age. — ~ करना, to separate, to remove (from); to conceal (in sthg). – अंतरकालीन, adj. = अंतःकालीन. अंतरतम, adj. & m. nearest, intimate; inner soul. अंतरपट, m. curtain, screen. अंतरराष्ट्रीय, adj. = अंतर्राष्ट्रीय. अंतरविरोध, m. internal conflict; mutual conflict; antagonism. अंतरस्थ, adj. internal. अंतरावरोध [°*ra*+*a*°], m. interception. °इत, adj. intercepted. अंतरोन्मुख [°*a*+*u*°], adj. introspective.

अंतरण *antaraṇ* [S.], m. **1.** spacing; displacement. **2.** transference (of assets, or ownership). **3.** transfer (to a new post).

अंतरा *antărā* [S., f. & adv.], m. & adj. **1.** [? × *antara*-[1]] m. second verse, or line, of a song. **2.** adj. intermediate; intermittent (fever). **3.** adv. *Pl.* occurring in the midst, or in the interval; nearly; nearby; except, without.

अँतरा *aṁtrā* [*antara*-[1], w. shortening of /ã/], adj. next but one.

अंतराल *antarāl*, m. & adj. see s.v. अंतर्-.

अंतरिक *antarik* [S.], m. one who transfers or makes over (property, &c).

अंतरिक्ष *antarikṣ* [S.], m. & adj. **1.** m. celestial space; outer space, cosmos. **2.** the sky, heavens. **3.** adj. transf. invisible, vanished. — अंतरिक्ष-मंडल, m. the universe. अंतरिक्ष-यात्री, m. astronaut. अंतरिक्ष-यान, m. spacecraft. अंतरिक्ष-विज्ञान, m. meteorology. °-वैज्ञानिक, m. meteorologist.

अंतरित *antarit* [S.], adj. **1.** interior. **2.** hidden. **3.** shifted, transferred.

अंतरिम *antarim* [Engl. *interim*: w. H. *antar*], adj. interim.

अँतरिया *aṁtriyā* [cf. H. *antarā*, *aṁtrā*], m. intermittent fever.

अंतरीय *antărīyă* [S.], adj. & m. **1.** adj. internal. **2.** m. an under-garment.

अँतरौटा *aṁtrauṭā* [**antarapaṭṭa*-], m. reg. garment worn beneath a fine sari, petticoat.

अंतश्- *antaś*- [S]. pref. inner (= अंतर्-). — अंतश्चेतन, adj. possessed of consciousness. अंतश्चेतना, f. the inner consciousness.

अंतस्- *antas*- [S]. pref. inner (= अंतर्-). — अंतस्तप्त, adj. heated, agitated within. अंतस्तल, m. depth, base; inner heart, soul. °ई, adj. deep- seated, inner (as emotions). अंतस्ताप, m. inward agitation, mental torment. अंतस्सत्ता, f. = अंतःकरण, 1.

अंतस्थ *antasth*, adj. & m. = अंतःस्थ s.v. अंतः-.

अंताराष्ट्रीय *antārāṣṭrīyă* [S.: -*ār*- ← °*ar*+*r*°], adj. = अंतर्राष्ट्रीय.

अंतिक *antik* [S.], adj. & m. **1.** adj. near. **2.** m. a neighbour.

अंतिम *antim* [S.], adj. last; final; ultimate.

अंते *ante* [cf. H. *anat*], adv. elsewhere.

अंतेवासी *antevāsī* [S.], m. a pupil who resides with his teacher.

अंत्य *antyă* [S.], adj. **1.** last, final. **2.** lowest (of caste, state). –. अंत्य-कर्म, m. = अंत्येष्टि-क्रिया. अंत्य-क्रिया, f. id. अंत्यज, adj. & m. born in the lowest caste(s), untouchable. अंत्य-लेख, m. concluding essay or remarks. अंत्याक्षरी, [°*ya*+*a*°], f. a pastime in which the participants recite verses in turn, the first word of each new verse being the same as the last of the verse preceding. अंत्येष्टि [°*ya*+*i*°], f. funeral sacrifice. अंत्येष्टि-क्रिया, f. funeral rites.

अंत्र *antră* [S.], m. intestines.

अंदर *andar* [P. *andar*], adv. **1.** within, inside. **2.** ppn. (usu. with के). within, inside (a space, or a period of time). **3.** under, within (a category). — ~ करना, to put in; to put inside; to put out of sight; to insert. ~ का, adj. inner, internal; hidden, secret.

अंदरसा *andarsā*, m. a kind of sweet made of rice flour and fried in *ghī*.

अंदरून *andărūn* [P. *andarūn*], m. interior; inner part of a dwelling.

अंदरूनी *andărūnī* [P. *andarūnī*], adj. **1.** interior, internal. **2.** intrinsic (quality). **3.** spiritual.

अंदाज़ *andāz* [P. *andāz*], m. **1.** rough estimate. **2.** conjecture, guess. **3.** manner, style; gait; gestures. **4.** affectation. — ~ **करना**, or **लगाना (का)**, to estimate; to evaluate; to conjecture. ~ **उड़ाना**, to imitate, to mimic. ~ **से**, adv. approximately, by guess. – **अंदाज़-पट्टी**, f. *Pl. HŚS.* estimate of the value of a standing crop (= **कनकूट**). **अंदाज़-पीटी**, f. *Pl. HŚS.* an over-adorned, or affected woman.

अंदाज़न *andāzan* [P. *andāz*+A. *-an*], adv. approximately, by guess.

अंदाज़ा *andāzā* [P. *andāza*], m. = **अंदाज़**, 1., 2.

अंदेशा *andeśā* [P. *andeśa*], m. **1.** consideration, reflection. **2.** anxious thought; concern. **3.** misgiving; apprehension; uncertainty. **4.** cause for apprehension: danger. — ~ **करना**, to feel anxiety or concern (for, about, **का**); to be apprehensive (of). – **अंदेशामंद** [P. *-mand*], adj. anxious, concerned.

अंदोह *andoh* [P. *andoh*], m. grief, anxiety, trouble.

अंध *andh* [S.], adj. & m. esp. in comp. **1.** adj. blind. **2.** benighted, ignorant. **3.** m. a blind man. **4.** a benighted person. **5.** darkness. — **अंधकार**, m. see hw. **अंध-कूप**, m. an overgrown, or dry, or filled-in well; thick darkness; blackout. °**ता**, f. benightedness. **अंध-खोपड़ी**, adj. block-headed. **अंध-तम**, m. = next. **अंध-तमस**, m. thick darkness. **अंधधुंध**, m. Brbh. = **अंधा-धुंध**, m. **अंध-भक्त**, m. a blind devotee, fanatic. °**इ**, f. blind devotion. **अंध-प्रज्ञा**, f. intuition (= **अंतर्ज्ञान**). **अंध-विश्वास**, m. superstition. °**ई**, adj. superstitious. **अंधानुकरण** [°*dha*+*a*°], m. blind imitation.

अंधकार *andhăkār* [S.], m. **1.** darkness. **2.** benightedness. **अंधकारमय**, adj. dark, &c.

अंधड़ *andhaṛ*, m. a violent dust-storm.

अंधता *andhătā* [S.], f. **1.** blindness. **2.** benightedness, folly.

अँधला *aṁdhlā*, adj. reg. = **अंधा**.

अंधा *andhā* [*andha-*], adj. & m. **1.** blind. **2.** benighted, foolish. **3.** hoodwinked, deceived. **4.** dim (as a lamp, a room, a bad mirror, or a dry or overgrown well). **5.** transf. filled in (a well). **6.** m. a blind man. — ~ **करना**, to blind; to blindfold; to trick, to deceive. ~ **कुआँ**, m. a dried-up well. ~ **दरबार**, m. a corrupt court, government or office; misgovernment. ~ **बनना**, = ~ **होना**. ~ **तारा**, m. blind star: the planet Neptune. ~ **होना**, to be or to become blind; to be blinded; to shut (one's) eyes (to), to connive (at). **अंधी सरकार**, f. a corrupt government, &c. (= ~ **दरबार**). **अंधे के हाथ बटेर लगना**, fig. to have a windfall. – **अंधा-कुप्प**, adj. & m. pitch-black (night); blackout. **अंधा-धुंध**, adj. excessive; unbridled, violent; wild, headlong, rash; in commotion; m. thick darkness; rashness; violence; commotion. **अंधाधुंध जमाना (पर)**, to belabour (one). **अंधा-धुंध रोना**, to weep bitterly; to sob violently. **अंधा-धुंध लुटाना**, to squander outrageously.

अंधापन *andhāpan* [cf. H. *andhā*], m. **1.** blindness. **2.** benightedness, folly. **3.** darkness, dimness.

अँधियार *aṁdhiyār* [*andhakāra-*, **andhĭkāra-*], adj. & m. Brbh. Av. = **अँधेरा**.

अँधियारा *aṁdhiyārā*, adj. & m. = **अँधेरा**.

अँधियारी *aṁdhiyārī* [*andhakāra-*, **andhĭkāra-*], f. Brbh. Av. **1.** darkness. **2.** storm.

अँधियाला *aṁdhiyālā*, adj. = **अँधेरा**.

अँधियाव *aṁdhiyāv* [**andhikavāta-*], m. reg. = **आँधी**.

अँधेर *aṁdher* [**andhĭkāra-*], m. **1.** arbitrary or tyrannical act: wrong, injustice. **2.** lawlessness, misrule. **3.** disorder; violence. — ~ **करना**, or **मचाना**, to commit an outrage (on, **पर**), to do violence (to); to oppress. **अँधेर-खाता**, m. irregularity (properly, in accounts or business); state of lawlessness, or chaos. **अँधेरगर्दी** [P. *-gardī*], f. id., 2. **अँधेर-नगरी**, f. benighted town: place in which lawlessness or chaos prevails.

अँधेरा *aṁdherā* [**andhĭkāra-*], adj. & m. **1.** adj. dark; dim. **2.** m. darkness, &c.; shadow. **3.** haze, mist. — ~ **करना**, to make dark, to darken, to overshadow; to extinguish (a light). **अँधेरी कोठरी**, f. a cell, &c.; a hidden room or place. ~ **छोड़ना**, to keep out of the light (of anyone). ~ **गुप**, adj. colloq. black as pitch. ~ **घुप्प**, adj. id. ~ **हो चलना**, darkness to come on. **अँधेरे घर का उजाला**, the light of a dark house: an only son; a beautiful child or person. **अँधेरे मुँह**, or **मुँह अँधेरे**, adv. where there is insufficient light to see (the face) clearly: at first light. — **अँधेरे-उजाले**, adv. at whatever time (of day or night); at early dawn.

अँधेरी *aṁdherī* [cf. H. *aṁdherā*], f. **1.** darkness, obscurity; dark night. **2.** storm. **3.** blinkers (for a horse). — ~ **झुकना**, to be overcast; to become dark. ~ **देना**, or **डालना**, to blindfold, to put blinkers (on); to hoodwink.

अँधौरी *aṁdhaurī* [? conn. **pūlikā-*], f. prickly heat.

अंब *amb* [*āmra-*], m. Brbh. = आम.

अंबक *ambak* [S.], m. Av. the eye.

अँबती *aṁbătī*, f. *Pl.* = अँबोती.

[1]**अंबर** *ambar* [S.], m. **1.** covering; clothing. **2.** the sky; the atmosphere. **3.** clouds. — अंबर-डंबर, m. red sky at sunset. अंबर-पुष्प, m. flower(s) from heaven (thrown by the gods): figment(s) of the imagination. अंबर-बेलि, f. = आकाश-बेल.

[2]**अंबर** *ambar* [A. *'ambar*], m. **1.** amber. **2.** a perfume, ambergris. — अंबर-पुष्प, m. amber-flower: a figment of imagination.

[3]**अंबर** *ambar*, m. = अंबार.

अँबराई *aṁbărāī*, f. reg. = अमराई.

अंबरी *ambarī* [P. *'ambarī*], adj. resembling ambergris; ash-coloured; fragrant.

अंबल *ambal*, m. = आँवल.

अंबा *ambā* [S.], f. **1.** mother. **2.** the goddess Durgā (= Devī).

अंबाड़ा *ambāṛā* [conn. *āmravāṭaka-*], m. the hog-plum, *Spondias mangifera*.

अंबार *ambār* [P. *ambār*], m. **1.** heap, pile. **2.** store. **3.** storehouse; granary.

अंबारी *ambārī* [f. P. *'am(m)ārī*], f. a howdah with canopy.

अंबालिका *ambālikā* [S.], f. mother: a title of the goddess Pārvatī.

अँबासना *aṁbāsnā*, v.t. reg. **1.** to season a new vessel by letting water remain in it. **2.** to rinse.

अंबिका *ambikā* [S.], f. **1.** mother. **2.** a title of the goddess Durgā, or of Pārvatī.

अँबिया *aṁbiyā* [cf. *āmra-*], f. a small unripe mango.

अंबु *ambu* [S.], m. **1.** water. **2.** *med.* plasma. **3.** (in chronograms) the figure four. — अंबुचर, m. Brbh. an aquatic creature. अंबुज, m. water-born: a lotus. अंबुद, m. water-giving: a cloud. अंबुधर, m. water-holder: a cloud. अंबुधि, f. ocean. अंबुनेत्रा, adj. f. having tear-filled eyes. अंबुपति, m. Av. the ocean. अंबुपालिका, f. a woman carrying water.

अँबोती *aṁbotī* [conn. *amlapattra-*], f. reg. a species of sorrel, *Oxalis corniculata*.

अंबोह *amboh* [P. *anboh*], adj. & m. **1.** adj. abundant. **2.** m. crowd; abundance.

अंभ *ambh* [S.], m. water: — अंभोज [°*bhas+ja*], m. water-born: the lotus.

अँभौरी *aṁbhaurī* [MIA *ambha-*+? **pūlikā-*], f. watery pustules; prickly heat.

अंश *aṃś* [S.], m. **1.** part, portion; Brbh. part or member of the body. **2.** section, division; group; digit (of the moon). **3.** share; inheritance. **4.** *fin.* a share. **5.** stake, bet. **6.** an amount due, fee. **7.** extent, degree. किसी ~ तक, or में, to some extent. **8.** degree (of rotation, temperature). **9.** numerator (of a fraction). **10.** pith, marrow; substance. अभी गेहूँ में ~ नहीं पड़ा, the wheat has no fullness as yet. **11.** strength, vigour. उसका तो ~ निकल गया, he became exhausted. — अंशकालिक, adj. working part-time. अंशतः, adv. in part, partly. अंश-दाता, m. inv. contributor. °-दान, m. due contribution (as to a fund). °-दायी, adj. contributory. अंशधर, m. = next. अंशधारी, m. a shareholder; an incarnation. अंश-पत्र, m. deed of partition of an estate; share certificate. अंशांश [°*śa+a*°], m. share of a share, fractional part. अंशांकन [°*śa+a*°], m. graduating, calibrating. अंशांकित, adj. graduated, &c. अंशावतार [°*śa+a*°], m. partial incarnation.

अंशक *aṃśak* [S.], m. **1.** a share. **2.** shareholder.

अंशी *aṃśī* [S.], m. **1.** a sharer; partner. **2.** one holding a share; a co-heir.

अंशुमान *aṃśumān* [S.], m. = अंशुमाली.

अंशुमाली *aṃśumālī* [S.], f. the sun.

अंस *aṃs* [S.], m. poet. shoulder, shoulder-blade.

अ- *a-* [S.; and *a-*], neg. pref. (found before consonants.) not; without; un-, in-, non-; wrong, bad (e.g. अपरिचित, adj. unacquainted; अभागी, adj. unlucky; अबोल, adj. speechless). — अकाज, m. Av. a bad action: frustration of a purpose, &c. (see s.v). अबार, m. Brbh. delay, lapse of time. अहिंदी-भाषी, adj. not having Hindi as mother-tongue (a person, a region).

अऊत *aūt* [*aputra-*], adj. & m. 19c. **1.** adj. having no son, or child. **2.** m. a man who dies childless.

अकंटक *a-kanṭak* [S.], adj. **1.** without thorns. **2.** without difficulties, or obstacles; unimpeded.

अकंपन *a-kampan* [S.], adj. firmness, steadiness.

अकंपित *a-kampit* [S.], adj. unshaken; firm.

-अक *-ak* [S. & H.], suffix (forms chiefly m. agent nouns from verb stems, e.g. लेखक, m. writer: fem. °इका; बैठक, f. sitting-room, session, &c.; also forms diminutives, e.g. संपुटक, m. small casket).

अकज- *akaj-* [cf. H. *akāj*], v.i. Av. **1.** to suffer harm, a wrong. **2.** to die.

अकड़ *akaṛ* [cf. H. *akaṛnā*], f. twist, distortion: **1.** stiffness, hardness. **2.** crookedness. **3.** constipation. **4.** stubborness. **5.** ostentation. **6.** arrogance, conceit; brashness. — **अकड़-तकड़, अकड़म-तकड़म**, f. colloq. = **अकड़बाज़ी**. **अकड़-फूँ**, f. id. **अकड़बाज़** [P. *-bāz*], m. an ostentatious or arrogant person. °**ई**, f. = **अकड़**, 4., 5. **अकड़-बाई** [*-vāta-*, or *-vāyu-*[1]], f. cramps, convulsions.

अकड़ना *akaṛnā* [cf.**ākkaḍa-*], v.i. **1.** to become twisted or crooked; to shrivel. **2.** to become distorted; to suffer a cramp or spasm. **3.** to become stiff or hard; to become numb or frozen; to become paralysed. **4.** transf. to be affected or ostentatious. **5.** to be arrogant, or conceited; to be insolent. **6.** to be displeased (at, **पर** or **में**).

अकड़ाना *akṛānā* [cf. H. *akaṛnā*], v.t. **1.** to distress. **2.** to obstruct, to impede.

अकड़ू *akṛū* [cf. H. *akaṛ*], m. = **अकड़बाज़**.

अकड़ैत *akṛait* [cf. H. *akaṛnā*], m. reg. an ostentatious person.

अकती *aktī*, f. = **अगती**.

अकथ *a-kath*, adj. see **अकथ्य**.

अकथनीय *a-kathănīyă* [S.], adj. = **अकथ्य**.

अकथित *a-kathit* [S.], adj. unspoken.

अकथ्य *a-kathyă* [S.], adj. **1.** not to be mentioned. **2.** inexpressible, indescribable.

अकधक *akdhak* ? f. hesitation.

अकन- *akan-* [*ākarṇayati*], v.t. Brbh. Av. to hear; to listen for (a sound).

अकबक *akbak* [cf. H. *akbakānā*], f. chatter, nonsense.

अकबकाना *akbakānā*, v.i. = **हकबकाना**.

अकबत *akabat*, f. E.H. see **आक़बत**.

अकबरी *akbarī* [A. *akbarī*], adj. & f. **1.** *hist.* having to do with the emperor Akbar. **2.** *HŚS.* unequal (a marriage). **3.** f. *Pl. HŚS.* a kind of sweet made of rice flour and sugar.

[1]**अकर** *a-kar* [S.], adj. **1.** without hands. **2.** exempt from taxes; duty-free.

[2]**अकर** *a-kar*, adj. **1.** not worth doing, useless. **2.** *HŚS.* difficult.

अकरण *a-karaṇ* [S.], m. & adj. **1.** m. non-performance, omission (as of a task). **2.** adj. = **अकरणीय**. **3.** difficult of accomplishment.

अकरणीय *a-karăṇīyă* [S.], adj. not to be done, not proper.

[1]**अकरा** *akrā*, adj. Brbh. Av. **1.** costly. **2.** of high quality, genuine.

[2]**अकरा** *akrā* [? conn. *aṅkura-*], m. **1.** a wild grass, *Vicia sativa*, which chokes young wheat. 2. = **आँवला**.

अकरी *akrī* [cf. H. [1]*akrā*], f. *Pl.* **1.** (time of) high prices. **2.** bad season, dearth.

अकर्म *a-karm* [S.], m. **1.** evil action. **2.** wickedness; sin; vice. **3.** absence of *karma*: inaction.

अकर्मक *a-karmak* [S.], adj. *gram.* intransitive.

अकर्मण्य *a-karmanyă* [S.], adj. **1.** idle. **2.** useless.

अकर्मण्यता *a-karmaṇyătā* [S.], f. **1.** idleness. **2.** uselessness.

अकर्मा *a-karmā* [S.], adj. m. inv. = **अकर्मण्य**.

अकर्मी *a-karmī* [S.], m. a wicked, or wretched person; sinner.

अक़ल *aql*, m. see **अक़्ल**.

अकलंक *a-kalaṅk* [S.], adj. **1.** without stain; unblemished; pure. **2.** guiltless.

अकलंकता *a-kalaṅkătā* [S.], f. spotlessness, purity.

अकलंकित *a-kalaṅkit* [S.], adj. = **अकलंक**.

अकलंकी *a-kalaṅkī* [S.], m. a person without guilt, or free of blame.

अकल- *akal-* [**ekkala-*: Pk. *ekkalla-*]. alone: — **अकल-सुरा**, m. an unsociable or solitary person; an envious person.

अकल्पनीय *a-kalpănīyă* [S.], adj. unimaginable.

अकल्पित *a-kalpit* [S.], adj. **1.** unimagined. **2.** not imaginary; not artificial; natural, real.

अकल्याण *a-kalyāṇ* [S.], m. & adj. **1.** m. an unlucky or unpropitious circumstance. **2.** adj. unpropitious; ominous. **3.** disconsolate.

अक़वाम *aqvām* [A. *aqvām*, pl. of *qaum*], m. U. peoples, nations; communities.

अकसर *aksar* [A. *akṣar*], adv. **1.** usually. **2.** for the most part, generally. **3.** often. — **~ करके**, adv. = ~.

अकसरियत *aksariyat* [A. *akṣarīya*: P. *akṣariyat*], f. greater part, majority.

अकसीर *aksīr* [A. *iksīr*], m. & adj. **1.** m. the philosopher's stone. **2.** panacea. **3.** adj. transf. very effective (as a medicine, a treatment).

अकस्मात् *a-kasmāt* [S.], adv. **1.** suddenly, unexpectedly. **2.** by chance.

अकाज *a-kāj* [cf. H. *kāj*], m. **1.** damage, harm. **2.** improper action; frustration of a purpose. **3.** uselessness. — **~**, adv. uselessly, in vain.

अकाजी *akājī* [cf. H. *akāj*], adj. causing damage or harm; obstructive; useless.

अकाट्य *a-kāṭyă*, adj. incontrovertible.

अकादमी *akādmī* [Engl. *academy*; ? ← Fr.], f. academy.

अकाम *a-kām* [S.], adj. without desire.

अकामता *a-kāmătā* [S.], f. freedom from desire.

अकामी *a-kāmī* [S.], adj. free from desire.

अकार *a-kār* [? cf. H. *akārath*, and P. (*be*)*kār*], adj. ineffectual.

अकारण *a-kāraṇ* [S.], adj. **1.** causeless; useless, senseless. **2.** spontaneous.

अकारत *a-kārat*, adj. see अकारथ.

अकारथ *a-kārath* [ad. *kṛtārtha-*: ? × P. (*be*)*kār*], adj. unprofitable; vain; useless. — ~ करना, to make useless; to mar, to ruin; to squander; to spend in vain. ~ जाना, to be useless, wasted, or in vain.

अकाल *a-kāl* [S.], m. & adj. **1.** m. an inopportune time. **2.** a bad season; drought; dearth. **3.** famine. **4.** adj. untimely, inopportune; out of season. **5.** premature.

अकासनीम *akāsnīm*, m. a parasitic plant found on the *nīm* tree.

अकिंचन *a-kiñcan* [S.], adj. & m. **1.** adj. poverty-stricken, destitute. **2.** m. poverty. **3.** a pauper.

अक़ीक़ *aqīq* [A. *'aqīq*], m. cornelian.

अक़ीदत *aqīdat* [A. *'aqīda*: P. *'aqīdat*], f. **1.** faith, belief (in, से). **2.** a faith. — अक़ीदतमंद [P. *-mand*], adj. having faith, believing.

अक़ीदा *aqīdā* [A. *'aqīda*], m. = अक़ीदत, 1.

अकीर्ति *a-kīrti* [S.], f. infamy; disgrace; bad reputation. — अकीर्तिकर, adj. shameful, dishonourable.

अकुंठ *a-kuṇṭh* [S.], adj. not blunt: **1.** keen, sharp. **2.** active, vigorous.

अकुल *a-kul* [S.], adj. & m. **1.** adj. without family. **2.** not of high birth. **3.** m. humble family or birth.

अकुलाना *akulānā* [cf. *ākula-*; Pa. *akkula-*], v.i. **1.** to be agitated; to be uneasy. **2.** to tire (of, से); to become averse (to). **3.** to be restless (for, के लिए). **4.** to feel nausea or sickness.

अकुलाहट *akulāhaṭ* [cf. H. *akulānā*], f. **1.** agitation; unease. **2.** weariness (of); aversion (to).

अकुली *akulī* [S.], adj. = अकुलीन.

अकुलीन *a-kulīn* [S.], adj. & m. **1.** adj. not of high family or birth. **2.** m. a low-born person.

अकुशल *a-kuśal* [S.], m. & adj. **1.** m. misfortune. **2.** adj. unlucky, inauspicious. **3.** unskilled.

अकृत *a-kṛt* [S.], adj. **1.** not done. **2.** not carried through, badly done. **3.** not made: uncreated.

अकृतकार्य *a-kṛtăkāryă* [S.], adj. unsuccessful; unskilled.

अकृतज्ञ *a-kṛtajñă* [S.], adj. ungrateful.

अकृतज्ञता *a-kṛtajñătā* [S.], f. ingratitude.

अकृतार्थ *a-kṛtârth* [S.], adj. = अकृतकार्य.

अकृती *a-kṛtī* [S.], adj. **1.** incapable. **2.** idle.

अकृत्य *a-kṛtyă* [S.], adj. & m. **1.** adj. not to be done, wrongful. **2.** m. a wrongful act.

अकृत्रिम *a-kṛtrim* [S.], adj. **1.** not artificial; genuine; natural. **2.** not forced (manner); candid.

अकेला *akelā* [**ekkalla-*: Pk. *ekkalla-*], adj. & m. **1.** adj. single, sole. **2.** singular, unique. **3.** solitary; alone; isolated. **4.** lonely. **5.** adv. singly, on own's own; alone; simply, merely. **6.** m. a solitary place. — ~ दम, m. a single breath: state of being single or alone. हम तो अकेले दम हैं, we're on our own. हमारा तो ~ दम है, id. अकेली कहानी, f. one side of a story or case. अकेले में, adv. = अकेले, 2. – अकेला-दुकेला, adj. one or two, a few only; solitary; lonely; adv. singly; in ones or twos.

अकेलापन *akelāpan* [cf. H. *akelā*], m. **1.** loneliness. **2.** singleness: celibacy. **3.** singularity.

[1]**अकोर** *akor*, m. Brbh. = अँकोर.

[2]**अकोर** *akor* [**utkoṭa-*: Pk. *ukkoḍa-*], m. reg. (W.) bribe: coaxing (of a cow that has lost her calf, to give milk); lure.

अकोल *akol* [*aṅkolla-*], m. arch. reg. (Bihar) a plant of the genus *Alanguin* (rubbing oil from its nuts on the skin was supposed to make a person invisible).

अकौड़ा *akauṛā*, m. reg. = आक.

-अक्कड़ *-akkaṛ* suffix (forms adjectives and nouns from verb stems, e.g. भुलक्कड़, adj. forgetful, absent-minded).

अक़्क़ल-बार *aqqal-bār*, f. reg. (S. India). *Pl.* the Indian shot-plant, *Canna indica*.

अक्खड़ *akkhaṛ*, adj. & m. **1.** adj. unyielding: uncouth, rough, awkward; uncivilised.

2. boorish. 3. self-willed; stubborn; perverse. 4. haughty. 5. truculent. 6. m. an uncouth person; boor.

अक्खड़पन *akkhaṛpan* [cf. H. *akkhaṛ*], m. 1. uncouthness, &c. (see अक्खड़). 2. self-will, &c. 3. haughtiness. 4. truculence.

अक्खड़पना *akkhaṛpanā*, m. = अक्खड़पन.

अक्खाह *akkhāh*, interj. oh! (expresses astonishment).

अक्तूबर *aktūbar* [Pt. *outubro*: w. Engl. *October*], m. October.

अक्रूर *a-krūr* [S.], adj. not cruel; gentle.

अक़्ल *aql* [A. *'aql*], f. understanding, good sense; mind; wisdom. — ~ का पुतला, m. colloq. a brainy person. ~ का दुश्मन, m. colloq. a stupid person. ~ का पूरा, m. iron. id. ~ काम न करना, the mind not to work; to be at a loss. ~ के पीछे लट्ठ, or लाठी, लिए फिरना, to chase (away) good sense: to act in a wilfully or grossly foolish way. ~ ख़र्च करना, to expend thought, to ponder (over, पर). ~ चक्कर में आना, the mind to be in a whirl, to be distracted; to be at one's wit's end. ~ चकराना, to allow oneself to be distracted or confused. ~ चरने जाना, fig. to be at one's wit's end; to be woolgathering. ~ जाती रहना, to lose one's wits, or senses. ~ ठिकाने होना, to have one's wits about one. ~ देना (को), to instruct, to teach sense (to). ~ दौड़ाना, = ~ ख़र्च करना. ~ पर पत्थर पड़ना, fig. to be dumbfounded, stupefied. ~ पर परदा पड़ना, fig. to have lost one's wits. ~ मारी जाना, to lose one's wits, or senses. ~ में आना, to get sense, to understand. ~ से बाहर, or दूर, adv. inconceivable; unreasonable; nonsensical. – अक़्ल-दाढ़, f. a wisdom tooth. अक़्लमंद [P. *-mand*], adj. intelligent; of good sense, wise. °ई, f.

अक़्ली *aqlī* [A. *'aqlī*], adj. having to do with mind or intelligence. — ~ गद्दा लगाना, colloq. to make a (mere) conjecture.

अक्ष *akṣ* [S.], m. 1. a die. 2. spot (as on a die). 3. an axle; axis. 4. yoke. 5. *geog.* latitude. — अक्ष-कर्ण, m. *HŚS.* hypotenuse. अक्षांश [°*ṣa+a*°], m. a degree of latitude.

अक्षत *a-kṣat* [S]. 1. adj. whole, entire; undivided; intact. 2. m. whole grains of rice (used in religious ceremonies). 3. fried grain. 4. barley. — अक्षत-तिलक, f. ceremonial placing of grains of rice on the forehead of an idol, a brāhmaṇ, or a worshipper. अक्षतयोनि, adj. & f. virgin; a virgin. – अक्षता, f. id.

अक्षम *a-kṣam* [S.], adj. incompetent.

अक्षमता *a-kṣamătā* [S.], f. incompetence.

अक्षय *a-kṣay* [S.], adj. 1. undecaying, imperishable. 2. external; permanent, durable. — ~ तूणीर, m. a quiver never empty. ~ नीवी, f. a permanent endowment. ~ वट, m. the 'undecaying banyans' (of Allahabad and Gayā). - अक्षय-कोश, m. a safe (for perishable food). अक्षय-तृतीया, f. = अखय-तीज. अक्षय-लोक, m. the eternal world, heaven.

अक्षयता *a-kṣayătā* [S.], f. imperishability; durability.

अक्षय्य *a-kṣayyă* [S.], adj. = अक्षय.

अक्षर *a-kṣar* [S.], adj. & m. 1. adj. imperishable; unchangeable. 2. m. a character of a syllabary or other writing system; a syllable; letter. 3. pl. a writing system, syllabary, alphabet. — ~ घोंटना, to learn one's alphabet. ~ ~ पूरा करना, to carry out to the letter. ~ ~ बयान, m. colloq. a full account. – अक्षर-ज्ञान, m. literacy. अक्षर-माला, f. a syllabary; alphabet. अक्षर-विन्यास, m. orthography; syllabification. अक्षरशः, adv. syllable by syllable; literally; to the letter, in full. अक्षर-शोधन, m. proof-reading. अक्षर-संयोजन, m. type-setting. अक्षरानुवाद [°*ra+a*°], m. a literal translation. अक्षरारंभ [°*ra+ā*°], m. first steps towards literacy. अक्षरार्थ [°*ra+a*°], m. literal sense.

[1]**अक्षरी** *akṣarī* [cf. H. *akṣar*], adj. & m. 1. adj. having good handwriting. 2. m. one having good handwriting.

[2]**अक्षरी** *akṣarī* [cf. H. *akṣar*], f. spelling.

अक्षरौटी *akṣarauṭī* [**akṣaravr̥tta-*; and ad.], f. 1. syllabary, alphabet. 2. handwriting.

अक्षि *akṣi* [S.], f. 1. the eye. 2. (in chronograms) the number two.

अक्षीय *akṣīyă* [S.], adj. axial.

अक्षुण्ण *a-kṣuṇṇ* [S.], adj. unbroken; continuing.

अक्षेम *a-kṣem* [S.], m. & adj. 1. m. misfortune. 2. adj. unfortunate, wretched.

अक्षोनि *akṣoni* [ad. *akṣauhiṇī-*], f. Brbh. an army.

अक्षोहिणी *akṣohiṇī* [ad. *akṣauhiṇī-*], f. an army.

अक्स *aks* [A. *'aks*], m. reverse, counterpart; reflection (= परछाई). — ~ उतारना, to trace an outline (of, का); to photograph. ~ करना (का), = prec., 1.

अक्सर *aksar*, adv. see अकसर.

अखंड *a-khaṇḍ* [S.], adj. 1. unbroken, undivided, entire; unlimited. 2. uninterrupted, continuous. 3. indivisible, indestructible.

अखंडता *a-khaṇḍătā* [S.], f. wholeness, entirety; integrity.

अखंडनीय *a-khaṇḍănīyă* [S.], adj. **1.** not to be broken, or divided. **2.** indivisible, indestructible. **3.** irrefutable; incontestable.

अखंडित *a-khaṇḍit* [S.], adj. **1.** unbroken; unlimited. **2.** continuous. **3.** not refuted.

अखंड्य *a-khaṇḍyă* [S.], adj. = अखंडनीय.

अखज *akhaj* [conn. *khādya-*], adj. unfit to be eaten; distasteful. — अखज-अदावत, f. hostility, ill-will.

अखड़ाना *akhṛānā* [cf. H. *akkhaṛ*], v.i. **1.** to be rough, coarse, rude. **2.** to be quarrelsome. — अखड़ाना-बखड़ाना, = ~.

अखड़ैत *akhṛait*, m. = अखाड़िया.

अख़नी *akhnī* [P. *yakhnī*], f. a broth made from the juice of boiled meat. — अख़नी-पुलाव, m. a rice dish with a meat broth or gravy.

अख़बार *akhbār* [A. *akhbār*, pl. of *khabar*], m. a newspaper. — अख़बार-नवीस [P. *-navīs*], m. a journalist; reporter. °ई, f. journalism. अख़बारवाला, m. a newspaper seller, editor or proprietor; a journalist, or reporter.

अख़बारी *akhbārī* [cf. H. *akhbār*], adj. having to do with newspapers, or with journalism. – ~ भाषा, f. newspaper language; specif. a heavily Sanskritised style of Hindi (as liable to be used in newspapers, or in news bulletins); journalese.

अखय *akhay*, adj. undecaying (see अक्षय). — अखय-तीज, m. *hind.* a festival observed on the third day of the bright half of Baisākh (when accounts are settled for expenses of the spring crop.)

अखरना *akharnā*, v.i. **1.** to be disagreeable; to irritate. **2.** to be burdensome.

अखरोट *akhroṭ* [conn. *akṣoṭa-*], m. walnut (tree and nut).

अख़रोट *akhroṭ*, m. pronun. var. = अखरोट.

अख़लाक़ *akhlāq* [A. *akhlāq*, pl. of *khulq*], m. **1.** morals, ethics; morality; virtues. **2.** friendliness.

अखाड़ा *akhāṛā* [*akṣavāṭa-*], m. **1.** wrestling ground; arena, ring; courtyard. **2.** sports ground. **3.** gymnasium. **4.** place of assembly (as of a *pañcāyat*, or of musicians or *sādhus*). **5.** band, company, group. — ~ गरम होना, to be crowded, bustling (a place of assembly). ~ जमना, a group, &c. to assemble. अखाड़े का, adj. athletically built. अखाड़े में आना, or उतरना, to step into an arena, into contention. — अखाड़ेबाज़ [P. *-bāz*], m. a wrestler; an athlete; transf. an intriguer, manoeuvrer. °ई, f. wrestling; manoeuvring.

अखाड़िया *akhāṛiyā* [cf. H. *akhāṛā*], m. **1.** a wrestler. **2.** athlete; gymnast. **3.** transf. a manoeuvrer, intriguer.

अखाद्य *a-khādyă* [S]. **1.** adj. not to be eaten. **2.** inedible. **3.** m. unlawful food.

अखिल *akhil* [S.], adj. whole, entire; all. — ~ भारतीय, adj. all-Indian. – अखिलेश्वर [°*la*+*ī*°], adj. lord of all: a title applied to Rām, Śiva, &c. as supreme deity.

अख़ीर *akhīr* [A. *akhīr*], adv. = आख़िर.

अख़्तियार *akhtiyār* [A. *ikhtiyār*], m. **1.** authority, power; right or freedom of action; jurisdiction. **2.** privilege. **3.** option, choice; preference. — ~ करना (का), to choose, to elect, to accept; to adopt (as an attitude); to take up (work, activity). ~ मिलना (को), to be given authority, &c. (to, का); to obtain authority. ~ में होना, to be subject to (one's, के) authority or discretion; to be in (one's) power. ~ रखना, to have authority, &c. (to, की).

अख्यात *a-khyāt* [S.], adj. **1.** unknown, obscure. **2.** infamous.

अख्याति *a-khyāti* [S.], f. **1.** infamy. **2.** obscurity.

अग *a-g* [S.], adj. & m. Brbh. Av. **1.** adj. unable to move. **2.** m. a mountain. **3.** a tree.

अगड़धत्त *agaṛdhatt*, adj. colloq. stalwart, sturdy.

अगड़-बगड़ *agaṛ-bagaṛ*, adj. & m. f. **1.** adj. confused, jumbled. **2.** worthless. **3.** m.f. confusion, jumble; odds and ends, junk. **4.** idle talk; aimless activity.

अगड़म-बगड़म *agaṛam-bagaṛam*, m. = अगड़-बगड़, 3.

अगणनीय *a-gaṇănīyă* [S.], adj. = अगण्य.

अगणित *a-gaṇit* [S.], adj. uncounted.

अगण्य *a-gaṇyă* [S.], adj. **1.** innumerable. **2.** incalculable. **3.** not to be taken account of, insignificant.

अगत *a-gat* [? ad. *agati-*], f. & adj. **1.** reg. the future, the hereafter. **2.** *HŚS.* bad state, plight. **3.** adj. *HŚS.* = अगम्य.

अगति *a-gati* [S.], f. & adj. **1.** f. helpless state. **2.** *hind.* disembodied state (as of a spirit, following improperly performed rites). *3. motionlessness, inertness. **4.** adj. inert. **5.** helpless.

अगतिक *a-gatik* [S.], adj. **1.** having no shelter, or recourse; helpless. **2.** *HŚS. hind.* whose last rites have not been properly performed.

अगती *agtī* [*agasti-*], f. the agatya tree, *Sesbana* (or *Aeschynomene*) *grandiflora*.

अगत्तर *agattar*, adj. reg. coming, future.

अगन *agan*, m. a kind of lark.

¹अगम *a-gam*, adj. = अगम्य.

²अगम *agam*, m. reg. = आगम.

अगम्य *a-gamyă* [S.], adj. **1.** inaccessible, unattainable; incomprehensible. **2.** impenetrable. **3.** unfathomable (as ocean); unbounded (in limits).

¹अगर *agar* [*agaru-*: ← Drav.], m. the aloe-tree and its wood. — अगरदान [P. *-dān*], m. a vessel for holding *agar* or perfumes. अगरबत्ती, f. an incense stick.

²अगर *agar* [P. *agar*], conj. if. — अगर-मगर, m. ifs and buts: hesitation; evasion, prevarication. अगर-मगर करना, to argue; to hesitate; to prevaricate.

अगरचे *agarce* [P. *agarce*], conj. although; even if.

अग़ल-बग़ल *agal-bagal* [f. H. *bagal*], adv. **1.** to this side and that, here and there. **2.** all around; nearby. — ~ का, adj. found all around, &c. ~ में, adv. = अग़ल-बग़ल. – ~ रखना, to put aside; to put away.

अगला *aglā* [cf. *agra-*], adj. & m. **1.** foremost, front; first. **2.** former, last; old; old-fashioned. **3.** recent (times, period). **4.** following, next; future; impending. **5.** chief, principal. **6.** m. leader, chief. **7.** another person, or party. **8.** forefathers. **9.** descendants, posterity. — ~ जन्म, m. a former birth; a future birth. अगले साल, m. next year. अगले ज़माने का, adj. of a former age, or generation; simple, straightforward.

अगवाई *agvāī*, f. = ¹अगवानी.

अगवाड़ा *agvāṛā* [**agravāṭa-*], m. **1.** front (of a house). **2.** space in front of a house.

¹अगवान *agvān*, f. Brbh. Av. = ¹अगवानी.

²अगवान *agvān*, m. Av. one who goes forward in welcome (see ²अगवानी).

¹अगवानी *agvānī* [conn. *agrayāvan-*], f. going or sending forward (to receive a guest): reception, welcome. — ~ करना (की), to go to (meet a visitor, a bridegroom and his party); to escort to one's home.

²अगवानी *agvānī*, m. Brbh. **1.** a forerunner, emissary. **2.** one who leads the way forward.

अगवार *agvār*, m. reg. first corn taken from a heap of newly threshed grain; corn lost during winnowing.

अगस्त *agast* [Pt. *agosto*: w. Engl. *August*], m. the month of August.

अगस्ति *agasti*, m. = अगस्त्य.

अगस्त्य *agastyă* [S.], m. **1.** *mythol.* name of a sage. **2.** the star Canopus. **3.** name of a tree, *Aeschynomene grandiflora* (= अकती, अगती).

अगहन *ag'han* [*agrahāyaṇa-*], m. the ninth lunar month of the Hindu year (November-December).

अगहनिया *ag'haniyā* [cf. H. *ag'han*], adj. = अगहनी.

अगहनी *ag'hanī* [cf. H. *ag'han*], adj. & f. **1.** having to do with the month Ag'han (as crops). **2.** f. that part of the *kharīf* crop harvested in Ag'han.

अगाऊ *agāū* [cf. H. *āgā*], m. & adj. **1.** m. an advance (of money). **2.** adj. advanced. **3.** adv. in advance, in front. **4.** beforehand.

अगाड़ी *agāṛī* [cf. H. *āgā*], f. **1.** front, forepart. **2.** first action, first attack (= आगा, 2). **3.** fore-fetters of a horse. **4.** *Pl.* advance (as of pay). **5.** adv. in front; ahead. — अगाड़ी-पिछाड़ी, f. the front and rear, first and last parts.

अगाध *a-gādh* [S.], adj. bottomless, unfathomable; profound.

अगाधता *agādhătā* [S.], f. bottomlessness; profundity.

अगास *agās*, m. = आकाश.

अगासी *agāsī* [cf. H. *agās*], f. reg. **1.** an upper verandah. **2.** *HŚS.* ? a kite (= चील).

अगिया *agiyā* [cf. H. *āg*], f. dimin. = आग. — अगिया-बैताल, m. name of a demon ruling over fire.

अगियाना *agiyānā* [cf. *agni-*[1]], v.i. & v.t. reg. **1.** v.i. to feel a burning sensation. **2.** to burn with anger. **3.** v.t. to set alight, on fire. **4.** to burn, to heat, to bake, to fire. **5.** *Pl.* to clean (metal vessels) by burning.

अगियारी *agiyārī* [*agnikārya-*], f. **1.** kindling the sacred fire. **2.** a receptacle for the sacred fire.

अगुआ *aguā* [*agregū-*], m. **1.** a guide. **2.** leader. **3.** match-maker.

अगुआई *aguāī* [cf. H. *aguā*], f. the lead (in an activity). — ~ करना, to take the lead.

अगुण *a-guṇ* [S.], adj. & m. **1.** without good qualities. **2.** *philos.* unqualified (the ultimate being). **3.** m. defect, fault, vice.

अगुणी *a-guṇī* [S.], adj. = अगुण, 1.

अगुवा *aguvā*, m. see अगुआ.

अगूढ़ *a-gūṛh* [S.], adj. **1.** not concealed, manifest; not recondite. **2.** open, straightforward (of disposition).

अगोचर *a-gocar* [S.], adj. & m. **1.** adj. not perceptible; unseen, not evident; mysterious. **2.** m. the invisible supreme being.

अगोट- *agoṭ-* [conn. H. *agornā*], v.t. Brbh. to check, to confine; to reject (sthg. said).

अगोत्री *a-gotrī* [S.], adj. belonging to a different *gotra*.

अगोरा *agorā* [H. *agornā*], m. one who watches over crops.

अगोरना *agornā*, v.t. **1.** to watch, to guard. **2.** to watch for, to wait for.

अगौनी *agaunī* [**agragamana-*], f. = [1]अगवानी.

अगौर *agaur*, m. reg. advance of rent paid by the cultivator to the land-holder in the months of Jeṭh and Asāṛh. — अगौर-बटाई, f. division of the crop in previously agreed proportions between landlord and tenant.

अग्ग्रास *aggrās* [ad. *agragrās-*], m. food offered in oblations, sacrifices, &c. to the gods.

अग्नि *agni* [S.], f. **1.** fire, &c. (= आग). **2.** (esp. in comp.) digestion. **3.** (in chronograms) the number three. — अग्नि-कर्म, m. cremation; = अग्नि-होत्र. अग्नि-कांड, m. conflagration. अग्नि-कुंड, m. a fire-pit. अग्नि-कोण, m. the south-east. अग्नि-क्रिया, f. cremation. अग्नि-क्रीड़ा, f. a partic. firework; firework display. अग्नि-चक्र, m. wheel of fire (as the sun). अग्नि-ज्वाला, f. a flame, tongue of flame. अग्नि-दाह, m. cremation; torment. अग्नि-निरोधक, adj. fire-resistant. अग्नि-परीक्षा, f. ordeal by fire; a difficult ordeal; assaying by fire (a precious metal). अग्नि-प्रस्तर, m. fire-stone: flint. अग्नि-बम, m. incendiary bomb. अग्निवर्धक, adj. digestive (a medicine). अग्नि-वर्षा, f. rain of fire, bombardment. अग्नि-शामक, m. fire-extinguisher. अग्नि-शाला, f. place for keeping a sacrificial fire. अग्नि-शिखा, f. = अग्नि-ज्वाला. अग्नि-शुद्धि, f. purification by fire; = °-परीक्षा. अग्नि-संस्कार, m. funeral ceremonies; any ceremony performed with consecrated fire. अग्निसह, adj. fire-resistant. अग्निसात्, adj. burned to ashes. अग्नि-होत्र, m. oblation to a sacrificial fire; a sacrificial fire. अग्नि-होत्री, m. one who keeps up a sacrificial fire. अग्न्यस्त्र [°*ni*+*a*°], m. a firearm. अग्न्याशय [°*ni*+*ā*°], m. the pancreas.

अग्र *agră* [S.], adj. & m. **1.** adj. front, foremost; first. **2.** prior. **3.** prominent, chief; best. **4.** m. foremost, or upper part. **5.** beginning. — अग्र-गण्य, adj. = ~, 3. अग्र-गति, f. forward movement; progress. अग्रतः, adv. in front; from the front; previously. अग्र-गामी, adj. & m. preceding; leading; avant-garde; a forerunner; leader. अग्रज, m. & adj. elder brother, first born; predecessor; elder, eldest. °-जा, f. अग्र-दूत, m. a herald, forerunner. अग्र-लेख, m. leading article. अग्रवर्ती, adj. & m. in a forward or leading position; leader. अग्रसर, adj. & m. preceding; leading; progressive; beginning, under way; one in the forefront, a leader. °ता, f. अग्रसारण, m. forwarding. °-सारित, adj. अग्र-सोची, adj. possessing foresight, or caution. अग्रहायण, m. the ninth lunar month of the Hindu calendar. अग्रहार, m. gift of land, or produce, to brāhmaṇs. अग्रांश [°*ra*+*a*°], m. front, or foremost part. अग्रामात्य [°*ra*+*a*°], m. chief minister.

अग्रणी *agrăṇī* [S.], adj. & m. **1.** adj. leading, advanced. **2.** m. a leader.

अग्रता *agrătā* [S.], f. priority, precedence.

अग्राह्य *a-grāhyă* [S.], adj. **1.** not to be received or taken, unacceptable; unwelcome. **2.** inadmissible (evidence, &c).

अग्रिम *agrim* [S.], adj. & m. **1.** adj. first in order or rank. **2.** forward (of position). **3.** early, prior. **4.** forthcoming, future. **5.** advanced (a sum of money). **6.** pressing (as thanks). **7.** m. an advance (of money). — ~ भुगतान, m. advance payment.

अघ *agh* [S.], m. **1.** sin; guilt; wickedness; crime. **2.** suffering. — अघकारी, m. a sinner, &c. अघनाशक, adj. sin-destroying. °-नासी, adj. Brbh. id. अघरूप, adj. Av. sinful. अघहर, adj. Brbh., sin-destroying. °-हरन, adj. id. °-हरनी, adj. f. id. अघारि [°*gha*+*a*°], m. Av. an enemy of sin.

अघट *a-ghaṭ* [S.], adj. = अघटित.

अघटित *a-ghaṭit* [S.], adj. & m. **1.** adj. which has not happened; unprecedented. **2.** improbable. **3.** Brbh. unfit, unworthy. **4.** m. Brbh. the unknown future.

[1]**अघाई** *aghāī* [cf. H. [1]*aghānā*], f. **1.** surfeit, fullness. **2.** adv. to the full; severely, harshly.

[2]**अघाई** *aghāī* [cf. H. [1] [2]*aghānā*], adj. **1.** surfeited, replete. **2.** satisfied, contented.

[1]**अघाना** *aghānā* [*āghrāpayati*], v.i. & v.t. **1.** v.i. to be surfeited or sated (with, से). **2.** to be satisfied, contented. **3.** to grow tired (of). **4.** to display pride or complacency. **5.** v.t. to fill, to satisfy. **6.** to glut, to cloy.

[2]**अघाना** *aghānā* [*āghrāṇa-*], adj. sated, &c. (cf. [1]अघाना).

अघोर *a-ghor* [S.], adj. **1.** not terrible: a title of Śiva. **2.** fine, splendid (as Kṛṣṇa's flute). **3.** (reinterpretation) terrible, fearsome. **4.** name of a Śaiva community of beggars.

— अघोर-पंथ, m. the *aghor* community. °ई, m. a member of the *aghor* community; a glutton.

अघोरी *aghorī* [S.], adj. & m. **1.** adj. foul, unclean. **2.** m. = अघोर-पंथी.

अघोरीपन *aghorīpan* [cf. H. *aghorī*], m. **1.** foulness, uncleanness. **2.** greed.

अघोरीपना *aghorīpanā*, m. = अघोरीपन.

अघोष *a-ghoṣ* [S.], adj. **1.** noiseless, without sound. **2.** *ling.* voiceless.

अचंचल *a-cañcal* [S.], adj. **1.** unmoved. **2.** firm, fixed. **3.** steady, constant; not fickle, not volatile (temperament).

अचंड *a-caṇḍ* [S.], adj. not fierce; gentle; tractable.

अचंभा *acambhā* [*ācchambha-], m. **1.** astonishment; bewilderment. **2.** a wonder, a marvel. — ~ करना, to marvel (at, से), to be astonished (at). अचंभे का, adj. strange, extraordinary. अचंभे में आना, to be astonished, astounded. अचंभे में डालना, to amaze, to astonish. अचंभे होना, = अचंभे में आना.

अचंभित *acambhit* [cf. H. *acambhā*], adj. astonished, astounded; bewildered; alarmed.

अच- *ac-* [cf. H. *acav-*], v.t. Brbh. = आचमन करना.

¹अचक *acak*, f. astonishment.

²अचक *acak* [? conn. H. *cakācak*], adj. **1.** brim-full. **2.** abundant.

अचक- *acak-* [? = H. ¹*acak*], adv. suddenly: — अचक-अचानक, adv. id.

अचकचाना *ackacānā* [cf. H. ¹*acak*], v.i. **1.** to be taken aback, astonished. **2.** to start.

अचकचाहट *ackacāhaṭ* [cf. H. *ackacānā*], f. **1.** astonishment. **2.** start, shock.

अचकन *ackan*, m. f. a long, single-breasted coat.

अचक्षु *a-cakṣu* [S.], adj. without eyes; blind.

अचतुर *a-catur* [S.], adj. not clever, or cunning, &c. (see s.v. चतुर).

अचपल *a-capal* [S.], adj. not unsteady: grave, calm, still.

अचपल *acpal* [conn. *capala-*], adj. = चपल.

अचपलता *acpaltā* [conn. *capalatā-*], f. = अचपलापन.

अचपला *acpalā* [? ad. *capala-*], adj. = चपल.

अचपलापन *acpalāpan* [cf. H. *acpalā*], m. restlessness; inconstancy, &c. (cf. चपलता).

अचपली *acpalī* [cf. H. *acpal*], f. reg. playfulness; flirtatiousness.

अचर *a-car* [S.], adj. **1.** immovable. **2.** inanimate.

अचरज *acăraj* [ad. *āścarya-*], m. & adj. **1.** m. a wonder, a miracle. **2.** surprise, astonishment. **3.** adj. wonderful, remarkable; surprising. — ~ आना, or होना (को), to be astonished. ~ करना, to perform a feat, a miracle.

अचरा *acrā* [*añcala-*], m. Brbh. border, hem (of a woman's garment). (cf. अँचरा).

अचल *a-cal* [S.], adj. & m. **1.** adj. not moving; not able to move. **2.** immovable; firm; fixed. **3.** changeless; constant. **4.** m. a mountain.

अचला *a-cālā* [S.], f. the earth.

अचव- *acav-* [*ācāmati*: w. *-cc-*], v.t. Brbh. **1.** to rinse the mouth and hands before or after eating. **2.** to sip water.

अचवन *acvan* [*ācamaṇa-*: w. *-cc-*], m. **1.** rinsing the mouth and hands after eating. **2.** sipping water (= *ācaman*, 2).

अचवाना *acvānā* [cf. *ācāmati*], v.t. **1.** to cause to be rinsed (the mouth and hands, before or after eating); to rinse the mouth. **2.** to give to be drunk (by, से). **3.** to sip (water).

अचांचक *acāñcak*, adv. 19c. = अचानक.

अचाका *acākā*, adv. Av. = अचानक.

अचानक *acānak*, adv. suddenly; unexpectedly; by chance, inadvertently.

अचाना *acānā* [*ācāmati*], v.t. *Pl.* = अचवाना.

¹अचार *acār* [P. *acār*], m. pickle. — ~ करना (का), colloq. to beat severely, to make (one) smart. ~ डालना, to pickle. ~ बनाना, to make pickles; to pickle (sthg., का).

²अचार *acār*, m. Av. = आचार.

अचिंत *a-cint* [S.], adj. **1.** free of care. **2.** heedless.

अचिंतनीय *a-cintănīyă* [S.], adj. = अचिंत्य.

अचिंता *a-cintā* [S.], f. **1.** freedom from care. **2.** heedlessness, disregard.

अचिंतित *a-cintit* [S.], adj. not thought of; disregarded.

अचिंत्य *a-cintyă* [S.], adj. unimaginable, inconceivable.

अचिकित्स्य *a-cikitsyă* [S.], adj. incurable.

अचिर *a-cir* [S.], adj. **1.** not of long duration; impermanent; brief. **2.** not of long date, recent; near (future). **3.** adv. soon, quickly.

अचीता *a-cītā* [cf. H. ¹*cītnā*], adj. **1.** not thought of; not desired. **2.** [×H. *cetnā*] Brbh. free of care.

अचूक *a-cūk* [cf. H *cūknā*], adj. **1.** unfailing, unerring; faultless. **2.** certain, infallible.

अचेत *a-cet* [S.], adj. **1.** without consciousness; unconscious, fainting; inanimate, inert. **2.** thoughtless; heedless, unconcerned; not alert, inattentive; careless. **3.** not discerning; stupid.

अचेतन *a-cetan* [S.], adj. & m. **1.** adj. = अचेत, 1. **2.** subconscious. **3.** m. inert matter. **4.** the subconscious. — अचेतनावस्था [°*na*+*a*°], f. state of unconsciousness.

अचेतनता *a-cetanătā* [S.], f. unconsciousness.

अचेतपना *acetpanā* [cf. H. *acet*], m. **1.** unconsciousness. **2.** obliviousness; inattention.

अचेष्ट *a-ceṣṭ* [S.], adj. inert.

अचैतन्य *a-caitanyă* [S.], adj. & m. **1.** adj. = अचेत, 1. **2.** m. absence of consciousness: unconsciousness, faint; inanimate nature.

अचैन *a-cain* [cf. H. *cain*], adj. & m. **1.** adj. restless, uneasy. **2.** m. restlessness, &c.

अचौन *acaun* [*ācamana-*: w. *-cc-*], m. Brbh. = आचमन, or (?) आचमनी.

¹**अच्छ** *acch* [ad. *akṣi-*], f. Brbh. **1.** the eye. **2.** a rosary.

²**अच्छ** *acch*, adj. Brbh. = अच्छा.

अच्छत *acchat* [ad. *akṣata-*], m. = अक्षत.

अच्छर *acchar* [ad. *akṣara-*], m. Av. a syllable; letter, character (of script).

अच्छरी *acchrī*, f. Brbh. = अप्सरा.

अच्छा *acchā* [*accha-*¹: ← Panj.], adj. **1.** good; excellent; pleasant; fine, nice; healthy (climate, locality). **2.** serviceable; useful. **3.** sound; healthy, well; fit; recovered. **4.** genuine; unadulterated; of high quality. **5.** virtuous; kind, benevolent, humane; well-behaved. **6.** skilful (in or at, में). **7.** proper, suitable, fitting; favourable, propitious; matching (as colours). **8.** fortunate; prosperous; happy. **9.** adv. well; very well, &c. ~ गाना, to sing well. **10.** m. pl. the good: senior or distinguished men; forefathers. **11.** interj. good! very good! well! oh! is that so? all right! — ~ आना, to suit, to go with (को); to turn out well; to arrive fortuitously. ~ करना, to do good; to act well; to make well, to cure. ~ कहना, to say yes; to describe as good; to speak well (of, को). ~ लगना, to be pleasing (to, को), to please; to look well, or attractive; to become, to suit (one, को); to have a good effect. ~ होना, to recover (health); to be cured; to be in good health. अच्छी कटना, time, or life, to be well or agreeably spent (by, की). अच्छी तरह (से), adv. well, &c.; adequately; abundantly. – अच्छा-ख़ासा, adj. very good, fine; excellent.

अच्छाई *acchāī* [cf. H. *acchā*], f. **1.** good quality; excellence; beauty. **2.** use, benefit; advantage.

अच्छापन *acchāpan* [cf. H. *acchā*], m. virtue, quality; excellence.

अच्युत *a-cyut* [S.], adj. & m. not fallen: **1.** adj. fixed; imperishable, permanent; immortal; eternal. **2.** m. title of Viṣṇu, and esp. of Kr̥ṣṇa. अच्युत-कुल, m. the Vaiṣṇava community.

अछ- *ach-* [*ākṣeti*], v.i. Brbh. Av. to be, to exist; to remain; to be alive.

अछत *a-chat* [ad. **achatra-*], adj. Av. crownless (a fallen or deposed king).

अछताना-पछताना *achtānā-pachtānā* [cf. H. *pachtānā*], v.t. **1.** to repent; to regret. **2.** to grieve.

अछरी *acharī*, f. Av. = अप्सरा.

अछरौटी *achrauṭī* [conn. *akṣara-*], f. Brbh. **1.** the (Devanāgarī) alphabet or syllabary, with its sounds. **2.** *Pl.* a way of playing a stringed instrument so as to express the mood of a song.

अछवानी *achvānī* [conn. H. *ajvāyn*], f. a warm drink containing *ajvāyn*, ginger and other spices, given to women after childbirth.

अछूत *a-chūt* [*acchupta-*], adj. & m. untouched: **1.** adj. not to be touched, untouchable. **2.** m. an untouchable (caste, person). — अछूतोद्धार [°*a*+*u*°], m. improvement of the condition of the scheduled castes.

अछूता *a-chūtā* [*acchupta-*], adj. **1.** untouched; undefiled; pure; unused; virgin; not to be touched (as food for religious persons). **2.** not taken up, or tried (a topic, or activity).

अछेद *a-ched* [ad. *acchedya-*], adj. Brbh. Av. indivisible.

अछेव *a-chev* [cf. *cheda-*], adj. Brbh. = अछेद.

अछेह *acheh* [cf. *cheda-*], adj. Brbh. indivisible (= अछेद).

अजंट *ajanṭ* [Engl. *agent*], m. an agent.

अज *a-j* [S.], adj. & m. not born: a title of the self-existent deity Brahmā. — °आ, f. poet. *philos.* = प्रकृति or ¹माया, 4.

अज़ *az* [P. *az*], prep. from, of (corresponds to से in certain expressions, e.g. कम ~ कम, at least).

अज- *aj-*. Brbh. Av. = आज.

अजगर *ajăgar* [S.], m. goat-swallower: **1.** a large snake, a python. **2.** fig. a ponderous or unwieldy object.

अजगरी *ajăgarī* [cf. H. *ajgar*], f. an indolent life (as that of the python which lives on the prey which comes its way).

अजगव *ajgav* [ad. *ajagava-*], m. *mythol.* Śiva's bow.

अजगुत *ajgut* [ad. *ayukta-*], adj. & m. Brbh. **1.** adj. strange, marvellous. 2. = अयुक्त, 1., 2. **3.** m. a wondrous thing.

अजदहा *ajdahā* [P. *azhdahā*], m. = अजगर.

अजनबी *ajnabī* [A. *ajnabī*], m. & adj. **1.** m. a stranger. **2.** a foreigner. **3.** adj. strange. **4.** foreign.

अजनबीपन *ajnabīpan* [cf. H. *ajnabī*], m. strangeness; unusual characteristics.

अजनबीयत *ajnabīyat* [P. *ajnabīyat*], f. = अजनबीपन.

अजन्म *a-janm* [S.], adj. unborn, unbegotten.

अजन्मा *a-janmā* [S.], adj. inv. m. unborn, unbegotten.

अजब *ajab* [A. *'ajab*], m. & adj. **1.** m. astonishment. **2.** adj. astonishing, strange.

अज़मत *azmat* [A. *'aẓama*: P. *'aẓamat*], f. 19c. greatness; grandeur; pomp.

अजमूद *ajmūd*, m. **1.** celery. **2.** *Pl.* = अजमोद.

अजमोद *ajmod*, m. **1.** a plant resembling *ajvāyn* (its seeds are used as a spice, and medicinally). **2.** *Pl.* a type of lovage (= अजवायन).

अजमोदा *ajmodā*, m. reg. parsley.

अजय *a-jay* [S.], adj. & m. **1.** adj. not victorious. **2.** unvanquished; invincible. **3.** m. defeat.

अजर *a-jar* [S.], adj. not subject to age or decay; unchanging; ever young. — अजर-अमर, adj. changeless and immortal: a title of the supreme being. अजरामर [°*ra+a*°], adj. id.

अजरायल *ajarāyal*, adj. Brbh. = अजर.

[1]**अजल** *ajal* [A. *ajal*], f. U. death, the appointed hour of death.

[2]**अजल** *a-jal* [S.], adj. waterless. — अजलचर, adj. Brbh. not aquatic.

अजवाइन *ajvāin*, f. see अजवायन.

अजवायन *ajvāyn* [*yavānī-*], f. a type of dill (*Ligusticum ajowan*), or of lovage (*Carum copticum*), and their seeds (used medicinally).

अजस्र *a-jasră* [S.], adj. **1.** unbroken, continual; perpetual. **2.** adv. for ever.

अज़ा *azā* [A. *'azā*], f. U. mourning.

[1]**अजात** *a-jāt* [S.], adj. **1.** unborn. **2.** undeveloped.

[2]**अजात** *a-jāt* [ad. *ajāti-*], adj. & m. **1.** adj. having lost caste membership. **2.** having no caste. **3.** m. one who has lost caste membership, &c.

अजाति *a-jāti* [S.], adj. 1. = [2]अजात. **2.** of low caste status.

अजाती *ajātī* [ad. *ajāti-*], m. = [2]अजात.

अजान *a-jān* [cf. H. *jānnā*], adj & m. **1.** adj. unknowing; ignorant; simple, innocent; heedless, careless. **2.** foolish. **3.** m. an ignorant, or foolish person, &c. **4.** ignorance. — ~ में, adv. in ignorance, without realising (sthg).

अज़ान *azān* [A. *aẕān*], m. *isl.* call to prayer (esp. as chanted by a muezzin from the turret of a mosque). — ~ देना, to call to prayer; to crow (a cock).

अजानपन *a-jānpan* [cf. H. *ajān*], m. **1.** ignorance; innocence. **2.** foolishness.

अजाना *a-jānā* [cf. H. *jānnā*], adj. unknown.

अजानी *a-jānī* [cf. H. *ajān*, adj.], f. ignorance; innocence; heedlessness.

अज़ाब *azāb* [A. *'aẕāb*], m. 19c. **1.** punishment. **2.** suffering; troublesome matter.

अजायब *ajāyb* [A. *'ajā'ib*, pl.], m. pl. esp. in comp. wonders. — अजायब-ख़ाना, m. = next. अजायब-घर, m. museum.

अजार *ajār*, m. Brbh. illness, sickness (= आज़ार).

अजित *a-jit* [S.], adj. **1.** unconquered; unsurpassed. **2.** invincible.

अजिन *ajin* [S.], m. Av. the hide of an antelope, tiger, &c.

अजिर *ajir* [S.], m. Brbh. a courtyard.

अजी *ajī*, interj. **1.** expression used in calling a person's attention without mentioning his or her name. **2.** expression of astonishment, or of disapproval.

अज़ीज़ *azīz* [A. *'azīz*], adj. & m. **1.** adj. valued. ***2.** dear, beloved. **3.** m. a dear friend.

4. a relative. — ~ **जानना**, or **रखना**, to value highly; to hold dear. – **अज़ीज़दार** [P. *-dār*], m. U. a close friend or relative. °**ई**, f. close relationship.

अज़ीज़ी *azīzī* [P. *'azīzī*], f. close or affectionate relationship.

अजीत *a-jīt* [ad. *ajita-*, × *jīta-* 'oppressed'], adj. = **अजित**.

अजीब *ajīb* [A. *'ajīb*], adj. evoking wonder or admiration: **1.** extraordinary, strange. **2.** wonderful; rare, unique. — **अजीबो-ग़रीब**, adj. = ~.

अज़ीम *azīm* [A. *'aẓīm*], adj. esp. U. great, large, vast. — **अज़ीमुश्शान** [A. *-ul-śān*], adj. vast, imposing.

अजीरन *a-jīran* [ad. *ajīrṇa-*], m. = **अजीर्ण**, 3.

अजीर्ण *a-jīrṇ* [S.], adj & m. **1.** unimpaired, new, fresh; hardy, strong. **2.** unwholesome. ***3.** m. surfeit: indigestion.

अजीव *a-jīv* [S.], m. **1.** adj. lifeless. **2.** m. an inanimate object.

अजूठा *a-jūṭhā* [cf. H. *jūṭhā*], adj. untouched (food).

अजूबा *ajūbā* [A. *'ujūba*], adj. inv. & m. **1.** adj. wonderful. **2.** m. a miracle. **3.** object, or person, of great interest or admiration.

अजूरा *ajūrā* [conn. A. *ajar*; ? ← M.], m. E.H. remuneration, wages, hire (of day-labour).

अजोड़ *a-joṛ* [cf. H. *joṛnā*], adj. **1.** unjoined, disconnected. **2.** not matching; inharmonious; asymmetrical. **3.** matchless, incomparable.

[1]**अजोत** *a-jot* [cf. H. *jotnā*], adj. reg. uncultivated (land).

[2]**अजोत** *a-jot* [cf. H. [1]*jot*], adj. not bright; dull, dim.

अजौरी *ajaurī* f. *hist.* advances, esp. to farm workers.

अजौली *ajaulī*, f. *Pl.* **1.** a quantity as much as will fill the hollowed palms. **2.** gleanings from the threshing-floor.

अज्ञ *a-jñă* [S.], adj. = **अजान**.

अज्ञता *a-jñătā* [S.], f. = **अज्ञानता**.

अज्ञात *a-jñāt* [S.], adj. **1.** unknown; unexpected. **2.** unknowing; unsophisticated, simple. — **अज्ञातयौवन**, adj. f. Brbh. = next. °**आ**, adj. f. Brbh. (a girl) surprised at the symptoms of her adolescence. **अज्ञातकुल**, adj. of unknown family; of nondescript kind. **अज्ञात-वास**, m. residence in a secluded, or secret, place.

अज्ञान *a-jñān* [S.], m. & adj. **1.** m. lack of knowledge, non-cognizance; ignorance. **2.** stupidity. **3.** adj. ignorant. **4.** stupid. — **अज्ञानतः**, adv. out of ignorance; not on purpose.

अज्ञानता *a-jñānătā* [S.], f. **1.** ignorance. **2.** stupidity.

अज्ञानपन *a-jñānpan*, m. = **अज्ञान**.

अज्ञानी *a-jñānī* [S.], adj. & m. **1.** adj. ignorant. **2.** foolish. **3.** m. an ignorant person, &c.

अज्ञेय *a-jñey* [S.], adj. unknowable. — **अज्ञेयवाद**, m. agnosticism. °**ई**, m. an agnostic.

अटंबर *aṭambar*, m. Brbh. a crowd, multitude.

[1]**अट-** *aṭ-* [ad. *aṭati*], v.i. Brbh. to go about; to wander.

[2]**अट-** *aṭ-* [? f. H. *aṭaknā*], v.i. Brbh. to be sheltered.

अटक *aṭak* [cf. H. *aṭaknā*], f. **1.** obstacle, hindrance; stoppage; check, restraint. **2.** prohibition. **3.** hesitation; doubt. **4.** entanglement, liaison, affair.

अटकना *aṭaknā* [**aṭṭakk-*], v.i. **1.** to be stopped, hindered or checked; to be withheld (as pay). **2.** to hesitate, to falter (as in speech). **3.** to delay, to linger. **4.** to stick, to catch. **5.** Brbh. to be caught (by, **सौं**). **6.** to be fastened, attached (to **में** or **पर**). **7.** to be entangled, or infatuated (with or by, **से**); to have an affair (with, **से**). **8.** fig. to be dependent (on, **से**); to be under the control (of).

अटकर *aṭkar*, f. Brbh. = **अटकल**.

अटकल *aṭkal* [**aṭṭakkalā-*], f. guessing (at sthg.); an unsupported estimate, conjecture. — ~ **लगाना**, to make a guess, &c. (at, as to, **पर**). ~ **से**, adv. by guess; at random; approximately. – **अटकल-पच्ची**, adj. & m. = next. **अटकल-पच्चू**, adj. & m. random, conjectural (a statement or guess); a conjecture; adv. by guess; at random. **अटकलबाज़** [P. *-bāz*], adj. shrewd. °**ई**, f. shrewdness; a guess, conjecture.

अटकलना *aṭkalnā*, v.t. = **अटकल करना**.

[1]**अटका** *aṭkā*, m. = **अटक**.

[2]**अटका** *aṭkā*, m. **1.** *Pl.* earthen vessel in which food is prepared for the public at the door of the Jagannāth temple in Puri. **2.** transf. *HŚS.* cooked rice or money offered at the temple of Jagannāth.

अटकाना *aṭkānā* [cf. H. *aṭaknā*], v.t. to cause to stick or to be caught: **1.** to obstruct, to hinder; to stop, to check, &c. **2.** to postpone. **3.** to fasten, to join. — **टाई अटकाए होना**, to wear a tie undone; to sport a tie. रोड़ा ~, to put a stumbling-block in (one's) way.

अटकाव *aṭkāv* [cf. H. *aṭkānā*], m. **1.** obstruction, hindrance; prevention; restraint. **2.** postponement.

अटन *aṭan* [S.], m. going about, wandering; journey, travels.

अटना *aṭnā* [conn. *aṭṭ-[1]], v.i. **1.** to be held or contained (in, में); to go or to fit (into). **2.** to be filled up.

अटपट *aṭpaṭ*, adj. & f. **1.** adj. agitated, confused, restless. **2.** incoherent, disjointed; nonsensical. **3.** f. random remarks. **4.** nonsense. — ~ बोलना, or बकना, to speak at random, &c.

अटपटाँग *aṭpaṭāṁg* [cf. H. *aṭpaṭ*], adj. = ऊटपटाँग.

अटपटा *aṭpaṭā*, adj. = अटपट.

अटपटाना *aṭpaṭānā*, v.i. **1.** to be agitated; to be confused, restless; to be tired; **2.** to hesitate, to delay. **3.** to speak incoherently; to talk nonsense.

अटपटी *aṭpaṭī*, f. Brbh. naughtiness.

अटम *aṭam*, m. heap, pile.

अटम-पटम *aṭam-paṭam*, adj. colloq. inappropriate (as words, dress).

अटल *a-ṭal* [cf. H. *ṭalnā*], adj. **1.** immovable; firm; stationary; permanent. **2.** not to be moved or shaken; inviolable, ineluctable (as a law). **3.** unwavering, steadfast (in, पर); resolute; stubborn; inflexible.

अटवाटी-खटवाटी *aṭvāṭī-khaṭvāṭī*, f. *Pl. HŚS.* bed and belongings. — ~ लेकर पड़ना, to take to one's bed (in a sulk).

अटवी *aṭavī* [S.], f. grove, forest; wild region.

अट-सट *aṭ-saṭ*, adj. & m. = अट्ट-सट्ट.

अटा *aṭā* [*aṭṭa-*[2]: Pk. *aṭṭa-*], m. **1.** reg. (W.) heap, pile. **2.** an upper room (= अटारी).

अटाटूट *aṭāṭūṭ* [H. *aṭnā*, H. *aṭūṭ*], adj. also transf. unbroken.

अटाना *aṭānā* [cf. *aṭṭ-[1]], v.t. to fix or to fit (into, में); to fasten (on, में), to join (to).

अटारी *aṭārī* [*aṭṭālikā-*], f. **1.** an upper room or building on the roof of a house; pent-house; attic. **2.** balcony.

अटाल *aṭal* [*aṭṭala-*], m. reg. (W.) heap, pile (as of grain).

अटाला *aṭālā* [*aṭṭāla-*], m. pile: goods, miscellaneous effects; lumber.

अटिया *aṭiyā* [cf. H. *aṭā*], f. dimin. a small thatched room on the roof of a house.

अटूट *a-ṭūṭ* [cf. H. *ṭūṭnā*], adj. **1.** unbroken. **2.** unbreakable. **3.** inexhaustible; unfailing, continuous.

अटेक *a-ṭek* [cf. H. *ṭek*], adj. unsupported.

अटेरन *aṭeran* [*āvr̥ttikaraṇa-*], m. a hollow stick or reed on which thread is wound before spinning; reel, bobbin, distaff. — ~ कर देना, colloq. to give no rest (to); to make (one) thin (see next). ~ हो जाना, to become as thin as a rake.

अटेरना *aṭernā* [cf. *āvr̥ttikara-*], v.t. to wind thread, to make skeins of thread.

अटोक *a-ṭok* [cf. H. *ṭoknā*], adj. Brbh. **1.** unencumbered (an entrance). **2.** uninterrupted, unbroken (activity).

अट्ट *aṭṭ* [S.], m. = अट्टालिका.

अट्ट-सट्ट *aṭṭ-saṭṭ* [cf. H. *aṇṭ*], adj. & m. **1.** adj. confused, &c. (= ऊटपटाँग). **2.** incoherent; nonsensical. **3.** m. nonsense.

अट्टहास *aṭṭăhās* [S.], m. loud laughter; a belly-laugh.

अट्टा *aṭṭā* [*aṭṭa-*[2]], m. an upper room; attic.

अट्टालिका *aṭṭālikā* [S.], f. **1.** a high, imposing building. 2. = अटारी.

अट्टी *aṭṭī* [*aṭṭa-*[3]], f. **1.** a bundle, hank, skein. **2.** a sheaf.

अट्ठा *aṭṭhā* [*aṣṭaka-*], m. an aggregate of eight; an eight (as in cards or at dice).

अट्ठाईस *aṭṭhāīs* [*aṣṭāviṁśati-*], adj. twenty-eight.

अट्ठानवे *aṭṭhānve* [*aṣṭānavati-*], adj. ninety-eight.

अट्ठावन *aṭṭhāvan* [*aṣṭāpañcāśat-*], adj. fifty-eight.

अट्ठासी *aṭṭhāsī* [*aṣṭāśīti-*], adj. eighty-eight.

अठ- *aṭh-*, adj. eight: — अठकोन, adj. Brbh. = next. अठकोनी, adj. octangular. अठगुना, adj. eight-fold. अठ-ताल, m. Brbh. a musical measure. अठन्नी, f. an eight-anna piece, half a rupee. अठपहरी, m. one constantly on duty (as watching over crops). अठपूष्ठी, adj. = next. अठपेजी, adj. octavo. अठमाशी, f. a weight of eight *māśās*; a gold coin weighing eight *māshās*. अठमासा, adj. & m. of eight months; a child born after eight months; a ceremony held in the eighth month of pregnancy. अठवाँसा, adj. & m. id. अठवाड़ा, m. = next. अठवारा, m. the eighth day following; a period of eight days, a week.

अठखेलपन *aṭhkhelpan* [cf. H. *aṭhkhelī*], m. playfulness, &c; flirtatiousness.

अठखेलपना *aṭhkhelpanā*, m. = अठखेलपन.

अठखेली *aṭhkhelī*, f. **1.** playfulness, merry-making. **2.** a flirtatious act or gesture; pl. airs, graces. — **अठखेलियाँ करना**, to disport (oneself); to flirt.

अठन्नी *aṭhannī*, f. see s.v. अठ-.

अठल *aṭhal*, m. *Pl.* the act and the ceremony of bathing a bride and bridegroom on the third day after marriage.

अठवारा *aṭhvārā*, m. see s.v. अठ-.

अठहत्तर *aṭhhattar* [*aṣṭāsaptati-*], adj. seventy-eight.

अठारह *aṭhārah* [cf. *aṣṭādaśa-*], adj. eighteen.

अठारहवाँ *aṭhārahvāṁ* [cf. H. *aṭhārah*], adj. eighteenth.

अठेल *a-ṭhel* [cf. H. *ṭhelnā*], adj. not to be pushed out of place, or pushed about; firm, stalwart.

अठौड़ी *aṭhauṛī* [cf. *aṣṭapada-*], f. reg. a tick or similar parasite.

अड़ँग-तड़ँग *aṛaṁg-taṛaṁg*, f. *Pl.* nonsensical talk, gibberish; folly.

अड़ँग-बड़ँग *aṛaṁg-baṛaṁg*, adj. E.H. at odds, incoherent (the mind or spirit).

अड़ंगा *aṛaṅgā*, m. **1.** tripping with the leg (in wrestling). **2.** an obstruction, obstacle. **3.** interference. — **~ डालना**, or **लगाना** (**में**), to place an obstacle (in the way of), to hinder. **~ मारना**, or **लगाना**, to trip up; to create obstacles. **अड़ंगे पर चढ़ाना**, to bring into a vulnerable position, to gain an advantage over. **अड़ंगे पर मारना**, or **दे मारना**, to throw (one), to trip (one). – **अड़ंगेबाज़** [P. *-bāz*], m. an obstructive, or interfering person. °**ई**, f. obstructiveness.

अड़ *aṛ* [cf. H. *aṛnā*: ← Drav.], f. **1.** obstinacy; contention, dispute. **2.** fig. obstruction, stoppage; barrier (cf. **आड़**, 2). — **~ पकड़ना**, to grow, or to be, stubborn; to be obstructive. – **अड़दार** [P. *-dār*], adj. stubborn.

अड़गोड़ा *aṛgoṛā* [H. *āṛ*+H. *goṛā*], m. reg. (W.) a piece of wood tied to the neck of cattle (to prevent them straying).

अड़चन *aṛcan*, f. obstacle, hindrance, difficulty (in the matter of, **में**).

अड़चल *aṛcal*, f. reg. (Raj.) = **अड़चन**.

अड़ड़ाना *aṛṛānā*, m. = **अरराना**.

अड़तालीस *aṛtālīs* [*aṣṭācatvāriṁśat-*], adj. forty-eight.

अड़तीस *aṛtīs* [*aṣṭātriṁśat-*], adj. thirty-eight.

अड़ना *aṛnā* [**aḍ-*], v.i. **1.** to come to a stop, to stop; to stick. **2.** to be obstinate; to jib; to be obstructive. **3.** to intervene, to interfere (in, **में**). **4.** to be determined (on, **पर**). **5.** to be or to become jammed, locked, wedged, or entangled. **6.** to knock, to jostle (against, **से**). **7.** to be in pawn. — **अड़-फँसकर रहना**, to be unresolved (a matter).

अड़प-झड़प *aṛap-jhaṛap* [cf. H. *jhaṛapnā*], f. a scuffle, tussle; scramble.

अड़बंगा *aṛbaṅgā* [cf. H. *aṛ*; *vaṅka-*[1]], adj. & m. Brbh. **1.** adj. crooked, uneven; contrary, perverse. **2.** m. obstruction, obstacle.

अड़बंद *aṛband*, m. E.H. = **आड़बंद**.

अडर-उडर *aḍar-uḍar* [conn. H. *āṛ*], m. reg. ditch and mound (forming a field boundary).

अड़वा *aṛvā*, m. E.H. a scarecrow.

अड़वाड़ *aṛvāṛ*, m. reg. a thick beam or pillar for supporting a roof.

अडसट्टा *aḍsaṭṭā*, m. *hist.* (W.) estimate, rough calculation, &c. (see **अरसट्टा**).

अड़सठ *aṛsaṭh* [*aṣṭāṣaṣṭi-*], adj. sixty-eight.

अड़हाया *aṛ'hāyā*, m. *Pl.* weeds, tares; oats.

अड़हुल *aṛ'hul*, m. the shoe-flower, *Hibiscus syriacus.*

अड़ा *aṛā* [cf. **aḍḍ-*: ← Drav.], m. Av. a birds' perch, roost.

[1]**अड़ाड़** *aṛāṛ* [conn. H. *aṛrānā*, *arrānā*], ? f. crashing or rumbling sound.

[2]**अड़ाड़** *aṛāṛ* [? conn. **aḍ(ḍ)-* (← Drav.): H. *aṛnā*], m. reg. an enclosure or shelter in shrub or jungle country where cattle are collected overnight, or where *mahuā* flowers are collected and dried.

अड़ाना *aṛānā* [cf. H. *aṛnā*], v.t. **1.** to cause to stop; to stop, to check; to obstruct. **2.** to ram, to thrust (into, **में**); to push, to shove (against, **से**). **3.** to stop up, to plug, to cork. **4.** to jam, to wedge (objects together); to give support to. **5.** to use pressure or force; to compel. **6.** to suspend, to postpone. — **अड़ाकर**, adv. by force.

[1]**अड़ार** *aṛār* [? conn. *aṭṭāla-*], m. Brbh. Av. a heap, pile.

[2]**अड़ार** *aṛār*, ? m. reg. (Bihar) **1.** a cattle-enclosure (= [2]**अड़ाड़**). **2.** pasture-land.

अड़ारी *aṛārī*, f. dimin. Brbh. heap, pile, mass (cf. [1]*aṛār*).

अडिग *a-ḍig* [cf. H. *ḍignā*], adj. immovable, unshakable; firm.

अड़ियल *aṛiyal* [cf. H. *aṛnā*], adj. **1.** obstinate, stubborn; obstructive, perverse. **2.** lazy.

अड़ी *aṛī* [cf. H. *aṛnā*], f. E.H. a check, stop, halt.

अड़ुआ *aṛuā*, adj. reg. (W.) obstinate, mulish; jibbing (as a horse); (= अड़ियल).

अड़सा *aṛusā* [*aṭaruṣaka-*], m. a shrub, *Adhatoda vasica*, used medicinally (= [2]रूस).

अड़ैंच *aṛaiṁc*, f. **1.** perversity. **2.** obstacle; objection. **3.** dislike, antipathy. — ~ निकालना (में), to throw obstacles (in the way); to object (to); to find fault (with). ~ रखना (से), to have dislike, &c. (for); to bear a grudge (against).

अडोल *a-ḍol* [cf. H. *ḍolnā*], adj. not shaking or swinging; motionless; firm, unshaken.

अड़ोस-पड़ोस *aṛos-paṛos* [cf. *prativeśa-*], m. & adv. **1.** m. neighbourhood, vicinity. **2.** adv. nearby.

अड़ोसी-पड़ोसी *aṛosī-paṛosī* [cf. **prativeśiya-*], m. a neighbour.

अढ़तिया *aṛhatiyā*, pronun. var. = आढ़तिया.

अड्डा *aḍḍā* [cf. **aḍḍ-*: ← Drav.], m. **1.** a place or an area serving a particular purpose: meeting-place; working-place, site; stand, station (vehicles); stall (vendors'); centre; an airfield; airport; field (of battle). **2.** *mil.* a base. **3.** a perching-place, perch (birds). **4.** square frame for embroidery. — ~ जमाना, to settle down (in a place); to take up a position.

अढ़ाई *aṛhāī* [*ardhatr̥tīya-*], adj. **1.** two and a half (= ढाई). **2.** (with सौ, हज़ार, and higher nouns of number) two and a half times.

अढाना *aḍhānā*, m. *Pl.* name of a *rāgiṇī*.

अढ़िया *aṛhiyā* m. reg. (Bihar) a small vessel of wood, metal or stone.

अढ़ैया *aṛhaiyā* [cf. H. *aṛhāī*], f. m. **1.** a weight or measure of two and a half seers. **2.** the two and a half times multiplication table.

अढ़ौना *aṛhaunā* [cf. *ādhāpayati*], m. reg. (E.) an assigned task.

अणि *aṇi* [S.], f. point or edge of a sharp instrument or weapon.

अणिमा *aṇimā* [S.], f. (m., *Pl.*). the power of making oneself infinitesimally small; state of invisibility (as assumed by a god, or attainable by austerities or by magic).

अणु *aṇu* [S.], m. & adj. **1.** m. a particle, fragment, tiny amount; speck. **2.** an atom. **3.** a molecule. **4.** adj. minute, microscopic. — अणु-कण, m. particle; *biol.* corpuscle. अणुगत, adj. atomic. अणु-चालित, adj. driven by atomic energy. अणु-जीव, m. a microbe: = जीवाणु. °विज्ञान, m. microbiology. अणु-जैविकी, f. id. अणु-तरंग, adj. *techn.* micro-wave. अणु-परमाणु, m. = ~, 1., 2. अणुबद्ध, adj. atomic (as a reaction). अणु-बम, m. atomic bomb. अणु-भट्टी, f. atomic reactor. अणुवाद, m. *philos.* atomism; *vaiśeṣika* doctrine. °ई, m. & adj. an atomist, &c. अणु-वीक्षण, m. minutest scrutiny. अणवस्त्र [°*ṇu*+*ā*°], m. atomic weapon. अणु-शक्ति, f. atomic energy.

अणुक *aṇuk* [S.], adj. **1.** minute, microscopic. **2.** atomic.

-अत *-at* [A. *-a(t)*: P. *-at*], suffix (forms f. abstract nouns, e.g. तबीयत, state of health).

अत- *at-*, adj. E.H. = इतना.

अतत्ताही *atattāhī*, m. pronun. var. *Pl.* = आततायी.

अतनु *a-tanu* [S.], m. **1.** adj. bodiless. **2.** the bodiless one: Kāmdev, the god of love.

अतर *atar*, m. = इत्र.

अतरपाल *atarpāl* [? cf. *antara-*], m. *hist.* E. land formerly cultivated, then abandoned.

अतरसों *atarsoṁ* [**ātriśvas*], adv. in three days' time; three days ago.

अतर्क *a-tark* [S.], adj. illogical. — ~ वर्णव्यवस्था, f. illogical arrangement or disposition (as of items of clothing).

अतर्क्य *a-tarkyā* [S.], adj. beyond thought or reason (as the supreme being).

अतल *a-tal* [S.], adj. & m. **1.** adj. bottomless; unfathomable. **2.** m. depth, depths. **3.** *mythol.* one of the seven *pātālas*, subterrestrial regions.

अतलस *atlas* [A. *aṭlas*], f. m. satin.

अतलसी *atlasī* [A. *aṭlasī*], adj. *Pl.* made of satin; like satin.

अतसी *atsī* [S.], f. Brbh. flax. — ~ कुसुम, m. the blue flower of flax.

अता *atā* [A. *'aṭā*], f. U. gift, grant. — ~ करना, or फ़रमाना, to give (to), to grant.

[1]**अताई** *atāī*, f. pronun. var. = आततायी.

[2]**अताई** *atāī* [P. *'aṭā'ī*], m. 19c. a self-taught singer, musician or dancer.

अता-पता *atā-patā* [f. H. *patā*], m. colloq. **1.** whereabouts. **2.** trace, track; clue.

अति *ati* [S.], adj. & f. chiefly in comp. **1.** adj. very much, very great. **2.** excessive. अत्युत्पादन, m. over-production. **3.** beyond (in point of time or place). अतीत, adj. past, former, beyond (see hw). **4.** f. excess, immoderateness.

अतिकाय *ati-kāy* [S.], adj. of huge size, gigantic.

अतिकाल *ati-kāl* [S.], m. Brbh. protracted time.

अतिक्रमण *ati-kramaṇ* [S.], m. going beyond: transgression.

अतिचार *ati-cār* [S.], m. **1.** rapid motion (as of a planet). **2.** excessive motion; unwarranted behaviour, transgression; trespass.

अतिजीवन *ati-jīvan* [S.], m. very long life; survival.

अतिजीवित *ati-jīvit* [S.], adj. = अतिजीवी.

अतिजीवी *ati-jīvī* [S.], adj. & m. **1.** adj. living very long; surviving. **2.** m. one who lives very long; a survivor.

अतिथि *atithi* [S.], m. a guest. — अतिथि-गृह, m. = अतिथि-शाला. अतिथि-धर्म, m. the obligations of hospitality. अतिथि-पूजा, f. guest-worship: fitting hospitality. अतिथि-शाला, f. accommodation for guests, a guest-house. अतिथि-सत्कार, m. honourable treatment of a guest: hospitality. अतिथि-सेवा, f. attention paid to a guest, hospitality. °-सेवी, adj. hospitable.

अतिदान *ati-dān* [S.], m. **1.** a munificent gift. **2.** munificence.

अतिपातक *ati-pātak* [S.], m. a heinous sin, or crime.

अतिबल *ati-bal* [S.], adj. very powerful.

अतिबार *ati-bār* [S.], adv. very frequently.

अतिबेल *ati-bel* [*ati*+*velā*-], adj. *Pl. HŚS.* extreme, excessive, unlimited.

अतिभार *ati-bhār* [S.], m. great, or excessive, burden.

अतिरंजन *ati-rañjan* [S.], m. exaggeration.

अतिरंजित *ati-rañjit* [S.], adj. exaggerated.

अतिरिक्त *ati-rikt* [S.], adj. **1.** exceeding, extra; additionally; reserve. **2.** excessive; surplus. **3.** adv. in addition (to, के); apart (from).

अतिरेक *ati-rek* [S.], m. excess, surplus.

अतिरोग *ati-rog* [S.], m. *Pl. HŚS.* tuberculosis.

अतिवक्ता *ati-vaktā* [S.], m. inv. a great talker, loquacious person.

अतिवाद *ati-vād* [S.], m. extremism.

अतिवादी *ati-vādī* [S.], adj. & m. extremist.

अतिवानी *ativānī*, adj. Av. very much, extreme.

अतिविष *ati-viṣ* [S.], m. an antidote to poison (= निरबिसी).

अतिशय *ati-śay* [S.], adj. & m. **1.** adj. very much. **2.** excessive. **3.** m. excess, extra. — अतिशयार्थक [°*ya*+*a*°], adj. *gram.* intensive. अतिशयोक्ति [°*ya*+*u*°], f. exaggeration; hyperbole.

अतिशयता *ati-śayătā* [S.], f. **1.** abundance. **2.** excess.

अतिशयी *ati-śayī* [S.], adj. abundant; vast; pre-eminent.

अतिशीत *ati-śīt* [S.], adj. excessively; unbearably cold.

अतिशीतन *ati-śītan* [S.], m. super-cooling.

अतिसार *ati-sār* [S.], m. dysentery; diarrhoea.

अतींद्रिय *atīndriyă* [S.], adj. & m. **1.** adj. beyond the range of the senses; metaphysical; supernatural; ineffable. **2.** m. the soul.

अतीत *atît* [S.], adj. & m. **1.** adj. past, elapsed. **2.** former. **3.** detached, free (from, से). **4.** in comp. beyond, surpassing. गुनातीत, adj. Brbh. *philos.* beyond the *guṇas* or constituents of the phenomenal world (the supreme being). **5.** beyond, ahead (of, के). **6.** m. the past. **7.** Brbh. *philos.* that which is beyond knowledge, the supreme being. **8.** E.H. an ascetic.

अतीत- *atīt-* [cf. *atīta*-], v.i. E.H. to elapse.

अतीव *atîv* [S.], adj. extreme; excessive.

अतीस *atīs*, m. an aconite, *A. heterophyllum*, or *palmatum*, and its root (used medicinally).

अतुरा- *aturā-* [ad. *ātura*-], v.i. Brbh. to be restless, impatient, &c.

अतुराई *aturāī*, f. Brbh. = आतुरता.

अतुल *a-tul* [S.], adj. unweighed, or unweighable: immeasurable; unequalled, incomparable.

अतुलनीय *a-tulănīyă* [S.], adj. = अतुल.

अतुलित *a-tulit* [S.], adj. = अतुल.

अतुल्य *a-tulyă* [S.], adj. **1.** unweighable; immeasurable; unequalled, incomparable. **2.** dissimilar.

अतृप्त *a-tṛpt* [S.], adj. **1.** unsatisfied; restless. **2.** dissatisfied.

अतृप्ति *a-tṛpti* [S.], f. **1.** lack of satisfaction or fulfilment; restlessness. **2.** dissatisfaction.

अतोल *a-tol* [cf. H. *tolnā*], adj. = अतुल.

अत्तार *attār* [A. *'aṭṭār*], m. **1.** perfume-seller. **2.** druggist.

अत्तारी *attārī* [P. *'aṭṭārī*], f. the business of a perfume-seller or druggist.

अत्यंत *aty-ant* [S.], adj. **1.** extreme; vast; excessive. **2.** endless. ***3.** adv. extremely, &c.

अत्यंतता *aty-antătā* [S.], f. extremeness; superabundance, excess (= अत्यधिकता).

अत्यधिक *aty-adhik* [S.], adj. very much; extreme; excessive.

अत्यधिकता *aty-adhikătā* [S.], f. superabundance, excess.

अत्यय *aty-ay* [S.], m. passing away; death.

अत्यर्थ *aty-arth* [S.], adj. exorbitant, excessive.

अत्यल्प *aty-alp* [S.], adj. very little, very few, very small.

अत्याचार *aty-ā-cār* [S.], m. **1.** transgression (of rules, propriety). **2.** excess, outrageous action; atrocity. **3.** tyranny.

अत्याचारी *aty-ā-cārī* [S.], adj. & m. **1.** adj. tyrannical, oppressive. **2.** m. a tyrant; oppressor.

अत्यानंद *aty-ā-nand* [S.], m. ineffable bliss, ecstasy.

अत्यावश्यक *aty-āvaśyak* [S.], adj. vitally important; extremely urgent.

अत्युक्ति *aty-ukti* [S.], f. exaggeration; hyperbole.

अत्युत्तम *aty-uttam* [S.], adj. exceedingly good, the very best.

अथ *ath* [S.], adv. & m. **1.** adv. thus, so, further. **2.** m. beginning. — ~ से अंत तक, from beginning to end. – अथच [← B.], adv. poet. however. अथवा, adv. see s.v.

अथक *a-thak* [cf. H. *thakna*], adj. **1.** unwearied. **2.** unwearying, vigilant. **3.** indefatigable.

अथमना *athamnā* [*astamayana-*: w. H. *athava-*; *-m-* ad.], m. *Pl. HŚS.* sunset; the west.

अथर्वनी *atharvănī* [ad. *atharvaṇi-*], m. E.H. a brāhmaṇ versed in the Atharva Veda.

अथव- *athava-* [cf. *asta-*], v.i. Brbh. Av. to set (the sun).

अथवा *athăvā* [S.], conj. or.

अथाई *athāī* [*āsthāyikā-*, Pk. *atthāiyā-*], f. Brbh. Av. a meeting-place, place for conversation or discussion.

अथाह *a-thāh* [*asthāgha-*], adj. & m. **1.** adj. bottomless, unplumbed. **2.** beyond a man's depth, unfordable (water, a river). **3.** fig. imponderable. **4.** m. a depth, abyss.

अथित *a-thit* [ad. *sthita-*], adj. *Pl.* unsteady; wavering.

अथिर *a-thir* [ad. *asthira-*], adj. E.H. unfixed, vacillating.

अदंड *a-daṇḍ* [S.], adj. not deserving, or exempt from, punishment; unpunished.

अदंडनीय *a-daṇḍănīyă* [S.], adj. not to be punished.

अदंड्य *a-daṇḍyă* [S.], adj. = अदंडनीय.

अदत्त *a-datt* [S.], adj. **1.** not given. **2.** not properly given: unjustly given; unpaid for.

अदद *adad* [A. *'adad*], m. **1.** a number; a figure. **2.** a unit, piece (of a type of object).

अदना *adnā* [A. *adnā*], adj. (inv., U.) lower, lowest: **1.** low. **2.** humble, insignificant; trifling. **3.** mean, base.

अदब *adab* [A. *adab*], m. **1.** good manners, politeness; civility; urbanity. **2.** belles-lettres. — ~ करना, to show deference or respect (to, का). ~ दिखाना (को), id. ~ से, adv. politely; respectfully.

अदबदकर *adbadkar* adv. 19c. = अदबदाकर, see s.v. अदबदाना.

अदबदाना *adbadānā*, v.i. to be agitated, uneasy, to be perplexed; to waver. — अदबदाकर, adv. uneasily; helplessly; certainly, definitely.

अदम *adam* [A. *'adam*], m. U. lack, want: non-existence.

अदम्य *a-damyă* [S.], adj. irrepressible.

अदय *a-day* [S.], adj. merciless, unfeeling, cruel.

अदरक *adrak* [ad. *ārdraka-*], m. green ginger.

अदरकी *adrakī* [cf. H. *adrak*], f. *Pl. HŚS.* ginger pieces cooked in sugar.

अदरख *adrakh*, m. = अदरक.

अदरावन *adrāvan* [conn. H. *ādar*], m. reg. (E.) conciliation, persuasion (of another, to do sthg).

अदर्श *a-darś* [S.], adj. unseen.

अदर्शन *a-darśan* [S.], m. **1.** invisibility, non-appearance. **2.** disappearance.

अदल *adal* [A. *'adl*], m. Av. justice.

अदल-बदल *adal-badal* [cf. H. *badal*], m. = अदला-बदला.

अदला-बदला *adlā-badlā*, f. = अदला-बदली.

अदला-बदली *adlā-badlī* [cf. H. *badalnā*], m. & adv. **1.** m. exchange, interchange; substitution; transfer. **2.** alteration; transmutation. **3.** bartering. **4.** sthg. given in exchange. **5.** vice versa. — ~ करना, to exchange, &c.; ~ करके, adv. making changes; making due changes, *mutatis mutandis*.

अदली-बदली *adlī-badlī*, f. = अदला-बदली.

अदवाइन *advāin*, f. = अदवान.

अदवान *advān* [*antadāmanī-; ← Panj.], f. the strings at the foot of a bedstead, by which the cross-strings are tightened or braced. — ~ कसना or खींचना, to tighten the strings of a bedstead.

अदहन *ad'han*, m. water being heated, or boiling, for cooking.

अदा *adā* [A. *adā*], f. **1.** completing, performing; fulfilling. **2.** due payment (as of a debt, a rent; or of a wage). **3.** grace, elegance, charm; accomplishment. **4.** flirtatious gestures or manner. — ~ करना, to perform, to accomplish (a task, a duty); to fulfil (an obligation); to discharge (as a debt); to pay out; to perform in due manner, to observe (a form, a ritual). - अदाकार, m. one who performs, accomplishes: an actor; artist. °ई, f. (manner of) performing, performance.

अदाता *a-dātā* [S.], adj. m. inv. not a giver: niggardly, mean.

अदानी *a-dānī* [S.], adj. not generous, miserly (= अदाता).

अदायगी *adāygī* [A. *adā*+P. *-gī*], f. 1. = अदा, 2. **2.** a charge made, a levy. **3.** due observance (of a custom). — नमक की ~, f. payment in kind.

अदालत *adālat* [A. *'adāla*: P. *'adālat*], f. court of law. — ~ करना, to take (a matter) to court, to use the courts; colloq. to try (cases, suits). ~ के ज़रिए से, adv. judicially; by a power of the court. दीवानी ~, f. civil court. फ़ौजदारी ~, f. criminal court. फ़ौजी ~, f. a military court. – अदालत-अपील, f. appeal court. अदालतबाज़ी [P. -*bāzī*], f. litigiousness.

अदालती *adālătī* [A. *'adālatī*], adj. **1.** judicial, legal. **2.** civil (marriage). **3.** actionable (a matter).

अदावत *adāvat* [A. *'adāva*: P. *'adāvat*], f. malice, ill-will; hatred. — ~ रखना, to bear ill-will, &c. (to, से, के साथ). ~ से, adv. maliciously.

अदावती *adāvătī* [A. *'adāvatī*], adj. malicious; hostile.

अदिति *a-diti* [S.], f. *mythol.* free, boundless: **1.** name of a goddess. **2.** the earth.

अदिन *a-din* [S.], m. an inauspicious or unlucky day; a time of misfortune.

अदिष्ट *a-diṣṭ* [ad. *adr̥ṣṭa-*], m. Brbh. fate; misfortune.

अदिस्टि *a-disṭi* [ad. *adr̥ṣṭi-*], adj. Av. invisible.

अदृढ़ *a-dr̥ṛh* [ad. *adr̥ḍha-*], adj. not firm or fixed, &c. (see दृढ़).

अदृश्य *a-dr̥śyă* [S.], adj. not to be seen, invisible; unperceived.

अदृश्यता *a-dr̥śyătā* [S.], f. invisibility.

अदृष्ट *a-dr̥ṣṭ* [S.], adj. & m. **1.** adj. unseen; invisible; vanished. **2.** m. sthg. unforeseen (as a danger, calamity). **3.** fate. — अदृष्टफल, adj. having consequences not yet evident.

अदेय *a-dey* [S.], adj. not to be given, or transferred; improper or unfit to be given.

अदेस *ades* [ad. *ādeśa-*], m. Av. respectful greeting (cf. आदेश, 3).

अदोष *a-doṣ* [S.], adj. **1.** faultless. **2.** guiltless, blameless; irreproachable.

अदौड़ी *adauṛī* [*ārdrakavaṭikā-], f. small lumps of pulse and spices fried in *ghī* and dried in the sun (used in curries).

अदौरी *adaurī*, f. = अदौड़ी.

अद्धा *addhā* [*arddha-*], m. a half: **1.** a half-bottle; a drink. **2.** a half piece. **3.** counterfoil (of a document). **4.** a half-hour chime.

अद्धी *addhī* [cf. *ardha-*], f. half a *damṛī* (an old coin of nominal value), or half a *pāī*; fig. a farthing.

अद्भुत *adbhut* [S.], adj. & m. **1.** adj. wonderful, astonishing, remarkable. **2.** strange; supernatural. **3.** m. surprise. **4.** a wonder, a marvel. — अद्भुत-कर्मा, m. inv. a performer of miracles. अद्भुत-रस, m. *rhet.* the savour, or mood, of wonder (as characterising a literary work or passage).

अद्भुतत्व *adbhutatvă* [S.], m. **1.** wondrous quality, &c. (see अद्भुत). **2.** strangeness.

अद्य *adyă* [S.], adv. today; now. — अद्यापि [°*ya*+*a*°], adv. 19c. even today, up until today. अद्यावधि [°*ya*+*a*°], adv. even today.

अद्यतन *adyatan* [S.], adj. **1.** of today. **2.** of the present time; up-to-date.

अद्रि *adri* [S.], m. **1.** rock, stone. **2.** mountain.

अद्रोह *a-droh* [S.], m. absence of ill-will, or enmity; peaceability; moderation.

अद्रोही *a-drohī* [S.], adj. & m. **1.** adj. peaceable, moderate. **2.** innocuous. **3.** m. a peaceable person, &c.

अद्वितीय *a-dvitīyă* [S.], adj. without a second: **1.** unique. **2.** unequalled, incomparable. **3.** supreme (a deity, or the ultimate *brāhmaṇ*).

अद्वेष *a-dveṣ* [S.], adj. & m. **1.** adj. not having ill-will. **2.** m. peaceableness, good will.

अद्वेषी *a-dveṣī* [S.], adj. = अद्वेष.

अद्वैत *a-dvait* [S.], adj. & m. **1.** adj. = अद्वितीय. ***2.** m. *philos.* non-duality; monism. — अद्वैतवाद, m. = ~, 2. °ई, adj. & m. monistic; a monist.

अधः- *adhaḥ-* [S.], pref. down, downward, below. — अधःपतन, m. falling down: decline; degenerate state. °-पतित, adj. in decline; degenerate. अधःपात m. = अधःपतन.

[1]**अध-** *adh-* [*arddha-*], adj. half: — अधकच्चरा, adj. raw, green; under-cooked; immature; undeveloped, uneducated. अधकट, adj. half worn-out. अधकपारी [cf. *kapāla-*], f. migraine. अधकहा, adj. half-told; spoken *sotto voce*. अधखिला, adj. half-open (as a flower); half-developed. अधखुला, adj. half-opened (as a door); half-developed, immature. अधगला, adj. half-cooked. अधगोहुआँ, adj. a mixture of half wheat and half barley. अधचक्कर, m. a semi-circle. अधचंद्र, adj. a half-moon; crescent. अधचरा, adj. half-grazed. अधजमा, adj. half-frozen (water); half-set (as jelly, or cement). अधजल, adj. half-full of water. अधजला, half-burnt. अधनंगा, adj. half-naked. अधन्ना, m. a half anna (copper). °ई, f. a half anna (nickel). अध-पई, f. a weight of half a *pāv*. अधपका, adj. half-ripe; half-cooked; immature. अधपक्का, adj. id. अधपेट, adj. half the stomach: half-fed. अधपेट खाना, not to get enough to eat. अधपौवा, m. = अध-पई. अधबँहिया, adj. inv. short-sleeved. अधबना, adj. half-made; half-formed, incomplete. अधबर, adv. 19c. half-way, midway; in the middle. अधबीच, adv. id.; during completion. अधमना, m. a weight of half a maund (twenty seers). अधमरा, or -मुआ, adj. half-dead. अधसेरा, m. a weight of half a seer.

[2]**अध-** *adh-*, adj. = अधस्-, अधः-, अधो-. — अधगो, m. Av. sexual drive; sensual impulses.

अधन *a-dhan* [S.], adj. Av. not having wealth; needy, destitute (= निधन).

अधन्ना *adhannā*, m. see s.v. [1]अध-.

अधम *adham* [S.], adj. & m. **1.** adj. base, vile. **2.** inferior; lowly; wretched. **3.** m. a base person, &c. — अधमाधम [°*ma*+*a*°], adj. lowest of the low.

अधमता *adhamătā* [S.], f. **1.** vileness, &c. **2.** lowliness, wretchedness.

[1]**अधर** *a-dhar* [cf. H. *dharnā*], adj. **1.** not caught or held. **2.** not able to be caught, &c.

[2]**अधर** *adhar* [ad. *adhara-*], m. & adj. lower part: **1.** m. the lower lip; the lip. **2.** the space between earth and sky: mid-air; empty or intervening space; **3.** adj. low, base. — ~ उठा लेना, to lift up in the air. ~ में, adv. in the middle, midway; in the midst (of). – अधर-पान, m. drinking the lip: kissing. अधर-बिंब, m. Brbh. a full, red lip. अधरबुद्धि, f. Av. of unfixed mind. अधरांग [°*ra*+*a*°], m. the lower body. अधरामृत [°*ra*+*a*°], m. nectar of the lips. अधरासव [°*ra*+*ā*], m. draught or potion of the lips.

अधर्म *a-dharm* [S.], m. **1.** unrighteousness; immorality, wickedness; sin; guilt; crime. **2.** irreligiosity, impiety. — ~ से, adv. unjustly, wrongfully.

अधर्मपना *a-dharmpanā* [cf. H. *adharm*], m. = अधर्म.

अधर्मिष्ठ *a-dharmiṣṭh* [S.], adj. = अधर्मी.

अधर्मी *a-dharmī* [S.], adj. & m. **1.** adj. unrighteous; immoral, wicked; sinful; criminal. **2.** irreligious. **3.** m. an unrighteous, or irreligious person, &c.

अधस्- *adhas-* [S.], pref. down, downward, below: — अधस्तल, m. lower level.

[1]**अधारी** *adhārī* [ad. *ādhāra-*], f. dimin. Brbh. Av. support, prop, rest; an ascetic's portable seat or tripod.

[2]**अधारी** *a-dhārī* [cf. H. *-dhārī*], m. reg. (W.) a bullock not broken in (that does not work).

अधार्मिक *a-dhārmik* [S.], adj. **1.** unjust, unrighteous; wicked; sinful. **2.** irreligious. **3.** not having to do with religion, secular.

अधि- *adhi-* [S.], pref. **1.** above, over (e.g. अधिराज्य, m. supreme sway). **2.** additional (e.g. अधिसंख्य, adj. supernumerary). **3.** particular, formal (e.g. अधिपत्र, m. a warrant).

अधिक *adhik* [S.], adj. **1.** increased, exceeding; more (than, से); many; much; very much, or many; great; abundant. **2.** excessive; too much, too many. **3.** additional. — ~ से ~, adv. at most. और ~, adj. still more. कहीं ~, adj. very much more. बहुत ~, adj. very much, &c.; too much. बहुत ही ~, adj. too much; very much, &c. – अधिकांश [°*ka*+*a*°], m. & adj. greater part; majority; the greater part of; the majority of; adv. chiefly; on the whole; often. अधिकांशतः, adv. = अधिकांश. अधिकाधिक [°*ka*+*a*°], adj. most of all; more and more.

अधिकतम *adhikătam* [S.], adj. **1.** greatest; maximum. **2.** vast, huge.

अधिकतर *adhikătar* [S.], adj. **1.** greater, preponderant; very many or much, &c. (see अधिक). **2.** adv. to a great extent; much; frequently; usually. — ~ लोग, m. pl. most of the people (involved).

अधिकता *adhikătā* [S.], f. **1.** great amount, abundance. **2.** increase. **3.** excess.

अधिकरण *adhi-karaṇ* [S.], m. support, base: **1.** section, article (as of a treaty); point (of an agreement). **2.** title, heading. **3.** a tribunal, commission. **4.** *gram.* locative case.

अधिकर्मी *adhi-karmī* [S.], m. superintendent, overseer.

अधिका- *adhikā-* [ad. *adhika-*], v.i. Brbh. to increase.

अधिकाई *adhikāī* [cf. H. *adhik*], f. Brbh. Av. **1.** great amount, abundance. **2.** greatness, supremacy.

अधिकार *adhi-kār* [S.], m. **1.** authority, power; government, rule; freedom of action. **2.** a right; pl. rights. **3.** a prerogative. **4.** possession, proprietorship (of, पर); control. **5.** right, entitlement (to, पर). **6.** mastery, control (of or over, पर); competence. **7.** paragraph, section (of a regulation). — ~ करना, to exercise authority; to administer, to control, &c. ~ जमाना, to take possession, or to establish control (of or over, पर); to assert a right. ~ देना (को), to give authority (to). ~ रखना, to have authority (to, का); to have a right, or claim (to, पर). – अधिकार-क्षेत्र, m. area of authority, or competence; jurisdiction. अधिकारपूर्ण, adj. authoritative. अधिकारपूर्वक, adv. having authority; by right; authoritatively. अधिकारप्राप्त, adj. possessed of authority, or of rights. अधिकारयुक्त, adj. invested with authority; plenipotentiary; authoritative. अधिकारहीन, adj. not having authority, &c.; consultative. अधिकारारूढ़ [°*ra* + *ā*°], adj. ascended, or come, to power; possessed of power.

अधिकारक *adhi-kārak* [S.], adj. authoritative.

अधिकारिक *adhi-kārik* [S.], adj. official.

अधिकारिणी *adhi-kāriṇī* [S.], f. a woman possessing authority, &c. (cf. अधिकारी).

[1]**अधिकारी** *adhi-kārī* [S.], adj. & m. **1.** adj. possessing authority or entitlement; official. **2.** authoritative. **3.** m. one possessing authority: an official; a governor, ruler; authority (in a field); pl. an administering body. **4.** one possessing a right, title, &c.; a proprietor; an agent, deputy. **5.** one deserving (sthg). — अधिकारी-तंत्र, m. bureaucratic rule, bureaucracy. कर्म-अधिकारी, m. Brbh. one who acknowledges (and does not look beyond) the obligations of *karma*.

[2]**अधिकारी** *adhi-kārī* [cf. H. *adhikār*], f. the holding of authority, tenure of an official post.

अधिकृत *adhi-kr̥t* [S.], adj. **1.** under (one's) authority, or control; taken in occupation. **2.** authorised, official (as a statement, a channel, a language). **3.** authorised, empowered; chartered (an accountant).

अधिकृति *adhi-kr̥ti* [S.], f. possession of authority, or rights, &c.; official status.

अधिगत *adhi-gat* [S.], adj. obtained, acquired: attained to (knowledge); studied, learned.

अधिगम *adhi-gam* [S.], m. **1.** obtaining, acquiring; attainment (to). **2.** knowledge. **3.** finding, judgment (in law).

अधिगमन *adhi-gaman* [S.], m. 1. = अधिगम. 2. analysis, study.

अधिग्रहण *adhi-grahaṇ* [S.], m. requisitioning, commandeering.

अधित्यका *adhityǎkā* [S.], f. a plateau.

अधिदेश *adhi-deś* [S.], m. a mandate.

अधिदैविक *adhi daivik* [S.], adj. *philos.* fully spiritualised (doctrine of Vallabhācārya).

अधिनायक *adhi-nāyak* [S.], m. supreme or undisputed leader.

अधिनायकत्व *adhi-nāyǎkatvǎ* [S.], m. unquestioned leadership.

अधिनियम *adhi-ni-yam* [S.], m. *govt.* an act.

अधिनियमन *adhi-ni-yaman* [S.], m. *govt.* enactment (of legislation).

अधिनियमित *adhi-ni-yamit* [S.], adj. enacted (legislature). — ~ करना, to enact as law (a bill).

अधिप *adhi-p* [S.], m. = अधिपति, 1., 2.

अधिपति *adhi-pati* [S.], m. **1.** lord, master. **2.** king, prince. **3.** presiding officer; president, chairman.

अधिपत्र *adhi-patrǎ* [S.], m. a warrant (written document).

अधिप्रमाणित *adhi-pra-māṇit* [S.], adj. authenticated.

अधिभार *adhi-bhār* [S.], m. a surcharge.

अधिभौतिक *adhi-bhautik* [S.], adj. *philos.* pertaining to matter, material.

अधिमत *adhi-mat* [S.], m. verdict.

अधिमान *adhi-mān* [S.], m. preference (in law, finance).

अधिमास *adhi-mās* [S.], m. an intercalary month (added to the lunar calendar every three years to adjust it to the seasons: = मलमास).

अधिया *adhiyā* [*ardhika-*], f. **1.** a half. **2.** a half share of produce, half payment in kind; half an annual revenue payment.

अधियाना *adhiyānā* [cf. H. *ādhā*], v.t. & v.i. **1.** v.t. to halve; to divide. **2.** v.i. to be halved; to be divided.

अधियार *adhiyār* [*ārdhikakāra-, or *ardhi*°], m. reg. (W.) **1.** a man who holds and works land in two villages. **2.** holder of half a share.

अधियारी *adhiyārī* [cf. H. *adhiyār*], m. reg. (W.) division of crops into halves (as between landowner and farm worker).

अधिराज *adhi-rāj* [S.], m. a monarch; an emperor.

अधिराज्य *adhi-rājyă* [S.], m. **1.** supreme sway, empire; sovereignty. **2.** an empire.

अधिरोपण *adhi-ropaṇ* [S.], m. imposition (as of a charge).

अधिरोपित *adhi-ropit* [S.], adj. imposed (as a charge).

अधिवक्ता *adhi-vaktā* [S.], m. inv. an advocate (at law).

अधिवर्ष *adhi-varṣ* [S.], m. a leap year.

अधिवास *adhi-vās* [S.], m. **1.** residence. **2.** taking up residence (in another place). **3.** place of domicile.

अधिवासी *adhi-vāsī* [S.], m. **1.** a resident; one domiciled in a place. **2.** a farmer holding his land by right of residence.

अधिवेशन *adhi-veśan* [S.], m. session, sitting (of an assembly); meeting.

अधिशासी *adhi-śāsī* [S.], adj. executive.

अधिशेष *adhi-śeṣ* [S.], m. a surplus.

अधिष्ठाता *adhi-ṣṭhātā* [S.], m. inv. **1.** one who superintends or guides; a ruler; governor; founder. **2.** the supreme being. **3.** a protector.

अधिष्ठात्री *adhi-ṣṭhātrī* [S.], f. **1.** one who superintends or guides. **2.** a supreme or controlling principle (as nature).

अधिष्ठान *adhi-ṣṭhān* [S.], m. **1.** residence, abode. **2.** resting-place, site (as of an idol). **3.** basis, base. **4.** governing or superintending body.

अधिष्ठित *adhi-ṣṭhit* [S.], adj. residing, placed, &c. (see अधिष्ठान).

अधिसंख्य *adhi-saṅ-khyă* [S.], adj. **1.** supernumerary. **2.** very numerous.

अधिसूचना *adhi-sūcănā* [S.], f. formal notification.

अधिसूचित *adhi-sūcit* [S.], adj. formally notified.

अधीक्षक *adhīkṣak* [S.], m. superintendent.

अधीक्षण *adhīkṣaṇ* [S.], m. management, supervision, charge.

अधीत *adhīt* [S.], adj. E.H. read, studied.

अधीन *adhīn* [S.], adj. **1.** subject, dependent; subordinate. **2.** docile; subservient; humble. **3.** ppn. w. के. subject (to), dependent (on); under the authority, jurisdiction (of). — अधीनस्थ, adj. in a position of dependence, &c. अधीनीकरण, m. making subject, subjugation. निर्माणाधीन [°*a*+*a*°], adj. under construction.

अधीनता *adhīnătā* [S.], f. **1.** subjection, dependence; subordination. **2.** submissiveness, &c. **3.** condition of subjection to (laws, a court).

अधीनीकरण *adhīnīkaraṇ* [S.], m. see s.v. अधीन.

अधीर *a-dhīr* [S.], adj. **1.** unsteady, unstable; irresolute; fickle. **2.** restless, impatient. **3.** hasty. **4.** confused, distracted.

अधीरज *adhīraj* [ad. *dhairya-*, *dhīrya-*: H. *dhīr*], adj. & m. **1.** adj. = अधीर. **2.** m. unsteadiness, indecision; fickleness. **3.** restlessness, impatience. **5.** hastiness. **4.** confusion, distraction.

अधीरता *a-dhīrătā* [S.], f. unsteadiness, &c.

अधीश *adhīś* [S.], m. **1.** master, lord. **2.** ruler, king. — न्यायाधीश [°*ya*+*a*°], m. a judge.

अधीश्वर *adhīśvar* [S.], m. supreme lord or king; emperor.

अधुना *adhunā* [S.], adv. at the present time.

अधूरा *adhūrā* [*ardhapūraka-], adj. **1.** incomplete, unfinished; imperfect, not fully formed; immature (a foetus; an adolescent; a plant). **2.** ineffective. — ~ जाना (को), (a woman) to miscarry. ~ रहना, to remain unfinished, &c. अधूरी रहना, to miscarry (a woman).

अधेड़ *adheṛ* [? *ardhaveḍa-], adj. middle-aged. — ~ उमर का आदमी, m. a middle-aged man.

अधेड़पना *adheṛpanā* [cf. H. *adheṛ*], m. middle age.

अधेला *adhelā*, m. a small copper coin, equal to half a pice.

अधेली *adhelī*, f. a silver or nickel coin equal to half a rupee.

अधैर्य *a-dhairyă* [S.], adj. & m. = अधीरज.

अधो- *adho-* [S.], pref. down, downward, below: — अधोगति, f. descent; decline; degraded or wretched state. °-गमन, m. = prec., 1., 2. °-गामी, adj. descending; declining. अधोमुख, adj. having the face or head downwards; dejected; shamefaced; upside down. अधोरेखन, m. underlining (= रेखांकन). °-रेखा, f. an underline. अधोलिखित, m. written down, recorded. अधोहस्ताक्षरी, m. the undersigned.

अधोतर *adhotar* [conn. **dhotta-* or *dhotra-*], m. E.H. a coarse cloth.

अधौड़ी *adhauṛī* [**ardhapuṭa-*], f. *Pl. HŚS.* **1.** a half-hide (as of a bull, or buffalo). **2.** heavy leather (as used in soles of shoes, &c). **3.** the stomach.

अध्यक्ष *adhy-akṣ* [S.], m. a person having supervision or direction (of): **1.** master, proprietor. **2.** officer in charge: chairman; president; director; dean; superintendent; commandant. — **अध्यक्ष-पद**, m. position of chairman, &c. °**ईय**, adj. **अध्यक्षात्मक** [°*ṣa* + *ā*°], adj. presidential (in character). **अध्यक्षीय**, adj. chairman's, president's, &c.

अध्यक्षता *adhy-akṣătā* [S.], f. **1.** direction, supervision. **2.** chairmanship, &c. (see **अध्यक्ष**).

अध्यक्षत्व *adhy-akṣatvă* [S.], m. = **अध्यक्षता**.

अध्यक्षा *adhy-akṣā* [S.], f. a woman having supervision, &c. (see **अध्यक्ष**).

अध्ययन *adhy-ayan* [S.], m. **1.** reading. ***2.** study. — **अध्ययन-अध्यापन**, m. study and teaching, educational or academic work. **अध्ययन-मनन**, m. thoughtful study. **अध्ययन-वर्ष**, m. academical year. **अध्ययनशील**, adj. studious. °**ता**, f. **अध्ययनावकाश** [°*na* + *a*°], m. study leave.

अध्ययनीय *adhy-ayanīyă* [S.], adj. deserving study; under study.

अध्यवसाय *adhy-avă-sāy* [S.], m. effort, attempting: perseverance; assiduity.

अध्यवसायी *adhy-avă-sāyī* [S.], adj. persevering, assiduous.

अध्यात्म *adhy-ātm* [S.], m. & adj. **1.** m. the supreme spirit. **2.** relationship of identity (esp. according to Vedānta theory) of the soul with the supreme spirit; spiritual matters. **3.** adj. spiritual. — **अध्यात्म-ज्ञान**, m. knowledge of the identity of the soul with the supreme spirit. **अध्यात्मवाद**, m. belief in *adhyātma* (see 2. above). °**ई**, adj. & m. **अध्यात्म-विद्या**, f. = **अध्यत्म-ज्ञान**.

अध्यात्मिक *adhy-ātmik*, adj. corr. = **आध्यात्मिक**.

अध्यादेश *adhy-ā-deś* [S.], m. a directive, or ordinance.

अध्यापक *adhy-āpak* [S.], m. a teacher; instructor.

अध्यापकी *adhy-āpăkī* [cf. H. *adhyāpak*], f. the activity or calling of teaching (cf. **अध्यापन**).

अध्यापन *adhy-āpan* [S.], m. the act of teaching, instruction. — **अध्यापन-शास्त्र**, m. pedagogical theory.

अध्यापिका *adhy-āpikā* [S.], f. a lady teacher, mistress, instructress.

अध्याय *adhy-āy* [S.], m. section (of a book); chapter; lesson.

अध्यारोप *adhy-ā-rop* [S.], m. **1.** raising, placing (an object) upon another. **2.** wrong attribution (of qualities, &c).

अध्यारोपण *adhy-ā-ropaṇ* [S.], m. = **अध्यारोप**.

अध्यारोपित *adhy-ā-ropit* [S.], adj. superimposed.

अध्यास *adhy-ās* [S.], m. 1. = **अध्यारोप**, 2. **2.** error, illusion.

अध्यासीन *adhy-āsīn* [S.], adj. seated: presiding.

अध्याहार *adhy-ā-hār* [S.], m. inference.

अध्याहृत *adhy-ā-hr̥t* [S.], adj. **1.** supplied (a word, a sense). **2.** inferred.

अध्येता *adhy-etā* [S.], m. inv. a student, scholar.

अध्येय *adhy-ey* [S.], adj. deserving of study.

अध्रुव *a-dhruv* [S.], adj. **1.** unfixed, inconstant. **2.** uncertain, doubtful.

अन- *an-* [*an-*], pref. un-, in-; the negation of (e.g. **अनदेखा**, adj. unseen; **अनाचार**, m. improper conduct: as a prefix in *tatsama* words **अन-** is used only with words beginning with a vowel.)

अनंग *an-aṅg* [S.], adj. & m. **1.** adj. bodiless. **2.** m. *mythol.* a title of Kāmdev, the love-god. — **अनंग-रंग**, m. Brbh. mood or sentiment of love (physical or mystical). **अनंगीकार**, m. rejection (of a proposal); repudiation (of an obligation). **अनंगीकरण**, m. act of rejection, or repudiation.

अनंगी *an-aṅgī* [S.], adj. & m. **1.** adj. bodiless. **2.** limbless, maimed. **3.** m. = **अनंग**.

अनंगीकरण *an-aṅgīkaraṇ* [S]. see s.v. **अनंग**.

अनंगीकार *an-aṅgīkār* [S.], m. see s.v. **अनंग**.

अनंत *an-ant* [S.], adj. & m. **1.** without end. **2.** eternal. **3.** infinite. **4.** m. vastness (of extent or space), infinitude. **5.** an eternal being (title used of several Hindu deities). — **अनंत-काल**, m. eternity. **अनंत-चतुर्दशी**, f. the fourteenth day of the month of Bhādoṁ; a festival honouring Anant (Viṣṇu) held on that day. **अनंत-मूल**, m. Indian sarsparilla, *Hemidesmus indicus*. **अनंत-राशि**, f. *math.* an infinite quantity.

अनंतता *an-antătā* [S.], f. **1.** endlessness, boundlessness. **2.** eternity. **3.** vastness.

अनंतिम *an-antim* [S.], adj. not final: provisional.

अनंतर *an-antar* [S.], adj. & m. **1.** not separated; adjacent; unbroken, continuous. **2.** ppn. (with के.) immediately upon; not differently from, following from; after. **3.** m. proximity.

अनंतरित *an-antarit* [S.], adj. **1.** not separated, &c. (= अनंतर), 1. **2.** whole, entire.

अनंतरीय *an-antarīyă* [S.], adj. immediately following; following from, subsequent.

अनंतर्हित *an-antar-hit* [S.], adj. not placed separately, &c. (cf. अनंतरित).

अनंत्य *an-antyă* [S.], adj. & m. **1.** adj. = अनंत. **2.** m. eternity. **3.** infinity, infinitude.

अनंद *anand*, m. (f.) Brbh. & 19c. = आनंद.

अनंश *an-aṃś* [S.], adj. without a share: excluded from an inheritance.

[1]**-अन** *-an*, suffix (forms f. and m. nouns from H. and OIA verb roots or stems, e.g. सूजन, f. swelling; [1]जामन, m. rennet; भोजन, m. eating, meal, food; चलन, m. movement, behaviour).

[2]**-अन** *-an*, suffix. pronun. var. = -इन.

[3]**-अन** *-an* [A. *-an*, acc. case suffix], suffix (forms adverbs on nouns of Arabic origin, e.g. क़रीबन, approximately).

अनकना *ankanā*, adj. = अनमना, 2., 3.

अनक्षर *an-akṣar* [S.], adj. & m. *Pl. HŚS.* **1.** adj. illiterate (= निरक्षर). **2.** m. an illiterate person; an ignorant person.

अनख *anakh* [? *anakṣa-*], m. f. **1.** anger; displeasure. **2.** envy. **3.** malice.

अनखा- *ankhā-* [cf. H. *anakh*], v.i. Brbh. **1.** to be angry. **2.** to be displeased.

अनखाहट *ankhāhaṭ* [cf. H. *ankhā-*], f. Brbh. **1.** anger. **2.** displeasure.

अनखी *ankhī* [cf. H. *anakh*], adj. reg. angry, &c.

अनगढ़ *an-gaṛh* [cf. H. *gaṛhnā*], adj. **1.** unformed; unfinished, crude. **2.** misshapen. **3.** uncouth, awkward; uncultivated. **4.** not set (a stone, jewel). **5.** disorganised, incoherent (speech, argument).

अनगढ़त *an-gaṛhat* [cf. H. *gaṛhnā*], f. *Pl.* incoherent speech; nonsense.

अनगढ़पन *an-gaṛhpan* [cf. H. *angaṛh*], m. unfinished state: **1.** roughness, crudeness. **2.** awkwardness in manners. **3.** stupidity.

अनगढ़पना *an-gaṛhpanā*, m. = अनगढ़पन.

अनगणित *an-gaṇit* [cf. *gaṇita-*], adj. = अनगिनत.

अनगिनत *an-ginat* [H. *ginnā* × *gaṇita-*], adj. **1.** uncounted. **2.** innumerable.

अनगिना *an-ginā* [cf. H. *ginnā*], adj. **1.** uncounted. **2.** innumerable. — ~ महीना, m. euph. the eighth month of pregnancy.

अनगी *angī* [conn. H. [1]*ānā*], f. *Pl.* allowance or discount of one anna in the rupee.

अनघ *an-agh* [S.], adj. without sin; pure.

अनघड़ *an-ghaṛ*, adj. = अनगढ़.

अनघड़त *an-ghaṛat*, f. = अनगढ़त.

अनघड़पन *an-ghaṛpan*, m. see अनगढ़पन.

अनघड़पना *an-ghaṛpanā*, m. = अनगढ़पन.

अनचाहत *an-cāhat* [cf. H. *cāhnā*], adj. **1.** not desired. **2.** not wishing.

अनचाहा *an-cāhā* [cf. H. *cahnā*], adj. not desired. — अनचाहे, adv. involuntarily.

अनचित *an-cit*, adj. *Pl.* = अनचित्ता.

अनचित्ता *an-cittā* [cf. H. *cītnā*], adj. & m. **1.** adj. inattentive; absent-minded. **2.** unconscious. **3.** m. a slap or thump given unawares from behind. — अनचित्ते में, adv. unwittingly; unawares, unexpectedly.

अनचीत *an-cīt* [cf. H. *cītnā*], adj. Brbh. = अनचीता.

अनचीता *an-cītā* [cf. H. *cītnā*], adj. **1.** not thought of, unforeseen. **2.** not desired. **3.** sudden, unexpected.

अनचेना *ancenā*, m. *Pl.* valuation of a standing crop (= कनकूट).

अनछीला *an-chīlā* [cf. H. *chīlnā*], adj. **1.** unpeeled, unpared. **2.** transf. rough, uncouth.

अनछेड़ *an-cheṛ* [cf. H. *cheṛnā*], adj. **1.** untouched. **2.** unmolested.

अनजना *an-janā* [cf. H. *jannā*], adj. unborn.

अनजाई *an-jāī* [cf. *jātya-*, **jātiya-*], f. *Pl.* a hybrid animal; mongrel.

अनजान *an-jān* [cf. H. *jānnā*], adj. & m. **1.** adj. unknowing, ignorant. **2.** unintentional. **3.** unknown; unperceived. **4.** m. an ignorant person. **5.** an unknown person, stranger. **6.** forgetful or unconscious state. — ~ में, adv. ignorantly; unintentionally.

अनजानत *an-jānat*, adv. Brbh. Av. while in ignorance; imperceptibly.

अनजाना *an-jānā*, adj. & m. = अनजान, 2.-6. अनजाने, adv. = अनजान में. अनजाने में, adv. id.

अनजानी *an-jānī* [cf. H. *anjān*], f. *Pl.* ignorance; negligence.

अनजामा *an-jāmā* [cf. *janman-*], adj. *Pl.* barren, unproductive (soil).

अनझिप *an-jhip* [cf. H. *jhap*], adj. not blinking.

अनट *anaṭ* [*anartha-*], m. E.H. **1.** wrong-doing, injury (to another). **2.** childish pranks, naughtiness.

अनत *anat* [*anyatra-*], adj. Brbh. Av. elsewhere.

अनदेखा *an-dekhā* [cf. H. *dekhnā*], adj. **1.** unseen; unprecedented, unexampled. **2.** invisible. **3.** undiscovered, undetected. — ~ करना, to pretend not to see, to ignore.

अनदेखी *an-dekhī*, f. (sthg.) unseen, &c. (cf. अनदेखा).

अनधिकार *an-adhi-kār* [S.], adj. taking place without right or authority, unauthorised.

अनन्नास *anannās* [Pt. *ananás*], m. the pineapple plant and its fruit.

अनन्नासी *anannāsī* [cf. H. *anannās*], adj. having to do with the pineapple; resembling the pineapple (as in taste).

अनन्य *an-anyă* [S.], adj. **1.** having no other, being only one: single; undivided, whole. **2.** entirely devoted (as to a deity). **3.** incomparable; unique. **4.** inalienable. — अनन्यचित्त, adj. intent on, or engrossed in. अनन्यदेव, adj. having no other god. अनन्यपरता, f. exclusive loyalty. अनन्यवृत्ति, adj. = अनन्य-चित्त; having only one source of income. अनन्याधिकार [°*ya*+*a*°], m. sole or exclusive right; monopoly.

अनन्यता *an-anyătā* [S.], f. singleness (as of mind); absorption, engrossment.

अनपच *an-pac* [cf. H. *pacnā*], f. indigestion.

अनपढ़ *an-paṛh* [cf. H. *paṛhnā*], adj. illiterate; uneducated.

अनपढ़ता *an-paṛhtā* [cf. H. *anpaṛh*], f. illiteracy.

अनपढ़ा *an-paṛhā*, adj. = अनपढ़.

अनपराध *an-apă-rādh* [S.], adj. & m. **1.** adj. not guilty, innocent. **2.** m. innocence.

अनपराधी *an-apă-rādhī* [S.], adj. & m. **1.** adj. = अनपराध. **2.** m. an innocent person.

अनपरिचय *an-pari-cay* [cf. H. *aparicay*], m. non-acquaintance.

अनपाय *an-apây* [S.], adj. imperishable; indestructible; enduring.

अनपायी *an-apâyī* [S.], adj. = अनपाय.

अनपेक्ष *an-apêkṣ* [S.], adj. **1.** disregarding, indifferent. **2.** impartial, neutral. **3.** self-sufficient (a person).

अनपेक्षा *an-apêkṣā* [S.], f. **1.** disregard, indifference. **2.** impartiality, neutrality. **3.** self-sufficiency.

अनपेक्षित *an-apêkṣit* [S.], adj. **1.** not wished for. **2.** unexpected.

अनपेक्ष्य *an-apêkṣyă* [S.], adj. not to be wished for; not to be expected.

अनप्रतीती *an-pratîtī* [cf. S. *pratīti*], adj. reg. **1.** having no trust, unfriendly. **2.** faithless, unbelieving.

[1]**अनबन** *anban* [cf. H. *bannā*], f. discord; dispute; quarrel.

[2]**अनबन** *anban* [? cf. H. *bannā*; ×*varṇa-*], adj. Brbh. Av. various.

अनबिंधा *an-biṁdhā* [cf. H. *biṁdhnā*], adj. unpierced.

अनबूझ *an-būjh* [cf. H. *būjh*], adj. **1.** hard to understand (a riddle, &c). **2.** thoughtless.

अनबेधा *an-bedhā* [cf. H. *bedhnā*], adj. unpierced, unperforated.

अनबोल *an-bol* [cf. H. *bol(na)*], adj. & m. **1.** adj. speechless, silent. **2.** dumb. **3.** m. transf. broken relationship, estrangement.

अनबोला *an-bolā* [cf. H. *bolnā*], adj. **1.** unspoken. 2. = अनबोल.

अनबोया *an-boyā* [cf. H. *bonā*], adj. **1.** unsown. **2.** wild (plants).

अनब्याहा *an-byāhā* [cf. *vivāhita-*], adj. unmarried.

अनभल *an-bhal* [cf. H. *bhalā*], m. bad fortune. — ~ चाहना or ताकना (का), to wish (one) ill. ~ मन में आना, an unkind or malicious thought to cross (one's, के) mind (about, का).

अनभला *an-bhalā* [cf. H. *bhalā*], adj. E.H. bad, wicked.

अनभाया *an-bhāyā* [cf. H. *bhānā*], adj. displeasing, disagreeable.

अनभिज्ञ *an-abhi-jñă* [S.], adj. unaware, ignorant.

अनभिज्ञता *an-abhi-jñătā* [S.], f. unawareness, ignorance.

अनभिलाष *an-abhi-lāṣ* [S.], m. & adj. **1.** m. absence of desire; indifference. **2.** adj. lacking desire.

अनभिलाषी *an-abhi-lāṣī* [S.], adj. & m. **1.** adj. lacking desire; indifferent. **2.** m. one free from desire.

अनमन *an-man*, adj. = अनमना.

अनमना *an-manā* [cf. H. *man*], adj. **1.** distracted, preoccupied. **2.** dejected. **3.** indisposed.

अनमनाना *anmanānā* [cf. H. *anmanā*], v.i. **1.** to be distressed. **2.** to be dejected.

अनमनापन *an-manāpan* [cf. H. *anmanā*], m. **1.** distress of mind; distraction, preoccupation. **2.** dejection.

अनमनाहट *an-manāhaṭ* [cf. H. *anmanā*], f. = अनमनापन.

अनमिल *an-mil* [cf. H. *milnā*], adj. ill-assorted, unsuitable; inappropriate (= अनमेल).

अनमेल *an-mel* [cf. H. *melnā*], adj. **1.** unmatched, discordant, inharmonious. **2.** unsuitable, inappropriate. **3.** unmixed, unadulterated. **4.** disconnected, heterogeneous.

अनमोल *an-mol* [cf. *maulya-*], adj. **1.** priceless. **2.** very valuable; precious.

अनरखा *an-rakhā* [cf. H. *rakhnā*], adj. unguarded, unprotected.

अनरस *an-ras* [cf. H. *ras*], m. **1.** want of flavour or enjoyment. **2.** distaste. **3.** coolness, distance (between friends).

अनरीति *an-rīti* [S.], f. **1.** unmannerly conduct. **2.** improper conduct.

अनर्गल *an-argal* [S.], adj. **1.** unbarred, without restraint. **2.** uninhibited; licentious. **3.** incoherent (as remarks).

अनर्थ *an-arth* [S.], adj. & m. **1.** adj. useless, pointless, futile. **2.** groundless. **3.** meaningless, senseless. **4.** injurious. **5.** m. senselessness, absurdity. **6.** a senseless, wrong or improper act. **7.** harm, loss; damage. **8.** misfortune. — ~ **करना**, to cause injury (to, **का**); to do sthg. senseless, wrong, &c. ~ **ढाना**, id. – **अनर्थकारी**, adj. acting senselessly, or wrongly; causing loss or damage. **अनर्थदर्शी**, adj. ill-intentioned, malevolent.

अनर्थक *an-arthak* [S.], adj. = अनर्थ.

अनर्थकारी *an-arthkārī* [S.], adj. see s.v.

अनर्थी *an-arthī* [S.], m. a wrong-doer; transgressor.

अनर्हता *an-arhătā* [S.], f. state of disqualification.

अनल *anal* [S.], m. **1.** fire; flame. **2.** (in chronograms) the number three.

अनलसित *an-alăsit* [S.], adj. not fatigued or enervated, vigorous.

अनवकाश *an-avă-kāś* [S.], adj. & m. **1.** adj. not having free time, or opportunity. **2.** uncalled for, inopportune. **3.** m. want of free time, &c.

[1]**अनवट** *anvaṭ* [**andhapaṭṭa-*], m. *HŚS.* blinkers (for working oxen).

[2]**अनवट** *anvaṭ* [**anuvarta-*], m. Av. a toe-ring (esp. one having little bells attached).

अनवद्य *an-a-vadyă* [S.], adj. Av. blameless, faultless.

अनवधान *an-avă-dhān* [S.], adj. & m. **1.** adj. inadvertent, inattentive. **2.** m. inadvertence, inattention; indifference.

अनवधानता *an-avă-dhānătā* [S.], f. inadvertence, &c.

अनवधि *an-avă-dhi* [S.], adj. without limit (of time, or space); endless; not terminated.

अनवरत *an-avă-rat* [S.], adj. incessant, continuous.

अनवरोध *an-avă-rodh* [S.], adj. not subject to check or interference.

अनवसर *an-avă-sar* [S.], m. & adj. **1.** m. want of free time. **2.** inopportune, or ill-fated time. **3.** adj. *Pl.* having no leisure, busy.

अनवस्थ *an-ava-sth* [S.], adj. **1.** unstable, changeable, &c. (see अनवस्था). **2.** incontinent.

अनवस्था *an-avă-sthā* [S.], f. **1.** lack of fixity, instability; uncertainty; anxiety, impatience. **2.** disorder.

अनवस्थित *an-avă-sthit* [S.], adj. unstable, changeable &c. (see अनवस्था).

अनवाँसा *anvāṁsā*, [**aṇuvaṁśa-*], m. *HŚS.* **1.** sheaf of corn. **2.** first harvest.

अनवाँसी *anvāṁsī* [**aṇuvaṁśa-*], f. *Pl. HŚS.* a very small measure of land.

अनशन *an-ăśan* [S.], m. **1.** fasting. **2.** hunger strike. — **अनशनकारी**, m. & adj. faster, hunger-striker, &c.

अनश्वर *a-naśvar* [S.], adj. imperishable, eternal.

अनसमझ *an-samajh* [cf. H. *samajhnā*], adj. **1.** ignorant, inexperienced. **2.** foolish. **3.** thoughtless.

अनसिखा *an-sikhā* [cf. H. *sīkhnā*], adj. uneducated, untrained.

अनसुन *an-sun* [cf. H. *sunnā*], adj. = अनसुना.

अनसुना *an-sunā* [cf. H. *sunnā*], adj. **1.** unheard. **2.** disregarded. **3.** unprecedented. — (सुना) ~ करना, to pretend not to hear; to turn a deaf ear to, to disregard wilfully.

अनसुनी *an-sunī* [cf. H. *ansunā*], f. not hearing, disregarding: ~ करना, = अनसुना करना.

अनसूय *an-asūya* [S.], adj. not spiteful, not envious.

अनसोच *an-soc* [cf. H. *socnā*], adj. thoughtless, inattentive.

अनसोचा *an-socā* [cf. H. *socnā*], adj. unthought of, forgotten. — अनसोचे, adv. heedlessly, carelessly.

अनहंकार *an-ahankār* [S.], m. absence of pride, humility.

अनहित *an-hit* [cf. *ahita-*], m. & adj. Brbh. Av. **1.** m. disadvantage, misfortune. **2.** ill disposition. **3.** an ill-disposed person. **4.** adj. bringing misfortune, &c.: ill-disposed.

अनहितू *anhitū*, m. = अनहित, 3.

अनहोता *an-hotā* [cf. H. *honā*], adj. **1.** deprived, in want. 2. = अनहोना.

अनहोना *an-honā* [cf. H. *honā*], adj. not to be: unexampled; improbable; unpromising.

अनहोनी *an-honī* [cf. H. *honā*], f. sthg. improbable, or impossible.

अनाकानी *anākānī*, f. = आनाकानी.

अनाकार *an-ā-kār* [S.], adj. without form, shapeless.

अनाक्रमण *an-ā-kraman̥* [S.], m. non-aggression.

अनाक्रांत *an-ā-krānt* [S.], adj. not attacked.

अनाक्रांता *an-ā-krāntā* [S.], f. *bot. Pl.* a nightshade, *Solanum jacquini*.

अनागत *an-ā-gat* [S.], adj. **1.** not come. **2.** not having occurred; unusual. **3.** yet to come, future. **4.** not learnt; unknown. **5.** adv. suddenly. **5.** Brbh. a partic. musical beat. **6.** adv. suddenly.

अनागति *an-ā-gati* [S.], f. non-arrival, &c.

अनागम *an-ā-gam* [S.], m. non-arrival, non-appearance.

अनागम्य *an-ā-gamyă* [S.], adj. inaccessible, unattainable.

अनाचरण *an-ā-caran̥* [S.], m. **1.** non-performance; omission. 2. = अनाचार.

अनाचार *an-ā-cār* [S.], m. unprincipled, improper or dishonest conduct.

अनाचारिता *an-ā-cāritā* [S.], f. lack of principle; dishonesty; vice.

अनाचारी *an-ā-cārī* [S.], adj. & m. **1.** unprincipled; dishonest. **2.** m. an unprincipled person, &c.

अनाचित *anācit* [corr. H. *ancit*], adj. inattentive, heedless.

अनाचिती *anācitī* [cf. H. *anācit*], f. inattention, heedlessness.

अनाज *anāj* [*annādya-*], m. **1.** grain. **2.** food (in general). — ~ का कीड़ा, m. a weevil; fig. grain-worm: man, mankind. ~ का दुश्मन, m. fig. scoffer of food, glutton. – अनाज-पानी, m. fig. cooking arrangements (of a family).

अनाजी *anājī* [cf. H. *anāj*], adj. having to do with grain.

अनाड़ी *anāṛī* [*ajñānin-*], adj. & m. **1.** inexperienced; unskilful, awkward. **2.** ignorant; foolish. **3.** m. a novice; an inept person. **4.** an ignoramus.

अनाड़ीपन *anāṛīpan* [cf. H. *anāṛī*], m. **1.** inexperience, &c. **2.** ignorance.

अनाड़ीपना *anāṛīpanā*, m. = अनाड़ीपन.

अनातुर *an-ātur* [S.], adj. **1.** not distressed. **2.** not restless.

अनात्म *an-ātmă* [S.], adj. & m. not self: **1.** adj. inanimate. **2.** physical, material. **3.** not one's own. **4.** m. *philos.* matter. — अनात्मवाद, m. materialism. °ई, adj. & m.

अनात्मक *an-ātmak* [S.], adj. **1.** unreal. **2.** of short duration.

अनाथ *a-nāth* [S.], adj. **1.** without a lord, or master; orphaned; widowed. **2.** helpless; wretched. **3.** *Pl.* unclaimed (land). **4.** m. an orphan, &c. — अनाथालय [°*tha*+*ā*°], m. a shelter for the destitute; an orphanage. अनाथाश्रम [°*tha*+*ā*°], m. id.

अनाद *anād* [ad. *anādi-*, *anādya-*], adj. *Pl.* 1. = अनादि. **2.** not original, &c. ~ भूमि, f. land transferred by mortgage.

अनादर *an-ā-dar* [S.], m. **1.** disrespect. **2.** disparagement. **3.** affront, slight. — ~ करना, to show disrespect, &c. (to or for, का).

अनादरण *an-ā-daran̥* [S.], m. **1.** showing disrespect, &c. (see अनादर.) **2.** not honouring (a cheque, &c).

अनादरणीय *an-ā-darănīyă* [S.], adj. **1.** not to be respected, &c. (see अनादर.) **2.** unworthy, disreputable.

अनादरित *an-ā-dărit* [cf. H. *ādar*: w. S.], adj. = अनादृत.

अनादि *an-ādi* [S.], adj. **1.** without beginning; eternal; immemorial. — अनाद्यंत [°*di+a*°], adj. without beginning or end.

अनादिता *an-āditā* [S.], f. = अनादित्व.

अनादित्व *an-āditvă* [S.], m. eternity without beginning.

अनादृत *an-ā-dṛt* [S.], adj. **1.** not respected, &c. (see अनादर.) **2.** disparaged. **3.** affronted, slighted.

अनानास *anānās* [Pt. *ananás*], m. see अनन्नास.

अनाप-शनाप *anāp-śanāp* [cf. H. *nāpnā*], adj. & m. **1.** adj. without measure; excessive. **2.** m. nonsense. **3.** confusion.

अनाम *a-nām* [S.], adj. nameless, anonymous; obscure.

अनामक *a-nāmak* [S.], adj. = अनाम.

अनामय *an-āmay* [S.], adj. & m. **1.** adj. sound, healthy. **2.** without fault. **3.** m. health; well-being.

अनामिका *a-nāmikā* [S.], f. **1.** the ring finger. **2.** a nameless or unknown woman.

अनायक *a-nāyak* [S.], adj. *Pl. HŚS.* having no leader, or protector.

अनायास *an-ā-yās* [S.], m. & adj. **1.** m. absence of effort, ease. **2.** indolence. **3.** adj. done without effort. ***4.** adv. involuntarily. **5.** suddenly.

अनायासिक *an-ā-yāsik* [S.], adj. done without effort.

अनार *anār* [P. *anār*], m. **1.** pomegranate. **2.** transf. a type of firework. — दस्ती ~, m. hand grenade. – अनार-दाना, m. dried pomegranate seed.

अनारपन *anārpan*, m. Brbh. = अनाड़ीपन.

अनारी *anārī* [P.], adj. having to do with the pomegranate.

अनावरण *an-ā-varaṇ* [S.], m. unveiling.

अनावर्ती *an-ā-vartī* [S.], adj. non-recurrent.

अनावृ+ष्टि *an-ā-vṛ+ṣṭi* [S.], f. lack of rain, drought.

अनावृत *an-ā-vṛt* [S.], adj. **1.** uncovered; bare. **2.** unveiled (as a monument). **3.** open, not hidden. — अनावृतीकरण, m. uncovering; unveiling.

अनावृत्त *an-ā-vṛtt* [S.], adj. **1.** not turned back, not returned. **2.** not recurring.

अनावृत्ति *an-ā-vṛtti* [S.], f. non-return; release from rebirth.

अनाश्य *a-nāśyă* [S.], adj. indestructible, imperishable.

अनाहत *an-ā-hat* [S.], adj. unhurt, unwounded. — ~ नाद, m. (in yoga) the paradoxical 'unstruck sound' heard when the spirit merges with the absolute.

अनाहार *an-ā-hār* [S.], m. & adj. **1.** m. not eating; fast. **2.** starvation. **3.** adj. not having eaten, fasting. **4.** starving.

अनाहारी *an-ā-hārī* [S.], adj. & m. **1.** adj. fasting. **2.** m. one keeping a fast.

अनिंदनीय *a-nindănīyă* [S.], adj. blameless, irreproachable.

अनिंदित *a-nindit* [S.], adj. not blamed: = अनिंदनीय.

अनिच्छा *an-icchā* [S.], f. **1.** lack of desire. **2.** disinclination. **3.** indifference. — अनिच्छापूर्वक, adv. reluctantly.

अनिच्छित *an-icchit* [S.], adj. undesired.

अनिच्छु *an-icchu* [S.], adj. = अनिच्छुक.

अनिच्छुक *an-icchuk* [S.], adj. unwilling; disinclined, uninterested.

अनित्य *a-nityă* [S.], adj. **1.** impermanent; transient; temporary. **2.** occasional, particular (a rite, &c).

अनित्यता *a-nityătā* [S.], f. impermanence; transient existence.

अनिद्र *a-nidră* [S.], adj. sleepless, wakeful.

अनिद्रा *a-nidrā* [S.], f. sleeplessness.

अनिद्रित *a-nidrit* [S.], adj. sleepless, wakeful.

अनिपुण *a-nipuṇ* [S.], adj. unskilled, unproficient.

अनियमित *a-ni-yamit* [S.], adj. irregular.

अनियार- *aniyār-* [cf. *anīka-*], adj. Brbh. pointed (as shape of eyes).

अनिरुद्ध *a-ni-ruddh* [S.], adj. unobstructed, unrestrained.

अनिर्णय *a-nir-ṇay* [S.], m. indefiniteness, uncertainty.

अनिर्णीत *a-nir-ṇīt* [S.], adj. **1.** indefinite, undecided. **2.** drawn (a game).

अनिर्मल *a-nir-mal* [S.], adj. not pure; dirty.

अनिर्वचनीय *a-nir-vacănīyă* [S.], adj. = अनिर्वाच्य.

अनिर्वाच्य *a-nir-vācyă* [S.], adj. **1.** unutterable, inexpressible in words. **2.** not to be chosen; ineligible.

अनिल *anil* [S.], m. wind, air. — अनिल-वाह, m. the atmosphere (= वातावरण).

अनिवारित *a-ni-vārit* [S.], adj. unchecked, unopposed.

अनिवार्य *a-ni-vāryă* [S.], adj. **1.** not to be warded off: unavoidable, inevitable; irresistible. ***2.** compulsory. **3.** essential (for, in, के लिए). — ~ भरती, f. (military) conscription. – अनिवार्यतः, adv. necessarily; compulsorily; at all costs, unconditionally.

अनिवार्यता *a-ni-vāryătā* [S.], f. **1.** compulsory, or essential nature (of, की). **2.** inevitability.

अनिश *a-niś* [S], adv. continuing, constantly.

अनिश्चय *a-niś-cay* [S.], adj. & m. **1.** adj. uncertain, doubtful. **2.** m. uncertainty, doubt. **3.** indefiniteness. — अनिश्चयात्मक [°*ya*+*ā*°], adj. *gram.* indefinite.

अनिश्चित *a-niś-cit* [S.], adj. **1.** uncertain, doubtful. **2.** not decided, indefinite.

अनिषिद्ध *a-ni-ṣiddh* [S.], adj. not forbidden.

अनिष्ट *an-iṣṭ* [S.], adj. & m. **1.** adj. undesired; undesirable. **2.** harmful. **3.** m. harm, evil; misfortune. — अनिष्टकर, adj. causing harm, evil, &c. °-कारी, adj. id.

अनिष्ठा *a-ni-ṣṭhā* [S.], f. **1.** unfirmness, unsteadiness. **2.** lack of faith.

अनी *anī* [*anīka-*], f. **1.** sharp point (of spear, arrow, &c). **2.** end, tip. **3.** face, front. **4.** prow. — अनीदार [P. *-dār*], adj. pointed.

अनीक *anīk* [S.], m. (f., *Pl.*). point, edge: army; host.

अनीति *a-nīti* [S.], f. **1.** improper conduct; wickedness, immorality; impropriety, bad manners. **2.** injustice, wrong. — ~ करना, to do injustice or wrong (to, पर).

अनीह *an-īh* [S.], adj. Brbh. Av. **1.** without desire. **2.** apathetic; indifferent.

अनु- *anu-*, prep. **1.** after, according to (e.g. अनुमति, f. consent; अनुपद, adj. poet. following (one)). **2.** severally, each by each. **3.** in sequence (e.g. अनुकथन, m. conversation). **4.** repeatedly.

अनुकंपा *anu-kampā* [S.], f. compassion; sympathy.

अनुकंपित *anu-kampit* [S.], adj. moved by sympathy, or compassion.

अनुकथन *anu-kathan* [S.], m. **1.** conversation. **2.** narrative.

अनुकरण *anu-karaṇ* [S.], m. following the example (of), imitation; mimicry. — ~ करना (का), to imitate. – अनुकरण-कर्ता, m. inv. an imitator. अनुकरणवाचक, adj. onomatopoeic. अनुकरणात्मक, [°*ṇa*+*ā*°], adj. imitative.

अनुकरणीय *anu-karăṇīyă* [S.], adj. deserving to be followed, or emulated.

अनुकर्ष *anu-karṣ* [S.], m. = अनुकर्षण.

अनुकर्षण *anu-karṣaṇ* [S.], m. **1.** drawing, dragging. **2.** attraction; attractiveness. **3.** *phys.* attraction.

अनुकारक *anu-kārak* [S.], m. = अनुकारी.

अनुकारी *anu-kārī* [S.], adj. & m. acting in accordance with: **1.** adj. imitating. **2.** following. **3.** obeying. **4.** m. an imitator, &c.

अनुकाल *anu-kāl* [S.], adj. & m. **1.** adj. timely; appropriate. **2.** m. (*Pl.*) proper time, due season.

अनुकूल *anu-kūl* [S.], adj. **1.** conformable to; in accord with. **2.** favourable; helpful. **3.** well-disposed. **4.** ppn. (w. के). in accordance (with); according (to).

अनुकूल- *anukūl-* [ad. S. *anukūlayati*: w. H. *anukūl*], v.t. Brbh. to be well disposed (to).

अनुकूलता *anu-kūlătā* [S.], f. **1.** conformity; accord. **2.** favourable conditions; convenience, facilities. **3.** favour; assistance.

अनुकूलन *anu-kūlan* [S.], m. adaptation, adjustment.

अनुकूलित *anu-kūlit* [S.], adj. made suitable or convenient; adapted.

अनुकृति *anu-kr̥ti* [S.], f. imitation, replica.

अनुक्त *an-ukt* [S.], adj. **1.** unsaid; unexpressed, understood. **2.** not told.

अनुक्ति *an-ukti* [S.], f. **1.** silence. **2.** improper remarks.

अनुक्रम *anu-kram* [S.], m. **1.** order, succession. **2.** sequence, series.

अनुक्रमण *anu-kramaṇ* [S.], m. successive, or sequential movement.

अनुक्रमणिका *anu-kramăṇikā* [S.], f. ordered arrangement; index; table of contents.

अनुक्षण *anu-kṣaṇ* [S.], adv. **1.** every moment. **2.** continually; perpetually.

अनुगत *anu-gat* [S.], adj. **1.** followed; imitated. ***2.** following. **3.** -अनुगत. conformable (to), according (to).

अनुगति *anu-gati* [S.], f. **1.** following. **2.** imitation. **3.** transf. death.

अनुगम *anu-gam* [S.], m. **1.** going after, following. **2.** *logic.* induction.

अनुगमन *anu-gaman* [S.], m. **1.** going after, following; imitating; specif. the death by burning of a Hindu widow who has heard of her husband's death away from home (*Pl. HŚS.*) 2. = अनुगम, 2.

अनुगामी *anu-gāmī* [S.], adj. & m. **1.** adj. following, succeeding; consequent (on). **2.** imitating. **3.** obedient (to). **4.** m. a follower, &c. **5.** imitator. **6.** dependant; servant.

अनुगूँज *anu-gūṁj* [ad. *guñja-*: w. H. *gūṁj*], m. echo.

अनुगृहीत *anu-gṛhīt* [S.], adj. **1.** shown favour; obliged (to, का). **2.** dispensed from obligation, privileged, immune.

अनुग्रह *anu-grah* [S.], m. **1.** favour, kindness. **2.** patronage; support, assistance. — ~ करना, to do a favour (to, पर); to favour. मुझपर उसका ~ है, I am under an obligation to him. – अनुग्रह-काल, m. period of grace (for making a payment).

अनुग्रही *anu-grahī* [S.], m. = अनुग्राही.

अनुग्राहक *anu-grāhak* [S.], adj. & m. **1.** adj. showing favour, kind. **2.** m. patron, supporter.

अनुग्राही *anu-grāhī* [S.], adj. & m. = अनुग्राहक.

अनुग्राह्य *anu-grāhyă* [S.], adj. worthy of favour.

अनुचर *anu-car* [S.], m. **1.** a follower, adherent. **2.** servant. **3.** companion (in a venture).

अनुचरित *anu-carit* [S.], adj. followed, pursued; sought after.

अनुचार *anu-car* [cf. H. *anucārī*], m. adherence, allegiance.

अनुचारी *anu-cārī* [S.], m. = अनुचर.

अनुचित *an-ucit* [S.], adj. **1.** inappropriate, unsuitable. **2.** improper.

अनुचित्रक *anu-citrak* [S.], m. illustrator (of a book).

अनुच्छेद *anu-cched* [S.], m. section (of a document); paragraph, article.

अनुज *anu-j* [S.], adj. & m. **1.** adj. born afterwards, younger. **2.** m. a younger brother.

अनुजन्मा *anu-janmā* [S.], m. inv. having a following birth: = अनुज.

अनुजा *anu-jā* [S.], f. younger sister.

अनुजीवी *anu-jīvī* [S.], adj. & m. **1.** adj. living by or upon, dependent (on). **2.** following, adhering to. **3.** m. a dependent. **4.** an adherent.

अनुज्ञप्त *anu-jñapt* [S.], adj. **1.** sanctioned, permitted.

अनुज्ञप्ति *anu-jñapti* [S.], f. **1.** licence, sanction, permission. **2.** patent rights.

अनुज्ञा *anu-jñā* [S.], f. **1.** licence, sanction. **2.** order, command. **3.** patent rights. — अनुज्ञाधारी, m. a patent-holder. अनुज्ञा-पत्रित, adj. patented.

अनुज्ञात *anu-jñāt* [S.], adj. = अनुज्ञप्त.

अनुज्ञापक *anu-jñāpak* [S.], adj. granting sanction, or permission.

अनुज्ञापन *anu-jñāpan* [S.], m. = अनुज्ञा, 1., 2. **2.** making known, clarifying (a situation). **3.** expressing (apology, pardon).

अनुज्ञेय *anu-jñey* [S.], adj. deserving permission or sanction.

अनुताप *anu-tāp* [S.], m. **1.** remorse; repentance. **2.** distress.

अनुतापित *anu-tāpit* [S.], adj. troubled by remorse, &c.

अनुतापी *anu-tāpī* [S.], adj. & m. **1.** adj. remorseful, penitent; troubled. **2.** m. a penitent.

अनुत्तर *an-uttar* [S.], adj. **1.** having no superior: best, excellent. **2.** having no answer.

अनुदान *anu-dān* [S.], m. contribution (to finances); grant.

अनुदिन *anu-din* [S.], adv. **1.** daily. **2.** perpetually, always.

अनुदेश *anu-deś* [S.], m. instruction, directive.

अनुद्योग *an-ud-yog* [S.], m. & adj. **1.** m. indolence. **2.** adj. indolent.

अनुद्योगी *an-ud-yogī* [S.], adj. & m. **1.** adj. indolent. **2.** m. an indolent person.

अनुद्वाह *an-ud-vāh* [S.], m. non-marriage, celibacy.

अनुनय *anu-nay* [S.], m. **1.** conciliation; courtesy, kindness. **2.** entreaty. **3.** modest manner. — अनुनय-विनय, m. continuing entreaty.

अनुनयी *anu-nayī* [S.], adj. **1.** acting courteously. **2.** making entreaty. **3.** showing modesty.

अनुनाद *anu-nād* [S.], m. echo, resonance.

अनुनासिक *anu-nasik* [S.], adj. & m. **1.** adj. nasal (of sound). **2.** m. a script indication of vowel nasality (= *candrabindu*).

अनुनासिकता *anu-nāsikătā* [S.], f. nasality.

अनुनीत *anu-nīt* [S.], adj. courteous; deferential.

अनुन्नत *an-unnat* [S.], adj. not developed or uplifted: backward.

अनुन्नति *an-unnati* [S.], f. undeveloped state, backwardness.

अनुपकार *an-upă-kār* [S.], m. disservice, harm.

अनुपकारी *an-upă-kārī* [S.], adj. & m. **1.** adj. not assisting or benefiting, harmful. **2.** m. unserviceable, useless.

अनुपम *an-upa-m* [S.], adj. **1.** incomparable. **2.** excellent, best.

अनुपमित *an-upa-mit* [S.], adj. uncompared (= अनुपम).

अनुपमेय *an-upa-mey* [S.], adj. incomparable.

अनुपलक्षित *an-upă-lakṣit* [S.], adj. unnoticed, unknown.

अनुपलब्ध *an-upă-labdh* [S.], adj. **1.** not obtained. **2.** not extant.

अनुपलब्धि *an-upă-labdhi* [S.], f. non-availability.

अनुपस्थित *an-upă-sthit* [S.], adj. not present, absent.

अनुपस्थिति *an-upă-sthiti* [S.], f. non-attendance, absence.

अनुपात *anu-pāt* [S.], m. **1.** successive arrival or incidence. ***2.** proportion; ratio. **3.** arithmetical progression. — अनुपातहीनता, f. disproportion, imbalance.

अनुपातक *anu-pātak* [S.], m. a heinous offence.

अनुपातन *anu-pātan* [S.], m. grading, sorting.

अनुपाती *anu-pātī* [S.], adj. proportionate.

अनुपान *anu-pān* [S.], m. a drink taken with or after medicine.

अनुपूरक *anu-pūrak* [S.], adj. supplementary.

अनुप्राणित *anu-prāṇit* [S.], adj. inspired.

अनुप्रास *anu-prās* [S.], m. **1.** assonance; alliteration. **2.** repetition of words (in literary composition).

अनुबंध *anu-bandh* [S.], m. **1.** connection; relationship, correlation. ***2.** contract, agreement. **3.** stipulation. **4.** appendix (to a document). **5.** section (of a book). **6.** sequel, result.

अनुबंधक *anu-bandhak* [S.], m. party to an agreement.

अनुबंधन *anu-bandhan* [S.], m. **1.** binding, connection. **2.** entering into a contract, &c. **3.** unbroken succession, or series.

अनुबंधी *anu-bandhī* [S.], adj. & m. **1.** adj. connected with, attached. **2.** resulting. **3.** m. a party to a contract.

अनुबद्ध *anu-baddh* [S.], adj. **1.** connected, attached. **2.** stipulated.

अनुबल *anu-bal* [S.], m. extra or reserve force, reinforcement.

अनुभव *anu-bhav* [S.], m. **1.** perception; consciousness. **2.** feeling. ***3.** experience (of, का, से); impression (of). — ~ करना, to be conscious (of, का), to be alive (to); to experience. – अनुभवपरक, perceptive (as words, advice); conducive to (right) feeling or impression. अनुभवप्राप्त, adj. experienced. अनुभववाद, m. empiricism. °ई, adj. & m. empirical; empiricist. अनुभवसिद्ध, adj. established by experience, empirical. अनुभवशील, adj. experienced. अनुभवहीन, adj. inexperienced. °ता, f. अनुभवातीत [°*va*+*a*°], adj. beyond experience, transcendental. अनुभवोक्ति [°*va*+*u*°], f. aphorism.

अनुभवी *anu-bhavī* [S.], adj. perceptive; sensitive; experienced.

अनुभाजन *anu-bhājan* [S.], m. distribution, apportionment.

अनुभाव *anu-bhāv* [S.], m. **1.** dignity. **2.** authority, power; influence. **3.** *rhet.* sign, indication of feelings by look or gesture. **4.** firm opinion, conviction.

अनुभावक *anu-bhāvak* [S.], adj. causing to perceive, or to feel.

अनुभावन *anu-bhāvan* [S.], m. expression of the feelings by look or gesture.

अनुभावी *anu-bhāvī* [S.], adj. possessing experience (of sthg).

अनुभाव्य *anu-bhāvyă* [S.], adj. **1.** to be experienced. **2.** of worth, estimable.

अनुभूत *anu-bhūt* [S.], adj. **1.** perceived, realised, understood. ***2.** felt; experienced.

अनुभूति *anu-bhūti* [S.], f. **1.** perception. **2.** realisation. ***3.** feeling; sensitivity (of feeling). — अनुभूतिपूर्ण, adj. sensitive; emotive. अनुभूतिमय, adj. rich in feeling (a work, a poem). अनुभूतिमूलक, adj. based on perception, empirical.

अनुमत *anu-mat* [S.], adj. **1.** allowed, assented to; approved, agreeable. **2.** advised, counselled.

अनुमति *anu-mati* [S.], f. **1.** permission, assent; approval. **2.** advice, counsel. **3.** command, decree. — अनुमतिप्राप्त, adj. approved; *fin.* listed, quoted. अनुमत्यर्थ [°*ti*+*a*°], adj. *ling.* imperative.

अनुमरण *anu-maraṇ* [S.], m. *hist. Pl. HŚS.* following in death: death by burning of a Hindu widow.

अनुमान *anu-mān* [S.], m. **1.** inference. **2.** notion; opinion. **3.** conjecture; estimate; guess. — ~ करना, or लगाना, to conjecture; to suppose; to estimate. ~ से, adv. conjecturally; at an estimate. – अनुमानत:, adv. id.

अनुमान- *anumān-* [cf. H. *anumān*], v.t. Brbh. Av. to think, to consider.

अनुमानिक *anu-mānik* [S.], adj. **1.** conjectural; hypothetical; suppositious.

अनुमानित *anu-mānit* [S.], adj. conjectured, estimated.

अनुमानी *anu-mānī*, adj. & m. **1.** [cf. H. *anumān*] adj. = अनुमानिक. **2.** [S.] m. theoriser; guesser.

अनुमापक *anu-māpak* [S.], adj. giving rise to an inference.

अनुमापन *anu-māpan* [S.], m. titration.

अनुमित *anu-mit* [S.], adj. inferred.

अनुमोद *anu-mod* [S.], m. = अनुमोदन.

अनुमोदक *anu-modak* [S.], adj. &. m. **1.** adj. approving, &c. **2.** m. a supporter; advocate.

अनुमोदन *anu-modan* [S.], m. **1.** approval. **2.** encouragement, incitement. **3.** seconding (a motion).

अनुमोदित *anu-modit* [S.], adj. approved; given support (as a measure).

अनुयाचन *anu-yācan* [S.], m. canvassing.

अनुयायी *anu-yāyī* [S.], m. a follower; adherent.

अनुयोक्ता *anu-yoktā* [S.], m. inv. one who enquires, &c. (see अनुयोग).

अनुयोग *anu-yog* [S.], m. **1.** enquiry, query; examination. **2.** rebuke, reproof.

अनुयोगी *anu-yogī* [S.], adj. enquiring, &c.

अनुयोजन *anu-yojan* [S.], m. the act of enquiry, &c. (see अनुयोग).

अनुयोजित *anu-yojit* [S.], adj. enquired into; examined.

अनुरंजक *anu-rañjak* [S.], adj. **1.** conciliating, satisfying. **2.** diverting, delighting.

अनुरंजन *anu-rañjan* [S.], m. **1.** conciliating, satisfying. **2.** diverting, delighting. **3.** delight. **4.** attachment, devotion. **5.** love.

अनुरंजित *anu-rañjit* [S.], adj. **1.** conciliated, &c. **2.** diverted, &c.

अनुरक्त *anu-rakt* [S.], adj. **1.** attached (to, में), devoted (to). **2.** engrossed (in, में).

अनुरक्ति *anu-rakti* [S.], f. attachment, devotion.

अनुरक्षण *anu-rakṣaṇ* [S.], m. maintenance (of equipment).

अनुराग *anu-rāg* [S.], m. **1.** attachment, affection; devotion. **2.** love, passion.

अनुराग- *anurāg-* [cf. H. *anurāg*, S. *anurāga-*], v.i. Brbh. Av. to feel attachment, &c. (for).

अनुरागी *anu-rāgī* [S.], adj. & m. **1.** adj. attached (to, पर); devoted (to). **2.** loving, passionate. **3.** m. a devotee, lover.

अनुराधा *anu-rādhā* [S.], f. the seventeenth *nakṣatra* or lunar mansion; stars in Libra.

अनुरूप *anu-rūp* [S.], adj. & m. **1.** adj. similar. **2.** corresponding, conformable; convenient. **3.** m. resemblance. **4.** correspondence, conformity. **5.** ppn. (w. के). corresponding (to).

अनुरूपक *anu-rūpak* [S.], m. **1.** image. **2.** sthg. similar: one of a pair.

अनुरेखन *anu-rekhan* [S.], m. tracing, copying by line.

अनुरोध *anu-rodh* [S.], m. **1.** obligingness, kind service. **2.** consideration, respect. ***3.** insistent entreaty, appeal. **4.** E.H. check, obstacle. — अनुरोध-पत्र, m. memorandum; letter of request.

अनुरोधक *anu-rodhak* [S.], adj. & m. **1.** adj. = अनुरोधी. **2.** m. = अनुरोध-पत्र.

अनुरोधी *anu-rodhī* [S.], adj. **1.** insistent. **2.** acting in compliance (with, के); kind, considerate.

अनुलेप *anu-lep* [S.], m. **1.** anointing, smearing. **2.** a fragrant ointment.

अनुलेपन *anu-lepan* [S.], m. **1.** anointing. **2.** smearing.

अनुलोम *anu-lom* [S.], adj. & adv. with the hair, with the grain: in natural or regular order.

अनुवर्तन *anu-vartan* [S.], m. **1.** following. **2.** acting in accordance (with), compliance; obedience. **3.** outcome.

अनुवर्ती *anu-vartī* [S.], adj. & m. **1.** adj. following; adhering to (as to a leader, or view). **2.** esp. in comp. observing, obeying (a directive). **3.** resulting on, consequent. **4.** m. a follower, &c.

अनुवा *anuvā* [*anūpa-*], m. *Pl. HŚS.* **1.** place where one stands to throw water from a sling-basket, when irrigating. **2.** platform at a well (from which water is drawn). **3.** sling-basket.

अनुवाद *anu-vād* [S.], m. **1.** repetition of sthg. said: an interpretation. ★**2.** a translation.

अनुवादक *anu-vādak* [S.], m. a translator.

अनुवादित *anu-vādit* [S.], adj. translated (= अनूदित).

अनुवादी *anu-vādī* [S.], m. & adj. **1.** m. = अनुवादक. **2.** adj. replying (to), answering. (*Pl. HŚS.*)

अनुवाद्य *anu-vādyă* [S.], adj. **1.** requiring or deserving translation. **2.** translatable. **3.** in process of translation.

अनुवृत्त *anu-vr̥tt* [S.], adj. & m. **1.** adj. following; adhering (to). **2.** complying with, obeying. **3.** taken up, adverted to (remarks, &c). **4.** pensioned. **5.** m. pensioner.

अनुवृत्ति *anu-vr̥tti* [S.], f. **1.** following. **2.** compliance. **3.** taking up (remarks, &c). ★**4.** subsistence; pension; stipend. अनुवृत्तिधारी, m. pensioner.

अनुवृत्तिक *anu-vr̥ttik* [S.], adj. pensionable.

अनुवृत्ती *anu-vr̥ttī* [S.], m. = अनुवृत्त, 5.

अनुशासक *anu-śāsak* [S.], m. **1.** one in control; governor; administrator. **2.** preceptor. **3.** proctor.

अनुशासन *anu-śāsan* [S.], m. **1.** control; discipline. **2.** control, management. **3.** directive, precept. — ~ करना (का), to control, &c. – अनुशासनात्मक [°*a* + *ā*°], adj. disciplinary.

अनुशासनिक *anu-śāsănik* [S.], adj. disciplinary.

अनुशासित *anu-śāsit* [S.], adj. **1.** controlled; disciplined. **2.** controlled, directed.

अनुशीलन *anu-śīlan* [S.], m. **1.** (mental) reflection. **2.** continued study; practice.

अनुशीलित *anu-śīlit* [S.], adj. **1.** pondered over. **2.** studied constantly; practised.

अनुशोक *anu-śok* [S.], m. sorrow over sthg., remorse, regret.

अनुषंग *anu-ṣaṅg* [S.], m. **1.** connection, association. **2.** compassion.

अनुष्ठान *anu-ṣṭhān* [S.], m. **1.** carrying out, undertaking (an activity). **2.** beginning, inception. **3.** observance, rite, practice.

अनुष्ठित *anu-ṣṭhit* [S.], adj. **1.** begun, inaugurated. **2.** carried out.

अनुश्रुत *anu-śrut* [S.], adj. handed down by tradition: legendary.

अनुसंधाता *anu-san-dhātā* [S.], m. inv. an enquirer, researcher.

अनुसंधान *anu-san-dhān* [S.], m. **1.** search, enquiry; investigation. **2.** research. — अनुसंधान-कर्ता, m. inv. an enquirer, researcher.

अनुसंधानी *anu-san-dhānī* [S.], adj. & m. **1.** adj. searching, enquiring. **2.** curious (to learn). **3.** m. an enquirer, researcher.

अनुसंधायक *anu-san-dhāyak* [S.], m. an enquirer, researcher.

अनुसमर्थन *anu-sam-arthan* [S.], m. ratification.

अनुसर- *anusar-* [cf. H. *anusār-*], v.i. Brbh. Av. **1.** to follow; to be consequent (upon). **2.** to imitate.

अनुसरण *anu-saraṇ* [S.], m. **1.** following. **2.** pursuing. **3.** following out, acting in accordance with (a condition, &c). **4.** custom, practice. **5.** imitating. **6.** succession. — ~ करना, to follow, &c.

अनुसार *anu-sār* [S.], m. conformity to usage: **1.** ppn. (w. के). according, conformably (to); answering (to); following, like. **2.** adv. in comp. id. नियमानुसार, in accordance with rule or habit.

अनुसार- *anusār-* [? ad. *anusārayati*], v.t. Brbh. **1.** to follow. **2.** to follow (a norm, &c.); to act.

अनुसारी *anu-sārī* [S.], adj. **1.** following, attendant. **2.** serving.

अनुसूचित *anu-sūcit* [S.], adj. scheduled, listed.

अनुसूची *anu-sūcī* [S.], f. schedule. — ~ दर f. scheduled tariff.

अनुसोचक *anu-socak* [S.], adj. **1.** regretting. **2.** [? × *śocya-*] regrettable.

अनुसोचना *anu-socănā* [ad. *anuśocana-*], f. grief.

अनुस्वार *anu-svār* [S.], m. *gram.* after-sound: **1.** vowel nasality (as denoted in the Devanāgarī script by a superscript dot). **2.** a superscript dot used in the Devanāgarī script to denote vowel nasality or (frequently in writing Hindi) a homorganic or other nasal consonant.

अनुहर- *anuhar-* [ad. *anuharati*], v.t. Brbh. Av. **1.** to imitate; to resemble. **2.** to be pleasant, congenial; to enhance (as ornaments a wearer's beauty).

अनुहरण *anu-haraṇ* [S.], m. imitation; resemblance.

अनुहार *anu-hār* [S.], m. & adj. **1.** imitation; resemblance. **2.** manner, fashion; appearance. **3.** adj. Brbh. resembling.

अनुहार- *anuhār-* [cf. H. *anuhār*], v.t. Brbh. Av. to imitate; to resemble.

अनुहारक *anu-hārak* [S.], adj. & m. **1.** adj. imitating, copying. **2.** m. an imitator, &c.

अनुहारी *anu-hārī* [S.], adj. **1.** imitating; resembling. **2.** imitated, copied (from).

अनूठा *anūṭhā* [**anna-uṭṭha-*], adj. **1.** uncommon, unprecedented; strange. **2.** rare, wonderful.

अनूदित *anûdit* [S.], adj. translated.

[1]**अनूप** *anūp* [S.], adj. & m. **1.** adj. watery, wet (land). **2.** m. swamp.

[2]**अनूप** *anūp* [corr. (metr.) H. *anupam*: ×H. *anūṭhā*], adj. incomparable; peerless, splendid; best.

अनृणी *an-ṛṇī* [S.], adj. free from debt (= उऋण).

अनेक *an-ek* [S.], adj. not one: **1.** many; several. **2.** various. **3.** much, abundant. — अनेकचित्त, adj. inconstant of mind. अनेकधा, adv. in various ways; by different means. अनेकरूप, adj. of various forms; of various kinds; variable of mind, fickle. अनेकवाद, m. *philos.* pluralism. अनेकविध, adj. of various kinds. अनेकशः, adv. frequently; = अनेकधा. अनेकाकार [°*ka*+*ā*°], adj. of various forms. अनेकाक्षर [°*ka*+*a*°], adj. polysyllabic. अनेकानेक [°*ka*+*a*°], adj. many different; very many. अनेकार्थ [°*ka*+*a*°], adj. of more than one meaning (a word). °अक, adj. id. अनेकेश्वरवाद [°*ka*+*ī*°], m. polytheism. °वादी, adj. & m. polytheistic; polytheist.

अनेकता *anekătā* [S.], f. = अनेकत्व.

अनेकत्व *anekatvă* [S.], m. **1.** variety, diversity. **2.** abundance.

अनेला *anelā*, adj. naive (cf. अलबेला), gullible.

अनैक्य *an-aikyă* [S.], m. disunity; discord, disagreement.

अनैस *anais* [? ad. *anāyāsa-*], adj. *Pl. HŚS.* ? worthless, bad.

अनैसे *anaise* [? ad. *anāyāsa-*], adv. **1.** easily, &c. **2.** Av. involuntarily: moved by a feeling of ill-will.

अनैसो *an-aiso*, adj. Brbh. = अनैस.

अनोखा *anokhā* [*anapekṣa-*], adj. **1.** uncommon, unprecedented; strange. **2.** novel; unique. **3.** rare, wonderful.

अनोना *a-nonā* [cf. H. *non*], adj. unsalted.

अनौआ *anauā*, m. Bihar. = अनुवा.

अनौटा *anauṭā*, m. *Pl.* = [1]अनवट.

अन्न *ann* [S.], m. **1.** food; food supplies, provisions. **2.** grain. — ~ का कीड़ा, m. grain-worm: man, mankind. ~ लगना, fig. to put on weight. – अन्न-कूट, m. pile of grain: a festival celebrated on the day following Dīvālī by the placing of foodstuffs in front of an idol of Viṣṇu-Kṛṣṇa. अन्न-कोष्ठ, m. a food-store, granary. अन्न-चोर, m. a hoarder of food, speculator in foodstuffs. अन्न-जल, m. food and drink. अन्न-जल उठना, to have no means of sustenance (at or in, से). अन्न-दाता, m. inv. food-giver: provider; benefactor; master. अन्न-धन, m. food and wealth; the wealth which is in food, essentials of life. अन्नपूर्ण, fertile, abundant; °आ, f. title of Durgā. अन्न-प्राशन, m. the ceremony of giving rice boiled in milk to an infant for the first time (usually between the fifth and eighth month). अन्न-वस्त्र, m. food and clothing. अन्न-शाला, f. granary. अन्नोत्पादन [°*na*+*u*°], m. food-production.

अन्ना *annā*, f. *Pl. HŚS.* wet-nurse.

अन्नी *annī* [cf. H. [1]*ānā*: and *ikannī*], f. = इकन्नी.

अन्य *anya* [S]. adj. other; different. — ~ पुरुष, m. *gram.* third person. – अन्यतम, adj. best (of all); supreme. अन्यतर, adj. better (of two); other, another, a different. अन्यतः, adv. from elsewhere; otherwise. अन्यदेशी, adj. & m. foreign; foreigner. °-देशीय, adj. & m. idd.; alien. अन्यमनस्क, adj. absent-minded. °ता, f. अन्यसंगम, m. adultery. अन्यापदेश [°*nya*+*a*°], m. allegory. °इक, adj. अन्योन्य [°*ya*+*a*°], adj. mutual; reciprocal.

अन्यत्र *anyatră* [S.], adv. **1.** elsewhere. **2.** otherwise (than, से). — अन्यत्र-स्थित, adj. located elsewhere. °इ, f. alibi.

अन्यथा *anyăthā* [S.], adv. **1.** otherwise; contrarily. **2.** adj. contrary; improper, wrong. — ~ करना, to revoke, to set aside (an order, &c). – अन्यथाकारिता, f. contrariness, paradoxical nature. अन्यथाचार [°*thā*+*ā*°], m. improper or wrong course of action.

अन्याय *a-ny-āy* [S.], m. **1.** injustice, wrong. **2.** oppression, outrage.

अन्यायी *a-ny-āyī* [S.], adj. & m. **1.** adj. unjust, wrong. **2.** oppressive; wicked. **3.** m. an unjust person. **4.** a wrong-doer.

अन्योन्य *anyonyă* [S.], adj. see s.v. अन्य.

अन्वय *anv-ay* [S.], m. **1.** connection; relationship. **2.** *gram.* syntax. **3.** family, lineage. **4.** leisure.

अन्वयन *anv-ayan* [S.], m. establishing a connection: determination (as of a meaning).

अन्वयी *anv-ayī* [S.], adj. **1.** connected; related. **2.** related by blood or family.

अन्वित *anv-it* [S.], adj. **1.** joined to. **2.** -अन्वित. endowed (with), possessed (of). **3.** fraught (with: as with emotion).

अन्विति *anv-iti* [S.], f. **1.** connected nature; unity. **2.** *lit.* unity (as of time, place, action).

अन्वीक्ष *anv-īkṣ* [S.], m. microscope.

अन्वीक्षण *anv-īkṣaṇ* [S.], m. microscopic, or minute, investigation.

अन्वेषक *anv-eṣak* [S.], adj. & m. **1.** adj. carrying out investigation, &c. (see अन्वेषण.) **2.** m. an investigator, &c.

अन्वेषण *anv-eṣaṇ* [S.], m. **1.** enquiry, investigation. **2.** research. — अन्वेषण-कर्ता, m. inv. an investigator; researcher. अन्वेषणालय [°*ṇa* + *ā*°], m. a research institute; laboratory.

अन्वेषित *anv-eṣit* [S.], adj. investigated.

अन्वेषी *anv-eṣī* [S], adj. **1.** -अन्वेषी. = अनवेषक, 1. **2.** m. = अन्वेषक, 2.

अपंग *apaṅg* [ad. *apāṅga-*: cf. *aṅga-*], adj. **1.** maimed. **2.** infirm, helpless.

अपंथी *a-panthī* [S.], adj. & m. without a path, on a bad path: **1.** adj. astray, lost. **2.** heretical. **3.** m. a heretic.

अप- *apă-* [S.], pref. away, back; down (esp. expressing inferiority: e.g. अपमान, m. disgrace; अपशब्द, m. term of abuse).

अपक *a-pak* [ad. *apakva-*], adj. = अपक्व.

अपकर्म *apă-karm* [S.], m. bad deed, misdeed.

अपकर्ष *apă-karṣ* [S.], m. **1.** deterioration: state of deterioration or decline. **2.** disgrace; fall.

अपकलंक *apă-kalaṅk* [S.], m. an indelible disgrace.

अपकार *apă-kār* [S.], m. **1.** detriment; harm, injury; disservice. **2.** affront, offence. **3.** wrong action, misconduct.

अपकारक *apă-kārak* [S.], adj. = अपकारी.

अपकारिता *apă-kāritā* [S.], f. injuriousness; offensiveness.

अपकारी *apă-kārī* [S.], adj. & m. **1.** adj. injurious, harmful; offensive. **2.** hostile, inimical. **3.** wrong, censurable. **4.** m. one who acts injuriously, &c. — अपकारीचार, m. Av. a wrongdoer.

अपकीर्ति *apă-kīrti* [S.], f. disrepute, dishonour; infamy.

अपकृष्ट *apă-kr̥ṣṭ* [S.], adj. **1.** deteriorated: inferior. **2.** base, abhorrent.

अपकृष्टता *apă-kr̥ṣṭătā* [S.], f. **1.** deteriorated state: inferiority. **2.** baseness, meanness; vileness.

अपक्व *a-pakvă* [S.], adj. **1.** uncooked, raw. **2.** unripe. **3.** immature.

अपक्वता *a-pakvătā* [S.] f. **1.** rawness. **2.** unripeness. **3.** immaturity.

अपक्ष *a-pakṣ* [S.], adj. **1.** wingless. **2.** taking no side: impartial; uninvolved.

अपगत *apă-gat* [S.], adj. gone away or amiss: strayed.

अपगति *apă-gati* [S.], f. **1.** improper, or base behaviour. **2.** ill repute. **3.** dire condition, plight.

अपघर्षण *apă-gharṣaṇ* [S.], m. abrasion (= रगड़).

अपच *a-pac* [S.], m. indigestion.

अपचय *apă-cay* [S.], m. **1.** loss, damage; waste. **2.** reduction (as in price); decline.

अपछरा *apăcharā*, f. Av. = अप्सरा.

अपटु *a-paṭu* [S.], adj. not deft, awkward; unskilled.

अपटुता *a-paṭutā* [S.], f. awkwardness; lack of skill.

अपढ़ *a-paṛh* [cf. H. *paṛhnā*], adj. = अनपढ़.

[1]**अपत** *a-pat* [ad. *apattra-*], adj. Brbh. leafless.

[2]**अपत** *apat* [cf. H. *pat*], adj. & m. Brbh. Av. **1.** adj. base, shameful; wicked. **2.** m. shame, disgrace.

अपतुष्टि *apă-tuṣṭi* [S.], f. appeasement.

अपति *a-pati* [S.], adj. **1.** not having a husband (a woman). **2.** not having a master.

अपतिव्रता *a-pativratā* [S.], f. not keeping the marital vow: an unfaithful wife.

अपतुष्टि *apă-tuṣṭi* [S.], f. appeasement.

अपत्य *apatyă* [S.], m. offspring, descendant. — अपत्यवाचक, adj. *gram.* patronymic.

अपथ *a-path* [S.], m. Brbh. **1.** a bad or impassable road. **2.** a wrong course, improper path.

अपथ्य *a-pathyă* [S.], adj. unwholesome, indigestible.

अपदस्थ *a-padasth* [S.], adj. 1.dismissed. **2.** deposed.

अपन *apan*, pron. reg. I.

अपनपा *apanpā* [cf. H. *apnā*], m. reg. = अपनापन.

अपना *apnā* [*ātmanaka-: Pk. *appaṇaya-*], adj. **1.** adj. one's, one's own; (in most cases where a second reference to a possessor is made within a simple sentence or a clause) his, her, my, &c. **2.** personal, private, individual. **अपनी ओर से**, for one's own part. **3.** (intensive) one's own. **मेरी अपनी कहानी**, my own story. **4.** m. usu. pl. one's relatives, friends, circle. **5.** **अपने**, refl. pron. obl. oneself. **अपने तक रखना**, to keep (a matter) to oneself. **अपने से**, adv. for, on, one's own part. — ~ ~, each his own, various, respective; particular, individual. ~ **करना**, to make (a person or thing) one's own; to appropriate; to usurp; to embezzle; to gain an ascendancy over, to win over, to charm; to attach (a person) to oneself. ~ **किया पाना**, to reap the fruit of one's actions. ~ **पराया**, m. & adj. (usu. pl.) relations and strangers; friends and foes; one's own and another's, others'. ~ **बेगाना**, or **बिगाना**, id. ~ **होना**, to become one's own; to become attached to one; to become one's creature; to behave like a relation. **वह रिश्वत देने से ~ होता है**, he can be bribed. **अपनी अपनी पड़ना (को)**, to be concerned each with his own affairs. **अपनी करके**, adv. as, or as carefully as, one's own. **अपनी**, or ~, **गाना**, to sing one's own praises, to boast; to be full of one's own affairs. **अपनी नींद सोना**, to sleep as or when one pleases: to be one's own master; to be free of care. **अपनी बीती**, f. sthg. which has happened to oneself. **अपने आप**, refl. pron. oneself; adv. on one's own, &c. (= **आप से आप**, **आप ही आप**). **अपने से ज़्यादा करना**, to over-exert oneself (to do sthg.); to go out of one's way. **अपने हाथों**, adv. with one's own hands. **अपना-सा करना**, to do what one can; to do as one thinks best. **अपना-सा मुँह लेकर**, with a peculiar look: disappointedly, in chagrin; shamefacedly; foolishly. **अपनी-सी करना**, to do as one pleases.

अपनाना *apnānā* [cf. H. *apnā*], v.t. **1.** to make (a person or thing) one's own, &c. (= **अपना करना**). **2.** to follow, to adopt (an attitude or a course of action).

अपनापन *apnāpan* [cf. H. *apnā*], m. **1.** kinship. **2.** affinity, intimacy. **3.** self-respect.

अपनापा *apnāpā* [cf. H. *apnā*], m. = अपनापन.

अपनाम *apă-nām* [S.], m. bad name, ill repute.

अपनायत *apnāyat* [cf. H. *apnā*], f. **1.** kinship. **2.** intimacy, friendship.

अपनाहट *apnāhaṭ*, f. = अपनायत, 2.

अपभय *apă-bhay* [S.], Brbh. Av. fear; unreasoning or blameworthy fear.

अपभाषा *apă-bhāṣā* [S.], f. coarse or obscene language.

अपभ्रंश *apă-bhraṃś* [S.], m. f. **1.** m. degeneration, corrupt form (esp. of speech and grammar). **2.** m. f. specif. any late corrupt form or far-evolved form of Middle Indo-Aryan language.

अपभ्रष्ट *apă-bhraṣṭ* [S.], adj. degenerate, corrupt.

अपमान *apă-mān* [S.], m. **1.** disrespect; disparagement; slander. **2.** dishonour, disgrace; libel. **3.** insult. **4.** contempt. — **अपमानकारी**, adj. = अपमानी, 2. **अपमानजनक**, adj. shameful, humiliating. **अपमानसूचक**, adj. contemptuous; disparaging.

अपमान- *apă-mān-* [cf. *apamāna-*], v.t. Brbh. Av. to show disrespect, contempt.

अपमानित *apă-mānit* [S.], adj. **1.** shown disrespect, &c. **2.** dishonoured, shamed. **3.** insulted.

अपमानी *apă-mānī* [S.], adj. & m. **1.** adj. disrespectful, &c. **2.** dishonouring, dishonourable (as an action); humiliating. **3.** dishonourable, disreputable (a person). **4.** insulting. **5.** m. a dishonourable person, &c.

अपमान्य *apă-mānyă* [S.], adj. deserving disrespect, dishonour, &c.

अपमृत्यु *apă-mṛtyu* [S.], f. sudden or untimely death.

अपयश *apă-yaś* [S.], m. **1.** dishonour, disgrace, shame. **2.** infamy. — **अपयशस्कर**, adj. dishonourable, &c.

अपयशकर *apă-yaśkar*, adj. = अपयशस्कर, see s.v. अपयश.

अपयशी *apă-yaśī* [S.], adj. **1.** dishonoured, disgraced. **2.** infamous.

अपरंपार *a-parampār* [S.], adj. & m. boundless, infinite; the infinite.

अपर *apar* [S.], adj. **1.** later, latter; following. **2.** western. **3.** interior; lower (as this world compared to another). ***4.** other, another; a second. — **अपर-परागण**, m. cross-pollination.

अपरस *apăras* [ad. *sparśa-*, *spṛśya-*], adj. & m. **1.** adj. untouched. **2.** untouchable. **3.** m. pej. what is not to be touched (sthg. judged to be polluting). — ~ **छूत**, f. ritual pollution by touch or association.

अपराजित *a-parā-jit* [S.], adj. **1.** undefeated. **2.** invincible. — **अपराजिता**, f. undefeated: a title of Durgā.

अपराजेय *a-parā-jey* [S.], adj. invincible.

अपराध *apă-rādh* [S.], m. **1.** a fault, an offence; guilt (over an offence). **2.** a crime. **3.** sin. — ~ **करना**, to offend (against, **का**); to sin (against). ~ **लगाना**, to impute a crime, &c. (to, **पर** or **को**); to accuse (of, **का**); to defame, to slander. – **अपराध-विज्ञान**, m. criminology. **अपराधशील**, adj. of criminal tendencies.

अपराधिक *apă-rādhik* [S.], adj. corr. criminal.

अपराधिता *apă-rādhitā* [S.], f. criminality, crime.

अपराधी *apă-rādhī* [S.], adj. & m. **1.** adj. blameworthy, culpable; guilty (of an offence). **2.** criminal. **3.** m. a guilty person, transgressor. **4.** a criminal.

अपराह्न *aparâhnă* [S.], m. early afternoon (midday to about three p.m).

अपरिचय *a-pari-cay* [S.], m. lack of acquaintance or knowledge (with or of, **से**).

अपरिचित *a-pari-cit* [S.], adj. **1.** unacquainted (with, **से**); not conversant (with). **2.** unknown, unrecognised (a person). **3.** unknown, unfamiliar (a matter, a topic); distant (a glance).

अपरिमित *a-pari-mit* [S.], adj. unmeasured; unlimited.

अपरिहार्य *a-pari-hāryă* [S.], adj. **1.** unavoidable (reason, &c). **2.** obligatory (duty). **3.** inalienable (right).

अपरीक्षित *a-parîkṣit* [S.], adj. **1.** untested, unexamined. **2.** unproved.

अपरूप *apă-rūp* [S.], adj. deformed; distorted.

अपलक *a-palak* [cf. H. *palak*], adj. unblinking (eyes); fixed (gaze).

अपलक्षण *apă-lakṣaṇ* [S.], m. a bad omen; bad sign.

अपवंचन *apă-vañcan* [S.], m. evasion, avoidance (as of tax).

अपवचन *apă-vacan* [S.], m. **1.** abuse. **2.** slander.

अपवर्ग *apă-varg* [S.], m. completion, end: release (as from suffering, or rebirth), emancipation.

अपवर्जन *apă-varjan* [S.], m. getting rid of: exclusion.

अपवर्जित *apă-varjit* [S.], adj. got rid of: excluded.

अपवर्तक *apă-vartak* [S.], m. *math.* a factor.

अपवर्तन *apă-vartan* [S.], m. removal: forfeiture (= **ज़ब्ती**).

अपवर्त्य *apă-vartyă* [S.], m. *math.* a multiple.

अपवश *apă-vaś*, adj. not subject, independent.

अपवाद *apă-vād* [S.], m. **1.** censure, blame, reproach. **2.** complaint, accusation. **3.** *philos.* refutation. ***4.** an exception, a special case. — **अपवादस्वरूप**, adv. by way of exception.

अपवादक *apă-vādak* [S.], adj. = **अपवादिक**.

अपवादिक *apă-vādik* [S.], adj. corr. **1.** exceptional, occurring as a special case. 2. = **अपवादी**.

अपवादित *apă-vādit* [S.], adj. **1.** censured, &c. **2.** slandered. **3.** refuted; challenged (as testimony).

अपवादी *apă-vādī* [S.], adj. & m. **1.** adj. censuring, &c. ***2.** exceptional. **3.** complaining. **4.** m. a complainant, plaintiff.

अपवाह *apă-vāh* [S.], m. flowing down: catchment (area).

अपवित्र *a-pavitra* [S.], adj. unclean, impure; unholy.

अपवित्रता *a-pavitrătā* [S.], f. uncleanness, unholiness.

अपव्यय *apă-vy-ay* [S.], m. **1.** mis-spending, bad use (of money). ***2.** extravagance.

अपव्ययी *apă-vy-ayī* [S.], adj. extravagant (in expenditure).

अपशकुन *apă-śakun* [S.], m. a bad omen.

अपशब्द *apă-śabd* [S.], m. **1.** an ungrammatical usage. **2.** an echo word attached to another. ***3.** an abusive word; abuse.

अपसंचय *apă-sañ-cay* [S.], m. hoarding.

अपसामान्य *apă-sāmānyă* [S.], adj. abnormal.

अपस्मार *apă-smār* [S.], m. epilepsy (= **मिरगी**).

अपहर- *apa-har-* [ad. *apaharati*], v.t. Av. **1.** to carry off, to take as plunder. **2.** to alleviate (an adverse effect).

अपहरण *apă-haraṇ* [S.], m. **1.** carrying off, taking as plunder; kidnapping; hi-jacking. **2.** robbing, stealing. **3.** depriving (of rank, rights); loss. — **अपहरण-कर्ता**, m. inv. one who carries off, &c.

अपहरणीय *apă-harănīyă* [S.], adj. **1.** to be carried off, &c. **2.** to be withdrawn, reduced (as rights, rank).

अपहर्ता *apă-hartā*, m. inv. one who carries off, robs, &c. (see s.v. **अपहरण**).

अपहार *apă-hār* [S.], m. carrying off: 1. = अपहरण, 1. **2.** embezzlement.

अपहारित *apă-hārit* [S.], adj. = अपहृत.

अपहारी *apă-hārī* [S.], m. = अपहरण-कर्ता.

अपहृत *apă-hṛt* [S.], adj. carried off: **1.** abducted. **2.** plundered.

अपांग *apâṅg* [S.], adj. **1.** bodiless, disembodied (as Kāmdev, the god of love). **2.** maimed. — **अपांग-दर्शन**, m. an ogling glance, leer.

अपाक *a-pāk* [S.], adj. & m. **1.** adj. immature, not ripe. **2.** immaturity.

अपाढ़ *apāṛh*, adj. reg. (E.) difficult to perform.

अपात्र *a-pātr* [S.], m. & adj. **1.** m. an undeserving or worthless person. **2.** adj. undeserving, unworthy; ineligible.

अपात्रता *a-pātrătā* [S.], f. unworthiness, unsuitability; demerit(s).

अपादान *apâdān* [S.], m. **1.** taking away, removing. **2.** *gram.* the ablative case.

1**अपान** *a-pān* [*a-+pāna-*], adj. Brbh. not to be drunk.

2**अपान** *apān* [conn. *ātman-*], m. Brbh. Av. self, individuality; identity.

अपाप *a-pāp* [S.], adj. sinless, guiltless.

अपाय *apây* [S.], adj. & m. Brbh. Av. **1.** adj. injurious, destructive. **2.** m. destruction; harm, injury.

अपार *a-pār* [S.], adj. **1.** shoreless. **2.** unbounded; infinite. **3.** impassable. **4.** unsurpassed, incomparable. **5.** excessive. — **अपारदर्शिता**, f. opacity. °**-दर्शी**, adj. opaque.

अपावन *a-pāvan* [S.], adj. impure, not holy; polluting.

अपाश्रय *apâśray* [S.], adj. without support, or shelter, destitute; helpless.

अपाहज *apāhaj*, m. = अपाहिज.

अपाहिज *apāhij*, m. a disabled person: **1.** a cripple; a maimed person.

अपि *api* [S.], encl. Brbh. Av. even, although.

अपितु *api-tu* [S.], conj. **1.** but even so, nonetheless. **2.** but rather.

अपील *apīl* [Engl. *appeal*], m. an appeal (esp. in law). — ~ **करना**, to appeal (to, **से**). – **अपील कर्ता**, m. inv. appellant.

अपीली *apīlī* [cf. H. *apīl*], adj. having to do with appeals, or an appeal.

अपुच्छ *a-pucch* [S.], adj. tailless.

अपुण्य *a-puṇyă* [S.], adj. & m. **1.** adj. without merit, unholy; irreligious; wicked. **2.** m. sin; irreligiosity.

अपुत्र *a-putr* [S.], adj. & m. **1.** adj. not having a son, childless. **2.** m. a bad son, an undutiful child.

अपुत्रक *a-putrak* [S.], adj. & m. **1.** adj. = अपुत्र. **2.** m. a childless person.

अपुरुष *a-puruṣ* [S.], adj. **1.** effeminate. **2.** impotent.

अपुष्ट *a-puṣṭ* [S.], adj. **1.** unnourished; undernourished; lean. **2.** unconfirmed.

अपूजक *a-pūjak* [S.], adj. irreverent, irreligious.

अपूजा *a-pūjā* [S.], f. irreverence, lack of due respect.

अपूज्य *a-pūjyă* [S.], adj. **1.** not to be revered or respected. **2.** not to be worshipped.

अपूठ- *apūṭh-* [cf. **utpṛṣṭha-* or **āpṛṣṭha-*], v.t. to overturn.

अपूठा *a-pūṭhā* [cf. *pṛṣṭa-*1], adj. E.H. not asked: not taken notice of.

अपूठौ *a-pūṭhau* [*aspṛṣṭa-*], adj. Brbh. untouched: not attained to.

अपूत *a-pūt*, m. & adj. = अपुत्र.

अपूर्ण *a-pūrṇ* [S.], adj. **1.** not full. **2.** incomplete; *gram.* imperfective; continuous. **3.** insufficient.

अपूर्णता *a-pūrṇătā* [S.], f. **1.** incompleteness. **2.** insufficiency.

अपूर्व *a-pūrv* [S.], adj. **1.** unprecedented. **2.** uncommon, extraordinary; strange. **3.** novel, new.

अपूर्वता *a-pūrvăta* [S.], f. unprecedented nature, strangeness.

अपेख *a-pekh* [cf. H. *pekhnā*], adj. reg. unseen.

अपेय *a-pey* [S.], adj. not drinkable; not to be drunk.

अपेल *a-pel* [cf. H. *pelnā*], adj. Av. immovable; unalterable.

अपेक्षक *apêkṣak* [S.], adj. waiting for, &c.

अपेक्षण *apêkṣaṇ* [S.], m. = अपेकषा, 1.-3.

अपेक्षणीय *apêkṣănīyă* [S.], adj. to be looked or hoped for, to be expected.

अपेक्षया *apêkṣayā*, adv. see s.v. अपेक्षा.

अपेक्षा *apêkṣā* [S.], f. **1.** looking about: consideration, regard; reference, relation.

2. looking or waiting (for, **की**), expectation (of one, **से**); hope; wish. **3.** need, requirement. **4.** comparison. **5.** perspicacity. **6.** adv. (w. **की**.) in comparison (with), in relation (to).
— **~ करना** (**की**), to wait (for); to anticipate, to expect; to hope (for). **~ रखना** (**की**), to hope (for), to entertain a wish (for); to look (to); to need. – **अपेक्षया**, adv. = next. **अपेक्साकृत**, adv. comparatively, relatively.

अपेक्षित *apêkṣit* [S.], adj. **1.** expected, waited for, &c. **2.** due, requisite.

अपेक्ष्य *apêkṣyă* [S.], adj. = **अपेक्षणीय**.

अपौरुष *a-pauruṣ* [S.], m. unmanly, or not pertaining to man: **1.** cowardly; effeminate. **2.** impotent. **3.** supernatural.

अपौरुषेय *a-pauruṣeyă* [S.], adj. superhuman, beyond human powers.

अप्रकट *a-pra-kaṭ* [S.], adj. **1.** unmanifested; not apparent; concealed. **2.** unclear.

अप्रकाश *a-pra-kāś* [S.], adj. not evident; hidden, secret.

अप्रकाशित *a-pra-kāśit* [S.], adj. **1.** not illuminated. ***2.** unpublished.

अप्रचलन *a-pra-calan* [S.], m. non-currency, state of being obsolete.

अप्रचलित *a-pra-calit* [S.], adj. **1.** not current; not customary. **2.** obsolete.

अप्रतिबंध *a-prati-bandh* [S.], adj. & m. **1.** adj. not restricted, free, unencumbered; undisputed (as a title). **2.** m. absence of restriction, &c.

अप्रतिबद्ध *a-prati-baddh* [S.], adj. 1. = **अप्रतिबंध**, 1. **2.** whimsical, unbridled (fancy)

अप्रतिभ *a-prati-bh* [S.], adj. without brilliance: not lively (of manner); shy, bashful.

अप्रतिभट *a-prati-bhaṭ* [cf. H. *bhaṭṭ*], adj. incomparably brave.

अप्रतिम *a-prati-m* [S.], adj. without a likeness: incomparable, unique.

अप्रतिष्ठ *a-prati-ṣṭh* [S.], adj. = **अप्रतिष्ठित**.

अप्रतिष्ठा *a-prati-ṣṭhā* [S.], f. **1.** dishonour, disgrace; ignominy. **2.** lack of reputation; low esteem.

अप्रतिष्ठित *a-prati-ṣṭhit* [S.], adj. **1.** dishonoured, disgraced; disesteemed. **2.** obscure, unknown.

अप्रतिहत *a-prati-hat* [S.], adj. **1.** uninjured, undamaged. **2.** unrepelled, undefeated. ***3.** unimpeded, unchecked.

अप्रतीत *a-pratît* [S.], adj. **1.** not deserving credence; implausible; improbable. **2.** unclear, uncertain.

अप्रतीति *a-pratîti* [S.], f. **1.** lack of confidence; mistrust. **2.** implausibility.

अप्रत्यक्ष *a-praty-akṣ* [S.], adj. **1.** invisible, not evident. **2.** hidden, secret; devious (a procedure); indirect (as a charge).

अप्रत्यय *a-praty-ay* [S.], m. & adj. **1.** adj. distrust, disbelief. **2.** m. distrustful, disbelieving. **3.** *gram.* not having inflexions or suffixes.

अप्रत्ययी *a-praty-ayī* [S.], adj. & m. **1.** adj. distrustful, disbelieving; sceptical. **2.** m. a doubter, sceptic.

अप्रत्याशित *a-praty-āśit* [S.], adj. unexpected, unhoped for; suddenly occurring or existent.

अप्रधान *a-pra-dhān* [S.], adj. subordinate; secondary (in importance).

अप्रभावी *a-pra-bhāvī* [S.], adj. without effect, ineffectual.

अप्रमाण *a-pra-māṇ* [S.], adj. **1.** not being capable of proof, unsubstantiated; inauthentic. **2.** not reliable, unauthoritative.

अप्रवीण *a-pra-vīṇ* [S.], adj. **1.** unskilled. **2.** inexperienced.

अप्रवीणता *a-pra-vīṇătā* [S.], f. lack of skill, or experience.

अप्रशिक्षित *a-pra-śikṣit* [S.], adj. uninstructed, untrained.

अप्रसन्न *a-pra-sann* [S.], adj. **1.** displeased (with, **से**); dissatisfied. **2.** dejected. **3.** disagreeable; ungracious.

अप्रसन्नता *a-pra-sannătā* [S.], f. displeasure, dissatisfaction, &c.

अप्रसाद *a-pra-sād* [S.], m. disapprobation, disfavour.

अप्रसिद्ध *a-pra-siddh* [S.], adj. not celebrated; unknown; obscure.

अप्राकृतिक *a-prākṛtik* [S.], adj. **1.** not having to do with the natural, or the phenomenal, world. **2.** unnatural.

अप्राचीन *a-prācīn* [S.], adj. not old: modern, recent.

अप्राण *a-prāṇ* [S.], adj. **1.** inanimate. **2.** not conscious.

अप्राप्त *a-prâpt* [S.], adj. **1.** unobtained, unacquired. **2.** in comp. not having obtained. **3.** not in evidence, absent, lacking.
— **अप्राप्तयौवना**, adj. f. *rhet.* as yet immature (a girl).

अप्राप्ति *a-prâpti* [S.], f. non-attainment, non-acquisition.

अप्राप्य *a-prâpyă* [S.], adj. **1.** unattainable. **2.** not extant.

अप्रामाणिक *a-prāmāṇik* [S.], adj. not genuine; inauthentic.

अप्राविधिक *a-prāvidhik* [S.], adj. non-technical.

अप्रासंगिक *a-prāsaṅgik* [S.], adj. not to the matter (in hand), irrelevant.

अप्रिय *a-priyă* [S.], adj. **1.** unloved, disliked. **2.** unpleasant, unwelcome (to, को). **3.** unloving, unfriendly.

अप्रीति *a-prīti* [S.], f. **1.** lack of love, affection, or liking. **2.** enmity, hatred.

अप्रैल *aprail* [Engl. *April*], m. April.

अप्रौढ़ *a-prauṛh* [S.], adj. immature.

अप्सरा *apsarā* [S.], f. *mythol.* **1.** a dancing-girl at the court of Indra. **2.** fig. a beautiful woman.

अफ़ग़ान *afgān* [P. *afgān*], m. an Afghan.

[1]**अफ़ग़ानी** *afgānī* [P. *afgānī*], adj. & m. **1.** adj. Afghan. **2.** m. an Afghan.

[2]**अफ़ग़ानी** *afgānī* [P. *afgānī*], f. the Pushtu language.

अफरना *apharnā* [*āspharati], v.i. **1.** to swell out (the stomach, with wind). **2.** to become fat. **3.** to be filled, gorged (the stomach). **4.** to be sated with, tired of.

अफरा *aphrā* [cf. H. *apharnā*], m. = अफराई.

अफ़रा-तफ़री *afrā-tafrī* [A. *ifrāṭ-tafrīṭ*], f. excess, abundance: **1.** confusion. **2.** commotion. **3.** alarm; panic; stampede.

अफराई *aphrāī* [cf. H. *apharnā*], f. **1.** surfeit, over-eating; gluttony. **2.** swelling of the stomach.

अफराना *aphrānā* [cf. H. *apharnā*], v.t. to glut, to satiate.

अफल *a-phal* [S.], adj. **1.** unfruitful, barren. **2.** unproductive, fruitless; useless.

अफ़लातून *aflātūn* [A. *aflāṭūn*], m. **1.** prop. n. Plato. **2.** a boastful or haughty man. — ~ का नाती, m. Plato's grandson: = ~, 2. ~ का साला, m. Plato's brother-in-law: id.

अफलित *a-phalit* [S.], adj. not having borne fruit.

अफ़वाज *afvāj* [A. *afvāj*, pl. of *fauj*], f. U. armies.

अफ़वाह *afvāh* [A. *afvāh*, pl. of *fam* 'mouth'], f. rumour; hearsay. — ~ उड़ाना, to spread a rumour.

अफ़वाही *afvāhī* [A. *afvāh*+P. *-ī*], adj. rumoured.

अफ़शाँ *afśām̐*. see अफ़शान.

अफ़शान *afśān* [P. *afśān*]. U. **1.** -अफ़शान, adj. scattering. **2.** f. strip, shred (as of cloud, or tinsel, or spangle).

अफ़सर *afsar* [Engl. *officer*], m. **1.** an officer, official. **2.** *hist.* agent (of the crown). **3.** *mil.* officer. **4.** a superior. — अफ़सरशाह, m. a bureaucrat. °ई, adj. & f. bureaucratic; bureaucracy.

अफ़सराना *afsarānā* [Engl. *officer*+P. *-āna*], adj. inv. official; bureaucratic.

अफ़सरियत *afsariyat* [Engl. *officer*+A. *-īya*: P. *-iyat*], f. the bureaucracy (of a regime, &c).

अफ़सरी *afsarī* [cf. H. *afsar*], adj. & f. **1.** adj. having to do with an officer or official, or with officialdom; bureaucratic. **2.** f. the duties and position of an officer.

अफ़साना *afsānā* [P. *afsāna*], m. U. **1.** tale; romance. **2.** short story.

अफ़सोस *afsos* [P. *afsos*], m. **1.** sorrow. **2.** regret. — ~ आना, or होना, sorrow, &c. to be felt (by, को). ~ करना, to feel sorrow or regret (for, का or पर); to lament; to take to heart. ~ की बात, f. a pity.

अफ़ीम *afīm* [A. *afyūn*, P. *apyūn*: ← Gk.], f. opium.

अफ़ीमची *afīmcī* [H. *afīm*+T. *-cī*], m. opium-eater, opium addict.

अफ़ीमी *afīmī* [cf. H. *afīm*], adj. & m. **1.** adj. having to do with opium. **2.** m. = अफ़ीमची.

अफेन *a-phen* [S.], adj. not having froth or foam.

अफ़्रीक़ी *afrīqī* [cf. A. *ifrīqī*, *afrīqī*], adj. African.

अब *ab* [cf. *evaṃ*, Ap. *evvahi* 'now'; and *eṣa*[1], *eta-* (*a-* by anal. w. pron. bases *ta-*, *ka-*, *ja-*)], adv. **1.** at the present time; now, just now; nowadays. **2.** at an immediately past or future time (seen as an extension of the present): recently; presently, shortly; from now on. — ~ का, adj. of the present; the next, the coming; new, fresh. ~ की, adv. this time; the next time; for, as of now. ~ के, adv. id. ~ जाकर, adv. as of now, with the lapse of time. ~ तक, adv. up till now; by now; hitherto; all this time. ~ तब, adv. now and then; presently, shortly. ~ तब करना, to put off, to delay; to evade, to prevaricate. ~ तब लगना, or होना, to be at the point of death. ~ न तब, adv. at neither time; neither in this world nor in the next; never; nowhere. ~ भी, adv. even now, yet, as yet, still; despite this, even so. ~ से, adv. from now on, henceforward, in future.

अबड़-धबड़ *abaṛ-dhabaṛ*, adj. **1.** clumsy, crude. **2.** discordant, jarring (as music).

अबतर *abtar* [A. *abtar*], adj. U. **1.** ruined, spoiled; deteriorated. **2.** bad, base.

अबद्ध *a-baddh* [S.], adj. **1.** unbound, unrestrained. **2.** disorganised, disordered.

अबध्य *a-badhyă* [ad. *avadhya-*], adj. **1.** not deserving death: inviolable; sacred. **2.** not to be killed.

अबरक *abrak* [ad. *abhraka-*], m. **1.** mica. **2.** talc. **3.** make-up, cosmetic.

अबरस *abras* [A. *abraś*], adj. Av. dapple grey (a horse).

अबरा *abrā* [P. *abrā*], m. the outer fold of a garment of doubled material.

अबरी *abrī* [P. *abrī*], adj. & f. clouded: **1.** a partic. mottled, or marbled, glossy paper. **2.** *HŚS.* a yellow stone found in the Jaisalmer region (used in inlay work).

अबरू *abrū* [P. *abrū*], f. m. the eyebrow.

अबल *a-bal* [S.], m. & adj. **1.** m. weakness. **2.** adj. powerless, weak.

अबलक *ablak* [A. *ablaq*], adj. Av. piebald (a horse).

अबलख *ablakh* [A. *ablaq*], adj. Brbh. = अबलक.

अबलता *a-balătā* [S.], f. = अबल्य.

अबला *a-balā* [S.], f. delicate one: a woman.

अबलापन *a-balāpan* [cf. *abalya-*], m. weakness, frailty (= अबल्य).

अबलापा *a-balāpā*, m. = अबलापन.

अबल्य *a-balyă* [S.], m. weakness, frailty.

अबस *a-bas*, adj. Brbh. = अवश, 2., 3.

अबाध *a-bādh* [S.], adj. **1.** unconstrained, uninhibited (as a smile). **2.** unrestricted (as trade). **3.** unlimited (as power).

अबाध्य *a-bādhyă* [S.], adj. not to be checked: unchecked; unconstrained.

अबाबील *abābīl* [A. *abābīl*], f. a swallow.

अबार *a-bār* [*a-*+H. *bār*], f. Brbh. delay, lapse of time.

अबीज *a-bīj* [*a-*+H. *bīj*], m. reg. (W.) bad seed (that fails to germinate).

अबीर *abīr* [A. *'abīr*], m. *hind.* a powder, usu. red, which is thrown and sprinkled at the Holī festival (made from ground meal, or minerals, esp. mica).

अबीरी *abīrī* [cf. H. *abīr*], adj. having to do with *abīr*; of the colour of *abīr*, red.

अबुद्धि *a-buddhi* [S.], adj. & f. **1.** adj. = अबुध. **2.** f. want of understanding or sense: ignorance; foolishness.

अबुध *a-budh* [S.], adj. without understanding or sense: ignorant; foolish.

अबूझ *a-būjh* [cf. H. *būjh*], adj. **1.** without understanding, or good sense; ignorant; stupid. **2.** [× *buddhya-*] unknowable, unfathomable.

अबूझा *a-būjhā* [cf. H. *būjhnā*, or *buddhya-*], adj. not understood; incomprehensible.

अबे *abe*, interj. pej. you! you rascal! wretch! — अबे-तबे करना, to address with undue familiarity, or disrespectfully or rudely. अबे-तबे से पेश आना, id.

अबेर *a-ber* [cf. *velā-*], f. **1.** lateness, delay. **2.** adv. late, after time. — देर-अबेर, f. = ~.

अबोध *a-bodh* [S.], adj. & m. **1.** adj. of immature mind: undiscerning, innocent; puzzled, at a loss. **2.** ignorant, stupid. **3.** m. ignorance, stupidity.

अबोधगम्य *a-bodhăgamyă* [S.], adj. incomprehensible.

अबोधनीय *a-bodhănīyă* [S.], adj. unintelligible.

अबोध्य *a-bodhyă* [S.], adj. incomprehensible.

अबोल *a-bol* [cf. H. *bol*], adj. **1.** speechless; silent, mute. **2.** dumb.

¹अबोला *a-bolā* [cf. H. *bolnā*], adj. unspoken.

²अबोला *a-bolā* [cf. H. *abol*], adj. & m. **1.** adj. unspeaking: taciturn; reserved; vain. **2.** m. a dumb creature. **3.** one incapable of speaking clearly, a child, an infant.

अब्ज *abjă* [S.], m. Brbh. Av. water-born: a lotus.

अब्जद *abjad* [A. *abjad*], m. **1.** the original arrangement of the Arabic alphabet (starting with the letters, a, b, j, a, d). **2.** the numerical value given conventionally to Arabic letters in this arrangement.

अब्द *abd* [S.], m. chiefly in comp. giving water: **1.** a year; an era. **2.** Brbh. a cloud. — अब्द-कोश, m. year-book.

अब्धि *abdhi* [S.], m. sea, ocean.

अब्बा *abbā* [cf. A. *ab*], m. **1.** father. **2.** hon. term of address to an elderly man. — अब्बा-जान, m. dear father.

अब्र *abr* [P. *abr*], m. a cloud.

अभंग *a-bhaṅg* [S.], adj. **1.** unbroken; undestroyed. **2.** continuing; eternal.

अभंगी *a-bhaṅgī* [S.], adj. Brbh. not subject to impairment: complete, perfect.

अभंगुर *a-bhaṅgur* [S.], adj. **1.** unbreaking, unbreakable; indestructible. **2.** non-transient, lasting.

अभंगुरता *a-bhaṅgurătā* [S.], f. lastingness, permanence.

[1]**अभक्त** *a-bhakt* [S.], adj. undevout, wanting faith; impious.

[2]**अभक्त** *a-bhakt* [S.], adj. not divided.

अभक्ति *a-bhakti* [S.], f. **1.** lack of devotion or faith; impiety. **2.** disregard, indifference (towards, के प्रति).

अभक्ष्य *a-bhakṣyă* [S.], adj. & m. **1.** adj. not to be eaten; unlawful as food. **2.** m. prohibited food.

अभद्र *a-bhadră* [S.], adj. indecent, crude (as conduct, language).

अभय *a-bhay* [S.], adj. & m. **1.** adj. fearless. **2.** m. freedom from fear. — अभयकर, adj. allaying fear, reassuring. अभय-दान, m. grant of lack of fear: assurance of safety or protection; safe conduct. अभय-पत्र, m. id., 2.; a pass (as issued by an authority). अभय-वचन, m. promise of safety or protection.

अभाग *a-bhāg* [cf. *bhāgya-*[1]], m. misfortune, ill-fate.

अभागा *a-bhāgā* [cf. *bhāgya-*[1]], m. unfortunate, ill-fated; wretched.

अभागापन *a-bhāgāpan* [cf. H. *abhāgā*], m. misfortune, ill-fate.

अभागिनि *a-bhāgini*, adj. f. & f. = अभागी.

अभागी *a-bhāgī* [cf. *bhāgya-*[1 2]; and S.], adj. & m. **1.** adj. unfortunate, ill-fated; wretched. **2.** without a (due) share. **3.** m. an unfortunate person.

अभाग्य *a-bhāgyă* [S.], m. misfortune, ill-fate.

अभाज्य *a-bhājyă* [S.], adj. indivisible.

अभाय *a-bhāy* [ad. *abhāva-*], m. Brbh. = अभाव, 1.

अभाव *a-bhāv* [S.], m. **1.** non-existence. **2.** absence; lack. **3.** poverty, want. **4.** Brbh. ill-will. — अभाव-ग्रस्त, adj. poverty-stricken. अभावात्मक [°*va*+*ā*°], adj. negative, inconclusive; mortal, deadly.

अभावनीय *a-bhāvănīyă* [S.], adj. inconceivable, not to be imagined.

अभावी *a-bhāvī* [S.], adj. non-existent; not destined to exist.

अभाव्य *a-bhāvyă* [S.], adj. not to be, impossible; improper.

अभि- *abhi-* [S.], pref. **1.** towards (e.g. अभिसार, m. lovers' meeting). **2.** particular (e.g. अभिजात, adj. well-born; अभियोग, m. accusation).

अभिकथन *abhi-kathan* [S.], m. **1.** assertion. **2.** allegation.

अभिकथित *abhi-kathit* [S.], adj. asserted; alleged.

अभिकरण *abhi-karaṇ* [S.], m. agency, means; an agency.

अभिकर्ता *abhi-kartā* [S.], m. inv. an agent, intermediary.

अभिकलन *abhi-kalan* [S.], m. calculating, computation.

अभिकल्पन *abhi-kalpan* [S.], m. planning; designing.

अभिक्रम *abhi-kram* [S.], m. **1.** assault, attack. **2.** an undertaking, enterprise.

अभिक्रिया *abhi-kriyā* [S.], f. reaction (= प्रति-°).

अभिगम *abhi-gam* [S.], m. 1. = अभिगमन, 1. **2.** access.

अभिगमन *abhi-gaman* [S.], m. **1.** approach, arrival. **2.** cohabitation.

अभिग्रहण *abhi-grahaṇ* [S.], m. taking up (as of a procedure, an attitude); taking over, acquiring.

अभिचार *abhi-cār* [S.], m. **1.** recourse to incantations or spells for an ulterior purpose. **2.** a spell, &c. of malign effect; black magic.

अभिचारक *abhi-cārak* [S.], m. a magician, sorcerer.

अभिचारी *abhi-cārī* [S.], m. = अभिचारक.

अभिजात *abhi-jāt* [S.], adj. **1.** well-born, of high rank; noble, aristocratic. **2.** innate. **3.** *Pl.* fig. wise; learned. — अभिजात-तंत्र, m. aristocracy, government by an aristocracy. अभिजात-भवन, m. *govt.* (U.K.) House of Lords.

अभिजातता *abhi-jātătā* [S.], f. nobility of birth.

अभिजाति *abhi-jāti* [S.], f. high or noble birth.

अभिजात्य *abhi-jātyă* [S.], adj. of high or good birth.

अभिजित *abhi-jit* [S.], adj. conquered.

अभिज्ञ *abhi-jñă* [S.], adj. **1.** knowledgeable, versed (in, से); skilled. **2.** informed (of, से).

अभिज्ञा *abhi-jñā* [S.], f. **1.** recognition, identification. **2.** remembrance, recollection. **3.** supernatural knowledge.

अभिज्ञान *abhi-jñān* [S.], m. recognition (by a distinctive mark or token).

अभिज्ञेय *abhi-jñey* [S.], adj. recognisable.

अभिदान *abhi-dān* [S.], m. *fin.* subscription.

अभिधा *abhi-dhā* [S.], f. literal sense (of a word); purport (of a pen-name).

अभिधान *abhi-dhān* [S.], m. setting out, telling: **1.** title, designation. **2.** a vocabulary, or dictionary.

अभिधारणा *abhi-dhārăṇā* [S.], f. a postulate, hypothesis.

अभिनंदन *abhi-nandan* [S.], m. **1.** praise, applause. **2.** ceremonial greetings; commemoration. — **अभिनंदन-ग्रंथ**, m. a presentation or commemorative volume. **अभिनंदन-पत्र**, m. congratulatory address. **अभिनंदन-समारोह**, m. commemorative function.

अभिनंदनीय *abhi-nandănīyă* [S.], adj. **1.** praiseworthy. **2.** deserving greetings, or commemoration.

अभिनंदित *abhi-nandit* [S.], adj. **1.** praised. **2.** greeted.

अभिनंदी *abhi-nandī* [S.], adj. **1.** praising, laudatory. **2.** salutatory, commemorative.

अभिनंद्य *abhi-nandyă* [S.], adj. = अभिनंदनीय.

अभिनय *abhi-nay* [S.], m. acting (on the stage).

अभिनव *abhi-nav* [S.], adj. **1.** recent, very new. **2.** contemporary, modern.

अभिनवन *abhi-navan* [S.], m. innovation.

अभिनिविष्ट *abhi-ni-viṣṭ* [S.], adj. engrossed (in).

अभिनिषिद्ध *abhi-ni-ṣiddh* [S.], adj. proscribed.

अभिनिषेध *abhi-ni-ṣedh* [S.], m. proscription.

अभिनीत *abhi-nīt* [S.], adj. acted, staged (a drama).

अभिनेता *abhi-netā* [S.], m. inv. an actor.

अभिनेत्री *abhi-netrī* [S.], f. an actress.

अभिनेय *abhi-neyă* [S.], adj. stageable (a drama).

अभिन्न *a-bhinn* [S.], adj. **1.** undivided, unseparated; close (a connection); whole, entire. **2.** inseparable, intimate (as friendship). **3.** essential, organic, integral (as a member, a component); inalienable.

अभिन्नता *a-bhinnătā* [S.], f. unseparatedness: integral unity; identity.

अभिपुष्ट *abhi-puṣṭ* [S.], adj. confirmed.

अभिपूर्ति *abhi-pūrti* [S.], f. implementation.

अभिप्राय *abhi-prây* [S.], m. **1.** purport, sense; meaning. **2.** aim, purpose, intention. **3.** a motif.

अभिप्रेरण *abhi-prêraṇ* [s.], impulse, motivation.

अभिप्रेत *abhi-prêt* [S.], adj. **1.** intended, aimed for. **2.** implied.

अभिभावक *abhi-bhāvak* [S.], m. guardian (as of a minor).

अभिभावकता *abhi-bhāvakătā* [S.], f. status of guardian.

अभिभाषण *abhi-bhāṣaṇ* [S.], m. formal or ceremonial address.

अभिभूत *abhi-bhūt* [S.], adj. defeated; in subjection; overwhelmed.

अभिमंचन *abhi-mañcan* [S.], m. staging (of a drama).

अभिमंत्रण *abhi-mantraṇ* [S.], m. consecration.

अभिमत *abhi-mat* [S.], adj. & m. **1.** adj. desired. **2.** approved of, assented to. **3.** m. wish, desire. **4.** opinion, counsel.

अभिमतता *abhi-matătā* [S.], f. *Pl.* desire.

अभिमान *abhi-mān* [S.], m. **1.** pride. **2.** unjustifiable pride; arrogance, vanity, conceit. — ~ **करना**, to behave proudly, &c. ~ **गलाना (का)**, to humble (one); to get rid of (one's own) pride.

अभिमानी *abhi-mānī* [S.], adj. & m. **1.** adj. proud. **2.** arrogant, &c. **3.** m. a proud person. **4.** an arrogant person, &c.

अभिमुख *abhi-mukh* [S.], adj. **1.** turned towards, facing. 2. adv. in front (of, के); in the presence (of). **3.** towards.

अभियंता *abhi-yantā* [S.], m. inv. an engineer.

अभियंत्रण *abhi-yantraṇ* [S.], m. engineering.

अभियांत्रिक *abhiyāntrik* [S.], adj. having to do with engineering.

अभियांत्रिकी *abhiyāntrikī* [S.], f. engineering (esp. as a science or skill).

अभियान *abhi-yān* [S.], m. **1.** a campaign. **2.** an expedition.

अभियुक्त *abhi-yukt* [S.], adj. accused.

अभियोक्ता *abhi-yoktā* [S.], m. inv. an accuser, prosecutor.

अभियोग *abhi-yog* [S.], m. an accusation.

अभियोजन *abhi-yojan* [S.], m. accusing, prosecuting, prosecution.

अभिरक्षक *abhi-rakṣak* [S.], m. custodian.

अभिरक्षण *abhi-rakṣaṇ* [S.], m. keeping in custody.

अभिरक्षा *abhi-rakṣā* [S.], f. custody.

अभिराधन *abhi-rādhan* [S.], m. appeasement.

अभिराम *abhi-rām* [S.], adj. delightful; beautiful; charming.

अभिरुचि *abhi-ruci* [S.], f. **1.** interest (in, से); inclination (towards). **2.** desire (for).

अभिलषित *abhi-laṣit* [S.], adj. desired.

अभिलाष *abhi-lāṣ* m. (f. ← °*a.*) = **अभिलाषा**.

अभिलाषा *abhi-lāṣā* [S.], f. desire, longing.

अभिलाषित *abhi-lāṣit* [S.], adj. denied, longed for.

अभिलाषी *abhi-lāṣī* [conn. H. *abhilāṣā*], adj. & m. **1.** adj. desirous. **2.** m. one who desires or longs (for, का).

अभिलिखित *abhi-likhit* [S.], adj. recorded.

अभिलेख *abhi-lekh* [S.], m. a written record (of any matter or transaction). — **अभिलेखागार** [°*kha+ā*°], an archive, store of records.

अभिलेखितृ *abhi-lekhitṛ* [S.], m. recording apparatus.

अभिवक्ता *abhi-vaktā* [S.], m. inv. a speaker: pleader (at law).

अभिवचन *abhi-vacan* [S.], m. a plea (at law).

अभिवाद *abhi-vād*, m. = **अभिवादन**, 1.

अभिवादन *abhi-vādan* [S.], m. **1.** respectful greeting; ceremonial greeting. **2.** praise.

अभिवादित *abhi-vādit* [S.], adj. greeted respectfully.

अभिवाद्य *abhi-vādyă* [S.], adj. to be greeted respectfully, or warmly.

अभिवृद्धि *abhi-vṛddhi* [S.], f. growth, increase.

अभिव्यंजक *abhi-vy-añjak* [S.], adj. expressive.

अभिव्यंजना *abhi-vy-añjănā* [S.], f. expression. — **अभिव्यंजनावाद**, m. expressionism.

अभिव्यंजित *abhi-vy-añjit* [S.], adj. expressed (= **अभिव्यक्त**).

अभिव्यक्त *abhi-vy-akt* [S.], adj. made clear: expressed.

अभिव्यक्ति *abhi-vy-akti* [S.], f. **1.** a manifestation. ***2.** an expression.

अभिशंसा *abhi-śaṃsā* [S.], f. accusation: conviction (of an offence).

अभिशंसित *abhi-śaṃsit* [S.], adj. convicted (of an offence).

अभिशप्त *abhi-śapt* [S.], adj. accursed, cursed.

अभिशस्त *abhi-śast* [S.], adj. = **अभिशंसित**.

अभिशाप *abhi-śāp* [S.], m. a curse, dire curse.

अभिशासन *abhi-śāsan* [S.], m. governing, rule (over, का).

अभिशासित *abhi-śāsit* [S.], adj. governed, ruled.

अभिषद *abhi-ṣad* [S.], m. a syndicate.

अभिषिक्त *abhi-ṣikt* [S.], adj. **1.** besprinkled: anointed; baptised. **2.** inaugurated, enthroned, invested. **3.** irrigated.

अभिषेक *abhi-ṣek* [S.], m. **1.** sprinkling; anointing (usu. with sacred water). **2.** inauguration, consecration, investiture. **3.** religious ablutions; the ceremonial bathing of an idol; offering made in connection with bathing an idol.

अभिसंधि *abhi-san-dhi* [S.], f. deceit; pej. alliance. — **दुरभिसंधि**, f. plot.

अभिसमय *abhi-sam-ay* [S.], m. settlement (of a dispute); convention.

अभिसरण *abhi-saraṇ* [S.], m. convergence.

अभिसार *abhi-sār* [S.], m. **1.** meeting, rendezvous; specif. lovers' meeting or assignation. **2.** union. **3.** attack, battle.

अभिसारिका *abhi-sārikā* [S.], f. a woman who keeps a lovers' tryst.

अभिसारिणी *abhi-sāriṇī* adj. & f. **1.** adj. = **अभिसारी**, 1. 2. = **अभिसारी**, 2., 4.

अभिसारी *abhi-sārī* [S.], adj. & m. **1.** adj. keeping a tryst or assignation. **2.** m. a lover keeping a tryst, &c. **3.** *HŚS.* an attacker. **4.** an attendant, assistant.

अभिसूचक *abhi-sūcak* [S.], m. index.

अभिस्वीकृति *abhi-svīkṛti* [S.], f. due or formal acceptance (as of a gift).

अभिहित *abhi-hit* [S.], adj. called, named (as).

अभी *abhī* [H. *ab*+*hī*], adv. at this particular time; now, just now, immediately; yet, still. — ~ का, adj. & adv. recent, contemporary; immediately. ~ तक, adv. up till the present moment; as of this moment. ~ तो, adv. as of now, as yet. ~ से, adv. from now onwards, starting now. मैं ~ (तक) नहीं गया, I haven't gone yet. मैं ~ आया था, I had just arrived; I had already arrived. – अभी-अभी, adv. just recently, just (right) now.

अभीत *a-bhīt* [S.], adj. not fearful, fearless.

अभीति *a-bhīti* [S.], f. fearlessness.

अभीप्सा *abhîpsā* [S.], f. desire, longing.

अभीप्सित *abhîpsit* [S.], adj. desired, longed for.

अभीप्सी *abhîpsī* [S.], adj. desirous (of, का).

अभीप्सु *abhîpsu* [S.], adj. = अभीप्सी.

अभीष्ट *abhîṣṭ* [S.], adj. & m. **1.** adj. desired, longed for. **2.** m. sthg. desired, longed for; a treasured wish.

अभूत *a-bhūt* [S.], adj. not having been or happened: **1.** non-existent. **2.** not past, contemporary. **3.** improbable. — अभूतपूर्व, adj. unexampled, unprecedented.

[1]**अभेद** *a-bhed* [S.], m. & adj. **1.** m. absence of distinction or difference, similarity; identity. **2.** adj. not different; identical. **3.** not divided, unitary.

[2]**अभेद** *a-bhed* [ad. *abhedya-*], adj. unbreakable, impenetrable, unshakable (as conviction).

अभेद्य *a-bhedyă* [S.], adj. **1.** indivisible. **2.** unbreakable, impenetrable; unshakable (as conviction). **3.** impregnable (a stronghold).

अभेव *a-bhev* [*a-*+H. *bhev*], m. Brbh. = [1]अभेद.

अभोग *a-bhog* [S.], adj. & m. **1.** adj. unused, unenjoyed. **2.** m. deprivation.

अभोगी *a-bhogī* [S.], adj. & m. **1.** adj. not making use (of, का). **2.** not enjoying: indifferent to pleasures of the senses. **3.** m. a person indifferent to pleasures of the senses.

अभोजन *a-bhojan* [S.], m. not eating, fasting.

अभोजी *a-bhojī* [S.], adj. & m. **1.** adj. not eating, fasting. **2.** m. a faster.

अभोज्य *a-bhojyă* [S.], adj. & m. **1.** adj. not to be eaten; unlawful as food. **2.** m. prohibited food.

अभ्यंतर *abhy-antar* [S.], m. & adj. **1.** m. inner part; interior; middle, included space. **2.** fig. the heart. **3.** ppn. (with के.) within. **4.** adj. internal, interior.

अभ्यर्थन *abhy-arthan* [S.], m. = अभ्यर्थना.

अभ्यर्थना *abhy-arthănā* [S.], f. earnest request, entreaty; prayer (for, की).

अभ्यर्थित *abhy-arthit* [S.], adj. asked earnestly, or begged, for.

अभ्यर्थी *abhy-arthī* [S.], m. one seeking keenly: a candidate.

अभ्यर्पण *abhy-arpaṇ* [S.], m. surrender.

अभ्यसित *abhy-asit* [S.], adj. = अभ्यस्त, 2., 3.

अभ्यस्त *abhy-ast* [S.], adj. **1.** practised; drilled, repeated; learnt by heart. **2.** accustomed (to, का or से), inveterate. **3.** experienced (in, का or में).

अभ्यागत *abhy-ā-gat* [S.], adj. & m. **1.** adj. arrived. **2.** m. a guest, visitor; specif. a holy man, an ascetic.

अभ्यागम *abhy-ā-gam* [S.], m. **1.** arrival. **2.** presence, proximity.

अभ्यापत्ति *abhy-ā-patti* [S.], f. protest.

अभ्यारोपण *abhy-ā-ropaṇ* [S.], m. indictment.

अभ्यास *abhy-ās* [S.], m. throwing towards, adding: **1.** practice; drill, repetition; repeated reading, study. **2.** habit. **3.** familiarity (with, का). **4.** *mil.* manoeuvres; an exercise. — ~ करना (का), to practice, &c.; to acquire familiarity (with); to inure oneself (to).

अभ्यासी *abhy-āsī* [S.], adj. **1.** given to practising, industrious; studious. **2.** practised, skilled (in, का).

अभ्युत्थान *abhy-ut-thān* [S.], m. **1.** rising (as a mark of respect). **2.** rise, elevation (as in rank). **3.** rise, increase, progress. **4.** rise, revolt.

अभ्युत्थायी *abhy-ut-thāyī* [S.], adj. having risen, &c. (see अभ्युत्थान).

अभ्युत्थित *abhy-ut-thit* [S.], adj. risen, &c. (see अभ्युत्थान).

अभ्युदय *abhy-uday* [S.], m. rise.

अभ्र *abhră* [S.], m. **1.** a cloud. **2.** the sky. 3. = अभ्रक, अब्रक.

अभ्रक *abhrak* [S.], m. = अबरक.

अमंगल *a-maṅgal* [S.], adj. & m. **1.** adj. unlucky, inauspicious. **2.** disastrous, evil. **3.** m. misfortune, &c.; calamity. **4.** ill omen.

अमका-धमका *amkā-dhamkā* [conn. H. *im*], adj. *Pl. HŚS.* = फ़लाना.

अमचूर *amcūr* [*āmra-*+**cūra-*: Pk. *cūra-*], m. mango parings dried in the sun (used as a seasoning).

अमड़ा *amṛā* [*āmrātaka-*], m. the hog-plum, *Spondias mangifera.*

अमत *a-mat* [S.], adj. & m. **1.** adj. not approved, not accepted. **2.** m. non-approval, non-acceptance.

अमति *a-mati* [S]. **1.** lack of thought, or good sense. **2.** non-approval, non-acceptance.

अमत्त *a-matt* [S.], adj. **1.** not intoxicated, sober. **2.** not proud. **3.** prudent.

अमन *amn* [A. *amn*], m. tranquillity, peace. — **अमन-अमान**, m. peace and security; adv. in peace and security. **अमन-चैन**, m. peace and prosperity, contentment of life. **अमनपसंद**, adj. peaceful, peaceable; pacifist; a peaceful person, &c.

अमनुष्य *a-manuṣyă* [S.], adj. & m. **1.** adj. inhuman. **2.** m. one who is not a man; a coward; demon.

अमनुष्यता *a-manuṣyătā* [S.], f. inhumanity.

अमनोगत *a-manogat* [S.], adj. **1.** not consciously intended. **2.** not in mind.

अमनोज्ञ *a-manojñă* [S.], adj. disagreeable; uninteresting.

अमनोनिवेश *a-manoniveś* [S.], m. not settling the mind: inattention, carelessness.

अमनोनीत *a-manonīt* [S.], adj. disapproved of.

अमनोयोग *a-manoyog* [S.], m. inattention, lack of concentration.

अमनोयोगी *a-manoyogī* [S.], adj. inattentive, not showing concentration.

अमनोरथ *a-manorath* [S.], adj. not desirous (of, से), averse (to).

अमनोहर *a-manohar* [S.], adj. unattractive; disagreeable.

अमम *a-mam* [S.], adj. **1.** disinterested, unselfish. **2.** indifferent; stoical. **3.** unfeeling; cruel.

अममता *a-mamătā* [S.], f. disinterestedness, &c. (see **अमम**).

¹**अमर** *amr* [A. *amar*], m. U. **1.** order, command. ***2.** matter, topic, question. **3.** occurrence.

²**अमर** *a-mar* [S.], adj. & m. **1.** adj. immortal; eternal. **2.** m. a divine being. — ~ **होना**, to live for ever; to live long. **अमर-धाम**, m. = **अमर-लोक**. **अमर-पक्षी**, m. the phoenix. **अमर-पुर**, m. = **अमर-लोक**. **अमर-बेल**, m. a parasitical creeper (*Cassyta filiformis*). **अमर-बौर**, m. id. **अमर-राज**, m. Brbh. king of the gods: a title of Indra. **अमर-लोक**, m. abode of the gods: paradise. **अमर-वल्ली**, f. = **अमरबेल**. °**-वल्लरी**, f. id.

अमरई *amraī*, f. 19c. mango grove.

अमरण *a-maraṇ* [S.], adj. & m. **1.** adj. undying. **2.** m. deathlessness, immortality.

अमरता *a-marătā* [S.], f. immortality.

अमरत्व *a-maratvă* [S.], m. immortality. — **अमरत्व-प्रदान**, adj. conferring immortality.

अमरस *am-ras* [H. *ām*+H. *ras*], m. mango juice.

अमराई *amrāī* [**āmrarāji-*: w. H. *ām*], f. mango grove.

अमराय *amrāy*, f. Brbh. = **अमराई**.

अमरीकन *amrīkan* [Engl. *American*], adj. & m., f. **1.** adj. American. **2.** m., f. an American.

अमरीका *amrīkā* [Engl. *America*], m. America; the United States of America.

अमरीकी *amrīkī* [Engl. *America*+H. *-ī*], adj. American.

अमरूत *amrūt*, m. = **अमरूद**.

अमरूद *amrūd* [? conn. *amara-*], m. the guava tree, and its fruit.

अमर्त्य *a-martyă* [S.], adj. & m. **1.** immortal. **2.** m. an immortal.

अमर्याद *a-maryād* [S.], adj. **1.** without bounds, limits. **2.** going beyond limits; unconventional. **3.** disrespected, dishonoured.

अमर्यादा *a-maryādā* [S.], f. disrespect, dishonour; disrespectful conduct, &c.

अमर्यादित *a-maryādit* [S.], adj. shown disrespect, &c.

अमर्ष *a-marṣ* [S.], m. anger.

¹**अमल** *a-mal* [S.], adj. & m. **1.** adj. clean, pure; clear. **2.** without stain; guiltless; sinless. **3.** m. purity, &c.

²**अमल** *amal* [A. *'amal*], m. **1.** act, action. **2.** operation; effect (on, पर). **3.** use, application. **4.** 19c. = **अमलदारी**. **5.** stroke (of an hour). — ~ **करना**, to act (upon, पर); to operate, to take effect; to make use (of). ~ **में आना**, to come into operation (as a law). ~ **में लाना**, to bring into operation, to put into effect; to make use of; to set to work. **अमलदार** [P. *-dār*], m. one having authority, an administrative officer; a collector of revenue. °**ई**, f. government, administration; rule. **अमल-पट्टा**, m. a writ; deed.

अमलतास *amaltās*, m. the Indian laburnum.

अमलतासी *amaltāsī* [cf. H. *amaltās*], adj. orange-yellow.

[1]**अमलना** *amalnā*, v.i. *Pl.* to suffer distension of the veins of the stomach, esp. of the umbilical cord.

[2]**अमलना** *amalnā* [cf. *amla-*], v.i. *Pl.* to become blunt or deadened by acidity (the teeth).

अमल-पट्टी *amal-paṭṭī*, f. [*āmlikā-*, *amlikā-*+H. *paṭṭī*], *Pl.* a broad hem-stitch (resembling a leaf of the tamarind tree in appearance).

अमला *amlā* [A. *'amala*, pl.], m. pl. & sg. **1.** workers; establishment, staff. **2.** a staff member; clerk. — अमलासाज़ी [P. *-sāzī*], f. the bribing of officials.

अमलाक *amlāk* [A. *imlāk*], m. U. possessions; estates, lands.

अमलिन *a-malin* [S.], adj. **1.** free from dirt; clean, pure. **2.** without stain.

अमली *amălī* [A. *'amalī*], adj. **1.** practical (as a measure, a question). **2.** exercising an effect.

अमा *amā* [S.], f. = अमावस्या.

अमात्य *amātyă* [S.], m. **1.** minister (of a government). **2.** counsellor.

अमात्र *a-mātră* [S.], adj. without measure, limitless.

[1]**अमान** *amān* [A. *amān*], f. **1.** security, safety. **2.** assurance of safety; quarter, mercy. — ~ देना (को), to promise safety (to), to give protection (to). ~ में रखना, to shelter, to protect.

[2]**अमान** *a-mān* [S.], adj. & m. **1.** adj. not moved by pride, modest. **2.** [×S. *amānya-*] not shown respect, dishonourable. **3.** m. disrespect, &c.

[3]**अमान** *a-mān* [S.], adj. incalculable; vast.

अमानत *amānat* [A. *amāna*: P. *amānat*], f. **1.** sthg. entrusted, deposited or assigned; a deposit; a security. **2.** charge, trust, guardianship. — ~ में ख़यानत, f. breach of trust, embezzlement. ~ रखना (को), to entrust (to), to deposit; to pawn. – अमानतख़ाना, m. a depository; pawnshop. guardianship, trusteeship. अमानतनामा, m. a deed of trust, or deposit. अमानतवाला, m. one who has deposited or assigned (goods, property).

अमानती *amānătī* [A. *amānat*+P. *-ī*], adj. **1.** adj. entrusted, deposited, &c. **2.** f. sthg. entrusted, &c.

अमाननीय *a-mānănīyă* [S.], adj. = अमान्य, 3.

अमाना *amānā* [**unmāyate*], v.i. reg. to go into, fit, be held (in, में).

[1]**अमानी** *a-mānī* [S.], adj. & m. **1.** adj. without pride, unassuming. **2.** not respected, not honoured. **3.** m. an unassuming person, &c.

[2]**अमानी** *amānī* [P. *amānī*], f. **1.** *Pl.* = [1]अमान. **2.** *Pl.* = अमानत. **3.** land held, or work done, under direct government supervision or control. **4.** ? work paid by the day. **5.** the levying of a rent adjusted to take account of seasonal variations in crop yield.

अमानुष *a-mānuṣ* [S.], adj. & m. **1.** adj. not human. **2.** inhuman. **3.** m. a non-human creature; monster; supernatural being.

अमानुषता *a-mānuṣătā* [S.], f. inhumanity.

अमानुषिक *a-mānuṣik* [S.], adj. = अमानुषी.

अमानुषी *a-mānuṣī* [S.], adj. **1.** not human. **2.** inhuman. **3.** superhuman; supernatural. **4.** having no human beings, unpopulated.

अमानुषीय *a-mānuṣīyă* [S.], adj. = अमानुषी.

अमान्य *a-mānyă* [S.], adj. **1.** not be be believed, or credited; not grantable or allowable (a petition; a goal). **2.** not acceptable (a decision, &c). **3.** not to be respected or honoured.

अमामा *amāmā* [A. *'imāma*], m. a large turban.

अमार *amār* [P. *ambār*], m. heap, pile.

अमावट *amāvaṭ* [*āmrāvarta-*], m. inspissated mango-juice.

अमावस *amāvas* [*amāvāsyā-*], f. the last day of the dark fortnight of a lunar month, the night of the new moon.

अमावस्या *amāvasyā*, f. = अमावस.

अमिट *a-miṭ* [cf. H. *miṭnā*], adj. **1.** not erased; indelible; indestructible. **2.** immutable; irrevocable (as a divine ordinance).

अमित *a-mit* [S.], adj. not measured: immeasurable, incalculable. अमितव्ययिता, f. unthriftiness, excessive expenditure. °-व्ययी, adj. & m. अमिताभ [°*ta*+*ā*°], adj. supremely brilliant, magnificent.

अमितता *a-mităt*ā [S.], f. unmeasured or boundless nature or state.

अमिता *a-mitā* [S.], f. immeasurability, immensity.

अमिति *a-miti* [S.], f. lack of measure or proportion; limitlessness.

अमिय *amiyă* [*amṛta-*], m. Brbh. Av. nectar. — अमिय-मूरि, f. = संजीवनी मूरि.

अमिया *amiyā*, f. dimin. a mango; an unripe mango.

अमी *amī* [*amṛta-*], f. **1.** nectar. **2.** transf. sweet one, darling.

अमीन *amīn* [A. *amīn*], m. **1.** a government officer concerned with investigation of land or revenue claims, surveying and apportioning land, collecting revenues, and enforcing judgements: commissioner; arbitrator; auditor; trustee. **2.** a community name (esp. W. India).

अमीनी *amīnī* [A. *amīn*+P. *-ī*], f. **1.** the position of an *amīn*. **2.** trust, guardianship, custody.

अमीर *amīr* [A. *amīr*], adj. & m. **1.** of rank or distinction. **2.** rich, wealthy. **3.** m. a person of rank or distinction: prince; nobleman; commander. **4.** a wealthy person. **5.** transf. a large-hearted, or munificent person. — **अमीर-उमरा**, m. chief of the nobles, chief minister; pl. the nobility. **अमीरज़ादा** [P. *zāda*], m. the son of a person of rank; man of noble birth. °**-ज़ादी**, f.

अमीराना *amīrānā* [P. *amīrāna*], adj. **1.** noble, lordly. **2.** stately.

अमीरी *amīrī* [A. *amīr*+P. *-ī*], adj. & f. **1.** adj. having to do with an *amīr*. 2. = **अमीराना**. **3.** f. rank, distinction. **4.** wealth. **5.** lordship, power, sway. **6.** grandeur. — ~ **करना**, to live in splendour; to exercise authority or sway.

अमुक *amuk* [S.], adj. a certain (person or thing); (some) one or another.

अमुक्त *a-mukt* [S.], adj. not released; illiberal (in expenditure).

अमुख्य *a-mukhyă* [S.], adj. not pre-eminent; subordinate.

अमूमन *amūman*, adv. = **उमूमन**.

अमूर्त *a-mūrt* [S.], adj. **1.** formless. **2.** without body; disembodied; intangible. — ~ **कला**, f. non-plastic arts: literature; music.

अमूल *a-mūl* [S.], adj. **1.** rootless. **2.** baseless.

अमूलक *a-mūlak* [S.], adj. = **अमूल**.

अमूल्य *a-mūlyă* [S.], adj. **1.** priceless, invaluable. **2.** costing nothing, gratis.

अमृत *a-mṛt* [S.], m. & adj. **1.** m. *mythol.* the nectar of the gods (conferring immortality), ambrosia. **2.** transf. any pleasant drink. **3.** adj. immortal, imperishable. — **अमृत-पुत्र**, m. fig. a divinely gifted man. **अमृतबान** [f. *mṛttikā-*], m. a glazed earthenware jar (see **मरतबान**). **अमृत-लोक**, m. = **अमर-लोक**. **अमृताक्षर** [°*ta*+*a*°], m. syllables, or words, of eternal significance.

अमृतत्व *a-mṛtatvă* [S.], m. immortality; release from rebirth.

अमृत्यु *a-mṛtyu* [S.], adj. & f. **1.** adj. immortal. **2.** f. immortality.

अमेठना *ameṭhnā*, v.t. = **उमेठना**.

अमेध्य *a-medhyă* [S.], adj. & m. **1.** adj. ritually impure. **2.** m. an impure substance (as bodily excretions).

अमोघ *a-mogh* [S.], adj. unerring, unfailing (a stratagem, &c).

अमोट *amoṭ* [*āmrāvarta-*], m. reg. inspissated mango-juice.

अमोल *a-mol* [cf. H. *mol*], adj. = **अमूल्य**.

अमोलक *a-molak* [cf. H. *amol*], adj. Brbh. = **अमूल्य**, 1.

अमोला *amolā* [cf. *āmra-*], m. **1.** a mango seedling. **2.** child's whistle made from a mango stone.

अमौआ *amauā* [cf. *āmra-*], adj. & m. **1.** adj. mango-coloured: dark green. **2.** m. a type of dark green cloth.

अम्माँ *ammāṁ*, f. = **अम्मा**.

अम्मा *ammā* [*ambā-*], f. mother. — **अम्मा-जान**, f. mother-in-law; interj. mother dear!

अम्मी *ammī*, f. colloq. esp. *musl.* mother.

अम्र *amr* m. see [1]**अमर**.

अम्ल *amlă* [S.], adj. & m. **1.** adj. sour, acid. **2.** m. an acid substance. **3.** acidity. — **अम्लजन**, m. oxygen. **अम्ल-पित्त**, m. acidity; heartburn. **अम्ल-सार**, m. lemon extract.

अम्लता *amlătā* [S.], f. sourness, acidity.

अम्लान *a-mlān* [S.], adj. not faded or languid; clean, pure; radiant.

अम्लिमा *amlimā* [S.], f. acidity.

अम्लीय *amlīyă* [S.], adj. acidic.

अम्हौरी *amhaurī*, f. pronun. var. = **अँभौरी**.

अयश *a-yaś* [S.], m. **1.** disrepute; bad name; disgrace, odium. **2.** slander, detraction. **3.** a disreputable person, &c. — ~ **कमाना**, or **लेना**, to earn a bad name; to incur odium, &c.

अयशस्कर *a-yaśaskar* [S.], adj. = **अयशस्वी**.

अयशस्वी *a-yaśasvī* [S.], adj. disreputable; disgraced; infamous.

अयशी *a-yaśī* [S.], adj. = **अयशस्वी**.

अयस् *ayas* [S.], m. iron. — **अयस्कांत**, m. loadstone.

अयस्क *ayask* [S.], m. ore.

-अया *-aya* [S.], suffix (forms adverbs on nominal stems, e.g. **साधारणतया**, in general).

[1]**अयान** *ayān* [*ajānant-*], adj. Brbh. Av. ignorant; foolish.

²**अयान** *a-yān* [S.], m. not moving: natural disposition.

अयाना *ayānā* [*ajānant-*], adj. & m. **1.** adj. ignorant; foolish. **2.** m. a fool.

अयाल *ayāl* [P. *yāl*], f. **1.** mane. **2.** forelock (of horse).

अयुक्त *a-yukt* [S.], adj. **1.** ill-matched; incompatible. **2.** unfit, unsuitable; inappropriate. **3.** not connected, detached; disconnected, incoherent. **4.** not used.

अयुक्ति *a-yukti* [S.], f. **1.** unsuitability; incompatibility. **2.** incongruity. **3.** dissociation. — **अयुक्ति-युक्त**, adj. unsuitable, inappropriate.

अयुत *a-yut* [S.], m. ten thousand, a myriad.

अयोग *a-yog* [S.], m. **1.** separation, disjunction. **2.** inauspicious conjunction of planets; inauspicious time.

अयोग्य *a-yogyă* [S.], adj. **1.** unsuitable, inappropriate. **2.** incapable, incompetent; unqualified. **3.** not serviceable. **4.** undeserving.

अयोग्यता *a-yogyătā* [S.], f. **1.** unsuitability, &c. **2.** incapability; lack of qualifications. **3.** unserviceability. **4.** unworthiness.

अरंड *araṇḍ* [*eraṇḍa-*], m. the castor-oil bush, or tree, *Ricinus communis*. — **अरंड-ख़रबूज़ा**, m. = **पपीता**.

अरंडी *araṇḍī* [cf. H. *araṇḍ*], f. **1.** castor oil seed. **2.** a castor oil bush. — **~ का तेल**, m. castor oil.

¹**अरई** *araī*, f. reg. a goad (= ¹**आर**).

²**अरई** *araī*, f. *Pl.* a kind of grass used as cattle-fodder and for thatching.

अरक़ *arăq* [A. *'araq*], m. 'arrack': **1.** sap, juice. **2.** extract, essence; distillation.

अरकाट *arkāṭ*, m. the city of Arcot.

अरकाटी *arkāṭī* [cf. H. *arkāṭ*], adj. & m. **1.** adj. having to do with Arcot. **2.** m. a man of Arcot. **3.** *hist.* a recruiting agent for workers for Mauritius, &c. on indenture.

अरकोछ *arkoch*. reg. (Bihar) a dish of pulse flour cooked in an *arvī* leaf.

अरक्षित *a-rakṣit* [S.], adj. **1.** unprotected. **2.** undefended.

अरगजा *argajā*, m. a perfume, yellowish in colour, made from various ingredients (as sandal, rose-water, camphor, musk, ambergris).

अरगजी *argajī* [cf. H. *argajā*], adj. **1.** dyed with *argajā*, yellowish. **2.** scented with *argajā*.

अरगन *argan* [Engl. *organ*], m. **1.** an organ. **2.** an accordion.

अरगनी *arganī*, f. a rope or cord, or bamboo, stretched between two points of support for hanging clothes (= **अलगनी**); sthg. hanging: colloq. a dejected face.

अरगल *argal*, m. = **अर्गल**.

अरगा- *aragā-*, v.t. Brbh. Av. = **अलगाना**.

अरघा *arghā* [conn. *argha-*], m. **1.** reg. (W.) = **अर्घ**, 1. 2. = **अर्घ-पात्र**.

अरघान *arghān* [? ad. *āghrāṇa-*], f. fragrance.

अरड़ाना *araṛānā* [*āraṭati*], v.i. = **अरराना**.

अरण्य *araṇyă* [S.], m. wild region, scrub jungle; forest.

अरत *a-rat* [S.], adj. **1.** passionless, listless. **2.** detached, uninvolved (the mind).

अरति *a-rati* [S.], f. **1.** listlessness. **2.** detachment. **3.** apathy.

अरथ- *arth-* [ad. *arthayati*], v.t. Brbh. to explain.

अरथी *arthī* [cf. H. ²*rathī*], f. a bier. — **~ निकलना**, a (Hindu) funeral to take place, or to begin.

अरदब *ardab*, ? m. reg. a vexatious or frustrating situation.

अरदली *ardalī* [Engl. *orderly*], m. an orderly, an attendant.

अरदाबा *ardābā*, m. **1.** reg. (Bihar) a mash of parched and bruised grain (fed to horses and cattle). **2.** Av. a mash having fish as main ingredient.

अरदास *ardās*, f. Av. **1.** petition, request; entreaty. **2.** offering to a deity.

अरना *arnā* [*araṇa-*], m. a wild buffalo.

¹**अरनी** *arnī* [*araṇa-*], f. a wild buffalo cow.

²**अरनी** *arnī* [? ad. *araṇī-*], f. *HŚS.* name of a small tree (a source of timber) found in the Himālayas.

अरप- *arp-* [ad. *arpayati*], v.t. Brbh. to present (an offering, &c.: see **अर्पण**).

¹**अरब** *arab* [A. *'arab*], m. **1.** Arabia. **2.** an Arab.

²**अरब** *arăb* [ad. *arbuda-*: w. *kharva-*, anal.], m. a hundred million; a myriad. — **अरब-खरब**, m. a myriad (of).

अरबरा- *arbarā-*, v.i. Brbh. = **हड़बड़ाना**.

¹**अरबी** *arbī* [A. *'arbī*], adj. & m. **1.** adj. Arabian. **2.** Arabic. **3.** m. an Arabian horse.

²**अरबी** *arbī* [A. *'arabīya*: P. *'arabī*], f. the Arabic language.

अरमनी *armanī* [P. *armanī*], adj. & m. **1.** adj. Armenian. **2.** m. an Armenian.

अरमान *armān* [P. *armān*], m. heartfelt wish, desire, longing; earnest hope. — ~ निकलना, or पूरे होना, to be satisfied; to be gratified. ~ निकालना, to fulfil (one's, के) wishes or hopes. ~ रह जाना, one's wishes, &c. to be unfulfilled.

अरर *arar*, interj. oh! (expressing dismay). — ~ यह कैसे हुआ? why (is he) taken aback like this?

अररा- *ararā-* [cf. H. *arrānā*], v.i. Brbh. metr. = अरराना.

अरराना *arrānā* [*āraṭati*], v.i. to fall with a crash (as a building, a tree); to rumble (as machinery).

अरराहट *arrāhaṭ* [cf. H. *arrānā*], f. crash, roar, rumble.

अरवन *arvan* [**ālavana-*], reg. (W.) **1.** first cutting of the crop (offered to family gods and brāhmaṇs). **2.** grain cut when still unripe.

अरविंद *arvind* [S.], m. a lotus.

अरवी *arvī* [*ālukī-*], f. a plant of the arum family, and its root (used as a vegetable).

¹**अरस** *a-ras* [S.; and H. *ras*], adj. **1.** without juice or sap. **2.** tasteless; insipid. **3.** jejune, vapid.

²**अरस** *aras*, m. Brbh. languor, &c. (= अलस).

³**अरस** *aras* [A. *'arś*], m. Brbh. **1.** roof, canopy. **2.** highest heaven.

अरस- *aras-* [cf. *alasa-*], v.i. Brbh. to be languid (the body).

अरसट्टा *arsaṭṭā* [conn. M. *aḍsaṭṭā*], m. *hist.* (W.) **1.** estimate, rough calculation. **2.** specif. monthly account of receipts and expenses.

अरस-परस *aras-paras* [*sparśa-*], m. **1.** touching, physical contact. **2.** a game: blind man's buff.

अरसा *arsā* [A. *'arṣa*], m. a space of time (esp. regarded as elapsed); interval. — ~ लगाना, to take a long time (in doing sthg). अरसे तक, adv. for some time (ahead). अरसे से, adv. for some (past) time. इस अरसे में, adv. in the meanwhile.

अरसिक *a-rasik* [S.], adj. not savouring (the essential quality of sthg.); dull (of nature).

अरसीलो *arsīlo* [H. *alas* × H. *rasīlā*], adj. Brbh. languid (the body).

अरस्तू *arastū* [P. *ariṣṭū*], m. Aristotle.

अरहट *arhaṭ* [*araghaṭṭa-*], m. a Persian wheel (for raising water from a well).

अरहर *arhar* [conn. *āḍhakī-*], f. a type of pulse (*Cajamus indicus*). — ~ की दाल, f. = अरहर.

अराजक *a-rājak* [S.], adj. **1.** not having a ruler. **2.** anarchical.

अराजकता *a-rājakătā* [S.], f. anarchy. — अराजकतावादी, m. a supporter of anarchy, anarchist.

अराज़ी *arāzī* [A. *arāẓī*, pl. of *arẓ*], f. pl. *Pl. HŚS.* lands; detached portions of land.

अराति *a-rāti* [S.], m. **1.** enemy, foe. **2.** the six 'enemies' or deadly sins: lust, anger, greed, error, pride and envy. **3.** (in chronograms) the number six.

अराबा *arābā* [P. *'arāba*], m. Brbh. a cart; gun-carriage.

अरार *arār*, m. reg. (E.) = ²अड़ाड़.

अरारा *arārā* [? conn. *aṭṭa-*²], m. reg. (W.) a high river bank or bluff.

अरारूट *arārūṭ* [Engl. *arrowroot*], m. arrowroot.

अराल *arāl* [S.], adj. poet. crooked.

अरिंदम *arindam* [S.], adj. poet. destroying the enemy: victorious.

¹**अरि** *ari* [S.], m. an enemy, foe.

²**अरि** *ari* [S.], m. *Pl. HŚS.* a wheel.

अरिनी *a-rinī*, adj. Brbh. out of debt.

अरिष्ट *a-riṣṭ* [S.], m. not hurt: name of a demon killed by Kr̥ṣṇa.

अरी *arī*, interj. (used to girls or women). = अरे.

अरीति *a-rīti* [S.], f. improper, or impolite, behaviour.

अरुंधती *a-rundhatī* [S.], f. *astron.* Arundhatī, the small star Alcor in the Plough.

अरु *aru* [*apara-*], conj. Brbh. = और.

अरुचि *a-ruci* [S.], f. **1.** dislike, aversion. **2.** lack of interest. **3.** lack of appetite. — अरुचिकर, adj. causing dislike, &c.; not awakening interest; unappetising.

अरुझ- *arujh-*, v.i. Brbh. Av. = उलझना.

अरुझा- *arujhā-*, v.t. & v.i. Brbh. Av. **1.** v.t. = उलझाना. **2.** v.i. = उलझना.

अरुण *aruṇ* [S.], adj. & m. **1.** adj. reddish brown; tawny. **2.** m. the sun. **3.** reddish glow, flush (of dawn); red or tawny colour. **4.** dawn. — अरुणचूड़, m. Av. red-crest: a cock. अरुण-शिखा, f. Av. id. अरुणाभ [°*ṇa* + *ā*°], adj. glowing red, reddish. अरुणोदय [°*ṇa* + *u*°], m. early dawn. अरुणोपल [°*ṇa* + *u*°], m. a ruby.

अरुणता *aruṇătā* [S.], f. = अरुण, 3.

अरुणित *aruṇit* [S.], adj. caused to glow, reddened; glowing red.

अरुणिमा *aruṇimā* [S.], f. reddish glow, flush.

अरुंतुद *arun-tud* [S.], adj. poet. striking a wound: causing increased pain.

अरुना- *arunā-* [cf. *aruṇa-*], v.i. & v.t. Brbh. **1.** v.i. to grow red; to grow bloodshot (the eyes). **2.** v.t. to cause (the eyes) to grow red (from crying).

अरुनाई *arunāī* [cf. *aruṇa-*, H. *arunā-*], f. Brbh. = अरुणता.

अरुनारा *arunārā* [**aruṇatara-*], adj. Brbh. Av. reddish, tawny.

अरुस *arus* [conn. *aṭarūṣa-*], m. *Pl.* the bush *Adhatoda vasica* (used medicinally).

अरूप *a-rūp* [S.], adj. & m. **1.** adj. formless. **2.** ill-formed, ugly. **3.** m. absence of form. **4.** shapelessness; ugliness.

अरूस *arūs* [A. *'arūs*], f. U. a bride.

अरे *are* [*are*], interj. (used to men). **1.** I say! hullo! (attracting attention). **2.** oh! (expressing astonishment, or concern).

अरे-परे *are-pare* [cf. Panj. *pare*, and H. *ār-pār*], adv. on this side and that; right and left.

अरोंधना *aroṁdhnā* [**ārundhati*], v.t. *Pl.* to strangle.

अरोग *a-rog* [S.], adj. & m. **1.** adj. free of disease, healthy. **2.** m. freedom from disease, health. **3.** a healthy person.

अरोगी *a-rogī* [S.], adj. = अरोग.

अरोग्य *a-rogyă* [S.], adj. = अरोग.

अरोग्यता *a-rogyătā* [S.], f. healthy state, health.

अर्क *ark* [S.], m. **1.** the sun. **2.** swallow-wort.

अर्क़ *arq*, m. see अरक़.

अर्गल *argal* [S.], m. **1.** a wooden bar or bolt, esp. for fastening a door. **2.** fig. an impediment.

अर्गला *argălā* [S.], f. = अर्गल.

अर्घ *argh* [S.], m. **1.** a respectful offering, to a deity or to an honoured guest, of water (in which substances such as rice, curds, or milk may be mixed); a libation. **2.** respectful reception of a guest. **3.** worth, value, price. — ~ चढ़ाना, or देना, to make an offering or oblation (to, को). – अर्घ-दान, m. presentation of an offering. अर्घ-पतन, m. decline in value; fall in prices. अर्घ-पात्र, m. a vessel in which water is offered to a deity, or to an honoured guest on his arrival. अर्घासन [°*gha* + *ā*°], m. a guest's seat of honour.

अर्घ्य *arghyă* [S.], adj. **1.** respected, honoured. **2.** costly, of worth. **3.** article offered respectfully to a deity, or to a guest (see *argh*).

अर्चक *arcak* [S.], adj. & m. **1.** adj. worshipping, adoring. **2.** m. a worshipper.

अर्चन *arcan* [S.], m. worship, adoration; homage.

अर्चना *arcănā* [S.], f. = अर्चन.

अर्चा *arcā* [S.], f. **1.** worship, adoration. **2.** *Pl. HŚS.* an image of a deity.

अर्चि *arci* [S.], f. (m., *Pl.*) **1.** flame. **2.** light, radiance.

अर्चित *arcit* [S.], adj. worshipped, adored.

अर्ज़ *arz* [A. *'arẓ*], m. breadth, width: representation, petition; request. — ~ करना, to report; to apply (for), to request; U. to say (to a superior), to submit (a viewpoint).

अर्जन *arjan* [S.], m. **1.** acquiring, acquisition. **2.** earnings; profits. **3.** accumulating.

अर्जनीय *arjănīyă* [S.], adj. worth earning (as money, reputation).

अर्जित *arjit* [S.], adj. **1.** acquired; earned, gained. **2.** accumulated. — ~ करना, to acquire; to earn.

अर्ज़ी *arzī* [P. *'arẓī*], f. *law.* representation, petition; submission. — ~ दाख़िल करना, or देना, to file a petition. ~ लगाना, to file a petition (against, पर), to sue. ~ लेना, to receive a petition; to entertain a case.

अर्जुन *arjun* [S.], m. a large deciduous tree, *Terminalia arjuna* (source of timber and gum, and used medicinally).

अर्णव *arṇav* [S.], m. ocean, sea.

अर्थ *arth* [S.], m. **1.** object, purpose; motive; interest. **2.** advantage, profit. ***3.** sense, meaning. ***4.** substance, wealth; assets; worldly prosperity; finance, finances; in comp. economy (of a state). **5.** *gram.* mood. **6.** (in comp.) for the purpose, or the sake, of. **7.** for the sake (of, के). — ~ देना, or रखना, to express or to contain a meaning. ~ निकालना, to make out or to perceive the meaning (of, का). सच्चे, or सही, अर्थों में, in the full sense (of a word, or phrase); truly, really. – अर्थकर, adj. useful; advantageous. अर्थगत, adj. semantic. अर्थ-गर्भित, adj. pregnant with meaning, meaningful. अर्थ-दंड, m. a fine (= जुरमाना). अर्थ-नीति, f. economic practice or policy: economics. अर्थनैतिक, adj. economic. अर्थ-न्यायालय, m. a civil court. अर्थपूर्ण, adj. meaningful. अर्थ-प्रक्रिया, f. civil proceedings. अर्थप्रधान, adj. concerned characteristically with finance, financial. अर्थ-बंध, m. = अर्थानुबंध. अर्थ-भेद, m. distinction in meaning. अर्थ-विचार, m. semantics. अर्थ-विज्ञान, m. semantics; the science of economics. अर्थ-विधान, m. semantics. अर्थ विधि, f. civil law. अर्थ-विवाद, m. a civil dispute, case. अर्थ-व्यवस्था, f. arrangement of finances: economy (as of a state); management of an economy. अर्थ-व्यवहार, m. id. अर्थ-शास्त्र, m. economics. °ई, m. economist. अर्थ-संबंधी, adj. economic. अर्थ-सिद्धि, f. achievement of a purpose, success; acquisition of wealth. अर्थहीन, adj. senseless, nonsensical; without resources; unsuccessful. अर्थागम [°*tha*+*ā*°], m. receipt or collection of income. अर्थाधिकारी [°*tha*+*a*°], m. a financial officer, or authority. अर्थानुबंध, [°*tha*+*a*°], a financial or economic agreement, or transaction. अर्थापन [°*tha*+*ā*°], m. obtaining a sense (from): interpretation. °आपित, adj. – अर्थतः, adv. in fact, in reality. अर्थात्, adv. see s.v.

अर्थात् *arthāt* [S.: abl. case of *artha*-], adv. that is to say, in other words.

अर्थिक *arthik* [S.], m. one having an object, or interest.

अर्थित *arthit* [S.], adj. sought after; requested; demanded.

अर्थिया *arthiyā* [cf. H. *arthī* 'petitioner'], m. **1.** one who has an object or interest; dependant, client. **2.** corr. agent (= अढ़तिया).

अर्थी *arthī* [S.], adj. & m. **1.** esp. in comp. adj. seeking after (sthg.); having an object or interest. **2.** wealthy. **3.** m. a petitioner; suitor, plaintiff; prosecutor. **4.** a wealthy person. **5.** a needy person.

अर्द्ध *arddh*, adj. & m. see अर्ध.

अर्ध *ardh* [S.], adj. & m. **1.** adj. अर्ध-. half, semi, hemi; partial. **2.** m. a half. — अर्ध-कुंभ, m. the 'minor' Kumbh melā (held every alternate sixth year). अर्ध-ग्रीष्म, adj. semi-tropical. अर्ध-चक्र, m. a semi-circle; *arch.* a semi-circular moulding. अर्ध-चंद्र, m. half-moon; a crescent; the markings on a peacock's tail. अर्ध-नयन, m. third eye (in the brow) of a deity. अर्धनारीश्वर, m. lord who is half woman: a title of Śiva. अर्ध-भाग, m. a half portion. °इक, m. one performing half a task, or entitled to a half share. अर्धवयस्क, adj. middle-aged. अर्ध-वर्ष, m. a half-year. °-वार्षिक, adj. half-yearly. अर्ध-विराम, m. a comma. अर्ध-वृत्त, m. a semi-circle. °आकार, adj. अर्ध-व्यास, m. a radius. अर्ध-शासकीय, adj. = next. अर्ध-सरकारी, adj. semi-official. अर्ध-सैनिक, adj. paramilitary. अर्ध-स्वर, m. *ling.* a semi-vowel. अर्धांग [°*dha*+*a*°], m. half, or one side of, the body; paralysis affecting one side of the body. °घात, m. id., 2. °ई, adj. & m. hemiplegic; a hemiplegic. अर्धांगिनी, f. she who sits at (one's) side: a wife. अर्धांशी [°*dha*+*a*°], m. one entitled to a half share. अर्धार्ध [°*dha*+*a*°], m. a quarter. अर्धाशन [°*dha*+*a*°}, m. insufficiency of food. अर्धासन [°*dha*+*ā*°], m. seat of honour (beside or shared with a host). अर्धीकरण, m. dividing in half.

अर्धाली *ardhālī* [? **ardhatāla*-: ad. *ardha*-], f. a single line of a *caupāī* couplet.

अर्धीकरण *ardhīkaraṇ* [S.], m. see s.v. अर्ध.

अर्पण *arpaṇ* [S.], m. **1.** delivering, entrusting. **2.** placing in or upon. **3.** an offering; sacrifice; gift. — ~ करना, to present, to offer (a gift, &c.); to devote (to, को); to dedicate (to).

अर्पित *arpit* [S.], adj. **1.** delivered, entrusted. **2.** presented, offered; sacrificed. — ~ करना, to present, &c.

अर्ब *arb*, m. = [2]अरब.

अर्बुद *arbud* [S.], m. = [2]अरब.

अर्भक *arbhak* [S.], m. Av. small: **1.** child, boy. **2.** young (of an animal).

अर्राटा *arrāṭā*, m. *Pl.* a prolonged rumbling sound (as of gunfire, or the fall of a building).

अर्श *arś* [A. *'arś*], m. U. **1.** highest heaven. **2.** throne.

अर्हंत *arhant*, m. = अर्हत.

अर्हत *arhat* [S.], m. a Buddha; a Jain saint, or deity.

अर्हता *arhătā* [S.], f. qualification.

अलंकरण *alaṅ-karaṇ* [S.], m. ornamenting, ornamentation, &c.; decoration.

अलंकार *alaṅ-kār* [S.], m. **1.** ornament, embellishment. **2.** *rhet.* an ornament of sound or sense; figure of speech. **3.** a decoration (military, civil). — अलंकार-शास्त्र, m. the science or art of rhetoric.

अलंकारिक *alaṅ-kārik* [S.], adj. ornamental, decorative.

अलंकृत *alaṅ-kr̥t* [S.], adj. ornamented, adorned, &c.; decorated.

अलंकृति *alaṅ-kr̥ti* [S.], f. an ornament, &c. — अलंकृतिप्रधान, adj. decorative (of style).

अलंग *alaṅg*, m. Brbh. Av. **1.** side, direction. **2.** length, extent (as of a rampart).

अलक *alak* [S.], f. a lock of hair.

अलका *alăkā* [S.], f. *mythol.* name of the residence (in the Himālayas) of Kuvera; transf. poet. Tibet.

अलक्तक *alaktak* [S.], adj. poet. lac-coloured, red.

अलक़तरा *alqatrā* [A. *al-qaṭrān*], m. tar.

अलकसाना *alkasānā* [cf. H. *ālkas*], v.i. = अलसाना.

अलकसाहट *alkasāhaṭ* [cf. H. *alkasānā*], f. = आलकस.

अलक्षण *a-lakṣaṇ* [S.], adj. & m. **1.** adj. without distinguishing marks. **2.** inauspicious. **3.** m. bad sign, ill omen. **4.** absence of distinguishing marks, characteristics.

अलक्षणी *a-lakṣăṇī* [S.], adj. & m. **1.** adj. unfortunate, ill-fated. **2.** m. unlucky person.

अलक्षित *a-lakṣit* [S.], adj. **1.** unseen, unobserved; not noted. **2.** invisible, indistinguishable.

अलक्ष्मी *a-lakṣmī* [S.], adj. & f. **1.** adj. not prosperous, unfortunate; poor. **2.** f. misfortune.

अलक्ष्य *a-lakṣyă* [S.], adj. **1.** invisible; imperceptible. **2.** unobserved.

अलख *a-lakh* [*alakṣya-*], adj. & m. **1.** adj. invisible; imperceptible (as the ultimate being). **2.** m. the ultimate being. — ~ जगाना, to call on, or to ask alms in the name of, God. ~ पुरुष, m. = ~. — अलखधारी, m. a member of a sect of yogīs. अलख-नामी, m. id.

अलग *a-lag* [*alagna-*], adj. **1.** detached, separate (from, से); loose, free (from a restraint). **2.** removed (as from a post); excluded (as from caste or other contacts). **3.** disengaged; not involved; aloof (from). **4.** set apart, or aside; safe, secure. **5.** different, distinct. **6.** singular, unusual. **7.** lonely, solitary. **8.** adv. apart, separately; unseen. **9.** at a distance; at liberty. — ~ करना, to separate; to unfasten; to set free; to remove, &c.; to set apart; to get rid of; to divorce; to sift, to select. ~ रहना, to remain separate, or uninvolved, &c. ~ होना, to be separated, &c.; to be removed; to part; to withdraw; to become aloof. — अलग-अलग, adj. = ~; adv. one by one, separately, individually. अलग-थलग, adj. delicate, fine, soft; adv. softly, tenderly; = ~.

अलगना *alagnā*, v.i. reg. *Pl.* (?) = अलग होना.

अलगनी *alagnī* [cf. **ālagyati*: Pa. *ālaggeti*], f. a rope or bamboo pole used to hang clothes on.

अलग़रज़ *algarz* [A. *al-garẓ*], adj. the essence is: in short; finally.

अलग़रज़ी *algarzī* [A. *al-garẓ*+P. *-ī*], f. **1.** heedlessness, unconcern (sc. for others). **2.** self-interest.

अलगा *algā* [*alagna-*], adj. separate: — अलगा-गुज़ारी, f. separation; split, breakup (as of a family).

अलगाना *algānā* [cf. H. *alag*], v.t. = अलग करना.

अलगाव *algāv* [cf. H. *alag*, *algānā*], m. **1.** separate state. **2.** detachment, aloofness. **3.** apathy. **4.** alienation (from, से). **5.** segregation; isolation.

अलग़ोज़ा *algozā* [P. *algoza*], m. flute, pipe.

अलगौझा *algaujhā*, m. reg. = अलगा-गुज़ारी.

अलग्योझा *alagyojhā* [f. *alagnā* or a reg. form of *algā*, adj.; ? conn. H. *algā-guzārī*], m. reg. = अलगा-गुज़ारी.

अलड़ *alaṛ*, m. = अल्हड़. — अलड़-बलड़, f. childish talk, silly prattle.

अलता *altā* [*alakta-*], m. **1.** lac dye (used by women to stain their feet red). **2.** varnish (as used on the fingernails).

अलपीन *alpīn*, m. = आलपीन.

अलफ़ाज़ *alfāz* [A.: pl. of *lafẓ*], m. pl. U. words.

अलबत्ता *albattā* [A. *al-batta*], adv. **1.** however. **2.** certainly, undoubtedly; indeed, to be sure.

अलबल *albal*, adj. reg. **1.** very strong; almighty. **2.** adv. quickly.

अलबाल *albāl*, m. Brbh. = [6]आला.

अलबिलल *albilal*, adj. **1.** very foolish. **2.** fruitless, vain.

अलबेट *albeṭ*, f. turn, twist, bend. — ~ देना, v.t. to twist, to wind.

अलबेला *albelā*, adj. **1.** charming, beautiful, handsome. **2.** showy (in dress, manner). **3.** strange, odd.

अलबेलापन *albelāpan* [cf. H. *albelā*], m. charm, &c. (see अलबेला).

अलभ्य *a-labhyă* [S.], adj. **1.** unattainable. **2.** rare, precious (as a talent).

[1]**अलम्** *alam* [S.], adj. or adv. poet. enough.

[2]**अलम** *alam* [A. *'alam*], m. banner: — अलमबरदार [P. *-bardār*], m. standard-bearer.

अलमस्त *almast* [P. *al-mast*], adj. **1.** drunk. **2.** lustful. **3.** furious, infuriated. **4.** mad, crazed. ***5.** transf. carefree.

अलमारी *almārī* [Pt. *armario*], f. **1.** cupboard. **2.** wardrobe. **3.** bookcase.

अलमास *almās* [P. *almās*], m. U. diamond.

अलल *alal* [**alala-*], adj. chiefly in comp. cheerful, frisky: — अलल-टप्पू, adj. & m. thoughtless; frivolous; irregular, absurd; a thoughtless person, &c.; adv. by guess. अलल-

बछेड़ा, m. a frisky calf; a giddy youth. अलल-हिसाब, adj. forgetful of payment.

अललाना *allānā*, v.i. reg. see अल्लाना.

अलल्ले-तलल्ले *alalle-talalle* [cf. **alala-*], m. **1.** delight. **2.** festivity, revelry. **3.** show, ostentation; extravagance. **4.** voluptuousness. — ~ करना, to make merry, &c.; to give oneself up to pleasure; to squander.

अलवान *alvān* [A. *alvān*: pl. of *laun* 'colour'], m. shawl cloth, shawl (of wool).

अलवाया *alvāyā*, adj. reg. **1.** soft, gentle, tender. **2.** adv. with a light hand or touch.

अलविदा *alvidā* [A. *al vidā'*], m. inv. U. **1.** the last Friday in Ramaẓān. **2.** interj. goodbye!

अलस *alas*, m. & adj. Brbh. = आलस्य, आलसी.

अलसाना *alsānā* [cf. H *ālas*], v.i. 1., to be lazy. 2., to be slack, inert or languid; to be drowsy.

अलसानि *alsāni* [cf. H. *alsānā*], f. Brbh. languor.

अलसी *alsī* [cf. *atasī-*: Pk. (Ś.) *alusī-*], f. **1.** linseed. **2.** flax. — ~ का तेल, m. linseed oil.

अलसेट *alseṭ*, f. *Pl.* **1.** deception, duplicity. **2.** discrepancy (in an account).

अलसेटिया *alseṭiyā* [cf. *ālasya-*: ?+**paṭṭu-* ← *paṭu-*] , adj. & m. *Pl.* **1.** crafty. **2.** lazy, idle. **3.** slow (in paying debts).

अलसौंह- *alsaumh-*, adj. Brbh. languid (look, glance).

अलहदा *alahdā* [A. *alā ḥida*], adj. separate, distinct; apart.

अलाई *alāī*, f. reg. (Raj.) = अम्हौरी.

अलान *alān* [*ālāna-*], m. Av. **1.** a post for tying an elephant to. **2.** chain or rope used to tie an elephant. **3.** a fetter, tie.

अलाप *alāp* [*ālāpya-*], m. = आलाप.

अलापना *alāpnā* [**ālapyati*], v.t. **1.** to converse. **2.** to warm up the voice before singing. **3.** to pitch or to raise the voice. **4.** to moan, to groan. — अपना राग अलापते जाना, to harp on the same theme.

अलाभ *a-lābh* [S.], m. non-acquirement: unprofitability; loss.

अलामत *alāmat* [A. *'alāma*: P. *'alāmat*], f. U. mark, sign.

अलाय-बलाय *alāy-balāy* [cf. H. *balā*], f. & adj. **1.** f. trouble, misfortune. **2.** adj. wretched, unfortunate.

अलाव *alāv* [*alāta-*], m. a fire lit in the open (as on winter nights, for warmth).

अलावा *alāvā* [A. *'ilāva*], adv. (as ppn. often inverted.) sthg. laid on top: **1.** in addition (to, के), over and above. **2.** apart (from); moreover.

अलाहदा *alāhdā* [P. *'alā ḥida*], adj. = अलहदा.

अलिंद *alind* [S.], m. poet. terrace; balcony.

अलि *ali* [S.], m. **1.** a large black bee. **2.** the Indian cuckoo, or koel.

अलिक *alik* [S.], m. Brbh. the forehead.

अलिनी *alinī* [S.], f. Av. a bumble bee (= अलि).

अलिफ़ *alif* [A.], m. & adj. **1.** the first letter of the Arabic alphabet. **2.** adj. transf. alone, friendless; destitute. — ~ बे, f. the ABC, the alphabet. ~ नंगा, adj. stark naked.

1**अली** *alī* [*alin-*], m. a black bee.

2**अली** *alī* [**alikā-*], f. a woman's female friend (= 2आली).

अलीक *alīk* [S.], adj. & m. **1.** adj. false, not genuine. **2.** disagreeable, displeasing. **3.** m. falsehood. **4.** anything disagreeable.

अलील *alīl* [A. *'alīl*], adj. unwell, ill.

अलेख *a-lekh* [**alekhya-*], adj. indescribable, incalculable; unknowable (as a deity).

अलेखा *a-lekhā*, adj. = अलेख.

अलैया-बलैया *alaiyā-balaiyā*, f. 1. = अलाय-बलाय. **2.** fig. offering, sacrifice.

1**अलोक** *a-lok* [*alokya-*], adj. & m. **1.** adj. invisible. **2.** m. the other world.

2**अलोक** *a-lok* [S.], adj. without people, deserted, desolate.

अलोकना *aloknā* [? ad. H. *ālok*; w. *ālokate*], v.i. & v.t. **1.** v.i. to be illuminated. **2.** v.t. to illuminate. **3.** Brbh. to see.

अलोकनीय *a-lokănīyă* [S.], adj. invisible.

अलोकित *a-lokit* [S.], adj. unseen, unnoticed.

अलोना *alonā* [*alavaṇa-*], adj. **1.** not salty, unsalted. **2.** tasteless, insipid. **3.** unattractive.

1**अलोप** *alop* [cf. **ālopyate*], adj. **1.** disappeared; concealed; invisible. **2.** vanished, extinct. — अलोप-अंजन, m. an ointment, said to make one invisible when applied to the eyes.

2**अलोप** *a-lop* [S.], adj. not concealed; visible, apparent.

अलोप- *alop-* [cf. H. 1*alop*], v.i. & v.t. Av. **1.** v.i. to be concealed. **2.** v.t. to conceal.

अलोभ *a-lobh* [S.], m. freedom from covetousness.

[1]**अलोल** *alol* [**āloḍa-*: Pa. *āloḷa-*], m. **1.** friskiness (esp. of a horse). **2.** frolicsomeness; flirtatiousness. ~ **करना**, to frisk, to frolic, &c. — **अलोल-कलोल**, m. = ~.

[2]**अलोल** *a-lol* [S.], adj. Brbh. not shaking, steady, firm.

अलौकिक *a-laukik* [S.], adj. **1.** unearthly, supernatural; superhuman, transcendental. **2.** strange, rare.

अलौह *a-lauh* [S.], adj. non-ferrous.

अल्प *alp* [S.], adj. **1.** small; little (of amount), few; short. **2.** insignificant, unimportant. **अल्पकालिक**, adj. short-lived; short-term, temporary. °**-कालीन**, adj. id. **अल्पजीवी**, adj. = °-**आयु**. **अल्पज्ञ**, adj. ignorant; foolish. **अल्प-तंत्र**, m. rule of the few: oligarchy. **अल्प-तनु**, adj. small, or frail of body; dwarfish. **अल्पतम**, adj. least, minimum; minimal. **अल्पदृष्टि**, adj. of little vision: unenlightened; unforeseeing. **अल्पप्रमाण**, adj. of little authority; based on little evidence. **अल्पप्राण**, adj. *ling.* non-aspirate. °**ईकरण**, m. de-aspiration. **अल्पबल**, adj. feeble. **अल्पबुद्धि**, adj. foolish, silly. **अल्प-मत**, m. minority opinion. **अल्पवयस्क**, adj. of young years; not adult, minor. **अल्प-विराम**, m. a comma. **अल्पशः**, adv. by degrees, gradually. **अल्पसंख्यक**, adj. small in numbers, or population; forming a minority. **अल्पांश** [°*pa*+*a*°], m. a small part; minority. **अल्पायु**, adj. [°*pa*+*ā*°] of young years; short-lived. **अल्पार्थक** [°*pa*+*a*°], adj. *ling.* diminutive. **अल्पावस्था** [°*pa*+*a*°], f. young age, tender years. **अल्पाहार** [°*pa*+*ā*°], m. moderation in eating; abstemiousness; a light meal. °**ई**, adj.

अल्पक *alpak* [S.], adj. & m. **1.** adj. very small; minimum; minimal. **2.** m. *ling.* a diminutive.

अल्पता *alpătā* [S.], f. **1.** small size or amount. **2.** insignificance, &c.; inferiority.

अल्पत्व *alpatvă* [S.], m. = **अल्पता**.

अल्पित *alpit* [S.], adj. made small: reduced; contracted; shortened.

अल्लम-गल्लम *allam-gallam*, m. **1.** trash, rubbish. **2.** nonsense. **3.** *Pl.* pretext, idle excuse. **4.** misappropriation; embezzlement. — ~ **खाना**, to (be ready to) eat anything at all. ~ **बकना**, to talk nonsense, to talk wildly.

अल्ल *all*, f. = [3]**आल**.

अल्लाना *allānā*, v.i. to cry out loudly; to scream, to shriek; to groan; to wail.

अल्लाह *allāh* [A. *allāh* ← *al-ilāh* 'the God'], m. Allah. — ~ ~, interj. (of surprise, approval, &c.) good heavens! ~ ~ **करना**, to call on God; to say (one's) prayers. ~ **आमीन**, interj. Allah amen: so be it. ~ **आमीन का लड़का**, a child granted after many prayers. ~ **आमीन से**, adv. with great care, anxiously (*Pl.*). ~ **का नाम**, the name of God; nothing whatever, not a bit. ~ **का नाम लेना**, to have the fear of God (in one: used in rebuking one who has lied). ~ **का नूर**, m. the light of God: a gift from God (as a beard, &c.); a very beautiful person; iron. a very ugly person. ~ **ताला** [A. *ta'ālā*, inv.], m. God the All-high. ~ **पीर मनाना**, to propitiate God and the saints. ~ **मियाँ**, m. the good Lord. ~ **मियाँ की गाय**, f. euphem. a simple person, simpleton; a snail. ~ **ही** ~, interj. God alone (is sure); = ~ ~. **अल्लाहो अकबर**, interj. God is great.

अल्हड़ *alhaṛ* [**allaḍa-*: ? × *āhlādayati*, H. *āhlānā*], adj. & m. **1.** childish. **2.** youthful, inexperienced. **3.** ignorant: untrained. **4.** carefree. **5.** m. pej. child, mere boy.

अल्हड़पन *alhaṛpan* [cf. H. *alhaṛ*], m. **1.** childishness. **2.** inexperience, &c. **3.** carefreeness, gaiety.

अव- *ava-* [S.], pref. away, down (e.g. **अवनति**, f. decline).

अवकलन *avă-kalan* [S.], m. **1.** observation; ascertainment. **2.** collecting, collection.

अवकलित *avă-kalit* [S.], adj. **1.** seen, observed; ascertained. **2.** collected.

अवकाश *avă-kāś* [S.], m. **1.** space, room; scope. **2.** opportunity. ***3.** leisure; vacation. **4.** retirement. **5.** E.H. the heavens; space. — **अवकाश-गृहण**, m. retirement. **अवकाशप्राप्त**, adj. retired. **अवकाश-यान**, m. space-craft.

अवकेशी *avă-keśī* [S.], adj. *Pl. HŚS.* unfruitful, barren (as a tree, or vine).

अवगत *avă-gat* [S.], adj. **1.** known; comprehended. **2.** apprised, informed (of, **से**). **3.** knowledgeable (in a topic). **4.** gone down, declined.

अवगति *avă-gati* [S.], f. **1.** knowledge, awareness; comprehension. **2.** decline, deterioration.

अवगाह *avă-gāh* [S.], adj. & m. Av. **1.** adj. deep, bottomless. **2.** unattainable. **3.** m. bathing. **4.** plunge, dive. **5.** immersion (as in thought).

अवगाहन *avă-gāhan* [S.], m. = **अवगाह**.

अवगीत *avă-gīt* [S.], m. & adj. **1.** m. a badly sung song. **2.** an indecent song. **3.** criticism; satire; lampoon. **4.** adj. *Pl. HŚS.* blamed; detested.

अवगुंठन *avă-guṇṭhan* [S.], m. a veil.

अवगुण *avă-guṇ* [S.], m. **1.** defect, fault. **2.** vice.

अवचेतन *avă-cetan* [S.], adj. sub-conscious.

अवच्छद *avă-cchad* [S.], m. *Pl. HŚS.* cover, covering.

अवच्छेद *avă-cched* [S.], m. **1.** part, section. ***2.** division; boundary, limit; distinction. **3.** distinguishing feature.

अवच्छेदक *avă-cchedak* [S.], adj. **1.** dividing; determining a boundary. **2.** distinguishing.

अवच्छेदन *avă-cchedan* [S.], m. **1.** dividing. **2.** section, division. **3.** determination of a boundary.

अवज्ञा *avă-jñā* [S.], m. disregard, disrespect (as for a person, or an order); neglect; contempt.

अवज्ञात *avă-jñāt* [S.], adj. disregarded; neglected, &c. (see **अवज्ञा**).

अवज्ञेय *avă-jñey* [S.], adj. deserving to be disregarded.

अवडेर- *avăḍer-*, v.t. reg. to abandon, to forsake.

अवढर *avaḍhar*, adj. poet. see **औढर**.

अवतंस *avă-taṃs* [S.], m. **1.** garland. ***2.** ornament, adornment. **3.** crest; diadem.

अवतत *avă-tat* [S.], adj. widely spread (over, or downwards).

अवतमस *avă-tamas* [S.], m. dusk.

अवतर- *avătar-* [ad. *avatarati*], v.i. Brbh. to descend (esp. as an incarnation of a deity); to be born, to appear.

अवतरण *avă-taraṇ* [S.], m. **1.** descending, descent. **2.** landing (of an aircraft). **3.** crossing (a river, &c). **4.** means of descent: steps, &c. **5.** incarnation. **6.** an extract, citation. — **अवतरण-छत्र**, m. parachute. **अवतरण-चिह्न**, m. quotation mark.

अवतरणिका *avă-tarăṇikā* [S.], f. introduction (to a book); preface.

अवतरित *avă-tarit* [S.], adj. **1.** descended. **2.** landed; crossed over. **3.** incarnate. **4.** excerpted.

अवतल *avă-tal* [S.], adj. concave.

अवतार *avă-tār* [S.], m. **1.** descent (esp. of a deity from heaven); incarnation. **2.** birth, appearance in the world. **3.** fig., often euphem. a pious or distinguished person. — ~ **करना**, or **लेना**, to become incarnate. ~ **कर-**, Brbh. to bring to birth in the world, to create.

अवतार- *avătār-* [S. *avatārayati*: w. H. *avatār*], v.t. Brbh. Av. to give birth to, to produce.

अवतारण *avă-tāraṇ* [S.], m. causing to descend: descent; incarnation.

अवतारणा *avă-tārăṇā* [S.], f. **1.** descent; incarnation. **2.** occurrence (of an incident). **3.** representation (as of an idea in artistic form). **4.** an extract, citation. **5.** introduction (to a book).

अवतारी *avă-tārī* [S.], adj. **1.** descending, descended; incarnate. **2.** possessing divine or supernatural qualities.

अवतीर्ण *avă-tīrṇ* [S.], adj. **1.** descended. **2.** crossed over. **3.** become incarnate. **4.** failed (examination). **5.** excerpted, cited.

अवदात *avă-dāt* [S.], adj. & m. **1.** adj. bright, white; yellow. **2.** m. a bright colour; whiteness, yellowness.

अवधान *avă-dhān* [S.], m. **1.** attention, due care; feat (of concentration). **2.** care, caution; vigilance. **3.** Av. = **औधान**.

अवधानी *avă-dhānī* [S.], adj. & m. **1.** adj. attentive; careful. **2.** m. an attentive person, &c.

अवधार- *avădhār-* [cf. *(ava)dhārayati*], v.t. Av. to hold, to take; to accept.

अवधारक *avă-dhārak* [S.], adj. considering carefully (a topic).

अवधारण *avă-dhāraṇ* [S.], m. **1.** ascertainment, accurate determination. **2.** definition (of a sense); specification. **3.** consideration (of a topic). **4.** conception. — **अवधारणबोधक**, adj. indicating a specification of sense (as a verbal auxiliary). **अवधारणात्मक** [°*a* + *ā*°], adj. conceptual.

अवधारणा *avă-dhārăṇā* [S.], f. conception, idea; an achievement.

अवधारणीय *avă-dhārăṇīyă* [S.], adj. to be ascertained, or reflected upon (a matter, a topic).

अवधारित *avă-dhārit* [S.], adj. **1.** ascertained. **2.** determined, decided.

अवधार्य *avă-dhāryă* [S.], adj. = **अवधारणीय**.

[1]**अवधावन** *avă-dhāvan* [S.], m. running or following after.

[2]**अवधावन** *avă-dhāvan* [S.], m. washing out, cleansing.

अवधि *avă-dhi* [S.], f. **1.** extent, limit. **2.** set time, period, term. — **अवधिसूचक**, adj. *gram.* durative. **अवधि-बाधित**, adj. having a limitation of time. **अवधि-भूत**, adj. *philos.* limited, qualified.

अवधूत *avă-dhūt* [S.], adj. & m. **1.** adj. shaken off, discarded. **2.** m. one who has renounced the world, an ascetic, a yogī.

अवधूपन *avă-dhūpan* [S.], m. perfuming with incense.

अवधूपित *avă-dhūpit* [S.], adj. perfumed, made fragrant.

अवध्य *a-vadhyă* [S.], adj. see अबध्य.

अवनत *avă-nat* [S.], adj. bowed down.

अवनि *avani* [S.], f. the earth, the world. — अवनि-तल, m. the surface of the earth. अवनिप, m. Av. lord of the earth: a king. अवनीश [°*ni*+*ī*°], m. id.

अवनी *avănī* [S.], f. the earth, the world. — अवनीप, m. Brbh. protector, or lord, of the earth: a king.

अवम *avam* [S.], adj. lowest; inferior; base.

अवमानता *avă-mānătā* [S.], f. disregard, downgrading (for, of, की).

अवमूल्यन *avă-mūlyan* [S.], m. devaluation.

अवयव *avă-yav* [S.], m. **1.** a limb, member; organ (of the body). **2.** component part.

अवयवी *avă-yavī* [S.], m. having members: **1.** the body. **2.** sthg. consisting of individual parts.

अवर *avăr* [S.], adj. **1.** low; subordinate; minor. **2.** *law.* minor; lower (court). **3.** rear. **4.** base, mean. — अवरज, adj. & m. born after, junior; younger brother.

अवरुद्ध *avă-ruddh* [S.], adj. **1.** restrained, obstructed. **2.** blocked, choked. **3.** confined; blockaded. **4.** subject to control; kept secret.

अवरोध *avă-rodh* [S.], m. **1.** obstacle; blockage. **2.** confinement, restriction; siege, blockade. **3.** women's quarters.

अवरोधक *avă-rodhak* [S.], adj. **1.** blocking, checking, &c. **2.** confining, &c.

अवरोधन *avă-rodhan* [S.], m. = अवरोध.

अवरोधित *avă-rodhit* [S.], adj. = अवरुद्ध.

अवरोधी *avă-rodhī* [S.], adj. & m. **1.** adj. = अवरोधक. **2.** m. sthg. which is an obstacle, &c. (see अवरोध).

अवरोह *avă-roh* [S.], m. descent; *mus.* descending scale.

अवरोहण *avă-rohaṇ* [S.], m. descending, descent.

अवर्ग *a-varg* [S.], adj. not belonging to a class or group.

अवर्गीय *a-vargīyă* [S.], adj. *gram.* not belonging to any of the classes (*varg*) of consonants: esp. to the guttural, palatal, retroflex, dental or labial classes (a sound).

अवलंब *avă-lamb* [S.], m. **1.** support. **2.** shelter, protection.

अवलंबन *avă-lamban* [S.], m. **1.** depending (on), supporting oneself (on): dependence; support. **2.** in comp. adopting (a course of action: e.g. मौनावलंबन, keeping silent).

अवलंबित *avă-lambit* [S.], adj. **1.** depending on; supported (by, पर; from, से). **2.** trusting (to, पर). **3.** protected, cherished.

अवलंबी *avă-lambī* [S.], adj. & m. **1.** adj. depending on; supported (by, का). **2.** giving support. **3.** m. a dependant.

अवलक्षण *avă-lakṣaṇ* [S.], adj. **1.** of ill omen; unfortunate. **2.** ill-favoured.

अवली *avalī* [*āvalī-*], f. Brbh. flock (of birds: = आवली).

अवलेह *avă-leh* [S.], m. jelly (medicinal).

अवलोकक *avă-lokak* [S.], adj. & m. **1.** adj. observing, &c. (see अवलोकन). **2.** m. one who observes, &c.

अवलोकन *avă-lokan* [S.], m. looking at; view, inspection; scrutiny. — अवलोकनार्थ [°*na*+*a*°], adv. for inspection, or perusal.

अवलोकना *avălokănā* [cf. *avalokayati*], v.t. to observe; to inspect; to scrutinise.

अवलोकनीय *avă-lokănīyă* [S.], adj. worth looking at, deserving inspection or scrutiny.

अवलोकित *avă-lokit* [S.], adj. looked at, inspected.

अवश *a-vaś* [S.], adj. **1.** not under control, unsubmissive. ***2.** in subjection, powerless; without choice; unavailing. **3.** adv. Brbh. in vain, to no avail.

अवशिष्ट *avă-śiṣṭ* [S.], adj. & m. **1.** adj. left over, remaining; residual. **2.** m. residue.

अवशेष *avă-śeṣ* [S.], m. **1.** remainder; remains, residue. **2.** mortal remains. **3.** surplus. **4.** end.

अवशेषित *avă-śeṣit* [S.], adj. Av. remaining, left over.

अवश्य *a-vaśyă* [S.], adj. **1.** unrestrained, uncontrolled. **2.** adv. necessarily, without doubt; at all costs; without fail. **3.** certainly, of course.

अवश्यम- *avaśyam-* [S.], adv. = **अवश्य** :— **अवश्यमेव**, adv. id. **अवश्यंभावी**, adj. bound to occur, inevitable.

अवसर *avă-sar* [S.], m. **1.** occasion, opportunity; fit or proper time. **2.** leisure time. **3.** (particular) moment, time. — ~ **आना**, or **पड़ना**, or **मिलना**, an opportunity, &c., to occur. ~ **ताकना**, = next. ~ **देखना**, to watch for an opportunity, &c.; to bide one's time. **इस** ~ **पर**, adv. on this occasion. – **अवसर-ग्रहण**, m. taking retirement. **अवसरप्राप्त**, adj. retired (from work). °**इ**, f. **अवसरवाद**, m. opportunism. °**ई**, adj. & m. opportunist; an opportunist.

अवसादी *avă-sādī* [S.], adj. *geol.* sedimentary.

[1]**अवसान** *avă-sān* [S.], m. **1.** end, completion; conclusion. **2.** death. **3.** boundary, limit.

[2]**अवसान** *avăsān*, m. Brbh. = [1]**औसान**.

अवसानक *avă-sānak* [S.], adj. & m. **1.** adj. leading to an end; terminal. **2.** m. extreme point, limit.

अवसेर *avăser*, f. see **औसेर**.

अवसेर- *avăser-* [? conn. *apasmarati*], v.i. Av. = **उसेर-**.

अवसेरी *avăserī*, adj. & f. Brbh. Av. **1.** adj. filled with care; anxious. **2.** delayed. **3.** f. Brbh. delay.

अवस्तु *a-vastu* [S.], adj. & m. **1.** adj. unreal, insubstantial. **2.** inessential; trivial. **3.** m. sthg. worthless.

अवस्तुता *a-vastutā* [S.], f. **1.** unreality. **2.** non-essential nature.

अवस्था *avă-sthā* [S.], f. **1.** state, condition; circumstances, situation. **2.** stage (of life, progress); age.

अवस्थान *avă-sthān* [S.], m. **1.** situation. **2.** stage. **3.** stopping place, halt (of train). **4.** dwelling-place.

अवस्थापन *avă-sthāpan* [S.], m. **1.** settling, determining (a matter). **2.** establishing (a foundation). **3.** place of settlement, residence.

अवस्थित *avă-sthit* [S.], adj. **1.** situated. **2.** *HŚS.* present (= **उपस्थित**).

अवस्थिति *avă-sthiti* [S.], f. situation.

अवहेलना *avă-helănā* [S.], f. neglect, indifference.

अवहेला *avă-helā* [S.], f. = **अवहेलना**.

अवांतर *avântar* [S.], adj. intermediate.

[1]**अवाई** *avāī* [cf. H. [1]*āvā*], f. arrival.

[2]**अवाई** *avāī* [*apavāda-*, or **āvāda-*], f. reg. **1.** rumour, hearsay. **2.** [× [1]*avāī*] report of approach or arrival.

[3]**अवाई** *avāī*, f. *Pl.* **1.** saddlecloth with fringes. **2.** [? = [4]*avāī*] a kind of pickaxe.

अवाक् *avāk* [S.], adj. **1.** speechless. **2.** taken aback, nonplussed.

अवाच्य *a-vācyă* [S.], adj. **1.** not to be uttered; not to be spoken of. **2.** inexpressible.

अवाम *avām* [A. 'avāmm, pl.], m. pl. the common people. — ~ **के सामने होना**, to be in the public eye.

अवामी *avāmī* [A. 'avāmm, pl. + -ī], adj. having to do with the common people (a movement, &c).

[1]**अवार** *avār* [S.], m. near bank (of river); near side.

[2]**अवार** *avār*, f. *Pl.* = **अबेर**.

अवि *avi* [S.], m. the sun.

अविकल *a-vi-kal* [S.], adj. **1.** unimpaired, without defect; complete, entire; exact (a copy). **2.** regular, orderly.

अविकल्प *a-vi-kalp* [S.], adj. **1.** without hesitation or doubt. ***2.** not subject to doubt; definite, decided. **3.** fixed, not subject to alteration.

अविकार *a-vi-kār* [S.], adj. not subject to change, unchanging.

अविकारी *a-vi-kārī* [S.], adj. & m. **1.** unchanging; constant, faithful (a person). **2.** not causing change: not harmful. **3.** *gram.* indeclinable; invariable. **4.** *gram.* absolutive. **5.** m. someone, or sthg., not subject to change or variation.

अविकार्य *a-vi-kāryă* [S.], adj. = **अविकार**.

अविगत *a-vi-gat* [S.], adj. not gone away; present; existent. — **अविगत-गति**, f. Brbh. the nature of the ultimate being.

अविचल *a-vi-cal* [S.], adj. **1.** motionless. **2.** unmoved, unshaken; resolute.

अविचलित *a-vi-calit* [S.], adj. = **अविचल**.

अविचार *a-vi-cār* [S.], adj. & m. **1.** adj. thoughtless. **2.** m. thoughtlessness. **3.** wrong thought; ill-advised or improper action.

अविचारित *a-vi-cārit* [S.], adj. **1.** not considered (a matter). **2.** ill-considered (a course of action).

अविचारी *a-vi-cārī* [S.], adj. & m. **1.** adj. thoughtless. **2.** wanting in judgment. **3.** m. a thoughtless person, &c.

अविचार्य *a-vi-cāryă* [S.], adj. unthinkable, unimaginable.

अविच्छिन्न *a-vi-cchinn* [S.], adj. without interval, undivided; uninterrupted, continuous.

अविच्छिन्नता *a-vi-cchinnătā* [S.], f. non-interruptedness, continuity.

अविच्छेद *a-vi-cched* [S.], adj. & m. **1.** adj. undivided; uninterrupted. **2.** m. lack of division or interval.

अविच्छेद्य *a-vi-cchedyă* [S.], adj. indivisible; undetachable; inalienable.

अविजित *a-vi-jit* [S.], adj. unconquered.

अविजेय *a-vi-jey* [S.], adj. **1.** unconquerable; indomitable. **2.** unimpugned (authority).

अविज्ञ *a-vi-jñă* [S.], adj. ignorant; illiterate.

अविज्ञात *a-vi-jñāt* [S.], adj. **1.** not understood. **2.** not known (a fact, a circumstance); little known (a person, a thing).

अविज्ञेय *a-vi-jñey* [S.], adj. not distinguishable, or to be known.

अविदित *a-vidit* [S.], adj. not known; not evident; mysterious.

अविद्या *a-vidyā* [S.], f. **1.** ignorance. **2.** false understanding, error. **3.** transf. illiteracy. **4.** stupidity. — **अविद्यामूलक**, adj. based on error.

अविनय *a-vi-nay* [S.], adj. & m. **1.** adj. ill-mannered. **2.** m. want of manners, discourtesy; brashness, indecorum.

अविनयी *a-vi-nayī* [S.], adj. wanting good manners, or behaviour (= **अविनीत**).

अविनाश *a-vi-nāś* [S.], m. indestructibility, imperishability.

अविनाशी *a-vi-nāśī* [S.], adj. **1.** indestructible, imperishable. **2.** everlasting, immortal. **3.** entire.

अविनीत *a-vi-nīt* [S.], adj. ill-mannered, misbehaving: discourteous; immodest.

अविनीता *a-vi-nītā* [S.], f. an immodest, or unfaithful, woman or wife.

अविभक्त *a-vi-bhakt* [S.], adj. **1.** undivided. **2.** joint (as property, share). **3.** not sharing.

अविभाजित *a-vi-bhājit* [S.], adj. = **अविभक्त**.

अविभाज्य *a-vi-bhājyă* [S.], adj. indivisible (as property, at law).

अविरल *a-vi-ral* [S.], adj. **1.** uninterrupted. **2.** close, dense. **3.** coarse.

अविरुद्ध *a-vi-ruddh* [S.], adj. **1.** unobstructed, unimpeded. **2.** permitted. **3.** not discordant or at variance; favourable, benign.

अविरोध *a-vi-rodh* [S.], m. **1.** absence of impediment. **2.** concurrence. **3.** harmony, peace.

अविरोधी *a-vi-rodhī* [S.], adj. & m. **1.** adj. not combative or truculent; peaceable, quiet. **2.** m. a peaceable person, &c.

अविलंब *a-vi-lamb* [S.], adj. & m. **1.** adj. not delaying, prompt. **2.** adv. without delay, promptly. **3.** m. promptness, despatch. — ~ **राशि**, f. sum payable on demand.

अविलंबित *a-vi-lambit* [S.], adj. not delaying, prompt.

अविवाद *a-vi-vād* [S.], adj. & m. **1.** adj. not contentious; peaceful; conciliatory. **2.** m. concord, harmony.

अविवादी *a-vi-vādī* [S.], adj. & m. **1.** adj. = **अविवाद**. **2.** m. a peaceable person, &c.

अविवाहित *a-vi-vāhit* [S.], adj. unmarried, single.

अविवेक *a-vi-vek* [S.], adj. & m. **1.** adj. = **अविवेकी**. **2.** m. lack of judgment, &c. **3.** imprudence; folly. — **अविवेकपूर्ण**, adj. ill-judged; indiscreet.

अविवेकता *a-vi-vekătā* [S.], f. = **अविवेक**.

अविवेकी *a-vi-vekī* [S.], adj. without judgment, not discriminating; imprudent.

अविशेष *a-vi-śeṣ* [S.], adj. & m. **1.** adj. not different; uniform. **2.** m. non-difference, similarity, &c.

अविशेषित *a-vi-śeṣit* [S.], adj. not distinguished; not particularised.

अविश्वसनीय *a-vi-śvasănīyă* [S], adj. not to be trusted in: **1.** untrustworthy. **2.** unbelievable; implausible.

अविश्वस्त *a-vi-śvast* [S.], adj. not trusted in: untrustworthy, unreliable.

अविश्वास *a-vi-śvās* [S.], m. **1.** mistrust, disbelief. **2.** suspicion. — **अविश्वास-पात्र**, m. one not trusted, &c. **अविश्वास-प्रस्ताव**, m. motion of no confidence.

अविश्वासता *a-vi-śvāsătā* [cf. H. *viśvās*], f. = **अविश्वास**.

अविश्वासपन *a-vi-śvāspan* [cf. H. *viśvās*], m. = **अविश्वास**.

अविश्वासी *a-vi-śvāsī* [S.], adj. & m. **1.** adj. not having confidence, distrustful. **2.** doubting, incredulous; suspicious. **3.** m. a distrustful person, &c.

अविष *a-viṣ* [S.], adj. **1.** not poisonous. **2.** anti-toxic.

अविषय *a-viṣay* [S.], adj. & m. **1.** adj. unacquainted with objects of sense: not of sensuous, or sensual temperament. **2.** m. indifference to objects of sense. **3.** imperceptibility: disappearance.

अविसन *a-visan* [ad. *vyasana-*], adj. **1.** unindustrious. **2.** without desire, indifferent.

अवीर *a-vīr* [S.], adj. helpless, weak; impotent.

अवीरा *a-vīrā* [S.], f. a childless widow.

अवेर *aver*, f. = अबेर. — अवेर-सवेर, adv. late and early, at all hours; late or early.

अवेरी *averī*, f. = अवेर: — अवेरी-सवेरी, f. = अवेर-सवेर.

अवैध *a-vaidh* [S.], adj. illegal.

अवैया *avaiyā* [cf. H. *ānā*], adj. & m. **1.** adj. coming, future. **2.** m. a coming. — अवैया-गवैया, m. coming and going.

अव्यक्त *a-vy-akt* [S.], adj. **1.** unmanifested; unknown. **2.** unclear. **3.** imperceptible.

अव्यय *a-vy-ay* [S.], adj. & m. **1.** adj. not liable to change. **2.** eternal. **3.** unexpended. **4.** m. *gram.* an indeclinable word; a particle.

अव्ययी *a-vy-ayī* [S.], adj. *gram.* indeclinable; relating to an indeclinable word. — अव्ययीभाव, m. an indeclinable (Sanskritic) compound word.

अव्यवस्था *a-vy-avă-sthā* [S.], f. lack of organisation; disorder.

अव्यवस्थित *a-vy-avă-sthit* [S.], adj. **1.** disorganised (a situation); confused; badly arranged or planned. **2.** confused, unsettled (in mind). — अव्यवस्थित-चित्त, adj. = ~, 2.

अव्यसन *a-vy-asan* [S.], adj. & m. **1.** adj. without desires, without vices. **2.** m. absence of vices.

अव्याकुल *a-vy-ākul* [S.], adj. not disturbed, calm.

अव्यापक *a-vy-āpak* [S.], adj. not pervading the whole; limited, restricted.

अव्याप्त *a-vy-āpt* [S.], adj. not pervading, not diffused.

अव्याप्ति *a-vy-āpti* [S.], f. insufficiency (as of a definition).

अव्याप्य *a-vy-āpyă* [S.], adj. = अव्यापक.

अव्यावहारिक *a-vyāvăhārik* [S.], adj. impracticable.

अव्यावहारिकता *a-vyāvăhārikătā* [S.], f. impracticability.

अव्याहत *a-vy-ā-hat* [S.], adj. **1.** Av. unchecked, unrestrained. **2.** unrepelled; not refuted. **3.** unrestricted (as a right). **4.** unbroken, intact. **5.** unalarmed, not disconcerted.

अव्वल *avval* [A. *avval*], adj. & m. **1.** first. **2.** chief. **3.** best; excellent. **4.** m. beginning. — ~ आना, or रहना, to come first (in a class, a competition). ~ दरजे का, first class, first rate. ~ से आख़िर तक, adv. from beginning to end.

अव्वलन *avvalan* [A. *avvalan̲*], adv. first, first of all.

अव्वलियत *avvaliyat* [A. *avvalīya*: P. *avvaliyat*], f. priority, pre-eminence.

अव्वलीन *avvalīn* [A. *avvalīn*], adj. first; former, ancient.

अशंक *a-śaṅk* [S.], adj. **1.** fearless. **2.** undoubting, confident.

अशंकित *a-śaṅkit* [S.], adj. **1.** = अशंक. **2.** not apprehended or suspected.

अशकुन *a-śakun* [S.], m. an ill omen.

अशकुनी *a-śakunī* [S.], adj. of ill omen.

अशक्त *a-śakt* [S.], adj. **1.** powerless, helpless. **2.** weak. **3.** incapable.

अशक्ति *a-śakti* [S.], f. **1.** powerlessness. **2.** weakness. **3.** incapability.

अशक्य *a-śakyă* [S.], adj. beyond the power of, impossible; impracticable.

अशन *aśan* [S.], m. **1.** eating. **2.** food.

अशनि *aśani* [S.], f. poet. a thunderbolt.

अशरण *a-śaraṇ* [S.], adj. without protection or shelter; helpless.

अशरफ़ *aśraf* [A. *aśraf*], adj. U. nobler; very noble, eminent.

अशरफ़ी *aśrafī* [P. *aśrafī*], f. var. /əśərfī/. a gold coin formerly current worth variously between sixteen and twenty-five rupees.

अशरा *aśrā* [A. *'aśra*], m. *isl.* the first ten days of the month of Muḥarram.

अशराफ़ *aśrāf* [A. *aśrāf*, pl. of *śarīf*], m. pl. & adj. U. **1.** m. pl. persons of aristocratic or eminent family. **2.** adj. = भलामानस.

अशरीर *a-śarīr* [S.], adj. bodiless; disembodied.

अशरीरी *a-śarīrī* [S.], adj. bodiless; disembodied.

अशनाया *aśănāyā* [S.], f. desire to eat: hunger.

अशांत *a-śānt* [S.], adj. not at peace, restless; disturbed.

अशांति *a-śānti* [S.], f. **1.** restlessness, anxiety; concern. **2.** disturbance; disturbed situation. — **अशांतिकारक**, adj. causing anxiety, &c.; causing disturbance.

अशास्त्रीय *a-śāstrīyă* [S.], adj. contrary to the *śāstras*; unscriptural.

अशिक्षा *a-śikṣā* [S.], f. **1.** lack of education. **2.** ignorance.

अशिक्षित *a-śikṣit* [S.], adj. **1.** uneducated. **2.** ignorant.

अशिव *a-śiv* [S.], adj. **1.** inauspicious; malign. **2.** not prosperous; wretched.

अशिष्ट *a-śiṣṭ* [S.], adj. **1.** uncouth, crude; impolite. **2.** uncultivated.

अशिष्टता *a-śiṣṭătā* [S.], f. **1.** uncouthness; impoliteness. **2.** lack of cultivation.

अशील *a-śīl* [S.], adj. **1.** of bad character. **2.** badly behaved.

अशुच *a-śuc* [ad. *aśuci*], adj. impure.

अशुचि *a-śuci* [S], adj. & f. (m., *Pl.*) **1.** adj. impure; polluted; base. **2.** f. impurity, &c.

अशुद्ध *a-śuddh* [S.], adj. **1.** impure. **2.** imperfect, faulty; incorrect, corrupt (as language or style). **3.** not refined or purified (a substance).

अशुद्धता *a-śuddhătā* [S.], f. **1.** impurity. **2.** imperfection.

अशुद्धि *a-śuddhi* [S.], f. **1.** impurity. **2.** imperfection. **3.** a fault, error. — **अशुद्धि-पत्र**, m. table of errors.

अशुभ *a-śubh* [S.], adj. & m. **1.** adj. inauspicious, unlucky; sinister. **2.** m. misfortune; calamity; evil. — **अशुभ-चिंतक**, adj. & m. ill-willed, malign; a malevolent person.

अशेष *a-śeṣ* [S.], adj. without remainder: 1. complete, entire. **2.** without end, vast, infinite.

अशोक *a-śok* [S.], m. & adj. **1.** m. freedom from care or sorrow; *hist.* name of the emperor Aśoka. **2.** the tree *Jonesia asoka* (known esp. for its red flowers). **3.** adj. free from care or sorrow. — **अशोकाष्टमी** [°*ka*+*a*°], m. *Pl. HŚS.* the eighth day in the first (light) half of the month Cait (when a festival in honour of Viṣṇu, involving drinking water with *aśoka* buds or leaves in it, is observed).

अशोभन *a-śobhan* [S.], adj. = **अशोभनीय**.

अशोभनीय *a-śobhănīyă* [S.], adj. **1.** unattractive; boding ill; dire (as circumstances). **2.** unseemly.

अशौच *a-śauc* [S.], m. **1.** impurity (esp. as arising in a household from a birth or a death). **2.** *Pl.* mourning.

अश्क *aśk* [P.], m. U. a tear.

अश्रद्धा *a-śraddhā* [S.], f. **1.** disbelief, want of faith. **2.** lack of reverence or esteem.

अश्रद्धेय *a-śraddheyă* [S.], adj. unworthy of respect or esteem.

अश्रु *aśru* [S.], m. a tear. — **अश्रु-पात**, m. the shedding of tears. **अश्रु-मुख**, adj. tear-faced: tearful.

अश्रुत *a-śrut* [S.], adj. **1.** unheard. **2.** unheard of, unprecedented. **3.** unskilled, inexperienced. — **अश्रुतपूर्व**, adj. unprecedented.

अश्रुति *a-śruti* [S.], adj. & f. **1.** adj. deprived of hearing. **2.** f. deafness.

अश्लील *a-ślīl* [S.], adj. wretched, base: indecent.

अश्लीलता *a-ślīlătā* [S.], f. indecency.

अश्लेष *a-śleṣ* [S.], adj. Brbh. without a double meaning.

अश्लेषा *a-śleṣā* [S.], f. (m. *Pl.*) the ninth lunar mansion (five stars in Cancer).

अश्व *aśvă* [S.], m. a horse. — **अश्व-गंधा**, m. = **असगंध**. **अश्व-चिकित्सक**, m. a veterinary surgeon. °-**चिकित्सा**, f. veterinary science. **अश्वपति**, m. an owner of horses; a horseman; person commanding or attended by horsemen. **अश्व-पालन**, m. horse-breeding. **अश्वमेध**, m. a Vedic horse-sacrifice (performed chiefly by kings: often in assertion of a king's dominion over his territory). **अश्वयुज**, m. *astrol.* the first lunar mansion. **अश्व-शक्ति**, f. horsepower. **अश्व-शाला**, f. a stable. **अश्वारूढ़**, [°*va*+*ā*°], adj. mounted on horseback. **अश्वारोही** [°*va*+*ā*°], adj. & m. mounted; a horseman. **अश्वारोही सेना**, f. a cavalry force.

अश्वतर *aśvătar* [S.], m. a mule.

अश्वत्थ *aśvatth* [S.], m. the sacred fig tree (*Ficus religiosa*).

अश्वा *aśvā* [S.], f. a mare.

अश्विनी *aśvinī* [S.], f. *astrol.* the first lunar mansion (in Aries).

अष्ट *aṣṭ* [S.], adj. eight. — **अष्टकोण**, adj. & m. octangular; an octagon. **अष्ट-छाप**, m. the eight seals or insignia: a group of eight Kṛṣṇa poets, all said to be disciples of Vallabhācārya or Viṭṭhalnāth, and to have lived at Govardhan in the later sixteenth century. **अष्टधातु**, f. m. the eight metals: bell-metal, alloy. **अष्टपदी**, f. a song or poem of eight verses. **अष्ट-प्रहर**, m. all twenty-four hours of the day; adv. night and day incessantly. **अष्टबाहु**, adj. & m. eight-armed; an octopus. **अष्टभुज**, adj. & m. eight-armed; an octagon. °**आ**, f. *hind.* a title of Durgā. **अष्ट-सिद्धि**, m. the eight *siddhis*: supernatural powers said to be obtainable by perfection of techniques of yoga. **अष्टांग** [°*ṭa*+*a*°], m. & adj. the eight parts of the body (which touch the ground in an elaborate obeisance): hands, thighs, breast, eyes and forehead; having, or consisting of eight members or parts. **अष्टावक्र**, m. *mythol.* name of a person born seriously crippled (as the result of a curse).

अष्टक *aṣṭak* [S.], m. an entity having eight parts; octet.

अष्टम *aṣṭam* [S.], adj. eighth.

अष्टमी *aṣṭămī* [S.], adj. the eighth day of a lunar fortnight.

अष्टादश *aṣṭādaś* [S.], adj. **1.** eighteen. **2.** eighteenth.

अष्टि *aṣṭi* [S.], f. a fruit stone, kernel.

असंख्य *a-saṅ-khyă* [S.], adj. countless, innumerable.

असंख्यक *a-saṅ-khyak* [S.], adj. unnumbered, countless.

असंख्यात *a-saṅ-khyāt* [S.], adj. unnumbered, countless.

असंख्येय *a-saṅ-khyeyă* [S.], adj. innumerable, countless.

असंगत *a-saṅ-gat* [S.], adj. **1.** not connected: incoherent; inconsistent; bizarre. **2.** senseless; absurd. **3.** inappropriate.

असंगति *a-saṅ-gati* [S.], f. **1.** incoherence; inconsistency; contradiction. **2.** absurdity. **3.** inappropriateness.

असंतति *a-san-tati* [S.], adj. childless.

असंतान *a-san-tān* [S.], adj. childless.

असंतुष्ट *a-san-tuṣṭ* [S.], adj. dissatisfied; discontented; displeased.

असंतुष्टि *a-san-tuṣṭi* [S.], f. = **असंतोष**.

असंतोष *a-san-toṣ* [S.], m. dissatisfaction; displeasure. — **असंतोषजनक**, adj. unsatisfactory.

असंतोषी *a-san-toṣī* [S.], adj. dissatisfied, discontented.

असंदिग्ध *a-san-digdh* [S.], adj. **1.** undoubted, unquestionable; unambiguous. **2.** authentic.

असंपूर्ण *a-sam-pūrṇ* [S.], adj. **1.** incomplete. **2.** imperfect, defective.

असंबद्ध *a-sam-baddh* [S.], adj. **1.** not connected. **2.** disconnected, disjointed; incoherent.

असंभव *a-sam-bhav* [S.], adj. **1.** impossible. **2.** inconceivable; improbable.

असंभावना *a-sam-bhāvănā* [S.], f. **1.** impossibility. **2.** inconceivability; improbability. **3.** Av. wretchedness.

असंभावनीय *a-sam-bhāvănīyă* [S.], adj. = **असंभाव्य**.

असंभावित *a-sam-bhāvit* [S.], adj. **1.** impossible. **2.** inconceivable.

असंभावी *a-sam-bhāvī* [S.], adj. not to happen: improbable, impossible.

असंभाव्य *a-sam-bhāvyă* [S.], adj. inconceivable; improbable; impossible.

असंयत *a-saṃ-yat* [S.], adj. unrestrained; unbridled.

असंयम *a-saṃ-yam* [S.], m. **1.** lack of self-restraint. **2.** indulgence of the senses.

असंयमित *a-saṃ-yamit* [S.], adj. unrestrained; indisciplined.

असंयमी *a-saṃ-yamī* [S.], adj. & m. **1.** adj. unrestrained, &c. **2.** m. an unrestrained or intemperate person.

असंयुक्त *a-saṃ-yukt* [S.], adj. not connected; separate.

असंयोग *a-saṃ-yog* [S.], m. **1.** want of opportunity. **2.** separation.

असंशय *a-saṃ-śay* [S.], adj. & m. **1.** adj. undoubting. **2.** undoubted. **3.** m. freedom from doubt.

असकत *askat* [cf. H. *sakat*], f. inactivity; laziness.

असकताना *askatānā* [cf. H. *askat*], v.i. *Pl.* to be inactive; to be lazy; to take it easy.

असकती *askatī* [cf. H. *askat*], adj. & m. **1.** adj. inactive, lazy. **2.** m. a lazy person, &c.

असगंध *asgandh* [ad. *aśvagandhā*-], m. a medicinal plant, *Physalis flexuosa*.

असगुन *asagun*, m. = **अशकुन**.

असज्जन *a-sajjan* [S.], adj. **1.** not virtuous, not honourable; disreputable. **2.** uncouth, coarse (of manner).

असत् *a-sat* [S.], adj. & m. **1.** adj. not existent, unreal; unfounded; illusory. **2.** untrue. **3.** not good, unrighteous; ungodly. **4.** m. untruth, falsehood.

असती *a-satī* [S.], adj. f. & f. **1.** adj. disloyal, unfaithful. **2.** f. a disloyal wife. **3.** a dissolute woman.

असत्कार *a-satkār* [S.], m. wrong or improper treatment; dishonour (as to a guest).

असत्कृत *a-satkṛt* [S.], adj. ill-treated, &c. (see असत्कार).

असत्ता *a-sattā* [S.], f. non-existence.

असत्ती *asattī* [cf. H. *sat(t)*], adj. & m., f. *Pl.* powerless; a helpless person, poor creature.

असत्य *a-satyă* [S.], adj. & m. **1.** adj. untrue, false; unfaithful. **2.** unrighteous; ungodly. **3.** m. untruth, falsehood. **4.** unrighteousness.

असत्यता *a-satyătā* [S.], f. **1.** falsehood; faithlessness. **2.** unrighteousness.

असद *asad* [A. *asad*], m. U. **1.** lion. **2.** the sign Leo (of the zodiac).

असबाब *asbāb* [A. *asbāb*: pl. of *sabab* 'cause'], m. **1.** goods, effects, property; things; wares. **2.** baggage; stores; equipment. **3.** cargo.

असभ्य *a-sabhyă* [S.], adj. **1.** uncouth; rude, impolite. **2.** uncivilised.

असभ्यता *a-sabhyătā* [S.], f. **1.** uncouthness; rudeness. **2.** uncivilised state.

असमंजस *a-sam-añjas* [S.], m. **1.** uncertainty; hesitation; suspense. **2.** difficult situation. **3.** disparity, disharmony.

असम *a-sam* [S.], adj. **1.** unequal **2.** dissimilar. **3.** uneven, not level. **4.** odd (a number).

असमझ *a-samajh* [cf. H. *samajh*], adj. & f. **1.** adj. without understanding: thoughtless; foolish; ignorant. **2.** f. lack of understanding, &c.

असमता *a-samătā* [S.], f. **1.** inequality. **2.** dissimilarity. **3.** unevenness.

असमय *a-sam-ay* [S.], m. & adj. **1.** m. a time of misfortune. **2.** an unsuitable time. **3.** adj. ill-timed, untimely. — ~ का, adj. untimely; premature. ~ में, adv. at an unsuitable time.

असमर्थ *a-sam-arth* [S.], adj. **1.** incapable, unable; powerless, weak; helpless. **2.** unfit, incompetent.

असमर्थता *a-sam-arthătā* [S.], f. **1.** inability; powerlessness. **2.** helplessness. **3.** incapacity.

असमान *a-samān* [S.], adj. **1.** unequal. **2.** dissimilar (to, से); disproportionate. **3.** not even; variable. **4.** incomparable.

असमानता *a-samānătā* [S.], f. l. inequality. **2.** dissimilarity. **3.** unevenness.

असम्मत *a-sam-mat* [S.], adj. **1.** not in agreement, dissenting. **2.** not approved of, rejected (a motion, plan).

असम्मति *a-sam-mati* [S.], f. **1.** disagreement, dissent. **2.** disapproval.

असमाप्त *a-sam-āpt* [S.], adj. unfinished, incomplete.

असमाप्ति *a-sam-āpti* [S.], f. incompleteness.

असम्मान *a-sam-mān* [S.], m. **1.** disrespect. **2.** disgrace.

असम्मित *a-sam-mit* [S.], adj. asymmetrical.

असर *asar* [A. *aṣr*], m. footprint: **1.** effect. **2.** impression; influence. — ~ करना (पर or में), to have an effect (on), to be effective. ~ पड़ना, id. – असरकारी, adj. = next. असरदार [P. *-dār*], adj. effective.

असल *asl* [A. *aṣl*], m. f. & adj. **1.** m. f. origin, base, source. **2.** substance, essence; original or real nature. **3.** stock, lineage. **4.** m. a man of good family. **5.** an original (document, &c). **6.** principal (amount: as opposed to interest). 7. adj. = असली, 1.-3. — ~ में, adv. in fact; positively, absolutely. दर ~, adv. id.

असलियत *asliyat* [A. *aṣlīya*: P. *aṣliyat*], f. **1.** reality. **2.** essential quality. **3.** originality. **4.** genuineness; purity.

असली *aslī* [A. *aṣlī*], adj. **1.** original; primary, basic; primitive; indigenous. **2.** real, essential; actual. **3.** genuine; unadulterated, pure. **4.** inherent, innate.

असवार *asvār*, m. pronun. var. = सवार.

असवारी *asvārī*, f. pronun. var. = सवारी.

असहन *a-sahan* [S.], adj. & m. **1.** adj. impatient, intolerant. **2.** unbearable. **3.** m. impatience, &c. — असहनशील, adj., impatient, &c.

असहनीय *a-sahănīyă* [S.], adj. unbearable, intolerable.

असहयोग *a-sah-yog* [S.], m. non-cooperation. — ~ आंदोलन, m. *hist.* the (Indian) non-cooperation movement.

असहाय *a-sahây* [S.], adj. without help or assistance; friendless.

असहायता *asahâyătā* [S.], f. helpless state.

असह्य *a-sahyă* [S.], adj. unbearable, intolerable.

असाँचा *a-sāṁcā*, adj. Av. metr. = असच, असत्य.

असाइत *asāit* [*a-*+A. *sā'at*], f. an unlucky, inauspicious moment.

असाक्षात् *a-sâkṣāt* [S.], adj. **1.** not before the eyes: not visible; unperceived. **2.** adv. in the absence (of, के); unperceived (by).

असाक्षिक *a-sâkṣik* [S.], adj. not having supporting witness or testimony.

असाक्षी *a-sâkṣī* [S.], m. **1.** one not a witness. **2.** one whose evidence or testimony is inadmissible.

असाक्ष्य *a-sâkṣyă* [S.], m. lack of evidence or testimony.

असाढ़ *asāṛh* [*āṣāḍha-*], m. the fourth month (lunar) of the Hindu year: June-July.

असाढ़ी *asāṛhī* [*āṣāḍhīya-*], adj. having to do with the month of Asāṛh (as moon, or crop).

असादृश्य *a-sādṛśyă* [S.], adj. & m. **1.** adj. dissimilar. **2.** m. dissimilarity; incomparability.

असाध *a-sādh* [ad. *asādhu-*], adj. = असाधु, 1.

असाधपन *a-sādhpan* [cf. H. *asādh*], m. unrighteousness, &c. (see असाध).

असाधारण *a-sādhāraṇ* [S.], adj. **1.** unusual. **2.** special, particular; exceptional; additional (an issue of a magazine); extraordinary (a session).

असाधु *a-sādhu* [S.], adj. **1.** unrighteous; wicked; immoral. **2.** not proper, corrupt (a word or usage).

असाधुता *a-sādhutā* [S.], f. unrighteousness, &c. (see असाधु).

असाधुत्व *a-sādhutvă* [S.], m. = असाधुता.

असाध्य *a-sādhyă* [S.], adj. **1.** not realisable, not attainable. **2.** incurable. **3.** irretrievable (a situation). — असाध्य-साधन, m. achievement of the impossible.

असाध्वी *a-sādhvī* [S.], f. an unrighteous or immoral woman.

असामंजस्य *a-sāmañjasyă* [S.], m. **1.** disharmony; disproportion. **2.** incompatibility.

असामयिक *a-sāmăyik* [S.], adj. untimely.

असामर्थ्य *a-sāmarthyă* [S.], f. = असमर्थता.

असामान्य *a-sāmānyă* [S.], adj. **1.** uncommon, unusual. **2.** particular, peculiar (an asset, a virtue). **3.** abnormal.

असामी *asāmī* [A.: pl. of *ism* 'name'], m. (f., *Pl.*) **1.** a person, an individual; party (partic. person in question). **2.** a tenant. **3.** a client, customer. **4.** a servant. **5.** *Pl.* office, post, appointment. — ~ बनाना, to make a fool of, to cheat. बड़ा ~, m. an important person (for some partic. purpose).

असाम्य *a-sāmyă* [S.], m. dissimilarity; disparity.

असार *a-sār* [*asāra-*], adj. **1.** not having sap, or pith. **2.** without content, empty; senseless; facile; vain (as the world).

असारता *a-sārătā* [S.], f. emptiness; senselessness; vanity.

असार्वजनिक *a-sārvăjanik* [S.], adj. not public, or governmental: private (as industry, finance).

असावधान *a-sâvă-dhān* [S.], adj. **1.** careless. **2.** inattentive. **3.** neglectful.

असावधानता *a-sâvă-dhānătā* [S.], f. = असावधानी.

असावधानी *a-sâvă-dhānī* [cf. H. *asāvdhān*], f. **1.** carelessness. **2.** inattention. **3.** neglect, negligence. — ~ से, adv. carelessly, &c.

असावरी *asāvărī*, f. = आसावरी.

असाहस *a-sāhas* [S.], m. lack of courage, cowardice; fear.

असाहसी *a-sāhăsī* [S.], adj. & m. **1.** adj. without courage, cowardly. **2.** m. a coward.

असि *asi* [S.], f. a sword; scimitar. — असि-धारा, f. the edge or blade of a sword. °-व्रत, m. fig. an extremely difficult task.

असित *asit* [S.], adj. **1.** adj. black; dark. **2.** m. black (colour). **3.** the dark half of the lunar month (full to new moon).

असिद्ध *a-siddh* [S.], adj. **1.** unaccomplished, unachieved; incomplete. **2.** unripe, raw, not cooked. **3.** not proven; invalid.

असिद्धि *a-siddhi* [S.], f. **1.** lack of success; incompleteness. **2.** lack of proof.

असीम *a-sīm* [S.], adj. unlimited, boundless; absolute.

असीमित *a-sīmit* [S.], adj. unlimited, unrestricted.

असील *asīl* [A. *aṣīl*], adj. **1.** of good origin; well-born. **2.** of good pedigree; pure-bred. **3.** without vices (an animal).

असीस *asīs* [cf. *āśiṣ-*, *āśīr-*], f. blessing, benediction.

असीसना *asīsnā* [cf. H. *asīs*], v.t. to bless.

[1]असु *asu* [S.], m. Brbh. vital breath, life, spirit.

[2]असु *asu* [ad. *aśva-*], m. Av. a horse.

असुख *a-sukh* [S.] **1.** adj. suffering, afflicted. **2.** causing distress. **3.** difficult, troublesome. **4.** m. unhappiness; suffering.

असुखी *a-sukhī* [S.], adj. unhappy; distressed.

असुर *asur* [S.], m. an evil spirit, demon. — असुराधिप [°*ra*+*a*°], m. Av. king of the demons. असुरारि [°ra + a°], m. Av. enemy of the *asuras*: a title of Viṣṇu.

असुरी *asurī* [S.], f. *Pl.* a demoness.

असुविधा *a-su-vi-dhā* [S.], f. inconvenience; trouble.

असूझ *a-sūjh* [cf. H. *sūjh*], adj. **1.** not discernible. **2.** unmanageable (a task, problem). **3.** Av. unimaginably large, huge.

असूया *asūyā* [S.], f. **1.** calumny; malice. **2.** jealousy.

असृज *asṛj* [S.], m. *Pl.* blood.

असेवन *a-sevan* [S.], m. disregard, neglect.

असेवा *a-sevā* [S.], f. disregard, neglect.

असेवित *a-sevit* [S.], adj. **1.** disregarded, neglected. **2.** unused.

असेसर *asesar* [Engl. *assessor*], m. an assessor; *Pl.* a juryman; an inspector.

असों *asoṁ*, adv. this year.

असोकी *a-sokī*, adj. Av. = अशोक.

असोग *a-sog* [ad. S. *aśoka-*], adj. & m. **1.** adj. reg. = अशोक. **2.** m. a tree, also called *devadāru.*

असोच *a-soc* [cf. H. *soc*], adj. & m. **1.** adj. carefree; thoughtless, heedless. **2.** inconceivable. **3.** m. absence of care; contentment.

असोची *a-socī* [cf. H. *soc*], adj. *Pl.* = असोच.

असोच्य *a-socyă* [S.], adj. not to be grieved for,

असोज *asoj* [ad. *aśvayuja-*], m. reg. the month Āśvin; the month Kvār.

अस्त *ast* [S.], m. & adj. **1.** m. home: setting (a heavenly body). **2.** fall, decline. **3.** the west. **4.** adj. setting (a heavenly body). **5.** set. — ~ होना, to set (the sun, &c). – अस्त-काल, m. time of setting; period of decline. अस्ताचल [°ta + a°], m. *mythol.* the western mountain (behind which the sun is supposed to set).

अस्तबल *astabal* [Pt. *estábulo*; A. *iṣṭabal*: ← L., Gk.], m. **1.** stable. **2.** lumber-room, junk-room.

अस्तब्ध *a-stabdh* [S.], adj. not firm, unsteady.

अस्तर *astar* [P. *astar*], m. **1.** lining (of a garment). **2.** petticoat. **3.** coating; coat (of paint, plaster). — ~ चढ़ाना, or लगाना, to sew a lining (into, में); to apply (a coating). – अस्तरकारी [P. *-kārī*] f. applying a lining, or coating.

अस्त-व्यस्त *asta-vyast* [cf. H. *vyast*], adj. **1.** scattered, in disorder. **2.** disorganised, preoccupied. **3.** perturbed. **4.** dishevelled (hair).

अस्तव्यस्तता *astavyastătā* [cf. H. *ast-vyast*], f. **1.** disorder. **2.** preoccupation. **3.** perturbation.

अस्ति *asti* [S.], f. existence, present reality.

अस्तित्व *astitvă* [S.], m. existence. — अस्तित्ववाद, m. existentialism. °ई, m. existentialist.

अस्तु *astu* [S.], interj. so be it; very well.

अस्तुति *a-stuti* [S.], f. not praising: speaking ill or slanderously (of one); (a person's) state of disgrace.

अस्त्र *astră* [S.], m. **1.** a weapon (esp. any missile: spear, arrow, &c.) **2.** armament. **3.** transf. means, resources. — ~ चलाना, to hurl, or to fire, a weapon. – अस्त्रकार, m. a maker of arms, or armaments. अस्त्रजीवी, m. one living by arms, a soldier. अस्त्रधारी, adj. & m. bearing arms; an armed man. अस्त्र-विद्या, f. military science. अस्त्र-शस्त्र, m. weapons, arms (whether thrown, or wielded). अस्त्र-शाला, f. an armoury, arsenal. अस्त्रागार [°ra + ā°], m. id. अस्त्रीकरण, m. arming, providing with arms. अस्त्रीकृत, adj. provided with arms.

अस्थल *asthal*, m. Brbh. = स्थल.

अस्थावर *a-sthāvar* [S.], adj. not fixed, movable.

अस्थायी *a-sthāyī* [S.], adj. **1.** unfixed, impermanent; of short duration. **2.** small (works).

अस्थि *asthi* [S.], f. **1.** a bone. **2.** pl. remains. — अस्थि-पंजर, m. a skeleton; fig. an emaciated body. अस्थि-प्रवाह, m. the consigning of human remains to a sacred river. अस्थि-भंग, m. fracture of a bone, or bones. अस्थिमय, adj. bony. अस्थिमाली, m. *hind.* having a necklace of skulls: a title of Śiva. अस्थि-विसर्जन, m. = अस्थि-प्रवाह. अस्थि-संचय, m. collection of remains after cremation.

¹अस्थित *a-sthit* [S.], adj. unfixed, unsettled.

²अस्थित *asthit*, adj. Brbh. = स्थित.

अस्थिति *a-sthiti* [S.], f. **1.** unfixed or unsettled state. **2.** *HŚS.* lack of cultivation or good manners.

अस्थिर *a-sthir* [S.], adj. **1.** unsteady, unstable. **2.** uncertain, undecided; fickle; restless, troubled. — अस्थिरवासी, adj. of unfixed abode.

अस्थिरता *a-sthirătā* [S.], f. **1.** unsteadiness, instability. **2.** uncertainly; fickleness.

अस्थि-समर्पण *asthi-samarpaṇ*, m. = अस्थि-प्रवाह.

अस्थैर्य *a-sthairyă* [S.], f. = अस्थिरता.

अस्निग्ध *a-snigdh* [S.], adj. = अस्नेह, 2.

अस्नेह *a-sneh* [S.], m. & adj. 1. m. unkindness, want of feeling. **2.** adj. unkind, unfeeling.

अस्पताल *aspatāl* [Pt. Engl. *hospital*], m. hospital.

अस्पर्श *a-sparś* [S.], m. *hind.* non-contact: prohibition of physical contact (of one who has washed, before worship or eating, and of a woman in her period).

अस्पर्शनीय *a-sparśănīyă* [S.], adj. not to be touched (see अस्पृश्य).

अस्पष्ट *a-spaṣṭ* [S.], adj. **1.** unclear, indistinct. **2.** not understood.

अस्पष्टता *a-spaṣṭătā* [S.], f. lack of clarity, indefiniteness.

अस्पृश्य *a-spr̥śyă* [S.], adj. not to be touched; impure, untouchable.

अस्पृश्यता *a-spr̥śyătā* [S.], f. *hind.* untouchability.

अस्पृष्ट *a-spr̥ṣṭ* [S.], adj. **1.** untouched. **2.** pure, virgin.

अस्पृह *a-spr̥h* [S.], adj. without desire, disinterested.

अस्फुट *a-sphuṭ* [S.], adj. **1.** indistinct (as speech); unclear. **2.** not blossomed (a flower).

अस्मत *asmat* [A. *'iṣmat*], f. defence: honour, integrity (esp. of a woman). — ~ बिगाड़ना, to take the virginity (of, की).

अस्मरण *a-smaraṇ* [S.], m. **1.** forgetfulness. **2.** oblivion.

अस्मिता *asmitā* [S.], f. one's self.

अस्मृति *a-smr̥ti* [S.], f. oblivion.

अस्र *asră* [S.], m. sthg. thrown: a tear.

अस्वाँसी *asvāṁsī*, f. *Pl.* = अनवाँसी.

अस्वामिक *a-svāmik* [S.], adj. = अस्वामी, 1.

अस्वामी *a-svāmī* [S.], adj. **1.** without master, or owner. **2.** having no right or title (of ownership). — ~ बिक्री, f. *Pl.* sale without ownership, illegal sale.

अस्वार्थ *a-svârth* [S.], adj. & m. **1.** adj. = अस्वार्थी. **2.** m. unselfishness.

अस्वार्थी *a-svârthī* [S.], adj. & m. **1.** adj. unselfish; disinterested. **2.** m. an unselfish or disinterested person.

अस्वीकरण *a-svīkaraṇ* [S.], m. not accepting, etc. (= अस्वीकार).

अस्वीकार *a-svīkār* [S.], m. **1.** non-acceptance, dissent. **2.** refusal; denial. — ~ करना, to refuse, &c. – अस्वीकारात्मक [°*ra*+*ā*°], adj. negative (response, &c.)

अस्वीकार्य *a-svīkāryă* [S.], adj. unacceptable.

अस्वीकृत *a-svīkr̥t* [S.], adj. not accepted; refused; declined.

अस्वीकृति *a-svīkr̥ti* [S.], f. = अस्वीकार.

अस्सी *assī* [*aśīti-*], adj. eighty.

अहं *ahaṃ* [*aham, ahaṃ-*], pron. **1.** the self, the ego. **2.** m. egoism. — अहंकार, m. sense of self, egoism; pride; arrogance; self-respect. °ई, adj. °कृति, f. = अहंकार. अहंतंत्र, m. autocracy; autarchy. अहंभाव, m. egoism; self-centredness. अहंमति, f.id. अहंमन्य, adj. egotistical. °ता, f. egoism; self-concern, spiritual ignorance. अहंवाद, E.H. = prec.

अहंता *ahaṃtā* [S.], f. = अहंकार.

[1]**अह** *ah*, interj. exclamation of astonishment, or of distress, pain, &c.

[2]**अह** *ah*, m. *Pl.* = अहं.

[3]**अह** *ah* [ad. *ahar-*], m. in comp. a day. — अहरह, adv. day by day.

अहत *ahat* [A. *aḥad*], m. E.H. ? unity; one.

अहद *ahd* [A. *'ahd*], m. **1.** contract; promise. **2.** time, period; lifetime; reign (of a king).

अहदी *ahdī* [cf. A. *aḥad*], m. one in league, collaborator: **1.** *hist.* Brbh. one of a class of veterans of Akbar's time, liable to be called on for military or other service; a bailiff, rent-collector. **2.** pej. an idle fellow. — जम ~, Brbh. death, the (all-powerful) bailiff.

अहम *ahm* [A. *ahamm*], adj. important.

अहमक़ *ahmaq* [A. *aḥmaq*], adj. & m. **1.** adj. foolish. **2.** m. a fool. — ~ की दुम, m. colloq. fool's tail: an out-and-out fool. ~ बनाना, to make a fool of; to fool, to cheat.

अहमक़पन *ahmaqpan* [cf. H. *ahmaq*], m. folly, stupidity.

अहमक़ी *ahmaqī* [A. *aḥmaq*+P. *-ī*], f. = अहमक़पन.

अहमिति *ahamiti* [*ahaṃmati*], f. Brbh. Av. = अहंमति, see s.v. अहं.

अहमियत *ahmiyat* [A. *ahmīya*: P. *ahmiyat*], f. importance. — ~ देना (को), to treat as important; to stress. ~ रखना, to have importance (a matter, a topic).

अहर- *ahar-* [S.], m. day: — अहरह, adv. day by day. अहर्निश, adj. occurring by day and night, constant, continual (as endeavours, &c).

अहरन *ahran*, m. reg. = अहेरन.

अहरिमन *ahriman* [P. *ahriman*], m. = अहरिमान.

अहरिमान *ahrimān* [P. *ahrimān*], m. the devil, Satan.

अहरी *ahrī* [S. *ādhāra-*], f. reg. a small tank or pond.

अहर्ष *a-harṣ* [S.], adj. & m. **1.** adj. not happy, sorrowful. **2.** m. sorrow.

अहर्षित *a-harṣit* [S.], adj. unhappy, sorrowful.

अहल *ahl* [A. *ahl*], m. used often with the extension -ए/-इ (*izāfā*). U. people, particular people (as members of a community, profession, household). — अहले-क़लम, m. a literary man. अहलकार, m. clerk; an agent, officer. अहले-ज़बान, m. those regarded as the custodians of good usage (of a language); poets, orators. अहले-वतन, m. members of a single nation, compatriots.

अहल- *ahl-* [**āhallati*: Pk. *ahallai*], v.i. reg. to move, to shake. — अहले-गहले, adv. joyfully, in a carefree way.

अहला *ahlā*, m. reg. = आहला.

अहवाल *ahvāl* [A. *aḥvāl*, pl. of *ḥāl*], m. **1.** state, condition; circumstances. **2.** account, narrative.

अहसान *ahsān*, m. = एहसान.

अहसास *ahsās* [A. *iḥsās*], m. **1.** perception; realisation. **2.** a feeling. — ~ करना, to feel. ~ दिलाना, to get (one, को) to realise.

अहसि *ahasi*, v.i. Av. = है, 2.

अहह *ahah* [S.], interj. exclamation of astonishment, awe, grief, pain, &c.

अहा *ahā*, interj. exclamation of pleasure; also (*Pl.*) pain, pity, &c.

अहाता *ahātā* [A. *iḥāṭa-*], m. **1.** an enclosed space: premises, precincts, a compound. **2.** an enclosure, enclosing fence, &c. — ~ घेरना, to surround, to enclose; to determine the limits (of, का).

¹अहार *ahār*, m. Av. = आहार.

²अहार *ahār*, m. *Pl.* starch; glue, paste.

अहारना *ahārnā*, v.t. *Pl. HŚS.* to starch; to paste.

अहिंसक *a-hiṃsak* [S.], adj. = अहिंसात्मक.

अहिंसा *a-hiṃsā* [S.], f. non-violence. — अहिंसात्मक [°*sā*+*ā*°], adj. of non-violent character or nature. अहिंसा-नीति, f. non-violent policy. अहिंसावाद, m. doctrine or profession of non-violence. °ई, adj. & m.

अहि *ahi* [S.], m. a snake. — अहि-नाह, *mythol.* Av. lord of serpents: the snake Śeṣ. अहि-पति, m. Av. id. अहि-फेन, f. m. snake's venom; [×P. *apyūn*] opium. अहि-राइ, m. Brbh. king of serpents: = अहि-नाह, m. अहि-सेज, m. *mythol.* the snake-bed of Viṣṇu: the snake Śeṣa.

अहित *a-hit* [S.], adj. & m. **1.** adj. harmful; inimical. **2.** m. harm, injury; evil. **3.** enmity. — अहितकर, adj. = next. अहितकारी, adj. & m. inimical; malign; an ill-wisher. अहित-चिंतक, m. id., 3.

अहिनी *ahinī* [S.], f. Brbh. Av. a female snake.

अहिवात *ahivāt* [**avidhavātva-*], m. Brbh. Av. married state (of a woman whose husband is alive); married happiness.

अहिवाती *ahivātī* [cf. H. *ahivāt*], f. a woman whose husband is alive.

अहीटा *ahīṭā* [*adhiṣṭhāyaka-*], m. *Pl.* a field watchman (who supervises crops until they are threshed, to ensure that dues are paid).

अहीर *ahīr* [*ābhīra-*], m. **1.** a community or tribe of herdsmen. **2.** an *ahīr* man; a herdsman.

अहीरन *ahīran* [cf. H. *ahīr*], m. an *ahīr* woman; a herdsman's wife.

अहे *ahe*, interj. 1. = अहो, 1. **2.** oh! (expressing sorrow, or aversion, &c).

अहेड़ *aheṛ* [*ākheṭa-*], m. f. **1.** hunting. **2.** game.

अहेड़ी *aheṛī* [cf. H. *aheṛ*; or conn. *ăkheṭika-*], m. a hunter; a fowler.

अहेतु *a-hetu* [S.], adj. **1.** without cause or motive. **2.** disinterested (an action). **3.** without result, vain.

अहेतुक *a-hetuk* [S.], adj. = अहेतु.

अहेर *aher*, m. Brbh. = अहेड़.

अहेरन *aheran* [*adhikaraṇī-*], m. reg. anvil.

अहेरी *aherī*, m. Brbh. Av. = अहेड़ी.

अहेरु *aheru* [S.], f. *Pl. HŚS.* the plant *Asparagus racemosus*.

अहइ *ahaï*, v.i. Av. = है.

अहै *ahai*, v.i. Brbh. = है.

अहो *aho*, interj. **1.** I say! (attracting attention). **2.** oh! (expressing sudden emotion: as sorrow, joy).

अहो- *aho-* [S.: for *ahā* before *r*]. day: — अहोरात्र, m. & adv. day and night.

अहोई *ahoī* [? *ābhoga-* or *āhava-*[1]], f. *Pl. HŚS.* name of a rite held before Divālī, when women pray for children (= होई).

अहोभाग्य *ahobhāgyă* [? H. *aho*, interj]. adj. & m. **1.** adj. fortunate. **2.** *Pl.* unfortunate. **3.** m. good fortune. **4.** *Pl.* ill fortune.

अह्वान *ahvān*, m. pronun. var. = आह्वान.

आ

आ *ā*, the second vowel of the Devanāgarī syllabary. — **आकार**, m. the sound /a/; the letter **आ**.

आँक *āṁk*, m. = **अंक**, 1.-3., 5. — **आँकबंदी**, f. *Pl.* adjustment of rents.

आँकड़ा *āṁkṛā* [*aṅka-*], m. esp. pl. **1.** a figure; estimate. ***2.** figures, statistics; rate (as of birth, death).

आँकना *āṁknā* [*aṅkayati*], v.t. **1.** to value, to appraise, to assess (weight, measure, number, condition). **2.** to mark, to stamp. **3.** to outline, to draw. **4.** to number (as pages). — **कम करके** ~, to underestimate.

आंकिकी *āṁkikī* [S.], f. statistics.

[1]**आँख** *āṁkh* [*akṣi-*], f. **1.** the eye. **2.** sight. **3.** look, glance; discernment, judgment. **4.** transf. eye (of needle). **5.** fig. emotions, mood; regard, favour. — ~ **अटकना**, to fall in love (with, **में**). ~ **आना** (**को**), to have an inflammation of the eyes; the eyes to run (a disorder). ~ (or **आँखें**) **उठना**, one's eye(s) to be raised; = ~ **आना**. ~ (or **आँखें**) **उठाना**, to raise the eyes; to look angrily or covetously (at, **की ओर**); to look boldly (at, **के सामने**); to give up, to leave off. ~ **उठाकर न देखना**, not to notice, to treat (one) with disdain; to be abashed; to be humble, or diffident. ~ (or **आँखें**) **उलटना**, the eyes to turn upwards (at death). ~ **का अंधा**, m. a benighted, foolish person. ~ (or **आँखों**) **का काँटा**, sthg. vexatious, a thorn in the side. ~ (or **आँखों**) **का काजल चुराना**, fig. to be a practised or inveterate thief. ~ **का जाला**, m. cataract of the eye. ~ **का तारा**, or **तिल**, m. the pupil of the eye; the apple of (one's) eye. ~ (or **आँखों**) **का तेल निकालना**, fig. to strain the eyes. ~ **का पानी उतरना**, or **ढलना**, or **मारना**, to lose honour, to be or to become shameless. ~ **की किरकिरी**, f. grit in the eye; = ~ **का काँटा**. ~ **की पुतली**, f. = ~ **का तारा**. ~ **के तले ख़ून उतरना**, to become bloodshot (the eyes). ~ (or **आँखें**) **गड़ना**, the eye(s) to be irritated; the sight to be set (on, **की ओर**), to desire. ~ **गरम करना**, to warm the eyes: to feast the eyes (with the sight of); to be comforted or consoled (by one). ~ **गुद्दी में रहना**, to be inattentive. ~ **घुड़कना**, to glare (at). ~ (or **आँखें**) **चढ़ना**, the eyes to be heavy (from, **से**); the eyes to flash with anger. ~ (or **आँखें**) **चढ़ाना**, = **आँख-भौंह चढ़ाना**; to be intoxicated (see ~ **चढ़ना**), 1. ~ (or **आँखें**) **चमकाना**, to make the eyes flash, or roll (in anger, or flirtatiously). ~ **चीर-चीर देखना**, = ~ **फाड़-फाड़कर देखना**; to look through (one). ~ (or **आँखें**) **चुराना**, to avert the eyes (from, **से**); to shun; to disregard, to leave unattended. ~ **चूकना**, the attention to wander, supervision to relax. **आँखें छत से लगना**, the eyes to look upwards (in expectation); the eyes to be turned upwards (in death). ~ (or **आँखें**) **छिपाना**, = ~ **चुराना**. ~ **झपकना**, to blink; to doze; to be dazzled; to be timid. ~ (or **आँखें**) **झमकाना**, = ~ **चमकाना**. ~ (or **आँखें**) **टँगना**, = ~ **उलटना**; the gaze to be directed upwards. ~ **टेढ़ी करना**, to look angry; to look angrily (at). ~ (or **आँखें**) **ठंडी होना**, sight to be assuaged: to be content, satisfied; to be pleased. ~ **डालना**, to throw a glance (towards, **पर**); to look lustfully (at). ~ (or **आँखें**) **तरेरना**, to glare (at). ~ **तले आना**, to come into view, the eye to fall (on); to be pleasing (to, **को**). ~ **दिखाना**, to look angry or threatening; to frown. ~ **देखकर**, adv. at a hint or a sign (from, **की**). ~ **देखना**, to look (to, **की**: for guidance, &c.) ~ (or **आँखें**) **दौड़ाना**, to cast the eyes about (eagerly or anxiously); to ogle. ~ (or **आँखें**) **नचाना** = **आँख चमकाना**; to delight (one, **की**). ~ **नाक से डरना**, fig. to fear God. ~ (or **आँखें**) **निकालना**, to put out the eye(s) (of, **की**), to blind; to glare (at); to threaten. ~ **पड़ना**, the eye, or gaze to fall (on, **पर**). ~ **पलटना**, the mood to change (esp. for the worse). ~ **पसारना**, to look far, or further, off; fig. to welcome elaborately (a guest). ~ **फटना**, the eye to burst (with pain); to be utterly astonished; to be consumed with envy or jealousy. ~ **फड़कना**, the eyelid to twitch (as an omen, twitching of the right eye has been regarded as auspicious in men; of the left, in women). ~ (or **आँखें**) **फाड़ फाड़कर देखना**, to look (at) with strained and eager eyes; to stare (at); to look (at) in astonishment. ~ (or **आँखें**) **फिरना**, affection or favour to be withdrawn (from, **से**). ~ **फूटना**, the eye to burst: to lose an eye; to lose one's sight; fig. to feel dislike (at the sight of). ~ **फूटी पीर गई**, 'the eye out, and the pain gone' (said of relief gained at too high a price). ~ (or **आँखें**) **फेरना**, to withdraw affection or favour (from, **से**). ~ **फैलाना**, to stare; to look astonished; to be discerning; = ~ **पसारना**. ~ (or **आँखें**) **फोड़ना**, to make blind; to ruin the eyes; fig. to study hard; to watch or to expect in vain. ~ (or **आँखें**) **बंद करना**, to close the eyes; fig. to die; to turn (from, **से**), to neglect, to ignore; to withdraw (from). ~ **बंद होना**, to faint. ~ **बचना**, to be distracted (from, **से**). ~ **बचाना** (**से**), to avoid the eye (of); to slip away; to avert the eyes (from), to pretend not to see. ~ **बदलना**, (one's, **की**)

favour or disposition (towards another) to change. ~ बनना, sight to be restored. ~ (or आँखें) बराबर करना, to look straight in the eyes. ~ बराबर रखना, to keep friendship or regard unaltered. ~ (or आँखें) बहाना, to weep. ~ बिगड़ना, sight to be impaired. ~ (or आँखें) बिछाना (के आगे), fig. to receive with respect or honour; to cherish, to esteem. ~ भर आना, the eyes to fill with tears. ~ भर, or भरकर, देखना, to stare hard and long (at, की ओर), to look one's fill; to look angrily or threateningly (at); to look lovingly or flirtatiously (at). ~ (or आँखें) भर लाना, tears to come to the eyes, to be ready to cry. ~ मारना, to wink, to give a wink; to ogle. ~ मिच जाना, the eye to close; to die. ~ मिचकाना, to blink; to wink. ~ मिलना, = ~ लड़ना. ~ मिलाना, to look full in the face (of, की); to exchange glances (with); to form friendship, &c. (with). ~ मीचना, or मिचाना, to close the eyes; = ~ मिचकाना; to connive (at); to blindfold. ~ (or आँखें) मूँदकर, adv. with eyes shut; blindly, thoughtlessly. ~ में आँखें पड़ना, eyes to meet: to fall in love. ~ में सील न होना, the eyes not to be moist: to be cold or hard hearted; to be bold, brazen. ~ रखना, to look hopefully (to, पर); to stare in admiration (at); to attend to, to oversee; to look wantonly (at). ~ रोशन करना, to delight the eyes (with a sight of). ~ लगना, to fall asleep, to doze; to feel love or affection (for, से). ~ लगाना, to fix the eyes (on, से); to form an attachment (to), to fall in love (with). ~ लजाना, the eyes to be lowered out of shame or modesty. ~ लड़ना, to meet the eyes (of, से): to exchange loving glances; to fall in love (with). ~ लड़ाना, to look steadfastly (at, से); to exchange glances. ~ लेना, to avert the eyes (from, से); to withdraw favour (from). ~ (or आँखें) लाल करना, to redden the eyes: to glare furiously. ~ (or आँखें) सुरख़ करना, = ~ लाल करना. ~ सेंकना, to rejoice the eyes (with a sight of); to derive pleasure or comfort (from, से). ~ से उतरना, or गिरना, to fall in the regard (of, की); to be in disgrace. आँखें ओझल, adv. out of (one's) sight, in one's absence. आँखें चार होना, to look into each other's eyes. आँखें दो चार होना, to talk intimately. आँखें न देखना, not to look, not to take notice (of, की). आँखें नीली-पीली करना, to grow livid with anger. आँखें रोशन होना, the eyes to be bright: to be joyful (at the sight of); to reach maturity (a young woman). आँखें सफ़ेद होना, or होने को आना, to grow blind with weeping and vain expectation. आँखें सीधी करना, to make peace (with), to reconcile (oneself). आँखें होना, to have eyes; to have or to acquire discernment; to have inner vision. आँखों की सुइयाँ निकालना, fig. to complete a task at little cost to oneself after another has worked at it; to take credit for another's work. आँखों के तारे छूटना, fig. the eyes to blaze (as in anger, indignation). आँखों के बल, adv. willingly; carefully. आँखों को खो बैठना, to lose (one's) sight; the sight to be much impaired. आँखों (or आँखों से) देखना, to see with (one's) own eyes. आँखों पर आइए, fig. you are heartily welcome. आँखों पर ठीकरे, or ठीकरी, रखना, fig. to be shameless, or unfeeling. आँखों पर तिनका रखना, fig. to see sthg. unclearly. आँखों पर पट्टी बँधना, fig. to be blind to a situation or a reality. आँखों पर परदा पड़ना, id.; fig. to go astray; the eyes to be darkened: to grow faint. आँखों पर बिठाना, fig. to treat with esteem or honour; to value; to hold dear. आँखों पर बैठिए! fig. be heartily welcome! आँखों पर रखना, = आँखों पर बिठाना. आँखों में, adv. by a movement or glance of the eye. आँखों में आना, to 'go to the head', to intoxicate; to be intoxicated. आँखों में कच्चा बैठना, sl. to become blind. आँखों में काजल घुलना, the eyes to be heavily made up. आँखों में ख़ार होना to be a thorn in the eye: to be a painful or unpleasant sight or matter (to, की). आँखों में ख़ून उतरना, the eyes to be bloodshot (with rage). आँखों में घर करना, to be always in the mind's eye; to win the affections (of, की). आँखों में चढ़ना, to be pleasing, attractive (to, की). आँखों में चरबी छाना, to be blinded by pride, vanity, lust, &c.; to be wilfully blind, to pretend not to know (one). आँखों में चुभना, to pierce the eyes, to irritate; fig. to strike, to charm. आँखों में टेसू (or सरसों) फूलना, fig. to be indifferent to the troubles of others, not being involved oneself. आँखों में धूल डालना, or झोंकना, to make blind (fig.): to cheat; to impose upon; to pilfer or snatch away. आँखों में न ठहरना, to appear worthless, to be thought little of; to be disapproved of. आँखों में नमक, or नोन, झोंकना, = आँखों में धूल झोंकना. आँखों में बसना, = आँखों में घर करना. आँखों में भंग घुटना, fig. to be drunk. आँखों में रात काटना, or ले जाना, to pass the night awake, to have sleepless nights. आँखों में सलाई फेरना, to put out the eyes (of, की). आँखों से मिलाना, or घुलना, to be in love (a couple). आँखों से लगाना, or लगाकर रखना, to lift to the eyes: = आँखों पर बिठाना. – आँख-ढक्का, m. goggles. आँख-ताँख निकल जाना, colloq. to give up the ghost. आँख-फोड़ टिड्डा, m. a midge that flies into the eyes; an ungrateful person. आँख-फोड़ा, m. id. आँख-भौंह, m. eye and brow: आँख-भौंह चढ़ाना, to look angry, to frown; to show dislike, disdain, &c. in one's expression. आँख-मिचौनी, f. = next. आँख-मिचौली, f. blind man's buff. आँख-मुंदाई, f. closing the eyes (in death). आँख-लगा, m. a lover. आँख-लगी, f. आँखवाला, adj. clever, quick.

[2]**आँख** *āṁkh* [*akṣa-*[3]], m. f. sprout, shoot; sprout in a sugar-cane joint; eye (of potato, &c).

आँग *āṁg*, m. Brbh. Av. = अंग.

आँगन *āṁgan* [*aṅgana-*], m. **1.** courtyard (of a house). **2.** court, area, quadrangle.

आँगा *āṁgā* [*anga-*[1]], m. *Pl.* **1.** a double armful. **2.** axle (of a cart). **3.** hire, fare.

आँगी *āṁgī*, f. reg. (Bihar) = अँगिया.

आँगुल *āṁgul* [*angula-*], m. a finger's breadth.

आँच *āṁc* [*arcis-*], f. **1.** flame, blaze. **2.** heat. **3.** brilliance. **4.** transf. burden, difficulty; misfortune. **5.** peril. **6.** sexual desire. — ~ आना (को), to suffer distress, or misfortune. ~ खाना, to be heated (a metal, a liquid); to grow angry. ~ दिखाना (को), v.t. to heat. साँच को ~ क्या? what has truth to fear from the fire (of an ordeal)?

आँचल *āṁcal* [*añcala-*], m. **1.** the border or hem at the end of a sari, or shawl, &c. **2.** the end of a sari, &c. (which usually covers a woman's breast). **3.** fig. breast, bosom. 4. = अंचल, 2. — ~ दबाना, fig. to suck at the breast. ~ देना, to give the breast (to an infant). ~ पर बैठाना, f. = बिछाना. ~ पसारना, or फैलाना (के आगे), to entreat (one's) favour or assistance. ~ फाड़ना, to put the *āṁcal* aside (from the head): to converse with a man not of (one's) family. ~ बिछाना, fig. to receive (a guest) with elaborate hospitality. ~ में बाँधना, to bear in mind (as of a knot tied in the *āṁcal*). ~ लेना, to cover the breast; to touch the border or hem of a women's garment in respectful welcome. ~ सिर पर डालना, to draw the sari over the head; fig. to marry (of a woman). – आँचल-पल्लू, m. the embroidered hem of a sari, &c.

आंचलिक *āṁcalik* [S.], adj. **1.** having to do with the end or edge of a sari. ★**2.** having to do with a region; specif. *lit.* regional (fiction).

आँचू *āṁcū* [*ākṣika-; ācchuka-*], m. reg. **1.** raspberry. **2.** blackberry, bramble. — काला ~, m. *Pl.* = ~, 2.

आँजन *āṁjan*, m. reg. (E.) = [1]अंजन.

आँजना *āṁjnā* [*añjati*], v.t. to apply collyrium, or lampblack, &c. to the eyes.

आंजनेय *āñjăney* [S.], m. *mythol.* a title of Hanumān.

आँजि *āṁji*, f. *Pl.* selvage, hem.

आँट *āṁṭ* [*āvr̥tti-*], f. **1.** twist, turn, fold (e.g. of cloth at the waist of the *dhotī*). **2.** catch, entanglement; hold (as in wrestling). **3.** antagonism; grudge; envy; misunderstanding. **4.** joint (of a finger, &c). **5.** transf. bundle. **6.** scratch made on silver or gold (to test its purity). — ~ पर चढ़ना, to be caught, held (as in wrestling); to come under (one's) power. ~ पड़ना (में), to become knotted or entangled; to feel antagonism, &c. (for). – आँट-साँट, f. intrigue, plot, collusion; *Pl.* rambling speech; evasive answer.

आँट- *āṁṭ-*, v.i. Av. = अँटना.

आँटी *āṁṭī* [**aṇṭa-*], f. **1.** twist, bunch (of fibre, grass). **2.** fold (of material, serving as a pocket: cf. आँट). **3.** hank, skein (of thread, &c). **4.** bundle (of grass, wood); sheaf. **5.** a 'leg trick' (in wrestling); kick. — ~ गरम करना, to warm the pocket: to give a bribe (to, की).

आँठी *āṁṭhī* [*aṣṭi-*], f. E. **1.** kernel, pip. **2.** clot (as of curds); knot, nodule. **3.** nipple.

आँड *āṁḍ* [*āmaṇḍa*], m. = [2]अंड.

आँड़ *āṁṛ* [*āṇḍa-, aṇḍa-*], m. = [1]अंड, 2 (and अंडा).

आँड़ू *āṁṛū* [cf. H. *āṁṛ*], adj. **1.** having testicles; (livestock) entire. **2.** having large testicles.

आँड़े-बाँड़े *āṁṛe-bāṁṛe* [? cf. H. *hāṁṛnā*], m. pl. reg. strolling, rambling. — ~ खाना, to take a stroll, to ramble.

आँत *āṁt* [*āntra-*], f. entrails; intestines; bowels. — ~ उतरना, a hernia to occur. ~ का बढ़ आना, m. a hernia. ~ गिरना, to pass loose white stools. ~ में बल पड़ना, the stomach to ache. आँतें गले में (or मुँह में) आना, fig. to be in desperate straits. आँतें समेटना, to contract the stomach: to go without food. ज़मीन की ~, f. the bowels of the earth.

आंतरिक *āntărik* [S.], adj. inner, internal.

आँद *āṁd* [?? **anda-*[1] × *ārdra-*], m. reg. mud, mire.

आंदन *āṁdan* [?? cf. **anda-*[1]: × *ārdra-*], m. *Pl.* = आँद.

आँदू *āṁdū* [*andŭka-*], m. Brbh. fetter (for elephants); anklet.

आंदोलन *āndolan* [S.], m. swinging: a movement (political, &c.)

आँधी *āṁdhī* [*andhikā-*, Pa. *andhikā-*], f. **1.** a dust-storm, whirlwind. **2.** a storm. — ~ आना, or उठना, a storm to come on. ~ उठाना, to create a storm, or a stir. ~ के आम, m. pl. windfallen mangoes: things obtained easily, cheaply, or free; things not lasting long. ~ चलना, a storm to rage. ~ होना, a tempest to rage; to be very active and ardent. गरज की ~, f. a thunderstorm.

आँब *āṁb* [*āmra-*: Pa. *amba-*], m. = आम.

आँबी *āṁbī* [*an-*+H. *bī(j)*], *Pl.* unsown, wild (of plants).

आँयबाँय *āṁy-bāṁy* [cf. H. *bāyāṁ*], adv. (going) in all directions.

आँव *āṁv* [*āma-*], m. looseness of the bowels: dysentery; diarrhoea. — ~ आना (को), to suffer from dysentery, &c. ~ गिरना, or पड़ना, or बैठना, id.

आँवन *āṁvan* [*āmocana-*], m. iron band round the nave of a wheel.

[1]**आँवल** *āṁval* [cf. *āma-*], m. placenta. — आँवल-झाँवल, m. pl. reg. twins. आँवल-नाल, f. umbilical cord.

[2]**आँवल** *āṁval*, m. = आँवला. — आँवल-गट्टा, m. a dried myrobalan, or a windfallen one.

आँवला *āṁvlā* [*āmalaka-*], m. the tree emblic myrobalan (*Phyllanthus emblica*) and its fruit. — आँवला-सार, m. purified sulphur.

आँवले *āṁvle* [cf. H. *āṁval*], m. pl. *Pl.* twins.

आँवा *āṁvā* [*āpāka-*, Pk. *āvāga-*], m. a potter's kiln; kiln; furnace.

आँसू *āṁsū* [*aśru-*], m. a tear. — ~ आना, चलना, or बहना, tears to come, or to flow: to weep. ~ गिराना, or बहाना, or ढालना, to shed tears; to pretend to weep. ~ टपकना, tears to drop: to weep. ~ ढलकाना, = ~ गिराना. ~ पी जाना, or पीकर रह जाना, to repress (one's) tears. ~ भर आना, tears to well (into the eyes, में). ~ भर लाना, to let tears well up: to begin to cry. आँसुओं का तार बँधना, (one's) tears to fall incessantly. आँसुओं से मुँह धोना, fig. to shed floods of tears. आठ आठ ~ रोना, to shed a flood of tears. – आँसू-ढाल, f. watering of the eyes (in horses).

-आ *-ā* [S.], suffix. **1.** forms f. nouns, and adjectives as used with nouns in more formal style (e.g. छात्रा, f. a girl or woman student; सुशीला स्त्री, a woman of good moral character; अपरा, f. not other: the earth, this world).

आ- *ā-* [S.], pref. up to, as far as, until (e.g. आजीवन, adv. as long as life remains). — आनील, adj. bluish. आबाल, m. one still a child.

आइंदा *āindā* [P. *āyanda*], adj. & m. **1.** adj. coming, future. **2.** adv. in future. **3.** m. the future. — आइंदे को, or के लिए, or में, adv. = ~.

आइ *āi*, f. Brbh. = [2]आई.

-आइन *-āin* [ad. *ānī-*], suffix (forms feminines for some m. nouns, e.g. सुहुआइन, merchant's wife).

[1]**आई** *āī* [cf. H. *ānā*], f. reg. coming, approach.

[2]**आई** *āī* [cf. *āyu-*], f. **1.** Brbh. period of life. **2.** appointed hour, death. — अपनी ~ करना, to bring about one's end, to seal one's fate.

-आई *-āī*, suffix (forms f. nouns from verb and nominal stems, e.g. पढ़ाई, reading, study; चौड़ाई, width, extension; ठकुराई, status of *ṭhākur*).

आईन *āīn* [P. *ā'īn*], m. **1.** regulation, statute. **2.** law. **3.** edict. **4.** constitution. — आईनदान, or -दां [P. *-dān*], m. one versed in the law; (*Pl.*) a rogue.

आईना *āīnā* [P. *ā'īna*], m. & adj. **1.** m. a mirror. **2.** adj. inv. fig. mirror-like: clear, bright, polished; transparent. — ~ दिखाना, to hold up a mirror (to, को), to show (a person) what he is. ~ देखना, to look in a mirror; to consider one's capacity (to perform a task). ~ होना, to be clear (a matter: to, पर). – आईनादार [P. *-dār*], m. mirror-holder: a barber. आईनासाज़ [P. *-sāz*], m. a mirror-maker. °ई, f.

आईनी *āīnī* [P. *ā'īnī*], adj. **1.** legal. **2.** constitutional.

आउ *āu* [*āyuṣ-*], f. m. Av. span of life, age.

-आऊ *-āū*, suffix (forms adjectives of quality from verb stems, e.g. उपजाऊ, fertile; फिसलाऊ, slippery).

आऊस *āūs* [**āvr̥ṣa-*: conn. H. *pāus*], m. *Pl. HŚS.* rice sown in April-June (Bengal).

आकंप *ā-kamp* [S.], m. shaking, trembling.

आकंपन *ā-kampan* [S.], m. shaking, trembling.

आकंपित *ā-kampit* [S.], adj. shaking, trembling.

आक *āk* [*arka-*?], m. swallow-wort, *Calotropis gigantea* (a medicinal plant = मदार). — ~ की बुढ़िया, pith of the āk plant; *fig.* a frail old woman.

आकन *ākan*, m. *Pl. HŚS.*. grass or weeds collected from a ploughed field.

आकर *ā-kar* [S.], m. **1.** a mine. **2.** a rich source; store; treasury. **3.** Av. type, variety (as of caste group).

आकरी *ākărī* [cf. H. *ākar*], f. E.H. mining, excavating.

आकर्ष *ā-karṣ* [S.], m. **1.** attraction; fascination. **2.** *phys.* attraction. **3.** lodestone; magnet.

आकर्षक *ā-karṣak* [S.], adj. **1.** drawing, attracting. **2.** attractive.

आकर्षण *ā-karṣaṇ* [S.], m. **1.** attracting, attraction. **2.** attractiveness, charm. — आकर्षण-परिधि, f. *phys.* field of attraction. आकर्षण-शक्ति, f. attractive force; charm.

आकर्षिक *ā-karṣik* [S.], adj. = आकर्षक.

आकर्षित *ā-karṣit* [S.], adj. drawn, attracted; fascinated.

आकर्षी *ā-karṣī* [S.], adj. = आकर्षक.

आकलन *ā-kalan* [S.], m. **1.** a collection. **2.** appraisal, evaluation.

आकला *āklā* [*ākula-*; Pk. *akkula-*], adj. *Pl.* peevish.

आकली *āklī* [*ākula-*; Pk. *akkula-*], f. **1.** agitation; motion (as of a vehicle). **2.** nausea.

आकस्मिक *ākasmik* [S.], adj. **1.** unexpected, sudden; casual (leave). **2.** occurring by chance. — ~ छुट्टी, f. special leave, casual leave. ~ निधि, f. contingency fund.

आकस्मिकता *ākasmikătā* [S.], f. **1.** suddenness, unexpected nature. **2.** chance nature. **3.** a contingency.

आकस्मिकी *ākasmikī* [S.], f. a chance event.

आकांक्षक *ā-kāṅkṣak* [S.], adj. = आकांक्षी.

आकांक्षा *ā-kāṅkṣā* [S.], f. **1.** wish, desire; ambition. **2.** intention. **3.** hope, expectation. — ~ ढोना, to cherish a desire, &c.

आकांक्षित *ā-kāṅkṣit* [S.], adj. **1.** desired, aspired towards. **2.** expected.

आकांक्षी *ā-kāṅkṣī* [S.], adj. & m. **1.** adj. desirous, aspiring. **2.** hopeful, expecting. **3.** m. one desirous of sthg.

आक़बत *āqabat* [A. *'āqiba*: P. *'āqibat*], f. following: end; the future life.

आक़ा *āqā*, m. see आग़ा.

[1]**आकार** *ā-kār* [S.], m. **1.** appearance. **2.** form, shape; a statue. **3.** expression (of the features). **4.** type; way, manner. **5.** size; bulk. **6.** format (of a book). — आकार-पत्र, m. a form, pro-forma. आकार-प्रकार, m. appearance; form; type; size, dimensions; ways, nature. आकार-रेखन, m. sketching, outlining. आकार-रेखा, f. a sketch, outline. आकार-विज्ञान, m. *biol.* morphology. आकारहीन, adj. formless, amorphous. आकारांत [°*ra*+*a*°], m. ending in *-ā* (a word).

[2]**आकार** *ā-kār* [S.], m. see s.v. आ.

आकारण *ā-kāraṇ* [S.], m. invitation.

आकारित *ā-kārit* [S.], adj. given form; sketched, outlined.

आकारी *ā-kārī* [S]. adj. possessed of form; well-built, shapely.

आकाश *ā-kāś* [S.], m. **1.** space. **2.** the sky; the heavens. ~ की ओर, towards the horizon. **3.** air. **4.** the cosmos. — ~ के कुलाबे मिलाना, = ~ पाताल एक करना. ~ खुलना, the sky to clear; conditions or circumstances to become favourable. ~ चूमना, or छूना, to kiss, or to touch, the sky: to be lofty; to show overweening conceit. ~ पर दिया जलाना, id., 2. ~ पाताल एक करना, to make great efforts; to make a great to-do, be boastful. ~ पाताल का फ़रक़, m. fig. a world of difference. ~ बाँधना, to talk wildly, to romance; to perform the impossible. ~ से बातें करना, = आसमान से बातें करना. – ~ आकाश-कुसुम, m. flower of heaven: sthg. wonderful. आकाश-गंगा, f. the Milky Way; *mythol.* the heavenly Ganges. आकाशगामी, adj. = next. आकाशचारी, adj. & f. moving through the heavens, or sky; a heavenly body; a bird. आकाश-चोटी, f. the zenith. आकाश-दीप, m. = next. आकाश-दीया, m. a lamp or torch attached to a pole; such a lamp, &c. lit in honour of Lakṣmī or Viṣṇu at the Dīvālī festival; *Pl.* a beacon. आकाश-धुरी, f. *astron.* axis of the heavenly sphere. आकाश-फल, m. fruit of heaven: offspring. आकाश-बेल, m. a rootless creeper, a parasite. आकाश-मंडल, m. = आकाश, 2., 3. आकाशवर्ण, adj. sky-blue. आकाशवाणी, f. a voice from heaven; radio; a radio station. आकाश-वृत्ति, f. & adj. precarious existence; an existence dependent on fortune. आकाश-सेना, f. air force.

आकाशी *ā-kāśī* [S.], adj. **1.** having to do with space, or with the sky; heavenly (a body, &c.); celestial. **2.** atmospheric. **3.** aerial.

आकाशीय *ā-kāśīyă* [S.], adj. = आकाशी.

आकिंचन *ākiñcan* [ad. *ākiñcanya-*], m. & adj. Av. **1.** m. poverty. **2.** adj. poverty-stricken.

आकिंचन्य *ākiñcanyă* [S.], m. poverty.

आकुल *ākul* [S.], adj. **1.** agitated; anxious, eager; uneasy; confused. **2.** distressed.

आकुलता *ākulătā* [S.], f. **1.** agitation, &c. (see आकुल). **2.** distress.

आकुलित *ākulit* [S.], adj. made agitated, &c.: = आकुल.

आकृति *ā-kṛti* [S.], f. **1.** form, shape. **2.** likeness, image. **3.** bodily appearance; features. **4.** a shape, figure. — आकृति-प्रधान, adj. formalistic.

आकृष्ट *ā-kṛṣṭ* [S.], adj. = आकर्षित.

आक्रम *ā-kram* [S.], m. **1.** entering upon; ascending. **2.** invading, invasion. **3.** seizing. **4.** *Pl.* superiority.

आक्रमण *ā-kramaṇ* [S.], m. **1.** an attack. **2.** aggression; invasion. — ~ करना (पर), to attack. – आक्रमणकारक, adj. used in attack, assault (a vehicle); aggressive, hostile; *mil.* offensive. °-कारी, adj. & m. attacking, aggressive; an aggressor, invader. आक्रमणमूलक, adj. being the source of an attack: aggressive. आक्रमणशील, adj. whose nature is to attack: aggressive, hostile.

आक्रमित *ā-kramit* [S.], adj. attacked.

आक्रम्य *ā-kramyă* [S.], adj. liable, predisposed (to infection).

आक्रम्यता *ā-kramyătā* [S.], f. predisposition (to infection).

आक्रांत *ā-krānt* [S.], adj. **1.** attacked, assailed; beleaguered. **2.** overpowered. **3.** agitated (as by emotion).

आक्रांति *ā-krānti* [S.], f. **1.** rising, mounting. **2.** attack, assault. **3.** overpowering.

आक्रामक *ā-krāmak* [S.], adj. & m. **1.** adj. attacking; aggressive. **2.** m. aggressor.

आक्रोश *ā-kroś* [S.], m. **1.** scolding, abuse. ***2.** resentment.

आक्षिप्त *ā-kṣipt* [S.], adj. thrown away.

आक्षेप *ā-kṣep* [S.], m. throwing away: **1.** censure, criticism (of, पर); aspersion (against, पर). **2.** accusation, charge (against, पर). **3.** implication. — ~ द्वारा, by implication.

आक्षेपक *ā-kṣepak* [S.], adj. **1.** throwing away. **2.** critical, condemnatory.

आक्षेपण *ā-kṣepaṇ* [S.], m. the act of throwing away (= आक्षेप).

आक्षेपी *ā-kṣepī* [S.], adj. = आक्षेपक.

आखत *ākhat* [*akṣata-*; and ad. S.], m. E.H. = अक्षत.

आख़-थू *ākh-thū* [onom.: H. *thūknā*], m. coughing and spitting.

आखर *ākhar*, m. Brbh. Av. = अक्षर.

आख़िर *ākhir* [A. *ākhir*], adj. & m. **1.** adj. last, final; latter. ***2.** adv. finally, at last; eventually; in the end, after all. **3.** m. end. **4.** outcome. — ~ को, and में, adv. = ~. ~ होना, to come to an end, to be over; to come last; to die. – आख़िरकार, adv. = ~.

आख़िरी *ākhirī* [A. *ākhirī*], adj. **1.** last, final, having to do with the end; latter. **2.** final, irrevocable. — ~ बहार, f. the end of spring; end of the harvest, or fruit season; end of youth; the eleventh hour.

आखु *ākhu* [S.], m. a mouse, rat.

आखेट *ā-kheṭ* [S.], m. **1.** hunting, the chase. **2.** fright, terror. — ~ करना, to hunt.

आखेटक *ā-kheṭak* [S.], m. **1.** a hunter. **2.** a hunting dog.

आखेटिक *ā-kheṭik* [S.], adj. hunting, chasing.

आखेटी *ā-kheṭī* [cf. *ākheṭa-*: ad.], adj. & m. **1.** adj. having to do with hunting, used for hunting (as a dog). **2.** m. a hunter. **3.** a hunting dog.

आख़ोर *ākhor* [P. *ākhor*], m. & adj. **1.** m. refuse, leavings; litter; filth. **2.** adj. decaying, rotten. **3.** trashy.

आख्या *ā-khyā* [S.], f. **1.** name, title. **2.** fame, renown. **3.** account, report.

आख्यात *ā-khyāt* [S.], adj. **1.** declared, made known; uttered. **2.** named. ***3.** celebrated.

आख्याता *ā-khyātā* [S.], m. inv. narrator (of a legend, or tale).

आख्याति *ā-khyāti* [S.], f. **1.** report. ***2.** fame, renown.

आख्यान *ā-khyān* [S.], m. **1.** tale, account, narrative. *2. a legend.

आख्यानक *ā-khyānak* [S.], m. a short tale, &c. — आख्यानक-गीति, f. ballad.

आख्यानिक *ā-khyānik* [S.], adj. legendary.

आख्यापित *ā-khyāpit* [S.], adj. announced.

आगंतुक *āgantuk* [S.], m. a newcomer.

आग *āg* [*agni-*], f. **1.** fire; a fire; a flame. **2.** heat. **3.** passion, anger; pangs (of love, jealousy, grief); lust. **4.** quarrel; ill-will. **5.** pangs of hunger. **6.** fire (of a weapon). **7.** venereal disease. **8.** adj. burning hot (an object: as the hand, brow). **9.** colloq. very expensive, or scarce. ~ के मोल, adv. at a fiendish price. — ~ उठाना, to stir up a quarrel (among or between, में), to create turmoil; to enrage, to provoke. ~ करना, to make a fire; to heat very hot; to excite anger or envy. ~ का पुतला, an energetic, or alert person; an irritable person. ~ का बाग़, m. a partic. firework. ~ खाना, to eat fire: to act in an exaggerated way; to cause a scandal. ~ जलाना, to light a fire. ~ जोड़ना, = ~ सुलगाना. ~ झाड़ना, to strike fire (from flint); to shake the ash from live coals, to stir up a fire. ~ दिखाना (को), to warm; to dry; to cause to ignite. ~ देना (को), to set alight; to set fire (to); specif. to light a cremation fire; to consume, to destroy. ~ धोना, = ~ झाड़ना. ~ पड़ना, to be very hot (climate, season); to feel burning heat; to feel pangs (as of grief, or of hunger); to rise high (prices). ~ पर लोटना, to roll on fire: to suffer torment or distress. ~ फाँकना, to eat fire; to attempt the impossible; to exaggerate greatly; to fabricate. ~ फूँकना, to blow or to fan a fire, or flame; to cause a burning sensation (in, में); to stir up a quarrel, &c.; to incite to anger, jealousy, &c. ~ बरसना, = ~ पड़ना, 1.; to rain down (of enemy fire). ~ बरसाना (पर), to bombard; to rake with fire; to call down imprecations. ~ बुझाना, to extinguish a fire; to satisfy (hunger, thirst); to pacify (a quarrel); to assuage. ~ भड़कना, to flare up (as fire, or emotions). ~ भड़काना, to fan or to blow a fire, or flame; to stir up (a quarrel, or emotions). ~ में झोंकना, fig. to thrust into a dire situation. ~ में पानी डालना, to quench a fire; to pacify (a quarrel, or emotions). ~ लगना (में), to be set on fire; to catch fire; to be very hot; to smart (a wound); to burn with emotion; to suffer pangs of hunger; to be destroyed (as hopes); to be blighted, to wither; to become scarce and expensive. ~ लगने पर कुआँ खोदना, fig. to shut the stable door after the horse is stolen. ~ लगाकर पानी को दौड़ना, to run for water after causing the fire: to make a show of remedying a dire situation caused by oneself. ~ लगाना (में or को), to set on fire; to burn; to kindle (as strife, strong emotion); to make mischief, to cause trouble; to destroy; to discard; to squander; to cause loss (to); to make a great display, to do wonders; to buy at too high a price. ~ लगे, interj. may it burn! the devil take it! ~ लेने आना, to come for fire: to pay a flying visit. ~ सुलगाना, to kindle a fire; to stir up strife, &c.; to incite. ~ से पानी हो जाना, to recover one's equanimity (as after sudden anger,) ~ होना, to become very hot; to be enraged (at, पर). — आगजनी, f. arson. आग-पानी का बैर, m. fig. natural antagonism; mortal enmity. आग-बगूला (or बबूला) होना, to be in a whirlwind of passion: to be enraged. आग-बोट, m. a steamer. आग-रुई, f. fire-cotton: tinder.

¹**आगत** *ā-gat* [S.], adj. & m. **1.** arrived; present. **2.** happened. **3.** m. a newcomer; guest. **4.** in comp. entered into (e.g. क्रमागत, adj. consecutive). — आगत-सत्कार, m. hospitality. आगत-स्वागत, m. welcome to a guest, hospitality.

²**आगत** *ā-gat* [ad. *āgati-*], f. reg. **1.** income, wealth. **2.** courtesy, consideration.

आगति *ā-gati* [S.], f. arrival.

आगम *ā-gam* [S.], m. **1.** coming, approach; entry; appearance. **2.** the future, the hereafter. **3.** a sacred text, esp. a Veda; a text containing spells and incantations; a *tantra*. **4.** document, deed. **5.** income. — ~ बाँधना, to determine the future, to foretell; to plan for the future. ~ बात, f. prophecy. – आगम-पत्र, m. title-deed. आगम-वक्ता, m. inv. one who foretells the future; an astrologist. आगम-शुल्क, m. customs or import duties.

आगमन *ā-gaman* [S.], m. **1.** coming, arrival; approach; appearance. **2.** origin. **3.** *logic.* induction. **4.** sexual intercourse. — आगमनात्मक [°*na*+*ā*°], adj. inductive.

आगमित *ā-gamit* [S.], adj. learned, mastered (a topic).

¹**आगर** *āgar* [ad. *ākara-*], m. **1.** a mine. **2.** a salt-pit. **3.** a store; treasury. **4.** fig. E.H. a wise or skilled person.

²**आगर** *āgar* [ad. *āgāra-*], m. abode.

आगल *āgal* [**argaḍa-*, *argala-*], m. f. reg. bar or bolt (of a door or window: = अर्गल).

आगा *āgā* [*agra-*], m. **1.** front, forepart; prow (of a ship); van (of an army); forehead; face; the genitalia. **2.** assault, onset. **3.** open space in front of a house. **4.** the future. — ~ भारी होना, colloq. to be pregnant; to be rough or dangerous (a road). - आगा-तागा लेना, to look after, to attend to; to question, to call to account. आगा-पीछा, m. front and rear; circumstances (of a matter); hesitation, vacillations. आगा-पीछा करना, to hesitate (in, में); to demur; to follow (one, का) continuously or remorselessly, to dog the footsteps (of). आगा-पीछा देखना to be cautious; to consider carefully (a matter and its consequences, का). आगा-पीछा सोचना (का), id.

आग़ा *āġā* [T. *āğā*], m. **1.** lord and master; owner. **2.** a *kābulī*, trader from Afghanistan. **3.** transf. dear (senior) friend.

आगाध *ā-gādh* [S.], adj. = अगाध.

आग़ाज़ *āġāz* [P. *āġāz*], m. U. beginning.

आगामी *ā-gāmī* [S.], adj. coming; impending, future.

आगामी *āgāmī* [cf. *āgama-*], m. a fortune-teller, seer; one versed in the *āgamas*.

आगार *ā-gār* [S.], m. **1.** dwelling, house. **2.** building or premises devoted to a particular purpose: e.g. institute; hall, chamber. **3.** receptacle, store; treasury.

आगारी *āgārī*, f. reg. = अगाड़ी, 4.

आगाह *āgāh* [P. *āgāh*], adj. **1.** informed (of, से), acquainted (with); forewarned. **2.** knowing, well-informed. — ~ करना (को), to inform (of, से); to report; to caution, to forewarn.

आगाही *āgāhī* [P. *āgāhī*], f. information, knowledge; foreknowledge. — ~ होना, to learn (of, से).

आगिल *āgil*, adj. Av. = अगला.

आगी *āgī*, f. metr. Av. = आग.

आगुआ *āguā*, m. pommel (of saddle, sword).

आगे *āge* [*agre*, *agreṇa*], adv. **1.** in front, out in front; ahead; further, further on. **2.** confronting; opposite; in view, in sight. **3.** in the future; again, in future. **4.** next (in time or place); afterwards, later. **5.** previously, first; already; formerly. **6.** furthermore. **7.** (w. के or से.) in front, out in front (of), &c.; confronting, &c.; in the presence (of); in the lifetime (of). — ~ ~, adv. ahead; later; with time; gradually. ~ आना, to approach; to confront; to come to pass; to come to light; to be received (by, के: of consequences or retribution). ~ करना, to place in front (of, के); to bring forward, to adduce; to promote. ~ का उठा खानेवाला, a hanger-on, dependant. ~ का कपड़ा, m. veil; = आँचल. ~ का क़दम पीछे पड़ना, to fall back after advancing; to recoil. ~ को, adv. in the future; in future; ahead. ~ चलकर or जाकर, adv. id. ~ डोलना, = ~ होना, 2. ~ देखना, to look before; to act prudently or carefully; to look to the future. ~ धरना, to place before (one, के), to put forward; to offer; to keep in sight or in view. ~ बढ़ना, to go forward; to progress; to go beyond, to surpass (one, से), to excel; to confront (one, के). ~ पीछे, adv. one after the other; front and rear, fore and aft; sooner or later; in one way or the other; straggling, in disorder; surrounded (by, के). ~ से, adv. from in front of, &c.; in the future; beforehand; from previously, for some time. ~ से लेना, to go out to receive, or to escort (an honoured visitor). ~ होना, = ~ बढ़ना; to succeed (one, के: as offspring). ~ होकर लेना, = ~ से लेना.

आग़ोश *āgoś* [P. *āgoś*], f. embrace.

आग्नेय *āgneyă* [S.], adj. **1.** having to do with fire or with the Vedic god Agni; fiery, glowing. **2.** volcanic; igneous (rock). **3.** incendiary (weapon). **4.** south-eastern. — ~ अस्त्र, m. a firearm. ~ काँच, m. burning-glass, magnifying glass. – आग्नेयास्त्र [°*ya*+*a*°], m. = ~ अस्त्र.

आग्रह *ā-grah* [S.], m. **1.** insistence, pertinacity. **2.** assiduity, zeal; enthusiasm. — ~ करना, to insist (on, पर or का). ~ से, adv. zealously. – आग्रहपूर्ण, adj. insistent; assiduous, &c. आग्रहपूर्वक, adv. insistently; assiduously, &c.

आग्रहण *ā-grahaṇ* [S.], m. drawing out (money from an account).

आग्रहायण *āgrahāyaṇ* [S.], m. 1. = अग्रहायण, अगहन. **2.** the day of full moon in the month Ag'han.

आग्रही *ā-grahī* [S.], adj. = आग्रहपूर्ण.

आघात *ā-ghāt* [S.], m. **1.** a blow; shock; gust; blast. **2.** injury. **3.** killing, slaughter. **4.** *ling.* stress.

आघातक *ā-ghātak* [S.], m. firing-pin.

आघार *ā-ghār* [S.], m. **1.** placing sacred food in front of an idol. **2.** libation of *ghī* made at certain sacrifices.

आचमन *ā-căman* [S.], m. **1.** rinsing the mouth. **2.** sipping water from the palm of the right hand (as a ritual purification: before meals, or religious ceremonies). — ~ करना, to rinse the mouth, &c.

आचमनी *ā-cămanī* [ad. *ācamanīya-*], f. a small spoon or ladle used in performing *ācaman* rites.

आचर- *ā-car-* [ad. *ācarati*], v.i. Av. = आचरण करना.

आचरण *ā-caraṇ* [S.], m. **1.** conduct, behaviour. **2.** custom, usage; rule or norm of conduct. **3.** religious observance. — ~ करना, to behave; to act; to make a practice (of, का). – आचरण-पंजी, f. report, notes (as on conduct). आचरण-पुस्तिका, f. report-book. आचरणशील, adj. of good or virtuous conduct.

आचरणीय *ā-carăṇīyă* [S.], adj. to be performed; meritorious (an action).

आचरित *ā-carit* [S.], adj. **1.** performed, carried out. **2.** customary, established.

आचार *ā-cār* [S.], m. **1.** manner of life; conduct, behaviour; good or virtuous conduct. **2.** custom, usage; tradition. **3.** rite, ceremony. **4.** interchange (as of letters). — आचारवान, adj. of good or virtuous conduct. °-वती, f. आचार-विचार, m. conduct, or behaviour, and views. आचार-व्यवहार, m. = ~, 1. आचार-शास्त्र, m. ethics. °ईय, adj. ethical. आचारहीन, adj. of bad conduct; depraved.

आचारिक *ā-cārik* [S.], adj. customary; traditional.

आचारी *ā-cārī* [S.], adj. = आचारवान.

आचार्य *ā-căryă* [S.], m. **1.** a spiritual preceptor or guide. **2.** a founder, or leader of a sect. **3.** (esp. as title) a man of distinguished learning; a senior professor; principal, &c.

आचार्या *ā-căryā* [S.], f. **1.** a spiritual preceptress or guide (see s.v. आचार्य). **2.** the wife of an *ācārya*.

आचार्यानी *ācāryānī* [S.], f. the wife of an *ācārya*.

आच्छन्न *ā-cchann* [S.], adj. = आच्छादित.

आच्छादन *ā-cchādan* [S.], m. **1.** covering. **2.** a covering.

आच्छादित *ā-cchādit* [S.], adj. **1.** covered; shaded; protected. **2.** concealed.

आछ- *āch-* [*ākṣeti*], v.i. Brbh. Av. = अछ-.

आज *āj* [*adya*], adv. **1.** today. **2.** at this time, now. — ~ का, adj. today's; recent; modern, contemporary. ~ के दिन, adv. this day, today. ~ तक, adv. until today, until now; as yet. ~ दिन को, adv. today; this afternoon. ~ शाम को, adv. this evening. – आज-कल, adv. nowadays; recently, of late; in a few day's time; today or tomorrow. आज-कल करना, or बताना, colloq. to procrastinate; to evade, to prevaricate. आज-कल का, adv. = ~ का, 2., 3. आज-कल में, adv. these days; soon, shortly. आज-कल लगना, death to draw near.

आजन्म *ā-janm* [S.], adj. existing from birth, enduring lifelong.

आज़माइश *āzmāiś* [P. *āzmā'iś*], f. test, trial; examination; assay (of a standing crop). — ~ करना, to test, &c.

आज़माइशी *āzmāiśī* [P. *āzmā'iśī*], adj. testing, investigatory, probing; experimental.

आज़माई *āzmāī* [P. *āzmā'ī*], f. = आज़माइश.

आज़माना *āzmānā* [cf. P. *āzmā*, pres. stem], v.t. **1.** to test, to try; to examine. **2.** to try conclusions with (a person).

आज़मूदा *āzmūdā* [P. *āzmūda*], adj. inv. tested, tried, proved.

आजा *ājā* [*āryaka-*¹], m. paternal grandfather. — आजा-गुरु, m. (one's) guru's guru.

आज़ाद *āzād* [P. *āzād*], adj. **1.** free, unrestrained; independent (a country). **2.** liberated, released. **3.** carefree, light-hearted. — आज़ाद-ख़याल, adj. free-thinking; of independent mind.

आज़ादगी *āzādgī*, f. = आज़ादी.

आज़ादी *āzādī* [P. *āzādī*], f. **1.** freedom; independence. **2.** release, deliverance; discharge; emancipation.

आज़ार *āzār* [P. *āzār*], m. **1.** sickness, disease. **2.** trouble, distress.

आजिज़ *ājiz* [A. *'ājiz*], adj. **1.** helpless; exhausted; overcome. ***2.** baffled, frustrated. **3.** despairing. **4.** submissive, humble. — ~ करना, to make helpless, &c. ~ आना, or रहना, to be helpless (against, से); to be unequal (to), to fall short; to despair (of).

आजिज़ी *ājizī* [P. *'ājizī*], f. **1.** helplessness, &c. (see आजिज़). **2.** humility. — ~ करना, to make entreaty (to, से). ~ से, adv. with humility.

आजी *ājī* [*āryikā-*], f. reg. paternal grandmother.

आजीवन *ā-jīvan* [S.], adj. lifelong.

आजीविका *ā-jīvikā* [S.], f. means of subsistence; livelihood.

आजू-बाजू *ājū-bājū* [cf. P. *bāzū*], adv. round about, about, nearby.

आज्ञप्ति *ā-jñăpti* [S.], f. an order, decree.

आज्ञा *ā-jñā* [S.], f. **1.** command, order; rule, sway, writ. **2.** commandment, precept. **3.** permission, leave. — ~ करना, to command; to rule; to give an order (for, की); to carry out an order. ~ देना, id., 3.; to dismiss, to allow to leave. ~ माँगना, to ask for permission. ~ लेना, to ask for and receive permission. ~ से, adv. in accordance with an order. (आपकी) जैसी ~, adv. as, or however, (you) wish. – आज्ञाकारक, adj. & m. commanding, &c.; a commander; ruler. °-कारिता, f. obedience to orders, ready compliance. °-कारी, adj. & m. obedient; a servant. आज्ञाधीन [°*ā*+*a*°], adj. amenable to authority, tractable. आज्ञानुसार [°*ā*+*a*°], adv. in accordance with orders. आज्ञा-पत्र, m. written order, or authority; edict; pass, warrant. आज्ञापालक, adj. & m. having regard for orders, obedient; a servant. °-पालन, m. carrying out orders, obedience; discipline. आज्ञा-भंग, m. breaking an order, disobedience; insubordination. °ई, adj. & m. disobedient, &c.; a disobedient person. आज्ञार्थ [°*ā*+*a*°], adj. & m. = next. °अक, adj. & m. *gram.* imperative. आज्ञासूचक, adj. *gram.* imperative.

आज्ञान *ā-jñān* [S.], m. perception.

आज्ञापक *ā-jñāpak* [S.], adj. & m. **1.** adj. commanding. **2.** m. commander, lord, master.

आज्ञापित *ā-jñāpit* [S.], adj. ordered, enjoined (a person, or a task).

आज्ञ *ājñă* [S.], m. poet. *ghī* (as used in a sacrifice).

आटना *āṭnā* [*aṭṭ-*¹], v.t. & v.i. **1.** v.t. = अटाना. **2.** to fill full. **3.** v.i. = अटना.

आटा *āṭā* [*ārta-*²], m. flour, meal; a substance of floury consistency. — ~ करना, to grind, to pound, to reduce to powder. ~ गीला करना, to moisten and leaven flour, to make dough. ग़रीबी में ~ गीला होना, colloq. to be plunged into increased difficulties or trouble. आटे में नमक, or नून, as much as gives flavour to flour: a little, a pinch. आटे में नमक बराबर, like salt in flour: like a drop in the ocean. – आटा-दाल, f. flour and lentils; fig. daily bread. आटे-दाल का भाव, m. fig. the way of the world; आटे-दाल का भाव मालूम होना, to know, or to learn, how hard life is; to know the ways of the world.

आटोप *āṭop* [S.: w. *ṭoppa-*¹, or H. *ṭopnā*], m. **1.** covering. **2.** pomp, show.

आठ *āṭh* [*aṣṭā*], adj. eight. — ~ ~ आँसू रोना, to shed floods of tears. आठों पहर, adv. eight watches: twenty-four hours a day, day and night. – आठ-अठारह होना, to be in disorder; to be scattered, dispersed; to be confused, perplexed; to be disturbed, distressed.

आड *āḍ* [*āḍi-*², f.], ? m. reg. (Raj.) a ditch full of water.

आड़ *āṛ* [cf. *aḍḍ-*: ← Drav.], f. **1.** covering, screen; shelter; protection; refuge. **2.** obstruction, &c. **3.** support. **4.** chock (for wheels). **5.** an ornament or decoration (worn on the forehead by women): an elongated spangle, or transverse marking. — ~ देना (को), to give shelter (to). ~ पकड़ना, or लेना, to take shelter. ~ में, adv. under cover (of, की); in ambush; under pretext or pretence (of); across, athwart, transversely. ~ में आना, to come in the way (of, की), to bar the way; to conceal oneself. – आड़बंद [P. *-band*], m. reg. (W.) the knot tying a loin-cloth; a tightly tied loin-cloth.

आडंबर *āḍambar* [S.], m. a kind of drum: **1.** ostentation, show. **2.** pretension, arrogance. — ~ करना, or बढ़ाना, to make, or to foist, pretensions; to be ostentatious, &c.

आडंबरी *āḍambărī* [S.], adj. **1.** ostentatious. **2.** pretentious, arrogant.

आड़ना *āṛnā* [**aḍḍ-*: ← Drav.], v.t. **1.** to stop, to check; to obstruct. **2.** to support, to prop. **3.** to shelter. **4.** to forbid. **5.** to put in pawn. — आड़े आना, to serve as support; to come in aid.

आड़ा *āṛā* [**aḍḍa-*: ← Drav.], adj. **1.** transverse, oblique, diagonal; crooked. **2.** horizontal. **3.** causing obstruction; interposed. — ~, or आड़े, आना, to come between; to obstruct, to hinder (one, or sthg., के: from or in, में); to shield (one, के). ~, or आड़े, पड़ना, id. आड़ी करना, or डालना, to obstruct; to oppose, to thwart (one, की). आड़े वक़्त, adv. in time of difficulty, adversity. आड़े हाथ, or हाथों, लेना, to fold in the arms (obs.): to embrace, to clutch; to overcome (as in wrestling); to speak with emphasis (sc. gesticulating): to give a good talking to, to rebuke. आड़े होना, to become crooked or bent; to bend oneself (over). – आड़ा-टेढ़ा, adj. id. आड़ा-तिरछा, adj. cross, peevish; displeased.

[1]**आड़ी** *āṛī* [cf. H. *āṛ*], m. a fellow-member of a team.

[2]**आड़ी** *āṛī* [? cf. H. *āṛnā*], f. *Pl. HŚS.* a kind of musical rhythm (*tāl*) in which certain beats are brought out fully.

[3]**आड़ी** *āṛī* [*āṭi-, āḍi-*], f. a coot.

आड़ी-टेढ़ी *āṛī-ṭeṛhī* [cf. H. *āṛā, ṭeṛhā*], f. **1.** obstinacy. **2.** crossness.

आड़ू *āṛū* [**āḍu-*], m. a peach. — ~ बुख़ारा, m. a large kind of plum (cf. [2]आलू).

[1]**आढ़** *āṛh*, f. *Pl. HŚS.* a kind of fish.

[2]**आढ़** *āṛh*, f. Brbh. ? a hidden movement; dissembling.

आढ़त *āṛhat* [cf. *ādhāpayati*; MIA **ādhapta-*], f. **1.** an agency, brokerage business. **2.** warehouse (esp. for grain). **3.** goods held by an agent. **4.** agent's commission, brokerage.

आढ़तिया *aṛhatiyā* [cf. H. *āṛhat*], m. a broker, agent (esp. in grain) working on commission.

आढ़ा *āṛhā* [*āḍhaka-*], reg. (Bihar) a measure of grain (16 cups).

आढ़े *āṛhe* [**āḍhiya-* or *āḍhya-*], adj. pl. hon. Av. rich, respected.

आढ्य *āḍhyă* [S.], adj. chiefly in comp. rich in, abounding in. — धनाढ्य, adj. wealthy.

आणविक *āṇăvik* [S.], adj. atomic; molecular.

आतंक *ā-taṅk* [S.], m. **1.** apprehension; fear; awe. **2.** terror. — ~ दिखाना (को), to overawe, to intimidate; to make fearful. ~ जमाना, or बैठाना (पर), to establish, or to inspire, fear or awe (in). – आतंकवाद, m. terrorism. °ई, adj. & m. terrorist; a terrorist.

आतंकित *ā-taṅkit* [S.], adj. **1.** apprehensive; fearful; awe-struck. **2.** terror-stricken.

आत *āt*, m. the custard-apple (= सीताफल).

-आत् *-āt* [S.: an abl. case ending], suffix (forms some adverbial expressions of cause, e.g. दैवात्, by chance or fate; दुर्भाग्यवशात्, by misfortune).

आततायी *ā-tătāyī* [S.], m. one whose bow is drawn: **1.** one intent on violence: a dangerous criminal (as a murderer, poisoner, incendiary). **2.** a tyrant; oppressor.

आतप *ā-tap* [S.], m. heat of the sun; burning heat.

आतम *ātam*, Brbh. Av. (chiefly in comp.) = आत्मा.

आतश *ātaś*, f. = आतिश.

आता *ātā*, m. *Pl.* = आत.

आतिथेय *ātitheyă* [S.], adj. & m. **1.** adj. proper for a guest. **2.** attentive to a guest. **3.** m. a host.

आतिथ्य *ātithyă* [S.], m. hospitality. — ~ करना, to show hospitality (to, का). – आतिथ्यकारी, adj. hospitable. आतिथ्य सत्कार, m. the forms of hospitality.

आतिश *ātiś* [P. *ātiś*], f. **1.** fire, flame. **2.** heat. — ~ का परकाला, m. a spark; a flame; fig. an active and energetic person. – आतिश-ख़ाना, m. a fireplace; fire temple. आतिशदान [P. *-dān*], m. a fireplace; grate; brazier (as for roasting corn). आतिशबाज़ [P. *-bāz*], m. a maker of fireworks. °ई, f. a firework. आतिशमिज़ाज, m. of fiery temperament.

आतिशक *ātiśak* [P. *ātiśak*], f. venereal disease, syphilis.

आतिशी *ātiśī* [P. *ātiśī*], adj. **1.** having to do with fire; fiery. **2.** heat-resistant. — ~ शीशा, m. a burning glass; magnifying glass.

आती-पाती *ātī-pātī* [cf. H. *ānā, pānā*], f. a game similar to hide-and-seek.

आतुर *ā-tur* [S.], adj. **1.** afflicted, distressed; desirous (of, को, के लिए). **2.** restless, impatient; hasty; quick, active.

आतुरता *ā-turătā* [S.], f. **1.** affliction, &c.; keen desire. **2.** restlessness, impatience, &c.

आतुरताई *ā-turătāī* [cf. H. *āturtā*], f. Brbh. = आतुरता.

आत्म- *ātm-*, in comp. see s.v. आत्मा.

-आत्मक *-ātmak* [S.], adj. formant. having the nature or character of (e.g. निश्चयात्मक, decisive).

आत्मनेपद *ātmanepad* [S.], m. *gram.* middle voice.

आत्मा *ātmā* [S.], f. (in cpds., आत्म-) **1.** soul, spirit; the self, the individual; the mind, the heart. **2.** the ultimate being. **3.** the body. — ~ की आँच, f. mother love. ~ ठंडी होना, a longing or craving to be satisfied. ~ मसोसना, to suffer distress; to repress wishes or longings. ~ में आग लगी होना, to feel pangs (of hunger, love). ~ सताना, to mortify the body; to inflict pain (on, की). – आत्मकथा, f. an autobiography. °-कथात्मक, adj. autobiographical. आत्मकहानी, f. id. आत्मगत, adj. internal; subjective. आत्मगौरव, m. self-respect, self-esteem. आत्मग्लानि, f. languor of spirit: depression. आत्मघात, m. suicide. आत्मघात करना, to commit suicide. °ई, adj. & m. committing suicide; a suicide. आत्मघोष, adj. & m. voicing one's own praises: one who sings his own praises. आत्मचरित, m. = आत्मकथा. आत्मचिंतन, m. self-analysis; deep thought. आत्मचेतना, f. self-consciousness. आत्मज, adj. & m. born from or begotten by oneself; one's own offspring. °जा, f. आत्मजात, m. id. आत्मजीवनी, f. = आत्मकथा. आत्मज्ञान, m. self-knowledge; knowledge of the soul or the supreme spirit. आत्मतुष्टि, f. self-satisfaction. आत्मत्याग, m. self-sacrifice. °ई, adj. self-sacrificing. आत्मनिर्भर, adj. self-sufficient; independent. आत्मनिवेदन, m. self-sacrifice; self-dedication. आत्मनिष्ठ, adj. concerned with the self (and its relation to the ultimate being); subjective. °ता, f. concern with the self; subjectivity. आत्मपीड़न, m. self-torment. आत्मप्रशंसा, f. self-praise. आत्मबल, m. spiritual strength; strength of character. आत्मबलिदान, m. self-sacrifice. आत्मबुद्धि, f. = आत्मज्ञान. आत्मबोध, m. = आत्मज्ञान. आत्मभरित, adj. self-sufficient. आत्मभू, adj. & m. self-born or mind-born: a title of Brahmā, Viṣṇu, Śiva, Kāmdev; a son. आत्मरक्षण, m. defending oneself, = next. °-रक्षा, f. self-defence. आत्मवंचक, adj. deceiving oneself. °-वंचना, f. self-deception. आत्मविचार, m. reflection on the soul and its relation to the ultimate being; self-examination. आत्मविद्या, f. knowledge of the soul and its relation to the ultimate being. आत्मविश्लेषण, m. self-analysis. आत्मविश्वास, m. self-confidence. °ई, adj. आत्मविस्मृत, adj. forgetful of self, oblivious to self. °इ, f. आत्मशक्ति, f. strength of mind; inner or spiritual strength. आत्मशासन, m. autonomy. °-प्राप्त, adj. having achieved autonomy, independent. आत्मश्लाघा, f. self-praise, egoism; vanity. आत्मसंयम, m. self-control; restraint. °ई, adj. आत्मसंवेदन, m. = आत्मज्ञान. आत्मसंदेह, m. self-doubt, lack of self-confidence. आत्मसंस्कार, m. self-improvement. आत्मसमर्पण, m. devoting oneself (to an aim); entrusting, or surrendering oneself. °-समर्पित, adj. utterly devoted (to), &c. आत्मसम्मान, m. self-respect. आत्मसात्, adj. absorbed, assimilated; appropriated. आत्मसात् करना, to absorb, &c. आत्म-सिद्ध, adj. self-evident. °इ, f. realisation of the self: attainment to release from rebirth. आत्मसुख, m. one's own pleasure or happiness. आत्महत्या, f. suicide. आत्महत्या करना, to commit suicide. आत्महन्, m. a suicide (person). आत्महिंसा, f. suicide. आत्महित, m. benefiting self; one's own benefit. आत्माधिक [°*ma*+*a*°], adj. more or dearer than self, or than life. आत्माभिमान [°*ma*+*a*°], m. self-respect; conceit. °ई, adj. आत्माराम [°*ma*+*ā*°], m. one rejoicing in knowledge of the self, esp. a yogī; the soul; the supreme being. आत्मार्थी [°*ma*+*a*°], adj. self-interested. आत्मावलंबन [°*ma*+*a*°], m. self-support, independence. आत्मावलंबी, adj.

आत्मिक *ātmik* [S.], adj. **1.** having to do with the self, or with the soul. **2.** spiritual.

आत्मिकता *ātmikătā* [S.], f. intimate nature, intimacy.

आत्मिकी *ātmikī* [S.], f. study of the psyche.

आत्मीय *ātmīyă* [S.], adj. & m. **1.** adj. one's own; special. **2.** related. **3.** close, intimate. **4.** m. a relative. **5.** a close friend.

आत्मीयता *ātmīyătā* [S.], f. **1.** relationship. **2.** feelings of kinship or intimacy.

आदत *ādat* [A. *'āda*: P. *'ādat*], f. **1.** habit. **2.** manner; knack. **3.** custom. — ~ करना, to make a habit (of, की). ~ पकड़ना, to acquire a habit. ~ पड़ना, or लगना, a habit to be acquired (by, को); the manner or knack (of, की) to be acquired (by); to be used (to, की).

आदतन *ādatan* [A. *'ādatan̲*], adv. from habit, habitually.

आदती *ādătī* [P. *'ādatī*], adj. customary, habitual.

आदम *ādam* [A. *ādam*], m. **1.** Adam. **2.** in comp. man. — आदमक़द, adj. of a man's height. आदमख़ोर [P. *-k̲h̲or*], m. a cannibal. °ई, f. cannibalism.

आदमियत *ādmiyat* [A. *ādamīya*: P. *ādamiyat*], f. **1.** humanity. **2.** compassion. **3.** civilisation. — ~ उठ जाना, to be bereft of (one's) humanity;

to behave in a cruel, unreasoning or unworthy way. ~ पकड़ना, to acquire civilisation; to recover (one's) reason, or senses. ~ में लाना, to civilise; to bring to reason, or to (one's) senses. ~ सीखना, = ~ पकड़ना. ~ सिखाना, = ~ में लाना.

आदमी *ādmī* [A. *ādamī*], m. **1.** a descendant of Adam: a man; a person; an adult (male). **2.** mankind. **3.** a husband. **4.** a servant. **5.** member of a team, crew, group. — ~ पीछे, adv. per man, individually. ~ बनाना, to educate; to civilise. ~ होना, to attain to manhood; to become a worthy human being, to become civilised.

आदमीयत *ādmīyat*, f. = आदमियत.

आदर *ā-dar* [S.], m. **1.** respect, esteem; honour; reverence. **2.** respectful treatment; notice, attention; deference. — ~ करना, to show respect, or attention, &c. (to, का). ~ देना (को), = ~ करना. ~ पाना, to meet with respect, or attention, &c.; to receive honours. ~ मिलना (को), id. ~ से, or के साथ, adv. respectfully, with honour, &c. – आदरपूर्वक, adv. respectfully, &c. आदरप्रदर्शक, adj. honorific. आदर-भाव, m. = ~. आदर-सत्कार, m. respectful treatment; fitting hospitality. आदर-सत्कार करना (का), to treat with respect, or with all due hospitality. आदर-सम्मान, m. = ~.

आदर- *ā-dar-* [cf. *ādara-*], v.t. Av. = आदर करना.

आदरणीय *ā-darăṇīyă* [S.], adj. to be respected, esteemed; revered.

आदरा *ādrā*, m. = आर्द्रा.

आदर्श *ā-darś* [S.], m. & adj. **1.** m. a mirror. **2.** sthg. which illustrates: a commentary. **3.** an exemplar; prototype. ***4.** an ideal. ***5.** adj. ideal; classic. — आदर्शवाद, m. idealism. °ई, adj. & m. idealistic; an idealist. आदर्शीकरण, m. idealisation. आदर्शोन्मुख [°*śa*+*u*°], adj. envisaging an ideal: idealistic.

आदर्शित *ā-darśit* [S.], adj. shown, pointed out; presented as an ideal.

आदर्शीकरण *ā-darśīkaraṇ* [cf. H. *ādarś*], m. idealisation.

आदा *ādā* [*ārdraka-*], m. reg. fresh (undried) ginger.

आदान *ā-dān* [S.], m. **1.** taking, receiving, accepting. **2.** receipt, acceptance (as of taxes, fees). — आदान-प्रदान, m. taking and giving: interchange, exchange.

आदाब *ādāb* [A. *ādāb*], m. & interj. **1.** m. good manners, courtesy. **2.** courteous greeting. **3.** interj. = ~ अर्ज़. — ~ अर्ज़ [A. *'arẓ*], interj. greetings! good morning!, &c. ~ अर्ज़ करना, to greet; to take (one's) leave. ~ करना, or बजाना, to greet with due courtesy, or respect; to use complimentary expressions; to acknowledge (one) as superior; to take one's leave.

आदि *ādi* [S.], m. & adj. **1.** m. beginning; origin. **2.** adj. first, prior; primary; original. **3.** primeval; early; primitive. **4.** pre-eminent. **5.** in comp. beginning with, and so on. इत्यादि, etcetera. **6.** adv. etcetera. — आदि-कर्ता, m. inv. creator. आदि-कवि, m. the first poet: a title of Vālmīki (to whom the Sanskrit *Rāmāyaṇa* is attributed). आदि-कारण, m. primary cause. आदि-काल, m. an ancient, or early period. °ईन, adj. आदि-काव्य, m. the first poem: a title of the *Rāmāyana*. आदि-ग्रंथ, m. the first book: a title given to the main scripture of the Sikhs. आदि-पुरुष, m. the first man; a title of Viṣṇu; *philos.* the impersonal *brahman*. आदिवासी, m. & adj. original inhabitant: a member of an indigenous tribe (as opposed to later settlers); indigenous, aboriginal.

आदिक *ādik* [S.], adj. **1.** having to do with the first, or the beginning (see आदि). **2.** beginning with, from the first onwards (as of the individuals of a group): e.g. सनकादिक, m. pl. Av. Sanak and the other (brothers).

आदित्य *ādityă* [S.], m. *mythol.* **1.** one of various deities, sons of Aditi; a deity. **2.** the sun. — आदित्य-मंडल, m. the sphere or region of the sun; the sun's orbit.

आदिम *ādim* [S.], adj. **1.** first, prior: original. **2.** primitive.

आदिल *ādil* [A. *'ādil*], adj. Av. just, upright.

[1]**आदी** *ādī* [A. *'ādī*], adj. **1.** accustomed (to, का). **2.** habitual. — ~ करना, to accustom (to, का). ~ होना, to be or to become accustomed (to); to be familiar (with: as with a subject).

[2]**आदी** *ādī* [*ārdraka-*], f. ginger (cf. आदा).

आदेश *ā-deś* [S.], m. **1.** pointing out, instruction. ***2.** order, directive; instruction; injunction, writ; mandate. **3.** (आदेस.) respectful greeting, or farewell. — आदेश-देय, adj. payable on demand. आदेशपूर्ण, adj. instructive, edifying.

आदेशक *ā-deśak* [S.], adj. directing, instructing, &c.

आदेशन *ā-deśan* [S.], m. directing, instructing, &c.

आदेशी *ā-deśī* [S.], m. one who directs, &c.; a fortune-teller.

आद्य *ādyă* [S.], adj. = आदि, 2.-4.

आधा *ādhā* [*ardha-*[2]], adj. & m. **1.** adj. half. **2.** m. a half. — ~ करना, to halve; to cut off half (of, का), to reduce by half. ~ तीतर ~ बटेर, half partridge, half quail: neither fish nor fowl.

~ होना, to be or to become half (of, का); to grow thin, to waste away. आधी बात कहना, to tell half a story, to keep sthg. back. आधी बात न पूछना, not to take the slightest notice (of a person: से). आधी रात, f. midnight. आधे आध, adv. half and half; in two (equal parts). आधे कान सुनना, to lend half an ear (to sthg. being said). आधे पेट, adv. half fed. आधे पेट खाना, not to have enough to eat. – आधा-सीसी, f. a migraine. आधों-आध, adv. = आधे आध.

आधान *ā-dhān* [S.], m. **1.** placing, depositing; 19c. conception. **2.** receiving. **3.** a receptacle. **4.** deposit, surety. — कर-आधान, m. taxation.

आधार *ā-dhār* [S.], m. **1.** base, foundation. **2.** basis; premise. ~ पर, on the basis (of, के). **3.** support, prop; object (as of a remark); fig. supporter, patron. **4.** a hollow (for water) made round the foot of a tree; water-channel. — आधारभूत, adj. having a base; well-grounded; basic. आधारहीन, adj. baseless.

आधारित *ā-dhārit* [S.], adj. based, supported, &c. — ~ करना, to base, &c. (on, पर, के ऊपर).

-आधारी *-ā-dhārī* [S.], adj. & m. formant. supported by, living on (e.g. दूध-आधारी, m. one who lives on milk).

¹आधि *ā-dhi* [S.], f. (m., *Pl.*) **1.** anxious thought; distress. **2.** expectation.

²आधि *ā-dhi*, f. (m., *Pl.*) *Pl. HŚS.* **1.** pawn, pledge. **2.** site, location.

आधिकारिक *ādhikārik* [S.], adj. having authority, official.

आधिक्य *ādhikyă* [S.], m. **1.** excess, surplus. **2.** abundance.

आधिपत्य *ādhipatyă* [S.], m. **1.** lordship, governorship; authority, control. **2.** supremacy, sovereignty; rule. **3.** control, mastery (as of an instrument). **4.** *mil.* occupation.

आधीन *ādhīn*, adj. = अधीन.

आधुनिक *ādhunik* [S.], adj. modern; of the present day; new, recent.

आधुनिकतम *ādhunikătam* [S.], adj. most recent, up to the minute; contemporary.

आधुनिकता *ādhunikătā* [S.], f. modernity. — आधुनिकतावाद, m. modernism. °ई, adj. & m.

आधुनीकरण *ādhunīkaraṇ*, [S.], m. modernisation.

आध्यात्मिक *ādhyātmik* [S.], adj. spiritual.

आध्यात्मिकता *ādhyātmikătā* [S.], f. spirituality.

¹आन *ān* [*āṇi-*], f. boundary: **1.** way, manner; rule or custom. **2.** honour, reputation; respectability; modesty. **3.** dignity, self-respect; pride. **4.** grace, elegance. — ~ तोड़ना, to infringe a custom (of, की); to abandon self-respect. ~ पर मर मिटना, to die for one's honour. ~ फेरना, to vaunt one's own merits. ~ मानना, to recognise the superiority (of, की); to yield (to, की, के सामने). ~ में आना, to behave modestly, to feel shyness. ~ रखना, to maintain one's honour, &c.; to keep self-respect. – आन-तान, f. pride; stubbornness. आन-बान, f. way, manner; = ~, 4., 2.; splendour, pomp; pride. °-शान, f. id., 3. आन-मान, m. respect, honour, consideration.

²आन *ān* [*ājñā-*], f. **1.** vow, oath; promise. **2.** forswearing: a promise not to do sthg. **3.** sthg. forbidden. — ~ तोड़ना, to break a vow. ~ मानना, to swear allegiance (to, की). ~ रखना, to keep a vow. तुझे क्या उसके घर जाने की ~ है? have you sworn not to go to his house? तुम्हें भगवान की ~ है ..., as God is your oath: I (or we) beseech you to ...

³आन *ān* [*anya-*], adj. **1.** other. **2.** second.

⁴आन *ān* [A. *ān*], f. moment, instant. — ~ कान में [← next], adv. in the space of a moment, forthwith. ~ की ~, adv. id. पल में ~, adv. id.

⁵आन *ān* [*āpayati*, w. *ānayati*], abs. poet. and U. = आ, आकर.

¹-आन *-ān*, suffix (forms m. and f. nouns from verb stems, e.g. उड़ान, f. flight).

²-आन *-ān* [P. *-ān*], suffix (forms plurals, e.g. मालिकान, m. masters). U.

आनंद *ā-nand* [S.], m. **1.** joy, delight; bliss. **2.** enjoyment; contentment. — ~ आना, or मिलना (को), to feel delight (in, में), to be delighted (to). ~ करना (से), to rejoice (at); to enjoy. ~ के तार बजाना, to sound the strings of joy: to enjoy oneself greatly, to revel. ~ मनाना to be joyful, to celebrate; (with का) to celebrate (an occasion). ~ लूटना, or लेना (का), to enjoy to the full; to revel (in). ~ से होना, to be very well, to be flourishing. — आनंद-घन, adj. compact of, or instinct with bliss. आनंद-पट, m. robe of joy: wedding attire (of bride). आनंदप्रद, adj. joy-giving; conducive to bliss. आनंद-बधाई, f. joyful celebrations; congratulations. आनंद-बधावा, m. id. आनंद-मंगल, m. joyfulness; revelry; flourishing state. आनंदमय, adj. blissful, blessed. आनंदवाद, m. the theory of attainment to spiritual bliss after death; hedonism. आनंदातिरेक [°*da*+*a*°], ecstasy.

आनंद- *ānand-* [ad. *ānandayati*: w. H. *ānand*], v.i. Brbh. to feel joy, &c.

आनंदता *ā-nandătā* [S.], f. *Pl.* state of joy or bliss.

आनंदित *ā-nandit* [S.], adj. joyful, delighted; blissful.

आनंदी *ā-nandī* [S.], adj. & m. **1.** adj. joyful, &c. **2.** m. a happy or cheerful person.

आन- *ān-* [*ānayati*], v.i. **1.** reg. to bring. **2.** chiefly reg. to come.

आनक *ānak* [S.], m. Brbh. a large military drum, kettledrum.

आनन *ānan* [S.], m. **1.** face. **2.** mouth.

आनन-फ़ानन *ānan-fānan* [A. *ānan-fānan*], adv. in the space of a moment, forthwith. — ~ में, adv. id.

आनर्त *ā-nart* [S.], m. a dancing-room.

[1]**आना** *ānā* [**āṇvaka-*], m. **1.** an anna (a coin equal to one sixteenth of a rupee; obs. since 1975). **2.** a sixteenth part or share. — पंद्रह आने, adv. fifteen annas (out of sixteen): to a great extent. सोलहों आने, adv. (all) sixteen annas: completely, one hundred per cent.

[2]**आना** *ānā* [*āpayati; āgata-*], v.i. **1.** to come; to approach; to arrive; to reach (a place, or point). **2.** to enter; to appear. **3.** to be acquired (skill, knowledge: by, को). मुझे हिंदी आती है, I know Hindi. **4.** to be perceived or felt (by, को: thoughts, emotions). मुझे ख़याल आया, the thought struck me. **5.** to come to pass, to befall. **6.** to grow, to develop (as crops, fruit); to come into vogue (a word or usage); to be inflamed (as a boil). **7.** to take on a form or guise. बड़ा आया दफ़्तर में काम करनेवाला! what airs you've assumed now you work in an office! **8.** to rise, to overflow. **9.** to sit well (on, में), to fit. **10.** to beseem, to grace (one, को). **11.** to be intent (on, पर). **12.** to issue, or to be voided. **13.** to be completed, perfected (a dish; a work). **14.** to be contained, held (in, में); fig. to be taken in, deceived (by). **15.** to be obtained; to be purchased (for a price: में, or को). **16.** m. coming, arrival. — आ कूदना or धमकना, to burst in (as into a room). आ टपकना [f. Engl.], to drop in. आ निकलना, to appear unexpectedly, to turn up. आ पड़ना (पर), to come down (on), to descend (upon); to fall (upon), to attack; to befall (misfortune); to be acquired; to appear; to take up (one's) quarters or station. आ पहुँचना, to arrive (at); to make one's way (to). आ बनना, to happen (to, पर), to come upon, to afflict (one). आ मिलना, to meet (with, से), to unite (with); to visit. आ रहना, to fall down (from, से); to fall in (a building); to come and live (in); to befall (a lasting misfortune). आ लगना (पर), to halt (at a due stopping-place); to moor; to be impending, to come (a time); to beset, to fall (upon). आइए, interj. come!; come on! (a request for cooperation). आए दिन, adv. (during) these days, at the present time. – आई-गई बात, f. a dead issue. आना-जाना, to pass to and fro; to circulate (vehicles); m. circulation; communication; contact, intercourse.

[3]**आना-** *ānā-* [*-ăpayati*], suffix (forms transitive verbs having causative force from intransitives or from other transitives; also denominative verbs, many esp. colloq., or reg. or poet.; e.g. जलाना, to burn; पढ़ाना, to teach; कराना, to cause to be done; सुस्ताना, to rest; ठंडाना, to grow cool.

[4]**-आना** *-ānā* [P. *-āna*], suffix (forms adjectives, mostly invariable, and nouns from nouns, e.g. मरदाना, male; राजपूताना, m. Rajasthan; रोज़ाना, adv. daily).

आनाकानी *ānākānī* [conn. *ākarṇayati*], f. **1.** turning a deaf ear; not acknowledging (one); showing reserve. **2.** overlooking, conniving. **3.** excuse, pretence. **4.** Brbh. whispering. — ~ करना, to turn a deaf ear (to, की); to overlook, to disregard; to make excuses.

-आनी *-ānī* [S.], suffix (forms feminines for m. nouns expressing occupation or status, (e.g. क्षत्राणी, wife of a kṣatriya; देवरानी, junior sister-in-law).

आनुपातिक *ānupātik* [S.], adj. proportional.

आनुपूर्व *ānupūrv* [S.], m. regular order, sequence.

आनुपूर्वी *ānupūrvī* [S.], adj. & f. **1.** adj. in regular order, successive. **2.** f. = आनुपूर्व.

आनुवंशिक *ānuvaṃśik* [S.], adj. hereditary.

आनुषंगिक *ānuṣaṅgik* [S.], adj. **1.** concomitant, connected; inherent. **2.** consequent (upon); incidental (to).

आनेयार *āneyār*, m. *Pl.* the time given to farm work in the hot season (viz. dawn till noon).

[1]**आप** *āp* [*ātman-*], pron. **1.** self, -self: oneself; myself, &c.; adv. by oneself. **2.** hon. you. **3.** hon. he, she, they. — ~ ~, pron. & adv. each one; each by or for himself. ~ ~ में, adv. mutually; among one another. ~ से ~, adv. of one's own accord; automatically, without more ado; voluntarily; spontaneously, without cause; untended, working automatically (a machine). ~ ही ~, adv. id.; quite alone, on one's own. – आप-बीती, f. what has befallen oneself, the story of one's own experiences. आपरूप, adj. & pron. having a (prestigious) form of one's own; of the form or nature of the absolute; iron. one's good self.

[2]**आप** *āp* [S.], m. Brbh. water.

आपत् *ā-pat*, f. misfortune, disaster (cf. आपत्ति, 1). — आपत्-काल, m. a time of disaster, or of distress; an emergency. °ईन, adj.

आपत्ति *ā-patti* [S.], f. **1.** a happening: misfortune; adversity. ***2.** an objection; a query. — आपत्तिजनक, adj. objectionable.

आपत्य *āpatyă* [S.], adj. **1.** having to do with offspring; parental. **2.** *gram.* patronymic.

आपद् *ā-pad* [S.], m. misfortune, disaster (cf. आपत्ति, 1). — आपद्-ग्रस्त, adj. beset by disaster, afflicted by misfortune.

आपदा *ā-pădā* [S.], f. **1.** misfortune, disaster (cf. आपत्ति, 1). **2.** distress.

आपन *āpan*, adj. Brbh. Av. = अपना.

आपनिक *ā-panik* [S.], m. *Pl. HŚS.* an emerald.

आपनौ *āpnau*, adj. Brbh. = अपना.

आपन्न *ā-pann* [S.], adj. afflicted (cf. आपद्).

आपराधिक *āpărādhik* [S.], adj. criminal.

आपस *āpas* [cf. *ātman-*], f. kindred, brotherhood; intimate group. — ~ का, adj. private, family; mutual. ~ में, adv. among themselves; mutually; reciprocally; in common; in concert. ~ में रहना, to live in harmony; to live as man and wife. – आपसदारी [P. *-dārī*], f. kinship, relationship. आपसदारी का, adj. having to do with a partic. group: mutual, collective.

आपा *āpā* [*ātman-*], pron. self, oneself, &c. — ~ खोना, = ~ तजना; = आपे से बाहर होना. ~ तजना, to sacrifice one's self, one's self-interest, or pride. ~ सँभालना, to take charge of oneself: to reach years of discretion. आपे में आना, to come to one's senses (as after a fit of anger); to become sober; to recover from exhaustion; to recover consciousness. आपे से बाहर करना, to drive (one) to distraction. आपे से बाहर होना, to be beside oneself (with emotion). – आपा-धापी, f. self-seeking; competition (among, में); free-for-all.

-आपा *-āpā*, m. suffix. = -पा.

आपात *ā-pāt* [S.], m. falling upon: **1.** attack; effect. **2.** an emergency.

आपानक *ā-pānak* [S.], m. a drinking-bout.

आपूर्ति *ā-pūrti* [S.], f. supply.

आपेक्षिक *āpêkṣik* [S.], adj. relative.

आप्त *āpt* [S.] reached, obtained: — आप्तवाक्य, adj. whose speech is fit or true: speaking credibly, trustworthy.

आप्रवास *ā-pra-vās* [S.], m. immigration.

आप्रवासी *ā-pra-vāsī* [S.], adj. & m. **1.** adj. immigrant; living abroad. **2.** m. an immigrant; one living abroad.

आप्लव *ā-plav* [S.], m. being bathed, or drenched.

आप्लावन *ā-plāvan* [S.], m. inundation.

आप्लावित *ā-plāvit* [S.], adj. **1.** immersed; inundated, flooded. **2.** bathed (in or by, से). **3.** drenched. **4.** flooded, overwhelmed (as by emotion, or a thought).

आप्लुत *ā-plut* [S.], adj. = आप्लावित, 2.-4.

आफ़त *āfat* [A. *āfa*: P. *āfat*], f. **1.** misfortune; disaster; trouble, turmoil. **2.** hardship, misery. — ~ आना, or टूटना, or पड़ना (पर), disaster, &c., to befall (one). ~ उठाना, to suffer misfortune, &c.; to endure misfortune, &c.; to cause trouble, disturbance. ~ का, adj. sl. damned great, the devil of a (thirst, &c.) ~ का टुकड़ा, m. = next. ~ का परकाला, m. spark of misfortune: one who brings trouble on others by his actions or attitude. ~ की पुड़िया, f. bundle of trouble: id. ~, or आफ़तें, डालना, to cause or to inflict trouble or suffering. ~ ढाना, to cause or to inflict trouble or suffering. ~ मोल लेना, to bring misfortune, &c. upon oneself needlessly. अपने सिर, or सिर पर, ~ लाना, id. – आफ़त-भरा, adj. woeful, miserable.

आफ़ताब *āftāb* [P. *āftāb*], m. the sun, sun's heat. — अफ़ताब-ज़दा [P. *-zada*], adj. inv. U. struck, or burnt by the sun. अफ़ताबरू, adj. U. glittering, blinding.

आफ़ताबा *āftābā* [P. *āftāba*, for *āb-tāba*], m. a water-pot.

आफ़ताबी *āftābī* [P. *āftābī*], adj. & f. **1.** adj. of, or like the sun. **2.** faded by the sun, yellow. **3.** f. a type of firework. **4.** a parasol; sunshade.

आफ़रीन *āfrīn* [P. *āfirīn*], interj. bravo!

आफ़ियत *āfiyat* [A. *'āfiya*: P. *'āfiyat*], f. well-being.

आब *āb* [P. *āb*], m. **1.** water; fig. alcohol. **2.** quality, purity; water (of a gem); temper (as of steel); sparkle, lustre. **3.** f. m. splendour; dignity; honour, reputation. — ~ ~ करना, to say 'water, water': (one's) neglect to be a reproach (to another). ~ उतरना, to lose lustre, to become dull; to fade; to be disgraced. ~ चढ़ाना (पर), to make bright, to polish; to temper (as steel). ~ जाना, = ~ उतरना. ~ रखना, to defend one's honour. – आबकार [P. *-kār*], m. a distiller, or seller, of alcoholic drink. °ई, f. & adj. the trade of a distiller; a distillery; liquor-shop; excise duty on alcohol; alcoholic (drink). आबगीर [P. *-gīr*], m. a water reservoir, pond, ditch; a weaver's brush (for sprinkling water on warp threads). आब-जोश, m. the juice of cooked meat, broth, gravy. आब-ताब, f. brightness; splendour; honour; majesty. आब-दस्त, m. washing (esp. after defecation); the water so used. आब-दस्त

करना, or लेना, to wash after defecation. आब-दाना, m. water and grain: food; livelihood; lot, destiny. आबदार [P. *-dār*], adj. bright; of good water (as gems) or temper (as steel). °ई, f. brightness, brilliance; sharpness (as of a sword); purity. आबरू, f. brightness of face: honour; reputation. आबरू उतारना (की), to disgrace, to dishonour; to vilify. आबरू का लागू होना, = next. आबरू के पीछे पड़ना, to be intent on ruining (one's, की) character or reputation. आबरू पैदा करना, to achieve dignity, rank, reputation. आबरू पर पानी फिरना, water to be cast on (one's, की) honour: to be dishonoured, &c. आबरू बनाना, to defend (one's, की) honour, &c. आबरू में फ़र्क़ आना, = next. आबरू में बट्टा लगना (की), to be impaired in reputation, stained in character. आबरू बिगाड़ना, or लेना, = आबरू उतारना. आब-शार [P. *-śār*], m. a waterfall. आबोहवा [P. *-o-*], f. climate; fig. atmosphere. आबे-कौसर [P. *-e-*, A. *kauṣar*], m. *mythol. isl.* the water of the river Kausar (of paradise): nectar.

आबद्ध *ā-baddh* [S.], adj. bound, constrained (as by one's word).

आबनूस *ābnūs* [P. *ābnūs*], m. ebony.

आबनूसी *ābnūsī* [P. *ābnūsī*], adj. **1.** made of ebony. **2.** black.

आबरू *ābrū*, f. see s.v. आब.

आबाद *ābād* [P. *ābād*], adj. **1.** settled (as a colony, a town); under cultivation (land). **2.** prosperous, flourishing; full, abundant. **3.** inhabited, populous. — ~ करना, to settle, to found; to cultivate (land); to build up (as a town, or a couple); to cause (the heart) to rejoice. ~ रहना, to be flourishing, or prosperous. ~ होना, = ~ रहना; to be occupied (a house); to have the prospect of children (a family).

-आबाद *-ābād* [P. *-ābād*], suffix (forms place names of settlements, e.g. इलाहाबाद, m., made populous by Allāh: Allahabad).

आबादानी *ābādānī* [P. *ābādānī*], f. **1.** a settled, or cultivated place. **2.** a prosperous, or pleasant place. **3.** prosperity. **4.** advancement, civilisation.

आबादी *ābādī* [P. *ābādī*], f. **1.** an inhabited, or settled, place. **2.** a settlement; colony, new quarter (of a town). **3.** population. **4.** prosperity.

आबी *ābī* [P. *ābī*], adj. **1.** having to do with water. **2.** aquatic. **3.** pale, watery (of colour).

आबेरवाँ *āberăvāṁ* [P. *āb-e-ravān*], m. flowing water: a fine muslin.

आबोताब *ābotāb*, f. = आब-ताब, s.v. आब.

आबोदाना *ābodānā* m. = आब-दाना, s.v. आब.

आबोहवा *ābohavā*, f. see s.v. आब.

आब्दिक *ābdik* [S.], adj. annual.

आभरण *ā-bharaṇ* [S.], m. filling: **1.** ornament, decoration. **2.** pl. jewels, jewellery. **3.** maintenance, support.

आभा *ā-bhā* [S.], f. **1.** light, splendour; beauty. **2.** gleam. **3.** tinge, nuance.

आभार *ā-bhār* [S.], m. **1.** burden; responsibility. **2.** obligation; debt; gratitude.

आभारी *ā-bhārī* [S.], adj. obliged, indebted (to, का; for, के लिए); grateful (to).

आभास *ā-bhās* [S.], m. **1.** splendour, light. **2.** appearance, likeness. **3.** false appearance or impression; semblance, shadow. **4.** suggestion, implication; inkling. **5.** intention, purpose.

आभासित *ā-bhāsit* [S.], adj. shining, bathed in light.

आभास्वर *ā-bhāsvar* [S.], adj. shining, radiant.

आभीर *ābhīr* [S.], m. **1.** a cowherd (= अहीर). **2.** *hist.* a nomadic pastoral tribe of north-west India.

आभूषण *ā-bhūṣaṇ* [S.], m. **1.** a piece of jewellery; pl. jewels (as decoration). **2.** an ornament, decoration; pl. finery.

आभूषित *ā-bhūṣit* [S.], adj. decorated, adorned.

आभोग *ā-bhog* [S.], m. **1.** enjoyment, comfort. **2.** completion: *mus.* last line of a verse (of early poetry).

आभोग्य *ā-bhogyă* [S.], adj. unfit for use, not to be used.

आमंत्रित *ā-mantrit* [S.], adj. invited (applications).

¹**आम** *ām* [*āmra-*], m. the mango tree, and its fruit. — ~ के ~, गुठली के दाम, to have the mango at the price of the stone: to kill two birds with one stone. आम खाने (से काम), या पेड़ गिनने (से)? if it's the mangoes you want, why (bother to) count the trees?: don't beat about the bush. आम-रस, m. inspissated mango juice.

²**आम** *ām* [A. *'āmm*], adj. & m. **1.** adj. common, general; everyday. **2.** ordinary. **3.** public (as a meeting, an election). **4.** m. the general population, common people. — ~ तौर पर, adv. usually; in general. ~ तौर से, adv. id. ~ देखा जाता है कि ..., it is generally observed that ... ~ में, adv. in public. – आम-फ़हम, adj. generally intelligible (as language); popular (a work).

[3]**आम** *ām* [S.], m. uncooked, undigested: constipation. — **आम-वात**, m. flatulence; constipation. **आम-शूल**, m. colic. **आमातिसार** [°*ma*+*a*°], m. dysentery. **आमान्न** [°*ma*+*a*°], m. uncooked food. **आमाशय** [°*ma*+*ā*°], m. the stomach.

आमद *āmad* [P. *āmad*], m. **1.** coming, approach, arrival. **2.** income, receipts. **3.** import, importation. — **ख़ुशामद से ~**, flattery brings financial rewards. – **आमद-ख़र्च**, m. receipts and outgoings. **आमद-रफ़्त**, coming and going; traffic, passage; way; communication, intercourse; transportation. **आमदवाला**, m. wholesaler in imported goods.

आमदनी *āmdanī* [P. *āmadanī*], f. **1.** income; revenue. **2.** proceeds, profit. **3.** imports, importation. — **आमदनी-रफ़्तनी**, f. U. turnover (of trade); imports and exports.

आमदिया *āmădiyā* [cf. H. *āmad*], m. **1.** one whose income is large. **2.** a wholesaler in imported goods.

[1]**आमन** *āman*, m. **1.** reg. the winter rice crop. **2.** *HŚS.* a field bearing only one crop per year.

[2]**आमन** *āman*, f. *Pl.* a large oval mango.

आमना-सामना *āmnā-sāmnā* [cf. H. *sāmnā*], m. **1.** confronting, confrontation. **2.** adv. opposite, facing; face to face. — **~ करना (का)**, to confront, to oppose. **आमने-सामने करना**, to bring face to face; to put side by side, to compare. **आमने-सामने का**, adj. opposite, facing.

[1]**आमनिया** *āmniyā*, f. *Pl.* land on which the winter rice crop (*āman*) is sown.

[2]**आमनिया** *āmniyā*, adj. var. /amənya/. reg. husked, cleaned (grain, &c).

आमय *āmay* [S.], m. sickness, disease.

आमर्ष *ā-marṣ* [S.], m. **1.** intolerance, envy; rancour. **2.** anger.

आमलक *āmălak* [S.], m. Brbh. Av. **1.** myrobalan (= **आँवला**). **2.** fig. sthg. small or trivial.

आमला *āmlā*, m. = **आँवला**.

आमलिका *āmălikā* [S.], f. = **इमली**.

आमात्य *āmātyă*, m. = **अमात्य**.

आमादा *āmādā* [P. *āmāda*], adj. come: **1.** prepared, ready (to, **पर**); roused, alert. **2.** disposed (to). — **~ करना**, to prepare, &c.; to arouse, to incite; to abet.

आमाल *āmāl* [A. *aʿmāl*, pl. of *ʿamal*], m. pl. U. acts, doings.

आमालक *āmālak* [S.], m. land near a mountain.

आमिल *āmil* [A. *ʿāmil*], m. Brbh. **1.** agent; executive officer, authority. 2. = **ओझा**.

आमिष *āmiṣ* [S.], m. **1.** meat. **2.** object of enjoyment; prey. — **आमिषभोजी**, adj. flesh-eating; non-vegetarian. **आमिषभोगी**, adj. bloodthirsty. **आमिष-लोलुप**, adj. eager for meat, &c.

आमीं *āmīṁ*, adv. = **आमीन**.

आमीन *āmīn* [A. *āmīn*], interj. so be it, amen. — **~ करनेवाला**, m. a yes-man.

आमुख *ā-mukh* [S.], m. preface, introduction.

आमूल *ā-mūl*, [S.], adv. from, or to, the root.

आमोख़्ता *āmokhtā* [P. *āmokhta*], adj. U. learnt.

आमोद *ā-mod* [S.], m. **1.** pleasure, amusement; diversion, pastime. **2.** Brbh. fragrance. — **आमोद-आलाप**, m. an entertaining conversation. **आमोद-प्रमोद**, m. diversion, pastime (usu. pl.); joking, bantering. **आमोद-यात्रा**, f. a journey, trip for pleasure.

आमोदन *ā-modan* [S.], m. pleasing, amusing (oneself or others).

आमोदित *ā-modit* [S.], adj. **1.** pleased, amused. **2.** delighted (by a fragrance).

आम्र *āmră* [S.], m. the mango (= [1]**आम**).

आम्ल *āml* [S.], m. acidity.

आय *āy* [S.], f. (m., *Pl.*) income; revenue; receipts; profit. — **आय-कर**, m. income tax. **आय-व्यय**, m. income and expenditure; budget. °**अक**, m. estimate; budget.

आयँती-पायँती *āyaṁtī-pāyaṁtī*, f. the head and foot of a bed.

आयंदा *āyandā*, adv. see **आइंदा**.

[1]**आयत** *āyat* [A. *āya*: P. *āyat*], f. **1.** token, mark; wonder, paragon. ***2.** a sentence or verse from the Qur'ān. — **आयतुल्लाह**, m. an ayatollah.

[2]**आयत** *ā-yat* [S.], adj. & m. **1.** adj. lengthened, stretching; extensive; broad. **2.** rectangular; oblong. **3.** m. a rectangle; parallelogram.

[3]**आयत** *āyat* [*ātapta-*], m. *Pl.* sunshine.

आयतन *ā-yatan* [S.], m. **1.** resting-place, abode; temple. **2.** extent. **3.** capacity, volume. — **~ में**, adv. in extent.

आयत्त *ā-yatt* [S.], adj. dependent on, subject to.

-आयन *-āyan* [S.], suffix (forms a few patronymics, e.g. **वात्स्यायन**, m. descendant of Vātsya; **कामायनी**, f. woman of the Kāma lineage (*gotra*)).

आयस *āyas* [*ādeśa-*], m. Av. command, directive.

[1]**आया** *āyā* [cf. H. *ānā*], part. adj. come. — आए दिन, adv. daily; constantly. – आया-गया, adj. come and gone: finished, (over and) done with (sthg. unpleasant); (only) slightly known (a person). आया-गया करना, to treat as (over and) done with. आए-गए, m. pl. unexpected guests.

[2]**आया** *āyā* [Pt. *aia*], f. an ayah, children's nurse; lady's maid.

[3]**आया** *āyā* [P. *āyā*], interrog. part. marking a following question (= sentence initial क्या). U.

आयात *ā-yāt* [S.], adj. & m. **1.** adj. imported. **2.** m. imported goods. — ~ करना, to import. – आयत-कर, m. import duty. आयात-निर्यात, m. import(s) and export(s). °-संतुलन, m. trade balance.

आयातक *ā-yātak* [S.], m. an importer.

आयातित *ā-yātit* [S.], adj. imported.

आयाम *ā-yām* [S.], m. **1.** extent (in space or time); length; breadth. **2.** scope, dimensions.

आयामन *ā-yāman* [S.], m. extending, extension.

आयास *ā-yās* [S.], m. **1.** effort, exertion. **2.** a laborious task. **3.** transf. fatigue.

आयासी *ā-yāsī* [S.], adj. taking pains; labouring long or hard.

आयीता *āyītā* [conn. *āyatta-*], adj. *Pl.* ready, prepared.

आयु *āyu* [ad. *āyuṣ-*], f. **1.** span of life, age; long life. **2.** period of time; term. — ~ सिरा-, v.i. Brbh. death to be near.

आयुक्त *ā-yukt* [S.], m. **1.** adj. commissioned. **2.** m. one appointed, or commissioned.

आयुध *ā-yudh* [S.], m. **1.** weapon. **2.** pl. arms; armament. **3.** armour. — आयुधकार, m. manufacturer of arms. आयूधजीवी, m. one living by arms, a serving soldier.

आयुधीय *ā-yudhīyă* [S.], adj. & m. **1.** adj. having to do with arms, or munitions. **2.** m. military equipment; munitions.

आयुर्- *āyur-* [S]. = आयु: — आयुर्विज्ञान, m. = next. आयुर्वेद, m. traditional Indian science of health or medicine. °इक, adj. °ई, m. an Ayurvedic practitioner. °ईय, adj. = °इक.

आयुष्- *āyuṣ-* [S]. = आयु: — आयुष्कर, adj. prolonging life. आयुष्मन, adj. (voc.) long-lived: venerable. आयुष्मान, adj. id. °-मती, f.

आयुष्य *āyuṣyă* [S.], f. long life (= आयु).

आयोग *ā-yog* [S.], m. *admin.* a commission.

आयोजक *ā-yojak* [S.], m. organiser, convener.

आयोजन *ā-yojan* [S.], m. **1.** organising, convening; arranging. **2.** organisation, &c.

आयोजना *ā-yojănā* [S.], f. 1. = आयोजन, 1. **2.** a project; function. — ~ करना (की), to organise.

आयोजित *ā-yojit* [S.], adj. organised, &c. (see आयोजन).

आरंभ *ā-rambh* [S.], m. beginning, commencement; start. — ~ करना, to begin; to undertake; to initiate (an activity, an attitude). ~ होना, to begin, to start; to become current. – आरंभ-कर्ता, m. inv. beginner, initiator. आरंभत:, adv. from the beginning; anew. आरंभ-शूर, m. a brave beginner: one who undertakes many things but carries none through.

आरंभक *ārambhak* [S.], m. = आरंभ-कर्ता.

आरंभिक *ā-rambhik* [S.], adj. **1.** initial. **2.** introductory, preparatory. **3.** elementary (level), primary. **4.** unadvanced, undeveloped (state).

आरंभी *ā-rambhī* [S.], adj. initiating, beginning.

[1]**आर** *ār* [*ārā-*], f. reg. **1.** a pointed implement; a goad; awl, bodkin; spike. **2.** a spoke (= तीली). **3.** 19c. sting. **4.** spur (of a cock).

[2]**आर** *ār*, m. f. *Pl. HŚS.* a kind of ladle used in sugar-making.

[3]**आर** *ār* [? H. *āṛ* ← **aḍḍ-*], f. Brbh. an ornament, or ornamental mark, worn by women on the forehead; a streak of sandalwood paste.

[4]**आर** *ār* [H. *āṛ*]. reg. a boundary between fields.

आरक्त *ā-rakt* [S.], adj. reddish; red.

आरक्षक *ā-rakṣak* [s.], m. providing protection or security: a guard.

आरक्षण *ā-rakṣaṇ* [S.], m. **1.** reserving (of a seat, a berth). **2.** reservation.

आरक्षा *ā-rakṣā* [S.], f. protection, security.

आरक्षित *ā-rakṣit* [S.], adj. **1.** reserved, held in reserve. **2.** kept safe or secure. **2.** reserved (as a seat). — ~ क्षेत्र, m. a (nature) reserve.

आरक्षी *ā-rakṣī* [S.], m. = आरक्षक.

आरज *āraj* [ad. *ārya-*], m. & adj. an Aryan (= आर्य).

आरज़ा *ārzā* [A. *'āriẓa*], m. a sickness.

आरज़ू *ārzū* [P. *ārzū*], f. **1.** wish, longing; eagerness; hope. **2.** eager request, entreaty. — ~ करना, to wish, &c.; to request; to entreat. ~ निकालना, or मिटाना, to satisfy a wish.

आरण्य *āraṇyă* [S.], adj. having to do with a wild region.

आरण्यक *āraṇyak* [S.], adj. & m. **1.** adj. = आरण्य. **2.** m. the name of a class of Vedic literature closely connected with the Brāhmaṇas. **3.** one living in a forest, &c.

आरती *ārătī* [*ārātrika-*], f. **1.** a ceremony performed in worshipping a god: a dish holding a lamp, burning *ghī*, incense or other articles, is moved in a series of circles in front of the idol. **2.** the dish used in the ceremony of *ārtī*. **3.** a hymn of praise; prayer. — ~ उतारना, or करना, to perform the ceremony of *ārtī*. ~ लेना, to put (one's) hands to the flame of the lamp, then to (one's) face, on completing the ceremony of *ārtī*.

आर-पार *ār-pār* [*āra-*[1]; *pāra-*], m. & adv. **1.** m. the nearer and further sides (of sthg.); total width or extent. **2.** adv. right across. **3.** right through, through and through. — ~ करना, to pierce right though, to penetrate (sthg., के). ~ की लड़ाई, f. conclusive battle. ~ दिखाई देना (के), to be transparent.

आरभती *ā-rabhătī* [S.], f. Brbh. a highly ornate style of composition; a bombastic style of language.

आरव *ā-rav* [S.], m. loud noise.

आरसी *ārsī* [*ādarśa-*, Pk. *ādarisa-*], f. **1.** a mirror. **2.** thumb-ring containing a mirror (rather than a stone). — हाथ कंगन, तो ~ क्या? fig. that is (sthg.) self-evident.

आरस्य *ārasyă* [S.], m. **1.** insipidity. **2.** spiritlessness, dullness (of nature).

आरा *ārā* [*āra-*[2]], m. **1.** reg. a spoke (= तीली). ***2.** [? × *ārā-*] a saw. **3.** a shoemaker's knife or awl. — ~ खींचना, or चलाना (पर), to saw. ~ सिर पर चलना, fig. to be tortured, to suffer great pain. आरे से काटना, to saw. – आराकश [P. -*kaś*], m. a sawyer.

आराइश *ārāiś* [P. *ārā'iś*], f. **1.** preparation, good arrangement. ***2.** decoration, embellishment. — ~ देना (को), to adorn, &c.

आराइशी *ārāiśī* [P. *ārā'iś*+H. -*ī*], adj. decorative.

आराति *ārāti* [S.], m. enemy, foe.

आराध- *ā-rādh-* [ad. *ārādhayati*], v.t. Brbh. Av. **1.** to worship, to adore. **2.** to propitiate; to gratify.

आराधक *ā-rādhak* [S.], adj. & m. **1.** adj. worshipping, adoring. **2.** propitiating; gratifying. **3.** m. a worshipper.

आराधन *ā-rādhan* [S.], m. = आराधना.

आराधना *ā-rādhănā* [S.], f. **1.** worship, adoration. **2.** propitiation.

आराधनीय *ā-rādhănīyă* [S.], adj. = आराध्य.

आराध्य *ā-rādhyă* [S.], adj. to be worshipped, adored, &c.

[1]**आराम** *ārām* [P. *ārām*], m. **1.** rest, repose; ease, comfort, contentment; leisure; convenience. **2.** well-being; restored health; relief (from pain or suffering). — ~ करना, to rest, to relax; to cure, to heal (one, को). ~ का, adj. giving comfort, &c.; comfortable; convenient; restful. ~ देना (को), to give repose, ease, &c. (to); to relieve, to assuage; to comfort; to cure, to heal. ~ पहुँचाना, id. ~ पाना, to find rest or peace; to find relief, comfort; to recover (health). ~ फ़रमाना, = ~ करना, 1. ~ लेना, id. ~ से, adv. at ease, in comfort; at leisure or convenience; contentedly; undisturbed; without difficulty. – आराम-कुरसी, f. an easy chair, arm-chair. आराम-गाह, f. a place to rest; a bedroom. आरामतलब [A. -*ṭalab*], adj. seeking or fond of comfort; disliking inconvenience; indolent. °ई, f. आरामदेह [P. -*deh*], adj. comfortable.

[2]**आराम** *ā-rām* [S.], m. a pleasure-place; grove; garden.

आरास्तगी *ārāstagī* [P. *ārāstagī*], f. **1.** well-ordered state. **2.** decoration, embellishment.

आरास्ता *ārāstā* [P. *ārăsta*], adj. **1.** well-arranged, well-ordered. **2.** decorated, embellished.

आरिफ़ *ārif* [A. *'ārif*], m. 19c. a wise man, holy man.

आरिया *āriyā*, m. *Pl. HŚS.* a kind of gourd producing small fruit.

[1]**आरी** *ārī* [A. *'ārī*], adj. U. naked: **1.** helpless (= आजिज़). **2.** tired or sick (of, से).

[2]**आरी** *ārī* [cf. H. *ārā*], f. **1.** a small saw. **2.** a shoemaker's awl.

आरूँधना *ārūṁdhnā* [**ārundhati*], v.t. *Pl.* to strangle (= अरोंधना).

आरूढ़ *ā-rūṛh* [S.], adj. **1.** mounted (on); ensconced in (power: a government). **2.** holding to (a statement, a promise); firm (in the matter of, पर).

आरोग्य *ārogyă* [S.], m. & adj. **1.** m. freedom from disease, health. **2.** adj. free of disease. — आरोग्यकारी, adj. curative, restorative. आरोग्यलाभ, m. restoration of health. आरोग्यलाभ करना, to be restored to health.

आरोग्यता *ārogyătā* [S.], f. healthy state, health. — आरोग्य-शाला, f. a sanatorium. आरोग्य-शास्त्र, m. hygiene (as a branch of science).

आरोप *ā-rop* [S.], m. **1.** placing or fixing (on). **2.** transplanting. **3.** attributing (to, पर). **4.** allegation, accusation, charge. — ~ करना, or लगाना, to make an allegation, &c. (against, पर).

आरोपक *ā-ropak* [S.], adj. one who alleges, or charges, &c.

आरोपण *ā-ropaṇ* [S.], m. = आरोप.

आरोपित *ā-ropit* [S.], adj. **1.** placed or fixed (on); imposed. **2.** transplanted. **3.** attributed (to, पर); *lit.* contrived (a character). **4.** alleged.

आरोह *ā-roh* [S.], m. 1. = आरोहण. **2.** development, evolution. **3.** *mus.* an ascending scale.

आरोह- *ā-roh-* [*ārohati*], v.i. E.H. to mount.

आरोहण *ā-rohaṇ* [S.], m. **1.** rising, ascending; mounting, climbing. **2.** growing (new shoots, or plants). — ~ करना, to ascend; to mount, to climb (a horse, a peak: पर).

आरोहित *ā-rohit* [S.], adj. **1.** mounted (upon, पर); ascended, climbed. **2.** shot, sprouted (new growth).

आरोही *ā-rohī* [S.], m. **1.** आरोही. one who ascends, or mounts. **2.** *mus.* an ascending scale. — पर्वतारोही, m. a mountaineer.

आर्जव *ārjav* [S.], m. *Pl. HŚS.* honesty, sincerity; candour.

आर्त *ārt* [S.], adj. **1.** afflicted, distressed; wretched. **2.** hurt, injured. — आर्त-नाद, m. a cry of distress, or of pain.

आर्ति *ārti* [S.], f. **1.** affliction, distress. **2.** pain.

आर्थिक *ārthik* [S.], adj. **1.** financial. **2.** economic. **3.** monetary.

आर्द्र *ārdră* [S.], adj. **1.** wet; moist. **2.** humid.

आर्द्रता *ārdrătā* [S.], f. **1.** moisture. **2.** humidity.

आर्द्रा *ārdrā* [S.], f. *astrol.* a lunar mansion (its occupation coincides usually with the month *Asāṛh* and traditionally with the beginning of the rains).

आर्य *āryă* [S.], adj. & m. **1.** adj. Aryan; honourable; noble; excellent. **2.** *ling.* Indo-European; Indo-Aryan. **3.** an Aryan. **4.** voc. particle. (early Indian contexts) good sir! **5.** a member of the Ārya Samāj. — आर्यभाषी, adj. speaking an Indo-European language. आर्यसमाजी, m. & adj. a member of the Ārya Samāj; having to do with the Ārya Samāj. आर्यावर्त [°*ya*+*ā*°], m. land of the Aryans: north and central India. आर्येतर [°*ya*+*i*°], adj. non-Aryan; non-Indo-European; non-Indo-Aryan.

आर्ष *ārṣ* [S.], adj. having to do with a sage (*ṛṣi*): sanctified by origin.

आलंग *ālaṅg*, f. heat (of a female animal). — ~ पर आना, to be in heat; to be lustful.

आलंब *ā-lamb* [S.], m. **1.** support, prop. **2.** base, foundation. **3.** protection, shelter.

आलंबन *ā-lamban* [S.], m. **1.** support, prop; maintenance. **2.** dependence. **3.** transf. a supporter, protector. **4.** *rhet.* an object or person serving as the stimulus of a particular *rasa*.

1**आल** *āl* [? *ārdrya-*, **ārdlya-*], f. m. **1.** moisture. **2.** tears.

2**आल** *āl* [**allā-*], f. **1.** name of a tree or plant, *Morinda citrifolia*, from the root of which a red dye is prepared. **2.** a pumpkin. **3.** a green stalk of onion.

3**आल** *āl* [A. *āl*], f. family, family line or name; sub-division of a community. — आल-औलाद, f. children, descendants.

आलकस *ālkas* [? conn. *ālasa-*], m. f. inactivity, &c. (= आलस्य).

अलक्षणी *a-lakṣăṇī* [S.], adj. & m. **1.** adj. unfortunate, ill-fated. **2.** m. unlucky person.

आलत *ālat* [A. *āla*: P. *ālat*], f. *Pl.* implement, apparatus, equipment.

आलता *āltā*, m. = अलता.

आलन *ālan* [**ālāpana-*[2]: Pk. *ālāvaṇa-*], m. **1.** a mixture of dough and lentils. **2.** straw, &c. mixed with mud (for brick-making, building, plastering).

आलपीन *ālpīn* [Pt. *alfinete* (← A.): ? × Engl. *pin*], m. a pin.

आलबाल *ālbāl* [P. *-bālā*], m. poet. = 3आला.

आलम *ālam* [A. *'ālam*], m. **1.** the world, the universe. **2.** state, condition. **3.** fig. loveliness. — आलमारा [P. *-ārā*], adj. inv. world-adorning; world-regulating.

आलमी *ālămī* [P. *'ālamī*], adj. of the world.

आलय *ālay* [S.], m. esp. in comp. house, abode, place.

आलस *ālas* [*ālasya-*], m. & adj. = आलस्य, आलसी.

आलसी *ālsī* [cf. *ālasya-*], adj. & m. **1.** adj. lazy. **2.** inactive, inert; drowsy. **3.** m. a lazy person.

आलसीपन *ālsīpan* [cf. H. *ālsī*], m. laziness, &c.

आलसीपना *ālsīpanā*, m. = आलसीपन.

आलस्य *ālasyă* [S.], m. **1.** laziness. **2.** inactivity, inertia; drowsiness.

[1]**आला** *ālā* [A. *a'lā*], adj. inv. higher, highest; supreme; best; chief. — ~ **दरजे का**, adj. of the best kind, or type.

[2]**आला** *ālā* [A. *āla*], m. tool, implement.

[3]**आला** *ālā* [A. *'alā*], adj. inv. very high, most high; exalted.

[4]**आला** *ālā* [**ālla-*: Pa. *alla-*], adj. reg. **1.** wet, saturated (esp. with rain). **2.** fresh, green.

[5]**आला** *ālā* [*ālaya-*], m. niche in a wall or pillar.

[6]**आला** *ālā* [**āla-*[2]: Pk. *āla-*], m. hollow for water around the foot of a tree.

आलात *ālāt* [ad. *ālāta-*], m. **1.** a firebrand. **2.** a glowing coal.

आलान *ālān* [S.], m. = अलान.

आलाप *ā-lāp* [S.], m. **1.** speaking; conversation. **2.** modulation of the voice in singing. **3.** prelude to a song. **4.** warbling of birds. — **आलाप-कलाप**, m. conversation. **आलापचारी**, f. modulating the voice before singing.

आलापक *ā-lāpak* [S.], adj. **1.** making conversation. **2.** preparing to sing.

आलापना *ālāpnā*, v.t. = अलापना.

आलिंगन *ā-lingan* [S.], m. embracing, embrace. — ~ **करना (का)**, to embrace. – **आलिंगन-पाश**, m. the arms folded in an embrace.

आलिंगित *ā-lingit* [S.], adj. embraced.

आलिंगी *ā-lingī* [S.], adj. & m. **1.** embracing. **2.** one who embraces.

आलि *āli* [S.], f. **1.** a (woman's) female friend (= [2]आली). **2.** f. m. a black bee (= अलि).

आलिम *ālim* [A. *'ālim*], m. U. knowing; learned: a learned man.

[1]**आली** *ālī* [A. *'ālī*], adj. exalted, high; noble. — **आलीजाह** [A. *jāh*], adj. high-ranking. **आलीशान**, adj. magnificent, splendid; stately; high-ranking.

[2]**आली** *ālī* [*ālĭ̄-*[3]], f. a woman's female friend.

[3]**आली** *ālī* [**āḍi-*: Pk. *ālī-*], f. reg. **1.** row, line; dividing ridge between fields. **2.** bed (of flowers or vegetables).

[1]**आलू** *ālū* [*āluka-*], m. potato. — ~ **गाच**, m. the potato plant; *Pl.* the tapioca shrub. ~ **दम**, m. a dish of steamed potatoes.

[2]**आलू** *ālū* [P. *ālū*], m. a plum: — ~ **बुख़ारा** [P. *bukhāra*], m. Bactrian plum: a prune.

आलूचा *ālūcā* [P. *ālūca*], m. a type of small plum.

आलूदा *ālūdā* [P. *ālūda*], adj. U. soiled, stained, smeared.

आलेख *ā-lekh* [S.], m. written display (as a notice, &c.); diagram.

आलेप *ā-lep* [S.], m. **1.** liniment. **2.** plaster.

आलेपन *ā-lepan* [S.], m. **1.** smearing, applying (embrocation, &c). **2.** plastering.

आलोक *ā-lok* [S.], m. **1.** seeing, vision; view, regard. ***2.** light, splendour. **3.** aspect, appearance. **4.** transf. chapter (of a book). **5.** a note, comment. — **आलोक-गृह**, m. lighthouse. **आलोक-पत्र**, m. memorandum; report. **आलोक-स्तंभ**, m. lighthouse.

आलोकन *ā-lokan* [S.], m. **1.** looking, observation; scrutiny. **2.** illumination. **3.** showing.

आलोकनीय *ā-lokănīyă* [S.], adj. deserving examination or scrutiny.

आलोचना *ā-locănā* [S.], f. considering: assessment, criticism. — **आलोचनात्मक** [°*nā*+*ā*°], adj. critical.

आलोचित *ālocit* [S.], adj. considered, reviewed.

आलोच्य *ā-locyă* [S.], adj. to be considered: under consideration, or review.

आलोड़न *ā-loṛan* [S. *āloḍana-*], m. **1.** churning up. **2.** agitation, perturbation. **3.** turning over, cogitating upon (a matter).

आलोड़ना *āloṛnā* [*āloḍayati*], v.t. to stir, to churn.

आलोड़ित *ā-loṛit* [S. *āloḍita-*], adj. **1.** churned up. **2.** agitated. **3.** thought through, revolved (a matter).

आल्हा *ālhā*, m. **1.** name of a legendary hero of Mahoba, of the 12th century A.D.; name of a ballad cycle about Ālhā. **2.** name of a Hindi metre containing thirty-one *mātrās* to the line. ~ **गाना**, to tell a long saga; to blow one's own trumpet.

आवंटन *ā-vaṇṭan* [S.], m. allocation.

-आव *-āv*, suffix (forms m. nouns from verb stems, e.g. **घेराव**, encirclement, siege).

आव- *āv-* [*āpayati*], v.i. Brbh. Av. to come.

आवक *āvak*, adj. arriving; incoming (as of supplies).

आवज़ *āvaj*, m. *hist.* a hemispherical drum resembling the *tāśā*.

-आवट *-āvaṭ*, suffix (forms f. nouns from verb stems, e.g. **रुकावट**, obstacle).

आवन *āvan* [*āpana-*], m. Brbh. coming; approach. — **आवन-जान**, m. coming and going: the cycle of birth and death.

आवभगत *āvbhagat* [? H. *āvā*+*bhagat* ad. *bhakti-*[1]], f. courteous or warm welcome; hospitality. — ~ **करना** (**की**), to welcome courteously.

आवभाव *āv-bhāv*, m. = **आव-भगत**.

आवरण *ā-vǎraṇ* [S.], m. **1.** covering, cover. **2.** protection, shield. **3.** obstruction. **4.** curtain, veil. — **आवरण-पत्र**, m. dust-jacket (of a book). **आवरण-पृष्ठ**, m. id.

आवर्जन *ā-varjan* [S.], m. poet. bending down. — **आवर्जना मूर्ति**, f. embodiment of humility.

आवर्त *ā-vart* [S.], m. **1.** turning motion; turn; returning. **2.** cyclical movement or progress. **3.** whirlpool, eddy. **4.** 19c. an edition.

आवर्तक *ā-vartak* [S.], adj. recurring, recurrent.

आवर्तन *ā-vartan* [S.], m. **1.** turning motion, rotation; turn; return. **2.** recurrence.

आवर्तित *ā-vartit* [S.], adj. **1.** turned, rotated, revolved. **2.** recurred.

आवर्ती *ā-vartī* [S.], adj. recurring, recurrent.

आवलि *avăli* [S.], f. = [1]**आवली**.

[1]**आवली** *āvălī* [S.], f. **1.** a row, line; rank; series. **2.** family line.

[2]**आवली** *āvlī*, f. *Pl. HŚS.* a mode of estimating crops, the produce of a small area (*bīsvā*) being taken as a measure of the whole.

[3]**आवली** *āvlī*, f. reg. **1.** calamity, disaster. **2.** mortal danger.

आवले *āvle*, m. pl. *Pl.* = **आँवले**.

आवश्यक *āvaśyak* [S.], adj. **1.** necessary; indispensable. **2.** inevitable. **3.** urgent (as a letter).

आवश्यकता *āvaśyakătā* [S.], f. **1.** necessity, need; requirement; demand; indispensability. **2.** inevitability. **3.** urgency (as of a letter). — **मुझे आपकी सहायता की ~ होगी**, I shall require your assistance. – **आवश्यकतानुसार** [°*tā*+*a*°], adv. according to need; according to demand. **आवश्यकतावश**, adv. of necessity.

आवश्यकीय *āvăśyăkīyă* [S.], adj. indispensable (= **आवश्यक**).

[1]**आवा** *āvā* [cf. *āpayati*], m. **1.** coming, approach. **2.** ? one coming or arriving. — **आवागमन**, m. = s.v. **आवा-जावा**, m. = next. **आवा-जाही**, f. coming and going; intercourse, communication; visiting; access.

[2]**आवा** *āvā*, m. = **आँवा**.

-आवा *-āvā*, suffix (forms m. nouns from verb stems, e.g. **दिखावा**, evidence, display).

आवागमन *āvāgaman* [H. *āvā*+S. *gamana-*], m. **1.** coming and going; arrival and departure. **2.** intercourse, communication. **3.** birth and death, transmigration.

आवाज़ *āvāz* [P. *āvāz*], f. var. /əvaz/. **1.** sound; noise; echo. **2.** voice; tone. **3.** call, cry. **4.** report, fame; rumour; innuendo. — ~ **उठाना**, to raise the voice, to speak out; to strain the voice; to spread a report. ~ **ऊँची करना**, id., 1. ~ **करना**, to emit a sound. ~ **कसना**, to speak out (against sthg.); to utter slander or innuendo (against, **पर**). ~ **देना** (**को**), to call out, to shout (to). ~ **निकालना**, = ~ **करना**; to utter (words or sounds); to speak. ~ **पड़ना**, *Pl. HŚS.* the voice to be hoarse, to lose (one's) voice. ~ **पर कान धरना**, or **रखना**, or **लगाना**, to lend an attentive ear (to, **की**). ~ **पर लगना**, to answer to or to obey a call (from, **की**). ~ **फटना**, the voice to be hoarse. ~ **में** ~ **मिलाना**, to sing in harmony (with, **की**); to agree automatically with what is said. – **आवाज़-बैठा**, adj. hoarse. **आवाज़-रोक**, adj. & m. sound-proof; a silencer, muffler.

आवाज़ा *āvāzā* [P. *āvāza*], m. 1. = **आवाज़**, 1., 4. **2.** taunting, jeers. – **आवाज़ा-तवाज़ा**, m. = ~, 4.; innuendoes.

आवाती *āvātī* [cf. H. [1]*avāī*], f. *Pl.* **1.** approach. **2.** season in which merchandise is expected.

आवारगी *āvārăgī* [P. *āvāragī*], f. **1.** wandering, vagrancy. **2.** transf. dissoluteness.

आवारा *āvārā* [P. *āvāra*], adj. & m. **1.** adj. separated from family, without house and home: wandering, vagrant; astray; stray (an animal); abandoned. **2.** dissolute. **3.** m. a wanderer, vagabond, &c. — ~ **फिरना**, to wander about; to go astray; to loaf about. – **आवारागिर्द** [P. *-gard*], adj. wandering, vagrant; dissolute. °**ई**, f.

आवास *ā-vās* [S.], m. **1.** place of residence or abode, habitation. **2.** housing. — **आवास-भत्ता**, m. residential allowance (additional to salary).

आवासन *ā-vāsan* [S.], m. immigration.

आवासिक *ā-vāsik* [S.], adj. residing, in residence.

आवासित *ā-vāsit* [S.], adj. resident.

आवासी *ā-vāsī* [S.], adj. residing, resident.

आवासीय *ā-vāsīyă* [S.], adj. residential.

आवाह- *āvāh-* [*āvāhayati*], v.t. Brbh. to call, to summon.

आवाहन *ā-vāhan* [S.], m. **1.** calling, summons. **2.** invitation; an appeal. **3.** invocation.

आविर्भाव *āvir-bhāv* [S.], m. **1.** appearance, manifestation. **2.** emergence, rise (of a sect, a person, a tendency).

आविर्भूत *āvir-bhūt* [S.], adj. appeared, manifest; emerged; risen.

आविल *āvil* [S.], adj. poet. muddied, impure.

आविष्करण *āviṣ-karaṇ* [S.], m. inventing, invention.

आविष्कर्ता *āviṣ-kartā* [S.], m. inv. inventor.

आविष्कार *āviṣ-kār* [S.], m. **1.** discovery. **2.** invention. — ~ **करना (का)**, to discover; to invent.

आविष्कारक *āviṣ-kārak* [S.], adj. & m. **1.** adj. inventive. **2.** m. inventor.

आविष्कारी *āviṣ-kārī* [S.], adj. inventing, inventive.

आविष्कृत *āviṣ-kr̥t* [S.], adj. **1.** discovered; made known. **2.** invented.

आविष्ट *ā-viṣṭ* [S.], adj. **1.** possessed (as by an evil spirit). **2.** engrossed (as by an idea). **3.** charged (with electricity).

आवृत *ā-vr̥t* [S.], adj. **1.** covered, covered over. **2.** enclosed, surrounded.

आवृत्त *ā-vr̥tt* [S.], adj. **1.** occurred. **2.** repeated; recurred.

आवृत्ति *ā-vr̥tti* [S.], f. **1.** recurrence, repetition. **2.** rehearsing, learning by heart (a lesson, &c). **3.** new edition (of a book).

आवेग *ā-veg* [S.], m. haste: fit (of anger, &c.); surge.

आवेज़ा *āvezā* [P. *āveza*], m. *Pl. HŚS.* pendant, ear-ring.

आवेदक *ā-vedak* [S.], m. an applicant.

आवेदन *ā-vedan* [S.], m. announcing, informing: submitting (a request); putting forward (a matter, for consideration). — **आवेदन-पत्र**, m. an application (form).

आवेश *ā-veś* [S.], m. access (of emotion); frenzy; fit.

आशंसा *ā-śaṃsā* [S.], f. hope, desire.

आशंकनीय *ā-śaṅkănīyă* [S.], adj. **1.** to be feared. **2.** to be doubted, suspected.

आशंका *ā-śaṅkā* [S.], f. **1.** fear. **2.** apprehension; doubt. **3.** awe. **4.** danger. — ~ **करना**, to be apprehensive (of, **की**), &c. ~ **आशंकाजनक**, adj. giving rise to fear, alarm, &c.; dangerous.

आशंकित *ā-śaṅkit* [S.], adj. **1.** fearful, alarmed. **2.** apprehended; suspected; feared.

आशना *āśnā* [P. *āśnā*], m. inv., f. **1.** an acquaintance; a friend. **2.** a lover; a mistress.

आशनाई *āśnāī* [P. *āśnā'ī*], f. **1.** acquaintance; friendship. **2.** liaison.

आशय *ā-śay* [S.], m. **1.** resting-place. ***2.** sense, purport. **3.** intention. **4.** scope. **5.** in comp. vessel, receptacle. — **आमाशय** [°*ma*+*ā*°], m. the stomach. **जलाशय** [°*la*+*ā*°], m. a reservoir; an expanse of water. **महाशय** [°*hā*+*ā*°], m. a gentleman.

आशा *āśā* [S.], f. **1.** hope, expectation; prospect. **2.** trust, reliance (on, **पर** or **की**). **3.** wish, desire. — ~ **करना (की)**, to hope (for); to expect; to desire; to place hope (in); to rely (on). ~ **छोड़ना**, to give up hope. ~ **टूटना**, or **छूटना**, hope to be lost, or given up. ~ **देना**, or **दिलाना (को)**, to give hope, or encouragement (to). ~ **पूरी करना (की)**, to gratify (one's) wish; to fulfil (one's) hope, expectation. ~ **बाँधना**, to form or to cherish a hope. ~ **रखना (की)**, = ~ **करना**. ~ **लगाना (पर**, or **से)**, = ~ **करना**, 2., 3. ~ **होना (को)**, to hope (for, **की**); to expect. – **आशाजनक**, adj. giving cause for hope, promising. **आशातीत** [°*śā*+*a*°], adj. beyond (all) hopes, or expectations. **आशान्वित** [°*śā*+*a*°], adj. accompanied by, or possessed of, hope: encouraged. **आशापूर्ण**, adj. = **आशा-भरा**. **आशाप्रद**, adj. = **आशाजनक**. **आशा-भरा**, adj. filled with hope. **आशामय**, adj. = **आशाजनक**. **आशावाद**, m. optimism (esp. *philos*). °**इता**, f. optimism (an attitude). °**ई**, m. & adj. an optimist; optimistic. **आशावान**, adj. hoping, hopeful; expecting. **आशाहीन**, adj. without hope, despairing.

आशिक़ *āśiq* [A. *'āśiq*], m. loving: a lover. — ~ **होना**, to be or to fall in love (with, **पर**). – **आशिक़-जार** [= *yār*], m. pl. 19c. lovers. **आशिक़-माशूक़**, m. pl. lover and beloved, lovers. **आशिक़-मिज़ाज**, m. amorous by disposition.

आशिक़ा *āśiqā* [A. *'āśiqa*], f. sweetheart, mistress.

आशिक़ाना *āśiqānā* [P. *'āśiqāna*], adj. inv. **1.** loving; amorous. **2.** erotic. — ~ **ख़त**, m. love letter.

आशिक़ी *āśiqī* [A. *'āśiqī*], f. state of being in love; courtship. — ~ करना, to court.

आशियाँ *āśiyāṁ* [P. *āśiyān*], m. = आशियाना.

आशियाना *āśiyānā* [P. *āśiyāna*], m. **1.** nest. **2.** fig. small dwelling.

आशिष *ā-śiṣ* [S.; stem form], m. blessing, benediction (= असीस).

आशीर्वचन *ā-śīrvacan* [S.], m. = आशीर्वाद.

आशीर्वाद *ā-śīrvād* [S.], m. blessing, benediction. — ~ करना (का), = next. ~ देना (को), to bless.

आशीष *āśīṣ* [S.], f. blessing (= आशिष).

आशु- *āśu-* [S.], adv. swiftly: — आशु-कवि, m. extempore poet. आशुतोष, adj. easily pleased; soon appeased. आशु-पत्र, m. express letter. आशु-लिपि, f. shorthand; °क, m. stenographer.

आश्चर्य *āścaryă* [S.], m. astonishment, surprise; wonder. — ~ करना, to feel astonishment (at, पर, से). ~ होना (को), to be astonished (at). — आश्चर्यकारक, adj. astonishing. °-कारी, adj. id. आश्चर्य-चकित, adj. struck with wonderment. आश्चर्यजनक, adj. astonishing, striking. आश्चर्यान्वित [°*ya*+*a*°], adj. experiencing astonishment, astonished.

आश्चर्यित *āścaryit* [S.], adj. astonished.

आश्रम *ā-śram* [S.], m. **1.** abode (as of a hermit or devotee); refuge; sanctuary. **2.** *hind.* a stage (of which there are four) in the life of a brāhmaṇ. — आश्रम-धर्म, m. the duties of each stage of life. आश्रमवासी, m. resident of an *āśram*, an ascetic.

आश्रमी *ā-śramī* [S.], adj. **1.** passing through one of the stages of life (see *āśram*). **2.** having to do with an *āśram*; living in an *āśram*.

आश्रय *ā-śray* [S.], m. **1.** refuge, shelter; abode. **2.** support; patronage. **3.** hope, trust. **4.** dependence (on, का), addiction (to). **5.** *rhet.* an exponent (of a particular emotion). — ~ करना, to give support, aid, or patronage (to, का). ~ लेना, to trust (in, का); to seek the support (of); to take refuge (in or with). – आश्रयदाता, m. inv. protector, patron. आश्रयहीन, adj. without shelter or support, helpless.

आश्रयी *ā-śrayī* [S.], adj. **1.** seeking refuge or support. **2.** under the protection (of, के), enjoying the support (of).

आश्रित *ā-śrit* [S.], adj. & m. resorting to: **1.** adj. supported (by). **2.** dependent (on, पर). **3.** relying (on, पर); finding sanctuary (with). **4.** m. a dependant; a servant; ward; adherent.

आश्लेष *ā-śleṣ* [S.], m. **1.** embrace. **2.** intimate connection.

आश्वस्त *ā-śvast* [S.], adj. reassured.

आश्वास *ā-śvās* [S.], m. **1.** breath, breathing. **2.** comfort, consolation. **3.** chapter, section (as of a romance).

आश्वासक *ā-śvāsak* [S.], adj. **1.** reassuring. **2.** consolatory.

आश्वासन *ā-śvāsan* [S.], m. **1.** assurance (of something); reassurance. **2.** comfort, consolation. — ~ देना, or दिलाना (को), to assure (one) of; to comfort, to console. – आश्वासन-पत्र, m. congratulatory address.

आश्वासनीय *ā-śvāsănīyă* [S.], adj. deserving confirmation, or to be the subject of reassurance (a matter).

आश्वासित *ā-śvāsit* [S.], adj. **1.** reassured. **2.** comforted, consoled.

आश्वासी *ā-śvāsī* [S.], adj. = आश्वासक.

आश्वास्य *ā-śvāsyă*, [S.], adj. = आश्वासनीय.

आश्विन *āśvin* [S.], m. the seventh month of the lunar calendar (= क्वार).

आषाढ़ *āṣāṛh*, m. = असाढ़.

आसंग *ā-saṅg* [S.], m. **1.** association, contact. **2.** attachment. **3.** instrumentality, means, help. **4.** [? f. *śakti-* w. *āsakti*] f. *Pl.* power, ability.

आस *ās* [*āśā-*], f. hope, &c. (= आशा). — ~ पूज-, v.i. Av. (one's) wish or desire to be satisfied.

-आस *-ās*, suffix (forms f. nouns, usually desideratives, from verb stems, e.g. *mutās*, micturition; *miṭhās*, sweetness).

आसकत *āskat* [conn. H. *askat*: ? × H. *ālas*], f. = असकत.

आसकताना *āskatānā*, v.i. see असकताना.

आसकती *āskatī* [cf. H. *āskat*], adj. & m. reg. = असकती.

आसक्त *ā-sakt* [S.], adj. **1.** strongly attached (to, से); engrossed (in). **2.** devoted (to); infatuated (with).

आसक्ति *ā-sakti* [S.], f. **1.** attachment, attraction (to, से). **2.** devotion (to); infatuation (with).

आसन *āsan* [S.], m. **1.** sitting; posture. **2.** a seat; mat of cloth, grass or skin (as used to sit on in prayer). **3.** place, seat (as of an ascetic). **4.** a posture (as in yoga). — ~ उखड़ना, one's seat, or posture, to be disturbed or shaken. ~ करना, to adopt yoga postures. ~ जमाना, to sit firmly, to take a firm seat (as on a horse).

~ जोड़ना, to adopt a squatting posture. ~ डिगाना, to shake the position (of, का); to unsettle the mind (of), to tempt, to seduce. ~ डोलना, id.; *hind.* to move, to act (a holy man, invoked by someone). ~ तले आना, to be ridden or mounted (a horse); to be enjoyed sexually (a woman); to fall into the power (of, के). ~ देना, to receive hospitably. ~ मारना to squat (on the haunches); to sit down, or to settle (in a place). ~ लगाना, id.; to sit obstinately until one's demands are satisfied.

आसनी *āsănī* [S.], f. a small carpet or skin (to sit on when praying).

आसन्न *ā-sann* [S.], adj. **1.** near, adjacent. **2.** approaching; impending. — ~ काल, m. early morning; the hour of death. ~ कोण, m. *math.* an adjacent angle. ~ भूत-काल, *gram.* perfect tense.

आस-पास *ās-pās* [cf. H. *pās*], adv. **1.** round about; near. **2.** all around. **3.** ppn. w. के. in the vicinity (of), round about; all around. — ~ का, adj. adjacent; neighbouring.

आसमान *āsmān* [P. *āsmān*], m. the sky; the heavens. — ~ के तारे तोड़ना, to shatter the stars: to be very skilled in a difficult activity; to attempt, or to achieve, the impossible. ~ ज़मीन एक करना, = next. ~ ज़मीन के क़ुलाबे मिलाना, to boast wildly; to make wildly ambitious plans. ~ झाँकना, or ताकना, to have a high opinion of oneself; to be in fine fettle (as a fighting cock). ~ टूटना, the sky to fall in (on one): to be overtaken or overwhelmed (by misfortune). ~ दिखाना (को), to throw (one) flat on one's back (as in wrestling; also fig). ~ पर उड़ना, to boast wildly; to behave haughtily. ~ पर क़दम रखना, to be of exuberant morale. ~ पर चढ़ाना, to extol; to flatter, to wheedle. ~ पर थूकना, to spit at the sky: to demean oneself by expostulation or criticism. ~ फट पड़ना, = ~ टूटना. ~ सिर पर उठाना, to cause a hullabaloo; to stir up a scandal; to make gigantic efforts. ~ में थेगली लगाना to put a patch on the sky: = ~ के तारे तोड़ना. ~ से गिरना, to be obtained unexpectedly, or without effort; to be undervalued. ~ से टक्कर खाना, or लेना, ~ से बातें करना, to reach to the sky, to be lofty. दिमाग़ ~ पर चढ़ना, or होना, (one's, का) mood, or morale, to be inflated; to give oneself airs. – आसमान-खोंचा, sthg. very high or tall (as a pole, a man). आसमान-ज़मीन का फ़रक़, a world of difference. आसमान-फाड़, adj. ear-splitting (as laughter).

आसमानी *āsmānī* [P. *āsmānī*], adj. l. having to do with the sky; aerial. **2.** light blue. **3.** heavenly, celestial. **4.** proceeding from fate or chance, unexpected.

आसरतू *āsartū* [cf. *āśrita-*], m. reg. = *āśrit.*

आसरा *āsrā* [**āśara-*], m. **1.** refuge; shelter; safeguard. **2.** support. **3.** fig. means of subsistence. **4.** patron. **5.** hope, trust, expectation. **6.** dependence. — ~ करना, to rely (on); to hope, to expect; to be dependent (on); to trust (in). ~ ढूँढ़ना, or ताकना, or देखना, to look for help, support (from, का); to expect help, &c. (from). ~ टूटना (का), hope, &c. to be lost; to despair. ~ देना (को), to give hope, &c.; to console; to reassure; to encourage. लेना, to trust (in, का, में); to seek the support (of); to take refuge (in).

आसरैत *āsrait* [cf. *āśraya-*], adj. & m. = आश्रित.

आसव *ā-sav* [S.], m. **1.** decoction, distillate; liquor. **2.** potion.

आसवन *ā-savan* [S.], m. distilling; distillation.

आसवनी *ā-savănī* [cf. H. *āsavan*], f. a distillery.

आसवित *ā-savit* [S.], adj. distilled.

आसा *āsā* [A. *'asā*], m. Brbh. rod, mace.

आसान *āsān* [P. *āsān*], adj. **1.** easy; simple. **2.** manageable; convenient.

आसानी *āsānī* [P. *asānī*], f. ease. — ~ से, adv. easily; simply; without difficulty, or inconvenience.

आसाम *āsām*, m. Assam.

1**आसामी** *āsāmī*, adj. & m. **1.** adj. Assamese. **2.** m. an Assamese.

2**आसामी** *āsāmī*, f. the Assamese language.

3**आसामी** *āsāmī*, m. = असामी.

आसार *āsār* [A. *āṣār*, pl. of *aṣar*], m. **1.** tracks, traces. ***2.** signs, indications; symptoms. **3.** relics, monuments. **4.** foundation (as of a building). **5.** breadth (of a wall).

आसावरी *āsāvărī*, f. **1.** *mus.* name of a *rāgiṇī*; a kind of tune. **2.** a type of silken cloth. **3.** a type of cotton cloth.

आसिन *āsin*, m. pronun. var. = आशविन.

आसीन *āsīn* [S.], adj. **1.** seated. **2.** installed, ensconced (in, पर); occupying (a post).

आसीस *āsīs*, f. *Pl. HŚS.* = असीस.

आसीस- *āsīs-*, m. 19c. = उसीसा, 1.

आसुर *āsur* [S.], adj. & m. **1.** adj. pertaining to an evil spirit. **2.** m. an evil spirit. — आसुर-विवाह, m. *hind.* a marriage in which the bride is purchased from her father and paternal relatives.

1**आसुरी** *āsurī* [cf. *āsura-*], adj. = आसुर.

²आसुरी *āsurī* [S.], f. *Pl. HŚS.* a trad. division of medicine, surgery.

आसोज *āsoj*, m. reg. = असोज.

आस्तान *āstān* [P. *āstān*], m. U. threshold; entrance to a shrine.

आस्तिक *āstik* [S.], adj. & m. **1.** believing, devout; religious. **2.** m. a believer, &c. — आस्तिकवाद, m. theism. °ई, adj. & m. theistic; a theist.

आस्तिकता *āstikătā* [S.], f. belief, piety.

आस्तिक्य *āstikyă* [S.], m. = आस्तिकता.

आस्ति *āsti* [conn. *asti*], f. a (financial) asset.

आस्तीन *āstīn* [P. *āstīn*], m. **1.** sleeve. **2.** cuff. — ~ चढ़ाना, to roll up the sleeves; fig. to make ready (for); to bully, to menace (one: पर). ~ का साँप, m. an enemy in the guise of a friend.

आस्ते *āste*, adv. = आहिस्ता.

आस्त्र *āstră* [S.], adj. armed.

आस्थगन *ā-sthagan* [S.], m. postponement.

आस्था *ā-sthā* [S.], f. standing (close) to, consideration: **1.** faith, belief. **2.** regard, respect. **3.** a session.

आस्थान *ā-sthān* [S.], m. **1.** place of assembly. **2.** session. **3.** temple, shrine.

आस्थानी *ā-sthānī* [S.], f. auditorium.

आस्थापन *ā-sthāpan* [S.], m. **1.** setting up, establishing. **2.** dedicating. **3.** a fortifying medicine, tonic.

आस्थित *ā-sthit* [S.], adj. staying, remaining.

आस्पद *ā-spad* [S.], m. **1.** place, situation; abode. **2.** status, rank; *hind.* community. — हास्यास्पद [°*ya*+*ā*°], adj. whose place is laughter: laughable, ridiculous.

आस्रताई *āsratāī* [cf. *āśrita-*]. the business of an *āśrit*; the privileges of an *āśrit*.

आस्वाद *ā-svād* [S.], m. taste; flavour; savour, relish.

आस्वादन *ā-svādan* [S.], m. **1.** tasting, trying. **2.** relishing.

आस्वादनीय *ā-svādănīyă* [S.], adj. appetising.

आस्वादित *ā-svādit* [S.], adj. **1.** tasted. **2.** relished.

आह *āh*, interj. & f. **1.** interj. oh! (expressing grief, unpleasant surprise, &c). **2.** f. a sigh. — ~ करना, or ~ भरना, to heave a sigh; to sigh. ~ खींचना, or मारना, or निकालना, to heave a sigh. ~ पड़ना, (another's) sighs to fall (on one): to bear the burden, or suffer the consequences, of distress (one) has caused. ~ लेना, to cause distress (to, की).

आहक *āhak* [P. *āhak*], m. **1.** quicklime; lime; plaster. **2.** *Pl.* cement.

आहट *āhaṭ* [cf. *āghaṭṭayati*], f. **1.** the sound of footsteps. **2.** light sound, noise. — ~ पाना, to hear footsteps, &c. ~ लेना or लेते रहना, to be listening (for, की: as for the sound of a person approaching).

-आहट *-āhaṭ*, suffix (forms f. nouns from verb and nominal stems, e.g. घबराहट, confusion; कड़वाहट, bitterness).

आहत *ā-hat* [S.], adj. struck; hurt; wounded (also fig).

¹आहन *āhan* [P. *āhan*], m. U. iron. — आहनगर [P. *-gar*], m. blacksmith.

²आहन *āhan*, m. chopped straw mixed with earth (used in building).

आहनी *āhănī* [P. *āhan*+-*ī*], adj. made of iron.

¹आहर *āhar* [*ādhāra-*], m. **1.** reservoir, pond. **2.** pile of cow-dung cakes.

²आहर *āhar*, m. Av. = आहार.

आहर-जाहर *āhar-jāhar*, m. reg. coming and going.

आहल *āhal*, m. *Pl.* freshness of soil.

आहला *āhlā*, m. reg. flooding.

आहलाना *āhlānā* [*āhlādayati*], v.i. to rejoice.

आहार *ā-hār* [S.], m. **1.** food; foodstuffs, food and drink. **2.** nourishment. — ~ करना, to eat; to take a meal. – आहार-विहार, m. essential needs (as food, drink).

आहारी *ā-hārī* [S.], m. **1.** an eater. **2.** in comp. eating (e.g. शाकाहारी, m. & adj. vegetarian).

आहार्य *ā-hāryă* [S.], adj. to be accepted: edible.

आहिस्तगी *āhistagī* [P. *āhistagī*], f. slowness, &c. (see आहिस्ता).

आहिस्ता *āhistā* [P. *āhista*], adj. **1.** slow. **2.** gentle, soft. **3.** lax, sluggish; lazy; late. — ~ ~, adv. slowly; gradually; gently, &c.; leisurely; sluggishly, &c.

आहुति *ā-huti* [S.], f. oblation; burnt offering; sacrifice.

आह्निक *āhnik* [S.], adj. & m. **1.** adj. daily, performed daily. **2.** m. daily work, or observance. **3.** daily wage.

आह्लाद *ā-hlād* [S.], m. **1.** joy, delight; merriment. **2.** exultation.

आह्लादक *ā-hlādak* [S.], adj. causing joy, &c.

आह्लादित *ā-hlādit* [S.], adj. made joyful, &c. (see आह्लाद).

आह्लादी *ā-hlādī* [S.], adj. 1. = आह्लादित. 2. = आह्लादक.

आह्वान *ā-hvān* [S.], m. call (to), summons; cry.

इ

इ *i*, the third vowel of the Devanāgarī syllabary. — इकार, m. the sound /i/; the letter इ.

इंगलिसिया *iṅglisiyā* [cf. Engl. *English*], m. *hist. Pl.* an invalided soldier (in receipt of a pension or an allotment of land); pensioner.

इंगलिस्तान *iṅglistān*, m. = इंग्लिस्तान.

इंगित *iṅgit* [S.], m. **1.** inner impulse. ***2.** suggestion; hint. **3.** gesture.

इंग्लिस्तान *iṅglistān* [Engl. *English*+P. *-i-stān*], m. England; Britain.

इंग्लिस्तानी *iṅglistānī* [cf. H. *iṅglistān*], adj. English; British.

इंच *iñc* [Engl. *inch*], m. an inch.

इँचना *iṁcnā* [cf. H. *aiṁcnā*], v.i. **1.** to be pulled, drawn; to be tightened. **2.** to be attracted. **3.** to be extracted. **4.** to be sucked up, or in. **5.** to hold oneself aloof.

इँचाव *iṁcāv* [cf. H. *aiṁcnā*], m. pulling, drawing, attraction.

इंजन *iñjan* [Engl. *engine*], m. **1.** an engine, motor. **2.** a railway engine.

इंजबार *iñjbār*, m. = अंजबार.

इंजर-पिंजर *iñjar-piñjar*, m. = अंजर-पंजर.

इंजीनियर *iñjīniyar* [Engl. *engineer*], m. an engineer.

इंजीनियरी *iñjīniyarī* [cf. H. *iñjīniyar*], f. engineering.

इंजील *iñjīl* [A. *injīl*: ← Gk.], m. **1.** the New Testament. **2.** the Bible.

इँड़ुआ *iṁṛuā*, m. = ईँडुरी.

इंतक़ाम *intaqām* [A. *intiqām*], m. revenge; retaliation; reprisal. — ~ लेना, to take revenge (for, का), &c.

इंतक़ाल *intaqāl* [A. *intiqāl*], m. **1.** transportation, transfer. ***2.** death.

इंतख़ाब *intakhāb* [A. *intikhāb*], m. U. **1.** selection, choice. **2.** election.

इंतज़ाम *intazām* [A. *intiẓām*], m. **1.** arrangement. **2.** order, method; discipline. **3.** organisation. — ~ करना (का), to arrange; to arrange for; to manage; to plan. ~ देना (को), to impart order (to): to arrange, to regulate. ~ रखना, to keep order, &c. — इंतज़ामकार [P. *-kār*], m. organiser.

इंतज़ार *intazār* [A. *intiẓār*], m. expecting, waiting (anxiously). — ~ करना, to wait (for, का). ~ देखना, to be on the watch (for, का).

इंतज़ारी *intazārī* [A. *intiẓār*+P. *-ī*], f. reg. = इंतज़ार.

इंतहा *intahā* [A. *intihā*], f. **1.** end, limit. **2.** utmost extent. — ~ का, adj. extreme; consummate. – इंतहापसंद, adj. & m. extremist.

इंतहाई *intahāī* [A. *intihāī*], adj. extreme.

इंतिक़ाल *intiqāl*, m. = इंतक़ाल.

इंतिख़ाब *intikhāb*, m. = इंतख़ाब.

इंतिज़ाम *intizām*, m. = इंतज़ाम.

इंतिज़ार *intizār*, m. = इंतज़ार.

इंतिहा *intihā*, f. = इंतहा.

इँदारा *iṁdārā* [**indrāgāra-*], m. reg. a large masonry well.

इंदिरा *indirā* [S.], f. **1.** a name of Lakṣmī (regarded as the goddess of wealth and prosperity). **2.** beauty, splendour.

इंदीवर *indīvar* [S.], m. the blue lotus; a lotus.

इंदु *indu* [S.], m. **1.** the moon. **2.** transf. month. **3.** camphor. — इंदु-कर, m. a moonbeam. इंदुवार, m. Monday.

इंदुर *indur* [*undura-*, *indūra-*: ← Austro-as.], m. a rat; a mouse.

इंद्र *indră* [S.], m. var. /indər/. the Vedic god Indra (god of rain, later regarded as king of the gods excepting Brahmā, Viṣṇu and Śiva). — ~ का अखाड़ा, m. the celestial court of Indra: a place of amusement and pleasure. ~ की परी, f. an *apsarā*; a divinely beautiful woman. – इंद्र-जाल, m. illusion; sorcery; deception. °ई, adj. °अक, m. magician. इंद्र-जौ, m. the seed of a medicinal plant, *Nerium antidysentericum*, or *Wrightia tinctoria*; black cumin (*Nigella*). इंद्र-धनु, m. = next. इंद्र-धनुष, m. the bow of Indra: the rainbow. °ई, adj. इंद्र-ध्वज, m. the banner of Indra; a festival honouring Indra as rain-god, held on the twelfth day of the bright fortnight of Bhādoṁ. इंद्र-नील, m. sapphire; emerald. इंद्र-पुरी, f. the heaven of Indra. इंद्र-प्रस्थ, m. name of the ancient Pāṇḍava capital near the present site of Delhi. इंद्र-लोक, m. the paradise of Indra.

इंद्र-वधू, f. the wife of Indra; the red-velvet insect (*bīr-bahūṭī*). इंद्र-सभा, f. = ~ का अखाड़ा. इंद्रायुध [°*a*+*ā*°], m. Indra's weapon: the rainbow. इंद्रासन [°*a*+*ā*°], m. the throne of Indra, or of any king.

इंद्राणी *indrāṇī* [S.], f. **1.** the wife of the god Indra; a title of the goddess Durgā. **2.** a kind of creeper (= इंद्रायन). **3.** *Pl.* name of a medicine or plant, *Vitex negundo.*

इंद्रायन *indrāyan* [f. *indrāṇī*-], m. a wild gourd, *Cucumis colocynthis*, and its attractive but bitter-tasting fruit; a beautiful but worthless person.

इंद्रिय *indriyă* [S.], m. **1.** the senses. **2.** the organs of sense. **3.** the genitals. — इंद्रिय-गोचर, adj. perceptible by the senses. इंद्रियज, adj. arising from the senses. इंद्रिय-जन्य, adj. id. इंद्रियजित, adj. having subdued the senses. इंद्रियजीत, adj. Av. id. इंद्रिय-ज्ञान, m. knowledge derived from the senses; perception. इंद्रियवाद, m. sensuousness (as a style or characteristic); hedonism. इंद्रिय-संवेदना, m. sense perception. °-संवेद्य, adj. perceptible by the senses. इंद्रियार्थ [°*ya*+*a*°], m. an object perceived by the senses.

इंद्री *indrī*, m. pronun. var. = इंद्रिय. — ~ जुलाब, m. a diuretic medicine.

इंधन *indhan* [S.], m. **1.** firewood. **2.** fuel.

इंसाफ़ *iṃsāf*, m. see इनसाफ़.

-इ *-i* [S.], suffix (forms nouns, chiefly abstract and with few exceptions f., e.g. कृषि, f. cultivating, agriculture; पाणि, m. f. hand).

-इक *-ik* [S.], suffix (forms adjectives and derived agent nouns from nominal roots, with *vṛddhi* of root or initial vowel, e.g. धार्मिक, adj. religious; दैनिक, adj. daily; सैनिक, adj. & m. military, soldier; (सम)सामयिक, adj. contemporary).

इक- *ik-* [**ekka*-], adj. one: — इकछत, adj. undisputed (rule, sway); universal. इकछत्ता, adj. & m. having one wing (an aircraft); a monoplane. इकटक, adj. fixed, staring (look, eyes). इकठौरा, adj. in one place, assembled together. इकतरफ़ा [cf. A. *-ṯaraf*], adj. one-sided, unbalanced. इकतार, adj. continuous; monotonous. इकतारा, m. a single-stringed musical instrument. इकपेचा, m. a kind of head ornament. इकबारगी, adv. see एक-बारगी. इकबारा, adj. happening once or by chance. इकरंगा, adj. of one colour, monotone. इकलड़ा, adj. one-stringed (necklace). इकसार, adj. even, level; equal, the same. इकसार करना, to level (a surface); to cultivate (land).

इकट्ठा *ikaṭṭhā* [*ekastha*-], adj. **1.** collected, assembled; (gathered) together. **2.** taken together, totalled. — ~ करना, to collect; to accumulate; to call together, to convene; to sum up, to total; to concentrate, to consolidate (as resources).

इकतालीस *iktālīs* [*ekacatvāriṁśat*-], adj. forty-one.

इकत्तीस *ikattīs* [*ekatriṁśat*-], adj. var. /iktīs/. thirty-one.

इक़दाम *iqdām* [A. *iqdām*], m. U. going forward: endeavour, effort.

इक़बाल *iqbāl* [A. *iqbāl*], m. **1.** admission; confession, acknowledgement. **2.** acceptance. **3.** prestige; prosperity. — इक़बाल-दावा, m. admission of a claim. इक़बालमंद [P. *-mand*], adj. fortunate; prosperous.

इक़बालिया *iqbāliyā* [A. *iqbālīya*], adj. including a confession (a statement).

इक़बाली *iqbālī* [A. *iqbālī*], adj. accepting, confessing (responsibility, or guilt: a statement, &c).

इकराम *ikrām* [A. *ikrām*], m. **1.** honouring, complimenting; respect. **2.** remuneration.

इक़रार *iqrār* [A. *iqrār*], m. **1.** promise; settlement, agreement. **2.** consent, acquiescence. **3.** confirmation; assertion, declaration. **4.** confession, acknowledgement. — ~ करना to promise; to undertake (a task); to agree; to declare; to confess. – इक़रार-नामा, m. a written agreement, contract.

इक़रारी *iqrārī* [A. *iqrārī*], adj. **1.** promissory. **2.** assenting. **3.** confirmatory. **4.** acknowledging.

¹इकलाई *iklāī* [cf. H. *ikallā*], f. a single fold of material, single sheet; a variety of cotton *dhotī*.

²इकलाई *iklāī* [cf. H. *ikallā*], f. reg. = अकेलापन.

इकलौता *iklautā* [**ekkalaputra*-], adj. only, sole (a child). — ~ बेटा, m. only son.

इकल्ला *ikallā*, adj. = अकेला.

इकसठ *iksaṭh* [*ekaṣaṣṭi*-], adj. sixty-one.

इकहत्तर *ik'hattar* [*ekasaptati*-], adj. seventy-one.

इकहरा *ikahrā* [cf. **ekadhā*-, *-dhāra*-], adj. **1.** single, of one layer or piece; simple (rather than complex); single (journey); unitary. **2.** lean; thin.

-इका *-ikā* [S.], f. suffix (forms f. agent nouns from verb stems and dimin. nouns from nominal stems, e.g. लेखिका, woman writer; पेटिका, small box).

इकाई *ikāī* [cf. **ekka-*], f. **1.** a unit. **2.** one constituent of a whole. **3.** a single group, or a group having a specific purpose; detachment; unit.

इकादसी *ikādasī*, f. = एकादशी.

इकानवे *ikānve*, adj. = इक्यानवे.

इकावन *ikāvan*, adj. = इक्यावन.

इकासी *ikāsī*, adj. = इक्यासी.

-इकी *-ikī* [S.], suffix (forms f. nouns serving esp. as names of sciences and technical fields, e.g. भाषिकी, linguistics).

इकौंज *ikaumj* [cf. H. *ek*, *ik-* and H. [1]*hū*, 2.], f. reg. (W.) a woman who has borne only one child.

इकौना *ikaunā* [*ekavarṇa-*: MIA *-kk-*], adj. reg. of one kind, pure.

इक्कस *ikkas* [? conn. *īrṣyā-*: ad.], f. reg. envy; jealousy.

इक्का *ikkā* [**ekka-*], adj. & m. **1.** adj. single. **2.** solitary. **3.** unique. **4.** m. a one-horse vehicle. **5.** a single or lone individual; straggler. **6.** the ace (at cards).

इक्कीस *ikkīs* [*ekaviṁśati-*], adj. twenty-one. — ~ रहना, to be twenty-one (to another's twenty): to get the better (of, पर), to overcome.

इक्यानवे *ikyānve* [*ekanavati-*], adj. ninety-one.

इक्यावन *ikyāvan* [*ekapañcāśat-*], adj. fifty-one.

इक्यासी *ikyāsī* [*ekāśīti-*], adj. eighty-one.

इक्षु *ikṣu* [S.], m. (f., *Pl.*) sugar-cane.

इख़लाक़ *ikhlāq*, m. corr. see अख़लाक़.

इख़लाक़ी *ikhlāqī* [A. *akhlāqī*], adj. corr. moral, ethical.

इख़लास *ikhlās* [A. *ikhlāṣ*], m. Brbh. pure (unsullied) affection, friendship, or love.

इख़वान *ikhvān* [A. *ikhvān*, pl.], m. *isl.* brothers; co-religionists.

इख़्तियार *ikhtiyār*, m. see अख़्तियार.

इख़्तियारी *ikhtiyārī* [A. *ikhtiyārī*], adj. U. **1.** voluntary. **2.** optional.

इख़्तिलाफ़ *ikhtilāf* [A. *ikhtilāf*], m. discord; opposition.

इगर-दिगर *igar-digar* [f. P. H.-U. *dīgar*], adj. *Pl.* **1.** disarranged, in disorder. **2.** spoiled.

इगारह *igārah*, adj. pronun. var. reg. = ग्यारह.

इच्छा *icchā* [S.], f. **1.** wish, desire. **2.** will. — ~ करना (की), to wish, to desire. ~ रखना (की), = ~ करना; to be ambitious (of). ~ मारना, to subdue desire. ~ लगना (को), to long (for, की). – इच्छाचारी, adj. Av. pleasing oneself. इच्छानुसार [°*ā*+*a*°], adv. according to (one's, की). इच्छान्वित [°*ā*+*a*°], adj. desirous. इच्छापूर्ण, adj. desirous. इच्छापूर्वक, adj. voluntary; deliberate. इच्छामय, adv. Av. by or according to one's (own) wish. इच्छा-मरण, m. Av. finding death at the time one wishes. इच्छारूप, adj. wilful.

इच्छित *icchit* [S.], adj. **1.** wished for. **2.** intended.

इच्छुक *icchuk* [S.], adj. & m. **1.** adj. desirous. **2.** m. one desirous (of sthg.: का).

इज़तिराब *iztirāb* [A. *iẓṭirāb*], m. U. anxiety, distress.

[1]**इजरा** *ijrā* [A. *ijrā*], m. causing to circulate: issuing, or giving effect to (as to a decree). — ~ करना, to issue; to execute.

[2]**इजरा** *ijrā*, m. *HŚS.* = इजरान.

इजरान *ijrān*, m. reg. (W.) land left fallow to recover its fertility.

इजलास *ijlās* [A. *ijlās*], m. **1.** sitting, session (as of a court or committee). **2.** a court.

[1]**इज़हार** *izhār* [A. *iẓhār*], m. **1.** disclosure, display; declaration. **2.** *law.* evidence, statement. — ~ करना, to make known; to declare; to express; to describe, to explain. ~ देना, to testify. ~ लेना, to record a statement; to examine (a witness). – इज़हारे तहरीरी, m. written evidence, deposition.

[2]**इज़हार** *izhār* [A. *iḥẓār*], m. U. causing to appear: summoning, summons.

इजाज़त *ijāzat* [A. *ijāza*: P. *ijāzat*], f. **1.** permission, leave; leave to depart, dismissal (from one's presence). **2.** authority (to do sthg.); sanction. — ~ देना (को), to grant leave, &c. (to do sthg., की); to allow to go (from one's presence); to grant, to concede; to authorise, to sanction; to empower.

इज़ाफ़त *izāfat* [A. *iẓāfa*: P. *iẓāfat*], f. increment: **1.** *gram.* the linking vowel *i* or *e* (as used in nominal constructions in Arabic, Persian and Urdu). **2.** generic name of the above constructions.

इज़ाफ़ा *izāfā* [A. *iẓāfa*], m. **1.** increase; additional amount. **2.** surplus, excess. — ~ करना, to increase. – इज़ाफ़ा-लगान, f. an increase in rent.

इज़ार *izār* [P. *izār*], f. trousers (= पायजामा). — इज़ारबंद [P. *-band*], m. draw-string of trousers. इज़ारबंद का ढीला, adj. lecherous.

इजारा *ijārā* [A. *ijāra*], m. **1.** leasing, letting, renting. **2.** a contract of lease or rental. **3.** land, or a house, &c., taken on lease or rented. **4.** right, title (as arising from lease or contract); monopoly. — ~ **करना**, to make a contract (to, **का**). ~ **देना** (**को**), to lease out, &c. (to). ~ **लेना**, to take on lease, &c. **इजारे पर लेना**, id. – **इजारेदार** [P. *-dār*], m. & adj. lease-holder, &c.; holder of a monopoly; monopolistic. °**ई**, f. monopoly.

इज़्ज़त *izzat* [A. *'izza*: P. *'izzat*], f. honour; good name; esteem. — ~ **उतारना** or **खोना**, or **बिगाड़ना** (**की**), = ~ **लेना**. ~ **करना** (**की**), to honour; to show respect (to). ~ **के पीछे पड़ना**, to be intent on ruining the honour or name (of, **की**). ~ **देना** (**को**), to honour. ~ **पर पानी फेरना**, = ~ **लेना**, 1. ~ **में फ़र्क़ आना**, or **बट्टा लगना**, honour or reputation to be sullied. ~ **रखना** (**अपनी**), to preserve (one's) honour; to be respected or honoured. ~ **लेना**, or **लूटना**, (**की**), to deprive (one) of honour or reputation, to treat with dishonour; to insult; to violate (a woman). (**दो**) **कौड़ी की** ~ **कर देना**, to heap insults or disgrace (on, **को**). – **इज़्ज़तदार** [P. *-dār*], adj. honoured, respected; holding high rank. **इज़्ज़तवाला**, adj. id.

इठलाना *iṭhlānā*, v.i. **1.** to walk affectedly, or flirtatiously; to give oneself airs. **2.** to speak other than in a normal way (as pertly, irritably, rudely); to drawl; to speak indistinctly. **3.** to avoid giving a direct answer; to feign ignorance.

इडली *iḍlī*, f. a steamed rice-cake (south Indian).

इड़ा *iṛā* [S.], f. **1.** *mythol.* a goddess, daughter of Manu, or of man. **2.** (in yoga) the left of three vessels running from the loins to the head.

इत *it*, adv. here; hither. — ~ **उत**, adv. = **इधर उधर**.

-इत *-it* [S.], suffix (forms passive past participial adjectives from verb roots and from modified forms of verb stems, e.g. **परिचित**, acquainted; **क्रोधित**, angered, angry).

इतक *itak*, adj. *Pl.* so much, this much.

इतना *itnā* [cf. *iyattaka-*], adj. as much as this, as many as this. — ~ **ही नहीं**, adv. not only this (but). **इतना-सा मुँह निकल आना** (**का**), to look taken aback, or disconsolate; fig. (the face) to have grown thin. **इतनी-सी बात पर**, adv. on (account of) so small a matter. **इतने पर भी**, adv. despite this. **इतने में**, adv. in the meantime; with this, with that. – **इतना-उतना**, m. a small quantity; a trifle.

इतबार *itbār*, m. = **एतबार**.

इतमाम *itmām* [A. *itmām*], m. completion, accomplishment.

इतमीनान *itmīnān* [A. *iṯmīnān*], m. **1.** content; repose, calm. *2. assurance; confidence; reliance. — ~ **करना**, to trust (in, **का** or **पर**), to rely (on); to give credence (to); to feel assurance (of). ~ **दिलाना** (**को**), id.; to cause (one) to be assured. ~ **देना** (**को**), to assure (one: of, **का**). ~ **रखना**, to feel content, to feel assurance (of). ~ **से**, adv. with assurance; with composure; contentedly.

इतमीनानी *itmīnānī* [A. *iṯmīnān*+P. *-ī*], adj. trustworthy, reliable.

इतर *itar* [S.], adj. **1.** other; remaining. **2.** inferior. — **इतर-भाषा**, f. specif. an Indian language other than Hindi. **इतरेतर** [°*ra*+*i*°], adj. mutual; reciprocal; respective.

इतराना *itrānā* [cf. *itvara-*], v.i. **1.** to behave with pride, or conceit, or arrogance, or affectation. **2.** pej. to exult (at, **पर**). **3.** to strut, to swagger (cf. **इठलाना**).

इतवार *itvār* [? conn. *āditya-*: anal. H. *ravivār*], m. Sunday.

इताअत *itāat* [A. *iṯā'a*: P. *iṯā'at*], f. U. **1.** obedience, submission; homage.

इतस्ततः *itastataḥ* [S.], adv. hither and thither.

इति *iti* [S.], adv. & f. **1.** adv. this much; thus. **2.** f. end, conclusion (as of a book, or letter). — ~ **करना** (**की**), v.t. to bring to an end, to conclude. – **इति-कर्तव्य**, m. a clear duty, or obligation. **इति-वृत्त**, m. a narrative; chronicle. **इतिवृत्तात्मक** [°*tta*+*ā*°], adj. narrative. **इत्यलम** [°*ti*+*a*], adv. and so to finish; the end. **इत्यादि** [°*ti*+*ā*], conj. etcetera. **इत्यादिक**, adj. pl. suchlike, similar, of such a group.

इतिहास *iti-hâs* [S.], m. thus indeed it was: history, annals; tradition; account. — **इतिहासकार**, m. a historian. **इतिहासज्ञ**, m. one versed in history; a historian. **इतिहासविद्**, m. id. **इतिहास-वेत्ता**, m. inv. id.

इतेक *itek*, adj. Brbh. = **इतना**.

इतै *itai* [cf. H. *it*], adv. Brbh. hither.

इतौ *itau*, adj. Brbh. = **इतना**.

इत्तफ़ाक़ *ittafāq* [A. *ittifāq*], m. **1.** concurrence: concord, harmony. **2.** confederation; conspiracy. ***3.** coincidence, chance; incident, affair. — ~ **करना**, = ~ **रखना**. ~ **पड़ना**, to happen, to chance. ~ **बनना**, agreement to exist (between, **में**); to agree; to suit, to be opportune. ~ **रखना**, to be in accord (with, **से**); to be on good terms (with); to live peaceably (with). ~ **से**, adv. by chance; unexpectedly.

इत्तफ़ाक़न *ittafāqan* [A. *ittifāqan*], adv. by chance; unexpectedly.

इत्तफ़ाक़िया *ittafāqiyā* [A. *ittifāqīya*], adj. inv. chance, accidental; unexpected.

इत्तफ़ाक़ी *ittafāqī* [A. *ittifāqī*], adj. = इत्तफ़ाक़िया.

इत्तला *ittalā* [A. *ittilā'*], f. var. (U.) /ittila/. **1.** information; notification; report. **2.** declaration, announcement. — ~ करना, to inform (of, से), to report; to announce. ~ देना (को), id. – इत्तला-नामा, m. a written notice; summons or citation. इत्तलामंद [P. *-mand*] adj. acquainted (with), apprized (of).

इत्तलाई *ittalāī* [cf. H. *ittalā*], adj. informing, notifying.

इत्तहाद *ittahād* [A. *ittiḥād*], m. U. union, league.

इत्ता *ittā*, adj. reg. = इतना.

इत्तिफ़ाक़ *ittifāq*, m. = इत्तफ़ाक़.

इत्तिला *ittilā*, f. = इत्तला.

इत्यादि *ity-ādi*, conj. see s.v. इति.

इत्र *itr* [A. *'itr*], m. **1.** fragrant essence, attar. **2.** perfume. **3.** incense. — ~ खींचना, or निकालना, to extract an essence. ~ मलना (पर), or लगाना (में), to rub scent on (body or clothes). – इतरदान [P. *-dān*], m. container for perfume, &c.

इदमित्थं *idamittham* [S.], adv. truly, indeed.

इदर *idar*, adv. pronun. var. = इधर.

इधर *idhar* [cf. H. [1]*dhār*], adv. **1.** hither; over here, on this side; on the one hand. **2.** recently; at the present time; towards a time in question. **3.** here. — ~ का, adj. belonging to this place, time or group. ~ का उधर होना, to be transformed; to be overturned. ~ की उधर करना, or लगाना, to distort, to misrepresent. ~ से उधर करना, to disarrange, to throw into disorder. ~ से उधर होना, to be disarranged, disordered; to be turned upside down; to be subverted; to be scattered, dispersed; to have vanished. – इधर-उधर, adv. hither and thither; here and there; around; anywhere, any place at all. इधर-उधर करना, to temporise; to shilly-shally; to disarrange; to dissipate (funds); to scatter, to disperse. इधर-उधर का, adj. various; unspecific, casual, desultory (remarks, conversation). इधर-उधर की लगाना, = इधर-उधर करना, 1. इधर-उधर की हाँकना, to talk boastfully. इधर-उधर रहना (के), to shadow, to tail (one). इधर-उधर में रहना, to spend time on this and that (not on the matter which should be in hand).

इन *in*, pl. obl. base. see यह 'this'.

-इन *-in* [*-inī-*], suffix (forms feminines of m. nouns referring to animate beings, e.g. लोहारिन, blacksmith's wife; दुल्हिन, bride; बाघिन, tigress).

इनक़लाब *inqalāb* [A. *inqilāb*], m. change, turn: **1.** revolution. **2.** transformation.

इनकार *inkār* [A. *inkār*], m. **1.** denial; objection (as to an argument); contradiction. **2.** refusal; rejection. — ~ करना (से), to deny; to contradict; to refuse (to); to reject.

इनकारी *inkārī* [cf. A. *inkār*], adj. & f. **1.** adj. expressing denial, refusal, &c.; negative (an answer). **2.** f. the act of denying, refusing, &c.; rebuttal.

इनक़िलाब *inqilāb*, m. see इनक़लाब.

इनफ़िसाल *infisāl* [A. *infiṣāl*], m. U. *law.* decision (of a case: cf. फ़ैसला).

इनशाल्लाह *inśāllāh* [A. *in śā' allāhu*], adv. if God wills.

इनसान *insān* [A. *insān*], m. **1.** a man, human being. **2.** mankind.

इनसानियत *insāniyat* [A. *insānīya*: P. *insāniyat*], f. **1.** human nature, humanity. **2.** human kindness, humanity.

इनसानी *insānī* [A. *insānī*], adj. **1.** human. **2.** humane (= मानवी).

इनसाफ़ *insāf* [A. *inṣāf*], m. **1.** justice, equity; impartiality. **2.** fair decision. — ~ करना, to act justly, to do right; to see justice done; to decide (a suit). ~ चाहना, to seek justice, or redress. ~ चुकाना, = ~ करना. ~ से, adv. justly, rightly; fairly. – इनसाफ़-तलब [A. *-ṭalab*], adj. U. seeking justice. इनसाफ़पसंद, adj. just, impartial.

इनसाफ़ी *insāfī* [cf. H. *insāf*], adj. just, impartial.

इनहिसार *inhisār* [A. *inḥiṣār*], m. U. encirclement, blockade.

इनाम *inām* [A. *in'ām*], m. **1.** a gift, favour. **2.** a prize, reward. **3.** a gratuity, tip. **4.** grant of rent-free land. — ~ देना (को) to give a reward, &c. (to). – इनाम-इकराम, m. reward and honour; gratuities. इनामदार [P. *-dār*], m. recipient of an award, or of a grant of rent-free land.

इनामी *ināmī* [A. *in'āmī*], adj. **1.** serving as a prize, &c. **2.** having prizes (a competition).

इनायत *ināyat* [A. *'ināya*: P. *'ināyat*], f. favour, kindness. — ~ करना, to show favour, &c. (to, पर). ~ रखना, id.

इनायती *ināyatī* [P. *'ināyatī*], adj. bestowed (a gift); favoured.

इनार *inār*, m. reg. = इँदारा.

-इनी *-inī* [S.], suffix (forms feminines, see s.v. -ई, 1).

इन्कार *inkār*, m. see इनकार.

इफ़रात *ifrāt* [A. *ifrāṯ*], f. ? m. (*Pl.*) excess, abundance. — ~ से होना, to abound. – इफ़रात-तफ़रीत, f. = अफ़रा-तफ़री.

इबरत *ibrat* [A. *'ibra*: P. *'ibrat*], f. U. warning; example.

इबरानी *ibrānī* [A. *'ibrānī*], adj. U. Jewish.

इबलीस *iblīs* [A. *iblīs*], m. Av. the devil, Satan.

इबादत *ibādat* [A. *'ibāda*: P. *'ibādat*], f. divine worship. — ~ करना (की), to worship (Allah). – इबादत-ख़ाना, m. mosque. इबादत-गाह [P. *-gāh*], f. id.

इबारत *ibārat* [A. *'ibāra*: P. *'ibārat*], f. **1.** article, essay. **2.** sentence structure. **3.** diction, style.

इब्तिदा *ibtidā* [A. *ibtidā*], f. beginning. — ~ करना, to begin; to inaugurate.

इब्तिदाई *ibtidāī* [A. *ibtidā'ī*], adj. introductory, elementary; primary, prior.

इब्रानी *ibrānī*, adj. Jewish; Hebrew.

इभ *ibh* [S.], m. Brbh. **1.** an elephant. **2.** (in chronograms) the number eight.

इम *im*, adv. = इमि.

इमकान *imkān* [A. *imkān*], m. U. **1.** capacity, power. ***2.** possibility, practicability.

इमदाद *imdād* [A. *imdād*], adj. U. **1.** help, assistance; subsidy. **2.** donation.

इमदादी *imdādī* [A. *imdād*+*-ī*], adj. U. **1.** assisted (as with funds); subsidised. **2.** auxiliary, supporting; relief (service).

इमरती *imartī* [? ad. *amṛta-*], f. **1.** a sweet made from pulse (fried in *ghī*: resembling the *jalebī*). **2.** reg. a small type of melon. **3.** *Pl.* small vessel for drinking from.

इमला *imlā* [A. *imlā*], m. **1.** correct writing, orthography. **2.** dictation. — ~ बोलना, to dictate. ~ लिखना, to take dictation.

इमली *imlī* [*āmla-*, Pk. *aṁbiliyā-*], f. the tamarind tree and its fruit. — ~ घोंटाना, rubbing with tamarind: a partic. marriage rite.

इमाम *imām* [A. *imām*], m. a religious leader; patriarch; priest. — इमाम-बाड़ा, m. a place where the *tāziyā* is kept by Shī'a Muslims during the month of Muḥarram; a building in which services commemorating the death of 'Alī and his sons Ḥasan and Ḥusain are held, in Muḥarram, a shrine; mausoleum.

इमामत *imāmat* [A. *imāma*: P. *imāmat*], f. the office of an *imām*.

इमामदस्ता *imām-dastā* [f. P. *hāvan-dasta*], m. mortar and pestle.

इमामा *imāmā*, m. = अमामा.

[1]**इमारत** *imārat* [A. *'imāra*: P. *'imārat*], f. building: **1.** a building. **2.** structure; superstructure (as of belief).

[2]**इमारत** *imārat* [A. *amāra*: P. *amārat*], f. emirate: command, power, authority.

इमारती *imārătī* [A. *'imāratī*], adj. having to do with building; used in building (materials).

इमि *imi*, adv. Brbh. Av. in this way (= ऐसे).

इम्तहान *imtahān* [A. *imtihān*], m. examination; test. — ~ देना, to take (to undergo) an examination. ~ लेना (का), to examine, to test (pupils, candidates).

इम्तियाज़ *imtiyāz* [A. *imtiyāz*], m. U. **1.** distinction, discrimination. **2.** discernment.

इम्तिहान *imtihān*, m. – इम्तहान.

-इयत *-iyat* [A. *-īya(t)*], suffix (forms f. abstract nouns, e.g. ख़ैरियत, f. well-being).

इयत्ता *iyattā* [S.], f. scope, extent.

-इया *-iyā*, suffix. **1.** [chiefly *-ika-*] forms chiefly agent nouns (e.g. डाकिया, m. postman; सुखिया, adj. happy). **2.** [*-ikā-*] forms feminines and diminutives, chiefly f. (e.g. बुढ़िया, old woman; डिबिया, small box). **3.** [*-ika-*] forms inv. adjectives of the sense 'having to do with, belonging to' (e.g. कलकतिया, of or belonging to Calcutta).

इरशाद *irśād* [A. *irśād*], m. U. direction, instruction; order.

इरसाल *irsāl* [A. *irsāl*], m. U. **1.** sending, despatch. **2.** sthg. sent, a remittance.

इरसी *irsī*, f. *Pl. HŚS.* axle-tree, axle.

इराक़ी *irāqī* [A. *'irāqī*], adj. & m. **1.** adj. Iraqi. **2.** m. an Iraqi. **3.** an Arab horse.

इरादतन *irādatan* [A. *irādatan̲*], adv. intentionally.

इरादा *irādā* [A. *irāda*], m. **1.** desire. ***2.** intention. — ~ करना, to intend (to, का); to aim (for: as for a goal). ~ होना, an intention to exist (on the part of, का: to, का). इरादे से, adv. intentionally; with the intention (of, के).

इर्द-गिर्द *ird-gird* [cf. P. *gird*], adv. **1.** all around, around; round about, in the vicinity. **2.** ppn. w. के. all around, &c.

इलज़ाम *ilzām* [A. *ilzām*], m. **1.** accusation, charge. **2.** censure; disgrace. **3.** calumny, libel.

— ~ देना, or लगाना (को), to accuse, to charge (with, का); to denounce. ~ धरना, to find fault (with, पर); to accuse (of).

इलाक़ा *ilāqā* [A. *'alāqa*], m. attachment, connection: **1.** a district; region. **2.** estate, holding. **3.** Brbh. connection.

इलाज *ilāj* [A. *'ilāj*], m. **1.** medical treatment. **2.** a remedy, cure. — ~ करना (का), to treat; to cure; colloq. to punish.

इलायची *ilāycī* [P. *ilācī*, conn. *elā-*: ← Drav.], f. var. /ilacī/. cardamom. — ~ बाँटना, *musl.* to distribute cardamoms: to invite to a marriage. – इलायची-दाना, m. a cardamom seed; a partic. sweet, cardamoms coated with sugar.

इलाही *ilahī* [A. *ilāhī*], adj. & m. **1.** having to do with God; divine, heavenly. **2.** m. Allah. **3.** interj. Oh God!

इल्तमास *iltamās* [A. *iltimās*], m. petition, request. — ~ करना (से), to petition, to request.

इल्तिजा *iltijā* [A. *iltijā*], f. U. entreaty, petition. — ~ करना, to make entreaty (of, से).

इल्तिफ़ात *iltifāt* [A. *iltifāt*], f. U. attention, regard; courtesy.

इल्म *ilm* [A. *'ilm*], m. **1.** knowledge. **2.** science.

इल्मी *ilmī* [A. *'ilmī*], adj. U. having to do with knowledge: scientific; literary; learned.

इल्लत *illat* [A. *'illa*: P. *'illat*], f. **1.** a fault, defect. **2.** a bad habit. **3.** sthg. bad or worthless. **4.** U. charge, indictment. — ~ लगाना, to acquire a bad habit. ~ में गिरफ़्तार होना, to be arrested and charged (with, की).

इल्ला *illa*, m. reg. a wart.

इल्ली *illī*, f. a caterpillar that attacks *arhar*.

-इश *-iś* [P. *-iś*], suffix (forms f. abstract nouns, e.g. गुंजाइश, space, scope).

इशरत *iśrat* [A. *'iśra*: P. *'iśrat*], f. enjoyment, pleasure.

इशारत *iśārat* [A. *iśāra*: P. *iśārat*], f. U. = इशारा.

इशारा *iśārā* [A. *iśāra*], m. **1.** sign; nod, wink, nudge. **2.** indication; allusion; hint; insinuation. — ~ करना, to make a sign, &c.; to point (at, पर), to point (out); to allude (to); to hint; to insinuate. – इशारेबाज़ी [P. *-bāzī*], f. conducting a mute dialogue (of gestures, glances).

इश्क़ *iśq* [A. *'iśq*], m. **1.** love, passion (for, से). **2.** passion, craze (for, का). — ~ लड़ाना, to have a love affair. — इश्क़-पेचाँ, m. = next. इश्क़-पेचा, m. a red-flowering twining plant; American jasmine, *Ipomœa quamoclit*, or *Q. vulgaris*. इश्क़बाज़ [P. *-bāz*], adj. & m. amorous; a ladies' man. °ई, f. flirtation.

इश्क़िया *iśqiyā* [cf. H. *iśq*], adj. inv. amatory; erotic.

इश्क़ी *iśqī* [P. *'iśqī*], adj. = इश्क़िया.

इश्तआल *iśtaāl* [A. *iśti'āl*], m. U. inflaming: causing (a dispute, an offence).

इश्तहार *iśtahār* [A. *iśtihār*], m. **1.** announcement, notification. **2.** an advertisement; a poster. **3.** a notice; leaflet. — ~ करना, to announce, to make public. ~ देना, id. – इश्तहार-नामा, m. an advertisement; poster. इश्तहारबाज़ी [P. *-bāzī*], f. advertising.

इश्तहारी *iśtahārī* [cf. A. *iśtihār*], adj. notified: advertised for, wanted.

इषा *iṣā* [S.], f. *Pl. HŚS.* pole, shaft (of plough, or vehicle).

इष्ट *iṣṭ* [S.], adj. & m. **1.** adj. desired. **2.** cherished; favourite. ~ मित्र, m. a close friend. **3.** revered. **4.** m. an object of desire, love or reverence; a favoured deity; a beloved person; one favoured by a deity. **5.** faith, trust, love. **6.** aim, goal. — इष्ट-काल, m. *astrol.* favourable moment. इष्ट-देव, m. the favoured deity of a family, or of an individual.

इष्टका *iṣṭakā* [S.], f. **1.** a brick. **2.** a brick used in building a Vedic sacrificial altar.

इष्टता *iṣṭātā* [S.], f. **1.** desirable or lovable quality. **2.** worthiness of reverence.

इष्टि *iṣṭi* [S.], f. **1.** desire. **2.** an object of desire.

इस *is* [*eṣa*[1], gen. sg. *etasya*], sg. obl. base. this (see यह). — ~पर भी, adv. despite this. इसलिए, adv. for this reason; and so, therefore. इसलिए कि, adv. for the reason that, because.

इसपरमूल *isparmūl*, m. *Pl.* a shrub, the Indian birthwort, *Aristolochia indica* (said to be an antidote to snake poison).

इसपात *ispāt*, m. = इस्पात.

इसबग़ोल *isbagol*, m. horse's ear: seed of the fleawort (a plant of the genus *Plantago*).

इसमाईली *ismāīlī* [A. *ismā'īlī*], m. name of a partic. Muslim community; a man of that community.

इसराईली *isrāīlī* [A. *isrā'īlī*], adj. & m., f. **1.** adj. Jewish; Israeli. **2.** m., f. a Jew; an Israeli.

इसराज *isrāj*, m. a kind of lute.

इसराफ़ *isrāf* [A. *isrāf*], m. excess, extravagance.

इसरार *isrār* [A. *iṣrār*], m. insistence, perseverance.

इसलाम *islām* [A. *islām*], m. Islam.

इसलामी *islāmī* [A. *islāmī*], adj. & m. **1.** adj. Islamic. **2.** m. a Muslim.

इसलाह *islāh* [A. *iṣlāḥ*], f. U. **1.** improvement; revision. **2.** reform.

इसी *isī*, sg. obl. base emphat. this (very). — **~से**, adv. for this very reason. **इसीलिए**, adv. id.

इस्टंट *isṭanṭ* [Engl. *assistant*], m. pronun. var. assistant.

इस्टाम *isṭām* [Engl. *stamp*], m. pronun. var. stamp: 1. postage stamp. **2.** stamp duty.

इस्टेशन *isṭeśan*, m. = **स्टेशन**.

इस्तक़बाल *istaqbāl* [A. *istiqbāl*], m. reception, welcome. — **~ करना (का)**, to receive, to welcome (a visitor, guest).

इस्तग़ासा *istagāsā* [A. *istigāsa*], m. U. calling for help: **1.** demanding justice; complaint, suit. **2.** *law.* the prosecution.

इस्तदुआ *istaduā* [conn. A. *istid'ā*: w. H. *duā*], f. corr. request; entreaty.

इस्तरी *istrī* [cf. Pt. *estirar*], f. **1.** an iron. **2.** ironing. — **~ करना**, to iron.

इस्तिंजा *istiñjā* [A. *istinjā*], m. *musl.* washing or wiping the private parts after satisfying nature. — **~ करना**, to wash, &c.; to urinate.

इस्तिक़बाल *istiqbāl*, m. see **इस्तक़बाल**.

इस्तिरी *istirī*, f. see **इस्तरी**.

इस्तिलाह *istilāh* [A. *iṣṭilāḥ*], f. U. **1.** phrase, idiom, usage. **2.** a technical term.

इस्तिसनाई *istisnāī* [A. *istiṣnāī*], adj. U. exceptional.

इस्तिस्नाय *istisnāy* [A. *istiṣnā*], m. *Pl. HŚS.* making a second: exclusion, exception.

इस्तीफ़ा *istīfā* [A. *isti'fā, istīfā*], m. seeking to be excused (from): **1.** resignation. **2.** abdication. — **इस्तीफ़ा देना**, to resign, &c. (from, **से**).

इस्तेदाद *istedād* [A. *isti'dād*], m. U. readiness: capacity, abilities.

इस्तेमाल *istemāl* [A. *isti'māl*], m. **1.** use, operation. **2.** practice, exercise (at, **का**: as at a sport). **3.** usage, custom; vogue. — **(का) ~ करना**, to use, to employ. **~ में आना**, to come into use; to be used. **~ में लाना (को)**, to bring into use, operation, &c. **~ में होना**, to be used.

इस्तेमाली *istemālī* [A. *isti'mālī*], adj. **1.** used, made use of. **2.** worn, second-hand (clothes). **3.** customary.

इस्पात *ispāt* [Pt. *espada*], m. steel.

इस्पाती *ispātī* [cf. H. *ispāt*], adj. **1.** made of steel. **2.** tempered.

इस्म *ism* [A. *ism*], m. U. name.

इस्लाम *islām*, m. see **इसलाम**.

इस्लामी *islāmī*, adj. & m. see **इसलामी**.

[1]**इह** *ih* [S.], adv. & m. **1.** adv. in this place; in this world. **2.** m. this world. — **इह-काल**, m. time here: this life. **इह-लोक**, m. this world.

[2]**इह** *ih*, pron. Brbh. = **यह**.

इहलौकिक *ihlaukik* [S.}, adj. of this world: worldly.

इहाँ *ihāṁ*, adv. Brbh. Av. = **यहाँ**.

इहि *ihi*, pron. Brbh. = **यह, इस**.

इहै *ihai*, pron. Brbh. = **यही**.

ई

ई *ī*, the fourth vowel of the Devanāgarī syllabary. — **ईकार**, m. the sound /ī/; the letter **ई**.

ईंगुर *ĩmgur* [*hiṅgula-*], m. red lead, vermilion.

इंघे *iṅghe*, adv. reg. here, hither.

ईंट *ĩmṭ* [*iṣṭ(ak)ā-*], f. **1.** a brick. **2.** an ingot. **3.** a tile. **4.** diamond (at cards). — **~ का घर मिट्टी करना**, to destroy a brick house: to destroy (one's) prosperity. **~ का जवाब पत्थर से देना**, to give a stone for a brick: to return with interest (a blow, an insult). **~ की चुनाई**, f. brick-laying; brickwork. **~ से ~ बजना**, brick to ring on brick: to be demolished; to be utterly ruined; to become public (a scandal or quarrel: between, **की**). **~ से ~ बजाना**, to raze to the ground; to lay in ruins. **डेढ़**, or **ढाई**, **~ का मसजिद अलग बनाना**, esp. pej. to make a little mosque of one's own: to differ from others (in thoughts or actions); to stand aloof. – **ईंटकारी** [P. *-karī*], f. brickwork. **ईंट-टाइल**, f. a tile. **ईंट-पत्थर**, m. brick and stone; sthg. of no intrinsic worth. **ईंटबंदी** [P. *-bandī*], f. brickwork; a brick structure.

ईंटा *ĩmṭā*, m. = **ईंट**.

ईंटाया *ĩmṭāyā* [cf. H. *aiṁṭhā*], m. *Pl.* the ring-dove, *Turtur cambayensis*.

ईंडुआ *ĩmḍuā*, m. = **ईंडुरी**.

ईंडुरी *ĩmḍurī* [**iṇḍuva-*: Pk. *aṇḍuva-*], f. a roll, coil or ring of cloth, straw or rope, on which sthg. is carried on the head, or on which round-bottomed vessels may be rested.

ईंदुर *ĩndur* [*indūra-*, Pk. *iṁdura-*: ← Austro-as.], m. **1.** rat; mouse. **2.** mole.

ईंधन *ĩndhan* [S.], m. fuel (wood, mineral, chemical). — **आण्विक ~**, m. atomic energy.

-ई *-ī*, suffix. **1.** [S.] forms m. nouns, and adjectives from nominal forms (e.g. **अधिकारी**, m. an official; **सुखी**, adj. happy; **कुचाली**, adj. of bad conduct; feminines often in *-इनी*).
2. [H. *-ī*, f.: × 3. below, and S.] forms f. nouns from nouns and verbs (e.g. **फेरी**, f. circuit; **बोली**, f. speech, language; dimin. **पहाड़ी**, f. hill; **देवी**, f. goddess; **रस्सी**, f. rope, string).
3. [P.: × 2. above] forms abstract nouns and adjectives from nominal forms and present stems of Persian verbs, of the sense 'connected with, belonging to' (c.g. **दोस्ती**, f. friendship; **हिंदी**, Hindi; **ख़ुशी**, f. happiness; **डाक्टरी**, f. study or practice of medicine; **(समझ)दारी**, f. intelligence).

-ईकरण *-ī-karaṇ* [S.], suffix (forms m. nouns having the force 'transformation into ..., -isation', e.g. **आधुनीकरण**, modernisation; **सरकारीकरण**, taking under government control).

-ईकृत *-ī-kṛt* [S.], suffix (forms adjectives having the force 'made into ..., -ised', e.g. **स्वीकृत**, adj. made one's own: accepted).

ईक्षण *īkṣaṇ* [S.], m. **1.** sight. **2.** the eye. **3.** looking at, viewing.

ईक्षणिक *īkṣaṇik* [S]., m. an astrologer.

ईख *īkh* [*ikṣu-*], f. sugar-cane.

-ईचा *-īcā* [P. *-īca*], suffix (forms m. dimin. nouns, e.g. **बाग़ीचा**, **बग़ीचा**, garden).

ईज़ा *īzā* [A. *īzā*], f. E.H. harm, injury; molestation.

ईजाद *ījād* [A. *ījād*], m. sthg. created: an invention, contrivance. — **~ करना**, to invent; to design; to discover. **~ होना**, to be invented, developed, &c.

ईज़ाद *īzād* [conn. P. *ziāda*], m. increase; addition. — **~ करना**, to increase, &c. (= **ज़्यादा करना**).

ईजादी *ījādī* [A. *ījādī*], adj. inventive.

ईठ *īṭh* [*iṣṭa-*], adj. Brbh. = **इष्ट**.

ईठि *īṭhi* [*iṣṭi-²*], f. Brbh. **1.** affection. **2.** desire. **3.** a woman's female friend (= **सखी**).

ईठी *īṭhī* [*ṛṣṭi-*], f. *Pl. HŚS.* spear, lance.

ईति *īti* [S.], f. Brbh. any seasonal disaster (as drought, flood, plague of insects); distress, suffering.

ईद *īd* [A. *'īd*], f. **1.** a festival. **2.** specif. *musl.* either of two festivals: (a) that of the breaking of the fast of Ramaẓān, held on the day after the new moon of that month, or (b) the sacrificial festival held in the month of *zu'l ḥijja*. — **~ का चाँद**, m. an *īd* moon: sthg. or someone rarely seen. – **ईद-गाह** [P. *-gāh*], f. a site (usu. enclosed) where *īd* and other Muslim celebrations are held. **बक़र-ईद**, f. = ~, 2(b).

ईदी *īdī* [P. *'īdī*], adj. **1.** adj. of or having to do with *īd*. **2.** f. a gift made at *īd*; money given to children at *īd*.

ईदुज़्ज़ोहा *īduzzohā* [A. *'īdu'ẓ-ẓŏhā*], f. = ईद, 2(b).

ईदुलफ़ितर *īdulfitr* [A. *'īdu'l fiṭr*], f. = ईद, 2(a).

ईदृश *īdṛś* [S.], adj. = ऐसा.

-ईन *-īn* [A. *-īn*], suffix (forms adjectives from nouns, e.g. शौक़ीन, eager, cultivated).

ईप्सित *īpsit* [S.], adj. desired, longed for.

ईफ़ाय *īfāy* [A. *īfā* (w. *izāfat*)], f. U. fulfilling (a promise); observing (an undertaking).

-ईभूत *-ī-bhūt* [S.], suffix (forms adjectives having the force 'become or changed into ..., -ised', e.g. घनीभूत, grown dense, or perceptible).

ईमान *īmān* [A. *īmān*], m. **1.** belief (esp. in God); faith, creed. **2.** good faith: honesty; trustworthiness; integrity. **3.** honour. **4.** conscience. — ~ का, adj. honest; trustworthy; fair; conscientious. ~ की कहना, to speak the truth. ~ की बात, f. sthg. said in good faith; the truth. ~ ठिकाने न होना, honesty to be absent: to have acted dishonestly or unscrupulously. ~ देना, to give up honesty: to act dishonestly, &c. ~ बेचना, to break one's word, or faith; to sell one's honour. ~ में फ़रक़ आना = ~ ठिकाने न होना. ~ रखना, to believe (in, पर). ~ लाना, to believe (in, पर); to become converted (to); to place confidence (in); to believe, to credit. ~ से, adv. faithfully; honestly; solemnly (of an assertion, &c.); conscientiously. — ईमानदार [P. *-dār*], adj. believing, feeling faith; faithful; righteous, guided by conscience; honest; trustworthy. °ई, f. faith (in God); fidelity; honesty, trustworthiness.

ईमानी *īmānī* [A. *īmān*+P. *-ī*], adj. faithful.

-ईय *-īyă* [S.], suffix (forms adjectives, e.g. भारतीय, Indian).

ईरान *īrān* [P. *īrān*], m. Iran.

[1]**ईरानी** *īrānī* [P. *īrānī*], adj. & m. **1.** adj. Iranian. **2.** m. an Iranian.

[2]**ईरानी** *īrānī* [P. *īrān*+H. *-ī*], f. the Persian language (incorrectly for फ़ारसी).

ईर्षा *īrṣā* [S.], f. see ईर्ष्या.

ईर्ष्या *īrṣyā* [S.], f. **1.** envy. **2.** jealousy. **3.** spite, ill-will. — ~ करना, or रखना, to be envious, &c., of (से, a person; की, a thing). ~ लगना (को), to feel envious, &c. – ईर्ष्या-द्वेष, m. envy and malice. ईर्ष्यावान, adj. envious, &c. (= ईर्ष्यालु).

ईर्ष्यालु *īrṣyālu* [S,], adj. **1.** envious. **2.** jealous. **3.** spiteful, malevolent.

-ईला *-īlā*, suffix (forms adjectives from nouns and verb stems (e.g. रसीला, juicy; नशीला, intoxicating; चमकीला, bright, shining).

ईश *īś* [S.], m. **1.** lord, master. **2.** the supreme spirit. **3.** ruler; king. **4.** husband.

ईशता *īśătā* [S.], f. = ईश्वरता.

ईशत्व *īśatvă* [S.], m. = ईश्वरता.

ईशना *īśănā* [S.], f. desire, inclination, choice.

ईशा *īśā* [S.], f. power, dominion.

ईशान *īśān* [S.], m. *Pl. HŚS.* 1. = ईश्वर, 1.; *mythol.* a title of Śiva. **2.** the north-east. — ईशान-कोण, m. id.

ईशिता *īśitā* [S.], f. *Pl. HŚS.* supremacy; divine or supernatural power.

ईशित्व *īśitvă* [S.], m. *Pl. HŚS.* = ईशिता.

ईश्वर *īśvar* [S.], m. **1.** lord; master. **2.** God. **3.** ruler; king. — ईश्वर-निष्ठ, adj. believing in God, religious, devout. ईश्वर-भक्त, m. a worshipper of God, pious person. ईश्वरवाद, m. theism. °ई, adj. & m. theistic; a theist. ईश्वराधीन [°*ra*+*ā*°], adj. & m. subject to or dependent on God; one accepting God's will, a servant of God. ईश्वरोपासक [°*ra*+*u*°], adj. worshipping god, devout.

ईश्वरता *īśvarătā* [S.], f. **1.** supremacy, lordship. **2.** divine nature; divine or almighty power.

ईश्वरत्व *īśvarătvă* [S.], m. = ईश्वरता.

ईश्वरी *īśvărī* [S.], f. **1.** mistress. **2.** goddess; title of goddesses and *śaktis*, esp. of Durgā and Lakṣmī.

ईश्वरीय *īśvărīyă* [S.], adj. of God, divine.

ईषत् *īṣat* [S.], adj. **1.** a little, somewhat. **2.** ईषत्-. semi-. ईषत्स्पृष्ट, adj. *ling.* semi-vocalic.

ईषद् *īṣad*, adj. in comp. = ईषत्, 2.

ईषद- *īṣad-* [S.], adj. Brbh. = ईषत्, 2: — ईषदहास, m. a slight smile.

ईसर *īsar*, m. Av. = ईश्वर.

ईसवी *īsvī* [A. *'īsavī*], adj. Christian. — ~ सन or शताब्दी, m. the Christian era. सन् ~, m. id.

ईसा *īsā* [A. *'īsā*], m. inv. Jesus. — ~ पूर्व, adv. before Christ, B.C. ~ मसीह, m. Jesus the Messiah, Jesus Christ.

ईसाई *īsāī* [P. *'īsāī*], adj. & m. **1.** adj. Christian. **2.** m. a Christian. — ~ **धर्म**, m. Christianity.

ईसार *īsār* [A. *īṣār*], m. U. presenting (a gift); an offering.

ईस्वी *īsvī*, adj. see **ईसवी**.

ईहाँ *īhāṁ*, adv. Brbh. = **यहाँ**.

ईहा *īhā* [S.], f. Brbh. **1.** desire. **2.** attempt, exertion.

ईहित *īhit* [S.], adj. **1.** desired. **2.** obtained by effort.

उ

उ *u*, the fifth vowel of the Devanāgarī syllabary. — **उकार**, m. the sound /*u*/; the letter उ.

उँ *uṁ* [onom.], interj. exclamation expressing interrogation; or petulance, displeasure, &c. eh? oh! — ~ ~ **करना**, to be petulant; to whimper.

उँकारी *uṁkārī* [? **udaṅkakāra*-], f. curve: a curved mark resembling the Arabic letter *re*, used esp. formerly in writing prices to denote rupees, also (obs.) with abbreviation marks denoting additional amounts of four annas.

उँगनी *uṁgnī* [cf. *upāṅga*-], f. greasing, smearing (as of axle of a cart).

उँगली *uṁglī* [*aṅguli*-], f. **1.** the finger. **2.** a finger's breadth. — ~ **उठना**, the finger to be raised (at, **पर**, **की ओर**): to be an object of vilification, or of notoriety. ~ **उठाना**, to point a finger (at): to call censure or contempt (upon). ~ **करना**, sl. to vex, to plague. ~ **काटना**, to gnaw the nails; to be dumbfounded. ~ (or **उँगलियाँ**) **चटकाना**, to snap the fingers; to crack the finger-joints. ~ (or **उँगलियाँ**) **तोड़ना**, id. ~ **दिखाना**, = ~ **उठाना**. ~ **रखना** (**पर**), to place the finger (on); to find fault (with). ~ **लगाना**, to lay a finger (on, **को**), to strike. **कन की** ~, f. = next. **कान** ~, f. the little finger. **डैनी** ~, f. middle finger (the touch of which is supposed to be a bad omen). **दाँतों में** (or **तले**) ~ **दबाना**, to bite the finger between the teeth: to be utterly astonished; to be stricken (as with grief). **पाँव की** ~, f. the toe. **पूजा** ~, f. the finger used to apply sandalwood; the ring finger. **बत** ~, f. the index finger. **उँगलियाँ तोड़ना**, to crack the finger-joints. **उँगलियों पर नचाना**, to cause to dance to (one's, **की**) playing: to do as one pleases with (one); to trifle with; to harass, to distress. **उँगलियों पर नाचना**, to dance at one's bidding, &c.

उँघाई *uṁghāī*, f. = **ऊँघाई**.

उँघाना *uṁghānā*, v.i. to be drowsy, to doze (= **ऊँघना**).

उँघास *uṁghās*, f. = **ऊँघाई**.

उँचान *uṁcān* [cf. H. *ūṁcā*], f. (m., *Pl.*) reg. = **ऊँचाई**.

उँचाना *uṁcānā* [cf. H. *ūṁcā*], v.t. to raise.

उँचाव *uṁcāv* [cf. H. *ūṁcā, uṁcānā*], m. = **ऊँचाई**.

उँचास *uṁcās*, f. reg. height.

उँचाहट *uṁcāhaṭ* [cf. H. *ūṁcā*], f. reg. = **ऊँचाई**.

उँजरी *uṁjrī*, f. *Pl. musl.* a small heap of corn set apart at harvest time, in honour of some saint.

उँजाला *uṁjālā*, m. pronun. var. = **उजाला**.

उँजियार *uṁjiyār*, m. Av. = **उजियार**.

उँजियारा *uṁjiyārā*, adj. & m. Av. = **उजियारा**.

उँजेला *uṁjelā*, m. pronun. var. = **उजेला**.

उँडलना *uṁḍalnā*, v.t. reg. = **उड़ेलना**.

उँड़ेलना *uṁṛelnā*, v.t. = **उड़ेलना**.

उऋण *uṛṇ* [*udṛṇin*-], adj. out of debt (to, **से**).

उकटना *ukaṭnā* [**utkartati*: Pk. *ukkattaï*], v.t. to cut out: **1.** to dig up, to root up; to unearth. **2.** to unearth (a secret). **3.** to return to, to hark back to (a matter). **4.** to abuse, to revile. — **उकट डालना**, to tear up; to destroy utterly. – **उकटा पुरान**, m. an old matter brought into the open again.

उकटवाना *ukaṭvānā* [cf. H. *ukaṭnā*], v.t. to cause to be dug up, &c.

उकड़ूँ *ukṛūṁ* [*utkuṭaka*-, Pk. *ukkuḍuya*-], adj. squatting with the feet flat on the ground. — ~ **बैठना**, to squat.

उकड़ू *ukṛū*, adj. see **उकड़ूँ**.

उकताना *uktānā*, v.i. **1.** to grow tired (of, **से**); to lose all relish (for). **2.** to be irritated (by, **से**); to fret, to chafe (at). **3.** to become irksome. — **पढ़ते जी** ~, to be bored with reading.

उकतारना *uktārnā*, v.t. reg. **1.** to stir up, to incite. **2.** to abet. **3.** to forward, to promote.

उकतारू *uktārū* [cf. H. *uktārnā*], m. *Pl.* instigator, plotter.

उकताहट *uktāhaṭ* [cf. H. *uktānā*], f. boredom, &c. (cf. **उकताना**).

उकलना *ukalnā* [**utkalati*], v.i. reg. **1.** to boil up or over. **2.** to be unfolded; to open (a flower).

उकलाना *uklānā* [? H. *ukalnā* × H. *akulānā*], v.i. to vomit.

उकवाँ *ukvāṁ* [? *upakrama-*], adv. reg. at a guess, roughly.

उकसना *ukasnā* [*utkasati*, or *utkarṣati*], v.i. **1.** to be raised, to rise. **2.** to be stirred, roused; to spring up (in, में). **3.** to give trouble (as the tonsils).

उकसवाना *ukasvānā* [cf. H. *uksānā*], v.t. to cause to be stirred up, &c. (by, से).

उकसाई *uksāī* [cf. H. *uksānā*], f. **1.** arousing; arousal. **2.** provocation.

उकसाना *uksānā* [cf. H. *ukasnā*], v. t. **1.** to raise, to lift. **2.** to turn up (a lamp); to fan, to blow (flame, &c.) **3.** to stir up, to rouse; to incite; to provoke.

उकसाव *uksāv* [cf. H. *ukasnā*], m. **1.** stimulation. **2.** instigation, provocation. — उकसाव-भरा, adj. provocative.

उकसावा *uksāvā* [cf. H. *ukasnā*], m. = उकसाव.

उकसाहट *uksāhaṭ* [cf. H. *uksānā*], f. **1.** stirring up, rousing; arousal. **2.** provocation.

उकेरना *ukernā* [**utkerayati*; Pk. *ukkiraï*], v.t. reg. to carve out.

उकेलना *ukelnā* [**utkelyate*: cf. Pk. *ukkellāviya-*], v.t. **1.** to undo, to unravel. **2.** to tear off or open; to flay.

उक्त *ukt* [S.], adj. **1.** spoken, said. **2.** aforesaid. — उक्त-प्रत्युक्त, m. speech and reply: conversation.

उक्ति *ukti* [S.], f. **1.** speech; language. **2.** utterance. **3.** story, invention. — उक्ति-युक्ति, f. a measure deliberated upon, a considered course of action.

उखट- *ukhaṭ-*, v.t. reg. to break off, to tear off.

उखटना *ukhaṭnā* [conn. **utkartati*, H. *ukaṭnā*: ? × H. *ukhāṛnā*], v.i. to stumble.

उखड़ना *ukhaṛnā* [cf. **utskṛta-*], v.i. **1.** to be rooted up; to be torn up or off; to be taken out (as a thorn); to be dug up. **2.** to be eradicated. **3.** to become detached, or removed; to come out (as a screw, or a stone from its setting). **4.** to be dislocated (a bone). **5.** to become indifferent (the heart): to become displeased or offended. **6.** to be driven away; to be diverted or dissuaded (from, से). **7.** to become scattered, dispersed. **8.** to be demolished; to be devastated or destroyed. **9.** to break up (a meeting); to be struck (a tent). **10.** to come undone, to unravel. **11.** to fall off, to decline. **12.** to lose credit (one's word, &c). **13.** to be unsteady, indistinct, irregular (as handwriting); to be out of tune (a singer). **14.** colloq. to slip or to slink away. यहाँ से उखड़ो! sl. clear out! **15.** to be carved, engraved, stamped (on, पर). — उखड़ा, adj. unsteady, indistinct, irregular; disturbed (sleep); dry, or harsh, or caustic (language). उखड़ी उखड़ी बातें सुनाना, to speak drily, &c. (to, को). उखड़ा-पुखड़ा, adj. = उखड़ा.

उखड़वाना *ukhaṛvānā* [cf. H. *ukhāṛnā*], v.t. to cause to be uprooted, &c.

उखड़ाना *ukhṛānā* [cf. H. *ukhaṛnā*], v.t. to cause to be uprooted (by, से).

उखल *ukhal*, m. = उखली.

उखली *ukhlī* [**udukkhala-*: Pk. *ukkhalu-*], f. a small wooden or stone mortar.

उखाड़ *ukhāṛ* [cf. H. *ukhāṛnā*], f. rooting up, eradication. — उखाड़-पछाड़, f. turmoil, uncertain situation; captious criticism.

उखाड़ना *ukhāṛnā* [cf. H. *ukhaṛnā*], v.t. **1.** to root up, to tear up or off; to take out (as a thorn, or a tooth); to dig up. **2.** to detach, to dislodge; to disperse. **3.** to dislocate (a bone). **4.** to alienate; to attract (from another allegiance). **5.** to overturn; to subvert. **6.** to demolish; to devastate.

उखाड़ी *ukhāṛī* [**ikṣuvāṭa-*], f. reg. a field of sugar-cane.

उखाड़ू *ukhāṛū* [cf. H. *ukhāṛnā*], adj. & m. **1.** adj. rooting up, eradicating, &c. (see उखाड़ना). **2.** m. a ravager, &c.

उखेड़ *ukheṛ* [cf. H. *ukheṛnā*], f. to be disturbed (in mood), displeased. — ~ बताना, to be cross (with, को); to be displeased or cool (towards).

उखेड़ना *ukheṛnā* [cf. **utskṛta-*: Pa. *ukkheṭita-*], v.t. = उखाड़ना.

उगटना *ugaṭnā*, v.t. reg. to abuse, to revile.

उगत *ugat* [ad. *udgati-*], f. **1.** growing, springing up. **2.** production. **3.** [? × *yukti-*] inventive power, ingenuity.

उगना *ugnā* [*udgāti*, v.i.: w. *-ā-* shortened in H. to allow differentiation from *ugānā*, v.t.], v.i. **1.** to spring up, to grow; to shoot, to sprout; to appear. **2.** to rise (a heavenly body). **3.** to begin, to set in; to dawn. — उग आना (पर), to grow up, or over (as plants over masonry).

उगलना *ugalnā* [**udgalati*[2]], v.t. **1.** to spit out. **2.** to vomit. **3.** to bring up (food) from the stomach or gullet (as cattle, birds). **4.** to disgorge, to restore (sthg. misappropriated). **5.** to blurt out, to reveal. — उगल-उगलकर खाना, to force oneself to eat. ज़हर ~, to spit poison: to show, or to betray, rancour.

उगलवाना *ugalvānā* [cf. H. *ugalnā*]. to cause to be disgorged (by, से); to extort.

उगहना *ugahnā* [cf. H. *ugāhnā*], v.i. to be collected, gathered, &c.

उगाई *ugāī* [cf. H. *ugānā*], f. **1.** growing, producing (crops). **2.** wages or payment for growing.

उगाना *ugānā* [**udgāti*, v.i.: Pk. *uggei*, *uggaï*], v.t. to cause to grow, to produce (as crops).

उगारना *ugārnā* [**udgālayati*²], v.t. **1.** *Pl. HŚS.* to clean the sediment from a well. **2.** *HŚS.* E.H. to save, to rescue.

उगाल *ugāl* [**udgāla*-²: Pk. *uggāla*-], m. **1.** remains of betel leaf, &c. spat out after chewing. **2.** *HŚS.* colloq. cast-off clothes. — **उगालदान**, m. a spittoon. °**ई**, f. id.

उगालना *ugālnā* [**udgālayati*²], v.t. **1.** to spit out. **2.** *Pl.* to chew the cud.

उगाला *ugālā* [cf. H. *ugārnā*], m. colloq. reg. (W.) waterlogged land.

उगाहना *ugāhnā* [*udgrāhayati*], v.t. to gather, to collect (as rent, revenue); to raise (funds).

उगाही *ugāhī* [*udgrāhita*-], f. **1.** collecting (as rent, revenue). **2.** monies raised, or levied; proceeds, revenue. **3.** payment by instalments.

उग्र *ugră* [S.], adj. & m. **1.** adj. fierce, terrible; cruel. **2.** harsh, dire; overpowering (as an odour). **3.** over-intense, extreme. **4.** *pol.* radical, of the far left. **5.** m. anger, fury. — **उग्रदली**, adj. = ~, 4. **उग्रवाद**, m. extremism. °**ई**, adj. & m. extremist.

उग्रता *ugrătā* [S.], f. **1.** fierceness, fury; cruelty. **2.** direness. **3.** over-intensity (as of conviction).

उग्रह *ugrah* [ad. *udgraha*-], m. the ending of an eclipse.

उघड़ना *ugharṇā* [**udghaṭati*, °*ita*-], v.i. **1.** to be uncovered, exposed; to be laid bare; to be unsheathed (a weapon). **2.** to be revealed.

उघाड़ना *ughāṛnā* [*udghāṭayati*], v.t. **1.** to uncover, to expose; to bare (the body); to unsheathe (a weapon). **2.** to reveal; to betray (a secret, &c).

उचकन *uckan* [conn H. *ucaknā*, *uckānā*], m. reg. a support, prop.

उचकना *ucaknā* [cf. *ucca*-], v.i. **1.** to be lifted up. **2.** to be jerked up. **3.** to spring up, to jump up. **4.** to stand on tiptoe to see (= **उझकना**).

उचकाना *uckānā* [cf. H. *ucaknā*], v.t. **1.** to lift up. **2.** to jerk up; to shrug (the shoulders).

उचक्का *ucakkā* [cf. *ucca*-: H. *uckānā*], m. **1.** a pickpocket; pilferer. **2.** a cheat, swindler.

उचक्कापन *ucakkāpan* [cf. H. *ucakkā*], m. **1.** pilfering, thieving. **2.** swindling, defrauding.

उचक्कापना *ucakkāpănā*, m. = **उचक्कापन**.

उचटना *ucaṭnā* [**uccaṭyate*], v.i. **1.** to go or to turn away (from, **से**); to withdraw (from); to be scared away. **2.** to rebound, to glance; to ricochet; to splash or to fly up (water, sparks); Brbh. to fly open (as a door). **3.** to be separated, detached; to be dropped, or lost; to come off (as plaster); to peel, to become chapped (skin). **4.** to be alienated (from); to be dissuaded (from); to be offended (with). **5.** to be weary (of); to be disgusted (by).

उचटाना *ucṭānā* [cf. H. *ucaṭnā*], v.t. = **उचाटना**.

उचड़ना *ucaṛnā* [*uccaṭati*], v.i. **1.** to be separated, detached, &c. (= **उचटना**, 3.) **2.** colloq. to clear out (to go promptly away).

उचरंग *ucraṅg* [? cf. **ucchalana*-], m. *Pl. HŚS.* a moth (= **पतंग**).

उचर- *ucar*- [*uccarati*], v.t. Brbh. = **उच्चारण करना**.

उचलना *ucalnā* [**uccalyati*; Pk. *uccallaï*], v.i. to be separated; to peel (as skin, scales).

उचलाना *uclānā* [cf. H. *ucalnā*], v.t. reg. to cause to be separated.

उचा- *ucā*- [cf. *ucca*-], v.t. Brbh. to raise.

उचाट *ucāṭ* [**uccāṭya*-], adj. & m. f. **1.** adj. driven or turned away. **2.** wild-looking; scared; bewildered. **3.** alienated; offended. **4.** indifferent (to, **से**), weary (of); disgusted (by). **5.** m. f. driving away. **6.** wild look; fear, &c. **7.** alienation; estrangement. **8.** indifference, weariness; disgust. — **आँखों से नींद ~ हो गई**, (his) sleepiness vanished.

उचाटना *ucāṭnā* [cf. H. *ucaṭnā*], v.t. **1.** to drive or to turn away (from, **से**); to scare away. **2.** to cause to rebound, to deflect; to cause to splash. **3.** to separate, to detach. **4.** to alienate (the heart, **जी**, from); to dissuade (from). **5.** to dishearten; to sadden, to make anxious.

उचाड़ना *ucāṛnā* [cf. H. *ucaṛnā*], v.t. reg. to tear (sthg.) off.

उचापत *ucāpat*, f. *Pl. HŚS.* taking of goods on credit; a credit account (with a tradesman or grain merchant) (W.); goods taken on credit.

उचापति *ucāpti* [cf. **uccāpyate*], f. Brbh. credit, &c. (= **उचापत**). — **~ कर-**, v.t. to take or to give goods on credit.

उचार *ucār* [*uccāra*-], m. E.H. utterance, voicing (of a name).

उचार- *ucār-* [**uccālayati*, Pk. *uccālei*], v.t. Av. to shake loose, or to knock out (as teeth, with a blow).

उचारना *ucārnā* [*uccārayati*], v.t. = उच्चारण करना.

उचावा *ucāvā* [conn. **utsvāpa-*], m. talking in one's sleep; nightmare.

उचित *ucit* [S.], adj. **1.** proper, right, fitting; appropriate; justifiable; acceptable. **2.** expedient; necessary.

उचितता *ucitătā* [S.], f. = औचित्य.

उचेलना *ucelnā* [conn. H. *ucalnā*], v.t. **1.** to separate (one thing from another). **2.** to peel off (as skin, scales); to pare.

उच्च *ucc* [S.], adj. **1.** high, lofty. **2.** higher, upper; superior. — ~ कुल का, adj. well-born, of good or aristocratic family. ~ कोटि का, adj. of high class or quality. – उच्चतर, adj. higher, &c. उच्चतम, adj. highest, &c.; supreme. उच्च-मान, m. a record (as in sport). उच्च-शिक्षा, f. higher education. उच्च-स्तर, m. high rank; high level; °ईय, adj. उच्चाकांक्षा [°*a*+*ā*°], f. lofty ideal(s); ambition. उच्चाकांक्षी, m. an ambitious person. उच्चाधिकारी [°*a*+*a*°], m. a high official. उच्चायुक्त [°*a*+*ā*°], m. *govt.* High Commissioner. उच्चायोग, m. High Commission.

उच्चत *uccat*, adv. *Pl.* on high, aloft.

उच्चता *uccătā* [S.], f. height, high level or position; excellence.

उच्चर- *uccar-* [*uccarati*], v.t. Av. = उच्चारण करना.

उच्चरित *uc-carit* [S.], adj. uttered, pronounced.

उच्चाटन *uccāṭan* [S.], m. **1.** driving away (by magical means). **2.** alienating; estranging.

उच्चान *uccān* [cf. *ucca-*], f. height, elevation.

उच्चार *uc-cār* [S.], m. pronunciation; utterance.

उच्चारण *uc-cāraṇ* [S.], m. **1.** pronunciation, enunciation, expression; *ling.* articulation. **2.** utterance. — ~ करना (का), to pronounce, &c.

उच्चारणीय *uc-cārăṇīyă* [S.], adj. = उच्चार्य.

उच्चारना *uc-cārnā* [ad. *uccāraṇa-*; w. H. *ucārnā*] v.t. = उचारना.

उच्चारित *uc-cārit* [S.], adj. pronounced, uttered; *ling.* articulated.

उच्चार्य *uc-cāryă* [S.], adj. to be pronounced, &c. (see उच्चारण); pronounceable.

उच्चैः *uccaiḥ* [S.], adv. aloud. — उच्चैश्रवा (for उच्चैःश्रवस्), m. inv. *mythol.* the horse of Indra, produced at the churning of the ocean.

उच्छिन्न *uc-chinn* [S.], adj. torn up, uprooted; destroyed.

उच्छिष्ट *uc-chiṣṭ* [S.], adj. & m. **1.** adj. left over (as food), rejected. **2.** sullied, defiled. **3.** m. remains of food.

उच्छू *ucchū*, m. *Pl. HŚS.* choking; cough made to clear the throat.

उच्छृंखलता *uc-chr̥ṅkhalătā* [S.], f. lack of restraint, abandon.

उच्छेदन *uc-chedan* [S.], m. extirpation, removal.

उच्छ्वास *uc-chvās* [S.], m. **1.** breathing out, a breath; a sigh. **2.** division of a book (esp. a romance).

उछंग *uchaṅg* [*utsaṅga-*], m. Brbh. = उत्संग.

उछटना *uchaṭnā* [**ucchaṭṭa-*: Pk. *ucchaṭṭa-*], v.i. reg. to withdraw (from, से). (cf. उचटना.)

उछल-कूद *uchal-kūd*, f. leaping and jumping: gambolling, playing; bustling about.

उछलना *uchalnā* [**ut-śalati*: Pk. *ucchalaï*], v.i. **1.** to spring up, to leap, to bound; to spring (upon, पर); to fly (at). **2.** to fly up; to splash up or out; to gush or to spurt up or out. **3.** to fly into a passion: to dance (with rage, or joy: से). **4.** to be evident, to leave a mark; to come to light. — जिस खूँटे से वह उछल रहा था, वह उखड़ गया है, the linchpin on which he has depended (for support) has torn out.

उछलाना *uchlānā* [cf. H. *uchālnā*], v.t. to cause to be thrown up (by, से).

उछाल *uchāl* [cf. H. *uchālnā*], f. **1.** an upward spring, bound; leap. **2.** tossing up or about. — ~ खाना, to rise sharply (prices). ~ भरना, or मारना, to leap, to bound. – उछाल-दीदा [P. *-dīda*], f. a woman with a wanton or roving eye.

उछालना *uchālnā* [**ut-śālayati*: Pk. *ucchālei*], v.t. **1.** to throw up, to toss up. **2.** to toss about: to treat with disrespect; to bring discredit on. — नाम ~ (का), to disgrace (one's) name. पगड़ी ~ (की), fig. to treat (one) disrespectfully.

उछाह *uchāh* [*utsāha-*], m. Brbh. Av. **1.** enthusiasm, eager desire. **2.** glad occasion, festival.

उजड़ना *ujaṛnā* [**ujjaṭati*], v.i. **1.** to be rooted up: to be laid waste; to be plundered; to be demolished, razed. **2.** to fall into ruin or decay. **3.** to be or to become deserted, desolate; to be depopulated. **4.** to be squandered, dissipated. **5.** fig. to perish, to die. **6.** to be ruined, dishonoured (a girl). — ~ घर बसाना, fig. to remarry. – उजड़ा-पुजड़ा, adj. in ruins; desolate.

उजड़वाना *ujaṛvānā* [cf. H. *ujāṛnā*], v.t. to cause to be laid waste, &c. (by, से).

उजड्ड *ujaḍḍ* [cf. **jaḍḍa-*: Pk. *jaḍḍa-*], adj. unfeeling, inert: **1.** stupid, senseless; obtuse. **2.** uncouth; coarse; loutish.

उजड्डपन *ujaḍḍpan* [cf. H. *ujaḍḍ*], m. **1.** stupidity. **2.** uncouthness, &c.

उजरत *ujrat* [A. *ujra*], f. remuneration.

उजला *ujlā* [*ujjvala-*], adj. **1.** bright, radiant; lovely, splendid; fair (as fame); well-lit (a room). **2.** clean, white (as clothes); polished, shining. **3.** enlightened (mind). — ~ मुँह होना, honour to be re-established or vindicated.

उजलाई *ujlāī* [cf. H. *ujlā*, *ujlānā*], f. **1.** brightness; cleanness. **2.** price paid for cleaning.

उजलाना *ujlānā*, v.t. = उजालना.

उजलापन *ujlāpan* [cf. H. *ujlā*], m. **1.** brightness, &c. **2.** cleanness, whiteness. **3.** enlightenment.

उजवाना *ujvānā*, v.t. *Pl.* **1.** to cause a person to pour (water, &c). **2.** to cause to be emptied; to empty (a container).

उजागर *ujāgar*, adj. **1.** bright, shining; splendid, gaudy. **2.** manifest; celebrated; pej. notorious. — ~ करना, to make famous (as one's name); to make notorious.

उजाड़ *ujāṛ* [**ujjāṭa-*], adj. & m. **1.** adj. laid waste, devasted; ruined. **2.** deserted, desolate. **3.** m. devastation. **4.** a ruined place, ruin. **5.** a deserted place, wilderness.

उजाड़ना *ujāṛnā* [**ujjāṭayati*: Pk. *ujjāḍia-*], v.t. **1.** to lay waste, to devastate; to plunder; to demolish, to raze; to ruin. **2.** to make desolate, to depopulate. **3.** to squander (money, health).

उजाड़ू *ujāṛū* [cf. H. *ujāṛnā*], adj. & m. **1.** adj. laying waste, &c.; destructive. **2.** squandering, wasteful. **3.** m. a plunderer, &c.

उजान *ujān* [conn. **ujjavana-*: Pa. *ujjavanikāya*, and *udyāti*], adv. *Pl. HŚS.* upstream.

उजालना *ujālnā* [**ujjvālayati*: Pa. *ujjāleti*], v.t. **1.** to make bright, or radiant; to clean, to polish; to cleanse. **2.** to light, to light up (a lamp).

उजाला *ujālā* [**ujjvālaka-*], m. & adj. **1.** m. light; daylight; daybreak, day; light of moon or stars. **2.** brightness, splendour; glory. **3.** adj. light, moonlit, clear (night). **4.** bright, radiant. — उजाले का तारा, m. the morning star, Venus.

उजास *ujās*, f. light, gleam.

उजियार *ujiyār*, m. Brbh. Av. = उजाला.

उजियारा *ujiyārā*, m. & adj. Brbh. Av. = उजाला.

उजियारिया *ujiyāriyā*, f. dimin. Brbh. = उजियारा.

उजियाला *ujiyālā* [**ujjvālaka-*, × *andhakāra-*], m. = उजाला.

उजियाली *ujiyālī*, f. = उजियाला.

उजूबा *ujūbā*, adj. & m. = अजूबा.

उजेला *ujelā*, m. = उजियाला, उजाला.

उज्जल *ujjal*, adj. = उजला.

उज्जागरी *ujjāgarī* [cf. H. *ujāgar*], adj. f. Brbh. = उजागर, 2.

उज्ज्वल *uj-jval* [S.], adj. **1.** bright, radiant; brilliant; lovely, splendid. **2.** fervent, ardent (as love, or ecstatic devotion). **3.** clean, white; unstained, without reproach.

उज्ज्वलता *uj-jvalătā* [S.], f. **1.** brightness, brilliance, &c. (see उज्ज्वल). **2.** cleanness, whiteness, &c.

उज्ज्वलन *uj-jvalan* [S.], m. **1.** blazing, burning; radiance, &c. **2.** making clean, causing to shine.

उज्ज्वलित *uj-jvalit* [S.], adj. **1.** made bright, radiant, &c. (see उज्ज्वल). **2.** made clean, made to shine.

उज़्र *uzr* [A. *ʻuzr*], m. **1.** excuse, apology; pretext. **2.** objection. — ~ करना, to offer an excuse; to object (to, की). ~ होना, objection to be raised (by, को; to, पर or में). – उज़्रदार [P. -*dār*], m. an objector.

उझकना *ujhaknā* [? H. *ucaknā* × H. *jhām̐knā*; also × *jhakk-*[1 4]], v.i. **1.** to raise oneself on tiptoe so as to see; to peep; to spy. **2.** to jump up, to spring up.

[1]**उझर-** *ujhar-*, v.i. Brbh. to flow; to flood (rain: = उझलना).

[2]**उझर-** *ujhar-* [cf. **ujjhāṭayati*], v.i. Brbh. to be lifted, to move (the hem of a garment).

उझलना *ujhalnā* [**ujjhalati*: Pk. *ujjhalia-*], v.i. reg. to flow, to be poured from one container into another.

उझालना *ujhālnā* [**ujjhālayati*], v.t. *Pl. HŚS.* to pour out.

उझिलना *ujhilnā* [**ujjhalati*: Pk. *ujjhalia-*], v.i. reg. 1. = उझलना. **2.** to be thrown down, or levelled (soil). — उझिला, m. earth taken from high places in a field and used to fill in hollows (E.); mustard seed cooked, or crushed for rubbing on the body.

उझेल *ujhel* [cf. H. *ujhilnā*], ? f. Brbh. pouring.

उझेलना *ujhelnā* [cf. H. *ujhilnā*], v.t. reg. to pour.

उटंगन *uṭaṅgan* [**uṭṭaṅgana-*], m. *Pl. HŚS.* a kind of nettle and its seed.

उटंग *uṭaṅg* [**uṭṭaṅga-*: *ṭaṅka-*³], adj. high on the leg, not long enough (trousers).

उटक- *uṭak-*, v.t. Brbh. to guess, to guess at.

उटक्कर-लैस *uṭakkar-lais* [? cf. H. *uṭak-*], adj. & m. **1.** adj. thoughtless. **2.** casual, random. **3.** *Pl.* nonsensical, absurd. **4.** m. one who guesses or conjectures (as in finding the way).

उटज *uṭaj* [S.], m. poet. a hut made of leaves.

उट्ठक-बैठक *uṭṭhak-baiṭhak*, f. **1.** rising and squatting: knee-bends (the exercise; also a school punishment). **2.** standing and kneeling alternately at prayer.

उठँगन *uṭhaṁgan*, m. reg. (Bihar) prop, support; wedge (used to raise sthg).

उठँगना *uṭhaṁgnā* [**upaṭṭhiṅga-*], v.i. *Pl. HŚS.* to rest (on or against, से); to depend (on) for support.

उठंगल *uṭhaṅgal*, adj. reg. dull-witted, stupid.

उठगन *uṭhgan*, m. *Pl.* = उठँगन.

उठना *uṭhnā* [**ut-sthāti*: Pk. *uṭṭhaï*], v.i. **1.** to rise, to rise up; to stand up; to get up; to recover, to convalesce. **2.** to ascend, to mount; to soar; to rise (a river). **3.** to rise to leave; to be ready, prepared; to move (from a house); to depart (from the world). **4.** to spring up, to shoot; to grow; to rise, to bloom (as youth, or new growth); to develop (the breasts). **5.** to be lifted (an object). **6.** to work, to ferment (leaven). **7.** to be exhausted, spent (as money to be expended); to be wasted, squandered; to be disposed of (a body). **8.** to be finished, over, ended. **9.** to be effaced, erased. **10.** to be abolished, or obsolete; to be discontinued; to be closed (premises, an institution). **11.** to be carried away, removed; to be withdrawn; to be carried off, stolen. **12.** to be displayed, exhibited; to stand out in relief or silhouette. **13.** to be brought into being; to be constructed, built; to be made, formed; to be built up, developed (as an institution); to develop, to progress (a country, a project). **14.** to be reared or fostered; to be hatched, or bred, to be brought up; to be trained; to be educated. **15.** to arise (as storm, disturbance); to break out (as epidemic, riot); to come on (as pain, illness); to come to mind; to come up (a topic, a dispute). **16.** to proceed (from, से); to originate, to emanate; to result. **17.** to be derived, obtained, enjoyed (advantage, happiness); to arise, to accrue (profit); to be recovered, reclaimed (land). **18.** to be made available (for a purpose); to be taken (as a loan, or on hire or lease). **19.** to be taken in (harvest). — **उठ खड़ा होना,** to rise or to jump to one's feet. **उठ बैठना,** to start up suddenly or involuntarily: to jump up, to sit up; to awake; to revive, to recover. – **उठते-बैठते,** adv. easily, gently, gradually; endlessly, continually; quickly, in a trice. **उठना-बैठना,** v.i. & m. to get up and sit down: to associate (with, के साथ); association, dealings (with); deportment, manners. **उठा-बैठी,** f. restlessness, fidgetiness, agitation; fuss, turmoil; = उट्ठक-बैठक.

उठ-बैठ *uṭh-baiṭh*, f. = उठा-बैठी, see s.v. उठना.

उठल्लू *uṭhallū*, adj. **1.** not having any fixed abode. **2.** movable. **3.** m. a wanderer, vagrant. — **~ चूल्हा,** m. a wandering stove: a vagrant, wanderer. **~ का चूल्हा,** m. id.

उठवाना *uṭhvānā* [cf. H. *uṭhānā*], v.t. to cause to be lifted, raised, removed, &c. (by, से).

उठवैया *uṭhvaiyā* [cf. H. *uṭhānā, uṭhvānā*], m. one who raises or helps to raise (a load, &c).

उठाईगीर *uṭhāīgīr*, m. = उठाईगीरा.

उठाईगीरा *uṭhāīgīrā* [cf. H. *uṭhānā*: P. *-gīr*], m. a pilferer, petty thief; a rascal.

उठाऊ *uṭhāū* [cf. H. *uṭhānā*], adj. & m. **1.** adj. extravagant, lavish. **2.** portable. **3.** m. an extravagant person; a spendthrift.

उठान *uṭhān* [**ut-sthāna-*; and H. *uṭhnā*], f. **1.** rise, ascent; act of appearance. **2.** beginning, commencement. **3.** height, elevation; attitude. **4.** stature; build, size. **5.** growth; swelling of the breasts (in adolescence). **6.** summit, height.

उठाना *uṭhānā* [**ut-sthāpayati*: Pa. *uṭṭhāpeti*], v.t. **1.** to lift, to raise; to pick up; to pack up (one's things); to finish (a term of work); to start, to set off. **2.** to rear, to foster; to hatch; to breed; to bring up; to train; to educate. **3.** to bring into being; to devise; to construct, to build; to build up, to develop. **4.** to arouse, to awaken; to cause to get up; to arouse (a feeling). **5.** to bear (a burden, a responsibility); to be responsible for (an enterprise); to undertake (a task). **6.** to undergo, to experience (suffering); to incur (as risk, debt). **7.** to derive, to obtain, to enjoy (advantage, happiness). **8.** to take in (harvest). **9.** to cause to disappear: to consume; to waste, to squander; to dispose of (as of a body). **10.** to efface, to erase. **11.** to abolish; to discontinue (an action, a case); to close (premises). **12.** to take away, to remove (from, से); to withdraw (from); to remove from (the world); to carry off, to steal. **13.** to raise (a matter, an objection); to start (a quarrel); **14.** to neglect, to leave undone (esp. neg. in उठा न रखना). **15.** to display, to exhibit; to bring out clearly. **16.** to work or to ferment in (as leaven). **17.** to throw up, to cause to fly (a kite, a bird). **18.** to set aside or to designate (for a purpose); to give, to bestow. **किराए पर उठा देना**, to lease, to rent (to, को). **19.** to take up in the hand (anything held sacred): to swear by (as by sacred water). — **उठा ले जाना**, to take away; to abscond with; to abduct, to kidnap.

उठा-बैठी *uṭhā-baiṭhī*, f. see s.v. उठना.

उठाव *uṭhāv* [cf. H. *uṭhnā, uṭhānā*], m. a rise, or high(er) ground.

उठावनी *uṭhāvnī*, f. = उठौनी, 1.-3., 5.

उठौनी *uṭhaunī* [*ut-sthāpana-: Pk. *uṭṭhăvaṇa-*], f. **1.** lifting, raising. **2.** money or food set apart to be offered to a deity. **3.** an advance; deposit. **4.** inauguration (of a task, an activity). **5.** *hind.* any of certain funerary rites, performed variously between the second and fourth days after a cremation.

उड़ंत *uṛant* [cf. H. *uṛnā*], adj. Av. flying, having the power of flight.

उड़का *uṛkā* [cf. H. *uṛhaknā*], adj. wedged or hooked open (a door).

उड़द *uṛad* [*uḍidda-: Pk. *uḍida-*], m. a pulse. — **~ की दाल**, f. = ~. **~ पढ़कर मारना (पर)**, to throw *uṛad* (at one) after pronouncing a spell over it: to enchant; to exorcise. **~ पर सफ़ेदी**, adv. (as much as) the white spot on *uṛad*: very little.

उड़न *uṛan* [cf. H. *uṛnā*], f. & adj. **1.** f. flying. **2.** adj. in comp. flying; flying off, vanishing. **3.** raging, spreading. — **उड़न-खटोला**, m. flying bedstead: a 'magic carpet'. **उड़न-घाई**, f. trickery, deceit. **उड़न-छू**, adj. flown off as if by enchantment: gone with the wind. **उड़न-झाई**, f. trickery, blandishment. **उड़न-फल**, m. an imaginary fruit giving the power of flight. **उड़न-बीमारी**, f. = उड़नी बीमारी, see s.v. उड़ना. **उड़नशील**, adj. volatile (a liquid).

उड़ना *uṛnā* [*uḍḍayate*], v.i. & adj. **1.** v.i. to fly; to fly up, to soar; to take flight. **2.** to move or to go rapidly; to dart; to fly, to rush (at). **3.** to disappear, to vanish: to be lost (as a page from a book); to be exhausted (a supply); to fade (colour); to turn pale (the face, from emotion); to evaporate or to dry in the sun (dew); to be lost (the senses: esp. w. जाना). **4.** to be carried off, stolen. **5.** to be squandered; to be consumed or spent lavishly (food, resources). **6.** to be indulged (the senses). **7.** to be wielded (as fists, a cane, a shoe). **8.** to be scattered (as papers); to take flight. **9.** to blow up, to explode. **10.** to be effaced, obliterated. **11.** to be worn out. **12.** to be knocked off; to be cut off (the head); to be torn off, or away. **13.** to waft, to spread (a fragrance); to become current (news, rumour). **14.** to unfurl, to fill (sails); to flap, to flutter (sails, garments). **15.** (w. चलना) to be vain, or conceited. **16.** to be tricked, deceived (by, से). **17.** adj. flying, darting: spreading, raging. — **उड़नी बीमारी**, f. an infectious or contagious disease. – **उड़ चलना**, to fly off, to dart away; to make extremely quick progress. **उड़ता बनना**, colloq. to depart quickly, to vanish. **उड़ती ख़बर**, f. a quickly-spreading rumour. **उड़ती चिड़िया पहचानना**, colloq. to know a villain when one sees him.

उड़प *uṛap* [ad. *uḍupa-*: ← Drav.], m. **1.** a raft. **2.** the moon. **3.** *HŚS.* a kind of dance.

उड़सना *uṛasnā* [*uddaśati], v.t. **1.** to pierce, to penetrate; to insert, to fold in. **2.** Av. colloq. to fold up: to finish.

उड़ाऊ *uṛāū* [cf. H. *uṛānā*], adj. & m. **1.** adj. extravagant, wasteful. **2.** pej. dispensable. **3.** m. a spendthrift. — **उड़ाऊ-खाऊ**, adj. = ~.

उड़ाक *uṛāk* [cf. H. *uṛnā*], adj. & m. = उड़ाका.

उड़ाका *uṛākā* [cf. H. *uṛāk*], adj. & m. **1.** adj. able to fly, fledged. **2.** fig. swift. **3.** m. a pilot. — **~ दल**, m. flying squad.

उड़ाकू *uṛākū* [cf. H. *uṛāk*], adj. & m. = उड़ाका.

उड़ान *uṛān* [cf. H. *uṛnā*], f. **1.** flying, flight. **2.** a flight. **3.** a leap, bound. — **~ करना**, to make a flight, to fly. **~ पर**, adv. in flight; at a distance by air, or flight time (of, की). **~ भरना**, to make a flight; to leap. **~ मारना**, id., 2. **उड़ान-छू**, adj. = उड़न-छू. **उड़ान-फर**, m. Av. = उड़न-फल.

उड़ाना *uṛānā* [*uḍḍāpayati*], v.t. **1.** to cause to fly: to fly (a kite; an aircraft); to let fly (a bird); to let free. **2.** to drive hard, or fast (as a horse, or car). **3.** to make off with; to rob (of). **4.** to squander; to consume or to spend lavishly (food, resources). **5.** to indulge (the senses). **मज़ा, or मौजें ~**, to amuse oneself (idly: with, by, at, में or के साथ). **6.** to disregard (advice). **7.** to conceal (from, से: as a secret). **8.** to wield effectively (an implement). **9.** to scatter (husk, papers); to frighten away (birds, enemies). **10.** to blow up; to destroy; to explode (a bomb). **11.** to efface, to obliterate; to remove (as a mark). **12.** to knock off (an upper portion); to cut off (the head). **13.** to spread, to circulate (a rumour). **14.** to unfurl (a sail, or flag). **15.** to get rid of, to dismiss. **16.** to take off, to mimic; to copy. **17.** to play upon, to deceive. **18.** to send flying: to throw (in wrestling). — उड़ा ले जाना, to carry off, to kidnap; to entice away. हाथ ~ (पर), to strike (violently).

उड़िया *uṛiyā* [**audrika-*: Pk. *oḍḍia-*], adj. inv. & f. **1.** adj. having to do with Orissa. **2.** f. the Oriya language.

उड़ीसा *uṛīsā*, m. Orissa.

उड़ीक *uṛīk*, f. = उढ़ीक.

उड़प *uṛup* [ad. *uḍupa-*], m. Brbh. lord of the stars: the moon.

उड़प *uṛup* [S.], m. = उड़प.

उड़ेख *uṛekh*, m. reg. (W.) the hind prop of a cart. (cf. उढ़ीक.)

उड़ेलना *uṛelnā* [**ullaṇḍati*: Pk. *ullaṁḍiya-*], v.t. **1.** to pour out, to empty (the contents of a vessel). **2.** fig. to pour out (as emotions). **3.** to flay.

उड़ेलवाना *uṛelvānā* [cf. H. *uṛelnā*], v.t. to cause to be emptied, &c. (by, से).

उढ़क *uṛhak* [? cf. H. *uṛhaknā*], f. *Pl.* wailing, crying (of a child).

उढ़कन *uṛhkan* [cf. H. *uṛhaknā*], m. *Pl. HŚS.* a support; ? a wedge.

उढ़कना *uṛhaknā*, v.i. **1.** to overturn; to tilt. **2.** to be supported, to rest (on or against).

उढ़काना *uṛhkānā* v.t. to support; to close (a door: with a wedge or hook).

उढ़री *uṛhrī* [cf. H. *oṛhnā*], f. pej. **1.** a woman taken by a man to live with. **2.** a second wife.

उढ़ाना *uṛhānā* [cf. H. *oṛhnā*], v.t. = ओढ़ाना.

उढ़ावनि *uṛhāvni* [cf. H. *uṛhānā*], f. 19c. a shawl.

उढ़ीक *uṛhīk*, ? m. a support, prop; ? wedge.

उत *ut*, adv. there; thither.

उत्- *ut-* [S.], pref. (before voiceless consonants) upwards, &c. (= उद्-: e.g. उत्पादन, m. protection.

उतना *utnā* [cf. *iyattaka-*, and *asau*, &c.: anal.], adj. as much as that, as many as that. — ~ ही, adj. just as much as that, &c.

उतंग *utraṅg*, m. *Pl. HŚS.* the wooden arch surmounting a door; lintel of a door.

उतरन *utran* [cf. H. *utarnā*], f. **1.** sthg. taken off: worn-out or second-hand clothes. **2.** a fragment.

उतरना *utarnā* [*uttarati*], v.i. **1.** to come down, to descend; to alight, to dismount, to disembark. **2.** to make one's appearance (in, में: as in a place, on a scene); to be born; to be incarnated; to become involved (in, में or पर: as in an activity, a war, a struggle); to become determined (to, पर). **3.** to pass over or across. **4.** to be taken down, lowered, set down; to be dismantled; to be demolished. **5.** to be taken off; to be cut, stripped, torn or broken off; to be dislocated (a bone). **6.** to be drawn out or off (a liquid); to fade (as dye); to be extracted (an essence, a dye); to be infused (tea). हाथों की मेंहदी ~, fig. (a woman's) wedding to be over, to be newly married. **7.** to be lowered, to decrease; to fall, to sink, to slip, to decline; to subside (as flood, fever, a fit of anger); to wane (as the moon); to ebb; to go off, to pass its peak (perishable goods or produce); to rot, or to decay; to grow insipid; to fade or to grow wan; to be drawn (a face). **8.** to be abased, or dishonoured; to be demoted; to be dethroned. **9.** to be freed (as from debt, obligation, oath; or from possession by an evil spirit). **10.** to halt; to encamp, to take up quarters; to settle. **11.** to grow slack; to go out of tune (a musical instrument). **12.** to pass the lips, to be consumed (food, drink); to be absorbed, understood (a matter). **13.** to be disconcerted; to fall (the face). **14.** to be taken down, recorded (an entry); to be registered (a mental impression). **15.** to be fashioned, produced; to be ready (a product, a dish); to be made (as a copy, a drawing). **16.** to be collected, levied. **17.** (in chess) to be exchanged (a piece reaching the last row of the board). **18.** to be managed (by, से); to be within the scope (of). **19.** to turn out to be, to prove (as of an amount or total). **20.** to end, to pass (a period of time); to pass away, to die. उतरती ~, f. declining years.

उतरवाना *utarvānā* [cf. H. *utarnā*], v.t. to cause to be brought down, lowered, &c. (by, से).

उतरहा *utarhā*, adj. northern.

उतराई *utrāī* [cf. H. *utarnā*, *utārnā*], f. **1.** coming down, alighting; coming down to the plains (from the hills). **2.** slope, descent. **3.** decline (of life). **4.** conveying across, ferrying; disembarkation. **5.** ferriage, toll. **6.** discharge (of a debt).

उतराना *utrānā* [cf. *uttarati*, and *uttārayati*], v.i. & v.t. **1.** v.i. to float (on, पर); to rise to the surface (as of water); fig. to wander about. **2.** Brbh. to boil up or over. **3.** v.t. = उतरवाना.

उतरायल *utrāyal* [cf. H. *utarnā*], adj. reg. second-hand.

उतान *utān* [*uttāna-*], adj. = उत्तान.

उतार *utār* [*uttāra-*], m. **1.** descent, decline; slope. **2.** landing-place; ford, ferry; ferriage, toll. **3.** decrease, reduction; fall (as of prices, or flood-water); ebb; abatement, alleviation (as of fever, or intoxication, or pride, anger). **4.** counter-measure, antidote. **5.** decay, deterioration. **6.** lower reach (of a river). — ~ पर होना, to decline, to subside, &c. दूसरा ~, m. *math.* square root. – उतार-चढ़ाव, m. descent and ascent; rise and fall; ebb and flow; undulation; fluctuation (as of prices, fortune); profit and loss; variability (of thought or emotion); shift, trickery, deception.

उतारन *utāran* [*uttāraṇa-*], m. (f., *Pl.*) discarded objects (esp. clothes).

उतारना *utārnā* [*uttārayati*], v.t. **1.** to cause to descend or to alight; to set down (as passengers, luggage, burden); to disembark; to help to dismount; *hind.* to send down (an *avatār*, into the world). **2.** to take across; to ferry across. **3.** to take down or off; to cut, to tear, to strip or to break off; to remove, to shed (clothes); to throw off (restraint, or shame). **4.** to draw, to run off (a liquid); to channel (water); to extract (an essence, a colour); to distil. **5.** to lower, to decrease; to depress (as prices); to assuage (a fever, or intoxication, or a fit of anger); to treat successfully (snake-bite); to vent (ire, spleen: on, पर). **6.** to abase, to lower; to detract from (honour, ritual purity); to make impure; to cause to lose caste status (esp. उतार देना); to demote; to dethrone. **7.** to exorcise; to draw down and confine (an evil spirit). **8.** to repay (a debt, an obligation); to fulfil (a vow, an oath). **9.** to lodge (a traveller, a guest). **10.** to lay (in a grave). **11.** to relax, to loosen (tension); to uncock (a firearm). **12.** to dispense, to distribute (food, alms). **13.** to swallow, to gulp down (esp. उतार जाना). **14.** to cause (one's face) to fall; to disconcert, to cause to blush (esp. उतार देना). **15.** to dislocate (a bone: esp. उतार देना). **16.** to record, to enter, to insert (in, में: esp. उतार लेना); to imprint (a matter, on one's mind). **17.** to produce (an artefact), to make (a copy, a drawing); to make (an imitation, or impersonation); to take (a photograph). **18.** to perform (a rite: as *ārtī*). **19.** to collect (a payment due). **20.** (in chess) to exchange (a piece reaching the last row of the board). — उतारा हुआ, adj. dismounted; fig. desperately engaged (in), firmly resolved (as cavalry dismounting to fight on foot).

उतारा *utārā* [cf. H. *utārnā*], m. **1.** descent (to a river). **2.** landing-place. **3.** crossing, passage (of a river, or pass); ferriage, toll. **4.** dismounting; halt; halting-place. **5.** delivery from possession by spirits, or from sickness; articles used in exorcising a spirit, or in removing a sickness (e.g. food, drugs and charmed substances, passed over or around the subject's body). **6.** an offering to evil spirits (often left at a crossroads). **7.** second-hand goods. — उतारे का माल, m. = ~, 7.

उतारू *utārū* [cf. H. *utārnā*], adj. stooping, lowering (oneself): **1.** bent on (a course of action, esp. an improper one), hell-bent. **2.** ready (for, पर). **3.** sloping downwards (as terrain). — ~ होना, to descend, to stoop; to be ready (for, पर); to engage, to embark (on).

उतावल *utāval*, f. Brbh. = उतावलापन.

उतावला *utāvlā* [**uttāpala-*: Pk. *uttāvala-*], adj. **1.** speedy. **2.** eager; hasty; impatient; rash. — ~ रहना, to be in haste, eager, &c.

उतावलापन *utāvlāpan* [cf. H. *utāvlā*], m. **1.** speediness. **2.** eagerness; hastiness; impatience; rashness.

उतावली *utāvlī* [cf. H. *utāvlā*], f. = उतावलापन.

उतू *utū*, Brbh. metr. = उत्तू.

उतृण *utr̥ṇ* [S.], adj. corr. freed from obligation, out of debt.

उतै *utai* [cf. H. *ut*], adv. Brbh. thither.

उत्कंठ *ut-kaṇṭh* [S.], adj. = उत्कंठित.

उत्कंठा *ut-kaṇṭhā* [S.], f. eager desire, longing. — उत्कंठातुर [°*ṭhā* + *ā*°], adj. tormented by desire.

उत्कंठित *ut-kaṇṭhit* [S.], adj. eagerly desirous; longing (for, के लिए, का).

उत्कट *ut-kaṭ* [S.], adj. **1.** exceeding the usual measure; vast (as fame, reputation). **2.** abounding in (emotions): ardent, passionate; frenzied.

उत्कर्ण *ut-karṇ* [S.], adj. having the ears raised or cocked (an animal).

उत्कर्ष *ut-karṣ* [S.], adj. **1.** elevation: eminence, excellence; superiority. **2.** rise, increase. **3.** excess. — उत्कर्षापकर्ष [°*ṣa* + *a*°], m. rise and fall, progress and decline.

उत्कर्षक *ut-karṣak* [S.], adj. **1.** raising, elevating. **2.** increasing. **3.** developing.

उत्कर्षता *ut-karṣātā* [S.], f. **1.** excellence. **2.** high level. **3.** excessiveness.

उत्कलित *ut-kalit* [S.], adj. loosened, unbound: blossoming.

उत्कीर्ण *ut-kīrṇ* [S.], adj. carved, engraved, cut.

उत्कोच *ut-koc* [S.], m. a bribe.

उत्कृष्ट *ut-kr̥ṣṭ* [S.], adj. eminent, excellent; superior.

उत्कृष्टता *ut-kṛṣṭătā* [S.], f. excellence; superiority.

उत्खनन *ut-khanan* [S.], m. excavation (= खुदाई).

उत्तप्त *ut-tapt* [S.], adj. **1.** heated. **2.** excited, agitated; angered; anxious; distressed.

उत्तम *uttam* [S.], adj. **1.** highest; supreme; best. **2.** choice, excellent. **3.** last. — **उत्तम-गंधा**, f. Brbh. jasmine. **उत्तम-पुरुष**, m. *gram.* first person. **उत्तमावस्था** [°*ma*+*a*°], f. *gram.* superlative degree. **उत्तमोत्तम** [°*ma*+*u*°], adj. the very best.

उत्तमता *uttamătā* [S.], f. **1.** excellence; worth. **2.** superiority.

उत्तर *uttar* [S.], adj. & m. **1.** adj. further. **2.** following, subsequent; late (as a period of time). **3.** last; future. **4.** upper; outer (garment). **5.** surpassing, best. **6.** answering. ***7.** northerly. ***8.** m. answer; conclusion, result (as of a calculation). **9.** fig. defence, justification. **10.** return, requital. ***11.** the north. — **~ देना (को)**, to answer. – **उत्तर-काल**, m. the future. **उत्तर-दाता**, m. inv. a person responsible (for, **का**). **उत्तर-दान**, m. a bequest. **°-दायक**, adj. answering; responsible. **°-दायित्व**, m. responsibility. **°-पूर्ण**, adj. = next. **उत्तरदायी**, adj. responsible, answerable. **उत्तर-पक्ष**, m. refutation, opposite case (of an argument). **उत्तर-पश्चिम**, adj. & m. north-west. **°ई**, adj. id. **उत्तर-पूर्व (पूरब)**, adj. & m. north-east. **°ई**, adj. id. **उत्तर-प्रत्युत्तर**, m. argument; altercation; pleading (at law). **उत्तर-प्रदेशीय**, adj. having to do with the state of U.P. **उत्तर-माला**, f. table of answers (in a text-book). **उत्तरवर्ती**, adj. subsequent; northern. **उत्तराधिकार** [°*ra*+*a*°], m. right of sucession; inheritance, succession. **°ई**, adj. & m. inheriting, succeeding; heir, successor. **°इणी**, f. **उत्तरायण** [°*ra*+*a*°], m. the summer solstice; the sun's northward progress. **उत्तरार्ध** [°*ra*+*a*°], m. latter or last part: upper part; northern part; further end. **उत्तरावस्था** [°*ra*+*a*°], f. *gram.* comparative degree. **उत्तरोत्तर** [°*ra*+*u*°], adj. & m. more and more; higher and higher; further and further; gradual(ly); continuous(ly); *Pl.* a rejoinder.

उत्तरण *uttaraṇ* [S.], m. taking over or across (to the far bank); landing.

उत्तराहा *uttarāhā* [*uttarāpatha-*], adj. northern.

उत्तरी *uttărī* [cf. H. *uttar*], adj. northern.

उत्तरीय *uttărīyă* [S.], m. & adj. **1.** m. an upper or outer garment; a shawl. **2.** adj. = **उत्तरी**.

उत्तरोत्तर *uttarôttar* [S.], adj. see s.v. **उत्तर**/.

उत्तल *ut-tal* [S.], adj. convex.

उत्ता *uttā*, adj. reg. = **उतना**.

उत्तान *ut-tān* [S.], adj. **1.** lying on the back. **2.** upside down, inverted.

उत्ताल *ut-tāl* [S.], adj. huge, towering (as a wave, a peak).

उत्तीर्ण *ut-tīrṇ* [S.], adj. **1.** crossed over (a river or sea); landed. **2.** liberated. **3.** passed, successful (in an examination: **में**). — **~ करना**, to pass (an examination).

उत्तुंग *ut-tuṅg* [S.], adj. lofty.

उत्तू *uttū*, m. esp. U. **1.** an appliance for crimping or marking cloth. ***2.** decorative marks or folds made in, or on, cloth. **3.** a welt, wale (caused by beating). — **~ करना**, to crimp, to mark (cloth); colloq. to berate, to vilify. **मारकर ~ बनाना**, to beat (one) black and blue. **~ होना**, fig. to become stupefied (as from drink).

उत्तेजन *ut-tejan* [S.], m. = next.

उत्तेजना *ut-tejănā* [S.], f. excitement, stimulation; encouragement.

उत्तेजित *ut-tejit* [S.], adj. excited, stimulated.

उत्तोलन *ut-tolan* [S.], m. raising, lifting; hoisting. — **पटोत्तोलन** [°*ṭa*+*u*°], m. raising of a curtain (at a theatre).

उत्तोलित *ut-tolit* [S.], adj. raised (as a flag).

उत्थल *utthal*, adj. reg. = **उथला**.

उत्थान *ut-thān* [S.], m. **1.** rising up. **2.** awakening; reinvigoration, advance (as of a people); *hind.* the awakening of Viṣṇu (on the eleventh day of the bright half of Kārttik). **3.** introductory or initial section (of a literary work). — **उत्थानोन्मुख** [°*na*+*u*°], adj. progressive.

उत्थानक *ut-thānak* [S.], adj & m. raising; advancing, progressive.

उत्थापन *ut-thāpan* [S.], m. **1.** raising up, erecting. **2.** tossing up. **3.** *hind.* arousing: installing (an idol for the observances of the day). **4.** launching (a rocket).

उत्पत्ति *ut-patti* [S.], f. **1.** origin. **2.** birth. **3.** produce. **4.** production; articulation (of a sound).

उत्पन्न *ut-pann* [S.], adj. **1.** arisen (from, **से**). **2.** produced; born. — **~ करना**, to create; to give rise to; to give birth to; to produce; to evoke. **~ होना**, to be created, &c.; to result, to occur.

उत्पल *ut-pal* [S.], m. a species of blue lotus; a lotus.

उत्पाटन *ut-pāṭan* [S.], m. uprooting; eradication.

उत्पाटित *ut-pāṭit* [S.], adj. uprooted; eradicated.

उत्पात *ut-pāt* [S.], m. **1.** natural disaster. **2.** confusion, turmoil. **3.** violence; injury, mischief. — ~ **करना**, or **मचाना**, to create turmoil, to wreak havoc.

उत्पाती *ut-pātī* [S.], adj. & m. **1.** adj. violent, destructive. **2.** m. a stirrer of commotion, or violence.

उत्पाद *ut-pād* [S.; w. H. *utpādan*], m. a product.

उत्पादक *ut-pādak* [S.], adj. & m. **1.** adj. producing. **2.** productive. **3.** having to do with production. **4.** m. a producer; manufacturer.

उत्पादकता *ut-pādakătā* [S.], f. productivity.

उत्पादन *ut-pādan* [S.], m. **1.** production. **2.** a (commercial) product. ~ **करना** (**का**), to produce. – **उत्पादन-क्षमता**, f. productivity. **उत्पादन-शक्ति**, f. productive capacity. **उत्पादन-शुल्क**, m. excise duty.

उत्पादित *ut-pādit* [S.], adj. produced.

उत्पादी *ut-pādī* [S.], adj. **1.** producing. **2.** productive.

उत्पाद्य *ut-pādyă* [S.], adj. to be produced.

उत्पीड़क *ut-pīṛak* [S.], m. an oppressor.

उत्पीड़न *ut-pīṛan* [S.], m. oppression; harassment.

उत्पीड़ित *ut-pīṛit* [S.], adj. oppressed.

उत्प्रवास *ut-pra-vās* [S.], m. emigration.

उत्प्रेक्षा *ut-prêkṣā* [S.], f. **1.** comparison, illustration; simile; metaphor. **2.** conceit, fancy.

उत्प्रेरक *ut-prêrak* [S.], m. a catalyst.

उत्फुल्ल *ut-phull* [S.], adj. fully open (a flower); wide open (the eyes); radiant (the face).

उत्स *uts* [S.], m. poet. a spring.

उत्संग *ut-saṅg* [S.], m. **1.** hip (of a woman who carries an infant); lap. **2.** flat surface or level (as of a roof). **3.** slope or upper part (of a mountain). **4.** inner or middle part. **5.** layer, stratum.

उत्संगित *ut-saṅgit* [S.], adj. taken in the lap; embraced.

उत्सर्ग *ut-sarg* [S.], m. pouring out, letting loose: **1.** abandoning. **2.** granting. **3.** dedicating (oneself, one's assets, to an aim). **4.** a sacrifice, offering; gift. **5.** a dedication. — ~ **करना**, to donate; to devote; to sacrifice.

उत्सर्गी *ut-sargī* [S.], adj. **1.** dedicating, devoting. **2.** self-sacrificing.

उत्सव *ut-sav* [S.], m. **1.** rejoicing, festivity. ***2.** festival. **3.** ceremony. — ~ **मनाना**, to celebrate a festival.

उत्साह *ut-sāh* [S.], m. strength, effort: **1.** enthusiasm; zeal. **2.** morale. — **उत्साहपूर्वक**, adv. enthusiastically, &c. **उत्साहवर्धक**, adj. encouraging; inspiring.

उत्साहक *ut-sāhak* [S.], adj. encouraging; inspiring.

उत्साहित *ut-sāhit* [S.], adj. = **उत्साही**, 2.

उत्साही *ut-sāhī* [S.], adj. **1.** energetic; persevering. ***2.** enthusiastic. **3.** encouraged; inspired.

उत्सुक *ut-suk* [S.], adj. restless: eager, keen.

उत्सुकता *ut-sukătā* [S.], f. restlessness: eagerness, keenness.

उथलना *uthalnā* [**utthalyati*: Pk. *utthalaï*], v.i. **1.** to move, to be movable. **2.** to be upset, overturned. — **उथलना-पुथलना**, v.i. to be thrown into confusion or disorder; to be upset, overturned.

उथल-पुथल *uthal-puthal* [cf. H. *uthalnā*], adj. & f. **1.** adj. in complete confusion; upset, overturned. **2.** confusion, disorder; upheaval. — **उथल-पुथल करना**, to throw into confusion or disorder; to overturn. **उथल-पुथल मचाना**, to cause confusion; to cause a sensation.

उथला *uthlā* [**ut-sthala-*], adj. **1.** shallow. **2.** low-lying. **3.** superficial, facile.

उथलापन *uthlāpan* [cf. H. *uthlā*], m. shallowness, &c.

उड्डयन *uḍḍayan* [S.], m. **1.** flying, flight. **2.** aviation.

उद्- *ud-* [S.], pref. (before voiced sounds). **1.** upwards; over, above (e.g. **उद्घाटन**, m. opening, inauguration). **2.** from, away from (e.g. **उद्भव**, m. origin).

उदक *udak* [S.], m. **1.** water. **2.** *Pl.* the pouring of water (a funeral rite).

उदजन *udăjan* [Engl. *hydrogen*: S.], m. water-born: hydrogen. — **उदजन-बम**, m. hydrogen bomb.

उदड़-गुदड़ *udaṛ-gudaṛ* [cf. H. *gūdṛī*], f. tattered clothes, rags.

उदधि *uda-dhi* [S.], m. holding water: the ocean.

उदमद *ud-mad*, adj. & m. corr. **1.** adj. Brbh. = उन्मत्त (?). **2.** m. E.H. = उन्माद.

उदय *ud-ay* [S.], m. **1.** rising, rise (esp. of heavenly bodies); ascent; the east. **2.** appearance, advent. **3.** light, splendour. **4.** rise, progress; prosperity. — ~ से अस्त तक, adv. from sunrise to sunset; from east to west, all over the world. ~ होना, to rise; to appear; to begin, to arise; to spring up. — उदयास्त [°*a*+*a*°], m. rising and setting; fig. rise and fall.

उदयी *ud-ayī* [S.], adj. **1.** rising. **2.** prospering, in the ascendant.

[1]**उदर** *udar* [S.], m. **1.** the abdomen; stomach; bowels; womb. **2.** cavity, interior. — ~ जिला-, Brbh. to fill the belly (with food). ~ भरना, id.; to support oneself. – उदरपूर्ति, f. filling the belly: finding nourishment; satisfying (one's) wants. उदर-भरण, m. id.

[2]**उदर** *udar*, adv. pronun. var. = उधर.

उदरीय *udărīyă* [S.], adj. abdominal.

उदात्त *ud-ātt* [S.: for *udādatta-*], adj. & m. **1.** adj. high, lofty; high or sharp (tone, accent). **2.** great, illustrious. **3.** generous, liberal. **4.** beloved. **5.** m. a high or sharp tone, or accent.

उदार *ud-ār* [S.], adj. **1.** noble, illustrious. **2.** generous, liberal. **3.** munificent. **4.** *pol.* liberal; moderate. — ~ दल, m. a liberal group or party. – उदारचरित, adj. noble, generous or liberal (in disposition or action). उदारचित्त, adj. high-minded; generous, liberal. उदारदली, adj. & m. liberal; a liberal.

उदारता *ud-ārătā* [S.], f. **1.** nobleness. **2.** generosity, liberality. — उदारतापूर्वक, adv. nobly; generously, &c. उदरतावाद, f. liberalism; °ई, adj. & m. liberal; a liberal.

उदास *ud-ās* [S.], adj. sitting apart, being indifferent: **1.** indifferent; apathetic; lack (of activity). ***2.** dejected, sad, forlorn; sullen. **3.** sombre (of colour), faded. — ~ बैठना, or होना, to be sorrowful, &c.; to be cool (towards, से); to be displeased (with); to be apathetic (towards). ~ पड़ना, to become downcast, &c.; to become indifferent, &c.

[1]**उदासी** *ud-āsī* [cf. H. *udās*], f. **1.** indifference. ***2.** dejection. **3.** dullness.

[2]**उदासी** *ud-āsī* [S.], m. & adj. **1.** m. an ascetic. **2.** name of a Sikh sect. **3.** a member of the Udāsī sect. **4.** adj. = उदास, 1., 2. **5.** solitary, withdrawn.

उदासीन *ud-āsīn* [S.], adj. & m. **1.** adj. indifferent (towards, से), detached; cool; apathetic; inert, passive. **2.** uninvolved, not participating; neutral. **3.** m. one detached from the world; a stoically indifferent person. **4.** a non-participant.

उदासीनता *ud-āsīnătā* [S.], f. indifference, &c. (see उदासीन).

उदाहट *udāhaṭ* [cf. H. *ūdā*], f. purple (colour).

उदाहरण *ud-ā-haraṇ* [S.], m. an example. — ~ के लिए, adv. for example. उदाहरणतः, adv. by way of example. उदाहरणार्थ [°*ṇa*+*a*°], adv. id.

उदित *udit* [S.], adj. **1.** risen (as the sun). **2.** evident; conspicuous. — उदितयौवना, f. *rhet.* Brbh. a young heroine (*nāyikā*) who has not yet completely outgrown childhood.

उदीयमान *udīyămān* [S.], adj. rising; promising.

उदुंबर *udumbar* [S.: ? ← Austro-as.], m. the fig-tree *Ficus glomerata*, and its fruit (= गूलर).

उदूखल *udūkhal* [S.], m. *Pl. HŚS.* a heavy wooden mortar used for pounding rice (= ऊखल).

उदोत *udot* [ad. *uddyota-*], m. Brbh. light, moonlight; radiance.

उदोति *udoti* [H. *udot* × H. *joti*], ? f. Brbh. = उदोत.

उदोती *udotī*, ? f. Av. metr. = उदोति.

उद्गत *ud-gat* [S.], adj. arisen, sprung up; emerged.

उद्गम *ud-gam* [S.], m. **1.** rising up, appearance. **2.** rise, origin; source.

उद्गार *ud-gār* [S.], m. **1.** welling up, boiling up or over. **2.** venting (feelings). **3.** an expression of strong feeling.

उद्ग्रहण *ud-grahaṇ* [S.], m. a levy.

उद्ग्रीव *ud-grīv* [S.], adj. with neck raised; with head held high.

उद्घाटन *ud-ghāṭan* [S.], m. **1.** disclosing, revealing; raising (a stage curtain). **2.** opening, inauguration. — ~ करना (का), to open, to inaugurate.

उद्घाटित *ud-ghāṭit* [S.], adj. **1.** disclosed, revealed. **2.** opened, inaugurated.

उद्दंड *ud-daṇḍ* [S.], adj. holding a raised staff: **1.** arrogant; insolent. **2.** wilful, refractory. **3.** rebellious, in revolt.

उद्दाम *ud-dam* [S.], adj. unrestrained; self-willed.

उद्दीपक *ud-dīpak* [S.], adj. **1.** blazing, glowing, &c. **2.** stimulating, exciting; provoking.

उद्दीपन *ud-dīpan* [S.], m. **1.** blazing, glowing. **2.** illumination. **3.** exciting (zeal, passion); provoking (anger). **4.** *rhet.* stimulus (to a particular emotion).

उद्दीप्त *ud-dīpt* [S.], adj. **1.** lit up, illuminated. **2.** fired (as with zeal); inflamed (as with passion).

उद्देश्य *ud-deśyă* [S.], m. **1.** anything referred to; *gram.* a subject. ***2.** intention, purpose, object. **3.** motive. **4.** sense, gist; indication. **5.** direction, tendency. — ~ से, adv. on purpose. – उद्देश्यहीन, adj. aimless, &c.

उद्दोत *uddot*, m. E.H. light, radiance (cf. उदोत).

उद्धत *ud-dhat* [S.], adj. **1.** puffed up, arrogant, haughty; vain. **2.** rude, insolent. **3.** wild, dishevelled (hair). **4.** eager, intent (on doing sthg., के लिए).

उद्धरण *ud-dharaṇ* [S.], m. taking up or out: an extract; a quotation.

उद्धव *ud dhav* [S.], m. **1.** sacrificial fire. **2.** *mythol.* name of a friend of Kṛṣṇa. — उद्धव-भूमि, f. fig. no man's land.

उद्धार *ud-dhār* [S.], m. raising, removing: **1.** deliverance; salvation. **2.** release, discharge (from debt). **3.** amelioration. **4.** *Pl. HŚS.* debt; credit. — उद्धार-विक्रय, m. sale on credit.

उद्धारक *ud-dhārak* [S.], m. a deliverer; saviour.

उद्बोध *ud-bodh* [S.], m. **1.** awakening, enlightening; enlightenment. **2.** recollection.

उद्बोधक *ud-bodhak* [S.], adj. **1.** awakening, enlightening. **2.** arousing, inciting.

उद्बोधन *ud-bodhan* [S.], m. **1.** awakening, enlightenment. **2.** arousing, inciting. — उद्बोधन-भाषण, m. keynote address.

उद्भट *ud-bhaṭ* [S.], adj. eminent, weighty (as in learning).

उद्भव *ud-bhav* [S.], m. **1.** birth, production. **2.** origin; source. **3.** springing up, appearance.

उद्भावना *ud-bhāvănā* [S.], f. imagining, fancy.

उद्भासित *ud-bhāsit* [S.], adj. shining forth: **1.** suffused (with light), illuminated. **2.** evident, visible.

उद्भिज *ud-bhij*, adj. & m. = उद्भिज्ज.

उद्भिज्ज *ud-bhijj* [S.], adj. & m. **1.** adj. sprouting, germinating. **2.** vegetable (in nature). **3.** m. a plant.

उद्भौति *ud-bhauti* [f. *adbhuta-*], f. corr. Brbh. a marvel, miracle.

उद्भ्रांत *ud-bhrānt* [S.], adj. astray; erring; confused.

उद्यत *ud-yat* [S.], adj. **1.** raised, held up. **2.** prepared, ready (to, को or के लिए); eager. **3.** active, assiduous (in, में).

उद्यम *ud-yam* [S.], m. raising, undertaking: **1.** effort, exertion; toil. **2.** employment, vocation. **3.** an enterprise. — ~ करना, to exert oneself, to endeavour; to labour; to follow a vocation. – उद्यम-कर्ता, m. inv. a tradesman; a businessman; manufacturer, industrialist.

उद्यमी *ud-yamī* [S.], adj. & m. **1.** adj. active, energetic. **2.** industrious. **3.** engaged in trade, commerce or industry. **4.** m. = उद्यम-कर्ता.

उद्यान *ud-yān* [S.], m. **1.** a park; a garden. **2.** Brbh. wild region, forest.

उद्यापन *ud-yāpan* [S.], m. **1.** bringing to a conclusion. **2.** concluding ceremony; dedication of a temple, or tank, on completion.

उद्यापित *ud-yāpit* [S.], adj. brought to a conclusion, &c. (see उद्यापन).

उद्योग *ud-yog* [S.], m. **1.** effort, exertion. **2.** attempt, endeavour. **3.** industry. — ~ करना, to endeavour (to, का). – उद्योग-धंधा, m. industrial activity; a particular industry, or trade. उद्योग-पति, m. industrialist. उद्योगप्रधान, adj. predominantly industrial (as production). उद्योग-शाला, f. a workshop; factory. उद्योगशील, adj. = उद्योगी. उद्योगीकरण, m. industrialisation. उद्योगीकृत, adj. industrialised.

उद्योगी *ud-yogī* [S.], adj. **1.** active, energetic; persevering; industrious. **2.** occupied (in, में), concerned (with).

उद्योगीकरण *ud-yogīkaraṇ* [S.], m. see s.v. उद्योग.

उद्योगीकृत *ud-yogīkṛt* [S.], adj. see s.v. उद्योग.

उद्योत *ud-yot* [ad. *uddyota-*], m. **1.** light. **2.** radiance, lustre.

उद्विग्न *ud-vign* [S.], adj. anxious, perturbed; confused; dejected.

उद्विग्नता *ud-vignătā* [S.], f. anxiousness, perplexity, &c. (see उद्विग्न).

उद्वेग *ud-veg* [S.], m. going quickly, or upwards: **1.** agitation of feelings; anxiety; unease. **2.** consternation, fear; bewilderment. **3.** dejection. **4.** haste, impetuosity. **5.** access of emotion; passion, heat; temper.

उद्वेगी *ud-vegī* [S.], adj. **1.** agitated, perturbed, &c. **2.** bewildered. **3.** dejected. **4.** hasty, precipitate. **5.** prone to fits of emotion.

उद्वेलित *ud-velit* [S.], adj. made to overflow; fig. stirred up (emotion).

उधड़ना *udhaṛnā* [cf. *uddhṛta-*, Pk. *uddhaṭa-*], v.i. **1.** to become unrolled or unravelled; to come undone (as stitching). **2.** to be torn off, or open; to be flayed (skin).

उधर *udhar* [cf. H. [1]*dhār*], adv. **1.** thither; over there, on that side; on the other hand. **2.** there. — ~ से, adv. from that side, thence; in that direction.

उधली *udhlī* [conn. H. *udhaṛnā*], adj. f. lustful.

उधार *udhār* [*uddhāra-*], m. **1.** a loan. **2.** a debt; credit. — ~ खाना, to live on credit. ~ खाए बैठना, fig. to be intent (on, के लिए, or पर), to wait intently (for, पर); to become (one's) mortal enemy. ~ देना (को), to lend; to sell on credit; to discharge a debt. ~ माँगना, to borrow. ~ लाना, to borrow. ~ लेना, to borrow; to buy on credit. ~ होना, to be on loan; to have been borrowed, to be owing (by).

उधार- *udhār-* [*uddhārayati*], v.i. Brbh. to deliver, to extricate (from, से).

उधेड़ *udheṛ* [cf. H. *udheṛnā*], f. **1.** unravelling, unpicking. **2.** laying open, &c. — उधेड़-बुन, f. unpicking and (re-)weaving: perplexity, dilemma; confusion; continuing concern; unease, distress; deliberation; an involved scheme.

उधेड़ना *udheṛnā* [cf. H. *udhaṛnā*], v.t. **1.** to undo; to unravel; to unpick; to pull to pieces; to squander (money, &c). **2.** to lay open; to strip off; to flay; to bark (a tree); to take off an upper part (as the roof of a house). **3.** to disclose, to expose (a deficiency, a secret). **4.** to open (a grave).

उन *un*, pl. obl. base. see वह 'that'.

उन्- *un-* [S.], pref. (before nasal consonants). upwards, &c. (= उद्-: e.g. उन्नति, f. rise, progress).

उनचास *uncās* [*ūnapañcāśat-*], adj. forty-nine.

उनतालीस *untālīs* [*ūnacatvāriṁśat-*], adj. thirty-nine.

उनतीस *untīs* [*ūnatriṁśat-*], adj. twenty-nine.

उनसठ *unsaṭh* [*ūnaṣaṣṭi-*], adj. fifty-nine.

उनहत्तर *unhattar* [*ūnasaptati-*], adj. sixty-nine.

उनाह *unāh* [*uṣṇa-*[1]], m. *Pl.* steam. — ~ लेना, to take a steam bath.

उन्नत *un-nat* [S.], adj. **1.** elevated; high, tall; well-developed. **2.** advanced, developed (as industry, society); prosperous. **3.** progressive (policy, &c). **4.** lofty (as ideals).

उन्नति *un-nati* [S.], adj. **1.** ascent. *****2.** advance, development; prosperity. **3.** improvement, progress. — ~ करना, to develop; to prosper; to progress. – उन्नतिशील, adj. developed; progressive. उन्नतोदर [°*ta*+*u*°], adj. protruding; convex.

उन्नयन *un-nayan* [S.], m. raising: development; uplift.

उन्नाब *unnāb* [A. *'unnāb*], m. the jujube fruit and tree.

उन्नाबी *unnābī* [P. *'unnābī*], adj. jujube-coloured, dark red.

उन्नायक *un-nāyak* [S.], m. uplifter, reformer; leader (of a country, a community).

उन्नायन *un-nāyan* [S.], m. = उन्नयन.

उन्नासी *unnāsī* [*ūnāśīti-*], adj. seventy-nine.

उन्निद्र *un-nidră* [S.], adj. sleepless. — ~ रोग, m. insomnia.

उनींदा *unīṁdā* [*unnidra-*], adj. **1.** sleepless (*Pl.*). *****2.** sleepy, drowsy.

उन्नीस *unnīs* [*ūnaviṁśati*], adj. nineteen. — ~ होना, fig. to be slightly inferior (i.e. as compared with 'twenty'); to deteriorate; to lessen. उन्नीस बीस का, adj. (only) slightly different. उन्नीस-बीस होना, to be almost alike, equal, &c.; to be almost evenly balanced (probabilities); sthg. untoward or unwelcome to happen.

उन्मत्त *un-matt* [S.], adj. & m. **1.** adj. insane. **2.** frenzied; intoxicated; lustful. **3.** m. a madman, &c. — उन्मत्त-लिंगी, m. one pretending madness.

उन्मत्तता *un-mattătā* [S.], f. = उन्माद.

उन्मन *un-man* [S.], adj. **1.** disturbed in mind. **2.** m. (in yoga) a supra-conscious state of mind, in which the spirit approaches to or attains oneness with the absolute.

उन्माद *un-mād* [S.], m. **1.** madness. **2.** frenzy; passion.

उन्मादक *un-mādak* [S.], adj. **1.** making frenzied. **2.** intoxicating.

उन्मादी *un-mādī* [S.], adj. = उन्मत्त.

उन्मान *un-mān* [S.], m. a measure (of size, weight or amount).

उन्मुक्त *un-mukt* [S.], adj. **1.** freed, released; unrestrained; unconstrained; free. **2.** made loose, opened; undone (as hair).

उन्मुक्ति *un-mukti* [S.], f. **1.** freedom; lack of constraint. **2.** release (of a prisoner). **3.** immunity.

उन्मुख *un-mukh* [S.], adj. **1.** raising the face, looking upwards. **2.** aspiring (towards, की ओर); tending towards. **3.** awaiting intently.

— आदर्शोन्मुख [°śa+u], adj. having an idealist tendency (a viewpoint).

उन्मुखर *un-mukhar* [S.], adj. ringing, noisy.

उन्मुद्र *un-mudră* [S.], adj. unsealed: beside oneself (with joy).

उन्मूलन *un-mūlan* [S.], m. rooting up: eradicating; abolishing.

उन्मेष *un-meṣ* [S.], m. 1.opening the eyes, looking at. **2.** manifestation, appearance; upsurge (of emotions). **3.** a twinkling of an eye: an instant of time.

उन्हार *unhār* [*anuhāra-*, Pk. *aṇuhāri-*], f. 19c. kind, type; appearance.

उपंग *upaṅg* [ad. *upāṅga-*], m. Brbh. Av. a type of musical instrument.

उप- *upă-* [S.], pref. **1.** near to (e.g. उपकार, m. sthg. supplied: a benefit, a service). **2.** resembling (esp. in a subordinate or inferior sense: e.g. उपभाषा, f. a dialect; उपराष्ट्रपति, m. vice-president; उपसंपादक, m. sub-editor; उपमार्ग, m. by-road).

उपकथा *upă-kathā* [S.], f. episode (in a larger story).

उपकरण *upă-karaṇ* [S.], m. **1.** instrument, apparatus; implement; utensil; equipment; means, device. **2.** materials. **3.** *hist.* insignia (of royalty).

उपकार *upă-kār* [S.], m. **1.** beneficence; kindness; favour. **2.** benefit, help; protection, preservation. — ~ करना, to show kindness (to, का or पर). ~ मानना, to feel or to express gratitude (to, का: as for a kindness).

उपकारक *upă-kārak* [S.], adj. & m. = उपकारी.

उपकारिता *upă-kāritā* [S.], f. **1.** kindliness, &c. **2.** beneficiality; efficacy (of medicine).

उपकारी *upă-kārī* [S.], adj. & m. **1.** adj. beneficent; good, kind. **2.** beneficial, helpful; furthering, conducive (to). **3.** m. a benefactor, &c.

उपकूल *upă-kūl* [S.], m. bank, shore.

उपकेंद्रीय *upă-kendrīyă* [S.], adj. centrifugal.

उपक्रम *upă-kram* [S.], m. **1.** preparatory or initial stage; preparation (for, का); beginning. **2.** an undertaking, enterprise. **3.** an expedient.

उपक्रमणिका *upă-kramaṇikā* [S.], f. = अनुक्रमणिका.

उपगत *upă-gat* [S.], adj. **1.** approached; turned, or fled, to. **2.** obtained. **3.** grasped, comprehended. **4.** incurred (as expense). **5.** accepted, agreed.

उपगति *upă-gati* [S.], f. **1.** approach. **2.** obtaining. **3.** comprehension. **4.** acceptance, &c.

उपगम *upă-gam* [S.], m. approach, &c. (= उपगति).

उपगमन *upă-gaman* [S.], m. = उपगति.

उपग्रह *upă-grah* [S.], m. **1.** *astron.* a satellite; *aeron.* an artificial satellite. **2.** encouragement, assistance.

उपग्रहण *upă-grahaṇ* [S.], m. **1.** holding (as in the hand). **2.** seizing, detaining. **3.** traditional study of sacred texts.

उपचार *upă-cār* [S.], m. **1.** service, attendance; traditional, or formal usage (as that of welcoming a guest). **2.** any of various individual rites in worship; a magical practice. **3.** treatment (of a patient); nursing; medical care; remedy. **4.** a process of treatment (as of raw materials).

उपचार- *upăcār-* [cf. *upacāra-*], v.t. Brbh. Av. **1.** to serve, to tend. **2.** to perform (as a traditional or formal usage, or as a rite).

उपचारक *upă-cārak* [S.], adj. & m. **1.** adj. serving, attending. **2.** treating. **3.** m. an attendant, &c.; a male nurse.

उपचारिका *upă-cārikā* [S.], f. a nurse.

उपचारी *upă-cārī* [S.], adj. 1. = उपचारक. **2.** performed as a traditional, or formal usage.

उपज *upaj* [cf. H. *upajnā*], f. **1.** produce. **2.** production (of goods, assets). **3.** crop; yield. **4.** productivity. **5.** original idea; invention; fancy. **6.** *mus.* Brbh. variations on a melody.

उपजना *upajnā* [*utpadyate*], v.i. to grow: **1.** to originate, to be born. **2.** to be produced; to spring up, to shoot, to sprout. **3.** to happen; to appear. **4.** to occur (to the mind: में).

उपजाऊ *upjāū* [cf. H. *upjānā*], adj. **1.** fertile, rich (soil, land). **2.** productive. — ~ करना, to fertilise (fields). – ~ शक्ति, f. fertility.

उपजाऊपन *upăjāūpan* [cf. H. *upjāū*], m. fertility (as of soil).

उपजाना *upjānā* [cf. H. *upajnā*], v.t. to cause to grow: **1.** to produce; to cultivate (a crop, as for sale). **2.** to create; to devise, to invent. **3.** to suggest (an idea).

उपजीवन *upă-jīvan* [S.], m. 1. = उपजीविका. **2.** dependence on another for support.

उपजीविका *upă-jīvikā* [S.], f. **1.** livelihood, means of support. **2.** subsidiary source of income.

उपजीवी *upă-jīvī* [S.], adj. & m. **1.** adj. dependent for support (on, का). **2.** m. a dependent.

उपटन *upṭan*, m. pronun. var. = उबटन.

उपटना *upaṭnā* [cf. H. *upāṭ-*], v.i. reg. to be uprooted, or removed.

उपड़ना *upaṛnā* [cf. H. *upāṛna*], v.i. **1.** to be uprooted. **2.** to be skinned. **3.** to be marked, or imprinted (a footprint, &c).

उपत्यका *upatyakā* [S.], f. land at the foot of a mountain, low land.

उपदंश *upă-daṃś* [S.], m. **1.** Brbh. relish, flavour; an appetiser. **2.** venereal disease; syphilis.

उपदान *upă-dān* [S.], m. a grant, subsidy; allowance.

उपदेश *upă-deś* [S.], m. indicating, instructing: **1.** advice, counsel. **2.** spiritual instruction. — ~ करना, to counsel; to exhort. ~ देना (को), id. – उपदेशात्मक [°*śa* + *ā*°], adj. instructive; didactic.

उपदेशक *upă-deśak* [S.], adj. & m. **1.** adj. instructive; didactic (= उपदेशात्मक). ***2.** m. a counsellor; preceptor, mentor. **3.** a missionary.

उपदेशी *upă-deśī* [S.], adj. & m. **1.** adj. giving counsel; wise, sage. **2.** m. (-देसी). Av. = उपदेशक.

उपदेश्य *upă-deśyă* [S.], adj. **1.** deserving instruction, &c. **2.** suitable to be taught, propounded.

उपदेष्टा *upă-deṣṭā* [S.], m. inv. = उपदेशक.

उपद्रव *upă-drav* [S.], m. **1.** sudden disturbance, commotion; turmoil. **2.** riot. **3.** uprising, revolt. **4.** sudden complication or relapse (in an illness). — उपद्रवकारी, adj. making trouble; causing turmoil, riot, &c.

उपद्रवी *upă-dravī* [S.], adj. & m. **1.** adj. turbulent. **2.** violent. **3.** rebellious, disaffected. **4.** m. a turbulent person, trouble-maker.

उपद्वीप *upă-dvîp* [S.], m. a small island.

उपधा *upă-dhā* [S.], f. fraud.

उपधान *upă-dhān* [S.], m. **1.** a support. **2.** a pillow, cushion.

उपनगर *upă-nagar* [S.], m. a suburb.

उपनगरीय *upă-nagārīyă* [S.], adj. suburban.

उपनयन *upă-nayan* [S.], m. *hind.* ceremony of investiture with the sacred thread (*janeū*).

उपनाम *upă-nām* [S.], m. **1.** nickname. **2.** pseudonym.

उपनामी *upă-nāmī* [cf. H. *upanām*], adj. having the nickname, pseudonym, &c., of.

उपनिवेश *upă-ni-veś* [S.], m. **1.** settlement. ***2.** colony.

उपनिवेशन *upă-ni-veśan* [S.], m. colonising.

उपनिवेशित *upă-ni-veśit* [S.], adj. colonised.

उपनिवेशी *upă-ni-veśī* [S.], adj. & m. **1.** adj. colonial. **2.** m. a colonist.

उपनिषद *upă-ni-ṣad* [S.], m. session (of a pupil with a teacher), and the knowledge there given: an *upaniṣad* (any of various philosophical works attached to the Brāhmaṇas, and expounding the inner meaning of the Vedas).

उपनीत *upă-nīt* [S.], adj. brought near: acquired, earned; invested with the sacred thread (cf. उपनयन).

उपन्यस्त *upă-ny-ast* [S.], adj. **1.** placed, brought near; given in keeping. ***2.** mentioned, told; specif. told in the form of a novel, given novel form.

उपन्यास *upă-ny-ās* [S.], m. placing near or together: a novel.

उपन्यासकार *upă-ny-āskār* [S.], m. a novelist.

उपपति *upăpati* [S.], m. lover (of a married woman).

उपपत्नी *upă-patnī* [S.], f. a mistress; concubine.

उपपातक *upă-pātak* [S.], m. a crime or sin which can be expiated.

उपबंध *upă-bandh* [S.], m. provision (of regulations, &c).

उपभाषा *upă-bhāṣā* [S.], f. a dialect.

उपभोग *upă-bhog* [S.], m. consumption (as of goods); enjoyment.

उपभोक्ता *upă-bhoktā* [S.], m. inv. a consumer.

उपमहाद्वीप *upă-mahādvîp* [S.], m. sub-continent.

उपमा *upă-mā* [S.], f. **1.** comparison; similarity; a simile. 2. = उपमान, 2. — ~ देना (की), to compare (with, से); to liken (to).

उपमान *upă-mān* [S.], m. **1.** comparison, similarity. **2.** *rhet.* an object of comparison.

उपमेय *upă-mey* [S.], adj. & m. **1.** adj. to be compared, comparable. **2.** m. *rhet.* the subject of a comparison.

उपयंता *upă-yantā* [S.], m. inv. one who takes hold: husband.

उपयुक्त *upă-yukt* [S.], adj. fit, proper; suitable; appropriate; worthy (as of a post).

उपयुक्तता *upă-yuktătā* [S.], f. suitability, &c.

उपयोग *upă-yog* [S.], m. **1.** application; use, service; usefulness. **2.** availability, validity. — ~ करना (का), to use, to employ.

उपयोगिता *upă-yogitā* [S.], f. **1.** usefulness, suitability for use. **2.** validity. — **उपयोगितावाद**, m. utilitarianism. °ई, adj. & m. utilitarian; a utilitarian.

उपयोगी *upă-yogī* [S.], adj. **1.** useful, serviceable. **2.** available, valid.

उपर *upar*, adv. Brbh. = उपरि.

उपरना *uparnā*, m. a shawl.

उपरला *uparlā* [**upparalla*-: Pk. *uppalla*-; and **uppari*], adj. **1.** upper. **2.** outer, exterior; superficial.

उपरांत *upărânt* [S.], adv. **1.** after. **2.** ppn. w. के. after.

उपराग *upă-rāg* [S.], m. **1.** colour, coloration. **2.** Av. darkening: eclipse.

उपराज- *uparāj-* [? ad. *upārjati*], v.t. Brbh. Av. **1.** to produce. **2.** to create. **3.** to acquire, to earn.

उपराजदूत *upa-rājdūt* [S.], m. chargé d'affaires.

उपराना *uprānā*, v.i. reg. = उपलाना.

उपराला *uprālā*, m. Brbh. help, support.

उपराष्ट्रपति *upă-rāṣṭrapati* [S.], m. vice-president (of a state).

उपरि *upari* [S.], adv. esp. in comp. above, over, upon. — **उपरि-निर्दिष्ट**, adj. referred to, or indicated, above. **उपरि-लिखित**, adj. written, or mentioned, above. **उपरोक्त** (for °युक्त), adj. corr. = next. **उपर्युक्त**, adj. above-mentioned.

उपरी-उपरा *uprī-uprā* [cf. H. *ūpar(ī)*], m. Brbh. rivalry.

उपरोक्त *uparokt*, adj. corr. see s.v. उपरि.

उपरोध *upă-rodh* [S.], m. **1.** obstacle, impediment; hindrance; disturbance. **2.** *HŚS.* protection, shelter.

उपरोधक *upă-rodhak* [S.], adj. obstructing, &c.

उपरोधन *upă-rodhan* [S.], m. obstruction, impediment.

उपरोधी *upă-rodhī* [S.], adj. obstructing, &c.

उपरोहित *upă-rohit* [f. *purohita*-], m. Av. = पुरोहित.

उपर्युक्त *upary-ukt*, adv. see s.v. उपरि.

उपल *upal* [S.], m. **1.** a stone. **2.** a hailstone (= ओला). **3.** a precious stone.

उपलक्ष *upă-lakṣ*, m. = उपलक्ष्य.

उपलक्षण *upă-lakṣaṇ* [S.], m. **1.** *rhet.* a type of metaphorical or elliptical expression; synecdoche. **2.** a sign, indication.

उपलक्षित *upă-lakṣit* [S.], adj. **1.** perceived. **2.** distinguished, marked; characterised.

उपलक्ष्य *upă-lakṣyă* [S.], m. **1.** sign, implication. ***2.** occasion. — ~ में, adv. on the occasion (of, के); in recognition (of).

उपलब्ध *upă-labdh* [S.], adj. **1.** obtained; achieved (by, को). **2.** to be had, available (to, को).

उपलब्धि *upă-labdhi* [S.], f. an achievement, or attainment.

उपला *uplā* [**utpala*-[2]], m. a dried cake of cow-dung (fuel).

उपलाना *uplānā* [**utplāvayati*: Pk. *uppilāvei*], v.i. *Pl.* to rise to the surface (of water), to float.

उपली *uplī* [cf. H. *uplā*], dimin. f. = उपला.

उपलेप *upă-lep* [S.], m. **1.** smearing, plastering: plastering with cow-dung. **2.** anointing. **3.** a substance smeared, spread, &c.

उपलेपन *upă-lepan* [S.], m. = उपलेप, 1., 2.

उपवन *upă-van* [S.], m. a grove, a garden.

उपवाद *upă-vād* [S.], m. censure, blame (= अपवाद).

उपवास *upă-vās* [S.], m. fasting; a fast; hunger-strike. — ~ करना, to fast. ~ रखना, to keep a fast.

उपवासी *upă-vāsī* [S.], adj. & m. **1.** adj. fasting, &c. **2.** m. one who fasts, &c.

उपविधि *upă-vidhi* [S.], f. a bye-law.

उपविष *upă-viṣ* [S.], m. *Pl. HŚS.* a narcotic; a drug.

उपविष्ट *upă-viṣṭ* [S.], adj. seated, sitting.

उपवीत *upă-vīt* [S.], m. invested with the thread: **1.** sacred thread (= जनेऊ). **2.** transf. investiture with the sacred thread (= उपनयन).

उपवेद *upă-ved* [S.], m. a class of writings dealing with four branches of knowledge, attached to and subordinate to the four Vedas.

उपवेशन *upă-veśan* [S.], m. the act of sitting.

उपशम *upă-śam* [S.], m. **1.** becoming calm or stilled (the aroused senses). **2.** tranquillity, calm; patience.

उपशमन *upă-śaman* [S.], m. calming, stilling; appeasing; allaying.

उपशांत *upă-śānt* [S.], adj. calm, pacified; appeased; allayed.

उपशांति *upă-śānti* [S.], f. tranquillity, calm.

उपशामक *upă-śāmak* [S.], adj. calming, pacifying, allaying.

उपसंजात *upă-sañ-jāt* [S.], adj. appeared, appearing (in a court).

उपस *upas*, f. *Pl. HŚS.* reg. bad smell, &c. (cf. उबसना).

उपसर्ग *upă-sarg* [S.], m. *gram.* a prefix; preposition (= पूर्वसर्ग).

उपस्कर *upă-skar* [S.], m. an appliance: equipment.

उपस्थ *upa-sthă* [S.], m. lower part: genitalia (male or female).

उपस्थित *upa-sthit* [S.], adj. **1.** present; arrived; ready (as to assist in a task). **2.** at hand, near; impending. **3.** actual, existing. **4.** presented, made, proposed (a deposition, a motion). — ~ करना, to present, to show, &c. ~ होना, to be present, &c.; to arise; to occur.

उपस्थिति *upa-sthiti* [S.], f. **1.** presence; attendance. **2.** attendance (as of participators, audience). — उपस्थिति-पंजी, f. attendance register. उपस्थिति-पत्र, m. a summons (at law).

उपहार *upă-hār* [S.], m. a complimentary gift. — ~ में देना (को), to present (to).

उपहास *upă-hās* [S.], m. **1.** laughter. *****2.** ridicule. — ~ करना (का), to deride (one). – उपहास-चित्र, m. a caricature. उपहासात्मक [°*a*+*ā*°], adj. mocking. उपहासास्पद [°*sa*+*ā*°], adj. ridiculous, ludicrous.

उपांत्य *upântyă* [S.], adj. penultimate.

उपा- *upā-* [*utpādayati*], v.t. Brbh. Av. **1.** to produce, to create. **2.** to devise.

उपाख्यान *upâkhyān* [S.], m. **1.** a legend, tale. **2.** episode (of a narration).

उपाट- *upāṭ-* [**utpaṭyati*, v.i.], v.t. Brbh. Av. = उपाड़ना.

उपाड़ *upāṛ* [cf. H. *upāṛnā*], m. ? *Pl.* pulling up or out by the root.

उपाड़ना *upāṛnā* [*utpāṭayati*], v.t. to uproot, to eradicate.

उपादान *upâdān* [S.], m. **1.** taking away. **2.** acquisition of knowledge; study. **3.** withdrawal (of the senses from the outer world). **4.** cause, motive. **5.** substance, raw material.

उपादेयता *upâdeyătā* [S.], f. usefulness.

उपाधि *upâdhi* [S.], f. sthg. put in the place (of sthg. else): **1.** *philos.* distinguishing property, attribute. *****2.** title, rank; decoration; degree, diploma. **3.** nickname. — उपाधिधारी, m. title-holder; graduate. उपाधि-पत्र, m. diploma (certificate).

उपाधी *upâdhī* [cf. H. *upādhi*], adj. Brbh. ? having the characteristics (of): prime, egregious (a ruffian).

उपाध्याय *upâdhy-āy* [S.], m. **1.** a teacher, preceptor (in traditional knowledge). **2.** name of a partic. brāhmaṇ sub-community. **3.** a man of that community.

उपाध्यायानी *upâdhy-āyānī* [S.], f. **1.** the wife of an *upadhyāy*. **2.** a teacher, preceptress.

उपाय *upây* [S.], m. **1.** means, recourse; scheme, plan; device; measure. **2.** *med. ayur.* treatment. — ~ करना, to devise a scheme; to try an expedient.

उपार्जन *upârjan* [S.], m. acquisition; earning; amassing. — ~ करना, to acquire, to earn, &c.

उपार्जित *upârjit* [S.], adj. acquired; earned; amassed. — ~ करना, to earn; to amass.

उपालंभ *upâlambh* [S.], m. **1.** reproach, complaint. **2.** railing, scolding.

उपास *upās*, m. = उपवास.

उपासक *upâsak* [S.], m. a worshipper, devotee.

उपासन *upâsan* [S.], m. **1.** sitting by the side of; attending, serving. **2.** worship.

उपासना *upâsănā* [S.], f. sitting near: **1.** attendance, service. *****2.** worship, adoration; reverence.

उपासनीय *upâsănīyă* [S.], adj. = उपास्य.

उपासा *upāsā* [ad. *upavāsa-*], m. *Pl..* fasting, keeping fast.

उपासी *upâsī* [S.], adj. & m. **1.** adj. worshipping. **2.** m. = उपासक.

उपास्य *upâsyă* [S.], adj. & m. **1.** adj. worthy of adoration, reverence. **2.** m. an object of reverence.

उपाहार *upâhār* [S.], m. a snack.

उपेक्षणीय *upêkṣăṇīyă* [S.], adj. to be neglected, negligible.

उपेक्षा *upêkṣā* [S.], f. **1.** neglect; indifference. **2.** contempt.

उपेक्षित *upêkṣit* [S.], adj. **1.** neglected; treated with indifference. **2.** scorned.

उपेक्ष्य *upêkṣyă* [S.], adj. = उपेक्षणीय.

उपोषण *upôṣaṇ* [S.], m. a fast.

उफ़ *uf* [A. *uf*], interj. **1.** oh! (expressing distress, regret, irritation, pain, &c). **2.** colloq. something trivial (as dust, or a puff of breath). — ~ करना, to express distress, &c., by saying '*uf*'. ~ कर देना, to reduce to dust, to destroy. ~ न करना, not to show distress, &c.: to endure, to allow to pass in silence; to show indifference. ~ न निकालना, id. ~ हो जाना, to be swept away as nothing, to be ruined or destroyed.

उफनना *uphannā* [**utphaṇati*], v.i. **1.** to boil up; to boil over. **2.** to froth, to foam.

उफान *uphān* [**utphāṇa-*], m. **1.** boiling up, or over; fig. surge. **2.** froth, foam. **3.** turmoil (of mind); burning eagerness.

उबकना *ubaknā* [cf. **ubbakka-*: Pk. *uvvakka-*], v.i. to vomit.

उबका *ubkā* [cf. H. *ubuknā*], m. reg. (W.) a slip-knot (as tied round the neck of a vessel used for drawing water).

उबकाई *ubkāī* [cf. H. *ubaknā*], f. vomiting.

उबकाना *ubkānā* [cf. H. *ubaknā*], v.t. to cause (one) to vomit.

उबटन *ubṭan* [*udvartana-*], m. a paste (made up of meal, turmeric, oil and perfume) rubbed on the body when bathing to clean and soften the skin; an ointment. — ~ करना, or मलना, or लगाना, to apply *ubṭan*.

उबटना *ubaṭnā* [*udvartayati*], v.t. to apply *ubṭan* to the body.

उबना *ubnā* [*udvapati*], v.i. to germinate, to shoot; to grow.

[1]**उबरना** *ubarnā* [cf. H. *ubārnā*], v.i. **1.** to be saved, delivered (from, से). **2.** (उबर पाना.) to get over (a reverse. से).

[2]**उबरना** *ubarnā* [cf. **urvara-*: Pk. *uvvaria-*], v.i. **1.** to be left over; to exceed. **2.** to be kept in reserve, to be put by.

उबराना *ubrānā*, v.t. = उबारना.

उबलना *ubalnā* [**ubbal-*], v.i. **1.** to boil, to boil up. **2.** to boil over; to overflow. **3.** to boil or to swell with emotion (as with rage, pride); to fume. — उबल पड़ना, fig. to turn angrily (on, पर).

उबलाना *ublānā*, v.t. = उबालना.

उबवाना *ubvānā* [cf. H. [2]*ubānā*], v.t. to cause to be sown (by, से).

उबसना *ubasnā* [**udvāsyate*], v.i. **1.** to smell unpleasant; to rot; to become stale, rancid, mouldy, mildewed; to become sticky or viscous. **2.** to ferment. **3.** to be weary, or out of patience.

उबसाना *ubsānā* [cf. H. *ubasnā*], v.t. **1.** to cause to rot, or to ferment. **2.** to allow to rot, &c.

उबाऊ *ubāū* [cf. H. *ubānā*], adj. tiring; boring.

उबाकना *ubāknā* [**ubbakka-*: Pk. *uvvakka-*], v.t. to vomit, to reject.

उबाकी *ubākī* [cf. H. *ubāknā*], f. vomiting.

[1]**उबाना** *ubānā* [cf. H. *ūbnā*], v.t. to tire, to wear out. — जी उबानेवाला, adj. boring, depressing.

[2]**उबाना** *ubānā* [*udvāpayati*], v.t. **1.** to sow, to plant. **2.** to cause to grow (crops).

उबार *ubār* [**udvāra-*], m. release, deliverance.

उबारना *ubārnā* [**udvārayati*: Pk. *uvvārei*], v.t. to release, to deliver (from, से).

उबाल *ubāl* [**ubbāl-*], m. **1.** boiling. **2.** fig. rage, fury. — ~ आना, to boil up. ~ खाना, to become enraged.

उबालना *ubālnā* [cf. **ubbāl-*], v.t. **1.** to boil (water, &c). **2.** to cook by boiling. — उबाला, adj. boiled; specif. boiled merely in water, unseasoned, tasteless; bleached.

उबासी *ubāsī*, f. a yawn. — ~ लेना, to yawn.

उभय *ubhay* [S.], adj. both. — उभयचर, adj. amphibious. उभयनिष्ठ, adj. *Pl.* regarding or respecting both sides: common to both sides. उभय-पक्ष, m. pl. the two sides or parties (to a question, a dispute). °ईय, adj. common to both sides, &c.; bilateral. उभयलिंग, m. *gram.* common gender. उभयसंकट, m. dilemma, quandary.

उभरना *ubharnā* [*udbharati*], v.i. **1.** to rise, to swell; to fill; to be developed, to become prominent (the breasts). **2.** to spring up; to shoot; to flourish, to increase, to rise; to appear, to develop (a pain, symptoms). **3.** to overflow. **4.** to become excited, stirred (as by passion). **5.** to be puffed up, conceited, vain. **6.** to be restored (to health, or from misfortune); to convalesce; to rally (in illness). **7.** to come to light; to become evident. **8.** to rise (in opposition, revolt).

उभराना *ubhrānā* [cf. H. *ubharnā*], v.t. = उभारना.

उभाड़ना *ubhāṛnā* [cf. **udbhṛta-*: Pk. *ubbhaḍa-*], v.t. = उभारना.

उभाना *ubhānā* [**udbhāyayati*], v.t. *Pl. HŚS.* to alarm, to disturb (as by gestures or movements).

उभार *ubhār* [**udbhāra-*: Pk. *ubbhāra-*], m. **1.** rising, swelling; plumpness; fullness (as of the breasts). **2.** prominence. **3.** *geog.* relief. — उभारदार [P. *-dār*], adj. prominent, raised; relief (map).

उभारना *ubhārnā* [**udbhārayati*: Pk. *ubbhālia-*], v.t. **1.** to raise up; to cause to swell. **2.** to rouse, to incite. **3.** to bring out, to highlight. **4.** to save, to liberate (= उबारना). — उभार लाना, to induce, to win over, to seduce.

उभिट- *ubhiṭ-* [cf. **upadviṣṭa-*], v.i. Brbh. to be hateful, unpleasant, or no more liked.

उभियाना *ubhiyānā* [cf. *ūrdhva-*; or H. [1]*ūbh*], v.i. reg. to rise up.

उमँग *umaṁg* [**unmagna-*: Pa. *ummagga-* (*ummaṅga-*)], f. **1.** height of feeling: elation, rapture; exultation. **2.** strong desire, ambition. — ~ पर होना, to run high, to be climactic (emotions). ~ लेना, to rejoice.

उमँगी *umaṁgī* [cf. H. *umaṁg*], adj. **1.** elated, &c. (see उमँग). **2.** desirous, ambitious.

उमँग- *umaṁg-* v.i. Brbh. = उमग-.

उमग- *umag-* [cf. **unmagna-*: Pa. *ummagga-*], v.i. Av. **1.** to be elated, or exultant. **2.** to swell, to flow.

उमड़ *umaṛ* [cf. H. *umaṛnā*], f. **1.** rising, swelling; overflowing; flooding. **2.** gathering (of clouds). **3.** overflowing (of emotion).

उमड़ना *umaṛnā* [**ummaḍḍ-*], v.i. var. /umənḍna/. **1.** to rise, to swell; to well up; to overflow; to gush out or forth. **2.** to grow dense, to gather (a crowd, clouds). **3.** to be affected, moved (the heart).

उमड़ाना *umṛānā* [cf. H. *umaṛnā*], v.t. **1.** to cause to overflow. **2.** to flood; to submerge.

उमदा *umdā*, adj. see उम्दा.

उमर *umr*, f. see उम्र.

उमरा *umarā* [A.: pl. of *amīr*], m. pl. persons of high birth or rank (esp. collectively, referring to a Muslim court or to Muslim society).

उमराव *umrāv* [f. H. *umarā*: A. *umarā'*], m. pl. U. = उमरा.

उमस *umas* [*ūṣman-*: Pa. *usumā-*], f. humid heat.

उमसना *umasnā*, v.i. to rot, &c. (= उबसना).

उमह- *umah-* [*unmathayati*], v.i. Brbh. **1.** to swell. **2.** to well up. **3.** fig. to exult.

उमूमन *umūman* [A. *'umūman*], adv. U. commonly, generally.

उमेठन *umeṭhan* [*udveṣṭana-*], f. twist, contortion.

उमेठना *umeṭhnā* [*udveṣṭate*], v.t. to twist.

उम्दगी *umdagī* [P. *'umdagī*], f. worth, excellence.

उम्दा *umdā* [A. *'umda*], adj. inv. excellent, fine; splendid, grand. — ~ बात, f. sthg. splendid, or wonderful.

उम्मीद *ummīd* [P. *um(m)īd*], f. var. /umīd/. **1.** hope; expectation. **2.** trust, dependence. — ~ करना, to hope. ~ दिलाना, or दिलवाना (को), to give hope (to); to assure. ~ पर, or में, adv. in hope, or expectation (of, की). ~ पर पानी फिर जाना, (one's) hopes to be disappointed. ~ बर आना, a hope to be realized. ~ बाँधना, or रखना, to hope (for, की); to place one's hopes (on, पर); to depend (on, पर). ~ से, adj. expecting, pregnant. मुझे ~ है कि..., I hope that... उम्मीदें लगाना (पर), = ~ बाँधना, 2.

उम्मीदवार *ummīdvār* [P. *ummīd*+P. *-var*], adj. & m. **1.** adj. hopeful; expecting. **2.** m. an applicant; candidate (for a post, or in an election); suitor. **3.** a dependant; pupil, apprentice.

उम्मीदवारी *ummīdvārī* [P. *ummīdvār*+*-ī*], f. **1.** hopefulness; expectancy. **2.** candidature. **3.** dependence. **4.** apprenticeship. **5.** course of pregnancy.

उम्मेद *ummed*, f. = उम्मीद.

उम्र *umr* [A. *'umr*], f. **1.** life, lifetime. **2.** age. उसकी ~ दस साल की, or दस साल, है, he is ten years of age. — ~ काटना, or गुज़ारना, or बिताना, to spend (one's) life. ~ भर, adv. all (one's) life. ~ भर का, adj. lifelong; sufficient for a lifetime. – उम्र-क़ैद, f. life imprisonment. °ई, m. f. a life prisoner. उम्र-रसीदा [P. *-rasīda*], adj. inv. U. advanced in years.

उर *ur* [S.], m. the breast; the heart. — ~ लाना, to clasp to the breast or heart. ~ में लगाना, id.

उरग *urag* [S.], m. breast-goer: a snake.

उरगिनी *uraginī* [S.], f. Brbh. a snake.

उरद *urad* [**uḍidda-*: Pk. *uḍida-*], m. = उड़द.

उरम- *uram-* [*avalambate*, and H. *urmā-*], v.i. Brbh. to hang down.

उरमा- *urmā-* [*avalambayati*], v.t. Brbh. to hang, to suspend (ornaments).

उरला *urlā* [*apāra-*], adj. **1.** belonging to this side. **2.** ? boundless: strange, mysterious.

उरस *urs* [A. *'urs*], m. *musl.* a ceremony celebrating the mystic union of the soul of a deceased *pīr* or saint with the supreme being.

उरस *uras* [**udrasa-*], adj. tasteless.

उरस् *uras* [S.], m. = उर. — उरसिज, m. produced on the chest: the female breast; nipple. उरोज [°*as*+°*-j*], m. id.

उरस- *uras-*, v.t. Brbh. = उड़सना, 1.

उरहन *urhan*, m. Brbh. reproach.

उरहना *urahnā* [**upālabhana-*] m. Brbh. reproach (= उलाहना).

उरु *uru* [S.], adj. broad, ample; vast.

उरूस *urūs*, f. U. = अरूस.

उरेह- *ureh-* [**udrikhati*, *ullikhati*, cf. **udrekha-*], v.t. Av. **1.** to draw, to trace out. **2.** to apply (collyrium to the eyes).

उर्दू *urdū* [T. *ordu*], m. f. **1.** army. **2.** *mil.* camp, encampment; camp market. **3.** f. Urdu: the distinctively Persianised form of Khaṛī bolī speech, as used both at more formal or literary levels, and more colloquially.

उर्दूपन *urdūpan* [cf. H. *urdū*], m. Urdu characteristics (as in Hindi usage).

उर्फ़ *urf* [A. *'urf*], adj. common parlance: known as; alias.

उर्वर *urvar* [ad. *urvarā-*], adj. fertile (of soil). — उर्वरीकरण, m. fertilisation.

उर्वरक *urvărak* [cf. H. *urvar*], m. fertiliser.

उर्वरता *urvarătā* [cf. H. *urvar*], f. fertility.

उर्वरा *urvărā* [S.], f. fertile soil; the earth (as a source of plenty). — उर्वरा-शक्ति, f. fertility.

उर्वी *urvī* [S.], f. wide: the earth, ground.

उलंग *ulaṅg* [**unnagna-*], adj. reg. naked.

उलँग- *ulaṁg-* [*ullaṅghayati*], v.t. Brbh. = उलंघना.

उलंघना *ulaṅghnā* [*ullaṅghayati*], v.t. to jump over or across.

उलचना *ulacnā* [*udricyate*], v.t. **1.** to throw out, to pour off (water); to drain. **2.** to bale out.

उलझन *uljhan* [cf. H. *ulajhnā*], f. **1.** tangled state, tangle. **2.** complication; twist, turn; problem. **3.** perplexity; anxiety; embarrassment. **4.** confusion, disorder. **5.** entanglement, embroilment. — उलझनदार [P. *-dār*], adj. tangled; intricate.

उलझना *ulajhnā* [*uparudhyate*], v.i. **1.** to be tangled, twisted. **2.** to be complicated, intricate (a matter). **3.** to be perplexed; to be embarrassed. **4.** to become entangled, involved, or embroiled (in a matter); to fall foul (of, से); to carp, to cavil (at, पर). **5.** to interfere (in, में: as in a dispute). **6.** to be disordered, disarranged. **7.** esp. उलझ रहना: to stick, to be unable to proceed (as in a matter, a lesson); to be delayed, detained. **8.** to be engaged, or engrossed (in, में). **9.** to be drawn (to), captivated (by, से). **10.** colloq. to be engaged, or married (to, से). — उलझना-उलझाना, m. interference, meddling. उलझना-पुलझना, v.i. = उलझना.

उलझाना *uljhānā* [cf. H. *ulajhnā*], v.t. **1.** to make tangled. **2.** to make complicated or intricate (a matter). **3.** to perplex, to confuse; to deceive; to seek to shake off (a pursuer). **4.** to divert, to distract (agreeably). **5.** to involve, to entangle (in a matter); to ensnare; to embroil (in a quarrel); to implicate. **6.** to intertwine, to fasten (to, से); to connect (with); to unite (by marriage).

उलझाव *uljhāv* [cf. H. *ulajhnā*], m. = उलझन.

उलझेड़ा *uljheṛā*, m. entanglement (= उलझन, 5).

उलझेड़िया *uljheṛiyā*, m. a quarrelsome person.

उलट *ulaṭ* [cf. H. *ulaṭnā*], m. f. **1.** overturning, upsetting; inversion; reversal. **2.** the wrong side (of sthg.) **3.** change. — उलट-पलट, m. f. & adj. transformation; confusion; deception; overturned; transformed; confused. उलट-पलट करना, to overturn, &c. उलट-पुलट, m. f. = उलट-पलट. उलट-पेंच, f. *Pl.* = *ulaṭ-pher*. उलट-फेर, m. change (of state or fortune); perplexity; intricacy, difficulty; deception, trickery. उलट-फेर का, adj. perplexing; involved, devious (conduct, language). उलट-बँसी, f. a suggestive paradox throwing light (in E.H. poetry) on the relationship of the soul to the ultimate being.

उलटना *ulaṭnā*, v.t. & v.i. **1.** v.t. [**ullaṭati* (w. *-ṭ-* ← v.i.)], esp. with *denā*, and *ḍālnā*: to reverse; to turn back to front, or inside out; to put back (as hands of a clock); to transpose, to transfer. **2.** to upset, to overturn; to capsize; to turn upside down (a glass, &c., having drained it). **3.** to lift back or up (as a curtain). **4.** to throw down; to overthrow; to destroy, to ruin; to subvert. **5.** to make drunk. **6.** to transform. **7.** to misrepresent (a meaning, intention); to misconstrue. **8.** to rebut, to contradict; to reverse or to negate the effect of (an order, a decision; or a charm). **9.** to turn over (papers, pages). **10.** to dig or to plough (soil). **11.** to repeat. **12.** to translate, to render. **13.** to vomit up. **14.** v.i. [**ullaṭyate*: Pk. *ullaṭṭa-*] to turn round, to be reversed, &c.; to return. **15.** to be overturned. उलटी खाट, f. a bed stood on end (after a death). **16.** to be transformed. **17.** to be ruined, &c.; to be done for, to die. **18.** to be disturbed (equilibrium): to be perturbed, agitated (the heart); to become proud; to lose one's sanity. **19.** उलट जाना. to faint; to grow drunk. **20.** उलट पड़ना. to fall (upon, पर), to turn (on), to assail. — उलटना-पलटना, to reverse; to overturn; to transform; to turn over (pages). उलटना-पुलटना, id.

उलटवाँसी *ulaṭvāṁsī*, f. E.H. a suggestive paradox.

उलटा *ulṭā* [cf. H. *ulaṭnā*], adj. & m. **1.** adj. reversed; back to front; upside down; confused, topsy-turvy; out of order or sequence. **2.** contrary, opposite. **3.** left (hand). **4.** wrong-headed, perverse. **5.** wrong, amiss. **6.** m. the reverse, the contrary. **7.** adv. on the contrary; notwithstanding. **8.** wrongly, wrong-headedly; unjustly. — ~ जवाब, m. a perverse, devious, or cheeky answer; retort. ~ तवा, m. colloq. a very dark-complexioned person. ~ धड़ बाँधना, to attach a counterweight: to counteract; bring a counteraction; to deceive. ~ भाड़ा, m. return fare. उलटी खोपड़ी का, m. wrong-headed, perverse. उलटी गंगा बहाना, to make the Ganges flow backward; to go against traditions or norms; to do sthg. unheard of. उलटे चलना, or फिरना, = उलटे पाँव फिरना. उलटे छुरे से मूँड़ना, to shave with the back of a knife: to cheat blatantly; to fleece. उलटी पट्टी पढ़ाना, to teach a wrong slate(-full): to misguide. उलटी माला फेरना, to count (one's) beads backwards: to invoke a curse (on). उलटी साँस चलना, to breathe one's last. उलटी साँस लेना, to gasp (for breath). उलटे काँटे, adv. *Pl.* short of the mark (i.e. of a scale indicator, in weighing goods for sale). उलटे पाँव फिरना, to retrace one's steps; to return forthwith. उलटे बाँस बरेली, bamboos back to Bareilli: coals to Newcastle. उलटे मुँह गिरना, to fall flat on the face; to fall into a trap prepared for another. उलटे मुल्क का, of a contrary country: perversely misunderstanding plain facts or simple matters. उलटे लटक जाना, to try desperately. उलटे होकर टँगना, colloq. to bend over backwards (in trying: = उलटे लटक जाना. – उलटा-पलटा, or उलटा-पुलटा, adj. confused, garbled (facts, situation). उलटा-सीधा, adj. half wrong and half right: mixed up, tangled; imperfect; improper. उलटी सीधी समझाना, to garble facts (as in an explanation): to give a garbled version, a confused argument. उलटी सीधी सुनाना, to heap abuse on, to vilify.

उलटा-पलटापन *ulṭā-palṭāpan* [cf. H. *ulṭā-palṭā*], m. confusion (of facts, or a situation).

उलटाव *ulṭāv* [cf. H. *ulaṭnā*], m. **1.** *Pl.* overturning. **2.** overturned or confused state; inversion; subversion.

उलटी *ulṭī* [cf. H. *ulṭā*], f. usu. pl. **1.** vomiting; nausea. **2.** somersault. — उलटियाँ होना (को), to vomit, &c.

उलड़ना *ulaṛnā* [**ullaṭati* × **ullaṭyate*, v.i.], v.t. & v.i. = उलटना.

उलथना *ulathnā* [**utthalyati*: metath.], v.i. to be stirred up (as the ocean by storms).

उलथा *ulthā* [cf. H. *ulathnā*], m. **1.** a type of dance incorporating rhythmical leaping movements. **2.** capsizing; a somersault. **3.** a translation (= उल्था). — ~ मारना, to capsize.

उलफ़त *ulfat* [A. *ulfa*: P. *ulfat*] love, affection; friendship.

उलमा *ulamā* [A. *'ulamā*, pl. of *'alim*], m. pl. U. the learned, jurists and theologians (of Islam).

उलह- *ulah-*, v.i. esp. Brbh. **1.** to spring up, to shoot (vegetation). **2.** to swell, to thrill (with emotion). **3.** to be reproachful.

उलाहना *ulāhnā* [**upālābhayati*], m. **1.** reproach; complaint, accusation. **2.** taunt. — ~ देना (को), to reproach, &c.

उलिचना *ulicnā* [cf. H. *ulīcnā*], v.i. to be poured or drained off (water); to be baled.

उलीचना *ulīcnā* [*udricyate*], v.t. **1.** to pour off, to drain off (water, &c). **2.** to bale.

उलू *ulū*, m. Brbh. Av. = उल्लू.

उलूक *ulūk* [S.], m. an owl.

उलूखल *ulūkhal* [S.], m. **1.** a mortar (for crushing or cleaning rice, grinding ingredients). **2.** an aromatic resin (= गुग्गुल).

उलेंडना *uleṇḍnā* [**ullaṇḍati*: Pk. *ullaṁdiya-*], v.t. **1.** to turn upside down (as a pot, to empty out its contents). **2.** to pour out (water, &c).

उल्का *ulkā* [S.], f. **1.** a meteor; comet. **2.** a spark. **3.** flame, fire. — उल्का-पात, m. the falling of a meteor, or of a meteor shower. °ई , adj. उल्का-पाषाण, m. meteorite.

उल्था *ulthā* [cf. H. *ulathnā*: ? × H. *ulṭā*], m. translation, version (esp. of a poetic text).

उल्लंघन *ul-laṅghan* [S.], m. **1.** leaping over or across. **2.** overstepping, transgression; violation (of a right, or a frontier,). — ~ करना (का), to leap over; to transgress. – उल्लंघन-कर्ता, m. inv. a transgressor, &c.

उल्लंघित *ul-laṅghit* [S.], adj. **1.** leapt over, crossed. **2.** overstepped, transgressed; violated.

उल्लास *ul-lās* [S.], m. **1.** radiance, splendour. ***2.** joy, delight, rapture. **3.** a section of a book (esp. a romance).

उल्लासित *ul-lāsit* [S.], adj. joyful, rapturous.

उल्लासी *ul-lāsī* [S.], adj. joyful, rapturous.

उल्लिखित *ul-likhit* [S.], adj. mentioned above.

उल्लेख *ul-lekh* [S.], m. mention, account (of, का). — ~ करना, to give an account, &c. (of).

उल्लेखनीय *ul-lekhănīyă* [S.], adj. deserving mention, notable.

उल्लू *ullū* [*ulūka-*[1]], m. **1.** an owl. **2.** fig. a simpleton, fool. ~ का पट्ठा, or बच्चा, m. a young owl: an out-and-out fool. ~ का मांस खाना, to eat owl's flesh; to act idiotically. ~ फँसाना, to catch a simpleton: to make an idiot (of). ~ बनना, or होना, to make a fool of oneself; to be roundly cheated. ~ बनाना, to make a fool of; to cheat. अपना ~ समझाना, to take for a fool: to cheat. अपना ~ सीधा करना, = ~ बनाना.

उल्लूपन *ullūpan* [cf. H. *ullū*], m. owlishness: stupidity.

उवार *uvār*, m. *Pl.* ploughing up a standing crop.

उशीर *uśīr* [S.], m. *khas* grass (used for making screens, &c).

उषस् *uṣas* [S.], f. = उषा; (in Vedic religion) dawn, personified.

उषसी *uṣăsī* [S.], f. twilight, dawn.

उषा *uṣā* [S.], f. dawn. — उषा-काल, m. daybreak.

उष्ट्र *uṣṭră* [S.], m. a camel.

उष्ण *uṣṇă* [S.], adj. & m. **1.** adj. hot; warm. **2.** fiery (of temperament). **3.** m. heat; warmth. **4.** the hot season. — उष्णांक [°*ṇa+a*°], m. *chem.* calorie.

उष्णक *uṣṇak* [S.], m. the hot season. **2.** *HŚS.* fever.

उष्णता *uṣṇătā* [S.], f. heat; warmth.

उष्णीष *uṣṇīṣ* [S.], m. **1.** turban. **2.** crown; diadem.

उष्म *uṣmă* [S.], m. 1. = उष्मा. **2.** the hot season. **3.** उष्म-. thermo- (e.g. उष्मगतिक, adj. thermodynamic). — उष्म-काल, m. the hot season. उष्मज, m. heat-born: insects (as flies, bugs, mosquitoes).

उष्मता *uṣmătā* [S.], f. heat.

उष्मा *uṣmā* [S.], f. **1.** heat. **2.** anger. — उष्मागतिकी, f. thermodynamics.

उष्मिक *uṣmik* [cf. H. *uṣma*], adj. thermal.

उस *us*, sg. obl. base. that (see वह). — ~में, adv. on that, on it; in the meantime.

उसनना *usannā* [cf. H. *usānnā*; or **ut-śrīṇati*], v.i. & v.t. **1.** v.i. to be boiled; to simmer. **2.** v.t. to boil, &c.

उसरना *usarnā* [*utsarati*], v.i. reg. **1.** *Pl.* to retreat, to recede. *2. to be finished or completed quickly; to be raised, built. **3.** to be passed or spent (time). **4.** to be scattered; to be agitated.

उसरबगेरी *usarbagerī* [? conn. **bakatara-*], f. Av. a kind of bird.

उसल-फुसल *usal-phusal* [? cf. H. *usarnā*], adj. confused, disordered; agitated. — ~ जाना, to be tossed, disordered, etc.

उसस- *usas-* [**ut-śvasiti*: Pk. *usasaï*], v.i. Brbh. to breathe; to sigh.

उसाँस *usāṁs*, f. pronun. var. = उसास.

उसानना *usānnā* [cf. **ut-śrāṇa-*], v.t. *Pl.* to boil (as some types of rice before husking).

उसाना *usānā* [**apaśrāpayati*], v.t. reg. to winnow (grain).

उसारना *usārnā* [*avasārayati* or *apasārayati*], v.t. to remove, to displace; to exceed (as in beauty).

उसारा *usārā*, m. = ओसारा.

उसास *usās* [**ut-śvāsa-*: Pk. *ussāsa-*], f. (m., *Pl.*) **1.** breath, breathing. **2.** a sigh; groan. **3.** a respite, spell; breather. — ~ छोड़ना, to breathe out; Av. to snort (horses); to heave a sigh. ~ भरना, or लेना, to heave a sigh; to breathe (in).

उसिजना *usijnā* [cf. H. *usījnā*], v.i. **1.** to bubble up, to boil. **2.** to simmer (water, or sthg. being boiled).

उसिनना *usinnā* [**ut-śrīṇāti*], v.i. reg. = उसनना.

उसी *usī*, sg. obl. base emphat. that (very).

उसीजना *usījnā* [**ut-śrīyate*[2]] to boil, to simmer (sthg).

उसीझना *usījhnā* [**utsidhyati*], v.t. = उसीजना.

उसीर *usīr*, m. = उशीर.

उसीसा *usīsā* [**ut-śīrṣa-*: Pa. *ussīsaka-*], m. **1.** a pillow. **2.** head of a bed.

उसूल *usūl* [A. *uṣūl*, pl. of *aṣl*], m. **1.** principles; essentials. **2.** doctrines. **3.** breeding, manners.

उसेर *user* [cf. H. *user-*], f. reg. **1.** remembering with regret; pining, yearning. **2.** *Pl.* anxiety, solicitude.

उसेर- *user-* [conn. *upasmarati*], f. reg. **1.** to pine, to yearn. **2.** [? × *apa-*] to delay.

उस्तरा *ustrā* [P. *usturā*], m. a razor. — उलटे उस्तरे से मूँड़ना, to cheat (one) blatantly; to fleece. कोरे उस्तरे की धार से मूँड़ना, id.

उस्ताद *ustād* [P. *ustād*], m. **1.** a teacher. **2.** a skilled craftsman; master (of an art). **3.** pej. a rogue. — ~ **होना**, to be or to become skilled (in, में).

उस्तादी *ustādī* [P. *ustādī*], f. & adj. **1.** f. mastery, skill; craftsmanship. **2.** pej. roguery, cunning. **3.** the duties or position of a teacher. **4.** adj. masterly, skilful.

उस्तानी *ustānī* [cf. H. *ustād*], f. **1.** the wife of a teacher. **2.** a woman teacher.

उस्तुरा *usturā*, m. see उस्तरा.

उस्र *usră* [S.], m. *Pl. HŚS.* **1.** a ray of light. **2.** a bull.

उह *uh*, pron. Brbh. = वह.

उहाँ *uhāṁ*, adv. Brbh. Av. = वहाँ.

उहाड़ *uhāṛ*, m. *Pl.* = ओहार.

उहार *uhār*, m. Av. = ओहार.

उहि *uhi*, pron. Brbh. = वह, उस.

ऊ

ऊ *ū*, the sixth vowel of the Devanāgarī syllabary. — **ऊकार**, m. the sound /ū/; the letter ऊ.

ऊँ *ūṁ*, interj. = उँ.

ऊँग *ūṁg*, f. pronun. var. = ऊँघ.

ऊँगन *ūṁgan*, f. pronun. var. = ऊँघन.

ऊँघ *ūṁgh* [cf. H. *ūṁghnā*], f. drowsiness; sleepiness. — **~ आना (को)**, to become drowsy.

ऊँघन *ūṁghan* [cf. H. *ūṁghnā*], f. dozing, drowsiness (= ऊँघ).

ऊँघना *ūṁghnā* [**uṅghati*: Pk. *uṁghaï*], v.i. to feel drowsy or sleepy; to doze.

ऊँघाई *ūṁghāī* [cf. H. *ūṁghnā*], f. drowsiness, dozing.

ऊँच *ūṁc* [*ucca-*], adj. **1.** high. **2.** upper, superior (rank, birth). — **ऊँच-नीच**, adj. & f. high and low; uneven, rough (ground); undulating; superior and inferior; f. unevenness; undulating ground; good and bad (aspects); varied or comprehensive particulars; inequality (social or ritual); vicissitudes (of life).

ऊँचा *ūṁcā* [*ucca-*], adj. **1.** high; tall. **2.** upper, superior (rank, birth, quality). **3.** great, high (as talents). **4.** high (pitch or volume); loud (voice). **5.** worn short (a garment). — **~ करना**, to raise; to elevate. **~ क़द**, m. tall stature. **~ चढ़ना**, to mount high; to rise to eminence. **~ बोल**, m. loud speech; proud or bold words. **~ सुनना**, or **सुनाई देना**, to be hard of hearing. **~ हाथ रहना (का)**, (one's) power or position to continue; to dominate; to excel. **ऊँचे सुर से** adv. in a high key. **ऊँचे बोल का मुँह नीचा** 'how are the mighty fallen'. **ऊँची दूकान**, f. a grand or fine shop, a great display. – **ऊँचाकानी**, f. see hw. **ऊँचा-नीचा**, adj. = ऊँच-नीच. **ऊँचा-नीचा दिखाना**, to deceive. **ऊँची-नीची सुनाना**, to give a dressing down, to berate.

ऊँचाई *ūṁcāī* [cf. H. *ūṁcā*], f. **1.** height. **2.** stature. **3.** eminence. **4.** high pitch or volume (sound).

ऊँचाकानी *ūṁcākānī*, f. reg. deafness.

ऊँचान *ūṁcān*, f. = ऊँचाई.

ऊँचास *ūṁcās*, f. = ऊँचाई.

ऊँचाहट *ūṁcāhaṭ*, f. = ऊँचाई.

ऊँछना *ūṁchnā* [*uñchati*], v.t. to comb (the hair).

ऊँजरी *ūṁjrī*, f. *Pl.* = उँजरी.

ऊँट *ūṁṭ* [*uṣṭra-*], m. **1.** a camel. **2.** (in chess) the bishop. — **~ बिठाना**, to make a camel lie down (in order to load it). **~ किस करवट बैठता है?** on which side will the camel sit?: let us see how the matter turns out. **~ के ~ ही रहे**, once a camel, always a camel: you can't make a silk purse out of a sow's ear. **~ के मुँह में जीरा** cumin in a camel's mouth: half a mouthful for a starving man. **~ की चोरी सिर पर खेलना**, fig. to risk everything by an outrageous theft. **शहर में ~ बदनाम**, the camel is vilified throughout the town: give a dog a bad name and hang him. – **ऊँट-कटारा**, a thistle, *Echinops echinatus*, of which camels are fond. **ऊँटवान** [P. *vān*], m. camel-driver.

ऊँटनी *ūṁṭnī* [cf. H. *ūṁṭ*], f. a she-camel.

ऊँठा *ūṁṭhā*, adj. *Pl.* = हूँठा.

ऊँह *ūṁh*, interj. exclamation expressing reservation, disapproval, &c.

ऊँहूँ *ūṁhūṁ*, interj. exclamation expressing refusal or denial, or reservation (as to sthg. said).

-ऊ *-ū* [MIA *-uka-*], suffix (forms chiefly adjectives and nouns of agentive force on verb stems, e.g. खाऊ, adj. fond of eating; उतारू, adj. bent upon, determined, ready; झाड़ू, m. broom; ढालू, adj. sloping; पिछलग्गू, m. a hanger-on; बाज़ारू, adj. of the bazaars, coarse; बुढ़ऊ, m. esp. pej. old man).

ऊई *ūī*, interj. expression of pleasure, pain, fear, surprise, &c (used by women).

ऊक *ūk* [cf. H. *ūk-*], f. E.H. omission, error.

ऊक- *ūk-* [*utkramati*: ? × *cukk-*], v.i. Brbh. to fall short, to fail; to miss, to err. — **ऊके-चूके**, adv. inadvertently; now and then, occasionally.

ऊख *ūkh* [*ikṣu-*], m. f. sugar-cane. — **~ का रस**, m. sugar-cane juice. **ऊख-रस**, m. id.

ऊखल *ūkhal* [**udukkhala-*: Pk. *udukkhala-*], m. a mortar (for husking grain in). — **~ में सिर देना**, fig. to put oneself in jeopardy, to invite disaster.

ऊजड़ *ūjaṛ* [**ujjaṭa-*: Pk. *ujjaḍa-*], adj. laid waste; ruined; desolate, deserted.

ऊझड़ *ūjhaṛ*, adj. E.H. = ऊजड़.

ऊटक *ūṭak*: — ऊटक-नाटक, m. a pointless or misconceived task or project; haphazard, unconstructive work.

ऊटपटाँग *ūṭpaṭāṁg* [?? cf. H. *ulṭā-palṭā*] adj. & m. **1.** adj. confused, contrary (as words). **2.** nonsensical, absurd. **3.** crabbed, difficult (as style). **4.** m. sthg. confused, nonsensical, &c.

ऊटपटाँगी *ūṭpaṭāṁgī* [cf. H. *ūṭpaṭāṁg*], m. one who speaks incoherently, or nonsensically; a confused or crazy person.

ऊड़ा *ūṛā*, m. *Pl.* = ²ओड़ा.

ऊढ़- *ūṛh-* [cf. *ūḍha-*], v.t. Av. to cause to be led (home): to marry (a wife).

ऊत *ūt* [*aputra-*], m. **1.** a man who dies childless; an unhoused spirit (= प्रेत). **2.** a fool.

ऊतक *ūtak* [cf. S. *ūti-*], m. *biol.* tissue. — ऊतक-विज्ञान, m. histology.

ऊतपटाँग *ūtpaṭāṁg*, adj. & m. (*Pl.*). = ऊटपटाँग.

ऊतरपातर *ūtar-pātar* [cf. *uttara-*], adj. *Pl.* disposed, paid off (accounts).

ऊद *ūd* [*udra-*], m. **1.** an otter. **2.** a fool. — ऊद-बिलाव, m. = ऊद.

ऊदा *ūdā* [**uddāta-*: Pk. *uddāyaï*], adj. & m. **1.** adj. purple; grey; brown. **2.** m. a purplish colour, &c.

ऊदी *ūdī* [cf. H. *ūdā*], f. a light shade of blue or grey, or of purple.

ऊदेस *ūdes* [*uddeśa-*], m. *Pl.* pointing out: track; search. — ~ करना, to search for.

ऊधम *ūdham* [*uddhama-*], m. usu. /udhɔm/. uproar; commotion. — ~ उठाना, or करना, or मचाना, to cause an uproar, &c.

ऊधमी *ūdhămī* [cf. H. *ūdham*], adj. **1.** rowdy, turbulent. **2.** quarrelsome, truculent.

¹**ऊन** *ūn* [*ūrṇā-*], f. wool. — ~ का, adj. woollen.

²**ऊन** *ūn* [*ūnaka-*], adj. **1.** deficient, defective. **2.** less, minus. **3.** Av. displeased, disaffected (towards). — ऊनवाचक, adj. *gram.* diminutive.

¹**ऊना** *ūnā*, adj. = ²ऊन.

²**ऊना** *ūnā* [cf. H. ¹*ūnā*], f. Brbh. a small sword.

¹**ऊनी** *ūnī* [cf. H. ¹*ūn*], adj. woollen.

²**ऊनी** *ūnī* [cf. H. ²*ūn*], f. **1.** deficiency. **2.** distress, displeasure.

ऊपर *ūpar* [**uppari*: Pk. *upparim̐*], adv. **1.** on top, above. **2.** over, up above; overhead. **3.** upwards. **4.** above, previously (referring to a preceding text). **5.** on the surface; superficially. **6.** extra, additionally. **7.** ppn. (w. के or से) on, on top of. **8.** over, up, above. **9.** upon, over, concerning. **10.** more than (in amount). — ~ ~, adv. over, all the way overhead; externally; without effect; hastily; superficially. ~ ~ का, adj. superficial; specious. ~ ~ से, adv. superficially; with a light hand, gently. ~ का, adj. external; superficial; additional; miscellaneous; clandestine (an extra payment, or a bribe); of top rank or grade; fine, first-rate. ~ को, adv. upwards, &c. ~ का दम भरना, to pretend affection or regard; to breathe one's last. ~ को दम भरना, id. ~ से ~, adv. from the very top: first of all; stealthily. अपने ~ लाना, to take on oneself (as a task). – ऊपर-तले के बच्चे, m. pl. children born in quick succession. ऊपरवाला, adj. & m. above: above-mentioned; situated above; dwelling above, or on high; a superior; colloq. the supreme being; an outsider, stranger; one not directly concerned: bystander, spectator.

ऊपरी *ūpărī* [cf. H. *ūpar*], adj. **1.** upper. **2.** outer, external. **3.** superficial; artificial (display, &c.); (merely) formal. **4.** not meeting a partic. need, deficient. **5.** extra, additional (as expenses). **6.** not having a partic. identity, belonging elsewhere; foreign, strange.

ऊफन- *ūphan-*, v.i. Brbh. = उफनना.

ऊब *ūb* [cf. H. *ūbnā*], f. dispiritedness, &c.

ऊबट *ūbaṭ* [*udvartman-*], m. Brbh. a rough road.

ऊबड़ *ūbaṛ* [? conn. *udvartman-*], adj. **1.** rough, uneven (as terrain); impassable (a road). **2.** inaccessible. — ऊबड़-खबाड़, adj. = ~; rugged, hilly.

ऊबना *ūbnā* [*udvijate*], v.i. to be dispirited; to be bored.

¹**ऊभ** *ūbh* [*ūrdhva-*], adj. Av. high. — ऊभ-चूभ, f. rising and sinking (in water).

²**ऊभ** *ūbh* [**ubbā-*: Pk. *uvvā-*; ? × *ŭ̄şman-*], f. m. **1.** sultry heat. **2.** languor, inertia.

¹**ऊभना** *ūbhnā* [cf. *ūrdhva-*], v.i. to rise.

²**ऊभना** *ūbhnā* [cf. H. ²*ūbh*], v.i. to suffer from the heat, to feel languid. — ऊभा-साँसी, f. the heaving of sighs: distress.

ऊमरी *ūmărī* [*udumbara-*], f. E.H. the fig-tree *Ficus glomerata*.

ऊमह- *ūmah-*, v.i. = उमह-.

ऊमी *ūmī* [*umbī-*], f. reg. an ear of half-ripe corn.

ऊरु *ūru* [S.], m. poet. the thigh.

ऊर्जा *ūrjā* [S.], f. power, energy.

ऊर्जस्वल *ūrjasval* [S.], adj. powerful.

ऊर्जस्वित *ūrjasvit* [ad. *ūrjasvat*], adj. vigorous.

ऊर्जित *ūrjit* [S.], adj. = ऊर्जस्वित.

ऊर्णनाभ *ūrṇanābh* [S.], m. poet. wool-bodied: a spider.

ऊर्ध्व *ūrdhvă* [S.], adj. **1.** raised, erect; vertical. **2.** high. **3.** upper. — **ऊर्ध्व-गमन**, m. ascending; ascent. **ऊर्ध्वदृग**, adj. having the eyes raised, looking upwards. **ऊर्ध्व-पातन**, m. sublimation. **ऊर्ध्व-पुंड्र**, m. a vertical sectarian mark (drawn on the forehead with vermilion, by Vaiṣṇavas). **ऊर्ध्वबाहु**, adj. having the arms raised. **ऊर्ध्व-बिंदु**, f. zenith. **ऊर्ध्वमुख**, adj. having the face raised, looking upwards. **ऊर्ध्व-श्वास**, m. gasp, sigh; last breath. **ऊर्ध्वाधर** [°*va*+*a*°], adj. vertical. **ऊर्ध्वोन्मुख** [°*va*+*u*°], adj. directed upwards; progressive.

ऊर्मि *ūrmi* [S.], f. a wave.

ऊर्मिल *ūrmil* [cf. H. *ūrmi*], adj. rough with waves (sea).

ऊलना *ūlnā*, v.i. poet. to be active, spirited.

ऊल-जलूल *ūl-jalūl*, adj. **1.** silly, stupid (an action); pointless. **2.** awkward, uncouth (a person). **3.** slovenly, untidy.

ऊषण *ūṣaṇ* [S.], m. **1.** *Pl. HŚS.* black pepper. **2.** *HŚS.* dry ginger.

ऊषर *ūṣar*, adj. *Pl.* = ऊसर.

ऊष्म- *ūṣm-* [S]. = उष्म, उष्ण.

ऊष्मा *ūṣmā* [S.], f. = उष्मा.

ऊसर *ūsar* [*ūṣara-*], adj. & m. **1.** adj. barren (land). **2.** m. barren soil; saline soil. — **ऊसर-अल्ली**, f. *Pl.* = next. **ऊसर-साँड़ा**, m. *Pl. HŚS.* a kind of large lizard found in sandy soil.

ऊष्म *ūṣmă* [S.], m. = उष्म. — **ऊष्मांक** [°*a*+*a*°], m. calorie.

[1]**ऊह** *ūh*, interj. exclamation of pain, distress, &c.; or of astonishment, or of indifference.

[2]**ऊह** *ūh* [S.], m. reasoning, deliberation; inference. — **ऊहापोह**, m. inferring and denying: uncertainty, indecision.

ऊहा *ūhā*, m. = [2]ऊह.

ऋ

ऋ *r̥*, the seventh vocalic sound of the Devanāgarī syllabary. — ऋकार, m. the sound /ri/; the letter ऋ.

ऋक् *r̥k* [S.], m. 1. = ऋचा. 2. = ऋग्वेद.

ऋक्ष *r̥kṣ* [S.], m. **1.** a bear. **2.** a star; a constellation.

ऋग्- *r̥g-* [S]. = ऋक्: — ऋग्वेद, m. the Ṛgveda or Veda of hymns, the first and most important of the original four Vedic texts.

ऋचा *r̥cā* [S.], f. **1.** a verse; a sacred verse praising a deity. **2.** the Ṛgveda. **3.** a magical invocation.

ऋजु *r̥ju* [S.], adj. **1.** direct, straight. **2.** honest.

ऋजुता *r̥jutā* [S.], f. **1.** directness, simplicity (of manner). **2.** honesty, uprightness.

ऋण *r̥ṇ* [S.], m. (for collocations see similar expressions s.v. क़र्ज़). **1.** a debt; credit (as extended to a borrower); debit (in an account). **2.** an obligation. **3.** *math. phys.* a negative quantity. — ऋण-ग्रस्त, adj. plagued by debt. ऋण-ग्राहक, m. a borrower. ऋण-दाता, m. inv. a creditor. ऋण-मुक्त, adj. free from debt, &c. ऋण-पत्र, m. *fin.* a bond. ऋण-शोध, m. clearance of a debt, &c. ऋणात्मक [°*ṇa*+*ā*°], adj. negative (as a charge).

ऋणी *r̥ṇī* [S.], adj. & m. **1.** adj. indebted (to, का). **2.** under obligation (to). **3.** m. a debtor.

ऋत *r̥t* [S.], m. a fixed order; cosmic order.

ऋतु *r̥tu* [S.], f. m. **1.** season. **2.** weather (as typical of a partic. season). — ऋतु-नाथ, m. Brbh. lord of the seasons: spring. ऋतु-पति, m. Brbh. id. ऋतुमती, adj. f. of (marriageable) age. ऋतु-राज, m. king of the seasons: spring. ऋतु-वर्णन, m. *rhet.* a description (in largely conventional terms) of one or more of the seasons of the year.

ऋद्ध *r̥ddh* [S.], adj. prosperous.

ऋद्धि *r̥ddhi* [S.], f. prosperity; success.

ऋषभ *r̥ṣabh* [S.], m. **1.** a bull. **2.** the second note of the Indian musical scale. **3.** fig. -ऋषभ. the best of (one's) kind (sc. male).

ऋषि *r̥ṣi* [S.], m. **1.** a sage (esp. any of the seven Vedic hymn-singers known as *r̥ṣi*); a seer. **2.** transf. a saint, an ascetic. **3.** symbol for the number seven. **4.** *astron.* the Great Bear. — ऋषि-ऋण, m. debt owing to the *r̥ṣis*: the study of the Vedas. ऋषि-पत्नी, f. a *r̥ṣi's* wife. ऋषीश्वर [°*ṣi*+*ī*°], m. chief of the *r̥ṣis*: the *r̥ṣi* Atri (later thought of as one of the four sons of Brahmā).

ऋष्टि *r̥ṣṭi* [S.], f. *Pl. HŚS.* **1.** sword. **2.** weapon.

ए

ए *e*, the eighth vocalic sound of the Devanāgarī syllabary as used in writing Hindi. — **एकार**, m. the sound /e/; the letter ए.

एंच-पेंच *eṁc-peṁc* [H. *aiṁc* × H. *aiṁth*, + P. *pec*], m. **1.** twist. **2.** entanglement. **3.** wiles, cunning.

[1]**ए** *e*, interj. = हे.

[2]**ए** *e*, pron. reg. = यह, इस. — **ए दम**, adv. this instant.

एक *ek* [*eka-*: Pk. *ekka-*; also P. *yak*], adj. **1.** one. **2.** single, sole; alone. **3.** the same, identical. **4.** united; at one, in harmony. **5.** unique. **6.** pre-eminent. **7.** adv. approximately. **पाँच ~**, half a dozen; **दो ~**, a couple, a very few; **कुछ ~**, some, a few. **8.** **एक-**. one, uni-, mono- (see also s.v. **इक-**, and separate hww). — **~ ~**, each; one by one; one after the other. **~ ~ करके**, adv. one by one. **~ ~ के दो दो**, two for one, twice as much (of time, number, price; or of effort, &c). **~ अंदाज़ से**, adv. after the same manner; equal, uniform. **~ आँख (से) देखना**, to look impartially on. **~ आँख न भाना**, the sight (of) to be intolerable (to, को). **~ आध**, adj. one or two, a few. **~ आवाज़**, adv. with one voice, unanimously. **~ और ~ ग्यारह**, fig. two heads are better than one. **~ क़लम**, adv. at a stroke of the pen. **~ चने के दो दाल**, the two halves of a gram seed: two equal shares; blood brothers. **~ चने से भाड़ नहिं फूटता**, one grain of gram won't burst the oven: a single error, or misfortune, will not bring disaster. **~ जगह**, adv. in one place, together. **~ ज़बान**, adv. with one voice; unanimously. **~ जान दो क़ालिब**, one soul, two bodies: close friends. **~ जैसा**, adj. of similar kind. **~ ढंग से**, adv. after the same manner or order; symmetrically. **~ तरफ़**, adv. on one side; apart. **~ तो**, on the one hand; for one thing (as opposed to another). **~ न एक**, adj. one or the other, either. **~ न चलना**, not to succeed: **उसकी ~ नहीं चलती**, nothing he does succeeds. **~ पंथ दो काज**, one road, two tasks: killing two birds with one stone. **~ पर ~**, adv. one over or above the other; one better than the next; one after the other. **~ बात**, f. one and the same thing, all one; one unvarying price; sthg. uttered and then held to (as faith, promise). **~ बार**, adv. once. **~ भाव**, adv. at the same rate or price. **~ में**, adv. at one, united. **~ लाठी हाँकना** to drive with the same stick: to treat all alike. **~ वक़्त**, adv. at one time, simultaneously. **~ संग**, adv. = next. **~ साथ**, together, in a body; simultaneously; suddenly. **~ से इक्कीस होना**, one to become twenty-one, to multiply, to flourish. **~ से ~ बढ़िया**, or **बढ़कर**, adj. one better than another. **~ होना**, to be united; to be at one; to stand alone, to be unique. **~ होकर**, adv. together, united (with, **के साथ**). – **एक-चश्म**, m. one-eyed: a profile. **एकचित्त**, adj. single-minded; attentive; of one mind. **एकछत्र**, adj. (symbolised by) a single (royal) parasol: sole, undisputed (sway, right). **एकज**, adj. & m. *HŚS.* single; once-born: a śūdra; a king. **एकजात**, adj. of one parentage; (× Ar. *zāt*) = **एकजाति**. **एकजाति**, adj. of one caste, family, or sort. **एकजातिक**, adj. = next. **एकजातीय**, adj. of one community; of one nation, national. **एकजान**, adj. having one soul or heart, united; true, sincere; homogeneous. **एकजुट**, adv. linked into one, united. °**ता**, f. **एकजुट होकर**, as one. **एकटंगा**, adj. one-legged. **एकटक**, m. a fixed gaze; adv. (w. **देखना**, &c.) steadily, fixedly. **एकडाल**, adj. made of one piece (as a knife). **एकत:**, adv. from one side; in one quarter; in one way. **एकतंत्र**, adj. single (of rule, control); autocratic, absolute. **एकतरफ़ा** [A. *ṭaraf*], adj. inv. one-sided; one-way (ticket); unilateral. **एकतल्ला**, adj. one-storeyed. **एकतान**, adj. closely attentive, absorbed (to or in, **में**); f. m. *mus.* harmony, unison. **एकतारा**, m. a single-stringed instrument. **एकदंत**, adj. Brbh. one-toothed; single-tusked (a title of the god Gaṇeś). **एकदरा** [P. *dar*], adj. having a single door; m. room; hallway. **एकदलीय**, adv. consisting of, or concerning, a single party; totalitarian. **एकदलवाद**, m. belief in a one-party system; °**ई**, adj. & m. **एकदिल**, adj. of one heart, or mind; unanimous, at one. °**ई**, f. **एकदेशीय**, adj. having to do with a single or the same country or region: internal (to a nation); regional; m. a compatriot. **एकनयन**, adj. having a single eye: *mythol.* a title of Śiva, and of Kuvera; a crow. **एकनिष्ठ**, adj. devoted to, or believing in, a single entity (deity, person, thing) only. °**आ**, f. **एकपत्नी**, f. a faithful wife. °**-व्रत**, m. vow of faithfulness to (one's) wife. **एकप्राण**, adj. of one soul or being (with, **से**). **एकबारगी** [P. *yak bāragī*], adv. at once, simultaneously; suddenly; quite, completely. **एकबारी**, adv. id. **एकमंज़िला** [P. *-manzil*], adj. single-storeyed. **एकमत**, adj. of one opinion, agreed. °**इ**, f. unanimous. **एकमहला** [A. *-maḥalla*], adj. single-storeyed. **एकमात्र**, adj. single, only. °**इक**, adj. *pros.* consisting of one metrical instant. **एकमुँह**, adj. being of one voice: agreeing; unanimous. °**आ**, adj. id. **एकभाषी**, adj.

monolingual. एकमुट्ठ, adv. as a handful; as one quantity or amount. एकमुश्त [P. *yak muśt*], adj. lump sum (a payment); = prec. एकरंग, adj. of one colour; of one sort or character, similar, uniform. एकरदन, adj. Brbh. = एकदंत. एकरस, adj. of one flavour, or character; monotonous; pleased with one thing only, unchanging, constant. °ता, f. एकरुख़ा [P. *rukh*], adj. inv. having a single face or side: worked or usable on one side only. एकरूप, adj. of the same form or appearance, similar. °ता, f. एकलव्य, m. *mythol.* name of a king of the Niṣadas (an enemy of Kṛṣṇa). एकवचन, m. *gram.* singular. एकविवाह, m. monogamy. एकवेणी, f. singly braided (a widow's hair). एकसत्तात्मक [°*tā*+*ā*°], adj. totalitarian. एकसत्ताधारी, m. dictator. एक-समान, adj. = एक-सा. एक-सां [P. *yak-sān*], adj. = next. एक-सा, adj. similar; identical. एक-से दिन न रहना, times to change (esp. for the better). एक-सार [P. *yak-sār*], adj. = एक-सा. एकसाला [P. *yak-sāla*], adj. inv. of one year's duration. एकसुरा, adj. constant, or monotonous of sound. एकसूत्र, adj. connected together, connected directly; of similar type; m. a small drum (= डमरू). एकस्वरता, f. unison. एकहत्था, adj. one-handed; controlled by one person. एकहत्था करना, to monopolise (trade, &c). एकांकी [°*ka*+*a*°], adj. & m. f. one-act; a one-act play. एकांग [°*ka*+*a*°], adj. having only one limb or member: mutilated, deformed; one-sided. एकांग घात, m. stroke affecting one side of the body. एकांगी, adj. one-sided; uniform. एकाक्षर [°*ka*+*a*°], adj. monosyllabic. एकात्म [°*ka*+*ā*°], adj. of one nature or essence; single, undivided. °अक, adj. unitary; °अकता, f. unitary state; identity. एकाधिक [°*ka*+*a*°], adj. more than one. एकाधिकार [°*ka*+*a*°], m. sole right; monopoly. °ई, adj. exclusive; monopolistic. एकाधिकृत [°*ka*+*a*°], adj. monopolised. एकाधिप [°*ka*+*a*°], m. sole, or supreme monarch. एकाधिपति, m. id. एकाधिपत्य, m. absolute power, sway (over, पर); exclusive right (to). एकांतर [°*a*+*a*°], adj. alternate; returning on alternate days (a fever). एकांतिक [°*a*+*a*°], adj. (?) applying particularly to, exclusive (as a right); having to do with one locality: regional, local. एकानन [°*ka*+*ā*°], m. having one face (human beings as opposed to gods). एकान्विति [°*ka*+*a*°], f. state of unity. एकार्थ [°*ka*+*a*°], adj. of the same sense, synonymous; having the same aim or object. °अक, adj. id. एक-आवाज़, adv. with one voice, as one. एकाह [°*ka*+*a*°], adj. performed during one day. एकीकरण, m. unification, union. एकीकृत, adj. unified, united. एकीभूत, adj. unified; integral (as a part). एकेश्वरवाद [°*ka*+*ī*°], m. monotheism. °ई, adj. & m. monotheistic; a monotheist. एकोत्तर [°*ka*+*u*°], adj. greater by one; (?) more than one.

एकंतरा *ekantărā* [ad. *ekāntara-*], adj. *Pl. HŚS.* next but one, alternate.

एकक *ekak* [S.], m. a unit (of enumeration, measurement).

एकठा *ekṭhā*, m. *Pl. HŚS.* a small boat rowed by sculling.

एकड़ *ekaṛ* [Engl. *acre*], m. an acre.

एकड़ा *ekṛā* [*eka-*: Pk. *ekka-*], m. the figure 1.

एकता *ekătā* [S.], f. **1.** sameness, identity. **2.** unity; harmony. — एकतावाद, m. monism. °ई, adj. & m. monistic, monist.

एकत्तरा *ekattarā*, adj. *Pl.* = एकांतर (see s.v. एक).

एकत्र *ekatr* [S.], adj. in one place: **1.** collected together; accumulated. **2.** concentrated (thoughts, emotions). — ~ करना, to collect, &c. एकत्रीकरण, m. collecting, amassing; assembling. एकत्रीभूत, adj. = एकत्र.

एकत्रित *ekatrit* [cf. H. *ekatr*], adj. **1.** collected together, &c. (= एकत्र, 1.); assembled (as a crowd). 2. = एकत्र, 2. — ~ करना, to collect, &c.

एकत्रीकरण *ekatrīkaraṇ* [S.] m. see s.v. एकत्र.

एकत्व *ekatvă* [S.], m. **1.** unity. **2.** a unit.

एकदम *ekdam* [H. *ek*+P. *dam*], adv. **1.** in a breath, in a moment; (all) at once; immediately. **2.** quite, completely.

एकदा *ekădā* [S.], adv. **1.** once, at one time. **2.** on one occasion. **3.** at once.

एकमेक *ekăm-ek* [S.], adj. **1.** homogeneous, quite one. **2.** mixed, jumbled; confused.

एकमेव *ekam-evă* [S.], adj. single, only.

एक़रार *eqrār*, m. = इक़रार.

एकल *ekal* [**ekkalla-*: Pk. *ekkalla-*], adj. **1.** alone. **2.** single. ~ मैच, m. a singles match (as tennis).

एकला *ekălā*, adj. = अकेला.

एकलौता *eklautā* [**ekkalaputra-*], adj. only, single (a child).

एकविंश *ekaviṃśa* [S.], adj. twenty-first.

एकविंशति *ekaviṃśati* [S.], adj. twenty-one.

एकस्व *ekasvă* [S.], m. patent.

एकहरा *ekahrā*, adj. = इकहरा.

एकांत *ekânt* [S.], adj. & m. **1.** adj. secluded, lonely. **2.** private; secret. **3.** unaccompanied. **4.** being exclusive: extreme; excessive. **5.** m. a secluded place, &c.; the inner heart. **6.** privacy. — ~ आवश्यक, adj. absolutely essential. ~ कारावास, m. solitary confinement. ~ में, adv. apart, alone, &c. – एकांत-वास, m. seclusion; residence or life in seclusion; confinement. °ई, adj. & m.

एकांतिक *ekântik* [S.], adj. **1.** directed towards one object (as love, or zeal). **2.** pertaining to one place or region.

एकांती *ekântī* [S.], adj. & m. **1.** adj. withdrawn, solitary (by temperament). **2.** m. an ascetic (esp. one devoted to a particular view, see एकांतिक).

एका *ekā* [*aikya-*], m. **1.** unity; unanimity. **2.** union; combination; league. **3.** conspiracy. **4.** a unit (organisational). — ~ करना, to act together; to form a group, a united body.

एकाई *ekāī* [cf. H. *ekā*], f. **1.** a unit (detachment, special group). **2.** a unit (of enumeration, measurement).

एकाएक *ek-ā-ek* [P. *yak-ā-yak*], adv. suddenly; unexpectedly.

एकाकी *ekākī* [S.], adj. **1.** alone, solitary. **2.** single; isolated. — एकाकीकरण, m. separating, isolating.

एकाकीकरण *ekākīkaraṇ* [S.], adj. see s.v. एकाकी.

एकाग्र *ekâgră* [S.], adj. intent on one point: **1.** attentive; concentrating. **2.** single-minded. — एकाग्रचित्त, adj. of intent mind, &c. (= एकाग्र).

एकाग्रता *ekâgrătā* [S.], f. intentness, concentration (upon, पर). — ~ से, adv. intently.

एकाग्रित *ekâgrit* [S.], adj. concentrated (the attention).

एकादश *ekādaś* [S.], adj. eleventh. — एकादशाह [°*sa*+*a*°], m. the eleventh day after a death; a rite performed on that day.

एकादशी *ekādăśī* [S.], f. the eleventh day of a lunar fortnight (traditionally kept as a fast among Hindus).

एकायन *ekâyan* [S.], m. & adj. *HŚS.* path for one, strait way: **1.** m. singleness of thought, or aim. **2.** lonely place. **3.** adj. single, undivided.

एकीकरण *ekīkaraṇ* [S.], m. see s.v. एक.

एकीकृत *ekīkṛt* [S.], adj. see s.v. एक.

एकीभूत *ekībhūt* [S.], adj. see s.v. एक.

एकोतरसो *ekotarso* [ad. *ekottara-*; w. H. *sau*], adj. reg. (E.) one hundred and one.

एजेंट *ejenṭ* [Engl. *agent*], m. an agent.

एड़ *eṛ* [**eḍḍi-*: ← Drav.], f. **1.** heel. **2.** transf. spur. — ~ करना, to spur, to incite; to put obstacles in (one's) way. ~ करो! colloq. be off! clear out! ~ टहलो! id. ~ देना, or लगाना, or मारना (को), to spur (a horse); to incite.

एड़क *eṛak* [ad. *eḍaka-*], m. *Pl. HŚS.* **1.** a ram. **2.** a kind of firework.

एड़-गज *eṛ-gaj*, m. *Pl.* the medicinal plant *Cassia tora* or *alata* (used in treating ringworm).

एड़ी *eṛī* [**eḍḍi-*: ← Drav.], f. **1.** heel. **2.** heel (of footwear). — ~ चोटी का पसीना एक करना, to sweat from head to heel: to make huge efforts. ~ चोटी पर (से) क़ुरबान करना, or वारना, *musl.* to turn (one) head over heels in sacrificing (one): to see to the devil. ~ से चोटी तक, adv. from head to heel. एड़ियाँ घिसना, or रगड़ना, to drag or to scuff the heels in walking; to go to much trouble, to make great efforts; to be in distress (as in illness, or death), or in agony; to have become poor.

एढ़ा-टेढ़ा *eṛhā-ṭeṛhā* [cf. H. *ṭeṛhā*], adj. & m. **1.** adj. crooked, &c. (= टेढ़ा). **2.** inconsiderate, thoughtless. **3.** m. crookedness, &c. (= टेढ़ापन).

एतक़ाद *etqād* [A. *i'tiqād*], m. confidence, faith (= एतबार).

एतक़ादी *etqādī* [A. *i'tiqādī*], adj. having faith in, believing.

एतद्- *etad-* [S.], adj. this: — एतदर्थ, adv. for this reason. एतदवधि, adj. up till the present. एतद्देशीय, adj. of this country. एतद्द्वारा, adv. by this means. एतद्विषयक, adj. dealing with this (matter).

एतना *etnā*, adj. Av. = इतना.

एतबार *etbār* [A. *i'tibār*], m. **1.** confidence; reliance; faith, belief. **2.** credit. **3.** regard, view. — ~ करना, to have confidence (in, पर, का); to rely (on); to be confident (of). ~ खोना, to lose credit, or credibility. ~ रखना, = ~ करना. इस ~ से, adv. from this point of view.

एतबारी *etbārī* [A. *i'tibārī*], adj. **1.** trustworthy; worthy of confidence. **2.** credible (as news, &c.)

एतमाद *etmād* [A. *i'timād*], m. U. reliance, trust, faith.

[1]**एतराज़** *etrāz* [A. *i'tirāẓ*], m. **1.** opposition; objection. **2.** criticism, fault-finding. — ~ करना, to object (to, पर).

[2]**एतराज़** *etrāz* [A. *iḥtirāz*], m. **1.** guarding against, abstaining (from). **2.** restraint; abstinence.

एतराज़ी *etrāzī* [A. *i'tirāz*+P. *-ī*], adj. objecting, dissentient.

एतवार *etvār*, m. = इतवार.

एतादृश *etādṛś* [S.], adj. = ऐसा.

एतादृशता *etādṛśătā* [S.], f. similarity.

एतादृशी *etādṛśī* [S.], adj. = एतादृश.

एतावता *etāvătā* [S.], adv. from this much.

एतौ *etau*, adj. Brbh. = इतना.

-एन *-enă* [S.: an instr. case ending], suffix (forms some adverbial expressions of manner, e.g. पूर्णरूपेण, completely).

एरंड *eraṇḍ* [S.], m. the castor-oil plant.

एरंडी *eraṇḍī* [cf. H. *eraṇḍ*, ¹*aṇḍī*], f. = एरंड.

एर-फेर *er-pher* [cf. H. *her-pher*], m. **1.** exchange; barter. **2.** collusion.

-एरा *-erā*, adj. & n. formant. **1.** [*-tara-*] expresses connection of sense with a stem nominal form (e.g. सँपेरा, m., snake-charmer; बघेरा, m., leopard; बहुतेरा, adj. much, pl. many, frequent; बछेड़ा, m. calf). **2.** [*-kăra-*] agentive (e.g. चितेरा, m. painter). **3.** [*-era-*] patronymic (e.g. चचेरा, adj. related through a paternal uncle).

एरा-ग़ैरा *erā-gairā*, m. = ऐरा-ग़ैरा.

एरा-फेर *erā-pher*, m. = एर-फेर.

एरा-फेरी *erā-pherī* [cf. H. *phernā*; also *hernā*], f. **1.** exchange, barter. **2.** (= हेरा-फेरी) wandering about; frequenting a partic. locality.

एरी-फेरी *erī-pherī*, f. = एर-फेर.

एलची *elcī* [P. *elcī*], m. U. envoy, ambassador. — एलचीपना, m. office or status of an ambassador, &c.

एला *elā* [S.: ← Drav.], f. cardamom.

एलान *elān* [A. *iʿlān*], m. **1.** declaration; announcement, proclamation. **2.** manifesto. **3.** slogan. — ~ करना, to announce, &c. – एलान-नामा, m. manifesto.

एलानची *elāncī* [A. *iʿlān*+T. *-cī*], m. crier (of news); announcer.

एलानिया *elāniyā*, adj. 1. open, public. **2.** adv. publicly, etc.

एलुआ *eluā* [*eluka-*], m. aloe(s) (a fragrant resin or wood; also a genus of plants, the source of a drug.)

एवं *evaṁ* [S.], adv. /evəm/. **1.** thus, so. *__2.__ and. — एवमेव, adv. exactly so.

एव *evă* [S.], adv. **1.** as you like. **2.** even so, indeed, exactly. **3.** only, still, just, also.

एवज़ *evaz* [A. *ʿivaẓ*], m. & ppn. **1.** m. a substitute. **2.** exchange; return, requital. *__3.__ ppn. w. के. in return, or exchange (for, में).

एवज़ी *evăzī* [P. *ʿivazī*], adj. & m. **1.** adj. substituting (for); officiating; held in reserve. **2.** m. a substitute, &c. — एवज़ीदार [P. *-dār*], m. a substitute.

एवड़ *evaṛ* [*avikaṭa-* × **ajakaṭa-*], m. reg. a flock of goats or sheep.

एवारा *evārā* [**avivāṭa-*], m. *Pl.* a shed for livestock in scrub country.

एषणा *eṣăṇā* [S.], f. poet. desire.

एहतमाम *ehtamām* [A. *ihtimām*], m. /ɛhtəmam/. U. **1.** care, solicitude. **2.** supervision, management, charge.

एहतियात *ehtiyāt* [A. *iḥtiyāṭ*], f. **1.** care. caution; vigilance. **2.** a precaution. — ~ करना, to exercise caution (in, में); to take precautions. ~ से, adv. cautiously, circumspectly, &c.

एहतियातन *ehtiyātan* [A. *iḥtiyāṭan*], adv. cautiously, &c.

एहतियाती *ehtiyātī* [A. *iḥtiyāṭī*], adj. **1.** cautious; vigilant. *__2.__ precautionary (a measure).

एहद *ehd*, m. = अहद.

एहसान *ehsān* [A. *iḥsān*], m. **1.** beneficence, benefaction; favour; kindness. **2.** sense of obligation, gratitude. — ~ करना, to do a kindness (to, पर); to show a favour (to). ~ का बदला, m. return of a favour; grateful acknowledgement. ~ का बोझ (किसी पर) लादना, to cause (a person) to feel obligation. ~ मानना, to feel obliged or grateful for kindness, &c. (from, का). ~ रखना, to show a favour (to, पर); to place (one) under obligation. ~ लेना, to accept a kindness, &c. (from, से); to be under obligation (to). – एहसान-फ़रामोश [P. *-farāmoś*], adj. forgetful of favours, &c.: ungrateful. °ई, f. एहसानमंद [P. *-mand*], adj. grateful; obliged. °ई, f. gratefulness; sense of obligation.

एहसानात *ehsānāt* [A. *iḥsānāt*, pl.], m. pl. U. favours, kindnesses, &c. (see एहसान).

ऐ

ऐ *ai*, the ninth vocalic sound of the Devanāgarī syllabary as used in writing Hindi. — ऐकार, m. the phoneme /əi/; the letter ऐ.

ऐंच *aiṁc* [cf. H. *aiṁcnā*], f. **1.** pulling, dragging. **2.** stretching, tightening. **3.** scarcity, dearth. **4.** holding aloof. **5.** delay. 6. = ऐंचा-तानी, 2., 3., s.v. ऐंचना. **7.** *Pl.* levying, recovery (from a tenant, of that part of a revenue demand due from him).

ऐंचन *aiṁcan* [cf. H. *aiṁcnā*], f. **1.** pulling, dragging. 2. = ऐंचा-तानी, 2., 3., s.v. ऐंचना.

ऐंचना *aiṁcnā* [**atiyañcati*: Pk *aïṁcaï*], v.t. **1.** to pull, to drag; to draw (a sword). **2.** to draw (a line); to write, to scribble; to sketch. **3.** to hang, to execute. **4.** to winnow (grain). **5.** to take in, to absorb (e.g. as lime does moisture). **6.** to inhale. **7.** to extort, to exact (a levy, &c). **8.** to take upon oneself (a duty, &c). **9.** to draw back or away. — ऐंची आँखवाला, adj. squint-eyed. – ऐंच-तानकर, adv. with effort, by hook or by crook. – ऐंचा-ताना, adj. pulled askew. ऐंचा-तानी, f. tugging and pulling, effort; tussle, struggle; entanglement, toils.

ऐंचाव *aiṁcāv* [cf. H. *aiṁcnā*], m. pulling, etc. (= इँचाव).

ऐंचीला *aiṁcīlā* [cf. H. *aiṁc*], adj. elastic.

ऐंठ *aiṁṭh* [cf. H. *aiṁṭhnā*], f. **1.** a twisting, twist; turn, coil; fold. **2.** tightening. **3.** stiffness, rigidity. **4.** transf. strutting; affectation. **5.** obstinacy. **6.** pride, arrogance. — ऐंठदार [P. *-dār*], adj. twisted; haughty. ऐंठबाज़ [P. *-bāz*], adj. = अकड़बाज़.

ऐंठन *aiṁṭhan* [*āveṣṭana-*], f. **1.** twist (as of strands). **2.** turn, coil (as of rope). **3.** tension (as of rope). **4.** contortion; spasm; colic. — रस्सी जल गई, ~ नहीं गई, the rope is burnt, but not its coils (said of one defeated who does not accept his defeat).

ऐंठना *aiṁṭhnā* [*āveṣṭyate, āveṣṭate*], v.i. & v.t. **1.** v.i. to be twisted. **2.** to writhe, to wriggle. **3.** to be cramped, or contorted. **4.** to become rigid, stiff, &c. **5.** to strut, &c. (= अकड़ना). **6.** v.t. to twist; to wind; to spin (as wool). **7.** to make crooked: to distort. **8.** to squeeze, to wring. **9.** to extort. — कान ~, to twist the ear (of, का: by way of punishment). – ऐंठकर, adv. stiffly; affectedly.

ऐंठनी *aiṁṭhnī* [cf. H. *aiṁṭhnā*], f. reg. **1.** peevishness. **2.** pride.

ऐंठवाना *aiṁṭhvānā* [cf. H. *aiṁṭhnā*], v.t. **1.** to cause to be twisted, &c. (by, से). 2. = ऐंठाना, 2., 3.

ऐंठा *aiṁṭhā* [cf. H. *aiṁṭhnā*], m. reg. **1.** twist, turn (= ऐंठ, ऐंठन); hank, skein. 2. = ऐंठ, 4.-6. **3.** *Pl., HŚS.* string of a spinning-wheel. **4.** a snail.

ऐंठाना *aiṁṭhānā* [cf. H. *aiṁṭhnā*], v.t. **1.** to twist, &c. **2.** to cause to writhe, &c. **3.** to cause to strut, &c.

ऐंठू *aiṁṭhū* [cf. H. *aiṁṭhnā*], adj. & m. **1.** adj. proud, haughty. **2.** affected. **3.** m. an extortionist, blackmailer.

ऐंठूपन *aiṁṭhūpan* [cf. H. *aiṁṭhū*], m. **1.** pride, hauteur. **2.** affectation.

ऐंठूपना *aiṁṭhūpanā* [cf. H. *aiṁṭhū*], m. = ऐंठूपन.

ऐंड़ *aiṁṛ* [cf. H. *aiṁṛnā*], f. & adj. **1.** f. Brbh. = ऐंठ. **2.** a whirlpool. **3.** adj. idle, useless, worthless.

ऐंड़ना *aiṁṛnā* [*āveṣṭate*], v.i. 1. = ऐंठना, 1.-3., 5. **2.** to roll or to turn from side to side (as in bed). **3.** to stagger, to reel. **4.** to loll about idly.

[1]**ऐंड़ा** *aiṁṛā* [cf. H. *aiṁṛnā*], part. adj. **1.** twisted, contorted. **2.** crooked, zigzag. **3.** staggering, reeling. **4.** transf. swaggering. **5.** haughty. **6.** coarse, crude (speech). — ऐंड़ी-बेंड़ी सुनाना, to abuse, to call names.

[2]**ऐंड़ा** *aiṁṛā*, m. a weight (for scales); make-weight (*Pl.*).

ऐंड़ाना *aiṁṛānā* [cf. H. *aiṁṛnā*], v.i. & v.t. **1.** v.i. = ऐंड़ना, 1. **2.** [cf. H. [2]*aiṁṛā*] v.t. to put in the scale, to weigh roughly. **3.** reg. to cause to roll or to sway from side to side, &c.

ऐंड़ालना *aiṁṛālnā*, v.t. *Pl.* = ऐंड़ाना.

ऐंद्रजालिक *aindrajālik* [S.], adj. & m. **1.** adj. magical; deceptive, illusory. **2.** m. a magician. **3.** a juggler.

ऐंद्रियक *aindriyak* [S.], adj. **1.** having to do with the senses. **2.** perceived through the senses.

ऐ *ai*, interj. = हे.

ऐकमत्य *aikmatyă* [S.], m. sameness of opinion, agreement; concurrence; unanimity.

ऐकाहिक *aikâhik* [S.], adj. lasting one day, ephemeral.

ऐक्य *aikyă* [S.], m. unity, &c. (= एकता).

ऐक्यता *aikyătā* [S.], f. *Pl.* = ऐक्य.

ऐगुन *aigun*, m. Av. = अवगुण.

ऐच्छिक *aicchik* [S.], adj. according to wish, voluntary.

ऐतिहासिक *aitihāsik* [S.], adj. **1.** historical. **2.** history-making (event).

ऐन *ain* [A. *'ain* 'eye'], adj. exact, precise (esp. of time). — ~ **मौक़े पर**, adv. just when needed; in the nick of time. ~ **वक़्त पर**, adv. id.; punctually to the dot. **यह आपकी ~ मेहरबानी है**, this is really very kind of you.

ऐनक *ainak* [P. *'ainak*], f. glasses (for vision).

ऐब *aib* [A. *'aib*], m. **1.** a fault, shortcoming; defect. **2.** a vice. — ~ **निकालना**, to find fault(s) (with or in, **में**). ~ **पकड़ना**, to find a fault. ~ **लगाना**, to impute fault(s) (to, **पर**, **को**); to blame. ~ **लाना**, to have a vice (as a horse). – **ऐबदार** [P. *-dār*], adj. flawed; defective.

ऐबी *aibī* [P. *'aibī*], adj. & m. **1.** adj. flawed; defective. **2.** vicious. **3.** m. a vicious person, a bad character.

-ऐया *-aiyā*, suffix (forms nouns, chiefly m., having dimin. or agentive force, e.g. **रहैया**, m. colloq. resident; **भूलभुलैया**, f. a maze).

ऐयार *aiyār* [A. *'aiyār*], m. **1.** a cunning person; villain. ***2.** a person possessing magical powers (as of becoming invisible, or taking a different human form); a wizard.

ऐयारपन *aiyārpan* [cf. H. *aiyār*], m. **1.** cunning; villainy. **2.** a wizard's magical power.

[1]**ऐयारी** *aiyārī* [P. *'aiyārī*], f. **1.** cunning; villainy. ***2.** imposture, deception (by magical means).

[2]**ऐयारी** *aiyārī* [H. *aiyār*], adj. dealing with magical events (a novel).

ऐयाश *aiyāś* [A. *'aiyāś*], adj. & m. **1.** adj. fond of luxury. **2.** voluptuous; sensual. **3.** m. a voluptuous person.

ऐयाशी *aiyāśī* [P. *'aiyāśī*], f. **1.** love of pleasure, or luxury. **2.** voluptuousness.

ऐरा-ग़ैरा *airā-gairā* [cf. H. *gair*], adj. & m. **1.** adj. this and the other, nondescript, so-so. **2.** of no account. **3.** m. a stranger. **4.** a nobody. — ~ **नत्थू ख़ैरा**, m. colloq. everyone and his brother. ~ **पँचकल्यान**, m. id. **ऐरी-ग़ैरी फ़सल बहुतेरी**, fig. (I'll) find something or other to eat without trouble.

ऐरावत *airāvat* [S.], m. **1.** *mythol.* the name of Indra's elephant. **2.** a thunder-cloud.

ऐल-फ़ैल *ail-fail* [f. A. *al-fi'l*], m. reg. **1.** abusive language. **2.** chatter, babble.

ऐलान *ailān*, m. = एलान.

ऐवान *aivān* [P. *aivān, ivan*], m. **1.** palace (esp. royal). **2.** hall, chamber; gallery; portico.

ऐश *aiś* [A. *'aiś*], m. life, way of life: **1.** life of pleasure and enjoyment; delight; luxury. **2.** voluptuousness; sensuality. — ~ **करना**, or **उड़ाना**, or **लूटना**, to live a life of pleasure. – **ऐश-आराम**, m. comfort of life; luxury. **ऐश आराम से होना**, to be nicely off, living comfortably. **ऐश-गाह** [P. *-gāh*], f. place of pleasure: inner or women's quarters (see **ज़नाना**, 1). **ऐशो-आराम**, m. = **ऐश-आराम**.

ऐश्वर्य *aiśvaryă* [S.], m. **1.** supremacy, dominion. **2.** superhuman power or quality; divine majesty. **3.** grandeur, pomp; majesty. **4.** prosperous state. — **ऐश्वर्य-प्रेम**, love of grandeur, ostentation. **°ई**, adj. **ऐश्वर्यवान**, adj. prosperous, affluent. **ऐश्वर्यशाली**, adj. id.

ऐश्वर्यीय *aiśvaryīyă* [S.], adj. endowed with superhuman qualities; grand, majestic.

ऐसा *aisā* [*īdṛśaka-*; × *tādṛśa-*, &c.], adj. & m. **1.** adj. of this sort. **2.** m. such a thing (as this). ~ **नहीं होने का**, this is impossible. **3.** ppn. like. **मर्द ~**, like a man. **4.** adv. in this way; as though. — **ऐसे में**, adv. at such a juncture, with this. **ऐसे ही**, adv. just so, precisely; as if, as though; casually, thoughtlessly. – **ऐसा-तैसा**, adj. = **ऐसा-वैसा**. **ऐसी-तैसी**, euph. disgrace, infamy; sthg. unmentionable. **ऐसी-तैसी करना**, to make a mockery (of, **की**). **ऐसा-वैसा**, adj. so-so; indifferent, inferior, bad; nondescript; euph. indecent; m. wretch.

ऐहलौकिक *aihlaukik* [S.], adj. of this world (cf. **ऐहिक**).

ऐहिक *aihik* [S.], adj. of this place: terrestial; worldly; secular; local. — **ऐहिकीकरण**, m. secularisation.

ऐहिकीकरण *aihikīkaraṇ* [S.], m. see s.v. **ऐहिक**.

ओ

ओ *o*, the tenth vocalic sound of the Devanāgarī syllabary as used in writing Hindi: — ओकार, m. the sound /o/; the letter *o*.

ओंकार *oṁkār* [S.], m. the sound ओम् (q.v).

ओंटना *oṁṭnā*, v.i. = औटना.

ओंटाना *oṁṭānā*, v.t. = औटाना.

ओंठ *oṁṭh* [*oṣṭha-*], m. the lip (= होंठ).

ओंध *oṁdh* [*avabandha-*], m. reg. the cord with which rafters or frames for thatching are fastened until the roof is finished.

-ओ- *-o-* [P. *-o-*], encl. and (= व: links nouns and adjectives in expressions of Persian origin, e.g. बंदोबस्त, m. arrangement; कमोबेश, adv. more or less).

[1]**ओक** *ok* [**audakya-*], m. **1.** the palm hollowed to drink from. **2.** water, &c. drunk from the hollowed palm.

[2]**ओक** *ok* [cf. H. *oknā*], f. vomiting; nausea.

[3]**ओक** *ok* [S.], m. Brbh. **1.** house, dwelling; dwelling-place. **2.** refuge.

ओकना *oknā* [**okk-*: Pk *okkia-*], v.i. to vomit.

ओखली *okhlī*, f. a small mortar (cf. ऊखल).

ओखा *okhā* [? *apakṣa-*], adj. **1.** inferior; bad; useless, ineffective. **2.** disagreeable.

ओग *og*, m. Brbh. levy, tribute. — ओग-दुवास, m. a Hindu festival held on the twelfth day of the dark fortnight of the month Bhādoṁ.

ओगरा *ogrā* [**oggara-*: ← T.], m. *Pl.* a kind of gruel, pottage.

ओगल *ogal* [cf. *avagalati*; anal.: ? ← G. or M.], m. *Pl.* moisture in the soil.

ओगार *ogār* [**avagāla-*; anal.], m. Brbh. juice (as of *pān*), running from the mouth.

ओगारना *ogārnā*, v.t. reg. to drain, or to clean, a well.

ओघ *ogh* [S.], m. **1.** stream, torrent. **2.** multitude; collection; heap.

ओघरा *oghrā*, m. *Pl.* = ओगरा.

ओछा *ochā* [**occha-*: Pk. *uccha-*], m. **1.** empty; shallow; vain. **2.** small, trifling; frivolous; facile. **3.** absurd. **4.** mean, base; worthless; degrading. — ~ पड़ना, to be or to prove ineffective (a blow, an attempt).

ओछाई *ochāī* [cf. H. *ochā*], f. = ओछापन.

ओछापन *ochāpan* [cf. H. *ochā*], m. **1.** emptiness, shallowness, &c. **2.** triviality, &c. **3.** absurdity. **4.** baseness.

ओज *oj* [S.], m. **1.** light. **2.** splendour, lustre. **3.** brilliance, fervour. — ओजपूर्ण, adv. shining, resplendent; brilliant (esp. of poetic quality or style).

[1]**ओजना** *ojnā* [**avatudyate*], v.t. to ward off (a blow).

[2]**ओजना** *ojnā* [?? = [1]*ojnā*], v.t. reg. to pour out.

ओजस्विता *ojasvitā* [S.], f. **1.** splendour. **2.** brilliance (esp. of poetic quality or style).

ओजस्वी *ojasvī* [S.], adj. – ओजपूर्ण.

ओझ *ojh* [*ūbadhya-*], m. entrails; paunch.

ओझड़ी *ojhṛī* [*ubadhya-*], f. reg. = ओझ.

ओझर *ojhar* [*ubadhya-*], m. reg. = ओझ.

ओझल *ojhal* [**ojjhalla-*], m. **1.** m. screen, shelter; concealment. **2.** adj. screened, hidden (by, के). **3.** disappeared, vanished. — ~ करना, to cause to disappear; to hide; to spirit away. आँख ~, पहाड़ ~, fig. out of sight, out of mind.

ओझा *ojhā* [*upādhyāya-*], m. **1.** a country doctor; sorcerer, wizard. **2.** name of a sub-community of brāhmaṇs. **3.** a member of the *ojhā* sub-community.

ओझाइन *ojhāin* [cf. H. *ojhā*], f. **1.** the wife of an *ojhā*. **2.** a sorceress, witch.

ओझाई *ojhāī* [cf. H. *ojhā*], f. the practice of sorcery. — ओझाईगीरी [P. *-gīrī*], f. id.

ओट *oṭ* [**oṭṭā-*], f. **1.** covering, screen; shelter. **2.** place of concealment; ambush. **3.** chock (for a wheel). — ~ करना, to cover, to conceal. ~ में, adv. concealed (by, की). ~ होना, to be concealed, &c. परदे की ~ में, adv. secretly, furtively. – ओटबंदी [P. *-bandī*], f. payment of a fixed amount (to cover use of a plough and pair of bullocks).

ओटन *oṭan* [cf. H. *oṭnā*], m. an appliance for cleaning cotton.

ओटना *oṭnā* [**avavartayati*: Pk. *ovaṭṭei*], v.t. **1.** to separate cotton seed, to clean cotton. **2.** fig. to utter repeatedly (a viewpoint), to insist upon. **3.** Brbh. to take upon oneself: to ward off (a blow).

ओटनी *oṭnī*, f. = ओटन.

ओटल *oṭal* [cf. H. *oṭ*], f. = ओट, 1., 2.

[1]**ओटा** *oṭā* [cf. H. *oṭ*], m. **1.** a partition wall or screen. **2.** a side wall; wall of a porchway. **3.** platform of bricks or earth. **4.** E.H. dike. **5.** *Pl.* ball, lump (as of mud).

[2]**ओटा** *oṭā* [cf. H. *oṭnā*], m. *Pl. HŚS.* a cleaner of raw cotton.

ओठ *oṭh*, m. = ओंठ, होंठ.

ओड़ *oṛ* [cf. H. *oṛnā*], f. protection (as from a blow). — हवा के सामने ~ लगाना, to shelter from the wind.

ओड़न *oṛan* [cf. **oḍḍā-*], m. Av. shield.

ओड़ना *oṛnā* [**oḍḍā-*], v.t. **1.** to cover (oneself) with a shield. ***2.** to ward off (a blow). **3.** to spread out (the arms).

[1]**ओड़ा** *oṛā*, [? conn. *oḍra-*[1]], m. reg. **1.** basket (used in field-work). **2.** hole in house wall (made by burglar: = सेंध).

[2]**ओड़ा** *oṛā*, m. lack, scarcity, want.

ओड़ी *oṛī* [cf. H. *oṛā*], f. reg. a small basket.

ओढ़ना *oṛhnā* [**oḍḍh-* (← Drav.): Pk. *oḍḍha-*], v.t. **1.** to cover with, to wrap round. **2.** to put on; to wear. **3.** to take on, to take upon oneself (a duty, a responsibility). **4.** m. a covering; sheet; blanket; shawl; veil. — ~ उतारना (का), to remove a covering, &c., to unveil; to expose, to defame. ~ ओढ़ाना, to cover with a sheet or mantle; to marry (a widow). ~ गले में डालना, to seek justice from (as a woman was supposed to do from one who had insulted her, by throwing the end of her shawl round his neck to drag him to the king's court). ~ बिछौना बनाना, to use a shawl as bedding: to use sthg. carelessly, to misuse. – ओढ़ना-बिछौना, m. coverings, bedding.

ओढ़नी *oṛhnī* [cf. H. *oṛhnā*], f. a woman's sheet or shawl. — ~ की बतास लगना, the wind from a woman's shawl to strike (one): to be under a woman's, or women's, influence.

ओढा *oḍhā* [? *apoḍha-*; Pk. **avavuḍḍha-*], m. *Pl.* double armful of corn (perquisite of village accountant).

[1]**ओत** *ot* [*avāpti-*], f. **1.** gain, advantage; benefit. **2.** surplus. **3.** recovery (from sickness). — ~ पड़ना, a profit, &c. to be made. – ओत-कसर, f. profit and loss.

[2]**ओत** *ôt* [S.], adj. & m. **1.** adj. woven. **2.** m. warp. — ओत-प्रोत, adj. crosswise and lengthwise, warp and woof; through and through.

ओता *otā*, adj. Av. = उतना.

ओद *od* [? *odman-*], m. Brbh. wetness, moistness.

ओद- *od-* [? *odman-*], adj. Brbh. wet, moist, damp.

ओदन *odan* [S.], m. Brbh. Av. boiled rice; food.

ओध- *odh-* [cf. *ābaddha-*], v.t. Av. to bind, to join (as battle).

ओधा *odhā* [A. *'uhda*], m. *HŚS.* office, post, position.

ओधे *odhe* [? conn. H. *odhā*], adj. & m. *Pl. HŚS.* **1.** adj. possessing a right or title. **2.** m. proprietor; master.

ओप *op* [cf. H. *opnā*], f. lustre, polish.

ओपना *opnā* [**opp-*: Pk. *oppa-*], v.i. & v.t. **1.** v.i. to be polished; to be lustrous, or beautiful. **2.** v.t. to polish, &c.

ओपनी *opnī* [cf. H. *opnā*], f. Brbh. a polishing stone.

[1]**ओबरा** *obrā*, adj. *Pl.* excessive.

[2]**ओबरा** *obrā*, adj. *Pl.* tasteless, insipid.

ओबरी *obrī* [*apavaraka-*], f. Brbh. a hut, shack; room.

ओभी *obhī*, f. *Pl.* ? a pit for catching wild animals.

ओम् *om* (= ॐ, the usual representation), m. a sacred syllable uttered or written in various contexts (as at the beginning and end of a reading of the Veda; before prayer; at the beginning of a text); a mystic name for the triad of deities Brahmā, Viṣṇu and Śiva.

ओर *or* [*avarā-*[1]], f. **1.** side, direction. **2.** end, limit; boundary; extreme. **3.** ppn. (w. की) in the direction (of), towards. — ~ आना, (one's, की) end to arrive, to meet one's death or end. ~ करना, to take the part (of, की); to be partial (to). ~ न छोर, adv. neither one end nor another: sthg. endless. ~ निभाना (अपनी), to do (one's) part; to do (one's) best; to carry out to the end. अपनी ~ देखना, to respect oneself, to consider one's own dignity. उस ~, adv. on that side; that way. चारों ~, adv. on all four sides, all around. के चारों ~, ppn. all around. – ओर-छोर, m. one end and the other: bearings, orientation (in a matter, का).

ओरमा *ormā*, m. (*Pl.*) f. (*HŚS.*) **1.** hem-stitching; seam; hem. **2.** *Pl.* felling (a seam).

ओरमा- *ormā-* [cf. *avalambayati*], v.t. E.H. to hang (sthg.) down.

ओरहन- *orhan-*, m. Brbh. = उरहना.

¹**ओरी** *orī* [? incorr. f. H. *oṛ*], m. reg. protector; supporter.

²**ओरी** *orī* [? cf. *avacūḍa-*], f. reg. **1.** eaves (of house). **2.** bank (of pond or stream).

¹**ओल** *ol* [*olla-*³: Pk. *ulla-*], f. **1.** security (as against loss), guarantee. **2.** bail. **3.** pledge, pawn. **4.** hostage. — ~ में देना, to give as a guarantee; to give as a hostage; to release on bail.

²**ओल** *ol* [*olla-*¹], m. a pungent, edible root, *Arum campanulatum* (= सूरन). — ओल-कोबी, f. *Pl.* a vegetable formerly called 'Knolecole'.

ओल- *ol-*, v.t. Brbh. **1.** [? cf. *avacūḍa-*] to shelter. **2.** to ward off. **3.** to take upon oneself; to bear, to endure.

ओलट *olaṭ* [*oṭal* (= *oṭ*)] f. = ओट.

ओलती *oltī* [cf. H. *ol-*, v.t.], f. eaves (of thatch).

ओलन *olan* [? cf. *avacūḍa-*, H. *ol-*], , m. a plumb-line.

ओलमा *olmā* [? cf. *avalambate*], m. *Pl.* an animal or bird killed and scalded to remove hair or feathers.

¹**ओला** *olā* [*upalaka-*], m. & adj. **1.** m. hailstone; hail. **2.** a loaf-sugar ball (type of candy). **3.** adj. transf. cold (as hail, ice). — ~ (or ओले) पड़ना, or गिरना, or बरसना, to hail. ~ होना, to be or to become cold. सिर मुँड़ाते ही ओले पड़े, hail fell as soon as he had shaved his head: misfortune overtook him at the outset.

²**ओला** *olā* [**avalaya-*], m. *Pl. HŚS.* **1.** screen. **2.** fig. secrecy.

ओली *olī* [*avacūḍa-*], f. **1.** Brbh. the hem of a garment (= आँचल). **2.** fig. bosom. **3.** Brbh. a hanging wallet, satchel, &c. — ~ ओड़ना, to spread out the skirt: to bow in humble entreaty. ~ लेना, to adopt.

ओष्ठ *oṣṭh* [S.], m. the lip.

ओष्ठी *oṣṭhī* [S.], f. **1.** *Pl. HŚS.* a creeper, *Coccinia grandis*, having a red flower with which the lip is compared. **2.** *HŚS.* the red gourd, *Momordica monodelpha.*

ओष्ठ्य *oṣṭhyă* [S.], adj. *ling.* labial (sound, letter).

ओस *os* [*avaśyā-*], f. dew. — ~ पड़ना, dew to fall (on, पर): to be blighted, to fade; to languish; to feel embarrassment. ~ का मोती, m. a dew-drop; sthg. ephemeral.

ओसनना *osannā* [**avaślakṣṇayati*: Pa. *osaṇheti*], v.t. reg. to knead (dough).

ओसर *osar* [**upasariyā-*, *upasaryā-*], f. a heifer.

ओसरा *osrā* [*avasara-*], m. Brbh. time, turn.

ओसाना *osānā* [**apaśrāpayati*], v.t. reg. = उसाना.

ओसार *osār* [**avasāra-*: Pk. *osāra-*], adj. & m. **1.** adj. wide. **2.** m. width.

ओसारा *osārā* [**avaśāra-*: Pa. *osāraka-*], m. **1.** a verandah. **2.** a porchway.

ओहदा *ohdā* [A. *'ōhda*], m. an office, duty; position. — ~ पाना, to obtain the post (of, का). – ओहदेदार [P. *-dār*], adj. & m. holding office; an office-holder.

ओहार *ohār* [**apaghāṭa-*: Pk. *ohāḍaṇa-*], m. Brbh. Av. covering; curtain of a litter (for protection, or concealment).

औ

औ *au*, the eleventh vocalic sound of the Devanāgarī syllabary as used in writing Hindi: — औकार, m. the phoneme /əu/; the letter *au*.

औंगन *aumgan* [cf. H. *aumgan*], m. axle-grease.

औंगना *aumgnā* [cf. *upāṅga-*], v.t. to grease (the axle of a cart).

औंगी *aumgī* [**āguṅga-*], f. reg. dumbness, silence.

औंडा *aumḍā* [**avoṇḍa-*], adj. deep; sunk.

औंडाई *aumḍāī* [cf. H. *aumḍā*], f. depth.

औंठी *aumṭhī*, f. reg. (E.), f. = अँगूठी.

औंधना *aumdhnā* [cf. H. औंधाना], v.i. **1.** to be overturned, &c. **2.** to be emptied, &c. **3.** Brbh. = औंधाना, 1. **4.** *Pl.* to lower (the sky with clouds).

औंधा *aumdhā* [*avamūrdha-*], adj. & m. **1.** adj. face down; upside down. **2.** overturned; in utter confusion, ruined; 'fallen flat'. **3.** crooked, wrong; adverse (as fortune). **4.** m. a fool. — ~ बख़्त, m. adverse fortune. औंधी खोपड़ी, f. wrong-head(ed): a fool. औंधी पेशानी, f. (whose) brow (is) marked with an adverse (sign): unlucky, ill-fated; not having foresight. औंधे मुँह, adv. face down, head down; head-first. औंधे मुँह दूध पीना, to suck with the face down: to be silly, or ignorant.

औंधाना *aumdhānā* [cf. H. *aumdhā*], v.t. **1.** to overturn; to upset. **2.** to empty (a vessel); to pour out (water). **3.** Brbh. to hang down (the head).

औ *au* [*aparam*], conj. & adv. poet. = और.

औकल *aukal* [*kalya-*[1]; ? pref. *au-* ← *ava-*], adj. *Pl.* restless, uneasy.

औकली *aukālī* [cf. H. औकल], f. *Pl.* restlessness, uneasiness.

औक़ात *auqāt* [A.: pl. of *vaqt*], f. **1.** times, life, days. **2.** circumstances; state, condition. **3.** capacity; means, resources. — ~ बसर करना, to pass (one's) days; to subsist (on or by, से); to earn a livelihood. – औक़ात-बसरी, f. passing (one's) days; subsisting, subsistence; livelihood.

औकान *aukān*, m. reg. pile of grain and chaff ready for winnowing.

औकाल *aukāl* [*kalya-*[3]; ? pref. *au-* ← *ava-*], adj. *Pl.* untimely; premature.

[1]**औगी** *augī*, f. *Pl. HŚS.* **1.** a whip made of twisted cord. **2.** ornamental edging (on shoes). **3.** *Pl.* reel or skein. **4.** *HŚS.* stick, goad.

[2]**औगी** *augī*, f. *Pl. HŚS.* ? pit for catching large animals.

औगुन *augun*, m. = अवगुण.

औगुनी *augunī*, adj. & m. **1.** adj. worthless; vicious, corrupt, depraved. **2.** m. a worthless person, &c.

औघट *aughaṭ* [ad. *avaghaṭṭa-*], adj. **1.** rough, impassable (as a road). **2.** inaccessible; unfrequented.

औघड़ *aughaṛ* [cf. H. *gaṛhnā*], adj. **1.** misshapen. **2.** awkward, ungainly; uncouth. **3.** strange.

औचक *aucak*, adj. & adv. unexpected(ly), suddenly. — ~ निरीक्षण, m. an unannounced inspection.

औचट *aucaṭ*, adv. 1. = औचक. **2.** f. Brbh. difficulty, predicament.

औचित्य *aucityă* [S.], m. **1.** appropriateness; suitability. **2.** propriety, rightness.

औछ *auch* [conn. *ākṣika-*, *ācchuka-*], m. *Pl. HŚS.* a plant (*Morinda tinctoria*, or *citrifolia*) from the root of which an orange dye is extracted. (? = दारुहल्दी).

औज़ार *auzār* [A.: pl. of *vizr*], m. burdens: **1.** tool, implement. **2.** *Pl.* tools, implements; equipment. **3.** arms.

औज़ारी *auzārī* [H. *auzār*+-*ī*], adj. having to do with equipment, &c.

औझड़ *aujhaṛ*, m. & adj. E.H. **1.** *Pl.* knock, blow; kick (of a fighting cock). **2.** adj. thoughtless, impulsive. **3.** adv. uninterruptedly.

[1]**औटन** *auṭan* [cf. H. *auṭnā*], f. m. Av. boiling; heat.

[2]**औटन** *auṭan*, f. *Pl. HŚS.* knife for cutting tobacco leaves.

औटना *auṭnā* [*āvartayati*], v.t. & v.i. **1.** v.t. to boil. **2.** to boil down, to evaporate. **3.** v.i. [← v.t. or *auṭānā*] to be boiled, &c. **4.** fig. to boil with anger.

औटाना *auṭānā* [cf. H. *auṭnā*], v.t. **1.** to cause to boil (as milk). **2.** to boil down (as milk). **3.** to heat.

औटावनी *auṭāvnī* [cf. H. *auṭānā*; +*tāpana-*], f. reg. earthen vessel in which milk is boiled.

औढर *auḍhar*, adj. & m. Brbh. Av. **1.** adj. consulting one's own inclination. **2.** m. compassion for the lowly. — **औढर-दानी**, adj. giving at (one's) will: a title of the god Śiva.

औत्कर्ष्य *autkarṣyă* [S.], m. excellence; superiority.

औत्सर्गिक *autsargik* [S.], adj. coming about by nature, natural.

औत्सुक्य *autsukyă* [S.], m. **1.** keen desire; impatience; anxiety. **2.** curiosity, interest.

औदुंबर *audumbar* [S.], adj. & m. *HŚS.* **1.** adj. made of fig wood. **2.** made of copper. **3.** m. fig wood. **4.** copper. **5.** a vessel of fig wood, or of copper.

औदसा *audăsā* [ad. **apadaśā-*], f. *HŚS.* dire state; calamity.

औदान *audān* [ad. *apadāna-*], m. *Pl. HŚS.* sthg. thrown in, given gratis.

औदार्य *audāryă* [S.], m. **1.** generosity (of spirit); nobility. **2.** liberality, munificence.

औदासीन्य *audāsīnyă* [S.], m. = **उदासीनता**.

औदास्य *audāsyă* [S.], m. 1. = **उदासीनता**. **2.** loneliness, solitude.

औदेस *audes* [ad. *avadeśa-*], m. reg. foreign country or region.

औद्योगिक *audyogik* [S.], adj. industrial.

औद्योगिकी *audyogikī* [S.], f. ? technology.

औधान *audhān* [ad. **avadhāna-*], m. E.H. womb.

औनापौना *aunā-paunā* [= H. *ānā, pānā*], adj. **1.** little (of amount). **2.** deficient. — **औने-पौने बेचना**, to sell for what one can get.

औनी *aunī*, f. Brbh. = **अवनी**.

औने-पौने *aune-paune* [cf. H. *ānnā, pānā*]. bringing and getting, haggling (over a price): — **~ करना**, to haggle.

औपचारिक *aupăcārik* [S.], adj. formal. — **~ रूप से**, adv. formally.

औपनिवेशिक *aupăniveśik* [S.], adj. colonial.

औरंग *auraṅg* [P. *aurang*], m. U. throne. — **औरंगज़ेबी** [P. *-zīb-*], f. a kind of cloth. **औरंगशाही** [P. *-śāh-*], f. a kind of silk.

और *aur* [*apara-*], conj. & adv. **1.** conj. and; moreover. **2.** but, still. **3.** adv. besides, additionally; further, again. **4.** otherwise, else. **5.** adj. other, different. **6.** extra, additional. — **~ ~**, adj. others besides; various, different. **~ एक**, adj. another. **~ का ~**, adv. quite different; quite changed; contrary, reversed. **~ कुछ**, something different; something further, some more. **~ कोई**, another, a different; someone else. **~ कहीं**, adv. elsewhere. **~ क्या**, adv. what else? of course! you know! **~ तो ~**, adv. others apart; what of others? **~ भी**, adv. again, further; still more; furthermore. **~ ही**, adj. quite different. **~ ही कुछ**, sthg. quite new, unexampled.

औरत *aurat* [A. *'aura*: P. *'aurat*], f. private: **1.** a woman. **2.** wife. — **~ की ज़ात**, f. womankind. – **औरत-ज़ात**, f. id.

औरताना *aurătānā* [P. *'auratāna*], adj. inv. of women; womanly.

औरस *auras* [S.], adj. & m. **1.** adj. legitimate (of birth). **2.** m. a legitimate son.

औरस-चौरस *auras-cauras* [? cf. H. *cauras*], adv. **1.** all around. **2.** adj. *Pl.* level, even; smooth.

औरसी *aurăsī* [S.], f. a legitimate daughter.

औरी-बौरी *aurī-baurī* [cf. H. *baurā, bāvlā*], adj. reg. mad, crazy.

औरेब *aureb*, adj. & m. **1.** adj. *Pl. HŚS.* crooked, misshapen. **2.** m. crookedness, &c. **3.** Brbh. trickery, deceit.

औल *aul*, m. *Pl. HŚS.* a calamity; outbreak of disease.

औल-फ़ौल *aul-faul*, m. abusive language (= **ऐल-फ़ैल**).

औलाद *aulād* [A.: pl. of *valad*], f. children; offspring; descendants.

औला-दौला *aulā-daulā*, adj. reg. unthinking, casual (as in patronage).

औला-मौला *aulā-maulā* adj. reg. = **औला-दौला**.

औलिया *auliyā* [A.: pl. of *valī*], m. inv. **1.** a saint. **2.** pl. saints, holy men. **3.** euph. a godless person.

औली *aulī*, f. reg. = [1]**आवली**. — **औली-सौली**, adv. in a row.

औलू *aulū* [*apūrva-*: **apuluva-*], adj. & m. **1.** adj. strange, unusual. **2.** unpleasant. **3.** uneasy. **4.** m. strangeness, &c.

औषध *auṣadh* [S.], m. f. medicine, &c. (= **औषधि**). — **औषध-निर्माण-शास्त्र**, m. pharmaceutics. **औषध-विज्ञान**, m. pharmacology. **°ई**, m. pharmacologist. **औषधालय** [°*dha*+*ā*°], m. dispensary; pharmacy.

औषधि *auṣadhi* [S.], f. medicine, medication; herb; drug.

औषधीय *auṣadhīyă* [S.], adj. medicinal.

औसत *ausat* [A. *ausaṯ*], adj. & m. **1.** adj. middle; medium. **2.** average. **3.** m. middle, &c. **4.** average.– ~ निकालना, or लगाना (का), to average. ~ (रूप से), adv. on average.

औसतन *ausatan* [A. *ausaṯan*], adv. on average.

औसती *ausatī* [A. *ausaṯ*+*-ī*], adj. = औसत.

औसना *ausnā*, v.i. **1.** [**apavāsyate*] to grow musty. **2.** to grow sticky; to ferment. **3.** [**āvāsayati*] to grow stale; to stink. **4.** [**ātāpasyati*] to suffer from heat. **5.** to ripen (as fruit kept under straw).

1**औसान** *ausān* [*avasāna-*], m. Brbh. the senses: self-possession, calmness. — ~ *bhūl-*, to lose one's presence of mind; to be stunned, aghast. ~ से, adv. calmly.

2**औसान** *ausān*, m. reg. (E.) = अहसान.

औसाना *ausānā* [cf. H. *ausnā*], v.t. reg. to ripen (produce) by covering it with straw, &c.

औसुच *ausuc*, adj. *Pl.* inconsiderate, heedless.

औसेर *auser* [cf. H. *avaser-*], f. Brbh. Av. **1.** care, solicitude. **2.** anxiety. **3.** delay.

क

क *ka*, the first consonant of the Devanāgarī syllabary. **ककार**, m. the sound /k/; the letter **क**.

कंक *kaṅk* [S.], m. Brbh. **1.** a partic. flesh-eating bird, the white kite (? white vulture). **2.** a heron.

कंकड़ *kaṅkaṛ* [cf. *karkara-*²], m. **1.** a nodule of limestone. **2.** a stone; pl. stones, gravel. **3.** a hard piece, fragment. **4.** an uncut jewel. — ~ **का**, m. made of limestone; metalled (a road). – **कंकर-पत्थर**, m. pebbles and stones, shingle, gravel; fig. rubbish.

कंकड़ी *kaṅkăṛī* [cf. **karkara-*²], f. **1.** a small stone. **2.** gravel. **3.** small fragment (as of sugar, salt).

कँकड़ीला *kaṁkṛīlā* [cf. H. *kaṅkaṛ*], adj. stony; gravelly (soil, or a road).

कँकड़ीलापन *kaṁkṛīlāpan* [cf. H. *kaṁkṛīlā*], m. stoniness (of soil).

कंकण *kaṅkaṇ* [S.], m. **1.** a metal bracelet. **2.** a dagger.

कंकर *kaṅkar*, m. = **कंकड़**.

कंकरा *kaṅkrā* [cf. H. *kaṅkar*], m. reg. a marble. — **कंकरे का आज़ार**, m. stone (in kidney, &c).

कंकरीट *kaṅkrīṭ* [Engl. *concrete*], m. concrete.

कँकरीला *kaṁkrīlā*, adj. = **कँकड़ीला**.

कंकरोल *kaṅkrol*, m. *Pl.* a kind of gourd.

कंकल *kaṅkal* [S.], m. a skeleton. — **कंकालकाय**, adj. having the body wasted to a skeleton. **कंकालशेष**, adj. remaining only as a skeleton: id.

कंकालिन *kaṅkālin* [ad. *kaṅkālinī-*], f. a witch, hag.

कंकालिनी *kaṅkālinī* [S.], f. Brbh. = **कंकालिन**.

कंगन *kaṅgan* [*kaṅkaṇa-*; ← Panj.], m. **1.** a bangle, bracelet of precious metal (worn by women). **2.** an iron bangle (worn by Sikh men). 3. = **कँगना**, 2. — **हाथ** ~, **तो आरसी क्या?** fig. that is totally self-evident.

कँगना *kaṁgnā* [ad. *kaṅkaṇa-*, or ← Panj.], m. 1. = **कंगन**, 1. **2.** a thread or string tied round the right wrist of a bridegroom and the left of a bride at the marriage ceremony. **3.** a song sung at the tying of a *kaṁgnā*. — ~ **खोलना**, the marriage ceremony of untying the *kaṁgnā*.

¹**कँगनी** *kaṁgnī* [cf. H. *kaṁgnā*], f. **1.** a small bracelet, or bangle of glass or lac. **2.** [? × *kaṅkaṭa-*] = **कँगूरा**, 1. **3.** [? × *kaṅkaṭa-*] a scalloped or toothed edge.

²**कँगनी** *kaṁgnī* [ad. *kaṅgunī-*], f. a millet, *Panicum italicum*.

कंगला *kaṅglā* [cf. H. *kaṅgāl*], adj. & m. **1.** adj. = **कंगाल**. **2.** m. a pauper; a beggar.

कंगाल *kaṅgāl* [ad. **kaṅkāla-*², or ← Panj.], adj. **1.** poor. **2.** wretched. — ~ **का** ~, adj. poorest of the poor.

कंगालपन *kaṅgālpan* [cf. H. *kaṅgāl*], m. **1.** poverty. **2.** wretched state.

¹**कंगाली** *kaṅgālī* [cf. H. *kaṅgāl*], adj. & m. **1.** adj. = **कंगाल**. **2.** m. a pauper.

²**कंगाली** *kaṅgālī* [cf. H. *kaṅgāl*], f. = **कंगालपन**.

कँगूरा *kaṁgūrā* [P. *kungura*], m. **1.** *arch.* upper moulding or ornamentation; cornice. **2.** parapet (wall). **3.** battlement (of a castle). **4.** pinnacle; turret. **5.** crest (of bird, or helmet). **6.** jewel or ornament (in a crown). — **कँगूरेदार** [P. *-dār*], adj. ornamented, &c.

कंघा *kaṅghā* [conn. **kaṅkaśa-*], m. a comb.

कंघी *kaṅghī* [cf. H. *kaṅghā*], f. a comb; a small comb. — **बालों में** ~ **करना**, to comb the hair. — **कंघी-चोटी**, f. doing the hair (a woman).

कँघेरा *kaṁgherā*, m. a maker of combs.

कंचन *kañcan* [ad. *kāñcana-*], m. gold.

कंचनी *kañcănī* [cf. H. *kañcan*], f. obs. a dancing-girl; a prostitute.

कँचली *kaṁclī* [conn. *kañculikā-*], f. a snake's slough (= **केंचुली**).

कंचुक *kañcuk* [S.], m. a bodice, brassiere; a women's jacket.

कंचुकी *kañcukī* [S.], f. = **कंचुक**.

कँचेरा *kaṁcerā* [**kāccakara-*], m. a glass-worker.

कंज *kañj* [S.], m. **1.** hair (of the head). **2.** a lotus.

कंजड़ *kañjaṛ*, m. reg. = **कंजर**.

कंजर *kañjar*, m. & adj. **1.** a scattered itinerant community, the members of which make and sell string, metal goods, &c. **2.** a member of this group; a tinker, gipsy. **3.** pej. a dirty, uncouth person. — **कंजरों की बोली**, the Romany language.

कंजरपन *kañjarpan* [cf. H. *kañjar*], m. uncouthness, &c. (see **कंजर**).

कंजरी *kañjrī* [cf. H. *kañjar*], f. **1.** a *kañjar* woman. **2.** a *kañjar*'s wife. **3.** a type of song sung by *kañjrīs*. **4.** reg. (N.) a prostitute.

कंजा *kañjā* [? conn. *kañc-* 'to shine'], adj. having light-coloured eyes.

कंजूस *kañjūs* [? H. *kān*+H. *cūs-*], m. & adj. **1.** m. a miser, skinflint. **2.** adj. miserly, niggardly.

कंजूसपन *kañjūspan* [cf. H. *kañjūs*], m. = **कंजूसी**.

कंजूसी *kañjūsī* [cf. H. *kañjūs*], f. miserliness, stinginess.

कंटक *kaṇṭak* [S.], m. & adj. **1.** m. a thorn. **2.** fig. a source of hurt or trouble; a troublesome person. — **कंटकाकीर्ण** [°*ka*+*ā*°], adj. scattered with thorns (a path): thorny, troublesome.

कंटकित *kaṇṭakit* [S.], adj. thorny.

कंटकी *kaṇṭakī* [S.], adj. thorny.

कँटार *kaṁṭār* [**kaṇṭāla-*], adj. reg. (Raj.) thorny.

कँटिया *kaṁṭiyā* [cf. H. *kāṁṭā*], f. *Pl. HŚS.* **1.** a hook. **2.** a fish-hook.

कँटीला *kaṁṭīlā* [cf. *kaṇṭin-*], adj. **1.** thorny, prickly; barbed. **2.** prickly, difficult (of temperament). **3.** long and shapely (eyes). — **~ तार**, m. barbed wire.

कंठ *kaṇṭh* [S.], m. **1.** the neck, throat. **2.** the Adam's apple. **~ निकलना**, the Adam's apple to develop: to arrive at puberty. **3.** fig. the voice. **~ फूटना**, a voice, or the sound of singing, to be suddenly heard. **~ रुँधना**, the voice to be choked. — **~ करना**, to memorise. **~ बैठना**, the throat to become hoarse. **~ लगाना (को)**, to embrace (one: = **गले लगाना**). **~ होना**, to be memorised. **उसे बहुत-सी कविताएँ ~ हैं**, he knows many poems by heart. – **कंठगत**, adj. in (one's) throat: **उसका हृदय कंठगत हो गया था**, his heart was in his mouth. **कंठ-तालव्य**, adj. *gram. Pl. HŚS.* gutturo-palatal or mid-front (vowel sounds: viz. /e/, /əi/). **कंठ-मणि**, f. a jewel worn at the throat. **कंठ-माला**, f. a necklace; reg. an infection, or other complaint, of the throat. **कंठस्थ**, adj. known by heart. **कंठाग्र** [°*ṭha*+*a*°], m. learned by heart. **कंठौष्ठ्य** [°*ṭha*+*o*°], adj. *gram. Pl. HŚS.* gutturo-labial or mid-back (vowel sounds: viz. /o/, /əu/).

कंठला *kaṇṭhlā* [cf. *kaṇṭhaka-*], m. **1.** a necklace of pieces of gold or silver, &c. **2.** such a necklace as put on children to avert evil (= **कंठी**).

कंठा *kaṇṭhā* [*kaṇṭhaka-*], m. a gold necklace; a necklace (of large beads).

कंठी *kaṇṭhī* [cf. H. *kaṇṭhā* (or *kaṇṭhikā-*)], f. a necklace of small beads; a Vaiṣṇava rosary.

कंठ्य *kaṇṭhyă* [S.], adj. & m. **1.** adj. having to do with the throat, guttural; velar. **2.** m. a velar sound or letter. **3.** a central vowel sound or letter (/ə/, /a/). — **कंठ्याक्षर** [°*ya*+*a*°], m. a letter denoting a velar sound.

कंडा *kaṇḍā* [? *kāṇḍa-*], m. **1.** a piece of dry dung (to be distinguished from *uplā*, a dung-cake). 2. = **उपला**.

कंडाल *kaṇḍāl*, m. **1.** *HŚS.* a wide-mouthed vessel of brass or iron. **2.** *Pl. HŚS.* a musical instrument made of brass.

[1]**कंडी** *kaṇḍī* [cf. H. *kaṇḍā*], f. 1. = **कंडा**. **2.** reg. a container for burning cow-dung fuel, a stove.

[2]**कंडी** *kaṇḍī* [*karaṇḍa-*[1]], f. a basket; a long, deep basket.

कंडील *kaṇḍīl* [A. *qandīl* ×Engl. *candle*], f. a lampshade.

कंडु *kaṇḍu* [S.], m. f. itching; a skin complaint.

कंडुआ *kaṇḍuā*, m. reg. a fungus that attacks cereals: rust; ergot.

कंडौरा *kaṇḍaurā* [conn. H. *kaṇḍā*], m. **1.** a place where cow-dung is kept, or where cow-dung cakes are made. **2.** a pile of cow-dung cakes.

कंत *kant* [S.], m. lover, dear husband.

कंथा *kanthā* [S.], f. a patched cloth or garment (associated with yogis and ascetics); = **गुदड़ी**. — **कंथाधारी**, adj. wearing a *kanthā*; a yogī, &c.

कंद *kand* [S.], m. a bulbous root; an onion; a partic. root, *Arum campanulatum* (*Pl*). **2.** Brbh. a lump, or sthg. round. — **कंद-मूल**, m. roots of different sorts; a partic. vegetable. **आनंद-कंद**, m. root, or source, of bliss.

क़ंद *qand* [A. *qand*, ← P.], m. U. white crystallised sugar.

कंदन *kandan*, m. *Pl. HŚS.* extirpating, destroying (cf. **निकंदन**).

कंदर *kandar* [S.], m. Av. a cave, cavern.

कंदरा *kandără* [S.], f. a cave, cavern; abyss.

कंदर्प *kandarp* [S.], m. *hind.* a title of Kāma, the god of love.

कंदल *kandal* [S.], m. **1.** Brbh. war, battle. **2.** 19c. young shoot or sprig.

कंदला *kandlā*, m. *Pl. HŚS.* **1.** an ingot of gold or silver. **2.** gold or silver wire.

कंदसार *kandsār* [cf. *sāra-*: ? conn. H. *kānh*], m. *Pl. HŚS.* a stag, a deer.

कंदा *kandā* [*kanda-*: ? ← Drav.], m. a bulbous root; a squill, *Scilla indica*, or *Urginea indica*.

क़ंदील *qandīl*, f. = क़िंदील.

कंदुक *kanduk* [S.], m. a ball.

कँदूरी *kaṁdūrī* [conn. *kandūraka-*], f. reg. = कुंदुर.

कंधर *kandhar* [S.], m. Av. the neck.

कंधा *kandhā* [*skandha-*], m. the shoulder. — ~ डालना, to throw off the yoke (an ox); fig. to give way, to lose heart. ~ देना, to take (a corpse on its bier: को) on the shoulder; to lend a shoulder, or hand (in, में). ~ लगना, a shoulder (of an animal, को) to be galled. कंधे चढ़ाना, to place (a child) on one's shoulder. कंधे से ~ छिलना, shoulders to be peeled: a dense crowd to form. कंधे से ~ भिड़ाना, or मिलाना, or लगाना, fig. to join forces, to work together. कंधे से लगाना, to lay (a child) against one's shoulder.

कँधियाना *kaṁdhiyānā* [cf. H. *kandhā*], v.t. to shoulder (sthg).

कँधेला *kaṁdhelā* [cf. *skandha-*], m. **1.** Brbh. the end of a sari worn over the shoulder. **2.** *Pl.* saddle-cloth; pack-saddle.

कंप *kamp* [S.], m. trembling, shaking; tremor. — कंपमान, adj. tremulous, shaking.

कँपकँपी *kaṁpkaṁpī* [cf. H. *kăṁpnā*], f. a shivering, shiver.

कंपन *kampan* [S.], m. a trembling, shaking, quivering; shivering.

कँपना *kaṁpnā* [*kampate*], v.i. to tremble (= काँपना).

कंपनी *kampănī* [Engl. *company*], f. **1.** a company. **2.** specif. *hist.* The East India Company. **3.** company, companionship. — कंपनी-बाग़, m. botanical gardens; a public garden, domain. कंपनी-राज, ~ का राज, m. *hist.* the (East India) Company's rule.

कंपा *kampā* [*kampa-*], m. a long stick, or the end section of a long rod, on which bird-lime is smeared (used by fowlers); a snare. — ~ मारना, or लगाना, to catch (birds) with a *kampā*; to ensnare.

कँपाना *kaṁpānā* [cf. H. *kāṁpnā*], v.t. to cause to tremble, or to shake.

कंपायमान *kampāyămān* [S.], adj. trembling; tremulous.

कंपास *kampās* [Engl. *compass*], m. **1.** a compass, pair of compasses; a theodolite, or similar instrument. **2.** a magnetic compass. — ~ लगाना, to set up a theodolite, &c.; to make a survey (of, का). ~ का महकमा, m. *hist.* the Indian land survey department. – कंपासवाला, m. a surveyor.

कंपित *kampit* [S.], adj. **1.** made to tremble or to shake; trembling; tremulous. **2.** fear-stricken, fearful.

कंपू *kampū* [Engl. *camp*: ? *-ū-* ← H. *urdū*], m. obs. *mil.* a camp. — ~ चढ़ाना, to strike camp.

कंबल *kambal* [*kambala-*[1]: ? ← Austro-as.], m. a blanket. — ~ डालकर, adv. under the blanket: (doing sthg.) surreptitiously. काले ~ पर रंग चढ़ाना, to attempt the impossible; to waste one's time or efforts.

कंबु *kambu* [S.], m. a conch shell. — कंबुकंठ, adj. & m. having a neck marked with three auspicious lines or folds suggestive of a conch shell; a neck so marked. °-धर, adj. Brbh. id.

कंबोज *kamboj* [S.], m. **1.** the region of Kamboj, Cambay. **2.** *mus.* the name of a *rāg*.

कँवल *kaṁval*, m. = कमल. — कँवल-बाई, f. reg. jaundice.

कँसताल *kaṁstāl* [H. *kāṁsā*+H. *tāl*], m. Brbh. cymbals.

कँसार *kaṁsār* [conn. *kāṁsyakāra-*], m. reg. an engraver on metal.

कँसुआ *kaṁsuā* [cf. *kāśa-*], m. reg. a caterpillar that attacks young shoots of sugar-cane.

-क *-kă*, adv. encl. Brbh. Av. indeed. — कबहुं ~, adv. sometimes, indeed.

कई *kaī* [*katipaya-*], pron. & adj. several, a few. — ~ एक, pl. some few (particular ones). ~ बार, several times.

ककड़ासिंगी *kakṛāsiṅgī*, f. = काकड़ासिंगी.

ककड़ी *kakṛī* [*karkaṭikā-*], f. a type of cucumber, or melon resembling the cucumber, *Cucumis utilissimus*. — ककड़ी-खीरा समझना, to think of (one) as insignificant or contemptible.

ककना *kaknā* [*kaṅkaṇa-*], m. reg. **1.** a metal bangle. **2.** (Bihar) a partic. weed which chokes crops.

ककनूँ *kaknūṁ* [A. *qaqnūs*], m. Av. the phoenix (bird).

ककमारी *kakmārī*, f. *Pl. HŚS.* the plant *Anamirta cocculus* (the seeds of which yield a poison that can be used to kill fish).

ककहरा *kakahrā* [? cf. H. [1]*kakkā*], m. the Indian syllabary; the alphabet, ABC.

ककुभ *kakubh* [S.], m. poet. sthg. high, or projecting; a part of a vīṇā.

ककोड़ा *kakoṛā* [*karkoṭaka-*], m. a cucurbitaceous plant resembling the *parval*, of which the fruit is red when ripe.

ककोरना *kakornā*, v.t. reg. to scratch; to scoop out (= कुरेदना).

कक्कड़ *kakkaṛ*, m. *Pl.* **1.** cut tobacco. **2.** a kind of hookah.

[1]**कक्का** *kakkā* [cf. *ka-kāra-*], m. reg. (N). = ककार s.v. क.

[2]**कक्का** *kakkā*, m. reg. (N). = काका.

कक्ष *kakṣ* [S.], m. **1.** the armpit or adjoining area. ***2.** a private room, or quarters, within a house or other building; the women's quarters of a house. **3.** a public room in a large building. व्याख्यान ~, m. lecture room. **4.** ? a porch, or other outbuilding attached to a house.

कक्षा *kakṣā* [S.], f. **1.** orbit (of a heavenly body). ***2.** a class (school, university, &c). **3.** rank, class: similarity, comparison.

कखरी *kakhrī* [cf. *kakṣā-*], f. reg. the armpit.

कखौरी *kakhaurī* [? *kakṣapuṭa-*], f. a boil or other swelling in the armpit.

कगार *kagār*, f. **1.** overhanging section (as of a cliff or bank, or of an arch); cornice. **2.** raised section (as of a wall or roof); a parapet. **3.** a slope, incline.

कगारा *kagārā*, m. = कगार, 1.

[1]**कच** *kac* [S.], m. the hair (of the head).

[2]**कच** *kac*, m. **1.** sound of cutting, cleaving (as of a blade into fruit, or flesh). **2.** squelching sound (as of a foot in mud).

[3]**कच-** *kac-*. = कच्चा: — कचदिला, adj. irresolute; cowardly. °-दिली, f. कचपेंदिया, m. without a stable base: an unstable person; a weak, fickle or undependable person. कच-बच, m. colloq. children, kids. कचलोहा, m. iron ore; pig-iron. कचलोंदा, m. an unworked lump (as of dough).

कचक *kacak* [cf. H. *kacaknā*], f. *Pl. HŚS.* **1.** a jerk, shock; shooting pain. **2.** a strain, or sprain.

कच-कच *kac-kac*, f. **1.** grating sound; crunching sound. **2.** chatter, hubbub; wrangling. — ~ करना, to wrangle; to chatter.

कचकचाना *kackacāna* [cf. H. *kac-kac*], v.i. v.t. **1.** v.i. to be or to feel gritty, to grate. **2.** to chatter (as voices); to wrangle. **3.** v.t. to grate, to grind (the teeth).

कचकचाहट *kackacāhaṭ* [cf. H. *kackacānā*], f. wrangling, altercation; confusion.

कचकना *kacaknā* [cf. **kacc-*[1]], v.i. **1.** to be jerked. **2.** to be sprained; to be twisted.

कचकाना *kackānā* [cf. H. *kacaknā*], v.t. reg. **1.** to jerk, to twist. **2.** to break or to snap (a small branch).

कचकेला *kackelā*, m. reg. a kind of plantain grown for its half-ripe fruit (used as a vegetable).

कचकोल *kackol* [P. *kackūl*], m. f. *Pl. HŚS.* a beggar's cup or bowl.

कचड़ा *kacṛā*, m. = [1]कचरा, 2., 3.

कचनार *kacnār* [*kāñcanāra-*: Pk. *kaṁcaṇāra-*], m. **1.** a moderate-sized deciduous tree, *Bauhinia variegata*. **2.** an erect shrub, *Bauhinia tomentosa*.

कच-पच *kac-pac* [cf. **kacc-*[2]: Pk. *kacc-*], m. f. & adj. **1.** m. a crowd, dense mass. **2.** adj. packed, crowded, crammed together.

कचपचिया *kacpaciyā* [cf. H. *kac-pac*], adj. crowded together: — ~ नक्षत्र, m. the Pleiades.

कचपची *kacpacī* [cf. H. *kacpaciyā*], f. Brbh. Av. the Pleiades.

कचपन *kacpan*, m. reg. = कच्चापन.

कचमच *kacmac*, f. colloq. babble, gibberish.

कचर-कचर *kacar-kacar*, f. **1.** the sound of sthg. juicy being eaten. **2.** fig. aimless chatter, or quarrelling.

कचरना *kacarnā*, v.i. **1.** to be trampled. **2.** to be mixed in (as flour into liquid).

[1]**कचरा** *kacrā* [conn. *karcūraka-*], m. **1.** an aromatic root of the genus *Curcuma*, zedoary. **2.** [× H. *kaccā*] a small unripe melon (*Cucumis momordica*, = फूट). **3.** [× H. *kaccā*] an unripe cucumber.

[2]**कचरा** *kacrā* [*kaccara-*[1]], m. **1.** rubbish, sweepings, straw; husks. **2.** *Pl. HŚS.* a pod of the cotton-tree (*semal*).

कचरी *kacrī* [*karcūra-*], f. 1. = [1]कचरा, 1. **2.** [? × H. *kaccā*] a small green and yellow striped melon.

कचलोन *kaclon* [cf. *lavaṇa-*], m. *Pl. HŚS.* black salt (= काली नमक).

कचवा- *kacvā-* [? cf. H. *kaccā*], v.i. Brbh. ? to be irritated.

कचवाट *kacvāṭ* [cf. H. *kacvā-*], f. reg. irritation; aversion.

कचहरिया *kacahriyā* [cf. H. *kacahrī*], adj. having to do with a court.

कचहरी *kacahrī* [**kr̥tyagharikā-*], f. **1.** a court. **2.** a public office. **3.** the people assembled, esp. in a court, or office: a crowd; company, group. **4.** the business of a court, or office. — ~ करना, to hold a court; to carry on official work. ~ का, adj. pertaining to a court or office; official. ~ चढ़ना, to go to court. ~ बरख़ास्त करना, to close, or to adjourn a court, &c. ~ लगना, a court to be established; colloq. a crowd to collect. ~ लगाना, to make a great to-do, or a great case (of sthg).

कचाई *kacāī* [cf. H. *kaccā*], f. unripeness, &c. (see कच्चा).

[1]**कचाकच** *kacākac* [cf. **kacc-*[2]: Pk. *kacc-*], adj. densely packed, crowded (= खचाखच).

[2]**कचाकच** *kacākac* [cf. **kacc-*[1]], f. reg. a pulling: squabble, brawl.

कचालू *kacālū*, m. **1.** a kind of *arvī*, or *baṇḍā* (qq. v). **2.** a salad. — ~ बनाना, colloq. to beat to a pulp.

[1]**कचिया** *kaciyā* [conn. H. *kaccā*], adj. reg. timid; shy.

[2]**कचिया** *kaciyā*, m. *Pl. HŚS.* a sickle.

कचियाना *kaciyānā* [cf. H. [1]*kaciyā*], v.i. reg. to be timid, or shy; to draw back (from).

कचूमर *kacūmar*, m. **1.** sliced mango or other fruit (for pickling). **2.** sweet fruit pickle. — ~ करना, or निकालना, colloq. to make mincemeat (of, की), to beat to a pulp; to ruin (through misuse). ~ निकलना, fig. to be at one's wits' end.

कचूर *kacūr* [conn.*karcūra-*], m. & adj. **1.** m. the tuberous plant zedoary (= जदवार). **2.** adj. dark green; reddish green.

कचूरना *kacūrnā*, v.t. reg. **1.** to crush; to pound. **2.** to cut up, to slice. **3.** to pull or to pick to pieces.

कचोका *kacokā*, m. *Pl.* piercing; stab, blow.

कचोट *kacoṭ*, f. vexation, galling feeling.

कचोटना *kacoṭnā*, v.i. & v.t. **1.** v.i. to feel vexation. **2.** v.t. to vex, to gall.

कचोना *kaconā* [? Panj. *kacoṇā*], v.t. *Pl. HŚS.* to pierce; to stab.

कचौड़ी *kacauṛī* [**kaccapūpaḍa-*], f. a kind of *pūrī* having a filling of lentils or vegetables, and deep-fried.

कचौरी *kacaurī* [**kaccapūra-*], f. = कचौड़ी.

कच्चा *kaccā* [**kacca-*[1]], adj. & m. **1.** adj. uncooked; untreated, raw (as unfired brick, unslaked lime). ~ माल, m. raw material(s). **2.** unripe, green (as fruit, wood). ~ फोड़ा, m. a boil not come to a head. **3.** crude, partly processed (as paper, raw sugar, pig-iron). **4.** immature, crude; undigested. ~ चिट्ठा, m. a rigmarole; ~ चिट्ठा खोलना, to tell a whole (discreditable) story. ~ बच्चा, m. a very young child. ~ हाल, m. an unvarnished story; a *bona fide* account. कच्ची उमर, f. immature age, or years. कच्चे दिन, m. pl. the first four or five months of pregnancy. **5.** rough, sketchy; preliminary, provisional. कच्ची आमदनी, f. gross proceeds. कच्ची बही, f. rough book; कच्ची सिलाई, f. tacking, basting (of a garment). **6.** unfinished, incomplete. कच्ची सड़क, f. an unmetalled or unsealed road. **7.** imperfectly known or acquired, or skilled. कच्चे अक्षर, m. pl. poorly formed characters (script); unpractised writing. अँग्रेज़ी में ~, inexperienced in using English; weak in English. **8.** inexperienced, simple; stupid. **9.** deficient; not fast (dye); not permanently confirmed (in tenure: a cultivator); undependable (a person). **10.** unsound, false; incorrect, unreliable (as advice); invalid (a document); discreditable (remarks). ~ पड़ना, to turn out incorrect (a statement, &c). **11.** unsteady, unstable. ~ करना, to make angry, to irritate; to discourage, to dissuade (from a purpose, से); to shame; to frighten. **12.** timid; tender. ~ जी, m. a faint heart; tender heart. **13.** m. preliminary work: a plan, sketch, draft; basting stitch. — ~ खाना, to eat raw; fig. to eat (one) alive. ~ कोढ़, m. reg. syphilis. कच्ची गोटी, or गोटियाँ, खेलना, to play with earthen pieces: = next. कच्ची गोली, or गोलियाँ, खेलना, to play with earthen marbles: to do sthg. childish; to act in an immature way. – कच्चा-पक्का, adj. half-cooked or prepared; half-ripe; built partly of baked bricks and partly of mud; partly finished (work); crude; conjectural, uncertain. कच्चा-पक्का करना, to cook or to prepare partially; to leave incomplete; to spoil. कच्ची-पक्की, f. abuse; a mixture of things of different quality. कच्चे-पक्के दिन, m. pl. = कच्चे दिन.

कच्चापन *kaccāpan* [cf. H. *kaccā*], m. unripeness, &c. (see कच्चा).

कच्चावट *kaccāvaṭ* [cf. H. *kaccā*], f. = कच्चाहट.

कच्चाहट *kaccāhaṭ* [cf. H. *kaccā*], f. unripeness, &c. (see कच्चा).

कच्चू *kaccū* [? ad. *kacu-*], m. a tuberous arum plant, taro (*Colocasia antiquorum*: = अरवी).

[1]**कच्छ** *kacch* [S.], m. Brbh. low-lying ground (by a river, or the sea).

[2]**कच्छ** *kacch* [ad. *kaccha(pa)-*], m. Brbh. = कच्छप.

[3]**कच्छ** *kacch* [ad. *kakṣyā̆-*], m. reg. the end of the *dhotī* drawn between the legs.

कच्छप *kacchap* [S.], m. **1.** a tortoise, turtle. **2.** the second or tortoise avatār of Viṣṇu.

कच्छपी *kacchapī* [S.], f. a female tortoise.

कच्छा *kacchā* [*kakṣyā-*], m. reg. a tight loin-cloth.

कच्छी *kacchī* [cf. H. [1]*kacch*], adj. & f. **1.** adj. of or belonging to Cutch. **2.** f. the speech of Cutch.

कछ *kach* [ad. *kakṣa-*], m. reg. side; flank.

कछना *kachnā*, m. 1. = कछनी. **2.** shorts.

कछनी *kachnī* [cf. *kakṣyā-*], f. the *dhotī*, worn drawn up round the thighs. — ~ काछे, adv. with *dhotī* worn drawn up high.

कछवारा *kachvārā* [*kaccha-+vāṭa-*[1]], m. reg. market gardeners' land.

कछवाह *kachvāh*, m. Brbh. = कछवाहा.

कछवाहा *kachvāhā*, m. *hist.* name of a Rājpūt community.

कछार *kachār* [cf. *kaccha-*], m. **1.** low, wet land (by a river). **2.** bank (of a river). **3.** alluvial land.

कछारना *kachārnā*, v.t. to wash; to rinse.

[1]**कछारी** *kachārī* [cf. H. *kachār*], adj. alluvial (land).

[2]**कछारी** *kachārī*, f. reg. a water-pot having a wide mouth; churning-pot.

कछियाना *kachiyānā*, m. *Pl. HŚS.* = कछवारा.

कछु *kachu* [conn. *kaścid*], pron. & adj. Brbh. Av. = कुछ.

[1]**कछुआ** *kachuā* [*kacchapa-*], m. a tortoise, turtle.

[2]**कछुआ** *kachuā* [*kakṣa-*[1]; ? w. H. [1]*kachua*], m. *Pl.* a side; one side or half (of a yoke).

कछुई *kachuī* [cf. H. *kachuā*], f. a female tortoise.

कछुक *kachuk*, pron. and adv. Brbh. = कुछ.

कचछौटा *kacchauṭā* [**kakṣapaṭṭa-*: Pk. *kachoṭī-*], m. the *dhotī*, worn drawn up round the thighs. — ~ खोलकर भाग जाना, fig. to take to one's heels.

कछौहा *kachauhā*, m. reg. land in low situations.

कज *kaj* [P. *kaj*], adj. & m. **1.** adj. crooked; awry. **2.** m. crookedness. **3.** fault. **4.** hang, lurk (in cloth). — ~ निकालना (का), to straighten, to straighten out. – कज-अदाई, f. U. perverseness; cross mannerism, crossness. कज-फ़हमी, f. 19c. U. stupidity.

कजरा *kajrā* [cf. H. *kajlā*], adj. & m. **1.** adj. soot-coloured, black. **2.** having black applied to the eyes. **3.** m. lampblack, &c. (= काजल).

कजरारा *kajrārā*, adj. **1.** soot-coloured, black (eyes, clouds). **2.** painted with lampblack, &c. (the eyes).

कजरी *kajrī*, f. Brbh. = कजली.

कजरीवन *kajrīvan* [f. *kadalī-* (← Austro-as.): cf. P. *zulmāt*, pl. 'dark place'], f. Av. name of a legendary forest where ascetics lived, and where the water of life was said to be found.

कजला *kajlā*, m. = काजल.

कजलाना *kajlānā* [cf. H. *kājal*], v.i. & v.t. **1.** v.i. to be dark (as from application of lampblack). **2.** fig. to die (a fire); to smoulder. **3.** to moulder; to become mildewed. **4.** v.t. to apply lampblack (to the eyes).

कजली *kajlī* [H. *kajlā*], f. a type of song song in the month Sāvan.

कजलौटा *kajlauṭā* [**kajjalavarta*], m. a pot for lampblack.

कजलौटी *kajlauṭī* [**kajjalavarta-*], f. a small pot for lampblack.

क़ज़ा *qazā* [A. *qaẓā*], m. U. **1.** decree. **2.** fate; death.

क़ज़ाक़ *qazāq* [T. *kazàk*], m. Brbh. cossack: a robber, bandit.

क़ज़ाक़ी *qazāqī* [P. *qazzāqī*], f. Brbh. robbery.

क़ज़िया *qaziyā* [A. *qaẓīya*], m. a dispute; a legal case.

कजी *kajī* [P. *kajī*], f. Brbh. crookedness: fault, deficiency.

कज्जल *kajjal*, m. = काजल.

कट- *kaṭ-*, pronun. var. = कठ-.

कटक *kaṭak* [S.], m. **1.** Brbh. Av. an army, host. **2.** Brbh. bracelet.

कटकट *kaṭkaṭ*, f. m. **1.** knocking together: chattering (of teeth); clicking, tapping, &c. **2.** wrangling, squabbling. — ~ करना, to chatter, to tap, &c.

कटकटाना *kaṭkaṭānā* [cf. **kaṭṭ-*], v.t. & v.i. **1.** v.t. = किटकिटाना. **2.** v.i. reg. to knock together: to chatter (the teeth).

कटकटी *kaṭkaṭī* [cf. **kaṭṭ-*], f. **1.** grating, grinding (the teeth). **2.** colloq. reg. trouble.

कटकना *kaṭkanā*, m. **1.** reg. model, pattern (to copy). **2.** *hist.* a sub-lease. **3.** reg. art, skill.

कटकरंज *kaṭkarañj*, m. the fever-nut, *Caesalpinia bonducella* (a thorny bush, the seeds of which are used in treating fever).

कटका *kaṭkā*, m. reg. pecking (at sthg). — ~ **भरना**, to peck (at).

कटकाई *kaṭkāī* [? cf. H. *kaṭak*], f. Av. army.

कटकेना *kaṭkenā*, m. *hist.* = **कटकना**, 2.

कटखना *kaṭkhanā* [? H. *kāṭnā*, *khānā*], adj. liable to bite.

1**कटड़ा** *kaṭṛā* [cf. *kaṇṭa-*2], m. **1.** *hist.* an enclosed and inhabited piece of land; market town belonging to a fort. ***2.** market, local bazaar.

2**कटड़ा** *kaṭṛā* [cf. **kaṭṭa-*2], m. a buffalo calf.

कटना *kaṭnā* [cf. H. *kāṭnā*], v.i. **1.** to be cut; to be harvested (grain). **2.** to be cut off, or cut away; to be written out (a cheque). **3.** to be killed (as in battle); to be killed (as by a train); to be slaughtered. **4.** to be deducted (from, **से**). **5.** to be removed (from, **से**: as a name from a list). **6.** to be squandered (money). **7.** to be spent (time); to be endured, lived through. **8.** to be ended (as tribulations). **9.** to disappear, to be removed; to be effaced; to be faded, bleached (colour); to be annulled (sins). **10.** to be countered or made ineffective (as a playing card when trumped). **11.** to avoid, to shun (another). **कटकर चला जाना**, id. **12.** to run off, to diverge (from, **में से**: a branch road, or canal). **13.** to be divisible (a number by, **से**, another). **14.** fig. to be hurt, wounded; to be ashamed, or humiliated. **मैं मन में कटा जा रहा था**, I felt greatly hurt, &c. — **कटा**, m. a cut, wound; cutting; bloodshed, slaughter, massacre. **कटा कर-**, Brbh. to kill (heartlessly). **कटा-कटी**, f. cutting and trimming; retrenchment; = **कटा**, 3. **कटा-छँटा**, adj. cut and cleared: pruned. **कटा-छनी** [H. *channā*], f. fierce fighting, carnage. **कटा-फटा**, adj. mutilated. **कटा-मारी**, f. carnage (= **कटा**, 3).

कटनास *kaṭnās*, m. Av. a kind of bird (? a jay).

1**कटनी** *kaṭnī* [*kartana-*1], f. **1.** cutting, esp. harvesting. **2.** harvest-time. **3.** wages for harvesting. — ~ **करना (की)**, to harvest. ~ **मारना**, to cut or to dig out weeds (in a field, before ploughing).

2**कटनी** *kaṭnī* [? H. *kaṭarnī*], f. reg. a knife; a potter's tool.

कटर *kaṭar*, m. = **कुटर**.

कटरा *kaṭrā*, m. = 1 2**कटड़ा**.

कटवाँ *kaṭvāṁ* [cf. H. *kaṭnā*], adj. formed by cutting: **1.** cut up, split up. **2.** figured (ornamentation); notched, toothed (as an arch). **3.** deducted.

कटवाँसी *kaṭvāṁsī* [**kāṣṭhavaṁśa-*], f. reg. (W). a knotty bamboo.

कटवाना *kaṭvānā* [cf. H. *kāṭnā*], v.t. to cause to be cut, &c. (by, **से**).

कटहरा *kaṭahrā*, m. = **कठघरा** (see s.v. **कठ-**).

कटहल *kaṭ'hal* [conn. *kaṇṭaphala-*], m. the Indian bread-fruit tree, or jack-fruit.

कटहा *kaṭ'hā*, adj. liable to bite.

कटा *kaṭā*, m. see s.v. **कटना**.

1**कटाई** *kaṭāī* [cf. H. *kaṭānā*], f. **1.** cutting; reaping; mowing. **2.** harvest-time. **3.** price, or dues paid, for cutting, &c. **4.** cutting off, trimming (a coin). — ~ **करना (की)**, to cut, &c. ~ **के दिनों में**, adv. at harvest-time. – **कटाई-छँटाई**, f. cutting back, pruning.

2**कटाई** *kaṭāī*, f. *Pl. HŚS.* a tall thorny shrub having a purple flower (= **भटकटैया**).

कटाऊ *kaṭāū* [cf. H. *kaṭānā*], adj. reg. cutting, biting; sharp (as remarks).

कटाक्ष *kaṭākṣ* [S.], m. **1.** a sidelong glance (at, **पर**). **2.** a flirtatious glance. **3.** fig. an aspersion. — ~ **करना**, to look sidelong, or askance (at).

कटान *kaṭān* [cf. H. *kaṭānā*], f. **1.** cutting; cut, style. 2. = **कटाव**, 4.

कटाना *kaṭānā* [cf. H. *kāṭnā*], v.t. to cause to be cut, &c. (by, **से**). — **टिकट कटा लाना**, to go and get a ticket.

कटार *kaṭār* [**karttāra-*: Pk. *kaṭṭārī-*], f. a dagger. — ~ **उतारना (में)**, to stab with a dagger. ~ **मारना (को)**, id.

कटारा *kaṭārā* [*kaṇṭakāra-*], m. plant of the genus *Echinops* or ? *Agave*.

कटारी *kaṭārī* [**karttāra-*: Pk. *kaṭṭārī-*], f. a small dagger.

कटाव *kaṭāv* [cf. H. *kaṭānā*], m. **1.** cutting, reaping. **2.** harvest, crop (= 1**कटाई**). **3.** cutting, section. **4.** erosion; breach. **5.** bank (as of a river). **6.** terseness (of language); tenseness (of manner). **7.** cutting or sarcastic quality (of speech). **8.** tracery, floral patterning (on cloth, or stone). **9.** serration (of a leaf, a hem). — **कटावदार** [P. *-dār*], adj. serrated.

कटास *kaṭās* [conn. *khaṭṭāśa-*], m. *Pl. HŚS.* an animal of the weasel family (= 2**खटास**).

कटाह *kaṭāh* [S.], m. = **कड़ाह**.

कटि *kaṭi* S.], f. the waist; the loins. — **कटि-ज़ेब** [P. *-zeb*], f. Brbh. waist ornament: woman's belt, girdle. **कटि-बंध**, m. belt, girdle; *geog.* zone, area. कटिबद्ध, adj. having the loins girt: ready, prepared.

¹**कटिया** *kaṭiyā*, f. reg. **1.** a small vessel of wood (cf. कठिया) or earth. **2.** [× *kanṭha-*] a milk-can having a long neck. **3.** a buffalo calf (cf. ²कटड़ा). **4.** reg. (E.) = ¹कटनी, 2.

²**कटिया** *kaṭiyā* [cf. H. *kāṁṭā*], f. a fishing-hook.

कटी *kaṭī* [cf. H. *kāṭnā*], f. a slashing stroke (with a sword).

¹**कटीला** *kaṭīlā*, adj. = कँटीला.

²**कटीला** *kaṭīlā*, adj. reg. cutting: **1.** sharp-edged. **2.** caustic. **3.** ardent, active (soldier, or army).

कटु *kaṭu* [S.], adj. **1.** pungent, sharp. **2.** bitter. **3.** keen, sharp (as a pang). **4.** cutting (a remark, criticism); harsh.

कटुआ *kaṭuā* [cf. H. *kaṭnā*], m. reg. **1.** Bihar. husks, or cut stalks used for fodder. **2.** W. a beetle that attacks rice. **3.** irrigation done by breaching the bank of a water-channel.

कटुता *kaṭutā* [S.], f. **1.** pungency, sharpness. **2.** bitterness. **3.** keenness (as of regret). **4.** severity (of a remark, a criticism). **5.** antagonism, enmity.

¹**कटैया** *kaṭaiyā* [cf. H. *kāṭnā*], m. Brbh. one who cuts, cutter.

²**कटैया** *kaṭaiyā* [*kanṭakita-*], m. reg. **1.** a prickly shrub. **2.** a coarse grass growing on waste land. — बन-कटैया, m. *Pl.* a thistle-like plant. भट-कटैया, m. a tall prickly shrub having a purple flower.

कटोरदान *kaṭordān* [H. *kaṭorā*+P. *-dān*], m. a metal vessel with a cover.

कटोरा *kaṭorā* [**kaṭṭora-*: Pk. *kaṭṭoraga-*], m. **1.** a shallow metal cup, or bowl. **2.** cup (of a flower). — ~ चलाना, reg. to make a cup turn round (by magic, to find out the identity of a thief).

कटोरी *kaṭorī* [cf. H. *kaṭorā*], f. **1.** a small shallow metal cup, or bowl. **2.** cup (of a flower). **3.** cup (of brassiere); gusset.

कटौती *kaṭautī* [? cf. H. *kaṭā(v)nā*], f. **1.** a cut (in any amount); reduction (in a rate, level). **2.** discount.

कटौवल *kaṭauval* [? cf. H. *kaṭā(v)nā*], f. esp. in comp. killing, slaughtering. — मार-कटौवल, f. id.

कटौसी *kaṭausī* [**kāṣṭhavaṁśa-*], f. reg. = कटवाँसी.

कट्टर *kaṭṭar* [? conn. H. *kaṭṭā*], adj. **1.** unyielding; strict (esp. in belief or practice); strictly orthodox (a Hindu). **2.** bigoted; fanatical. **3.** inveterate (as enmity). — कट्टर-पंथी, m. a fanatic.

कट्टरता *kaṭṭartā* [cf. H. *kaṭṭar*], f. = कट्टरपन.

कट्टरपन *kaṭṭarpan* [cf. H. *kaṭṭar*], m. **1.** strictness (of view or practice). **2.** bigotry. **3.** inveteracy; fanaticism.

¹**कट्टा** *kaṭṭā*, adj. **1.** strong, sturdy. **2.** hard, stiff. **3.** fig. determined; implacable. — हट्टा-कट्टा, m. = ~, 1.

²**कट्टा** *kaṭṭā*, m. reg. a big fat louse.

कट्ठा *kaṭṭhā*, m. reg. **1.** a measure of land (80 sq. yds). **2.** a corn measure of five *ser*.

कठंदर *kaṭhandar*, m. swelling of the stomach.

कठ- *kaṭh-*. **1.** having to do with, or like, wood; wooden. **2.** pej. unfeeling, insensitive; stultified. — कठ-केला, m. reg. a kind of wild plantain. कठघरा, m. a large wooden cage; railing; witness-box, dock. कठ-पुतली, f. a wooden doll, puppet; a frail girl. कठ-पुतली का नाच, m. a puppet show. हाथ की कठ-पुतली, f. a puppet in the hand (of, के). कठफोड़ा, m. a woodpecker. कठबढ़ैया [cf. H. *baṛhaī*], f. id. कठबेल, m. the wood-apple (= कैथ). कठबोली [ad. *ṣaḍ-*], f. a crude jargon. कठमस्त, adj. sturdy, burly; crassly overbearing. °आ, adj. reg. id. कठमुल्ला, m. an ignorant mullah or schoolteacher; a bigot. कठवैद्य, m. an ignorant doctor.

कठरा *kaṭhrā* [cf. *kāṣṭha-*], m. 1. = कठघरा (see s.v. कठ-). **2.** reg. a wooden platter, pot, or trough; wooden board, or block. **3.** reg. a wooden saddle for a camel.

कठारी *kaṭhārī*, f. an ascetic's wooden water-pot with a spout (= कमंडल).

कठिन *kaṭhin* [S.], adj. **1.** hard; sharp (a blade, &c). **2.** harsh. **3.** difficult; burdensome.

कठिनता *kaṭhinătā* [S.], f. = कठिनाई.

कठिनाई *kaṭhināī* [cf. H. *kaṭhin*], f. **1.** hardness; sharpness. **2.** harshness. ***3.** difficulty; burdensomeness. **4.** difficult situation.

कठिया *kaṭhiyā* [cf. H. *kāṭh*], m. & adj. reg. **1.** m. a wooden platter. **2.** a snare, trap. **3.** adj. made of wood.

कठोर *kaṭhor* [S.], adj. **1.** hard. ***2.** harsh (of manner); unfeeling. **3.** uncouth. **4.** arduous (penance, toil).

कठोरता *kaṭhorătā* [S.], f. hardness, harshness, &c. (see कठोर).

कठोरपन *kaṭhorpan* [cf. H. *kaṭhor*], m. = कठोरता.

कठौती *kaṭhautī* [*kāṣṭhapātra-], f. a wooden bowl; small wooden tub, or pot; wooden platter.

कठौवा *kaṭhauvā* [? *kāṣṭhamaya-*], m. = कठौता.

कड़ *kaṛ* [*karaṭa-*], f. the seed of safflower, *Carthamus tinctorius.*

कड़क *kaṛak* [cf. *kaḍati*: H. *kaṛaknā*], f. **1.** a loud sound or report; a crack or peal of thunder; crashing (as of drums). **2.** an ache, continuing pain. **3.** intensity; excess. – **~ चाय,** strong tea.

कड़कड़ *kaṛkaṛ* [cf. H. *kaṛkaṛānā*], adj. crackling, crunching; with a crackling or crunching sound. — **~ चबाना,** to chew, to crunch noisily.

कड़कड़ाना *kaṛkaṛānā* [cf. *kaṭakaṭā-*; also *kiṭakiṭāyate*], v.i. & v.t. **1.** v.i. to crackle (as oil or *ghī* when boiling). **2.** v.t. to cause to crackle: to boil (oil or *ghī*; to melt down (fat). 3. = **किड़किड़ाना.**

कड़कना *kaṛaknā* [*kaṭakka-], v.i. **1.** to crackle, to crash; to thunder; to roar, to growl; to burst into a rage. **2.** to split, to tear. **3.** colloq. to be off ('like a shot'). — **कड़ककर बोलना,** to shout, to rage.

[1]**कड़का** *kaṛkā* [cf. H. *kaṛak*], m. crack, report, crash, &c.

[2]**कड़का** *kaṛkā* [cf. H. *kaṛkī*], adj. colloq. broke.

कड़की *kaṛkī* [M. *kaḍkī*, *kaḍkā*: cf. H. *kaṛaknā*], f. colloq. severity: high prices. — **~ के दिन,** m.pl. hard times.

कड़खा *kaṛkhā* [Pk. *kaḍakkiya-* × *khaṭakh(aṭāyate)*; ? also *ākhyā-*], m. Brbh. a martial song in a partic. metre of long lines, to encourage soldiers at the time of battle; an exultant song or shout; commemoration of the deeds of former heroes. (cf. **करखा**).

कड़खैत *kaṛkhait* [cf. H. *kaṛkhā*], m. Brbh. a singer of *kaṛkhā* songs or exhortations (in Indian armies); a bard (*bhāṭ*); a woman minstrel (*ḍhāṛhī*).

कड़छी *kaṛchī*, f. reg. = **करछी.**

कड़ड़ा *kaṛṛā* [cf. H. [1]*kaṛā*], adj. = [1]**कड़ा.**

कड़ना *kaṛnā* [? conn. *kālayati*[2]], v.t. *Pl.* to pierce, to perforate.

कड़मड़ *kaṛmaṛ* [cf. *kaṭṭ-], m. *Pl.* **1.** a grating or cracking sound (as of a dog gnawing a bone); crunching. **2.** murmuring, grumbling.

कड़मड़ाना *kaṛmaṛānā*, v.i. & v.t. reg. **1.** v.i. to crackle (see **कड़कड़ाना**). **2.** to murmur, to grumble, &c. (see **कुड़कुड़ाना**). **3.** v.t. to gnaw; to crunch.

कड़रबून *kaṛarbūn* [conn. *karaṭa-*[2]: Pk. *karaḍa-*], m. *Pl.* a kind of safflower.

[1]**कड़वा** *kaṛvā* [*kaṭu-*], adj. **1.** bitter; acrid, pungent, sharp; saline, brackish. **2.** disagreeable; harsh, strong; impetuous (of temper), ardent; sour, morose; angry, displeased; coarse, crude. — **~ करना,** to embitter; fig. to squander. **~ ज़हर,** adj. bitter poison: bitter as gall. **~ तेल,** m. fatty oil made from mustard or rape seed. **~ दिल करना,** to grieve (for, **के बारे में**); to show a brave, or a hard, heart; to bear or to suffer without complaint. **~ नीम,** adj. = **~ ज़हर. ~ लगना (को),** to taste bitter, &c.; to be disagreeable (to). **~ होना,** or **हो जाना,** to be or to become bitter; to be or to become surly, displeased, or angry. **कड़वी रोटी,** f. *hind.* the food sent for three days by the relatives of a family in which a death has occurred. **कड़वा-कसैला** (or **कसेला**), adj. bitter and astringent; adverse. **कड़वे-कसैले दिन,** harsh times or days; the days at the change of seasons, or of late pregnancy.

[2]**कड़वा** *kaṛvā* [*kaṭu-*], m. myrrh (= **गुग्गुल**).

कड़वाट *kaṛvāṭ*, f. pronun. var. = **कड़वाहट.**

कड़वाना *kaṛvānā* [cf. H. *kaṛvā*], v.i. reg. **1.** to become bitter, &c.; to feel sore, or to sting (the eyes, as from want of sleep). **2.** to feel bitterness or anger (towards, **से**); to be averse (to), to dislike.

कड़वापन *kaṛvāpan* [cf. H. *kaṛvā*], m. bitterness, pungency, &c.

कड़वास *kaṛvās* [cf. H. *kaṛvā*], f. *Pl.* = **कड़वाहट.**

कड़वाहट *kaṛvāhaṭ* [cf. H. *kaṛvā*], f. bitter taste; bitterness, pungency, &c.

कड़वी *kaṛvī*, f. = **करबी.**

[1]**कड़ा** *kaṛā* [cf. *kaḍḍati*], adj. **1.** hard, stiff; firm, tight; tough. **2.** strong, powerful; hardy, vigorous. **3.** harsh, severe; rigorous; austere. **4.** firm, resolute; inflexible; hard to deal with, grudging. **5.** difficult; grievous; burdensome (prices); strong (as tea). — **~ करना,** v.t. to harden, to toughen, &c.; to embolden. **~ दिल करके देना,** m. to give grudgingly. **कड़ी कहना,** to speak harshly (to, **को**), to berate. **कड़ी झेलना,** v.i. to suffer distress or hardship. **कड़ी (कड़ी) सुनाना,** = **कड़ी कहना.**

[2]**कड़ा** *kaṛā* [*kaṭa-*[1]], m. **1.** a heavy ring of metal or other material, worn on the wrists or ankles; a bangle, bracelet; anklet. **2.** anything

resembling a ring or bracelet in form; link (of a heavy chain, cf. [1]कड़ी); handle (of a door); hilt (of a sword). **3.** reg. a verse or line (of Hindi poetry).

[3]**कड़ा** *kaṛā* [*kaṭa-*[3], H. [2]कड़ी], m. a heavy beam or rafter.

कड़ाई *kaṛāī* [cf. H. *kaṛā*], f. **1.** hardness, firmness, toughness. **2.** harshness, sternness; strictness. **3.** firmness, resolution. **4.** difficulty, burdensomeness. — ~ करना, v.t. to practise severity, &c.; to be austere, to retrench (financially), to be resolute; to be obdurate.

कड़ाकड़ *kaṛākaṛ* [cf. *kaṭakaṭa-*], adj. producing a continued or repeated cracking or succession of loud sounds.

कड़ाका *kaṛākā* [**kaṭakka-*], m. **1.** a loud cracking sound, a crash (as of anything breaking or falling heavily). **2.** severity, intensity (as of heat, cold, famine, or epidemic). **3.** colloq. a strict fast. — ~ गुज़रना (पर), to suffer a hard time, or severely: to fast long or rigidly; to go without food, to starve. कड़ाके का, adj. sharp, fierce, severe, rigorous.

कड़ाड़ा *kaṛāṛā*, m. reg. (W.) = कड़ारा.

कड़ापन *kaṛāpan* [cf. H. *kaṛā*], m. hardness, stiffness, firmness, &c.

कड़ाबीन *kaṛābīn* [f. P. *qarābīn*: ← F.], f. a carbine.

कड़ारा *kaṛārā* [*kaḍāra-*], m. steep, high bank (of a river, tank); a precipice.

कड़ावा *kaṛāvā*, m. S.H. *Pl.* care, charge, trust (= ज़िम्मा).

कड़ाह *kaṛāh*, m. reg. = कड़ाहा.

कड़ाहा *kaṛāhā* [*kaṭāha-*[1]], m. var. /kəṛhaya/ a shallow widemouthed metal pan or cauldron (for boiling or frying). — ~ पूजन, m. the ceremony of worshipping the boiling pan on its first use on some festive occasion. कराहे की पूजा, f. id.

कड़ाही *kaṛāhī* [cf. H. *kaṛāhā*], f. **1.** a small pan or frying pan. **2.** anything cooked in a *kaṛāhī* (as *kacaurī*, *pūrī*, *halvā*). — ~ चढ़ना, the pan to be put on the fire: preparation to be made (for a feast). ~ चाटना, to lick the pot: to eat straight from the pot (said to bring about the ill luck of a fall of rain during the wedding procession of a person who does so). ~ में हाथ डालना, to put the hand in a pan of boiling oil: to submit to an ordeal.

कड़ियल *kaṛiyal* [cf. H. *kaṛā*], adj. Brbh. hard, harsh, stiff, or tough of nature.

कड़िहार *kaṛihār* [? *kaṭi-*, or **kaḍḍhati*, w. H. *-hār*], m. E.H. **1.** one who rescues (from danger). **2.** ? a steersman.

[1]**कड़ी** *kaṛī* [*kaṭa-*[1]], f. **1.** a ring or circle of metal; link (of a chain); window-hook, door-hook; a staple. **2.** a bridle (with linked bit). **3.** a handcuff; fetter. **4.** a verse, or the chorus (of a song). **5.** connection, sequence (as of events).

[2]**कड़ी** *kaṛī* [*kaṭa-*[3]], f. a beam; a squared rafter.

कड़ेर *kaṛer*, adj. reg. (E.) hard, stiff, &c. (= [1]कड़ा).

कड़ोड़ा *kaṛoṛā*, m. *Pl. HŚS.* = [2]करोड़ा.

कड़ोर *kaṛor*, m. E.H. corr. = करोड़.

कड्डी *kaḍḍī*, f. *Pl.* a metal pin or nail.

कढ़ना *kaṛhnā* [cf. H. *kāṛhnā*], v.i. **1.** to be drawn, drawn out, extracted. **2.** to be boiled down, thickened (milk). **3.** to be outlined, drawn, painted; to be embroidered. **4.** to rise, become prominent. **5.** to slip away, to elope. — कढ़ा-कढ़ाया, adj. newly drawn (milk); newly embroidered, &c.

कढ़वाना *kaṛhvānā* [cf. H. *kāṛhnā*], v.t. **1.** to cause to be drawn or pulled out, or off. **2.** to have or to get drawn, or painted; to have or to get embroidered. **3.** to cause to slip away, to spirit away.

[1]**कढ़ाई** *kaṛhāī*, f. pronun. var. = कड़ाही.

[2]**कढ़ाई** *kaṛhāī* [cf. H. *kāṛhnā*, *kaṛhānā*], f. **1.** pulling or drawing out. **2.** embroidery. **3.** payment for embroidery.

कढ़ाना *kaṛhānā* [cf. H. *kāṛhnā*], v.t. = कढ़वाना.

कढावनी *kaḍhāvnī* [cf. *kvathati*], f. reg. (W.) a vessel in which milk is boiled, or butter clarified.

कढावली *kaḍhāvlī* [cf. *kvathati*], f. reg. (W.) = कढावनी.

कढ़ी *kaṛhī* [*kvathita-*; Pk. *kaḍḍhia-*], f. a particular dish, pulse meal with spices and sour milk (*dahī*).

कढ़ुआ *kaṛhuā* [cf. H. *kaṛhnā*], m. *Pl. HŚS.* **1.** sthg. taken out: a loan, debt; deduction from a sum lent. **2.** reg. (E.) food kept over from an evening meal until the next day. **3.** a container used for ladling.

कढेलड़ *kaḍhelaṛ* [conn. H. *kaṛhnā*, or Panj. *kaḍḍhṇā*], m. reg. a child born to a widow who has remarried.

कण *kaṇ* [S.], m. **1.** a particle, small fragment, granule; a grain, seed; drop. **2.** facet (of a cut stone). — ~ मात्र, adv. merely a fragment, or particle (of). – ~ ~ में समा जाना, to pervade every atom (of, के).

कणिका *kaṇikā* [S.], f. small fragment; a grain (as of corn).

कत *kat* [conn. *kutaḥ*; Pk. *katt-*, Ap. *kattha*], adv. Brbh. Av. **1.** ? where, whither? **2.** rhetor. why?; by no means.

क़त *qat* [A. *qaṯṯ*], m. cutting: nib (of a pen).

क़तई *qataī* [A. *qaṯ'ī*], adj. & adv. **1.** adj. final. **2.** adv. completely, absolutely. उसे यह ~ पसंद नहीं, he will on no account allow this.

कतना *katnā* [cf. H. *kātnā*], v.i. to be spun.

कतनी *katnī* [cf. H. *katnā*], f. reg. **1.** spinning. **2.** a small straw basket.

कतर *katar* [cf. H. *katarnā*], f. esp. कतर-. cutting, clipping. — कतर-छाँट, f. cutting and trimming. कतर-ब्योंत, f. id.; cutting out (clothes); retrenchment, economies; thrift; small deductions (from an amount); peculation(s); fig. contriving (an expedient). कतर-ब्योंत करना (की), to cut out; to make economies; to make deductions, &c.; to plan, to contrive. कतर-ब्योंत से, adv. by cutting and trimming, &c.

कतरन *katran* [cf. H. *katarnā*], f. **1.** cutting, trimming. **2.** a cutting, clipping; a piece.

कतरना *katarnā* [cf. *kartari-*], v.t. **1.** to cut, to trim; to cut out (as cloth, paper); to cut up (as straw). **2.** fig. to interrupt (words, speech).

कतरनी *katarnī* [cf. *kartari-*], f. **1.** scissors. **2.** shears.

कतरवाँ *katarvāṁ*, adj. crooked, zigzag (course).

कतरवाई *katarvāī* [cf. H. *katarvānā*], f. price paid for or cost of cutting out.

कतरवाना *katarvānā* [cf. H. *katarnā*], v.t. to cause to be cut, trimmed, &c. (by, से).

कतरा *katrā* [cf. H. *katarnā*], m. **1.** a clipping, paring. **2.** chip, fragment (as of stone). **3.** a piece (as of sweet).

क़तरा *qatrā* [A. *qaṭra*], m. a drop (of liquid). — ~ – ~, adv. drop by drop.

कतराई *katrāī* [cf. H. *katarnā*, *katrānā*], f. **1.** cutting out. **2.** price paid for or cost of cutting out.

कतराना *katrānā* [cf. H. *katarnā*], v.t. & v.i. **1.** v.t. to cause to be cut, trimmed; to cause to be cut out. **2.** v.i. to avoid, to shun (a person, से); to slip away (from). **3.** to turn aside (from a main road, a direct course); to go by a roundabout route.

क़तल *qatl* [A. *qatl*], m. **1.** killing, slaughtering; carnage. **2.** murder; assassination. **3.** execution. — ~ करना, to kill, &c. – क़तलगाह [P. *-gāh*], f. place of execution; gallows. क़तले-आम, m. a massacre.

कतला *katlā* [cf. *karta-*[2]], m. a slice, piece (of food). — कतले करना, to slice (sthg., के).

कतवाई *katvāī* [cf. H. *katvānā*], f. = कताई.

कतवाना *katvānā* [cf. H. *kāṭnā*], v.t. to cause to be spun (by, से).

क़ता *qatā* [A. *qaṭ'*], f. cutting: **1.** Brbh. kind, type. **2.** U. cut (of garment), style.

कताई *katāī* [cf. H. *kātnā*, *katānā*], f. **1.** spinning. **2.** payment for or cost of spinning.

कतान *katān* [A. *kattān*: P. *katān*], f. *Pl. HŚS.* a kind of fine linen cloth.

कताना *katānā* [cf. H. *kātnā*], v.t. = कतवाना.

क़तार *qatār* [A. *qiṭār*], f. **1.** a line, row. **2.** series, order. — ~ बाँधना (की), to place in a row, to line up; to place in order. ~ में, adv. in a line; in order.

कतारा *katārā* [*kāntāraka-*], m. 19c. a tall, red variety of sugar-cane.

कति *kati* [S.], adj. Brbh. = कितना. — कतिपय, adj. several, a few.

कतीरा *katīrā*, m. a large deciduous tree, *Sterculia urens*, and an insoluble gum obtained from its bark.

कतुआ *katuā* [× H. *katnā*], m. pronun. var. (metath). = टकुआ.

कत्तर *kattar*, m. reg. (W.) = कत्तल.

कत्तल *kattal* [? = H. *katar*], m. reg. (W.) a chip, small piece (as of stone).

क़त्ताल *qattāl* [A. *qattāl*], m. U. a murderer.

कत्ती *kattī* [**karta-*[3]], f. **1.** a small sword. **2.** a knife; dagger.

कत्थई *katthaī* [cf. H. *katthā*], adj. dark red in colour.

कत्थक *katthak*, m. = कथक, 3., 4.

कत्था *katthā*, m. an astringent and narcotic vegetable extract from the plant or tree *Acacia catechu* (eaten in betel leaf with lime, which it turns red).

क़त्ल *qatl*, m. see क़तल.

कथ- *kath-* [ad. *kathayati*], v.t. Brbh. Av. **1.** to tell; to recite; to expound. **2.** to compose (oral poetry). **3.** to reproach.

कथक *kathak* [S.], m. **1.** narrator; specif. public narrator and expounder of sacred legends. **2.** *drama.* the speaker of a prologue, an actor. **3.** a community of singers and dancers. **4.** name of a style of dance.

कथड़ी *kathṛī* [cf. *kanthā*-[2]], f. a patched or tattered garment, or quilt.

कथन *kathan* [S.], m. **1.** narrating. **2.** a narrative; an account; statement. **3.** utterance, words. **4.** a type of literary composition, unbroken narrative by a single speaker. — **उनके अपने कथनानुसार** [°*na+a*°], adv. as he himself says, would say, &c.

कथनीय *kathănīyă* [S.], adj. **1.** to be said, uttered; able to be said. **2.** fit or deserving to be said.

कथा *kathā* [S.], f. **1.** sthg. said. **2.** story, tale; legend; specif. sacred legend or tale. **3.** narration. **4.** report, news. **5.** rumour. — **~ बखानना**, = ~ next. **~ बाँचना**, to read or to recite a tale (esp. scriptural). **~ बैठाना**, v.t. to arrange for the telling of a sacred legend by a professional narrator. – **कथाकार**, m. narrator; novelist. **कथात्मक** [°*thā+ā*], adj. narrative (as gifts, skill). **कथानक**, m. narrative, plot; a short story. **कथा-वस्तु**, f. subject-matter of a narrative. **प्रधान कथावस्तु**, f. central theme, leitmotiv. **कथा-वार्ता**, f. conversation, discussion, talk. **कथोपकथन** [°*thā+u*°], m. id.; dialogue.

कथाकली *kathākalī*, f. a style of classical Indian dance.

कथिक *kathik*, m. = **कथक**.

कथित *kathit* [S.], adj. **1.** said, uttered; narrated. **2.** spoken (language).

कथ्य *kathyă* [S.], adj. = **कथनीय**.

क़द *qad* [A. *qadd*], m. height, stature. — **क़ददार** [P. -*dār*], adj. of good stature. **क़दावर, क़द्दावर,** [P. -*āvar*], adj. tall. °**ई**, f. **आदमक़द**, adj. of a man's height.

[1]**कद** *kad* [A. *kadd*], f. **1.** importuning; persistence (in), insistence (on or about, **की**). **2.** envy, rancour. — **~ रखना**, to feel envy, &c. (of, **की**).

[2]**कद** *kad* [ad. *kadā*: ← Panj., Raj.], adv. reg. = **कब**.

कद- *kad-* [S.] useless, bad, defective: — **कदन्न**, m. poor quality grain. **कदर्थ**, m. sthg. useless. **कदर्थना**, f. trouble, plight. **कदर्य**, adj. miserly, avaricious; mean, sordid (as an attitude). °**ता**, f. **कदाकार**, adj. misshapen, ugly. **कदाचार**, m. bad, wicked, or depraved conduct.

कदंब *kadamb* [S.], m. **1.** the tree *Nauclea cadamba*. **2.** Brbh. Av. assembly, crowd; a number (of).

कदन *kadan* [S.], m. Brbh. destroying, destruction; slaughter.

क़दम *qadm* [A. *qadam*], m. **1.** the foot; the sole; a foot's length. **2.** a pace, step. **3.** fig. step, measure. — **~ उखड़ना**, colloq. to clear out. **~ उठाना**, to step out, to walk fast; to make quick progress; to take steps or measures; to undertake (an activity). **~ गाड़ना**, to plant the foot firmly (on); to secure one's footing. **~ छूना**, to touch the feet (of, **के**: reverentially, or imploringly). **~ दिखाना**, to show the paces (as of a horse); colloq. to make tracks, to be off. **~ पर ~ रखना**, to follow in the footsteps (of, **के**). **~ बक़दम** [P. *ba-*], adv. in step; step by step, by degrees. **~ बढ़ाना**, to extend the pace, to step out; to progress. **~ में ~ मिलाते चलना**, to keep in step. **~ रखना**, to set foot (in, **में**; on, **पर**); to venture (upon). **~ लेना** (**के**), esp. euph. to acknowledge a master, to yield to (as in villainy). – **~ ~**, adv. step by step; at an easy pace. **~ ~ पर**, adv. hard on the heels (of, **के**). **क़दमबाज़** [P. -*bāz*], m. a pacer (horse). **क़दमबोसी** [P. -*bos-*], f. kissing the feet (of, **की**: in respect or homage).

क़दमचा *qadamcā* [P. *qadamca*], m. **1.** step, footboard (as of a carriage). **2.** place for feet (in lavatory).

क़दर *qadr* [A. *qadr*], f. **1.** merit, worth. **2.** estimation; value set (upon, **की**). **3.** measure, extent, degree. **किस ~?** to what extent? — **~ करना** (**की**), to appreciate justly, to value. – **क़दरदान** [P. -*dān*], adj. & m. appreciating, valuing; a good judge (of). °**ई**, f. just appreciation (of), discernment.

कदर्य *kad-aryă* [S.], adj. see s.v. **कद-**.

कदर्यता *kad-aryătā* [S.], f. see s.v. **कद-**.

कदली *kadălī* [S.], f. the plantain, or banana.

कदा *kadā* [S.], adv. when? — **कदाचित**, adv. see s.v. **कदापि** [°*dā+a*°], adv. see s.v.

कदाच *kadāc* [S.], adv. Brbh. = **कदाचित्**.

कदाचित् *kadâcit* [S.], adv. **1.** at some time; hardly ever. **2.** perhaps.

कदापि *kadâpi* [S.], adv. in neg. contexts. sometimes; at all, on any account. — **~ नहीं**, adv. never; by no means, absolutely not.

क़दीम *qadīm* [A. *qadīm*], adj. ancient, former (time, age, ways).

कदीमा *kadīmā*, m. reg. (Bihar) **1.** the pumpkin *Cucurbita pepo*. **2.** *Pl.* a crowbar.

क़दीमी *qadīmī* [P. *qadīmī*], adj. of old: = **क़दीम**.

कद्दू *kaddū* [P. *kad(d)ū*], m. a pumpkin, gourd. — कद्दूकश [P. *-kaś*], m. an appliance for cutting and grating pumpkins.

क़द्र *qadr*, m. see क़दर.

कधी *kadhī* [? ad. *kadā*: × H. *kabhī*], adv. E.H. = कभी.

कन *kan* [*kaṇa-*], m. **1.** a particle, small fragment, &c. (= कण, 1., 2). **2.** reg. = कनकूत; division of crops between landlord and tenant. **3.** reg. (E.) a shoot (of a plant). — ~ की उँगली, f. the little finger. – कनकूत, f. appraisal or valuation of a standing crop.

कन- *kan-* [*karṇa-*]. the ear: see s.vv.

कनक *kanak* [S.], m. **1.** gold. **2.** Brbh. the thorn-apple (धतूरा).

कनकटा *kankaṭā* [H. *kān*+H. *kăṭnā*], adj. earless; having the ears cut off; (for कन-काटा) one who cuts off the ears (of another).

कनकटी *kankaṭī* [H. *kān*+H. *kaṭnā*], f. an inflammation of the ear.

कनकनाना *kankanānā*, v.i. **1.** to tingle. **2.** to feel on edge.

कनकी *kankī* [*kaṇika-*, **kaṇikka-*], f. a piece of broken rice; scrap, fragment.

कनकूत *kankūt*, m. see s.v. कन.

कनकौवा *kankauvā* [? H. *kān*+H. *kauvā*], m. **1.** a large square paper kite. **2.** a herb of the genus *Ipomoea*. — ~ बढ़ाना, to let a kite rise. ~ लड़ाना, to fly kites against each other (hoping to cut a rival's line).

कनखजूरा *kankhajūrā* [H. *kān*+H. *khajūrā*], m. a centipede.

कनखी *kankhī* [**karṇākṣi-*], f. **1.** a side-glance; wink. **2.** a leer, ogling. — ~ मारना, to wink (at). कनखियों से देखना, to look surreptitiously at, &c.

कनछेदन *kanchedan* [H. *kān*+H. *chednā*], m. *hind.* the ceremony of piercing a child's ears.

कनटोप *kanṭop* [H. *kān*+H. *ṭop*], m. a cap with flaps covering the ears.

कनपटी *kanpaṭī*, f. the temple; the area between the temple and the ear.

कनपेड़ *kanpeṛ* [H. *kān*+H. *peṛ* 'lump'], m. a swelling of the glands between ear and throat; mumps.

कनपेड़ा *kanpeṛā*, m. = कनपेड़.

कनफटा *kanphaṭā* [H. *kān*+H. *phaṭnā*], adj. slit-eared: a designation of members of the Nāth yogī sect.

कनफुकवा *kanphukvā* [H. *kān*+H. *phūm̐knā*], m. colloq. one who whispers *mantras* into another's ear (cf. ओझा).

कनफेड़ *kanpheṛ*, m. reg. = कनपेड़.

कनरस *kanras* [H. *kān*+H. *ras*], m. pleasure in hearing (music, &c.), a taste for music.

कनरसिया *kanrasiyā* [cf. H. *kanras*], m. one who enjoys music.

कनस्तर *kanastar* [Engl. *canister*], m. canister.

कनवा *kanvā*, m. a measure of capacity or weight, (?) one sixteenth of a seer.

कनवाई *kanvāī* [**karṇavyādhikā-*], f. *Pl.* piercing the ears.

कनसलाई *kansalāī* [H. *kān*+H. [2]*silāī*], f. a kind of centipede.

कनसुई *kansuī* [? **karṇaśūcikā-*], f. eavesdropping. — कनसुइयाँ लेना, to eavesdrop.

कनहरि *kanhari* [**karṇadhara-*], f. Brbh. helmsman, boatman.

कनहरी *kanharī* [cf. H. *kanhari*], f. E.H. steering, piloting (a boat).

कनहरीला *kanharīlā* [cf. H. *kanhār*], m. *Pl.* helmsman.

कनहाई *kanhāī* [cf. H. *kanihā*], f. valuation of a standing crop.

कनहार *kanhār* [*karṇadhāra-*], m. Av. helmsman.

कनहारा *kanhārā* [*karṇadhāra-*], m. Av. helmsman, boatman.

कनहारू *kanhārū*, m. Av. = कनहारा.

कना *kanā* [*kanyā-*: cf. *kanyā-gata-*], f. *astron.* the dark fortnight of the month of Āśvin. — कनागत, m. the position of a planet (esp. Jupiter) in the sign of Virgo: the period marked by this position, the dark half of Āśvin (auspicious for religious rites); a *śrāddh* or religious ceremony performed daily during this period in honour of deceased ancestors.

क़नात *qanāt* [? A. *qanāh*; P. *qanāt*], f. **1.** the wall of a tent. **2.** a canvas screen.

क़नाती *qanātī* [P. *qanātī*], adj. enclosed or surrounded by screening. — ~ मसजिद, f. *musl.* a screened-off area used as a place of worship.

कनिको *kaniko* [*kaṇika-*, **kaṇikka-*], m. Brbh. a tiny piece, little bit.

कनियाँ *kaniyām̐* [cf. *karṇikā-*], f. Brbh. the lap.

कनिया *kaniyā*, f. 19c. = कनियाँ.

कनियाना *kaniyānā* [cf. H. *kannī*], v.i. **1.** to avoid, to steer clear (of a person, से). 2. = कन्नी खाना.

कनियाहट *kaniyāhaṭ* [cf. H. *kaniyānā*], f. **1.** avoiding. **2.** transf. shyness, timidity.

कनिष्ठ *kaniṣṭh* [S.], adj. **1.** smallest; little (finger). **2.** youngest; younger (brother); junior.

कनिष्ठा *kaniṣṭhā* [S.], f. 1. = कनिष्ठिका. **2.** a junior wife. **3.** a less-favoured wife.

कनिष्ठिका *kaniṣṭhikā* [S.], f. the little finger.

कनिहा *kanihā* [? **kaṇikabhāvaka-*], m. reg. valuer or appraiser of a crop.

कनी *kanī* [*kaṇikā-*], f. **1.** a fragment; broken piece (as of grain); blob (of *ghī*, &c). **2.** a small piece (of crystal, diamond). **3.** a hard or uncooked grain (as of rice). — ~ खाना, or चाटना, to swallow a sharp fragment of diamond (so as to end one's life).

कनीनिका *kanīnikā* [S.], f. pupil of the eye.

कनीज़ *kanīz* [P. *kanīz*], f. a servant-girl.

कनीर *kanīr*, m. E.H. ? = कनेर.

कने *kane* [*karṇa-*], adv. Brbh.; U. (obs). **1.** beside, near (to, के). **2.** in the possession (of). **3.** at the house (of). **4.** m. side, direction. इस ~, adv. on this side.

कनेठा *kaneṭhā* [H. *kānā*+H. *aiṁṭhnā*], adj. **1.** squint-eyed. **2.** one-eyed. — काना-कनेठा, adj. = ~.

कनेठी *kaneṭhī* [H. *kān*+H. *aiṁṭhnā*], f. twisting the ear (as a punishment). — ~ खाना, to have one's ear twisted. ~ देना, to twist the ear (of, को). ~ लगाना, id.

कनेर *kaner* [*karavīra-*; Pk. *kaṇavīra-*], m. oleander, *Nerium odorum.*

कनेरिया *kaneriyā* [cf. H. *kaner*], adj. dark red.

कनोखी *kanokhī* adj. reg. 1. = कनखी, 1. **2.** squint-eyed.

कनौजिया *kanaujiyā* [cf. H. *kanauj*], adj. usu. inv. & m. **1.** adj. of or belonging to Kanauj. **2.** m. an inhabitant of Kanauj.

कनौड़ *kanauṛ* [**karṇamarda-*], f. **1.** shame; stigma (see कनौड़ा). **2.** shyness, diffidence.

कनौड़ा *kanauṛā* [**karṇamarda-*], adj. touching the ears as a sign of disgrace or repentance: **1.** ashamed. **2.** disgraced. **3.** shy, diffident. **4.** insignificant.

कनौती *kanautī* [*karṇapattraka-*], f. **1.** the ear of an animal. **2.** pricking up the ear(s) (a horse). — कनौतियाँ उठाना, or खड़ी करना, or बदलना, to prick up the ears.

कन्ना *kannā* [*karṇaka-*], m. a projecting edge, end or rim; a lug or projecting part. — कन्नों से उखड़ना or उखड़ जाना or कटना, to be torn right away (as a kite from its string); fig. to turn away in a huff. पतंग का ~, m. the two parts of a kite-string which are tied to the kite.

[1]**कन्नी** *kannī* [*karṇikā-*], f. **1.** outer edge. **2.** hem (of a garment). **3.** balancing strip, make-weight (attached to the edge of a kite). — ~ काटना, to steer clear (of, से) to avoid (a person); to undermine (one: की), to ruin. ~ खाना, to heel in flight (a kite).

[2]**कन्नी** *kannī*, f. pronun. var. = करनी.

कन्या *kanyā* [S.], f. **1.** an unmarried girl, or woman. **2.** a daughter. **3.** the sign Virgo (of the zodiac). — कन्या-कुमारी, f. name of Cape Comorin. कन्याकुब्ज, m. the city and region of Kanauj. कन्या-धन, m. property belonging to a girl before her marriage. कन्या-दान, m. the giving of (one's) daughter in marriage; a partic. marriage rite. कन्यावस्था [°*yā*+*a*°], f. girlhood.

कन्हाई *kanhāī*, m. = कन्हैया.

कन्हैया *kanhaiyā* [cf. *kṛṣṇa-*], m. dimin. **1.** dear Kānh: a name of Kṛṣṇa. **2.** fig. Brbh. a beloved person (male).

कप *kap*, m. trembling (= काँप). — कपकपी, f. = कँपकँपी.

कपट *kapaṭ* [S.], m. **1.** insincerity, dissembling. **2.** deceit. **3.** trickery; trick. — ~ करना (के साथ), to dissemble; to deceive (one). ~ रखना, to harbour deceitful intentions (against, से). ~ से, adv. falsely; deceitfully. – कपट-वेष, m. a disguise; an assumed character; hypocrisy. कपट-वेश, m. id.

कपटी *kapăṭī* [S.], adj. & m. **1.** adj. insincere, dissembling. **2.** designing, deceitful. **3.** malicious. **4.** m. a dissembler, &c.

कपड़- *kapaṛ-*. = कपड़ा: — कपड़-कीड़ा, m. a clothes-moth. कपरछन, adj. strained or sifted through cloth, fine (as a powder). कपड़छन करना, to sift, &c. कपड़छान, adj. id.

कपड़ा *kapṛā* [*karpaṭa-*: ← Austro-as.], m. **1.** cloth. **2.** clothing, clothes. **3.** garment. — कपड़े से, or में, होना, to be menstruating. – ~ पहनना, to put on a garment. कपड़े पहनना, to dress. कपड़े रँगना, to dye cloth, or clothes; to become an ascetic. – कपड़ा-लत्ता, m. clothes, clothing. कपड़ावाला, m. cloth-merchant, draper.

कपड़ाहंद *kapṛāhand* [**karpaṭagandha-*], f. the smell of burnt cloth.

कपड़ौटी *kapṛauṭī* [? *karpaṭa-*+*āvṛti-*× *āvṛtti-*], f. **1.** *Pl.* straining through cloth. **2.** reg. covering the mouth of a vessel with a cloth.

कपर्दिनी *kapardinī* [S.], *mythol.* name of a goddess.

कपाट *kapāṭ* [S.], m. **1.** a door. **2.** leaf of a door. **3.** a valve.

कपाल *kapāl* [S.], m. **1.** the skull; head. **2.** the brow. **3.** fig. what is written on the brow: destiny. **4.** a broken water-pot; potsherd. **5.** a beggar's bowl. — ~ खुलना (का), (one's) fortune to take a favourable turn. ~ फूटना (का), the skull to be broken; to be unfortunate. – कपाल-क्रिया, f. ceremonial breaking of the skull of a corpse at cremation (performed by a son or the nearest relative).

कपालिका *kapālikā* [S.], f. wearing skulls as a necklace: a title of the goddess Kālī.

कपाली *kapālī* [S.], adj. & m. **1.** adj. wearing skulls as a necklace. **2.** m. a title of Śiva.

कपास *kapās* [*karpāsa-*, °*sī-*: ← Austro-as.], f. **1.** the cotton plant. **2.** cotton (uncarded).

कपासी *kapāsī* [cf. H. *kapās*], adj. **1.** made of cotton. **2.** of the colour of the cotton plant, or its flower: light green, yellow.

कपि *kapi* [S.], m. **1.** a monkey. **2.** a title of Viṣṇu. — कपि-ध्वज, monkey-bannered: a title of Arjun. कपींद्र [°*pi+i*°], m. lord of the monkeys: a title of Viṣṇu, and of Hanumān.

कपित्थ *kapitth* [S.], m. the wood-apple tree, and its fruit (= कैथ).

कपिल *kapil* [S.], adj. & m. Av. **1.** adj. monkey-coloured: brown, reddish. **2.** m. Brbh. name of a sage, founder of the Sāṅkhya system of philosophy.

कपिश *kapiś* [S.], adj. monkey-coloured: brown, reddish.

कपूत *kapūt* [H. *ku-*; *putra-*], m. & adj. **1.** m. a bad son. **2.** adj. bad (a son).

कपूती *kapūtī* [cf. H. *kapūt*], f. badness (in a son).

कपूर *kapūr* [*kapūra-*], m. camphor. — ~ खाना, to take camphor: to take poison.

कपूरा *kapūrā*, m. testicles (of a buffalo, ram, goat, &c).

कपूरी *kapūrī* [cf. *karpūra-*: ? ← Austro-as.], adj. & f. camphor-like: **1.** adj. yellowish. **2.** fragrant. **3.** f. a yellowish type of betel leaf.

कपोत *kapot* [S.], m. a pigeon. — कपोत-वृत्ति, f. fig. meek acceptance (of what life brings).

कपोती *kapotī* [cf. H. *kapot*], f. a hen pigeon.

कपोल *kapol* [S.], m. the cheek. — कपोल-कल्पना, f. figment of imagination. °-कल्पित, adj. fabricated, imaginary.

कप्तान *kaptān* [Engl. *captain*], m. **1.** captain (of a crew, a team). **2.** *mil.* captain.

कप्तानी *kaptānī* [cf. H. *kaptān*], f. captaincy. — ~ करना (की), to captain (a crew, &c).

कफ *kaph* [S.], m. **1.** phlegm. **2.** (in Indian medicine) one of the constituent humours (*dhātu*) of the body.

[1]**कफ़** *kaf* [S.; and P. *kaf*], m. (N., f). **1.** phlegm, mucus. **2.** *ayur.* one of the humours of the body. **3.** reg. froth, foam. — ~ निकालनेवाला, adj. & m. *med.* expectorant. ~ निस्सारक adj. & m. id. – कफ़-क्षय, m. the mucus of a tubercular person. कफ़गीर [P. *-gīr*], m. reg. (Bihar) skimmer; stirrer. कफ़ोत्सारक [°*fa+u*°], adj. & m. = ~ निकालनेवाला.

[2]**कफ़** *kaf* [Engl. *cuff*], m. cuff (of clothing). — कफ़दार [P. *-dār*], adj. having cuffs.

कफ़चा *kafcā* [P. *kafca*], m. reg. (Bihar) a skimmer, or stirrer.

कफ़न *kafan* [A. *kafan*], m. a shroud. — ~ को कौड़ी न रखना, not to save or to put aside a penny. ~ फाड़कर उठना, to rise from the dead; to appear suddenly. ~ फाड़कर चिल्लाना, to give a terrifying shriek. ~ सिर से बाँधना, or लपेटना, to tie or to wrap one's shroud round one's head: to engage in a risky enterprise; to risk life, to court death. – कफ़न-खसोट, m. shroud-snatcher: a shameless thief. कफ़न-चोर, m. stealer of grave-clothes: a base person. कफ़न-दफ़न, m. pej. burial, funeral. इस मामले को उसने कफ़न-दफ़न कर दिया, he suppressed, concealed this matter.

कफ़नाना *kafnānā* [cf. H. *kafan*], v.t. U. to wrap (a dead body) in a shroud.

कफ़नी *kafnī* [P. *kafanī*], f. an ascetic's unsewn garment.

क़फ़स *qafas* [A. *qafaṣ*], m. **1.** U. a birds' cage. **2.** 19c. a cell; imprisonment.

कफ़ाई *kafāī* [cf. H. [1]*kaf*], f. reg. (W). scum (as produced in an indigo vat during fermentation).

कफी *kaphī* [cf. H. *kaph*], adj. **1.** filled with phlegm or mucus. **2.** *ayur.* characterised by phlegm (a complaint).

कबंध *kabandh* [S.], m. **1.** cask, barrel. **2.** the belly. **3.** fig. a headless trunk. **4.** *mythol.* name of a demon.

कब *kab* [cf. Ap. *kabbe*: for S. *kadā*], adv. **1.** when? **2.** rhetor. when, indeed? (= never). — ~ ~, adv. occasionally, rarely. ~ का, adj. of what time? rhetor. adj. & adv. of long ago; long since; for a long time. नहीं ~ का लखनऊ चला आया होता, otherwise I would have come over to Lucknow long ago. ~ का ... ~ का, adv. as of one time ... as of another. ~ को, adv. = ~. ~ तक, adv. up till when? for how long? ~ से, adv. since when? for how long? आप ~ से यहाँ हैं? how long have you been here?

कबक *kabak* [P. *kabak*], m. a kind of partridge, or quail (= चकोर).

कबड्डी *kabaḍḍī*, f. a game in which each player in turn, shouting '*kabaḍḍı kabaḍḍī*', tries to touch one or more opponents in his territory and to return uncaught to his own before running out of breath.

क़बर *qabr*, f. see क़ब्र.

कबरा *kabrā* [*karbara-*: ← Austro-as.], adj. spotted, speckled; greyish.

कबहुँ *kab'huṁ*, adv. Av. = कभी.

क़बा *qabā* [A. *qabā'*], f. U. a long robe open at the skirt and chest.

कबाड़ *kabāṛ*, m. **1.** heap, collection (of odds and ends); scrap, rubbish. **2.** old or broken furniture. — कबाड़-ख़ाना, m. lumber-room; scrap-merchant's shop or premises.

कबाड़ा *kabāṛā* [cf. H. *kabāṛ*], m. 1. = कबाड़. **2.** colloq. sthg. ruined or botched.

कबाड़िया *kabāṛiyā* [cf. H. *kabāṛ*], m. a dealer in old or broken furniture, scrap-merchant.

कबाड़ी *kabāṛı*, m. = कबाड़िया.

कबाब *kabāb* [P. *kabāb*], m. roasted meat; specif. pieces of meat roasted on a spit. — ~ होना, to be roasted; to be scorched; to burn (as with envy or anger). जलकर ~ होना, id., 3.

कबाब-चीनी *kabāb-cīnī* [cf. P. *kabāba*], m. cubeb, *Piper cubeba* (a Javan shrub, used medicinally and the source of a resin).

कबाबी *kabābī* [P. *kabābī*], m. & adj. **1.** m. a seller of roast meat. **2.** pej. a meat-eater. **3.** adj. reg. fit for roasting (meat, poultry).

क़बायली *qabāylī* [A. *qabā'il*, pl.+P. *-ī*], m. tribesman (of N.W. Frontier).

कबारू *kabārū* [? P. *kārobār*], m. Av. metr. work, occupation (as of a boatman).

क़बाहत *qabāhat* [A. *qabāḥa*: P. *qabāḥat*], f. U. inconvenience, difficulty.

कबीर *kabīr* [A. *kabīr*], adj. & m. **1.** adj. U. great; noble. **2.** m. a type of indecent song sung at the Holī festival. **3.** name of a north Indian *sant* poet of the late 15th century. — कबीर-पंथ, m. the sect or followers of Kabīr. °ई m. a follower of Kabīr.

क़बीला *qabīlā* [A. *qabīla*], m. **1.** a tribe. **2.** family.

क़बीली *qabīlī* [P. *qabīlī*], adj. tribal. — ~ क्षेत्र, m. tribal area.

क़बुली *qabulī* [P. *qabūlī*], f. Av. metr. a sacrificial animal.

कबूतर *kabūtar* [P. *kabūtar*], m. a pigeon. — ~ उड़ाना, to fly pigeons. ~ की तरह लोटना, fig. to be very restless, agitated. – कबूतर-ख़ाना, m. a dovecot. कबूतरबाज़ [P. *bāz*], m. a pigeon-fancier; colloq. a ladies' man. °ई, pigeon-fancying.

कबूतरी *kabūtărī* [cf. H. *kabūtar*], f. **1.** a hen pigeon. **2.** colloq. an attractive woman; a village dancing-girl.

क़बूल *qabul* [A. *qabūl*], m. **1.** acceptance. **2.** consent; agreement. **3.** recognition, sanction. **4.** acknowledgment, admission. **5.** approval; choice. — ~ करना, to accept, &c. ~ होना (को), to be acceptable, &c. (to).

क़बूलना *qabūlnā* [cf. H. *qabūl*], v.i. = क़बूल करना.

क़बूलियत *qabūliyat* [A. *qabūlīya*: P. *qabūliyat*], f. **1.** acceptance. **2.** document of acceptance (as of a lease).

क़बूली *qabūlī* [P. *qabūlī*], f. acceptable: **1.** Av. see क़बुली. **2.** *reg.* a dish of boiled rice and gram.

क़ब्ज़ *qabz* [A. *qabẓ*], f. seizing, taking possession: constipation. — ~ करनेवाला, adj. *med.* astringent. ~ होना (को), to be constipated.

क़ब्ज़ा *qabzā* [A. *qabẓa*], m. **1.** grasp; clutch. **2.** seizure. **3.** possession; occupancy. **4.** occupation by force. **5.** handle; hilt. **6.** a hinge. **7.** the upper arm. — ~ करना (पर), to seize; to take possession, &c. (of); to usurp. ~ देना (को), to yield or to make over possession (to). ~ रखना, to seize hold (of, पर); to keep hold (of). क़बज़े में लाना, to get into one's grasp, or power; to seize, &c. – क़ब्ज़ादार [P. *-dār*], m. & adj. occupant, tenant; hinged. °ई, f. occupancy.

क़ब्ज़ियत *qabziyat* [cf. A. *qabẓ*: P. *qabẓiyat*], f. constipation.

क़ब्र *qabr* [A. *qabr*], f. **1.** grave. **2.** tomb (= मक़बरा). — ~ का मुँह झाँकना, to look into (one's) grave, to be all but dead. ~ के मुरदे उखाड़ना, to dig up the dead from the grave: to rake up old grievances. ~ में पाँव लटकाना, to hang a foot in the grave: to be on the point of death. – क़बरगाह [P. *-gāh*], f. burial-ground. क़ब्रिस्तान [P. *-stān*], m. id. °ई, adj.

कभी *kabhī* [cf. H. *kab*], adv. **1.** sometimes; at any time. **2.** at one time, long ago. — ~ कभार, adv. = next. ~ ~, adv. from time to time, sometimes. ~ ... ~, adv. at one time ... at another time. ~ का, adj. of sometime; adj. & adv. rhetor. of long ago; long since. ~ तो,

adv. = next. ~ न ~, adv. sometime or another, sooner or later; seldom. ~ नहीं, or ~ ... नहीं, adv. never.

कमंद *kamand* [P. *kamand*], f. scaling-ladder; rope, lasso.

कमंडल *kamaṇḍal* [*kamaṇḍalu-*[1]], m. **1.** an earthen or wooden water-pot used by ascetics, and by other devout persons. **2.** a vessel having a spout. — **दंड-कमंडल**, m. staff and water-pot, worldly goods (of an ascetic or hermit).

कमंडलु *kamaṇḍalu* [S.], m. see **कमंडल**.

कम *kam* [P. *kam*], adj. & adv. **1.** adj. little, few, small (of amount or quantity); deficient, scanty. **2.** less (than, **से**). ~ **अज़** ~ (U.), ~ **से** ~, less than little: the least, the fewest. **3.** adv. little; seldom. **वह ~ सुनता है**, he is hard of hearing. ~ **अज़** ~, ~ **से** ~, at least. ~ ~, adv. little by little. – ~ **करना**, to reduce, to decrease; to moderate, to relax; to deduct, *math.* to subtract. ~ **होना**, to lessen, to decrease, to abate; to be deficient, to fail. – **कमअक़्ल**, adj & m. of weak understanding, stupid, foolish; a stupid person, &c. °**ई**, f. stupidity. **कमउम्र**, adj. of young age. **कमख़र्च**, adj. thrifty; parsimonious; economical (to run). **कमख़र्च बाला-निशीन** [P. *bālā*, adj., P. *niśīn*], spending little but seated high: doing well without effort or expense. °**ई**, f. thriftiness; stinginess. **कमज़ात**, adj. of low caste. **कमज़ोर**, adj. see hw. **कमज़ोरी**, f. see hw. **कमतर** [P. *-tar*], adj. less. °**ईन**, adj. least. **कमनज़र**, adj. weak-sighted. **कमबख़्त** [P. *-bakht*], adj. & m. unfortunate; wretched; a wretch. °**ई**, f., misfortune; calamity. **कमबख़्ती आना (पर)**, to be overtaken by misfortune. **कमबख़्ती का मारा**, adj. & m. afflicted, wretched, accursed; a wretched person. **कमबेश** [P. *-beś*], adv. more or less. **कममेहनती**, f. & adj. laziness; lazy. **कमसिन** [A. *-sin*], adj. of young years, young. °**ई**, f. youth. **कमहिम्मत**, adj. of little courage; cowardly. °**ई**, f. & adj. cowardice; cowardly. **कमहैसियत**, adj. of small means; mean, beggarly. **कमो-बेश** [P. *-o-*], adv. = **कमबेश**.

कमकर *kamkar* [cf. H. *kam*], adj. deprived.

कमचोर *kamcor*, m. = **कामचोर** (see s.v. **काम**).

कमज़ोर *kamzor* [P. *kamzor*], adj. **1.** weak, feeble. **2.** deficient, ineffectual. — ~ **करना**, to weaken, to enfeeble; to impoverish, to exhaust.

कमज़ोरी *kamzorī* [P. *kamzorī*], f. **1.** weakness, enfeeblement. **2.** debility. **3.** deficiency.

कमठ *kamaṭh* [S.], m. a tortoise, turtle.

कमठा *kamṭhā* [**kammaṭṭha-*: ad. *kamaṭha-*: ← Austro-as.], m. reg. a bow; cotton-carder's bow.

कमतर *kamtar*, adj. see s.v. **कम**.

कमताई *kamtāī* [cf. H. *kam*], f. a state of diminution or reduction; shortage, scarcity.

कमती *kamtī* [cf. H. *kam*], f. **1.** f. diminution. **2.** scarcity, lack. **3.** adj. reg. little, few, &c. (see s.v. **कम**). — **कमती-बढ़ती**, f. fluctuation (as of prices); adv. more or less (see **कम-बेश**).

कमनीय *kamănīyă* [S.], adj. desirable, desired; pleasing, beautiful, lovely.

कमनैत *kamnait* [cf. H. *kamān*], m. Brbh. **1.** a bowman. **2.** *Pl.* beater (in a hunt).

कमनैती *kamnaitī* [cf. H. *kamnait*], f. Brbh. archery.

कमर *kamar* [P. *kamar*], f. **1.** the waist, the loins. **2.** waist (of a garment).
— ~ **कसना**, = ~ **बाँधना**. ~ **झुकना**, to walk with a stoop. ~ **टूटना**, the loins or back to be broken: to be feeble or exhausted (by work or privation); to give way, to sink (under a blow or loss); to lose confidence or courage; to lose the support of friends. ~ **तोड़ना**, to break the back (of, **की**); to deprive of hope, to discourage; to alienate (friends or supporters). ~ **थामना**, to seize (one) by the waist; fig. to prosecute a claim (against one); to support, to back, to encourage. ~ **पकड़ना**, see ~ **थामना**. ~ **बाँधना**, to get ready, to prepare, to arm (for, **पर, के लिए**); to resolve, to be intent (on, **पर**). ~ **बैठ जाना**, = ~ **टूटना**. ~ **मज़बूत करना**, to find courage or heart (for a task). ~ **रह जाना**, the loins or back to give way: to have a pain, or stiffness, in the back (as from long standing, or unaccustomed work); the back to be paralysed. ~ **सीधी करना**, to stretch oneself out to rest, to lie down. – **कमरतोड़**, adj. & m. back-breaking, difficult; burdensome; a partic. hold in wrestling. **कमर-पट्टी**, f. = next. **कमरबंद** [P. *-band*], m. a waistband, sash; belt; draw-string (as for pājāmā, śalvār).

क़मर *qamar* [A. *qamar*], m. U. the moon.

कमरक *kamrak*, m. pronun. var. = **कमरख**.

कमरख *kamrakh* [conn. *karmaraṅga-*: ? × H. *rukh*], m. a partic. small tree, *Averrhoa bilimbi*, and its sour, astringent fruit (used in pickles, medicinally, and in dyeing).

कमरा *kamrā* [Pt. *camara*], m. **1.** a room. **2.** hall, chamber (of a public building). **3.** compartment. — **बंद कमरे में**, adv. *law.* in camera.

कमरिया *kamriyā*, f. dimin. a small blanket (= **कमली**).

कमरी *kamrī* [P. *kamarī*], adj. having to do with the waist or loins. — ~ **अंगरखा**, m. a short jacket.

कमल *kamal* [S.: ← Drav.], m. a lotus (*Nelumbium speciosum*, or *Nymphæa nelumbo*). — कमल-कंद, m. lotus root (eaten as a vegetable). कमल-ककड़ी, f. lotus stalk. कमल-गट्टा, m. a lotus seed (used medicinally). कमल-नयन, adj. = कमलाक्ष. कमल-नाभ, m. lotus-navel: a title of Viṣṇu. कमल-नाल, m. = कमल-ककड़ी. कमल-पत्र, m. a lotus leaf. कमलबाई, f. see s.v. कमल-वन, m. a lotus thicket. कमलाकर [°*la*+*ā*°], adj. abounding in lotuses. कमलाकार [°*la*+*ā*°], adj. lotus-shaped. कमलाक्ष [°*la*+*a*°], adj. lotus-eyed, having beautiful eyes. कमलासन [°*la*+*ā*°], m. a posture in *yoga*.

कमलबाई *kamalbāī* [cf. *vāta-*, or *vāyu-*: ad. *kamala-*], f. *Pl. HŚS.* a form of jaundice.

[1]**कमला** *kamlā* [S.], f. a title of the goddess Lakṣmī. — कमला-कांत, m. beloved of Kamalā: a title of Viṣṇu. कमला-पति, m. lord of Kamalā: a title of Viṣṇu.

[2]**कमला** *kamlā* [? *kapanā-*; cf. *kambalin-*], m. a palmer-worm: the caterpillar or larva of a brown moth which attacks vegetation; its bristles irritate the skin (cf. गिंदर). — कमला-गिंदर, m. a palmer-worm.

कमलिनी *kamalinī* [S.], f. dimin. **1.** a lotus. **2.** a cluster of lotuses. **3.** a place abounding in lotuses. **4.** *rhet.* a woman of the first and best of four traditionally distinguished classes (= पद्मिनी).

कमली *kamlī* [*kambalikā-*: ? ← Austro-as.], f. a small blanket; an ascetic's blanket. — अपनी ~ में मस्त होना, to glory, or to revel, in what one has; to be indifferent to others. – कमली-कीड़ा, m. a palmer-worm, see [2]कमला. काली कमलीवाला, an ascetic.

कमवाना *kamvānā* [cf. H. *kamānā*], v.t. **1.** to cause to earn, to cause to work. **2.** to cause to be earned; to earn (cf. कमाना).

कमांडर *kamāṇḍar* [Engl. *commander*], m. *mil.* commander.

कमाई *kamāī* [cf. H. *kamānā*], f. **1.** the act of earning or acquiring. **2.** earnings, gain, profits. **3.** due recompense, or retribution. — ~ करना, to earn, to work. ~ पूत, m. a son who is working. गाढ़ी ~ के पैसे, money bitterly earned, a bitter recompense. गाढ़े (वक़्त) की ~, sthg. won or earned with difficulty, or bitterly.

कमाऊ *kamāū* [cf. H. *kamānā*], adj. **1.** capable of earning; earning one's living. **2.** (rare) productive of gain, profitable. — ~ पूत, m. a son who is working. ~ बीबी, f. a wife who is working. – कमाऊ-खाऊ, adj. earning and eating: in work and prospering.

कमाची *kamācī*, f. reg. = खपच्ची.

[1]**कमान** *kamān* [P. *kamān*], f. **1.** a bow. **2.** the sign Sagittarius (of the zodiac). **3.** an arch. — ~ खींचना (रस्सी से), to draw a bow. ~ चढ़ना (की), to enjoy pre-eminence, supremacy, or victory; fig. to bend the brows, to scowl. ~ चढ़ाना, to draw a bow. ~ तानना, id. – कमानगर [P. *-gar*], m. reg. (Bihar) bow-maker. कमानदार [P. *-dār*], adj. armed with a bow; arched.

[2]**कमान** *kamān* [Engl. *command*], f. **1.** a command, instruction. **2.** *mil.* a particular command or force. **3.** a position, or the status, of command. — ~ पर होना, to be on military service. हाई (मुख्य) ~, m. *mil.* High Command. – कमान-अफ़सर, m. obs. commanding officer (cf. कमांडर).

कमानचा *kamāncā* [P. *kamānca*], m. a small bow.

कमानची *kamāncī* [cf. H. *kamāncā*], f. dimin. hoop (of a cask).

कमाना *kamānā* [**karmāpayati*], v.t. **1.** to earn. **2.** to acquire; to save, to accumulate. **3.** to work (sthg.): to treat, to tend, to service. चमड़ा ~, to tan, or to clean or curry leather. पाख़ाना ~, to clean a lavatory. — अपना नाम ~, to make one's name. – कमा खाना, to live by one's earnings, to support oneself.

कमानी *kamānī* [P. *kamānī*], f. & adj. **1.** f. a spring (in a mechanism). बड़ी ~, f. main-spring; बाल ~, f. hair-spring. **2.** a folding portion (of an appliance: as the legs of a pair of spectacles). **3.** adj. bent, arched. — कमानीदार [P. *-dār*], adj. having a spring, or springs (as a bed-frame, or a mattress).

कमार *kamār* [*karmāra-*], m. reg. (Bihar) a blacksmith.

कमाल *kamāl* [A. *kamāl*], m. & adj. **1.** m. excellence, perfection. **2.** something wonderful; a great achievement; a miracle. **3.** adj. very great, extreme. — ~ करना, to do something wonderful; to succeed to perfection. ~ को पहुँचना, to attain perfection (as an artistic performance). ~ रखना (में), to be perfect (in), a master (of). ~ दिखाना, to show consummate skill or power; to work wonders, or miracles.

कमासुत *kamāsut*, m. an earner.

कमिश्नर *kamiśnar* [Engl. *commissioner*], m. a commissioner.

कमिश्नरी *kamiśnarī* [cf. H. *kamiśnar*], f. **1.** the status or work of a commissioner. **2.** a commissioner's office.

कमी *kamī* [P. *kamī*], f. **1.** deficiency, shortage; want, lack; shortfall, deficit. **2.** diminution, decline; reduction (as of prices). **3.** shortcoming, fault. — कमी-बेशी, f. fluctuation; profit and loss.

क़मीज़ *qamīz* [A. *qamīṣ*], f. a shirt.

कमीन *kamīn* [P. *kamīn*], adj. low, base (= कमीना).

कमीनपन *kamīnpan* [cf. H. *kamīn*], m. see कमीनापन.

कमीनपना *kamīnpanā* [cf. H. *kamīn*], m. = कमीनापन.

कमीना *kamīnā* [P. *kamīna*], adj. & m. **1.** adj. low, base. **2.** m. a base person; person belonging to a community of low status.

कमीनापन *kamīnāpan* [cf. H. *kamīnā*], m. lowness, baseness.

कमीला *kamīlā*, m. *Pl.* = कमेला.

कमीशन *kamīśan* [Engl. *commission*], m. **1.** a commission (cf. आयोग). **2.** commission; brokerage. **3.** remission, reduction, discount (as on a charge or price). — ~ देना, to allow commission or discount (to, को; for, को or के लिए). ~ बैठना, a commission to sit or to be held. ~ लेना, to charge commission, &c.

कमेटी *kameṭī* [Engl. *committee*], f. a committee.

कमेड़ी *kameṛī* [f. A. *qumrī*], f. reg. (Raj.) a dove; ? the ring-dove.

कमेरा *kamerā* [*karmakara-*], m. a workman, labourer; *hist.* a hired labourer.

कमेला *kamelā* [*kāmpīla-*[1]], m. a drug obtained from the capsules of *Mallotus philippinensis* (see कमोद, 2).

कमोद *kamod* [ad. *kumuda-*; w. *moda-*], m. Brbh. **1.** the white water-lily or lotus (the seeds of which are said to have aphrodisiac properties). **2.** ? the tree called *kamelā Mallotus philippinensis*: source of a dye, and formerly used medicinally.

कमोदनी *kamodnī* [cf. H. *kamod*], f. E.H. the white water-lily (= कमोद).

कमोदी *kamodī* [cf. H. *kamod*], f. reg. (Bihar) a sweet rice.

कमोरा *kamorā*, m. reg. an earthenware vessel (cf. कमोरी).

कमोरी *kamorī*, f. Brbh. a small, wide-mouthed earthenware pot (as used for making curds in).

कम्मल *kammal*, m. pronun. var. = कंबल.

क़याम *qayām* [A. *qiyām*], m. U. **1.** state of rest; stay, halt; residence. **2.** stability; permanence. **3.** certainty.

क़यामत *qayāmat* [A. *qiyāma*: P. *qiyāmat*], f. & adj. **1.** f. the resurrection; doomsday. **2.** calamity. **3.** fig. lamentation; commotion. **4.** adj. astounding; dire. — ~ उठाना, or मचाना, to make an appalling commotion. ~ करना, = ~ तोड़ना, 2. ~ का, adj. = ~, 4. ~ झूठ बोलना, to be an appalling liar. ~ तोड़ना, to bring calamity (upon, पर); to oppress harshly.

क़यास *qayās* [A. *qiyās*], m. measuring: **1.** thought, conception; conjecture. **2.** imagining, fancy.

करंक *karaṅk* [S.], m. skull, head; a water-cup made from a coconut; bones of the body, skeleton.

करंग *karaṅg* [ad. *karaṅka-*], m. *Pl.* = करंक.

करंजवा *karañjvā* [cf. H. *karañjā*], m. reg. **1.** an unwanted shoot springing from the base of a plant (as sugar-cane). **2.** smut (in cereal crops).

[1]**करंजा** *karañjā* [*karãnja(ka)-*], m. **1.** the fever-nut, *Caesalpinia bonducella* (= कटकरंज: a thorny bush, the seeds of which are used medicinally). **2.** the tree *Pongamia glabra*. **3.** a brown colour (see करंजोई).

[2]**करंजा** *karañjā* [*karañja(ka)-*], adj. having light-coloured eyes (= कंजा).

करंजोई *karañjoī* [cf. *karañja(ka)-*], f. a brown colour obtained from the *karañjā*, q.v.

[1]**कर** *kar* [*kara-*[2]], m. tax; tribute; toll. — ~ उगाहना, to collect a tax, &c. ~ लगाना, to impose a tax (on, पर), to tax. – करदाता, m. inv. taxpayer. करदेय, adj. taxable. कर-मुक्त, adj. exempt from tax. कर-योग्य, adj. taxable. कराधान [°*ra+ā*°], m. imposing of tax, taxation.

[2]**कर** *kar* [S.], m. doer, maker: **1.** hand. **2.** trunk (of elephant). **3.** beam (of sun, moon). — ~ गहना (का), to take the hand (of): to shelter, to protect; to marry. - कर-ग्रहण, m. taking the hand: marriage. करतल, m. the palm of the hand. °अमलक, m. fig. Brbh. sthg. small or insignificant. °ध्वनि, f. clapping, applause. °ई, f. = करतल, करतलध्वनि. कर-ताल, m. clapping, applause; a kind of small cymbal. °ई, f. beating time by clapping the hands; = करताल. कर-पीड़न, m. hand-pressing: marriage. करबद्ध, adj. with hands folded: earnest (entreaty). कर-माला, f. the hands used as a rosary (the finger-joints corresponding to the beads). कर-सेवक, m. one offering service with or by the hand: specif. adherent of a conservative Hindu group. कराघात [°*ra+ā*°], m. blow with the hand.

[3]**कर** *kar*, ppn. Av. करि, f. = का.

[1]**करई** *karaī*, f. reg. (Bihar) a small earthen pot with a spout (cf. करवा).

[2]**करई** *karaī*, m. *Pl.* a granary, storehouse.

[1]करक *karak* [cf. H. *karaknā*], f. a sharp stinging pain, ache.

[2]करक *karak* [S.], m. the drinking-pot of an ascetic, or student.

[3]करक *karak* [S.], m. hailstone, hail.

करकच *karkac*, ? m. **1.** sea-salt, made by evaporation. **2.** Brbh. a fragment.

करकना *karaknā* [cf. H. *kaṛaknā*], v.i. **1.** to pain, to ache. **2.** to rankle. **3.** Brbh. to clash, to resound. **4.** to break, to snap.

[1]करकरा *karkarā* [*karkaṭa-*], m. **1.** the demoiselle (black-headed) crane, *Anthropoides virgo*. **2.** *HŚS.* the sarus crane (= सारस).

[2]करकरा *karkarā*, adj. = कुरकुरा.

करकराना *karkarānā* [*kaṭakaṭa-*; also *kiṭakiṭāyate*], v.i. **1.** to creak (as of branches); to crackle; to sound harshly (speech). **2.** [cf. H. *karaknā*] to ache (as the eye). **3.** to scratch, to scrabble. **4.** reg. (E.) to cackle (as a hen).

करकराहट *karkarāhaṭ* [cf. H. *karkarānā*], f. **1.** cracking, snapping, crackling. **2.** creaking, grating. **3.** reg. (E.) squabbling, quarrelling.

करका *karkā* [cf. H. [3]*karak*], m. (poet. also f.) hail.

करकाना *karkānā* [? cf. H. *karaknā*], v.t. **1.** to break, to snap. **2.** to bend, to twist, to sprain.

करख- *karakh-*, v.t. Brbh. to incite.

करखा *karkhā*, m. = कड़खा.

करगता *kargatā* [*kaṭi-* (← Drav.); ad. *gata-*], m. *Pl. HŚS.* **1.** a string worn round the waist; a waistband or belt (= करधनी). **2.** a cloth tied round the loins.

करगस *kargas* [ad. *karkaśa-*], m. E.H. a kind of arrow.

करगह *kargah*, m. see करघा.

करगही *kargahī*, f. [P. *kargah*], f. *hist.* a tax on weavers, loom-tax.

करगा *kargā*, m. pronun. var. = करघा, करगह.

करग्रहण *kargrahaṇ*, m. see s.v. [2]कर.

करघा *karghā* [cf. P. *kārgāh*], m. **1.** a weaver's shop. ***2.** a loom. **3.** the hollow in the ground in which a weaver's feet work the treadle.

करछा *karchā*, m. a large ladle (cf. करछी).

करछाल *karchāl*, f. 19c. spring, bound.

करछी *karchī* [cf. H. *karchā*, and *karchul*], f. **1.** a ladle. **2.** a skimmer.

करछुल *karchul* [cf. **kaṭacchu-*: Pa. *kaṭacchu-*], f. **1.** a ladle. **2.** reg. (Bihar) a stoker's shovel.

करछुली *karchulī*, f. = करछुल.

करण *karaṇ* [S.], m. **1.** making, doing. **2.** an action. **3.** *gram.* the instrumental case. **4.** an instrument, implement.

[1]करणी *karāṇī* [S.], f. *math.* a surd, or surd root.

[2]करणी *karṇī*, f. E.H. = करनी.

करणीय *karăṇīyă* [S.], adj. to be done or made; practicable; proper or lawful to be done; necessary to be done.

करड़ी *kurăṛī*, f. the safflower *Carthamus tinctorius* (source of a cooking oil).

करतब *kartab* [ad. *kartavya-*], m. **1.** exploit, feat. **2.** art, skill; sleight of hand. **3.** a bad or wrong action. — ~ दिखाना, to show (one's) skill (in, का).

करतबी *kartabī* [cf. H. *kartab*], adj. performing feats; skilled, adroit.

करतूत *kartūt* [? ad. *kartavyatā*], f. **1.** deed, action; doing(s); trickery. **2.** 19c. art, skill.

करदा *kardā*, m. reg. (W). deduction made from a measured amount to allow for a shortfall in the measurement (as caused by chaff included in grain for sale).

करधनी *kardhanī* [**kaṭabandhana-*], f. **1.** an ornamental belt made of gold or silver links or segments. **2.** a belt of several strands of cotton, girdle. — ~ टूटना, to grow weak; to lose heart; to lose means, to grow poor.

करनल *karnal* [Engl. *colonel* (← *coronel*)], m. colonel.

करना *karnā* [cf. *karoti*], v.t. **1.** to do, to act, to perform, to carry out; to work through (as a sum, a problem); to engage in, to study (as a subject). **2.** to transact, to conduct (business). कचहरी ~, to hold a court. दूकान ~, to keep a shop. **3.** to feel (emotions, desires). मेरा जी बाहर जाने को कर उठा, I suddenly felt a longing to get away. **4.** to put, to place (often कर देना); to arrange, dispose of: to apply; to set up, to establish; to convey. वापस ~, to return (sthg). उसने पानी घड़े में कर दिया, he poured the water into the pot. दीवार पर रंग करो! paint the wall! **5.** to attend to. चौका(-बरतन) ~, to do the dishes. **6.** to make use of, to avail oneself of. रिकशा ~, to go by rickshaw. दवा ~, to take medicine. धोती करना, reg. (N.) to wear a *dhotī*. **7.** to make, to form, to produce; to devise, to contrive (usu. कर लेना); to work (an appliance). चोटी ~, to do one's hair (a woman). रोटी ~, to make the bread, to do the cooking. **8.** to appoint (to a post). **9.** to impart, to bestow. **10.** to render, to cause to be or to become (often कर देना); to turn or to change (into).

11. to effect, to bring about (upon a person: को). **12.** to take over, to make (one's) own. उसने दूसरी कर ली है, he's taken a mistress, or, a second wife. — कर गुज़रना, to carry through; to accomplish. कर देखना, to try, to test. कर लाना, to effect, to accomplish, to execute. करके, adv. having done, doing; = -कर, abs.; for the reason (of). हम यहाँ आ करके बैठ गए, we made our way here and sat down.

क़रनाई *qarnāī* [P. *qar(n)nāy*], f. a horn, trumpet.

करनी *karnī* [*karaṇīya-*], f. **1.** an action, act; a deed. ~ का फल, the fruit of acts, reward or retribution. **2.** a misdemeanour, prank. **3.** a bricklayer's trowel.

करबर *karbar* [ad. *karbara-*: ← Austro-as.], m. Brbh. speckled: the cheetah.

करबला *karbalā* [A. *karbalā*], f. m. *isl.* **1.** name of the place in Iraq where Ḥusain, the younger son of 'Alī, was killed and buried. **2.** place where a *tāziyā* is buried; a Muslim shrine or burying-place.

करबी *karbī* [*kaḍamba-*], f. Brbh. the hollow stalk of a plant (esp. of a fodder plant).

[1]**करम** *karam* [A. *karam*], m. generosity; kindness; grace, favour.

[2]**करम** *karam*. see कर्म, क्रम.

[3]**करम** *karam*. see कर्म, क्रम.

करमकल्ला *karamkallā* [P. *karamb* + *karĭra-*[1]], m. a cabbage; a dwarf-cabbage.

[1]**करवट** *karvaṭ* [**kaṭavr̥tti-*], f. the side (of the body) on which one rests; the position of lying or sleeping on the side. — ~ तक न लेना, not to bestir oneself. ~ बदलना, to turn over while resting or sleeping; to turn to new interests, friends, &c. उसके भाग्य ने ~ बदली है, his fortunes have improved. ~ लेना, = ~ बदलना; to turn over (of a ship). करवटें बदलना, to toss and turn, to be restless. करवटों में काटना, to pass (time) restlessly, in agitation. ऊँट किस ~ बैठता है? colloq. how will the matter turn out?

[2]**करवट** *karvaṭ* [*karapattra-* (? × *paṭṭa-*); w. infl. from H. [1]*karvaṭ*], m. a saw. — काशी-करवट लेना, to die in Banaras, to meet one's death in Banaras (and to gain merit thereby).

करवर *karvar* [*kali-*[1] + *bala-*, *mala-*], f. Brbh. Av. distress, trouble, disaster.

करवाँसी *karvāṁsī*, f. *Pl.* the twentieth part of a *bisvāṁsī*.

करवा *karvā* [cf. *karaka-*[1]], m. **1.** an earthen pot with a spout. **2.** reg. a pod or seed-vessel. — ~ चौथ, f. *hind.* a festival (in the month Kārttik) at which married women observe a fast and worship the *karvā* filled with water (or make an offering of a *karvā* filled with sweets).

करवानक *karvānak* [P. *karvānak*], m. Brbh. Av. **1.** the stone curlew. **2.** *Pl.* a bustard; a crane.

करवाना *karvānā* [cf. *kārayati*], v.t. to cause to be done, to effect, to bring about, to have or to get done (by, से): = कराना.

करवार *karvār* [*karapāla-*], m. Brbh. Av. **1.** a sword. **2.** an oar, paddle; pole used as a rudder.

करवारा *karvārā* [*karapāla-*], m. *Pl.* the bucket attached to a *ḍheṁklī* (lever with fulcrum and counterpoise, used for raising water from a well); (?) the beam of a *ḍheṁklī*.

करवाल *karvāl* [*karapāla-*], m. *Pl. HŚS.* = करवार.

करवीर *karvīr* [S.], m. the fragrant oleander, *Oleander* or *Nerium odorum*.

करवैया *karvaiyā* [cf. H. *karnā*], m. one who brings about or effects an action; causer, doer.

करश्मा *karaśmā*, m. = करिश्मा.

करष *karaṣ*, f. Av, hostility; anger; envy.

करष- *karaṣ-* [ad. *karṣati*], v.i. Av. to be drawn, attracted, captivated.

करसायल *karsāyal* [f. *kr̥ṣṇasāra-*], m. poet. Brbh. an antelope, black buck.

करसी *karsī* [S. *karīṣa-*], f. a piece of dry cow-dung. — ~ ले-, Brbh. Av. to sit by a penance-fire.

करह *karah* [*karabha-*], m. E.H. a camel.

करहा *karhā* [*karabha-*], m. E.H. a camel.

कराँकुल *karāṁkul* [*kalāṅkura-*], m. Brbh. **1.** a crane, *Ardea sibirica*. **2.** *Pl.* the black curlew, *Grus cinerea*.

कराँत *karāṁt* [conn. *karapattra-*], m. a saw.

[1]**कराँती** *karāṁtī* [cf. H. *karāṁt*], f. a small saw.

[2]**कराँती** *karāṁtī* [cf. H. *karāṁt*], m. reg. a sawer, sawyer.

[1]**कराई** *karāī* [cf. H. *karānā*], f. cost of getting sthg. done.

[2]**कराई** *karāī* [*kalāya-*], f. reg. **1.** Bihar. gram (*Phaseolus radiatus*). **2.** E. chaff of pulse.

कराकुल *karākul*, m. 19c. = कराँकुल.

कराना *karānā* [cf. H. *karnā*], v.t. to cause to be done (by, से); to effect (as an introduction, a change); to perform (a sacrifice, &c).

करामत *karāmat* [A. *karāma*: P. *karāmat*], f. a miracle performed by a saint or a righteous man.

करामात *karāmāt* [A. *karāmāt*, pl.], f. marvellous deeds: exploit, feat. — ~ दिखाना, to perform an exploit.

करामाती *karāmātī* [A. *karāmāt*+P. *-ī*], adj. & m. **1.** adj. miraculous, marvellous. **2.** m. a person having supernatural power; magician.

करायजा *karāyjā*, m. *Pl. HŚS.* the plant *Nerium antidysentericum* (= इंदर-जौ, and कोरैया).

करायल *karāyal*, m. *Pl. HŚS.* resin.

क़रार *qarār* [A. *qarār*], m. resting, staying: **1.** fixed state; state of rest; permanence. **2.** stability (of mind); tenacity (of purpose). **3.** settlement, determination. **4.** agreement, engagement. **5.** rest, peace (of mind). — ~ आना (को), to be at rest, or at ease. ~ देना (को), to establish, to settle (a doubtful matter); to lay down, to decree; to adjudge; to accept (as correct). ~ पाना, to be or to become fixed, or settled, or at rest. – क़रार-नामा, m. a written agreement.

करारा *karārā*, adj. **1.** hard, firm. **2.** strong, sturdy. **3.** well-baked (as bread); crisp. **4.** colloq. high-priced; heavy (as price). **5.** of full weight (coin). **6.** harsh (as a rebuff); decisive (a defeat). **7.** sound (a beating).

क़रारी *qarārī* [P. *qarārī*], adj. **1.** fixed, settled. **2.** agreed.

कराल *karāl* [*kaḍāra-*], adj. having projecting teeth: **1.** fearsome, dreadful; loathsome. **2.** high, towering (as a cliff).

कराव *karāv* [cf. H. *karānā*], m. reg. the marriage of a widow (esp. with the former husband's younger brother).

क़रावल *qarāval* [T. *qarāghol*], m. **1.** vanguard. **2.** sentry; guard. **3.** watchman. **4.** hunter.

कराह *karāh* [cf. H. *karāhnā*], f. a moan, groan.

कराहत *karāhat* [A. *karāha*: P. *karāhat*], f. U. dislike, disgust, aversion.

कराहना *karāhnā* [?? conn. **kārayati*[2]], v.i. **1.** to moan, to groan. **2.** to grieve; to sigh.

करिणी *kariṇī* [S.], f. a she-elephant.

करिन *karin* [S.], m. having a hand or trunk: an elephant.

करिया *kariyā* [cf. H. *kālā*], adj. reg. black.

करियात *kariyāt*, f. *Pl.* = किरयात.

[1]**करिल** *karil* [*karira-*[1]], m. Av. a shoot, sprout.

[2]**करिल** *karil* [conn. Pk. *kaḍilla-*], m. Av. = कड़ाह.

[3]**करिल** *karil*, m. Av. = कुरुल.

करिवर *karivar* [S.], m. a splendid elephant (cf. करी).

करिश्मा *kariśmā* [P. *kiriśma*], m. wink, glance: **1.** wonderful deed; a wonder, phenomenon. **2.** talisman, charm; charisma. — ~ दिखाना, to perform a feat.

करिहाँ *karihām̐*, f. Brbh. = करिहाँव.

करिहाँव *kurihām̐v* [**kaṭibhāga-* (× *-sthāna-*)], m. f. reg. the loins; waist; buttocks.

करी *karī* [S.], m. having a hand or trunk: an elephant. — करिवदन, m. elephant-faced: = next. करिवर, m. Av. splendid elephant (a title of Gaṇeś).

क़रीना *qarīnā* [P. *qarīna*], m. **1.** connexion, context. **2.** way, manner, system; proper way (of acting). ***3.** arrangement, order; symmetry. — क़रीने से, adv. from context; by analogy; in proper order. क़रीने से रखना, or लगाना, to put in order.

क़रीब *qarīb* [A. *qarīb*], adj. **1.** near (in time, place, or connexion). **2.** adv. approximately. ~ ~, adv. id. **3.** nearly, almost. **4.** ppn. w. के. near (to), &c.

क़रीबन *qarīban* [A. *qarīban*], adv. = क़रीब, adv.

करीम *karīm* [A. *karīm*], adj. **1.** generous; benign, gracious; forgoing. **2.** a title of God: the Merciful Being.

[1]**करीर** *karīr* [*karīra-*[1]], m. the shoot of a bamboo plant.

[2]**करीर** *karīr* [*karīra-*[2]], m. a thorny leafless shrub, the caper bush, *Capparis aphylla* (which grows in deserts, and is eaten by camels).

करील *karīl*, m. Brbh. = [2]करीर.

करुणा *karuṇā* [S.], f. **1.** compassion, pity. **2.** mercy, tenderness. — करुणागार [°*ā*+*ā*°], m. store of compassion; one very compassionate. करुणात्मक [°*ā*+*ā*°], adj. compassionate nature. करुणार्द्र [°*ā*+*ā*°], adj. moved or melted by compassion. करुणासन [°*ā*+*ā*°], m. mercy-seat, throne of grace. करुणाकर [°*ā*+*ā*°], adj. mine of compassion (= करुणागार). करुणात्मक [°*ā*+*ā*°], adj. touching, pathetic. करुणायतन, m. abode of compassion: one supremely compassionate. करुणानिधान, treasury of compassion: a title of the supreme being as worshipped with devotion. करुणानिधि, f. id. करुणापर [°*ā*+*a*°], adj. (whose nature is) inclined towards compassion. करुणामय, adj. compassionate, tenderhearted, gentle. करुणावान, adj. compassionate.

करेरा *karerā*, adj. reg. hard, stiff; vehement.

करेला *karelā* [*kāravella-*: ← Drav.], m. **1.** a bitter-tasting gourd, *Momordica charantia*. **2.** *Pl. HŚS.* a kind of firework. — ~ नीम चढ़ा a *karelā* creeper climbing a *nīm* tree: an unpleasant (bitter) situation made worse.

करेली *karelī*, f. reg. a variety of bitter gourd (see करेला).

करैत *karait* [cf. H. *kālā*], m. name of a black, very poisonous snake.

करैला *karailā*, m. reg. = करेला.

करैली *karailī*, f. reg. = करेली.

करो- *karo-*, v.t. Brbh. = किरोलना.

करोड़ *karoṛ* [conn. *koṭi-*[2]: ← Austro-as.], m. ten millions, a crore. — करोड़पति, m. possessor of a crore of rupees, of vast wealth. करोड़खुख, m. tale-teller, empty liar.

[1]**करोड़ा** *karoṛā* [? *kali-*[1] + *mala-*], m. distress, trouble, disaster; famine; drought. (cf. करतर).

[2]**करोड़ा** *karoṛā* [? cf. *kara-*[2]; also H. *karoṛ*], m. N. joc. tax-gatherer; inspector, overseer (as of a market).

करोड़ी *karoṛī* [cf. H. *karoṛ*], m. **1.** an extremely wealthy person, a millionaire. 2. = [2]करोड़ा.

करोनी *karonī* [cf. H. *karo-*, *kironā*], f. reg. **1.** milk that sticks to the bottom of a pot after boiling; scrapings (of a pot). **2.** a scraper.

करौंट *karauṁṭ*, f. reg. (Bihar) = करवट.

करौंदा *karauṁdā* [*karamarda-*], m. the corinda bush, *Carissa carandas*, and its small acid fruit.

करौंदिया *karauṁdiyā* [H. *karauṁdā*], adj. reg. reddish (the colour of *karauṁdā* berries).

करौत *karaut* [*karapattra-*], m. a saw.

करौल *karaul*, m. Brbh. a hunter (= क़रावल).

करौली *karaulī*, f. a dagger.

कर्क *kark* [S.], m. **1.** a crab. **2.** *astron.* the sign Cancer. — कर्क-राशि, f. = ~, 2. कर्क-रेखा, f. tropic of Cancer.

कर्कट *karkaṭ* [S.], m. **1.** a crab. **2.** *astron.* the sign Cancer. **3.** *Pl. HŚS.* the demoiselle crane (= [1]करकरा).

कर्कश *karkaś* [S.], adj. & m. **1.** adj. hard, harsh, rough; sharp, piercing. **2.** quarrelsome; violent. **3.** unfeeling. **4.** m. a harsh or violent person, &c.

कर्कशता *karkaśātā* [S.], f. **1.** harshness; quarrelsomeness; harsh or piercing sound. **2.** insensitivity.

कर्केतर *karketar* [ad. *karketana-*], m. *Pl. HŚS.* a kind of quartz.

कर्कोटक *karkoṭak* [S.], m. *Pl. HŚS.* the bael tree, *Aegle marmelos*, and its fruit (*śrīphal*).

क़र्ज़ *qarz* [A. *qarz*], m. **1.** a debt. **2.** a loan. — ~ उठाना, to take on a debt (of, का). ~ उतारना, or अदा करना, or चुकाना, to pay a debt. ~ काढ़ना, or लेना, to take a loan (from, से), to borrow. ~ खाना, to live on money borrowed (from, का), to be dependent financially (on). ~ देना, to lend (to, को). – क़र्ज़दार [P. *-dār*], adj. & m. indebted, owing; a debtor. °ई, f. indebtedness.

क़र्ज़ा *qarzā* [A. *qarza*], m. = क़र्ज़.

कर्ण *karṇ* [S.], m. **1.** the ear; the sense of hearing. **2.** a handle; helm, rudder. **3.** *geom.* hypotenuse (of a triangle); diagonal (of a quadrilateral); chord, secant. **4.** *pros.* spondee. — कर्ण-कटु, adj. harsh to the ear (a sound). कर्णगोचर, adj. perceptible to the ear. कर्णधार, m. steersman, boatman. कर्ण-नाद, m. a ringing in the ears. कर्ण-फल, m. *Pl.* a sort of fish, *Ophiocephalus kurrawey*; (local) a citron. कर्ण-पाली, f. the lobe, or the outer edge of the ear; a garland, or string of jewels, hanging from the ear. कर्णपुर, m. an ancient name for Bhagalpur. कर्णफोन, m. an earphone. कर्णभेदी, adj. piercing the ears (a sound). कर्णफूल, m. an ear pendant or stud. कर्ण-मूल, m. *Pl HŚS.* the root of the ear; a swelling of the glands near the ear. कर्णमोटी, f. *Pl.* a title of Devī or Durgā. कर्णवेध, m. the ceremony of piercing the ears. कर्ण-शूल, m. earache. कर्ण-स्राव, m. discharge from the ear. कर्णाधार [°*ṇa* + *ā*], m. = कर्णधार.

कर्णकटु *karṇkaṭu* [S.], adj. see s.v. कर्ण.

कर्णाट *karṇāṭ* [S.], m. **1.** the Karnataka region (in early times the central districts of the Deccan peninsula, including Mysore). **2.** a person from the Karnataka region. **3.** *mus.* name of a *rāga*.

कर्णाटक *karṇāṭak* [S.], m. the Karnataka region of south India.

कर्णाटी *karṇāṭī*, f. *mus.* name of a *rāgiṇī* (associated with the *rāga* Mālava).

कर्णिका *karṇikā* [S.], f. **1.** an ear ornament, ear-ring. **2.** the middle finger. **3.** the pericarp of a lotus. **4.** a fruit-stalk.

कर्णिकार *karṇikār* [S.], m. a species of *campā* flower (*Michelia*).

कर्णी *karṇī* [S.], adj. & m. *Pl. HŚS.* **1.** adj. having ears or projections; having large ears. **2.** m. *mythol.* name of a mountain; one of the seven principal ranges of mountains which divide the universe.

कर्तन *kartan* [S.], m. cutting.

कर्तनी *kartanī* [S.], f. scissors.

कर्तरी *kartărī* [S.], f. *Pl. HŚS.* scissors; shears.

कर्तव्य *kartavyă* [S.], m. to be done: **1.** duty. **2.** task. – कर्तव्य-निष्ठ, adj. dutiful. °आ, f. कर्तव्यपरायण, adj. conscientious. कर्तव्य-मूढ़, adj. uncertain what to do. कर्तव्य-विमूढ़, adj. id. कर्तव्यशील, adj. conscientious.

कर्तव्यता *kartavyătā* [S.], f. sense of duty.

कर्ता *kartā* [S.], m. inv. **1.** doer; performer; specif. *hind.* chief mourner at a cremation. **2.** maker; composer. **3.** creator of the world, God. **4.** master, proprietor; manager. **5.** husband. **6.** *gram.* nominative (case). **7.** *gram.* subject. — कर्ता-धर्ता, m. inv. the head of a household; = ~, 3., 4. कर्ताप्रधान, adj. *gram.* active (voice). कर्तावाच्य, m. *gram.* active voice.

कर्तापन *kartāpan* [cf. H. *kartā*], m. authorship, &c.

कर्तार *kartār* [S.], m. Brbh. Av. = कर्ता, 1.-3.

कर्तृ *kartr̥* [S.], m. esp. कर्तृ-. = कर्ता. — कर्तृप्रधान, adj. *gram.* active (a verb). करतृवाचक, adj. *gram.* id.; denoting a subject. °-वाची, adj. denoting a subject. °-वाच्य, m. *gram.* active voice. कर्तृवाच्य क्रिया, f. a transitive verb.

कर्तृत्व *kartr̥tvă* [S.], m. state of acting: agency, action; management; rule. — कर्तृत्व-शक्ति, f. power to act, &c., freedom as an agent.

कर्द *kard* [S.], m. mud, mire.

कर्दम *kardam* [S.], m. **1.** mud, mire. **2.** fig. defilement; sin. **3.** Brbh. *mythol.* name of a *prajāpati.*

कर्पास *karpās* [S.], m. = कपास.

कर्पूर *karpūr* [S.], m. camphor. — कर्पूर-वर्ति, f. a taper of camphor and *ghī.* कर्पूर-श्वेत, adj. yellowish-white.

कर्म *karm* [S.], m. **1.** action (with its fruit, and implications of merit); an act, deed; work, occupation; function. **2.** (moral) duty or obligation. **3.** a religious observance, action or rite (as sacrifice, ablution, funeral obsequies). **4.** fate (as the consequence of previous acts); fortune, lot. **5.** result, effect. **6.** (*gram.*) an object; the accusative case. — ~ का लिखा, m. what is marked or written by fate, destiny. ~ का हेठा, adj. abased by fate, wretched. ~ जागना, (one's, का or के) fortune to take a favourable turn, to be in luck. ~ ठोकना, fig. to bewail one's (अपना, अपने) fate or lot. ~ फूटना, fate to prove adverse, to have bad luck. – कर्मकर्ता, m. inv. an agent, deputy; priest. कर्म-कांड, m. see s.v. कर्मकार, m. obs. a workman; reg. blacksmith. कर्मकारक, m. *gram.* accusative case. कर्म-क्षेत्र, m. see s.v. कर्मगति, f. the effects of (one's) *karma*. कर्मचांडाल, m. one debased by his actions. कर्मचारी, m. an employee, worker; post-holder, staff member; obs. collector of revenue from a partic. division of a village. कर्मच्युत, adj. obs. dismissed from office. कर्मज, adj. arising from *karma* (as merits). कर्मनाश, var. करमनासा, f. name of a river which joins the Ganges east of Banaras (so called because contact with its water is supposed to destroy the merit of works). कर्मनिष्ठ, adj. seeking to follow one's proper *karma*; believing in the efficacy of *karma*. कर्म्प्रधान, adj. concerned primarily with *karma* (as an attitude); transf. objective, physically verifiable; *gram.* passive (a verb). कर्म-फल, m. the fruits of actions (esp. with regard to reincarnation of the spirit). कर्म-फोड़, adj. destroying one's destiny: unlucky, unfortunate. कर्मभूमि, f. the region of religious actions: *mythol.* an epithet of Bhārata, Airāvata, and Videha; India, the world. कर्मभोग, m. the fulfilling of destiny, experiencing the consequences of actions. कर्म-मीमांसा, f. see s.v. कर्मयोग, m. the disinterested performance of one's proper *karma.* कर्म-रेखा, f. see s.v. कर्मवाच्य, adj. & m. *gram.* passive. कर्मवीर, m. hero of *karma*: one performing a noble task or performing duty nobly. कर्मशील, adj. dutiful, conscientious; disinterested (in results of actions). कर्मशूर, m. = कर्मवीर. कर्मसिद्धि, f. accomplishment of an act, success. कर्मस्थान, m. = कर्मभूमि. कर्मागत [°*a*+*ā*°], adj. descended, or inherited, in regular succession; traditional. कर्माचल [°*a*+*a*°], m. = कर्मभूमि. कर्माधीन [°*a*+*ā̆*°], adj. subject to destiny, fated, destined. कर्मेंद्रिय [°*a*+*i*°], m. one of the five 'organs of action' (opp. to *buddhīndriya* or 'organs of sense'): the hand, foot, larynx, and organs of generation and excretion.

कर्म-कांड *karmă-kāṇḍ*, [S.], m. **1.** that part of the Veda which relates to ceremonial acts and sacrificial rites. ***2.** the body of religious ceremonies enjoined by Hindu law or established by custom.

कर्म-क्षेत्र *karmă-kṣetr* [S.], m. 1. = कर्मभूमि, see s.v. कर्म. **2.** sphere of functions or duties.

कर्मचारी *karmcārī* [S.], m. see s.v. कर्म.

कर्मठ *karmaṭh* [S.], adj. **1.** industrious, assiduous. 2. = कर्मनिष्ठ (see s.v. कर्म).

कर्मणा *karmaṇā* [S.], adv. & adj. **1.** by actions. **2.** arising through actions or deeds.

कर्मण्य *karmaṇyă*, adj. **1.** industrious, energetic. **2.** enjoined by *dharma* or scripture.

कर्मण्यता *karmaṇyătā* [S.], f. industry, energy.

कर्मत *karmat*, m. obs. *Pl.* a name of the letter ओ (ओकार).

कर्म-मीमांसा *karmă-mīmāṃsā* [S.], f. the prior or practical division of the *mīmāṃsā* philosophy (relating to works, or to religious observances undertaken for specific works).

कर्म-रेखा *karmă-rekhā* [S.], f. mark or line of fate (esp. on the brow): destiny, fate, lot.

कर्मशील *karmăśīl* [S.], adj. see s.v. कर्म.

कर्मी *karmī* [S.], adj. & m. **1.** adj. performing one's *karma*, or religious rites. **2.** engaged in work of a particular nature. **3.** m. a person employed to perform particular tasks.

कर्रवाई *karravāī*, f. = काररवाई.

कर्रा *karrā*, adj. = कड़ा.

कर्राहना *karrāhnā*, v.i. pronun. var. reg. = कराहना.

कर्ष *karṣ* [S.], m. pulling, attraction; astringency. — कर्ष-फल, m. = आँवला, and बहेड़ा.

कर्षक *karṣak* [S.], m. a ploughman; a farmer.

कर्षण *karṣaṇ* [S.], m. **1.** pulling, drawing; haulage. **2.** attracting; attraction.

कर्षी *karṣī* [S.], adj. & m. *Pl. HŚS.* **1.** adj. dragging, drawing, attracting; attractive. **2.** m. a ploughman.

कलंक *kalaṅk* [S.], m. **1.** a spot, mark; disfigurement. **2.** blemish, disgrace. **3.** fig. accusation, suspicion, aspersion. — ~ का टीका लगना (को), to be branded, disgraced, &c. ~ लगाना (को), to brand, to stigmatise. चाँद का ~, m. the man in the moon (cf. लांछन, 2).

कलंकित *kalaṅkit* [S.], adj. blemished, disgraced; defamed, made suspect, or reproachable. — ~ करना, to disgrace, &c.

कलंकी *kalaṅkī* [S.], adj. & m. **1.** adj. blemished, disgraced; defamed, suspect, reproachable. **2.** one having a blemished character, &c.

कलंगी *kalaṅgī*, f. = कलगी.

क़लंदर *qalandar* [P. *qalandar*], m. **1.** an itinerant Muslim ascetic. **2.** a bear-dancer, or monkey-dancer.

क़लंदरी *qalandarī* [P. *qalandarī*], adj. & f. **1.** adj. of or having to do with a *qalandar*. **2.** f. the life of a *qalandar*.

[1]**कल** *kal* [S.], adj. soft, low, sweet (of a sound); delightful, charming. — कल-कल, m. a continuous indistinct noise; murmur, buzz, hum; gurgle; wrangling, quarrelling. कल-कल करना, to make an indistinct noise; to wrangle, &c. — कल-कंठ, m. & adj. a sweet voice; sweet-voiced. कल-धौत, m. gold and silver. कल-रव, m. sweet sound (as of birds). कल-हंस, m. a kind of duck or goose: ? the whistling teal; a title of the supreme being.

[2]**कल** *kal* [*kalya-*[3]], m. & adv. **1.** yesterday; the recent past. ~ का आदमी, a man of yesterday; a recent arrival; an upstart. **2.** tomorrow; the near future. ~ को, in the future, as for the future. — ~ का दिन, yesterday; tomorrow. ~ कलाँ को, adv. at some (indefinite) future time. ~ की बात, something which happened yesterday; a recent occurrence. ~ रात (को), or ~ की रात, last night; tomorrow night. – आज-कल, adv. nowadays.

[3]**कल** *kal* [*kalā-*[2]: ← Drav.], f. **1.** a device, an instrument; a machine; a water pipe or tap. **2.** a part or component (= कल-पुरज़ा); a part of the body, side. मेरी ~-~ में दर्द है, or मेरी ~-~ टूट रही है, my whole body aches. देखिए ऊँट किस ~ बैठेगा, (fig.) let's see how the matter turns out. **3.** a skill; a stratagem. कल-बल-छल, m. shrewdness, strength and cunning: all means (to an end). — ~ उमेठना, or घुमाना, or फेरना (की), to bring under control, to check or to discipline. उसकी ~ आपके हाथ में है, he is in your power, at your disposal. – कल-कारख़ाने, m. pl. factories. कलदार [P. *-dār*], adj. & m. reg. (Bihar) machined; a coin having a milled edge.

[4]**कल** *kal* [*kalya-*[1]], f. ease; peace, quiet; relief, repose. — ~ आना (को), or ~ पड़ना (को), or ~ पाना, to be at ease, to obtain ease or relief. ~ से, adv. at ease, &c. ~ (से) बे-कल होना, to become ill at ease or disturbed.

[5]**कल** *kal* [*kali-*[2]], f. = कली.

[6]**कल** *kal* [*kali-*[1]], m. = [2]कलि.

क़लई *qalaī* [A. *qal'ī*], f. **1.** tin. ***2.** tinning (of utensils); tin-plate; gilding. **3.** whitewashing. **4.** fig. veneer, specious gloss. — ~ उखड़ना, or उधड़ना, or खुलना, a veneer to be removed: the real qualities (of, की) to be exposed. ~ करना (पर), to tin; to whitewash. ~ का चूना, m. lime. ~ खोलना, to unmask the real qualities (of, की). ~ न लगना, a veneer not to stick: the real quality (of, की) not to be obscured. – क़लईगर [P. *-gar*], m. a tinsmith. °ई, f. the business of tinning. क़लईदार [P. *-dār*], adj. tin-plated.

क़लक़ *qalaq* [A. *qalaq*], m. keen regret; distress. — ~ रहना, regret to rankle. ~ होना (को), to feel regret, or distress; to pine.

कलकी *kalkī* [S.], m. the name of the tenth and future avatār of Viṣṇu as destroyer of the wicked and liberator of the world, at the end of the *kali yuga*.

कलक्टर *kalakṭar* [Engl. *collector*], m. **1.** *admin.* collector, chief administrative officer of a district. **2.** a collector (generally).

[1]**कलक्टरी** *kalakṭarī* [cf. H. *kalakṭar*], adj. *admin.* having to do with a collector. — ~ कचहरी, f. *law.* collectorate court.

[2]**कलक्टरी** *kalakṭarī* [cf. H. *kalakṭar*], f. *admin.* **1.** a collector's activity or rank. **2.** collector's office(s).

कलगा *kalgā*, m. = कलगी.

कलगी *kalgī* [ad. P. *kal(a)kī, kalgī*: ← T.], f. **1.** comb (of a cock); crest (of a bird). **2.** an ornament attached to a turban: crest, plume; jewel, &c. **3.** the peak of a (Sikh's) turban. — कलगीदार [P. *-dār*], adj. crested, plumed, &c.

कल-जिभा *kal-jibhā* [H. *kālā*+H. *jībh*], adj. & m. **1.** adj. black-tongued: evil-tongued; whose curses are fulfilled, ill-omened. **2.** esp. -जिभी, f. such a person.

कलत्र *kalatr* [S.], f. wife.

कलना *kalănā* [cf. [3]*kal*], f. poet. sthg. created, creation.

कलपना *kalapnā* [cf. H. [2]*kalāp*], v.i. **1.** to be distressed or in pain. **2.** to lament.

कलपाना *kalpānā* [cf. H. *kalapnā*], v.t. to grieve, distress, pain.

कलफ़ *kalaf* [P. *kalaf*], m. starch. — ~ लगाना (को), to starch. – कलफ़दार [P. *-dār*], adj. starched.

कलबंदा *kalbandā*, m. *Pl.* a variety of aloe.

कलबूत *kalbūt* [cf. P. *kālbūd*, for *kalbūt*], m. **1.** Brbh. shoemaker's last. **2.** mould, frame. **3.** body, frame (of a man or animal).

कलबूद *kalbūd*, m. E.H. = कलबूत, 3.

कलभ *kalabh* [S.], m. a young elephant.

कलम *kalam* [*kaḍamba-*; × H. *qalam*], f. **1.** a reed (for writing with). **2.** reg. (Bihar) a shoot, or seedling (of indigo, or betel).

क़लम *qalam* [A. *qalam*], f. m. **1.** a pen. **2.** a painter's brush. **3.** f. [× H. *kalam*] a cutting (for planting or grafting). **4.** the tapering part of a pointed beard; a side-lock of hair. **5.** [? × H. *kalam*] *chem.* a crystal. **6.** fig. penmanship; style of writing, or of painting. – ~ करना, to cut; to cut off; to prune. ~ घसीटना, to scribble. परकार की ~, f. a compass (for drawing). ~ जारी रहना (की), (one's) writ or authority to continue. ~ चलाना, to write. ~ फेरना, or मारना, to cross (out or through, पर); fig. to cancel. ~ बनाना, to make or to mend a pen; to shave the upper part of the beard. ~ लगाना, to plant (cuttings); to graft (on to, में). – क़लमकार, m. a writer, pen-pusher; engraver; painter. °ई, f. writing; engraving; painting. क़लमघसीट, m. pen-puller: a hack writer. कलमजीवी, m. one who lives by the pen: a literary man; journalist. क़लमतराश [P. *-tarāś*], m. a pen-knife. क़लम-दवात, f. pen and ink(well). क़लमदान [P. *-dān*], m. pen-holder. क़लमबंद [P. *-band*], adj. written down; recorded.

कलमल *kalmal* [cf. *kalate*], f. agitation, restlessness, disquiet.

कलमलाना *kalmalānā* [cf. H. *kalmal*], v.i. to fidget, to move restlessly or uneasily; to writhe, or wriggle; to flounder.

कलमा *kalmā* [A. *kalima*: P. *kalma*], m. **1.** a word, speech; saying, discourse. **2.** *isl.* the Muslim confession of faith (i.e. *lā ilāha illa'l-lāh* 'there is no god but God ...'). — ~ पढ़ाना, to make (one) repeat the *kalmā*, to convert (one) to Islam. ~ पढ़ना, to repeat the *kalmā*; to acknowledge the superiority (of, का); iron. to follow servilely (in one's words).

कलमी *kalmī* [*kaḍambī-*], f. tops of the plant *Convolvulus repens* (used as a vegetable).

क़लमी *qalămī* [P. *qalamī*], adj. **1.** grafted. **2.** crystalline (saltpetre, &c).

कलमुँहा *kalmuṁhā* [H. *kālā*+H. *muṁh*], adj. & m. black-faced: **1.** adj. of forbidding or ill-omened features. **2.** pej. disgraced; wretched. **3.** m. a forbidding-looking, or opprobrious person.

कलवल *kalval*, f. = करवर.

कलवार *kalvār* [*kalyapāla-*: Pk. *kallā-* ← Drav.], m. **1.** a distiller of spirits; a collector of toddy-juice from palm trees; one belonging to the *kalvār* community. **2.** a seller of spirits, &c.; liquor-shop keeper, innkeeper. — कलवार-ख़ाना, m. liquor-shop, drinking-house.

कलवारिन *kalvārin* [cf. H. *kalār*], f. **1.** a woman of the *kalvār* community. **2.** the wife of a *kalvār*. **3.** a woman who keeps a liquor-shop, &c.

[1]**कलवारी** *kalvārī* [cf. H. *kalvār*], f. **1.** the occupation or activity of a *kalvār*. **2.** the place of work or business of a *kalvār*.

[2]**कलवारी** *kalvārī* [cf. H. *kalvār*], adj. & m. **1.** adj. having to do with a *kalvār*, or *kalvārs*. **2.** m. = कलवार.

कलश *kalaś* [S.], m. = कलसा.

कलस *kalas*, m. = कलश.

कलसना *kalasnā*, v.i. = किलसना.

कलसा *kalsā* [*kalaśa-*], m. **1.** a water-pot, pitcher, jar. **2.** a rounded pinnacle or a ball, &c., on the top of a dome; crest, finial. — ~ थापन करना, to offer to a deity a jar of water in which twigs from sacred trees have been placed.

कलसी *kalsī* [*kalása-*], f. dimin. = कलसा.

कलह *kalah* [S.], m. quarrel, strife. — कलहप्रिय, adj. quarrelsome.

कलहंस *kalhaṃs* [S.], m. a partic. goose or duck: ? the whistling teal (see [1]कल).

कलहटी *kalahṭī* [? conn. *kalā-*[2]], f. *Pl.* tumbling, acrobatics.

कलहारी *kalhārī* [*kalahakāra-*], f. *Pl. HŚS.* a quarrelsome woman.

कलाँ *kalām̐*, adj. pronun. var. = कलान.

कला *kalā* [S.], f. **1.** a small part of anything. **2.** specif. a sixteenth part: a digit of the moon. **3.** an art; a skill or accomplishment; trick; juggling. ~ करना, to perform a trick or feat; to play a trick (on, पर) (= ~ खेलना). **4.** art; a person's art or skill. — कला-कृति, f. an artistic work or creation. कला-कुशल, adj. artistic, skilled in art, or in an art. कला-कौशल, m. art, skill in art. कला-नाथ, m. the moon; a fine artist. कला-निधि, f. the moon. कलानेत्री, f. see s.v. कलापूर्ण, adj. artistic. कलाबाज़ [P. *-bāz*], m. an acrobat. °ई, f.: acrobatics, somersaulting. कलाबाज़ी करना or खाना, to tumble, to somersault; to perform acrobatics. कलावंत, m. an acrobat. कलावान, adj. artistic; skilled in art, or in an art.

[1]**कलाई** *kalāī* [*kalācī-*], f. **1.** the wrist. **2.** *Pl.* fetlock (of a horse).

[2]**कलाई** *kalāī* [*kalāya-*], f. a pulse, *Phaseolus roxburghii* or *Ph. radiatus* (= उड़द or मूँग).

कलाक़ंद *kalāqand* [cf. P. *qand*], m. a sweet made of *khoā* or *chenā* with sugar.

कलाकार *kalākār* [cf. *kalā-*[2]], m. f. an artist, one skilled in an art; a skilled performer; an actor.

कलाकारिता *kalākāritā* [cf. *kalā-*[2]], f. artistry.

कलाकारी *kalākārī* [cf. *kalā-*[2]], f. = कलाकारिता.

कलान *kalān* [P. *kalān*], adj. large, great. — कलान-रास, adj. large- or long-headed: of good breeding, pedigree (a horse).

कलाना *kalānā* [*kalayati*[2]], v.t. reg. (N. or Panj.) to shake up, to shake together; to winnow.

कलानेत्री *kalānetrī* [cf. *kalā-*, and H. *(abhi)netrī*], f. a woman artist.

[1]**कलाप** *kalāp* [S.], m. totality, mass (of a number of separate things). — क्रिया-कलाप, works (as of an author); one's activity, doings. उनका क्या ~ रहता है आज-कल? what's he doing nowadays?

[2]**कलाप** *kalāp* [? conn. *lāpā-*], m. lamentation, sorrow.

कलापी *kalāpī* [S.], m. poet. having a mass of (tail-)feathers: a peacock.

कलाबतून *kalābatūn*, m. reg. = कलाबत्तू.

कलाबत्तू *kalābattū* [S. *kalā-*[2]; ? with *vr̥tta-/varta-*], m. silk thread around which is twisted gold or silver thread or wire; silk and silver or gold thread twisted together; gold or silver thread, or fringe.

कलाम *kalām* [A. *kalām*], m. **1.** word, speech, discourse; a complete sentence, or proposition. **2.** a composition, work. — ~ करना, to speak, to relate. – तकिया-कलाम, m. prop for speech: a word or phrase repeatedly or habitually used in speech (as 'actually' or 'I mean' in English).

कलार *kalār*, m. = कलवार, कलाल.

कलाल *kalāl* [**kallāla*], m. = कलवार.

कलावा *kalāvā* [cf. H. [1]*kalāī*], m. **1.** a thread of red and yellow strands, worn on the wrist on auspicious occasions (= मौली, 2). **2.** *Pl. HŚS.* the rope round an elephant's neck (in loops of which the mahout places his feet).

कलिंग *kaliṅg* [S.], m. *hist.* **1.** Kalinga, the name of a region along the S.E. coast of India extending from near Cuttack to near Madras. **2.** the *karañjā* tree (*Pongamia glabra*).

कलिंद *kalind* [S.], m. *mythol.* Brbh. name of the mountain on which the river Jumna rises.

कलिङ्दा *kaliṅdā* [*kālindaka-*], m. water-melon (= तरबूज़).

[1]**कलि** *kali* [S.], f. a flower bud.

[2]**कलि** *kali* [S.], m. *mythol.* **1.** name of the last and worst of the four *yugas* or ages, the present or iron age, at the end of which the world is to be destroyed. **2.** dissension, strife, quarrelling. — कलि-काल, m. the *kali* age. कलि-मल, m. impurity, guilt, sin. कलि-युग, m. the *kali* age. °ई, adj. having to do with the *kali* age.

कलिका *kalikā* [S.], f. a bud (cf. कली).

कलित *kalit* [S.], adj. made with art or skill.

क़लिया *qaliyā* [A. *qaliya*], m. boiled or fried meat with any dressing; a meat curry.

कलियाना *kaliyānā* [cf. H. *kalī*], v.i. to bud, to blossom.

कली *kalī* [*kalikā-*], f. **1.** a flower bud. कच्ची ~, an unopened bud. **2.** fig. a delicate or innocent-looking girl. **3.** a gusset (in clothing). 4. = ~ का चूना. — ~ का चूना, unslaked lime. पान, ~, दली, *pān*, lime, *supārī* (ingredients of made-up betel leaf). बंद ~, f. a virgin. कलियाँ आना (में), to begin to bud or to blossom.

कलीसा *kalīsā* [P. *kalīsă*: ← Gk.], m. a church.

कलुष *kaluṣ* [S.], adj. & m. **1.** adj. dirty, dirtied. **2.** foul, impure; sinful; base. **3.** m. dirt; impurity; sin, &c. — कलुष-भेद, m. foul discrimination.

कलुषित *kaluṣit* [S.], adj. dirtied; defiled, debased, &c. (cf. कलुष).

कलुषी *kaluṣī* [cf. H. *kaluṣ*], m. a base or sinful person, &c. (cf. कलुष).

कलूटा *kalūṭā* [cf. H. *kālā*], adj. pej. **1.** dark-complexioned. **2.** base, wretched.

कलेउ *kaleu*, m. = कलेवा.

कलेजा *kalejā* [*kāleyaka-*], m. **1.** the liver (esp. of a human being). **2.** the vitals: specif. heart, liver and lungs; the heart. **3.** courage, vitality; the heart, stomach, emotions. — ~ उछलना, the heart to leap (as with joy); the heart to palpitate. ~ उड़ा जाना, to lose heart, to be anxious. ~ उलटना, the heart to rise to the mouth; to be exhausted by vomiting. ~ काटना, fig. to do sthg. resolutely at great cost or sacrifice. ~ काँपना, the heart to tremble: to be afraid; to feel very cold. ~ खाना, to gnaw one's heart: to afflict, to burden. ~ छलनी होना, the heart to be pierced (like a sieve: as by afflictions). ~ जलना, the heart to burn: to grieve, to mourn; to burn with envy. ~ टुकड़े-टुकड़े होना, the heart to be broken; courage or morale to fail. ~ टूटना, id. ~ ठंडा करना, to assuage (one's, का) heart: to obtain one's wish; to obtain relief. ~ तर होना, the heart to be fresh: to be at ease, to relax. ~ थामकर बैठ जाना, or रह जाना, to be suddenly frightened, the heart to miss a beat. ~ दहलना, the heart to quake. ~ पक जाना, fig. to reach limits of endurance. ~ फटना, the heart to burst: to be grief-stricken; to be consumed with envy or jealousy. ~ बढ़ना, the heart to rise: to be emboldened. ~ मलना, to feel frustrated, or jealous. – ~ मसोसकर रह जाना, to remain with heart wrung: to feel a continuing helplessness or frustration. ~ मुँह को आना, = ~ उलटना; to be grief-stricken; to be filled with loathing. ~ सुलगना, the heart to be burning (as with grief or malice). कलेजे का टुकड़ा, m. fig. a person or thing supremely dear. कलेजे पर चोट लगना (के), to be wounded at the heart: to suffer a dire shock or blow. कलेजे पर साँप फिरना, or लोटना, fig. to suffer jealousy or envy. कलेजे पर हाथ धरकर, or रखकर, देखना, to consider (sthg.) with hand on heart: to consider objectively or justly. कलेजे में आग लगना, to feel a burning thirst. कलेजे में ठंडक पहुँचना (को), to feel relieved, &c. कलेजे से लगाना, or लगा रखना, to hold very dear, to cherish; to embrace. पत्थर का ~, m. a heart of stone.

कलेजी *kalejī* [cf. H. *kalejā*], f. **1.** the liver (of an animal). **2.** the liver, lungs and heart (or 'pluck': of an animal).

कलेवर *kalevar* [S.], m. **1.** the body, frame; carcass. **2.** fig. framework. — ~ बदलना, *hind.* to pass (by transmigration) from one body to another.

कलेवा *kalevā* [cf. **kālyaka-*] **1.** a light morning meal. **2.** a light meal taken at other times, esp. a lunch carried by travellers, labourers, &c. **3.** a particular meal, taken by a bridegroom and his party in the bride's house. — ~ करना, to breakfast, &c.

कलेशियाया *kaleśiyāyā* [cf. *kleśa-*: ad.], adj. & m. **1.** adj. quarrelsome, truculent. **2.** m. a quarrelsome person.

कलेस *kales* [*kleśa-*: Pa. *kilesa-*], m. = क्लेश.

कलेसहाया *kaleshāyā* [? *-bhāva-*], adj. & m. = कलेशियाया.

कलैंडर *kalaiṇḍar* [Engl. *calendar*], m. a calendar.

कलैया *kalaiyā* [cf. *kalā-*²: H. ³*kal*], f. a somersault. — ~ खाना, to turn a somersault.

कलोंजी *kaloṁjī*, f. = कलौंजी.

कलोर *kalor* [? cf. *kalya-*²: Pk. *kalhoḍa-*], f. a heifer.

कलोल *kalol* [*kallola-*: ← Drav.], m. gambolling, sport, play; frolicsomeness, wantonness. — ~ करना, to frolic, to gambol, &c.

कलौंजी *kalauṁjī* [**kālakuñjikā-*], f. **1.** black cumin, *Nigella indica* (used medicinally: ? = इंदर-जौ). **2.** stuffed, spiced lady's-fingers (*bhiṇḍī*) or egg-plant. **3.** a spiced mango chutney.

कलौंस *kalaums*, f. **1.** blackness, darkness; dark stain or spot. **2.** fig. = कलंक.

कल्प *kalp* [S.], m. rule, practice; age: **1.** *mythol.* an aeon: the period of a day of Brahmā, 1, 000 *yugas* or 4, 320, 000, 000 years, measuring the duration of the world. **2.** an age, era. — कल्प-तरु, m., or कल्प-द्रुम, m., or कल्प-लता, f., = कल्प-वृक्ष. कल्प-वास, m. residence as an ascetic on the banks of the Ganges during the month of Māgh. कल्प-वृक्ष, m. *mythol.* one of the fabulous plants or trees of Indra's or of Kṛṣṇa's paradise, a tree that grants all desires. कल्पांत [°*pa*+*a*°], m. the end of a *kalpa*. कल्पांतर [°*pa*+*a*°], m. another *kalpa*; a new age.

कल्पना *kalpănā* [S.], f. making, forming: **1.** imagination. **2.** something imagined: a figment of imagination; a conjecture; hypothesis. — ~ करना (की), to imagine; to contrive (as ideas, plans); to suppose, &c. ~ से, adv. conjecturally. – कल्पनातीत [°*nā + a*°], adj. beyond imagination; inconceivable. कल्पना-शक्ति, f. imaginative power. कल्पनाशील, adj. imaginative (a person).

कल्पनीय *kalpănīyă* [S.], adj. imaginable, conceivable.

कल्पित *kalpit* [S.], adj. formed, fabricated; artificial, contrived, false; supposed, assumed.

क़ल्ब *qalb* [A. *qalb*], m. U. the heart; inner part, core.

कल्मष *kalmaṣ* [S.], m. **1.** stain. **2.** sin.

कल्याण *kalyāṇ* [S.], m. **1.** welfare, prosperity; good fortune. **2.** a virtuous or auspicious action. **3.** *mus.* name of a *rāg* (sung at night). — ~ करना, to bring about (one's) well-being or salvation. ~ होना, to be prosperous, to be propitious. – कल्याणकर, adj. = next. °-कारी, adj. auspicious, conducive to one's well-being, &c. कल्याणकारी राज्य, m. welfare state. कल्याण-कोष, m. welfare fund.

कल्याणी *kalyāṇī* [S.], adj. & m. **1.** adj. auspicious, prosperous, &c. (see कल्याण); euph. blessed. **2.** a prosperous, or blessed person.

कल्लर *kallar*, adj. & m. reg. **1.** adj. barren, sterile. **2.** barren or saline soil.

1कल्ला *kallā* [*karĭra-*1], m. **1.** shoot, sprout. **2.** a cabbage (= करमकल्ला).

2कल्ला *kallā* [P. *kalah*], m. **1.** the upper jaw, cheek. **2.** fig. boasting. — ~ बैठना, to be deflated (a boaster).

कल्लाना *kallānā*, v.i. to burn, to sting. — जी ~, to feel vexation or a sense of hurt.

कल्लाल *kallāl* [**kallāla-*], m. reg. (W). = कलवार.

कल्लोल *kallol* [S.], m. **1.** a wave. **2.** joy, delight.

कल्लोलिनी *kallolinī* [S.], f. having waves: a river.

कवच *kavac* [S.], m. **1.** armour; coat of mail. **2.** an amulet, lucky charm. **3.** armour-plating. — कवचधारी, adj. carrying armour, armoured. कवच-पत्र, m. birch-tree leaf inscribed with a number (see ~, 2).

कवचित *kavăcit* [S.], adj. **1.** clad in armour. **2.** armoured (a vehicle).

कवची *kavăcī* [S.], adj. wearing armour.

कवयित्री *kavayitrī* [S.], f. a poetess.

कवर *kavar* [S.], m. *Pl. HŚS.* braid or cluster (of hair); bundle, bunch.

कवरी *kavărī* [S.], f. poet. a braid of hair.

कवल *kavăl* [S.], m. **1.** a mouthful (of food). 2. = कुल्ली.

कवाच्छ *kavācch*, m. reg. (Bihar) = केवाँच.

क़वायद *qavāyd* [A. *qavā'id*, pl.], f. var. /qəvait/. rules: **1.** m. U. grammatical rules; grammar. **2.** f. *mil.* drill; parade. **3.** manoeuvres (= युद्धाभ्यास). — ~ करना, to perform drill (soldiers); to walk in step. ~ सिखाना (को), to drill (soldiers); colloq. to pace (restlessly) about. ~ लेना (से), id. फ़ौजी ~, f. = ~, 2.

कवि *kavi* [S.], m. a poet. — कवि-सम्मेलन, m. a gathering at which poets recite their works. कवीश्वर [°*i + ī*°], m. lord of poets: eminent poet.

कविता *kavitā* [S.], f. **1.** poetry. **2.** a poem.

कविताई *kavitāī* [cf. H. *kavitā*], f. **1.** poetry-making, composition of poetry. 2. = कविता, 1.

कवित्त *kavitt* [ad. *kavitva-*], m. **1.** poetry; a poem. **2.** a Hindi syllabic metre having four lines with thirty-one syllables per line. 3. = छप्पय.

कवित्व *kavitvă* [S.], m. poetic quality; poetic insight.

कव्य *kavyă* [S.], m. 19c. offering of food to dead ancestors.

क़व्वाल *qavvāl* [A. *qavvāl*], m. speaking (by occupation): a musician (usu. a Muslim) who sings religious songs to an accompaniment (as on the *sāraṅgī* or *tānpūrā*); a professional story-teller.

क़व्वाली *qavvālī* [A. *qavvālī* and H. *qavvāl*], f. **1.** singing and playing by one or more *qavvāls*. ***2.** the type of songs sung by *qavvāls*. **3.** [H.] occupation of a *qavvāl*.

कश *kaś* [P. *kaś*], m. **1.** a drawing, pulling. 2. draw, inhaling (of a cigarette, hookah, &c). **3.** -कश. adj. & m. formant. drawing, pulling; enduring. — ~ खींचना, or लेना, or लगाना, to take a puff (at, का). – दिलकश, adj. attractive, interesting. मेहनतकश, adj. & m. enduring (or one who endures) difficulty. कशाकशी [P. *-ā-*], f. a pulling to and fro; jostling, turmoil; dilemma, perplexity; struggle, conflict. कशमकश [P. *-ma-*], f. = कशाकशी.

कशा *kaśā* [ad. *kaśā̆-*], m. f. a whip, lash.

कशिश *kaśiś* [P. *kaśiś*], f. **1.** attraction, attractive power. **2.** attractiveness, charm.

कशीदगी *kaśīdăgī* [P. *kaśīdagī*], f. U. tension; ill-feeling.

कशीदा *kaśīdā* [P. *-kaśīda-*], m. pulled, stretched: a kind of needlework, embroidery. — ~ काढ़ना, to embroider.

कश्ती *kaśtī* [P. *kaśtī*], f. **1.** a boat, (small) vessel; a canoe, or skiff. **2.** a long, narrow tray, or drawer. **3.** (in chess) the castle, rook (syn. हाथी).

कश्मीर *kaśmīr* [S.], m. Kashmir.

कश्मीरनी *kaśmīrnī* [cf. H. *kaśmīr*], f. a Kashmiri woman.

[1]**कश्मीरी** *kaśmīrī* [cf. H. *kaśmīr*], adj. & m. **1.** adj. having to do with Kashmir. **2.** m. a man born in Kashmir.

[2]**कश्मीरी** *kaśmīrī* [cf. H. *kaśmīr*], f. the Kashmiri language.

कश्यप *kaśyap* [S.], m. *mythol.* **1.** name of a deified sage, son of Marīci, husband of Diti and Aditi, and father of the Daityas and Ādityas. **2.** name of a brāhmaṇ *gotra*.

कश्शाफ़ *kaśśāf* [A. *kaśśāf*], adj. very clear, explicit.

कष्ट *kaṣṭ* [S.], m. **1.** difficulty, trouble; inconvenience; labour, effort. **2.** wretchedness, hardship, want. **3.** pain, suffering; affliction. — ~ उठाना, or सहना, to suffer difficulty, distress, &c. ~ करना, to make an effort, to take pains or trouble. ~ देना (को), to trouble, to inconvenience; to molest. ~ पाना, = ~ उठाना. – कष्टकर, adj. causing difficulty, suffering, &c. कष्टदायक, adj. id. कष्टसाध्य, adj. to be accomplished with effort or difficulty.

[1]**कस** *kas* [*kaṣa-*], m. **1.** assaying, testing, proving. **2.** means of assaying: touchstone. **3.** the outcome of an assay: virtue, quality; temper (of a sword). — कसदार [P. *-dār*], adj. active, vigorous.

[2]**कस** *kas* [cf. *karṣati*], m. **1.** a means of binding; a fastening, or tie; tether. *__2.__ strength, tenacity; power. — कसबल, m. reg. (E.) vigour, virility.

[3]**कस** *kas* [conn. *kaṣāya-* or ? *kaṣa-*], m. *Pl. HŚS.* **1.** a decoction. **2.** astringency.

[4]**कस** *kas*, Brbh. Av. = कैसे, कैसा.

[5]**कस** *kas* [conn. *karṣaka-*], m. reg. (W). a small mattock, or pickaxe.

कसक *kasak* [cf. *kaṣati*], f. **1.** an ache; a nagging or recurrent pain; stitch (in the side). **2.** pang (as of the heart). **3.** fig. sympathy, compassion. **4.** rancour; chagrin. — ~ निकालना or मिटाना, to relieve the pain or distress (of, की).

कसकना *kasaknā* [cf. *kaṣati*]. **1.** to ache; to feel a nagging or recurrent pain. **2.** to feel a pang (as of the heart).

कसकुट *kaskuṭ* [cf. *kāṁsya-*; ?+H. *kūṭnā*], m. an alloy of copper, tin and zinc.

कसन *kasan* [cf. H. *kasnā*], f. **1.** the process of tightening, tying. इस खाट की ~ बहुत अच्छी है, this bed is well made (tightly joined and strung). **2.** reg. (W.) ? m. tie, fastening, thong. **3.** transf. strain; suffering.

[1]**कसना** *kasnā* [*karṣati*], v.t. **1.** to tighten, to draw tight. **2.** to tie, to fasten, to bind; to harness (a horse). **3.** to press down or against; to constrict (as the body by an ill-fitting garment). **4.** to cram or to pack (into a container or vehicle); to load (a firearm); colloq. to land (a blow). **5.** to restrain, to discipline. उसे ~ पड़ेगा, he'll have to be brought under control. — कसकर, कसके, abs. tightly; forcibly; sparingly. बारिश कसके हो रही थी, it was raining heavily. – कसा-कसाया, adj. made completely ready; tight, compact.

[2]**कसना** *kasnā* [*kaṣati*], v.t. to rub: **1.** to assay, to test, to examine; to put to proof. **2.** to grate (as vegetables). कसी-कसाई गरी, grated coconut.

कसबन *kasban*, f. pronun. var. = कसबिन.

क़सबा *qusbā* [A. *qaṣba*], m. a small town; a large village.

क़सबाती *qasbātī* [P. *qaṣbātī*], adj. of or belonging to a town, or a large village.

कसबिन *kasbin* [A. *kasb*+H. *-in*], f. reg. (W). = कसबी.

कसबी *kasbī* [A. *kasb*+P. *-ī*], f. reg. (E). one who earns or gains: specif. a prostitute.

क़सम *qasam* [A. *qasm*], f. an oath. — ~ उतारना, to free oneself of a sworn obligation; to carry out a obligation nominally only. ~ खाना, m. to swear an oath. ~ खाने के लिए, adv. = next. ~ खाने को, adv. (enough) to meet an obligation (sc. to take an oath upon: of sthg. in short supply). हमारे पास ~ खाने को एक पैसा नहीं है, I haven't a *paisā*, I swear. ~ खिलाना (को), to make (one) swear; to put (one) on oath. ~ तोड़ना, to break an oath. ~ दिलाना (को), = next. ~ देना (को), to administer an oath (to); to adjure (one). ~ रखना (पर), to make (one) swear. ~ रखाना (से), id. ~ लेकर कहना, to say on oath. ~ लेना, to put (one, से) on oath. ~ से? adv. colloq. seriously? you don't mean it! घर में खाना था, तो उनके लिए काम करने की ~ थी, if there was any food in the house, that was enough for them to swear not to work. तुम्हें … की ~ है, [I] implore you by ….

कसमस *kasmas*, f. = कसमसाहट.

कसमसाना *kasmasānā* [cf. *kaṣati, maṣati*], v.i. **1.** to stir, be agitated; to wriggle; to fidget. **2.** to be stirred (to do sthg). वह उनसे मिलने के

लिए कसमसा उठा, he felt an anxious desire to meet, or to see, them.

कसमसाहट *kasmasāhaṭ* [cf. H. *kasmasānā*], f. agitation, restlessness; fidgeting, wriggling.

क़समी *qasmī* [P. *qasmī*], adj. **1.** sworn (as a statement). **2.** bound by oath (a person).

कसर *kasr* [A. *kasr*], f. **1.** a want, defect; shortcoming, shortfall; difficulty, estrangement (in a relationship). मियाँ बीबी में ~ पड़ गई, husband and wife fell out. **2.** loss, damage. — ~ उठाना or उठा रखना, to accept or suffer a loss; neg. not to tolerate a defect. उसने कोइ ~ उठा न रखी, he left nothing undone. ~ करना (में), to allow a shortcoming (in); to make a deduction. ~ छोड़ना, to cause sthg. to fall short, be wanting; neg. = ~ न उठाना. ~ निकालना, to make good a loss; to be revenged, to get even (with one). अच्छे नंबर पाकर पिछले साल की ~ निकाल ली, (he) made up for the previous year's bad marks. ~ पड़ना, loss or shortfall to be suffered (by, को); a flaw or deficiency to develop (in, में). ~ रखना, – ~ छोड़ना. ~ रहना, to fall short, &c.; सब्ज़ी में कुछ नमक की ~ रह गई है, there's not enough salt in the vegetables.

[1]**कसरत** *kasrat* [A. *kaṣrat*], f. U. **1.** abundance; excess. **2.** majority. — ~ से, adv. in abundance.

[2]**कसरत** *kasrat* [A. *kasra*: P. *kasrat*], f. **1.** exercise (usu. bodily exercise); training, practice. **2.** an individual physical exercise. — ~ करना, to train, to practise (a bodily or athletic skill).

कसरती *kasratī* [cf. H. *kasrat*], adj. inv. **1.** taking physical or athletic exercise. **2.** developed (the body) by training or exercise; athletic, gymnastic. — ~ आदमी, one accustomed to physical exercise. ~ बदन, m. a well-developed body or build.

कसवाना *kasvānā* [cf. H. *kasnā*], v.t. **1.** to have or to get tied, &c. **2.** to have or get tested, &c.; to have or to get grated (as coconut).

क़साइन *qasāin* [cf. H. *qasāī*], f. a butcher's wife, &c. (see क़साई).

कसाई *kasāī* [cf. *kasnā*], f. **1.** tightening, tightness, tension. **2.** control, discipline. ~ के साथ रखना, to keep under good discipline. **3.** restriction, limitation.

क़साई *qasāī* [cf. A. *qaṣṣāb*], m. & adj. **1.** m. a butcher. **2.** a merciless person; a brute. **3.** adj. cruel, murderous. — ~ का पिल्ला, m. pej. butcher's pup: smug person. ~ की नज़र देखना, to look fiercely (at), to glare. ~ के खूँटे से बँधना, to be tied to a butcher's stake: to be handed over helpless to a brute. – क़साई-ख़ाना, m. slaughter-house.

[1]**कसाना** *kasānā* [cf. H. [1]*kasnā*], v.t. to cause to be tightened; to draw tight (with a cord, &c).

[2]**कसाना** *kasānā* [cf. H. [2]*kasnā*], v.t. to cause to be tested, assayed, or put to proof.

[3]**कसाना** *kasānā* [cf. H. *kāṁsā*], v.i. reg. to acquire a metallic taste (as curds left standing in a metal container).

कसार *kasār* [**kaṁsāra*-: Pk. *kaṁsāra*-], m. a sweet made of flour fried in *ghī*, with sugar.

कसाला *kasālā* [A. *kasāla*], m. toil, labour, pains.

कसाव *kasāv* [cf. H. *kasnā*], m. **1.** tightness, or tension (as a state or condition). **2.** attractive or good physical build.

कसावट *kasāvaṭ* [cf. H. *kasnā*], f. tightness; tension.

कसावर *kasāvar* [cf. H. *kāṁsā*], m. a metal plate, struck with a stick: cymbal, gong.

कसी *kasī* [*karṣaka*-], f. *Pl.* Raj. Panj. a mattock.

क़सीदा *qasīdā* [A. *qaṣīda*], m. a type of Urdu or Persian poem of the form of the *gazal*, but of greater length.

कसीर *kasīr* [A. *kaṣīr*], adj. U. **1.** numerous. **2.** abundant. — ~ को, adv. 19c. quite, absolutely.

कसीला *kasīlā* [cf. H. *kasnā*], adj. well built, strong (a person or animal).

कसीस *kasīs* [*kāsīsa*-], m. iron sulphate, green vitriol.

क़सूर *qasūr* [A. *quṣūr*], m. **1.** fault (of omission or commission), error; shortcoming. — ~ करना, to fall short, to be neglectful; to commit a fault. ~ बतलाना, to point out faults, to find fault (in or with, में). – क़सूरमंद [P. -*mand*], = next. क़सूरवार [P. -*vār*], adj. at fault.

कसेरा *kaserā* [*kāṁsyakāra*-], m. **1.** a coppersmith, brazier, worker in pewter; a plumber. **2.** a man belonging to the *kaserā* community. **3.** a seller of metal vessels. — कसेर-हट, m. a brazier's quarter (in a village or town). °-हट्टा, m. id.

कसेरिन *kaserin* [cf. H. *kaserā*], f. wife of a *kaserā*.

कसेरू *kaserū* [*kaśeruka*-], m. **1.** a kind of grass, *Scirpus kysoor*. **2.** ? the edible tuber of *Cyperus tuberosus* (*C. rotundus*).

क़सैया *qasaiyā* [cf. H. *qasāī*], adj. butcher's, butcher-like.

कसैला *kasailā* [[cf. H. [2]*kasānā*; MIA *-illa-*], adj. astringent; pungent; fig. irritated (the mind).

कसैलापन *kasailāpan* [cf. H. *kasailā*], m. astringency; pungency.

कसोरा *kasorā*, m. an earthen bowl.

कसौंजी *kasauñjī*, f. **1.** [**kāsamārja-*] = कसौंदा. **2.** reg. (Bihar) must (for fermentation).

कसौंदा *kasaumdā* [*kasamarda-*], m. Av. name of a shrub, *Cassia sophora* or *C. occidentalis*, of which the seeds have medicinal uses.

कसौंदी *kasaumdī*, f. *Pl. HŚS.* **1.** *HŚS.* = कसौंदा. **2.** an oil pickle.

कसौ *kasau* [*kīdṛśa-*: anal.], adj. Brbh. what sort of? (= कैसा).

कसौटी *kasauṭī* [conn. *kaṣapaṭṭikā-*], f. **1.** a touchstone. **2.** test, proof, criterion. — ~ पर चढ़ाना, or कसना, or लगाना, to assay, to test, to prove.

कस्तूरा *kastūrā* [cf. H. *kastūrī*], m. 1. = कस्तुरी, 2., 3. **2.** the Malabar whistling thrush.

कस्तूरी *kastūrī* [ad. *kastūrikā-*], f. **1.** musk. **2.** the musk deer (a small brownish-grey deer). **3.** the Indian blackbird, *Turdus merula* (a greyish bird).

क़स्द *qasd* [A. *qaṣd*], m. U. intention, resolve; attempt; wish. — ~ करना, to determine, to resolve.

क़स्बा *qasbā*, m. see क़सबा.

कस्सन *kassan* [*-ss-* ad. *karṣati*], f. reg. (W.) = कसन, 2.

कस्सा *kassā*, m. *Pl. HŚS.* bark of the *babūl* tree; a liquid extract from the bark of this tree (cf. [3]कस).

क़स्साब *qassāb* [A. *qaṣṣāb*], m. E.II. a butcher. — क़स्साब-ख़ाना, m. slaughter-house.

क़स्साबी *qassābī* [P. *qaṣṣābī*], f. butcher's trade, butchery.

कहं *kahaṁ* [*kakṣam*], ppn. Brbh. Av. = को.

क़हक़ह *qahqah*, m. = क़हक़हा.

क़हक़हा *qahqahā* [A. *qahqaha*], m. a loud laugh; burst of laughter. — ~ उड़ाना, or मारना, or लगाना, or लेना, to roar with laughter.

क़हत *qaht* [A. *qaḥṯ*], m. U. famine.

कहन *kahan* [*kathana-*], m. sthg. said: — कहन-सुनन, m. words, an altercation, &c. (= कहा-सुनी).

कहना *kahnā* [*kathayati*], v.t. & m. **1.** v.t. to speak, to say (to, से; reg. often को); to tell; to utter; to declare, to relate; to say to be; to compose (a poem). **2.** to order (sometimes with को rather than से); to advise; to rebuke. **3.** m. something said, a remark, comment; an account. राजपूतों की विरता के क्या कहने! what tales there are of the Rājpūts' valour! **4.** an order; an assertion; advice; rebuke. आपका ~ बजा है, what you have said, urged is to the point. — ~ करना, to carry out the instructions (of, का). कहने की बातें, mere words. कहने को, adv. for the sake of talking; according to reports. कहने पर जाना, or चलना, to follow (one's, के) instructions, advice, &c. कहने में रहना or होना, id. कह सुनाना, to relate (sthg.: to, को). कहूँ तो मा मर जाएगी, न कहूँ तो बाप कुत्ता खा जाएगा, colloq. if I speak my mother will die, if I don't my father will eat dog-meat (an acute dilemma). – कहना-बदना, to determine on; to promise. कहना-सुनना, m. dispute, wrangling. कहने-सुनने को, adv. by all accounts. कहा, m. see s.v.

कहनावट *kahnāvaṭ* [cf. H. *kahnā*], f. a saying, proverb.

क़हर *qahr* [A. *qahr*], m. sthg. violent or dire: **1.** calamity. **2.** rage, fury. — ~ करना, to treat (one, पर) with extreme harshness or violence. ~ का, adj. U. fearful, ruinous, dire; fig. striking. ~ टूटना, a disaster to befall (one, पर). ~ ढाना, or तोड़ना, to bring a disaster (on, पर); fig. to slay (by her beauty: a woman); to rage (at, पर). ~ है! damn it!

कहर- *kahar-*, v.i. Brbh. = कराहना.

कहलवाना *kahalvānā* [cf. H. *kahnā*], v.t. **1.** to cause to be called or named; to cause to be designated. **2.** to cause to be spoken, said or told. (= कहवाना).

कहलाना *kahlānā* [cf. H. *kahnā*], v.i. & v.t. **1.** v.i. to be called or named; to be designated. **2.** to be said to be. **3.** v.t. to cause (one) to speak or to say; to cause to tell. — कहला भेजना, to send to tell, to send word (to, को).

क़हवा *qahvā* [A. *qahva*], m. coffee. — क़हवा-ख़ाना, m. coffee-house.

कहवाना *kahvānā* [cf. H. *kahnā*], v.t. to cause to be spoken or said; to cause (sthg.) to be told.

कहवैया *kahvaiyā* [cf. H. *kahnā*], m. a speaker, &c.

कहाँ *kahāṁ* [cf. H. *yahāṁ*, *vahāṁ*], adv. **1.** where? **2.** rhetor. in what (possible) case? how? इन दिनों मैं वहाँ ~ जाता हूँ, I never go there nowadays. मैं यह काम ~ करूँ? how am I to do this work? **3.** whither? — ~ … ~ …, where (on the one hand) … where (on the other): what a difference between … and …. ~ का, of what place?; strange, unusual; of no sort. ~ का ~, from where to where?: where, indeed?

extremely, intensely; far. ~ तक, how far? how long? to what extent? ~ पर, at, or to, what (particular) place? ~ से, whence?; how?; how, indeed? अभी ~ का ~ पहुँचा होगा, he will already have gone a long way. दाम ~ के ~ पहुँच गए, how very much prices rose! यह ~ की वारदात है! what an unusual occurrence this is!

[1]**कहा** *kahā* [conn. *kasya*], interr. pron., &c. Brbh. **1.** what? which? **2.** rhetor. how? why?

[2]**कहा** *kahā* [H. *kahnā*], m. something said: **1.** a remark; remarks. **2.** advice. **3.** an order. — ~ करना, to carry out the instructions (of, का). ~ मानना (का), to obey. – कहा-कही, f. exchange of words. कहा-सुना, m. = next. कहा-सुनी, f. dispute, wrangle.

क़हाक़ा *qahāqā*, m. = क़हक़हा.

कहाना *kahānā* [cf. H. *kahnā*], v.t. = कहवाना.

कहानी *kahānī* [H. **kahānā*, Brbh. *kahāno*], f. **1.** tale, story. **2.** a short story.

कहानो *kahāno* [*kathānaka-*], m. Brbh. tale, story.

कहार *kahār* [**kācahāra-*: Pk. *kāhāra-*], m. **1.** a water-drawer, &c. (= धीवर), and carrier of palanquins (*pālkī*). **2.** one belonging to a *kahār* community.

कहारिन *kahārin* [cf. H. *kahār*], f. **1.** a woman of a *kahār* community. **2.** the wife of a *kahār*. **3.** a female *kahār*.

कहारी *kahārī* [cf. H. *kahār*], f. = कहारिन.

कहालत *kahālat* [P. *kahālat*; cf. H. *kāhil*], f. inactivity, sloth; remissness.

कहावत *kahāvat* [**kathāvārttā-*], f. a proverb, saying.

कहीं *kahīṁ* [H. *kahāṁ*+H. *hī*], adv. **1.** somewhere; anywhere. ~ भी, anywhere at all. **2.** by some chance; anyhow; perhaps. **3.** rhetor. by no means. ~ जाड़े में लू होती है? can the *lū* wind blow in winter? **4.** w. neg. may it not happen that; lest. ~ वह अभी न आए, don't let him come now! (मैं डड़ता हूँ कि) कहीं बारिश न आ जाए, I'm afraid it may rain. **5.** rhetor. to how great an extent: greatly. आप उनसे ~ अधिक जानते हैं, you know far more than he. — बड़ा आया नवाब ~ का! iron. what a *navāb* (how high and mighty) he has become! – ~ और, somewhere else. ~ ~, adv. here and there; at times; at intervals. ~ ... ~, adv. in one place ... in another; now ... now; at intervals. ~ का, adj. belonging to somewhere (see 5. above). ~ का ~, adv. here and there; now here, now there; from one state or place to another, quite transformed. ~ का ~ पहुँचना, to make great strides, or progress. ~ नहीं, adv. nowhere. ~ पहुँचना, to reach great heights. ~ से, adv. from somewhere; from anywhere. किसी को ~ का न छोड़ना, to leave one (in peace) nowhere: to pursue relentlessly. जहाँ ~, adv. wherever. हर ~, adv. everywhere.

[1]**कहुं** *kahuṁ* [*kakṣam*], ppn. Brbh. Av. = को.

[2]**कहुं** *kahuṁ* adv. Brbh. Av. = कहूँ.

कहूँ *kahūṁ*, adv. Brbh. Av. somewhere; anywhere at all.

काँइया *kāṁiyā*, adj. & m. cunning; a rogue.

काँकड़ी *kāṁkṛī* [*karkara-*], f. a small stone.

काँ-काँ *kāṁ-kāṁ*, f. pronun. var. = काँव-काँव.

कांक्षा *kāṅkṣā* [S.], f. desire, longing.

कांक्षित *kāṅkṣit* [S.], adj. **1.** desired, longed for. **2.** desirous.

कांक्षी *kāṅkṣī* [S.], adj. & m. **1.** desiring, desirous. **2.** m. one desirous (of sthg).

काँख *kāṁkh* [*kakṣā-*], f. **1.** armpit. **2.** side (of the body). — ~ में दबाना, = बग़ल में दबाना. ~ आना, a swelling to arise in or near the armpit.

काँखना *kāṁkhnā* [*kāṅkṣati*], v.i. **1.** to strain. **2.** to grunt, to groan. — काँख-कूँखना, colloq. = काँखना.

काँखा *kāṁkhā* [cf. H. *kāṁkhnā*], m. colloq. **1.** violent effort, straining. **2.** grunt, groan.

काँगड़ी *kāṁgṛī* [conn. **kāṅgārikā-*], f. an earthenware pot of coals (carried slung from the neck by Kaśmīrīs, and worn under the outer garment, to provide warmth).

काँगनी *kāṁgnī* [*kaṅgunī-*], f. reg. (W). a millet, *Setaria italica*.

काँग्रेसी *kāṁgresī* [H. *kāṅgres*: ← Engl.], adj. & m. **1.** adj. having to do with a congress, specif. pol. with the Indian Congress party. **2.** m. a member of the Congress party or of one of its sections.

[1]**काँच** *kāṁc* [**kācca-*: Pk. *kacca-*], m. **1.** glass. **2.** crystal. **3.** a type of impairment of sight in which the eye remains clear.

[2]**काँच** *kāṁc*, m. prolapse of the rectum. — ~ निकालना (का), colloq. to beat to a jelly.

कांचन *kāñcan* [S.], m. & adj. **1.** m. gold. **2.** adj. made of gold, golden.

काँचा *kāṁcā*, adj. reg. = कच्चा.

कांची *kāñcī* [S.], f. Brbh. a woman's belt having small bells, &c. attached.

काँचुली *kāṁculī* [conn. *kañculikā-*], f. reg. **1.** a bodice. **2.** a snake's slough (= केंचुली).

काँजी *kāṁjī* [*kāñjika-*], f. **1.** a kind of vinegar made from rice, or mustard seed. **2.** rice-water. — **काँजी-हौस**, or °-**हौद** [A. *-hauẓ*], m. rice-water trough (hence) regimental cells or lock-up: a pound for cattle.

काँटा *kāṁṭā* [*kaṇṭaka-*], m. **1.** thorn. **2.** sting; spur (of cock); quill (of porcupine). **3.** bone (of fish). **4.** nail; firing-pin (of gun). **5.** hook; fish-hook; button-hook. **6.** needle, pointer (of a balance); hand (of a clock); tongue (of a buckle); bolt (of a lock); a balance. **7.** fork. **8.** a pitchfork. **9.** fig. dryness (as of the tongue from thirst); dehydration (after fever). **10.** a thorn in the side; inconvenience, impediment (as to progress); cause of care or suffering. **11.** antagonism. **काँटे की कुश्ती**, f. a bitter struggle (in wrestling). **12.** *math.* a mark made in verifying multiplication; verification. — ~ **निकालना**, to remove a thorn; to give relief (to, **का**: as from pain). ~ **होना**, to become like a thorn: to become very thin, to waste away. **काँटे की तौल होना**, to be exactly weighed (as seen from a scale): to be spoken or done with precision (words, acts). **काँटे की लड़ाई**, f. an even match, or contest. **काँटे बोना**, to plant thorns: to sow troubles. **काँटे में तुलना**, to be weighed out to the mark (on a scale): to be precious (a commodity). **काँटों का चूहा**, m. reg. a hedgehog. **काँटों का सूअर**, m. reg. a porcupine. **काँटों पर घसीटना**, to drag among thorns; to cause mortification (as by undeserved or excessive praise). **काँटों पर लोटना**, to roll on thorns: to suffer pangs (as of envy, or remorse). – **काँटा-सा खटकना**, to prick as a thorn (in, **में**): to rankle (in). **काँटेदार** [P. *-dār*], adj. thorny; barbed. **काँटेदार तार**, m. barbed wire.

काँटी *kāṁṭī* [cf. H. *kāṁṭā*], f. **1.** small thorn, prickle. **2.** small scales. **3.** small hook, or nail, &c. (see **काँटा**). **4.** a fetter. **5.** *Pl.* cotton refuse.

काँठा *kāṁṭhā* [*kaṇṭha-*], m. **1.** Av. throat. **2.** [*kaṇṭhaka-*] red and blue ring round a parrot's throat. **3.** Brbh. edge, shore.

कांड *kāṁḍ* [S.], m. **1.** single joint (of cane, stalk). ***2.** section, part; section of a book. **3.** incident: unfortunate or dire event.

काँड़- *kāṁṛ-* [*kaṇḍayati*], v.t. Brbh. **1.** to trample. **2.** to pound, to crush (as grain).

काँड़ली *kāṁṛlī*, f. *Pl.* purslane.

काँड़ा *kāṁṛā*, adj. pronun. var. reg. = **काना**.

काँड़ी *kāṁṛī* [*kāṇḍa-*: ? ← Drav.], f. **1.** Bihar. a wooden pail. **2.** hollow (of a mortar). **3.** a hollow stalk. **4.** [? × **kāmuṭha-*], reg. yoke.

कांत *kānt* [S.], adj. & m. **1.** adj. beloved. **2.** lovely, pleasing. **3.** m. lover; specif. a title of Kṛṣṇa; husband.

कांता *kāntā* [S.], f. a beloved or beautiful woman; sweetheart; wife.

कांतार *kāntār* [S.], m. a forest, or desolate region.

कांति *kānti* [S.], f. **1.** loveliness. **2.** lustre, splendour (as of a woman's attire). — **कांतिहीन**, adj. dull, lacklustre.

काँदा *kāṁdā* [*kanda-*: ? ← Drav.], m. **1.** an edible root or bulb. **2.** an onion.

काँदु *kāṁdu* [*kandu-*], m. *hist.* a sugar-boiler; sweet-maker.

काँदो *kāṁdo* [*kardama-*], m. reg. mud, mire.

काँध *kāṁdh*, m. Brbh. Av. = **कंधा**.

काँध- *kāṁdh-* [*skandhayati*], v.t. Brbh. Av. to lift, to raise; to assume; to accept.

काँधर *kāṁdhar*, m. reg. the neck.

काँप *kāṁp* [cf. H. *kāṁpnā*], m. reg. **1.** an ear ornament. **2.** shaky muddy soil.

काँपना *kāṁpnā* [*kampate*], v.i. **1.** to tremble; to quiver. **2.** to shiver.

काँव-काँव *kāṁv-kāṁv*, f. a cawing sound. — ~ **करना**, to caw.

काँवड़ *kāṁvaṛ*, f. = **काँवर**.

काँवर *kāṁvar* [conn. **kāmaṭha-*: ← Austro-as.], f. a bamboo, or other pole, having slings or baskets suspended at each end for carrying loads.

काँवरा *kāṁvrā*, adj. excited, wild, frenzied.

काँवरी *kāṁvrī* [cf. H. *kāṁvar*], m. a porter who uses a sling-pole.

काँस *kāṁs* [*kāśa-*], m. f. a tall grass, *Saccharum spontaneum*, used as a thatching material and for making ropes, mats, &c. — ~ **में तैरना**, fig. to make one's way ahead facing difficulties or uncertainty.

काँसा *kāṁsā* [*kāṁsyaka-*], m. any alloy of copper and tin, or copper and zinc; bell-metal; brass; bronze.

काँसी *kāṁsī* [cf. H. *kāṁsā*], f. = **काँसा**.

कांस्य *kāṁsyă* [S.], adj. & m. **1.** adj. made of *kāṁsā*. **2.** m. = **काँसा**.

[1]**का** *kā* [conn. *kṛta-*], ppn. **1.** of; belonging to. **उस ~ एक घर था**, he had, owned a house. **उस ~ घर**, m. his house. **उसकी सिर्फ़ एक ही आँख है**, he has only one eye. **उस संदूक़ ~ ताला नहीं है**, that box has no lock. **गाँव के लोग**, m. pl. village people. **पीने ~ पानी**, m. drinking water. **भारत ~ सबसे बड़ा शहर**, m. the biggest city in India. **यहाँ ~ मौसम**, m. the weather here. **राम दस बरस ~ है**, Rām is ten years old. **हिंदी की एक किताब**, f. a

Hindi book. **2.** concerning. उसके यहाँ ठहरने की बात, f. the question of his staying here. **3.** made or consisting of. ईंटों ~ मकान, m. a brick-built house. **4.** in respect of, per. लकड़ियाँ एक रुपया गट्ठर की हैं, the wood costs one rupee a bundle. **5.** के, adv. obl. related to, connected with. उसके एक बहन है, he has a sister. **6.** के, adv. obl. = को, 4. उसके चोट लगी, he got hurt. – अरे दामू के बच्चे! hey there, you Dāmū! राम का-सा मेहनती किसान, m. a farmer as hard-working as Rām. सारे ~ सारा, adj. the entire amount of, all of.

²**का** *kā*, interr. pron. & adj. Brbh. Av. **1.** what? which? (= क्या, कौन). **2.** obl. (= किस) whom? which? what?

काई *kāī* [? conn. P. H. *kāhī*], f. **1.** scum on stagnant water. **2.** mould on walls and pavements; moss. **3.** rust. **4.** [× *kāsīsa-*] verdigris. — काई-सा फट जाना, to be dispersed or scattered like scum on water (clouds, or a crowd); to be dispersed temporarily.

काऊ *kāū* [conn. *kasya*], adv. (w. coalesced encl.) Av. = कभी, or कभी भी.

¹**काक** *kāk* [S.], m. **1.** a crow. **2.** a cunning fellow. — काक-भुशुंडि, m. *mythol.* name of a devotee of Rām who was cursed by the sage Lomaśa for the imperfections of his belief, and turned into a crow.

²**काक** *kāk* [Engl. *cork*], m. cork; a cork.

काकड़ा *kākṛā* [*kakkaṭa-*²], m. *Pl.* stiff leather; a large or stiff wick.

काकड़ासिंगी *kākṛāsiṅgī* [*karkaṭaśr̥ṅgikā-*], f. the tree *Pistacia integerrima*, and the galls formed on its leaves and petioles (used medicinally).

काकली *kākălī* [S.], f. a low, soft sound.

काकलोद *kāklod*, f. *Pl.* reg. attachment, longing.

काका *kākā* [**kākka-*: ← Drav.], m. inv. senior male relative: **1.** a father's younger brother. **2.** term of address to an elder brother, or cousin, &c.

काकातुआ *kākātuā* [Ind. *kakatua*], m. cockatoo.

काकातूआ *kākātūā*, m. = काकातुआ.

काकिनी *kākinī* [ad. *kākiṇī-*], f. Brbh. a partic. small coin.

काकी *kākī* [cf. H. *kākā*], f. senior female relative: **1.** aunt. **2.** mother.

¹**काकु** *kāku*, m. = काका.

²**काकु** *kāku* [S.], m. (metr. *-ū-*) Av. secret jibe or taunt; sarcasm.

काकुन *kākun* [**kaṅkunī-*], f. reg. (W). a millet, *Panicum italicum*.

काकुल *kākul* [P. *kākul*], m. lock (of hair).

काख *kākh* [*kakṣa-*¹], m. the armpit.

¹**काग** *kāg* [*kāka-*: +*-g-* onom.], m. **1.** a crow. **2.** transf. the uvula. — ~ उठाना, to raise the uvula (of an infant, का). — काग-भुसुंड, m. a crow like Bhuśuṇḍi (see s.v. ¹काक): a big crow. काग-भुसंड, m. id.

²**काग** *kāg* [Engl. cork], m. cork; a cork.

काग़ज़ *kāgaz* [P. *kāgaẕ*: for orig. *kāgad*], m. **1.** paper. **2.** a paper, document. **3.** an account. **4.** *fin.* bond, note. **5.** a newspaper. — ~ काला करना, to blacken paper: to write (esp. to little point). ~ की नाव, f. a paper boat: sthg. which will not survive long. ~ के घोड़े दौड़ाना, colloq. to keep up an active correspondence. ~ खोलना, to open the papers (of, के); to expose the misdeeds (of). चिट्ठी का ~, m. writing-paper. – काग़ज़-क़लम, m. f. paper and pen(s), stationery. काग़ज़-पत्र, m. pl. papers; documents. काग़ज़-फ़रोश [P. *-farośʼ*], m. a paper-seller, stationer.

काग़ज़ात *kāgăzāt* [P. *kāgaẕāt*: A. f. pl. suffix], m. pl. papers; documents, records.

काग़ज़ी *kāgăzī* [P. *kāgaẕī*], adj. & f. **1.** adj. made of paper. **2.** done on paper. ~ काररवाई, f. paper-work. **3.** thin, soft (as skin of a nut, or rind); delicate. — ~ सबूत, m. documentary evidence.

कागद *kāgad* [P. *kāgad*: → *kāgaẕ*], m. obs. = काग़ज़.

कागर *kāgar* [P. *kāgaẕ*: G. or Raj. *kāgaḷ*], m. **1.** Brbh. Av. = काग़ज़. **2.** Brbh. wing.

कागा *kāgā* [*kāka-*: +*-g-* onom.], m. = ¹काग. — कागा-रोल, m. the cawing of crows; chattering, din. कागा-रौल, m. id.

कागौर *kāgaur* [H. ¹*kāg*+H. *kaur*], f. reg. (W). crow's morsel: the remains of bread-cakes from a *śrāddh* ceremony (thrown away mixed with buttermilk, for crows to eat).

काच *kāc*, m. = ¹काँच. — काच-लवन, m. *Pl.* *HŚS*. black salt (= काला नमक). काच-मणि, m. crystal; quartz.

काछ *kāch* [*kakṣyā-*; *kakṣa-*, m.], m. 1. = धोती, esp. the end of the *dhotī* tucked in at the waist behind. **2.** reg. shorts. **3.** [transf. or × *kakṣa-*¹], the loins. — ~ काछना, to wear a *kāch*; fig. to play a role. ~ खोलना, colloq. to have sexual intercourse. ~ मारना, to put on a *kāch*.

काछन *kāchan* [cf. H. *kāchī*], f. a *kāchī* woman; wife of a *kāchī*.

[1]**काछना** *kāchnā*, m. = काछ.

[2]**काछना** *kāchnā* [cf. H. *kāch*], v.t. to put on (a *kāch* or *dhotī*).

[3]**काछना** *kāchnā*, v.t. reg. **1.** to skim (milk, &c). **2.** to collect (exudation of opium).

काछनी *kāchnī* [cf. H. *kāch(nā)*], f. 1. = काछ (esp. as tightly worn). **2.** cloth worn over a *kāch*.

काछा *kāchā*, m. = काछ. — ~ कसना, to put on a *kāch*; to gird the loins, to prepare.

काछी *kāchī* [cf. *kaccha-*], m. **1.** a community of market gardeners. **2.** a member of the *kāchī* community.

[1]**काज** *kāj* [*kārya-*], m. **1.** task, work; activity. **2.** occupation. **3.** matter, affair; a matter in hand; feast (esp. one given on the death of an old person). **4.** purpose, point. — ~ सँवारना, to achieve a goal or purpose; to complete a task. – काजे, adv. for the purpose (of, के); on account (of).

[2]**काज** *kāj*, m. button-hole stitch, button-hole.

काजल *kājal* [*kajjala-*: ? ← Drav.], m. lampblack (applied medicinally and as a cosmetic to the eyes); soot. — ~ का तिल, m. beauty-spot. ~ की ओबरी, or कोठरी, f. lampblack-room, cellar; a place, or (fig.) an affair, from which one cannot emerge without a stain on one's character. ~ डालना, or देना, or लगाना, or सारना, to apply lampblack (to, में: the eyes).

काजी *kājī* [cf. H. [1]*kāj*], adj. & m. **1.** adj. active, industrious. **2.** employed, working. **3.** m. an industrious person, &c. **4.** a workman.

क़ाज़ी *qāzī* [A. *qāẓī*], m. *musl.* a judge or magistrate. — ~ जी दुबले क्यों, शहर के अंदेशे से, iron. if the qāẓī is thin it's because of his (officious) worries about the city.

काजू *kājū*, m. the cashew-nut.

काजू-भोजू *kājū-bhojū* [? conn. H. [1]*kāj*], adj. showy but insubstantial (as cheap jewellery).

[1]**काट** *kāṭ* [cf. H. *kāṭnā*], f. **1.** cutting. **2.** separation, disconnection. **3.** a cut, slash. **4.** a wound; bite. **5.** slice, piece, bit; chip; cut, section. **6.** erasure, deletion; removal (as of dirt). **7.** trimming; cut, style (of clothes). **8.** channel (cut by water); erosion. **9.** damage, loss. **10.** a cut (in expenditure), retrenchment; deduction. **11.** a defensive move (as in wrestling); fig. refutation (in argument). **12.** deceit. **13.** fig. pungency; corrosiveness; virulence. **14.** reg. scum, dirt, dregs. — ~ करना, to make a cut, &c. (in); to corrode; to destroy. — काट-कपट, m. = ~, 11. काट-कूट, f. = next. काट-छाँट, f. cutting and clipping; pruning, lopping; deletion; cuttings (as of fabric); economies (in expenditure). काट-छाँट करना, to cut and chip, &c. काट पीट, f. cancellations, corrections. काट-फाँस, f. dividing off and ensnaring: manoeuvring, double-dealing. काट-फाँस करना, to cut and chip; to speak maliciously (about one), to intrigue.

[2]**काट** *kāṭ* [? cf. H. *kāṭnā*], f. reg. edge (of a blade).

काटन *kāṭan* [cf. H. *kāṭnā*; and *kartana-*[1]], m. **1.** cutting, clipping; cutting off, or out. **2.** a clipping, trimming.

काटना *kāṭnā* [*kartati*[1]], v.t. **1.** to cut; to cut into; to carve, to saw; to cut (a crop); to write (a cheque); to cut (cards); to book (a ticket). **2.** to cut apart, to divide; to cleave (as waves); *math.* to cut (one line with another); *arith.* to divide (one number into another). **3.** to bite into (food). **4.** to bite (of an animal, a snake); to sting. **5.** to gnaw; to eat away (as ants). **6.** to wound; to chafe (against, में: as a shoe the foot). **7.** to cut out, to erase; to wash out (dirt, or sin); to delete; to cancel (a ticket, or an item from a programme); to abolish. **8.** to disconnect (as a carriage from a train). **9.** to cut away, to erode. **10.** to spend (time, life); to while away (time); to complete (a term). **11.** to make, to drive (a road, &c.); to lay out (road, garden). **12.** to cross (one's path). **13.** to block (a road, &c). **14.** to cause inconvenience (to); to interrupt (an activity). **15.** to surmount (a difficulty); to make (a distance). **16.** to refute (words, an opinion). **17.** to settle, to adjust (as a dispute). **18.** to deduct. **19.** cause one to suffer (shame, distress). **20.** to carp at, to find fault with (argument). **21.** colloq. to make away with (goods); to make or to gain (money). **22.** to be sharp; to be pungent; to be corrosive, or virulent; to sting (as cold wind). — काट खाना, to bite. काटा, m. one who is bitten (by, का); reg. a bite. काटा-काटी [× *karta-*[2]], f. cutting and hacking; slaughter, massacre. काटे खाना (को), to be oppressive, to torment (as remorse or longing).

[1]**काटू** *kāṭū* [cf. H. *kāṭnā*], adj. **1.** adj. prone to bite (an animal). **2.** irritable. **3.** stinging; pungent; corrosive.

[2]**काटू** *kāṭū*, m. *HŚS.* the cashew-nut tree, *Anacardium occidentale.*

काठ *kāṭh* [*kāṣṭha-*], m. **1.** wood. **2.** a piece of wood or timber; log; beam. **3.** stocks. — ~ का उल्लू, m. wooden owl: a blockhead, idiot. ~ का घोड़ा, m. a wooden horse; colloq. crutch. ~ की भंबो, f. a puppet; a stupid person, stupid woman. ~ की हाँड़ी, f. a wooden pot: anything to be used once and not again. ~ मारना (को), to be thunderstruck. ~ में पाँव देना, or ठोकना, to put (one's, के) legs in the stocks; to encumber (oneself). ~ होना, to become a log: to lose consciousness; to stand stock-still (as in fear or astonishment); to become hard, dry (an object), or insensitive (a person). – काठ-कबाड़, m. old or broken furniture, lumber. काठ-कीड़ा, m. a bug. काठ-कोयला, m. charcoal.

काठिन्य *kāṭhinyă* [S.], m. = कठिनाई.

काठी *kāṭhī* [*kāṣṭhikā-*], f. **1.** the body, frame; bodily strength. **2.** wooden saddle for a horse or camel. — ~ कसना, or धरना (पर), to saddle (an animal).

काड़ा *kāṛā* [**kaḍḍa-*], m. reg. (Bihar) a buffalo calf (= ²पाड़ा).

काड़ी *kāṛī*, f. reg. (W). a dry stalk (as of corn).

काढ़न *kāṛhan* [cf. H. *kaṛhnā*], f. embroidery.

काढ़ना *kāṛhnā* [**kaḍḍhati*: Pa. *kaḍḍhati*], v.t. **1.** to pull, to pull out or off; to pull across (a curtain, veil); to strip off (skin, &c). **2.** to take out; to draw (water, or milk from a cow); to draw off (liquid); to spread (its hood: a snake). **3.** to boil down, to thicken (milk). **4.** to drive out or away. **5.** to draw (letters, lines); to trace, to sketch. **6.** to embroider (on cloth or other material). **7.** to contrive; to get, to obtain (from, से); to borrow (money). **8.** to drag out (days, life). **9.** to search out (an error).

काढ़ा *kāṛhā* [cf. H. *kāṛhnā*], m. a medicinal extract.

कात *kāt* [**karta-³*], m. reg. a cutting or paring tool.

कातना *kātnā* [**kartati²*: Pk. *kattaï*], v.t. **1.** to spin (cotton, thread, cord). **2.** to twist or to wrap round. — महीन ~, to spin fine: to spin a story (pej.) – काता, adj. spun. बुढ़िया का काता, m. old woman's spinning: a sweet made from shredded pumpkin.

कातर *kātar* [S.], adj. **1.** timid; cowardly; submissive. **2.** distressed, agitated; dejected.

कातरता *kātarătā* [S.], f. timidity, &c. (see कातर).

काता *kātā* [**karta-³*], m. *Pl. HŚS.* reg. (E). a knife used (as by cremation-workers) for cutting or paring bamboos.

कातिक *kātik*, m. = कार्त्तिक.

कातिब *kātib* [A. *kātib*], m. U. writer, scribe; clerk.

क़ातिल *qātil* [A. *qātil*], adj. & m. **1.** adj. killing, murderous; cruel (a lover). **2.** captivating (a woman's beauty). **3.** m. a murderer.

क़ातिलाना *qātilānā* [P. *qātilāna*], adj. murderous (assault, &c).

काती *kātī* [*karttrī-*], f. **1.** *Pl. HŚS.* goldsmith's scissors or pincers. **2.** Brbh. a knife; a short sword.

कादंबरी *kādambarī* [S.], f. wine; the moon.

कादंबिनी *kādambinī* [S.], f. a bank of clouds.

काद *kād* [*karda-*], m. Brbh. mud.

कादर *kādar* [ad. *kātara-*], adj. Brbh. = कातर.

कादा *kādā* [*karda-*], m. reg. (W). mud: alluvial deposit.

क़ादिर *qādir* [A. *qādir*], adj. E.H. mighty; omnipotent.

कादो *kādo* [*kardama-*], m. Brbh. mud.

¹कान *kān* [*karṇa-*], m. **1.** the ear. **2.** hearing. **3.** projecting part; handle (as of a pot); helm or rudder (of a ship). **4.** ragged end (of cloth). **5.** pan (of a musket). **6.** an ornament worn over the ear (rather than hung from the lobe). — ~ उठाना, to prick up the ears. ~ उड़ना, the ears to fail (one): to be deafened (by noise), to be no longer sensitive (as to remonstration). ~ उमेठना, to twist the ears (of, के: in punishment). अपना ~ उमेठना, fig. to be contrite. ~ ऊँचे करना, = ~ उठाना. ~ कतरना, = ~ काटना. ~ करना, = ~ धरना. ~ खड़े करना, = ~ उठाना. ~ का परदा, m. the eardrum. ~ का कच्चा, or पतला, adj. credulous. ~ काटना, to cut off the ears (of, के); to get the better (of), to outwit; to surpass (in, में). ~ खाना, to vex the ears (of, के: with noise, or pestering). ~ खोलना, to open the ears (of, के), to inform (of); to warn (of). ~ गरम होना, to give a talking-to; to berate. ~ गूँगे होना, to have a buzzing in the ears; to become partially deaf. ~ दबाकर, or दबाए, चला जाना, fig. to slink away. ~ दबाना, fig. to act submissively. ~ दिखाना, to show the ears: to have the ears cleaned. ~ देना, or धरना, to give ear (to, पर), to pay attention. ~ न दिया जाना, listening to be impossible (because of a din). ~ न हिलाना, not to move the ears; to make no sign; to be tamed, docile. ~ पकड़ना (अपना), to hold one's ear (in contrition); to forswear (doing sthg., से); to confess inferiority. ~ पकड़कर उठाना बिठाना, to make (one) get up and sit repeatedly while holding the ear(s): to have (a person) under one's thumb. ~ पड़ना, to be audible (to, के); to come to the ears (of). ~ पर जूँ, or जूँ तक, न रेंगना, a louse not to crawl on the ear(s): no heed to be taken (of sthg.: by, के); no effect to be produced (on). ~ पर हाथ देना, or धरना, to place the hands on the ears; not to wish to hear, or to comply, &c. ~ पारि सुन-, Brbh. to listen attentively. ~ फटना, the ears to be deafened; the ears to be slit (as for a *sādhu's* ear ornament). ~ फाड़कर सुनना, to strain the ears, to listen attentively. ~ फूँकना, to whisper into the ear (of, के: as tales, slander); to tutor, to school (a follower). ~ फूटना, to be or to become deaf; to be deafened (by). ~ बजना, the ears to ring, or to tingle; to imagine that one hears a sound. ~ बहना, a discharge to come from the ear. ~ बहरे कर देना (अपने), to shut one's ears (to); to turn a deaf ear. ~ भरना, v.i. the ears to be full, to have heard enough; v.t. to fill or to poison the ear (of, के: against another). ~ में आवाज़ पड़ना, words, or remarks, to be overheard; to be heard, reported. ~ में उँगली दे रहना, fig. to turn a deaf ear (to). ~ में खटकना, to grate on the ear (of, के). ~ में डालना, or कहना, to whisper into the ear (of, के: as a warning, a hint). ~ में तेल डालकर बैठना, or सोना, fig. to turn a deaf ear; to be inattentive or negligent. ~ में रूई डालकर बैठना, fig. id. ~ रखना, = ~ लेगाना. ~ लगना, to get into the confidence (of, के); to be attentive. ~ लगाना, to lend an ear, to listen (to, पर); to be attentive. ~ होना, to have ears: to be able to learn from experience. - कानों-कान कहना, to whisper. कानों-कान न जानना, not to know or to have heard a whisper (of). कानों-कान न सुनना, not to hear at all.

²**कान** *kān*, f. **1.** modesty, shame. **2.** respect. — ~ छोड़ना, to behave immodestly, or disrespectfully.

³**कान** *kān*, pronun. var. Brbh. = कान्ह, and कांत, 3.

कानन *kānan* [S.], m. **1.** forest; grove. **2.** house.

¹**काना** *kānā* [*kāṇa-*], adj. **1.** one-eyed. **2.** having a hole (as a fruit, a cowrie); worthless, useless. **3.** marked, spotted (fruit). **4.** having a rotten kernel, or no kernel. — काना-कुतरा, adj. disfigured (a person); spoiled (as fruit).

²**काना** *kānā* [*karṇaka-*], adj. distorted in shape (as a *cārpāī*).

कानाकानी *kānākānī* [cf. H. *kān*], f. = कानाफूसी.

कानाफूसी *kānāphūsī* [cf. H. *kān*, H. *phusphusānā*], f. **1.** whispering; whispered words; tales, intrigue. **2.** a sudden noise made in a child's ear. — ~ करना, to whisper, &c.

कानाबाती *kānābātī* [cf. H. *kān*, H. *bāt*], f. = कानाफूसी.

कानि *kāni*, f. Brbh. = ²कान.

¹**कानी** *kānī* [*kanya-*], f. the little finger. — ~ उँगली, f. id.

²**कानी** *kānī*, f. reg. *Pl.* resentment, rancour.

क़ानून *qānūn* [A. *qānūn*], m. **1.** a law; regulation. **2.** law (in general). — क़ानूनगो [P. -*go*], m. law-speaker; register of lands of a *parganā*; superintendent of village accountants. क़ानूनदाँ [P. -*dān*], m. law-knower: jurist.

क़ानूनन *qānūnan* [A. *qānūnan*], adv. by law, legally.

क़ानूनियत *qānūniyat* [A. *qānūnīya*: P. *qānūniyat*], f. legality.

क़ानूनिया *qānūniyā* [cf. H. *qānūn*], m. a legalistic or litigious person.

क़ानूनी *qānūnī* [P. *qānūnī*], adj. **1.** legal. **2.** juridical. ~ स्वीकृति, f. acceptance *de iure*. **3.** legislative. **4.** controversial (matter). **5.** litigious (person).

कान्यकुब्ज *kānyakubjă* [S.], m. name of a community of brāhmaṇs.

कान्ह *kānh* [*kṛṣṇa-*], m. dark blue, black: Kṛṣṇa (the *tadbhava* form of this name, as applied to the god).

कान्हड़ा *kānhṛā*, m. *mus. Pl. MŚS.* name of a *rāg*.

कापट्य *kāpaṭyă* [S.], m. **1.** wickedness. **2.** deceit; fraud.

कापना *kāpnā*, v.i. = काँपना.

कापालिक *kāpālik* [S.], m. having to do with a skull: name of a type of Śaiva ascetic.

कापी *kāpī* [Engl. *copy(-book)*], f. **1.** an exercise book, notebook. **2.** a copy (= प्रति).

कापुरुष *kā-puruṣ* [S.], m. base wretch; coward.

काफल *kāphal* [*kaṭphula-*: ← Pk. *kapphala-*, **kāipphala-*], m. = कायफल.

क़ाफ़िया *qāfiyā* [A. *qāfiya*], m. rhyme, rhyming syllable (the penultimate in Urdu poems using double rhyme). — ~ तंग होना (का), to be hard pressed for a rhyme; fig. to be faced with difficulties. – क़ाफ़ियाबंदी [P. -*bandī*], f. making rhymes; playing the poet.

काफ़िर *kāfir* [A. *kāfir*], adj. & m. **1.** adj. not believing (esp. in Islam); impious. **2.** m. an unbeliever, infidel. **3.** pej. base person, wretch; villain.

काफ़िराना *kāfirānā* [P. *kāfirāna*], adv. as an unbeliever; basely.

काफ़िरी *kāfirī* [P. *kāfirī*], adj. & f. **1.** adj. pertaining to an unbeliever. **2.** m. unbelief, impiety.

क़ाफ़िला *qāfilā* [A. *qāfila*], m. caravan (of vehicles); convoy.

काफ़ी *kāfī* [A. *kāfī*], adj. **1.** enough, sufficient. **2.** a fair or considerable amount of. **3.** adv. quite, fairly. — दिल्ली के ~ पास, adv. quite near Delhi. बहुत ~, adj. more than enough, ample.

काफ़ूर *kāfūr* [P. *kāfūr*], m. camphor. — ~ हो जाना, fig. to take to one's heels; to vanish (a person). होश ~ हो जाना, to lose consciousness.

काबर *kābar* [*karbara-*: ← Austro-as.], adj. & m. *Pl. HŚS.* mottled: **1.** adj. grayish. **2.** m. reg. (W.) a clay soil containing sand. **3.** a speckled bird.

क़ाबला *qāblā* [P. *qābila*], m. a bolt.

काबा *kābā* [A. *kaʻba*], m. the 'cubical' shrine at Mecca (chief goal of Muhammadan pilgrimage).

क़ाबिज़ *qābiz* [A. *qābiẓ*], adj. taking, seizing; possessing; occupying.

क़ाबिल *qābil* [A. *qābil*], adj. **1.** capable (of, के). **2.** fit, qualified (a person). **3.** worthy, deserving (of). **4.** appropriate, suitable (as an occasion: for an action). — क़ाबिल-दीद, adj. 19c. worth seeing. क़ाबिल-तर्क, adj. 19c. deserving discussion. क़ाबिले-दाद, adj. praiseworthy.

क़ाबिलीयत *qābilīyat* [A. *qābilīya*: P. *qābilīyat*], f. **1.** capability. **2.** fitness, suitability; qualification.

काबीना *kābīnā* [P. *kābīna*: ← F.], m. *govt.* U. cabinet.

काबुक *kābuk* [P. *kābuk*], f. pigeon-house, dovecot.

[1]**काबुली** *kābulī* [P. *kābulī*], adj. & m. **1.** adj. of or belonging to Kabul. **2.** produced in Kabul (as gram, dried fruit). **3.** m. an inhabitant of Kabul; one born in Kabul.

[2]**काबुली** *kābulī* [P. *kābulī*], f. the language of Kabul.

क़ाबू *qābū* [P. *qābū*], m. **1.** hold, grasp. **2.** possession. **3.** control, authority (over, पर); power. **4.** command (of a language, पर). — ~ पाना, to obtain power (over, पर); to obtain an opportunity. ~ में करना, or लाना, to bring under control or subjection; to bring into (one's) possession; to acquire ascendancy over. ~ में रखना, to keep under control.

[1]**काम** *kām* [*karman-*[1]], m. **1.** action, act. **2.** work, task. **3.** occupation; business. **4.** matter, business in hand; purpose. **5.** a feat. **6.** service, use; need (of, से). **7.** workmanship; manufacture. **8.** needlework. — ~ आना, to be of use (to, के); to serve a purpose; to come into use; to be used, or spent (in, में); euph. to fall (in battle). ~ का, adj. of work; useful, serviceable (to, से); ~ का दिन, m. a working day. ~ करना, to work (as, का); to act; to act (upon, पर), to have effect; colloq. to settle the hash (of); to kill. ~ की बात होना, to require hard work (a task, an activity). ~ के सिर होना, = ~ में लगना. ~ खुलना, a task to be begun; a business to be started. ~ चलना, work to progress. ~ चलाना, to keep a task going, progressing; to make do (by means of, से). ~ चढ़ाना, to put a task or matter in hand; to set (a machine, का) going. ~ तमाम करना, to finish a task or business; euph. to put an end (to one, का), to kill. ~ देखना, to see to the work (of, का). अपना ~ देखो! do your work properly! ~ देना, to give work (to, को); to give good service (to); (a thing) to be of use, or to perform a function. ~ निकलना, work to be got out (of, से); a purpose, or a result, to be achieved. ~ निकालना, to achieve (one's) purpose. ~ पड़ना = ~ आना, 1.; to have business (with, से); to be in need (of). ~ पर जाना, to go to work; to go on duty. ~ पर लगाना, to put (one, को) to work, to give work (to). ~ पर होना, to be at work; to have work. ~ बढ़ाना, to increase the work (of, का); to stop work. ~ बनना, a purpose, or success, to be achieved. ~ बिगाड़ना, to spoil the work, or any concern (of, का); to put a spoke in the wheel (of), to foil; to ruin the reputation (of). ~ में ~ निकालना, to kill two birds with one stone. ~ में देह चुराना, to shirk work. ~ में लगना, to be of use; to be busy (in, or with). ~ में लाना, to bring into use; to have recourse to. ~ लगना, work to begin; work to be found (by, को). ~ लगाना, to begin work; to put work in hand. ~ लेना, to set to work; to make use (of, से). ~ सरना, = ~ निकलना, 2. ~ से ~ रखना, to mind (one's, अपने) own business. ~ से जाता रहना, to become unusable; to give up (one's) work; to be dismissed. ~ होना, work, or a purpose, to exist; euph. life to come to an end. ~ हो गया, the task or purpose was (or is) achieved. – काम-काज, m. work, business, tasks. °ई, adj. & m. working, active; having responsible work, superintending; a worker; superintendent. कामगार [P. *-gār*], m. & adj. a labourer; working, having work. काम-चलाऊ, adj. which lets work go on: serviceable (as a makeshift). कामचोर, adj. & m. work-thief: idle; a shirker. °ई, slacking, idleness. काम-दानी [P. *-dānī*], f. a type of embroidery on net or muslin (small flowers worked in gold or silver thread). [1]कामदार [P. *-dār*], adj. worked, decorated (with, का); embroidered. [2]कामदार [P. *-dār*], m. a manager, agent. कामदिलाऊ, adj. giving work, or information about work (as a bureau). काम-धंधा, = ~, 3. काम-धाम, m. = काम-काज.

[2]**काम** *kām* [S.], m. **1.** desire. **2.** sexual desire; passion; lust. **3.** the object of desire, &c. **4.** = कामदेव. **5.** -काम. desirous of (e.g. सत्यकाम, adj. desirous of truth, righteous). — काम-कला, f. Av. the skill or wiles of Kāmdev. काम-केलि, f. flirtation, love-making. कामग, adj. Brbh. following (one's) desires; lustful. कामकूट, adj. lustful. काम-कृत, adj. Av. created by Kāmdev;

having achieved one's desire. काम-केलि, f. amorous play; love-making. कामद, adj. Av. granting desires. कामदेव, m. *mythol.* name of the god of love. काम-धुज, m. Brbh. the banner of Kāmdev. काम-धेनु, f. *mythol.* the cow of plenty, a fabulous cow produced at the churning of the ocean and supposed to yield whatever is requested of her. काम-प्रिय, adj. lustful, wanton. कामरूप, adj. taking any shape at will: lovely, pleasing; name of the region of western Assam. °ई, adj. id. कामवती, adj. f. = next. कामवान, adj. passionate, amorous. काम-वासना, f. passion of love; lust. काम-सूत्र, m. name of several Sanskrit works on sexual love, esp. that of Vātsyāyana. कामांध [°*ma*+*a*°], adj. blinded by desire, or lust. कामातुर [°*ma*+*ā*°], adj. love-sick; lustful. कामार्त [°*ma*+*ā*°], adj. id. कामार्थी [°*a*+*a*°], adj. *Pl. HŚS.* lustful, wanton. कामोत्तेजक [°*ma*+*a*°], adj. stirring up passion. कामोद [°*ma*+*u*°], m. *mus.* name of a *rāg* (sung at night). कामोद्दीपक [°*ma*+*u*°], adj. kindling passion, erotic; aphrodisiac. कामोन्माद [°*ma*+*u*°], m. frenzy of love.

काम- *kām-* [P. *kām*]. desire: — कामयाब [P. -*yāb*], adj. obtaining one's desire: successful. °ई, f. success.

क़ामत *qāmat* [A. *qāma*: P. *qāmat*], m. 19c. stature, bodily shape.

कामना *kāmănā* [S.], f. **1.** desire. **2.** lust.

कामयिता *kāmayitā* [S.], m. inv. one who desires, &c. (see ²काम).

कामरि *kāmri*, f. Brbh. = कमली.

कामरी *kāmrī*, f. Brbh. a blanket (= कमली).

कामायनी *kāmāyanī* [S.], f. see s.v. -आयन.

कामिनी *kāminī* [S.], f. desirous: **1.** an amorous woman; a loving woman. **2.** an attractive woman.

कामिल *kāmil* [A. *kāmil*], adj. U. perfect, complete: accomplished, capable.

¹**कामी** *kāmī* [*karmika-*], adj. active, busy (a person).

²**कामी** *kāmī* [S.], adj. & m. **1.** adj. desirous (of, का), amorous. **2.** lustful. **3.** m. a lascivious man.

³**कामी** *kāmī* [cf. H. ¹*kām*], f. reg. materials for work: **1.** an ingot of precious metal. **2.** W. twigs for basket-making.

कामुक *kāmuk* [S.], adj. desirous, amorous; sensual.

कामुकता *kāmukătā* [S.], f. amorous desire; sensuality.

कामुकी *kāmukī* [S.], f. a sensual woman.

काम्य *kāmyă* [S.], adj. **1.** desirable. **2.** beautiful, lovely. **3.** self-interested (action, observance).

काम्यता *kāmyătā* [S.], f. desirability.

काय *kāy*, m. esp. in comp. the body, &c. (= काया).

कायक *kāyak* [S.], adj. having to do with the body; bodily (as sensations); physical (life).

कायथ *kāyath*, m. = कायस्थ.

कायथी *kāythī*, f. = कैथी.

क़ायदा *qāydā* [A. *qā'ida*], m. **1.** regulation, rule; law. **2.** custom, practice, way; habit. **3.** regularity; uniformity. **4.** precept, principle. **5.** manners, etiquette. **6.** a primer, reader. **7.** *gram.* a rule. — ~ से, adv. in accordance with rule, or custom, &c.; properly. – क़ायदे-क़ानून, m. pl. rules and regulations.

कायनात *kāynāt* [A. *kā'ināt*, pl.], f. U. **1.** existing things; the world. **2.** possessions, stock, capital.

कायफल *kāyphal* [*kaṭphala-*: ← MIA *kapphala-*, **kāipphala-*], m. a small prickly tree, *Fragraria vesca*, the aromatic bark and seeds of which are used in perfumery and medicine; wild nutmeg, *Myrica sapida*.

क़ायम *qāym* [A. *qā'im*], adj. standing: **1.** fixed, established; set up. **2.** lasting; remaining in force. **3.** stable. **4.** steadfast (in respect of, पर). — ~ करना, to set up, to establish; to make permanent; to uphold, to support; to appoint (to, पर). ~ रखना, = ~ करना, 1., 3.; to keep up, to preserve. ~ रहना, to continue; to remain in operation, or in force; to survive; to stand firm; to persist (in, पर: as in a view, a resolve).

कायर *kāyar* [*kātara-*], adj. & m. **1.** adj. cowardly; timid. **2.** m. a coward, &c.

कायरता *kāyarătā* [cf. H. *kāyar*], f. cowardice; timidity.

कायरपन *kāyarpan* [cf. H. *kāyar*], m. cowardice.

कायरी *kāyrī* [cf. H. *kāyar*], adj. cowardly.

क़ायल *qāyl* [A. *qā'il*], adj. & m. saying: agreeing (to); convinced. — ~ करना (को), to convince (one; of, का). ~ होना, to be convinced (of), to acknowledge; to acquiesce (in: as in one's fate).

कायस्थ *kāyasth* [S.], m. **1.** name of a Hindu community regarded as of mixed origin, the writer caste. **2.** a man of the Kāyasth community.

काया *kāyā* [S.], f. **1.** the body. **2.** body (of an object); trunk (of a tree). **3.** outer form, appearance. **4.** [Engl. *body*] an incorporated body. — **काया-कल्प**, m. rejuvenation (esp. by magical means). **काया-पलट**, f. transformation, metamorphosis; change of body, rebirth; recovery of health (after illness); an elixir of youth.

कायिक *kāyik* [S.], adj. **1.** performed by the body (acts, sins). **2.** ? = **कायक**.

कार *kār* [P. *kār*], m. in comp. act; work, occupation; affair, matter. — **कारामद**, adj. [P. -*āmada*] come into use; available; serviceable. **कारामद करना**, to make available, or of use. **कारकुन** [P. -*kun*], m. doer of work: agent, manager; representative. **कारख़ाना**, m. factory; workshop; business, activity. °**-ख़ानेदार** [P. -*dār*], m. factory-owner, industralist. **कारख़ाना करना**, to open, or to run, a factory. **कारगर** [P. -*gar*], adj. doing the work: practical; successful. **कारगुज़ार** [P. -*guzār*], adj. skilful in work, expert; business-like. °**ई**, f. performance of work. **कार-चोब**, m. an embroidery frame; embroidery; embroiderer. °**ई**, adj. embroidered; embroidery with gold and silver thread. **कार-नामा**, m. record of deeds: chronicle, history; a deed, exploit. **कारबार** [P. -*bār*], m. dealings, business; trade; occupation. **कारबार करना**, to trade (in, **का**). °**ई**, m. & adj. a businessman; tradesman; business-like. **काररवाई** [P. -*ravāī*], f. working, operation (as of a business); management (of a business); step(s) taken, measure(s); proceedings (of a meeting), legal proceedings; activity. **काररवाई करना**, to take steps, or action; to be active; to hold proceedings. **कारसाज़** [P. -*sāz*], adj. dextrous, skilful, clever. °**ई**, skilfulness, &c.; pej. cleverness, cunning. **कारस्तानी** [P. -*istānī*], f. pej. a blunder, mistake; a cunning or devious act, or course of action.

-कार -*kār* [S., and P. -*kār*], suffix (forms agent nouns from nominal stems, e.g. **साहित्यकार**, m. writer, literary man; **काश्तकार**, m. cultivator, farmer).

कारक *kārak* [S.], adj. & m. **1.** adj. **-कारक**. doing, acting; causing. e.g. **हितकारक**, adj. beneficent. **2.** m. doer; agent or causative factor. **3.** *gram.* case. — **कारक-रचना**, f. *gram.* formation of cases, declension.

कारकुन *kārkun*, m. see s.v. **कार**.

कारख़ाना *kārkhānā*, m. see s.v. **कार**.

कारण *kāraṇ* [S.], m. **1.** cause; means, instrument. **2.** motive, purpose; reason. **3.** prime cause; source, basis. **4.** (in tantric ritual; and transf.) alcoholic drink. **5.** adv. & ppn. w. **के**. because (of); on account (of), for the sake (of). — **हिंदी जानने के ~ ...**, adv. because (he, they, &c.) knew (or know) Hindi .... **इस ~ (से)**, adv. for this reason; by this means. – **किसी कारणवश**, adv. for some, or a particular, reason. – **कारणात्मक** [°*na* + *ā*°], adj. causal.

कारणिक *kārăṇik* [S.], adj. having a cause.

कारणिकता *kārăṇikătā* [S.], f. causality.

कारतूस *kārtūs* [Fr. *cartouche*], m. a cartridge.

कारबार *kārbār*, m. see s.v. **कार**.

काररवाई *kārravāī*, f. see s.v. **कार**.

कारवाँ *kārvāṁ* [P. *kārvān*], m. a convoy, caravan (of travellers). — **कारवाँ-सराय** [P. -*sarāy*], m. an inn, caravanserai.

कारा *kārā* [S.], f. prison. — **कारागार** [°*rā* + *ā*°], m. place of imprisonment, prison. °**इक**, adj. & m. having to do with a prison; jailer. **कारा-गृह**, m. = **कारागार**. **कारा-दंड**, m. imprisonment as a punishment. **सश्रम कारा-दंड**, m. hard labour. **कारा-पाल**, m. jailer. **कारा-वास**, m. living in prison: imprisonment. °**ई**, m. prisoner.

कारिंदा *kārindā* [P. *kārandu*], m. an agent, manager; factor.

कारी *kārī* [P. *kārī*], adj. Av. operating, effective: **1.** piercing, penetrating (as a sound). **2.** mortal (as a wound).

[1]**-कारी** -*kārī* [S.], adj. formant. doing, making, performing (e.g. **कार्यकारी**, performing an act; executive).

[2]**-कारी** -*kārī* [P. *kārī*], f. formant. work (e.g. **दस्तकारी**, f. handicraft).

कारीगर *kārīgar* [P. *kārīgar*], m. a craftsman.

कारीगरी *kārīgarī* [P. *kārīgarī*], f. **1.** workmanship, craftsmanship; skill. **2.** skilled work; artistic work (as inlaying, &c).

कारु *kāru* [S.], m. poet. a maker, craftsman.

कारुणिक *kāruṇik* [S.], adj. compassionate, tender; kind.

कारुण्य *kāruṇyă* [S.], m. compassion; kindness.

क़ारूँ *qārūṁ* [A. *qārūn*], m. the cousin of Moses (proverbial for avarice).

कारोबार *kārobār* [P. *kār-o-bār*], m. = **कार-बार** (see s.v. **कार**).

कार्कश्य *kārkaśyă* [S.], m. = **करकशता**.

कार्तिक *kārtik*, m. corr. see **कार्त्तिक**.

कार्त्तिक *kārttik* [S.], m. the eighth month of the Hindu lunar year (October-November).

कार्त्तिकी *kārttikī* [S.], adj. & f. **1.** adj. having to do with the month Kārttik. **2.** f. the day of full moon in the month Kārttik.

कार्त्तिकेय *kārttikeyă* [S.], m. *mythol.* name of the god of war (son of Śiva: reared by the six *kr̥ttikās* or Pleiades).

कार्पण्य *kārpaṇyă* [S.], m. **1.** wretchedness, poverty. ***2.** miserliness.

कार्पास *kārpās* [S.], m. & adj. **1.** m. cotton. **2.** adj. made of cotton.

कार्मिक *kārmik* [S.], adj. & m. **1.** m. adj. working. **2.** m. a worker; pl. personnel.

कार्मुक *kārmuk* [S.], m. poet. a bow.

कार्य *kāryă* [S.], m. **1.** action, act; activity. **2.** work, task, duty; function, role. **3.** occupation. **4.** business, matter (in hand); agenda. — **कार्यकर**, adj. useful, effective. **कार्य-कर्ता**, m. inv. worker, or official; manager, executive. °**-कर्त्री**, f. **कार्य-कारण**, m. an effect with its cause: cause and effect. **कार्यकारिणी**, adj. f. = next. **कार्यकारी**, adj. performing an act, acts: executive; acting, temporary. **कार्यक्रम**, m. programme; timetable; a scheduled activity. **आपका आज क्या कार्यक्रम है?** what's on your timetable today? °**-क्रमण**, m. programming. **कार्य-क्षम**, adj. capable, competent. °**ता**, f. **कार्य-क्षेत्र**, m. field, or sphere of activity or authority. **कार्य-दूत**, m. chargé d'affaires. **कार्यदर्शी**, m. supervisor. **कार्य-परायण**, adj. devoted to one's work, or to a task. **कार्यपाल**, m. an executive. °**इका**, f. & adj. **कार्यभार**, m. burden of responsibility; °**ई**, adj. bearing a partic. responsibility, in charge. **कार्यरूप**, m. real form, reality. **कार्यरूप में परिणत करना**, to realise (an ambition, &c). **कार्यरूपेण**, adv. in reality, *de facto*. **कार्यवाहक**, adj. officiating, acting. °**-वाही**, adj. & f. managing; = **कारवाई**. **कार्यवश**, adv. because of some business or activity; (away) on business. °**आत्**, adv. id. **कार्य-विधि**, f. method of acting, procedure. **कार्य-विवरण**, m. account of actions, proceedings. **कार्यशील**, adj. active; energetic. **कार्य-समिति**, f. executive committee; working committee. **कार्य-सूची**, f. agenda. **कार्य-स्थगन**, m. adjournment of a matter. **कार्य-हेतु**, m. *law.* cause of action. **कार्याधिकारी** [°*a*+*a*°], m. one in charge of a partic. activity. **कार्यान्वयन** [°*ya*+*a*°], m. implementation (as of a policy). **कार्यान्वित** [°*ya*+*a*°], adj. brought about, realised (hopes, &c.); implemented, created. **कार्यालय** [°*ya*+*ā*°], m. office, offices; administrative or government department. **कार्यावली** [°*ya*+*ā*°], f. acts, activities: agenda.

कार्यालीन *kāryālīn*, adj. official in style, used in offices.

कालंगड़ा *kālaṅgṛā*, m. *mus.* a kind of *rāg* or song.

[1]**काल** *kāl* [*kāla-*[2]], m. **1.** time. **2.** a time; season; age. **3.** [also ad. *kāla-*[2]] *gram.* tense, time reference. **4.** suitable occasion. **4.** eventual destiny, fate; (time of) death; a title of Yama, the king of the dead; the messenger of death. — **~ काटना**, or **बिताना**, to pass time; to while away time. **~ का टूटा**, or **मारा**, adj. & m. famine-stricken; a victim of famine. **~ के बस होना**, to be subject to time; to be in death's clutches. **~ के मुँह**, or **के गाल, जाना**, to enter death's maw, to die. **सिर पर ~ नाचना** (**के**), fig. death to be impending. – **काल-क्रम**, m. lapse, process or sequence of time; chronology. **काल-क्रम से**, adv. with time; in sequence. °**-क्रमिक**, adj. chronological; *ling.* diachronic. **काल क्षेप**, m. allowing time to pass, delay; spending time. **काल-गूदड़ी**, f. the quilt of time: **काल-गुदरियाँ सी-**, Brbh. fig. to waste one's life. **काल-चक्र**, m. the wheel of time; a cycle, epoch. **काल-ज्ञान**, m. secular (as opposed to spiritual) knowledge. **काल-दर्श**, m. calendar. **काल-दोष**, m. time-fault: an anachronism. **काल-धर्म**, m. the law of time: death, dying; process of time; an event occurring in due season. **काल-नेमि**, m. *mythol.* name of a demon who took on the disguise of an ascetic with the intention of killing Hanumān; (°**-नेम**) Brbh. name of a demon killed by Kr̥ṣṇa. **काल-बस**, adv. in death's clutches. **काल-रात्रि**, f. night of the dissolution of the world. **काल-वाचक**, adj. *gram.* denoting time. °**वाची**, adj. id. **काल-विपाक**, m. fullness of time. **कालहीन**, adj. timeless, eternal. **कालांतर** [°*la*+*a*°], m. another age or time; intervening time, interval. **कालांतर में**, adv. in the course of time. °**इत**, adj. superseded. **कालावधि** [°*la*+*a*°], f. period of time; a term, limit.

[2]**काल** *kāl* [ad. *akāla-*; also H. [1]*kāl*], m. & adj. bad time: **1.** m. famine. **2.** adj. inauspicious, dire. **3.** unseasonable. — **~ पड़ना**, famine to occur, or to begin.

[3]**काल** *kāl*, adv. reg. = [2]**कल**.

काल- *kāl-*, adj. = **काला**. — **काल-कोठरी**, f. black room: cell, esp. as for solitary confinement.

कालकूट *kālăkūṭ* [S.], m. a deadly poison; specif. *mythol.* poison produced at the churning of the ocean (swallowed by Śiva and causing the blueness of his throat).

कालपनिकता *kālpănikătā* [S.], f. **1.** imaginary or hypothetical nature. **2.** *Pl.* contrivance, cunning.

कालबूत *kālbūt* [P. *kālbūd*, for *kalbūt*], m. **1.** Brbh. framework, structure (as for the building of an arch). **2.** see **कलबूत**.

कालविट *kālviṭ* [*kālapr̥ṣṭha-*], m. *Pl.* black-backed: the female black buck.

कालस *kālas* [cf. *kālā-*[1]], m. *Pl.* blackness.

काला *kālā* [*kāla-*[1]: ← Drav.], adj. **1.** black. **2.** wicked. **3.** fearful, dire. **4.** m. a title of

Kr̥ṣṇa. — ~ करना, to blacken; to scribble on (paper). ~ कौवा, m. a black crow. ~ चोर, m. a master thief, consummate villain. ~ जीरा, m. black cumin, *Nigella sativa*; ? = काली जीरी. ~ तिल, m. black-seeded sesame. ~ देव, m. a black god, or demon; a fiend; a very dark-complexioned man. ~ नमक, m. black salt (a factitious sulphide, used medicinally, and as a spice). ~ पहाड़, m. a black mountain or hill; colloq. an elephant; an insupportable burden. ~ बाज़ार, m. black market. ~ बाल, m. pubic hair. ~ भुजंग, adj. a black snake: jet-black. काली कुटकी, f. black hellebore. काली जीरी, f. black caraway, *Vernonia anthelmintica*. काली मिट्टी, f. black or rich soil. काली मिर्च, f. black pepper. काली सेम, f. a species of bean. काली हाँड़ी सिर पर धरना, to place a black pot on the head (of, के): to bring disgrace (on). काले कोसों, adv. long miles off, far off. काले बाल, m. pl. = ~ बाल. मुँह ~ करना, to blacken the face (of, का), to bring disgrace (on); to get rid (of). – काला-कलूटा, adj. coal-black (of complexion). काला-कोयला, adj. coal-black. काला पानी, m. black-water: transportation (to the Andaman Is. penal colony). काला-पानी भेजना, to deport to penal servitude. काला-बाज़ारी, f. dealing in a black market. काली-पीली आँखें करना, to glare (in anger).

कालापन *kālāpan* [cf. H. *kālā*], m. blackness; darkness of complexion.

कालिंदी *kālindī* [S.], f. Brbh. a name of the river Jumna (said to rise on a mountain called Kalinda).

कालि *kāli*, adv. Brbh. Av. = ²कल.

¹**कालिक** *kālik* [S.], adj. & m. **1.** adj. esp. -कालिक. pertaining to a partic. time. e.g. पूर्वकालिक, of former times. **2.** occurring in due time or season; periodical. **3.** *gram.* pertaining to tense or to time. **4.** m. a periodical publication.

²**कालिक** *kālik*, m. pronun. var. = कालिख.

कालिका *kālikā* [S.], f. var. /kalka/. **1.** blackness. **2.** a black or dark cloud. **3.** a title of the goddess Durgā.

कालिख *kālikh* [? cf. *kālaka-*], m. var. /kalakh/. blackness: **1.** lampblack, soot. **2.** a black mark or spot; mole, freckle. **3.** fig. disgrace, shame; fault, defect. — ~ लगाना (नाम पर), to give a bad name (to, के). ~ लगाना (मुँह, or मुँह में), to put to shame, to disgrace (one, के); to cause annoyance (to).

कालिमा *kālimā* [S.], f. (m., *Pl.*) var. /kalma/. blackness, &c. = कालिख.

¹**कालिया** *kāliyā* [*kālaka-*, *kālika-*], adj. black-complexioned.

²**कालिया** *kāliyā*, m. = ²काली.

¹**काली** *kālī* [S.], f. **1.** black colour or mark. **2.** [*kālikā-*] *mythol.* a title of the goddess Durgā.

²**काली** *kālī* [*kāliya-*], m. *mythol.* name of a snake that lived in the river Jumna, and was killed by Kr̥ṣṇa.

³**काली** *kālī*, adv. Av. metr. = कालि.

क़ालीन *qālīn* [P. *qālīn*], f. a carpet.

-कालीन *-kālīn* [S.], adj. formant. **1.** pertaining to a partic. time (e.g. मध्यकालिन, medieval). **2.** defining (an adj.) in respect of time (e.g. अल्पकालिन, of short duration).

कालुष्य *kāluṣyă* [S.], m. blackness: foulness, impurity.

कालौंच *kālauñc*, f. reg. = कलौंस.

कालौंछ *kālaum̐ch*, f. 19c. = कलौंस.

कालौंस *kālaum̐s*, f. reg. **1.** blackness. **2.** disgrace, shame.

काल्पनिक *kālpănik* [S.], adj. **1.** imaginary. **2.** hypothetical (a possibility).

कावर *kāvar*, m. pronun. var. reg. = काँवर.

कावा *kāvā* [P. *kāva*], m. *Pl. HŚS.* moving in a circle (a horse, on a rope). — ~ काटना, to canter in a circle.

काव्य *kāvyă* [S.], m. **1.** (Sanskrit) a literary composition in verse by a single author. **2.** a poem (esp. elaborate). **3.** poetry, belles lettres. — काव्यगत, adj. poetic (sensibility, or style). काव्यात्मक [°*ya*+*ā*°], adj. poetic (as sensibility, gifts). °ता, f.

काव्यत्व *kāvyatvă* [S.], m. poetic quality or style.

¹**काश** *kāś* [P. *kāś*], conj. would that. — ~ कि, conj. id. ~ मैं वहाँ जा सकता! how I wish that I might go there!

²**काश** *kāś* [S.], m. = काँस.

काशी *kāśī* [S.], f. shining: a name of the city of Banaras. — काशी-करवट लेना, to accept the saw at Banaras: to seek self-immolation at Banaras so as to gain merit; fig. to suffer extreme hardship. काशी-फल, m. a kind of pumpkin.

काश्त *kāśt* [P. *kāśt*], m. **1.** ploughing; cultivation, farming. **2.** cultivated land; field, farm. **3.** tenure of land. — ~ में लाना, to bring (land) under cultivation. ~ लगना, to gain tenure (of, पर). – काश्तकार [P. *-kār*], m. a tenant farmer. °ई, f. farming; rented farm land; tenancy, lease of farm land.

काषाय *kāṣāy* [S.], m. reddish-brown: a cloth or garment.

काश्मीर *kāśmīr* [S.], m. = कश्मीर.

काष्ठ *kāṣṭh* [S.], m. **1.** wood, &c. (= काठ). **2.** timber.

काष्ठा *kāṣṭhā* [S.], f. *HŚS.* **1.** mark, limit: goal; boundary. **2.** summit, peak.

काष्ठीय *kāṣṭhīyă* [S.], adj. **1.** of wood, wooden. **2.** having to do with wood or timber.

[1]**कास** *kās* [*kāśa-*], m. reg. = काँस.

[2]**कास** *kās* [S.], m. *Pl. HŚS.* cough, coughing.

कासनी *kāsnī* [P. *kāsnī*], f. & adj. **1.** f. endive; chicory. **2.** adj. chicory-coloured; lilac.

क़ासिद *qāsid* [A. *qāsid*], m. U. a messenger.

कासीस *kāsīs*, m. = कसीस.

काह *kāh* [? conn. H. *kāhe*], pron. Brbh. Av. = क्या.

काहल *kāhal*, adj. Brbh. = काहिल.

काहिल *kāhil* [A. *kāhil*], adj. languid, inert; indolent, slack; negligent.

काहिली *kāhilī* [A. *kāhil*+P. *-ī*], f. languor; indolence; remissness. — ~ करना, to be indolent, slack, &c.

काही *kāhī* [P. *kāhī*], adj. & f. **1.** adj. grass-coloured, greenish. **2.** f. a greenish colour. **3.** reg. = काई.

[1]**काहू** *kāhū* [conn. *kasya*], obl. pron. stem (w. coalesced encl). Brbh. Av. = किसी.

[2]**काहू** *kāhū* [P. *kāhu*], m. reg. a kind of lettuce.

काहे *kāhe* [conn. *kasya*], obl. pron. stem (w. coalesced suffix). Brbh. Av. & colloq. 1. = किस. **2.** adv. why? — ~ को, adv. id.

किंकर *kiṁ-kar* [S.], m. a servant.

किंकरता *kiṁkarătā* [S.], f. Brbh. service, bondsmanship.

किंकर्तव्यविमूढ़ *kiṁkartătavyavimūṛh* [S.], adj. uncertain what to do.

किंकिणी *kiṅkiṇī* [S.], f. **1.** a small bell. **2.** a woman's or children's belt of small bells, or any tinkling ornaments.

किंगरी *kiṅgrī* [P. *kingrī*], f. Av. *mus.* a stringed instrument of medium size having a box-like wooden frame.

किंचित् *kiñcit* [S.], adv. & adj. **1.** adv. a little, somewhat. **2.** adj. small, little.

किंजल्क *kiñjalk* [S.], m. lotus tendril or (?) pollen.

किंतु *kin-tu* [S.], conj. but, however; still, nevertheless.

क़िंदील *qindīl* [A. *qindīl*], f. **1.** a candle. **2.** a light, esp. one with protecting paper; lampstand; shade. **3.** chandelier.

किंवदंती *kiṃvadantī* [S. *kiṃvadantĭ*], f. what do (they) say?: a rumour; hearsay.

किंवा *kiṃ-vā* [S.], conj. or, or else; otherwise.

किंशुक *kiṃśuk* [S,], f. the tree *Butea frondosa*, and its red flowers.

कि *ki* [P. *ki*], conj. & adv. **1.** conj. (introducing nominal clauses.) that. उसे अफ़सोस था ~ ..., he was sorry that .... बात यह है ~ ..., the thing is that .... मैंने उससे पूछा ~ ..., I asked him if, whether .... **2.** when (of a sudden, new development.) वह भारत जानेवाली थी ~ बीमार पड़ गई, she was about to go to India when she fell ill. **3.** in order to (= ताकि). **4.** adv. [× *kim*] or. जाओगे ~ नहीं? will you go or not? बनारस जाओगे ~ इलाहाबाद? will you go to Banaras or Allahabad? **5.** (pleonastically: esp. w. relative words, which it usually follows.) जैसे ~ मैं कह रहा था ..., as I was saying ....

किकियाना *kikiyānā* [cf. **kīkkati*], v.i. to screech, to scream, to chatter (as a monkey); to shout or to wail unrestrainedly.

किच-किच *kic-kic*, f. = कच-कच.

किचकिचाना *kickicānā*, v.i. **1.** to grate, to grind the teeth. **2.** to clench the teeth. — किचकिचाकर दाँत काटना, to bite with (one's) full strength.

किचकिचाहट *kickicāhaṭ* [cf. H. *kickicānā*], f. **1.** grating the teeth. **2.** clenching the teeth.

किचकिचिया *kickiciyā* [cf. H. *kickicānā*], m. colloq. **1.** a wrangler. **2.** a chatterbox.

किचकिची *kickicī*, f. = किचकिचाहट. — ~ बाँधना, to grate the teeth habitually or continuously.

किचड़ा *kicṛā*, m. = कीचड़.

किचड़ाना *kicṛānā* [cf. H. *kīcaṛ*], v.i. & v.t. **1.** v.i. to secrete matter (the eyes). **2.** v.t. to cause (the eyes) to secrete matter (a medicine).

किचड़ाहा *kicṛāhā* [cf. H. *kīcaṛ*], adj. muddy.

किच-पिच *kic-pic* [? cf. H. *kīc*], f. mud, mire.

किचर-पिचर *kicar-picar* [cf. H. *kicpic*], adj. **1.** muddy. **2.** unclear (as writing); confused.

किटकिटाना *kiṭkiṭānā* [*kiṭakiṭāyate* × **kaṭṭa-*[1]], v.t. & v.i. **1.** v.t. to grate (the teeth: in frustration, &c). **2.** to clench (the teeth). **3.** v.i. to feel gritty (the teeth).

किटकिटी *kiṭkiṭī*, f. = कटकटी.

[1]**किट्ट** *kiṭṭ* [S.], m. *Pl. HŚS.* a secretion; sediment (= [1]कीट); excreted substance.

[2]**किट्ट** *kiṭṭ*, m. *Pl.* a kind of sour dish.

किड़- *kiṛ-* [H. *kīṛā*]. a worm: — किड़-खाया, adj. worm-eaten.

किड़किड़ाना *kiṛkiṛānā* [*kiṭakiṭāyate*], v.t. to grind or to gnash the teeth.

किण्व *kiṇvă* [S.], m. *Pl. HŚS.* drug or seed used as a ferment in making spirits.

कित *kit* [conn. *kutra*], adv. **1.** Brbh. where, whither? **2.** rhetor. Av. why?; by no means.

कितना *kitnā* [cf. **kiyatta*-: and Pa. *kittaka*-], adj. **1.** how much? **2.** pl. how many? **3.** rhetor. how! ~ अच्छा आदमी है! how fine a man he is! **4.** adv. rhetor. very much. उसे ~ समझाया, पर वह न माना, (I) urged him time and again but he didn't agree. — ~ ही (... क्यों न), adj. however much. उसके पास ~ ही पैसा (क्यों न) हो, however much money he may have. कितने एक, adj. some few, several.

क़िता *qitā* [A. *qiṭ'a*], m. U. a cut-off portion: **1.** a piece; plot (of ground). **2.** (w. numbers) a unit. 3. = क़ता, 2.

किताब *kitāb* [A. *kitāb*], f. **1.** a book. **2.** a sacred book, scripture (esp. Muslim; also Christian, Hebrew). — ~ पर चढ़ाना, to enter in a book, to note. – किताब-ख़ाना, m. (for कुतुब-ख़ाना) a library. किताब-घर, m. bookshop. किताब-फ़रोश [P. *farosh*], m. book-seller.

किताबत *kitābat* [A. *kitāba*: P. *kitābat*], f. **1.** writing. **2.** sthg. written: an inscription; an epitaph.

किताबी *kitābī* [A. *kitāb*+P. *-ī*], adj. **1.** pertaining to a book or to books; derived from books (knowledge, &c.); bookish (a person). **2.** book-shaped, oblong; elongated. — ~ कीड़ा, m. book-worm (also fig). ~ चेहरा, m. a long or oval face.

कितीक *kitīk* adj. pl. f. Brbh. = कितेक.

कितेक *kitek* [H. *kittau*+H. *ek*], adj. pl. m. Brbh. how many (particular items)? (= कितने).

कितौ *kitau*, adj. Brbh. = कित्तौ.

कित्त *kitt*, adv. Av. = कित, 2.

कित्तौ *kittau*, adj. Brbh. = कितना.

किदार *kidār* [ad. *kedāra*-], m. = केदार. — किदार-बसंत, m. *mus.* name of a *rāg*.

किदारा *kidārā* [ad. *kedāra*-], m. *mus.* name of a *rāg* sung at midnight in summer.

किधर *kidhar* [conn. H. [1]*dhār*], adv. **1.** whither? **2.** where? — ~ से, adv. from where?

[1]**किन** *kin*, pron. obl. pl. base. see कौन.

[2]**किन** *kin* [*kiṇa*-], m. Brbh. a wound, scar.

किनार *kinār* [P. *kanār*, *kinār*]. side, edge: — दर ~ [P. *dar*], adv. (leaving) aside; not to mention.

किनारा *kinārā* [P. *kanāra*; and *kanār*, *kinār*], m. **1.** side, edge, margin; end, limit. **2.** shore, bank, beach. **3.** a border, hem. — ~ करना, to hold (oneself) aloof (from, से); to abstain, or to refrain (from). ~ खींचना, = ~ करना. – किनारे किनारे, adv. all along the bank, &c.; alongside (of, के). किनारे, किनारे पर, ppn. & adv. by the side (of, के), alongside; on the bank (of); ashore, on land; aside, out of the question, not to speak of (= दर किनार). किनारे पर लगना, to be brought to shore. किनारे पहुँचना, to reach the end or conclusion (of, के). किनारे बैठना, to remain aloof or uninvolved. किनारे रहना (से), = ~ करना. किनारे लगना, to reach the shore, to put to shore; to reach the end (of, के). किनारे लगाना, to put to shore, to beach (a boat); to moor; to lay to (a ship); fig. to conclude (a task). किनारे होना, to move or to step aside; to turn aside (from, से). – किनाराकशी [P. *-kaśī*], f. holding aloof (from). किनारेदार [P. *-dār*], adj. having a border, edged (material).

किनारी *kinārī* [H. *kinārī*, → P.], f. edging, trimming (of gold or silver).

किन्नर *kinnar* [S.], m. **1.** *mythol.* a being with a human body and horse's head, reckoned among the *gandharvas* (as divine musicians or singers). **2.** *mythol.* a class of demigods attached to Kuvera, the god of wealth. **3.** name of a community of singers and musicians.

किफ़ायत *kifāyat* [A. *kifāya*: P. *kifāyat*], f. sufficiency, abundance: **1.** profit, advantage (by saving). आपको ~ रहेगी, you'll benefit (by sthg). ***2.** economy, thrift; an economy, saving; retrenchment. ~ में मिलना, to be had cheaply, advantageously. पचास रुपए की ~, a saving of fifty rupees. **3.** parsimony; reluctance. आपको पैसे ख़र्च करने में ~ क्यों? why are you reluctant to spend money? — ~ करना, to economise; to suffice; to beat down (a price); to lower (a price). ~ से, economically, &c. – किफ़ायतशार [P. *-śār*], adj. thrifty.

किफ़ायती *kifāyătī* [cf. H. *kifāyat*], adj. & f. **1.** adj. thrifty, economical. **2.** parsimonious. **3.** cheap; inexpensive to maintain. **4.** f. a sufficiency; an abundance, &c. (cf. किफ़ायत).

क़िबला *qiblā* [A. *qibla*], m. sthg. opposite: **1.** the direction of Mecca (to which Muslims turn their faces to pray). **2.** fig. any venerated person: a father; a king.

किम् *kim* [*kim*], pron. & adv. what? why? how? — किमपि, adv. Brbh. Av. anything at all (= कुछ भी).

किमख़ाब *kimkhāb* [P. *kamkhvāb*], m. silk or satin worked with gold or silver flowers, brocade.

किमख़ाबी *kimkhābī* [cf. P. *kamkhvābī*], adj. brocaded; embroidered.

किया *kiyā* [*kṛta-*], perf. part. & m. **1.** done, performed. **2.** sthg. done. — अपने किए का फल, m. the just reward of (one's) deeds.

किरकिटी *kirkiṭī* [*kiri-*; ?+*kiṭṭa-*], f. Brbh. dust or dirt fallen into the eye.

किरकिर *kirkir* [cf. *kiṭakiṭāyate*], f. **1.** grittiness; the sound of anything gritty under the teeth. **2.** reg. grating, creaking (as of a door). — ~ करना, to grate under the teeth.

किरकिरा *kirkirā* [cf. *kiṭakiṭāyate*], adj. gritty, sandy; spoiled, marred. — ~ करना, to make gritty; to spoil. ~ ताश, m. a kind of brocade. सारा मज़ा ~ हो गया, all the fun was spoiled.

किरकिराना *kirkirānā* [*kiṭakiṭāyate*], v.i. **1.** to sound or to be gritty; to grate; to be painful (as the eye). **2.** reg. (E.) to crackle.

किरकिरापन *kirkirāpan* [cf. H. *kirkirā*], m. grittiness.

किरकिराहट *kirkirāhaṭ* [cf. H. *kirkirānā*], f. = किरकिर, and करकराहट.

किरकिरी *kirkirī* [cf. H. *kirkir*], f. **1.** grittiness, sandiness, &c. **2.** a piece of grit, sand. **3.** colloq. disgrace; loss of prestige.

किरकी *kirkī*, f. *Pl. HŚS.* pendant to a nose-ring.

किरच *kirc*, f. **1.** a splinter (of glass, metal); fragment. **2.** a bit, grain. **3.** fig. a straight sword (for thrusting with). — ~ का गोला, m. *mil.* grenade.

किरचा *kircā*, m. = किरच, 1., 2. — किरचे-किरचे करना, to cut to pieces.

किरण *kiraṇ* [S.], f. (m). **1.** a ray, beam; a sunbeam, moonbeam; an electromagnetic ray. **2.** a tassel (of gold or silver). — ~ फूटना, day to break, or dawn. – किरणमय, adj. radiant.

किरतनिया *kirtaniyā* [cf. H. *kīrtan*], m. a singer of devotional songs (= कीर्तनिया).

क़िरतास *qirtās* [A. *qirṭās*], m. S.H. paper.

किरदार *kirdār* [P. *kirdār*], m. U. character (of a literary work).

किरन *kiran*, f. see किरण.

किरना *kirnā* [*kirati*], v.i. reg. (E.) to fall off: **1.** to decay, to moulder; to crumble; to wear out. **2.** to be blunted (as a knife); to feel shame (at, से), to be shy (of).

किरम *kirm* [P. *kirm*], m. = कृमि.

किरमिच *kirmic*, m. canvas.

क़िरमिज़ *qirmiz* [A. *qirmiz*], m. cochineal (the insect: a former source of scarlet and crimson dye).

क़िरमिज़ी *qirmizī* [P. *qirmizī*], adj. & m. **1.** adj. crimson; scarlet. **2.** m. crimson or scarlet colour.

किरयात *kiryāt* [*kirātatikta-*], f. a bitter shrub, *Andrographis paniculata*, source of a household medicine. (see चिरायता).

किरवान *kirvān* [*kṛpāṇa-*], m. Brbh. a sword, scimitar.

किराँची *kirāṁcī* [Pt. *carraguem*], f. reg. (W.) a two-wheeled covered cart.

किरात *kirāt* [S.], m. name of a mountain tribe.

[1]**किराना** *kirānā* [ad. *krayāṇaka-*], m. things sold: groceries; spices.

[2]**किराना** *kirānā* [cf. H. *kirnā*; or **kerayati*], v.t. to sift.

किरानी *kirānī*, m. & adj. **1.** m. a clerk. **2.** arch. a Eurasian; a Christian. **3.** adj. arch. Eurasian, European; Christian. — किरानी-ख़ाना, m. an office.

किराया *kirāyā* [P. *kirāya*], m. charge or payment for hire, rent, or lease; freight charge. — ~ उतारना, to collect a rental payment. ~ करना, to hire out, &c. (= किराए पर देना). किराए देना, to take (sthg.) on hire or rent. किराए का, adj. rented, rental; hired. किराए का टट्टू, m. a hireling; a hired hack. किराए पर देना, to hire out, to rent out, to lease out. किराए पर लेना, to take on hire, rent or lease. – किराएदार [P. -*dār*], m. one who takes on hire, rent or lease. किराया-नामा, m. deed of lease.

किराव *kirāv*, m. reg. (E.) a small type of pea (= केराव).

किरासन *kirāsan* [Engl. *kerosene*], m. kerosene, paraffin.

किरीट *kirīṭ* [S.], m. a tiara, diadem, crest; any ornament used as a crown.

किरीटी *kirīṭī* [S.], adj. & m. **1.** adj. decorated with a diadem; crested; crowned. **2.** m. one decorated with a diadem: a king; a title of Arjuna.

किरोना *kironā* [H. ²*kirānā* × H. *rolnā*], v.t. reg. *Pl.* = किरोलना.

किरोलना *kirolnā* [H. ²*kirānā* × *rolnā*, *kurednā*], v.t. reg. **1.** to winnow, to pick out. **2.** to scrape, to scratch up (= कुरेलना).

किरौना *kiraunā* [cf. *kīṭa-*], m. reg. (Bihar) **1.** a flying insect that attacks cereals, chiefly millets. **2.** a worm; a snake.

क़िर्मिज़ *qirmiz*, m. see क़िरमिज़.

क़िर्मिज़ी *qirmizī*, adj. & m. see क़िरमिज़ी.

किलक *kilak*, f. = किलकार.

किलकना *kilaknā* [cf. *kilakilāyati*], v.i. to shout in delight (= किलकारना).

किलकार *kilkār*, m. = किलकारी.

किलकारना *kilkārnā* [cf. H. *kilkār*], v.i. to shout or to cry out aloud (as in delight or exultation); to chorus (birds).

किलकारी *kilkārī* [cf. *kilikilā-*], m. **1.** shouting or crying aloud (in excitement, in delight, or in triumph). — ~ भरना, or मारना, to shout, to scream, &c.

किलकिल-काँटा *kilkil-kāṁṭā*, m. Śiva's fork: a boys' game (one boy draws several lines on a stone and hides it; the others search for it, calling out '*kilkil-kāṁṭā*').

¹**किलकिला** *kilkilā* [? conn. *kilakilāyati*], m. **1.** the white-breasted kingfisher. **2.** *Pl.* the grey babbler.

²**किलकिला** *kilkilā*. *mythol.* Av. name of an ocean.

किलनी *kilnī*, f. a tick (insect found on animals).

किलबिलाना *kilbilānā*, v.i. to creep.

किल्बिषी *kilbiṣī* [S.], adj. culpable; sinning.

किलवाई *kilvāī* [cf. H. *kilvānā*], f. reg. a large rake (for gathering grass, &c.; also for spiking ground after rain or irrigation).

किलवाना *kilvānā* [cf. H. *kīlnā*], v.t. *Pl. HŚS.* to cause to be set with nails (as a piece of wood, to make a rake).

किलस *kilas* [cf. H. *kilasnā*], f. distress, grief. — तुम्हें क्यों ~ हो रही है? what's the matter? (to one crying).

किलसना *kilasnā* [*kliśyate*: Pa. *kilissati*], v.i. **1.** to curse. **2.** to weep. **3.** to feel pain.

किलसाना *kilsānā* [cf. H. *kilasnā*], v.t. to cause to weep.

किल्विषी *kilviṣī*, adj. see किल्बिषी.

क़िला *qilā* [A. *qal'a*], m. a fort; a castle. — ~ टूटना, a fort to be taken; a cause of difficulty to be eliminated; a feat to be successfully performed. ~ फ़तेह करना, to take a fort; to achieve sthg. difficult. ~ बनाना, to build a fort; to fortify (a place). ~ बाँधना, id., 2. – क़िलाबंद [P. *-band*], adj. shut up in a fort. °ई, f. defending, defence of a fort; defensive works, defences. क़िलेदार [P. *-dār*], m. commandant of a garrison or fort.

किलिक *kilik* [P. *kilk*], f. a piece of reed, reed pen.

किलोल *kilol*, f. pronun. var. = कलोल.

क़िल्लत *qillat* [A. *qilla*: P. *qillat*], f. **1.** deficiency, scarcity. **2.** difficulty. **3.** want, poverty. — ~ से, adv. because of a scarcity (of, की); with difficulty.

¹**किल्ला** *killā* [*karīra-*¹], m. a bud, sprout.

²**किल्ला** *killā*, m. = कीला.

किल्लाना *killānā* [*kilakilāyati*], v.i. *reg.* to shriek, to scream (= चिल्लाना).

¹**किल्ली** *killī* [**kīlla-*], f. **1.** a peg. **2.** a rod. **3.** a handle. — ~ ऐंठना, or घुमाना, or दबाना (की), to move or to turn a control: colloq. to pull strings; to induce or to incite (one, की). — धुर-किल्ली, f. axle-pin.

²**किल्ली** *killī* [cf. H. *killānā*], f. a scream, shriek. — ~ मारना, to scream, to shriek.

किवाँच *kivāṁc*, f. m. pronun. var. = केवाँच.

किवाड़ *kivāṛ* [*kavāṭa-*: ? ← Drav.], m. **1.** leaf of a door. **2.** door. — ~ देना, or भिड़ाना, or लगाना, to draw door-leaves to, to close a door.

किवाड़ी *kivāṛī* [*kapāṭikā-*], f. a small door; a door.

किशन *kiśan* [ad. *kṛṣṇa-*], m. = कृष्ण, 3.

किशमिश *kiśmiś* [P. *kiśmiś*], f. a small dried grape; raisin, currant.

किशमिशी *kiśmiśī* [P. *kiśmiśī*], adj. **1.** made with raisins. **2.** of the colour or taste of raisins.

किशोर *kiśor* [S.], m. **1.** a youth; teenager. **2.** a minor, one under eighteen (earlier, fifteen). — ~ अवस्था, f. adolescence; minority. – युगल-किशोर, m. *hind.* a title of Kṛṣṇa as thought of in conjunction with Rādhā, his consort.

किशोरी *kiśorī* [S.], f. an adolescent girl; a young woman.

¹**किश्त** *kiśt* [P. *kiśt*], f. **1.** (in chess) check. — ~ देना (को), to put in check. ~ लगना, to be in check.

²**किश्त** *kiśt*, f. = क़िस्त.

किश्ती *kiśtī*, f. = कश्ती.

किष्किंध *kiṣkindh*, m. *mythol.* the name of a mountain in the south of India (in northern Mysore) containing a cave, the residence of the monkey-king Bali. — ~ कांड, m. title of the fourth book or section of the *Rāmāyaṇa*.

किस *kis*, interr. pron. base. see कौन.

किसन *kisan* [ad. *kṛṣṇa-*], m. = कृष्ण, 3.

किसब *kisab* [cf. A. *kasb*], m. Brbh. acquirement, gain: craft, trade.

किसबी *kisbī* [cf. H. *kisab*], m. reg. (E). a craftsman.

क़िसमत *qismat*, f. see क़िस्मत.

किसलय *kisălay* [S.], m. sprout or shoots of new foliage.

किसान *kisān* [*kṛṣāṇa-*], m. a cultivator, farmer.

किसानी *kisānī* [cf. H. *kisān*], f. farmer's work, farming.

क़िस्त *qist* [A. *qisṭ*], f. **1.** an instalment, due portion. **2.** instalment payment. **3.** agreed conditions of payment by instalments. **4.** episode (of a serial). — ~ पर, adv. by instalments. ~, or क़िस्तें, बाँधना, to arrange to pay (a debt, की), by instalments. – क़िस्तकार, m. one who pays by instalments. क़िस्तबंदी [P. -*bandī*], f. payment by instalments; arranging to pay by instalments. क़िस्तवार, adv. by instalments.

क़िस्म *qism* [A. *qism*], m. kind, type; partic. variety. — किस ~ का? what sort of? – क़िस्मवार [P. -*vār*], adv. according to kind or type; classed, classified.

क़िस्मत *qismat* [A. *qisma*: P. *qismat*], f. division: fate, destiny; lot. — ~ उलटना, or पलटना, or फूटना, (one's) fortune to take a turn for the worse. ~ आज़माना, to try one's fortune or luck. ~ का धनी, m. a lucky person. ~ का लिखा, m. the decree of fate; lines of fate (on the brow). ~ का हेठा, m. one who has been unfortunate, an unlucky person. ~ की बात, f. a fated thing; a lucky thing. ~ खुलना, or चमकना, or जागना, or फिरना (की), (one's) fortune to take a favourable turn. ~ लड़ना (की), (one's) fortune to be in the balance (against others'); to have a good run of luck. ~ से पहले, adv. before fate decrees: before one deserves (sthg). – क़िस्मतवाला, adj. lucky, fortunate.

क़िस्सा *qissā* [A. *qiṣṣa*], m. **1.** a tale, story. **2.** account (of some matter); news. **3.** transf. a matter, business. **4.** dispute, quarrel. — ~ उठाना, or खड़ा करना, to start a dispute or quarrel. ~ करना, colloq. to wrangle or to quarrel. ~ कोताह करना, (with, से) to shorten a story: to cut a matter short (see below). ~ पाक करना, to settle a dispute, or an outstanding matter; colloq. to see the end of, to kill. – क़िस्सा-कहानी, f. a tale from start to finish: sthg. imagined or make-believe; pl. tales and stories. क़िस्सा-कोताह [P. -*kotāh*], adv. (to make the) story short: to finish the story. क़िस्सागो [P. -*go*], m. U. story-teller. °ई, f. story-telling.

कीक *kīk* [cf. H. *kīknā*], f. scream, cry.

कीकना *kīknā* [**kīkkati*], v.i. reg. to scream, to cry out shrilly.

कीकर *kīkar* [**kikkara-*], m. the acacia, *A. arabica* (a small tree found chiefly in dry regions: = बबूल).

कीकरी *kīkrī* [cf. H. *kīkar*], f. *Pl. HŚS.* a wavy border or edging of cloth. = कीचड़.

कीचड़ *kīcaṛ* [cf. *cikka-*[2]: ← Drav. and Austro-as.], m. (f., *Pl.*) **1.** gummy matter in the eyes. ***2.** mud, mire, ooze.

[1]**कीट** *kīṭ* [*kiṭṭa-*], m. *Pl. HŚS.* sediment, dregs.

[2]**कीट** *kīṭ* [S.], m. an insect. — कीट-नाशक, adj. & m. insecticide. कीट-विज्ञान, m. entomology. कीटाणु [°*ta*+*a*°], m. a microbe, germ.

कीड़-खाया *kīṛ-khāyā* [cf. H. *kīṛā*], adj. worm-eaten; decayed (a tooth).

कीड़ा *kīṛā* [*kīṭa-*], m. **1.** an insect. **2.** a worm; a grub. **3.** (see also किड़-.) canker, mildew, rot (on vegetation). — ~, or कीड़े, लगना, to be worm-eaten. कीड़े पड़ना, worms to appear (in, में) or to infest. रेशम का ~, m. a silk-worm. – कीड़े-मकोड़े, m. pl. insects.

कीड़ा-कीड़ी *kīṛā-kīṛī* [**krīḍākrīḍita-*], f. play and frolicking: a partic. childrens game.

कीड़ी *kīṛī* [cf. H. *kīṛā*], f. a worm; a small insect.

कीन *kīn*, perf. Brbh. = किया.

कीनना *kīnnā* [*krīṇāti*], v.t. reg. (Bihar) to buy.

कीना *kīnā* [P. *kīna*], m. rancour, malice, spite; grudge. — ~ रखना, to feel rancour, &c.; to nurse a grudge. कीने से, adv. maliciously.

कीन्ह *kīnh*, perf. Brbh. Av. = किया.

क़ीमत *qīmat* [A. *qīma*: P. *qīmat*], f. **1.** price. **2.** value, worth. **3.** cost. — ~ कम करना, to beat down a price. ~ चुकाना, to pay the price (for sthg., की); to fix a price. ~ लगाना, to fix the price (of, की); to make an offer.

क़ीमती *qīmtī* [P. *qīmatī*], adj. **1.** expensive. **2.** valuable; precious.

क़ीमा *qīmā* [A. *qīma*], m. **1.** minced meat. **2.** a meat curry. — ~ **करना**, to chop up (meat) fine; colloq. to hack, to mangle.

कीमिया *kīmiyā* [A. *kīmiyā*: ← Gk.], m. U. **1.** alchemy. **2.** chemistry (= **रसायन**).

कीर *kīr*, [S.], m. Brbh. Av. a parrot.

कीर्तन *kīrtan* [S.], m. mentioning, praising, celebrating: group singing of hymns (*bhajan*) to a deity. — **कीर्तनकार**, m. a singer of *bhajans*; devotional singing.

कीर्तनिया *kīrtaniyā* [cf. H. *kīrtan*], m. = **कीर्तनकार**.

कीर्ति *kīrti* [S.], f. mention: fame; glory. — ~ **करना**, to make a name, to acquire fame. – **कीर्ति-मान**, m. esp. *athl.* a record. **कीर्ति-लेखा**, m. *archaeol.* inscription praising (a king, &c). **कीर्ति-स्तंभ**, m. monument (as to a person, or to a dynasty).

कील *kīl* [*kīla*-[1]], m. **1.** a nail; tack. **2.** spike, peg. **3.** a nose-pin or stud. **4.** core (of a boil). — **कील-काँटा**, m. colloq. equipment, tools, accessories; get-up, attire; fig. bad handwriting, scribbling; = **किलकिल-काँटा**).

कीलक *kīlak* [S.], m. a peg, pin; pivot.

कीलना *kīlnā* [*kīlati*], v.t. **1.** to pin, to fasten together. **2.** to spike (a cannon). **3.** to close up (the mouth), to silence (one). **4.** to rivet or to bind (one) by a spell; to destroy (as insect pests) by magic.

कीला *kīlā* [*kīlaka*-], m. a large nail; spike, peg.

कीलिया *kīliyā* [cf. H. *kīlī*], m. reg. (W.) the man who works the oxen at a well.

कीली *kīlī* [cf. H. *kīlā*], f. **1.** peg, pivot, axis. **2.** reg. (W.) spike in the yoke of a harness; the system of working a well for irrigation with two pairs of oxen (which are changed by removing the spike in the yoke).

कीलित *kīlit* [S.], adj. pinned, spiked, &c. (see **कीलना**).

कीश *kīś* [S.], m. poet. an ape.

कुं *kuṁ*, ppn. E.H. = **को**.

कुँकुआना *kuṁkuānā*, v.i. to whimper.

कुंकुम *kuṅkum* [S.], m. **1.** saffron. 2. = **रोली**.

कुंकुमा *kuṅkumā*, m. **1.** a container for *gulāl*, or *rolī*. **2.** Av. = **कुंकुम**.

कुंचित *kuñcit* [S.], adj. crooked; curved, curled; contracted.

कुंज *kuñj* [S.], m. **1.** an arbour, bower. **2.** a grove.

कुँजड़न *kuṁjṛan* [cf. H. *kuṁjṛā*], f. **1.** a *kuṁjṛā* woman. **2.** a *kuṁjṛā's* wife. **3.** a woman who sells vegetables, &c.

कुँजड़ा *kuṁjṛā* [cf. *kuñja*-], m. **1.** name of a community of vegetable-sellers and market gardeners. **2.** a man of that community; a greengrocer, fruiterer. — **कुँजड़े का ग़ल्ला**, a *kuṁjṛā's* drawer: a mess; disorder. **कुँजड़े की लड़ाई**, f. fig. a quarrel over nothing.

कुंजर *kuñjar* [S.], m. Av. an elephant.

कुंजी *kuṁjī* [*kuñcikā*-[1]], f. **1.** a key. **2.** key, fair version (as of a text).

कुंठा *kuṇṭhā* [S.], f. **1.** bluntness. **2.** dullness, stupidity. **3.** frustration.

कुंठित *kuṇṭhit* [S.], adj. **1.** blunted, blunt. **2.** dull, stupid. **3.** concealing (one's) true feelings: frustrated. ~ **भाव से**, in frustration.

कुंड *kuṇḍ* [S.], m. **1.** a wide-mouthed, deep basin. **2.** pit (as for sacrificial fire). **3.** a pool. **4.** tank (as consecrated to a person or deity); a tank encompassed by tall flights of steps.

कुंडड़ा *kuṇḍṛā* [cf. *kuṇḍa*-[3]: ← Drav.], m. reg. (W.) a stack (as of corn); heap, pile.

कुंडरा *kuṇḍrā* [cf. H. *kuṇḍ*], m. Brbh. a large vessel.

कुंडल *kuṇḍal* [S.], m. **1.** a large ear-ring (as worn by yogīs). **2.** ring, hoop; circular rim. **3.** any ring-shaped ornament (as a metal bangle). **4.** coil (as of rope, wire); snake's coil. **5.** *electr.* a coil. **6.** a circle. **7.** a halo. — **कुंडलाकार** [°*la* + *ā*°], adj. ring-shaped; coiled; spiral.

कुंडलिनी *kuṇḍalinī* [S.], f. coiled (goddess: as awakened in *haṭha yoga*). — ~ **शक्ति**, f. the vital energies.

कुंडलिया *kuṇḍāliyā* [cf. H. *kuṇḍal(ī)*], f. a six-line stanza consisting of a *dohā* followed by two *kāvyas*, or *rolās*; the last foot of the *dohā* is repeated as the first of the following couplet, and the last two syllables of the stanza must be the same as the first two syllables.

कुंडली *kuṇḍālī* [S.], f. **1.** a small ear-ring, &c. (see **कुंडल**, 1., 2). **2.** a circular figure or diagram; horoscope. **3.** coil (of a snake). **4.** ringlet, curl. — ~ **बनाना**, to make a circular figure, &c. ~, or **कुंडलियाँ**, **मारना**, to coil itself up (a snake).

[1]**कुंडा** *kuṇḍā*, m. staple (of a door-fastening); hasp.

[2]**कुंडा** *kuṇḍā* [ad. *kuṇḍa*-: H. *kūṁṛā*], m. a large earthenware bowl.

[1]**कुंडी** *kuṇḍī* [cf. H. [1]*kuṇḍā*], f. **1.** a hasp; staple (of a door-fastening). **2.** chain (for fastening a door); door-catch. **3.** bolt, bar (of a door). — ~ **बंद करना**, or **मारना**, or **लगाना**, to fasten a door (with chain, hasp or bolt).

[2]**कुंडी** *kuṇḍī* [cf. H. [2]*kuṇḍā*], f. an earthenware or stone pot.

[3]**कुंडी** *kuṇḍī* [cf. H. *kuṇḍ*], f. a pot (as for *ghī*, chutney, *bhāṁg*).

कुंत *kunt* [S.], m. a spear, a lance.

कुंतल *kuntal* [S.], m. the hair of the head; a lock, or locks, of hair.

कुंती *kuntī* [S.], f. (in the *Mahābhārata* legends) name of a wife of Pāṇḍu, mother of the five Pāṇḍava princes by five gods.

[1]**कुंद** *kund* [P. *kund*], adj. & m. **1.** adj. blunt. **2.** dull, obtuse (of intelligence or wits). **3.** m. Brbh. a lathe (cf. **कुंदा**). — **ज़हन**, or **अक़्ल**, ~ **हो जाना**, to be, or to have become, stupid.

[2]**कुंद** *kund* [S.], f. a jasmine.

कुंदन *kundan*, m. & adj. **1.** m. pure gold, fine gold; gold leaf. **2.** adj. colloq. brilliant, best, finest. ~ **माल**, m. choice goods. — **शरीर** ~ **हो जाना**, fig. to be restored (after illness) to perfect health.

कुँदरू *kuṁdrū*, m. the creeper ivy gourd, *Tricosanthes*, and its fruit.

कुंदा *kundā* [P. *kunda*], m. **1.** a log; block of wood. **2.** stock (as of a rifle); transf. wooden rifle (used by recruits in training); handle (of an implement); stirring stick. **3.** heavy wooden fetter, stocks. **4.** a heavy beam. **5.** wooden working surface (as for laundering, chopping). **6.** gusset (in trousers). **7.** a bird's wing, or wings. **8.** ? corr. = [1]**कुंडा**. — ~, or **कुंदे**, **झाड़ना**, to flap the wings (a bird). **लकड़ी का** ~, m. = ~, 1.

कुंदी *kundī*, f. *Pl. HŚS.* calendering or fulling (cloth). — **कुंदीगर** [P. *-gar*], m. a fuller of cloth.

कुंदुर *kundur* [ad. *kunduru-*], m. gum-resin of trees of the genus *Boswellia*: imported olibanum.

कुंबल *kumbal*, m. = **कूम्हल**.

कुंबी *kumbī* [*kuṭumbin-*], m. **1.** name of a partic. community of cultivators. **2.** a man of that community.

कुंभ *kumbh* [S.], m. **1.** a water-pot, jar. **2.** the sign Aquarius (of the zodiac). **3.** the festival (*melā*) held every twelfth January-February at Allahabad, Hardvār and other centres (so called because the sun is then in Aquarius). **4.** the lobe on the upper part of an elephant's forehead. — **कुंभकर्ण** or °-**करण**, m. *mythol.* pot-eared: name of a *rākṣas*, the brother of Rāvaṇ. **कुंभकार**, m. = **कुम्हार**. **कुंभज**, adj. *mythol.* pot-born: a name of the sage Agastya, and of others. **कुंभ-राशि**, f. the constellation Aquarius.

कुंभनी *kumbhnī* [ad. *kumbhinī-*], f. E.H. a small jar; ? a ditch full of water.

कुँभलाना *kuṁbhlānā*, v.i. pronun. var. see **कुम्हलाना**.

कुंभार *kumbhār*, m. E.H. = **कुम्हार**.

कुंभिका *kumbhikā* [S.], f. a type of quickly growing water-weed or grass.

कुँभिला- *kuṁbhilā-*, v.i. Brbh. = **कुँभलाना**.

[1]**कुंभी** *kumbhī* [S.], f. **1.** a small pot or jar. **2.** a name of the Ardha-kumbh melā, held every sixth year between Kumbh melās (see s.v. **कुंभ**). — **कुंभी-पाक**, m. name of a hell in which the wicked are baked, or cooked.

[2]**कुंभी** *kumbhī* [S.], m. name of several trees, esp. *Careya arborea* (source of a resin and a fibre; also used medicinally).

कुंभीर *kumbhīr* [S.], m. *Pl. HŚS.* = [1]**घड़ियाल**.

कुँवर *kuṁvar* [conn. *kumāra-*], m. **1.** a boy, youth; specif. an unmarried youth. **2.** a son. **3.** a prince. — ~ **साहब**, m. young gentleman (usu. a term of address or personal reference).

कुँवरी *kuṁvarī* [conn. *kumārī*], f. Brbh. **1.** young girl; unmarried girl. **2.** daughter. **3.** princess.

कुँवार *kuṁvār* [*kumāra-*], m. = **कुमार**.

कुँवारपन *kuṁvārpan* [cf. H. *kuṁvār*], m. **1.** young manhood. **2.** bachelordom.

कुँवारा *kuṁvārā* [*kumāra-*], adj. & m. **1.** adj. unmarried. **2.** m. a young bachelor. — ~ **नाता**, m. pre-marital sexual relationship.

कुँहड़ा *kuṁhṛā*, m. = **कुम्हड़ा**.

कु *ku*, adv. encl. Brbh. Av. indeed (= **-क**).

कु- *ku-* [*ku-*; also, and more usually, S.], pref. var. (as H. form) *ka-*. bad, useless, defective (e.g. **कुचाली**, adj. of bad conduct; **कुरूप**, adj. ill-formed; **कपूत**, **कुपुत्र**, m. a bad son).

कुआँ *kuāṁ* [*kūpa-*[1]], m. a well. — ~ **खोदना**, to dig a well; to lay a trap (for, **के लिए**). ~ **चलाना**, to work a well; to irrigate from a well. **कुएँ झाँकना**, to look into a well (for): to search high and low; to go to all efforts. **कुएँ का मेंढक**, m. frog in a well: a person of circumscribed views, unenlightened attitudes, or restricted experience. **कुएँ में गिरना**, to fall into a well: to come to disaster. **कुएँ**, or **कुओं**, **में बांस डालना**, to put a bamboo into a well, &c.: to probe, to search thoroughly. **कुएँ में भाँग पड़ना**, fig. one and all (in a group) to have taken leave of their senses. तेल का ~, m. an oil-well.

कुआर *kuār*, m. = क्वार.

कुई *kuīṁ* [*kumudikā*-], f. water-lily; white lotus.

कुक-कुक *kuk-kuk* [onom.], f. the clucking of a hen.

कुकड़ी *kukṛī*, f. reg. **1.** W. hank, skein (of string or thread). **2.** Bihar. thread on the spindle of a spinning-wheel.

कुकड़ूँकूँ *kukṛūṁkūṁ* [onom.], f. the crow of a cock.

कुकरोंदा *kukroṁdā* [*kukkuramardaka*-], m. = कुकरौंधा.

कुकरौंधा *kukrauṁdhā*, m. the plant *Celsius*, and its fruit (used medicinally).

कुकर्म *ku-karm* [S.], m. a bad or wicked action; misconduct, villainy, vice, sin; fornication.

कुकर्मी *ku-karmī* [S.], adj. & m., f. **1.** adj. wicked, villainous, vicious, &c. (cf. कुकर्म). **2.** m., f. a wicked person.

कुकुर *kukur* [ad. *kukkura*-], m. a dog. — कुकुर-खाँसी, f. a barking cough; whooping-cough. कुकुर-दंत, m. an impacted tooth. °ई, m. a person having impacted teeth.

कुकुरमुत्ता *kukurmuttā* [*kukkura*-, *mūtra*-], m. a mushroom (cf. [1]खुंभी); a toadstool.

कुक्कुट *kukkuṭ* [S.], m. a cock. — कुक्कुट-पालन, m. poultry farming. कुक्कुटासन [°*ṭa*+*ā*°], m. a posture in yoga.

कुक्कुटी *kukkuṭī* [S.], f. a hen.

कुक्कुर *kukkur* [S.: ← *kurkura*-], m. a dog.

कुक्षि *kukṣi* [S.], f. womb.

कुख्याति *ku-khyāti* [S.], f. infamy, disrepute.

कुच *kuc* [S.], m. f. **1.** the female breast. **2.** nipple. — कुचाग्र [°*ca*+*a*°], m. id.

कुचंदन *ku-candan* [S.], m. *Pl. HŚS.* **1.** red sandalwood. **2.** sappan-wood (= बक्कम).

कुचकुचवा *kuckucavā*, m. reg. an owl.

कुचकुचिया *kuckuciyā*, m. a species of bird: (*Pl.*) the red-headed Trogon.

कुचक्र *ku-cakr* [S.], m. bad circle: a plot, or intrigue.

कुचक्री *ku-cakrī* [cf. H. *kucakr*], m. a plotter; conspirator.

कुचलना *kucalnā* [cf. **kucyate*: *kucati*], v.t. & v.i. **1.** v.t. to crush, to pound. **2.** to trample on. **3.** to beat to pulp. **4.** v.i. to be crushed, &c.

कुचला *kuclā*, m. the snakewood tree, *Strychnos nux-vomica* (source of strychnine).

कुचलाई *kuclāī* [cf. H. *kucalnā*], f. crushing, pounding.

कुचाल *ku-cāl* [S.], f. & adj. **1.** f. misconduct; wicked or depraved conduct. **2.** adj. of bad conduct, &c.

कुचाली *ku-cālī* [S.], adj. of bad conduct, &c. (see कुचाल).

कुचेल *ku-cel* [S.], m. & adj. **1.** m. bad clothing; coarse cloth. **2.** adj. poorly clad.

कुचेलना *kucelnā*, v.t. = कुचलना.

कुचैन *ku-cain* [cf. H. *cain*], m. Brbh. unease, restlessness; distress.

कुचैल *ku-cail*, adj. = कुचैला.

कुचैला *kucailā* [ad. *kucela*-; ? × H. *mailā*], adj. **1.** poorly clad (a person). **2.** ragged, tattered (clothes). — मैला-कुचैला, adj. id.

कुछ *kuch* [conn. *kiṁcid*], pron. & adj. & adv. **1.** pron. something; anything. वह ~ नहीं जानता, he doesn't know anything. **2.** a little, some (of a partic. amount). मुझे ~ दीजिए, please give me some. **3.** fig. sthg. particular. ~ कहना, or कह बैठना, to make a pointed, or unpleasant, remark (to, से). **4.** adj. some; any. वह ~ हिंदी जानता है, he knows some Hindi. **5.** a few (not particularised). ~ आदमी, m. pl. a few men, some people. **6.** adv. somewhat, a little; at all. — ~ एक, adj. & adv. a few (partic. ones); somewhat; a little. ~ ऐसा, adj. of the sort (which). ~ ऐसी किताबें लाओ जो ..., bring some books which .... ~ और, sthg. further, some more; sthg. different. ~ कर देना, to make sthg. else of, to transform; to bewitch. ~ का ~, sthg. quite different; greatly improved; in quite another manner; quite otherwise. ~ का ~ समझना, to take (a matter) quite the wrong way. ~ ~, adv. somewhat, rather. ~ डर नहीं (है), there's nothing to fear; don't worry. ~ तुमने ख़्वाब देखा? have you dreamt sthg.?: are you out of your senses? ~ तो, adv. just a little; sthg. indeed. ~ न ~, pron., adj. & adv. sthg. or other; some or other(s); somewhat, a little. ~ न पूछिए, don't ask at all. ~ परवा(ह) नहीं, it doesn't matter, never mind. (यह) ~ बात नहीं, it's nothing, it doesn't matter; (this) is irrelevant; (this) will not do (as a reason, argument). ~ भी, pron. & adj. whatever; any(thing) at all. ~ हो जाना, to become sthg., or someone; to be quite transformed (a person); euph. to be possessed by an evil spirit. ऐसी हवा बाँधी कि ~ न पूछिए, he went to unheard of lengths (of ceremony, or exaggeration). और ~, sthg.

different, sthg. else; sthg. further, some more. जो ~, pron. & adj. whatever. बहुत ~, pron. & adv. a large amount; a great deal. सब ~, everything.

कुज *kuj* [S.], m. Brbh. the planet Mars.

कुजात *ku-jāt* [ad. *kujāti-*], adj. & f., m. **1.** adj. of low birth, or caste. **2.** f. = कुजाति, 1. **3.** m. = कुजाति, 2., 3.

कुजाति *ku-jāti* [S.], f. & m. **1.** f. low birth, or caste. **2.** m. a man of low caste. **3.** an outcaste.

कुज्जी *kujjī*, f. an unglazed earthenware cup.

कुट *kuṭ* [*kuṣṭha-*[1]], m. a tall herb, *Costus speciosus* (of which the root is used medicinally).

कुटका *kuṭkā*, m. a piece, fragment.

[1]**कुटकी** *kuṭkī*, f. **1.** a small millet, *Panicum miliare*. **2.** [? = [3]*kuṭkī*] a medicinal plant, *Helleborus niger*; aconite.

[2]**कुटकी** *kuṭki*, f. reg. **1.** cutting, cutting off. **2.** a gnat. **3.** separation, estrangement.

कुटकुट *kuṭkuṭ*, ? f. m. sound of nibbling, or of munching.

कुटना *kuṭnā* [*kuṭṭanī-*], m. **1.** a pimp, pander. **2.** a go-between; fig. mischief-maker.

कुटनाई *kuṭnāī* [cf. H. *kuṭnā*], f. **1.** pimping, pandering. **2.** pimp's wages.

कुटनापा *kuṭnāpā* [cf. H. *kuṭnā*], m. **1.** pimping, pandering. **2.** cuckolded state (of a husband).

कुटनी *kuṭnī* [*kuṭṭanī-*], f. a bawd. — ~ का घर, m. a brothel.

कुटम्मस *kuṭammas* [cf. H. कूटना], f. **1.** a beating, beating-up. **2.** fig. rough reception.

कुटवाना *kuṭvāna* [cf. H. *kūṭnā*], v.t. to cause to be hammered, pounded, &c. (by, sē).

कुटाई *kuṭāī* [cf. H. *kuṭānā*], f. **1.** pounding; bruising (grain). **2.** price paid for pounding, &c.

कुटिर *kuṭir*, m. = कुटीर.

कुटिल *kuṭil* [S.], adj. **1.** crooked. **2.** devious; guileful. **3.** wicked.

कुटिलई *kuṭilaī* [cf. H. *kuṭil*], f. Av. = कुटिलता.

कुटिलता *kuṭilătā* [S.], f. crookedness, &c. (see कुटिल).

कुटिलपन *kuṭilpan* [S.], m. = कुटिलता.

कुटी *kuṭī* [S.], f. cottage, hut (esp. remote); hermitage.

कुटीर *kuṭīr* [S.], m. cottage, hut (esp. remote).

कुटुंब *kuṭumb* [S.], m. **1.** family; family line. **2.** relatives. — कुटुंब-क़बीला, m. the members of (one's) family.

कुटुंबी *kuṭumbī* [S.], adj. & m. **1.** adj. having to do with a family. **2.** having a family. **3.** m. head of a family. **4.** family member, relative.

कुटुम *kuṭum*, m. pronun. var. = कुटुंब.

कुटुर *kuṭur*, m. a crunching or munching sound. — कुटुर-कुटुर, m. id.

कुटेव *ku-ṭev*, f. Brbh. a bad habit.

कुट्टनी *kuṭṭănī* [S.], f. a bawd.

कुट्टा *kuṭṭā*, m. *Pl. HŚS.* **1.** a bird with clipped wings. **2.** a decoy bird.

कुट्टी *kuṭṭī* [**kuṭṭa-*[2]: Pa. *kuṭṭa-*], f. **1.** chopped straw or fodder. **2.** papier mâché. **3.** fig. severing friendship (with, से). — ~ करना, to break off (friendship: with).

कुठला *kuṭhlā* [cf. *koṣṭha-*[2]], m. **1.** a large earthen bin for grain. **2.** *Pl. HŚS.* lime-kiln. — कुठला-सा, adj. fat, bulky.

[1]**कुठार** *kuṭhār* [S.], m. **1.** an axe; hatchet. **2.** reg. a sort of hoe or spade.

[2]**कुठार** *kuṭhār*, m. reg. = कुठियार.

[1]**कुठारी** *kuṭhārī* [cf. H. [1]*kuṭhār*: and *kuṭhārikā-*], f. Av. a small axe, hatchet.

[2]**कुठारी** *kuṭhārī*, f. reg. a crucible for melting metals.

कुठाली *kuṭhālī*, f. a jeweller's crucible (= [2]कुठारी).

कुठिया *kuṭhiyā* [cf. *koṣṭha-*], f. (m., *Pl.*) m. an earthen grain-bin.

कुठियार *kuṭhiyār* [*koṣṭhāgāra-*], m. a storehouse; granary.

कुठियारी *kuṭhiyārī* [cf. H. *kuṭhiyār*], m. reg. keeper of a storehouse.

कुठौर *ku-ṭhaur* [H. *ku*+H. *ṭhaur*], m. **1.** m. bad place, wrong place. **2.** adj. out of place, misplaced.

कुड़क *kuṛak* [cf. *kuṛaknā*], f. clucking (of a hen); a hen that has finished laying; a clucking hen.

कुड़कना *kuṛaknā*, v.i. & v.t. **1.** v.i. to cackle, to cluck, (= कुड़कुड़ाना). **2.** to crack, to crackle; to clatter (= कड़कना). **3.** to murmur, to grumble. **4.** v.t. to crunch, to munch.

कुड़कुड़ *kuṛkuṛ* [cf. H. *kuṛkuṛānā*], m. **1.** a sound of rumbling or grumbling. **2.** clucking (of a hen).

कुड़कुड़ाना *kuṛkuṛānā*, v.i. & v.t. **1.** v.i. to rumble (as the bowels). **2.** to grumble, to murmur (in irritation or anger). **3.** to cackle, to cluck (as a hen). **4.** *HŚS.* v.t. to scare birds by shouting.

कुड़कुड़ी *kuṛkuṛī* [cf. H. *kuṛkuṛānā*], f. a rumbling in the bowels.

कुड़बुड़ाना *kuṛbuṛānā*, v.i. to grumble, to murmur unhappily.

कुड़मा *kuṛmā* [*kuṭumba-*], m. reg. (N). **1.** family, kindred, dependants. **2.** caste, tribe.

कुड़माई *kuṛmāī* [cf. H. *kuṛmā*], f. reg. (N). engagement, betrothal; the celebration of an engagement.

कुड़मुड़ *kuṛmuṛ*, m. *Pl.* = कड़मड़.

कुड़मुड़ाना *kuṛmuṛānā*, v.i. = कुड़बुड़ाना, and कड़मड़ाना.

कुड़ी *kuṛī* [*kuṭī-*], f. reg. (N). **1.** a hut. **2.** a hearth; *hist.* hearth-tax.

कुड़ुक *kuṛuk* [cf. *kuṭi-*], f. *Pl.* a coil (of string or rope); a wire.

कुड़ुम- *kuṛum-* [cf. H. *kuṛmā*], f. reg. (N). family: — कुड़ुमचोदी, f. incest.

कुडौल *ku-ḍaul* [H. *ku*+H. *ḍaul*], adj. **1.** ill-shaped. **2.** shapeless.

कुढंग *ku-ḍhaṅg* [H. *ku*+H. *ḍhaṅg*], adj. & m. **1.** adj. ill-mannered; uncouth. **2.** depraved. **3.** m. bad way, or ways.

कुढंगा *ku-ḍhaṅgā* [cf. H. *kuḍhaṅg*], adj. 1. = कुडंग. **2.** ugly.

कुढंगी *ku-ḍhaṅgī* [cf. H. *kuḍhaṅg*], f. = कुढंग, 3.

कुढ़क *kuṛhak*, f. *Pl.* = कुढ़न.

कुढ़न *kuṛhan* [cf. H. *kuṛhnā*], f. **1.** vexation; resentment; jealousy. **2.** disgust. **3.** distress, sorrow; fretting.

कुढ़ना *kuṛhnā* [cf. *kruddha-*], v.i. **1.** to be vexed or chagrined, or resentful (with or over a thing, से; with a person, पर); to be jealous. **2.** to be disgusted. **3.** to grieve or to be distressed (for); to mourn; to fret. **4.** to be angry.

कुढब *ku-ḍhab* [H. *ku*+H. *ḍhab*], adj. **1.** ill-shaped, misshapen. **2.** ill-mannered; uncouth.

कुढ़ाना *kuṛhānā* [cf. *kruddha-*], v.t. **1.** to irritate; to make jealous. **2.** to tease, to worry, to molest. **3.** to distress (one).

कुढ़ानी *kuṛhānī* [cf. H. *kuṛhānā*], f. *Pl.* vexing, annoying; teasing.

कुढ़ापन *kuṛhāpan*, m. *Pl.* vexed or jealous state: cf. कुढ़न.

कुढ़ापा *kuṛhāpā*, m. *Pl.* = कुढ़ापन.

कुतना *kutnā* [cf. H. *kūtnā*], v.i. reg. to be estimated (as revenue, produce).

कुतरन *kutran* [cf. H. *kutarnā*], f. a piece gnawed or bitten off.

कुतरना *kutarnā*, v.t. **1.** to gnaw; to nibble. **2.** to peck. — कुतरा, part. adj. colloq. marked by smallpox.

कुतरवाना *kutarvānā* [cf. H. *kutarnā*], v.t. to cause to be gnawed, &c.

कुतर्क *ku-tark* [S.], m. **1.** wrong reasoning. **2.** false doctrine.

कुतिया *kutiyā* [cf. H. *kuttā*], f. a bitch. — ~ का पिल्ला, m. a puppy; pej. a bastard son.

कुतुब *kutub* [A. *kutub*, pl.], f. pl. U. books. — कुतुब-ख़ाना, m. library.

क़ुतुब *qutub* [A. *quṭb*], m. the pole star. — क़ुतुबनुमा [P. *-numā*], m. inv. a compass.

कुतूहल *kutūhal* [S.], m. **1.** curiosity; eager interest (in sthg. unusual). **2.** anything curious or interesting; a show, spectacle, event; sport (of Kṛṣṇa with the cowherd girls).

कुतूहली *kutūhālī* [S.], adj. **1.** curious, inquisitive. **2.** fond of a show or spectacle; sportive (see कुतूहल).

कुत्त *kutt* [ad. *kutra*], adv. reg. where? whither?

कुत्ता *kuttā* [**kutta-*[1]: Pk. *kutta-*], m. **1.** a dog. **2.** catch, pawl (in mechanism); trigger. **3.** latch. — कुत्ते की दुम, f. a dog's tail (never straight): a person incorrigible in bad ways. कुत्ते की नींद, f. a light sleep.

कुत्ती *kuttī* [cf. H. *kuttā*], f. a bitch (= कुतिया).

कुत्सा *kutsā* [S.], f. **1.** censure; calumny. **2.** contempt.

कुत्सित *kutsit* [S.], adj. **1.** blamed, censured. **2.** base. — ~ मंडली, f. a disreputable group.

कुथरा *kuthrā* [cf. **kuttha-*[1]: Pk. *kutthaï*], m. rotting; filth.

कुथुआ *kuthuā*, m. reg. an inflammation of the eyelids (in children).

कुदकना *kudaknā* [cf. *kūrdati*], v.i. to leap, to jump; to caper, to gambol.

कुदक्कड़ा *kudakkaṛā* [cf. H. *kūdnā*, *kudaknā*], m. caper, frisking, gambolling.

क़ुदरत *qudrat* [A. *qudra*: P. *qudrat*], f. **1.** divine power. **2.** the creation; nature.

क़ुदरती *qudratī* [P. *qudratī*], adj. **1.** occurring or found naturally, natural. **2.** innate. **3.** instinctive. — ~ अमर है, U. it's a natural thing (that).

कुदरा *kudrā*, m. = कुदाल.

कुदवाना *kudvānā* [cf. H. *kūdnā*], v.t. to cause to leap, &c. (see कूदना).

कुदशा *ku-daśā* [S.], f. dire state.

कुदाँव *ku-dāṁv* [H. *ku*+H. *dāṁv*], m. **1.** treacherous trick, or blow. **2.** vulnerable spot (of an enemy).

कुदाई *kudāī* [cf. H. *kūdnā*, *kudānā*], f. jumping.

कुदान *kudān* [cf. H. *kūdnā*], f. act of jumping; jump. — ~ भरना, or मारना, to make, or to achieve, a jump.

कुदाना *kudānā* [cf. H. *kūdnā*], v.t. **1.** to cause to jump; to spur (a horse). **2.** to dandle (a child). **3.** to bounce (a ball).

कुदाल *kudāl* [*kuddāla*-: ? ← Drav.], f. m. **1.** a grub-hoe; a spade. **2.** a one-sided pickaxe.

कुदाली *kudālī* [*kuddāla*-: ? ← Drav.], f. a small hoe or narrow-bladed spade, &c. (see कुदाल).

कुदृष्टि *ku-dṛṣṭi* [S.], f. **1.** evil eye. **2.** malicious glance. **3.** lascivious glance.

क़ुद्दूस *quddūs* [A. *quddūs*], adj. U. pure, holy.

कुधातु *ku-dhātu* [S.], f. Av. base metal: iron.

-कुन *-kun* [P. *kardan*: present stem], adj. formant. doing (e.g. कारकुन, m. agent, estate-manager).

कुनकुना *kunkunā*, adj. lukewarm (= गुनगुना).

कुनबा *kunbā* [*kuṭumba*-], m. family, kindred. — ~ इकट्ठा करना, to establish a family, to produce children. ~ जोड़ना, id. कुनबे का, or की, m., f. a relative. – कुनबेवाला, a relative; family man.

कुनमुनाना *kunmunānā*, v.i. **1.** to whine, to whimper. **2.** to be restless, or agitated. **3.** to demur.

कुनह *kunh*, f. (m., *Pl.*) grudge, spite, malice.

कुनही *kunhī* [cf. H. *kunh*], adj. spiteful, vindictive.

कुनाई *kunāī* [? cf. H. *konā*], f. *Pl. HŚS.* a bit, corner, scrap.

कुनामी *ku-nāmī* [S.], adj. & m. **1.** adj. of bad name, infamous, disreputable. **2.** a person of bad name.

कुप *kup* [*kūpya*-: Panj. *kupp*], m. **1.** pile (of hay, straw); stack. **2.** heap (of chaff, &c).

कुपंथ *ku-panth* [S.], m. bad way or course; bad conduct.

कुपढ़ *ku-paṛh* [H. *ku*+H. *paṛhnā*], adj. illiterate; uneducated.

[1]**कुपथ** *ku-path* [S.], m. **1.** bad road or way. **2.** bad ways, conduct. — कुपथगामी, adj. going on a bad course; heading for ruin; depraved, immoral.

[2]**कुपथ** *ku-path*, m. Brbh. = कुपथ्य.

कुपथ्य *ku-pathyă* [S.], adj. & m. **1.** adj. belonging to a bad way: unwholesome (as food). **2.** m. unwholesome food.

कुपात्र *ku-pātr* [S.], adj. & m. **1.** adj. unworthy. **2.** m. an unworthy person.

कुपित *kupit* [S.], adj. angered.

कुपुत्र *ku-putr* [S.], m. a bad son.

कुपूती *ku-pūtī* [cf. H. *kuputr*], f. mother of an unworthy son.

कुप्पा *kuppā* [**kuppa*-], m. **1.** a large leather container for oil, *ghī*, &c. **2.** colloq. a portly person. — ~ लुढ़कना, the vessel to overturn: to die (a king, &c.) ~ हो जाना, to become very fat; to swell. मुँह ~ बनाए बैठना, to sulk. मुँह फुलाकर ~ हो जाना, id.

कुप्पी *kuppī* [**kuppa*-], f. a leather bottle for oil, &c.

कुफ़्र *kufr* [A. *kufr*], m. E.H. unbelief; impiety.

कुफ़रान *kufrān* [A. *kufrān*], m. E.H. unbelief; blasphemy.

कुफ़राना *kufrānā* [A. *kufr*+P. *-āna*], adv. E.H. as an unbeliever, impiously.

कुफ़ुर *kufur*, m. pronun. var. Av. = कुफ़्र.

क़ुफ़्ल *qufl* [A. *qufl*], m. U. a lock.

कुब *kub* [**kubba*-], m. a hump on the back.

कुबड़ *kubaṛ* [cf. **kubba*-], m. a hump on the back.

कुबड़ा *kubṛā* [cf. **kubba*-], adj. & m. **1.** adj. hunchbacked. **2.** crooked, deformed. **3.** m. a hunchback.

कुबड़ी *kubṛī* [cf. H. *kubṛā*], f. a hunchbacked woman.

कुबुद्धि *ku-buddhi* [S.], adj. & f. **1.** adj. foolish. **2.** wicked. **3.** f. stupidity. **4.** wickedness.

कुब्ज *kubj* [S.], adj. **1.** hunchbacked. **2.** crooked, deformed.

कुब्जा *kubjā* [S.], f. a hunchbacked woman.

कुब्बा *kubbā* [*kubba-], adj. **1.** hunchbacked. **2.** crooked, deformed.

कुमंत्रणा *ku-mantraṇā* [S.], f. bad advice, evil counsel; intrigue.

कुमक *kumak* [P. *kumak*], f. **1.** *mil.* reinforcements, assistance. **2.** help, aid, support. — ~ देना (को), to reinforce; to aid, &c.

कुमकुम *kumkum*, m. **1.** saffron (*Crocus sativus*). ***2.** a red preparation used in making the cosmetic mark called *bindī*, and also certain sectarian markings, on the forehead.

क़ुमक़ुमा *qumqumā* [A. *qumquma*], m. **1.** a container made of lac, used for the *abīr* and *gulāl* powder thrown at the Holī festival. **2.** a round ornamental shade or lantern.

कुमत *ku-mat*, f. Brbh. Av. = कुमति.

कुमति *ku-mati* [S.], f. & adj. **1.** f. a base thought or sentiment. **2.** stupidity, folly. **3.** adj. wicked, vicious, cruel. **4.** stupid.

कुमया *kumayā* [? ad. *kumāyā-], f. metr. Brbh. harshness, severity.

क़ुमरी *qumrī* [A. *qumrī*], f. E.H. whitish: a turtle-dove; wood-pigeon.

कुमार *kumār* [S.], m. **1.** a youth; a young unmarried man. **2.** a prince (= राज-कुमार). **3.** a child, boy (of very young age). — कुमार-व्रत, m. a vow of celibacy.

कुमारपन *kumārpan* [cf. H. *kumār*], m. **1.** the time or condition of youth; youthfulness. **2.** bachelorhood.

कुमारी *kumārī* [S.], f. **1.** a young unmarried girl; a virgin girl. **2.** a title of an unmarried girl: 'miss'.

कुमार्ग *ku-mārg* [S.], m. **1.** a bad road. **2.** a wrong course, bad ways.

कुमुद *kumud* [S.], m. a water-lily, *Rottlera tinctoria*; the lotus, esp. the white lotus or water-lily, *Nymphæa esculenta*, and the red lotus, *Nymphæa rubra*.

कुमुदिनी *kumudinī* [S.], f. dimin. **1.** a lotus. **2.** a cluster of lotus flowers. **3.** place abounding in lotuses (as a tank).

कुमेरु *ku-meru* [S.], *mythol.* the South Pole.

कुमैत *kumait* [A. *kumait*], adj. & m. Brbh. **1.** adj. bay-coloured (a horse). **2.** m. a bay horse.

कुम्हड़ा *kumhṛā* [*kuṣmāṇḍa-*], m. the white gourd-melon, *Benincasa cerifera* (= पेठा).

कुम्हलाई *kumhlāī* [cf. H. *kumhlānā*], f. **1.** fading, withering, drooping. **2.** blighted, or scorched, state. **3.** fig. dejected appearance.

कुम्हलाना *kumhlānā* [cf. *komh-], v.i. & v.t. **1.** v.i. to fade, to wither, to droop. **2.** to be blighted, scorched, frosted. **3.** fig. to sink (as the heart). **4.** v.t. to cause to wither, or fade; to blight.

कुम्हार *kumhār* [*kumbhakāra-*], m. **1.** a potter. **2.** a man of the *kumhār* community. — ~ का चाक, a potter's wheel.

कुम्हारगिरी *kumhārgirī* [H. *kumhār*+P. *-garī*], f. a potter's work or activity.

कुम्हारन *kumhāran* [cf. H. *kumhār*], f. **1.** a potter's wife. **2.** a woman of the *kumhār* community.

कुम्हारनी *kumhārnī* [cf. H. *kumhār*], f. = कुम्हार.

[1]**कुम्हारी** *kumhārī* [*kumbhakārikā-*], f. = कुम्हारन.

[2]**कुम्हारी** *kumhārī* [cf. H. *kumhār*], f. **1.** a potter's work or activity. **2.** pottery.

[3]**कुम्हारी** *kumhārī* [cf. H. *kumhār*], f. a wasp-like insect which builds its nest of clay.

कुरंग *kuraṅg* [S.], m. & adj. **1.** m. an antelope or deer. **2.** adj. Av. dark bay-coloured (a horse).

कुरंड *kuraṇḍ* [*kuruvinda-*], m. corundum stone, *Adamantinus corundum*; a whetstone.

कुरक़ी *qurqī*, f. & adj. see कुर्क़ी.

कुरकुट *kurkuṭ* [*kura-; ?+*kuṭṭana-*], f. reg. (E). scraps, crumbs, fragments.

कुरकुटा *kurkuṭā* [cf. H. *kurkuṭ*], m. reg. (E). scraps, crumbs, fragments.

कुरकुर *kurkur*, m. a crunching or munching sound.

कुरकुरा *kurkurā*, adj. **1.** crisp, dry; brittle. **2.** *Pl.* counterfeit (a coin).

कुरकुराना *kurkurānā*, v.i. = करकराना.

कुरता *kurtā* [P. *kurta*], m. a collarless shirt.

कुरती *kurtī* [cf. H. *kurtā*], f. **1.** blouse. **2.** brassiere.

क़ुरबान *qurbān* [A. *qurbān*], m. **1.** f. a sacrifice; an offering. **2.** devotion. — ~ करना, to sacrifice; to devote. ~ जाना, or होना, to be sacrificed; to feel devotion (for or to, पर).

क़ुरबानी *qurbānī* [P. *qurbānī*], adj. & f. **1.** adj. sacrificed, devoted. **2.** a sacrifice; victim. — ~ करना (की), to sacrifice.

कुरम-कुरम *kuram-kuram* [onom.], f. **1.** the sound produced in biting anything hard or crisp, crunching; munching (= कुरकुर). **2.** adv. with a crunching sound, &c.

कुरमुर *kurmur* [cf. H. *kuṛkuṛī*; **murumura-*], f. reg. (E). murmuring; rumbling (of the bowels).

कुररी *kurarī* [S.], f. poet. an osprey, bird of prey.

कुरलना *kuralnā*, v.i. to call, to warble (birds).

कुरलाना *kurlānā* [P. *kurlāuṇā*], v.i. reg. (N.) = कुरलना.

कुरव *kurav* [*kuraba-*], m. = कुरवक.

कुरवक *kuravak* [ad. *kurabaka-*], m. the red amaranth; barleria flowers of different species.

कुरसी *kursī* [A. *kursī*], f. **1.** chair; seat. **2.** throne. **3.** (in law) bench. **4.** base (as of a pillar); raised foundation, plinth. **5.** genealogy. — ~ का अहमक़, m. pej. a downright fool. ~ का है, pej. he's from Kursī (a place near Lucknow): he is a stupid person. ~ तोड़ना, colloq. to break (one's) chair: to be very idle. ~ देना (को), to give (one) a chair, a seat. ~ पर बैठना, to be installed in a seat (of authority). – कुरसी-नामा, m. family tree. आराम-कुरसी, f. an easy chair. आराम-कुरसी पर बैठना, to sit in an easy chair.

कुरा *kurā*, m. 19c. the crimson amaranth (= कुरवक).

कुराई *kurāī*, f. *Pl. HŚS.* a beam (?): stocks (for the feet).

क़ुरान *qurān* [A. *qur'ān*], m. the Qur'ān. — ~ उठाना, to raise the Qur'ān: to swear by the Qur'ān. ~ का जामा पहनना, to wear a garment made of the leaves of the Qur'ān: to swear by God excessively, and implausibly. ~ पर हाथ धरना, or रखना, to place the hand on the Qur'ān: to swear by the Qur'ān. – क़ुरान-शरीफ़, m. noble Qur'ān: = ~.

कुराह *ku-rāh* [H. *ku*+H. *rāh*], f. wrong or improper course.

कुराही *ku-rāhī* [cf. H. *kurāh*], m. one on a wrong course: a bad or depraved person.

कुरिया *kuriyā* [*kulikā-*; ? × *kuṭī-*], f. reg. a lady; proprietress. — कुरिया-रूपी, adj. & adv. lady-like; in the manner of a lady.

कुरियाल *kuriyāl* [**kura-*+*kāra-*], f. Brbh. Av. state of a bird sitting at ease and preening its wings with its beak; tranquillity; security, confidence. — ~ में गुल्ला लगना (को), to be struck by the pellet (of misfortune) in a moment of security: to be disappointed when sure of success.

कुरी *kurī* [S.], f. reg. a millet (= चेना); pigeon-pea (= अरहर).

कुरीज़ *kurīz* [P. *kurīz*], ? f. Brbh. moulting (of birds). — ~ करना, to moult.

कुरीति *ku-rīti* [S.], f. misconduct, an improper practice or custom.

कुरु *kuru* [S], m. var. /kurū/. **1.** the name of an ancient king of Delhi and of the surrounding region; name of that region and of its people. **2.** *mythol.* the most northerly of the four *Mahādvīpas* or chief divisions of the known world (otherwise considered to be one of the nine *varṣas* or divisions of the known world). — कुरुक्षेत्र, m. field of the Kurus: the name of a region near Karnal (north of Delhi), the scene of the legendary battle between the Kauravas and the Pāṇḍavas. कुरुवंश, m. the race of Kuru. °ई, adj. & m. belonging to that race; a man of that race.

कुरुचि *ku-ruci* [S.], f. **1.** depraved inclination; perversion. **2.** distaste, aversion.

कुरुल *kurul* [S.], m. *Pl. HŚS.* a curl, lock (of hair).

कुरुविल्ल *kuruvill* [*kuruvinda-*], m. *Pl.* a ruby.

कुरुविल्व *kuruvilva* [cf. H. *kuruvill*], m. corr. *Pl.* a ruby.

कुरूप *ku-rūp* [S.], adj. & m. **1.** adj. ill-formed, deformed; ugly. **2.** m. deformity, ugliness.

कुरूपता *ku-rūpătā* [S.], f. ugliness.

कुरूपा *ku-rūpā* [S.], f. an ugly or deformed woman.

कुरूपी *ku-rūpī* [S.], adj. = कुरूप, 1.

कुरेदना *kurednā* [cf. **kura-*], v.t. **1.** to scrape, to scratch; to rake, to stir (as a fire); to preen (a bird); to scrape or to scratch up. **2.** colloq. to explore, to go over (a matter). जान ~, to vex or to irritate (one).

कुरेदनी *kurednī* [cf. H. *kurednā*], f. **1.** an instrument for scraping, or poking. **2.** E. a scoop. — दाँत-कुरेदनी, a toothpick.

कुरेलना *kurelnā* [cf. **kura-* (? **kurīkaroti*)], v.t. reg. = कुरेदना.

कुरेलनी *kurelnī*, f. reg. = कुरेदनी.

कुरोचना *kurocnā* [**kura-*; cf. H. *khuracnā*], v.t. = खुरचना.

क़ुर्क़ *qurq* [T.], adj. confiscated, attached (property). — ~ करना, to seize, to attach. – क़ुर्क़-अमीन, m. court officer employed to attach property, bailiff. क़ुर्क़-नामा, m. = क़ुर्क़ी का परवाना.

क़ुर्क़ी *qurqī* [P. *qurqī*], f. & adj. **1.** f. attachment (of property). **2.** adj. = क़ुर्क़. — ~ उठाना, to remove an attachment. ~ का परवाना, m. writ of attachment. ~ बैठाना, to set a guard over attached property; to block exit (as from a house); = कुर्क़ करना. ~ भेजना, to send a bailiff (to attach property).

कुर्बान *qurbān*, m. see क़ुरबान.

कुर्म-मोर *kurm-mor* [*mayūra-*], m. *Pl.* ? the white-crested Kalij pheasant (of the sub-Himālayas), *Gallophasis albocristatus*. (see [1]खर).

कुर्मी *kurmī* [*kuṭumbin-*], m. **1.** a community of agriculturalists in eastern and central north India (also sometimes known as *gr̥hasthas*; essentially the same as the *kumbīs* of the west and south). **2.** a man of that community.

कुर्री *kurrī*, f. *Pl.* gristle, cartilage.

कुर्सी *kursī*, f. see कुरसी.

[1]**कुल** *kul* [*kula-*], m. **1.** a herd, troop, multitude. ***2.** a tribe; community, sect. वल्लभ ~, the Vallabhan community. **3.** a family, house; lineage. **4.** transf. good lineage or pedigree. — ~ उछालना, to disgrace one's family. ~ का, having to do with a family, caste, &c.; in respect of family, &c. – कुल-उछाल, m., one who disgraces his family. °आ, m. id. कुल-कंटक, m. = कुल-उछाल. कुल-कर्म, m. the practice or observance followed by a family, &c. कुल-कलंक, m. stain on family (honour): = कुल-उछाल. कुल-कानि, f. Brbh. family prestige or honour. कुल-जात, adj. of good family; born in a particular family, &c. कुल-तंत्र, m. rule of a particular group, oligarchy. कुल-तारण, m. one who saves, or is a credit to, his family, &c. कुल-देव, m. family god or object of worship. कुल-देवता, f. a family god; pl. the principal deities worshipped by a family. कुल-देवी, f. family goddess. कुल-धर्म, m. the duties and obligations of a family; a family's tradition or honour. कुल-नाम, m. family name, 'surname'. कुल-नाश, m. a disgrace to (one's) family; fig. black sheep. कुल-पति, m. the head of a family; patriarch; chancellor, or vice-chancellor (of a university). कुल-परिवार, m. (extended) family. कुल-मर्यादा, f. family honour or respectability; = कुल-कर्म. कुल-रीति, f. = कुल-कर्म. कुल-वधू, f. a woman of good or noble family. कुलवान, adj. of good or noble family. °-वती, f. कुलाचार [°*la*+*ā*°], m. the particular duty of a family, caste, &c. (= कुल-धर्म). कुलाचार्य [°*la*+*ā*°], m. a family teacher or priest; one knowing the genealogies of particular families and employed to arrange marriages between them. कुलाधिपति [°*la*+*a*°], m. a chancellor (= कुलपति).

[2]**कुल** *kul* [A. *kull*], m. & adj. **1.** m. the whole (of); total, or gross, amount. ~ मिलाकर कितने लोग थे? how many people were there altogether? **2.** adj. all, entire. यह ~ ख़ुराफ़ात उन्हीं की है, it's they who have caused all this trouble. **3.** adv. altogether. ~ कोई दस आदमी थे, there were about ten men altogether. — ~ आय, f. total income. ~ जमा, m. sum total. ~ नफ़ा, m. gross profit.

कुलंग *kulaṅg* [conn. *kuraṅkara-*], m. Brbh. a crane (= सारस).

कुलंजन *kulañjan* [S.], m. **1.** the plants called galangal (*Alpinia galanga*, and *A. officinarum*: used medicinally). **2.** *Pl.* fennel or cumin seed (*Nigella sativa*). **3.** *Pl.* betel (*Piper betle*) root.

कुलकुलाना *kulkulānā* [? cf. **kulati*], v.i. **1.** to be restless or fidgety (to do sthg). **2.** to giggle. **3.** colloq. to itch.

कुलकुली *kulkulī* [cf. H. *kulkulānā*], f. **1.** restlessness, fidgetiness. **2.** giggling. **3.** itching.

कुलक्षण *ku-lakṣaṇ* [S.], m. & adj. **1.** m. an evil or unlucky mark or sign or omen; ominous characteristic; ugly appearance. **2.** adj. showing evil marks or signs: ominous; of forbidding appearance.

कुलचा *kulcā* [P. *kulīca*], m. a small round bread-roll made of flour, milk and butter.

कुलटा *kulăṭā* [S.], f. a promiscuous woman.

कुलथी *kulthī*, f. reg. (W.) a kind of black, or grey-seeded, gram of the genus *Dolichos*: horse-gram.

कुलफ़ी *qulfī* [P. *quflī*], f. **1.** a mould (as for jellies, ice-cream). ***2.** ice-cream.

कुलबुलाना *kulbulānā* [cf. H. *kurmur*], v.i. **1.** to fidget, to be restless; to writhe, to wriggle; to creep (a snake); to itch, to be irritated; to rumble (the bowels). **2.** to toss about (restlessly or in distress). **3.** to occur to the mind (an uncomfortable thought).

कुलबुलाहट *kulbulāhaṭ* [cf. H. *kulbulānā*], f. **1.** fidgeting, wriggling, &c. **2.** itchiness, irritation. **3.** restlessness, distress.

कुलह *kulah*, f. Av. hood; cowl (of falcon) (= कुलाह).

कुलाँच *kulāṁc* [? cf. *kūrdati, laṅgha-*], f. a bound; leap, bounce. — ~ मारना, id. ~ (कुलाँचें) भरना, to bound, to skip, &c.

कुलाबा *qulābā* [A. *qulāba*], m. **1.** a hook. **2.** an iron ring; link, hasp. **3.** hinge. **4.** handle (as of a cup). — ज़मीन-आसमान के कुलाबे मिलाना, to close the hinge of earth and sky: to build castles in the air.

कुलाल *kulāl*, m. a potter.

कुलाह *kulāh* [P. *kulāh*], f. hat, cap, hood.

कुलिंजन *kuliñjan*, m. pronun. var. = कुलंजन.

कुलिश *kuliś* [S.], m. *mythol.* the thunderbolt of Indra.

कुलिया *kuliyā* [cf. *kuṭa-*[1]], m. a tall, narrow vessel with a cap (for oil, &c.)

क़ुली *qulī* [T.], m. **1.** a porter. **2.** a labourer. — क़ुली-कबाड़ी, m. pl. pej. id. क़ुलीगीरी [P. *-gīrī*], f. portering; labouring.

कुलीन *kulīn* [S.], adj. & m. **1.** adj. of good family; of good or noble descent. **2.** m. a person of good family. **3.** *hind.* a kulīn (Bengali) brāhmaṇ.

कुलीनता *kulīnătā* [S.], f. **1.** respectability of family. **2.** rank, nobility of descent. **3.** *hind.* a partic. brahminical status (see कुलीन, 3).

कुलेल *kulel* [H. *kalol* × H. *khel*, or *keli*], f. Brbh. = कलोल.

कुल्या *kulyā* [S.], f. channel, stream.

[1]**कुल्ला** *kullā* [**kullī-*], m. rinsing the mouth; gargling. — ~ करना, to rise the mouth, to gargle. – कुल्ला-मंजम करना, to brush the teeeth and rinse the mouth.

[2]**कुल्ला** *kullā*, m. a savoury: boiled or fried potatoes stuffed with spices.

[3]**कुल्ला** *kullā*, m. reg. **1.** W. a shoot, sprout. **2.** E. a light watering given to sugar-cane when it sprouts.

कुल्ली *kullī* [**kullī-*], f. rising the mouth; gargling. — ~ करना, to rinse the mouth; to gargle.

कुल्हड़ *kulhaṛ* [cf. **kulla-*[3] (← Drav.), *kulha*(*rī-*)], m. an earthenware cup.

कुल्हाड़ा *kulhāṛā* [*kuṭhāra-*], m. an axe.

कुल्हाड़ी *kulhāṛī* [*kuṭhāra-*], f. a hatchet.

कुल्हिया *kulhiyā* [cf. **kulla-*[3] (← Drav.), *kulha*(*rī-*)], f. a small earthenware cup.

कुवलय *kuvalay* [S.: ← Drav.], m. **1.** the blue water-lily; the night-lotus. **2.** the earth, globe.

कुविचार *ku-vicār* [S.], m. wicked thought.

कुवेर *kuver* [S.], m. *hind.* the god of wealth. — कुवेरोचित [°*ra*+*u*°], adj. befitting Kuvera; befitting a very wealthy man.

कुवेला *ku-velā* [S.], f. **1.** an unsuitable time. **2.** a bad time; hard times. — वेला ~, adv. at good times and bad: rain or shine.

क़ुव्वत *quvvat* [A. *quvva*: P. *quvvat*], f. U. strength, power.

कुश *kuś* [S.], m. **1.** a sacred grass used in brahmanical ceremonies, *Poa cynosuroides*; a seat or mat made from *kuś* grass. **2.** *mythol.* name of a son of Rām. — कुश-कन्या, f. a girl who is to be married. कुशाग्र [°*a*+*a*°], adj. sharp (as points of *kuśa* grass), shrewd.

कुशल *kuśal* [S.], adj. & f. m. **1.** adj. skilful, deft, expert. **2.** healthy. **3.** happy; prosperous. **4.** f. m. health, well-being. **5.** good fortune; safety, happiness, prosperity. — ~ यह थी कि ..., it was fortunate that .... ~ हुआ, that is fortunate (of some newly learned event). शेष ~ है, everything else is going well (used at the end of a letter). – कुशल-आनंद, m. welfare, prosperity. कुशल-क्षेम, m. health and well-being. कुशलदायक, adj. affording happiness or well-being. कुशलपूर्वक, adj. safely, successfully; skilfully. कुशल-प्रश्न, m. enquiry for a person's health or welfare; friendly greeting. कुशल-मंगल, m. = कुशल-क्षेम. कुशल-मंगल है? is everything going well? कुशल-समाचार, m. news of a person's well-being.

कुशलता *kuśalătā* [S.], f. **1.** skilfulness, expertness, deftness. **2.** well-being, welfare.

कुशलात *kuśalāt* [cf. H. *kuśalatā*], f. Brbh. Av. = कुसलात.

कुशा *kuśā* [ad. *kuśa-*[1]], m. = कुश, 1.

-कुशा *-kuśā* [P. *kuśā*], adj. formant. U. expanding. — दिलकुशा, adj. inv. heart-expanding, delightful.

कुशील *ku-śīl* [S.], adj. & m. **1.** adj. of bad disposition, or character. **2.** of bad temper or manners; rude, uncouth, badly behaved. **3.** m. a person of bad disposition, &c.

कुशीलता *ku-śīlătā* [S.], f. **1.** bad disposition or character. **2.** bad temper, manners.

कुश्तम-कुश्ता *kuśtam-kuśtā* [cf. H. *kuśtī*; P. *-ma-*], m. brawl, fracas.

कुश्ता *kuśtā* [P. *kuśta*], m. a mercury compound (used as a tonic).

कुश्ती *kuśtī* [P. *kuśtī*], f. wrestling; struggling. — ~ करना, or खेलना, to wrestle, to struggle (with, से). ~ बदना (से), to challenge to wrestle; to agree (with one, से) to fight or to wrestle. ~ माँगना (से), to challenge to wrestle. ~ में मारना, to pin down, to win a fall. ~ लड़ना, = ~ खेलना. – कुश्तीगर [P. *-gar*], m. a wrestler. कुश्तीबाज़ [P. *-bāz*], m. a wrestler.

कुष्ठ *kuṣṭh* [S.], m. leprosy. — कुष्ठ-रोग, m. leprosy; °ई, m. a leper.

कुष्ठित *kuṣṭhit* [S.], adj. leprous.

कुष्मांड *kuṣmāṇḍ* [S.], m. a kind of pumpkin, *Benincasa cerifera* (= कुम्हड़ा).

कुसंकट *ku-saṅkaṭ* [S.], m. dire misfortune, or peril.

कुसंग *ku-saṅg* [S.], m. Brbh. Av. bad company.

कुसंगत *ku-saṅgat* [ad. *kusaṅgati*], f. = कुसंगति.

कुसंगति *ku-saṅgati* [S.], f. bad company.

कुसमय *ku-samay* [S.], m. **1.** bad or inopportune time or moment. **2.** time of trouble or distress.

कुसलात *kusalāt* [cf. H. *kuśaltā*: ? w. A. pl. suffix], f. Brbh. well-being, prosperity.

कुसवाना *kusvānā* [cf. H. *kosnā*], v.t. to cause to be cursed, &c.

कुसुंभ *kusumbh* [S.], m. safflower (see ²कुसुम).

कुसुंभी *kusumbhī* [cf. H. *kusumbh*], f. cloth dyed with safflower.

¹**कुसुम** *kusum* [S.], m. a flower. — कुसुम-चाप, m. having flowers for his bow: the god Kāmdev. कुसुम-पंचक, m. the five flowery arrows of Kāmdev. कुसुम-बाण, m. armed with flowery arrows: Kāmdev. कुसुमांजलि [°*ma*+*a*°], f. a handful, offering of flowers. कुसुमाकर [°*ma*+*ā*°], m. Brbh. abundance of flowers: the spring. कुसुमायुध [°*ma*+*ā*°], m. *mythol.* armed with (arrows of, or tipped with) flowers: a title of Kāmdev. कुसुमावलि (°*ma*+*ā*°), f. a cluster of flowers.

²**कुसुम** *kusum* [*kusumbha-*: Pa. *kusumbha-*], m. reg. **1.** safflower, *Carthamus tinctorius* (source of an oil and a dye). **2.** the red or reddish yellow dye of safflower.

कुसुमित *kusumit* [S.], adj. in flower, flower-covered.

कुसुमी *kusumī* [cf. *kusumbha-*], adj. reddish-yellow.

क़ुसूर *qusūr*, m. see क़सूर.

कुस्वप्न *ku-svapn* [S.], m. bad dream, nightmare.

कुस्वभाव *ku-svabhāv* [S.], m. a bad or wicked nature.

कुस्वभावी *ku-svabhāvī* [S.], m. a person of bad or wicked nature.

कुहँकुहँ *kuhaṁkuhaṁ*, m. Av. = कुमकुम.

कुहक *kuhak* [S.], m. deception; = ¹माया, 2.

कुहनी *kuhnī* [*kaphoṇī-*: Pk. *kuhanī-*], f. the elbow. — ~ मारना, to strike (one) with the elbow. कुहनियाँ टेकना, to lean on the elbows. – कुहनीदार [P. *-dār*], adj. having arms (a chair).

कुहर *kuhar* [S.], m. a cavity; hole, tear; chasm.

कुहरा *kuhrā* [cf. **kuha-*²], m. **1.** mist; haze. **2.** fog.

कुहराम *kuhrām* [A. *qahr ʻām*], m. weeping and wailing, lamentation.

कुहासा *kuhāsā* [**kubhāṣma-*], m. mist; fog.

कुहुक *kuhuk* [cf. H. *kuhuknā*], f. the cry of a bird (esp. *koel*, cuckoo, or peacock).

कुहुकना *kuhuknā* [cf. *kuhu-*], v.i. to cry (a bird, esp. *koel*, cuckoo, and peacock).

कुहूक *kuhūk*, f. = कुहुक.

कुहेलिका *kuhelikā* [S.], f. mist, haze, fog.

कुहेसा *kuhesā*, m. reg. = कुहासा.

कूँखना *kūṁkhnā* [H. *kūṁthnā* ×H. *kāṁkhnā*], v.t. to give a hollow groan, or grunt.

¹**कूँच** *kūṁc* [**kuñca-*¹], f. reg. the Achilles tendon; hough (of a quadruped).

²**कूँच** *kūṁc* [**kuñca-*²: ← Drav.], m. the small red seed of *Abrus precatorius* (used as a jewellers' weight, and also as an animal poison).

³**कूँच** *kūṁc*, m. reg. a weaver's brush (= कूची).

कूँचा *kūṁcā* [*kūrca-*: ? ← Drav.], m. reg. (Bihar) a broom.

कूँची *kūṁcī*, f. reg. = कूची.

कूँज *kūṁj*, f. the demoiselle crane.

कूँड़ा *kūṁṛā* [*kuṇḍaka-*: ← Drav.], m. **1.** an earthen or wooden vessel (for kneading bread in, or for washing clothes); tub, trough. **2.** a large pot (as for flowers). **3.** ring of earth round a tree (to hold water).

कूँड़ी *kūṁṛī* [*kuṇḍikā-*: ← Drav.], f. **1.** a small tub, &c. (see कूँड़ा). **2.** a small stone mortar (for grinding *bhāṁg*, &c.

कूँथना *kūṁthnā* [*kunthati*], v.i. to groan, to strain (at sthg).

कूईं *kūīṁ*, f. = कुईं.

¹**कूक** *kūk* [cf. H. ¹*kūknā*], f. **1.** shrill cry (as of a peacock, or cuckoo); shriek. **2.** sobbing, wailing. **3.** calling (of birds).

²**कूक** *kūk* [cf. H. ²*kūknā*], f. winding up (a clock, &c). — ~ देना (को), to wind, to wind up.

कूकड़ी *kūkṛī* [*kurkura-*], f. a bitch (= कुत्ती, कुतिया).

¹**कूकना** *kūknā* [**kūkkati*: Pk. *kukkaï*], v.i. **1.** to utter a shrill cry (as a peacock or cuckoo); to scream. **2.** to sob, to wail. **3.** to call out (as birds); to call, to shout.

²**कूकना** *kūknā* [cf. **krukna-*: *krukta-*], v.t. to wind, to wind up (as a watch).

कूकर *kūkar* [*kurkura-*], m. a dog.

कूकाहट *kūkāhaṭ* [cf. H. ¹*kūknā*], f. reg. sobbing, crying; shrieking.

कू-कू *kū-kū*, f. cooing sound.

कूच *kūc* [P. *kūc*], m. departure. ~ **करना**, to depart; to make a march (as an army); fig. to die. ~ **बोलना**, to sound the departure (of a troop).

कूचा *kūcā* [P. *kūca*], m. often /kũca/. a lane, alley. — **कुचागर्दी** [P. *-gardī*], f. wandering, idling (about a town).

कूचिया *kūciyā* f. reg. the tamarind tree.

कूची *kūcī* [*kūrca-*: ? ← Drav.], f. **1.** a large brush (for applying paint, plaster, &c). **2.** reg. a small broom. **3.** a fine brush; artist's brush. — ~ **करना** (**को**), = ~ **फेरना**. ~ **देना**, to apply (paint, &c.: to, **में**). ~ **फेरना** (**पर**), to brush, to clean; to plaster, &c.

कूजन *kūjan* [S.], m. calling (of birds).

कूजना *kūjnā* [ad. *kūjati*], v.i. to call, to cry (birds).

कूज़ा *kūzā* [P. *kūza*], m. **1.** an earthen water-pot with a short neck. **2.** sugar crystallised in an earthen pot. — **मिसरी का** ~, m. a cup-shaped or globular piece of sugar candy.

¹**कूट** *kūṭ* [S.], m. **1.** [*kūṭa-*⁴] a peak, summit. **2.** [*kūṭa-*²] a heap (as of grain). **3.** [*kūṭa-*⁶] a puzzling question; enigma. **4.** a verse of obscure meaning. **5.** [× Engl. *code*] a code. **6.** a concerted scheme or plot; *Pl. HŚS.* trap, snare. **7.** f., *Pl.* [? infld. *nīti-*] deceit; falsehood. — **कूट-कर्म**, m. deceit. **कूट-नीति**, f. diplomacy. °**-नीतिक**, adj. = **कूटनैतिक**. °**-नीतिज्ञ**, m. a diplomat. **कूटनैतिक**, adj. diplomatic.

²**कूट** *kūṭ* [cf. H. *kūṭnā*], f. papier mâché.

कूटना *kūṭnā* [*kuṭṭayati*], v.t. **1.** to pound. **2.** to crush. **3.** to thresh (corn). **4.** to beat, to thrash. — **कूट-कूटकर भरा होना**, to be crammed (into, **में**): to be abundantly characteristic of (as a quality); to be possessed in great measure.

कूटी *kūṭī*, f. *Pl. HŚS.* sarcasm, innuendo; satire.

कूड़ा *kūṛā* [*kūṭa-*²], m. **1.** rubbish, sweepings; dirt. **2.** useless object(s), rubbish. — **कूड़ा-करकट**, m. = ~. **कूड़ा-ख़ाना**, m. public rubbish-dump. **कूड़ेदान** [P. *-dān*], m. rubbish-bin.

कूढ़ *kūṛh* [**kuḍḍha-*: cf. Pk. *kuḍhiya-*], adj. stupid, foolish. — ~ **के** ~, m. pl. supremely foolish (people). – **कूढ़-मग़ज़**, adj. dull-witted (= **कूढ़**).

कूत *kūt* [**kutta-*²: Pk. *kutta-*], m. **1.** valuation, appraisal. **2.** conjecture.

कूतना *kūtnā* [cf. H. *kūt*], v.t. to estimate, to appraise.

कूद *kūd* [cf. H. *kūdnā*], f. **1.** jumping. **2.** a jump, spring. — ~ **मारना**, to jump, to spring. – **कूद-फाँद**, f. = ~, 1.; skipping, gambolling.

कूदना *kūdnā* [*kūrdati*: ? ← Drav.], v.i. **1.** to jump, to leap. **2.** to hop. **3.** fig. to rejoice. **4.** colloq. to appear (suddenly: a person). **5.** colloq. to interfere (in, **में**). — **बल पर** ~, fig. to depend (on, **के**) for one's success. – **कूदना-फाँदना**, to jump about; to dance (for joy); to gambol. – **कूद पड़ना**, to jump, &c.; to jump down. **कूदकर पार करना**, to jump across (sthg).

कूप *kūp* [S.], m. **1.** a well. **2.** a hole, pit. **3.** an oil-well. — **कूप मंडूक**, m. a frog in a well; = **कुएं का मेंढक**.

कूपी *kūpī* [cf. H. *kūp*; or S.], f. *Pl. HŚS.* a small well or pit.

कूबड़ *kūbaṛ* [cf. **kubba-*], m. a hump, hunched back.

कूबड़ा *kūbṛā* [cf. **kubba-*], adj. hunchbacked; crooked.

कूम्हल *kūmhal* [*kumbhila-*], m. **1.** a hole made by a thief in the wall of a house (= **सेंध**). **2.** housebreaking, burglary. — ~ **देना** (**में**), = **सेंध लगाना**.

¹**कूर** *kūr* [*krūra-*], adj. = **क्रूर**.

²**कूर** *kūr* [P. *kūr*], adj. Brbh. **1.** blind. **2.** fig. benighted.

कूर्म *kūrm* [S.], m. **1.** a tortoise, turtle. **2.** the second avatār or incarnation of Viṣṇu (his descent in the form of a tortoise to support the mountain Mandara at the churning of the ocean). — ~ **पुराण**, m. *hind.* the fifteenth Purāṇa (which contains the history of the tortoise incarnation of Viṣṇu).

कूल *kūl* [*kūla-*¹], m. **1.** bank, shore. **2.** pond, lake.

¹**कूला** *kūlā*, m. pronun. var. = **कूल्हा**.

²**कूला** *kūlā* [*kulyā-*], m. an irrigation channel.

कूल्हा *kūlhā* [**kulla-*¹: Pk. *kulla-*], m. **1.** the hip. **2.** the buttocks.

कूवत *kūvat*, f. = **कुव्वत** (see also s.v. **ला-**).

कूहड़ *kūhaṛ*, adj. rough, uneven (a road or path).

कृच्छ *kṛcch* [S.], adj. 19c. = **कृच्छ्र**.

कृच्छ्र *kṛcchră* [S.], adj. **1.** causing trouble or pain. ***2.** bad, wicked. ***3.** wretched.

कृत *kṛt* [S.], adj. **1.** done; performed. **2.** made; prepared; composed. **3.** m. *mythol.* the first of the four ages (*yuga*) of the world, the golden age. — कृतकर्म, adj. who has performed a task or duty: = next. °-कार्य, adj. who has attained his object: successful; able. °-कृत्य, adj. who has accomplished a task, or a purpose: successful; contented. कृतघ्न, adj. destroying what has been done (for one): ungrateful. °ता, f. कृतज्ञ, adj. acknowledging what has been done: grateful. °ता, f. कृत-निंदक, adj. Av. = कृतघ्न. कृतविद्य, adj. who has knowledge: learned. कृतसंकल्प, adj. resolved, decided. कृतहस्त, adj. dextrous, skilful. कृतात्मा [°*ta*+*ā*°], m. inv. one whose spirit is controlled, or purified. कृतार्थ [°*ta*+*a*°], adj. who has accomplished a purpose: successful; contented.

कृतक *kr̥tak* [S.], adj. **1.** made or done artificially. **2.** feigned, false.

कृति *kr̥ti* [S.], f. **1.** acting, action. **2.** a work; a composition; work of art.

कृती *kr̥tī* [S.], adj. **1.** skilful. **2.** successful. **3.** satisfied, contented.

कृते *kr̥te* [S. (loc.)], adv. on behalf of, on the authority of.

कृत्तिका *kr̥ttikā* [S.], f. the third lunar mansion, the Pleiades.

कृत्य *kr̥tyă* [S.], m. sthg. to be done: **1.** an act. **2.** a service, function. **3.** a rite.

कृत्या *kr̥tyā* [S.], f. Brbh. a female deity or demoness to whom sacrifices are offered for magical purposes.

कृत्रिम *kr̥trim* [S.], adj. **1.** made, man-made; synthetic (a product). **2.** artificial; forged, counterfeit; factitious. **3.** forced (as manner); feigned. **4.** obs. adopted (a son).

कृत्रिमता *kr̥trimătā* [S.], f. man-made, or artificial, quality, &c. (see कृत्रिम).

कृदंत *kr̥dant* [S.], m. *gram.* a nominal form made by addition of a primary affix to a verbal root; specif. a participle. — पूर्वकालिक ~, m. an absolutive. भूत, or भूतकालिक, ~, m. past, or perfective participle. वर्तमान, or वर्तमानकालिक ~, m. present, or imperfective participle.

कृदंती *kr̥dantī* [cf. H. *kr̥dant*], adj. *gram.* participial.

कृदंतीय *kr̥dantīyă* [S.], adj. *gram.* = कृदंती.

कृपण *kr̥paṇ* [S.], adj. & m. **1.** adj. miserly. **2.** miserable, wretched. **3.** m. a miser.

कृपणता *kr̥paṇătā* [S.], f. **1.** miserliness; avarice. **2.** wretchedness.

कृपया *kr̥payā* [S.], adv. = कृपा करके.

कृपा *kr̥pā* [S.], f. **1.** grace, favour. आपकी ~ से, or है, it is by your kindness (that I am well: said in answer to an enquiry on meeting, &c). **2.** compassion. **3.** mercy; forgiveness. — ~ करना, to show grace, favour, &c. (to, पर). ~ करके, adv. of your grace: please, kindly. – कृपाकांक्षी [°*ā*+*ā*°], adj. desiring the favour (of a person, की). कृपा-दृष्टि, f. a look of favour. कृपादृष्टि करना, to look with favour (on, पर). कृपा-निधान, m. store of grace: a title of the supreme being; your honour. कृपा-पात्र, m. recipient of favour. °ई, f. कृपापूर्वक, adv. of (one's) grace, kindly. कृपायतन [°*ā*+*ā*°], m. abode of grace: a title of the supreme being.

कृपाण *kr̥pāṇ* [S.], m. **1.** a dagger. **2.** a sword.

कृपाणी *kr̥pāṇī* [S.], f. a small dagger.

कृपालु *kr̥pālu* [S.], adj. **1.** showing favour; kind. **2.** compassionate. **3.** merciful.

कृपालुता *kr̥pālutā* [S.], f. **1.** compassionateness. **2.** mercifulness.

कृमि *kr̥mi* [S.], m. **1.** a worm. **2.** any small insect. **3.** *med.* worms. **4.** *Pl. HŚS.* lac (a red dye produced by insects). — कृमिघ्न, adj. & m. worm-destroying; *Pl.* a shrub, *Erycibe paniculata* (used as a vermifuge, and called *bairaṅg*). कृमिज, adj. & m. *Pl.* produced by worms; Agallochum. कृमिनाशक, m. antidote to worms. कृमि-विज्ञान, m. helminthology.

कृमिल *kr̥mil* [S.], adj. *Pl. HŚS.* having worms, wormy.

कृमी *kr̥mī* [S.], adj. *Pl.* having worms, wormy.

कृश *kr̥ś* [S.], adj. **1.** emaciated, wasted. **2.** weak, feeble. **3.** *Pl. HŚS.* minute, fine; slender (of build). — कृशकाय, adj. very thin, or wasted in body.

कृशता *kr̥śătā* [S.], f. thinness, weakness, &c. (see कृश).

कृशानु *kr̥śānu* [S.], m. a title of the Vedic fire-god, Agni: fire.

कृशित *kr̥śit* [S.], adj. **1.** emaciated. **2.** enfeebled.

कृषि *kr̥ṣi* [S.], f. **1.** agriculture. **2.** ploughing, cultivation; sowing (crop). **3.** harvest.

कृषी *kr̥ṣī* [S.], m. *Pl. HŚS.* = कृषक.

कृष्ट *kr̥ṣṭ* [S.], adj. ploughed.

कृष्ण *kr̥ṣṇ* [S.], adj. & m. **1.** adj. black, dark, dark blue. **2.** fig. black, bad (a deed). ***3.** m. name of the eighth avatār of Viṣṇu. 4. = कृष्ण-पक्ष. — कृष्ण-पक्ष, m. the 'dark half' of a lunar month, period of a waning moon. कृष्ण-सार, m. the black buck. कृष्णागरु [°*ṇa*+*a*°], m. black aloe. कृष्णाष्टमी [°*ṇa*+*a*°], m. = जन्माष्टमी.

कृष्णता *kr̥ṣṇătā* [S.], f. blackness.

कृष्णत्व *kr̥ṣṇatvă* [S.], m. = कृष्णता.

कृष्णा *kr̥ṣṇā* [S.], f. **1.** the river Kistna. **2.** Brbh. name of a companion (*sakhī*) of Rādhā.

केंकड़ा *keṁkṛā*, m. pronun. var. = केकड़ा.

कें-कें *keṁ-keṁ* [onom.], m. plaintive sound of birds calling.

केंचुआ *keṁcuā* [**keñcuka-*: *kiñculaka-*], m. **1.** an earthworm. **2.** an intestinal worm.

केंचुल *keṁcul*, f. = केंचुली.

केंचुली *keṁculī* [conn. *kañculikā-*], f. skin or slough (of a snake). — ~ **छोड़ना**, or **डालना**, to shed its skin (a snake). ~ **बदलना**, to change (its) skin; to be a turncoat.

केंद्र *kendră* [S.: ← Gk.], m. centre; middle part. — **केंद्र-बिंदु**, f. centre point. **केंद्र-सरकार**, f. *admin.* the centre, central government (of India). **केंद्रस्थ**, adj. situated at the centre, or centrally. **केंद्रापसारी** [°*a*+*a*°], adj. centrifugal. **केंद्राभिसारी** [°*a*+*a*°], adj. centripetal. **केंद्रीकरण**, m. centralisation. **केंद्रीकृत**, adj. centralised. **केंद्रीभूत**, adj. centred, focused (as attention).

केंद्रित *kendrit* [S.], adj. centred (on, **पर**).

केंद्रीकरण *kendrīkaraṇ* [S.], m. see s.v. केंद्र.

केंद्रीकृत *kendrīkr̥t* [S.], adj. see s.v. केंद्र.

केंद्रीय *kendrīyă* [S.], adj. central.

केउ *keu* [cf. *ka-*[2]], pron. Av. = कोई.

केकड़ा *kekṛā* [*karkaṭa-*[1]], m. **1.** a crab. **2.** the sign Cancer (of the zodiac).

केका *kekā* [S.], m. peacock's cry. — **केका-रव**, m. noise of peacocks crying.

केकिनी *kekinī* [S.], f. a peahen.

केकी *kekī* [S.], m. Brbh. a peacock.

केड़ा *keṛā* [**keḍa-*], m. **1.** a sapling. **2.** 19c. a shoot (from the family tree): a youth. **3.** reg. (Bihar) a small bundle of crop given to village workmen on the occasion of a marriage.

केत *ket* [S.], m. Brbh. = केतु, 3.

केतकी *ketăkī* [S.], f. = केवड़ा.

केतन *ketan* [S.], m. poet. flag, banner.

केतली *ketlī* [Engl. *kettle*], f. a kettle.

केतिक *ketik*, pron. & adj. Brbh. = कितना.

केतु *ketu* [S.], m. sign, mark: **1.** flag, banner. **2.** a comet, or meteor. **3.** *mythol.* name of a demon, supposed (with Rāhu) to cause eclipses by devouring the sun or moon.

केदार *kedār* [S.], m. a field: **1.** a name of Śiva. **2.** *mus.* name of a *rāg*. — **केदारनाथ**, m. name of a place of pilgrimage at Kedar in the Himālayas; = ~, 1.

केबिस *kebis*, f. reg. (Bihar) a red clay.

केयूर *keyūr* [S.], m. an armlet (worn on the upper arm).

केर *ker* [**kārya-*: Pa. *kāriya-*, *kayira-*], ppn. Av. = का.

केराव *kerāv* [**kerāva-*: cf. *kalāya-*], m. reg. (Bihar) a small type of pea (often sown with other crops).

केला *kelā* [*kadala-*: ← Austro.-as.], m. **1.** the plantain, *Musa sapientum*. **2.** a banana.

केलि *keli* [S.], f. **1.** amorous play, dalliance. **2.** sexual intercourse.

केवट *kevaṭ* [*kevarta-*], m. a boatman (= खेवट).

केवड़ा *kevṛā* [*ketaka-*: ← Drav.], m. **1.** the screwpine, *Pandanus odoratissimus*, and its fragrant flower. **2.** scent made from the *kevṛā* flower.

केवल *keval* [S.], adj. & adv. **1.** adj. exclusively (one's) own, sole; one and only, absolute. **2.** adv. only; solely, merely.

केवली *kevălī* [S.], m. **1.** one who believes in an absolute unity of spirit. **2.** specif. a Jain saint or deity (*arhat*).

केवाँच *kevāṁc* [*kapikacchū-*], m. a medicinal plant, *Mucuna pruriens*, the pods of which have stinging hairs.

केवाँछ *kevāṁch* [*kapikacchū-*], m. reg. = केवाँच.

केवाड़ी *kevāṛī*, f. reg. a small door (see किवाड़).

केवार *kevār*, m. reg. = किवाड़.

केश *keś* [S.], m. hair (of the head).

केशर *keśar* [S.], m. = केसर.

केशव *keśav* [S.], m. having long, or much, or beautiful, hair: a title of Viṣṇu/Kr̥ṣṇa.

केशी *keśī* [S.], m. *mythol.* hairy: name of an *asura* (demon) killed by Kr̥ṣṇa.

केसर *kesar* [*kesara-*], m. **1.** the stigma or pistil of a flower, specif. of the crocus (*Crocus sativus*). **2.** filament of a lotus. ***3.** saffron. **4.** saffron or yellow colour.

केसरिया *kesriyā* [cf. H. *kesrī*], adj. dimin. & f. = केसरी.

[1]**केसरी** *kesărī* [*kesarin-*], m. maned: a lion.

[2]**केसरी** *kesrī* [cf. H. *kesar*], adj. & f. **1.** adj. saffron-coloured; dyed with saffron. **2.** f. saffron colour, yellow colour.

केहरी *kehărī* [*kesarin-*; ? ← Panj.], m. Brbh. Av. a lion.

केहुनी *kehunī*, f. = कुहनी.

कैंड़ा *kaiṁṛā*, m. reg. measure, cut; type.

क़ैंची *qaiṁcī* [? T.], f. **1.** scissors. **2.** shears. **3.** fig. boards, &c. fastened in the form of an oblique cross. **4.** a leg hold (in wrestling). — ~ करना, colloq. = ~ लगाना. ~ काटना, colloq. to slip away (= कतराना). ~ लगाना, to apply scissors, or shears (to, में): to cut, to trim (hair, or vegetation).

क़ै *qai* [A. *qai*], f. **1.** vomiting; vomit. **2.** nausea. — ~ आना (को), to feel nausea; to be sick or disgusted (of, with or at, से). ~ करना, to vomit. ~ लेना, to induce vomiting. ~ लानेवाला, adj. emetic. – क़ै-दस्त, f. vomiting with diarrhoea; cholera.

[1]**कै** *kai* [*kati*], adj. how many?

[2]**कै** *kai* [? *kim*, or H. *ki*, +H. (*h*)*ī*], conj. Brbh. or. — ~ … ~, either … or; whether … or.

[3]**कै** *kai*, ppn. Av. = की.

[4]**कै** *kai* [H. *kari*], abs. Av. = करके.

कैटभ *kaiṭabh* [S.], m. Brbh. *mythol.* name of an *asura* (demon) killed by Viṣṇu.

कैथ *kaith* [*kapittha-*], m. the wood-apple, *Feronia elephantum*, and its small, hard fruit. — हाथी के खाए कैथ, m. pl. *kaith* fruit eaten by elephants: sthg. indigestible, or of no real use.

कैथी *kaithī* [cf. *kāyastha-*], f. a modified form of the Devanāgarī script used esp. in Bihar.

क़ैद *qaid* [A. *qaid*], f. **1.** imprisonment, confinement. **2.** control; restriction, limitation. **3.** an obligation. — ~ करना, to imprison; to secure (in bonds); to capture. ~ काटना, or भुगतना, to undergo a term of imprisonment. ~ रखना, to keep in custody. ~ रहना, to remain in custody. ~ लगाना, to impose a restriction, &c. (on, की; to, में); to attach conditions (to). सख़्त ~, f. rigorous imprisonment. – क़ैद-ख़ाना, m. a jail. क़ैद-तन्हाई [P. *-tanhāī*], m. solitary confinement.

क़ैदिन *qaidin* [cf. H. *qaid*], f. a female prisoner.

क़ैदी *qaidī* [P. *qaidī*], m. **1.** a prisoner; convict. **2.** a captive.

कैन *kain*, f. *Pl. HŚS.* a bamboo twig.

कैफ़ियत *kaifiyat* [A. *kaifiya* 'how': P. *kaifiyat*], f. quality, nature, condition: **1.** account, details, particulars (of sthg). **2.** state of affairs, situation. — ~ देना, to give an account, &c. (of, की); to describe (a situation).

कैरव *kairav* [S.], m. Av. a white water-lily, or lotus.

कैरा *kairā*, adj. **1.** [*kekara-*] *Pl.* squint-eyed. **2.** [? *karĭra-*[1]] *Pl. HŚS.* light-blue, grey (eyes: = कंजा).

कैरी *kairī* [? *karīra-*[1]], f. **1.** a small unripe mango. **2.** a locket made in the shape of a mango.

कैरु *kairu* [*kavala-*], m. Brbh. = कौर.

कैल *kail*, adj. reg. (E). yellowish grey or cream-coloured (of cattle: cf. कैरा, 2).

कैलाश *kailaś*, m. pronun. var. = कैलास.

कैलास *kailās* [S.], m. *mythol.* name of a mountain supposed to be located in Tibet near the Mānsarovar Lake, and regarded as the home of Kuvera and main abode of Śiva.

कैली *kailī*, f. reg. (Bihar) = [1]करिल.

कैवल्य *kaivalyă* [S.], m. *philos.* absolute singleness of state, or unity; state of oneness with the absolute being.

क़ैसर *qaisar* [A. *qaiṣar*: ← Gk.], m., f. Caesar: **1.** m. an emperor. **2.** f. an empress.

कैसा *kaisā* [*kīdr̥śa-*: Ap. *kaïsa-*], adj. & adv. **1.** adj. of what kind? what sort of? in what condition? **2.** adv. how? why? — ~ ही, adj. & adv. of whatever sort; in whatever way. आप कैसे हैं? how are you (m.)? आप कैसी हैं? how are you (f.)? — कैसी-कैसी सुनाना (को), to give a straight talking-to.

कोंच *koṁc* [cf. H. *koṁcnā*], f. prick; stab.

कोंचना *koṁcnā* [**kocc-*], v.t. **1.** to pierce. **2.** to stab, to wound. **3.** fig. to cause distress to. — कोंचा-काँची, f. squabbling, sparring.

कोंछना *koṁchnā* [? H. *kāchnā* × H. *khoṁsnā*], v.t. **1.** to draw round and tuck in (the end of a *dhotī* or sari). **2.** to tie (sthg.) in the hem of one's *dhotī* or sari and tuck it into the waist.

[1]**कोंढ़ा** *koṁṛhā*, m. reg. metal ring; hasp.

[2]**कोंढ़ा** *koṁṛhā*, m. कुम्हड़ा.

कोंत *koṁt* [*kunta-*[1]; Pk. *konta-*: ? ← Gk.], m. ? f. *Pl.* a spear, barb.

कोंपल *koṁpal* [*kuṭmala-*], f. a new leaf, sprout, shoot.

कोंपली *koṁplī*, f. reg. = कोंपल.

कोंहड़ा *koṁhṛā*, m. = कुम्हड़ा.

¹को *ko* [*kakṣam*], ppn. marker of oblique case in a preceding form; functions are: **1.** specifier of a definite direct object. दर्ज़ी ~ बुलाओ, call the tailor. इस ~ क्या कहते हैं? what is this called? **2.** marker of an indirect object. उस ~ किताब दीजिए, please give him a book. **3.** marker of an adverbial expression. तीन मई ~, on the third of May. बुधवार ~, on Wednesday. वह अपने देश (~) लौटा, he returned to his country. सुबह ~, in the morning. आगे ~, afterwards; in the future. **4.** marker of a structural relationship between two nominal forms in a sentence: the second form usually denotes an abstract quality or condition characterising the referend of the first (which is marked by को); also in analogous expressions. मुझ ~ खुशी है (कि ...), I am happy (that ...). उस ~ मालूम है (कि ...), he knows (that ...). उस ~ हिंदी आती है, he knows Hindi. उस ~ जाने में एक घंटा लगा, it took him an hour to get there. उस ~ यहाँ रहना होगा, or पड़ेगा, he must stay here. उस ~ क्या चाहिए? what does he want? **5.** in other cases को has the general sense 'with regard to, in respect of' and is often (but not when followed by होना alone) interchangeable with के लिए, e.g. क्या आप जाने ~ तैयार हैं? are you ready to go? — उसने उससे आने ~ कहा, he asked him to come. वह बाहर जाने ~ था, he was about to go out. वह हिंदी सीखने ~ भारत गया, he went to India to learn Hindi.

²को *ko*, pron. Brbh. = कौन.

³को *ko*, ppn. Brbh. 1. = का. 2. = कौं.

¹कोई *koī* [*kaścid*, Pa. *koci*], pron. & adj.: almost always sg. (but see 3. and further below). **1.** someone; anyone. **2.** some; any; a certain. **3.** (with numerals) some, approximately. ~ दस ऊँट, some ten, a dozen camels. **4.** rhetor. what? (= क्या). लड़की, ~ तेरी अक़्ल मारी गई? have you lost your senses, girl? — ~ और, pron. & adj. someone else; another, a different. ~ ~, pron. & adj. some, some few. ~ ~ आपको बता देगा ..., a few people will tell you .... ~ न ~, pron. & adj. someone or another; some, one or another. ~ नहीं, pron. & adj. no one; not any. गाँव में ~ तालाब नहीं है, there's no tank in the village. ~ भी आपको बता देगा, anyone at all will tell you. ~ है? is anyone there? जो ~, pron. & adj. whoever, whichever. जिस किसी का जो जी चाहे, whatever anyone may wish for. सब ~, pron. everyone. हर ~, pron. id. – कोई-सा, adj. any (out of a number). कोई-से तीन विषय, any three subjects.

²कोई *koī* [*kaumudika-*], f. = कुई.

कोउ *kou*, pron. Brbh. = कोई.

¹कोक *kok* [S.], m. 1. = कोकिल. **2.** Brbh. = चकवा. — कोक-नद, m. flower of the red water-lily.

²कोक *kok* [S.], m. = कोक-शास्त्र. — कोक-शास्त्र, m. a treatise on sex, attributed to Koka.

कोकटी *kokṭī*, f. reg. (Bihar) a kind of cotton having a reddish colour (source of a fine cloth).

कोकनी *koknī*, colloq. *Pl. HŚS.* small, inferior.

कोका *kokā* [**kokka-*: Pk. *kokk(āsa)-*], m. **1.** nail, tack; spike. **2.** small thorn, prickle. **3.** spike (of a plantain); bud.

कोकाह *kokāh* [S.], m. Av. a white horse.

कोकिल *kokil* [S.], m. the black cuckoo, *Cuculus indicus.* — कोकिल-कंठ, adj. cuckoo-throated: sweet-voiced. °ई, adj. id. कोकिल-बैनी, adj. Av. sweet-voiced.

कोकिला *kokilā* [S.: or H. *kokil*], f. the black cuckoo (= कोकिल).

कोको *koko*, m. colloq. cawing sound (of a crow).

कोख *kokh* [*kaukṣa-*], m. **1.** the abdomen. ***2.** the womb. — ~ उजड़ना, fig. a woman's child or children to die. ~ की आँच, f. maternal grief. ~ खुलना, the womb to be opened: (a woman) to conceive after long waiting. ~ मारी जाना, the womb to be stricken: to be infertile. – कोख-जली, adj. whose womb has caused (her) suffering: (a woman) whose child or children have not survived. कोख-माँग से ठंडी, or भरी-पूरी, होना, to be satisfied in womb and (hair)-parting: to be blessed (a married woman).

कोखा *kokhā* [*kaukṣa-*], m. = कोख.

कोचना *kocnā* [**kocc-*], v.t. to pierce, &c. (= कोंचना).

¹कोट *koṭ* [S.], m. **1.** a fort. **2.** wall, rampart (of fort or city). **3.** palace. — कोट-पाल, m. commandant of a fort.

²कोट *koṭ* [Engl. *coat*], m. coat: **1.** jacket. **2.** overcoat. — कोट-पतलून, m. coat and trousers: European men's dress.

कोटपीस *koṭpīs*, f. name of a card game.

कोटर *koṭar* [S.], m. hollow (prop. in a tree).

कोटला *koṭlā* [cf. H. *koṭ*], m. **1.** a small fort. **2.** *Pl.* muniments room (of a temple).

कोटवाल *koṭvāl* [*koṭṭapāla-*], m. = कोतवाल.

कोटा *koṭā* [Engl. *quota*], m. quota.

कोटि *koṭi* [S.], f. **1.** [*koṭi-*¹] top, point, end (esp. curved, as of a bow). **2.** category; grade, standard. **3.** [*koṭi-*²: ← Austro-As.] = करोड़. — उच्च ~ का, adj. of high standard, or quality. – कोटि-क्रम, m. sequential development. कोटि-बंध, m. grading, classing. °-बद्ध, adj. graded, &c.

कोटिक *koṭik* [S.], adj. millions, myriads (of); innumerable.

कोठ *koṭh* [**koṭṭha-*²: Pk. *koṭṭha-*], m. *Pl. HŚS.* a kind of leprosy with large round spots.

कोठरी *koṭhrī* [cf. *koṣṭha-*²] **1.** small or dark room (of a house). **2.** store-room; granary; shed. **3.** cell (of a prison). **काली ~**, f. solitary confinement cell.

कोठा *koṭhā* [*koṣṭhaka-*], m. **1.** granary; storehouse. **2.** a large (inner) room. **3.** the flat top or a roof of a house; room built on a roof, or in an upper storey. **4.** a brothel. **5.** fig. the stomach, bowels; womb. **6.** square (as of a games board). — **कोठे पर बैठना**, to sit in an upper room: to become a prostitute. – **कोठेवाली**, f. a prostitute.

कोठार *koṭhār* [*koṣṭhāgāra-*], m. = **कुठियार**.

कोठारी *koṭhārī* [*koṣṭhāgārika-*], m. = **कुठियारी**.

कोठी *koṭhī* [*koṣṭha-*²], f. **1.** a large house of brick or stone, a bungalow. **2.** transf. a mercantile firm. **3.** a bank. **4.** storehouse (= **कोठा**, 1.); hold (of a ship). **5.** womb. — **~ खोलना**, to start a business; to set up as a banker, or money-lender. **~ बैठना**, a house to collapse; a business to fail. — **कोठीवाल**, m. businessman, merchant; money-lender.

कोडंड *koḍaṇḍ*, m. Brbh. = **कोदंड**.

कोड़ना *koṛnā* [*koṭayate*], v.t. reg. to dig up or out, to scrape out; to carve.

कोड़ा *koṛā* [**koraḍa-*], m. **1.** a whip. **2.** fig. urging, incitement. — **~ मारना**, or **लगाना (को)**, to whip. – **कोड़ेबाज़** [P. *-bāz*], m. one who whips. **°ई**, f. whipping.

कोड़ाई *koṛāī* [cf. H. *koṛnā*], f. reg. cost of digging out, &c.

कोड़ाना *koṛānā* [cf. H. *koṛnā*], v.t. reg. **1.** to cause to be dug out. **2.** to have (sthg.) carved or engraved.

कोड़ी *koṛī* [**koḍi-*: ← Austro-as.], f. a score, twenty.

कोढ़ *koṛh* [*kuṣṭha-*²], m. leprosy. — **~ में खाज**, itch on leprosy: one disaster upon another. **~ चूना**, or **टपकना**, leprous wasting to occur.

कोढ़िन *koṛhin* [cf. H. *koṛhī*], f. a female leper.

कोढ़ी *koṛhī* [cf. H. *koṛh*], adj. & m. **1.** adj. leprous. **2.** m. a leper.

कोण *koṇ* [S.], m. an angle.

कोणिक *koṇik* [S.], adj. **1.** having corners. **2.** angular (as measurement, movement).

कोणीय *koṇīyă* [S.], adj. angular (as measurement, movement).

कोतल *kotal* [P. or T. *kutal*], m. **1.** Av. a led horse, spare horse. **2.** *Pl.* anything held in reserve (as an army, a force).

कोतवाल *kotvāl* [P. *kotvāl*], m. chief police officer of a town or city; deputy superintendent of police; officer in charge of a police station.

कोतवाली *kotvālī* [P. *kotvālī*], f. **1.** position and duties of a *kotvāl*. **2.** a *kotvāl's* office, chief police station.

कोताह *kotāh* [P. *kotāh*], adj. U. **1.** small. **2.** deficient.

कोताही *kotāhī* [P. *kotāhī*], f. U. **1.** deficiency, shortcoming. **2.** fig. miserliness. — **~ करना**, to be lacking (in, **में**); to be miserly.

कोथमीर *kothmīr* [**kostambarī-*], f. *Pl. HŚS.* coriander (= **धनिया**).

कोथला *kothlā* [**kotthala-*: Pk. *kotthala-*], m. **1.** a large bag, sack. **2.** the stomach.

कोथली *kothlī* [cf. H. *kothlā*], f. **1.** a small bag; a deep money-bag. **2.** bag of sweets (sent as a gift).

कोदंड *kodaṇḍ* [S.], m. **1.** a bow. **2.** fig. an eyebrow.

कोदों *kodoṁ* [*kodrava-*], m. a kind of small millet that grows readily on poor soil, *Paspalum scrobiculatum.* — **~ दलाना**, to cause millet to be ground (by, **से**): to set (one) a hard or impossible task. **~ देकर पढ़ना**, to give (only) millet in return for learning: to be content with a poor education.

कोदो *kodo*, m. = **कोदों**.

कोना *konā* [*koṇa-*: ← Drav.], m. **1.** a corner, an angle; point (as of a geometrical figure). **2.** an angular piece; sliver, splinter (as of glass). **3.** fig. quiet place, corner. — **~ झाँकना**, to look aside, to avert the eyes (in embarrassment or confusion). **देश के कोने कोने में**, adv. in every part of the country. – **कोनेदार** [P. *-dār*], adj. having corners, angular.

कोप *kop* [S.], m. anger; rage. — **~ करना**, to become angry (with, **पर**). – **कोप-भवन**, m. Av. boudoir.

कोप- *kop-* [**kopyate*: Pk. *koppaï*], v.i. Brbh. Av. to be or to become angry.

कोपल *kopal*, f. pronun. var. = **कोंपल**.

कोपित *kopit* [S.], adj. angered, enraged.

¹**कोपी** *kopī* [S.], adj. angry; irascible.

²**कोपी** *kopī* [cf. S. *ko'pi*], pron. Av. metr. = **कोई**.

कोफ़्त *koft* [P. *koft*], f. a blow: **1.** sadness. **2.** vexation; tedium. **3.** great fatigue, distress.

4. inlaying of gold or silver (on steel, &c). — कोफ़्तगरी [P. *-garī*], f. steel work inlaid with gold or silver.

कोफ़्ता *koftā* [P. *kofta*], m. beaten, pounded: chopped or spiced meat or vegetable.

कोब *kob* [P. *kob*], m. reg. (W). a small mallet.

कोबी *kobī* [? ← B. *kopi*], f. *Pl. HŚS.* = गोभी.

कोमल *komal* [S.], adj. **1.** soft, tender; delicate. **2.** supple. **3.** soft (the voice); flat (in tone). **4.** mild, gentle (as temperament). **5.** *mus.* flattened (a note). — कोमलांग [°*la*+*a*°], adj. soft-limbed, tender, lovely. °ई, f. a lovely woman.

कोमलता *komalătā* [S.], f. softness, tenderness, &c. (see कोमल).

कोमलताई *komalătāī* [cf. H. *komaltā*], f. Av. = कोमलता.

कोयर *koyar*, m. reg. **1.** vegetables. **2.** green fodder.

कोयरी *koyrī*, m. reg. a cultivator: a gardener (= काछी).

कोयल *koyl* [*kokila-*[1]], m. the black cuckoo (= कोकिल).

कोयला *koylā* [*kokila-*[2], MIA *kōila-*: ← Austro.-as.], m. **1.** charcoal; coal. **2.** a live coal. — कोयले की खान, f. a coal mine. जलकर ~ हो जाना, to glow with anger, to become furious.

कोया *koyā* [**koya-*], m. stone or pulp of fruit: **1.** pulp (of the jack fruit). **2.** eyeball. **3.** corner of the eye. **4.** cocoon (of the silkworm).

[1]**कोर** *kor* [*koṭi-*[1]], f. **1.** point, tip. **2.** edge. **3.** small piece split or broken off (from anything); obs. thorn. **4.** ill-will (= खोड़). **5.** a small defect or shortcoming.

[2]**कोर** *kor* [*kora-*; or S.], m. a joint (as of the fingers).

कोर- *kor-* [*koṭayate*], v.t. Brbh. = कोड़ना.

कोरक *korak* [S.], m. Brbh. a bud; ? sepals; ? a blossom.

क़ोरमा *qormā* [T. *qavurma*], m. a lightly spiced fried curry.

कोरा *korā* [**kora-*], adj. **1.** unused, new; unbleached; blank (paper). **2.** plain, undyed (silk). **3.** neglected, unoiled (hair). **4.** unversed, unskilled (in, का). **5.** ignorant, stupid. **6.** mere, simple. **7.** blunt; fig. flat (refusal). **8.** unsuccessful, unsatisfied (in a request); disappointed (in a hope). — ~ बचना, to escape unhurt or unscathed. ~ रह जाना, to get nothing, to be disappointed. ~ लौटना, to return empty-handed. ~ सिर, m. an untended head, neglected hair.

कोरापन *korāpan* [cf. H. *korā*], m. **1.** newness, freshness, &c. (see कोरा). **2.** virginity.

कोरी *korī*, m. reg. a weaver (= कोली).

कोरैया *koraiyā*, m. 19c. the plant *Nerium antidysentericum*, or *Wrightia* (cf. इंदर-जौ).

कोरो *koro*, m. reg. a bamboo rafter, or pole; a prop.

कोर्ट *korṭ* [Engl. *court*], m. **1.** a court (of law). **2.** court (as for tennis).

[1]**कोल** *kol* [*kroḍa-*: MIA *kola-*], m. the breast, lap; embrace.

[2]**कोल** *kol* [*kola-*[1]]. m. name of a tribe of central India.

[3]**कोल** *kol*, m. Brbh. a hog.

कोल- *kol-* [*koṭayate*, or **korati*], v.t. Brbh. **1.** to hollow out. **2.** to crush; to confuse (the mind).

कोलतार *koltār* [Engl. *coal tar*], m. coal tar.

[1]**कोला** *kolā* [*kroḍa-*], m. reg. (E). a small field (esp. one beside a house or enclosed on two or three sides by water).

[2]**कोला** *kolā* [*kroṣṭra-*], m. reg. (S.) a jackal.

कोलाहल *kolāhal* [S.], m. **1.** uproar, din; shouting. **2.** noise of festivities. — ~ करना, to make an uproar, &c.

कोलाहली *kolāhălī* [S.], adj. noisy (as a place, an occasion).

कोलिन *kolin* [cf. H. [2]*kol*], f. a Kol woman.

कोलिया *koliyā*, m. *Pl. HŚS.* a narrow lane.

कोलियाना *koliyānā* [cf. H. [1]*kol*], v.t. to embrace.

कोली *kolī* [*kolika-*: ← Drav. or Austro-as.], m. **1.** a Hindu community of weavers. **2.** a weaver.

कोल्हाड़ *kolhāṛ*, m. reg. site of a sugar-mill (press and boiling-house).

कोल्हू *kolhū* [**kolhu-*: Pk. *kolhua-*], m. a press, mill (for sugar-cane or oil-seeds). — ~ का बैल, m. fig. a plodding, or a stupid ox. ~ के बैल की तरह पिलना, to work like a galley-slave. ~ काटकर मोगरी बनाना, to break up a press to make a mallet: to lose much and gain little. ~ में डालकर पेरना, to crush in a press; fig. to torment.

कोविद *kovid* [S.], m. versed, learned: an experienced person; a scholar.

कोविदार *kovidār* [S.], m. = कछनार.

कोश *koś* [S.], m. **1.** store-room. **2.** treasury. **3.** treasure; store. **4.** a dictionary. 5. = अंड-कोश. **6.** cocoon (of a silkworm). — **कोश-कर्ता**, m. inv. = **कोशकार**. **कोश-कला**, f. lexicography (as a skill or art). **कोशकार**, m. a lexicographer. **कोशागार** [°*śa* + *ā*°], m. store-room; treasury. **कोशाध्यक्ष** [°*śa* + *a*°], m. treasurer.

कोशिका *kośikā* [S.], f. *biol.* cell.

कोशिश *kośiś* [P. *kośiś*], f. effort, attempt. — ~ **करना** (**की**), to try.

कोष *koṣ* [S.], m. = **कोश**; specif. a fund.

कोष्ठ *koṣṭh* [S.], m. **1.** an enclosed place (as a granary, or inner room). **2.** any abdominal organ (esp. the stomach, intestines, bowels). **3.** column (of items in a composite list). — **कोष्ठ-बद्धता**, f. constipation. **कोष्ठाग्नि** [°*ṭha* + *a*°], f. stomach-fire: the digestion.

कोष्ठक *koṣṭhak* [S.], m. **1.** brackets (in punctuation). **2.** table (of figures, &c).

कोस *kos* [*krośa-*], m. a measure of distance (approx. two miles). — **कोसों दूर**, adv. miles away. **काले** ~, m. pl. black leagues: a long, or hard, distance.

कोसन *kosan* [cf. H. *kosnā*], f. cursing, curse(s).

कोसना *kosnā* [*krośati*], v.t. & m. **1.** v.t. to curse; to abuse. **2.** m. a curse. — **कोसने देना**, to call down curses (on, **को**). – **कोसा**, m. a curse. **कोसा-काटी**, f. id. **कोसा-कासी**, f. id. **कोसा-कासी करना**, = **कोसना**.

कोसली *koslī* [cf. *kośa-*], m. *Pl.* a new leaf just shooting.

¹**कोसा** *kosā*, m. see s.v. **कोसना**.

²**कोसा** *kosā* [*kauśa-*], m. a kind of silk manufactured in Madhya Pradesh.

³**कोसा** *kosā* [*kośa-*], m. **1.** reg. pod (of a leguminous plant); (Bihar) husk (of an ear of corn). **2.** reg. large earthenware saucer (as used to cover water-jars, or to hold food).

कोफ़्त *koft*, f. [P.*koft*], beating: grief, anguish.

¹**कोह** *koh* [*krodha-*], m. Brbh. Av. anger.

²**कोह** *koh* [P. *koh*], m. U. a mountain, hill. — **कोह-नूर**, m. mountain of light: the Koh-i-noor diamond. **कोहिस्तान**, m. mountainous region. °**ई**, adj. & m. mountainous; a hill-man.

³**कोह** *koh* [*kūpa-*³: × *guhā-*¹], m. reg. (Bihar) a pot; trough; basket.

कोहड़ *kohaṛ* [**kūpaghaṭa-*], m. frame at the mouth of a well.

कोहनी *kohnī*, f. pronun. var. = **कुहनी**.

कोहर *kohar* , m. Raj. a well.

कोहरा *kohrā*, m. pronun. var. = **कुहरा**.

कोहराना *kohrānā* [cf. H. *kohrā*], v.i. to be indistinct, or in a haze.

कोहराम *kohrām*, m. = **कुहराम**.

कोहा- *kohā-* [cf. H. *koh-*], v.i. Av. to be angry, or displeased.

कोहान *kohān* [P. *kohān*], m. hump (of bull, camel).

¹**कोही** *kohī* [cf. H. ¹*koh*], adj. Brbh. Av. angry, displeased; ill-disposed.

²**कोही** *kohī* [P. *kohī*], adj. & m. **1.** adj. mountainous; hilly. **2.** of or belonging to a hilly region. **3.** m. a hill-man.

³**कोही** *kohī* [P. *kohī*], f. *Pl. HŚS.* the shahin falcon.

कौं *kaum̆*, prep. Brbh. = **को**.

कौंचा *kaum̆cā* [f. P. *kafca*], m. reg. (W). a ladle, skimmer; stirrer.

कौंदना *kaum̆dnā*, v.i. pronun. var. = **कौंधना**.

कौंध *kaum̆dh* [cf. H. *kaum̆dhnā*], f. flash (as of lightning); sudden dazzling light.

कौंधना *kaum̆dhnā*, v.i. to flash (as lightning).

कौंधा *kaum̆dhā* [cf. H. *kaum̆dhnā*], m. flash of lightning.

कौंला *kaum̆lā* [*kamala-*¹], m. reddish: a type of large, sweet orange, *Citrus aurantium*.

कौंसिल *kaum̆sil* [Engl. *council*], f. council.

कौटुंबिक *kauṭumbik* [S.], adj. **1.** pertaining to a family. **2.** forming a family. **3.** having a family.

कौड़ा *kauṛā*, m. a fire lit in the open to give warmth (= **अलाव**).

कौड़ियाला *kauṛiyālā* [cf. H. *kauṛī*], adj. & m. **1.** adj. coloured, or marked, like a cowrie; braided; spotted. **2.** m. colloq. a kind of braided or spotted snake.

कौड़िल्ला *kauṛillā* [conn. H. *kauṛiyālā*], m. a kind of kingfisher.

कौड़ी *kauṛī* [*kapardikā-*: ← Drav.], f. **1.** a small shell, a cowrie (formerly in use as a barter token of very low value). **2.** colloq. a small amount of money. **3.** a gland; a hard swelling. **गले में** ~ **निकल आना**, the Adam's apple to develop. **4.** a white mark on the finger nail. — ~ **का**, adj. = **दो** ~ **का**. ~ **के तीन तीन होना**, to be selling at, or worth, three cowries each: to be of no real value. ~, or **कौड़ियों**, **के मोल**, adv. dirt cheap. ~ **को तंग**, or **मुहताज**, or **हैरान**, **होना**, to be hard pressed for every farthing. ~ को न पूछना, not to make the least enquiry after; to hold in no esteem. ~ ~, f. & adv. every last cowrie, the full amount. ~ ~ भर पाना, to receive payment to the last farthing. ~ ~ लेना, to exact payment in full. ~ भर, adv. a very little. कानी, or फूटी, ~, f. a broken cowrie, bad cowrie; fig. a farthing. दो ~ का, adj. worthless (a person); of no account. दो ~ की इज़्ज़त करना (की, अपनी), to dishonour (one); to cheapen (oneself).

कौणप *kauṇap* [S.], m. poet. a demon or goblin.

कौतुक *kautuk* [S.], m. **1.** eager curiosity. **2.** any event arousing curiosity or interest; a show, spectacle; festive activity. **3.** trick, prank; wile (as of the love-god).

कौतुकी *kautukī* [S.], adj. **1.** festive, merry; cheerful. **2.** having an interesting art or skill (as a juggler, or dancer). **3.** mischievous.

कौतूहल *kautūhal* [S.], m. = कुतूहल.

कौन *kaun* [*kaḥ punar*], pron. & adj. **1.** pron. who? **2.** adj. which? (used of persons or of particular things). ये ~ किताबें हैं? which books are these? — ~? who's there? (in response to a knock or call). कौन-सा, adj. which? (of a set range of possibilites). आज कौन-सा दिन है? what day is today? मैं प्रसाद बोल रहा हूँ … कौनसे? this is Prasād speaking. … which Prasād?

कौपीन *kaupīn* [S.], m. (f., *Pl.*) **1.** loin-cloth (of an ascetic). **2.** transf. the genitals.

क़ौम *qaum* [A. *qaum*], f. **1.** a people; a nation. **2.** tribe. **3.** species; race. — क़ौमपरस्त [P. -*parast*], adj. & m. nationalist. °ई, f.

कौमार *kaumār* [S.], adj. & m. *Pl. HŚS.* **1.** adj. pertaining to a youth, or to a young girl. **2.** pertaining to sexual abstinence or to celibacy. **3.** m. childhood. — कौमार-व्रत, m. vow of celibacy.

कौमार्य *kaumāryă* [S.], m. state of youthfulness: virginity.

क़ौमियत *qaumiyat* [A. *qaumīya*: P. *qaumīyat*], f. nationality.

क़ौमी *qaumī* [A. *qaumī*], adj. **1.** national. **2.** tribal.

कौमुदी *kaumudī* [S.], f. **1.** moonlight (which causes the night-lotus, *kumuda*, to blossom). **2.** the day of full moon in the month Kārttik. **3.** fig. elucidation: commentary, guide (to a text or topic).

कौमोदकी *kaumodăkī* [S.], f. *Pl. HŚS. mythol.* the club of Viṣṇu/Kṛṣṇa.

कौर *kaur* [*kavala-*: ? ← Drav.], m. a mouthful (of food). — ~ करना, 19c. to eat. मुँह का ~, m. the food one eats (or needs, to survive).

कौरव *kaurav* [S.], adj. & m. *mythol.* & *hist.* **1.** adj. connected with Kuru, or the Kurus. **2.** m. a descendant of Kuru.

कौरा *kaurā* [? *kroḍa-*], m. Brbh. side, recess, corner (of a room, a door). — कौरैं, adv. at the side, by the door.

क़ौल *qaul* [A. *qaul*], m. sthg. said: **1.** U. assertion. **2.** promise, word. — ~ का पक्का, or पूरा, or सच्चा, m. true to one's word. ~ तोड़ना, to break one's word. ~ देना (को), to give one's word (to). ~ से फिरना, to go back on one's word. ~ हारना, U. id. – बक़ौल [P. *ba-*], adv. according to the saying (of, के).

[1]**कौल** *kaul* [S.], adj. & m. **1.** adj. of good family. **2.** m. a well-born man.

[2]**कौल** *kaul* [S.: *kola-*[4]], m. *hind.* a follower of Śākta beliefs or practices.

कौली *kaulī* [? *kola-*[2]], f. **1.** bosom; lap; embrace. **2.** armful. — ~ भरना, to embrace.

कौवा *kauvā* [*kāka-*], m. **1.** a crow. **2.** fig. a cunning fellow. **3.** the uvula. — कौवा-डोंडी, f. reg. = घुँघची; a species of Agallochum. कौवा-लुकान, adj. reg. hiding a crow: several inches high (a young crop).

क़ौवाल *qauvāl*, m. see क़व्वाल.

क़ौवाली *qauvālī*, f. see क़व्वाली.

कौश *kauś* [S.], adj. silken (= कौशेय).

कौशल *kauśal* [S.], m. **1.** skill; dexterity. **2.** a craft; handicraft. कला-कौशल, m. id. **3.** craft, cunning. **4.** welfare, prosperity.

कौशल्या *kauśalyā* [S.], f. name of the wife of Daśarath, and mother of Rām.

कौशेय *kauśey* [S], adj. silken.

कौस्तुभ *kaustubh* [S.], m. *mythol.* name of the jewel worn by Kṛṣṇa on his breast.

क्या *kyā* [cf. *kim*], pron. & adj. **1.** (non-initial in sentence) what? यह ~ है? what is this? **2.** (marker of interrogation) is it that…? **3.** rhetor. what a …! how …! — ~ अच्छा! how good! how fine! ~ … ~, whether … or, irrespective of … or. ~ कुछ, what all? what not? sthg. extraordinary. ~ ख़ूब, how splendid! ~ जाने, how can one know? who knows? heaven knows. ~ बात है? what is it? what is the matter? ~ मजाल है, what power has he? (he can do, or dare do, nothing). ~ मुँह लेकर आया? with what face did he come: how dared he come? ~ हुआ? what has happened? what is the matter? आप उनसे ~ ~ कहेंगे? what (various things) will you say to them? और ~? what else; naturally, of course. राजपूतों के ~ कहने हैं! what things there are to tell about the Rajputs! वह ~ जाएगा! iron. he won't go! he'll never go! हिंदी तो ~, वह तमिल भी जानते हैं, what of Hindi, he also knows Tamil. यह ~? why this? why is this so? यह ~ चीज़ है? pej. what (sort of) thing is this? यह एक ही ~, सभी अच्छे हैं! what of this (single) one, all are good!

क्यारी *kyārī* [*kedārikā-*], f. **1.** a bed (of vegetables or flowers); a border. **2.** reg. (W.) a field plot banked up for irrigation.

क्यों *kyoṁ* [*kim*: Ap. *kiṁva*], adv. & interj. **1.** adv. why? **2.** interj. why! — उसके के पास (चाहे) कितना ही पैसा ~ न हो, (फिर भी) उसका कोई आदर नहीं करता, however much money he may have, no one respects him. और जाएँ ~ न, जब कि उन्हें फ़ुरसत हो? and why shouldn't they go, when they have the time?

क्योंकर *kyoṁkar* [H. *kyoṁ*+E.H. *kari*], adv. how? by what means? for what reason, why?

क्योंकि *kyoṁki* [H. *kyoṁ*+H. *ki*], conj. because.

क्योंके *kyoṁke*, adv. = क्योंकर.

क्योड़ा *kyoṛā*, m. pronun. var. = केवड़ा.

क्रंदन *krandan* [S.], m. weeping, lamenting. — ~ करना, to weep.

क्रकच *krakac* [S.], m. *Pl. HŚS.* a saw.

[1]**क्रम** *kram* [S.], m. **1.** a step, pace. **2.** degree, stage; position in a series. **3.** uninterrupted or regular progress; order, succession, sequence. **4.** due method (of procedure). **5.** *rhet.* name of an *alaṅkāra*. **6.** *Pl.* power, strength (= पराक्रम). — ~ (से), turn by turn; gradually, by degrees; in due course or order. ~ करके, obs. gradually; in order; respectively. – क्रम-चय, m. *math.* a permutation. क्रम-बद्ध, adj. ordered, sequential; graded. °ता, f. क्रमशः, adv. gradually, by due stages.

[2]**क्रम** *kram*, m. corr. = कर्म.

क्रव्य *kravyă* [S.], m. poet. flesh: — क्रव्याद [°*a*+*a*°], adj. carnivorous.

क्रय *kray* [S.], m. buying, purchase. — क्रय-विक्रय, m. buying and selling, traffic, trade. क्रय-शक्ति, f. purchasing power.

क्रांत *krānt* [S.], adj. **1.** gone over or across. **2.** surpassed. **3.** overcome; defeated. **4.** checked; suppressed (an uprising).

[1]**क्रांति** *krānti* [S.], f. **1.** revolution. **2.** progress, course (of the sun on the ecliptic). – क्रांतिकारी, adj. & m. revolutionary; a revolutionary. क्रांतिबिंदु, f. critical or decisive point; crisis. क्रांतिवादी, adj. urging revolution, revolutionary.

[2]**क्रांति** *krānti*, f. Brbh. corr. = कांति.

क्रिया *kriyā* [S.], f. **1.** an action, act, deed. **2.** a religious act or ceremony; a pious act, duty; obsequies; an oath. **3.** *gram.* a verb. **4.** obs. business; work, labour; a literary work. — ~ करना, to perform the obsequies (of, की). ~ खाना, to take an oath, to swear (by, की). नित्य ~, f. the recurring functions: excretion; other toilet functions; daily worship. – क्रिया-कर्म, m. religious service or duty, daily observance (as oblations, prayer); funeral ceremonies. क्रिया-कलाप, m. the body of actions enjoined by religion, or performed by an individual. क्रियात्मक [°*ā*+*ā*°], adj. of use, practical. क्रिया-द्योतक, adj. = क्रियावाचक. क्रियानिष्ठ, adj. orthodox (in religious observance). क्रियापद, m. *gram.* a verbal form or construct. क्रिया-भंग, m. the rendering ineffective of a religious act. क्रियार्थक [°*ā*+*a*°] adj. *gram.* verbal. क्रियावाचक, adj. *gram.* verbal. क्रियाविशेषण, m. *gram.* an adverb. क्रियाशील, adj. active, energetic. क्रियेंद्रिय [°*ā*+*i*°], m. an organ of action (= कर्मेंद्रिय, see s.v. कर्म).

क्रिस्तान *kristān* [Pt. *cristão*; × H. *musalmān*, P. *naṣrān*], m., f. a Christian. — ~ हो जाना, to become a Christian.

क्रिस्तानी *kristānī* [cf. H. *kristān*], adj. Christian.

क्रीट *krīṭ*, m. Brbh. = किरीट.

क्रीड़ा *krīṛā* [S.], f. **1.** sport, play; pleasure, amusement. **2.** specif. the sport or pleasure (*līlā*) of Kṛṣṇa as an avatār. — ~ करना, v.t., to play, to sport, &c. – क्रीड़ांगन [°*a*+*ā*°], m. sportsground; stadium. क्रीड़ास्थल, m. the site of Kṛṣṇa's *līlā*; a playground. क्रीड़ित, adj. enacted, played; characterised by *krīṛā* (childhood, youth). जल-क्रीड़ा, f. water-games: Kṛṣṇa's frolics in the Jumna river with the herdgirls of Braj.

क्रीडितृ *krīḍitṛ* [S.], m. *Pl.* a player, one who sports; a gambler.

क्रीत *krīt* [S.], m. bought, purchased. — क्रीत-दास, m. a bought slave.

क्रुद्ध *kruddh* [S.], adj. **1.** angered, angry. **2.** fierce.

[1]**क्रूर** *krūr* [S.], adj. **1.** cruel, harsh; fierce, terrible. **2.** inauspicious (as in epithets of the planets Saturn and Mars). **3.** base, vile; insensitive. — क्रूरकर्म, adj. performing cruel or terrible deeds; unrelenting. क्रूरकोष्ठ, m. *Pl. HŚS.* sluggish bowels. क्रूरचरित, adj. of cruel or harsh conduct. क्रूरदृष्टि, f. malignant glance (as of the evil eye).

[2]**क्रूर** *krūr*, m. Brbh. a contraction of the name Akrūr.

क्रूरता *krūrătā* [S.], f. cruelty, harshness; fierceness, &c. (see [1]क्रूर).

क्रूस *krūs* [Pt. *cruz*], m. a cross.

क्रेता *kretā* [S.], m. inv. a buyer, purchaser.

क्रोड *kroḍ* [S.], f. **1.** the lap. **2.** the interior (of anything); a hollow, cavity. **3.** the open arms, embrace. — क्रोड-पत्र, m. marginal addition; supplement; postscript.

क्रोड़ *kroṛ*, m. see क्रोड.

क्रोध *krodh* [S.], m. anger; rage; resentment. — ~ करना, to be angry (with, पर). ~ दिलाना, to make (one) angry. ~ में आना, to become angry, enraged. – क्रोध-भवन, m. *HŚS.* = कोप-भवन. क्रोधमय, adj. angry, wrathful. क्रोधमान, adj. angry. क्रोधवंत, adj. Brbh. id. क्रोधवश, adj. & m. overpowered by anger, passionate; one prone to anger. क्रोधवान, adj. angry. क्रोधानल [°*dha*+*a*°], m. the fire of (one's) anger.

क्रोधन *krodhan* [S.], m. *Pl. HŚS.* being angry, anger.

क्रोधित *krodhit*, adj. angry, enraged; irritated.

क्रोधी *krodhī* [S.], adj. & m. **1.** adj. angry, hot-tempered. **2.** m. a man prone to anger.

क्रोश *kroś*, m. = कोस.

क्रौंच *kraum̐c* [S.], m. **1.** a wading bird: a kind of bittern, heron, or curlew; ? the Demoiselle crane. **2.** a mountain, part of the Himālaya range (north of Assam). **3.** *mythol.* one of *dvīpas* or principal divisions of the world. **4.** name of a *rākṣas* or demon. **5.** Brbh. name of a weapon.

क्लर्की *klarkī* [cf. H. *klark*: ← Engl.], f. clerk's post or duties.

क्लांत *klānt* [S.], adj. tired, wearied; languid.

क्लांति *klānti* [S.], f. fatigue, weariness; languor.

क्लास *klās* [Engl. *class*], f. m. a (school) class.

क्लासिकी *klāsikī* [Engl. *classical*], adj. classical.

क्लिष्ट *kliṣṭ* [S.], adj. **1.** distressed, sufffering; wretched. **2.** difficult to grasp (as the meaning of a word, or a style of language).

क्लिष्ठता *kliṣṭhătā* [S.], f. distress, &c.; difficulty, unintelligibility (see क्लिष्ट).

क्लीव *klīv* [S.], adj. impotent.

क्लीवता *klīvătā* [S.], f. impotence.

क्लेश *kleś* [S.], m. **1.** affliction, suffering; anguish. **2.** strife, quarrelling. — ~ करना (को), to afflict, to distress. ~ करना (से), to strive (with), quarrel (with); to grieve or to mourn (at). ~ देना (को), = ~ करना (को). ~ मचाना, to stir up strife, &c. – क्लेशमय, adj. full of or consisting of suffering, &c.

क्लेशित *kleśit* [S.], adj. & m. **1.** adj. afflicted, distressed, anquished. **2.** care-worn. **3.** m. an afflicted or suffering person.

क्लैव्य *klaivyă* [S.], m. = क्लीवता.

क्वणित *kvaṇit* [S.], adj. sounded: resounding.

क्वाँरा *kvām̐rā* [*kumāra-*], adj. **1.** young, unmarried. **2.** single; lonely.

क्वाँरी *kvām̐rī* [*kumārikā-*], f. an unmarried girl.

क्वाथ *kvāth* [S.], m. decoction, infusion (as of a herbal medicine).

क्वार *kvār* [*kumāra-*], m. a name of the seventh lunar month (= Āśvin: September-October).

क्वारछल *kvārchal*, m. virginity. — ~ उतरना, virginity to be lost.

क्वारपना *kvārpanā*, m. = क्वारापन.

क्वारा *kvārā*, adj. = क्वाँरा.

क्वारापन *kvārāpan* [cf. H. *kvām̐r*], m. virginity.

क्षण *kṣaṇ* [S.], m. **1.** a moment, an instant; a leisure moment; suitable moment. **2.** the moment or time of a particular event. — ~ ~, adv. moment by moment, from moment to moment; continually, uninterruptedly; gradually. ~ भर (के लिए), adv. for just a moment. ~ भर में, adv. in the space of a moment. ~ मात्र, adv. for just a moment, no more than a moment. – क्षण-भंगुर, adj. ephemeral. क्षणांतर [°*ṇa*+*a*°], adv. a moment afterwards, thereupon.

क्षणिक *kṣaṇik* [S.], adj. momentary, temporary, transitory, fleeting.

क्षत *kṣat* [S.], adj. **1.** wounded, hurt. **2.** damaged; having suffered loss or damage. — क्षत-विक्षत, adj. extensively wounded, &c.

क्षति *kṣati* [S.], f. **1.** damage, loss, detriment. **2.** injury; destruction. — ~ देना, or पहुँचाना, to do damage (to, को). – क्षति-ग्रस्त, adj. damaged. क्षति-पूर्ति भत्ता, m. compensatory allowance, compensation.

क्षत्राणी *kṣatrāṇī* [ad. *kṣatriyāṇī-*], f. **1.** a woman of the kṣatriya caste group. **2.** the wife of a kṣatriya, or of a khatrī.

क्षत्रिय *kṣatriyă* [S.], m. a member of the second *varṇa* (q.v.) of later Indo-Aryan society.

क्षत्रियता *kṣatriyătā* [S.], f. the status or condition of a kṣatriya.

क्षपा *kṣapā* [S.], f. night.

क्षम- *kṣam-* [ad. *kṣamayati*], v.t. Brbh. to pardon, to forgive.

क्षमता *kṣamătā* [S.], f. ability; capacity, fitness.

क्षमा *kṣamā* [S.], f. forgiveness, pardon, absolution. — **~ करना (को)**, to forgive, to pardon, to excuse. – **क्षमा-याचना**, f. entreaty for forgiveness. **क्षमा-योग्य**, adj. pardonable, venial. **क्षमावान**, adj. forgiving. **क्षमा-शील**, adj. of forgiving disposition. **°ता**, f. **क्षमा-सागर**, m. ocean of forgiveness: title of a deity viewed as supreme being.

क्षमित *kṣamit* [S.], adj. pardoned. — **~ कर देना**, to pardon.

क्षमी *kṣamī* [S.], adj. Brbh. of a forgiving nature, &c. (see **क्षमा**).

क्षम्य *kṣamyă* [S.], adj. forgivable, excusable.

क्षय *kṣay* [S.], m. **1.** decline, decrease; loss, wane. **2.** destruction; end, termination (esp. of the world or universe). ***3.** decay, wasting. **4.** tuberculosis. — **क्षय-काल**, m. *hind.* the *pralay* or end of the world. **क्षय-पक्ष**, m. fortnight of the waning moon. **क्षय-रोग**, m. tuberculosis. **°ई**, adj. & m. consumptive; one suffering from tuberculosis.

क्षयिष्णु *kṣayiṣṇu* [S.], adj. prone or fated to decline or to decay.

क्षयी *kṣayī* [S.], adj. declining, decaying.

क्षर *kṣar* [S.], adj. & m. **1.** adj. perishing, impermanent. **2.** m. anything which must perish.

क्षरण *kṣaraṇ* [S.], m. **1.** a flowing, distilling, dropping. **2.** erosion. **3.** corr. ? an alkaline product.

क्षांत *kṣānt* [S.], adj. patient, enduring, forbearing.

क्षांति *kṣānti* [S.], f. patience, endurance, forbearance.

क्षात्र *kṣātr* [S.], adj. & m. **1.** adj. having to do with the kṣatriya caste group. **2.** m. the kṣatriya caste group.

क्षार *kṣār* [S.], adj. & m. **1.** adj. salty. **2.** alkaline. **3.** caustic, corrosive; pungent. **4.** m. any corrosive substance, esp. an alkali; caustic soda or potash; burnt lime (**चूने का ~**). 5. = **काला नमक**. **6.** borax. **7.** salt. **8.** ashes.

क्षारक *kṣārak* [S.], adj. caustic.

क्षिति *kṣiti* [S.], f. the earth. — **क्षितिज**, m. earth-born: the horizon. **क्षितितल**, m. surface or region of the earth.

क्षिप्र *kṣipră* [S.], adj. swift.

क्षीण *kṣīṇ* [S.], adj. **1.** diminished, reduced. **2.** wasted, decayed; destroyed, lost. **हमारा बुधि-बल ~**, our wisdom and strength are gone (poet). **3.** enfeebled; thin, wasted. **4.** slight, slender; subtle. **चाँद का ~ प्रकाश**, the moon's faint light. **5.** miserable, poor. — **क्षीणकर**, adj. causing diminution, wasting, &c. **क्षीणकाय**, adj. of very slight or frail build. **क्षीण-चंद्र**, m. the early waxing or late waning moon. **क्षीणमन**, adj. of weak mind; of decayed mental powers; of subtle intellect. **क्षीण-रोग**, m. a wasting sickness.

क्षीणता *kṣīṇătā* [S.], f. **1.** a reduced or wasted state. **2.** feebleness. **3.** slenderness, frailty; subtlety.

क्षीयमाण *kṣīyămāṇ* [S.], adj. wasting away, perishing.

क्षीर *kṣīr* [S.], m. **1.** milk. **2.** thickened milk (cf. **खीर**). **3.** the milky juice or sap of plants. — **क्षीर-निधि**, f. *mythol.* the ocean of milk. **क्षीर-नीर**, m. milk and water, milk mixed with water. **क्षिर-नीर करना**, to discriminate (as between good and bad). **क्षीर-पाक**, adj. & m. cooked in milk; an Ayurvedic medicine, prepared with milk. **क्षीरमय**, adj. composed of or consisting of milk. **क्षीर-व्रत**, m. a fast or observance during which only milk is taken. **क्षीर-सागर**, m. = **क्षीर-निधि**.

क्षुद्र *kṣudră* [S.], adj. **1.** small, minute; trifling. ***2.** mean, base; contemptible. **3.** niggardly. **4.** poor. — **~ जीव**, m. a lower animal, brute beast.

क्षुद्रता *kṣudrătā* [S.], f. **1.** meanness, pettiness, &c. **2.** inferiority, insignificance.

क्षुधा *kṣudhā* [S.], f. hunger, appetite; desire. — **क्षुधार्त** [°*dhā* + *ā*°], adj. pained by, or faint with, hunger.

क्षुधालु *kṣudhālu* [S.], adj. hungry.

क्षुधित *kṣudhit* [S.], adj. hungry.

क्षुब्ध *kṣubdh* [S.], m. agitated, &c. (see **क्षोभ**).

क्षुर *kṣur* [S.], m. a hoof.

क्षेत्र *kṣetr* [S.], m. **1.** a region, zone, or area; locality, district; precinct. **2.** land; an enclosed plot of land, a field. **3.** extent, area (= **क्षेत्रफल**). **4.** any sphere of action or operation; a partic. topic or area. **5.** *philos.* the body (considered as the field of the indwelling and working of the soul). **6.** *geom.* a figure, diagram. — **क्षेतरज्ञ**, m. *philos.* the soul. **क्षेत्रफल**, m. area, extent. **क्षेत्र-पाल**, m. one who oversees or guards a field. **क्षेत्र-सीमा**, f. the boundaries of a field, or of a sacred place. **क्षेत्राधिकार** [°*ra* + *a*°], m. *law.* jurisdiction.

क्षेत्रीय *kṣetrīyă* [S.], adj. having to do with a locality, &c. (see क्षेत्र).

क्षेप *kṣep* [S.], m. **1.** a throw, cast (as of a net, or a load being carried). **2.** a trip, journey (with a load); turn. **3.** a load.

क्षेपक *kṣepak* [S.], m. an additional quantity: interpolation (in a text).

क्षेपण *kṣepaṇ* [S.], m. a casting, throwing, impelling.

क्षेम *kṣem* [S.], m. & adv. **1.** m. easy or comfortable state, well-being; tranquillity, security. **2.** safety, happiness, prosperity. **3.** adv. (rare) at ease, secure, &c. — **वे कुशल-क्षेम से हैं**, they are well, thriving.

क्षोभ *kṣobh* [S.], m. **1.** agitation, disturbance (of mind). **2.** distress, anguish. **3.** ill-will, malice.

क्षौर *kṣaur* [S.], m. *hind.* shaving of the head (or beard) (= **मुंडन**). — **~ कर्म**, m. the ceremony of shaving the head.

ख

ख *kha*, the second consonant of the Devanāgarī syllabary. — **खकार**, m. the sound /kh/; the letter **ख**. **खगोल**, m. see s.v. **खद्योत**, m. see s.v.

खँख *khaṁkh*, adj. reg. = **खँखड़**.

खँखड़ *khaṁkhaṛ* [conn. *khakkhaṭa-*], adj. & m. **1.** adj. hard; dry and crackling; shrivelled, withered. **2.** m. anything hard, &c.; a skeleton.

खँखार *khaṁkhār* [**khaṅkhār-*], m. **1.** the sound of clearing the throat. **2.** phlegm; spittle.

खँखारना *khaṁkhārnā* [cf. **khaṁkhār-*], v.i. **1.** to clear the throat. **2.** to spit or to cough up mucus.

खंग *khaṅg* [S.], m. = **खड्ग**.

खंगड़ *khaṅgaṛ*, m. any hard or dry object, or substance (= **खँखड़**).

खँगालना *khaṁgālnā* [**khaṅkhālayati*], v.t. **1.** to wash, to wash out; to rinse. **2.** colloq. to make a clean sweep (thieves, of a house). **3.** fig. to plumb, to probe.

खँचिया *khaṁciyā* [cf. **khañca-*], f. reg. a small wicker basket.

खंजन *khañjan* [S.], m. a wagtail.

ख़ंजर *k͟hañjar* [A. *k͟hanjar*], m. a curved dagger.

[1]**ख़ंजरी** *k͟hañjărī* [P. *k͟hanjarī*], f. a small tambourine.

[2]**ख़ंजरी** *k͟hañjărī* [A. *k͟hanjar*+P. *-ī*], f. *Pl.* a kind of striped silk.

[1]**खंड** *khaṇḍ* [ad. *khaṇḍa-*[1]], m. **1.** a piece, fragment; part. **2.** a division; floor, or apartment (of a house); region (of a country, or of the world); section, segment; chapter; fascicule. — ~ **करना**, to smash to pieces, to demolish. – **खंड-कथा**, f. an episodic narrative; episode in a narrative. **खंड-काव्य**, m. a narrative poem not dealing with a heroic or sacred subject. **खंड-ग्रहण**, m. a partial eclipse. **नव-खंड**, m. nine continents: the nine fabled regions of the world.

[2]**खंड** *khaṇḍ* [S.], m. Brbh. coarse sugar (= **खाँड़**). — **खंडसारी**, f. = ~.

खंडन *khaṇḍan* [S.], m. **1.** breaking into pieces; destroying; dividing; interrupting; preventing. **2.** refuting, contradicting; belying; revoking. — ~ **करना**, to break, to divide; to refute, to prove wrong. – **खंडन-मंडन**, m. refutation and elaboration (of a topic under discussion): arguing for and against.

खंडनीय *khaṇḍănīyă* [S.], adj. to be rejected, or refuted.

खंडर *khaṇḍar*, m. pronun. var. = **खंडहर**.

खँड़र *khaṁṛar*, m. pronun. var. = **खंडहर**.

खँडरा *khaṁḍrā* [cf. *khaṇḍa-*[2]], m. Av. a kind of sweet made from pulse and flour.

खंडरीच *khaṁḍărīc* [ad. *khañjarīṭa-*: metath.], m. reg. a wagtail.

खंडहर *khaṇḍhar* [**khaṇḍaghara-*], m. & adj. **1.** m. a ruin, ruined building. **2.** a dilapidated building. **3.** sg. or pl. mass of ruins (as of a village or town). **4.** adj. ruined; dilapidated.

खँड़हर *khaṁṛ'har*, m. = **खंडहर**.

खंडा *khaṇḍā* [*khaṇḍa-*[1]], m. E.H. broken rice; reg. (E.) a fragment.

खंडित *khaṇḍit* [S.], adj. **1.** broken into pieces; destroyed; split, divided; interrupted, broken off (as proceedings). **2.** made imperfect; refuted; contradicted; impugned; disappointed (as trust, hope). — ~ **करना**, to break, to destroy, &c.

खंडिता *khaṇḍitā* [S.], f. *rhet.* a woman whose husband or lover has been unfaithful.

ख़ंदक़ *k͟handaq* [A. *k͟handaq*], f. **1.** ditch, moat. **2.** *mil.* trench; shelter.

ख़ंदाँ *k͟handāṁ* [P. *k͟handān*], adj. S.H. smiling, laughing.

खंधक *khandhak*, m. pronun. var. = **ख़ंदक़**.

खंबा *khambā*, m. pronun. var. = **खंभा**.

खंभा *khambhā* [*skambha-*[1]], m. a pillar; pole, post, stake. — **बिजली का** ~, m. an electric light pole. **खंभे**, pl. specif. the two perpendiculars supporting the cross-beam or rod over a well-mouth.

खंभार *khambhār*, m. Brbh. distress, anguish.

खँभार *khaṁbhār* [? **skambhabhāra-*], m. Brbh. concern; distress.

खकारना *khakārnā*, v.i. pronun. var. = **खँखारना**.

खक्खा *khakkhā* [cf. *khakkhati*], m. loud laughter. — ~ मारना, or लगाना, to guffaw.

खखार *khakhār*, m. pronun. var. = खँखार.

खखोलना *khakholnā* [?? conn. **khokkha-*], v.t. to search for, to search out (among many objects).

खग *khag* [S.], m. moving in the air or sky: a bird; a heavenly body; a divine or semi-divine being; a cloud. — खग-केतु, m. id. खग नाथ, m. = खगेस. खग-पति, m. id. खगेस [°*a*+*ī*°], m. Brbh. Av. lord of birds: Garuṛ, the vehicle of Viṣṇu.

खगहा *khag'hā* [cf. *khaḍga-*], m. a rhinoceros.

खगोल *khagol* [S.], m. **1.** the vault or sphere of the heavens. **2.** a planet. — खगोल-मिति, f. measuring or mapping the heavens. खगोल-विद्या, f. astronomy.

खगोलक *khagolak*, [S.], m. = खगोल.

खग्ग *khagg*, m. reg. = खड्ग.

खच-खच *khac-khac* [onom.], f. a splashing or squelching noise (= पच-पच).

खचड़ा *khacṛā* [cf. H. [1]*khacnā*], adj. ? crowded.

[1]**खचना** *khacnā* [**khacyate*], v.i. & v.t. **1.** v.i. to be fastened or joined; to be set (in); to be studded (with); to be inlaid. **2.** to be crowded, packed (into); to be packed out (as seating-space). **3.** v.t. to set (of jewels), to inlay. — खचाखच, adj. crowded, packed tightly. गाड़ी खचाखच भरी थी, the train was packed full. तलवारें खचाखच चलने लगीं, swords began to be wielded furiously.

[2]**खचना** *khacnā* [cf. H. [1]*khāṁcnā*], v.t. to be cut, or engraved (as lettering in rock).

खचर-खचर *khacar-khacar*, m. खच-खच.

ख़चर-ख़चर *k͟hacar-k͟hacar*, m. a splashing, or squelching sound (= खचर-खचर).

खचित *khacit* [S.], adj. **1.** fastened; set (into, में), inlaid (of jewels). **2.** crowded, packed (with, से).

खचेड़ना *khaceṛnā* [cf. **khañca-*], v.t. to drag, to drag along.

ख़च्चर *k͟haccar*, m. a mule.

खजला *khajlā*, m. = खाजा.

ख़ज़ानची *k͟hazāncī* [P. *k͟hizāncī*], m. **1.** treasurer. **2.** cashier.

ख़ज़ाना *k͟hazānā* [A. *k͟hizāna*], m. **1.** treasury; store. **2.** finance, revenue. **3.** a treasure. — खुले ख़ज़ाने, adv. openly, publicly.

खजुरा *khajurā*, m. reg. = खजूरा.

खजूर *khajūr* [*kharjūra-*], m. **1.** the date-palm; the wild date. **2.** a date. **3.** a sweet made of wheat flour (shaped like a date).

[1]**खजूरा** *khajūrā* [*kharjūra-*], m. *Pl. HŚS.* ridgepole of a thatched house.

[2]**खजूरा** *khajūrā* [*kharjūraka-*], m. *Pl. HŚS.* a centipede (= कनखजूरा).

खजूरी *khajūrī* [*kharjūraka-*], adj. **1.** having to do with the date-palm. **2.** made of date leaves (as a fan, a basket), or resembling them in shape. **3.** plaited, twisted.

खट *khaṭ* [cf. H. *khaṭkhaṭānā*], f. the sound of knocking, &c.; noise. — खट-खट, f. repeated knocking; noise, clatter; wrangling. खट-खट करना, to knock, to make a clatter, &c. °इया, adj. & m., f. noisy; restless, fidgety; quarrelsome; a noisy person, &c.; °इया पावड़ी, wooden-soled sandals (= खड़ाऊँ). खट-पट, f. noise, clatter, clashing; wrangling, quarrel. °-पटिया, adj. & m. noisy; quarrelsome; a noisy person, &c.; wooden-soled sandals. — खटखटा, m. a rattle (to scare away birds); wrangling, discord; colloq. trouble, troublesome matter; care, anxiety. खटाखट, adv. forcefully and continuously; quickly. काम खटाखट हो रहा है, work is in full swing. खटापटी, f. = खट-पट.

[1]**खट-** *khaṭ-* [H. *khāṭ*], f. bedstead, bed: — खटबुना, m. a stringer of beds. खटमल, m. a bed-bug. °ई, adj. pej. of a purplish colour. खट-मुत्ता, m. a bed-wetter.

[2]**खट-** *khaṭ-* [S. *ṣaṭ*], adj. six: — खटपद, m. an insect: type of large black bee. °ई, f. खट-रस, m. the six literary savours (*ras*). खटराग, m. discordant singing; discord; assortment of belongings. खटराग लाना, to make a noise or row; to create discord. क्या खटराग जमा किया है आपने? what's all this collection of things?

[3]**खट-** *khaṭ-*, adj. = खट्टा.

खटक *khaṭak*, f. = खटका.

खटकना *khaṭaknā* [cf. H. *khaṭ*], v.i. **1.** to sound, to rattle. **2.** to be a cause of unease, misgivings, or hesitation (to, को). यह प्रयोग ज़रा खटकता है, this usage does not seem quite right. उसे कुछ ऐसा खटक रहा है कि ..., he is rather concerned that ... **3.** to be inconvenient or burdensome (to, को); to rankle (in, में), to be cause for quarrel, or dissension.

खटका *khaṭkā* [cf. H. *khaṭ*], m. **1.** the sound of knocking, rattling, &c.; sound of footsteps. **2.** device making such a sound; a bolt or catch (as of a door, a rifle); a switch; winder (of a watch); a scarecrow which is made to rattle by pulling a string. **3.** unease (of mind);

misgiving; scruple; anxiety, care; apprehension. — ~ लगना (को), to feel misgivings, &c.

खटकाना *khaṭkānā* [cf. H. *khaṭaknā*], v.t. **1.** to make a sound of knocking or rattling; to knock at, to slam, to rattle (as a door). **2.** to cause unease, misgivings, &c.

खटखटाना *khaṭkhaṭānā* [conn. *khaṭakhaṭāyate*], v.t. to make a knocking or rattling noise. — दरवाज़ा ~, to knock at a door. उसे खटखटाए चलो, colloq. jog his memory.

खटना *khaṭnā* [*khaṭṭayati*], v.i. **1.** to continue, or to hold fast (in a burdensome activity); to work hard or doggedly. **2.** to remain over; to be earned. — सुबह से शाम तक ~, to toil from morning to evening.

खटरिया *khaṭariyā* [? **khaṭvāripu-*], m. *Pl. HŚS.*. a kind of insect, or bug.

खटला *khaṭlā* [?? conn. **ṣaṭ-rāga-*], m. *Pl. HŚS.* wife and family, household, baggage.

खटवाँस *khaṭvāṁs*, m. retiring (sulkily or angrily) to bed.

खटवाट *khaṭvāṭ* [**khaṭvāpaṭṭa-*], m. Av. bed-board(s), bed.

खटवारी *khaṭvārī*, f. reg. (W.) a manure pit.

खटाई *khaṭāī* [cf. H. *khaṭṭā*], f. **1.** sourness, acidity or tartness. **2.** any acid substance; a particular spice. — ~ करना (की), to spoil, to turn sour (as pleasure). ~ खाना, v.t. to take sour substances; to be or to become pregnant. ~ में डालना, to place in acid; to lay aside (a matter); to keep (a person) in suspense. ~ में पड़ना, to be placed in acid (for cleaning); to be put aside, left undecided (a matter).

खटाक *khaṭāk* [cf. H. *khaṭ*], m. a crashing noise. — ~ से, adv., with a crash, or a rush.

खटाका *khaṭākā*, m. = खटाक.

[1]**खटाना** *khaṭānā* [cf. H. *khaṭṭā*], v.i. to become sour, acid or tart.

[2]**खटाना** *khaṭānā* [conn. *khaṭṭayati*], v.i. Brbh. to find a resting-place or support; to maintain oneself, to exist.

[1]**खटास** *khaṭās* [cf. *khaṭṭa-*[1]], f. sourness, acidity, tartness of taste.

[2]**खटास** *khaṭās* [*khaṭṭāśa-*], m. an animal of the weasel family.

खटिक *khaṭik*, m. **1.** a seller of vegetables and fruit; reg. a distiller. **2.** a member of the *khaṭik* community.

खटिका *khaṭikā* [S.], Brbh. chalk (= खड़िया).

खटिया *khaṭiyā* [cf. H. *khāṭ*], f. a small bedstead or bed.

खटीक *khaṭīk*, m. **1.** Raj. Panj. a dealer in hides, a tanner; butcher. **2.** *Pl.* a hunter. **3.** *Pl.* a keeper of pigs and poultry.

खटोलना *khaṭolnā*, m. reg. **1.** = खटोला. **2.** transf. *Pl.* a kind of net or snare.

खटोला *khaṭolā* [cf. *khaṭvā-*], m. a small bedstead, or bed. — उड़न-खटोला, m. flying bedstead: magic carpet.

खट्टा *khaṭṭā* [*khaṭṭa-*[1]], adj. & m. **1.** adj. acid, sour, tart. **2.** m. a citron. — जी (or मन) ~ होना, to be displeased, or depressed. दाँत खट्टे करना (के), fig. to give a reverse (to), to discomfit. मन ~ करना, to disappoint (one). – खट्टा-चूक, adj. very sour. खट्टा-मीठा or °मिट्ठा, adj. & m. sour and sweet; a mixed taste; a pleasant taste. खट्टे-मीठे दिन, good and bad times. खट्टा-मीठा खाना, to take the good with the bad.

खट्टापन *khaṭṭāpan* [H. *khaṭṭā*], m. sourness, acidity, tartness.

खट्टिक *khaṭṭik*, m. *Pl. HŚS.* = खटीक.

खट्टू *khaṭṭū* [cf. H. *khaṭnā*], adj. colloq. industrious.

खड्ग *khaḍgă* [S.], m. a sword.

खड़ *khaṛ* [*khaṭa-*, *khaḍa-*: ← Drav.], f. reg. (Bihar) grass, straw; long thatching grass; grass and trees (cf. [3]खर). — खड़-बीहड़, adj. rough (ground, or way).

खड़ंक *khaṛaṅk*, adj. dry, dried up (as bread, &c).

खड़ंख *khaṛaṅkh*, adj. pronun. var. = खड़ंक.

खड़ंजा *khaṛañjā*, m. reg. (W.) a row of bricks (esp. as laid in a floor or on the ground).

[1]**खड़क** *khaṛak* [cf. H. *khaṛaknā*], f. **1.** the sound of knocking, &c. (= खटक). **2.** a shooting pain (= कसक).

[2]**खड़क** *khaṛak* [? conn. *khaḍaka-*, H. *khaṛā*], m. reg. (W.) **1.** a hurdle used as a door. **2.** cow-shed; pen, pound.

खड़कना *khaṛaknā*, v.i. = खटकना.

[1]**खड़का** *khaṛkā*, m. = खटका.

[2]**खड़का** *khaṛkā*, m. *Pl.* a stalk; toothpick (cf. खरका).

खड़काना *khaṛkānā* [cf. H. *khaṛaknā*], v.t. = खटकाना.

खड़खड़ *khaṛkhaṛ* [cf. H. *khaṛkhaṛānā*], f. = खड़खड़ाहट. — ~ शब्द, m. sound of the rustling of fallen leaves.

खड़खड़ाना *khaṛkhaṛānā* [*khaṭakhaṭāyate*], v.i. & v.t. **1.** v.i. to knock, to rattle; to clatter; to rustle (dry leaves). **2.** v.t. to make a knocking or rattling sound, to make a noise or clatter with; to brandish (a sword; sc. to draw with a rasping sound). **3.** to grind (the teeth).

खड़खड़ाहट *kharkharāhaṭ* [cf. H. *kharkharānā*], f. a knocking, or rattling sound, &c.; a rustling sound (as of fallen leaves).

खड़खड़िया *kharkhariyā* [cf. H. *kharkharānā*], m. colloq. a dummy cart (used in training horses); a rattle-trap.

खड़ग *kharag*, m. = खड्ग.

खड़बड़ *kharbar* [cf. *khaṭakhaṭāyate*, and H. *khalbal*], f. noise, tumult; confusion.

खड़बड़ा *kharbarā* [cf. H. *kharbar*], adj. noisy, tumultuous; confused.

खड़बड़ाना *kharbarānā* [cf. H. *kharbar*], v.i. & v.t. **1.** v.i. to be noisy, tumultuous, or confused. **2.** v.t. to stir up noise, &c.

खड़बड़ाहट *kharbarāhaṭ* [cf. H. *kharbarānā*], f. = खड़बड़.

खड़मंडल *kharmaṇḍal*, m. confusion; wrangling.

खड़ल *kharal*, f. ? m. *Pl.* = खरल.

खड़सान *kharsān*, m. *Pl. HŚS.* a whetstone (= खरसान).

खड़ा *kharā* [*khaḍaka-*], adj. & m. **1.** adj. standing, erect; perpendicular; steep. ~ **खेत**, m. a standing, or ripe, crop; *geom.* a vertical plane. **खड़ी पाई**, f. the *daṇḍa* or vertical mark of punctuation. **2.** abrupt. ~ **जवाब**, m. a blunt answer; an unceremonious refusal. **3.** stationary; parked, moored; aground; inert, stagnant. ~ **पानी**, stagnant water. **4.** on call, waiting; ready (as cash); continual, constant; awaiting completion, or processing. ~ **चना**, m. whole grain. **खड़ी दाल**, m. uncooked or half-cooked lentils. **5.** final. ~ **दाँव**, m. the last stake. **6.** m. a perpendicular. — ~ **करना**, to set up, to erect; to lift up; to raise (a question); to institute, to initiate; to instigate; to obtain (as money, for a purpose); to bring to a stop (as a vehicle); to fix, to station; to prepare. ~ **रखना**, to support, to maintain. ~ **रहना**, to remain standing; to stay, to wait. ~ **होना**, to stand; to stand up; to rear up; to be set up, &c. (cf. ~ **करना**). **खड़ी लगाना**, to tread water (in swimming). **खड़े पाँव**, adv. immediately, without delay. **बिगड़ ~ होना**, to bridle (at sthg., **पर**), to take strong exception (to). **भाग ~ होना**, to halt after fleeing: to escape successfully. – **खड़े-खड़े**, adv. standing all the while: immediately, promptly, forthwith; within a short while.

खड़ाऊँ *kharāūṁ* [conn. **kāṣṭhapādukā-*: MIA **khaḍa-*], m. a wooden-soled sandal.

खड़ाका *kharākā*, m. = खटाक.

खड़ापन *kharāpan* [cf. H. *kharā-*] erectness, uprightness; steepness; abruptness.

¹खड़िया *khariyā* [*khaṭikā-*], f. **1.** white clay (= ~ **मिट्टी**). **2.** chalk.

²खड़िया *khariyā* [cf. H. *khar*], f. net for a load (as of grass, straw).

खड़ुवा *kharuvā* [*khaḍū-²*], m. a type of women's metal bracelet.

खड्ग *khaḍgă* [S.], m. a sword, scimitar. — ~ **मारना (को)**, to strike (one) with a sword. – **खड्गहस्त**, adj. having sword in hand.

खड्गी *khaḍgī* [S.], adj. & m. **1.** adj. armed with a sword. **2.** m. a person armed with a sword.

खड्ड *khaḍḍ* [**khaḍḍa-*], m. **1.** a pit; a gap. **2.** low ground between hills; a pass, saddle. **3.** ravine.

खड्डा *khaḍḍā* [**khaḍḍa-*], m. reg. **1.** a pit; hollow. **2.** dimple.

ख़त *k͟hat* [A. *k͟hatt*], m. line, mark: **1.** a letter. **2.** handwriting. **3.** m. f. down on the face; sideburns, beard. — ~ **आना**, a letter to arrive; down to appear (on the face); sideburns to grow. ~ **निकलना**, id., 2., 3. ~ **बनाना**, to trim sideburns. – **ख़तकशी** [P. *-kaśī*], f. fine writing, calligraphy. **ख़त-किताबत**, f. correspondence.

ख़तना *k͟hatnā* [A. *k͟hatna*], m. *musl.* circumcision. — ~ **करना (का)**, to circumcise.

ख़तम *k͟hatm*, m. see ख़त्म.

ख़तरनाक *k͟hatarnāk* [P. *k͟haṭarnāk*], adj. dangerous; risky.

ख़तरा *k͟hatrā* [A. *k͟hatra*], m. danger; risk. — ~ **मोल लेना**, to court danger; to incur risk gratuitously. **ख़तरे की ज़ंजीर**, f. emergency chain. **ख़तरे में डालना**, to expose (as life) to danger.

ख़ता *k͟hatā* [A. *k͟hatā*], f. **1.** a mistake; slip, oversight. **2.** miss (as of an arrow). **3.** fault. — ~ **करना**, to err, to be at fault; to miss (a mark). ~ **खाना**, to suffer, to pay for an error. – **ख़तावार** [P. *-vār*], adj. U. at fault, guilty.

खतियाना *khatiyānā* [cf. H. *khātā*], v.t. to enter in an account-book or ledger.

खतौनी *khataunī* [cf. **khatāvnā*, v.t., H. *khātā*], f. **1.** a ledger, account-book; a volume or paper containing separate accounts or items. **2.** a paṭvārī's roll or list of village lands with details of distribution and assessment. **3.** the entering of accounts.

खत्तरी *khattrī*, m. see खत्री.

खत्ता *khattā* [*khātra-*: ← Drav.], m. **1.** a pit (esp. for storing grain, &c). **2.** a granary, or receptacle for storage. **3.** reg. (Bihar) a ditch (serving as boundary).

खत्ती *khattī*, f. = खत्ता. — खत्ती-भरा अनाज, m. grain stored away in the granary.

ख़त्म *khatm* [A. *khatm*], m. & adj. **1.** m. end. **2.** adj. finished, completed, done; exhausted (as a commodity). — ~ करना, to finish; euph. to do for, to kill. ~ होना, to come to an end, to finish, to stop; to be finished, exhausted.

खत्रानी *khatrānī* [*kṣatriyāṇī-*], f. **1.** a woman of the kṣatriya caste group. **2.** the wife of a kṣatriya, or of a khattrī.

खत्री *khatrī* [*kṣatriya-*: Panj. *khattrī*], m. a member of the khattrī community (merchants and traders).

खदखदाना *khadkhadānā*, v.i. = खदबदाना.

खदबद *khadbad* [onom.], f. the sound of bubbling or boiling. — ~ करना, to boil, to simmer.

खदबदाना *khadbadānā* [cf. H. *khadbad*], v.i. to boil, to simmer; to bubble. (also transf.)

खदर-बदर *khadar-badar*, f. = खदबद, q.v.

खदान *khadān*, f. an excavation; a clay-pit.

खदिर *khadir* [S.], m. the tree *Mimosa catechu* (= खैर).

खदेड़ *khadeṛ* [cf. H. *khadeṛnā*], f. chase, pursuit.

खदेड़ना *khadeṛnā* [**khadd-*], v.t. **1.** to drive away. **2.** to chase, to pursue; to hunt.

खदेरना *khadernā*, v.t. = खदेड़ना.

खद्दर *khaddar* [**khaddara-*: Panj. *khaddar*], m. = खादी.

खद्योत *khadyot* [S.], m. a light in the sky: a firefly.

[1]**खन** *khan* [*kṣaṇa-*], m. Brbh. Av. **1.** a moment, an instant. **2.** a particular day of the lunar fortnight.

[2]**खन** *khan* [? *khaṇḍa-*[1] × P. *khāna*], m. division, partition; storey, floor (of a house).

[3]**खन** *khan* [cf. *khaṇakhaṇāyate*], f. chink, jingle. — खन-खन, f. a tinkling sound, &c.

खनखनाहट *khankhanāhaṭ* [cf. H. [3]*khan*], f. chinking, jingling.

खनक *khanak* [cf. H. *khanaknā*], f. **1.** a ringing, clinking or jingling sound. **2.** a clashing or clanking sound; clattering (as of dishes).

खनकना *khanaknā* [cf. *khaṇakhaṇāyate*], v.i. **1.** to clink, to jingle. **2.** to clash; to clatter.

खनकाना *khankānā* [cf. H. *khanaknā*], v.t. **1.** to cause to clink, or to jingle. **2.** to cause to clash, or to clatter.

खनकार *khankār* [cf. H. *khankhanānā*], m. the sound *khan-khan*.

खनखनाना *khankhanānā* [*khaṇakhaṇāyate*], v.i. & v.t. **1.** to clink, to jingle. **2.** to clash; to clatter.

ख़नख़नाना *khankhanānā*, v.i. to speak through the nose.

खनकौआ *khankauā* [cf. H. *khankānā*], adj. ringing true (a coin).

खनता *khantā* [*khanitraka-*], m. reg. a digging implement: crowbar; shovel.

खनती *khantī* [*khanitra-*], f. reg. dimin. = खनता.

खनन *khanan* [S.], m. digging; excavating.

खनना *khannā* [*khanati*], v.t. to dig; to excavate.

खनिज *khanij* [conn. Pk. *khaniya-*], adj. & m. **1.** adj. mineral. **2.** m. a mineral.

खनी *khanī* [*khani-*], f. a pit in which grain is stored.

खपचा *khapcā*, m. 19c. = खपच्ची.

खपची *khapcī*, f. = खपच्ची.

खपच्ची *khapaccī*, f. **1.** a splinter, sliver (of wood or bamboo); skewer. **2.** a lath; splint. **3.** transf. reg. screen.

खपड़ा *khapṛā* [conn. *kharpara-*: MIA *-ḍ-*], m. **1.** a tile (esp. for roofing). **2.** a potsherd; the bottom portion of an earthenware vessel. **3.** colloq. skull; cranium. — खपड़े छाना, to lay tiles (on, पर), to tile.

खपड़ैल *khapṛail* [conn. *kharpara-*: MIA *-ḍ-*], m. a tiled roof. — ~ डालना (पर), to roof with tiles.

खपत *khapat* [cf. H. *khapnā*], f. & adj. **1.** f. consumption, using up; demand (for goods). **2.** *Pl. HŚS.* selling off (of goods), sale. **3.** fitting, accommodating; fit or proper place. उसकी इस जगह में अच्छी ~ है, he has fitted into this place well. **4.** adj. consumed, expended. **5.** [conn. *kṣipta-*: ← Panj.] *Pl.* deranged.

खपती *khaptī* [cf. H. *khapat*], adj. & m. **1.** adj. determined, dogged. **2.** [conn. *kṣipta-*: ← Panj.] *Pl.* deranged. **3.** m. a determined person, &c.

खपना *khapnā* [*kṣapyate*], v.i. **1.** to be consumed, to be used up; to be sold out (an object or commodity). **2.** to be taken in or into; to be absorbed (in or by, में); to be assimilated; to be mixed (into or with); to adjust. **वह यहाँ के जीवन में खप गया है,** he has adjusted to life here. **3.** to fit, to be fitted (into). **4.** to be destroyed, or ruined. **5.** fig. to be afflicted, taxed or exhausted. — **मर खपना,** to be exhausted; to die, to perish.

खपरैल *khaprail*, m. reg. = खपड़ैल.

खपाच *khapāc*, f. *Pl.* = खपच्ची.

खपाट *khapāṭ*, m. **1.** *Pl.* a large piece of split wood; branch broken off a tree. **2.** reg. (W.) wooden side-piece of a bellows.

खपाना *khapānā*, [cf. H. *khapnā*], v.t. **1.** to cause to be exhausted, to exhaust; to use up; to waste. **2.** to take in or into; to absorb; to assimilate; to mix (into, with, में). **3.** to put or to fit (into). **4.** to make an end of, to destroy; to ruin. **5.** fig. to afflict. — **सिर ~ (का),** v.t. fig. to try, to be a trial (to).

खपाव *khapāv* [cf. H. *khapānā*] **1.** consumption, use, expenditure. **2.** absorption, assimilation; adjustment (as to a new situation). **3.** destruction, &c.

खप्पर *khappar* [*kharpara-*], m. **1.** gourd, coconut or other vessel used as a begging bowl or dish. **2.** skull. — **~ भरना (का),** to give alms to (a yogī, in the name of Śiva).

ख़फ़गी *khafgī* [P. *khafagī*], f. displeasure (with, से or पर). — **~ करना,** to be angry (with, पर).

ख़फ़ा *khafā* [P. *khafa*], adj. inv. displeased, angry (with, से). — **~ करना,** to make (one, को) displeased, or angry.

ख़बर *khabar* [A. *khabar*], f. **1.** news; information. **2.** report, notification; message. **3.** rumour. **4.** fig. heed, care, attention. **5.** fig. good judgment or sense. — **~ उड़ाना,** to spread a rumour, or rumours. **~ करना (को),** to inform (of, की); to report (to). **~ देना (को),** to inform (of, की). **~ मिलना,** news to be received (by, को). **~ रखना,** to be informed (of, की), to bear in mind; to be on the alert. **~ लगाना,** to search (for, की), to trace (as stolen goods). **~ लेना,** to pay heed (to, की); to be mindful (of); to look (after); to watch (over); to enquire (into, or about); to look (up), to visit; colloq. to account for, to settle the hash (of). **~ होना (को),** to have knowledge (of, की). **~ है कि ...** it is learned that .... – **ख़बरगीर** [P. *-gīr*], m. an informer, spy. **°ई,** f. informing. **ख़बरदार** [P. *-dār*], adj. & interj. watchful, careful; be careful! **ख़बरदार करना,** to forewarn. **°ई,** f. watchfulness, care; charge, care, guardianship; guard. **ख़बरदारी करना,** to take care, &c. (of, की). **ख़बर-नवीस** [P. *-navīs*], m. informer, spy, agent. **°ई,** f. spying.

ख़बीस *khabīs* [A. *khabīṣ*], adj.& m. **1.** adj. bad, wicked. **2.** foul. **3.** m. wretch; villain; miser. **4.** an evil spirit.

ख़ब्त *khabt* [A. *khabṭ*], m. **1.** madness. ***2.** obsession; craze; whim. — **~ चढ़ना,** or **सवार होना (पर),** an obsession to seize (one). – **ख़ब्तुलहवास,** adj. = ख़ब्ती. **°ई,** f.

ख़ब्ती *khabtī* [P. *khabṭī*], adj. mad, crazy.

खब्बा *khabbā* [*kharva-*], adj. & m. N. **1.** adj. left (hand). **2.** m. a left-handed person.

खभार *khabhār*, m. Av. concern, distress (= खँभार).

ख़म *kham* [P. *kham*], m. **1.** bend; curve. **2.** coil, curl. **3.** sthg. bent or crooked. **4.** reverse, defeat. — **~ ठोंकना,** to slap the hands on the arms (as showing readiness to fight, or to set to). **~ बजाना,** or **मारना,** id. – **ख़मदार** [P. *-dār*], adj. U. bent, crooked.

खमस *khamas* [?? ad. *ūṣmā-*], adj. & m. **1.** adj. humid. ***2.** m. humidity.

ख़मियाज़ा *khamiyāzā* [P. *khamiyāza*], m. stretching: punishment. — **~ उठाना,** or **खींचना,** or **भरना,** to reap the (bitter) fruit (of, का).

ख़मी *khamī* [P. *khamī*], f. crookedness.

ख़मीर *khamīr* [A. *khamīr*], m. **1.** leaven; yeast. **2.** kneaded and leavened dough. **3.** fig. the stuff of (one's) nature. — **~ उठना,** to ferment; to rise (dough).

ख़मीरा *khamīrā* [A. *khamīra*], m. & adj. **1.** m. = ख़मीर. **2.** a thick syrup (medicinal). **3.** a fragrant tobacco. **4.** adj. leavened.

ख़मोश *khamoś*, adj. pronun. var. = ख़ामोश.

ख़मोशी *khamośī*, f. pronun. var. = ख़ामोशी.

खम्माच *khammāc*, f. *mus.* name of a *rāgiṇī* (attached to Mālkos *rāg*).

खम्माज *khammāj*, f. = खम्माच.

खम्हाउर *khamhāur* reg. (Bihar) a yam.

ख़यानत *khayānat* [A. *khiyāna*: P. *khiyānat*], f. breach of trust. — **~ करना,** to be unfaithful to a trust.

ख़याल *khayāl* [A. *khayāl*], m. usu. /xjal/, /xijal/. **1.** thought, idea. **2.** opinion. **3.** notion, fancy. **4.** fig. the mind. **5.** regard, attention (to someone or sthg.); care. **6.** ghost, phantom. **7.** *mus.* a north Indian style of singing, or instrumental music, said to date from the 15th century, consisting of variations on a short phrase. — **~ आना,** a thought to occur (to, को).

~ करना, to think (of, का), to consider; to imagine, to fancy; to attend (to), to take care or heed (of). ~ न रहना, to be forgotten, to escape memory. ~ पड़ना, to occur (to, को), to seem; the mind to be fixed or set (on). ~ बाँधना, to form an idea (of or about, का), to imagine; to build castles in the air; to arrange one's thoughts. ~ में न लाना, to give no thought (to, को); to disregard; to take no notice or heed (of). ~ में रहना, to be always thinking (of sthg). ~ रखना, to bear in mind; to pay due attention (to, का), fig. to keep one's eye (on). ~ से उतरना, to slip from mind, or from memory. ~ से बाहर, adj. beyond imagination, inconceivable.

ख़यालात *khayālāt* [A. *khayālāt*, pl.], m. pl. thoughts; ideas, attitudes.

ख़याली *khayālī* [A. *khayālī*], adj. **1.** imaginary. **2.** fanciful. **3.** illusory. — ~ पुलाव पकाना, to indulge in vain imaginings; to build castles in the air.

ख़र *khar* [P. *khar*], m. a donkey (= [1]खर). — ख़रगोश, m. see s.v. ख़रदिमाग़, adj. donkey-brained, stupid; ill-tempered; proud; boastful. °ई, f.

[1]**खर** *khar* [*khara-*[1]], m. **1.** an ass, donkey. **2.** a mule. — ~ मोर, m. the lesser florican, *Sypheotides indica.* (?)

[2]**खर** *khar* [S.], adj. harsh, severe; hot; biting.

[3]**खर** *khar* [*khaṭa-*: ← Drav.], m. reg. (E.) grass, straw; long grass for thatching (= खड़).

खरका *kharkā* [cf. *khaṭa-*, *khaḍa-*], m. a straw; a toothpick. — ~ करना, to use a toothpick.

ख़रख़र *kharkhar*, m. = ख़ुरख़ुर.

खरखरा *kharkharā* [? *khara-*[2], redupl.], adj. & m. **1.** adj. rough, uneven. **2.** m. a curry-comb (= खरहरा).

ख़रख़रा *kharkharā*, m. = ख़रख़र.

ख़रख़शा *kharkhaśā* [P. *kharkhaśa*], m. quarrel, wrangle.

ख़रगोश *khargoś* [P. *khargoś*], m. donkey-eared, or large-eared: a hare, a rabbit.

ख़रच *kharc*, m. see ख़र्च.

खरछरा *kharcharā*, adj. rough, uneven (= खरखरा).

खरतल *khartal* [cf. *khara-*[2]], adj. **1.** candid, open, frank (in speech or manner). **2.** Av. harsh, sharp.

[1]**खरपा** *kharpā*, m. *Pl. HŚS.* side seam (of a garment).

[2]**खरपा** *kharpā*, m. reg. (Bihar) a woman's shoe.

खरब *kharb* [ad. *kharva-*], m. ten thousand millions; a very large number.

ख़रबूज़ा *kharbūzā* [P. *kharbūza*], m. the sweet melon, *Cucumis melo.*

ख़रबूज़ी *kharbūzī* [cf. H. *kharbūzā*], adj. coloured or streaked like the *kharbūzā.*

खरभर *kharbhar* [**khalabhala-*: Pk. *khalabhaliya-*], f. Av. confusion, commotion.

खरल *kharal* [**kharalla-*], f. ? m. *Pl.* a mortar or stone for grinding on.

खरसान *kharsān* [*khara-*[2] + *śāṇa-*[2]], m. Brbh. a whetstone.

खरसैला *kharsailā*, adj. scabby, mangy (of animals).

खरहक *kharhak*, ? m. **1.** *hist.* portion of grain given at the end of harvest to village servants. **2.** reg. (W.) fee to a blacksmith for work done on the occasion of a marriage.

खरहरा *kharahrā* [? H. *kharakharā*], m. a curry-comb. — ~ करना (को), to curry-comb.

खरहा *kharhā* [cf. *khaṭa-*, *khaḍa-*: ← Drav.], m. living in long grass: **1.** a hare; rabbit. **2.** reg. (E.) an unbroken ox.

खरहारना *kharhārnā*, v.t. to sweep.

खरही *kharhī*, f. reg. (W.) a stack, or heap (of grass, straw).

खरा *kharā* [*khara-*[2]], adj. **1.** genuine, real, true; good; pure; honest, trustworthy; candid. **2.** fair, right; full, standard (as weight); fixed, settled. — ~ खोटा, adj. & m. good and bad; the good and the bad. ~ खोटा सुनाना, = खरी खरी सुनाना. ~ असामी, m. a good tenant: one who pays in cash. खरी खरी सुनाना, to speak candidly (to, को); to reprimand. खरी खोटी सुनाना, = खरी खरी सुनाना; to speak abusively or harshly. रुपए खरे होना, to have received (one's) money, to see the colour of one's money.

खराई *kharāī* [cf. H. *kharā*] **1.** genuineness, trueness; virtue; purity; honesty, trustworthiness; candour. **2.** justness, fitness, exactness.

ख़राद *kharād* [P. *kharrād*], m. a lathe. — ~ पर उतरना, or चढ़ना, to be put on the lathe; fig. to be polished, or improved.

ख़रादना *kharādnā* [cf. H. *kharād*], v.t. **1.** to turn (on a lathe). **2.** to trim.

ख़रादी *kharādī* [P. *kharādī*], m. a turner; machinist.

खरापन *kharāpan* [cf. H. *kharā*], m. genuineness, goodness, &c. (see खरा).

ख़राब *kharāb* [A. *kharāb*], adj. **1.** bad, worthless; inferior. **2.** spoiled; contaminated. **3.** ruined; destroyed. **4.** wretched, miserable (state). **5.** corrupt, depraved; indecent; wicked. **6.** violated (a woman). — ~ करना, to spoil, &c.; to ruin, &c.; to corrupt; to violate.

ख़राबी *kharābī* [P. *kharābī*], f. **1.** defect, deficiency; a (moral) vice. **2.** harm, injury; loss. **3.** ruin, destruction. **4.** bad state; trouble, difficulty. — ~ देखना, to experience or to suffer ruin, or harm. ~ निकालना, to seek wilfully for faults.

ख़रामाँ *kharāmāṁ* [P. *khirāmān*], adj. inv. U. often redupl. **1.** walking in a stately or graceful way. **2.** strutting. — ~ ~ चाल, f. stately gait.

ख़राश *kharāś* [P. *kharāś*], f. **1.** scratch, scraping; clawing. **2.** hoarseness or irritation of the throat.

ख़राशना *kharāśnā* [cf. H. *kharāś*], v.t. to scratch, to scrape; to claw.

खराहंद *kharāhand* [? *khara-*[2], or *kṣāra-*, + *gandha-*], f. the smell of urine; an offensive smell.

खरिका *kharikā*, m. reg. (Bihar) a piece of leaf fibre (cf. खरका).

खरिहान *kharihān*, m. E.H. = खलियान.

खरी *kharī* [cf. H. [1]*khar*], f. a female donkey.

ख़रीता *kharītā* [A. *kharīṭa*], m. U. pouch, purse: bag (for letters).

ख़रीद *kharīd* [P. *kharīd*], f. **1.** buying, purchase. **2.** a thing bought. **3.** reg. cost, price. **4.** demand, need. — ख़रीददार [P. *-dār*], m. incorr. = ख़रीदार, s.v. °ई, f. ख़रीद-बेच, f. buying and selling, trading. ख़रीद-नामा, m. deed of purchase, title-deed. ख़रीद-फ़रोख़्त, [P. *farokht*], f. buying and selling: dealings, trading. ख़रीद-फ़रोख़्त करना, to buy and sell, &c. ख़रीदो-फ़रोख़्त, f. U. id.

ख़रीदना *kharīdnā* [cf. H. *kharīd*], v.t. **1.** to buy. **2.** fig. to bring upon oneself (= मोल लेना).

ख़रीदार *kharīdār* [P. *kharīdār*], m. **1.** purchaser. **2.** customer.

ख़रीदारी *kharīdārī* [P. *kharīdārī*], f. purchasing. — ~ अच्छी चलना (की), to sell well (an item or commodity).

ख़रीफ़ *kharīf* [A. *kharīf*], f. the autumn harvest; autumn crops.

ख़रीफ़ी *kharīfī* [P. *kharīfī*], adj. maturing in the autumn; having to do with the autumn harvest.

खरोंच *kharoṁc* [cf. H. *kharoṁcnā*], f. **1.** scratching. **2.** a scratch; graze. — ~ आना (को), to receive a scratch, to be grazed. ~ मारना (पर), to scratch.

खरोंचना *kharoṁcnā*, v.t. = खुरचना.

खरोंट *kharoṁṭ*, f. = खरोंच.

खरोंटना *kharoṁṭnā* = खुरचना.

खरोचना *kharocnā*, v.t. = खुरचना.

खरोटना *kharoṭnā*, v.t. = खुरचना.

ख़र्च *kharc* [P. *kharc*], m. **1.** outgoings: expenditure, expenses. **2.** expense, cost. **3.** debit side (of an account). ~ में लिखना, to enter as a debit. — ~ आना, to (fall to) be spent. ~ उठाना, to bear an expense. ~ करना, to spend. ~ पड़ना, to be spent, expended. ~ में पड़ना, to be debited (a sum). ~ में डालना, to involve (one) in expense; to write down (a sum) to expenses. ~ होना, to be spent; to be taken up (time); to be consumed (a purchased quantity). अपने ~ पर, adv. at one's own expense.

ख़र्चना *kharcnā* [cf. H. *kharc*], v.t. 1. = ख़र्च करना. **2.** to use, to bring into use.

ख़र्चा *kharcā* [P. *kharca*], m. a partic. expense, outlay or cost (cf. ख़र्च, 1). — ~ दिलाना, to award costs (in law).

ख़र्ची *kharcī* [P. *kharcī*], f. **1.** a provision of expenses, an allowance. **2.** charge, or earnings, of a prostitute. — ~ कमाना, to live on the wages of prostitution. ~ जाना, euph. to go out for wages: to become a prostitute.

ख़र्चीला *kharcīlā* [cf. H. *kharc*], adj. **1.** extravagant (a person). **2.** expensive (an object).

ख़र्चू *kharcū* [cf. H. *kharc*], adj. & m. **1.** adj. extravagant (with money). **2.** m. a spendthrift. **3.** a lavish spender.

खर्जूर *kharjūr* [S.], m. = खजूर.

खर्ब *kharb*, m. see खरब.

खर्व *kharv* [S.], adj. poet. maimed.

खर्रा *kharrā* [? *khara-*[2]], m. **1.** a schedule, memorandum; a roll. **2.** a curry-comb (= खरहरा).

खर्रट *kharraṭ*, adj. forceful, vigorous.

खर्राटा *kharrāṭā* [? onom.], m. snoring. — खर्राटे भरना, or मारना, to snore. खर्राटे लेना, id.; colloq. to sleep soundly.

खलंगा *khalaṅgā*, m. reg. (E.) a reception area (near a house: for male visitors).

[1]**खल** *khal* [*khala-*[2]], adj. & m. **1.** adj. base, vile; wicked; deceitful; cruel. **2.** mischievous. **3.** m. a base person, &c. — खल-नायक, m. the villain (as of a story, or film).

[2]**खल** *khal* [*khala-*[5]] oil-cake, residue (from the pressing of oil-seeds).

ख़लक़ *khalq* [A. *khalq*], m. f. E.H. creation, the world.

खलखल *khalkhal* [cf. H. *khalkhalānā*], f. esp. adv. **1.** a sound of rumbling or bubbling. **2.** a sound of laughter (= खिलखिल). 3. = खलबल.

खलखलाना *khalkhalānā* [*khalakhalāyate*], v.i. & v.t. **1.** v.i. to make a rumbling or bubbling sound. **2.** to rattle or to chink (as money). **3.** v.t. to cause (a liquid) to bubble or boil.

खलड़ी *khalṛī* [cf. H. [2]*khāl*], f. a small hide or skin (as of a sheep).

खलता *khalătā* [S.], f. **1.** wickedness; villainy. **2.** malice.

खलना *khalnā* [*khalati*], v.i. **1.** Brbh. to grind (in a mortar); to destroy. **2.** fig. to wound, to hurt (a person).

खलबल *khalbal* [**khalabhala-*: Pk. *khalabhaliya-*], f. **1.** confusion, disturbance; agitation. **2.** noise, commotion. — ~ डालना (में), to throw into confusion, or panic. ~ पड़ना (में), or ~ मचना, to be in confusion, &c.

खलबलाना *khalbalānā* [cf. **khalabhala-*], v.i. **1.** to be agitated; to be excited. **2.** to bubble (boiling liquid).

खलबलाहट *khalbalāhaṭ* [cf. H. *khalbalānā*], f. confusion, agitation; commotion.

खलबली *khalbalī*, f. 1. = खलबल. **2.** a partic. disturbance. पेट में ~, an upset stomach.

ख़लल *khalal* [A. *khalal*], m. **1.** breach; interruption. **2.** disorder, confusion; misunderstanding. **3.** upset (of body or mind). — ~ आना, disorder or disturbance to arise (in, में). ~ डालना, to obstruct, to interfere (in, में). – ख़ललंदाज़ [P. *-andāz*], m. a disturber of the peace. ख़ललदिमाग़, adj. & m. crazy; hot-headed; disturbance of mind.

खलसा *khalsā*, m. a kind of fish, *Trichopodus colisa.*

खला- *khalā-* [cf. H. *khālī*], v.t. Brbh. to empty; fig. to voice (inner thoughts).

खलाना *khalānā* [cf. H. *khālī*], v.t. reg. to empty.

खलार *khalār* [cf. *khalla-*[2]], m. reg. (Bihar) low ground.

ख़लास *khalās* [A. *khalāṣ*], adj. & m. **1.** adj. freed; released. **2.** needy, poor. **3.** m. deliverance, release; discharge (as from service). **4.** relief (from any burden). — ~ करना, to release, &c. (from, से). ~ होना, to be freed, released; to obtain relief (from any burden).

[1]**ख़लासी** *khalāsī* [P. *khalāṣī*], f. = ख़लास.

[2]**ख़लासी** *khalāsī* [P. *khalāṣī*], m. **1.** a sailor, crew member. **2.** tent-pitcher, porter.

खलियान *khaliyān* [*khaledhānī-*], m. **1.** threshing-floor. **2.** granary. **3.** store of unthreshed corn.

खलियाना *khaliyānā* [cf. H. *khāl*], v.t. reg. **1.** to flay. **2.** colloq. to make a killing (as when gambling).

ख़लिश *khaliś* [P. *khaliś*], f. pricking or tingling sensation.

खलिहान *khalihān*, m. reg. = खलियान.

खली *khalī* [*khala-*[5]], f. oil-cake; scented oil-cake (cf. खलेल).

ख़लीज *khalīj* [A. *khalīj*], m. U. gulf, bay.

ख़लीफ़ा *khalīfā* [A. *khalīfa*], m. successor: **1.** a caliph. **2.** senior person (*musl.*: esp. in hon. reference to one providing services, as a cook, barber, &c). **3.** fig. rascal, villain.

खलु *khalu* [S.], adv. Av. indeed, truly.

खलेटी *khaleṭī* [cf. H. *(tal)aiṭī*, °*haṭī*], f. reg. (E.) ? = खलार.

खलेल *khalel*, m. Brbh. scented oil.

खल्लड़ *khallaṛ* [cf. *khalla-*[3]], m. a mortar for grinding drugs, &c.

खल्ला *khallā* [*khalla-*[2], Pk. *khalla-*], m. reg. (W.) low ground.

ख़ल्लासी *khallāsī*, m. = [1]ख़लासी.

खल्वाट *khalvāṭ* [S.], adj. bald.

खवा *khavā*, m. the shoulder; shoulder-blade; upper arm. — खवे से ~ छिलना, to be crowded together uncomfortably tightly, to be cheek by jowl (with).

ख़वातीन *khavātīn* [A. *khavātīn*, pl.], f. pl. U. ladies.

खवाना *khavānā* [cf. H. *khānā*], v.t. to cause to eat; to feed (one, को).

ख़वास *khavās* [A. *khavāṣṣ*], m. **1.** U. personal servant, attendant (as of a king). **2.** concubine.

ख़वासी *khavāsī* [P. *khavāṣī*], f. Brbh. **1.** office or duty of an attendant. **2.** attendant's seat behind a dignitary in a howdah.

ख़वैया *khavaiyā* [cf. H. *khavānā*], m. one who feeds, or offers food (to others).

ख़शख़श *khaśkhaś* [P. *khaśkhāś*], m. poppy; poppy-seed.

ख़स *khas* [P. *khas*], f. **1.** the grass *Andropogon muraticum*. **2.** a curtain or hanging made of *khas* (= टट्टी).

खस- *khas-* [**khasati*[1]: Pk. *khasaï*], v.i. Brbh. Av. to sink, to fall, to slip off.

खसकंत *khaskant* [cf. H. *khasaknā*], f. reg. *Pl. HŚS.* slipping, or slinking, away.

खसकना *khasaknā*, v.i. = खिसकना.

खसकाना *khaskānā*, v.t. = खिसकाना.

खसखस *khaskhas* [P. *khaśkhaś*], f. **1.** a poppy. ***2.** a poppy-head, or its seeds.

खस-खस *khas-khas* [**khasa-*[2]], f. a sound of grating, chewing, &c.

खसखसा *khaskhasā* [cf. H. *khaskhas*], adj. having to do with poppy-seed: **1.** granular (as sand). **2.** greyish (as hair, beard).

खसखसी *khaskhasī* [cf. H. *khaskhas*], adj. & f. **1.** adj. greyish white (as poppy-seed). **2.** f. a greyish white colour.

ख़सम *khasm* [A. *khaṣm*], m. master: husband. — ~ करना, to marry (a woman). – ख़समवाली, f. a woman whose husband is alive.

ख़सरा *khasrā* [P. *khasra*: ? ← Drav.], m. a village book-keeper's list of fields; surveyor's field-book.

खसरा *khasrā* [*khasa-*[1]], m. a skin complaint; ringworm. — उसे ~ निकल आया है, he has ringworm.

ख़सी *khasī*, m. & adj. see ख़स्सी.

ख़सीस *khasīs* [A. *khasīs*], adj. base: mean, stingy.

खसोट *khasoṭ* [cf. H. *khasoṭnā*], m. **1.** a plucking or tearing out. **2.** a scratch, tear. — कफ़न-खसोट, adj. colloq. shroud-snatcher: shameless wretch.

खसोटना *khasoṭnā* [**khass-*], v.t. **1.** to pull out; to pluck out or off. **2.** to scratch, to tear. **3.** to snatch; to pilfer; to plunder.

ख़स्तगी *khastagī* [P. *khastagī*], f. **1.** fragility, brittleness. **2.** crispness (as of pastry).

ख़स्ता *khastā* [P. *khasta*], adj. wounded, broken: **1.** fragile, brittle. **2.** crisp (as pastry). **3.** tired. **4.** bad, dire (state). — ~ हाल, m. bad (personal) state or circumstances. – ख़स्तादिल, adj. U. heart-broken.

ख़स्सी *khassī* [A. *khaṣī*], m. & adj. **1.** m. a castrated animal (esp. a goat). **2.** adj. castrated. — ~ करना, to castrate.

ख़ाँ *khāṁ*, m. pronun. var. see ख़ान.

खाँखर *khāṁkhar*, adj. **1.** hollow. **2.** holey (a pot).

खाँग *khāṁg* [*khadga-*[1]], m. **1.** horn of a rhinoceros. **2.** spike; spur (of cock, &c.); tusk (of boar).

खाँच *khāṁc* [cf. H. *khāṁcnā*], f. reg. the action of drawing, tracing, or of drawing together; a mark drawn or traced.

[1]**खाँचना** *khāṁcnā* [**khañc-*], v.t. **1.** to scratch a line, or groove; to draw; to mark. **2.** to scribble.

[2]**खाँचना** *khāṁcnā* [cf. **khañca-* and ? **khacyate*], v.t. to set together; to weave, to set in.

[1]**खाँचा** *khāṁcā* [**khañca-*], m. **1.** a basket (woven from twigs, stalks or split bamboo). **2.** a coop, cage.

[2]**खाँचा** *khāṁcā* [cf. H. [1]*khāṁcnā*], m. a groove. — खाँचेदार [P. *-dār*], adj. grooved.

खाँड़ *khāṁṛ* [*khaṇḍu-*[1]], f. coarse sugar (obtained by boiling down and drying the residue of sugar-cane juice). — ~ गलाना, to boil down or to crystallise sugar. कच्ची ~, f. raw (uncrystallised) sugar. – खाँड़-सारी, a refiner of sugar. खाँड़-साल, f. a sugar refinery.

खाँड़- *khāṁṛ-* [*khaṇḍate*], v.t. Brbh. Av. **1.** to break to pieces. **2.** to chew; to bite.

खाँड़ा *khāṁṛā* [**khaṇḍaka-*], m. Av. **1.** a double-edged sword; cutlass. **2.** *Pl.* a cleaver.

खाँटी *khāṁṭī*, adj. real, thorough. — ~ बनारसी, m. a true Banārasī.

खाँप *khāṁp* [**phakk-*[1]], f. a piece, slice (of fruit: = फाँक).

खाँसी *khāṁsī* [*kāsikā-*], f. a cough. — ~ आना (को), to cough. काली ~, f. whooping-cough. तर ~, f. a loose cough. पुरानी ~, f. a chronic cough. – कुक्कुर-खाँसी, f. = काली ~.

खाई *khāī* [*khātikā-*, Pk. *khāi-*], f. **1.** a ditch, trench; moat; drain. **2.** gulf, distance (between dissimilar things).

खाऊ *khāū* [*khāduka-*], adj. & m. **1.** adj. voracious; gluttonous. **2.** m. a voracious person, &c. **3.** one who takes bribes. — खाऊ-उड़ाऊ, adj. & m. extravagant, prodigal; an extravagant person, &c.

ख़ाक *khāk* [P. *khāk*], f. **1.** dust; earth. **2.** ashes. **3.** fig. nothing at all; sthg. useless.

क्या ~ है, it's of no use at all. ~ जानता है, he knows absolutely nothing. संदूक़ क्या, ~ बनाकर गया होगा, far from finishing (making) the box, he'll have left without starting it. **4.** fig. curse, damnation. ~ ऐसी ज़िंदगी पर! a curse on this life! — ~ करना, to reduce to dust, to raze, to destroy. ~ चाटना, to lick the dust, to abase oneself. ~ छानना, to sift dust: to toil to no purpose; to rack the brains vainly; to roam (about or through, की). ~ डालना, to throw dust (on, पर); to bury (as a quarrel); to conceal (sthg. discreditable); to heap curses (on). ~ फाँकना, to eat the dust: to wander, to roam; fig. to deal in lies. ~ में मिलना, to be reduced to dust or ashes, to be ruined; to perish. ~ में मिलाना, = ~ करना. ~ सियाह कर देना, to lay waste (a territory) with fire. ~ होना, = ~ में मिलना. – ख़ाकसार, adj. & m. like dust: humble; a humble petitioner (self-deprecatory). °ई, f. self-abasement. ख़ाक-पत्थर, m. fig. dust and stones: sthg. of no interest or importance.

ख़ाका *khākā* [P. *khāka*], m. **1.** outline, tracing; diagram; map. **2.** plan; draft. **3.** graph. **4.** model (as of a site). **5.** estimate. — ~ उड़ाना (का), to caricature; to make fun (of); to vilify. ~ उतारना (का), to trace, to outline; to sketch. ~ खींचना, to sketch out a plan; to outline (a situation). ~ बनाना, to make a plan, or sketch; to make a model.

ख़ाकी *khākī* [P. *khākī*], adj. & f. & m. **1.** adj. dust- or earth-coloured. **2.** f. the colour of dust or earth. **3.** m. khaki (uniform) cloth.

[1]**खाखर** *khākhar*, m. खड़खड़.

[2]**खाखर** *khākhar*, m. Av. name of a bird.

खाज *khāj* [*kharju-*: ← Drav.], f. **1.** the itch, a skin complaint. **2.** eczema. **3.** mange. — ~ उठना, an itch, &c. to break out (on, में). कोढ़ की ~, or कोढ़ में ~, itch on leprosy: one trouble on top of another.

खाजा *khājā* [*khādya-*], m. a kind of sweet made from fried pastry.

खाट *khāṭ* [*khaṭvā-*], f. a bedstead, bed. — ~ कटना, colloq. to be confined to bed; to be bedridden. ~ पकड़ना, to take to bed, to be ill. ~ पर पड़ा होना, to be bedridden. ~ बिछाना, to make up a bed. ~ से उतारना, to take (a dying man) from his bed. ~ से लगना, = ~ पर पड़ा होना. – खाट-खटोला, m. goods and chattels.

खाड़ी *khāṛī* [**khāḍa-*], f. **1.** a bay, gulf; specif. the Persian Gulf. **2.** an inlet (of the sea).

खात *khāt* [*khātra-*], m. f. **1.** m. pit (for compost); excavation (as for a tank or well). **2.** f. manure, dung (= [1]खाद). — ~ देना or ~ डालना (में), to manure (land).

खाता *khātā* [*kṣatra-*], m. **1.** a ledger, account-book. **2.** an individual account. **3.** a budget, estimated account. — ~ खोलना, to open an account. खाते बाक़ी, f. the balance of an account. चालू ~, m. a current account. – खातेदार [P. *-dār*], m. an account-holder; a landholder paying rent to a paṭvārī. °ई, f. a system of tenure of land by rent. बही-खाता, f. a book of cumulated accounts.

ख़ातिर *khātir* [A. *khāṭir*], f. what occurs to the mind: **1.** regard, respect. **2.** considerate attention; hospitality. **3.** ppn. out of consideration (for, की). — ~ करना, to show regard, &c. (for, की). ~ में न लाना, to show no regard or esteem (for). – ख़ातिरजमा रखना, to be composed, or assured. – ख़ातिरदारी [P. *-dārī*], f. showing regard, or consideration; entertainment, hospitality. ख़ातिरदारी करना, to show consideration (for, की); to receive respectfully, or hospitably.

खाती *khātī* [*kṣattr̥-*], m. Av. a carpenter; carver.

ख़ातून *khātūn*, [T. *hātùn*, f. lady (title occurring finally in many Muslim female names).

[1]**खाद** *khād* [*khātikā-*, MIA **khaddha-*], m. f. **1.** m. reg. (Bihar) pit (for storing grain or manure); temporary planting site (for cane seedlings). ***2.** f. (m.) manure.

[2]**खाद** *khād* [ad. *khādya-*], m. *hist.* an advance of money (to farmers) for food.

[1]**खादर** *khādar* [? cf. H. [1]*khād*; × *kardaṭa-*], f. low alluvial land near water (fit for rice cultivation, or offering good grazing).

[2]**खादर** *khādar* [**khaddara-*], f. = खादी.

ख़ादिम *khādim* [A. *khādim*], m. **1.** a servant. **2.** *musl.* attendant, officiant at a mosque or shrine.

ख़ादिमा *khādimā* [A. *khādima*], m. a female servant.

खादी *khādī* [**khadda-*], f. a thick, coarse type of cotton cloth.

खाद्य *khādyă* [S.], adj. & m. **1.** adj. edible; to be eaten. **2.** food. — खाद्य-पदार्थ, m. usu. pl. foodstuffs. खाद्य-संकट, m. shortage of food. खाद्य-संवितरण, m. food rationing. खाद्याखाद्य [°*ya*+*a*°], m. lawful and unlawful food. खाद्यानुभाजन [°*ya*+*a*°], m. food rationing. खाद्यान्न [°*ya*+*a*°], m. food (as a resource: esp. grain). खाद्योत्पादन [°*ya*+*u*°], m. production of food.

खान *khān* [*khāni-*, Pk. *khāṇī-*], f. **1.** a mine, a quarry; source. **2.** a store; treasury. **3.** ample store, abundance.

ख़ान *khān* [P. *khān*], m. **1.** lord, prince: a title of Muslim nobles (esp. those of Paṭhān descent). **2.** honorific used esp. with Paṭhān names. **3.** a chief headman of several villages. — ख़ानक़ाह [P. *gāh*: Ar. *-q-*], f. a ṣūfī residential establishment; monastery. ख़ान-सामाँ, m. see s.v.

खानक *khānak* [S.] a digger; a miner.

ख़ानगी *khāngī* [P. *khānagī*], adj. & f. **1.** adj. domestic, household. **2.** private (any matter). **3.** f. a prostitute.

ख़ानदान *khāndān* [P. *khānadān*], m. **1.** family; family line. **2.** dynasty.

ख़ानदानी *khāndānī* [P. *khāndānī*], adj. **1.** family, familial. **2.** hereditary. **3.** of good family.

खान-पान *khān-pān* [H. *khānā*+H. ²*pān-*; or ad. *pāna-*], m. **1.** eating and drinking. **2.** customs of eating; types of food. — ~ खान-पान करना, to eat, to take a light meal. ~ खान-पान का संबंध, m. a tie of commensality (with, के साथ).

खानवाँ *khānvāṁ* [*khāni-*: Pk. *khāṇī-*], m. reg. (E.) a trench, drainage ditch (round a field).

ख़ानसामाँ *khānsāmāṁ* [P. *khānsāmān*], m. master of the stores: **1.** steward, butler; waiter. **2.** cook. **3.** storekeeper, warehouseman.

ख़ानसामा *khānsāmā*, m. see ख़ानसामाँ.

खाना *khānā* [*khādati*], v.t. & m. **1.** v.t. to eat. **2.** to consume; to swallow; to inhale; to devour. **3.** to take, to take in, to accept. क़सम ~, to swear an oath. रिश्वत ~, to take a bribe. **4.** (esp. खा लेना) to embezzle. **5.** to suffer, to endure. मार ~, to suffer a beating. सरदी ~, to endure the cold. मुँह की ~, to suffer shame for one's damaged reputation. **6.** m. eating; food. — ~ न पचना (का), fig. (one) to be concerned or uneasy. जान, or दिमाग़, ~ (की), to harass (one). मुँह की ~, to be struck in the face. खा जाना, to eat up, to consume. खा डालना, colloq. to rob, to make a clean sweep (in robbing); to fleece, to defraud. खा पका जाना, colloq. to squander or to go through (all one's wealth or resources). – खाना-कमाना, to earn one's living. खाना-पीना, m. food and drink; board. – खाता-पीता, adj. well-nourished; well-off, flourishing.

ख़ाना *khānā* [P. *khāna*], m. **1.** esp. -ख़ाना. house, dwelling; place (of business). डाक-ख़ाना, m. post office. **2.** compartment (as of a carriage); division (as of a drawer, book-case); pigeon-hole; case (for glasses). **3.** square (of a games board). **4.** column (of a table, or page); heading; box (of a form). **5.** check (in a pattern). — ख़ाना-ख़राबी, f. ruin of a family. ख़ाना-तलाशी, f. search of a house. ख़ानापुरी, f. filling in sections (of a form). ख़ानाबदोश [P. -ba-dos], adj. & m. with house on back: nomadic; a wanderer, nomad. °ई, f. wandering or nomadic life.

खानि *khāni* [S.], f. a mine, &c. (= खान).

¹खाप *khāp* [? cf. H. **khāpnā*, v.t.: H. *khapnā*, v.i.], f. reg. a blow.

²खाप *khāp* [conn. H. *khapānā*], m. *Pl.* **1.** sheath; stalk, stem (of plantain). **2.** tribe, group. **3.** [× H. *phāṁk*] a slice of fruit.

खापट *khāpaṭ* [? conn. H. *khapnā*], adj. & f. **1.** adj. *Pl.* old, worn out. **2.** f. reg. (W.) a whitish, heavy and unproductive clay soil having traces of iron.

ख़ाब *khāb*, m. see ख़्वाब.

खाबड़ *khābaṛ*, adj. reg. rough, uneven (ground). — खाबड़-खूबड़, adj. id.

खाम *khām* [*skambha-*¹], m. reg. (W.) a post, pillar.

ख़ाम *khām* [P. *khām*], adj. **1.** unripe, immature. **2.** reg. (W.) gross (receipts). — ख़ाम-ख़याली, f. wrong or foolish idea.

ख़ामी *khāmī* [P. *khāmī*], f. rawness, immaturity; defect, fault, flaw.

ख़ामोश *khāmoś* [P. *khāmoś*], adj. **1.** quiet, silent. **2.** calm (of temperament, or of the world of nature). **3.** uncomplaining (as at injustice).

ख़ामोशी *khāmośī* [P. *khāmośī*], f. **1.** quietness. **2.** calm.

ख़ार *khār* [P. *khār*], m. **1.** a thorn. **2.** cock's spur. **3.** fig. rancour; envy; jealousy. — ~ आँखों का, m. sthg. disagreeable to sight, an eyesore. ~ खाना, or खाए बैठना, to feel rancorous or jealous (of, पर). ~ निकालना, to vent rancour. ~ होना, to be an irritant, to rankle; to be an eyesore. – ख़ारदार [P. *-dār*], adj. thorny; bristly; barbed; troublesome.

¹खार *khār* [*kṣāra-*¹], m. **1.** an alkali; potash; caustic potash or soda. **2.** saltiness, brackishness; salinity (of land). **3.** saline land or soil.

²खार *khār*, m. rough or difficult ground (as a stony beach, or ground cut up by rain).

खारा *khārā* [*kṣāra-*¹], adj. **1.** alkaline; hard (water). **2.** saline, brackish. — ~ नमक, m. alkaline salt: sodium sulphate, Glauber's salt. ~ नोन, m. id. खारी मिट्टी, f. saline soil.

खारापन *khārāpan* [cf. H. *khārā*], m. **1.** alkalinity. **2.** salinity, brackishness.

ख़ारिज *khārij* [A. *khārij*], adj. being out of: **1.** excluded. **2.** rejected. — ~ करना, to exclude;

to eject; to reject; to dismiss (a case). ~ करके, adv. excluding, excepting. ~ होना, to be excluded, &c.; to fail (a line), to become extinct.

ख़ारिश *kh̲āriś* [P. *kh̲āriś*], f. **1.** an itch; hoarseness (of the throat). **2.** mange.

खारी *khārī* [cf. H. [1]*khār*], adj. inv. **1.** salty, brackish. **2.** alkaline: impregnated esp. with potassium salts (soil).

खारीपन *khārīpan* [cf. H. *khārī*], m. saltiness, brackishness.

खारुआ *khāruā* [**khāru-*], m. a kind of coarse cotton cloth, dyed red with *āl* (*Morinda*) dye.

[1]**खाल** *khāl* [*khalla-*[2], Pk. *khalla-*], f. **1.** a canal, watercourse. **2.** moat, trench. **3.** reg. (Bihar) low-lying land.

[2]**खाल** *khāl* [*khalla-*[1]], f. **1.** skin, hide. **2.** reg. a bellows. — ~ उड़ाना (की), or उधेड़ना, or खींचना, to flay; to thrash. अपनी ~ में मस्त होना, to be self-content, carefree.

ख़ालसा *kh̲ālsā* [A. *kh̲ālṣa*], adj. & m. **1.** adj. = ख़ालिस. **2.** *hist.* exchequer, revenue department. **3.** *hist.* crown or government lands. ***4.** m. the Sikh order or brotherhood established by Guru Govind. — ख़ालसे लगना, *hist.* to be appropriated or confiscated (by government).

खाला *khālā*, adj. & m. **1.** adj. *HŚS.* low. **2.** m. reg. = [1]खाल.

ख़ाला *kh̲ālā* [A. *kh̲āla*], f. maternal aunt. — ~ का, or ~ जी का, घर, m. aunt's house: a place of comfort and security. – ख़ाला-मामा का घर, m. id. ख़ालाज़ाद [P. *-zād*] भाई, m. maternal cousin.

ख़ालिक़ *kh̲āliq* [A. *kh̲āliq*], m. E.H. the Creator.

ख़ालिस *kh̲ālis* [A. *kh̲āliṣ*], adj. pure, unadulterated; genuine.

ख़ाली *kh̲ālī* [A. *kh̲ālī*], adj. **1.** empty. **2.** blank (a page, form). **3.** unobstructed (path, way). **4.** not busy, free (a person, a time). **5.** not in use (an object, an appliance). **6.** vacant (a post). **7.** devoid (of, से), without. **8.** useless, ineffective. वार ~ जाना, a blow to miss its mark, a scheme to misfire. **9.** pure, unmixed. **10.** adv. only, merely. **11.** alone. — ~ करना, to empty (of, से); to clear or to rid (of); to vacate; to make available (as for use). ~ पेट, adv. on, or with, an empty stomach. ~ हाथ, adv. empty-handed; unarmed; penniless.

ख़ाविंद *kh̲āvind* [P. *kh̲āvand*], m. **1.** lord, master. ***2.** husband. — ~ करना, to take a husband.

खास *khās*, f. reg. (W.) a square-cut bag; a load, bagful.

ख़ास *kh̲ās* [A. *kh̲āṣṣ*], adj. **1.** particular, special; distinct; express (as a stipulation). **2.** specific; personal, private (as a house, a servant, a session). **3.** choice, best (as goods). **4.** main, chief (in standing or importance). **5.** U. noble. — ~ अपना, adj. distinctive; all one's own (= ~, 2). ~ अपने लिए, adv. all for oneself (as a possession, or a service). ~ करके, adv. = ख़ासकर (see s.v). ~ तौर पर, or से, adv. in particular, especially. – ख़ास-पसंद, adj. 19c. appealing to the cultivated, or to connoisseurs. ख़ासमख़ास [P. *-ma*], m. colloq. a protégé. ख़ासो-आम, [P. *-o-*], m. the select and the common: one and all, the public.

ख़ासकर *kh̲āskar* [cf. H. *kh̲ās*], adv. in particular, especially.

ख़ासा *kh̲āsā* [A. *kh̲āṣṣa*], adj. & m. **1.** adj. = ख़ास, 1., 2. **2.** good, fine; pleasing. **3.** adv. particularly, very. इधर ~ गरम (ख़ासी गरमी) है, it's very hot here. **4.** m. = ख़ासियत. **5.** Brbh. a kind of fine cloth, muslin. — अच्छा ~, adj. = ~, 2.

ख़ासियत *kh̲āsiyat* [A. *kh̲āṣīya*: P. *kh̲āṣiyat*], f. quality, special property; special nature.

ख़ाहमख़ाह *kh̲āhmăkh̲āh*, adv. see s.v. ख़्वाह.

ख़ाहिश *kh̲āhiś*, f. see ख़्वाहिश.

खिंच *khiṁc* [cf. H. *khiṁcnā*], f. pulling; a pull.

खिंचना *khiṁcnā* [cf. H. *khīṁcnā*], v.i. **1.** to be pulled; to be stretched, to stretch; to be tightened, to tighten; to be extracted; to be drawn to, or attracted. **2.** to be drawn (as a sword); to be sketched; to be taken (a photo). **3.** to continue, to be protracted; to draw away from, to keep aloof from.

खिंचवाई *khiṁcvāī* [cf. H. *khiṁcnā*], f. the cost of pulling, extracting, sketching, &c.

खिंचवाना *khiṁcvānā* [cf. H. *khīṁcnā*], v.t. to cause to be pulled, stretched, &c.

खिंचाई *khiṁcāī* [cf. H. *khiṁcnā*], f. **1.** the act or process of drawing, pulling. **2.** cost of or charge for pulling.

खिंचाव *khiṁcāv* [cf. H. *khiṁcnā*], m. **1.** drawing, pulling; tightness; tension; attraction; magnetic power. **2.** discord, contention; strain (in relationships).

खिंचावट *khiṁcāvaṭ*, f. = खिंचाव, and खिंचाई, 1.

खिंडना *khiṇḍnā* [**khiṇḍ-*], v.i. reg. to be scattered, or spread: to be wasted.

खिंडवाना *khiṇḍvānā* [cf. H. *khiṇḍnā*], v.t. to cause to be scattered, &c.

खिंडाना *khiṁḍānā* [cf. H. *khiṇḍnā*], v.t. to scatter, to spread; to waste.

खिचड़ा *khicṛā* [cf. *khiccā-*], m. a dish made with rice and different types of pulse, &c., boiled together.

खिचड़ी *khicṛī* [cf. *khiccā-*], f. **1.** a dish of rice and pulse boiled together, with *ghī* and spices. **2.** a mixture; hotch-potch. ~ **बाल**, m. greying hair. ~ **भाषा**, f. mixed language, a jargon. **3.** *hind.* the *makar-saṅkrānti* festival (when *khicṛī* is eaten, and uncooked *khicṛī* given out to brāhmaṇs). **4.** the eating of *khicṛī* as a marriage custom. ~ **करना**, to make a mess or a hash (of doing sthg., **की**). ~ **पकना**, a scheme or plot to be hatched. ~ **पकाना**, to scheme or to plot together. **ढाई चावल की ~ अलग पकाना**, fig. to go against general opinion in one's acts or intentions. **बीरबल की ~**, sthg. concocted by Bīrbal: something impossible.

खिचना *khicnā*, v.i. pronun. var. = **खिंचना**.

खिचवाई *khicvāī*, f. pronun. var. = **खिंचवाई**.

खिचवाना *khicvānā*, v.t. pronun. var. = **खिंचवाना**.

खिचाना *khicānā*, v.t. = **खिंचाना**.

खिजना *khijnā*, v.i. = **खीजना**.

खिजलाना *khijlānā* [cf. H. *khījnā*], v.t. & v.i. **1.** v.t. = **खिजाना**. ***2.** v.i. to be irritable; to grow angry.

खिजलाहट *khijlāhaṭ* [cf. H. *khijlānā*], f. irritation, vexation.

ख़िज़ाँ *k͟hizāṁ* [P. *k͟hizān*], m. U. autumn.

खिजाना *khijānā* [cf. H. *khījnā*], v.t. **1.** to irritate, to vex. **2.** to tease, to provoke.

ख़िज़ाब *k͟hizāb* [A. *k͟hiẓāb*], m. **1.** dyeing the hair (esp. the beard); painting the nails. **2.** a hair-dye. — ~ **लगाना**, to apply dye (to, **में**).

खिजावट *khijāvaṭ* [cf. H. *khijānā*], f. irritation, vexation.

खिझना *khijhnā*, v.i. = **खीजना**.

खिझाना *khijhānā*, v.t. = **खिजाना**.

खिड़की *khiṛkī* [*khaḍakkikā-*, Pk. *khaḍakkī-*], f. sthg. made of matting: **1.** a window. **2.** a shutter. — ~ **खोलना**, or **निकालना**, to open a window. ~ **फोड़ना**, to throw open a window. – **खिड़कीदार** [P. *-dār*], adj. having a window; or having an opening (as an *aṁgarkhā* or turban).

ख़िताब *k͟hitāb* [A. *k͟hiṭāb*], m. **1.** title (of rank). **2.** *athl.* a prize.

ख़िताबी *k͟hitābī* [P. *k͟hiṭābī*], adj. titled.

ख़िदमत *k͟hidmat* [A. *k͟hidma*: P. *k͟hidmat*], f. **1.** service. **2.** employment, work. **3.** a service, favour. — ~ **करना** (**की**), to serve; to wait (on); to attend (to one); colloq. to give a beating (to). ~ **में**, adv. at, or in, the service (of, **की**). – **ख़िदमतगार** [P. *-gār*], m. a servant. °**ई**, f. service, attendance; readiness to serve. **ख़िदमतगुज़ार** [P. *-guzār*], adj. & m. ready to serve, attentive; an attentive servant.

ख़िदमती *k͟hidmatī* [P. *k͟hidmatī*], adj. & m. **1.** adj. attentive in service. **2.** granted in reward for service (as an estate). **3.** m. servant, attendant (esp. at a mosque).

खिन्न *khinn* [S.], adj. **1.** depressed, distressed; uneasy. **2.** fatigued, exhausted. — **खिन्नमन**, adj. dejected, &c.

खिन्नता *khinnătā* [S.], f. dejected or depressed state.

[1]**खियाना** *khiyānā* [cf. H. *khānā*], v.t. reg. to cause to eat; to feed, &c. (= [1]**खिलाना**).

[2]**खियाना** *khiyānā* [*kṣīyate*], v.i. reg. to be worn, worn out.

खिरनी *khirnī* [*kṣīriṇī-*, Pk. *khīriṇī-*], f. the tree *Mimusops kauki*, and its fruit (= *kṣīrī*), or *Wrightia* (source of a rubber).

ख़िराज *k͟hirāj* [P. *k͟harāj*], m. a tax, tribute.

खिरिसा *khirisā* [*kṣīraśāka-*], m. Av. a dish (usu. curds) made with beestings.

खिलक्कड़ *khilakkaṛ* [cf. H. *khelnā*], adj. playful (as a child, a cat).

खिलखिल *khilkhil* [cf. H. *khilnā*], f. **1.** a sound of laughter; a burst of laughter. **2.** tittering, giggling.

खिलखिलाना *khilkhilānā* [cf. H. *khilkhil*], v.i. **1.** to laugh aloud, to burst out laughing. **2.** to titter, to giggle. **3.** fig. to gleam in the sun. — **खिलखिलाके हँसना**, to laugh aloud; to burst out laughing.

खिलखिलाहट *khilkhilāhaṭ* [cf. H. *khilkhilānā*], f. a peal of laughter.

ख़िलअत *k͟hil'at* [A. *k͟hil'a*: P. *k͟hil'at*], f. a robe of honour (presented to office-holders, or as a mark of distinction).

खिलना *khilnā* [**khil-*], v.i. **1.** to open, to expand; to bloom; to burst, to swell, to crack (as roasted grain, or plaster, or a wall). **2.** to be radiant (in manner); to be delighted or exhilarated. **3.** to be striking or attractive (as clothing, or colours). **4.** to burst out laughing.

खिलवाड़ *khilvāṛ* [cf. **khel-*, &c.], m. & adj. **1.** m. diversion, amusement. **2.** an easy or trivial matter; child's play. **3.** a plaything. **4.** adj. = खिलाड़ी, 4. — ~ करना, to toy (with, से).

खिलवाड़ी *khilvāṛī* [cf. **khel-*, &c.], m. & adj. **1.** m. one who enjoys diversions or amusements; one who toys (with others' feelings). **2.** adj. enjoying diversions, &c.

¹**खिलवाना** *khilvānā* [cf. H. *khānā*], v.t. to cause (one) to eat: to get or to have (one) fed by (से) another.

²**खिलवाना** *khilvānā* [cf. H. *khelnā*], v.t. to cause to be played with: to cause to be amused or diverted by (से) another.

³**खिलवाना** *khilvānā* [cf. H. *khilnā*], v.t. to cause to be made to expand, &c., by (से) another.

खिलाई *khilāī* [cf. H. ¹*khilānā*], f. **1.** feeding. **2.** the cost of or charge for feeding. — खिलाई-पिलाई, f. maintenance; cost of maintenance.

खिलाऊ *khilāū* [cf. H. ¹³*khilānā*], adj. & m. **1.** adj. providing food, or support. **2.** causing to bloom, &c. **3.** m. one who feeds, or supports.

खिलाड़िन *khilāṛin* [cf. H. *khilāṛī*], f. a playful, or wanton, woman.

खिलाड़ी *khilāṛī* [cf. **khel-*, &c.], m. & adj. **1.** m. one who plays: a sportsman; athlete. **2.** one who displays striking skills (a magician, snake-charmer, &c). **3.** adj. fond of or skilled at games or sports. **4.** playful; facetious; mischievous.

खिलाड़ीपन *khilāṛīpan* [cf. H. *khilāṛī*], m. sportsmanship.

¹**खिलाना** *khilānā* [cf. H. *khānā*], v.t. **1.** to cause to eat, to feed. **2.** to cause to take (as medicine, or the air, or an oath). **3.** to entertain (to a meal).

²**खिलाना** *khilānā* [cf. H. *khelnā*], v.t. to cause to play; to give opportunity to play; to dandle; to divert (a child).

³**खिलाना** *khilānā* [cf. H. *khilnā*], v.t. to cause to bloom; to cause to expand or to spread; to cause to burst or to crack, &c. — काँच का गिलास ~, to crack a glass. दाने ~, to make popcorn.

ख़िलाफ़ *k͟hilāf* [A. *k͟hilāf*], m. & adj. succession, opposition: **1.** m. contrary, opposite. **2.** opposition. **3.** adj. contrary; opposed. ***4.** ppn. w. के. in opposition (to), against; contrary (to).

ख़िलाफ़त *k͟hilāfat* [A. *k͟hilāfa*: P. *k͟hilāfat*], f. succession: **1.** caliphate; the office or title of caliph. **2.** *hist.* a political movement of the years around 1920, originating in the Indian Muslims' concern over the Turkish caliphate. **3.** [× H. *k͟hilāf*] opposition.

खिलौना *khilaunā* [cf. **khel-*, &c.: H. ²*khilānā*], m. **1.** a thing to amuse; a plaything, toy. **2.** a trifling thing. — हाथ का ~, fig. a puppet, or plaything, in (one's) hands.

¹**खिल्ली** *khillī* [**khill-*], f. fun; a joke. — ~ उड़ाना, to make fun (of, की); to make a fool (of). ~ करना, to joke (with, से); to flirt (with). ~ में उड़ाना, to treat as a joke; to make a laughing-stock of. — खिल्लीबाज़ [P. *-bāz*], adj. & m. fond of joking; a joker.

²**खिल्ली** *khillī* [**khilli-*], f. betel leaf made up for chewing. पान की ~, f. id.

खिसकना *khisaknā* [cf. **khis-*, **khasati*¹], v.i. **1.** to move away; to slip or to slink away. **2.** to be displaced; to be put back, postponed.

खिसकाना *khiskānā* [cf. H. *khisaknā*], v.t. **1.** to move away, to remove; to drive away. **2.** to cause to be shifted, to displace; to put back, to postpone, to carry away.

खिसकू *khiskū* [cf. H. *khisaknā*], m. colloq. one who slips or slinks away.

¹**खिसा-** *khisā-*, v.i. Brbh. = खिसियाना.

²**खिसा-** *khisā-*, v.t. reg. (Raj.) = खिसकाना.

खिसारी *khisārī* [**khesārī-*] f. reg. the chickling vetch (= लतरी).

खिसियानपट *khisiyānpaṭ*, f. = खिसियानपन.

खिसियानपन *khisiyānpan* [cf. H. *khisiyānā*], m. shamefacedness, mortification, &c.

खिसियाना *khisiyānā* [**khiss-*], v.i. & adj. **1.** v.i. to be ashamed; to be abashed, or mortified; to grin (as with embarrassment); to be riled. **2.** to look blank or foolish. **3.** to grind the teeth (in anger). **4.** adj. ashamed; abashed, &c.; disconcerted; riled. — ~ करना (को), to abash, &c. खिसियानी बिल्ली खंभा नोचे, prov. the angry cat scratches the pillar: anger is often vented on one not responsible.

खिसियाहट *khisiyāhaṭ*, f. = खिसियानपन.

खींच *khīṁc* [cf. H. *khīṁcnā*], f. a pulling, drawing, &c. — खींच-तान, f. pulling and tugging; mutual tension. °ई, f. id.

खींचना *khīṁcnā* [**khiñc-*], v.t. **1.** to pull; to drag. **2.** to draw (as a sword). **3.** to draw, to attract. **4.** to draw (a line, a picture); to take (a photograph). — खींचा-तानी [H. *tānnā*], f. pulling and tugging; competition.

खीचना *khīcnā*, v.t. pronun. var. = खींचना.

खीज *khīj* [cf. H. *khījnā*], f. **1.** irritation, vexation; fretfulness. **2.** a cause of irritation;

teasing. — ~ उठना (को), to feel irritation (about sthg). ~ निकालना, to take out one's irritation (on, पर); to make fun (of).

खीजना *khījnā* [*kṣīyate* × *krudhyati*], v.i. **1.** to be irritated or vexed. **2.** to be teased.

खीझ *khījh*, f. = खीज.

खीझना *khījhnā*, v.i. = खीजन.

खीर *khīr* [*kṣīra-*], f. a dish of rice boiled in milk, with sugar. — ~ के मोल, adv. colloq. very cheaply. ~ चटाना, to give (a child) *khīr* for the first time. ~ में नोन, salt in the *khīr*: something ruined. टेढ़ी ~, f. fig. a difficult matter, or task. – ~ चटाई, f. giving a child *khīr* for the first time; the ceremony of *ann-prāśan*.

खीरा *khīrā* [conn. *kṣīraka-*], m. a cucumber, *Cucumis sativus*, or *C. utilissimus*. — खीरे के मोल, adv. colloq. very cheaply, dirt cheap. – खीरा-ककड़ी समझना, to think of, or to treat as worthless or insignificant.

खीरी *khīrī*, f. Av. = खिरनी.

1**खील** *khīl* [cf. **khill-*] parched grain, or rice.

2**खील** *khīl* [*khīla-*], f. a small piece, or fragment. — ~ ~ करना, to break to pieces.

खीली *khīlī* [**khilli-*], f. *Pl. HŚS*. a betel leaf made up with its ingredients.

1**खीस** *khīs* [? *kṣī(ra)rasa-*], f. beestings.

2**खीस** *khīs* [**khiss-*], f. **1.** a grin or grimace (as of embarrassment, or anger). **2.** abashment, mortification. **3.** chattering (as a monkey). **4.** the tusks of a boar. — ~ or खीसें काढ़ना, or निकालना, to put on a grin; to grin.

खीसा *khīsā* [P. *kīsa*], m. **1.** a small bag, purse. ***2.** pocket.

खुँडला *khum̐ḍlā*, m. *Pl. HŚS*. a ruin; ruined house.

खुँदलना *khum̐dalnā* [*kṣundati*], v.t. to trample, to tread (on); to crush; to work with the feet.

खुंबी *khumbī*, f. pronun. var. = 1खुंभी.

1**खुंभी** *khumbhī* [conn. *kumbha-*], f. a mushroom; toadstool, fungus.

2**खुंभी** *khumbhī* [**khumbha-*], f. **1.** Brbh. a gold band (on an elephant's tusk). **2.** Av. gold stud, or ear ornament.

खुखरी *khukhrī*, f. a kukri, Gurkha's knife.

खुक्खल *khukkhal*, adj. = खोखला.

खुचर *khucar*, f. a defect. — ~ निकालना, to make captious criticisms.

खुजलाना *khujlānā*, v.t. to scratch (an itchy place).

खुजलाहट *khujlāhaṭ* [cf. H. *khujlānā*], f. **1.** scratching. **2.** itchiness.

खुजली *khujlī* [*kharju-*1: ← Drav.], f. **1.** itchiness. **2.** mange. — ~ उठना, or मचना, or होना (में), to be itchy; to have an itch.

खुजवाना *khujvānā* [cf. H. *khujānā*], v.t. to cause to be scratched or to be itchy.

खुजाना *khujānā* [*kharju-*1: ← Drav.], v.t. & v.i. **1.** v.t. to scratch (with the nails). **2.** v.i. to feel itchy. — हड्डी ~, the bones to itch: to anticipate a beating.

खुट *khuṭ* [**khuṭyate*], f. usu. in comp. pecking, tapping. — खुट-खुट, f. a tapping sound. – खुट-बढ़ैया [? by variation of H. *kaṭh*], f. colloq. a woodpecker.

1**खुटक** *khuṭak* [cf. H. *khuṭaknā*], f. pecking, tapping.

2**खुटक** *khuṭak* [? = 1*khuṭak*], f. Brbh. = खटक.

खुटकना *khuṭaknā* [cf. **khuṭyate*], v.t. **1.** to peck; to break its shell (a hatching bird). **2.** to nibble; to peel (as rind) with the teeth.

खुटका *khuṭkā*, m. = खटका.

खुट-चाल *khuṭ-cāl* [H. *khoṭa*+H. *cāl*], f. Brbh. wrong or vicious conduct.

खुटाई *khuṭāī* [cf. H. *khoṭā*], f. wickedness; faithlessness; dishonesty; insincerity; malice.

खुटिला *khuṭilā*, m. ? Brbh. a kind of ear-ring.

खुड़खुड़ *khuṛkhuṛ*, f. = खड़खड़ाहट.

खुड्डी *khuḍḍī* [? **khuṭati*: Pk. *khuḍia-* × **khaḍḍa-*, Pk. *khaḍḍa-*], f. **1.** a gap, opening; gap between two teeth. **2.** hole, or foot-rests, in a latrine.

ख़ुतबा *khutbā* [A. *khuṭba*], f. *musl.* recitation: a public prayer or encomium offered at a mosque for a reigning king; praise. — ~ पढ़ना, to proclaim the accession (of: के नाम का).

ख़ुतूत *khutūt* [A. *khuṭūt*], m. pl. U. **1.** lines. **2.** letters. (see ख़त).

ख़ुद *khud* [P. *khvud*], refl. pron. self (myself, himself, itself, &c). — ख़ुद-इख़्तियारी, f. self-control. ख़ुद-काश्त, f. & m. land cultivated by its owner; a farmer who owns his land. ख़ुदकुशी [P. *-kuśī*], f. suicide. ख़ुदकुशी करना, to commit suicide. ख़ुदग़र्ज़, adj. self-interested, selfish. °ई, f. ख़ुदपसंद, adj. self-satisfied. ख़ुदपरस्त [P. *-parast*], adj. self-worshipping: selfish; opinionated. °ई, f. ख़ुद-बख़ुद [P. *ba-*], adv. of or by oneself, &c.; of one's own accord. ख़ुदमुख़्तार, adj. independent in action, not subject to restraint; °ई, f. ख़ुदराय, adj. self-willed, headstrong, opinionated.

खुदना *khudnā* [cf. H. *khodnā*], v.i. **1.** to be dug; to be excavated. **2.** to be engraved; to be carved.

खुदनी *khudnī* [cf. H. *khodnā*], f. **1.** an engraving tool. **2.** an implement for picking or poking with; reg. (W.) a wooden poker. **3.** reg. (Bihar) a digging implement, a metal-tipped spade.

खुदरा *khudrā*, adj. pronun. var. खुरदरा.

ख़ुदरा *khudrā* [P. *khurda*], adj. & m. **1.** adj. small (in size or quantity). **2.** m. retail (of goods). ~ करना, or बेचना, to sell in small lots, or retail. **3.** a bit, fragment, something trifling; small coin, or change. दस रुपए का ~, change for ten rupees. — ख़ुदराफ़रोश [P. *-farośh*], m. a pedlar.

खुदवाई *khudvāī* [cf. H. *khudvānā*], f. the cost of or charge for digging, &c.

खुदवाना *khudvānā* [cf. H. *khodnā*], v.t. to cause to be dug, or engraved, &c.

ख़ुदा *khudā* [P. *khudā*], m. the supreme being, God. — ~ उठा ले! may God remove him (by death)! the devil take him! ~ का घर, m. the abode of God: heaven; a mosque. ~ का नाम लेना, to act justly, to do justice. ~ की पनाह, God preserve (me, &c.)! ~ की मार, f. divine wrath. ~ ~ करके, with much prayer: with great difficulty. ~ जाने, God (above) knows. ~ न करे, God forbid! ~ न ख़्वास्ता [P. *-khvāsta*], id. ~ हाफ़िज़, God (be your) protector! goodbye! उन्हें ~ से काम पड़ ही गया, he (finally) turned to God for help. – ख़ुदापरस्त [P. *-parast*], adj. God-worshipping, devout. °ई, f.

खुदाई *khudāī* [cf. H. *khudānā*], f. **1.** digging; excavating; engraving; carving. **2.** the cost of or charge for digging, &c. **3.** colloq. investigating (a matter).

ख़ुदाई *khudāī* [P. *khudāī*], adj. & f. **1.** adj. belonging to God; divine. **2.** f. divinity; divine power. **3.** creation, the world.

खुदाना *khudānā* [cf. H. *khodnā*], v.t. to cause to be dug; to cause to be engraved, or carved.

ख़ुदावंद *khudāvand* [P. *khudāvand*], m. **1.** lord, master. **2.** voc. lord! master! sir! **3.** God.

खुदावट *khudāvaṭ*, f. = खुदाई.

ख़ुदी *khudī* [P. *khvudī*], f. selfishness; egoism; pride.

खुद्दी *khuddī* [*kṣudra-*], f. **1.** a small piece, fragment. **2.** remains, lees.

खुधा *khudhā* [ad. *kṣudhā-*: ? ← B.], f. E.H. = क्षुधा.

ख़ुनकी *khunkī* [P. *khunukī*], f. coolness, slight chill (in air).

खुनखुना *khunkhunā*, m. reg. a child's toy, rattle (= झुनझुना).

खुनस *khuns*, f. m. dislike; animosity; spite, ill-will; envy.

खुनसाना *khunsānā* [cf. H. *khuns*], v.i. to feel dislike or ill-will; to be spiteful; to be envious.

खुनसी *khunsī* [cf. H. *khuns*], adj. & m. **1.** adj. filled with ill-will, &c. **2.** m. a person bearing ill-will.

ख़ुफ़िया *khufiyā* [A. *khufya*], adj. inv. secret; clandestine. — ~ पुलिस, f. secret police. ~ विभाग, m. Secret Branch.

खुबना *khubnā*, v.t. pronun. var. = खुभना.

खुभना *khubhnā* [**skubhyate*: Pk. *khubbhaï*], v.t. **1.** to pierce, to prick. **2.** to stir, to affect.

ख़ुम *khum* [P. *khum*], m. a large jar; wine-jar.

ख़ुमार *khumār* [P. *khumār*], m. **1.** intoxication. **2.** hangover. **3.** drowsiness; languor (of love). **4.** religious ecstasy. **5.** power to charm. — ~ चढ़ना, drink to take effect (on, को); drowsiness, &c. to be felt.

ख़ुमारी *khumārī* [P. *khumārī*], f. & adj. **1.** f. = ख़ुमार, 1.-3. **2.** adj. languishing.

खुमी *khumī*, f. = [1]खुंभी.

खुरंड *khuraṇḍ*, m. the crust or scab on a healing wound.

खुर *khur* [*khura-*], m. **1.** a hoof. **2.** the foot (sc. leg) of a bed.

खुरखुर *khurkhur* [? onom.], f. coughing; rattling of the throat. — ~ करना, to cough.

ख़ुरख़ुर *khurkhur*, m. **1.** snoring (= ख़र्राटा). **2.** purring (of a cat). **3.** rattle (of the throat); coughing, hawking. — ~ करना, to snore, &c.

खुरखुरा *khurkhurā* [? *kṣur(ita-)*, redupl.], adj. rough, uneven.

खुरखुराना *khurkhurānā*, v.i. to make a rattling sound, or sound of clearing the throat.

ख़ुरख़ुराहट *khurkhurāhaṭ* [cf. H. *khurkhur*], f. hoarseness, coughing.

खुरचन *khurcan* [cf. H. *khuracnā*], f. **1.** scraping. **2.** scrapings (as of a pot). **3.** a kind of sweet (*rabṛī*) made from scrapings.

खुरचना *khuracnā* [cf. *kṣurati*], v.t. to scrape; to scratch; to gouge. — बदन ~ (का), colloq. to flay.

खुरचनी *khurcanī* [cf. H. *khuracnā*], f. **1.** a scraper; an eraser; a scoop or shovel. **2.** a kind of sweet made of scrapings of boiled milk.

ख़ुरजी *khurjī* [? cf. A. *khurj*], f. a saddle-bag; sack or bag for goods or equipment.

खुरट *khuraṭ*, m. = खुरपका, खुरहा.

खुरदरा *khurdarā*, adj. rough, uneven.

खुरदरापन *khurdarāpan* [cf. H. *khurdarā*], adj. roughness.

खुर-पका *khur-pakā* [H. *khur*+H. *paknā*], m. a complaint of hooved animals (cf. खुरहा).

खुरपना *khurapnā* [cf. H. *khurpā*], v.t. to scrape up (as grass); to hoe (as weeds).

खुरपा *khurpā* [*kṣurapra-*], m. a flat-bladed tool for scraping up grass, or for weeding.

खुरपी *khurpī*, f. = खुरपा.

ख़ुरमा *khurmā* [P. *khurma*], m. **1.** a date (tree, fruit). **2.** a kind of sweet (shaped like a date).

ख़ुरमा *khurmā* [P. *khurmā*], m. **1.** a date. **2.** a sweet (shaped like a date).

खुरराँटा *khurrāṁṭā*, m. pronun. var. = खर्राटा.

खुरहा *khurhā* [**khuraghāta-*], m. reg. (E). foot and mouth disease (in cattle).

खुराँट *khurāṁṭ*, adj. colloq. **1.** very old; worn, ragged . **2.** experienced; crafty, cunning.

ख़ुराक *khurāk* [P. *khvurāk*], f. **1.** food, provisions. **2.** daily rations. **3.** partic. type of food (of a person), diet. **4.** single dose (of medicine). — ख़ुराकबंदी [P. *-bandī*], f. food rationing.

ख़ुराकी *khurākī* [P. *khvurākī*], f. 1. = ख़ुराक, 2. **2.** daily allowance (to purchase food); subsistence allowance. **3.** m. colloq. one who is fond of food.

ख़ुराफ़ात *khurāfāt* [A. *khurāfāt*, pl.], f. superstitions, fables: **1.** senseless words, nonsense. **2.** foul language, abuse. **3.** an outrageous matter or incident; uproar. — ~ बकना, to talk nonsense; to speak abusively.

ख़ुराफ़ाती *khurāfātī* [P. *khurāfāt*+H. *-ī*], adj. & m. **1.** adj. trouble-making, mischievous. **2.** m. a trouble-maker, &c.

खुरिया *khuriyā*, f. **1.** a cup-shaped container. **2.** the knee-bone.

खुरी *khurī* [cf. H. *khur*], f. hoof-mark.

खुरेंच *khureṁc*, f. = खरोंच.

खुरेंचना *khureṁcnā*, v.t. = खुरचना.

ख़ुर्द *khurd* [P. *khurd*], adj. U. **1.** little. **2.** young. — ख़ुर्दबीन [P. *-bīn*], f. microscope.

ख़ुर्दा *khurdā* [P. *khurda*], m. a small quantity, or piece (cf. खुदरा). — ~ पकड़ना, to carp, to cavil. ~ बेचना, to sell in small amounts, or retail.

ख़ुर्रम *khurram* [P. *khurram*], adj. U. glad.

खुर्रा *khurrā* [? H. *khurkhurā*], adj. ? inv. rough, uneven; coarse (as stringing, fibre).

खुर्राट *khurrāṭ*, adj. & m. colloq. **1.** adj. pej. long-experienced. **2.** shrewd, cunning. **3.** m. a shrewd old man.

खुर्राटा *khurrāṭā*, m. = खर्राटा.

ख़ुर्शंद *khurśand* [P. *khursand*], adj. corr. *HŚS.* contented, happy.

खुलना *khulnā* [cf. H. *kholnā*], v.i. **1.** to be open, to come loose, to unravel; to be untied or unfastened; to be disentangled; to be scattered (as clouds). **2.** to be uncovered, or laid bare; to become clear (the sky); to be light (a colour). **3.** to be cleared (as a drain); to be removed (an obstruction); to be broadened (the mind). **4.** to be laid, or split, open; to be dissected; to be analysed. **5.** to be freed of restraint (as hand or tongue); to be loosed (as a hawk); to be resolved (a fear, an inhibition). **6.** to be solved, or explained; to be made known, to become evident (to, पर). अब उसका भेद उनपर खुल गया है, now they know his secret (or, his real nature). **7.** to be opened, to be set up (as of a show, institution, exhibition). **8.** to get under way (as work). **9.** to be started (as a car); to be turned or switched on (as a radio). **10.** to leave (as a train). **11.** to be dismantled (a mechanism). **12.** to dilate (upon, पर). **13.** to develop (an activity, in scope). **14.** to be intimate or familiar (with, पर); to become favourable (fortune). — किसी का हुक़्क़ा ~, fig. to be accepted into, or allowed to return to, the social life of one's community. – खुला मकान, m. a house in an open situation. खुले आम, adv. openly, for all to see. खुले ख़ज़ाने, adv. in the open treasury: openly, publicly; fearlessly. खुले बाज़ार, adv. = prec. खुले मैदान, adv. = खुले ख़ज़ाने; in an open space. – खुलकर, abs. openly, freely, uninhibitedly; publicly; at leisure, in comfort. – खुला-खुला, adj. thoroughly open; plain, straightforward; wide apart; distinct (as handwriting). खुले-खुले, adv. openly, &c.

खुलबंदी *khulbandī* [H. *kholnā*+P. *bandī*], f. *Pl.* reshoeing (a horse, with its old shoes).

खुलवाई *khulvāī* [cf. H. *khulvānā*], f. causing to be open; getting (sthg.) opened.

खुलवाना *khulvānā* [cf. H. *kholnā*], v.t. to cause to get open; to have or to get opened (by another).

खुलाई *khulāī* [cf. H. *khulānā*], f. causing to be open, opening.

खुलाना *khulānā* [cf. H. *kholnā*], v.t. to cause to be open.

ख़ुलासा *khulāsā* [A. *khulāṣa*], m. & adj. **1.** m. substance, essence; gist. **2.** abstract, abridgment. **3.** outcome. **4.** adj. free, unencumbered; spacious, open; unchecked (dysentery). **5.** plain, evident; explicit. — ~ हाल, m. the gist of a (present) situation.

ख़ुश *khuś* [P. *khvuś*], adj. **1.** pleased, glad; happy. **2.** flourishing; well (of health); prosperous. **3.** cheerful (of temperament). **4.** pleasing; good. — ~ करना, to please; to amuse; to gratify. तबीयत ~ होना, to feel refreshed; to feel bodily and mental well-being. – ख़ुशक़िस्मत, adj. fortunate; °ई, f. good fortune. ख़ुशक़िस्मती से, adv. fortunately. ख़ुशख़त, m. & adj. good handwriting; having good handwriting. °ई, f. id., 1. ख़ुशख़बरी, f. good news. ख़ुश-ख़ुश, adv. = ख़ुशी से. ख़ुशगवार [P. *-gavār*], adj. agreeable. ख़ुशगुलू, adj. 19c. sweet-throated; sweet-voiced. ख़ुशदिल, adj. contented, happy. °ई, f. ख़ुशनवीस [P. *-navīs*], m. a good handwriter; calligrapher. °ई, f. calligraphy. ख़ुशनसीब, adj. fortunate. °ई, f. ख़ुशनीयत, adj. well-disposed; honest. °ई, f. ख़ुशनीयती से, adv. in good faith. ख़ुशनुमा [P. *-numā*], adj. inv. attractive, pretty. ख़ुशबयान, adj. eloquent. °ई, f. ख़ुशबू [P. *-dār*], f. fragrance. °दार, adj. ख़ुशमिज़ाज, adj. of cheerful temperament. ख़ुशहाल, adj. in good or satisfactory circumstances: happy; fortunate, prosperous. °ई, f. ख़ुशामद [P. *-āmad*], m. flattery; fawning. ख़ुशामद करना (की), to flatter, &c.; to curry favour (with). °ई, f. ख़ुशामदी टट्टू, m. pej. sycophant.

ख़ुशाल *khuśāl*, adj. pronun. var. see ख़ुशहाल s.v. ख़ुश.

ख़ुशी *khuśī* [P. *khvuśī*], f. **1.** happiness; pl. happy times. **2.** pleasure. **3.** cheerfulness; gaiety. **4.** consent. — ~ करना, to make merry; to do the will or pleasure (of, की). ~, or ख़ुशियाँ, मनाना, to rejoice, to celebrate. ~ में आना, to become pleased. ~ से, adv. with pleasure, gladly; willingly, readily; at (one's, अपनी) own convenience. ~ ~, adv. id. मुझे बड़ी ~ है, I'm very pleased, delighted.

ख़ुश्क *khuśk* [P. *khuśk*], adj. **1.** dry. **2.** parched (as land). **3.** dried (as fruit); withered. **4.** dry (manner, or subject-matter). **5.** adv. only, merely. उसे ~ चार रुपए मिलते हैं, he gets a bare four rupees. — ~ राह से, adv. by land, overland. प्राण ~ होना, fig. to be terrified. ख़ुश्कदिमाग़, adj. sorrowful; °ई, f. grief. ख़ुश्कसाली, f. U. drought.

ख़ुश्की *khuśkī* [P. *khuśkī*], f. **1.** dryness. **2.** dry land. **3.** drought. **4.** dandruff. **5.** dryness (of manner). — ~ की राह से, adv. by land; overland.

खुस-खुस *khus-khus*, f. reg. see खुसर-फुसर, खुस-पुस.

खुसटिया *khusaṭiyā*, f. dim. an owl (= खूसट).

खुस-फुस *khus-phus*, f. = खुसर-फुसर.

खुसफेली *khusphelī* [cf. P. *khvuś*; ? A. *fiʿl*], adj. reg. (E.) ease, comfort.

खुसर-फुसर *khusar-phusar* [onom.], f. whispering. — ~ करना, to whisper. ~ लगाना, to start whispering.

ख़ुसूसन *khusūsan* [A. *khuṣūṣan*], adv. U. especially.

ख़ुसूसियत *khusūsiyat* [cf. A. *khuṣūṣī*: P. *khuṣūṣiyat*], f. particular feature; characteristic.

ख़ूँख़्वार *khūṁkhvār*, adj. = ख़ून-°, see s.v.

[1]**खूँट** *khūṁṭ* [**khunṭa-*[2]], m. **1.** direction, quarter. **2.** corner, angle. **3.** corner-stone (of a foundation). **4.** part, share; a fried bread cake offered to a goddess. **5.** Av. an ear ornament. — चारों ~, m. pl. the four corners (of the world). – चौखूँट, m. id.

[2]**खूँट** *khūṁṭ*, f. (m., *Pl.*) ear-wax.

खूँटना *khūṁṭnā* [**khunṭati*], v.t. **1.** to pluck. **2.** Brbh. to vex, to tease.

खूँटा *khūṁṭā* [**khunṭa-*[1]], m. **1.** a stake, peg. **2.** a post; pile. **3.** a stump. **4.** a wooden handle, or shaft. **5.** support, protection. — खूँटे के बल उछलना, to leap as far as stake (and tether) allow: to depend or to presume on (another's) protection or support. ~ गाड़ना, to determine a boundary point, or (fig.) the limits or scope of sthg. क़साई के खूँटे से बाँधना, to tie (one) to a butcher's stake: to put (one) in, or to expose one to, the direst danger.

खूँटी *khūṁṭī* [cf. H. *khūṁṭā*], f. 1. = खूँटा, 1. **2.** stubble. **3.** Av. = खूँटा, 5.

खूँदना *khūṁdnā* [**kṣundati*: Pk. *khuṁdaï*], v.t. **1.** to trample (with hooves, or feet). **2.** to dig or to paw up (ground).

खूट *khūṭ*, m. pronun. var. = खूँट.

खूट- *khūṭ-*, v.t. Brbh. = खूँटना.

खूटा *khūṭā*, m. pronun. var. = खूँटा.

खूटी *khūṭī*, f. pronun. var. = खूँटी.

खूड़ *khūṛ*, m. reg. (W.) a furrow.

खूद *khūd* [*kṣudra-*], f. *Pl. HŚS.* dregs, refuse.

ख़ून *khūn* [P. *khūn*], m. **1.** blood. **2.** fig. killing; murder; a murder. — ~ (आँखों में) उतरना, (the eyes) to become bloodshot. ~ करना, to shed blood, to kill, to murder; to assassinate; fig. to squander. ~ का जोश, m. love of family, family feeling. ~ का जोश तो होता ही है, blood is thicker than water. ~ का प्यासा, adj. bloodthirsty; desirous of killing (one, के). ~ ख़ुश्क होना, the blood to run dry (from fear). ~ पीना, to drink the blood (of, का): to bring about the death (of); to cause dire suffering (to); to restrain or to suppress emotion. ~ लेना, to bleed (one, का). ~ सफ़ेद करना, to turn the blood white: to act unkindly or unfeelingly. ~ सफ़ेद हो जाना, to lack natural feeling. ~ सिर चढ़ना, to be set on the murder (of, का); to have blood on one's head. ~ सिर पर सवार होना, id., 1. – ख़ून-ख़च्चर, m. bloodshed, bloody fighting (= next). ख़ून-ख़राबा, m. bloodshed, bloody fighting. °-ख़राबी, f. id. ख़ूनख़ोर [P. -*khor*], adj. & m. bloodthirsty, murderous; a bloodthirsty person. ख़ूनख़्वार [P. -*khvār*], adj. blood-drinking: bloodthirsty, murderous. °ई, f. murderousness; slaughter, bloodshed. ख़ूनरेज़ [P. -*rez*], adj. & m. U. bloodshedding: murderous; a murderer. °ई, f. bloodshed, slaughter.

ख़ूनी *khūnī* [P. *khūnī*], adj. & m. **1.** adj. having to do with blood, or with murder. **2.** bleeding, blood-stained. **3.** bloody (as a battle). **4.** m. a murderer; assassin.

ख़ूब *khūb* [P. *khūb*], adj. **1.** fine, splendid; lovely, charming. **2.** adv. very much, lots (of); very well; fine, splendidly. — क्या ख़ूब! how fine! how splendid! wonderful! ख़ूबसूरत, adj. of beautiful face or form: beautiful; handsome. °ई, f. beauty; handsomeness.

ख़ूबानी *khūbānī* [P. *khūbānī*], f. a dried apricot or fig.

ख़ूबी *khūbī* [P. *khūb*], f. **1.** excellence, virtue. **2.** beauty. — ~ से, adv. splendidly, excellently. बख़ूबी [P. *ba-*], id. adv.

खूसट *khūsaṭ*, adj. & m. **1.** adj. dry, decrepit; old, worn out (a person). **2.** useless, worthless. **3.** m. pej. a dry old person. **4.** Av. an owl.

खेई *kheī*, f. reg. dry brambles or thorns; brushwood.

खेकसा *kheksā*, m. reg. (Bihar) a creeping plant having fruit resembling those of the *parval*.

खेखसा *khekhsā*, m. = खेकसा.

खेचना *khecnā*, v.t. = खींचना.

खेचर *khecar* [S.], m. something moving in the sky: **1.** a bird; a heavenly body. **2.** a demigod, or spirit.

खेचरी *khecarī* [S.], m. (in yoga) spirit of the invisible ultimate being. — खेचरी-मुद्रा, f. seal or symbol of the ultimate being.

¹खेटक *kheṭak* [S.], m. reg. (Raj.) a shield.

²खेटक *kheṭak* [S.], m. a village.

³खेटक *kheṭak* [ad. *kheṭaka-*], m. reg. (Raj.) hunting.

खेड़ा *kheṛā* [*kheṭa-²*], m. **1.** a small village. **2.** *archaeol.* a mound, the site of an ancient settlement. — खेड़े की दूब, village grass: something of little worth.

¹खेड़ी *kheṛī* [cf. H. *khernā*], f. afterbirth; placenta. — ~ गिराना, to cause an abortion.

²खेड़ी *kheṛī* [H. *kheṛī* (place name)], f. a locally made steel.

खेत *khet* [*kṣetra-*], m. **1.** a field. **2.** harvest, crop. **3.** ground, land; region; field (of battle). — ~ आना, to fall (in battle). ~ कमाना, to manure, or to work, land. ~ करना, to cultivate land; to fight or to contend (with). ~ काटना, to reap a crop. ~ रहना, to fall (in battle). — खेतदार [P. -*dār*], m. owner or occupier of a field.

खेतिया *khetiyā* [cf. H. *khet*], m. a cultivator, farmer.

खेतिहर *khetihar* [**kṣetriyadhara-*], m. a cultivator, a farmer.

खेती *khetī* [*kṣetriya-*], f. **1.** cultivation, tillage. **2.** farming, agriculture. **3.** a corn field; sown land. **4.** a crop; produce. — ~ करना, to cultivate the soil; to be a farmer. ~ सँभालना, to work as a farmer. – खेती-बारी, f. = next. खेती-बाड़ी, f. farming; agriculture.

खेद *khed* [S.], m. depression; lassitude; grief; distress; regret. — ~ करना, to grieve (over, का); to regret. ~ होना (को), to grieve; to regret. – खेदजनक, adj. to be (much) regretted.

खेदा *khedā* [**khedd-*], m. **1.** a drive, hunt (of elephants, or other wild animals). **2.** a stockade (for catching elephants, &c).

खेदाई *khedāī* [cf. H. *khedā*], f. having to do with an elephant drive, or with a stockade.

खेदना *khednā* [**khedd-*], v.t. to drive, to hunt (animals).

खेदित *khedit* [S.], adj. grieved; distressed.

खेदी *khedī* [cf. H. *khed*], adj. & m. = खेदित.

खेना *khenā* [*kṣepayati*], v.t. **1.** to row; to punt. **2.** to pass through, to endure (suffering, &c). — बुरे दिन ~ डालना, fig. to make one's way through a difficult time.

खेप *khep* [*kṣepya-*], f. **1.** a load; a consignment, cargo. **2.** a supply (regularly renewed); an assortment. **3.** a round journey; a single time or occasion, turn. — ~ भरना, or लादना, to load; to carry a load; to perform a trip.

खेपना *khepnā*, v.t. reg. (Bihar) to spend (time).

खेपिया *khepiyā* [cf. H. *khep*], m. *Pl.* one who makes a trip.

खेम *khem* [ad. *kṣema-*], m. well-being, &c. (see क्षेम). — हेम-खेम, m. Brbh. = कुशल-क्षेम.

खेमटा *khemṭā*, m. a partic. metre; a kind of song.

ख़ेमा *khemā* [A. *khaima*], m. a tent.

खेरना *khernā* [conn. **kṣirati*], v.i. reg. (Raj.) to run, to flow.

खेरा *kherā*, m. Av. = खेड़ा.

खेरी *kherī* [cf. **kṣirati*], f. afterbirth (= [1]खेड़ी).

[1]**खेल** *khel* [**khel(l)-*: Pk. *khelaï*], m. **1.** play; sport; amusement; dallying. **2.** a game. **3.** sthg. easy or unimportant: a trifle. **4.** a wonder, a spectacle. **5.** showing (as of a film). — ~ करना, to play (with, से). ~ खिलाना, to play with (one, को), to lead (one) on; to harass (one). ~ खेलना, to play a game. ~ बिगाड़ना, to spoil (one's) business, or game. ~ मचाना, to play, to get a game under way. – खेल-खेल में, adv. lightly, casually. खेल-कूद, m. games, playing; sport; athletics.

[2]**खेल** *khel*, m. *Pl. HŚS.* a trough (for watering livestock).

खेलत *khelat* [cf. H. *khelnā*], adj. reg. playing: sportive.

खेलना *khelnā* [**khel(l)-*], v.i. & v.t. **1.** v.i. to play; to sport, to amuse oneself; to dally. **2.** v.t. to play (at). **3.** to act (a part); to perform. **4.** to employ, to turn to (cunning, &c). — जान पर, or जी पर, ~, to risk one's life (to do sthg., के लिए). जान से खेल जाना, to be done with life. – खेला, adj. experienced, knowing. खेला-खाया, adj. pleasure-seeking.

खेलवाड़ *khelvāṛ*, m. = खिलवाड़.

खेलवाना *khelvānā*, v.t. = [2] [3]खिलवाना.

खेला *khelā* [cf. H. *khelnā*], m. colloq. performance (of dance, drama).

खेलाड़ी *khelāṛī*, m. pronun. var. = खिलाड़ी.

खेलाना *khelānā*, v.t. = [2] [3]खिलाना.

खेलौना *khelaunā*, m. reg. = खिलौना.

खेवक *khevak* [ad. *kṣepaka-*: w. H. *khe(v)nā*], m. Av. rower, boatman.

[1]**खेवट** *khevaṭ* [*kevarta-*], m. a fisherman, a boatman.

[2]**खेवट** *khevaṭ* [? conn. **kṣepapaṭṭa-*], m. a village register of land holdings and rents due.

खेवना *khevnā*, v.t. = खेना.

[1]**खेवा** *khevā* [*kṣepaka-*], m. **1.** a boatman. **2.** a boat; an oar or pole.

[2]**खेवा** *khevā* [*kṣepa-*], m. **1.** Av. crossing (of a river). **2.** reg. (Bihar) fare for a river crossing.

खेवैया *khevaiyā* [cf. H. *khe(v)nā*], m. a rower, boatman.

खेस *khes* [**kheśśa-*], m. **1.** a kind of heavy patterned cloth. **2.** a shawl of such cloth.

खेसारि *khesāri*, f. = खिसारी.

खेह *kheh*, f. Brbh. Av. dust.

खैंचना *khaiṁcnā*, v.t. = खींचना.

खै *khai* [*kṣati-*], f. reg. dirt; dust, ashes.

खैनी *khainī* [conn. *khādati*], f. chewing tobacco, mixed with lime.

ख़ैमा *khaimā*, m. a tent (= ख़ेमा). — ख़ैमागाह, f. a camp-place, camp.

खैर *khair* [*khadira-*; and *khādira-*], m. **1.** the plant or tree *Acacia catechu* (= खदिर: a source of gum, timber and the astringent extract used with *pān* leaves). **2.** catechu extract (= कत्था).

ख़ैर *khair* [A. *khair*], f. & interj. **1.** f. well-being, welfare. **2.** interj. indeed! really! **3.** well then, in that case. **4.** in fact, I suppose that ... (qualifying a previous remark). — ~ मनाना, or माँगना, to hope for the well-being (of, की), to wish (one) well; to seek (one's own: अपनी) peace of mind, or welfare. ~ से, adv. in good condition, well, safely; peacefully. ~ है, it is well; is all well? ~ हुई, it was well (that, कि). अपनी ~ मनाओ! look after yourself! – ख़ैर-आफ़ियत, f. well-being, welfare (= कुशल-क्षेम). ख़ैर-ख़बर, f. news, good news. ख़ैरख़ाह [P. *-khvāh*], adj. & m. well-wishing; a well-wisher. °ई, f. good will.

खैरा *khairā* [*khadiraka-*], adj. & m. **1.** adj. of the colour of catechu, brown; bluish grey. **2.** m. a bird or animal of brown or bluish-grey colour.

ख़ैरात *khairāt* [A. *khairāt*, pl.], f. **1.** alms. **2.** donation (for any charitable purpose).

ख़ैराती *khairātī* [A. *khairāt*+P. *-ī*], adj. charitable (a gift, a service).

ख़ैरियत *khairiyat* [A. *khairiya*: P. *khairiyat*], f. **1.** well-being (= कुशल-क्षेम). **2.** good fortune. — ~ यह हुई कि ..., it was lucky that ....

खैला *khailā*, m. reg. (W.) a calf; young bullock (not yet working).

खोंखना *khoṁkhnā* [**khokkh-*: Pk. *khokkhaï*], v.i. to cough; to clear the throat of phlegm.

खोंच *khoṁc* [cf. H. *khoṁcnā*], f. **1.** a scratch, tear. **2.** a puncture; stab. — ~ आना or लगना (को, or में), to be scratched, torn, &c.

खोंचड़ *khoṁcaṛ* [cf. *khoṁcnā*], m. a lazy or idle fellow; rascal.

खोंचना *khoṁcnā* [**khoṅc-*], v.t. **1.** to scratch, to tear. **2.** to puncture; to pierce. **3.** to thrust, to stuff (into, में: = खोंसना).

खोंचा *khoṁcā* [cf. H. *khoṁcnā*], m. **1.** a thrust; a stab, prick. **2.** a pole (as used smeared with bird-lime by fowlers).

खोंची *khoṁcī* [cf. H. *khoṁcnā*, and *khoṁsnā*], f. **1.** a small amount of grain taken as payment for a service, or given to a beggar. **2.** a protruding part or section. **3.** reg. (Bihar) a pole with net attached (for collecting fruit).

खोंट *khoṁṭ* [cf. H. *khoṁṭnā*], f. breaking off; pruning.

खोंटना *khoṁṭnā* [**khuṇṭati*, **khoṭayati*: Pk. *khoḍaya-*], v.t. to break off, to prune.

खोंडर *khoṁḍar*, m. reg. (W). gleanings or leavings on the threshing floor.

खोंता *khoṁtā*, m. reg. a bird's nest.

खोंप *khoṁp*, m. = ¹खोप.

¹**खोंपा** *khoṁpā* [**khompa-*], m. reg. (Bihar) a storehouse (for straw).

²**खोंपा** *khoṁpā* [**khoppa-*⁴: ← Drav.], m. a woman's hair tied up on top of the head (= ²खोप).

खोंसना *khoṁsnā* [**skoṣati*], v.t. **1.** to push or to thrust into; to tuck in. **2.** to cram in.

खो *kho*, f. pronun. var. = खोह.

¹**खोआ** *khoā* [**khova-*], m. thickened milk.

²**खोआ** *khoā* [*kṣoda-*], m. *Pl. HŚS.* pounded bricks, mortar, plaster.

खोइया *khoiyā*, f. a marriage dance or play performed at the bride's house by the women of a bridegroom's party.

खोई *khoī* [*kṣapita-*], f. **1.** crushed sugar-cane (from which the juice has been pressed). **2.** reg. (E.) an empty cob or shell; husk.

खोखला *khokhlā* [**khokkha-*], adj. & m. **1.** adj. hollow; empty; excavated. **2.** cracked, not watertight (a vessel). **3.** decayed; worm-eaten. **4.** m. something hollow (as a tree, or a tooth).

¹**खोखा** *khokhā* [? conn. *naukṣaka-*: × **chokkara-*], m. reg. a boy.

²**खोखा** *khokhā* [**khokkha-*], m. sthg. hollow: **1.** a paper bag or wrapper. **2.** reg. a paid bill or draft.

खोखी *khokhī* [? conn. *kaukṣaka-*: × **chokkara-*], f. a girl.

खोज *khoj* [**khojja-*], f. (m., *Pl.*). **1.** search, searching out. **2.** enquiry, investigation; research. **3.** mark, trace, clue. — ~ करना, to search (for, की); to search out. ~ निकालना, to find the track (of), or a clue (to); to trace. ~ मलिया-मेट करना, or मिटाना, to wipe out all trace (of, की). ~ मिलना, to obtain, or find, the track (of); to get an inkling (of). ~ में रहना, to be on the look out for faults (on the part of, की). ~ लगाना, to set up a search (for, की). – खोज-ख़बर, f. enquiry. खोज-ख़बर लेना, to enquire (about one, की). खोज-खाज, f. enquiry; close search; effort.

खोजक *khojak* [cf. H. *khojnā*], m. a searcher, investigator.

खोजना *khojnā* [**khojjati*: Pk. *khojja-*], v.t. **1.** to search for, to search out. **2.** to enquire, to investigate; to explore.

ख़ोजा *k͟hojā* [P. *k͟hvāja*], m. **1.** a eunuch. **2.** name of a west Indian Muslim community. **3.** *HŚS.* = ख़्वाजा.

खोजाना *khojānā* [cf. H. *khojnā*], v.t. to cause to be searched for; to cause enquiry to be made, &c.

खोजी *khojī* [cf. H. *khoj*], adj. & m. **1.** adj. searching, enquiring. **2.** m. one who searches, &c.

खोट *khoṭ* [**khoṭṭa-*], m. (f., *Pl*). **1.** fraud, falsehood; unfaithfulness, insincerity. **2.** wickedness, vice. ***3.** fault, defect; adulteration. **4.** hurt, harm; loss (in trade). — ~ करना, to practise fraud, &c.; to commit a fault; to injure, to cause loss (to, का or की). ~ मिलाना (में), to adulterate. ~ निकालना (में), to detect faults (in); to find fault (with).

खोटा *khoṭā* [**khoṭṭa-*], adj. & m. **1.** adj. false, fraudulent; treacherous; insincere. **2.** wicked, vicious, bad. ***3.** defective: adulterated; counterfeit. **4.** m. a false person, &c. — खोटी कहना (को), = खोटी-खरी सुनाना. – खोटा-खरा, m. bad and good. खोटी-खरी सुनाना (को), to abuse, to use bad language (to); to speak harshly or severely (to). खोटी बात, f. foul language.

खोटाई *khoṭāī* [cf. H. *khoṭā*], f. = खोटापन.

खोटापन *khoṭāpan* [cf. H. *khoṭā*], m. **1.** fraudulence, baseness; deceit, &c. **2.** fault, flaw, &c.

खोड़ *khoṛ* [**khoṭi-*: Pk. *khoḍi-*], f. Brbh. **1.** the anger or curse of a god or spirit. **2.** an unlucky moment.

खोडर *khoḍar* [*koṭara-* (← Drav.) × **khola-*²], m. *Pl.* a hollow in a tree.

खोड़ौ *khoṛau*, adj. Brbh. = खोटा.

खोद *khod* [cf. H. *khodnā*], f. **1.** digging. **2.** fig. investigation.

खोदना *khodnā* [**khodd-*], v.t. **1.** to dig; to excavate; to undermine, to dig (sthg.) out. **2.** to carve; to engrave. **3.** to investigate, to probe. — खोदकर पूछना (से), to question closely.

खोदनी *khodnī*, f. = खुदनी.

खोदवाना *khodvānā*, v.t. = खुदवाना.

खोदाई *khodāī*, f. = खुदाई.

खोदाना *khodānā*, v.t. = खुदाना.

ख़ोनचा *khoncā* [P. *khvānca*], m. a hawker's tray or case.

ख़ोन्चा *khoncā*, m. see ख़ोनचा.

खोना *khonā* [*kṣapayati*], v.t. **1.** to lose. **2.** to cause to be lost or destroyed; to waste. इस हरकत ने उसकी इज़्ज़त खो दी है, this act has cost him his honour. उसने घर की दौलत खो दी, he squandered his family's money. **3.** fig. to be preoccupied, lost in thought.

¹**खोप** *khop* [**khoppa-*²], m. a hole, tear (as in material to be sewn). — ~ भरना (की), to sew (together) with long stitches, to baste.

²**खोप** *khop* [**khoppa-*⁴: ← Drav.], m. Av. a woman's hair tied up behind.

खोपड़ी *khopṛī* [**khoppaḍa-*], f. **1.** a shell (as of a coconut, or a tortoise). **2.** colloq. the skull. **3.** colloq. the head. — ~ खा जाना, or चाटना, to plague, to worry (one, की); to torment; to eat up (another's) resources. ~ खुजलाना, to bring a beating upon one's head. ~ गंजी करना, to beat (one's, की) skull bare, to beat soundly.

खोपरा *khoprā* [**khoppara-*], m. **1.** coconut kernel, or shell. **2.** colloq. the brain; the skull. — खोपरे का तेल, m. coconut oil.

¹**खोपा** *khopā* [**khoppa-*¹], m. *Pl. HŚS.* coconut kernel.

²**खोपा** *khopā* [**khoppa-*³: ? ← Drav.], m. *Pl. HŚS.* corner (of a thatch, or a house).

खोबार *khobār* [?? P. *khok*+H. *bāṛ*, f. ← *vāṭikā-*], m. reg. (E.) a pigsty.

खोया *khoyā*, m. see खोआ.

खोर *khor* [**khora-*² or **khola-*²], f. *Pl.* a hollowed-out place; a cavern; (sunken) lane or alley.

-ख़ोर *-khor* [P. *khor*], adj. & m. formant. eating (e.g. मुफ़्तख़ोर, m. one who eats without paying, a sponger).

खोरा *khorā* [*khora-*¹], adj. Av. lame.

¹**खोरी** *khorī* [**khora-*² or *khola-*²], f. Brbh. **1.** a (sunken) lane or alley. **2.** a narrow valley.

²**खोरी** *khorī*, f. Brbh. = खोट.

¹**खोल** *khol* [cf. H. *kholnā*], f. the act of opening, &c.

²**खोल** *khol* [conn. *kholi-*], m. **1.** an outer covering; shell (as of a snail, mollusc; a cloth, a case or cover; crown (of a tooth); reg. cloth sheet, garment. **2.** a sheath; scabbard. **3.** reg. (Bihar) blinkers.

³**खोल** *khol* [**khola-*²] **1.** reg. a hollow; cavity. **2.** reg. (Bihar) a slot; mortice.

खोलना *kholnā* [**kholl-*], v.t. **1.** to open; to loosen; to unfasten, to untie; to unmoor; to unlock; to take off, to remove (as a *dhotī*). **2.** to disentangle; to unravel. **3.** to uncover; to lay open. **4.** to clear, to unblock. **5.** to solve; to explain, to display, to disclose (to, पर). आपने उसका भेद मुझपर खोल दिया है, you have revealed the truth about him to me. **6.** to bring to an end (as a fast). **7.** to inaugurate, to establish. **8.** to start, to set in action (as a radio, or a car). **9.** to dismantle (an apparatus). — खोलकर, adv. openly, plainly; warmly. जी खोलकर, openly; unrestrainedly; to one's heart's content; gladly.

खोसना *khosnā*, v.t. = खोंसना.

खोली *kholī* [**kholla-*¹: Pk. *kholla-*], f. a small room.

खोह *khoh* [conn. *goha-*; ? ×*khani-*], f. **1.** a cave; den (of a wild beast). **2.** a chasm. **3.** a pit, hole.

खौंखी *khaumkhī* [cf. *khaum-khaum*], f. reg. coughing; a cough.

खौं-खौं *khaum-khaum* [onom.], f. the sound of coughing. — ~ करना, to cough.

ख़ौफ़ *khauf* [A. *khauf*], m. fear. — ~ करना, to be afraid (of, से). ~ खाना, to be in fear (of, का). ~ दिखाना, or देना (को), to frighten, to terrify; to threaten. ~ में डालना, to intimidate; to alarm. ~ रखना, to be in fear (of, का). – ख़ौफ़नाक [P. -*nāk*], adj. fearsome, terrifying; afraid.

¹**खौर** *khaur*, m. reg. (W.) a Śaiva (crescent-shaped) *tilak*.

²**खौर** *khaur*, m. reg. (W.) a funnel-shaped fishing net.

खौरा *khaurā*, m. **1.** *HŚS.* mange. **2.** [**khora-*²] *Pl.* rot (among sheep).

खौलन *khaulan* [cf. H. *khaulnā*], f. the act of boiling.

खौलना *khaulnā* [*kha-ul], v.i. **1.** to boil, to grow hot. **2.** fig. to be enraged.

खौलाना *khaulānā* [cf. H. *khaulnā*], v.t. **1.** to cause to be boiled; to make boiling hot. **2.** fig. to infuriate, to enrage.

ख्यात *khyāt* [S.], adj. & f. **1.** adj. celebrated; well known. **2.** named, called. **3.** m. a type of chronicle celebrating the history of states and dynasties, deeds of kings, &c.

ख्याति *khyāti* [S.], f. **1.** fame, renown; reputation. **2.** designation.

ख़्याल *khyāl*, m. see **ख़याल**.

ख्रीष्ट *khrīṣṭ* [B.: ← Engl. *Christ*], m. obs. Christ.

ख़्वाजा *khvājā* [P. *khvāja*], m. usu. /xaja/. **1.** man of distinction or rank. **2.** *musl.* a venerable ascetic. **3.** chief of a household establishment; butler.

ख़्वाब *khvāb* [P. *khvāb*], m. usu. /xab/. **1.** dream. **2.** vision. — ~ **देखना**, to have a dream. ~ **में आना**, to appear (to one, **को**) in a dream.

ख़्वार *khvār* [P. *khvār*], adj. usu. /xar/. **1.** base, vile. **2.** wretched.

ख़्वारी *khvārī* [P. *khvārī*], f. usu. /xarī/. **1.** baseness. **2.** wretchedness.

ख़्वाह *khvāh* [P. *khvāh*], conj. usu. /xah/. wishing: either, or; whether. — ~ ... ~, conj. whether ... or. ~ **म** ~ [P. *-ma-*], adv. willy-nilly; of necessity. – **ख़्वामख़्वाह**, adv. id.

ख़्वाहिश *khvāhiś* [P. *khvāhiś*], f. usu. /xahiś/. **1.** wish, desire. **2.** request. — ~ **करना**, or **रखना**, to have a desire (for, **की**). – **ख़्वाहिशमंद** [P. -*mand*], adj. desirous, solicitous; curious.

ग

ग *ga*, the third consonant of the Devanāgarī syllabary. — **गकार**, m. the sound /g/; the letter **ग**.

गंग *gaṅg* [*gaṅgā*], f. the river Ganges. — **गंग-गति लेना**, to die. **गंग-बरार** [P. *bar-ār*], m., f. *Pl. HŚS.* alluvial land recovered from a river.

गंगा *gaṅgā* [S.], f. the river Ganges. — **गंगा-यमुना**, f. the Ganges and Jumna rivers. – ~ **उठाना**, to swear by the (water of) the Ganges. ~ **जी**, f. hon. the Ganges; fig. an expanse of water (as caused by flooding). ~ **दुहाई**, (I swear) by the Ganges; (I call upon) the Ganges: heaven help (us)! ~ **नहाना**, to bathe in the Ganges; to be freed from sin and go to heaven; to be finally freed from cares, to reach (one's) goal. ~ **पार**, adv. across, or beyond the Ganges. ~ **पार करना**, to send away (from a locality); to send abroad. ~ **माई**, or ~ **माता**, f. Mother Ganges, the sacred Ganges. **उलटी** ~ **बहाना**, fig. to attempt the impossible; to achieve sthg. almost impossible. **बहती** ~ **में हाथ धोना**, to 'take the current when it serves'. **भरी** ~ **में (खड़ा होकर) कहना**, to swear implicitly by the Ganges. – **गंगा-गति**, f. going to the Ganges (to die), death; death and release from the cycle of rebirth. **गंगा-जमनी**, adj. inv. & f. mixed, composite; of whitish grey colour; made of alloy; an alloy; an ear-ring of alloy. **गंगा-जल**, m. Ganges water. °**ई**, f. a container for Ganges water. **गंगाजली उठाना**, to swear by the water of the Ganges. **गंगा-द्वार**, m. a name of the town of Hardvar (where the Ganges reaches the plains). **गंगाधर**, m. upholder of the Ganges: a title of Śiva. **गंगा-पूजा**, f. worship by a newly married couple at the bank of a river or tank. **गंगा-प्राप्ति**, f. fig. dying on the banks of the Ganges. **गंगा-यात्रा**, f. pilgrimage to the Ganges. **गंगा-लाभ**, m. fig. death. **गंगावतरण** [°*gā+a*°], m. *mythol.* the descent of the Ganges to earth. **गंगावतार** [°*gā+a*°], m. id. **गंगा-सागर**, m. the place where the Ganges reaches the sea; a metal water-pot with a spout (for carrying sacred water to be used in worship). **गंगा-स्नान**, m. bathing in the Ganges; name of a bathing festival held on the Ganges on the last day of the month of Kārttik. **गंगोतरी** [°*gā+u*°: for °*ttrī*], f. the place in the Himālayas where the Ganges rises. **गंगोदक** [°*gā+u*°], m. Ganges water. **आकाश-गंगा**, f. the Milky Way; *mythol.* the heavenly Ganges.

गंगाल *gaṅgāl*, m. a large metal vessel for holding water.

गंगाला *gaṅgālā*, m. *Pl. HŚS.* land subject to flooding of the Ganges.

[1]**गंज** *gañj* [conn. *gañja-*[2] (← Ir.) [3]; ? ← Panj.; and P.], m. f. a store, hoard: **1.** a grain market. **2.** a market. **3.** heap, pile.

[2]**गंज** *gañj*, m. *Pl. HŚS.* **1.** baldness. **2.** a complaint of the scalp.

गंजन *gañjan* [ad. *gañjana-*; cf. H. [1]*gaṁjnā*], m. Av. **1.** contempt; disrespect. **2.** destruction. **3.** fig. one who destroys.

[1]**गँजना** *gaṁjnā* [**gañj-*: Pk. *gaṁjaï*], v.t. **1.** to treat with contempt, or disrespect; to abuse. **2.** Brbh. to destroy.

[2]**गँजना** *gaṁjnā* [conn. **gañja-*[3]], v.t. to pile up (= [1]*gāṁjnā*).

गंजा *gañjā*, adj. bald.

गँजाई *gaṁjāī* [cf. H. [2]*gaṁjnā*], f. heaping or piling up.

गँजिया *gaṁjiyā*, f. reg. a saddle-bag; a coarse bag of hemp fibre.

[1]**गंजी** *gañjī* [cf. H. [1]*gañj*], f. heap. pile.

[2]**गंजी** *gañjī* [Engl. *Guernsey*], f. a woollen vest.

गंजीफ़ा *gañjīfā* [P. *ganjīfa*], m. *Pl. HŚS.* **1.** a pack of cards. **2.** a kind of card game (played with a pack of ninety-six cards, 12 per suit).

गँजेड़ी *gaṁjeṛī* [cf. H. *gāṁjā*], m. one addicted to hemp (cannabis).

गँजेरी *gaṁjerī* [cf. *gañjā-*], f. reg. (W.) = **गँजिया**, 2.

गँठ- *gaṁṭh-* [H. *gāṁṭh*]. = **गाँठ**. — **गँठकटा**, m. a pickpocket. **गँठजोड़**, m. joining a knot: making an alliance. °**आ**, m. tying the (marriage) knot (in the clothing of bride and bridegroom). **गँठ-बंधन**, m. id.; union, alliance. **गँठलगू**, m. colloq. a constant attendant or hanger-on.

गँठना *gaṁṭhnā*, v.i. = **गठना**.

गँठिया *gaṁṭhiyā*, adj. **गठिया**.

गँठी *gaṁṭhī* [cf. *granthi-*; *grathna-*], f. a root or flake (as of an onion); a clove (of garlic) (see **गट्ठा**).

गँठीला *gaṁṭhīlā* [cf. H. *gāṁṭh*], adj. knotted, knotty.

गंड *gaṇḍ* [S.], m. the cheek; the temple. — **गंड-स्थल**, m. id.

गंडा *gaṇḍā* [*gaṇḍaka-*: ← Austro-as.], m. **1.** an aggregate of four: the number four; counting by fours. **2.** a knot. ***3.** a cord or piece of cotton consisting usu. of coloured threads knotted together, tied round the neck, wrist or ankle (as a charm to avert the evil eye). **4.** a cord, or string of shells, or metal plates, fastened round animals' necks as an ornament or charm. — **गंडा-तावीज़**, m. amulet, charm.

गँडासा *gaṁḍāsā*, m. pronun. var. = **गँड़ासा**.

गँड़ासा *gaṁṛāsā* [**gaṇḍāsi-*], m. **1.** a chopper for crop stalks. **2.** a long-handled chopper or axe (serving as a weapon).

गँड़ासी *gaṁṛāsī* [**gaṇḍāsi-*], f. a small chopper (= **गँड़ासा**).

गंडी *gaṇḍī* [*gaṇḍikā-*; or cf. H. *gaṇḍā*], m. *Pl.* a magic circle (to ward off danger).

गँडेरी *gaṁḍerī*, f. pronun. var. = **गँड़ेरी**.

गँड़ेरी *gaṁṛerī* [cf. *gaṇḍa-*[2]], f. a section of sugar-cane (between two knots).

गंतव्य *gantavyă* [S.], adj. & m. **1.** adj. to be gone (by), or traversed (as a road). **2.** m. destination.

गंद *gand* [P. *gand*; cf. H. *gandh*], m. **1.** a smell, stench. **2.** filth. — **~ बकना**, to use foul language.

गंदक *gandak* [P. *gandak*], f. pronun. var. = **गंधक**.

गंदगी *gandagī* [P. *gandagī*], f. **1.** dirt, filth. **2.** fig. obscenity. **3.** a smell, stench.

गँदलाहट *gaṁdlāhaṭ* [cf. H. *gaṁdlā*], f. dirtiness; pollution.

गंदा *gandā* [P. *ganda*], adj. **1.** dirty, filthy. **2.** fig. obscene. **3.** vile, bad (of temper). **4.** stinking, rotten; rancid. — **~ करना**, to make foul; to pollute; to disgrace. **~ बिरोज़ा** [P. *fīroza*], m. resin (of *Boswellia*, or of pine).

गंदुम *gandum* [P. *gandum*], m. U. wheat.

गंदुमी *gandumī* [P. *gandumī*], adj. U. wheat-coloured.

गंध *gandh* [S.], f. **1.** smell; fragrance; scent. **2.** a scented substance; perfume. **3.** a bad smell, stench. **4.** fig. a whiff, trace. — **~ देना**, to smell bad. – **गंधकारिता**, f. the making of perfumes. **गंध-जल**, m. perfumed water. **गंध-तैल**, m. perfumed oil. **गंध-निवारक**, m. a deodorant. **गंध-पत्र**, m. the white tulsī plant. **गंध-बिलाव**, m. *HŚS.* a civet cat (? the small Indian civet). **गंध-मृग**, m. the musk deer. **गंध-राज**, m. sandalwood; any fragrant flower, esp. those of *Gardenia florida* and *Jasminum zambac*. **गंधवाह**, m. poet. fragrance-bearing: the wind. **गंध-सार**, m. id.

गंधक *gandhak* [S.], f. sulphur. — **~ का तेज़ाब** or **~ का तेल**, m. sulphuric acid. – **गंधक-वटी**, f. sulphur pill (a digestive). **गंधकाश्म** [°*ka*+*a*°], m. a sulphurous mineral; brimstone.

गंधकी *gandhăkī* [cf. H. *gandhak*; or ad. *gandhakīya-*], adj. & m. **1.** adj. sulphur-coloured; sulphurous. **2.** sulphuric. **3.** m. an unpleasant-smelling flying bug; a green fly that attacks rice, millets and young pulse.

गंधर्व *gandharv* [S.], m. **1.** *mythol.* a heavenly minstrel or musician; a demigod of the heaven of Indra. **2.** *hind.* a community, of which the women are singers and dancers. — **गंधर्व-लोक**, m. realm of the *gandharvas*, the heaven of Indra. **गंधर्व-विद्या**, f. the science or art of music. **गंधर्व-विवाह**, m. *hind.* marriage by mutual agreement, without any marriage ceremony.

गँधला *gaṁdhlā*, adj. = **गदला**.

गँधाना *gaṁdhānā* [conn. H. *gandh*], v.i. to smell (of, **से**).

गंधार *gandhār* [ad. *gāndhāra-*], m. **1.** the Gāndhāra region. **2.** *mus.* name of a *rāg*.

गंधी *gandhī* [cf. H. *gandh*], m. **1.** a maker or seller of perfumes. **2.** reg. (Bihar) = **गंधकी**.

गंधीला *gandhīlā* [cf. H. *gandh*], adj. **1.** fragrant. **2.** malodorous.

गंभीर *gambhīr* [S.], adj. **1.** deep; low (a sound). **2.** profound; unfathomable. **3.** serious; thoughtful; earnest (a person); solemn; dignified.

गंभीरता *gambhīrătā* [S.], f. **1.** depth. **2.** profundity, &c. (see **गंभीर**). **3.** gravity, &c.

गँवई *gaṁvaī* [cf. H. *gāṁv*], adj. & f. **1.** adj. having to do with a village or villages; rustic. **2.** pej. = **गँवार**, 2. **3.** f. a small village.

गँवर- *gaṁvar-* [cf. H. *gaṁvār*]. uncouth, &c.: — **गँवर-दल**, m. & adj. a group or crowd of yokels; uncouth, boorish, &c.

गँवाऊ *gaṁvāū* [cf. H. *gaṁvānā*], adj. & m. **1.** adj. wasteful; prodigal. **2.** m. a waster, spendthrift.

गँवाना *gaṁvānā* [cf. *gamayati*], v.t. **1.** to allow to be lost; to lose (a thing). **2.** to lose, to miss (a road). **3.** to waste, to squander (as money, time, opportunity).

गँवार *gaṁvār* [**grāmadāra-*: Pk. *gavāra-*], m. & adj. **1.** m. a villager: an uncouth, or ignorant person. **2.** adj. boorish, uncouth; uneducated.

गँवारपन *gaṁvārpan* [cf. H. *gaṁvār*], m. boorishness; uncouthness.

गँवारी *gaṁvārī* [cf. H. *gaṁvār*], adj. & f. pej. **1.** adj. rustic. (= गँवारू.) **2.** f. boorishness, uncouthness. **3.** a village speech, or style of speech. 4. = गँवार, 1.

गँवारू *gaṁvārū* [cf. H. *gaṁvār*], adj. & m. pej. rustic: **1.** adj. unrefined, uncouth; boorish. **2.** m. an uncouth person.

गंस *gaṃs* [conn. H. *gāṁsnā*], m. Brbh. ill-will.

गऊ *gaū* [**gavu-*: Pa. *gavuṁ*], f. reg. (E.) = गाय.

गगन *gagan* [S.], m. **1.** the sky, the heavens. **2.** the regions beyond the world, space.

गगरा *gagrā* [*gargara-*²: ? ← Austro-as.], m. a large water-pot.

गगरी *gagrī* [*gargara-*²: ? ← Austro-as.], f. a water-pot.

¹**गच** *gac* [**gacca-*], m. **1.** mortar, cement; plaster (esp. for mosaic work). **2.** a plastered floor. — गचकारी, f. *Pl. HŚS.* plastering; building, brick laying.

²**गच** *gac* [**gacc-*], adj. crowded together. — गच-पच, adj. crowded, packed, squashed all together; jumbled together (= गिच-पिच).

³**गच** *gac* [? onom.], m. the sound of squelching, or of piercing or puncturing.

ग़ची *gacī*, f. reg. = ग़चू.

ग़चू *gacū*, m. reg. a small hole made in the ground (by boys, in playing *gullī-ḍaṇḍā*).

गच्चा *gaccā*, m. reg. (E.) a setback. — ~ खाना, to incur dishonour.

गज *gaj* [S.], m. **1.** an elephant. **2.** *mythol.* the eight elephants of the quarters of the world. **3.** (in chronograms) the number 8. **4.** bow (as of a *sāraṅgī*). — गज-गति, f. a stately gait; a (woman's) graceful gait. °-गामिनी, adj. walking majestically; walking gracefully. गज-गाह [*grāha-*], m. Av. a decorative fringe or hanging tied round an elephant's neck. गज-दंत, m. ivory; an impacted tooth. °ई, adj. of ivory. गज-दान, m. the gift of an elephant (an act of very great merit). गज-पति, m. a large or noble elephant; a rajah owning many elephants. गज-पाल, m. a mahout. गज-मुख, adj. & m. = गजानन. गज-मोती, m. a large pearl (as supposed to be found in elephants' heads). गज-राज, m. = गजेंद्र; the leader of a herd of elephants. गजवदन, adj. & m. = गजानन. गजानन [°*ja*+*ā*°], adj. & m. elephant-faced: an epithet of Gaṇeś. गजेंद्र [°*ja*+*i*°], m. a large or noble elephant.

गज़ *gaz* [P. *gaz*], m. **1.** a measure of length, formerly of approximately 33 inches; a yard; obs. a timber-merchants' yard (24 inches). **2.** an instrument for measuring; a yard measure. **3.** *mus.* bow for a *sāraṅgī*.

गज़क *gazak* [P. *gazak*], m. **1.** a snack (e.g. of pastries, fruit or sweets) taken with wine, opium or hemp. **2.** a sweet made from sesame and sugar.

गजगजाना *gajgajānā* [cf. *garjati*], v.i. **1.** to sound, to rattle. **2.** to buzz, to hum.

ग़ज़ब *gazab* [A. *gazab*], m. & adj. anger; violence: **1.** m. a disaster; a dire or disastrous thing. **2.** sthg. extreme, or excessive. ~ की प्यास, f. a terrible thirst. **3.** adj. extreme; stupendous; splendid; extraordinary; terrible; harmful (to, के हक़ में). **4.** excessive. — ~ करना, to do sthg. wonderful; to do sthg. outrageous; to tyrannise (over, पर). ~ गरमी पड़ रही है, colloq. it's devilish hot. ~ टूटना (पर), disaster to befall (one). ~ ढाना, or तोड़ना (पर), to wreak vengeance (on); to oppress; to ravage (a lover's heart). ~ बनके निकले (or निकली) हो! colloq. you're looking splendid!

¹**गजर** *gajar* [? cf. *garjā-*: and Pk. *gajjira-*], m. **1.** chimes. **2.** the four a.m. chimes. — ~ बजे, adv. at early dawn.

²**गजर** *gajar* [? cf. H. *gājar*], f. reg. (Bihar) a mixed crop (? comprising peas with a cereal). — गजर-बजर [H. *bājrā*], m. pej. poor-quality food.

गजरा *gajrā* [*gārjara-*, Pk. *gajjara-*], m. **1.** Brbh. a bracelet (? cut or decorated to resemble carrot leaf, or root). **2.** reg. (W.) a wrist ornament. **3.** a garland of flowers (worn on the wrist).

ग़ज़ल *gazal* [A. *gazal*], f. a poem of partic. metrical type on, or including conventionally, an amatory theme.

गजा *gajā*, f. Av. a drum-stick.

गजाल *gajāl*, m. *Pl. HŚS.* a kind of fish.

गज़ी *gazī* [P. *gazī*], f. a type of coarse cotton cloth.

गज्जर *gajjar*, m. reg. (W.) swampy ground.

गज्झा *gajjhā* [*grāhya-*], m. a heap, pile. — ~ मरना, colloq. to make a pile (of money).

गझिन *gajhin*, adj. thick (as cloth, or beard); tangled (vegetation).

गट *gaṭ* [? onom.], m. the sound of gulping, or of gurgling. — ~ ~, m. & adv. continued gulping, or gurgling; with a gulping noise, &c. ~ से, adv. with a gulp; all at once. – गटागट, adv. id.

गटकना *gaṭaknā* [? conn. H. *gaṭ*], v.i. **1.** to gulp down, to bolt (food). **2.** colloq. to embezzle.

ग़टरग़ूँ *gaṭargūm̐*, m. = गुटरगूँ.

गट्टा *gaṭṭā* [**gaṭṭa-*], m. **1.** a hard lump; a sweet. **2.** a corn. **3.** a large seed, or corm. **4.** a stopper, plug (as the padding round the tube of a hookah, which fixes into the mouth of the bowl). **5.** the wrist joint, or the ankle joint; pastern (of a horse). — **गट्टे पड़ना**, calluses to form (on the feet, &c).

गट्ठर *gaṭṭhar* [cf. H. *gaṭṭhā*], m. a large bundle; a bale; a large package, parcel.

गट्ठा *gaṭṭhā* [*grathna-*, or cf. *granthayati*], m. **1.** a large bundle; a load. **2.** a bulbous root (as of onion or turmeric); a clove (of garlic). **3.** the wrist joint, or the ankle joint; a horse's pastern (= गट्टा, 5). **4.** [?] a measure of length, one twentieth of a *jarīb*.

गट्ठी *gaṭṭhī* [*grathna-*, or cf. *granthayati*], f. a small bundle; pack, bale; pad (for a pack-animal's back).

गठ- *gaṭh-*. = गँठ-.

गठड़ी *gaṭhṛī*, f. reg. (Raj.) = गठरी.

गठन *gaṭhan* [S.], m. structure, build; construction.

गठना *gaṭhnā* [cf. H. *gām̐ṭhnā*], v.i. **1.** to be joined together; to be connected; to be built (esp. the body). **2.** to come together; to plot, to collude; to be joined (in friendship, or as allies). — **गठा हुआ शरीर**, a strongly built body.

गठरी *gaṭhrī* [cf. H. *gaṭṭhar*], f. **1.** a bundle; a package; parcel. **2.** fig. (one's) money-bag, or wealth. **3.** fig. a person lying inert, or helpless. — **~ करना**, or **बनाना**, to pack up or to bundle together; to tie (sthg., or someone) up; to double up (an opponent, in wrestling). **~ बाँधना**, to pack (one's, **की**) things; to prepare for a journey. **~ मारना**, to rob (one, **की**).

गठवाई *gaṭhvāī* [cf. H. *gam̐ṭhvānā*], f. **1.** causing to be mended, &c. **2.** the cost or charge for getting (sthg.) mended.

गठवाना *gaṭhvānā* [cf. H. *gām̐ṭhnā*], v.t. to cause to be joined or fastened, &c.; to cause to be strung or threaded; to have mended (as shoes).

गठाना *gaṭhānā*, v.t. = गठवाना.

गठाव *gaṭhāv* [cf. H. *gaṭhnā*], m. manner of structure (= गठन).

गठिया *gaṭhiyā* [cf. H. *gaṭṭhī*], f. rheumatism; gout. — **गठिया-बाई**, f. rheumatism.

गठियाना *gaṭhiyānā*, [cf. H. *gaṭṭhī*], v.t. to pack or to wrap up, to bundle up.

गठीला *gaṭhīlā* [cf. *grantha-*], adj. **1.** knotty. **2.** compact, well-built (of a person).

गठौंद *gaṭhaund* [**granthabandha-*], m. reg. (E.) money tied up in a bag or bundle, cash to be deposited.

गड़ंग *gaṛaṅg*, m. *Pl. HŚS.* reg. a store-room, arsenal.

गड़ंत *gaṛant* [cf. H. *gaṛnā*], m. *Pl. HŚS.* an object over which an incantation is uttered and which is then buried (in the hope of achieving some end by magical means).

गड़ *gaṛ*, m. pronun. var. = गढ़.

गड़क *gaṛak* [ad. *gaḍaka-*], m. *Pl. HŚS.* a kind of goldfish.

गड़गड़ *gaṛgaṛ* [**gaḍagaḍa-*: Pk. *gaḍayaḍa-*], f. **1.** gurgling. **2.** *HŚS.* a rumbling in the stomach (= गुड़गुड़).

गड़गड़ा *gaṛgaṛā* [cf. H. *gaṛgaṛ*], m. colloq. gurgler: a hookah.

गड़गड़ाट *gaṛgaṛāṭ*, f. pronun. var. = गड़गड़ाहट.

गड़गड़ाना *gaṛgaṛānā* [cf. H. *gaṛgaṛ*], v.i. & v.t. **1.** v.i. to gurgle. **2.** to rumble (as clouds). **3.** v.t. to cause to gurgle, &c.

गड़गड़ाहट *gaṛgaṛāhaṭ* [cf. H. *gaṛgaṛānā*], f. **1.** a gurgling sound. **2.** a rumbling sound.

गड़गड़ी *gaṛgaṛī* [cf. H. *gaṛgaṛ*], f. E.H. a small drum.

गड़-गूदड़ *gaṛ-gūdaṛ* [cf. H. *gūdaṛ*], f. rags, tatters.

गड़ना *gaṛnā* [cf. H. *gāṛnā*], v.i. **1.** to penetrate or to be driven (in or into, **में**); to be fixed (in); to stick (into), to pierce. **2.** to sink (into). **3.** to be put (into the ground); to be buried. **4.** fig. to be a source of irritation (as a speck of dirt in the eye).

गड़प *gaṛap* [? onom., conn. H. [2]*gap*], m. **1.** the noise of falling into water or mud; splash, splosh. **2.** a gulp. — **~ करना**, transf. to embezzle. **~ (से) खा जाना**, to gobble up, to wolf (food).

गड़बड़ *gaṛbaṛ* [**gaḍḍa-baḍḍa-*], f. m. & adj. **1.** f. disorder, confusion, muddle; disturbance, uproar. **2.** agitation (of mind), bewilderment; alarm. **3.** adj. confused. — **~ करना**, to confuse, to mix up; to make a mess of. **~ पड़ना (में)**, to be interfered with, adversely affected. – **गड़बड़-घोटाला**, m. colloq. shady dealings, a scandal; row. **गड़बड़-झाला** [M. *jhālā*], m. = prec.

गड़बड़ाना *gaṛbaṛānā* [cf. H. *gaṛbaṛ*], v.i. & v.t. **1.** v.i. to get into a state of confusion, or muddle. **2.** to be disturbed; to be alarmed. **3.** v.t. to confuse. **4.** to disturb; to alarm.

गड़बड़ाहट *gaṛbaṛāhaṭ* [cf. H. *gaṛbaṛānā*], f. **1.** confusion. **2.** disturbance, uproar. **3.** agitation; alarm.

गड़बड़ी *garbarī* [cf. H. *garbar*], f. = गड़बड़, गड़बड़ाहट. — ~ में पड़ना, to fall into confusion, &c.

गडमड *gaḍmaḍ*, f. & adj. = गड़बड़; awry.

गडरिया *gaḍariyā*, m. = गड़ेरिया.

गड़रिया *garariyā* [cf. *gaḍḍara-*], m. = गड़ेरिया.

गड़वाना *garvānā* [cf. H. *gārnā*], v.t. **1.** to cause to be driven or fixed (in or into, में); to cause to be stuck or sunk (into). **2.** to cause to be buried.

गड़हा *gar'hā* [H. *gaḍḍhā*], m. **1.** a hole, a pit (= गड्ढा). **2.** a hollow; crater. — ~ आँटना, or भरना, to fill up a hole or hollow. आँख का ~, m. the eye-socket.

गड़ाना *garānā* [cf. H. *gārna*], v.t. **1.** to cause to penetrate or to be driven (into, में); to push or to stick (into); to pierce. **2.** to put (into the ground); to bury.

गड़ाप *garāp*, m. = गड़प, 1.

गड़ारा *garārā* m. reg. (W.) a cart-track.

गड़ारी *garārī*, f. **1.** an instrument for twisting thread or string. **2.** a pulley, or block (as for a well-rope). **3.** a groove; rut or track (for a rope or wheel). — गड़ारीदार [P. *-dār*], adj. *HŚS.* milled (a coin); zigzag (a line).

गड़ुवा *garuvā* [conn. *gaḍuka-*], m. **1.** a water-pot having a spout. **2.** a narrow-mouthed pot. **3.** a drinking-mug.

गडेरिया *gaḍeriyā*, m. = गड़ेरिया.

गड़ेरिया *gareriyā*, m. **1.** a shepherd; goatherd; cowherd. **2.** one of a partic. community of herdsmen. — गड़ेरिया-पुराण, m. shepherds' tales: village tales and notions.

गड़ेरी *garerī*, f. pronun. var. = गँड़ेरी.

गड़ोना *garonā*, v.t. = गड़ाना.

गड़ोलना *garolnā*, m. *Pl. HŚS.* a child's go-cart.

गड्ड *gaḍḍ* [**gaḍḍa-*[2]], m. a bundle, bunch; collection. — ~ का ~, adv. the whole lot, or bunch. – गड्ड-मड्ड, adj. jumbled up, in a confused mass (papers).

गड्डी *gaḍḍī* [**gaḍḍa-*[2]], f. **1.** a bundle, bunch; wad (of notes); pack (of cards). **2.** a heap, pile.

गड्ढा *gaḍḍhā* [**khaḍḍa-* (Pk. *khaḍḍā-*); ? × **gaḍḍa-*[1]], m. **1.** a ditch, hole; a pit; crater. **2.** a sunken area (as of ground, or of the cheeks). **3.** a pitfall. — आँख का ~, the eye-socket.

गढ़ंत *garhant* [cf. H. *garhnā*], adj. & f. **1.** adj. fabricated; artificial; imaginary. **2.** f. sthg. fabricated; an imitation; a fiction. 3. = गढ़न. — मन-गढ़ंत बात, f. sthg. made up; a figment of imagination.

गढ़ *garh* [*gaḍha-*], m. **1.** a fort; a stronghold; castle. **2.** socket (of the eye). — ~ जीतना or तोड़ना, to capture or to reduce a fort; fig. to accomplish a difficult feat. – गढ़-पति, m. commander of a fort; a rajah. गढ़वाल, m. = गढ़-पति.

गढ़ई *garhaī* [cf. H. *garhā*], f. dimin. a pit; a small pond or tank.

गढ़त *garhat* [cf. H. *garhnā*], f. *Pl. HŚS.* structure, construction.

गढ़न *garhan* [cf. H. *garhnā*], f. **1.** making, fashioning. **2.** make or style (of sthg.), workmanship.

[1]**गढ़ना** *garhnā* [**gaṭhati*: Pk. *gaḍhai*; and *ghaṭate*], v.t. & v.i. **1.** v.t. to make, to shape; to forge, to cast; to mould. **2.** to make with craftsmanship; to engrave; to carve; to smoothe, to plane; to create. **3.** to fabricate (as a tale). **4.** v.i. to be made or shaped (esp. by beating or hammering); to be fashioned, forged, &c.

[2]**गढ़ना** *garhnā*, v.i. reg. = गड़ना.

गढ़ा *garhā*, m. see गड़हा.

[1]**गढ़ाई** *garhāī* [cf. H. [1]*garhānā*], f. **1.** making, shaping, fashioning; workmanship. **2.** the cost or charge of making, &c.

[2]**गढ़ाई** *garhāī* [cf. H. [2]*garhānā*], f. reg. **1.** burying. **2.** the cost or charge of burying.

[1]**गढ़ाना** *garhānā* [cf. H. *garhnā*], v.t. to cause to be made or shaped (esp. by beating or hammering); to fashion.

[2]**गढ़ाना** *garhānā*, v.t. reg. = गड़ाना.

[1]**गढ़िया** *garhiyā*, f. **1.** [cf. H. *garh*] = गढ़ी. **2.** [cf. H. *garhā*] reg. = a small pond or tank.

[2]**गढ़िया** *garhiyā* [cf. H. *garhnā*], m. a craftsman: a goldsmith, jeweller, &c.

गढ़ी *garhī* [cf. H. *garh*], f. a small fort; fortification.

गढ़ैया *garhaiyā* [cf. H. *garhnā*], m. Brbh. Av. a craftsman, artificer.

गण *gaṇ* [S.], m. **1.** a group, troop, company; tribe. **2.** pl. dependants, servants; attendant deities. **3.** a genus, or broad category. **4.** *pros.* a group of *mātrās* comprising a foot. **5.** *gram.* a collective plural marker. — गणतंत्र, m. a republic. °वादी, adj. & m. republican; a republican. °आत्मक, adj. republican. °ई, adj. &

m. = °वादी. गण-नाथ, m. lord of the attendants (minor deities): the god Gaṇeś. °-नायिका, f. the goddess Durgā. गण-पति, m. = गण-नाथ. गणपूरक, m. = next. गण-पूर्ति, f. a quorum. गण-मुख्य, m. the leader of a group, &c. गणराज्य, m. = गणतंत्र. गणसंख्या, f. a collective numeral. गणाधिप [°ṇa + a°], m. chief of the *gaṇas*: the god Gaṇeś. गणाध्यक्ष [°ṇa + a°], m. id. गणेश [°ṇa + ī°], m. lord of the attendant (minor deities): the god Gaṇeś. °-चतुर्थी, f. a festival observed on the fourth of any of several months, in honour of Gaṇeś. °-चौथ, f. id. गोबर-गणेश, m. Gaṇeś of dung: a fat, useless person; a complete fool.

गणक *gaṇak* [S.], adj. & m. **1.** adj. calculating. **2.** m. one who calculates: specif. an astrologer. ~ यंत्र, m. a calculating machine; computer.

गणन *gaṇan* [S.], m. counting, calculation.

गणना *gaṇănā* [S.], f. counting. — जन-गणना, f. census.

गणनीय *gaṇănīyă* [S.], adj. **1.** able to be counted, calculable. **2.** needing counting; worthy of account.

गणिका *gaṇikā* [S.], f. a prostitute; a dancing-girl.

गणित *gaṇit* [S.], m. **1.** arithmetic. **2.** mathematics. — गणितकार, m. = next. गणितज्ञ, m. a mathematician. गणित-ज्योतिष, m. astronomy. गणित-विद्या, f., or °-शास्त्र, m. mathematics.

गण्य *gaṇyă*, [S.], adj. **1.** able to be counted. **2.** needing counting; worthy of account. (= गणनीय.) — गण्य-मान्य, adj. distinguished, prestigious.

¹गत *gat* [S.], adj. **1.** gone, departed; previous; last. ~ वर्ष, last year. **2.** -गत. come to, located in, concerned with, having properties of. व्यक्तिगत, adj. personal (as characteristics, circumstances). — गतप्राय, adj. near its conclusion. गतांक, [°ta + a°], m. previous number (of a journal). गतांत [°ta + a°], adj. having reached, or approaching, its conclusion. गतागत [°ta + ā°], adj. gone and returned; reversible (a line of verse). °इ, f. going and returning; death and reincarnation. गतानुगत [°ta + a°], m. the observance of custom. °इक, adj. (blindly) conventional. गतार्थ [°ta + a°], adj. meaningless; of reduced means.

²गत *gat* [*gati-*], f. a going: **1.** situation, condition; aspect; plight. **2.** recourse; utility. **3.** a type of action in dancing; a type of song and esp. its accompaniment. — ~ करना, to make use (of, की); euph. to beat; to perform the last rites (of). ~ का, adj. of good quality; useful (as goods, produce). ~ पर नाचना, to dance to music. ~ बनाना, colloq. to beat. ~ भरना, = ~ पर नाचना. ~ लेना, to dance in a particular way. –

गतका *gatkā*, m. *HŚS.* a wooden stick or blunt sword (used in fencing).

गति *gati* [S.], f. **1.** going, movement; course, motion; progress, development. **2.** ending; death (and transmigration). वीर ~ पाना, to die a hero's death. **3.** situation, condition; a period of time. **4.** manner, way of acting; scope, reach. **5.** means, recourse; shelter, protection (as offered by a god to a devotee). — गतिज, adj. kinetic. गतिपूर्ण, adj. active, dynamic (= क्रियाशील). गतिमान, adj. in motion; movable; dynamic. गतिरोध, m. hindrance to movement, or to the progress (of); an obstacle. गतिविज्ञान, m. dynamics. गतिविद्या, f. id. गतिविधि, f. manner of acting, procedure, activity. गतिशील, adj. = गतिमान. गतिहीन, adj. motionless; inert.

गतिक *gatik* [S.], adj. & m. **1.** adj. dynamic. **2.** m. = गति, 1.

गतिकी *gatikī* [cf. H. *gati*, w. *gatik*], f. dynamics.

गते गते *gate gate* [cf. H. ²*gat*], adv. reg. (E.) slowly, by degrees.

गत्ता *gattā* [*gātraka-*: ← P.], m. pasteboard, cardboard.

¹गद *gad* [S.], m. **1.** a disease. **2.** *mythol.* name of a monkey in Rāma's army.

²गद *gad* [cf. H. *gādnā*], f. a thudding sound.

गदका *gadkā*, m. reg. (W.) = गतका.

गदगद *gadgad* [ad. *gadgada-*], adj. inarticulate from emotion; faltering; stammering; ecstatic.

गदगोल *gadgol*, [cf. **gadda-*¹], m. a stirring up: turmoil.

गदबदा *gadbadā*, adj. plump.

गदबदाना *gadbadānā* [? conn. H. *gadgad*], v.i. to rejoice.

ग़दर *gadr* [A. *gadr*], m. faithlessness: rebellion; revolt; disturbance. — ~ मचाना, to revolt, &c.

गदरा *gadrā* [cf. **gadda-*²], adj. **1.** not fully ripe (fruit or corn). **2.** ripening: plump, well-developed.

गदराना *gadrānā* [cf. H. *gadrā*], v.i. **1.** to ripen, to be ripening; to bloom; to develop. **2.** to become inflamed (as the eye).

गदराहट *gadrāhaṭ* [cf. H. *gadrānā*], f. near ripeness (of fruit).

गदला *gadlā* [cf. **gadda-*¹], adj. **1.** muddy (as water); dirty. **2.** foul, impure. — ~ करना, to muddy, to stir up.

गदलापन *gadlāpan* [cf. H. *gadlā*], m. muddiness; impurity.

गदहा *gad'hā*, m. = गधा.

गदहूल *gad'hūl* [*gadda-[1] + phulla- or *hūl-, H. *hūl-*], m. Brbh. a lotus.

[1]**गदा** *gadā* [S.], f. **1.** a mace; a club. **2.** dumb-bells. — गदाधर, adj. club-bearing: title of Kṛṣṇa.

[2]**गदा** *gadā* [P. *gadā*], m. E.H. a beggar.

गदाई *gadāī* [cf. H. [2]*gadā*], adj. pej. of no account, wretched.

गदागद *gadāgad* [cf. H. *gad*], adv. one after another; helter-skelter; all at once, or in a rush.

गदेल *gadel* [? conn. H. *gadrā*, or H. *god*], m. reg. (E.) a baby.

[1]**गदेला** *gadelā* [cf. *garda-[2]: ? ← Drav.], m. **1.** a large padded mattress (to sit on). **2.** reg. (Bihar) saddle-pad of a camel; howdah-pad of an elephant. **3.** reg. padded roofing (on an *ikkā* or bullock-cart).

[2]**गदेला** *gadelā*, m. reg. (W.) a small pickaxe; *Pl.* crowbar.

गद्दा *gaddā* [*garda-[2]: ? ← Drav.], m. a mattress; a large padded cushion. — गद्देदार [P. *-dār*], adj. padded, soft.

ग़द्दार *gaddār* [A. *gaddār*], m. **1.** a traitor; rebel. **2.** an apostate.

ग़द्दारी *gaddārī* [P. *gaddārī*], f. a traitor's, or rebel's, act; treachery, &c.

गद्दी *gaddī* [*garda-[2]: ← Panj.], f. **1.** a cushion. **2.** a throne, royal seat; (family's or ancestors') native seat. **3.** the seat or cushion from which a money-lender, merchant, &c. conducts business. **4.** transf. sectarian leadership, or status; office. **5.** something stuffed or padded; a pack-saddle; a bandage or pad; pessary. **6.** something bulky, a large bundle of paper; a sheaf. — ~ पर बैठना, to rule, to hold authority. ~ पर विराजमान होना, id. ~ रखना, to put a bandage (on, पर or में); to use a pessary. ~ से उतारना, to remove from a throne, or from office. – गद्दीनिशीन [P. *-niśīn*], adj. the incumbent of a seat of office; a regent, vice-regent. °ई, f. accession to office.

गद्य *gadyă* [S.], m. prose. — गद्य-पद्य, m. prose and verse. गद्य-काव्य, m. a prose poem. गद्यात्मक [°*ya* + *ā*°], adj. consisting of or characterised by prose (a work, a style); prosaic.

गधा *gadhā* [*gardabha-*], m. **1.** an ass, donkey. **2.** transf. an ass-load. **3.** a fool. — गधा-पच्चीसी, f. the years of indiscretion, years up to twenty-five. गधा-लोटन, m. an asses' wallowing-hole (place to be avoided). गधे पर चढ़ाना, to mount (one) on an ass: to expose to disgrace. – गधा-चंद, m. a stupid fellow, donkey.

गधापन *gadhāpan* [cf. H. *gadhā*], m. foolishness, asininity.

गधी *gadhī* [*gardabha-*], f. a she-ass.

गनना *gannā*, v.i. = गिनना.

गनहेल *ganhel*, ? m. a kind of oats, *Avena sativa*.

ग़नी *ganī* [A. *ganī*], adj. & m. Brbh. Av. **1.** adj. rich. **2.** m. a rich person.

[1]**गनी** *ganī* [cf. H. *gannā*], f. Brbh. counting; estimate; worth, account.

[2]**गनी** *ganī* [conn. *gōṇī-*: ‹ Drav.], f. coarse sacking, 'gunny'.

ग़नीमत *ganīmat* [A. *ganīma*: P. *ganīmat*], f. booty: **1.** a piece of good fortune. **2.** abundance. — ~ जानना, to prize, to value. ~ समझना, to regard as good fortune: to be pleased (about sthg). ~ है कि ..., it's a lucky thing that ....

गन्ना *gannā* [*gaṇḍa-*], m. sugar-cane.

[1]**गप** *gap* [*gappa-; and cf. *jalpati*], f. **1.** casual talk, gossip. **2.** baseless or exaggerated remarks; rumour. — ~ उड़ाना, to spread baseless notions, &c. ~ छाँटना, to indulge in gossip, &c. ~ मारना, to talk idly (about, की). ~ लड़ाना, to gossip. – गप-शप, f. = ~.

[2]**गप** *gap* [? onom.], m. **1.** the sound of gulping or swallowing. **2.** the sound of pricking or puncturing. — ~ से, adv. voraciously; swiftly, deftly (as of the administering of an injection). – गप-गप, m. & adv. the sound of gulping down, &c. गप-गप खाना, to eat voraciously. – गपागप खाना, id. गपागप पढ़ना, to devour (a book).

गपकना *gapaknā* [cf. H. [2]*gap*], v.t. **1.** to gulp, to bolt (food). **2.** to take in, to usurp. **3.** to catch, to snap up (as a ball).

गपका *gapkā* [cf. H. *gapaknā*], m. **1.** a gulping, bolting (of food). **2.** reg. a bribe. **3.** *Pl.* a soft-sounding thrust, or blow.

गपड़-चौथ *gapaṛ-cauth*, m. colloq. golden chance (sc. as at a festival) for gossiping.

गपड़-शपड़ *gapaṛ-śapaṛ*, f. = [2]गप.

गपोड़ा *gaporā* [cf. H. [1]*gap*], m. = [1]गप, 2.

गपोड़िया *gaporiyā*, m. = गप्पी.

गप्पी *gappī* [cf. H. [1]*gap*], adj. & m. **1.** adj. fond of gossip. **2.** m. a gossip; an idle talker.

गफ़ *gaf* [P. *gaf*], adj. thick, of close texture (material).

ग़फ़ *gaf* [P. *gaf*], adj. thick, heavy (of cloth).

ग़फ़लत *gaflat* [A. *gafla*: P. *gaflat*], f. **1.** neglect; forgetfulness. **2.** inattention. **3.** heedlessness. **4.** soundness (of sleep); unconsciousness. **5.** a fainting fit. — ~ **करना** (**से**), to neglect; to disregard. ~ **की नींद**, f. the sleep of the just. ~ **से**, adv. negligently; thoughtlessly; carelessly.

ग़फ़लती *gaflatī* [P. *gaflatī*], adj. neglectful, &c. (see **ग़फ़लत**).

गब-गब *gab-gab* [onom.], m. & adv. the sound of gulping or gobbling.

गबदा *gabdā* [H. *gadbadā*], adj. colloq. plump.

ग़बन *gabn* [A. *gabn*], m. defrauding, misappropriation; embezzlement.

गबर-गबर *gabar-gabar*, m. & adv. = **गब-गब**.

गबरू *gabrū* [*garbharūpa-*], adj. & m. **1.** adj. youthful, juvenile. **2.** m. a teenager; young man. **3.** reg. (Bihar) a bridegroom.

गब्भा *gabbhā* [*garbha-*], m. *Pl. HŚS.* a quilt.

गभीर *gabhīr*, adj. = **गंभीर**.

ग़म *gam* [P. *gam*], m. **1.** sadness; sorrow. **2.** care, concern. — ~ **करना**, or **मनाना**, to grieve (for, **पर**). ~ **खाना**, to suffer grief; to feel sympathy (for, **का**); to bear grief. ~ **ग़लत करना** (**अपना**), to distract (oneself) from sorrow, to console (oneself). ~ **होना**, to be regretful (of or about, **का**). – **ग़मख़ोर** [P. *-khor*], adj. suffering patiently; meek. °**ई**, f. **ग़मगीन** [P. *-gīn*], adj. sad; dejected; depressed. °**ई**, f. **ग़मज़दा** [P. *-zadā*], adj. inv. & m. sorrow-stricken, suffering grief; a griever. **ग़मनाक** [P. *-nāk*], adj. causing sadness; = **ग़मगीन**.

गमक *gamak* [S.], m. **1.** deep tone or sound (as of a *vīṇā*, or a drum). **2.** shake or trill (in music); grace note. **3.** fragrance, aroma.

गमकना *gamaknā* [cf. H. *gamak*], v.i. to be fragrant.

गमकीला *gamkīlā* [cf. H. *gamak*], adj. fragrant, aromatic; spicy.

गमछा *gamchā*, m. reg. a cloth or towel (= **अँगोछा**).

गमत *gamat* [ad. *gamatha-*], m. *Pl. HŚS.* a path, way.

गमन *gaman* [S.], m. **1.** the act of going. **2.** gait. **3.** sexual relations. — **गमनागमन** [°*na*+*ā*°], m. going and coming; leaving and arriving; circulation (of traffic); transportation.

गमनीय *gamănīyă* [S.], adj. **1.** passable. **2.** to be crossed or traversed. **3.** accessible, attainable.

गमला *gamlā*, m. a wide-mouthed jar or pot (as for plants).

ग़मज़ *gamz* [A. *gamz*], m. U. a wink; flirtatious glance.

गमाना *gamānā*, v.t. pronun. var. = **गँवाना**.

गमार *gamār*, adj. pronun. var. (E.) = **गँवार**.

ग़मी *gamī* [P. *gamī*], f. time of sorrow: **1.** death. **2.** mourning. — **शादी-ग़मी**, f. times of joy and sorrow: times of marriage and death.

गम्मत *gammat*, f. reg. amusement; object of amusement or liking.

गम्य *gamyă* [S.], adj. accessible, attainable; practicable.

गम्यता *gamyătā* [S.], f. accessibility; practicability.

गयंद *gayand* [*gajendra-*], m. an elephant, a fine or noble elephant.

[1]**गया** *gayā* [*gata-*], perf. part. **1.** gone, past. **2.** Av. corrupt, dissolute. — **गई करना**, to overlook (an offence, &c.) to connive at; to neglect (to do sthg). **गए दरजे**, adv. at most; at least. – **गया-गवाया**, adj. lost and gone, stolen. **गया-गुज़रा**, adj. past; destroyed, broken down; corrupt, worthless. **गया-बीता**, adj. past (as days); outdated (a person, or an attitude).

[2]**गया** *gayā*, f. the city of Gaya in Bihār (an important place of Hindu pilgrimage). — ~ **करना**, to visit Gaya to worship ancestors. — **गयावाल**, m. a resident, or a brahmaṇ keeper of community records, of Gaya.

गयाल *gayāl* [conn. *gata-*], m. reg. **1.** W. a person who dies without an heir. **2.** *hist.* a co-tenant's land when not claimed after his death, or when left unworked. **3.** a bad (unpaid) debt.

गर *gar*, conj. U. (in poetry) = **अगर**.

गरंड *garaṇḍ* [? **gārakhaṇḍa-*], m. reg. **1.** an enclosure of mud or earth; an embankment. **2.** W. mud base (for the lower of two grindstones).

-गर *-gar* [P. *gar*], suffix (forms m. agent nouns from nouns, e.g. **जादूगर**, magician).

गरई *garaī* f. reg. (Bihar) a kind of fish.

ग़रक़ *garq* [A. *garq*], adj. **1.** drowned. **2.** sunk; immersed. — ~ **करना**, to drown; to immerse.

गरकट *garkaṭ* [H. *galā*+H. *kāṭnā*], m. a cut-throat: murderer, assassin.

ग़रक़ी *garqī* [P. *garqī*], adj. & f. **1.** adj. flooded (land). **2.** f. flooding (of land). **3.** flooded land. **4.** sinking (of a boat). — ~ **में आना**, to be flooded; to be liable to flood.

गरगज *gargaj* [cf. H. *gaṛh*], m. Av. a raised structure, scaffolding: specif. a tall movable gun-platform (part of the defences of a fort).

ग़रग़रा *gargarā* [A. *gargara*], m. **1.** gargling. **2.** bubbling (as boiling water). **3.** rattling sound in the throat; death-rattle.

गरगराना *gargarānā*, v.i. reg. = **गड़गड़ाना**.

गरज *garaj* [cf. H. *garajnā*], f. **1.** the noise of thunder. **2.** a roaring, bellowing.

ग़रज़ *garz* [A. *garẓ*], f. & adv. **1.** f. motive; purpose. **2.** need, desire. **3.** interest, concern. **4.** purport, gist. ~ **यह कि** ..., the fact of the matter is, in short. **5.** adv. in short, in a word. — ~ **का बावला**, obsessed by (one's) passions or desires. ~ **का यार**, m. a self-interested friend. ~ **निकालना (अपनी)**, to achieve (one's) purpose or desire. ~ **पड़ना**, to have need (of, **की**: as of assistance). ~ **रखना**, to have an interest (in, **की**); to cherish a desire, to aim (at). – **ग़रज़मंद** [P. -*mand*], adj. self-interested; needy. °**ई**, f.

गरजना *garajnā* [ad. *garjati*: w. H. *gājnā*], v.i. to thunder; to roar, to bellow.

गरजाहट *garjāhaṭ* [cf. H. *garajnā*], f. the rumbling of thunder.

ग़रज़ी *garzī* [P. *garẓī*], f. self-interested.

गरट्ट *garaṭṭ* [ad. *granthi*-, m.], m. Brbh. a group.

गरदन *gardan* [P. *gardan*], f. **1.** the neck; the throat. **2.** neck (as of a flask). — ~ **उठाना**, fig. to resist; to rise, to rebel. ~ **उड़ाना (की)**, to behead. ~ **उतारना**, or ~ **काटना**, id. ~ **झुकाना**, to bow the neck: to submit; to defer (to); to be ashamed. ~ **ढलना** or **ढलकना**, fig. to be near (one's) end. ~ **न उठाना**, to be laid low (by illness); to be docile (under some compulsion). ~ **नापना**, to take (one, **की**) by (sc. around) the throat. ~ **पर छुरी फेरना**, to put to the knife: to kill; to harass. ~ **पर जुआ रखना**, to yoke (one): to take, or to give (one) a burden or responsibility. ~ **पर सवार होना**, to ride on the neck (of): to tyrannise, to domineer; to dominate. ~ **पर होना**, to be laid at (one's) door, on one's conscience. ~ **फँसाना**, to involve (one, **की**) in difficulty; colloq. to give, or to incur, responsibility. ~ **मरोड़ना**, to wring (one's) neck, to strangle; to plague, to torment. ~ **में हाथ डालना**, to take by the throat. – **गरदन-घुमाव**, m. neck-twister: a wrestling hold. **गरदनतोड़**, adj. & m. neck-breaking: causing an excruciating headache (a partic. infectious fever: ? meningitis); a wrestling hold.

गरदनी *gardnī* [P. *gardan*], f. **1.** a blow on the neck. **2.** reg. (W.) covering for the neck and upper body of a horse. — ~ **लगाना**, to strike (one, **को**) on the neck.

गरदानना *gardānnā* [P. *gardānīdan*: *gardān*, pres. stem], v.t. to go through or over, to repeat (as a lesson).

गरम *garm* [P. *garm*], adj. **1.** hot; warm. **2.** ardent; zealous; quick (of temper); agitated; sensuous. **3.** active, brisk; burning, topical (an issue); live (an electric wire). – ~ **करना**, to heat, to warm; to excite; to stimulate; to warm up, to exercise (a horse). ~ **बोलना**, to speak heatedly; to speak with feeling and effectively. – ~ **ख़बर**, f. 'hot news'; a current rumour. ~ **दल**, m. *pol.* an activist group (*hist.*); an extremist group. ~ **पड़ना**, to become angry, to be ready to quarrel (with, **से**). ~ **पानी**, m. wine; tea. ~ **मसाला**, m. the various common spices used in cooking (collectively): a partic. mixture of spices. ~ **होना**, to be or to become hot; to become excited, or stimulated; to become angry, to be ready to quarrel (with, **से**); to be brisk, busy; to be rife. – **गरम-गरम**, adj. all hot, piping hot; new, fresh; spontaneous, extempore. **गरम-जोशी**, f. enthusiasm, zeal; warmth of affection. **गरम-बाज़ारी**, f. activity (in a market), brisk demand, or good sale; high value or estimation (of, **की**). **गरम-मिज़ाज**, adj. quick-tempered. **गरम-सर्द**, or **गरमो-सर्द**, adj. hot and cold; lukewarm. – **गरमागरम**, adj. id. °**ई**, f. heat (of an argument). °**ई से**, adv. eagerly; zealously.

गरमाई *garmāī* [cf. H. *garm*], f. **1.** becoming hot or warm. **2.** heat.

गरमाना *garmānā* [cf. H. *garm*], v.i. & v.t. **1.** v.i. to become hot, to become warm; to be warmed up. **2.** to become angry; to become enlivened, or enthusiastic. **3.** v.t. to heat, to warm; to warm up. **4.** to make angry; to enliven, &c. — **जेब** ~, to warm (one's) pocket: to give a consideration; to bribe.

गरमाहट *garmāhaṭ* [cf. H. *garm*], f. **1.** becoming hot, or warm. **2.** heat, warmth.

गरमी *garmī* [P. *garmī*], f. **1.** heat; warmth. **2.** usu. pl. the hot weather. **3.** venereal disease. **4.** ardour; zeal, enthusiasm; quickness (of temper); volatility (of emotion); sexual passion. **5.** activity, briskness: topicality. — ~ **करना (में)**, to heat, to warm; to become angry (with, **से**). ~ **की हद**, f. *Pl.* boundary-line of the heat: the tropics. **(अपनी)** ~ **निकालना**, to satisfy (one's) sexual desire. ~ **पड़ना**, to be hot (the weather). ~ **होना (को)**, to suffer from the heat; to have a veneral disease. – **ठंडी-गरमी**, f. variability (of feeling); indifference.

गरल *garal* [*garala*-], m. poison. — **गरलधर**, adj. poison-holding: poisonous.

गराँव *garāṁv*, m. reg. (E.) = **गलाँवन**.

गरामी *garāmī* [P. *garāmī*], adj. esp. in comp. respected, of high repute. — **नामी-गरामी**, adj. id.

[1]**ग़रारा** *ġarārā* [? A. *ġargara*], m. gargling; a gargle. — ~ **करना**, to gargle.

[2]**ग़रारा** *ġarārā* [P. *ġarāra*], m. **1.** loose trousers (women's). **2.** a large sack, tent-bag. — **ग़रारेदार** [P. *-dār*], adj. baggy, loose (trousers).

गरारी *garārī*, f. reg. (Bihar) = **गड़ारी**.

गराव *garāv* [? ad. *grāha-*], m. reg. (W.) **1.** a sheaf, bundle of fodder. **2.** a chopper (= **गँड़ासा**).

गरावा *garāvā* [? conn. *galati*[1]], m. reg. (W.) a light friable soil.

गरास- *garās-* [ad. *grāsayati*; H. *grās*], v.t. Brbh. Av. to swallow, to devour.

गरिमा *garimā* [S.], f. **1.** weight: dignity, prestige; excellence; importance. **2.** self-importance, vanity.

गरियार *gariyār* [cf. *guḍi-*, Pk. *gali-*], adj. & m. **1.** adj. Av. stubborn (as an ox). **2.** m. reg. (W.) a stubborn ox (that will not move).

गरियारी *gariyārī* [cf. H. *gariyār*], f. *Pl.* stubbornness, obstinacy.

गरिष्ठ *gariṣṭh* [S.], adj. **1.** weighty. **2.** indigestible.

गरी *garī* [**garu-*[2]], f. **1.** kernel (of a nut or seed). **2.** pulp, flesh (as of a fruit). — ~ **का तेल**, m. coconut oil.

-गरी *-garī* [P. *-garī*], f. noun formant. practice (of), trade, work (e.g. **जादूगरी**, f. magic, magic skill).

ग़रीब *ġarīb* [A. *ġarīb*], adj. & m. **1.** adj. poor. **2.** humble, modest. ~ **ख़ाना**, m. humble dwelling: my house. **3.** mild (as the glance). **4.** m. a poor man. — ~ **करना**, to impoverish. – **ग़रीबपरवर** [P. *-parvar*], m. supporter, or cherisher of the poor. **ग़रीबनवाज़** [P. *-navāz*], adj. & m. kind, or hospitable to the poor; one who treats the poor kindly (a lord, or deity). °**ई**, f. kindness to the poor. **ग़रीबनिवाज़**, adj. & m. = **ग़रीबनवाज़**.

ग़रीबाना *ġarībānā* [P. *ġarībāna*], adj. like a poor person.

ग़रीबी *ġarībī* [P. *ġarībī*], f. **1.** poverty. **2.** humility, lowliness. — ~ **आना (पर)**, to be reduced to poverty. ~ **में आटा गीला**, wet flour in poverty: the poor must endure everything.

गरुआ *garuā* [*guru-*], adj. Av. **1.** weighty, grave. **2.** proud.

गरुआई *garuāī* [cf. H. *guru*], f. Av. **1.** weight. **2.** load, mass, vastness.

गरुड *garuḍ*, m. pronun. var. = **गरुड़**.

गरुड़ *garuṛ* [S.], m. *mythol.* name of a bird, the vehicle of Viṣṇu. — **गरुड़गामी**, m. he who rides on Garuṛ: Viṣṇu. **गरुड़-घंटा**, m. a bell surmounted by an image of Garuṛ (rung in worship by devotees of the Vaiṣṇava deity Ṭhākur jī). **गरुड़-व्यूह**, *hist.* name of a partic. military formation, with main strength in the centre. **गरुड़-सिंह**, m. *mythol.* a griffin.

ग़रूर *ġarūr* [A. *ġurūr*], m. **1.** (false) pride. **2.** vanity. — ~ **करना**, to behave haughtily. ~ **होना (को)**, to be proud, &c.

गरेबान *garebān* [P. *garebān*], m. var. /gireban/. a collar. — ~ **पकड़ना**, to take (one, **का**) by the collar, or by the neck. **(अपने)** ~ **में मुँह डालना**, to be introspective; to be conscious or ashamed of one's faults. ~ **में हाथ डालना**, = ~ **पकड़ना**.

गरेर- *garer-*, v.t. Av. to surround; to lay siege to.

गरेरा *garerā* [cf. H. *garer-*], adj. Av. winding, spiral (flight of steps).

गरोह *garoh*, m. pronun. var. = **गिरोह**.

ग़र्क़ *ġarq*, m. see **ग़रक़**.

गर्गरी *gargarī* [S.], f. a water-pot.

गर्ज़ *garz*, f. see **ग़रज़**.

गर्जन *garjan* [S.], m. **1.** the sound of thundering or rumbling. **2.** roaring, bellowing. — ~ **करना**, to thunder, to bellow, &c. – **गर्जन-तर्जन**, m. storming, shouting (in anger).

गर्त *gart* [S.], m. a pit; a ditch; gulf, chasm.

गर्द *gard* [P. *gard*], f. dust. — ~ **उड़ना (की)**, dust to fly about; (fig.) to be or to become ruined or desolate (a place). ~ **उड़ाना (की)**, to raise dust; to ruin, to lay waste. ~ **फाँकना**, fig. to wander aimlessly (in or about, **की**), to idle about. ~ **होना**, to be or to become dust; to be worthless; pej. to be very easy. – **गर्दख़ोर** [P. -*khor*], adj. dust-absorbent: not dirtying easily (fabric). **गर्द-गुबार**, or **गर्दो-गुबार**, m. dust, clouds of dust; turmoil.

गर्दभ *gardabh* [S.], m. an ass, a donkey.

गर्दा *gardā* [P. *gardah*], ? f. Av. metr. see **गर्द**.

गर्दिश *gardiś* [P. *gardiś*], f. a going round, or about: **1.** wandering aimlessly. ***2.** adversity. **3.** *pol.* a revolution. — ~ **में आना**, to fall on hard times; to fall into a state of turmoil, or of revolution.

गर्दी *gardī* [P. *-gardī*], f. wandering; revolution: change; turmoil; affliction. — ~ **के दिन**, m.pl. times of turmoil. — **गुंडागर्दी**, f. trouble-making by hooligans.

गर्भ *garbhă* [S.], m. **1.** the womb. **2.** the belly. **3.** conception, pregnancy. **4.** foetus, embryo. — ~ गिरना, to miscarry. ~ गिराना, to carry out an abortion. ~ रहना (को), to become pregnant. ~ से होना, to be or to become pregnant. – गर्भकारी, adj. impregnating, causing conception. गर्भ-काल, m. period of pregnancy; time of delivery. गर्भ-केसर, m. *bot.* pistil, or carpel. गर्भ-कोश, m. womb. गर्भ-क्लेश, m. birth pains. गर्भ-गृह, m. an inner room; shrine; confinement room. गर्भ-धारण, m. conception; pregnancy. गर्भ-नाड़ी, f. umbilical cord. गर्भ-नाल, m. id. गर्भ-निरोध, m. contraception. °अक, adj. & m. contraceptive. गर्भ-निस्रव, m. afterbirth, placenta. गर्भ-पात, m. miscarriage. गर्भ-पात करना, to cause a miscarriage. °अक, °ई, adj. inducing miscarriage. गर्भ-पातन, m. abortion. गर्भ-भवन, m. = गर्भ-गृह. गर्भ-मास, m. month of delivery. गर्भ-वास, m. gestation of an embryo; the womb. गर्भ-विज्ञान, m. embryology. गर्भस्थ, adj. being carried (a child in the womb). गर्भ-स्थापन, m. fertilisation. गर्भ-स्राव, miscarriage; abortion. °अक, m. an abortionist. °ई, adj. inducing miscarriage. गर्भांक [°*bha+a*°], m. an act (in a play); a scene, episode. गर्भाधान, [°*bha+ā*°], m. fertilisation; a ceremony performed after menstruation to favour conception; (esp.) a ceremony performed on the first indications of pregnancy. गर्भावस्था [°*bha+a*°], f. the state of pregnancy. गर्भाशय [°*bha+ā*°], m. the womb.

गर्भवती *garbhăvatī* [S.], adj. f. pregnant.

गर्भिणी *garbhiṇī* [S.], adj. f. pregnant.

गर्म *garm*, adj. see गरम.

[1]**गर्रा** *garrā*, adj. reddish (as plumage); bay-coloured (a horse); iron-grey (a horse).

[2]**गर्रा** *garrā*, m. reg. (Bihar) = गारा.

गर्री *garrī* [? conn. H. *gaṛārī*], f. **1.** *Pl. HŚS.* an instrument for twisting thread or string. **2.** reg. (W.) a cylindrical roller (for field-work).

गर्व *garv* [S.], m. **1.** pride. **2.** arrogance. **3.** vanity; conceit; self-satisfaction. — ~ करना, to be proud (of, पर); to be haughty; to be conceited (about). – गर्वप्रद, adj. forming a source of pride, glorious. गर्वशील, adj. proud; haughty, &c. गर्वोक्ति [°*va+u*°], f. an arrogant remark or remarks, &c. गर्ववंत, adj. Brbh. proud; haughty, &c.

गर्वित *garvit* [S.], adj. given cause for pride, proud; haughty, &c.

गर्वीला *garvīlā* [cf. H. *garv*], adj. proud; haughty, &c.

गर्हण *garhaṇ* [S.], m. *Pl. HŚS.* censuring; censure, reproach.

गर्ह्य *garhyă* [S.], adj. & m. **1.** adj. censurable, base; detestable. **2.** m. a censurable, or base person.

गर्हित *garhit* [S.], adj. = गर्ह्य, 1.

[1]**गल-** *gal-* [cf. H. *galā*]. the throat; the neck: — गल-कंबल, m. dewlap. गल-गंड, m. goitre. गल-ग्रंथि, f. the thyroid gland. गल-घोंटू, adj. causing choking, suffocating. गल-थना, m. dewlap. गल-फाँसी, f. a noose (for the neck); fig. dire predicament. गल-बाहीं, f. embracing, an embrace: गल-बाहीं डालना, or करना, to put (one's) arm round (another's) neck.

[2]**गल-** *gal-* [cf. H. *gāl*]. the cheek: — गल-गुच्छा, m. see गल-मुच्छा. गलगुथना, adj. plump-cheeked, plump. गल-तकिया, m. a small pillow or cushion for the cheek when resting. गल-थैली, f. *zool.* pouch (as in a monkey's mouth). गल-फड़ा, m. see s.v. गल-फूला, adj. chubby-cheeked; chubby. गल-मुच्छा, m. sideboards (on the cheeks); a florid moustache. गल-शोथ, m. inflammation of the throat. गल-सुआ, m. mumps.

[1]**गलका** *galkā* [cf. H. *galna*], m. E.H. a sweet made from raw fruit, with spices.

[2]**गलका** *galăkā* [cf. *gala-*[2]], m. reg. (E.) a swelling, or boil in the neck.

[1]**गलगल** *galgal* [cf. H. *gaṛgaṛ*], f. a gurgling or gulping sound. — ~, adv. with a gurgle, or a gulp.

[2]**गलगल** *galgal* [P. *galgal*], m. **1.** a citron. **2.** a particular bird (? a stork: cf. लगलग).

गलगला *galgalā* [cf. *galati*[1]], adj. Brbh. damp; tear-filled (eyes).

गलगलाना *galgalānā* [cf. *galati*[1]], v.i. & v.t. reg. **1.** v.i. to be damp, to be moist; to be softened. **2.** to be moved (with emotion). **3.** v.t. to soften. **4.** to mollify.

गलगलाहट *galgalāhaṭ* [cf. H. *galgalānā*], f. reg. the act or process of softening; softness.

ग़लत *galat* [A. *g̱alaṭ*], adj. **1.** incorrect, wrong (as a sum, a conclusion). **2.** untrue (a remark, &c). — ~ करना, to determine or to regard as wrong; to annul; to disregard. ~ समझना, to misunderstand. – ग़लत-नामा, m. list of errata. ग़लतबयानी, f. false witness. ग़लतफ़हमी, f. wrong understanding; misconception.

गलतंस *galtaṃs* [ad. *galitavaṃśa-*], adj. *hist.* dying without issue.

ग़लतान *galtān* [P. *g̱alṭān*], adj. E.H. rolling, wallowing.

ग़लती *galtī* [P. *g̱alatī*], f. **1.** wrong procedure or conclusion, mistake, error; inaccuracy; misconception. **2.** misstatement. **3.** oversight, slip. — ~ करना, to make a mistake, &c. ~ में पड़ना, to fall into an error.

गलन *galan* [cf. H. *galnā*], f. melting, decaying, &c.

गलना *galnā* [*galati*[1]], v.i. **1.** to melt; to dissolve; to become soft. **2.** to waste, to decay; to become emaciated; to become numbed. **3.** to rot. **4.** to fall, to fall away; to be lost, to vanish; to be forfeited (as a piece in a game). — (किसी की) दाल न ~, (one's) lentils not to cook: not to achieve a purpose.

गलफड़ा *galphaṛā* [H. [1]*gal-* or *gal*+H. *phāṛnā*], m. **1.** gill (of a fish). **2.** *Pl. HŚS.* corner of the mouth, cheek.

गलवाना *galvānā* [cf. H. *galnā*], v.t. to cause to be melted; to cause to be dissolved, or softened.

गलही *galhī*, f. reg. bow (of a boat).

गलाँवन *galāṁvan* [**galadāmana-*[2]], m. reg. neck-rope, halter.

गला *galā* [*gala-*[2], *galaka-*], m. **1.** the throat; the neck; gullet. **2.** fig. the voice. **3.** neck or collar (of clothes). — ~ आना, the throat or tonsils to be sore or inflamed. ~ उठाना, to lift the uvula (in treating the throat); to paint or to treat the throat. ~ करना (का), id. ~ काटना, to cut (one's, का) throat; fig. to do violence (to); to do wrong (to); to overcharge, to cheat; to sting the throat (as a sharp taste). ~ खुलना, the throat or voice to be relaxed. ~ घुटना, the throat to be choked; one to feel suffocated. ~ घोंटना, to choke (one, का); to strangle. ~ छुड़ाना, to extricate (one, का: from a danger or a predicament). ~ छूटना, the neck to be safe, or not at risk, from (से). ~ जोड़ना, to become intimate (with, से). ~ दबाना, = ~ घोंटना; to put pressure upon (one). ~ पकड़ना, to take (one) by the throat; to turn upon (one); to turn to (demanding redress); to force, to compel; to sting (one's) throat (= ~ काटना). ~ पड़ना = ~ आना. ~ फँसना, (one) to be firmly caught, or trapped; to be implicated (in, में). ~ फटना, the throat to become hoarse. ~ फट जाना, the voice to break (at adolescence). ~ फाड़ना, to make (oneself) hoarse (with shouting). ~ फूलना, the throat, or the glands of the neck, to swell. ~ बंद होना, to be choked or suffocated. ~ भर आना, the voice to choke (with emotion). ~ बैठना, the throat to become hoarse; to lose one's voice. ~ रेतना, to file the throat: to cause great distress or suffering (to, का). गले उतारना, fig. to make (sthg.) acceptable (to one reluctant to accept it), to convince one (of). गले का हार होना, to be a garland round (one's) neck: to be dearly loved; to be burdensome; iron. to lavish unwelcome attention; to be importunate. गले के नीचे उतरना, fig. to be readily acceptable, or comprehensible (to, or by, से). गले चिपकाना, to fasten upon the neck (of, के): to lay to (one's) charge; to foist upon one (a wrong accusation); to oblige (one) to accept (sthg). गले डालना, id. गले पर छुरी फेरना, to put to the knife: to kill; to harass. गले बाँधना, = गले चिपकाना. गले लगना, to embrace (one, के); to urge, to importune; to be burdensome. गले मँढना, = गले चिपकाना. गले मिलना, to embrace (= गले लगना). गले में, adv. at (one's) throat: (being worn) on the upper body. गले लगाना, to embrace (one, के); fig. to feel warmly towards; to force (sthg.) upon (one) (= गले चिपकाना). गले से उतरना, to be swallowed. गले से लगना, = गले लगना. बंद ~, a closed collar. बात गले तक आना, a matter to threaten to overwhelm one. – गला-तोड़, m. a stiff or twisted neck.

गलाई *galāī* [cf. H. *galānā*], f. dissolving; melting, &c. (= गलावट, 1).

गलाऊ *galāū* [cf. H. *galānā*], adj. **1.** soluble; liable to melt, &c. **2.** dissolving, solvent.

ग़लाज़त *galāzat* [A. *gilāẓa*: P. *gilāẓat*], f. U. **1.** grossness, coarseness. **2.** filth.

गलाना *galānā* [cf. H. *galnā*], v.t. **1.** to cause to be melted, to melt; to dissolve; to soften; to smelt (iron). **2.** to cause to be wasted; to mortify; to benumb (of cold); to emaciate. **3.** to cause to rot. — गलानेवाला, adj. & m. dissolving; a solvent.

गलार *galār*, m. reg. **1.** the rose-ringed parakeet. **2.** ? S. a species of mynah.

गलाव *galāv* [cf. H. *galānā*], m. solution (of a solid in a liquid).

गलावट *galāvaṭ* [cf. H. *galānā*], f. **1.** the act or process of dissolving; melting, &c. **2.** a solution (= गलाव).

गलित *galit* [S.], adj. **1.** melted, dissolved. **2.** wasted away; impaired. **3.** vanished, fallen away. — ~ कुष्ठ, m. an aggravated type of leprosy. – गलितयौवना, adj. f. & f. whose youth has passed; a woman whose youth has passed.

गलियाना *galiyānā* [cf. H. *gālī*], v.t. to utter abuse (= गाली देना).

गलियारा *galiyārā* [? **galīkāra-*], m. **1.** a passage, path; lane. **2.** passageway, corridor.

गली *galī* [**galī-*], f. **1.** a lane, alley. **2.** a partic. small section, quarter (of a village). — ~ कमाना, to work as a sweeper. गलियाँ छानना, to wander through, or to scour, the lanes (of, की). बंद ~, f. a cul-de-sac, or blind alley. – गली-गली, adv. in every lane; from lane to lane. गली-कूचा, m. lane or alley; pl. lanes and alleys (of a village or town).

गलीचा *galīcā*, m. = ग़ालीचा.

ग़लीज़ *galīz* [A. *galīẓ*], adj. & f. U. **1.** adj. dirty; impure. **2.** f. rubbish; filth.

गल्प *galp* [H. ¹*gap*, B. *gappa*; ? × *jalpati*], m. a tale, story.

गल्ला *gallā* [P. *ga(l)la*], m. a flock, herd.

ग़ल्ला *gallā* [P. *galla*], m. **1.** grain. **2.** daily proceeds of sales of produce. 3. = गुल्लक. **4.** reg. (Bihar) sheaves piled ready for threshing. — ~ भरना, to put grain in store; to hoard grain. – ग़ल्लाफ़रोश [P. *-faroś*], m. a grain-merchant.

गवँ *gavaṁ*, f. Av. = गौं.

गवन *gavan* [*gamana-*], m. Brbh. Av. = गमन.

गवाक्ष *gavākṣ* [S.], m. a small window; skylight.

गवाना *gavānā* [cf. H. *gānā*], v.t. to cause (a song) to be sung.

-गंवार *-gavār* [P. *guvār*], adj. digestible: acceptable, tolerable.

गवारा *gavārā* [P. *guvārā*], adj. **1.** digestible, palatable. ***2.** acceptable, agreeable (to, को). — ~ करना, v.t. to take (upon oneself, अपने ऊपर); to endure, to stomach; to make tolerable (to oneself); to adjust (to sthg).

गवाह *gavāh* [P. *gavāh*], m. a witness (as of an event, or to a statement). — ~ करना, to make (one) a witness; to bring forward as a witness. ~ ठहराना, to make or to name (one) a witness. ~ बनाना, id. ~ लाना, to bring evidence (in the form of a witness or witnesses). ~ होना, to be a witness (of or to, का).

गवाही *gavāhī* [P. *gavāhī*], f. testimony, evidence. — ~ करना (पर, or की), to witness (a document). ~ देना, to give evidence, to testify (to, पर or की). ~ लिखना, = ~ करना. झूठी ~, f. false witness; perjury.

गवेषना *gavêṣănā* [S.], f. investigation; research.

गवेषी *gavêṣī* [S.], m. investigator; researcher.

गवैया *gavaiyā* [cf. H. *gānā*], m. a singer.

गव्य *gavyă* [S.], m. sthg. produced by a cow: milk; butter; *ghī*; urine; dung. — पंच-गव्य, m. pl. the five products of a cow.

ग़श *gaś* [A. *gaśś*], m. fainting fit. — ~ आना (को), to faint. ~ खाना, id. ~ होना, to swoon (over, पर): to be infatuated (with), or fascinated (by).

ग़शी *gaśī* [P. *gaśī*], f. a fainting fit.

गश्त *gaśt* [P. *gaśt*], f. **1.** going round, patrolling (as of guards). **2.** a round, a beat. — ~ लगाना (में), to go one's rounds; to patrol (an area). – मटरगश्त, f. wandering here and there; a walk.

गश्ती *gaśtī* [P. *gaśtī*], m. & adj. **1.** m. a watchman, guard; one on patrol. **2.** adj. going round, circulation; being on watch, or on patrol. ~ हुकम, a circular order. **3.** mobile (as a library). — मटरगश्ती करना, to go about or around, to go for a stroll, to wander.

गस्सा *gassā* [**grāsya-*], m. a mouthful (of food); a bite, morsel. — ~ तोड़ना, to take a bite (of, का).

गह *gah* [*graha-*], f. *Pl. HŚS.* a handle.

गहक *gahak* [cf. H. *gahaknā*], f. **1.** a strong desire. ***2.** exhilaration; warmth, fervour.

गहकना *gahaknā* [? **gṛdhati* (Pk. *gahia-*) × **grahati* (Pk. *gahaï*], v.i. **1.** to feel a strong desire. ***2.** to be exhilarated, ecstatic. — गहककर बोलना, to speak warmly or fervently.

गहकी *gahkī* [? cf. H. *gāhak*], m. E.H. a customer.

गहगह *gahgah*, adj. = गहगहा.

गहगहा *gahgahā* [cf. H. *gahgahānā*], adj. Brbh. Av. rapturous, excited; festive.

गहगहाना *gahgahānā* [cf. H. *gahaknā*], v.i. & v.t. **1.** v.i. to be enraptured or exhilarated. **2.** v.t. to make delighted, &c.

¹**गहन** *gahan* [*grahaṇa-*, and H. *gahnā*], m. f. **1.** a seizing. **2.** an eclipse. — ~ पड़ना, or लगना, an eclipse to occur; to be eclipsed.

²**गहन** *gahan* [S.], adj. & m. **1.** adj. thick, dense (as of a forest, or darkness); impenetrable; inaccessible. **2.** deep; profound (of thought). **3.** obscure. **4.** active, intensive (as a process). **5.** m. a dense or deep place; a thicket; forest; impenetrable darkness. **6.** a secret or inaccessible place; hiding-place; cave.

गहनता *gahanătā* [S.], f. **1.** thickness, denseness. **2.** impenetrability. **3.** obscurity.

¹**गहना** *gahnā* [*grahaṇa-*], m. **1.** an ornament; a jewel; pl. jewellery; trinkets. **2.** a pledge, pawn. — गहने रखना (को), to pawn (valuables); to mortgage.

²**गहना** *gahnā* [**grahati*: Pk. *gahaï*], v.t. & m. **1.** v.t. to seize; to lay hold of, to take up (as a weapon). **2.** to turn to (as to a course of action). **3.** m. reg. (W.) a grass rake.

गहनि *gahani* [cf. *grahaṇa-*, and H. *gahnā*], f. Brbh. seizing, taking.

¹**गहनी** *gahnī* [cf. H. ¹*gahan*], f. having to do with an eclipse: **1.** *Pl.* a calf born malformed. **2.** *HŚS.* a disease affecting animals' gums.

[2]**गहनी** *gahnī* [cf. H. [2]*gahnā*], f. *HŚS.* a light grass rake (cf. [2]गहना).

[3]**गहनी** *gahnī*, f. **1.** caulking. **2.** reg. (Bihar) hemp used in caulking.

[4]**गहनी** *gahnī* [cf. H. [1]*gahan*], adj. pawned. — ~ धरना, to place in pawn.

गहमा-गहमी *gahmā-gahmī* [cf. H. *ghamāgham*], f. **1.** commotion, bustle; liveliness. **2.** an angry quarrel.

गहरवार *gaharvār*, m. name of a Rājpūt community of the Banaras region.

[1]**गहरा** *gahrā* [*gabhīra-*], adj. **1.** deep; intimate (of feelings); sound (sleep); strong (drink); dark; viscous; heavy (with sleep). **2.** profound; grave, weighty. **3.** harsh, cruel (a blow). — ~ असामी, m. colloq. a wealthy person. ~ पेट, m. one who keeps his feelings hidden, a 'deep' person. ~ हाथ, m. a cruel blow; a good stroke (of business). गहरी घुटना, to prepare strong liquor (with, से); to be intimate with. गहरी छनना, = prec.; to have a great fight (with, से). गहरे में, adv. clandestinely. गहरे होना, to prosper; to fatten; to gain. उसके गहरे हैं, he is doing very well.

[2]**गहरा** *gahrā* [cf. *graha-*], m. reg. (W.) **1.** a sheaf. **2.** a bundle of sheaves, or thatching grass.

गहराई *gahrāī* [cf. H. [1]*gahrā*], f. **1.** depth; profundity, &c. **2.** a deep place; cavity; depth, gulf.

गहराना *gahrānā* [cf. H. [1]*gahrā*], v.t. & v.i. **1.** v.t. to make deep, to deepen. **2.** v.i. to be deep.

गहरापन *gahrāpan* [cf. H. *gahrā*], adj. depth; profundity, &c.

गहराव *gahrāv*, m. = गहराई, 1.

गहरी *gahrī* [H. [1]*gahrā*], f. *Pl.* low swampy ground (as for rice cultivation).

गहरु *gaharu* [? conn. *graha-*, *grahila-*], m. Brbh. Av. holding back: delay; neglect.

गहल *gahal* [cf. *graha-*], f. reg. a bunch, cluster (as of bananas).

गहवारा *gahvārā* [P. *gahvāra*], *Pl. HŚS.* a cradle.

गहूँ *gahūṁ*, m. pronun. var. = गेहूं.

गहूरी *gahūrī*, f. *Pl. HŚS.* demurrage.

गह्वर *gahvar* [S.], adj. & m. **1.** adj. deep. **2.** dense; impenetrable. **3.** obscure, secret. **4.** m. a depth; abyss. **5.** a wood, thicket. **6.** a cave, den. **7.** socket (of the eye).

गाँकर *gāṁkar*, m. reg. (W.) damper: bread-cakes made of coarse grain such as *arhar*, and cooked in ashes.

गाँगन *gāṁgan*, f. a blind boil.

[1]**गाँजना** *gāṁjnā* [conn. *gañja-*[2] [3]], v.t. to collect, to pile up.

[2]**गाँजना** *gāṁjnā* [**gañj-* 'press, ram': Pk. *gaṁjaï*], v.t. *Pl.* to stir, to churn.

गाँजर *gāṁjar*, f. *Pl.* a kind of grass.

गाँजा *gāṁjā* [*gañjā-*: Pk. *gaṁja-*], m. **1.** hemp, *Cannabis sativa.* **2.** hemp leaves, flower heads, or buds. — गाँजे का दम लगाना, to smoke cannabis. – गाँजेवाला, m. a seller of hemp, or of *bhāṁg.*

गाँठ *gāṁṭh* [*granthi-*], f. **1.** a knot; a fastening. **2.** a knot (in wood); joint (as in a reed, or of the body). **3.** a hardened or enlarged gland; tumour. **4.** a bundle, parcel; bale; a bunch. **5.** knot (as in a *dhotī*): fig. purse, pocket. **6.** a contract, agreement. **7.** fig. a complication; a misunderstanding; ill-feeling; guile. — ~ कटना, to have (one's) purse stolen, (one's) pocket picked; to be robbed. ~ कतरना or काटना, to be robbed. ~ का, one's own (as money in the pocket); private. ~ का खोना, to waste one's money; to act to one's disadvantage; to incur loss. ~ का पूरा, adj. & m. well-off; a wealthy person. ~ खोलना, to untie a knot; to disentangle; to spend freely; to remove a complication, &c. ~ जोड़ना, to knot (esp. the ends of the clothes of a bride and bridegroom); to become intimate. ~ देना, to tie a knot (in, में: often as a reminder). ~ पड़ना (में), (sthg.) to become knotted or entangled; misunderstanding to arise (in the heart). ~ बाँधना, = ~ देना; (w. लेना) to arrange or to contract for or about (sthg.); मन की ~ बाँधना, to harbour ill-feeling, &c. ~ से जाना, to be lost (a thing). ~ (से) बाँध लेना, to accept implicitly, to assimilate (an idea). अपनी ~ की एक चीज़, f. sthg. bought with (one's) own money. डेढ़ ~, f. a slip-knot. – गाँठकट, m. a pickpocket. गाँठ-गठीला, adj. knotted; knotty (of wood); compactly built. गाँठदार [P. *-dār*], adj. knotted; knotty. गाँठ-भरा, adj. full of knots; intricate; having the pocket full (of money). गुर-गाँठ, f. a tight knot.

गाँठना *gāṁṭhnā* [*granthayate*], v.t. **1.** to knot, to fasten; to string or to thread. **2.** to join; to mend (as shoes, fabric). **3.** to arrange, to dispose; to compose (i.e. to arrange words or ideas). **4.** to take on, to assume (as an air, an attitude). **5.** w. लेना. to win to (one's) side, to ally with oneself; to take (sthg.) over, or to appropriate. **6.** to reduce to subjection; to intimidate.

गांड *gāṇḍ*, f. pronun. var. = गाँड़.

गाँड़ *gāṁṛ* [*gaṇḍa-*[1]], f. anus. — ~ फटना (की), vulg. to be helpless with fright. ~ फाड़ना (की), to terrify (one). ~ मारना, to commit sodomy (with, की). अपनी ~ मराना, to suffer sodomy. – गाँड़-मरानी, f. a prostitute.

गाँडर *gāṁḍar* [conn. *gaṇḍālī-*], f. a long grass, *Andropogon muraticum*, (used in thatching; its roots are used in making screens); ? a sweet-scented medical grass (*Cymbopogon*).

गाँडीव *gāṁḍīv* [S.], m. *mythol.* the bow of Arjun.

गाँडू *gāṁḍū*, m. pronun. var. = गाँड़ू.

गाँड़ू *gāṁṛū* [*gaṇḍa-*[1]], m. vulg. **1.** a male homosexual. **2.** an impotent man. **3.** fig. a timid, or wretched person.

गांधर्व *gāndharv* [S.], adj. & m. **1.** adj. belonging to or connected with the *gandharvas*. **2.** m. the art of the *gandharvas*: song, music, dance. **3.** *hind.* a form of marriage requiring only the parties' mutual agreement.

गांधार *gāndhār* [S.], m. **1.** the region of Gāndhāra. **2.** a man from Gāndhārā. **3.** *mus.* the third note of the Indian heptatonic scale. — गांधार-भैरव, m. *mus.* the name of a mixed *rāg*.

गांधारी *gāndhārī* [cf. *gāndhāra-*], adj. & f. **1.** adj. belonging to or connected with Gāndhāra. **2.** f. a Gāndhāra woman; name (in the *Mahābhārata* story) of the wife of Dhṛtarāṣṭra. **3.** *mus.* name of a *rāgiṇī*.

गाँधी *gāṁdhī* [*gāndhika-*], m. **1.** a perfume-seller. **2.** name of a Gujarati trading community.

गांभीर्य *gāmbhīryă* [S.], m. **1.** depth. **2.** thoughtfulness, profundity. **3.** seriousness.

गाँव *gāṁv* [*grāma-*], m. **1.** a village. **2.** obs. a site, place. — ~ मारना, to raid a village (bandits).

गाँवटी *gāṁvṭī* [cf. H. *gāṁv*], adj. reg. (W.) of or belonging to a village.

गाँस *gāṁs* [cf. H. *gāṁsnā*], f. **1.** an arrow-head, spear-head, &c. **2.** a rankling urge or desire; ill-will. — ~ निकालना, to find comfort (as in settling a score).

गाँसना *gāṁsnā* [? *grāsayati*], v.t. **1.** to take in, to draw in, or close; to hem in. **2.** to pierce, to bore. **3.** to string, to thread. — गाँसकर रखना, colloq. to retain, not to forget (sthg).

गाँसी *gāṁsī*, f. Brbh. = गाँस, 1.

गाँहक *gāṁhak*, m. pronun. var. = गाहक.

गागर *gāgar* [*gargara-*[2]], f. a water-pot. — ~ में सागर, the ocean in a pot: much said, or sthg. completely expressed, in few words.

गागरी *gāgrī*, f. = गागर.

गाछ *gāch* [**gakṣa-*: Pa. *gaccha-*], m. reg. a bush; a tree.

[1]**गाछी** *gāchī*, f. *Pl. HŚS.* **1.** a pad for a beast of burden. **2.** saddle-bag, &c. (= ख़ुरजी).

[2]**गाछी** *gāchī* [cf. H. *gāch*], f. reg. (E.) **1.** a grove of trees. **2.** a nursery for rice.

[1]**गाज** *gāj* [**gajja-*], f. foam, froth; scum.

[2]**गाज** *gāj* [*garjā-*], f. **1.** the noise of thunder. **2.** roaring; anger. **3.** thunderbolt; lightning. — ~ पड़ना, lightning to strike. – गाज-मारा, adj. & m. afflicted, unfortunate.

[3]**गाज** *gāj*, f. *Pl. HŚS.* a glass bangle.

गाजना *gājnā* [*garjati*], v.i. reg. **1.** to thunder, to rumble. **2.** to roar; to sound. **3.** to revel; to be delighted.

गाजर *gājar* [*gārjara-*, Pk. *gajjara-*], f. (m., *Pl.*) a carrot. — ~ की शकल का, adj. tapering; conical. गाजर-मूली समझना, to think of, or to treat, as worthless or insignificant.

गाजा-बाजा *gājā-bājā* [H. *gājnā*+H. *bājā*, or *bǎjnā*], m. **1.** the sound of musical instruments. **2.** a band. **3.** singing and music.

ग़ाज़ी *gāzī* [A. *gāzī*], m. a victor over (non-Muslim) unbelievers; a hero.

गाटा *gāṭā*, m. reg. (W.) **1.** [H. *gāṁṭh*] the yoking of bullocks (as for work in a mill). **2.** [**gaṭṭa-*] a plot of land.

[1]**गाड़** *gāṛ* [**gaḍḍa-*[1]: Pk. *gaḍḍa-*], f. **1.** Brbh. Av. a pit, ditch. **2.** reg. (W.) low land (on which water does not lie long). **3.** *HŚS.* a pit for food storage.

[2]**गाड़** *gāṛ* [**gaḍḍa-*[4]], f. reg. (W.) = गाडर.

गाड़ना *gāṛnā* [**gaḍḍ-*[1]], v.t. **1.** to drive (into or into, में); to embed. **2.** to plant. **3.** to cover over (a fire) with ashes. **4.** to bury. — खोदकर गाड़ देना, fig. to see the end of (one).

गाडर *gāḍar* [*gaḍḍara-*], f. Brbh. Av. a sheep; a ewe.

[1]**गाड़ा** *gāṛā*, m. reg. a large cart.

[2]**गाड़ा** *gāṛā*, m. *Pl. HŚS.* 1. = [1]गाड़. **2.** pronun. var. = गाढ़ा, 7. **3.** [×H. *gāṛhā*] = गारा.

गाड़ी *gāṛī* [**gāḍḍa-*: Pk. *gaḍḍi-*], f. a conveyance: **1.** cart; carriage. **2.** car, truck, bus; bicycle. **3.** train. **4.** railway carriage, or truck. — ~ छूटना, a train to leave. ~ जहाँ पहले थी, वहाँ अब भी है, fig. no progress has been made. ~ भर, adj. & m. a cart-load (of); ~ भर रास्ता, a road wide enough for a cart. ~ पकड़ना, to catch a train. ~ पकड़ने से रह जाना, to miss a train. — गाड़ीवान [P. *-vān*], m. a carter; driver, &c. डाक-गाड़ी, f. a mail train. माल-गाड़ी, f. a goods train. सवारी गाड़ी, f. a passenger train.

[1]**गाढ़ना** *gāṛhnā* [**gāṭhayati*], v.t. to shape, to forge, to hammer out.

[2]**गाढ़ना** *gāṛhnā*, v.t. reg. = गाड़ना.

गाढ़ा *gāṛhā* [*gāḍha-*], adj. & m. **1.** adj. thick, dense, viscous. **2.** muddy; strong (as tea); deep (as colour). **3.** coarse, heavy (as cloth). **4.** close, intense (as a friendship or enmity). **5.** bitter (experience). गाढ़ी कमाई, f. hard-won earnings. **6.** bold; abrasive; shrewd, smart. **7.** m. a type of coarse, thick cloth. **8.** harsh or bitter times. — गाढ़ी छनना, strong *bhāṁg* to be taken; a matter to be discussed intimately; a close friendship to exist. गाढ़ी नींद, f. deep sleep.

गाढ़ापन *gāṛhāpan* [cf. H. *gāṛhā*], m. thickness, closeness, &c.

गात *gāt* [*gātra-*], m. the body.

[1]**गाता** *gātā* [S.], m. inv. a singer.

[2]**गाता** *gātā*, m. *Pl. HŚS.* = गत्ता.

गाती *gātī* [cf. H. *gāt*], f. Brbh. a cloth garment worn over one shoulder and under the other armpit.

गात्र *gātr* [S.], m. the body.

गाथ *gāth* [ad. *gāthā-*: w. H. [4]*gāh*], f. a song; song of praise.

गाथक *gāthak* [S.], m. *Pl. HŚS.* a singer, musician; chanter of scriptural texts.

गाथा *gāthā* [S.], f. **1.** a song or chant. **2.** a narrative poem; a ballad. **3.** a partic. classical metre.

गाद *gād* [**gadda-*[1]], f. reg. sediment; mud. — ~ उठाना, to stir up sediment, or mud.

गादर *gādar* [**gaddara-*], m. reg. (Bihar) = गादा.

गादा *gādā* [**gadda-*[2]], m. reg. (E.) unripe cereal, or peas (cut and cooked in the ear).

गादुर *gādur*, m. *Pl. HŚS.* the flying fox (a bat) or flying squirrel.

गान *gān* [*gāna-*], m. **1.** singing. **2.** a song. — ~ करना, to sing. – गान-विद्या, f. the theory of vocal music.

गाना *gānā* [*gāpayati*], v.t., v.i. & m. **1.** v.t. to sing; to chant; to sing the praises of. **2.** v.i. to sing. **3.** m. singing, &c. **4.** a song. — ~ ~, to sing a song. अपनी ही ~, to sing one's own praises. – गाना-बजाना, m. singing and playing, song and music.

ग़ाफ़िल *gāfil* [A. *gāfil*], adj. **1.** negligent, neglectful (of, से); remiss. **2.** heedless. — ~ रहना, to be neglectful, &c. (of).

गाब *gāb* [*garbha-*], m. a dense evergreen tree *Diospyros embryopteris* (its fruit-pulp yields a gum and a tar).

गाबदू *gābdū*, adj. stupid.

गाभ *gābh* [*garbha-*], m. Av. young shoot, or leaf.

गाभिन *gābhin* [*garbhiṇī-*], adj. pregnant (esp. an animal).

गाम *gām* [*grāma-*], m. a village.

-गामिनी *-gāminī*, adj. & f. = -गामी.

-गामी *-gāmī* [*gāmin-*], adj. & m. **1.** adj. going; moving on, or in, or towards, or in a particular manner. **2.** m. one who goes, &c.

गाय *gāy* [*gāvī-*], f. **1.** a cow. **2.** fig. a gentle or tractable person.

गायक *gāyak* [S.], m. a singer.

ग़ायत *gāyat* [A. *gāya*: P. *gāyat*], adj. extreme; consummate; inordinate. — ~ दरजे का पाजी, an egregious rascal.

गायत्री *gāyatrī* [S.], f. **1.** a Vedic metre. **2.** the name of a particularly sacred verse of the R̥gveda. **3.** a name of Durgā, and of the Ganges.

गायन *gāyan* [S.], m. singing.

ग़ायब *gāyb* [A. *gā'ib*], adj. absent; disappeared, vanished. — ~ करना, to make off (with sthg.); to hide (sthg.) away. घर में पैसे ~ थे, there was no money at all in the house. – ग़ायब-गुल्ला, adj. colloq. = ग़ायब.

गायिका *gāyikā* [S.], f. a singer.

गार *gār*, m. = गारा.

ग़ार *gār* [A. *gār*], m. sunken place: **1.** cave, den, lair. **2.** pit (? = H. [1]गाड़).

-गार *-gār* [P. *-gār*], suffix (forms m. agent nouns from nouns, e.g. गुनाहगार, sinner).

ग़ारत *gārat* [A. *gāra*: P. *gārat*] f. plunder, pillage; devastation. — ~ होना, to be laid waste, or devastated. – ग़ारतगर [P. *-gar*], m. a plunderer. °ई, f. plundering; laying waste. ग़ारत-पीटा, adj. trashy, worthless; decrepit.

गारना *gārnā* [*gālayati* or *gāḍayati*], v.t. **1.** to squeeze or to wring out; to milk; to rub, to press. **2.** to cause to drip out (as tears). **3.** to cause to be wasted or destroyed.

गारा *gārā* [**gāra-*], m. **1.** thick mud. **2.** mortar; plaster. — ~ **करना**, to prepare mud for building or plastering.

गारुड़ *gāruṛ* [*gāruḍa-*], adj. & m. Brbh. **1.** adj. *mythol.* having to do with Garuṛ. **2.** m. a *mantra* against snake-bite or snake poison.

गारुड़ी *gāruṛī* [*gāruḍika-*], m. Brbh. **1.** one who administers *mantras* against snake-bite, &c. **2.** reg. (Raj.) a snake-charmer.

गार्ड *gārḍ* [Engl. *guard*], m. a guard.

गार्हस्थ्य *gārhasthyă* [S.], adj. & m. **1.** adj. having to do with a householder; domestic. **2.** m. domestic life.

गाल *gāl* [*galla-*: ← Drav.], f. **1.** the cheek. **2.** Av. cheek, presumption. — ~ **पर** ~ **चढ़ना**, (one's) cheeks to grow fat. ~ **फुलाना**, to puff out the cheeks; to sulk; to be haughty. ~ **बजाना**, to talk haughtily; to boast; to blow air from the cheeks by striking them: as done in recognition of Śiva (the sound produced is called *bam-bam*). ~ **सेंकना**, to warm, or to foment, the cheek(s). **काल के ~ में जाना**, to pass into death's maw, to perish.

गाला *gālā* [P. *gāla*], m. **1.** a flock of cotton; a ball of carded cotton. **2.** a pod of cotton. — **राई का** ~, m. fig. sthg. very white, or bright.

ग़ालिब *gālib* [A. *gālib*], adj. Brbh. **1.** overcoming; triumphant (over, **पर**); excelling. **2.** U. probable. — ~ **आना (पर)**, U. to overcome; to surpass.

ग़ालिबन *gāliban* [A. *gāliban*], adv. **1.** most probably. **2.** for the most part, chiefly.

गाली *gālī* [*gāli-*], f. **1.** abusive language, abuse. **2.** a type of indecent song sung at weddings. — ~ **खाना**, to endure abuse. ~ **देना**, to abuse, to revile. **गालियों पर उतरना**, to come down to name-calling. – **गाली-गलौज**, f. mutual abuse, railing. **गाली-गुफ़्तार** [P. *-guftār*], f. or **गाली-वाली**, id.

ग़ालीचा *gālīcā* [A. *gālī*+P. *-ca*], m. a small carpet.

गालू *gālū* [H. *gāl*], adj. colloq. garrulous, boastful.

गाव *gāv* [**gāva-*; P. *gāv*], m. an ox: — **गाव-तकिया**, m. a large pillow or bolster (to lean against).

गावदी *gāvdī* [P. *gāvdī*], adj. & m. **1.** adj. bovine, stupid. **2.** m. a stupid person.

गावना *gāvnā*, v.i. & v.t. reg. see **गाना**.

[1]**गाह** *gāh* [P. *gāh*], f. esp. in comp. **1.** a place. **2.** a time, occasion. — **गाहबगाहे, गाहेबगाहे, गाह-गाह**, adv. at times; repeatedly; often.

[2]**गाह** *gāh* [*grāha-*], m. **1.** Av. one who seizes. **2.** Av. a crocodile.

[3]**गाह** *gāh* [cf. H. *gahnā*], f. Brbh. seizing; striking.

[4]**गाह** *gāh* f. Brbh. = **गाथा**.

गाहक *gāhak* [ad. *grāhaka-*: w. H. [1]*gāhnā*], m. one who takes, receives or values sthg.; a customer. — **जी**, or **प्राण**, **का** ~, m. one plotting to take (another's, **के**) life.

गाहकी *gāhăkī* [cf. H. *gāhak*], f. sale, selling; a transaction of selling and buying.

[1]**गाहन** *gāhan* [cf. H. *gāhnā*], m. reg. (W.) a harrow for clearing grass from ploughed land.

[2]**गाहन** *gāhan* [S.], m. E.H. plunging; investigating.

[1]**गाहना** *gāhnā* [*gāhate*], v.t. **1.** to plunge into; to investigate. **2.** to thresh, to tread out (grain).

[2]**गाहना** *gāhnā* [*grāhayati*], v.t. to catch, to seize.

गाहा *gāhā* [*gāthā-*], f. Av. = **गाथा**.

गाही *gāhī* [*grāha-*], f. a group of five. — **दस** ~ **आम**, fifty mangoes.

गिंजना *gimjnā* [cf. H. *gīmjnā*], v.i. to be crumpled (as clothes).

गिंजाई *gimjāī* [? cf. **giñjakā-*: Pa. *giñjaka-*], f. a type of centipede common in the rainy season.

गिंजोलना *gimjolnā*, v.t. *Pl.* reg. = **गींजना**.

गिंडुरी *gimḍurī* [cf. H. *īmḍurī*; ? × *genḍu-*], f. a rope of grass or twine (coiled to support a round-bottomed jar). (= **ईंडुरी**).

गिंदर *gindar*, m. reg. (W.) an insect which attacks growing cereal crops.

गिंदौड़ा *gimdauṛā* [**gendavaṭaka-*], m. a flat, round cake of sugar.

गिच-पिच *gic-pic* [cf. H. **gicc-*: ← Drav.], adj. crowded or jumbled together.

गिजगिजा *gijgijā* [**gijj-*: ← Drav.], adj. soft and juicy (as ripe fruit).

गिजबिजा *gijbijā*, adj. = **गिजगिजा**.

ग़िज़ा *gizā* [A. *gizā*], m. **1.** food. **2.** diet.

गिटकिरी *giṭkirī*, f. a trill (in singing).

गिटगिरी *giṭgirī*, f. 19c. = **गिटकिरी**.

गिटपिट *giṭpiṭ*, f. colloq. chit-chat.

गिट्टक *giṭṭak* [cf. **giṭṭa-*], m. a piece, fragment (of stone or metal).

गिट्टा *giṭṭā* [**giṭṭa-*], m. & adj. **1.** m. a hard lump, piece. **2.** the ankle joint (cf. गट्टा, 5). **3.** m. a dwarf. (cf. गुट्टा). **4.** adj. = गुट्टा, 3.

गिट्टी *giṭṭī* [**giṭṭa-*, or H. *giṭṭā*], f. **1.** rubble; ballast; broken pottery. **2.** a reel (as for thread).

गिड़गिड़ाना *giṛgiṛānā*, v.i. to whine, to be tearful; to entreat abjectly.

गिड़गिड़ाहट *giṛgiṛāhaṭ* [cf. H. *giṛgiṛānā*], f. whining; abject entreaty.

गिड़ुरी *giṛurī*, f. reg. (E.) = गिंडुरी.

गिद्ध *giddh* [*gṛdhra-*], m. **1.** a vulture. **2.** fig. one who is cunning, or rapacious.

गिनती *gintī* [cf. H. *ginnā*], f. **1.** counting; calculation; enumeration. **2.** reckoning, account. — ~ करना, to count. ~ के, adj. countable: a few, only a few. ~ गिनना, to count by numbers. ~ गिनने, or गिनाने, के लिए, a few, a small number only. ~ में आना, to be noteworthy; to have to be reckoned with, to deserve inclusion (in a group). ~ में लाना, or लेना, or समझना, to take account of; to think notable.

गिनना *ginnā* [*gaṇayati*: MIA *giṇ-*, &c.], v.t. **1.** to count, to calculate. **2.** [×H. *gunnā*] to consider, to estimate, to evaluate. **3.** to consider of account. — गिन-गिनकर, adv. one by one: painstakingly, thoroughly; prudently. गिना-गिनाया, adj. ready counted. गिने-चुने, adj. pl. selected, singled out. इने-गिने, adj. pl. few, numbered.

गिनवाना *ginvānā* [cf. H. *ginnā*], v.t. to cause to be counted (by, से).

गिनाना *ginānā* [cf. H. *ginnā*], v.t. & v.i. **1.** v.t. to cause to be counted. **2.** v.i. reg. to be counted; to be considered.

गिमटी *gimṭī* [Engl. *dimity*], f. a heavy, figured cotton cloth (used for bedding, &c).

गिरई *giraī*, f. reg. (E.) = गरई.

गिरगिट *girgiṭ*, m. a chameleon. — ~ के-से रंग बदलना, to change colour like a chameleon; to flush or to turn pale (as with anger).

गिरगिरी *girgirī*, f. Brbh. a child's fiddle, a toy.

गिरजा *girjā* [Pt. *igreja*], m. a church; chapel. — गिरजा-घर, m. a church.

गिरदा *girdā* [P. *girda*], m. anything round: **1.** Brbh. a round pillow. **2.** reg. (N.) a round flat bread-cake.

गिरदावर *girdāvar* [P. *-āvar*], m. a superintendent.

गिरना *girnā* [**girati*[1]], v.i. **1.** to fall; to fall down, or over; to collapse. **2.** to fall, to drop (on or on top of, पर); to rush (upon, पर), to attack. **3.** to fall (price); to decline (an activity, or health); to drop (heat, wind). **4.** to debouch (a river); to be cast (a vote). **5.** to befall (a calamity). **6.** to be disgraced; to be ruined; to fall (from, से: as from esteem). — गिर-पड़कर, adv. with tottering steps; with much difficulty; all of a scramble. गिरते-पड़ते, adv. id.

गिरफ़्त *giraft* [P. *girift*], f. **1.** seizing, capture. **2.** grasp, clutch; power. **3.** a handle. — ~ में आ जाना, to be taken into custody. भय की ~ में होना, to be seized with fear.

गिरफ़्तार *giraftār* [P. *giriftār*], adj. **1.** arrested, seized. **2.** assailed or beleaguered by (troubles, or emotions). — ~ करना, to arrest, to seize.

गिरफ़्तारी *giraftārī* [P. *giriftārī*], f. arrest, detention; imprisonment. — ~ निकलना, a warrant for (one's, की) arrest to be issued.

[1]**गिरमिट** *girmiṭ* [Engl. *agreement*], m. *hist.* esp. Fiji. agreement: contract by indenture (to work on cane plantations).

[2]**गिरमिट** *girmiṭ* [Engl. *gimlet*], m. a gimlet.

गिरमिटिया *girmiṭiyā* [cf. H. [1]*girmiṭ*], adj. *hist.* indentured labourer.

गिरवाना *girvānā* [cf. H. *girnā*, and *girānā*], v.t. **1.** to cause to be knocked down, or felled. **2.** to cause to be dropped. **3.** to cause to be overthrown.

गिरवी *girvī* [P. *giravī*], adj. & f. **1.** adj. pledged, pawned. **2.** f. sthg. pawned, a surety. **3.** a mortgage. — ~ धरना or रखना, to pawn. ~ धरनेवाला or रखनेवाला, m. pawnbroker. ~ से छुड़ाना, to redeem, to recover from pawn; to pay off a mortgage (on). – गिरवी-गट्टा, m. pawnbroking. गिरवी-ग्राही, m. a mortgagee. गिरवीदार [P. *-dār*], m. a mortgagor. गिरवि-नामा, m. a mortage deed. गिरवी-पत्र, m. id.

गिरस्ती *girastī*, f. pronun. var. = गृहस्थी.

गिरह *girah* [P. *girih*], f. **1.** a knot. **2.** the end of a garment, knotted (to hold money, or as a reminder). **3.** transf. a pocket. **4.** three finger-breadths; one sixteenth of a *gaz*. — ~ पड़ना, a misunderstanding to arise. ~ बाँधना to note and remember (sthg). – गिरहकट, m. a cutpurse, pickpocket. गिरहदार [P. *-dār*], adj. knotty, knotted; jointed.

गिरहस्त *girhast*, m. Av. = गृहस्थ.

गिरा *girā* [S.], f. **1.** speech; voice. **2.** things said: poetry. **3.** *hind.* a name of Sarasvatī, the goddess of speech. — गिरा-पति, m. a name of Brahmā.

गिराऊ *girāū* [cf. H. *girānā*], adj. **1.** fit to be pulled down, or felled. **2.** to be pulled down; ready to fall.

गिराना *girānā* [cf. H. *girnā*], v.t. **1.** to cause to fall; to throw or to knock down; to fell; to bring down; to shed (blood). **2.** to allow to fall; to drop; to spill; to shed (tears); to lower, to reduce (as prices). **3.** to overthrow, to destroy; to debase; to disgrace.

गिरानी *girānī* [H. *girānā*], f. a time of reduced prosperity.

गिरावट *girāvaṭ* [cf. H. *girnā*], f. a falling, fall.

गिरि *giri* [S.], m. a mountain, a hill. — **गिरिजा**, f. the mountain-born one: a name of Pārvatī. **गिरिजा-कुमार**, m. a name of Kārttikeya. **गिरिजा-पति**, m. a name of Śiva. **गिरिधर**, m. the mountain-holder: a name of Kṛṣṇa. **गिरि-धरन**, **गिरि-धारन**, m. Brbh. who holds up a mountain: id. **गिरिधारी**, m. = **गिरिधर**. **गिरि-नाथ**, m. a name of Śiva, or of the Himālayas, or of Govardhan Hill. **गिरि-पथ**, m. a mountain valley or pass. **गिरि-माला**, f. a mountain range. **गिरि-राज**, m. a name of the Himālayas, of Govardhan Hill, of mount Sumeru, or of Kṛṣṇa. **गिरि-राय**, m. id. **गिरिवर**, m. an imposing mountain. **गिरि-शिखर**, m. a mountain peak. **गिरींद्र** [°*ri*+*i*°], m. a large mountain; the number 8. **गिरीश** [°*ri*+*ī*°], m. a large mountain, a name of Śiva; or of the Himālayas, or of Govardhan hill.

गिरिफ़्त *girift*, f. = **गिरफ़्त**.

-गिरी *-girī*, f. noun formant. = **-गरी**.

गिरो *giro*. reg. (E.) = **गिरवी**.

गिरोह *giroh* [P. *guroh*], m. f. a group, party, band (of people).

गिर्द *gird*, adv. round, around: see s.v. **इर्द-गिर्द**. — **गिर्दागिर्द**, adv. round about; all around. **गिर्दावर** [P. *-āvar*], m. an inspector of customs, or of financial records.

गिल *gil* [P. *gil*], f. earth, clay. — **गिलकार**, m. a plasterer; °**ई**, f. plastering.

गिलगिला *gilgilā* [? conn. **grilla*-: Pk. *gilla*-; also *galati*[1]], adj. **1.** wet, moist; clammy. **2.** viscous, slimy. **3.** soft, pulpy (as over-ripe fruit; = **गिजगिजा**).

गिलट *gilaṭ* [Engl. *gilt*], f. gilt; gilding; chromium or metal plating of any kind.

गिलटी *gilṭī* [cf. **giḍa*- (? ← Drav.): *gaḍula*-], f. **1.** a gland. **2.** a swelling of the glands; a tumour. — ~ **निकलना** (**के**), (one) to suffer an illness in which the glands are affected.

गिलना *gilnā* [*gilati*], v.t. reg. to swallow.

गिलहरा *gilahrā*, m. reg. (W.) a betel-box.

गिलहरी *gilahrī*, f. a squirrel.

गिला *gilā* [P. *gilā*], m. **1.** complaint; lamentation. **2.** reproach; accusation. — ~ **करना** (**का**), to complain (of). – **गिला-शिकवा**, m. complaint, &c. (= ~).

ग़िलाफ़ *gilāf* [A. *gilāf*], m. **1.** covering, cover; pillow-case; quilt. **2.** sheath.

गिलास *gilās* [Engl. *glass*], m. a glass, a tumbler (glass or metal); a mug.

गिलोय *giloy* [*guḍūcī*-], f. a particular creeper; a medicine derived from this, used against fevers.

गिलौंदा *gilaundā*, m. reg. (W.) the flower or pod of the *mahuā* tree.

गिलौ *gilau*, m. *Pl.* = **गिलोय**.

गिलौड़ी *gilauṛī*, f. reg. = **गिलौरी**.

गिलौरी *gilaurī*, f. a folded betel leaf with its contents, ready for eating (= **बीड़ा**).

ग़िल्ला *gillā*, m. = **गुल**.

गिल्ली *gillī*, f. = **गुल्ली**.

गींजना *gīṁjnā* [**gijj*-: ← Drav.], v.t. to crumble, or to crumple, with the hand.

गीत *gīt* [S.], m. **1.** song; a song. **2.** a song of praise. — ~ **गाना**, to sing a song; fig. to tell a long tale. ~ **गाना** (**का** or **के**), to sing the praises (of). **राष्ट्रीय** ~, m. national anthem. – **गीतकार**, m. a song composer or writer. **गीत-क्रम**, m. melody. **गीतात्मक** [°*ta*+*ā*°], adj. having to do with singing; musical. **गीतायन** [°*ta*+*a*°], m. home of melody: a musical instrument.

गीता *gītā* [S.], f. **1.** a song; an episode (in a poetic work). ***2.** specif. the *Bhagavadgītā* (an episode of the *Mahābhārata*).

गीति *gīti* [S.], f. a song, singing: — **गीति-काव्य**, m. a lyrical poem, or poetry.

गीदड़ *gīdaṛ* [**gidda*-[1]], m. **1.** a jackal. **2.** pej. a coward. — **गीदड़-भभकी**, f. jackal's threat: bluster, bravado.

गीदड़ी *gīdṛī* [cf. H. *gīdaṛ*], f. a jackal (female).

गीध *gīdh*, m. = **गिद्ध**.

गीधना *gīdhnā* [cf. *gṛddha*- or *gṛdhra*-], v.i. **1.** to be or to become greedy (for). **2.** to be attracted (as an animal by food).

-गीर *-gīr* [P. *gīr*], adj. & m. formant. seizing; conquering (e.g. **जहानगीर**, world-conquering or -conqueror).

-गीरी *-gīrī* [P. *gīrī*], noun formant, f. a taking, taking up or on (of an activity: e.g. **गुमाश्तागीरी**, activity, or commission, of an agent).

गीला *gīlā* [? **grilla-*: Pk. *gilla-*], adj. **1.** wet; damp, moist. **2.** humid.

गीलापन *gīlāpan* [cf. H. *gīlā*], m. **1.** wetness; dampness, moistness. **2.** humidity.

गुँगा *gumgā*, adj. pronun. var. = गूँगा.

गुँगाई *gumgāī* [cf. H. *gūmgā*], f. **1.** dumbness. **2.** speechlessness.

गुंचा *guñcā* [P. *gunca*], m. **1.** a bud; blossom. **2.** fig. enjoyment. — ~ खिलना, a bud to open; to become radiant (the face); to be catching (a mood of delight).

1**गुंज** *guñj* [*guñja-*1], f. **1.** a humming or murmuring sound. **2.** an echo. **3.** the sound of birds' singing.

2**गुंज** *guñj*, m. = गुंजा.

गुंजन *guñjan* [S.], m. = 1गुंज.

गुँजना *gumjnā*, v.i. pronun. var. = गूँजना.

गुंजलक *guñjalak* [cf. *guñja-*2, Pk. *guñjellia-*], f. coil (of a snake).

गुंजा *guñjā* [ad. *guñjā-*: ← Drav.], f. the smallest of a jeweller's weights, a grain (the berry of the shrub *Abrus precatorius*).

गुंजान *guñjān*, adj. thick, dense, compact.

गुंजाइश *guñjāiś* [P. *gunjā'iś*], f. **1.** space, room; scope, opportunity. **2.** margin; profit. — ~ रखना, to have room (for, की). – गुंजाइशवाला, adj. capacious; profitable.

गुंजार *guñjār* [cf. *guñja-*1], m. poet. = 1गुंज.

गुँजिया *gumjiyā*, f. reg. (W.) a woman's ear-ring.

गुँझिया *gumjhiyā*, f. reg. (W.) a sweet made of wheat flour containing a filling (? = गुझिया, 2).

गुंठित *gunṭhit* [S.], adj. poet. veiled.

गुंडई *gunḍaī* [cf. H. *gunḍā*], f. hooliganism.

गुंडा *gunḍā* [conn. *gonḍa-*1], m. **1.** a dissolute person. ***2.** lout, bully.

गुँथवाना *gumthvānā* [cf. H. *gūmthnā*], v.t. to cause to be strung; to cause to be plaited, &c.

गुँधना *gumdhnā* [cf. H. *gūmdhnā*, and *gūmthnā*], v.i. **1.** to be kneaded. **2.** to be plaited, braided.

गुँधवाना *gumdhvānā* [cf. H. *gūmdhnā*, and H. *gūmthnā*], v.t. **1.** to cause to be kneaded. **2.** to cause to be plaited, &c.

गुँधाई *gumdhāī* [cf. H. *gūmdhnā*, and H. *gūmthnā*], f. 1. = गुँधावट, 1., 2. **2.** cost of, or payment for kneading, or for plaiting.

गुँधावट *gumdhāvaṭ*, f. **1.** [cf. H. *gūmdhnā*] kneading. **2.** [cf. H. *gūmthnā*] plaiting, braiding.

गुंफन *gumphan* [S.], m. twining, stringing together.

गुंफा *gumphā* [S.], f. = गुफा.

गुंफित *gumphit* [S.], adj. twined, strung, woven.

गुंबज *gumbaj*, m. = गुंबद.

गुंबद *gumbad* [P. *gumbad*], m. an arch: **1.** a dome, cupola. **2.** tower, bastion. — गुंबददार [P. *-dār*], adj. domed; convex.

गुंबदी *gumbadī* [cf. H. *gumbad*], adj. & f. **1.** adj. domed, dome-shaped. **2.** f. a circular vaulted chamber (with central pillar).

गुआ *guā*, m. Av. = गुवा.

गुइयाँ *guiyām* [? conn. P. *gū* (← *guftan*)], f. m. **1.** f. a (woman's) female friend or companion. **2.** m. partner (in a game); fellow team-member. **3.** a friend.

गुग्गुल *guggul* [*gulgulu-*], m. a thorny tree, *Amyris agallochum*, and its fragrant resin.

गुच्ची *guccī*, f. **1.** a small hole (esp. as dug by children in playing *gullī-ḍaṇḍā*). **2.** a pit. — गुच्ची-पाला, m. a game in which cowries, &c. are thrown into a hole; the game of tip-cat. गुच्ची-सी आँखें, tiny eyes.

गुच्छ *gucch* [S.], m. a cluster, bunch.

गुच्छा *gucchā* [*guccha-*: ← Drav.], m. **1.** anything of which the parts are drawn or gathered together: a cluster, bunch; a skein, hank. **2.** a tangle (as of hair). **3.** a tassel. **4.** a collection (of short stories). — गुच्छेदार [P. *-dār*], adj. clustered, tufted, tasselled.

गुज़र *guzar* [P. *guzar*], m. **1.** passage, passing; access. **2.** the passage of time; life, existence. — ~ करना, v.i. to spend one's time; to make do, to get by. – गुज़र-बसर, m. subsisting, getting by.

गुज़रना *guzarnā* [cf. P. *guzar*], v.i. **1.** to pass, to make one's way (past). **2.** to elapse (time); to befall, to happen (to, पर). **3.** (esp. गुज़र जाना.) to pass by; to pass away, to die. — वह गाँव के पास से गुज़रा जा रहा था, he was making his way past the village. – गुज़रा, m. the past.

गुजरात *gujarāt* [**gurjaratrā-*: Pk. *gujjarattā-*], m. the state or region of Gujarāt.

1**गुजराती** *gujarātī* [cf. H. *gujarāt*], adj. & m. **1.** adj. of or belonging to Gujarat. **2.** m. a man of Gujarat.

²गुजराती *gujarātī* [cf. H. *gujarāt*], f. the Gujarati language.

गुजरिया *gujriyā* [cf. H. *gūjrī*], f. **1.** one who takes the part of a woman in a dance. **2.** an earthen image representing a milkmaid (a young girl's toy).

गुजरी *gujrī*, f. = गूजरी, 3., 4.

गुज़श्ता *guzaśtā* [P. *guzaśta*], m. the past.

गुजाई *gujāī*, f. reg. a mixture of wheat and barley sown together (= गोजरा).

गुज़ार *guzār* [P. *guzār*], adj. formant. causing to pass; performing; paying.

गुज़ारना *guzārnā* [cf. P. *guzār*], v.t. **1.** to cause to pass; to spend (time, or one's life); to complete. **2.** to lay (a gift, &c.) before (one).

गुज़ारा *guzārā* [P. *guzāra*], m. **1.** a passing over, crossing. **2.** life, existence; the spending of time. **3.** the means of existence; subsistence, maintenance. — **~ करना**, to live, to exist (on, or by means of, से). **थोड़े में ~ करना**, to get by on little (expenditure). — **गुज़ारेदार** [P. *-dār*], m. one having a subsistence allowance.

गुज़ारिश *guzāriś* [P. *guzāriś*], f. a petition, request. — **ख़िदमत में ~ करना**, to present or to represent (a matter: to, की). – **गुज़ारिश-नामा**, m. a (written) petition, entreaty.

-गुज़ारी *-guzārī* [P. *guzārī*], noun formant, f. passing: performance (as of duty); payment (as of rent).

गुजिया *gujiyā*, f. pronun. var. = गुझिया.

गुज्झा *gujjhā* [*guhya-*], adj. & m. **1.** adj. E.H. secret, hidden. **2.** m. a dowel.

गुझिया *gujhiyā* [? conn. H. *gūṁdhnā*], f. **1.** a kind of small pastry. **2.** a sweet, made with *khoā*.

गुट *guṭ*, m. a group; a faction.

¹गुटकना *guṭaknā* [? cf. H. *gaṭaknā*], v.t. to gulp, to bolt (= गटकना).

²गुटकना *guṭaknā* [? = H. ¹*guṭaknā*], v.i. to coo (as a dove).

गुटका *guṭkā* [cf. H. *guṭṭā*; ? ad. *guṭikā-*], m. **1.** a small ball; a pill having magical effect (= गुटिका). **2.** a lump or chunk; a wedge (as inserted in door-frames to hold a door open, or as used to tune a *tablā*). **3.** a small book; handbook, manual; anthology.

गुटरगूँ *guṭargūṁ*, m. sound of cooing.

गुटरगूं *guṭargūṁ*, m. = गुटरगूँ.

गुटिका *guṭikā* [S.], f. **1.** a small globe or ball; a pill having supposed magical effects. 2. = गुटका, 3.

गुट्टा *guṭṭā* [conn. **goṭṭa-* (? ← Drav.); **guṭṭha-*¹], m. & adj. **1.** m. a lump; a lump of gum-lac (as used in a children's game). **2.** a dwarf. **3.** adj. chunky, short of stature.

¹गुठला *guṭhlā* [cf. **guṭṭha-*¹: Pk. *guṭṭha-*], m. a large lump; cyst.

²गुठला *guṭhlā* [cf. **guṭṭha-*³], adj. *Pl. HŚS.* blunted.

गुठली *guṭhlī* [cf. **guṭṭha-*¹: Pk. *guṭṭha-*], f. **1.** lump, mass; clot. ***2.** stone (of a fruit), kernel. **3.** a gland.

गुड़ *guṛ* [*guḍa-*²], m. raw sugar; boiled sugar-cane juice. — **~ की भेली**, f. a lump of raw sugar. **~ की-सी बातें**, f. pl. sweet words (that stop short of deeds). **~ गोबर कर देना**, to ruin (sthg. promising. **~ दिखाकर ढेला मारना**, fig, to disappoint (one's, को) hopes after raising them. — **गुड़-अंबा** or **गुड़-आंबा**, m. mangoes boiled with flour and sugar. **गुड़-च्यूँटा होना**, to be inseparable (as sugar and ants). **गुड़-धानी**, f. parched wheat and sugar.

गुड़गुड़ *guṛguṛ* [conn. **guḍuguḍa-*], ? m. **1.** a bubbling sound (as of a hookah). **2.** a rumbling sound (as of the stomach).

गुड़गुड़ाना *guṛguṛānā* [cf. H. *guṛguṛ*], v.i. & v.t. **1.** v.i. to bubble. **2.** to rumble. **3.** to cause to bubble, &c.; colloq. to smoke (a hookah).

गुड़गुड़ाहट *guṛguṛāhaṭ* [cf. H. *guṛguṛānā*], f. **1.** a bubbling sound. **2.** a rumbling sound.

गुड़गुड़ी *guṛguṛī* [cf. H. *guṛguṛ*], f. 1. = गुड़गड़ाहट. **2.** a small hookah.

गुड़च *guṛac*, ? f. *Pl. HŚS.* = गुरुच.

गुडरू *guḍrū*, m. Av. a partic. bird: ? the bustard-quail.

गुड़हल *guṛ'hal*, m. reg. (E.) the shoe-flower, *Hibiscus syriacus* (= अड़हुल).

गुड़ाई *guṛāī* [cf. H. *goṛnā*], f. **1.** hoeing. **2.** cost of or charge for hoeing.

गुड़ाकू *guṛākū* [H. *guṛ* × H. *tambākū*], m. a mixture of tobacco and raw sugar for smoking.

गुड़िया *guṛiyā* [**guḍḍa-*], f. **1.** a doll. **2.** a puppet. **3.** a beautiful-looking girl. — **~ का खेल**, m. an easy matter, child's play. **~ सी**, f. tiny, dainty. **गुड़ियों का ब्याह**, m. dolls' wedding: a poor man's wedding (involving small expense, or small dowry). **राम की ~**, f. = इंद्रवधू.

गुड़ी *guṛī*, f. Brbh. = गुड्डी, 1.

गुड्डा *guḍḍā* [**guḍḍa-*], m. **1.** a doll; a puppet. **2.** an effigy (of a man). **3.** an object of scorn or infamy. — **~ बनाना**, to make an effigy (of, का); to cause fun to be made of.

[1]**गुड्डी** *guḍḍī* [**guḍḍa-*], f. **1.** a paper kite. **2.** a doll (= गुड़िया). **3.** colloq. a lovely girl or daughter.

[2]**गुड्डी** *guḍḍī* [**goḍḍa-* (Pk. *goḍḍa-*) × **guṭṭha-*[2]], f. the knee-bone. — हड्डी-गुड्डी तोड़ना, to break all (one's, की) bones, to beat soundly.

गुढ़ा *guṛhā*, m. reg. (W.) thwarts (of a boat).

गुण *guṇ* [S.], m. var. /gũṛ/. **1.** a quality, a property. **2.** *ling.* (in Sanskrit grammar) a partic. vowel grade. **3.** *philos.* each of the three constitutents of nature (viz. *sattva* 'goodness', *rajas* 'passion' and *tamas* 'darkness'). **4.** a symbol for the number three. **5.** a good quality, a virtue; a skill, aptitude; a talent. **6.** (with numerals.) a multiplicative suffix: -fold, times. — ~ गाना, to sing the praises (of, के). ~ मानना (के), fig. to acknowledge a favour; to be grateful (to one) for. – **गुणकारक**, adj. productive of good qualities: profitable, effective. °-**कारी**, adj. id. **गुण-खान**, f. a mine of virtues: an excellent, or talented person. **गुणगत**, adj. qualitative. **गुण-गाथ**, f. singing of the praises (of a person or thing, की); appraising the qualities (of). °-**गाथा**, f. id. **गुण-गान**, m. = गुण-गाथ. **गुण-गान करना**, to eulogise (one, का). **गुण-ग्राहक**, adj. & m. appreciating or discerning the virtues (of); patronizing learning; one who appreciates merit, &c. °-**ग्राही**, adj. & m. id. **गुण-घाटी**, adj. & m. ungrateful, uncognisant; such a person. **गुण ज्ञाता**, m. inv. one who recognises merit. **गुण-दोष**, m. pl. virtues and vices. **गुण-धर्म**, m. a virtue or a duty which is an aspect of the possession of particular qualities. **गुणनाशक**, adj. & m. destroying qualities, &c.; an antidote. **गुण-निधान**, m. treasury of virtues: = गुण-खान. **गुणमान**, m. standard quality (as of materials). **गुणवंत**, adj. = गुणवान. **गुणवाचक**, adj. *ling.* qualitative (of an adjective). **गुणवान**, adj. & m. endowed with virtues, &c.; an admirable, or a talented person. **गुण-सागर**, m. ocean of virtues: a supremely meritorious person; a title of the supreme being (seen as the possessor of all qualities). **गुण-स्तुति**, f. encomium, panegyric. **गुणहीन**, adj. without virtues; without properties. **गुणांक**, [°*ṇa + a*°], m. *math.* a multiplier or coefficient. **गुणाढ्य** [°*ṇa + ā*°], adj. richly endowed with qualities. **गुणातीत** [°*ṇa + a*°], adj. beyond the *guṇas*: a title of the unqualified supreme being. **गुणात्मक** [°*ṇa + ā*°], adj. qualitative. **गुणानुवाद** (°*ṇa + a*°), m. relating, or glorifying the virtues (of, का). **गुणानुवाद करना**, to eulogize. **गुणान्वित**, adj. possessed of qualities; well-qualified.

गुणक *guṇak* [S.], m. *math.* a multiplier.

गुणन *guṇan* [S.], m. **1.** multiplying; multiplication. **2.** counting (= गणन). **3.** supposing, estimating.

गुणा *guṇā* [*guṇaka-*: and ad.], m. **1.** multiplication. **2.** (with numerals) a multiplicative suffix: -fold, times. (= गुना.) — ~ करना (को), to multiply (by, से).

गुणी *guṇī* [S.], adj. & m. **1.** adj. having good qualities; having skills or talents; excellent, worthy. **2.** m. a good, skilled or worthy person. **3.** Brbh. a magician, sorcerer.

गुण्य *guṇyă* [S.], adj. & m. **1.** adj. able to be multiplied. **2.** m. a multiplicand.

गुत्थम-गुथा *gutthaṃ-guthā* [cf. H. *guthnā*], m. **1.** a brawl, struggle (esp. wrestling). **2.** confusion, entanglement.

गुत्थी *gutthī* [cf. **guptha-*; H. *guthnā*], f. **1.** an entangled mass (as of string). **2.** a confused situation or problem; puzzle, knotty problem. **3.** a psychological problem, or fixation.

गुथना *guthnā* [cf. H. *gūthnā*], v.i. **1.** to be strung, to be threaded. **2.** to be plaited or braided. **3.** to be tangled; to catch (in). **4.** to be entangled (in, में); to close (with an antagonist, से; = जुटना).

गुथवाँ *guthvāṃ* [cf. H. *guthnā*], adj. **1.** strung together; plaited, interlaced, &c. **2.** entangled.

गुथवाना *guthvānā* [cf. H. *guthnā, gūṃthnā*], v.t. to cause to be knotted, strung, plaited, &c.

गुद *gud* [S.], m. anus.

गुदकारा *gudkārā*, adj. = गुदगुदा.

गुदगुदा *gudgudā* [? cf. H. *gūdā*], adj. **1.** plump, fleshy. **2.** soft.

गुदगुदाना *gudgudānā*, v.t. **1.** to tickle. **2.** to incite, to stimulate.

गुदगुदाहट *gudgudāhaṭ* [cf. H. *gudgudanā*], f. = गुदगुदी.

गुदगुदी *gudgudī* [cf. H. *gudgudānā*], f. **1.** tickling; tingling. **2.** stimulation; itch. — ~ लगाना, or करना (को), to tickle, &c.

गुदड़िया *gudaṛiyā* [cf. H. *gūdṛī*], f. dimin. patched or tattered clothes. — ~ पीर, m. *Pl. HŚS.* a tree outside a town or village on which people tie rags as votive offerings.

गुदड़ी *gudṛī* [cf. **gudda-*], f. **1.** a quilt, or bedding of rags. **2.** a tattered garment. — ~ का लाल, a jewel in rags. ~ बाज़ार, m. a second-hand clothes market.

गुदना *gudnā* [cf. H. *godnā*], v.i. & m. **1.** v.i. to be pricked or punctured. **2.** to be tattooed. **3.** m. tattooing; a tattoo. — ~ गुदाना (में), to get (oneself) tattooed.

गुदवाना *gudvānā* [cf. H. *godnā*], v.t. to cause to be tattooed.

गुदा *gudā* [*guda-*, Pk. *guda-*], m. anus.

गुदाज़ *gudāz* [P. *gudāz*], adj. soft, plump, fleshy.

गुदाना *gudānā*, v.t. = गुदवाना.

गुदाम *gudām*, m. = गोदाम.

गुदार *gudār* adj. reg. soft (= गूदेदार).

गुदारा *gudārā* [P. *guzāra*], m. Av. crossing (of a river).

गुदी *gudī*, f. *Pl. HŚS.* reg. a sheltered place for repairing boats, a small dock (= गोदी).

गुद्दा *guddā*, m. reg. large branch (of a tree).

गुद्दी *guddī* [conn. **gudda-*: ← Panj.], f. the nape of the neck. — अक़्ल, or आँखें, ~ में होना or चली जाना, to be or to become inattentive.

गुन *gun*, m. Brbh. Av. = गुण. — गुनमय, adj. composed of *guṇas*; meritorious.

गुनगुन *gungun* [**gunaguna-*], f. **1.** buzzing, humming. **2.** mumbling, muttering. **3.** singing softly, humming. — ~ करना, to buzz, &c.

गुनगुना *gungunā* [cf. H. *gungun*], adj. & m. **1.** adj. lukewarm, tepid (= कुनकुना). **2.** speaking nasally. **3.** m. lukewarmness, &c.

गुनगुनाना *gungunānā* [**gunaguna-*], v.i. **1.** to buzz, to hum. **2.** to simmer (as water). **3.** to mumble, to mutter. **4.** to sing softly, to hum.

गुनगुनापन *gungunāpan* [cf. H. *gungunā*], m. tepidity.

गुनगुनाहट *gungunāhaṭ* [cf. H. *gungunānā*], f. = गुनगुन.

गुनना *gunnā* [*guṇayati*[1 2]], v.t. **1.** to consider, to estimate; to ponder. **2.** to consider highly; to praise. **3.** to multiply (by, से). — पढ़ना और ~, m. reading and evaluating, or digesting.

गुनहगार *gunahgār* [P. *gunahgār*], m. see s.v.

गुना *gunā* [*guṇaka-*], m. inv. & adj. **1.** m. a multiplicative quantity. कई ~ अधिक, several times larger, or greater. **2.** adj. (with numerals) a multiplicative suffix: -fold, times. दुगुना, twice as much (as, से).

गुनाह *gunāh* [P. *gunāh*], m. **1.** sin; fault, offence; vice. **2.** guilt. — ~ करना, to sin; to incur guilt. ~ रखना, to impute a sin or fault (to, पर); to accuse wrongly (of). – गुनाहकार, m. *Pl.* a sinner, &c. °ई, f. = गुनाहगारी. गुनाहगार [P. -*gār*], m. a sinner, &c. °ई, f. sinfulness; guiltiness.

गुनिया *guniyā* [P. *gūniyā*: ← Gk.], m. a carpenter's square.

गुन्नी *gunnī* [conn. *guṇa-*], f. reg. a light whip of twisted cloth with which people beat each other at the Holī festival.

गुप *gup* [H. *gupt*], adj. **1.** hidden, secret. **2.** dark; blind. — ~ अँधेरा, m. thick darkness. गुप-चुप, adj. & f. secret; secretly; secrecy; silence.

गुप-चुप *gup-cup*, m. a boys' game (in which one puffs out his cheeks, and another strikes them with both hands so as to produce a sound).

गुपाल *gupāl*, m. pronun. var. = गोपाल.

गुप्त *gupt* [S.], adj. & m. **1.** adj. hidden, secret; kept secret; confidential. **2.** m. name of a north Indian community. **3.** m. a dissembler, hypocrite. — ~ करना, to conceal. ~ रहना, to remain hidden. ~ आमदनी, f. an undisclosed income. ~ दान, m. a secret gift or donation. ~ माल, m. hidden wealth or treasure. ~ रूप, adv. secretly. – गुप्त-चर, m. a scout, spy. °ई, f. espionage. गुप्तचर्या, f. espionage.

गुप्ती *guptī* [cf. H. *gupt*], f. a sword-stick.

गुप्फा *gupphā* [**guppha-*], m. *Pl. HŚS.* tassel; wreath; bunch (as of flowers).

गुफा *guphā* [cf. **gupphā-*], f. a cave; place of retreat.

गुफ़्तगू *guftgū* [P. *guftgū*], f. conversation; a conversation. — ~ करना, to hold a conversation (esp. an intimate one).

गुफ़्तार *guftār* [P. *guftār*], f. esp. in comp. speaking. — गाली-गुफ़्तार, f. mutual abuse.

गुबरैला *gubrailā* [cf. *gorvara-*, Pk. *gov(v)ara-*], m. a type of black beetle which lives in dung.

गुबार *gubār* [A. *gubār*], m. **1.** dust; dust-storm. **2.** fig. bad feeling. **3.** affliction, grief. **4.** perplexity. — ~ निकालना (अपना), to vent or to work out ill-feeling, &c.; to take revenge.

गुबारा *gubārā*, m. = गुब्बारा.

गुब्बारा *gubbārā* [P. *gubbāra*], m. **1.** a balloon (vehicle). **2.** a balloon (plaything, decoration). **3.** a kind of firework that bursts in the air.

गुभना *gubhnā* [*cubhyate* × **goḍḍ-*], v.i. = खुभना, चुभना.

गुभाना *gubhānā* [cf. H. *gubhnā*], v.t. = चुभाना.

गुभी *gubhī* [? *garbha-* × **gudda-*], f. Brbh. shoot, sprout.

गुम *gum* [P. *gum*], adj. **1.** lost. **2.** wanting, missing (as alertness, intelligence). **3.** absent; hidden. — ~ करना, to lose; to hide. – गुमनाम,

adj. whose name is lost: of no repute; anonymous; inglorious. °ई, f. गुमनाम पत्र, m. an anonymous letter. गुमराह, adj. & m. losing the way, wandering; misled; gone astray; one who has lost his way. °ई, f. being lost or astray; error; apostasy; depravity. गुमराह करना, v.t. to lead astray, &c. गुमशुदा, adj. inv. lost, &c. °-शुदगी [P. *-śudagī*], f. state of being lost or astray. गुमसुम [A. *ṣumm*], adj. quite still or quiet. गुमहोश, adj. unconscious.

गुमटा *gumṭā*, m. = गुमड़ा.

गुमटी *gumṭī*, f. **1.** a workmen's cabin. **2.** a stall.

गुमड़ा *gumṛā* [cf. *gulma-*], m. **1.** a swelling, lump; tumour. **2.** a bruise.

गुमड़ी *gumṛī* [cf. H. *gumṛā*], f. a small lump, &c.

गुमान *gumān* [P. *gumān*], m. **1.** conjecture, supposition. **2.** distrust, suspicion. ***3.** pride; haughtiness. — ~ करना, to imagine, to suppose; to mistrust; to be proud, or conceited. ~ लाना, = ~ करना. ~ है, it is supposed, &c. – गुमान भरा, adj. proud; conceited.

गुमानी *gumānī* [P. *gumānī*], adj. & m. **1.** suspicious, doubting. **2.** proud.

गुमाश्ता *gumāśtā* [P. *gumāśta*], m. a deputed agent, business representative; accountant (of a business); authorised buyer and seller of goods. — ~ करना, to appoint as an agent, &c. – गुमाश्तागीरी [P. *-gīrī*], f. commission; the business or status of an agent, &c.

गुम्मा *gummā*, m. reg. a piece of brick.

गुर- *gur-*. pronun. var. = गुरु.

गुरगा *gurgā*, m. **1.** a servant. **2.** a rascal.

गुरगाबी *gurgābī*, f. **1.** a toeless shoe. **2.** reg. (W.) a kind of shoe or slipper having the toe turned up.

गुरदम *gurdam*, m. reg. (Bihar) a stirrer for sugar during boiling (? = ²गुरदा).

¹**गुरदा** *gurdā* [P. *gurda*], m. a kidney. — गुरदे की सूजन, f. inflammation of the kidney. – गुरदानुमा [P. *-numā*], adj. kidney-shaped. गुरदेवाला, adj. fig. having spirit or courage.

²**गुरदा** *gurdā* [cf. *guḍa-²*: ?+H. *dā*], m. reg. (W.) a scraper used to prevent sugar from burning as it is being boiled.

गुरबत *gurbat* [A. *gurba*: P. *gurbat*], f. **1.** the state of a stranger, or foreigner; wretched or helpless state; poverty. **2.** humility.

गुरबना *gurabnā*, v.t. reg. (W.) to dig, to dig up; to hoe, to weed.

गुरसी *gursī*, f. reg. (W.) a fireplace, grate (cf. बुरसी).

गुरिया *guriyā* [*guḍikā-*], f. reg. (E). a glass bead.

गुरु *guru* [S.], adj. & m. **1.** adj. heavy. **2.** *ling. pros.* long. **3.** weighty; momentous. **4.** venerable, honoured. **5.** m. a spiritual guide, mentor. **6.** a teacher. **7.** pej. scoundrel. **8.** a name of the god Bṛhaspati, or of the planet Jupiter. — गुरु-कुल, m. guru's place of residence; a school, seminary. गुरुगत, adj. acquired from a guru. गुरु-घंटाल, adj. an egregious rascal. गुरु-जन, m., esp. pl. venerable or eminent persons; elders. गुरु-दक्षिणा, f. gift or fee to a guru by an initiate. गुरु-देव, m. respectful term of address to a guru. गुरुद्वारा, m. guru's residence; a Sikh temple. गुरु-पूर्णिमा, f. the full moon of Asāṛh (when a guru is venerated). गुरु-भाई, m. pl. pupils of the same guru; fellow-disciples. गुरु-मंत्र, m. the *mantra* received from a guru; an efficacious means (to sthg., का). गुरुमुख, m. one initiated by a guru as his pupil. °ई, f. The Gur(u)mukhī script (of the Sikh scriptures, and of Panjabi). गुरुवार, m. Thursday.

गुरुआई *guruāī* [cf. H. *guru*], f. **1.** the position or activity of a guru. **2.** iron. cunning.

गुरुआनी *guruānī* [cf. H. *guru*], f. a guru's wife; female mentor or guide.

गुरुच *guruc* [ad. *guḍūcī-*], f. *Pl. HŚS.* a self-rooting creeper, *Menispermum glabrum* (found growing in trees).

गुरुता *gurutā*, f. = गुरुत्व.

गुरुत्व *gurutvă* [S.], m. **1.** weight; length (as of a vowel or a phonetic quantity). **2.** gravity. **3.** substance, importance. **4.** the position or effectiveness of a religious leader, or of a mentor. — गुरुत्व-केंद्र, m. centre of gravity. गुरुत्वाकर्षण [°*tva+ā*°], m. gravitation.

गुरुवार *guruvār* [S.], m. see s.v. गुरु.

गुरूब *gurūb* [A. *gurūb*], m. U. setting (of the sun).

गुरेज़ *gurez* [P. *gurez*], f. flight, escape (from, से). — ~ और परहेज़, m. = ~.

गुरेट *gureṭ*, m. *HŚS.* a roller attached to a handle, used to stir sugar during refining.

गुर्गा *gurgā*, m. see गुरगा.

गुर्जर *gurjar* [S.], m. & adj. **1.** m. the state or region of Gujarat. **2.** a person from Gujarat. **3.** a *gūjar*, q.v. **4.** adj. of or belonging to Gujarat.

गुर्जरी *gurjarī* [S.], f. **1.** a woman from Gujarat. **2.** a *gūjar* woman.

गुर्दा *gurdā*, m. see [1]गुरदा.

गुर्राना *gurrānā* [conn. P. *gurrīdan*], v.i. **1.** to growl (at, पर); to roar. **2.** to snarl, to speak angrily (at or to).

गुर्री *gurrī*, f. *Pl. HŚS.* parched barley.

गुर्विणी *gurviṇī* [S.], adj. f. E.H. pregnant.

गुल *gul* [P. *gul*], m. **1.** a rose; a flower. **2.** sthg. burned: esp. a burnt wick, or its ash. — ~ करना, to extinguish (a candle, a lamp). ~ खिलना, to flower; to come to light (sthg. strange, or interesting). ~खिलाना, to cause to happen (sthg. strange; also iron.); to cause disturbance; to poke fun at. ~ होना, to go out; to be put out (as a candle). – गुल-क़ंद, m. sugared rose-leaves dried in the sun (an aperient). गुलकार, m. a floral decorator. °ई, f. floral decoration. गुल-चमन, m. a flower garden; flower-bed; a meadow of flowers.

गुलचाँदनी *gul-cāṁdnī*, f. a white flower that opens at night, *Calonyction roxburghii*. गुलछर्रा, m. a scattering of flowers: a life given over to pleasures. गुलछर्रे उड़ाना, to live a high life. गुलज़ार [P. *-zār*], m. & adj. a garden, or a bed, of roses or flowers; blooming, flourishing. गुलदस्ता, m. a bunch of flowers; collection, garland (of choice or attractive objects). गुल-दाउदी, = °. दावदी. गुलदार, adj. flowering; flower-bearing; ornamented with flowers, or with floral designs. गुल-दान [P. *-dār*], m. a flower-vase. गुल-दाना, m. a particular sweet (बुंदिया). गुल-दावदी [P. *-dāvūdī*], f. the Indian chrysanthemum. गुल-नरगिस, f. the narcissus flower; a kind of creeper. गुल-नार, m. the pomegranate flower; a red colour. गुल-फानूस, m. a partic. large flowering tree. गुल-फ़ाम [P. *-fām*], adj. & f. rose-coloured; a mistress. गुल-बकावली, f. a plant of the type of turmeric, and its flowers. गुल-बदन, adj. & f. having a body like the rose: delicate, graceful; a beautiful woman. गुल-मेहंदी, f. the balsam, *Impatiens balsamina*, and its flower. गुल-रोग़न, f. oil of roses. गुलशन [P. *-śan*], m. a flower garden or rose garden; a flower-bed, &c.; a delightful spot. गुलिस्तान, m. see s.v.

गुल *gul* [P. *gul*], m. noise, din. — ~ करना, or मचाना, to make a din, &c. – गुल-गपाड़ा, outcry, uproar. शोर-गुल, m. id.

[1]**गुलगुला** *gulgulā* [conn. *guḍa-*[1] or *guḍa-*[2]], m. a sweet, spiced cake or dish made from wheat flour and sugar fried in *ghī*.

[2]**गुलगुला** *gulgulā*, adj. soft; plump, sleek.

[1]**गुलगुली** *gulgulī*, f. tickling, tingling (= गुदगुदी).

[2]**गुलगुली** *gulgulī* [*guḍa-*[1 2]], f. a dish of balls of rice and molasses.

गुलगोथना *gulgothnā*, adj. = गलगुथना (s.v. [2]गल-).

गुलझटी *guljhaṭī*, f. *Pl. HŚS.* **1.** a tangle (as of string). **2.** perplexity; unease (of mind).

गुलझड़ी *guljhaṛī*, f. *Pl. HŚS.* = गुलझटी.

गुलड़ी *gulṛī* [cf. *guḍa-*[1]; *gola-*[1]], f. a small ring-shaped cake of cow-dung.

गुलत्थी *gulatthī* [cf. *guḍa-*[1]], adj. & f. **1.** adj. soft and lumpy (as boiled rice). **2.** f. *Pl.* watery boiled rice, salted (taken for dysentery). **3.** a lump (as of boiled rice).

गुलहरी *gulahrī*, f. = गुलड़ी.

गुलाई *gulāī*, f. = गोलाई.

गुलाब *gulāb* [P. *gulāb*], m. **1.** rose-water. ***2.** a (red) rose. — गुलाब-जल, m. rose-water. गुलाब-जामुन, m. a sweet made from *khoā* and soft milk cheese, fried in *ghī* and soaked in syrup; the rose-apple, *Eugenia jambolana*.

गुलाबी *gulābī* [P. *gulābī*], adj. & f. **1.** adj. having to do with roses. **2.** pink. **3.** delicate, small, light. **4.** f. a flush. — ~ आँख, f. an eye flushed with wine. ~ आना, a flush to rise (to the cheeks: पर). ~ जाड़ा, m. a mild winter; the warmer weather following winter.

गुलाम *gulām* [A. *gulām*], m. a boy, youth: **1.** a slave. **2.** a servant. **3.** the jack (in cards). — ~ करना, or बनाना, to enslave. – गुलाम-चोर, m. a partic. card game. गुलाम-ज़ादा [P. *-zāda*], m. son of a slave; my son (self-deprecatory). गुलामशाही [P. *-śāhī*], f. enslavement (to).

गुलामी *gulāmī* [P. *gulāmī*], f. slavery. — ~ करना, to be slave (to, की); to slave (for).

गुलाल *gulāl* [? conn. *guṇḍaka-*: cf. Pk. *guṁḍana-*], m. the powder (usu. red) thrown and sprinkled by participants in the Holī festival. — ~ उड़ाना, or ~ फेंकना, to throw, to sprinkle or to rub *gulāl* (on one).

गुलिस्तान *gulistān* [P. *gulistān*], m. a rose-garden, flower-garden: name of a famous Persian composition in prose and verse by Sa'dī of Shiraz.

गुलू *gulū* [P. *gulū*], m. the neck, throat. — गुलू-बंद, m. a scarf; a type of close-fitting necklace.

गुलेल *gulel* [P. *gulel*], f. a pellet-bow; catapult. — गुलेलबाज़ [P. *-bāz*], m. one who shoots with a catapult. °ई, f. firing a catapult.

गुलेलची *gulelcī* [P. *gulelcī*], f. = गुलेलबाज़.

गुलेला *gulelā* [cf. H. *gulel*], m. a pellet, shot (for a *gulel*).

गुलेला *gulelā* [P. *gulela*], m. a pellet.

गुलौरा *gulaurā* [**guḍavaṭaka-*], m. reg. = [1]गुलगुला.

गुल्म *gulm* [S.], m. **1.** a thicket. **2.** a bush. — लता-गुल्म, m. vegetation, undergrowth.

गुल्लक *gullak* [P. *gullak*], m. **1.** container for ready money, cash-box. **2.** a niche in a wall used for keeping money in.

गुल्ला *gullā* [*guḍa-*[1]], m. **1.** a ball; a pellet (for shooting). **2.** reg. (E.) a small piece of sugar-cane. **3.** reg. (E.) short axle (of a lever-beam).

गुल्ली *gullī*, f. **1.** any small globular, or round object, a lump, or piece. **2.** peg, short stick; specif. the short stick struck by the longer *ḍaṇḍā* in the game *gullī-ḍaṇḍā* ('tip-cat'); bail (in cricket). — गुल्ली-डंडा खेलना, to play at *gullī-ḍaṇḍā*; to waste (one's) time.

गुवा *guvā* [conn. *guvāka-*], m. Av. betel nut.

गुसैयाँ *gusaiyāṁ*, m. = गोसाईं.

गुसैल *gusail*, adj. pronun. var. = गुस्सैल.

गुस्ताख़ *gustākh* [P. *gustākh*], adj. arrogant, brash; insolent, rude.

गुस्ताख़ाना *gustākhānā* [P. *gustākhāna*], adv. U. arrogantly; brashly; rudely.

गुस्ताख़ी *gustākhī* [P. *gustākhī*], f. arrogance; brashness; audacity; rudeness. — ~ करना, to presume (on); to be arrogant, &c. ~ से, arrogantly, &c.

गुस्ल *gusl* [A. *gusl*], m. bathing, washing. — ~ करना, to wash. – गुस्ल-ख़ाना, m. washing enclosure, bathroom.

गुस्सा *gussā* [A. *guṣṣa*], m. & adj. **1.** m. anger; rage. **2.** adj. colloq. angry. ~ आना (को), to grow angry. ~ उतारना, to take out (one's) anger (on, पर). ~ करना, to be angry (with, पर). ~ खाना, or थूक देना, to eat, or to spit out, (one's) anger: to suppress anger. ~ दिलाना (को), to anger; to provoke. ~ नाक पर रहना, or होना, to be quick-tempered, or irritable. ~ पीना, to drink (one's) anger: = ~ खाना. ~ मारना, to suppress anger. गुस्से, adv. in anger; because of anger. गुस्से में, adv. id., 1. गुस्से में भर जाना, to become enraged. गुस्से में लाना, = ~ दिलाना. गुस्से से, or के मारे, भूत हो जाना, to grow frantic with rage. गुस्से होना, to be angry (with, पर). – गुस्सेवर [P. *guṣṣevar*], adj. U. quick-tempered.

गुस्सैल *gussail* [cf. H. *gussā*], adj. quick-tempered.

गुह *guh* [*gūtha-*, Pk. *gūha-*], m. excrement. — ~ उछालना, to throw dung about (on, पर): to sully (one's) name; to revel in publicising unsavoury truths. ~ उठाना, fig. colloq. to be a menial servant (of, का). ~ खाना, to do sthg. vile or shameful. ~ में घसीटना, to treat vilely or shamefully. मुँह में ~ देना, to heap shameful reproach (on, के). – गुह-मूत, m. excrement and urine. गुह-मूत करना (का) to rear, to tend (as infant); to do very dirty work.

गुह- *guh-* [*guphati*], v.t. Brbh. to thread, &c. (= गूँथना).

गुहा *guhā* [S.], f. **1.** a cave. **2.** a den, lair. **3.** a secret or mysterious place. **4.** cavity.

गुहार *guhār*, f. = [1]गोहार.

गुहारना *guhārnā*, v.i. = गोहारना.

गुहेरा *guherā* [conn. *gaudhera-*], m. reg. a kind of poisonous lizard (cf. गोह).

गुह्य *guhyă* [S.], adj. **1.** requiring, or able to be, hidden. **2.** secret, mysterious; esoteric.

गूँगा *gūṁgā* [**guṅga-*], adj. **1.** dumb. **2.** without the power of (adequate) speech. — गूँगे का गुड़ खाना, to eat *gur* as a dumb man: to experience feelings inexpressible in words. गूँगे का सपना देखना, to dream, but be dumb: id. गूँगी पहेली, f. a riddle asked by means of gestures only. – गूँगा-बहरा, adj. deaf and dumb.

गूँगापन *gūṁgāpan* [cf. H. *gūṁgā*], m. dumbness.

[1]गूँच *gūṁc* [**kuñca-*[2]: ← Drav. × H. *guñjā*], m. *Pl. HŚS.* (E.) = गुंजा.

[2]गूँच *gūṁc* [? conn. *ku(ñ)cikā-*], f. *Pl. HŚS.* a kind of fish (? freshwater shark).

गूँज *gūṁj* [*guñja-*], f. **1.** humming, buzzing. **2.** reverberation, resonance; echo. **3.** roaring, growling.

गूँजना *gūṁjnā* [*guñjati*], v.i. **1.** to hum, to buzz. **2.** to resound; to echo. **3.** to roar, to growl.

गूँथना *gūṁthnā* [*guphati* × *granthayati*], v.t. **1.** to string, to thread. **2.** to plait, to braid. **3.** to stitch; to tack.

गूँदना *gūṁdnā*, v.t. pronun. var. = गूँधना.

गूँधना *gūṁdhnā* [*guphati* × *bandhati*], v.t. **1.** to knead (dough). **2.** to plait, to braid.

गू *gū* [*gūtha-*], f. = गुह.

गूगल *gūgal* [*gulgulu-*], m. the tree *Commiphora mukul*, and its fragrant resin; bdellium.

गूजर *gūjar* [*gurjara-*], m. **1.** the name of a Rājpūt community (chiefly agricultural). **2.** a man of the *gūjar* community; a cowherd; milkman.

गूजरनी *gūjarnī*, f. = गूजरी, 1., 2.

गूजरी *gūjrī* [cf. H. *gūjar*], f. **1.** a woman of the *gūjar* community. **2.** the wife of a *gūjar*; a cowgirl; milkmaid. **3.** a heavy, toothed metal anklet or bracelet. **4.** *mus.* name of a *rāgiṇī*.

गूझा *gūjhā*, m. = गुझिया.

गूढ़ *gūṛh* [S.], adj. **1.** hidden, secret. **2.** mysterious. **3.** abstruse. — ~ पत्र, m. a ballot-paper. ~ पथ, m. a hidden passage. ~ पुरुष, m. *Pl.* a secret emissary. ~ मार्ग, m. = ~ पथ. ~ लेख, m. a code. गूढ़ार्थ [°*ṛha+a*°], m. & adj. a hidden meaning; of hidden meaning. गूढ़ोक्ति [°*ṛha+u*°], f. a remark, or words, of hidden sense. गूढ़ोत्तर [°*ṛha+u*°], m. a Delphic answer.

गूढ़ता *gūṛhătā* [S.], f. **1.** secret nature; enigmatic nature. **2.** abstruseness.

गूढ़त्व *gūṛhatvă* [S.], m. = गूढ़ता.

गूढ़ा *gūṛhā*, m. reg. (Bihar) thwarts (of a boat: = गुढ़ा).

गूथना *gūthnā*, v.t. = गूँथना.

गूदड़ *gūdaṛ* [cf. **gudda-*], m. **1.** old cotton; the padding from a quilt. **2.** old tattered clothes or rags. — ~ गाँठना, to sew old rags into a garment. – गूदड़-गादड़, m. rags and tatters.

गूदड़ी *gūdṛī*, f. = गुदड़ी.

गूदर *gūdar*, m. = गूदड़.

गूदा *gūdā* [**gudda-*], m. **1.** pith, marrow; pulp. **2.** flesh (of a fruit). **3.** *Pl. HŚS.* transf. the brain. **4.** substance, essence. — गूदे की हड्डी, f. a marrow-bone. बात का ~ निकालना, to get to the heart of a matter. – गूदेदार [P. *-dār*], adj. having marrow or pith.

¹गून *gūn* [? conn. *guṇa-*, **gauṇa-*], m. reg. tow-rope, hawser (of a boat).

²गून *gūn*, m. = गोन.

गूमड़ा *gūmṛā* [cf. *gulma-*], m. = गुमड़ा.

गूमा *gūmā* [P. *gūma-*], m. *Pl. HŚS.* the plant *Pharnaceum mollugo*, and its fruit (used medicinally).

गूल *gūl*, f. reg. (W.) an irrigation channel.

गूलड़ *gūlaṛ*, f. = गूलर.

गूलर *gūlar* [**gullara-*], f. the wild fig, *Ficus glomerata*, and its fruit. — ~ का कीड़ा, m. *HŚS.* fig. a person of limited vision and experience. ~ का फूल, m. sthg. inconceivable; sthg. very unlikely to be obtained.

गूलू *gūlū*, m. a large deciduous tree, *Sterculia urens*.

गूह *gūh*, f. = गू.

गूहड़िया *gūhṛiyā* [**gūthaghaṭita-*], m. *Pl.* a manure-heap.

गृध्र *gr̥dhră* [S.], m. & adj. **1.** m. a vulture. **2.** adj. vulturine, rapacious.

गृध्रसी *gr̥dhrasī* [S.], f. *HŚS.* sciatica.

गृह *gr̥h* [S.], m. **1.** house, dwelling; home. **2.** building or room assigned to a special purpose (e.g. प्रतीक्षागृह, m. waiting-room). **3.** गृह-. the sphere of house or home, domestic sphere. — गृह-उद्योग, m. cottage industry; domestic crafts. गृह-कर्म, m. the activities and responsibilities of a householder. गृह-कलह, m. a domestic, or an internal dispute. गृह-कार्य, m. the activities of a householder. गृह-जन, m. the members of a household. गृहत्याग, m. leaving, or running away from, home. °ई, m. गृह-दाह, m. the burning down of a house; a destructive family quarrel. गृह-देवता, m. , °-देवी, f. a god or goddess in whose tutelage particular household tasks are performed. गृह-पति, m. a householder; head of a family. गृह-पत्नी, f. the lady of a house; housewife. गृह-पशु, m. a domestic animal. गृह-पाल, m. a watchman; a dog. गृह-प्रवेश, m. ceremonial entry to a new house. गृह-भेद, m. domestic quarrelling. °ई, adj. & m. prying (or one who pries) into domestic secrets; causing (or a causer of) family quarrels. गृह-मंत्री, m. *govt.* Home Minister. °-मंत्रालय [°*tra+ā*°], Home Ministry. गृह-युद्ध, m. civil war. गृह-रक्षक, m. *mil.* Home Guard; a member of the Home Guard. गृह-लक्ष्मी, f. the lady of a house (seen as the source of its prosperity). गृह-सचिव, m. *govt.* Home Secretary. गृहस्थ, adj. & m. being a householder; a householder; a brāhmaṇ carrying out the obligations of domestic life. °ई, adj. & m. domestic; a household; householder. गृहस्थाश्रम [°*stha+ā*°], m. the second or domestic stage of life, as laid down for a brāhmaṇ. °ई, m. one in this stage. गृह-स्वामी, m. the head of a household. °-स्वामिनी, f. the lady of a house. गृहागत [°*ha+ā*°], adj. & m. visiting a house; a guest. गृहासक्त [°*ha+ā*°], adj. & m. homesick; one who is homesick. गृहोद्योग [°*ha+u*°], m. = गृह-उद्योग.

गृहिणी *gr̥hiṇī* [S.], f. lady, or mistress of a house.

गृही *gr̥hī* [S.], m. a householder.

गृहीत *gr̥hīt* [S.], adj. **1.** seized, taken; caught; attacked, prey to. **2.** accepted; acquired; grasped, understood. — गृहीतार्थ [°*ta+a*°], m. accepted meaning; obs. one who grasps a meaning.

गृहीता *gr̥hītā* [S.], m. inv. *fin.* receiver.

गृह्य *gr̥hyă* [S.], adj. **1.** domestic; internal; domesticated, tame. **2.** to be taken; to be received; acceptable; obtainable.

गेंगला *gemglā*, adj. & m. **1.** adj. simple, silly. **2.** m. a silly person. **3.** a child.

गेंगलापन *gemglāpan* [cf. H. *geglā*], m. simplicity, silliness.

[1]**गेंडुआ** *gemduā* [*genḍuka-*: ← Drav.], m. Brbh. Av. **1.** a pillow, bolster. **2.** E. = गेंड़ुरी, 2.

[2]**गेंडुआ** *genḍuā* [*gandūpada-*], m. reg. W. a round worm or caterpillar which attacks millets.

गेंड़ुरी *gemṛurī* [conn. **guṇḍala-*: ← Drav.], f. **1.** a coil (= गेंडुली). **2.** specif. rope coil used for placing a pot, &c. on.

गेंडुली *gemdulī* [conn. **guṇḍala-*: ← Drav.], f. coil (of a snake, or a rope). — ~ मारना, to coil (itself) up (a snake).

गेंद *gemd* [*genduka-*: ← Drav.], f. a ball. — ~ खेलना, to play at, or with, a ball. – गेंदंदाज़ [P. *-andāz*], m. = गेंदबाज़. गेंद-बल्ला, m. bat and ball. गेंदबाज़ [P. *-bāz*], m. bowler (cricket). °ई, f.

गेंदई *gemdaī* [cf. H. *gemdā*], adj. & f. **1.** adj. marigold-coloured: yellow, golden. **2.** yellow colour.

गेंदा *gemdā* [*genduka-*: ← Drav.], m. a marigold.

गेंदुआ *gemduā*, m. Brbh. a pillow, bolster.

गेगला *geglā*, adj. reg. = गेंगला.

गेड़ी *geṛī* [? conn. *genḍu-*], f. *Pl. HŚS.* ? E. a boy's game (knocking a stick across a line by throwing another stick at it).

गेदा *gedā*, m. *Pl. HŚS.* **1.** an unfledged bird; nestling. **2.** fig. an infant.

गेरना *gernā* [cf. H. *girnā*], v.t. **1.** to cause to fall; to throw (as in wrestling). **2.** to throw about, to scatter. **3.** reg. to apply (as collyrium to the eyes). **4.** reg. to prepare, to make (as pickle).

गेरुआ *geruā* [cf. H. *gerū*], adj. & m. **1.** adj. ochre-coloured, red; reddish; yellowish. **2.** coloured or dyed with red ochre. **3.** m. ochre dye. — ~ बाना, m. the reddish-yellow robe of ascetics.

गेरुई *geruī* [cf. H. *gerū*], f. *Pl. HŚS.* a red blight (affecting corn).

गेरू *gerū* [cf. *gairikā-*], m. **1.** red ochre; raddle. **2.** reg. (Bihar) a red clay soil.

गेसू *gesū* [P. *gesū*], m. a ringlet, lock (of hair).

गेह *geh* [S.], m. house; home.

गेही *gehī* [S.], m. poet. householder.

गेहुँअन *gehuman* [cf. H. *gehūm*], m. *HŚS.* name of a partic. (very poisonous) snake having a light brown skin.

गेहुआँ *gehuām* [cf. H. *gehūm*], adj. wheat-coloured; like wheat.

गेहूँ *gehūm* [conn. *godhūma-*], m. wheat.

गैंड़ा *gaimṛā* [**gayaṇḍa-*] a rhinoceros.

गैंता *gaimtā*, m. reg. (W.) a pickaxe.

गैंती *gaimtī*, f. a pickaxe.

[1]**गैन** *gain* [cf. *gagana-*], m. Brbh. the sky.

[2]**गैन** *gain* [? *gajendra-*], m. E.H. a large or mighty elephant.

[3]**गैन** *gain* [? *gamana-* × *gati-*], m. Brbh. a pace, a step. — ~ कर-, Brbh., to make (one's) way.

गैना *gainā* [*grahaṇa-*], m. reg. **1.** a small breed of bullock. **2.** reg. (W.) a malformation or growth in cattle (making them unfit for field-work).

गैनी *gainī* [cf. H. *gainā*], f. *Pl.* = गैना, 1.

ग़ैब *gaib* [A. *gaib*], m. E.H. the invisible; the hidden world.

ग़ैबी *gaibī* [P. *gaibī*], adj. Brbh. invisible; hidden.

गैया *gaiyā* [cf. H. *gāy*], f. dimin. a cow.

ग़ैर *gair* [A. *gair*], adj. & m. **1.** adj. other. **2.** non-related. **3.** unknown, strange (person, region); foreign. **3.** ग़ैर-. not; non-, un-, in-, anti-, extra-, de-, &c. **4.** m. a non-relative; an outsider. — ~ करना, to treat (one, को), like a stranger. – ग़ैर-आबाद [P. *-ābād*], adj. unpopulated, unsettled. ग़ैर-इंसाफ़, adj. unjust. °ई, f. ग़ैरक़ानूनी, adj. unlawful; illegal. °-क़ानूनियत, f. ग़ैरजानकारी, f. lack of knowledge or familiarity. ग़ैरज़िम्मेदार [P. *-dār*], adj. not responsible; irresponsible. °ई, f. ग़ैरनिवासी, adj. & m. non-resident. ग़ैरमामूली, adj. out of the ordinary. ग़ैर-मिसिल [A. *-misl*], adj. Brbh. dissimilar: unfitting, improper. गैरमुकम्मल, adj. incomplete. ग़ैरमुनासिब, adj. inappropriate. ग़ैरमुमकिन, adj. impossible. ग़ैरमुल्की, adj. & m. foreign; a foreigner. ग़ैरवाजिब, adj. improper, wrong. °ई, adj. id. ग़ैरसरकारी, adj. non-governmental; private (sector, &c.); unofficial. ग़ैरहाज़िर, adj. absent; °ई, f. absence; non-appearance, default.

ग़ैरत *gairat* [A. *gaira*: P. *gairat*], f. **1.** shame. **2.** a just sense of honour or self-respect. **3.** bashfulness. — ~ खाना, to feel shame, &c. ग़ैरतमंद [P. *-mand*], adj. having a proper sense of self-respect, &c.

गैरिक *gairik* [S.], m. = गेरू.

ग़ैरियत *gairiyat* [A. *gairiya*: P. *gairiyat*], f. strangeness.

गैरी *gairī* [cf. *graha-*], f. reg. a pile of corn-stalks (? = [2]गहरा, 2).

[1]**गैल** *gail* [cf. *gati-*], f. reg. road, path.

[2]**गैल** *gail*, f. reg. = गहल.

गैलड़ *gailaṛ*, m. reg. the son of a woman by a former marriage, a stepson.

गैलहू *gailahū* [cf. H. [1]*gail*], m. reg. (W.) a traveller; a passer-by.

गोंइड़ *goṁir* [**godaṇḍa-*], m. the outskirts of a village; fields near a village.

गोंचड़ी *goṁcṛī* [?? conn. H. *joṁk*], f. *Pl.* a tick (on cattle).

गोंठ *goṁṭh*. **1.** m. *Pl.* a kind of wide stitch or sewing. **2.** f. *HŚS.* a fold or folds made in the cloth of a *dhotī*, at the waist.

गोंठा *goṁṭhā* [conn. *goviṣṭhā-*], m. reg. (W.) dried cow-dung.

गोंड *goṁḍ* [*goṇḍa-*[1]], m. **1.** a tribe living chiefly in the Vindhya range in Madhya Pradeś. **2.** a man of that tribe, a Gond. — गोंडवाना [? *-vanya-*], m. *Pl. HŚS.* the Gond region.

गोंद *goṁd* [*gundra-*], f. **1.** gum; glue. **2.** *Pl.* a gelatinous sweet. **3.** *Pl. HŚS.* a reed or rush. — गोंददानी [P. *-dānī*], f. a gum- or glue-bottle. गोंद-पंजीरी, f. a preparation chiefly from sugar, *ghī* and flour, with *goṁd*, given to women after childbirth. गोंद-पाग, m. Brbh. = ~, 2.

[1]**गोंदनी** *goṁdnī*, f. *Pl. HŚS.* = गोंदी.

[2]**गोंदनी** *goṁdnī* [cf. *gundra-*], f. *Pl.* a reed or rush (used in making mats).

गोंदरी *goṁdrī* [cf. *gundra-*], f. reg. a reed mat.

गोंदा *goṁdā*, m. *Pl. HŚS.* a soft dough (made from meal of parched gram) fed to birds. — ~ दिखाना, to incite (birds) to flight by throwing food among them.

गोंदी *goṁdī* [*gundra-*], f. *Pl. HŚS.* **1.** a tree of the genus *Cordia*, and its plum-like fruit. 2. = हिंगोट.

[1]**गो** *go* [*go-*; *gava-*], f., m. **1.** a cow. **2.** a bull, or ox. **3.** Brbh. the power of speech. **4.** the senses. **5.** the earth, world. **6.** *Pl. HŚS.* light. — गोकुल, m. a herd of cattle; name of a village near Mathura, and its vicinity (*mythol.* the scene of Kṛṣṇa's childhood). °नाथ, m. Lord of Gokul: title of Kṛṣṇa. °पति, m. id. गो-कुशी [P. -*kuśī*], f. battle, slaughter; the killing of a cow. गो-खुर, m. a cow's hoof, or hoof-mark. गो-गृह, m. = गो-शाला. गो-ग्रास, m. food for cows (set aside from a meal). गो-घात, m. cattle-slaughter, the killing of a cow. °अक, m. one who kills a cow; a butcher. °ई, m. id. गो-चंदन, m. a type of sandalwood. गोचर, m. & adj. pasturage for cows; *philos.* an object perceptible by the senses; the field of sensory perception, or range of comprehension; field of action. °भूमि, f. pasture land. गो-चारण, m. the tending of cattle. गो-जल, m. cows' urine. गो-दान, m. the gift of a cow (to a brāhmaṇ). गो-दोहन, m. milking a cow. गो-धन, m. wealth in cattle; a herd of cattle. गोधूलि, f. earth-dust: twilight (when a mist may rise from the earth, and when dust may be stirred up by cattle returning to their village). गोधौरी, f. reg. (W.) earth-whiteness: id. गो-धेनु, f. a cow with a calf, giving milk. गोप, m. see hw. गो-पति, m. lord of cattle: a title of Kṛṣṇa; a cowherd. गो-पद, m. a cattle-pen; a cow's hoof, or hoof-mark; ruts worn by hooves. गोपाल, m. a cowherd; protector of the earth: a king; a title of Kṛṣṇa. °अक, m. a cowherd. °इका, °ई, f. id. °-पालन, m. the raising or keeping of cattle. गोपुर, m. main gate or entrance (of a town, a fort, a temple). गो-प्रवेश, m. = गोधूलि. गो-बंधन, m. a halter for a cow. गो-मल, m. cow-dung. गो-मांस, m. cow's flesh, beef. गो-मुख, m. a cow's muzzle, or expression; iron. hole or breach made in a wall. °ई, f. a Himālayan gorge through which the Ganges flows; a bag in which a rosary is kept concealed. गो-मृग, m. an antelope, the *nīl-gāy*. गो-मेद, m. cow-fat: the name of several precious stones (as topaz, zircon, onyx). °अक, m. id. गो-रक्ष, m. the protection of cattle; a cowherd. °अक, adj. protecting cattle; m. a cowherd. °ई, adj. id. गो-रज, f. dust stirred up by the hooves of cattle. गो-रस, m. milk; yogurt; buttermilk. गो-रोचन, m. a partic. bright yellow pigment. गोलोक, m. the heaven of Kṛṣṇa; paradise. गो-वध, m. = गो-घात. गोवर्धन, m. Govardhan hill, near Vṛndāvan (*mythol.* lifted by Kṛṣṇa to shelter the people of Braj and their herds from rains sent by Indra); the name of a festival observed on the day following Dīvālī. °-धारी, m. supporter of Govardhan: a title of Kṛṣṇa. °-नाथ, m. lord of Govardhan: id. गोविंद, m. a title of Viṣṇu-Kṛṣṇa. गो-व्रत, m. an observance of expiation for the killing of a cow. गो-शाला, f. cattle-stall, byre. गोसाईं, m. see hw. गोसइयाँ, m. dimin. see गो-साईं, 1., 2. गो-स्वामी, m. see hw. गो-हत्या, f. the killing of a cow.

[2]**गो** *go* [P. *go* ← *guftan* 'to speak'], conj. although; notwithstanding (that).

गोइंठा *goiṁṭhā* [*goviṣṭhā-*], m. reg. cow-dung; a cow-dung cake.

गोइयाँ *goiyāṁ*, f. m. = गुइयाँ.

गोईं *goīṁ*, f. reg. **1.** a pair (or yoke) of oxen. **2.** pair (as of people working together).

-गोई *-goī* [P. *-goī*], f. speaking.

गोकि *goki* [P. *go kĕ*], conj. = गो.

गोखरू *gokhrū* [*gokśura-*], m. cow's hoof: **1.** the plant *Ruellia longifolia* and its fruit. **2.** the plant *Tribulus lanuginosus* and its thorny seed. **3.** an ear-ring shaped like *gokhrū* seed. **4.** an anklet with ornaments shaped like *gokhrū* seed. **5.** narrow twisted lace; a braided ornament of lace of gold thread.

[1]**गोचना** *gocnā*, v.t. *Pl. HŚS.* to catch, to seize, to stop.

[2]**गोचना** *gocnā* [H. *gohūṁ* + H. *canā*], m. reg. (W.) a field or crop of wheat and gram sown together.

गोजई *gojaī* [cf. H. *gohūṁ*, H. *jau*], f. reg. = गोजरा.

गोजर *gojar*, m. f. a centipede.

गोजरा *gojrā* [cf. H. *gohūṁ*, H. *jau*], m. reg. (W.) a mixture of wheat and barley; a crop of wheat and barley (? or barley and gram) sown together.

गोजाई *gojāī*, f. reg. = गोजरा.

गोजी *gojī*, f. reg. (Bihar) a light staff or stick.

गोझा *gojhā*, m. *Pl. HŚS.* a thorny grass which springs up during the rainy season.

गोट *goṭ* [**goṭṭa-*: ← Drav.], f. **1.** hem or border (of a garment); edging; braid; gold or silver lace. **2.** a piece, counter (in a game: = गोटी). ~ बनाना (को), to treat (one) as a pawn in a game. ~ मारना, or पीटना, to capture a piece. **3.** Av. = गोटा, 3.

गोटा *goṭā* [**goṭṭa-*: ← Drav.], m. **1.** gold or silver lace (see गोट, 1). **2.** a name given to several preparations or substances consisting of separate fragments, or lumps: roasted coriander seeds; cardamoms and *supārī*; grated coconut or portions of coconut kernel. **3.** Av. a ball; a cannon-ball. — गोटा-किनारी, f. edging of gold or silver lace.

गोटिया *goṭiyā*, f. dimin. = गोटी. — गोटिया-चाल, f. the moving of pieces: a carefully laid plan.

गोटी *goṭī* [**goṭṭa-*: ← Drav.], f. **1.** a small round stone. **2.** a piece, a man (in a game). — ~ जमना, a move, or an action, to succeed or to promise well. ~ पिटना, a piece to be taken. ~ पीटना, to capture a piece. ~ बिठाना, to carry through (one's) scheme or purpose. ~ बैठना, = ~ जमना. ~ मरना, a piece to be taken. ~ हाथ से जाना, a piece to be lost; a plan to fail.

गोड़ *goṛ* [**goḍḍa-*: Pk. *goḍḍa-*], m. the foot; leg, knee. — ~ गिरना, or पड़ना, or लगना (के), to touch (a person's) feet reverentially; to fall at the feet (of). ~ टूटना, the leg(s) to break, or to hurt, or to give way; hope to be disappointed. ~ पसारना, to stretch out (in comfort); to prosper.

गोड़ना *goṛnā* [**goḍḍ-*], v.t. to hoe, to break up (ground: = गोढ़ना).

गोड़ी *goṛī*, f. *Pl. HŚS.* booty.

गोड़ैत *goṛait* [cf. H. *goṛ*], m. a village watchman, and messenger.

गोढ़ना *goṛhnā* [**goḍḍ-*: ? × H. *kāṛhnā*], v.t. **1.** to scrape, to scratch (= गोड़ना). **2.** to scrape out, to hollow out. **3.** to dig, to excavate.

गोढर *goḍhar* [? **goḍḍ-*: **gauḍḍyaphala-*], m. reg. (W.) weeds picked up in a field (by a harrow, *Pl*).

गोढ़ा *goṛhā* [**grāmārdha-*: Pk. *gāmaddha-*], m. reg. (W.) the innermost circle of the lands of a village.

गोत *got* [*gotra-*], m. **1.** *gotra*, an exogamous sub-division of a caste group. **2.** family, lineage, stock.

गोतम *gotam* [S.], m. **1.** *mythol.* name of a *ṛsi*, the husband of Ahalyā (whom he cursed and turned to stone for her infidelity). **2.** the name of the founder of the Nyāya philosophy.

गोता *gotā* [*gotra-*], m. reg. (W.) a cattle-enclosure.

ग़ोता *ġotā* [A. *ġoṭa*], m. diving, plunging; a plunge. — ~ खाना, to be immersed; to sink; to dive (as a kite); to be lost (as in a difficult subject). ~ देना (को), to immerse, to dip. ~ मारना, or लगाना, to plunge (into, में); to throw oneself (into: as into a subject). – ग़ोताख़ोर [P. *-khor*], adj. & m. diving; a diver. ग़ोताख़ोर बमवर्षक, m. dive-bomber. °ई, f. diving; being dipped or plunged. ग़ोताबाज़ [P. *-bāz*], m. a diver.

गोतिया *gotiyā*, adj. & m. = गोती.

गोती *gotī* [*gotrin-*], adj. & m. **1.** adj. belonging to the same *gotra*. **2.** m. one of the same *gotra* (as, का).

गोत्र *gotră* [S.], m. an exogamous sub-division of a caste group. — गोत्रकार, m. nominal founder of any particular *gotra*. गोत्रज, adj. born in the same *gotra*. गोत्र-प्रवर्तक, m. = गोत्रकार.

गोथ *goth*, m. ? reg. (Raj.) a yoke, or yoke-pin.

गोद *god* [**goddī-*], f. **1.** lap. **2.** bosom; embrace. **3.** inner part, enclosure. **4.** fig. adoption. **5.** name given to a token gift of a coconut, rice, &c. made to a bride, and taken from her after a year of marriage. — ~ का बच्चा, m. a child in arms. ~ देना (को), to give (one's child) to be adopted. ~ पसारना, (अपनी), to spread out (one's) skirt, or garment (to receive sthg., in begging or entreating). ~ फैलाना, id. ~ बैठना, to be adopted (a child). ~ भरना (की), (a woman) to have a child or children; to be pregnant. ~ में खिलाना (को), to nurse; to bring up. ~ में डालना, to give a child for adoption (to, की). ~ में लेना (को), to take on one's knees, &c. ~ लेना (को), to take on one's knees, or in one's arms; to adopt (a child). ~ सूनी रह जाना, to be childless (a woman). मंदिर की ~, f. the inner part of a temple. – गोद-भरी, adj. f. having a child in arms, or in the lap; with child.

गोदना *godnā* [**godd-*], v.t. & m. **1.** v.t. to pierce, to puncture, to jab. **2.** to tattoo. **3.** to scratch; to vaccinate. **4.** to wound (the feelings); to rouse; to goad. **5.** m. tattooing.

गोदनी *godnī* [cf. H. *godnā*], f. an instrument used in tattooing.

गोदा *godā* [cf. H. *godnā*], m. reg. (E.) a branding-iron.

गोदाम *godām* [B. *gudām*: ← Ind. *gudang*; ? ← S. India], m. **1.** a warehouse, depot, 'godown'. **2.** a store, heap. — ठंडा ~, m. a cold store.

गोदी *godī* [cf. H. *god*], f. **1.** the lap (= गोद). **2.** a dockyard; customs warehouse. — ~ कर्मचारी, or मज़दूर, m. a dock-worker.

गोधूलि *godhūli* [S.], f. see s.v. गो.

गोधौरी *godhaurī* [cf. H. *go*, H. *dhaur*], f. reg. (W.) see s.v. गो.

गोन *gon* [*goṇī-*: ← Drav.], f. **1.** a saddle-bag (for carrying grain in sacks). **2.** a heavy sack.

गोप *gop* [S.], m. **1.** a cowherd. **2.** the leader of a group of cowherds. **3.** a community of cowherds (= ग्वाला); a man of that community. — गोपाष्टमी [°*pa+a*°], f. *hind.* the eighth day of the light half of the month Kārttik (when cows are especially worshipped, Kṛṣṇa being said to have become a cowherd on that day). गोपेंद्र [°*pa+i*°], m. lord of the herdsmen: a title of Kṛṣṇa; a title of Nand, the leader of the herdsmen of Gokul. गोपेश्वर [°*pa+ī*°], m. lord of the herdsmen: a title of Śiva, and of Kṛṣṇa.

गोपन *gopan* [S.], m. **1.** guarding; protection. ***2.** hiding, concealing. **3.** a hidden or secret place. — ~ करना, to hide, to conceal.

गोपनीय *gopănīyă* [S.], adj. **1.** needing to be protected, or preserved. ***2.** needing to be kept secret, or hidden; confidential. — ~ रखना, to keep, or to treat as, confidential.

गोपिका *gopikā* [S.], f. = गोपी.

गोपिन *gopin* [? cf. H. *gop*], f. = गोपी.

गोपी *gopī* [*gopikā-*], f. **1.** the wife of a cowherd (*gop*). **2.** a herdgirl; milkmaid. **3.** specif. *mythol.* any of the herdgirls of Braj (who were in love with Kṛṣṇa). — गोपी-चंदन, m. a partic. type of white clay, or an imitation, used in making sectarian markings on their faces by Vaiṣṇavas. गोपी-नाथ, m. lord of the herdgirls: a title of Kṛṣṇa.

गोप्य *gopyă* [S.], adj. **1.** needing to be protected, or preserved. ***2.** needing to be kept secret, or hidden. (= गोपनीय).

गोफन *gophan* [**gopphanā-*: Pk. *gophaṇā-*], f., m. reg. (W.) a sling (as used in scaring birds away from crops).

गोफना *gophnā*, m. = गोफन.

गोबर *gobar* [*gorvara-*, Pk. *gov(v)ara-*], m. cow-dung. — ~ करना, to excrete dung (a cow, &c). ~ की कंडी, f. a piece of dry cow-dung. ~ खाना, to eat cow-dung: to repent (an action); to continue in very reprehensible ways. ~ पाथना, to make dung-cakes (for fuel). ~ लीपना, to plaster with dung (as floors). – गोबर-गणेश, m. an (image of) Gaṇeś in cow-dung: a fat, useless creature; a complete fool.

गोबरी *gobrī* [cf. *gorvara-*, Pk. *gov(v)ara-*], f. **1.** *Pl. HŚS.* plaster made of cow-dung and mud. **2.** reg. (W.) a cake of cow-dung.

गोबरैला *gobrailā*, m. a dung-beetle (= गुबरैला).

गोबी *gobī*, f. pronun. var. = गोभी.

गोभी *gobhī* [*gojihvikā-*], f. **1.** a cauliflower (= फूल-गोभी). **2.** a cabbage. — बंद ~, f. a cabbage.

गोयंदा *goyandā* [P. *goyanda*], m. U. informer, spy.

गोया *goyā* [P. *goyā*, ← *guftan*], adv. so to speak: as if, as though.

गोर *gor* [P. *gor*], f. **1.** a grave. **2.** a tomb. — ~ बनाना, to make a grave (for, की); fig. to bring about the ruin (of).

गोरखधंधा *gorakhdhandhā* [H. *gorakh* (= °*nāth*)+H. *dhandhā*], m. **1.** a complicated task or problem. **2.** fig. a trying existence. **3.** a difficult puzzle; an intricate toy, or machine; a labyrinth, maze.

गोरखनाथ *gorakhnāth* [H. *gorakh*) (= °*nāth*)+S.], m. name of a legendary yogī, founder of the Gorakh panth, or community bearing his name.

गोरखपंथ *gorakhpanth* [H. *gorakh*+S.], m. the sect or community of Gorakhnāth.

गोरखपंथी *gorakhpanthī* [cf. H. *gorakhpanth*], adj. & m. **1.** adj. having to do with the community of Gorakhnāth. **2.** m. a member of that community.

गोरखा *gorkhā* [*gorakṣa-*], m. a Gurkha.

गोरा *gorā* [*gaura-*], adj. & m. **1.** adj. fair-complexioned; attractive. **2.** light-skinned. **3.** m. a Caucasian. — गोरा-चिट्टा, adj. = ~, 2. गोरा-भभूका, adj. reddish white.

गोराई *gorāī*, f. = गोरापन.

गोरापन *gorāpan* [cf. H. *gorā*], m. **1.** fairness of complexion. **2.** whiteness (of skin).

गोरी *gorī* [cf. H. *gorā*], f. **1.** a fair-complexioned woman; a beautiful woman. **2.** a Caucasian woman.

गोरू *gorū* [*gorūpa-*], m., f. **1.** an ox. **2.** a cow. ***3.** pl. cattle.

ग़ोल *gol* [P. *gol*], m. crowd, flock, herd. — ~ के ~, m. pl. whole crowds, masses.

¹**गोल** *gol* [*gola-¹*], m. & adj. **1.** m. anything round; a circle. **2.** a sphere, a ball. **3.** a lump. **4.** in comp. = गोला. **5.** adj. round; circular; annular. **6.** spherical, globular. **7.** cylindrical. **8.** colloq. a zero, sthg. absent or wanting. — ~ करना, to purloin, to filch. ~ दरवाज़ा, m. a revolving door. ~ बाँधना, to form a circle. ~ बात, f. an empty or over-general remark; an ambiguous remark; an entangled or doubtful matter. ~ मिर्च, f. black pepper. ~ रहना, to remain silent, to make no response; to be absent (when one should have been present). ~ होना, colloq. to slip away, to make oneself scarce. – गोलंदाज़ [P. *-andāz*], m. a gunner. °ई, f. gunnery; shelling. गोल-गप्पा, m. a round puffed cake fried in *ghī*. गोल-गोल, adj. quite round; adv. in round terms, in outline. गोलचला, m. = गोलंदाज़. गोल-चक्कर, m. a traffic circle. गोल-दायरा, m. a circle; traffic circle. गोल-मटोल, adj. fat and squat of build; confused, unclear. गोलमाल, m. things lumped together: confusion, mess. गोलमाल करना, to make a mess (of, का); to purloin, to embezzle. गोल-मोल, adj. colloq. unclear; fudged (an issue). गोल-मेज़, adj. round-table (conference). गोल-योग, m. *astron.* an unlucky positioning of the planets. गोलाकार [°*la* + *ā*°], m. of round, spherical or cylindrical shape. गोलार्द्ध, m. a hemisphere.

²**गोल** *gol* [*gola-²*], m. a large globular earthenware water-jar.

³**गोल** *gol* [Engl. *goal*], m. a goal. — ~ उतारना, to score, or to achieve, a goal. ~ करना, to score a goal.

गोलक *golak* [S.], m. **1.** a round lump. **2.** Brbh. Av. eyeball, eye. **3.** Brbh. vault (of the sky).

ग़ोलक *golak* [P. *golak*], m. a bag or box for keeping money in.

गोलची *golcī* [H. ³*gol* + P. *-cī*], m. a goalkeeper.

गोला *golā* [*gola-*], m. **1.** a round lump; ball. **2.** a cannon-ball; *mil.* a shell; *athl.* a shot. **3.** a coconut shell; coconut kernel. **4.** the round parapet of a well. **5.** a grain market. **6.** a swollen stomach; colic. **7.** [cf. H. ¹*gol*, 7.] reg. a round beam or pole (as used in house-building); prop (for earthen walls). — गोले चलाना, or दाग़ना, or फेंकना (पर), to bombard. गोले बरसाना, id. ~ भरना (में), to load (a heavy firearm). तोप का ~, a shell. – गोला-बाड़ी, f. a storehouse, warehouse. गोलाबारी [P. *-bār*], f. a bombardment. गोला-बारूद, f. shot and powder; stored ammunition.

गोलाई *golāī* [cf. H. *gol*], f. **1.** roundness; curvature (as of a circle or sphere). **2.** a circular surround.

गोली *golī* [*golikā-*], f. **1.** a round lump, ball; a marble; globule. **2.** a bullet; (piece of) shot. **3.** a pill. — ~ खाना, to be struck by a bullet. ~ चलाना, or दाग़ना, or फेंकना, to fire a shot, or shots. ~ भरना, to load (as a rifle: में). ~ मारना, to hit (one, को) with a bullet, to shoot; to shoot (one) dead; to shoot (at, पर). ~ मारो! colloq. to hell with (one, को)! ~ लगना, a shot to hit (sthg., को). गोलियाँ खेलना, to play at marbles. कच्ची गोलियाँ न खेलना, fig. not to be bluffing. – गोली-कांड, m. an incident involving shooting; small arms fire. गोली-गट्ठा, m. = गोली-बारूद. गोली-चालन, m. small arms fire. गोली-प्रहार, m. a burst, or bursts, of small arms fire. गोलीबारी [P. *-bārī*], f. small arms fire. गोली-बारूद, f. shot and powder: stored ammunition. गोलीमार, m. one firing, a rifleman. गोलीरोक, adj. bullet-proof. गोलीसह, adj. id.

गोव- *gov-* [*gopayati*], v.t. Brbh. Av. to hide, to conceal.

गोवर्धन *go-vardhan*, m. see s.v. गो.

गोवा *govā* [*gomaya-*], m. *Pl.* cow-dung, manure.

गोवारी *govārī* [cf. *govāṭa-*], f. reg. (W.) a cow-enclosure.

गोशा *gośā* [P. *gośa*], m. **1.** U. corner. **2.** Brbh. horn (of a bow).

गोश्त *gośt* [P. *gośt*], m. **1.** meat, flesh. **2.** a soup made with meat.

गोष्ठ *goṣṭh* [S.], m. a cow-pen, byre.

गोष्ठी *goṣṭhī* [S.], f. **1.** an assembly, meeting; symposium. **2.** a society, association. **3.** discussion, deliberation (of a group). — ~ जमना, a meeting to be convened.

गोष्पद *goṣpad* [S.], m. poet. cow's hoof: a small amount.

गोसाईं *gosāīṁ* [*gosvāmin-*], m. *hind.* lord of cows: **1.** a title of the supreme being. **2.** a holy man, an ascetic; honorary title prefixed to personal names; title given to leaders of the Vallabhan community. **3.** name of a brāhmaṇ sub-community, descendants of Caitanya; a man of this sub-community. **4.** name of a partic. community of yogīs.

गोस्वामी *gosvāmī*, m. = गोसाईं.

गोह *goh* [*godhā*-], f. a type of large lizard.

[1]**गोहन** *gohan* [? *godhana*-], m. Brbh. Av. **1.** one making up a group; associate, companion. **2.** adv. in the company (of), as one of a group.

[2]**गोहन** *gohan* [? *godhana*-], m. reg. (W.) sloping path (for bullocks drawing water) at a well.

गोहर *gohar*, m. reg. (W.) **1.** a pathway for cattle. **2.** a cowshed.

[1]**गोहरा** *gohrā*, m. reg. (W.) = गोहर.

[2]**गोहरा** *gohrā*, m. a dried cow-dung cake.

गोहरा- *gohrā*- [cf. H. *gohār(nā)*], v.i. E.H. to call to, to call out to.

गोहरौर *gohraur*, m. reg. (Bihar) a pile of cow-dung cakes.

गोहाई *gohāī* [?? *goghāta*-], f. reg. (W.) the treading out of grain by bullocks.

गोहानी *gohānī* [cf. H. *gauhān*], m. *Pl.* land near a village, well-manured land.

[1]**गोहार** *gohār*, m. **1.** a cry, shout; a call for help. **2.** an uproar. — ~ मचाना, or मारना, or लगाना, to cry for help.

[2]**गोहार** *gohār*, *hist.* reg. (Bihar) services performed for a landlord by tenants.

गोहारना *gohārnā* [cf. H. *gohār*], v.i. & v.t. to call out, to shout (to); to call for help.

गोहाल *gohāl* [conn. *gośālā*-], m. reg. (E. Bihar) cowshed.

गोहुवन *gohůvan*, m. *HŚS.* a large snake; ? boa constrictor.

गोहूँ *gohūṁ* [*godhūma*-], m. wheat.

गोहूना *gohūnā*, m. *Pl.* ? = गोहुवन.

गौं *gauṁ* [*gama*-], f. Brbh. **1.** going, way of going; purpose. **2.** occasion, opportunity; advantage.

गौंछी *gaumchī*, f. **1.** *Pl.* a hole; pit. **2.** reg. (Bihar) low, waterlogged land.

[1]**गौंडा** *gaumḍā* [**godaṇḍa*-], m. reg. **1.** a country road. **2.** [× **grāmārdha*-] the near vicinity of a village. **3.** alms distributed on the arrival of a marriage party at the bride's village.

[2]**गौंडा** *gaumḍā* [conn. *govr̥nda*-], m. reg. (W.) a cattle-pen.

गौ *gau* [**gavu*-: Pa. *gavaṁ*], f. Brbh. = गो, 1.

गौख *gaukh* [*gavākṣa*-], m. **1.** gallery (esp. on an upper floor), verandah (= छज्जा, 1). **2.** a small window; skylight.

गौखा *gaukhā*, m. = गौख.

ग़ौग़ा *gaugā* [P. *gauga*], m. noise, uproar.

गौड़ *gauṛ* [S.], m. **1.** *hist.* a partic. grouping of brāhmaṇ communities. ***2.** a partic. brāhmaṇ sub-community. **3.** a partic. kāyasth sub-community. **4.** member of a Gauṛ community. **5.** *hist.* the region of Gauṛ (central West Bengal). **6.** *mus.* name of a *rāg*.

गौड़ी *gauṛī* [*gauḍa*-: and ad.], f. **1.** spirits distilled from *guṛ*, raw sugar; rum. **2.** *mus.* the name of a *rāgiṇī*.

गौड़ीय *gauṛīyă* [S.], adj. & m. **1.** adj. *hist.* having to do with the region of Gauṛ. **2.** m. a man from the region of Gauṛ. **3.** a follower of the philosopher Caitanya.

गौण *gauṇ* [S.], adj. **1.** secondary, subsidiary. **2.** inferior. **3.** figurative or transferred (a meaning).

गौतम *gautam* [S.], adj. & m. **1.** adj. having to do with, or descended from, Gotama. **2.** Brbh. = गोतम. **3.** name of the Buddha. **4.** name of a brāhmaṇ community.

गौतमी *gautămī* [cf. H. *gautam*], f. *HŚS. mythol.* name of Ahalyā, the wife of Gotama.

गौन *gaun* [*gamana*-], m. Brbh. a going; advance (as in a campaign); departure (= गौना).

गौनहाई *gaunhāī* [cf. *gamana*-], f. Brbh. a young wife, when first brought to her husband's home (see गौना).

गौना *gaunā* [*gamana*-], m. *hind.* ceremonial bringing of a wife from her father's to her husband's home (on reaching puberty, or after marriage). — ~ करा लाना (का), to bring (one's wife) home to one's parents' house. ~ माँगना (को), to ask for (one's wife) from her father.

गौनावली *gaunāvlī* [cf. *gamana*-; ?+H. -*vālā*], f. a child-bride (when brought to her husband's house).

ग़ौर *gaur* [A. *gaur*], m. **1.** deep thought, deliberation. ***2.** close attention, care. — ~ करना, to reflect (upon, पर); to look (upon: as with favour). ~ से, adv. attentively; minutely. – ग़ौरतलब [A. *ṭalab*], adj. requiring, or deserving, attention.

[1]**गौर** *gaur* [S.], adj. & m. **1.** adj. white, pale; pale red. ***2.** fair-complexioned. **3.** m. the gaur (a wild ox). — **गौरांगी** [°*ra*+*a*°], f. a fair-complexioned, esp. Caucasian, woman.

[2]**गौर** *gaur* [*gaurī-*], f. *hind.* **1.** a name of the goddess Pārvatī. **2.** a ceremony in which a girl whose marriage has been arranged is worshipped by her near relatives.

गौरव *gaurav* [S.], m. having to do with a guru: **1.** weight, gravity. **2.** dignity; venerability. ***3.** honour; repute, prestige. **4.** grandeur. — **गौरव-ग्रंथ**, m. a leading work (of a literature); a classic. **गौरवशाली**, adj. grand, splendid; glorious. **गौरवान्वित** [°*va*+*a*°], adj. attended by glory: honoured; glorious.

गौरवित *gaurăvit* [S.], adj. invested with gravity: **1.** dignified; venerable. **2.** honoured; of repute. **3.** grand, splendid; solemn.

[1]**गौरा** *gaurā* [S.], f. = **गौरी**.

[2]**गौरा** *gaurā*, m. *Pl.* a cock-sparrow.

गौरी *gaurī* [S.], f. a name of the goddess Pārvatī. — **गौरी-चंदन**, m. red sandalwood. **गौरीपति**, m. the lord of Gaurī: title of Śiva. **गौरीश** [°*rī*+*ī*°], m. = **गौरीपति**.

गौरैया *gauraiyā* [cf. H. [2]*gaurā*], f. a sparrow.

गौहर *gauhar* [P. *gauhar*], m. U. essence, hidden virtue: a pearl.

गौहान *gauhān* [**grāmadhāna-*: Pk. *gāmahaṇa-*], m. **1.** reg. (W.) the circle of lands of a village adjoining the village site. **2.** *hist. Pl.* a village made over (to one) as a permanent settlement.

गौहारी *gauhārī* [? **grāmādhāra-*], f. *hist.* rich, manured land.

ग्यारह *gyārah* [conn. *ekādaśa*[1]], adj. eleven.

ग्यारहवाँ *gyārahvāṁ* [cf. H. *gyārah*], adj. eleventh.

ग्रंथ *granth* [S.], m. **1.** a knot. ***2.** a literary work; a book, treatise. **3.** specif. the Ādi Granth (the sacred scriptures of the Sikhs). — **~ साहब**, m. = ~, 3. – **ग्रंथ-कर्ता**, m. inv. the writer or compiler of a book. **ग्रंथकार**, m. id. **ग्रंथ-माला**, f. a (published) series of volumes. **ग्रंथ-रचना**, f. composition of a work. **ग्रंथालय** [°*tha*+*ā*°], m. a library, reading-room. **ग्रंथावली** [°*tha*+*ā*°], f. collected works.

ग्रंथि *granthi* [S.], f. **1.** a knot. **2.** *anat.* constriction. **3.** a gland. **4.** a fixation, complex. — **~ सुलझाना**, to resolve a difficulty. – **ग्रंथि-बंधन**, m. bringing together, associating, uniting; = **गैंठ-बंधन**. **ग्रंथि-मूल**, m. a root vegetable.

ग्रंथित *granthit* [S.], adj. knotted; tied.

ग्रंथिल *granthil* [S.], adj. knotty, knotted.

ग्रथित *grathit* [S.], adj. **1.** strung; tied; connected. **2.** arranged; composed. **3.** constructed.

ग्रस- *gras-* [cf. *grasati*], v.t. Brbh. Av. to devour.

ग्रसित *grasit*, adj. = **ग्रस्त**.

ग्रस्त *grast* [S.], adj. **1.** seized, taken; possessed by. **2.** swallowed, devoured. **3.** -**ग्रस्त**. affected by; influenced by; involved in.

ग्रह *grah* [S.], m. seizing: **1.** an eclipse (= **ग्रहण**). ***2.** a planet (as influencing men's destinies). **3.** a symbol for the number nine (corresponding to the nine heavenly bodies, including the sun, Rāhu and Ketu, which were recognised as planets). **4.** an artificial satellite. **5.** name of evil spirits influencing the body and mind of man, to cause insanity, &c. — **~ आना** (**पर**), to come under the influence of an evil star; to be possessed of an evil spirit. **~ देखना**, to consult (one's) horoscope. **~ बिगड़ना**, one's star to change, one's fortune to decline. **~ मिलना**, horoscopes (of a proposed bride and groom) to agree. **अच्छे ~**, favourable stars, good fortune. – **ग्रह-कुंडली**, f. a horoscope. **ग्रह-चिंतक**, m. an astrologer. **ग्रह-दशा**, f. *astron.* position of the planets; one's fortune, as determined by this. **ग्रह-दृष्टि**, f. the interaction of planets as envisaged in a horoscope. **ग्रह-नक्षत्र**, m. the planets and other heavenly bodies. **ग्रहनाश**, adj. countering a planetary influence. **ग्रह-पीड़ा**, f. a baleful planetary influence. **ग्रह-बाधा**, f. id. **ग्रह-यज्ञ**, m. a sacrifice intended to countervail inauspicious planetary influences. **ग्रह-योग**, m. conjunction of planets. **ग्रह-शांति**, f. *hind.* an observance intended to appease inauspicious planetary influences; such appeasement. **ग्रहाधीश** [°*ha*+*a*°], m. lord of the planets, the sun.

ग्रहण *grahaṇ* [S.], m. **1.** seizing, grasping; seizure. **2.** *mythol.* eclipse (seizure of sun or moon by the demon Rāhu). **3.** taking, accepting; acquisition; perception, grasp. **4.** overshadowing, effacement. — **~ करना**, to seize; to receive, to accept; to obtain; to accede to; to grasp, to comprehend. **~ पड़ना**, or **लगना**, an eclipse to occur; to be eclipsed. **आंशिक ~**, m. a partial eclipse. **पूर्ण ~**, m. a full eclipse. – **ग्रहण-स्नान**, m. *hind.* bathing at the time of an eclipse.

ग्रहणीय *grahăṇīyă* [S.], adj. to be taken, or accepted; acceptable.

[1]**ग्राम** *grām* [S.], m. **1.** -**ग्राम**. a collection; a group, troop. ***2.** a village. — **ग्राम-गीत**, m. a village song, a folk-song. **ग्राम-दान**, m. the *grām-dān* movement of Vinoba Bhave (which aimed

at bringing privately owned sections of land into village ownership). **ग्राम-देवता**, m. a village deity. **ग्राम-पंचायत**, f. a village panchayat, or council. **ग्राम-पुरोहित**, m. a village priest. **ग्रामवासी**, adj. & m. living in a village, or in villages; a villager. **ग्राम-सुधार**, m. village reform, improvement of village life and conditions. **ग्राम-सेवक**, m. a village servant: a worker for improvement of village life and conditions. **ग्रामाचार** [°*ma*+*ā*°], m. pl. village customs or practices. **ग्रामाधिकारी** [°*ma*+*a*°], m. headman of a village. **ग्रामोद्योग** [°*ma*+*u*°], m. village industry.

[2]**ग्राम** *grām* [Engl. *gramme*], m. a gramme.

ग्रामिक *grāmik* [S.], adj. & m. **1.** adj. = **ग्रामीण**. **2.** m. *Pl. HŚS.* headman of a village.

ग्रामी *grāmī* [S.], adj. = **ग्रामीण**.

ग्रामीण *grāmīṇ* [S.], adj. & m. **1.** adj. of or having to do with a village: rustic, rural. **2.** m. a villager.

ग्रामोफोन *grāmophon* [Engl. *gramophone*], m. a gramophone.

ग्राम्य *grāmyă* [S.], adj. & m. **1.** adj. having to do with a village; used in, or produced in a village; rustic, rural. **2.** pej. clownish; uncouth. **3.** m. an uncouth person, &c.

ग्रास *grās* [S.], m. **1.** a mouthful; a morsel. **2.** fig. an eclipse. — **~ करना**, v.t. to swallow, to devour.

ग्राह *grāh* [S.], m. **1.** a crocodile. **2.** a seizing, taking.

ग्राहक *grāhak* [S.], m. one who takes, receives or values sthg.: a customer; a subscriber.

ग्राही *grāhī* [S.], adj. taking, receiving; valuing.

ग्राह्य *grāhyă* [S.], adj. **1.** to be taken or received; worthy of acceptance, or of emulation. **2.** perceptible (to the senses).

ग्रीव *grīv* [S.], f. m. the neck; nape of the neck.

ग्रीवा *grīvā* [S.], f. the neck; nape of the neck.

ग्रीष्म *grīṣmă* [S.], m. **1.** the hot season (corresponding approximately to the months Jeṭh and Asāṛh). **2.** heat, warmth. — **ग्रीष्म-ऋतु**, m. the hot season. **ग्रीष्म-काल**, m. id. **°ईन**, adj. having to do with the hot season. **ग्रीष्मावकाश** [°*ṣma*+*a*°], hot weather, or summer, vacation.

ग्रैव *graiv* [S.], adj. having to do with the neck.

ग्रैष्म *graiṣmă* [S.], adj. of or relating to the hot season.

ग्लानि *glāni* [S.], f. **1.** languour; fatigue. **2.** depression; remorse. **3.** aversion, disgust (from, or at, **पर**).

ग्वार *gvār* [*gopālī-*, Pk. *govālī-*], f. the plant *Dolichos fabaeformis*, and its bean.

ग्वाल *gvāl*, m. = **ग्वाला**.

ग्वालन *gvālan*, f. = **ग्वालिन**.

ग्वाला *gvālā* [*gopāla-*], m. **1.** a cowherd; a milker, milkman. **2.** a man of the *gvālā* community. — **ग्वाल-बाल**, m. pl. a cowherd's, or cowherds' children. **ग्वाला-बाल**, m. pl. id.

ग्वालिन *gvālin* [cf. H. *gvāl*], f. **1.** a cowgirl; milkmaid. **2.** the wife of a *gvālā*. **3.** a woman of the *gvālā* community. **4.** name of a small bird having black and white stripes on its wings and supposed to call '*dahī dahī*'.

ग्वाली *gvālī*, f. *Pl. HŚS.* = **ग्वालिन**.

ग्वैंड़ो *gvaiṁṛo*, m. Brbh. = **गोंइड़**. — **ग्वैंड़े**, adv. near by; near (to, **के**).

घ

घ *gha*, the fourth consonant of the Devanāgarī syllabary. — **घकार**, m. the sound /gh/; the letter **घ**.

घँगोल *ghaṁgol*, m. a water-lily, or white lotus.

घँघरा *ghaṁghrā*, m. reg. (E.) = **घघरा**.

घँघरी *ghaṁghrī*, f. reg. (E.) = **घघरी**.

घँघोरना *ghaṁghornā*, v.t. = **घँघोलना**.

घँघोलना *ghaṁgholnā* [**ghaṅgholayati*], v.t. **1.** to stir round, to stir up; to make muddy (water). **2.** to rinse. **3.** to stir or mash together.

घंटा *ghaṇṭā* [*ghaṇṭā-*], m. **1.** a bell; a clock; gong, chime. **2.** an hour; a period, or session, of one hour. **3.** glans penis. — **~ दिखाना (को)**, to give a vulgarly contemptuous answer (to one making a request). **~ भर पहले**, adv. an hour ago. **घंटों**, adv. for hours. – **घंटा-घर**, m. a clock-tower.

घंटिका *ghaṇṭikā* [S.], f. **1.** a small bell. **2.** Brbh. a jar for water.

घंटी *ghaṇṭī* [*ghaṇṭā-*], f. **1.** a small bell; a bell. **2.** the sound of a bell. **3.** a small metal pot. **4.** the uvula.

घँसना *ghaṁsnā*, v.i. & v.t. = **घिसना, घस-**.

[1]**घई** *ghaī*, f. reg. (W.) a platform of earth on which corn is stacked.

[2]**घई** *ghaī*, f. E.H. **1.** a whirlpool, depth. **2.** reg. (Bihar) a deep furrow.

घघरा *ghaghrā*, m. = **घाघरा**.

घघरी *ghaghrī*, f. reg. = **घाघरा**.

घचाघच *ghacāghac*, adj. **1.** pronun. var. = **खचाखच**. **2.** [? onom.] the sound of sthg. hard or sharp biting into or piercing sthg. soft.

[1]**घट** *ghaṭ* [cf. H. *ghaṭnā*], adj. & f. **1.** adj. small, little (of amount, or prestige); inferior. **2.** f. decrease; loss. — **घट-बढ़**, f. & adv. falling and rising, fluctuation; 'less or more', approximately.

[2]**घट** *ghaṭ* [S.], m. **1.** a large water-jar. **2.** fig. the body. **3.** m. f. the mind; the heart, the soul. — **~ में बसना**, or **बैठना**, to dwell in the heart (of, **के**). **मंगल ~**, m. a vessel filled with water for an auspicious occasion. – **घट-घट**, m. the entire body or soul (as pervaded by the supreme being). **घटज**, m. *mythol.* pot-born: a title of the sage Agastya.

घटक *ghaṭak* [S.], m. accomplishing: **1.** a marriage broker or go-between; messenger, representative. **2.** *math.* factor. **3.** ? = **गुट**.

घटकना *ghaṭaknā*, v.t. = **घुटकना**.

घटन *ghaṭan* [S.], m. **1.** happening, occurring; an occurrence. **2.** forming, making; accomplishing.

घटना *ghaṭănā* [S.], f. a happening; incident; event. — **~ घटित होना**, an event, or incident, to take place. – **घटना-क्रम**, m. a series of events, or incidents. **घटनापूर्ण**, adj. eventful. **घटना-स्थल**, m. place, or site, of an incident or accident.

[1]**घटना** *ghaṭnā* [**ghaṭṭati*: Pk. *ghaṭṭaï*], v.i. **1.** to decrease; to lessen, to be reduced; to fall. **2.** to be deducted (from, **से**); *math.* to be subtracted. **3.** to deteriorate; to decline.

[2]**घटना** *ghaṭnā* [**ghaṭyate*], v.i. **1.** to come about, to happen. **2.** to be formed, made.

घटनीय *ghaṭănīyă* [S.], adj. able or likely to happen: possible, probable.

घटवाना *ghaṭvānā* [cf. H. [1]*ghaṭnā*], v.t. to cause to be decreased, &c.

घटवार *ghaṭvār* [**ghaṭṭapāla-*], m. **1.** a collector of ferry charges; ferryman. **2.** a collector of bathing charges (from pilgrims or other worshippers).

घटा *ghaṭā* [S.], f. **1.** lowering clouds; a dense cloud. **2.** a troop, a forbidding assemblage. — **~ उठना**, or **छाना**, heavy clouds to overspread (the sky). **घटाटोप** [°*ṭā*+*ā*°], m. dense, lowering clouds; canopy (as of a palanquin).

[1]**घटाना** *ghaṭānā* [cf. H. [1]*ghaṭnā*], v.t. **1.** to cause to be lessened: to lessen; to reduce (as prices); to alleviate. **2.** to deduct (from, **से**); *math.* to subtract. **3.** to cause to deteriorate; to impair. — **घटाकर बोला जाना**, to be quoted at a reduced price (a commodity).

[2]**घटाना** *ghaṭānā* [cf. H. [2]*ghaṭnā*], v.t. to cause to happen.

घटाव *ghaṭāv* [cf. H. [1]*ghaṭānā*], m. **1.** a decrease; a lessening, reduction. **2.** *math.* subtraction. **3.** deficiency; decline. — **घटाव-चढ़ाव**, m. fall and rise, fluctuation.

घटिका *ghaṭikā* [S.], f. *Pl. HŚS.* **1.** a jar, water-jar; water-clock. **2.** *astron.* a partic. short period of time (twenty-four or forty-eight minutes).

[1]**घटित** *ghaṭit* [S.], adj. decreased, lessened, &c.

[2]**घटित** *ghaṭit* [S.], adj. **1.** happened, taken place. **2.** formed, made; accomplished.

घटिया *ghaṭiyā* [cf. H. [1]*ghaṭnā*], adj. inv. inferior, of poor quality.

[1]**घटिहा** *ghaṭihā* [cf. H. *ghāṭ*], m. reg. (W.) **1.** a collector of ferry charges. **2.** a boat.

[2]**घटिहा** *ghaṭihā* [H. *ghaṭiyā*], adj. inv. *HŚS.* dishonest; cunning.

घटी *ghaṭī* [cf. H. [1]*ghaṭnā*], f. decrease.

[1]**घट्टा** *ghaṭṭā* [? conn. H. [1]*ghaṭnā, ghaṭṭā*], m. reg. **1.** a shortfall, loss. **2.** a breach, gap; a wound.

[2]**घट्टा** *ghaṭṭā*, m. reg. a callus (= गट्टा).

घट्टी *ghaṭṭī* [conn. H. [1]*ghaṭnā*], f. **1.** a decreasing; a reduction; fall (as of water level). **2.** a deficiency; decline. **3.** a loss; deficit. — ~ से, adv. at a loss.

घड़घड़ाना *ghaṛghaṛānā* [**ghaḍaghaḍa-*], v.i. to rumble; to thunder.

घड़घड़ाहट *ghaṛghaṛāhaṭ* [cf. H. *ghaṛghaṛānā*], f. rumbling; thundering.

घड़त *ghaṛat*, f. pronun. var. = गढ़त.

घड़ना *ghaṛnā*, v.i. pronun. var. = गढ़ना.

घड़वाई *ghaṛvāī*, f. pronun. var. = [1]गढ़ाई.

घड़ा *ghaṛā* [*ghaṭa-*[1]], m. an earthen water-pot. — घड़ों पानी पड़ना, to be deluged with water: (one, को) to feel shame (at, से). चिकना ~, m. a smooth vessel: a brazenly shameless person.

घड़ाई *ghaṛāī*, f. pronun. var. = [1]गढ़ाई.

घड़ाना *ghaṛānā*, v.t. pronun. var. = [1]गढ़ाना.

घड़िया *ghaṛiyā* [cf. H. *ghaṛā*], f. dimin. **1.** a small earthen pot; crucible. **2.** *Pl. HŚS.* honeycomb.

[1]**घड़ियाल** *ghaṛiyāl* [cf. *ghanṭika-*], m. the Ganges crocodile, or gavial.

[2]**घड़ियाल** *ghaṛiyāl* [**ghaṭītāḍa-*], m. f. a gong; a bell; a wall clock.

[1]**घड़ियाली** *ghaṛiyālī* [cf. H. [2]*ghaṛiyāl*], m. *Pl. HŚS.* a man who strikes the hours on a gong.

[2]**घड़ियाली** *ghaṛiyālī* [cf. H. [2]*ghaṛiyāl*], f. a small bell (as used in worship).

[1]**घड़ी** *ghaṛī* [*ghaṭikā-*], f. **1.** a small space of time; specif. a period of twenty-four minutes. **2.** a particular moment, or short period of time; a moment, an occasion. **3.** an instrument to measure time; a watch; a clock. — ~ पहर, m. a short space of time. ~ भर, adv. for a moment. ~ भर में, adv. in a moment; within a moment's space. ~ में ... ~ में, adv. now ... now. ~ में तोला, ~ में माशा, now an ounce, now a grain: (blowing) now hot, now cold. कलाई की ~, f. a wrist watch. जगानेवली ~, f. an alarm clock. – घड़ी-घड़ी, adv. every now and again; repeatedly; constantly. घड़ीसाज़ [P. *-sāz*], m. a watchmaker. °ई, f. watchmaker's trade or craft. धूप-घड़ी, f. sundial.

[2]**घड़ी** *ghaṛī* [*ghaṭita-*], adj. folded, wrapped (as clothes or cloth).

घड़ोला *ghaṛolā* [cf. *ghaṭa-*[1]], m. *Pl. HŚS.* a small earthen pot.

घड़ौंची *ghaṛaumcī* [**ghaṭamañca-*], f. a stand for pots.

घतिया *ghatiyā* [H. [2]*ghāt*], f. Brbh. attack, blow.

घन *ghan* [*ghana-*[2]], adj. & m. **1.** adj. solid, dense; hard; coarse, heavy; thick, viscous; impenetrable (= घना). **2.** deep (of colour, or sound). **3.** massed (as clouds). **4.** adv. very, much. **5.** m. a compact mass or substance: a cloud, cloud-bank; an anvil; a heavy hammer or club. **6.** collection, group. **7.** *math.* cube (of a number). — घन-क्षेत्र, m. cubic measurements. घन-गरज, m. & adj. the noise of thunder; thunderous. घन-घटा, f. a heavy cloud or cloud-bank. घनघोर, adj. very dense, heavy; fearsome, terrible. घन-चक्कर, m. sthg. which spins or turns: a top; a Catherine wheel; fig. an inconstant, fickle or foolish person; predicament, difficulty. घन-चक्कर में आना, to get into a predicament. घन-नाद, m. the rumbling of thunder. घन-पति, m. *mythol.* lord of the clouds: a title of Indra. घन-फल, m. cube; cubic capacity. घन-मान, m. cubic measurements. घन-मूल, m. cube root. घन-श्याम, adj. & m. cloud-dark: very dark; a title of Kr̥ṣṇa. घनसार, m. camphor. घनाक्षरी (°*na*+*a*°), f. polysyllabic: name of a Hindi metre (= कवित्त). घनात्मक [°*na*+*ā*°], adj. cubical. घनीभूत, adj. grown dense, &c.: intruding into consciousness (as grief).

घनघनाना *ghanghanānā* [**ghanaghana-*: Pk. *ghaṇa-*], v.i. & v.t. **1.** v.i. to jingle, to clink. **2.** to rumble (as machinery); to murmur. **3.** v.t. to cause to jingle, or to rumble, &c.

घनघनाहट *ghanghanāhaṭ* [cf. H. *ghanghanānā*], f. **1.** jingling, clinking. **2.** rumbling; murmuring.

घनता *ghanătā* [S.], f. **1.** thickness, denseness; firmness, hardness. **2.** impenetrability. **3.** *phys.* = घनत्व.

घनत्व *ghanătvă* [S.], m. density.

घना *ghanā* [*ghana-*[2]], adj. **1.** (cf. घन) thick, dense; coarse, heavy. **2.** impenetrable. **3.** close, intimate. **4.** intensive, active.

घनापन *ghanāpan*, m. = घनता, 1.

घनिष्ठ *ghaniṣṭh* [S.], adj. very close; intimate.

घनिष्ठता *ghaniṣṭhătā* [S.], f. closeness, intimacy.

घनेरा *ghanerā* [*ghanatara-], adj. Brbh. Av. much, many.

घपची *ghapcī*, f. reg. a grasp, clutch with both hands.

घपला *ghaplā*, m. **1.** confusion; discrepancy (in an account). **2.** fraud. — ~ डालना (में), to confuse, to obscure; to fudge (as an account).

घबड़ाना *ghabṛānā*, v.i. & v.t. = घबराना.

घबराना *ghabrānā*, v.i. & v.t. **1.** v.i. to be confused; to be flustered; to be embarrassed. **2.** to be perplexed. **3.** to be perturbed, or alarmed. **4.** v.t. to confuse (a person); to fluster; to embarrass. **5.** to perplex. **6.** to alarm, to dismay, &c.

घबराहट *ghabrāhaṭ* [cf. H. *ghabrānā*], f. **1.** confusion; embarrassment. **2.** perplexity. **3.** agitation, alarm.

घमंड *ghamaṇḍ*, m. **1.** pride, arrogance; conceit. **2.** vanity. — ~ करना, to be proud, &c. (of, पर). ~ पर आना, or होना, id.

घमंडी *ghamaṇḍī* [cf. H. *ghamaṇḍ*], adj. & m. **1.** adj. proud, arrogant, conceited. **2.** vain. **3.** m. such a person.

घमघमाना *ghamghamānā* [conn. H. *ghamāgham*], v.t. to make the sound of blows falling; to strike (one).

घमरौल *ghamraul*, f. *Pl. HŚS.* crowd; affray; turmoil, confusion.

घमस *ghamas*, f. = घमसा.

घमसा *ghamsā* [cf. *gharma-*], m. humidity, closeness.

घमसान *ghamsān*, m. = घमासान.

घमाघम *ghamāgham* [cf. *gharma-*: P. *garmāgarm*], f. **1.** sound of repeated blows; sound of lively activity. **2.** adv. resoundingly.

घमाना *ghamānā* [cf. H. *ghām*], v.i. & v.t. **1.** v.i. to warm (oneself) in the sun; to enjoy the sun. **2.** v.t. to warm, or to air, in the sun.

घमासान *ghamasan*, m. & adj. **1.** m. a fierce fight or battle; slaughter. **2.** adj. fierce, murderous (as a battle). — ~ करना, to wreak havoc (in, or among, में).

घमोई *ghamoī*, f. reg. (E.) a kind of prickly plant having yellow flowers (? = मकोय).

घमौरी *ghamaurī* [cf. *gharma-*; ? infld. H. *rasaulī*], f. prickly heat.

घर *ghar* [*ghara-*], m. **1.** a house; living quarters, residence. **2.** home; household; family. **3.** a partic. building. डाक ~, m. post office; पुतली ~, m. textile factory. **4.** a particular room or place in a house. रसोईघर, m. kitchen, cooking area; पूजा ~, m. place set aside for worship. **5.** a particular or characteristic place; native place; place of abode; resting place; sign (of the zodiac); square (as of a chess-board, or in an almanac); section (as of a cupboard or drawer). **6.** a housing, or setting; frame; container. चश्मे का घर, m. a spectacle-case. **7.** a recourse; a practice; subterfuge. कुश्ती के ~, m. pl. fig. the (inventory of) tricks or holds of wrestling. — ~ आबाद करना, to set up house (on marriage); to produce children; to make a home prosperous or happy. ~ करना, to establish a home; to settle (in, में); to find a home (as in a person's heart). ~ का, adj. having to do with a house; domestic; one's own; family, private. ~ का ~, an entire household. ~ का भेदी, m. one who knows the affairs of a household. ~ का रास्ता नापना, or पकड़ना, or लेना, to take the road home; fig. to keep to oneself. ~ के ~, adv. (restricted to) within the household, privately. ~ के ~ होना, to be all square, to be even. ~ ~, adv. to, in, or at every house; from house to house. ~ चलाना, to run a household; to support a household. ~ जमाना, to establish a household. ~ डूबना, a household to be ruined. ~ तक पहुँचना (के), to come down to personal remarks (about family members). ~ पड़ना (के), to be taken into a man's house or establishment (of a woman, as his mistress; of goods, for sale, &c). ~ पीछे, adv. per house. ~ फोड़ना, to sow dissension in a household. ~ फूँक(कर) तमाशा देखना, to set fire to (one's) house and watch the fun: to waste one's resources foolishly. ~ बनाना, to build a house; to make a home. ~ बसना, a home to be set up (on marriage). ~ बिगड़ना, a household to be ruined, or to be torn (as by quarrels). ~ बैठना, a house to collapse; (a person) to sit at home; to be out of work; = ~ पड़ना, 1.; a household to be ruined. ~ बैठे, adv. without stirring from home: easily. ~ बैठे की नौकरी, f. a sinecure. ~ में, in (one's) house: one's wife; one's husband. ~ में डालना (को), to keep (a woman as a mistress). ~, or ~ को, सिर पर उठाना, to take responsibility for a household upon oneself; to set a house, or household, in turmoil. ~ से, from (one's) house: = ~ में. ~ से बाहर पाँव, or पैर, निकालना, to set foot outside the house: to leave the straight and narrow path. ~ से बेघर करना (को), to turn (one) out of one's house. – घर-गृहस्थ, m. a householder. °ई, f. a household (its members and effects). घर-घराना, m. = घराना. घर-घाट, m. fig. home and background: essential character (esp. of a person); type, kind. घर-घाल, m. Av. destruction of a household. °अक, m. the destroyer of a household. घर-घुसड़, °-घुसना, °-घुसा, or °-घुस्सू, pej. = घर-बसा. घर-जाया, m. Brbh. Av. a servant, slave. घर-जुगत, f. means of economising in housekeeping. घरदारी [P. *-dārī*], f. household work. घर-दासी, f. the lady of a house. घर-द्वार, m. = घरबार. घर-पोई, adj. f. Av. cooked at home. घर-फोड़ा, m. one who creates dissension in a household. °ई, f. घरबंद [P. *-band*], adj. under house arrest; monopolised (by, का or की). °ई, f. house arrest. घर-बसा m. Brbh. a stay-at-home; an ineffectual person. घरबार, m. house and premises; household goods; family. घरबार आबाद होना, or बसना, a house to be inhabited; to have a wife. घरबार बसाना, to take a wife; to consummate a marriage. °ई, m. & adj. = घर-गृहस्थ; domestic. घरवाला, m. householder; husband; occupant of a house; °ई, f. – घरबघर [P. *-ba-*], adv. = ~ ~.

घरऊ *gharaū* [cf. H. *ghar*], adj. reg. (E.) = घरू.

घरघर *gharghar* [**gharaghara-*], m. **1.** a rattling or rumbling sound. 2. = घुरघुर.

घरघराना *ghargharānā* [cf. **gharaghara-*], v.i. **1.** to rattle, to rumble; to be hoarse, or wheezy (the voice). **2.** to growl, to snarl.

घरड़ *gharaṛ*, m. *Pl.* chopped *moṭh*, or gram fodder.

घरनई *gharnaī* [**ghaṭanāvikā-*], f. reg. (W.) = घरनाव.

घरनाव *gharnāv* [**ghaṭanāvā-*], f. Brbh. a small raft or float supported by earthenware vessels.

घरनी *gharnī* [**ghariṇī-*], f. lady of a house; wife.

घराती *gharātī* [cf. H. *ghar*; w. H. *barātī*], adj. & m., f. colloq. belonging to a bride's wedding party; one of that party.

घराना *gharānā* [**gharāyatana-*], m. **1.** family, household. **2.** house, lineage. **3.** school (of music, dance).

घरू *gharū* [cf. H. *ghar*], adj. having to do with a household or family; domestic; personal.

घरेलू *gharelū* [cf. H. *ghar*], adj. having to do with a household or family; domestic (as of family or national affairs, or of crafts, or of animals); personal. — ~ लड़ाई, f. civil war. ~ साधन, m. (internal) national resources.

घरौंदा *gharaum̐dā*, m. a small or frail house; a play house (built by children).

घरौंधा *gharaum̐dhā* [**gharabandha-*], m. Brbh. = घरौंदा.

घर्घर *gharghar* [S.], m. a rattling sound.

घर्माक्त *gharmâkt* [S.], adj. poet. heat-besmeared: suffering from the heat.

घर्रा *gharrā* [cf. **gharaghara-*], m. death-rattle, death agony. — ~ चलना (को), a death-rattle to arise (in the throat).

घर्राटा *gharrāṭā* [cf. H. *gharrā*], m. **1.** a rattling. **2.** a snore, snoring. **3.** a snorting.

घर्षण *gharṣaṇ* [S.], m. **1.** rubbing; rubbing or grinding down smooth. **2.** friction.

घलुआ *ghaluā* [cf. H. *ghāl*], m. sthg. given a buyer additional to his purchase (= घाल).

घस- *ghas-*, v.t. Brbh. to rub (= घिसना).

घसियारा *ghasiyārā*, m. a cutter or scraper of grass; seller of grass.

घसियारिन *ghasiyārin* [cf. H. *ghasiyārā*], f. **1.** the wife of a grass-cutter. **2.** a woman who works as a seller of grass.

घसीट *ghasīṭ* [cf. H. *ghasīṭnā*], f. **1.** dragging. **2.** track, trace (of sthg. dragged along). **3.** scribbled writing, scrawl.

घसीटना *ghasīṭnā* [cf. *gharṣati*, *ghṛṣyate*], v.t. **1.** to drag; to drag along; to haul. **2.** to drag (the hand or pen): to scribble, to scrawl. **3.** to draw (into, में), to involve; to implicate. — धर ~, to catch hold of and pull, to haul away. घसीटकर चलाना, to drag (sthg.) away, or along; to drag out, to protract. – घसीटा-घसाटी, f. mutual, or many-sided, tugging: a scuffle, scramble.

घसेरा *ghaserā*, m. = घसियारा.

घहर *ghahar* [? conn. **gharaghara-*], m. rumbling (as of thunder). — ~, m. continuous rumbling.

घहराना *ghahrānā* [cf. H. *ghahar*], v.i. **1.** to thunder. **2.** to rumble; to roar, to bellow. **3.** to roll, to surge (of clouds).

घहरानि *ghahrāni* [cf. H. *ghahar*], f. Brbh. rumbling (of clouds).

घाँ *ghām̐*, f. = घाई.

घाँगरा *ghām̐grā*, m. pronun. var. = घाघरा.

घाँघर *ghām̐ghar*, m. reg. = घाघरा.

घाँघरा *ghām̐ghrā*, m. pronun. var. = घाघरा.

घाँटी *ghām̐ṭī*, f. = घंटी.

घाँस *ghām̐s*, f. reg. (W.) = घास.

घाईं *ghāīṃ*, f. Brbh. **1.** a time; a turn. (= ²घात.) **2.** side, direction (= ओर).

¹**घाई** *ghāī* [cf. H. *gahnā*], f. **1.** the angle or space between two fingers or toes. **2.** hob of an oven. **3.** pronun. var. = गाही.

²**घाई** *ghāī*, f. = ¹घात.

घाई-घप *ghāī-ghap* [conn. *ghāta-*; cf. H. *gapaknā*, *gapāgap*], adj. & m. **1.** adj. gulping in: misappropriating; embezzling. **2.** living precariously, or from hand to mouth; cunning. **3.** squandering. **4.** m. one who misappropriates, &c.

घाग *ghāg*, m. pronun. var. = घाघ.

घाघ *ghāgh*, adj. & m. **1.** adj. knowing, experienced; shrewd. **2.** cunning, wily. **3.** m. a shrewd old man; a wily old rascal.

घाघरा *ghāghrā* [*ghargharī-*], m. an ample, ankle-length skirt. — घाघरा-पलटन, f. colloq. *hist.* a group or troop of kilted soldiers; women-folk (as a group).

घाघरी *ghāghrī* [H. *ghāghrā*], f. a small *ghāghrā*.

घाट *ghāṭ* [*ghaṭṭa-*¹], m. **1.** a landing-place; wharf. **2.** a slope to water, a river bank; a ford. **3.** a flight of steps to water; embankment. **4.** a place (as at a river bank) for washing clothes. **5.** a mountain pass. — ~ नहाना, to perform a bathing observance after a death. ~ लगना, to come to shore, or to a bank, &c. (a boat, or persons about to embark); to find a refuge. ~ ~ का पानी पीना, fig. to have seen many a harbour: to have experienced much. ~ मारना, to avoid a toll; to smuggle. न घर का, न ~ का, neither of home nor workplace: a jack-of-all-trades (said of the washerman's dog). – घाट-कप्तान, m. harbourmaster; ferrymaster. घाटबंदी [P. *-bandī*], f. closure of a port; an embargo; the building of a *ghāṭ*. घाटवाल, m. = घाट-कप्तान; a brāhmaṇ superintending a *ghāṭ*.

घाटा *ghāṭā* [cf. **ghaṭṭati*: Pk. *ghaṭṭaï*], m. **1.** a decrease, decline. **2.** a reduction, fall (of prices). **3.** shortfall, deficit; loss. — ~ उठाना, to suffer a loss. ~ पड़ना, or आना, or होना, a loss to befall, to be suffered (by, को). ~ भरना, to make good a loss, or a deficit. घाटे में चलना, to trade at a loss.

घाटिया *ghāṭiyā* [cf. H. *ghāṭ*], m. = घाटवाल, see s.v. घाट.

घाटी *ghāṭī* [cf. H. *ghāṭ*], f. **1.** a valley. **2.** a mountain pass; a slope.

¹**घात** *ghāt* [S.], m. **1.** killing; murder; destruction. **2.** striking down, wounding. **3.** a blow. **4.** *math.* power (of a number). — ~ करना (का), to kill; to destroy.

²**घात** *ghāt* [cf. Pk. *ghatt-*; ? × *ghāta-*], f. **1.** a proper or suitable time; opportunity. **2.** design, intention. **3.** ambush, trap; treachery; trickery. **4.** cover, concealment. — ~ चलाना, to practise treachery, to be a trickster. ~ ताकना, to look for an opportunity (to, की). ~ मिलना, an opportunity to be found (to, की). ~ लगना, id. ~ लगाना, = ~ ताकना. ~ में फिरना, or रहना, or होना, to look for a chance to attack (one), &c.

घातक *ghātak* [S.], adj. & m. **1.** adj. killing: murderous (as a blow). **2.** damaging, destructive; savage (an animal), wounding. **3.** hostile. **4.** inauspicious, malign. **5.** m. a murderer; executioner; butcher; one who wounds or maims.

घातन *ghātan* [S.], m. killing, murdering.

घाता *ghātā* [cf. Pk. *ghatt-*], m. sthg. additional: sthg. thrown in additional to a buyer's purchase. — घाते में, adv. over and above, into the bargain.

घातिनी *ghātinī* [S.], f. & adj. Brbh. Av. = ¹घाती.

¹**घाती** *ghātī* [S.], m. & adj. **1.** m. a killer; destroyer. **2.** adj. esp. in comp. killing; destroying, destructive (e.g. आत्मघाती, suicidal).

²**घाती** *ghātī* [cf. H. ²*ghāt*], adj. *Pl. HŚS.* lying in wait, lurking.

घान *ghān* [**ghāna-*: Pk. *ghāṇa-*], m. a quantity of material (as for milling or grinding, or baking) to be processed at one time; a batch. — ~ उतरना, a batch to be finished, processed. ~ डालना, to throw in a batch (to an oven, or a machine); to begin processing material. ~ पड़ना, or लगना, a batch to be put under processing (in, में).

घाना *ghānā*, m. reg. (W.) = घान.

घानी *ghānī* [cf. H. *ghān*], f. **1.** a pressing, crushing or grinding machine (as for oil-seeds, sugar-cane, grain). **2.** a mill. 3. = घान. — ~ करना, to crush, to press, to grind.

घाम *ghām* [*gharma-*], m. f. **1.** heat and light of the sun. **2.** sunstroke; glare. **3.** sultriness. **4.** oppressiveness; difficulty, trouble. — ~ खाना, to enjoy, or to warm oneself in, the sun. ~ लगना (को), to be overcome by heat. ~ लेना, = ~ खाना. ~ सेंकना, to bask in the sun.

घामड़ *ghāmaṛ*, adj. out of (one's) senses, stupid.

घाय *ghāy*, m. = घाव.

घायल *ghāyal* [cf. *ghāta-*], adj. **1.** wounded. **2.** hurt, injured; smitten (by, से). — ~ करना, to wound, &c.

घाल *ghāl* [cf. H. *ghālnā*], f. m. **1.** a throwing, throwing down; a blow. **2.** confusion, commotion; jumble. **3.** sthg. given to a buyer additional to his purchase. — **घाल-मेल**, m. a thorough mixture; jumble; liaison, affair. **घाल-मेल करना**, to mix up; to jumble; to shuffle (cards). **घाल-मेल रखना**, to be on intimate terms (with, **से**).

घालक *ghālak* [cf. H. *ghālnā*], m. & adj. Brbh. Av. **1.** m. one who destroys or lays waste. **2.** a killer. **3.** adj. destructive; murderous.

घालना *ghālnā* [**ghalyati*], v.t. **1.** to throw, to throw down. **2.** Av. to set, to place (upon or in). **3.** to ruin; to lay waste. **4.** to strike down, to kill.

घाव *ghāv* [*ghāta-*], m. **1.** a wound; a bruise. **2.** a sore. — **~ करना (में)**, to wound. **~ खाना**, to receive a wound. **~ पूजना**, or **पुरना**, a wound to heal. **~ पूरा होना**, or **भरना**, v.i. id. **~ लगाना**, to wound (one, **को**). **~ हरा हो आना**, an old wound to be reopened; a lingering sorrow to revive. **~ पर नमक (नोन) छिड़कना**, to rub salt in a wound.

घास *ghās* [*ghāsa-*], f. grass; fodder; hay; straw. — **~ काटना**, or **खोदना**, or **छीलना**, fig. to do sthg. trivial or pointless. **~ खाना**, to live on grass; to take cannabis; to lose one's wits or senses. – **घास-खोदा**, m. one who scrapes up grass for fodder. **घास-पात**, m. grass and leaves; vegetation; (vegetable) refuse. **घास-फूस**, m. grass and straw; weeds; refuse. **घास-भूसा**, m. grass and chaff, fodder; refuse.

घासलेट *ghāsleṭ*, m. **1.** kerosene oil. **2.** transf. an inferior product.

घासलेटी *ghāsleṭī* [cf. H. *ghāsleṭī*], adj. colloq. inferior (a product).

घिग्घी *ghigghī* [? **gheggha-*], f. **1.** the larynx. **2.** ? a choking sensation in the throat, speechlessness (as from joy, fear, weeping). — **~ बँधना**, or **बंद होना**, the voice to fail or falter (from emotion).

घिघियाना *ghighiyānā* [cf. H. *ghigghī*], v.i. **1.** to be unable to speak (from emotion). **2.** to whine, to whimper (in entreaty); to beseech; to fawn.

घिच-पिच *ghic-pic*, adv. = **गिच-पिच**.

घिचोलना *ghicolnā* [cf. **ghīcc-*], v.t. to rub (with the hands); to squeeze or to squash (= **गिंजना**).

घिन *ghin* [*ghṛṇā-*], f. **1.** aversion; abhorrence. **2.** nausea. — **~ आना (को)**, to feel aversion, disgust (for or with, **से**); to feel nausea. **~ करना**, to feel aversion, disgust (for or with, **से**). **~ लगना**, = **~ आना**.

घिनघिनाना *ghinghinānā* [cf. H. *ghin*], v.i. to be disgusted (with, **से**).

घिनाना *ghinānā* [cf. H. *ghin*], v.i. & adj. **1.** v.i. to make (one) feel disgust, &c. (for, **को**). **2.** adj. = **घिनौना**.

घिनौना *ghinaunā* [cf. H. *ghināvnā*], adj. disgusting, loathsome; obnoxious; very ugly.

घिनौनापन *ghinaunāpan* [cf. H. *ghinaunā*], m. loathsomeness, &c.

घिया *ghiyā*, m. = **घीया**.

घिरका *ghirkā* [cf. H. *ghirnā*], m. *Pl.* a kind of roundabout made with two poles (for children to play on).

घिरना *ghirnā* [**ghir-*: ? ← Drav.], v.i. **1.** to be surrounded or enclosed (by, **से**). **2.** to be collected around, to gather (as clouds).

घिरनी *ghirnī* [cf. H. *ghirnā*], f. **1.** a pulley. **2.** a wheel or instrument for twisting ropes. **3.** the tumbling pigeon. — **~ खाना**, to revolve, to whirl; to tumble over and over.

घिराई *ghirāī* [cf. H. *ghirnā*], f. **1.** causing (sthg.) to be surrounded, or guarded; grazing (cattle). **2.** the cost or charge of enclosing (cattle, &c).

घिराना *ghirānā* [cf. H. *ghirnā*], v.t. to cause to be surrounded or enclosed.

घिरायँद *ghirāyaṁd*, f. stench of urine.

घिराव *ghirāv* [cf. H. *ghirnā*], m. 1. = **घिराई**, 1. 2. = **घेराव**.

घिस *ghis*, f. = **घिस्सा**.

घिसटना *ghisaṭnā* [conn. H. *ghasīṭnā*], v.i. **1.** to be dragged; to drag, to trail. **2.** to be involved or implicated (in, **में**: a matter).

घिसन *ghisan* [cf. H. *ghisnā*], f. **1.** rubbing; friction. 2. damage.

घिसना *ghisnā* [*ghṛṣyate*], v.i., v.t. & adj. **1.** v.i. to be rubbed; to be worn; to be worn down or smooth; to be scoured (clean). **2.** v.t. to rub; to rub down, to grind; to scour. **3.** to groom (a horse). **4.** adj. liable, or apt, to be worn by rubbing (as cloth). — **घिस-घिसकर चलना**, v.i. to rub or to drag along; to wear well (as shoes). – **घिसा-पिटा**, adj. hackneyed, flat, jejune.

घिसनी *ghisnī* [H. *ghisnā*], f. rubbing.

घिस-पिस *ghis-pis*, f. colloq. close contact (cf. **घिच-पिच**).

घिसाना *ghisānā* [cf. H. *ghisnā*], v.t. to cause to be rubbed, or worn.

घिसाव *ghisāv* [cf. H. *ghisnā*], m. friction, abrasion; attrition.

घिस्सम-घिस्सा *ghissam-ghissā* [cf. H. *ghisnā*, *ghissā*], m. repeated or continuous rubbing: rubbing shoulders, jostling.

घिस्सा *ghissā* [cf. H. *ghisnā*; *ghr̥syate*], m. **1.** rubbing; friction; abrasion, wear. **2.** a glancing blow (in wrestling). — ~ लगना (को), to be rubbed or worn.

घी *ghī* [*ghr̥ta-*], m. *ghī*, clarified butter. — ~ का कुप्पा लुढ़कना, the *ghī*-vessel to overturn: the death to take place (of a wealthy or important person); a loss to be sustained. ~ के दिए, or चिराग़, जलाना, or भरना, to burn, or to prepare lamps of *ghī*: to delight in (one's) success; to prosper. पाँचों उँगलियाँ ~ में होना, to have one's whole hand in the *ghī*: to revel in wealth, or in material comforts. – घी-खिचड़ी, adj. & m. f. like *ghī* and *khicaṛī*: intimate friends.

घीकुवाँर *ghīkuvāṁr* [*ghr̥ta-*; w. *kumārī-*], m. ? f., *Pl.* the aloe plant, or a partic. variety of it (cf. घृत-कुमारी).

घीया *ghīyā*, m. the bottle-gourd, *Cucurbita lagenaria*. — मीठा ~, m. a sweet pumpkin. लंबा ~, m. a bottle-gourd. – घीयाकश, m. = कद्दूकश. घीया-तोरी, f. the gourd *Luffa pentandra*. °-तुरई, f. id.

घुँगची *ghuṁgcī*, f. pronun. var. = घुँघची.

घुँगरू *ghuṁgrū*, m. pronun. var. = घुँघरू.

घुँघची *ghuṁghcī*, f. var. reg. /ghumcī/. the berry of the shrub *Abrus precatorius*.

घुँघनी *ghuṁghnī*, f. *Pl. HŚS.* = घूँघनी.

घुँघराला *ghuṁghrālā*, adj. curly (of hair).

घुँघरू *ghuṁghrū* [**ghuṅghura-*], m. **1.** a small bell. **2.** a string of small bells worn round the wrist or ankle. — ~ बाँधना, fig. to prepare (oneself) to dance. – घुँघरूदार [P. *-dār*], adj. hung with small bells.

घुंघुना *ghunghuna* [conn. *ghuṁghrū*], m. reg. a child's rattle.

घुँटाना *ghuṁṭānā*, v.t. = घुटाना.

घुंडी *ghuṇḍī* [**ghuṇṭa-*[2]], f. **1.** a button (esp. of cloth); a knot, or tag. **2.** nipple. **3.** fig. a difficulty, or frustration. — ~ लगाना, to button (a garment, की); to put a button (on, में). मन की ~ खोलना, to unburden (one's) heart.

घुइयाँ *ghuiyāṁ*, f. the tuberous herb *Colacasia antiquorum* (= कच्चू, अरवी).

घुग्घू *ghugghū*, m. **1.** an owl. **2.** fig. a stupid person.

घुघुआ *ghughuā*, m. dimin. = घुग्घू.

घुटकना *ghuṭaknā* [cf. **ghuṭṭ-*], v.t. **1.** to gulp down, to bolt. **2.** fig. to embezzle.

घुटन *ghuṭan* [cf. H. *ghuṭnā*], f. **1.** choking, suffocation. **2.** oppressiveness; sultriness.

[1]**घुटना** *ghuṭnā* [**ghuṭṭa-* or *ghuṇṭa-*[1] (← Drav.)], m. the knee; region of the knee. — ~, or घुटने, टेकना, to kneel; to kneel in submission, or entreaty (to, के आगे or के सामने). घुटने के बल चलना, to crawl. घुटने में सिर देना, to lower the head to the knees (as in shame or grief, or in thought).

[2]**घुटना** *ghuṭnā* [cf. H. *ghoṭnā*], v.i. **1.** to be rubbed; to be polished; to be ground. **2.** to be shaved clean. **3.** to be constricted (the throat, or the breath); to feel tension. **4.** to be well mixed (in, or with, में); to be well cooked; to be well practised or versed (in sthg). **5.** to be close friends (with, में). — आजकल उन दोनों में ख़ूब घुट रही है, the two of them are very close these days. – घुट-घुटकर मरना, to die a lingering or hard death.

घुटन्ना *ghuṭannā* [cf. H. *ghuṭnā*], m. shorts reaching to (and tight about) the knees.

घुटाई *ghuṭāī* [cf. H. *ghuṭānā*], f. **1.** polishing; polish; smoothness. **2.** shaving clean. **3.** cost or charge of polishing, or shaving. **4.** strangling.

घुटाना *ghuṭānā* [**ghoṭṭ-*], v.t. **1.** to cause to be rubbed clean or polished. **2.** to cause to be shaved clean. **3.** to cause to be stifled or choked.

घुट्टी *ghuṭṭī* [cf. **ghuṭṭ-*: Pk. *ghuṭṭai*], f. a digestive medicine given to infants. — ~ में पड़ना, fig. to be imbibed or acquired from infancy (an attitude, a trait).

घुड़- *ghuṛ-* [cf. H. *ghoṛā*]. a horse: — घुड़चढ़, m. horse-riding. °-चढ़ा, m. a horseman. °-चढ़ी, f. horse-riding; the bridegroom's riding on horseback in a marriage procession. घुड़दौड़, f. a horse's galloping; swift gait; a horse race; a racecourse. घुड़दौड़ का घोड़ा, m. a race-horse. घुड़नाल, f. m. a cannon or gun carried on a horse. घुड़सवार, adj. & m. mounted; a horseman. °ई, f. riding. घुड़साल, f. a stable.

घुड़कना *ghuṛaknā* [conn. *ghurati*[1], × **ghūra-*], v.t. **1.** to frighten by one's tone of voice, to growl or to snarl at. ***2.** to scold; to reprimand. **3.** to frown at; to threaten; to browbeat.

घुड़की *ghuṛkī* [cf H. *ghuṛaknā*], f. **1.** growling, snarling. ***2.** scolding, rebuke, reprimand. **3.** frown; browbeating. — ~ खाना, to suffer a scolding. ~ देना, = घुड़कना, 2.

घुड़घुड़ाना *ghuṛghuṛānā*, v.i. = घुरघुराना.

घुणाक्षर *ghuṇâkṣar* [S.], m. worm-holes (traced in wood). — ~ न्याय से, adv. like tracery of worms in wood: as an unsuspected, adverse development.

घुन *ghun* [*ghuṇa-*], m. **1.** a woodlouse. **2.** a weevil. **3.** fig. gnawing grief, or disease. — ~ लगना (को), to be attacked by insect pests; to be worm-eaten; to waste away (from disease, or sorrow).

घुनना *ghunnā* [cf. H. *ghun*], v.i. **1.** to be attacked by weevils, or by wood-worm. **2.** to be consumed (as by illness, grief).

घुन्ना *ghunnā*, adj. **1.** malicious; spiteful. **2.** sullen; designing; secretive.

घुपाना *ghupānā*, v.t. colloq. = गुभाना.

घुप्प *ghupp*, adj. dense, thick (of darkness).

घुमंतू *ghumantū* [cf. H. *ghūmnā*], adj. poet. always moving; restless.

घुमक्कड़ *ghumakkaṛ* [cf. H. *ghūmnā*], adj. roving, wandering.

घुमटा *ghumṭā*, m. giddiness.

घुमड़ *ghumaṛ* [cf. H. *ghumaṛnā*], f. gathering, massing (of clouds).

घुमड़ना *ghumaṛnā* [cf. H. *ghūmnā*], v.i. to gather, to grow thick (as of clouds).

घुमड़ी *ghumṛī* [cf. H. *ghūmnā*], f. **1.** turning, spinning. **2.** giddiness; faintness. **3.** a whirlpool.

घुमरी *ghumrī*, f. reg. = घुमड़ी.

घुमवाना *ghumvānā* [cf. H. *ghūmnā*], v.t. **1.** to cause to revolve, &c. **2.** to cause to go round, or about, &c.

घुमाना *ghumānā* [cf. H. *ghūmnā*], v.t. **1.** to cause to revolve; to turn round; to roll. **2.** to whirl round; to brandish. **3.** to cause to go round or about; to take round, to show round; to take out or to exercise (an animal). **4.** to send round, to circulate. **5.** to lead astray; to beguile. **6.** colloq. to whisk away: to pinch (sthg). — उसने उसे लंदन (or लंदन में) घुमाया, he showed him round London. – घुमाना-फिराना, to lead (one) a round, or dance.

घुमाव *ghumāv* [cf. H. *ghūmnā*], m. **1.** a turning around, &c. **2.** a bend, turn (as of a road, river). **3.** a twist, complication; a trick, a snare. **4.** reg. (W.) turning over (of ground, in ploughing). — घुमाव-फिराव, m. = घुमाव, 1.; deviousness, prevarication. – घुमावदार [P. *-dār*], adj. turning, winding; spiral; complicated, tricky; over-elaborate (language).

घुरघुर *ghurghur* [cf. *ghuraghurāyate*], m. **1.** a rumbling (= घरघर, 1). **2.** growling or snarling; snorting. **3.** purring.

घुरघुरा *ghurghurā*, m. *Pl. HŚS.* **1.** a kind of cricket. **2.** the yellow-fronted pied woodpecker (= कठफोड़ा). **3.** a kind of ulcer.

घुरघुराना *ghurghurānā* [*ghuraghurāyate*], v.i. **1.** to rumble, to grumble (= घरघराना, 1). **2.** to growl, to snarl; to snort. **3.** to purr.

घुरत *ghurat*, m. reg. (E.) a cattle-pen.

घुरना *ghurnā*, v.i. reg. to growl, or to rumble.

घुर्राना *ghurrānā* [conn. *ghuraghurāyate*], m. to growl, to snarl.

घुलन *ghulan* [cf. H. *ghulnā*], f. melting; dissolving; mixing. — घुलनशील, adj. soluble. °ता, f.

घुलना *ghulnā* [cf. H. *gholnā*], v.i. **1.** to melt; to soften; to mellow; to ripen. **2.** to be dissolved; to waste (the body); to become lean; to suffer. **3.** to be mixed (with, में); to be intimate (with). — घुल-घुलकर बात करना, to speak intimately, or amorously (to, से). घुल-घुलकर मरना, to die wretchedly (as after long illness). घुल-मिलकर रहना, to be on very intimate terms (with, से); to live in union, or in harmony (with). – घुला-मिला, adj. in union; close, intimate.

घुलवाना *ghulvānā* [cf. H. *ghulnā*], v.t. **1.** to cause to be melted, dissolved. **2.** to cause to be mixed.

घुलाना *ghulānā* [cf. H. *ghulnā*], v.t. **1.** to cause to be melted, or softened; to move, to affect. **2.** to cause to be dissolved; to suck (sthg. sweet). **3.** to cause to be mixed (in or with, में). **4.** to cause to waste (away); to afflict.

घुलावट *ghulāvaṭ* [cf. H. *ghulnā*], f. **1.** melting, softening; softness, mellowness. **2.** dissolving. **3.** mixing; mixture.

घुस *ghus* [cf. H. *ghusnā*], f. esp. in comp. entering, pushing (into). — घुस-पैठ, f. entry, right of entry: pushing or penetrating, or infiltrating (into, में); experience or knowledge of (a subject). °इया, m. an infiltrator; undercover agent.

घुसड़ना *ghusaṛnā*, v.i. colloq. = घुसना.

घुसड़-फुसड़ *ghusaṛ-phusaṛ* [cf. H. *ghusaṛnā*], f. cramming or stuffing in.

घुसना *ghusnā* [**ghuss-*[1]], v.i. **1.** to penetrate; to thrust in; to enter forcibly. **2.** to enter uninvited, or surreptitiously; to creep, to slink (into, में). **3.** to interfere (in). **4.** to vanish, to evaporate (a feeling, an attitude). — घुसकर बैठना, to sit squeezed close together; to squeeze in; to sit hidden away (somewhere).

घुसाना *ghusānā* [cf. H. *ghusnā*], v.t. **1.** to cause to enter or to penetrate; to thrust or to force (into, में); to cram (in). **2.** to insinuate, or to introduce (surreptitiously).

घुसायन *ghusāyan*, f. *Pl.* a woman of the ghosī (*ahīr*) community.

घुसेड़ना *ghuseṛnā* [cf. *ghuss-[1]], v.t. **1.** to cause to penetrate; to thrust or to force (into, में); to cram (in). **2.** to insinuate (= घुसाना).

घूँगची *ghūṁgcī*, f. pronun. var. = घुँघची.

घूँगट *ghūṁgaṭ*, f. m. pronun. var. = घूँघट.

घूँगनी *ghūṁgnī*, f. pronun. var. = घूँघनी.

घूँगर *ghūṁgar*, m. pronun. var. = घूँघर.

घूँगरू *ghūṁgrū*, m. pronun. var. = घुँघरू.

घूँघची *ghūṁghcī*, f. = घुँघची.

घूँघट *ghūṁghaṭ* [cf. *ghumbapaṭṭa-], f. m. the end of the sari, or other cloth, used (by a woman) to hide the face; a veil. — ~ उठाना, or खोलना, to raise a covering (from the face); to unveil. ~ उलटना, to raise a veil (from the face). ~ ओढ़ना, = next. ~ करना (पर), to hide or to veil (the face). ~ काढ़ना, or निकालना, or लेना, or मारना (पर), id. ~ की ओट में चोट, fig. riding rough-shod over a woman's feelings.

घूँघनी *ghūṁghnī* [*ghuṅgana-], f. wheat, gram or peas, soaked and boiled with spices.

घूँघर *ghūṁghar* [*ghuṁghura-: ← Drav.], m. **1.** a curl. **2.** very curly hair. — ~ करना, to curl (the hair).

घूँघरू *ghūṁghrū*, m. = घुँघरू.

घूँट *ghūṁṭ* [*ghuṭṭ-: Pk. ghuṭṭai], m. **1.** a gulp, a swallow. **2.** a pull (as at a pipe). — ~ ~ करके, adv. by (small) mouthfuls, by sips. – ~ पीना, or भरना, or लेना, to take a mouthful; to draw (as on a pipe). ख़ून, or लहू, का ~ पीना, to drink a mouthful of blood: to show forbearance; to suffer a bitter, or humiliating experience.

घूँटना *ghūṁṭnā* [*ghuṭṭ-: Pk. ghuṭṭai], v.t. to gulp, to swallow.

घूँस *ghūṁs*, f. see [2]घूस.

घूँसा *ghūṁsā* [*ghūssa-], m. **1.** a blow with the fist. **2.** the fist. — ~ खाना, to be struck with the fist. ~ जमाना, or पिलाना, or मारना, or लगाना (को), to strike with the fist. ~ लड़ाना, to box (with, से). — घूँसेबाज़ [P. -*bāz*], m. a boxer. °ई, f. boxing.

घूआ *ghūā*, m. **1.** the ends of reeds (source of a coarse cotton fibre). **2.** Bihar. the hair on a corn-cob. **3.** *Pl. HŚS.* an insect found in water or marshy land.

घूघस *ghūghas*, m. *Pl. HŚS.* reg. a bastion; outwork.

घूघू *ghūghū*, m. pronun. var. = घुग्घू.

घूटी *ghūṭī*, f. reg. land which has been cropped for rice.

घूम *ghūm* [cf. *ghummati: w. H. ghūmnā], m. **1.** a turning round; revolution. **2.** a going round or encircling (sthg). **3.** Brbh. drowsiness. — घूम-घुमार-, adj. Brbh. drowsy, heavy (of the eyes, as with sleep or alcohol); full, wide (as a skirt).

घूमना *ghūmnā* [*ghummati: Pk. ghummaï], v.i. **1.** to revolve; to spin, to whirl. **2.** to move in a circle; to go round or about; to travel; to wander. **3.** to turn, to bend (as a road). **4.** to turn round (a person). **5.** to be or to become dizzy; to swim (the senses). — सिर ~, to be dizzy; to be drowsy; to be tipsy. – घूमना-घामना, colloq. to wander about.

घूमर- *ghūmra-* [cf. H. ghūmnā], adj. Brbh. turning round: blowing (in the wind: trees).

[1]**घूर** *ghūr* [*ghūḍa-], m. **1.** rubbish, trash. **2.** a rubbish heap. **3.** reg. (W.) loose sandy soil. **4.** reg. a manure pit; a fire of dung or rubbish. — घूर-बरार [P. *barār*], m. *hist.* dues levied on sharers and under-tenants in proportion to the total village expenses of the year (Bundelkhand).

[2]**घूर** *ghūr* [*ghūra-], m. **1.** a stare. **2.** a glare, frown. — घूरा-घारी, f. exchange of flirtatious glances.

घूरना *ghūrnā* [*ghurati[2] × *ghūra-], v.i. & v.t. **1.** v.i. to go or to roll round, to look round or about. **2.** v.t. to glare at. **3.** to stare intently at; to ogle. — घूर-घूरके देखना, = ~, 2., 3.

घूरा *ghūrā* [*ghūḍa-], m. 1. = [1]घूर. **2.** a dung-heap. **3.** a temporary fireplace; stove.

घूर्ण *ghūrṇ* [S.], adj. poet. whirling, rolling.

[1]**घूस** *ghūs* [cf. H. ghusnā], f. the bandicoot rat, or mole-rat.

[2]**घूस** *ghūs* [*ghūssā-], f. a bribe; a gift, consideration. — ~ खाना, or लेना, to take a bribe, or bribes. ~ देना (को), to bribe. – घूसख़ोर [P. -*khor*], m. one who takes bribes.

घूसा *ghūsā*, m. the fist (= घूँसा). — घूसम-घूसा, m. fisticuffs; brawl.

घृणा *ghṛṇā* [S.], f. **1.** aversion; hatred, abhorrence. **2.** contempt, disdain.

घृत *ghṛt* [S.], m. clarified butter, *ghī*. — घृत-कुमारी, f. the aloe plant, or a partic. variety of it.

घेंट *gheṁṭ*, m. reg. the throat; neck.

घेंटा *gheṁṭā*, m. reg. a piglet.

घेघरा *gheghrā*, m. reg. sthg. swollen: an unripe pod.

घेघा *gheghā* [*gheggha-], m. reg. a swelling in the neck: goitre.

घेतला *ghetlā*, m. reg. a slipper having a curled toe.

घेपना *ghepnā* [*ghṛpta-: Pk. *ghettuṁ* (H. *-p-* anal.)], v.t. reg. **1.** to take up (with the fingers, or hand, or a spoon, &c). **2.** to stir, to mix together (as with the fingers). **3.** colloq. to pinch, to purloin. **4.** to scrape.

घेर *gher* [cf. H. *ghernā*], m. & adj. **1.** m. the act of surrounding, encircling. **2.** sthg. which encloses, a circle, ring; boundary. **3.** circumference. **4.** fullness (as of a skirt). **5.** adj. loose, full (as of a skirt). **6.** adv. around. — **घेर-घार**, m. = **घेर**, 1.-3. **घेर-घार करना**, to surround; to enclose; to hem in, to beset. – **घेरदार** [P. *-dār*], adj. ample, roomy (of a garment).

घेरना *gherna* [*gher-: ? ← Drav.], v.t. **1.** to surround, to encircle. **2.** to hedge in, to confine. **3.** to overspread (the sky: of clouds). **4.** to beset; to besiege; to blockade. **5.** to importune (as with requests). **6.** to contain, to include; to occupy (space).

घेरनी *ghernī* [cf. H. *ghernā*], f. reg. (W.) **1.** a handle for turning a spinning-wheel. **2.** *Pl.* a winch.

घेरवा *ghervā* [H. *girvī* × H *ghernā*], m. *hist.* a mortgage in which land is held as security, and in payment of the interest.

घेरा *gherā* [cf. H. *ghernā*], m. **1.** sthg. which encloses; a circle, ring; boundary; wall. **2.** perimeter; circumference. **3.** orbit (planetary, &c). **4.** encirclement, a siege; a blockade. **5.** an enclosed space. **6.** ampleness, size (of a garment). **7.** *Pl.* giddiness, vertigo. — **~ उठाना (का)**, to raise the siege (of). **~ डालना (पर)**, to surround; to lay siege (to); to blockade; to picket. **घेरे में पड़ना**, to be surrounded (by, **के**). **घेरे में फँसना**, id.; to go into orbit. – **घेराबंदी** [P. *-bandī*], f. encirclement (= ~, 4).

घेराव *gherāv* [conn. H. *ghernā*], m. encirclement; besieging or blockading (esp. of the house or office of an official, to gain political or other demands).

घेवर *ghevar* [*ghṛtapūra-*], m. a kind of sweet made of flour, *ghī* and sugar.

घोंगा *ghoṁgā*, m. pronun. var. = **घोंघा**.

घोंघा *ghoṁghā* [*ghoṅgha-*], m. & adj. **1.** m. a snail-shell; a snail; cockle, cockle shell. **2.** husk (of grain). **3.** a worthless person, or thing. **4.** adj. stupid. — **~ बसंत**, m. an out-an-out idiot.

घोंघाई *ghoṁghāī* [cf. H. *ghoṁghā*], m. the jungle babbler, *Turdoides striatus*.

घोंघी *ghoṁghī*, f. dimin. a snail (= **घोंघा**).

घोंटना *ghoṁṭnā*, v.t. = **घोटना**.

घोंपना *ghoṁpnā* [*ghopp-], v.t. colloq. to thrust in (a knife, &c).

घोंसला *ghoṁslā* [conn. *ghuss-¹], m. **1.** a nest. **2.** fig. little house, hut.

घोंसुआ *ghoṁsuā*, m. = **घोंसला**.

घोघा *ghoghā*, m. pronun. var. = **घोंघा**.

घोट *ghoṭ* [cf. *ghoṭnā*], f. **1.** polish. **2.** a sense of suffocation.

घोटक *ghoṭak* [S.], m. a horse.

घोटना *ghoṭnā* [*ghoṭṭ-], v.t. & m. **1.** v.t. to rub, to rub down; to polish; to grind. **2.** to shave clean. **3.** to squeeze (the throat), to choke. **4.** to mix, to dissolve; to boil or to cook well. **5.** colloq. to go over mechanically (a lesson to be learned by heart). **6.** m. an instrument for rubbing, grinding, &c. — **गला ~ (का)**, to choke, to strangle. – **घोट-घोटकर मारना**, to beat mercilessly.

घोटा *ghoṭā* [cf. *ghoṭṭ-], m. **1.** a polishing or grinding stone, or implement. **2.** an instrument used to rub cloth being dyed. **3.** *HŚS.* dyed cloth. **4.** *HŚS.* shaving, being shaved. — **~ लगाना**, colloq. to learn by heart or mechanically (a lesson).

घोटाई *ghoṭāī* [cf. H. *ghoṭā*], f. **1.** polishing or grinding. **2.** payment for polishing, &c.

घोटाला *ghoṭālā* [conn. M. *gho(ṁ)ṭāḷā*], m. disorder, confusion (in affairs); scandal.

घोटू *ghoṭū* [cf. H. *ghoṭnā*], adj. & m. colloq. **1.** adj. **-घोटू**. choking, suffocating (e.g. **दमघोटू**, id). **2.** m. one who learns (lessons) by rote.

घोड़- *ghoṛ-*. = **घुड़-**.

घोड़ा *ghoṛā* [*ghoṭaka-*: ? ← Drav.], m. **1.** a horse. **2.** (in chess) the knight. **3.** a catch, trigger; hammer (of a gun). — **~ कसना**, to saddle a horse. **~ खोलना**, to unsaddle, or to untie a horse; to turn a horse loose. **~ चढ़ाना (का)**, to cock (a gun). **~ छोड़ना**, to pull a trigger; to release a catch; to gallop a horse (after, **के पीछे**); = **~ खोलना**, 2. **~ दबाना**, = **~ छोड़ना**, 2. **~ निकालना**, to break in a horse; to bring a horse forward, into the lead. **~ बेचकर सोना**, colloq. to sleep in peace, to be relieved of care. **~ मर जाना**, a horse to give out, to fail. **घोड़े पर चढ़े आना**, colloq. to hasten back; to be in haste (to complete a task).

घोड़ी *ghoṛī* [*ghoṭa-*: ? ← Drav.], f. **1.** a mare. **2.** the ceremonial arrival on horseback of a bridegroom at the bride's home. **3.** marriage songs sung by the groom's party. — ~ **चढ़ना**, to ride to one's bride's home on the wedding day.

घोपा *ghopā*, m. reg. (W.) a way of folding a blanket over the head against rain or cold.

घोर *ghor* [S.], m. **1.** terrible, frightful; awesome. **2.** extreme, intense; deep (sleep); heavy (as rain); huge. **3.** violent, vehement; harsh.

घोर- *ghor*, v.i. Brbh. to make a rumbling sound.

घोरता *ghorătā* [S.], f. **1.** frightfulness; awesomeness. **2.** intensity. **3.** vehemence.

घोरी *ghorī*, adj. = **अघोरी**.

घोल *ghol* [cf. H. *gholnā*], m. sthg. dissolved: a solution. — **घोल-मेल**, m. mixing; a mixture.

घोलना *gholnā* [*gholayati*], v.t. **1.** to mix in (with a liquid, **में**); to stir; to shake. **2.** to dissolve; to melt. — **काम में ज़हर** ~, fig. to put a spanner in the works. **घोलकर पी जाना**, fig. to have done with, to cast off (as inhibiting feelings).

घोष *ghoṣ* [S.], m. **1.** sound, noise; outcry; roar; slogan. **2.** voice; Brbh. = **घोषणा**. **3.** *ling.* a voiced sound. **4.** a settlement or encampment of cowherds. **5.** name of a Bengali community.

घोषक *ghoṣak* [S.], m. an announcer.

घोषण *ghoṣaṇ* [S.], m. proclaiming, voicing.

घोषणा *ghoṣăṇā* [S.], f. **1.** a declaration; announcement; manifesto. **2.** proclamation. — ~ **करना**, to proclaim, to announce. – **घोषणा-पत्र**, m. a (written) announcement; manifesto.

घोषित *ghoṣit* [S.], adj. announced; proclaimed.

घोसला *ghoslā*, m. = **घोंसला**.

घोसिन *ghosin* [cf. H. *ghosī*], f. **1.** the wife of a herdsman. **2.** a milkwoman.

घोसी *ghosī* [cf. *ghoṣa-*], m. **1.** a cowherd; milkman. **2.** a man of the Ghosī community.

घौद *ghaud*, f. reg. ? bunch, cluster (of grapes, dates, bananas).

घौरी *ghaurī*, f. Av. a cluster, bunch (= **घौद**).

-घ्न *-ghnă*, adj. formant. striking, killing; destroying, removing (e.g. **कृतघ्न**, not acknowledging sthg. done: ungrateful.

घ्राण *ghrāṇ* [S.], m. **1.** smelling. **2.** fragrance. **3.** E.H. transf. the nose. — ~ **करना**, v.t. to smell. – **घ्राणेंद्रिय** [°*ṇa+i*°], m. the organ of smell, nose; the sense of smell.

घ्रात *ghrāt* [S.], adj. smelt; smelled at, sniffed.

च

च *ca*, the sixth consonant of the Devanāgarī syllabary. — **चकार**, m. the sound /c/; the letter च.

चंग *caṅg* [P. *cang*], m. sthg. crooked or bent: **1.** a musical instrument resembling a tambourine; Jew's harp. **2.** reg. a paper kite; streamer attached to a kite.

चंगा *caṅgā* [*caṅga-*], adj. **1.** sound, good; pure, right (the heart, or way of thought). **2.** well, healthy; cured, recovered. — **~ करना (को)**, v.t. to cure, to heal. **~ बनाना (को)**, to put to rights, to correct; euph. to punish. **~ होना**, v.i. to be cured, to recover; to be convalescent.

चंगुल *caṅgul* [P. *cangul*], m. **1.** claws (of a wild beast), talons (of a bird of prey). **2.** clutch, grasp; clutching hands. **3.** a handful (as scooped up with bent fingers). — **~ में पड़ना**, or **फँसना (के)**, to fall into the clutches (of).

चँगेर *caṁger*, f. Brbh. a small basket.

चँगेरी *caṁgerī*, f. dimin. Brbh. = **चँगेर**.

चंचरीक *cañcarīk* [S.], m. Av. a bee.

चंचल *cañcal* [S.], adj. & m. **1.** adj. moving, shaking, trembling; quick, active. ***2.** unsteady, restless; inconstant, fickle; giddy, flirtatious; playful; naughty. **3.** transient, ephemeral. **4.** volatile (of temperament). **5.** m. an unsteady or inconstant person, &c.

चंचलता *cañcalătā* [S.], f. **1.** moving or unsteady state; variability, capriciousness; flirtatiousness; playfulness; naughtiness. **2.** transitoriness. **3.** volatility.

चंचलत्व *cañcalatvă* [S.], m. = **चंचलता**.

चंचलपन *cañcalpan* [cf. H. *cañcal*], m. = **चंचलता**.

चंचला *cañcalā* [S.], f. **1.** lightning. **2.** a title of Lakṣmī, the goddess of good fortune.

चंचलाहट *cañcalāhaṭ* [cf. H. *cañcal*], f. *Pl. HŚS.* = **चंचलता**.

चंचु *cañcu* [S.], f. beak, bill (of a bird).

चंट *canṭ*, adj. **1.** cunning, sly. **2.** villainous.

चंड *canḍ* [S.], adj. & m. **1.** adj. fierce, violent; strong; harsh. **2.** hot; passionate; raging; wounding, stinging. **3.** m. heat. **4.** anger, fury.

चंडता *canḍătā* [S.], f. Brbh. **1.** fierceness; strength. **2.** passion.

चंडा *canḍā* [S.], f. **1.** a passionate or enraged woman. **2.** a title of the goddess Durgā.

चंडाल *canḍāl*, m. = **चांडाल**. — **चंडाल-चौकड़ी**, f. colloq. a bunch of idlers, useless lot.

चंडालिन *canḍālin*, f. = **चांडालिन**.

चंडालिनी *canḍālinī*, f. = **चांडालिन**.

चंडिका *canḍikā* [S.], f. = **चंडा**, 1.

चंडी *canḍī* [S.], f. **1.** a title of the goddess Durgā. **2.** fig. a passionate or enraged woman. 3. = **~ सप्तशती** (a popular Sanskrit work). — **~ कुसुम**, m. *Pl. HŚS.* red oleander (= **कनेर**).

चंडू *canḍū*, m. a mixed preparation of opium (of Chinese type) for smoking. — **चंडू-ख़ाना**, m. an opium-smokers' den. **चंडूबाज़** [P. *-bāz*], m. an opium addict.

चंडूल *canḍūl*, m. the crested lark. — **पुराना ~**, m. pej. an old fool.

चंडोल *canḍol*, m. reg. **1.** a palanquin having two poles. **2.** E.H. a child's toy consisting of several small earthen pots joined together.

[1]**चंद** *cand* [P. *cand*], adj. some, a few; several. — **~ एक**, adj. one or two, a very few. – **चंदरोज़ा** [P. *-roza*], adj. inv. of or for a few days; transitory, ephemeral; temporary. **~ दर ~**, adj. 19c. several, various, one or the other.

[2]**चंद** *cand* [ad. *candra-*], m. the moon.

चंदन *candan* [S.], m. **1.** the sandal tree, *Santalum album* (source of white and yellow sandal); sandalwood. **2.** the red sandal, *Pterocarpus santalinus* or *Caesalpinia sappan*, and its wood. **3.** scented oil of sandalwood; sandalwood paste (used as a cosmetic, &c).

चंदनहार *candanhār*, m. reg. = **चंद्र-हार**, see s.v. **चंद्र**.

चंदनी *candănī* [cf. H. *candan*], adj. **1.** having to do with sandalwood. ***2.** of the colour of sandalwood.

चँदला *caṁdlā* [cf. *candra-*], adj. bald.

[1]**चँदवा** *caṁdvā* [*candrodaya-*], m. **1.** a small canopy, or awning. **2.** crown, top (as of a hat).

[2]**चँदवा** *caṁdvā* [cf. *candra-*], m. reg. (Bihar) handle or grip of a plough-shaft.

[1]**चंदा** *candā* [*candra-*], m. **1.** the moon. **2.** a round piece or slice.

[2]**चंदा** *candā* [P. *candā*], m. **1.** a contribution; donation (sometimes euph). **2.** a subscription. — ~ **करना**, to raise or to collect a subscription. ~ **देना (को)**, to pay a subscription; to make a contribution (to).

चंदावल *candāval* [? conn. H. [1]*caṁdvā* (*caṁdoā*)], m. rearguard (of an army); camp followers.

चँदिया *caṁdiyā* [cf. H. *cāṁd*], f. dimin. colloq. the crown of the head. — ~ **पर बाल तक न छोड़ना (की)**, to leave not a hair on one's head; to thrash (one); to rob, to despoil (one) utterly. ~ **मूड़ना (की)**, to shave the head (of); id.

चँदेरी *caṁderī*, f. = **चँदेली**.

चंदेल *candel*, m. *hist.* = **चंदेला**.

चंदेला *candelā*, m. *hist.* name of a Rājpūt tribe.

चँदेली *caṁdelī* [cf. H. *candelā*], f. a fine and costly cotton cloth (made originally at Candel or Canderi, in Bundelkhand).

चंदोल *candol*, m. Brbh. = **चंदावल**.

चंद्र *candră* [S.], m. **1.** the moon. **2.** a moon-shaped mark or spot (as on a peacock's tail, or in the script sign *candrabindu*). — **चंद्र-अभियान**, m. an expedition to the moon. **चंद्र-अवतरण**, m. moon landing. **चंद्र-कक्षा**, f. lunar orbit. **चंद्र-कला**, f. a digit (one sixteenth) of the moon's disc; a crescent moon; moonlight. **चंद्रकांत**, m. & adj. moon-stone (a translucent felspar: supposed to dissolve in the moon's beams); lovely as the moon. °**आ**, f. the beloved of the moon: night. **चंद्र-कांति**, f. moonlight. **चंद्र-क्षय**, m. the period of the new moon. **चंद्र-गृह**, m. *astrol.* the sign Cancer. **चंद्र-गोल**, m. disc of the moon. **चंद्र-ग्रह**, m. = next. **चंद्र-ग्रहण**, m. an eclipse of the moon. **चंद्रचूड़**, m. moon-crested: a title of Śiva. **चंद्र-जोत**, f. moonlight. **चंद्र-तल**, m. lunar surface. **चंद्र-द्युति**, f. moonlight. **चंद्रधर**, adj. & m. holding or wearing the moon: a title of Śiva. **चंद्र-पंचांग**, m. a lunar almanac. **चंद्र-परिक्रमा**, f. lunar orbit. **चंद्र-प्रभा**, f. moonlight. **चंद्र-बिंदु**, m. *gram.* moon and dot: a sign used (in Hindi and Bengali) to mark vowel nasality. **चंद्रभागा**, f. Brbh. a name of the river Chenab. **चंद्रभाल**, adj. & m. having the moon on (one's) forehead: a title of Śiva. **चंद्रभूषण**, adj. & m. whose ornament is the moon: id. **चंद्र-मंडल**, m. orb or disc of the moon. **चंद्र-मणि**, f. = **चंद्रकांत**. **चंद्र-मल्लिका**, f. jasmine. **चंद्र-माला**, f. = **चंद्र-हार**. **चंद्र-मास**, m. = **चांद्र-मास**. **चंद्रमुकुट**, adj. & m. crowned with the moon: a title of Śiva. **चंद्रमुख**, adj. moon-faced: fair of face. °**ई**, adj. id. **चंद्रमौलि**, adj. & m. moon-crested: a title of Śiva. **चंद्र-यान**, m. moon-craft, space vehicle; lunar module. **चंद्र-रत्न**, m. a pearl. **चंद्र-रेख**, f. = **चंद्र-कला**. **चंद्र-ललाम**, adj. & m. decorated with, or as beautiful as, the moon: a title of Śiva. **चंद्र-लेखा**, f. = **चंद्र-कला**. **चंद्र-लोक**, m. the sphere or heaven of the moon. **चंद्र-वंश**, m. *mythol.* the lunar race: a kṣatriya dynasty (in which Kṛṣṇa and Bharata were both born) claiming descent from the moon. °**ई**, adj. & m. having to do with the lunar race; one of that race. **चंद्रवदन**, adj. = **चंद्रमुख**. °**ई**, adj. id. **चंद्र-वधु**, f. E.H. bride of the moon: the insect called *bīr-bahūṭī*. **चंद्रवार**, m. Monday. **चंद्रवेष**, adj. & m. Brbh. clothed with, wearing the moon: a title of Śiva. **चंद्रशेखर**, adj. & m. = **चंद्रमुकुट**. **चंद्र-सौध**, m. moonlight; an uppermost apartment or balcony, open to the moon. **चंद्र-हार**, m. a necklace made of circular, and semi-circular pieces of material. **चंद्रहास**, m. Av. deriding the moon: a glittering sword; the sword of Rāvaṇa. **चंद्रार्ध** [°*ndra*+*a*°], m. a half moon. **चंद्रालोक** [°*ndra*+*ā*°], m. moonlight. °**इत**, adj. moonlit. **चंद्रावतरण** [°*ndra*+*a*°], m. = **चंद्र-अवतरण**. **चंद्रोदय** [°*ndra*+*u*°], m. moonrise.

चंद्रमा *candrămā* [S.], m. inv. the moon. — ~ **बलवान होना**, fig. to have good fortune in all (one) does.

चंद्रायण *candrâyaṇ* [S.], m. a religious observation or penance, in which the amount of food taken daily is reduced gradually to zero, and then increased, in step with the waning and waxing moon.

चंद्रिका *candrikā* [S.], f. **1.** moonlight; a moonbeam. **2.** Brbh. the 'eye' in a peacock's tail.

चँप- *caṁp-* [cf. H. *cāṁpnā*, *capnā*], v.i. **1.** E.H. to be pressed or trodden down. **2.** *Pl.* to lie hidden; to crouch; to creep.

चंपई *campaī* [cf. *campaka-*], adj. & f. **1.** adj. having the colour of the *campā* flower: yellowish, golden, orange. **2.** f. yellowness, &c.; brightness (of sunlight).

चंपक *campak* [S.], m. = **चंपा**. — **चंपक-माला**, f. a garland of *campā* flowers; a necklace (= **चंपा-कली**).

चंपत *campat* [cf. H. *cāṁpnā*, *capnā*], adj. **1.** lying concealed, invisible. **2.** vanished. — ~ **होना** or **हो जाना**, colloq. to vanish, to make oneself scarce.

चंपा *campā* [*campaka-*], m. the tree *Michelia campaca*, and its fragrant yellowish-white flower. — **चंपा-कली**, f. a necklace of small ornaments shaped like buds of the *campā*. **चंपा-केला**, m. a variety of plantain (small, scented and very sweet). °**-केली**, f.

चँपी *caṁpī* [cf. H. *caṁp-*], f. shampoo, massage.

चंपू *campū* [S.], f. a type of composition treating the same subject in alternate passages of prose and verse.

चंबल *cambal*, m. **1.** a beggar's bowl, or shell. **2.** reg. (W.) wooden trough (used in raising water for irrigation).

चँबेली *caṁbelī*, f. reg. = चमेली.

चँवर *caṁvar* [*camara-*], m. **1.** the yak. **2.** yak's tail: a flywhisk. **3.** Av. crest (as carried by a war-horse, or elephant). — ~ डुलाना, or हिलाना, to whisk away flies.

[1]**चक** *cak* [ad. *cakra-*], m. **1.** a wheel. **2.** *mythol.* discus (of Viṣṇu). 3. = [1]चकई. **4.** landed property; a holding; a piece of assigned or rent-free land. **5.** the detached or unconsolidated fields of a village; a village. **6.** a sub-division of land (as of a *parganā*, &c). — ~ काटना, v.t. to assign boundaries to a section of land; to divide up land. – चक-डोरी, f. wheel and string: a toy resembling a top, or a yo-yo (= [1]चकई and चकडोर). चकबंदी [P. -*bandī*], f. defining or marking the boundaries of a section of land; division of holdings; consolidation of holdings. चकबस्त [P. -*bast*], m. name of a Kashmiri brāhmaṇ community.

[2]**चक** *cak* [cf. **cakyate*: Pa. *cakita-*], adj. abundant; ample, a lot (of); sufficient.

चक- *cak-*, v.i. Brbh. to be astonished, or startled.

[1]**चकई** *cakaī* [cf. *cakra-*, or H. [1]*cak*], f. a child's toy resembling a yo-yo.

[2]**चकई** *cakaī* [*cakravāka-*], f. the female *cakvā* bird. — चकई-चकवा, m. male and female *cakvās*; a pair of *cakvās*.

चकचका *cakcakā* [? conn. H. [2]*cak*], adj. colloq. glittering, bright, shining (colours, &c).

चकचकाना *cakcakānā* [? cf. H. *cakcakā*], v.i. *HŚS.* to be replete: to ooze.

चक़चक़ी *caqcaqī* [T.], f. a type of cymbals made of wood.

चकचौंध *cakcaumdh*, f. = चकाचौंध.

चकडोर *cakḍor* [*cakra-*; *davara-*], m. wheel and string: a toy of the kind of a top, or a yo-yo (= [1]चकई).

चकता *caktā*, m. = चकत्ता.

चकती *caktī* [cf. H. *cakattā*], f. **1.** a round or squarish piece (as of cloth, leather, metal); a patch; plate; lump. **2.** a shred, scrap.

चकत्ता *cakattā* [cf. *cakra-*], m. **1.** a round blotch or mark (on the skin); a scar; cut, scratch. **2.** a piece of cut turf. **3.** a slab. **4.** colloq. patch, small area (as of sunlight).

चकनाचूर *caknācūr* [**cakkana-*; **cūra-* (Pk. *cūra-*)], adj. & m. **1.** adj. broken to pieces, shattered. **2.** exhausted, tired out (the body); racked (with pain). **3.** m. fragments, scraps; filings; atoms. — ~ करना, v.t. to shatter, to pulverise.

चक़मक़ *caqmaq* [T. *çaqmaq*], m. f. flint; a flint. — ~ करना, to strike fire (with flint and steel). ~ झाड़ना, id.

चकमा *cakmā* [? **cakrakarma-*], m. cheating, trickery; deception. — ~ खाना, to be cheated, or deceived (by, का). ~ देना (को), to cheat, to trick or to deceive (one). चकमे में आना, or पड़ना (के), to fall a victim to (one's) trickery, to be deceived, &c.

चक़माक़ *caqmāq*, m. f. = चक़मक़.

चकरबा *cakarbā* [?? conn. *cakravāta-*: w. H. *cakkar*, and reg. *jhagaṛvā*], m. *Pl. HŚS.* uproar; quarrel.

चकराना *cakrānā* [cf. H. *cakkar*, *cakr*], v.i. & v.t. **1.** v.i. to revolve; to spin, to whirl. **2.** to go around, to wander about. **3.** to be perplexed; to be confused or bewildered; to be agitated, disturbed. **4.** v.t. to cause to revolve; to spin, to whirl; to make (one's head) giddy. **5.** to make perplexed; to confuse; to bewilder; to agitate, to disturb. — सिर ~, the head to be in a whirl; to be confused, &c.

चकरानी *cakrānī* f. pronun. var. a woman servant (= चाकरानी).

चकरी *cakrī* [cf. H. *cakr*, *cakkar*], f. Brbh. a wheel, &c.

चकला *caklā* [**cakrala-*: Pk. *cakkala-*], m. **1.** a circular object: a round, broad stone, or flat board or plate (on which dough is rolled out); a log of wood. **2.** a mill (for grinding pulse). **3.** a district; section (of a town, esp. a prostitutes' quarter). **4.** brothel. — चकलेदार [P. -*dār*], m. the administrator and collector of revenues of a *caklā*.

चकली *caklī* [cf. H. *caklā*], f. **1.** a small flat stone, &c. on which cosmetics or spices are ground (cf. चकला, 1). **2.** a pulley.

चकल्लस *cakallas*, f. turmoil, uproar; fuss, to-do.

चकवँड़ *cakvaṁṛ* [*cakramarda-*: ← Drav.], m. a shrub, *Cassia tora* (used medicinally, e.g. in treating ringworm, and formerly also in processing indigo).

चकवँढ़ *cakvaṁṛh*, m. pronun. var. reg. (E.) = चकवँड़.

चकवा *cakvā* [*cakravāka-*], m. a large orange-brown duck, the sheldrake, or Brahminy duck, *Anas casarca* (trad. supposed to be separated from its mate at night).

चकवी *cakvī*, f. the female *cakvā* bird.

चकाचक *cakācak* [cf. H. ²*cak*], adj. **1.** abundant, plentiful. **2.** drenched, soaked. **3.** brilliant (a picture, a scene). — ~ खाना, v.t. to eat well or abundantly, to have a splendid meal.

चकाचौंध *cakācaumdh* [? H. *cakācak*+H. *caumknā*×*cundhā*], f. **1.** a dazzling light. **2.** the state of being dazzled, dazed or giddy. — ~ करना, to blind, to dazzle; to confuse. ~ में आना, or पड़ना (से), to be dazzled (by); to be bewildered (by). ~ लगना (से), id.

चकाचौंधी *cakācaumdhī*, f. = चकाचौंध. — ~ मारना, v.t. to dazzle; to daze; to make giddy.

चकावल *cakāval* [cf. *cakra-*], m. reg. a bony deposit, causing lameness, on the pastern of a horse.

चकित *cakit* [S.], adj. **1.** alarmed, frightened. **2.** astonished, confused.

चकोतरा *cakotrā*, m. the shaddock (a partic. citrus tree, *Citrus decumana*) and its fruit.

चकोर *cakor* [S.], m. a type of partridge, *Perdix rufa* or *Tetrao rufus* (trad. supposed to live on moonbeams).

चकोरी *cakorī* [cf. H. *cakor*], f. a female partridge (see चकोर).

चकौंध *cakaumdh*, f. = चकाचौंध.

चक्कर *cakkar* [ad. *cakra-*], m. 1. = चक्र, 1.-8. **2.** a curve, bend. **3.** a round journey. **4.** fig. perplexity, confusion; trouble, inconvenience. — ~ आना, to grow dizzy, to feel faint. ~ काटना, to revolve; to wander; to make a round trip. ~ खाना, to be made to revolve; to wind (as a road); to wander; to be dizzy, to faint. ~ देना, to confuse, or to deceive (one, को). ~ पड़ना, a perplexity to arise: to lose (one's) way. ~ मारना, to revolve; to make a round trip; to take a walk. ~ में आना, v.i. to be involved or entangled in difficulties; to be confused, or uncertain; to be misled. ~ में डालना, v.t. to involve in difficulties; to perplex; to mislead. ~ में पड़ना, v.i. = ~ में आना. ~ लगाना, v.t. = ~ मारना, 2., 3.; to go a round, or a circuit; to make an orbit. – चक्करदार [P. *-dār*], adj. circular, round; circuitous, round-about; involved, complicated. चक्करदार सीढ़ी, f. a spiral staircase.

चक्का *cakkā* [*cakra-*], m. **1.** a wheel. **2.** any round, flat object; a clod of earth, piece (of brick, stone); a flat piece (as of turf); a round or a square pile (as of bricks). **3.** *athl.* discus. — चक्केबाज़ी [P. *-bāzī*], f. throwing brickbats.

चक्की *cakkī* [*cakra-*], f. **1.** a millstone. **2.** a pair of millstones; a mill. **3.** a grindstone. —~ का पाट, m. the face of a millstone: the upper or lower millstone of a pair. ~ चलाना, v.t. to work a mill; to work at a laborious task; colloq. to do hard labour. ~ पीसना, v.t. to grind in a mill; to work a mill. ~ फेरना, v.t. = ~ चलाना. ~ में जुटना, to be yoked in a mill: to slave, to sweat. चलती ~, f. turning millstones: the world. – चक्की-घर, m. a mill. चक्की-चूल्हा, m. millstone and stove: a woman's domestic tasks.

चक्कू *cakkū*, m. pronun. var. = चाकू.

चक्र *cakr* [S.], m. **1.** a wheel; a potter's wheel. **2.** a circular object: Catherine wheel; *mythol.* discus (of Viṣṇu). **3.** mill or press (oil, or cane) driven by a revolving beam. **4.** a circular shape: circle, ring; circumference. **5.** *mil.* a ring-shaped formation of troops. **6.** a group, circle. **7.** circular motion; a turn, revolution; a circuit, round; a cycle; whirlwind; whirlpool, eddy. **8.** giddiness; derangement. **9.** [Engl. *round*] a round (of ammunition, or of a competition). **10.** a medal, decoration. — चक्र-क्रम, m. rotation; cyclic order. चक्र-गति, f. circular motion; id., 1. चक्रधर, adj. & m. discus-holder: a title of Viṣṇu or of Kṛṣṇa; a ruler; a snake. °-धारी, m. id. चक्र-पाल, m. the ruler of a region. चक्र-यान, m. a wheeled vehicle. चक्रवत्, adj. revolving, rotating. चक्रवर्ती, m. ruler of a wide region or country; a mighty or supreme king, an emperor. °इनी, f. चक्रवाक, m. the *cakvā* bird (the ruddy sheldrake, or Brahminy duck). चक्र-वात, m. a whirlwind. चक्र-व्यूह, m. (troops) drawn up in a circular formation (see ~, 5). चक्रांकित [°*kra*+*a*°], adj. marked or stamped with a circle or ring-shaped mark. चक्राकार [°*kra*+*ā*°], adj. of circular shape, round; ring-shaped. चक्रायुध [°*kra*+*ā*°], adj. & m. armed with a discus: a title of Viṣṇu.

चक्रावल *cakrāval*, m. reg. = चकावल.

चक्रीय *cakrīyă* [S.], adj. **1.** circular; ring-shaped. **2.** cyclical.

चक्षु *cakṣu* [S.], m. the eye. — चक्षुःपथ, m. field of vision. चक्षुरिंद्रिय, m. the organ of sight; the sense of sight. चक्षुर्मल, m. secretion from the eye. चक्षु-रोग, m. eye disease, ophthalmia.

चक्षुः- *cakṣuḥ-*. see s.v. चक्षु.

चक्षुर्- *cakṣur-*. see s.v. चक्षु.

चख *cakh* [ad. *cakṣus-*], m. Brbh. Av. the eye. — चख-पूतरि, f. apple of the eye: a dearly loved person.

चख़ *cakh* [P. *cakh*], f. quarrelling; uproar. — चख़-चख़, f. dispute, wrangling. चख़ाचख़ी, f. id.

चखना *cakhnā* [cf. **cakṣati*: Pk. *cakkhaï*], v.t. **1.** to taste, to eat; to try (of food); to partake; to relish. **2.** fig. to experience; to suffer. — मज़ा

~ (का), to taste the pleasure (of): to experience the pain or tribulation (of).

चखाना *cakhānā* [cf. H. *cakhnā*], v.t. **1.** to cause to taste; to give as food (to, को); to regale (with). **2.** to give a taste of (to, को); to cause to suffer, or to experience; to inflict (punishment).

चखाहा *cakhāhā*, m. reg. colloq. a herdsman.

चखौती *cakhautī* [cf. H. *cakhănā*], f. a tasty or savoury morsel, delicacy.

चघड़ *caghaṛ*, adj. colloq. cunning, rascally.

चचर *cacar*, adj. & f. *Pl. HŚS.* **1.** adj. ploughed after lying fallow (land). **2.** f. fallow land, when first ploughed (cf. [2]चाँचर).

चचा *cacā*, m. pronun. var. = चाचा.

चचिया *caciyā* [cf. H. *cācā*, *cācī*], adj. inv. of the nature of a paternal aunt or uncle. — ~ ससुर, m. father-in-law's brother, husband's uncle. ~ सास, f. father-in-law's brother's wife, wife's aunt.

चचींड़ा *cacīṁṛā* [*ciciṇḍa-*], m. reg. a vine and its gourd: **1.** *Bela vulgaris.* **2.** the snake-gourd, *Trichosanthes anguina.*

चची *cacī*, f. pronun. var. = चाची.

चचेरा *cacerā* [cf. **cācca-*], adj. descended from a paternal uncle. — ~ भाई, m. a male cousin on the father's side. चचेरी बहन, f. a female cousin on the father's side.

चचोड़ना *cacoṛnā*, v.t. to suck, to suck at (particularly at sthg. dry).

चच्चा *caccā*, m. pronun. var. = चाचा.

चच्ची *caccī*, f. pronun. var. = चाची.

[1]**चट** *caṭ* [**caṭa-*], f. **1.** a cracking or snapping sound. **2.** a cracking of the finger-joints. **3.** adv. quickly; instantly. — ~ से, adv. id. ~ मँगनी पट ब्याह, no sooner engaged than married (also transf). – चट-चट, f. & adv. the sound of repeated cracking, snapping, crackling, or striking (of blows). चट-चट बलैयाँ लेना, to crack the finger-joints (as a charm to avert misfortune, esp. from children). चटपट, adv. quickly; instantly; suddenly. चटपट हो जाना, to die suddenly. °ई, f. quickness, briskness; eagerness; raciness (of style). – चटाचट, m. & adv. the sound of repeated cracking, snapping or striking (of blows); repeatedly; in quick succession. चटापटी, f. quickness, briskness; suddenness; sudden death; a number of deaths in rapid succession.

[2]**चट** *caṭ* [? cf. H. *cāṭnā*; × H. [1]*caṭ*, 3.], adj. consumed. — ~ करना, v.t. to eat up; to devour, to consume; to dissipate; to expropriate, to embezzle. ~ होना, v.i. to be eaten up; to be consumed; to be dissipated; to be embezzled, &c.

[1]**चटक** *caṭak* [**caṭa-*], f. & adj. **1.** f. a crack, snap; crash; a smack. **2.** quickness, briskness. **3.** brightness, brilliance; prime (of life). **4.** pungency (of spices). **5.** adj. quick; sharp, intelligent. **6.** bright, brilliant. — ~ से, adv. briskly; cleverly, adroitly. – चटक-मटक, f. mincing or wanton gait; modish life-style.

[2]**चटक** *caṭak* [S.], m. a sparrow.

चटकना *caṭaknā* [cf. **caṭa-*], v.i. **1.** to make a snapping or cracking sound; to crack; to crackle. **2.** to break with a crack, &c.; to split; to burst; to explode. **3.** to burst open (a bud); to bloom. **4.** to be suddenly irritated or angry; to go away suddenly. **5.** to burst out, to develop (between, में: a dispute, dissension). — उनकी आपस में चटक गई, they fell out.

चटकनी *caṭkanī* [cf. H. *caṭaknā*], f. the bolt of a door. (= चिटकनी.)

चटकल *caṭkal* [cf. B. *caṭ*], f. (jute) sacking factory.

चटका *caṭkā* [**caṭa(kka-)*], m. **1.** a snapping or crackling. **2.** [? × **caṭṭ-*] eagerness, desire. — ~ लगना (को), to desire eagerly.

चटकाना *caṭkānā* [cf. H. *caṭaknā*], v.t. **1.** to cause to make a snapping or cracking sound; to snap (the fingers); to crack (a whip); to cause to creak (shoes); to crack the finger-joints (by bending the fingers). **2.** to break with a snap; to split.

चटकारना *caṭkārnā* [cf. H. *caṭkārā*], v.t. **1.** to smack (the lips); to clack (the tongue). **2.** to crack (the finger-joints by bending them). **3.** fig. to dismiss (a challenge).

चटकारा *caṭkārā* [conn. *caṭatkāra-*], m. a smacking of the lips, or of the tongue against the palate. — चटकारे का, adj. tasty, luscious. चटकारे भरना, or मारना, or लेना, to smack the lips, &c. चटकारे से, adv. with relish.

चटकारी *caṭkārī* [cf. H. *caṭkārā*], f. **1.** a clacking of the tongue (as in urging cattle, or relishing food). **2.** cracking the finger-joints.

चटकीला *caṭkīlā* [cf. H. *caṭak*], adj. **1.** bright; brilliant; splendid; charming, delightful. **2.** gaudy, showy; meretricious. **3.** pungent; tasty; sharp, strong (of taste).

चटकीलापन *caṭkīlāpan* [cf. H. *caṭkīlā*], m. **1.** brightness, &c. **2.** pungency, &c.

चटखना *caṭakhnā*, v.i. = चटकना.

चटखनी *caṭkhanī*, f. = चिटखनी.

चटखारना *caṭkhārnā*, v.t. = चटकारना.

चटखारा *caṭkhārā*, m. = चटकारा.

चटख़ारा *caṭkhārā*, m. pronun. var. = चटखारा, चटकारा.

चटचटा *caṭcaṭā* [cf. **caṭa-*], adj. & m. **1.** adj. making a repeated cracking, or crackling sound. चटचटी लकड़ी, f. colloq. firewood. **2.** m. the sound of repeated cracking, &c.

चटचटाना *caṭcaṭānā* [cf. H. *caṭcaṭā*], v.i. & v.t. **1.** v.i. to make a repeated cracking, or crackling noise. **2.** to snap, to break. **3.** v.t. to cause to crack, or to crackle.

चटना *caṭnā* [cf. H. *cāṭnā*], v.i. & adj. **1.** v.i. to be tasted, &c. **2.** adj. colloq. voracious.

चटनी *caṭnī* [cf. H. *caṭnā*], f. **1.** a sweet pickle or sauce. **2.** any seasoning or relish. **3.** sthg. chopped, mashed or bruised (as *caṭnī* in preparation). — ~ करना, or बनाना (को), to reduce to a pulp; to bruise, &c. ~ होना, or हो जाना, to be reduced to a pulp, &c.; to be eaten with relish; to be completely consumed or exhausted.

चटपट *caṭpaṭ* [cf. H. *caṭpaṭānā*], adv. quickly, smartly.

चटपटा *caṭpaṭā* [**caṭa-*; *paṭ-*²], adj. & m. **1.** adj. hot, spicy; savorous. **2.** brisk, lively. **3.** m. a savoury.

चटपटाना *caṭpaṭānā* [cf. H. *caṭpaṭā*], v.i. *Pl. HŚS.* to move briskly (in haste, or agitation).

चटपटी *caṭpaṭī*, f. see s.v. ¹चट.

चटर-चटर *caṭar-caṭar*, f. a clacking sound (of wooden shoes).

चटरी *caṭrī*, f. *Pl. HŚS.* ? the chickling vetch (= खिसारी, लतरी).

चटवाना *caṭvānā* [cf. H. *cāṭna*], v.t. to cause to be tasted, &c.

चटसाल *caṭsāl* [H. ¹*cāṭī*, ¹*caṭṭā* + *śālā-*], f. Brbh. a school.

¹**चटाई** *caṭāī* [**caṭṭa-*], f. a mat of interwoven strips of leaf, or bamboo. — चटाईदार [P. *-dār*], adj. woven (as a चटाई).

²**चटाई** *caṭāī* [cf. H. *cāṭnā*, *caṭānā*], f. **1.** tasting. **2.** causing (sthg.) to be tasted, &c.

चटाक *caṭāk* [**caṭakka-*], f. **1.** a crack, or crackling sound; a smack. **2.** a crash; sound of an explosion. — चटाक-चटाक, loud reports, &c. चटाक-पटाक, adv. quickly; instantly; suddenly.

चटाका *caṭākā* [**caṭakka-*], m. = चटाक. — चटाके का, adj. loud, violent; harsh, strong, extreme.

चटाख *caṭākh*, f. = चटाक.

चटाना *caṭānā* [cf. H. *cāṭnā*], v.t. & m. **1.** v.t. to cause to taste, or to lick; to cause to lap; to give to eat (to, को). **2.** to give as a bribe (to, को). **3.** colloq. to give a taste of (a whip, &c.); to cause (one) to bite (the dust). **4.** m. the ceremony of feeding a child for the first time (*ann-prāśan*).

चटिया *caṭiyā*, m. reg. = ¹चट्टा.

चटुल *caṭul* [S.], adj. restless; tremulous.

चटोर *caṭor*, adj. & m. = चटोरा.

चटोरा *caṭorā* [cf. H. *cāṭnā*], adj. & m. **1.** adj. greedy, gluttonous. **2.** fond of sweet or delicate food. **3.** m. a glutton. **4.** a person with a sweet tooth.

चटोरापन *caṭorāpan* [cf. H. *caṭorā*], m. **1.** greed. **2.** fondness for sweet food.

¹**चट्टा** *caṭṭā*, m. *Pl. HŚS.* a school pupil.

²**चट्टा** *caṭṭā*, m. *Pl. HSS.* a red mark, or pimple.

चट्टान *caṭṭān*, f. **1.** a crag; a rock. **2.** rock; a piece of rock or mineral. **3.** *geol.* a seam, stratum. — तेलवाली ~, f. oil-bearing rock.

चट्टा-बट्टा *caṭṭā-baṭṭā* [cf. H. ¹*caṭ*, and **varta-*³], m. a child's toy: a number of painted wooden balls suspended from a flat or saucer-shaped piece of wood, which rattle when shaken. — चट्टे-बट्टे लड़ाना, to stir up trouble by carrying tales. एक ही थैले के चट्टे-बट्टे, fig. several of a kind, horses from the same stable.

¹**चट्टी** *caṭṭī*, f. an open-heeled sandal.

²**चट्टी** *caṭṭī*, f. **1.** shortcoming, lack. **2.** Panj. loss (as in trade). **3.** injury, damage; expense, charge, fine.

³**चट्टी** *caṭṭī*, f. a halting- or camping-place.

चड़ *caṛ* [**caṭa-*], f. m. a cracking or crackling sound (as of breaking or burning wood); a sound of tearing (cloth, &c). — चड़-चड़, f. m. a continued or repeated sound of breaking, tearing, &c.; idle chatter. – चड़ाचड़, f. id.

चड़चड़ाना *caṛcaṛānā* [cf. H. *caṛ*], v.i. to crack, to crackle, &c.

चड़-बड़ *caṛ-baṛ* [cf. H. *caṛ*], f. chattering, babbling (of voices). — ~ करना, or बोलना, v.i. to chatter, to jabber.

चड़बड़िया *caṛbaṛiyā* [cf. H. *caṛ-baṛ*], adj. & m. **1.** adj. talkative, gossiping. **2.** m. a chatterer, &c.

चड़ाक *caṛāk* [conn. H. *caṭāk*], adj. snapped, broken.

चड्डा *caḍḍā*, m. *HŚS.* the upper thigh.

चड्डी *caḍḍī* [Panj.], f. a type of loin-cloth, or underwear.

चड्ढी *caḍḍhī* [conn. H. *caṛhnā*], f. reg. mounting, riding: a childrens' game of piggy-back, in which winners ride on the backs of losers. — ~ खिलाना, to take (one, को) for a ride (on a motorcycle). ~ गाँठना (पर), to ride on the back (of). ~ देना (को), to take (one) on one's back.

चढ़ती *caṛhtī* [cf. H. *caṛhnā*], f. **1.** rise, increase; advance. **2.** superiority.

चढ़न *caṛhan* [cf. H. *caṛhnā*], f. **1.** ascending. &c. **2.** mounting, &c.

चढ़ना *caṛhnā* [**caḍhati*: Pk. *caḍhaï*], v.i. **1.** to rise, up, to mount; to climb; to mount (on, पर); to ride (on); to embark; to rise (prices, a river); to increase, to grow; to wax (moon, season); to mount up, to be in arrears (as pay). **2.** to be mounted or set (on or around, पर); to be placed (upon); to be applied or attached (to, पर); to be fitted (to); to be adjusted or set (a bow-string, or the tension of a drum); to be set (a bone); to be spread; to be overlaid (as metal in electrolysis). **3.** to be entered (items in a ledger). **4.** to be raised up; to be shortened (a lower hem). **5.** to be elevated, or promoted; to be exalted. **6.** to be offered (in devotion, or as a sacrifice: to, को). **7.** to advance, to proceed; to go (for a purpose: to, पर); to be taken or conveyed (to); to progress, to be advanced (of time). (उसे) तीसरा महीना चढ़ चुका था, she was three months pregnant. **8.** to march (against, पर); to attack; to assail; to invade. **9.** to take effect, to be rampant (as poison, intoxicants, fever); to be dominant (over, पर), to possess or to obsess (emotions). **10.** to be superior; to excel. – चढ़ बनना, v. i. *Pl.* to advance, to gain ground; to get the better (of); to prosper. उनकी चढ़ बनी है, he is rising fast, doing well. चढ़ बैठना (पर), v.i. to mount, to ride (upon); to overcome, to subjugate. चढ़कर, adv. with a rise or increase; baldly, confessedly; by design; excellently, in a superior way or degree. चढ़-चढ़कर बोलना, to speak in a raised or high-pitched voice. चढ़ता भाव, m. a rising price or rate. चढ़ता होना, v.i. to be rising, &c.; to be superior (to, से); to excel. चढ़ा-ऊपरी, f. vying, competing (with).

चढ़वाना *caṛhvānā* [cf. H. *caṛhnā*], v.t. to cause to be raised up, &c.; to have or to get (sthg.) raised (by another, से).

चढ़वैया *caṛhvaiyā*, m. = चढ़ैया.

चढ़ाई *caṛhāī* [cf. H. *caṛhnā, caṛhānā*], f. **1.** ascending, rising, mounting; rising movement (as of prices); embarkation. **2.** attack, assault (upon, पर); invasion, incursion. **3.** a height, high place or region; an ascending slope. **4.** price or cost of ascending, riding, &c.; fare. **5.** causing to rise; giving as an offering; affixing; adjusting; embellishing. — ~ करना (पर), to climb; to attack.

चढ़ाऊ *caṛhāū* [cf. H. *caṛhānā*], adj. capable of being climbed.

चढ़ाना *caṛhānā* [cf. H. *caṛhnā*], v.t. **1.** to cause to rise up, to raise; to lift up (upon, पर); to place (upon, पर, के ऊपर); to roll up (sleeves). **2.** to apply (to or upon, पर: as paint, dye); to affix, to attach, to fit (to); to adjust or to set (a bow-string, or the tension of a drum). **3.** to put away, to replace (an object in its container). **4.** to enter (as in a ledger). **5.** to offer (to, को: as to a deity); to dedicate; to sacrifice; to devote. **6.** to elevate (a person's grade or rank), to promote; to exalt. **7.** to cause to advance; to lead in an attack (against, पर). **8.** to cause to increase, to cause to swell (cf. बढ़ाना); to incite (a person).

चढ़ाव *caṛhāv* [cf. *caṛhnā, caṛhānā*], m. **1.** ascent, rise; rise (as in prices), increase; swelling, flooding. **2.** an attack, assault; an access, fit; dominance (of alcohol: over: पर). **3.** elevation; promotion, advancement. **4.** sthg. applied, fitted or adjusted (as a bow-string); decoration, embellishment. **5.** an offering (as to a deity). **6.** *math.* raising to a power. — चढ़ाव-उतार, m. rise and fall, increase and decrease; ebb and flow, or flood (tide); ups and downs. (*math.*) involution and evolution; (*mus.*) a rising and descending scale.

चढ़ावा *caṛhāvā* [cf. H. *caṛhānā*], m. **1.** anything presented in sacrifice; any religious offering or gift. **2.** a present of jewellery or clothes from a bridegroom to his bride, to be worn at the wedding. **3.** incitement, encouragement. — ~ चढ़ाना, to present or to make a religious offering (to, को).

चढ़ैत *caṛhait* [cf. H. *caṛhnā*], m. *Pl. HŚS.* one who mounts: a horseman; a mounted soldier; an expert horseman.

चढ़ैता *caṛhaitā* [cf. H. *caṛhnā*], m. *Pl. HŚS.* = चढ़ैत.

चढ़ैया *caṛhaiyā* [cf. H. *caṛhnā, caṛhānā*], m. **1.** one who ascends, or mounts, a horseman; a climber. **2.** one who lifts: weigher of goods, grain, &c. in a scale.

चढ़ौवा *caṛhauvā* [cf. H. *caṛhānā*], m. *Pl. HŚS.* a shoe having a high heel.

चताख *catākh*, f. pronun. var. = चताक.

चताख़ *catāk͟h*, f. pronun. var. = चताक.

चतुर *catur* [S.], adj. **1.** quick, active. **2.** clever, skilful, adroit. **3.** sagacious, shrewd; cunning.

चतुर- *catur-* [S.], adj. & n. formant. four: — चतुरंग, adj. & m. of four parts; chess (the ancient Indian form of the game); a quartet (singers and instrumentalist). °ई, adj. id. चतुरानन, adj. & m. having four faces; a title of Brahmā. चतुराश्रम, m. the four stages of life (according to brahmanical teaching). चतुर्गुण, adj. fourfold. चतुर्दश, adj. fourteen. °ई, f. *hind.* the fourteenth day (of the light or dark half of the month). चतुर्दिक्, adj. & adv. facing the four quarters (of the compass); many-sided; on all sides. चतुर्दिश, m. pl. the four quarters (of the world). चतुर्धाम, m. pl. *hind.* the four abodes or pilgrimage places: see चारों धाम. चतुर्बाहु, adj. & m. four-armed; a title of Viṣṇu and Śiva. चतुर्भुज, adj. & m. four-armed; quadrilateral; a title of Viṣṇu. °ई, f. a title of Durgā. चतुरमास, m. *hind.* the period of four months between the eleventh of the bright halves of Asāṛh and Kārttik. चतुरमुख, adj. having four faces; facing all directions; multi-sided. °ई, adj. id. चतुर्युग, adj. & m. pl. having to do with the four ages; the four ages. °ई, f. a cycle of the four ages. चतुर्वर्ग, m. pl. the four goals of life (*arth*, *kām*, *dharm* and *mokṣa*). चतुर्वर्ण, m. pl. the four classes (of Aryan society). चतुर्विद्या, f. fourfold knowledge (of the Vedas). चतुर्वेद, m. pl. the four Vedas. °ई, m. one knowing the four Vedas; the name of a brāhmaṇ sub-community.

चतुरता *caturătā* [S.], f. = चतुराई.

चतुराई *caturāī* [cf. H. *catur*], f. **1.** quickness, alertness. **2.** cleverness; skill; dexterity. **3.** shrewdness; cunning. — ~ छोलना or तौलना, to deal in cunning; to act shrewdly.

चतुर्थ *caturth* [S.], adj. fourth. — ~ काल, m. the fourth watch (of the day): evening. ~ आश्रम, m. the fourth of the brahmanical stages of life: life as an ascetic. चतुर्थांश [°*tha*+*a*°], m. a fourth part.

चतुर्थी *caturthī* [S.], f. **1.** *hind.* the fourth day of a lunar fortnight. **2.** *gram.* dative case.

चतुष्- *catuṣ-* [S.], adj. & n. formant. four, quadri-: — चतुष्पद, m. quadruped (= चौपाया).

चतुष्तय *catuṣtăyă* [S.], m. sthg. having four parts, folds, &c.; a quartet.

चद्दर *caddar*, f. pronun. var. = चादर.

[1]**चनक** *canak* [cf. H. *canaknā*], f. reg. **1.** bursting (as of a bud or pod); cracking. **2.** pain (in the back). — चनक-बाई, f. *Pl. HŚS.* rheumatism (in the back).

[2]**चनक** *canak* [ad. *caṇaka-*], m. E.H. = चना.

चनकना *canaknā*, v.i. *Pl. HŚS.* **1.** to burst (as a pod); to crack. **2.** to be irritated or irritable.

चनचनाना *cancanānā* [cf. H. *canaknā*], v.i. **1.** to crackle; to sputter. **2.** to crack (as glass); to split (ripe pods). **3.** to throb, to shoot.

चनचनाहट *cancanāhaṭ* [cf. H. *cancanānā*], f. **1.** crackling, &c. **2.** throbbing, shooting.

चनसुर *cansur* [conn. *candraśūra-*], m. a kind of cress, *Lepidum sativum.*

चना *canā* [*caṇa-*], m. the chick-pea, or gram (*Cicer arietenum*). — लोहे के चने चबाना, to chew iron gram: to carry out a difficult task.

चनार *canār* [P. *canār*], m. **1.** the plane tree. **2.** the poplar.

चनी *canī* [cf. H. *canā*], f. reg. a small variety of gram.

चनेठ *caneṭh*, m. (f., *Pl.*) *Pl. HŚS.* name of a grass resembling the chick-pea (source of a drug given to cattle).

चपकन *capkan* [cf. H. *capaknā*], f. *Pl. HŚS.* a close-fitting jacket.

चपकना *capaknā*, v.i. = चिपकना.

चपकाना *capkānā*, v.t. reg. = चिपकाना.

चपटना *capaṭnā* [cf. **capp-* (Pk. *cappaï*); **carpaṭṭa-*], v.i. to be pressed flat, or even.

चपटा *capṭā* [**carpaṭṭa-*], adj. & m. **1.** adj. pressed flat, flat; level; shallow and broad. **2.** m. a flat-nosed person. **3.** a large flat earthen vessel.

चपटाना *capṭānā* [cf. H. *capaṭnā*], v.t. to press flat, or even.

चपटी *capṭī* [cf. H. *capaṭnā*], f. **1.** reg. (W.) a small flat earthen vessel. **2.** a kind of tick (on cattle). **3.** colloq. vulva.

चपड़क़नाती *capaṛqanātī* [? cf. H. *capaṛnā* or *cupaṛnā*+A. *qanā'a*: P. *qanā'at*], adj. & m. **1.** adj. unctuous, sycophantic. **2.** m. an unctuous flatterer.

चपड़-चपड़ *capaṛ-capaṛ* [? cf. H. *cabhnā*], f. & adv. **1.** f. the sound of chewing or eating. **2.** the sound of lapping. **3.** adv. noisily (of eating or drinking).

चपड़ना *capaṛnā*, v.i. reg. to slip away, to evade.

[1]**चपड़ा** *capṛā*, m. lac.

[2]**चपड़ा** *capṛa*, m. reg. (Bihar) a tough, quickly spreading grass resembling twitch.

चपड़ासी *capṛāsī* [? f. P. *caprāst*, H. *capṭā*], m. = चपरासी.

चपत *capat* [cf. **carpa-*], f. (m., *Pl*). a slap, a thump. — ~ जमाना, or झड़ना, or लगाना (को), to slap. ~ दे मारना (को), v.t. id. ~ पड़ना, transf. a loss to befall (one).

चपना *capnā* [cf. H. **capp-*: Pk. *cappaï*], v.i. **1.** to be pressed, compressed; to be squeezed; to be crushed. **2.** to be abashed; to be intimidated.

चपनी *capnī*, f. *Pl. HŚS.* flat lid or cover of a pot.

चपरास *caprās* [? P. *caprāst*], f. **1.** metal badge or plate (worn as identification by messengers or orderlies). **2.** belt-clasp, buckle.

चपरासी *caprāsī* [cf. H. *caprās*], m. an orderly, or official messenger; peon.

चपरि *capari* [ad. *capalam*, adv.], adv. Brbh. Av. quickly, instantly.

चपरी *caprī*, f. *Pl. HŚS.* a small pulse (resembling gram).

चपल *capal* [S.], adj. & m. **1.** adj. tremulous, unsteady; restless. **2.** active; agile, swift. **3.** inconstant, fickle; volatile. **4.** m. an unsteady person, &c.

चपलता *capalătā* [S.], f. **1.** activity; quickness, agility. **2.** unsteadiness, restlessness. **3.** inconstancy; volatility.

चपला *capălā* [S.], f. **1.** lightning. **2.** the goddess Lakṣmī.

चपलाई *capălāī* [cf. H. *capal*], f. Brbh. = चपलता.

चपाती *capātī* [conn. **carpa-*], f. a thin cake of unleavened bread.

चपाना *capānā* [cf. H. *capnā*], v.t. **1.** to press, to press down; to squeeze; to crush. **2.** *HŚS.* to splice (the strands of a rope). **3.** to abash; to intimidate.

चपेकना *capeknā* [cf. H. *cipaknā*, *capaknā*], v.t. reg. 1. = चिपकाना, 1. **2.** to force (sthg.) on (a person).

चपेट *capeṭ* [**cappeṭṭa-*: ← Drav.], m. **1.** a slap. **2.** a blow. **3.** fig. attack; sudden blow or shock; range, reach (of sthg. harmful). — ~ में आना, to be threatened (by, की: as by sthg. dangerous); to fall victim (to).

चपेटना *capeṭnā* [cf. H. *capeṭ*], v.t. **1.** to attack, to assail. **2.** fig. to berate.

चपेटा *capeṭā*, m. = चपेट.

चप्पल *cappal* [cf. **carpa-*], f. a sandal; an open-heeled slipper.

चप्पल-सेहुँड़ *cappal-sehuṁṛ*, f. the prickly pear, *Opuntia dillenii* (= नाग-फनी).

चप्पा *cappā* [? *catv(ara-)*], m. four (fingers') breadth: a span, small amount, of land. — चप्पा-चप्पा, m. every inch of ground.

चप्पी *cappī*, f. *Pl. HŚS.* massaging the limbs.

चप्पू *cappū* [**carpa-*], m. a paddle; an oar. — ~ मारना, or चलाना, to row.

चबक *cabak* [cf. H. *cabaknā*], f. *Pl. HŚS.* a throb or shoot of pain.

चबकना *cabaknā*, f. *Pl. HŚS.* to throb or to shoot with pain.

चबना *cabnā* [cf. *cabānā*], v.i. to be chewed. — चबनी हड्डी, f. *Pl. HŚS.* gristle, cartilage.

चबर-चबर *cabar-cabar* [cf. H. *cabnā*], f. jabber, chatter.

चबवाना *cabvānā* [cf. H. *cabānā*], v.t. to cause to be chewed.

चबाई *cabāī* [cf. H. *cabānā*], f. chewing, &c.

चबाना *cabānā* [cf. *carvati*], v.t. **1.** to chew; to gnaw; to crunch. **2.** to bite (the lip: in amazement, perplexity or mortification). **3.** to cause to chew. — चबाने का दाँत, m. a molar tooth. – चबा-चबाकर बातें करना, to speak indistinctly; to speak slowly or hesitantly; to speak affectedly, or haughtily. - चबा डालना, colloq. to chew (one) up, to eat (one) alive. चबे को, or चबाई बातें, ~, to go over old ground.

चबूतरा *cabūtrā* [? cf. **caturvṛtta-*], m. **1.** a platform; base (as of a temple, or mosque). **2.** a terrace; an open raised area. — ~ बाँधना, to construct a platform, &c.

चबेना *cabenā* [cf. *carvati*, *carvayati*], m. something to be chewed: parched grain (as food).

चबेनी *cabenī* [cf. H. *cabenā*], f. 1. = चबेना. **2.** a light midday snack (as grain, sweets).

चबोड़ *caboṛ* [cf. H. *cabānā*, *cabonā*], adj. & f. *Pl.* **1.** adj. crushed, bruised. **2.** f. a joke.

चभक *cabhak*, f. pricking, stinging.

चभच्चा *cabhaccā*, m. pronun. var. = चहबच्चा.

चभड़-चभड़ *cabhaṛ-cabhaṛ* [cf. H. *căbhnā*], f. = चपड़-चपड़.

चभना *cabhnā* [cf. H. *cābhnā*], v.i. reg. to be chewed or crushed.

चमक *camak* [**cammakka-*: Pk. *camakka-*], f. **1.** sparkle, glitter. **2.** a flash, gleam; brilliance, splendour. **3.** a sudden or startled impulse (as of fear). **4.** a shooting pain. — ~ देना, to gleam, to glitter. – चमक-चोट, f. bedazzling: duping. चमक-दमक, f. glitter; brilliance; splendour. चमकदार [P. *-dār*], adj. glittering, gleaming; brilliant, splendid. चमकदार गोली, f. a tracer bullet.

चमकना *camaknā* [*cammakka-] **1.** to shine, to sparkle; to glitter; to glow; to glare; to gleam (as metal, or light); to be polished. **2.** to be dazzled, or screwed up (the eyes, in strong light). **3.** to be attractive, or seductive. **4.** to prosper, to flourish (as an enterprise); to be brisk (as trade), to go well; to be prominent. **5.** to go to the head (alcohol). **6.** to be strongly aroused (the emotions); to become enraged. **7.** to be startled, to start; to shy (a horse); Brbh. to scatter, or to rush away (to safety).

चमकवाना *camakvānā* [cf. H. *camaknā*], v.t. to cause to shine, &c.; to get made bright, to have polished, &c. (by another, से).

चमकाना *camkānā* [cf. H. *camaknā*], v.t. **1.** to cause to shine or to glitter; to cause to flash or to gleam; to cause to glow; to display, to make brilliant or attractive; to burnish, to polish; to brandish, to flourish (as a sword). **2.** to flash (the eyes, or glance). **3.** to cause to prosper; to make prominent or celebrated. **4.** to rouse, to stir up (emotions: in, में); to irritate; to provoke. **5.** to startle; to cause to shy (a horse).

चमकारा *camkārā* [cf. *camakka-], adj. E.H. dazzling; brilliant.

चमकारी *camkārī* [? *camatkāritā-], f. E.H. brilliance.

चमकी *camkī* [cf. H. *camaknā*], f. tinsel, a spangle; foil.

चमकीला *camkīlā* [cf. H. *camaknā*], adj. **1.** sparkling, glittering. **2.** brilliant, splendid.

चमकीलापन *camkīlāpan* [cf. H. *camkīlā*], m. **1.** sparkle, glitter. **2.** brilliance.

चमकौवल *camkauval* [cf. H. *camkānā*], adj. & f. **1.** adj. *Pl.* shining, &c. (= चमकीला). **2.** f. *HŚS.* causing to shine; ogling, or seductive gesturing.

चमक्को *camakko* [cf. H. *camaknā*], f. **1.** a seductive woman. **2.** a brazen or shameless woman.

चमगादड़ *camgādaṛ*, m. **1.** a bat. **2.** a flying fox. **3.** fig. one without principles (who moves at random in different directions).

चम-चम *cam-cam* [cf. H. *camcamānā*], adv. = चमाचम.

चमचमाना *camcamānā* [cf. *camma(kka)-], v.i. & v.t. **1.** v.i. to shine, to sparkle; to glitter. **2.** v.t. to make shiny, &c.; to clean well; to polish.

चमचमाहट *camcamāhaṭ* [cf. H. *camcamānā*], f. brightness, sparkle; glitter.

चमचा *camcā*, m. **1.** a large spoon. **2.** a ladle. **3.** pej. a yes-man; flatterer. — ~ भर, m. a spoonful.

चम-चिच्चड़ *cam-ciccaṛ* [H. *cām*+H. *cicṛī*], m. colloq. one who sticks to the skin like a tick: an unwanted attendant or hanger-on.

चमची *camcī* [cf. H. *camcā*], f. **1.** a small spoon. **2.** spatula.

चमड़ा *camṛā* [cf. *carman-*], m. **1.** hide; skin. **2.** leather. **3.** colloq. condom. — ~ उतारना, or उधेड़ना, or खींचना, or निकालना (का), to skin, to flay: colloq. to tan the hide (of), to beat badly. ~ कमाना, to process or to tan hide(s). ~ सिझाना, id.

चमड़ी *camṛī* [cf. H. *camṛā*], f. **1.** skin (of the human body). **2.** hide (= चमड़ा).

चमत्कार *camatkār* [S.], m. **1.** sthg. astonishing; sthg. splendid; a spectacle; miracle. **2.** wonderful quality, or achievement. **3.** amazement, astonishment. — चमत्कारपूर्ण, adj. astonishing; splendid, wonderful.

चमत्कारक *camatkārak* [cf. H. *camatkār*], m. *HŚS.* = चमत्कारी, m.

चमत्कारिक *camatkārik* [S.], adj. = चमत्कारी.

चमत्कारित *camatkārit* [S.], adj. astonished.

चमत्कारिता *camatkāritā* [S.], f. astonishing nature, or quality.

चमत्कारी *camatkārī* [S.], adj. & m. **1.** adj. astonishing; splendid, wonderful. **2.** m. an astonishing or wonderful person.

चमत्कृत *camatkṛt* [S.], adj. astonished.

चमत्कृति *camatkṛti* [S.], f. astonishment.

चमन *caman* [P. *caman*], m. **1.** a flower garden. **2.** a place lush or abounding in flowers. **3.** fig. a flourishing place.

चमर *camar* [S.], m. **1.** the yak. **2.** a yak's tail: a flywhisk. — चमर-गाय, f. a yak cow. चमर-पुच्छ, adj. & m. having a flowing tail; a fly-whisk. चमर-बगली, f. the small green (crested) bittern. चमर-बैल, m. a yak bullock. चमर-शिखा, f. ornamental crest (fixed over a horse's head).

चमर- *camar-* [H. *camār*]. = चमार: — चमर-चलाक, adj. deceitful, cunning. °ई, f.

चमरख *camrakh* [*carmarakṣā-], f. reg. **1.** the pieces of leather forming the bearings of the axle of a spinning-wheel. **2.** *Pl.* the leather strap which goes round a spinning- wheel. **3.** fig. sthg. dried or wizened. चमरौधा, adj. & f. reg. **1.** adj. made of leather: of heavy or country make (shoes). **2.** f. *HŚS.* a heavy country-made shoe.

चमरस *camras* [cf. *carma-*], m. *Pl. HŚS.* a sore place on the foot caused by chafing of a shoe.

चमरावत *camrāvat*, f. reg. (W.) a leather-worker's fee or payment in kind.

चमरी *camrī* [S.], f. **1.** a yak cow. **2.** a flywhisk (cf. **चमर**).

चमला *camlā*, m. *Pl. HŚS.* = **चंबल**.

चमाइन *camāin*, f. reg. = **चमारिन**; a village midwife.

चमाऊ *camāū*, m. (? f., *Pl.*) reg. = **चमौवा**.

चमाचम *camācam*, adv. with a flash or glitter, brightly.

चमार *camār* [*carmakāra-*], m. **1.** a leather-worker; a tanner; shoemaker. **2.** a man belonging to the *camār* or leather-workers' community. **3.** fig. a base person.

चमारन *camāran*, f. = **चमारिन**.

चमारनी *camārnī*, f. = **चमारिन**.

चमारिन *camārin* [cf. H. *camār*], f. a woman of the *camār* community; the wife of a leather-worker.

चमारी *camārī*, f. & adj. 1. = **चमारिन**. **2.** the occupation of a *camār*. **3.** adj. having to do with a *camār*, or *camārs*.

चमूकन *camūkan* [**carmotkuna-*], m. *Pl. HŚS.* a louse; a tick (on cattle).

चमेली *camelī* [**campavelli-*] the jasmine, *Jasminium grandiflorum*, and its flower.

चमोकन *camokan* [**carmotkuna-*], m. reg. a body louse; a tick (on cattle).

चमोटा *camoṭā* [*carmapaṭṭa-*], m. a leather strap; strop.

चमोटी *camoṭī*, f. dimin. reg. = **चमोटा**.

चमौवा *camauvā*, m. *HŚS.* = **चमरौधा**.

चम्मच *cammac*, m. a spoon. — **चम्मच-बोजा** [P. *-būza*], m. the spoonbill.

चयन *cayan* [S.], m. selection.

[1]**चर** *car* [S.], adj. & m. **1.** adj. moving, going; movable, shifting. **2.** animate. **3.** m. a spy. **4.** an agent, emissary. — **चराचर** [°*ra*+*a*°], adj. & m. animate and inanimate; the world, or creation, in their entirety; the heavens.

[2]**चर** *car* [**caṭa-*], f. m. the sound made by tearing cloth, breaking wood, &c.; a crackling sound (= **चड़**). — **चर-चर**, f. see s.v.

चरक *carak*, m. white leprosy.

चरकटा *carkaṭā* [H. *cārā*+H. *kāṭnā*], m. **1.** one who cuts fodder. **2.** one who does menial work.

चरका *carkā* [conn. H. *carak*], m. U. **1.** a slight wound. **2.** trickery. — **उसके चरके में मत आओ**, don't be taken in by him.

चरख़ *carkh* [P. *carkh*], m. **1.** a wheel; a potter's wheel. **2.** a lathe. **3.** a spinning-wheel. — ~ **चढ़ाना**, v.t. to turn (on a lathe). ~ **चढ़ना**, to be turned (as on a lathe). – **चरख़-चूँ**, m. the creaking of a wheel.

चरख़ा *carkhā* [P. *carkha*], m. **1.** a wheel; pulley; reel, bobbin; spindle. ***2.** a spinning-wheel. **3.** any machine for twisting thread, wire, &c. **4.** a machine for pressing sugar-cane. **5.** colloq. a nag; a frail old person; a rickety cart. **6.** fig. a round of work, or burdensome task. — ~ **कातना**, to spin. ~ **चलाना**, id.; fig. to spin a long story. – **चरख़ा-पूनी**, °**-पोनी**, f. spinning and carding.

चरख़ी *carkhī* [H. *carkhā*], f. 1. = **चरख़ा**, 1.-3. **2.** a potter's wheel. **3.** an instrument for separating cotton from the seed. **4.** a firework, Catherine wheel. **5.** chamber (of a revolver).

चरग *carg* [ad. P. *carkh*], m. E.H. a falcon.

चरच- *carac-* [cf. *carcā-*], v.t. Av. **1.** to smear (upon); to anoint. **2.** to adopt, to take up. **3.** *Pl. HŚS.* to worship.

चर-चर *car-car* [**caṭa-*], f. **1.** sound of talking; chatter, gabble. **2.** a crackling sound; creaking (of shoes); tearing (of cloth); scratching (of a pen); grating, rough sound (of a voice); rattling sound (of a cart).

चरचरा *carcarā* [cf. H. *car-car*], adj. & m. 1. = **चरपरा**. **2.** *HŚS.* a bird resembling the *muniyās* (? = **चरचरी**).

चरचराना *carcarānā* [cf. H. *car-car*, *carcarā*], v.i. & v.t. **1.** v.i. to make a cracking or crackling sound; to crack; to creak (as shoes); to scratch (as a pen); to tear (as cloth); to sputter; to break with a crack. **2.** to smart, to burn (as a wound); to tingle. **3.** v.t. to break (sthg.) with a crack.

चरचराहट *carcarāhaṭ* [cf. H. *car-car*, *carcarā*], f. **1.** a cracking or crackling sound, &c. **2.** a smarting, or burning.

चरचरी *carcarī* [H. *carcarā*], f. the Indian pipit (*Anthus novaeseelandiae*).

चरचूँ *carcūṁ* [H. *car*; onom.], m. **1.** creaking sound (as of a cart-wheel). **2.** idle chatter.

चरट *caraṭ* [S.], m. *Pl. HŚS.* a wagtail.

चरड़-चरड़ *carar̤-carar̤* [cf. H. *car*], f. = चर-चर.

चरण *caraṇ* [S.], m. **1.** usu. pl. and hon. foot; feet. **2.** a quarter; section; phase, stage. **3.** a foot (of verse); single line (of verse). **4.** fig. proximity; attendance; dependence. — ~ छूना (के), to touch (a person's) feet in respect. ~ देना (के), to set foot, to be an auspicious guest or visitor. ~ पड़ना (के), to appear as an auspicious guest or visitor. ~ लेना (के), = ~ छूना. चरणों पड़ना (के), to fall at (one's) feet (as in respect, love, or entreaty). चरणों में चढ़ाना, to offer (to a deity, or to a loved or respected person). चरणों में प्रणाम करना (के), = ~ छूना. चरोणों में रहना (के), to remain near (one); to attend, to serve (as a devotee). – चरण-कमल, m. pl. (hon.) lotus feet. चरण-चिह्न, m. pl. foot-prints; representations of the feet of a deity. चरण-दास, m. servant, attendant (of a revered personage). °ई, f.; a subservient wife. चरण-पादुका, f. a wooden sandal; pl. = चरण-चिह्न, 2. चरण-पूजा (की), f. worship of (a person's) feet; ceremonial salutation (of). चरण-युग, m. pair of feet: the feet of a deity or of a revered person. चरण-रज, f. the dust of the feet of a revered person. चरण-वंदना, f. = चरण-पूजा. चरण-सरोज, m. pl. = चरण-कमल. चरण-सेवा, f. massaging the feet; = चरण-पूजा. °-सेवी, m. one who massages another's feet, &c. चरण-स्पर्श, m. = चरण-पूजा; = चरण-सेवा. चरणांबुज [°*ṇa*+*a*°], m. pl. = चरण-कमल. चरणामृत [°*ṇa*+*a*°], m. foot-nectar: the water in which the feet of an idol or of a respected personage have been washed; a mixture of milk, curds, *ghī*, sugar and honey, considered sacred, and used in the tending of idols and sacred objects. चरणामृत लेना (का), to sip the water in which the feet of an idol, &c., have been washed; to sip. चरणार्ध [°*ṇa*+*a*°], m. a half foot (of verse). चरणार्विंद [°*ṇa*+*a*°], m. pl. = चरण-कमल. चरणोदक [°*ṇa*+*u*°], m. = चरणामृत.

चरत *carat* [H. *calnā*: ? w. H. *vrat*], m. a day not laid down as one for fasting.

चरती *cartī* [cf. H. *carat*], m. one who does not keep a fast.

¹**चरना** *carnā* [*carati*], v.i. & v.t. **1.** v.i. to graze. **2.** to wander. **3.** v.t. to graze; to eat in a crude way. — आँखें ~, colloq. to be blind to sthg. happening before (one's) eyes.

²**चरना** *carnā* [*caraṇa*-: ? ad. G.], m. 19c. shorts. — ~ काछना, to put on shorts.

चरनी *carnī* [cf. H. *carnā*], f. Brbh. forage.

चरन्नी *caranni*, f. reg. = चवन्नी.

चरपरा *carparā*, adj. hot, pungent (food); acrid.

चरपराना *carparānā* [cf. H. *carparā*], v.i. **1.** to taste sharp, hot (food). **2.** to smart, to burn (as a wound); to tingle.

चरपराहट *carparāhaṭ* [cf. H. *carparā*], f. **1.** sharp or pungent taste. **2.** stinging pain, ache; tingling.

चरफरा- *carpharā*-, v.i. Av. to be restless, restive.

चरबाँक *carbāṁk* [P. *carb*, H. *cal*-+H. *bāṁk*], adj. **1.** smooth-spoken, plausible; unctuous. **2.** quick-tongued, clever; glib. **3.** brazen, shameless. — चरबाँकदीदा, adj. inv. brazen, wanton.

चरबी *carbī* [P. *carbī*], f. fat; grease; suet; tallow. — ~ चढ़ना (शरीर पर), to grow fat. ~ छाना, v.i. to grow fat; to grow self-centred, or domineering. – चरबीदार [P. *-dār*], adj. fat; sleek; fatty; greasy.

चरम *caram* [S.], adj. **1.** ultimate, final; last. **2.** supreme. — ~ सीमा, f. ultimate limit: climax, perfection. — चरम-पंथ, m. the final way or recourse: an extremist attitude. °ई, adj. & m. extremist.

चरमर *carmar*, f. & adj. = चर-चर.

चरवाई *carvāī* [cf. H. *carvānā*], f. = चरवाही, 1., 2.

चरवाना *carvānā* [cf. H. *carnā*], v.t. **1.** to cause to graze. **2.** to cause to be grazed.

चरवाहा *carvāhā*, m. a herdsman, shepherd.

चरवाही *carvāhī* [cf. H. *carvānā*; ? ×H. *bāhnā*], f. **1.** the work of looking after grazing animals. **2.** price paid for grazing, or for pasturage. — ~ करना (की), to tend grazing animals.

चरवैया *carvaiyā* [cf. H. *carvānā*], m. = चरवाहा.

चरस *caras* [**carassa*-], m. **1.** reg. a large leather bag or bucket (for drawing water from wells). ***2.** a resinous preparation of hemp, cannabis (= गाँजा: but ? orig. denoted imported hemp).

चरसा *carsā* [**carassa*-], m. a large leather bag or bucket (= चरस).

चरसिया *carsiyā* [cf. H. *caras*], m. **1.** the man who empties well-water from a *caras* or leather bag into an irrigation channel. 2. = चरसी.

चरसी *carsī* [cf. H. *caras*], m. one addicted to smoking hemp.

चरा *carā* [P. *carā*], m. grazing, pasturing; pasture. — चरा-गाह, f. grazing-ground, pasture; a meadow.

चराई *carāī* [cf. H. *carānā*], f. **1.** sending animals out to graze; pasturing. **2.** grazing land, pasturage. **3.** price paid for grazing; rent for pasturage.

चराक *carāk*, m. *Pl.* an animal that grazes.

चरान *carān* [? conn. Panj. *carānd*; (Bihar) *carāṁṭ*], m. *Pl.* pasture land.

चराना *carānā* [cf. H. *carnā*], v.t. **1.** to tend (grazing animals); to graze; to feed (animals). **2.** transf. to have (a person) under (one's) command or control. **3.** to lead (by the nose), to make a fool of.

चराव *carāv* [cf. H. *carānā*], m. pasture-ground.

चरिंदा *carindā* [P. *carinda*], m. U. grazing: an animal (esp. herbivorous).

चरित *carit* [S.], m. **1.** behaviour, practice; acts, deeds. **2.** narrative of a person's life; a biography. **3.** an institutionalised observance. **4.** disposition of mind, character. — **चरित-नायक**, m. the subject of a biography. **चरितार्थ** [°*ta*+*a*°], adj. attaining one's object, successful; realised, effected. °**ता**, f. attainment of one's object, &c.

चरित्र *caritr* [S.], m. **1.** behaviour, conduct; manner; ways. **2.** an account of a person's life; a biography. **3.** character; nature. **4.** a character (as of a novel: = पात्र). — **चरित्र-चित्रण**, m. character portrayal. **चरित्र-नायक**, m. = चरित-नायक. **चरित्र-भ्रष्ट**, adj. of degenerate character. **चरित्रवान** adj. °-**वती**, f. of good character, virtuous. **चरित्र-वैचित्र्य**, m. a peculiarity of character. **चरित्रहीन**, adj. characterless; of base character. **चरित्रांकन**]°*tra*+*a*°], m. character portrayal.

[1]**चरी** *carī* [S.], f. = चर, 1.

[2]**चरी** *carī* [cf. *carā*-], f. green stalks (of *jvār* grass) cut for fodder.

चरुआ *caruā* [cf. *caru*-], m. a large earthen pot.

चरैया *caraiyā*, m. = चरवाहा.

चर्चा *carcā* [S.], f. (m., U.) repetition: **1.** discussion, consideration, reflection; argument; talk, mention. **2.** rumour, gossip. **3.** smearing (as the body with ointment), anointing. — **~ उठना**, discussion to arise (of, की); mention to be made (of). **~ करना**, to make mention (of, की), &c. **~ चलाना** (की), to spread, or to deal in, rumours (about, की). **~ होना** (की), to be mentioned, talked of, or discussed; to be reported, announced.

चर्चित *carcit* [S.], adj. **1.** smeared; anointed. **2.** -चर्चित. discussed, &c.

चर्म *carm* [S.], m. **1.** skin, hide; leather. **2.** parchment. — **चर्मकार**, m. a worker with leather or hides. °**ई**, f. working with leather or hides. **चर्मकार्य**, m. working with leather or hides. **चर्म-चक्षु**, m. *philos.* the eyes of the material body (as opposed to those of the spirit). **चर्म-वाद्य**, m. any percussion instrument having a leather membrane. – **चर्ममय**, adj. made of skin or leather; covered with leather.

चर्मार *carmār* [H. *camār*: ad. *carma*-], m. *HŚS*. = चमार.

चर्मी *carmī* [S.], adj. **1.** having a hide or skin; covered with hide, or parchment. **2.** made of leather.

चर्या *caryā* [S.], f. **1.** an activity or routine (esp. one prescribed or sanctioned by religion or custom); manner of behaviour. **2.** work, occupation; service.

चर्रमर्र *carrmarr* [cf. **caṭa*-; onom.], f. & adj. **1.** f. = चर-चर. **2.** gabbling (of conversation). **3.** adj. crackling, &c.

चर्राना *carrānā* [cf. H. [2]*car*, *car*(*r*-)], v.i. **1.** to make a tearing, cracking or crackling noise. **2.** to smart, to ache; to throb. **3.** to be felt (as desire, or longing).

चर्वण *carvaṇ* [S.], m. **1.** chewing. **2.** sthg. to be chewed (esp. grain).

चल *cal* [*cara*-[1 2], *cala*-[1 2]], adj. & m. **1.** adj. moving. **2.** unsteady, restless; disturbed, confused; fickle, inconstant; volatile. **3.** movable (assets). **4.** transient, ephemeral. **5.** m. movement. **6.** unsteadiness; mobility. **7.** *math.* a variable. — **चल-चलाव**, m. = चलाचल, m. **चलचित्त**, adj. & m. feeble-minded, inconstant; a fickle or changeable person, &c. **चल-चित्र**, m. a fleeting glimpse; a movie film. °-**चित्रण**, m. filming. °-**चित्रित**, adj. filmed. **चल-मुद्रा**, f. currency. **चल-विचल**, adj. & f. m. unsteady, unstable; displaced, disordered; unsteadiness, &c.; disorder, confusion. **चलाचल** [°*la*+*a*°], adj. & m. movable and immovable; unsteady, restless; variable; stir, bustle; preparation (as for departure); impending death; final departure. °**ई**, f. id.

चलंता *calantā* [cf. H. *calnā*], adj. **1.** valid, current (as coin). **2.** saleable (= चलता).

[1]**चलता** *caltā* [cf. H. *calnā*], adj. **1.** moving, in motion; mobile (as a service). **2.** current, in vogue, customary; in use (as land, an account, coin, a road); in demand (goods); popular. **3.** active, brisk; efficient; thriving (as a business). — **~ करना**, to dismiss, to despatch; to set going; to get (sthg.) working; to originate, to introduce; to carry through. **~ पुरज़ा**, m. colloq. a smooth customer, a shrewd operator. **~ बनना**, to slip away; to slink

away. ~ होना, to be in motion, &c.; to be issued, sent out; = ~ बनना. चलती सीढ़ी, or सीढ़ियाँ, f. an escalator.

²**चलता** *caltā*, m. name of a partic. tree (? *Dillenia indica* or *speciosa*) having a hard strong wood and acid, glutinous fruit.

चलती *caltī* [cf. H. *calnā*], f. sphere of action; authority, influence.

चलतू *caltū* [cf. H. *caltā*], adj. colloq. **1.** current, commonplace (language, matters); hackneyed. **2.** cunning, shrewd (a person: cf. चलता पुरज़ा).

चलन *calan* [S.], m. **1.** going, moving, proceeding, gait; mien. **2.** trembling, unsteadiness. ***3.** currency (of money), circulation (of goods, money); demand (for goods). ***4.** (occasionally f.) procedure; conduct, behaviour; way, manner; habit, custom; fashion. **5.** a ceremony, rite. — ~ करना (का), to introduce, to institute; to make current or fashionable. ~ से, adv. in good manner, well, properly.

चलना *calnā* [*calati*], v.i. & v.t. **1.** v.i. to go, to move, to work (a machine or appliance); to turn (a wheel); to sail (a ship); to blow (the wind); to flow, to run (water, or a water-channel). **2.** to set out, to depart; to start; to be discharged (a weapon); to be used, employed; to be wielded (a weapon). **3.** to progress, to advance; to flourish (a business, a task); to be satisfactory, to work, to serve. उसका काम चल रहा है, his work is going well, or satisfactorily. उसकी चल रही है, he is getting on well. उसकी एक, or कुछ, नहीं चलती, nothing succeeds for him. **4.** to be begun, to be current, or in vogue; to be topical; to be prominent (a reputation); to be in force; to be in use (as a road, a canal); to be offered, or served (successive courses of food). चलते मूड में लिखना, to write as the mood takes (one). **5.** to be exchanged, to be felt (animosity). उनमें ख़ूब चल रही है, they are quarrelling, at sixes and sevens. **6.** to continue, to endure; to be handed down (as a tradition). **7.** to be able to be coped with, or completed (by, से). उससे एक पूड़ी और नहीं चलती, he can't manage (to eat) another *pūṛī*. मुझसे उसकी लिखावट नहीं चलती, I can't (manage to) read his writing. **8.** to conduct oneself, to behave; to be averse or ill-willed; to turn (away from, से); to be deceitful. **9.** to move towards an end; to be decrepit, or worn out; to be finished, done. **10.** v.t. to move (a piece, a counter); to make a move, to take a step. — पेट ~ (का), (one's) stomach to be kept going: an existence to be eked out; a living to be made. मन ~ (का), to be covetous, or eager (of or for, पर), to be attracted (to). चल जाना, to begin to move, to get under way; to be worn out, finished; to die; to be (mentally) disturbed or deranged. चल देना, to leave, to depart; to slip away. चल निकलना, to make good progress (in, में); to go well, to thrive; to be excessive. चल पड़ना, to begin to move, to get under way. चल बसना, to depart for another life: to die. – चला आना, to approach; to return; to be long current (as a tradition). चला चलना, to go, to go one's way. चला जाना, to go, to proceed, &c.; to go away. – चलें, or चलो, imp. interj. come on! let's get going! चलो चलें! id. अपने चलते, adv. to the best of one's ability. यों ही चलते, adv. by the way, by the bye. चलते चलते, adv. while going, on the way; gradually.

चलवाना *calvānā* [cf. H. *calnā*, *calānā*], v.t. **1.** to cause to go, to proceed, &c. **2.** to cause to be driven, &c. (by another: से).

चलवैया *calvaiyā* [cf. H. *calnā*, *calānā*], m. **1.** one who moves, &c.; one who walks or goes about much. **2.** one who causes to move, drives, &c.

चलाऊ *calāū* [cf. H. *calnā*, *calanā*], adj. **1.** lasting, durable. **2.** allowing completion (as of a task): serving, adequate; makeshift. — काम-चलाऊ, adj. serviceable, &c.

चलान *calān*, f. = चालान.

चलाना *calānā* [cf. H. *calnā*], v.t. **1.** to cause to move or to go, to set or to keep in motion; to make (one) go; Av. to send. **2.** to train, to bring up (a child). **3.** to impel, to urge; to drive (a vehicle); to work (a machine, an implement); to wind (a watch); to stir, to agitate (a liquid). **4.** to discharge (a weapon); to fire, to shoot (at, पर); to throw (as a stone). **5.** to use, to employ; to wield (as a weapon or fists); to turn to, to take up (as guile, fraud, force). **6.** to give currency to, to put in circulation; to originate; to publicise or to propagandise for; to talk about (की). किसी की चलाना, to talk (frequently) about, to make play of (a connection or relationship). **7.** to give effect to, to enforce (as an order); to inaugurate, to establish (as a society); to institute (a law-suit); to serve, to offer (food). **8.** to conduct; to transact, to direct; to run (as a firm, a household); to deal (with a person, के साथ). **9.** to carry out, to perform (a task); to manage well or satisfactorily; to puzzle out, to bring to a solution (a difficult matter). **10.** to cause to be finished: to ruin. — पेट ~, to keep one's stomach going: to eke out an existence; to make a living. मन ~, to feel envy or rancour (of or against, पर). हाथ ~, to raise (one's) hand against (पर), to strike. चलाए चलना, to get along, to get by (as with work).

चलायमान *calāyămān* [conn. H. *calnā*], adj. **1.** in motion, newly under way (as a vehicle). **2.** unsteady, inconstant.

चलाव *calāv* [cf. H. *calnā, calānā*], m. **1.** motion, movement; departure. **2.** procedure, conduct; custom.

चलावा *calāvā* [cf. H. *calānā*], m. custom; a partic. custom.

चलित *calit* [S.], adj. **1.** gone, departed; in motion. **2.** unfixed, unsteady. ***3.** current, in vogue, customary.

चलौना *calaunā* [H. *calānā*], m. reg. **1.** a ladle (for stirring). **2.** a stick (for turning a spinning-wheel).

चवन्नी *cavannī* [H. *cau*+H. *ānā*], m. a four-anna piece.

चवाई *cavāī* [cf. **caturvāda-*], m. Brbh. a slanderer.

चवालीस *cavālīs* [*catuścatvāriṁśat-*], adj. forty-four.

चशमा *caśmā*, m. see चश्मा.

चश्म *caśm* [P. *caśm*], f. the eye. — ~, or चश्मे, बद दूर, may the evil eye be far removed (expresses wish for good fortune): evil be to him who evil thinks. - चश्मदीद [P. *-dīd*], adj. seen with (one's) own eyes; having seen with (one's) own eyes. चश्मदीद गवाह, m. an eye-witness. °ई, f. the evidence of an eye-witness.

चश्मा *caśmā* [P. *caśma*], m. **1.** a spring, source; fountain. **2.** glasses. — ~ चढ़ाना, = ~ लगाना. ~ लगना (को), (one) to wear, or to need, glasses. ~ लगाना, to wear, or to put on, glasses. चाँदी का ~ लगाना, to wear silver glasses: to take bribes.

चषक *caṣak* [S.], m. a drinking-vessel; wine-cup.

चस- *cas-* [? cf. H. *cāsnā*], v.i. Brbh. to be split, or divided.

चसक *casak* [**cassakk-*], f. a shooting or throbbing pain; an ache; stitch.

चसकना *casaknā* [**cassakk-*], v.i. to shoot with pain, to throb; to palpitate.

चस्का *caskā* [cf. H. *casaknā*], m. **1.** taste (for, का); inclination, relish. **2.** ardent desire, addiction (to, का); temptation. **3.** habit, vice. — ~ पड़ना or लगना (को), (one) to acquire a habit or taste (of or for, का). ~ होना (को), (one) to have a habit (of), or to be tempted (to).

चस्पाँ *caspāṁ* [P. *caspān*], adj. adhering; sticking or stuck (to, पर). — ~ करना, to affix; to paste (on or to).

चस्पा *caspā*, adj. = चस्पाँ.

चह *cah*, m. *Pl. HŚS.* a platform; pier-head (at a river crossing).

चहक *cahak* [cf. H. *cahaknā*], f. warbling, singing, &c. (birds).

चहक- *cahak-* [**cahakk-*], v.t. Brbh. to burn, to blister; to brand.

चहकना *cahaknā*, v.i. **1.** to warble, to sing (as birds); to chirp; to whistle. **2.** fig. to sing one's own praises, to talk boastfully.

चहका *cahkā* [cf. H. *cahak-*], m. **1.** a burning, or sthg. burning: *HŚS.* a firebrand; reg. (Bihar) a kind of firework. **2.** *Pl. HŚS.* layer of stone or cement on a mud floor.

चहकार *cahkār* [cf. H. *cahkārnā*], f. the sound of (birds) warbling, singing, &c.

चहकारना *cahkārnā* [cf. H. *cahaknā*], v.i. to warble, to sing, &c.

चहचहा *cahcahā*, m. **1.** warbling, singing (of birds); chirping. **2.** chatter, merriment; loud laughter. — चहचहे करना, or मारना, to warble, &c.

चहचहाना *cahcahānā* [cf. H. *cahcahā*], v.i. **1.** to warble, to sing (as birds), to chirp. **2.** to chatter, to make merry.

चहचहाहट *cahcahāhaṭ*, f. = चहचहा.

चहचहिया *cahcahiyā* [cf. H. *cahcahā*], m. *Pl.* a warbler, whistler.

चहना *cahnā*, v.t. pronun. var. = चाहना.

चहबच्चा *cahbaccā* [cf. P. *căh*], m. **1.** a ditch, drainage pit, sump. **2.** reg. (W.) storage-pit (for grain). **3.** reg. vat (as for indigo, or raw sugar).

¹चहल *cahal*, f. merriment, festivity. — ~ करना, to be cheerful; to make merry. — चहल-पहल, f. = ~; bustle, activity. चहल-पहल मचाना, to make merry; to create a bustle or stir. चहलबाज़ [P. -*bāz*], adj. merry, amusing.

²चहल *cahal* [**cakhalla-*], f. reg. a moist loam; a heavy damp soil not needing ploughing.

चहल- *cahal-* [P. *cihal*], adj. forty: — चहल-क़दमी, f. a short walk, a stroll.

चहला *cahlā* [**cakhalla-*], m. Brbh. mud; ooze (cf. ²चहल).

चहली *cahlī*, f. *Pl. HŚS.* reg. pulley for a well-rope.

चहार- *cahār-* [P. *cahār*], adj. four: — चहारदीवारी, f. an enclosing wall (= चारदीवारी).

चहुँ *cahuṁ* [cf. H. *cau-*], adj. = चारों: — ~ ओर, adv. on (all) four sides, all around.

चहूँ *cahūṁ*, adj. = चहुँ.

चहेता *cahetā*, m. desired: dear one, darling.

चहोड़- *cahoṛ-* [? = H. *choṛnā*], v.t. E.H. ? orthogr. var. **1.** to remove (sthg.) to a place of safe keeping. **2.** *Pl. HŚS.* to transplant (rice).

चाँक *cāṁk*, f. reg. **1.** a wooden stamp. **2.** mark or inscription (fixed on a heap of grain, to ward off the evil eye and protect from theft: = थाप).

चाँक- *cāṁk-*, v.t. Brbh. to stamp, to mark (= H. चाक-).

चाँगला *cāṁglā* [cf. *caṅga-*], adj. **1.** sound, healthy, active. **2.** pej. smart, shrewd.

[1]**चाँचर** *cāṁcar*, m. *Pl. HŚS.* 1. = चाचरि. **2.** reg. (Bihar) a cowherds' song; song sung while working in rice-fields.

[2]**चाँचर** *cāṁcar* [?? conn. H. *cāpaṛ*], m. reg. **1.** land left unploughed for a year or more. **2.** a poor clay soil.

चाँचरि *cāṁcari* [*carcarī-*], f. Av. = चाचरि.

चाँचरी *cāṁcrī*, f. reg. (W.) grains or corn left in the ear after treading out.

चांचल्य *cāñcalyă* [S.], m. = चंचलता.

चाँटा *cāṁṭā*, m. a slap, a blow. — ~ जमाना, or मारना, or लगाना (पर), to slap; to strike.

[1]**चाँटी** *cāṁṭī*, f. Av. an ant.

[2]**चाँटी** *cāṁṭī*, f. *hist.* a tax extorted from tradesmen and others.

चाँड *cāṁḍ*, m. pronun. var. = [1]चाँड़.

[1]**चाँड़** *cāṁṛ* [*caṇḍa-*[1]], adj. Brbh. **1.** strong. **2.** fierce, arrogant.

[2]**चाँड़** *cāṁṛ*, f. **1.** *Pl. HŚS.* a pillar, prop. **2.** Brbh. Av. a desire (= चाड़). — ~ सर-, v.i. a desire to be satisfied. ~ सरा-, v.t. to satisfy a desire.

चांडाल *cāṇḍāl* [S.], m. **1.** the lowest of the original mixed Aryan communities. **2.** a man of this group. **3.** an outcaste. **4.** fig. a wretch.

[1]**चाँद** *cāṁd* [*candra-*], m. **1.** the moon. **2.** a moon-shaped (round, semi-circular, or crescent) mark. **3.** a target, mark. **4.** an ornament having a moon-like shape, worn on the head; a large flat spangle set with stones. — ~ का कुंडल, or मंडल (बैठना), a halo round the moon (to form). ~ का टुकड़ा, m. piece of the moon: a lovely, or a handsome person. ~ चढ़ना, the moon to rise; good fortune to dawn. ~ देखना, to be on the watch for, or to see, the new moon as soon as it is visible; to anticipate a welcome event. ~ पर थूकना, to spit at the moon: to bring disgrace on oneself (as by slandering another). ~ पर धूल डालना, = id. आज किधर ~ निकला? rhetor. where has (the present) moon appeared? (expressing surprise or delight at an unexpected arrival, or development). चार ~ लगना (को), to have a splendid or beautiful appearance; to be raised to a high position. – चाँद-बाला, m. an ornament shaped like a half-moon, suspended from the ear. चाँदमारी, f. target practice; a rifle range. चाँदमारी करना, to practise shooting. चाँदमारी का मैदान, m. rifle range. चाँद-सा मुखड़ा, m. a lovely face. चाँद-सूरज, m. an ornament worn in the hair.

[2]**चाँद** *cāṁd* [*candra-*], f. **1.** the crown of the head. **2.** top, summit. — ~ निकल आना, (one, के) to grow bald. ~ पर बाल न छोड़ना, not to leave a hair on one's head: to beat soundly; to despoil (as of goods).

चाँदना *cāṁdnā* [**cāndraṇa-*], m. **1.** moonlight. **2.** light, brilliance.

चाँदनी *cāṁdnī* [**cāndraṇa-*], f. **1.** moonlight; a moonbeam. **2.** a white or shining object; a partic. white flower, *Tabernaemontana coronaria*; a white cloth spread over a carpet. **3.** an awning, canopy. — ~ खिलना, the moonlight to be bright. ~ चौक, m. a splendid public place or market; a partic. wide street in Delhi. ~ छिटकना, = ~ खिलना. ~ रात, f. a moonlit night. चार दिन की ~, f. a short-lived happiness, good fortune or success.

चाँदला *cāṁdlā* [cf. *candra-*], adj. & m. **1.** adj. crescent-shaped. **2.** bald. **3.** m. reg. (W.) a round flat spangle worn on the forehead.

चाँदा *cāṁdā* [H. *cāṁd*], m. **1.** *Pl. HŚS.* a particular marked point: a theodolite or trigonometrical station. **2.** *Pl. HŚS.* observation point (on a rifle range); a butt. **3.** (from its shape) a protractor.

चाँदी *cāṁdī* [*candrikā-*], f. **1.** silver; money, wealth. **2.** income; fig. windfall, good luck. **3.** the crown of the head. **4.** a silvery or whitish object; ash. — ~ कर डालना, or देना, to turn to profit; to burn to ash; to consume. ~ का जूता, m. colloq. silver shoe: a bribe. ~ काटना, v.t. usu. pej. to be coining money. आजकल उनकी ~ है, he is flourishing nowadays.

चाँदीला *cāṁdīlā* [cf. *candra-*], m. Brbh. a bald person.

चांद्र *cāndra* [S.], adj. & m. **1.** adj. lunar. **2.** m. a lunar month. **3.** *Pl.* the fortnight of the waxing moon. **4.** moonstone (a pearly felspar). — चांद्र-मस, adj. & m. lunar; name of a lunar mansion, the constellation Mṛgaśiras. चांद्र-मास, m. a lunar month.

चाँप *cāṁp*, f. = [1]चाप.

चाँपना *cāṁpnā* [**camp-*: Pk. *caṁpai*], v.t. **1.** to press, to squeeze; to put pressure (on). **2.** to press in, to thrust, to cram. — सिर ~, to massage the scalp.

चाँय-चाँय *cāṁy-cāṁy* [onom.], f. noise (as of birds): chirping; cawing; chatter, gabble.

चाँव-चाँव *cāṁv-cāṁv*, f. chattering.

चाँवल *cāṁval*, m. = चावल.

चा *cā*, f. reg. = चाय.

चाइयाँ *cāiyāṁ* [cf. H. *cāīṁ*], adj. & m. pej. **1.** adj. tricky (customer). **2.** m. a trickster.

[1]**चाईं** *cāīṁ* [? *cyāvita-*], f. scab, scurf; mange.

[2]**चाईं** *cāīṁ*, m. *Pl. HŚS.* **1.** name of a community of low status. **2.** a cunning trickster.

चाक़ *cāq* [P. *cāq*: ← T.*çaka*], adj. **1.** trim, smart. **2.** active, vigorous. — चाक़-चौबंद, adj. id.; in good order and condition.

[1]**चाक** *cāk* [*cakra-*], m. **1.** a wheel; potter's wheel; grindstone; pulley. **2.** a ring-shaped or circular object. **3.** a mill. — ~ पूजना, m. *hind.* worshipping the potter's wheel (a marriage ceremony).

[2]**चाक** *cāk* [P. *cāk*], m. & adj. **1.** m. a tear; a slit, cut (as in clothes or cloth). **2.** adj. torn. — ~ करना, v.t. to destroy (as dreams).

[3]**चाक** *cāk* [Engl. *chalk*], m. chalk.

चाक- *cāk-* [cf. H. [1]*cāk*], v.t. Brbh. to encircle or otherwise to mark (as a pile of grain, to discourage theft).

चाकर *cākar* [P. *cākar*], m. a servant.

चाकरानी *cākrānī* [cf. H. *cākar*], f. a woman servant.

चाकरी *cākrī* [P. *cākarī*], f. **1.** service, employment; duty. **2.** a grant (of land) for personal service. — ~ करना, or बजाना (की), to serve, to attend.

चाका *cākā*, m. reg. = [1]चाक.

चाकी *cākī*, f. reg. = चक्की.

चाक़ू *cāqū* [T. *çakı*], m. a pocket-knife.

चाक्षुस *cākṣus* [S.], adj. **1.** having to do with sight, or the eye; visual. **2.** visible. — ~ गवाह, m. an eye-witness.

चाख *cākh* [*cakṣus-*], f. reg. or poet. the eye.

चाखना *cākhnā*, v.t. = चखना.

चाचरि *cācari* [*carcarī-*], f. Brbh. **1.** a kind of song sung with dancing at the Holī festival. **2.** *mus.* the name of a *rāg*. **3.** merry-making at the Holī festival.

चाचा *cācā* [**cācca-*], m. **1.** paternal uncle, father's younger brother. **2.** term of address to a senior or elderly man. **3.** colloq. culprit, villain. — चाचाज़ाद भाई [P. *-zād*], m. a brother fathered by an uncle: a cousin.

चाची *cācī* [**cācca-*], f. **1.** paternal aunt, father's younger sister. **2.** term of address to a senior or elderly woman.

चाट *cāṭ* [cf. H. *cāṭnā*], f. **1.** licking, tasting. **2.** a taste (of sthg). **3.** taste, relish; taste for (sthg.); inclination, propensity. **4.** an appetiser, savoury (as *cole*, *dahī baṛe*); a delicacy (as a spiced fruit or vegetable salad).– ~ पड़ना (की), to get a taste (for). ~ लगना (को), id.

चाटना *cāṭnā* [**caṭṭ-*: Pk. *caṭṭei*], v.t. **1.** to taste, to lick; to lap. **2.** colloq. to try (as a new activity). **3.** to eat greedily, to devour. **4.** to eat away (of insects); to squander. **5.** to burn momentarily without catching (a flame). — किताब ~, colloq. to devour a book. चाट पोंछकर खाना, to eat (sthg.) up with relish.

चाटा *cāṭā*, m. *Pl. HŚS.* vessel used to collect sugar-cane juice (as the cane is crushed).

[1]**चाटी** *cāṭī* [cf. *chāttra-*; ? × *ceṭa-*, H. *celā*], m. a pupil. — चेले-चाटी, m. pl. pupils.

[2]**चाटी** *cāṭī* [cf. H. *cāṭā*], f. dimin. *Pl. HŚS.* an earthen vessel; pitcher; churn.

चाटु *cāṭu* [S.], m. flattery. — चाटुकार, m. a flatterer. °ई, f. flattery. चाटु-पटु, m. a skilled flatterer. चाटूक्ति [°*ṭu*+*u*°], f. flattering words.

चाटू *cāṭū* [cf. H. *cāṭnā*], adj. & m. colloq. **1.** adj. greedy, gluttonous. **2.** discriminating (in food). **3.** m. a gluttonous person. **4.** an epicure. **5.** fig. one who takes bribes.

चाड़ *cāṛ* [? conn. *cāṭu-*: M. *cāḍ*], f. Brbh. love, desire.

चाड़ी *cāṛī* [cf. *cāṭu-*], f. reg. slander.

चातक *cātak* [S.], m. the pied cuckoo or *papīhā*, *Cuculus melanoleucus* (supposed to live only on rain-drops, esp. those falling in the autumn asterism *svāti*).

चातुर *cātur* [S.], adj. clever, &c. (= चतुर).

चातुर- *cātur-* [S.], adj. four: — चातुर्दश, adj. having to do with the fourteenth (of the lunar month). चातुर्मास, m. a period of four months (of the year). चातुर्वर्ण्य, m. the four original social groups taken collectively; their traditionally prescribed activities. चातुर्विद्य, m. one versed in the four Vedas; the four Vedas. चातुर्होत्र, m. a sacrifice performed by four priests.

चातुरी *cāturī* [S.], f. **1.** cleverness, accomplishment; skill. **2.** shrewdness.

चातुर्य *cāturyă* [S.], m. = चातुरी.

चादर *cādar* [P. *cādar*], f. **1.** a sheet; coverlet. **2.** a woman's light shawl. **3.** sheet (of metal). — ~ उतारना (का), to take off (a woman's) shawl: to insult or to disgrace (a woman). ~ ओढ़ाना (को), to give a shawl to wear: to marry (a widow). ~ करना, reg. (N.) to wear a shawl. ~ काली होना, the shawl to be(come) black: to be shamed. ~ चढ़ाना, to offer a *cādar* (at the tomb of a saint). ~ से बाहर पाँव फैलाना, to put (one's) feet out beyond one's shawl: to undertake more than (one's) capacities or resources allow. – चादर-जोड़ा, m. a pair of shawls.

चादरा *cādarā* [P. *cādara*], m. a shawl worn by men (covering head and shoulders down to the waist).

[1]**चाप** *cāp* [cf. **capp-*: Pk. *cappaï*], f. **1.** pressing, pressure. **2.** footsteps, the sound of footsteps.

[2]**चाप** *cāp* [S.], m. a bow. — ~ चढ़ाना, to set (an arrow) to a bow, to bend a bow.

[3]**चाप** *cāp* [cf. H. *cāṁpnā*], m. *Pl.* fibre of the jujube (बेर, झड़बेरी) ? after extraction of the pulp.

चापट *cāpaṭ* [? conn. **carpaṭṭa-*], f. *Pl. HŚS.* husk, bran.

चापड़ *cāpaṛ* [*carpaṭa-*], f. & adj. reg. **1.** f. hard, crusty or stony soil. **2.** a flat expanse of land. **3.** m. reg. (Raj.) husk or flake: bran. **4.** adj. *Pl. HŚS.* laid flat (as buildings, in storm or flood).

चापना *cāpnā* [**capp-*], v.t. **1.** to press. **2.** to clasp (in an embrace).

चापलूस *cāplūs* [P. *cāplūs*], m. a flatterer; sycophant.

चापलूसी *cāplūsī* [P. *cāplūsī*], f. flattery; sycophancy.

चापल्य *cāpalyă* [S.], m. **1.** mobility; quickness of movement. **2.** fickleness. **3.** volatility (of temperament).

चापी *cāpī* [S.], m. *Pl. HŚS.* bowman, archer.

चाफंद *cāphand*, m. *Pl. HŚS.* a kind of fishing-net.

चाबना *cābnā* [*carvati*], v.t. **1.** to chew; to press with the teeth (as the lip), to bite; to crunch; to gnaw; to champ. **2.** colloq. to gobble up, to embezzle.

चाबी *cābī* [Pt. *chave*], f. **1.** a key. **2.** a wedge. — ~ देना, or भरना, or लगाना (में), to wind up (as a clock); to lock.

चाबुक *cābuk* [P. *cābuk*], m. **1.** a whip. **2.** fig. incitement (to, के लिए). — ~ फटकारना, to crack a whip. ~ मारना or लगाना (को), to whip.

चाबू *cābū* [cf. H. *cābnā*], m. a chewer, &c.

चाभना *cābhnā* [*carvati*: MIA *cabbh-*], v.t. reg. = चाबना.

चाभी *cābhī*, f. = चाबी.

चाभुक *cābhuk*, m. pronun. var. = चाबुक.

चाम *cām* [*carman-*], m. **1.** skin, hide. **2.** leather. — ~ के दाम, m. *hist.* leather money (introduced by Nizām the *bhiśtī*, during his three days' rule in the time of Humāyūn). ~ के दाम चलाना, to introduce a leather currency: to stretch temporary authority to the limit; colloq. to work as a prostitute. – चाम-चोर, m. an adulterer. °ई, f. adultery.

चामर *cāmar* [S.], m. a fly-whisk.

चामीकर *cāmīkar* [S.], m. gold.

चामुंडा *cāmuṇḍā* [S.], f. a form of the goddess Durgā.

चाय *cāy* [P. *cā'e*], f. tea. — चाय-ख़ाना, m. a tea-shop, or stall. चाय-घर, m. id. चायदान, m. = next. °ई, f. a teapot. चाय-पान, m. the drinking of tea. चाय-पानी, m. refreshments (including tea). चायफ़रोश [P. *-faroś*], m. a seller of tea.

[1]**चार** *cār* [conn. *catvāri*], adj. **1.** four. **2.** a few; a number (of). ~ आदमियों के सामने, adv. in public. ~ दिन में ही, adv. very shortly. उनके पास ~ पैसे हैं, he has quite a bit of money. — ~ उँगल, or अँगुल, m. the breadth of four fingers, a palm's breadth. °ई, f. id. ~ के कंधों पर चढ़ना, or चलना, or जाना, to mount or go on one's bier: to depart this life. ~ चाँद लगना (में), to have fourfold, or heightened, beauty, or success, or prosperity. ~ टूक, adj. broken into four pieces, completely broken or smashed. ~ तरफ़, adv. = चारों तरफ़. ~ दिन का, adj. fleeing, transient; (one) not long for this world. ~ दिन के मेहमान, m. pl. guests for a few days: transient inhabitants (of this world). ~ दिन की चाँदनी, f. a nine days' wonder. ~ नज़र (नज़रें), f. (pl.) = ~ आँखें. ~ पथ, m. pl. a crossroads. ~ पाँच करना, to talk about this and that; to hedge, to prevaricate. ~ पैसे, m. pl. four pice: a small amount of money; minimal sum (for a purpose). ~ पैसे भी नहीं, hardly any money at all. ~ लोगों का यह कहना है, reg. a number of people say (or, have said) this. ~ सौ बीस, m. colloq. a smart operator (who risks infringing article 420 of the criminal code). आँखें ~ करना, to bring four eyes together: to meet the glance (of, से); to meet (privately: as lovers). चारों ओर,

adv. = चारों तरफ़. चारों ख़ाने चित, or चित्त, गिरना, to fall flat on (one's) back; colloq. to be quite disconcerted or demoralised, or dejected. चारों चूल बराबर, adv. all square (as carpentry work). चारों तरफ़, adv. on all sides, all around, everywhere. चारों दिशा, or दिशाएँ, adv. id. चारों धाम, m. *hind.* the four abodes: the pilgrimage-places Pūrī, Rāmeśvaram, Dvārkā and Badarikāśram. चारों पदार्थ, m. pl. *hind.* the four (chief) things or objects (of life), viz. *arth*, *kām*, *dharm* and *mokṣa*. चारों मग़ज़, m. pl. the pulp of four seeds, used in medicine: *kakṛī*, *kaddū*, *kharbūzā* and *khīrā*. चारों युग, m. pl. *hind.* the four epochs of the world, viz. *satya* or *kṛt*, *tretā*, *dvāpar* and *kali*. – चारख़ाना, adj. & m. see s.v. चार-खूँट, m. the four quarters of the globe, the whole world. चार-चश्म, adj. shameless, brazen; unfaithful, disloyal. चार-जामा, m. a saddle made with four folds of cloth; a garment. चारतार, m. having four strings: a lute with four strings. चारदीवारी, f. an enclosure, courtyard; an enclosing wall (round a house and garden, or a town); ramparts. चारपाई, f. see s.v. चारपाय, or चारपाया, m. a quadruped. चार-बाग़, m. a rectangular garden laid out in four equal and rectangular sections; a cloth or shawl so patterned. चार-यार, m. pl. *musl.* the four successors of Muḥammad, viz. Abū-bakr, 'Umr, 'Us̤mān and 'Alī. °ई, f. a meeting of, or the friendship of, four persons; a Muslim sect which honours equally the four successors of Muḥammad.

[2]चार *cār* [*cāra-*[2]], m. **1.** Brbh. a ceremony or custom. **2.** a present on a festive occasion. — चार-तार, m. finery (of a woman).

[3]चार *cār* [S.], m. Av. a spy or secret agent.

चारख़ाना *cārkhānā* [H. *cār*+P. *khāna*], adj. & m. **1.** adj. chequered; consisting of lines intersecting at right angles (a design). **2.** m. chequered marking; chequered cloth. — चारख़ानेदार [P. *-dār*], adj. chequered.

चारण *cāraṇ* [S.], m. a bard; singer. — चारण-भाट, m. pl. bards and minstrels.

चारपाई *cārpāī* [H. *cār*+P. *pā'e*], f. a bedstead; a bed. — ~ धरना, or पकड़ना, or लेना, = next. ~ पर पड़ना, to take to one's bed; to be confined to bed. ~ बिछाना, to spread or to make a bed. ~ से (पीठ) लगना, = ~ पर पड़ना.

[1]चारा *cārā* [*cāra-*[2]], m. **1.** fodder. **2.** bait. — ~ डालना, to give fodder (to, को); to bait. – चारागाह, f. grazing land.

[2]चारा *cārā* [P. *cāra*], m. **1.** an expedient, a recourse. **2.** a remedy, cure.

चारु *cāru* [S.], adj. **1.** agreeable, welcome. ***2.** lovely, elegant; graceful.

चारुता *cārutā* [S.], f. loveliness, elegance; grace.

चारोली *cārolī* [cf. *cāra-*], f. *Pl. HŚS.* kernel (? esp. of *ciraumjī*).

चार्वाक *cārvāk* [S.], m. speaking agreeably: **1.** the name of a materialistic philosopher. **2.** a follower of Cārvāka. **3.** the views of Cārvāka, atheistic views.

[1]चाल *cāl* [**calyā-*], f. **1.** motion, movement; gait. **2.** pace. **3.** Av. moment of departure. **4.** a move (as in chess). **5.** procedure, method; an action; behaviour; courtesy. **6.** practice, custom; fashion; vogue. नई ~, modern ways, or style. **7.** a means; a scheme; trick; stratagem. — ~ चलना, to act, to conduct oneself; to practise trickery or deception (on, से). ~ दिखाना, to show the paces (of, की); to show one's heels, to be off. ~ पकड़ना, to pick up speed; to become current; to follow the course, or custom (of, की). ~ में आना, or फँसना, to be tricked or deceived (by, की). ~ में ~ मिलाना, to keep step with (one, की). दोहरी ~, f. a quick march, or pace. – चाल-चलन, m. (f.) conduct, behaviour. चाल-ढाल, f. manner, procedure, behaviour; demeanour. चालबाज़ [P. *-bāz*], adj. & m. deceitful, fraudulent; a deceitful person, &c. °ई, f. deceit, fraud; intrigue.

[2]चाल *cāl* [*cāla-*[3]], m. roof, or thatch; house providing cheap rented quarters for tenants.

चालक *cālak* [cf. H. *cāl*], adj. & m. **1.** adj. driving, impelling; motive (force). **2.** *phys.* conducting. **3.** E.H. fraudulent. **4.** a driver; pilot. **5.** *phys.* a conductor. — चालक-मंडल, m. crew (as of an aircraft).

चालन *cālan* [S.: w. H. *cālnā*], m. **1.** causing to move, driving, impelling. **2.** husk, remnant (from sieving or straining). — चालनहार, m. one who drives, or transports; one who sifts.

चालना *cālnā* [*cālayati*], v.t. **1.** to drive, to impel. **2.** to transport, to convey; to remove. **3.** to perform; to direct; to instigate. ***4.** to shake; to sift; to winnow.

चालनी *cālnī*, f. reg. (Bihar) = छलनी.

चालनीय *cālănīyă* [S.], adj. ready or fit to be moved, shaken, &c.

चाला *cālā* [conn. *cāla-*[2]], m. **1.** departure. **2.** an auspicious moment or day for departure. **3.** specif. the departure of a bride for her husband's home on marriage; a bride's return to her father's home, shortly after marriage.

चालाक *cālāk* [P. *cālāk*], adj. **1.** active, quick. **2.** dextrous, clever. ***3.** astute, cunning; vigilant.

चालाकी *cālākī* [P. *cālākī*], f. **1.** activity, quickness. **2.** dexterity, skill. ***3.** cunning; vigilance. **4.** a trick; stratagem. — ~ **करना**, to practise guile (upon, **से**); to deceive. ~ **खेलना**, id. ~ **से**, adv. cunningly, craftily; by unfair means.

चालान *cālān* [cf. H. *calānā*], f. **1.** despatch, consignment; transportation (of goods); transfer (of money). **2.** an invoice; bill of lading. **3.** a remittance; memorandum of financial transactions. **4.** clearance (as of customs). **5.** the sending forward or up, committal (of a case, or a prisoner); colloq. booking. — ~ **करना (की)**, to send up, to commit (for trial); to forward.

चालीस *cālīs* [*catvāriṁśat-*], adj. forty.

चालीसा *cālīsā* [cf. H. *cālīs*], m. & adj. **1.** m. the fortieth year of an era, or of a century. **2.** *hist.* the Indian famine of 1783 (*saṃvat* 1840). ***3.** an aggregate of forty (as days, or verses, or constituents of a medicine); *musl.* a rite performed forty days after a death. **4.** the *Hanumān-cālīsā* (a Brajbhāṣā poem). **5.** adj. numbering forty years.

चालू *cālū* [cf. H. *calnā*, *cāl*], adj. **1.** current, in force; continuing, in progress (as a show, a term). **2.** in working order, active; on, available (a service). **3.** frequented, busy (a street). **4.** pej. cunning. — ~ **हालात में**, adv. in good working order.

चाव *cāv* [cf. **cāh-*], m. **1.** active wish, desire; a need; eagerness, longing; zeal. **2.** cordiality. — ~ **पूरा होना**, a wish, &c. to be satisfied. ~ **में आना (के)**, to become well liked (by), a favourite (of). ~ **से**, adv. with relish; eagerly. **(अपना)** ~ **निकालना**, to satisfy (one's) desire. – **चाव-चोचला**, m. endearment; caress.

चावल *cāval* [**cāmala-* or **cāvala-*: Pk. *cāul*], m. **1.** rice; husked rice. **2.** cooked rice. **3.** a grain (as of rice, or other cereal); the weight of a grain of rice. — ~ **चबवाना (से)**, to make (one) chew rice (in the belief that a thief will be revealed by bleeding from the mouth, or by not salivating, when chewing rice over which an incantation has been uttered). ~ **भर**, m. & adv. a tiny fragment, or amount.

चाशनी *cāśnī* [P. *cāśnī*], f. **1.** a syrup. **2.** a taste, flavour (as of one substance with another). **3.** relish (for, **की**). — ~ **देखना**, to watch (boiling) syrup; to await fruition of (a plan, a plot).

चाष *cāṣ* [S.], m. Av. the blue jay.

चास *cās* [**carṣa-*: Pk. *cāsā-*; or cf. H. *cāsnā*], f. reg. (E.) ploughing; one ploughing (of a field). — ~ **करना**, to plough.

चासना *cāsnā* [**carṣati*], v.t. *Pl. HŚS.* to plough.

चासा *cāsā* [cf. H. *cāsnā*], m. *Pl. HŚS.* a ploughman, cultivator.

[1]**चाह** *cāh* [**cāh-*], f. **1.** wish, desire; need; eagerness, longing; choice, fancy. **2.** will, volition. **3.** affection, fondness. — ~ **से**, adv. with pleasure, or relish; eagerly; lovingly; voluntarily. ~ **होना (की)**, to feel a desire, &c. (for); to be in request or demand.

[2]**चाह** *cāh* [P. *căh*], m. reg. a reservoir: well, pit (cf. **चहबच्चा**).

चाहक *cāhak* [cf. H. *cāhnā*], adj. & m. *Pl. HŚS.* **1.** adj. loving, affectionate. **2.** m. a lover.

चाहत *cāhat* [cf. H. *cāhnā*], f. desire, &c. (cf. [1]**चाह**).

चाहता *cāhtā* [cf. H. *cāhnā*], adj. & m. **1.** adj. owing, due. **2.** m. a due.

चाहना *cāhnā* [**cāh-*], v.t. & f. **1.** v.t. to wish, to desire; to ask for; to be inclined (to); to choose, to approve, to prefer. **2.** to need; to demand; to entreat. **3.** to intend; to attempt. **4.** to like, to love. **5.** to look forward to. **6.** (w. perf. part.) to be about to. **7.** Av. to look at; to look for. **8.** f. (cf. [1]**चाह**.) a wish.

चाहा *cāhā* [*cāṣa-*[1]], m. a snipe; sandpiper.

चाहिए *cāhie* [cf. H. *cāhnā*], v.i., usu. inv. is wanted (by, **को**); is needful (to or for); should, ought. — **मुझे उन्हें पढ़ना** ~, I ought to read them. **मुझे पानी** ~, I need (or want) some water. **मुझे पानी ~ था**, I needed water. **मुझे यहाँ रहना** ~, I ought to stay here. **मुझे ये किताबें पढ़नी** ~, I ought to read these books. **ये किताबें यहाँ रहनी चाहिए**, these books should (or ought to) stay here.

चाही *cāhī* [cf. H. *cāhā*], f. a snipe or sandpiper (the hen bird).

चाहीता *cāhītā*, m. = **चहेता**.

चाहे *cāhe* [cf. H. *cāhnā*], conj. though, even if. — ~ **कितना … क्यों न** …, id. ~ **जितना**, however great, however much. ~ **जो**, whoever; whichever. – ~ … ~, either … or; whether … or. ~ … **पर** (or **तो भी**), though … still, yet.

चाहो *cāho* [cf. H. *cāhnā*], conj. (2 pers. pl. contexts). though, even if. — ~ … ~, either … or; whether … or.

चिंगड़ा *ciṅgṛā* [conn. *ciṅgaṭa-*], m. a shrimp; a prawn.

चिंगड़ी *ciṅgṛī*, f. dimin. = **चिंगड़ा**.

चिंगारी *ciṅgārī*, f. = **चिनगारी**.

चिंघाड़ *cinghāṛ* [**cinghāṭa-*], f. scream, screech, trumpeting (of an elephant); reg. shrieking, screaming. — ~ **मारना**, to scream, to shriek, &c.

चिंघाड़ना *cinghāṛnā* [cf. **cinghāṭa-*], v.i. to scream, to shriek, &c.

चिंचा *ciñcā* [S.], f. the tamarind tree, or its seed (= **चियाँ**).

चिंचिनी *ciñcinī* [ad. *ciñciṇī*], f. E.H. = **चिंचा**.

चिंतक *cintak* [S.], m. & adj. **1.** m. a thinker. **2.** one feeling concern, &c. **3.** adj. in comp. thinking. — **शुभ-चिंतक**, m. a well-wisher.

चिंतन *cintan* [S.], m. **1.** thought, the process of thought. **2.** thinking, reflecting, meditating (over or upon, **का**). — ~ **करना** (**का**), to think over; to ponder (on). – **चिंतनगत**, adj. characterised by thought, or by an attitude; ideological. **चिंतन-धारा**, f. outlook, attitude; ideology. **चिंतनशील**, adj. meditative, reflective. **चिंतन-स्वतंत्रता**, f. independence of mind or thought.

[1]**चिंतना** *cintnā*, v.t. **1.** to think (about); to ponder (over). **2.** to be concerned (about).

[2]**चिंतना** *cintănā* [cf. H. *cintan*], f. 1. = **चिंतन**. 2. = **चिंता**, 2.

चिंतनीय *cintănīyă* [S.], adj. **1.** to be thought about, to be considered. **2.** giving cause for concern, &c.; serious.

चिंता *cintā* [S.], f. **1.** thought, consideration, reflection. **2.** care, concern; attention; anxiety; apprehension. **3.** a matter for thought or concern; risk; danger. — ~ **करना** (**की**), to think (about), to reflect (upon), to ponder; to be anxious or uneasy (about). ~ **लगना**, concern to be felt (by, **को**, about, **की**). **कुछ**, or **कोई**, ~ **नहीं**, there's nothing to worry about; it doesn't matter. – **चिंताकुल** [°*tā*+*ā*°], adj. perturbed by care, &c. **चिंता-ग्रस्त**, adj. consumed or devoured by care, &c. **चिंताजनक**, adj. causing concern, &c.; grave. **चिंतातुर** [°*tā*+*ā*°], adj. distressed by cares. **चिंता-धारा**, f. flow or sequence of thought; outlook, attitude. **चिंतापर**, adj. thoughtful, serious (a person); anxious. **चिंतापूर्ण**, adj. thoughful, serious (a person, or a book, &c.); pensive. **चिंता-मणि**, f. jewel of thought: a supposed jewel granting its possessor all desires; an object infinitely precious to its possessor. **चिंता-मग्न**, adj. immersed in thought, &c. **चिंता-मुक्त**, adj. freed from care, &c. **चिंता-व्यथित**, adj. tormented by care, &c. **चिंताशील**, adj. thoughtful, serious by temperament; attentive; concerned; of powerful intellect.

चिंतायमान *cintāyămān* [cf. H. *cintā*], adj. thoughtful, immersed in thought.

चिंतित *cintit* [S.], adj. **1.** preoccupied; perplexed. **2.** concerned; anxious.

चिंत्य *cintyă* [S.], adj. = **चिंतनीय**.

चिंदी *cindī*, f. a piece, fragment, scrap, rag. — ~ ~ **करना** (**की**), to break (sthg.) to pieces; to tear to shreds, &c.

चिउँटा *ciumṭā*, m. = **चींटा**.

चिउँटी *ciumṭī*, f. = **चींटी**.

चिउड़ा *ciuṛā*, m. = **चिड़वा**.

चिउरा *ciurā*, m. E.H. = **चिड़वा**.

चिक़ *ciq* [T.], f. a hanging screen or blind (made of split bamboo, or of reeds, placed horizontally and strung together).

[1]**चिक** *cik* [? **cikk-*], f. a twinge of pain in the back.

[2]**चिक** *cik*, m. reg. a butcher (of sheep or goats).

चिकट *cikaṭ*, adj. pronun. var. = **चिक्कट**.

चिकटना *cikaṭnā*, v.i. **1.** to be sticky (as the hair). **2.** to be dirty, filthy, greasy, matted.

चिकटा *cikṭā*, adj. = **चिक्कट**.

चिकन *cikan* [P. *cikan*], f. muslin or other cotton cloth embroidered with raised patterning of flowers, vines, &c.; embroidery, needlework. — **चिकनकारी**, f. *cikan* work.

चिकना *ciknā* [*cikkaṇa-*], adj. & m. **1.** adj. oily, greasy; fatty, fat; rich (food). **2.** (of soil) heavy, clayey; loamy. **3.** smooth, glossy; sleek; polished, gleaming; slippery. **4.** bland; unctuous, plausible. **5.** m. oil or grease; fat. — ~ **करना**, to oil, to grease; to smoothe; to polish. ~ **काग़ज़**, m. glossy paper. ~ **घड़ा**, m. a greasy pot: an intractable person; an incorrigible, shameless or debauched person. ~ **देखकर फिसल पड़ना**, to slip at the (very) sight of grease: not to see beyond an (inviting) outward appearance. **चिकनी छालिया**, f. betel nut boiled in milk (eaten chopped up, with betel leaf). **चिकनी डाली**, f. = **चिकनी छालिया**. **चिकनी मिट्टी**, f. potter's clay; clay soil, heavy loam. **चिकनी सुपारी**, f. = **चिकनी छालिया**. **चिकने घड़े पर पानी पड़ना**, water to fall upon (and not to clean) a greasy pot: no good effect to be forthcoming. – **चिकना-चुपड़ा**, adj. oily, greasy; fatty; unctuous, obsequious; plausible, specious; sleek or spruce in dress. **चिकनी-चुपरी बातें करना**, or **बनाना**, to speak plausibly; to cajole; to flatter.

चिकनाई *ciknāī* [cf. H. *ciknā*], f. = **चिकनाहट**.

चिकनाना *ciknānā* [cf. H. *ciknā*], v.t. & v.i. **1.** v.t. to oil, to grease. **2.** to smoothe, to polish; to clean; to make sleek. **3.** v.i. to be or to become oily or fatty, &c. **4.** to be or to become smooth, or sleek, or slippery, &c. **5.** to be or to grow plump; to put on weight. — बात चिकनाकर कहना, to speak in an emollient, or placatory way.

चिकनापन *ciknāpan* [cf. H. *ciknā*], m. = चिकनाहट.

चिकनाहट *ciknāhaṭ* [cf. H. *ciknā*], f. **1.** oiliness, fattiness, &c. **2.** oil, grease; fat; butter. **3.** smoothness; cleanness, polish, &c.

चिकनिया *cikăniyā* [cf. H. *ciknā*], adj. Brbh. spruce, well-groomed.

चिकसा *ciksā*, m. reg. (Bihar) flour, meal.

[1]**चिकारा** *cikārā* [*chikkāra-*: ← Drav.], m. the ravine deer (found in rough terrain on the banks of the river Jumna).

[2]**चिकारा** *cikārā* [*cītkāra-*], m. a two-stringed, bowed instrument of the type of the *sāraṅgī*.

चिकारी *cikārī* [? cf. *cītkāra-*], f. reg. a gnat, mosquito.

चिकित्सक *cikitsak* [cf. *cikitsā-*], m. one who gives medical treatment, a doctor; a *vaidya*. — चिकित्सकीय, adj. medical, medically certified (leave).

चिकित्सा *cikitsā* [S.], f. medical treatment; healing; therapy. — चिकित्सालय [°*sā*+*ā*°], m. hospital; sanatorium; clinic. चिकित्सावकाश [°*sā*+*a*°], m. leave on medical grounds. चिकित्सा-शास्त्र, m. medical science. चिकित्सा-सेवा, f. medical treatment.

चिकित्सित *cikitsit* [cf. *cikitsā-*], adj. treated; cured.

चिकित्स्य *cikitsyă* [S.], adj. treatable, curable.

चिकुर *cikur* [S.], m. the hair of the head; a lock of hair.

चिकोटना *cikoṭnā*, v.i. to nip, to pinch.

चिकोटी *cikoṭī* [? conn. H. *cuṭkī*], f. a pinch (with the fingers). — ~ काटना (में), to pinch.

चिक्कट *cikkaṭ* [cf. *cikka-*[2]: ← Drav.], adj. **1.** sticky; viscous. **2.** greasy, oily; dirty, filthy; shiny, black.

चिक्कणी *cikkaṇī* [S.], f. *Pl. HŚS.* betel nut.

चिक्करना *cikkarnā* [**cītkaroti*], v.i. to cry out loudly; to scream.

चिक्का *cikkā*, m. reg. a children's game resembling *kabaḍḍī*.

चिखर *cikhar*, m. reg. husk of gram (used as cattle-fodder).

चिखवाना *cikhvānā* [cf. H. *cīkhnā*], v.t. to cause to scream, &c.

चिखुर *cikhur*, m. E.H. a squirrel.

चिखुरन *cikhuran*, m. sthg. weeded, a weed.

चिखुरना *cikhurnā* [**cikṣurati*], v.t. to weed (esp. by hand).

चिखौना *cikhaunā*, m. = चखौती.

चिचड़ी *cicṛī*, f. a tick, a louse. — ~ होकर लिपटना (में), to cling like a louse (to).

चिचरा *cicrā*, m. the ḍhāk tree (*Butea frondosa*).

चिचिंडा *ciciṇḍā*, m. reg. = चचींड़ा.

चिचियाना *ciciyānā* [**cicc-*: Pk. *cicci-*], v.i. to utter a high-pitched cry: to scream, to shriek; to squeal; to bleat; to squeak.

चिट *ciṭ* [cf. **caṭyate*], f. **1.** a piece, bit, chip, shred. **2.** specif. a piece of paper, esp. one written on; a chit. — ~ उखड़ना (की), a small piece to be knocked off: to be chipped, to splinter. ~ लगाना (में), to stick a piece (of paper, &c., on); to affix a patch. ~ लेना (की), to take a chit or receipt (in exchange for); to register, &c.

चिटकनी *ciṭhanī*, f. = चटकनी, and चिटखनी.

चिटकना *ciṭaknā*, v.i. = चटकना.

चिटखनी *ciṭkhanī*, f. the bolt of a door.

चिट्टा *ciṭṭā*, adj. **1.** bright, clear; white. **2.** light-coloured.

चिट्ठा *ciṭṭhā* [**ciṣṭa-*], m. **1.** an account (as of revenues, expenditure, lands); roll (as of pay, rent). **2.** transf. pay, stipend (as an outgoing). **3.** a memorandum, list; an estimate; a draft; a note. — ~ उतारना, to prepare an account; to record in an account, to take account of (a payment). ~ बाँटना (को), to distribute pay (to), to pay. ~ बाँधना (का), to draw up a memorandum or account (of); to calculate, to estimate. कच्चा ~, m. a preliminary account, or balance-sheet. कच्चा ~ खोलना, to reveal dubious dealings or actions (on the part of, का). पक्का ~, m. a final balance; a bank statement. – चिट्ठा-बही, f. a rough account or balance-sheet; an account; estimate.

चिट्ठी *ciṭṭhī* [**ciṣṭa-*], f. **1.** a letter; a note; an invoice. **2.** a bill, order, draft, promissory note. **3.** a ballot; a vote. — ~ करना, v. t. *HŚS.* to write or to issue an order (to one's account, के नाम). ~ डालना, or छोड़ना, to post a letter. ~ भरना (की), to pay a bill or an order; to meet (another's) debt. गश्ती ~, f. a circular letter. गुमनाम ~, f. an anonymous letter. रजिस्ट्री ~, f. a registered letter. सिफ़ारिशी ~, f. letter of recommendation or introduction. – चिट्ठी-पत्री, f. correspondence. चिट्ठी-बही, f. a ledger of (registered) letters. चिट्ठी-रसाँ [P. *-rasān*], m.

deliverer of a letter: postman. चिट्ठी-हुंडी, f. bills of exchange.

चिड़ *ciṛ* [**ciḍ-*], f. pronun. var. = चिढ़.

चिड़चिड़ा *ciṛciṛā* [cf. **ciḍ-*], adj. **1.** irritable; touchy, fretful. **2.** short-tempered.

चिड़चिड़ाना *ciṛciṛānā* [cf. H. *ciṛciṛā*; × **caṭa-* or H. *caṛ*], v.i. **1.** to crackle (as burning wood, oil being heated); to creak (as boards, shoes). **2.** to be irritable; to fret. **3.** to be short-tempered. **4.** to be irritated (the skin).

चिड़चिड़ापन *ciṛciṛāpan* [cf. H. *ciṛciṛā*], m. = चिड़चिड़ाहट.

चिड़चिड़ाहट *ciṛciṛāhaṭ* [cf. H. *ciṛciṛā*], f. **1.** irritability; touchiness; fretfulness. **2.** short temper. **3.** irritation (of the skin).

चिड़ना *ciṛnā*, v.t. pronun. var. = चिढ़ना.

चिड़वा *ciṛvā* [*cipiṭa-*], m. rice boiled, pounded and roasted.

चिड़ा *ciṛā* [**ciṭaka-*: Pk. *ciḍiga-*], m. a cock bird; a cock-sparrow.

चिड़ाना *ciṛānā* [cf. **ciḍ-*], v.t. pronun. var. = चिढ़ाना.

चिड़ालू *ciṛālū* [cf. **ciḍ-*, H. *ciṛānā*], adj. & m. **1.** adj. irritating, angering. **2.** m. an irritating person.

चिड़िया *ciṛiyā* [**ciṭaka-*: Pk. *ciḍiga-*], f. **1.** a bird; a sparrow, a hen sparrow. **2.** a shuttlecock. **3.** (in cards) a club, clubs. **4.** fig. a valuable prize, quarry. — ~ का, adj. pej. term of abuse. ~ का दूध, bird's milk: sthg. impossible or absurd. ~ चुनगुन [cf. H. *cunnā*], colloq. small bird(s). सोने की ~, f. a golden bird: = ~, 4. – चिड़िया-ख़ाना, m. aviary; zoo. चिड़िया-घर, m. id. चिड़ियावाला, m. pej. a stupid person.

चिड़ी *ciṛī* [**ciṭaka-*: Pk. *ciḍiga-*], f. **1.** a hen bird, a hen sparrow. **2.** a bird. **3.** (in cards) a club, clubs. — चिड़ीमार, m. bird-hunter, fowler.

चिढ़ *ciṛh* [cf. H. *ciṛhnā*], f. **1.** irritation, vexation (at or with, से); offence, huff. **2.** dislike, aversion (to, से). **3.** a matter of dislike; provocation. **4.** mocking, jeering; a vexatious nickname. — ~ निकालना (की), to irritate; to provoke; to mock, to banter.

चिढ़ना *ciṛhnā* [**ciḍh-*], v.i. **1.** to be irritated (with, से); to take offence, to be wilfully displeased or provoked (at, or by, पर). **2.** to dislike, to be averse (to, से).

चिढ़वाना *ciṛhvānā* [cf. H. *ciṛhnā*], v.t. to cause (one, को) to be irritated, &c. (by another, से).

चिढ़ाना *ciṛhānā* [cf. H. *ciṛhnā*], v.t. **1.** to cause to be irritated, &c.; to irritate; to offend; to provoke. **2.** to cause (one, को) to dislike, to create aversion (to, से). **3.** to mock, to jeer (at, को). — मुँह ~, to mock (one, का).

चित *cit* [**citta-*[2]], adj. lying flat on the back. — ~ करना, to throw (an adversary) on the back; fig. to overthrow; to take aback, to foil. ~ गिराना, id. ~ पड़ना, to fall, or to lie, on the back. ~ लेटना, to lie flat on the back. ~ होना or हो जाना, to be thrown, or to lie, flat on the back; to faint, to collapse; to be laid low. चारों खाने ~, adj. flat on the back, spread-eagled. – चित-पट, f. heads or tails (a game); wrestling.

चित- *cit-* [cf. *citta-*[1]], v.i. Brbh. Av. to look, to gaze.

चितकबरा *citkabrā* [*citra-* + *karbara-* (← Austro-as.)], adj. spotted, speckled, dappled; variegated.

चित्कार *citkār*, m. pronun. var. = चीतकार.

चितना *citnā* [cf. *citrayati*], v.i. *Pl.* to be drawn or painted.

चितला *citlā* [*citrala-*], adj. *Pl. HŚS.* = चितकबरा.

चितवन *citvan* [cf. H. *citavnā*], f. a look, glance. — ~ चढ़ाना, to frown (rare: = त्योरी चढ़ाना).

चितवना *citavnā* [cf. *citta-*[1]], v.t. to look (at, की ओर), to gaze (at).

चितवनि *citvani*, Brbh. Av. = चितवन.

चिता *citā* [S.], f. a funeral pyre. — ~ चुनना, or सजाना, to build a funeral pyre. ~ पर चढ़ना, (one's body) to be placed on a pyre; to mount the pyre (a widow, in self-sacrifice). – चिता-पिंड, m. an offering of cakes, rice, milk, &c. to the spirits of one's ancestors at a cremation. चिता-भूमि, f. a cremation-ground. चितारोहण [°*tā* + *ā*°], m. mounting the pyre (in self-immolation).

चिताखा *citākhā*, m. reg. (W.) = चिता.

चिताना *citānā*, v.t. = चेताना.

चिति *citi* [S.], f. mind, understanding.

चितेरा *citerā* [*citrakara-*], m. a painter, an artist; an engraver.

चितेरिन *citerin* [cf. H. *citerā*], f. a woman painter, artist, &c.

चित्त *citt* [*citta-*[1]], m. **1.** the understanding; the mind. **2.** thought, reflection. **3.** the soul; the heart. — ~ उचटना (से), (the mind) to be bored (with), indifferent (to). ~ करना, the heart to long (to, को, के लिए). ~ चुराना, to steal (one's, का) heart. ~ देना, to give one's mind (to, को), to be attentive; to set the heart (on). ~ धरना, id. ~ पर चढ़ना, to be impressed upon, or to obsess, the mind. ~ बँटना, the mind to be distracted. ~ बँटाना, to divide or to distract the attention. ~ भंग होना, the mind to be broken: to be distracted; to be indifferent. ~ में जमना, or बैठना, to form in the mind (a resolve). ~ में बैठाना, to instil in the mind. ~ लगना (the mind) to be attached, attentive (to, से). ~ लगाना, to apply the mind (to, से). ~ लाना, id. ~ से उतरना, to escape the mind, to be overlooked or neglected. ~ से न टलना, to be ever-present to the mind. – चित्त-चेत, adj. mindful, observant, cautious. चित्त-चोर, adj. & m. heart-stealing; one who delights the heart (esp. Kṛṣṇa). चित्त-निवृत्ति, f. inactivity, or repose, of mind or spirit. चित्त-प्रसन्नता, f. contentment of mind; happiness. चित्तवान, adj. possessed of reason; kind-hearted, amiable. चित्त-विश्लेषण, m. psychoanalysis. चित्त-वृत्ति, f. state of mind; trend of thought; inclination. चित्ताकर्षक [°*tta*+*ā*°], adj. interesting; fascinating.

चित्तरसारी *cittarsārī* [*citraśālikā*-; ad. *citra*-], f. Av. a picture gallery (= चित्र-शाला).

चित्तल *cittal*, m. pronun. var. = चीतल.

चित्ती *cittī* [*citra*-] **1.** a spot, mark, stain; freckle; scar. **2.** a speckled cowric shell. **3.** dot, spot (as on dice, dominoes). **4.** a small white-specked bird (= ¹लाल, मुनिया). **5.** mildew or rot (as in cloth). — ~ खाना, to become mildewed or rotted. ~ पड़ना, a spot, &c. to appear (on, पर or में). – चित्तीदार [P. *-dār*], adj. spotted, speckled, &c.

चित्र *citr* [S.], m. **1.** a picture; a painting; drawing; sketch. **2.** a photograph. **3.** cine film. — ~ उतारना or बनाना, to draw or to paint a picture; to take a photograph. ~ लिखना, *HŚS.* to draw or to paint a picture; to draw a sketch. ~ लेना, to take a photograph. रंगीन ~, m. a coloured picture; a film in colour. – चित्र-कला, f. the art of painting, &c.; graphic art. चित्रकार, m. a painter, artist. °ई, f. the art, or the work of painting, &c.; ornamenting; decoration. चित्र-तल, m. a surface for painting, canvas. चित्र-पट, m. id.; a hanging, roll-painting; screen; cine film. चित्र-बद्ध, adj. depicted, portrayed. चित्र-लिखित, adj. presented as in a picture; attractive; motionless. चित्र-लिपि, f. picture-writing; writing in ideographs. चित्र-लेखक, m. an artist. °-लेखन, m. the painting of pictures, &c.; °ई, f. an artist's brush. चित्रवत्, adj. (motionless) as a picture, stock-still. चित्र-विचित्र, adj. multi-coloured. चित्र-विद्या, f. = चित्र-कला. चित्र-शाला, f. an art studio; picture gallery; a sumptuously decorated room. चित्रस्थ, adj. present in a picture, having been drawn; = चित्रवत्. चित्र-सारी, f. = चित्र-लेखन; Brbh. a picture gallery. चित्रांकन [°*tra*+*a*°], m. = चित्र-लेखन. °आंकित, adj. = चित्र-लिखित. चित्रांग [°*tra*+*a*°], adj. spotted; dappled; striped. चित्रात्मक [°*tra*+*ā*°], adj. picturesque, vivid. °ता, f. picturesqueness. चित्राधार [°*tra*+*ā*°], m. an album; a support for a picture. चित्रालय [°*tra*+*ā*°], m. = चित्र-शाला. चित्रीकरण, m. illustrating (as a book); embellishment. चित्रोत्तर [°*tra*+*u*°], m. *rhet.* an ingenious answer to a question, couched partly in the words of the question itself.

चित्रक *citrak* [S.], m. **1.** a painter, artist. **2.** *HŚS.* an ornamental or sectarian mark on the forehead.

चित्रण *citraṇ* [S.], m. drawing, tracing; delineating (as a character in a novel).

चित्रा *citrā* [S.], f. *astron.* **1.** the star Spica. **2.** the fourteenth lunar mansion.

चित्रिणी *citriṇī* [S.], f. *rhet.* the second division of women; a woman of talent and beauty (cf. *padminī*).

चित्रित *citrit* [S.], adj. **1.** drawn, traced, delineated. **2.** illustrated (as a book); decorated with pictures.

चिथड़ा *cithṛā* [cf. **citth*-], m. & adj. **1.** m. a rag, a tatter. **2.** adj. torn, tattered. — चिथड़े लगना (लग जाना), to be in rags. चिथड़े चिथड़े करना (कर देना), to tear to shreds or to pieces. – चिथड़े-गुदड़े, m. pl. rags, tatters; scattered clouds.

चिथड़िया *cithaṛiyā* [cf. H. *cithṛā*], adj. & m. **1.** adj. ragged. **2.** clothed in rags. **3.** m. a person wearing rags.

चिथाड़ना *cithāṛnā* [cf. **citth*-], v.t. **1.** to tear to rags. **2.** colloq. to scold severely; to humiliate; to vilify.

चिथेड़ना *citheṛnā*, v.t. = चिथाड़ना.

चिद्- *cid-* [S]. see s.v. चित्त. — चिदात्मा, f. the principle of thought, pure intelligence; the supreme being, seen as pure intelligence. चिदानंद, m. intelligence and bliss, as attributes of the supreme being. चिद्घन, adj. compact with, or instinct of, thought: an attribute of the supreme being, or of the supernatural Vṛndāvan (Golok). चिद्रूप, adj. & m. of the nature of or consisting of intelligence; the supreme being. चिद्विलास, m. (the lord's) delight in thought: *māyā*, or the illusory nature of the world.

चिन्- *cin-* [S]. = चिद्-: — चिन्मय, adj., consisting of thought; (truly) alive.

चिनक *cinak*, f. **1.** a stinging, or burning sensation; pain felt when urinating. **2.** irritation, inflammation.

चिनग *cinag*, f. 1. = चिनक. **2.** Brbh. a spark.

चिनगना *cinagnā*, v.i. *Pl.* **1.** to sting, to burn. **2.** to be inflamed.

चिनगारी *cingārī* [cf. H. *cinag*; ? w. *-kārita-*], f. a spark. — ~ छूटना, or निकलना, sparks to be emitted (from, से); (the eyes) to flash. ~ छोड़ना, to emit sparks; to flash (the eyes); to say stinging or wounding things. ~ डालना, to shed sparks; to put a light (to, में), to kindle; to sow discord or confusion (in, में).
~ लगाना, = ~ डालना, 2., 3. ~ लगानेवाला, m. an incendiary.

चिनगी *cingī*, f. a spark (= चिनगारी: also fig).

चिनना *cinnā* [*cinoti*], v.t. = चुनना.

चिनार *cinār*, m. = चनार.

[1]**चिनिया** *ciniyā* [cf. H. *cīnī*], adj. inv. & m. **1.** adj. made of sugar. **2.** sugary, sweet. **3.** white. **4.** m. Bihar. a soft, large, whitish sugar-cane.

[2]**चिनिया** *ciniyā* [*cūrṇita-*], adj. inv. small; young. — ~ केला, m. a very small, sweet banana (*Musa champa*). ~ बतक, f. a duck.

चिनौती *cinautī*, f. = चुनौती.

चिन्ह *cinh*, m. = चिह्न.

चिन्हवाना *cinhvānā* [cf. H. *cīnhnā*], v.t. to cause to be recognised, or distinguished (by another, से); to have marked, stamped, &c.

चिन्हाना *cinhānā* [cf. H. *cīnhnā*], v.t. to cause to be recognised, or recognisable; to mark out, to distinguish.

चिन्हानी *cinhānī* [cf. H. *cinhānā*], f. *Pl. (HŚS)*. a mark, sign, token.

चिन्हार *cinhār* [**cihnadhāra-*], m. *Pl. HŚS.* an acquaintance.

चिन्हारी *cinhārī* [**cihnakāra-*], f. Av. recognition.

चिपक *cipak* [cf. H. *cipaknā*], f. **1.** adhesion: cohesion. **2.** stickiness, &c. (= चिपचिपाहट).

चिपकना *cipaknā* [cf. **cippa-*; **cimb-*; *picc-*], v.i. **1.** to stick, to adhere; to jam, to be tight (as a door); to crowd, to pack (together). **2.** to cling (to, से). **3.** to be involved (with, से); to have an affair (with). **4.** to be absorbed (in or by, में).

चिपकवाना *cipakvānā* [cf. H. *cipaknā*], v.t. to cause to be stuck, &c.

चिपकाना *cipkānā* [cf. H. *cipaknā*], v.t. **1.** to cause to adhere; to stick (on, पर). **2.** to embrace. **3.** colloq. to get (one) into a job or post.

चिपकू *cipkū* [cf. H. *cipaknā*], adj. & m. hanging on; a hanger-on.

चिपचिपा *cipcipā* [cf. H. *cipaṭnā*], adj. sticky; clinging; viscous; slimy.

चिपचिपाना *cipcipānā* [cf. H. *cipcipā*], v.i. to be sticky, to cling (as a wet garment), &c.

चिपचिपाहट *cipcipāhaṭ* [cf. H. *cipcipā*], f. stickiness, &c.

चिपटना *cipaṭnā* [cf. **cippa-*; **cimb-*; *picc-*, **cippiṭṭa-*], v.i. **1.** to stick, to adhere. **2.** to cling (to, से); to embrace. **3.** to be flattened.

चिपटा *cipṭā* [**cippiṭṭa-*; cf. **cippa-*], adj. **1.** flattened. चिपटी नाक, f. a flat nose. **2.** stuck (see चिपटना); clinging (to, से).

चिपटाना *cipṭānā* [cf. H. *cipaṭnā*], v.t. **1.** to cause to adhere; to stick (sthg.) on; to lay close or flat (against sthg). **2.** to embrace.

चिपटापन *cipṭāpan* [cf. H. *cipṭā*], m. **1.** flatness. **2.** adhesiveness.

चिपड़ी *cipṛī* [cf. H. *cipaṭnā*], f. a thin, small cake of cow-dung.

चिप्पड़ *cippaṛ* [? conn. H. *cipaṭnā*], m. a piece, patch.

चिप्पी *cippī* [**cippa-*], f. a piece (stuck on to sthg.); a patch.

चिबिल्ला *cibillā*, adj. = चिलबिला.

चिबुक *cibuk* [S.], f. the chin.

चिमटना *cimaṭnā* [cf. **cimb-*], v.n. **1.** to adhere (to, से); to be pasted, stuck; to cling (to, से). **2.** to be embraced closely. **3.** to attach (oneself) closely (to, से); to be in attendance; to dog (one's steps); to persecute. — चिमट रहना, to stick or to cling close (to, से).

चिमटा *cimṭā* [cf. **cimb-*], m. tongs; pincers; forceps.

चिमटाना *cimṭānā* [cf. H. *cimaṭnā*], v.t. **1.** to cause to adhere, &c. **2.** to embrace closely.

चिमटी *cimṭī* [cf. H. *cimṭā*], f. **1.** pincers, &c. **2.** a nip, pinch. –

चिमड़ा *cimṛā*, adj. reg. = चीमड़.

चियाँ *ciyāṁ*, m. a tamarind seed.

चिरं *ciraṁ* [S.], adv. long, for a long time; long since. — चिरंजीव, adj. & m. long-lived; immortal; a son. °-जीवी, adj. id.

चिरंजी *ciraṅjī*, adj. = चिरंजीव.

चिरंजीवी *ciraṅjīvī*, adj. see s.v. चिरं.

चिरंतन *cirantan* [S.], adj. old, of long standing, ancient.

चिर *cir* [S.], adj. & m. **1.** adj. long, long-lasting; of long standing, ancient. **2.** adv. long, for a long time. **3.** long since. **4.** m. ? a long period. — चिर-काल, m. & adv. a long period; for a long time. चिर-काल से, adv. id.; long since, long ago. चिरकालिक, adj. existing for a long time, ancient. °-कालीन, adj. id. चिर-कुमार, adj. & m. a confirmed bachelor. चिर-जीवन, m. long life; immortality. °-जीवी, adj. long-lived; immortal. चिरतुषार-रेखा, f. snow-line. चिर-नवीन, adj. ever new. चिर-परिचित, adj. of very long acquaintance. चिर-प्रतीक्षित, adj. long awaited. चिर-पोषित, adj. long-nurtured. चिर-मान्य, adj. long-honoured. चिर-रोगी, adj. & m. (one) chronically ill; (one) long ill. चिर-समाधि, f. an eternal trance or sleep; death. चिर-स्थायी, adj. of long-standing existence, or currency. चिर-स्मरणीय, adj. long memorable, never to be forgotten. चिरायु [°ra + ā°], adj. = °जीवी.

चिरकना *ciraknā* [cf. P. *cirk*], v.i. *Pl. HŚS.* to pass excreta in small amounts.

चिरकुट *cirkuṭ* [cf. H. *cīrnā*; **kuṭṭa*-[2] (Pa. *kuṭṭa*-)], m. Av. a bit, piece, rag; a tattered garment.

चिरचिटा *circiṭā*, m. **1.** a kind of grass (it resembles young *bājrā* or millet, and its grain can be eaten). **2.** a thorny shrub, *Lycium europaeum* (its fruit can be eaten, and it has medicinal uses).

चिरचिरा *circirā* [? conn. H. *circiṭā*], m. the plant *Acyranthes aspera* (a source of pearl-ash).

चिरना *cirnā* [cf. H. *cīrnā*], v.i. to be split, cut or torn; to split, to splinter; to tear.

चिरमिराना *cirmirānā*, v.i. to smart, to burn; to tingle.

चिरमिराहट *cirmirāhaṭ* [cf. H. *cirmirānā*], f. smarting, burning; tingling.

चिरवाई *cirvāī* [cf. H. *cirvānā*], f. **1.** causing (sthg.) to split, to be cut, &c. **2.** price paid for having wood split.

चिरवाना *cirvānā* [cf. H. *cīrnā*], v.t. to cause to split, to be cut or to tear; to have or to get split, &c. (as wood, cloth: by, से).

चिराँद *cirāṁd* [cf. *gandha*-], f. the smell of burning leather, flesh, &c. (= चिरायंद).

चिराई *cirāī* [cf. H. *cīrnā*], f. **1.** sawing. **2.** cost of, or price paid for, sawing or splitting (wood).

चिराग़ *cirāg* [P. *cirāg*], m. a lamp, a light. — ~ गुल होना, a lamp to go out, or to be put out; a family line to be extinguished. ~ जले, adv. at lighting-up time, with the fall of darkness. ~ ठंडा करना, to put out a lamp. ~ तले अँधेरा होना, darkness to be found at the base of a lamp: unpleasant things to co-exist with what is good or splendid. ~ बढ़ाना, to put out a lamp. ~ बुझना, = ~ गुल होना. ~ में बत्ती पड़ना, fig. darkness to come on. ~ रौशन होना, a lamp to burn, to be lit. ~ लेकर ढूँढ़ना, to search with a lamp: to search with care. ~ से ~ जलना, a lamp to be lighted from another: to derive profit from each, or one another. ~ से, or का, फूल झड़ना, a lamp to shed sparks (a good omen). ~ हँसना, id. घी के ~ जलना, lamps to burn with *ghī*: to live in high style; to make great rejoicing. – चिराग़-गुल, m. blackout. चिराग़-दान [P. *-dān*], m. a lamp-stand; candlestick. चिराग़-बत्ती, f. a wick for a lamp; a lamp and wick; चिराग़-बत्ती करना, to prepare lamps for lighting, to light the lamps. चिराग़-बत्ती का समय (का वक़्त), m. twilight; dark; evening.

चिरातन *cirātan* [*cirantana*- × *purātana*-], adj. Brbh. old, ancient.

चिराना *cirānā* [cf. H. *cīrnā*], v.t. to cause to be torn; to cause to tear, to split, &c.

चिरायंद *cirāyand* [cf. *gandha*-], f. the smell of burning leather, flesh, &c.

चिरायता *cirāytā* [conn. *cirātikta*-], m. a type of gentian used medicinally, *Gentiana cherayta*.

चिराव *cirāv* [cf. H. *cirānā*], m. **1.** a tear, slit, or cut. **2.** split wood (for fuel).

चिरौंजी *ciraumjī* [cf. *cāra*-[3]], f. the tree *Buchanania latifolia*, and its nut.

चिरौटा *ciraụṭā*, m. reg. a cock bird.

चिरौरी *ciraurī* [?? cf. *cāṭupaṭu*-,], f. ingratiating entreaty.

चिर्क *cirk* [P. *cirk*], m. U. dirt, filth.

चिर्मिठी *cirmiṭhī*, f. *Pl.* wild liquorice.

चिलक *cilak* [cf. **cilla*-[2]], f. **1.** glitter, brilliance. **2.** a shooting pain; a stitch (from running).

चिलकना *cilaknā* [cf. **cilla*-[2]], v.i. **1.** to glitter, to sparkle. **2.** to shoot with pain, to ache.

चिलकी *cilkī* [cf. H. *cilaknā*], f. sthg. glittering, or brilliant: **1.** colloq. a silver coin; a rupee. **2.** a silken, or glossy garment.

चिलग़ोज़ा *cilgozā* [**cillā*- (Pk. *cilla*-) + P. *goza*], m. **1.** the seed or kernel of the Himālayan pine *Pinus gerardiana*; a cone of this tree. **2.** the tree *Pinus gerardiana*.

चिलचिल *cilcil* [cf. H. *cilcilānā*], f. reg. glittering: mica.

चिलचिलाना *cilcilānā* [**cilla*-[2]: Pk. *cillaa*-], v.i. to burn, to blaze (as of the sun's heat, or light).

चिलड़ा *cilṛā*, m. reg. (W.) a fried pulse cake.

चिलबिल *cilbil*, m. a kind of large tree, or plant.

चिलबिला *cilbilā*, adj. boyish, childish; boisterous, uncouth.

चिलबिलापन *cilbilāpan* [cf. H. *cilbilā*], m. boyishness, childishness, &c.

चिलबिल्ला *cilbillā*, adj. = चिलबिला.

चिलम *cilam*, f. a clay bowl with or without stem, in which tobacco, &c. is smoked. — ~ चढ़ाना (की), to fill or to prepare a *cilam* (for); to serve or wait upon (one). ~ पीना, to smoke a *cilam*. ~ भरना (की), = ~ चढ़ाना. – चिलमचट, m. an avid smoker. चिलम-तंबाकू, m. *cilam* and tobacco, makings (of a smoke). चिलम-तंबाकू बंद करना, fig. to outcaste (a man) from his community. चिलमबरदार [P. *-bardār*], m. one who prepares a *cilam*, or a hookah. °ई, f. colloq. menial work. चिलमपोश [P. *-poś*], m. the lid of a *cilam*.

चिलमची *cilamcī* [H. *cilam*+P. *-cī*], f. a metal basin used for washing the hands, &c. (as after a meal).

चिलमन *cilman*, f. a curtain or hanging screen made of split bamboo, or of reeds (= चिक़, चिलवन).

चिलवन *cilvan*, f. Brbh. a screen; a hanging screen of reeds or split bamboo; such a screen, or sieve, used to catch fish. (= चिलमन.)

चिलवाई *cilvāī*, f. reg. (W.) muddy place (as at a well-mouth).

चिलवाना *cilvānā* [cf. H. *cillānā*], v.t. to cause a shout, &c. to be uttered (by, से).

चिलहला *cilahlā* [cf. **cikhalla-*: Pk. *cikhalla-*], adj. *Pl.* muddy.

चिल्लड़ *cillaṛ*, m. a louse (= चील्हड़).

चिल्लपों *cillpoṁ* [cf. H. *cillānā*], f. clamour, hubbub.

चिल्लर *cillar*, m. a louse (= चील्हड़).

[1]**चिल्ला** *cillā* [P. *cilla*], m. a bow-string.

[2]**चिल्ला** *cillā* [cf. P. *cihal*; and P. *cillā*], m. a period of forty days: the coldest period of winter (beginning with the second half of the month of Pūs). — चिल्ले का जाड़ा, m. bitter cold.

चिल्लाना *cillānā*, v.t. **1.** to cry out loudly, to shout; to scream (at, पर); to yelp; to whine (as dogs). **2.** to make an outcry. — चिल्लाकर कहना, v.t. to shout, &c.

चिल्लाहट *cillāhaṭ* [cf. H. *cillānā*], f. **1.** a cry, scream. &c. **2.** outcry, clamour.

चिल्हवाँस *cilhvāṁs* [? conn. **cillipāśa-*], m. Av. snare for a bird (sc. a kite).

चिवाना *civānā* [*citādhāna-*], m. reg. (W.) a cremation site.

चिहाना *cihānā* [*citādhāna-*], m. reg. (W.) a cremation site.

चिहुँकना *cihuṁknā*, v.i. pronun. var. = चौंकना.

चिह्न *cihn* [S.], f. **1.** a mark; spot, scar, stain; print, impression (as of the feet). **2.** a sign, mark; a symbol; badge; emblem. **3.** a symptom; a characteristic. — ~ चढ़ाना (पर), to mark, to brand; to stigmatise.

चिह्नित *cihnit* [S.], adj. marked, distinguished; known, recognised. — ~ करना (को), to mark out, to make recognisable.

चीं *cīṁ* [onom.], f. chirping; chattering, murmuring; squealing; squeaking. — ~ ~ करना, to chirp, to chatter, &c. ~ बुलाना, to cause to admit defeat, &c. ~ बोलना, to utter a cry (as of helplessness, submission); to admit defeat. – चीं-चख, f. hooting (of an owl). चीं-चपड़, f. hesitant or mild objection, colloq. a squeak; impudence.

चींगा *cīṁgā* [**ciṅga-*], m. *Pl.* a young bird.

चींटा *cīṁṭā* [cf. **cimb-*, H. *cimaṭnā*], m. a large ant (black or red). — गुड़ चींटे होना, pej. to consort closely: to be as thick as thieves.

चींटी *cīṁṭī* [cf. **cimb-*, H. *cimaṭnā*], f. an ant. — ~ की चाल चलना, to proceed slowly, or hesitantly.

चींथना *cīṁthnā*, v.t. = चीथना.

चींदी *cīṁdī* [H. *cindī*], f. reg. a washer of leather or other material (on a wheel).

-ची *-cī* [P. *-cī*; ← T. *-ci*], suffix (forms chiefly agent nouns e.g. बावरची, m. cook).

चीकट *cīkaṭ* [cf. *cikka-*[2]: ← Drav.], adj. & m. (f., *Pl.*) **1.** adj. greasy, dirty (as cloth: = चिक्कट). **2.** m. grease, oil, dirt; the deposit of an oil lamp. **3.** *Pl.* a clay soil.

चीख़ *cīkh* [cf. H. *cīkhnā*], f. a scream, shriek; screech. — ~ मारना, to scream, &c. चीख़-पुकार, f. screaming and crying out.

चीखना *cīkhnā* [? **cakṣati*: Pk. *cakkaï* infld. by H. *pīnā*], v.t. = चखना.

चीख़ना *cīkhnā*, v.i. to scream, to shriek; to howl.

चीखल *cīkhal* [**cikkhala-*: Pk. *cikhalla-*], m. mud, mire.

चीखुर *cīkhur*, m. *Pl.* *HŚS.* a squirrel.

चीज़ *cīz* [P. *cīz*], f. **1.** a thing, an article; an item, component. **2.** a commodity, product. **3.** a precious object. **4.** a literary or musical work. — चीज़ें, pl. things, goods.

चीड़ *cīr* [*cīḍā-*], f. a pine or fir tree.

¹**चीतना** *cītnā* [cf. *citta-*¹], v.t. **1.** to think; to think of. **2.** to desire.

²**चीतना** *cītnā* [*citrayati*], m. **1.** to draw, to paint. **2.** to scrawl, to scribble.

चीतल *cītal* [*citrala-*, Pk.*cittala-*], m. **1.** the axis or spotted deer (also called *jhāṁk*, q.v). **2.** *Pl. HŚS.* a large spotted snake resembling the python. **3.** reg. name of the fish called *phalkī.*

¹**चीता** *cītā* [*citraka-*], m. a leopard; cheetah.

²**चीता** *cītā* [*citta-*¹], m. **1.** consciousness. **2.** the faculties; the heart.

चीत्कार *cītkār* [S.], m. a shriek, scream.

चीथड़ा *cīthṛā*, m. = चिथड़ा.

चीथना *cīthnā* [**citth-*], v.t. **1.** to tear to pieces. **2.** to crush.

¹**चीन** *cīn* [S.], m. the country of the Chinese, China. — चीनांशुक [°*na*+*a*°], m. poet. a cloth of Chinese origin.

²**चीन** *cīn* [*cīna-*²], m. a kind of small millet (cf. ²चीना).

चीनना *cīnnā*, v.t. = चीन्हना.

¹**चीना** *cīnā* [*cīnaka-*¹], adj. inv. Chinese: — ~ ककड़ी, f. a type of small cucumber. ~ बदाम (or बादाम), m. the peanut.

²**चीना** *cīnā* [*cīnaka-*²], m. a kind of millet, *Setaria italica* or *Panicum frumentaceum.*

चीनिया *cīniyā* [cf. H. *cīnī*], adj. inv. = चीनी, adj.

¹**चीनी** *cīnī* [cf. H. ¹*cīn*], adj. & m. f. **1.** adj. Chinese. **2.** m. f. a Chinese. **3.** f. sugar. **4.** china, porcelain. — ~ का बरतन, m. a china vessel. ~ मिट्टी, f. porcelain clay.

²**चीनी** *cīnī*, f. the Chinese language.

चीन्हना *cīnhnā* [*cihnayati*], v.t. to recognise.

चीन्हा *cīnhā* [cf. *cihnayati*], m. an acquaintance.

चीपड़ *cīpaṛ* [? cf. **cippa-*], f. secretion of the eye.

चीमटा *cīmṭā*, m. = चिमटा.

चीमड़ *cīmaṛ*, adj. tough, tenacious; inflexible.

चीयाँ *cīyāṁ*, m. a tamarind seed (= चियाँ).

¹**चीर** *cīr* [*cīra-*: ← Drav.], m. **1.** a strip of material. **2.** a rag, tatter. **3.** clothing. — चीर-हरण, m. stealing or taking away clothes (specif. *mythol.* in reference to Duḥśāsana's removing the clothes of Draupadī, and Kṛṣṇa's taking away those of the herdgirls).

²**चीर** *cīr* [cf. H. *cīrnā*], f. **1.** splitting, tearing, cutting, &c. **2.** a split, tear, &c. — चीर-फाड़, f. = ~, 1.; dissecting; *med.* the carrying out of an operation, surgery.

³**चीर** *cīr*, f. = चीड़.

चीरना *cīrnā* [**cīrayati*], v.t. **1.** to split; to tear; to cut; to saw. **2.** *med.* to lance. **3.** to form, to create. **4.** colloq. to acquire by dubious means, to get away with (goods, money).

¹**चीरा** *cīrā* [*cīra-*: ← Drav.], m. a cut, incision; wound. — ~ उतारना, or तोड़ना, to take the virginity (of a girl, का).

²**चीरा** *cīrā* [*cīra-*: ← Drav.], m. reg. (W). a turban (of cloth of striped or wavy pattern).

चीरी *cīrī*, f. Brbh. = चिड़िया.

चीरू *cīrū*, m. *Pl.* (*HŚS*). red thread.

चील *cīl* [*cillā-*], f. a kite (the bird). — ~ के घोंसले में माँस, meat in a kite's nest: sthg. bound to vanish quickly. – चील-झपटा, चील-झपट्टा, m. kite's swoop: violent snatch; a boys' game.

चीलड़ *cīlaṛ* [*cillaḍa-*], m. a louse.

चीलर *cīlar*, m. = चीलड़.

चीला *cīlā*, m. a fried cake of pulse-meal.

चीलू *cīlū*, m. a fresh apricot (or similar fruit).

चील्ह *cīlh* [*cillā-*], f. Av. = चील.

चील्हड़ *cīlhaṛ*, f. a louse (= चीलड़).

चीवर *cīvar* [S.], m. garment of an ascetic (esp. the upper garment of a Buddhist).

चीस *cīs* [**cīssa-*], f. a shooting or throbbing pain (= टीस). — ~ मारना, to shoot with pain, to throb, to ache.

चुँगना *cuṁgnā*, v.t. pronun. var. = चुगना.

चुंगल *cuṅgal*, m. = चंगुल.

चुंगी *cuṅgī* [**cuṅga-*: ← Drav.], f. a portion of produce: duty, levy or toll on produce (esp. that entering a town). — ~ लगाना, to impose a levy. – चुंगी-कचहरी, f. customs office. चुंगी-घर, m. toll-house.

चुंधला *cundhlā*, adj. = चुंधा.

चुँधलाना *cuṁdhlānā* [cf. H. *cundhlā*], v.i. & v.t. = चौंधियाना.

चुंधा *cundhā* [*culla-*¹ × *andha-*], adj. & m. **1.** adj. weak-sighted. **2.** m. one dazzled by strong light. **3.** one having small eyes.

चुँधियाना *cuṁdhiyānā*, v.i. & v.t. = चौंधियाना.

चुंबक *cumbak* [S.], m. **1.** a lodestone. **2.** a magnet.

चुंबकत्व *cumbakatvă* [S.], m. magnetism.

चुंबकीय *cumbakīyă* [S.], adj. magnetic (pole, field; mine). — ~ आकर्षण, m. magnetic attraction.

चुंबन *cumban* [S.], m. kissing; a kiss. — ~ करना, v.t. to kiss.

चुंबा *cumbā* [*cumbă-*], m. a kiss (= चूमा).

चुंबित *cumbit* [S.], adj. kissed.

चुआन *cuān* [? **cyutadhāna-*], m. dripping, draining: **1.** 19c. a tank, reservoir. **2.** reg. a surface depression, into which water drains. **3.** reg. (W.) water table (as measured from a well).

चुआना *cuānā* [cf. H. *cūnā*], v.t. & m. **1.** to cause to drop or to drip; to drain; to distil; to filter. **2.** reg. leaking (of a roof).

चुक़ंदर *cuqandar* [P. *cuqandar*], m. beetroot. — चीनीवाला ~, m. sugar-beet.

चुकटा *cukṭā* [? H. *bukṭā* × II. *cuṭkī*], m. reg. a handful.

चुकटी *cukṭī*, f. a pinch, &c. (= चुटकी).

चुकता *cuktā* [cf. H. *cuknā*], adj. & m. **1.** adj. being settled, being adjusted, &c.; discharged, paid (a debt); balanced (an account); made good. **2.** wholesale. **3.** m. the paid portion of an account.

चुकती *cuktī* [cf. H. *cuktā*], f. **1.** reg. (W.) settlement (as of rent). **2.** *Pl.* sentence (of a court).

चुकना *cuknā* [**cukk-*: Pk. *cukkaï*], v.i. **1.** to be finished, to be completed; to come to an end; to be exhausted (as a supply). **2.** to be settled; to be fixed or agreed (as a price, a rate); to be adjusted (an account, a law-suit, a difference or dispute). **3.** to fall short (of, से). — चुक चलना, to be over and done (as a season). चुक जाना, = चुकना.

चुकरी *cukrī* [cf. H. *cukr*], f. reg. rhubarb.

चुकाई *cukāī* [cf. H. *cukānā*], f. **1.** settlement, adjustment; discharge; compensation. **2.** assigning, allocation.

चुकाना *cukānā* [**cukkaï*], v.t. **1.** to finish, to complete. **2.** to settle; to fix (as a price, a rate); to adjust (a law-suit, an account, a difference or dispute); to discharge (a debt); to make good (damage); to make or to pay (a charge, or compensation: to, को). **3.** to assign, to allot; to exact (payment, requital).

चुकौता *cukautā* [**cukk-*+*pattra-*], m. **1.** settling, payment, adjustment (as of a debt, an account, a law-suit); an agreed sum in settlement. **2.** a receipt.

चुकौती *cukautī*, f. = चुकौता.

चुक्कड़ *cukkaṛ*, m. reg. **1.** a small earthen vessel, a drinking-cup. **2.** a pit; a small tank or pond.

चुक्र *cukr* [S.], m. sourness; a sour substance.

चुग़द *cugd* [P. *cugd*], m. **1.** an owl. **2.** a fool.

चुगना *cugnā* [**cugyati*], v.t. **1.** to peck; to pick at, to feed on (of birds). **2.** to gather; to pick out, to select, to cull.

चुग़ल *cugal* [P. *cugal*], m. **1.** a slanderer. **2.** a tale-bearer; informer. — चुग़लख़ोर [P. *-khor*], m. one who deals in slander, &c., = ~. °ई, f. slander, &c.

चुग़ली *cuglī* [P. *cuglī*], f. **1.** slander. **2.** tale-bearing, informing. — ~ खाना, or लगाना (की), to slander (one); to inform (about one).

चुगवाना *cugvānā* [cf. H. *cugnā*], v.t. to cause to peck, &c.; to have or to get fed (fowl, &c., by another: से); to cause to gather, or to cull.

चुगा *cugā* [cf. H. *cugnā*], m. food scattered for birds, pickings.

चुगाई *cugāī* [cf. *cugnā, cugānā*], f. **1.** pecking, picking, feeding (of birds). **2.** causing (birds) to feed. **3.** the cost of or wages for supervising fowl when feeding.

चुगाना *cugānā* [cf. H. *cugnā*], v.t. **1.** to cause to peck or to feed. **2.** to feed (grain, &c. to fowl).

चुचकारना *cuckārnā*, v.t. to coax, to fondle (= चुमकारना, पुचकारना).

चुचकारी *cuckārī* [cf. H. *cuckārnā*], f. coaxing, fondling.

चुचवाना *cucvānā* [cf. H. *cucānā*], v.t. to cause to be wet, &c.

चुचाना *cucānā*, v.i. *Pl. HŚS.* **1.** to drop, to drip; to leak; to ooze, to exude, to be distilled. **2.** to be dripping wet. **3.** to be bursting (of ripe fruit, or opening flowers).

चुचियाना *cuciyānā*, v.i. ? = चुचाना.

चुचुकना *cucuknā*, v.i. to dry up, to be parched; to wither.

चुटकना *cuṭaknā* [cf. **cuṭṭ-*, *cuṇṭati*], v.t. & v.i. **1.** v.t. to nip; to pinch; to bite (of a snake). **2.** to break, to pluck. **3.** to whip. **4.** v.i. to snap (the fingers).

चुटकी *cuṭkī* [cf. H. *cuṭaknā*], f. **1.** a pinch (small quantity); the tips of thumb and first finger (placed together). **2.** a snap of the fingers; sthg. insignificant, a trifle. **3.** a knot, twist, constriction (in cloth). **4.** rebuke; sarcasm; innuendo. — ~ काटना, to pinch; to wound or to hurt; to nettle. ~ देना (को), to snap the fingers (at). ~ बजाते, adv. in a trice; easily. ~ बजाना (को), = ~ देना. ~ भर, m. a pinch. ~ भरना, = ~ काटना. ~, or चुटकियों में, adv. = ~ बजाते. ~ लेना, to make fun of, to be sarcastic at (one's) expense. चुटकियों पर काम करना, to perform a task easily, deftly. चुटकियों में उड़ाना, to pass off as a trivial matter; to pass off in a light-hearted manner; to make fun of.

चुटकुला *cuṭkulā*, m. **1.** a joke; joking. **2.** a witticism; a humorous story; pun; riddle. **3.** a mischievous joke, prank. — ~ छेड़ना, or छोड़ना, to tell a joke, a humorous story, &c. – चुटकुला-सा, adj. amusing; facetious.

चुटपुट *cuṭpuṭ*, adj. & f. pronun. var. = छुटफुट.

चुटपुटिया *cuṭpuṭiyā*, m. reg. a children's firework.

चुटला *cuṭlā*, m. = [1] [2]चुटीला.

चुटिया *cuṭiyā* [cf. H. *coṭī*], f. **1.** a lock of hair left on the otherwise shaven head (men). **2.** a coil of hair, top-knot (women).

[1]**चुटीला** *cuṭīlā* [cf. H. *coṭ*], adj. wounding, sharp (as speech).

[2]**चुटीला** *cuṭīlā* [conn. *coṭṭa-[1]: ? ← Drav.], m. **1.** the hair, or a lock of hair, worn behind the head; a ribbon with which the hair is tied or braided. **2.** an ornament for the hair when worn plaited or tied behind the head.

चुटैल *cuṭail* [cf. H. *coṭ*], adj. *Pl. HŚS.* hurt, wounded.

चुट्टा *cuṭṭā* [conn. *coṭṭa-[1]: ? ← Drav.], m. a large coil of hair, or top-knot.

चुड़ *cuṛ* [*cuḍa-: ? ← Drav.], f. vulva.

चुड़ैल *cuṛail* [cf. H. *cuṛ*], f. **1.** the ghost of a woman who dies while pregnant, or in childbirth. **2.** reg. (Bihar) an evil spirit imagined to sit in the shape of a bird on the roof of a house where a woman is pregnant, and to harm the child. ***3.** pej. a witch, hag; bitch. — ~ मँडराना, fig. a spirit to possess (one, के सिर).

चुड्ड *cuḍḍ* [*cuḍḍa-: ? ← Drav.], f. reg. (Panj.) vulva, vagina.

चुड्डो *cuḍḍo*, f. pej. a whore.

चुदक्कड़ *cudakkaṛ* [cf. H. *codnā, cudānā*], adj. & m. pej. **1.** adj. wanting sexual intercourse constantly. **2.** m. one who wants sexual intercourse constantly.

चुदना *cudnā* [cf. H. *codnā*], v.i. (a woman) to have sexual intercourse with (से) a man.

चुदवाई *cudvāī* [cf. H. *cudānā*], f. money earned by prostitution.

चुदवाना *cudvānā* [cf. H. *codnā*], v.t. = चुदाना.

चुदवास *cudvās* [cf. H. *cudvānā*], f. desire for sexual intercourse with a man.

चुदवैया *cudvaiyā* [cf. H. *codnā*], adj. & m. = चुदक्कड़.

चुदाई *cudāī* [cf. H. *codnā, cudānā*], f. **1.** sexual intercourse. **2.** money earned by prostitution (= चुदवाई). — ~ खाना (की), to live on the wages of prostitution.

चुदाना *cudānā* [cf. H. *codnā*], v.t. **1.** to incite or to allow (a man) to have sexual intercourse (with one, को). 2., to procure (a woman) for immoral purposes.

चुदानी *cudānī* [cf. H. *cudānā*], f. vulva, vagina.

चुदास *cudās* [cf. H. *codnā*], f. desire for sexual intercourse. — ~ लगना, sexual desire to be felt.

चुदासा *cudāsā* [cf. H. *cudās*], adj. desirous of having sexual intercourse.

चुनचुना *cuncunā*, m. & adj. **1.** m. an intestinal worm, thread-worm. **2.** adj. causing an itch. — चुनचुने लगना, to have worms; to be irritated or stung (by, से: as by crabby remarks).

चुनचुनाना *cuncunānā*, v.i. to itch. to sting.

चुनचुनी *cuncunī* [cf. H. *cuncunā*], f. **1.** itchiness. **2.** unease.

चुनट *cunaṭ* [cf. H. *cunnā*], f. = चुनावट.

चुनन *cunan* [cf. H. *cunnā*], f. **1.** choosing, selecting. **2.** a portion chosen or picked out; a portion picked out and rejected (as from grain); culling. **3.** a gather, tuck; a crease, pleat; wrinkle.

चुनना *cunnā* [*cinoti*: Pk. *cuṇaï*], v.t. **1.** to choose, to select; to pluck, to gather; to glean; to pick or to peck at; to discard, to cull. **2.** to elect. **3.** to arrange; to set out. **4.** to build up (as a wall); to wall up; to immure (in, में). **5.** to gather, to tuck; to crimp; to crease, to pleat.

[1]**चुनरी** *cunrī* [cf. H. *cunnā*], f. **1.** partly dyed (usu. red) cloth (of which portions have escaped the dyeing process by being twisted or knotted together). **2.** the process of dyeing *cunrī* cloth.

[2]**चुनरी** *cunrī* [? ad.*cūrṇita-*], f. a garnet.

चुनवाँ *cunvāṁ* [cf. H. *cunnā*], adj. gathered, picked, chosen; choice.

चुनवाई *cunvāī* [cf. H. *cunvānā*], f. **1.** causing to be picked, gathered, built up, &c. **2.** cost of or charge for getting (sthg.) picked, or built (as a wall), &c.; the wages of bricklayers or masons.

चुनवाना *cunvānā* [cf. H. *cunnā*], v.t. **1.** to cause to be chosen, selected, &c. (by, से). **2.** to cause (a person) to be immured (in, में).

चुनाँचे *cunāṁce* [P. *cunānce*], conj. since, because.

चुनाई *cunāī* [cf. H. *cunnā*], f. **1.** picking out, selecting; collecting. **2.** arranging, ordering. **3.** building up (as a wall); piling up. **4.** filling up (a hole); walling up (a gap in masonry). **5.** masonry-work. **6.** cost of or charge for masonry-work. — **कच्ची ~**, f. building in brick without mortar. **पक्की ~**, f. building in brick with mortar.

चुनानचे *cunānce* [P. *cunān-cĕ*], adv. **1.** U. for this reason, accordingly. **2.** for the reason that, since.

चुनाना *cunānā* [cf. H. *cunnā*], v.t. **1.** to cause to be chosen, selected, &c. (by, से). **2.** to cause to be arranged, or put in order. **3.** to dress or to array (oneself, को, in, में).

चुनाव *cunāv* [cf. H. *cunnā*], m. **1.** a choice, selection; a thing or person chosen, or selected. **2.** an election. **3.** a frill; tuck; crimping. — **~ में जीतना**, v.t. to win an election. **~ लड़ना**, to fight an election. **आम ~**, m. a general election. – **चुनाव-अभियान**, m. election campaign. **चुनाव-निरीक्षक**, m. returning officer. **चुनाव-याचिका**, f. petition that an election result be set aside.

चुनावी *cunāvī* [cf. H. *cunāv*], adj. electoral.

चुनावट *cunāvaṭ* [cf. H. *cunnā*], f. **1.** a tuck, gather (in cloth); a frill. **2.** a crease, rumple; a wrinkle.

चुनिंदा *cunindā* [cf H. *cunnā*, P. *cinīda*], adj. inv. **1.** chosen, selected. **2.** choice, select. **3.** gathered, picked.

चुनिया *cuniyā* [? H. ²*ciniyā*; × H. *muniyā*], f. *Pl.* a finch (= मुनिया).

चुनी *cunī* [cf. H. *cūnī*], f. = चुन्नी. — **चुनी-भूसी**, f. a coarsely ground, unsieved flour.

चुनौटिया *cunauṭiyā*, adj. Brbh. gathered, pleated, tucked (cloth).

चुनौटी *cunauṭī* [**cūrṇavarta-*], f. a small box for holding the lime which is eaten with betel leaf or tobacco.

चुनौती *cunautī* [cf. H. *cunnā*], f. selecting (the fittest men for a task): **1.** a challenge. **2.** incitement, encouragement, instigation. — **~ देना (को)**, to challenge (one); to defy.

चुन्नट *cunnaṭ*, f. a gathering (in cloth: = चुनट). — **चुन्नटदार** [P. *-dār*], adj. gathered, tucked.

चुन्ना *cunnā*, interj. an exclamation used in calling small children.

चुन्नी *cunnī* [conn. *cūrṇita-*], f. small fragments: **1.** bruised or broken grain. **2.** bran, sawdust. **3.** a small ruby. **4.** Av. tinsel, spangle (as a women's ornament).

चुप *cup* [**cuppa-*¹], f. & adj. **1.** f. silence; quiet. **2.** adj. silent; quiet. **3.** adv. silently; quietly. — **~ करना**, v.t. to keep silent, not to allow to be heard. **~ रहना** or **लगाना**, to remain quiet; to keep silence. **~ लगना (को)**, to be struck dumb. **~ साधना**, = ~ रहना; to practise silence. **~ होकर**, in silence. – **चुप-चाप**, adj. & adv. continously silent, quite silent or still; quite silently; furtively, secretly; inertly. **चुप-चुप**, adj. & adv. id.

चुपकी *cupkī* [cf. **cuppa-*¹], f. silence; quiet. — **~ लगना (को)**, to be struck dumb.

चुपके *cupke* [cf. **cuppa-*¹], adv. **1.** silently; quietly. **2.** stealthily. — **~ से**, adv. silently, &c.; in a low voice.

चुपचुपाना *cupcupānā* [cf. H. *cup*], v.i. **1.** to keep quite silent. **2.** to move quietly or stealthily. — **चुपचुपाते**, adv. quite silently, &c.

चुपड़ना *cupaṛnā* [**cuppa-*²: Pk. *cuppa-*], v.t. **1.** to oil, to grease; to smear; to baste; to lubricate. **2.** to anoint. **3.** to varnish. **4.** to foist upon, to attribute wrongly (to, के सिर). **5.** to smoothe or to gloss over; to palliate. — **चुपड़ी बात**, f. unctuous words, flattery. – **घी-चुपड़ी रोटी**, a *roṭī* rubbed over with, or dipped in, *ghī*. **चिकना-चुपड़ा**, adj. oily; unctuous; specious.

चुपड़वाँ *cupaṛvāṁ* [cf. H. *cupṛā*], adj. oiled, oily, greasy, &c.

चुप्पी *cuppī* [**cuppa-*¹], f. silence; quiet. — **~ चुप्पी लगाना**, to be or to keep silent.

चुबलाना *cublānā* [? conn. H. *cabānā*: w. MIA **cobb-*, **cabbh-*], v.t. colloq. to chew or to savour (food) without swallowing it.

चुभकना *cubhaknā* [? cf H. *cubhnā*], v.i. to plunge; to duck (as a water bird).

चुभकी *cubhkī* [cf. H. *cubhnā*], f. Brbh. a plunge, dive; ducking under the water.

चुभन *cubhan* [cf. H. *cubhnā*], f. **1.** a piercing, pricking. **2.** a piercing pain. **3.** colic.

चुभना *cubhnā* [**cubhyate*], v.i. **1.** to be thrust (into, में); to pierce; to penetrate; to sting (a wound, or tears). **2.** to be pierced; to be stabbed; to be stung. **3.** to be struck vividly or fascinated (by, से). **4.** to be sharply disagreeable (to, को). **5.** to strike (the mind, fancy or imagination). — **चुभता मज़ाक़**, m. a witticism. **चुभती कहना**, to speak wittily; to speak cuttingly.

चुभलाना *cubhlānā*, v.t. colloq. = चुबलाना.

चुभवाना *cubhvānā* [cf. H. *cubhnā*], v.t. to cause to be pierced, &c.

चुभाना *cubhānā* [cf. H. *cubhnā*], v.t. to cause to pierce: to thrust (into, में); to pierce; to stab; to sting.

चुभोना *cubhonā*, v.t. = चुभाना.

चुमकार *cumkār* [cf. *cumbă*-], f. (m., *Pl.*) **1.** a kissing sound. **2.** sound made with the lips to coax, call or reassure children or animals.

चुमकारना *cumkārnā* [cf. H. *cumkār*], v.t. **1.** to make a kissing sound. **2.** to coax, to reassure. **3.** to speak or to murmur lovingly to.

चुमकारी *cumkārī*, f. = चुमकार. — ~ देना (को) = चुमकारना.

चुमाना *cumānā* [cf. H. *cūmnā*], v.t. to cause to kiss.

चुम्मा *cummā* [*cumbŭ*-], m. a kiss. — चुम्मा-चाटी, f. kissing and caressing.

चुर *cur* [cf. H. *cūr*-], f. the sound of crunching or crackling (dry or brittle objects).

चुरकुट *curkuṭ* [cf. H. *cūr*; **kuṭṭa*-[2] (Pa. *kuṭṭa*-)], m. & adj. Brbh. **1.** sthg. ground up, small pieces; a powder. **2.** adj. disconcerted; distressed.

चुरचुरा *curcurā* [cf. H. *cur*], adj. & m. **1.** adj. crisp, crunchy; crumbling. **2.** m. a crunchy or crumbly substance.

चुरचुरी *curcurī* [H. *curcurā*], f. dregs; sediment.

[1]**चुरना** *curnā* [cf. *corayati*], v.t. to be stolen.

[2]**चुरना** *curnā* [? conn. *cūr*-], v.i. reg. to cook; to boil (as rice, lentils).

चुर-मुर *cur-mur* [c & adj. H. *cur*; and onom.], m. f. **1.** m. a crunching or crackling sound. **2.** adj. [H. *cūr*] crushed, pulverised. — ~ बोलना, to make a crunching sound. &c.

चुरमुरा *curmurā* [cf. H. *cur-mur*], adj. & m. **1.** adj. making a crunching or crackling sound. **2.** [cf. H. *cūr*] m. cleaned rice, soaked, flattened and roasted (to chew).

चुरमुराना *curmurānā* [cf. H. *cur-mur*], v.i. & v.t. **1.** v.i. to crunch or to crackle; to rustle (leaves). **2.** v.t. to cause to crunch, &c. (by crushing, or roasting). — मन ~, to be or to become fretful, or irritated.

चुरवाना *curvānā* [cf. H. *curānā*], v.t. to cause to be stolen (by, से).

चुरस *curas*, f. (? m.) *Pl. HŚS.* a crease, wrinkle.

चुराना *curānā* [cf. *corayati*], v.t. **1.** to steal; to captivate (as the heart). **2.** to hide away, to conceal; to withhold; to withdraw or to turn away (the eyes). — आँख चुराकर देखना, to steal a glance (at, की ओर), to look furtively (at). चित्त ~ (का), to steal (one's) heart; to beguile (one). समय ~, to snatch or to make available time (from, से).

चुरी *curī* [*cūḍa*-[2]], f. Brbh. a bracelet, bangle.

चुर्र-मुर्र *curr-murr*, f. & adj. = चुर-मुर.

चुर्री *currī* [? conn. H. *curcurī*], f. dregs, sediment.

चुल *cul* [cf. **cul*-], f. **1.** itching; fidgetiness. **2.** lust. — ~ मिटाना, to satisfy a craving, or lust (for, के लिए).

चुलचुलाना *culculānā* [cf. **cul*-], v.i. to itch.

चुलबुल *culbul* [cf. **cul*-: Pk. *culuculaï*], f. **1.** restlessness, fidgetiness. **2.** liveliness. **3.** flirtatiousness.

चुलबुला *culbulā* [cf. H. *culbul*], adj. **1.** restless, fidgety. **2.** lively. **3.** flirtatious.

चुलबुलाना *culbulānā* [cf. H. *culbulā*], v.i. to be restless or fidgety; to roll or to toss about (as in fever).

चुलबुलापन *culbulāpan* [cf. H. *culbulā*], m. = चुलबुल.

चुलबुलाहट *culbulāhaṭ* [cf. H. *culbulā*], f. = चुलबुल.

चुलबुलिया *culbuliyā*, adj. = चुलबुला.

चुलाव *culāv* [? cf. [2]*curnā*], m. *Pl. HŚS.* a rice dish (cf. पुलाव) without meat.

चुल्ली *cullī*, f. under-support (as for a stack of grain).

चुल्लू *cullū* [*culu*-], m. **1.** the palm of the hand hollowed (as to hold water); a mouthful of water. **2.** rinsing of the mouth with water sipped from the hand (as done before meals or religious ceremonies). — ~ भर, m. as much water, &c. as can be held in the hollowed hand. ~ भर पानी में डूब मरना, iron. to drown oneself in a handful of water: to be greatly embarrassed or ashamed. ~ भर लहू, or ख़ून, पीना (का), fig. to avenge oneself (upon), to see the utter defeat (of). चुल्लुओं लहू, or ख़ून, पीना (का), id. ~ से पीना, to drink from the hollowed palm. – चुल्लू-चुल्लू साधना, to sip, to take by degrees; to grow gradually rich.

चुवाना *cuvānā*, v. t. see चुआना.

चुसकी *cuskī* [cf. H. *cūsnā*], f. a mouthful of water or other liquid; a sip, suck; pull (as at a pipe). — ~ लगाना, or लेना, to take a sip, &c. (of or from, में).

चुसक्कड़ *cusakkaṛ* [cf. H. *cūsnā*], m. **1.** one who is in the habit of sucking. **2.** a tippler, drinker.

चुसना *cusnā* [cf. H. *cūsnā*], v.i. **1.** to be sucked, or drained; to be emptied; to be exploited. **2.** to be absorbed (by, से, or into, में).

चुसनी *cusnī* [cf. H. *cūsnā*], f. sthg. to be sucked; a baby's bottle, or gratifier.

चुसाना *cusānā* [cf. H. *cūsnā*], v.t. to cause to be sucked (by, से).

चुस्त *cust* [P. *cust*], adj. **1.** quick, brisk; active, alert. **2.** clever, ingenious, smart; adroit. **3.** close, narrow, tight-fitting (of clothes). **4.** sound, not deficient; excellent. — ~ नाप-काट पग, adj. of attractive cut, stylish. गवाह ~, मुद्दई सुस्त, fig. (one who is) no longer active when his activity is most needed. — चुस्त-चालाक, adj. = ~, 1., 2.

चुस्ती *custī* [P. *custī*], f. **1.** quickness, alertness, &c. (cf. चुस्त). **2.** ingenuity, dexterity, &c. **3.** close cut (of clothes); elegance. **4.** soundness, good quality.

चुहचुहा *cuhcuhā*, adj. **1.** lively, bright. **2.** warm, deep (of colours); glowing.

चुहचुहाना *cuhcuhānā*, v.i. **1.** to be brilliant (as a verse). **2.** to glow (as colours). 3. = चहचहाना.

चुहल *cuhal*, f. **1.** merriment (= [1]चहल). **2.** naughtiness (of behaviour). — ~ बंद करो! stop being a nuisance! – चुहलबाज़ [P. *bāz*], adj. merry, light-hearted; amusing; naughty, &c. °ई, f.

चुहलिया *cuhliyā* [cf. H. *cuhal*], adj. comical, funny (a person).

चुहिया *cuhiyā* [cf. H. *cūhā*], f. dimin. a small rat; a female rat.

चूँ *cūṁ* [onom.], f. a slight noise or sound; a squeak; creak; chirp, twitter; the noise of passing wind. — ~ न करना, not to make the slightest sound; to acquiesce cravenly without protest. – चूँ-चूँ, f. squeaking; creaking; chirping, twittering; a squeaking toy. चूँ-चहाट, or चूँ-चाँ, f. = चूँ-चूँ, 1.-3.

चूँकि *cūṁki* [P. *cūnki*], conj. since, because.

चूँची *cūṁcī*, f. pronun. var. = चूची.

चूँट- *cūṁṭ-* [*cuṇṭati*], v.t. Brbh. to nip, to break; to pluck.

चूँटा *cūṁṭā* [cf. **cimb-*], f. reg. (Bihar) pincers; small tongs.

चूँटी *cūṁṭī* [cf. **cimb-*], f. reg. (Bihar) small pincers, or tongs.

चूँदर *cūṁdar*, f. = [1]चुनरी.

चूँदरी *cūṁdrī*, f. = [1]चुनरी.

चूँसना *cūṁsnā*, v.t. pronun. var. = चूसना.

[1]**चूक** *cūk* [cf. H. *cūknā*], f. **1.** shortcoming; mistake, blunder, fault. **2.** omission; oversight.

[2]**चूक** *cūk* [*cukra-*], m. **1.** an acidic medicinal preparation (made esp. from lemon juice). **2.** sourness, acidity. **3.** a bitter-tasting plant: sorrel, *Rumex vesicarius*, or *R. montanus*.

चूकना *cūknā* [**cukk-*: Pk. *cukkaï*], v.i. to fall short: **1.** to make a mistake, or blunder; to err. **2.** to go astray, to stray (from, से). **3.** to fail, to omit (to do sthg., से); to miss (a target, &c.); not to achieve (an aim). **4.** to be deficient (in, में); to be omitted (from, से). **5.** E.H. to be finished (= चुकना, 1).

[1]**चूका** *cūkā* [*cukra-*], m. *Pl. HŚS.* wild sorrel (see [2]चूक).

[2]**चूका** *cūkā*, m. reg. (Bihar) a kind of large earthen milk-pot (capacity about five litres).

चूख- *cūkh-*, v.t. E.H. = चूसना.

चूची *cūcī* [**cucci-*; Pk. *cucuya-*], f. **1.** nipple. **2.** the female breast. — ~ पीना, or लेना, to suck, to take the breast.

चूज़ा *cūzā* [P. *cūza*], m. a chicken.

[1]**चूड़ा** *cūṛā* [*cūḍa-*[1]: ← Drav.], f. **1.** the ceremony of shaving the head. **2.** a single lock or tuft of hair left unshaven on the top of the head. **3.** crest (as of a bird). — चूड़ाकरण, m. the ceremony of first shaving a child's head. चूड़ा-कर्म, m. the rite of tonsure (cf. चूड़ाकरण). चूड़ा-मणि, f. a jewel or ornament worn on the top of the head; the chief, best, supreme (of a kind).

[2]**चूड़ा** *cūṛā* [*cūḍa-*[2], Pk. *cūḍa-*], m. a bracelet, bangle.

[3]**चूड़ा** *cūṛā*, m. = चिड़वा.

चूड़ाल *cūṛāl* [*cūḍāla-*], adj. & m. **1.** *Pl. HŚS.* having a single lock of unshaven hair on the crown of the head. **2.** m. the chickling vetch, *Lathyrus sativus*.

चूड़ाला *cūṛālā*, m. **1.** *Pl. HŚS.* a kind of sedge (*Cyperus*). **2.** *HŚS.* ? an aconite (= जदवार).

चूड़िया *cūṛiyā* [cf. H. *cūṛī*], m. a kind of striped cloth.

चूड़ी *cūṛī* [*cūḍa-*[2]: Pk. *cūḍa-*], f. **1.** a bangle, bracelet (as of glass, lac, plastic: not of metal).

2. a gather, tuck (in material). 3. transf. spiral grooving; rifling. — चूड़ियाँ टूटना, (a married woman's) bangles to be broken: to become a widow. चूड़ियाँ ठंडी करना, to put off one's bangles; euph. to break one's bangles (on the death of one's husband). चूड़ियाँ पहनना, to put on bangles: to behave effeminately; to remarry (of a widow). चूड़ियाँ पहनाना (को), to marry (a widow); to arrange the marriage of (a widow). चूड़ियाँ फोड़ना, or बँधाना, or बढ़ाना, = चूड़ियाँ ठंडी करना. – चूड़ीदार [P. -*dār*], adj. gathered, drawn together into rumples or pleats. चूड़ीदार पायजामा, m. narrow-legged cotton trousers with gatherings running down the length of the lower leg.

चूड़ीहारा *cūṛīhārā* [cf. H. *cūṛī*], m. a maker of bangles.

चूत *cūt* [**cutta*-: ? ← Drav.], f. vulva. — चूत-मरानी, f. a prostitute.

चूतड़ *cūtaṛ* [**cutta*-: ? ← Drav.], m. colloq. buttocks; rump. — ~ के बल बैठना, to sit on one's backside: to be badly disconcerted or at a loss. ~ दिखाना, to turn tail. ~ पीटना, = next; to lament, to grieve. ~ बजाना, to slap the backside as an expression of emotion: to be overjoyed. ~ सिकोड़ना, to hold in the backside: to loiter, to hang back.

चूतिया *cūtiyā* [cf. H. *cūt*], m. & adj. pej. an immoral person: 1. m. a contemptible wretch. 2. an idiot, fool. 3. adj. idiotic, stupid. — चूतिया-चक्कर, m. = ~, m.; a stupid or pointless quarrel, or tangle. चूतिया-चंपई, m. id. चूतिया-पंथी, f. idiotic conduct, &c.

चूतियापन *cūtiyāpan* [cf. H. *cūtiyā*], m. idiocy, folly.

चून *cūn* [*cūrṇa*-], m. 1. flour, meal. 2. powder; filings. 3. lime. — लोह ~, m. iron filings.

चूनर *cūnar*, f. = [1]चुनरी.

चूनरी *cūnrī*, f. = [1]चुनरी.

[1]**चूना** *cūnā* [*cūrṇa*-], m. lime; slaked lime. — ~ फेरना (पर), to whitewash. ~ बुझाना, to slake lime. ~ लगाना (में), to whitewash; fig. to do down, to cause harm (to); to defame. चूने का पत्थर, m. limestone. चूने की भट्टी, f. a lime-kiln. कच्चा ~, m. quicklime. बुझा ~, m. slaked lime.

[2]**चूना** *cūnā* [**cyutati*], v.i. & adj. 1. v.i. to drop, to drip (liquid); to leak; to ooze; to be distilled, secreted. 2. to fall (fruit). 3. to leak (a vessel, a roof). 4. adj. leaking, dripping; leaky.

चूनी *cūnī* [*cūrṇa*-], f. fragments of bruised or coarsely ground grain. — चूनी-भूसी, f. a coarse flour, with its bran.

चूभ *cūbh* [cf. H. *cūbhnā*], m. a piercing, prick.

चूमन *cūman* [cf. H. *cūmnā*], f. Brbh. kissing.

चूमना *cūmnā* [*cumbati*], v.t. to kiss. — चूमकर छोड़ देना, to give up lightly a cherished object, or goal, to kiss goodbye (to); to give up a difficult task with equanimity. चूम-चाटकर छोड़ देना, id.

चूमनि *cūmani* [*cumbana*-], f. Brbh. kissing.

चूमा *cūmā* [*cumbǎ*-], m. a kiss. — ~ देना (को), to kiss. ~ लेना (का), to take a kiss (from), to kiss. – चूमा-चाटी, f. kissing and caressing.

चूर *cūr* [**cūra*-: Pk. *cūra*-], m. & adj. 1. m. powder; filings; particles, fragments; crumbs; atoms. 2. adj. crushed. 3. incapacitated, distracted. exhausted (as by work); intoxicated; absorbed (by or in, में); besotted (by, में); obsessed. — ~ करना, v.t. to smash, to shatter; to pulverise. ~ होना, to be smashed, &c.; to be distracted, &c. ~ हो रहना, = ~ होना, 2. नशे में ~, adj. dead drunk. – चूर-चार, m.pl. & adj. fragments; crumbs; = next. चूर-चूर, adj. crushed, shattered. चूर-मूर, adj. id.; Brbh. relieved (care).

चूर- *cūr*- [**cūrayati*: Pk. *curei*], v.t. Brbh. Av. to crush; to smash, to break.

चूरकी *cūrkī* [cf. *cūḍa*-[1]: ← Drav.], f. reg. lock (of hair).

चूरन *cūran*, m. = चूर्ण, 2.

चूरमा *cūrmā*, m. a sweet: crumbled bread or breadcrumbs (*cūr*) fried in *ghī*, and mixed with sugar.

चूरा *cūrā* [**cūra*-: Pk. *cūra*-], m. 1. powder; filings; sawdust. 2. fragments; bruised grain. — ~ करना, to crush, to pulverise; to bruise (grain). चूरा-मन, broken-hearted; contrite, repentant.

चूरी *cūrī* [conn. *cūlikā*-], m. a cake made of crumbled bread with *ghī*.

चूर्ण *cūrṇ* [S.], m. & adj. 1. m. any ground, or minutely fragmented substance; powder; flour. 2. specif. a digestive powder (composed of ground spices, dried mangoes, limes, &c). 3. adj. crushed, pulverised; smashed, ruined. — चूर्ण-मन, adj. broken-hearted.

चूर्णिका *cūrṇikā* [S.], f. fried, or pounded rice or grain (= सत्तू).

चूर्णित *cūrṇit* [S.], adj. crushed, powdered; smashed, ruined.

[1]**चूल** *cūl* [*cūḍa*-[1]: ← Drav.], m. 1. top, crest. 2. the hair of the head.

[2]**चूल** *cūl* [*cūḍa*-[1]: ← Drav.], f. 1. pivot (as of a door, in its socket on a threshold). 2. (in

carpentry) a tenon; a dovetail; wedge. — ~ न बैठना, (fig.) to be out of joint: not to go well (an enterprise, or a relationship). चूलें उखड़ना, the joints to become dislocated, or loose: to be tried, taxed; to be worn out, exhausted (as with work). चूलें ढीली करना, to tax; to wear out. चूलें ढीली होना, = चूलें उखड़ना.

चूल्हा *cūlhā* [*cullī-*: ← Drav.], m. a stove; hearth. — ~ जलना, a stove to be lit; food to be cooked. ~ झोंकना, to light, or to feed, a stove. ~ न्यौतना, (*Pl.*) *HŚS.* to invite (an entire household) to a meal. चूल्हे में जाना, to be consumed, destroyed; to go to the devil. चूल्हे में डालना, or झोंकना, to abandon to one's destruction: to throw to the wolves. चूल्हे में पड़ना, = चूल्हे में जाना, 1. – चूल्हा-चक्की, f. stove and grindstone: household chores. चूल्हा-भाड़, stove and oven: चूल्हे-भाड़ में जाओ! go to the devil!

चूसन *cūsan* [cf. H. *cūsnā*], f. suction.

चूसना *cūsnā* [*cūṣati*], v.t. **1.** to suck; to draw in; to soak up, to absorb. **2.** (esp. चूस डालना, or लेना.) to drain, to exhaust. **3.** to expropriate, to exploit (wrongfully).

चूहड़ा *cūhṛā* [**cūhaḍa-*], m. **1.** a sweeper; an outcaste. **2.** a base or villainous person. — चूहड़ा-चमार, pej. a man of low caste.

चूहा *cūhā* [**cūha-*], m. **1.** a rat; a mouse. **2.** colloq. dry mucus (of the nose). — ~ चूहे का बिल, m. a refuge, bolt-hole. ~ चूहा-दंती, f. rat's teeth: a bracelet made of pieces of gold or silver wire. चूहादान, m. = next. चूहेदान, [P. *-dān*], m. a rat-trap, mouse-trap. चूहेमार, m. a sparrow-hawk.

चूही *cūhī* [cf. H. *cūhā*], f. a mouse; a rat.

चें *cem̐*, f. = चीं.

चेंगड़ा *cem̐gṛā* [cf. **ceṅga-*], m. *HŚS.* reg. a young child.

चेंच *cem̐c*, m. ? f. reg. (Bihar) a grass which springs up in the rainy season (used as fodder).

चेंचला *cem̐clā*, m. an unfledged bird, nestling (= चेंचुआ).

चेंचुआ *cem̐cuā* [?? cf. H. *cem̐*], m. an unfledged bird.

चेंड़ा *cem̐ṛā* [cf. **ceṅga-*], adj. *Pl.* young, little.

चेंप *cem̐p*, f. pronun. var. = चेप.

चेक *cek* [Engl. *cheque*], m. a cheque. — ~ काटना, to write a cheque. ~ भुनाना, to cash a cheque.

चेचक *cecak*, f. small-pox. — छोटी ~, f. measles. – चेचकरू, adj. having the face marked by smallpox.

¹चेटक *ceṭak*, m. f. Brbh. Av. a miraculous deed; magic, illusion.

²चेटक *ceṭak*, f. *Pl.* thought, care, anxiety. — ~ लगना (की), to think (of), to feel anxiety (for).

चेत *cet* [ad. *cetas-*], m. **1.** consciousness. **2.** wits, senses. **3.** alertness; caution. **4.** memory, recollection. — ~ करना, to bear in mind. ~ में आना, to recover consciousness.

चेतन *cetan* [S.], adj. & m. **1.** adj. conscious, aware. **2.** rational. **3.** alert, vigilant. **4.** m. consciousness; the soul (= चैतन्य). **5.** intelligence. **6.** a living and sentient being. — ~ करना (को) *Pl.*, to make conscious; to rouse, to awake; to bring (one) to (one's) senses; to make conscious (of, के प्रति); to warn (of).

चेतनता *cetanātā* [S.], f. **1.** a state of consciousness. **2.** rationality. **3.** the possession of a soul. **4.** awareness or consciousness (as of an issue, a viewpoint).

¹चेतना *cetănā* [S.], f. **1.** consciousness; intelligence. **2.** recollection. 3. = चेतनता, 4.

²चेतना *cetnā* [cf. *cettṛ-*], v.i. & v.t. **1.** v.i. to be or to become conscious. **2.** to be aroused, to awake. **3.** to be or to become aware (of, के प्रति). **4.** to be alert, to have one's wits about one. **5.** v.t. to think, to reflect (upon).

¹चेता *cetā* [cf. H. *cetnā*], m. 1. = चेत. 2. = चित्त.

²चेता *cetā* [ad. *cettṛ-*: w. H. ²*cetnā*], m. one who thinks, reflects or is conscious.

चेताना *cetānā* [cf. H. *cetnā*], v.t. **1.** to draw (one's) attention (to sthg.); to remind (one). **2.** to advise, to suggest. **3.** to caution, to warn.

चेतावनी *cetāvnī* [cf. H. *cetanā*], f. **1.** a warning: caution. **2.** reminder.

चेना *cenā*, m. a millet (= ²चीना).

चेप *cep* [**ceppa-*], f. **1.** stickiness. **2.** a sticky substance: gum; resin; bird-lime. **3.** gummy secretion (in the eye). **4.** matter, pus. — चेपदार [P. *-dār*], adj. sticky, viscous.

चेपना *cepnā* [cf. **ceppa-*], v.t. to stick on.

चेपा *cepā* [? **ceppa-*], m. *Pl.* a disease which affects standing crops.

चेपी *cepī* [cf. H. *cep*], f. a piece stuck on; a patch.

चेरा *cerā* [*ceṭa-*], m. **1.** a servant. **2.** a pupil, disciple.

चेराई *cerāī* [cf. H. *cerā*], f. Brbh. service, attendance (upon, की).

चेरी *cerī* [*ceṭa-*], f. a woman servant.

चेला *celā* [**cella-*, and *ceṭa-*], m. a pupil, disciple; an attendant. — ~ करना, to make a disciple or convert of. – चेले-चाटी, चेले-चाटे, pl. pupils, &c.

चेली *celī* [**cella-*], f. a female pupil; female attendant.

चेष्टा *ceṣṭā* [S.], f. **1.** action or movement of the body; activity; gesture. **2.** impulse; expression (of the features). **3.** effort, exertion; attempt, endeavour. — ~ करना, to attempt.

चेष्टित *ceṣṭit* [S.], adj. **1.** characterised by activity, striving for. **2.** undertaken, striven for.

चेस्टर *ceṣṭar* [Engl. *Chesterfield*], m. ? obs. a kind of overcoat.

चेहरा *cehrā* [P. *cĕhra*], m. **1.** face, features; likeness. **2.** expression (facial). **3.** face, front part. **4.** mask. — ~ उतरना, the face to fall. ~ बुझना, fig. id. ~ भाँपना (का), to read (one's) expression. गैस-रक्षक ~, m. gas-mask. – चेहरा-मोहरा, m. facial expression.

चेहलुम *cehlum* [P. *cihalum*], m. *musl.* fortieth: **1.** the fortieth day of mourning. **2.** an observance carried out on the fortieth day after a death, or after the burial of the *tāziyā* in the month of Muḥarram.

चैत *cait* [*caitra-*], m. **1.** the first month (lunar) of the Hindu year (the full moon of which is in the constellation *citrā*), March-April. **2.** a song sung in the month of Cait. — ~ की फ़सल, f. the spring crop. ~ खेलना, to join in the songs and sports of Cait.

चैतन्य *caitanyă* [S.], m. & adj. **1.** m. consciousness; the soul. **2.** rationality, intelligence; perception. **3.** the ultimate being (considered as the essence of all consciousness). **4.** adj. conscious; percipient. **5.** rational. — चैतन्यात्मक [°*nya*+*ā*°], adj. characterised by rationality, consciousness, &c.

चैतन्यता *caitanyatā* [S.], f. state or faculty of consciousness.

चैतवाड़ा *caitvāṛā* [H. *cait*+H. *-vāṛā*], m. the season or time of Cait, q.v.

चैती *caitī* [cf. H. *cait*], adj. & f. **1.** adj. having to do with the month of Cait. **2.** the spring (*rabī*) crop or harvest. 3. = चैत, 2.

चैत्र *caitr* [S.], m. = चैत.

चैन *cain* [cf. *cakati*], m. ease of mind, contentment; quiet, peace; repose. — ~ आना, or पड़ना (को), (one) to be at ease, contented. ~ उड़ाना, to enjoy oneself, to be contented. ~ करना, to relax, to take pleasure. ~ की बंसी बजना the flute of contentment to be heard: a contented life to be led. ~ से, adv. at ease, contentedly. – चैन-चान, m. = ~ .

[1]**चैल** *cail* [S.], m. *Pl. HŚS.* clothing.

[2]**चैल** *cail*, ? m. reg. (W.) land twice ploughed.

चैला *cailā* [**cavilla-*], m. a piece of split wood (for burning).

चैली *cailī* [**cavilla-*], f. **1.** a splinter or chip of wood. **2.** reg. (Bihar) a wedge.

चोंक *comk*, adj. sharp: — ~ करना, to sharpen (a pencil, a blade).

चोंकीला *comkīlā* [cf. H. *comk*], adj. sharp, abrasive (as manner).

चोंगा *comgā* [**conga-*], m. **1.** section of bamboo (used as a container for oil, salt, &c., or as a tube or funnel). **2.** a cylindrical case. **3.** a cylindrical object; telephone receiver (handset).

चोंगी *comgī*, f. dimin. reg. = चोंगा.

चोंच *comc* [**coñca-*: ← Drav.], f. **1.** beak, bill. **2.** pej. & dimin. mouth. **3.** spout. — ~ बंद कराना, to get (one, की) to hold his tongue. ~ मारना, to peck. ~ मिलाना, to join beaks, to bill and coo. ~ लड़ाना, fig. to squabble. ~ सँभालो! hold your tongue! — दो-दो ~ होना, to squabble (with, से); a squabble to break out (between, से).

चोंचला *comclā*, m. pronun. var. = चोचला.

चोंटी *comṭī*, f. reg. (Bihar) a wedge (= [2]चूल).

चोंड़ा *comṛā* [**conda-*: ← Drav.], m. **1.** head, crest. **2.** coil of (a woman's) hair; top-knot (esp. that of an old woman; cf. जूड़ा). — ~ मुँडवाना (का), to cause (one's) head to be shaved; to incur disgrace. चोड़े पर चढ़कर (के), despite, in defiance (of). धूप में ~ सफ़ेद करना, to let one's hair grow white in the sun (rather than by maturing during life): to idle one's life away.

चोंथ *comth*, m. cow-dung, excreted at a single time.

चोंप *comp*, f. = [1]चोप.

चोआ *coā* [cf. H. *cuānā*], m. **1.** a substance or object which drips, oozes, or drains; Av. a fragrant paste of four ingredients. **2.** a windfall (fruit). **3.** dribble; a filtrate, distillation. **4.** reg. (W.) = चुआन, 2.

चोई *coī*, f. husk of lentils, &c.

चोकड़ *cokaṛ*, m. = चोकर.

चोकर *cokar* [cf. **cokka-*], m. husks or refuse of wheat, barley, &c.; bran.

चोखा *cokhā* [*cokṣa-*], adj. & m. **1.** adj. pure, genuine. **2.** good, excellent; delightful; beautiful. **3.** sound, honest; sincere. **4.** sharp (as a knife). **5.** keen, pungent; high, clear (a sound). **6.** m. a spiced dish of roasted or fried vegetables (= भुरता). — मज़ा ~ आना, colloq. a good time to be had.

चोखाई *cokhāī* [cf. H. *cokhā*], f. = चोखापन.

चोखापन *cokhāpan* [cf. H. *cokhā*], m. **1.** genuineness. **2.** good quality, &c. **3.** sharpness; pungency.

चोगा *cogā*, m. *Pl. HŚS.* = चुगा.

चोग़ा *cogā* [T. *çoga*], m. a long, loose knee-length cloak.

चोचला *coclā*, m. **1.** artfulness, playfulness; whimsy. **2.** archness, flirtatiousness. **3.** affectation, foible. — चोचले दिखाना, or बघारना, to be whimsical, arch, &c.; to be affected.

चोज *coj* [*codya-*], m. sthg. wonderful or admirable (esp. a remark); a subtle, or pointed, remark; an epigram.

चोजी *cojī* [cf. H. *coj*], adj. inv. *Pl.* subtle, nice (a remark, &c).

चोट *coṭ* [**coṭṭ-*], f. **1.** blow; wound; injury, hurt, knock; bruise; damage. **2.** shock, blow, impact. **3.** rivalry, competition. **4.** loss (as in trade). — ~ आना (को), a blow, or a wound, to be received (by). ~ उभरना, a wound to be reopened or revived. ~ करना (पर, or में), to strike (at), to make an attack (on); to do hurt (to), to wound; to cast a spell (on or over). ~ का, adj. equal to, able to withstand, or to be compared with (one, की). ~ खाना, to suffer a blow, or a wound; to suffer loss or injury. ~ जमाना (पर), to strike (at), to make an attack (on). ~ देना, or पहुँचाना, or लगाना (को), id. ~ पड़ना, a blow to fall. ~ पर ~, blow upon blow, a succession of misfortunes. ~ बचाना, to ward off a blow. ~ मारना, = ~ करना; to hammer in (a nail, &c). ~ लगना (को), a blow, or a wound, to be received; to be hurt; to be wounded; to feel pain. – चोट-चपेट, f. a wound, injury.

चोटा *coṭā*, m. reg. molasses; treacle.

चोटार *coṭār*, adj. **1.** Brbh. violent (a blow). **2.** reg. (E.) prone to bite or to butt (an animal).

चोटी *coṭī* [**coṭṭa-*[1]: Pk. *coṭṭī-*], f. **1.** a lock of hair left unshaven on the crown of the head; top-knot. **2.** a pigtail. **3.** coil of (a woman's) hair; a woman's top-knot; ornament for (a woman's) hair. **4.** crest (of a bird). **5.** summit, apex; peak, crest (of a mountain); pinnacle; vertex. — ~ कटाना, fig. to renounce the world, to become a holy man. ~ करना (की), to plait (one's) hair; to do one's hair (a woman). ~ का, adj. the highest, the best; the acme or essence of. ~ गूँथना, = ~ करना. ~ दबना, to be in a subservient position (to, के नीचे). ~ रखना, to wear or to keep a lock of unshaven hair. ~ हाथ में आना, or होना, one's top-knot to come into, or be in (another's) hand: to come into or to be in another's power, to become or to be subservient to (another). - चोटीदार [P. *-dār*], adj. having a top-knot, &c.; crested; peaked; tapering.

चोट्टा *coṭṭā* [**coṭṭa-*[2]: ← Drav.], m. a pilferer.

चोत *cot*, m. reg. (E.) = चोंथ.

चोदना *codnā* [**coddati*], v.t. to have sexual intercourse with (of a man).

चोदू *codū* [cf. H. *codnā*], adj. & m. **1.** adj. constantly wanting sexual intercourse; lascivious. **2.** m. a lascivious man.

चोद्दू *coddū*, adj. & m. = चोदू.

[1]**चोप** *cop*, m. Brbh. **1.** desire; avidity. **2.** delight; enthusiasm.

[2]**चोप** *cop*, f. pronun. var. = चोब.

चोब *cob* [P. *cob*], f. **1.** a mace. **2.** a drum-stick. — चोबदार [P. *-dār*], m. mace-bearer. °ई, f. mace-bearer's work or function.

चोबा *cobā* [? H. *cobhā*], m. a small iron nail, tack, &c.

चोभ *cobh*, f. = चोब.

चोभा *cobhā* [cf. H. *cubhānā*], m. **1.** *Pl.* piercing, pricking. **2.** *HŚS.* a spiked implement used to shred or to pulp fruit in making preserves. **3.** a small iron nail, tack, &c. **4.** reg. (Bihar) a lancet.

चोर *cor* [*cora-*[1]], m. & adj. **1.** m. a thief; a robber. **2.** one who is 'he' or 'it' in a children's game. **3.** a hidden abscess (as in a healed wound, or under a tooth); an ulcer. **4.** an ulterior motive or intention. **5.** adj. hidden, secret (as a room, compartment, door, or way); false, misleading; deceptive, treacherous. — ~ गढ़ा, m. a pit-fall, trap. ~ ज़मीन, f. quagmire. ~ पेट, m. inconspicuous stomach (of a pregnant woman); a bottomless stomach. ~ पैर, m. pl. noiseless feet. ~ बाज़ार, m. black market. °ई, f. black market dealings. ~ बालू, m. = ~ ज़मीन. ~ महल, m. apartment or apartments for concubines; a secret apartment. ~ लगना, v.i. (a place) to be infested by thieves. ~ शिकारी, m. a poacher. – चोरकट, m. a thief, pilferer. चोर-चकार, m. id. चोर-चमार, m. a thief, villain. चोर-छेद, m. a gap, crack, hole (as in a roof, through which water can enter). चोर-थन, adj. withholding milk in the udder (a cow, goat or buffalo). चोर-दंत, m. a tooth additional to the normal number. चोर-बदन, adj. of deceptively sturdy build.

चोरी *corī* [*caurikā-*], f. **1.** theft; robbery. **2.** stealth; concealment. — ~ करना, to steal. ~ का, adj. stolen; secret, furtive. ~ जाना, to be stolen. ~ (में) जाना, to be stolen. ~ लगना (को), to be accused of, or charged with, theft; to be seen to be guilty of theft. ~ लगाना (को), to accuse of, or to charge with, theft. – चोरी-चोरी (से), adv. by stealth, clandestinely. चोरी-छिपे, adv. id.

चोला *colā* [*coḍa-*[1]], m. **1.** a long gown or cloak; a bride's garment. **2.** a baby's first (ceremonial) garment. **3.** fig. the body; guise, outward appearance. — ~ छोड़ना, to leave the body: to die. ~ बदलना, v.t. to change the body: (the soul) to transmigrate.

चोली *colī* [cf. H. *colā*], f. **1.** a bodice, blouse. **2.** a brassiere. — चोली-दामन का नाता, m. relationship of bodice and hem (of lower garment): a close or intimate relationship. चोली-दामन का साथ, m. id.

चोषण *coṣaṇ* [S.], m. sucking, draining; suction.

चोष्य *coṣyă* [S.], adj. able to be sucked.

चोहला *cohlā*, m. reg. (W.) a large peg; wooden balk (tied to necks of dangerous cattle).

चौंक *caurìk* [cf. H. *caurìknā*], f. a sudden start; a shudder, shiver.

चौंकना *caurìknā* [**camakka-*: Pk. *camakka-*], v.i. **1.** to be startled, to start; to be greatly astonished; to shudder, to shiver; to wince. **2.** to be roused (from sleep). **3.** to be vigilant, on the alert. — चौंक उठना, id. (often expressing a stronger degree of suddenness, reflex action, &c. than *caurìk parnā*): to start violently, to start up. चौंक पड़ना, to start, &c.; to wake with a start.

चौंकाना *caurìkānā* [cf. H. *caurìknā*], v.t. **1.** to cause to be startled, to startle. **2.** to arouse, to waken. **3.** to put on the alert.

चौंड़ू *caurìṛū*, m. an idiot, fool.

चौंतरा *caurìtrā*, m. Brbh. = चौतरा, चबूतरा.

चौंतीस *caurìtīs* [*catustrirìśat-*], adj. thirty-four.

चौंथना *caurìthnā*, v.t. to snatch or to tear away.

चौंध *caurìdh*, f. state of being dazzled.

चौंधला *caurìdhlā*, adj. = चुँधला.

चौंधलाना *caurìdhlānā*, v.i. & v.t. = चुँधलाना, and चौंधियाना, q.v.

चौंधा *caurìdhā* [H. *caurìknā* × H. *andhā*], adj. **1.** dazzled. **2.** weak-sighted.

चौंधियाना *caurìdhiyānā* [cf. H. *caurìdhā*], v.i. & v.t. **1.** v.i. to be dazzled. **2.** to have weak sight. **3.** to be greatly astonished, or bewildered; to be frightened out of one's senses. **4.** v.t. to dazzle.

चौंधी *caurìdhī*, f. = चौंध.

चौंर *caurìr*, m. see चँवर.

चौंरी *caurìrī* [*camara-*], f. a fly-whisk (cf. चँवर).

चौंषरौं *caurìṣaraurì* [? **catuṣkara-*], m. Brbh. /cəũkh-/. ? quadruped: a rat.

चौंसठ *caurìsaṭh* [*catuḥṣaṣṭi-*], adj. sixty-four. — ~ घड़ी, adv. all the time, constantly. ~ सीढ़ियाँ, f. pl. E.H. the sixty-four steps: a partic. tantric or Nāth Śaiva progression.

चौंसर *caurìsar*, m. pronun. var. = चौसर.

चौ- *cau-* [*catur-*, &c.], adj. four: — चौकोन, चौकोना, adj. & m. four-cornered; square; a square. चौकोर, m. id. चौखंड, adj. & m. four-storeyed; a four-storeyed building; a fourth storey. °आ, adj. & m. id. चौख़ाना, adj. = चारख़ाना. चौखूँट, m. & adv. the four points of the compass; the four quarters of the world; on all sides. °आ, adj. four-cornered; square. चौखूँटा कोष्ठक, m. square brackets. चौगड़ा, m. pronun. var. = चौघड़ा. चौगिर्द [P. *-gird*], adv. on all sides, all around. चौगुन, adj. four-fold. °आ, adj. id. मन ~ बढ़ना, fig. to be extremely encouraged. चौगून, f. *mus.* increasing the speed or volume of singing four-fold towards a climax. चौगोड़ा, adj. & m. four-footed; a quadruped. चौघड़ा, m. an object having four compartments, or sections: a box for *pān*, spices, &c.; a candle-holder of four sections. चौघड़िया, adj. inv. of four hours: short, fleeting (a favourable moment). चौजुगी, adj. & m. *mythol.* having to do with the four ages; a cycle of the four ages. चौतरफ़ा [P. *-taraf*], adj. inv. four-sided. चौताल, m. *mus.* a drumming or clapping rhythm of four beats; a song to this rhythm. °आ, adj. four-beat. चौदंता, adj. having four teeth; young (an animal). चौपई, f. see s.v. चौपग, m. a quadruped. चौपतिया, adj. inv. having, or characterised by, four leaves or petals. चौपत्ती, f. a brochure. चौपथ, m. a crossroads. चौपद, m. a quadruped; a quatrain. °आ, m. = चौपद, 2. चौपन्ना, m. a pamphlet, brochure. चौपहरा, adj. lasting twelve hours; complete in twelve hours; day-long, night-long. चौपहल, adj. four-sided. °आ, adj., °ऊ, adj. id.

चौपहिया, adj. inv. & m. four-wheeled; a four-wheeled vehicle. चौपही, f. see s.v. चौपाई, f. see s.v. चौपाया, adj. & m. four-footed; a quadruped; a four-footed piece of furniture. चौपेजी, adj. of four pages; quarto. चौपैया, m. a partic. type of quatrain having 30 *mātrās* per line. चौफला, adj. four-bladed. चौफेर, adj. & adv. all round, on all sides. °ई, f. & adv. circuit (around, की); id. चौबंदी [P. *-bandī*], f. binding, attaching at four points; shoeing (a horse); a bodice or jacket having four tie-straps. चौबंदी बाँधना (पर), to shoe (a horse). चौ-बग़ला, adj. four-sided; on all sides. चौबरसी, f. a festival commemorating a particular event every fourth year; a commemorative rite taking place four years after a death. चौबार, m. = next. [1]चौबारा, m. a room with four doors (properly one in each side): an assembly-room, &c.; an upper porch. [2]चौबारा, adv. four times. चौबोला, m. a verse of four lines, used in drama; the metre of this verse; singer or accompanist of *caubolās*. चौमंज़िला, adj. four-storeyed. चौमसिया, adj. inv. & m. having to do with a period of four months, esp. that from Asāṛh to Kārttik; a worker hired for that period. चौमहला, adj. four-storeyed. चौमार्ग, m. a crossroads. चौमास, m. = चौमासा, m. चौमासा, m. & adj. the four rainy months from Asāṛh to Kārttik; a song about love, set in the conventional context of the rainy season; having to do with the rainy season. °-मासी, f. = चौमासा, 2. चौमुख, adj. having four faces, facing four ways; many-sided; on all sides. °आ, adj. id. चौमुखी, adj. id. चौमुहानी, f. a crossroads. चौरंग, adj. & m. of four colours; a slashing stroke (with a sword). °आ, = चौरंग, adj. चौरस्ता, m. = next. चौरास्ता, m. a crossroads. चौराहा, m. id. चौलड़ा, adj. & m. of four strings or strands; a necklace of four strands. °ई, f. चौवाई, f. see s.v. चौसिंगा, adj. & m. four-horned; a four-pointed antelope. चौसिंघा, adj. & m. id. चौहट, m. Brbh. Av. = चौहट्टा. चौहट्ट, m. id. चौहट्टा, m. a market at a crossroads, a market square. चौहद्दी, f. boundary, boundaries of an area. चौहरा, adj. see s.v.

चौक *cauk* [*catuṣka-*], m. **1.** a quadrangle; courtyard. **2.** a square; market-place; market. **3.** main street, or central area of a city. **4.** a crossroads. **5.** a ceremonial square: an ornamented, patterned square of coloured flour, *gulāl*, &c. in which a bride and bridegroom sit at their marriage, as well as during preliminary ceremonies; a similar square filled with sweets, or with precious stones. **6.** the number four; an aggregate of four. — ~ पूजना, to perform a particular act of worship in the eighth month of pregnancy; reg. = ~ पूरना. ~ भरना, or पूरना, v.t. to form or to lay out a ceremonial square; to fill such a square with sweets, &c. चारों चौक, adv. on all four sides; Av. thoroughly. – चौक-चकनी, f. reg. a festival held on the fourth of the light fortnight in Bhādoṁ when school pupils worship Gaṇeś.

चौकड़ा *caukṛā* [cf. *catuṣka-*], m. **1.** a group or total of four. 2. = चौका, 4. **3.** *hist.* division of a crop between tenant and landowner in proportions of one quarter and three-quarters.

चौकड़ात *caukṛāt* [cf. H. *caukṛā*], f. an assembly of four: a council of arbitration.

चौकड़ी *caukṛī* [cf. H. *caukṛā*], f. **1.** a group or total of four (objects, or people). **2.** fourfold construction (as of the stringing of a bedstead). **3.** a bound, leap (as of a deer, with all four legs together); a bounce. — ~ भरना, to bound, to spring; to bounce. ~ भूलना (अपनी), colloq. to lose (one's) dash. ~ मारना, id. ~ मारकर बैठना, to squat with legs folded, drawn up. ~ लगाना, = ~ मारना.

चौकन्ना *caukannā* [*catuṣkarṇa-*], adj. **1.** vigilant, alert, wary. **2.** sly. — ~ होना, or रहना (से), to be on one's guard (against).

चौकस *caukas*, adj. **1.** watchful, alert; careful. **2.** good, proper, fine (as of quality, or weight). — ~ करना (से), to alert one (to). ~ रहना (से), to be on one's guard (against); to be careful.

चौकसाई *cauksāī*, f. = चौकसी.

चौकसी *cauksī* [cf. H. *caukas*], f. watchfulness; watch, guard (over, पर); care. — ~ करना (की), to watch (over), to guard; to be careful (about), to be alert.

चौका *caukā* [*catuṣka-*], m. **1.** an aggregate of four; a four (as in cards, cricket). **2.** a square piece of ground; a cooking area; an eating area. **3.** a square slab (of marble or other stone). **4.** a vessel divided into a number of compartments. — ~ लगाना (पर or में), to make clean an area (as for cooking, or worship) by smearing it with earth and cow-dung. चौके पर राँड़ होना, fig. to be widowed immediately after marriage. – चौका-बरतन, m. cleaning the cooking or eating area, and the utensils, after a meal; washing up. चौका-बरतन करना, to wash up.

चौकी *caukī* [*catuṣka-*], f. **1.** a low, rectangular, four-legged seat; stool; bench. **2.** a dais, platform; throne; shrine; seat of an important person. **3.** a kneading-board (= चकला). **4.** a site, station or base; post (as of a guard; or of police or customs). **5.** a watch-post; an outpost. **6.** guard, watch. — ~ बदलना, v.i. & v.t. a guard to be changed; to change guard. ~ बैठना, to be on watch. ~ बैठाना, to station a guard or watch. ~ भरना, v.t. to make an offering to a deity; to keep watch. – चौकी-घर, m. a guard-house, watch-post. चौकीदार [P. -*dār*], m. a watchman; guard; local policeman.

°ई, f. the work, position or pay of a watchman, &c.; rate levied for watch or guard duties. चौकी-पहरा, m. turn of watch or guard duty.

चौकोन *caukon*, adj. & m. **1.** adj. four-cornered; square. **2.** a square.

चौखट *caukhaṭ* [**catuṣkāṣṭha-*: Pk. *caükkaṭṭhī-*], f. (also m., *Pl.*) **1.** a door-frame; door-sill and lintel. **2.** threshold.

चौखटा *caukhṭā* [cf. H. *caukhaṭ*], m. frame (as of a picture).

चौखा *caukhā* [**catuṣkhāta-*], m. reg. a place where four boundaries meet.

चौगान *caugān* [P. *caugān*], m. **1.** a polo stick. ***2.** polo. **3.** a polo field; fig. arena.

चौड़ा *cauṛā* [**ca-uḍa-*], adj. & m. **1.** adj. wide, broad; ample. **2.** an open, or a remote area. — ~ करना, v.t. to widen; to enlarge; to extend, to expand. चौड़े में, adv. in the open, openly. चौड़े में बैठा रह जाना, to be left desolate, to be quite forsaken; to be ruined.

चौड़ाई *cauṛāī* [cf. H. *cauṛā*], f. **1.** width, breadth; extent. **2.** latitude. **3.** [× H. *cauṛāna*] being extended: extension, expansion.

चौड़ान *cauṛān* [cf. H. *cauṛā*, or *cauṛānā*], f. width, breath.

चौड़ाना *cauṛānā* [cf. H. *cauṛā*], v.t. & v.i. **1.** v.t. to widen, to broaden. **2.** to enlarge, to expand. **3.** v.i. to grow wide, to widen.

चौड़ापन *cauṛāpan* [cf. H. *cauṛā*], m. width, breadth, &c.

चौड़ाव *cauṛāv* [cf. H. *cauṛā*], m. width, breadth.

चौतरा *cautrā* [cf. H. *caurā*, and *catura-*[2]], m. = चबूतरा.

चौतरिया *cautariyā*, m. dimin. = चौतरा.

चौतीस *cautīs*, adj. pronun. var. = चौंतीस.

चौथ *cauth* [*caturtha-*], f. **1.** a fourth part. **2.** *hist.* a tribute levied by the Marāṭhās on north Indian rulers. **3.** the fourth day of a lunar fortnight. — ~ का चाँद, m. the moon on the fourth night of a fortnight: esp. that of the bright fortnight of Bhādoṁ (supposed to bring reproach or disgrace on one who looks at it).

चौथपन *cauthpan* [cf. H. *cauth*], m. the fourth stage of life (supposed to begin from the seventy-fifth year).

चौथा *cauthā* [*caturtha-*], adj. & m. **1.** adj. fourth. **2.** m. an observance taking place on the fourth day after a death, when gifts of clothes or money are given to the widow or son of the deceased.

चौथाई *cauthāī* [cf. *caturtha-*], f. a quarter; a quarter (of). — तीन ~ दुनिया, three-quarters of the world.

चौथिया *cauthiyā* [cf. H. *cauth*], m. *Pl.* **1.** holder of a fourth share. **2.** a quartan fever.

चौथी *cauthī* [H. *cauthā*], f. the fourth day: an observance taking place on the fourth day of marriage (signalising formal completion of the ceremony).

चौदश *caudaś*, f. = चौदस.

चौदस *caudas* [cf. *caturdaśa-*[2]], f. the fourteenth day of the lunar fortnight.

चौदह *caudah* [*caturdaśa*[1]], adj. fourteen. — ~ खंड, m. pl. E.H. = ~ भुवन. ~ चंदा, m. pl. E.H. the fourteen moons: = ~ विद्या. ~ ठहर, m. pl. E.H. = next. ~ भुवन, m. pl. *mythol.* the fourteen worlds: the earth and the six heavenly regions above it, with the seven regions below. ~ रत्न, m. pl. *mythol.* the fourteen treasures produced at the churning of the ocean. ~ लोक, m. pl. = ~ भुवन. ~ विद्या, f. pl. fourteen traditional divisions of knowledge, incl. the Vedas, various classes of auxiliary works, and the Purāṇas.

चौदहवाँ *caudahvāṁ* [cf. *caturdaśa-*[2]], adj. fourteenth. — चौदहवीं रात, a night on which the moon is full. चौदहवीं (रात) का चाँद, m. a full moon; a lovely face.

चौधराई *caudhrāī* [cf. H. *caudhrī*], f. the work, position, or status of a *caudhrī*.

चौधराना *caudhrānā* [H. *caudhrī*+P. *-āna*], m. = चौधराई.

चौधरानी *caudhrānī* [cf. H. *caudhrī*], f. wife of a *caudhrī*.

चौधरी *caudhrī* [conn. *caturdhara-*], m. **1.** the leader of a community or occupational group. **2.** the headman of a village. **3.** an honorific title.

चौपई *caupaī* [*catuṣpadikā-*], f. a partic. type of quatrain having fifteen *mātrās* per line.

चौपट *caupaṭ* [cf. **catuṣpaṭṭa-*], adj. & f. **1.** adj. open all round; wide open. **2.** levelled, razed, laid waste; ruined. **3.** fig. depraved, ruined. **4.** f. a waste; a ruin. — ~ करना, to level; to demolish; to ruin; to corrupt.

चौपड़ *caupaṛ* [*catuṣpuṭa-*], m. **1.** a game like *causar*, played with dice on a cloth or board of cross-shaped layout. **2.** a *caupaṛ* cloth (or board). **3.** transf. the form of a cross; a temple courtyard. — ~ का, adj. cruciform. ~ का बाज़ार, or ~ बाज़ार, m. a market or bazaar area formed around a crossroads. – चौपड़बाज़ [P. *-bāz*], m. a *caupaṛ* player.

चौपही *caupahī*, f. Brbh. = चौपई.

चौपाई *caupāī* [**catuṣpādikā-*], f. a quatrain (usually printed as two rhyming lines of verse, each containing sixteen *mātrās* or metrical instants).

[1]**चौपाल** *caupāl* [cf. *catur-*; **palla-*[3]], m. **1.** an assembly-room, or covered assembly-place (in a village). **2.** a verandah.

[2]**चौपाल** *caupāl* [? = H. [1]*caupāl*], m. reg. (E.) a litter or palanquin open at the sides.

चौपाला *caupālā*, m. a closed litter or palanquin.

चौपैया *caupaiyā*, f. see s.v. चौ-.

चौबच्चा *caubaccā*, m. = चहबच्चा.

चौबर *caubar*, adj. sturdy, stout; bold.

चौबा *caubā*, m. = चौबे.

चौबाइन *caubāin* [cf. H. *caube*], f. **1.** a woman of the Caube brāhmaṇ community. **2.** the wife of a Caube.

चौबीस *caubīs* [*caturviṁśati-*], adj. twenty-four.

चौबे *caube* [*caturveda-*], m. **1.** a partic. brāhmaṇ community. **2.** a man of that community.

चौर *caur* [**ca-uḍa*], m. reg. **1.** an open space in forest land. **2.** Bihar. an underground pit for storing grain.

चौरंग *caurang* [*caturaṅga-*], m. cutting off four, or several, things (as the four legs of an animal) with a single sword stroke. — ~ काटना (के), to cut off cleanly with one stroke. ~ मारना (के), to hamstring (an animal).

चौरस *cauras* [*caturaśra-*], adj. **1.** level, even; flat. **2.** square. **2.** adv. on all four sides alike, all round. — ~ करना, to make even, to level.

चौरसाई *caursāī* [cf. H. *cauras*], f. *Pl. HŚS.* **1.** evenness. **2.** levelling (of ground).

चौरसाना *caursānā* [cf. H. *cauras*], v.t. to make level or even.

चौरसी *caursī* [cf. H. *cauras*], f. levelling, planing.

चौरा *caurā* [*catura-*[2]], m. **1.** a platform (= चबूतरा). **2.** specif. platform or plinth of masonry worshipped as the abode of a deity, saint or spirit. **3.** a place of sacrifice; altar.

चौरानवे *caurānve* [*caturnavati-*], adj. ninety-four.

[1]**चौरासी** *caurāsī* [*caturaśīti-*], adj. **1.** eighty-four. **2.** an aggregate of eighty-four; Av. small ankle-bells worn by dancing-girls; *hist.* a sub-division of a *parganā* comprising eighty-four villages. **3.** an aggregate of eighty-four lacs: *hind.* the endless succession of transmigrations. — ~ में पड़ना, to be caught up in the cycle of transmigration.

[2]**चौरासी** *caurāsī* [*caturaśra-*], f. reg. a kind of chisel, file or plane.

चौराहा *caurāhā* [H. *cau-*+P. *rāh*], m. a crossroads.

चौरी *caurī*, f. dimin. = चौरा.

चौर्य *cauryă* [S.], m. theft.

चौल-कर्म *caul-karm* [S.], m. *hind.* the ceremony of tonsure: shaving the head of a child three years old, leaving only one lock on the crown.

चौला *caulā*, m. *Pl.* reg. (W.) a kind of bean (= लोबिया).

चौलाई *caulāī* [**catūrāji-*], f. name of several plants of the species *Amaranthus* (two varieties being called *lāl caulāī* (*lāl sāg*) and *harī caulāī*) whose leaves are boiled for food.

चौवन *cauvan* [*catuṣpañcāśat-*], adj. fifty-four.

चौवा *cauvā* [? *caturvaya-*], m. **1.** an aggregate of four; a four (as at cards, dice, cricket). **2.** four fingers' breadth, a palm's breadth. — ~ लगाना, to hit a four.

चौवाई *cauvāī* [**caturvāta-*], f. a wind (blowing) from all quarters: a gentle breeze.

[1]**चौस** *caus*, m. *Pl. HŚS.* powder; flour, meal.

[2]**चौस** *caus*, m. reg. (W.) land four times ploughed (cf. *causarī*).

चौसठ *causaṭh*, adj. pronun. var. = चौंसठ.

चौसर *causar*, m. **1.** a game played by two players with sixteen counters each, using three dice, on a cloth or board of cross-shaped layout (= चौपड़). **2.** a *causar* cloth or board.

चौसरी *causărī* [**catuḥsara-*], f. *Pl.* **1.** a women's ornament worn tightly round the neck and hooked behind. 2. = [2]*caus.*

चौहत्तर *cauhattar* [*catuḥsaptati-*], adj. seventy-four.

चौहरा *cauhrā*, [cf. *cau-*], adj. having four folds; fourfold.

चौहान *cauhān*, m. **1.** name of a Rājpūt community. **2.** a man of that community.

च्यंत- *cyant-*, E.H. = चिंत-.

च्यवन *cyavan* [S.], m. a trickling, flowing; distilling. — **च्यवन-प्राश**, m. *ayur.* A partic. tonic medicine.

च्युत *cyut* [S.], adj. **1.** fallen (from, **से**). **2.** deviated, strayed (from, **से**). **3.** depraved, corrupt. — **च्युताधिकार** [°*ta*+*a*°], adj. discharged or dismissed from (one's) position, deprived of authority.

च्युति *cyuti* [S.], f. **1.** a falling; a flowing out or down. **2.** a falling short, failing. **3.** discharge, dismissal; demotion. **4.** want, lack.

च्यूँटा *cyūṁṭā*, m. = **चींटा**.

च्यूँटी *cyūṁṭī*, f. = **चींटी**.

छ

छ *cha*, the seventh consonant of the Devanāgarī syllabary. — ~ छकार, m. the sound /ch/; the letter छ.

छँकाना *caṁkānā*, v.t. ? to cause to strain, or to filter.

छंगा *caṅgā* [*ṣaḍaṅga-*: w. H. *chah*], adj. & m. **1.** adj. having six fingers, or six toes. **2.** m. a person having six fingers or toes.

छँगुली *chaṁgulī*, f. sixth finger; little finger.

छँटना *chaṁṭnā* [cf. H. *chāṁṭnā*], v.i. **1.** to be cut, to be pared; to be trimmed; to be cut down, or cut to pieces. **2.** to be cut back, or curtailed; to diminish. **3.** to be picked out, to be selected; to be cleared (as weeds, dirt); to be separated, sifted; to be cleaned or rinsed out. छँटा हुआ बदमाश, m. an out-and-out villain. **4.** to hold back, to hold oneself aloof. **5.** to reduce, to grow thin; to lessen. — छँटते छँटते क्षीण हो जाना, to diminish progressively (as in numbers). छँटे छँटे फिरना, or रहना (से), to avoid contact (with), to hold oneself aloof (from).

छँटनी *chaṁṭnī* [cf.H. *chaṁṭnā*], f. cutting back, retrenchment.

छँटवाई *chaṁṭvāī* [cf. H. *chāṁṭnā*], f. **1.** causing to be cut, &c. **2.** causing to be picked out, &c. 3. = छँटाई, 3.

छँटवाना *chaṁṭvānā* [cf. H. *chāṁṭnā*], v.t. **1.** to cause to be cut, trimmed, &c. (by, से). **2.** to cause to be separated, sifted, &c. (by).

छँटा *chaṁṭā* [H. *chaṁṭnā*], adj. picked, sorted, &c.; utter, out-and-out (a scoundrel).

छँटाई *chaṁṭāī* [cf. H. *chāṁṭnā*], f. **1.** cutting, trimming, &c. **2.** picking out, selecting; separating, sifting; cleaning. **3.** the cost of, or wages for, cutting or picking, &c.

छँटाना *chaṁṭānā* [cf. H. *chāṁṭnā*], v.t. 1. = छँटवाना. 2. = छाँटना.

छँटाव *chaṁṭāv* [cf. H. *chāṁṭnā*], m. **1.** cutting, paring, &c. **2.** cutting back, retrenchment; redundancy. **3.** picking out, selection; separating, sifting, &c. **4.** siftings, refuse. **5.** a detachment (from a main body).

छँड़ना *chaṁṛnā* [conn. H. *chāṛnā*], v.i. *Pl. HŚS.* to vomit.

[1]**छंद** *chand* [ad. *chandas-*[1]; or ← Panj.], m. Brbh. Av. **1.** deceit, trickery. **2.** ingenuity. — छंद-कपट, m. deceit; cunning.

[2]**छंद** *chand* [ad. *chandas-*[2]], m. *pros.* metre. — छंद-मुक्त, adj. free, non-metrical (verse). छंद-विधान, m. prosody. छंद-व्यवस्था, f. id. छंद-शास्त्र, m. poetics. छंदात्मक [°*as*+*ā*°], adj. poetic, in verse.

[3]**छंद** *chand* [S.], m. a wrist ornament.

[1]**छँदना** *chaṁdnā* [cf. H. [2]*chand*: ? × H. *chāṃdnā*], v.t. to compose verse.

[2]**छँदना** *chaṁdnā* [cf. H. *chāṃdnā*], v.i. *Pl. HŚS.* to be fettered, hobbled (an animal).

छंदी *chandī* [cf. H. [1]*chand*], adj. & m. **1.** adj. deceitful, &c. **2.** m. a deceiver, trickster.

छंदो- *chando-*. = [2]छंद: — छंदोदोष, m. a metrical irregularity. छंदोबद्ध, adj. having verse form. छंदोभंग, m. = छंदोदोष. छंदोयोजना, f. poetic composition.

छँहा- *chaṁhā-* [cf. H. *chāṁh-*], v.i. Brbh. to be shaded: to rest in the shade.

छ- *cha-*, adj. six: — छकोना, छकोनिया, adj. hexagonal. छगुना, adj. sixfold. छदाम, m. a coin of the value of about a quarter of a pice; 'a farthing'. छमाही, adj. & f. six-monthly; a period of six months; wages, &c. for six months; a ceremony, &c. occurring once every six months. छ-रस, m. pl. *rhet.* the six tastes.

[1]**छई** *chaī* [cf. H. *chay*], m. & adj. **1.** reg. tuberculosis. **2.** adj. tubercular.

[2]**छई** *chaī* [conn. **chāpa-*: Pa. *chāpa-*], f. *Pl.* children: the young generation.

छः *chaḥ*, adj. = छह.

छकड़ा *chakṛā* [**chakkaṭa-*], m. a two-wheeled bullock-cart; a cart.

छकड़ी *chakṛī*, f. = छक्का, 1., 2.

[1]**छकना** *chaknā* [cf. H. [1]*chakānā, chāk-*] **1.** to be satiated; to be intoxicated. **2.** to be fully satisfied; to be gratified. **3.** iron. to get as one's portion; to be tricked. — छककर खाना, to eat one's fill.

[2]**छकना** *chaknā* [conn. **chakka-*[1]] **1.** to be astonished, to be taken aback. **2.** to be harassed or afflicted.

[1]**छकवाना** *chakvānā* [cf. H. [1]*chakānā*], v.t. to cause to be satiated, &c.

[2]**छकवाना** *chakvānā* [cf. H. [2]*chakānā*], v.t. to cause to be astonished, &c.

छकाछक *chakāchak* [cf. H. [1]*chaknā*], adj. **1.** satisfied, sated; brim-full; intoxicated. **2.** adv. completely, thoroughly. — ~ करना, to satiate; to fill full (with, or of, से).

[1]**छकाना** *chakānā* [cf. *chakka-*[2]], v.t. **1.** to satiate. **2.** to satisfy fully; to gratify. **3.** to punish soundly; to inflict a reverse (on).

[2]**छकाना** *chakānā* [cf. H. [2]*chaknā*], v.t. to astonish, &c.

छकुर *chakur*, m. *Pl. HŚS.* a division (as of crops), with one-sixth assigned to the landholder.

छक्का *chakkā* [*ṣaṭka-*], m. **1.** a group or total of six; a six (in cards, dice, cricket). **2.** sthg. having six sections; a group having six members. **3.** the faculties, the wits (the five senses with *man*, heart or intellect); cunning. — छक्के छुड़ाना (के), to disconcert, to bewilder (one); fig. to take the wind from (one's) sails. छक्के छूटना, (के), to be disconcerted, bewildered. — छक्का-पंजा, m. sixes and fives: trickery, deceit; plotting. छक्का-पंजा भूलना, to be at a loss (as to what to do). – छक्केबाज़ [P. *-bāz*], m. a wily person.

छगड़ा *chagṛā* [ad. **chaggala-*; cf. Raj. *chagal*], m. E.H. a goat.

छगन- *chagan-* [? conn. **chadyati*: anal. MIA *-gg-*], v.t. *Pl.* to taste, &c. (= चखन).

छगरा *chagrā* [**chaggala-*], m. reg. (W.) a goat.

छगरी *chagrī* [**chaggala-*], f. reg. a small goat.

छछिया *chachiyā* [cf. H. *chāch*], f. a skimmer (as for buttermilk).

छछूँदर *chachūṁdar* [*chucchundari-*: ← Drav.], f. the musk rat.

छज्जा *chajjā* [*chādya-*], m. **1.** a balcony, a gallery. **2.** eaves; an overhang (in building), projection. **3.** the roof of a porch. **4.** reg. the bottom of a cart. — छज्जेदार [P. *-dār*], adj. having a balcony, &c.

छटँकी *chaṭaṁkī* [cf. H. *chaṭāṁk*], f. a weight of approx. two ounces.

छटकना *chaṭaknā* [? conn. **chaṭṭ-*[1]], v.i. to slip (from the hand or grasp).

छटना *chaṭnā*, v.i. = छँटना.

छट-पट *chaṭ-paṭ* [cf. **chaṭṭa-*[1]], f. **1.** tossing about, floundering. **2.** agitation, restlessness; haste, impatience. — ~ करना, to flounder.

छटपटाना *chaṭpaṭānā* [cf. H. *chaṭ-paṭ*], v.i. **1.** to toss about, to flounder. **2.** to be agitated, restless; to be in haste.

छटपटाहट *chaṭpaṭāhaṭ* [cf. *chaṭpaṭānā*], f. a state of floundering, or of agitation, &c.; = छट-पट.

छटपटी *chaṭpaṭī* [cf. H. *chaṭpaṭānā*], f. = छट-पट.

छटाँक *chaṭāṁk* [**ṣaṭṭaṅka-*], f. a sixteenth of a *ser* (approx. two ounces). ~ भर, adv. a tiny amount (of a substance).

छटाँकी *chaṭaṁkī*, f. = छटँकी.

छटा *chaṭā* [S.], f. splendour, brilliance, lustre.

छठ *chaṭh* [*ṣaṣṭhī-*], f. the sixth day of the lunar fortnight.

छठवाँ *chaṭhvāṁ* [cf. *ṣaṭ-*], adj. sixth (= छठा).

छठा *chaṭhā* [*ṣaṣṭha-*], adj. sixth. — छठे, adv. in sixth place. छठे छहमास, छठे छमाहे, adv. colloq. every sixth six months: once in a blue moon.

छठी *chaṭhī* [H. *chaṭhā*], f. 1. = छठ. **2.** the sixth day after the birth of a child (when ceremonial observances, incl. the naming of the child, are performed). — ~ का खाना, food prepared and eaten on the sixth day after the birth of a child. ~ का खाया-पिया निकालना, colloq. to punish (one). ~ का दूध याद आना, fig. to be in a very helpless and painful situation. ~ का दूध याद दिलाना, to reduce (one) to complete helplessness, to beat (one) severely.

[1]**छड़** *chaṛ* [**chaṭa-*], f. m. **1.** a pole, rod; staff; bar. **2.** a fishing-rod. **3.** *Pl.* stem, stalk, stubble.

[2]**छड़** *chaṛ*, [? = [1]*chaṛ*], f. *Pl.* a fragrant grass.

छड़ना *chaṛnā* [**chaṭ-*: Pk. *chaḍā-*], v.t. **1.** to separate husk from grain by beating or pounding. **2.** colloq. to thrash.

छड़वाना *chaṛvānā* [cf. H. *chaṛnā*], v.t. to cause (grain) to be husked (by, से).

छड़ा *chaṛā* [cf. H. *chaṛnā*], adj. & m. **1.** adj. separate, apart; single. **2.** m. a single (unmarried) man. **3.** a single ornament having several or many parts: a kind of silver anklet; a chain or bunch of pearls. **4.** reg. (Bihar) a single leather thong or tie. — छड़े-छटाँक, and छड़े-छटाँक, adv. on one's own, keeping to oneself; unencumbered.

छड़ी *chaṛī* [**chaṭa-*], f. **1.** stick, cane, rod; switch; walking stick. **2.** *hind.* a ceremony taking place on the fourth day of a wedding in which the bride and bridegroom playfully beat each other with flower-covered sticks.

छड़ीला *chaṛīlā*, m. **1.** *Pl.* a kind of fragrant moss. **2.** reg. (Bihar) a spice used in manufacturing tobacco.

[1]**छत** *chat* [**chatti-*], f. **1.** a roof. **2.** a ceiling. **3.** a deck. — ~ डालना, to build a roof (on, &c., पर). ~ पाटना, or बनाना, to make a ceiling (to, की).

[2]**छत** *chat* [ad. *kṣata-*], adj. & m. Brbh. Av. **1.** adj. wounded, hurt. **2.** m. a wounded place, wound.

छतनार *chatnār* [cf. *chattra-*[1], or ← Panj.], adj. umbrella- or mushroom-shaped: flattish.

छतरी *chatrī* [ad. *chattra-*[1]], f. **1.** an umbrella; a small umbrella; bamboo frame set on a pole (as a perch for doves). **2.** a covering, canopy; hood (of a vehicle); poop, uppermost space (of a vessel). **3.** an ornamental pavilion (on the uppermost level of a building, or over a burial place or cenotaph). — ~ फ़ौज, f. a parachute division or force. ~ सैनिक, m. paratrooper. — छतरीदार [P. *-dār*], adj. having a covering, canopy, or pavilion. छतरीधारी, adj. *mil.* equipped with parachute(s). छतरीबाज़ [P.*-bāz*], m. a parachutist.

छताँ *chatāṁ* [*ākṣeti*], part. E.H. being, existing.

छति *chati* [ad. *kṣati-*], f. Av. harm, loss; damage.

छतियाना *chatiyānā* [cf. H. *chātī*], v.t. colloq. *Pl. HŚS.* to raise (a firearm) to the shoulder.

छत्तर *chattar* [*chattvara-*], m. *Pl.* = छत्रा.

छत्ता *chattā* [*chattra-*[1]], m. **1.** a wasp's nest, beehive. **2.** a covered way, or passage. **3.** umbrella (= छाता). **4.** reg. (Bihar) cluster, group (as of buds). **5.** pericarp of a lotus.

छत्तीस *chattīs* [*ṣattriṁśat-*], adj. thirty-six.

छत्तीसा *chattīsā* [cf. H. *chattīs*], adj. possessing thirty-six arts or skills: **1.** cunning; dissembling. **2.** licentious, lewd.

[1]**छत्र** *chatr* [ad. *chattra-*[1]], m. **1.** a parasol, an umbrella (esp. as held over kings or their thrones, or over idols). **2.** a mushroom. — छत्र-छाँह, f. = next. छत्र-छाया, f. protection, shelter; patronage. छत्रधर, m. = °-धारी; an attendant holding a royal parasol. °-धार, m. E.H. = next. °-धारी, m. holding a parasol: a king. छत्र-पति, m. a king dignified by the emblem of a parasol: a great king.

[2]**छत्र-** *chatr-* [ad. *kṣatr(iya-), kṣātra-*], m. Brbh. Av. a kṣatriya: — छत्र-पूत, m. a Rājpūt. छत्र-बंधु, m. pej. one whose relatives are kṣatriyas.

छत्रक *chatrak* [ad. *chattraka-*], m. **1.** a mushroom. **2.** a fungus.

छत्रा *chatrā* [*chattvara-*], m. reg. (W.) house or shelter used for distributing cooked food to beggars.

छत्रिनी *chatrinī* [cf. H. [2]*chatrī*, and *kṣatriyāṇī-*], f. = क्षत्रानी.

छत्री *chatrī* [ad. *kṣatriya-*], m. a man of the kṣatriya caste group.

छद *chad* [S.], m. Brbh. **1.** a covering. **2.** a leaf. **3.** a wing.

छद्म *chadmă* [S.], m. a covering over: **1.** a disguise; masquerade. **2.** dissembling, a pretext. — छद्म-तापस, m. a false ascetic, a religious impostor. छद्म-नाम, m. a pseudonym. छद्म-युद्ध, *mil.* manoeuvres. छद्म-वेश, m. a disguise. °ई, m. a disguised person; a dissembler.

छद्मी *chadmī* [S.], m. = छद्मवेशी, s.v. छद्म.

[1]**छन** *chan* [conn. **channa-*[2]], m. f. **1.** a hissing or sizzling sound (of water falling on a hot surface, or of cooking). **2.** a jingling sound. **3.** a bracelet (worn between bangles).

[2]**छन** *chan* [ad. *kṣaṇa-*], m. = क्षण.

छनक *chanak* [cf. H. *chanchanānā*], f. a tinkling or jingling sound.

छनछन *chanchan* [cf. **channa-*[2]], f. & adv. **1.** a jingling, clinking or tinkling sound. **2.** a hissing or sizzling sound (of water heating, or of cooking). — ~ करना, to jingle, to chink, &c.

छनछनाना *chanchanānā* [cf. **channa-*[2]], v.i. & v.t. **1.** v.i. to jingle, to clink; to tinkle. **2.** to hiss, to simmer, to sing (a kettle); to sizzle (as food being fried). **3.** v.t. to cause to make a jingling, hissing or sizzling sound; to heat; to fry.

छनछनाहट *chanchanāhaṭ* [cf. H. *chanchanānā*], f. **1.** jingling, clinking; tinkling. **2.** hissing, simmering; sizzling.

[1]**छनना** *channā* [**kṣaṇati*], v.i. **1.** to be sifted; to be winnowed. **2.** to be strained, or filtered. **3.** colloq. to be consumed (intoxicants). **4.** fig. to be intimate. उनमें गहरी छनता है, they are on very close terms. **5.** to filter (through, से: as of sunlight or moonlight through trees). **6.** to be separated out; to be discarded; to be decided (a quarrel, a fight). **7.** to be perforated, torn (the body with wounds). **8.** to be closely searched, to be investigated (a matter).

[2]**छनना** *channā* [cf. **channa-*[2]], v.i. colloq. to be fried.

[3]**छनना** *channā* [**kṣāṇana-*: Pk. *chāṇaṇa-*], m. a strainer; straining-cloth; sieve.

छननी *channī* [cf. H. [3]*channā*], f. dimin. a strainer, &c.

छनवाना *chanvānā* [cf. H. [1]*channā, chānnā*], v.t. **1.** to cause to be sifted, strained, &c. (by). **2.** to cause to be investigated (by, से).

छनाक *chanāk* [**chanakka-*], m. 1. = [1]छन, 2. 2. = झन.

छनाना *chanānā* [cf. H. [1]*channā, chānnā*], v.t. **1.** to cause to be sifted, strained, &c. (by, से). **2.** to cause to be drunk (by, से: an intoxicant such as *bhāṅg*, which is strained).

छनिक *chanik* [ad. *kṣaṇika-*], adj. = क्षणिक.

छन्न *chann* [S.], adj. covered; concealed.

छन्ना *channā* [? cf. H. *chanchanānā*], m. reg. (N.) a vessel made of bell-metal (which rings when struck); a large *kaṭorā*.

छप *chap* [? onom.], f. **1.** splashing, or squelching sound (as of an object falling into water or mud). **2.** washing, splattering (of rain). **3.** splashing (of water). — छपाछप, f. = ~ ; the sound of panting accompanying bodily exertion.

छपक *chapak* [cf. H. *chapaknā*], f. a splash, splashing sound (= छप). — ~से, adv. with a splash. — ~ ~ करना, to make a splashing sound; to splash.

छपकना *chapaknā* [cf. H. *chap*], v.i. **1.** to be dashed or thrown (water). **2.** to be splashed, bespattered.

छपकली *chapkalī*, f. = छिपकली.

छपका *chapkā* [cf. H. *chapakna*], m. **1.** a splash (of water, &c.); spatter (as on clothing).

छपकाना *chapkānā* [cf. H. *chapaknā*], v.t. **1.** to dash or throw (water). **2.** to splash, to bespatter (as with water).

छपना *chapnā* [cf. H. *chāpnā*], v.i. **1.** to be stamped; to be marked, to be printed (cloth). **2.** to be printed (a book); to be published.

छपरा *chaprā* [*chattvara-*], m. a thatch; a hut.

छपरी *chaprī*, f. E.H. = छपरा.

छपवाई *chapvāī* [cf. H. *chapvānā*], f. **1.** causing to be printed. **2.** cost of, or wages for, printing.

छपवाना *chapvānā* [cf. H. *chāpnā*], v.t. to cause to be printed, &c. (by, से).

छपाई *chapāī* [cf. H. *chāpnā, chapānā*], f. **1.** printing. **2.** a printing, an impression. **3.** style of print or type-face. **4.** cost of, or wages for, printing.

छपाका *chapākā* [cf. H. *chap*], m. = छप.

छपाछप *chapāchap*, adj. see s.v. छप.

छपाना *chapānā* [cf. *chāpnā*], v.t. to cause to be printed, &c. (by, से).

छपैया *chapaiyā* [cf. H. *chapānā*], m. a printer.

छप्पन *chappan* [*ṣaṭpañcāśat-*], adj. fifty-six. — ~ छुरी, f. colloq. fifty-six knives: a dangerous woman. ~ पकवान, m. pl. colloq. all the food one could possibly want (see next). ~ भोग, m. *hind.* fifty six dishes (as offered to the Vallabhan deity Ṭhākurjī).

छप्पय *chappay* [*ṣaṭpada-*], m. a partic. six-line stanza of composite structure based on the *rolā* and *ullāla* metres.

छप्पर *chappar* [*chattvara-*], m. **1.** a thatched roof. **2.** a thatched building; a hut; a shed. ~ छाना, or डालना, to build a thatch; to make a home, to reside. ~ टूट पड़ना, the roof to fall in: a sudden calamity to befall one. ~ पर धरना, or रखना, to place on the thatch: to treat as worthless or trivial. ~ फाड़कर देना (को), fig. to give from on high (in an unexpected, or miraculous way). — छप्पर-खट, f. a bedstead with curtains and upper covering.

छब *chab*, f. = छवि.

छबड़ा *chabṛā*, m. **1.** a basket made of twigs, or reeds. **2.** a hawker's display case.

छबड़ी *chabṛī*, f. dimin. see छबड़ा.

छबि *chabi* [ad. *chavi-*], f. 1. = छवि. **2.** [× Ar. *śabīh*] a likeness; portrait; a photograph. — ~ उतारना (की), to draw a portrait (of); to take a photograph (of).

छबीला *chabīlā* [? conn. *chavi-*, or *chādmika-*], adj. **1.** graceful, shapely (a woman); handsome (in a feminine way). **2.** foppish, modish (of attire).

छबीलापन *chabīlāpan* [cf. H. *chabīlā*], m. foppishness, modishness.

छब्बीस *chabbīs* [*ṣadviṁśati-*], adj. twenty-six.

छब्बीसी *chabbīsī* [cf. H. *chabbīs*], f. a way of counting as used by fruit-sellers, in which twenty-six fives are reckoned as one hundred.

छम- *cham-* [ad. *kṣamā-*, *kṣamate*], v.i. Av. to forgive, to pardon.

छम-छम *cham-cham* [cf. **chamma-*], f. & adv. **1.** f. a jingling sound (as of anklets, bells). **2.** the sound of heavy rain. **3.** adv. with a jingling sound; with a drumming sound (rain).

छमछमाना *chamchamānā* [cf. **chamma-*], v.i. **1.** to jingle. **2.** to drum, to beat (rain). **3.** to glitter, to flash.

छमा *chamā* [ad. *kṣamā-*], f. = क्षमा.

छय *chay* [ad. *kṣaya-*], m. = क्षय.

छरछराहट *charcharāhaṭ*, f. a burning sensation.

छरहरा *charahrā*, adj. **1.** lean, spare (of build). **2.** Brbh. slender, graceful (a woman). **3.** lively, active (as of animals).

छरहरापन *charahrāpan* [cf. H. *charahrā*], m. leanness, &c.

छरिंदा *charindā*, adj. *Pl. HŚS.* = छरीदा.

छरीदा *charīdā*, adj. *Pl. HŚS.* separate, alone, single.

छर्रा *charrā* [? cf. **chaṭ*-: Pk. *chaḍā*-], m. **1.** a small stone; piece of shot. **2.** a charge of shot; shower (esp. of stones, &c). छर्रे चलना, shot to fly; repartee to be exchanged.

छल *chal* [*chala*-[1]], m. **1.** deceit; fraud; dissembling, pretence. **2.** pretext. **3.** trick, stratagem; manoeuvre; trickery. — ~ करना, to deceive, &c. ~ में आना (के), to be deceived (by), &c.; to be imposed on (by). – छल-कपट, m. deceit; cunning. छल-छिद्र, m. Av. deceit; dissembling; trickery. छल-बट्टा, m. fraud and harm: deceit, &c. छल-बल, m. fraud and force: trickery, stratagem, &c. °इया, adj. fraudulent, &c. छल-विद्या, f. (Brbh.) a deceitful skill or art.

छलक *chalak* [cf. H. *chalaknā*], f. splashing, overflowing; a splash, &c.

छलकना *chalaknā* [**chalakka*-], v.i. **1.** to be spilt, to spill; to splash. **2.** to overflow; to brim (as with tears: the eyes). **3.** to ripple (flowing water).

छलकाना *chalkānā* [cf. H. *chalaknā*], v.t. to cause to overflow, or to spill.

छलछल *chalchal* [cf. **chala*-[2]], f. the sound of splashing, rippling or overflowing.

छलछलाना *chalchalānā*, v.i. = छलकना.

छलछलाहट *chalchalāhaṭ* [cf. H. *chalchalānā*], f. the sound of splashing, rippling or overflowing.

छलन *chalan* [S.], m. **1.** deceiving, &c. (cf. छल). **2.** tricking, cheating, &c.

[1]**छलना** *chalnā* [*chalayati*], v.t. **1.** to deceive; to defraud; to delude. **2.** to trick, to cheat; to outwit.

[2]**छलना** *chalnā* [conn. *cālana*-; H. *chalnī*], m. **1.** a large sieve. **2.** a large strainer.

[3]**छलना** *chalănā* [S.], f. deceit; an appearance, a fiction.

छलनी *chalnī* [*cālana*-: w. H. [3]*channā*], f. & adj. **1.** f. a sieve. **2.** a strainer. **3.** adj. colloq. riddled (with holes). **4.** battered. — ~ करना, to riddle; to batter. ~ होना, to be pierced repeatedly; to be riddled with holes; to be battered; to be worn out (as the feet with walking).

छलहाया *chalhāyā* [cf. *chala*-], adj. deceiving, faithless.

छलाँग *chalāṁg* [cf. H. *chalāṁgnā*], f. **1.** a leap, bound; spring. **2.** *athl.* a jump. — ~, or छलाँगें, भरना, or मारना, to leap, to bound (as a stag).

छलाँगना *chalāṁgnā* [? **ut-śal-*+*laṅghati*], v.i. to leap, to bound; to spring.

छलावा *chalāvā* [cf. H. *chalnā*], m. **1.** an apparition. **2.** will o' the wisp.

छलिया *chaliyā* [cf. H. *chal*], adj. & m. = छली.

छली *chalī* [S., and cf. H. *chal*], adj. & m. **1.** adj. deceitful; false; faithless. **2.** colloq. tricky, slippery. **3.** m. a deceiver. **4.** a trickster, cheat.

छल्ला *challā*, m. **1.** a plain ring, usu. of metal. **2.** a ring-shaped object; ringlet, lock (of hair). **3.** [Panj.] a kind of song. — छल्लेदार [P. *-dār*], adj. having rings, or ringlets; annular; having spots of grease or oil on the surface (as soup, water)

[1]**छल्ली** *challī*, f. **1.** a small basket or container made of woven twigs, grasses, &c. **2.** an ear of maize.

[2]**छल्ली** *challī* [conn. *challī̆*-], f. skin; bark.

छल्लू *challū*, adj. reg. boyish, silly (cf. छलछिलाना).

छवाँ *chavāṁ* [cf. H. *chah*: anal.], adj. sixth (= छठा).

छवाना *chavānā* [cf. H. *chānā*], v.t. to cause to be covered or thatched (by, से).

[1]**छवि** *chavi* [S.], f. **1.** beauty; grace, charm; graceful form. **2.** brilliance; lustre; splendour. **3.** image, picture (of a person: see छबि; also fig). छवि-कंद, m. Brbh. a person of abundant or supreme beauty.

[2]**छवि** *chavi* [Panj.], f. a spear (= *barchī*).

छवैया *chavaiyā* [cf. H. *chānā, chavānā*], m. a thatcher.

छह *chah* [**kṣaṭ*: Pa. *cha*], adj. six.

छहरना *chaharnā* [conn. Pk. *chuha*-], v.i. to be scattered, dispersed.

छाँट *chāṁṭ* [cf. H. *chāṁṭnā*], f. **1.** cutting, paring; trimming. **2.** picking, sorting out. **3.** cut, fashion. **4.** a cutting; a scrap; scraps; refuse, rubbish; vomit(ing). **5.** an excerpt. — छाँट-छँटाव, m. = next. छाँट-छूट, f. cutting off, cutting down; trimming, pruning; cuttings; retrenchment, saving; savings. छाँट-छूट करना, to cut off, &c.; to retrench; to save.

छाँटना *chāṁṭnā* [**chāṇṭ*-], v.t. **1.** to cut, to pare; to trim; to prune; to dress; to cut off, to cut through; to cut to pieces (as an army). **2.** to cut back; to curtail; to abridge; to retrench. **3.** to take or to pick out, to select; to separate (as husk from grain, by pounding); to sift, to sieve. **4.** to pick out and reject; to clear, to remove (as weeds, dirt, seeds). **5.** fig. to wash lightly; to rinse. **6.** to discuss (a topic) in a desultory way. **7.** to parade, to display (knowledge or learning).

छाँड़ना *chāṁṛnā* [**chṛndati*: Pk. *chaṁḍaï*], v.t. **1.** = छोड़ना. **2.** *Pl. HŚS.* to vomit.

छाँद *chāṁd* [**chanda-*[3]], f. E.H. a hobble (for animals).

छाँदना *chāṁdnā* [**chandati*], v.t. *Pl. HŚS.* to fasten, to tie; to hobble (an animal).

छांदिक *chāndik* [S.], adj. metrical; rhythmical.

छाँव *chāṁv*, f. = छाँह.

छाँह *chāṁh* [*chāyā-*, × *ābhā-*: Pk. *chāhā-*], f. **1.** shade. **2.** shadow. **3.** reflection. **4.** fig. protection, shelter. — ~ न छूने देना, fig, not to allow (one) to come near. छाँह-गीर [P. *-gīr*], m. Brbh. a parasol (emblem of royalty).

छाईं *chāīṁ* [*chāyā-*], f. **1.** shade. **2.** shadow. **3.** reflection.

छाई *chāī* [*chādi-*], f. ashes, ash.

[1]**छाक** *chāk* [**chakka-*[2]], f. 19c. a quantity (esp. of food) sufficient for one time: **1.** lunch, &c. (as taken by labourers to work). **2.** *Pl. HŚS.* cakes of refined flour (sent as a marriage gift). **3.** a turn, occasion; milking-time; milking.

[2]**छाक** *chāk* [**chakka-*[1]], f. Brbh. intoxication.

छाक- *chāk-* [**chakka-*[2]1], v.i. Brbh. Av. to be satiated; to be intoxicated.

[1]**छागल** *chāgal* [S.], m. & f. *Pl. HŚS.* **1.** m. a goat. **2.** f. reg. (W.) an earthen water-pot with a spout (orig. of goat-skin); a water-bag.

[2]**छागल** *chāgal*, m. reg. an anklet with bells.

छाछट *chāchaṭ*, pronun. var. = छियासठ.

छाछ *chāch* [**chācchī-*], f. buttermilk.

छाज *chāj* [**chajja-*: Pk. *chajjiā-*], m. a flat winnowing basket or fan.

छाजन *chājan* [cf. H. *chājnā*], f. m. **1.** thatching, covering in. **2.** Av. thatch. **3.** eczema. **4.** transf. esp. in comp. clothing, garments.

[1]**छाजना** *chājnā* [**chādyate*], v.t. to thatch.

[2]**छाजना** *chājnā* [**chadyati*: Pk. *chajjaï*], v.i. Brbh. Av. to be becoming (to); to grace (a scene).

छाड़ *chāṛ* [cf. H. *chāṛnā*], f. reg. (W.) leaving: land gained by the retreat of a river.

छाड़ना *chāṛnā* [*chardati*], v.t. = छाँड़ना.

छात *chāt* [*chattra-*], m. Av. **1.** parasol (as an emblem of royalty). **2.** fig. protection.

छाता *chātā* [*chattra-*], m. **1.** a parasol. **2.** an umbrella. — छाताधारी सैनिक, m. paratrooper. साँप का ~, m. reg. (E.) mushroom.

छाती *chātī* [**chātti-*], f. **1.** breast, chest; bosom. **2.** breast(s) (of a woman). **3.** fig. heart, spirit, courage; emotions. — ~ उड़ी जाना, the heart to be overwhelmed (with apprehension, or premonitions). ~ उभरना, the breasts to swell. ~ उमगना, or उमड़ना, to be strongly moved, deeply touched; to rejoice. ~ का जम, m. fig. a heavy burden; a nuisance. ~ का पत्थर, or पहाड़, m. id. ~ कूटना, = ~ पीटना. ~ के किवाड़ खुलना, the heart's doors to be open: to be overwhelmed with emotion (as feelings of joy, or envy); one's intimate thoughts to be revealed; to become enlightened (as to sthg). ~ के किवाड़ खोलना, to open one's heart.
~ गदराना, = ~ उभरना. ~ जलना, the heart to burn (as with grief, envy, rancour); to suffer heart-burn. ~ जलाना (की), to distress (one); to vex; to wound the feelings (of). ~ छुड़ाना (से), to wean (a baby, or animal). ~ जुड़ाना, v.i. the heart to be cooled, set at rest; to be comforted; to become contented. ~ ठंडी होना, v.i. id. ~ तले रखना, to guard, to cherish (in the heart: an emotion, a precious secret). ~ थमना, the heart to be benumbed (as with grief).
~ थामना, = ~ पकड़ना. ~ देना (को), to give the breast (to). ~ निकलकर चलना, to strut, to stalk. ~ पकड़के रह जाना, to grieve in silence; to be left helpless, without recourse. ~ पकना, to feel wounded, hurt or vexed. ~ पत्थर की करना, to harden the heart; to harden one's resolve. ~ पर चढ़ना (की), to be a torment, to obsess (one: a thought); to plague (one). ~ पर झेलना, v.t. to bear (a sorrow, a vexation). ~ पर पत्थर रखना, to hold the emotions in check: to endure patiently. ~ पर बाल होना, fig. to be large-hearted, generous of nature; to be able to be relied upon. ~ पर मूँग (or दाल, or कोदों) दलना, v.t. to grind pulse on the breast (of, की): deliberately to cause pain or vexation (to). ~ पर साँप फिरना, or लोटना, a snake to writhe in (one's) heart: to burn with envy or rancour.
~ पिलाना (को), = ~ देना. ~ पीटना, to beat the breast; to lament, to grieve. ~ फटना, the heart to be torn: to grieve; to feel sympathy or compassion. ~ फुलाना, to puff out the chest: to be cocky, haughty or pretentious. ~ भर, adj. breast-high. ~ भरना, or भर आना, the breast to swell (with emotion): to be greatly moved; to weep. ~ मसोसना, to keep (one's) feelings in check; to bear patiently; to grieve. ~ लगाना, to

lament, to grieve. ~ से लगाना (को), to embrace (one).

छात्र *chātr* [S.], m. a student; a pupil. — छात्रवृत्ति, f. a scholarship, grant for study. छात्रालय, m. = next. छात्रावास [°*tra*+*ā*°], m. a student hostel.

छात्रा *chātrā* [S.: cf. H. *chātr*], f. a student; a pupil.

छादन *chādan* [S.], m. **1.** covering; sheltering; concealing. **2.** a covering; clothing.

छादित *chādit* [S.], adj. covered; sheltered.

[1]**छान** *chān* [**channi*-], f. Brbh. Av. a thatch; a frame for thatching; a thatched building.

[2]**छान** *chān* [cf. H. *chānnā*], f. straining, sifting. — छान-बीन [H. [1]*bīnnā*], f. sifting and culling: close search; examination; analysis. छान-बीन करना (की), to search or examine closely; to analyse.

छानना *chānnā* [**kṣāṇayati*], v.t. **1.** to sift; to winnow. **2.** to strain, to filter; transf. to take (habitually: *bhāṁg*). **3.** to select. **4.** to search closely, to search through; to examine; to investigate. — ~ मारना, = ~, 4.

छानस *chānas* [cf. H. *chānnā*], f. chaff, husk.

छाना *chānā* [*chādayati*[1]], v.t. & v.i. **1.** v.t. to cover; to thatch, to roof. **2.** to spread, to erect (an awning, &c., as a shelter). **3.** to shade (a place); to shelter. **4.** v.i. to be spread, to spread; to be diffused. **5.** to settle (over), to cast a shadow (over); to overcast; to weigh (upon). **6.** to settle or to swarm (upon). **7.** to be shaded (a place). — घर, झोंपड़ी or डेड़ा ~, v.t. to put up a house, hut or tent. रोब ~ (की), v.i. (one's) presence or authority to be evident. छा रहना, v.i. to cover completely, to line; to settle (in a place).

छानि *chāni* [**channi*-], f. Brbh. thatch.

छानी *chānī* [**channi*-], f. reg. **1.** thatch, roofing. **2.** transf. a hut.

छाप *chāp* [cf. **chapp*-], f. **1.** a stamp, impression; imprint; mark; sectarian mark. **2.** an instrument for stamping; a seal; signet. **3.** fig. impression, influence, effect. — ~ करना, to put a seal or stamp on (पर, or में). ~ डालना, to make an impression (on, पर); to exercise an influence (on or over, पर). ~ पड़ना (की), an influence to be felt (on, पर, by or from, की). ~ लगाना, to put a seal or stamp on (में).

छापना *chāpnā* [**chapp*-], v.t. **1.** to stamp; to mark; to print (cloth). **2.** to seal. **3.** to print (a book). **4.** to make an imprint, to copy through, to trace. **5.** to make an impression (on, पर); to exercise an influence (upon, पर).

छापा *chāpā* [cf. H. *chāpnā*], m. **1.** a stamp, impression; imprint, copy; sectarian or decorative mark or design. **2.** an instrument for stamping; a wooden stamp; seal. **3.** a printing press. **4.** the press (as an institution). छापे की आज़ादी, f. freedom of the press. **5.** stamped or printed material; an edition (of a paper). **6.** a sudden attack or raid ; specif. a night attack; a police search. — ~ करना, v.t. = छापना. ~ डालना, = next. ~ मारना (पर), to attack, or to take, by surprise; to raid. ~ छापा लगाना (में, or पर), to put a stamp or seal (on), to stamp, &c. छापे में, adv. in print. पत्थर का ~-, m. lithography. — ~ छापा-ख़ाना, m. a printing firm; printing works. छापामार, m. a sudden assailant; guerrilla; commando. °ई, f. & adj. the mounting of sudden attacks; guerrilla warfare. छापेख़ाना, m. = छापा-ख़ाना. छापेमार, m. = छापामार. छापेवाला, m. or छापेख़ानेवाला, m. a printer.

छापित *chāpit* [cf. H. *chāpnā*], adj. Brbh. printed, impressed.

छाबड़ी *chābṛī* [cf. Pk. *chabba*-], f. a hawker's tray or case.

छाया *chāyā* [S.], f. **1.** shade; a shady place. **2.** shadow; darkness, obscurity. **3.** reflection. **4.** fig. protection, shelter. **5.** imitation: a rendering (of a text); a faint image or resemblance; travesty (of, की). **6.** an apparition, spectre. — छायाकार, m. photographer. छाया-ग्राहिनी, f. *mythol.* Brbh. title of a demoness who was duped into seizing a false image of Hanumān. छाया-चित्र, m. a photograph. छाया-तरु, m. a large shady tree. छाया-दान, m. offering up one's reflection (to avert the influence of evil spirits): making an offering of a cup of *ghī* or oil into which one has first glanced. छाया-नाट्य, m. a shadow theatre. छाया-पथ, m. the Milky Way. छाया-लोक, m. world of shades: a world other than the phenomenal world. छायावाद, m. a viewpoint (dominant in Hindi poetry in the years 1918-35) which stressed the importance of expression of the poet's individual sensibility; the movement espousing this viewpoint. °ई, adj. & m. having to do with *chāyāvād*; an adherent of *chāyāvād*.

छायी *chāyī* [conn. *kṣaya*-], f. ash.

[1]**छार** *chār* [*kṣāra*-[1]], m. & adj. **1.** m. ash, ashes. **2.** alkali. **3.** transf. dust. **4.** adj. corrosive. **5.** sharp, pungent. **6.** saline. — छार-खार करना, to reduce to ashes, or ruins.

[2]**छार** *chār* [? conn. *chaṭā*-], f. *Pl.* a mass, lump; clod.

छारी *chārī* [? conn. *chaṭā*-], f. *Pl.* a small lump (of precious metal).

[1]छाल *chāl* [*challi-*], f. **1.** bark. **2.** skin, rind, peel. — ~ उतारना (की), to skin, to peel. — छाल-छबीला, m. *Pl.* a species of fragrant moss.

[2]छाल *chāl* [**challa-*], m. spray; wave.

[3]छाल *chāl*, f. Av. ? a sweet (? w.r. for [1]छाक).

छालनी *chālnī*, f. reg. (W.) = छलनी.

छाला *chālā* [*challi-*], m. **1.** skin, hide. **2.** a blister; a pustule. — ~ पड़ना, a blister to form (on, में).

छाली *chālī* [cf. H. *chālā*], f. betel-nut.

छावणो *chāvṇo*, v.t. reg. (Raj.) = छाना.

छावन *chāvan* [*chādana-*], m. Brbh. thatch.

छावनी *chāvnī* [*chādana-*: reformed on caus. in MIA], f. **1.** reg. thatching, roofing. ***2.** a hutment, cantonment (for troops, or police); barracks. — ~ डालना, to set up an encampment.

छावर- *chāvr-*, m. Brbh. young (of an animal: cf. छावा).

छावा *chāvā* [**chāpa-*: ? conn. *śāvaka-*], m. reg. (Bihar) a young pig.

छिंकना *chiṁknā* [cf. H. *cheknā*], v.i. **1.** to be stopped, checked; to be taken (as a place, or as a partner). **2.** to be surrounded.

[1]छिंकवाना *chiṁkvānā* [cf. H. *chīṃknā*], v.t. to cause to sneeze.

[2]छिंकवाना *chiṁkvānā* [cf. H. *cheṁknā*], v.t. = [2]छिंकाना.

छिंकाई *chiṁkāī* [cf. H. *chīṃknā*], f. sneezing.

[1]छिंकाना *chiṁkānā* [cf. H. *chīṁknā*], v.t. to cause to sneeze.

[2]छिंकाना *chiṁkānā* [cf. H. *cheṁknā*], v.t. **1.** to cause to stop. **2.** to cause to seize, to have (one) detained.

छि *chi*, interj. = छी.

छिउल *chiul*, m. pronun. var. = छीउल.

छिकना *chiknā*, v.i. pronun. var. = छिंकना.

छिछड़ा *chichṛā*, m. = छीछड़ा.

छिछला *chichlā*, adj. & m. **1.** adj. shallow. **2.** m. a shallows; bank, shoal.

छिछलाई *chichlāī* [cf. H. *chichlā*], f. shallowness.

छिछलापन *chichlāpan* [cf. H. *chichlā*], m. shallowness.

छिछली *chichlī* [H. *chichlā*], f. a skipping-stone.

छिछोरपन *chichorpan* [cf. H. *chichorā*], m. **1.** shallowness, superficiality; pettiness, frivolity. **2.** triviality, worthlessness.

छिछोरा *chichorā*, adj. **1.** shallow, superficial: petty (as an attitude); frivolous. **2.** trivial; worthless, base.

छिछोरापन *chichorāpan* [cf. H. *chichorā*], m. = छिछोरपन.

छिजना *chijnā*, v.i. reg. = छीजना.

छिजाना *chijānā* [cf. H. *chījna*], v.t. to cause to waste or wear away, to decrease, to lessen.

छिटकना *chiṭaknā* [**chiṭṭ-*], v.i. **1.** to be scattered; to be sprinkled or sprayed; to be splashed or spattered; to be spread. **2.** to be dispersed; to become separated (from, से); to be diffused (light); to be bright. **3.** to be disarranged or displaced; to be dishevelled (hair). **4.** to spring back (as a door-bolt, a catch). **5.** to be disturbed.

छिटका *chiṭkā* [cf. H. *chiṭaknā*], m. a splash, drop.

छिटकाना *chiṭkānā* [cf. H. *chiṭaknā*], v.t. **1.** to scatter; to sprinkle, to spray; to splash, to spatter. **2.** to disperse; to dissipate. **3.** to disarrange; to displace. **4.** to snap back (a door-bolt, rifle-bolt).

छिटकी *chiṭkī* [cf. H. *chiṭaknā*], f. a splash; a speck, spot. — ~ करना, to spot, to fleck, to mark with strokes or touches. ~ डालना (पर), to splash. ~ देना, or लगाना (पर or में), = ~ करना.

छिटपुट *chiṭpuṭ* [cf. H. *chiṭaknā*], adj. dispersed; straggling (clouds); miscellaneous.

[1]छिटवा *chiṭvā*, m. reg. (E.) broadcast sowing.

[2]छिटवा *chiṭvā*, m. *HŚS.* a bamboo basket.

छिड़कना *chiṛaknā* [**chiṭ-*], v.t. **1.** to sprinkle. **2.** to spray; to pour. **3.** to scatter. — घाव पर नोन, or नमक, ~, to rub salt in a wound.

छिड़कवाना *chiṛakvānā* [cf. H. *chiṛaknā*], v.t. to cause to be sprinkled, &c. (by, से).

छिड़काई *chiṛkāī* [cf. H. *chiṛaknā*], m. sprinkling, watering.

छिड़काना *chiṛkānā* [cf. H. *chiṛaknā*], v.t. to cause to be sprinkled (by, से).

छिड़काव *chiṛkāv* [cf. H. *chiṛaknā*], m. sprinkling, watering (esp. as a process, or a routine).

छिड़ना *chiṛnā* [cf. H. *cheṛnā*], v.i. **1.** to be touched; to be played on (a stringed instrument); to be tuned. **2.** to break out (as a war, or a quarrel); to begin; to be stirred up, to arise (a matter); to be heard, to ring out (a melody, an instrument).

छिड़वाना *chiṛvānā* [cf. H. *cheṛnā*], v.t. **1.** to cause to be touched, &c. **2.** to cause to break out, &c.

छितनी *chitnī*, f. *Pl. HŚS.* **1.** a small shallow basket. **2.** reg. a broken basket.

छितरना *chitarnā* [**chitr-*; ? ← Panj.], v.i. = छितराना, 1., 2.

छितर-बितर *chitar-bitar* [cf. **chitr-*; ? w. *vistarati*], adj. **1.** scattered. **2.** dispersed.

छितराना *chitrānā* [cf. **chitr-*], v.i. & v.t. **1.** v.i. to be scattered, or diffused; to be sprinkled, sprayed; to be spread, to spread. **2.** to be dispersed. **3.** v.t. to scatter; to sprinkle, to spray; to spread. **4.** to disperse.

छितराव *chitrāv* [cf. *chitrānā*], m. the state of being scattered, &c. ; dispersal. — ~ कर देना (का), to scatter, &c.

छिति *chiti* [ad. *kṣiti-*], f. Brbh. **1.** the earth; the ground. **2.** (in chronograms) the number one. — छिति-छान, adj. *Pl.* covering the earth; scattered, dispersed across the earth; prostrate.

छिदना *chidnā* [cf. H. *chednā*], v.i. to be pierced.

छिदवाई *chidvāī* [cf. H. *chidvānā*], f. **1.** causing to be pierced, &c. **2.** cost of or charge for piercing, &c.

छिदवाना *chidvānā* [cf. H. *chednā*], v.t. to cause to be pierced, &c. (by, से).

छिदाना *chidānā* [cf. *chednā*], v.t. to cause to be pierced, &c. (by, से).

छिद्र *chidră* [S.], m. **1.** a hole; an opening, a gap; crack. **2.** a pore. **3.** in comp. a defect. — छिद्रकरण, adj. having the ears pierced. छिद्रदर्शी, adj. & m. given to fault-finding; a captious critic. छिद्रान्वेषण [°*dra*+*a*°], m. captious criticism. °-आन्वेषी, m. a captious critic.

छिद्रित *chidrit* [S.], adj. **1.** pierced, perforated. **2.** having gaps. **3.** *HŚS.* having faults.

छिन *chin* [ad. *kṣaṇa-*], m. = क्षण. — ~ एक, m. & adv. = छिनक.

छिनक *chinak* [cf. H. *chin*], m. & adv. **1.** an instant. **2.** in (the space of) an instant.

छिनकना *chinaknā*, v.i. **1.** to blow the nose. **2.** colloq. to go away in a huff.

छिनना *chinnā* [cf. H. *chīnnā*], v.i. to be snatched, to be seized (from).

छिनरा *chinrā* [cf. H. *chināl*], m. *Pl. HŚS.* a man of bad character.

छिनवाना *chinvānā* [cf. H. *chīnnā*], v.t. to cause to be snatched, &c. (by, से).

छिनाना *chinānā* [cf. H. *chīnnā*], v.t. **1.** to cause to be snatched away, &c. (by, से). **2.** to snatch away (from, से).

छिनाल *chināl* [**chinnāli-*: Pk. *chinnālia-*], f. & adj. pej. **1.** f. a loose woman; prostitute. **2.** adj. adulterous, wanton (esp. a woman).

छिनालपन *chinālpan* [cf. H. *chināl*], m. adultery (of a woman); prostitution.

छिनालपना *chinālpanā*, m. = छिनालपन.

छिनाला *chinālā*, f. = छिनाल.

छिन्न *chinn* [S.], adj. **1.** cut; torn; damaged. **2.** divided off, separated. **3.** destroyed. — छिन्न-भिन्न, adj. cut or broken into pieces; pierced through and through; scattered; destroyed. छिन्न-संशय, adj. whose doubt is removed: free from doubt.

छिपकली *chipkalī* [cf. *śepyā-*; Pk. *chippa-*], f. a lizard: the common house-lizard.

छिपकी *chipkī*, f. = छिपकली.

छिपटी *chipṭī*, f. a chip, shaving, splinter. — छिपटी-सा, adj. thin, delicate.

छिपना *chipnā* [**chipp-*; cf. H. *chupnā*], v.i. **1.** to be hidden; to hide; to lurk; to be veiled, or masked; to be obscure. **2.** to become hidden; to set (the sun); to elude observation or pursuit. — दिन ~, day to end, dark to come. छिपकर, adv. stealthily, secretly. छिप रहना, to go into hiding. छिपा रहना, to remain hidden; to be hidden or obscure (from or to, पर: a fact, a truth). छिपते फिरना, to skulk about, to be in hiding. छिपे छिपे, = छिपा-छिपी (adv.) — छिपा-छिपी, f. & adv. secreting away; furtive behaviour; secretly, underhandedly.

छिपाना *chipānā* [cf. H. *chipnā*], v.t. to cause to be hidden; to hide, to conceal; to cover. — छिपाकर, adv. secretly, stealthily. सिर छिपाए, adv. *id.*

छिपाव *chipāv* [cf. *chipnā*], m. concealment; secrecy.

छिमा *chimā* [ad. *kṣamā-*], f. = क्षमा.

छिम्मी *chimmī* [**chimba-*], f. reg. (Bihar) a pod.

छिया *chiyā*, m. Brbh. excrement. — छिया-छरद कर-, to act in a vile way.

छियानवे *chiyānve* [*ṣaṇṇavati-*], adj. ninety-six.

छियालीस *chiyālīs* [*ṣaṭcatvāriṁśat-*], adj. forty-six.

छियासठ *chiyāsaṭh* [*ṣaṭṣaṣṭi-*], adj. sixty-six.

छियासी *chiyāsī* [*ṣaḍaśīti-*], adj. eighty-six.

छिलका *chilkā* [cf. **chilla-*[2]], m. **1.** skin, shell, husk, peel. **2.** bark, rind. **3.** crust, scale. — ~ उतारना (का), to shell, to husk, to peel.

छिलछिला *chilchilā*, adj. shallow, rippling (water).

छिलना *chilnā* [cf. H. *chīlnā*], v.i. **1.** to be shelled, husked or peeled. **2.** to be barked; to be rough or sore (the throat). **3.** to be flayed. **4.** to be scraped or scratched; to be erased.

छिलनी *chilnī* [cf. H. *chilnā*], f. a scraper.

छिलवाई *chilvāī* [cf. H. *chīlnā*], f. **1.** peeling, paring, husking, &c. **2.** cost of, or wages for, peeling, &c.

छिलवाना *chilvānā* [cf. H. *chīlnā*], v.t. to cause to be peeled, pared, &c. (by, से).

छिलाना *chilānā* [cf. H. *chilnā*], v.t. to cause to be pared, &c. (by, से).

छिलौरी *chilaurī*, f. a blister.

छिल्लड़ *chillaṛ* [cf. **chilla-*[2]], m. *Pl. HŚS.* husk. (= छिलका).

छिहत्तर *chihattar* [*ṣaṭsaptati-*], adj. seventy-six.

छींक *chīṁk* [*chikkā-*, Pk. *chikkā-*], f. sneezing; a sneeze. — ~ आना (को), to sneeze. ~ पड़ना, or होना, to sneeze (a bad omen).

छींकना *chīṁknā* [cf. *chikkā-*], v.i. to sneeze.

छींका *chīṁkā* [**chikya-*], m. **1.** a net, or hanging basket (for food). **2.** a rope bridge (= झूला). **3.** a muzzle (for cattle).

छींचना *chīṁcnā*, v.t. = सींचना.

छींट *chīṁṭ* [cf. H. *chīṁṭnā*], f. **1.** a splash, drop; a spattering. **2.** a spot, stain. **3.** floral or figured patterning (orig. painted). **4.** chintz, printed calico.

छींटना *chīṁṭnā* [**chiṇṭ-*], v.t. **1.** to sprinkle. **2.** to scatter.

छींटा *chīṁṭā* [cf. H. *chīṁṭnā*], m. **1.** a splash, drop; pl. a slight shower, bespattering. **2.** a scattering; sowing (broadcasting); interspersal (of one crop with another). **3.** dose, fix (as of opium). **4.** spot, stain. **5.** aspersion; ridicule. — ~ कसना, or छोड़ना, or फेंकना (पर), to cast aspersions (on); to ridicule. ~ देना, or मारना, to sprinkle, to splash. — छींटाकशी [P. *-kaśī*], f. casting aspersions, ridiculing.

छींबी *chīṁbī* [**chimba-*], f. a pod.

छी *chī*, [*chi-*], interj. expressing disgust or dislike, & f. **1.** interj. ugh! shame! **2.** f. transf. excrement. — ~ ~, = ~. ~ ~ करना, to express dislike, &c.

छी- *chī-* [*chupati*? × *kṣipati*], v.t. Brbh. = छूना.

छीउल *chīul*, ? m. **1.** the tree *Butea frondosa* (= ढाक, पलाश). **2.** *Pl.* the Indian butter-tree, *Bassia butyracea.*

छीउली *chīulī*, f. *Pl.* = छीउल, 2.

छीका *chīkā*, m. pronun. var. = छींका.

छीछड़ा *chīchṛā*, m. **1.** membrane, skin. **2.** pej. a scrap of flesh. — ~ करना, to flay; to tear to pieces.

छीछालेदर *chīchāledar*, f. colloq. a bad situation: trouble, predicament, mess.

छीज *chīj* [cf. H. *chījnā*], f. **1.** wasting or wearing away; swindling; deterioration. **2.** damage, loss. — छीज-बट्टा, m. wear and tear.

छीजना *chījnā* [*chidyate*], v.i. **1.** to waste or to wear away; to dwindle; to be effaced; to deteriorate. **2.** to be damaged.

छीट *chīṭ*, f. = छींट.

छीटना *chīṭnā*, v.t. = छींटना.

छीदा *chīdā* [*chidra-*], adj. thin, sparse (of texture or composition); widely separated.

छीन *chīn* [ad. *kṣīṇa-*], adj. = क्षीण.

छीनकर *chīnkar*, m. *Pl.* acacia (= कीकर; बबूल).

छीनना *chīnnā* [cf. *chinna-*], v.t. **1.** to snatch away; to tear, to pluck, or to wrench away. **2.** to seize; to usurp; to confiscate. — छीन-झपट, f. snatching away; snatching or scrabbling for from different directions. – छीना-खसोटी, f. id., 2. छीना-छानी, f., छीना-छीनी, f. id. छीना-छानी करना, to scrabble, &c. (for, के लिए). छीना-झपटी, f. = छीन-झपट, 2.

छीप *chīp* [cf. H. *chīpnā*], f. **1.** whitish spots or discoloration (of the skin). **2.** reg. a mark, impression.

छीपना *chīpnā* [**chipp-*], v.t. to print (cloth).

छीपी *chīpī* [cf. H. *chīp, chīpnā*], m. a cloth-printer.

छीमी *chīmī*, f. = छींबी.

[1]**छीर** *chīr* [ad. *kṣīra-*], m. = क्षीर.

[2]**छीर** *chīr*, m. *hist.* land cultivated by a proprietor or lessee himself.

छीलन *chīlan* [cf. H. *chīlnā*], f. **1.** paring, scraping, &c. **2.** parings, scrapings, shavings.

छीलना *chīlnā* [cf. **chilla-*[1]: Pk. *chillia-*], v.t. **1.** to skin, to peel, to pare; to bark (a tree). **2.** to scratch, to scrape; to scratch out, to erase. **3.** to shave, to plane; to turn (on a lathe). **4.** to sharpen (a pencil). **5.** to irritate (the throat, &c).

छुँगली *chuṁglī*, f. colloq. the little finger.

छुआई *chuāī* [cf. H. *chūnā*], f. **1.** touching. **2.** causing to be touched. — चूना ~, f. whitewashing.

छुआछूत *chuāchūt* [H. *chūnā, achūt*], f. touched and untouched: restrictions on touching, or contact.

छुआना *chuānā*, v.t. = छुलाना.

छुई-मुई *chuī-muī* [cf. H. *chūnā*, H. *muā*, adj.], f. **1.** the sensitive plant, *Mimosa pudica*. **2.** colloq. a sensitive or irritable person. **3.** a delicate or frail thing.

छुचकारना *chuckārnā*, v.t. *Pl.* = छुछकारना.

छुच्छ *chucch*, adj., E.H. empty, hollow (= छूछा).

छुच्छी *chucchī* [cf. H. *chūchā*], f. reg. (Bihar) sthg. hollow or having a hole: **1.** a hollow tube. **2.** a washer.

छुछकारना *chuchkārnā*, v.t. *Pl. HŚS.* to set on or to encourage (a dog).

छुछमछली *chuchmachlī* [H. *chūchā*+H. *machlī*], f. *HŚS.* a tadpole.

छुछूँदर *chuchūṁdar*, f. 1. = छछूँदर. **2.** reg. (Bihar) a partic. firework.

छुट *chuṭ* [cf. **kṣutyate: Pk. chuṭṭa-*; Panj. *chuṭṭ*], conj. Brbh.; 19c. apart from, except for.

छुट- *chuṭ-* [cf. H. *choṭā*], adj. little, small. — छुटफुट, adj. see s.v.

छुटका *chuṭkā* [cf. H. *choṭā*], adj. & m. **1.** adj. little, small. **2.** lesser, junior. **3.** m. a little or junior one.

छुटका- *chuṭkā-* [cf. **kṣutyate*: Pk. *chuṭṭa-*], v.t. Brbh. Av. **1.** to release. **2.** to open, to undo. **3.** to leave, to slip from.

छुटकारा *chuṭkārā* [cf. H. *chūṭnā*], m. **1.** release; deliverance, relief (from danger, or distress). **2.** discharge, acquittal; exemption. **3.** escape. — ~ देना (को), to release (from, से); to acquit; to exempt. ~ पाना, to obtain release, &c. (from, से); to be freed; to get free from, to be rid of.

छुटपन *chuṭpan* [cf. H. *choṭā*], m. **1.** childhood. **2.** infancy.

छुटपना *chuṭpanā* [cf. H. *chuṭpan*], m. = छुटपन.

छुटफुट *chuṭphuṭ* [cf. H. *choṭā, phūṭnā*], adj. & f. **1.** adj. miscellaneous, (expenses, contingencies); occasional, sporadic; petty. **2.** f. sundry expenses, &c.

छुटभैया *chuṭbhaiyā*, m. pej. a person of little importance.

छुटवाना *chuṭvānā* [cf. H. *chūṭnā*], v.t. = छुड़वाना.

छुटाई *chuṭāī*, f. = छोटाई.

छुटाना *chuṭānā*, v.t. = छुड़ाना.

छुटापा *chuṭāpā* [cf. H. *choṭā*], m. = छुटपन.

छुटौती *chuṭautī* [cf. H. *chūṭnā*], f. **1.** remission (of a sum due). **2.** a ransom.

छुट्टा *chuṭṭā* [cf. **kṣutyate*: Pk. *chuṭṭa-*], adj. & m. **1.** adj. untethered, unrestrained. **2.** detached, single; unencumbered; mere, simple. **3.** miscellaneous. **4.** m. small change. — छुट्टे हाथ, adv. with empty hands: unarmed.

छुट्टी *chuṭṭī* [cf. **kṣutyate*: Pk. *chuṭṭa-*], f. **1.** release; permission to go; discharge, acquittal; respite. **2.** leave; holiday, vacation; break (during the day's work); leisure time. **3.** a statutory holiday. ~ देना (को), to give leave (to); to release; to let go, to dismiss. ~ पर, adv. on holiday, &c. ~ मनाना, to spend a holiday, to be on holiday. स्कूलों में ~ है, the schools are on holiday.

छुड़वाना *chuṛvānā* [cf. H. *choṛnā*], v.t. **1.** to cause to be released, &c. (by, से). **2.** to cause to be loosened, or removed, or set aside, or discharged, &c. (by, से).

छुड़ाई *chuṛāī* [cf. H. *choṛnā, chuṛānā*], f. **1.** setting free, releasing; discharging; rescuing. **2.** liberation; discharge, dismissal; rescue; ransom.

छुड़ाना *chuṛānā* [cf. H. *choṛnā*], v.t. **1.** to cause to be freed (by, से); to effect the release of; to get (one) discharged, or acquitted. **2.** to cause to be free, to release; to discharge (an offender); to dismiss; to acquit; to rescue, to extricate. **3.** to redeem (a pledge). **4.** to cause to be loose; to get undone (a knot, or bond); to break or to work free from (an animal from a tether, or a force from its attackers). **5.** to get rid of (as a habit). **6.** to remove (as a cover, seal, stamp; or as a stain). **7.** to cause to be set aside; to except, to exclude; to deduct (a sum). **8.** to cause to be discharged (a firearm, or fireworks).

छुड़ाव *chuṛāv* [cf. H. *choṛnā, chuṛānā*], m. **1.** a state of abandonment, &c. **2.** a state of liberation, emancipation, rescue, &c.

छुड़ौती *chuṛautī* [cf. H. *churānā*], f. **1.** ransom. **2.** remission (of a payment).

छुतहरा *chutahrā* [cf. **chupta-*: Pk. *chutta-*], adj. *Pl.* ceremonially impure: used (a dish).

छुतहा *chut'hā* [cf. **chupta-*: Pk. *chutta-*], adj. **1.** contagious. **2.** unclean, (ceremonially); not usable or touchable.

छुधा *chudhā*, f. Brbh. Av. = क्षुधा.

छुधित *chudhit*, adj. Brbh. Av. = क्षुधित.

छुपना *chupnā* [**chupp-*], v.i. = छिपना.

छुरा *churā* [*kṣura-*], m. a large knife; dagger; blade. — उलटे छुरे से मूड़ना, to shave with the back of a blade: to treat as an utter idiot; to hoodwink completely. — छुरा-छुरी, f. fighting with knives.

छुरी *churī* [*kṣurikā-*], f. a knife; dagger; scalpel. — ~ चलाना, or फेरना, to use a knife (on): to cause harm (to); to cause pain, or suffering (to). ~ देना (को), colloq. to stab, to knife. ~ मारना (को), to stab. मीठी ~, f. sweet knife: cold steel; a secret enemy. मन में ~, f. a knife (kept ready) in the heart: a secret enmity.

छुलकना *chulaknā*, v.i. *Pl. HŚS.* = छुलछुलाना.

छुलछुला *chulchulā* [cf. *kṣulla-*], adj. dribbling.

छुलछुलाना *chulchulānā* [cf. *kṣulla-*], v.i. to pass urine slowly, or involuntarily.

छुलाई *chulāī* [cf. H. *chūnā*], f. touching (= छुआई).

छुलाना *chulānā* [cf. H. *chūnā*], v.t. to cause to be touched, or felt (by, से).

छुहना *chuhnā* [cf. H. *chūnā*; × **kṣubhati*], v.i. **1.** to be touched. **2.** Brbh. to be affected, moved (by).

छुहारा *chuhārā* [**chohāra*], m. a dried, sweet date.

छुहावट *chuhāvaṭ* [cf. H. *chūnā*], f. touching, touch.

छूँछा *chūm̐chā*, adj. pronun. var. = छूछा.

छूँछी *chūm̐chī*, f. pronun. var. *Pl. HŚS.* = छूछी.

छू *chū* [onom.] m. (f., *Pl.*) **1.** a blowing or breathing sound. **2.** blowing or breathing after a prayer or incantation. **3.** sound used in setting a dog (on sheep, &c). — ~ करना, to pronounce an incantation and blow (on, पर); to conjure (a deity); to exorcise. ~ होना, to vanish, to disappear suddenly. – छू-छू, m. = ~, 2.; conjury, magic. छू-मंतर, m. an incantation, charm; interj. hey presto! छू-मंतर करना, = ~ करना. छूआछू, m. repeated sound of blowing or panting (from exertion).

छूई-मूई *chūī-mūī*, f. = छुई-मुई.

छूछ *chūch* [*tucchya-*: Pk. *chuccha-*], adj. & f. **1.** adj. = छूछा. **2.** f. refuse (esp. that of pressed sugar-cane).

छूछक *chūchak*, m. **1.** a ceremony observed after childbirth (when the mother visits her father, generally forty days after the birth, and returns with gifts of clothes, money, &c). **2.** gifts given on this occasion.

छूछा *chūchā* [*tucchya-*: Pk. *chuccha-*], adj. **1.** empty. **2.** without substance; shallow; facile. **3.** base, contemptible. — छूछे हाथ, adv. empty-handed; unarmed.

छूछी *chūchī* [H. *chūchā*], f. reg. **1.** a thin tube. **2.** needlecase. **3.** reg. (W.) socket (for a screw).

छूट *chūṭ* [cf. H. *chūṭnā*], f. **1.** deliverance, freedom (from, से), escape. **2.** freedom, liberty (to, की). **3.** exemption (from, से); remission; deduction, discount. **4.** separation (from, से). **5.** leavings, refuse; grain left on the threshing-floor. **6.** releasing, letting go.

छूटना *chūṭnā* [**kṣuṭyate*: Pk. *chuṭṭa-*], v.i. **1.** to be released, to be let go; to be discharged, acquitted; to be redeemed (a pledge). **2.** to come loose; to be loose, or free; to be wielded, brought into play (as fists, or reinforcements). **3.** to be free (from, से), to escape; to be rid (of, से). **4.** to be omitted; to be given up, or abandoned. **5.** to come out or forth; to spurt out (liquid); to come off (dye, paint); to be got rid of (an infection, a cough). **6.** to be lost (courage, patience, wits); to end (life). **7.** to leave, to depart (a train, &c.); to start. उससे गाड़ी छूट गई, he missed the train. **8.** to fall back, to fall behind; not to prosper. **9.** to discharge; to fire, to be shot (a weapon, a syringe); to play (a fountain).

छूत *chūt* [**chupti-*], f. **1.** the touch of sthg. ritually impure; ritual contamination. **2.** the notion of untouchability. **3.** impurity. **4.** contagious infection. **5.** malignant influence (of a spirit). — ~ उतारना (की), to remove the effect of contact with sthg. impure. ~ का, or की, adj. contagious (a disease, &c). ~ छुड़ाना (की), to free oneself (from an evil or unwelcome presence or association). – छूत-छात, f. = ~, 2.

छूना *chūnā* [*chupati*], v.t. & m. **1.** v.t. to touch; to feel. **2.** to smear, to smear over (of whitewash). **3.** to handle, to take up. **4.** m. touching, touch, contact.

[1]**छूही** *chūhī*, f. reg. (Bihar) **1.** a pile of cow-dung. **2.** E.H. sthg. worthless.

[2]**छूही** *chūhī*, f. reg. (W.) ? chalk (soil).

छेंक *cheṁk* [cf. H. *cheṁknā*], f. **1.** stopping, checking. **2.** detaining. **3.** confiscating.

छेंकन *cheṁkan* [cf. H. *cheṁknā*], f. **1.** stoppage, interruption. **2.** detention. **3.** confiscation.

छेंकना *chemknā* [cf. *cheda(-kka-)*; ? × **chindati*], v.t. **1.** to stop, to check; to bar; to surround. **2.** to detain. **3.** to confiscate. **4.** to cut out, to score out; to cancel (a written entry or record).

छेंकवैया *chemkvaiyā* [cf. H. *chemknā*], m. one who detains or stops, &c.

छेंकाव *chemkāv* [cf. H. *chemknā*], m. state of stoppage, interruption, &c. (cf. छेंक).

[1]**छेक** *chek* [cf. *cheda(-kka-)*], m. **1.** E.H. a cut; a wound. **2.** pronun. var. = छेंक.

[2]**छेक-** *chek-* [S.], adj. clever, urbane:— छेकानुप्रास [°*ka*+*a*°], m. a type of alliteration involving single repetitions of several consonants. छेकोक्ति [°*ka*+*u*°], f. insinuation, double entendre.

छेकना *cheknā*, v.t. pronun. var. = छेंकना.

छेकला *cheklā*, m. *Pl.* a hole, &c. (= छेक, छेद).

छेड़ *cheṛ* [cf. H. *cheṛnā*], f. **1.** touching, handling; adjusting, tuning (an instrument). **2.** activating, instigating; beginning (a war, a quarrel); stirring up (a matter); striking up, beginning (music, singing). **3.** meddling, interference; molesting. **4.** irritating, provoking, inciting; teasing. — छेड़-खानी, f. = next. छेड़-छाड़, f. repeated, or mutual, touching, or interaction; = ~, 3., 4.

छेड़ना *cheṛnā* [**cheḍ-*²; ? × **kṣeḍati*, Pk. *kheḍaï*], v.t. **1.** to touch, to handle; to adjust, to tune (an instrument). **2.** to activate, to instigate; to begin (a war, a quarrel); to stir up, to raise (a matter); to strike up, to begin (music, singing). **3.** to meddle, to interfere with; to molest. **4.** to irritate, to provoke, to incite; to tease.

छेड़ा *cheṛā* [cf. H. *cheṛ*], m. touch; provocation, &c.

छेत्र *chetr* [ad. *kṣetra-*], m. = क्षेत्र.

छेद *ched* [*chidra-*; × *cheda-*], m. **1.** a hole. **2.** an opening; gap, crack. **3.** [*cheda-*] cutting, cutting off. **4.** a cut, section; incision.

छेदक *chedak* [ad. *chedaka-*: w. H. *ched*], m. a tool for boring or piercing; an auger; drill; punch.

छेदन *chedan* [S.], m. **1.** a boring, a piercing. **2.** cutting off.

छेदना *chednā* [cf. *chidra-*, *cheda-*], v.t. **1.** to bore, to pierce. **2.** to cut off; to pare.

छेदा *chedā*, m. reg. a grain weevil, *Calandria granaria*.

[1]**छेना** *chenā* [**styainya-*], m. **1.** thick curdled milk, curds. **2.** a sweet made of curds. — छेना-बड़ा, m. = ~, 2.

[2]**छेना** *chenā* [Panj. *chaiṇā*], m. *Pl.* a small kind of cymbal.

छेनी *chenī* [*chedana-*], f. a chisel; a gouge.

छेम *chem* [ad. *kṣema-*], m. = क्षेम. — छेमकरी, f. Av. the white or Brahminy kite (a bird of good omen). – छेम-कुशल, f. = कुशल-क्षेम.

छेर *cher* [*chagala-*], m. reg. a goat.

छेरना *chernā* [cf. **chakara-*], v.i. reg. to have diarrhoea (esp. an animal).

छेरी *cherī* [*chagalikā-*], f. reg. a nanny-goat.

छेरुआ *cheruā* [cf. H. *cher*], m. reg. (Bihar) a castrated animal (specif. a goat).

छेव *chev* [*cheda-*], m. *Pl.* **1.** a cut (made as in earth with a spade); spade's depth. **2.** a mark made by cutting. **3.** a piece (as of wood, or earth) cut off. — ~ मारना, to make a cut (in, में).

छेवना *chevnā*, v.t. **1.** to cut; to pierce, to lance. **2.** Brbh. Av. to wound. **3.** *Pl.* to bleed (a palm tree).

छेवनी *chevnī*, f. *Pl. HŚS.* a tool for piercing, or notching; a chisel (= छेनी).

छेवर *chevar*, m. *Pl. HŚS.* skin.

छेवा *chevā* [*cheda-*], m. *Pl. HŚS.* **1.** mark (for, or of, cutting). **2.** stroke, line (in writing). **3.** obs. inoculation, vaccination (= [1]टीका, 5).

छै *chai*, adj. = छह.

छैना *chainā* [? H. *chījnā* × H. *chay*], v.i. *Pl. HŚS.* **1.** to be worn out, or away; to fray. **2.** to go bad, to turn (as milk).

छैया *chaiyā* [cf. **chāpa-*], m. Brbh. child, boy.

छैल *chail*, adj. & m. = छैला. — छैल-चिकनिया, E.H. = ~ . छैल-छबीला, adj. & m. = ~ .

छैला *chailā* [*chavilla-*], adj. & m. **1.** adj. modish; fine-looking, handsome. **2.** m. a modishly dressed person, a dandy.

छैलापन *chailāpan* [cf. H. *chailā*], m. **1.** modishness (of attire). **2.** jauntiness, airs.

छोआ *choā*, m. reg. (W.) molasses (? = चोआ).

छोकड़ा *chokṛā* [cf. H. *chokrā*; or **chokka-*], m. a boy, lad.

छोकरा *chokrā* [**chokkara-*], m. a boy, lad.

छोकरी *chokrī* [**chokkara-*], f. a girl, lass.

छोटा *choṭā* [**choṭṭa-*], adj. **1.** small. **2.** lesser: junior, younger; subordinate; minor. **3.** trivial, insignificant. **4.** inferior; pej. contemptible. — ~ **भाई**, m. younger brother. – **छोटे-बड़े**, pl. great and small; young and old; varied, various. **छोटा-मोटा**, adj. little, small; = ~, 3.

छोटाई *choṭāī* [cf. H. *choṭā*], f. = **छोटापन**, 1.

छोटापन *choṭāpan* [cf. H. *choṭā*], m. **1.** smallness. **2.** triviality; insignificance.

छोड़कर *choṛkar*, abs. conj. except for, apart from (see **छोड़ना**).

छोड़ना *choṛnā* [*kṣoṭayati*], v.t. **1.** to let go, to release. **2.** to set free; to discharge; to pardon. **3.** to leave; to defer (until, **पर**). **4.** to put in and leave; to deliver or to post (a letter); to hide (sthg.) away; to add (an ingredient). **5.** to leave alone; to abandon. **6.** to give up, to renounce; to resign (a post). **7.** to omit, to overlook; to disregard (a matter); to leave (sthg.) out. **8.** to take off (clothes). **9.** to discharge (a weapon, a firework). **10.** to emit, to give out; to pour out; to spread (manure); to play (a fountain). **11.** to set in motion, to start up (an engine, a car). **12.** to assign, to detail (one, to do sthg.: **के लिए**). — **छोड़ आना**, to leave (as a person or a thing) at a distant place. **छोड़कर**, abs. conj. apart from, except for.

छोड़ाना *choṛānā*, v.t. = **छुड़ाना**.

छोत *chot* [cf. H. *chūt*], f. 1. = **छूत**. **2.** malignant influence (esp. on the eyes). — ~ **झाड़ना (की)**, to attempt to cure eye disease (attributed to malignant influence) by the use of a charm or incantation.

छोनि- *choni-*, f. metr. Av. the earth (= **छोनी**): — **छोनिप**, m. lord of the earth: a king.

छोनी *chonī* [ad. *kṣoṇi-*], f. Av. the earth.

छोप *chop* [cf. H. *chopnā*], m. **1.** plastering; filling up, making good. **2.** coat (of plaster, paint). — ~ **चढ़ाना**, to apply a coat (of plaster, &c). – **छोप-छाप**, m. colloq. plastering, &c. **छोप-छाप करना**, to plaster, &c.

छोपना *chopnā* [**chopp-*], v.t. **1.** to apply a coat (as of plaster, or paint); to paint. **2.** to repair, to make good (as by plastering).

छोभ *chobh*, m. Av. = **क्षोभ**.

छोर *chor* [?? cf. H. *choṛnā*], m. **1.** border edge; side; end. **2.** bank, shore. **3.** summit, brow (of a hill). **4.** boundary, limit. **5.** [? = H. [2]*chor*] reg. (Bihar) short rope attached to a bucket, &c.

छोर- *chor-* [*chorayati*; ? × H. *choṛnā*], v.t. Brbh. **1.** to free, to release. **2.** to take off, to put aside (a garment). **3.** *HŚS.* to seize, to snatch. (?)

छोरा *chorā* [**chokara-*: Pk. *choyara-*], m. a boy, lad.

छोरी *chorī* [**chokara-*: Pk. *choyara-*], f. a girl.

छोल *chol* [cf. H. *cholnā*], f. (m. *Pl.*) **1.** a scraping, a shaving. **2.** a scratch, graze. **3.** flap, covering. — **छोलकट**, adj. pej. circumcised.

छोलदारी *choldārī* [H. *chol*, 3.+H. *-dārī*], f. a small gable tent.

छोलना *cholnā* [**choll-*], v.t. **1.** to cut, to lop. **2.** to skim, to peel, to scrape, to pare. **3.** Brbh. to reveal.

छोलनी *cholnī* [cf. H. *cholnā*], f. a scraper.

छोला *cholā* [? cf. H. *cholnā*], m. **1.** *Pl.* gram, chick-pea (in the pod). ***2.** boiled and spiced gram. **3.** reg. (W.) a worker who strips and prepares sugar-cane for pressing.

छोह *choh* [conn. *kṣobha-*], m. love, affection.

छोहरा *chohrā* [**chokhara-*: Pk. *chohara-*], m. reg. (W.) = **छोकरा**.

छोहरी *chohrī* [**chokhara-*: Pk. *chohara-*], f. reg. (W.) = **छोकरी**.

छोहा- *chohā-* [cf. H. *choh*], v.t. Brbh. to feel affection or love.

छोही *chohī* [cf. H. *choh*], adj. affectionate.

छौंक *chaumk*, f. **1.** seasoning; taste, flavour. **2.** spices for seasoning food. — **छौंक-बघार**, f. seasoning, making spicy (a dish, or a narrative).

छौंकन *chaumkan*, m. = **छौंक**, 2.

छौंकना *chaumknā*, v.t. to throw in seasoning, to season.

छौना *chaunā* [cf. **chāpa-*], m. **1.** the young of any animal. **2.** reg. a child, boy.

[1]**छौर** *chaur*, m. = **क्षौर**.

[2]**छौर** *chaur*, m. reg. stalks of fodder plants: a large stack of fodder plants.

ज

ज *ja*, the eighth consonant of the Devanāgarī syllabary. — जकार, m. the sound /j/; the letter ज.

ज़ंग *zaṅg* [P. *zang*], m. rust. — ~ लगना (में), to rust.

[1]**जंग** *jaṅg* [P. *jang*], f. war; battle; fight. ~ करना, to make or to wage war. – जंगावर [P. *-āvar*], adj. = next. जंगजू [P. *-jū*], adj. seeking fight: warlike, aggressive. जंगबाज़ [P. *-bāz*], m. a warlike person. °ई, f. war-mongering.

[2]**जंग** *jaṅg*, f. *HŚS.* a large, wide boat.

जंगम *jaṅgam* [S.], adj. & m. **1.** adj. moving, not stationary; living. **2.** movable. **3.** wandering, itinerant (as a beggar). **4.** m. name of a Śaiva community.

जंगल *jaṅgal* [*jaṅgala-*], m. & adj. **1.** m. jungle: forest, woods; wooded, or scrub country; a wild or uninhabited region. **2.** a thicket; overgrown ground. **3.** adj. wild, desolate; lonely. — ~ जाना, or फिरना, colloq. to go to open country (to relieve oneself). – जंगल-जलेबी, f. a thorny shrub, *Sida carpinifolia* or *rhombifolia*, the source of a fibre, and its flower; colloq. a small pile of droppings.

जंगला *jaṅglā*, m. **1.** a grating; a lattice; lattice window. **2.** a railing. **3.** a partic. kind of ornamented cloth. — जंगले का कपड़ा, m. = ~, 3.

जंगली *jaṅglī* [cf. H. *jaṅgal*], adj. & m. **1.** adj. having to do with forest, &c. **2.** forested, wooded, wild (a region). **3.** wild (animals, plants). **4.** uncouth, uncivilised. **5.** m. an uncouth person, &c.

जंगलीपन *jaṅglīpan* [cf. H. *jaṅglī*], m. **1.** wildness, wild state. **2.** uncouthness, &c.

ज़ँगाना *zaṁgānā* [cf. H. *zaṅg*], v.i. reg. ? to rust.

ज़ंगार *zaṅgār* [P. *zangār*], m. verdigris, copper acetate.

ज़ंगारी *zaṅgārī* [P. *zangārī*], adj. of the colour of verdigris, green.

जंगी *jaṅgī* [P. *jangī*], adj. **1.** having to do with war; military; naval. **2.** turbulent, aggressive. **3.** vast, extensive. — ~ लाट, m. commander-in-chief.

जंघा *jaṅghā* [S.], f. = जाँघ.

जँचना *jaṁcnā* [cf. H. *jāṁcnā*], v.i. **1.** to be examined, to be investigated. **2.** to be tested, to be appraised, evaluated. **3.** to be rated, or judged; to seem; specif. to seem good (to, को, or की नज़र में); to be liked (by). **4.** to be verified. — जँचा-तुला, adj. balanced, careful (as words, opinion).

जँचवैया *jaṁcvaiyā* [cf. H. *jāṁcnā*], m. examiner, tester, appraiser, &c.

जँचा *jaṁcā* [H. *jaṁcnā*], adj. **1.** tried, proved. **2.** skilled. — ~ हाथ, m. a practised hand.

जँचाई *jaṁcāī* [cf. H. *jāṁcnā*], f. **1.** examining, examination; investigation, &c. **2.** appraising, appraisal.

जँचावट *jaṁcāvaṭ*, f. = जँचाई.

[1]**जंजाल** *jañjāl* [H. *jan*+H. *jāl*], m. snare(s) of the world: **1.** entanglement(s), trouble(s), care(s). **2.** colloq. trouble, bother. **3.** fig. a troublesome person. — ~ में फँसना, to fall into difficulties, to get into trouble, or a mess. जी का ~, m. fig. a troublesome matter, or person.

[2]**जंजाल** *jañjāl* [f. P. *jazā'il*], m. a muzzle-loading firearm, small cannon.

जंजालिया *jañjāliyā* [cf. H. [1]*janjāl*], adj. = जनजाली.

जंजाली *jañjālī* [cf. H. [1]*janjāl*], adj. & m. causing trouble (a person).

ज़ंजीर *zañjīr* [P. *zanjīr*], f. **1.** a chain. **2.** a fetter, fetters.

ज़ंजीर *zañjīra* [P. *zanjīra*], m. chain-stitch.

ज़ंजीरी *zañjīrī* [P. *zanjirī*], adj. chained.

जंट *janṭ* [Engl. *adjutant*], adj. joint (superintendent, &c.)

जंत *jant* [ad. *yantra-*], m. reg. rope, thong, tie (as used in lashing timbers, or bamboos).

जंतर *jantar* [ad. *yantra-*], m. **1.** an instrument; an appliance, apparatus; a machine; obs. an observatory. **2.** an astrological or magic diagram. **3.** amulet, charm. **4.** magical skill or art: juggling. — जंतर-मंतर, m. casting spells, working charms; ceremonies involving spells or charms; an observatory.

[1]**जंतरी** *jantrī* [cf. H. *jantar*], m. **1.** a conjurer, juggler, wizard. **2.** E.H. a musician.

[2]**जंतरी** *jantrī* [cf. H. *jantar*], f. **1.** an almanac. **2.** an appliance for drawing gold or silver wire; a pincers.

जँतसर *jaṁtsar*, m. reg. = जँतसारी.

जँतसार *jaṁtsār* [**yantraśālā-*], f. *Pl. HŚS.* a place where grinding (of meal) is done.

जँतसारी *jaṁtsārī* [cf. **yantraśālā-*], f. reg. a kind of song sung by women while grinding grain.

[1]**जंता** *jantā* [ad. *yantr̥-*], m. inv. Brbh. **1.** one who subdues, the master (of). **2.** a charioteer.

[2]**जंता** *jantā* [ad. *yantra-*; w. H. *jāṁtā*], m. reg. **1.** an appliance for making wire. **2.** a grindstone.

जँताना *jaṁtānā* [cf. *yantra-*], v.i. *Pl. HŚS.* to be ground, or crushed.

जंती *jantī*, f. dimin. reg. = [2]जंता.

जंतु *jantu* [S.], m. an animal; a creature; an insect, &c. — जंतुघ्न, adj. & m. = next. जंतु-नाशक, adj. & m. *Pl. HŚS.* vermifuge; insecticide; asafoetida. जंतु-फल, m. *Pl. HŚS.* the fig-tree *Ficus glomerata*, and its fruit. जंतु-शाला, f. a zoo (= चिड़िया-घर). जंतु-शास्त्र, m. zoology. जंतु-विज्ञान, m. id.

जंदरा *jandrā* [*yantra-*; ← Panj.], m. reg. a kind of rake; a board as used in trenching up earth.

जंबक *jambak* [ad. *jambuka-*], m. E.H. a jackal.

जंबीर *jambīr* [S.], m. *Pl. HŚS.* **1.** a sour lime (*Citrus acida*), and its fruit. **2.** *Pl. HŚS.* a basil having white or light-coloured flowers, and small leaves.

जंबु *jambu* [S.], f. Brbh. Av. = जंबू. — जंबु-द्वीप, m. *mythol.* the central one of the seven continents surrounding mount Meru; the central division of the known world, including (or co-extensive with) India.

जंबुक *jambuk* [S.], m. Av. a jackal.

जंबू *jambū* [ad. *jambu-*], f. the rose-apple (= जामुन). — जंबू-द्वीप, m., = जंबु-द्वीप.

ज़ंबूरक *zambūrak* [P. *zambūrak*], f. *Pl. HŚS.* a small gun or cannon carried on a camel.

जँभाना *jaṁbhānā* [*jr̥mbhate*], v.i. to yawn.

जँभाई *jaṁbhāī* [cf. H. *jaṁbhānā*], f. a yawn.

जंभीर *jambhīr* [S.], m. Brbh. = जंबीर.

जँवाई *jaṁvāī*, m. pronun. var. = जमाई.

-ज *-jă* [S.], v. suffix (forms adjectives and nouns). born (in or from)... (e.g. जलज, m. water-born: lotus; pearl; conch shell).

जई *jaī* [? *yaviya-*], f. **1.** oats. **2.** a small species of barley. **3.** young shoots of barley (considered auspicious: offered to patrons, and worn in turbans during the Daśahrā festival). — ~ डालना, to plant seed for germination.

ज़ईफ़ी *zaīfī* [P. *ẓa'īfī*], f. 19c. feebleness; old age.

ज़क *zak* [A.], f. U. **1.** defeat. **2.** disgrace, humiliation. **3.** injury, loss. — ~ उठाना, to suffer humiliation, &c.

[1]**जक** *jak* [H. *jakh*], m. pronun. var. = यक्ष; a guardian of buried treasure; a miser.

[2]**जक** *jak* [? cf. **jhakk-*[4]], f. Brbh. obsession, fascination (= [1]झक).

जकड़ *jakaṛ* [cf. H. *jakaṛnā*], f. **1.** tightness, constriction. **2.** clutch (of a cold, or rheumatic pain).

जकड़ना *jakaṛnā* [cf. *yata-*, MIA **yakka-*], v.t. & v.i. **1.** v.t. to pull tight, to tie tightly; to bind. **2.** to constrain. **3.** v.i. to be tightly bound, or constrained. **4.** to stiffen (joints). **5.** to be numb (with cold). — जकड़कर बाँधना, to tie tightly.

ज़कात *zakāt* [A. *zakāt*], f. **1.** *musl.* portion of property given as alms. **2.** tax, levy.

जख *jakh*, m. = यक्ष.

ज़ख़म *zak͟hm* [P. *zak͟hm*], m. a wound; an injury. — ~ खाना, to suffer a wound. ~ ताज़ा, or हरा, होना, a wound to reopen; old grief to be felt anew. ~ देना, to wound (one, को). ~ पर नमक छिड़कना, to sprinkle salt on a wound.

ज़ख़मी *zak͟hmī* [P. *zak͟hmī*], adj. wounded; hurt, injured. — ~ करना, to wound, &c.

ज़ख़ीरा *zak͟hīrā* [A. *zak͟hīra*], m. **1.** sthg. hoarded, a treasure; stock, store. **2.** storehouse, store. गेहूँ का ~, m. granary. **3.** provisions, stores. — ज़ख़ीरेदार [P. *-dār*], m. a hoarder. °ई, f. hoarding.

ज़ख़्म *zak͟hm*, m. see ज़ख़म.

ज़ख़्मी *zak͟hmī*, adj. see ज़ख़मी.

[1]**जग** *jag* [ad. *jaga-*, also *jagat-*], m. (for some cpds. see those listed s.v. जगत्, जगज्, जगद्, जगन्) the world; the universe. — जगकर्ता, m. inv. creator of the universe: the god Brahmā. °-कर्तार, m. id. जगकारन, m. Av. cause of the universe: the supreme being. जग-जननी, f. Av. mother of the world: any chief goddess (as Pārvatī, &c). जग-जाना, adj. known to the world: famous, celebrated. जगजामिनी, f. Av. the night of worldly existence. जग-जाल, m. Av. the snare(s) of the world. जग-ज़ाहिर, adj. evident to the world: self-evident. जग-जीता, adj. victorious over the world. जग-जीव, m. a living creature.

°-जीवन, m. life of the world: a title of the supreme being as giver of life. जग-जोनि, f. Av. source of the world: the god Brahmā. जग-तारक, m. saviour of the world. °-तारण, m., °-त्राता, m. inv. id. जग-निवास, m. Av. abode of the world: Viṣṇu or Kr̥ṣṇa. जग-पति, m. lord of the world: the supreme being. °नी, f. Brbh. hon. wife of a *jajmān*. जगबंद [ad. *vandhya-*], adj. Brbh. deserving honour in the world. जग-बीता, adj. experienced by, or in the world. जग-बीती कहानी, f. story or account of things that have happened (other than to the narrator). जग-बीती, f. the way, or experience, of the world. जग-सूर, m. Av. world-hero: a king. जग-हँसाई, f. a cause of general laughter, laughing-stock. जग-हँसाई करना (की), to make (one) a laughing-stock. जगेश्वर [°*ga*+*ī*°], m. lord of the world: title of Viṣṇu, and of Śiva.

²जग *jag*, m. = यज्ञ.

जगज्- *jagaj-*. see s.v. जगत्. — जगज्जयी, adj. having conquered the world: all-conquering.

जगजगाना *jagjagana* [cf. **jag-*], v.i. to give a dazzling light (= जगमगाना): to flash; to glitter.

जगजगाहट *jagjagāhaṭ* [cf. H. *jagjagānā*], f. dazzling light, &c.

जगण *jagaṇ* [cf. *gaṇa-*], m. *pros.* a foot consisting of a short, a long and a short syllable, in that order: an amphibrach.

जगत *jagat*, f. the plinth of masonry or cement, or wooden framework, built round a well-mouth.

जगत् *jagat* [S.], m. (for some collocations see those of similar sense listed s.v. ¹जग.) **1.** the world, the universe. **2.** created things; mankind. — जगत्तारणी, f. the salvation of the world. जगत्पालक, m. preserver of the world: the supreme being. जगत्प्राण, m. life of the world: the supreme being. जगत्सेठ, m. an important merchant, banker, &c.; a very wealthy man. जगत्स्वामी, m. lord of the world: the supreme being.

जगती *jagătī* [S.], f. = जगत्. — जगतीचर, m. one who walks the earth: man. जगती-तल, m. the surface of the earth; the earth.

जगद्- *jagad-*. = जगत्. — जगदंबा, f. mother of the world: a title of Durgā, or Pārvatī. °अंबिका, f. id. जगदात्मा, f. soul of the universe: the supreme spirit. जगदाधार, m. support of the universe: the supreme being. जगदीश, m. lord of the world: the supreme being; Viṣṇu. °-ईश्वर, m. id. जगद्गुरु, m. mentor of the world: title of Viṣṇu, and also of other deities; a widely revered teacher. जगद्धाता, m. inv. creator of the world: Brahmā, or Viṣṇu. °-धात्री, f. a title of Durgā, or of Sarasvatī. जगद्वंद्य, adj. to be honoured by the world: a title of Kr̥ṣṇa. जगद्वासी, m. an inhabitant of the world. जगद्विनाश, m. the destruction of the world. जगद्व्यापी, adj. diffused or current throughout the world.

जगन्- *jagan-*. see s.v. जगत्. — जगन्नाथ, m. lord of the world: a title of Viṣṇu or of Kr̥ṣṇa; specif. the idol and temple of Viṣṇu at Puri; the district of Puri. जगन्माता, f. mother of the world: a title of Durgā.

जगना *jagnā* [cf. H. *jāgnā*], v.i. **1.** to wake up. **2.** to be awake. **3.** to burn (a flame).

जगमग *jagmag* [cf. H. *jagmagānā*], f. & adj. **1.** f. dazzling light, &c. **2.** adj. dazzling, &c. — ~ करना, v.t. to make bright, or splendid.

जगमगा *jagmagā* [cf. H. *jagmajānā*], adj. = जगमग, 2.

जगमगाना *jagmagānā* [cf. **jag-*], v.i. & v.t. **1.** v.i. to emit a dazzling light, to flash; to glitter. **2.** to be splendid, brilliant. **3.** v.t. to cause to flash, or to glitter.

जगमगाहट *jagmagāhaṭ* [cf. H. *jagmagānā*], f. **1.** dazzling light, flash, glare; glitter. **2.** brilliance, splendour.

जगर-मगर *jagar-magar*, adj. Brbh. = जगमग.

जगवाना *jagvānā* [cf. H. *jāgnā*], v.t. to cause to wake, or to be aroused, alert, &c. (by, से).

जगह *jagah* [P. *jā'egāh*], f. **1.** place, particular place, locality. **2.** proper place or time. **3.** post, appointment; a vacancy. **4.** room, space; seat, place. — ~ छोड़ना, to leave a place; to leave space. ~ देना (को), to make room (for); to place (one). ~, or ~ में, ppn. & adv. instead, in place (of, की). ~ सिर होना, or ~ से होना, to be opportune, or proper. – जगह-जगह, adv. here and there; everywhere. जगहबजगह [P. *-ba-*], adv. here and there.

जगहा *jag'hā*, f. pronun. var. = जगह.

-जगा *-jagā*, adj. = जागा.

जगा-जोत *jagā-jot* [cf. H. *jāgnā*, 4.], f. brightness, brilliance, splendour.

जगात *jagāt*, m. Brbh. = ज़कात.

जगाना *jagānā* cf. H. *jāgnā*], v.t. **1.** to cause to be awake, to awaken; to rouse. **2.** to make conscious or alert; to stimulate. **3.** to kindle, to revive (as a flagging fire).

जग्य *jagyă*, [ad. *yajña-*], m. = यज्ञ.

जघन *jaghan* [S.], m. buttocks, rump, haunches.

जघन्य *jaghanyă* [S.], adj. & m. **1.** adj. low, vile, base. **2.** m. a low-born person.

जघन्यता *jaghanyătā* [S.], f. baseness.

जच- *jac-*, pronun. var. = जँच-.

ज़चा *zacā*, f. = जच्चा.

जच्चा *jaccā* [P. *zaca, zaja*], f. a woman who has recently given birth. — जच्चा-ख़ाना, m. place of confinement, lying-in room. जच्चा-बच्चा, m. pl. mother and (newborn) child.

ज़च्चा *zaccā* [P. *zaca*], f. a woman who has recently given birth.

जच्छ *jacch*, m. Av. = यक्ष.

जज *jaj* [Engl. *judge*], m. a judge.

जज़बात *jazbāt* [A. *jazbāt*, pl.], m. pl. **1.** feelings; mood. **2.** desire, longing. — °ई, adj. moved by feelings, emotional.

जजमान *jajmān* [ad. *yajamāna-*], m. **1.** one who requests and pays for the performance of a sacrifice. **2.** one who pays for services traditionally given (as by brāhmaṇs, or tradespeople).

जजमानी *jajmānī* [cf. H. *jajmān*], f. **1.** the status or activity of a *jajmān*. **2.** the fee paid by a *jajmān*.

जज़िया *jaziyā*, m. = जिज़िया.

जजी *jajī* [cf. H. *jaj*], f. judge's position, activity or status.

जज़ीरा *jazīrā* [P. *jazīra*], m. an island.

जजु *jaju* [cf. *yajuḥ-*], m. Av. the Yajurveda.

जज़्ब *jazb* [A. *jazb*], m. **1.** absorption. **2.** misappropriation. — ~ करना, to absorb; to expropriate; to misappropriate.

जज़्बा *jazbā* [A. *jazba*], m. **1.** emotion, feeling. **2.** passion.

जज़्बात *jazbāt* [A. *jazbāt*, pl.], m. pl. emotions, feelings.

जज़बाती *jazbātī* [cf. H. *jazbāt*], adj. emotional.

जट *jaṭ*, f. E.H. = जटा.

जटना *jaṭnā*, v.t. *Pl. HŚS.* to snatch away; to pilfer.

जटमलंग *jaṭmalaṅg*, m. *Pl.* the prickly amaranth (*Amarantus spinosus*).

जटल *jaṭal*, f. *Pl. HŚS.* an idle or nonsensical story, tale, yarn. — ~ मारना or हाँकना, to chatter on.

जटवाड़ा *jaṭvāṛā* [H. *jāṭ* or Panj. *jaṭṭ*+H. *vāṛā*], m. a Jāṭ district, or quarter.

जटा *jaṭā* [S.], f. **1.** matted hair (as worn by ascetics, and attributed to the god Śiva); a mass of twisted or braided hair. **2.** sthg. tangled or fibrous; tangled roots or suckers. — जटा-जूट, adj. = ~, 1. जटाधर, °-धारी, adj. & m. wearing matted hair, &c.; an ascetic; a beggar; a title of Śiva. °-धारी, f. the cockscomb flower (an amaranth), *Celosia cristata*. जटामांसी, f. spikenard (a perennial herb of the Himālayas, *Nardostachys jatamansi*), or a fragrant grass (*Cymbopogon*). जटामासी, f. id.

जटाऊ *jaṭāū*, m. E.H. = जटायु.

जटायु *jaṭāyu* [S.], m. *mythol.* name of the king of the vultures.

जटित *jaṭit*, adj. **1.** [conn. *jaṭā-*] *Pl.* matted, tangled. ***2.** [conn. **jaḍita-*: H. *jaṛnā*] set or studded with jewels.

जटिल *jaṭil* [S.], adj. **1.** tangled, matted (as hair). ***2.** involved, complicated.

जटिलता *jaṭilătā* [S.], f. involved nature, complication.

जटी *jaṭī* [S.], adj. & m. **1.** adj. having matted hair. **2.** m. an ascetic.

जट्टी *jaṭṭī*, f. charred tobacco (as in a *cilam*).

जठर *jaṭhar* [S.], m. the stomach; the abdomen. — जठराग्नि [°*ra*+*a*°], f. fire of the stomach: digestive power. जठरामय [°*ra*+*ā*°], m. dropsy (= जलोदर).

जठेरा *jaṭherā* [*jyeṣṭhatara-*], adj. & m. **1.** adj. elder, eldest; senior. **2.** m. a senior (brother, &c).

[1]**जड़** *jaṛ* [*jaṭā-*], f. **1.** root. **2.** basis, foundation; basic or essential aspect. **3.** origin, cause. — ~ उखाड़ना (उखेड़ना) (की), to uproot; to eradicate; to damage severely. ~ काटना (की), to cut the root (of): to destroy utterly; to undermine, to damage. ~ खोदना (की), = ~ उखाड़ना. ~ जमना, to take root. ~ जमाना (की), to lay the foundation (of), to establish; to consolidate. ~ पकड़ना, = ~ जमना. ~ में लगना (की), fig. to threaten the complete destruction (of). ~ से, adv. by the root, root and all. परवत की ~, f. foothills (of a mountain range). जड़ों में तेल देना, fig. to harm roots, or growth. – जड़-मूल से, adv. = ~ से.

[2]**जड़** *jaṛ* [*jaḍa-*], adj. & m. **1.** adj. lifeless, inert; unfeeling. **2.** composed of lifeless matter, material. **3.** senseless, stupid. **4.** cold, numb. **5.** m. an inanimate or inert body; lifeless matter. **6.** a stupid person. — ~ हो जाना, fig. to be numbed (by shock), or frozen (into immobility). - जड़-बुद्धि, f. & m. dullness of intellect, stupidity; a stupid person. जड़वाद, m. materialism. °ई, adj. & m. materialistic; a materialist. जड़-विज्ञान, m. physics.

जड़ता *jaṛătā* [S.], f. **1.** lifelessness; inertness; insensibility. **2.** senselessness, stupidity. **3.** torpor, apathy.

जड़त्व *jaṛatvă* [S.], m. = जड़ता.

जड़न *jaṛan* [cf. H. *jaṛnā*], f. the act of setting (jewels).

जड़ना *jaṛnā* [**jaḍati* (← Drav.): Pk. *jaḍia-*], v.t. & v.i. **1.** v.t. to attach, to fix on; to stick on. **2.** to fix or to stick in (as a nail). **3.** to set (jewels); to inlay; to mount. **4.** to deliver (a blow, a slap); to make (a cutting remark). **5.** to complain (of, की: to, से); to speak ill (of). **6.** v.i. to be joined, attached; to adhere.

जड़वट *jaṛvaṭ* [cf. H. [1]*jaṛ*], f. *Pl.* trunk (of a tree).

जड़वत *jaṛvat* [cf. H. [1]*jaṛ*], adj. E.H. inert.

जड़वाई *jaṛvāī* [cf. H. *jaṛvānā*], f. **1.** causing jewels to be set, &c. **2.** the cost of, or charge for, getting jewels set.

जड़वाना *jaṛvānā* [cf. H. *jaṛnā*], v.t. to cause jewels, &c., to be set, studded or mounted (by, से).

जड़वी *jaṛvī* [**jāḍyavīja-*], f. *Pl. HŚS.* reg. (W.) shoots of rice when first springing from the ground; rice seed germinated after being soaked (= जड़हन).

जड़हन *jaṛ'han* [**jāḍyadhānya-*], m. rice sown in seed-beds at the beginning of the rainy season, and later transplanted.

जड़ाई *jaṛāī* [cf. H. *jaṛnā*], v.t. **1.** the act of setting jewels; jeweller's work. **2.** setting, mount (for jewels). **3.** cost of, or charge for setting jewels.

जड़ाऊ *jaṛāū* [cf. H. *jaṛnā*], adj. set or studded with jewels or precious metal; inlaid.

जड़ान *jaṛān* [cf. H. *jaṛnā*], f. = जड़ाई.

[1]**जड़ाना** *jaṛānā* [cf. H. *jāṛā*], v.i. to be cold; to grow cool.

[2]**जड़ाना** *jaṛānā* [cf. H. *jaṛnā*], v.t. to cause (jewels or precious metal) to be set, studded or mounted (by, से).

जड़ाव *jaṛāv* [cf. H. *jaṛnā*], m. setting, mounting (of jewels).

जड़ावट *jaṛāvaṭ* [cf. H. *jaṛnā*], f. **1.** a setting, mount (for jewels). **2.** the act of setting jewels.

जड़ावर *jaṛāvar* [cf. H. *jāṛā*], m. winter clothes.

जड़ित *jaṛit* [cf. **jaḍati*], adj. set, studded, inlaid.

जड़िया *jaṛiyā* [cf. H. *jaṛnā*], m. a jeweller; goldsmith.

जड़ी *jaṛī* [cf. H. *jaṛ*], f. any root used medicinally. — जड़ी-बूटी, f. roots and herbs used medicinally; medicines, drugs.

जड़ीला *jaṛīlā* [cf. H. *jaṛ*], adj. having a root.

जड़ुल *jaṛul* [*jaṭula-*], m. *Pl. HŚS.* a freckle or mark on the skin.

जत *jat* [ad. *yati-*], f. *Pl. HŚS.* a musical rhythm (used in singing at the Holī festival).

जतन *jatan*, m. = यत्न.

जतनी *jatnī* [cf. *yatna-*], adj. energetic, industrious.

जतरिया *jatriyā* [conn. *yantra-*], f. reg. (W.) a small grindstone for crushing pulse.

जतरी *jatrī* [conn. *yantra-*], f. pincers.

जतलाना *jatlānā* [cf. H. *jatānā*], v.t. = जताना.

जताना *jatānā* [cf. *jñapta-*, *janati*], v.t. **1.** to cause to be known, or understood (to, or by, को). **2.** to cause to be perceived; to make felt (as status or position); to evince; to display (as feelings). **3.** to point out, to inform (of); to warn.

जती *jatī* [ad. *yati-* or *yatin-*], m. Brbh. = [2]यति.

जतु *jatu* [S.], m. lac, shellac. — जतु-गृह, m. the house daubed with lac, built (according to the *Mahābhārata* story) by Duryodhana as a fire-trap for the Pāṇḍavas.

जतुक *jatuk* [S.], m. **1.** lac, shellac. **2.** asafoetida.

जत्था *jatthā*, m. a group, party; band, gang; flock. — ~ बाँधना, to form a group or band, &c. – जत्थेदार [P. *-dār*], m. leader of a group or band. जत्थेबंद, adv. formed into a group or band. °ई, f. often pej. formation into a group or band. जत्थेबंदी करना, to form into groups, &c.

जत्रु *jatru* [S.], m. Brbh. the collar-bone.

[1]**जद** *jad*, adv. Brbh. Raj. = जब.

[2]**जद-** *jad-* [A. *jidd*]. effort, exertion: — जदोजहद [P. *-o-*], f. id.

जदपि *jadapi*, conj. Brbh. Av. = यद्यपि.

जदवार *jadvār* [P. *zadvār*; A. *jadvār*], m. **1.** zedoary (*Curcuma zedoaria*): a herb used medicinally, and as a spice. **2.** a substance (? *Aconitum palmatum*) used as an antidote to poison (= निर्विषी).

जदीद *jadīd* [A. *jadīd*], adj. U. newly cut off: new, recent, modern.

जदुईस *jaduīs*, m. Brbh. lord of the Yadus (= यदुनाथ).

जद्दी *jaddī* [cf. A. *jadd*], adj. reg. (Bihar) ancestral (estate).

जन *jan* [*jana-*], m. a living being: **1.** a man; a person. **2.** an attendant, servant; adherent (of a leader, or a deity). **3.** (pl. and in comp.) people, folk; community, a group. — जन-गणना, f. a census. जन-चर्चा, f. a matter of common knowledge or belief. जन-जागरण, m. general awareness (of a situation, a topic), enlightened knowledge. जन-जाति, f. a tribe. जन-तंत्र, m. a democracy; a republic. °-वाद, m. practice of, or belief in democracy. °ई, m. & adj. a democrat; democratic. °ईय, adj. id. जनतंत्रात्मक [°*tra* + *ā*°], adj. democratic. °-तांत्रिक, adj. democratic. जन-त्राता, m. inv. Av. a saviour of his people, or servants. जन-धन, m. manpower. जन-निदेश, m. a referendum. जनपद, m. a community, people; the territory of a country as a whole (as contrasted with the seat of government); a particular province, or district. °ई, m. a regional governor. °ईय, adj. regional. जनप्रिय, adj. popular. जन-मत, m. popular opinion; a vote of the people, plebiscite. जन-मर्यादा, f. popular custom, or convention. जन-यात्रा, f. a popular demonstration, march supporting a cause. जन-रंजन, m. delight of the people: one who pleases the people. जन-रव, m. noise of voices, clamour; rumour, report; calumny. जन-वध, m. genocide. जन-वल्लभ, m. one dear to the people. जनवाद, m. the practice of, or belief in, democracy. °ई, m. & adj. a democrat; democratic. जन-वास, m. residence, quarters; quarters for the bridegroom's party at a wedding. जन-वासा, m. Av. id. जन-शक्ति, f. manpower. जन-शून्य, adj. empty of people, deserted. जन-श्रुत, adj. heard of among men: celebrated. °इ, f. hearsay, rumour; tradition. जन-संख्या, f. number of people, or residents; population. जन-समाज, m. society with its members, society in general. जन-समुदाय, m. a community. जनसाधारण, m. generality of people: the public; the average man. जनसामान्य, m. = जन-साधराण. जन-हित, m. the people's, or public, well-being. जनाकर [°*na* + *ā*°], m. a throng of people. जनाकीर्ण [°*na* + *ā*°], adj. densely populated; crowded with people. जनाचार [°*na* + *ā*°], m. = जन-मर्यादा. जनाधिक्य [°*na* + *ā*°], m. over-population. जनाश्रम [°*na* + *ā*°], m. an inn; a shelter. जनाश्रय [°*na* + *ā*°], m. id. जनेंद्र [°*na* + *i*°], m. lord of men: a king, rajah. जनेश [°*na* + *ī*°], m. lord of men: id. जनोन्मुख [°*na* + *u*°], adj. turned towards, attentive or sympathetic to, the people. जनोपयोगी [°*na* + *u*°], adj. useful to the people, of general utility.

ज़न *zan* [P. *zan*], f. S.H. a woman.

-जनक *-janak* [S.], adj. formant & m. **1.** adj. formant. causing producing (e.g. संतोषजनक, satisfactory). **2.** m. father, progenitor.

ज़नख़दाँ *zanakhdāṁ* [P. *zanakhdān*], m. U. the chin.

ज़नख़ा *zankhā* [? P. *zanka*], adj. & m. **1.** adj. effeminate; impotent. **2.** m. a eunuch. **3.** a dancing-boy.

जनता *janătā* [S.], f. people, populace, population; the public. — आम ~, f. the common people.

जनन *janan* [S.], m. **1.** producing. **2.** reproduction; propagation. **3.** genesis, birth, origin.

जनना *jannā* [*janayati*], v.t & ? v.i. **1.** v.t. to give birth to (a child, or young). **2.** to beget. **3.** v.i. *Pl.* to be born.

जननी *janănī* [S.], f. mother, progenitrix.

जनब *janab*, m. reg. the plant *Crotalaria juncea* (a source of fibre: = [1]सन).

जनमना *janamnā* [cf. H. *janm*], v.i. to be born, to come into existence.

जनमाना *janmānā* [cf. H. *janm*], v.t. **1.** to give birth to, to produce (a child: the mother). **2.** to cause, to give rise to (as a belief).

जनयिता *janayitā* [S.], m. inv. father, progenitor.

जनरल *janral* [Engl. *general*], m. a general.

जनवरी *janvarī* [Engl. *January*], f. January.

जनवाँसा *janvāṁsā* [**janyavāsa-*], m. = जनवासा.

जनवाई *janvāī* [cf. H. *janvānā*], f. = जनाई, 1., 2.

जनवाना *janvānā* [cf. H. *jannā*], v.t. to cause to be born (= जनाना).

जनवासा *janvāsā* [**janyavāsa-*], m. living quarters of the bridegroom's party (at the time of a wedding).

जना *janā* [*jana-*], m. a man, a person (= जन).

जनाई *janāī* [cf. H. [1]*janānā*], f. **1.** midwifery. **2.** cost of, or payment for, a midwife's services. **3.** a midwife.

जनाज़ा *janāzā* [A. *jināza*, *janāza*], m. a bier, with corpse; bier; coffin. — ~ उठना, the bier to be raised; a funeral to begin, or to take place. ~ निकलना, a funeral to take place. जनाज़े का जलूस, m. funeral procession. जनाज़े की गाड़ी, f. hearse.

ज़नानख़ाना *zanānkhānā* [P. *zanān*, pl. + P. *khāna*], m. women's apartments.

ज़नाना *zanānā* [P. *zanāna*], adj. inv. & m. f. **1.** adj. women's (rooms, compartment, work, institution). **2.** feminine, womanly. **3.** gynaecological. **4.** effeminate. **5.** m. an effeminate man; colloq. a woman. **6.** women's apartments.

[1]**जनाना** *janānā* [cf. H. *jannā*], v.t. to deliver (a child: a midwife). (= **निकालना**).

[2]**जनाना** *janānā* [cf. H. *jānnā*], v.t. **1.** to cause to be known (to, **को**). **2.** to point out (to), to inform of.

ज़नानापन *zanānāpan* [cf. H. *zanānā*], m. effeminacy.

ज़नानी *zanānī* [P. *zanānī*], adj. women's, feminine. — ~ **धोती**, f. a woman's *dhotī*.

जनाब *janāb* [A. *janāb*], m. a title of respect (also euph.): your honour, your excellency; his honour, his excellency. — **जनाब-आली**, m. exalted sir: = **जनाब**. **जनाबे मन**! my dear sir!

[1]**जनाव** *janāv* [cf. H. [1]*janānā*], m. delivery (of a child: by a midwife).

[2]**जनाव** *janāv* [cf. H. *jānnā*], m. Brbh. Av. information, knowledge.

जनावर *janāvar*, m. corr. = **जानवर**.

[1]**जनि** *jani* [*yathā na*], neg. adv. Brbh. Av. not.

[2]**जनि** *jani* [S.], f. **1.** birth, genesis. **2.** Brbh. = **जनी**, 1.

जनित *janit* [S.], adj. produced, engendered; caused (by, **से**).

जनिता *janitā* [S.], m. inv. father, progenitor.

जनित्री *janitrī* [S.], f. mother, progenitrix.

जनी *janī* [*jani-*], f. **1.** a woman; a mother; a daughter, daughter-in-law. **2.** a woman servant.

जनु *janu* [? *yat+na*], conj. Brbh. Av. as if.

जनुक *januk*, conj. w. encl. *Pl. HŚS.* = **जनु**.

जनून *janūn* [A. *junūn*], m. **1.** possession by a *jinn*: madness; mental disturbance. **2.** transf. a craze (for sthg.: cf. **सनक**). — ~ **चढ़ना** (**पर**), madness to possess (one); to be mentally disturbed. ~ **की हालत में**, adv. in a state of insanity or derangement.

जनूनी *janūnī* [A. *junūnī*], adj. insane; mentally disturbed.

जनूब *janūb* [A. *janūb*], m. U. the south.

जनूबी *janūbī* [A. *janūbī*], adj. U. southern.

जनेऊ *janeū* [*yajñopavīta-*], m. *hind.* **1.** a sacred thread worn from adolescence by males of the upper three community groups. **2.** investiture (of a person, **का**) with the sacred thread.

जनेत *janet* [*janyayātrā-*], f. E.H. bridegroom's procession or journey to the bride's house.

जनेवा *janevā*, m. **1.** a hardy fodder grass (*Andropogon annulatus*: used in land reclamation). **2.** ? *Pl.* a kind of fragrant grass which grows with *kharīf* crops.

जनौं *janauṁ* [H. *na jānauṁ*], adv. rhetor. neg. Av. I do not know: heaven knows.

जन्नत *jannat* [A. *janna*: P. *jannat*], f. paradise.

जन्नती *jannatī* [A. *jannatī*], adj. of paradise, heavenly.

जन्म *janm* [S.], m. **1.** birth. **2.** origin; emergence. **3.** existence: lifetime; incarnation. — ~ **गँवाना**, to waste (one's) life: to live in a way unworthy of a man. ~ ~ **का**, adj. existing from life(time) to life(time), or eternally. ~ **डुबोना**, to ruin (one's) life ~ **देना** (**को**), to give birth to; to create, to give rise to (a belief, or a misconception). ~ **बिगड़ना**, (one's) life to be ruined; to become a widow. ~ **बिगाड़ना**, = ~ **डुबोना**. ~ **लेना**, to be born; to become incarnate (a deity); to appear, to emerge. ~ **से**, adv. by, or from birth. ~ **से प्राप्त**, adj. hereditary. ~ **हारना**, to lose (the benefit of) birth as a human being. – **जन्म-जन्म**, or **जन्म-आजन्म**, adv. from birth to birth: for ever. **जन्म-कुंडली**, f. a horoscope. **जन्म-क्षेत्र**, m. place or region of birth. **जन्मगत**, adj. hereditary; congenital. **जन्म-गाँठ**, f. an anniversary; a birthday. **जन्म-ग्रहण**, m. = ~, 1., 2. **जन्म-ग्रहण करना**, to take birth. **जन्म-जला**, pej. burnt or spoiled from birth: originally bad; unfortunate, wretched. **जन्मजात**, adj. inborn; instinctive; hereditary; congenital. **जन्म-तिथि**, f. date of birth. **जन्म-दर**, f. birth-rate. **जन्म-दाता**, m. inv. progenitor, father. °-**दात्री**, f. mother. **जन्म-दिन**, m. birthday. **जन्म-दिवस**, m. id. **जन्म-नक्षत्र**, m. *astrol.* planet or constellation in the ascendant at the time of a birth. **जन्म-नियंत्रण**, m. lowering of the birth-rate. **जन्म-पंजी**, f. register of births. **जन्म-पत्र**, m., °-**पत्रिका**, f., = next. **जन्म-पत्री**, f. a horoscope; fig. detailed account. **जन्म-प्रमाणक**, m. birth certificate. **जन्म-बावला**, m. pej. a born idiot. **जन्म-भूमि**, f. region of birth; native land. **जन्म-मरण**, m. eternal death; life and death. **जन्म-योग**, m. *astrol.* a position of the planets from which the birth of a child can be foretold. **जन्म-राशि**, f. = **जन्म-नक्षत्र**. **जन्म-रोगी**, m. one ailing from birth. **जन्म-शती**, f. the centenary of a birth. **जन्म-सिद्ध**, adj. determined by birth: innate, hereditary; having realised life's goal: successful. **जन्म-स्थान**, m. birth-place. **जन्मांतर** [°*nma+a*°], m. another birth, the next life. °**ईय**, adj. pertaining to another birth, &c. **जन्मांध** [°*nma+a*°], adj. & m. blind from birth; one blind from birth. **जन्माष्टमी** [°*nma+a*°], f. *hind.* the eighth day of the dark half of the month Bhādoṁ, the birth-day of Kṛṣṇa; the festival held on that day. जन्मोत्तर [°*nma+u*°], adj. post-natal. जन्मोत्सव [°*nma+u*°], m. celebration of a birth; celebration of a birthday; the *janmāṣṭamī* festival, see above.

जन्मना *janmanā* [S.], adv. by or through (one's) birth.

जन्माना *janmānā* [cf. H. *janm*], v.t. **1.** to give birth to. **2.** to assist at a birth.

जन्मी *janmī* [S.], m. a living creature.

जन्य *janyă* [S.], adj. & m. **1.** adj. having to do with men, or with a people. **2.** -जन्य. produced (by, or from); caused by.

जप *jap* [conn. *japya-*], m. **1.** repetition in a low tone of an incantation, or the name of a deity; counting silently the beads of a rosary, &c. **2.** a muttered prayer or spell. **3.** meditation on the name of a deity. — ~ करना, to mutter prayers, &c. ~ कराना, to have prayers said, or beads counted, for a sick person (by, से). – जप-तप, m. devotion, worship, the performance of religious observances. जप-माल, or °-माला, f. a rosary.

जपजी *japjī* [← Panj.], f. a religious text of the Sikhs.

जपना *japnā* [conn. *japyati*: w. Panj. *japṇā*], v.t. **1.** to repeat in a low tone an incantation, or the name of a deity. **2.** to meditate on the name of a deity. **3.** to count (one's beads).

[1]**जपा** *japā* [S.], f. Brbh. the China rose (= [3]जवा).

[2]**जपा** *japā* [cf. H. *japnā*], m. Av. one who recites incantations, &c. — जपा-तपा, m. = जपी-तपी.

जपी *japī* [cf. H. *japnā*], m. one who repeats incantations, &c. — जपी-तपी, m. colloq. a devout person.

जफ़ा *jafā* [A. *jafā*], f. roughness, rudeness: oppression, harshness, cruelty; injustice.

ज़फ़ीर *zafīr* [? A. *zafīr*, w. A. *ṣafīr*], f. a whistling sound.

ज़फ़ील *zafīl* [? A. *zafīr*, w. A. *ṣafīr*], f. reg. a whistling sound (as made while flying pigeons); a whistle.

जब *jab* [cf. H. *kab*, and *ab*: anal.], adv. & conj. **1.** when, at the time when; while. **2.** whereas. — ~ कभी, adv. wherever. ~ का, adj. of that time, of the time when: past, previous, last. ~ का ~, or ~ का तब, adv. at the proper moment. ~ कि, conj. = ~. ~ ~, conj. whenever. ~ तक, conj. as long as; (with neg.) until; by which time, by that time. ~ तब, adv. sometimes, occasionally. ~ तलक (chiefly reg.), = ~ तक. ~ भी, conj. whenever. ~ लग, or ~ लों (लौं), conj. reg. = ~ तक. ~ से, conj. from the time when, since. ~ ही, conj. as soon as, at the very moment. जभी, adv. colloq. hence, therefore, as a result. जभी तो वह नाराज़ हुआ, that's the reason he got angry.

जबड़ा *jabṛā* [cf. *jambha-*], m. the jaw; the jaws.

ज़बर *zabar* [P. *zabar*], adj. upper, superior; great, larger. — ज़बरदस्त, adj. having the upper hand: strong; high-handed, overbearing; oppressive (as rule); overwhelming (as superiority); strict (an order); colloq. tough (a question); colloq. vast, massive. °ई, f. & adv. force, compulsion; high-handedness, oppression; forcibly; unjustly; arbitrarily. ~ करना, to use force (with or towards, पर), to compel; to oppress. ~ से, adv. = ज़बरदस्ती, adv. जबरजंग, adj. colloq. = ज़बरदस्त/.

जबर *jabr* [A. *jabr*], m. force; compulsion.

जबरन *jabran* [A. *jabran*], adv. forcibly; by compulsion. — ~ भरती करना, to enrol or to enlist by force, to press into service.

जबराइल *jabrāil* [A. *jibrā'īl*], m. the archangel Gabriel.

जबरी *jabrī* [cf. H. *jabran*], adj. forced, compulsory.

ज़बह *zabah* [A. *ẕabḥ*], m. usu. /zibəh/. slaughtering (an animal for food). — ~ करना, to slaughter; specif. to slaughter in accordance with Muslim law.

ज़बान *zabān* [P. *zabān*], f. **1.** tongue. **2.** a language, tongue; speech. **3.** fig. word, promise. — ~ आना (को), (a person) to find (his) tongue. ~ का, adj. unwritten, oral (as an agreement). ~ का पक्का, adj. true to one's word. ~ का मीठा, adj. sweet-tongued. ~ काटना, to interrupt the speech (of, का); to check (one's own, अपने) tongue (as in remorse). ~ के चटकारे लेना, to smack the lips; to have a sweet tooth. ~ के नीचे ~ होना, to say different things to different people, to say one thing and mean another. ~ के मज़े लेना, to have a sweet tooth. ~ खोलना, to unloose the tongue, to speak out. ~ चलना, the tongue to be busy. ~ चलाना, to talk much, or too much; to be abusive; to make good use of (one's, अपनी) tongue. ~ दबाकर कहना, to speak in a whisper. ~ देना, to give (one's) word. ~ निकालना, colloq. to use foul language. ~ पकड़ना (की), to prevent (one) from speaking; to interrupt; to cavil at the words (of). ~ पर, or में, ताला लगना, fig. to keep silent (as from constraint); colloq. to have nothing to say. ~ पर मोहर लगना, the tongue to be sealed: id. ~ पर चढ़ना, to be much talked about; to be on the tip of the tongue, to be well-learned. ~ पर रखना, to taste. ~ पर लाना, to utter, to say, to mention. ~ पर होना, to be subject of talk, not to be forgotten. ~ पलटना, or फेरना, or बदलना, colloq. to change (one's) tune. ~ बंद होना, to be speechless; to be silenced, or at a loss; to have lockjaw. ~ बिगड़ना (की), the tongue to be spoiled: to use bad language; sense of taste to be lost. ~ मुँह में रखना, to hold (one's) tongue. ~ सँभालना, to mind one's tongue; to hold one's tongue; to speak with all care. ~ से निकलना, to escape the lips (of, की); to be uttered. ~ से निकालना, to be uttered, or pronounced. ~ हारना, to give (one's, अपनी) word. ~ हिलाना, to wag the tongue, to speak; to make a request. लंबी ~, f. a long tongue (attribute of a talkative, or of an abusive, person). — ज़बान-दराज़ [P. *-darāz*], adj. long-tongued: impudent; abusive. °ई, f. ज़बानबंदी [P. *-bandī*], f. written testimony, affidavit. ज़बानबंदी करना, to take down a statement.

ज़बानी *zabānī* [P. *zabānī*], adj. **1.** oral. **2.** unwritten; traditional. — ~ जमाख़र्च, m. mere words (as opposed to deeds). ~ याद होना, (sthg.) to be known by heart.

जबार *jabār* [A. *javār*], m. reg. (Bihar) neighbourhood.

ज़बून *zabūn* [P. *zabūn*], adj. E.H. bad, deficient.

ज़ब्त *zabt* [A. *ẓabṭ*], m. & adj. **1.** m. control, restraint (as over emotions). **2.** taking possession (of), seizing. **3.** confiscation. **4.** adj. confiscated. — ~ करना, to control, to restrain; to seize (property, &c.); to confiscate. ~ किए रहना, to restrain (one's) emotions. — ज़ब्तशुदा [P. *-śuda*], adj. inv. confiscated.

ज़ब्ती *zabtī* [P. *ẓabṭī*], f. seizure, confiscation. — ~ में आना, to be seized, or confiscated.

जब्बार *jabbār* [A. *jabbār*], adj. E.H. mighty, conquering.

जभी *jabhī*, conj. & adv. **1.** conj. = जब भी, see s.v. जब. **2.** adv. see s.v. जब; also = जब ही.

जम *jam*, m. = यम.

जमकना *jamaknā*, v.i. **1.** [cf. **jamm-*] *Pl. HŚS.* = चमकना. **2.** *Pl.* = [1]जमना.

जमकूड़ा *jamkūṛā*, m. reg. (W.) a mat worn over the shoulders to keep off rain.

जमघट *jamghaṭ* [cf. H. *jamnā*; **ghaṭṭa-*[3]], m. a gathering, a dense crowd.

जमघटा *jamghaṭā*, m. = जमघट.

ज़मज़म *zamzam* [A. *zamzam*], m. *musl.* name of a famous well at Mecca.

[1]**जमना** *jamnā* [*yamyate*], v.i. **1.** to become firm, or fixed; to fit in place (in or on, पर); to stand firm; to be transfixed, rooted (to a spot). **2.** to settle (in a place or spot). **3.** to become hard or firm; to congeal; to be frozen, to freeze; to curdle, to clot (as milk, blood); to be deposited, to settle. **4.** to sprout, to shoot; to germinate; to take root (a seed); to grow (hair). **5.** colloq. to be delivered, planted (a blow). **6.** to be collected, to collect (as a crowd). **7.** to be established, or consolidated (a position, an activity, an ascendancy); to thrive. **8.** to be impressed (upon, पर or को); to be effective, or memorable. **9.** to take a stand (on, पर): to persist, to insist. **10.** to pace (a horse).

[2]**जमना** *jamnā*, f. = यमुना.

जमनिका *jamănikā* [ad. *yavanikā-*], f. **1.** E.H. = यवनिका. **2.** reg. (Bihar) musical prologue (to a drama).

जमनौता *jamnautā* [H. *zāmin*+H. *-autā* ← *vṛtti-*], m. a small percentage paid to one who is surety for some amount.

जमहूर *jamhūr* [A. *jamhūr*], m. **1.** a community, a populace. **2.** a state, nation.

जमहूरियत *jamhūriyat* [A. *jamhūrīya*: P. *jamhūriyat*], f. **1.** a democracy. **2.** a republic.

जमा *jamā* [P. *jam'*], f. & adj. inv. **1.** f. a collection. **2.** a gathering, assembly. **3.** an amount; a total, a whole. **4.** capital; principal; assets; stock; credit (as opposed to debit), receipts. **5.** a deposit. **6.** *math.* addition. **7.** adj. collected, gathered together. **8.** deposited; standing to credit. **9.** added (to). तीन ~ एक चार, three and one are four. — ~ करना, to collect, to amass; to deposit; to credit (a payment); to raise (money); to add. ~ मारना, to misappropriate, to embezzle (a sum of money). – जमाकरता, m. inv. a depositor. जमा-ख़र्च, m. income and expenditure; current account. °ई, f. cash flow. जमा-ख़र्च करना, or मिलाना, to make up, or to balance, an account. जमा-ख़ाता, m. a (bank) account. जमाख़ोर [P. *-khor*], m. a hoarder; speculator. °ई, f. hoarding; speculation. जमादार [P. *-dār*], m. one in immediate charge of a body of men: a corporal; junior officer of police, customs, &c.; a head guide, or messenger; voc. a sweeper. °ई, f. the office, work or status of a *jamādār*. जमा-पूँजी, f. capital, assets. जमाबंदी [P. *-bandī*], f. revenue accounts; government revenue from land; land dues. जमामार, m. an embezzler; one who extorts money.

जमाई *jamāī* [*jāmātṛ-*], m. a son-in-law.

जमाऊ *jamāū* [cf. H. *jamānā*], adj. able to be fixed, or stuck; fixed; enduring.

जमात *jamāt* [A. *jamā'a*: P. *jamā'at*], f. **1.** a class (school). **2.** a community, group. **3.** transf. line, row.

जमादार *jamādār*, m. see s.v. जमा.

ज़मानत *zamānat* [A. *ẓamāna*: P. *ẓamānat*], f. **1.** surety. **2.** bail. — ~ दाख़िल करना, to enter bail (= next). ~ देना, to furnish surety, to put up bail. ~ पर छोड़ना, or रिहा करना, to release on bail. ~ पर लेना, to bail (a person) out. ~ लेकर छोड़ना, = ~ पर छोड़ना. – ज़मानतदार [P. *-dār*], m. a guarantor. ज़मानत-नामा, m. bail bond, deed of surety.

ज़मानतन *zamānatan* [A. *ẓamānatan*], adv. by way of surety.

ज़मानती *zamānatī* [P. *ẓamānatī*], adj. & m. **1.** adj. *law.* having to do with bail; bailable (an offence). **2.** m. *Pl. HŚS.* one who gives bail or surety. — ~ रुपया, or धन, m. deposit as surety, caution money.

जमाना *jamānā* [cf. H. [1]*jamnā*], v.t. **1.** to cause to be fixed, or to adhere; to set or to lay in place (as a brick); to spread (a layer). **2.** to cause to congeal; to freeze (water); to clot, to coagulate (milk, blood). **3.** to cause to take root, to plant. **4.** to fix, to lay down; to measure out (a distance). **5.** colloq. to deliver (a blow, a slap); to hit (a score: cricket). **6.** to collect, to amass. **7.** to establish, to consolidate (a position, an activity, an ascendancy). **8.** to impress (upon, पर: as one's words, or authority). — दृष्टि ~ (अपनी), to fix (one's) eyes, or gaze (on, पर). बर्फ़ ~, to make ice. रंग, or प्रभाव, ~ (अपना), to make an impression or to consolidate (one's) influence (upon, पर). हाथ ~ (अपना), to acquire a skill, or knack; to form a hand (in writing).

ज़माना *zamānā* [P. *zamāna*], m. **1.** time, period; the times; an age. **2.** the world. — ~ देखे होना, to have seen, or to know, the world. ~ पलटना, or बदलना, times to change, a situation to change. ज़माने भर का, adj. the whole world's: an inordinate amount of. उस ज़माने में, adv. during that period, or era. – ज़मानासाज़ [P. *-sāz*], m. an opportunist; a turncoat. °ई, f.

जमाल *jamāl* [A. *jamāl*], m. beauty, charm, elegance.

जमाल-गोटा *jamāl-goṭā*, m. a small cultivated tree, *Croton tiglium*, and its nut (used as a purgative).

जमाव *jamāv* [cf. H. [1]*jamnā*], m. **1.** state of adhesion, consolidation, &c.; state of being frozen. **2.** a gathering, mass.

जमावट *jamāvaṭ* [cf. H. *jamnā*], f. **1.** consolidation, thickening, collecting, &c. **2.** sthg. thickened, or collected; *min.* a deposit.

जमावटी *jamāvṭī* [cf. H. *jamāvaṭ*], adj. colloq. thickened (milk).

जमावड़ा *jamāvṛā* [cf. H. *jamāv*], m. a gathering, assembly.

ज़मीं- *zamīṁ-*, f. earth, &c. (see ज़मीन): — ज़मींक़ंद [P. *-qand*], m. a kind of sweet potato. ज़मींदार [P. *-dār*], m. landowner, landlord; zamindar (responsible for ground rents to government). °ई, f. landed estate; freehold; position or tenure of a zamindar; the system of collecting land revenue through zamindars.

ज़मीन *zamīn* [P. *zamīn*], f. **1.** earth, ground; soil. **2.** land, tract; terrain. **3.** background (as to a picture). **4.** foundation, groundwork. **5.** the earth, world. — ~ आसमान एक करना, to unite heaven and earth: to make untold efforts; to create utter confusion. ~ आसमन का फ़रक़, a whole world of difference. ~ आसमान के कुलाबे मिलना, U. the hinges of earth and sky to close: a dire happening to occur. ~ आसमान के कुलाबे मिलाना, fig. to boast wildly. ~ दिखाना, to show the ground (to, को): to lay low; to get the better (of). ~ पकड़ना, to take root; to be rooted to a spot; fig. to hold one's ground, to persevere obstinately. ~ पर पैर न रखना, to walk above the earth: to be vainglorious; to exult (esp. in pride). ~ बाँधना, to prepare a background (for a painting). ~ में गड़ना, or समाना, to sink into the ground (with shame, embarrassment). – ज़मीनदोज़ [P. *-doz*], adj. level with the ground, razed; subterranean.

ज़मीन- *zamīn-*. see ज़मीं-, and s.v. ज़मीन.

ज़मीनी *zamīnī* [P. *zamīnī*], adj. having to do with the earth, earthly, terrestrial.

जमीयत *jamīyat* [A. *jam'īya*: P. *jam'īyat*], f. a collected party, or body: association, society; assembly.

ज़मीर *zamīr* [A. *ẓamīr*], m., f. heart, mind; thoughts.

जमैयत *jamaiyat* [? = *jama'īyat*, corr.], f. pronun. var. = जमीयत.

जमोआ *jamoā*, m. *hist.* indigo sown in spring and ready to cut in August.

जमोग *jamog*, m. *hist.* reg. (E.) transfer of liabilities by mutual consent; aggregated yearly payments of rent or revenue; a conditional mortgage.

जमोगा *jamogā*, m. *Pl.* a children's complaint, wind.

जमोट *jamoṭ* [**jambukāṣṭha-*], m. reg. wooden cylinder used in forming the foundation of a masonry well (often made of *jāmun* wood).

जम्हाई *jamhāī*, f. = जँभाई.

जम्हाना *jamhānā*, v.i. = जँभाना.

जयंती *jayantī* [S.], f. **1.** a jubilee. **2.** a birthday celebration. **3.** a flag, banner. **4.** a victorious woman: title of Durgā, and of Pārvatī.

जय *jay* [*jaya-*], f. & interj. **1.** f. victory; triumph. **2.** interj. long live! hail (to, की); hurrah! — ~ करना, or पाना, to obtain a victory (over, पर), to defeat. ~ गोपाल! hail to Gopāl (Kr̥ṣṇa)!: greetings! ~ बोलना, or मनाना, to wish prosperity (to, की). – जय-घोष, m. shout of victory. जय-चिह्न, m. a trophy, prize. जय-जयकार, m. a shout, or shouts, of victory or triumph; exultation. जय-जयजार करना, to shout in triumph; to rejoice. जय-जयवंती, f. *mus.* name of a *rāgiṇī*. जय-जीव, interj. Av. hail and long live: greetings. जय-दुंदुभी, f. victory drum(s). जय-ध्वज, m. victory flag. जय-ध्वनि, f. = जय-घोष. जय-नाद, m. = जय-जयकार. जय-पत्र, m. letter accepting a defeat (in battle) or confirming a victory (in a legal case). जय-पाल, m. guardian of victory: a king. जय-मंगल, m. fig. a royal elephant. जय-मल्लार, m. *mus.* name of a *rāg*. जय-माल, f. garland of victory; garland placed round a bridegroom's neck by his bride. °आ, f. id. जय-यज्ञ, m. victory sacrifice: the Aryan *aśvamedha* or horse sacrifice. जय-लेख, m. = जय-पत्र. जय-शब्द, m. shout or song of victory. जय-श्री, f. victory; the goddess of victory; *mus.* = जैत-स्री, name of a *rāgiṇī*. जय-स्तंभ, m. a victory column. जयोल्लास [°*ya+u*°], m. exultation of victory.

जय- *jay-* [cf. *jayati*], v. t. Av. to conquer.

जयक *jayak* [S.], adj. *HŚS.* victorious.

जयचंदी *jaycandī*, f. like Jaycand (*hist.* the Gāhaḍavāla ruler of Banaras): treacherous.

जयत-कल्याण *jayat-kalyāṇ* [S.], m. *mus.* name of a mixed *rāg*.

जयति *jayati* [? f. *jayantī-*], m. *mus.* name of a mixed *rāg*. — जयति-श्री, ? f. name of a *rāgiṇī* (= जैत-स्री).

जयन *jayan* [S.], m. Brbh. conquest.

जया *jayā* [S.], f. the victorious one: a title of several deities, incl. Durgā, and Pārvatī.

जयिष्णु *jayiṣṇu* [S.], adj. victorious.

जयी *jayī* [S.], adj. victorious. — कालजयी, adj. timeless (as an achievement).

ज़र *zar* [P. *zar*], m. **1.** U. gold; silver. **2.** money, wealth. — ज़र-ख़रीद, adj. bought with one's own money (as a slave). ज़रख़ेज़ [P. -*khez*], adj. gold-producing: fig. fertile. ज़रगर [P. -*gar*], m. goldsmith; jeweller. ज़रतारी, adj. embroidered with gold wire. ज़रदार [P. -*dār*], adj. wealthy, rich. ज़रदोज़ [P. -*doz*], m. an embroiderer (who works with gold or silver thread). °ई, f.

[1]**जर** *jar* [*jvara-*], m. Av. a fever.

[2]**जर** *jar*, f. Brbh. Av. a root (= जड़). — जरकट्टा, m. reg. (Bihar), cutting a crop at the root.

[1]**जर-** *jar-*, v.i. Brbh. Av. = जलना.

[2]**जर-** *jar-*, v.i. Av. = जड़ना.

जरजर *jarjar*, adj. = जर्जर.

जरठ *jaraṭh* [S.], adj. **1.** old, infirm; decrepit, decayed. **2.** harsh, cruel. — जरठपन, m. Av. old age.

ज़रद *zard* [P. *zard*], adj. **1.** yellow. **2.** pale. — ~ पड़ना, to turn pale. ज़रदरंग, adj. yellow-coloured; fig. bashful. ज़रदाड़ू, m. = next. ज़रदालू, m. apricot.

ज़रदा *zardā* [P. *zarda*], m. **1.** tobacco for chewing (with *pān*, or alone). **2.** a sweet *pulāv* coloured with saffron. 3. = ज़रदी, 3.

ज़रदी *zardī* [P. *zardī*], f. **1.** yellowness. **2.** paleness. **3.** jaundice. **4.** yolk of an egg. — ~ छाना (पर), the face to grow pale.

जरना *jarnā* [*jvarati*], v.i. *Pl.* to be feverish; to suffer from fever.

जरनि *jarani* [cf. H. *jalan*], f. Brbh. Av. **1.** a burning sensation, pain. **2.** a pang.

ज़रब *zarab* [A. *ẓarb*], f. **1.** Brbh. blow, stroke. **2.** *math.* multiplication. — ~ करना, to multiply. ~ देना, to strike; to multiply.

ज़रबीला *zarbīlā* [cf. P. *ẓarb*], adj. Brbh. striking, splendid (as a sight).

ज़रर *zarar* [A. *ẓarar*], m. E.H. harm, damage.

जरवा- *jarvā-*, v.t. E.H. = जलवाना.

जरा *jarā* [S.], f. old age: infirmity, decrepitude. — जरा-ग्रस्त, adj. assailed by age, infirm. जरा-जीर्ण, adj. made frail by age. जरातुर [°*rā+ā*°], adj. afflicted by age, decrepit, senile.

ज़रा *zarā* [A. *ẕarra*], adj. inv. **1.** adj. esp. ~ सा, a little (of). ~ सी चीनी, f. a little sugar. **2.** unimportant, insignificant; trivial. ~ सी लड़की, f. a slip of a girl. **3.** adv. a little. **4.** just: would you mind, please. ~ यहाँ आइए, would you just come over here. — ~ भी नहीं, adv. not in the slightest. ~ सुनूँ, adv. rhetor. are you telling me (that) …? ~ ~, adv. little by little; every little bit. ~ ~ करके, adv. id.

जरा- *jarā-*, v.t. Brbh. Av. = जलाना.

जराइ *jarāi*, f. Brbh. = जड़ाव.

ज़राफ़त *zarāfat* [A. *ẓarāfa*: P. *ẓarāfat*], f. U. wit; facetiousness.

जरायम *jarāym* [A. *jarā'im*, pl. of *jarīma*]. crimes, offences: — जरायमपेशा, m. one who lives by crime, a criminal.

जरायु *jarāyu* [S.], m. (? f., *Pl.*) **1.** caul (the membrane enveloping a foetus). **2.** placenta. — जरायुज, adj. & m. viviparous, mammalian; a mammal.

जराव *jarāv*, m. Brbh. = जड़ाव.

जराह *jarāh*, m. pronun. var. = जर्राह.

ज़रिया *zariyā* [A. *zarī'a*], m. **1.** means; agency, cause; source. **2.** connection, influence (with one: के यहाँ). **3.** ppn w. के. by means (of); through the agency or intervention (of); in or by virtue (of). – ज़रिए से, adv. by means, &c. (of, के: = ~, 3).

¹**जरिया** *jariyā* [cf. H. *jalnā*], adj. burnt, made by boiling (as saltpetre).

²**जरिया** *jariyā*, f. *Pl.* the support for the pivot on which the lever-beam of a well works.

ज़री *zarī* [P. *zarī*], f. **1.** gold thread. **2.** gold brocade.

जरीब *jarīb* [A. *jarīb*], f. a surveyor's measuring chain (of fifty-five yards). — ~ डालना, to measure by chain, to survey (land).

जरीबाना *jarībānā*, m. corr. = जुरमाना.

जरुथ *jaruth* [ad. *jarūtha-*], m. *Pl.* skinniness; loose or flabby flesh.

ज़रूर *zarūr* [A. *ẓarūr*], adv. **1.** certainly, of course. **2.** without fail; at all costs. — ~ से ~, adv. = next. उनको जाना ~ है, he must certainly go. – ज़रूर-ज़रूर, adv. quite certainly; without fail; most urgently.

ज़रूरत *zarūrat* [A. *ẓarūra*: P. *ẓarūṛat*], f. **1.** need, necessity, want; lack. — ~ पड़ना or होना (की), (sthg.) to be needed, or wanted (by, को). ~ पड़ने पर, adv. at need. ~ में काम आना, to prove useful (to, को) in time of need. ~ से, adv. necessarily. ~ से ज़्यादा, more than needed. – ज़रूरतमंद P. *-mand*], adj. needy.

ज़रूरियात *zarūriyāt* [A. *ẓarūrīyāt*, pl.], f. pl. necessities.

ज़रूरी *zarūrī* [A. *ẓarūrī*], adj. **1.** necessary; important; indispensable. **2.** urgent; special (a meeting, session). **3.** unavoidable. — उनका जाना ~ है, he must certainly go.

जरेला *jarelā*, m. *Pl.* reg. a kind of rice (cf. जड़हन).

जर्जर *jarjar* [S.], adj. **1.** decrepit, decayed; archaic. **2.** broken down; broken to pieces. **3.** old.

जर्जरता *jarjarătā* [S.], f. decrepitude, &c. (see जर्जर).

जर्जरित *jarjarit* [S.], adj. decrepit; dilapidated.

ज़र्द *zard*, adj. see ज़रद.

ज़र्दा *zardā*, m. see ज़रदा.

ज़र्दी *zardī*, f. see ज़रदी.

ज़र्रा *zarrā* [A. *zarra*], m. particle; atom. — ~ भर, m. a tiny amount: speck, pinch, &c. — ज़र्रानवाज़ी [P. *-navāzī*], f. gratitude for small favours.

जर्राह *jarrāh* [A. *jarrāḥ*], m. a surgeon.

¹**जर्राही** *jarrāhī* [A. or P. *jarrāhī*], adj. surgical.

²**जर्राही** *jarrāhī* [cf. H. *jarrāh*], f. surgery.

जल *jal* [*jala-*], m. **1.** water. **2.** (in chronograms) a symbol for the number four. — जल-अलि, m. E.H. a water-beetle, or insect. जल-कंटक, m. the water-chestnut (= सिंघारा); the water plant *jal-kumbhī*. जल-कर, m. water tax or rate. जल-कल, m. a water-main; water-supply. जल-कल अधिकरण, m. Water Board. जल-कुक्कुट, m. a water-hen, coot or (?) teal. °ई, f. id.; the black-headed gull. जल-कुक्कुभ, m. a partic. water-bird. जल-कुंड, m. a pool of water. जल-कुंभी, f. a type of water-weed. जल-केलि, f. = जल-क्रीड़ा. जल-कौआ, m. water-crow: a water ouzel; the little cormorant. जल-क्रिया, f. the offering of a libation of water to gods, or to dead relatives. जल-क्रीड़ा, f. sporting or frolicking in water; water sports. जल-घुमर, m. a whirlpool. जल-घेरा, m. a sea blockade. जलचर, adj. & m. Av. moving on water: aquatic; amphibious; an aquatic, or amphibious animal. °ई, f. m.? id.; a fish. जल-चादर, f. Brbh. sheet of water: a cascade. जलचारी, m. = जलचर. जल-चालित, adj. water-powered. जल-चिह्न, m. water-mark. जल-जंतु, m. an aquatic animal. जलज, m. water-born: a lotus; a pearl; a conch shell. जल-जात, adj. produced from, growing or living in water; a lotus. जल-जोनि, f. Brbh. fire. जल-डमरूमध्य, m. *geog.* a strait. जल-डाकू, m. a pirate. जल-तरंग, m. a harmonica (a series of metal cups filled with water, and producing different notes when struck); the sound of a harmonica. जल-तोड़, m. a breakwater. जल-थल, m. land and water, land and sea; low-lying, wet ground. जल-थंभ, m. diking, damming (a flow of water); Brbh. checking the flow of water by magic. जलद, m. water-giving: a cloud. जलद-काल, m. the rainy season. जलदागम [°*da* + *ā*°], m. the approach of clouds, or of the rainy season. जल-दस्यु, m. a pirate. °ता, f. piracy. जल-दान, m. = जल-क्रिया. जल-देव, m. god of the waters: the Vedic deity Varuṇa. °ता, m. inv. id. जलधर, m. holding water: a cloud; the ocean. °ई, f. the vessel or hollow in which a *lingam* is mounted. जल-धार, m. a flood of water; heavy rain. जल-धारा, f. stream or current of water. जलधि, m. receptacle of water: the ocean. जल-निकासी, f. drainage. जल-निधि, m. wealth or store of water: the ocean. जल-निवास, m. a lake-dwelling. जल-पक्षी, m. an aquatic bird. जल-पति, m. = जल-देव. जल-पथ, m. = जल-मार्ग. जल-परी, f. a mermaid. जल-पाटल, m. Brbh. lampblack, collyrium. जल-पान, m. the drinking of water: a snack, refreshment; breakfast. जल-पान करना, to take refreshment, &c. जल-पान का अड्डा, m. refreshment stall. जल-पान-गृह, or -घर, m. a cafeteria. जल-पिंड, m. fire. जल-पिप्पली, f. = next. जल-पीपल, f. an aquatic plant (the berries of which are used medicinally). जल-पोत, m. water-floater: boat, vessel. जल-प्रपात, m. a waterfall. जल-प्रलय, m. *mythol.* destruction of the world by flood. जल-प्रवाह, m. a current, or stream, of water. जल-प्रांगन, m. territorial waters. जल-प्रांत, m. an area near water: a bank, shore. जलप्राय, adj. having abundant water. जल-प्लावन, m. an inundation. °-प्लावित, adj. inundated. जल-बंधक, m. a dam; dike. जल-बम, m. depth-charge. जल-बिजली, f. electricity produced by water-power. °-घर, m. a hydro-electric power station. जल-भौंरा, m. a water-beetle. जल-मग्न, adj. immersed in water. जलमय, adj. consisting of, or filled with, water. जल-मल, m. foam; scum. जल-मापक, m. a hydrometer. जल-माया, f. a mirage. जल-मार्ग, m. a waterway; sea-passage; channel, drain, &c. जलमुक, m. Brbh. shedder of water: a cloud. जल-मुर्ग़ा, m. water-fowl: moorhen. °ई, f. जल-यंत्र, m. any machine or appliance worked by, or delivering, water. जल-यात्रा, f. a journey by water, voyage. जल-यान, m. water-vehicle: a boat, vessel. जल-रंग, m. (pl.) water-colours: (sg.) a water-colour; painting in water-colours. जल-राशि, f. a quantity, or expanse of, water; the ocean. जल-रुद्ध, adj. cut off by water; watertight; waterproof. जलरुह, m. growing in water: a lotus. जल-रोधक, adj. = जल-रुद्ध, 2., 3. जल-वायु, m. climate. जल-वाष्प, m. water-gas. जल-वास, m. abiding in water: a period of immersion in water. जलवाह, m. carrying water: a cloud. जल-विद्युत, m. = जल-बिजली. °ईय, adj. hydro-electric. जल-विभाजक, adj. forming a watershed. °-विभाजन, m. watershed. जल-विश्लेषण, m. hydrolysis. जल-विहार, m. an excursion or outing by boat; = जल-क्रीड़ा. जल-व्याल, m. a water-snake. जलशायी, m. resting on water: a title of Viṣṇu. जल-समाधि, f. loss of life by drowning. जल-समाधि देना, euph. to place (a dead body) in a river. जल-सिंह, m. sea-lion. जल-सुत, m. Brbh. water-born: a pearl. जल-सूखा, m. drought. जल-सेना, f. a fleet; navy. जल-सेना का अड्डा, m. naval base. जल-सैनिक, adj. & m. naval; a member of a navy, sailor. जल-स्तंभ, m. a water-spout. जल-स्तंभन, m. = जल-थंभ, 2. जल-स्पर्श, m. the touching of water (esp. Ganges water) for religious purposes. जलहीन, adj. without, or deprived of, water; arid. जलांक [°la+a°], m. = जल-चिह्न. जलांचल [°la+a°], m. a canal. जलांजलि [°la+a°], f. an offering of water in the cupped hands (to ancestors, &c.; see जल-क्रिया). जलागार [°la+ā°], m. a reservoir. जलाचमन [°la+ā°], m. rinsing the mouth with water. जलातंक [°la+ā°], m. hydrophobia. जलाधार [°la+ā°], m. body of water: lake, reservoir, &c. जलार्द्र [°la+ā°], adj. wet, heavy with moisture. जलावतरण [°la+ā°], m. launching (of a ship). जलावर्त [°la+ā°], m. a whirlpool. जलाशय [°la+ā°], m. = जलाधार. जलेश्वर [°la+ī°], m. = जल-देव. जलोत्सर्ग [°la+u°], m. reg. the symbolic marriage ceremony of a well or a tank to a nearby image. जलोदर [°la+u°], m. dropsy.

जलंधर *jalandhar* [*jalaṁ+dhara-*], m. dropsy (= जलोदर).

ज़लज़ला *zalzalā* [A. *zalzala*], m. earthquake.

जलजलाना *jaljalānā* [cf. **jhal-*³; ? × **jag-*], v.i. to glare, to shimmer (= झलझलाना).

जलजलाहट *jaljalāhaṭ* [cf. H. *jaljalānā*], f. glare, shimmer.

जलन *jalan* [cf. H. *jalnā*]. f. **1.** burning. **2.** inflammation; stinging, smarting; itching. **3.** fig. inflammation (of the feelings); distress. **4.** envy; jealousy; spite. **5.** irritation; anger. **6.** hatred, aversion, animosity. जलनशील, adj. inflammable.

जलना *jalnā* [*jvalati*], v.i. **1.** to burn, to be burnt; to be lit (a lamp, a stove); to be on a fire (a cooking utensil); to be scorched, or singed; to be dried up, parched by the sun (as fields). **2.** to be on fire; to be burnt down (a building). **3.** to be cremated (a body). **4.** to burn, to sting, to smart. **5.** to be inflamed (the feelings); to feel duress. **6.** to feel envy, or jealousy. **7.** to feel irritation, exasperation, anger. — जल मरना, to be seared by emotion; to die by fire. – जलती आग में कूदना, fig. to court, or to incur, danger, or dire difficulties. जलती आग में घी डालना, fig. to add fuel to a fire. जला, adj. & m. see s.v.

जलपाई *jalpāī*, f. a small Himālayan tree, *Elaeocarpus serratus*, and its fruit, the wild olive.

जलवा *jalvā* [A. *jalva*], m. making clear: splendour, lustre; beauty.

जलवाना *jalvānā* [cf. H. *jalnā*], v.t. to cause to be burnt, &c. (by, से).

जलवैया *jalvaiyā* [cf. *jalvānā*], m. one who burns (sthg).

जलसा *jalsā* [A. *jalsa*], m. **1.** a sitting, session; meeting (of a body). **2.** a gathering, function (social or formal).

जलहर *jalhar* [*jaladhara-*], m. Brbh. **1.** a cloud. **2.** a tank, pond.

जलहरि *jalhari* [cf. *jaladhara-*], f. dimin. E.H. = जलहर.

जला *jalā* [cf. H. *jalnā*], adj. & m. **1.** adj. burnt, &c. **2.** m. a burn, a burnt place. — मन

~ ह्वोना, fig. to feel anger, resentment or ill-will. जले को जलाना, to burn a burn: to reopen a wound. जले पर नोन (or नमक) छिड़कना, to sprinkle salt on a burn: to rub salt on a wound. जले फफोले फोड़ना (के), fig. to add one grief or vexation to another. – जला-भुना, adj. burnt and roasted: inflamed with anger; filled with irritation, resentment or ill-will जली-कटी, f. caustic and cutting words; acrimony, bitterness. जली-कटी पर आना, to descend to acrimony. जली-कटी सुनाना, to make acrimonious, or personal remarks.

जलाऊ *jalāū* [cf. H. *jalnā, jalānā*], adj. **1.** combustible. **2.** intended for burning (as firewood).

जलाना *jalānā* [cf. H. *jalnā*], v.t. **1.** to burn; to kindle, to light (a lamp, a stove). **2.** to set on fire; to burn down. **3.** to burn off, or out; to cauterise. **4.** to inflame (feelings); to cause distress (to); to excite envy or jealousy (in); to irritate, to exasperate, to anger.

जलापा *jalāpā* [cf. H. *jalā*], m. rancour; envy; jealousy; spite.

जलाल *jalāl* [A. *jalāl*], m. majesty, splendour, glory.

¹**ज़लालत** *zalālat* [A. *zalāla*: P. *zalālat*], f. **1.** baseness, abjectness; obsequiousness. **2.** abasement, humiliation. **3.** indignity, insult.

²**ज़लालत** *zalālat* [A. *ẓalāla*: P. *ẓalālat*], f. error, fault, vice.

जलाली *jalālī* [A. *jalālī*], adj. illustrious, glorious.

जलावतन *jalā-vatan* [A.: P. *jalā-vaṭan*], m. & adj. **1.** m. leaving one's country; expulsion, banishment. **2.** an exile. **3.** adj. banished, exiled. — ~ करना (को), to exile (one). ~ होना, to have left one's country, to be exiled.

जलावतनी *jalāvatănī* [P. *jalāvaṭanī*], f. expulsion from one's country: exile, banishment.

जलावन *jalāvan* [cf. H. *jalānā*], m. f. reg. fuel.

जली-कटी *jalī-kaṭī*, f. see s.v. जला, adj.

जलीय- *jalīyă-* [S.], adj. having to do with, or characterised by, water: of water, aqueous, hydro-; aquatic.

ज़लील *zalīl* [A. *zalīl*], adj. **1.** base, abject. **2.** dishonoured, humiliated; insulted. — ~ करना, to humiliate; to insult.

जलूस *jalūs*, m. = जुलूस.

जलेबा *jalebā*, m. a large *jalebī*.

जलेबी *jalebī* [A. *zalābiya*, P. *zalībiya*], f. **1.** a sweet (in shape resembling a pretzel: made of flour soaked in syrup and fried). **2.** a type of firecracker.

जलैया *jalaiyā* [cf. H. *jalānā*], m. one who inflames or excites.

जलोदर *jalôdar* [S.], m. see s.v. जल.

जल्द *jald* [A. *jald*], adj. & f. **1.** adj. quick, swift. **2.** brisk. **3.** impetuous. **4.** f. speed, swiftness, &c. — ~, adv. quickly; hastily; soon. ~ से ~, adv. as soon as possible. जल्दबाज़ [P. -*bāz*], m. a brisk, hasty, or impetuous person. °ई, f. briskness; haste; impetuosity.

जल्दी *jaldī* [A. *jald*+P. *ī*], f. & adv. **1.** speed, swiftness. **2.** briskness; haste. **3.** impetuosity. — ~ करना, to hurry; to be hasty; to be impetuous. ~ मचाना, id., 2., 3. ~ से, or ~, adv. quickly; hastily; soon. ~ से ~, adv. as soon as possible.

जल्प *jalp* [S.], m. talk, chatter; wrangling discussion.

जल्प- *jalp-* [cf. *jalpati*], v.i. Av. to chatter; to brag.

जल्पक *jalpak* [S.], m. Av. a chatterer; wrangler.

जल्लाद *jallād* [A. *jallād*], m. flayer: **1.** an executioner. **2.** fig. a harsh or merciless person.

जल्लादी *jallādī* [A. or P. *jallādī*], f. cruelty, mercilessness; villainy.

जल्वा *jalvā*, m. see जलवा.

जवन *javan*, m. = यवन.

जवनिका *javănikā*, f. = यवनिका.

¹**जवाँ** *javāṁ* [*yamaka-*], adj. & m. **1.** adj. twin. **2.** m. a twin.

²**जवाँ** *javāṁ*, adj. & m. pronun. var. = जवान. — जवाँमर्द, adj. & m. manly, courageous; large-hearted: generous, magnanimous; a manly person, &c.; a soldier, warrior. °ई, f. manliness, courage, &c. जवाँ-मौत, f. an untimely, or premature death. जवाँ-मौत मरना, to die prematurely.

¹**जवा** *javā* [*yavaka-*], adj. & m. **1.** adj. of the size or shape of a barley-corn. **2.** m. a grain of barley. **3.** a clove of garlic. **4.** a partic. type of stitch. — जवेदार [P. -*dār*], adj. made with small golden pieces (a chain, &c).

²**जवा** *javā* [? **jabu-*], m. reg. (E.) a cattle muzzle (= जाब).

³**जवा** *javā* [S.], m. the China rose (an ornamental plant having orange flowers).

जवाद *javād*, adj. Brbh. = ज़्यादा.

जवान *javān* [P. *javān*], adj. & m. **1.** adj. young, youthful. **2.** vigorous, in one's prime. **3.** bold, brave. **4.** m. a young adult; a youth. **5.** an able-bodied man: a soldier, warrior; a police officer. — जवान-जहान, adj. in the bloom of youth.

जवानपन *javānpan*, m. = जवानी.

जवानपना *javānpanā*, m. = जवानी.

[1]**जवानी** *javānī* [P. *javānī*], f. youth; early adulthood; adolescence; the years of youth, &c. — ~ उठना (में), young adulthood, or adolescence, to begin. ~ उतरना, or ढलना, youth to pass. ~ उभड़ना (में), = ~ उठना; the body to develop in adolescence. ~ चढ़ना (पर), = ~ उठना; youthful passion to dominate (one). ~ का आलम, m. the season, or years, of youth. ~ का फल, m. the fruit or enjoyment of youth. ~ की नींद, f. the sleep of the just. ~ पर आना, to reach puberty; to attain full vigour; to bloom. ~ पूरी बहार पर होना, youth to be in full flower.

[2]**जवानी** *javānī*, f. corr. = अजवायन (*Carum copticum* or *Ammī perpusillum*).

जवाब *javāb* [A. *javāb*], m. **1.** an answer. **2.** dismissal, discharge (from, से); refusal, rejection (as of a proposition). **3.** a counterpart; an equal, double, complement. — ~ तलब करना, to request, or to demand an answer or account (from, से). ~ देना (को), to answer; to be answerable or responsible for; to discharge, to dismiss; to resign; to refuse, to reject; to desert, to forsake. ~ पाना, to be discharged, dismissed. ~ मिलना, id. — जवाब-तलबी, f. requiring or compelling an answer. जवाब-तलबी करना, to call to account. जवाबदार [P. *-dār*], adj. = जवाबदेह. °ई, f. = जवाबदेही. जवाबदेह [P. *-deh*], adj. & m. responsible, accountable; a person responsible; respondent, defendant (at law). °ई, f. responsibility; liability; defence. जवाब-सवाल, m. question and answer; dialogue; dispute; cross-examination. जवाब-सवाल करना, (parties) to argue, to dispute; to participate in an interrogation.

जवाबी *javābī* [A. *javābī*], adj. & m. **1.** adj. having to do with an answer: given in answer; counter (as a blow); reply-paid (a telegram). **2.** complimentary. **3.** m. one answering; a respondent, defendant (at law).

जवारा *javārā* [*yavākāra-*], m. **1.** large millet; barley, &c. **2.** a blade or shoot of barley. **3.** *Pl.* maize.

जवारी *javārī* [? cf. H. *juvār*], f. *Pl. HŚS.* **1.** *mus.* bridge (of a *sitār*, &c). **2.** a thread stretched over the bridge of a musical instrument, beneath the strings.

जवाल *javāl* [cf. A. *javvāl*], m. Brbh. going about: the world and its burdens (cf. जंजाल).

ज़वाल *zavāl* [A. *zavāl*], m. Brbh. declining: harm, misery, wretchedness.

जवाली *javālī*, f. barley mixed with wheat, or gram, for fodder.

जवास *javās*, m. = जवासा.

जवासा *javāsā* [*yavāsaka-*], m. a thorny shrub or grass, *Alhagi maurorum* or *Hedysarum alhagi* (used for coarse grazing, and medicinally; it loses its leaves in the rainy season).

जवाहर *javāhar* [A. *javāhir*, pl. & sg.], m. pl. & sg. **1.** pl. jewels, precious stones. **2.** sg. jewel. — जवाहर-ख़ाना, m. *hist.* depository for jewels.

जवाहरात *javāharāt* [A. *javāhirāt*], f. = जवाहर, 1.

जवाहिर *javāhir*, m. = जवाहर.

जशन *jaśan* [P. *jaśn*], m. **1.** a celebration, festival. **2.** a banquet. **3.** an entertainment of singing and dancing (esp. to conclude a celebration). **4.** rejoicing, joy. — ~ करना (*HŚS.*), or मनाना, to hold a celebration, &c.; to rejoice.

[1]**जस** *jas*, adj. Brbh. Av. = जैसा. — ~ का तस, adj. = जैसे का तैसा.

[2]**जस** *jas*, m. = यश.

जसु *jasu*, f. Brbh. = यशोदा.

जसुदा *jasudā*, f. Brbh. = यशोदा.

जसुमति *jasumati* [ad. *yaśomatī-*], f. Brbh. = यशोदा.

जसोदा *jasodā*, f. Brbh. = यशोदा.

जसोवै *jasovai* [*yaśomatī-*], f. Av. = यशोदा.

[1]**जस्त** *jast* [conn. *jasada-*], m. **1.** zinc. **2.** pewter. — ~ चढ़ा (हुआ), adj. zinc-plated.

[2]**जस्त** *jast* [P. *jast*], f. a leap, spring. — ~ मारना, to leap, to spring.

जस्तई *jastaī* [cf. H. *jast(ā)*], adj. **1.** of, or made of, zinc. **2.** of, or made of, pewter. **3.** greyish-coloured.

जस्ता *jastā*, m. = [1]जस्त.

जहँ *jahaṁ*, adv. Brbh. Av. = जहाँ.

जहद *jahd* [A. *jahd*], m. E.H. toil, exertion.

जहन्नुम *jahannum* [A. *jahannam*], m. hell; damnation.

जहन्नुमी *jahannumī* [A. *jahannamī*], adj. having to do with hell; hellish, infernal.

ज़हमत *zahmat* [A. *zaḥma*: P. *zahmat*], f. **1.** unease, discomfort. ***2.** trouble, difficulty. — ~ उठाना, to suffer distress, or serious difficulty.

ज़हर *zahr* [P. *zahr*], m. **1.** poison. **2.** fig. anything very disagreeable. — ~ उगलना, to vomit poison: to say venomous or poisonous things; to sneer (at). ~ करना, colloq. to turn to poison: to ruin or to spoil (as food, or pleasure). ~ का घूँट पीना, to take a swallow of poison: to endure a bitter reverse or frustration. ~की गाँठ, f. poison-knot: bundle of trouble (= आफ़त की पुड़िया). ~ खाना, to take poison (on account of, पर). ~ खिलाना (को), to poison. ~ मारना, to act as an antidote. ~ लगना, to seem hateful (to, को). ~ होना (के लिए), id. – ज़हरदार [P. *-dār*], adj. poisonous. ज़हर-बाद, m. poison-air: swelling and inflammation. ज़हरमार, adj. & m. anti-toxic; antidote. ज़हर-मोहरा, m. bezoar stone (an antidote to poison).

ज़हरी *zahrī* [P. *zahrī*], adj. = ज़हरीला.

ज़हरीला *zahrīlā* [cf. H. *zahr*], adj. poisonous.

¹जहाँ *jahāṁ* [conn. H. *yahāṁ*], rel. adv. **1.** where, in the place where or which. **2.** whereas. — ~ कहीं, adv. wherever; everywhere. ~ का तहाँ, adv. in the same place, where it was, &c.; everywhere. ~ तक, adv. as far as; to the point where. ~ तक हो सके, as far as possible. ~ तहाँ, adv. here and there, all about; in some few places. ~ ... वहाँ, or वहीं, in the place where ... there; whereas ... nonetheless. ~ से, adv. whence. – जहाँ-जहाँ, adv. wherever.

²जहाँ *jahāṁ*, m. pronun. var. = जहान.

जहाज़ *jahāz* [A. *jahāz*], m. a ship; a vessel, craft (see also हवाई ~). — ~ का ~, m. a real ship: sthg. of great size. ~ पर, adv. on board ship, aboard. – जहाज़-गोदी, f. a shipyard. जहाज़-घाट, m. a dock. जहाज़मार, adj. anti-aircraft: जहाज़मार तोप, f. an anti-aircraft gun. जहाज़रान [P. *-rān*], m. the captain of a ship. °ई, f. shipping, navigation.

जहाज़ी *jahāzī* [A. *jahāzī*], adj. marine; naval; nautical. — ~ अड्डा, m. a naval base. ~ डाकू, m. a pirate. ~ बेड़ा, m. a fleet. ~ लोग, m. pl. sailors; crew (of a ship).

जहान *jahān* [P. *jahān*], m. the world (cf. ²जहाँ). — जहानारा [P. *-ārā*], adj. world-adorning. जहाँगीर [P. *-gīr*], adj. & m. seizing (conquering) the world; name of the fourth Mughal emperor. जहाँदीद [P. *-dīd*], adj. = next. -दीदा [P. *-dīda*], adj. & m. one who has seen the world: an experienced person. जहाँपनाह [P. *-panāh*], m. one who provides protection for the world: title given to a powerful king.

जहालत *jahālat* [A. *jahāla*: P. *jahālat*], f. **1.** imperfect knowledge, ignorance; reg. illiteracy. **2.** barbarousness.

जहीं *jahīṁ*, adv. w. encl. in the very place (where) (see s.v. जहाँ).

ज़हीन *zahīn* [A. *ẕahīn*], adj. intelligent; quick-witted.

जहेज़ *jahez* [f. A. *jahāz*], m. a bride's goods, or dowry (= दहेज़).

जह्नु *jahnu* [S.], m. *mythol.* name of an ancient king and sage, who drank up the waters of the Ganges on their being brought down from heaven, and then released them from his ears: the Ganges (*jāhnavī*) is regarded as his daughter.

जाँगर *jāṁgar* [conn. *jaṅghā-*], m. the thigh and leg: **1.** the body. **2.** bodily energy, vigour. जिसका ~, उसकी धरती, might is right. **3.** Brbh. grain-stalks empty after threshing. — जाँगर-चोर, adj. lazybones.

जांगल *jāṁgal* [S.], m. *Pl.* a wild bird: the grey or francoline partridge.

जांगली *jaṅgāli* [S.], f. *Pl. HŚS.* the plant cowhage (= केवाँच).

जाँगलू *jāṁglū* [cf. *jaṅgala-*], adj. *Pl. HŚS.* wild, savage; uncouth (a person).

जाँघ *jāṁgh* [*jaṅghā-*], f. the thigh. — अपनी ~ उघाड़ना, or नंगी करना, colloq. to show one's thigh: to reveal what should be hidden.

जांघिक *jāṁghik* [S.], adj. having to do with the thigh, femoral.

जाँघिया *jāṁghiyā* [conn. *jāṅghika-*], m. shorts.

जाँघिल *jāṁghil* [cf. H. *jāṁgh*], m. colloq. *Pl. HŚS.* long-shanks: the painted stork.

जाँच *jāṁc* [*yācnā-*], f. **1.** examination, investigation; enquiry; interrogation. **2.** test; appraisal, evaluation. **3.** verification. **4.** research, analysis. — जाँच-आयोग, m. commission of enquiry. जाँच-कर्ता, m. inv. an investigator, appraiser, &c. जाँच-परख, f. careful scrutiny, &c. जाँच-पड़ताल, f. any process of examining, appraising, &c. जाँच-समिति, f. committee of enquiry.

जाँचना *jāṁcnā* [*yācyate*], v.t. **1.** to examine, to investigate; to enquire into; to interrogate. **2.** to test; to appraise, to evaluate. **3.** to verify. **4.** to research, to analyse. — जाँचना-परखना, to undertake a thorough examination, &c. (of); to scrutinise.

जाँत *jāṁt* [*yantra-*], m. f. **1.** Av. a hand-mill (for grinding corn). **2.** reg. a millstone. — जाँतपट, m. surface of a millstone.

जाँता *jāṁtā* [*yantraka-*], m. = जाँत.

जाँती *jāṁtī*, f. *Pl.* dimin. = जाँता.

जाँब *jāṁb* [*jamba-*], m. Av. the rose-apple tree, *Eugenia jambolana*, and its fruit.

जॉब *jāb* [Engl. *job*], m. a job.

जांबव *jāmbav* [S.], m. *Pl. HŚS.* fruit of the rose-apple tree (जामुन).

[1]**जा** *jā*, obl. base. Brbh. the one which, or who (see जो).

[2]**जा** *jā* [P. *jā*], f. place. — ~ बजा [P. *ba-*], adv. here and there; everywhere. ~ बेजा, adv. in place and out of place: appropriate and inappropriate. – जा-नमाज़, जाय नमाज़, f. *musl.* prayer-mat, or cloth. बजा [P. *ba-*], adj. inv. in place: proper, fit; right, true.

जा- *jā-* [cf. *jāta-*], v.t. Brbh. Av. to give birth to.

जाई *jāī* [cf. H. [1]*jāyā*], f. E.H. a daughter.

जाकड़ *jākaṛ* [? H. *rokaṛ* × H. *jānā*], m. **1.** deposit (on goods taken from a seller on approval, or for use if required). **2.** a conditional purchase. **3.** goods taken on approval, &c.

ज़ाकिर *zākir* [A. *ẕākir*], adj. U. remembering, praising.

जाकेट *jākeṭ* [Engl. *jacket*], f. a jacket.

जाख *jākh* [*yakṣa-*], m. Brbh. a living supernatural being; one of a class of semi-divine beings.

जाखन *jākhan*, m. reg. (W.) the wooden wheel-shaped foundation of the brickwork of a well.

जाखिनी *jākhinī* [*yakṣiṇī-*: ad. *-inī*], f. Av. a female supernatural being.

[1]**जाग** *jāg* [conn. H. *jagah*], f. Brbh. place.

[2]**जाग** *jāg* [ad. *yāga-*], m. Brbh. Av. sacrifice; offering.

[3]**जाग** *jāg* [cf. H. *jāgnā*], f. reg. awakening.

जागता *jāgtā* [H. *jāgnā*], adj. **1.** waking. **2.** watchful. **3.** fully efficacious (as a deity's influence), potent; manifest. — जागते रहो! keep alert! (the night watchman's cry).

जागना *jāgnā* [*jāgrati*], v.i. **1.** to wake up. **2.** to be awake. **3.** to be alert, vigilant. **4.** to be on the ascendant (as fortune); to be prominent (a reputation). **5.** to be efficacious, &c. (see जागता).

जागर *jāgar* [S.], m. **1.** wakefulness. **2.** awareness.

जागरण *jāgaraṇ* [S.], m. **1.** wakefulness. **2.** vigil. **3.** awareness.

जागरी *jāgrī* [Kan.: ← *śarkarā-*[2]], f. jaggery, coarse sugar (properly palm sugar).

जागरूक *jāgărūk* [S.], adj. alert; aware.

जागरूकता *jāgărūkătā* [S.], f. alertness; awareness.

जागा *jāgā* [*jāgrat-*], m. keeping awake throughout the night (as an aspect of a religious observance).

जागीर *jāgīr* [P. *jā-gīr*], f. an estate, a freehold (as formerly given by government, in return for services). — जागीरदार [P. *-dār*], m. the holder of a *jāgīr*.

जागीरी *jāgīrī* [cf. H. *jāgīr*], adj. & f. **1.** adj. having to do with a *jāgīr*. **2.** f. the position or status of a *jāgīr*.

जागृत *jāgr̥t* [ad. *jāgrat-*], adj. 1. = जाग्रत्. **2.** awake. **3.** watchful, vigilant.

जागृति *jāgr̥ti* [ad. *jāgarti-*], f. = जाग्रति.

जाग्रत् *jāgrat* [S.], adj. = जागृत.

जाग्रति *jāgrati* [ad. *jāgarti-*], f. **1.** wakefulness, being awake. **2.** alertness, vigilance. **3.** awareness.

जाजन *jājan* [ad. *yājana-*], m. E.H. causing a sacrifice to be performed (for others).

जाजम *jājam*, f. = जाजिम.

जाज़िब *jāzib* [A. *jāẕib*], adj. U. **1.** drawing, attracting. **2.** absorbent.

जाजिम *jājim* [P. *jājim*], f. a chequered or figured linen cloth spread over a floor, or over a carpet.

जाजुलन *jājulan* [ad. **jājvalana-*], m. *Pl.* rage.

जाजुलित *jājulit* [ad. **jājvalita-*], m. reg. (Raj.) enraged.

जाज्वल्यमान *jājvalyămān* [S.], adj. burning, raging.

जाट *jāṭ* [**jaṭṭa-*[2]], m. **1.** the name of a north-west Indian community (chiefly of cultivators). **2.** a man of that community.

जाटलि *jāṭali* [S.], f. *HŚS.* name of a tree similar to the *ḍhāk* tree.

जाठ *jāṭh* [*yaṣṭi-*], f. **1.** vertical axis (of a roller in an oil- or sugar-mill). **2.** vertical pole (marking a dedication or consecration: as in a tank).

जाठर *jāṭhar* [S.], adj. **1.** having to do with the stomach. **2.** the stomach. **3.** appetite.

जाड़ *jāṛ* [**jāṭā-*: ← Drav.], f. *Pl.* reg. root (of the teeth): a molar tooth.

जाड़ा *jāṛā* [*jāḍya-*], m. **1.** cold. **2.** (also pl.) the cold season. — **~ खाना**, to suffer from cold. **~ लगना (को)**, cold to be felt (by, **को**). **जाड़ों में**, adv. during the cold season.

जाड्य *jāḍyă* [S.], m. **1.** coldness, numbness. **2.** inertness, sluggishness, insensibility. **3.** stolidity; boorishness. **4.** stupidity.

ज़ात *zāt* [A. *z̲āt*], f. **1.** nature, essence. **2.** the person, the self. **3.** [× H. [2]*jāt*] breed, kind; community, caste; sex. — **~ गँवाना**, to give up (one's) community (as by breaking a commensality rule). **~ जाना**, (one's) community standing to be lost. **~ छोड़ना**, to renounce (one's) community. **~ से ख़ारिज करना**, to outcaste. **~ से निकालना**, id.

[1]**जात** *jāt* [ad. *jāta-*], adj. born; produced. — **जात-कर्म**, m. *hind.* a ceremony performed at the birth of a child, before the cutting of the umbilical cord. **जात-क्रिया**, f. id. **जातदंत**, adj. (a child) whose teeth have grown in. **जातरूप**, adj. Av. brilliant; golden. **जातवेदस्**, m. fire.

[2]**जात** *jāt* [ad. *jāti-*], f. birth, &c. (see **जाति**, **ज़ात**). — **~ का ब्राह्मण**, a brāhmaṇ by caste. – **जात-पाँत**, f. lineage, family; community, caste. **जात-बिरादरी**, f. caste community or fellow community members. **जातवाला**, m. a person of high caste; a caste-fellow.

जातक *jātak* [S.], m. **1.** a newborn child. **2.** a story dealing with an episode from a former life of the Buddha. — **जातक-माला**, f. an anthology of Buddhist stories.

जाति *jāti* [S.], f. **1.** birth. **2.** position fixed by birth; community or caste group. **3.** good birth, high caste. **4.** kind, race; genus, species; nationality. **5.** community; nation; tribe; family, lineage. — **~ बाहर होना**, to be (an) outcaste. **जाति-कर्म**, m. corr. = **जात-कर्म**, s.v. [1]**जात**. **जातिगत**, adj. having to do with community or race, &c.; communal. **जातिच्युत**, adj. outcast. **जाति-धर्म**, m. caste duties; caste law, or usage. **जाति-पाँति**, f. = **जात-पाँत**, s.v. [2]**जात**. **जाति-बहिष्कार**, m. outcasting. °**-बहिष्कृत**, adj. **जाति-बिरादरी**, f. = **जात-बिरादरी**. **जाति-भाई**, m. a caste-fellow, a man of the same community. **जाति-भेद**, m. discrimination by community or race. **जातिभ्रष्ट**, adj. & m. fallen from caste, outcast; an outcaste. **जाति-मिश्रण**, m. hybridisation, miscegenation. **जाति-लक्षण**, m. distinguishing mark of caste, genus, species, &c. **जातिवाचक**, adj. generic. **जातिवाचक संज्ञा**, f. a generic name, common noun. **जातिवाद**, m. nationalism; racialism. **जाति-वैर**, m. racial or communal hostility; xenophobia. **जाति-शास्त्र**, m. ethnography. **जातिसंकर**, adj. of mixed caste, parentage, &c. **जातिहीन**, adj. of low caste; outcaste.

जातित्व *jātitvă* [S.], m. **1.** distinction of community; community identity. **2.** generic property.

ज़ाती *zātī* [A. *z̲ātī*], adj. **1.** U. essential, intrinsic. **2.** personal (affairs, matters). — **~ तौर पर**, adv. personally. **~ मामला**, m. a personal matter.

[1]**जाती** *jātī* [cf. H. [2]*jāt*], adj. having to do with community, kind, race, family, &c.

[2]**जाती** *jātī* [S.], f. *Pl. HŚS.* **1.** jasmine (= **चमेली**, **मालती**). **2.** nutmeg (= **जायफल**).

जातीय *jātīyă* [S.], adj. having to do with community, nation, or race.

जातीयता *jātīyătā* [S.], f. **1.** communal, national or racial identity. **2.** communalism, racialism.

जातुधान *jātudhān* [ad. *yātudhāna-*], m. a kind of evil spirit or demon.

जात्य *jātya* [S.], adj. **1.** of the same community or family, &c.; related. **2.** of good family, well-born.

जादुई *jāduī* [cf. H. *jādū*], adj. magical. — **~ छड़ी**, f. magic wand.

जादू *jādū* [P. *jādū*], m. **1.** magic; a spell, charm. **2.** enchantment. **3.** transf. sleight-of-hand: conjury; juggling. — **~ उतारना**, to break a spell, to disenchant. **~ करना (पर)**, to bewitch, to enchant. **~ चलाना**, or **जगाना** (*HŚS.*), or **मारना**, id. – **जादूगर** [P. *-gar*], m. a magician, wizard; conjurer, juggler. °**नी**, f. sorceress, witch. °**ई**, f. magic, sorcery; sthg. miraculous. **जादू-टोना**, m. the practice of magic; magical arts. **जादूनज़र**, adj. (one) whose glance captivates, or fascinates. **जादूफ़रेब**, adj. seductive, alluring.

जादो *jādo* [ad. *yādava-*], m. = **यादव**, 3.

[1]**जान** *jān* [P. *jān*], f. & adj. **1.** f. life, spirit; animating force (expressions showing **जान**, f. in this sense often coexist with equivalents containing **जी**, m). **2.** vitality, vigour. **3.** essential quality, essence. **4.** adornment, grace, beauty. **5.** sweetheart, darling. **6.** adj. dear, beloved. — **~ आँखों में आ जाना**, to be on the point of death. **~ आना**, life to revive (in, **में**); the spirits to be refreshed, or restored. **~ का**, adj. mortal. **~ का गाहक (की)**, m. one seeking (another's) life: a mortal enemy; iron. one who is a harassment, or a great nuisance. **~ का जंजाल**, m. harassment to the spirit: a source of distress, or of worry. **~ का लागू** *Pl. HŚS.*, m. = **~ का गाहक**. **~ का लेवा**, m. id. **~ की अमान**, f. safety of (one's) life, quarter. **~ की ख़ैर मनाना**, fig. to succeed in escaping. **~ की पड़ना**, fear for (one's) life to be felt (by, **को**). **~ के लाले पड़ना**, to come into mortal peril; to despair of

life. ~ को ~ न समझना, fig. not to spare oneself (as in efforts). ~ को पड़ना, fig. to plague (one, की), to pester. ~ खपाना (अपनी), to exhaust, or to over-exert (oneself). ~ खाना (की), to plague, to torment; to distress; to bore. ~ खोना (अपनी), to sacrifice, or to give up, (one's) life (for, के लिए). ~ चुराना (अपनी), to shrink (from, से); to shirk. ~ छुड़ाना (की, or अपनी), to escape with life; to save or to extricate oneself, &c. (from, से). ~ छुपाना, = ~ चुराना. ~ जाना, the soul to depart. ~ दूभर होना, = ~ भारी होना. ~ देना (के पीछे, or के लिए), to exhaust, or over-exert oneself. ~ देना (पर), = ~ खोना; to be devoted (to). ~ निकलना, life to depart, to die. ~ पड़ना, = ~ आना; to become animated, lively. ~ पर आना, or आ बनना, life to be in imminent danger. ~ पर खेलना (अपनी), to risk life; to lose (one's) life in a hazardous action; to court death. ~ पर नौबत आना, = ~ पर आना. ~ पर बनना, = ~ पर आना. ~ प्यारी, f. esp. voc. dear love. ~ बचाना (की, अपनी), to save the life (of); to shrink, to skulk (in safety). ~ भारी होना (पर), life to be burdensome (upon); to be weary of life. ~ लड़ाना, to make great efforts. ~ मारना (की, अपनी), to kill; to distress, to worry; to exert (oneself) to the utmost. ~ में ~ आना, to be revived, or refreshed; to be comforted. ~ सूखना, to be terror-stricken, (the throat) to be dry (with fear). ~ से गुज़र जाना, or ~ से जाना, to depart life, to die. ~ से मारना, to deprive of life, to kill. ~ से हाथ धोना (or धो बैठना), to wash one's hands of life, to give up or to despair of life. ~ हथेली पर लेना, fig. to risk one's life. ~ हलकान करना (की, अपनी), to distress; to work (one, oneself) to death. ~ है तो जहान है, while there's life there's hope. अब्बा ~, m. esp. voc. father, dear father. – जान-जोखिम, °-जोखों, f. & adv. risk or danger to life; at risk, in danger. जान-तोड़, adj. soul-destroying, heart-breaking (toil: = जी-तोड़). जानदार [P. *-dār*], adj. & m. having life or strength; vigorous; spirited, vital; a living creature, an animal (usu. implying strength). जान-बख़्शी, f. pardon; assurance of pardon. जानबर [P. *-bar*], adj. U. surviving: जानबर होना, to survive, to outlive. जानबाज़ [P. -*bāz*], adj. risking (one's) life; intrepid; foolhardy. °ई, f. courage, valour. जान-बीमा, m. life assurance (= जीवन-°). जानलेवा, adj. mortal, deadly.

[2]**जान** *jān* [*jñāna*-: w. *jānāti*], f. (m.) **1.** knowledge; acquaintance. **2.** understanding; opinion. — मेरी, or मेरे, ~ में, adv. in my opinion. जानकार, adj. & m. acquainted, informed, specialist; familiar (with, से); an acquaintance; an informed person, expert. °ई, f. acquaintance; informed knowledge. जानकारी कराना, or देना (की), to make (one) acquainted, or informed (with or about, से). – जान-पहचान, f. acquaintance, familiarity (with, से). °ई, m. an acquaintance.

जानकारी *jānkārī*, f. see s.v. [2]जान.

जानकी *jānakī* [S.], f. *mythol.* daughter of Janaka: title of Sītā.

जाननहार *jānanhār* [cf. H. *jānnā*], m. Brbh. Av. one who knows, &c.

जानना *jānnā* [*jānāti*], v.t. **1.** to know. **2.** to understand. **3.** to ascertain, to learn. **4.** to perceive; to recognise. **5.** to suppose, to consider. **6.** to know how to (do sthg). — जान पड़ना (को), to be perceived (by): to appear or to seem (to); to occur (to); to seem good (to). जान रखना, to bear in mind. – जानकर, abs. knowingly, deliberately. जान-बूझ, जान-बूझकर, adv. knowingly; advisedly; intentionally, deliberately.

जानवर *jānvar* [P. *jānvar*], m. **1.** a living creature, an animal; a beast. **2.** pej. a fool; a boor.

जानहु *jānahu*, conj. Brbh. Av. = जानो.

जाना *jānā* [*yāti*], v.i. **1.** to go; to depart; to travel; to issue (from, से); to go, to lead (to: as a road); to be sent, despatched (as a telegram); to go on, to continue; to turn (to, पर: as the thoughts); to act, to proceed. **2.** to pass, to pass away; to elapse; to be lost; to be spent; to be destroyed or ruined. हमारा क्या जाता है? what have we to lose? what does it matter to us? **3.** to diminish. जाता रहना, to dwindle, to evaporate (as courage, patience), to vanish; to be gone for good. **4.** euph. to die. **5.** to be forgotten, or passed over; to be overlooked (as an offence). **6.** to be without, or deprived (of, से). — जा निकलना, or पड़ना, to turn up, to appear (by chance, or suddenly). जाने देना, to allow to go, &c.; to drop (a matter); to overlook (an offence, &c).

जानिब *jānib* [A. *jānib*], f. side, direction. — की ~, ppn. towards. – जानिबदार [P. *-dār*], adj. & m. partial; a supporter; patron (= तरफ़दार). °ई, f. support; partiality. जानिबदारी करना (की), to take the side or part (of); to be partial (to).

जानी *jānī* [cf. P. *jān*], adj. & f. m. **1.** adj. cordial; beloved; intimate (a friend). **2.** mortal, deadly (an enemy). **3.** *Pl. HŚS.* f. m. darling.

[1]**जानु** *jānu* [S.], m. the knee. — जानु-पानि, adv. Av. on hands and knees.

[2]**जानु** *jānu*, conj. Av. = जानो.

जाने *jāne* [H. *jāne*, 3. sg. subj.], conj. & adv. **1.** as if. **2.** rhetor. one may know: who knows?; heaven knows. — कौन ~, who knows? क्या ~, what, or how, does one know?: who knows? ख़ुदा ~, God knows. न ~, one cannot know: who knows? – जाने-अनजाने, adv. wittingly or unwittingly.

जानो *jāno* [cf. H. *jānnā*, and Brbh. Av. 2 pl. subj.-pres. and **3.** sg. imp. forms], conj. **1.** it seems as if. **2.** as if.

जाप *jāp* [*jalpa-*, *jāpya-*], m. **1.** repeating an incantation, or the name of a deity (= जप). **2.** Av. a rosary.

जापक *jāpak* [S.], m. one who repeats an incantation, or the name of a deity.

जापन *jāpan* [? conn. H. *jāp*], m. repeating an incantation, or the name of a deity.

जापा *jāpā* [*jātatva-*, or **jāp-*], m. **1.** childbirth, delivery. **2.** place of confinement.

जापान *jāpān* [Engl. *Japan*], m. Japan.

[1]**जापानी** *jāpānī* [cf. H. *jāpān*], adj. & m. f. **1.** adj. Japanese. **2.** m. f. a Japanese.

[2]**जापानी** *jāpānī*, f. the Japanese language.

जापी *jāpī* [cf. H. *jāp*], m. = जापक.

जापू *jāpū* [cf. H. *jāp*], m. reg. = जापक.

ज़ाफ़रान *zāfrān* [A. *za'farān*], m. f. saffron.

ज़ाफ़रानी *zāfrānī* [A. *za'frānī*], adj. **1.** of saffron. **2.** saffron-coloured, yellow.

जाफ़री *jāfrī* [A. or P. *ja'farī*], f. a bamboo screen or lattice; lattice-work.

जाफ़ा *jāfā*, m. reg. increase (= इज़ाफ़ा).

जाब *jāb* [**jabbu-*], m. reg. a rope muzzle (for cattle).

ज़ाबित *zābit* [A. *ẓābiṭ*], adj. U. practising self-restraint; strict; punctual; enduring.

जाबिर *jābir* [A. *jābir*], adj. despotic, tyrannical.

जाबी *jābī* [cf. H. *jāb*], f. reg. **1.** *Pl.* muzzle (for small cattle). **2.** W. a child's network purse (tied to the waist).

ज़ाब्ता *zābtā* [A. *ẓābiṭa*], m. U. **1.** procedure, practice; usage. **2.** a procedure; formality. **3.** regulation, ordinance; code (as of practice, or law).

[1]**जाम** *jām* [P. *jām*], m. a goblet, drinking-vessel. — ~ चलना, the goblet to be passed: drinking to be going on.

[2]**जाम** *jām*, m. = [1]याम.

[3]**जाम** *jām* [*janman-*], m. a son.

[4]**जाम** *jām* [Engl. *jam(med)*], adj. jammed, blocked (a road).

[1]**जाम-** *jām-* [cf. *janman-*: Pk. *jammaï*], v.i. Av. to arise, to be produced, to germinate.

[2]**जाम-** *jām-* [*yamyate*], v.i. reg. = [1]जमना.

जामदानी *jāmdānī* [P. *jāma*+P. *dānī*], f. **1.** a box, trunk (for clothes). **2.** a type of embroidered cloth (usu. muslin) in which the flowers are woven rather than stitched.

[1]**जामन** *jāman* [cf. H. [2]*jām-*], m. sour milk used as a coagulant, rennet.

[2]**जामन** *jāman*, m. pronun. var. = जामुन.

[1]**जामा** *jāmā* [A. *jāmi'*], adj. collective, universal: — ~ मसजिद, f. a congregational mosque (in which Muslims gather to hear Friday prayers).

[2]**जामा** *jāmā* [P. *jāma*], m. a garment; a long gown; wedding robe (worn by a bridegroom). — असली ~ पहनाना, to transform (sthg., को) into reality. जामे से बाहर होना, to be beside oneself (with emotion, esp. anger). जामे में फूला न समाना, fig. to be beside oneself (with delight, &c). जामादार [P. *-dār*], m. a guard, a keeper (prop. of a wardrobe). °ई, f. guarding, guard duty.

जामाता *jāmātā* [ad. *jāmātṛ-*], m. inv. a son-in-law.

जामिक *jāmik* [ad. *yāmika-*], m. E.H. watchman, guard.

ज़ामिन *zāmin* [A. *zāmin*], m. guarantor; surety. — ज़ामिनदार [P. *-dār*], m. a person having a guarantor; (in law) one who is bailed.

जामुन *jāmun* [**jambūna-*], m. the rose-apple (*gulāb jāmun*) tree, *Eugenia jambolana*, or *Syzygium jambolanum*, and its fruit.

ज़ायक़ा *zāyqā* [A. *zā'iqa*], m. taste; flavour; savour. — ~ लेना (का), to taste, to savour. – ज़ायक़ेदार [P. *-dār*], adj. tasty.

जायज़ *jāyaz* [A. *jā'iz*], adj. **1.** allowable; right, proper. **2.** lawful, authorised; valid. — ~ क़रार देना, to decide to be lawful, &c.; to legalise; to be upheld.

जायज़ा *jāyzā* [*jā'iza*], m. **1.** examination, scrutiny. **2.** verification, checking. **3.** account, report. — ~ देना, to undergo examination or scrutiny; to give an account, accounting (of, का). ~ लेना (का), to examine, to check.

जायदाद *jāydād* [P. *jā'edād*], f. **1.** estate, property. **2.** effects. **3.** assets, resources; wealth.

जायफल *jāyphal* [*jātiphala-*: *-ph-* ad.], m. nutmeg; mace (= जावित्री, q.v).

जायमान *jāyămān* [S.], adj. poet. bringing to birth.

[1]**जाया** *jāyā* [*jāta-*: H. *jā-*], adj. & m. **1.** adj. born. **2.** m. reg. a son.

[2]**जाया** *jāyā* [S.], f. Brbh. a wife. — जायापती, pl. wife and husband.

[3]**जाया** *jāyā* [A. *ẕāi'*], adj. inv. perishing: — ~ करना, to waste.

ज़ार *zār* [P. *zār*], m. groan, lament. — ~ ~ रोना, to weep bitterly.

[1]**जार** *jār* [*jāra-*], m. a lover (adulterous). — जार-कर्म, m. adultery. जारज, adj. & m. born of adultery, illegitimate; an illegitimate child. °आ, f. °ता, f. illegitimacy. जारजन्मा, adj. m. born of adultery. जारजात, adj. id.

[2]**जार** *jār* [**jvāra-*], m. *Pl.* vehemence, violence, virulence.

जारक *jārak* [S.], adj. **1.** adj. consuming, burning. **2.** digestive.

जारण *jāraṇ* [S.: ? × H. *jāran*], m. consuming, burning.

जारन *jāran* [**jvālana-*], m. reg. **1.** burning. **2.** reg. (W.) firewood.

जारना *jārnā* [*jvālayati*], v.t. reg. = जलाना.

जारल *jāral*, m. a tree, *Lagerstroemia reginae* (timber tree of north-east India).

[1]**जारी** *jārī* [A. *jārī*], adj. **1.** progressing, current, continuing. **2.** in use, in force; legal (as tender). **3.** prevalent; rife. — ~ करना, to make current, to circulate; to issue (as a draft, or a journal); to institute (a practice); to enact, to bring into force; to exercise (a right). ~ रखना, v.t. to carry on, to continue, to maintain. ~ रहना, v.i. to go on, to continue, to remain in force.

[2]**जारी** *jārī* [cf. H. [1]*jār*], f. adultery.

[1]**जाल** *jāl* [*jāla-*], m. **1.** a net. **2.** a lattice grating; lattice window. **3.** network, mesh. **4.** a web. **5.** fig. a tangle. **6.** illusion, deception. — ~ डालना, to cast a net; to set a trap. ~ फैलाना, or बिछाना, to spread a net; to lay or to set a trap (for, के लिए). ~ में डालना, or फँसाना, or लाना, to take in a net; to ensnare. – जालदार [P. *-dār*], adj. & m. consisting of mesh, network; a cloth or garment having network embroidery.

[2]**जाल** *jāl* [A. *ja'l*], m. a fabrication, forgery: — जालसाज़ [P. *-sāz*], m. a forger. °ई, f. forgery.

जालना *jālnā* [*jvālayati*], v.t. reg. = जलाना.

जाला *jālā* [*jālaka-*], m. **1.** a web. **2.** *med.* cataract. — ~ पड़ना (आँख में), a cataract to develop (in the eye).

जालिका *jālikā* [S.], f. E.H. a fine net, network; filigree (of moonbeams).

ज़ालिम *zālim* [A. *ẕālim*], adj. & m. f. acting wrongfully: **1.** adj. wicked; unjust; tyrannical. **2.** cruel. **3.** m. a tyrant. **4.** a cruel person; f. fig. an unrelenting mistress.

ज़ालिमाना *zālimānā* [P. *ẕālimāna*], adj. inv. tyrannous; cruel.

ज़ालिमी *zālimī* [P. *ẕālimī*], f. = ज़ुल्म.

[1]**जालिया** *jāliyā* [*jālika-*], m. *HŚS.* net-man: a fisherman.

[2]**जालिया** *jāliyā* [cf. H. [2]*jāl*], m. a forger.

[1]**जाली** *jālī* [*jālikā-*], f. **1.** network, netting, criss-cross; a net; muzzle (for a bullock). **2.** material of open weave: muslin, gauze; lace. **3.** a lattice, trellis; grating; screen. — जालीदार [P. *-dār*], adj. provided with netting, netted material, &c.

[2]**जाली** *jālī* [A. *ja'lī*], adj. **1.** forged, counterfeit. **2.** false, spurious; fictitious; perjured (testimony).

जावक *jāvak*, m. *Pl. HŚS.* the red colour obtained from the lac insect (= अलता).

जावित्री *jāvitrī* [*jātipattrī-*: ad.], f. mace (fibrous covering of the nutmeg, used as an aromatic spice and also medicinally).

जासूस *jāsūs* [A. *jāsūs*], m. **1.** a spy. **2.** *mil.* a scout. **3.** a detective.

[1]**जासूसी** *jāsūsī* [A. *jāsūsīya*], f. **1.** espionage. **2.** reconnaissance. **3.** detective work. — ~ करना, to spy; to reconnoitre; to investigate (a crime).

[2]**जासूसी** *jāsūsī* [A. *jāsūsī-*], adj. having to do with espionage, reconnaissance or detective work. — ~ उपन्यास, m. a detective novel.

ज़ाहिद *zāhid* [A. *zāhid*], m. U. one who abstains: a devout person, a recluse; zealot.

ज़ाहिर *zāhir* [A. *ẕāhir*], adj. **1.** evident, apparent. **2.** conspicuous. **3.** outward, obtensible. — ~ करना, to make (sthg.) clear; to reveal, to disclose (to, से); to publish; to expose; to make a show of, to affect. ~ में, adv. openly; in public; ostensibly. ~ है कि ..., it is clear that ....

ज़ाहिरा *zāhirā* [for A. *ẕāhiran*], adv. = ज़ाहिर में.

ज़ाहिरी *zāhirī* [P. *ẕāhirī*], adj. = ज़ाहिर.

जाहिल *jāhil* [A. *jāhil*], adj. & m. **1.** adj. ignorant; illiterate; foolish. **2.** uncivilised, barbarous; boorish. **3.** m. an ignorant person, &c.

ज़ाहिल *zāhil* [A. *ẕāhil*], adj. U. forgetful, negligent.

जाहिली *jāhilī* [A. *jāhil*+P. *-ī*], f. ignorance, &c.

जाहिलीयत *jāhilīyat* [A. *jāhilīya*: P. *jāhiliyat*], f. ignorance, a state of ignorance, &c.

जाही *jāhī* [*jātī-*], f. *Pl. HŚS.* **1.** a jasmine (cf. जूही). **2.** a firework.

जाह्नवी *jāhnăvī* [S.], f. daughter of Jahnu: a title of the river Ganges.

ज़िंदगानी *zindagānī* [P. *zindagānī*], f. **1.** = ज़िंदगी. **2.** livelihood.

ज़िंदगी *zindagī* [P. *zindagī*], f. life; lifetime.

ज़िंदा *zindā* [P. *zinda*], adj. inv. **1.** living, alive. **2.** full of life; active. — ~ करना, to revive; to put life into. ~ रहना, to live; to survive. – ज़िंदादिल, adj. lively; cheerful. °ई, f. ज़िंदाबाद [P. -*bād*], interj. may (he) live: long live …!

जिंस *jiṃs* [A. *jins*], f. **1.** kind, species: merchandise, goods, wares. **2.** grain, crop, produce. **3.** movable articles, things. — जिंसवार [P. *-vār*], adj. & m. according to kind or species ; a headman's list of the crops of a village.

जि- *ji-*, obl. base. Brbh. = जिस, see s.v. जो.

जिआ- *jiā-*, v.t. Brbh. Av. = जिला-.

ज़िक्र *zikr* [A. *ẕikr*], m. **1.** mention; report, account. **2.** remembrance, thinking of God (in Sufism). — ~ करना (का), to mention, to speak (of). ~ छिड़ना, to be broached (a matter: का).

जिगजिगिया *jigjigiyā*, m. a flatterer.

जिगजिगी *jigjigī* f. *Pl.* coaxing, beseeching; flattery.

जिगर *jigar* [P. *jigar*], m. **1.** the liver; the vitals. **2.** the heart, spirit; fig. dear one, darling. **3.** courage, vitality, pluck. — ~ का टुकड़ा, m. fig. a dear one; a son.

जिगरा *jigrā* [cf. H. *jigar*], m. strength, vitality; courage, pluck.

जिगरी *jigrī* [cf. H. *jigar*], adj. **1.** having to do with the liver. **2.** touching or concerning the heart. **3.** close, intimate (a friend).

जिच *jic*, adj. & m. **1.** adj. helpless. **2.** tired, weary (of, से). **3.** m. helplessness. ***4.** deadlock; stalemate. ~ पकड़ना, to be at loggerheads.

जिजिया *jijiyā*, f. = जीजी.

जिज़िया *jiziyā* [A. *jizya*], m. *hist.* a poll-tax, levied on non-Muslims living under Muslim government (as during the Delhi Sultanate, and most of the Mughal Empire).

जिजीविषा *jijīviṣā* [S.], f. desire to live.

जिज्ञासा *jijñāsā* [S.], f. **1.** desire to know: curiosity; inquisitiveness. **2.** enquiry, investigation.

जिज्ञासित *jijñāsit* [S.], adj. **1.** forming an object of curiosity, or of enquiry (on the part of, से). **2.** sought after.

जिज्ञासु *jijñāsu* [S.], adj. & m. **1.** adj. curious, inquisitive. **2.** m. an enquirer, investigator.

जिज्ञास्य *jijñāsyă* [S.], adj. to be enquired into, worthy of or needing investigation.

जिठानी *jiṭhānī*, f. = जेठानी.

[1]**जित** *jit* [S. *jita-*], adj. conquered; subdued. — जितात्मा [°*ta*+*ā*°], adj. & m. inv. whose self is subdued; one who has subdued his passions. जितेंद्रिय [°*ta*+*i*°], adj. & m. whose senses or passions are subdued; an ascetic.

[2]**जित** *jit* [conn. *yatra*[1]], adv. Brbh. Av. **1.** where. **2.** whither; whithersoever. — ~ कित, adv. wherever; whithersoever.

जितक *jitak*, adj. Brbh. = जितेक.

[1]**जितना** *jitnā* [conn. *iyattaka* : anal.], adj. & adv. as much as; as many as; however much, however many. — ~ … उतना (ही), as much, or as many as … (just) so much, or so many. दिल्ली की आबादी कलकत्ते जितनी बड़ी नहीं है, the population of Delhi is not as large as that of Calcutta.

[2]**जितना** *jitnā* [cf. H. *jītnā*], v.i. to be conquered or subdued; to be won.

जितलाना *jitlānā*, v.t. = जिताना.

जितवाना *jitvānā* [cf. H. *jītnā*], v.t. to cause to be conquered, &c. (by, से).

जितवैया *jitvaiyā* [cf. H. *jītnā*], m. & adj. **1.** m. a victor, winner. **2.** adj. victorious.

जिताना *jitānā* [cf. H. *jītnā*], v.t. to cause to conquer or to subdue; to cause to win.

जितीक *jitīk*, adj. Brbh. = जितेक.

जितेक *jitek* [conn. *iyattaka-*: anal.], adj. Brbh. = जितना.

जितो *jito*, adj. Brbh. = जितना.

जित्ता *jittā*, adj. = जितना.

जित्वर *jitvar* [S.], adj. & m. **1.** adj. victorious. **2.** m. a victor, conqueror.

ज़िद *zid* [A. *ẓidd*], f. **1.** stubbornness, obstinacy. **2.** doggedness, persistence; insistence. — ~ करना, to be stubborn; to be refractory (a child); to persist; to insist (on, की). ~ आना, or चढ़ना (को), to be or to become stubborn; to insist (on). ~ पर, adv. so as to spite (another, की), perversely. ~ पकड़ना, or

बाँधना, = ~ आना (को). ~ रखना, to harbour spite or malice (towards, की); to be persistent or importunate.

ज़िदियाना *zidiyānā* [cf. H. *zid*], v.i. colloq. = ज़िद करना.

ज़िद्द *zidd*, f. see ज़िद.

ज़िद्दी *ziddī* [P. *ẓiddī*], adj. **1.** stubborn, obstinate; wilful. **2.** persistent.

जिधर *jidhar* [conn. H. [1]*dhār*], adv. **1.** in which(ever) direction, whither(soever). **2.** in which(ever) place, where(soever). — ~ ... उधर, adv. where(ever), whither(soever) ... there, thither. – जिधर-तिधर, adv. here and there; all around, everywhere.

[1]**जिन** *jin*, obl. pl. base. the one which (see जो).

[2]**जिन** *jin*, जिनि, neg. adv. = [1]जनि.

[3]**जिन** *jin* [S.], m. a chief saint of the Jains; a Buddha.

[4]**जिन** *jin*, m. = जिन्न.

ज़िना *zinā* [A. *zinā*], f. adultery.

जिन्न *jinn* [A. *jinn*], m. **1.** a jinn, demon. **2.** fig. a headstrong or resolute person. — ~ उतारना, to cast out a jinn (from, से); to exorcise. ~ चढ़ना, or सवार होना (पर), (one) to be possessed by a demon; to be in a frenzy of rage; to be obsessed. ~ पकड़ना, to capture a jinn; to exorcise.

जिन्नी *jinnī* [A. *jinnīya*], adj. having to do with a *jin*.

ज़िबह *zibah*, m. = ज़बह.

जिब्भा *jibbhā* [cf. *jihvā-*], adj. & m. **1.** adj. in comp. having a tongue (e.g. कलजिब्भा, adj. & m. black-tongued: foul-tongued; m. one whose curses are feared). **2.** m. colloq. reg. (Bihar) a kind of wide flat vessel.

जिमख़ाना *jimkhānā*, m. **1.** ? a gymkhana. **2.** [× Engl.] a gymnasium.

जिमाना *jimānā* [cf. H. *jīmnā*], v.t. **1.** to feed. **2.** to receive to a meal, to entertain.

जिमि *jimi* [Ap. *jima*; ? × *katham*, Ap. *kimi*], adv. & conj. Av. like, as, just as.

ज़िम्मा *zimmā* [A. *zimma*], m. **1.** responsibility. **2.** charge, trust. — ~ पड़ना, responsibility to fall (on, पर). ~ लेना (अपने ऊपर), to assume responsibility (for, का). ज़िम्मे, ppn. w. के, also prep. in the charge (of, के); being the responsibility (of). ज़िम्मे आना, or निकलना, or होना, to be outstanding (as a debt: to the account of, के). ज़िम्मे करना, to entrust (to, के: a task, responsibility); to take upon (oneself, अपने). ज़िम्मे लेना, = ज़िम्मे करना, 2. – ज़िम्मेदार [P. *-dār*], adj. & m. responsible (for, का, के लिए); liable (as at law); a person having responsibility, guarantor, surety; trustee. °ई, f. responsibility, obligation; liability; trust, charge, keeping. ज़िम्मेवार [P. *-vār*], adj. & m. = ज़िम्मेदार. °ई, f. = ज़िम्मेदारी.

ज़िम्मादार *zimmādār*, adj. = ज़िम्मेदार.

ज़िम्मादारी *zimmādārī*, f. = ज़िम्मेदारी.

ज़िम्मावार *zimmāvār*, adj. = ज़िम्मेदार.

ज़िम्मावारी *zimmāvārī*, f. = ज़िम्मेवारी.

ज़िम्मेदार *zimmedār*, adj. & m. see s.v. ज़िम्मा.

ज़िम्मेदारी *zimmedārī*, f. see s.v. ज़िम्मा.

ज़िम्मेवार *zimmevār*, adj. & m. see s.v. ज़िम्मा.

ज़िम्मेवारी *zimmevārī*, f. see s.v. ज़िम्मा.

जियरा *jiyrā* [cf. *jīva-*], m. E.H. life, soul (= जीव).

जिया- *jiyā-*, v.t. Brbh. Av. = जिलाना.

ज़ियाफ़त *ziyāfat* [A. *ẓiyāfa*: P. *ẓiyāfat*], f. U. **1.** a feast. **2.** hospitality. — ~ करना, to feast (one, की).

ज़िरह *zirah* [P. *zirah*], f. *Pl. HŚS.* chain-mail (see ज़ीर).

ज़ियारत *ziyārat* [A. *ziyāra*: P. *ziyārat*], f. visiting (a shrine, &c.); pilgrimage.

जिरह *jirah* [A. *jarḥ*], m. cross-questioning: wrangle; a provocation.

ज़िला *zilā* [A. *zila'*], m. an administrative district. — ज़िलाधीश [°*lā* + *a*°], m. district judge. ज़िलाबंदी [P. *-bandī*], f. the division of a province into districts; restriction on movement (of produce) from a district. ज़िलेदार [P. *-dār*], m. *hist.* superintendent of a district; a district revenue officer. °ई, f. office or post of *ziledār*. ज़िलेवार [P. *-vār*], adj. pertaining to a district.

ज़िलादार *zilādār*, m. see ज़िलेदार s.v. ज़िला.

ज़िलादारी *zilādārī*, f. see ज़िलेदारी s.v. ज़िला.

जिलाना *jilānā* [cf. *jīvala-*], v.t. **1.** to give life to; to animate; to revive. **2.** to allow to live, to preserve alive. **3.** to keep (an animal).

ज़िलावार *zilāvār*, adj. see ज़िलेवार s.v. ज़िला.

जिल्द *jild* [A. *jild*], f. **1.** the skin. **2.** cover or binding of a book. **3.** transf. volume. — ~ चढ़ाना (पर), to bind (a book). ~ बनाना, or बाँधना (की), id. — जिल्दगर [P. *-gar*], m. a book-binder. जिल्दबंद [P. *-band*], m. a book-binder. °ई, f. book-binding; cost of, or payment for, book-binding. जिल्दसाज़ [P. *-sāz*], m. = जिल्दबंद. °ई, f. = जिल्दबंदी. सजिल्द, adj. with binding: bound.

जिल्दी *jildī* [A. *jildī*], adj. having to do with the skin, cutaneous.

ज़िल्लत *zillat* [A. *zillat*], f. = ज़लालत. ~ उठाना, to suffer humiliation, or insult (at the hands of, से). ~ देना (को), to insult, to dishonour.

जिवा- *jivā-*, v.t. Brbh. = जिलाना.

जिस *jis*, obl. base. the one which (see जो). — ~ पर, adv. upon whom, or which; whereupon. ~ पर भी, adv. despite which. ~ समय, adv. at the time when, when. ~ से, adv. from whom, or which; by means of which; because of which. – जिस-तिस, obl. base. whomever; whatever; someone or other.

जिस्म *jism* [A. *jism*], m. the body.

जिस्मानी *jismānī* [A. *jismānī*], adj. having to do with the body, bodily; physical. — ~ मेहनत, f. physical effort. ~ सज़ा, f. corporal punishment.

जिस्मी *jismī* [A. *jismī*], adj. having to do with the body, bodily.

ज़िहन *zihn*, m. see ज़ेहन.

जिहाद *jihad* [A. *jihad*], m. **1.** a war fought by Muslims against unbelievers. **2.** a religious war; a crusade.

जिह्वा *jihvā* [S.], f. the tongue. — जिह्वाग्र [°*vā*+*a*°], m. & adj. the tip of the tongue; on the tip of the tongue: known by heart. जिह्वा-मूल, m. the root of the tongue. जिह्वामूलीय, adj. *ling.* uvular; guttural.

जींगन *jīṁgan*, m. Brbh. = जुगनू.

[1]**जी** *jī* [*jīva-*[1]], m. (with expressions showing जी there often co-exist equivalents showing जान, f., or दिल, m.; and sometimes मन, m). **1.** life, spirit; inner self; mind; heart, feelings. **2.** spirits, courage, morale. **3.** bodily state; health; vigour. **4.** affection, regard. — ~ अच्छा होना, to be in a state of well-being. ~ आना (पर), to be attracted (to); to fall in love (with), to long (for: a person or thing). ~ उकटाना, or उचटना (से), to be weary (of), to be disgusted (with). ~ उठाना, to withdraw (one's) affection (from, से). ~ उड़ जाना, or उड़ा जाना, to be confused, or disconcerted; to lose (one's) head. ~ उलझना, to be anxious; to be alarmed. ~ उलट जाना, (one's) mood, or mind, to change; the senses to become confused, or lost. ~ ऊब जाना, to grow bored. ~ कच्चा करना, to lose heart. ~ करना, to desire, to long (for, का). ~ काँपना, to shudder (at, से); to be terrified (of or at, से). ~ का, adj. courageous. ~ का गाहक, m. = जान का ~. ~ का जंजाल, m. fig. someone or sthg. very burdensome. ~ का बुख़ार निकालना, to give release to a pent-up anger or sorrow. ~ की, or का, जी में रहना, a desire, or ambition, to remain unfulfilled. ~ की निकालना, to realise a desire, or an ambition; = ~ का बुख़ार निकालना; to vent anger, or to take revenge (upon, पर). ~ की पड़ना, to fear for (one's) life. ~ को ~ समझना, to treat (one, के) with humanity, or consideration. ~ को मारना, to subdue the self: to repress a desire, or a discontent. ~ को लगना, to touch the heart: to be agreeable (to, के); to make an impression (on); to be importunate, burdensome; to wound, to hurt. ~ खट्टा करना, to make (one's) heart bitter: to turn (one: का) against (another, से, or की ओर से); to harden one's heart against (another). ~ खपाना, to exhaust (one's) life: to overwork, to work (oneself, अपना, or another, का) to death. ~ खरा-खोटा होना, to vacillate, to be torn by good and bad impulses. ~ खोलकर, adv. openly, frankly; unrestrainedly; to one's heart's content; gladly. ~ घबराना, to be uneasy; to be disturbed, agitated; to be bewildered. ~ चलना, to desire, or to long (for, पर); to go out of one's senses. ~ चलाना, to hanker (after, पर), to long (for); to venture, to dare. ~ चाहना, the heart to wish: to long (for, का). ~ चुराना (का), to steal (one's) heart. ~ चुराना (से), to shirk or to neglect (work, &c). ~ छुपाना, colloq. = ~ चुराना. ~ छूटना, to lose heart, to be faint-hearted; to become tired (of, से); to become free (of a burden). ~ छोटा करना, to become discouraged; to give play to meaner, or ungenerous, instincts. ~ छोड़ना, to lose heart, to become demoralised. ~ जलना, to feel veneration, or envy; to be wounded, hurt (in mind). ~ जलाना, to inflame the mind (of, का): to vex; to wound; to plague; to arouse warm emotion in the heart (of), to befriend. ~ जानता है, the heart knows (describing an unanalysable feeling). ~ जाने, id. ~ टँगा, or लगा, रहना, to feel a continuing suspense, or preoccupation (about or with, की ओर). ~ टूट जाना, the spirit to be broken, to despair. ~ ठंडा करना, to assuage (one's) heart (by achieving an objective). ~ ठंडा होना, to be finally satisfied. ~ डालना (में), to restore to life; to encourage; to save from death; to become attached to, to set one's heart on (one). ~ डूबना, the spirits to sink, to be depressed; to be sunk in meditation; to faint. ~ ढहा जाना = id., 1. ~ तरसना, the spirit to long, or to thirst (for, के लिए); to be in dire want (of). ~ तोड़कर, adv. with all one's might. ~ दान करना, to grant life, to pardon (one, का: of a capital crime). ~ दुखी होना, the spirit to grieve: to be distressed, troubled. ~ धँसना, = ~ डूबना, 1. ~ धड़कना, the heart to palpitate: to tremble, to shudder. ~ निकलना, to expire, to die; to be in mortal fear (of); to be dying for (पर), to desire extremely, or excessively. ~ निढाल होना, = ~ डूबना, 1., 3. ~ पड़ना, life to arise (in, में): to be quickened, or encouraged; to become maggoty or wormy. ~ पर आ बनना, (one's) life to come into question, to be at risk. ~ पर खेलना, to risk life.

~ पर चलना, to follow the pleasure, or wish (of, के). ~ पसीजना, or पिघलना, the heart to melt: to feel pity, compassion, or affection. ~ पीछे पड़ना, the mind to be distracted (as from preoccupations). ~ फट जाना, the heart to break; the heart to be filled with disaffection, rancour. ~ फटा जाना, id., 2. ~ फिरना (से), (to) turn (from); to be satiated (with); to be averse to. ~ फीका होना, affection to fail: to become indifferent (to, की ओर से); to turn against. ~ बँटना, the mind to be divided: to be unsettled, disconcerted. ~ बढ़ाना, to encourage, to inspire (one, का). ~ बहलाना (का, or अपना), to divert, to amuse. ~ बुरा करना, to fill (one, का) with ill-will, &c. (against, की ओर से); to take offence; to give offence (to, का). ~ बैठ जाना, the heart to sink; to feel faint. ~ भर आना, the heart to fill: to be deeply moved; to be seized with grief. ~ भर जाना, to be contented (with, से) to be satiated (with); to have grown tired (of). ~ भरकर, adv. to one's heart's content. ~ मचलाना, or मतलाना, to feel nausea. ~ मारना, = ~ को मारना. ~ मिलना (से), the heart to be attached (to): to be congenial (to). ~ में आना, to come into the mind, to arise (a thought or feeling); to occur (to, के). ~ में चुभना, or गड़ना, to make an impression on the mind, or heart. ~ में जलना, to be consumed with envy, jealousy, &c. ~ में ~ आना, to be revived, or refreshed; to be reassured, or comforted. ~ में ~ डालना, to encourage, to fortify; to reassure; to comfort. ~ में डालना, to form in the mind, to conceive (esp. a wrong notion, or a casual intention). ~ में बैठना, to be impressed on, or fixed in, the mind; to be believed implicitly. ~ में लगना, = ~ को लगना, 2. ~ रखना, to have a mind (to, का); to gratify, to satisfy (one, का). ~ लगना, the heart to be set (on, पर or से): to be drawn to, to love; to be absorbed (in, में or की ओर), intent (on). ~ लगाना, to set one's heart (on, से), to love; to become absorbed (in, में or की ओर), intent (on). ~ ललचना, to desire eagerly, to hanker (after, पर or के लिए). ~ ललचाना, to arouse desire in (का). ~ लुभाना, to awaken desire (in, का); to captivate the heart. ~ लेना, to plumb the mind or heart (of, का); to take the life (of). ~ लोटना, to be very fond (of, पर), devoted (to). ~ से उतर जाना, to fall in (one's) esteem, to lose the regard or favour (of, के); to lose all heart or morale. ~ से, adv. with all one's heart, with a will. ~ से जाना, to give up life, to die. ~ से मारना, to kill (= मार डालना). ~ हट जाना, the heart or mind to turn away (from): to become averse (to, से). ~ हलका होना, to find relaxation, reassurance or relief. ~ हाथ में रखना, to keep (one, का) well-disposed, content. ~ हारना, to lose heart, to be discouraged; to be depressed. ~ हिलना, to feel fear (at, से); to be moved (by or at). ~ ही ~ में, adv. in one's inmost soul; to oneself. ~ होना, to have a desire (for, का). – जी-चला, adj. & m. = मन-चला. जी-जान, f. life and spirit: जी-जान लड़ाना, to put heart and soul (into, में); जी-जान से, adv. with all one's soul; with all one's might. जी-तोड़, adv. heart-breaking (of effort, or struggle).

²**जी** *jī* [*jīva-²*, *jīvatu*], hon. **1.** an expression of respect or of affection (used with proper names). **2.** an expression of assent: yes; true; very good (= ~ हाँ). **3.** an expression of enquiry: yes? what is it? — ~ हाँ, interj. = ~, 2. — जी-हुज़ूर, m. a yes-man. °ई, f. flattery.

जीजा *jījā* [**jījja-*], m. an elder sister's husband.

जीजी *jījī* [**jījja-*], f. **1.** an elder sister-in-law. **2.** voc. form of address to a senior lady (women). **3.** elder sister.

जिट *jiṭ*, f. reg. boasting. — ~ उड़ाना, to boast (about, की).

जीत *jīt* [cf. H. *jītnā*], f. winning, victory; a win; a success.

जीतना *jītnā* [cf. *jita-*: Pk. *jitta-*], v.t. & v.i. **1.** v.t. overcome, to defeat (an enemy); to conquer; to beat. **2.** to win (a battle, contest, prize). **3.** to win the favour of, to win (one) over. **4.** v.i. to be won, to be successful (a case, a suit).

जीतव *jītav* [cf. H. *jītā*, and S. *jīvitavya-*], m. E.H. life, lifetime.

जीता *jītā*, adj. & m. see s.v. जीना.

जीतिया *jītiyā* [cf. H. *jīnā*], ? f. reg. *hind.* a fast, with worship of Durgā, kept by mothers who have lost children.

जीतू *jītū* [cf. H. *jīt*], m. colloq. victor.

ज़ीन *zīn* [P. *zīn*], m. **1.** saddle. **2.** a kind of strong cotton cloth. — ~ कसना, or खींचना, or बाँधना (का or पर), to saddle (a horse, &c). – ज़ीनपोश [P. *-poś*], m. a saddle-cloth. ज़ीनसाज़ [P. *-sāz*], m. saddler. ज़ीन-सवारी, f. riding with saddle: use (of a horse) for riding. ज़ीन-सवारी में रहना, to be kept for riding (a horse).

ज़ीनत *zīnat* [A. *zīna*: P. *zīnat*], f. U. **1.** beauty, elegance. **2.** ornament, decoration.

जीना *jīnā* [*jīvati*], v.i. **1.** to be alive, to live; to exist. **2.** to enjoy life. — जी उठना, to be revived; to be enlivened. – जीता, adj. & m. living, alive; reg. (W.) mutual assistance with ploughing. जीते जी, adv. living, alive; in the lifetime (of, के); to the length of (one's) life. जीते जी मरना, to die a living death; to suffer extreme misery or anguish. जीते रहना, to remain alive; to enjoy a long life, to prosper. – जीता-जागता, adj. living and healthy; flourishing; lively (an account, &c.); striking, graphic.

ज़ीना *zīnā* [P. *zīna*], m. **1.** ladder. **2.** a flight of stairs, or of steps.

जीब *jīb*, f. pronun. var. = जीभ.

जीभ *jībh* [*jihvā*-], f. **1.** the tongue. **2.** a flat, projecting part: tongue (of a shoe); nib (of a pen). — ~ **काटना (की)**, to stop (one) speaking (by making signs), to get one to be silent. ~ **चलाना**, to boast (to, पर). ~ **थोरी कर-**, Brbh. to speak little. ~ **दाँतों तले दबाना**, to catch the tongue under the teeth: to bite the tongue in amazement, fear. ~ **दाबके बात कहना**, to speak hesitantly, or with reserve; to speak quietly. ~ **दूजी कर-**, Av. to speak further. ~ **निकालना**, to poke out the tongue; to be exhausted, or very thirsty; to tear out the tongue. ~ **पकड़ना (की)**, to interrupt, to silence (one); to criticise in detail; to compel (one) to make good a promise. ~ **हिलाना**, to raise the voice, to speak. **छोटी** ~, f. uvula.

जीभड़िया *jībhṛiyā* [cf. H. *jībh*], f. dimin. E.H. = जीभ.

जीभी *jībhī* [cf. H. *jībh*], f. & adj. **1.** f. a tongue-scraper. **2.** scraping of the tongue. **3.** nib (of a pen). **4.** adj. having to do with the tongue; tongue-shaped; lingual.

जीमड़ *jīmaṛ*, m. a partic. tree (Bihar).

जीमना *jīmnā* [**jimyati* or **jimmati*], v.i. **1.** to partake of food. **2.** colloq. to receive money wrongfully (a bribe, embezzled funds).

ज़ीर *zīr*, f. Brbh. = ज़िरह.

जीरक *jīrak* [S.], m. = जीरा.

जीरा *jīrā* [*jīraka*-: w. P. *zīra*], m. the cumin plant, and its seed. — **ऊँट के मुँह में** ~, fig. sthg. utterly insufficient. **जीरे का पानी**, cumin-water (a mixture of spices and other ingredients in water: taken to aid digestion).

ज़ीरा *zīrā* [P. *zīra*], m. = जीरा.

जीर्ण *jīrṇ* [S.], adj. old: **1.** worn out, decrepit; decayed. **2.** frail with age. **3.** outworn, outmoded (an opinion, a custom). **4.** continuing, lingering (a fever). — **जीर्ण-ज्वर**, m. a fever which continues for some time. **जीर्ण-शीर्ण**, adj. decrepit, ancient (as clothing, &c). **जीर्णावस्था** [°*ṇa*+*a*°], f. years of infirmity, old age. **जीर्णोद्धार** [°*ṇa*+*u*°], m. repair, restoration (as of a building).

जीर्णता *jīrṇātā* [S.], f. **1.** decrepitude, decay. **2.** frailty, infirmity (of age).

जील *jīl* [P. *zer*], f. *mus.* **1.** *Pl.* a high note or tone; the treble. **2.** *HŚS.* a soft, or low note.

जीव *jīv* [S.], m. **1.** the soul; the individual soul (as distinguishable from the supreme soul, *paramātmā*); life. **2.** a living creature. **3.** any partic. form of life. — **जीव-कोष**, m. *biol.* a cell. **जीव-जगत**, m. the world of living creatures. **जीव-दंड**, m. death penalty. **जीव-दया**, f. tenderness or regard for animal life. **जीव-दान**, m. the gift of life: sparing, or saving, a life. **जीव-धन**, m. wealth in livestock. **जीव-धातु**, m. protoplasm. **जीवधारी**, adj. & m. possessing life; assuming life; = ~, 2. **जीव-योनि**, f. born containing a soul: = ~, 2. **जीव-लोक**, m. the world of living beings; living things; mankind. **जीव-विज्ञान**, m. biology. °**ईय**, adj. biological. **जीव-वृत्ति**, f. the characteristics of a living creature; livelihood as earned by rearing cattle. **जीव-वैज्ञानिक**, m. a biologist. **जीव-संक्रमण**, m. transmigration of the soul. **जीव-हत्या**, f. the taking of life. **जीव-हिंसा**, f. violence to living beings; = prec. **जीवाणू** [°*va*+*a*°], a microbe, bacteria; embryo. **जीवात्मा** [°*va*+*ā*°], f. the individual soul (= ~, 1). **जीवाधार** [°*va*+*ā*°], m. support of the soul: the heart; the world. **जीवावशेष** [°*va*+*a*°], m. a fossil. **जीवाश्म** [°*va*+*a*°], m. id. °-**विज्ञान**, m. palaeontology. **जीवेश** [°*va*+*ī*°], m. lord of living creatures: the supreme being.

जीवंत *jīvant* [S.], adj. living, alive.

जीवक *jīvak* [S.], m. **1.** a living creature; an animal. **2.** a career, course of life.

जीवट *jīvaṭ*, adj. & m. f. **1.** adj. bold; resolute. **2.** m. f. courage, spirit; resolution.

जीवड़ा *jīvṛā* [cf. *jīva*-], m. E.H. life; the soul.

जीवत् *jīvat* [S.], adj. **1.** living, alive; for or during life. **2.** [×H. जीवित] lively (a person). — **जीवन्मुक्त** [°*t*+*mu*°], adj. & m. released, while living, from future birth; one so released. °**मुक्ति**, f. release from future birth; residence of the soul with *brāhmaṇ*. **जीवन्मृत** [°*t*+*mṛ*°], adj. dead while living: moribund; inert.

जीवन *jīvan* [S.], m. **1.** life; existence; lifetime; livelihood. **2.** 19c. water. — ~ **चलाना (अपना)**, to lead (one's) life. ~ **बिताना (अपना)**, to spend (one's) life. ~ **भरना (अपना)**, to live out (one's) life. — **जीवन-चरित**, m. a biography. °-**चरित्र**, m. id. **जीवन-जगत**, m. the world of living things, of nature. **जीवन-तत्त्व**, m. a vitamin. **जीवन-तरु**, m. Av. tree of life: source of life, most precious object. **जीवन-तल**, m. level of life, standard of living. **जीवन-दर्शन**, m. view of life. **जीवन-दान**, m. gift of life: pardon (of a capital offence). **जीवन-नौका**, f. lifeboat. **जीवन-पर्यंत**, adv. for the length of life, until death. **जीवनप्रद**, adj. life-giving. **जीवन-प्रमाणक**, m. document attesting a person to have been alive on a particular date. **जीवन-बूटी**, f. life-giving root: a plant supposed to provide a drug restoring life; sthg. supremely precious. **जीवन-मरण**, m. life and death; transmigration of the soul. **जीवन-मान**, m. standard of life. **जीवन-मूरि**, f. Brbh. = जीवन-बूटी. **जीवन-मूलि**, f. Brbh. id. **जीवन-यापन**, m. way or pattern of life. **जीवनरक्षी**,

adj. life-saving; जीवनरक्षी पेटिका, f. a life-belt. जीवन-लीला, f. a life, one's life and acts. जीवन-वृत्त, m. a biography. °-वृत्तांत, m. id. जीवन-शक्ति, f. life force. जीवन-स्तर, m. standard of living; level of life. जीवनांत [°*na*+*a*°], m. the end of life, death. जीवनोपाय [°*na*+*u*°], m. means of subsistence, livelihood. जीवनोपार्जन [°*na*+*u*°], m. the earning of a livelihood. जीवन-औषध, m. a life-restoring drug (cf. जीवन-बूटी). जीवन-मुक्त, °-मुक्ति, °-मृत: see s.v. जीवत्.

जीवनमुक्त *jīvanmukt*, adj. Av. see s.v. जीवत्.

जीवनमृत *jīvanmr̥t*, adj. see s.v. जीवत्.

जीवनी *jīvănī* [cf. H. *jīvan*], f. a biography.

जीवनीय *jīvănīyă* [S.], adj. **1.** able to live. **2.** life-giving.

जीविका *jīvikā* [S.], f. livelihood; means of subsistence; occupation. — ~ अर्जित करना, or चलाना, to earn one's livelihood. ~ लगाना, to provide a livelihood (for).

जीवित *jīvit* [S.], adj. & m. **1.** adj. restored to life. ***2.** living, alive. **3.** live (as a wire: = गरम). **4.** m. life, existence. — जीवित-काल, m. life-time.

जीवी *jīvī* [S.], adj. & m. **1.** adj. -जीवी. living, alive; living on or by means of (e.g. बुद्धिजीवी, m. an intellectual). **2.** m. *Pl. HŚS.* one having a soul, or life: a living being.

जीह *jīh* [*jihvā*-], f. Av. the tongue.

जुंग *jung*, f. emotion, impulse.

जुंबिश *jumbiś* [P. *jumbiś*], f. moving, movement; shaking. — ~ खाना, to move, to stir.

जुआँ *juāṁ* [*yūka*-], m. a (large) louse (see जूँ).

[1]**जुआ** *juā* [*yuga*-], m. a yoke. — ~ उतारना, to throw off a yoke. ~ बाँधना (को, or पर), to yoke (as a beast).

[2]**जुआ** *juā* [*dyūta*-], m. gambling; a wager; a gamble. — ~ खेलना, to gamble; to stake a bet, to take a chance. ~ जीतना, to win a gamble, or a gambling game. – जुआ-ख़ाना, m. a gambling-house. जुआबाज़ [P. -*bāz*], m. a gambler.

जुआठ *juāṭh* [**yugakāṣṭha*-], m. reg. a yoke of two bars (for oxen).

जुआरी *juārī* [**dyūtakārin*-], m. a gambler.

जुईं *juīṁ* [cf. H. *juāṁ*], f. dimin. a louse.

जुई *juī*, f. reg. (W.) an insect destructive to certain crops (as beans, peas, pulse).

ज़ुकाम *zukām* [A. *zukām*], m. a cold (in throat or head). — ~ होना (को), to catch or to have a cold.

जुखना *jukhnā* [cf. H. *jokhnā*], v.i. to be weighed, or measured.

जुखाई *jukhāī* [cf. H. *jokhnā*, *jukhānā*], f. **1.** causing to be weighed or measured: weighing, measuring. **2.** cost of, or charge for weighing, &c.

जुखाना *jukhānā* [cf. H. *jokhnā*], v.t. to cause to be weighed, or measured (by, से).

जुग *jug* [ad. *yuga*-; and *yugma*-], m. & adj. **1.** m. = युग. **2.** 19c. adj. paired, twin. — ~ फूटना, a pair to be parted: to quarrel (friends). – जुग-जोड़, adj. with the two (hands) joined: earnest (as an appeal).

जुगत *jugat*, f. = युक्ति.

जुगति *jugati*, f. Brbh. = युक्ति.

जुगती *jugătī* [cf. H. *jugat*], adj. & m. **1.** adj. clever, skilful; resourceful. **2.** economical. **3.** m. a resourceful person. **4.** an economical person.

जुगनी *jugnī*, f. **1.** a jewel worn at the neck; pendant to a necklace. 2. = जुगनूँ, 1.

जुगनूँ *jugnūṁ*, m. **1.** a firefly; glow-worm. 2. = जुगनी, 1.

जुगनू *jugnū*, m. = जुगनूँ.

जुगा- *jugā*- [cf. *yogyā*-], v.t. E.H. **1.** to keep with care, to guard. **2.** *Pl.* to assist (one) in his work (expecting that the assistance will in due course be returned). — जुगाकर रखना, *Pl.* to gather together, to collect.

जुगाड़ *jugāṛ*, f. provision, means of providing (for, की).

जुगाल *jugāl* [cf. H. *jugālnā*], m. cud (of ruminants).

जुगालना *jugālnā*, v.t. to chew the cud.

जुगाली *jugālī* [cf. H. *jugāl*], f. chewing the cud. — ~ करना, to chew the cud; to chew over (a matter).

जुगुप्सा *jugupsā* [S.], f. **1.** disgust, loathing. **2.** *Pl. HŚS.* censure, abuse.

जुगुप्सित *jugupsit* [S.], adj. **1.** disgusting, detested. **2.** *Pl. HŚS.* censured.

जुज़ *juz* [A. *juz'*], m. 19c. a part, piece; a section, amount (esp. of printing paper). — जुज़ो-कुल, m. U. part and all, the whole. जुज़बंदी [P. -*bandī*], f. book-binding.

जुज्झ *jujjh* [**yudhya*-], f. E.H. battle.

जुझ *jujh* [conn. **yudhya*-: ? w. H. *jūjhnā*], m. *Pl.* battle.

जुझना *jujhnā*, v.i. = जूझना.

जुझाऊ *jujhāū* [cf. H. *jū̆jhnā*], adj. **1.** truculent, quarrelsome. **2.** martial, military.

जुझार *jujhār* [cf. H. *jū̆jhnā*], m. a warrior.

जुझारा *jujhārā* [cf. H. *jū̆jhnā*], m. Av. = जुझार.

जुट *juṭ* [cf. H. *juṭnā*], m. **1.** a pair, paired object; reg. (W.) yoke (of oxen). **2.** colloq. bundle, group, set (of objects).

जुटना *juṭnā* [**yuṭyati*], v.i. **1.** to join; to adhere; to heal, to close (a wound). **2.** to be adjoining, or adjacent. **3.** to close (with, से: in fight). **4.** to be involved or absorbed (in, में, or के पीछे: as in a task). **5.** to be collected, to collect; to come together, to assemble; to get together (as to plot or to intrigue).

जुटाना *juṭānā* [cf. H. *juṭnā*], v.t. to cause to collect, or to combine: to collect; to amass, to obtain.

जुटाव *juṭāv* [cf. H. *juṭnā*], m. collecting, amassing.

जुट्टी *juṭṭī* [conn. H. *juṭnā*], f. *Pl. HŚS.* **1.** small bundle (as of grass). **2.** pile (of flat objects).

जुठारना *juṭhārnā* [cf. *juṣṭa-*], v.t. reg. to taste food (and so to make it impure for others). (= [1]झुटालना, झुटाना).

जुड़ना *juṛnā* [cf. H. *joṛnā*], v.i. **1.** to be joined, to be attached; to be added, appended. **2.** to cause to be mended, repaired. **3.** to be collected (= जुटना); to come together, to assemble. **4.** to be available (to, को). **5.** to be fastened, to be yoked (= जुतना); to be stuck together.

जुड़पित्ती *juṛ-pittī*, f. a skin complaint causing itching and blotchiness.

जुड़वाँ *juṛvāṁ* [cf. H. *joṛā*], adj. inv. & m. **1.** adj. twin, paired. **2.** m. a twin; twins.

जुड़वाई *juṛvāī* [cf. H. *juṛvānā*], f. **1.** causing to be joined, &c. **2.** cost of, or charge for, having (sthg.) repaired, &c.

जुड़वाना *juṛvānā* [cf. H. *joṛnā*], v.t. **1.** to cause to be joined, &c. (by, से). **2.** to cause to be mended. **3.** to cause to be coupled or paired; to cause to be compared (as horoscopes).

जुरहा *jur'hā*, m. ? pronun. var. *Pl.* twins (= जुड़वाँ).

जुड़ा- *juṛā-* [cf. H. [2]*jūṛā*; × H. *juṛānā*], v.t. & v.i. Brbh. Av. **1.** v.t. to cool, to assuage (as the heart, or sight). **2.** v.i. to be cooled, &c.

[1]**जुड़ाई** *juṛāī* [cf. H. *juṛā-*], f. Brbh. Av. **1.** cold, coolness. **2.** relief, comfort, satisfaction.

[2]**जुड़ाई** *juṛāī*, f. joinery (= जोड़ाई).

जुड़ाना *juṛānā* [cf. H. *joṛnā*], v.t. **1.** to cause to be joined (by the agency of, से); to cause to adhere. **2.** to cause to be mended. **3.** to cause to couple or to pair; to bring together, to compare.

-जुत *-jut* [ad. *yuta-*], adj. formant. *Pl. HŚS.* joined (to), possessed (of).

जुतना *jutnā* [cf. *jotnā*], v.i. **1.** to be attached; to be yoked (to, में). **2.** fig. to toil, to drudge (at, में). **3.** to be ploughed.

जुतवाना *jutvānā* [cf. H. *jotnā*], v.t. **1.** to cause to be joined or yoked (by, से). **2.** to cause to be ploughed (by).

जुताई *jutāī* [cf. H. *jutānā*], f. **1.** ploughing, cultivation. **2.** cost of, or wages for, ploughing.

जुताऊ *jutāū* [cf. H. *jutānā*], adj. arable.

जुताना *jutānā* [cf. *yukta-*; H. *jotnā*], v.i. **1.** to cause to be fastened; to cause to be yoked. **2.** to cause to be ploughed (land).

जुतियाना *jutiyānā* [cf. H. *jūtā*, *jūtī*], v.t. **1.** to beat with a shoe or slipper. **2.** fig. to affront, to outrage.

जुत्तम-जुत्ता *juttam-juttā*, m. flailing of shoes: a scuffle, brawl.

जुदा *judā* [P. *judā*], adj. prop. inv. **1.** separate, separated, apart. **2.** distinct, different. — ~ करना, to separate (from, से); to part; to detach; to sever; to distinguish, to identify; to dismiss (from a post). ~ ~, adj. & adv. various, distinct; separately, severally.

जुदाई *judāī* [P. *judā'ī*], f. **1.** separation, parting; absence. **2.** estrangement. **3.** distinction, difference.

जुनरी *junrī*, f. = जुन्हरी.

जुनून *junūn*, m. = जनून.

जुन्हरी *junhrī* [*yavanāla-*; H. *junhār*], f. **1.** millet (= [2]ज्वार). **2.** maize.

जुन्हाई *junhāī* [cf. *jyotsnā-*], f. Brbh. moonlight; the moon.

जुन्हार *junhār* [*yavanāla-*], m. reg. (W.) **1.** millet (= [2]ज्वार). **2.** maize.

जुन्हैया *junhaiyā* [cf. H. *junhāī*], f. dimin. = जुन्हाई.

जुमला *jumlā* [A. *jumla*], m. a sentence; a clause.

जुमा *jumā* [P. *jum'a*], m. day of the congregation: Friday.

जुमेरात *jumerāt* [A. *juma'*+H. *rāt*], f. the eve of Friday: Thursday. — काली ~, f. Black Thursday: doomsday.

जुर- *jur-*, v.t. Brbh. Av. = जुड़ना.

जुरमाना *jurmānā* [P. *jurmāna*], m. a fine, penalty. — ~ **करना**, to impose a fine. ~ **देना**, or **भरना**, to pay a fine. ~ **मुआफ़ (माफ़) करना (का)**, to remit a fine. ~ **लगना**, to fine to be incurred (by, **को**).

जुराब *jurāb*, m. pronun. var. = जुर्राब.

जुर्म *jurm* [A. *jurm*], m. an offence; crime; sin. — ~ **क़बूल करना**, or **क़बूलना**, to admit an offence; to plead guilty. — **जुर्म-संगीन**, m. heavy or grave offence: a capital crime.

जुर्माना *jurmānā*, m. see जुरमाना.

जुर्रत *jurrat* [A. *jur'at*], f. courage, daring. — **तुम्हारी ~ कैसी पड़ी?** how dared you?

जुर्रा *jurrā* [P. *jurra*], m. 19c. active, quick: a male falcon.

जुर्राब *jurrāb* [T. *çorab*], m. a stocking; a sock.

जुल *jul*, m. deceit, swindling, trickery. — ~ **खेलना**, to behave deceitfully; to cheat. ~ **देना (को)**, to deceive; to cheat. ~ **में आना (के)**, to fall into the toils (of), to be cheated (by). – **जुलबाज़** [P. *-bāz*], m. a cheat, trickster. °**ई**, f. trickery, &c.

जुलना *julnā* [cf. **yuṭati*], v.i. in comp. w. **मिलना**. to be joined, to meet; to be harmonious, to agree.

ज़ुलम *zulm*, m. see ज़ुल्म.

ज़ुलमियत *zulmiyat* [P. *ẕulmiyat*], f. oppression, tyranny.

जुलाई *julāī* [Engl. *July*], f. the month of July.

जुलाब *julāb* [A. *julāb*: ← P. *gulāb*], m. a purgative.

जुलाहा *julāhā* [cf. P. *jŭlāh*], m. a weaver (usu. applied to a Muslim).

जुलाहिन *julāhin* [cf. H. *julāhā*], f. a weaver's wife; female weaver.

जुलूस *julūs* [A. *julūs*], m. **1.** a procession. **2.** a demonstration. — ~ **निकलना**, a procession to move off; a demonstration to be made. ~ **निकालना**, to organise a procession, or a demonstration.

ज़ुल्फ़ *zulf* [P. *zulf*], f. U. lock (of hair); locks, hair.

ज़ुल्फ़ी *zulfī* [? H. *zulf*], f. *HŚS.* = ज़ुल्फ़.

ज़ुल्म *zulm* [A. *ẕulm*], m. **1.** wrong-doing, wickedness; injustice; tyranny. **2.** an outrageous act (of wickedness), an excess. **3.** oppression; extortion. **4.** cruelty. — ~ **करना**, to do wrong (to, **पर**); to tyrannise (over); to oppress. ~ **ढाना (पर)**, to perpetrate wrong (against), to oppress. ~ **तोड़ना**, to commit a wrongful or outrageous act (against, **पर**).

ज़ुल्मत *zulmat* [A. *ẕulma*: P. *ẕulmat*], f. 19c. darkness.

ज़ुल्मी *zulmī* [P. *ẕulmī*], adj. **1.** doing wrong, unjust; wicked; tyrannical. **2.** cruel.

जुव- *juv-* = युव-.

जुवा *juvā*, adj. & m. inv. (Brbh., incorr. f.) = युवा.

जुवार *juvār* [*yugadhāra-*], m. *Pl.* a yoke for oxen (= [1]जुआ).

जुवारा *juvārā* [*yugadhāra-*], m. reg. **1.** a yoke, pair (of oxen). **2.** W. as much land as a pair of bullocks can plough in a day.

जुस्तजू *justjū* [P. *justojū*], f. searching, search; enquiry, investigation. — ~ **करना**, to search, &c.

जुहार *juhār* [? **juyakāra-*], f. **1.** greeting, salutation. **2.** a formal mode of salutation, or obeisance; specif. *Pl.* falling at the feet (of).

जुहारना *juhārnā* [cf. H. *juhār*], v.t. to salute, to make obeisance to; to address reverentially.

जुही *juhī*, f. = जूही.

जूँ *jūṁ* [*yūkā-*], f. **1.** a louse. **2.** fig. a tiny object. — ~ **की चाल चलना**, fig. to move at the speed of a tortoise. ~ **दिखाना (को)**, to get (one) to search for lice. ~ **देखना**, to search for lice. ~ **पड़ना (में)**, lice to appear, &c.: to become infested with lice (a garment, a person). ~, or **जुएँ, मारना**, to kill lice: to dilly-dally, to dawdle. **मरी ~**, f. pej. dead louse: a sluggish or inert person. **कानों पर**, or **में**, ~ **तक न रेंगना**, fig. to be deaf to argument, or entreaty. – **जूँ-मुँहा, जू-मुहाँ**, adj. small-mouthed: smooth-tongued, hypocritical.

जू *jū*, m. reg. = [2]जी.

जूआ *jūā*, m. = [1 2]जुआ.

जूझ *jūjh* [cf. H. *jūjhnā*; and **yudhya-*], f. m. fighting, struggle, battle; war.

जूझना *jūjhnā* [*yudhyate*], v.i. **1.** to fight (with, **से**), to wage war (with). **2.** to struggle, to contend (with). **3.** Av. to die fighting. — **जूझ मरना**, to die fighting.

जूट *jūṭ* [S.], m. the matted or twisted hair of an ascetic, or of the god Śiva.

जूठ *jūṭh*, m. f. = जूठा, जूठन.

जूठन *jūṭhan* [cf. H. *jūṭh*], f. **1.** remnants of food. **2.** an object previously used by another (and so made impure and unfit for use).

जूठा *jūṭhā* [*juṣṭa-*], adj. & m. **1.** adj. touched, tasted (food): left uneaten. **2.** used, made impure (utensils, cooking vessels); unfit for another's use. **3.** remnants of food (= जूठन).

जूड़ *jūṛ* [**jūḍa-*], m. E.H. cold.

[1]**जूड़ा** *jūṛā* [*jūṭa-*], m. the hair coiled or tied up behind.

[2]**जूड़ा** *jūṛā* [**jūḍa-*], adj. cold.

जूड़ी *jūṛī* [**jūḍa-*], f. a shivering fit; an ague, fever. — ~ आना (को), a fever to be felt coming on (by). – जूड़ी-ताप, = ~, 2.

जूतंपैज़ार *jūtampaizār*, f. = जूत-पैज़ार s.v. जूत.

जूत *jūt* [*yukta-*], m. chiefly in comp. a shoe, slipper (= जूता). — जूत-ख़ोरा [P. *-khora-*], adj. & m. beaten with shoes; mean, base; one who has suffered a shoe-beating, &c. जूत-पैज़ार [P. *-paizār*], f. shoes-and-slippers: fighting with shoes.

जूता *jūtā* [*yuktaka-*], m. **1.** a pair of shoes, shoes; slippers; sandals. **2.** a shoe, &c. **3.** fig. blow or beating with a shoe; disgrace; a grievous blow. ~ उछलना, = ~ चलना. ~ उछालना (पर), = ~ मारना. ~ उठाना, to pick up a shoe (to beat one); to perform degrading tasks (for, का). ~ काटना, a shoe to pinch. ~ खाना, to suffer a shoe-beating; to be treated insultingly. ~ गाँठना, to mend a shoe; to do unclean or debasing work. ~ चलना, shoes to be in play: a fracas, or vindictive quarrel, to occur (among, (आपस में). ~ चलाना (पर), = ~ मारना. ~ चाटना (का), to lick the shoes (of): to fawn, to abase oneself. ~ देना (को), = ~ मारना. ~ पड़ना (पर), shoes to fall (upon); = ~ खाना; to receive a humiliating rebuff. ~ बरसना (पर), id., 1. ~ मारना (को), to give (one) a shoe-beating; to treat contemptuously; to give a humiliating rebuff. ~ लगना (को), = ~ पड़ना; ~ लगना (पाँव में), a shoe to pinch. ~ लगाना (को), = ~ मारना, 1. जूते का आदमी, or जूते का यार, m. one only fit to be beaten. जूते सिर पर रखकर भागना, fig. to take off (one's) shoes and run ignominiously: to take to one's heels. जूते सीधे करना (के), iron. to set (another's) shoes straight: to fawn (upon). जूते (जूतों) से ख़बर लेना, to let one's shoe(s) do the listening: = ~ मारना, 1. जूते (जूतों) से बात करना, to let one's shoe(s) do the talking: = ~ मारना, 1. चाँदी का ~, m. silver shoe: a bribe. मारो ~ इसे! colloq. to the devil with it! forget about it! हवादार ~, m. an open sandal. – जूताख़ोर [P. *-khor*], adj. & m. pej. beaten with shoes; mean, base; one who has suffered a shoe-beating, &c. °ई, f. जूता-जूती पर आना, to come to blows.

जूती *jūtī* [cf. H. *jūtā*], f. a small shoe; specif. a woman's shoe, slipper, or sandal. — ~ की नोक पर मारना, = जूतियाँ मारना. ~ की नोक से, adv. = ~ से. ~ के बराबर, adj. base, contemptible; of no worth. ~ पर ~ चढ़ना, one shoe to (be found) lying on top of another (regarded as the sign of an impending journey). ~ पर रखकर रोटी देना (को), to support (one) while treating (him or her) with contempt, &c. मेरी ~ से, adv. pej. it concerns (only) my shoes: as far as I am concerned, for all I care. जूतियाँ उठाना (की), to pick up the shoes (of): to perform menial or degrading tasks (for). जूतियाँ खाना, to suffer a shoe-beating; to be treated insultingly; to remain in an abject state of submission. जूतियाँ चटकाते फिरना, to walk about making the shoes creak: to walk about idly, or not knowing what to do. जूतियाँ चलना (में, or आपस में), shoes to be in play: a fracas to occur (among). जूतियाँ पड़ना (पर), shoes to fall (upon): to receive a shoe-beating. जूतियाँ मारना (को), to give (one) a shoe-beating; to treat contemptuously; to speak harshly to, to give a humiliating rebuff. जूतियाँ लगना (को), shoes to fall (upon): = जूतियाँ पड़ना. जूतियाँ सिर पर रखना (की), to place (another's) shoes on one's head: to abase oneself, to grovel. जूतियाँ सीधी करना (की), iron. to set (another's) shoes straight: to fawn (upon). – जूतीख़ोर [P. *-khor*], adj. & m. beaten with slippers, &c. (= जूताख़ोर). जूती-छिपाई, f. the hiding of a bridegroom's shoes by the bride's sisters and friends; money which he gives to recover them. जूती-पैज़ार [P. *paizār*], f. a fight with shoes; fracas.

जूथ *jūth*, m. Brbh. Av. = यूथ.

[1]**जून** *jūn* [*jīrṇa-*], adj. & m. **1.** adj. Av. old. **2.** m. time; a particular time, a meal-time. — दोनों ~ खाना, to have enough for two meals a day.

[2]**जून** *jūn* [Engl. *June*], m. June.

[3]**जून** *jūn* [*yoni-*], f. **1.** birth; form of existence or station fixed by birth. **2.** the body (as the abode of the soul). — ~ बदलना, to change births, to transmigrate. ~ पाना, to be born, or reborn (as, की). ~ पूरी करना, to live out (one's) allotted life.

[1]**जूना** *jūnā* [*yūna-*], m. **1.** a grass rope. **2.** a bundle of grass (for cleaning vessels).

[2]**जूना** *jūnā* [cf. *jīrṇa-*], adj. old, worn, decayed; thin.

[1]**जूप** *jūp* [**dyūtatva-*], m. Brbh. gambling: a game of dice played by a newly wed couple as part of the wedding ceremony.

[2]**जूप** *jūp*, m. = यूप.

जूरी-मारी *jūrī-mārī*, f. reg. *hist. Pl.* (land) brought under cultivation: land actually in possession (as distinct from that to which a man is entitled by descent).

जूला *jūlā* [*yugala-*], m. *hist.* reg. (N.) a tract of land sixteen *bīsīs* in area.

जूलाई *jūlāī*, f. = जुलाई.

जूस *jūs* [*yūṣa-*], m. **1.** broth. **2.** cooking-water from vegetables. **3.** juice from cooked fruit.

जूसताख *jūstākh* [P. *juft*+P. *ṭāq*], m. Brbh. evens and odds: name of a game.

जूसी *jūsī* [? cf. H. *jūs*], f. sugar-cane juice (before boiling).

[1]**जूह** *jūh* [conn. *yuga-*], m. *Pl.* a yoke (= [1]जुआ).

[2]**जूह** *jūh*, m. = जूथ.

जूहड़ *jūhaṛ*, m. *Pl.* a yoke attached to a plough.

जूही *jūhī* [*yūthikā-*], f. **1.** a jasmine (*Jasminum auriculatum*: cf. चमेली, मोतिया). **2.** reg. a kind of firework.

जृंभ *jṛmbh* [S.], m. yawning, gaping.

जृंभित *jṛmbhit* [S.], adj. yawning, gaping, agape.

जेंवन *jemvan* [*jemana-*], m. **1.** food. **2.** eating, partaking of food.

जेंवना *jemvnā* [*jemati*], v.i. = जीमना.

जेंवनार *jemvnār*, m. E.H. = जेवनार, ज्योनार.

जेंवाना *jemvānā* [cf. H. *jemvnā*], v.t. **1.** to feed. **2.** to entertain to a meal.

जे *je*, pl. rel. pron. Brh. Av. = जो.

जेट *jeṭ*, f. a heap, pile.

[1]**जेठ** *jeṭh* [*jyeṣṭha-*], adj. & m. **1.** adj. eldest, senior. **2.** m. a husband's elder brother.

[2]**जेठ** *jeṭh* [*jyaiṣṭha-*], m. the third month (lunar) of the Hindu year, May-June.

जेठरा *jeṭhrā* [cf. H. *jeṭhā*, *jeṭh*], adj. & m. reg. **1.** adj. = जेठा, 1. **2.** m. = [1]जेठ.

जेठा *jeṭhā* [*jyeṣṭha-*], adj. **1.** eldest, senior; very old. **2.** best, chief; most excellent.

जेठानी *jeṭhānī* [**jyeṣṭhajāni-*: Pk. *jiṭṭhāṇi-*], f. the wife of a husband's elder brother.

जेठी *jeṭhī* [cf. H. [2]*jeṭh*], adj. having to do with the month Jeṭh; a partic. crop (cotton, rice) maturing in Jeṭh.

जेठौत *jeṭhaut* [**jyeṣṭhaputra-*], m. son of a husband's elder brother.

जेता *jetā* [conn. *iyattaka-*: Pa. *ettaka-*; anal.], adj. Av. = जितना.

जेतिक *jetik*, adj. Brbh. = जितना.

जेब *jeb* [A. *jaib*, P. *jeb*], f. m. breast; opening (of garment) at the neck: a pocket. — ~ कतरना, or काटना, to pick the pocket (of, की). ~ गरम होना, to have money in (one's) pocket. – जेब-कट, m. = next. जेब-कतरा, m. a pickpocket. जेब-ख़र्च, m. money for out-of-pocket expenses. जेब-घड़ी, f. a pocket-watch.

-ज़ेब *-zeb* [P. *zeb*], nominal formant. U. adorning, becoming (e.g. पाज़ेब, f. foot ornament, anklet; औरंगज़ेब, m. adornment of the throne).

जेबी *jebī* [H. *jeb*], adj. having to do with the pocket, small, personal. — ~ किताब, f. a (small) note-book. ~ घड़ी, f. a pocket-watch. ~ रूमाल, m. a handkerchief. ~ संस्करण, m. pocket edition.

जेय *jey* [S.], adj. able to be conquered, or captured.

जेर *jer* [*jarāyu-*], m. *Pl. HŚS.* the membrane enclosing a foetus; afterbirth.

ज़ेर *zer* [P. *zer*], adv. **1.** under, below. **2.** adj. inferior; subject; defeated. — ज़ेरबारी, f. burdens, expenses.

[1]**जेल** *jel* [Engl. *jail*], m. a prison, jail. — ~ काटना, or भोगना, to endure, or to suffer imprisonment. — जेल-ख़ाना, m. = ~.

[2]**जेल** *jel*, m. reg. = जेली.

[3]**जेल** *jel*, m. **1.** *Pl.* a row, string, line. **2.** reg. (Bihar) a flock of sheep or goats.

जेलर *jelar* [Engl. *jailer*], m. a jailer.

जेली *jelī*, f. reg. (W.) a kind of pitchfork made of wood (used in turning over sheaves of corn in threshing).

जेवड़ा *jevṛā* [cf. *jīvā-*], m. a rope, cord.

जेवड़ी *jevṛī* [cf. *jīvā-*], f. dimin. a string, cord.

[1]**जेवनार** *jevnār*, f. = ज्योनार.

[2]**जेवनार** *jevnār*, f. reg. (W.) land left uncultivated for a year.

ज़ेवर *zevar* [P. *zevar*], m. ornament, piece of jewellery.

ज़ेवरात *zevarāt* [P. *zevarāt*, pl.], pl. ornaments, jewellery.

[1]**जेष्ठ** *jeṣṭh* [S. *jyeṣṭha-*, H. [1]*jeṭh*], adj. eldest, senior (= [1]जेठ, [1]ज्येष्ठ).

[2]**जेष्ठ** *jeṣṭh* [S. *jyaiṣṭha-*, H. [2]*jeṭh*], m. the month Jeṭh (= [2]जेठ, [2]ज्येष्ठ).

जेष्ठा *jeṣṭhā*, f. = ज्येष्ठा.

जेह *jeh*, f. Brbh. **1.** a bow-string (esp. the middle portion). **2.** thickened plaster-work on the lowest portion of a wall.

जेहड़ *jehaṛ*, f. reg. a pile of water-pots carried one on top of the other on a woman's head.

ज़ेहन *zĕhn* [A. *ẕĕhn*], m. intelligence, wits; mind. — ~ लड़ाना, to set the mind to work: to consider, to ponder (sthg. difficult). – ज़ेहनकुंद, adj. dull-witted. ज़ेहनदार [P. *-dār*], adj. intelligent.

ज़ेहनी *zĕhnī* [A. *ẕĕhnī*], adj. intelligent (= ज़हीन).

जेहरि *jehri*, f. Brbh. an ornament worn on the feet or ankles (a chain with small bells).

जै *jai*, pl. rel. adj. Brbh. = जितने.

[1]**जैत** *jait* [ad. *jaitra-*], m. the plant *Sesbenia aculeata* (source of a fibre).

[2]**जैत** *jait* [ad. *jaitra-*], m. *mus.* name of a musical mode. — जैत-स्री, m. & (?) f. = श्री (राग); name of a *rāgiṇī*.

जैती *jaitī*, f. *Pl. HŚS.* a weed of the genus *Euphorbia* which springs up with *rabī* crops.

ज़ैतून *zaitūn* [A. *zaitūn*], m. the olive tree; an olive.

जैत्र *jaitr* [S.], adj. & m. **1.** adj. victorious. **2.** m. conqueror, victor. — ~ रथ, m. triumphal car, chariot.

जैन *jain* [S.], m. **1.** a Jain. **2.** the Jain community. — जैन-मत, m. Jain doctrine or belief.

जैनी *jainī* [cf. H. *jain*], adj. & m. **1.** adj. having to do with the Jain community or Jain beliefs. **2.** m. a Jain.

जैफर *jaiphar*, m. Av. nutmeg (= जायफल).

ज़ैल *zail* [A. *ẕail*], m. U. rear or lower part. — ~ में, adv. as follows, as below.

जैव *jaiv* [S.], adj. **1.** pertaining to living creatures. **2.** *chem.* organic. — जैव-रसायन, m. biochemistry; organic chemistry. जैवरासायनिक, adj. biochemical.

जैविकी *jaivikī* [S.], f. biology.

जैसा *jaisā* [*yādṛśa-*], rel. adj. & pron. **1.** of such a sort as. **2.** (as ppn.) like, similar to. उन जैसी औरतें, women like them. **3.** that which; the kind of ... which. — ~ कि, conj. just as; as though. जैसे का तैसा, adj. as (sthg. was) before, unchanged. जैसी की तैसी करना (की), to put (one) in one's place. जैसे को तैसा, like for like, tit for tat. – जैसा-तैसा, adj. ordinary, average, humdrum. जैसा-तैसा कर डालना, to make (sthg.) ordinary, not to do credit (to); to ruin (a joke). जैसी-तैसी करना, to do disreputable or sordid things.

जैसे *jaise* [cf. H. *jaisā*], adv. **1.** in the way in which, just as. **2.** for instance. **3.** as if. — ~ बने, adv. as well as may be; somehow or other. ~ ही, conj. as soon as; precisely in the way in which. – जैसे-जैसे, adv. in proportion as, just as. जैसे-तैसे, adv. somehow or other, by hook or by crook, with difficulty.

जोंक *jonk* [**jonkā-*], f. a leech. — ~ लगाना, to apply leeches. ~ होकर, or ~ की तरह, लिपटना, to cling like a leech (and suck blood).

जोंग *jong*, m. *Pl. HŚS.* aloe wood.

[1]**जो** *jo* [*ya-*], rel. pron. & adj. the one who, or which. — ~ कि, rel. conj. = ~. ~ कुछ, pron. & adj. whatever, whichever. ~ कोई, pron. & adj. whoever; whatever, whichever. ~ ~, pron. & adj. whoever; whatever, whichever. ~ ... सो ..., the one who, or which ... he, &c. (esp. in concise, or gnomic expressions). ~ ... वह ..., the one who, or which ... he, &c. कि ~, rel. conj. = ~ कि.

[2]**जो** *jo* [*yataḥ*], conj. **1.** if; although. **2.** when. — ~ पैं, or पै, conj. Brbh. but if; even if.

जो- *jo-*, v.t. Brbh. = जोहना.

जोई *joī* [*yuvati-*], f. Brbh. a wife.

जोख *jokh* [cf. H. *jokhnā*], f. esp. in comp. weighing, measuring; weight. — उसकी ~ दो सेर है, it weighs two seers.

जोखना *jokhnā* [**yokṣati*], v.t. **1.** to weigh, to measure. **2.** to assess, to calculate.

-जोखा *-jokhā* [cf. H. *jokhnā*], m. **1.** weighing, measuring (cf. लेखा-जोखा). **2.** assessment, calculation.

जोखाई *jokhāī*, f. = जोखाई.

जोखिम *jokhim* [*yogakṣema-*], f. **1.** risk, danger. **2.** a hazardous undertaking. **3.** sthg. risked, or at risk. **4.** loss. — ~ उठाना, to run the risk (of, की: by, में or से); to suffer loss. ~ का, adj. risky, dangerous. ~ में डालना, to put at risk, to endanger. ~ में पड़ना, to run a risk, to fall into danger.

जोखिमी *jokhimī* [cf. H. *jokhim*], adj. & m. **1.** adj. risky, dangerous. **2.** m. a venturesome, or foolhardy person.

जोखों *jokhoṁ*, f. pronun. var. = जोखिम.

[1]**जोग** *jog*, m. = योग.

[2]**जोग** *jog*, adj. 1. = योग्य. **2.** colloq. intended for, directed to (a letter).

जोगव- *jogav-* [cf. *yogyā-*], Brbh. Av. **1.** to attend to; to be intent on. **2.** to guard, to tend; to be devoted to.

जोगिन *jogin*, f. a female ascetic (= योगिनी).

जोगिनी *joginī*, f. = जोगिन.

जोगिया *jogiyā* [cf. H. *jogī*], adj. &·m. **1.** adj. having to do with a yogī. **2.** ochre-coloured (as a yogī's garment). **3.** m. a yogī. **4.** ochre colour. **5.** *mus.* name of a *rāg*.

जोगी *jogī*, m. = योगी.

जोटा *joṭā* [cf. H. *joṛā* and *juṭnā*, *juṭānā*], m. Av. a pair.

जोड़ *joṛ* [H. *joṛnā*], m. **1.** a join; union, connection; joint; patch; seam. **2.** joint (of the body). **3.** a part added, an addition. **4.** *math.* addition; total. **5.** pair, mate; equal, match (of or for, का). **6.** *athl.* a match. **7.** a rhyme (between words). **8.** a set, suit (of clothes, = जोड़ा). — ~ का, adj. equal; similar; identical. ~ देना (में), = ~ लगाना. ~ बैठाना, to fit a joint (into, में), to dovetail. ~ लगाना, to put a patch or piece (in or on, में or पर); to add up (a sum). कुल ~, m. a total (amount). – जोड़-जाड़, m. savings, amounts scraped together; scraps. जोड़-तोड़, m. a makeshift; device; cunning, craft; manipulation. जोड़-तोड़ करना, to exercise ingenuity, or cunning. जोड़दार [P. *-dār*], adj. having joins or joints. जोड़-पत्र, m. an addendum. जोड़-मेल, f. harmony, agreement.

जोड़ती *joṛtī* [cf. H. *joṛnā*], f. reg. adding, addition; counting.

जोड़न *joṛan* [cf. H. *joṛnā*], f. m. **1.** f. joining, &c. **2.** m. a joining agent: solder. **3.** a coagulant; rennet.

जोड़ना *joṛnā* [**yoṭayati*: Pk. *joḍei*], v.t. **1.** to join; to unite, to connect, to attach. **2.** to lay (bricks); to set (type); to solder; to set (a bone); to assemble (components); to mend, to patch; to stitch together; to bind up, to heal (a wound, a broken heart). **3.** to gather together, to amass; to save up (money); to compile, or compose (a literary work). **4.** to make an addition; to add; to count up. **5.** to harness (as to a horse: से). **6.** to match, to mate. **7.** to put a light to: to light (a fire, a lamp). **8.** to form, to strike up (a connection, relationship). — जोड़ना-जाड़ना, v.t. to scrape together (as savings: see ²जोड़ा).

जोड़ला *joṛlā* [cf. H. *joṛnā*], adj. reg. twin (brother or sister).

जोड़वाँ *joṛvāṁ*, adj. & m. f. = जुड़वाँ.

¹**जोड़ा** *joṛā* [cf. H. *joṛ*, and *joṛnā*], m. **1.** a pair, a couple (objects, persons, animals). **2.** one of a pair, a counterpart; partner, mate; consort (wife or husband). **3.** an equal, a match. **4.** set or suit (of clothes). — एक ~ जूता (जूते), a pair of shoes. ~ खिलाना, v.t. to cause to mate (animals). ~ बनाने का मौसम, m. breeding season. – जोड़ा-जामा, m. suit of clothes (esp. as given to a bridegroom by his father-in-law).

²**जोड़ा** *joṛā* [cf. H. *joṛnā*], adj. joined, &c. — जोड़ा-जाड़ा, colloq. much mended, or patched; scraped together piecemeal (as savings).

जोड़ाई *joṛāī* [cf. H. *joṛnā*], f. **1.** joining, laying, patching, &c. **2.** joinery. **3.** cost of, or payment for, joining, &c.

जोड़िया *joṛiyā* [cf. H. *joṛnā*, and *joṛī*], m. colloq. **1.** a twin. **2.** mate, companion (= जोड़ीदार).

जोड़ी *joṛī* [cf. H. ¹*joṛā*], f. 1. = ¹जोड़ा. **2.** a vehicle drawn by two horses or bullocks. — जोड़ीदार [P. *-dār*], m. a mate, partner, colleague; an equal.

¹**जोत** *jot* [ad. *jyoti-*], f. **1.** light; brilliance, splendour. **2.** a beam or ray of light; the light or flame of a lamp or candle; a halo. **3.** a lamp, &c. (as placed before an idol). **4.** a glance (of the eye); sight. **5.** the soul. — ~ चढ़ाना, to light a lamp (before an idol). ~ में ~ समाना, the human soul to merge or to be united with the ultimate being.

²**जोत** *jot* [*yoktra-*; cf. H. *jotnā*], f. **1.** a fastening; cord, rope; trace (of a harness); strap fastening a yoke to the neck of an animal. **2.** yoking (draught animals). **3.** ploughing; ploughed land; a cultivator's holding. **4.** tenure of, or rent paid by, a cultivator.

जोतन *jotan* [cf. H. *jotnā*], m. reg. (W.) ploughing.

जोतना *jotnā* [*yoktrayati*], v.t. **1.** to yoke (animals to a plough, mill, cart, &c.); to harness. **2.** to plough, to cultivate; fig. to reclaim (land). **3.** to force (one) (to, में: as to a task). **4.** to have (a mare) put (to a stallion). — अपनी ही ~, to plough one's own furrow, to work or to act alone. घोड़ी को (घोड़े से) ~, to put a stallion to a mare.

जोता *jotā* [conn. *yoktra-*, or H. *jotnā*], m. a ploughman; cultivator. — हल-जोता, m. a ploughman.

जोताई *jotāī* [cf. H. *jotnā*], f. **1.** ploughing. **2.** cost of, or payment for, ploughing.

जोताऊ *jotāū* [cf. H. *jotnā*], adj. arable.

जोति *joti* [ad. *jyoti-*], f. Brbh. light, &c. (= ¹जोत).

जोतिया *jotiyā*, m. dimin. = जोता.

जोती *jotī* [*yoktra-*], f. reg. cord, string, or strap (as for suspending the scale of a balance, or for fastening a bullock yoke to the animal's neck).

जोधा *jodhā*, m. inv. Brbh. = योद्धा.

जोधापन *jodhāpan* [cf. H. *jodhā*], m. soldiering; bravery.

जोनि *joni*, f. = योनि.

जोबन *joban* [*yauvana-*], m. **1.** youth; adolescence; the years of youth, &c. **2.** youthful vigour, beauty or bloom. **3.** transf. a young woman's breasts. — ~ उभरना (में), the age of adolescence, or of young adulthood, to begin; the body to develop in adolescence. ~ उतरना, or ढलना, the years of youth to pass. ~ पर आना, to reach puberty; to bloom; to attain full vigour. ~ लूटना (अपना or का), to revel in (one's) youth; to enjoy, esp. sexually, a young woman. ~ निकालना, = ~ लूटना, 1.

ज़ोम *zom* [A. *zu'm*], m. **1.** assertion; presumption. **2.** arrogance.

ज़ोर *zor* [P. *zor*], m. & adv. **1.** m. strength, power. **2.** effort, exertion; strain. **3.** force (as of water, wind). **4.** weight, emphasis; stress. **5.** potency (as of drugs, alcohol). **6.** power (over, पर); authority; improper influence; coercion. **7.** threat, attack (on, पर: as in chess). **8.** support, new strength. **9.** adv. extremely. — ~ आना (को), to acquire or to gain strength. ~ करना, to use force; to exert oneself; to compel (one, पर); to gather strength. ~, or ज़ोरों, का, adj. strong; severe, violent; intense. ~ चलना, to have power, &c. (over, पर). ~ चलाना, to use force, or violence (against, पर). ~ डालना, to put pressure (on, पर); to tax, to strain. ~ देना, to give strength or support (to, को); to press (upon, पर); to lay stress (on, पर); to corroborate. ~ देकर, adv. with force or pressure; with emphasis. ~ पकड़ना, to gain in strength or intensity. ~ पड़ना (पर), to be strained (as the eyes); to be compelled. ~पहुँचाना, = ~ डालना. ~ बाँधना, to gain in strength or intensity; to gather momentum. ~ भरना, to gain strength; to attain full strength. ~ में आना, to attain strength. ~ लगाना, or मारना, to apply force; to make efforts, to strive. ज़ोरों पर चढ़ा होना, to be in one's prime, at one's best. ज़ोरों पर होना, to be intense, or at its height (as a fashion); to rage (a disease, an epidemic). ~ से, adv. by force; severely, violently; intensely. ज़ोरों से, or के साथ, adv. = ~ से, 2., 3. – ज़ोर-आज़माई [P. *-āzmāī*], f. trial of strength. ज़ोर-ज़बरदस्ती, adv. by force. ज़ोरदार [P. *-dār*], adj. powerful; forcible; emphatic; massive. ज़ोर-ज़ुल्म, m. violence, repressive measures. ज़ोर-शोर से, adv. with great force; with much pomp. ज़ोरा-ज़ोरी, adv. & f. by force, violently; force, coercion. ज़ोरावर [P. *-āvar*], adj. strong, powerful. °ई, f. force, compulsion.

जोरू *jorū* [**yuvatirūpa-*], f. a wife. — ~ का गुलाम, m. a dominated, or hen-pecked husband. – जोरू-जाँता, m. wife and hand-mill: house and home.

जोली *jolī* [*yugala-*], m. esp. in comp. **1.** a partner, mate. **2.** an equal, contemporary.

जोव- *jov-*, v.t. Brbh. Av. = जोहना.

जोश *jośa* [P. *joś*], m. **1.** boiling. **2.** heat, excitement; passion; ardour, enthusiasm; rage; frenzy. — ~ आना, passion to be aroused (in, को). ~ खाना, to boil, to boil up. ~ दिलाना, to incite (against, के ख़िलाफ़). ~ देना (को), to cause to boil. ~ पर होना [← Engl.], to be on the boil. ~ में आना, to boil up; to grow heated, &c. ~ में लाना, to anger, to enrage. ख़ून का ~, m. family pride or sense of honour. – जोश-ख़रोश, m. = ~, 2. जोशपूर्ण, adj. passionate, ardent, &c.

जोशन *jośan* [A. *jauśan*], m. **1.** Brbh. armour, coat of mail. **2.** a silver or gold ornament, or armlet.

जोशाँदा *jośāṁdā* [P. *jośānda*], m. a brew or decoction of medicinal herbs (= काढ़ा).

जोशी *jośī*, m. = जोषी.

जोशीला *jośīlā* [cf. H. *joś*], adj. passionate; ardent, zealous, &c.

जोशीलापन *jośīlāpan* [cf. H. *jośīlā*], m. passion; ardour, zeal, &c.

जोषी *joṣī* [*jyautiṣika-*: *-ṣ-* ad.], m. **1.** name of a brāhmaṇ sub-community. **2.** a man of that community. 3. = ज्योतिषी.

जोहड़ *johaṛ*, m. reg. (W.) small lake or pool (esp. as formed in a dry river-bed).

ज़ोहरा *zohrā* [A. *zuhra*: P. *zŏhra*], f. U. the planet Venus.

जोहन *johan* [cf. H. *johnā*], f. gazing, looking longingly; a longing glance.

जोहना *johnā* [conn. *dyotate*], v.t. **1.** to look at, to see. **2.** to watch for; to long for the coming (of). **3.** to search for.

जौं *jauṁ*, conj. Brbh. Av. = [2]जो.

जौंकना *jauṁknā*, v.t. *Pl. HŚS.* to scold, to abuse.

जौंची *jauṁcī*, f. reg. a smut in barley and wheat which prevents the grains developing.

जौंडा *jauṁḍā*, m. reg. (W.) a high platform used for keeping watch on crops.

जौंड़ा *jauṁṛā*, m. reg. (Bihar) payment of village servants in kind.

जौंरा-भौंरा *jauṁrā-bhauṁrā*, m. *Pl. HŚS.* a vault, treasure-room.

[1]**जौ** *jau* [*yava-*], m. **1.** barley. **2.** millet. **3.** a grain of barley. **4.** transf. a measure of weight, or length; a jot. — **~ बराबर**, adv. equal to a barley-corn (in weight, or length): a tiny amount, or space. – **जौ-जौ हिसाब लेना**, to make a strict accounting, to exact the last farthing, &c. **जौ-भर**, m. the tiniest amount, a jot.

[2]**जौ** *jau*, conj. Brbh. Av. = [2]**जो**.

ज़ौक़ *zauq* [A. *zauq*], m. U. taste: pleasure, delight (in, **से**). — **ज़ौक़-शौक़**, m. great pleasure, delight.

जौन *jaun* [H. *jo* × H. *kaun*], rel. pron. & adj. Brbh. = [1]**जो**.

[1]**जौनार** *jaunār*, f. reg. (N.) a feast (= **ज्योनार**).

[2]**जौनार** *jaunār* [? conn. *yavanāla-*], m. reg. (W.) land used for a crop of sugar-cane following a barley crop.

जौर *jaur* [A. *jaur*], m.f. U. wrong-doing, injustice, violence. — **जौरो जफ़ा**, f. id.

जौलानी *jaulānī* [A. *jawalān*+P. *-ī*], f. 19c. quickness, alertness.

[1]**जौहर** *jauhar* [**jatughara-*], m. **1.** pyre (for a suicide). **2.** taking one's own life by fire (as formerly by Rājpūt women facing capture by a conqueror). **3.** the practice (*hist.* attributed to Rājpūts) of taking the life of one's wife and children before fighting to the death. — **~ करना**, to kill oneself sacrificially. **~ होना**, to die on a pyre.

[2]**जौहर** *jauhar* [P. *gauhar*: A. P. *jauhar*], m. (and f., *Pl.*) **1.** essential quality, worth; excellence, virtue; particular skill, merit or quality. **2.** a precious stone. **3.** marks or grain (showing the temper of a sword). — **~ खुलना** (**का**), (one's) abilities or virtues to appear. **~ दिखाना (अपना)**, fig. to show (one's) mettle, or what one is worth.

जौहरी *jauhrī* [A. *jauhrī*], m. **1.** a jeweller; appraiser (of precious stones). **2.** an expert, connoisseur.

-ज्ञ *-jñă* [S.], v. suffix (forms adjectives and nouns). knowing (e.g. **अभिज्ञ**, adj. knowledgeable, versed (in)).

ज्ञपित *jñapit* [S.], adj. **1.** made known. **2.** taught, expounded.

ज्ञप्ति *jñapti* [S.], f. **1.** making known, notifying. **2.** sthg. made known, the subject of an announcement.

ज्ञात *jñāt* [S.], adj. **1.** known (a matter: to, **को**); understood. **2.** perceived, apparent, evident.

ज्ञातव्य *jñātavyă* [S.], adj. **1.** requiring to be known: deserving study or enquiry; to be considered (as). **2.** perceptible, comprehensible.

ज्ञाता *jñātā* [S.], adj. & m. inv. **1.** adj. knowledgeable (about, **का**), versed (in); learned. **2.** m. a knowledgeable person; an expert; scholar.

ज्ञाति *jñāti* [S.], m. *hind.* a kinsman; one of the same *gotra*.

ज्ञान *jñān* [S.], m. **1.** knowledge; understanding; wisdom. **2.** learning. **3.** consciousness. **4.** *philos.* understanding of the identity of the self with the ultimate *brāhmaṇ*. — **~ छाँटना**, to sift (one's) knowledge: to show off (one's) learning. **~ दौड़ाना (अपना)**, to exercise the understanding; to meditate deeply. **~ बघारना**, to stir (one's) knowledge: = **~ छाँटना**. **~ में आना (के)**, to be apprehended or comprehended by. **साधारण ~**, m. the rudiments of knowledge. **सामानय ~**, m. general knowledge. – **ज्ञान-कांड**, m. *philos.* the part of the Veda dealing with knowledge of the ultimate being. **ज्ञान-कोश**, m. an encyclopedia. **ज्ञान-गम्य**, m. accessible to knowledge; comprehensible. **ज्ञान-गोचर**, adj. id. **ज्ञान-चक्षु**, m. the sight or vision (born of) true knowledge; a learned or wise person. **ज्ञान-चर्चा**, f. religious or philosophical discussion. **ज्ञानतः**, adv. with foreknowledge. **ज्ञानदा**, f. she who gives knowledge: a title of the goddess Sarasvatī. °**-दाता**, m. inv. a giver of knowledge: teacher, preceptor. °**-दात्री**, f. a title of the goddess Sarasvatī. **ज्ञान-पीठ**, f. an educational establishment. **ज्ञानपूर्वक**, adv. = **ज्ञानतः**. **ज्ञानमय**, adj. consisting of knowledge: knowing, wise. **ज्ञान-मूढ़**, adj. foolish in (one's) wisdom: behaving foolishly while knowing better. **ज्ञान-योग**, m. *philos.* the yoga leading to true knowledge (see ~, 4). **ज्ञानवान**, adj. °**-वती**, f. knowledgeable; learned; wise. **ज्ञान-विज्ञान**, m. knowledge of different sorts; range of knowledge. **ज्ञान-संस्थान**, m. an educational establishment, institute. **ज्ञान-साधन**, m. a means of knowledge. **ज्ञानार्जन** [°*na*+*a*°], m. acquisition of knowledge, education. **ज्ञानालय** [°*na*+*ā*°], m. id. **ज्ञानाश्रयी** [°*na*+*ā*°], adj. inv. based on knowledge; dealing with ultimate knowledge and its attainment (literary works). **ज्ञानासन** [°*na*+*ā*°], m. a posture in yoga. **ज्ञानेंद्रीय** [°*na*+*i*°], f. the organs of sense. **ज्ञानोदय** [°*na*+*u*°], m. rise of knowledge, enlightenment.

ज्ञानिक *jñānik* [S.], adj. having to do with knowledge or learning: academic.

ज्ञानी *jñānī* [S.], adj. & m. **1.** adj. knowing; learned. **2.** wise; judicious. **3.** possessing true knowledge (see **ज्ञान**, 4). **4.** m. a wise man; a sage. **5.** specif. a Sikh who is an authority on Sikh scripture.

ज्ञापक *jñāpak* [S.], adj. & m. **1.** adj. making known: notifying, communicating. **2.** informative. **3.** m. one who announces, or proclaims.

ज्ञापन *jñāpan* [S.], m. a making known: announcement; notification; memorandum.

ज्ञापित *jñāpit* [S.], adj. made known: announced; notified; revealed.

ज्ञाप्य *jñāpyă* [S.], adj. worth making known.

ज्ञेय *jñeyă* [S.], adj. knowable.

ज्या *jyā* [S.], f. **1.** a bow-string. **2.** *math.* chord of an arc. — ज्या-मिति [Engl. *geometry*], f. geometry. °इक, adj.

ज़्यादती *zyādatī* [P. *ziyādatī*], f. **1.** increase; addition. **2.** excess, surplus. **3.** an excess, wrongful or oppressive act.

ज़्यादा *zyādā* [A. *zyāda*], adj. inv. **1.** more; very many, a lot, much (of). **2.** too many. **3.** adv. much; very much, very often, a lot. **4.** too much. — ~ करना, v.t. to increase. ~ लीजिए, please take a larger helping, a lot. ~ होना, to abound; to be in excess. इतना ~, adj. & adv. as much as this. कहीं ~, adv. how much more! very much more. ~ से ~, adj. & adv. more than many, or much: most of; overmuch; at most. – ज़्यादातर [P. *-tar*], adj. & adv. most (of); most commonly, very often; for the most part.

ज्यामिति *jyāmiti*, f. see s.v. ज्या.

[1]**ज्येष्ठ** *jyeṣṭh* [S.], adj. **1.** eldest, senior; elderly. **2.** best, chief, most excellent.

[2]**ज्येष्ठ** *jyeṣṭh* [cf. *jyaiṣṭha-*], m. the month Jeṭh, May-June.

ज्येष्ठता *jyeṣṭhătā* [S.], f. seniority.

ज्येष्ठा *jyeṣṭhā* [S.], f. **1.** an elder sister, or senior female relative. **2.** a favourite, or an elder, wife. **3.** the middle finger.

ज्यों *jyoṁ* [conn. *eva*[1]: Ap. *jiṁva*], adv. in the way in which; just as; like. — ~ का त्यों, adj. unaltered, the very same; in its entirety, &c. ~ का त्यों रखना, to keep as it was, &c.; to keep intact, or safe. ~ ही (correl. त्यों ही), conj. at the moment when, as soon as; just as if. – ज्यों-ज्यों, conj. in proportion as. ज्यों-त्यों, adv. somehow or other; with difficulty. ज्यों-त्यों करके, adv. = ज्यों-त्यों.

ज्योति *jyoti* [S.], f. light; brilliance, radiance. — ज्योति-शास्त्र, m. Brbh. see ज्योतिःशास्त्र s.v. ज्योतिः-.

ज्योतिः- *jyotiḥ-*. = ज्योति. — ज्योतिःशास्त्र, m. astrology; astronomy.

ज्योतित *jyotit* [S.], adj. illuminated, given light, or lustre.

ज्योतिर्- *jyotir-*. = ज्योति. — ज्योतिरिंगण, m. moving light: a firefly. ज्योतिर्मंडल, m. sphere of lights: the heavens; ? galaxy. ज्योतिर्मय, adj. consisting of light: brilliant; starry. ज्योतिर्लिंग, m. a title of Śiva; one of several chief Śiva *liṅgas* (said to number twelve). ज्योतिर्विद्, m. = ज्योतिषी, see s.v. ज्योतिर्विद्या, f. = ज्योतिष, see. s.v.

ज्योतिश्- *jyotiś-*. = ज्योति.– ज्योतिश्चक्र, m. circle of (heavenly) lights: the zodiac. ज्योतिश्छाया, f. light and shade.

ज्योतिष *jyotiṣ* [ad. *jyautiṣa-*], m. **1.** astrology. **2.** astronomy. — ज्योतिष्पथ, m. path of lights: the heavens. ज्योतिष्मान, adj. °-मती, f. brilliant, radiant; celestial.

ज्योतिषिक *jyotiṣik* [ad. *jyautiṣika-*; or S.], adj. & m. **1.** adj. astrological. **2.** astronomical. **3.** m. an astrologer.

ज्योतिषी *jyotiṣī* [ad. *jyautiṣika-*; w. H. *joṣī*], m. **1.** an astrologer. **2.** an astronomer.

ज्योत्स्ना *jyotsnā* [S.], f. **1.** moonlight. **2.** a moonlit night. — ज्योत्स्नेश [°*nā*+*ī*°], m. lord of the moonlight: the moon.

ज्योनार *jyonār* [**jemanakāri-*], f. feast, banquet (as at a wedding, or as given to brāhmaṇs). — ~ बैठना, to sit down to a feast.

ज्वर *jvar* [S.], m. fever; a high temperature. — ~ आना (को), a fever to come on. ~ उतरना, a fever to subside. – ज्वर-ग्रस्त, adj. attacked by, laid low by fever. ज्वर-नाशक, adj. febrifuge. ज्वराक्रांत [°*ra*+*ā*°], adj. = ज्वर-ग्रस्त. ज्वराग्नि [°*ra*+*a*°], f. a fit, paroxysm of fever.

ज्वरित *jvarit* [S.], adj. suffering from fever; feverish.

ज्वरी *jvarī* [S.], adj. *Pl. HŚS.* suffering from fever.

ज्वलंत *jvalant* [S.], adj. **1.** burning, blazing. **2.** brilliant; highly convincing (an example, a proof); splendid (an achievement).

ज्वलका *jvalăkā* [S.], f. a tongue of flame.

ज्वलन *jvalan* [S.], m. **1.** a burning, blazing; conflagration. **2.** burning feeling: an outburst (as of anger). — ज्वलनशील, adj. inflammable; combustible. °ता, f.

ज्वलित *jvalit* [S.], adj. **1.** set alight, burning; blazing. **2.** brilliant (as light). **3.** burnt, consumed.

ज्वाइन *jvāin*, f. = अजवायन.

[1]**ज्वार** *jvār* [**javacāra-*], m. flood-tide; tide. — ज्वार-भाटा, m. flood and ebb tides; the tide.

[2]ज्वार *jvār* [*yavākāra-*], Pk. *juāri-*], f. millet.

ज्वाल *jvāl* [S.], m. = ज्वाला.

ज्वाला *jvālā* [S.], f. **1.** flame, blaze; light; heat. **2.** a burning or searing pain. **3.** intense distress or passion. — **ज्वालामुखी**, m. & adj. a volcano; volcanic.

झ

झ *jha*, the ninth consonant of the Devanāgarī syllabary. — झकार, m. the sound /jh/; the letter झ.

झं *jhaṁ* [S.], m. *HŚS.* = झन.

झँकाना *jhaṁkānā* [cf. H. *jhāṁknā*], v.t. to cause to peep, to spy, &c.

झंकार *jhaṁkār* [*jhaṅkāra-*; or S.], f. **1.** a ringing sound (= झनक, 1.); resonance (as of a *sitār* string). **2.** chirping (as of a cricket). **3.** sharp cry (as of a peacock).

झंकारना *jhaṁkārnā* [cf. H. *jhaṁkār*], v.i. & v.t. **1.** v.i. to ring; to clink, to jingle; to rattle; to clang; to resound (the string of a musical instrument). **2.** to chirp (as a cricket). **3.** v.t. to cause to ring or to resound; to pluck (a string).

झंकृत *jhaṃkr̥t* [S.], adj. resounding. — ~ करना, to cause to resound.

झँख- *jhaṁkh-*, v.i. Av. = झींखना.

झंखाड़ *jhaṁkhāṛ* [cf. **jhaṅkh-*²], m. **1.** a dense thicket; thorny undergrowth. **2.** a leafless tree.

झँगा *jhaṁgā*, m. = झगा.

झँगिया *jhaṁgiyā*, f. = झगा.

झँगुला *jhaṁgulā*, m. = झगा.

झँगुलिया *jhaṁguliyā*, f. pronun. var. = झगा.

झँगुली *jhaṁgulī*, f. Brbh. pronun. var. = झगा.

झंझकार *jhaṁjhkār*, m. E.H. a ringing, or resonance.

झंझट *jhañjhaṭ*, f. m. **1.** perplexity, worry; difficulty; trouble. **2.** wrangling, wrangle. — ~ उठाना, to suffer difficulties, &c. ~ मोल लेना, to involve oneself in difficulties.

झंझटिया *jhañjhaṭiyā* [cf. H. *jhañjhaṭ*], adj. & m. **1.** adj. = झंझटी, 2. **2.** m. a quarrelsome person.

झंझटी *jhañjhaṭī* [cf. H. *jhañjhaṭ*], adj. **1.** perplexing, worrisome, difficult (a matter). **2.** quarrelsome.

झंझर *jhañjhar*, m. = झज्झर.

झँझरी *jhaṁjhrī*, adj. & f. = झझरी.

झंझा *jhañjhā* [S.], f. **1.** wind and heavy rain; a storm; squall. **2.** a clanging sound; rattling; jingling. — झंझानिल [°*ñjhā*+*a*°], m. violent wind and rain. झंझा-वात, m. id.

झँझिया *jhaṁjhiyā* [cf. H. *jhāṁjh*], f. a small cymbal.

झँझोड़ना *jhaṁjhoṛnā*, v.t. **1.** to shake, to give a shaking to. **2.** to pull and tear, to worry (as an animal its prey).

झंडा *jhaṇḍā* [**dhvajadaṇḍa-*], m. a flag; banner; standard. — ~ खड़ा करना, to raise a flag. ~ गाड़ना, to plant a flag (on or over, पर). ~ पहराना, id.; fig. to urge the cause (of, का), to make propaganda (for). झंडे तले आना, to come under the flag (of, का; to adhere to the cause (of). झंडे तले के दोस्ती, f. a casual or passing acquaintance. झंडे पर चढ़ना, to be hoist on a flagpole: to be shown as infamous or unworthy. झंडे पर चढ़ाना, to expose as infamous, &c. – झंडाभिवादन [°*ḍā*+*a*°], m. saluting the flag. झंडोत्तोलन [°*ḍā*+*u*°], m. the hoisting of a flag.

झंडी *jhaṇḍī* [cf. H. *jhaṇḍā*], f. dimin. a flag; signal-flag. — झंडीदार [P. *-dār*], adj. having a flag, &c.

झँडूल- *jhaṁḍūl-* [cf. **jhaṇṭa-*: Pk. *jhaṁṭī-*], adj. Brbh. **1.** having a still unshaven head (a child). **2.** pl. as yet uncut (a child's hair). **3.** *Pl. HŚS.* having thick foliage (a tree).

¹**झँपना** *jhaṁpnā* [**jhamp-*¹], v.i. **1.** to close (the eyelids); to doze. **2.** to spring (upon, पर).

²**झँपना** *jhaṁpnā* [cf. **jhamp-*² (Pk. *jhaṁpaï*) and H. *jhāṁpnā*], v.i. & v.t. **1.** v.i. to be covered over; to be hidden. **2.** v.t. to cover over, to close; to conceal.

झँपान *jhaṁpān*, m. *Pl. HŚS.* a kind of covered sedan chair.

झँवा *jhaṁvā*, m. Brbh. = झाँवाँ.

झँवाना *jhaṁvānā* [cf. H. *jhāṁvāṁ*], v.i. & v.t. **1.** v.i. to darken in the sun (complexion). **2.** to dry up, to wither; to fall. **3.** to burn away, to smoulder; to go out. **4.** to be cleaned by rubbing with *jhāṁvāṁ* (as the feet). **5.** v.t. to burn, to heat. **6.** to cause to dry up, &c. **7.** to cause to burn away, &c. **8.** to clean by rubbing with *jhāṁvāṁ* (as the feet).

झईं *jhaīṁ*, f. Av. = झाँई.

झई *jhaī*, f. Brbh. = झाँई.

[1]**झक** *jhak*, [*jhakk-[4]], f. obsession, craze; whim, caprice. — ~ चढ़ना, or सवार होना (पर), an obsession or craze to dominate (one: for or about, का); to be obstinate. ~ मारना [× H. [1]*jhakh*], to babble; to boast. – झक-झक, f. = ~ झक-झक बंद करो! stop (your nonsensical) chatter, or objections!

[2]**झक** *jhak* [*jhakk-[3]], adj. **1.** bright, shining. **2.** clear, clean, white. — ~ करना, *Pl.* to polish, to shine (= झलकाना). – झक-झक, adj. shining, glittering. झकाझक, adj. id.

झक- *jhak-* [conn. *jhakkh-: Pk. *jhakkhia-*], v.i. Brbh. to babble, to chatter; to complain, or to regret, constantly.

झकझका *jhakjhakā* [cf. H. [2]*jhak*], adj. = [2]झक.

झकझकाना *jhakjhakānā* [cf. H. [2]*jhak*], v.i. to shine, to glitter.

झकझकाहट *jhakjhakāhaṭ* [cf. H. *jhakjhakānā*)], f. **1.** brightness, radiance **2.** clearness, cleanness.

झकझोर *jhakjhor* [*jhakk(ol)-, and cf.*jholayati*], m. & adj. **1.** m. shaking, jolting; a blast (of wind). **2.** pulling and tugging: wrangling, squabbling; frolicking. **3.** adj. violent, tempestuous (as wind).

झकझोरना *jhakjhornā* [cf. H. *jhakjhor*], v.t. to shake violently.

झकझोरा *jhakjhorā* [cf. H. *jhakjhor*], m. a jolt, blow.

झकड़ी *jhakṛī*, f. reg. earthen vessel used in milking.

झकरी *jhakrī*, f. reg. = झकड़ी.

झकोर *jhakor* [cf. H. *jhakornā*; or *jhakkol-], f. m. shaking; a blast of wind.

झकोरना *jhakornā* [cf. *jhakkol-], v.t. to shake, to set in motion (as trees by wind); to drive, to beat (wind or rain).

झकोरा *jhakorā* [cf. H. *jhakor*], m. **1.** shaking (as of a tree by wind); a gust, blast (of wind); a heavy shower; squall; a large wave. **2.** an impulse; blow, impact. — ~ खाना, to be buffeted, shaken or tossed. ~ देना, to shake, to buffet (as wind a tree).

झकोल *jhakol* [*jhakkol-], f. m. 1. = झकोर. **2.** Brbh. a wind; puff (of a breeze).

झकोलना *jhakolnā* [*jhakkol-], v.t. 1. = झकोरना. **2.** to dash, to beat (as waves on a boat); to splash.

झकोला *jhakolā* [cf. *jhakkol-], m. = झकोरा.

[1]**झक्कड़** *jhakkaṛ* [*jhakk-[1]], m. a blast, squall; violent storm. — ~ उठना, a storm to rise. ~ चलना, a storm to rage.

[2]**झक्कड़** *jhakkaṛ* [*jhakk-[4]], adj. stubborn, perverse.

[1]**झक्की** *jhakkī* [cf. *jhakk-[4]], m. a person driven by an obsession or craze.

[2]**झक्की** *jhakkī* [cf. *jhakkh-: Pk. *jhakkhia-*], m. **1.** a chatterer. **2.** one who talks to himself.

झक्कीपन *jhakkīpan* [cf. H. [1]*jhakkī*], m. craziness, obsessiveness.

[1]**झख** *jhakh* [conn. *jhakkh-: Pk. *jhakkhia-*], f. incoherent speech, babble; foolish speech, nonsense. — ~ मारकर, adv. despite all one can do. willy-nilly. ~ मारना, to (sit and) babble, or chatter: to do little or nothing (cf. [1]झक).

[2]**झख** *jhakh* [ad. *jhaṣa-*], m. Brbh. Av. a fish; the sign Pisces (of the zodiac).

झख- *jhakh* , v.i. Brbh. Av. = झक-, and झींखना.

झगड़ना *jhagaṛnā* [*jhaggaḍ-], v.i. to quarrel: to wrangle; to squabble; to argue. — झगड़ा-झगड़ी, f. wrangling, quarrelling.

झगड़ा *jhagṛā* [*jhaggaḍ-], m. a quarrel; dispute, row; fight, brawl; quarrelling. — ~ उठाना, to start or to cause a quarrel (among, में). ~ करना, to quarrel, &c. ~ कराना, = ~ उठाना. ~ ख़रीदना, or मोल लेना, to take a quarrel upon oneself. – झगड़ा-झगड़ी, f. see s.v. झगड़ना. झगड़ा-झंझट, f. quarrelling, wrangle. झगड़ा-टंटा, m. id. झगड़ा-फ़साद, m. id. झगड़ा-रगड़ा, id.

झगड़ाउ *jhagṛāu* [cf. H. *jhagṛā*], adj. quarrelsome, &c. (= झगड़ालू).

झगड़ाना *jhagṛānā* [cf. H. *jhagaṛnā*], v.t. to cause to quarrel, &c.

झगड़ालिन *jhagṛālin*, adj. f. & f. **1.** adj. f. = झगड़ालू. **2.** f. a quarrelsome woman.

झगड़ालू *jhagṛālū* [cf. *jhaggaḍ-], adj. & m. **1.** adj. quarelsome, truculent; litigious. **2.** m. a quarrelsome person.

झगड़ालूपन *jhagṛālūpan* [cf. H. *jhagṛālū*], m. quarrelsomeness, truculence.

झगड़ू *jhagṛū*, adj. reg. = झगड़ाऊ.

झगा *jhagā* [? *adhyaṅgaka-], m. a long, loose garment (specif. as worn by very young children).

झगुलिया *jhaguliyā*, f. = झगा.

झगुली *jhagulī*, f. Brbh. = झगा.

झजरी *jhajrī*, f. pronun. var. = झझरी.

झज्झर *jhajjhar* [*jharjhara-*²], m. a porous water-jug.

झझक *jhajhak*, f. 1. = झिझक. **2.** an unpleasant smell.

झझकना *jhajhaknā*, v.i. = झिझकना.

झझका- *jhajhkā-* [cf. H. *jhijhaknā*], v.t. Brbh. to cause (one) to feel a sudden hesitation, fear, &c.

झझकार- *jhajhkār-* [cf. H. *jhijhak*, *jhajhak*], v.t. Brbh. **1.** to rebuke. **2.** to set back or to humble (as pride or self-esteem).

झझरी *jhajhrī* [cf. *jharjhara-*²], adj. & f. **1.** adj. perforated. **2.** porous. **3.** grated, latticed. **4.** f. a porous jug (cf. झज्झर). **5.** fire-bars. **6.** a lattice, screen. — झझरीदार [P. *-dār*], adj. = ~, 1.-3.

झझलका *jhajhalkā*, m. *Pl.* break of day, early dawn.

झट *jhaṭ* [cf. **jhaṭṭ-*], m. & adj. **1.** m. quickness. **2.** adj. quick; adv. quickly, at once. — ~ से, adv. = ~. – झटपट, adv. this very moment, = ~.

झटक *jhaṭak* [cf. **jhaṭṭ-*], f. a jerk, wrench, shake; a toss, throw; gust (of wind).

झटकना *jhaṭaknā* [cf. **jhaṭṭ-*], v.t. & v.i. **1.** v.t. to jerk, to jolt, to wrench, to shake; to shake off. **2.** to snatch or to tear away (from, से). **3.** v.i. to be shaken; to be worn, or set back (by grief or illness); to be lost, or shed (as weight).

¹**झटका** *jhaṭkā* [cf. H. *jhaṭaknā*], m. **1.** a jerk, wrench, shake; spasm, tremor; twitch, stitch (in the side). **2.** gust (of wind). **3.** blow (as of misfortune). **4.** (electric) shock. — ~ खाना, to be jerked, wrenched, &c. ~ देना (को), to jerk, &c.; to jolt, to jostle. झटके का माल, m. colloq. plunder, booty.

²**झटका** *jhaṭkā* [cf. H. *jhaṭaknā*], adj. & m. **1.** adj. slaughtered with a single knife-stroke (an animal). **2.** m. an animal so slaughtered.

झटकाना *jhaṭkānā* [cf. H. *jhaṭaknā*], v.t. = झटकारना.

झटकारना *jhaṭkārnā* [cf. H. *jhaṭak*], v.t. to jerk, to twist, to shake, &c.

झटास *jhaṭās*, f. reg. squall, driving rain.

झटिति *jhaṭiti* [S.], adv. Av. = झट.

झड़ *jhaṛ*, f. = झड़ी.

झड़- *jhaṛ-* [*jhāṭa-*, Pk. *jhaḍa-*]. a bush: — झड़-बेर, m. the fruit of the wild jujube tree. °ई, f. the wild jujube tree; = झड़-बेर. झड़-बेरी का काँटा, m. fig. a person dificult to deal with.

झड़कना *jhaṛaknā*, v.i. pronun. var. = झिड़कना.

झड़झड़ाना *jharjhaṛānā* [cf. **jhaṭ-*, and **jhaṭati*: Pk. *jhaḍaï*], v.t. & v.i. **1.** v.t. to shake, to jerk, to flap. **2.** to overturn. **3.** v.i. to shake, to rustle, to flap.

झड़झड़ाहट *jharjharāhaṭ* [cf. H. *jharjharānā*], f. shaking and rustling (as of a tree); flapping (of wings: cf. झाड़ना).

झड़न *jhaṛan* [cf. H. *jhaṛnā*], f. **1.** falling down, off, or out; shedding; moulting. **2.** shavings, sweepings; rubbish.

झड़ना *jharnā* [**jhaṭati*: Pk. *jhaḍaï*], v.i. **1.** to fall down, off or out; to be shed, or poured; to be discharged or ejaculated. **2.** [×H. *jhāṛnā*] to be shaken, to be swept off, brushed, or dusted; to be beaten (carpets, furniture); to be winnowed; to be sifted. **3.** to shake. **4.** to wither, to decline. — झड़ा-झड़, adv. continuously, heavily (of rain, gunfire); in quick succession.

झड़प *jhaṛap* [cf. **jhaṭ-*], f. **1.** sparring, fighting; a fight, brawl; a cock-fight. **2.** an acrimonious squabble or quarrel.

झड़पना *jharapnā* [cf. H. **jhaṭ-*], v.i. & v.t. **1.** v.i. to spar, to fight (as cocks); to rush frantically or to fall (upon, पर). **2.** to squabble. **3.** v.t. to snatch aggressively away. — झड़पा-झड़पी, f. contention, sparring; squabbling.

झड़पाना *jharpānā* [cf. H. *jharapnā*], v.t. **1.** to cause to fight (esp. cocks). **2.** to cause to squabble.

झड़वाना *jharvānā* [cf. H. *jhāṛnā*], v.t. to cause to fall, or to be shaken, &c. (by, से).

झड़ाक *jharāk* [cf. **jhaṭ-*], adv. reg. (Raj.) quickly, at once.

झड़ाना *jharānā* [cf. H. *jhāṛnā*], v.t. **1.** to cause to be swept, shaken, &c. (by, से). **2.** to cause to be cast out (an evil spirit).

झड़ी *jhaṛī* [**jhaḍī-* (← Drav.): Pk. *jhaḍī-*], f. **1.** a shower. **2.** continuous rain. **3.** fig. shower (as of complaints, questions). — ~ बँधना, or लगना, rain to set in.

झन *jhan* [cf. *jhaṇ-*], f. (m., *Pl.*) ringing, clashing (of metallic objects); jingling; rattling; clanking. — ~ से, adv. with a clash, &c. – झनझन, f. & adj. clashing, &c. झनझन करना, to clash, &c.

झनक *jhanak* [cf. H. *jhanaknā*], f. **1.** ringing, a ringing sound; clinking; jingling; rattling; clanging. **2.** tingling; pricking. **3.** vexation, irritation. — झनक-मनक, f. Brbh. tinkling, jingling (of small bells, ornaments).

झनकना *jhanaknā* [cf. **jhaṇatka-*], v.i. to ring, to resound (= झंकारना). — झनकना-पटकना, m. shouting and flailing: a tantrum.

झनकाणा *jhankāṇā* [cf. **jhanatka-*], v.t. to cause to ring, or to clink, &c. (see झंकारना).

झनकार *jhankār* [*jhanaṭkāra-*], m. Brbh. = झंकार.

झनझनाना *jhanjhanānā* [*jhaṇajhaṇāyate*, and H. *jhan*], v.i. **1.** to ring, to resound; to jingle; to rattle; to clash. **2.** colloq. to be irritable, or suddenly angry (= झुँझलाना). **3.** to tingle, to become numb (the limbs) (= झुनझुनाना).

झनझनाहट *jhanjhanāhaṭ* [cf. H. *jhanjhanānā*], f. **1.** ringing, resounding, &c. **2.** irritation, or anger (= झुँझलाहट). **3.** tingling, numbness (of the limbs).

झनझनी *jhanjhanī* [cf. H. *jhanjhan*, s.v. *jhan*, and H. *jhanjhanānā*], f. tingling, numbness (of the limbs).

झनाका *jhanākā* [cf. H. *jhan*], m. a clashing, clanking or ringing sound.

झन्नाना *jhannānā*, v.i. = झनझनाना.

झन्नाहट *jhannāhaṭ* [cf. H. *jhannānā*], f. **1.** resounding, tinkling. ***2.** tingling, numbness.

झप *jhap* [**jhapp-*[1]], m. & adj. **1.** m. a sudden movement: a spring, dart; a tumble, fall. **2.** adj. quick, sudden; adv. quickly, in a moment's space. — ~ ~, adv. all in a moment, = ~. ~ से, adv. = ~. – झपा-झप, adv. id.

झपक *jhapak* [cf. H. *jhapaknā*], f. **1.** a closing or lowering of the eyelids; a nod (in drowsiness). **2.** a blink of the eye; a moment, twinkling of the eye. **3.** swinging, swaying (as of a fan). **4.** a gust (of wind).

झपकना *jhapaknā* [cf. **jhapp-*[1]], v.i. **1.** to close (the eyes); to nap, to doze. **2.** to be lowered (the eyes: as in embarrassment, shame). **3.** to blink (the eyes). **4.** to move to and fro (a fan).

झपकाना *jhapkānā* [cf. H. *jhapaknā*], v.t. to blink (the eyes).

झपकी *jhapkī* [cf. **jhapp-*[1] and (for senses 1. and 2.) H. *jhapaknā*], f. **1.** drowsiness; a nap, doze. **2.** blinking (of the eyes). **3.** reg. (W.) a cloth in which grain is winnowed. — ~ आना (को), (one) to feel drowsy. ~ लगाना, or लेना, to doze, to nod.

झपट *jhapaṭ* [cf. **jhapp-*[1]], f. **1.** a spring, leap; swoop (of a beast or bird of prey); rush, dash, pounce. **2.** shock, impact (of an attack). **3.** a brush, encounter; round (in a fight).

झपटना *jhapaṭnā* [cf. **jhapp-*[1]], v.i. & v.t. **1.** v.i. to spring, to pounce, or to swoop (at or on, पर); to snatch or to snap (at, पर). **2.** to rush or to fly (at, पर). **3.** colloq. to go quickly, or with all speed. **4.** v.t. to seize and carry off; to snatch or to snap up.

झपटाना *jhapṭānā* [cf. H. *jhapaṭnā*], v.t. to cause to run or to go quickly; to despatch (one) with all speed.

झपट्टा *jhapaṭṭā* [cf. **jhapp-*[1]], m. 1. = झपट, 1. **2.** fig. violent effect (of an attack, a calamity, an epidemic); malign influence (of a spirit). — ~ मारना (पर), to spring, to swoop or to rush (upon); to dive (upon: an aircraft); to snatch (at, or away). झपट्टे में आना (के), to fall into the clutches (of); to be possessed (by: an evil spirit). – झपट्टामार, adj. swooping upon, &c. झपट्टामार हवाई जहाज़, m. a dive-bomber.

झपना *jhapnā* [conn. H. *jhapaknā*], v.i. to close (the eyes).

झपनी *jhapnī*, [cf. H. ?*jhampnā*], f. a cover, lid.

झपाक *jhapāk* [cf. **jhapp-*[1]], f. & adv. **1.** f. quickness, haste; activity, agility. **2.** adv. quickly, in a flash. — ~ से, = ~.

झपाका *jhapākā* [cf. **jhapp-*[1]], m. & adv. = झपाक. — झपाके से, adv. = झपाक से.

झपाटा *jhapāṭā*, m. = झपट्टा.

झपाना *jhapānā* [cf. H. *jhapnā*], v.t. to allow to close (the eyes); to nap, to doze.

झपास *jhapās* [cf. **jhapp-*[1]], f. reg. a downpour.

झपेट *jhapeṭ* [cf. H. *jhapeṭnā*], f. = झपट, 1., 2., झपट्टा.

झपेटना *jhapeṭnā* [cf. H. *jhapaṭnā*], v.i. to spring, or to swoop (upon, पर); to launch a sudden attack (on).

झपेटा *jhapeṭā* [cf. H. *jhapeṭnā*], m. = झपट्टा.

झप्पान *jhappān*, m. *Pl. HŚS.* = झँपान.

झबरा *jhabrā*, adj. hairy, shaggy (an animal).

झबरापन *jhabrāpan* [cf. H. *jhabrā*], m. shagginess.

झबिया *jhabiyā*, m. reg. (Bihar) a woman's arm ornament.

झबूक- *jhabūk-*, v.i. E.H. = चमकना, झमकना.

झब्बा *jhabbā*, m. a tassel, pendant; cluster. — झब्बेदार [P. *-dār*], adj. tasselled, &c.

झब्बुआ *jhabbuā*, adj. reg. (W.) long-haired (= झबरा).

झमक *jhamak* [cf. H. *jhamaknā*], f. **1.** radiance, glitter, flash. **2.** jangle, clash (as of anklets).

झमकड़ा *jhamakṛā* [cf. H. *jhamak*], m. 19c. = झमक, 1.

झमकना *jhamaknā* [cf. *jhamm-[1 3 4]], v.i. **1.** to glitter, to flash. **2.** to jangle, to clash. **3.** Brbh. to beat, to blow (wind or rain).

झमकाना *jhamkānā* [cf. H. *jhamaknā*], v.t. **1.** to cause to glitter; to flash (the eyes). **2.** to cause to jangle or to clash.

झमकार- *jhamkār-*, adj. Brbh. shedding rain (clouds).

झम-झम *jham-jham* [*jhamm-[1 3 4]], m. & adj. **1.** m. = झमाका, 1., 2. **2.** sparkle: gleam. **3.** adj. & esp. adv. dashing, pattering (of heavy or steady rain). **4.** clashing, jangling (as of ornaments). **5.** sparkling, gleaming. — झमाझम, m. & adj. the beating of steady or heavy rain; heavily and continuously (raining); radiantly.

झमझमाना *jhamjhamānā* [cf. H. *jham-jham*], v.i. & v.t. **1.** v.i. to dash, to patter (heavy or steady rain). **2.** to sparkle, to gleam. **3.** to clash, to jangle. **4.** to tingle. **5.** v.t. to cause to sparkle or gleam.

झमझमाहट *jhamjhamāhaṭ* [cf. H. *jhamjhamānā*], f. **1.** a dashing, or pattering. **2.** sparkling, gleaming.

झमाका *jhamākā* [cf. *jhamm-[1 4]], m. **1.** dashing, or pattering sound (of steady rain). **2.** clashing or jangling (as of ornaments). **3.** crash (as of breaking glass).

झमाझम *jhamājham*, m. & adv. see s.v. झम-झम.

झमूरा *jhamūrā*, adj. & m. **1.** adj. hairy, shaggy. **2.** m. a shaggy animal; a bear. **3.** *HŚS.* an unkempt or long-haired child.

झमेला *jhamelā* [cf. *jhamm-[2]], m. **1.** entanglement, mess; difficulty, trouble. **2.** a row, wrangle.

झमेलिया *jhameliyā* [cf. H. *jhamelā*], f. a troublesome person; mischief-maker; quarrelsome person.

[1]**झर** *jhar*, f. = झल.

[2]**झर** *jhar* [S.], m. **1.** a waterfall. **2.** a spring (of water). **3.** a torrent (as of water, rain; or of anger).

झरझर *jharjhar* [cf. *jharati[1]: Pk. *jharaï*], f. the sound of gurgling, rushing, or roaring (water, wind).

[1]**झरना** *jharnā* [*jharati[1]: Pk. *jharaï*], v.i. & adj. **1.** to run, to flow; to cascade. **2.** to trickle; to drip, to ooze. **3.** to cascade in showers (as flowers from heaven). **4.** adj. *HŚS.* flowing, cascading.

[2]**झरना** *jharnā* [*jharaṇa-*[1]], m. **1.** m. a cascade, waterfall. **2.** a spring. **3.** a kind of weave incorporating a wavy pattern of threads. **4.** [cf. *jharjhara-*[2]] a perforated skimmer. **5.** a kind of sieve.

झरबेरी *jharberī*, f. reg. = झड़-बेरी (see s.v. झड़-).

झरी *jharī* [cf. H. *jharnā*], f. **1.** waterfall, cascade, &c. (= झड़ी). **2.** *HŚS.* levy made on hawkers and small tradesmen by landowners or contractors.

झरुआ *jharuā*, m. *Pl. HŚS.* a nutritious grass.

झरोखा *jharokhā*, m. **1.** a small barred window; lattice window; skylight. **2.** a loop-hole.

झल *jhal* [*jhalā-*, also *jhal-[3], *jhall-[2]], f. m. **1.** heat; radiance; glare. **2.** sharpness (taste, smell). **3.** fierce emotion: strong desire; frenzy; obsession, craze (= [1]झक).

झलक *jhalak* [cf. H. *jhalaknā*], f. **1.** brightness, radiance; a gleam; reflection. **2.** a glimpse. **3.** a suffused glow; aura.

झलकना *jhalaknā* [cf. *jhal-[3]], v.i. **1.** to shine, to glitter; to gleam; to be reflected. **2.** transf. to become evident.

झलका *jhalkā* [cf. *jhal-[3]], m. Av. a blister.

झलकाना *jhalkānā* [cf. H. *jhalaknā*], v.t. **1.** to cause to shine, or to gleam, &c. **2.** to polish, to burnish. **3.** to cause to appear, to imply; to suggest.

झलकी *jhalkī* [cf. H. *jhalak*], f. 1. = झलक. **2.** a short radio play, or dramatic sketch.

झलझल *jhaljhal* [cf. *jhal-[3]], f. m. & adj. **1.** f. m. glitter, brilliance. **2.** adj. glittering, brilliant; adv. radiantly. — झलाझल, adj. = ~.

झलझलाना *jhaljhalānā* [cf. *jhal-[3]], v.i. & v.t. **1.** v.i. to glitter, to sparkle. **2.** to burn, to smart. **3.** to become enraged. **4.** v.t. to cause to glitter, &c.

झलझलाहट *jhaljhalāhaṭ* [cf. H. *jhaljhalānā*], f. **1.** glittering, brilliance, radiance. **2.** burning, smarting.

[1]**झलना** *jhalnā* [cf. H. *jhālnā*], v.i. to be soldered, to be repaired (metal).

[2]**झलना** *jhalnā* [*jhal-[2]], v.t. to move to and fro (as a fan); to flap, to swing, to wave.

झलमल *jhalmal*, m. = झलझल.

झलवाई *jhalvāī* [cf. H. *jhalvānā*], f. **1.** causing to be soldered. **2.** cost of, or price paid for soldering.

¹**झलवाना** *jhalvānā* [cf. H. *jhālnā*], v.t. to cause to be soldered, or repaired (by, से).

²**झलवाना** *jhalvānā* [cf. H. ²*jhalnā*], v.t. to cause to be moved to and fro, &c. (by, से); to have (one) fanned.

झलहाया *jhalhāyā*, adj. & m. burning with strong emotion: **1.** adj. envious, covetous. **2.** jealous, suspicious. **3.** lustful. **4.** obsessed. **5.** m. an envious, or jealous person, &c.

झला *jhalā* [cf. H. ²*jhalnā*], m. reg. a shower of rain.

झलाई *jhalāī* [cf. H. *jhālnā*, *jhalānā*], f. **1.** soldering. **2.** cost of, or price paid for soldering.

झलाझल *jhalājhal*, adj. see s.v. झलझल.

¹**झलाना** *jhalānā* [cf. H. *jhālnā*], v.t. to cause to be soldered (by, से): to solder, to repair.

²**झलाना** *jhalānā* [cf. H. ²*jhalnā*], v.t. to cause to be moved (by, से: as a fan); to cause to flap, to swing, to wave.

झलाबोर *jhalābor* [? conn. H. *jhalājhal*], m. 19c. glitter, radiance. — ~ का, adj. glittering (material).

¹**झल्ला** *jhallā*, m. a large basket.

²**झल्ला** *jhallā* [cf. **jhall-*¹], m. a shower of rain.

³**झल्ला** *jhallā* [**jhall-*²: Pk. *jhala-*], adj. hot, hot-tempered; crazed.

झल्लाना *jhallānā* [cf. **jhall-*²: Pk. *jhala-*], v.i. & v.t. **1.** v.i. to become enraged. **2.** v.t. ? to enrage.

झल्ली *jhallī* [cf. H. ¹*jhallā*], f. dimin. a basket.

झष *jhaṣ* [S.], m. see ²झख.

झहरा- *jhaharā-*, v.i. Brbh. Av. **1.** to make a rumbling, gurgling, dashing or loud rustling sound. **2.** to feel strong emotion: to be angry; to be irritated.

झाँई *jhāṁī* [*jhāmaka-*; Pk. *jhāmia-*], f. dark colour, darkness: **1.** shadow; reflection, gleam. **2.** dark or worn spot (in a mirror). **3.** a freckle, or dark spot on the skin. **4.** deception, trickery. **5.** echo. — ~ आना (को), a darkness to come over (one's) eyes, everything to go black. ~ देना, or बताना (को), to deceive; to coax, to cajole (= झाँसा देना). – झाँई-झप्पा, m. trickery. झाँई-माँई, f. a children's game (dancing in a circle and shouting or singing).

झाँक *jhāṁk* [cf. H. *jhāṁknā*], f. peeping, spying; a peep. — झाँक-झूँक, f. the act of peeping, &c.

झाँक- *jhāṁk-*, v.i. Brbh. Av. = झख-, झीखना.

झाँकना *jhāṁknā* [**jhaṅkh-*¹], v.t. **1.** to peep, to peer, to spy. **2.** to glance; to put one's head out (from a door or window). **3.** to look in (briefly), to pay a brief visit (to, के यहाँ).

झाँकर *jhāṁkar* [cf. **jhaṅk-*¹], m. = झंखाड़.

झाँकी *jhāṁkī* [cf. H. *jhāṁknā*], f. **1.** a glimpse, view. **2.** trans. brief account (of a topic, की). **3.** a sight: an exhibition, display (esp. one representing the birth of Kr̥ṣṇa, at the time of the janmāṣṭamī festival).

झाँख *jhāṁkh*, m. the *cītal* or spotted deer (*Axis axis*).

झाँझ *jhāṁjh* [**jhāñjha-*], f. **1.** a cymbal; cymbals. **2.** [*jhañjhā-*] colloq. *Pl. HŚS.* raging anger. **3.** [? conn. *jharjhara-*²] transf. reg. (Bihar) a colander. **4.** = *jhāṁjhan.*

झाँझन *jhāṁjhan* [cf. **jhāñjha-*], f. reg. a tinkling (hollow) anklet.

झाँझर *jhāṁjhar* [**jharjhara-*²], adj. & m. Av. **1.** adj. leaky, perforated. **2.** m. sthg. perforated, or shot through (as the heart, by arrows of a lady's beauty).

झाँझरी *jhāṁjhrī*, f. Brbh. = झाँझन.

झाँझिया *jhāṁjhiyā* [cf. H. *jhāṁjh*], m. one who plays the cymbals.

झाँझी *jhāṁjhī* [conn. *jharjhara-*², or cf. H. *jhāṁjh*], f. **1.** a perforated pot or vessel. **2.** a procession of young girls (at night in the month of Āśvin; they carry on their heads perforated earthen pots with lamps inside, and sing songs, while going from house to house, where they receive money or food). **3.** the kind of song sung on this occasion.

झाँट *jhāṁṭ* [**jhaṇṭa-*: Pk. *jhaṁṭī-*], f. **1.** pubic hair. **2.** colloq. a worthless or trivial object. — ~ जलना, to feel malice. ~ बराबर, adj. worthless, trifling. ~ की झँटुल्ली, f. the most worthless of objects.

झाँप *jhāṁp* [**jhamp-*²: Pk. *jhaṁpaï*], f. (m., *Pl.*) **1.** cover (as of a basket). **2.** a matwork shade, screen or shutter.

झाँपना *jhāṁpnā* [**jhamp-*²: Pk. *jhaṁpaï*], v.t. to cover; to conceal, to screen.

¹**झाँपा** *jhāṁpā* [**jhamp-*³], m. reg. (Bihar) a kind of basket having a lid.

²**झाँपा** *jhāṁpā* [**jhamp-*²], m. a large basket lid.

झाँवर *jhāṁvar*, f. marshy land (= झाबर).

झाँवर- *jhāṁvar-* [cf.*jhāma-*[1]: Pa. *jhāma-*], adj. Brbh. **1.** dark-coloured, black. **2.** gloomy (mood).

झाँवली *jhāṁvlī*, f. *Pl. HŚS.* a sidelong look, flirtatious look.

झाँवाँ *jhāṁvāṁ* [*jhāmaka-*], m. pumice stone; overburnt brick (used esp. to clean the feet).

झाँस *jhāṁs*, f. pungency.

झाँसना *jhāṁsnā*, v.t. **1.** to deceive, to trick. **2.** to coax, to cajole.

झाँसा *jhāṁsā*, m. **1.** deception, trickery; hoax. **2.** coaxing, cajoling. — ~ देना, or बताना (को), to deceive, to hoodwink; to cajole. झाँसे में आना (के), to be taken in (by); to be talked into (sthg.) (by). – झाँसा-पट्टी, f. deceit; bluff; cajolery. झाँसा-पट्टी उजागर करना, to call (one's) bluff. झाँसेबाज़ [P. *-bāz*], m. a tricky customer; one who cajoles, &c.

झाँसू *jhāṁsū*, m. **1.** a deceiver, cheat. **2.** a coaxer, cajoler.

झाईं *jhāīṁ*, f. see झाँईं.

झाऊ *jhāū* [*jhāvu-*: Pa. *jhāvuka-*], m. the tamarisk (*Tamarix*) shrub or tree (a source of twigs for making baskets, brooms, wattles).

झाग *jhāg* [**jhaggā-*], f. m. foam; froth; scum.

झाझर *jhājhar* [*jharjhara-*[1]], m. *Pl.* = झाँझ, झाँझरी.

[1]**झाड़** *jhāṛ* [*jhāṭa-*, Pk. *jhāḍa-*], m. **1.** a bush. **2.** bushes, undergrowth, brambles; scrub; vegetation. **3.** a chandelier. **4.** a type of firework. — ~ का काँटा, m. a bramble-thorn; fig. a troublesome person. – झाड़ खंड, m. a scrub or forest region; dense forest, &c. झाड़-झंखाड़, m. a tangled thicket of brambles, &c.; a pile of junk (as discarded wood, furniture). झाड़-झूर, m. id. झाड़दार [P. *-dār*], adj. & m. having bushes, &c.; thick, dense (growth); thorny; patterned (cloth); a type of embroidery with floral ornamentation.

[2]**झाड़** *jhāṛ* [cf. H. *jhāṛnā*], f. causing to drop or to fall, shaking down: **1.** sweeping, cleaning. **2.** sweepings. **3.** casting out by means of charms or incantations (a sickness, esp. the effect of snake-bite; or an evil spirit). **4.** scolding, berating. — ~ पिलाना (को), to scold (one). – झाड़-झूड़, f. colloq. sweeping and cleaning, brushing, &c. झाड़-पोंछ, f. id. झाड़-फ़ानूस, m. a lantern shedding its light: a chandelier. झाड़-फूँक, f. = ~, 3. झाड़-बुहार, f. = झाड़-झूड़.

झाड़न *jhāṛan* [cf. H. *jhāṛna-*], f. (? m.) **1.** sweepings, dust, rubbish. **2.** a duster, cloth, &c.

झाड़ना *jhāṛnā* [**jhāṭayati*], v.t. **1.** to cause to drop or to fall; to shake off; to knock down, to shed (feathers). **2.** to shake, to sweep off; to brush; to dust; to beat (carpets, furniture); to sift, to winnow; colloq. to comb (the hair). **3.** to sweep, to dash, to strike; to flap (wings); to brandish (a weapon); to deliver (a blow). **4.** colloq. to air (knowledge). **5.** to cast out (an evil spirit, &c., see [2]झाड़, 3). **6.** to give a shaking to: to scold, to berate. **7.** to extract, to extort (money). — झाड़-पछोड़कर देखना, to sift and winnow (a matter): to investigate in detail. झाड़ना-पोंछना, to sweep, to clean, to dust, &c. झाड़ना-फूँकना, = ~, 5. झाड़ा, m. colloq. shit.

[1]**झाड़ा** *jhāṛā* [*jhāṭa-*, Pk. *jhāḍa-*], m. ? a bush; bushes. — ~ फिरना, colloq. to go to defecate.

[2]**झाड़ा** *jhāṛā* [cf. *jhāṛnā*], m. sweeping, cleaning: **1.** sweepings, rubbish. **2.** incantation (see [2]झाड़, 3). **3.** shaking down: minute search (of the clothes and person of one suspected of stealing). — ~ देना, to submit (one, को) to a minute search.

झाड़ी *jhāṛī* [*jhāṭa-*, Pk. *jhāḍa-*], f. **1.** a shrub. **2.** bushes, undergrowth, &c. (= [1]झाड़, 2).

झाड़ू *jhāṛū*, m. a broom. — ~ देना (में), to sweep (a room, &c.); to make a clean sweep, to spare nothing. ~ फिरना (में), fig. to be swept clean (as a room); to be swept away (as savings). ~ फेरना (में), to go over (a floor) with a broom. ~ मारना (को), to belabour with a broom, to chase off. ~ लगाना (में), to sweep (a room). – झाड़ूबरदार [P. *-bardār*], m. a sweeper. झाड़ू बुहारी, f. colloq. sweeping.

झापड़ *jhāpaṛ*, m. a blow with the open hand.

झापा *jhāpā*, m. *Pl.* ? a narrow-mouthed basket.

झाबर *jhābar*, f. low land, marsh, swamp.

झाबा *jhābā*, m. a large basket woven of straw.

[1]**झाम** *jhām* [**jhamm-*[1 3]], m. Brbh. a tassel, or ornament (that swings, or glitters).

[2]**झाम** *jhām*, m. reg. a large mattock or shovel (as used in dredging or excavating wells).

[1]**झामर** *jhāmar* [cf. **jhamm-*[3 4]], m. reg. (W.) an anklet. — झामर-झूमर, m. attraction, or blandishment(s) (of the world).

[2]**झामर** *jhāmar* [S.], m. *Pl. HŚS.* a small whetstone (as for spindles, needles).

झामा *jhāmā*, m. pumice (see झाँवाँ).

झार *jhār* [**jhāla-*[2]], f. ? m. Brbh. Av. heat, burning (= [2]झाल).

झारना *jhārnā* [**jhārayati*], v.t. *Pl.* (*HŚS*). **1.** to sift. **2.** to winnow. **3.** colloq. to comb out (the hair).

[1]**झारा** *jhārā* [cf. H. *jhārnā*, and *jhāṛnā*], m. reg. (W.) a sieve.

[2]**झारा** *jhārā*, f. metr. Av. heat, burning (= [2]झाल).

झारी *jhārī* [**jhārikā-*], f. a pitcher having a long neck and a spout.

[1]**झाल** *jhāl* [**jhāla-*[1]], f. **1.** fusing, soldering; welding. **2.** solder.

[2]**झाल** *jhāl* [**jhāla-*[2]], f. sharpness, pungency.

[3]**झाल** *jhāl* [cf. *jhallī-*], ? f. reg. (Bihar) cymbals (as used in temple worship).

झालना *jhālnā* [**jhālayati*], v.t. **1.** to solder. **2.** to seal up (a container).

[1]**झालर** *jhālar* [*jhallarī-*[1]], f. a fringe; border, edging. — झालरदार, adj. having a fringe, &c.

[2]**झालर** *jhālar* [*jhallarī-*[2]], ? f. reg. (W.) small cymbals.

[1]**झालरी** *jhālrī* [? conn. *jhallarī-*[1]], f. Brbh. a garland.

[2]**झालरी** *jhālrī* [*jhallarī-*[2]], f. Brbh. cymbals.

झाला *jhālā*, m. resonance (of a stringed instrument).

झिंगवा *jhiṁgvā*, m. a shrimp (= झींगा).

झिंगा *jhiṁgā*, m. E.H. = झींगा.

झिंगारना *jhiṁgārnā*, v.i. *Pl. HŚS.* = झंकारना.

झिंझिना *jhiṁjhinā*, adj. = झीना.

झिंझी *jhiṁjhī*, f. *Pl. HŚS.* a cowrie shell having the top worn away or broken off.

झिंझोटी *jhiṁjhoṭī*, f. *mus.* name of a *rāgiṇī*.

झिंझोड़ना *jhiṁjhoṛnā*, v.t. = झँझोड़ना.

झिंटी *jhiṇṭī*, f. *Pl. HŚS.* name of a shrub, *Barleria cristata* (? = कटसरैया).

झिक- *jhik-*, v.i. Brbh. to look, to glance.

झिक-झिक *jhik-jhik* [cf. H. *jhīṁknā*], f. fretting, whining, complaining.

झिख-झिख *jhikh-jhikh* [cf. H. *jhīṁkhnā*], f. = [1]झख, and cf. झींखना.

झिजक *jhijak*, f. pronun. var. = झिझक.

झिजकना *jhijaknā*, v.i. pronun. var. = झिझकना.

झिझक *jhijhak*, f. a sudden start (of the emotions): **1.** being at a loss, hesitation; fear; shyness, reserve; timidity. **2.** an impulse of anger. — ~ निकलना, hesitation to vanish; anger to subside. ~ निकालना (की), to allay (hesitation); to calm (anger).

झिझकना *jhijhaknā*, v.t. to feel a sudden start (of the emotions): **1.** to be at a loss, to shrink, to hesitate; to be afraid; to be shy, or reserved; to be timid. **2.** to shy (a horse). **3.** to have a fit of anger.

झिड़क *jhiṛak* [cf. H. *jhiṛaknā*], f. **1.** a pull, jerk. ***2.** a rebuke; threat (= झिड़की). **3.** an augury.

झिड़कना *jhiṛaknā* [cf. **jhaṭati*: Pk. *jhaḍaï*], v.t. **1.** to shake, to jerk. **2.** to drive away; to throw aside, or down. ***3.** to snap at (one); to rebuke; to browbeat.

झिड़कवाना *jhiṛakvānā* [cf. H. *jhiṛaknā*], v.t. **1.** to cause to be shaken, &c. (by, से). **2.** to cause to be scolded, &c. (by).

झिड़काना *jhiṛkānā* [cf. H. *jhiṛaknā*], v.t. 1. = झिड़कना. 2. = झिड़कवाना.

झिड़की *jhiṛkī* [cf. H. *jhiṛaknā*], f. snapping at (one); scolding; rebuke; threat. — ~ खाना, to suffer a scolding, &c. ~, or झिड़कियाँ, देना (को), to snap at (one); to scold; to rebuke; to threaten.

झिपना *jhipnā* [cf. H. *jhapnā*], v.i. to be closed (eyes); to be hidden.

झिरझिर *jhirjhir* [cf. H. *jhirnā*], adj. **1.** trickling, splashing. **2.** blowing gently, wafting.

झिरझिरा *jhirjhirā* [cf. **jhirati*[2]], adj. **1.** worn, thin. **2.** flimsy, badly woven (cloth).

झिरझिराना *jhirjhirānā* [cf. H. *jhirjhir*], v.i. to flow gently, to trickle; to waft.

झिरी *jhirī*, f. **1.** a crack, chink, slit. **2.** a small source or spring (of water). **3.** reg. (W.) grain, esp. wheat, damaged by frost.

झिलँगा *jhilaṁgā*, adj. & m. **1.** adj. worn, ragged. **2.** m. an old bed with loose or broken stringing.

झिलना *jhilnā* [cf. H. *jhelnā*], v.i. **1.** to be sensed, or experienced. **2.** to be borne, carried.

झिलम *jhilam*, f. Av. chain-mail attached to a helmet as protection for the neck, hauberk.

झिलमिल *jhilmil* [cf. **jhil-*], f. m. & adj. **1.** f. m. sparkling, shimmering; flashing; twinkling. **2.** flickering. **3.** indistinct light (of dawn or dusk). **4.** Av. a type of finely woven cloth, muslin. **5.** Av. armour: ? coat of mail. **6.** adj. = झिलमिला.

झिलमिला *jhilmilā* [cf. H. *jhilmil*], adj. **1.** sparkling, &c. (cf. झिलमिल, 1., 2). **2.** fine (of texture: as muslin). **3.** indistinct (light); vague (as an allusion).

झिलमिलाना *jhilmilānā* [cf. H. *jhilmil*], v.i. & v.t. **1.** v.i. to sparkle, to shimmer; to twinkle. **2.** to flicker. **3.** v.t. to cause to sparkle.

झिलमिलाहट *jhilmilāhaṭ* [cf. H. *jhilmilānā*], f. = झिलमिल, 1., 2.

झिलमिली *jhilmilī* [cf. H. *jhilmil*], f. **1.** f. a shutter or venetian blind. **2.** a screen. **3.** a type of ear-ring. **4.** sparkle, shimmer, &c.

झिल्लड़ *jhillaṛ*, adj. **1.** thin (of material). **2.** open (of weave: = झिलमिला, 3).

[1]**झिल्ली** *jhillī*, f. **1.** a membrane; lining; film. **2.** *med.* cataract. **3.** a chrysalis. **4.** parchment. — झिल्लीदार [P. *-dār*], adj. having a membrane, &c.

[2]**झिल्ली** *jhillī* [S.], f. a cricket.

झींखना *jhīṁkhnā*, v.t. **1.** to grieve, to regret; to lament. **2.** to fret, to complain.

झींगर *jhīṁgar*, m. pronun. var. = झींगुर.

झींगा *jhīṁgā* [**jhiṅga-*], m. **1.** a shrimp, prawn. **2.** [× H. *jhīṁgur*] reg. (E.) an insect which attacks cotton crops.

झींगुर *jhīṁgur* [**jhiṅgura-*: Pk. *jhiṁgira-*], m. a cricket.

झींसी *jhīṁsī*, f. drizzle, light rain. — ~ पड़ना, light rain to fall.

झीखना *jhīkhnā*, v.i. = झींखना.

झीना *jhīnā* [**jhīna-*: Pk. *jhīṇa-*], adj. **1.** worn, wasted. **2.** thin. **3.** delicate, slender; fine (texture); subtle.

झीमना *jhīmnā*, v.t. = झूमना.

झील *jhīl* [**jhilla-*[1]: Pk. *jhillī-*], f. **1.** a lake. **2.** a pool.

झीलर *jhīlar* [cf. H. *jhīl*], m. a small lake, or pool.

झीसी *jhīsī*, f. = झींसी.

झुंगी *jhuṅgī*, f. Panj. = झुगिया.

झुँझलाना *jhuṁjhlānā*, v.i. **1.** to be irritable, to snap (at). **2.** to flare up in anger.

झुँझलाहट *jhuṁjhlāhaṭ* [cf. H. *jhuṁjhlānā*], f. **1.** irritability. **2.** sudden anger, loss of temper.

झुंड *jhuṇḍ* [**jhuṇḍra-*], m. **1.** a flock (of animals or birds); a troop; herd; swarm. **2.** a crowd, band. **3.** clump. — ~ के ~, m. entire flocks; dense flocks.

झुकना *jhuknā* [**jhukkati*], v.i. **1.** to be bent down, to bend; to droop; to lean, to incline; to sink; to be lowered, to drop (a flag, or the eyes); to nod, to sink (the head). **2.** to bend down, to stoop; to crouch. **3.** to submit, to yield (to, के सामने, के आगे); to pay homage (to). **4.** to be perplexed (the mind). **5.** to incline (towards, की ओर); to show an interest (in), or a proclivity (for). **6.** to round, to turn (on, पर, or की ओर). **7.** colloq. to be spent or thrown away (in or on, में). — झुककर बैठना, to crouch.

झुकाना *jhukānā* [cf. H. *jhuknā*], v.t. **1.** to cause to bend downwards, to bend; to cause to sink, to lower (as a flag, or the eyes); to nod, to incline (the head). **2.** to cause to bow or to stoop; to subjugate; to cause to acquiesce. **3.** to turn (one) (towards, की ओर); to cause (one) to accept; to force (one) (into, में: a subordinate post, or position). **4.** colloq. to pour (as a commodity from its container: = डालना).

झुकाव *jhukāv* [cf. H. *jhuknā*], m. **1.** the property or state of being bent down, bowed, &c.; slope; curvature. **2.** stoop. **3.** bend; tilt, incline; list. **4.** inclination (towards, की ओर); proclivity.

झुकावट *jhukāvaṭ* [cf. H. *jhuknā*], f. **1.** bending downwards; stooping, nodding. **2.** the state of being bent downwards, &c.

झुगिया *jhugiyā* [cf. H. *jhuṅgī*; Panj. *jhuggī*], f. Brbh. a hut, &c. (= झुँगी).

झुटपुट *jhuṭpuṭ*, m. = झुटपुटा.

झुटपुटा *jhuṭpuṭā* [? H. *jhūṭh* + H. [1]*phūṭ*], m. twilight: dawn; dusk.

झुटाना *jhuṭānā* [cf. H. *jūṭh*], v.t. **1.** to pollute (food, or utensils) by touching or tasting. **2.** to leave (uneaten food).

[1]**झुटालना** *jhuṭālnā* [cf. H. *jhūṭ*], v.t. = झुटाना.

[2]**झुटालना** *jhuṭālnā*, v.t. pronun. var. = झुठलाना.

झुट्ठल *jhuṭṭhal* [cf. H. *jhūṭhā*, *jhuṭhālnā*], adv. in pretence, or in fun.

झुठलाना *jhuṭhlānā* [cf. H. *jhūṭhā*], v.t. **1.** to cause to appear false, or wrong; to cast doubt on. **2.** to show to be false, or wrong; to disprove; to belie. **3.** to misrepresent, to falsify.

झुठाई *jhuṭhāī*, f. = झूठापन.

झुठाना *jhuṭhānā*, v.t. = झुठलाना.

झुठालना *jhuṭhālnā*, v.t. = झुठलाना.

झुनझुना *jhunjhunā*, m. a child's rattle.

झुनझुनाना *jhunjhunānā* [cf. H. *jhanjhanānā*], v.i. & v.t. **1.** v.i. to ring, to resound; to jingle; to rattle; to clash. **2.** to tingle, to become numb (the limbs). **3.** v.t. to cause to ring, resound, &c.

झुनझुनी *jhunjhunī* [cf. H. *jhanjhanī*, *jhunjhunānā*], f. **1.** tingling, numbness (of the limbs). **2.** *Pl.* an anklet, or anklets (with bells). — ~ **चढ़ना** or **पड़ना**, to feel numbness, pins and needles (in a limb).

झुन्नी *jhunnī*, f. = **झुनझुनी**.

झुमका *jhumkā* [cf. **jhumma-*], m. **1.** a bell-shaped pendant (of an ear-ring). **2.** cluster. — **झुमकेदार** [P. *-dār*], adj. having a pendant; clustering.

झुमकी *jhumkī*, f. dimin. = **झुमका**, 1.

झुरकट *jhurkaṭ*, adj. *Pl.* = **झुरकुट**.

झुरकुट *jhurkuṭ*, [cf. H. *jhurnā*], adj. **1.** withered. **2.** thin, wasted.

झुरझुरी *jhurjhurī*, f. a shivering fit; the onset of fever; tremor, thrill.

झुरना *jhurnā* [**jhurati*²], v.i. **1.** to shrivel, to waste away; to wither, to fade. **2.** to pine, to grieve; to endure suffering.

झुरमुट *jhurmuṭ*, m. **1.** a dense crowd; large gathering. **2.** dense undergrowth, a thicket.

झुरा- *jhurā-* [cf. H. *jhūr-*], v.i. Av. to waste away, to be dried up; to pine.

झुर्री *jhurrī*, f. a wrinkle, fold, pucker.

झुलना *jhulnā*, m. = **झूलना**.

झुलस *jhulas* [cf. H. *jhulasnā*], f. = **झुलसन**.

झुलसन *jhulsan* [cf. H. *jhulasnā*], f. **1.** scorching, &c. **2.** being scorched, &c. **3.** scorching heat.

झुलसना *jhulasnā*, v.i. & v.t. **1.** v.i. to be scorched; to be charred, blackened; to be singed; to be branded. **2.** to be parched, to wither. **3.** v.t. to scorch, &c.

झुलसाना *jhulsānā* [cf. H. *jhulasnā*], v.t. to cause to be scorched, singed or branded (by, **से**).

झुलाना *jhulānā* [cf. H. *jhūlnā*], v.t. **1.** to cause to swing or to sway (an object). **2.** to swing, to rock (a person). **3.** to dangle, to hang. **4.** to keep (one) running to and fro, or active (at, **में**). **5.** to keep one waiting anxiously.

झूँगा *jhūṁgā*, m. reg. (W.) brushwood; scrub.

झूँझल *jhūṁjhal*, f. = **झुँझलाहट**.

झूँठ *jhūṁṭh*, m. & adj. pronun. var. **1.** m. = **झूठ**. **2.** adj. = ¹**झूठा**.

झूँठर *jhūṁṭhar*, f. *hist.* fields yielding a double crop (= ²**झूठन**).

झूंदी *jhūṁdī*, f. *hist.* a lot or parcel of land as part of a coparcenary tenure; the revenue assessed on such a lot.

झूठ *jhūṭh* [**jhūṭṭha-*: Pk. *jhuṭṭha-*], m. & adj. **1.** m. a lie; falsehood. **2.** adj. lying, false (= ¹**झूठा**). — ~ **जानना**, to regard as a lie, to disbelieve. ~ **पकड़ना (का)**, to detect falsehood; to convict (one) of a lie. ~ **बनाना**, to invent a lie, or a deception. ~ **बोलना**, to tell a lie; not to speak the truth. ~ **लगाना**, to speak untruth (of, **को**); to calumniate. **सफ़ेद** ~, m. a white lie; a brazen (if condonable) lie. – **झूठ-बयानी करना**, to give false evidence, &c. **झूठ-भरा**, adj. false, spurious; mendacious. **झूठ-बयानी**, f. false testimony; perjury. **झूठ-मूठ**, m. & adv. lying, falsehood; falsely, fraudulently; vainly; with no good reason or basis, in fun. **झूठ-सच**, m. falsehood and truth: misrepresentation; calumny. **झूठ-सच जोड़ना**, to join falsehood and truth: to embroider on the truth; to misrepresent. **झूठ-सच लगाना (को)**, to misrepresent; to calumniate.

¹**झूठन** *jhūṭhan*, f. = **जूठन**.

²**झूठन** *jhūṭhan* [H. *jūṭhan* × H. ¹*jhūṭhan*], f. *hist.* land yielding a second crop.

¹**झूठा** *jhūṭhā* [**jhūṭṭha-*: Pk. *jhuṭṭha-*], adj. & m. **1.** adj. lying; false. **2.** insincere, hypocritical. **3.** illusory, unsound (belief); vain. **4.** counterfeit, forged, spurious. **5.** impure (metal, alloy, commodity). **6.** unreliable, defective; useless. **7.** m. a liar, a false person. &c. **झूठों का पीर**, m. fig. a consummate liar. — ~ **पड़ना**, to be proved, or to prove, false, untrustworthy, &c.; to fail, to be useless (as a limb, a tool, a weapon). ~ **बनाना**, = **झुठलाना**, 1., 2. **झूठे**, adv. uselessly, in vain, needlessly. **झूठों**, adv. falsely; as a pretence; as a formality. – **झूठी-सच्ची**, f. = **झूठ-सच**.

²**झूठा** *jhūṭhā*, adj. & m. pronun. var. = **जूठा**. — **झूठा-झाटा**, m. leavings (= **जूठा**).

झूठापन *jhūṭhāpan* [cf. H. *jhūṭhā*], m. falsehood.

झूठियाइल *jhūṭhiyāil*, f. *hist.* = ²**झूठन**.

झूड़ *jhūṛ* [**jhūṭa-*¹], m. *Pl.* a bush; brushwood.

झूना *jhūnā* [**jhūrṇa-*], adj. **1.** Brbh. = **झीना**. **2.** *Pl.* a kind of muslin.

झूपा *jhūpā* [**jhuppa-*²], m. reg. (W.) collection, heap, pile.

झूम *jhūm* [cf. H. *jhūmnā*], f. swaying, swinging.

झूमक *jhūmak* [cf. *jhumma-*], m. **1.** Brbh. Av. = **झूमर**, 2., 3. **2.** reg. (Bihar) an ear ornament, pendant.

झूमना *jhūmnā* [? conn. **kṣumbhati, kṣubh-*; ×**jhaṭ-* or **jhamp-*[1]], v.i. **1.** to sway, to wave; to rock; to stagger, to reel; to nod (from sleep). **2.** to move imposingly (a person, or an animal). **3.** fig. to be delighted, or triumphant. **4.** to gather, to lower (clouds). — **दरवाज़े पर हाथी ~**, an elephant to sway at one's gate: to live in great prosperity and contentment.

झूमर *jhūmar* [cf. *jhumma-*], m. **1.** an ornament for the forehead or side of the head (a number or a series of chains, forming a fringe). **2.** a ring-dance (by a group of women). **3.** a type of song (as accompanying this dance, or sung at marriages, or at the Holī festival).

[1]**झूर** *jhūr* [**jhūṭa-*[1]], m. reg. brushwood.

[2]**झूर** *jhūr* [cf. H. *jhūr-*], adj. & ? m. **1.** adj. Av. dry. **2.** ? m. reg. (W.) drought, &c. (= **झूरा**).

झूर- *jhūr-* [**jhūrati*: Pk. *jhūraï*], v.i. Brbh. Av. to waste away, to wither; to pine.

झूरा *jhūrā* [cf. H. *jhūr-*], m. reg. (W.) drought; famine.

झूल *jhūl* [cf. H. *jhūlnā*], f. **1.** swinging. **2.** [A. *jull*], a horse-cloth; caparisoning. **3.** colloq. an over-loose garment.

झूलन *jhūlan* [cf. H. *jhūlnā*], f. **1.** swinging. **2.** *hind.* name of a festival held in the month of Sāvan (when idols of Kṛṣṇa and Rādhā are swung in swings).

झूलना *jhūlnā* [**jhulyati*: Pk. *jhullaï*], v.i. & m. **1.** v.i. to swing, to sway; to dangle. **2.** to swing (for amusement or exercise). **3.** fig. to be in suspense. **4.** m. a hanging bridge (= **झूला**, 5). **5.** *pros.* name of a metre.

झूला *jhūlā* [cf. H. *jhūlnā*], m. **1.** a swing; a swinging-rope. **2.** transf. a type of song sung by women when swinging. **3.** a hammock. **4.** a cradle. **5.** a hanging bridge. — **~ झूलन**, to swing; to rock. **~ डालना**, to put up or to hang a swing, &c. (in or from, **में**).

झूली *jhūlī* [cf. H. *jhūlā*], f. reg. (W.) **1.** a cloth used as a winnowing fan. **2.** a hammock.

झेंपना *jheṁpnā*, v.i. to feel embarrassment or shame.

झेर *jher*, m. Brbh. = **झेरा**.

झेरा *jherā* [**adhyākara-*], m. reg (W.) **1.** an old well-shaft. **2.** a Brbh. pit-fall; difficulty, trouble.

झेलना *jhelnā* [**jhelati*], v.t. **1.** to endure, to bear; to tolerate. **2.** to undergo, to experience; to receive, to digest (as information, an experience).

झोंक *jhoṁk* [conn. **jhuṅkati*], f. **1.** gust, blast (of wind). **2.** impulse, impetus; colloq. a go, turn. **3.** impact, influence (as of alcohol, or of sleep); a fit, access; heat, frenzy (of action or emotion); blow, shock. **4.** momentum, onrush. **5.** weight, pressure (as of a wall on a buttress); burden. **6.** [×H. *jhuknā*] dip, inclination (of a scale). — **~ में आकर करना**, to carry out (as a task) with speed and singlemindedness. **~ में पड़ना**, to gather momentum, to get under way.

झोंकना *jhoṁknā* [conn. **jhuṅkati*], v.t. & m. **1.** v.t. to throw, to toss (into, **में**); to throw in (fuel), to stoke; to pour in or down (in quantity); to heat (a furnace, an oven). **2.** to push, to impel. **3.** to squander (in or on, **में**). **4.** to foist (upon, **पर** or **के ऊपर**: a task); to impute (to). **5.** m. colloq. fuel (as for a furnace).

झोंका *jhoṁkā* [cf. H. *jhoṁknā*], m. **1.** a gust, puff, blast (of wind). **2.** a downpour (rain). **3.** a wave, roller. **4.** sudden drowsiness, a nap. **5.** a blow, shock; a hold (in wrestling). **6.** swaying, swinging. — **~ खाना**, to suffer a shock, to receive a blow; to heel (a ship in a storm); to veer (off course).

झोंकाना *jhoṁkānā* [cf. H. *jhoṁknā*], v.t. to cause to be thrown, tossed, &c. (by, **से**).

झोंकिया *jhoṁkiyā* [cf. H. *jhoṁknā*], m. stoker (of a furnace).

झोंझ *jhoṁjh*, m. reg. **1.** nest (of a bird); fig. refuge. **2.** paunch; swelling.

झोंटा *jhoṁṭā* [**jhoṇṭa-*], m. **1.** coil, bunch (esp. of a woman's hair, = **झोंपा**); top-knot; pigtail. **2.** reg. (W.) a male buffalo (so called on account of its hump). **3.** swing, swaying. — **झोंटा-झोंटी**, f. mutual pulling and tugging at the hair of the head, a scuffle. **झोंटा-झोंटी करना**, to fight, to scuffle. **झोंटी-झोंटा**, m. = **झोंटा-झोंटी**.

झोंटी *jhoṁṭī* [**jhoṇṭa-*], f. dimin. 1. = **झोंटा**, 1., 2. **2.** reg. (W.) a buffalo calf.

झोंपड़ा *jhoṁpṛā* [**jhompa-*], m. a hut (built of earth or clay, and roofed with thatch, reeds, &c.); a shed.

झोंपड़ी *jhoṁpṛī* [cf. **jhompa-*], f. = **झोंपड़ा**.

झोंपा *jhoṁpā*, m. **1.** a coil, bunch (esp. of hair on a woman's head, = **झोंटा**). **2.** Av. a bunch, cluster.

झोकंड *jhokaṇḍ* [cf. H. *jho(ṁ)knā*], m. reg. (W.) fireplace (of a sugar-boiling house).

झोक *jhok*, f. pronun. var. = **झोंक**.

झोकट *jhokaṭ*, m. reg. (W.) = **झोकंड**.

झोकना *jhoknā*, v.t. = **झोंकना**.

झोकवाह् *jhokvāh*, m. reg. (E.) a stoker (= झोंकिया).

झोकिया *jhokiyā*, m. pronun. var. a stoker (= झोंकिया).

झोझ *jhojh*, m. = झोंझ.

झोटा *jhoṭā*, m. = झोंटा.

झोना *jhonā* [? **adhyāvahati*; ← Panj. *jhoṇā*], v.t. reg. to set in motion (as a wheel, or a process).

झोरना *jhornā* [**jhoṭati*: Pk. *jhoḍaï*], v.t. reg. **1.** to shake, to shake off, or down; to beat soundly. **2.** colloq. to amass (money).

[1]**झोल** *jhol* [**jhola*-[1]: Pk. *jholiā*-], m. **1.** m. bagginess, puckering; a rumple, pucker, tuck. **2.** free or swinging end (as of a sari). **3.** Brbh. a screen, curtain. **4.** sac, membrane; womb. — ~ **खाना**, to pucker; to hang, to sag. ~ **डालना**, to make baggy; to make a tuck, &c. (in, **में**). ~ **निकालना**, to remove bagginess, or a tuck, &c. (from, **में से**). – **झोल-झाल**, m. & adj. bagginess; loose. – **झोलदार** [P. *-dār*], adj. loose, &c.

[2]**झोल** *jhol* [**jhola*-[2]], m. broth, soup; juice, gravy. — **झोलदार** [P. *-dār*], adj. having a juice.

[3]**झोल** *jhol* [? conn. **jhoṭati*, H. *jhornā*], ? m. Brbh. Av. ashes, dust.

[1]**झोला** *jholā* [**jhola*-[1]: Pk. *jholiā*-], m. **1.** a bag, sack (esp. one closed with a draw-string). **2.** a case (as of cloth, canvas).

[2]**झोला** *jholā* [? conn. **jholayati*], m. Av. a blast of wind (either hot or cold, harmful to crops and vegetation).

झोली *jholī* [**jhola*-[1]: Pk. *jholiā*-], f. **1.** a bag, sack (cf. [1]**झोला**). **2.** a pouch, wallet. **3.** the loose portion of a garment (held out to receive sthg). — ~ **डालना**, or **फैलाना**, to hold out the skirt of one's garment (as to receive alms). ~ **भरना**, to give alms, &c. (to, **की**).

झौंकना *jhaumknā*, v.t. reg. (W.) to butt, to gore.

झौंर *jhaumr*, f. m. Brbh. Av. **1.** a bunch, cluster (as of fruit). **2.** a thicket. **3.** a group. **4.** an ornament worn on the head.

झौंरी *jhaumrī*, f. reg. (W.) handful or bundle (of dry weeds, cleared from a field).

-झौंसा *-jhaumsā*, adj. formant. scorched (e.g. **मुँह-झौंसा**, adj. colloq. pej. wretched, confounded).

झौ *jhau*, f. reg. *Pl.* fire, flame, heat.

झौड़ *jhauṛ* [**jhapaḍ*-], f. a quarrel, row; clash.

झौना *jhaunā* [cf. H. *jhāū*], m. a large open basket (made of tamarisk twigs; used for carrying earth, &c).

झौवा *jhauvā* [*jhāvu*-, Pa. *jhāvuka*-], m. reg. = **झौना**.

ट

ट *ṭa*, the eleventh consonant of the Devanāgarī syllabary. — **टकार**, m. the sound /ṭ/; the letter ट.

[1]**टंकी** *ṭaṅkī* [Engl. *tank*], f. a tank, pond; reservoir.

[2]**टंकी** *ṭaṅkī* [S.], f. *mus.* name of a *rāgiṇī*.

टंकक *ṭaṅkak* [S.], m. a typist.

टंकण *ṭaṅkaṇ*, m. typing. — **टंकण-यंत्र**, m. a typewriter.

टँकना *ṭaṁknā* [*ṭaṅkati*], v.i. **1.** to be stitched; to be sewn on. **2.** to be joined, or attached.

टंका *ṭaṅkā* [*ṭaṅka-*[1]: ← central Asia], m. *hist.* = **टका**, 1.

टँकाना *ṭaṁkānā* [cf. H. *ṭāṁknā*], v.t. = **टँकवाना**.

टंकार *ṭaṅkār* [*ṭaṅkāra-*], f. **1.** twang, twanging; a ringing sound. **2.** cry, howl.

टँकारना *ṭaṁkārnā* [cf. H. *ṭaṅkār*], v.i. to twang; to ring; to strike (a clock, gong).

टँकोर *ṭaṁkor*, f. m. **1.** Av. twang (of a bow). **2.** Brbh. a light blow (= **टकोर**).

टँगड़ी *ṭaṁgṛī* [cf. *ṭaṅga-*[3]], f. the leg; the lower leg.

टँगना *ṭaṁgnā* [cf. H. *ṭāṁgnā*], v.i. & m. **1.** v.i. to hang, to be suspended, hung. **2.** to be hanged. **3.** m. a line, cord or pole (for hanging clothes, &c).

टँगवाना *ṭaṁgvānā* [cf. H. *ṭāṁgnā*], v.t. to cause to be suspended (by, **से**).

टँगाना *ṭaṁgānā* [cf. H. *ṭāṁgnā*], v.t. **1.** to cause to be suspended (by, **से**). **2.** to suspend, to hang (= **टाँगना**).

टँगारी *ṭaṁgārī*, f. reg. (W.) a carpenter's axe.

टँगाव *ṭaṁgāv* [cf. H. *ṭaṁgānā*], m. hanging, suspension.

टंच *ṭañc*, adj. reg. *Pl. HŚS.* miserly.

टँच *ṭaṁc* [cf. H. *ṭāṁcnā*], f. Brbh. sewing, stitching.

टंटा *ṭaṇṭā* [**ṭaṇṭa-*], m. **1.** wrangling, squabble, row. **2.** turmoil, confusion. **3.** difficulty, trouble; rigmarole. — **~ मचाना**, to stir up a quarrel, &c. – **टंटेबाज़** [P. *-bāz*], adj. & m. quarrelsome; a quarrelsome person.

टंटाल *ṭaṇṭāl*, m. = **टंटा**.

टक *ṭak* [cf. H. *ṭaknā*], f. a gaze, stare. — **~ बाँधना** or **लगाना** (**पर**), to fix the gaze (on); to aim (at); to look for support (to). – **टक-टक देखना**, **~ बाँधना**, 1.

टकटकाना *ṭakṭakānā* [conn. **ṭhakk-*[1]], v.t. & v.i. **1.** v.t. to knock, to rap. **2.** v.i. to knock, to rattle.

टकटकी *ṭakṭakī* [cf. H. *ṭak*], f. a fixed stare. — **~ बाँधना**, or **लगाना** (**पर**), = **~ बाँधना**, 1. **~ लगना**, to stare, to be wide open (the eyes).

[1]**टकना** *ṭaknā*, v.i. = **तकना**.

[2]**टकना** *ṭaknā*, m. pronun. var. = **टखना**.

टकराना *ṭakrānā* [cf. H. *ṭakkar*], v.i. & v.t. **1.** v.i. = **टक्कर खाना**. **2.** to collide (with, **से**). **3.** to oppose, to confront. **4.** v.t. to knock together, or against; to dash together, or against; to butt. **5.** to bring into conflict. — **माथा ~**, to bow the head (to the ground in obeisance); to make great efforts.

टकसाल *ṭaksāl* [*ṭaṅkaśālā-*], f. a mint, assay office. — **~ चढ़ाना**, to assay.

टकसालिया *ṭaksāliyā* [cf. H. *ṭaksāl*], m. = **टकसाली**.

टकसाली *ṭaksālī* [cf. H. *ṭaksāl*], adj. & m. **1.** adj. having to do with a mint. **2.** tried, tested, of true ring; genuine, sound. **3.** m. *Pl. HŚS.* superintendent of a mint.

टकसालीपन *ṭaksālīpan* [cf. H. *ṭaksālī*], m. **1.** genuineness, currency (as of language). **2.** good quality (as of language).

टकही *ṭak'hī* [cf. *ṭaṅka-*[1]: ← central Asia], f. reg. (Bihar) an accountant's commission.

टका *ṭakā* [*ṭaṅka-*[1]], m. **1.** *hist.* a copper coin worth two former pice. **2.** *ayur.* a weight (three *tolās*). **3.** Brbh. Av. a rupee. **4.** money. — **टके का**, adj. poor; of no worth or account (a person). **टके को न पूछना**, fig. not to take any notice (of, **से**). **टके कोस का दौड़नेवाला**, m. fig. one ready to work excessively hard for little reward. **टके गज़ की चाल**, f. a slow or ineffective way of proceeding. – **टका-भर**, adj. a little, just a little. **टका-सा जवाब**, adj. a short answer; a blunt refusal. **टका-सा मुँह लेकर रह जाना**, to be speechless from shame or embarrassment. **टका-सी जान**, f. = next. **टकी-सी जान**, f. fig. one powerless, or of little account; *Pl. HŚS.* a single, or isolated life: a person having no relatives. दो टके का, adj. worthless, trashy.

टकुआ *ṭakuā* [*tarku-*] **1.** a spindle. **2.** a pointed instrument; an awl.

टकैत *ṭakait* [cf. H. *ṭakā*], adj. *Pl. HŚS.* moneyed, rich.

टकैया *ṭakaiyā* [cf. H. *ṭakā*], adj. pej. cheap.

टकोर *ṭakor* [cf. H. *ṭakornā*], f. m. *Pl. HŚS.* **1.** a poultice. **2.** a light blow, tap; drum-beat.

टकोरना *ṭakornā*, v.t. *Pl. HŚS.* **1.** to foment. **2.** to strike lightly.

टक्कर *ṭakkar* [*ṭakkarā-*], f. **1.** striking, knocking (against, से); impact. **2.** a collision (between, में or की). **3.** competition, rivalry (between, में); conflict, clash. — ~ का, adj. equal, comparable. ~ खाते, or मारते, फिरना, to wander aimlessly, or in a wretched state. ~, or टक्करें खाना (से), to knock (against), to suffer an impact; to collide (with); to be dashed (against); to stumble; to vie (with). ~ खिलाना, v.t. to knock or to dash (against, से), &c. ~ मारना, to butt; to strive; to endeavour; to strive in vain. ~ लगना (से), to knock (against), &c. (= ~ खाना). ~ लगाना, to compete, to clash (with, से). ~ लेना (से), to confront, to contend (with). पहाड़ से ~ लेना, to face up to an opponent of much superior strength.

टखना *ṭakhnā*, m. the ankle.

टखनी *ṭakhnī* [cf. H. *ṭakhnā*], f. dimin. = टखना.

टगर *ṭagar*, f. a kind of tree having white flowers.

टघरना *ṭagharnā*, v.i. reg. to melt.

टघराना *ṭaghrānā*, v.t. reg. to melt (= पिघलाना).

टटका *ṭaṭkā*, adj. reg. fresh, new, recent.

[1]**टटरी** *ṭaṭrī*, f. a fence, hedge, screen (see टट्टी).

[2]**टटरी** *ṭaṭrī* [cf. H. *ṭāṁṭ*], f. crown (of the head).

टटवानी *ṭaṭvānī* [cf. H. *ṭaṭṭū*], f. reg. a pony mare.

टटाना *ṭaṭānā* [cf. **taṭṭ-*], v.i. **1.** *Pl. HŚS.* to be dried. **2.** reg. (E.) to ache (the limbs or body).

टटिया *ṭaṭiyā*, f. Brbh. = टट्टी.

टटिहरी *ṭaṭihrī* [*ṭiṭṭibha-*; ← Panj. *ṭaṭīhrī*], m. = टिटिहरी.

टटीरी *ṭaṭīrī*, f. = टिटिहरी.

टटोना *ṭaṭonā*, v.t. = टटोलना.

टटोल *ṭaṭol* [cf. H. *ṭaṭolnā*], f. feeling, groping.

टटोलना *ṭaṭolnā*, v.t. **1.** to feel, to feel for, to grope. **2.** to test by feeling. **3.** colloq. to investigate, to sound out, to test, to try.

टट्टर *ṭaṭṭar* [cf. **traṭṭa-*], m. **1.** a bamboo or wickerwork frame, or screen. **2.** a shutter. **3.** a hiding-place. — ~ देना, or लगाना (पर), to screen; to enclose.

टट्टी *ṭaṭṭī* [**traṭṭa-*: Pk. *ṭaṭṭī-*], f. sthg. woven: **1.** a bamboo framework, trellis. **2.** a screen (esp. of khas grass: kept wet, it cools the air entering a building); shutter. **3.** transf. a lavatory. **4.** excrement. — ~ करना, to defecate. ~ की आड़ में, or से, शिकार खेलना, to hunt or to shoot from shelter; to be an unseen enemy. ~ की ओट में, or से, शिकार खेलना, id. ~ की ओट बैठना, to sit behind a screen; to act secretly. ~ जाना, to go to relieve oneself. ~ लगना, to wish to defecate. ~ लगाना, to put up a screen or shutter. धोखे की ~, f. a cover for deceit; a camouflage.

टट्टू *ṭaṭṭū* [**ṭaṭṭu-*], m. a pony. — अड़ियल ~, m. a stubborn, mulish person. किराए, or भाड़े का ~, a hireling.

टठिया *ṭaṭhiyā*, f. reg. *Pl. HŚS.* a flat metal (? or earthen) dish (= थाली).

[1]**टन** *ṭan*, m. f. a ringing sound, clang, clash; twang. — टन-टन, f. ringing, clanging, &c.

[2]**टन** *ṭan* [Engl. *ton*], m. a ton.

टनक *ṭanak* [cf. H. *ṭanaknā*], f. **1.** a clashing or ringing sound. **2.** a jingling, tinkling.

टनकना *ṭanaknā*, v.i. to clash, to ring (= टन-टन करना).

टनटनाना *ṭanṭanānā* [cf. H. *ṭan-ṭan*], v.i. & v.t. **1.** v.i. to ring, to resound (a bell, a gong). **2.** v.t. to ring, to strike. **3.** colloq. to tune (an instrument).

टना *ṭanā*, m. clitoris (= टन्ना).

टनाका *ṭanākā* [cf. H. *ṭan*], m. a loud ringing, clanging.

टन्ना *ṭannā*, m. = टना.

[1]**टप** *ṭap* [onom.], m. **1.** the sound of dropping or dripping (as of rain). **2.** the sound of a soft object (as fruit) falling to the ground. — ~ से, adv. all of a sudden; quickly. – टप-टप, adv. in continuous drops; in a shower (as rain, tears, bullets); continuously. टपाटप, adv. = id.

[2]**टप** *ṭap*, m. hood, roof (of a vehicle).

टपक *ṭapak* [cf. H. *ṭapaknā*], f. **1.** dropping, dripping. **2.** sound of dripping.

टपकना *ṭapaknā* [*ṭapp-], v.i. **1.** to drop, to drip; to dribble; to exude; to leak. **2.** to fall (fruit). **3.** to appear (suddenly). **4.** to be evident (emotion, or a disposition). **5.** to be abundant in, to suffuse (as youth the body). **6.** to long or to yearn (the heart).

टपका *ṭapkā* [cf. H. *ṭapaknā*], m. **1.** dropping, dripping. **2.** a drop, drip. **3.** transf. a throbbing pain. **4.** a windfall (fruit; esp. a mango). — टपके का, adj. fallen, ripe (fruit). – टपका-टपकी, f. continuous dropping or dripping; a trickle; drizzle.

टपकाना *ṭapkānā* [cf. H. *ṭapaknā*], v.t. to cause to drop, or to drip; to distil.

टपकाव *ṭapkāv* [cf. H. *ṭapaknā*], m. **1.** dripping. **2.** causing to drip; distilling.

टपना *ṭapnā* [cf. H. *ṭāpnā*], v.i. **1.** to leap, to jump (over or across). **2.** to wait (unfed, or with hopes unfilfilled).

टपाना *ṭapānā* [cf. H. *ṭāpnā*], v.t. **1.** to cause to leap, or to bound. **2.** to keep (one) waiting. **3.** colloq. to filch; to smuggle (sthg.) away.

टप्पर *ṭappar* [cf. *tarpa-[1]], m. reg. **1.** a thatch; W. thatched house. **2.** canopy (of a cart). **3.** Bihar. matting.

टप्पा *ṭappā* [cf. *tarpati], m. **1.** the distance of a leap or bound. **2.** a rebound, bounce; ricochet. **3.** range (as of a shot); intervening space; stretch (of terrain). **4.** a type of folk song (Panjab). — ~ खाना, to rebound, to bounce; to ricochet. ~ देना, to leap, to bound.

टब्बर *ṭabbar* [? ← Panj. *ṭabbar*], m. reg. (N.) a family, household.

टमकी *ṭamkī*, f. *Pl. HŚS.* a small drum; a gong.

[1]**टमटम** *ṭamṭam* [? Engl. *tandem*], f. a one-horse carriage (in which two passengers sit in front and two at the rear).

[2]**टमटम** *ṭamṭam*, f. the sound of a drum.

टमाटर *ṭamāṭar* [Engl. *tomato*], m. tomato.

टर *ṭar*, f. a cry; croak (of a frog); chatter; scream; shout. — टर-टर, f. crying out; croaking, chattering, &c.; grumbling; insistence. टर-टर करना, or लगाना, to croak, to chatter, &c.; to be insistent, or obstinate.

टर- *ṭar-* [*ṭarati*], v.i. Brbh. Av. = टलना.

टरकना *ṭaraknā* [cf. *ṭarati*], v.i. = टलना.

टरकाना *ṭarkānā* [cf. H. *ṭaraknā*], v.t. = टालना.

टरटराना *ṭarṭarānā* [cf. H. *ṭar-ṭar*, see s.v. *ṭar*], v.i. = टर्राना.

टर्रटर्र *ṭarr-ṭarr*, f. = टर-टर, see s.v. टर.

टर्रा *ṭarrā*, adj. **1.** refractory, stubborn; insistent (on a point, a view). **2.** vicious (a horse). — टर्रैबाज़ी [P. *-bāzī*], f. insistence, obstinacy.

टर्राना *ṭarrānā* [cf. H. *ṭarrā*], v.i. **1.** to cry out, to croak; to chatter; to scream. **2.** to be insistent or obstinate.

टर्रापन *ṭarrāpan* [cf. H. *ṭarrā*], m. = टर्रैबाज़ी, see s.v. टर्रा.

टर्रू *ṭarrū* [cf. H. *ṭarrānā*], m. *Pl. HŚS.* a child's toy which makes a croak like a frog's.

टलना *ṭalnā* [*ṭalati*], v.i. **1.** to be moved, to move away; to retire, to withdraw; not to appear. **2.** to give way; to draw back (from, से: as from a commitment); to shrink (from). **3.** to turn (from, से), to give up (as a habit). **4.** to pass over, or away (as a period of time, or a danger); to be endured. **5.** to be averted or deflected. **6.** to be postponed, deferred (an event). **7.** to be put off, not acted upon (as a request, a command).

टलमल *ṭalmal*, adj. reeling, trembling.

टलमलाना *ṭalmalānā* [cf. H. *ṭalmal*, and ? *ṭalati*], v.i. & v.t. **1.** v.i. to totter. **2.** v.t. to excite desire or longing in, to tantalise.

टलहा *ṭalhā*, adj. reg. of poor quality (metal).

टल्ला *ṭallā*, m. a shock, blow. — टल्ले मारना, to fritter away time, to wander aimlessly. – टल्ले-नवीसी, f. = टिल्ले-°.

टस *ṭas*, ? f. sound of sthg. heavy being moved. — ~ से मस न होना, not to move, or to yield, the slightest bit; (a situation) to be unchangeable.

टसक *ṭasak* [cf. H. [2]*ṭasaknā*], f. a shooting or throbbing pain; a stitch.

[1]**टसकना** *ṭasaknā*, v.i. **1.** to move; to stir, to shake. **2.** to be moved; to shed tears. **3.** to be ripe (fruit).

[2]**टसकना** *ṭasaknā*, v.i. to shoot with pain, to throb.

टसकाना *ṭaskānā* [cf. H. [1]*ṭasaknā*], v.t. **1.** to move; to stir, to shake. **2.** to disconcert.

टसना *ṭasnā*, v.i. *Pl. HŚS.* to burst, to split apart.

टसर *ṭasar* [conn. *tasara-*; Pk. *ṭasara-*], m. coarse silk, tussore.

टसुआ *ṭasuā* [cf. H. [1]*ṭasaknā*], m. a tear.

टहक *ṭahak* [cf. H. *ṭahaknā*], f. a shooting or throbbing pain (= टसक).

टहकना *ṭahaknā*, v.i. to throb, to shoot with pain; reg. to melt (cf. टपकना).

टह्ना *ṭahnā*, m. a branch (cf. H. टह्नी).

टह्नी *ṭahnī*, f. a small branch, twig.

टहल *ṭahal* [cf. H. *ṭahalnā*], f. **1.** walking to and fro: service, task, duty. **2.** attendance, care; household work. — टहल-टई, f. ? E.H. service, attendance.

टहलना *ṭahalnā* [**ṭahall-*], v.i. to walk up and down; to go for a walk; to saunter.

टहलनी *ṭahalnī* [cf. H. *ṭahalnā*], f. a woman servant, maidservant.

टहलाना *ṭahlānā* [cf. H. *ṭahalnā*], v.t. to cause to walk up and down; to send, or to take for a walk, to lead about.

टहलुआ *ṭahluā* [cf. H. *ṭahal*], m. a servant, attendant.

टहोका *ṭahokā*, m. **1.** a light blow or kick; slap; nudge. **2.** an impulse, shock. — ~ खाना, to suffer a blow, &c. ~ देना, or मारना, to strike, to kick, &c.

टाँक *ṭāṁk* [cf. H. *ṭāṁknā*], f. Brbh. **1.** a metal pin, point; nib. **2.** *Pl. HŚS.* assessment, valuation. **3.** Av. a partic. small weight.

टाँकन *ṭāṁkan* [cf. H. *ṭāṁknā*], f. **1.** stitching; joining. **2.** riveting. **3.** soldering.

टाँकना *ṭāṁknā* [*ṭaṅkati*[1]], v.t. **1.** to join, to fasten; to stitch, to sew on; to rivet; to solder. **2.** to attach, to tack on. **3.** to record, to jot down (a note).

टाँका *ṭāṁkā* [cf. *ṭaṅkati*[1]], m. **1.** a stitch; a join; seam; stitching. **2.** a rivet, split-pin. **3.** solder. **4.** Av. a cauldron. — ~ चलाना, to baste, to tack. ~ देना, or लगाना (में), to stitch; to rivet, to solder; to join. ~ भरना (में), id. टाँके उखड़ना, or उधड़ना, stitches, &c. to loosen, or to come undone; fig. to be ruined. टाँके खुलना, id., 1.; fig. secrets to be exposed or betrayed. टाँके लगाना (में), = ~ लगाना, 1., 2.; to put stitches in (a wound).

टाँकी *ṭāṁkī* [*ṭaṅka-*[2]], f. **1.** a cold chisel. **2.** a piece cut or scooped out (as from a fruit) as a sample.

टाँग *ṭāṁg* [*ṭaṅga-*[3]], f. the leg; the lower leg. — ~ अड़ाना, to interfere (in, में). ~ उठाना, = colloq. to move oneself, to hurry. ~ की राह निकलना, = ~ तले से निकलना. ~ तले से निकलना, to come from under the legs (of, की): to yield (to), to admit defeat. ~ तोड़ना (की), to cripple; to make ineffective; colloq. to murder (a language). ~ लड़ाना, to trip up. टाँगें टूटना, the legs to fail (from fatigue). टाँगें पसारना (अपनी), to stretch out (one's) legs; to be at one's ease. टाँगें रह जाना, the legs to give way, to fail.

टाँगना *ṭāṁgnā* [**ṭaṅg-*], v.t. **1.** to hang up (on, पर), to suspend (from, में or से). **2.** to hang (a person).

[1]**टाँगा** *ṭāṁgā*, m. = ताँगा.

[2]**टाँगा** *ṭāṁgā* [**ṭaṅga-*[2]], m. reg. (Bihar) an adze (= टाँगी).

टाँगी *ṭāṁgī* [**ṭaṅga-*[2]], f. reg. (Bihar) an adze or axe.

टाँच *ṭāṁc* [cf. H. *ṭāṁcnā*], f. **1.** tortuous behaviour. **2.** troublesome or annoying behaviour.

टाँचना *ṭāṁcnā* [**ṭañcati*; ? ← G. *ṭāṁcvuṁ*], v.t. **1.** to stitch (*HŚS.*); to patch. **2.** ? *Pl.* to move crookedly, or obliquely. **3.** *Pl.* to cajole, to hover.

टाँचा *ṭāṁcā* [cf. H. *ṭāṁcnā*], m. reg. (W.) contraction of the leg sinews (in cattle).

टाँची *ṭāṁcī*, f. a long narrow bag; a sewn water-bag.

टाँट *ṭāṁṭ*, m. f. crown of the head; skull, cranium. — ~ के बाल उड़ जाना, fig. to be in a state of deprivation. ~ के बाल उड़ाना, to beat the hair from (one's) skull: to beat mercilessly. ~ खुजलाना, fig. to earn a thrashing. ~ गंजी होना, = ~ के बाल उड़ जाना.

ठाँठी *ṭhāṁṭhī* f. reg. (Bihar) = टठिया, थाली.

टाँड़ *ṭāṁṛ* [*tandra-*], m. **1.** reg. (W.) a scaffolding, platform (in a field, from which crops can be watched). **2.** a shelf. **3.** reg. (Bihar) a drill (for sowing seed).

टाँड़ो *ṭāṁṛo* [*tandra-*], m. Brbh. **1.** file or line (as of cattle); train (of dependants or devotees); caravan (of merchants). **2.** goods, baggage (of merchants).

टाँयटाँय *ṭāṁy-ṭāṁy*, f. chatter, &c. (cf. चाँय-चाँय). — ~ फिस्स, colloq. a flop.

टाँस *ṭāṁs*, f. cramp.

टाट *ṭāṭ* [**tratta-*: Pk. *taṭṭī-*], m. sacking; a piece of sacking; matting. — ~ में मूँज का बखिया, m. grass stitching in sackcloth: poor goods poorly packaged.

टाटक *ṭāṭak*, adj. = टटका.

टाटर *ṭāṭar*, m. Av. crown of the head (= टाँट).

टाटी *ṭāṭī*, f. = टट्टी.

टाड़ *ṭāṛ* [?? conn. *ṭal-*[2], or ← Panj.], f. Brbh. an ornament worn on the upper arm.

टाड़ा *ṭāṛā*, m. reg. (Bihar) a pot for ghī.

[1]**टाप** *ṭāp* [**ṭappa-*[2]], f. **1.** hoof (of a horse). **2.** sound of hooves. — ~ मारना, to paw, or to beat the ground (a horse, with its hooves).

[2]टाप *ṭāp* [**tarpa-*[1], **ṭappa-*[1]], reg. (Bihar) a bamboo basket, or net (for catching fish, or for weeding).

टापना *ṭāpnā* [**tarpati*; cf. **ṭappa-*[2]], v.i. & v.t. **1.** v.i. to paw, or to beat the ground (a horse). **2.** to stamp (as in impatience, pain, despair). **3.** v.t. to jump over (a wall, &c.)

टापरा *ṭāprā* [cf. **tarpa-*[1]: *talpa-*[1]], m. reg. (W.) a thatched house, or hut.

[1]टापा *ṭāpā* [cf. **tarpati*], m. E.H. a leap, spring. — ~ दे-, to jump (ahead, away).

[2]टापा *ṭāpā* [**tarpa-*[1]], m. reg. (Bihar) a bamboo basket (for catching fish).

टापू *ṭāpū* [**ṭāppuka-*], m. an island; shoal (in a river).

टाबर *ṭābar*, m. E.H. Raj. **1.** a household. ***2.** a child.

टामक *ṭāmak*, m. Brbh. a large drum.

टार *ṭār-*, v.t. Brbh. Av. = टालना.

[1]टाल *ṭāl* [**ṭalla-*[1], *aṭṭāla-*], f. **1.** a stack, heap or pile (as of wood, stone, straw). **2.** a place or depot where wood, &c. is stored, and sold. — ~ करना, to set up, or to run, a wood-store, &c.

[2]टाल *ṭāl* [cf. H. *ṭālnā*], f. **1.** deferring, postponing. **2.** turning away, deterring; evasion; prevarication, excuse. — टाल-टूल, f. = next. टाल-मटोल, टालम-टोल, टाल-मटाल, f. postponement: evasion; prevarication, excuse. टालमटोल करना, to put off, to defer; to practise evasion; to prevaricate.

टालना *ṭālnā* [*ṭālayati*], v.t. **1.** to turn (sthg.) away; to prevaricate, to make excuse. **2.** to turn (one) away, to send away. **3.** to avert (a development); to prevent; to avoid; to deflect, to make light of (an insinuation, a joke made against one). **4.** to impose or to foist (as a task: upon, पर). **5.** to defer, to postpone (until, पर or तक); to neglect, to fail to act (on). **6.** to tolerate, to allow (as misconduct); to endure (lapse of time). — टाला-टूली, or °-टोली, f. = टाल-मटोल.

टाली *ṭālī* [conn. **ṭal-*[2]: Pk. *ṭalaṭalaï*], f. Brbh. a cow-bell; a calf.

टिंडा *ṭiṇḍā* [*tinduka-*], m. a creeper and its fruit, used as a vegetable; a kind of gherkin.

टिकट *ṭikaṭ* [Engl. *ticket*], f. m. **1.** a ticket. **2.** a stamp. **3.** a label. **4.** a badge, insignia. — तीन ~ महा-बिकट, colloq. when three go together, there is trouble. – टिकट-घर, m. ticket office or booth. टिकटदार [P. *-dār*], adj. stamped (a letter). टिकट-परीक्षक, m. ticket inspector. टिकट-बाबू, m. booking clerk.

[1]टिकटिक *ṭikṭik*, f. a clacking of the tongue (to urge on an animal).

[2]टिकटिक *ṭikṭik* [Engl. *tick*], f. ticking (as of a watch).

टिकटिकी *ṭikṭikī*, f. = टकटकी.

टिकठी *ṭikṭhī* [cf. *kāṣṭha-*], f. **1.** a three-legged stool, or table. **2.** a framework of bamboo, &c.; bier (= अरथी). **3.** triangular framework (to which a person is tied to be flogged).

टिकड़ा *ṭikṛā* [cf. **ṭikka-*[1 3]], m. **1.** a round flat object (as an ornament, a spangle). **2.** a round flat cake.

टिकड़ी *ṭikṛī*, f. dimin. = टिकड़ा, 2.

टिकना *ṭiknā* [cf. **ṭikk-*], v.i. **1.** to stop; to be detained. **2.** to remain, to stay; to lodge, to put up. **3.** to be fixed, set (in place); to be supported (by, से); to lean (against). **4.** to last, to endure; not to change, to spoil or to wear out quickly. **5.** to be concentrated, intent (the mind).

[1]टिकरी *ṭikrī* [cf. **ṭikka-*[1 3]], f. 1. = टिकिया. **2.** a fried savoury pastry. 3. = टिकली.

टिकली *ṭiklī* [cf. **ṭikk-*[1 3]], f. **1.** a spangle of foil, or glass, worn on the forehead as an ornament. **2.** a small round piece of metal. **3.** reg. (W.) a small round cake.

टिकाउ *ṭikāu* [cf. H. *ṭiknā*], adj. **1.** fixed, firm, stable. **2.** lasting, durable; firm (a colour).

टिकाऊपन *ṭikāūpan* [cf. H. *ṭikāū*], m. durability, &c.

टिकान *ṭikān* [cf. H. *ṭiknā*], f. halting-place; stopping-place.

टिकाना *ṭikānā* [cf. H. *ṭiknā*], v.t. **1.** to cause to stop; to detain; to check. **2.** to cause to remain; to lodge, to place; to put (one) up. **3.** to fix, to set (in place); to lean (against, से or के साथ). **4.** to support, to prop up. **5.** colloq. to hand or to slip (to).

टिकानी *ṭikānī* [cf. H. *ṭikānā*], f. reg. (W.) **1.** the cross-bars of a cart frame. **2.** *Pl.* prop (as used to support the shafts or pole of a cart).

टिकाव *ṭikāv* [cf. H. *ṭiknā*], m. **1.** stability, firmness. **2.** durability, permanence.

टिकिया *ṭikiyā* [cf. **ṭikka-*[3]], f. **1.** a flattened, round object (as of dough ready for baking): a small flat cake of bread. **2.** a small cake, or pellet (as of charcoal). **3.** a pill, pastille.

टिकुली *ṭikulī*, f. = टिकली.

टिकैत *ṭikait* [cf. H. [1]*ṭīkā*], m. a prince, heir.

टिकोरा *ṭikorā*, m. reg. (E.) a small unripe mango.

टिकौना *ṭikaunā* [cf. H. *ṭikānā*], m. reg. base, support.

टिक्कड़ *ṭikkaṛ* [cf. **ṭikka-*[3]], m. a thick, flat cake of bread.

टिक्कस *ṭikkas* [Engl. *tax*], m. **1.** 19c. a tax, duty. **2.** a stamp; a ticket.

टिक्की *ṭikkī* f. a round, flat piece; a small bread-cake.

टिचन *ṭican* [? Engl. *attention*], adj. colloq. obs. ready and correct.

टिटकारना *ṭiṭkārnā*, v.t. to urge on (an animal) by clacking the tongue.

टिटकारी *ṭiṭkārī*, f. clacking of the tongue (as to urge on a horse). — ~ भरना, to clack the tongue.

टिटिहरी *ṭiṭihrī* [*ṭiṭṭibha-*], f. a sandpiper, or lapwing (pewit).

टिटिहा *ṭiṭihā* [*ṭiṭṭibha-*], m. a male sandpiper, or pewit. — टिटिहा-रोर, m. the cry of the sandpiper, &c.; a plaintive sound.

टिट्टिभ *ṭiṭṭibh* [S.], m. a sandpiper, or lapwing.

टिड्डा *ṭiḍḍā* [**ṭiḍḍa-*, **triḍḍa-*: Pk. *tiḍḍa-*], m. a grasshopper.

टिड्डी *ṭiḍḍī* [**ṭiḍḍa-*, **triḍḍa-*: Pk. *tiḍḍī-*], f. a grasshopper, or locust. — टिड्डी-दल, m. swarm of locusts.

टिपका *ṭipkā*, m. E.H. = टपका, 1., 2.

टिपारी *ṭipārī* [H. [1]*piṭārī*], f. Brbh. a basket, or box.

टिपोर *ṭipor*, m. reg. boasting.

टिप्पणी *ṭippaṇī* [S.], f. **1.** a commentary. **2.** a remark, observation; comment, note.

टिप्पस *ṭippas*, m. f. a scheme, trick; manoeuvre. — ~ जमाना, or भिड़ाना, or लगाना, to lay a plan, &c.

टिब्बा *ṭibbā* [**ṭibba-*; ? ← Panj.], m. reg. rising ground; a hill.

टिमटिम *ṭimṭim*, adj. & m. **1.** adj. twinkling. **2.** m. twinkling. **3.** a soft sound. — ~ करना, = टिमटिमाना.

टिमटिमाना *ṭimṭimānā*, v.i. **1.** to twinkle. **2.** to flicker; to flare up (a light, before going out).

टिमटिमाहट *ṭimṭimāhaṭ*, f. twinkling, flickering.

टिमाक *ṭimāk*, f. **1.** finery. **2.** airs, ostentation.

टिल्ला *ṭillā*, m. a shock, blow, thrust: — टिल्ले-नवीसी [P. *-navīsī*], f. pej. frivolous or degrading activity.

टीक *ṭīk* [**ṭikka-*[1]: Pk. *ṭikka-*], m. reg. **1.** an ornament of stamped or inlaid metal worn on the neck or head. **2.** a mark.

[1]**टीका** *ṭīkā* [**ṭikka-*[1]: Pk. *ṭikka-*], m. **1.** a round ornamental or sectarian mark (or marks) made on the forehead; an ornamental patch of tinsel or precious metal, or a jewel or ornament, worn on the forehead. **2.** ceremony where a *ṭīkā* is imprinted (as a betrothal, or investiture). **3.** mark of investiture, or pre-eminence (also iron.); adornment, glory (of, का). **4.** a dowry, wedding gifts. **5.** transf. vaccination. — ~ भेजना, to send wedding gifts (to, को). ~ लगाना (को), to vaccinate or to inoculate.

[2]**टीका** *ṭīkā* [S.], f. a commentary; a sub-commentary. — टीका-टिप्पणी, f. extensive commentary or discussion (on or of, पर or की). – टीकाकार, m. a commentator.

टीड़ी *ṭīṛī*, f. Av. Brbh. = टिड्डी.

टीप *ṭīp* [cf. H. *ṭīpnā*], f. **1.** pressing, squeezing; pressing into place (mortar, plaster); a fingerprint. **2.** massaging. **3.** a note, sthg. recorded; document; horoscope. **4.** a draft, sketch. **5.** a high note, high pitch. — ~ लगाना, to press, to squeeze. – टीप-टाप, f. finishing touches: pointing (with mortar, plaster); splendour, pomp; ostentatious manner.

टीपना *ṭīpnā* [**ṭipp-*[1]; ? = **ṭippati*], v.t. & f. **1.** v.t. to press, to squeeze; to press in (mortar, plaster). **2.** to massage. **3.** to note. **4.** to draft, to sketch (as an outline, a horoscope). **5.** f. [cf. *janmapatrī*, f.] a horoscope. — गला ~, to seize or to take (one) by the throat.

टीबा *ṭībā* [**ṭibba-*], m. reg. (Raj.) rising ground; sand bank.

टीम-टाम *ṭīm-ṭām*, m. pomp, show, ostentation.

टीम-टिमाक *ṭīm-ṭimāk*, m. = टीम-टाम.

टीला *ṭīlā* [**ṭilla-*], m. a hillock; mound.

टील्हा *ṭīlhā*, m. reg. (Bihar) a hillock, mound (= टीला); broken ground, ground cut by ravines.

टीस *ṭīs*, f. a shooting or throbbing pain; a stitch. — ~ उठना, a shooting pain to be felt. ~ मारना, to shoot with pain, to throb (in, में).

टीसना *ṭīsnā*, v.i. *Pl. HŚS.* to shoot with pain, to throb.

टुँगाना *ṭuṁgānā*, v.t. ? to nibble.

टुंच *ṭuñc* [conn. **ṭuṇṭa-, tucchya-*], adj. & f. **1.** adj. very small. **2.** very little (in quantity). 3. = टुच्चा. **4.** f. a tiny amount (of money). — ~ भिड़ाना, or लड़ाना, to work with small sums of money; to play for low stakes; to amass (money) gradually.

टुंटा *ṭuṇṭā*, m. = टुंडा.

टुंड *ṭuṇḍ* [**ṭuṇḍa-*[2]], m. **1.** stump (of a branch, a tree, a limb); a leafless branch or tree. **2.** a person, or animal, mutilated or physically defective. **3.** a hand, branch, &c. that has been cut off.

टुंडा *ṭuṇḍā* [**ṭuṇḍa-*[2]], adj. & m. **1.** adj. mutilated or physically defective (a person, or an animal). **2.** lopped, cut back drastically (a tree). **3.** m. a lazy person. **4.** a stump (= टुंड).

टुंडी *ṭuṇḍī* [conn. *tundi-*: **ṭuṇḍi-*], f. **1.** the navel. **2.** *Pl. HŚS.* stump of an arm, the arm excluding the hands.

टुइयाँ *ṭuiyāṁ*, adj. & f. **1.** adj. very small, tiny. **2.** reg. a small spouted drinking-pot.

टुक *ṭuk* [**ṭukka-*], adj. & adv. **1.** adj. little. **2.** adv. a little; just.

टुक-टुक *ṭuk-ṭuk*, adv. = टुकुर-टुकुर.

टुकड़- *ṭukaṛ-*. a piece, scrap: — टुकड़-तोड़, m. one who lives on scraps (provided by another), a dependant, hanger-on.

टुकड़ा *ṭukṛā* [cf. **ṭukk-*], m. **1.** a piece, bit; scrap; fragment. **2.** a part, section. **3.** a piece of bread: subsistence. — ~ ~, or टुकड़े टुकड़े, करना, to break, to tear, to pull or to cut to pieces. टुकड़े उड़ाना (के), to shred; to shatter. टुकड़े करना (के), to break into pieces; to divide. टुकड़े तोड़ना (के), fig. to live as a dependant or hanger-on (of). टुकड़ों पर पड़ना, or पलना (के), id. चाँद का ~, m. fig. a lovely creature. – टुकड़ा-तोड़ जवाब, m. a curt answer; a rebuff. टुकड़ा-सा जवाब, m. id.

टुकड़ी *ṭukṛī* [cf. H. *ṭukṛā*], f. **1.** a small piece; fragment. **2.** a small group; a band, party; unit. **3.** flock (of birds).

टुकुर-टुकुर *ṭukur-ṭukur* [? cf. H. *ṭak*], adv. intently (gazing). — ~ ताकना, or देखना, to look intently at.

टुच्चा *ṭuccā* [conn. **ṭuṇṭa-, tucchya-*], adj. & m. **1.** adj. base, worthless. **2.** degrading. **3.** m. a base, or dissolute person.

टुटका *ṭuṭkā*, m. reg. = टोटका.

टुटपूँजिया *ṭuṭpūṁjiyā* [cf. H. *pūṁjī*], m. & adj. **1.** m. a small merchant or trader. **2.** adj. of small means.

टुटरूँ-टूँ *ṭuṭrūṁ-ṭūṁ* [onom.], m. & adj. **1.** m. the cooing of a dove. **2.** adj. colloq. alone, forlorn.

टुटहा *ṭuṭ'hā* [cf. H. *ṭūṭnā*], adj. reg. broken.

टुनकार *ṭunkār* [cf. H. *ṭunṭunānā*], f. chiming (of a clock).

टुनटुन *ṭunṭun*, f. = टन-टन, see s.v. [1]टन.

टुनटुनाना *ṭunṭunānā*, v.i. & v.t. = टनटनाना.

टुनिहाई *ṭunihāī*, f. Brbh. = टोनहाई, 2.

टुन्ना *ṭunnā* [**ṭunna-*], m. = टना.

टुसियाना *ṭusiyānā*, v.i. poet. to bud.

टूँ *ṭūṁ*, f. m. sound of making wind.

टूँग *ṭūṁg* [cf. H. *ṭūṁgnā*], f. pecking.

टूँगना *ṭūṁgnā*, v.t. **1.** to nibble (grass, shoots). **2.** to pick at (food); to take a quick taste. — टूँगा-टाँगी, f. nibbling, pecking.

टूँडी *ṭūṁḍī* [**ṭuṇḍi-*], f. navel.

टूक *ṭūk* [**ṭukka-*], m. a piece, fragment. — दो ~ करना, to break, to divide in two. दो ~ जवाब, m. a short answer, a flat refusal. दो ~ बात कहना, not to mince words. – टूक-टूक करना, = टुकड़ा टुकड़ा करना. टूक-सा, adj. & m. = थोड़ा-सा.

टूट *ṭūṭ* [cf. H. *ṭūṭnā*], f. **1.** breaking, fracture. **2.** a fragment. **3.** breach, rupture (as between friends). **4.** loss. **5.** Av. error, defect (as in a text). — टूट-फूट, f. (pl.) pieces, fragments; tatters; (sg.) scrap metal; a break, something amiss (as in a machine).

टूटन *ṭūṭan* [cf. H. *ṭūṭnā*], f. **1.** breaking, fracture; fragmentation. **2.** a fragment. **3.** *Pl. HŚS.* an omission (from a text) supplied in the margin.

टूटना *ṭūṭnā* [*truṭyati*], v.i. **1.** to be broken, to break; to break off; to be cracked; to snap; to burst; to be damaged; to be demolished; to be ruined. **2.** to become separated (from, से: an animal from a flock, a member from a community). **3.** to be broken off (a relationship). **4.** to come to an end; to fail, to collapse (a firm, an institution); to subside (a fever, a price); to be in short supply. **5.** to happen, to be committed (an outrage, a crime). **6.** to fall (upon, पर), to rush (upon); to attack. **7.** to go as a crowd, to congregate (at, पर). **8.** to fall in torrents; to be abundant. **9.** to be changed (a note, a coin); to be exchanged (a draft). **10.** to be ruined, reduced to poverty. **11.** to become weak, infirm; to feel pains in the bones or joints. **12.** to be afflicted, to pine. — आ ~, to appear suddenly or unexpectedly. दम ~, to be out of breath. – टूटे दम (खेल) खेलना,

to play (a game) without enthusiasm or hope. — टूटा-फूटा, adj. broken to pieces; extensively damaged; broken (speech); of wretched state.

टूम *ṭūm* [← Panj.], f. reg. an ornament; finery.

टूमना *ṭūmnā*, v.t. to push gently, to nudge.

टूसा *ṭūsā* [*ṭūssa-], m. **1.** shoot, sprout. **2.** reg. (W.) fibre: awn (on cereal ears). **3.** *Pl. HŚS.* fruit of the *āk*, *Calotropis gigantea.*

टूसी *ṭūsī* [cf. H. *ṭūsā*], f. *Pl. HŚS.* a bud.

टेंगनि *ṭeṁgăni*, f. Av. a fish (cf. टेंगरा).

टेंगरा *ṭeṁgrā*, m. reg. (Bihar) a catfish.

टेंट *ṭeṁṭ*, f. reg. ? sthg. small and round: **1.** a fold or tuck made in the *dhotī* at the waist, to hold money, &c. **2.** a cotton pad; a ripe *karīl* fruit. — ~ ढीला करना, to open (one's) purse, to come forth with money. ~ में एक ढेला नहीं होना, colloq. not to have a penny on one.

टेंटा *ṭeṁṭā*, m. *HŚS.* a large bird (? the grey hornbill).

टेंटी *ṭeṁṭī* [cf. H. *ṭeṁṭ*: Pl. *ṭeṁṭā*], f. Brbh. the *karīl* tree, and its fruit.

टेंटुआ *ṭeṁṭuā*, m. the windpipe, the throat. — ~ दबाना (का), to throttle, to strangle.

टें-टें *ṭeṁ-ṭeṁ*, f. **1.** screeching; screech, cry (as of a parrot). **2.** babbling, chattering. — ~ करना, to screech; to babble. ~ फिस्स कर जाना, colloq. not to be able to sustain an effort.

टेक *ṭek* [cf. H. *ṭeknā*], f. **1.** a support; a prop; a rest; a supporting beam. **2.** means or source of support. **3.** fig. a matter of importance (to one, की), sthg. on which one insists. **4.** refrain (of a song). — ~ गहना, or पकड़ना, to insist (as upon a viewpoint); to be stubborn. ~ निभाना (की), to carry out (one's) firm intention; to win acceptance for (one's) viewpoint. ~ पूरी होना (की), (one's) object to be gained. ~ लगाना (में or को), to support, to prop up. ~ रहना, = ~ पूरी होना.

टेकन *ṭekan*, m. a prop, support.

टेकना *ṭeknā* [*ṭekk-], v.t. **1.** to support, to prop up. **2.** to lean on, to support (oneself) on. **3.** to maintain strongly, to insist upon (as upon a viewpoint). — घुटने ~, to bow the knee. माथा ~, to bow the forehead.

टेकनी *ṭeknī* [cf. H. *ṭekan*], f. dimin. reg. = टेकन.

टेकर *ṭekar* [cf. *ṭekka-], m. reg. a hillock, rising ground.

टेकरा *ṭekrā* [cf. *ṭekka-], m. reg. a hillock, rising ground.

टेकरी *ṭekrī* [cf. *ṭekka-], f. dimin. a hillock, rising ground.

टेकी *ṭekī* [cf. H. *ṭek*], adj. reg. reliable, trustworthy.

टेकुरी *ṭekurī*, f. reg. an awl, a jeweller's tool.

टेघरना *ṭegharnā*, v.i. reg. to melt (= टघरना, पिघलना).

टेटी *ṭeṭī*, f. Brbh. pride; ? displeasure, haughty behaviour.

टेटुआ *ṭeṭuā*, m. 19c. = टेंटुआ.

टेड़ा *ṭeṛā*, m. *Pl. HŚS.* the trunk of a tree.

टेढ़ *ṭeṛh*, adj. & f. **1.** adj. reg. = टेढ़ा. **2.** f. twist, bend; crookedness. **3.** contrariness; haughtiness.

टेढ़ा *ṭeṛhā* [*treḍḍha-], adj. **1.** crooked; bent; twisted, twisting; zigzag; awry. **2.** slanting; diagonal. **3.** unfavourable, adverse; ill-tempered, cross; intractable; rude. **4.** difficult, complicated; vexatious. — ~ करना, to make crooked, to bend; to distort. ~ पड़ना, or होना, to be displeased (with, से); to be at odds (with). टेढ़ी आँख से देखना, to look askance, or with displeasure (at). टेढ़ी खीर, f. fig. sthg. difficult or complicated; a trial. टेढ़ी ज़बान, f. a harsh tongue. टेढ़ी सुनाना (को), to speak harshly (to); to be impertinent or rude (to); to rebuke. टेढ़े, adv. crookedly; sidelong; slantwise. टेढ़े टेढ़े चलना, to behave deviously, or truculently. – टेढ़ा-मेढ़ा, adj. = ~, 1., 4.; slipshod (work). टेढ़ी-सीधी सुनाना, = टेढ़ी सुनाना.

टेढ़ाई *ṭeṛhāī* [cf. H. *ṭeṛhā*], f. = टेढ़ापन.

टेढ़ापन *ṭeṛhāpan* [cf. H. *ṭeṛhā*], m. **1.** crookedness. **2.** obliqueness, slant. **3.** crossness, ill-humour. **4.** complication (as of a task).

टेना *ṭenā*, v.t. reg. to sharpen, to whet.

टेनी *ṭenī* [? = H. *ṭahnī*], f. little, small: **1.** the little finger. **2.** reg. (Bihar) fresh shoots near the base of a regenerating plant. — ~ मारना, colloq. to put (one's) little finger on the scales): to give light weight.

टेम *ṭem*, f. 19c. flame, light (of candle or lamp).

[1]**टेर** *ṭer* [cf. H. *ṭernā*], f. **1.** a call, shout. **2.** a high-pitched note (in singing). — ~ लगाना, to raise the voice, to call, &c.; to implore.

[2]**टेर** *ṭer*, adj. *Pl. HŚS.* passed, spent.

टेरना *ṭernā* [*ṭer-], v.t. **1.** to call out, to shout; to scream; to roar. **2.** to sing, to chant. **3.** ? to sound (as a flute).

टेरनि *ṭerni* [cf. *ṭer-], f. Brbh. calling, &c. (cf. टेर, 1).

टेरा *ṭerā* [conn. *ṭeraka-*], adj. *Pl. HŚS.* squint-eyed.

टेला *ṭelā*, m. marriage custom, marriage ceremony.

टेव *ṭev* [cf. *ṭev-: ? conn. *ṭipp-[1]], m. a habit, a way.

टेवकी *ṭevkī*, f. reg. prop, support (= टेक).

टेवा *ṭevā* [cf. *ṭev-], m. **1.** sketch or outline of a horoscope. **2.** reg. (W.) letter from a prospective bride's father announcing the marriage.

टेसू *ṭesū*, m. **1.** the *palāś* tree, *Butea frondosa*, and its flower. **2.** *hind.* the *ṭesū* festival of the tenth day of the bright half of the month Āśvin (when boys go from house to house singing songs, and receive gifts of money or grain); a song sung at, or an effigy made for, this festival.

टेहला *ṭehlā*, m. *Pl. HŚS.* = टेला.

[1]**टोंक** *ṭoṁk*, f. pronun. var. = टोक.

[2]**टोंक** *ṭoṁk* [*ṭoṅka-], m. *Pl. HŚS.* beak, point; end, tip (of a piece of land).

टोंट *ṭoṁṭ* [*ṭoṇṭa-[3]], f. E.H. beak, bill (of a bird).

[1]**टोंटा** *ṭoṁṭā* [*ṭoṇṭa-[1 3]], m. **1.** a tube; spout. **2.** a cartridge case.

[2]**टोंटा** *ṭoṁṭā* [*ṭoṇṭa-[2]], m. handless.

टोंटी *ṭoṁṭī* [*ṭoṇṭa-[3]], f. **1.** a spout. **2.** a tap. — टोंटीदार [P. *-dār*], adj. having a spout.

टोआ *ṭoā* [cf. *ṭoh-], m. feeling, groping (= टोह). — टोआ-टोआ, f. feeling, groping (for, की).

टोई *ṭoī*, f. *Pl. HŚS.* joint of a reed (= पोरी).

टोक *ṭok* [cf. H. *ṭoknā*], f. **1.** checking; obstruction; interference. **2.** interruption: questioning. **3.** influence of the evil eye. — ~ लगना, interference to occur (on the part of, की); malign influence to fall (on, को).

[1]**टोकना** *ṭoknā* [*ṭokk-], v.t. **1.** to challenge; to interrupt: to question. **2.** to check; to obstruct; to interfere; to raise an objection to. **3.** to regard with an evil eye. — टोका-टोकी, f. hindrance, prevention.

[2]**टोकना** *ṭoknā* [cf. *ṭokk-[1]], m. **1.** a wide-mouthed brass or copper vessel (for water). **2.** reg. a basket.

टोकनी *ṭoknī* [cf. *ṭokka-[1]], f. 1. = [2]टोकना, 1. **2.** reg. a basket. **3.** (Bihar) blinkers (for cattle).

टोकरा *ṭokrā* [cf. *ṭokka-[1]], m. a large basket.

टोकरी *ṭokrī* [cf. *ṭokka-[1]], f. a basket.

टोटका *ṭoṭkā* [? cf. *ṭoṭṭa-[1]], m. **1.** a magical practice; reg. a black earthen pot (placed in a field to avert the evil eye). **2.** a charm, spell; amulet.

[1]**टोटा** *ṭoṭā* [*ṭoṭṭa-[1 2]], m. **1.** *Pl. HŚS.* a hollow tube or stump; a section of bamboo (cf. [1]टोंटा). ***2.** a cigarette end.

[2]**टोटा** *ṭoṭā* [? *ṭoṭṭa-[2]], m. **1.** loss, damage. **2.** deficiency, lack. — ~ उठाना, to suffer loss, or damage. ~ पड़ना, a loss to be incurred. ~ भरना, to make good a loss, &c.; to compensate, to indemnify.

टोटि *ṭoṭi* [cf. H. [2]*ṭoṭā*], f. Brbh. a shortcoming, deficiency.

टोडर *ṭoḍar*, Av. a long necklace.

[1]**टोड़ा** *ṭoṛā* [conn. H *ṭoḍar*], m. **1.** reg. (W.) a neck chain; a bag or purse. **2.** reg. (Bihar) a wrist ornament. **3.** *Pl.* an anklet with bells.

[2]**टोड़ा** *ṭoṛā*, m. reg. projecting part of a roof, or wall; eaves; roof-battens.

टोड़ी *ṭoṛī* [*troṭaka-*], f. *mus.* name of a *rāgiṇī*.

टोनहा *ṭonhā*, m. a sorcerer.

टोनहाई *ṭonhāī* [cf. H. *ṭonā*], f. **1.** sorcery. **2.** a sorceress.

[1]**टोना** *ṭonā* [*ṭona-], m. **1.** a charm, spell; sorcery. **2.** fascination, charm. **3.** a marriage-song. — ~ चलाना, to practise sorcery. — टोना-टनमन, m. sorcery. टोना-टोटका, m. id. टोना-टोटका करना, to practise sorcery. टोनेबाज़ [P. *-bāz*], m. a sorcerer; conjurer.

[2]**टोना** *ṭonā*, v.t. = टोहना.

टोप *ṭop* [*ṭoppa-[1]], m. **1.** a large hat; hood. **2.** a helmet. **3.** a thimble.

टोपा *ṭopā* [*ṭoppa-[1]], m. = टोप, 1.

टोपी *ṭopī* [*ṭoppa-[1]], f. **1.** a hat; cap; hood. **2.** a cover, lid, cap; stopper; crown (of a tooth). **3.** a thimble. **4.** a percussion cap, detonator. **5.** glans penis. — ~ उछालना (की), to knock off (one's) hat: to put (one) to public shame. ~ बदलना (से), to exchange hats (with): to be on intimate terms (with). – टोपीदार [P. -*dār*], adj. wearing a hat.

टोभ *ṭobh*, m. Brbh. joining; ? stitching.

टोल *ṭol* [*ṭola-], m. Brbh. **1.** a group, party, band. **2.** quarter (of a village).

टोला *ṭolā* [*ṭola-], m. **1.** quarter (of a town or village). **2.** a set, assortment.

टोली *ṭolī* [**ṭola-*], f. dimin. **1.** a group, party, band; flock. **2.** quarter (of a town or village).

टोह *ṭoh* [cf. H. *ṭohnā*], f. **1.** feeling (for); touching. **2.** searching out, investigating. **3.** information. **4.** care (of or for), supervision. — ~ मिलना, information to come to light (about, की). ~ लगाना, or लेना (की), to search out, &c. ~ रखना (की), to watch over, &c. – टोह-उड़ान, f. a reconnaissance flight.

टोहना *ṭohnā* [**ṭoh-*], v.t. **1.** to feel for, to grope; to touch, to feel. **2.** to search for, to search out. — टोहा-टाई, f. prolonged or detailed search.

टौरिया *ṭauriyā*, m. reg. a hillock.

ठ

ठ *ṭha*, the twelfth consonant of the Devanāgarī syllabary. — **ठकार**, m. the sound /ṭh/; the letter ठ.

ठंड *ṭhanḍ*, f. = ठंढ.

ठंडई *ṭhanḍaī* [? H. *ṭhanḍā*], f. a cold drink.

ठंडक *ṭhanḍak*, f. = ठंढक.

ठंडा *ṭhanḍā*, adj. = ठंढा.

ठंडाई *ṭhanḍāī*, f. = ठंढाई.

ठंडी *ṭhanḍī*, f. colloq. *Pl. HŚS.* smallpox (= शीतला).

ठंढ *ṭhanḍh* [*stabdha-*; **ṭhanḍha-* w. *-n-* ← Drav.], f. coldness, cold; coolness. — ~ **पड़ना**, to grow cold (weather, season). ~ **लगना (को)**, to feel cold (a person); to catch a cold.

ठंढक *ṭhanḍhak* [cf. H. *ṭhanḍh*], f. **1.** coldness; coolness. **2.** relief from heat. **3.** satisfaction (of a desire); comfort; relief; fig. sthg. bringing relief. **4.** abatement (of turmoil, or an epidemic); calm; lull. — ~ **पड़ना**, to grow cold (weather, season); to be refreshed; to be satisfied (a desire); to abate.

ठंढा *ṭhanḍhā* [*stabdha-*; **ṭhanḍha-*], adj. **1.** cold; cool; chill. **2.** cooled; frozen. **3.** refreshing, cooling. **4.** refreshed. **5.** satisfied (as the heart); placated; soothed. **6.** calm, quiet, placid; collected (the thoughts, emotions). **7.** abated, subdued (as pangs); dejected (as a sigh); without desire; inert, inactive (as business); not live (a wire); lifeless. — ~ **करना**, to make cold, or cool; to extinguish (a light); to refresh; to quench; to assuage; to placate; to deflate, to reduce (enthusiasm, or arrogance); to finish with, to destroy. ~ **पड़ना**, to become cold, or cool; to abate, or to become extinguished (as desires). **ठंढी आग**, f. colloq. snow; frost. **ठंढे ठंढे**, adv. in the cool of the day (morning or evening); quietly, peaceably.

ठंढाई *ṭhanḍhāī* [cf. H. *ṭhanḍhā*], f. **1.** a cooling drink or potion containing certain ground spices, seeds, &c. **2.** an infusion of *bhāṁg* with these substances.

[1]**ठक** *ṭhak* [*ṭhakk-*[1]], f. the sound of knocking or hammering. — **ठक-ठक**, f. repeated knocking, &c. **ठक-ठक की आवाज़**, f. a hard, insistent voice.

[2]**ठक** *ṭhak*, adj. 19c. astonished, amazed.

ठकठकाना *ṭhakṭhakānā* [cf. H. *ṭhak-ṭhak*], v.i. & v.t. **1.** v.i. to knock, to rattle. **2.** v.t. to knock, to rattle.

ठकठकिया *ṭhakṭhakiyā* [cf. H. *ṭhakṭhak*], m. a stickler; one who insists on his point.

ठकुआ *ṭhakuā*, m. reg. (Bihar) a kind of sweetened puri.

ठकुर- *ṭhakur-*. = ठाकुर. — **ठकुर-सुहाती**, f. fawning, flattery.

ठकुराइत *ṭhakurāit*, f. Brbh. = ठकुरायत.

ठकुराइन *ṭhakurāin* [cf. H. *ṭhākur*], f. the wife of a *ṭhākur*.

ठकुराई *ṭhakurāī* [cf. H. *ṭhākur*], f. **1.** the rank, office or status of a *ṭhākur*. **2.** supremacy; authority.

ठकुरानी *ṭhakurānī* [cf. H. *ṭhakur*], f. the wife of a *ṭhākur*.

ठकुरायत *ṭhakurāyat* [cf. H. *ṭhākur*], f. 1. = ठकुराई. **2.** estate, landed property.

ठग *ṭhag* [cf. **ṭhagg-*: Pk. *ṭhaga-*], m. **1.** a cheat, swindler; villain. **2.** a robber. **3.** *hist.* a thug: member of a secret gang of robbers and murderers. — **ठगबाज़ी** [P. *-bāzī*], f. the practice of cunning, imposture or fraud. **ठग-मूरी**, f. thug-root: an intoxicating or stupefying drug. **ठग-मोदक**, m. Brbh. a drugged sweet. **ठग-विद्या**, f. the art of, skill in, trickery or fraud.

ठगना *ṭhagnā* [**ṭhagg-*: Pk. *ṭhagiya-*], v.t. & v.i. **1.** v.t. to cheat, to dupe. **2.** to rob. **3.** fig. to charm. **4.** v.i. to be cheated. **5.** to be robbed. **6.** fig. to be charmed. — **ठगा-ठगी**, f. = ठगबाज़ी. **ठगा-सा**, adj. robbed, cheated, &c.; charmed; taken aback, at a loss.

ठगनी *ṭhagnī* [cf. H. *ṭhag*], f. **1.** a woman who deceives, &c.; a seductive woman. **2.** the wife of a robber, &c.

ठगपना *ṭhagpanā* [cf. H. *ṭhag*], m. **1.** deceit, fraud. **2.** thievishness.

ठगवाना *ṭhagvānā* [cf. H. *ṭhagnā*], v.t. to cause to be cheated or robbed (by, से).

ठगाई *ṭhagāī* [cf. H. *ṭhagānā*], f. reg. = ठगपना.

ठगाना *ṭhagānā* [cf. H. *ṭhag*], v.i. & v.t. reg. **1.** v.i. to be duped, deceived. **2.** fig. to be charmed. **3.** v.t. to dupe, &c. **4.** to cause to be duped, &c. (= ठगवाना).

ठगिनी *ṭhaginī*, f. = ठगनी.

ठगी *ṭhagī* [cf. H. *ṭhag*], f. **1.** cheating, imposture. **2.** robbing, robbery. **3.** *hist.* thuggery (see ठग, 3). **4.** fascination, enchantment.

ठगोरी *ṭhagorī* [*ṭhagg-+? *mūla-* or *kavala-*], f. **1.** charm, spell. **2.** cheating, imposture. — ~ डालना, or लगाना (पर), to cast a spell (on); to cheat. ~ ला-, Brbh. id.

ठगौरी *ṭhagaurī*, f. = ठगोरी.

ठघाई *ṭhaghāī*, f. reg. = ठगपना.

ठट *ṭhaṭ*, m. **1.** 19c. a crowd, throng (cf. ठाठ). **2.** Brbh. array.

ठटना *ṭhaṭnā*, v.i. & v.t. pronun. var. = ठठना.

ठटोली *ṭhaṭolī*, f. = ठठोली.

ठट्ट *ṭhaṭṭ*, m. 19c. a crowd, company; community (= ठट).

ठट्टा *ṭhaṭṭā*, m. Av. metr. a crowd (= ठट, ठट्ट).

ठट्ठर *ṭhaṭṭhar* [cf. *ṭhaṭṭha-*[1]], m. **1.** a roofing framework (= ठाठ, 1). **2.** a skeleton (= ठठड़ी).

ठट्ठा *ṭhaṭṭhā* [*ṭhaṭṭha-*[2]], m. **1.** a joke; joking, bantering. **2.** a laugh, guffaw. **3.** transf. a trifle; an easy matter. — ~ उड़ाना, to laugh (at, का), to make fun. ~ करना, to joke (with, से or के साथ). ~, or ठट्ठे, मारना, to make fun (of, पर, का/के). ~ लगाना, to make a joke; to make fun (of, का). ठट्ठे में उड़ाना, to pass off with a joke; = ~ उड़ाना. – ठट्ठे-मिज़ाज, adj. & m. jocular, facetious; a joker. ठट्ठेबाज़ [P. *-bāz*], adj. & m. = prec. °-बाज़ी, f. joking, bantering, &c.

ठठना *ṭhaṭhnā*, v.i. & v.t. **1.** v.i. to be fixed; to be firm. **2.** Av. to be decked, arrayed. **3.** v.t. Brbh. to fix; to make firm; to make definite. **4.** Av. to adorn.

ठठरी *ṭhaṭhrī* [cf. *ṭhaṭṭha-*[1]], f. **1.** a skeleton. **2.** colloq. a very thin person. **3.** bamboo framework (as for a thatched roof). **4.** a bier (= अरथी). — ठठरियाँ निकल आना, (a creature) to be mere skin and bone.

[1]**ठठाना** *ṭhaṭhānā* [cf. H. *ṭhaṭṭhā*], v.i. to guffaw. — ठठाकर हँसना, = ~.

[2]**ठठाना** *ṭhaṭhānā* [cf. H. *ṭhāṭh*], v.i. to be rampant, to hold sway (as chaos).

ठठेर *ṭhaṭher*, m. reg. = ठाठ, 1.

ठठेरा *ṭhaṭherā* [*ṭhaṭṭhakara-*], m. a coppersmith, tinsmith, brazier.

ठठेरी *ṭhaṭherī* [cf. H. *ṭhaṭherā*], f. & adj. **1.** f. a coppersmith's or brazier's wife. **2.** a female brazier. **3.** adj. having to do with braziers. — ~ बाज़ार, m. braziers' lane or quarter (in a bāzār).

ठठोल *ṭhaṭhol*, adj. & m. **1.** adj. jocular, facetious. **2.** m. a joker, (= ठट्ठेबाज़). **3.** joking, a joke. — ठठोलबाज़, = ठठोल, adj. °-बाज़ी, f. joking (= ठट्ठेबाज़ी).

ठठोलपन *ṭhaṭholpan* [cf. H. *ṭhaṭhol*], m. = ठठोली.

ठठोलिया *ṭhaṭholiyā* [cf. H. *ṭhaṭhol*], adj. & m. = ठठोल, 1., 2.

ठठोली *ṭhaṭholī* [cf. H. *ṭhaṭhol*], f. joking, a joke. — ~ करना, to joke, to banter. ठठोलियाँ मारना, id.

ठड्डा *ṭhaḍḍā* [*stabdha-*], m. reg. (E.) **1.** a framework. **2.** the lengthwise stick of a paper kite. **3.** the backbone.

ठढ़ौ *ṭhaṛhau*, adj. Brbh. metr. = ठाढ़ा.

ठन *ṭhan* [onom.], f. a ringing sound. — ठनकार, f. = ~. ठन-ठन, f. a repeated or continuous ringing, clashing, clanging, or jingling. ठन-ठन गोपाल, m. iron. a pauper; a trivial or worthless person. ठनाठन, f. = ठन-ठन.

ठनक *ṭhanak* [cf. H. *ṭhan*], f. **1.** a ringing sound. **2.** the sound of a drum.

ठनकना *ṭhanaknā* [onom.: cf. H. *ṭhan*], v.i. **1.** to ring, to resound; to clink; to jingle. **2.** to beat, to sound (a drum). **3.** to throb, to shoot (pain). — माथा ~, sudden anxiety to be felt.

ठनकाना *ṭhankānā* [cf. H. *ṭhanaknā*], v.t. **1.** to cause to ring, to resound, to clink (metal). **2.** to beat (a drum).

ठनठनाना *ṭhanṭhanānā* [cf. H. *ṭhan-ṭhan*], v.i. & v.t. **1.** v.i. to clash, to clang, &c. repeatedly or continuously. **2.** v.t. to cause to clash, &c.

ठनना *ṭhannā* [cf. H. *ṭhānnā*], v.i. **1.** to be determined on, resolved (a matter). **2.** to be launched, to break out; to begin; to arise, to appear. — उनमें ठनी हुई है, trouble has broken out between them.

ठनाका *ṭhanākā* [cf. H. *ṭhan*], m. a clanging sound; clatter.

ठपना *ṭhapnā* [cf. H. *ṭhappā*], v.t. colloq. **1.** to close or to clap shut. **2.** to clap, to pat (as a dung-cake on a wall); to stamp. **3.** to finish up (work).

ठपवाना *ṭhapvānā* v.t. colloq. to cause to be closed, &c. (see ठपना).

ठप्प *ṭhapp* [? H. *ṭhapnā*], colloq. a conclusive ending: — ~ पड़ना, or हो जाना, to come to an end.

ठप्पा *ṭhappā* [cf. *ṭhapp-], m. **1.** a stamp, die; printer's block; type. **2.** an impression, print (of hand, foot, paw). **3.** mould (as for working metal). **4.** a kind of broad printed lace.

— ~ लगाना (पर), to stamp, to print; to assign a partic. character (to, को).

ठमकना *ṭhamaknā* v.i. to stop, to hesitate.

ठरमरुआ *ṭharmaruā* [H. *ṭhirnā*; H. *marnā*], adj. colloq. half-dead with cold.

ठरिया *ṭhariyā*, m. reg. (Bihar) a simple kind of hookah having a short, straight stem.

ठर्रा *ṭharrā*, m. an intoxicant made from fruit of the *mahuā* tree.

ठलुआ *ṭhaluā* [cf. **ṭhalla-*], adj. & m. **1.** adj. out of work. **2.** m. an idle person.

[1]**ठस** *ṭhas* [? conn. **ṭhass-*], m. a dull sound (as of a failed explosion, or a falling sack, or as made by a bad coin).

[2]**ठस** *ṭhas* [**ṭhass-*: cf. H. *ṭhāṁsnā*], adj. **1.** pressed down, crammed (in). **2.** hard, firm; solid, substantial (construction); heavy; thick (weave, fabric). **3.** grave, serious (as a mood). **4.** dense, stupid. **5.** stubborn. **6.** lazy. **7.** stingy. — ठसाठस, adj. crammed full; crowded.

[1]**ठसक** *ṭhasak* [cf. **ṭhas-*], f. pride, vanity; ostentation. — ठसकदार [P. *-dār*], adj. haughty, vain; ostentatious.

[2]**ठसक** *ṭhasak*, f. = ठसका.

ठसका *ṭhaskā*, m. a dry cough.

[1]**ठस्सा** *ṭhassā*, m. 19c. = [1]ठसक.

[2]**ठस्सा** *ṭhassā* [cf. **ṭhass-*], m. reg. (Bihar) a mould for shaping metal.

ठहर *ṭhahar*, m. Brbh. a place, spot.

ठहरना *ṭhaharnā* [cf. **stabhira-*], v.i. **1.** to stand still, to be stationary; to stop; to pause; to rest; to remain; to cease (as rain). **2.** to be set in place or position; to be fixed. **3.** to stand firm, to resist; not to deteriorate, to keep well (as perishable goods, cloth). **4.** to stay, to lodge; to take up quarters. **5.** to wait, to remain; to be delayed (the rains); to linger (an illness). **6.** to settle, to be deposited (a solid in a liquid). **7.** to be arranged, settled, determined; to improve (health). **8.** to be ascertained, established, proved (a fact, a case). **9.** to prove to be, to turn out; to have the position or status of. — मन ~, the heart to be calm; to be self-assured, self-possessed.

ठहराऊ *ṭhahrāū* [cf. H. *ṭhaharnā*], adj. **1.** fixed, firm, stable. **2.** lasting, durable.

ठहराना *ṭhahrānā* [cf. H. *ṭhaharnā*], v.t. **1.** to cause to stay, or to stop; to bring to a halt. **2.** to set in place or position; to fix. **3.** to provide accommodation (for, को). **4.** to arrange, to settle (a matter); to determine (as a price). **5.** to ascertain, to establish, to prove (a fact, an argument); to deduce, to conclude. **6.** to decree, to adjudge; to appoint (as).

ठहराव *ṭhahrāv* [cf. H. *ṭhaharnā*, *ṭhahrānā*], m. **1.** stability (as of a situation). **2.** permanence, durability. **3.** pause; halt; cessation; *econ.* recession. **4.** stopping-place, a stop. — सूरज का ~, m. solstice.

ठहाका *ṭhahākā*, m. a loud laugh, guffaw. — ~ मारना, or लगाना, to burst out laughing.

ठाँ *ṭhāṁ*, f. m. 1. = ठाँव. 2. = ठाँय.

ठाँई *ṭhāṁī*, m. Brbh. = ठाँव.

ठाँठा *ṭhāṁṭhā*, adj. reg. healthy, fit.

ठाँय *ṭhāṁy* [onom.], f. sound of a bang, crash, or shot. — ~ ~, f. id.

ठाँव *ṭhāṁv* [*sthāman-*], m. f. **1.** place, partic. or proper place, site; place of work or residence; halting-place. **2.** Av. occasion. — ठाँव-ठाँव, adv. from place to place; in different places; here and there.

ठा- *ṭhā-* [*sthāpayati*], v.t. Brbh. Av. = ठानना.

ठाउं *ṭhāuṁ*, m. Brbh. Av. = ठाँव.

ठाकुर *ṭhākur* [*ṭhakkura-*], m. **1.** an idol. **2.** a deity; the supreme deity. **3.** a lord, or chief; landed proprietor; headman; a person of rank or position. **4.** an honorific title or form of address. — ~ जी, m. title of supreme deity (used by members of the Vallabhan community, and others). – ठाकुर-द्वारा, m. a temple. ठाकुर-प्रसाद, m. an offering of food to an idol. ठाकुर-बाड़ी, f. reg. (E). a temple. ठाकुर-शाही, f. dominance of the landed class. ठाकुर-सेवा, f. service of an idol, or god; support for a temple establishment.

ठाकुराइन *ṭhākurāin*, f. = ठकुराइन.

ठाकुराई *ṭhākurāī*, f. = ठकुराई.

ठाकुरानी *ṭhākurānī*, f. = ठकुराइन.

ठाट *ṭhāṭ*, m. pronun. var. = ठाठ.

ठाट- *ṭhāṭ-* [conn. H. *ṭhāṭh*], v.i. Av. to be harnessed, provided with (as a vehicle with animals to pull it).

ठाटर *ṭhāṭar* [cf. **thaṭṭha-*[1]], m. **1.** a framework of bamboo (cf. टट्टी). **2.** fig. Av. the body.

ठाठ *ṭhāṭh* [**thaṭṭha-*[1 2]], m. **1.** a framework (as of bamboo, for a thatch); a skeleton, or structure; Av. bare branches of a tree. **2.** Av. means, scheme, arrangement. **3.** 19c. goods, equipment. **4.** fashion, cut, style; adornment, array. **5.** pomp, splendour. **6.** a stance (in wrestling). **7.** *mus.* a scale. — ~ से adv. in ease, or comfort: in splendour; &c. – ठाठ-बाट, f. ease, comfort; pomp, splendour.

ठाठा *ṭhāṭhā* [? **thaṭṭha-*[1]], m. reg. (W.) hump (of a bull).

ठाड़ा *ṭhāṛā*, adj. pronun. var. = ठाढ़ा.

ठाढ़ा *ṭhāṛhā* [*stabdha-*], adj. **1.** fixed, stationary; standing. **2.** perpendicular; steep. **3.** whole, unground (grain).

ठान *ṭhān* [cf. H. *ṭhānnā*], f. **1.** plunging into (an activity). **2.** a firm resolve.

ठानना *ṭhānnā* [cf. **sthānya-*], v.t. **1.** to resolve, to determine on; to be intent on. **2.** to plunge into (an activity).

[1]**ठार** *ṭhār* [? H. *ṭhaur* × H. *ṭhāṁv*], m. Brbh. a place (= ठौर).

[2]**ठार** *ṭhār* [**sthāra-*: Pk. *thāra-*], m. reg. (E.) frost.

ठाला *ṭhālā* [**ṭhalla-*: Pk. *ṭhalla-*], m. & adj. **1.** m. unemployment. **2.** slackness, inertness. **3.** reg. unoccupied, idle.

ठाली *ṭhālī* [**ṭhalla-*], adj. unoccupied, idle.

ठाव *ṭhāv*, m. f. pronun. var. = ठाँव.

ठाहर *ṭhāhar* [? **sthāvira-*], m. Brbh. Av. = ठाँव, 1.

ठिंगना *ṭhiṁgnā* [cf. **thiṅga-*[2]], adj. unusually short of stature.

ठिंगनाई *ṭhiṁgnāī* [cf. H. *ṭhiṁgnā*], f. unusual shortness of stature.

ठिकरी *ṭhikrī*, f. reg. = ठीकरी.

ठिकाना *ṭhikānā* [? cf. **ṭhikka-*], m. **1.** fixed place, or abode; site; residence; living quarters. **2.** particular or proper place; beat (as of a street barber); refuge; employment, position. **3.** certain knowledge; authenticity; reliability; fixed limit, or extent. इसका क्या ~? how can this be relied on? **4.** consistency, good sense; appropriateness (as of conduct, speech). **5.** basis, foundation (for sthg.); means; arrangement. **6.** fixed goal; objective. — ~ करना (का), to put in (its) proper place; to find a place (for); to arrange; to find a post (for); to find a match (for); to take account (of); to find an explanation (for); to settle, to encamp. ~ लगाना (का), to verify; to establish (as a fact). ठिकाने का, adj. consistent, balanced; appropriate; sensible. ठिकाने आना, to return, to be restored (the senses); to come to one's senses; to come to the heart of a matter. ठिकाने पहुँचाना, to carry through (a task); colloq. to dispose of, to kill (a person). ठिकाने लगना, to be of use, to bear proper fruit; to be despatched, killed; to be terminated. ठिकाने लगाना (को), to make use of, to put to good use; to put to bad use, to squander, to run through (money); to settle, to arrange; to deliver; to give work (to); to give refuge (to); to dispose of, to kill; to terminate. ठिकाने रहना, to remain stationary, or stable; to pursue a fixed course.

ठिगना *ṭhignā*, adj. = ठिंगना.

ठिटरना *ṭhiṭarnā*, v.i. pronun. var. = ठिठरना.

ठिठक *ṭhiṭhak* [cf. H. *ṭhiṭhaknā*], f. **1.** stopping suddenly. **2.** being taken aback. **3.** hesitation, reluctance.

ठिठकना *ṭhiṭhaknā*, v.i. **1.** to stop suddenly; to stand still. **2.** to be taken aback. **3.** to shrink, to hesitate; to shy (a horse).

ठिठर *ṭhiṭhar* [cf. H. *ṭhiṭhurnā*], f. numbness, chill.

ठिठरना *ṭhiṭharnā*, v.i. = ठिठुरना.

ठिठिरना *ṭhiṭhirnā*, v.i. = ठिठुरना.

ठिठुरन *ṭhiṭhuran* [cf. H. *ṭhiṭhurnā*], f. numbness, chill; shivering.

ठिठुरना *ṭhiṭhurnā* [cf. *sthira-*], v.i. **1.** to be numbed, or chilled; to be frozen; to shiver. **2.** to be checked (growth, by cold).

ठिठुराहट *ṭhiṭhurāhaṭ* [cf. H. *ṭhiṭhurnā*], f. numbness; shivering.

ठिठोली *ṭhiṭholī* [conn. H. *ṭhī-ṭhī*], f. joking, laughing.

ठिनक *ṭhinak* [cf. H. *ṭhinaknā*], f. **1.** a sob; a whimper. **2.** fretfulness; sulkiness.

ठिनकना *ṭhinaknā*, v.i. **1.** to sob; to whimper. **2.** to be fretful; to sulk; to whine.

ठिया *ṭhiyā* [*stibhi-*, or **stṛta-*], m. reg. **1.** W. a boundary mark. **2.** resting-place, destination. **3.** Bihar. a carpenter's block (working surface).

ठिर *ṭhir* [*sthira-*], f. cold weather, or spell.

ठिरना *ṭhirnā* [cf. H. *ṭhir*], v.i. to be chilled; to freeze; to shiver.

ठिराना *ṭhirānā* [cf. H. *ṭhirnā*], v.t. **1.** to cause to freeze. **2.** to cause to congeal.

ठिलना *ṭhilnā* [cf. H. *ṭhelnā*], v.i. to be pushed, &c.

ठिलिया *ṭhiliyā*, m. reg. **1.** an earthenware water-pot. **2.** [cf. H. *ṭhelnā*] trailer (of truck or tractor).

ठिलुआ *ṭhiluā*, m. 19c. = ठलुआ.

ठिव्व *ṭhivv*, m. Brbh. a place.

ठिहुनी *ṭhihunī*, f. reg. = ठेहुना.

ठीक *ṭhīk* [**ṭhīkka-*], adj. **1.** right, true. **2.** fit, proper, appropriate; satisfactory; in good condition; well-fitting (clothing). **3.** correct; exact. **4.** regular, in order; harmonious. **5.** certain, established, fixed (an arrangement). **6.** adv. exactly, just; correctly; just so. **7.** in a proper manner, fittingly. — ~ आना (को), to answer (a requirement); to prove true. ~ करना, to make right, to correct; to improve; to arrange, to adjust; to settle, to determine; to arrange for, to appoint; to ascertain, to establish; colloq. to put to rights, to punish. ~ बनाना, to make right or exact, &c. (= ~ करना). ~ होना, to be well, fine, or all right; to suit (a person, को: clothing); to fit; = ~ आना. – ठीक-ठाक, adj. & adv. = ~. ठीकम-ठीक, adj. & adv. quite true; quite correct; in perfectly good condition; quite truly, &c.

ठीकम-ठीक *ṭhīkam-ṭhīk*, adj. & adv. see s.v. ठीक.

ठीकर *ṭhīkar* [cf. H. *ṭhīkrā*], m. *hist.* turn or duty (in a rota determined by drawing potsherd lots) to keep a village watch.

ठीकरा *ṭhīkrā* [**ṭhikkara-*: Pk. *ṭhikkariā-*], m. **1.** a potsherd. **2.** a begging bowl. **3.** fig. a worthless object. — ~ फोड़ना, fig. to slander, to defame (one, का). ~ समझना, to treat as of no value.

ठीकरी *ṭhīkrī* [**ṭhīkkara-*: Pk. *ṭhikkariā-*], f. **1.** = ठीकरा. **2.** a flat earthenware plate placed over a *cilam.*

ठीका *ṭhīkā* [**ṭhīkka-*], m. **1.** a contract (= ठेका, 1.); contract work (by a builder, a supplier of produce); piece-work. **2.** a licence, a lease. **3.** a place of licensed sale (as of alcohol, or *bhāṁg*). **4.** onus, responsibility. — ~ देना, = ठेका देना. ~ लेना, to take responsibility (for, का); = ठेका लेना. – ठीका-पत्र, m. a deed of contract, or lease. ठीकेदार [P. -*dār*], m. a contractor, &c.

ठी-ठी *ṭhī-ṭhī*, f. giggling, tittering. — ~ करना, to giggle, to titter.

ठीहा *ṭhīhā*, m. reg. = ठिया.

ठुँसवाना *ṭhuṁsvānā*, v.t. = ठुसवाना.

ठुँसाना *ṭhuṁsānā*, v.t. = ठुसाना.

ठुकना *ṭhuknā* [cf. H. *ṭhoknā*], v.i. **1.** to be knocked, hammered; to be hammered in, or on. **2.** to be beaten, thrashed; to be defeated. **3.** colloq. to be lost, spent to no point (money).

ठुकराना *ṭhukrānā* [cf. H. *ṭhokar*], v.t. **1.** to kick against, to kick away. **2.** to reject, to rebuff; to spurn.

ठुकवाना *ṭhukvānā* [cf. H. *ṭhoknā*], v.t. to cause to be hammered, beaten, &c. (by, से).

ठुकाई *ṭhukāī* [cf. H. *ṭhoknā, ṭhuknā*], f. beating, hammering; colloq. a beating.

[1]**ठुड्डी** *ṭhuḍḍī* [**ṭhuḍḍa-*], f. the chin. — ~ पकड़ना (की), to take by the chin: to caress; to humour, to coax; to appease.

[2]**ठुड्डी** *ṭhuḍḍī*, f. **1.** a cob of corn with the grains removed. **2.** a grain of corn unburst on roasting.

ठुनक *ṭhunak*, f. = ठिनक.

[1]**ठुनकना** *ṭhunaknā*, v.i. = ठिनकना.

[2]**ठुनकना** *ṭhunaknā*, v.t. = ठोंकना.

ठुनुकना *ṭhunuknā*, v.i. = [1]ठुनकना.

ठुमक *ṭhumak* [cf. H. *ṭhumaknā*], f. an affected gait (as in dancing, or of children), strutting; mincing; stately gait. — ~ चाल, f. = ~.

ठुमकना *ṭhumaknā*, v.i. to move with an affected gait; to strut; to mince; to toddle.

ठुमका *ṭhumkā*, m. 1. = ठुमक. **2.** a jerk (as on a kite-string).

ठुमकाना *ṭhumkānā* [cf. H. *ṭhumaknā*] **1.** to cause to move with an affected gait, &c. **2.** to jerk (a kite-string).

ठुमकारना *ṭhumkārnā* [cf. H. *ṭhumaknā*], v.t. = ठुमकाना, 2.

ठुमकी *ṭhumkī* [cf. H. *ṭhumkā*], f. = ठुमका.

ठुमरी *ṭhumrī* [cf. **stumbha-*[1]], f. a type of song for two voices; *hist.* a type of courtesans' song.

[1]**ठुर्री** *ṭhurrī*, f. (E.) = [1]ठुड्डी.

[2]**ठुर्री** *ṭhurrī*, f. reg. grain which has not burst while being parched (cf. [2]ठुड्डी).

ठुस *ṭhus*, m. = [1]ठस.

ठुसकना *ṭhusaknā* [cf. **ṭhuss-*], v.i. **1.** to weep softly or silently. **2.** to sob.

ठुसकी *ṭhuskī*, f. sound of making wind.

ठुसना *ṭhusnā* [cf. H. *ṭhūṁsnā*], v.i. to be crammed (in).

ठुसवाना *ṭhusvānā* [cf. H. *ṭhūṁsnā*], v.t. to cause to be crammed full (by, से).

ठुसाना *ṭhusānā* [cf. H. *ṭhūṁsnā*], v.t. = ठुसवाना.

ठूँठ *ṭhūṁṭh* [**ṭhunṭha-*: Pk. *ṭhuṁṭha-*], m. **1.** stump (as of a branch, an arm); trunk (of a tree); a stunted tree. **2.** an amputated hand or arm. **3.** a person having an amputated hand or arm. **4.** stubble.

ठूँठा *ṭhūṁṭhā* [**ṭhunṭha-*: Pk. *ṭhuṁṭha-*], adj. **1.** reduced to a stump, or trunk (as an arm, or a tree); having lopped or bare branches; having the hand or arm amputated. **2.** empty.

ठूँसना *ṭhūṁsnā*, v.t. **1.** to force down or in, to thrust or to cram in. **2.** colloq. to eat greedily, to pack in (food).

ठूरी *ṭhūrī*, f. reg. (Bihar) grain which has not burst while being parched (cf. ²ठुड्डी).

ठूसना *ṭhūsnā*, v.t. = ठूँसना.

ठेंगना *ṭheṁgnā* [cf. **ṭheṅga-*], adj. *Pl. HŚS.* very short of stature (cf. ठिंगना).

ठेंगा *ṭheṁgā* [**ṭheṅga-*], m. **1.** a cudgel, a stick. **2.** the thumb. **3.** sl. penis. — ~ दिखाना, to show the thumb: to make a contemptuous gesture, or retort. मेरे ठेंगे से, adv. by my thumb: pej. for all I care (= बला से).

ठेंगुनी *ṭheṁgunī* [cf. H. *ṭheṁgā*], f. reg. (Bihar) a thick stick.

ठेंघुनी *ṭheṁghunī*, f. reg. (Bihar) = ठेंगुनी.

ठेंठ *ṭheṁṭh*, adj. pronun. var. = ठेठ.

ठेंठा *ṭheṁṭhā* [? conn. *sthesṭha-*], m. stubble (of a crop).

ठेंठी *ṭheṁṭhī*, f. **1.** sthg. plugging the ear; an ear-plug; ear-wax. **2.** a plug, stopper.

ठें-ठें *ṭheṁ-ṭheṁ*, f. gleeful or malicious laughter (cf. ठी-ठी).

ठेक *ṭhek* [**ṭhekk-*; cf. H. *ṭek*], f. **1.** a support, prop (as for a load). **2.** *Pl. HŚS.* a wedge inserted below sthg. **3.** bottom, base. **4.** reg. (W.) enclosed space (as made with *ṭaṭṭīs*) for storing grain. **5.** reg. (E.) ferrule (as on a walking-stick).

ठेका *ṭhekā* [cf. **ṭhīkka-*; and **ṭhekk-*], m. **1.** a contract, &c. (= ठीका, 1.-3). **2.** an auxiliary drum played with the left hand along with a *tablā*. **3.** muted accompaniment of a singer (on drums). — ~ देना (को), to give a contract (to); to lease (to). ~ देनेवाला, a lessor, granter of a contract. ठेके की मियाद, f. the term (period) of a contract or lease. ठेके पर देना (को), to lease (to). ठेके पर, or में, adv. by the job, by piece-work. ~ लेना, to make a contract (for, का), to take on contract; to lease, to take on licence. – ठेका-पट्टा, m. a deed of lease. ठेका-पत्र, m. a deed of contract, or lease. ठेकाबंदी [P. *-bandī*], f. a lease; a leased property. ठेकेदार [P. *-dār*], m. a contractor, a lessee; a piece-worker.

ठेकी *ṭhekī* [cf. H. *ṭhek*], f. **1.** *Pl. HŚS.* supporting, propping up (a load, while in the course of carrying it). **2.** reg. (Bihar) a wedge.

ठेठ *ṭheṭh* [*sthesṭha-*], adj. **1.** pure, genuine; real, true, actual. **2.** specif. unmixed with loanwords (a style of language); informal, idiomatic (speech).

ठेपी *ṭhepī*, f. **1.** a stopper, a cork. **2.** a small lid. — ठेपीदार [P. *-dār*], adj. having a stopper; corked.

ठेल *ṭhel* [cf. H. *ṭhelnā*], f. (m., *Pl.*) pushing, shoving; a push; impulse. — ठेल-ठाल, f. continuous pushing, &c.

ठेलना *ṭhelnā* [**ṭhell-*], v.t. **1.** to push, to shove; to jostle. **2.** to propel; to shoot (a goal). — ठेला-ठेल, f. shoving, shouldering, jostling. °-ठेली, f. id.

ठेलम-ठेल *ṭhelam-ṭhel*, f. & adv. **1.** f. = ठेला-ठेली, see s.v. ठेलना. **2.** adv. with much shoving, &c.

ठेला *ṭhelā* [cf. **ṭhell-*], m. **1.** a cart, trolley; wheelbarrow. **2.** a push, a shove. — ठेला-गाड़ी, f. a cart, a trolley; truck, wagon.

ठेवना *ṭhevnā*, f. the knee (= घुटना).

ठेस *ṭhes* [**ṭhess-*], f. **1.** a knock, blow; shove. **2.** fig. a blow, shock. — ~ देना, or पहुँचाना, or लगाना (को), to strike, to hurt. ~ लगना (को), to receive a blow, a shock, &c. ~ लगाकर बैठना (से), to sit with the back against (sthg).

ठेसना *ṭhesnā* [**ṭhess-*], v.t. **1.** to knock, to strike against; to shove. **2.** to thrust in, to cram in (= ठूँसना). **3.** colloq. to eat greedily (= ठूँसना).

ठेसरा *ṭhesrā*, m. reg. (? W.) a jeer, taunt.

ठेहुना *ṭhehunā*, f. reg. the knee (cf. ठेवना).

ठोंक *ṭhoṁk*, f. = ठोक.

ठोंकना *ṭhoṁknā*, v.t. = ठोकना.

ठोंग *ṭhoṁg* [**ṭhoṅga-*], f. **1.** a peck, pecking. **2.** a beak, bill. **3.** a blow struck with the (bent) fingers.

ठोंगना *ṭhoṁgnā* [cf. **ṭhoṅga-*], v.t. **1.** to peck. **2.** to strike with the (bent) fingers.

ठोंगा *ṭhoṁgā* [**ṭhoṅga-*], m. a peck, pecking (= ठोंग, 1).

ठोंठ *ṭhoṁṭh* [**ṭhonṭha-*¹], f. beak, bill.

ठोंसा *ṭhoṁsā*, m. reg. (Bihar) a stamp or mould for making metal ornaments (cf. ²ठस्सा).

ठो *ṭho*, encl. reg. (E.) a particle used with cardinal numerals preceding nouns, where individual units are referred to. — दो-ठो पान, two *pān* leaves.

ठोक *ṭhok* [cf. H. *ṭhoknā*], f. a blow.

ठोकना *ṭhoknā* [**ṭhokk-*], v.t. **1.** to drive in (as a peg); to hammer home; to strike; to tap. **2.** to kick, to score (a goal). **3.** to strike against (sthg.); to slap (as the back); to beat (a drum); to clap (the hands); to hammer on (fetters); to pound, to knead. **4.** colloq. to beat, to punish.

5. to test, to examine (as goods). **ठोक-बजाकर,** adv. after striking and sounding: after close scrutiny; openly, publicly. **6.** to advance, to urge (a claim against someone). — **ताल ~,** to clap the palms (on the thighs, in challenge or preparation for fight). **ताला ~,** to make a lock fast (of or on, **का**); to lock or to shut up.

ठोकर *ṭhokar* [**ṭhokkarā-*], f. **1.** striking (esp. with the foot) against sthg.; tripping, stumbling; a kick; a blow. **2.** a knock, blow (suffered); injury. **3.** a cause of stumbling, obstacle (on a path or road). **4.** fig. a blow, reverse. — **~ खाना,** to trip, to stumble; to suffer loss, or misfortune. **ठोकरें खाना,** id.; to be roughly treated. **~ देना (को),** to kick, to beat; to cause loss or damage (to); to insult, to injure. **~ मारना,** to knock, to kick (against, **पर**). **~ लगना,** to knock (against, **की**); to trip, to stumble; to suffer damage. **~ लेना,** = **~ खाना,** 1. **ठोकरों पर पड़ा रहना,** to suffer indignities while dependent (on, **की**).

ठोकवा *ṭhokvā* [cf. H. *ṭhoknā*], m. colloq. a pancake (as flattened by hand).

ठोट *ṭhoṭ* [**ṭhoṭṭha-*], adj Brbh. stupid.

ठोड़ी *ṭhoṛī* [**ṭhoḍḍa-*], f. the chin (= [2]**ठुड्डी**).

ठोढ़ी *ṭhoṛhī*, f. = **ठोड़ी.**

ठोप *ṭhop*, m. reg. a drop. — **~ ~ गिरना,** to drip.

ठोर *ṭhor* [**ṭhoḍa-*[1]], f. beak, bill; spout.

ठोस *ṭhos*, adj. **1.** solid, dense. **2.** firm, sound, serving as a basis; substantial (as a work, a proof); real, true, genuine. **3.** dense, obtuse.

ठोसा *ṭhosā* [cf. H. *ṭhos*], m. the thumb (= **ठेंगा,** 2., 3).

ठोसाई *ṭhosāī* [cf. H. *ṭhos*], f. **1.** solidity. **2.** firmness, soundness, &c.

ठौर *ṭhaur* [*sthāvara-*], m. a fixed or particular place; locality; place of residence; a place, part (of the body). — **~ न आना,** to stay far (from), to hold aloof (from). **~ रहना,** to remain fixed or stationary. – **ठौर-कुठौर,** adv. = next. **ठौर-ठिकाना,** m. place of residence; locality; whereabouts. **ठौर-ठौर,** adv. in various places; in certain parts. **ठौर-बेठौर,** adv. in any place indiscriminately (as of falling blows); in a vital part; out of place, untimely.

ड

ड *ḍa*, the thirteenth consonant of the Devanāgarī syllabary. — **डकार**, m. the sound /ḍ/; the letter **ड**.

डंक *ḍaṅk* [conn. *ḍaṅk-: Pk. *ḍaṁka-*], m. **1.** a sting. **2.** fig. a cutting or wounding remark. **3.** Brbh. point, nib (of a pen). — **~ मारना (को)**, to sting. **~ लगना (को)**, to be stung (by, **का**). – **डंकदार** [P. *-dār*], m. having a sting.

डंका *ḍaṅkā* [**ḍaṅka-*: Pk. *ḍakka-*], m. a drum; a kettledrum. — **~ पीटना (का)**, to announce openly, to proclaim. **~ बजना (का)**, to be proclaimed; to be celebrated, or notorious. **~ बजाना (का)**, to beat a drum; to proclaim (as one's authority); to exercise authority, to rule; to glory (in); to rejoice. **डंके की चोट पर**, adv. fig. with fanfare, ostentatiously. **डंके की चोट कहना**, = **~ पीटना**. – **डंका-निशान**, m. drum and standard: van (as of a royal procession).

डँकिनी *ḍaṁkinī* [**ḍāṅkinī-*], f. = **डाकिनी**.

डँकियाना *ḍaṁkiyānā* [cf. **ḍaṅk-*], v.t. to sting.

डँकीला *ḍaṁkīlā* [cf. **ḍaṅk-*], adj. having a sting.

डँगवारा *ḍaṁgvārā*, m. *hist.* mutual assistance between farmers (consisting in the loan of oxen and ploughs without charge).

डंगू *ḍaṅgū*, m. 19c. a fever (? dengue fever).

डंठल *ḍaṇṭhal* [cf. **ḍaṇṭha-*], m. stalk, stem (of cereals, grasses).

डँठला *ḍaṁṭhlā*, m. reg. (W.) stalks (of a grain crop: = **डंठल**).

डँठा *ḍaṁṭhā*, m. reg. (W.) stalks (of a grain crop: = **डंठल**).

डँठी *ḍaṁṭhī*, f. reg. stalks (of a grain crop: = **डंठल**).

डंड *ḍaṇḍ* [*daṇḍa-*; Pk. *ḍaṇḍa-*], m. **1.** Av. a stick, rod. **2.** the upper arm. **3.** *athl.* a press-up. **4.** punishment; penalty; fine. **5.** compensation. — **~ डालना**, to impose a fine, &c. (on, **पर**). **~ देना**, = **~ भरना**. **~ पेलना**, to practise press-ups. **~ भरना**, to pay a penalty, &c. (for, **का**); to pay damages. **~ लेना (से)**, to fine. — **डंड-पेल**, m. a gymnast; one who keeps fit.

डँडना *ḍaṁḍnā* [*daṇḍayati*], v.t. reg. to fine, to punish.

डँडवत *ḍaṁḍvat*, f. Av. = **दंडवत**.

डंडा *ḍaṇḍā* [*daṇḍaka-*], m. **1.** a staff, a pole; bar, beam (of a pair of scales); rod; wand. **2.** rung (of a ladder). **4.** a long block, bar (as of soap). **4.** transf. a boundary wall. — **~ खाना**, to suffer a beating. **~ चलाना (पर)**, to beat, to belabour. **डंडे के ज़ोर से**, adv. by force. **डंडे बजाते फिरना**, colloq. to wander idly about. **डंडे बजाना**, to play or to fight with staves. **डंडे से बात करना**, to have recourse to force (rather than to argument). – **डंडा-बेड़ी**, f. *Pl. HŚS.* fetters with metal bars attached. **डंडा-सा**, adj. stick-like; very thin.

डँड़िया *ḍaṁṛiyā* [cf. H. *ḍaṇḍī*], f. a striped sari (as worn at the Holī festival).

1**डंडी** *ḍaṇḍī* [cf. *daṇḍin-*], m. one carrying a staff (esp. an ascetic).

2**डंडी** *ḍaṇḍī* [cf. H. *ḍaṇḍā*], f. **1.** a stick; cane; rod. **2.** beam (of a pair of scales). **3.** shaft (of a vehicle). **4.** handle; lever. **5.** stalk, stem; shoot. **6.** a line, stripe. **7.** sl. penis. — **~ मारना**, to press down the beam of a balance: to give short weight. – **डंडीदार** [P. *-dār*], m. one who weighs (goods, produce). **डंडीमार**, m. one who gives short weight.

डँवरुआ *ḍaṁvăruā*, m. Brbh. gout.

डँसना *ḍaṁsnā*, v.t. = **डसना**.

डकडकाना *ḍakḍakānā*, v.i. to make a noise in swallowing; to take large gulps. — **डकडकाके पीना**, to gulp noisily, or gulp in greedily.

डकराना *ḍakrānā*, v.i. to bellow; to roar; to low.

डकार *ḍakār* [cf. H. *ḍakārnā*], f. **1.** a belch. **2.** bellowing; roaring; lowing. — **~ लेना**, to belch. **~ तक न लेना**, iron. to carry out an action inconspicuously (esp. embezzlement).

डकारना *ḍakārnā* [cf. **ḍakkāra-*], v.i. & v.t. **1.** v.i. to belch. **2.** to bellow; to roar; to low. **3.** v.t. to gulp down, to swallow. **4.** to embezzle.

डकैत *ḍakait* [cf. **ḍākka-*[1]], m. a robber; one of a band of robbers.

डकैती *ḍakaitī* [cf. H. *ḍakait*], f. robbery, banditry.

डग *ḍag* [conn. **ḍag-*[2]], f. a step, or stride. — **~ दे-**, Brbh. = next. **~ भरना**, or **धरना**, to step out, to stride. ~ मारना, to stride swiftly, or with long steps.

डग-डग *ḍag-ḍag* [cf. H. *ḍagḍagānā*], adj. & m. swaying, lurching, &c. (= डगमग, and डगमगाहट).

डगडगाना *ḍagḍagānā* [cf. **ḍag-*[1]: Pk. *ḍagamagaï*], v.i. to sway, to lurch, &c. (= डगमगाना).

डगमग *ḍagmag* [cf. H. *ḍagmagānā*], adj. **1.** rocking, swaying; trembling. **2.** tottering (gait). **3.** rolling. **4.** wavering (in faith or opinion).

डगमगाना *ḍagmagānā* [cf. **ḍag-*[1]: Pk. *ḍagamagaï*], v.i. & v.t. **1.** v.i. to rock, to sway; to tremble. **2.** to totter, to stagger. **3.** to walk ostentatiously (a woman); to roll (a boat). **4.** to waver (as in faith). **5.** v.t. to cause to shake, &c.

डगमगाहट *ḍagmagāhaṭ* [cf. H. *ḍagmagānā*], f. **1.** swaying, &c. **2.** tottering, lurching. **3.** wavering.

डगर *ḍagar* [cf. **ḍag-*[2]], f. a road, track; path. — ~ बताना, to point out a road or way (to, को), to direct; to lead. हर ~ राम की, (one's) every act depends on God.

डगर- *ḍagar-*, v.i. Brbh. to totter; to lurch.

डगरना *ḍagarnā*, m. reg. (Bihar) a wooden platter.

डगरा *ḍagrā*, m. reg. **1.** a large open woven basket (used to hold rice, flour, &c., and for winnowing). **2.** Bihar. a large flat wooden dish.

[1]**डगरी** *ḍagrī* [cf. H. *ḍagar*], f. way, path.

[2]**डगरी** *ḍagrī* [cf. H. *ḍagrā*], f. dimin. reg. a small woven basket.

डगरो *ḍagro*, m. Brbh. = डगर.

डटना *ḍaṭnā* [cf. H. [1]*ḍāṭnā*], v.i. **1.** to be or to become fixed or firm; to stay in place; to stay in or at a place. **2.** to be restrained, checked. **3.** to come to a halt. **4.** to be determined, resolved (a person); to be stubborn; to resist stubbornly. **5.** to be settled, agreed on. **6.** to endure. — डटकर, adv. stubbornly, &c.; vigorously, uninhibitedly. पाँव ~, to plant the feet firmly.

डटाना *ḍaṭānā* [cf. H. [1]*ḍaṭnā*], v.t. **1.** to set in place, to fix; to push forward (as to a set place); colloq. to consume, to account for (food). **2.** to restrain, to check. **3.** to bring to a halt.

डट्टा *ḍaṭṭā* [cf. H. *ḍāṭ*: Pk. *-daṭṭa-*], m. reg. a stopper, plug; door-stop.

डढ़- *ḍaṛh-* [cf. *dagdha-*], v.i. Brbh. to burn, to be burnt.

डढ़ियल *ḍaṛhiyal* [cf. H. *ḍāṛhī*], f. bearded; having a long beard.

डपट *ḍapaṭ* [cf. H. *ḍapaṭnā*], f. **1.** shouting, rebuking; a rebuke. **2.** rushing forward; galloping.

डपटना *ḍapaṭnā* [cf. **drapp-*; also *darpa-*, and **dabb-*, **ḍabb-*], v.t. & v.i. **1.** v.t. to shout at, to rebuke. **2.** to rush at, to assault. **3.** to urge (a horse). **4.** v.i. to rush forward; to gallop.

डपटाना *ḍapṭānā* [cf. H. *ḍapaṭnā*], v.t. to ride hard (a horse); to charge on horseback (against, पर).

डपोर-संख *ḍapor-saṅkh*, m. & adj. pej. big conch shell: **1.** a loud talker (who does nothing). **2.** a big, stupid person.

डप्पू *ḍappū*, adj & m. *Pl. HŚS.* **1.** adj. vast, huge. **2.** m. a huge man, or creature.

डफ *ḍaph* [A. *daff* × (?) *ḍamaru-*], m. a drum: tambourine used by *lāvnī* singers.

डफला *ḍaphlā*, m. = डफ.

डफली *ḍaphlī*, f. dimin. a tambourine.

डफार- *ḍaphār-*, v.i. Av. to make a great noise (in weeping).

डफ़ालची *ḍafālcī*, m. *Pl. HŚS.* = डफ़ाली.

डफाली *ḍaphālī*, m. *Pl. HŚS.* a drum player.

डफोर *ḍaphor-*, v.i. Brbh. to make a great outcry.

डब *ḍab* [conn. H. *ḍabbā*], m. *Pl. HŚS.* **1.** a pouch, pocket. **2.** leather (as used in making pots, or utensils).

डबका *ḍabkā*, m. reg. fear, apprehension.

डबकौंह- *ḍabkauṁh-* [cf. H. *ḍabḍabānā*], adj. Brbh. tearful.

डबडबाना *ḍabḍabānā*, v.i. **1.** to be filled with, or to overflow with, tears (the eyes). **2.** to brim, to flow (tears).

डबरा *ḍabrā* [cf. H. *ḍābar*], m. = डाबर.

[1]**डबरी** *ḍabrī* [**ḍabbara-*], f. a ditch, pool of water.

[2]**डबरी** *ḍabrī* [cf. **ḍabba-*[1]: ? ← Drav.], f. an earthen water-cup, bowl.

[3]**डबरी** *ḍabrī*, f. *hist.* division of profits among a village community according to members' respective shares.

डबल *ḍabal* [Engl. *double*], adj. double. — ~ रोटी, f. bread containing yeast; a loaf.

डब्बा *ḍabbā* [conn. **ḍabba*-[1]], m. **1.** a box, carton, container; a tin; reg. (W.) leather container for oil or *ghī*. **2.** a compartment. **3.** a railway carriage. **4.** a freight container. — ~ गोल होना, colloq. to be unsuccessful (in an examination). – डब्बाबंद [P. *-band*], adj. preserved, canned (food). °-बंदी, f. canning, preserving.

डब्बी *ḍabbī* [cf. H. *ḍabbā*], f. a small box.

डब्बू *ḍabbū* [cf. *darva*-], m. reg. a ladle.

डमरु *ḍamăru* [S.], m. = डमरू.

डमरू *ḍamrū* [ad. *ḍamaru*-], m. **1.** a small drum (having playing surfaces at both ends; its narrow middle part can be held in the hand). **2.** an object having a narrowed waist or middle part. — डमरूमध्य, m. an isthmus.

डयन *ḍayan* [S.], m. **1.** flight. **2.** fig. a litter (= पालकी).

डर *ḍar* [*dara*-; Pk. *ḍara*-], m. **1.** fear. **2.** awe. — ~ दिखाना (को), to frighten, to put in fear (of, का); to intimidate. ~ लगना (को), to feel fear, to be afraid (of, से). – डरपोक [cf. H. *poṁknā*], adj. & m. timid; cowardly; a timid person, &c. °ना, adj. 19c. id.

डरना *ḍarnā* [*darati*: Pk. *ḍaraï*], v.i. **1.** to be afraid (of or to, से); to be frightened (by, से). **2.** to feel reluctance (to, से), misgivings (about).

डरपना *ḍarapnā* [cf. *darati*: Pk. *ḍaraï*], v.i. = डरना.

डरपोक *ḍarpok*, adj. see s.v. डर.

डराऊ *ḍarāū* [cf. H. *ḍarnā*], adj. fearful, timid.

[1]**डराना** *ḍarānā* [cf. H. *ḍarnā*], v.t. **1.** to make (one) afraid; to frighten. **2.** to intimidate, to deter.

[2]**डराना** *ḍarānā*, adj. = डरावना.

डरावना *ḍarāvnā* [H. *ḍarānā*-], adj. **1.** causing fear, fearsome; formidable. **2.** intimidating, deterrent.

डरावा *ḍarāvā* [cf. H. *ḍarānā*], v.t. intimidation, threat. — ~ दिखाना (को), to threaten, &c.

डरीला *ḍarīlā* [cf. H. *ḍar*], adj. reg. = डरावना.

डरेस *ḍares*, adj. & m. = दरेस.

डरैला *ḍarailā* [cf. H. *ḍar*], adj. = डरावना.

डलना *ḍalnā* [cf. H. *ḍālnā*], v.i. **1.** to be thrown down. **2.** to be poured. **3.** to be put, placed, or laid; to be imposed. **4.** to be laid down (arms). **5.** to be put on (clothing). **6.** to be noted down, recorded. **7.** to be suspended, hung.

डलवाना *ḍalvānā* [cf. H. *ḍālnā*], v.t. to cause to be thrown down, &c. (by, से).

[1]**डला** *ḍalā* [**ḍala*-], m. a piece, lump; clod.

[2]**डला** *ḍalā* [conn. **ḍalla*-[2]: Pk. *ḍalla*-], m. = [2]डाली.

डलाना *ḍalānā*, v.t. = डलवाना.

डलिया *ḍaliyā* [cf. **ḍalla*-[2]: Pk. *ḍalla*-], f. a small basket.

डली *ḍalī* [**ḍala*-], f. **1.** a small piece, bit; a lump. **2.** a betel nut (= सुपारी).

डल्ला *ḍallā* [**ḍalla*-[2] ? ← Panj.], m. = [2]डला.

डस *ḍas*, f. **1.** reg. (Raj.) the string by which a scale is held (in weighing). **2.** [conn. *daśā*-] *Pl.* unwoven threads at the end of the warp (in a piece of cloth).

डसना *ḍasnā* [*daṁśati*: Pk. *ḍaṁsaï*], v.t. to bite, to sting (as a snake, a scorpion).

[1]**डसाना** *ḍasānā* [cf. **dhvāsayati*], v.t. to spread, to make (a bed).

[2]**डसाना** *ḍasānā* [cf. H. *ḍasnā*], v.t. reg. to cause to bite.

डहँक- *ḍahaṁk*-, v.t. Av. = [2]डहकना.

डहक- *ḍahak*-, v.i. Brbh. **1.** to break down (as in tears); to sob. **2.** to cry out, to roar.

[1]**डहकना** *ḍahaknā* [conn. H. *ḍahḍahānā*], v.i. **1.** to blossom. **2.** to be radiant, splendid.

[2]**डहकना** *ḍahaknā*, v.t. to deceive; to disappoint, to tantalise.

डहका- *ḍahkā*-, v.t. Brbh. Av. to deceive.

डहडहा *ḍahḍahā*, adj. Brbh. **1.** blossoming, flourishing (vegetation); delightful. **2.** glowing, radiant (as eyes, or the moon).

डहडहाना *ḍahḍahānā*, v.i. & v.t. **1.** v.i. to blossom, to flourish; to be delightful. **2.** to glow, to be radiant. **3.** v.t. reg. to make fertile or flourishing.

डहर *ḍahr*, m. reg. a path (= डगर).

[1]**डहरा** *ḍahrā*, m. E.H. = डहर.

[2]**डहरा** *ḍahrā*, m. low, marshy ground.

डहरा- *ḍahrā*- [cf. H. *ḍahr*], v.t. Brbh. to turn (the eyes) towards (one).

डहरी *ḍahrī* [cf. H. [2]*ḍahrā*], adj. reg. wet, waterlogged (ground).

[1]**डाँक** *ḍāṁk*, f. pronun. var. = [1]डाक.

[2]**डाँक** *ḍāṁk*, m. Av. a drum (= डंका).

[3]**डाँक** *ḍāṁk*, m. Brbh. = डंक.

डाँक- *ḍāṁk-* [conn. H. [1]*ḍāknā*, v.i.], v.t. E.H. to leap across or over.

डाँकिनी *ḍāṁkinī*, f. E.H. = डाकिनी.

डाँकू *ḍāṁkū*, m. pronun. var. = डाकू.

1**डाँग** *ḍāṁg* [**ḍaṅga-*[1]: Pk. *ḍaṅgā-*], f. m. a short, heavy stick.

2**डाँग** *ḍāṁg* [**ḍaṅga-*[3]], f. m. ridge (of a mountain); hilly land; severely eroded ground (as found along the lower Jumna).

डाँगर *ḍāṁgar* [*ḍaṅgara-*[2]], adj. & m. **1.** adj. pej. useless; half-starved (an animal). **2.** m. a thin animal (esp. horned cattle).

डाँट *ḍāṁṭ* [cf. H. [1]*ḍāṁṭnā*], f. **1.** restraining, checking. **2.** browbeating, threatening; a threat, or threatening gesture. **3.** rebuking, scolding. — ~ पड़ना (को), to suffer a scolding; to be threatened. ~ देना, or बताना, or सुनाना (को), to scold, to threaten (one). ~ में रखना (को), to keep (one) in check, obedient; to cow (one). ~ रखना (पर) id. ~ लगाना, = ~ बताना. – डाँट-डपट, f. = ~, 2.; an attack, assault (on, पर). डाँट-फटकार, f. = ~, 3.

1**डाँटना** *ḍāṁṭnā* [**dranṭ-*], v.t. **1.** to restrain, to check; to curb. **2.** to browbeat, to threaten. **3.** to scold; to punish.

2**डाँटना** *ḍāṁṭnā*, v.t. pronun. var. = [1]डाटना.

डाँठ *ḍāṁṭh*, m. reg. **1.** a cut crop; stalks (of a grain crop: डंठल). **2.** refuse of a crop after threshing.

डाँड़ *ḍāṁṛ* [*daṇḍa-*; Pk. *ḍaṇḍa-*], m. **1.** E. a stick, staff, pole; bar, beam. **2.** an oar. **3.** transf. a fine, punishment; forfeiture. **4.** indemnity. — ~ खेना, or चलाना, or लगाना, to row. ~ भरना, to pay a fine, penalty, or indemnity. ~ मारना, = ~ चलाना; to measure, to survey. ~ लगाना, to fine (one, को). ~ लेना, to exact a penalty, &c. (from, से). – डाँड़-मेंड़, f. = डाँड़ा, 3.

डाँड़- *ḍāṁṛ-* [*daṇḍayati*], v.t. Brbh. Av. **1.** to punish, to fine. **2.** to take revenge on.

डाँड़ा *ḍāṁṛā* [*daṇḍaka-*], m. **1.** reg. a pole. **2.** an oar. **3.** boundary line or mark. होली का ~, m. materials collected at a village boundary, &c., and burnt at the Holī festival. — डाँड़ा-मेंड़ा, m. a boundary line.

1**डाँड़ी** *ḍāṁṛī* [*daṇḍika-*], m. a rower.

2**डाँड़ी** *ḍāṁṛī* [*daṇḍa-*; Pk. *ḍaṇḍa-*], f. **1.** a beam, rod; the beam of a pair of scales. **2.** Av. a stalk. **3.** *hist.* a kind of hammock hung from a pole and carried by porters. — ~ मारना, to give short measure (by weight).

डाँवरी *ḍāṁvrī* [conn. **ḍambha-*], f. Brbh. a girl, daughter.

डाँवरू *ḍāṁvrū* [conn. **ḍambharūpa-*], m. reg. a tiger cub.

डाँवाँडोल *ḍāṁvāṁḍol*, adj. & m. **1.** adj. shaken; unsteady (as gait). **2.** unsettled, vacillating (mind). **3.** uncertain, uneasy (a situation). **4.** m. tremor (as of an earthquake). — ~ फिरना, to wander about aimlessly.

डाँवाँडोली *ḍāṁvāṁḍolī* [cf. H. *ḍāṁvāṁḍol*], f. shaken, unsettled or uncertain state.

डाँस *ḍāṁs* [*daṁśa-*], m. reg. (E.) a large mosquito; a gad-fly.

-ड़ा *-ṛā* [MIA *-ḍa-*], suffix (forms nouns having potentially dimin. force, e.g. मुखड़ा, m. little face, sad face; तुकड़ा, m. piece).

डाइन *ḍāin* [*ḍākinī-*], f. **1.** a demoness; witch, hag. **2.** pej. a shrewish or ugly old woman.

1**डाक** *ḍāk* [**ḍakka-*[1] ? conn. **ḍakk-*[1]], f. **1.** the postal service. **2.** post, mail. — ~ की (or का) टिकट, f. m. a postage stamp. ~ में डालना, to post (a letter, &c). ~ से, adv. by post. – डाक-ख़र्च, m. postal expenses. डाक-ख़ाना, m. post office. डाक-गाड़ी, f. a mail train. डाक-घर, m. post office. डाक-टिकट, f. m. a postage stamp. डाक-तार, m. the post and telegraph service. डाक-तार विभाग, m. Post and Telegraph Department. डाक-बँगला, m. a circuit-house, inspection bungalow. डाक-महसूल, m. postal charges, postage. डाक-मुहर, f. postmark. डाक-व्यय, m. postal expenses. डाक-सेवा, f. the postal service. डाकवाला, m. a postman.

2**डाक** *ḍāk* [Engl. *dock*], m. a dock.

3**डाक** *ḍāk*, m. *Pl.* a piece of gold or silver leaf used as a foil for a gem.

4**डाक** *ḍāk* [cf. H. *ḍāknā*], f. *Pl. HŚS.* calling out, shouting; bidding (at auction).

डकटरी *ḍakṭarī*, adj. & f. **1.** adj. 19c. doctor's (medicine). **2.** f. medical studies. **3.** doctor's work or profession.

1**डाकना** *ḍāknā*, v.i. to step or to leap across (cf. डाँक-).

2**डाकना** *ḍāknā* [**ḍakk-*[1]], v.i. *Pl.* (*HŚS.*) to call out, to shout.

डाकर *ḍākar*, f. reg. a rich clay soil.

डाका *ḍākā* [**ḍākka-*], m. robbery; an attack by robbers. — ~ डालना, or मारना, to commit robbery (in a band). ~ पड़ना, an attack by robbers to be made (on, पर). – डाकाज़नी [P. *zadan*], f. robbery, dacoity.

1**डाकिन** *ḍākin* [cf. H. *ḍākū*], f. **1.** a female robber. **2.** a robber's wife.

[2]**डाकिन** *ḍākin*, f. = डाकिनी.

[3]**डाकिन** *ḍākin* [cf. H. *ḍākiyā*], f. a postman's wife.

डाकिनी *ḍākinī* [S.], f. **1.** a demoness; witch, hag. **2.** pej. a shrewish woman.

डाकिया *ḍākiyā* [cf. H. [1]*ḍāk*], m. a postman.

डाकू *ḍākū* [cf. **ḍākka-*[1]], m. a robber, one of a band of robbers.

डाकैत *ḍākait*, f. = डकैत.

डाकैती *ḍākaitī*, f. = डकैती.

डाक्टर *ḍākṭar* [Engl. *doctor*], m. a doctor, a person trained in western medicine.

डाक्टरी *ḍākṭarī* [cf. H. *ḍākṭar*], f. & adj. **1.** f. medicine, medical science. **2.** the profession or standing of a doctor. **3.** adj. medical. — ~ सीखना, to study medicine. ~ करना, to practise medicine.

डाचो *ḍācī* [? cf. Raj. *ḍāc* 'tooth'; ← Raj. or Panj.], f. a young female camel that has calved once.

डाट *ḍāṭ* [cf. H. [1]*ḍāṭnā*], f. **1.** a stopper, plug. **2.** a support; a spike (holding sthg. in place). **3.** keystone (of an arch). **4.** pronun. var. = डाँट. — ~ बैठाना, to set a support, &c. in place. ~ लगाना, to plug, &c.

[1]**डाटना** *ḍāṭnā* [**draṭ-*: Pk. *-daṭṭa-*], v.t. **1.** to stop up, to plug; to pack full, to cram (into, में). **2.** to eat greedily. **3.** to support, to hold in place. **4.** to display, to vaunt (dress, finery).

[2]**डाटना** *ḍāṭnā*, v.t. pronun. var. = डाँटना.

डाढ़ *ḍāṛh* [**dāṁṣṭra-*: Pk. *dāḍhā-*], f. **1.** a molar tooth. **2.** fang (of a wild animal). — अक़ल-डाढ़, f. wisdom tooth.

डाढ़ा *ḍāṛhā* [*dagdha-*; Pk. *ḍaḍḍha-*], m. Av. a fire, scrub fire.

डाढ़ी *ḍāṛhī*, f. = दाढ़ी.

[1]**डाब** *ḍāb* [**ḍabba-*[1]], m. a green coconut.

[2]**डाब** *ḍāb*, m. pronun. var. = [1]डाभ.

डाबर *ḍābar* [**ḍabbara-*], m. **1.** low ground where water collects; marshy ground. **2.** a pool of water; puddle. **3.** a small tank or ditch for water.

डाबी *ḍābī*, f. reg. a sheaf.

[1]**डाभ** *ḍābh* [*darbha-*], m. **1.** *kuśa* grass (used in sacrifices); a grass that spreads on waste land. **2.** Av. young mango shoots.

[2]**डाभ** *ḍābh*, m. a green coconut (= [1]डाब).

[1]**डामर** *ḍāmar*, m. **1.** resin, esp. of the *sāl* tree. **2.** pitch. **3.** reg. a torch (using pitch).

[2]**डामर** *ḍāmar*, m. = डाबर, 2.

डामाडोल *ḍāmāḍol*, adj. = डाँवाँडोल.

डायन *ḍāyan*, f. see डाइन.

[1]**डार** *ḍār*, f. Brbh. Av. = [1]डाल.

[2]**डार** *ḍār*, f. E.H. = डलिया.

[3]**डार** *ḍār* [?? cf. H. *ḍālnā*], f. *Pl.* file (of animals or birds); flock.

[1]**डाल** *ḍāl* [*ḍāla-*[1]], f. a branch. — ~ का टूटा, adj. plucked from the branch; fresh; fine, splendid. एक ~ पर रहना, fig. to be of congenial temperament (a couple, a group).

[2]**डाल** *ḍāl* [**ḍalla-*[2]: Pk. *ḍalla-*], f. **1.** a basket. **2.** transf. reg. a gift; gift to a bride.

डालना *ḍālnā* [**ḍāl-*], v.t. **1.** to throw down; to cast, to hurl; to sow, to scatter (seed). **2.** to pour; to put (as sugar in tea); to lay (upon, पर or के सिर: as of a burden, a responsibility). **3.** to put, to place, to consign (for safe keeping); to maintain (as a mistress). **4.** to put down, to lay before (one); to present; to lay down (arms). **5.** to put on (as shoes, bangles); to throw on (a garment). **6.** to spread (over, पर); to spread out. **7.** to put down, to record (as a note). **8.** to suspend, to hang. **9.** to cast off, to put aside. **10.** to cause, to occasion (in, में). **11.** to bring into line or file (as one horse behind another).

[1]**डाली** *ḍālī* [cf. **ḍāla-*[1]] a branch, a small branch.

[2]**डाली** *ḍālī* [**ḍalla-*[2]: Pk. *ḍalla-*], f. **1.** a wide, flat basket. **2.** a basket or tray of flowers, fruit, &c. sent as a present. — ~ भेजना, or लगाना, to send a complimentary gift (to).

डावाँदोल *ḍāvāṁdol*, adj. & m. = डाँवाँदोल.

डास- *ḍās-* [**dhvāsayati*], v.t. Av. to spread, to make (a bed).

[1]**डासन** *ḍāsan* [**dhvāsana-*], m. Av. bedding.

[2]**डासन** *ḍāsan* [cf. H. *ḍāṁsnā*], f. Av. biting.

डाह *ḍāh* [*dāha-*; ? × *dābha-*], f. **1.** heart-burning, jealousy, envy. **2.** malice, enmity; hatred. — ~ करना, to be jealous (of); to bear ill-will (to). ~ खाना, to feel jealousy, &c. – डाह-भरा, adj. = डाही.

डाहना *ḍāhnā* [*dāhayati*], v.t. & v.i. **1.** v.t. to cause to burn with jealousy, malice, &c. (see डाह). **2.** v.i. to burn with jealousy, &c.

डाही *ḍāhī* [cf. H. *ḍāh*], adj. **1.** jealous, envious. **2.** malicious; ill-willed.

डिंगल *ḍiṅgal*, f. an archaising form of early Mārvāṛī language, as used in Rājasthānī bardic poetry.

[1]**डिंभ** *ḍimbh* [S.], m. Brbh. a child.

[2]**डिंभ** *ḍimbh*, m. E.H. pride, vanity (cf. दंभ).

डिगना *ḍignā* [cf. **dig-*[1], and **giḍḍ-*], v.i. **1.** to shake, to move; to slip; to stumble; to fall. **2.** to shift, to be displaced. **3.** to be deflected (from, से: as from faith); to shrink, to flinch (from).

डिगमिगाना *ḍigmigānā* [cf. **ḍig-*[1]], v.i. = डगमगाना.

[1]**डिगरी** *ḍigrī* [Engl. *decree*], f. a decree; an injunction. — ~ जारी करना, to issue a decree, &c.; to enforce a decree. ~ देना, to grant a decree; to award (a sum). ~ होना, a decree, &c. to be granted (to, की). – डिगरीदार [P. *-dār*], m. one in whose favour a decree has been given.

[2]**डिगरी** *ḍigrī* [Engl. *degree*], f. **1.** a degree (of temperature, or arc). **2.** a degree (academic). — डिगरीधारी, adj. holding a degree, graduate. डिगरी-प्राप्त, adj. graduated, graduate.

डिगाना *ḍigānā* [cf. H. *ḍignā*], v.t. **1.** to cause to shake or to move; to cause to slip, or to stumble. **2.** to make loose, or unsteady. **3.** to shake (as one's faith).

डिग्गी *ḍiggī*, f. reg. = दिग्गी.

डिग्री *ḍigrī*, f. = [1] [2]डिगरी.

डिठियारो *ḍiṭhiyāro* [cf. *dṛṣṭi-*], adj. Brbh. possessing sight.

डिठौना *ḍiṭhaunā*, m. = दिठौना.

डिढ्या *ḍiḍhyā*, f. **1.** a covetous glance. **2.** eager desire. — ~ लगाना, to look covetously (at, पर); to covet, to desire.

डिप्टी *ḍipṭī* [Engl. *deputy*], m. esp. in comp. deputy, assistant (commissioner, &c).

डिबिया *ḍibiyā* [cf. H. *ḍibbā*], f. a small or miniature box or casket.

डिब्बा *ḍibbā* [conn. **ḍibba-*[1]], m. = डब्बा.

डिब्बी *ḍibbī* [cf. H. *ḍibbā*], f. a small box, case, or casket.

डिमडिमी *ḍimḍimī*, f. Brbh. = डुगडुगी.

डिसमिस *ḍismis* [Engl. *dismiss*], adj. dismissed (as an employee, a case). — ~ करना, to dismiss, &c.

डींग *ḍīṃg*, f. **1.** boasting. **2.** vanity. — ~ मारना, or हाँकना, to boast, to brag; to be vainglorious. – डींगमार, adj. & m. boastful; a boaster.

डींगिया *ḍīṃgiyā* [cf. H. *ḍīṃg*], m. a boaster.

डीठ *ḍīṭh* [*dṛṣṭi-*], f. **1.** look, glance. **2.** sight, vision. **3.** the evil eye. — ~ बाँधना, to enchant, to bewitch (one, की). ~ मारना, to cast a glance (at, पर). ~ लगाना, to cast a spell (on, पर).

डीठ- *ḍīṭh-* [cf. *dṛṣṭa-*], v.t. Av. to see.

डील *ḍīl* [**ḍilla-*], m. bulk, size; stature. — डील-डौल, m. size and shape, physical build.

डीह *ḍīh*, m. **1.** a settlement, village; reg. (Bihar) land adjoining a village. **2.** ruins of a deserted village; reg. (W.) mound or site of a village.

डीहा *ḍīhā*, m. reg. a mound; bank (cf. ढीह, ढूह).

डुक *ḍuk* [**ḍukka-*], m. reg. (Raj.) a blow with the fist.

डुकड़ी *ḍukṛī*, f. a two-horse cart.

डुकरिया *ḍukariyā* [cf. H. *ḍokrā*], f. dimin. pej. an old woman. — डुकरिया-पुरान, m. an old wives' tale.

डुकियाना *ḍukiyānā* [cf. H. *ḍuk*], v.t. *Pl. HŚS.* to strike or to thump (one) with the fist.

डुक्कर *ḍukkar*, m. reg. (Raj.) a boar.

डुगडुगाना *ḍugḍugānā* [cf. **ḍuggi-*], v.t. to beat (a drum).

डुगडुगी *ḍugḍugī* [**ḍuggi-*], f. a small kettledrum. — ~ पीटना, or फेरना, to proclaim by (beat of) drum, to make public. ~ बजाना, id.; to play the kettledrum.

डुग्गी *ḍuggī*, f. = डुगडुगी.

डुपट्टा *ḍupaṭṭā*, m. = दुपट्टा.

डुबकी *ḍubkī* [cf. H. *ḍūbnā*], f. **1.** a dive, plunge; ducking (under the water). **2.** fig. disappearance from sight, or mind. — ~ खाना, to be dipped; = ~ लगाना, 1. ~ देना (को), to dip, to immerse. ~ मारना, or लगाना, to plunge, to duck, to bob; not to turn up.

डुबना *ḍubnā*, v.i. *Pl.* = डूबना.

डुबवाना *ḍubvānā* [cf. H. *ḍūbnā*], v.t. to cause to be sunk, immersed, &c. (by, से).

डुबसी *ḍubsī* [cf. H. *ḍūbnā*; ? ← Panj.], f. reg. (W.) land liable to be flooded.

[1]**डुबाई** *ḍubāī* [cf. H. *ḍubānā*], adj. enough to sink or to drown in (water).

[2]**डुबाई** *ḍubāī* [cf. H. *ḍubānā*], f. *hist.* an unconditional bribe (not to be returned if a suit is lost).

डुबान् *ḍubān* [cf. H. *ḍubānā*], f. **1.** a deep place, depth. **2.** a plunge.

डुबाना *ḍubānā* [cf. H. *ḍūbnā*], v.t. **1.** to cause to sink; to immerse. **2.** to sink (a ship). **3.** to drown (one). **4.** to flood (as with water). **5.** fig. to ruin, to destroy.

डुबाव *ḍubāv* [cf. H. *ḍubānā*], m. **1.** state of immersion, sinking; drowning. **2.** depth of water sufficient to allow a person or thing to be completely immersed.

डुबोना *ḍubonā*, v.t. = डुबाना.

डुब्बी *ḍubbī* [cf. H. *ḍūbnā*], f. a dive, plunge (= डुबकी).

डुभा *ḍubhā*, m. reg. (Bihar) a large cup, or small vessel to eat from.

डुरी *ḍurī*, f. 19c. = ¹डोरी.

डुलना *ḍulnā* [cf. H. *ḍolnā*], v.i. 1. = डोलना. **2.** to walk with a swaying or enticing gait (a woman).

डुलाना *ḍulānā* [cf. H. *ḍolnā*], v.t. **1.** to cause to move, to move (a fan, &c.); to shake, to swing. **2.** to cause to move on, or away (a person, or an animal). **3.** to move or to agitate (the settled mind, or heart).

डूँगर *ḍūṁgar* [cf. **ḍuṅga-*: Pk. *duṁgara-*], m. a hill; hillock.

डूँगरी *ḍūṁgrī* [cf. H. *dūṁgar*], f. dimin. a small hill, hillock.

डूँगा *ḍūṁgā*, adj. & m. **1.** *Pl.* deep. **2.** *HŚS. mus.* a partic. note.

डूँड़ा *ḍūṁṛā* [**ḍuṇḍa-*²], m. & adj. **1.** m. a bullock with one horn, or with broken or defective horns. **2.** adj. having one horn, &c. **3.** impaired; in a sad state.

डूब *ḍūb* [cf. H. *ḍūbnā*], f. sinking, diving, &c.

डूबना *ḍūbnā* [**buḍyati*: MIA *buḍḍaï*], v.i. **1.** to sink; to set (the sun); to end (the day); to dive. **2.** to drown. **3.** to be immersed, flooded (ground). **4.** to be lost, ruined (as funds, reputation); to be sacrificed to no avail. **5.** to be engrossed (in, में: as in study, or activity); to be sunk (in: as in grief, or shame). — **डूब मरना**, to drown. **डूबती रक़म**, f. a lost sum: a bad debt.

डूमर *ḍūmar* [**ḍumbara-*: ? ← Austro-as.], m. the fig-tree *Ficus glomerata*, = गूलर (a large tree that loses its leaves in the rainy season: source of a gum).

डेंगी *ḍeṁgī* [**ḍeṅga-*¹], f. a small boat, rowing-boat, dinghy; canoe. — **डेंगीवाला**, m. a boatman.

डेग *ḍeg* [conn. **ḍig-*²], m. a step, pace.

डेढ़ *ḍeṛh* [**dvaiyardha-*], adj. **1.** one and a half. **2.** one and a half times. **~ सौ**, one hundred and fifty. — **अपनी ~ ईंट की मसजिद बनाना**, or **चुनना**, fig. to be intent on an inconsequential task. **~ चावल की खिचड़ी अलग पकाना**, fig. to hold to one's own (insignificant) opinion. **~ हड्डी का**, adj. colloq. wasted, emaciated. – **डेढ़-पौवा**, m. a weight equal to one and a half *pāv*.

¹**डेरा** *ḍerā* [**ḍera-*¹], m. **1.** a temporary dwelling, or shelter; a tent. **2.** a halting-place. **3.** abode, quarters. — **~ उखाड़ना**, to strike camp. **~ खड़ा करना**, to pitch a tent; to encamp. **~ डालना**, = **~ खड़ा करना**; to take up (one's) abode. **~**, or **डेरे**, **पड़ना**, to be encamped. – **डेरा-डंडा**, m. tent and poles: a tent with accessories, baggage.

²**डेरा** *ḍerā* [**ḍera-*²], adj. reg. (Bihar) crooked (as eyebrows).

डेल *ḍel* [**ḍella-*], m. lump, piece, clod.

डेला *ḍelā* [**ḍella-*], m. **1.** the eyeball; the white of the eye. 2. = ढेला, डेल.

डेली *ḍelī*, f. Av. a fowler's basket.

डेवढ़ा *ḍevṛha* [**dvaiyardha-* × **duvardha-*], adj. & m. **1.** adj. increased by a half, by fifty per cent; half as big or as much again (as). **2.** m. multiplication by one and a half; fifty per cent interest in kind (esp. on grain). — **~ करना**, to increase by a half, by fifty per cent. **~ साँप**, m. a water-snake. **~ सूद**, m. interest at fifty per cent. **डेवढ़ी गाँठ**, f. a slip-knot; a knot easily untied.

डेवढ़ी *ḍevṛhī*, f. = ड्योढ़ी.

डेहरी *ḍehrī*, f. **1.** threshold. **2.** reg. (E.) a household grain-store.

डेहली *ḍehlī*, f. reg. (Raj.) = डेहरी.

डैन *ḍain* [*ḍayana-*], m. E.H. a wing.

डैना *ḍainā* [*ḍayana-*], m. **1.** a wing. **2.** an oar. — **डैनेदार** [P. *-dār*], adj. having wings.

डैनी *ḍainī* [cf. H. *ḍāyan*], adj. reg. of evil omen, unlucky. — **~ उँगली**, f. the middle finger.

डोंगरा *ḍoṁgrā*, m. a shower before the beginning of the rainy season.

डोंगा *ḍoṁgā* [**ḍoṅga-*¹], m. **1.** a boat (esp. without sails); a canoe. **2.** a trough. **3.** reg. a ladle or stirrer.

डोंगी *ḍoṁgī* [cf. H. *ḍoṁgā*], f. a small open boat; a canoe.

डोंड़हा *ḍoṁṛ'hā* [conn. *dundubha-*], m. a water-snake.

डोंड़ा *ḍoṁṛā*, m. pronun. var. = ढोंढा.

¹**डोंड़ी** *ḍoṁṛī*, f. a small pod, or seed-capsule.

²**डोंड़ी** *ḍoṁṛī*, f. = डौंड़ी.

डोंब *ḍomb* [*ḍomba-*], m. Av. = डोम.

डोई *ḍoī*, f. reg. a wooden spoon or ladle.

डोकरा *ḍokrā* [**ḍokka-*[2]], m. colloq. or pej. **1.** an old man. **2.** father; grandfather (paternal).

डोकरी *ḍokrī* [cf. H. *ḍokrā*], f. dimin. colloq. or pej. **1.** old woman. **2.** mother; grandmother (paternal).

डोड़हा *ḍoṛ'hā*, m. *HŚS.* = डोंड़हा.

डोड़ा *ḍoṛā*, m. a pod, seed-capsule (esp. of the poppy, cotton or swallow-wort plants: cf. डोंड़ी).

डोनी *ḍonī* [*droṇa-*[1]], f. small boat.

डोब *ḍob* [cf. H. *ḍobnā*], m. reg. (W. and Raj.) dipping, soaking; dyeing. — ~ देना (को), to dye.

डोब- *ḍob-* [**ḍobb-*], v.t. E.H. to dip, to soak; to dye.

डोम *ḍom* [*ḍomba-*], m. **1.** *hind.* the name of a partic. community (makers of ropes, baskets, &c., workers at cremation-places). **2.** *musl.* the name of a community of musicians and dancers. **3.** a man of a *ḍom* community.

डोमनी *ḍomnī* [*ḍombinī-*], f. **1.** a woman of a *ḍom* community. **2.** the wife of a *ḍom*.

डोमपन *ḍompan* [cf. H. *ḍom*], m. also pej. qualities or activities associated with *ḍoms*.

डोमपना *ḍompanā* [cf. H. *ḍom*], m. = डोमपन.

डोर *ḍor* [*davara-*; Pk. *ḍora-*], f. **1.** thread, string, rope; line. **2.** attachment. — ~ पर लगाना, or लाना, to set on the track (to success, &c). ~ मज़बूत होना (की), (one) to be tenacious of life. ~ लगना, to be attached (to); to be absorbed (in).

[1]**डोरा** *ḍorā* [*davara-*; Pk. *ḍora-*], m. **1.** thread, string, rope; line. **2.** line, outline; trace, streak. आंख का ~, m. a bloodshot eye. **3.** edge (of a sword-blade). **4.** bond, tie (of affection, &c). **5.** prolonged note or call (of a bird). — ~ डालना (में), to string, to thread (as a needle). डोरे डालना (पर), to lay a snare (for); to be after (a girl). डोरे डालना (में), to stitch (as a quilt); to braid (the hair).

[2]**डोरा** *ḍorā*, m. *Pl. HŚS.* a large ladle, or scoop.

डोरिया *ḍoriyā* [cf. H. [1]*ḍorā*], m. striped material (esp. muslin).

डोरियाना *ḍoriyānā* [cf. H. [1]*ḍorī*], v.t. to tie with string or cord.

[1]**डोरी** *ḍorī* [cf. H. [1]*ḍorā*], f. **1.** string, cord; rope; surveyor's line. **2.** braid, piping. **3.** bond, tie (as of affection). — ~ ढीली करना, or छोड़ना, to relax discipline (over, की). ~ लगना, to be drawn by, to feel the pull of (home, &c). – डोरीवाला, m. rope-maker; rope-seller.

[2]**डोरी** *ḍorī*, f. reg. (W.) a ladle (as used in making sugar).

[1]**डोल** *ḍol* [*dola-*[1]; Pk. *ḍola-*]; m. & adj. **1.** a swinging, rocking. **2.** a swing. फूल-डोल, m. a swing made of, or ornamented with, flowers. **3.** adj. swinging, &c. — ~ ~, m. moving to and fro, roving.

[2]**डोल** *ḍol* [**dola-*[2]], m. a bucket, or large leather bag (for drawing water, or as used in irrigation).

डोलचा *ḍolcā* [H. [2]*ḍol*+P. *-ca*], m. a bucket.

डोलची *ḍolcī* [cf. H. *ḍolcā*], f. **1.** a small bucket. **2.** a small basket.

डोलना *ḍolnā* [*dolāyate*; cf. Pk. *ḍolāaṁta-*]; v.i. **1.** to swing, to rock; to sway. **2.** to move, to stir; to move about; to wander. **3.** to totter; to shake. **4.** to flinch, to waver (a viewpoint, a resolve). — डोलना-फिरना, to wander about.

डोला *ḍolā* [*dola-*[1]; Pk. *ḍola-*], m. **1.** a litter carried by porters (esp. as used to convey a bride to the house of her parents-in-law). **2.** a swing. **3.** a cradle.

डोलाना *ḍolānā*, v.t. = डुलाना.

डोली *ḍolī* [cf. H. *ḍolā*], f. = डोला, 1. उनकी ~ उठ गई, euph. he died. – डोली-डंडा, m. a game in which a boy is lifted on the crossed hands and arms of two others, or on two sticks.

डोसा *ḍosā*, m. a south Indian dish (rice pancake).

डोहरा *ḍohrā*, m. *Pl.* a large ladle or spoon.

डौंकना *ḍauṁknā*, v.i. to bellow.

डौंज *ḍauṁj*, m. **1.** reg. (W.) a boundary mark. **2.** *Pl.* a platform in a field (from which crops can be watched over).

डौंजा *ḍauṁjā*, m. reg. (W.) = डौंज.

डौंड़ी *ḍauṁṛī* [*ḍiṇḍima-*], f. **1.** a small kettledrum. **2.** proclamation by beat of drum. — ~ देना, or पीटना, or फेरना, to announce publicly, to proclaim. ~ बजना, fig. to be announced; to be proclaimed.

डौंरु *ḍauṁru*, m. Bibl. = डमरु.

डौढ़ा *ḍauṛhā*, adj. & m. pronun. var. = ड्योढ़ा.

डौढ़ी *ḍauṛhī*, f. pronun. var. = ड्योढ़ी.

डौल *ḍaul* [**ḍavala-*], m. **1.** shape, form; build; appearance. **2.** fashion, style; characteristic manner; proper manner. ~ **से** adv. in order; in due form; methodically. **3.** plan, scheme. **4.** likelihood. **5.** estimate (of revenue or assets). — ~ **बाँधना**, or **लगना** (**का**), to contrive to obtain. ~ **पर लाना**, to get (someone or sthg.) into shape, or into proper order. – **डौलदार** [P. -*dār*], adj. well-built. **डौल-डाल**, m. means, method.

डौला *ḍaulā* [Panj. *ḍaulā*], m. the wrist.

ड्योढ़ा *ḍyoṛhā*, adj. & m. = **डेवढ़ा**.

ड्योढ़ी *ḍyoṛhī* [**dehuḍī-*], f. threshold; porch; entrance, door. — **ड्योढ़ीदार** [P. -*dār*], m. door-keeper, porter. **ड्योढ़ीवान**, m. id.

ढ

ढ *ḍha*, the fourteenth consonant of the Devanāgarī syllabary. — **ढकार**, m. the sound /ḍh/; the letter **ढ**.

ढँकना *ḍhaṁknā*, v.t. & v.i. = [1]**ढकना**.

ढंग *ḍhaṅg*, m. **1.** particular nature or characteristic; way, style, manner. **2.** method, means, manner, way. **3.** kind, type. **4.** style of behaviour; manners. **5.** skill, accomplishment. **6.** transf. sign, prospect. — **~ का**, adj. suitable, appropriate; skilled. **~ पर लाना**, to gain acceptance of (one's, **अपने**) viewpoint or purpose (from, **को**); to bring about conformable behaviour, &c. (on the part of, **को**). **~ बरतना**, to comport oneself properly, to behave well; to conform (as to a fashion); to adapt oneself (to, **का**). **~ से**, adv. fittingly, properly. **अपने ~ का**, adj. individual; original; eccentric. **मोटे ~ से**, adv. in general; basically.

ढंढ-मंढ *ḍhaṇḍh-maṇḍh*, adj. colloq. crumbling (structure); insubstantial (remarks).

ढँढोई *ḍhaṁḍhoī*, f. reg. (W.) scum of boiling sugar-cane juice.

ढँढोर- *ḍhaṁḍhor-*, v.t. Brbh. Av. to search.

ढँढोरची *ḍhaṁḍhorcī* [cf. H. *ḍhaṁḍhorā*], m. a public crier.

ढँढोरा *ḍhaṁḍhorā*, m. **1.** drum (as used by a public crier). **2.** proclamation by beat of drum. — **~ पीटना**, or **फेरना**, to proclaim by beat of drum, to announce publicly.

ढँढोरिया *ḍhaṁḍhoriyā* [cf. H. *ḍhaṁḍhorā*], m. a public crier.

ढँपना *ḍhaṁpnā*, v.i. & v.t. = **ढपना**, [1]**ढकना**.

ढई *ḍhaī* [? conn. *ḍhāhnā*], f. **1.** *Pl. HŚS.* a strong shake or pull, a determined effort: staying overlong (as of a guest or visitor seeking some object). **2.** picketing. — **~ देना**, to force an invitation; to picket.

[1]**ढकना** *ḍhaknā* [cf. H. *ḍhakānā*, *ḍhāṁknā*], v.t. & v.i. **1.** v.t. to cover. **2.** to conceal. **3.** v.i. to be covered. **4.** to be concealed.

[2]**ढकना** *ḍhaknā* [cf. **ḍhakk-*: Pk. *ḍhakkaï*], m. = **ढक्कन**.

ढकनी *ḍhaknī* [cf. H. [2]*ḍhaknā*], f. a small cover or lid.

ढकवाना *ḍhakvānā* [cf. H. *ḍhāṁknā*, *ḍhaknā*], v.t. to cause to be covered (by, **से**).

ढका *ḍhakā* [cf. **dhakk-*], m. Brbh. a push, blow.

ढकाना *ḍhakānā*, v.t. = **ढकवाना**.

ढकेलना *ḍhakelnā* [cf. **dhakk-*], v.t. **1.** to shove, to push; to push over. **2.** to jostle. **3.** to push away; to dislodge. — **ढकेला-ढकेली**, f. pushing, shoving; a crush, crowd.

ढकोसना *ḍhakosnā*, v.t. to guzzle or to gulp (food or drink).

ढकोसला *ḍhakoslā*, m. pretence, deception, delusion.

ढक्कन *ḍhakkan* [cf. **ḍhakk-*: Pk. *ḍhakkiṇī-*], m. a cover, lid.

ढक्का *ḍhakkā* [S.], f. Brbh. a large drum.

ढचर *ḍhacar*, adj. & m. **1.** adj. fragile. **2.** m. a framework. **3.** plan (of a construction, task) (= **ढाँचा**). — **~ बाँधना**, or **खड़ा करना**, to make a plan.

ढचरा *ḍhacrā*, m. reg. = **ढाँचा**.

ढटींगड़ *ḍhaṭīṁgaṛ*, adj. & m. **1.** adj. sturdy, burly. **2.** fine (to outward appearances). **3.** m. a burly or hulking fellow.

ढटींगड़ा *ḍhaṭīṁgṛā*, adj. & m. = **ढटींगड़**.

ढड्ढो *ḍhaḍḍho*, f. *Pl.* a babbler: ? = the gregarious bird called *sāt bhāī*, *Turdoides striatus*.

ढनमना- *ḍhanmanā-* [conn. H. *ḍhalmalānā*], v.i. Av. to roll or to thrash about (on the ground).

ढप *ḍhap*, m. = **डफ**.

ढप-ढप *ḍhap-ḍhap*, m. a drumming sound: **~ करना**, to drum, to beat (on, **पर**).

ढपढपाना *ḍhapḍhapānā* [cf. H. *ḍhap-ḍhap*], v.t. to beat or to drum (on, **पर**).

[1]**ढपना** *ḍhapnā* [cf. H. *ḍhāṁpnā*], v.i. & v.t. **1.** v.i. to be covered. **2.** v.t. to cover. **3.** to conceal.

[2]**ढपना** *ḍhapnā* [cf. **ḍhamp-*], m. a covering; cover, lid.

ढपौना *ḍhapaunā* [cf. **ḍhamp-*], m. reg. (Bihar) a cover, lid (cf. [2]**ढपना**).

ढप्पू *ḍhappū* [cf. **ḍhappa-*], adj. *Pl. HŚS.* bulky, heavy (of build).

ढफ *ḍhaph*, m. = ढप, डफ.

ढब *ḍhab*, m. **1.** way, manner, means; proper manner. **2.** *HŚS.* proper conduct. — ~ का, adj. competent; skilful; suitable.

ढबकी *ḍhabkī*, f. reg. (W.) rope fastened to the end of the crusher in a sugar-cane mill.

ढब-ढब *ḍhab-ḍhab*, m. the sound of beating a drum.

ढबढबुआ *ḍhabḍhabuā* [cf. H. *ḍhab-ḍhab*], m. reg. (Bihar) a rattling scarecrow.

[1]**ढबरी** *ḍhabrī*, f. = ढिबरी.

[2]**ढबरी** *ḍhabrī* [conn. H. *ḍhābar*], f. reg. (Bihar) land lying under water for part of the year.

ढबीला *ḍhabīlā* [cf. H. *ḍhab*], adj. reg. graceful, elegant.

ढबुआ *ḍhabuā* [**ḍhabba*-: ? w. M. *ḍhabbū*], m. lump: **1.** obs. an unstamped piece of copper used as a coin. **2.** reg. (W.) thatch (on a field platform).

ढब्बूस *ḍhabbūs* [cf. H. *ḍhabuā*], adj. reg. heavy, fat; clumsy.

ढम-ढम *ḍham-ḍham*, m. a sound of drumming.

ढमलाना *ḍhamlānā*, v.i. *Pl. HŚS.* = ढलमलाना.

ढरक- *ḍharak-*, v.i. Brbh. Av. = ढलकना.

ढरकी *ḍharkī* [cf. H. *ḍharak-*], f. shuttle (of a loom).

ढर्रा *ḍharrā*, m. reg. way, manner, style; attitudes.

ढलक *ḍhalak* [cf. H. *ḍhalaknā*], f. **1.** spilling. **2.** rolling, rocking. **3.** inclining, tilting.

ढलकना *ḍhalaknā* [cf. **ḍhalati*: Pk. *ḍhalaï*], v.i. **1.** to flow down, to overflow; to be spilt, or shed; to be poured out. **2.** to fall or to hang down loosely. **3.** to roll; to slide.

ढलका *ḍhalkā* [cf. H. *ḍhalaknā*], m. **1.** running over, or spilling (as of a watering eye). **2.** reg. (W.) an eye complaint.

ढलकाना *ḍhalkānā* [cf. H. *ḍhalaknā*], v.t. **1.** to cause to overflow; to cause to spill; to pour out; to shed (tears). **2.** to cause to roll down; to roll (= ढुलकाना). **3.** to tilt; to overturn.

ढलना *ḍhalnā* [**ḍhalati*: Pk. *ḍhalaï*], v.i. **1.** to run down, to flow; to drop, to fall; to be spilt. **2.** to be poured out; to be cast (metal). **3.** to tilt, to incline (= ढुलना). **4.** to sink, to draw to a close (as day, or life).

ढलमल *ḍhalmal* [cf. H. *ḍhalnā*], adj. shaking, unsteady; tottering; wavering.

ढलमलाना *ḍhalmalānā* [cf. H. *ḍhalmal*], v.i. to sway, to be unsteady; to totter; to waver.

ढलवाँ *ḍhalvāṁ*, adj. = ढालवाँ, 1., 2.

ढलवाना *ḍhalvānā* [cf. H. *ḍhālnā*], v.t. to cause to be poured out (by, से); to cause to be cast, &c. (by).

ढलाई *ḍhalāī* [cf. H. *ḍhalānā*], f. **1.** pouring out, casting. **2.** cost of, or wages for, casting, &c.

ढलाऊ *ḍhalāū* [cf. H. *ḍhalnā*], adj. & m. **1.** adj. sloping. **2.** m. a slope.

[1]**ढलान** *ḍhalān* [cf. H. *ḍhalnā*], f. a slope, sloping ground.

[2]**ढलान** *ḍhalān* [cf. H. *ḍhālnā*], f. casting, pouring (metal).

ढलाना *ḍhalānā* [cf. H. *ḍhālnā*], v.t. to cause to be poured out, cast, &c. (by, से).

ढलाव *ḍhalāv* [cf. H. *ḍhalnā*], m. **1.** a slope. **2.** the process of pouring, casting, &c.

ढलुवाँ *ḍhaluvāṁ*, adj. see ढलवाँ.

ढलैत *ḍhalait* [cf. H. [2]*ḍhāl*], m. *Pl. HŚS.* shield-bearer: an armed soldier, or watchman.

ढलैया *ḍhalaiyā* [cf. H. *ḍhālnā*], m. a caster, foundryman.

ढवाना *ḍhavānā*, v.t. = ढहवाना.

ढहना *ḍhahnā* [cf. H. *ḍhāhnā*], v.t. **1.** to collapse, to fall to pieces (a building, &c). **2.** to be demolished, razed; to be destroyed or ruined.

ढहवाना *ḍhahvānā*, v.t. = ढहाना, 1.

ढहाना *ḍhahānā* [cf. H. *ḍhāhnā*], v.t. **1.** to cause to collapse; to break down, to knock down, &c. (= ढाहना). **2.** fig. to bring down, to lay low; to humble (one).

ढाँक *ḍhāṁk*, m. = ढाक.

ढाँकना *ḍhāṁknā* [**ḍhaṅk*-: Pk. *ḍhaṁk*-], v.t. = [1]ढकना, v.t.

ढाँग *ḍhāṁg* [? H. [2]*ḍāṁg* × H. *ḍhā(h)nā*], f. reg. a bluff, or cliff.

ढाँच *ḍhāṁc*, m. reg. = ढाँचा.

ढाँचा *ḍhāṁcā*, m. **1.** framework; structure; system. **2.** form, plan, style. **3.** skeleton.

ढाँपना *ḍhāṁpnā* [**ḍhamp*-], v.t. **1.** to cover; to shut, to close. **2.** to conceal (= [1]ढकना, v.t).

ढाँस *ḍhāṁs* [cf. H. *ḍhāṁsnā*], f. reg. a cough (in animals).

ढाँसना *ḍhāṁsnā*, v.i. *HŚS.* to cough (animals).

ढाँसी *ḍhāṁsī*, f. reg. = **ढाँस**.

ढाई *ḍhāī* [*ardhatr̥tīya-*], adj. **1.** two and a half. **2.** two and a half times. ~ **सौ**, two hundred and fifty. — ~ **दिन**, two and a half days: a short or fleeting period. ~ **बजे**, half past two; at half past two. **चेहरे पर** ~ **बजना**, colloq. to look downcast.

ढाक *ḍhāk* [*dhakṣu-*], m. the *ḍhāk* tree, *Butea frondosa* (= **पलाश**). — ~ **के तीन पात**, three *ḍhāk* leaves: a poor or helpless person or state.

ढाका *ḍhākā*, m. the city of Dhaka (Dacca).

ढाटा *ḍhāṭā*, m. a band of cloth worn (by men) round the cheeks and chin.

ढाटी *ḍhāṭī* [cf. H. *ḍhāṭā*], f. dimin. reg. (W.) an object fastened at an animal's mouth or nose (so as to stop it eating while working).

ढाठा *ḍhāṭhā*, m. = **ढाटा**.

ढाढ़स *ḍhāṛhas* [cf. *dhārṣṭya-*, or *dārḍhya-*], m. **1.** fortitude; courage; patience. **2.** encouragement; comfort. — ~ **देना**, or **दिलाना** (**को**), to encourage; to comfort. ~ **बाँधना**, to take heart, to have courage, &c. ~ **बँधाना** (**का**) or **को**), id.

ढाढ़िन *ḍhāṛhin*, f. **1.** a woman of the *ḍhāṛhī* community. **2.** the wife of a *ḍhāṛhī*.

ढाढ़ी *ḍhāṛhī* [? cf. **ḍhaḍḍha-*[3]: Pk. *ḍhaḍḍha-*], m. **1.** a community of itinerant singers and musicians (chiefly, but not entirely, a Muslim community). **2.** a man of the *ḍhāṛhī* community.

ढाना *ḍhānā* [cf. H. *ḍhāhnā*], v.t. **1.** to break down, to destroy (a building, &c.); to raze. **2.** to knock down, to lay low. **3.** fig. to cause to befall, to bring (trouble, &c.: on, **पर**). — **ग़ज़ब ढाना**, to cause a catastrophe; to wreak havoc.

ढापना *ḍhāpnā*, v.t. = **ढाँपना**.

ढाबर *ḍhābar*, m. Av. a pool of dirty water (? = **डाबर**).

ढाबा *ḍhābā*, m. broad eaves to a house (beneath which people can sit); a place where snacks or meals are sold.

[1]**ढार** *ḍhār*, m. f. Brbh. **1.** m. = [1] [2]**ढाल**. **2.** reg. (Bihar) an ingot mould. **3.** f. (W.) a kind of ear ornament.

[2]**ढार** *ḍhār* [H. *ḍhālnā*], m. reg. (W.) a heap of threshed corn before winnowing (= [2]**सिल्ली**).

ढार- *ḍhār-*, v.t. Brbh. Av. = **ढालना**.

ढारस *ḍhāras*, m. pronun. var. = **ढाढ़स**.

[1]**ढाल** *ḍhāl* [cf. H. *ḍhālnā*], f. m. (Brbh.) **1.** cast, mould, form; way, manner; habit. **2.** slope, incline.

[2]**ढाल** *ḍhāl* [conn. *ḍhāla-*], f. a shield. — **ढाल-तलवार**, f. shield and sword.

ढालना *ḍhālnā* [**ḍhālayati*: Pk. *ḍhālaï*], v.t. **1.** to pour out; to spill. **2.** to cast (metal), to mould; to mint (coin). **3.** to fashion, to form; to compose (a sentence, a verse). **4.** to aim, to direct (one's words: at, **पर**). **5.** to drink, to tipple.

ढालवाँ *ḍhālvāṁ* [cf. H. [1]*ḍhāl*, *ḍhālū*], adj. & m. **1.** adj. sloping. **2.** cast, moulded. **3.** m. a sloping place, slope. **4.** reg. (Bihar) diagonal rail or arm, support (as for the body of a cart on the axle).

ढालिया *ḍhāliyā* [cf. H. *ḍhālnā*], m. a caster, foundryman, moulder.

ढाली *ḍhālī* [cf. H. [2]*ḍhāl*], adj. & m. **1.** adj. carrying a shield. **2.** m. one carrying a shield.

ढालू *ḍhālū* [cf. H. [1]*ḍhāl*, *ḍhālnā*], adj. & m. **1.** adj. sloping. **2.** m. a caster, moulder, &c. **3.** slope, descent.

ढासना *ḍhāsnā* [Panj. *ḍhāsṇā*], m. support (for the back or body).

ढाह *ḍhāh* [cf. H. *ḍhāhnā*], ? m. reg. (Bihar) severely broken or eroded ground; a ravine.

ढाहना *ḍhāhnā* [cf. **dhvāsayati*], v.t. = **ढाना**.

ढाहा *ḍhāhā* [cf. H. *ḍhāhnā*], m. *Pl. HŚS.* steep slope or bank (as of a river).

ढिंढोर- *ḍhiṁḍhor-* [conn. Pk. *ḍhaṁḍholaï*], v.t. Brbh. to stir up; to search through.

ढिंढोरा *ḍhiṁḍhorā*, m. = **ढँढोरा**.

ढिकलना *ḍhikalnā* [cf. H. *ḍhakelnā*], v.i. reg. to be pushed.

ढिग *ḍhig* [**ḍhigga-*[2]], m. vicinity; quarter, side. — ~, ppn. near (to, **के**).

ढिगाड़ *ḍhigāṛ*, m. *Pl.* reg. (W.) heap, pile, store.

ढिठाई *ḍhiṭhāī* [cf. *dhr̥ṣṭa-*], f. **1.** brashness, presumptuousness. **2.** insolence. **3.** boldness, fearlessness. **4.** obstinacy, wilfulness. — ~ **करना**, to be bold, brash, &c.

ढिबरी *ḍhibrī* [cf. **ḍhibba-*], f. **1.** nut (of a bolt); a socket; a mould. **2.** a small lamp having a spout or housing for the wick.

ढिलमिल *ḍhilmil* [cf. H. *ḍhīlā*, and H. *ḍhalmal*], adj. **1.** lax (as measures). 2. = **ढलमल**.

ढिलाई *ḍhilāī* [cf. H. *ḍhīlā*], f. **1.** looseness, slackness. **2.** laziness. **3.** negligence.

ढिल्लड़ *ḍhillaṛ* [cf. **ḍhilla-*[2]: Pk. *ḍhilla-*], adj. & m. **1.** lazy. **2.** negligent. **3.** m. a lazy person, &c.

ढिसर- *ḍhisar-*, v.i. Brbh. to collapse, to be given up (a worthy intention).

ढींढ़ा *ḍhīṁṛhā* [*ḍhiṇḍha-[2]], m. reg. colloq. swollen stomach (of pregnancy).

ढीठ *ḍhīṭh* [*dhr̥ṣṭa-*], adj. **1.** brash, presumptuous. **2.** insolent, rude. **3.** bold, fearless. **4.** stubborn, wilful.

ढीठता *ḍhīṭhătā* [cf. H. *ḍhīṭh*], f. brashness, &c. (= ढिठाई).

ढीठपन *ḍhīṭhpan* [cf. H. *ḍhīṭh*], m. brashness, &c.

ढीठपना *ḍhīṭhpanā* [cf. H. *ḍhīṭh*], m. = ढीठपन.

ढीम *ḍhīm* [*ḍhīmma-], m. reg. (W.) a lump, clod.

ढील *ḍhīl* [*ḍhilla-[2]: Pk. *ḍhilla-*], f. & adj. **1.** f. looseness. **2.** slackness, laxity. **3.** negligence; laziness. **4.** adj. loose. — ~ करना, to be slack, negligent (in, में); to delay. ~ देना (को), to loosen; to relax (as restraint, control); to give rein (to). – ढील-ढाल, f. = ~, 2.-4.

ढीलना *ḍhīlnā* [cf. H. *ḍhīlā*], v.t. **1.** to loosen, to relax. **2.** Brbh. to let loose (animals).

ढीला *ḍhīlā* [*ḍhilla-[2]: Pk. *ḍhilla-*], adj. **1.** loose. **2.** slack, relaxed; flabby. **3.** unchecked, unrestrained. **4.** negligent, indifferent; slack, dilatory. **5.** weakened, indifferent (ardour, enthusiasm). **6.** thin, watery (a dish). **7.** Brbh. languid (a glance). — ~ छोड़ना, to leave unchecked, undisciplined. ~ पड़ना, to grow slack, &c.; to weaken (shares). — ढीला-ढाला, adj. relaxed, or slack, &c.

ढीलापन *ḍhīlāpan* [cf. H. *ḍhīlā*], m. looseness, slackness, &c.

ढीह *ḍhīh*, f. reg. **1.** a mound (cf. ढूह). **2.** high bank over a river.

ढीहा *ḍhīhā*, m. reg. = ढीह.

ढुँढ़वाना *ḍhuṁṛhvānā* [cf. H. *ḍhūṁṛhnā*], v.t. to cause to be searched for, searched out (by, से).

ढुक- *ḍhuk-* [*ḍhukyati: Pk. *ḍhukkaï*], v.i. Brbh. Av. **1.** ? to enter, to make one's way. **2.** to hide in wait, to lurk.

ढुकली *ḍhuklī*, f. reg. (W.) = ढेंकली.

ढुड़ *ḍhuṛ*, m. the hip. — ~ पर उठाकर दे मारना, to give one a cross-throw (in wrestling).

ढुलकना *ḍhulaknā* [cf. *ḍhulati], v.i. **1.** to fall over or down; to slip, to slide; to drop, to drip. **2.** to roll, to roll down.

ढुलकाना *ḍhulkānā* [cf. H. *ḍhulaknā*], v.t. **1.** to cause to fall; to cause to slip, or to slide; to cause to drop, or to drip. **2.** to cause to roll down; to roll. **3.** to tilt; to overturn. **4.** to incline (one) to; to incite (one).

[1]**ढुलना** *ḍhulnā* [*ḍhulati], v.i. **1.** to tilt, to incline. **2.** to move, to slip down or forward. **3.** to roll down; to roll. **4.** to be poured out; to be spilt (= ढलना). **5.** to yield, to sink (= ढलना). **6.** to shake, to wave.

[2]**ढुलना** *ḍhulnā* [cf. H. [2]*ḍhulānā*], v.i. to be carried, conveyed.

ढुलमुल *ḍhulmul* [cf. H. [1]*ḍhulnā*], adj. = ढलमल.

ढुलवाई *ḍhulvāī* [cf. H. *ḍhulvānā*], f. = ढुलाई.

ढुलवाना *ḍhulvānā* [cf. H. *ḍhonā*], v.t. to cause to be carried or conveyed (by, से).

ढुलाई *ḍhulāī* [cf. H. *ḍhulānā*], f. **1.** carrying, transporting (as of goods). **2.** cost of or payment for transporting.

[1]**ढुलाना** *ḍhulānā* [cf. H. [1]*ḍhulnā*], v.t. **1.** to cause to slope, or to tilt. **2.** to cause to overflow, to spill. **3.** to overturn. **4.** to cause to move, to wave, to shake.

[2]**ढुलाना** *ḍhulānā* [cf. H. *ḍhonā*], v.t. to cause to be carried, conveyed, &c. (by, से).

ढूँढ *ḍhūṁḍh*, m. reg. (W.) a dilapidated, or ruined, house.

ढूँढ़ *ḍhūṁṛh* [cf. H. *ḍhūṁṛhnā*], f. seeking, searching out. — ढूँढ़-ढाँढ़, f. continued or close search; investigation. ढूँढ़-ढाँढ़ करना, to search closely, &c.

ढूँढ़न *ḍhūṁṛhan* [cf. H. *ḍhūṁḍhnā*], m. = ढूँढ़.

ढूँढना *ḍhūṁḍhnā*, v.t. pronun. var. = ढूढ़ना.

ढूँढ़ना *ḍhūṁṛhnā* [*ḍhūṇḍh-: Pk. *ḍhuṁḍhullaï*], v.t. to look for; to search out, to find. — ढूँढ़ना-ढाँढ़ना, to make continued or close search for; to investigate. – ढूढ़ निकालना, to search out; to discover; to reveal. ढूढ़ लाना, to search out and bring: to find.

ढूँढार *ḍhūṁḍhār* [cf. H. *ḍhūṁṛhnā*], m. = ढूँढ.

ढूँढिया *ḍhūṁḍhiyā*, m. reg. a Jain devotee or ascetic.

ढूँढी *ḍhūṁḍhī*, f. 19c. ? the arm.

ढूँढेर *ḍhūṁḍher* [cf. H. *ḍhūṁṛhnā*], m. = ढूँढ.

ढूक- *ḍhūk-* [*ḍhukyati: Pk. *ḍhukkaï*], v.i. Brbh. **1.** to go into. **2.** to lurk; to peep; to eavesdrop.

ढूह *ḍhūh*, m. reg. **1.** a mound. **2.** ground intersected by ravines.

ढेंक *ḍheṁk* [*ḍheṅka-[3]: Pk. *ḍheṁka-*], m. **1.** a stork or crane (? the painted stork, *Ibis* *leucocephalus*). **2.** the ring-tailed fishing eagle, *Haliaetus leucoryphus*.

ढेंकली *ḍheṁklī* [cf. **ḍheṅka-*²: Pk. *ḍheṁkā-*], f. **1.** an apparatus for drawing water (lever supported on an upright, with a bucket attached to one end and a counterpoise weight at the other). **2.** lever, windlass (for raising weights). **3.** an apparatus for pounding grain, worked by the foot. **4.** colloq. a way of stitching pieces of cloth together with the patterning out of line. **5.** transf. a somersault. — ~ **खाना**, or **लगाना**, to turn a somersault. ~ **में डालना**, colloq. to put in a difficult situation, in a hot spot.

ढेंका *ḍheṁkā* [**ḍheṅka-*²: Pk. *ḍheṁkā-*], m. **1.** a machine for pounding oil-seeds, or husking grain, consisting of a lever with attached pestle and worked by the foot. **2.** a curved piece of wood which serves as the upper housing for the roller in an oil-mill or sugar-mill. **3.** reg. (Bihar) a beam serving as a door-bar.

ढेंकी *ḍheṁkī*, f. reg. (Bihar) **1.** a machine for husking grain (cf. **ढेंका**, 1). **2.** a lever used with a counterpoise weight for drawing water (= **ढेंकली**).

ढेंकुली *ḍheṁkulī*, f. pronun. var. = **ढेंकली**.

ढेंखर *ḍheṁkhar*, m. reg. (W.) a bundle of thorns tied together (used as a makeshift harrow, and in threshing grain).

ढेंगा *ḍheṁgā*, m. *Pl.* a heavy stick or piece of wood.

ढेंड़स *ḍheṁṛas*, m. the plant called okra, lady's fingers (= **भिंडी**).

ढेंड़ी *ḍheṁṛī* [**ḍheṇḍha-*¹], f. reg. **1.** Bihar. a pod or seed capsule (as of cotton, hemp, pulse). **2.** W. a capsule-shaped ear ornament.

ढेंढ *ḍheṁḍh*, m. E.H. = ²**ढेढ**, 2.

ढेंढी *ḍheṁḍhī*, f. E.H. = **ढेंड़ी**.

ढेंपी *ḍheṁpī*, f. reg. (Bihar) = **ढेपा**.

ढेंरा *ḍheṁrā* [conn. **ḍhera-*³], adj. cross-eyed, squinting (cf. **टेरा**, ²**डेरा**).

ढेक *ḍhek*, m. Av. a stork or crane (= **ढेंक**).

ढेकली *ḍheklī* [cf. **ḍhekka-*²], f. = **ढेंकली**.

ढेकुला *ḍhekulā* [cf. **ḍhekka-*²], m. reg. = **ढेंकुली**.

ढेकुली *ḍhekulī* [cf. **ḍhekka-*²], f. = **ढेंकुली**.

ढेड *ḍheḍ*, m. reg. (Raj.) = ²**ढेढ**, 2.

ढेड़ *ḍheṛ* [**ḍheḍḍha-*¹], m. a heap (= **ढेर**).

ढेड़ी *ḍheṛī* [cf. H. *ḍheṛ*], f. dimin. a small heap.

¹**ढेढ** *ḍheḍh*, m. reg. (Bihar) = **ढेढा**.

²**ढेढ** *ḍheḍh* [? ← Panj.], m. **1.** a crow. **2.** name of a community of low status whose members work with hides.

ढेढा *ḍheḍhā* [**ḍheḍḍha-*¹], m. *HŚS.* a pod or seed-capsule.

ढेन *ḍhen* [? *dhenu-* × H. *ḍhor*], f. reg. = **धेनु**.

ढेपा *ḍhepā*, m. reg. (W.) a lump (as of clay), a clod.

ढेबरी *ḍhebrī* [cf. **ḍhebba-*], f. = **ढिबरी**.

ढेर *ḍher* [**ḍhera-*¹], m. a heap, pile; abundance. — ~ **करना**, to make a heap (of, **का**); to amass; to strike down, to knock unconscious; to kill. ~ **सारे**, adj. pl. colloq. lots of. ~ **होना**, to become a heap: to lie in ruins, to fall (a building); to lie inert or unconscious; to lie dead, to be killed. – **ढेर-सा**, adj. & m. colloq. a great amount or number, heaps (of).

ढेरा *ḍherā* [**ḍhera-*³], m. reg. (W.) **1.** a wheel-shaped wooden framework having two, or three intersecting arms (used for twisting thread or twine). **2.** a framework used to hold open the mouth of a leather water-bucket.

¹**ढेरी** *ḍherī* [cf. H. *ḍher*], f. dimin. a small heap.

²**ढेरी** *ḍherī* [cf. H. *ḍher*], m. reg. (W.) a shareholder in a village or estate.

ढेलवाँस *ḍhelvāṁs* [**ḍhellapāśa-*], m. a sling.

ढेलवाँसी *ḍhelvāṁsī* [cf. H. *ḍhelvāṁs*], m. *Pl.* one who uses a sling.

ढेला *ḍhelā* [**ḍhella-*], m. a lump; clod; pellet. — **ढेला-चौथ**, m. the fourth day of the light half of the month Bhādoṁ (when earth and stones are liable to be thrown at neighbours' houses, as an effort to escape evil influence of the moon). – **ढेलाबाज़ी** [P. *-bāzī*], f. the throwing of stones; stoning.

ढैया *ḍhaiyā* [cf. H. *ḍhāī*], m. a measure of two and a half seers' weight.

ढोंकना *ḍhoṁknā*, v.t. to gulp, &c. (= **ढोकना**).

ढोंग *ḍhoṁg*, m. **1.** deceit, trickery. **2.** pretence, imposture; sanctimoniousness; unjustified airs or display; hypocrisy. — ~ **बाँध रखना**, to make a pretence or show (of, **का**), to practise deceit. – **ढोंगबाज़** [P. *-bāz*], m. a trickster, impostor, &c. °**-बाज़ी**, f. the practice of deceit, &c.

ढोंगिया *ḍhoṁgiyā* [cf. H. *ḍhoṁg*], adj. & m. = **ढोंगी**.

ढोंगी *ḍhoṁgī* [cf. H. *ḍhoṁg*], adj. & m. **1.** adj. deceitful. **2.** dissembling, fraudulent; hypocritical. **3.** m. a deceitful person, &c.

ढोंडी *ḍhoṁḍī*, f. reg. (W.) a grass which grows in rice-fields and chokes young plants.

ढोंड़ी *ḍhoṁṛī*, f. reg. a girl (= ढोटी).

ढोंढ *ḍhoṁḍh*, m. = ढोंढा.

ढोंढा *ḍhoṁḍhā*, m. a pod, or seed-capsule.

ढोंढी *ḍhoṁḍhī*, f. a small pod, or seed-capsule.

ढोआ *ḍhoā* [**ḍhauka-*; *ḍhaukana-*], m. reg. (W.) a present (as made by a tenant to a landlord) on festival days.

ढोक *ḍhok* [cf. H. *ḍhoknā*], m. a gulp, large mouthful.

ढोकना *ḍhoknā*, v.t. to gulp large amounts of, to gulp down.

ढोका *ḍhokā* [**ḍhokka-*[1 2]], m. reg. (E.) **1.** a small piece (as a lump of salt, or a flat piece of stone). **2.** a covering (placed in front of the eyes), blinkers.

ढोटा *ḍhoṭā*, m. a child, son.

ढोटी *ḍhoṭī*, f. a girl, daughter.

ढोड़ी *ḍhoṛī*, f. pronun. var. = ठोड़ी.

ढोना *ḍhonā* [*ḍhaukayati*], v.t. **1.** to carry, to convey (by means of, पर). **2.** to bear (as suffering); to suffer.

ढोबरा *ḍhobrā*, m. reg. **1.** hole (as in a pot, or in a wall). **2.** a broken pot.

ढोर *ḍhor* [? conn. **dhaura-*[2]], m. cattle. — **ढोर-डंगर**, or °-**डाँगर**, m. pl. cattle. **ढोर-पालक**, m. a raiser of cattle.

ढोरना *ḍhornā* [**ḍholayati*], v.t. **1.** Brbh. to put down or forward, to present. **2.** Brbh. to shed (tears). **3.** Brbh. to shake. **4.** to roll (the eyes).

ढोरा *ḍhorā*, m. reg. (W.) = [2]ढोला, 2.

ढोरी *ḍhorī*, f. Brbh. eagerness, ardour; ? ardent devotion.

ढोल *ḍhol* [*ḍhola-*], m. a large (elongated) drum. — ~ **पीटना** or **बजाना**, to proclaim by beat of drum; to announce publicly. – **ढोल-ढमक्का**, m. drums, &c.; drums and accompanying instruments; fanfare, display. **ढोल-मजीरा**, m. drums and cymbals; musical instruments.

ढोलक *ḍholak* [cf. *ḍhola-*], m. a small drum.

ढोलकिया *ḍholkiyā* [cf. H. *ḍholak*], m. a drummer.

ढोलकी *ḍholkī* [cf. *ḍhola-*], f. = ढोलक.

ढोलन *ḍholan*, m. E.H. lover; friend.

ढोलना *ḍholnā*, m. Brbh. an amulet, of the shape of a drum.

ढोलनी *ḍholnī* [? H. *ḍolnā* × H. [1]*ḍhulnā*], f. Brbh. corr. a cradle.

[1]**ढोला** *ḍholā*, m. **1.** reg. (W.) an earthen mound; earthen boundary marker. **2.** E.H. [? conn. H. *ḍhelā*] the body.

[2]**ढोला** *ḍholā*, m. reg. (W.) **1.** a partic. greenish caterpillar. **2.** a weevil that attacks grain.

[3]**ढोला** *ḍholā* [cf. Raj. *ḍholo*], m. reg. **1.** a lover: name of a legendary prince of Rajasthan. **2.** bridegroom; husband.

ढोलिया *ḍholiyā* [cf. H. *ḍhol*], m. a drummer.

ढोली *ḍholī*, f. a heap or bundle of about two hundred *pān* leaves.

ढौंचा *ḍhauṁcā* [**ardhapañcama-*: Pk. *addhapaṁcama-*], adj. & m. **1.** four and a half. **2.** the four and a half times table.

त

त *ta*, the sixteenth consonant of the Devanāgarī syllabary. — **तकार**, m. the sound /t/; the letter त.

तंग *taṅg* [P. *tang*], adj. **1.** contracted, cramped; narrow (as a lane). **2.** tight (clothing). **3.** wanting, scarce; stinted. **4.** stinting; miserly (hand, heart). **5.** in want (of, से). **6.** distressed, troubled; sad; vexed; put to trouble. **7.** burdensome; awkward (a time, an activity); demanding, severe. — ~ **आना**, to be distressed, &c.; to be in difficulty; to be tired, fed up (of or with, से). ~ **करना**, to tighten; to distress, &c.; to put pressure (on, को); to oppress. ~ **हाथ होना**, to be badly off. ~ **होना** (को), = ~ **आना**. – **तंगदस्त**, adj. poor, in want; miserly. °**ई**, f. poverty; parsimony. **तंगदिल**, adj. miserly; ungenerous of nature; pettifogging. °**ई**, f. parsimony; small-mindedness. **तंगमोहरी**, adj. colloq. tight-fitting (trousers). **तंगहाल**, adj. in straitened circumstances, in want; in difficult circumstances. °**ई**, f. poverty; adversity.

तँगियाना *taṁgiyānā* [cf. H. *taṅg*], v.t. to tighten (as the girth of a horse).

तंगी *taṅgī* [P. *tangī*], f. **1.** cramped conditions; narrowness. **2.** tightness (clothing). **3.** scarcity. **4.** stinginess. **5.** poverty, want. **6.** distress, suffering. **7.** difficulty. — ~ **उठाना**, to suffer poverty, &c.

तंज़ *taṃz* [A. *ṭanz*], m. U. mockery; sneer; taunt.

तंडुल *taṇḍul* [S.], m. grain (esp. rice) after threshing and winnowing.

[1]**तंत** *tant* [? conn. *tattva-*], m. Av. **1.** precise moment, moment of truth, nick of time. **2.** substance, essence (of a matter).

[2]**तंत** *tant* [*tanti-*, *tantu-*], m. f. **1.** thread, string, wire (of a musical instrument). **2.** Av. attachment: strong desire; Brbh. means.

तंति *tanti* [S.], m. **1.** cord, line; string (as of a bow). **2.** a weaver.

तंती *tantī*, f. E.H. a musician.

तंतु *tantu* [S.], m. **1.** thread, cord, wire, string, line. **2.** fibre. **3.** tendril, filament. **4.** cobweb. **5.** *electr.* filament. — **तंतु-कीट**, m. silk-worm; spider. **तंतुवाय**, m. web-weaver: a weaver; a spider.

तंत्र *tantră* [S.], m. warp (of cloth), weaving: **1.** essential part, basis; chief doctrine, theory. **2.** arrangement, system; structure; regular order of ritual. **3.** specif. a work teaching magical and mystical formulae for worship or the attainment of superhuman power. **4.** charm, spell; incantation; oath. **5.** means (cf. [2]तंत, 2). **6.** a thread, string. — **तंत्र-मंत्र**, m. charms, incantations. **तंत्रिका-तंत्र**, m. the nervous system.

तंत्रिका *tantrikā* [S.], f. a nerve.

[1]**तंत्री** *tantrī* [S.], adj & m. **1.** adj. having to do with a tantra. **2.** m. follower of a tantra; a musician, singer.

[2]**तंत्री** *tantrī* [S.], f. string (of a musical instrument).

तंदुरुस्त *tandurust* [P. *tandurust*], adj. of sound body: **1.** healthy. **2.** vigorous.

तंदुरुस्ती *tandurustī* [P. *tandurustī*], f. **1.** health. **2.** vigour.

तंदुल *tandul*, m. = तंडुल.

तंदूर *tandūr* [P. *tannūr*], m. a large earthen oven.

तंदूरी *tandūrī* [cf. P. *tannūr*], adj. cooked in an oven (*tandūr*).

तंद्रा *tandrā* [S.], f. **1.** lassitude. **2.** drowsiness, dozing. — **तंद्रालस** [°*rā* + *ā*° or *a*°], adj. & m. inert from sleep, only half awake; = तंद्रा.

तंद्रालु *tandrālu* [S.], adj. drowsy, sleepy; languid.

तंद्रित *tandrit* [S.], adj. = तंद्रालु.

तंबा *tambā* [P. *tambān*], m. Brbh. a kind of wide-legged trousers.

तंबाकू *tambākū* [P. *tambākū*], m. tobacco. — ~ **पीना**, to smoke; to have a smoke.

तंबिया *taṁbiyā* [*tāmrika-*], adj. & m. **1.** adj. made of copper. **2.** m. reg. (W.) a copper pan; (Bihar) a ladle used in stirring liquid sugar.

तँबियाना *taṁbiyānā* [cf. H. *tambiyā*], v.i. **1.** to become copper-coloured. **2.** to acquire a coppery taste or smell (food kept in a copper container).

तंबीह *tambīh* [A. *tanbīh*], f. making mindful: admonition, reproof.

तंबू *tambū* [P. *tambū*], m. a tent (esp. a large one); pavilion; canopy. — ~ उखाड़ना, to dismantle a tent. ~ खड़ा करना, or डालना, or तानना, to pitch a tent; to encamp.

तंबूरची *tambūrcī*, m. a *tambūrā* player.

तंबूरा *tambūrā* [P. *tambūra*], m. a stringed instrument used to accompany a singer (= तानपूरा).

तंबोल *tambol* [**tāmbola-* (← Austro-as.): Pk. *tambola-*], m. betel leaf.

तँबोलन *tambolan*, f. pronun. var. = तँबोलिन.

तँबोलिन *tambolin* [cf. **tāmbolika-*: Pk. *tambolia-*], f. **1.** a woman who sells betel leaf. **2.** wife of a seller of betel leaf.

तँबोली *tambolī* [**tāmbolika-*: Pk. *tambolia-*], m. a seller of betel leaf.

तँवा- *tamvā-* [cf. H. *tamvālā*], v.i. E.H. to have darkness before the eyes, to faint.

तँवाला *tamvālā* [**tamāla-*²], m. *Pl.* (*HŚS.*) darkness before the eyes, fainting.

तअज्जुब *taajjub*, m. = ताज्जुब.

तअल्लुक़ *ta'alluq*, m. = ताल्लुक़.

तअल्लुक़ा *ta'alluqā*, m. = ताल्लुक़ा.

तआरुफ़ *taāruf* [A. *ta'āruf*], m. U. mutual acquaintance.

तआला *ta'ālā* [A. *ta'ālā*], adj. inv. *isl.* exalted (God). — ख़ुदा ~, God the Most High.

¹**तईं** *taīṁ* [conn. *ta-*: ? *tāvat-*, Ap. *tāvamhiṁ*], ppn. w. के. reg. **1.** to, up to. **2.** concerning, in the matter of; for.

²**तईं** *taīṁ*, adv. reg. then.

तई *taī* [*tapaka-*], f. reg. a metal frying pan or griddle (as used by *halvāīs* in making sweets).

-तः *-taḥ* [S.], suffix (forms adverbs, e.g. अधिकांशतः, in general).

¹**तक** *tak* [*tāvatka-*], ppn. & adv. **1.** ppn. up to, as far as; as much as. **2.** until: जब ~, as long as … तब ~, until that time. **3.** by, before (of time). **4.** adv. even. उसे एक पैसा ~ न रहा, he didn't have even a pice left. — अब ~, up until now, up to the present. कब ~? until when? by when? कहाँ ~? how far? to what extent? यहाँ ~ कि …, up to the point that …, up to a point where …

²**तक** *tak*, f. E.H. = ताक.

³**तक** *tak* [*tarka-*], m. reg. **1.** a large pair of scales. **2.** Brbh. = तर्क.

तक़दीर *taqdīr* [A. *taqdīr*], f. measuring: fate, destiny, lot. — ~ का खोटा, or हेठा, adj. & m. having a wretched lot, dogged by misfortune; such a person. ~ का सिकंदर, m. an Alexander in fortune: a very lucky person. ~ खुलना (की), one's fortune to change for the better. ~ फूटना (की), one's fortune to change for the worse. ~ लड़ना (की), = ~ खुलना. ~ लड़ाना, to try one's luck. तक़दीरवर [P. *-var*], adj. having a lucky fate or destiny.

तक़दीरी *taqdīrī* [A. *taqdīr*], adj. (restricted) having to do with fortune or chance. — ~ मामला, m. a matter of luck.

तकना *taknā* [conn. *tarkayati*], v.t. & v.i. reg. **1.** v.t. = ताकना. **2.** v.i. to look, to stare. **3.** to take aim; to point (a dog). **4.** to be looked at, &c.

तकनीकी *taknīkī* [Engl. *technical*], adj. technical; technological.

तकब्बरी *takabbarī* [A. *takabbur*+P. *-ī*], f. Brbh. **1.** *Pl.* pride, arrogance. **2.** ? irresistible one: *HŚS.* a kind of sword.

तकरार *takrār* [A. *takrār*], f. repeating: dispute, wrangle. — ~ करना, to dispute, to quarrel (about, पर).

तकरारी *takrārī* [cf. A. *takrār*], adj. & m. **1.** adj. quarrelsome, disputatious. **2.** m. [P. *takrārī*], a quarrelsome person.

तक़रीबन *taqrīban* [A. *taqrīban*], adv. **1.** approximately, about; nearly. **2.** near, nearby.

तक़रीर *taqrīr* [A. *taqrīr*], f. **1.** speaking; speech, discourse; conversation. **2.** a speech; statement, account.

तक़रीरी *taqrīrī* [A. *taqrīr*+H. *-ī*], adj. **1.** having to do with speech, &c.; conversational; oral. **2.** forming a topic of discussion, or debate.

तकला *taklā* [cf. *tarku-*], m. a spindle; shaft.

तकली *taklī* [cf. H. *taklā*], f. dimin. a spindle.

तक़लीद *taqlīd* [A. *taqlīd*], f. 19c. imitation. — ~ करना (की), to imitate; to mimic, to ape.

तकलीफ़ *taklīf* [A. *taklīf*], f. taking care: **1.** trouble, difficulty; inconvenience. **2.** distress (emotional or physical); suffering. **3.** hardship. — ~ उठाना, to experience or to suffer difficulty, &c. ~ करना, to take the trouble, to trouble oneself (to do sthg). ~ देना, or पहुँचाना (को), to cause trouble (to); to cause distress, &c. (to). – ~ की बात, f. a troublesome matter. ~ में, adv. in distress or want, &c.

तकल्लुफ़ *takalluf* [A. *takalluf*], f. taking pains: formality of behaviour. — ~ करना, to behave with formality, to stand on ceremony. ~ का, adj. formal (in style or manner). –

तकल्लुफ़मिज़ाज, adj. formal, ceremonious in manner.

तकवा *takvā*, m. = तकला.

तकवाना *takvānā* [cf. H. *tāknā*], v.t. to cause to be watched or superintended (by, से).

तकवाहा *takvāhā* [cf. H. *tāknā*], m. watchman (over crops).

तकवाही *takvāhī* [cf. H. *takvāhā*], reg. watching (over, की), keeping an eye (on).

तक़सीम *taqsīm* [A. *taqsīm*], f. **1.** dividing, division; partition. **2.** distribution. **3.** *math.* division. — ~ करना, to divide; to distribute (among or over, में or पर).

तक़सीमी *taqsīmī* [cf. A. *taqsīm*], adj. **1.** divisible; liable to division (as land). **2.** divided according to an allocation.

तक़सीर *taqsīr* [A. *taqṣīr*], f. **1.** shortcoming; omission; failure. **2.** fault, mistake; offence.

तकाई *takāī* [cf. H. *tāknā*, *takānā*], v.t. **1.** looking (at), watching (over). **2.** spying (on); tracking, shadowing.

तक़ाज़ा *taqāzā* [A. *taqāẓā*], m. **1.** demand, request (as for immediate payment, or the performance of a necessary task); claim. **2.** requirement, exigency (as of a situation). — ~ करना (का), to demand (payment, &c.); to exact. उम्र का ~, m. the demands, or ways, of a (particular) age (of life); the claims of age (as to respect). तक़ाज़े का, adj. due to be returned or paid for; requisitioned.

तक़ाज़ाई *taqāzāī* [A. *taqāẓā*+P. -*ī*], adj. demanding, exacting; pressing, importunate.

तकाना *takānā* [cf. H. *tāknā*], v.t. **1.** to cause (one) to look at, or to watch over (as fields); to show (to, को). **2.** to cause (one) to wait, to keep (one) in hope.

तक़ावी *taqāvī* [A. *taqāvī*], f. strengthening: an advance, a loan (esp. to cultivators, for running expenses and improvements). — ~ बाँटना, to divide the amount of a loan (between, में).

तकिया *takiyā* [P. *takya*], m. **1.** a pillow; a small bolster; cushion. **2.** a prop, support; *mil.* supporting forces. — तकिया-कलाम, m. prop to speech: an expletive; a needless word or phrase used repeatedly. तकियादार [P. -*dār*], m. a *faqīr*.

तकुआ *takuā*, m. = तकला.

तक्र *takr* [S.], m. Brbh. buttermilk with water.

तक्षक *takṣak* [S.], m. **1.** a cutter (esp. of wood); a carver. **2.** a carpenter.

तक्षण *takṣaṇ* [S.], m. cutting; paring; planing; carving.

तखड़ी *takhṛī* [? ← Panj. *takkṛī*], f. *Pl. HŚS.* a pair of small scales.

तखन *takhan* [*tatkṣaṇa-*], adv. reg. (Bihar) at that time, then.

तख़मीनन *takhmīnan* [cf. A. *takhmīnan*], adv. at a guess, approximately.

तख़मीना *takhmīnā* [cf. A. *takhmīn*], m. **1.** a guess, a conjecture. **2.** an estimate, appraisal. — ~ करना, or लगाना, to make a conjecture or assessment (of, का).

तख़ल्लुस *takhallus* [A. *takhalluṣ*], m. a literary pseudonym.

तखान *takhān* [*takṣan-*: Pk. *takkhāṇa-*], m. reg. a carpenter.

तख़ैयुल *takhaiyul* [A. *takhaiyul*], m. fancy, imagination.

तख़्त *takht* [P *takht*], m. **1.** throne. **2.** seat. **3.** raised place; stage, platform. 4. = तख़्ता, 1., 5. — ~ छोड़ना, to abdicate a throne. ~ पर बिठाना, to enthrone. ~ पर बैठना, to ascend a throne; to reign. ~ या तख़्ता, throne or bier: victory or death. ~ से उतारना, to dethrone. – तख़्तताऊस, m. *hist.* the Peacock Throne (of India). तख़्तनशीन [P. -*niśīn*], adj. & m. sitting on a throne: reigning; a sovereign. °ई, f. accession to a throne; reign. तख़्तपोश [P. -*poś*], m. cloth or cushion placed on a throne, seat, &c.

तख़्ता *takhtā* [P. *takhta*], m. **1.** a plank, board. **2.** boarding, deck (of a ship). **3.** a hoarding. **4.** a blackboard. **5.** a bench; berth, colloq. bed. **6.** a sheet (of paper). — ~ हो जाना, to become wooden: to become hard, insensitive, inert. ~ उलटना, to overthrow (का: as a ruler, a government).

तख़्ती *takhtī* [P. *takhtī*], f. dimin. **1.** a small board. **2.** a child's writing-board.

तगड़ा *tagṛā* [cf. *targa-], adj. **1.** sturdy, robust; dependable. **2.** forceful, vigorous. **3.** valid, strong (an argument). — तगड़ी रक़म, f. colloq. a vast sum.

तगड़ी *tagṛī* [cf. *trāgga-, &c.: Pk. *tagga-*], f. **1.** a thread or cord worn round the waist. **2.** a chain, with bells attached, worn round the waist.

तगना *tagnā* [cf. H. *tāgnā*], v.i. to be stitched together, or quilted.

तग़मा *tagmā*, m. see तमग़ा.

तगवाई *tagvāī*, f. = तगाई.

तगाई *tagāī* [cf. H. *tagānā*], f. **1.** stitching together, quilting. **2.** cost of, or price paid for, stitching, &c.

तगादा *tagādā*, m. corr. = तक़ाज़ा.

तगाना *tagānā* [cf. H. *tāgnā*], v.t. to cause to be stitched together, or quilted (by, से).

तग़ाफ़ुल *taġāful* [A. *taġāful*], m. inattention, neglect.

तग़ार *taġār* [P. *taġār*], m. reg. **1.** a tub, pail (as for mixing mortar, or carrying lime); an earthen pan (as for kneading sweets). **2.** *Pl.* a mason's mud or lime pit.

तग़ारी *taġārī* [cf. P. *taġār*], f. dimin. reg. a small tub, pail, &c.

तगियाना *tagiyānā* [cf. H. *tāgā*], v.t. = तागना.

तग़ीर *taġīr* [A. *tagyīr*], f. Brbh. changing, change (for the worse).

तग़ीरी *taġīrī* [A. *tagyīr*+H. *-ī*], f. Brbh. state of change (for the worse).

तग़य्युर *tagaiyyur* [A. *tagaiyur*], m. 19c. becoming changed; deterioration.

तग्गा *taggā*, m. = तागा.

तग्गड़ *taggaṛ*, reg. (Bihar) a partic. flower.

तचना *tacnā*, v.i. **1.** to be heated, scorched; to be parched. **2.** to suffer distress.

तचाना *tacānā* [cf. H. *tacnā*], v.t. to heat, to scorch; to parch.

तज्- *taj-* [cf. *ta*], pron. & adj. that: — तज्जनित, adj. produced from that, arising therefrom.

तज़किरा *tazkirā* [A. *tazkira*], m. U. esp. *musl.* memory: a memoir, biography.

तजना *tajnā* [cf. *tyajati*], v.t. **1.** to abandon. **2.** to renounce.

तजरबा *tajrabā* [A. *tajriba*], m. experience. — ~ करना (का), to experience. – तजरबाकार, adj. & m. experienced; versed (in, का), expert (in); an expert. °ई, f. experience, practical knowledge.

तजर्बा *tajarbā*, m. = तजरबा.

तजल्ली *tajallī* [A. *tajallī*], f. E.H. clearness; brilliance, splendour.

तजवीज़ *tajvīz* [A. *tajvīz*], f. **1.** deliberation, investigation. **2.** opinion, judgment. ***3.** scheme, plan, proposal. — ~ होना, to be enquired into, investigated.

तजुरबा *tajurbā*, m. = तजरबा.

तज्ञ *tajñă* [ad. *tajjña-*], adj. Av. = तत्त्वज्ञ.

तट *taṭ* [S.], m. **1.** bank (of a river). **2.** shore; coast. — तटवर्ती, adj. lying near or at a bank, or shore, coastal. तटस्थ, adj. standing on a bank, or shore: impartial; abstaining, indifferent; neutral. °ता, f. impartiality; non-interference; neutrality. °वाद, m. a professed policy of neutrality, or of non-alignment. °ई, adj. & m. following a policy of neutrality, &c.

तटिनी *taṭinī* [S.], f. having banks: a river.

तटीय *taṭīyă* [S.], adj. having to do with a bank, coast or shore.

तड़ंगा *taṛaṅgā*, adj. in comp. sturdily built.

तड़ *taṛ* [*traṭ-*], m. **1.** a sound of snapping, cracking, bursting, tearing. **2.** a sound of striking, slapping. — तड़ातड़, m. & adv. a cracking sound, &c.; with a cracking sound; in quick succession.

[1]**तड़क** *taṛak* [cf. H. *taṛaknā*], f. **1.** cracking, snapping, &c. **2.** a crack, split. **3.** flash (as of lightning). — तड़क-भड़क, f. fig. splendour, show.

[2]**तड़क** *taṛak*, m. reg. (Bihar) **1.** roofing (of a cart). **2.** corner ridgepole (of a roof).

तड़कना *taṛaknā* [cf. *traṭ-*], v.i. & v.t. **1.** v.i. to crack, to snap; to split; to burst. **2.** to become suddenly angry, to snap (at, पर). **3.** v.t. to season (lentils, vegetables).

तड़का *taṛkā* [cf. *traṭ-*, H. *taṛaknā*], m. **1.** daybreak. **2.** seasoning. — ~ देना, or लगाना (में), to season (food). ~ होना, day to break; colloq. to be without money, to be 'broke'.

तड़काना *taṛkānā* [cf. H. *taṛaknā*], v.t. to cause to crack; to split with a crack; to burst; to snap.

तड़तड़ाना *taṛtaṛānā* [cf. *traṭ-*], v.i. **1.** to make a snapping or cracking sound; to burst (as thunder). **2.** to crackle (as hot *ghī*); to fizz; to whizz; to hiss; to ache, to throb. **3.** to patter, to clatter (as rain). **4.** to storm, to rage.

तड़तड़ाहट *taṛtaṛāhaṭ* [cf. H. *taṛtaṛānā*], f. **1.** a snapping, or cracking sound; clap (of thunder). **2.** crackling; fizzing, &c. **3.** pattering, clattering. **4.** storming, raging.

तड़प *taṛap* [cf. H. *taṛapnā*], f. **1.** tossing about, restlessness. **2.** agitation of feelings; anxiety; eagerness; throb, beat (as of the heart); suffering, agony. **3.** haste; sudden bound or spring. **4.** crack, report (of an explosion). **5.** flash, glitter (as of lightning, or of a jewel). — तड़प-झड़प, f. show, display.

तड़पना *taṛapnā* [cf. **taḍapphaḍ-*: Pk. *taḍapphaḍaï*], v.i. **1.** to toss about, to be restless; to flounder; to writhe. **2.** to be agitated; to be very anxious, eager (to, के लिए);

to throb, to beat (as the heart). **3.** to bound, to spring; to flare (as with sudden anger).

तड़पाना *taṛpānā* [cf. H. *taṛapnā*], v.t. **1.** to make restless. **2.** to make uneasy, agitated. **3.** to cause to stumble.

तड़फ *taṛaph*, f. = तड़प.

तड़फड़ाना *taṛphaṛānā* [**taḍapphaḍ-*: Pk. *taḍapphaḍaï*], v.i. & v.t. **1.** v.i. = तड़पना. **2.** v.t. = तड़पाना.

तड़फड़ाहट *taṛphaṛāhaṭ* [cf. H. *taṛphaṛānā*], f. **1.** tossing about, floundering; fluttering. **2.** agitation; anxiety.

तड़फना *taṛaphnā*, v.i. = तड़पना.

तड़फाना *taṛphānā*, v.t. = तड़पाना.

तड़ाक *taṛāk* [cf. *traṭ-*], f. & adv. **1.** f. = तड़. **2.** adv. with a crack, &c. **3.** noisily, boisterously. **4.** quickly, briskly. — ~ से, adv. with a crack or crash; smartly, quickly. – तड़ाक-फड़ाक, adv. in quick succession; without delay, at once (= prec).

तड़ाका *taṛākā* [cf. *traṭ-*], m. 1. = तड़ाक. **2.** banging, clattering. **3.** bustle, activity. **4.** intensity, severity (of heat, cold, storm). **5.** a cracker, banger. **6.** demand for, scarcity of (a commodity). — तड़ाके का, adj. violent (storm); intense (heat, &c.); active, brisk; gaudy; brilliant, splendid.

तड़ाग *taṛāg* [ad. *taḍāga-*], m. Brbh. Av. a pond, tank.

तड़ातड़ *taṛātaṛ*, adv. see s.v. तड़.

तड़ातड़ी *taṛātaṛī* [cf. H. *taṛātaṛ*], f. haste, hurry.

तड़ाभड़ी *taṛābhaṛī* [cf. H. *taṛ*], f. **1.** haste, hurry. **2.** a quick succession.

तड़ाया *taṛāyā* [? conn. H. *taṛākā*], m. *Pl.* showiness (as of dress).

तड़ावा *taṛāvā*, m. *HŚS.* = तड़ाया.

तड़ित *taṛit* [S.], f. lightning. — तड़ित-रक्षक, m. lightning conductor.

तड़ी *taṛī* [**taḍikā-*], f. **1.** a slap; punishment. **2.** esp. तड़ी-. colloq. trickery. — ~ जड़ना, or जमाना, or देना, or लगाना (पर), *HŚS.* to give a slap. – तड़ीबाज़ [P. *-bāz*], adj. colloq. tricky (a customer).

तत्- *tat-* [S.], adj. & pron. that. — तत्काल, adj. of the time concerned; immediate; adv. at the time concerned, &c. °ईन, adj. of the time concerned; topical, current. तत्क्षण, adj. immediate; adv. immediately; in an instant. तत्क्षेत्रीय, adj. local. ततच्छन, adv. 19c. = तत्क्षण. तत्पर, adj. having 'that' as an aim: in readiness (for, के लिए); intent (on, में); devoted, attentive (to). °ता, f. readiness, &c. तत्पश्चात, adv. thereafter. तत्पुरुष, m. & adj. *gram.* a determinative compound; determinative. तत्सम, adj. & m. *gram.* (in New Indo-Aryan languages) a loanword used in the same written form (and substantially similar spoken form) as in Sanskrit; a construct from Sanskrit roots, characterised by the same usage of script and pronunciation. तत्संबंधी, adj. connected with that: related, relevant. तत्सामयिक, adj. having to do with the time in question, contemporary.

ततखन *tatkhan*, adv. Av. = तत्क्षण, see s.v. तत्-.

ततरी *tatrī*, f. the wild varnish tree, *Rhus succedanea* (galls from which are used medicinally).

ततहड़ा *tatahṛā* [**taptaghaṭa-*], m. reg. (W.) a large vessel for heating water to wash in.

तताना *tatānā* [cf. *tapta-*], v.t. reg. to heat.

ततार *tatār* [**taptakāri-*], f. *Pl.* fomentation.

ततार- *tatār-* [cf. H. *tatār*], v.t. Brbh. to foment; to bathe with water.

ततैया *tataiyā*, m. a wasp, or hornet.

तत्ता *tattā* [*tapta-*], adj. hot, heated.

तत्त्व *tattvă* [S.], m. **1.** real state or nature; essence; the supreme spirit. **2.** one of the five traditionally distinguished elementary substances (ether, air, fire, water, earth). **3.** *chem.* an element. **4.** a basic principle; an axiom. **5.** an element, aspect or factor (in a system). **6.** *philos.* the real nature of the human soul (as identical with the all-pervading supreme spirit). — तत्त्वज्ञ, m. one who knows the real nature of things; a philosopher. तत्त्व-ज्ञान, m. knowledge of the real nature of things, or of any matter; philosophical knowledge. °ई, m. one who knows the real nature of things; a specialist; a philosopher. तत्त्वतः, adv. truly, really; essentially. तत्त्ववाद, m. a philosophical view, or system; adherence to a philosophical view. °ई, adj. & m. philosophical; a philosopher. तत्त्वविद्, m. = तत्त्वज्ञ. °-विद्या, f. philosophy. °-वेत्ता, m. inv. = तत्त्वज्ञ. तत्त्व-शास्त्र, m. philosophy. तत्त्व-शून्य, m. devoid of true worth or value. तत्त्व-संबंधी, adh. having to do with the real nature of things, &c. तत्त्वावधान [°*va*+*a*°], m. supervision, direction; aegis.

तत्पर *tatpar* [S.], adj. see s.v. तत्-.

तत्र *tatră* [S.], adv. there.

तत्व *tatva*, m. corr. = तत्त्व.

तथ *tath* [ad. *tathya-*: ? ← Panj. or Raj.], adj. & m. *Pl.* *HŚS.* = तथ्य or तत्त्व.

तथा *tathā* [S.], conj. & adv. **1.** conj. and. **2.** adv. in the same way as. — **तथाकथित**, adj. so-called. **तथागत**, m. who comes and goes in the same way : title of the Buddha. **तथापि** [°*thā*+*a*°], conj. nevertheless. **तथास्तु** [°*thā*+*a*°], so be it. **तथैव** [°*thā*+*e*°], adv. in just the same way (as). **तथोक्त** [°*thā*+*u*°], adj. = **तथाकथित**.

तथ्य *tathyă* [S.], m. sthg. which is so: **1.** a fact. **2.** a truth, a reality.

तत्थोथंभो *tattho-thambho*, m. colloq. maintaining (an existing position).

तद्- *tad-* [S.], adj. & pron. that: — **तदंतर**, adv. = next. **तदनंतर**, adv. immediately thereafter. **तदनुकूल**, adj. corresponding, conformable (to sthg.); appropriate (to). **तदनुरूप**, adj. of the same form (as sthg.); similar (to). **तदनुवर्ती**, adj. ensuing (upon, sthg). **तदनुसार**, adj. in accordance (with sthg.); conformably (to); accordingly. **तदपि**, conj. Brbh. Av. nevertheless (= **तो भी**). **तदर्थ**, adj. having a particular purpose (a sub-committee, &c). **°ई**, adj. synonymous (with). **°ईय**, adj. id. **तदाकार**, m. of the same form (as sthg.); similar (to). **तदुत्तर**, adv. thereafter. **तदुपरांत**, adv. id. **तदुपरि**, adv. in addition, over and above. **तद्गत**, adj. connected, concerned (with sthg.); contained in, diffused through. **तद्गुण**, m a figure of speech in which the qualities of one object are attributed to another. **तद्देशीय**, adj. of the same country (as). **तद्धित**, adj. & m. a suffix forming nouns from other nouns; a noun so derived. **°आंत**, adj. ending in a *taddhita* suffix. **तद्भव**, adj. & m. *gram.* of the nature of that: (in New Indo-Aryan languages) a word which has evolved organically from an early Indo-Aryan form (as distinct from a borrowing made at a later stage). **तद्यपि**, adv. = **तथापि**. **तद्रूप**, adj. of the same form (as sthg).

तदपि *tadapi* [S.], conj. poet. see s.v. **तद्-**.

तदबीर *tadbīr* [A. *tadbīr*], f. **1.** forethought, prudence. ***2.** expedient, plan; device; arrangement; means. — **~ करना**, to deliberate, to devise an expedient (for or against, **की**); to dispose (of).

तदा *tadā* [S.], adv. then.

तदीय *tadīyă*, adj. **1.** belonging to, connected with (sthg). **2.** 19c. concerned with ultimate questions, philosophical (as a society).

¹तन *tan* [*tanū*-, and P. *tan*], m. the body. — **~ कसना**, to subdue the body. **~ का ताप**, m. bodily distress or need (esp. hunger). **~ तोड़ना**, to stretch; to tax the body. **~ देना**, to apply oneself (to, **में**); to exert oneself, to take pains. **~ लगना**, to be felt (by, **के**), to come home (to); to be brought into use (by). – **तनदुरुस्त**, adj., **°ई**, f. see s.vv. **तनज़ेब** [P. *zeb*], m. a fine muslin, resembling *nainsukh*. **तन-मन**, m. body and soul, the whole self. **तन-मन से**, adv. with body and soul, heart and soul. **तन-मन मारना**, to restrain (one's) desires, or emotions; to concentrate the senses, to become oblivious to (one's) surroundings. **तन-मन-धन**, m. (one's) physical, mental and material resources, all one is and has. **तनसुख**, m. a fine muslin (cf. **तनज़ेब**, **नैनसुख**).

²तन *tan* [-*tanaḥ*, Ap. *taṇeṃ*], ppn. Brbh. towards.

तन्- *tan-* [S.], adj. & pron. that. — **तन्मय**, adj. consisting of that: absorbed, engrossed (in, **में**). **°ता**, f.

तनक *tanak*, adj. Brbh. = **तनिक**.

तनख़ाह *tankhāh* [P. *tankhvāh*], f. wages, pay, salary. — **~ देना (को)**, to pay wages, &c. (to). – **तनख़ाहदार** [P. *-dār*], m. a wage-earner, &c.

तनख़्वाह *tankhvāh*, f. see **तनख़ाह**.

तनतना *tantanā* [A. *ṭanṭana*], m. **1.** din, noise. **2.** fig. fame, report; pomp, splendour. **3.** arrogance, domineering.

तनतनाना *tantanānā* [cf. H. *tantanā*], v.i. **1.** to show overbearingness, arrogance. **2.** to show overbearing anger.

तनदुरुस्त *tandurust* [P. *tandurust*], adj. sound in body: healthy. — **~ करना**, to restore to health, to cure.

तनदुरुस्ती *tandurustī* [P. *tandurustī*], f. health.

तनना *tannā* [cf. H. *tānnā*], v.i. **1.** to be stretched; to be made taut, tight. **2.** to be spread, to spread. **3.** to be pitched (a tent). **4.** to hold oneself erect; to move or act in a stiff or pompous way. **5.** to be tense with emotion. **भौंहें ~**, the brows to be knitted (in anger, irritation). **6.** to be at the ready, raised to strike (swords, staves). **7.** [Engl.] to grow firm (prices).

तनय *tanay* [S.], m. a son.

तनया *tanayā* [S.], f. a daughter.

तनहा *tanhā* [P. *tanhā*], adj. **1.** solitary, lonely; alone. **2.** single; unique.

तनहाई *tanhāī* [P. *tanhāī*], f. **1.** loneliness, solitude. **2.** privacy. — **~ क़ैद**, f. solitary confinement. **क़ैदे ~**, f. U. id.

तना *tanā* [P. *tana*], m. **1.** trunk (of a tree). **2.** stalk, stem.

तनाज़ा *tanāzā* [A. *tanāzaʻa*], m. *Pl. HŚS.* a quarrel, dispute.

तनातनी *tanātanī* [cf. H. *tannā*], f. tension; strained relationship.

तनाना *tanānā* [cf. H. *tānnā*], v.t. to cause to be stretched, spread, &c. (by, से).

तनाब *tanāb* [A. *ṭunub*; *aṭnāb*, pl.: P. *ṭanāb*], f. a tent-rope; long rope.

तनाव *tanāv* [cf. H. *tannā*], m. **1.** tightness, tension. **2.** tension (nervous, emotional, &c). — ~ तना-, v.t. Brbh. to make fast (as tent-ropes: cf. तनाब).

तनिक *tanik* [cf. *tanu-*, *tanuka-*], adj. **1.** adj. little, slight; very little, the least. **2.** adv. a little, slightly; a little while. — तनिक-सी, adv. = ~.

तनिमा *tanimā* [S.], f. poet. thinness, slenderness.

तनिया *taniyā* [cf. *tanikā-*], f. Brbh. **1.** a narrow loin-cloth. **2.** *HŚS.* ? a bodice.

तनी *tanī* [*tanikā-*], f. string, cord or tape serving as a fastening (of a garment, a bag). — तनीदार [P. *-dār*], adj. having strings, &c.

¹**तनु** *tanu* [S.], adj. **1.** thin, slender. **2.** delicate, frail. **3.** slight, small, trivial.

²**तनु** *tanu* [cf. *tanū̆-*], f. the body. — तनुज, m. offspring, son. °आ, f. daughter. तनुधारी, adj. & m. Av. possessing a body: mortal; a living creature. तनु-पोषक, m. Av. one who attends to his or her material interests.

तनू *tanū* [S.], m. = ²तनु.

तन्नाना *tannānā*, colloq. = तनना.

तन्वी *tanvī* [S.], f. a delicate or graceful woman.

¹**तप** *tap* [S.], m. **1.** heat; the hot weather. **2.** fever. — ~ उतरना, heat to lessen; a fever to subside. – तपेदिक़ [A. *-diqq*], f. see s.v.

²**तप** *tap* [*tapas-*], m. ascetic fervour or practice; religious austerity; penance; mortification. — ~ करना, or साधना, to carry out ascetic practices. – तपोधन [°*as*+*dha*°], m. rich in penance: most pious; a great ascetic. °ई, m. id. तपोबल [°*as*+*ba*°], m. power deriving from ascetic practices. तपोलोक [°*as*+*lo*°], m. *mythol.* realm of asceticism: the sixth heavenly region above the earth. तपोवन [°*as*+*va*°], m. a grove in which ascetic practices are carried out. तपोवरण [°*as*+*va*°], adj. interfering with ascetic practice(s). तपोवृद्ध [°*as*+*vṛ*°], adj. = तपोधन. तपोव्रत [°*as*+*vr*°], m. penance and fasting.

तपक- *tapak-* [cf. **tapp-* (conn. **ṭapp-*)], v.i. Brbh. to throb, to palpitate.

तपकची *tapakcī*, m. *hist.* a chief revenue accountant.

तपड़ी *tapṛī*, f. *Pl. HŚS.* a mound; a raised boundary of earth (dividing plots of land).

¹**तपन** *tapan* [cf. H. *tapnā*], f. **1.** heat (= ताप, 1). **2.** the state of being hot, burning; pangs.

²**तपन** *tapan* [S.], m. the sun. — तपन-यौवन, m. the young sun, ardent heat.

तपना *tapnā* [cf. H. *tāpnā*], v.i. **1.** to be heated; to burn, to blaze. **2.** to suffer distress, grief, or pain; fig. to be self-sacrificing, to suffer in a cause. **3.** to be splendid or awe-inspiring (suggesting powers of an ascetic).

तपरिहाऊ *taprihāū* [cf. H. *tapṛī*], m. *hist.* plots of land cultivated in small patches among the uncultivated land of an estate.

तपस् *tapas* [S.], m. = ²तप.

तपसा *tapsā* [ad. *tapasyā-*], f. = तपस्या.

तपसी *tapăsī* [ad. *tapasvī-*], adj. & m. = तपस्वी.

तपस्या *tapasyā* [S.], f. ascetic fervour or practice, &c. (= ²तप).

तपस्विता *tapasvitā* [S.], f. quality of an ascetic, asceticism.

तपस्विनी *tapasvinī*, adj. f. & f. **1.** adj. f. = तपस्वी. ***2.** f. an ascetic. **3.** the wife of an ascetic.

तपस्वी *tapasvī* [S.], adj. & m. **1.** adj. ascetic, engaged in penance. ***2.** m. an ascetic; a yogī; a devotee.

¹**तपा** *tapā*, m. an ascetic.

²**तपा** *tapā*, m. the hot weather.

तपाक *tapāk* [P. *tapāk*], m. **1.** warmth, ardour; the anguish of love. **2.** affection; friendship; solicitude. **3.** transf. alacrity. — ~ से, adv. warmly, cordially, &c.; quickly, at once.

¹**तपाना** *tapānā* [cf. H. *tapnā*], v.t. **1.** to heat; to melt (as *ghī*). **2.** to test, to assay (metals by heat). **3.** to cause to suffer distress, grief; to mortify (the flesh).

²**तपाना** *tapānā* [cf. *tarpayati*], v.t. *Pl.* to make a libation to gods or ancestors.

तपाव *tapāv* [cf. H. *tapnā*], m. **1.** heat (as a quality or condition). **2.** making hot (as a process).

तपास *tapās* [cf. H. ¹*tap*, and H. *tapnā*], f. reg. sunshine, sun's heat.

तपिश *tapiś* [P. *tapiś*], f. **1.** heat. **2.** distress, suffering.

तपी *tapī* [cf H. ²*tap*], adj. & m. = तपस्वी.

तपेदिक़ *tapediq* [P. *tap-e-diq*], f. tuberculosis.

तपेला *tapelā*, m. a container for heating liquids.

तपो- *tapo-* [S]. asceticism, ascetic: see s.v. [2]तप.

तपौनी *tapaunī* [cf. H. [2]*tapānā*], f. molasses (as offered by robbers to Devī). — ~ का गुड़ खाना, fig. to have been irremediably corrupted.

तप्त *tapt* [S.], adj. **1.** heated, hot. **2.** distressed, suffering. — तप्त-कुंड, m. a hot spring.

तप्ति *tapti* [S.], f. heat.

तफ़क्कुर *tafakkur* [A. *tafakkur*], m. 19c. **1.** cogitation, reflection. **2.** anxiety.

तफ़तीश *taftīś* [A. *taftīś*], f. examination, scrutiny; investigation, search.

तफ़रीक़ *tafrīq* [A. *tafrīq*], f. *Pl. HŚS.* separation, division; distinction.

तफ़रीह *tafrīh* [A. *tafrīḥ*], f. gladdening: **1.** amusement, entertainment. **2.** walk, stroll. **3.** delight, fun; joking. — ~ करना, to amuse oneself; to stroll; to enjoy oneself, to laugh and joke.

तफ़रीहन *tafrīhan* [A. *tafrīhan*], adv. by way of amusement, &c.

तफ़र्क़ा *tafarqā* [A. *tafriqa*: ? w. H. *farq*], m. making a difference: discord, dissension.

तफ़सीर *tafsīr* [A. *tafṣīr*], f. U. an explanation (esp. of the Qur'ān).

तफ़सील *tafsīl* [A. *tafṣīl*], f. separating: **1.** explanation, detailed account; analysis. ***2.** particulars, details. **3.** list, specification. — ~ करना, to give the detail (of, की); to explain in detail; to specify.

तफ़ावत *tafāvat* [A. *tafāva*: P. *tafāvat*], m. U. distance; distinction, disparity.

तब *tab* [H. *ab*: anal.], adv. **1.** then, at that time. **2.** next, thereafter. **3.** therefore, that being so. — ~ का, adj. of that time. ~ तो, adv. then indeed, then; for that reason. ~ भी, adv. even then; even so. तभी, adv. at that very time; instantly; for just that reason.

तबक़ा *tabqā* [A. *ṭabqa*], m. **1.** U. storey, floor. **2.** *Pl. HŚS.* layer. ***3.** rank, order; class.

तबदील *tabdīl* [A. *tabdīl*], f. changing; change; transfer, substitution. — ~ करना (को), to change; to transfer.

तबदीली *tabdīlī* [A. *tabdīl*+P. *-ī*], f. **1.** change. **2.** transfer (as of officials). **3.** change, relief (of a watch). **4.** shifting, moving (as of a counter or piece).

तबर *tabar* [P. *tabar*], m. reg. (Raj.) an axe.

[1]**तबल** *tabal*, m. Brbh. an axe (= तबर).

[2]**तबल** *tabal*, m. Av. a drum (= तबला).

तबलची *tabalcī* [A. *ṭabl*+P. *-cī*], m. *tablā* player, drummer.

तबला *tablā* [A. *ṭabla*], m. a small drum. — ~ चढ़ाना, to tighten the membrane of a *tablā* (in tuning it). ~ मिलाना, to tune a *tablā*.

तबलिया *tabliyā* [cf. H. *tablā*], m. drummer (= तबलची).

तबस्सुम *tabassum* [A. *tabassum*], m. a smile.

तबाक़ *tabāq* [A. *ṭabāq*], m. **1.** reg. (W.) a broad, flat dish, platter; bowl. **2.** colloq. head, skull.

तबादला *tabādlā* [cf. A. *tabādul*], m. a transfer.

तबाह *tabāh* [P. *tabāh*], adj. **1.** ruined; laid waste. **2.** fig. wretched. — ~ करना, to ruin, to lay waste. – तबाह-हाल, adj. in ruined state; in wretched condition.

तबाही *tabāhī* [P. *tabāhī*], f. **1.** ruin; destruction. **2.** wretched or devastated state.

तबियत *tabiyat*, f. = तबीयत.

तबीअत *tabīat*, f. see तबीयत.

तबीब *tabīb* [A. *ṭabīb*], m. U. medical man (= हकीम).

तबीयत *tabīyat* [A. *ṭabī'a*: P. *ṭabī'at*], f. **1.** temperament. **2.** intrinsic quality. **3.** mind; state of mind, mood. **4.** state of health. — ~ आना, to be attached (to, पर), in love (with); to desire (sthg). ~ उधर थी, (he or she) longed (for sthg). ~ ख़राब होना, to feel unwell; to be unwell. ~ ख़ुश होना, to feel refreshed (mentally or physically). ~ ठीक होना, to be recovered (from illness); to feel better (after momentary indisposition). ~ ताज़ी होना, to feel refreshed. ~ पर ज़ोर डालना, to exert oneself. ~ फड़क उठना, to be thrilled (at a thought, or a prospect). ~ फिरना, to feel no affinity (for, से), to feel aversion (to). ~ बिगड़ना, to become ill-tempered; to become ill or sick; to lust. ~ भरना, v.i. the mind to be satiated (with, से); to cloy; v.t. to give (one, की or अपनी) full or ample satisfaction. ~ लगना (को), to feel interest (in, में), to take pleasure (in); to be attached (to); to long (for, से). ~ लड़ाना, to grapple (with, से: as with a difficulty); to tackle. तबीयतदार [P. *-dār*], adj. having good health; sociable, affable. °ई, f.

तबै *tabai*, adv. Brbh. = तभी, and तब भी.

तभी *tabhī* [H. *tab*+H. *hī*], adv. see s.v. तब.

तम *tam* [ad. *tamas-*], m. **1.** darkness, &c. (= तमस्). **2.** fig. shame, disgrace.

-तम *-tam* [S.], suffix (forms superlatives, e.g. नवीनतम, adj. most recent).

तमंचा *tamañcā* [T. *tabanca*], m. **1.** a pistol. **2.** sl. a girl. — ~ छोड़ना or दाग़ना, to fire a pistol (at, पर).

तमक *tamak* [cf. H. *tamaknā*], f. flushing with anger; sudden rage.

तमकना *tamaknā* [cf. *tāmrākṣa-*], v.i. to flush with anger; to become enraged.

तमग़ा *tamgā* [T. *damga*], m. **1.** a medallion, medal. **2.** brand (on an animal).

तमतमाना *tamtamānā* [conn. *tămra-*; ? w. H. *tamaknā*], v.i. **1.** to flush. **2.** to glow. **3.** to sparkle; to flash.

तमतमाहट *tamtamāhaṭ* [cf. H. *tamtamānā*], f. flushing, flush; glow.

तमन्ना *tamannā* [A. *tamannā*], f. desire, longing. — ~ करना, to long (for, की).

तमस् *tamas* [S.], m. **1.** darkness. **2.** *philos.* the quality (*guṇa*) of darkness or ignorance, as a constituent of all nature; gloom; inertness, indolence; anger, malice. — **तमस-आच्छन्न**, covered, hidden in darkness.

तमस्ख़ुर *tamaskhur* [A. *tamaskhur*], m. 19c. joking, buffoonery.

तमस्विनी *tamasvinī* [S.], f. night, dark night.

तमस्वी *tamasvī* [cf. H. *tamasvinī*], adj. dark, gloomy.

तमस्सुक *tamassuk* [A. *tamassuk*], m. *fin.* U. a promissory note, bond.

तमाँचा *tamāṁcā*, m. pronun. var. = तमाचा.

तमाइ *tamāi* [cf. A. *ṯama'*], f. Brbh. greed, strong desire.

तमाकू *tamākū*, m. pronun. var. = तंबाकू.

तमाचा *tamācā* [P. *ṯamā(n)ca*], m. a slap. — ~ जड़ना, or जमाना, or देना, or मारना (को), to slap, to strike.

तमाम *tamām* [A. *tamām*], adj. complete, entire; completed, finished. — ~ करना, to complete; to conclude. काम ~ करना, to put an end to (a matter: specif. euph. to kill one, का).

तमामी *tamāmī* [P. *tamāmī*], f. Brbh. brocade; fine gold cloth.

तमाल *tamāl* [S.], m. an evergreen tree, *Garcinia xanthocymus* (having dark bark, and white flowers: source of gum-resin, and of a yellow dye).

तमाश- *tamāś-*. see s.v. तमाशा.

तमाशा *tamāśā* [A. *tamāśī*: P. *tamāśā*], m. **1.** show, spectacle. **2.** amusement; fun; joke. **3.** transf. sthg. trivial. यह कोई ~ नहीं है, this is no laughing matter. **4.** sthg. astonishing or curious. — ~ करना, to put on a show; to act a part; to make fun (of, का). ~ दिखाना, to show (one, को) sthg. striking; fig. to give (one) a thrashing. ~ देखना, to see sthg. striking, a spectacle; to see what is to be seen, to see the fun. **तमाशे की बात**, f. a strange or interesting thing. – **तमाशगीर** [P. *-gīr*], m. keen spectator of diversions; a dissolute person (= next). **तमाशबीन** [P. *-bīn*], m. spectator of diversions, &c.; a dissolute person. °ई, f. fondness for diversions, &c.; debauchery.

तमाशाई *tamāśāī* [P. *tamāśāī*, m.], m. & adj. **1.** m. a spectator, onlooker. **2.** the organiser of a show, &c. **3.** adj. fit for a show or spectacle.

तमिस्र *tamisră* [S.], m. darkness.

तमिस्रा *tamisrā* [S.], f. a dark night, a night during the wane of the moon.

तमी *tamī* [S.], f. night, darkness. — **तमीचर**, m. Av. night-goer: a demon.

तमीज़ *tamīz* [A. *tamyīz*], f. **1.** discernment, discrimination. **2.** good sense. ***3.** courtesy, manners. — **तमीज़दार** [P. *-dār*], adj. discerning; judicious, sensible; discreet; courteous.

तमो- *tamo-* [S]. darkness: — **तमोगुण**, m. = तमस्, 2. °ई, adj. & m. dominated in temperament by the quality of *tamas*; an ignorant, morose, inert or malicious person.

तय *tay* [A. *ṯai*], m. folding, rolling up: **1.** finishing, concluding (a matter). **2.** deciding (a matter). — ~ करना, to conclude, to dispose of; to complete (a journey); to decide (sthg). ~ होना, to be concluded, or disposed of; to be decided. – **तयशुदा**, adj. inv. settled, decided.

तरंग *taraṅg* [S.], f. **1.** a wave. **2.** an undulating sound or rhythm. **3.** a swelling emotion; rapture, transport. **4.** whim, mood; fancy. **5.** transf. a chapter, or section (of a book). — ~ में आना, to be transported by emotion; to be attracted (to, की). ~ में होना, to be in the mood, in good form (a singer, &c). तरंगें मारना, to be stirred up, rough (water). तरंगें लेना, fig. to be sunk, or lost (as in sleep, or a stupor: की).

तरंगिणी *taraṅgiṇī* [S.], f. a river.

तरंगित *taraṅgit* [S.], adj. **1.** agitated by waves (water); washed over by waves. **2.** caused to swell, or to stir (sound, wind). **3.** stirred or agitated by emotion.

तरंगी *taraṅgī* [S.], adj. 1. = तरंगित, 1. ***2.** capricious. **3.** emotional.

[1]**तर** *tar* [P. *tar*], adj. **1.** wet, moist; saturated; juicy. **2.** luxuriant (of growth), fresh. **3.** cool, refreshing; alleviating fever. **4.** refreshed; gladdened. **5.** delighting, splendid, fine. **6.** flourishing, prosperous. — ~ करना, to wet,

to moisten, &c. तरबतर [P. *-ba-*], adj. soaked, drenched. तरो-ताज़ा [P. *-o-*], adj. moist and fresh: fresh (as fruit); ripe; flourishing. °-ताज़गी, f. freshness, &c.

²**तर** *tar* [conn. *tarhi*], conj. E.H. = तो.

³**तर** *tar*, adv. Brbh. Av. = तल.

-तर *-tar* [S. & P. *-tar*], adj. suffix (forms comparatives, e.g. उच्चतर, higher; बदतर, worse).

तरई *taraī* [cf. *tārā-*], f. dimin. Av. a star.

तरक *tarak*, m. reg. (W.) a rafter.

तरक- *tarak-* [ad. *tarkayati*], v.t. Brbh. Av. **1.** to deliberate, to discuss. **2.** to conjecture (about), to interpret.

तरकश *tarkaś* [P. *tarkaś*], m. a quiver. — तरकशबंद [P. *-band*], adj. wearing a quiver.

तरकारी *tarkārī* [cf. P. *tar(r)a*], f. **1.** green vegetables. **2.** a vegetable curry.

तरकी *tarkī*, f. reg. **1.** *Pl. HŚS.* a kind of ear-ring. **2.** reg. a broad metal plate worn as an ear ornament.

तरकीप *tarkīp*, m. Brbh. = तरकीब.

तरकीब *tarkīb* [A. *tarkīb*], f. **1.** form, structure, arrangement. **2.** means, plan, contrivance. — ~ करना (की), to construct; to organise. ~ देना (को) to form; to construct; to organise. ~ से, adv. in proper form, proportion or manner; economically. किसी ~ से, adv. by any means (at all). तरकीबें भिड़ाना, to scheme.

तरक़्क़ी *taraqqī* [A. *taraqqī*], f. ascending: **1.** progress; growth, development. **2.** promotion. — ~ करना, to make progress; to do well (in or at, में); to develop; to promote. ~ देना (को), to develop, to encourage (a field of activity). ~ पाना, to be developed, encouraged. ~ पर होना, to be progressing; to be developing.

तरच्छ *taracch* [ad. *tarakṣu-*], m. Brbh. a hyena.

तरजना *tarăjnā* [ad. *tarjati*: ? w. H. *garajnā*], v.i. **1.** 19c. to roar fearsomely (a tiger). **2.** Brbh. to threaten, &c. (see तर्जन).

तरजीला *tarjīlā* [cf. H. *tarajnā*], adj. **1.** prone to threaten, or to scold. **2.** prone to anger.

तरजीह *tarjīh* [A. *tarjīḥ*], f. **1.** superiority, excellence. ***2.** preference, precedence. — ~ देना, to give preference or priority (to, को; over, पर). ~ रखना (पर), to be superior (to), to surpass.

तरजुमा *tarjumā* [A. *tarjama*], m. translation; interpretation. — ~ करना (का, or को), to translate, &c. ~ होना, to be translated, &c. – तरजुमानवीस [P. *-navīs*], m. a translator.

तरजुमान *tarjumān* [A. *turjumān*: P. *tarjumān*], m. a translator; interpreter.

तरजुमानी *tarjumānī* [cf. P. *tarjumān*], f. the position and duties of an interpreter, &c.

तरण *taraṇ* [S.], m. **1.** crossing over (as a river). **2.** deliverance. — तरण-तारण, m. deliverance by crossing (the ocean of birth and rebirth): a title of the supreme being.

तरणि *taraṇi* [S.], f. the sun.

तरणी *tarăṇī* [S.], f. a boat.

तरतराना *tartarānā* [cf. H. ¹*tar*], v.i. to be soaked, drenched (as food in *ghī*).

तरतीब *tartīb* [A. *tartīb*], f. **1.** arranging. **2.** arrangement, disposition; order. — ~ देना (में), to arrange, to set in order. ~ से लगाना, to set in order, id. तरतीबवार [P. *-vār*], adj. orderly; methodical; adv. methodically.

तरतीबी *tartībī* [A. *tartīb*+P. *-ī*], adj. **1.** orderly. **2.** methodical.

तरद्दुद *taraddud* [A. *taraddud*], f. causing (sthg.) to return: indecision, perplexity; anxiety.

तरना *tarnā* [*tarati*], v.i. & v.t. **1.** v.i. to float. **2.** to cross over. **3.** to be saved (esp. from rebirth). **4.** v.t. to cross (by boat, or swimming).

तरन्नुम *tarannum* [A. *tarannum*], m. trilling, modulation; singing (of poetry).

तरफ़ *taraf* [A. *ṭaraf*], f. **1.** side, direction. **2.** edge, margin. **3.** side (of an object). **4.** side, party. **5.** leaning, bias (towards). **6.** ppn. w. की. in the direction (of), towards; to. — एक ~ ... दूसरी ~, adv. on the one hand ... on the other. अपनी ~ देखना, to respect oneself, to consider one's own dignity. अपनी ~ से, adv. on or from one's own side or account, as far as one is concerned; from one's own pocket. ~ होना, to be on the side (of, की). उसने मेरी ~ देखा, he looked at me. वह कार की ~ चला, he went towards the car; he went over to the car. – तरफ़दार [P. *-dār*], m. supporter, partisan. °ई, f. तरफ़दारी करना, to take the side (of, की); to favour.

तरफ़ैन *tarfain* [A. *ṭarafain*, dual], f. pl. the two parties (to a dispute).

तरब *tarb*, m. *HŚS.* additional strings laid below the fret of a *sāraṅgī* to enhance its tone.

तरबूज़ *tarbūz* [P. *tarbūz*], m. a water-melon.

तरबूज़ा *tarbūzā* [P. *tarbūza*], m. = तरबूज़.

तरल *taral* [S.], adj. **1.** tremulous; glittering, sparkling. **2.** unsteady, inconstant, fickle; volatile. **3.** of short duration. ***4.** liquid. — तरलीकृत, adj. liquefied.

तरलता *taralătā* [S.], f. **1.** tremulousness. **2.** unsteadiness, &c. ***3.** liquid quality, fluidity.

तरला *tarlā* [cf. *tala-*], m. *Pl. HŚS.* lower or under part: a bamboo pole supporting a thatch.

तरलित *tarălit* [S.], adj. **1.** stirred (water, by wind). **2.** stirred by emotion. **3.** made liquid.

तरलीकृत *taralīkr̥t* [S.], adj. see s.v. तरल.

तरवर *tarvar* [*taravaṭa-*: Pk. *taḍavaḍā-*], m. the shrub *Cassia auriculata* (the bark of which is used in tanning, and the seeds and leaves medicinally).

तरवरिया *tarvariya*, m. = तलवारी.

तरवारि *tarvāri* [S.], f. Brbh. Av. a sword (= तलवार).

तरशना *taraśnā* [cf. H. *tarāśnā*], v.i. to be pared, &c.

तरशवाना *taraśvānā* [cf. H. *tarāśnā*], v.t. to cause to be pared, &c. (by, से).

तरस *taras* [cf. H. *tarasnā*], m. compassion, pity; mercy. — ~ आना (को), to feel pity (for, का). ~ खाना, to be moved by pity (for, पर).

तरसना *tarasnā* [**tr̥ṣati* or *tr̥syati*], v.i. **1.** to long (for, के लिए). **2.** to be tantalised, or teased. **3.** to suffer (for want of, को).

तरसाना *tarsānā* [cf. H. *tarasnā*], v.t. **1.** to cause (one) to long (for, के लिए); to tantalise, to tease. **2.** to cause to suffer (for want of, को). — दाने दाने को ~, to grudge every grain, or the very means of existence, (to, को).

तरसों *tarsoṁ* [H. *atarsoṁ*], adv. in three days' time; three days ago.

तरसौंह- *tarsauṁh-* [cf. H. *taras*], adj. Brbh. longing, yearning.

तरह *tarah* [A. *ṭarḥ*], f. **1.** kind, type. इस ~ का, adj. this sort of. **2.** manner, mode, way. अच्छी ~ (से), adv. well; feeling well, or fit. किस ~? how? **3.** state, condition. **4.** U. a verse set, showing the metre in which a poem is to be composed. **5.** ppn. w. की. like, as, in the manner (of). — ~ ~ के, adv. pl. m. different sorts of, many kinds of, various. ~ देना (को), to put to one side, to overlook (a fault); to turn a deaf ear (to), to evade. कई ~ से, adv. in several ways, in many respects. पूरी ~ से, adv. fully, entirely. बुरी ~, adv. badly; severely (as of a beating); disgracefully. हर ~ से, adv. in every way, entirely.

तराइन *tarāin* [*tārāgaṇa-*], m. pl. Av. the stars.

तराई *tarāī* [cf. **tara-*³], f. **1.** low-lying land (esp. that at the foot of the Himālayas). **2.** an alluvial plain (as that of the Ganges).

तराज़ू *tarāzū* [P. *tarāzū*], m. a pair of scales, a balance.

तरान *tarān* [? cf. *tărnā*], m. reg. a tax, duty.

तराना *tarānā* [P. *tarāna*], m. **1.** a melody, song; anthem. **2.** a trill (of the voice); an exercise (in singing).

तराबोर *tarābor* [cf. H. *bor-*], adj. soaked, drenched (= सराबोर).

तरायल *tarāyal* [?? **talapalāla-*], reg. (W.) the lowest level of grass in a thatch (cf. ²तिरपाल).

तरार- *tarār-* [? conn. P. *ṭarrār*], adj. Brbh. quick, active; flooding (with tears).

तरावट *tarāvaṭ* [cf. H. *tar*], f. **1.** dampness, moisture; humidity. **2.** coolness (as of air), refreshing quality. — आँखों में ~ आना, (the sight of sthg.) to do (one's) eyes good.

तरावत *tarāvat* [A. *ṭarāva*: P. *ṭarāvat*; × P. *tar*], f. **1.** freshness, juiciness. **2.** greenness, luxuriance.

तराश *tarāś* [P. *tarāś*], f. & m. **1.** f. cutting; paring; carving; scratching out. **2.** cut, shape (of clothes); style. **3.** sculpture. **4.** m. in comp. a cutter, carver, &c. — तराश-ख़राश, f. shaping, forming; trimming; arranging (as dress); fine shape; elegance; erasing. तराश-ख़राश करना, to erase, &c.

तराशना *tarāśnā* [cf. H. *tarāś*], v.t. to cut; to pare; to carve; to scratch out.

तराशा *tarāśā* [P. *tarāśa*], m. a paring, shaving, chip, shred, scrap.

तरास- *tarās-* [ad. *trāsayati*], v.t. Av. to frighten.

तरिक *tarik* [S.], m. *Pl. HŚS.* **1.** a ferryman. **2.** a raft.

तरिवन *tarivan* [**tālaparṇa-*], m. Av. a kind of ear ornament.

¹**तरी** *tarī* [S.], f. a boat.

²**तरी** *tarī* [cf. P. *tar*], f. **1.** moistness, wetness; humidity. **2.** coolness.

तरीक़ा *tarīqā* [A. *ṭarīqa*], m. path: **1.** manner (of acting), practice; method. **2.** custom, usage; system (of procedure). **3.** manner, style (as of life). — तरीक़े से, adv. methodically.

-तरीन *-tarīn* [P. *-tarīn*], adj. suffix (superlative) best, choice (e.g. बेहतरीन, adj. id).

तरु *taru* [S.], m. a tree. — तरु-रोपण, m. tree-planting. तरुवर, m. best of trees: a large or fine tree; *mythol.* the *kalpa-vṛkṣ* or 'wishing-tree' of Indra's paradise.

तरुण *taruṇ* [S.], adj & m. **1.** adj. young; youthful. **2.** fresh, new (as foliage). **3.** m. a young man. — तरुणावस्था [°*ṇa*+*a*°], f. the years of youth, early adulthood.

तरुणता *taruṇătā* [S.], f. = तरुणाई.

तरुणाई *taruṇāī* [cf. H. *taruṇ*], f. youth, youthfulness; the years of youth.

तरुणी *taruṇī* [S.], f. a young woman.

तरुनापा *tarunāpā* [cf. *taruṇa-*], m. reg. = तरुणाई.

तरेंडा *tareṁḍā* [cf. *taraṇḍa-*: Ap. *taraṇḍaya-*], m. Av. a raft.

तरेरना *tarernā*, v.t. to glare (with the eyes). — आँखें ~, to glare.

[1]**तरैया** *taraiyā* [cf. H. *tārā*], f. dimin. a star.

[2]**तरैया** *taraiyā* [cf. H. *tarnā*, and *tārnā*], m. **1.** crossing over, &c. (see तरना). **2.** causing to cross over, &c. (see तारना).

तरोई *taroī*, f. = [1]तुरई.

तरोवर *tarovar*, m. Brbh. = तरुवर.

तर्क *tark* [S.], m. **1.** reasoning. **2.** deliberation, discussion. **3.** argument; objection. **4.** logic. — ~ उठाना, to raise an argument, or an objection. ~ करना (पर), to consider, to discuss. – तर्कपूर्ण, adj. making good sense; logical. तर्क-युक्त, adj. logical. तर्क-वितर्क, m. deliberation; arguing, argument. तर्क-विद्या, f. the science of reasoning: logic. तर्क-शास्त्र, m. id. तर्कसंगत, adj. in accordance with reason or logic, logical; rational. तर्क-सिद्ध, adj. logically proven, or deducible. तर्कातीत [°*ka*+*a*°], adj. beyond reason: irrational. तर्काभास [°*ka*+*ā*°], m. semblance of reason: specious reasoning, or argument.

तर्कित *tarkit* [S.], adj. **1.** deliberated, discussed. **2.** disputed.

तर्की *tarkī* [S.], m. one who adheres to logic or reason; a logician.

तर्कु *tarku* [S.] m. a spindle, distaff (= तकुआ).

तर्क्य *tarkyă* [S.], adj. to be discussed or reasoned about.

तर्ज़ *tarz* [A. *ṭarz*], f. **1.** form, fashion. **2.** U. manner, style. **3.** melody (of a song).

तर्जन *tarjan* [S.], m. **1.** threatening. **2.** scolding, admonishing. **3.** anger.

तर्जनी *tarjanī* [S.], f. threatening finger: the forefinger. — ~ दिखाना, or हिलाना, to reprove.

तर्जुमा *tarjumā*, m. see तरजुमा.

तर्पण *tarpaṇ* [S.], m. **1.** satisfaction; gratification. **2.** a religious observance: the offering of libations of water to the gods, or to (का) the spirits of one's ancestors.

तर्रार *tarrār* [A. *ṭarrār*], adj. sharp-tongued. — तेज़-तर्रार, adj. quick-tempered.

तर्रारा *tarrārā* [A. *ṭarrāra*], m. sharpness; activity, speed. — तर्रारे भरना, to go at full speed (as a horse).

तर्ष *tarṣ*, m. Brbh. = तृषा.

तर्षण *tarṣaṇ* [S.], m. **1.** thirsting, thirst. **2.** longing, desire.

तल *tal* [*tala-*], m. **1.** surface. **2.** level. **3.** lowest part, base; bottom; low ground. **4.** side, face (of an area). — के चारों ~, adv. on all four sides, or faces. – तल-ऊपर, adv. upside down; one over or upon another, topsy-turvy. तल-चुआ, m. *Pl.* light land on clay (quickly waterlogged during rainy periods). तल-छट, f. sediment, dregs, grounds. °ई, f. having, or to do with, sediment, &c. तलपट, adj. see s.v.

तलक *talak* [? *tāvatka-* or Brbh. *tā*: × H. *lăg*], ppn. = तक.

तलख़ *talkh* [P. *talkh*], adj. **1.** bitter; distasteful. **2.** acrimonious, rancorous. — तलख़मिज़ाज, adj. ill-tempered.

तलख़ी *talkhī* [P. *talkhī*], f. **1.** bitterness. **2.** acrimony, rancour.

तलना *talnā* [**talati*[2]: Pk. *talaï*], v.t. to fry.

तलपट *talpaṭ* [cf. H. *tal*; H. [1]*paṭ*], adj. levelled; flattened: ruined (as crops, possessions); thrown (a wrestler).

तलफ- *talaph-*, v.i. Brbh. Av. = तड़पना, तड़फना.

तलफ़्फ़ुज़ *talaffuz* [A. *talaffuz*], f. pronunciation.

तलब *talab* [A. *ṭalab*], f. search: **1.** wish, desire. **2.** craving. **3.** pay, wages. **4.** -तलब. a seeker, desirer (e.g. आराम-तलब, adj. fond of comfort). — ~ करना, to demand, to claim (from, से); to exact (a fine, &c.); to summon. जवाब ~ होना, an explanation or account to be given (to a superior). – तलबगार [P. *-gār*], adj. & m. seeking, desirous (of, का); a seeker, claimant.

तलबाना *talăbānā* [P. *talabāna*], m. a fee for presenting or serving a document.

तलबी *talăbī* [P. *ṭalabī*], f. **1.** summons, call (to appear); demand. **2.** mobilisation.

तलमलाना *talmalānā* [conn. **taḍa(pphaḍ-)*], v.i. **1.** to be restless, uneasy; to be agitated; to be impatient, or tantalised. **2.** to grieve. **3.** to toss about.

तलमली *talmalī* [cf. H. *talmalānā*], f. restlessness, &c. — ~ लगना (को), to feel restless, &c.

तलवरिया *talvariyā* [cf. H. *talvār*], m. a swordsman.

तलवा *talvā* [**talapāda-*], m. the sole of the foot. — तलवे चाटना, to lick the soles of the feet (of, के): to flatter abjectly; to ingratiate oneself (with). तलवे धो-धोकर पीना, fig. to perform humiliating services (for, के). तलवे सहलाना, to stroke the soles of the feet (of, के): = तलवे चाटना. तलवों टले मेटना, to trample underfoot; to treat with contempt, to spurn. तलवों से आग लगना, to feel the soles burning: to be furiously angry.

तलवार *talvār* [*taravāri-*], f. a sword; sword-blade. — ~ का पानी, m. the temper, quality of a sword-blade. ~ का पानी पिलाना (को), fig. to let (one, को) see (one's, अपनी) mettle, or taste one's sword. ~ की छाँह, or छाँहों, में, adv. under, or with, an armed guard. ~ की धार पर चलना, fig. to be in a precarious situation. ~ के घाट उतारना, to strike down with (one's) sword. ~ खींचना, to draw a sword. ~ तौलना, to raise a sword (to strike). ~ मारना, to strike with, or to use, a sword. ~ म्यान करना, to sheathe a sword. ~ म्यान में जाना, a sword to be sheathed. ~ से बात करना, to turn to (one's) sword (as despairing of argument, or to seek satisfaction). तलवारें खिंचना, swords to be drawn: fighting to break out. तलवारें चलना, swords to be at work, fighting to be going on.

तलवारी *talvārī* [cf. H. *talvār*], adj. having to do with a sword, or swords.

तलहटी *talhaṭī* [**talaghaṭṭikā-*], f. low land beneath mountains (= तराई).

तलही *talhī* [cf. *talla-*[1]], adj. reg. living in a pond or tank (a bird).

तला *talā* [*tala-*], m. **1.** lowest part, base; bottom. **2.** keel. **3.** sole (of a shoe). — तले, adv. & ppn. (often w. के.) at the bottom (of), at the foot (of); inside; under; under the authority or direction (of); born from, dropped by (an animal). तले आना, to come down; to suffer loss; to fall under, to be crushed (by); to take shelter (under). – तले-ऊपर, adv. upside down; one over or upon another; topsy-turvy, in confusion. तले-ऊपर करना, to turn upside down, &c. तले-ऊपरके बच्चे, m. colloq. children born at very short intervals.

[1]**तलाई** *talāī* [*taḍāga-*], f. a small tank, or pond.

[2]**तलाई** *talāī* [cf. H. *talnā*, *talānā*], f. **1.** frying. **2.** causing (sthg.) to be fried. **3.** charge for having (sthg.) fried.

तलाक़ *talāq* [A. *ṭalāq*], f. divorce. — ~ देना (को), to divorce. ~ लेना, to get a divorce, to become divorced. – तलाक़शुदा [P. *-śuda*], adj. inv. divorced.

तलाना *talānā* [cf. H. *talnā*], v.t. to cause to be fried (by, से).

तलाफ़ी *talāfī* [A. *talāfī*], f. making amends: reparation, compensation.

तलामली *talāmalī*, f. 19c. = तलमली.

[1]**तलाव** *talāv* [*taḍāga-*], m. tank, pond (= तालाब).

[2]**तलाव** *talāv* [cf. H. *talnā*], m. frying.

तलावरी *talāvrī* [cf. H. *talāv*], f. a small tank, or pond.

तलाश *talāś* [P. *talāś*], f. **1.** search. **2.** investigation. — ~ करना, to search (for, की or को). ~ में, adv. searching (for, की).

तलाशना *talāśnā*, v.t. = तलाश करना.

तलाशी *talāśī* [cf. H. *talāś*], f. **1.** searching. **2.** search (as of a person, a house). — ~ देना, to institute a search (of, की). ~ लेना, to search the person or house, &c. (of, की).

तली *talī* [**talikā-*: Pk. *taliyā-*], f. **1.** lowest part, bottom. **2.** sole (of a shoe). **3.** palm (of the hand). — तली-झाड़, f. a thorough cleaning out, a clean sweep.

तलुआ *taluā*, m. see तलवा.

तले *tale*, adv. & ppn. see s.v. तला.

तलैटी *talaiṭī* [H. *talhaṭī*], f. low-lying ground.

तलैया *talaiyā* [cf. H. *talāī*], f. a small tank, or pond.

तल्ख़ *talkh*, adj. see तलख़.

तल्ला *tallā* [*tala-*, or **talla-*[2]], m. storey; floor (of a building).

तल्ली *tallī* [cf. H. *talā*, or **talla-*[2]], f. a light shoe.

तव *tavă* [S.], adj. your; thy.

तवक़्क़ा *tavaqqā* [A. *tavaqqu'*], m. E.H. trust, reliance.

तवज्जह *tavajjah* [A. *tavajjuh*], f. turning the face (to): **1.** attention. **2.** favour. — ~ करना (का), to show attention (to). ~ देना (को), id.

तवनगरी *tavangarī*, f. 19c. = तवानगरी, see s.v. तवान.

तवस्सुत *tavassut* [A. *tavassuṭ*], m. being in the middle: mediation.

तवा *tavā* [**tapaka-*: Pk. *tavaya-*], m. **1.** a flat iron plate, griddle (as for baking bread-cakes); frying pan. **2.** colloq. a gramophone record. — ~ **सिर से बाँधना**, to steel oneself to receive a blow; to prepare to defend oneself. **उलटा** ~, m. the bottom side of a griddle: colloq. a person of jet-black complexion. **तवे का हँसना**, the glowing of a griddle (sc. of the soot on its underside, foretelling a family quarrel); sparks to fall from a griddle (a good omen). **तवे की बूँद**, f. sthg. of short duration, ephemeral; sthg. ineffectual, insignificant. **तवे-सा मुँह**, m. a black face; one besmirched, disgraced. **एक तवे की रोटी**, f. bread-cakes from the same griddle, birds of a feather.

तवाई *tavāī*, f. Brbh. corr. = **तबाही**.

तवाज़ा *tavāzā* [A. *tavāzu'*], m. **1.** hospitality. **2.** attention, courtesy (to a guest).

तवान *tavān* [P. *tavān*], m. *Pl.* power: — **तवानगर** [P. *-gar*], m. powerful; rich; °**ई**, f. power, wealth.

तवायफ़ *tavāyaf* [A. *ṭavā'if*, pl. 'bands, companies'], f. a dancing-girl; prostitute.

तवारीख़ *tavārīkh* [A. *tavārīkh*, pl.], f. **1.** dates, annals. ***2.** history.

तवारीख़ी *tavārīkhī* [A. *tavārīkh*+-*ī*], adj. historical.

तवालत *tavālat* [P. *ṭavālat*], f. prolonging, protractedness: bother, entanglement.

तवेला *tavelā* [A. *ṭavīla*], m. reg. **1.** a long rope used for tying cattle. **2.** a foot-rope, tether. **3.** stable, stall.

तवेली *tavelī* [cf. H. *tavelā*], m. reg. (W). = **तवेला**.

-तव्य *-tavyă* [S.], suffix (forms m. verbal nouns, e.g. **कर्तव्य**, duty).

तशख़ीस *taśkhīs* [A. *taśkhīṣ*], f. reg. (W.) valuing, valuation; a system of assessing land to be rented.

तशफ़्फ़ी *taśaffī* [A. *taśaffī*], f. alleviation, relief (of pain, or after anger: **को**).

तशरीफ़ *taśrīf* [A. *taśrīf*], f. (in address, or honorific reference) honouring: your honour; one's (good) self. — ~ **फ़रमाना**, to vouchsafe one's presence: to come; to go. ~ **रखिए**, please sit down. ~ **लाना**, to come. ~ **ले जाना**, to go, to depart.

तशवीश *taśvīś* [A. *taśvīś*], f. 19c. confusion: anxiety, alarm.

तशा *taśā*, m. pronun. var. = **तासा**.

तश्त *taśt* [P. *taśt*], m. **1.** a platter. **2.** a basin.

तश्तरी *taśtărī* [cf. P. *ṭaśt*, *taśtakī*], f. a small plate, saucer.

तसकीन *taskīn* [A. *taskīn*], f. calming: consolation; comfort. — ~ **देना (को)**, to console, to comfort.

तसदीक़ *tasdīq* [A. *taṣdīq*], f. speaking truth: attesting, confirming, verifying. — ~ **करना**, to confirm, &c.

तसद्दुक़ *tasadduq* [A. *taṣadduq*], m. *musl.* giving alms (cf. **सदक़ा**).

तसबी *tasbī* [A. *tasbīh*: × Guj. *bī*, H. *bīā*], m. E.H. glorifying: a rosary.

तसमा *tasmā* [P. *tasma*], m. **1.** a strap, thong. ***2.** a shoe-lace. — ~ **खींचना**, to draw a strap tight, &c. ~ **लगा न रखना**, colloq. to sever or to separate completely.

तसर *tasar* [? conn. *tasara-*: Pk. *tasara-*], m. coarse silk, tussore (= **टसर**).

तसलसुल *tasalsul* [A. *tasalsul*], m. linkage; sequence.

तसला *taslā*, m. a brass or iron vessel having steep sides (used in kneading dough or for boiling rice, &c).

तसली *taslī*, f. dimin. a small metal vessel (see **तसला**).

तसलीम *taslīm* [A. *taslīm*], f. making safe: **1.** acceptance (of a situation, a fact, a doctrine). **2.** salutation, obeisance. — ~ **करना**, to accept; to salute or to greet respectfully.

तसल्ली *tasallī* [A. *tasallī*], f. being diverted: consolation; comfort. — ~ **देना**, or **दिलाना (को)**, to console; to comfort. – **तसल्लीबख़्श**, adj. consolatory, comforting.

तसवीर *tasvīr*, f. see **तस्वीर**.

तसव्वुफ़ *tasavvuf* [A. *taṣavvuf*], f. **1.** Ṣūfī theology, Sufism. **2.** mysticism.

तसव्वुर *tasavvur* [A. *taṣavvur*], m. forming, fashioning: imagination. — ~ **करना**, to imagine. ~ **में लाना**, to conceive (a notion), to imagine.

तसू *tasū*, m. *Pl. HŚS.* a measure of length of about an inch, the twenty-fourth or twentieth part of a builder's yard (*gaz*).

तस्कर *taskar* [S.], m. **1.** a robber. ***2.** a smuggler. — **तस्कर-व्यापार**, m. contraband goods; traffic in contraband. °**ई**, m. a smuggler; dealer in contraband.

तस्करता *taskarătā* [S.], f. smuggling; life spent in smuggling.

तस्करी *taskarī* [S.], f. **1.** robbery. ***2.** smuggling.

तस्कीन *taskīn*, f. see तसकीन.

तस्फ़िया *tasfiyā* [A. *taṣfiya*], m. making (sthg.) clear: **1.** settling (as a dispute); disposal (of a case). **2.** reconciliation; compromise. — ~ करना (का), to reconcile; to effect a compromise (between); to settle, to dispose (of).

तस्मा *tasmā*, m. see तसमा.

तस्वीर *tasvīr* [A. *taṣvīr*], f. forming: **1.** a picture, drawing; painting; portrait. **2.** a photograph. — ~ बनाना, or खींचना, or उतारना (की), to paint a picture, to draw a sketch (of); to take a photograph (of). ~ लेना [f. Engl. *take*], id.

तह *tah* [P. *tah*], f. **1.** a fold. **2.** a layer, stratum; film. **3.** bottom, lowest level; foundation; basement. **4.** essential, or hidden meaning; profundity; subtleness. — ~ करना, to fold. ~ कर रखना, to keep folded up, to keep (sthg.) carefully; to leave undisturbed; not to reveal (sthg). ~ का, adj. deep, profound; mysterious; occult; real, genuine. ~ को, or तक, पहुँचना, to get to the bottom (of, की). ~ जमाना (की), to fold; colloq. to down glass after glass. ~ देना, to tinge (with, की). ~ लगाना (में), to fold, to fold up. – तह-ख़ाना, m. an underground room or dwelling: a cellar; basement, vault; pl. catacombs. तहदार [P. *-dār*], adj. having depth, or substance (as a remark, a poem).

तहँ *taham̐*, adv. Brbh. Av. = तहाँ.

तहक़ीक़ *tahqīq* [A. *taḥqīq*], f. ascertainment of the truth; investigation, enquiry; interrogation.

तहक़ीक़ात *tahqīqāt* [pl. of A. *taḥqīq*], f. enquiries, &c. (= तहक़ीक़).

तहज़ीब *tahzīb* [A. *tahẕīb*], f. improving, refining: refinement; culture. — तहज़ीब-याफ़्ता [P. *-yāfta*], adj. cultured; refined.

तहत *taht* [A. *taḥt*], m. **1.** m. subjection; authority, control. **2.** ppn. w. के. beneath, under; subject (to). — ~ में, adv. under the authority or control (of, के); in subjection (to).

तहमत *tahmat* [Panj. *tahimat*, *tahimad*], f. m. a cloth worn wrapped round the waist and falling to the ankles, by men (= लुँगी).

तहरीर *tahrīr* [A. *taḥrīr*], f. **1.** writing; hand, style of writing. **2.** sthg. written, a document. **3.** statement, declaration. **4.** transf. a writer's or recorder's fee. — ~ करना (की), to write; to describe; to record. ~ होना, to be written, &c.

तहरीरी *tahrīrī* [A. *taḥrīrī*], adj. written, written down (a submission, evidence).

तहलका *tahalkā* [A. *tahluka*], m. **1.** alarm, panic. **2.** confusion, consternation. **3.** excitement.

तहलील *tahlīl* [A. *taḥlīl*], f. 19c. untying, dissolving: digesting. — ~ करना, to digest.

तहस-नहस *tahs-nahs* [cf. A. *naḥs*], adj. ruined, quite destroyed. — ~ करना, to ruin, &c.

तहसीन *tahsīn* [A. *taḥsīn*], f. making or considering as good: approval, acclaim.

तहसील *tahsīl* [A. *taḥṣīl*], f. **1.** *admin.* a revenue district. **2.** the offices or court of a tahsīldār. — तहसीलदार, m. a sub-collector of revenue. °ई, f. the office or jurisdiction of a sub-collector; collecting the revenue.

तहसीलना *tahsīlnā* [cf. H. *tahsīl*], v.t. to collect (revenue).

तहाँ *tahām̐* [cf. *ta-*; and *iha-*], adv. **1.** there. **2.** thither. — जहाँ का ~, adv. in the very (same) place.

तहाना *tahānā* [cf. H. *tah*], v.t. **1.** to fold. **2.** to wrap (in, में).

तहीं *tahīm̐*, adv. Brbh. Av. = वहीं.

तहूर *tahūr* [A. *ṭahūr*], m. a means of purifying (see s.v. शराब).

ताँगा *tām̐gā*, m. a two-wheeled horse-drawn vehicle for passengers, a trap, tonga. — ताँगावाला, m. a tonga-driver.

तांडव *tāṇḍav* [S.], m. **1.** *mythol.* the dance of Śiva (as taking place at the dissolution of the world). **2.** frenzied dancing, frenzy.

ताँत *tām̐t* [*tanti-*], f. **1.** a sinew. **2.** catgut; string (of a musical instrument); string or leather strap (of a spinning-wheel). **3.** reg. (W.) a loom. — ~ बाँधना (की), colloq. to silence (a chatterer). — ताँत-सा, adj. thin, skinny.

ताँता *tām̐tā* [*tantu-*], m. **1.** a line, row. **2.** a series. **3.** sequence, continuation. — ~ बँधना, or लगना, a line, &c., to form; to continue in succession, or uninterruptedly.

[1]**ताँती** *tām̐tī* [cf. H. *tām̐t(ā)*], f. 1. = ताँता. **2.** E.H. = ताँत.

[2]**ताँती** *tām̐tī* [*tantrika-*], m. reg. a weaver.

तांत्रिक *tāntrik* [S.], adj. & m. **1.** adj. having to do with *tantras*. **2.** technical. **3.** m. a person versed in tantric knowledge.

ताँबई *tām̐baī* [cf. H. *tām̐bā*], adj. copper-coloured.

ताँबा *tām̐bā* [*tāmra-*], m. copper. — ताँबाकार, m. a coppersmith.

ताँबिया *tām̐biyā* [cf. H. *tām̐bā*], adj. **1.** adj. made of copper. **2.** copper-coloured. **3.** m. a small copper or brass pan, or ladle.

तांबूल *tāmbūl* [S.], m. betel, esp. betel leaf (= ¹पान); a rolled betel leaf. — तांबूल-पत्र, m. = ~. तांबूल-वल्ली, f. betel plant.

¹**तांबूली** *tāmbūlī* [S.], m. a betel-seller.

²**तांबूली** *tāmbūlī* [S.], f. Brbh. a betel plant.

ताँवत *tāṁvat*, adv. E.H. = तावत्.

ताँसना *tāṁsnā* [*trāsayati*], v.t. to intimidate; to treat harshly.

¹**ता** *tā*, obl. base, sg. Brbh. that, &c. (see वह).

²**ता** *tā* [P. *tā*], adv. until, as far as; as long as. — ता-ज़िंदगी, adv. during life. ताकि, conj. see s.v.

-ता *-tā* [S.], suffix. **1.** forms f. abstract nouns (e.g. वीरता, bravery, heroism). **2.** forms inv. m. agent nouns and some terms of relationship, f. as well as m. (e.g. करता, a doer, maker; पिता, m. father; माता, f. mother).

ताईं *tāīṁ*, ppn. w. के. E.H. **1.** up to, near, beside. **2.** (in expressions of speaking) to, with. **3.** for the benefit of.

ताई *tāī* [cf. H. *tāyā*], f. wife of a father's elder brother.

ताईद *tāīd* [A. *tā'īd*], f. strengthening: confirmation, corroboration.

ताऊ *tāū* [*tātagu-*], m. **1.** father's elder brother. **2.** colloq. a senior, superior. — बछिया का ~, m. colloq. calf's uncle: a complete fool.

ताऊन *tāūn* [A. *tā'ūn*], m. U. plague (the disease).

ताऊस *tāūs* [A. *ṭā'ūs*], m. 19c. a peacock. — तख़्त ~, m. the Peacock Throne (of Mughal India).

ताएरा *tāerā* [*tātatara-*], adj. having to do with, or related to, a father's elder brother. — ~ भाई, m. father's elder brother's son, cousin.

ताक *tāk* [cf. H. *tāknā*], f. **1.** look, glance. **2.** fixed look, stare; peep. **3.** watch, expectation (for: of an opportunity). **4.** view, aim (at, पर); scrutiny. — ~ बाँधना, to look fixedly (at, पर); to take aim (at). ~ रखना, or लगाना (पर), to keep (one) in sight, to keep an eye (on). ~ में बैठना, or रहना (की), to be on the watch (for); to lie in wait (for). – ताकाताक, f. = °-ई, see s.v. ताकना. ताक-झाँक, f. = ~, 2.; investigation.

ताक़ *tāq* [A. *ṭāq*], m. an arch: **1.** niche, recess. **2.** ledge, shelf. — ~ पर धरना, or रखना, to put on the shelf; to put aside, to shelve; to be neglectful of (as claims of friendship). ~ पर रहना, or होना, to be shelved (a matter); not to be implemented (a decision, &c.); colloq. to become ineffective (strength). ~ भरना, *musl.* to place a lighted lamp in a niche as a votive offering.

ताक़त *tāqat* [A. *ṭāqa*: P. *ṭāqat*], f. **1.** strength, power. **2.** ability, capability. **3.** power, energy (electric, &c). – ताक़तवर [P. *-var*], adv. strong, powerful.

ताकना *tāknā* [*tarkayati*], v.t. **1.** to look at, to look alertly at. **2.** to gaze at; to stare at; to peep at. **3.** to watch for (as for an opportunity); to look longingly at or to. **4.** colloq. to look into (a matter). **5.** Av. to think out, to ponder over. **6.** to search out. — ताका-झाँकी, f. = ताक-झाँक. ताकाताकी, f. exchange of glances, stares.

ताकि *tāki* [P. *tāki*], conj. so that, in order that.

ताकीद *tākīd* [A. *tākīd*], f. **1.** strict instruction; demand, request. **2.** compulsion, coercion. — ~ करना (से, or को), to enjoin, to instruct; to caution. ~ कामिल, f. 19c. strict instructions.

ताग *tāg* [**trāgga-*, &c.: Pk. *tagga-*], m. E.H. = तागा.

तागड़ी *tāgṛī* [cf. H. *tāgā*], f. = तगड़ी.

तागना *tāgnā* [cf. H. *tāg(ā)*], v.t. reg. to thread (a needle); to stitch.

तागा *tāgā* [**trāgga-*, &c.: Pk. *tagga-*], m. **1.** thread. **2.** string, cord. — ~ डालना, to put loose stitches (in, में: esp. in padded material). ~ पिरोना (में), to thread (as a needle).

ताज *tāj* [P. *tāj*], m. **1.** crown. **2.** diadem, tiara. **3.** crest, plume. **4.** *arch.* an ornamental turret. **5.** fig. supreme exemplar or exponent; paragon. — ताज-गुज़ारी, f. conferring a crown, crowning. ताजपोशी [P. *pośīdan*], f. coronation. ताजमहल, m. the Taj Mahal (tomb of the Mughal Empress Mumtāz Maḥal, at Agra). – ताजदार [P. *-dār*], adj. & m. crowned; diademed; crested; a reigning sovereign. °ई, f. sovereignty (over, की); royal status.

ताज़गी *tāzgī* [P. *tāzagī*], f. **1.** freshness; revival, refreshment. **2.** novelty. **3.** greenness, good condition (as of vegetables); tenderness.

ताजन *tājan* [*tarjana-*: w. P. *tāz(iy)āna*], m. Brbh. a whip.

ताज़ा *tāzā* [P. *tāza*], adj. **1.** fresh; refreshed, invigorated. **2.** flourishing, happy. **3.** new, recent; current (rate). **4.** young, tender. — ~ करना, to refresh; to renew. — ~ दम, adj. = ~, 1.

ताज़िया *tāziyā* [A. *ta'ziya*], m. *musl.* a representation of the shrines of Ḥasan and Ḥusain, sons of 'Alī (made of bamboo and paper, &c., and carried in procession during the month of Muḥarram, chiefly by Śī'as).

— ~ ठंढा करना, to bury a *tāziyā*, to throw a *tāziyā* into a river (on the last day of mourning in Muḥarram). ~ ठंढा होना, a *tāziyā* to be buried, &c. – ताज़ियादारी [P. *-dārī*], f. having a *tāziyā*: recognising the ritual or the symbolism of the *tāziyā*.

ताज़ियाना *tāziyānā* [P. *tāziyāna*], m. a whip.

ताजिर *tājir* [A. *tājir*], m. a merchant.

ताज़ी *tāzī* [cf. P. *tāz*, pres. stem of *tākhtan*], m. fast-running, fleet: an Arab horse.

ताज़ीम *tāzīm* [A. *ta'ẓīm*], f. esp. U. honouring: respect, reverence.

ताज़ीरात *tāzīrāt* [A. *ta'zīrāt*, pl.], f. punishment: criminal code.

ताज्जुब *tājjub* [A. *ta'ajjub*], m. **1.** surprise, astonishment. **2.** admiration. — ~ करना (पर), to be surprised, amazed (at); to admire. ~ में आना, to be surprised, &c. ~ में डालना, to surprise, &c.

ताटंक *tāṭaṅk* [S.], m. *Pl.* a kind of large ear-ring.

[1]**ताड़** *tāṛ* [**tāḍa-*[3]: Pk. *tāḍa-*], m. the palm tree *Borassus flabellifer* (fan-palm). — ताड़-पत्र, m. a palm-leaf prepared for writing on; a document written on palm leaves. ताड़-वन, m. a palm grove.

[2]**ताड़** *tāṛ* [cf. H. *tāṛnā*], f. perception, understanding. — ताड़बाज़ [P. *-bāz*], adj. of quick intelligence.

ताड़क *tāṛak* [ad. *taḍaka-*], m. one who punishes.

ताड़न *tāṛan* [S.], m. **1.** a beating, punishment. **2.** a scolding. — ~ करना (को, or का), to punish, &c.

[1]**ताड़ना** *tāṛnā* [*tāḍayati*[1]], v.t. & m. **1.** v.t. to beat, to punish. **2.** to scold. **3.** m. f. = ताड़न. — ~ देना (को), = ताड़न करना.

[2]**ताड़ना** *tāṛănā* [ad. *tāḍanā-*: w. H. *tāṛnā*], f. = ताड़न.

[3]**ताड़ना** *tāṛnā* [*tāḍayati*[2]], v.t. **1.** to perceive, to understand. **2.** to become aware of; to guess, to deduce. **3.** to look into, to examine (a matter).

ताड़नीय *tāṛănīyă* [S.], adj. deserving punishment; punishable.

ताड़ी *tāṛī* [*tāḍa-*[3]: Pk. *tāḍa-*], f. fermented juice of the palm tree, toddy. — ताड़ीवाला, m. an extractor of toddy-juice.

तात *tāt* [S.], m. **1.** father. **2.** a respected or venerable person. **3.** affectionate term of address, esp. to a junior person. — तात-मात, m. pl. parents.

तातल *tātal* [S.], adj. *Pl. HŚS.* hot, warm.

ताता *tātā* [*tapta-*], adj. Brbh. Av. heated, hot.

ताताथेई *tātātheī*, f. beating time (in music); beat or rhythm of the feet striking the ground (in dancing).

तातार *tātār* [P. *tātār*], m. & adj. **1.** m. a Tartar, a Mongol. **2.** *hist.* Mongol territory. **3.** adj. Tartar, Mongol.

तातारी *tātārī* [P. *tātārī*], adj. & m. **1.** adj. Tartar, Mongol; Scythian. **2.** m. = तातार, 1.

तातील *tātīl* [A. *ta'ṭīl*], m. discontinuing, freeing: a holiday, festival.

तात्कालिक *tātkālik* [S.], adj. **1.** of the particular moment, immediate, urgent. **2.** contemporary; topical. **3.** of a particular time, or age. **4.** simultaneous.

तात्त्विक *tāttvik* [S.], adj. having to do with reality or essence: essential; fundamental.

तात्पर्य *tātparyă* [S.], m. **1.** aim, reference to (से) an object; concern (with, से); intent. **2.** meaning, purport. — कहने का ~ यह है कि ..., what (I) mean is that .... तात्पर्यार्थ [°*ya* + *a*°], m. inner meaning.

तादात्म्य *tādātmyă* [S.], m. sameness of nature or character: identity; similarity.

तादाद *tādād* [A. *ta'dād*], f. numbering, count: amount, quantity, number(s). — बड़ी ~ में, adv. in great numbers, quantity.

तादृश *tādṛś* [S.], adj. like that, of that sort.

तान *tān* [cf. H. *tānnā*], f. **1.** stretching, tension. **2.** 19c. knitting (the eyebrows). **3.** *mus.* a tone, note; key-note. **4.** melody. **5.** a stay, guy; spoke (as of a bicycle wheel). — ~ उड़ाना, to sing, or to strike up, a melody, or a key-note. ~ तोड़ना, to spoil or to lose a melody. ~ भरना, = ~ उड़ाना. ~ लगाना, or लेना, to give inflections to the voice (in singing).

[1]**तानना** *tānnā* [*tānayati*], v.t. **1.** to stretch, to extend; to expand; to pull over (as a sheet). **2.** to tighten; to clench (fists); to draw (a bow); to knit (the brow). **3.** to pitch (a tent); to erect. **4.** to raise (a stick, the hand: in threat or violence); to aim (a weapon). — (पैर) तानकर सोना, to stretch out (the legs) and go to sleep.

[2]**तानना** *tānnā* [*tānyate*], v.i. **1.** to be stretched out, to lie full length; to sleep, to rest. **2.** fig. to die. — लंबी तानकर सोना, to sleep stretched out or comfortably. तानकर सोना, to sleep deeply, or untroubled (? see also s.v. [1]तानना).

तानपूरा *tānpūrā* [f. P. *tambūra*, H. *tambūrā*], m. stringed instrument used to accompany singers.

[1]**ताना** *tānā* [A. *ṭa'na*], m. taunt, jibe; ridicule. — ~, or ताने, देना (को), to taunt; to ridicule. ~, ताने, मारना (को), id. – ताना-तशना [A. *taśnī'*], m. pl. taunts; ridicule. ताना-तिचना, or °-तिशना, m. pl. id. तानाशाह, m. a despot, dictator. °ई, f. despotism, &c.

[2]**ताना** *tānā* [*tāna-*], m. **1.** warp (of a fabric). **2.** Av. tie (of a garment). — ताना-बाना, m. warp and woof.

[3]**ताना** *tānā* [*tāpayati*], v.t. reg. **1.** to heat; to melt. **2.** to temper (metal). **3.** to test, to assay.

तानी *tānī* [*tāna-*], f. *Pl.* **1.** warp (= [2]ताना); strand, length (of thread). **2.** price paid for weaving.

ताप *tāp* [S.], m. **1.** heat. **2.** burning; fever. **3.** passion; pain, suffering; grief. — ताप-क्रम, m. temperature. ताप-तिल्ली, f. enlargement of the spleen, with fever. ताप-चालक, m. *phys.* a conductor of heat. °ता, f. conductivity of heat. ताप-नाभिकीय, adj. thermo-nuclear. ताप-मान, m. temperature. ताप-मापक, m. measuring heat: °यंत्र, m. thermometer. तापहर, adj. assuaging pain, grief, &c.

तापक *tāpak* [S.], adj. heating; inflaming; distressing.

तापन *tāpan* [S.], adj. & m. **1.** adj. causing heat, heating. **2.** causing distress. ***3.** m. heating. **4.** inflaming. **5.** distressing.

तापना *tāpnā* [*tapyati*], v.i. & v.t. **1.** v.i. to warm oneself. **2.** to suffer heat (e.g. as an ascetic practising austerities). **3.** to suffer distress. **4.** v.t. to burn; to burn up. — आग, or अग्नि ~, to warm, or to heat, oneself at a fire.

तापस *tāpas* [S.], m. an ascetic.

तापसी *tāpăsī* [S.], f. **1.** a female ascetic. **2.** the wife of an ascetic.

तापस्य *tāpasyă* [S.], m. asceticism.

तापिच्छ *tāpicch* [S.], m. poet. = तमाल.

तापित *tāpit* [S.], adj. **1.** heated. **2.** inflamed. **3.** distressed, suffering.

तापी *tāpī* [S.], adj. **1.** heated, glowing. **2.** suffering heat. **3.** suffering distress.

ताफ़्ता *tāftā* [P. *tāfta*], m. twisted, woven: a kind of bright or glossy silk, taffeta.

ताब *tāb* [P. *tāb*], f. **1.** heat. **2.** passion; pain; grief; anger. **3.** light, lustre; honour. **4.** strength, vigour; ability; fortitude, endurance, patience. **5.** curling, twisting (by heat). — ~ खाना, to be twisted. ~ देना (को), to heat; to inflame; to give lustre, to polish; to sharpen. आब (न) देखना न ~, fig. to be heedless of reputation or honour. मूँछों पर ~ देना, to curl the moustaches: to preen oneself. – ताबदार [P. *-dār*], adj. warm, hot, burning; bright; curled, twisted.

ताबड़-तोड़ *tābaṛ-toṛ*, adv. **1.** in quick succession. **2.** in confusion, helter-skelter. **3.** forthwith.

ताबीर *tābīr* [A. *ta'bīr*], f. U. interpretation (esp. of dreams).

ताबुत *tābut* [A. *tābūt*], m. a coffin.

ताबे *tābe* [A. *tābe'*], adj. dependent (on, के); obedient (to, के): — ताबेदार [P. *-dār*], adj. & m. dependent; submissive, obedient; a servant. ताबेदार करना, to make an adherent (of, का); to make obedient (to, का). °ई, f. dependence; submissiveness, obedience; loyalty, fidelity.

[1]**ताम** *tām* [S.: w. *tāmasa-*, *tamas*], m. Brbh. **1.** suffering, distress. **2.** darkness.

[2]**ताम** *tām* [*tāmra-*], m. chiefly in comp. copper. — ताम-चीनी, f. enamel.

तामजान *tāmjān*, m. var. तामझाम. an open litter (पालकी).

ताम-झाम *tām-jhām*, m. colloq. **1.** pomp, show. **2.** pej. goods and chattels, clobber.

तामड़ा *tāmṛā* [cf. *tāmra-*], adj. & m. *Pl. HŚS.* **1.** adj. copper-coloured. **2.** m. a reddish-blue artificial stone.

तामड़ी *tāmṛī* [cf. *tāmra-*], f. a copper or brass vessel used for collecting water.

तामरस *tāmras* [S.], m. a lotus, red lotus.

तामलकी *tāmalăkī* [S.], f. **1.** *Pl.* the tree *Flacourtia cataphracta*. **2.** the small tree *Averrhoa bilimbi* (= कमरख). **3.** ? *HŚS.* = आँवला.

तामलेट *tāmleṭ*, m. = टामलोट.

तामलोट *tāmloṭ* [Engl. *tumbler* × H. *loṭnā*], m. a tumbler.

तामस *tāmas* [S.], adj. & m. **1.** adj. dark. **2.** *philos.* characterised by the *guṇa* or quality of *tamas*: inert; benighted, ignorant; angry; malevolent. **3.** m. darkness. **4.** the quality of *tamas*: ignorance, error; Brbh. anger. **5.** an ignorant person, a villain, &c.

तामसी *tāmăsī* [cf. H. *tāmas*], adj. = तामस, 1., 2.

तामा *tāmā*, m. = ताँबा.

तामिस्र *tāmisră* [S.], m. **1.** the dark half of the lunar month. **2.** anger, frustration.

तामीर *tāmīr* [A. *ta'mīr*], f. **1.** building, construction. **2.** rebuilding. **3.** a building, structure. — ~ करना, to build, &c.

तामील *tāmīl* [A. *ta'mīl*], f. **1.** putting into effect (as a decree). **2.** carrying out, executing (as an order). — ~ करना (की), to put into effect; to carry out; to serve (as notice).

ताम्मुल *tāmmul* [A. *ta'ammul*], m. consideration, deliberation. — ~ करना, to reflect, to deliberate.

ताम्र *tāmr* [S.], adj. & m. **1.** adj. coppery red. ***2.** m. copper. — ताम्रकार, m. a coppersmith. ताम्रचूड़, m. copper-crest: a cock. ताम्र-पट्ट, m. a copper plate (as used to record grants, inscriptions). ताम्र-पत्र, m. id. तम्र-पर्ण, m. a red leaf. ताम्र-युग, m. *archaeol.* the bronze age. ताम्र-वर्ण, adj. & m. copper-coloured, reddish; a coppery colour.

तायब *tāyb* [A. *tā'ib*], adj. E.H. penitent.

ताया *tāyā* [**tātiya-*], m. father's elder brother (= ताऊ).

[1]**तार** *tār* [*tāra-*: w. P. *tār*], m. f. **1.** m. thread, string. **2.** stringing; warp (of a loom). **3.** wire; line (telephone); string (of a musical instrument). **4.** the telegraph (system); a telegram; a cable. **5.** unbroken flow (as of rain, or tears). **6.** a bit, piece; streak; pej. piece of jewellery. **7.** f. Brbh. *mus.* a musical scale or sequence of notes; a high note or tone. — ~ का खंभा, m. telegraph pole. ~ जमना, or बैठना, or लगना, a chance of success or good fortune to arise (for, का). ~ टूटना, the continuity or sequence (of sthg., के) to be interrupted. ~ देना, to hand in, to send, a telegram. ~ निकलना, a clue to be found (to, का). ~ बँधना, a sequence (of activity, का or के) to continue unbroken. ~ बाँधना (का or के), to continue or to repeat (an act) without interruption. ~ भेजने का पता, m. telegraphic address. – तार-तार, adj. in pieces or shreds; piecemeal. तार-तार करना, to tear to pieces or shreds. – तारकश [P. *-kaś*], m. a maker of gold or silver wire. °ई, f. wire-drawing. तार-ख़ाना, m. telegraph office. तार-घर, m. id. तार-तोड़, m. a kind of open needlework, esp. with gold or silver thread. तार-पत्र, m. a letter telegram. तार-बाबू, m. colloq. telegraph clerk; telegraphist. तार-यंत्र, m. a telegraph (instrument). तारवाला, m. & adj. a telegraph boy; a telegraph employee; stringed (an instrument).

[2]**तार** *tār*, m. = [1]ताल.

[3]**तार** *tār* [H. [1]*tāṛ*], m. Brbh. Av. a palm leaf; an ear ornament (? shaped like a palm leaf).

तारक *tārak* [S.], m. **1.** deliverer, saviour. **2.** *HŚS.* name of a salvific invocation addressed to Rām. **3.** a star; a planet. **4.** pupil (of the eye). **5.** an asterisk. — तारकांकित [°*ka+a*°], adj. marked with an asterisk.

तारका *tārăkā* [S.], f. a planet; a star.

तारकित *tārăkit* [S.], adj. starry, bright with stars.

तारकी *tārăkī* [cf. H. *tārak*], adj. starry (= तारकित).

तारकोल *tārkol* [Engl. *coal-tar*], m. asphalt, tar.

तारण *tāraṇ* [S.], adj. & m. **1.** adj. causing or enabling to cross. **2.** granting salvation. **3.** m. means of crossing; a raft, vessel. **4.** means of deliverance; saviour (= Viṣṇu). **5.** crossing over. **6.** salvation. — ~ करना, to enable to cross; to save. – तारण-तरण, m. E.H. deliverance (by crossing the ocean of birth and rebirth): = ~, 4., 2.

तारतम्य *tārătamyă* [S.], m. **1.** comparability, proportion. **2.** distinction, difference. **3.** sequence.

तारना *tārnā* [*tārayati*], v.t. **1.** to enable to cross, to take (one) across. **2.** to save; specif. *hind.* to save from rebirth.

तारपीन *tārpīn* [Engl. *turpentine*], m. turpentine.

तारा *tārā* [*tāraka-*], m. (poet. also f.) **1.** a star; a planet; a meteor. **2.** pupil (of the eye); fig. apple of (one's) eye. **3.** fig. fate, destiny. — ~ टूटना, a meteor to fall. ~ हो जाना, fig. to recede to a great distance, to become unattainable; to reach a great height. तारे गिनना, to count stars, to be wakeful. तारे तोड़ लाना, fig. to perform a miracle, a very difficult task. तारे तोड़ना, fig. to impose (on), to deceive. तारे दिखाई देना, to see stars: to feel faint (from a blow, or from weakness). – तारा-ग्रह, m. *astron.* star-planet: one of the five 'lesser planets' (Mercury, Venus, Mars, Jupiter, Saturn). तारा-पथ, m. star-way: the heavens. तारा-पुंज, m. a constellation. तारा-मंडल, m. id. तारावली [°*rā+ā*°], f. collection of stars: = तारा-पुंज. – तारों-भरा, adj. starry.

तारामीरा *tārāmīrā*, m. a kind of brassica, *Eruca sativa.*

तारिका *tārikā* [S.], f. dimin. 1. = तारका. **2.** an asterisk (= तारक). **3.** a film-star.

तारिणी *tāriṇī*, adj. f. & f. **1.** adj. f. = तारी. **2.** f. a form of the goddess Durgā.

तारी *tārī* [S.], adj. & m. **1.** adj. causing or enabling to cross. **2.** m. a saviour.

तारीक *tārīk* [P. *tārīk*], adj. dark.

तारीकी *tārīkī* [P. *tārīkī*], f. darkness.

तारीख़ *tārīkh* [A. *tārīkh*], f. **1.** date. **2.** *law.* date of a court appearance. — ~ डालना, to set a date; to date (a document). अक्तूबर की पहली ~ को, on the first of October. – तारीख़वार [P. *-vār*], adj. dated.

तारीफ़ *tārīf* [A. *taʻrīf*], f. making known: **1.** praise. **2.** fig. merit. **3.** the facts which are to be known (about one): introduction (of a stranger). **4.** *hist.* table of rates and export duties (cf. Engl. *tariff*). — ~ करना (की) to praise. ~ के पुल बाँधना, to build bridges of praise: to praise to the skies.

तारुण *tāruṇ* [S.], adj. young.

तारुण्य *tāruṇyă* [S.], m. youth; youthfulness.

तार्किक *tārkik* [S.], adj. & m. **1.** adj. having to do with logic; reasoned, logical. **2.** m. a logician; a philosopher.

[1]**ताल** *tāl* [*tāḍa-*[1], *tāla-*[1]], m. f. **1.** clapping the hands, applause. **2.** beating time (in music); musical time; rhythm. **3.** cymbals. **4.** slapping the palms on the arms or thighs as a challenge (in wrestling). — ~ ठोंकना, or मारना, to slap the arms, &c. (see 4. above). ~ देना, to give or to beat time (in music); to chime (a clock). ~ से बेताल, adj. out of time (a beat, rhythm). – ताल-ठोंक, f. slapping (as of the hands on the arms, see **4.** above). तालपूर्ण, adj. rhythmical. ताल-बद्ध, adj. id. ताल-मेल, m. harmony; agreement; just proportion; favourable moment. ताल-मेल खाना, to be in harmony, &c. ताल-मेल बैठाना (में), to bring into harmony (as inconsistent facts, or activities); to adjust (to, से). ताल-युक्त, adj. rhythmical.

[2]**ताल** *tāl* [*talla-*[1]], m. a pond; tank.

[3]**ताल** *tāl* [**tāḍa-*[3], *tāla-*[2]], m. the palm tree, fan-palm. — ताल-पत्र, m. = ताड़-पत्र. ताल-रस, m. Brbh. palm-toddy. ताल-वन, m. a palm grove. ताल-वृंत, m. a palm-leaf fan.

[4]**ताल** *tāl* [*uttāla-*: aphet.], adj. high, huge.

तालक *tālak*, m. Brbh. = ताल्लुक.

तालमखाना *tālmakhānā*, m. reg. the water-lily, and its edible seed.

तालव्य *tālavyă* [S.], adj. & m. **1.** adj. palatal. **2.** m. *ling.* a palatal consonant; a front vowel.

ताला *tālā* [*tāḍa-*[2], *tāla-*], m. a lock; a padlock. — ~ जड़ना, or डालना (में), to fasten with a lock. ~ तोड़ना, to force (a lock); to break into (का: as into a house). ~ लगना (पर), = next, 1., 2. ~ लगना (में), to be locked, locked up; to be sealed (the lips); fig. to end (a family line). ताले में रखना, to keep locked. – ताला-कुंजी, f. lock and key. हाथ में ताला-कुंजी होना (के), to hold the purse-strings. तालाबंदी [P. *-bandī*], f. lockout (of a work-force).

तालाब *tālāb* [P. *tālāb*], m. a pond; tank; reservoir.

तालिका *tālikā* [S.], f. a list, table, schedule.

तालिब *tālib* [A. *ṭālib*], adj. U. seeking. — तालिब-इल्म, m. seeker of knowledge: a student. तालिबे-इल्म, m. id.

तालिबा *tālibā* [A. *ṭāliba*], f. U. a student.

[1]**ताली** *tālī* [*tāḍa-*[1], *tālikā-*], f. **1.** clapping the hands. **2.** applause. — ~ देना, to beat time (in music). ~ पिटना, fig. hands to be clapped: (one) to be mocked or derided. ~ पीटना, or बजाना, or मारना, to clap the hands (to attract attention, or to show delight, or approval, or derision). एक हाथ से ~ नहीं बजती, it takes two hands to clap: it takes two to make a quarrel.

[2]**ताली** *tālī* [cf. *talla-*[1]], f. Av. a small pond or tank.

[3]**ताली** *tālī* [cf. H. *tālā*], f. a key.

तालीम *tālīm* [A. *taʻlīm*], f. instructing, instruction; education. — ~ देना (को), to teach, to instruct. ~ पाना, to receive instruction; to be educated. आम ~, f. general education. – तालीमयाफ़्ता [P. *-yāfta*], adj. inv. educated.

तालीमी *tālīmī* [A. *taʻlīmī*], adj. educational, concerning education.

तालू *tālū* [*tāluka-*], m. **1.** the palate. **2.** fontanelle (of a newborn baby). — ~ उठाना (का), to lift the uvula (of a newly born baby). ~ चटकना, the palate to crack: to suffer (great thirst, or fever). ~ से जीभ न लगना, (one's) tongue never to be still.

ताल्लुक़ *tālluq* [A. *taʻalluq*], m. **1.** connection; relationship. **2.** concern, reference (with or to, से). — ~ रखना (से), to be connected (with); to concern, to have reference (to). – ताल्लुक़दार [P. *-dār*], m. = ताल्लुक़ेदार, see s.v. ताल्लुक़ा.

ताल्लुक़ा *tālluqā* [A. *taʻalluqa*], m. **1.** a landed estate. **2.** an administrative district. — ताल्लुक़ेदार [P. *-dār*], m. a large landholder, owner of an estate. °ई, f. the duties, or position of a *tālluqedār*; tenure of a *tālluqā*.

ताल्लुक़ात *tālluqāt* [pl. of A. *taʻalluq*], m. pl. connections, concerns, dependencies.

ताव *tāv* [*tāpa-*, and P. *tāv*], m. **1.** heat. **2.** passion; anger. **3.** strength; speed. **4.** fine or splendid state; dignity. **5.** twisting; coil, curl; roll. **6.** [P. *tā*] a large sheet of paper. — ~ आना, to be heated (as fabric, in ironing); ~ में आना, to become enraged. ~ खाना, to be heated; to suffer overheating, burning; to become enraged. ~ चढ़ना (को), to conceive a strong desire. ~ देना (को), to heat (sthg.); to twist, to curl. मूँछों पर ~ देना, to curl the moustaches: to feel smug satisfaction. – तावदार [P. *-dār*], adj. passionate, ardent (of temperament); fine, splendid. ताव-भाव, m. qualities, strengths (of a person); ostentation; manner.

ताव- *tāv-* [*tāpayati*], v.t. Brbh. to heat (= ³ताना).

तावत् *tāvat* [S.], adj. & adv. to that extent or amount; so much, so many; so long; so far.

तावा *tāvā*, m. = तवा.

तावान *tāvān* [P. *tāvān*], m. compensation.

तावीज़ *tāvīz* [A. *ta'vīz*], m. **1.** an amulet, charm. **2.** a locket.

ताश *tāś* [conn. P. *tās*], m. **1.** playing cards. **2.** a playing card. **3.** gold cloth, or brocade. — ~ का पत्ता, m. a playing card. ~ खेलना, to play cards.

ताशा *tāśā* [P. *tāsa*], m. a hemispherical drum (played with sticks).

तासा *tāsā* [P. *tāsa*], m. a small drum.

तासीर *tāsīr* [A. *tāsīr*], f. effect; action, manner of operation (as of a medicine).

ताहम *tāham* [P. *tā-ham*], conj. despite so much, nevertheless (cf. ²ता).

ताहिरी *tāhirī*, f. = तहरी.

तिंतिड़ी *tintiṛī* [*tintiḍī-*], f. the tamarind tree.

-ति *-ti* [S.], suffix (forms abstract nouns, normally f., e.g. प्रीति, love).

ति- *ti-* [*tri-*], adj. & n. formant. three, threefold. – तिरंगा, m. tricolour; the national flag of India.

तिकड़म *tikṛam*, f. m. manoeuvring; strategem.

तिकड़ी *tikṛī*, f. **1.** sthg. consisting of three parts. **2.** a triumvirate, troika.

तिकार *tikār* [cf. H. *ti-*], m. reg. a third ploughing.

तिकोणिया *tikoṇiyā* [cf. H. *tikon(ā)*], adj. & f. **1.** adj. = तिकोना. **2.** f. reg. a carpenter's square (*guniyā*).

तिकोन *tikon*, adj. & m. = तिकोना.

तिकोना *tikonā* [ad. *trikoṇa-*], adj. & m. **1.** adj. triangular. **2.** m. a triangle. **3.** a small triangular-shaped pastry (*samosā*).

¹**तिक्का** *tikkā* [P. *tikka*], m. a small piece of meat. — तिक्का-बोटी करना (की), to tear (prey) to pieces; colloq. to make mincemeat (of).

²**तिक्का** *tikkā*, m. a three (in cards).

तिक्त *tikt* [S.], adj. bitter, pungent. — तिक्ताक्ति [°*ta*+*a*°], f. ammonia.

तिक्तक *tiktak* [S.], adj. = तिक्त.

तिखना *tikhanā*, [cf. H. ²*khan*], m. third floor, storey.

तिखरा *tikhrā* [cf. H. *tikhārnā*], adj. *Pl. HŚS.* ploughed three times.

तिखार *tikhār*, m. reg. (W). a third ploughing (cf. तिकार).

तिखारना *tikhārnā*, v.t. **1.** *Pl.* to plough three times before sowing. **2.** [? **niḥkṣārayati* × *tīkṣṇa-*] *Pl. HŚS.* to enquire closely into.

तिखूँट *tikhūṁṭ* [*tri-*; **khuṇṭa-*²], f. a triangle. — तिखूँट-नाप, f. obs. trigonometry.

तिखूँटा *tikhūṁṭā* [*tri-*; **khuṇṭa-*²], adj. triangular.

तिगुना *tigunā* [ad. *triguṇa-*], adj. threefold.

तिग्म *tigm* [S.], adj. sharp, pungent; fiery, passionate.

तिजहर *tij'har* [*tritīya-*+*(pra)hara-*], m. reg. third watch of the day, afternoon.

तिजारत *tijārat* [A. *tijāra*: P. *tijārat*], f. **1.** trade; commerce. **2.** goods traded. — ~ करना, to trade (in, की). – तिजारत-ख़ाना, m. a commercial or mercantile firm.

तिजारती *tijāratī* [A. *tijāratī*], adj. having to do with trade; commercial; mercantile.

तिजारी *tijārī* [**tṛtīyakajvāra-*], f. *Pl.* (*HŚS.*) a fever recurring every third day.

तिड़ी-बिड़ी *tiṛī-biṛī*, adj. reg. = तितरबितर.

तिढ़- *tiṛh-*. = टेढ़ा: — तिढ़मुँहाँ, adj. wry-mouthed.

तित *tit*, adv. Brbh. **1.** there. **2.** thither.

तितनो *titno*, adj. Brbh. = उतना.

तितर-बितर *titar-bitar* [? conn. *vistarati*], adj. **1.** scattered, dispersed. **2.** thrown here and there; in disorder. — ~ करना, v.t. to disperse; to throw into disorder.

तितली *titlī*, f. **1.** a butterfly. **2.** colloq. a showily dressed or flirtatious woman. **3.** reg. name of a grass used as fodder and also medicinally.

तितिक्षा *titikṣā* [S.], f. endurance, forbearance.

तितौ *titau*, adj. Brbh. = उतना.

तित्तर-बित्तर *tittar-bittar*, adv. pronun. var. = तितर-बितर.

तित्तिर *tittir* [cf. *tittira-*], m. *Pl. HŚS.* a partridge (= तीतर).

तित्तिरी *tittirī* [cf. *tittirika-*], m. *Pl.* = तीतर.

तिथि *tithi* [S.], f. **1.** a lunar day. **2.** a date of a lunar or solar month. — तिथि-पत्र, m. an almanac (astrological).

तिथित *tithit* [S.], adj. dated.

तिदरा *tidarā* [**tridvaraka-*], adj. three-doored.

तिदरी *tidarī* [**tridvaraka-*], adj. three-doored.

तिधर *tidhar* [conn. H. [1]*dhār*], adv. reg. **1.** thither. **2.** there.

तिधारा *tidhārā* [ad. **tridhāra-*], m. confluence of three streams.

तिधारी *tidhārī* [cf. H. *tidhārā*], adj. & f. **1.** adj. having three lines, streams, or edges. **2.** f. three streams or lines.

तिन *tin* [*tṛṇa-*], m. = तिनका.

तिन *tin*, obl. base, pl. chiefly reg. see वह.

तिनकना *tinaknā* [cf. *tṛṇṇa-*], v.i. to flare up (in anger: at, पर).

तिनका *tinkā* [cf. *tṛṇa-*], m. **1.** grass, straw. **2.** a blade of grass; a straw; a shred, scrap. — ~ तोड़ना, to break off a connection (with, से); to ward off the evil eye (as in sorcery, by breaking a blade of grass). ~ दाँतों में (मुँह में) पकड़ना, or लेना, fig. to yield abjectly; to confess inferiority. ~ न रहना, not a shred or scrap to remain: to be swept clean; to be cleaned out (as of money). ~ हो जाना, to waste; to shrivel. तिनके का सहारा (डूबते को), a frail support, a straw (for a drowning man). तिनके की ओट पहाड़, fig. a large issue lurking behind a seemingly trivial question. तिनके को पहाड़ करना, fig. to make a mountain out of a molehill. तिनके चुनना, to pick straws: to be crazed (by grief).

तिपाई *tipāī* [cf. *tri-*; *pāda-*], f. a three-legged stool, or table.

तिपारी *tipārī*, f. reg. (E.) = मकोय.

तिफ़्ल *tifl* [A. *ṭifl*], m. U. a child.

तिफ़्ली *tiflī* [P. *ṭiflī*], f. U. childhood.

[1]**तिबारा** *tibārā* [*tri-*; *vāra-*[2]], adj. **1.** three times, thrice. **2.** adv. for a third time.

[2]**तिबारा** *tibārā* [*tri-*; *dvāra-*], m. a hall or room having three doors.

तिबारी *tibārī*, f. = [2]तिबारा.

तिबासी *tibāsī* [cf. **trivāsa-*], adj. three days old (food).

तिब्बी *tibbī* [A. *ṭibbī*], adj. medical; medicinal.

[1]**तिमि** *timi* [Ap. *tima*], adv. Av. in such a way (= वैसे).

[2]**तिमि** *timi* [S.], m. a fabulous fish of huge size. — तिमिंगिल, m. swallower of the *timi*: a huge fish, leviathan.

तिमिर *timir* [S.], m. **1.** darkness. **2.** a defect of the eyes. — तिमिरजा, adj. f. born of darkness. तिमिरजाल, m. net of darkness: enveloping darkness. तिमिर-नाशक, m. dispeller of darkness: an instructive work, illuminator (of a subject).

तिमुहानी *timuhānī*, f. Av. a confluence of three rivers; specif. *mythol.* that of Ganges, Jumna and Sarasvatī at Allahabad.

तिय *tiy* [*strī-*], f. Brbh. Av. = स्त्री.

[1]**तिया** *tiyā* [H. *tīyā*], adj. & m. **1.** adj. multiplied by three. **2.** m. a group of three. **3.** a three (in cards or at dice).

[2]**तिया** *tiyā* [*strī-*], f. Brbh. metr. = *tī*.

तिरंगा *tirangā*, m. see s.v. ति-.

तिरखूँट *tirkhūṁṭ* [ad. *tri-*; H. *khūṁṭ*], f. a triangle.

तिरखूँटा *tirkhūṁṭā* [cf. H. *tirkhūṁṭ*], adj. triangular.

तिरछा *tirchā* [*tiraśca-*], adj. **1.** slanting, oblique; crosswise. **2.** crooked, awry. — ~ करना, to place on a slant, or across. तिरछी आँखों, or निगाहों, से देखना, to look sidelong (at, की ओर); to look askance (at); to look angrily (at). तिरछी चितवन, or नज़र, f. a sidelong glance; ogling; a squint. तिरछी बात, f. a cutting remark; an oblique reference; a matter misconceived, or distorted. तिरछे, adv. aslant; obliquely; diagonally; crookedly; amiss.

तिरछाई *tirchāī* [cf. H. *tirchā*], f. = तिरछापन.

तिरछाना *tirchānā* [cf. H. *tirchā*], v.i. & v.t. **1.** v.i. *HŚS.* to be aslant, &c. **2.** to be crooked. **3.** v.t. to place aslant. **4.** to make crooked; to distort.

तिरछापन *tirchāpan* [cf. H. *tirchā*], m. **1.** slant, obliqueness. **2.** crookedness.

तिरछियाना *tirchiyānā* [cf. H. *tirchā*], v.i. to edge, to go sidelong or obliquely.

तिरना *tirnā* [*tirate*], v.i. **1.** to float. **2.** to swim (= तैरना). **3.** to cross over.

तिरप *tirap*, m. Brbh. a partic. gesture of the hand made in dancing with a partner.

तिरपट *tirpaṭ*, adj. reg. bent, crooked.

तिरपटा *tirpaṭā* adj. reg. squint-eyed.

तिरपन *tirpan* [*trayahpañcāśat-*], adj. fifty-three.

[1]**तिरपाल** *tirpāl* [f. Engl. *tarpaulin*], m. a tarpaulin.

[2]**तिरपाल** *tirpāl*, m. reg. (W.) bundles of grass placed beneath the tiles of a roof.

तिरपौलिया *tirpauliyā* [ad. *tri-*; *pratolī-*], m. a building having three doors or gates.

तिरबिद *tirbid* [P. *tirbid*, *turbad*: *trivṛtā-*], f. *Pl.* the root and skin of *Operculina turpethum* (used as a laxative: = तेवड़ी).

तिरमिरा *tirmirā* [cf. H. *tirmirī*], m. **1.** a sensation of dazzlement. **2.** a spot (as of oil or *ghī*) floating on water or other liquid. **3.** an extreme sensitivity of the eyes to strong light.

तिरमिराना *tirmirānā* [cf. H. *tirmirā*, *tirmirī*], v.i. **1.** to be dazzled. **2.** to glisten (as oil on water). **3.** to quiver, to vibrate. **4.** to be dizzy.

तिरमिराहट *tirmirāhaṭ* [cf. H. *tirmirānā*], f. **1.** a sensation of being dazzled, or dizzy. **2.** glistening. **3.** quivering, vibration.

तिरमिरी *tirmirī* [cf. **tirimiri-*], f. **1.** a sensation of being dazzled, or dizzy. **2.** dizziness.

तिरमुहानी *tirmuhānī* [ad. *tri-*; **mukhāyana-*], f. **1.** a junction of three roads. **2.** a confluence of three rivers (see तिमुहानी).

तिरसठ *tirsaṭh* [*trayaḥṣaṣṭi-*], adj. sixty-three.

तिरस्कार *tiras-kār* [S.], m. placing beyond or beside: **1.** censure; scolding; reproach. **2.** disrespect; disdain. — ~ करना, to express censure, &c. (of, को).

तिरस्कृत *tiras-kṛt* [S.], adj. **1.** censured; reproached. **2.** scorned; disdained.

तिरानवे *tirānve* [*trayonavati-*], adj. ninety-three.

तिराना *tirānā* [cf. H. *tirnā*, and *tarnā*], v.t. **1.** to cause to float; to cause to swim. **2.** to cause to cross over (water). **3.** to rescue, to save.

तिरासी *tirāsī* [*tryaśīti-*], adj. eighty-three.

तिराहा *tirāhā* [cf. *tri-*; H. *rāh*], m. an intersection of three roads.

तिरिया *tiriyā* [cf. *strī-*; ← Panj.], f. reg. a woman. — तिरिया-चरित्तर, m. women's ways; a woman's wiles, or trickery.

तिरेंदा *tireṁdā* [conn. H. *tareṁḍa-*: ? w. *tirate*], m. *Pl. HŚS.* float (of a fishing line); buoy (cf. तरेंडा).

तिरोधान *tirôdhān* [S.], m. *philos.* concealment (of things and properties by divine power).

तिरोभाव *tirôbhāv* [S.], m. *philos.* disappearance (of things and properties by divine power).

तिरोभूत *tirôbhūt* [S.], adj. *philos.* disappeared, vanished.

तिरोहित *tirôhit* [S.], adj. concealed; vanished.

तिर्यक् *tiryak* [S.], adj. **1.** slanting, oblique; crosswise. **2.** *HŚS.* crooked.

तिलंगा *tilaṅgā* [*tailaṅga-*, *tiliṅga-*], m. **1.** an inhabitant of the Telinga region (southwards from Orissa towards Madras). **2.** *hist.* an Indian soldier in a European-controlled army.

तिलंगाना *tilaṅgānā* [H. *tilaṅgā* + P. *-āna*], m. the Telugu-speaking region of India.

[1]**तिलंगी** *tilaṅgī* [*tailaṅga-*, *tiliṅga-*], m. = तिलंगा, 1., 2.

[2]**तिलंगी** *tilaṅgī* [*tailaṅga-*, *tiliṅga-*], f. the Telugu language.

तिल *til* [*tila-*[1]: ? ← Austro-as.], m. **1.** the sesame plant. **2.** sesame seed, oil-seed. **3.** a mole or black spot (on the face); a decorative mark made on the face (as with lampblack). **4.** the pupil of the eye. **5.** a tiny object, or least amount. **6.** a moment, an instant. — ~ का ताड़ करना, to make a mountain out of a molehill, to exaggerate (a matter). ~ की ओट पहाड़, a mountain hiding behind a sesame seed: a large question underlying one apparently trivial. ~ ~, adv. in small amounts, little by little, slowly. ~ ~ का हिसाब, m. a meticulous account. ~ भर, adv. a tiny amount; for a moment. ~ रखने, or धरने, की जगह नहीं, fig. (there is) no room, or space, (left) at all. इन तिलों में तेल नहीं है, there is no oil in these seeds: no benefit, or hope, in this quarter. तिलों से तेल निकालना, fig. to achieve a purpose with difficulty. – तिल-कुट, m. a kind of sweet made from pounded sesame seeds soaked in a syrup of molasses or sugar. तिल-खली, f. oil-cake of sesame seeds. तिल-चावली, f. a mixture of sesame seed and rice, or of black and white (as in greying hair). तिल-चूड़ी, *Pl.* = तिल-कुट. तिल-चूर्ण, m. = तिल-कुट. तिलदानी, f. see s.v. तिल-पट्टी, f. *HŚS.* a kind of sweet made from sesame seeds soaked in a syrup of sugar or molasses. तिल-पपड़ी, f. *HŚS.* id. तिल-पुष्प, m. the sesame flower. तिल-भुग्गा, m. = तिल-कुट. तिल-सुषमा, f. a splendour to which many sources contribute fragmentarily. तिलांजलि [°*la* + *a*°], f. = next. तिलांजली, f. a palm, or the cupped palms, full of water mixed with sesame seeds, offered to the spirit of a relative as part of the funeral rites. तिलांजली देना (को), to perform last rites, to part for ever (with); to make an end (of: as of a practice). तिलोदक [°*la* + *u*°], m. = तिलांजली.

तिलक *tilak* [S.], m. **1.** an ornament, adornment. **2.** ornamental mark made on the forehead. **3.** sectarian mark made (with saffron, sandal, &c.) chiefly on the forehead. **4.** mark made on the forehead of a newly engaged bridegroom. **5.** sign of consecration or investiture; transf. consecration, &c.; ceremony. **6.** commentary (on a text). **7.** name of a small tree having bright red or orange flowers (cf. कमेला). — ~ करना (का), to adorn with a *tilak*; to solemnise the engagement (of); to consecrate, to invest. ~ चढ़ाना (को), = ~ करना. ~ देना (को), or भेजना, to make a gift to a bridegroom on his betrothal (the bride's relatives). ~ लगाना (पर), = ~ करना, 1. – तिलक-कमोद, m. *mus.* name of a *rāg.* तिलकधारी, m. one who is marked with, or wears, a *tilak*. तिलक-मुद्रा, f. = ~, 3.

तिलचट्टा *tilcaṭṭā* [cf. H. *tel*; H. *cāṭnā*], m. a cockroach.

तिलड़ा *tilaṛā* [*tri-*; **laḍa-*], adj. having three strands (as a necklace, or garland).

तिलड़ी *tilaṛī* [cf. H. *tilaṛā*], f. a necklace or garland of three strands.

तिलदानी *tildānī* [H. *til*+P. *-dān(ī)*], f. reg. container for small objects: a sewing-bag.

तिलमिलाना *tilmilānā*, v.i. **1.** to become suddenly enraged. **2.** to be dazzled.

तिलवा *tilvā* [**tilapūpa-*], m. a sweet made from ground sesame and sugar.

तिलस्म *tilasm* [A. *ṯilism*], m. **1.** sthg. enchanted, the work or creation of magic; a magic spell. **2.** a talisman, charm. — ~ तोड़ना, to break a spell; to fathom the nature of sthg. magical.

तिलस्माती *tilasmātī* [A. *ṯilismāt*, pl.+P. *-ī*], adj. = तिलस्मी.

तिलस्मी *tilasmī* [P. *ṯilismī*], adj. **1.** magical, enchanted. **2.** dealing with mystery (as a detective story).

तिलहन *tilhan*, m. oil-seed; oil-crop.

तिलहा *tilhā* [cf. *taila-*], adj. oily.

तिलहाई *tilhāī* [cf. H. *tilhā*], f. oiliness.

तिला *tilā* [A. *ṯilā*], m. *HŚS.* an ointment (used as an aphrodisiac by men).

तिलाकार *tilākār* [cf. P. *ṯilā*], m. 19c. a gilder.

तिलावा *tilāvā* [A. *ṯalī'a*, pl. *ṯalā'e*: P. *ṯāva*], m. *Pl. HŚS.* a night-watch, patrol.

तिलियर *tiliyar*, m. = तिलेर.

तिलिस्म *tilism*, m. see तिलस्म.

तिली *tilī*, f. reg. = तीली.

तिलेती *tiletī*, f. reg. ? stubble of mustard or sesame.

तिलेर *tiler* [cf. *tila-*[1]], m. a speckled bird: the rose-coloured starling, *Sturnus roseus*; ? the spotted dove, *Streptopelia chinensis*.

तिलौंछ- *tilaumch-* [? conn. H. *tel*: Pk. *pumchaï*, H. *pomchnā*], v.t. Brbh. to rub (with oil).

तिल्ला *tillā* [P. *tila*, *ṯilā*], m. **1.** ornamentation (of a garment) with gold or silver thread. **2.** fringe or border of gold or silver thread (as to a turban or sari). — तिल्लेदार [P. *-dār*], adj. having a fringe of gold thread, &c.

[1]**तिल्ली** *tillī* [**tillikā-*[3]], f. the spleen.

[2]**तिल्ली** *tillī*, f. oil-seeds.

तिवाड़ी *tivāṛī*, m. = तिवारी.

तिवारी *tivārī* [*tripāṭhin-*], m. **1.** name of a brāhmaṇ sub-community (= त्रिपाठी). **2.** a man of that community.

तिस *tis* [*ta-* ×H. *jis*, *kis*], obl. base of the dem. pron. सो. chiefly reg. that; he, she, it. — ~ पर, adv. thereupon; that being so; moreover; upon that. ~ पर भी, adv. despite that, notwithstanding. ~ पर तुर्रा यह (है), colloq. to cap it all; into the bargain.

तिसरैत *tisrait* [cf. H. *tīsrā*], m. a mediator, arbitrator.

तिसा- *tisā-* [cf. *tr̥ṣā-*], v.i. Brbh. to be thirsty.

तिसायो *tisāyo* [cf. *tr̥ṣā-*: Pk. *tisāia-*, H. *tisā-*], adj. reg. (Raj.) thirsty.

तिसाला *tisālā* [cf. *tri-*; P. *sāla*], adj. **1.** three years old (an animal). **2.** lasting three years (as a lease, a post).

तिहत्तर *tihattar* [*trayaḥsaptati-*], adj. seventy-three.

तिहरा *tihrā*, adj. = तेहरा.

तिहवार *tihvār*, m. = त्योहार.

तिहाई *tihāī* [cf. *tribhāga-*], f. **1.** a third. **2.** a harvest, crop (of which either two-thirds or one third could be assigned to the cultivator).

तिहारा *tihārā*, pron. = तुम्हारा.

तिहिं *tihim* [Ap. *tahim*], pron. Brbh. 1. = उस. 2. = उसको.

तिहुं *tihum*, adj. Brbh. = तीनों.

तिहूं *tihūm*, adj. Brbh. 1. = तीनों. 2. = तीनों भी, तीनों ही.

ती *tī* [conn. *strī-*], f. Brbh. Av. **1.** a woman. **2.** a wife.

-ती *-tī* [H. *-tā*], suffix (forms a few f. abstract nouns on verb stems expressing action, or state arising from action, e.g. बढ़ती, rise, increase; भरती, enlisting, enlistment; पावती, receipt (of sthg.)).

तीकना *tīknā*, v.t. to aim at (cf. ताकना, तकना).

तीक्ष्ण *tīkṣṇ* [S.], adj. **1.** sharp, cutting; high (tone); shrill. **2.** hot, burning; corrosive. **3.** spiced, pungent. **4.** fine, thin (cloth). **5.** bright (light). **6.** passionate, ardent; angry. **7.** quick of mind; subtle. **8.** harsh. — **तीक्ष्णदंत**, adj. sharp-toothed. **तीक्ष्णदृष्टि**, adj. having sharp sight. **तीक्ष्णधार**, adj. & m. sharp-edged; a sword. **तीक्ष्णबुद्धि**, adj. sharp-witted, acute; shrewd.

तीक्ष्णता *tīkṣṇātā* [S.], f. **1.** sharpness, cutting quality; shrillness. **2.** heat. **3.** pungency. **4.** fineness, thinness. **5.** passion, ardour. **6.** quickness or sharpness of mind; shrewdness.

तीक्ष्णत्व *tīkṣṇatvā* [S.], m. = तीक्ष्णता.

तीखन *tīkhan* [ad. *tīkṣṇa-*], adj. Brbh. = तीक्ष्ण.

तीखा *tīkhā* [*tīkṣṇa-*], adj. **1.** sharp, &c. (= तीक्ष्ण, most senses; cf. तेज़). // 2. smart, sprightly; racy.

तीखापन *tīkhāpan* [cf. H. *tīkhā*], m. sharpness, &c.

तीखुरा *tīkhurā* [conn. *trikṣura-*], f. m. Indian arrowroot, *Maranta arundinacea*, and the starch obtained from it.

तीछन *tīchan* [ad. *tīkṣṇa-*], adj. Brbh. = तीक्ष्ण.

तीछा *tīchā* [ad. *tīkṣṇa-*], adj. Av. sharp: distressing.

तीज *tīj* [*tṛtīyā-*], f. **1.** the third day of a lunar fortnight. **2.** a festival held on the third day of a lunar fortnight, esp. in the month of Sāvan. — **तीज-त्योहार**, m. a festival.

तीजा *tījā* [*tṛtīya-*], adj. & m. **1.** adj. third (in number or rank). **2.** m. a third one.

तीजापन *tījāpan* [cf. H. *tījā*], m. E.H. the third stage of life, renunciation of domestic life.

तीत *tīt* [*tikta-*], adj. **1.** bitter. **2.** hot, pungent, acrid.

तीतर *tītar* [*tittira-*], m. a partridge; a guinea-fowl. — **आधा ~ आधा बटेर**, fig. neither fish nor fowl.

तीतरी *tītrī* [cf. H. *tītar*], f. a hen partridge.

तीता *tītā* [*tikta-*], adj. = तीत.

तीतिर *tītir*, m. pronun. var. = तीतर.

तीन *tīn* [*trīṇi-*], adj. three. — **~ काल**, m. pl. = त्रिकाल. – **तीन-छह का रिश्ता**, m. fig. a distant relationship. **तीन-तिताला**, m. the number three; an odd number. **तीन-तेरह**, adj. three and thirteen (regarded as unlucky numbers): scattered, dispersed; destroyed; squandered. **तीन-तेरह करना**, to scatter, &c. **तीन-तेरह बकना**, to talk incoherent nonsense. **तीन-पाँच**, f. three and five: squabbling; trickery, machination. **तीन-पाँच करना**, to dispute or to quarrel (with, से); to practise trickery, to prevaricate.

तीमन *tīman* [S.], m. basil.

तीमार *tīmār*, m. care, attendance (on the sick); nursing. — **तीमारदार** [P. *-dār*], m. an attendant, one who nurses. °**ई**, f. attendance, nursing.

तीय *tīy*, f. Brbh. Av. = स्त्री.

तीया *tīyā* [*trika-*], adj. & m. = [1]तिया.

तीरंदाज़ *tīrandāz*, m. see s.v. [2]तीर.

[1]**तीर** *tīr* [*tīra-*], m. & adv. **1.** m. shore, bank. **2.** margin, edge. **3.** vicinity. **4.** adv. near (to, के). — **~ पकड़ना**, or **लगना**, to come to the shore, &c. – **तीरवर्ती**, adj. situated on a shore, &c.; adjacent. **तीरस्थ**, adj. id.

[2]**तीर** *tīr* [P. *tīr*], m. **1.** an arrow. **2.** fig. a shot; a move, a telling step. — **~ चलाना**, or **छोड़ना**, or **फेंकना**, or **मारना**, to shoot an arrow (at, पर); to fire a shot (in argument); to make a good move (in one's affairs). **~ लगना**, an arrow to hit the mark; a move to succeed. – **तीरंदाज़** [P. *-andāz*], m. an archer. °**ई**, f. archery. **तीर-कमान**, f. arrows and bow, weapons. **तीर-तुक्का**, m. see s.v. तुक्का.

तीरथ *tīrath*, m. see तीर्थ.

तीर्ण *tīrṇ* [S.], adj. **1.** crossed, passed over. **2.** spread, expanded.

तीर्थ *tīrth* [S.], m. **1.** a place of pilgrimage (esp. partic. places along the course of sacred rivers, as the Ganges); a bathing place. **2.** pilgrimage. **3.** fig. a revered personage. — **~ करना**, to go on pilgrimage.- **तीर्थ-पति**, m. = °-राज. **तीर्थ-यात्रा**, f. a pilgrimage. °**-यात्री**, m., °**-यात्रिणी**, f. a pilgrim. **तीर्थ-राज**, m. king of pilgrimage-places: Allahabad or Prayāg (where the rivers Ganges and Jumna meet). **तीर्थ-सेवी**, m. one who resides at (devotes his life to residence at) a place of pilgrimage. **तीर्थ-स्थान**, m. = ~, 1. **तीर्थाटन** [°*tha*+*a*°], m. a pilgrimage. **तीर्थोदक** [°*tha*+*u*°], m. water taken from a place of pilgrimage.

तीर्थक *tīrthak* [S.], m. a brāhmaṇ priest attending a place of pilgrimage (= [1]पंडा).

तीली *tīlī*, f. **1.** a straw. **2.** a thin sliver, bar or wire (wood or metal); spoke; rod. — **दियासलाई**, or **माचिस**, **की ~**, f. a match-stick.

तीवन *tīvan* [**tīmana-*: Pk. *tīmaṇa-*], m. *Pl. HŚS.* a sauce or relish: lentils or vegetables with a sauce.

तीवरता *tīvrătā* [S.], f. **1.** intensity, &c. **2.** ardour, impetuosity. **3.** excess.

तीव्र *tīvră* [S.], adj. **1.** strong, intense; sharp, keen; pungent; harsh; swift; sharp (a musical note). **2.** ardent, impetuous. **3.** excessive. — **तीव्रीकरण**, m. intensification.

तीस *tīs* [*triṁśat-*], adj. thirty. — **तीस**, or **तीसों**, **दिन**, adv. the thirty days (of the month): every day. – **तीस-मार ख़ाँ**, m. iron. great warrior: big talker.

तीसरा *tīsrā* [**trihsara-*], adj. & m. **1.** adj. third. **2.** m. a third person; an uninvolved person; an arbitrator. — ~ **पहर**, m. the third watch: the time between noon and three p.m.; early afternoon. **तीसरे**, adv. thirdly.

तीसी *tīsī* [**tissi-*], f. linseed (the seed of flax); flax.

तुंग *tuṅg* [S.], adj. & m. **1.** adj. high, lofty; prominent. **2.** domineering. **3.** m. peak, summit.

तुंगता *tuṅgătā* [S.], f. height, loftiness.

तुंड *tuṇḍ* [S.], m. **1.** snout. **2.** beak; Brbh. point (of a sword).

तुंद *tund* [S.], m. the belly; a pot-belly (= **तोंद**).

तुंद- *tund-* [P. *tund*], adj. swift, sharp, fierce: — **तुंद-ख़ू**, adj. U. irascible.

तुंदिल *tundil* [S.], adj. pot-bellied.

तुंबा *tumbā* [*tumbaka-*: ← Austro-as.], m. a gourd (= **कद्दू**); a hollowed-out gourd (as used by ascetics to carry water).

तुंबी *tumbī*, f. dimin. = **तुंबा**.

तुक *tuk*, f. **1.** rhyme. **2.** *Pl. HŚS.* a line of verse. **3.** logic, sense, rhyme and reason. — ~ **जोड़ना**, or **बिठाना**, or **मिलाना**, to rhyme, to versify. ~ **में** ~ **मिलाना**, id.; to concert or to side (with, **से**); to agree abjectly (with). – **तुकबंद** [P. -*band*], m. a versifier. °-**ई**, f. versifying. **तुकबंदी करना**, = ~ **जोड़ना**.

तुकमा *tukmā* [P. *tukma*], m. *Pl. HŚS.* loop for a button.

तुकली *tuklī*, f. dimin. = **तुक्कल**.

तुक्कल *tukkal* [? ← Panj.], m. (*Pl.*) *HŚS.* a large paper kite.

तुक्का *tukkā* [P. *tukka*], m. an arrow without a head. — **तीर पर** ~, fig. a blunt retort (cf. **दो-टूक जवाब**). – **तीर-तुक्का जमाना**, colloq. to make uninformed remarks.

तुग़ियानी *tuġiyānī* [cf. A. *ṭugyān*], f. U. excess.

तुचा *tucā* [ad. *tvacā-*], f. Av. skin, shrivelled skin.

तुच्छ *tucch* [S.], adj. **1.** empty. ***2.** worthless, insignificant. **3.** base, contemptible. — ~ **जानना**, or **समझना**, to consider worthless; to despise. – **तुच्छातितुच्छ** [°*cha* + *a*°], adj. most worthless; most base. **तुच्छार्थक** [°*cha* + *a*°], adj. *gram.* diminutive. **तुच्छीकृत**, adj. 19c. considered as worthless.

तुच्छता *tucchătā* [S.], f. **1.** emptiness. ***2.** worthlessness. **3.** baseness.

तुच्छत्व *tucchatvă* [S.], m. = **तुच्छता**.

तुझ- *tujh-* [*tubhya(m)*], obl. base. see **तू**.

तुड़वाई *tuṛvāī* [cf. H. *tuṛvānā*], f. **1.** causing to be broken, &c. **2.** price paid for getting fruit picked, or money changed.

तुड़वाना *tuṛvānā* [cf. H. *toṛnā*], v.t. to cause to be broken, &c. (by, **से**).

तुड़ाई *tuṛāī* [cf. H. *tuṛānā*], f. **1.** causing to be broken, &c. **2.** price paid for, or cost of, picking fruit, or changing money.

तुड़ाना *tuṛānā* [cf. H. *toṛnā*], v.t. **1.** to cause to be broken (by, **से**); to break (as an animal its halter, a prisoner his chain). **2.** to change (a note or large coin). **3.** to pick (fruit).

तुतई *tutaī*, f. a small earthen or metal vessel with a spout.

तुतरा- *tutrā-*, v.i. Brbh. = **तुतलाना**.

तुतला *tutlā*, adj. = **तोतला**.

तुतलाई *tutlāī* [cf. H. *tutlānā*], f. **1.** lisping, speaking indistinctly. **2.** stammering, stuttering.

तुतलाना *tutlānā* [cf. H. *totlā*, *tutlā*], v.i. **1.** to lisp, to speak indistinctly (as a child). **2.** to stammer, to stutter.

तुतलापन *tutlāpan* [cf. H. *tutlānā*], m. **1.** lisping speech, &c. **2.** stammering speech, &c.

तुतलाहट *tutlāhaṭ* [cf. H. *tutlānā*], f. = **तुतलाई**.

तुत्थ *tutth* [S.], m. *Pl. HŚS.* copper sulphate (= **तूतिया**).

तुन *tun* [*tuṇi-*, *tunyu-*], m. the toon tree, *Cedrela toona* (a source of strong and durable timber).

तुनक *tunak*, adj. = **तुनुक**.

तुनकना *tunaknā*, v.i. = **तिनकना**.

तुनकी *tunkī*, f. reg. (W.) ? a thin, crisp bread-cake.

तुनतुनी *tuntunī*, f. a musical instrument (stringed).

तुनुक *tunuk* [P. *tunuk*], adj. **1.** delicate, sensitive. **2.** frail. — तुनुकमिज़ाज, adj. irritable of temperament; whimsical. °ई, f. irritability; whimsicality.

तुपक *tupak* [P. *tupak*], f. Brbh. a kind of musket.

तुपाना *tupānā*, v.t. = तोपना.

तुफ़ंग *tufaṅg* [P. *tufang*], m. Brbh. a tube through which sthg. is blown: a musket.

तुफ़ैल *tufail* [A. *t̤ufail*], m. companion: instrumentality. — ~ से, adv. by means (of, के); thanks (to).

तुफ़ैली *tufailī* [A. *t̤ufailī*], adj. sponging, parasitical.

तुम *tum* [*tuvam*, also *yuṣmad-*], pron. (reduced hon. grade). you. — ~ लोग, pron. you (specif. pl. reference).

तुमड़ी *tumṛī* [cf. *tumba-*[1]], f. a hollow gourd, &c. (= तुंबी).

तुमुल *tumul* [S.], m. & adj. **1.** m. tumult, din. **2.** confusion, tumultuous combat. **3.** adj. tumultuous. **4.** excited, confused.

तुम्हारा *tumhārā* [cf. *tuvam, yuṣmad-*], adj. your, yours.

तुरंग *turaṅg*, [S.], m. going quickly: a horse.

तुरंज *turañj* [P. *turanj*], m. **1.** a citron. **2.** embroidered work.

तुरंजी *turañjī* [P. *turanjī*], adj. citron-coloured, yellowish.

तुरंत *turant* [*turant-*], adv. **1.** quickly; in haste. **2.** at once. **3.** recently. — ~ का, adj. recent, new. ~ का जनमा, adj. new-born.

तुरंता *turantā* [cf. H. *turant*], m. colloq. quick (fix): cannabis (= गाँजा).

[1]**तुर** *tur* [*tura-*[1]], ? f. Brbh. speed.

[2]**तुर** *tur* [*turī-*, Pa. *tulikā-*], f. **1.** *Pl. HŚS.* a weaver's brush. **2.** *Pl.* fibrous stick used by weavers to clean and separate the threads of the woof. **3.** *HŚS.* stick or roller on which cloth from the loom, or braid, is rolled.

[1]**तुरई** *turaī*, f. a cucurbitaceous plant, *Luffa acutangula*, and its fruit.

[2]**तुरई** *turaī*, f. = तुरही.

तुरक *turk*, m. Av. see तुर्क.

तुरकाना *turkānā* [P. *turkāna*], adj. & m. **1.** adj. *Pl. HŚS.* Turkish, of Turkish type (see तुर्क). **2.** m. E.H. a Turk, a Muslim.

तुरकानी *turkānī* [P. *turkāna*+H. *-ī*], f. E.H. a Turkish or Muslim woman.

तुरकिन *turkin*, f. see तुर्किन.

तुरग *turag* [S.], m. Av. going quickly: a horse (= तुरंग).

तुरत *turat* [*turant-*], adv. = तुरंत. — तुरत-फुरत, m. swiftness; alacrity; activity; adv. quickly, &c. तुरतो शताब [P. *-o-śitāb*], adv. poet. colloq. = ~.

तुरतुरी *turturī*, f. *Pl.* a long trumpet or horn.

तुरन *turan*, adj. Brbh. = तूर्ण.

तुरपन *turpan* [cf. H. *turapnā*], f. hem-stitching, hemming. — तुरपन-बेल, f. embroidery of cloth with creepers and flowers.

तुरपना *turapnā* [conn. **trupyati*, or **trupnāti*], v.t. to hem-stitch, to hem.

तुरपवाना *turapvānā* [cf. H. *turapnā*], v.t. to cause to be hemmed (by, से).

तुरपाना *turpānā* [cf. H. *turapnā*], v.t. **1.** to cause to be hemmed (a garment). **2.** to hem (= तुरपना).

तुरबत *turbat* [A. *turba*: P. *turbat*], f. a grave, a tomb.

तुरम *turam* [? ← Panj. or Raj.], m. *Pl.* a trumpet (= तुरई).

तुरमती *turamtī* [? ad. **tvarāmatī*], f. Brbh. a kind of falcon (? the red-headed merlin).

तुरय *turay*, m. Brbh. see तुरै.

तुरही *turhī* [cf. *tūra-*], f. a trumpet; a horn.

तुरा *turā* [*tura-*[1], ? ad. Pk. *turā-*, or ad. *tvarā-*], f. Brbh. speed, quickness.

तुराई *turāī* [**tūlāvatī-*], f. Brbh. Av. **1.** a cotton-filled quilt. **2.** a mattress.

तुराय *turāy* [cf. *tura-*[1]], adv. Brbh. quickly (? or = v.i).

तुरावति *turāvati* [ad. *tvarāvat*], adj. f. Brbh. swift.

तुरिअ *turia* [*turaga-*], m. Av. a horse.

तुरित *turit* [? ad. *tvarita-*: H. *turat*], adv. Av. = तुरत.

तुरिय *turiyă*, adj. Brbh. = तुरीय.

[1]**तुरी** *turī* [**tūriya-*: Pk. *tŭria-*], f. = तुरही.

[2]**तुरी** *turī* [*turagī-*], f. Brbh. Av. a mare.

तुरीय *turīyă* [S.], adj. fourth. — तुरीयावस्था [°*ya*+*a*°], f. *philos.* the fourth state of the soul, in which the soul has become one with the supreme spirit.

तुरुक *turuk*, m. reg. = तुर्क.

तुरुप *turup* [Engl. *trump*], m. a trump (in cards). — ~ देना (को), to trump.

तुरुपना *turupnā*, v.t. pronun. var. = तुरपना.

तुरुष्क *turuṣkă* [S.], m. *hist.* **1.** a Scythian (of central Asia). **2.** a Turk.

तुरै *turai* [*turaga-*], m. Av. a horse.

तुर्क *turk* [P. *turk*], m. **1.** a Turk: an inhabitant of Turkestan, west central Asia. **2.** a Muslim solider, esp. one from Turkestan; pej. a plunderer. **3.** a Muslim. — तुर्क-मिज़ाज, adj. *Pl.* 'of Turkish temperament': ruthless, cruel.

तुर्किन *turkin* [cf. H. *turk*], f. **1.** a Turkish woman, a woman from Turkestan. **2.** a Muslim woman.

तुर्किस्तान *turkistān* [P. *turkistān*], m. **1.** Turkestan, west central Asia. **2.** Turkey.

तुर्की *turkī* [P. *turkī*], adj. & f. m. **1.** adj. Turkish: having to do with Turkestan. **2.** f. the Turkish language. **3.** m. 19c. a horse of central Asian breed. **4.** m. [× Engl. *Turkey*] = तुर्किसतान.

तुर्त *turt*, adv. = तुरंत.

तुर्रा *turrā* [A. *ṭurra*], m. curl: **1.** plume, crest. **2.** an ornament worn on the turban. **3.** fig. the best (of a matter). — ~ यह, कि ..., = next. उसपर, or तिसपर, ~ यह, कि ..., to cap it all; to add insult to injury.

तुर्श *turś* [P. *turś*], adj. **1.** sour, acid. **2.** ill-tempered. — तुर्शमिज़ाज, adj. ill-tempered. तुर्शरूई [P. *-rū*], f. sourness, or sternness of expression; ill-temper.

तुर्शाई *turśāī* [cf. H. *turś*], f. reg. **1.** sourness, acidity. **2.** ill-temper.

तुर्शाना *turśānā* [cf. H. *turś*], v.i. to become sour, acid.

तुर्शी *turśī* [P. *turśī*], f. **1.** sourness, acidity. **2.** ill-temper.

तुल *tul* [*tulya-*], adj. Brbh. = तुल्य.

[1]**तुलना** *tulnā* [*tulayati*], v.i. & v.t. **1.** v.i. to be weighed. **2.** to be balanced against, compared, appraised; to be comparable (with, के साथ). **3.** to be balanced, in equilibrium. **4.** to be suspended. **5.** to be drawn up (as confronting armies). **6.** to be resolved (upon, पर), to be bent (on). **7.** v.t. to weigh, to value, to appraise, &c.

[2]**तुलना** *tulănā* [S.], f. **1.** weighing against, comparison. **2.** equivalence, comparability. — ~ में, adv. in comparison (with, की). – तुलनात्मक [°*nā* + *ā*°], adj. comparative.

तुलनीय *tulănīyă* [S.], adj. comparable.

तुलवाई *tulvāī* [cf. H. *tulvānā*], f. **1.** getting (sthg.) weighed. **2.** price paid for having (sthg.) weighed.

तुलवाना *tulvānā* [cf. H. *tolnā*], v.t. to cause to be weighed, &c. (by, से).

तुलवैया *tulvaiyā* [cf. H. *tulvānā*], m. a weigher.

तुलसी *tulsī* [*tulasī-*], f. the sacred basil plant. — तुलसी-दल, m. a basil leaf. तुलसी-पत्र, m. id. तुलसी-वन, m. a thicket of basil shrubs.

तुला *tulā* [S.], f. **1.** a pair of scales; weighing as a test of guilt or innocence (see तुला-परीक्षा). **2.** the sign Libra (of the zodiac). **3.** a vessel for measuring grain; a measure of grain. — तुला-दंड, m. the beam of a balance. तुला-दान, m. traditional gift (to a brāhmaṇ) of one's body-weight of grain, cloth, &c. तुला-धार, m. & adj. the strings holding the scales of a balance; a merchant; holding a balance. तुला-पत्र, m. a balance sheet. तुला-परीक्षा, f. traditional test or ordeal by weighing (an accused being innocent if his weight at a second weighing, after prayers and ceremonies, is lighter than previously: otherwise guilty). तुला-मान, m. measure of weight; a weight.

[1]**तुलाई** *tulāī* [cf. H. *tulāna*], f. **1.** getting (sthg.) weighed. **2.** price paid for having (sthg.) weighed.

[2]**तुलाई** *tulāī* [cf. *tūla-*], f. Brbh. a light quilt stuffed with cotton.

तुलाना *tulānā* [cf. H. *tulnā*], v.t. to cause to be weighed (by, से), to cause to be valued, appraised.

तुलावा *tulāvā* [cf. H. [1]*tulnā*], m. reg. (Bihar) a strut, or other part of the woodwork transmitting the weight of a cart to its axle.

तुलित *tulit* [S.], adj. weighed.

तुल्य *tulyă* [S.], adj. equal; similar (to); comparable (in weight or significance). — तुल्यकक्ष, adj. of the same type.

तुल्यता *tulyătā* [S.], f. equality; similarity; comparability.

तुवर *tuvar* [*tubarī-*[2]], f. a pulse (= अरहर).

तुष *tuṣ* [S.], m. **1.** husk, chaff. **2.** dry straw.

तुषार *tuṣār* [S.], m. & adj. **1.** m. frost. **2.** snow. **3.** adj. frosty; cold. — तुषार-ऋतु, m. winter. तुषार-गिरि, m. the Himālayas. तुषार-रेखा, f. snow-line. तुषारावृत्त [°*ra* + *ā*°], adj. snow-covered.

तुष्ट *tuṣṭ* [S.], adj. **1.** satisfied, contented. **2.** pleased. — तुष्टीकरण, m. placating, appeasing; appeasement.

तुष्टता *tuṣṭătā* [S.], f. = तुष्टि.

तुष्टि *tuṣṭi* [S.], f. **1.** satisfaction. **2.** pleasure.

तुष्टीकरण *tuṣṭīkaraṇ* [S.], m. see s.v. तुष्ट.

तुस *tus* [*tuṣa-*], m. **1.** husk. **2.** awn (of grain).

तुहिन *tuhin* [S.], m. frost, ice, snow. — तुहिन-कण, m. particles of hoar-frost, &c. तुहिन-गिरि, m. Av. snowy mountain(s); the Himālayas.

तूँ *tūṁ* [cf. *tuvam*], pron. reg. you; thou. — तूं-ताँ करना, to dispute, to squabble; to hurl abuse.

तूँबा *tūṁbā* [*tumba-*¹: ← Austro-as.], m. a hollowed-out gourd; a container for water; a float. (= तुंबा).

तूँबी *tūṁbī* [*tumbikā-*: ← Austro-as.], f. dimin. a small gourd, &c. (see तूँबा).

तू *tū* [*tuvam*], pron. you; thou. (zero hon. grade: emphasises intimacy or informality, or reverence (for a deity); also pej., esp. in the usage of persons employing both *āp* and *tum*). — ~ ~ मैं मैं, f. wrangling, squabbling; mutual abuse. ~ ~ मैं मैं करना, to squabble; to hurl abuse. – तू-तड़ाक, f. rudeness of manner. तू-तड़ाक करना, to squabble; to hurl abuse. तू-तुकार, ? m. 19c. abuse, vituperation. तू-तू करना, id.

तूणीर *tūṇīr* [S]. a quiver.

तूत *tūt* [conn. *tūta-*], m. the mulberry, and its fruit.

तूता *tūtā*, m. reg. = तूतिया.

तूतिया *tūtiyā* [cf. **tūtta-*: ? ← Drav.], m. copper sulphate, blue vitriol.

तूती *tūtī* [P. *ṭūṭī*], f. **1.** esp. U. a parrot, parrakeet. ***2.** any of several small singing birds; the Indian rosefinch, *Carpodacus erythrinus*. ***3.** transf. a flute, pipe. **4.** fig. a sweet or eloquent speaker. — ~ बुलवाना (अपनी), to have (one's) pipe played: to win fame. ~ बोलना, to enjoy good repute or standing; to gain influence, or authority.

तू-तू *tū-tū* [onom.], f. interj. **1.** the call of the *koel*, cuckoo. **2.** a sound made in calling to a dog.

तूदा *tūdā* [P. *tūda*], m. U. heap, pile.

तूना *tūnā* [*trupati*], v.i. reg. to abort (esp. animals).

तूफ़ान *tūfān* [*ṭūfān*], m. **1.** a storm of wind and rain. **2.** a disastrous flood. **3.** fig. a calamity. **4.** fig. storm (of argument); flood (as of abuse, or slander); commotion. — ~ आना (में), a storm to strike, or to blow. ~ उठाना, or करना, to raise a commotion. ~ कड़ा करना, id.; = next. ~ बाँधना, or लेना (पर), to raise a storm: to defame, to slander. बर्फ़ की ~, f. a snow-storm.

तूफ़ानी *tūfānī* [P. *ṭūfānī*], adj. **1.** stormy (weather). **2.** boisterous (as a reception); stormy (as a meeting). **3.** mischief-making; slandering. **4.** stormy, truculent (of temperament). — ~ दस्ता, m. flying squad.

तूमड़ी *tūmṛī* [cf. *tumba-*¹: ← Austro-as.], f. **1.** = तूँबी. **2.** a pipe made from a gourd (used by snake-charmers, jugglers).

तूमना *tūmnā* [*tumbati*], v.t. to pull (as cotton or wool) to pieces, before combing and spinning; to clean (cotton).

तूमार *tūmār* [A. *ṭūmār*], m. a roll, scroll: a long-drawn-out story, rigmarole; palaver. — ~ खड़ा करना, or बाँधना, to make a long story (of); to make much (of little).

तूरान *tūrān* [P. *tūrān*], m. Transoxiania, Turkestan.

तूरानी *tūrānī* [P. *tūrānī*], adj. & m. **1.** adj. having to do with Transoxiania. **2.** m. a Transoxianian: a Turk; a Mongol.

तूर्ण *tūrṇ* [S.], adj. swift.

तूर्य *tūryă* [S.], m. a trumpet.

तूल *tūl* [A. *ṭūl*], m. **1.** length; extent. **2.** prolixity; diffuseness. — ~ पकड़ना, or खींचना, to be drawn out, to continue long (as a matter, or a disease); to extend far. ~ देना (को), to lengthen; to spin out (words, a story; a matter). – तूल-कलाम, m. verbosity. तूल-तवील, adj. U. drawn out (as a story).

¹तूल *tūl* [*tūla-*], m. **1.** cotton; cotton-like fibres (from *semal* and other pods). **2.** bright red cotton cloth. **3.** a red colour (bright, or dark).

²तूल *tūl* [*tulya-*], adj. Brbh. Av. = तुल्य.

तूलि *tūli* [S.], f. = तूली.

तूलिका *tūlikā* [S.], f. a painter's brush.

तूली *tūlī* [*tūlikā-*], f. a painter's brush.

तृतीय *tr̥tīyă* [S.], adj. third. — तृतीयांश [°*ya*+*a*°], m. a third part.

तृतीया *tr̥tīyā* [S.], f. **1.** the third day of a lunar fortnight. **2.** *gram.* instrumental case.

तृन *tr̥n* [S.], m. **1.** grass, herbaceous growth. **2.** a blade of grass; a straw (= तिनका). — ~ गहना, or पकड़ना, fig. to behave abjectly; to cringe; to grovel. ~ तोड़ना, to break off a connection (with, से); to ward off the evil eye (as by breaking a blade of grass). – तृणचर, adj. & m. herbivorous; a herbivorous animal. तृणजंभा, adj. id. तृणमय, adj. grassy; made of grass. तृणवत, adj. grass-like: insignificant, worthless.

तृप्त *tṛpt* [S.], adj. satisfied, sated.

तृप्ति *tṛpti* [S.], f. satisfaction, satiety; gratification.

तृषा *tṛṣā* [S.], f. **1.** thirst. **2.** desire, longing. — तृषातुर [°*ṣā* + *ā*°], adj. tormented by thirst, &c. तृषावंत, adj. Av. thirsty; longing (for).

तृषित *tṛṣit* [S.], adj. **1.** thirsty. **2.** longing (for); agitated.

तृष्णा *tṛṣṇā* [S.], f. **1.** thirst. **2.** desire, longing. — तृष्णाकुल [°*ṇā* + *ā*°], adj. distressed by thirst; tormented by desire. तृष्णार्त [°*ṇā* + *ā*°], adj. id.

तृष्णालु *tṛṣṇālu* [S.], adj. thirsty; filled with desire.

तेंतालीस *temtālīs* [*trayaścatvāriṁśat-*], adj. forty-three.

तेंतीस *temtīs* cf. *trayastriṁśat-*], adj. thirty-three.

तेंदुआ *tenduā*, m. a leopard.

तेंदुई *tenduī*, f. a female leopard.

तेंदू *tendū* [*tainduka-*], m. **1.** a small musk-melon (*Cucurbita moschata*). **2.** a variety of water-melon, *Citrullus var. fistulosus*. **3.** name of trees yielding ebony: *Diospyros melanoxylon* or *D. tomentosa*. **4.** a dense evergreen tree, *Diospyros embryopteris* and its large, resinous fruits (used in dyeing and tanning).

¹ते *te* [*ta-*], pron. pl. Brbh. Av. they; those.

²ते *te*, ppn. E.H. = तैं.

तेइ *tei*, pron. Brbh. = तिहिं, 2.

तेईस *teīs* [cf. *trayoviṁśati-*], adj. twenty-three.

तेकुना *tekunā*, m. reg. (Bihar) a sweet potato (white).

तेखी *tekhī* [cf. *taikṣṇya-*], adj. Brbh. angry.

तेग़ *teg* [P. *teg*], f. **1.** a sword; cutlass. **2.** a dagger.

तेग़ा *tegā* [P. *tega*], m. Brbh. a short sword.

तेज *tej* [ad. *tejas-*], m. **1.** spirit, energy; strength; ardour, fire. **2.** lustre, brilliance; splendour, majesty, dignity; awesomeness. — तेजधारी, adj. possessing energy, &c.: strong, brilliant; splendid. तेज-पत्ता, तेज-पत्र, m. = next. तेज-पात, m. bay-leaf, cassia. तेजमान, adj. = next. तेजवान, adj. energetic; strong; brilliant; splendid; majestic. °-वती, f.

तेज़ *tez* [P. *tez*], adj. **1.** sharp (as a blade); piercing (a glance); keen (sight); loud (voice). **2.** hot, burning; acrid; corrosive. **3.** sharp, spiced; pungent. **4.** bright, striking (colour). **5.** strong, effective (medicine). **6.** fiery, passionate, ardent; angry. **7.** quick, swift; agile; deft. **8.** inconstant, immature (as reactions, emotions). **9.** quick-witted, alert, keen; intelligent. **10.** high (price, rate). — तेज़अक़्ल, adj. of quick intelligence. तेज़क़दम, adj. swift of pace; brisk. तेज़-तर्रार, adj. sharp- or quick-tempered; fiery. तेज़नज़र, adj. sharp-sighted. तेज़निगाह, adj. sharp-sighted. तेज़-बारूद, f. dynamite. तेज़मिज़ाज, adj. quick-tempered. तेज़रफ़्तार, adj. of fast pace, rapid. °ई, f. rapidity. तेज़ाब, m. an acid. °इयत, f. acidity. °ई, adj. acidic; made or treated with acid (as high-carat gold).

तेज- *tej-*, v.t. E.H. = त्यजना.

तेजस् *tejas* [S.], m. esp. in comp. = तेज. — तेजस्कर, adj. irradiating; giving strength, or glory; invigorating. तेजस्करिय, adj. radio-active. °ता, f. radio-activity.

तेजसी *tejasī*, adj. Av. = तेजस्वी.

तेजस्विता *tejasvitā* [S.], f. energy, &c. (cf. तेजस्वी).

तेजस्विनी *tejasvinī* [S.], adj. f. = तेजस्वी.

तेजस्वी *tejasvī* [S.], adj. **1.** energetic, &c. (= तेजवान). **2.** gifted, brilliant.

तेज़ाब *tezāb*, m. see s.v. तेज़.

तेज़ाबी *tezābī*, adj. see s.v. तेज़.

तेज़ी *tezī* [P. *tezī*], f. **1.** sharpness, keenness. **2.** heat, warmth. **3.** sharp taste, spiciness. **4.** brightness (colour). **5.** potency (medicine). **6.** warmth of feeling, passion, ardour; anger. **7.** speed; agility; deftness. **8.** quick-wittedness. **9.** high price. — तेज़ी-मंदी [P. *-mandī*], f. fluctuation (as of price, rate, trade).

तेजो- *tejo-*. = तेजस्: — तेजोमय, adj. consisting of light: brilliant, glorious; ardent. तेजोरूप, adj. & m. whose form is light: consisting only of light; the supreme spirit, *brahman*. तेजोवान, adj. = तेजवान, °वती, f.

तेतिक *tetik*, adj. Brbh. = उतना.

तेतो *teto*, adj. Brbh. = उतना.

तेम *tem* [cf. *ta-*, and *eva*¹: Pk. *jev(v)a*, Ap. *jema*], conj. E.H. = ¹त्यों.

तेरस *teras* [cf. *trayodaśī-*], f. the thirteenth day of a lunar fortnight.

तेरह *terah* [**trayedaśa-*: Pk. *teraha-*], adj. thirteen.

तेरहीं *terahīṁ* [cf. H. *terahvāṁ*], f. the thirteenth day after a death (when the last of the funeral rites are performed, viz. the offering of food to ancestors, and to brāhmaṇs).

तेरही *terăhī* [cf. H. *terah*], adj. having to do with the thirteenth day. — ~ **चाँद**, m. a moon almost full.

तेरा *terā* [cf. *tuvam*], adj. your, thy (zero hon. grade); yours, thine. — **तेरा-मेरा**, m. squabbling, altercation. **तेरा-मेरा करना**, to squabble, to quarrel (over sthg). **तेरी-मेरी**, f. = **तेरा-मेरा**.

तेरिज *terij* [M. *terīj*: w. M. *berīj*, ← P. *barīz*], m. E.H. a summation (of amounts, or items). — **तेरिज-बेरिज** [M. *-berīj*], m. id.

तेल *tel* [*taila-*], m. **1.** vegetable oil (from sesamum, mustard, &c). **2.** mineral oil, petroleum; oil. **3.** petrol. **4.** grease. **5.** transf. a pre-marriage rite (in which the head, shoulders, hands and feet of the bride and groom are anointed with oil mixed with turmeric, some days before the marriage ceremony). **6.** sweat. — ~ **उबटन करना**, = next. ~ **चढ़ाना (पर)**, to anoint with oil (see 5. above). ~ **निकलना**, oil to be extracted (from, **का**); oil or grease to exude (from, **से**); to sweat profusely. ~ **निकालना**, or **पेरना**, to extract oil (from **का**). ~ **मलना**, to rub oil (on, **में**). ~ **में हाथ डालना**, to endure an ordeal (sc. of boiling oil). ~ **लगाना**, to apply oil (to, **में**); to anoint. **आँखों का** ~ **निकालना**, = ~ **निकलना**, 3. **कड़वा** ~, m. mustard oil. **मिट्टी का** ~, m. paraffin, kerosene. – **तेल-कारख़ाना**, m. an oil refinery. **तेल-कुआँ**, m. an oil-well. **तेल-कूप**, m. id. **तेलधारी**, adj. fatty, oily; oil-bearing. **तेल-फुलेल**, m. vegetable oils. **तेल-बीज**, m. oil-seed. **तेल-मालिश**, f. rubbing oil (into the skin), massaging with oil. **तेल-रोग़न**, m. oil paint. **तेल-वाहक**, adj. transporting oil (a vehicle); **तेल-वाहक जहाज़**, an oil tanker. **तेल-शोधन**, m. the refining of oil. **तेल-हँड़ा**, m. an earthenware oil-jar. **°ई** f.

तेलहन *telhan*, m. = **तिलहन**.

तेलाय *telāy* [*tailatāpaka-*], ? m. reg. (Bihar) an earthen vessel for heating oil or *ghī*.

तेलिन *telin* [cf. H. *telī*], f. **1.** an oil-miller's wife. **2.** a woman who prepares oil. **3.** a woman of the Telī community.

तेलिनी *telinī* [ad. *tailinī-*], f. *Pl. HŚS.* a wick.

तेलिया *teliyā* [**tailiya-*: Pk. *teliya-*], adj. & m. **1.** adj. oily. **2.** brownish and glossy; bay-coloured. **3.** having to do with oil-millers. **4.** m. *Pl. HŚS.* a dark glossy colour; a dark bay colour.

तेलिहर *telihar*, m. a partic. small bird (black, with white spots).

तेली *telī* [*tailika-*], m. & adj. **1.** m. an oil-miller; a seller of oil. **2.** a man of the Telī community. **3.** pej. an unclean or dirty person. **4.** having to do with oil; oily. — ~ **का बैल**, m. an oil-miller's ox: a drudging creature. – **तेली-तँबोली**, m. oil-millers and *pān*-sellers: low-caste people.

तेवड़ *tevaṛ*, adj. E.H. triple (as a moat).

तेवड़ी *tevṛī* [*trivṛtā-*], f. *Pl.* the plant *Operculina turpethum* (used as a laxative).

तेवन *tevan* [S.], m. *Pl. HŚS.* play, sport; a pleasure-garden.

तेवर *tevar* [*taimir-*], m. **1.** darkness before the eyes; giddiness, faintness. **2.** peculiar expression of the eyes: look, expression; attitude. **3.** fig. the brow. **4.** fig. anger. — ~ **चढ़ना**, or **तानना**, the brow to be knit (in a frown, or scowl). ~ **चढ़ाना** to knit the brow; to frown. ~ **बदलना**, to change (one's, **का**) expression, or conduct (towards another); to become ill-disposed (to, **के प्रति**, **की ओर**). ~ **बिगड़ना**, id.

तेवराना *tevrānā* [cf. H. *tevar*], v.i. **1.** to feel giddy; to feel faint. **2.** to be knit (the brows).

तेवरी *tevrī*, f. = **त्योरी**.

तेवहार *tevhār*, m. Av. = **त्योहार**.

तेसरी *tesrī* [conn. **triḥsara-*], f. *Pl.* **1.** thrice-ploughed land. **2.** reg. (Bihar) division of a crop into shares of one third to the landlord and two-thirds to the tenant.

तेह *teh* [*tejas-*], m. Brbh. **1.** brilliance (of the sun). **2.** anger, passion. **3.** vehemence: imperiousness, wilful or dogged pride. **4.** *Pl.* steadfastness.

तेहबार *tehbār* [ad. *-vāra*], m. Brbh. = **त्योहार**.

तेहर *tehar* [cf. H. *tehrā*], f. Brbh. a women's belt, or anklet (consisting of three light chains).

तेहरा *tehrā* [*traidha-*, **tridhāra-*], adj. **1.** threefold, treble; folded in three. **2.** triple (in number).

तेहराना *tehrānā* [cf. H. *tehrā*], v.t. **1.** to make threefold; to do (sthg.) three times over; to apply three layers or coats; to apply a third layer. **2.** to make in triplicate.

तेहा *tehā* [*tejas-*], m. = **तेह**, 2.-3.

तैं *taiṁ* [conn. *ta-*: ? **tatena*], ppn. Brbh. Av. = **से**.

[1]**तै** *tai*, m. see **तय**.

[2]**तै** *tai*, adj. pl. m. reg. = **उतना**, **तितना**.

तैतिल *taitil* [S.], m. a partic. auspicious period of the lunar fortnight.

तैनात *taināt* [A. *ta'aiyunāt*, pl.], adj. **1.** appointed, sent on duty. **2.** posted (on watch or duty). — ~ **करना**, to assign to a duty.

तैनाती *taināti* [P. *ta'ināti*], f. posted duty, watch.

तैयार *taiyār* [A. *ṭaiyār*: P. *taiyār*], adj. **1.** ready; prepared, in readiness; alert; available for use. **2.** finished, completed, made; prepared (as food). **3.** fully developed; plump, heavy (as an animal); pubescent; mature; ripe (fruit). **4.** trained, skilled. — ~ **करना**, to make ready, to prepare; to produce; to arrange, to put in order; to train. ~ **बैठना**, to be ready and waiting.

तैयारी *taiyārī* [P. *taiyārī*], f. **1.** readiness. **2.** preparation; preparations. **3.** construction, completion; manufacture; production. **4.** splendour, show.

तैरना *tairnā* [*tirate × pratirati*], v.i. & v.t. **1.** v.i. to swim; to float. **2.** v.t. to swim over or across. — **तैरा हुआ (में)**, adj. familiar (with), versed (in).

तैराई *tairāī* [cf. H. *tairnā, tairānā*], f. **1.** swimming. **2.** swimming over or across.

तैराक *tairāk*, m. a swimmer.

तैराकी *tairākī*, f. swimming.

तैराना *tairānā* [cf. H. *tairnā*], v.t. **1.** to cause to swim. **2.** to cause to float.

तैलंग *tailaṅg* [S.], m. *hist.* the Telinga region (southwards from Orissa to near Madras).

तैलंगा *tailaṅgā*, m. = तिलंगा.

तैलंगी *tailaṅgī*, adj. & m. **1.** adj. having to do with the Telinga region. **2.** m. = तिलंगा, 1.

तैल *tail* [S.], adj. & m. **1.** adj. made from sesame. **2.** m. sesame oil. 3. = तेल. — **तैल-इंजन**, m. a diesel engine. **तैल-जनित**, adj. produced from petroleum. **तैल-पोत**, m. an oil tanker. **तैल-यंत्र**, m. an oil-mill. **तैल-रंग**, m. oil paint. **तैलाक्त** [°*la* + *ā*°], adj. anointed with, redolent of, oil.

तैली *tailī*, m. = तेली.

तैश *taiś* [A. *ṭaiś*], m. **1.** rage. **2.** sulk, huff. — ~ **खाना**, or ~ **में आना**, to become enraged.

तैसा *taisā* [*tādṛśa-*], adj. **1.** of that sort, such. **2.** adv. = तैसे.

तैसे *taise* [cf. H. *taisā*], adv. in that way, so.

तोंद *tomd* [**tonda-*: Pk. *tumda-*], f. a large belly. — ~ **निकलना**, to grow fat.

तोंदल *tomdal* [cf. H. *tomd*], adj. pot-bellied. — **तोंदल-तुंदाला**, adj. = ~.

तोंदी *tomdī*, f. *Pl. HŚS.* the navel.

तोंदीला *tomdīlā* [cf. H. *tomd*], adj. pot-bellied.

तोंदैला *tomdailā* [cf. H. *tomd*], adj. pot-bellied.

तोंबा *tombā*, m. = तूँबा.

तोंबी *tombī*, f. dimin. = तूँबी.

तो *to* [*tatas*: ? × *tāvat*], conj. **1.** (initially in sentence or clause.) then, at that time; in that case. **2.** but, however. **3.** interj. well, now. ~ **मैं क्या कहूँ?** well, what am I to say? **4.** (non-initially: introduces an idea complementing, or at variance in some way with what precedes) in fact, actually, but. **बात ~ यह है कि** ..., the fact is that .... **5.** indeed, certainly, just. **खाओ ~!** please do eat! just eat this! **6.** at any rate, at least, just. **उसे ~ दो पैसे का दूध ~ चाहिए**, but he does need two pice worth of milk. **7.** moreover. — ~ **भी**, conj. even then, even so, yet, still, nevertheless. ~ **वह बोलते ~ सही**, then he would certainly have told you. ~ **सही**, adv. indeed, all right, certainly (more emphatic than ~ used alone). **तुम जाओ ~ सही**, by all means go. **खोलो ~ सही**, please do open (the door). **आप अच्छे ~ हैं?** are you well, all right? (a conventional question.) **नहीं (~)**, conj. otherwise.

तो- *to-* [*tava*], obl. base. Brbh. see तू.

तोई *toī*, f. reg. ornamental lace, edging.

तोखू *tokhū* [ad. *toṣa-*], m. Av. metr. = तोष.

तोड़ *toṛ* [**troṭa-*: Pk. *toḍa-*], m. **1.** m. breaking, a break; fracture; breach; split; cut (as in a dike). **2.** breaking or injuring power: force, velocity (as of current, wind); impact. **3.** check, counter; counter-blow or move; counter-effect; effective rejoinder. **4.** a countering agency, antidote. **5.** whey. **6.** breaking, destroying. **7.** resisting. — **तोड़-जोड़**, m. breaking and joining, dismantling and reassembling; forming altered liaisons; arrangement, construction; contriving, managing; planning; schemes, expedients. (see **जोड़-तोड़**.) **तोड़-ताड़**, m. = next, 1.-5. **तोड़-फोड़**, m. breaking to pieces; fracture; damage, destruction; breaching; demolition; sabotage. **तोड़-मरोड़**, m. breaking and wrenching: tearing to shreds; distorting; misinterpreting.

तोड़ना *toṛnā* [*troṭayati*], v.t. **1.** to break; to snap, to split; to burst; to tear; to sprain. **2.** to break into, to break open (a house, a lock); to break up (ground), to plough. **3.** to destroy, to demolish; to lay waste; to kill (a bird or small animal); to take, to capture (as a fort). **4.** to break, to reduce; to give change for (money); to factorise. **5.** to reduce, to beat down (a price). **6.** to ruin, to disgrace; to bankrupt (a person); to break down (a witness); to humble (pride). **7.** to exhaust; to exercise, to strain (the body); to run off, to drain away (water); to weaken. **हिम्मत ~**, to discourage, to depress. **8.** to break off, to tear off (from, **से**); to gather, to pluck; to pluck or to take out. **9.** to commit (an outrage, offence: against, पर). **10.** to break, to interrupt, to put an end to; to check, to discontinue, to dissolve, to sever (a process or activity, an enterprise, a group, a state, a relationship); to break (a promise). — कमर ~ (की), to break the back (of: also fig.); to render ineffective, to discourage; to alienate (a friend, supporter). दम ~ or तोड़ रहना, to be at the point of death. रोटी ~, euph. to be feckless, idle. – तोड़ना-ताड़ना, = next. तोड़ना-फोड़ना, to break to pieces; to demolish. तोड़ना-मरोड़ना, to break and wrench: to tear to shreds; to distort; to misinterpret.

तोडर *toḍar* [cf. H. *toṛā*], m. Av. a heavy gold or silver anklet.

तोड़वाई *toṛvāī*, f. = तुड़वाई.

तोड़वाना *toṛvānā*, v.t. = तुड़वाना.

[1]**तोड़ा** *toṛā* [**troṭa-*: Pk. *toḍa-*], m. **1.** break, fracture. ***2.** section, part. **3.** a gold or silver bracelet, or neck chain (made up of separate parts). **4.** scarcity, want. **5.** *Pl. HŚS.* bank, bar, island (formed by a current). **6.** *Pl.* mounting (of a ploughshare). **7.** *mus.* name of a *rāg.* **8.** 19c. match (of a firearm). — तोड़ेदार बंदूक़, f. a matchlock.

[2]**तोड़ा** *toṛā* [cf. **toba-*], m. **1.** a purse, money-bag. **2.** fig. pride. — ~ लगाना, to act in a haughty manner.

तोड़ाई *toṛāī*, f. = तुड़ाई.

तोड़ाना *toṛānā*, v.t. = तुड़ाना.

तोड़ी *toṛī* [**troṭikā-*], f. a kind of mustard (distinct from *rāī* and *sarsoṁ*).

तोतला *totlā* [cf. **totta-*[1]], adj. **1.** speaking indistinctly (as a child); lisping. **2.** stammering, stuttering.

तोतलाना *totlānā* [cf. H. *totlā*], v.i. = तुतलाना.

तोतलापन *totlāpan*, m. = तुतलापन.

तोता *totā* [? P. *tota*], m. **1.** a parrot. **2.** colloq. pet, darling. **3.** (from its shape) hammer (of a firearm). — तोता-सा बोलना, to talk sweetly or charmingly. तोते की तरह पढ़ना, to read or to repeat without understanding, to parrot (sthg). तोते की-सी (or की तरह) आँखें फेरना, or बदलना, to turn one's attentions elsewhere: to be faithless; to become indifferent (to). मुँह के तोते उड़ जाना, to be taken aback, speechless. हाथों के तोते उड़ जाना, to be confused, at a loss (what to do). – तोताचश्म, adj. parrot-eyed: faithless, false, treacherous. °ई, f. faithlessness, &c. तोतापंखी, adj. parrot-winged: golden, bright (as light). तोता-मैना, parrot and mynah: a loving but quarrelling pair.

तोती *totī* [cf. H. *totā*], f. a parrot, parrakeet: colloq. dear little girl.

तोप *top* [T. *top*], f. **1.** a field-gun, gun; cannon. **2.** colloq. a very fat person. **3.** sl. big shot. — ~, or तोपें, चलाना, or छोड़ना, or दाग़ना, to fire a gun (as in a barrage: at, पर). ~ के मुँह पर रखना, to place at the muzzle of a cannon: to execute. ~ पर रखना, id. ~ से उड़ाना, to blow from (in front of) a cannon: to execute; to condemn to be shot. तोपें मारना, = तोपें चलाना. बड़ी ~, f. a heavy gun. – तोप-ख़ाना, m. artillery; an artillery battery; an arsenal. तोप-गाड़ी, f. a gun-carriage.

तोपची *topcī* [T.], m. an artilleryman.

तोपना *topnā* [**topyate*], v.t. **1.** to cover over (as with a mound); to conceal. **2.** to fill in (a ditch).

तोपवाना *topvānā* [cf. H. *topnā*], v.t. **1.** to cause to be covered over (by, से). **2.** to cause to be concealed (by).

तोबड़ा *tobṛā* [conn. P. *tobra*], m. nose-bag.

तोबा *tobā* [A. *tauba*], f. & interj. **1.** f. abjuring sin. **2.** interj. good heavens! heaven forbid! — ~ करना, to vow to sin no more; to repent (of, पर or से); to recant. ~ करके कहना, to say in all earnestness, to swear. ~ कराना, to make (one, से) repent; to force (one) to recant. ~ तिल्ला करना, or मचाना, to vow humbly or abjectly not to sin. ~ बुलवाना, to force (one, से) to abjure sin, or to mend (one's) ways. – ~ ~, interj. = ~.

तोम *tom* [ad. *stoma-*[2]], m. Brbh. mass, bulk.

तोमड़ा *tomṛā*, m. = तूँबा.

तोमड़ी *tomṛī*, f. dimin. = तूँबी; = तूमड़ी.

तोमर *tomar* [S.], poet. a lance, javelin.

[1]**तोय** *toy* [S.], m. water. — तोय-कृच्छ्र, m. a penance in which only water is taken for a fixed period (sometimes a month). तोयद, adj. & m. water-giving; a cloud. तोयधर, m. water-holder: a cloud.

[2]**तोय** *toy* [*tava*+Ap. or E.H. *-hi*], obl. pron. Brbh. = तुझे.

तोर *tor* [cf. *tava*], pron. Brbh. Av. your; thy.

तोरण *toraṇ* [S.], m. **1.** an arched gateway. **2.** the ornamented arch of a gateway. **3.** decorations to a gateway (garlands, foliage).

तोरा *torā* [cf. *tava*], pron. reg. = तोर.

[1]**तोरी** *torī*, f. = [1]तुरई.

[2]**तोरी** *torī*, f. reg. (Bihar) an oil-seed crop (= [1]तोड़ी).

तोल *tol*, m. = तौल.

तोलना *tolnā* [*tolayati*], v.t. = तौलना.

तोला *tolā* [*tolaka-*], m. **1.** a measurement of twelve *māśās* (about 13g). **2.** a weight, of one *tolā*.

तोल्य *tolyă* [S.], adj. & m. *HŚS*. **1.** adj. to be weighed. **2.** m. weighing.

तोशक *tośak* [P. *tośak*], f. (m., *Pl.*) **1.** bedding; a quilt; mattress. **2.** effects (personal). — तोशक-ख़ाना, m. = तोशा-ख़ाना, see s.v. तोशा.

तोशदान *tośdān* [cf. P. *tośa*], m. **1.** a pouch, bag (as for provisions). **2.** [Engl. *cartouche* ← F.] a container for cartridges.

तोशा *tośā* [P. *tośa*], m. **1.** provisions for a journey. **2.** simple food. — तोशा-ख़ाना, m. 19c. a storeroom (for furniture and effects).

तोष *toṣ* [S.], m. **1.** satisfaction. **2.** gratification. **3.** happiness, contentment.

तोष- *toṣ-* [cf. *toṣayati*], v.t. to satisfy; to please.

तोषक *toṣak* [S.], adj. & m. **1.** adj. satisfying. **2.** gratifying. **3.** m. one who causes satisfaction, &c.

तोषण *toṣaṇ* [S.], adj. & m. **1.** adj. = तोषक. **2.** m. satisfying. **3.** satisfaction; gratification.

तोषित *toṣit* [S.], adj. **1.** satisfied; contented. **2.** gratified.

तोषी *toṣī* [S.], adj. & m. **1.** adj. satisfied, &c. (with, by). 2. = तोषक. **3.** m. a contented person, &c. 4. = तोषक.

तोहफ़ा *tohfā* [A. *tohfa*], m. a gift, a present.

तोहमत *tohmat* [A. *tuhma*: P. *tŏhmat*], f. **1.** false accusation. **2.** calumny, slander. — ~ करना, or देना, or धरना, or मढ़ना, or लगाना (पर), to accuse falsely, &c.

तोहमती *tohmatī* [A. *tuhma*+P. *-ī*], adj. & m. **1.** adj. slanderous. **2.** m. a false accuser. **3.** a slanderer.

¹तौं *tauṁ*, adv. Brbh. = ¹त्यों.

²तौं *tauṁ*, adv. Brbh. = तो.

तौंस- *tauṁs-* [*tapasyati*; ? ← Panj. *tauṁsṇā*], v.i. E.H. to be overcome by the sun's heat.

तौक़ *tauq* [A. *ṭauq*], m. **1.** neck-ring; metal collar. **2.** yoke (of subservience).

तौन *taun* [*ta-*; and H. *kaun*: anal.], pron. reg. = ¹सो.

तौबा *taubā*, f. = तोबा.

तौर *taur* [A. *ṭaur*], m. **1.** manner, way. **2.** state, condition. **3.** demeanour. — आम ~ पर, or से, adv. generally, usually. ठीक ~ से, adv. properly. मनमाने ~ पर, adv. wilfully; idiosyncratically. मोटे ~ पर, adv. roughly, approximately. – तौर-तरीक़ा, m. practice; method; manner, approach. तौर-बेतौर होना [P. *be-*], to be in a bad state; to be at death's door; to be badly treated.

तौफ़ीक़ *taufīq* [A. *taufīq*], f. making convenient: means, power; chance (to do sthg).

तौल *taul* [cf. H. *taulnā*], f. **1.** weighing. **2.** weight. — तौल-ताल, m. weighing and measuring, weighing out.

तौलना *taulnā* [conn. *tolayati*], v.t. **1.** to weigh. **2.** to balance, to compare. **3.** to assess, to gauge; to ponder (a matter); to weigh (words). **4.** to poise (a weapon, in preparing to strike or shoot). — तौल-तौलकर, adv. prudently, with an eye to the consequences.

तौलवाई *taulvāī*, f. = तौलाई, 2., 3.

तौलवाना *taulvānā* [cf. H. *taulnā*], v.t. to cause to be weighed (by, से).

तौला *taulā*, m. a small copper or earthen vessel (for measuring out liquids).

तौलाई *taulāī* [cf. H. *taulnā*, *taulānā*], f. **1.** weighing. **2.** getting (sthg.) weighed. **3.** cost of, or charge for, having (sthg.) weighed.

तौलाना *taulānā* [cf. H. *taulnā*], v.t. to cause to be weighed (by, से).

तौलिया *tauliyā* [Engl. *towel*], m. a towel.

तौली *taulī*, f. dimin. **1.** reg. (Bihar) a metal cooking-pot. **2.** an earthenware measuring cup (used in filling a storage container).

तौलैया *taulaiyā* [cf. H. *taulnā*], m. a weigher of grain.

तौल्य *taulyă* [S.], m. **1.** a weight. **2.** comparability, equivalence.

तौसन *tausan* [P. *tausan*], m. 19c. a young unbroken horse; a steed, charger.

तौहीन *tauhīn* [A. *tauhīn*], f. dishonour, disgrace.

त्यक्त *tyakt* [S.], adj. **1.** left, relinquished. **2.** abandoned. **3.** resigned, renounced; discarded.

त्यजना *tyajnā* [ad. *tyajati*], v.t. to leave, to abandon (= तजना, त्याग करना).

त्याग *tyāg* [S.], m. **1.** leaving, relinquishing. **2.** abandoning. **3.** renouncing; resignation; abdication. **4.** separation; divorce. — ~ करना, to give up; to abandon; to renounce (someone or sthg., का). ~ देना (को), to dismiss, = ~ करना.

– त्याग-पत्र, m. a letter of resignation, or dismissal; writ of divorce. त्यागशील, adj. self-denying; liberal, generous. °ता, f. self-abnegation; liberality.

त्यागना *tyāgnā* [ad. *tyāga-*: w. H. *tyāg*], v.t. = त्याग करना.

त्यागी *tyāgī* [S.], adj. & m. **1.** adj. abandoning, renouncing (as worldly life); self-denying. **2.** m. an ascetic.

त्याज्य *tyājyă* [S.], adj. to be given up, or abandoned; needful of being given up; capable of being given up.

[1]**त्यों** *tyoṁ* [conn. Ap. *tima*], adv. **1.** in the same way, thus, so. **2.** at the same time. — त्योंही, adv. just so; just then.

[2]**त्यों** *tyoṁ*, ppn. Brbh. ? towards (= [1]तईं).

त्योरस *tyoras*, m. the third year distant: the year before last; the year after next.

त्योरी *tyorī* [cf. H. *tevar*], f. **1.** peculiar expression of the eyes. **2.** fig. the brow (as contracted in a frown, or scowl). — ~ चढ़ना, the brow to be knit: to frown, to scowl. ~ चढ़ाना, to knit the brow, &c.; to glance angrily. ~ बदलना, id. ~ में बल पड़ना, = ~ चढ़ना.

त्योहार *tyohār* [**tithivāra-*], m. a festival.

त्योहारी *tyohārī* [cf. H. *tyohār*], f. **1.** a gift of money, or other present, given on the occasion of a festival. **2.** a meal, or food, given on such an occasion.

त्यौं *tyauṁ*, adv. = [1]त्यों.

त्यौनार *tyaunār*, m. Brbh. means, manner.

त्यौहार *tyauhar*, m. = त्योहार.

त्रपा *trapā* [S.], f. Brbh. shame.

त्रय *tray* [S.], adj. & m. **1.** adj. in comp. triple, threefold. **2.** m. a group of three, triad.

त्रयी *trayī* [S.], f. a group of three, a triad. — त्रयी-धर्म, m. the duties, forms of sacrifice, &c. laid down by the three Vedas.

त्रयोदश *trayodaś* [S.], adj. thirteenth.

त्रयोदशी *trayodăśī* [S.], f. the thirteenth day of a lunar fortnight.

त्रस्त *trast* [S.], adj. **1.** frightened, fearful. **2.** distressed, perturbed.

त्राण *trāṇ* [S.], m. **1.** protection; defence; shelter; armour. **2.** help. **3.** safety, deliverance. — ~ करना (का), to protect; to save. – त्राण-कर्ता, m. inv. a protector; deliverer, saviour.

त्राणक *trāṇak* [S.], adj. & m. **1.** adj. protecting. **2.** m. = त्राण-कर्ता.

त्राणी *trāṇī* [S.], adj. & m. = त्राणक.

त्राता *trātā* [S.], adj. & m. inv. **1.** adj. protecting. **2.** rescuing. **3.** m. a protector. **4.** a saviour.

त्रायन *trāyan* [cf. H. *tirānā*], ? f. E.H. crossing over (the ocean of existence).

त्रास *trās* [S.], m. **1.** fear, dread; alarm. **2.** distress, suffering.

त्रास- *trās-*, v.t. Brbh. Av. see तरास-.

त्रासक *trāsak* [S.], adj. & m. **1.** adj. causing fear, &c. **2.** destroying, removing (as the suffering of existence). **3.** m. one causing fear, &c.

त्रासदिक *trāsadik* [cf. H. *trāsadī*], adj. tragic.

त्रासदी *trāsadī* [f. Engl. *tragedy*], f. a tragedy.

त्रासन *trāsan* [S.], m. **1.** causing dread, alarm or distress (to). **2.** a cause of dread, &c. (to).

त्रासित *trāsit* [S.], adj. **1.** frightened, fearful; alarmed. **2.** suffering distress, or affliction.

त्रासी *trāsī* [S.], adj. & m. **1.** adj. fearful, timid. **2.** m. a fearful person.

त्राह *trāh*, exclam. = त्राहि.

त्राहि *trāhi* [S.], exclam. help! save (me, us)! — ~ ~ करना, or मचाना, to call repeatedly for help, or for mercy. ~ माम [S. *mām*]! save me!

त्रिंश *triṁś* [S.], adj. thirtieth.

त्रिंशत् *triṁśat* [S.], adj. thirty.

त्रि- *tri-* [S.], adj. & n. formant. three; triple, treble: — त्रिकाल, m. the three times or tenses: past, present and future; morning, noon and evening. °-ज्ञ, adj. omniscient. °-ज्ञता, f. omniscience. °-दर्शी, adj. seeing the three times: omniscient. त्रिकूट, adj. & m. having three peaks; such a mountain; *mythol.* name of several mountains, esp. that on which Laṅkā was situated. त्रिकोण, adj. & m. triangular; a triangle. °-घंटा, m. *mus.* a triangle. °-मिति, f. trigonometry. त्रिजग, त्रिजगत, m. = त्रिभुवन. त्रिदंडी, m. a *saṃnyāsī* who carries three long bamboo staves tied together; one who has control over his words, thoughts and actions. त्रिदल, m. a trefoil; a tripartite group. °ई, adj. tripartite. °ईय, adj. id. त्रिदश, adj. & m. thirty; Brbh. a deity (one of thirty, i.e. of the thirty-three deities excluding Brahmā, Viṣṇu and Śiva). त्रिदोष, m. Brbh. a triple disorder of bile, blood and phlegm. त्रिधा, adj. inv. triple; in three forms, or ways. त्रिदेव, m. triple deity: the gods Brahmā, Viṣṇu and Śiva. त्रिनयन, adj. & m. = त्रिलोचन. त्रिपट्ट, m. poet. three lines (on the forehead). त्रिपथ, m. an intersection of three roads; three paths or ways (as of the world and the regions above and below, or of action, knowledge and devotion). °आ, °गा, f. the Ganges. त्रिपद, adj. & m. three-footed; *math.* trinomial; a tripod; *HŚS.* a three-legged stool, table. °आ, f. the Gāyatrī verse of the Ṛgveda. त्रिपाठी, m. a brāhmaṇ who studies three Vedas; name of a brāhmaṇ community. त्रिपाद, adj. three-footed. त्रिपुंड, m. a set of three horizonal lines on the forehead, made with cow-dung ash, sandal, &c. by devotees of Śiva. °-पुंड्र, m. id. त्रिपौलिया, m. = तिर-°: see s.v. त्रिफला, m. a medicine used for eye complaints, made up of the three myrobalans *āṁvlā, baheṛā* and *haṛ.* त्रिबली, f. Brbh. three folds of skin (regarded as auspicious) over the navel. त्रिभंग, adj. & m. having three angles or bends; of angular posture (as Kṛṣṇa depicted playing the flute, with bent legs, hips and neck); one standing in such a posture. °ई, adj. & m. = prec. त्रिभुज, adj. & m. having three arms, or sides; a triangle. त्रिभुवन, m. the three worlds (heaven, earth and the lower regions); the universe. त्रिभुवन-नाथ, m. lord of the three worlds: a title of Viṣṇu. त्रिमात्रिक, adj. & m. *pros.* lengthened to the value of three *mātrās* or instants; a vowel so lengthened. त्रिमुकुट, adj. having three peaks (= त्रिकूट). त्रिमुख, m. having three faces, or mouths. त्रिमूर्ति, f. the triad of deities Brahmā, Viṣṇu and Śiva. त्रिमुहानी, f. = तिरमुहानी. त्रिरात्रि, f. the space of three successive nights. त्रिलोचन, adj. & m. three-eyed; a title of Śiva. त्रिलोक, m. the three worlds: sky, atmosphere and earth; heaven, earth and the lower regions; the universe. °-नाथ, m. lord of the three worlds: the title of several deities, incl. Rām, Kṛṣṇa and Viṣṇu. °पति, m. id. °ई-नाथ, m. = त्रिलोक-नाथ: a title of Viṣṇu. त्रिवर्ग, m. three things forming a class (e.g. the three goals of human life, viz. *dharm, arth* and *kām*, or the brāhmaṇ, kṣatriya and vaiśya community groups). त्रिविध, adj. of three kinds; threefold; in three ways. त्रिविध ताप, m. Av. threefold suffering (bodily, caused by fate, or by contact with the world). त्रिवेद, m. the three Vedas (*Ṛg, Yajus* and *Sāman*). °ई, m. one schooled in the three Vedas; name of a brāhmaṇ community. त्रिवेणी, f. *mythol.* triple-braid: the confluence at Allahabad of Ganges and Jumna with a subterranean river, called Sarasvatī. त्रिशिर, adj. & m. three-headed; *mythol.* name of a *rākṣas* killed by Rām; name of an *asur* killed by Viṣṇu. °आ, m. inv. id. त्रिशूल, m. a trident, esp. that of Śiva. °-धारी, m. the trident-bearer: title of Śiva. त्रिसंध्या, f. the three divisions of the day: early morning, noon, and evening or sunset. त्रिसूल, m. = त्रिशूल.

त्रिक *trik* [S.], adj. & m. **1.** adj. threefold. **2.** m. a triad.

त्रिकुटा *trikuṭā* [conn. *trikaṭu(ka)*-], m. *Pl. HŚS.* a mixture of three spices or ingredients, including ginger and pepper.

त्रिकुटी *trikuṭī* [S.], f. E.H. (in yoga.) ? a higher *cakra* situated at the level of the eyebrow (cf. *viśuddha cakra*).

त्रिगण *trigaṇ*, m. = त्रिवर्ग.

त्रिगुण *triguṇ*, m. & adj. *philos.* **1.** the three *guṇas*, qualities or constituents of nature (*prakṛti*), viz. *sattva, rajas* and *tamas*. **2.** adj. possessing the three *guṇas*; threefold. — त्रिगुणात्मक [°*ṇa*+*ā*°], adj. = ~.

त्रिगुणी *triguṇī* [S.], adj. = त्रिगुण.

त्रिज्या *trijyā* [S.], f. a radius.

त्रिपाठी *tripāṭhī* [S.], m. see s.v. त्रि-.

त्रिभंगी *tribhaṅgī* [S.], adj. & m. see s.v. त्रि-.

त्रिमूर्ति *trimūrti* [S.], f. see s.v. त्रि-.

त्रिया *triyā* [cf. *strī*-; ← Panj.], f. reg. = स्त्री

त्रिलोक *trilok* [S.], m. see s.v. त्रि-.

त्रिवर्ग *trivarg* [S.], m. see s.v. त्रि.

त्रिविध *trividh* [S.], adj. see s.v. त्रि-.

त्रिवेणी *triveṇī* [S.], f. see s.v. त्रि-.

त्रिवेदी *trivedī* [S.], m. see s.v. त्रि-.

त्रिशूल *triśūl* [S.], m. see s.v. त्रि-.

-त्री *-trī* [S.], suffix (forms feminines for m. nouns formed with *-tā*, e.g. अभिनेत्री, actress).

त्रुटि *truṭi* [S.], f. **1.** a defect. **2.** an error, mistake; misprint.

त्रेता *tretā* [S.], m. inv. *mythol.* the second of the four ages of progressive decline through which the world is considered to pass within each aeon (*kalpa*). — त्रेता-युग, m. the *tretā* age.

त्रै- *trai-* [S.], adj. formant. three, tri-: — त्रैवार्षिक, adj. triennial.

त्रोटक *troṭak* [S.], m. **1.** a type of drama, in which the hero (*nāyaka*) is a celestial being. **2.** *mus.* a name of a *rāg*.

-त्व *-tvă* [S.], suffix (forms m. abstract nouns from nouns and adjectives, e.g. पुरुषत्व, manliness; उत्तरदायित्व, responsibility).

त्वक्- *tvak-* [S.], m. **1.** the skin (= त्वचा). **2.** touch.

त्वचा *tvacā* [S.], f. **1.** skin. **2.** bark. **3.** rind, peel.

त्वरा *tvarā* [S.], f. **1.** speed. **2.** haste. — त्वरालिपि, f. shorthand.

त्वरित *tvarit* [S.], adj. **1.** speedy, quick. **2.** hasty.

त्वष्टा *tvaṣṭā* [S.], m. inv. *mythol.* carpenter, builder: a deity, the artificer of the gods.

थ

थ *tha*, the seventeenth consonant of the Devanāgarī syllabary. — **थकर**, m. the sound /th/; the letter **थ**.

थंब *thamb*, m. pronun. var. = **थंभ**.

थंभ *thambh* [*stambha*-], m. **1.** a pillar. **2.** a prop, support.

थँभना *thaṁbhnā* [cf. H. *thāṁbhnā*], v.i. reg. (W.) = **थमना**.

थँभाना *thaṁbhānā* [cf. H. *thāṁbhnā*], v.t. reg. (W.) to cause to be held, &c.

थई *thaī* [*stṛti*-], f. *Pl.* a mass, heap, pile.

थकन *thakan*, f. *HŚS.* growing tired (= **थकान**).

थकना *thaknā* [**sthakk*-: Pk. *thakkaï*], v.i. **1.** to tire; to be fatigued; to be exhausted. **2.** to grow weak; to flag. **3.** to be inert, sluggish. **4.** Brbh. to stop, to remain, to be still (as wind, or the moon in its course). — **थका-माँदा** [P. *-mānda*], adj. tired, tired out, &c. **थका-हारा**, adj. exhausted (by, **का**); dejected, disenchanted (with, **का**).

थकान *thakān* [cf. H. *thaknā*], f. **1.** tiredness, fatigue; exhaustion. **2.** lassitude.

थकाना *thakānā* [cf. H. *thaknā*], v.t. **1.** to tire, to fatigue; to exhaust. **2.** to harass.

थकावट *thakāvaṭ*, f. = **थकान**.

थकाहट *thakāhaṭ*, f. = **थकान**.

थकित *thakit* [cf. H. *thaknā*; ? ad. *sthagita*-], adj. tired, &c.

थक्का *thakkā*, adj. & m. **1.** adj. congealed, clotted (as curd); thick. **2.** m. a mass, lump; clod; clot. **3.** an ingot.

थन *than* [*stana*-], m. **1.** udder. **2.** teat. — **थनदार** [P. *-dār*], having an udder, a large udder; in milk.

थनी *thanī* [cf. H. *than*], f. *Pl. HŚS.* a fleshy growth (as found on the necks of goats).

थनेला *thanelā* [**stanapiḍaka*- or **stanakīla*-], m. reg. **1.** inflamed breast (of a woman); inflamed udder. **2.** a swelling or abscess in the breast.

थनैत *thanait* [cf. H. *thān*], m. reg. (E.) resident headman (of a village); landlord's agent, or manager.

थपक *thapak* [cf. H. *thapaknā*], f. a pat, a tap.

थपकना *thapaknā* [cf. H. [1]*thāpnā*], v.t. **1.** to pat, to tap; to caress. **2.** to soothe.

थपकी *thapkī* [cf. H. *thapaknā*], f. a pat.

थपड़ी *thapṛī* [cf. **thapp*-], f. *Pl. HŚS.* clapping of hands.

थपथपाना *thapthapānā*, v.t. = **थपकना**.

थपना *thapnā* [cf. H. [1]*thāpnā*], v.i. to be patted; to be patted into the shape of a cake.

थपनो *thapno* [cf. H. [2]*thāpnā*, v.t.], m. Brbh. fixed place, firm refuge.

थपेड़ा *thapeṛā* [cf. **thapp*-], m. **1.** slap, blow. **2.** buffet, impact (as of waves, wind).

थप्पड़ *thappaṛ* [cf. **thapp*-], m. a slap, blow. — ~ **मारना**, or **देना** (**पर**), to slap; to strike, to strike (at).

थमना *thamnā* [cf. H. *thāmnā*], v.i. **1.** to stand still, to stop; to be still, quiet. **2.** to cease. **3.** to be restrained, held in check (as the emotions). **4.** to be held, kept (in the hand). **5.** to be supported, to rest; to recover oneself (as after stumbling).

थमाना *thamānā* [cf. H. *thāmnā*], v.t. **1.** to cause to be stopped, &c. (by, **से**); to stop. **2.** to hand (sthg.) over. — **उत्तर** ~, colloq. to come out with a forthright answer.

[1]**थर** *thar* [*stara*-], m. reg. a layer.

[2]**थर** *thar*, m. Brbh. = **थल**.

थर-थर *thar-thar* [cf. H. *thartharānā*], adj. & f. (m., *Pl.*) **1.** adj. shaking, trembling. **2.** m. trembling (from fear). — ~ **करना**, or **काँपना**, to tremble.

थरथराना *thartharānā* [cf. *tharatharāyamāna*-], v.i. **1.** to shake, to tremble (with fear). **2.** to tremble, to quiver.

थरथराहट *thartharāhaṭ* [cf. H. *thartharānā*], f. trembling (from fear).

थरथराहा *thartharāhā* [cf. H. *thartharānā*], adj. trembling (with fear).

थरथरी *tharthari* [cf. H. *tharthar*], f. **1.** *Pl. HŚS.* = **थर-थर**. **2.** *Pl. HŚS.* fit of shivering.

थरहर- *tharhar*-, v.i. Brbh. = **थरथराना**.

थर्राना *tharrānā* [cf. *tharatharāyamāna-*], v.i. to shake, to tremble (with fear).

थल *thal* [*sthala-*], m. **1.** dry ground; land (as opposed to water). **2.** place, site. **3.** *Pl. HŚS.* lair (as of a tiger). — **थलचर**, adj. & m. moving on land, terrestrial; a land animal. °-**चारी**, adj. & m. id. **थलज**, adj. Brbh. land-born: living on land. **थल-पति**, m. a king. **थल-बेड़ा**, m. a mooring-place; wharf. **थल-सेना**, f. an army, land forces.

थलकना *thalaknā* [cf. **thal-*], v.i. **1.** to hang loosely, to shake, to quiver (= **थलथलाना**). **2.** to tremble, to throb.

थलथल *thalthal* [cf. **thal-*], adj. & f. **1.** adj. shaking: flabby (flesh). **2.** shakiness, quivering: flabbiness. — **~ करना**, to shake, to quiver.

थलथलाना *thalthalānā* [cf. H. *thalthal*], v.i. **1.** to become loose or flabby. **2.** to shake, to quiver (as a jelly).

थवई *thavaī* [*sthapati-*], m. reg. a mason, or carpenter.

थसथसाना *thasthasānā*, v.i. to become slow or sluggish.

थहराना *thahrānā*, v.i. = **थरथराना**.

थाँग *thāṁg* [**sthāghya-*: Pk. *thagghā-*], f. Brbh. exact place (of sthg. lost or sought): **1.** trace, track (of stolen property). **2.** *Pl. HŚS.* hiding-place (of thieves).

थाँगी *thāṁgī* [cf. H. *thāṁg*], m. *Pl. HŚS.* an informant (about a theft).

थाँभ- *thāṁbh-*, v.t. Av. = **थामना**.

थाँवला *thāṁvlā* [? *sthāla-* × *sthāman-*], m. = **थाला**.

था *thā* [cf. *sthita-*], v.i. imperf. was.

थाक *thāk* [cf. **sthagha-*: Pk. *thaha-*], m. **1.** reg. (Bihar) a heap, pile (as of grain). **2.** a boundary pillar.

थाक- *thāk-*, v.i. Brbh. = **थकना**.

थाती *thātī* [**sthāpti-*: Pk. *thattia-*], f. **1.** a pledge, sthg. promised. **2.** a pledge, sthg. given in trust.

थान *thān* [*sthāna-*], m. **1.** place, locality; site. **2.** abode. **3.** stable, stall, manger. **4.** breed (of animals); stock. **5.** piece, bolt (of cloth); reg. unit, item.

थानक *thānak* [ad. *sthānaka-*], m. reg. position, place.

थाना *thānā* [*sthānaka-*], m. 1. = **थान**, 1., 2. **2.** a police station, or post. — **थानेदार** [P. *-dār*], m. a police sergeant, superintendent of a police station or post. °**ई**, f. & adj. the position or rank of *thānedār*; having to do with the position of *thānedār*.

थानी *thānī* [cf. H. *thān*], m. E.H. a householder.

थाप *thāp* [cf. H. *thāpnā*], f. **1.** a pat, slap, blow. **2.** sound of a drum struck with the palm of the hand. **3.** authority, power; prestige. — **~ देना**, to pat, to slap, &c. **~ मारना**, to slap, &c.; to beat (a drum); to pat into cakes (cow-dung, to plaster a wall); to attack suddenly.

[1]**थापना** *thāpnā* [**thapp-*], v.t. **1.** to pat, to tap, to beat. **2.** to pat (cow-dung) into cakes (for fuel). **3.** to plaster (cow-dung, on a wall). **4.** to imprint, to stamp (as a palm-mark on a house wall, see **थाप**, or as an owner's mark on produce).

[2]**थापना** *thāpnā* [*sthāpyate*], v.t. to set up, to set in place; to erect (an idol, &c).

[3]**थापना** *thāpnā* [ad. *sthāpanā-*], f. setting up, erecting (as of an idol).

थापा *thāpā* [cf. H. *thāpnā*], m. **1.** mark, impression, stamp; distinguishing mark. **2.** mark made by the palm (dyed with henna, &c.) on the wall of a house (as on an auspicious occasion, or to mark the house out for robbery). **3.** a stamp (instrument). **4.** a pug mark. — **~ देना**, or **लगाना (पर)**, to mark with the hand; to mark.

थापी *thāpī* [cf. H. *thāpnā*], f. a wooden instrument for patting or beating (as used by potters, plasterers, stonemasons).

थाम *thām* [*stambha-*], m. a pillar.

थामना *thāmnā* [*stambhate*], v.t. **1.** to stop, to check; to restrain. **2.** to clutch, to seize. **3.** to prop, to support; to maintain; to assist. **4.** to undertake, to assume (a task, a burden).

थाल *thāl* [*sthāla-*], m. a large flat metal plate or dish, a tray.

थाला *thālā* [*sthāla-*], m. **1.** a trench dug round the base of a tree to hold water. **2.** a hole in the ground in which a tree is to be planted.

थाली *thālī* [cf. *sthālī-*], f. **1.** a flat metal plate or dish; platter. **2.** transf. present of sweets, fruits, &c. (made by relatives or friends on festive occasions). — **~ का बैंगन**, m. egg-plant on a tray: one whose opinions follow his self-interest. **~ बजाना**, to strike a *thālī*: to rejoice at the birth of a son; to work a charm against snake-bite.

थावर *thāvar* [*sthāvara-*], m. Brbh. stationary, immovable: any inanimate object. — **थावर-जंगम**, m. things inanimate and animate, all existent things.

थावस *thāvas*, f. reg. (Raj.) firmness, endurance, patience.

थाह *thāh* [*sthāgha-*, Pk. *thāgha-*], f. **1.** bottom; fig. limit (as of wealth). **2.** shallow water. **3.** depth; fig. innermost thoughts or feelings. — ~ लेना, or लगाना, to gauge the depth (of, की); to plumb, to assess (a matter, a person's attitude).

थाहना *thāhnā* [cf. H. *thāh*], v.t. to sound, to plumb.

थिगला *thiglā*, m. = थिगली.

थिगली *thiglī* [cf. **thigg-*: Pk. *thiggala-*], f. a patch. — ~ लगाना (में), to patch.

थिति *thiti* [cf. *sthiti-*], f. Av. stability, permanence.

थिर *thir* [*sthira-*], adj. **1.** fixed, firm. **2.** permanent, durable; settled. **3.** calm (as water, weather, temperament); equable.

थिरकना *thiraknā* [cf. *sthira-*], v.i. to move or to dance in a delicate or expressive manner; to mince; to hop or to walk (a bird); to flit (as shadows); to beat or to tap (the feet, in time to music).

थिरता *thirtā*, f. = स्थिरता.

थिरना *thirnā* [cf. *sthira-*], v.i. **1.** to grow calm or still (as water); to clear (liquid). **2.** to settle, to be precipitated (from a liquid).

थिराना *thirānā*, v.i. & v.t. **1.** v.t. to calm, to make calm or still (as water); to cause to clear (liquid). **2.** to precipitate (from a liquid). **3.** v.i. to grow calm.

थीकरा *thīkrā*, m. *Pl. HŚS.* ?? = ठीकर.

थुकाई *thukāī* [cf. H. *thūknā*], f. spitting.

थुकाना *thukānā* [cf. H. *thūknā*], v.t. **1.** to cause to spit. **2.** to cause (oneself) to be dishonoured, shamed, or disgraced.

थुक्कम-थुक्का *thukkam-thukkā*, m. see s.v. थुक्का.

थुक्का *thukkā* [cf. **thukk-*: Pk. *thukka-*], m. chiefly in comp. spittle. — थुक्का-फ़ज़ीहत, f. disgrace, a disgraceful matter; deplorable abuse, or quarrelling. °ई, f. id. थुक्कम-थुक्का, m. mutual reviling.

थुड़ी *thuṛī* [cf. *thūt*], f. & interj. **1.** f. spitting (at, पर; dishonour, shame; disgrace. **2.** interj. shame! — ~ ~ होना, to be dishonoured, &c.

थुत्कार *thutkār* [cf. H. *thut(h)kārnā*], f. = थुत्कारा.

थुत्कारा *thutkārā* [cf. *thūt*], m. the sound of spitting.

थुथकारना *thuthkārnā* [cf. *thukk-*, *thūt*], v.i. **1.** to spit; to splutter. **2.** to spit (at): to feel disgust or contempt (for, पर); to drive away scornfully.

थुथड़ा *thuthṛā* [cf. **thuttha-*], m. = थूथन.

थुथनी *thuthnī*, f. snout, muzzle.

थुथाना *thuthānā* [cf. **thuttha-*], v.t. to contort (the face, features). — मुँह ~, to grimace.

थुथारना *thuthārnā*, v.i. pronun. var. = थुथकारना.

थुनी *thunī*, f. Brbh. metr. = थूनी.

थुलमा *thulmā* [cf. *sthūla-*], m. reg. a kind of woollen cloth, or blanket.

थुरहथ- *thurhath-* [H. *thoṛā*+H. *hāth*], adj. Brbh. having small hands.

थुलथुल *thulthul* [cf. **thal-*, **thur-*], adj. = थलथल.

थूँबा *thūm̐bā*, m. *Pl.* a lump of earth or clay (used as a counterpoise).

थू *thū* [*thūt*], f. & interj. **1.** f. the sound of spitting. **2.** interj. shame! (= थुड़ी). — ~ ~ करना, to be always spitting; to spit (at, पर); to jeer (at). ~ ~ होना, to be jeered (at); to be scorned, &c.; = थुड़ी थुड़ी होना.

थूअड़ *thūaṛ*, m. reg. = थूहर.

थूअर *thūar*, m. reg. = थूहर.

थूक *thūk* [**thukk-*: Pk. *thukka-*], m. spittle; saliva.

थूकना *thūknā* [**thukk-*: Pk. *thukkaï*], v.i. & v.t. **1.** v.i. to spit (at, पर). **2.** to treat with contempt; to vilify. **3.** v.t. to spit out. **4.** to reject (as in disgust). — थूककर चाटना, fig. to eat (one's words); to retract (a promise); to break (a promise).

थूथन *thūthan* [cf. **thuttha-*], m. **1.** muzzle, snout. **2.** pej. ugly face, mug. — ~ फुलाना, to pout; to grimace.

थूथनी *thūthnī*, f. = थूथन.

थून *thūn*, m. E.H. = थूनी.

थूनिया *thūniyā*, f. dimin. = थूनी.

थूनी *thūnī* [*sthūṇa-*], f. **1.** a post, pillar. **2.** prop, vertical support (as for a roof, or the axle of a water-lever); upright at a well-mouth (supporting the windlass).

थूरना *thūrnā*, v.t. **1.** Brbh. to strike, to beat, to pound. **2.** colloq. to cram in (food).

थूवा *thūvā* [*stūpa-*], m. **1.** a heap, mound; mound of earth or clay (used to mark a field boundary). **2.** large clod or lump (of earth or clay).

थूहर *thūhar*, m. **1.** a spurgewort (*Euphorbia*: = सेहुँड़). **2.** a prickly spurgewort.

थूहा *thūhā* [**stūbha-*: Pk. *thū(b)ha-*], m. = थूवा.

थेई-थेई *theī-theī*, f. **1.** rhythmical beating of time with the foot. **2.** dancing with expressive action (cf. थिरकना).

थेगली *theglī*, f. = थिगली.

थैला *thailā* [cf. *sthavi-*, Pa. *thavikā-*], m. a large bag, a sack.

थैली *thailī* [cf. *sthavi-*, Pa. *thavikā-*], f. **1.** a bag, a sack. **2.** a small bag; purse; transf. an amount of money. — ~ **खोलना**, to open (one's) purse, to disburse (money). – **थैलीदार** [P. *-dār*], adj. one who holds money: a banker, cashier, treasurer. **थैली-पति**, m. a monied person.

थोक *thok* [*stabaka-*: Pk. *thavaya-*], m. **1.** mass, quantity; total amount. 2. wholesale goods, or trade. **3.** *Pl. HŚS.* a holding, local division (of an estate); sub-division in a coparcenary (*bhaiyācārī*) estate. — **थोक-ख़रीदार** [P. *-dār*], m. a wholesale purchaser. **थोक-फ़रोश** [P. *-faroś*], m. a wholesale dealer. **थोकदार**, m. id.; *Pl.* the holder of a *thok*.

थोड़ *thoṛ* [**thoḍa-*²], m. reg. the spathe (edible inner part) of a plantain stem.

थोड़ा *thoṛā* [cf. *stoka-*], adj. **1.** little, small (of amount); a little. **2.** few; a few; not many. **3.** insufficient, limited; slight; scarce; not enough. **4.** adv. little, rarely; a little, somewhat. — ~ ~, adj. a little bit (of). ~ ~ **करके**, adv. a little at a time, by degrees. ~ **ही**, **थोड़े ही**, adv. little indeed; by no means. **थोड़े दिनों से**, adv. of late, recently. – **थोड़ा-बहुत**, adj. a certain amount (of). **थोड़ा-सा**, adj. a small amount of.

थोता *thotā*, adj. pronun. var. = थोथा.

थोथ *thoth* [**thottha-*²], m. *Pl. HŚS.* hollowness, emptiness.

थोथनी *thothnī* [cf. **thottha-*¹], f. = थूथन.

थोथा *thothā* [**thottha-*²], adj. **1.** blunt. *****2.** worm-eaten, empty; hollow. **3.** meaningless, senseless.

¹**थोप** *thop*, m. reg. **1.** end or point (of an object): as of the apex of a wooden cart frame. **2.** [cf. H. *thopnā*] *Pl.* cap, top, mounting.

²**थोप** *thop* [cf. H. *thopnā*], m. colloq. a slap, thump.

³**थोप** *thop* [**stopya-*], m. mound: a Buddhist stupa.

थोपना *thopnā* [**stopyate*], v.t. **1.** to cover, to smear or to plaster (over, पर); to place (over or on). **2.** to lay (upon, पर or के सिर), to attribute (to: as a fault, an accusation, a shortcoming).

थोबड़ा *thobṛā* [**thobba-*], m. **1.** muzzle, snout. **2.** pej. ugly face, mug.

थोर *thor*, adj. Brbh. Av. = थोड़ा.

द

द *da*, the eighteenth consonant of the Devanāgarī syllabary. — **दकार**, m. the sound /d/; the letter **द**.

दंग *daṅg* [P. *dang*], adj. taken aback, dumbfounded. — **~ रह जाना**, to be astonished, &c. – **दंगो-दुवाल** [P. *-o-*], m. imposing pomp or grandeur.

दंगई *daṅgaī* [cf. H. *daṅgā*], adj. & m. = **दंगाबाज़**.

[1]**दंगल** *daṅgal* [P. *dangal*], m. **1.** an excited crowd. **2.** an arena (esp. for wrestling). **3.** contest (as wrestling, or reciting). — **~ बँधना**, or **जमना**, a crowd to be gathered (for a contest). **~ मारना**, to win a wrestling bout. **~ में उतरना**, to appear in an arena, to enter a fray. – **दंगलबाज़** [P. *-bāz*], m. contender, champion. **°ई**, f. contest in the arena.

[2]**दंगल** *daṅgal*, m. **1.** a padded cushion, or mattress. **2.** *Pl.* a kind of chair.

दंगली *daṅgălī* [P. *dangal*+*ī*], adj. **1.** having to do with a contest, &c. **2.** quarrelsome, aggressive; victorious.

दंगा *daṅgā*, m. **1.** wrangle; uproar. **2.** brawl, affray. **3.** riot. **4.** revolt. — **~ करना**, or **मचाना**, to create a disturbance, &c.; to riot. – **दंगा-फ़साद**, m. rioting, riot. **दंगाबाज़** [P. *-bāz*], adj. quarrelsome, pugnacious; turbulent, riotous; m. a quarrelsome person, &c. **°ई**, f.

दंगाई *daṅgāī* [cf. H. *daṅgā*], adj. & m. **1.** adj. quarrelsome, pugnacious. **2.** m. a quarrelsome or pugnacious person. **3.** a rioter.

दंगैत *daṅgait*, adj. & m. *Pl.* = **दंगाबाज़**.

दंड *daṇḍ* [S.], m. **1.** stick; staff, rod; beam; yoke; mast. **2.** mace. **3.** stem, handle. **4.** transf. punishment; penalty; fine. **5.** in comp. judicial procedure; the law. **~ न्यायालय**, m. criminal court. **6.** assault, violence. **7.** a partic. physical exercise. **~ पेलना**, to do *daṇḍas*. — **~ ग्रहण करना**, to take up the staff: to become a wandering ascetic. **~ डालना**, to impose a penalty or fine (on, **पर**). **~ देना (को)**, to punish. **~ पड़ना**, loss or damage to be incurred. **~ भरना**, to pay a penalty or fine. – **दंड-ढक्का**, m. *Pl. HŚS.* a kind of kettledrum, on which the hours were struck. **दंड-तामड़ी**, f. *Pl.* perforated copper or metallic vessel which, sinking in water at a pre-measured rate, could serve as a water clock. **दंडधर**, adj. holding a staff: a title of Yama, the god of death; m. ruler, governor; wandering ascetic. **°-धारी**, adj. id. **दंड-नायक**, m. *hist.* leader of an army; a legal official; administrator, governor. **दंड-नीति**, f. harsh policy (of a ruler); penal code. **दंड-पाल**, m. a door-keeper, porter. **दंड-प्रमाण**, m. = **दंडवत**. **दंड-प्राप्त**, adj. punished; sentenced, condemned. **दंडवत**, f. stick-like (posture): prostration (esp. as to an idol). **दंडवत करना**, to prostrate oneself. **दंड-विधान**, or **°-संग्रह**, m. = **दंड-संहिता**. **दंड-विधि**, f. id. **दंड-शास्त्र**, m. the law (esp. in its penal aspect). **दंड-संहिता**, f. penal code. **दंडाणु** [°*ḍa*+*a*°], m. bacillus. **दंडात्मक** [°*ḍa*+*ā*°], adj. punitive; penal. **दंडादेश** [°*ḍa*+*ā*°], m. *law.* sentence. **°इत**, adj. **दंडाधिकारी** [°*ḍa*+*a*°], m. magistrate.

दंड- *daṇḍ-* [*daṇḍayati*], v.t. Brbh. to punish; to fine.

दंडक *daṇḍak* [S.], m. 1. = **दंड**, 1., 2. **2.** a type of Hindi metre consisting of long lines. **3.** adj. punishing. — **दंडक-वन**, m. name of a forest in south India (in which according to tradition Rām resided for some time). **दंडकारण्य**, m. id.

दंडन *daṇḍan* [S.], m. punishing, punishment.

दंडनीय *daṇḍănīyă* [S.], adj. deserving punishment, punishable (a person, or an offence).

दंडा *daṇḍā* [*daṇḍa-*], m. stick; pole; stake (= **डंडा**). — **दंडा-डोली**, f. fighting with sticks.

दंडायमान *daṇḍāyămān* [S.], adj. standing upright.

दंडित *daṇḍit* [S.], adj. **1.** punished; fined. **2.** sentenced.

दंडी *daṇḍī* [S.], m. **1.** a mace-bearer. **2.** staff-holder: = **दंडधर**.

दंड्य *daṇḍyă* [S.], adj. = **दंडनीय**.

दंत *dant* [S.], m. esp. in comp. **1.** tooth. **2.** tusk. — **दंत-कथा**, f. a tradition; a legend; an assertion without textual support; a fiction. **दंतकार**, m. dental technician, dentist. **°ई**, dentistry. **दंत-कुरेदनी**, f. = next. **दंत-खोदनी**, f. toothpick. **दंत-चिकित्सक**, m. dentist. **°-चिकित्सा**, f. dental care. **दंत-तालव्य**, adj. *ling.* palato-dental. **दंत-धावन**, m. cleaning the teeth, rinsing the mouth; = **दातुन**. **दंत-पीड़**, f. toothache. **दंत-मंजन**, m. toothpaste. **दंत-मल**, m. tartar. **दंत-शूल**, m. toothache. **दंतोष्ठ्य** [°*ta*+*o*°], adj. *ling.* labio-dental.

दँतार *daṁtār*, adj. = **दंतुर**.

दँतारा *daṁtārā* [**dantākāra-*], m. reg. sthg. toothed: a large rake.

दँताली *daṁtālī* [*dantāli-*], f. row of teeth.

दँतावली *daṁtāvlī* [*dantāvala-*], f. *Pl.* a rake, a harrow.

दँतिया *daṁtiyā* [cf. H. *dāṁt*], f. child's first teeth.

¹**दंती** *dantī* [S.], adj. & m. **1.** adj. having large or projecting teeth. **2.** toothed, cogged; serrated. **3.** *ling.* dental. **4.** m. Brbh. an elephant. **5.** a boar.

²**दंती** *dantī* [S.], f. *Pl. HŚS.* a small tree, *Croton tiglium*, or *C. polyandrum*, the nuts from which can be used as a purgative.

दँतीला *daṁtīlā* [cf. H. *dāṁt*], adj. = ¹दंती, 1., 2.

दंतुर *dantur* [S.], adj. & m. *Pl. HŚS.* **1.** adj. having large or projecting teeth; tusked. **2.** m. an elephant. **3.** a boar.

दँतुला *daṁtulā* [cf. H. *dāṁt*], adj. = ¹दंती, 1., 2.

दँतुली *daṁtulī*, f. = दँतिया.

दँतुवा *daṁtuvā*, reg. *Pl.* = दँतावली.

दंतू *dantū* [cf. *danta-*], adj. having prominent teeth (a person).

दँतेला *daṁtelā* [cf. H. *dāṁt*], adj. = ¹दंती, 1., 2.

दंत्य *dantya* [S.], adj. **1.** having to do with the teeth. **2.** *ling.* dental. — दंत्योष्ठ्य [°*ta*+*o*°], adj. *ling.* labio-dental.

दंद *dand* [ad. *dvandva-*], m. **1.** quarrel, quarrelling. **2.** confusion, turmoil; uproar. — दंद-फंद, m. scheming, machination.

दंदान *dandān* [P. *dandān*], m. *Pl. HŚS.* tooth. — दंदानसाज़ [P. *-sāz*], m. dental technician.

¹**दंदाना** *dandānā* [P. *dandāna*], m. **1.** tooth (of a saw, &c). **2.** notch, jag. — दंदानेदार [P. *-dār*], adj. toothed, notched, &c.

²**दंदाना** *dandānā*, v.i. & v.t. reg. **1.** v.i. to be hot or warm. **2.** v.t. to make or to keep hot or warm.

दंदारू *dandārū*, m. *Pl. HŚS.* blister; pimple.

दंपति *dampati* [ad. *dampatī*], m. a married couple, husband and wife.

दंभ *dambh* [*dambha-*], m. **1.** pretence, hypocrisy; deceit. **2.** pride; arrogance. **3.** boasting; ostentation.

दंभी *dambhī* [cf. H. *dambh*: w. S. *dambhī*], adj. & m. **1.** adj. hypocritical. **2.** proud; arrogant. **3.** boastful. **4.** m. a hypocrite, &c.

दँवरी *daṁvrī* [*davara-*], f. reg. **1.** rope with which a string of cattle are tied together (as bullocks when threshing). **2.** transf. threshing grain with bullocks. **3.** fishing line. **4.** = ²दौर.

दंश *daṃś* [S.], m. **1.** biting; a bite. **2.** stinging; a sting (wound). **3.** a tooth. **4.** a sting. **5.** Av. a stinging fly.

दंशक *daṃśak* [S.], adj. & m. **1.** adj. biting, stinging. **2.** m. a creature that bites or stings (cf. दंश, 5).

दंशन *daṃśan* [S.], m. the act of biting, or stinging.

दंशित *daṃśit* [S.], adj. **1.** bitten. **2.** stung.

दँशूक *daṁśūk*, adj. *HŚS.* biting, stinging.

दँशेर *daṁśer*, adj. *Pl. HŚS.* biting, stinging.

दंष्टरा *daṃṣṭrā* [S.], f. **1.** large tooth; fang. **2.** tusk.

-द *-dă* [S.], v. suffix (forms adjectives and nouns). giving (e.g. जलद, m. cloud).

दई *daī* [*daiviya-*], m. f. **1.** the supreme being, God. **2.** fate; misfortune. **3.** f. godhead, divinity. — ~ ~ करना, to cry out 'Oh God', to bewail one's fate. ~ का दूसरा, m. euphem. a devil (= ²देव). ~ का मारा, adj. & m. stricken by fate: accursed, unlucky; an accursed or wretched person. ~ की घाली, adj. f. Brbh. id. ~ लगना (को), to suffer a stroke of misfortune.

दक़-लक़ *daq-laq* [? A. *dakk, lakk*: P. *daq-o-laq*], m. U. bare plain, desert.

दक़ियानूस *daqiyānūs* [P. *daqiyānūs*: ← L. *Decianus*, adj.], m. & adj. **1.** m. an old-fashioned or conservative person. **2.** adj. = दक़ियानूसी.

दक़ियानूसी *daqiyānūsī* [P. *daqiyānūs*+*-ī*], adj. pej. old-fashioned, conservative.

दक़ीक़ा *daqīqā* [A. *daqīqa*], m. U. **1.** sthg. small or trifling; small matter. **2.** transf. a minute.

दक्खिन *dakkhin* [*dakṣiṇa-*], adj. & m. **1.** adj. southern, south. **2.** m. the south. **3.** *geog.* the Deccan. — ~ जाना, euph. colloq. to die. ~ जाओ! go to hell!

दक्खिना *dakkhinā* [*dakṣiṇa-*; ad. *dakṣiṇā-*], adj. f. & f. *Pl.* **1.** adj. f. southern. **2.** f. southerly wind.

दक्खिनी *dakkhinī* [cf. H. *dakkhin*], adj. & m. & f. **1.** adj. southern, south; south Indian. **2.** f. the Hindi-Urdu of the Deccan (esp. the older language). **3.** m., f. a southerner; a south Indian.

दक्ष *dakṣ* [S.], adj. **1.** dextrous; skilled, clever (at or in, में); adroit, deft. **2.** competent, able; fit, qualified. **3.** Brbh. right (hand or side).

दक्षता *dakṣătā* [S.], f. dexterity, skill, &c. (see दक्ष).

दक्षिण *dakṣiṇ* [S.], adj. & m. **1.** adj. right (hand or side). **2.** southern, south. 3. = दक्ष, 1. **4.** righteous, honest; direct, sincere; (*Pl.*) polite, amiable. **5.** m. the right hand or side. **6.** the south; *geog.* the Deccan. **7.** *pol.* the right. — दक्षिण-पश्चिम, m. south-west. °ई, adj. दक्षिण-पूर्व, m. south-east. °ई, adj. दक्षिण-पंथ, m. *pol.* right wing. °ई, adj. दक्षिण-मार्ग, m. *pol.* right wing. दक्षिणाचल [°*ṇa*+*a*°], m. *mythol.* the Malaya or southern mountain. दक्षिणाभिमुख [°*ṇa*+*a*°], adj. facing the south. दक्षिणायण [°*ṇa*+*a*°], m. the sun's movement south of the equator; the winter half-year; the period between summer and winter solstices; the winter solstice. दक्षिणावर्त [°*ṇa*+*ā*°], adj. turning towards the right, or to the south; adv. clockwise; m. = ~, 6.

दक्षिणता *dakṣiṇătā* [S.], f. **1.** skilfulness, dexterity. **2.** uprightness, honesty. **3.** politeness, kindness.

दक्षिणा *dakṣiṇā* [S.], f. **1.** fee paid to a brāhmaṇ for performance of a sacrifice, or other religious service. **2.** donation; gratuity. **3.** the south. — दक्षिणा-पथ, m. way to the south; south India.

दक्षिणी *dakṣiṇī* [cf. H. *dakṣiṇ*], adj. & m. & f. **1.** adj. southern, south. **2.** m., f. a southerner. **3.** f. = दक्खिनी, 2.

दक्षिणीय *dakṣiṇīyă* [S.], adj. 1. = दक्षिणी. **2.** entitled to receive *dakṣiṇā*.

दक्षिणेन *dakṣiṇenă* [S.], adv. on the right (side).

दखना *dakhnā* [*dakṣiṇa*-; ad. *dakṣiṇā*-], adj. f. & f. *Pl.* = दक्खिना.

दखनाई *dakhnāī* [conn. **dakṣiṇavāta*-: ? × H. *cauvāī*], f. *Pl.* a southerly wind.

दख़मा *dakhmā* [P. *dakhma*], m. any tower or raised place where Pārsīs lay the bodies of their dead.

दख़ल *dakhl* [A. *dakhl*], m. **1.** entry, access; admission. **2.** entering (upon); possession, occupancy. **3.** progress (in a study); proficiency; grasp. **4.** reach, scope. **5.** influence; authority, jurisdiction. **6.** intrusion; interference. — ~ करना, to take possession (of, पर), to occupy; to encroach (upon); to have authority, &c. (over); to meddle, or to interfere (in, में). ~ देना, to allow (one) entry, or access (to, में); to intrude (in, में); to interfere, &c. ~ में, adv. in the possession (of, के); under the authority or jurisdiction (of). ~ पाना, to have access; to be versed or skilled (in, में). ~ रखना, to be proficient, or versed (in, में); to have access (to). ~ होना, (one, को) to be versed (in, में); an influence (of or from, का) to be dominant. – दख़ल-अंदाज़ी [P. *-andāzī*], f. interference. दख़लदार [P. *-dār*], m. one having admission; partner; accomplice. दख़ल-दिहानी [cf. P. *dihāndan*], f. the granting of possession (to a claimant at law). दख़ल-नामा, m. a writ of entrance or possession (of lands, &c).

दख़ील *dakhīl* [A. *dakhīl*], adj. & m. **1.** adj. allowed entrance, admitted. **2.** in occupation, possession (as of land). **3.** interfering. **4.** *Pl.* introduced, adopted (as a word). **5.** m. *Pl.* one introduced or involved (in a business or matter). — दख़ीलकार, adj. & m. having possession (esp. of land, on a hereditary basis or for a long term). °ई, f. possession, occupancy, extended lease; land so held.

दगड़ *dagaṛ*, m. a kettledrum.

दगड़ना *dagaṛnā*, v.i. reg. **1.** to rock; to roll (= डगरना). **2.** to be disbelieving, not to credit (sthg).

दगड़ा *dagṛā* [**dag*-²], m. road (= डगर).

दगड़ाना *dagṛānā* [cf. H. *dagaṛnā*], v.t. reg. **1.** to rock; to roll. **2.** to propel.

दगदगा *dagdagā*, adj. & m. **1.** adj. burning brightly; glowing, gleaming. **2.** m. a burning lamp.

दग़दग़ा *dagdagā* [A. *dagdaga*], m. **1.** perturbation; anxiety. **2.** alarm, fear. **3.** awe. **4.** suspicion, distrust.

दगदगाना *dagdagānā* [**dag*-¹; Pk. *ḍagamagaï*], v.i. **1.** to burn brightly; to glow, to gleam; to glitter. **2.** to be inflamed or red (as the eyes).

दगध- *dagadh-* [cf. *dagdha*-: ad.], v.t. & v.i. **1.** v.t. reg. to burn. **2.** to cause grief, &c.; to wound; to reproach; to threaten; to deceive. **3.** v.i. Av. to be burnt, &c.

दग़ना *dagnā* [cf. H. *dāgnā*], v.i. **1.** to be branded (with an iron); to be marked (as with smallpox). **2.** to be fired (a firearm).

दगमगाना *dagmagānā*, v.i. reg. = डगमगाना.

दग़ल *dagal* [A. *dagal*], m. deceit; villainy. — दग़ल-फ़सल [A. *faṣl*], f. deceit; depravity. दग़लबाज़, adj. = दग़ाबाज़.

दगला *daglā*, m. a quilted coat or jacket.

दग़ली *daglī* [P. *daglī*], adj. & f. *Pl.* **1.** adj. deceitful. **2.** f. deceit.

दग़ा *dagā* [P. *dagā*], f. **1.** deceit, imposture; fraud. **2.** treachery. — ~ **करना**, to act deceitfully, treacherously, &c. (towards, **से**, or **के साथ**). ~ **खाना**, to be deceived, betrayed or imposed on (by, **से**). ~ **देना (को)**, to deceive, &c. (= ~ **करना**); to let (one) down (a person or thing of which hope is held out), to delude. – **दग़ादार** [P. *-dār*], adj. = **दग़ाबाज़**. °**ई**, f. **दग़ाबाज़** [P. *-bāz*], adj. & m. deceitful, &c.; a cheat, impostor; traitor. °**ई**, f. deceit, fraud; treachery, villainy.

दग़ाई *dagāī* [cf. H. *dagānā*], f. price paid for branding or marking.

दग़ाना *dagānā* [cf. H. *dāgnā*], v.t. **1.** to cause to be branded or marked (by, **से**). **2.** to cause (a firearm) to be fired.

दग़ीला *dagīlā* [cf. H. *dāg*], adj. marked, spotted, stained (= **दाग़दार**).

दग़ैल *dagail* [cf. H. *dagā*], adj. 1. = **दग़ीला**. **2.** fig. Brbh. = **दग़ाबाज़**.

दग़ोलिया *dagoliya*, m. an impostor.

दग्ध *dagdh* [S.], adj. **1.** burnt; scorched. **2.** fig. tormented (as by grief); hurt, wounded; inflamed (with desire). **3.** unlucky, unpropitious. **4.** cunning. — **दग्धाक्षर** [°*dha* + *a*°], m. *rhet.* burnt letters: letters considered inauspicious in particular positions in a line of verse.

दच *dac*, ? m. reg. (E.) *Pl.* a homestead.

दच्छ *dacch*, adj. & m. Av. = **दक्ष**.

दच्छिन *dacchin*, m. Brbh. Av. = **दक्षिण**.

दच्छिना *dacchinā*, f. Brbh. = **दक्षिणा**.

दज्जाल *dajjāl* [A. *dajjāl*], m. **1.** a liar; deceiver. **2.** a one-eyed man.

दटना *daṭnā*, v.i. reg. = **डटना**.

दड़कना *daṛaknā*, v.i. reg. **1.** to split (= **दरकना**). **2.** to gape: to eat greedily.

दड़बड़ाना *daṛbaṛānā*, v.t. reg. **1.** to make out to be false, to misrepresent. **2.** to threaten, to intimidate.

दड़बा *daṛbā*, m. = **दरबा**.

दड़र *daṛar*, ? m. *Pl.* flood, torrent; waterfall.

दड़ाड़ *daṛāṛ*, f. reg. = **दराड़**, **दरार**.

दड़ूकना *daṛūknā*, v.i. *Pl. HŚS.* = **दड़ोकना**.

दड़ेड़ा *daṛeṛā* [conn. **daḍavaḍa-*: Pk. *daḍavaḍa-*], m. reg. **1.** impetuosity, violent attack. **2.** pelting rain.

दड़ोकना *daṛoknā*, v.i. reg. to bellow (cattle); to roar.

दढ़- *daṛh-*. beard: — **दढ़-मुँड़ा**, adj. having the beard shaven, beardless.

दढ़ियल *daṛhiyal* [cf. H. *dāṛhī*], adj. bearded.

दढ़ी *daṛhī*, f. a kind of carp (? barbel).

दत *dat*, interj. = **दुत**.

दत- *dat-*, v.i. Brbh. = **डटना**.

दतुवन *datuvan*, f. = **दातुन**.

दतून *datūn*, f. = **दातुन**.

दतोई *datoī*, f. *Pl.* land lately cropped with corn, millet or *jvār*.

दतौन *dataun*, f. = **दातुन**.

दत्त *datt* [S.], adj. & m. **1.** given. **2.** made over, assigned; paid. **3.** m. a gift. **4.** an adopted son (one who has 'given himself'). **5.** [× Engl. *data*] data. — **दत्तचित्त**, adj. devoted, zealous; attentive (to). **दत्तावधान** [°*ta* + *a*°], adj. = **दत्तचित्त**, 2.

दत्तक *dattak* [S.], m. **1.** an adopted son. **2.** a subsidy, grant. — **दत्तक-ग्रहण**, m. adoption (of a son). °**ग्राही**, adj. & m. adopting. **दत्तक-पिता**, m. adoptive father. **दत्तक-पुत्र**, m. = **दत्तक**.

दत्तकी *dattăkī* [S.], adj. *law.* adoptive.

ददरी *dadrī* [*dardara-*, Pa. *daddara-*], f. reg. unripe corn, cut and taken home unthreshed. — ~ **का मेला**, m. name of a yearly festival held in Ballia.

ददा *dadā*, m. Brbh. = **दादा**.

ददिया *dadiyā* [cf. H. *dādā*], adj. having to do with a paternal grandfather. — **ददिया-ससुर**, m. father-in-law's father. **ददिया-सास**, f. father-in-law's mother.

ददिहाल *dadihāl* [cf. H. *dadiyā*: ? + *āvali-*, *ālaya-*], m. **1.** paternal grandfather's house, or family. **2.** ancestors on the paternal grandfather's side.

ददोड़ा *dadoṛā* [cf. *dadru-*[1]], m. reg. a swelling (caused by an insect bite, or other irritation).

ददोरा *dadorā*, m. Brbh. = **ददोड़ा**.

दद्रु *dadru* [S.], m. a skin disease, rash; ringworm (= [2]**दाद**).

दद्रू *dadrū*, m. = **दद्रु**.

दधल *dadhal*, m. reg. *Pl. HŚS.* = **दलदल**.

[1]**दधि** *dadhi* [S.], m. = [1]**दही**. — **दधि-काँदो**, m. Brbh. a ritual celebration of Kṛṣṇa's birthday, involving the throwing of *dahī* mixed with turmeric or (?) orig. with clay. **दधि-दान**, m. tribute of *dahī* (as paid by the herdgirls to Kṛṣṇa). **दधि-मंथन**, m. the churning of *dahī*. **दधि-सुत**, m. Brbh. butter.

²**दधि** *dadhi*, m. Brbh. = उदधि. — दधि-सुत, m. born from ocean (or cloud or river): lotus; pearl; shell-fish; moon; poison.

दन *dan* [**dan-*], m. the sound of a shot, or of a gun being fired. — ~ से, adv. briskly, promptly.

दनदनाना *dandanānā* [cf. H. *dan*], v.i. & v.t. **1.** v.i. to ring, to reverberate (as a shot); to boom. **2.** to be brisk, active; to be in high spirits. **3.** v.t. to fire, to shoot off (a gun).

दनादन *danādan* [cf. H. *dan*], f. **1.** booming, reverberation. **2.** adv. with a reverberating noise. **3.** continuingly. **4.** briskly, quickly.

दनुज *danuj* [S.], m. *mythol.* Brbh. Av. son of Danu: a Dānava or demon. — दनुजारि [°*ja*+*a*°], m. enemy of demons: a title of Viṣṇu.

दन्न *dann*, m. = दन.

दप *dap*, m. Brbh. = दर्प.

दपट *dapaṭ* [cf. H. *dapaṭnā*], f. rebuke; censure.

दपटना *dapaṭnā* [cf. **drapp-*], v.t. **1.** to rebuke; to censure. **2.** *Pl.* to rush on, to attack (= डपतना).

दपदप *dapdap* [cf. H. *dapdapānā*], f. reg. shining. — ~ करना, to shine.

दपदपाना *dapdapānā*, v.i. reg. to shine.

दपदपाहट *dapdapāhaṭ* [cf. H. *dapdapānā*], f. reg. shining; brilliance, splendour.

दपू *dapū*, f. vulg. *Pl.* anus.

दफ़ *daf* [A. *daff*], m. a large tambourine (without cymbals).

दफ़तर *daftar*, m. see दफ़्तर.

दफ़न *dafn* [A. *dafn*], m. **1.** burying; burial. **2.** covering, concealing. — ~ करना, to bury; to conceal. ~ होना, to be buried.

दफ़नाना *dafnānā* [cf. H. *dafn*], v.t. to bury, &c.

दफ़लची *dafalcī* [H. *daf* × H. *tabalcī*], m. a tambourine player.

दफ़ला *daflā* [cf. H. *daf*], m. a small tambourine.

¹**दफ़ा** *dafā* [A. *daf'a*], f. **1.** time, occasion; moment. **2.** article, clause (of a law, an edict); section (of a document). **3.** a group, section; class (school). — ~ लगाना, to accuse (one, पर) under a clause or statute (concerning, की). एक ~, adv. on one occasion, once. जाती ~, adv. when leaving. — दफ़ादार [P. *-dār*], m. *mil.* one in command of a small body of men: a junior officer; a non-commissioned officer.

²**दफ़ा** *dafā* [A. *daf'*], m. inv. U. repelling, warding off. — ~ करना, to repel (as an attack), to ward off; to guard (oneself: against, से).

दफ़ाली *dafālī* [cf. H. *daf*], m. tambourine player; a *faqīr* who plays the tambourine.

दफ़ीना *dafīnā* [A. *dafīna*], f. buried treasure.

दफ़्तर *daftar* [A. *daftar*], m. **1.** a roll, list; volume (of documents). **2.** a record-office, archive. ***3.** an office, place of business; bureau. **4.** an extensive account; statement, report. — ~ खोलना, to give a circumstantial account (of, का). – दफ़्तर-ख़ाना, m. record-office. दफ़्तरनवीस [P. *-navīs*], m. 'document-writer': clerk. दफ़्तरशाही [P. *-śāhī*], f. bureaucracy.

दफ़्तरी *daftărī* [A. *daftar*+P. *-ī*], adj. & m. **1.** adj. having to do with an office, bureau, &c. **2.** bureaucratic. **3.** m. office employee. **4.** superintendent of office stores; book-binder. — दफ़्तरी-ख़ाना, m. book-bindery.

दफ़्ती *daftī* [P. *daftī(n)*: ? A. *daffatain*, dual of *dafa*], f. the cardboard covers of a book; cardboard.

दबंग *dabaṅg* [cf. **drapp-*; × **dabb-*], adj. & m. **1.** adj. blustering, brash. **2.** crude, uncouth. **3.** m. a bully; lout; clown.

दबंगपन *dabaṅgpan* [cf. H. *dabaṅg*], m. bluster, brashness. — ~ रखना, to bluster, &c.

दबंगा *dabaṅgā*, adj. reg. = दबंग.

दबक *dabak* [cf. H. *dabaknā*], f. 1. = दबकी. **2.** a wrinkle.

दबकई *dabkaī* [cf. H. *dabaknā*], f. **1.** the act of beating wire (as for embroidery). **2.** the business or craft of a wire-beater.

दबकन *dabkan* [cf. H. *dabaknā*], f. *Pl.* **1.** weight used to press down the small arm of a water-wheel (ढेंकली). **2.** place of ambush.

दबकना *dabaknā* [cf. **dabb-*], v.i. & v.t. **1.** v.i. to be covered or concealed. **2.** to lie hidden (as in ambush), to skulk. **3.** to crouch down; to set (as a dog). **4.** to be intimidated, or cowed. **5.** v.t. [conn. *dābnā*] to beat, to flatten (wire, metal). **6.** Brbh. to chide. — दबक रहना, to lie hidden (= ~, 2).

दबकाना *dabkānā* [cf. H. *dabaknā*], v.t. to press down: **1.** to stow away, to conceal, to hide. **2.** to chide, to scold; to browbeat; to intimidate.

दबकी *dabkī* [cf. H. *dabaknā*], f. **1.** the act of hiding; crouching; lurking. **2.** ambush. — ~ मारना, or लगाना, to hide, &c.; to lie in ambush.

दबकीला *dabkīlā* [cf. H. *dabak*], adj. *Pl.* = दबकेल.

दबकेल *dabkel* [cf. H. *dabaknā*], adj. & m. **1.** adj. lurking, skulking. **2.** m. skulker.

दबकैया *dabkaiyā* [cf. H. *dabaknā*], m. a wire-beater (of gold or silver wire, for embroidery).

दबगर *dabgar* [P. *dabba+gar*], m. a maker of leather bottles, &c.

दबड़ू-घुसड़ू *dabṛū-ghusṛū* [cf. H. *dabnā, ghusnā*], adj. & m. **1.** adj. skulking, hidden; cowardly. **2.** helpless, insignificant; dependent. **3.** m. a skulker, &c.

दबदबा *dabdabā* [A. *dabdaba*], m. **1.** noise, din. **2.** fig. state, pomp; majesty; dominant position. **3.** awesomeness. **4.** overbearingness.

दबना *dabnā* [**dabb-* (← Drav.): cf. H. *dābnā*], v.i. **1.** to be pressed down. **2.** to be squeezed; to be rubbed, massaged (the feet). **3.** to be crushed; to be buried. दब मरना, to be crushed to death. **4.** to subside; to yield (under weight, pressure). **5.** to be restrained; to be subdued; to be reluctant; to be furtive (in glance, step); to be repressed (feelings). दबकर चलना, = दबे पाँव चलना. **6.** to be oppressed; to submit (to control, authority); to yield (to force); to be intimidated, to cower; to be overshadowed (in importance). **7.** to die down (as fire, epidemic), to subside (as anger, or illness); to be forgotten, or shelved (a matter); to be retrenched (in scope). हाथ ~, (one's) circumstances to be reduced. **8.** to be concealed; to crouch down; to lurk; to be lost, to vanish (possessions). **9.** to be withheld, or usurped (a right, a possession); to fall short (an amount). — दबी ज़बान से, adv. in a subdued voice; in a reluctant voice. दबे पाँव चलना, to walk or to move stealthily. – दबा-दबाया, adj. covered, concealed; restrained, &c.

दबाई *dabāī* [cf. H. *dabānā*], f. **1.** pressing down, &c. (= दबाव). **2.** treading out corn (= [1]दावन, 1).

दबाऊ *dabāū* [cf. H. *dabānā*], adj. & m. **1.** adj. pressing down; pressing heavily on the shafts (as the weight of a badly loaded cart). **2.** burdensome, oppressive. **3.** m. an oppressor, &c.

दबाना *dabānā* [cf. H. *dābnā*], v.t. **1.** to press down, to press; to ring (an electric bell). **2.** to squeeze. **3.** to crush. **4.** to restrain; to curb, to repress (as feelings). **5.** to subdue; to oppress; to rule. **6.** to snub (a person); to intimidate. **7.** to dominate, to overshadow (in importance). **8.** to withhold, to usurp (a right, a possession); to encroach upon. **9.** to suppress (as news); to secrete; to embezzle. **10.** to sow (seed). — दबाकर, adv. pressing down, restraining, compelling, &c. दुम दबाकर भागना, to flee with (one's) tail between (one's) legs. हाथ दबाकर ख़र्च करना, to spend money carefully.

दबाव *dabāv* [cf. H. *dabānā*], m. **1.** pressing; pressure. **2.** restraint; repression (as of feelings). **3.** power, authority; influence. **4.** constraint, compulsion. **5.** oppression; domination. **6.** emphasis. — ~ देकर बोलना, to speak giving emphasis (to sthg). ~ मानना, to submit (to, का); to accept the ascendancy (of, का). ~ में आना, to come under a dominating influence (of or from, के).

दबाहट *dabāhaṭ* [cf. H. *dabānā*], f. reg. = दबाव.

दबिया *dabiyā* [cf. *darvi-*], m. *Pl.* a measure of about ten handfuls (of corn, &c).

दबीज़ *dabīz* [P. *dabīz*], adj. thick, strong, heavy (build, cloth).

दबीर *dabīr* [P. *dabīr*], m. U. writer, secretary.

दबीला *dabīlā* [cf. *darvi-*], m. *Pl.* a paddle, oar.

दबूचना *dabūcnā*, v.t. reg. = दबोचना.

दबूसा *dabūsā* [P. *dabūsa*], m. *Pl. HŚS.* rear cabin of ship; stern.

दबेहरा *dabehrā* [**darvaphālaka-* or °*-dhāraka-*], m. *Pl.* a large wooden ploughshare fixed behind the iron share.

दबेहरी *dabehrī* [cf. H. *dabehrā*], f. *Pl.* a light plough.

दबैल *dabail* [cf. H. *dabnā*], adj. & m. **1.** adj. subject, subordinate (to, का); oppressed. **2.** submissive, weak. **3.** m. one subject, or oppressed.

दबोचना *dabocnā*, v.t. **1.** to seize, to clutch; to swoop or to spring on. **2.** to press tight, to squeeze. **3.** to hide away.

दबोस *dabos*, m. *Pl. HŚS.* flint.

दबोसना *dabosnā*, v.t. reg. to be a (habitual) drinker.

दबौनी *dabaunī* [cf. H. *dabānī*], f. *Pl. HŚS.* **1.** a press (machine). **2.** a weight, added weight.

दब्बा *dabbā* [*darva-*], m. *Pl.* **1.** spoon, ladle (usu. of leather). **2.** leather bottle (for oil, &c).

दब्बू *dabbū* [cf. H. *dabnā*], adj. submissive, weak.

दब्बो दब्बो *dabbo dabbo* [cf. H. *dabnā*], adj. colloq. hushed up (a matter). — ~ करना, to hush up, to keep (sthg.) quiet.

[1]दम *dam* [P. *dam*], m. **1.** breath; life, spirit. **2.** breathing or blowing out; puff (as in casting a spell); blast (as of a furnace). **3.** draw, puff (as at a hookah); whiff. **4.** moment, instant. **5.** vitality, vigour; mettle; ambition. **6.** strength: quality (as of material); efficacy (as of medicine). **7.** sharp edge (of a blade). **8.** [? × *dambha-*] false hope. **9.** state of simmering (over a fire). — ~ **अटकना**, breathing to stop (as at death); to suffer from breathlessness. ~ **आना**, id. ~ **उलटना**, to gasp for breath; to be suffocated or choked; to breathe one's last; to be dumbfounded, confused. ~ **के** ~ **का**, adj. momentary. ~ **के** ~ **में**, adv. in (the space of) a moment. ~ **खाना**, to remain silent (as in confusion); to be disappointed or crestfallen; to bear patiently; to be simmered (vegetables, &c). ~ **खींचना**, to draw in the breath: to remain quiet or silent, to hold one's peace; to puff (at, **का**), to have a smoke. ~ **ख़ुश्क होना**, the throat to be dry (as with fear). ~ **घुटना**, to be suffocated, or choked. ~ **घुटनेवाला**, suffocating; stuffy (atmosphere). ~ **घोंटना**, to suffocate; to strangle; to plague, to persecute. ~ **चढ़ना**, to be out of breath, to pant. ~ **चुराना**, to hold the breath, to feign fainting or death; to shirk, to hold back (from, **से**). ~ **छोड़ना**, to expire; fig. to be very fearful. ~ **टूटना**, to be unable to hold the breath; to be out of breath; to be dying. ~ **तोड़ना**, or **तोड़ रहना**, to be dying. ~ **देना**, to give up life, to die; to die (for, **पर**), to be wildly in love (with); to simmer, to stew (vegetables, &c.); to give temper (to, **को**: steel). ~ **नाक में आना**, to be very distressed; to be plagued or worried to death; to be at the last gasp (of life). ~ **निकलना**, to expire; to long or to pine (for, **पर**); not to be able to bear (sthg., **में**). ~ **पर आ बनना**, one's life to be in dire danger; to be very nearly ready, or cooked (food). ~ **पर** ~, adv. moment by moment: constantly; regularly. ~ **फड़कना**, to be thrilled, delighted. ~ **फ़ना होना**, life to be extinguished: to lose consciousness; to freeze in fear. ~ **फूँकना**, to breathe (into, **में**); to inflate. ~ **फूलना**, to be out of breath, exhausted. ~ **बंद करना (का)**, to silence. ~ **बंद होना**, the breath to be held; (one) to be silenced. ~ **बढ़ाना**, to speak at undue length; to practise holding the breath. ~ **बना रहे!** long may you live! ~ **बाँधना**, to hold the breath; to be intent, very attentive; to risk, to dare. ~ **भर**, or ~ **भर (को)**, adv. for a moment. ~ **भर में**, adv. in (the space of) a moment. ~ **भरना**, to become breathless, or exhausted; to utter a word (neg. contexts); to sing the praises (of, **का**), to boast (of); to believe (in), to profess; to prolong (a sung note). ~ **मारना**, to utter a word (as in objection, or in casting a spell); to intervene (in a conversation); to smoke (hemp, &c.); to boast (of, **का**); to recover (from physical effort). ~ **में आना**, to be taken in or deceived (by, **के**); to turn to (as to drugs). ~ **में** ~ **आना**, to recover breath, to revive; to regain composure. ~ **में** ~ **रहना**, or **होना**, breath or life to remain: to remain alive. ~ **में लाना**, to delude; to entice, to entrap. ~ **रखना**, to hold one's peace, to be content with a little. ~ **रुकना**, to be suffocated, or choked. ~ **रोकना (का)**, to suffocate, to choke; to strangle. ~ **लगना**, to be desirous (of, **का**); to be affected by fumes (of); to have a smoke. ~ **लगाना**, to draw (at, **का**), to smoke ; to have a breather. ~ **लेकर बैठ रहना**, to be silent (in puzzlement or confusion). ~ **लेना**, to draw breath: to rest (from, **से**). ~ **साधकर रहना**, to hold the breath (as an austerity, or otherwise). ~ **साधना**, id. ~ **सूखना**, the throat to be dry (as with fear). ~ **ही** ~ **में रखना**, fig. to nourish a vain hope. ~ **होंठों पर**, or **लबों पर**, **आना**, to be on the point of death. ~ **होना**, to be stewed or simmered; to be kept warm on the fire. **हर** ~, adv. at every moment, always. – **दम-ख़म**, m. vigour, energy; endurance; edge, temper (of a blade); beauty. **दम-घोंटू**, adj. suffocating; oppressive. **दम-चूल्हा**, m. portable stove or oven. **दम-झाँसा**, m. coaxing; inveiglement. **दम-दमड़ी**, f. strength and money: personal or financial power. **दमदार** [P. *-dār*], adj. vigorous, long lived; strong; well-tempered, sharp (blade). **दम-दिलासा**, m. false hope; comfort; encouragement. **दम-पट्टी**, f. = **दम-झाँसा**. **दम-बदम** [P. *ba-*], adv. every moment; continually; repeatedly. **दमबाज़** [P. *-bāz*], adj. deceitful, treacherous; m. a plausible or untrustworthy person; a smoker of *gāṁjā*. °**ई**, f. **दममार**, m. a drug-addict. **दमसाज़** [P. *-sāz*], m. close companion; accompanist.

[2]**दम** *dam* [S.], m. **1.** subduing. **2.** subduing the feelings; self-control, restraint; mortification.

दमई *damaī*, f. *Pl.* rate or amount of assessment.

[1]**दमक** *damak* [cf. H. *damaknā*], f. **1.** glitter, brilliance; glow. **2.** heat, hot blast; warmth. **3.** flush, bloom. **4.** ardour. — **दमकदार** [P. *-dār*], adj. glittering; fig. clear, evident.

[2]**दमक** *damak* [S.], adj. *Pl. HŚS.* **1.** adj. taming, subduing. **2.** m. one who subdues his passions; a hero.

दमकड़ा *damakṛā*, m. reg. *Pl.* = **दमरखा**.

दमकना *damaknā*, v.i. **1.** to shine, to glitter; to glow; to flare up. **2.** to give out heat. **3.** to bloom.

दमकल *damkal* [cf. H. [3]*kal*], f. (m., *Pl.*) **1.** a pump. **2.** a fire-engine. **3.** jack or crane (for lifting weights); winch. — ~ **कर्मचारी**, m. a fireman. ~ **गाड़ी**, f. = ~, 2. ~ **घर**, m. fire station.

दमकला *damkalā* [cf. H. *damkal*], m. **1.** a syringe. 2. = **दमकल**. **3.** portable stove or oven.

दमका *damkā*, m. an inhabited village (Bihar); a hillock (*Pl.*; E. Avadh).

दमकीला *damkīlā* [cf. H. *damaknā*], adj. glittering, &c.

दमखड़ा *damakhṛā*, m. reg. *Pl.* = दमरखा.

दमड़ा *damṛā* [*dramma-*: ← Gk.], m. money, wealth. — दमड़े करना, to raise ready money by selling off, selling cheaply.

दमड़ी *damṛī* [*dramma-*: ← Gk.], f. a coin of nominal value (one eighth or one quarter of a *paisā*); a farthing. — ~ की, adj. worth a farthing: worthless. ~ के तीन होना, to be worth three farthings: to be worthless, useless; to be dirt cheap.

दमदमा *damdamā* [P. *damdama*], m. **1.** booming of a drum, or of cannon, &c. **2.** tumult, din. **3.** fig. pomp, show. **4.** transf. kettledrum (= दमामा). **5.** a mound, raised battery. **6.** rampart, defensive work. — ~ बाँधना, to fortify with outworks; to raise a battery.

दमदमाना *damdamānā*, v.t. to cause to move or to vibrate; to shake.

दमन *daman* [S.], m. **1.** subduing, repressing; repression (as of instincts). **2.** oppression. **3.** suppression, disciplining (as of unruly ways). **4.** *Pl. HŚS.* = दोना (*Artemisia*). — दमनकारी, adj. repressive (measures, &c.); punitive. दमन-चक्र, m. fig. continuing repressive acts or policy. दमनशील, adj. repressive by nature, tyrannical. दमनात्मक [°*na*+*ā*], adj. = दमनकारी.

दमनक *damănak* [S.], m. *Pl. HŚS.* = दमन, 4.

[1]**दमनी** *damănī* [S.], f. *Pl.* a courageous woman (cf. दमन, 1).

[2]**दमनी** *damănī* [S.], adj. Brbh. (self-)restrained: modest.

दमनीय *damănīyă* [S.], adj. to be restrained or suppressed; restrainable; tamable.

दममदार *dammadār*, m. reg. (W.) *Pl.* name of a festival honouring a Muslim saint called Śāh Madār.

दमरक *damrak*, m. reg. *Pl.* = दमरखा.

दमरका *damarkā*, m. reg. *Pl.* = दमरखा.

दमरखा *damarkhā* [?? conn. H. *camrakh*], m. reg. (W.) the piece of leather in a spinning-wheel which holds up the spun thread.

दमा *damā* [P. *dama*], m. **1.** breathlessness; asthma. **2.** a bellows. **3.** tuberculosis.

दमाद *damād*, m. pronun. var. = दामाद.

दमान *damān* [P. *damān*], adj. U. powerful; terrible; impetuous; fierce.

दमानक *damānak* [cf. P. *damān*], f. (m., *Pl.*) Brbh. a carbine; blunderbuss.

दमामा *damāmā* [P. *damāma*], m. **1.** a large drum. **2.** fig. noise, pomp.

दमित *damit* [S.], adj. **1.** repressed (as instincts). **2.** subdued, conquered. — दमित-शमित, adj. repressed and restrained (= दमित).

दमिरका *damirkā*, m. reg. (W.) = दमरखा.

दम्य *damyă* [S.], adj. 1. = दमनीय. **2.** tamed.

दया *dayā* [S.], f. **1.** compassion, pity; sympathy. **2.** mercy; clemency. **3.** kindness. — ~ आना, to feel compassion, &c. (for, पर). ~ करना, or रखना, or लाना, to feel compassion, &c. (for, पर, के ऊपर); to show mercy or kindness (to). – दयाकर, adj. Av. compassionate; merciful; kind. °-कृत, adj. compassionate (an act); kindly. °-कार, adj. id. दया-निधि, f. treasure of mercy: a supremely compassionate person; title of the supreme being. दयापूर्वक, adv. compassionately; mercifully; kindly. दयामय, adj. compassionate, &c. दयामान, adj. = दयाकर. दयामूर्ति, f. embodiment of compassion. दया-युक्त, adj. compassionate, &c. दया राम, m. a compassionate or sympathetic person. दयार्द्र [°*ya*+*ā*°], adj. fig. compassionate; tender-hearted. दयावान, adj. compassionate; merciful; kind. दयाशील, adj. compassionate by nature: id.; humane. दया-सागर, m. ocean of compassion: = दया-निधि. दयाहीन, adj. merciless, harsh.

दयानत *dayānat* [A. *diyānat*], f. **1.** honesty, integrity. **2.** conscientiousness. — दयानतदार [P. *-dār*], adj. honest, upright; conscientious; °ई, f. बददयानत, adj. dishonest; °ई, f.

दयार *dayār* [A. *diyār*, pl. of *dār*], m. region, province.

दयाल *dayāl* [*dayālu*], adj. **1.** compassionate. **2.** merciful. **3.** kind.

दयालु *dayālu* [S.], adj. = दयाल.

दयालुता *dayālutā* [S.], f. **1.** compassion. **2.** mercy. **3.** kindness.

दयित *dayit* [S.], adj. & m. **1.** adj. cherished, beloved. **2.** m. a loved one; husband.

दयिता *dayitā* [S.], f. Brbh. a loved one; wife.

दयौ *dayau*, Brbh. gave, given (= दिया).

[1]**दर** *dar* [P. *dar*], m. **1.** a door; entrance, threshold. **2.** gate. **3.** transf. place. — ~ ~ माँगना, to beg from door to door. दरो दीवार देखना [P. *-o-*], to look anxiously, or expectantly, around. – दर-दालान, m. an outer hall, antechamber. दर-(ब-)दर [P. *-ba-*], adv. from door to door; from place to place. दरबान [P. *-vān*] m. door-keeper, porter. दरवान, m. id.

²दर *dar* [P. *dar*], prep. in; on; at; by; concerning: — दरअसल, adv. = असल में. दरकिनार, adv. on one side, apart; aside, out of the way; out of the question. दरगुज़र, adj. passed over; set aside; excused. दरगुज़र करना (से), to pass by or over; to overlook, to excuse. दरपरदा, adv. secretly; privately; by implication, indirectly. दरपेश, adv. in front, forwards; under consideration, in hand; pending. दर-पेश करना, or लाना, to put forward. °ई, f. being before a court (a case). दरमाहा [P. *-māha*], m. monthly wage. दरहाल, adv. at present, just now.

³दर *dar*, f. **1.** price, rate (of sale or exchange); tariff. **2.** rate of interest. **3.** level (of market). **4.** worth, value, excellence. **5.** estimation, esteem. — निश्चित ~ पर, adv. at a fixed price or rate. फुटकर ~, f. retail price. दरबंदी [P. *-bandī*], f. fixing of a price or rate; rent rates (as the basis for village assessments); assessing the price or value of crops or produce, or the level of rates.

⁴दर *dar* [S.], m. Brbh. fear (= डर).

⁵दर *dar* [*dara-*³], m. reg. crack, crevice; hole.

⁶दर *dar* [? *dara-*²], f. Brbh. sugar-cane.

⁷दर *dar* [*dara-*], m. Brbh. Av. conch shell.

दरक *darak*, m. = दरका.

दरकना *daraknā* [cf. *darayati*], v.i. **1.** to be torn. **2.** to split, to crack. **3.** fig. to throb (the heart). **4.** Brbh. to be broken (as the heart).

दरका *darkā* [cf. H. *daraknā*], m. **1.** a tear. **2.** a crack. **3.** blow causing a tear or crack.

दरकाना *darkānā* [cf. H. *daraknā*], v.t. & v.i. **1.** v.t. to tear. **2.** to split, to crack. **3.** v.i. Brbh. = दरकना.

दरकार *dar-kār* [P. *darkār*], adj. & f. **1.** adj. needed, required. **2.** f. need.

दरकारी *dar-kārī* [P. *darkārī*], adj. = दरकार.

दरखाल *darkhāl*, ? m. reg. (E.) cattle enclosure (= नोहरा).

दरख़ास्त *dar-khāst* [P. *darkhvāst*], f. **1.** desire, request. **2.** demand, application. **3.** petition, appeal. — ~ करना (की), to request; to apply (for); to petition; to propose. ~ देना, to submit a request, &c. ~ पड़ना, a petition, &c. to be lodged (against, पर or के ऊपर).

दरख़्त *darakht* [P. *darakht*], m. a tree.

दरख़्वास्त *dar-khvāst*, m. see दरख़ास्त.

दरगाह *dar-gāh* [P. *dargāh*], f. **1.** portal, threshold. **2.** royal court. **3.** *musl.* shrine or tomb of a saint.

दरगाहा *dar-gāhā*, adj. *Pl.* having to do with a *dargāh*.

दरगुज़र *dar-guzar*, adj. see s.v. दर.

दरज़ *darz* [P. *darz*], f. E.H. **1.** a crack; split. **2.** a seam. **3.** sewing.

दरजा *darjā*, m. see दर्जा.

दरज़िन *darzin*, f. see दर्ज़िन.

दरज़ी *darzī*, m. see दर्ज़ी.

दरदरा *dardarā* [*darayati*: Panj. *dardarā*], adj. coarsely ground; crushed, bruised (grain); granulated.

दरदरापन *dardarāpan* [cf. H. *dardarā*], m. coarseness (of grain).

दरबरा- *darbarā-*, v.i. Brbh. to be restless, anxious.

दरबहरा *darbahrā*, m. *Pl. HŚS.* an intoxicating drink (made from rice, and other plants).

दरबा *darbā* [? conn. *dara-*³], m. **1.** a fowl-house; dovecot. **2.** a hollow, or nook used for nesting. **3.** pej. hole, place, room; cell.

दरबार *dar-bār* [P. *darbār*], m. **1.** a royal court; hall of audience. **2.** the holding of a court, levee; durbar. **3.** royal audience. — ~ करना, or लगाना, to hold a court or levee; to sit in a royal council; to hold audience. ~ बाँधना, euph. a bribe to be settled. ~ साहब, m. name of the Sikh temple in Amritsar where the sacred scripture *Granth Sāhab* is housed (= *harmindar: hari mandir*). – दरबारदारी [P. *-dārī*], f. attendance at court. fig. दरबारदारी करना (की), to attend court assiduously; to dance attendance (on), to be obsequious. दरबारे-आम [P. *-e-*], m. public audience; public hall of audience. दरबारे-ख़ास, m. private audience; private hall of audience.

दरबारी *dar-bārī* [P. *darbār*+*-ī*], adj. & m. **1.** adj. having to do with a royal court. **2.** courtly. **3.** m. a courtier; one entitled to a seat in a levee. **4.** *mus.* name of a *rāg*. — ~ ज़बान, f. court language; elegant language (esp. of the Mughal court).

दरमन *darman*, m. = दरमान: — दवा-दरमन, m. medicine, remedy.

दरमा *darmā* [*dāḍimba-*], m. reg. the pomegranate.

दरमान *darmān* [P. *darmān*], m. U. medicine, medical treatment.

दरमियान *dar-miyān* [P. *darmiyān*], m. var. /dərmiyā̃/. **1.** middle, midst; interval. **2.** adv. in the middle. **3.** ppn. w. के. in the middle of; between, among; mediating between; during; before, in view (of). — ~ का, adj. middle.

~ आना (के), to come between, to intervene; to take place between; to interrupt, to interfere. ~ लाना, to introduce (a matter); to include; to adduce. इस ~ में, in the meanwhile.

दरमियानी *dar-miyānī* [P. *darmiyānī*], adj. & m. **1.** adj. middle; intermediate; inner; included, contained. **2.** average, fair (of grade, rank). **3.** m. an intermediary; broker; arbitrator.

दरयाफ़्त *dar-yāft*, f. see दरियाफ़्त.

दरवाज़ा *darvāzā* [P. *darvāza*], m. **1.** a door; doorway, entrance. **2.** a gate; gateway, entrance; ceremonial gateway. — ~ ठोकना, to knock at a door. दरवाज़े की मिट्टी खोद, or ले, डालना, to wear away the ground at a doorway (by frequent visiting).

दरवेश *darveś* [P. *darveś*], m. a Muslim religious mendicant, dervish; beggar.

दरवेशी *darveśī* [P. *darveśī*], f. the way of life of a dervish; beggary.

दरस *dars* [A. *dars*], m. U. reading: a lesson.

दरस *daras* [ad. *darśa-*], m. **1.** sight; glimpse. **2.** seeing, meeting. — ~ दिखाना, to give a glimpse (of), to show (oneself, or one's face).

दरस- *daras-* [cf. H. *daras*], v.i. & v.t. Brbh. **1.** v.i. to be visible; to appear, to be seen. **2.** ? v.t. to see.

दरसनिया *darsaniyā* [cf. H. *darśan*], m. reg. = ओझा.

दरसनी *darsănī*, f. = दर्शनी.

दरहम *darham* [P. *dar-ham*], adj. intermixed, jumbled together; confused. — दरहम-बरहम, adj. = ~. दरहम-बरहम करना, to jumble up, to make disorganised.

दराँत *darāṁt* [*dātra-*²; Panj. *darātī*], m. **1.** a hooked knife. **2.** a sickle (= दराँती).

दराँती *darāṁtī* [**dātrī-*; Panj. *darātī*], f. **1.** a sickle. **2.** a kind of scythe. ~ पड़ना, the sickle to be taken (to, में): to be reaped, &c.

दरा *darā*, m. reg. = ¹दर्रा.

¹**दराज़** *darāz* [P. *darāz*], adj. long, extended. — ~ होना, to lie down, to stretch out at full length. – दराज़-दस्त, adj. *Pl. HŚS.* long-handed: tyrannical. गाल-दराज़, adj. sl. abusive.

²**दराज़** *darāz* [Engl. *drawers*], f. drawer (of a chest, &c).

दराज़ी *darāzī* [P. *darāzī*], f. length; extension.

दराड़ *darāṛ* [cf. *darayati*; +-*ăḍ-*], f. reg. = दरार.

दरार *darār* [**darākāra-*], f. **1.** a crack. **2.** gap, opening; crevasse. **3.** breach (as in a wall, a front).

दरिंदा *darindā* [P. *daranda-*], adj. & m. **1.** adj. rapacious, ferocious. **2.** m. a beast of prey.

दरिद्र *daridră* [S.], adj. & m. **1.** adj. poor, needy. **2.** wretched. **3.** m. a poverty-stricken person.

दरिद्रता *daridrătā* [S.], f. poverty.

दरिद्रनी *daridrănī* [ad. *daridriṇī-*], f. reg. a poor or wretched woman.

दरिद्रित *daridrit* [S.], adj. = दरिद्र.

दरिद्री *daridrī* [*daridrita-*: ad.], adj, Brbh. **1.** poor, needy. **2.** wretched.

दरिया *dariyā* [P. *daryā*], m. inv. **1.** the sea. ***2.** a river (large). — ~ को कूज़े में बंद करना, to enclose the sea in a jar: to be concise (in speech); to achieve the impossible. ~ पार, adv. on the far side of the river. – दरियादिल, adj. generous; munificent. °ई, f. दरिया-बरामद [P. *bar-āmad*], m. alluvial land; land reclaimed from a river. दरिया-बरार [P. *bar-ār*], m. id. दरिया-बुर्द [P. *-burd*], adj. carried or washed away by a river (as land). -ई, f.

¹**दरियाई** *dariyāī* [P. *daryāī*], adj. **1.** marine; seafaring; maritime. **2.** having to do with a river, or rivers; riverine (commerce, transportation); riparian (district). — ~ आदमी, m. seaman. ~ घोड़ा, m. hippopotamus. ~ तोता, m. *Pl.* 'river-parrot': ? flamingo.

²**दरियाई** *dariyai* [f. P. *dārāī*], f. satin.

दरियाफ़्त *dariyāft* [P. *daryāft*], f. **1.** investigation. **2.** ascertainment. — ~ करना, to enquire; to ascertain. ~ होना, to be enquired into; to be ascertained.

¹**दरी** *darī* [S.], f. **1.** cave. **2.** valley (= ¹*darrā*).

²**दरी** *darī* [P. *darī*], m. Brbh. having doors: — दरी-ख़ाना, m. house or room having doors on all sides.

³**दरी** *darī* [**darita-*], f. a carpet, matting (made of cotton).

दरीचा *darīcā* [P. *darīca*], m. **1.** a small door. **2.** a small window; casement.

दरीची *darīcī*, f. Brbh. a small door (= दरीचा).

दरीबा *darībā*, m. a stall in a market (esp. one where *pān* is sold).

दरूनी *darūnī*, adj. E.H. = अंदरूनी.

दरेग़ *dareg* [P. *dareg*], m. U. **1.** denial, withholding. **2.** disinclination; regret. **3.** *HŚS.* shortcoming. — ~ करना, to withhold (sthg., का:), to begrudge.

दरेज़ *darez* [? cf. Engl. *dress*], f. printed muslin, or other fine printed material.

दरेर *darer*, m. = दरेरो.

दरेरना *darernā*, v.t. reg. **1.** to rub. **2.** to grind.

दरेरो *darero* [conn. **daḍavaḍa*-: Pk. *daḍavaḍa*-, H. *daṛeṛā*], m. Brbh. onslaught.

¹**दरेस** *dares* [Engl. *dress*], f. 1. = दरेज़. **2.** dress.

²**दरेस** *dares* [Engl. *dressed*], adj. & m. **1.** adj. adjusted; in order. ***2.** ready-made. **3.** *Pl.* m. road; margin. — ~ करना, to adjust, to put in order or alignment; to level (a road surface); to dress (a wound).

दरेसी *daresī* [cf. H. ²*dares*]. **1.** f. *Pl. HŚS.* proper adjustment. **2.** state of good condition, or repair. **3.** m. *Pl.* a dresser (of wounds, &c.), orderly.

दरोग़ *darog* [P. *durog*], m. falsehood, lie. — दरोग़गोई [P. -*goī*], f. speaking falsehood. दरोग़-हलफ़ी [A. -*ḥalf*+P. -*ī*], f. perjury.

दर्ज *darj* [A. *darj*], m. & adj. **1.** m. insertion, entry (as in a list or file); inclusion. **2.** record, registration. **3.** adj. entered, recorded. — ~ करना, to insert, to enter, &c; to record, &c. ~ होना, to be inserted, or recorded, &c.

दर्जन *darjan* [Engl. dozen], f. a dozen.

दर्जा *darjā* [A. *daraja*], m. **1.** step, stage, degree (as in progress). **2.** grade, level (of attainment, &c.); extent. **3.** quality, standard (as of goods, materials, services); type. **4.** class (school). **5.** rank, standing (of post); class (in examinations). **6.** position, situation; plight. **7.** gradation, degree. **8.** compartment (as in a cupboard, or filing cabinet). — ~ उतारना, = next, 2. ~ घटाना, to reduce the quality (of, का); to reduce the standing (of), to demote. ~ चढ़ाना, to promote. अव्वल दर्जे का, adj. of fine quality, first class; high grade; egregious. ऊँचे दर्जे पर पहुँचना, to reach a high level. पहला ~, m. first class. पहला ~ रखना, to gain first place. – दर्जाबंदी [P. -*bandī*], f. classification; grading, evaluating. दर्जावार [P. -*vār*], adj. graded; adv. by stages.

दर्जावार *darjāvār*, adj. see s.v. दर्जा.

दर्ज़िन *darzin* [cf. H. *darzī*], f. **1.** a sempstress. **2.** a tailor's wife.

दर्ज़ी *darzī* [P. *darzī*], m. a tailor. — दर्ज़ीगिरी [P. -*garī*], f. tailors' craft or work, tailoring.

दर्द *dard* [P. *dard*], m. **1.** pain. **2.** specif. birth pains. **3.** fig. pangs, suffering. **4.** pity, compassion; sympathy. — ~ आना (को), to feel distress (at sthg.); to feel compassion. ~ उठना, pain to arise (in, में); = ~ लगना. ~ करना, to be sore; to ache. ~ का मारा, adj. & m. afflicted, suffering; a sufferer. ~ खाना, to feel compassion; = ~ लगना. ~ दिखाना, to show sympathy. ~ लगना, birth pains to begin. – दर्दतोड़, adj. alleviating pain (as a drug). दर्द-दिल, m. = दर्दे-दिल. दर्दनाक [P. -*nāk*], adj. painful; piteous, tragic. दर्दमंद [P. -*mand*], adj. afflicted; compassionate, sympathising. °ई, f. दर्दशरीक, adj. commiserating, sympathetic. दर्दसर, m. headache (= सरदर्द); fig. trouble, vexation. °ई, f. id. दर्दे-दिल [P. -*e*-], m. heartache: grief, anguish.

दर्दर *dardar* [S.], adj. *HŚS.* **1.** adj. = दरदरा. **2.** reg. coarse gravel. **3.** *Pl.* cinnabar (ore of mercuric sulphide).

दर्दीला *dardīlā*, adj. painful.

दर्दुर *dardur* [S.], m. **1.** a frog. **2.** a pipe or flute.

दर्द्रु *dardru*, m. *Pl. HŚS.* = दद्रु.

दर्द्रू *dardrū*, m. *Pl. HŚS.* = दद्रु.

दर्प *darp* [S.], m. **1.** pride; arrogance. **2.** conceit; boastfulness. **3.** pomp.

दर्पण *darpaṇ* [S.], m. a mirror.

दर्पा *darpā*, m. reg. = दर्प.

दर्पित *darpit* [S.], adj. filled with pride, &c. (= दर्पी).

दर्पी *darpī* [S.], adj. **1.** proud; arrogant. **2.** conceited; boastful. **3.** insolent.

दर्भ *darbh* [S.], m. a grass (esp. sacrificial *kuśa* grass).

¹**दर्रा** *darrā* [P. *darra*], m. **1.** a mountain pass; valley. **2.** a crack, fissure.

²**दर्रा** *darrā*, [? conn. H. *dardarā*], m. reg. **1.** coarse flour, meal. **2.** gravel.

दर्राना *darrānā*, v.i. to go straight and quickly; to go boldly forward.

दर्वी *darvī* [S.], f. **1.** *Pl. HŚS.* spoon, ladle. **2.** *HŚS.* transf. cobra's hood.

दर्श *darś* [S.], m. **1.** sight; glimpse. **2.** specif. the day of a new moon, or the day following.

दर्शक *darśak* [S.], adj. & m. **1.** adj. finally in comp. showing, pointing out. **2.** m. a spectator; observer; visitor (to an exhibition, &c). **3.** supervisor, person in charge. **4.** door-porter. — दर्शक-दीर्घा, f. spectators' or visitors' gallery.

दर्शन *darśan* [S.], m. **1.** seeing, observing; observation; inspection. **2.** sight. **3.** usu. pl. having sight (of); audience (with); visiting (a shrine); worshipping (before an idol). **4.** transf. seeing, meeting, visiting (a respected person). आपके ~ कब होंगे? when shall I (have the good fortune to) see you (again)? **5.** *law.* appearance (in court, of an accused). **6.** appearance, semblance. **7.** view (of sthg.); thought (as of a philosopher or sage); philosophy; specif. any of the six Hindu philosophical systems; contemplation, vision; vision, dream. गांधी (का) दर्शन, the thought of Gandhi. **8.** view, opinion. **9.** transf. mirror. — ~ करना (के), to visit, to have an interview (with); to visit a shrine (of). ~ देना (को), to appear before (a person); to grant an audience, or interview. ~ पाना, to obtain a sight (of, का or के), to be granted audience, &c. (with). – दर्शनकार, m. philosopher. दर्शनाभिलाषी [°*na*+*a*°], adj. & m., f. desirous of seeing (one: formula in use for concluding a letter). दर्शनेंद्रिय [°*na*+*i*°], m. the organ of sight, the eye; the sense of sight.

दर्शनी *darśănī* [ad. *darśanīya-*], f. a bill of exchange payable at sight. — ~ हुंडी, f. id.

दर्शनीय *darśanīya* [S.], adj. worthy of being seen, worth seeing; fine-looking; picturesque.

दर्शाना *darśānā* [ad. *darśayati*: w. H. *darś*, *darśan*], v.t. & v.i. **1.** v.t. to show; to exhibit. **2.** v.i. Brbh. to appear.

दर्शिका *darśikā* [S.], f. a spectator, &c. (cf. दर्शक, m).

दर्शित *darśit* [S.], adj. **1.** shown, exhibited. **2.** seen, understood; apparent.

दर्शी *darśī* [S.], adj. esp. finally in comp. & m. **1.** adj. seeing, observing. **2.** contemplating, reflecting upon (a field of thought, &c). **3.** m. one who sees; observer.

दल *dal* [*dala-* [1 4]], m. **1.** group, band; party (political, sectarian, &c.); detachment; expedition; team. **2.** army. **3.** flock, herd (of animals). **4.** leaf. **5.** petal. **6.** thickness, bulk, volume. — गरम ~, m. extremist party. नरम ~, m. moderate party. – दलदार [P. *-dār*], adj. thick, solid; fleshy, pulpy. दलबदलू, m. pej. one who changes party or affiliation, a 'vicar of Bray'. दलबादल, m. gathered clouds; fig. a vast army.

दलक *dalak* [cf. H. *dalaknā*], f. **1.** shaking, trembling; vibration; shock. **2.** a throbbing or shooting pain. **3.** *Pl.* glitter, splendour.

दलकना *dalaknā* [cf. **dal-*[2]], v.i. **1.** to shake, to tremble. **2.** to throb. **3.** to glitter, to sparkle.

दलदल *daldal* [cf. **dal-*[2]], f. m. **1.** marshy land; marsh, swamp; mire. **2.** fig. difficult situation.

दलदला *daldalā* [cf. H. *daldal*], adj. marshy, boggy.

दलदलाना *daldalānā* [cf. H. *daldal*], v.i. **1.** to shake, to quake. **2.** *Pl.* = थरथराना.

दलदलाहट *daldalāhaṭ* [cf. H. *daldalānā*], f. shaking, quivering; tremor.

दलदली *daldalī* [cf. H. *daldal*], adj. = दलदला.

दलन *dalan* [S.], m. **1.** breaking or tearing to pieces; destroying. **2.** crushing, trampling.

दलना *dalnā* [*dalati*], v.t. **1.** to grind coarsely (as grain); to split (pulse). **2.** to crush, to trample. — दल-मसल करना, to thrash, to beat; *Pl.* to rumple. – दले-पंज, m. *HŚS.* an old horse; *Pl.* old age (in a horse).

दलबा *dalbā*, adj. **1.** broken, crushed; dispirited. **2.** *Pl.* beaten, defeated (as a bird used in training another of its species to fight).

दलमल- *dalmal-* [H. *dalnā*+H. *malnā*], v.t. Brbh. Av. to crush, to trample; to destroy.

दलवाई *dalvāī* [cf. H. *dalvānā*], f. price paid for, or cost of, grinding grain, &c.

दलवाना *dalvānā* [cf. H. *dalnā*], v.t. to cause to be ground or split (grain, pulse: by से).

दलवैया *dalvaiyā* [cf. H. *dalnā*], m. a grinder of grain or pulse; a seller of ground grain or pulse.

दलहन *dalhan* [**daladhānya-*], m. pulse, pulse crop.

दलहरा *dalharā* [? cf. H. *dalnā*], m. *HŚS.* dealer in pulse.

दलहारा *dalhārā* [? cf. H. *dalnā*], m. *Pl.* dealer in pulse.

दलाना *dalānā* [cf. H. *dalnā*], v.t. to cause to be ground, or split (grain, pulse).

[1]दलाल *dalāl* [A. *dallāl*], m. **1.** a broker. **2.** an agent, go-between; salesman. — दलालबाज़ [? H. *dalālbāzī*], m. broker. दलालबाज़ी [P. *-bāzī*], f. brokerage; commission (= दलाली).

[2]दलाल *dalāl* [A. *dalāl*], m. *Pl.* coquettishness.

दलालत *dalālat* [A. *dalāla*: P. *dalālat*], f. **1.** S.H. guidance, sign. **2.** argument (for), proof.

दलाला *dalālā* [A. *dallāla*], f. go-between, procuress.

दलाली *dalālī* [cf. H. *dalāl*], f. **1.** the business of a broker, &c. **2.** brokerage; commission.

दलित *dalit* [S.], adj. **1.** broken or torn to pieces. **2.** crushed, ground; trampled. **3.** oppressed.

दलिद्दर *daliddar* [**daridriya-*: Pa. *daliddiya-*, m. **1.** poverty. **2.** transf. mess, rubbish, refuse.

दलिया *daliyā* [*dalita-*], m. **1.** coarsely ground grain; split pulse. **2.** a thin gruel.

दली *dalī* [cf. H. *dal*], adj. having to do with a group, &c. (= दलीय).

दलीय *dalīyă* [S.], adj. **1.** concerning a group, party, &c. (see दल). **2.** sectarian; factional.

दलील *dalīl* [A. *dalīl*], f. **1.** evidence, argument. **2.** demonstration, proof. — ~ करना, to argue (over, about, पर); to discuss, to debate (a matter); to give evidence (in court); to indicate (a necessary conclusion). ~ देना or पेश करना, or लाना, to put forward evidence, an argument, &c.

दलीली *dalīlī* [A. *dalīl*+P. *-ī*], adj. **1.** argumentative. **2.** good in arguing or in advocacy.

दलेंती *dalemtī*, f. = दलैंती.

दलेल *dalel* [Engl. *drill*], f. *mil.* drill. — ~ बोलना, to put (one) on drill fatigue.

दलैंती *dalaimtī* [**dalayantrikā-*], f. reg. a hand-mill for grinding grain.

दल्लाल *dallāl*, m. see [1]दलाल.

दव *dav* [S.], m. Brbh. Av. **1.** a forest fire; fire. **2.** in comp. a forest. — दवाग्नि [°*va*+*a*°], f. = दावाग्नि. दवारि [°*va*+*a*°], f. enemy of a forest: id. °ई, f. id. दवानल [°*va*+*a*°], f. = दावानल.

दवा *davā* [A. *davā*], f. **1.** medicine. **2.** treatment; remedy. — ~ करना (की), to treat; to cure; to obtain treatment (from, की). ~ खाना or पीना, to take medicine. ~ लगना (को), a medicine to take effect. – दवा-ख़ाना, m. a chemist's shop, dispensary. दवा-दरमन [P. *darmān*], m. f. = next. दवा-दारू, f. medicine(s), medical treatment. दवा-फ़रोश [P. *-faroś*], m. seller of medicines, chemist.

दवाई *davāī* [cf. H. *davā*], f. = दवा.

दवात *davāt* [A. *davāh*: P. *davāt*], f. inkwell.

दवाम *davām* [A. *davām*], m. **1.** continuance, permanence. **2.** adv. always; eternally.

दवामी *davāmī* [A. *davām*+*-ī*], adj. permanent (as a lease, a land settlement).

दव्वार *davvār*, m. Brbh. = दवारि (s.v. दव).

दश *daś* [S.], adj. chiefly in comp. **1.** ten. **2.** forming a tenth (of). — दशकंठ, m. ten-necked: a title of the demon Rāvaṇ. दशमुख, adj. ten-headed: a title of Rāvaṇ. दश-वार्षिक, adj. decennial. दशशीर्ष, m. ten-headed: a title of Rāvaṇ. दशांग [°*śa*+*a*°], m. a partic. incense supposed to have ten ingredients. दशाब्दी [°*śa*+*a*°], f. a decade. दशावतार [°*śa*+*a*°], m. having ten avatārs: a title of Viṣṇu. दशांश [°*śa*+*a*°], m. tenth part, tithe. दशाह [°*śa*+*a*°], m. ten days; = दसवाँ, 2., 3.

दशक *daśak* [S.], m. **1.** an aggregate of ten. **2.** a decade.

दशन *daśan* [S.], m. tooth.

दशम *daśam* [S.], adj. & m. **1.** adj. tenth. **2.** forming a tenth part. **3.** m. tenth part. — ~ द्वार, m. tenth door: (in yoga) the supposed tenth opening of the body, within the skull: through this opening the soul is said to escape to merge with the absolute. – दशम-लव, m. decimal point. °-पद्धति, f. decimal system. °ई, adj. decimal. °-ईकरण, m. decimalisation. दशमांश [°*ma*+*a*°], m. tenth part.

दशमिक *daśămik* [S.], adj. decimal.

[1]**दशमी** *daśămī* [S.], f. **1.** the tenth day of a lunar fortnight. 2. = विजया-दशमी (see s.v. दशहरा, 2). **3.** *Pl. HŚS.* the tenth decade or last stage of human life. **4.** *Pl.* the last ten years of a century. **5.** *HŚS.* death; release from rebirth.

[2]**दशमी** *daśămī* [S.], adj. & m. **1.** adj. aged between ninety and a hundred years; extremely old. **2.** m. an aged man.

दशहरा *daśahrā* [S. *daśaharā-*, f.], m. **1.** the tenth day of the bright half of the month Jeṭh; the festival in honour of the river Ganges held on that day (which is regarded as the birthday of Ganges). ***2.** the tenth day of the bright half of the month Āśvin; the celebrations in honour of Durgā held on this day (*vijayā-daśamī*) as a culmination of the Durgāpūjā festival; the celebration of the victory of Rām over the demon Rāvaṇ, held on the same day.

दशा *daśā* [S.], f. **1.** state, condition. **2.** situation, circumstances; period or stage of life. **3.** *astrol.* situation of heavenly bodies; conjunction, or influence. **4.** *HŚS.* wick (of lamp). — ऐसी ~ में, adv. in such circumstances; in these circumstances. — दशा-फल, m. result of circumstances or condition of life. दशाहीन, adj. unfortunate, wretched.

दशानिक *daśānik* [S.], m. *Pl. HŚS.* a small tree, *Croton polyandrum* or *C. tiglium* (*jamāl-goṭā*) which produces a medicinal oil.

[1]**दशी** *daśī* [cf. *daśa-*], f. = दशक.

[2]**दशी** *daśī* [S.], m. *hist.* superintendent of ten villages.

दश्त *daśt* [P. *daśt*], m. U. desert; arid or wild region.

दस *das* [*daśa-*], adj. **1.** ten. **2.** a significant number (of), various. ~ आदमी, m. pl. a good number of people. – दसों दिशा, f. the ten directions: eight points of the compass together with zenith and nadir. दसों द्वार, m. pl. the ten gateways: (in yoga) the nine openings of the body together with the *brahmarandhra* passage for the vital energies, which is said to open within the skull at the moment of union with the absolute.

[1]**दसना** *dasnā*, v.i. = दिसना.

[2]**दसना** *dasnā* [*dhvasyate, dhvasati*], v.i. & v.t. **1.** v.i. *Pl. HŚS.* to be spread. **2.** दस-, v.t. Brbh. to spread.

दसवाँ *dasvāṁ* [cf. H. *das*], adj. & m. **1.** adj. tenth. **2.** m. the tenth day after a death. **3.** prayers or offerings on the tenth day after a death.

दसवीं *dasvīṁ* [H. *dasvāṁ*], f. *Pl.* tenth day of a month, or of a lunar fortnight.

दसहरा *dasahrā*, m. = दशहरा.

दसा *dasā*, m. = दस्सा, 2.

दसी *dasī* [*daśā-*], f. E.H. the unwoven threads at the end of a piece of cloth; fringe.

दसीला *dasīlā* [cf. H. *daśā*], adj. *Pl.* in good circumstances, prosperous.

दसूठन *dasūṭhan* [**daśot-sthāna-*], m. *Pl.* bathing on the tenth day after childbirth.

दसोंखा *dasoṁkhā*, m. *Pl.* = दसोखा.

दसोखा *dasokhā* [? conn. *dhvasyate*, and *pakṣa-*], m. *Pl.* moulting. — ~ झाड़ना, to moult.

दसोतरा *dasotrā* [**daśottara-*], adj. & m. **1.** adj. plus ten. **2.** adv. at ten per cent. **3.** m. ten per cent; a tenth.

दसौंध *dasauṁdh* [*daśabandha-*], m. *Pl.* offering made to a goddess when a child reaches its tenth year.

दसौंधी *dasauṁdhī* [cf. *daśabandha-*], m. Brbh. Av. one entitled to a tithe, or portion: a panegyrist, bard.

दस्त *dast* [P. *dast*], m. **1.** chiefly in comp. the hand. **2.** diarrhoea. — ~ आना, or छूटना, or लगना (को), to have diarrhoea. हरे ~, m. dysentery. – दस्तंदाज़ [P. *-andāz*], adj. meddling, interfering. °ई, f. दस्तकार, adj. & m. dextrous, expert; a craftsman, tradesman. °ई, f. handicraft; craftsmanship. दस्तख़त, m. signature. दस्तख़त करना, to sign. दस्तख़त लेना, to get (a person's) signature. °ई, adj. signed; needing signature (a document); written with one's own hand; in manuscript. दस्त-गरदाँ [P. *-gardān*], adj. *Pl.* going from hand to hand: lent on short term (money); hawked about for sale. दस्तगीर [P. *-gīr*], m. Brbh. Av. helper; patron. °ई, f. aid. दस्त-दराज़, m. long-handed, long-armed: oppressor; pickpocket. °ई, f. दस्त-पनाह, m. *Pl. HŚS.* tongs. दस्त-बदस्त [P. *-ba-*], adv. & adj. hand in hand; from hand to hand; quick, deft. °ई, f. Brbh. hand-to-hand transaction, or encounter. दस्तबंद, m. a string of pearls or precious stones worn round the wrist; a gold or silver ornament worn on thc back of the hand. दस्तयाब [P. *-yāb*], adj. U. attained, acquired. दस्तावर [P. *-āvar*], adj. purgative. दस्तावेज़ [P. *-āvez*], f. a bond, deed; certificate, document. ° ई, adj. having to do with a bond, &c.

दस्तक *dastak* [P. *dastak*], f. **1.** knock (at a door). **2.** clapping of the hands (as to attract attention). **3.** a writ, summons; call-up notice. **4.** a levy, tax. **5.** permit, licence; pass. — ~ देना [P. *-ba-*], to knock (at, *par*); to clap the hands, ~ बाँधना, *Pl. HŚS.* to incur needless expenses. ~ माफ़ करना, to absolve from a duty, to forgive. ~ लगाना, to serve a writ, &c. (on, पर); to impose a tax (on); fig. to place a burden of expense (upon one, पर).

दस्तरख़ान *dastarkhān* [P. *dastārkhvān*], m. **1.** tablecloth. **2.** transf. table. — ~ की बिल्ली, f. 'cat at the table': an uninvited guest.

[1]**दस्ता** *dastā* [P. *dasta*], m. **1.** a handle; grip, hilt; butt (of rifle). **2.** a handful, bundle; skein; bunch (flowers); quire (of paper). **3.** small flower-bed. **4.** *mil.* unit, detachment; platoon; squadron; flight. पाँचवाँ ~, m. fifth column.

[2]**दस्ता** *dastā*, m. = जस्ता.

दस्ताना *dastānā* [P. *dastāna*], m. a glove.

दस्ती *dastī* [P. *dastī*], adj. & f. **1.** adj. manual. **2.** having a handle. **3.** held in, or conveyed in, the hand. **4.** f. a small handle. **5.** hand-lamp, torch. **6.** a pencil case; pen-holder. **7.** a gift (as made on the last day of the *daśahrā* festival). — ~ गोला, m. hand grenade.

दस्तूर *dastūr* [P. *dastūr*], m. custom, usage, practice; normal procedure, rule. — ~ है, it is the usual practice. – बदस्तूर [P. *ba-*], adv. according to custom, as is usual.

दस्तूरी *dastūrī* [P. *dastūrī*], adj. & f. **1.** adj. customary. **2.** f. a customary payment; payment to an intermediary; commission (as to a buyer's agent).

दस्यु *dasyu* [S.], m. **1.** an impious person; barbarian. **2.** a wrong-doer; bandit; thief.

दस्युता *dasyutā* [S.], f. **1.** villainy; banditry, robbery. **2.** barbarous ways.

दस्सा *dassā* [?? *dasyu-*], m. **1.** pej. a person of mixed caste. **2.** one of the two chief divisions of the Agravāl community.

[1]**दह** *dah* [*draha-*], m. Brbh. **1.** a deep pool. **2.** a tank. — काली-दह, m. *mythol.* Kāliya's pool.

[2]दह *dah* [P. *dah*], adj. Brbh. Av. ten.

दहक *dahak* [cf. H. *dahaknā*], f. **1.** burning, blazing; tongue of flame. **2.** a blaze; conflagration. **3.** fig. heat, fire (of ardour, or shame).

दहकना *dahaknā* [cf. *dahati*], v.i. **1.** to burn, to blaze. **2.** to be burnt, scorched. **3.** fig. to be consumed (as by grief, remorse).

दहकाना *dahkānā* [cf. H. *dahaknā*], v.t. **1.** to kindle, to light (a blaze). **2.** to provoke, to inflame (anger, &c).

दहड़-दहड़ *dahaṛ-dahaṛ* [*dṛḍha*-; ? × H. *dahnā*], adv. with a roaring, or crackling sound (as of a fire).

दहन *dahan* [*dahana*-], m. **1.** burning; chem. combustion. **2.** fire. **3.** reg. closeness, humidity. — दहनशील, adj. inflammable.

दहना *dahnā* [*dahati*], v.i. & v.t. **1.** v.i. to be burnt, to burn. **2.** to blaze (as with anger). **3.** v.t. Brbh. to burn, to consume. **4.** Brbh. to cause distress.

दहनीय *dahnīyă* [S.], adj. **1.** to be burnt, fit to be burnt. **2.** combustible.

दहम *dahm*, adj. reg. burnt out, extinguished (a fire).

दहरी *dahrī*, f. *Pl.* a heavy clay, waterlogged soil.

दहल *dahal* [cf. H. *dahalnā*], f. **1.** shaking, trembling. **2.** fear. **3.** *Pl.* transf. shifting sand; quicksand.

दहलना *dahalnā*, v.i. **1.** to shake, to tremble. **2.** to be alarmed, or terrified.

[1]दहला *dahlā* [cf. *daśa*-], m. the ten (at cards).

[2]दहला *dahlā* [*dehalī*-], m. reg. the hollow made round the trunk of a tree (to hold water: = थाला).

दहलाना *dahlānā* [cf. H. *dahalnā*], v.t. **1.** to cause to shake. **2.** to make afraid.

दहलीज़ *dahlīz* [P. *dahlīz*], f. threshold; porchway; vestibule. — ~ का कुत्ता, m. porch-dog: hanger-on, parasite. ~ की मिट्टी ले डालना, to wear away the earth of the threshold: to be always at (someone's) door. ~ न झाँकना (की), not to look at (one's) doorway: to cease to visit. ~ पर होना, to be on the doorstep, impending.

दहशत *dahśat* [A. *dahśa*: P. *dahśat*], f. **1.** fear, alarm. **2.** terror. — ~ खाना, to be frightened; to be terrified. ~ देना (को), to frighten, &c.; to intimidate; to terrorise. – दहशतंगेज़ [P. *-angez*], adj. & m. stirring up fear: terrifying; intimidating; m. a terrorist. °ई, f. intimidation; terrorism. दहशतगर्दी [P. *-gardī*], f. terrorising, terrorism. दहशतनाक [P. *-nāk*], adj. terrifying. दहशतज़दा [P. *-zada*], adj. terror-stricken.

दहा *dahā* [P. *dahā*], m. *musl.* **1.** the first ten days of the month of Muḥarram. **2.** models of the tombs of Ḥasan and Ḥusain (= ताज़िया). **3.** transf. the entire month of Muḥarram.

दहाई *dahāī* [cf. *daśaka*-], f. **1.** the figure ten. **2.** place of the tens (in numbers). **3.** tenth part. **4.** the (first) decimal place; a decimal.

दहाका *dahākā*, m. *Pl.* **1.** a collection of ten. **2.** *arith.* the tens.

दहाड़ *dahāṛ*, f. **1.** roaring. **2.** thunderous noise. **3.** any loud cry. — ~ (or दहाड़ें) मारना), or मारकर रोना, to sob, to wail.

दहाड़ना *dahāṛnā*, v.i. **1.** to roar. **2.** to thunder. **3.** to sob, to wail.

[1]दहाना *dahānā* [cf. H. *dahnā*], v.t. reg. to set fire to, to burn.

[2]दहाना *dahānā* [P. *dahāna*], m. **1.** mouth (as of a river, watercourse, drain). **2.** opening (as of a valley). **3.** mouth (of a receptacle). **4.** mouthpiece. **5.** bit (of a bridle). — ~ करना, sl. to urinate.

दहिंगल *dahiṁgal*, m. = ग्वालिन, 4.

दहित *dahit* [S.], adj. burnt, scorched.

दही *dahī* [*dadhi*-], m. thick sour milk, curds, yoghurt. — ~ का तोड़, m. whey. ~ ~ करना, to call 'curds, curds': to peddle one's wares. ~ जमना, to become coagulated (milk). ~ जमाना, to make curds. – दही-बड़ा, m. a partic. savoury: small lumps of fried pulse, with curds and spices.

दहेंडी *daheṁḍī*, f. pronun. var. = दहेंड़ी.

दहेंड़ी *daheṁṛī* [*dadhibhāṇḍa*-], f. reg. a pot in which milk is made into curds, or in which curds are kept.

दहेज़ *dahez* [P. *jahez* (A. *jihāz*, *jahāz*); ? × H. *daijā*], m. dowry. — ~ में देना, to give as dowry.

दहेज़ू *dahezū* [cf. H. *dahez*], adj. having to do with a dowry; colloq. pej. cheap, tawdry (*Pl.*).

दहेड़ *daheṛ*, m. *Pl.* name of several birds: raven, crow; *Coracias*; the magpie-robin, *Copsychus saularis*.

दहेला *dahelā*, m. the ten (in cards: = [1]दहला).

दहेल- *dahel*- [cf. H. *dahnā*], adj. Brbh. **1.** burnt. **2.** [× H. *duhelā*] tormented (by grief); suffering.

दहैंड़ी *dahaiṁṛī*, f. pronun. var. = दहेंड़ी.

दहोका *dahokā*, m. *Pl.* a measure of about ten (?) handfuls of grain.

दहोतरा *dahotrā* [**daśottara-*; w. P. *dah*], m. *Pl.* a tenth; an allowance or tax of ten per cent.

दाँ *dāṁ*, m. = दाँव. — एक ~, adv. obs. once.

[1]**दाँग** *dāṁg* [**daṅga-*], f. reg. **1.** hill; precipice. **2.** summit. **3.** high bank (of river).

[2]**दाँग** *dāṁg*, m. Av. ? a kettledrum.

[3]**दाँग** *dāṁg* [P. *dāng*], f. U. **1.** a sixth part; a minute weight, the equivalent of six *rattī* seeds. **2.** side, quarter.

दाँगर *dāṁgar* [**daṅgara-*[1]], m. reg. **1.** horned cattle (= डाँगर). **2.** pej. dolt, idiot.

दाँगी *dāṁgī* [cf. H. [1]*dāṁg*], adj. & m. reg. **1.** adj. of or belonging to hilly country. **2.** m. name given to Bundela Rājpūts.

दाँड़ *dāṁṛ* [*daṇḍ-*], m. = डाँड़.

दाँड़ना *dāṁṛnā* [*daṇḍayati*], v.t. **1.** to punish. **2.** to fine.

दांडिक *dāṇḍik* [S.], m. *Pl. HŚS.* punisher; executioner.

[1]**दाँड़ी** *dāṁṛī* [*daṇḍika-*], m. reg. rower, waterman.

[2]**दाँड़ी** *dāṁṛī* [*daṇḍikā-*], f. reg. a balance.

दाँत *dāṁt* [*danta-*], m. **1.** tooth. **2.** tusk. **3.** m. f. tooth, cog. **4.** notch. — ~ का दर्द, m. toothache. ~ (or दाँतों) उँगली काटना, or दबाना, = next. ~ (or दाँतों) में, or तले, उँगली दबाना, to bite the forefinger in astonishment or puzzlement; or in remorse; or as a sign of sympathy or sorrow; or in requesting silence. ~ कटकटाना, to grind the teeth (in anger); to cause the teeth to chatter (through cold). ~ करना, to teethe. ~ काटना, to bite; to seize in the teeth. ~ किचकिचाना, or किटकिटाना, = ~ कटकटाना, 1.; to grit the teeth, to strive. ~ किरकिराना, v.i. the teeth to feel gritty, on edge. ~ किरकिरे होना, fig. to suffer a rebuff or setback. ~ कुरेदने को तिनका न रहना, 'to lack a straw for a toothpick': not to have a penny to one's name. ~ खट्टे करना, to set the teeth on edge; to give a setback (to, के), to displease, to disconcert; to frustrate; to excite the envy or jealousy (of). ~ गड़ाना, = ~ लगाना, 1., 2. ~ चबाना, = ~ पीसना. ~ झड़ना, the teeth to fall out, or to be broken. ~ झाड़ना, to knock out a tooth; fig. to give a severe setback (to). ~ तेज़ करना, to bear a grudge (against, पर); to set one's heart (on). ~ तोड़ना, to break the teeth (of, के): to make powerless or harmless, to bring low. ~ निकालना, to show the teeth: to teethe; to laugh; to express helplessness, to gape; to whine, to cringe; fig. to be worn out (shoes). ~ निकोसना, or निपोड़ना, id., 4. ~ पर चढ़ाना, to detract from the virtues or praise (of, के). ~ पीसना, to grind or to grate the teeth; to grin. ~ बजना, the teeth to chatter; squabbling to go on. ~ बजाना, to squabble, to wrangle. ~ बाना, to show the teeth, &c. (= ~ निकालना). ~ बनानेवाला, m. a dentist. ~ बैठना or बैठ जाना, the teeth to be, or to become, clenched (as in lockjaw). ~ मारना (पर), to bite; fig. to obtain possession (of). ~ रखना (पर), to desire strongly, to covet; to be intent upon (as on revenge, &c). ~ लगना (पर), to be bitten (into); desire or greed to be felt (for); = ~ बैठना. ~ लगाना, to fix the teeth (into, पर); to set one's heart (on); to wear false teeth. ~ लगाए रहना = ~ लगाना, 2. ~ लाना, to teethe. ~ सलसलाना, the teeth to cause discomfort. ~ से ~ बजना, the teeth to chatter. ~ होना, = ~ रखना, 1. दाँतों का इलाज कराना, or करवाना, to obtain dental treatment, to go to the dentist. दाँतों का डाकटर, m. a dentist. दाँतों चढ़ना, fig. to provoke the envy or hatred (of). दाँतों ज़मीन पकड़ना, 'to seize the ground in the teeth': to be reduced to dire straits; to be in great pain. दाँतों तले उँगली दबाना, = ~ (तले) उँगली दबाना. दाँतों तले होंठ दबाना, to bite the lip (in anger, contrition). दाँतों पर न रखा जाना, fig. to be unbearable (of taste). दाँतों पर मैल न होना, 'no tartar to be on the teeth': to be poverty-stricken, to starve. दाँतों मारना = ~ पीसना. दाँतों में उँगली देना = ~ में उँगली दबाना. दाँतों में जीभ, or ज़बान (की तरह) होना, to be (as) the tongue between the teeth, to be unharmed among enemies. दाँतों में तिनका लेना, 'to take a piece of grass in the mouth (as a cow)': to show submissiveness in the face of displeasure. — दाँत-काटी रोटी खाना, fig. to be a close friend (of, की). दाँत-घुँघनी, f. *Pl. HŚS. musl.* a preparation of wheat flour, sugar and poppy-seed (eaten ceremonially when a child's first tooth appears). दाँत-दर्द, m. toothache. दाँतदार [P. *-dār*], adj. toothed (as a wheel); notched; having zigzag ornamentation. दाँत-भड़ाका, m. wrangling, quarrel. दाँत-विज्ञान, m. dentistry. दाँतसाज़ [P. *-sāz*], m. dental technician, dentist.

[1]**दांत** *dānt* [S.], adj. dental.

[2]**दांत** *dānt* [S.], adj. **1.** in subjection. **2.** repressed.

दाँतन *dāṁtan*, m. (? f.) = दातुन. — दाँतन-कुल्ला करना, to brush the teeth, and rinse the mouth.

दाँतना *dāṁtnā* [cf. H. *dāṁt*], v.i. *Pl. HŚS.* to get teeth (animals).

दाँतवन *dāṁtvan*, m. (? f.) = दातुन.

दाँता *dāṁtā* [*dantaka-*], m. **1.** tooth (of wheel, saw, comb); cog. **2.** a notch, jag. — दाँते पड़ना (में), to become notched or jagged. – दाँता-किटकिट, f. quarrelling; abuse. °-किलकिल, id. दाँतेदार [P. *-dār*], adj. toothed, cogged; serrated.

दांतिक *dāntik* [S.], adj. *Pl. HŚS.* made of ivory.

दाँतिया *dāṁtiyā* [cf. H. *dāṁt*], m. *Pl. HŚS.* a mixture of alkaline salts (*reh*) and tobacco, a tooth-powder.

[1]**दाँती** *dāṁtī* [cf. H. *dāṁtā*], f. = दाँता, 1. — ~ पड़ना, notches or serration to appear (in, में).

[2]**दाँती** *dāṁtī* [*dantin-*], m. & f. having teeth or tusks: **1.** m. a wild boar. **2.** f. *Pl.* a harrow. **3.** reg. (W.) a sickle (serrated). **4.** *HŚS.* a ravine.

[3]**दाँती** *dāṁtī* [**dantiya-*], f. **1.** the teeth, set of teeth (= बत्तीसी, 2). **2.** lockjaw. – ~ लगना, the teeth to be clenched; to have lockjaw.

दाँतू *dāṁtū* [cf. H. *dāṁt*], adj. reg. having prominent teeth.

दाँना *dāṁnā* [**dāmayati*], v.t. to tread out grain (from unthreshed corn: oxen).

दांभिक *dāmbhik* [S.], adj. & m. **1.** adj. proud; overbearing. **2.** hypocritical. **3.** deceitful. **4.** m. an overbearing person, &c. **5.** fig. a crane, heron (*Ardea nivea*).

दाँय *dāṁy*, f. Brbh. = [1]दावन.

दाँव *dāṁv* [*dātu-*, or *dāman-*[2]], m. **1.** time, turn; move, throw (in a game). **2.** opportunity. **3.** power, grasp, control. **4.** snare, trap; ambush. **5.** stroke, blow (as in a game or contest); hold, throw (as in wrestling). **6.** stake, wager; forfeit, penalty. — ~ करना, to use a trick, or hold; = ~ ताकना; = ~ खेलना. ~ कहना, to speak considering the occasion, to be a yes-man. ~ का दूना, adj. of twice face value (as a playing card). ~ खाना, to be tricked (by, से). ~ खेलना, to try cunning (on, के साथ). ~ चलना, to take one's turn, to make one's move (in a game); one's move to succeed. ~ चलाना, to make the most of an opportunity, to take advantage. ~ ताकना, to watch for (one's) opportunity; to lie in wait. ~ देना, to give (one) his turn; to trick, to take in; to pay a lost bet, or forfeit. ~ पकड़ना, to wrestle. ~ पड़ना, to be thrown (dice); to be thrown high (dice). ~ पर चढ़ना, to come into the control or power (of, के). ~ पर चढ़ाना, or लाना, to bring under (one's) power, to get a grip (of an opponent). ~ पर रखना, to stake, to wager. ~ पर लगाना, id. ~ (में) बैठना, to lie in ambush, to lurk. ~ में आना, to be tricked (by, के). ~ लगना, an opportunity to present itself. ~ लगाना, to set a trap, or ambush; to stake, to wager. ~ लेना, to take (one's) turn; to seize a chance; to exact a forfeit, or a penalty. – दाँव-घात, m. ambush; trick; opportunity (for an underhand manoeuvre). दाँव-पेंच, m. a trick; stratagem, manoeuvre.

दाँवनी *dāṁvnī*, f. reg. = दामनी, 2.

दाँवरी *dāṁvrī* [**dāmara-*], f. *Pl. HŚS.* **1.** rope; twine. **2.** specif. rope with which bullocks are tied together when treading out corn.

दाँहो *dāṁho* [? H. *dāṁv*, obl. pl.], adv. *Pl.* properly, well; thoroughly; to (one's) heart's content.

दा *dā* [*dātra-*[2]], m. reg. a sickle; cleaver.

दाईं *dāīṁ*, f. *Pl.* equality (of age or size); measure, size.

दाई *dāī* [cf. P. *dāya*], f. **1.** a wet-nurse; nurse. **2.** a midwife. **3.** a woman servant. — दाईगिरी [P. *-gīrī*], f. midwifery; a nurse's duties.

दाऊ *dāū* [? *dādda-* × *tātagu-*], m. **1.** elder brother. **2.** father.

दाऊद *dāūd* [A. *dā'ūd*], m. David (of Israel: one of the prophets of Islam). — दाऊद-ख़ानी, f. Av. a type of rice having a reddish husk; a type of short-bearded, high-grade wheat.

दाऊदी *dāūdī* [cf. A. *dā'ūd*], f. **1.** chain-mail. **2.** a shrub, *Chrysanthemum indicum*, and its flower. **3.** (*Pl. HŚS.*) = दाऊद-ख़ानी.

दाएँ *dāeṁ* [cf. H. *dāvnā*], f. *Pl.* tying bullocks together to thresh corn by treading; treading out corn; unthreshed corn.

दाक *dāk* [S.], m. *Pl. HŚS.* giver, donor (esp. to brāhmaṇs); commissioner of a brahminical sacrifice.

दाक्षायणी *dākṣāyaṇī* [S.], f. *Pl. HŚS.* daughter of Dakṣa: **1.** *astrol.* the lunar asterisms considered collectively as daughters of Dakṣa; name of partic. asterisms, esp. of Rohiṇī and Aśvinī. **2.** *Pl.* the plant *Croton polyandrum.*

दाक्षिणात्य *dākṣiṇātyă* [S.], m. poet. belonging to the south: the south.

दाक्ष्य *dākṣyă* [S.], m. **1.** dexterity, adroitness; skill. **2.** capability.

दाख *dākh* [*drākṣā-*], f. **1.** a grape. **2.** a raisin.

दाख़िल *dākhil* [A. *dākhil*], adj. & m. **1.** adj. entering; arriving. **2.** admitted to, joining (a group). **3.** entered (in a list); inserted, included. **4.** paid, paid over (as a fine). **5.** m. entering (upon), taking possession (of). **6.** entry (in a book, account). **7.** inclusion, incorporation. — ~ करना (में, के अंदर), to cause to enter, &c.; to cause to be entered (as in a list); to produce (as to a court); to include; to deposit; to pay over. ~ होना, to enter, &c.; to occupy; to be included (in, में); to be entered, paid, &c. – दाख़िल-ख़ारिज करना, to transfer land or property (in a register, by 'entering' and 'striking out' partic. details). दाख़िल-दफ़्तर करना, to file with the record (a paper, &c).

दाख़िला *dākhilā* [A. *dākhila*], m. **1.** entry; admission; admittance. **2.** entry fee. **3.** entry (in an account, &c). **4.** paying out (of money, &c). **5.** receipt, voucher.

दाख़िली *dākhilī* [A. *dākhilī*], adj. internal, interior.

दाग़ *dāg* [P. *dāg*], m. **1.** the mark of burning; a brand. **2.** a mark; spot, speck; stain; streak. **3.** freckle. **4.** scar. **5.** blemish; stigma, disgrace. **6.** transf. sorrow, grief. **7.** loss, injury, damage. — ~ खाना, to be wounded, or grieved (by, से). ~ चढ़ाना, = ~ लगाना, 3. ~ दिलाना, to set fire (to, में), to set alight. ~ देना (को), to mark, to scar; to brand. ~ लगाना, to brand; to mark; to defame. ~ लाना (में), id., 3. ~ ह्रोना, to be marked, scarred, &c. सफ़ेद ~, m. leprosy. – दाग़-बेल, f. the line of a road or of foundations, as marked out for construction. दाग़ बेल लगाना, to mark out; to take the first, or preliminary, steps. दाग़दार [P. *-dār*], adj. marked; scarred; streaked, striped; stained; blemished; shamed, disgraced.

दाग़ना *dāgnā* [cf. H. *dāg*], v.t. **1.** to burn, esp. with an iron; to brand; to cauterise. **2.** to mark. **3.** to fire (a firearm); to shoot (a goal). **4.** to detonate. **5.** to start (a combustion engine).

दाग़ी *dāgī* [P. *dāgī*], adj. **1.** marked, &c. (= दाग़दार); notorious. **2.** transf. doomed, condemned (to, का). — ~ करना, to mark, &c.

दाड़क *dāṛak* [S.], m. *Pl. HŚS.* = दाढ़.

दाड़िंब *dāṛimb* [*dāḍimba-*; Pk. *dāḍima-*], m. *Pl. HŚS.* = दाड़िम.

दाड़िम *dāṛim* [*dāḍimba-*, Pk. *dāḍima-*], m. the pomegranate tree, and its fruit. — दाड़िमप्रिय, m. *Pl. HŚS.* 'liking pomegranates': the parrot. दाड़िम-पुष्पक, m. name of a medicinal plant, *Soymida febrifuga* or *Amoora rohitaka*.

दाढ़ *dāṛh* [**dāṃṣṭra-*: Pk. *dāḍhā-*], f. **1.** a molar tooth. **2.** a tusk.

दाढ़ा *dāṛhā*, m. reg. 1. = दाढ़. **2.** *Pl.* a number, multitude.

दाढ़ी *dāṛhī* [**dāṃṣṭra-*: Pk. *dāḍhiā-*], f. **1.** beard. **2.** chin. — ~ घोटना, or मूँड़ना, to shave off the beard. ~ छोड़ना, to let the beard grow. ~ धूप में सफ़ेद करना, fig. to be wanting (through idleness or uninvolvement in affairs) in experience, or judgment, or wisdom. ~ बनाना, to shave the beard, to trim the beard. – दाढ़ीदार [P. *-dār*], adj. bearded. दाढ़ीजार, m. = दारी-जार.

दात *dāt* [*dātra-*[1], or *datta-*], m. Brbh. **1.** a gift. **2.** liberality.

दातव्य *dātavyă* [S.], adj. & m. **1.** adj. to be given or bestowed. **2.** m. sthg. to be given; donation; charity.

दाता *dātā* [S.], adj. & m. **1.** adj. liberal, generous. **2.** m. a liberal man; donor, benefactor. **3.** transf. the supreme being.

दातापन *dātāpan* [cf. H. *dātā*], m. liberality, beneficence; benevolence.

दातार *dātār* [**dātrakāra-*], m. Brbh. Av. = दाता.

दाति *dāti* [S.], f. E.H. giving, act of giving (? for दात, 2).

दातुन *dātun* [*dantapavana-*], f. **1.** a twig, esp. of the *nīm* or *babūl* tree, the frayed end of which is used to clean the teeth. **2.** cleaning the teeth. — ~ करना, to clean the teeth.

दातुवन *dātuvan*, f. = दातुन.

दातृत्व *dātṛtvă* [S.], m. liberality, beneficence.

दातोन *dāton*, f. = दातुन.

दातौन *dātaun*, f. = दातुन.

दात्र *dātră* [S.], m. *Pl. HŚS.* = दा.

[1]**दाद** *dād* [P. *dād*], f. **1.** justice; equity. **2.** due praise. — ~ देना (को), to give due praise (to); to appreciate. – दादो-फ़रियाद, m. appeal for justice or redress.

[2]**दाद** *dād* [*dadru-*[1]], m. **1.** ringworm. **2.** shingles.

दादनी *dadănī* [cf. P. *dādan*], f. E.H. **1.** advances of money or pay. **2.** debts.

दादरा *dādrā* [cf. H. *dādur*], m. a type of song to a quick melody (common in Agra district and Bundelkhand).

दादस *dādas*, f. reg. mother of a wife's or husband's mother-in-law (= ददिया-सास).

दादसरा *dādasrā* [**dāddaśvaśura-*], m. (*Pl.*) father of a wife's or husband's father-in-law.

दादसुसरा *dādsusrā*, m. *Pl.* = दादसरा.

दादा *dādā* [**dādda-*], m. inv. **1.** paternal grandfather. **2.** elder brother. **3.** respectful term of address to an older man. **4.** pej. bully, lout; gangster. — दादागिरी [P. *-gīrī*], f. pej. bullying, loutish behaviour.

[1]**दादी** *dādī* [**dādda-*], f. paternal grandmother.

[2]**दादी** *dādī* [P. *dādī*], m. *Pl. HŚS.* plaintiff, complainant.

दादुर *dādur* [*dardura-*[1]], m. a frog.

दादू *dādū* [cf. H. *dādā*], m.: term of address. 1. = दादा. **2.** 'brother, friend'. **3.** 'son'.

दाध *dādh* [**dagdhi-*], f. Av. burning; fire, heat.

दाध- *dādh-* [cf. *dagdha-*], v.t. & (*Pl.*) v.i. Av. to burn.

दान *dān* [*dāna-*[1]], m. **1.** giving; giving in marriage. **2.** a gift; donation; offering; grant; endowment. **3.** alms. **4.** Brbh. levy, tribute. **5.** exudation (from the temples of a rutting elephant). — ~ करना, = next. ~ देना, to give away, to bestow (a gift, offering, &c). — दान-कर्ता, m. inv. a donor. दान-दक्षिणा, f. a religious gift to a beggar; gift to a brāhmaṇ. दान-दाता, m. inv. = दान-कर्ता. दान-धर्म, m. the practice of liberality: almsgiving, charity. दान-पत्र, deed of gift; a will. दानपरायण, adj. generous, liberal. दान-पात्र, m. a beneficiary. दान-पुन, m. = next. दान-पूण्य, m. the merit arising from liberality: = दान-धर्म. दान-लीला, *mythol.* name given to Kṛṣṇa's exaction of tribute from the herdgirls of Braj as they go with their milk, &c. to market. दान-लेख, m. = दान-पत्र, 1., 2. दान-वीर, m. 'hero in giving': a very munificent person. दानशील, adj. of liberal nature, munificent. °ता, f.

-दान *-dān* [P. *-dān*], suffix. = -दानी.

दानता *dānătā* [S.], f. = दानपन.

दानपन *dānpan* [cf. H. *dān*], m. = दानशीलता.

दानव *dānav* [S.], m. & adj. **1.** m. *mythol.* a class of demons; a demon. **2.** adj. having to do with the *dānavas*; fiendish.

दानवी *dānăvī* [S.], f. & adj. **1.** f. demoness. **2.** adj. = दानव.

[1]**दाना** *dānā* [P. *dānā*], adj. inv. & m. **1.** adj. wise, learned. **2.** m. a wise man.

[2]**दाना** *dānā* [P. *dāna*], m. **1.** a grain; transf. crumb, speck. **2.** a single, small object; clove (of garlic); sthg. to be threaded (as a bead, a pearl). **3.** a pimple. **4.** fleck (on the skin: as a freckle, or a smallpox mark; or in cloth); dappling, stippling. **5.** grain, corn; food. **6.** seed-corn. — ~ जमाना (में), to sow seed (in); to bait (a hook). ~ डालना (के आगे, के सामने), to feed (fowls, &c). ~ देना (को), id. ~ भराना, to feed (its young: a bird). दाने दाने को तरसना, or मुहताज होना, 'to want for each crumb': to be in dire want. – दाना-चारा, m. fodder. दाना-पानी, m. food and drink; sustenance. दाना-पानी उठना, means of support or livelihood to be withdrawn. दाना-पानी छोड़ना, to fast. दाना-बदली करना, *Pl.*, to bill and coo (birds). दानाबंदी [P. *-bandī*], f. assessment of revenue made from a valuation of standing crops. दानेदार [P. *-dār*], adj. granulated; containing flecks, &c.; containing grain. दाने-दुनके, m. pl. crumbs, pickings.

[3]**दाना** *dānā* [*dānava-*], m. *mythol.* = दानव.

दानाई *dānāī* [P. *dānāī*], f. wisdom; knowledge.

दानिश *dāniś* [P. *dāniś*], f. **1.** knowledge. **2.** learning. — दानिशमंद [P. *-mand*], adj. & m. wise; learned; a wise or learned person. °ई, f.

[1]**दानी** *dānī* [S.], adj. & m. **1.** adj. liberal; beneficent, bountiful. **2.** m. generous person; benefactor.

[2]**दानी** *dānī* [? *dānīya-*], m. Brbh. Av. collector of a levy or tribute.

-दानी *-dānī* [cf. P. *-dān*], suffix (forms f. nouns having the sense 'container of or for ...', e.g. चायदानी, teapot).

दानीपन *dānīpan* [cf. H. [1]*dānī*], m. = दानशीलता.

दानीय *dānīyă* [S.], adj. to be given, due (a gift, a fee).

दाप *dāp* [*darpa-*], m. Brbh. Av. **1.** pride, arrogance. **2.** [? × H. *dāb*] power. **3.** anger. **4.** boastfulness; pomp, show. **5.** vanity, conceit.

दाब *dāb* [cf. **dabb-*: ← Drav.] f. (m., *Pl.*) **1.** pressure; weight. **2.** power, authority; control. **3.** awe. **4.** impression (in printing). **5.** paper-weight. — ~ दिखाना (को), = next; to overawe. ~ जमाना, or बैठाना, to exercise or to assert authority or control (over, पर). ~ में रखना, to keep under control, or in subjection (a child, a territory). – दाबदार [P. *-dār*], adj. powerful, mighty; awesome; oppressive.

दाबना *dābnā* [**dabb-*: ← Drav.], v.t. = दबाना.

दाबा *dābā* [cf. H. *dābnā*], m. weighing down: **1.** burden, exaction. **2.** reg. covering (a person suffering from fever) with a blanket (to induce sweating). **3.** *HŚS.* covering (a graft on a tree) with mud.

दाबी *dābī*, f. reg. **1.** beam used in pressing green indigo in vats. **2.** measure of about ten handfuls of autumn crop; bundle of sheaves. **3.** reg. (E.) sole (of plough). **4.** small scales.

दाभ *dābh* [*darbha-*], m. *kuśa* grass (= दर्भ).

दाभ्य *dābhyă* [S.], adj. *Pl. HŚS.* governable.

[1]**दाम** *dām* [*dramma-*: ← Gk.], m. **1.** Brbh. a coin of minute value (one twenty-fifth of a *paisā*). **2.** often pl. price; cost; value; rate (of purchase). **3.** money, funds. **4.** transf. shrewd expenditure to achieve a purpose. — ~ उठना, to be gained, made (money, by sale); to be spent (on a purchase). ~ करना, to settle, or to haggle

over, a price. ~ ~, m. the whole amount, last farthing (of). ~ देना, to pay (one, को) the price or value (of, का or के). ~ भर, m. the full price (of). ~ भरना, to pay the price or value (of: as damages, &c.); to make good. एक (ही) दाम, adv. at a fixed price. चाम के ~ चलाना, to circulate leather money: to act arbitrarily to gratify a whim. सस्ते ~, or दामों, पर, adv. cheaply.

²**दाम** *dām* [*dāman-*¹], m. **1.** a rope; cord; string. **2.** (= ³दाम) transf. Brbh. snare. **3.** Brbh. Av. garland.

³**दाम** *dām* [P. *dām* : ? × *dāman-*¹], m. Brbh. a snare. — ~ में लाना, to snare, to trap (one, को). – दामदारी [P. *-dārī*], f. the laying of nets; a branch of revenue arising from fowlers, players, musicians, &c. (*Pl.*).

दामचा *dāmcā*, m. reg. **1.** a field platform for watching crops. **2.** boundary mark (between fields).

दामन *dāman* [P. *dāman*], m. **1.** skirt (of a garment); petticoat. **2.** fig. lower slopes (of a mountain, or a range). **3.** outskirts (of a town). **4.** sheet (of a sail). — ~ छुड़ाना, to free (oneself, का, from, से): to shake off, to get rid (of, से); to escape (from). ~ झटक लेना, 'to snatch the skirt (from, से)': to refuse abruptly or churlishly. ~ झाड़कर उठना, 'to shake the skirt on rising': to leave in displeasure; to shake off connection (with a person or place). ~ तले छिपाना, to screen, to protect; to hide (a fault); to pass over (sthg. discreditable) in silence. ~ दबा बैठना, to intrude (upon, का). ~ पकड़ना, or थामना, to take refuge (with, का), to come under the protection (of); to throw oneself on the mercy (of); to become an adherent (of); to detain by holding the garment (of). ~ फैलाना, 'to spread the skirt (in bowing)': to supplicate; to desire. ~ से लगना, to cling to the skirt (of, का): to come under, or to claim, the protection (of); to depend (upon). – चोली-दामन का नाता, m. 'the relationship between bodice and skirt': intimate connection. चोली-दामन का साथ, m. id. दामनगीर [P. *-gīr*], adj. & m. clutching the skirt (of, का), depending (on); seeking justice, or redress (from); an adherent; plaintiff; claimant. °ई, f. dependence, &c.

दामनी *dāmnī* [**dāmana-*], f. 1.reg. part of a woman's dress: veil, mantle. **2.** Brbh. women's head ornament. **3.** reg. piece of a shroud (kept by the relatives of the deceased person). **4.** *Pl.* *HŚS.* saddle-cloth.

दामर *dāmar*, f. *HŚS.* = ¹डामर.

दामा *dāmā* [*dāman-*¹], m. *Pl.* *HŚS.* = ²दाम.

दामाद *dāmād* [P. *dāmād*], m. son-in-law.

¹**दामादी** *dāmādī* [P. *dāmādī*], f. state, relationship, or rights of a son-in-law. — ~ में लेना, to take (into one's family) as a son-in-law.

²**दामादी** *dāmādī* [cf. P. *dāmād*], adj. having to do with a son-in-law.

दामासाही *dāmāsāhī* [? *dāmāsāh*, prop. n.], f. obs. proportionate division of a bankrupt's estate among his creditors.

दामिनी *dāminī* [f. *saudāmanī-*, *saudāminī-*], f. Brbh. Av. lightning.

¹**दामी** *dāmī* [cf. H. *dām*], adj. & f. **1.** adj. costly, fine (as of clothes). **2.** f. *Pl.* *HŚS.* land valuation, assessment.

²**दामी** *dāmī* [P. *dāmī*], m. reg. a setter of snares: fowler; hunter.

दांपत्य *dāmpatyă* [S.], adj. having to do with married life or relationship.

दाय *dāy* [S.], m. **1.** sthg. to be given, gift; donation; marriage gift, dowry. **2.** inheritance. — दाय-भाग, m. share of inheritance. °ई m. heir. दायागत [°*ya*+*ā*°], m. obtained as an inheritance. दायाद [°*ya*+*ā*], m. *Pl.* *HŚS.* heir; claimant. °ई, f. दायाधिकारी [°*ya*+*a*°], m. one entitled to an inheritance, heir.

दायक *dāyak* [S.], m. & adj. finally in comp.; simplex Av. = दाता. — लाभदायक, adj. profitable, advantageous.

दायज *dāyăj* [*dāyādya-*], m. **1.** dowry, marriage gift.

दायजा *dāyjā* [*dāyādya-*], m. = दायज.

दायजो *dāyjo*, m. Brbh. = दायज.

दायम *dāym* [A. *dā'im*], adj. E.H. continuing, lasting (= दायमी).

दायमी *dāymī* [A. *dā'imī*], adj. E.H. lasting long, or for ever.

दायर *dāyr* [A. *dā'ir*], adj. going round: in process; instituted (proceedings, suit); filed (complaint). — ~ करना, to institute, &c. दायरो सायर [A. *sā'ir*], m. *Pl.* U. circuit (of judges, &c).

दायरा *dāyrā* [A. *dā'ira*], m. **1.** circle, ring; circumference. **2.** circuit. **3.** transf. sphere (of influence or effect, or of interests). **4.** group (of associates). **5.** vicinity. **6.** orbit. **7.** a tambourine. **8.** *musl.* monastery (= ख़ानक़ाह). — गोल-दायरा, m. traffic roundabout.

दायाँ *dāyāṁ*, adj. = दाहिना. — दाएँ-बाएँ करना, to prevaricate, to dissemble; to secrete, to conceal. दाएँ-बाएँ देखना, to keep sharp look-out, to be circumspect. दाएँ-बाएँ देकर निकल जाना, to dodge right and left, to get away.

[1]दाया *dāyā* [ad. *dayā-*], f. Brbh. = दया.

[2]दाया *dāyā* [cf. H. *dāī*], m. *Pl.* **1.** husband of a nurse (दाई). **2.** male nurse.

दायिता *dāyitā* [S.], f. **1.** charge, responsibility (cf. उत्तरदायित्व). **2.** payment, paying (as of dividends).

दायित्व *dāyitvă* [S.], m. liability (in law).

दायी *dāyī* [S.], adj. **1.** -दायी. = -दायक. 2. = उत्तरदायी.

[1]दार *dār* [P.: present stem of *dāštan*], adj. & m. in comp., esp. as second member forming adjectives and nouns. having, holding; possessor, &c. — दारमदार [P. *-ma-dār*], m. adjustment (of a dispute); settlement; dependence; protection, support. ज़मीनदार, m. landowner. समझदार, adj. discerning; intelligent.

[2]दार *dār* [S.], f. wife. — दार-कर्म, m. marriage.

[3]दार *dār* [*dāru-*[2]; w. P. *dār*], m. wood: impaling stake, gibbet; gallows. — ~ पर चढ़ाना, or खैंचना, to impale.

[4]दार *dār* [A. *dār*], m. U. house, dwelling. — दारुलहुकूमत, f. 'abode of government': capital city.

दारक *dārak* [S.], m. Brbh. **1.** a boy; son, child. **2.** *Pl. HŚS.* young animal.

दारचीनी *dārcīnī* [P. *dārcīn* ×H. *cīnī*], f. cinnamon.

दारन *dāran*, m. *Pl. HŚS.* the clearing-nut plant, *Strychnos potatorum.*

दारा *dārā* [cf. *dāra-*[2]], f. wife.

दारिका *dārikā* [S.], f. Brbh. a girl; daughter.

दारिद *dārid*, m. Brbh. Av. = दारिद्रय.

दारिद्र *dāridră*, m. Brbh. = दारिद्रय.

दारिद्री *dāridrī* [cf. H. *dāridra*], adj. = दरिद्री.

दारिद्रय *dāridryă* [S.], m. **1.** poverty. **2.** wretchedness.

दारी *dārī* [*dārikā-*, Pa. *dārikā-*], f. *Pl. HŚS.* 1. = दासी, 1. **2.** prostitute. दारी-जार, m. pej. husband of a prostitute or concubine; transf. bastard.

दारु *dāru* [S.], m. Brbh. Av. **1.** wood, timber. **2.** the deodar pine. — दारु-कदली, f. a kind of banana, wild banana. दारु-निशा, f. *Pl. HŚS.* the plant *Cucurma xanthorrhizon.* दारु-फल, m. pistachio nut. दारु-हल्दी, f. an evergreen bush, *Morinda angustifolia*, yielding a yellow dye; the plant *Cucurma xanthorrhizon* (*Pl.*).

दारुक *dāruk* [S.], m. Brbh. **1.** a wooden doll, puppet. 2. = दारु, 2. **3.** title of Yogācārya, an incarnation of Śiva.

दारुण *dāruṇ* [S.], adj. & m. **1.** adj. fearsome, terrible. **2.** cruel, painful (as suffering). **3.** harsh. **4.** piteous (plight). **5.** m. [*dāruṇya-*] harshness. **6.** cruelty. **7.** the plant lead-wort (*Plumbago zeylanica*).

दारू *dārū* [P. *dārū*], f. **1.** wine; liquor. **2.** medicine; drug. **3.** medical treatment. **4.** gunpowder. — ~ उतरना, (one) to sober up. — दारूकार, m. maker of wine. दारूख़ोर [P. *-khor*], m. a (habitual) drinker. °ई, f. drunken state. दारू-दरमन [P. *-darmān*], m. medicines; medication. दारूबंदी, f. prohibition of alcohol. दारू-सीसा, m. powder and lead: ammunition. दारूहा, m. reg. a habitual drinker.

दारूड़ा *dārūṛā* [cf. H. *dārū*], m. reg. = दारू.

दारूड़ी *dārūṛī*, f. = दारूड़ा.

दारोग़ा *dārogā* [P. *dāroga*], m. **1.** a police inspector or superintendent. **2.** superintendent (of tolls, or of a municipal or government department). — दारोग़ा-जेल, m. a jailer. दारोग़ा-जंगल, m. a forester.

दारोग़ाई *dārogāī* [cf. P. *dāroga*], f. the office, or duties, of a *dārogā.*

दारोमदार *dār-o-madār*, m. = दारमदार (see s.v. [1]दार).

दाढर्च *dārḍhyă* [S.], m. **1.** firmness, stability. **2.** strength.

दार्विका *dārvikā* [S.], f. *Pl. HŚS.* **1.** a collyrium made with *Cucurma xanthorrhiza.* **2.** a pot-herb.

दार्वी *dārvī* [S.], f. **1.** *HŚS.* = दारु-हल्दी. **2.** *Pl. HŚS.* = दार्विका.

दार्ष्टांत *dārṣṭānt* [S.], adj. *Pl. HŚS.* explained by an example or simile; illustrated by a metaphor or other figure of speech.

दार्शनिक *dārśănik* [S.], adj. philosophical.

दाल *dāl* [*dāla-*[2]], f. **1.** split pea, lentils; pulse. **2.** lentils boiled and spiced for eating. **3.** sthg. resembling *dāl* (in shape, colour, &c.): a focus (of light rays); a crust, scale, scab; a dark spot. — ~ गलना (की), (one's) *dāl* to soften (in boiling); to achieve one's purpose, to succeed; to have an advantage, to avail; to keep in (with, के साथ), to get on (with). ~ चप्पू होना, to cling, or to get stuck, together; to become entangled, or embroiled. ~ बँधना, a scab to form; a focus (of light) to be formed. ~ में कुछ काला, fig. sthg. suspicious, or amiss. ~ में मक्खी डालना, fig. to throw a spanner in the works. ~ में नोन, m. 'salt in the *dāl*': sthg. savourous. आटे ~ का भाव मालूम होना, m. the price of staple foods to become known (to, को): to learn what side one's bread is buttered on. जूतियों ~ बँटना, fig. parties (to a quarrel) to come to blows.

पतली ~ का खानेवाला, 'one who lives on watery lentils': a feeble person; pej. a baniyā. दाल-दलिया, f. 'lentils only': poor diet; pot luck. दाल-दलिया करना, to conclude (a matter) for better or worse. दाल-दलिया खाना, to take pot luck. दाल-भात, m. lentils and rice; = दाल-दलिया. दाल-भात में मसूर, fig. an unwelcome or disruptive presence. दाल-मोठ, f. 'various lentils': spiced fried lentils, as a savoury. दाल-रोटी, f. lentils and bread, adequate food; sustenance, livelihood. दाल-रोटी चलना, to have enough to live on.

दाला *dālā*, m. *Pl.* a partic. type of land tenure formerly current in the Doab.

दालान *dālān* [P. *dālān*], m. **1.** a hallway; corridor (in a house). **2.** a verandah. **3.** a balcony, gallery.

¹दाव *dāv* [S.], m. **1.** a forest fire. **2.** in comp. forest. **3.** fire, heat. — दावाग्नि [°*va*+*a*°], f. = next. दावानल [°*va*+*a*°], m. forest fire.

²दाव *dāv*, m. = दाँव.

³दाव *dāv* [*dātra*-²], m. reg. **1.** a hatchet having a hooked point. **2.** a sickle.

दावत *dāvat* [A. *daʻva*: P. *daʻvat*], f. a call: **1.** invitation (esp. to a meal). **2.** party; feast, banquet; reception. — ~ करना, to give a party, &c.; to invite. ~ खाना, to dine (as a guest). ~ देना (को), = ~ करना. ~ क़बूल करना (की), to accept (another's) invitation to a meal, &c. ~ में जाना, to go as a guest to a meal, &c. – दावत-नामा, m. letter or card of invitation.

दावती *dāvătī* [P. *dāvatī*], m. **1.** a guest (esp. at a meal, &c.: see दावत). **2.** an invoker of spirits, exorcist, magician.

¹दावन *dāvan* [cf. **dāmayati*²: H. *dāmnā*], m. **1.** the process of treading out corn. **2.** Brbh. Av. fig. destruction.

²दावन *dāvan*, m. reg. = ³दाव.

दावा *dāvā* [A. *daʻvā*], m. **1.** claim (on or to, पर). **2.** legal action, suit. **3.** pretension. **4.** contention, assertion; confidence. — ~ करना, to lay claim (to, का; against or from, पर); to sue; to have pretensions; to assert. ~ ख़ारिज करना, to dismiss a legal claim, or suit. ~ जताना, = ~ करना, 1. दावे के साथ कहना, to say with all confidence, to maintain. दावे से कहना, id.

दाश *dāś* [S.; ? = *dāsa*-], m. *Pl. HŚS.* **1.** fisherman; boatman. **2.** *HŚS.* servant.

दाश्त *dāśt* [P. *dāśt*], f. *Pl. HŚS.* keeping, caring for; bringing up.

दास *dās* [*dāsa*-], m. **1.** slave; transf. = शूद्र. **2.** servant. **3.** devotee (of a god). — दास-जन, m. Brbh. = दास. दास-भाव, m. = दास्य, 3. दासानुदास [°*sa*+*a*°], m. a servant of servants, humble servant.

दासता *dāsătā* [S.], f. **1.** the condition of a slave, servitude. **2.** service (to a master).

दासत्व *dāsatvă* [S.], m. = दासता.

दासपन *dāspan* [cf. *dāsatva*-], m. = दासता.

दासपुर *dāsăpur* [S.], m. *Pl. HŚS.* a fragrant grass, *Cyperus rotundus*.

दासा *dāsā* [**dāsaka*-], m. a supporting beam or piece of stone (as one projecting from a wall, beneath a thatch).

दासिका *dāsikā* [S.], f. = दासी.

दासी *dāsī* [S.], f. **1.** a female slave. **2.** female servant. **3.** temple servant; concubine. — दासी-पुत्र, m. son of a female slave; bastard.

दासीत्व *dāsītvă* [S.], m. = दासीपन.

दासीपन *dāsīpan* [cf. H. *dāsī*], f. the condition of a female slave, &c. (cf. *dāsătā*).

दास्ताँ *dāstām̐*, f. = दास्तान.

दास्तान *dāstān* [P. *dāstān*], f. **1.** a tale, story; a history. **2.** transf. fame, notoriety.

दास्य *dāsyă* [S.], m. **1.** slavery, servitude. **2.** service. **3.** humility (of worship, as a characteristic of devotion).

दाह *dāh* [*dāha*-], f. **1.** burning. **2.** conflagration, fire. **3.** cremation. **4.** burning sensation; inflammation; fever. **5.** fig. ardour, zeal. **6.** pangs (of envy, or jealousy). ~ करना, to burn; to cremate. ~ देना (को), to light (a pyre). ~ रखना, to bear envy, &c. (towards, की ओर). – दाह-कर्म, m. = next. दाह-क्रिया, f. the act, or ceremony, of cremation. दाह-गृह, m. crematorium. दाह-संस्कार, m. = दाह-क्रिया. दाह-सर, m. cremation site.

दाहक *dāhak* [S.], adj. & m. **1.** adj. burning. **2.** incendiary; ~ बम, m. incendiary bomb. **3.** inflammatory. **4.** m. the plant *Plumbo zeylanica*. **5.** an incendiary.

दाहन *dāhan* [S.], m. causing to burn, setting fire to (cf. दाह, 1., 2).

दाहना *dāhnā* [*dāhayati*], v.t. **1.** to burn; to set fire to. **2.** to cremate. **3.** fig. to cause pangs of suffering to.

दाहिना *dāhinā* [*dākṣiṇa*-], adj. **1.** right (hand). **2.** fig. well-disposed, favourable. **3.** auspicious (an omen: esp. one in which male persons or creatures are involved). — दाहिनी ओर, f. the right hand; on or to the right; दाहिनी ओर (के), adv. to the right (of). दाहिने पड़ना, to be found on the right (as a destination). – दाहिने-बाएँ, adv. on both sides, all round.

दाहिनी *dāhinī* [cf. H. *dāhinā*], f. circumambulation clockwise (as of a temple or idol). — ~ देना, to circumambulate.

[1]**दाही** *dāhī* [S.], adj. = दाहक.

[2]**दाही** *dāhī* [A. *dāhī*], adj. E.H. sagacious, shrewd.

दाह्य *dāhyă* [S.], adj. **1.** inflammable. **2.** to be burnt: awaiting cremation (a body).

दिआव- *diāv-*, v.t. Brbh. = दिलाना.

दिउला *diulā* [cf. *dīpa-*], m. reg. a small earthenware lamp.

दिउली *diulī* [cf. *dīpa-*], f. reg. 1. = दिउला. **2.** a scar; pock-mark. **3.** dandruff.

दिक़ *diq* [A. *diqq*], adj. & m. **1.** adj. troubled, disturbed. **2.** irritated, harassed; inconvenienced. **3.** unwell. **4.** m. tuberculosis (= तपेदिक़). ~ करना, to irritate; to tease; to plague, &c. ~ कर मारना, to worry (one) exceedingly; to pester, to torment.

दिक् *dik* [S.], f. chiefly in comp. direction, &c. (= दिशा). — दिक्पति, m. *mythol.* a regent or guardian deity of one of the ten points of the compass, or of a quarter of the world. दिक्पाल, m. id. दिक्शूल, m. an inauspicious planetary conjunction, &c. (= दिशा-शूल). दिक्सूचक, m. compass.

दिक़्क़त *diqqat* [A. *diqqa*: P. *diqqat*], f. **1.** suffering, distress. **2.** difficulty; perplexity; inconvenience, trouble. — ~ में पड़ना, to fall into difficulties or distress. ~ होना (को), to suffer (from, से: as from climate, or conditions); to be in difficulty, &c. (because of, से).

दिखना *dikhnā* [cf. H. *dīkhnā*], v.i. & v.t. **1.** v.i. = दीखना. **2.** v.t. Av. = देखना.

दिखलवाई *dikhalvāī* [cf. H. *dikhlānā*], f. = दिखाई, 2., 3.

दिखलवाना *dikhalvānā* [cf. H. *dikhlānā*], v.t. = दिखवाना.

दिखलाई *dikhlāī* [cf. H. *dikhlānā*], f. = दिखाई, 2., 3. — ~ देना, = दिखाई देना.

दिखलाना *dikhlānā* [cf. H. *dekhnā*], v.t. = दिखाना.

दिखलावा *dikhlāvā* [cf. H. *dikhlānā*], m. 1. = दिखावा. **2.** *Pl.* one who shows the way, a guide.

दिखवाना *dikhvānā* [cf. H. *dekhnā*], v.t. to cause to be shown (by, से; to, को).

दिखवैया *dikhvaiyā* [cf. H. *dikhānā*, *dekhnā*], m. **1.** one who shows. **2.** an onlooker, spectator.

दिखाई *dikhāī* [cf. H. *dikhnā*, *dikhānā*], f. **1.** seeing. **2.** showing; display. **3.** cost of, or payment for, showing. **4.** coming into view, appearance. — ~ देना (को), to come into sight, to appear (to); to be visible (to), to be seen; to seem (to). ~ पड़ना, id.; to seem.

दिखाऊ *dikhāū* [cf. H. *dikhnā*, *dikhānā*], adj. **1.** visible, to be seen; worth seeing. **2.** worth displaying, attractive. **3.** superficial, specious. **4.** showy, ostentatious.

दिखाना *dikhānā* [cf. H. *dekhnā*], v.t. to show (to, को); to demonstrate, to indicate; to reveal; to display, to present. — ~ दिखाना, to frighten.

दिखाव *dikhāv* [cf. H. *dekhnā*], m. **1.** sight. **2.** view, aspect, appearance.

दिखावट *dikhāvaṭ* [cf. H. *dikhānā*], f. **1.** showing, displaying. 2. = दिखावा.

दिखावटी *dikhāvăṭī* [cf. H. *dikhāvaṭ*], adj. **1.** specious. **2.** false, forged (papers, money).

दिखावा *dikhāvā* [cf. H. *dikhānā*], m. **1.** show, ostentation; pomp, pageantry. **2.** appearance: pretence, disguise. — मुँह-दिखावा, m. see s.v. मुँह.

दिग्- *dig-* [S.] = दिक्: – दिगंचल, m. distant quarter, far distance; Av. = दृग-अंचल. दिगंत, m. & adv. end of (any) direction: the horizon; far distance; in all directions. °-गामिनी, adj. reaching to the horizon, limitless. °-फलक [A. *falak*], m. sky on the horizon. दिगंबर, adj. having the regions (i.e. space) as clothing: naked; m. specif. a Digambar Jain; a naked ascetic. दिगंश, m. a degree of angle; azimuth. °ईय, adj. दिग्गज, m. & adj. *mythol.* elephant of the quarters: one of the elephants standing at the quarters of the sky and supporting the earth; mighty, great (as in learning, or authority). दिग्दर्शन, m. pointing out the way (ahead, or through a difficulty); orientation, survey; sample, specimen; extensive acquaintance (with a topic). °-दर्शक, m. guide, mentor. दिग्दाह, m. glow in the sky (esp. after sunset: considered a bad omen). दिग्बिंदु, cardinal point (of the compass). दिग्भ्रांति, f. confusion, disorientation. दिग्मंडल, m. = दिङ्मंडल. दिग्विजय, m. conquest of territory in all directions: conquest of the world; widespread fame. °ई, adj.

दिगदिगाना *digdigānā*, v.i. reg. to chatter (as the teeth, with cold).

दिग्गी *diggī* [*dīrghikā-*], f. reg. an oblong tank or pond.

दिघी *dighī*, f. reg. = दिग्गी.

दिङ्- *diṅ-* [S.] = दिक्: – दिङ्नाग, m. = दिग्गज, 1. दिङ्मंडल, circle of the quarters: the entire world. दिङ्मूढ़, adj. disoriented, astray; foolish.

दिठवन *diṭhvan* [f. H. *devṭhān*], m. = देवठान.

दिठौना *diṭhaunā* [cf. *dr̥ṣṭa-*], m. a patch, or a black mark made with lampblack on the forehead or cheek of a child (to avert the evil eye).

दिढ़ *diṛh* [*dr̥ḍha-*], adj. = दृढ़.

दिढ़ता *diṛhtā* [ad. *dr̥ḍhatā-*], f. = दृढ़ता.

दितिया *ditiyā*, f. *Pl.* = द्वितीया.

दिन *din* [*dina-*], m. **1.** a day. **2.** day, daytime. **3.** pl. days, time, period. **4.** life span; lot, fate. — ~ उतरना, day to end, dusk to fall. ~ आना, (one's: के) time to come, to be about to die. ~ काटना, to pass one's days with difficulty. ~ को, adv. by day; during the main part of the day (as opposed to early morning, evening). ~ को तारे दिखाई देना (को), fig. to be beaten severely (see next); to live a gloomy or wretched life. ~ को तारे दिखाना (को), to show (one) stars by daylight: to beat severely. ~ को ~ रात को रात न जानना or समझना, to take no note of day or night: to be utterly absorbed, engrossed. ~ खुलना, = ~ फिरना. ~ चढ़ना, day to advance, the sun to rise; the time of menopause to be reached; to conceive (a woman). ~ चढ़ाना, to allow time to pass (before acting), to delay. ~ चढ़े, adv. after dawn; in mid- or later morning. ~ छिपना, v.i. day to disappear, the sun to set. ~ जाते देर नहीं लगी, prov. time waits for no man. ~ डूबना, = next. ~ ढलना, day to close, the sun to sink, to grow late. ~ ~, adv. every day, daily, always. ~ ~ का, adj. daily, every day's. ~ दूना रात चौगूना बढ़ना, or होना, to develop or to progress at accelerating speed, by leaps and bounds. ~ निकलना, = ~ चढ़ना. ~ पर ~, adv. = ~ बदिन. ~ पूरे करना, to serve, or to live, one's full time; to go one's full time (in pregnancy); to drag out one's days. ~ पूरे होना, to be complete, to come to an end (one's days, a set or due period). ~ फिरना, (one's) fortune to take a turn (for the better). ~ फूलना, day to break. ~ बदिन [P. *ba-*], adv. day by day, from day to day. ~ बहुरना or भले आना, = ~ फिरना. ~ बिगड़ना, (one's) fortune to take a turn for the worse. ~ भर, adv. all day. ~ भरना, to spend the whole day (on sthg.); to spend, or to drag out, one's days. ~ मुँदना, day to draw to a close, = ~ छिपना. ~ लगना (को), to give oneself airs (= हवा लगना). ~ से, adv. during daytime, by day. ~ होना, day to dawn. दिनों का फेर, m. a change in fortunes (usu. for the worse). दिनों से उतरना, to leave (youth) behind. आए ~, adv. daily, always. आए ~ का, adj. कितने ~ (or दिनों) से, adv. since when? पूरे दिनों से होना, to have reached the full term of pregnancy. बड़ा ~, m. broad day; Christmas Day; adv. late in the morning. बहुत दिनों से, adv. for a long time (up to the present). — दिनकर, m. day-maker: the sun. दिन-चर्या, f. daily round; daily work, livelihood. दिन-दहाड़े, or -दिहाड़े, adv. in broad daylight; day in, day out. दिन-दिया, m. daylight. दिन-दिवाले, or -दिवाली, adv. = दिन-दहाड़े. दिन-दोपहर, or दिन-धौले, adv. = दिन-दहाड़े. दिन-नाथ, m. day-lord: the sun. दिन-पंजी, f. day-list, diary. दिन-पत्र, m. calendar. दिन-पात, m. sustenance, daily bread. दिन-प्रति, adv. daily (= प्रतिदिन). दिन-मणि, f. Brbh. Av. day-jewel: the sun. दिन-मान, m. measure, or length of a day (as this varies during the year). दिन-रात, adv. day and night; day or night; constantly. दिन-रैन, adv. Brbh. id. दिनांक [°*na*+*a*°], m. date. °इत, adj. dated. दिनांत [°*na*+*a*°], m. close of day, sunset, evening. दिनांध [°*na*+*a*°], m. a creature 'blind by day' (owl, bat). दिनातीत [°*na*+*a*°], adj. out of date, old-fashioned. दिनानुदिन [°*na*+*a*°], adv. day by day, from day to day. दिनाप्त [°*na*+*ā*°], adj. up to date, contemporary. दिनार्द्ध [°*na*+*a*°], m. midday. दिनों-दिन, adv. = ~ बदिन.

दिनाई *dināī*, f. **1.** *Pl. HŚS.* a skin disease, ringworm. **2.** Brbh. poison.

दिनाती *dinātī*, f. *Pl. HŚS.* **1.** a day's labouring work. **2.** day-wages.

दिनी *dinī* [cf. H. *din*], adj. Brbh. old (esp. of animals).

दिनौंध *dinauṁdh*, adj. blind by day.

दिनौंधा *dinauṁdhā*, adj. = दिनौंध.

दिनौंधी *dinauṁdhī*, f. blindness by day.

दिमाग़ *dimāg* [A. *dimāg*], m. **1.** brain. **2.** mind. **3.** transf. conceit; arrogance; disdain. **4.** fancy, whim. — ~ (सातवें) आसमान पर चढ़ना, or होना, pej. (one's) mind to be in the (seventh) heaven: to be very conceited, or haughty. ~ का अरक़ निचोड़ना, to wring out the brain: = ~ लड़ाना. ~ का पुरज़ा ढीला होना (के), sl. (one) to have a screw loose. ~ ख़राब कर देना, to spoil (a child). ~ ख़ाली करना, to beat or to rack (one's, अपना) brains ; to distract, &c. (cf. next). ~ ख़ाली होना, to be distracted, worried; to be plagued; to be bored. ~ गरम हो जाना, one's temper to grow hot, or to be lost. ~ चढ़ना, or चलना, the head to be turned: to become conceited, proud, &c. ~ चाटना, to distract, to plague; to bore. ~ झड़ना, pride to take a fall. ~ न(हीं) मिलना, or पाया जाना (का), (one's) pride to be unfathomable, or extreme. ~ में ख़लल होना (के), to be mentally deranged. ~ लड़ाना, to cudgel one's brains. — दिमाग़चट, adj. & m. distracting, plaguing; boring; a chatterer, a bore. दिमाग़दार [P. *-dār*], adj. conceited, arrogant; disdainful; fanciful; brainy, intelligent.

दिमाग़ी *dimāgī* [A. *dimāg*+P. *-ī*], adj. **1.** of the brain; mental (as work, activity); needing intelligence. 2. = दिमाग़दार. **3.** imaginary.

दिया *diyā*, m. = दीया.

दियानत *diyānat*, f. = दयानत.

दियारा *diyārā* [**dvīpākāra-*], m. reg. **1.** land adjoining a river, river bank. **2.** an island in a river.

दिरम *diram* [P. *diram*: ← Gk.], m. **1.** a silver coin of small value. **2.** money, coin. **3.** a measure of weight, drachma.

दिरमान *dirmān*, m. reg. = दरमान.

दिरमानी *dirmānī* [cf. H. *darmān*], m. E.H. 'provider of a cure': medical man.

दिरहम *dirham* [A. *dirham*, P. *diram*], m. = दिरम.

[1]**दिल** *dil* [P. *dil*], m. (alongside expressions with दिल equivalents with [1]जी, m. or जान, f., or मन, m. often coexist). **1.** heart. **2.** soul; spirit. **3.** fig. the feelings, emotions. — ~ अटकना, = ~ फँसना; to be obsessed (with, में). ~ आना, to fall in love (with, पर); to long (for). ~ उचटना, the heart to turn (from, से): to be weary (of); to be disgusted (with); to be alienated (from). ~ उचाट होना, id. ~ उलटना, the heart to be perturbed, or distracted. ~ कड़ा करना, to harden the heart. ~ कड़वा करना, to make the heart bitter: to steel oneself (to a task). ~ करना, the heart to be moved (to do sthg., के लिए). ~ का गुबार, or फफोला, or बुख़ार निकालना, = ~ के फफोले फोड़ना. ~ का बादशाह, m. one in command of his heart; a man of noble emotions. ~ की कली खिलना, the heart's bud to open: to be moved by delight, or rapture. ~ की गाँठ खोलना, = ~ के फफोले फोड़ना, 1. ~ की लगी बुझाना, to assuage or to satisfy (an emotion, a longing). ~ कुम्हलाना, the heart to wither: to grieve, to pine. ~ के ~ में, adv. in (one's) inmost heart. ~ के फफोले टूटना, heart's blisters to break: suffering of heart or mind to be relieved. ~ के फफोले तोड़ना, or फोड़ना, to relieve the mind (of pain, or of feelings of ill-will, revenge, &c.); to open old wounds. ~ को लगना, to affect the heart, to make an impression (on, के); to commend itself (to). ~ खटकना, to feel unease, or suspicion. ~ खट्टा करना (का), to turn (one's) heart against (another, से); to displease, to offend. ~ ख़ुश करना, to gladden; to amuse; to gratify. ~ खोलकर, adv. openly, without reserve; generously. ~ चलना, the heart to be set (on, पर). दिल, or दिलों, चुटकियाँ लेना, to make fun (of, की). ~ चुराना, m. to steal the heart (of, का); to turn one's interest or sympathies (from, से), to cool towards (a person, an enterprise); to be inattentive (to). ~ छोटा करना, to suppress feelings of, or no longer to feel, generosity, sympathy or interest (towards). ~ जमना, to become absorbed (in, पर); to be content (with, से). ~ जलना, the heart to burn: to feel anger, ill-will or envy; to feel vexation. ~ टूटना, the heart to be broken; to be be discouraged, to despair; affection or regard to be no longer felt. ~ ठहरना, the heart to be at rest: to be comforted, consoled; to become calm. ~ ठिकाने लगना, id. ~ ठिकाने लगाना, to comfort; to calm. ~ ठिकाने न होना, to be ill at ease, troubled in mind. ~ ठुकना, the heart to be tempered or made firm: to be assured, confident; to have faith (in, पर). ~ ठोककर, adv. boldly, taking one's courage in both hands. ~ डूबना, v.i. consciousness to be lost. ~ तोड़ना, to break the heart (of, का); to dishearten; to disappoint. ~ थामना, to hold or to clutch the heart: to be in suspense; to feel a pang; to steel the heart. ~ देखना, to study or to gauge the temperament (of, का); to ascertain the feelings or wishes (of). ~ पक जाना, feeling to come to a head: to be fed up. ~ पकड़ा जाना, (one's, का) feelings to be discovered, or detected. ~ पकड़े फिरना, fig. to be constantly affected by an emotion or mood. ~ पर चलना, to act according to the wishes (of, के). ~ पीछे पड़ना, the heart to turn back (from): to forget sorrow, to be consoled; to become composed. ~ फँसना, the heart to be ensnared, to fall in love. ~ फटना, the heart to be torn: love or regard to cool. ~ फिरना, to be tired (of, से), to be disgusted (with). ~ फीका होना, = ~ खट्टा होना. ~ फेरना, to turn the heart (from, से): to make disinclined, or disaffected (towards). ~ बढ़ाना (का), to encourage, to inspire. ~ बटोरना, to gather (one's, का) courage. ~ बुझना, the heart to be extinguished: feelings of warmth, or of enthusiasm, to die. ~ बुरा करना (अपना), to take offence (at, से), to become displeased. ~ बुरा होना, (one's) feelings or affections to become alienated (from, की ओर से); to feel unwell. ~ भर, adv. to one's heart's content. ~ भर आना, the heart to fill: to be deeply moved. ~ भर जाना, id.: to be satisfied; to be sated. ~ मज़बूत रखना, to keep a stout heart. ~ मसोसना, or मसोसकर रहना, to contain (one's) emotion, to bear silently or patiently. ~ माने, adv. to the heart's content. ~ में, adv. in the heart; to oneself (of unexpressed thoughts or feelings). ~ में आग लगाना, to cause anguish; to arouse envy, or jealousy. ~ में आना, to arise (thoughts, feelings); to win the affections (of, के). ~ में ~ डालना, to cause (one, के) to feel as oneself; to exercise influence (over); to possess the heart (of). ~ में गाँठ, or गिरह, पड़ना, ill-will or disaffection to arise. ~ में घर करना, to find a home in the heart (of, के): to become intimate (with); to win the heart (of); to be warmly accepted (by: as a thought, or an emotion). ~ में फ़रक़ आना, a coolness to be felt (by, के: in friendship or relationship). ~ में फ़रक़ होना, to feel distrustful (of, के), to suspect. ~ में बल पड़ना, = ~ में फ़रक़ आना. ~ मैला करना, to give (oneself) over to grief, vexation, &c.; to take to heart; to be displeased. ~ रखना, to possess the affections (of, का); to show consideration for

the feelings or wishes (of), to gratify; to conciliate; to comfort; to encourage. ~ लगना, the heart to be given (to): to be in love (with, पर); to be attached (to, पर, की तरफ़, से); to be attentive (to), engrossed (in, में). ~ लगाना, to be intent (on, में); to fall in love (with, से). ~ लेना, to win the heart (of, का); = ~ देखना, 2. ~ लोटना, to be utterly devoted (to, पर). ~ सँभालना, to take heart; to gather one's courage (for an effort). ~ से, adv. with all one's heart; heartily, with a will. ~ से उतरना, to fall from the heart: to be less esteemed (by, के); to be no longer felt (an emotion). ~ से गिरना, id.; to fall in the estimation (of, के). ~ हलका करना, to relieve the heart (of pent-up feelings); to unburden oneself. ~ हाथ में करना, or लेना, or रखना, to keep (one: का) well disposed towards oneself. ~ हिलना, the heart to shake, to feel fear (at, से); to be moved (by or at). ~ ही ~ में, adv. in one's inmost heart; to oneself, silently. एक ~ होकर, adv. with one heart; unanimously. ठंडे ~ से, adv. cold-heartedly; dispassionately. बड़ा ~ करना, to show generosity, or liberality. – दिलकश [P. *-kaś*], adj. heart-attracting: attractive; inviting; charming. °ई, f. दिलगीर [P. *-gīr*], adj. seizing the heart: filling with fear, or anguish; afflicted, depressed, sad. °ई, f. affliction, grief. दिल-गुरदा [P. *gurda*], m. heart and kidney: courage, pluck. दिल-चला, adj. persevering; enterprising, bold, resolute; generous; emotional, volatile. दिलचस्प [P. *-casp*], adj. interesting; attractive, pleasant (= दिलकश). °ई, f. °ई रखना, or लेना, to take an interest (in, से or में). दिलचोर, adj. heart-thieving: inattentive, idle; captivating the heart; *Pl.* timid. दिल-जमई [P. *-jam'ī*], f. ease of mind, assurance. दिल-जला, adj. & m. burning, or smitten, with love; a love-sick person. दिल-जोई [P. *-joī*], f. seeking to please; attention (to another); sympathy. दिल-दादा [P. *-dāda*], adj. inv. who has given his heart. दिलदार [P. *-dār*], adj. generous of heart, or of instincts; possessing the heart, charming; heartened. °ई, f. generosity, &c.; charm; consolation; encouragement. दिलपसंद, adj. pleasing, agreeable, desirable. दिलफ़रेब, adj. bewitching, enchanting. दिल-फेंक, adj. who gives his heart easily, easily attracted. दिलबर [P. *-bar*], adj. attractive, charming. °ई, f. charm; consolation, comfort. दिल-बहलाव, m. pastime, diversion. दिलरुबा [P. *-rubā*], adj. inv. heart-captivating; m. f. lover, beloved; m. *HŚS.* a type of stringed instrument. दिलावर [P. *-āvar*], adj. bold, intrepid. °ई, f. दिलासा [P. *-āsā*], m. inv. comfort, consolation; encouragement. दिलासा देना (को), to soothe, to console; to encourage. दिलो-जान [P. *-o-*], m. heart and soul; fig. tooth and nail. दिलो-जान से, adv. दिलो-दिमाग़, m. heart and brain: inner being; loftiness of soul; ambition; pride; stateliness. दिल्लगी, f. see s.v.

[2]**दिल** *dil* [**dilla-*], f. reg. *Pl.* hillock; site of an old village.

दिलवाना *dilvānā* [cf. H. *dilānā*], v.t. to cause to be given, &c. (= दिलाना).

दिलवैया *dilvaiyā* [cf. H. *dilvānā*], m. one who causes to be given, paid, &c.

दिलहा *dilhā*, m. *HŚS.* = दिल्ला.

दिलाना *dilānā* [cf. H. *denā*], v.t. **1.** to cause to be given (by, से, to, को); to assign; to consign. **2.** to put in possession (of); to occasion. इतमीनान ~, to give assurance (to, को). — दिला पाना, to get back, to recover.

दिलासा *dilāsā*, m. see s.v. [1]दिल.

दिली *dilī* [P. *dilī*], adj. of the heart: **1.** cordial, sincere (wishes). **2.** close, intimate (a friend).

दिलेर *diler* [P. *diler*], adj. **1.** bold. **2.** lively, animated. **3.** brash.

दिलेराना *dilerānā* [P. *dilerāna*], adv. boldly, &c.

दिलेरी *dilerī* [P. *dilerī*], f. **1.** boldness. **2.** brashness; presumption. — ~ करना, to be bold (in, में); to make bold (to).

दिल्लगी *dillagī* [cf. H. *dil*], f. **1.** application of heart or mind: attention (to); inclination. **2.** fun, joking. यह कोई ~ नहीं है, this is no laughing matter. **3.** making fun of, poking fun. **4.** attachment, friendship. — ~ में उड़ाना, to laugh off (a remark, &c). – दिल्लगीबाज़ [P. *-bāz*], m. a joker, light-hearted person. °ई, f.

दिल्ला *dillā*, m. panel (of a door). — दिल्लेदार, adj. panelled (a door).

दिल्ली *dillī* [? cf. H. [2]*dil*], f. Delhi. — ~ अभी दूर है, prov. [P. *dĕhlī hanoz dūr ast*], Delhi is still far off: there is still much to be done. – दिल्लीबाल, adj. = दिल्लीवाला; m. a type of slipper with a pointed, upturned toe. दिल्लीवाला, adj. having to do with Delhi; m. a resident of, or one born in, Delhi.

दिवंगत *divaṁgat* [S.], adj. gone to heaven: deceased.

दिव *div* [S.], m. (f., *Pl.*) **1.** heaven, sky. **2.** day. — दिव-राज, m. king of heaven: a title of the god Indra.

दिवस *divăs* [S.], m. a day; particular day, anniversary. — दिवसावसान [°*sa+a*°], m. end of day, evening.

-दिवसीय *-divăsīyă* [S.], adj. lasting … days.

दिवा *divā* [S.], m. day; daylight. — दिवांध [°*ā+a*°], adj. blind by day. °की, f. the musk rat. दिवाकर, m. day-maker: the sun. दिवारात्रि, f. day and night; adv. by day and by night, constantly. दिवा-स्वप्न, m. daydream; दिवास्वप्न देखना, to daydream.

दिवाना *divānā*, adj. = दीवाना.

दिवानापन *divānāpan*, m. = दीवानापन.

दिवाला *divālā* [cf. H. *divāliyā*], m. bankruptcy. — ~ निकलना (का), to become bankrupt. ~ पीटना, or निकालना, to declare bankruptcy.

दिवालिया *divāliyā* [cf. H. *dīvālī*], m. a bankrupt (at whose house one or more lamps, *diyā*, might be lit in daylight).

दिवालियापन *divāliyāpan* [cf. H. *divāliyā*], m. bankruptcy.

दिवि *divi* [S.], f. poet. the blue jay.

दिवैया *divaiyā* [cf. H. *denā*], m. a giver, bestower.

दिव्य *divyă* [S.], adj. & m. **1.** adj. divine. **2.** supernatural. **3.** wonderful; charming. **4.** m. an ordeal. **5.** an oath. — दिव्यचक्षु, m. one possessing supernatural vision or knowledge; one blind to the physical world, a blind man. दिव्य-दृष्टि, f. supernatural vision. दिव्यधर्मी, adj. divine of nature: righteous; agreeable. दिव्य-रत्न, m. divine gem: the gem *cintāmaṇi*. दिव्यांगना [°*ya*+*a*°], f. *mythol.* an *apsarā*.

दिव्यता *divyătā* [S.], f. **1.** divinity. **2.** supernatural quality. **3.** divine beauty.

दिशा *diśā* [S.], f. **1.** direction; course (as of an aircraft). **2.** quarter, region. **3.** point of the compass. **4.** colloq. = दिशा-फ़राग़त. **5.** -दिशि, adv. poet. in (or from) a partic. direction. — ~ फिरना, or जाना, euph. to go off in a certain direction: to obey a call of nature. – दिशा-निदेशक, m. guide. दिशा-फ़राग़त [P. *farāgat* 'rest'], f. a call of nature. दिशाकाश [°*śā*+*ā*°], m. the entire heavens, the wide sky. दिशावधि [°*śā*+*a*°], f. space and time. दिशा-शूल, f. *astrol.* an inauspicious planetary conjunction, or sign in the sky; an unlucky direction, or day, for travel.

दिशि *diśi*, f. corr. direction (see s.v. दिशा).

दिष्ट *diṣṭ* [S.], adj. & m. **1.** adj. indicated. **2.** determined. **3.** m. fate. **4.** counsel.

दिष्टि *diṣṭi* [S.], f. *HŚS.* good fortune.

दिसंबर *disambar* [Pt. *dezembro*: w. Engl. *December*], m. December.

दिसना *disnā* [*dr̥śyate*], v.i. & v.t. **1.** v.i. to be visible. **2.** to seem. **3.** v.t. to see. **4.** to show.

दिसावर *disāvar* [**deśāpara-*], m. **1.** a foreign country, or countries. **2.** market for exports; source of imports. — ~ आना, to be imported. ~ उतरना, to fall in price (imports or exports). ~ चढ़ना, to rise in price, to be in demand (as exports or imports).

दिसावरी *disāvărī* [cf. H. *disāvar*], adj. & m. **1.** adj. foreign; imported (goods). **2.** m. a foreigner.

दिहाड़ा *dihāṛā* [cf. *divasa-*; ? a NW form, or ?? × *ahar-*], m. **1.** (in comp. w. दिन.) a day; a hard or wretched day. **2.** plight, misery. — दिन-दिहाड़े लूटा जाना, to be looted day in, day out.

दिहाड़ी *dihāṛī* [cf. H. *dihāṛā*], f. **1.** a day. **2.** a day's work. दस रुपए ~, ten rupees a day. **3.** daily wage.

दीक्षक *dīkṣak* [S.], m. one who inducts, teaches.

दीक्षण *dīkṣaṇ* [S.], m. = दीक्षा, 2.

दीक्षा *dīkṣā* [S.], f. *hind.* **1.** preparation or consecration for a religious ceremony. **2.** instruction (esp. in disciplehood to a teacher, by reception from him of a partic. mantra); initiation; transf. esp. comp. education. **3.** undertaking religious observances, or austerities; offering sacrifice. **4.** self-dedication (to a purpose, a person). — दीक्षांत [°*ṣā*+*a*°], m. completion of *dīkṣā*: a ceremony concluding a sacrifice; a graduation ceremony. दीक्षा-प्राप्त, adj. initiated (into disciplehood); educated (as at a college, university).

दीक्षित *dīkṣit* [S.], adj. & m. **1.** adj. consecrated. **2.** instructed, initiated. **3.** m. an instructed person. **4.** name of a brāhmaṇ community.

दीगर *dīgar* [P. *dīgar*], adj. other; next, following.

दीघी *dīghī*, f. reg. = दिग्गी.

दीठ *dīṭh* [*dr̥ṣṭi-*], f. (syn. of दृष्टि, [1]नज़र, and [1]आँख in many usages) **1.** sight. **2.** vision. **3.** look, glance. **4.** view (of sthg.), viewpoint, regard. ~ बाँधना, to enchant. – दीठबंद [P. -*band*], m. magic. °ई, f. practice of magic; state of trance.

दीठना *dīṭhnā* [cf. *dr̥ṣṭa-*], v.i. reg. to be seen, to appear.

दीद *dīd* [P. *dīd*], f. sight. — ~ करना, to look (at, की); to inspect. – दीदबान [P. -*bān*], m. a watch, guard; °ई, f. S.H. observation, look-out.

दीदा *dīdā* [P. *dīda*], adj. & m. **1.** adj. U. seen. **2.** m. the eye. **3.** the sight. **4.** fig. forwardness, shamelessness. — ~ खोलकर देखना, to look with open eyes: to consider maturely, or attentively. ~, or दीदे, लगना, to have eyes fixed (on): to be intent (on, पर); to be drawn (to, में). ~ फोड़ना,

to strain the eyes. दीदे का पानी ढलना, modesty to be thrown away, to be brazen or shameless. दीदे का पानी मर जना, obs. id. दीदे धोकर पी जाना, = दीदे का पानी ढलना. दीदे निकालना, to glare (at, की तरफ़); to blind. दीदे फाड़कर देखना, to look steadfastly (at, की तरफ़). दीदे बदलना, a relationship to deteriorate. दीदे मटकाना, to make eyes (at). दीदे लाल-पीले, or नीले-पीले. होना, to get into a rage. – दीदा-धोई, f. a shameless woman. दीदा-दलेली [cf. A.P. *dalāl*, P. *dilāl*], f. *Pl.* shamelessness, wantonness. दीदा-फटी, adj. f. & f. having large staring eyes; shameless, wanton.

दीदार *dīdār* [P. *dīdār*], m. **1.** sight (= दीद). **2.** look, appearance; beauty, charm. **3.** transf. eye-to-eye encounter, interview. — दीदारबाज़ी [P. *-bāzī*], f. exchanging flirtatious glances.

दीदारी *dīdārī* [cf. H. *dīdār*], f. U. seeing, viewing.

दीदारू *dīdārū* [cf. H. *dīdār*], adj. reg. good to look at, attractive (a person).

दीदी *dīdī* [**diddā-*], f. elder sister.

दीधिति *dīdhiti* [S.], f. light; ray, beam.

[1]**दीन** *dīn* [S.], adj. **1.** needy; wretched, suffering. **2.** dejected. **3.** humble, meek; abject. — दीन-दयाल, adj. compassionate to the poor, &c.; a title of the supreme being. °उ, adj. id. दीन-दुखी, adj. wretched and distressed. दीन-बंधु, m. friend of the poor, &c.; a title of Viṣṇu/ Kṛṣṇa. दीनहित, adj. Av. beneficent to the poor, &c.

[2]**दीन** *dīn* [A. *dīn*], m. faith, religion. — ~ का, adj. having to do with religion, religious. ~ में मिलाना, to make a convert (of, को: to a religion). – दीन-इलाही, f. divine faith: the religion founded (A.D. 1582) by the emperor Akbar. दीनदार [P. *-dār*], adj. religious, devout. °ई, f. दीन-दुनिया, f. the next world and this; the entire world. दीन-दुनिया से जाना, to fail to win happiness in this world or the next.

दीनता *dīnătā* [S.], f. **1.** need, want; suffering. **2.** dejection. **3.** humility, meekness.

दीनताई *dīnătāī* [cf. H. *dīnătā*], f. = दीनता.

दीनत्व *dīnatvă* [S.], m. = दीनता.

दीनानाथ *dīnānāth* [H. *dīn-nāth*], m. lord or protector of the poor, &c.: a title of the supreme being.

दीनार *dīnār* [A. & P. *dīnār*: ← Gk.; S. *dīnāra-*], m. **1.** a gold coin. **2.** a gold ornament.

दीनौ *dīnau*, Brbh. gave, given (= दिया).

दीन्यौ *dīnyau*, Brbh. gave, given (= दिया).

दीन्ह *dīnh*, Brbh. Av. gave, given (= दिया).

दीन्हा *dīnhā*, Av. gave, given (= दिया).

दीन्हौ *dīnhau*, Brbh. = दीन्ह.

दीन्ह्यौ *dīnhyau*, Brbh. gave, given (= दिया).

[1]**दीप** *dīp* [ad. *dvīpa-*], m. an island. — ~ अंतर करना, *Pl.* to transport overseas.

[2]**दीप** *dīp*, m. = दीया. — दीप-दान, m. *hind.* lamp-offering: the rite of suspending a lamp, for ten days after the death of a relative, on a *pīpal* or other tree (to light the soul's journey to the abode of Yama); offering a lighted lamp to an idol. दीपदानी [P. *-dān*], f. a container for candles, wicks and lamp-oil. दीप-पुष्प, m. the plant *Michelia champaka* (= चंपा). दीप-माला, f. a row of lamps (lit in worship, or at the Dīvālī festival). °-मालिका, f. id. दीप-शिखा, f. flame of a lamp or candle; a torch, lamp. दीपाधार [°*pa* + *ā*°], m. the stand or stem of a lamp; a candlestick. दीपावली [°*pa* + *ā*°], f. = दीवाली.

दीपक *dīpak* [S.], adj. & m. **1.** adj. illuminating. **2.** transf. stimulating, exciting (as the feelings). **3.** m. = दीया. **4.** *mus.* name of a *rāga.* **5.** *Pl. HŚS.* a kind of firework.

दीपन *dīpan* [S.], m. **1.** setting light to (sthg.), kindling. **2.** illuminating. **3.** stimulating (as the feelings).

दीपना *dīpnā* [*dīpyate*], v.i. to be lit; to burn, to shine.

दीपिका *dīpikā* [S.], f. **1.** a small light, lamp. **2.** transf. commentary on a text.

दीपित *dīpit* [S.], adj. = दीप्त.

दीप्त *dīpt* [S.], adj. **1.** blazing. **2.** glittering. **3.** radiant, glowing; bright. **4.** illuminated.

दीप्ति *dīpti* [S.], f. **1.** light. **2.** radiance; glow, gleam; lustre. **3.** splendour. — दीप्तिमान, adj. having brightness: brilliant, &c.

दीप्य *dīpyă* [S.], adj. **1.** to be kindled, &c. (see दीपन). **2.** able to be illuminated; radiant. दीप्यमान, adj. = दीप्तिमान.

दीमक *dīmak* [P. *dīvak*], f. **1.** white ant. **2.** reg. weevil. **3.** *Pl.* moth. — ~ लगना (को, or में), to be infested by white ants; to be eaten by white ants. – दीमक-खाया, adj. eaten by white ants, full of holes; pock-marked.

दीया *dīyā* [*dīpaka-*], m. **1.** a light; a lamp, lantern; candle. **2.** the vessel holding the oil for a light (as used at Dīvālī, &c). — ~ जलाना, to light a lamp (at a bankrupt's door): to declare bankruptcy. ~ जले, adv. at dusk. ~ ठंडा होना, a light to go out: a death to occur in a family. ~ दिखाना (को), to illuminate with a lamp, &c. ~ बढ़ाना, or बुझाना, to extinguish a lamp.

~ बारना, v.t. to light a lamp. ~ लेकर ढूँढ़ना, to search with care. – दीया-बत्ती, f. lights, lamps; दीया-बत्ती करना, to prepare the lamps, &c.; to light the lamp(s). दीया-सलाई, f. a match. दियासलाई दिखाना, to put a match (to, को).

दीर्घ *dīrgh* [S.], adj. & m. **1.** adj. long (of a space or time); prolonged; elongated. **2.** high, tall; vast. **3.** grave, weighty. **4.** *pros. ling.* long. **5.** m. *ling.* a long vowel; diphthong. — दीर्घकाय, adj. tall; huge of stature; gigantic. दीर्घकालिक, adj. of long standing; long in progress. °-कालीन, adj. id. दीर्घजीवी, m. long-lived. दीर्घदर्शी, adj. long-sighted; far-seeing. दीर्घ-दृष्टि, adj. & f. id.; long sight; far-sightedness. दीर्घ-वृत्त, m. an ellipse. °-वृत्तीय, adj. दीर्घ-सूत्रता, f. dilatoriness, spinning (things) out (esp. by officials). °-सूत्री, adj. dilatory. दीर्घायु [°*gha*+*ā*°], adj. long-lived. दीर्घावधि [°*gha*+*a*°], f. a lengthy period of time. दीर्घीकरण, m. *ling.* lengthening.

दीर्घा *dīrghā* [S.], f. a gallery.

दीर्घीकरण *dīrghīharaṇ* [S.], m. see s.v. दिर्घ

दीर्ण *dīrṇ* [S.], adj. poet. torn, rent.

दीवट *dīvaṭ* [*dīpavarti-*], f. a lampstand.

दीवा *dīvā*, m. = दीया.

दीवान *dīvān* [P. *dīvān*], m. **1.** a royal court. **2.** council of state; tribunal (of justice or revenue). **3.** a minister of state; secretary; steward. **4.** the collected verse of a poet (esp. in Persian or Urdu). **5.** divan. — ~ आम [P. *dīvān e 'ām*], m. *hist.* public hall of audience; public reception. ~ आला [A. *'alā*], m. inv. chief minister. ~ ख़ास [P. *dīvān e khāṣṣ*], m. *hist.* privy council chamber; cabinet council. – दीवान-ख़ाना, m. hall of audience; public room (of a house). दीवान-ख़ालसा [P. *dīvān e khāliṣa*], m. *hist.* accountant-general of the royal revenue.

दीवानगी *dīvāngī* [cf. P. *dīvāna*], f. = दीवानापन.

दीवानपन *dīvānpan* [cf. H. *dīvānā*], m. = दीवानापन.

दीवाना *dīvānā* [P. *dīvāna*], adj. **1.** insane. **2.** possessed (by a frenzy); ecstatic; fanatical. — ~ बनाना, or करना, to make mad; to drive to frenzy.

दीवानापन *dīvānāpan* [cf. H. *dīvānā*], m. **1.** madness. **2.** frenzy; mania.

दीवानी *dīvānī* [P. *dīvānī*], adj. & f. **1.** adj. having to do with a tribunal, or a court; judicial; civil. **2.** f. *hist.* the office, duties or jurisdiction of a *dīvān*. **3.** a civil court. **4.** litigation.

दीवार *dīvār* [P. *dīvār*], f. **1.** a wall. **2.** embankment. **3.** outer, vertical portion (of sthg.); upper (of a shoe; rim of a plate). — ~ के भी कान हैं, walls have ears. दीवारें चाटना, fig. to come to the end of (one's) life. – दीवारगीर [P. *-gīr*], f. a wall-bracket; wall lamp. °ई, f. wall-bracket; tapestry, hanging.

दीवारी *dīvārī* [cf. H. *dīvār*], f. a small wall.

दीवाल *dīvāl*, f. = दीवार.

दीवाली *dīvālī* [*dīpāvali-*], f. row of lamps: a festival in honour of Lakṣmī, held at the new moon of the month Kārttik (when houses and buildings are illuminated).

दीस- *dīs-* [*dṛśyate*], v.i. Brbh. Av. to appear, to be visible.

दीसे *dīse*, adj. & adv. *Pl.* like; likely.

दुँगरी *duṁgrī*, f. *Pl.* a type of coarse cotton cloth, dungaree.

दुंगानी *duṅgānī*, f. *hist.* N. fractional division of an estate.

[1]**दुंद** *dund* [**duvaṁdva-*], m. **1.** quarrelling. **2.** noise, din, uproar. — ~ मचाना, to create an uproar, &c.

[2]**दुंद** *dund* [conn. *dundubhi-*], m. Av. a large drum.

दुंदका *dundkā*, m. *Pl.* a sugar-mill; the outlet for the smoke at a sugar-mill.

[1]**दुंदुभ** *dundubh* [ad. *dundubhi-*], m. *HŚS.* = दुंदुभि.

[2]**दुंदुभ** *dundubh* [S.], m. reg. a water-snake.

दुंदुभि *dundubhi* [S.], m. a large drum.

दुंदुभी *dundubhī* [ad. *dundubha-*: ← Austro-as.], f. Av. metr. = दुंदुभि.

दुंबा *dumbā* [P. *dumba*], m. a fat-tailed sheep.

दु- *du-* [**du-*[2]], adj. two. (for many cpds. in दु-, equivalents in दो- , q.v., are found; see also hww). — दुअन्नी, f. a two-anna coin. दुकेला, adj. see अकेला. दुकेले, adv. with another, as a pair. दुख़ाना, adj. having two compartments, or stories. दुगाड़ा, adj. & m. *Pl. HŚS.* double-barrelled; a double-barrelled firearm. दुघड़िया, adj. lasting two hours. दुचंद, adj. Brbh. double, twofold. दुचित, adj. = next. दुचित्ता, adj. of two minds: puzzled, doubtful; irresolute; absent-minded. दुछत्ता, adj. (house) having a double roof; having two wings (a biplane). दुज़बान, adj. two-tongued: deceitful of speech; equivocal. °ई, f. दुजायगी, f. separateness; alienation. दुतई (for दुतही), f. lined cloth; a piece of cloth of two breadths (used to lie on). दुतरफ़ा [A. *-ṭaraf*], adj. inv. having two sides, or aspects; mutual;

supporting both sides (in a dispute), deceitful. दुतारा, adj. having two strings, or threads; m. *mus.* a two-stringed instrument. दुदामी [P. *dām* 'thread'], f. muslin embroidered with flowers. दुदिला, adj. = दुचित्ता. दुधारा, adj. two-edged (a blade); m. a two-edged sword; ° -धारी, f. दुनाली, adj. double-barrelled; f. a double-barrelled gun. दुपटी, f. Brbh. = दुपट्टा, see s.v. दुपट्टी, f. double-sidedness: duplicity, hypocrisy. दुपलड़ी, adj. a cap made of two pieces of material (= दोपल्ली). -पल्लू, m. id. दुपल्ला, adj. having two folds; folded in two. दुपल्ली टोपी, f. a kind of wide-set forage cap. दुपहरिया, f. Brbh. a small flowering plant (of which the flowers open around mid-day). दुपहिया, adj. two-wheeled. दुपालिया, f. = दुपलड़ी. दुबारा, adj. performed twice, repeated; adv. twice; a second time. दुबाज़ [P. *-bāz*], m. *Pl.* a kind of pigeon; a paper kite; a kind of eagle. दुभाँतिया, adj. & m. deceitful; a hypocrite. दुभाषिया, m. speaking two languages: an interpreter. °-भाषी, m. id. दुभेसिया [f. *veṣa-* × *bheda-*], m. of two guises: a deceitful or hypocritical person. दुमंज़िला, adj. two-storeyed; two-decked (a ship, a bus); two-tiered. दुमहला, adj. id., 1., 2. दुमाहा [P. *-māha*], adj. inv. lasting two months; occurring every two months. दुमुँहा, adj. having two mouths, or faces; two-faced, deceitful. दुरंगा, adj. & m. of two colours; piebald; capricious; deceitful; hypocritical; a capricious person, &c. °पन, m. duplicity; hypocrisy. दुरंगी, f. id. दुराहा, m. a road branching into two; a crossroads. दुरुख़ा, adj. inv. & m. of the same face or appearance on both sides (as cloth); having two faces or aspects; = दुभेसिया. -रुखी, f. दुलड़ा, adj. & m. having two strings or hands of two rows; fig. having two strings to one's bow; necklace or belt, &c. of two strings or bands. °-लड़ी, f. id. दुलत्ती, f. a kick with the hind feet (as of a horse). दुलत्ती फेंकना, मारना or चलाना, to kick out. दुलाई, f. a quilted wrap or covering. दुशाखा, f. a forked stick, double support. दुशाला, m. a double shawl (= दुपट्टा). दुशाले में लपेटकर मारना, to soften the impact of an attack: to wrap up harsh criticism in kind or innocuous words. दुसाई, f. *Pl.* = दुसाहा. दुसाखी, f. *Pl.* id. दुसार, m. Brbh. piercing right through (sthg). दुसाला [P. *-sāla*], adj. inv. two years old; biennial. दुसाहा, m. reg. land which bears two crops a year. °-साही, f. id. (*Pl.*). दुसूती, f. a kind of cloth woven of double threads. दुसेजा, m. Brbh. a large bed. दुसेरा, m. a weight of two seers. °-सेरी, f. id. दुहत्थर, adj. see next. दुहत्थड़, adj. & f. m. held with both hands (a weapon, &c.); a blow struck with both hands. दुहत्था, adj. performed with both hands, with full force; two-handled. दुहाजू [**dubhārya-*], adj. m. & m. (a man) married a second time.

दुअन्नी *duannī*, f. see s.v. दु-.

[1]**दुआ** *duā* [A. *du'ā*], f. **1.** invocation: one's wish (for another); pej. ill wish. ***2.** prayer: supplication; benediction. ~ करना, or माँगना, to pray (for, की); to wish (for), to desire. ~ देना (को), to bless, to pray for. आपकी ~ से, adv. (it is) thanks (only) to your prayer (formula acknowledging a kind act, or interest). – दुआगो [P. *-go*], m. one who invokes or utters a blessing, a well-wisher. °ई, f. utterance of a blessing, &c.

[2]**दुआ** *duā*, adj. & m. *Pl.* **1.** adj. consisting of two. **2.** m. the two (cards, dice).

दुइ *dui*, adj. Brbh. Av. two.

दुई *duī* [cf. H. *do*], f. **1.** twofold nature, duality. **2.** a second, another. **3.** separation, estrangement.

दुः- *duḥ-* [S.], pref. = दुर्-. — दुःशासन, adj. & m. intractable; badly governed; misgovernment, maladministration. दुःशील, adj. of bad character, depraved. दुःसंग, m. bad company, or society. दुःसह, adj. difficult to be borne; intolerable. दुःसाध्य, adj. difficult to be accomplished; difficult to reach; difficult to deal with, or to cure. दुःसाहस, m. rashness; presumption; irreverence. °इक, adj. rash, &c. (an action). °ई, adj. दुःस्पर्श, m. 'difficult to be touched': name of several plants. दुःस्वप्न, m. bad dream, nightmare.

दुःख *duḥkh* [S.], m. = दुख. — दुःखकर, adj. causing grief, pain, or trouble, &c. दुःखद, adj. id. दुःख-दर्द, m. grief and pain: distress, troubles. दुःखदायक, adj. & m. = दुःखद; oppressor, persecutor, &c. id. °-दायी, adj. & m. id. दुःखप्रद, adj. = दुःखद. दुःखमय, adj. grievous, sad (as a time, an event); filled with sorrow (a person). दुःखवादी, adj. voicing sorrows: inclined to pessimism; m. a pessimist. दुःख-सागर, m. ocean of sorrows: the world; a sea of troubles. दुःख-सुख, m. pain and pleasure, sorrow and joy. दुःखात्मक [°*kha*+*ā*°], adj. tragic. दुःखांत [°*kha*+*a*°], adj. whose end is sorrow: tragic (a tale, a drama). °इका, f. *lit.* a tragedy.

दुःखित *duḥkhit* [S.], adj. **1.** afflicted by grief; sad. **2.** distressed; in misery or misfortune. **3.** suffering pain.

दुःखी *duḥkhī* [S.], adj. & m. = दुखी.

दुक- *duk-*, v.i. Brbh. to hide.

दुकड़ा *dukṛā*, adj. & m. **1.** paired. **2.** m. a pair. **3.** *Pl. HŚS.* a fourth part of a *paisā*.

दुकड़ी *dukṛī*, f. **1.** a pair; a paired or twin object; object with two links or rings (as a bridle, a vessel). **2.** a two-horse trap.

दुकान *dukān* [A. *dukkān*: P. *dūkān*], f. **1.** a shop; stall. **2.** a workshop. — ~ उठाना (की), to mar or to ruin the business (of); to close or to shift the shop or business (of); to close up a shop. ~ करना, to keep a shop; to open a shop. ~ चलना, a shop or business to flourish. ~ बढ़ाना, to close up a shop or stall. ~ लगाना, to set up or to open a shop or business; to display goods for sale. पान की ~, f. a betel shop or stall.

दुकानदार *dukāndār* [P. *dūkāndār*], m. a shopkeeper.

दुकानदारी *dukāndārī* [P. *dūkāndārī*], f. **1.** shopkeeping; business, trade. **2.** seeking to profit (from, की); dealing (in); pej. trickery. ~ चलाना, or करना, to keep shop; to trade.

दुकाल *dukāl* [*duṣkāla-*], m. bad time: famine.

दुकूल *dukūl* [S.], m. **1.** cloth woven from the inner bark of a partic. plant: fine cloth or clothing; linen. **2.** a shawl.

दुक्का *dukkā*, m. a pair; the two (cards, dice).

दुख *dukh* [*duḥkha-*], m. & adj. for most cpds. see s.v. दुःख. **1.** m. sorrow, grief; distress; dejection. **2.** regret. **3.** vexation, chagrin; annoyance. **4.** suffering; misfortune. **5.** trouble, difficulty. **6.** pain. **7.** adj. painful; troublesome. — ~ उठाना, to be afflicted, to suffer; to suffer difficulty, &c.; to take trouble, or pains. ~ का मारा, adj. wretched, miserable; m. a wretched person. ~ की बात, f. a matter for sorrow, or regret; unfortunate matter. ~ देना, or पहुँचाना, to cause pain or distress (to, को); to cause trouble (to). ~ पाना, to suffer grief, distress, &c. ~ भरना or भोगना, = ~ उठाना, 1., 2. ~ में डालना, to cause distress or suffering (to, को). ~ लगना (को), to be affected by grief, or regret; to suffer pain. ~ होना (को), grief, regret or pain to be felt; difficulty to be experienced. – दुखदाई, adj. Av. see दुःखदायी. दुख-दुंद, adj. Brbh. grief and contention: = दुःख-दर्द.

दुखड़ा *dukhṛā* [cf. *duḥkha-*], m. suffering, distress; misfortune; labour, toil. — ~ पीटना, or भरना, to live a life of toil and trouble. ~ रोना, to bewail (one's) woes, to tell (one's) sad story.

दुखना *dukhnā* [*duḥkhati*], v.i. **1.** to give pain, to ache. **2.** to feel compassion (for: as the heart). **3.** to feel compunction or remorse.

दुखहायौ *dukhhāyau*, adj. Brbh. grieved, sad.

दुखाना *dukhānā* [cf. *duḥkhati*: Pk. *dukkhāvei*], v.t. to cause suffering or pain; to pain, to wound. — जी, or दिल, ~, to pain the heart.

दुखारा *dukhārā*, adj. = दुखी.

दुखारी *dukhārī*, adj. = दुखी.

दुखित *dukhit*, adj. see दुःखित.

दुखिया *dukhiyā* [cf. *duḥkhita-*], adj. inv. = दुखी.

दुखियारा *dukhiyārā*, adj. = दुखी.

दुखी *dukhī* [*duḥkhita-*], adj. & m. **1.** adj. grieving, sad; sorry. **2.** suffering, distressed; wretched. **3.** suffering pain. **4.** m. a sorrowful or suffering person.

दुग-दुग *dug-dug*, [conn. **dhukk-*], adj. palpitating: — ~ काँपना, to shake with fear.

दुगदुगी *dugdugī*, f. **1.** reg. = धुकधुकी, 2. **2.** *HŚS.* = धुकधुकी, 3. — ~ में दम होना, the heart to be in the throat; to be on the point of death; fig. to enjoy excellent health although in advanced age.

दुगला *duglā*, m. *Pl.* = [2]दोगला.

दुगुना *dugunā* [H. *dūnā*; ad. **duguṇa-*], adj. & m. **1.** adj. twofold, double; twice as much or as many (as, से); twice as large (as). **2.** m. twice the amount (of, का). — दो ~ चार, twice two are four.

दुग्ध *dugdh* [S.], adj. & m. **1.** adj. milked. **2.** m. what is milked, milk. — दुग्ध-खाद्य, m. dairy produce. दुग्ध-पदार्थ, m. a milk product. दुग्ध-शाला, m. dairy. दुग्धाम्ल [°*dha*+*a*°], m. lactic acid.

दुग्धता *dugdhătā* [S.], f. milkiness.

दुग्धिका *dugdhikā* [S.], f. **1.** *Pl. HŚS.* = [1]दूधी. **2.** *HŚS.* a fragrant grass.

दुग्धिनिका *dugdhinikā* [S.], f. *Pl. HŚS.* a red species of *Achyranthes aspera*.

दुग्धी *dugdhī* [S.], adj. **1.** having milk (= दुधार). **2.** milky. **3.** *chem.* lactic.

दुज *duj* [ad. *dvija-*], m. **1.** twice-born: reg. a brāhmaṇ. **2.** Brbh. tooth. **3.** E.H. bird (as hatched from an egg previously laid).

दुत *dut*, interj. **1.** away (with you)! **2.** nonsense! — ~ करना, to reprimand; to drive away. – दुतकार, m. reproof; scolding. °ई, f.

दुति *duti* [ad. *dyuti-*], f. Brbh. Av. **1.** light; splendour. **2.** E.H. blank paper.

दुतिया *dutiyā*, f. = द्वितीया.

[1]**दुत्ता** *duttā* [cf. H. *dut*], m. reg. driving away by saying '*dut*'. — ~ देना (को), to drive away scornfully.

[2]**दुत्ता** *duttā* [conn. H. *dhuttā*], m. reg. trick, cheating. — ~ देना (को), to cheat.

दुद्धी *duddhī* [*dugdhikā-*], f. **1.** a kind of Asclepias. **2.** any of several kinds of Euphorbia, spurgewort (plants giving a milky juice). **3.** a whitish chalk. **4.** a kind of soft white stone.

दुधमुँहा *dudhmuṁhā*, adj. not weaned.

दुधार *dudhār* [conn. **dugdhahāra-*], adj. giving milk, milch (cow, goat, &c).

दुधारू *dudhārū*, adj. = दुधार.

दुधैल *dudhail*, adj. = दुधार.

दुनका *dunkā*, m. crumb, scrap (see s.v. [2]दाना).

दुनियाँ *duniyāṁ*, f. see दुनिया.

दुनिया *duniyā* [A. *dunyā*], f. **1.** the world; this world, or life: transf. worldly goods or pleasures. **2.** people. — **नई ~ बसाना**, to start life anew. **दुनियादार** [P. *-dār*], adj. & m. worldly; down-to-earth, practical; a worldly person; man of the world. °**ई**, f. worldliness, attention to or skill in worldly matters; worldly affairs, or goods; wife and children, family; outward courtesy, ceremony; sexual relations. **दुनियादारी की बातें**, f. pl. polite words; dissembling. **दुनियासाज़** [P. *-sāz*], adj. & m. = दुनियादार. °**ई**, f. worldliness; tact; dissembling.

दुनियाई *duniyāī* [A. *dunyāvī*: w. H. *-āī*], adj. = दुनियावी.

दुनियावी *duniyāvī* [A. *dunyāvī*], adj. belonging to the world, worldly; secular.

दुपट्टा *dupaṭṭā* [cf. *paṭṭa-*[2]], m. a shawl of doubled material; sheet, wrapper. — **~ हिलाना**, or **फहराना**, to wave a flag (of truce); to surrender (a fort). **मुँह पर ~ तानकर सोना**, to sleep with a sheet drawn over the head; to sleep in peace, or with the mind at ease.

दुपहर *dupahr*, f. = दोपहर.

दुपहरी *dupahrī*, f. = दोपहरी.

दुबकना *dubaknā*, v.i. to skulk (= दबकना).

दुबधा *dubdhā* [*dvidhā*, adv., Pa. *dveḷhaka-*, n.; and ad. *dvividha-*], m. ? f. dilemma, doubt; indecision; uncertainty. **~ करना**, to feel doubt; to mistrust. ~, or **दुबधे**, **में आना**, or **पड़ना**, to become uncertain, &c.

दुंबा *dumbā* [P. *dumba*], m. a fat-tailed sheep.

दुबकना *dubaknā*, v.i. = दबकना.

दुबधैल *dubdhail* [cf. H. *dubdhā*], adj. & m. reg. **1.** adj. being of two minds, perplexed, &c. (see दुबधा). **2.** m. a waverer.

दुबला *dublā* [*durbala-*], adj. **1.** thin; lean. **2.** weak, frail; infirm. — **दुबला-पतला**, adj. slight (of build); scrawny; weak, &c.

दुबलाई *dublāī* [cf. H. *dublā*], f. = दुबलापन.

दुबलाना *dublānā* [cf. H. *dublā*], v.i. & v.t. **1.** v.i. to become thin, &c. **2.** v.t. to cause to waste; to age (a person: of worry, &c).

दुबलापन *dublāpan* [cf. H. *dublā*], m. **1.** thinness, &c. **2.** weakness, &c.

दुबलापना *dublāpanā* [cf. H. *dublā*], m. = दुबलापन.

दुबलापा *dublāpā* [cf. H. *dublā*], m. = दुबलापन.

दुबसी *dubsī*, f. *Pl.* obs. 'two in twenty': percentage allowed to farmers on revenue paid to government.

दुबाइन *dubāin*, [cf. **duveda-*], f. **1.** a woman of the Dūbe caste. **2.** the wife of a Dūbe.

दुबिधा *dubidhā*, m. Brbh. = दुबधा.

दुबे *dube*, m. = दूबे.

दुम *dum* [P. *dum*], f. **1.** tail. **2.** end, rear or hind part. — **~ के पीछे फिरना**, to be in constant attendance (on, के); to be always at one's heels. **~ दबाकर भागना**, adv. to flee abjectly; to scuttle away (see next). **~ दबाना**, to put the tail between the legs: to turn tail. **~ में घुसना**, to creep under the tail (of, की: as pups under a bitch); to take refuge (with); to follow about, to cling to (servilely, or as a child to its mother). **~ हिलाना**, to wag the tail: to show childish delight; to fawn (before, के सामने). — **दुमकटा**, adj. docked, tailed (an animal). **दुमछल्ला**, tail (esp. of a paper kite); fig. a constant follower, or attendant. **दुमदार** [P. *-dār*], adj. having a tail. **दुमदार तारा**, m. a comet.

दुमची *dumcī* [P. *dumcī*], f. **1.** crupper. **2.** tail-bone, coccyx. — **~ की हड्डी**, f. = ~, 2.

दुमबाल *dumbāl* [P. *dumbāl*], m. **1.** tail. **2.** transf. hind or rear part; stern; end. **3.** rudder.

[1]**दुर** *dur* [*dūra-*], interj. be off! clear out! — **~ करना**, to drive away (as a dog); to send scornfully away. — **दुर-दुर फिट-फिट होना**, to be an object of scorn.

[2]**दुर** *dur* [A. *durr*], m. Brbh. Av. **1.** a pearl. **2.** an ear-ring set with a single pearl. **3.** a pearl pendant worn from the nose. **4.** fig. a kind of horse.

दुर्- *dur-* [S.], pref. **1.** bad; wrong; evil; wicked. **2.** base, contemptible. **3.** difficult, troublesome. **4.** inferior, deficient. **5.** wanting, without. — **दुरंत**, adj. endless, infinite; difficult of achievement; ending badly. **दुरभिग्रह**, m. the plant *Achyranthes aspera* (source of potash salts); °**आ**, f. the plant cowach, *Mucuna pruritus*; *Alhagi maurorum*. **दुरवस्थ**, adj. in a bad or wretched condition. °**आ**, f. **दुराक्रांत**, adj. unconquered, unconquerable. **दुराग्रह**, m. excessive stubbornness; misguided zeal. °**ई**, adj. & m. **दुराचार**, m. bad or improper conduct; wickedness; °**ई**, adj. & m. of bad conduct;

wicked; depraved; irreligious; wicked person, villain, &c. दुराधर्ष, adj. Brbh. hard to overcome; mighty. दुराराध्य, adj. difficult to propitiate, or to worship; worthy of conciliation or of devotion, despite the cost. दुरारूढ़, adj. difficult to master (as a style of language). दुराशा, f. Brbh. Av. a vain hope; a wrongful hope. दुरुत्साहन, m. incitement, instigation. दुरूह, adj. difficult to understand. दुर्गंध, f. bad smell. दुर्गत, adj. & f. in bad circumstances: unfortunate; needy; = next; °इ, f. misfortune; want; abjectness; cruel treatment; pangs of hell. दुर्गम, adj. difficult, or impassable (as a road); inaccessible; difficult to achieve; difficult to grasp, profound. दुर्घट, adj. difficult to be accomplished, unattainable. दुर्घटना, f. an accident; a disaster; outbreak of violence, incident. °ग्रस्त, adj. damaged in an accident; destroyed, wrecked. दुर्जन, m. a villain, scoundrel. दुर्जय, adj. difficult to defeat, invincible. °ता, f. दुर्जेय, adj. = दुर्जय. दुर्ज्ञेय, adj. difficult to be known or understood, incomprehensible. दुर्दंड, adj. inveterate, incorrigible. दुर्दमनीय, adv. hard to repress or to subdue, obstinate. दुर्दशा, f. evil plight, misery; unsteadiness. °ग्रस्त, adj. दुर्दशा करना (की), to reduce to dire straits, to ill-use. दुर्दांत, adj. uncontrolled, uncontrollable. दुर्दृष्ट, adj. unfortunate. दुर्दैव, m. misfortune; evil spirit. दुर्धर, adj. difficult to catch or to hold; powerful, mighty; incomprehensible. दुर्धर्ष, adj. unconquerable, indomitable. दुर्नाम, m. bad name, disrepute; slander. °आ, m. *Pl. HŚS.* haemorrhoids. दुर्बल, adj. weak; frail; nerveless, powerless; impotent. °ता, f. दुर्बुद्धि, adj. & m. f. foolish; ignorant; ill-disposed, perverse; a fool, &c.; foolishness, &c. दुर्बोध, adj. difficult to understand. °-बोध्यता, f. difficulty, obscurity (of sense). दुर्भर, adj. hard to lift or to bear. दुर्भाग्य, m. misfortune; ~ से, adv. unfortunately. दुर्भाग्यग्रस्त, adj. afflicted by misfortune. दुर्भाग्यवश, adv. = ~ से; दुर्भाग्यवशात्, adv. id. दुर्भाव, m. bad disposition: ill-will; ill-temper; bad behaviour or manners. दुर्भिक्ष, m. dearth, famine. दुर्मद, adj. intoxicated; crazy; overweeningly proud. दुर्मर, adj. dying hard. दुर्मर्ष, adj. intolerable. दुर्मिल, adj. = दुर्लभ. दुर्लभ, adj. difficult to find, or to obtain; difficult to attain, or to accomplish; fig. rare, choice, excellent; precious, beloved. दुर्ललित, adj. spoiled (a child); petulant, self-indulgent (a desire). दुर्वचन, m. harsh speech: reproach; abuse; slander; ill-omened utterance. दुर्वाच्य, m. = prec. दुर्वाद, m. = prec., 1.-3.; altercation; innuendo. दुर्वासना, f. wrongful desire; vain desire. दुर्विनीत, adj. uncultured. दुर्वीक्ष्य, adj. difficult to see, indistinct. दुर्वृत्त, adj. & m. of bad behaviour, base; wicked; a rogue, villain. °इ, f. bad circumstances; disreputable conduct or occupation; villainy. दुर्व्यसन, m. bad habit, vice. °ई, adj.

दुर- *dur-* [cf. *dūra-*], v.i. Av. **1.** to go out of the way, to disappear. **2.** not to be evident. **3.** to lie hidden.

दुरखा *durkhā*, m. *HŚS.* see s.v. दुरखी, f.

दुरखी *durkhī* [*dūrakṣya-*], f. reg. a kind of grasshopper harmful to indigo, tobacco, mustard, wheat and other crops.

दुरगत *durgat*, f. see दुर्गति s.v. दुर्-.

दुरजन *durjan*, m. Brbh. see दुर्जन s.v. दुर्-.

दुरदाम *durdām* [*durdamya-*: *dur-* ad.], adj. Brbh. obstinate, persistent.

दुरदुराना *durdurānā* [cf. H. *dŭr*], v.t. to drive or to send scornfully away.

दुरबरन *durbaran* [ad. *durvarṇa-*], m. Brbh. silver.

दुरमिस *durmis*, m. reg. = दुरमुट.

दुरमुट *durmuṭ*, m. reg. rammer (for pounding earth).

दुरमुस *durmus*, m. reg. = दुरमुट.

दुरा- *durā-* [cf. H. *dūr*], v.i. Brbh. to be absent, to have disappeared.

दुराज *durāj* [*-rājya-*], m. Brbh. **1.** [*dur-*] misgovernment, misrule. **2.** [*du-*] a jointly controlled state.

दुराना *durānā* [cf. H. *dūr*], v.t. **1.** to remove, to make away with. **2.** to put away (fear, &c.); to have done with. **3.** to conceal (a matter). — दुरादुरी, f. Av. secrecy, stealth. दुरादुरी करि, adv. secretly, stealthily.

दुराव *durāv* [cf. H. *durānā*], m. **1.** concealment. **2.** dissembling, hypocrisy. — ~ करना, to practise concealment: to attempt to deceive.

दुराव *durāv-*, v.t. Brbh. Av. = दुराना.

दुरित *durit* [S.], m. & adj. **1.** m. bad course: sin. **2.** adj. sinful. **3.** *Pl.* difficult. **4.** [× *durānā*] *Pl.* concealed.

दुरी *durī*, f. *Pl.* the two (on dice).

दुरुस्त *durust* [P. *durust*], adj. **1.** right; correct; precise, exact. **2.** in good condition or order; sound (of health). **3.** fit, proper. **4.** interj. right! exactly! — ~ आना, to turn out well (a plan, &c.); to suit (a purpose); to be applicable; to prove true. ~ करना, to put right; to adjust; to repair; to cure; euphem. to set (one) to rights. ~ रखना, = next, 1. ~ समझना, to admit, to allow (an argument, a case); to consider right or proper; to understand rightly, or justly. – दुरुस्त-अक़्ल, adj. of right mind, sane.

दुरुस्ती *durustī* [P. *durustī*], f. **1.** rightness, correctness, &c. **2.** good order, or repair; soundness (of health). **3.** fitness, appropriateness; justness. **4.** adjustment, correction; repair; reform.

दुरूद *durūd* [P. *durūd*], m. *isl.* benediction; praise (esp. of Muḥammad).

दुरूह *dur-ūh* [S.], adj. see s.v. दुर-.

दुरौंध *duraumdh* [**duvārabandha-*], m. *Pl. HŚS.* lintel of a door.

दुरौंधा *duraumdhā*, m. *HŚS.* = दुरौंध.

दुर्ग *dur-g* [S.], adj. & m. **1.** adj. difficult or impassable (a road; inaccessible; unattainable. ***2.** m. a fort, esp. a hill fort; stronghold. **3.** *mythol.* name of a demon killed by Durgā. दुर्ग-कर्म, m. difficult work: fortification.

दुर्गा *durgā* [S.], f. **1.** the goddess Durgā, consort of Śiva. — दुर्गा-नवमी, f. the ninth day of the light half of the month Kārttik (sacred to Durgā). दुर्गा-पूजा, f. Hindu festival celebrating Durgā, held during the first ten days of the light half of the month Āśvin; a less important celebration during the same period of the month Cait. दुर्गाष्टमी [°*gā*+*a*°], f. the eighth day of the light half of the months Āśvin and Cait.

दुर्दमता *dur-damătā* [cf. S. *durdama-, durdamya-,*], f. indomitability.

दुर्दम्य *dur-damyă* [S.], adj. indomitable.

दुर्रा *durrā* [P. *durra*], m. *Pl. HŚS.* a whip, scourge. — ~ मारना, to whip, to flog.

दुलकी *dulkī* [cf. **dulati*: Pk. *dulaï*], f. trotting (gait). — ~ जाना, or चलना, to trot. ~ चाल, f. = ~.

दुलखना *dulakhnā*, v.i. reg. **1.** to refuse stubbornly, to decline. **2.** to disobey.

दुलदुल *duldul* [A. *duldul*], m. **1.** *musl.* Muḥammad's mule (which he gave to his son-in-law 'Alī). ***2.** hedgehog.

दुलफ़ीन *dulfīn* [A. *dulfīn*: ← Gk.], m. dolphin.

दुलहन *dulhan* [cf. H. *dūlhā*], f. a bride; a young wife.

दुलहिन *dulhin*, f. see दुलहन.

दुलही *dulhī*, f. *Pl. HŚS.* = दुलहन.

दुलहेटा *dulheṭā* [*durlabha-*+**beṭṭa-*], m. reg. dear son, precious son.

दुला *dulā-*, v.t. Brbh. = डुलाना.

दुलार *dulār*, m. **1.** fondness, love. **2.** fondling, caressing. **3.** whim (as of a spoilt child). — ~ करना, to caress; to love.

दुलारना *dulārnā*, v.t. to fondle, to caress; to spoil by kindness (a child).

दुलारा *dulārā* [cf. H. *dulārnā*], adj. dear, darling.

दुलीचा *dulīcā* [? f. P. *gālīca*], m. E.H. a carpet.

दुल्हा *dulhā*, m. see दूलहा.

दुल्हैया *dulhaiyā*, f. Brbh. = दुलहन.

दुवाल *duvāl* [P. *duvāl*], f. **1.** leather strap; stirrup-leather. **2.** pomp, majesty (see s.v. दंग).

दुवाली *duvālī* [P. *duvālī*], f. leather strap. — दुवालीबंद [P. *-band*], m. obs. a uniformed soldier (with bandolier).

दुश्- *duś-* [S.], pref. = दुर्-. — दुश्चक्र, m. bad circle: embroilment, obsession; vicious circle. दुश्चर, adj. unattainable, inaccessible; difficult to accomplish. दुश्चरित, adj. & m. = next. दुश्चरित्र, adj. & m. doing wrong; wicked; depraved; bad character or conduct. दुश्चलन, m. bad or wicked conduct. दुश्चेष्टा, f. unworthy, or wicked, impulse, or endeavour.

दुशमन *duśman*, m. see दुश्मन.

दुश्मन *duśman* [P. *duśman*], m. enemy; adversary.

दुश्मनी *duśmanī* [P. *duśmanī*], f. enmity; hostility; animosity. — ~ डालना, to sow enmity or discord (between, में or के बीच).

दुश्वार *duśvār* [P. *duśvār*], adj. difficult; troublesome, burdensome (to, के लिए).

दुश्वारी *duśvārī* [P. *duśvārī*], f. difficulty; troublesomeness, &c.

दुष्- *duṣ-* [S.], pref. = दुर्-. — दुष्कर, adj. difficult to be accomplished, arduous. °-कर्म, m. wrong or wicked act; sin; crime. °ई, m. an evil-doer, &c. °-कृत, m. sthg. done wrongfully, = °-कर्म. °इ, f. = °-कर्म. °-कृत्य, m. = °-कर्म. दुष्पार, adj. hard to be completed. दुष्प्राप्त, adj. = next. °-प्राप्य, adj. difficult to be obtained; difficult to attain (to). दुष्प्रेक्ष्य, adj. difficult to be looked at, unclear; unpleasant to the sight; fearsome.

दुष्ट *duṣṭ* [S.], adj. & m. **1.** adj. corrupted, depraved. **2.** wicked; vicious; corrupt (as a witness); false. **3.** base. **4.** *HŚS.* vitiated, wrongful. **5.** m. a wicked person, &c. **6.** a villain; enemy. **7.** wretch. — दुष्ट-दलन, m. destroyer of the wicked: a title of Kṛṣṇa. दुष्टभाव, adj. of depraved or evil nature. दुष्टमति, adj. of evil mind, depraved, &c. दुष्टाचार [°*ṭa*+*ā*°], adj. of wicked conduct, &c. °ई, m. a wicked person. दुष्टात्मा [°*ṭa*+*ā*°], adj. & m. = दुष्टभाव.

दुष्टता *duṣṭātā* [S.], f. **1.** depravity. **2.** wickedness, &c. (see दुष्ट).

दुष्टताई *duṣṭātāī* [cf. H. *duṣṭātā*], f. = दुष्टता.

दुस्- *dus-* [S.], pref. = दुर्-. — दुस्तर, adj. difficult to be crossed; difficult to reach or to accomplish. °-तार adj. = prec., 1. दुस्सह, adj. = दुःसह. दुस्साहस, adj. = दुःसाहस.

दुसराँद *dusrāṁd*, m. colloq. fellow-lodger; chum, mate.

दुसराना *dusrānā* [cf. H. *dūsrā*], v.t. usu. abs. to repeat. — दुसराकर, adv. repeatedly; again, a second time. दुसरा-तिसराकर, adv. for a second and third time; over and over again.

दुसाध *dusādh*, m. name of a Hindu community who keep pigs and work as watchmen.

दुस्सर *dussar* [cf. H. *dūsrā*], m. *Pl.* double stakes (dice); double or quits.

दुस्सा *dussā* [*dūrśa-*], m. *Pl. HŚS.* = धुस्सा.

दुहता *duhtā* [*dauhitra-*], m. daughter's son, grandson.

दुहती *duhtī* [*dauhitrī-*], f. daughter's daughter, granddaughter.

दुहन *duhan*, m. *Pl.* milking, the act of milking.

दुहना *duhnā* [**duhati*: Pa. *duhati*], v.t. & v.i. **1.** v.t. to milk. **2.** to squeeze out. **3.** fig. to exploit. **4.** v.i. to be milked.

दुहनी *duhnī* [*dohanī-* × H. *duhnā*], f. milk-pail.

दुहनी *duhnī* [*dohana-*[1]; × H. *duhnā*], f. **1.** milking. **2.** a milk-pail.

दुहरा *duhrā*, adj. = दोहरा.

दुहराना *duhrānā*, v.t. = दोहराना.

दुहरित *duhrit* [H. *duhrānā* + S. *-ita-*], adj. doubled.

[1]**दुहाई** *duhāī*, f. a calling twice: **1.** announcement, proclamation. **2.** cry for help, mercy, or justice; appeal (to, की); complaint. **3.** exclamation; oath (upon, की). — ~ करना, or देना, to cry for help, mercy, or justice (to, की). ~ फिरना (की), to be proclaimed (as one's investiture, or fame). ~ दुहाई फेरना, to make known a proclamation, boast or challenge. – दुहाई-तिहाई करना, = ~ करना.

[2]**दुहाई** *duhāī* [cf. H. *duhnā*], f. **1.** milking. **2.** payment for milking.

दुहाजू *duhājū* [**dubhārya-*], m. see s.v. दु-.

दुहाना *duhānā* [cf. H. *duhnā*], v.t. **1.** to cause to be milked (an animal: by, से). **2.** fig. to exploit.

दुहाव *duhāv* [cf. H. *duhnā*], m. a landlord's perquisite (at festivals) of milk from cultivators' cows.

दुहि *duhi*, f. *Pl.* desire, lust.

दुहिता *duhitā* [S.], f. daughter.

दुहुँ *duhuṁ*, adj. Brbh. both (= दोनों).

दुहूँ *duhūṁ*, adj. Brbh. = दोनों.

दुहेला *duhelā* [cf. *duḥkha-*, × *sukha-*], adj. & m. Brbh. Av. **1.** adj. difficult, arduous. **2.** grieving, distressed. **3.** m. a difficult task, &c.

दुह्य *duhyă* [S.], adj. **1.** milkable, milk-giving. **2.** needing milking.

दूकान *dūkān*, f. = दुकान.

दूकानदार *dūkāndār*, m. = दुकानदार.

दूकानदारी *dūkāndārī*, f. = दुकानदारी.

दूखना *dūkhnā* [*duḥkhayati*], v.i. reg. = दुखना.

दूगला *dūglā*, m. *Pl.* = [2]दोगला.

दूज *dūj* [**dutīyā-*: Pa. *dutiya-*], f. second; specif. the second day of a lunar fortnight. — ~ का चाँद, m. the new moon; fig. an infrequent visitor. – दूज-बर, m. a man who marries a second wife.

दूजा *dūjā* [**dutīya-*: Pa. *dutiya-*], adj. **1.** second; other, another. **2.** secondary. **3.** *Pl.* second spirit or soul.

दूत *dūt* [S.], m. **1.** an envoy, messenger; negotiator. **2.** an ambassador. **3.** a secret messenger, spy. — दूतालय [°*ta* + *ā*°], m. = next. दूतावास [°*ta* + *ā*°], m. an embassy, high commission.

दूतता *dūtătā* [S.], f. = दूतत्व.

दूतत्व *dūtatvă* [S.], m. = दूताई, 2.

दूतनी *dūtnī* [cf. H. *dūt*], f. = दूती.

दूतपन *dūtpan* [cf. H. *dūt*], m. 1. = दूताई, 2. **2.** ambassadorship. **3.** spying.

दूताई *dūtāī* [cf. H. *dūt*], f. **1.** the business of an envoy, &c. **2.** the position, duties or status of an envoy, &c.

दूतिका *dūtikā* [S.], f. = दूती.

दूती *dūtī* [S.], f. **1.** a female envoy, &c. **2.** a procuress. **3.** a gossip, tale-bearer.

दूत्य *dūtyă* [S.], m. = दूतत्व.

दूध *dūdh* [*dugdha-*], m. **1.** milk. **2.** milky sap or juice (of certain plants). **3.** fig. family, race, caste, sect. — ~ उतरना, milk to come in (to the breasts, or udder). ~ और चीनी-सा मिलना, to mix well, and to good effect. ~ और जल-सा मिलना, to mix intimately. ~ का ~ (और) पानी का पानी करना, to distinguish milk from water (when the two have been mixed): to distinguish the good or true from the bad or false; to adjudicate unerringly. ~ का धुला, fig. beyond reproach. ~ का बच्चा, m. a nursing infant. ~ का-सा उबाल, m. a sudden fit or frenzy (as of anger, excitement). ~ की बू मुँह से आना, fig. to be still an infant; to be callow. ~ की मक्खी, f. a fly in the milk: sthg. both contemptible and troublesome. ~ की लाज, f. fig. family honour. ~ के दाँत, m. milk teeth. ~ के दाँत न टूटना, fig. not to have reached years of discretion. ~ चढ़ना, milk to be withheld (in the udder); = ~ उतरना. ~ चुराना, or चढ़ाना, to withhold milk. ~ छुड़ाना, or बढ़ाना (का), to wean. ~ देखना (का), to examine the milk of a pregnant woman (hoping to foretell the sex of the child from its thickness). ~ देनेवाला, milk-giving, dairy (animal). ~ पड़ना, or आना (में), the milk to form (in grain prior to its ripening). ~ पिलाना (को), to suckle, to nurse. ~ पीना, to drink milk; fig. to be in good hands, or well looked after (sthg. precious). ~ भर आना, milk to flow (into, में) or to fill (breasts, udder); to feel maternal affection. दूधों नहाओ, पूतों फलो! may you bathe in milk and be fruitful in sons: may you prosper in cattle and children! माँ का ~ लजाना, to shame (one's) family honour. – दूध-कटू, adj. weaned early (a child or an animal). दूधदानी, f. a vessel for milk. दूध-धारा, f. the Milky Way. दूध-धुला, adj. milk-washed: pure white. दूध-ख़ून का नाता, m. blood relationship. दूध-पदार्थ, m. pl. dairy produce. दूध-पीता, adj. nursing, still in infancy; fig. callow; colloq. interest-bearing (money). दूध-पूत, fig. cattle and sons: prosperous state. दूध-फेनी, f. a kind of vermicelli cooked in milk. दूध-बहन, f. foster-sister. दूध-भाई, m. foster-brother. दूध-भात, f. rice boiled in milk. °ई, f. see दूधा-भाती. दूध-माँ, f. foster mother. दूध-मूत, m. milk and urine: दूध-मूत करना (का), to care for (an infant). दूधवाला, adj. & m. selling milk; yielding milk, or sap; a milk vendor. दूधाधारी, adj. living on milk. °-आहारी, adj. id. दूधा-भाती, f. ceremonial supping of boiled rice and milk by a bride and bridegroom (each feeding the other) on the fourth day after marriage.

दूधा *dūdhā* [*dugdha-*], m. **1.** *Pl. HŚS.* a kind of high-quality rice. **2.** juice of unripe grain.

दूधार *dūdhār*, adj. = दुधार.

दूधिया *dūdhiyā* [cf. H. *dūdh*], adj. **1.** containing milk; made of milk; dairy (produce). **2.** milky (of colour). **3.** juicy, still green (grain). — ~ चाय, f. tea with milk. ~ पत्थर, m. chalk-stone; a pottery clay; opal.

[1]**दूधी** *dūdhī* [*dugdhin-*], adj. **1.** containing, or yielding, milk, &c. (see दूध). **2.** f. the breast (esp. of a mother or wet-nurse). **3.** starch.

[2]**दूधी** *dūdhī* [conn. *dugdhikā-*], f. name of several plants having milky sap (as various species of Asclepias, Echites, Euphorbia).

[1]**दून** *dūn* [**duguṇa-*: Pk. *duuṇa-*], adj. double, twofold (= दूना). — ~ की लेना or हाँकना, to boast, to brag. ~ की सूझना, to dream of sthg. beyond one's reach.

[2]**दून** *dūn* [*droṇī-*[2]], m. (f. *Pl.*) a tract of country lying at the foot of hills, a valley.

दूना *dūnā*, adj. = दुगुना. — ~ ~, adj. & adv. twice as much again; more and more.

दूब *dūb* [*dūrvā-*], f. any of several types of soft grass, as *Cynodon* or *Panicum dactylon* (commonly used as fodder). — खेड़े की ~, f. grass at a village site: fig. a poor man of no account (and liable to be trampled on).

दूबड़-घसड़ *dūbaṛ-ghasṛū*, m. *Pl.* one who slips away through weakness: a helpless or insignificant person.

दूबर *dūbar*, adj. reg. = दुर्बल, see s.v. दुर्-.

दूबरा *dūbrā*, adj. reg. = दुर्बल, see s.v. दुर्-.

दूबा *dūbā* [cf. H. *dūb*; S. *dūrvā-*], f. = दूब.

दूबिया *dūbiyā* [cf. H. *dūb*], adj. & m. **1.** adj. consisting of grass. **2.** green, grass-green. **3.** m. colloq. frequenting grass, or lawns: the hoopoe.

दूबे *dūbe* [**duveda-*], m. **1.** name of a brāhmaṇ sub-community. **2.** a man of the Dūbe sub-community.

दूभर *dūbhar* [*durbhara-*], adj. **1.** hard to be borne, burdensome; trying. **2.** hard to obtain (as a commodity).

दूम- *dūm-* [f. *druma-*], v.i. Brbh. to blow (in the wind: trees).

दूमा *dūmā*, m. obs. *Pl. HŚS.* a small leather case used for the transportation of tea.

दूर *dūr* [*dūra-*], adj. & f. (for some compounds, see separate hww.) **1.** adj. distant, remote. **2.** removed (as a difficulty). **3.** दूर- [S]. distant; tele-: e.g. दूर-संचार, m. telecommunications. **4.** adv. far, far off (from, से). **5.** f. distance, remoteness (= दूरी). — ~ करना, to put or to keep at a distance; to remove (from, से); to conceal; to efface (as a memory); to avert (a calamity); to dispel (a doubt); to solve (a difficulty); to get rid of, to dispossess ; to abolish. ~ का, adj. distant; future; distant (as a relative); far-reaching (as thought; far-fetched, wild (claim, boast); thorough-going (a scolding); requiring careful consideration (a topic). ~ की कौड़ी लाना, to propose sthg. impracticable or fanciful. ~ पर, adv. in the distance. ~ पार, adv. May it be far: God forbid! (esp. used by women). ~ भागना, or

रहना, to flee, or to remain, far (from, से); to abstain (from); to avoid, to shun. ~ से, adv. from afar. ~ हो, interj. colloq. clear out! – दूरंदेश [P. *-andeś*], adj. far-seeing, discerning; prudent. °ई, f. foresight; prudence, circumspection. दूरगामी, adj. going far, far-reaching. दूर-चित्रण, m. telephotography. दूर-दराज़ [P. *-darāz*], adj. far, very distant; long. दूर-नियंत्रण, m. remote control. दूर-प्रहारी, adj. having a long striking-power or range (as an aircraft, a gun). दूरबीन [P. *-bīn*], f. (m., *Pl.*) telescope; binoculars. दूरभाष, m. telephone. दूरमार, adj. = दूर-प्रहारी. दूर-मुद्रक, m. teleprinter. दूर-लेख, m. telegram. दूरवर्ती, adj. remotely situated; living at a distance; remote, ancient (as a period). दूरवासी, adj. living at a distance, or abroad; outlandish. दूर-वीक्षण, m. दूरदर्शन, s.v. दूरस्थ, adj. situated at a distance (in space or time), remote. दूरांतरित [°*ra*+*a*°], adj. removed far off (= ~). दूरागत [°*ra*+*ā*°], adj. come from afar. °-ईकृत, adj. removed. °-ईभूत, adj. distant, removed.

दूरता *dūrătā* [S.], f. – दूरत्व.

दूरत्व *dūratvă* [S.], m. remoteness, distance.

दूरदर्शक *dūrdarśak* [S.], adj. & m. **1.** adj. = दूरदर्शी. **2.** m. telescope. **3.** binoculars. — दूरदर्शक-यंत्र, m. id.

दूरदर्शन *dūrdarśan* [S.], m. **1.** far-sightedness. **2.** long-sightedness. **3.** foresight. ***4.** television. — दूरदर्शन-यंत्र, m. television set.

दूरदर्शिता *dūrdarśitā* [S.], f. foresight.

दूरदर्शी *dūrdarśī* [S.], adj. & m. **1.** adj. far-seeing, discerning. **2.** long-sighted. **3.** m. a learned or discerning man.

दूरी *dūrī* [cf. H. *dūr*; P. *dūrī*], f. distance away, or between, remoteness; separation. — ~ पर, adv. at a distance (of, की).

दूरीकरण *dūrīkaraṇ* [S.], m. see s.v. दूर.

दूरीकृत *dūrīkr̥t* [S.], adj. see s.v. दूर.

दूरीभूत *dūrībhūt* [S.], adj. see s.v. दूर.

दूर्वा *dūrvā* [S.], f. = दूब.

दूलम *dūlam* [**durlambha-*], m. reg. what is not attainable, or hard to obtain.

दूल्हा *dūlhā* [*durlabha-*], m. a bridegroom. — ~ देखना, to see or to meet a prospective bridegroom.

दूषक *dūṣak* [S.], adj. & m. **1.** adj. contaminating. **2.** transf. wicked; base. ***3.** attributing fault or blame. **4.** m. one who blames, &c. **5.** a wicked person, &c.

दूषण *dūṣaṇ* [S.], m. **1.** spoiling; contaminating; corrupting. **2.** censuring; disgracing; dishonouring. **3.** calumniating; calumny. 4. = दोष, 1.-3. — वायु-दूषण, m. atmospheric pollution.

दूषणीय *dūṣăṇīyă* [S.], adj. **1.** to be blamed, blameworthy. **2.** base; contemptible.

दूषित *dūṣit* [S.], adj. **1.** spoiled; contaminated; corrupted, corrupt. **2.** censured; disgraced; dishonoured. **3.** falsely accused. — ~ करना, to spoil, &c.

दूष्य *dūṣyă* [S.], adj. **1.** blameworthy. **2.** base; contemptible.

दूसरा *dūsrā* [**dviḥsara-*], adj. & m. **1.** adj. second. **2.** other, another; next. **3.** m. a second (person or thing); a match, equal. **4.** a duplicate. — ~ उतार, m. *math.* square root. ~ चढ़ाव, m. *math.* square. दूसरी बार, adv. a second time, again. दूसरी माँ, f. stepmother. दूसरे, adv. secondly. दूसरे दिन, adv. the next day.

दूहना *dūhnā*, v.t. = दुहना.

दूहिया *dūhiyā*, m. *Pl. HŚS.* double stove, or fireplace.

दृक् *dr̥k* [S.], m. **1.** the eye. **2.** sight (= दृष्टि). **3.** fig. inner perception; wisdom.

दृग *dr̥g* [S.], m. esp. in comp. the eye, &c. (= दृक्). — दृग-अंचल, m. E.H. eyelid; eyelash. दृगनवंत, adj. Brbh. having eyes (= आँखोंवाला). दृग-मिचाव, m. hide and seek.

दृढ़ *dr̥ṛh* [S.], adj. **1.** fixed, firm; hard, unyielding, tough; strong (of physique); tight (as a knot); close (an embrace); stiff. **2.** solid; compact. **3.** fixed, firm (a decision, intention, opinion); established (a basis); consolidated. **4.** steadfast; persevering; dependable. **5.** sound (health). **6.** severe, violent. — दृढ़कारी, adj. strengthening; resolute, hardy; persevering. दृढ़चित्त, adj. firm or resolute of mind, staunch. दृढ़चेता, adj. id. दृढ़निश्चय, adj. of firm intention; certain, undoubted (a matter). °ई, adj. of firm intention. दृढ़प्रतिज्ञ, adj. true to one's promise. दृढ़संकल्प, adj. of firm resolve. दृढ़ांग [°*ṛha*+*a*°], adj. firm-bodied, stalwart. दृढ़ायन [°*ṛha*+*a*°], m. confirmation, corroboration. दृढ़ायुध [°*ṛha*+*ā*°], adj. having strong weapons: strong in battle; m. a hero. दृढ़ीकरण, m. strengthening, consolidation.

दृढ़ता *dr̥ṛhătā* [S.], f. **1.** firmness; hardness; strength. **2.** steadfastness, resolution; conviction. **3.** confirmation, corroboration.

दृढ़त्व *dr̥ṛhatvă* [S.], m. = दृढ़ता.

दृढ़ाई *dr̥ṛhāī* [cf. H. *dr̥ṛh*], f. reg. = दृढ़ता.

दृढ़ाना *dr̥ṛhānā* [cf. H. *dr̥ṛh*], v.i. & v.t. **1.** v.i. *HŚS.* to be firm, strong, &c. (cf. दृढ़). **2.** to be fixed, confirmed. **3.** v.t. Brbh. Av. to strengthen. **4.** to confirm, to corroborate.

दृढ़ीकरण *dṛṛhīkaraṇ* [S.], m. see s.v. दृढ़.

दृप्त *dṛpt* [S.], adj. poet. proud, haughty.

दृश *dṛś* [S.], m. & f. **1.** m. seeing, observing. **2.** f. the eye.

दृश्य *dṛśyă* [S.], adj. & m. **1.** adj. to be seen, visible; evident. **2.** worthy of being seen; beautiful, pleasing; picturesque. **3.** perceptible; phenomenal (as the world). **4.** to do with sight, visual; optic. **5.** m. sthg. visible, or perceived. **6.** a sight, scene, view; scenery. **7.** a picture; view; sketch. **8.** scene (in a play). **9.** *math.* a given quantity. — **दृश्यगत**, adj. objective. **दृश्य-चित्र**, m. a landscape painting. **दृश्य-पट**, m. = next. **दृश्य-पटल**, m. tableau, panorama. **दृश्यमय**, adj. = next. **दृश्यमान**, adj. visible; evident; under inspection; attractive, picturesque. **दृश्य-श्रव्य**, adj. *techn.* audio-visual. **दृश्यांतर** [°*ya*+*a*°], m. change of scene (in a drama). **दृश्यावली** [°*ya*+*ā*°], f. a collection of pictures or views; panorama.

दृश्यत्व *dṛśyatvă* [S.], m. **1.** visibility; clarity (of detail). **2.** attractiveness to the eye (a scene, picture, play).

दृष्ट *dṛṣṭ* [S.], adj. **1.** seen, observed; known. **2.** visible, apparent. **3.** experienced; endured. — **दृष्ट-कूट**, m. *lit.* enigma, enigmatic style (in which meaning is concealed in coded usage). **दृष्टमान**, adj. Brbh. visible; m. the visible world. **दृष्टांत** [°*ṣṭa*+*a*°], adj. end of what is seen: example, illustration; instance, precedent, citation. °**परक**, adj. figurative; allegorical. °**रूप**, adj. id.

दृष्टि *dṛṣṭi* [S.], f. **1.** sight. **2.** look, glance; gaze; the eyes. **3.** eyesight, vision. **4.** view (of sthg.), viewpoint; regard; consideration. **इस ~ से**, adv. from this point of view; with this in mind. — **~ (में) आना**, to come into view, to appear. **~ उठाना**, to raise the eyes. **~ करना**, to look (at, **की** or **पर**); to take a view (of); = **~ डालना**. **~ डालना**, or **देना**, v.t. to cast a glance, to look (at, or over, **पर**); to consider. **~ पर चढ़ना**, to be pleasing in the eyes (of, **की**); to be vexing to the eyes (of). **~ फेरना**, to avert the eyes (from, **से**); to turn away (from: as in coldness, ingratitude). **~ बाँधना**, to enchant (one's sight: **की**). **~ भर देखना**, to look one's fill; to glance fleetingly at. **~ मारना**, to tip a wink, to give a sign by eye. **~ में रखना**, to keep in view, not to overlook. **~ लगाना**, to fix the eyes (on, **पर**); to be intent (on: an object). **~ से गिरना**, to fall in the eyes (of, **की**). – **दृष्टिकोण**, m. point of view, perspective. **दृष्टि-क्रम**, m. perspective. **दृष्टिगत**, adj. seen, visible. °**-गम्य**, adj. able to be seen. **दृष्टिगोचर**, adj. within range of sight: perceptible; evident. **दृष्टि-दोष**, m. sight defect; careless scrutiny; influence of the evil eye. **दृष्टि-निक्षेप**, m. casting a glance, = ~, 2. **दृष्टि-पटल**, m. retina. **दृष्टि-पथ**, m. field or range of vision. **दृष्टि-पात**, m. = ~, 2. **दृष्टि-बंध**, m. deception of the sight: magic; trickery. **दृष्टि-बंधक**, m. *Pl.* mortgage of real estate, without possession. **दृष्टिहीन**, adj. sightless.

देआड़ा *deāṛā* [f. *dehikā*-], f. reg. a white-ant hill.

देउहरा *deuharā*, m. pronun. var. = [1]देहरा.

देख *dekh* [cf. H. *dekhnā*], f. **1.** seeing, looking at, &c. **2.** consideration, observation. — **देख-भाल**, f. observation, scrutiny; supervision, care (of a child, a patient); investigation; reconnaissance. **देख-रेख**, f. = **देख-भाल**, 1., 2.

देखन *dekhan* [cf. H. *dekhnā*], f. = **देख**.

देखना *dekhnā* [**dṛkṣati*, **drakṣati*: Pa. *dakkhati*, × *prekṣate*], v.t. **1.** to see; to watch, to look at; to look on (as a spectator). **2.** to turn the eyes (towards, **की ओर**); to glance (at). **3.** to perceive, to observe. **4.** to consider, to think. **5.** to see to, to attend to (a matter); to superintend. **6.** to watch over, to guard; to guard against (sthg. happening), to take care. **7.** to inspect; to search, to scrutinise; to visit (as a patient). **8.** to examine, to test, to try. **9.** to look for, to search for. **10.** to experience. **11.** to tolerate (a situation, or a person). — **देखने में**, adv. to all appearances; superficially. **देखने में आना**, to be visible; to be evident, to appear; to be generally known (as a state of affairs). – **देखना-भालना**, = ~, 5.-8. **देखना-सुनना**, to make all prudent enquiry (about sthg). – **देखते**, adv. before the eyes (of, **के**), in the presence (of); through long or continued looking; compared (with). **देखते रह जाना**, to be able only to look on: to stand agape, or dejected. **देखा**, m. seeing, sight. **देखा-दिखाया**, adj. seen, and approved (by, **का**); inspected. **देखा-देखी**, f. & adv. looking at each other: confrontation (of two persons); imitation; rivalry; in sight (of, **की**); at the sight (of); in imitation (of); out of rivalry (with). **देखा-भाली**, f. looking, scanning, searching. **देखा-भूली**, f. deception (as by a conjurer); optical illusion; maze. **देखी-अनदेखी करना**, to overlook (one, **की**); to take no notice of (**को**).

देख-भाल *dekh-bhāl*, f. see s.v. **देख**.

देखवैया *dekhvaiyā* [cf. H. *dekhnā*], m. an observer, spectator.

देखा *dekhā* [cf. H. *dekhnā*], m. see s.v. **देखना**.

देखा-देखी *dekhā-dekhī* [cf. H. *dekhnā*], f. & adv. see s.v. **देखना**.

देखा-भाली *dekhā-bhālī*, f. = **देख-भाल**, see s.v. **देख**.

देग *deg* [P. *deg*], m. a large metal pot (esp. for cooking).

देगचा *degcā* [P. *degca*], m. a metal pot.

देगची *degcī* [cf. H. *degcā*], f. a small metal pot.

देदीप्यमान *dedīpyămān* [S.], adj. shining intensely, brilliant; radiant.

देन *den* [cf. H. *denā*], f. m. **1.** giving. **2.** a gift. **3.** an outgoing; a loan; debt, liability. **4.** a contribution; legacy (from the past). — देनदार [P. *-dār*], m. a debtor. °ई, f. = देन, 3. देन-लेन, f. dealings, transactions (= लेन-देन).

देना *denā* [*dadāti*: Pa. *deti*, infld. by *neti* ← *nayati*], v.t. & m. **1.** to give; to cause (as pain, trouble, hope, &c). **2.** (esp. w. देना.) to dispose of, to consign; to deliver. **3.** (esp. w. देना.) to grant, to bestow; to impart; to contribute; to make (a payment). **4.** to produce, to yield (as crops, milk); to lay (a bird). **5.** (with obl. inf.) to allow. **6.** to place, to put (on, in, or into, में, or पर); to apply; to put on (clothes). पौधों में पानी ~, to water plants. सिर पर टोपी ~, to put a hat on (one's) head. **7.** (esp. w. मारना.) to give, to strike (as a blow); to dash (down or against, पर); to throw; to stamp. **8.** to emit, to give forth (as a cry). **9.** to close (as a door); to do up (a lace, button). **10.** m. giving, paying. **11.** sthg. to be paid: a debt, liability. — दे जाना, to hand in, to leave behind (an object). – देना-पाना, m. assets and liabilities; profit and loss.

देय *dey* [S.], adj. **1.** to be given. **2.** proper for a gift. **3.** required, due (as payment, &c). **4.** to be granted, allowed. — देयादेय [°*ya*+*ā*°], m. debit and credit, income and expenditure. °-फलक, m. balance (of accounts). देयादेश, [°*ya*+*ā*°], m. order for payment.

देयक *deyak* [S.], m. a cheque.

देर *der* [P. *der*], f. & adv. **1.** f. a period or lapse of time, interval. **2.** delay; lateness; slowness. **3.** adv. delayed, late. ~ आना, to arrive late (as a train). — ~ करना, to delay; to be late; to be slow. ~ तक, adv. for some time (into the future); for a long time. ~ आए दुरुस्त आए, prov. what is long in coming will come right. ~ में, adv. after delay; late (of arrival, completion of a task, &c). ~ लगाना, to allow time to elapse (on purpose); to delay; to loiter. ~ से, adv. late; since or for some time (already past). ~ से आना, to arrive late. ~ होना (को), time to elapse; to be delayed; to be late. कितनी ~ में, adv. by when? how soon? कुछ ~ के बाद, adv. after some time. थोड़ी ~ में, adv. within a short while, soon. – देर-दार, f. colloq. = ~; delay, putting off, postponing (a matter). देर-सवेर, adv. = next. °-सवेरे, adv. sooner or later; now and again; at whatever time.

देरा *derā* [? H. [1]*dehrā*; P. *dera*], m. reg. 1. = [1]देहरा. 2. = डेरा.

देरी *derī* [P. *derī*], f. = देर. — ~ करना, to delay; to be late; to be slow. ~ लगना (को), time to elapse: to be late; to be long; to be slow.

[1]**देव** *dev* [S.], m. **1.** a god. **2.** title of a revered or greatly respected person, esp. of a brāhmaṇ, or of a king, &c. **3.** transf. idol. — देव-ऋण, m. *hind.* debt to a god, or gods: any observance due to a deity from a worshipper. देव-ऋषि, m. = देवर्षि. देव-कन्या, f. divine maiden; an *apsaras*. देव-कर्म, m. religious act or rite: a sacrifice to the gods. देव-गण, m. pl. the gods. देव-गति, f. Brbh. transition to paradise: death. देव-गिरि, f. *mus.* name of a *rāgiṇī*. देव-गांधारी, f. *mus.* name of a *rāgiṇī*. देव-गृह, m. abode of the gods: heaven, a heavenly sphere; a temple. देव-ठान, m. see hw. देव-तरु, m. tree at which village assemblies are held. देव-थान, f. m. (?) place of idols: a temple. देव-त्रयी, f. the triad of gods Brahmā, Viṣṇu and Śiva. देव-दत्त, adj. & m. god-given; given to the gods (as an offering, sacrifice); a gift of God. देवदार, m. the deodar pine or cedar. °-दारु, m. id. देव-दास, m. a devout person; a temple servant. °ई, f. a temple servant; a dancing-girl, temple prostitute. देवदानी, f. name given to a kind of creeper (= [1]तोरी, [1]तुरई). देव-दूत, m. a messenger of the gods, an angel. देव-दृष्टि, f. divine vision. देव-धान्य, m. millet (= [2]ज्वार). देव-नदी, f. divine river: the Ganges. देवनागरी, f. the Devanāgarī script. देव-निंदा, f. reviling the gods: blasphemy; heresy. °-निंदक, m. a blasphemer; heretic. देव-पति, m. lord of the gods: a title of Indra. देव-पथ, m. way of, or to, the gods: the sky, heaven. देव-पुरी, f. city of the gods: name of Indra's capital Amarāvatī. देव-पूजा, f. worship of the gods; idolatry, paganism. °-पूजक, m. *Pl.* idolater, &c. देव-भाषा, f. fig. the Sanskrit language. देव-मंदिर, m. = देवालय. देव-मास, m. the eighth month of pregnancy. देव-मूर्ति, f. an idol. देव-यान, m. the vehicle of a god; a means of access to paradise after death. देव-योनि, f. a being of divine birth, demigod (as *vidyādharas, kinnaras*, &c). देव-राज, m. ruler of the gods: a title of Indra. °आ, m. id. देवरूप, adj. of divine form, godlike. देवर्षि, m. a divine sage (as Nārada). देव-लोक, m. world of the gods: paradise; the sphere of a partic. deity; any of the worlds above the earth. देव-लोक को सिधारना, to depart to paradise, to die. देव-वधू, f. a god's wife; an *apsaras*. देव-वल्लभ, m. the tree *Mallotus philippinensis* (source of a dye and a drug called *kamelā, kamūd*). देववाद, m. theism. देव-वाणी, f. fig. the Sanskrit language; a prophecy. देवांगना [°*va*+*a*°], f. = देव-वधू. देवार्पण [°*va*+*a*°], m. sacrifice to a god, or gods. देवालय [°*va*+*ā*°], m. = देव-गृह, 2. देवासुर [°*va*+*a*°], m. gods and demons. देवाहुति [°*va*+*ā*°], f. an

oblation to the gods. देवेंद्र [°*va*+*i*°] chief of the gods: a title of Indra, and of Śiva. देवोत्थान [°*va*+*u*°], m. = देवठान. देवोन्माद [°*va*+*u*°], m. religious frenzy. देवोपमता [°*va*+*u*°], f. comparability with the gods, divine nature. देवोपासना [°*va*+*u*°], f. divine worship.

²**देव** *dev* [P. *dev*], m. **1.** a demon; ghost. **2.** a giant, monster. — ~ का ~, m. a monster indeed.

देवकीय *devăkıyă* [S.], adj. = दैविक, 1.

देवटी *devṭī* [**daipavarti-*], f. *Pl.* a lamp; a torch.

देवठान *devṭhān* [H. ¹देव+H. *uṭhān*], m. *hind.* the waking of Viṣṇu (on the eleventh of the bright half of the month Kārttik).

देवता *devătā* [S.], m. inv. **1.** a god. **2.** transf. an object of worship, or a person held to be sacred; an idol. **3.** a revered person.

देवतिन *devtin* [cf. H. *devătā*, and *daivat*], f. a goddess.

देवत्व *devatvă* [S.], m. divine character, divinity.

देवनी *devnī*, f. **1.** a goddess. **2.** a demoness.

देवर *devar* [*devara-*], m. husband's younger brother.

देवरानी *devrānī* [**devarajāṇī-*: Pk. *de(v)arāṇī-*], f. husband's younger brother's wife.

देवर्ण *devarṇ* [S.], m. = देव-ऋण.

¹**देवल** *deval* [*devakula-*], m. a temple; shrine.

²**देवल** *deval* [S.], m. one who tends an idol (= पुजारी); a devotee.

देवली *devlī* [*devakulikā-*], f. *Pl. HŚS.* a small temple or shrine made for an idol only.

देवहरा *devharā*, m. reg. = ¹देहरा.

¹**देवा** *devā* [cf. H. *denā*], adj. & m. **1.** adj. giving, paying, &c. **2.** m. a giver. — देवा-लेवा, m. barter; trading.

²**देवा** *devā* [*devatā-*], m. a god, a deity.

देवाल *devāl*, adj. & m. *Pl.* **1.** adj. giving, generous. **2.** able to give, or to pay. **3.** *HŚS.* m. a giver, liberal person.

देवाला *devālā*, m. 1. = देवालय. 2. = दिवाला.

देवालिया *devāliyā*, m. = दिवालिया.

देवी *devī* [S.], f. **1.** a goddess. **2.** consort of a god: esp. Durgā (wife of Śiva). **3.** a lady. देविओ और सज्जनो! ladies and gentlemen!

देवैया *devaiyā* [cf. H. *denā*], m. a giver, bestower.

देवोतर *devotar*, m. *Pl. HŚS.* land held in the name of deities.

देश *deś* [S.], m. **1.** place, quarter, region; province. **2.** country; nation. **3.** native land, or region. — ~ बदेश फिरना [P. *ba-*], to travel from country to country, to travel about. – देशगत, adj. (become) characteristic of a nation, &c.: national; regional. देशज, adj. id.; *ling.* regional (a term, in respect of its origin). देश-त्याग, m. voluntary exile; emigration. °ई, m. an exile; emigrant. देश-द्रोह, m. treason. °ई, m. a traitor. देश-धर्म, m. the customs of a country, or of a region. देश-निकाला, m. banishment, exile. देश-निकाला देना (को), to banish, &c. देश-निकासित, adj. banished, exiled. देश-निष्कासन, m. = देश-निकाला. °-निष्कासित, adj. = देश-निकासित. देश-प्रेम, m. patriotism. °ई, m. a patriot. देश-प्रत्यावर्तन, m. return to (one's) country: repatriation (cf. वापसी, 2). देश-बंधु, m. a fellow-countryman. देश-बहन, f. a fellow-countrywoman. देश-भक्त, adj. & m. patriotic; a patriot. °-भक्ति, f. patriotism. देश-भाई, m. a fellow-countryman. देशमुख, m. a prominent regional figure, leader. देशवाला, adj. & m. national; a national, citizen. देशवासी, adj. & m. living or settled in a country; a citizen, resident. देश-विदेश, m. & adv. one's own country and others; at home and abroad. देशस्थ, adj. situated, or living in, a country or region. देश-हितकर, adj. beneficial to a country (actions, service). °-हितैषी, m. a well-wisher of one's country, a patriot. देशांतर [°*śa*+*a*°], m. another, or foreign, country or region. °अण, m. emigration; exile. °इत, adj. °ई, adj. & m. foreign; foreigner. देशांश [°*sa*+*a*°], m. longitude. °ईय, adj. देशाचार [°*śa*+*ā*°], m. local or national custom. देशाटन [°*śa*+*a*°], m. a long journey through a country, or countries. देशाधिपति [°*śa*+*a*°], m. the ruler of a land; governor of a region. देशाधीश [°*śa*+*a*°], m. ruler of a land. देशानुराग [°*śa*+*a*°], = देशभक्ति. देशाहंकार [°*śa*+*a*°], m. blind patriotism, chauvinism. °ई, adj. & m. देशीकरण, m. naturalisation; assimilation (to a national norm). देशोन्नति [°*śa*+*u*°], f. national progress. देशोपकारक [°*śa*+*u*°], adj. = देश-हितकर.

देशाख *deśākh* [*deśākhya-*: and. ad.], m. *Pl. mus.* name of a *rāg* sung at noon in the spring.

देशाखी *deśākhī* [cf. *deśākhya-*], f. *HŚS. mus.* name of a *rāgiṇī* sung at noon in the spring.

देशावर *deśāvar*, m. = दिसावर.

देशावरी *deśāvărī*, adj. & f. = दिसावरी.

देशिनी *deśinī* [S.], f. *Pl. HŚS.* the index finger.

देशी *deśī* [S.], adj. & m. **1.** adj. of, made in, or belonging to a region or locality; regional, provincial; country, rural; pure (*ghī*). **2.** of, made in or belonging to a country; national; indigenous; internal (as opposed to foreign). **3.** m. an inhabitant of a region, or country.

देशीकरण *deśīkaraṇ* [S.], m. see s.v. देश.

देशीय *deśīy* [S.], adj. = देशी.

देश्य *deśyă* [S.], adj. = देशी.

देस *des* [*deśa-*], m. reg. **1.** region, country (= देश). **2.** *mus.* name of a *rāg* (sung at midnight). — देसवाल, adj. local (resident).

देसा *desā*, m. *Pl. musl.* an annual offering for the dead.

देसावर *desāvar*, m. = दिसावर.

देसावरी *desāvărī*, adj. & f. = दिसावरी.

देसी *desī* [cf. H. *des*; or ad. *deśī-*], adj. & m. reg. indigenous, &c. (= देशी).

देह *deh* [P. *dĕh*], m. a village. — देहक़ान, m. U. farmer; village. °ई, adj.

देह *deh* [*deha-*], f. m. **1.** the body. **2.** transf. life; birth in human form. — ~ छोड़ना, to leave the body, to die. ~ धरना, or लेना, to be born in human form. ~ बिसारना, to lose consciousness. ~ लगना, to nourish the body (food). ~ सँभालना, to steady oneself, to recover oneself. — देह-त्याग, m. relinquishing the body: death. देह-धारण, m. assumption of body, birth. °-धारी, adj. embodied, living; incarnate. देहवान, adj. & m. possessing a body; bodily; a living creature; human being. देहांत [°*ha*+*a*°], m. end of the body, death. देहांतर [°*ha*+*a*°], m. another body: a further incarnation. °अण, m. transmigration of the soul into another body. देहावसान [°*ha*+*a*°], m. = देहांत.

देहक *dehak* [S.], adj. of or belonging to the body.

[1]**देहर** *dehar*, m. reg. = [1]देहरा.

[2]**देहर** *dehar* [*dehalī-*], f. *Pl. HŚS.* low land liable to flooding (cf. [1]देहली).

[1]**देहरा** *dehrā* [**devaghara-*: Pk. *devahara-*], m. a temple.

[2]**देहरा** *dehrā* [cf. H. *deh*], m. E.H. the body.

देहरी *dehrī*, f. Brbh. = [1]देहली.

[1]**देहली** *dehlī* [*dehalī-*], f. threshold; door-step. देहली-दीपक, m. a light at the threshold (shining in all directions): an argument, &c. that can be used in more than one way.

[2]**देहली** *dehlī*, f. Delhi (= दिल्ली).

देहात *dehāt* [P. *deh*+A. pl. suffix], m. country, countryside.

देहातिन *dehātin* [cf. H. *dehātī*], f. a village woman.

देहाती *dehātī* [P. *dehātī*], adj. & m. **1.** adj. having to do with the country, or with a village; rural. **2.** m. a villager.

देही *dehī* [S.], adj. & m. **1.** adj. possessing a body. **2.** m. a living creature; human being. **3.** the soul.

दैजा *daijā* [*dāyādya-*], m. reg. = दहेज़.

दैत *dait*, m. Brbh. = दैत्य.

दैत्य *daityă* [S.], m. *mythol.* **1.** son of Diti: a demon. **2.** a giant. **3.** fig. monster.

दैनंदिन *dainaṁdin* [S.], adj. **1.** daily. **2.** adv. day by day, constantly.

दैनंदिनी *dainaṁdinī* [S.], f. a diary.

दैन *dain* [A. *dain*], m. S.H. a debt; a loan.

दैनिक *dainik* [S.], adj. **1.** daily. **2.** having to do with day, diurnal.

दैनिकी *dainikī* [S.], f. **1.** a day's hire or wages. **2.** a diary.

दैन्य *dainyă* [S.], adj. **1.** poverty; wretchedness. **2.** humility, meekness; abject state.

दैयड़ *daiyaṛ*, m. the magpie-robin, *Copsychus saularis* (cf. दहेड़).

दैयत *daiyat*, m. Brbh. = दैत्य.

दैया *daiyā*, f. **1.** mother. **2.** (children's language) home (as in hide and seek). — दैया-दहाड़, f. a loud cry; outcry.

दैव *daiv* [S.], adj. & m. **1.** adj. divine; heavenly. **2.** destined, fated. **3.** m. a deity; a heavenly being. ***4.** divine power; fate, destiny; God. — ~ बरसना, rain to fall. – दैव-गति, f. course of fate, lot; misfortune. दैवज्ञ, m. an astrologer; prophet. दैव-योग, m. intervention, or act of fate: fortune, chance. दैववश, adv. by chance, unexpectedly. दैव-वाणी, f. heavenly voice: divine revelation. दैववाद, m. fatalism. °ई, m.

दैवत *daivat* [S.], adj. & m. reg. **1.** adj. having to do with the gods: divine. **2.** unexpected. **3.** m. a god. — दैवत-पति, m. a title of Indra.

दैवात् *daivāt* [S.], adv. as fated; by chance; providentially.

दैविक *daivik* [S.], adj. **1.** having to do with a god, or gods; divine. **2.** divinely caused. **3.** happening by chance.

दैवी *daivī* [S.], adj. **1.** divine. **2.** fated. **3.** happening by chance. — ~ प्रेरणा से, adv. by a fated impulse. – दैवी-गति, f. what is to happen, the future.

दैव्य *daivyă* [S.], m. divine power or effect; fate; chance.

दैहिक *daihik* [S.], adj. of or belonging to the body.

दैहिकी *daihikī* [S.], f. physiology (= शरीर-विज्ञान).

दों *dom̐*, m. *Pl.* subdivision of an estate.

दो *do* [*dva-*: Pk. *do-*], adj. two. (for many compounds, equivalents in दु-, q.v., are found; see also hww. in दो-). — ~ आँसू गिराना, or बहाना, to shed a few tears. ~ एक, a (very) few. ~ करना, to divide in two; to bisect. ~ कौड़ी का, adj. worthless, trivial. ~ गाल बोलने का मौक़ा, m. a chance to talk briefly. ~ चार, adj. a few. ~ चार होना, to meet privately (with, से). ~ दिन का, adj. temporary, transient. ~ दिन का महमान, m. a fleeting guest (as beauty, life). ~ दिन न पकड़ना, not to live half of life, to die early. ~ ~ बातें करना, to discuss (sthg.) briefly and to the point. ~ बोल पढ़वाना, to get two words (of agreement): to obtain the assent of two contracting parties; to arrange a marriage quietly. ~ मुँह हँस लेना, to take, or to show, mild pleasure. ~ नावों पर पैर रखना, to have one's feet on two boats: to fall between two stools. ~ शब्द, m. pl. two words; a few words; foreword. किसके ~ सिर हैं? who has two heads?: who would be so rash as to throw away his life? – दोअक्की, f. reg. two-faced nature, duplicity. दो-अर्थी, adj. & m. ambiguous; equivocal; ambiguity. दोख़समी, f. a woman who marries a second time. दो-चित्ती, f. indecision; divided attention. दो-जीया, f. a pregnant woman. दो-टूक, adj. of two pieces: clear, plain; decisive; tersc. दो-टूक जवाब, m. a decisive answer; a terse answer; flat refusal or denial, rebuff. दो-टूक होना, to be adjusted, settled, completed. दो-तल्ला, adj. two-storeyed; of two tiers or layers. दोतही, f. a blanket of two thicknesses. दोपल्ली, f. a cap sewn out of two pieces of material. दोपस्ता [? P. *-pastā*], adj. f. pregnant. दो-पाटी, adj. of two breadths or folds. दोपाया [P. *-pāya*], adj. inv. & m. two-legged; biped. दोपौवा, m. two quarters: a half; a weight of half a seer; half a betel leaf. दोप्याज़ा, adj. a meat curry containing a double or large amount of onion. दोफला, adj. two-edged (a blade). दोफ़सली, adj. & m. yielding two crops per year; having two senses, ambiguous; land yielding two crops per year. दोबरसी, adj. biennial. दोबाला [P. *-bālā*], adj. twofold; twin. दोमुँहापन, m. duplicity. दोरसा, m. & adj. a mixture of two things of different qualities (as soil, tobacco); having two or contrary tastes (a substance) or tendencies. दोरसे दिन, m. the period of pregnancy. दोहगा, f. Brbh. a widow taken as concubine.

दोआब *doāb* [P. *do-āb*], m. a region lying between and reaching to the confluence of two rivers (esp. that between Ganges and Jumna).

दोआबा *doābā* [P. *do-āba*], m. = दोआब.

दोक *dok*, m. *Pl. HŚS.* a two-year-old horse or calf.

दोखी *dokhī*, f. *Pl.* raised mound indicating the junction between two boundaries.

[1]**दोगला** *doglā*, adj. & m. **1.** adj. of mixed blood, cross-bred; mongrel; illegitimate. **2.** hybrid. **3.** transf. two-faced, deceitful. **4.** m. a person or animal of mixed blood, &c. **5.** a hybrid. **6.** a deceitful person.

[2]**दोगला** *doglā*, m. *HŚS.* sling-basket (round and deep) used in irrigation.

दोज़ख़ *dozakh* [P. *dozakh*], m. **1.** hell. **2.** fig. the belly. — ~ भरना, pej. to fill the belly. पेट का ~ भरना, id.

दोज़ख़ी *dozakhī* [P. *dozakhī*], adj. & m. **1.** adj. of hell. **2.** damned; sinful. **3.** m. a dweller in hell. **4.** a sinner.

दोझा *dojhā*, adj. & m. *Pl.* **1.** adj. married to a second wife. 2. = दूज-बर (see s.v. दूज).

दोदना *dodnā*, v.t. reg. to deny.

दोधार *dodhār*, adj. ? = दुधार.

[1]**दोन** *don* [**daunada-*], m. **1.** land between two rivers. **2.** junction of two rivers.

[2]**दोन** *don*, m. (f., *Pl.*) = [2]दून.

दोना *donā* [*droṇa-*[1]], m. a leaf-basket; leaf-cup.

दोनों *donom̐* [cf. *dva-*], adj. the two, both. — ~ ओर, adv. on both sides; in both directions. ~ जून खाना, to eat twice a day, to have enough to eat. ~ वक़्त मिलना, day and night to mingle, dusk to fall. ~ हाथ ताली बजाना, to clap with both hands: to meet half-way (in cooperation); to give as good as one gets (in a quarrel).

दोपहर *dopahr* [cf. H. *pahr*], f. midday; the period around midday. — दोपहर का, adj. midday (meal, bell, &c). दोपहर ढलना, midday to be past. दोपहर ढले, adv. after the height of the day. ठीक ~, adv. at noon.

दोपहरिया *dopahriyā* [cf. H. *dopahr*], adj. & f. **1.** adj. = दोपहर का. **2.** f. reg. = दोपहर.

दोपहरी *dopahrī* [cf. H. *dopahr*], adj. & f. /dupɛhri/. **1.** adj. = दोपहर का. **2.** f. the period around midday; early afternoon.

दोबल *dobal* [*daurbalya-*], m. Brbh. weakness, shortcoming; offence.

दोयम *doyam* [P. *duvvum*], adj. **1.** second. **2.** second-rate, inferior.

दोर *dor* [*davara-*], m. reg. = ²दौर.

¹**दोल** *dol* [S.], m. Brbh. **1.** a swing; swinging cot, cradle. **2.** a litter. **3.** *Pl. HŚS.* swinging; name of a Kṛṣṇa swing festival held on the fourteenth of the month Phālgun. — **दोल-माल करना**, to hesitate.

²**दोल** *dol* [**dola-*²; or P. *dol* ? × A. *dalw* 'bucket' w. metath.], m. bucket.

दोलक *dolak* [S.], adj. & m. **1.** adj. swinging. **2.** m. pendulum.

दोलन *dolan* [S.], m. **1.** swinging, rocking. **2.** rippling, &c. (waves). **3.** vibration; oscillation. — **~ करना**, *phys.* to oscillate.

दोला *dolā* [*dola-*¹], m. **1.** swing; cradle. **2.** wavering, vacillation. — **दोला-यात्रा**, f. *Pl.* name of a swing festival in honour of Kṛṣṇa and Rādhā.

दोलायमान *dolāyămān* [S.], adj. **1.** swinging, rocking. **2.** rippling, &c. (waves). **3.** wavering, uncertain.

दोलायित *dolāyit* [S.], adj. swinging, rocking.

दोलिका *dolikā* [S.], f. a swing.

दोलित *dolit* [S.], adj. **1.** swinging, rocking. **2.** rippling, &c. (waves). **3.** wavering.

दोशीज़ा *dośīzā* [P. *dośīza*], adj. & f. adolescent (a girl); virgin.

दोष *doṣ* [S.], m. **1.** fault, defect; vice; sinfulness. **2.** blame; reproach. **3.** offence; sin; guilt; crime. **4.** damage, harm. **5.** disorder (bodily); disease. — **~ डालना**, to seek to attribute a fault, &c. (to, **पर**). **~ देना** or **लगाना**, to impute a fault, &c. (to, **को** or **पर**), to blame; to accuse; to calumniate. **~ निकालना**, to find fault (in or with, **में**). – **दोष-ग्रस्त**, adj. & m. involved in crime or guilt; convicted, guilty; a criminal, &c. **दोष-पूर्ण**, adj. faulty. **दोष-मुक्त**, adj. free of fault; innocent (of a charge). **दोष-युक्त**, adj. faulty. **दोषसिद्धि**, f. conviction (in law). **दोषारोप**, m. = next. **दोषारोपण** [°*sa*+*ā*°], m. attribution of fault, blame &c. (to, **पर**); accusation.

दोष- *doṣ-* [*doṣayati*], v.t. Av. **1.** to blame. **2.** to accuse. **3.** to calumniate.

दोषी *doṣī* [S.], adj. & m. **1.** adj. faulty, &c.; vicious, corrupt. **2.** blameworthy. **3.** guilty; sinful. **4.** m. a wicked, guilty or sinful person. — **~ ठहराना**, to find at fault; to find guilty.

दोसाही *dosāhī*, f. see s.v. **दु-**.

¹**दोसी** *dosī*, f. reg. curds.

²**दोसी** *dosī*, m. *Pl.* a man of a Muslim community of dairymen.

दोस्त *dost* [P. *dost*], m. **1.** a friend. **2.** a lover, sweetheart. — **दोस्त-अहबाब**, m. pl. U. friends, companions. – **दोस्तदार** [P. *-dār*], m. & adj. & adv. friend; friendly. °**ई**, f. friendship; love. **दोस्त-परवर** [P. *-parvar*], adj. cherishing friends: friendly.

दोस्ताना *dostānā* [P. *dostāna*], adj. & m. **1.** adj. friendly. **2.** m. friendly manner, friendliness. — **दोस्ताने अंदाज़ में**, adv. in a friendly way, as a friend.

दोस्ती *dostī* [P. *dostī*], f. **1.** friendship; affection. **2.** love. — **~ करना**, or **गाँठना**, to form a friendship (with, **से**); to form a liaison (with). **~ जोड़ना**, id. **~ का दम भरना**, to pretend friendship (for, **की**); to boast of friendship (with). – **दोस्ती-यारी**, f. closeness, intimate association (between, **से**). **दोस्ती-रोटी**, f. a bread-cake made in two layers.

दोह्ता *dohtā*, m. = **दुहता**.

दोहती *dohtī*, f. = **दुहती**.

दोहद *dohad* [S.], m. **1.** craving (as in pregnancy). **2.** an object of craving. **3.** transf. pregnancy. — **दोहदवती**, f. *Pl. HŚS.* woman feeling the craving of pregnancy.

दोहन *dohan* [S.], m. **1.** milking. **2.** fig. exploitation.

दोहना *dohnā*, v.t. = **दुहना**.

दोहनी *dohnī*, f. = **दुहनी**.

दोहर *dohar* [conn. **dudhāra-*], f. (*Pl.*, m.) **1.** a cloth of two folds, a double sheet. **2.** *Pl.* land bearing two crops a year. **3.** *Pl.* the old bed of a river. **4.** *Pl.* a sandy sub-soil.

दोहर- *dohar-* [cf. H. *dohrā*], adj. repeated. — **दोहर-कम्मा**, m. colloq. work needing to be redone.

दोहरना *doharnā* [cf. H. *dohrānā*], v.i. & v.t. **1.** v.i. to be repeated. **2.** to be doubled, folded. **3.** v.t. to repeat, &c.

दोहरा *dohrā* [*dvidhā*, **dudhāra-*], adj. & m. **1.** adj. double, twofold; twice as much. **2.** reduplicated. **3.** transf. ample, fat (of build). **4.** m. a doubled *pān* leaf. — **दोहरी चाल**, f. quickened pace. **दोहरी बात**, f. a *double entendre*.

दोहराई *dohrāī* [cf. H. *dohrānā*], f. **1.** repeating, repetition. **2.** revision. **3.** doubling, folding. **4.** reduplication.

दोहराना *dohrānā* [cf. H. *dohrā*], v.t. **1.** to repeat (sthg. said or done). **2.** to revise (a lesson, &c). **3.** to fold, to double. **4.** to reduplicate.

दोहराव *dohrāv* [cf. H. *dohrānā*], m. repetition (= दोहराई).

दोहल *dohal*, m. *Pl. HŚS.* = दोहद.

दोहली *dohlī*, f. obs. *Pl. HŚS.* lands granted rent-free, esp. for a public or charitable purpose.

दोहा *dohā* [*dvidhā*, *dvipatha-*; Ap. *duvahaa-*], m. a rhyming couplet, in which each line consists of half-lines made up of feet of 6+4+3 and 6+4+1 *mātrās* respectively.

दोहान *dohān* [**duhāyana-*], m. reg. a two-year-old bullock.

दोहाव *dohāv* [cf. H. *duhānā*], *Pl. HŚS.* landholder's portion of milk from tenants' cows.

दोहिया *dohiyā* [*dohin-*], m. milkman; cowherd.

दोही *dohī* [S.; or *dohin-*], m. = दोहिया.

दौंगड़ा *dauṁgṛā*, m. a heavy shower.

दौंजा *dauṁjā*, m. reg. a platform, scaffolding.

दौ *dau* [*dava-*], m. Brbh. **1.** a forest fire; fire. **2.** burning heat. — ~ लग-, to feel burning heat; to feel pangs (of love).

दौड़ *dauṛ* [cf. H. *dauṛnā*], f. **1.** running; a run; a gallop. **2.** (esp. in comp.) race. घुड़-दौड़, f. horse-race. **3.** course, career; distance to be traversed; flight (of fancy). **4.** range, scope, sphere. **5.** fig. hard effort, endeavour. **6.** raid, attack. **7.** *HŚS. naut.* capstan. — ~ मारना, or लगाना, to go at a run, &c.; to travel a given distance; to complete a given course. – दौड़-कूद, f. athletics. दौड़-धपाड़, f. = next. दौड़-धूप, f. scurrying, bustle, effort. दौड़-धूप करना, to run to and fro; to go to much effort. दौड़-भाग, m. = दौड़-धूप; flight, confusion; panic.

दौड़ना *dauṛnā* [cf. *dravati*], v.i. **1.** to run; to hasten; to gallop. **2.** to rush (at, upon, पर); to attack. **3.** to spread quickly (as news). **4.** to spread (over, पर; through, में: as a flush across the face, poison through the body). **5.** fig. to be obsessed (with, के पीछे); to try hard to obtain (sthg). **6.** to flow, to course (liquid, a current). **7.** to turn, to run (as the mind, or fancy, in a given direction). — दौड़ना-धूपना, to scurry, to go to effort. – दौड़ा-दौड़, f. = दौड़-धूप; adv. at a run, in haste. दौड़ा-दौड़ी, f. scurrying, bustle, haste; a running race.

दौड़ाई *dauṛāī* [cf. H. *dauṛnā*], f. **1.** running. **2.** scurrying, bustle (= दौड़-धूप).

दौड़ाक *dauṛāk* [cf. H. *dauṛnā*], m. a runner; athlete.

दौराकी *daurākī* [cf. H. *dauṛākī*], f. running; athletics.

दौड़ाना *dauṛānā* [cf. H. *dauṛnā*], v.t. **1.** to cause to run; to urge on, to drive (a horse). **2.** to despatch (a person) in haste. **3.** to impel; to move (as pen over paper); to run (the eyes in a given direction); to move quickly, to run (sthg. into a new position). **4.** to extend (as a canal, or electricity, to a new region). **5.** to give play to (thought, imagination).

दौड़ाहा *dauṛāhā*, m. reg. **1.** village messenger, runner. **2.** an itinerant official.

दौथाईं *dauthāīṁ*, m. *Pl.* day, dawn.

[1]**दौना** *daunā* [*damana-*[2]: ← Ir.], m. the plant *Artemisia indica* or *A. lactifolia*, or its flower; marjoram, rosemary.

[2]**दौना** *daunā*, m. = दोना.

[1]**दौर** *daur* [A. *daur*], m. **1.** revolving, revolution. **2.** passing round (as of wine). **3.** circle, orbit; transf. field of authority, sway. **4.** a round tour, circuit. **5.** passage or change of time, vicissitude; period of years, age, cycle. **6.** stage (of a continued process); progress. — ~ चलना (का), to be passed round (wine). – दौर-दौरा [A. *-daura*], m. field of authority, sway.

[2]**दौर** *daur* [*davara-*], m. reg. the strings used to sling a water-basket (in irrigation).

[1]**दौरा** *daurā* [A. *daura*], m. **1.** turn, revolution (= [1]दौर, 1). **2.** round, tour, circuit (= [1]दौर, 4). **3.** session (of circuit court). **4.** outbreak, ravages (of disease). **5.** fit, attack (of illness). — ~ करना, to go on a tour (of inspection, &c.); to hold sessions. – दौरे पर जाना, id. दौरे पर रहना, to be on tour, on circuit. दिल का ~, m. a heart attack. – दौरा-अदालत, f. court of session. दौरा-सुपुर्द, m. commitment for trial before court of session.

[2]**दौरा** *daurā* [? **dola-*[2] × *davara-*], m. reg. large basket (without a lid).

दौरात्म्य *daurātmyǎ* [S.], m. baseness of soul, wickedness.

दौरान *daurān* [A. *davarān*], m. **1.** revolving, turning; whirling. **2.** duration, period (= [1]दौर, 5). **3.** circulation (as of the blood). — ~ में, adv. in the course (of, के), during. सिर का ~, m. giddiness.

दौरी *daurī* [? **dola-*[2] × *davara-*], f. reg. **1.** small flat basket of bamboo or *mūṁj* grass (without a lid). **2.** sling-basket (used with rope in irrigation).

दौर्गंधि *daurgandhi* [S.], f. *Pl.* bad smell.

दौर्गंध्य *daurgandhyă* [S.], m. bad smell.

दौर्जन्य *daurjanyă* [S.], m. wickedness, malice.

दौर्बल्य *daurbalyă* [S.], m. weakness; debility.

दौर्भाग्य *daurbhāgyă* [S.], m. misfortune (= दुरभाग्य).

दौर्मद *daurmad* [S.], m. **1.** drunkenness. **2.** haughtiness.

दौर्हार्द *daurhārd* [S.], m. badness of heart or mind; enmity.

दौलत *daulat* [A. *daula*: P. *daulat*], f. prosperity; wealth. — **दौलत-ख़ाना**, m. prosperous house (polite form of reference to another's house).

दौलतमंद *daulatmand* [P. *daulatmand*], adj. prosperous; wealthy. — **~ करना**, to bless or to enrich (with, **से**).

दौलतमंदी *daulatmandī* [P. *daulatmandī*], f. prosperous state.

दौस *daus* [A. *daus*], m. *Pl.* **1.** treading, trampling. **2.** indulging sexual appetite.

दौहित्र *dauhitră* [S.], m. daughter's son, grandson.

दौहित्री *dauhitrī* [S.], f. daughter's daughter, granddaughter.

द्युति *dyuti* [S.], f. **1.** light, radiance; lustre. **2.** beauty. **3.** splendour, majesty. — **द्युतिमान**, adj. radiant, resplendent.

द्युतिमा *dyutimā* [S.], f. radiance, brilliance.

द्यूत *dyūt* [S.], m. gambling. — **द्यूत-पूर्णिमा**, f. the day of full moon in the month Kārttik (the night of which is devoted traditionally to gambling games in honour of Lakṣmī).

द्योतक *dyotak* [S.], adj. & m. **1.** adj. illuminating. **2.** clarifying (a meaning); indicating (a sense). **3.** m. an indicator; symptom. **4.** *gram.* a particle.

द्योतन *dyotan* [S.], m. illumination, &c.

द्योतित *dyotit* [S.], adj. **1.** illuminated, &c. **2.** signified, indicated (a sense).

द्यौरानी *dyaurānī*, f. = **देवरानी**.

द्रव *drav* [S.], adj. & m. **1.** adj. fluid, liquid. **2.** liquefied; melted. **3.** *ling.* liquid. **4.** m. running, flowing. **5.** fluid or liquid state. **6.** a fluid. 7. *Pl.* = **द्रव्य**, 1., 2. — **द्रव-इंजीनियरी**, m. fluid mechanics. **द्रव-गति-विज्ञान**, m. hydraulics. **द्रव-चालित**, adj. hydraulic.

द्रव- *drav-* [cf. H. *drav*: and ad. *dravati*], v.i. Brbh. Av. to be fluid: **1.** to melt; to dissolve. **2.** to be moved (as with pity); to show mercy.

द्रवक *dravak* [S.], adj. **1.** running, flowing. **2.** fluid.

द्रवण *dravaṇ* [S.], m. **1.** running, flowing (= **द्रव**, 1). **2.** melting; fusing. **3.** melting, softening (of the emotions). — **द्रवणशील**, adj. fluid, liquid; easily moved by emotion.

द्रवता *dravătā* [S.], f. liquid or fluid state.

द्रवत्व *dravatvă* [S.], m. fluid or liquid state.

द्रविड़ *draviṛ* [S.], adj. & m. **1.** adj. Dravidian. **2.** m. a Dravidian. **3.** the Dravidian region, esp. the Tamil-speaking part of it.

द्रवित *dravit* [S.], adj. **1.** made liquid, caused to flow or to melt. **2.** moved (the emotions).

द्रव्य *dravyă* [S.], m. **1.** substance, matter. **2.** a thing, object. **3.** a raw material; commodity. **4.** a chemical element. **5.** assets, wealth; money, friends. — **द्रव्य-मान**, m. *phys.* mass. **द्रव्यवाचक**, adj. *gram.* denoting quantity, or mass (a noun). **द्रव्यवान**, adj. wealthy.

द्रव्यत्व *dravyatvă* [S.], m. material nature (of a thing).

द्रष्टव्य *draṣṭavyă* [S.], adj. **1.** deserving inspection or scrutiny; notable. **2.** requiring attention, noteworthy.

द्रष्टा *draṣṭā* [S.], m. inv. one who sees.

द्राक्षा *drākṣā* [S.], f. a grape. — **द्राक्षा-शर्करा**, f. grape-sugar; glucose. **द्राक्षासव** [°*ṣā*+*ā*°], m. grape liquor.

द्राघिमा *drāghimā* [S.], f. **1.** length. **2.** longitude. **3.** apogee.

द्राव *drāv* [S.], m. running, flowing: 1. = **द्रावण**, 1., 2. **2.** exuding. 3. = **द्रावण**, 3. — **द्रावकर**, m. *Pl. HŚS.* borax; flux.

द्रावक *drāvak* [S.], adj. **1.** *HŚS.* causing to run, pursuing. ***2.** causing to dissolve, solvent. **3.** causing to melt, melting. **4.** fig. affecting, enchanting.

द्रावण *drāvaṇ* [S.], m. **1.** dissolving. **2.** melting; fusing. **3.** thawing. **4.** *Pl.* the fruit of *Strychnos potatorum*, used for purifying water. **5.** *HŚS.* the soap-nut (**रीठा**).

द्राविका *drāvikā* [S.], f. *Pl. HŚS.* saliva.

द्राविड़ *drāviṛ* [S.], adj. & m. **1.** adj. = **द्रविड़**. **2.** m. a south Indian sub-caste of brāhmaṇs.

द्राविड़ी *drāviṛī* [S.], adj & f. **1.** adj. having to do with the Dravidians, Dravidian; southern. **2.** f. a Dravidian woman. **3.** *Pl. HŚS.* = **इलायची**.

द्रुत *drut* [S.], adj. speedy, swift; runaway, escaped, flown. — **द्रुत-पद**, m. a quick step, fleet foot; adj. quick; quickly. **द्रुत-पाठ**, m. quick reading. द्रुत-विलंबित, m. quick and slow: name of a Sanskrit metre (used experimentally in early modern Hindi verse).

द्रुति *druti* [S.], f. *HŚS.* quickness, swiftness.

द्रुम *drum* [S.], m. **1.** a tree. **2.** *mythol.* a tree of Indra's or Kṛṣṇa's paradise (= पारिजात). — **द्रुम-पातन**, m. tree-felling. **द्रुम-सार**, m. Brbh. pomegranate tree. **द्रुम-आली**, f. a line of trees.

द्रोण *droṇ* [S.], m. **1.** a wooden vessel. **2.** a basket made of leaves. **3.** a crow. **4.** *mythol.* name of a teacher of the Kauravas and Pāṇḍavas, a Kaurava leader.

द्रोणा *droṇā* [S.], f. *Pl. HŚS.* a small shrub (= गूमा; ? = [1]दौना).

द्रोणी *droṇī* [S.], f. **1.** small boat. **2.** boat-shaped vessel; leaf-cup.

द्रोह *droh* [S.], m. **1.** hostility, enmity; ill-will; rancour. **2.** treachery. **3.** wrong, offence. — **~ करना**, to act in a hostile way, &c. (towards, से). – **द्रोह-चिंतन**, injurious or rancorous thought.

द्रोही *drohī* [S.], adj. & m. **1.** adj. hostile, inimical; rancorous. **2.** disaffected, treacherous. **3.** rebellious, mutinous. **4.** m. an enemy. **5.** a disaffected person; traitor. **6.** conspirator. **7.** rebel.

द्वंद्व *dvandvā* [S.], m. **1.** pair, couple; brace. **2.** a wedded or mated couple (persons, animals). **3.** a pair of complementary qualities or conditions (as heat and cold, joy and sorrow, the absolute and the qualified). **4.** hostility, conflict; quarrel; tension (as between antagonists). — **द्वंद्वज**, adj. arising from two, or from opposing, causes. **द्वंद्वमय**, adj. dual; antagonistic; contradictory. **द्वंद्वात्मक** [°*va* + *ā*°], adj. dialectic.

द्वय- *dvay-* [S]. a couple, a pair: — **द्वयक्षर**, adj. *ling.* disyllabic. **द्वयाग्नि** [°*ya* + *a*°], m. *Pl.* a tree, *Plumbago zeylanica*, from which potash is produced. **द्वयोष्ठ्य** [°*ya* + *o*°: for °*au*], adj. *ling.* bilabial.

द्वादश *dvādaś* [S.], adj. **1.** twelve. ***2.** twelfth.

द्वादशी *dvādăśī* [S.], f. the twelfth day of a lunar fortnight.

द्वापर *dvāpar* [S.], m. *mythol.* the third of the four ages of the world (*yugas*) which together make up one aeon (*kalpa*).

द्वार *dvār* [S.], m. **1.** door, gate. **2.** entrance; doorway, gateway, passage. **3.** access. **4.** means, expedient. **5.** (in yoga) opening (of the body). — **द्वार-चार**, m. marriage rite performed at the door of the bride's house. **द्वार-पंडित**, m. chief paṇḍit in a royal establishment; admissions officer (at a *gurukul*). **द्वार-पटी**, f. E.H. curtain or hanging in front of a door. **द्वार-पाल**, m. door-keeper, gate-keeper, porter; guard. °**-पालक**, id. **द्वार-पूजा**, f. = **द्वार-चार**. **दवारावती** [= *dvārăvatī*], f. = **द्वारका**, s.v.

द्वारका *dvārăkā* [S.], f. having many gates: name of the legendary capital of Kṛṣṇa, and, today, of a sacred place near the mouth of the Gulf of Kutch. — **द्वारका-नाथ**, m. a title of Kṛṣṇa.

[1]द्वारा *dvārā* [S. *dvārā*], ppn. **1.** by means (of, के), by the agency (of). **2.** (in the address of a letter) care of.

[2]द्वारा *dvārā*, m. E.H. door, &c. (= द्वार).

द्वारिका *dvārikā*, f. = **द्वारका**.

द्वि- *dvi-* [S.], adj. & n. formant. two, double, bi-, di-: — **द्विकर**, m. pl. the two hands. **द्विखंड**, adj. divided into, or having, two sections. °**ई**, adj. id. **द्विगु**, m. *gram.* a compound word, the first member of which is a numeral. **द्विगुण**, adj. = **दुगुना**. °**इत**, adj. id. **द्विज**, adj. & m. twice-born; a man of the Brāhmaṇ, Kṣatriya, Rājput or Vaiśya caste groups (regarded as reborn on investiture with the sacred thread at puberty); a brāhmaṇ; an oviparous creature (bird, snake, &c). °**ता**, f. twice-born, or brāhmaṇ, status. °**आ**, f. Brbh. a partic. creeper. °**-नारी**, f. a brāhmaṇ woman. **द्विजन्मा**, adj. & m. inv. = **द्विज**. **द्विजाति**, m. = **द्विज**. **द्विकल**, adj. having two leaves; bipartite; m. *bot.* dicotyledon. **द्विधा**, adv. & f. in two ways; in two parts; in two directions; = **दुबधा**. °**करण**, m. bisection. °**त्मक** [°*dhā* + *ā*°], adj. twofold, dual; of two kinds. °**र्थक**, adj. equivocal, ambiguous. **द्विधातु**, adj. & m. having two roots, or natures; an alloy of two metals. **द्विनेत्री**, adj. binocular (as vision, an instrument). **द्विपक्षीय**, adj. two-sided, bipartite, bilateral. **द्विपथ**, m. place where two roads meet. **द्विपद**, adj. having two feet; having two parts; *math.* binomial; m. a biped (as men, birds, gods); *ling.* a compound. °**ई**, f. a couplet. **द्विपाद**, adj. = **द्विपद**, and **द्विपदी**. **द्विभाजन**, m. division into two, bisection. **द्विभाव**, adj. & m. of two aspects: dissembling; hypocritical; deceitful; dissimulation, &c. **द्विमात्रिक**, adj. *pros.* of two *mātrās*; long (a vowel, a syllable). **द्विमुखा**, f. leech. °**-मुखी**, f. a cow in calf. **द्विरसना**, f. two-tongued: a snake (specif. female); a woman who equivocates. **द्विरेता**, m. inv. a hybrid (animal). **द्विरेफ**, m. making the sound 'r-r': a bee. **द्विलिंग**, adj. bisexual. **द्विवचन**, m. *gram.* dual number. **द्विवर्षीय**, adv. lasting, or occurring once in, two years. ° **वार्षिक**, adj. id. **द्विविध**, adj. of two kinds, or parts; adv. in two ways. **द्विविवाह**, m. bigamy. **द्विवेदी**, m. a particular brāhmaṇ sub-caste (= दुबे). **द्विशफ**, adj. cloven-hooved. **द्विशिर**, adj. having two heads (see s.v. दो). द्विसदनी, adj. bicameral. द्विस्वर, adj. *ling.* diphthongal.

द्वितीय *dvitīyă* [S.], adj. **1.** second. **2.** secondary. — द्वितीयाश्रम [°*ya*+*ā*°], m. the second of the traditional stages of a man's life (i.e. as husband and father).

द्वितीयक *dvitīyak* [S.], adj. 1. = द्वितीय. **2.** duplicate.

द्वितीया *dvitīyā* [S.], f. **1.** second day of a lunar fortnight. **2.** *gram.* accusative case.

द्वित्व *dvitvă* [S.], m. **1.** two-fold nature; duality. **2.** doubling, reduplication. — ~ करना (का), to double.

द्विर- *dvir-* [S.], adv. twice: — द्विरागमन, m. twice coming: ceremonial arrival of the bride at her father-in-law's house (to take up residence there with her husband). द्विरुक्त, adj. uttered twice, repeated; said or told in two ways; *ling.* reduplicated. °इ, f. repetition, tautology; reduplication.

द्वीप *dvîp* [S.], m. **1.** an island; land largely surrounded by water, peninsula. **2.** *mythol.* any of several terrestrial regions supposed to surround mount Meru (ring-shaped; usually seven were enumerated), e.g. जंबु-द्वीप, m. the central region of the world. — द्वीप-पुंज, m. = द्वीप-समूह. द्वीप-माला, f. = next. द्विप-समूह, m. archipelago.

द्वीपी *dvîpī* [S.], adj. & m. **1.** adj. having to do with an island; island-dwelling. **2.** m. an islander.

द्वीप्य *dvîpyă* [S.], adj. = द्वीपी.

द्वेष *dveṣ* [S.], m. hatred; aversion; spite; enmity. — द्वेषपूर्ण, adj. filled with ill-will, spiteful, hostile. द्वेष-भाव, m. attitude of hostility, &c.

द्वेषी *dveṣī* [S.], adj. & m. **1.** adj. hating; filled with aversion; hostile. **2.** m. one filled with ill-will; an enemy.

द्वेष्य *dveṣyă* [S.], adj. *Pl. HŚS.* hateful, detestable.

द्वेष्यता *dveṣyătā* [S.], f. *Pl.* **1.** detestability. **2.** detestation.

द्वै *dvai* [cf. *dvaya-*], m. *Brbh.* a pair, the two.

द्वै- *dvai-* [S.], adj. & n. formant. two, double, bi-, di-: — द्वैभाषिक, adj. bilingual. द्वैविध्य, m. duality, dual nature; uncertainty, indecision; duplicity. द्वैराज्य, m. *pol.* a jointly controlled state.

द्वैत *dvait* [S.], m. **1.** double nature or entity, duality; ambiguity. **2.** *philos.* dualism (esp. that between the ultimate being and the universe). **3.** Av. distinction, division. — द्वैतवाद, m. = ~, 2. °ई, adj.

द्वैध *dvaidh* [S.], m. **1.** double nature or existence. **2.** distinction, division. **3.** difference (of opinions, interests); conflict. **4.** duplicity. — द्वैध-शासन, m. diarchy. द्वैधीकरण, m. dividing, disuniting.

द्वैधीकरण *dvaidhīkaraṇ* [S.], m. see s.v. द्वैध.

द्वैप्य *dvaipyă* [S.], adj. = द्वीपी.

ध

ध *dha*, the nineeenth consonant of the Devanāgarī syllabary. — **धकार**, m. the sound /dh/; the letter **ध**.

धंधक *dhandhak* [cf. *dhandha-*], m. Av. = **धंधा**. — **धंधक-धोरी**, m. a toiler, drudge.

धंधका *dhandhkā*, m. *Pl. HŚS.* a kind of drum.

धँधला *dhaṁdhlā* [cf. *dhandha-*], m. trick, cheating; dissembling. — **धँधले आना** (**को**), to be skilled in cheating. **धँधले में आना**, to be duped (by, **के**). **धँधलेबाज़** [P. *-bāz*], m. a trickster, cheat, &c. °*ī*, f. trickery, &c.

धँधलाना *dhaṁdhlānā* [cf. H. *dhaṁdhlā*], v.t. to trick, to cheat, &c.

धंधा *dhandhā* [*dhandha-*], m. **1.** craft, occupation; trade; profession; business. **2.** work, activity; task. — **घरेलू धंधे**, m. pl. domestic crafts, village industries.

[1]**धँधार** *dhaṁdhār*, adj. Av. fire, tongue of flame.

[2]**धँधार** *dhaṁdhār*, adj. reg. lonely, solitary.

धँधारी *dhaṁdhārī* [cf. H. [2]*dhaṁdhār*], f. reg. loneliness, solitude.

धँधाला *dhaṁdhālā*, f. procuress, bawd.

धँधेला *dhaṁdhelā*, adj. *Pl.* deceitful.

धंस *dhaṃs*, m. Brbh. = **ध्वंस**.

धँसन *dhaṁsan* [cf. H. *dhaṁsnā*], f. **1.** sinking (into, **में**). **2.** piercing, being thrust (into).

धँसना *dhaṁsnā* [*dhvaṁsati*], v.i. **1.** to sink (into, **में**). **2.** to pierce, to stick (into, **में**). **3.** to penetrate; to be plunged (into water); to vanish (in a crowd). **4.** Brbh. to be lost (an idea). **5.** to subside (as a foundation); to be cratered (as ground by shell-fire). **6.** to be sunk (in thought).

धँसान *dhaṁsān* [cf. H. *dhaṁsnā*], f. & adj. **1.** f. sinking (as into soft ground: = **धँसन**). **2.** a swamp, bog. **3.** *hind.* immersion (of an idol in water). **4.** adj. swampy.

धँसाना *dhaṁsānā* [cf. H. *dhaṁsnā*], v.t. **1.** to cause to sink (into, **में**). **2.** to cause to pierce; to thrust (into).

धँसाव *dhaṁsāv* [cf. H. *dhaṁsnā*], m. 1. = **धँसन**. 2. = **धँसान**, 2. **3.** a pit.

धक *dhak* [**dhakk-*], f. (m., *Pl.*). **1.** shock. **2.** palpitation; anxiety. **3.** surge (of zeal, &c.) — **~ रह जाना**, to become motionless from fear, amazement, or consternation. **~ से रह जाना**, id. – **धकाधक**, adv. with a surge, impetus.

धक-धक *dhak-dhak* [cf. H. *dhak*, *dhakdhakānā*], f. m. **1.** beating, palpitation; tremor. **2.** perturbation. **3.** blaze (of fire). **4.** adv. a-tremble. **~ करना**, to beat fast (the heart); to be perturbed; to blaze.

धकधकाना *dhakdhakānā* [conn. **dhagg-*: Pk. *dhagadhagaï*], v.i. **1.** to beat, to palpitate (as the heart). **2.** to be perturbed. **3.** to blaze, to flare; to flash, to glitter.

धकधकाहट *dhakdhakāhaṭ* [cf. H. *dhakdhakānā*], f. = **धक-धक**.

धकधकी *dhakdhakī* [cf. H. *dhak-dhak*], f. = **धुकधुकी**.

धका- *dhakā-* [H. *dhakkā*]. shove, jolt: — **धका-पेल**, f. pushing and shoving; congestion (of traffic). °**ई**, f. id. **धकापेली करना**, to push and shove.

धकियाना *dhakiyānā*, v.t. reg. to shove or to elbow (one's way: = **धक्का देना**, 1).

धकेल *dhakel* [cf. H. *dhakelnā*], m. (f. ?). a shove, push. — **धकेल-गाड़ी**, f. a trolley, handcart.

धकेलना *dhakelnā* [cf. *dhakkayati*], v.t. **1.** to shove. **2.** to jostle.

धकेलवाँ *dhakelvāṁ*, adv. reg. plentifully, abundantly.

धकेलू *dhakelū* [cf. H. *dhakelnā*], adj. & m. **1.** shoving, &c. **2.** m. one who shoves, or jostles. **3.** sl. a lover.

धकैत *dhakait* [cf. H. *dhakkā*], m. Brbh. one who shoves or pushes.

धक्कम-पेल *dhakkam-pel*, f. = **धक्कम-धक्का** s.v. **धक्का**.

धक्का *dhakkā* [cf. *dhakkayati*], m. **1.** shove, jolt. **2.** shock; impact. **3.** blow of fate, unlucky chance; loss, damage. — **~ खाना**, to suffer a blow; to suffer misfortune, or loss. **~ देना** (**को**), to shove, &c.; to strike; to bring misfortune, or loss (on). **~ लगना** (**को**), to receive a blow; to experience misfortune, or loss. **धक्के खाना**, to be roughly treated; = **~ खाना**, 2. **दिनों को धक्के देना**, to get along (through life); to survive, to manage. बिजली का ~, m. an electric shock. – धक्कम-धक्का, m. = next. धक्का-धक्की, f. pushing and shoving, jostling. धक्कामार, adj. aggressive (physically); arrogant. धक्का-मुक्की, f. pushing and jostling.

धक्काड़ *dhakkāṛ* [cf. H. *dhakkā*], adj. whose view has an impact: **1.** influential; weighty, authoritative. **2.** prolific (a writer).

धगड़ *dhagaṛ*, m. = धगड़ा, 1. — धगड़बाज़ [P. *-bāz*], f. an adulteress. धगड़हाई, f. id.

धगड़ा *dhagṛā*, m. **1.** lover; adulterer. **2.** reg. master, superior.

धगड़ी *dhagṛī*, f. an adulteress.

धगधगाना *dhagdhagānā*, v.i. = धकधकाना.

धगोलना *dhagolnā*, v.i. reg. to roll, to wallow.

धचकना *dhacaknā*, v.i. **1.** to be jerked, shaken; to jolt, to shake. **2.** to give way under (one's) weight (as a swampy ground).

धचका *dhackā*, m. **1.** jolt, shock. **2.** loss, damage (= धक्का). — ~ उठाना, or खाना, to suffer a shock, or loss, &c. ~ लगना (को), shock, &c. to be felt.

[1]**धज** *dhaj* [**dhajja-*], f. **1.** splendid appearance, or attire. **2.** imposing manner or style. **3.** posture, attitude.

[2]**धज** *dhaj* [ad. *dhvaja-*], m. penis.

धजा *dhajā* [**dhajja-*], m. **1.** flag, pennant; strip of cloth (as flown over a shrine). **2.** pole with strip of cloth attached. 3. = [1]धज, 3.

धजीला *dhajīlā* [cf. H. [1]*dhaj*], adj. **1.** of good or attractive build (a person). **2.** personable. **3.** well-dressed, stylish.

धज्जी *dhajjī* [conn. **dhajja-*], f. strip, shred (as of cloth, paper). — ~ हो जाना, fig. to become emaciated, or frail. धज्जियाँ उड़ाना (की), to tear to shreds; to punish severely; to show to be worthless, or censurable (as statements, or a person's character). धज्जियाँ करना (की), id. धज्जियाँ लगना, to be reduced to poverty. धज्जियाँ लेना, to criticise severely.

धटींगर *dhaṭīṁgar*, adj. & m. *Pl.* = धतींगड़.

धड़ंग *dharaṅg*, adj. **1.** stalwart, strapping. **2.** esp. -धड़ंग. naked. — नंग-धड़ंग, adj. stark naked.

[1]**धड़** *dhaṛ* [**dhaḍa-*: Pk. *dhaḍa-*], m. **1.** the body, trunk; body, main part (of an object, or a group). **2.** trunk of a tree. — ~ में उतरना, or पड़ना, to be swallowed or gulped down. ~ में उतारना, or डालना, to swallow or to gulp down. ~ रह जाना, the body to be paralysed; the body to waste away. – धड़-भाई, m. one of a party or side, supporter, partisan.

[2]**धड़** *dhaṛ* [**dhaḍ-*: Pk. *dhaḍahaḍia-*; ? × *dṛḍha-*], f. m. **1.** a noisy sound, esp. as of a fal[l] or blow; bang, thud, &c. 2. = दहड़- (see दहड़-दहड़). **3.** transf. drum (as beaten when a wrestler wins a bout). — ~ से, adv. with a bang, crash, &c.; smartly, at once; boldly. – धड़-धड़, adv. & m. f. intensely, violently, noisily; a loud, repeated sound (as knocking, rattling). धड़-धड़ करना, to knock at, to rattle (a door, &c.); to beat (a drum). धड़-धड़ काँपना, reg. to shake or to shiver violently. धड़ाधड़, f. a succession of sharp sounds: rattling, thumping, banging; adv. with a loud, continued sound; fig. boldly; briskly (as progress of sales); without interruption (of speech, &c.) °ई, f. uninterrupted hammering, or firing, &c.; brisk activity; flow (as of speech).

[3]**धड़** *dhaṛ* [*dṛḍha-*], adj. **1.** firm, hard, strong. **2.** intense, fierce, severe.

धड़क *dharak* [cf. H. *dharaknā*], f. **1.** beating, throbbing (as of the heart: = धड़कन). **2.** fear, alarm.

धड़कन *dharkan* [cf. H. *dharaknā*], f. = धड़क.

धड़कना *dharaknā* [cf. **dhaḍ-*: Pk. *dhaḍahaḍia-*], v.i. **1.** to beat, to throb; to palpitate. **2.** to blaze up, to burn fiercely. **3.** to burn (as with anger, or in a fever). **4.** to tremble (with fear). **5.** to clatter, to crash.

धड़का *dharkā* [cf. H. *dharaknā*], m. 1. = धड़क, 1. **2.** state of suspense, alarm (cf. धड़क, 2). **3.** a rattle (to scare birds from crops). **4.** crash, peal (of thunder). **5.** shock, blow.

धड़काना *dharkānā* [cf. H. *dharaknā*], v.t. **1.** to cause to beat or to throb (as the heart). **2.** to frighten, to alarm. **3.** to cause to clatter or to crash, &c.

धड़क्का *dharakkā* [cf. H. *dharākā*], m. 1. = धड़ाका. **2.** sound of beating or hammering, &c. **3.** alarming, intimidating (someone); bravado. 4. = धड़का, 3. **5.** transf. an excited crowd. धूम-धड़क्का, m. excitement (of a crowd), hullabaloo.

धड़खा *dharkhā*, m. reg. **1.** alarm, fear. **2.** *Pl.* a scarecrow.

धड़धड़ाना *dhardharānā* [cf. H. [2]*dhaṛ*], v.i. **1.** to make a rattling or banging noise; to sound (a drum); to knock (at, पर). **2.** to throb, to palpitate. **3.** to move impetuously or boldly; to rush.

धड़ल्ला *dharallā* [cf. H. [2]*dhaṛ*], m. **1.** sound o[f] beating or hammering, &c. (= धड़क्का). **2.** impetuosity; boldness. धड़ल्ले से, adv. in full force, or flood. **3.** transf. a turbulent crowd.

धड़वा *dhaṛvā*, m. *Pl. HŚS.* a kind of *mainā* bird.

धड़वाई *dhaṛvāī* [cf. H. [1]*dhaṛī*], m. *Pl. HŚS.* weigher of grain brought into a market (at a fee of a *dhaṛī*'s weight of the amount).

धड़ा *dhaṛā* [*dhaṭaka-*], m. **1.** a weight (usu. four, or five, or ten seers); a counterpoise; the quantity corresponding to a weight. **2.** specif. a large weight made up by first counterbalancing stones, &c. against a small, known weight, then adding them to this as required. **3.** a balance, scales. **4.** a composite body; group, party. — ~ **उठाना** (**का**), to weigh. ~ **करना** (**का**), to balance (a weight in a scales). ~ **बाँधना**, id.; to make up a composite weight to weigh with. **धड़े बँधना**, or **पड़ना**, parties or factions to form (from or within a larger group). **उलटा** ~ **बाँधना**, fig. to bring a counter-charge.

धड़ाका *dhaṛākā* [cf. **dhaḍ-*: Pk. *dhaḍahaḍia-*], m. **1.** loud crashing sound; sound of a shot; explosion. **2.** rumble, roar (of thunder, or a storm); din (as of battle). **3.** transf. violence, impetuosity (as of an attack). **4.** boldness. — **धड़ाके से**, adv. with a crashing sound; impetuously.

धड़ाम *dhaṛām*, m. (? f., *Pl.*). any sudden loud sound; crash; thud; splash. — ~ **से**, adv. with a crash, &c.; with a rush.

[1]**धड़ी** *dhaṛī* [cf. H. *dhaṛā*], f. **1.** a weight (four, or five seers); any quantity corresponding to a weight. 2. = **धड़ा**, 2. — ~ ~ **करके लूटना**, to steal or to take all that one has. ~ **भरना**, to weigh. **धड़ियों**, adv. a substantial amount (of).

[2]**धड़ी** *dhaṛī* [**dhaṭa-*[3]], f. **1.** line, stripe. **2.** border, edge (as of cloth). — ~ **जमाना**, to apply cosmetic paste (*missī*) to the teeth or lips.

[1]**धत** *dhat*, f. a bad habit; a weakness; vice. — ~ **पड़ना**, or **लगना**, a habit (of, **की**) to grow (on one); to become addicted (to).

[2]**धत** *dhat*, interj. expression of reproof, contempt; clear out! cut it out! — ~ **करना** (**को**), to abuse; to drive away. ~ **तेरे की**! you rascal!; clear out!

धता *dhatā* [cf. H. [2]*dhat*], m. **1.** the act of driving away. **2.** evasion, escape (from importunity, &c.) — ~ **बताना** (**को**), to drive away; to have no more to do (with); to escape (from).

धतियल *dhatiyal*, adj. *Pl.* = **धत्ती**.

धतिया *dhatiyā*, adj. & m. = **धत्ती**.

धतींगड़ *dhatīṁgaṛ*, adj. & m. (*Pl.*) *HŚS.* **1.** adj. sturdy, bulky (of physique). **2.** *Pl.* bold, overbearing. **3.** base (of birth). **4.** m. a sturdy fellow, &c.

धतींगड़ा *dhatīṁgṛā*, adj. & m. *HŚS.* = **धतींगड़**.

धतूरा *dhatūrā* [*dhattūra-*], m. the thorn-apple (a narcotic). — ~ **तो नहीं खा गया है**? surely he is crazy? ~ **देना** (**को**), to drug or to poison with *dhatūrā*.

धतूरिया *dhatūriyā* [cf. H. *dhatūrā*], m. *hist.* one who drugs or poisons with *dhatūrā*.

धत्ती *dhattī* [cf. H. [1]*dhat*], adj. & m. **1.** adj. having a vice; addicted (to, **का**). **2.** m. a person addicted to any vice.

धधक *dhadhak* [cf. H. *dhadhaknā*], f. **1.** blazing, flaring. **2.** fierce heat of flames. **3.** tongue of flame.

धधकना *dhadhaknā* [**dhagg-*: Pk. *dhagadhagaï*], v.i. to blaze; to flare.

धधकाना *dhadhkānā* [cf. H. *dhadhaknā*], v.t. to cause to blaze (a fire); to kindle.

धधकार *dhadhkār* [cf. *dagdha-*; × H. *dhadhaknā*], m. E.H. flaring anger.

धधाना *dhadhānā*, v.i. reg. = **धधकना**.

धनंतर *dhanantar*, m. = [1] [2]**धनत्तर**.

[1]**धन** *dhan* [*dhana-*; and S.], m. **1.** property, assets; cattle, herds. ***2.** wealth, riches; money; funds, capital. **3.** treasure. **4.** mineral resources. **5.** *math.* an amount to be added so as to give a total. **चार** ~ **पाँच नौ**, four and five are nine. **6.** *math.* the sign +; *chem.*, &c. positive (pole). — **धन-चिह्न**, m. *math.* the sign +. **धन-जन**, m. wealth and people (of a country); **धन-जन का ह्रास**, m. decline in wealth and prosperity. **धन-तेरस**, m. the thirteenth day of the dark half of the month Kārttik; a festival honouring Lakṣmī held on that day. **धन-दंड**, m. money penalty, fine. **धनद**, wealth-giving; munificent. **धन-दौलत**, f. wealth and riches, accumulated wealth. **धन-धान्य**, m. money and food. **धनधारी**, m. Brbh. = **धन-पति**. **धन-पक्ष**, m. credit side (of an account). **धन-पति**, m. lord of riches: a very wealthy person; epithet of Kuvera. **धन-पत्र**, m. account-book; bank-note; *Pl.* inventory of property. **धनमान**, adj. = **धनवान**. **धन-मूल**, m. principal, capital. **धन-राशि**, f. a sum of money; riches. **धन-लोलुप**, adj. greedy for wealth. °**ता**, f. **धनवंत**, adj. Brbh. Av. = next. **धनवान**, adj. wealthy; m. a wealthy man. °**-वती**, f. **धन-संपत्ति**, f. accumulated wealth. **धन-सत्ता**, f. capitalism. °**वाद**, m., id. °**वादी**, adj. & m. capitalist, &c. **धन-सुँघा**, adj. colloq. having a nose for money. **धनहर**, m. Brbh. thief. **धनहीन**, adj. without wealth, poor. **धनाग्र** [°*na* + *a*°], m. *electr.* anode. **धनात्मक** [°*na* + *ā*°], adj. *chem.*, &c. positive. **धनादेश** [°*na* + *ā*°], m. money order. **धनाधिकार** [°*na* + *a*°], m. title or right to

property. °ई, m. an heir. धनाढ्य [°*na*+*ā*°], adj. abounding in wealth: very rich. °ता, f. opulence. धनाध्यक्ष [°*na*+*a*°], m. treasurer. धनांध [°*na*+*a*°], adj. blinded by weath. धनार्जन [°*na*+*a*°], m. = धनोपार्जन. धनार्थी [°*na*+*a*°], adj. seeking wealth. धनावह [°*na*+*ā*°], adj. wealthy. धनेश [°*na*+*ī*°], m. lord of riches: = धनपति; the hornbill. धनेश्वर [°*na*+*ī*°], m. = धनपति, 2. धनोपार्जन [°*na*+*u*°], m. acquisition of wealth, earning of money.

²**धन** *dhan* adj. Brbh. = धन्य.

³**धन** *dhan* [*dhanikā*-, Pk. *dhaṇiā*-: w. *dhanya*-], f. Brbh. Av. young woman, lady; beloved.

धनकटी *dhankaṭī* [H. *dhān*+H. *kaṭnā*], f. the season for cutting rice.

धनकना *dhanaknā*, v.i. reg. to be set on fire; to blaze.

धनकर *dhankar* [cf. H. *dhān*], m. *Pl. HŚS.* **1.** a heavy clay soil (low-lying). **2.** a field in which a rice crop has been grown; crop of sugar-cane sown after rice.

धनकुट्टी *dhankuṭṭī* [H. *dhān*+H. *kūṭnā*], f. **1.** the pounding of grain (esp. rice). **2.** a mechanically worked mallet for pounding grain raised by means of a beam worked on a fulcrum. **3.** reg. (E.) a small red flying insect with a black head. — धनकुट्टी करना, to give a beating (to), to thrash.

धनतहिया *dhantahiyā* [cf. H. *dhān*], m. *Pl.* a rice-field which has been cut.

¹**धनत्तर** *dhanattar* [ad. *dhanava(n)ttara*-], adj. *Pl.* **1.** very rich or powerful. **2.** a wealthy or influential person.

²**धनत्तर** *dhanattar* [ad. *dhanvantari*-], m. *mythol.* = धन्वंतरि (name of the physician of the gods).

धनथिया *dhanthiyā*, m. *Pl.* = धनतहिया.

धनवंत *dhanvant* [S.], adj. Brbh. Av. = धनवान, see s.v. ¹धन.

धनहर *dhanhar* [**dhānyabhara*-], adj. reg. (Bihar) rice-growing (land).

धनहा *dhanhā*, adj. & m. *Pl.* **1.** adj. rice-growing (land). **2.** m. a cultivator of rice.

धना *dhanā* [S.], f. reg. wife, mistress, lady.

धनाशरी *dhanāśrī* [S.], f. **1.** name of a *rāgiṇī*. **2.** colloq. a hold or trick in wrestling. — ~ सुनाना, colloq. to box (one's) ears, to make the ears ring.

धनिक *dhanik* [conn. *dhanya*-, cf. Pk. *dhaṇia*-], adj. & m. **1.** adj. wealthy. **2.** m. a rich man. **3.** a creditor, money-lender. **4.** husband.

धनिया *dhaniyā* [*dhāneyaka*-], m. f. coriander. — धनिये की खोपड़ी में पानी पिलाना, to give (one) a drink from a coriander husk: to tantalise; to kill by inches.

धनिष्ठा *dhaniṣṭhā* [S.], f. the twenty-third, or twenty-fourth, lunar mansion (the dolphin).

¹**धनी** *dhanī* [S.; cf. also *dhanya*-, see H. ²*dhanī*], adj. **1.** rich, wealthy. **2.** praiseworthy, virtuous. **3.** m. a rich man. **4.** proprietor, master. **5.** husband. — तलवार का ~, m. a brave or skilful swordsman. बात का ~, m. true to one's word; wise in counsel. — धनी-धोरी, m. a person of power or influence; master (as of a household). धनी-मानी, adj. rich and respected.

²**धनी** *dhanī* [*dhanikā*-, Pk. *dhaṇiā*-], f. **1.** mistress, proprietress. **2.** lady; young wife.

धनु *dhanu* [S.], m. **1.** a bow. **2.** the sign Sagittarius (of the zodiac). **3.** *math.* chord of a circle.

धनुक *dhanuk* [ad. *dhanuṣ*; or MIA *dhanukka*-], m. 1. = धनुष, 1., 2. **2.** fine narrow lace; embroidery. — धनुक-बाई [-*vāta*-], f. lockjaw, tetanus; the sensation of 'pins and needles' (*Pl.*)

¹**धनुकी** *dhanukī* [cf. H. *dhanuk*], f. reg. bow used for scutching or carding cotton (= धुनकी).

²**धनुकी** *dhanukī* [cf. H. *dhanuk*], adj. reg. bow-shaped.

धनुर्- *dhanur*- [S.], m. a bow: — धनुर्धर, adj. armed with a bow; m. an archer. °-धारी, m. an archer. धनुर्यज्ञ, m. any religious ceremony symbolically involving a bow; an archery contest. धनुर्विद्या, f. the art of archery.

धनुष *dhanuṣ* [S.] m. **1.** a bow. **2.** a rainbow. **3.** the sign Sagittarius (of the zodiac). **4.** a measure of length equalling about 1.75m. (viz. four *hastas*, representing the length of the forearm with the extended hand). **5.** an arc (of a circle). — ~ चढ़ाना, to draw a bow. ~ टूटना, a bow to be discharged. ~ तोड़ना, to break a bow; to shoot a bow. — धनुष-धरन, m. Brbh. = धनुर्धारी. धनुष-बान, m. bow(s) and arrow(s). धनुष-मख , m. Av. = धनुर्यज्ञ.

धन्नासेठ *dhannāseṭh* [*dhanya*-+H. *seṭh*], m. **1.** a wealthy or monied man. **2.** a banker.

धन्नासेठी *dhannāseṭhī* [cf. H. *dhannāseṭh*], f. possession of great wealth.

धन्नी *dhannī* [cf. H. *dharan*], f. *Pl.* beam.

धन्नोता *dhannotā* [conn. ²*dharaṇa*-], m. *Pl.* a cross-beam (= धरन).

धन्य *dhanyă* [S.], adj. & m. **1.** auspicious, blessed; lucky. **2.** praiseworthy, virtuous.

3. bringing wealth. 4. m. gratitude. 5. interj. blessings (on you)! — ~ कहना, to pronounce blessings on, to bless. ~ मानना, to express devout or heartfelt thanks (for, का). ~ मेरे भाग्य, how fortunate am I! — धन्य-भाग्य, m. good fortune. धन्यवाद, m. giving thanks; gratitude; praise; interj. thank you! धन्यवाद करना, to express gratitude (for, का); to praise. धन्यवाद कहना (से), id. धन्यवाद देना (को), id.

धन्यता *dhanyātā* [S.], f. good fortune, blessed state.

धन्याक *dhanyāk* [S.], m. coriander (= धनिया).

धन्वंतरि *dhanvantari* [S.], m. *mythol.* the physician of the gods (considered, in a rebirth as Divodās, king of Banaras, to be the founder of Indian medicine).

धन्वा *dhanvā* [S.], m. a bow. — धन्वाकार [°*vā*+*ā*°], adj. bow-shaped.

धन्वी *dhanvī* [S.], adj. & m. 1. armed with a bow. 2. cunning, shrewd. 3. m. bowman, archer.

धप *dhap*, f. m. 1. sound, noise, crack; clack (of a shoe); thud (= धब-धब). 2. thump, blow.

[1]**धपना** *dhapnā* [**dhapp*-: ? ← Austro-as.], v.i. reg. to rush (at), to spring (on).

[2]**धपना** *dhapnā* [cf. H. *dhāpnā*], v.i. reg. 1. to be filled, satisfied. 2. to be tired or sick (of), sated.

धपाड़ *dhapāṛ*, m. reg. running, race.

धपिया *dhapiyā* [cf. H. *dhāp*], f. reg. a short run, or distance.

धपियाना *dhapiyānā* [cf. H. *dhap*], v.t. reg. to slap, to strike.

[1]**धप्पा** *dhappā* [**dhapp*-: ? ← Austro-as.], m. 1. a slap, blow. 2. loss, damage. — ~ लगना (को), to be struck a blow; to suffer loss. ~ मारना (पर), to slap, to strike; to damage; to cheat.

[2]**धप्पा** *dhappā*, m. reg. distance, range, space, &c. (= धाप).

धब-धब *dhab-dhab* [cf. H. *dhabdhabānā*], f. (m., *Pl.*). 1. noise, thud (as of a heavy, soft object falling). 2. sound of heavy footsteps.

धबधबाना *dhabdhabānā*, v.i. to fall heavily (as footsteps).

धबला *dhablā*, m. a *dhotī*, or a long skirt of coarse, strong cloth. — तेरे धबले में ख़ाक! pej. dust on your dhotī! the devil take you!

धब्बल *dhabbal*, adj. & m. reg. 1. adj. heavy, thickset. 2. m. a thickset or sturdy person.

धब्बा *dhabbā* [**dhabba*-], m. 1. a blot, stain; dark patch. 2. blemish; slur, stigma. — ~ लगना, or पड़ना (में), to be stained, dirtied; to be disgraced (a person's name). ~ लगाना, or डालना (में), to stain, &c.; to disgrace (a person's name). – धब्बेदार [P. *-dār*], adj. spotted, stained, soiled.

धम *dham* [**dhamm*-: Pk. *dhamadhamaï*], f. a loud sound; bang, crash, thud. — ~ से, adv. with a loud noise; heavily; all at once; continuously (of noise). – धम-धम, f. a repeated loud sound (as of a drum, &c.); reverberation (as of footsteps, or hooves). धमाचौकड़ी, f. turmoil, row; brawl. धमाधम, f. = धम-धम; a fight, brawl; adv. with a loud noise; continuously (of noise, or beating).

[1]**धमक** *dhamak* [cf. H. *dhamaknā*], f. 1. drumming or thumping sound (as of heavy footsteps, or sthg. heavy falling). 2. shock; blow; blast.

[2]**धमक** *dhamak* [S.], m. *Pl. HŚS.* a blacksmith.

धमकना *dhamaknā* [cf. **dhamm*-: Pk. *dhamadhamaï*], v.i. 1. to make a loud sound (as footsteps, or sthg. falling). 2. to feel a shock, to shake; to throb; to palpitate; to beat (as drums). 3. to burst in (to, or upon); to make a dash or sally (against). 4. to flash; to glimmer.

धमका *dhamkā* [cf. H. [1]*dhamak*, *dhamaknā*], m. 1. sound of sthg. heavy falling. 2. shock; blow. 3. closeness, humidity. 4. threat, menace.

धमकाना *dhamkānā* [cf. H. *dhamaknā*], v.t. 1. to threaten; to menace. 2. to berate. 3. to terrorise.

धमकाहट *dhamkāhaṭ* [cf. H. *dhamkānā*], f. threatening, &c.

धमकी *dhamkī* [cf. **dhammakka*-], f. 1. threatening, threat. 2. rebuke, — ~ देना (को), to threaten, &c. ~ में आना, to be frightened or coerced by the threats (of, की). — धमकीबाज़ी [P. *-bāzī*], f. threatening behaviour, recourse to threats.

धमकीला *dhamkīlā* [cf. H. *dhamkī*], adj. & m. reg. 1. adj. glowing; glittering. 2. m. a bright colour.

धमधमाना *dhamdhamānā* [cf. H. *dhamdham*], v.i. 1. to stamp or to drum (with feet or hooves). 2. to make a thumping sound: a thump or blow to be delivered.

धमधमाहट *dhamdhamāhaṭ* [cf. H. *dhamdhamānā*], f. 1. stamping or drumming (with feet or hooves). 2. thumping, banging.

धमधूसर *dhamdhūsar*, adj. fat, obese.

धमन *dhaman* [S.], m. **1.** blowing with bellows. **2.** bellows; tube for blowing on a fire. — धमन-भत्ती, f. blast furnace.

धमना *dhamnā*, v.i. **1.** E.H. to blaze (a fire). **2.** *Pl.* to sigh, to be sad. **3.** *Pl.* to gasp (in amazement).

धमनि *dhamăni* [S.], f. = धमनी.

धमनी *dhamănī* [S.], f. **1.** artery; vein. **2.** nerve.

धमस *dhamas*, f. m. reg. = धम्मस.

धमाका *dhamākā* [*dhammakka-], m. **1.** a loud noise, crash. **2.** a hard blow or thump. **3.** transf. a small cannon (as carried formerly on an elephant). **4.** fig. a threat.

धमाचौकड़ी *dhamācaukṛī*, f. see s.v. धम.

धमाधम *dhamādham*, f. see s.v. धम.

धमार *dhamār*, f. (m., *Pl.*) **1.** a musical measure. **2.** a type of song sung during the Holī festival. **3.** great merriment, uproar; cavorting (of actors, faqīrs, &c). **4.** fire-walking (of ascetics).

धमारिया *dhamāriyā* [cf. H. *dhamār*], m. **1.** a singer of *dhamār* songs. **2.** a fire-walking ascetic.

धमूका *dhamūkā*, m. a blow with the fist.

धमोका *dhamokā*, m. *Pl.* a kind of tambourine.

धम्मस *dhammas* [cf. H. *dham*], f. m. **1.** *Pl.* rammer (for consolidating soil). **2.** pounding, blow(s). **3.** fig. sthg. burdensome.

धम्माल *dhammāl*, m. *Pl. HŚS.* = धमार.

धर *dhar* [S.], m. **1.** finally in comp. holding; wearing; having, keeping; supporting (e.g. भूधर, m. a mountain). **2.** m. Brbh. Av. the earth. **3.** a mountain.

धरण *dharaṇ* [S.], m. **1.** holding; supporting; possessing; placing; retaining, fastening. **2.** seizing. **3.** sthg. which holds: a support; fastening. **4.** *Pl. HŚS.* bank, dike. **5.** *Pl. HŚS.* the female breast.

धरणी *dharăṇī* [S.], f. **1.** the earth; the world. **2.** soil, land. **3.** a beam. **4.** *Pl. HŚS.* a blood-vessel. — धरणीधर, m. *mythol.* supporting the world: a title of the snake Śeṣnāg, and of Viṣṇu in his incarnations as a tortoise and a boar. धरणी-सुता, f. *mythol.* daughter of the earth: a title of Sītā. धरणीश्वर [°ṇī+ī°], m. *HŚS. mythol.* lord of the earth: a title of Viṣṇu, and of Śiva.

धरता *dhartā* [? cf. H. *dharnā*], m. discount, commission.

धरती *dhartī* [*dharitrī-*], f. **1.** the earth. **2.** earth, soil; land. — ~ का फूल, m. mushroom, toadstool. ~ के परदे पर, adv. on earth's surface, on the earth. ~ के लाल, m. pl. sons of the soil. ~ जोतना, or बाहना, to plough the soil; to labour. ~ पर पैर न रखना, to be haughty or conceited; to be beside oneself with joy. — धरती-माता, f. mother earth.

[1]**धरन** *dharan* [*dharaṇa-*[1]], m. = धरण.

[2]**धरन** *dharan* [cf. H. *dharnā*: × *dharaṇa-*[1], *dharaṇī-*], f. 1. = [1]धरन. **2.** beam. **3.** womb. **4.** *Pl. HŚS.* navel, umbilical cord. — ~ टलना, डिगना or हटना, a prolapse (of the uterus, &c.) to occur. ~ मिलाना, or लड़ाना, sl. to have sexual intercourse (with, से).

[1]**धरना** *dharnā* [*dharati*], v.t. **1.** to hold, to keep; to possess; to assume (as powers), to obtain; to fix, to determine (as a time); to suspend (as an undertaking); to hold (as an opinion). **2.** to seize; to detain; to restrain (see [2]धरना); to check, to counter (a stratagem, &c). **3.** to place, to put; to deposit; to pawn; to stake (a wager). **4.** to put on, to apply; to wear. **5.** to apply (as the mind, or ear). — धर दबाना, or दबोचना, to seize (as prey); to pin down (as an enemy), to overcome. धर धमकना, to come, or to go, in a rush, impetuously. धर पकड़कर, adv. forcibly. – धरा-ढका, adj. put safely away, secreted. धरा-ढका धन, m. (a) hidden treasure.

[2]**धरना** *dharnā* [*dharaṇa-*[1]], m. **1.** sitting constantly at the door of a person whose attention one is demanding (as that of a debtor, or of one from whom a favour is sought). **2.** fasting (as at the door of a temple) to obtain favours from the idol. **3.** picketing. — ~ देना (पर), to enforce payment of a debt or compliance with a demand by sitting constantly at the door (of); to extort favours (from an idol); to picket.

धरनेत *dharnet* [cf. H. [1] [2]*dharnā*], m. an insistent creditor or importunate petitioner (see [2]धरना).

धरनैत *dharnait*, m. *Pl.* = धरनेत.

धरवाना *dharvānā* [cf. H. [1]*dharnā*], v.t. to cause to be held, or seized, &c. (by, से).

धरसना *dharasnā* [*dharṣati*], v.t. **1.** to overpower; to exceed (as in splendour). **2.** to repress, to curb, to chide.

धरा *dharā* [S.], f. the earth; the world. — धरा-तल, m. surface of the earth; surface, level (in relation to a base line or height); level, standard (of achievement, &c.); area (in square measurement). °ईय, adj. धराधर, m. *mythol.* earth-supporter: title of the snake Śeṣa. धरा-पृष्ठ, m. surface of the earth. धराशायी, adj.

resting, or sleeping on the earth; fallen to the ground; laid low.

धराई *dharāī* [cf. H. *dharnā*], f. **1.** placing. **2.** holding, seizing.

धराऊ *dharāū* [cf. H. *dharnā, dharānā*], adj. **1.** kept, stored up (goods). **2.** kept for special occasions (as clothes, foodstuffs).

धराना *dharānā* [cf. H. *dharnā*], v.t. & v.i. **1.** v.t. to cause to be seized or held (by, से). **2.** to owe. **3.** to deposit (as funds, a pledge). **4.** to fix, to appoint (a date, a time, a name). **5.** v.i. reg. to be seized. — वह मेरे पैसे धराता है, he owes me money.

धरावट *dharāvaṭ* [cf. H. *dharānā*], f. *Pl. HŚS.* land ascertained and apportioned by estimate (not by measurement).

धरावना *dharāvnā*, f. reg. **1.** a woman married a second time. **2.** second marriage (of a woman).

[1]**धराहर** *dharāhar* [**dhavalaghara-*], m. Av. white(washed) house: **1.** balcony, terrace (of large house). **2.** minaret.

[2]**धराहर** *dharāhar* [**dharādhāra-*], m. reg. a depository.

धरिंगा *dhariṅgā*, m. reg. *Pl.* a kind of rice.

धरित्री *dharitrī* [S.], f. the earth.

धरेचा *dharecā*, m. (*Pl.*) *HŚS.* = धरेला.

धरेल *dharel* [cf. H. [1]*dharnā*], f. a mistress, concubine.

धरेला *dharelā* [cf. H. [1]*dharnā*], m. a lover.

धरोड़ *dharoṛ*, m. reg. *Pl. HŚS.* = धरोहर.

धरोत *dharot*, f. reg. = धरोहर.

धरोल *dharol*, m. *Pl.* = धरोहर.

धरोहर *dharohar* [cf. H.. *dharāv*; + *dhara-*], f. **1.** sthg. entrusted to another, a charge, trust; inheritance. **2.** a deposit; pledge; sthg. pawned. **3.** adv. in trust, serving as a deposit. — ~ रखना, to entrust (to); to deposit (with).

धरौकी *dharaukī*, f. *Pl.* determination by guess.

धरौत *dharaut*, f. reg. = धरोहर.

धर्ता *dhartā* [S.], m. inv. **1.** one who holds, supports, or preserves. **2.** one who assumes (a task, a responsibility). **3.** a debtor.

धर्म *dharm* [S.], m. **1.** what is to be held or kept: the complex of religious and social obligations which a devout Hindu is required to fulfil, right action, duty; morality; virtue, virtuous life; justice. **2.** customary observances of community or sect, &c. **3.** the prescriptions or sanctions of religion; moral law. **4.** religion. **5.** particular nature or character; walk of life; way of life (e.g. of a woman as opposed to a man, of a man as opposed to a youth); caste. **6.** spiritual merit, as deriving from the fulfilment of *dharma*. **7.** धर्म-. = ~, 1.-6.; fig. imposing, large. धर्म-घड़ी, f. a large clock (in a public place). — ~ उठाना, to swear by one's religion. ~ करना, to act rightly, or virtuously; to perform a duty; to give alms. ~ कमाना, to obtain the fruits of virtuous life (esp. rebirth as a man). ~ खाना, = ~ उठाना. ~ में आना, to be incumbent on one as an aspect of *dharma* (an action). ~ रखना, to maintain *dharma*: to act in accordance with *dharma*. ~ लगती कहना, to speak in good faith, in all honesty. ~ से, adv. in good faith; solemnly (of a statement sworn). – धर्म-कर्म, m. a duty or observance prescribed by religion; a virtuous act; righteous conduct. धर्म-क्षेत्र, m. the field of law, or morality; an area near Karnal credited with being the scene of the battle between the Kurus and Pāṇḍus described in the *Mahābhārata*. धर्म-गुरु, m. religious preceptor. धर्म-ग्रंथ, m. a sacred book, scripture. धर्म-चक्र, m. wheel of law: fig. the teachings of the Buddha; national symbol of modern India. धर्म-चर्या, f. righteous or devout conduct. °-चारी, adj. & m., f. observing *dharma*: righteous; moral; virtuous; a righteous or devout person; a faithful spouse. धर्मच्युत, adj. fallen, lapsed (in conduct or belief). धर्मज्ञ, adj. knowing *dharma*; m. one versed in moral and religious matters. °-ज्ञान, m. knowledge of moral and religious duty. धर्मतंत्र, m. theocracy. धर्मत्यागी, m. an apostate; renegade. धर्मदर्शन, m. theology. धर्म-दास, m. temple attendant. °ई, f. धर्म-दाय, m. a charitable endowment. धर्म-धक्का, m. sufferings in an altruistic cause. धर्म-ध्वज, m. iron. flaunter of righteousness, hypocrite. °ई, m. id. धर्म-निरपेक्ष, adj. secular. धर्म-निष्ठ, adj. devout, religious. °ता, f. धर्म-निष्पत्ति, f. fulfilment of moral or religious duty or observance. धर्म-पति, m. a lawfully married man; a righteous man. °-पत्नी, f. a lawfully married wife. धर्मपरायण, adj. devout, religious. °ता, f. धर्म-पालक, adj. fostering the law: dutiful. धर्म-पुत्र, m. a lawful son; adopted son. धर्म-प्रचारक, m. a missionary. धर्म-बाप, m. adopted father; godfather. धर्म-बेटा, m. adopted son; godson. धर्म-भीरु, adj. godfearing, devout; superstitious. धर्ममय, adj. consisting of *dharma*: righteous; moral; virtuous. धर्म-मूर्ति, f. image of righteousness: a respectful title. धर्म-याजक, m. a missionary. धर्म-युग, m. *mythol.* the first of the four ages of the world (= सत्य युग). धर्म-युद्ध, m. a religious war; crusade. धर्म-राज, m. a just ruler (as the Pāṇḍava King Yudhiṣṭhira); a judge; one who acts justly. धर्मरूप, adj. of the form of, or characterised by, righteousness, &c.: righteous; virtuous. °ई, adj. id. धर्मवाद, m. contention or discussion about religious matters. °-वादी, adj. धार्मवान, adj. righteous;

virtuous; just; devout. **धर्म-विवाह**, m. lawful marriage. **धर्म-वीर**, m. a supremely righteous or virtuous person, &c. **धर्म-वेत्ता**, m. inv. = **धर्मज्ञ**. **धर्म-विपर्यय**, m. conversion (of faith). **धर्मशाला**, f. a rest-house for travellers and pilgrims, or an alms-house (built as an act of religious merit). **धर्म-शास्त्र**, m. a body or code of precepts having religious sanction (as Hindu law). **°ई**, adj. & m. having to do with *dharm-śāstra*; lawful; a jurist (Hindu law). **°ईय**, adj. **धर्मशील**, adj. virtuous; devout. **°ता**, f. **धर्म-सभा**, f. court of justice; religious assembly, or society. **धर्म-सारी**, f. Brbh. = **धर्म-शाला**. **धर्म-स्थल**, m. a sacred place. **धर्मस्व**, m. a charitable gift or endowment; *HŚS.* philanthropic institution. **धर्महीन**, adj. unrighteous, irreligious. **धर्मांतरण** [°*ma*+*a*°], m. change of religion, conversion. **°आंतरित**, adj. & m. converted; apostate. **धर्मांध** [°*ma*+*a*°], adj. bigoted, fanatical; **°ता**, f. **धर्माचारी** [°*ma*+*ā*°], m. = **धर्मचारी**. **धर्मात्मा** [°*ma*+*ā*°], adj. & m. inv. righteous; virtuous; devout; a righteous person, &c.; a saint. **धर्मादा** [ad. *dāya-*], m. inv. religious endowment. **धर्माधर्म** [°*ma*+*a*°], m. righteousness and evil, right and wrong. **धर्माधिकरण** [°*ma*+*a*°], m. court chamber or place of session. **धर्माधिकारी** [°*ma*+*a*°], m. = **धर्माध्यक्ष**. **धर्माधिष्ठान** [°*ma*+*a*°], m. court room, court house. **धर्माध्यक्ष** [°*ma*+*a*°], one determining matters of *dharma*: officer of justice, judge. **धर्मानुयायी** [°*ma*+*a*°], m. adherent of a partic. religion. **धर्मानुराग** [°*ma*+*a*°], m. religious zeal. **°ई**, adj. & m. zealous in religion; pej. a zealot. **धर्माभिमानी** [°*ma*+*a*°], adj. & m. fanatical or chauvinistic in religion; pej. a fanatic, &c. **धर्मार्थ** [°*ma*+*a*°], adv. & m. for religious purposes (as a donation, &c.); charitable grant, religious endowment. **धर्मावतार** [°*ma*+*a*°], m. incarnation of *dharma*: respectful form of address to a holy man, a judge, &c. **धर्मावलंबी** [°*ma*+*a*°], adj. & m. righteous, religious; = **धर्मानुयायी**. **धर्मासन** [°*ma*+*ā*°], m. seat of justice, or judgment; the bench. **धर्मेतर** [°*ma*+*i*°], adj. worldly, secular. **धर्मोत्तर** [°*ma*+*u*°], adj. supremely righteous, just, &c.; glorious; pej. fanatical. **धर्मोपदेश** [°*ma*+*u*°], m. spiritual instruction. **धर्मोपदेशक** [*ma*+*u*°], m. spiritual preceptor.

धर्मता *dharmătā* [S.], f. **1.** righteousness, morality; devoutness. **2.** inherent nature or property (of sthg).

धर्मत्व *dharmatvă* [S.], m. *Pl.* = **धर्मता**.

-धर्मा *-dharmā* [S.], adj. inv. having a partic. *dharma*.

धर्मिष्ठ *dharmiṣṭha* [S.], adj. completely righteous, virtuous, devout, &c. (cf. **धर्म**).

धर्मी *dharmī* [S.], adj. **1.** following *dharma*: righteous; devout; godly; just. **2.** Brbh. *philos.* characterised by partic. attributes. **3.** **-धर्मी**. adhering to a partic. religion. **4.** characterised by a partic. quality. **5.** m. a righteous man, &c.

धर्ष *dharṣ* [S.], m. **1.** overbearing conduct; insolence; brashness; violence.

धर्षण *dharṣaṇ* [S.], m. behaving overbearingly.

धर्षणा *dharṣăṇā* [S.], f. = **धर्षण**.

धलधलाना *dhaldhalānā*, v.i. reg. to gush out, to gurgle.

धवनि *dhavni* [*dhamanī-*], f. Brbh. bellows.

धवल *dhaval* [S.], adj. & m. **1.** adj. white; dazzling; brilliant. **2.** handsome, beautiful. **3.** m. white (colour). 4. = [1]**धौ**. — **धवल-मृत्तिका**, f. white earth: chalk. **धवलीकृत**, adj. = **धवलित**.

धवलित *dhavălit* [S.], adj. made white, or brilliant, &c.

धवलीकृत *dhavălīkṛt* [S.], adj. = **धवलित**.

[1]**धवा** *dhavā* [*dhava-*], m. = [1]**धौ**.

[2]**धवा** *dhavā*, m. *hist. Pl.* A Muslim community, bearers of palanquins; a member of that community.

धस *dhas* [**dhvasa-*], m. **1.** Av. plunge, dive. **2.** *Pl.* steep slope; earthworks, fortification. **3.** reg. a red sterile soil.

[1]**धसक** *dhasak* [cf. H. [1]*dhasaknā*], f. sinking, subsiding.

[2]**धसक** *dhasak* [cf. H. *dhāṁsnā*], f. dry coughing, cough.

[1]**धसकना** *dhasaknā* [*dhvasati*], v.i. **1.** to sink, to subside. **2.** to slip (out of place); to give way (as a wall); to fall away. **3.** to pierce, to stick (into, **में**).

[2]**धसकना** *dhasaknā* [? = [1]*dhasaknā*], v.i. to cough.

धसका *dhaskā* [cf. H. [2]*dhasaknā*], m. coughing (of animals).

धसना *dhasnā* [*dhvasati*], v.i. = **धँसना**.

धसान *dhasān*, f. & adj. = **धँसान**.

धाँगर *dhāṁgar* [**dhaṅga-*], m. reg. a community whose work is as diggers of wells and tanks.

धाँधना *dhāṁdhnā*, v.t. **1.** to devour, to bolt (food). **2.** fig. to assail. **3.** to close, to stop up.

धाँधल *dhāṁdhal* [cf. *dhandha-*], f. **1.** cheating, trickery. **2.** disturbance; outcry, clamour. — ~ **करना**, or **मचाना**, to cheat, &c.; to make a disturbance, &c. **धाँधलबाज़** [P. *-bāz*], m. a cheat, trickster.

धाँधलपन *dhāṁdhalpan* [cf. H. *dhāṁdhal*], m. cheating, trickery; guile.

धाँधलपना *dhāṁdhalpanā* [cf. H. *dhāṁdhal*], m. = धाँधलपन.

¹**धाँधली** *dhāṁdhlī* [cf. H. *dhāṁdhal*], adj. & f. **1.** adj. wily, tricky (to deal with). **2.** f. = धाँधल.

²**धाँधली** *dhāṁdhlī* [H. *dhāṁdhal*], m. *Pl.* a cheat, trickster.

धाँय *dhāṁy*, f. **1.** banging, clattering, or booming sound (as of a gun, a drum). **2.** adv. with a bang, &c. — **धाँय-धाँय करना**, to bang, to boom; colloq. to jabber; to wrangle.

धाँस *dhāṁs* [cf. H. *dhāṁsnā*], f. irritation of the throat (caused by tobacco, spices, &c.); dry coughing, cough. — **उसे मिर्चों की ~ चढ़ गई है**, the peppers have made him cough.

धाँसना *dhāṁsnā*, v.i. to cough (esp. horses and cattle).

धाँसी *dhāṁsī* [cf. H. *dhāṁsnā*], f. coughing, cough.

धा- *dhā-* [*dhāvati*], v.i. Brbh. Av. **1.** to run. **2.** to scurry about; to toil, to drudge.

-धा *-dhā* [S.], suffix (forms multiplicatives or adverbs from numerals, e.g. **नवधा**, ninefold.)

¹**धाक** *dhāk* [**dhākka-*], f. **1.** renown, fame; prestige; notoriety. **2.** pomp. **3.** awe; dread. — **~ जमना**, or **बँधना**, the renown or prestige, &c. (of, **की**) to become established; to be held in awe, or in fear (by, **पर**, among, **में**). **धाक बैठना**, awe or fear (of, **की**) to spread or to settle (upon, **पर**).

²**धाक** *dhāk*, f. *Pl. HŚS.* a post.

धाकड़ *dhākaṛ* [cf. H. ¹*dhāk*], adj. **1.** famed; notorious. **2.** inspiring awe, dread. **3.** strong of body.

धाखा *dhākhā*, m. *Pl.* a swing.

धागा *dhāgā* [**dhāgga-*], m. **1.** thread. **2.** *Pl.* fig. bonds (of love, &c.) — **~ डालना (में)**, to thread (a needle, &c.); to quilt. **~ पिरोना (में)**, = **धागा डालना**. **~ भरना** or **मारना (में)**, to darn, to mend. **धागे धागे करना**, to tear to shreds.

¹**धाड़** *dhāṛ* [*dhāṭi-*: Pk. *dhāḍi-*], f. **1.** assault. **2.** band, gang (of robbers). — **~ पड़ना (पर)**, an attack to be made (upon: by robbers). – **मार-धाड़**, f. violence, affray.

²**धाड़** *dhāṛ*, f. = **दहाड़**.

धाड़ना *dhāṛnā* [**dhāṭayati*: Pk. *dhāḍei*], v.t. reg. **1.** to attack, to rob. **2.** *Pl.* to cast (metal).

धाड़ैत *dhāṛait* [cf. H. ¹*dhāṛ*], m. member of a (bandit) gang.

धातकी *dhātākī* [S.], f. **1.** a large deciduous shrub, *Woodfordia floribunda* (which yields a dye and a gum). **2.** *Pl. HŚS. Grislea tomentosa.*

धाता *dhātā* [S.], m. inv. **1.** establisher, creator. **2.** preserver; parent. **3.** a title of Brahmā, and of Viṣṇu; also of Śiva.

धातु *dhātu* [S.], f. (m., *Pl.*) **1.** a primary substance (viz. earth, fire, water, air, atmosphere (*ākāśa*): these comprising the *pañcabhūta*). **2.** *chem.* an element. **3.** an ore; mineral. ***4.** a metal. **5.** a bodily humour (phlegm, wind, bile). **6.** a secretion; semen. **7.** *gram.* a root; stem; base. — **धातु-उद्योग**, m. metallurgical industry. **धातु-कर्मी**, m. metallurgist. **धातु-पाक**, m. name of a disease of the uro-genital system. **धातु-पाषाण**, m. an ore. **धातु-पिंड**, m. ingot. **धातुमय**, adj. rich in minerals. **धातु-मारिणी**, f. *Pl.* dissolving metals: borax. **धातु-मिश्रण**, m. an alloy. **धातु-रूप**, m. a verb form; a verb stem or base. **धातुवाद**, m. alchemy. **°ई**, m. alchemist. **धातु-विज्ञान**, m. metallurgy; (?) mineralogy. **धातु-विद्या**, f. = prec . **धातु-शास्त्र**, m. = **धातु-विज्ञान**. **°-शास्त्री**, m. a metallurgist; mineralogist.

धात्र *dhātr* [S.], m. a vessel, container.

धात्रिका *dhātrikā* [S.], f. emblic myrobalan (= **आँवला**).

धात्री *dhātrī* [S.], f. **1.** a wet-nurse; foster-mother. **2.** midwife (= **दाई**). **3.** mother. **4.** title of the goddess Sarasvatī. 5. = **आँवला**. — **धात्री-विज्ञान**, f. obstetrics.

धान *dhān* [*dhānya-*], m. **1.** the rice plant; paddy. **2.** unhusked rice. — **की खीलें** or **खिलियाँ**, f. pl. swollen parched rice. **धान-कट्टी**, f. the harvesting of rice. **धान-काटी**, f. id. **धान-कुट्टा**, m. a pounder or thresher of rice. **°-कुट्टी**, f. pounding or threshing rice. **धान-पान**, m. & adj. rice-leaf: a slender, or delicate object or creature; slender, delicate.

धानवैया *dhānvaiyā* [cf. H. *dhān*], m. reg. **1.** thresher of rice. **2.** seller of rice or grain.

धाना *dhānā*, v.t. = **ध्याव-**.

¹**धानी** *dhānī*, f. **1.** unhusked rice. **2.** roasted wheat or barley. **3.** rice-land, good soil for rice or cereals.

²**धानी** *dhānī* [cf. H. *dhān*], adj. & f. **1.** adj. light green. **2.** f. a light green colour.

-धानी *-dhānī* [S.], f. **1.** place of, site of (e.g. **राजधानी**, capital). **2.** [H. *-dānī*] receptacle; stand.

धानुक *dhānuk* [**dhānuṣka-*], m. **1.** a bowman; one armed with a bow. **2.** cotton-carder.

धानुष्क *dhānuṣk* [S.], m. = धानुक, 1.

धान्य *dhānyă* [S.], m. **1.** rice (= धान). **2.** grain, corn. **3.** *Pl. HŚS.* coriander.

धाप *dhāp* [**dhapp-*], m. (f., *Pl.*) *Pl. HŚS.* **1.** distance traversible at a sprint, or rush (cf. [1]धपना), a short or medium distance. **2.** large expanse of low ground.

धापना *dhāpnā* [**dhrāpyate*; Pa. *dhāta-*], v.i. & v.t. **1.** v.i. Brbh. to be filled, satisfied. **2.** to be weary (of doing sthg). **3.** v.t. *Pl. HŚS.* to satisfy, &c.

धाबरी *dhābrī*, f. reg. **1.** *Pl.* fowl-house (= दरबा). **2.** *Pl. HŚS.* dovecot.

धाबा *dhābā*, m. **1.** a flat roof of earth or (?) thatch; a house so roofed. **2.** pent-house. ***3.** a cheap eating-place.

धा-भाई *dhā-bhāī* [cf. H. *dhāī*], m. foster-brother.

धाम *dhām* [S.], m. **1.** dwelling, abode. **2.** splendour, radiance. **3.** place of pilgrimage. **4.** fig. the body. — परम ~, m. Brbh. the supreme abode: the ultimate being; paradise.

[1]**धामन** *dhāman* [conn. *dharmaṇa-*[1]], m. *Pl. HŚS.* a large harmless snake.

[2]**धामन** *dhāman* [*dharmaṇa-*[2]: Pk. *dhammaṇa-*], m. *Pl. HŚS.* a kind of bamboo, *Grewia tiliaefolia* (from which bows are made).

[3]**धामन** *dhāman* [**dhārmaṇa-*], m. *Pl.* a grass of good quality.

धामनी *dhāmănī* [S.], f. *Pl. HŚS.* = धमनी.

धामा *dhāmā*, m. *Pl. HŚS.* an open basket made of cane or rattan.

धामिन *dhāmin*, m. = [1] [2]धामन.

धामी *dhāmī* [cf. H. *dhām*; or *dharmin-*] m. title of a member of the sect of Prāṇnāth (A.D. 1618-1694).

धाय *dhāy* [*dhātrī-*], f. **1.** wet-nurse (= दाई). **2.** foster-mother. **3.** midwife (= दाई).

[1]**धार** *dhār* [*dhārā-*[1] [2]], f. (m., *Pl.*) **1.** [*dhārā-*][1] flow, current, stream; channel (of a river); spring. **2.** downward flow; heavy shower (of rain). **3.** libation. **4.** [*dhārā-*[2]] edge (of blade). **5.** edge, end, limit; Brbh. direction. **6.** line, chain (as of mountains). — ~ चढ़ाना, to offer as a libation (milk, water); to sharpen (a blade). ~ देना, to give (a flow of) milk; to offer in sacrifice; to be of use. ~ धरना (पर or की), to sharpen. ~ निकालना (की), to milk; to sharpen. ~ पर मारना, fig. to treat, or to view, with contempt (cf. ~ मारना). ~ बँधना (की), to pour out in a flood; to charm and render harmless (an enemy's sword, &c). ~ मारना, colloq. to urinate (on, पर); fig. to treat with contempt. ~ रखना (की), to drink milk from the teat. ~ रखना (पर), to sharpen (a blade). – धार-धुर्रा, m. *Pl.* = next. धार-धूरा, m. reg. boundary formed by a stream or stream-bed.

[2]**धार** *dhār* [*dhāra-*[2]], m. *HŚS.* collected rainwater (for medicinal use: cf. [1]धार, 2).

धारक *dhārak* [S.}, adj. & m. **1.** adj. holding, containing. **2.** checking, detaining, restraining. **3.** m. one who holds, &c. **4.** *Pl. HŚS.* debtor.

धारण *dhāraṇ* [S.], m. **1.** holding, keeping; maintaining, preserving (as a vow, a memory). **2.** carrying. **3.** wearing. **4.** taking (as food, or medicine). **5.** taking on, assuming (a rank, a posture; a loan); acquiring. — ~ करना, to maintain, to wear, to assume, &c.

धारणा *dhārăṇā* [S.], f. **1.** holding in the mind; memory; aptitude (to learn). **2.** notion, conception (of sthg.); view. **3.** firmness, steadfastness.

धारणी *dhārăṇī* [S.], f. **1.** *Pl. HŚS.* a vessel or channel of the body. **2.** a charm, incantation.

धारना *dhārnā* [*dhārayati*], v.t. **1.** to hold; to carry. **2.** to put on, to wear. **3.** to support. **4.** to owe.

धारा *dhārā* [S.], f. 1. = [1]धार, 1., 2. **2.** current (electric). **3.** (esp. *law.*) section, article; paragraph. **4.** multitude, mass. 5. = [1]धार, 4. **6.** rim, circumference (of a wheel). — धाराप्रवाह, adv. in an unbroken stream, successively; freely. °ई, adj. धारा-यंत्र, m. fountain. धारावाहिक, adj. uninterrupted, continuous; free, flowing (as speech); serialised (publication). °ता, f. continuity. °-वाही, adj. id. धारासार, m. a heavy shower.

धारिणी *dhāriṇī* [S.], f. the earth, the world.

धारित *dhārit* [S.], adj. supported, maintained.

[1]**धारी** *dhārī* [*dhārā-*[2]], f. **1.** a line. **2.** a stripe (as in material); streak. **3.** a groove. **4.** a margin, border. — धारीदार [P. *-dār*], adj. lined; striped; streaked.

[2]**धारी** *dhārī*, f. *Pl.* **1.** the plant *Lythrum fruticosum* (used in dyeing). **2.** *Grislea tomentosa.*

-धारी *-dhārī* [S.], adj. & m. **1.** adj. wearing, carrying, &c. (cf. धारण). **2.** m. a wearer, &c.

धार्मिक *dhārmik* [S.], adj. having to do with *dharma*: **1.** righteous. **2.** religious. **3.** devout.

धार्मिकता *dhārmikătā* [S.], f. **1.** righteousness. **2.** religious quality; piety, devotion.

धार्य *dhāryă* [S.], m. sthg. to be borne: a task.

धाला *dhālā*, m. *hist. Pl.* a tax or rate levied on individuals (of about one anna in the rupee, or one seer per maund).

धाव- *dhāv-* [*dhāvati*], v.i. Brbh. Av. **1.** to run; to hasten. **2.** *Pl.* to roam. **3.** v.t. *Pl.* to pursue; to attack.

¹**धावक** *dhāvak* [S.], adj. & m. **1.** adj. running, swift. **2.** m. a runner, messenger. **3.** *athl.* runner.

²**धावक** *dhāvak* [S.], m. = **धोबी**.

¹**धावन** *dhāvan* [S.], m. **1.** running, moving swiftly. **2.** a runner, messenger.

²**धावन** *dhāvan* [S.], m. **1.** washing. **2.** *HŚS.* a cleansing agent or substance.

धावनि *dhāvani* [cf. *dhāvana-*], f. Brbh. 1. = ¹**धावन**, 1. **2.** attack.

धावनिका *dhāvănikā* [S.], f. *Pl. HŚS.* a kind of prickly nightshade.

धावनी *dhāvănī* [S.], f. *Pl. HŚS.* name of several plants.

धावमान *dhāvămān* [S.], adj. = ¹**धावक**.

धावा *dhāvā* [**dhāva-*: Pa. *dhāva-*], m. **1.** running; swift course. **2.** a swift, or forced march. **3.** an attack, incursion. — **~ करना (पर)**, to move quickly (upon), to attack; to surprise (an enemy). **~ बोलना**, to order an attack; = **~ करना**. **~ मारना**, to make a forced march; to make a sudden attack (on, **पर**).

¹**धावित** *dhāvit* [S.], adj. *Pl. HŚS.* **1.** run or gone away; running away. **2.** advanced towards, or against.

²**धावित** *dhāvit* [S.], adj. purified, cleansed.

धाह *dhāh*, f. cry; roar; yell. — **~ मारना**, to cry, to roar; to yell. **~ मेलना**, id.

¹**धिंगा** *dhiṁgā*, m. *Pl.* a kind of pitchfork or rake with curved tines, used on the threshing-floor.

²**धिंगा** *dhiṁgā*, adj. = **धींगा**.

धिंगाई *dhiṁgāī*, f. Brbh. **1.** trouble-making; harassing, teasing. **2.** brashness, brazenness.

धिंगाना *dhiṁgānā* [cf. H. *dhīṁgā*], v.t. reg. to harass, to tease.

धिंचा *dhiṁcā*, m. *Pl.* a kind of tamarind.

धिक *dhik* [S.], interj. & m. **1.** interj. shame! a curse on! **2.** m. curse. — **धिक्कार**, m. reproach; insult; curse. **°ई**, f. curse; cursed state, damnation. **धिक्कार करना**, or **देना**, to curse. **धिक्कृत**, adj. reproached; insulted; cursed.

धिक्कारना *dhikkārnā* [cf. H. *dhikkār*, S. *dhikkāra-*], v.t. to reproach; to insult; to curse.

धियानगी *dhiyāngī*, f. *Pl.* daily wages; day's work.

धियाना *dhiyānā* [? **duhitājana-*], m. reg. **1.** sons-in-law. **2.** brothers-in-law.

धियानी *dhiyānī* [cf. H. *dhiyānā*], f. reg. daughters, or sisters (of a family).

धिरकार *dhirkār*, m. reg. = **धिक्कार**.

धिरकाल *dhirkāl*, m. *Pl.* name of a community of bamboo-workers.

धिराना *dhirānā* [? cf. H. *dhirkār*], v.t. reg. to threaten, to bully.

धींग *dhīṁg*, adj. & m. **1.** adj. sturdy, stalwart. **2.** violent, turbulent. **3.** wicked, base. **4.** m. a sturdily built person, &c. — **धींग-धुकड़ी**, f. trouble-making; = **धींगा-मुश्ती**.

धींगड़ा *dhīṁgṛā*, adj. & m. = **धींग**.

धींगा *dhīṁgā* [S.], adj. = **धींग**. — **धींगा-धाँगी**, f. & adv. violence, harassing; brawl; by force. **धींगा-धींगी**, f. id. **धींगा-मुश्ती** [P. *-muśt*], f. fisticuffs, brawl.

धींवर *dhīṁvar*, m. Brbh. = **धीवर**.

¹**धी** *dhī* [S.], f. **1.** understanding, intelligence; sense. **2.** mind. — **धीमान**, adj. intelligent; sensible; wise.

²**धी** *dhī* [*duhitṛ-*], f. daughter; girl.

धीम *dhīm*, m. & adj. reg. = **धीमा**.

धीमर *dhīmar*, m. = **धीवर**.

धीमा *dhīmā* [**dhīmma-*], adj. **1.** slow, sluggish; lazy. **2.** subdued (as sound, voice); soft, low; faint. **3.** faint, dim (as light, colour); slight (in intensity), weak; low (as a fever). **4.** moderate; abated (as fever, or emotion). — **~ करना**, to slacken (as pace); to soften, to moderate; to allay. **~ पड़ना**, to grow sluggish, or faint, dim, &c.; to abate. **धीमे**, adv. slowly; softly, gently; gradually; faintly; &c. **धीमे से**, adv. id. **धीमे धीमे**, adv. id.

धीमाई *dhīmāī* [cf. H. *dhīmā*], adj. slowness, &c. (see **धीमा**).

धीमान *dhīmān* [S]. see s.v. ¹**धी**.

धीर *dhīr* [*dhīra-*; and S.], adj. & m. **1.** adj. steadfast, resolute; bold. **2.** patient; persevering. **3.** lasting, stable, constant. **4.** calm, self-possessed; sedate. **5.** solemn, grave; deep (voice). **6.** handsome, attractive. **7.** soft, gentle, mild. **8.** slow, sluggish. **9.** m. steadfastness, &c. **10.** patience, &c. **11.** calm, composure. **12.** solemnity, gravity. — **~ धरना**, &c. = **धीरज धरना**, &c. – **धीरोदात्त** [°*ra*+*u*°], adj. brave and noble.

धीरज *dhīraj* [ad. *dhīrya-*], m. = धीर. — ~ देना, = ~ बाँधना. ~ धरना, or रखना, or करना, to take courage; to be composed; to be consoled; to have patience or perseverance. ~ बाँधना, or बँधाना (को), to encourage; to raise morale; to comfort. – धीरजमान, adj. *Pl. HŚS.* possessing steadfastness, patience, &c. (= धीर). धीरजवान, adj. id.

धीरता *dhīrătā* [S.], f. = धीर.

धीरत्व *dhīratvă*, m. = धीर.

धीरा *dhīrā* [*dhīra-*], adj. & m. **1.** adj. = धीर. **2.** m. *HŚS.* = धैर्य. — धीरे, adv. slowly; gradually; deliberately (of speech); patiently; gently, softly, quietly. धीरे से, adv. id. धीरे धीरे, adv. = धीरे.

धीरिया *dhīriyā* [cf. H. *dhīr*], f. dimin. reg. dear daughter.

धीरी *dhīrī*, f. *Pl. HŚS.* the pupil of the eye.

धीवर *dhīvar* [S.], m. **1.** a fisherman. **2.** the caste of fisherman.

धीवरी *dhīvărī* [S.], f. a fisherman's wife.

धुंगार *dhuṁgār*, f. (m., *Pl*).) seasoning, spices.

धुँगारना *dhuṁgārnā* [? conn. H. *dhuāṁ*], v.t. to season, to spice.

धुंद *dhund*, m. reg. 1. = [1]दुंद. **2.** *Pl.* [? × H. [1]धुन] design, intention; idea.

धुंध *dhundh* [**dhūmāndha-*: Pa. *dhūmandha-*], f. (m., *Pl.*) **1.** haze, mist; fog. **2.** duliness, gloom; dust-cloud(s). **3.** weak sight. **4.** adj. hazy, &c. **5.** blurred (of the senses). — ~ करना, to make hazy, &c.; to make drunk or stupefied. ~ का पसारा, region of darkness: the world. – धुंधकार, m. mistiness; darkness, obscurity.

धुँधकिया *dhuṁdhkiyā*, adj. *Pl.* causing haziness. (see धुंध).

धुँधर *dhuṁdhar*, f. reg. dust in the air; darkness.

धुँधलका *dhuṁdhalkā* [cf. H. *dhuṁdhlā*], adj. & m. **1.** adj. = धुँधला. **2.** m. dawn, twilight; dim light. **3.** weakness of sight. — धुँधलके, adv. at dawn.

धुँधला *dhuṁdhlā* [cf. *dhūmāndha-*: Pa. *dhūmandha-*], adj. **1.** hazy, misty; foggy; cloudy. **2.** dimness, blurred quality (as of sight, memory). **3.** dull.

धुँधलाई *dhuṁdhlāī* [cf. H. *dhuṁdhlā*], f. haze, &c. (= धुँधलापन).

धुँधलाना *dhuṁdhlānā* [cf. H. *dhuṁdhlā*], v.i. **1.** to become hazy, &c. **2.** to become dull, or dim.

धुँधलापन *dhuṁdhlāpan* [cf. H. *dhuṁdhlā*], m. **1.** haziness, &c. **2.** weakness (of sight). **3.** dullness; pallor.

धुँधलाहट *dhuṁdhlāhaṭ* [cf. H. *dhuṁdhlā*], f. = haze, &c. (= धुँधलापन).

धुँधाना *dhuṁdhānā* [cf. H. *dhuṁdh*], v.i. **1.** to be gloomy. **2.** to be dirty (a window, &c.) — धुंधाती कुंठा, f. depression (of mind).

धुँधु *dhuṁdhu*, m. a kind of insect, the red-velvet insect (= बीर-बहूटी).

धुँधुआना *dhuṁdhuānā* [conn. *dhundhu-*], v.i. to be filled with smoke, to be very smoky.

धुँधुकार *dhuṁdhukār* [cf. *dhundhu-*], m. Brbh. **1.** darkness. **2.** heavy cloud or rain; gloom.

धुँधेरी *dhuṁdherī* [**dhūmāndhăkāra-*], f. Brbh. = धुंध, 1., 2.

धुँधेला *dhuṁdhelā*, adj. *Pl. HŚS.* = धँधेला.

धुँवारा *dhuṁvārā*, m. reg. **1.** see धुआँरा, **2.** adj. – धूमिल.

धुँवाराना *dhuṁvārānā*, v.t. *Pl.* to smoke.

धुआँ *dhuāṁ* [*dhūma-*], m. **1.** smoke. **2.** [× *dhūpa-*] vapour; wafted aroma or smell; gas. — ~ काढ़ना, v.t. to boast. ~ देना (को), to emit smoke, to smoke; to waft smoke or vapour (towards or over); to smoke (sthg.); to fumigate. ~ लेना, to inhale smoke, to draw (at, का). दिल का ~ शांत करना, to relieve strong feelings or emotion. धुएँ उड़ाना, to reduce to poverty; = धज्जियाँ उड़ाना. धुएँ के बादल उड़ाना, to talk grandly, but vaguely. धुएँ पानी का शरीक, 'sharer in smoke and water': an immediate neighbour. धुएँ बिखेरना, 'to scatter as smoke': to exhaust (one's resources); to shut (one) up, to silence (one). — धुआँदान, m. outlet (in a roof) for smoke; chimney. धुआँधार, adj. smoky; ponderous, oppressive: dense (clouds); torrential (rain); deep (intoxication); vigorous, active; furious. धुआँ-लपक, m. a sponger, hanger-on. धुआँ-सा, adj. smoky, smoked; grey, ashen (of complexion).

धुआँरा *dhuāṁrā* [? **dhūmākhara-*], m. hole for smoke; chimney.

धुआँसा *dhuāṁsā* [**dhūmāśa-*], adj. & m. **1.** adj. smoked, smoky. **2.** m. soot.

धुकड़-पुकड़ *dhukaṛ-pukaṛ* [cf. **dhukk-*], f. **1.** beating, palpitation. **2.** perturbation. **3.** wavering, indecision.

धुकड़ी *dhukṛī* [**dhokka-*[1]], f. *Pl. HŚS.* a purse, small bag of coarse material.

धुकधुकी *dhukdhukī* [cf. **dhukk-*: Pk. *dhukkādhukkaï*], f. 1. = धक-धक. **2.** the hollow at the base of the throat (= दुगदुगी). **3.** an ornament usu. worn at the base of the throat (= दुगदुगी). **4.** fig. intent consideration, reflection. — ~ लगाना, or समाना, one (को or में) to be very apprehensive.

धुगधुगी *dhugdhugī*, f. = धुकधुकी, 2., 3.

[1]**धुत** *dhut*, adj. steeped (in, में), intoxicated, besotted. — नशे में ~, adj. drunk.

[2]**धुत** *dhut*, interj. = [2]धत.

धुत्ता *dhuttā* [? cf. H. *dhūt-*], m. trickery, cheating. — ~ देना (को), to trick.

धुधुकार *dhudhukār* [cf. H. *dhū-dhū*], m. **1.** loud noise. **2.** roaring (of a conflagration).

[1]**धुन** *dhun* [*dhūni-*], f. **1.** ardent desire; obsession, craze. **2.** keenness; whim. **3.** diligence, perseverance. **4.** absorbing thought. **5.** *Pl.* a racking pain in the bones. — ~ आना (को), a wish to seize (one). ~ का पक्का, adj. intent on an ambition, &c. ~ लगना, an obsession, &c. to take possession (of one: को). ~ समाना, a wish, &c. to engross (one). ~ सवार होना, to be driven by an urge or passion (to, की). ~ होना (को), = ~ सवार होना.

[2]**धुन** *dhun* [ad. *dhvani-*], f. style, mode, partic. modulation (in singing); melody.

[1]**धुनकना** *dhunaknā* [cf. *dhūnoti*], v.t. to scutch or to card cotton.

[2]**धुनकना** *dhunaknā*, v.i. *Pl.* to sound, to boom (cannon).

धुनकारना *dhunkārnā*, v.i. *Pl.* (*HŚS.*) to roar, to bellow, to thunder.

धुनकी *dhunkī* [cf. H. *dhunaknā*], f. bow used for scutching or carding cotton (= [1]धनुकी).

धुनना *dhunnā* [*dhūnoti*], v.t. **1.** to scutch or to card (cotton). **2.** to beat (as the head or brow; or a person). **3.** to strive; to rack (the brains).

धुनाई *dhunāī* [cf. H. *dhunnā*], f. a beating, drubbing.

[1]**धुनि** *dhuni* [ad. *dhvani-*], f. reg. = ध्वनि.

[2]**धुनि** *dhuni* [S.], f. Brbh. river (= [3]धुनी).

धुनिया *dhuniyā* [cf. H. *dhunnā*], m. a cotton-carder.

धुनिहाव *dhunihāv* [conn. H. *dhunnā*], m. *Pl. HŚS.* a racking pain in the bones.

[1]**धुनी** *dhunī* [cf. H. [1]*dhun*], adj. persevering, assiduous; obsessed (cf. [1]धुन).

[2]**धुनी** *dhunī* [cf. *dhvani-*], f. reg. **1.** = ध्वनि. **2.** transf. frog.

[3]**धुनी** *dhunī*, [? S.; or ad. **dhvanin-*], f. reg. the roaring one: a river.

धुप्पल *dhuppal*, f. colloq. dodge, bluff.

धुपेली *dhupelī*, [cf. H. [2]*dhūp*] f. *Pl. HŚS.* prickly heat.

धुमपाल *dhumpāl*, adj. reg. extremely fat (= धमधूसर).

धुमला *dhumlā*, adj. **1.** *Pl.* smoky; hazy; dim, dark. **2.** *Pl. HŚS.* blind.

धुमलाई *dhumlāī*, f. *Pl. HŚS.* smokiness, &c. (see *dhumlā*).

धुमस *dhumas*, m. *Pl.* = धम्मस.

धुमैला *dhumailā* [cf. *dhūma-*], adj. hazy, indistinct.

धुरंधर *dhurandhar* [S.], adj. & m. **1.** bearing a yoke, a burden. **2.** strong in supporting: mighty, great (as a leader, scholar, &c). **3.** m. fig. prestigious leader, &c.

धुर *dhur* [*dhur-*], m. f. & adj. **1.** m. f. yoke; forepart of a shaft (where the yoke is fixed). **2.** load. **3.** axle. **4.** beginning; extremity, end. **5.** head place, place of honour. **6.** adj. extreme; remote, distant. **7.** firm. ~ ख़ामोशी, f. a heavy silence. **8.** adv. quite, purely, truly. — ~ ऊपर, adj. straight above; far above, at the very top. ~ सिर से, adv. from the very beginning. ~ से ~ तक, adv. from beginning to end, throughout, wholly.

धुरा *dhurā* [*dhur-*], m. **1.** an axle, axle-tree; axis. **2.** shaft. **3.** yoke. **4.** reg. border or limits (as of a village or field), boundary; landmark.

धुरिया-धुरंग *dhuriyā-dhurang*, adj. **1.** alone. **2.** unaccompanied (song).

धुरियाना *dhuriyānā* [cf. H. *dhūl*], v.t. & v.i. reg. **1.** v.t. to throw dust on; to conceal (a fault, &c). **2.** to sift; to winnow. **3.** v.i. to be covered with dust, &c.

धुरी *dhurī* [*dhur-*, *dhurā-*], f. **1.** pole; axle. **2.** axis. **3.** fig. firmness. धुरीहीन, adj. of weak will or character.

धुरीसाँझ *dhurī-sāṁjh* [H. *dhūli*], f. dusk, twilight.

धुरीण *dhurīṇ* [S.], adj. **1.** bearing (a burden). **2.** -धुरीण. transf. great, mighty; prominent (in affairs, &c).

धुरीय *dhurīyă* [S.], adj. able to bear a burden: leading, eminent.

धुर्रा *dhurrā*, m. **1.** small section or amount; shred (as of cloth); speck; sthg. trivial. **2.** a stupid person. — धुर्रे उड़ाना, = धज्जियाँ उड़ाना. गाँव का ~, m. a stupid or uncouth person.

[1]**धुलना** *dhulnā* [cf. H. *dhulānā*], v.i. **1.** to be washed. **2.** to be washed out or away; to be

eroded (land). **3.** fig. to be expunged (a sin, &c).

[2]**धुलना** *dhulnā*, v.i. reg. to swing; to roll.

धुलवाई *dhulvāī*, f. = धुलाई.

धुलवाना *dhulvānā* [cf. H. *dhulānā*], v.t. to cause to be washed (by, से); to get (sthg.) washed.

धुलाई *dhulāī* [cf. H. *dhulānā*], f. **1.** washing. **2.** sum paid for washing. — धुलाई-मशीन, f. washing machine. हाथ-धुलाई, f. (barber's) fee for washing the hands of the bride and bridegroom before the marriage feast.

धुलाना *dhulānā* [cf. H. *dhonā*], v.t. to cause to be washed (by, से); to get (sthg.) washed.

धुलेंडी *dhulem̐ḍī* [? *dhūli-*+**ullaṇḍati*], f. the second day of the Holī festival (when the participants throw *gulāl* powder and coloured water at one another).

धुवाना *dhuvānā* [cf. H. *dhonā*], v.t. = धुलाना.

धुस्तूर *dhustūr*, m. reg. = धतूरा.

धुस्सा *dhussā* [**dhūrśa-*: cf. *dūrśa-*], m. reg. a coarse woollen material; a blanket made of this material.

धूँ *dhūm̐*, f. **1.** explosion, report (of a gun). **2.** sound (of a drum, &c).

धूँका *dhūm̐kā*, m. *Pl.* = धुआँरा.

धूँधूँकार *dhūm̐dhūm̐kār*, m. *E.H.* = धुँधुकार.

धूँवर *dhūm̐var* [**dhūmara-*], adj. *Pl.* = *dhūmil.*

धूआँ *dhūām̐*, m. = धुआँ.

धूत *dhūt* [S.], adj. **1.** shaken; shaken off, removed. **2.** deserted, abandoned. **3.** judged. **4.** reproached.

धूत- *dhūt-* [cf. *dhūrtā-*[1]], v.t. Brbh. Av. to cheat, to deceive.

धू-धू *dhū-dhū*, m. the crackling or roaring of flames.

धूनक *dhūnak* [S.], m. *Pl. HŚS.* resin (esp. of the *sāl* tree).

धूना *dhūnā* [*dhūṇa-*], m. gum, resin (esp. of *Shorea robusta*).

धूनी *dhūnī* [*dhūpana-*], f. **1.** smoke. **2.** smoke-fire (as of an ascetic, who sits beside it as a penance, or as lit to extort compliance with demands). **3.** the burning of incense. **4.** fumigation. — ~ जगना, a *dhūnī* fire to be lit: (one, की) to become an ascetic. ~ देना (में or को), to smoke, to fumigate; to exorcise; to importune. ~ रमाना, to light a smoke-fire (as penance); to become a yogī. ~ लगना, = ~ जगना. ~ लगाना, to become a yogī; to extort compliance with a demand. ~ लेना (की), to inhale smoke (as a penance); to undergo fumigation. – धूनी-पानी का संजोग, m. *Pl.* the union of fire and water: close friendship or attachment (between persons thought of as having been in a relationship of guru and disciple in a former birth).

[1]**धूप** *dhūp* [S.], m. incense; fragrant gum or resin; aroma. — ~ चढ़ाना, to burn incense (as before an idol). — धूपदान, m. a censer; container for incense. °ई, f. id. धूप-दीप, m. offering of incense (to an idol).

[2]**धूप** *dhūp* [**dhuppā-*], f. light or heat of the sun; sunshine; the sun. — ~ खाना, to bask in the sun. ~ खिलाना, to place in the sun (to dry, &c). ~ चढ़ना, the sun to rise, or to be high. ~ दिखाना (को), to put in the sun (to dry, or to air). ~ देना (को), id. ~ पड़ना, the sun, or heat, to be very strong. ~ में चूड़ा, or बाल, सफ़ेद करना, to let one's hair grow white in the sun: to grow grey without gaining knowledge or wisdom from life. ~ लेना, = next. ~ सेंकना, to bask in the sun. बदली की ~, f. a clouded sun, a very hot sun. — धूप-छाँह, f. light and shade; variegated material (as shot silk). °ई, adj. variegated. धूप-स्नान, m. [Engl.] sunbathing, basking in the sun.

धूपना *dhūpnā* [cf. H. *dhūp*], v.t. **1.** to burn incense (to or before an idol); to perfume. **2.** to fumigate.

धूपित *dhūpit* [S.], adj. **1.** perfumed. **2.** tired, exhausted.

[1]**धूम** *dhūm* [? **dhunman-*], m. **1.** noise; uproar; turmoil. **2.** display, ostentation. **3.** report, fame. — ~ मचना, or पड़ना, to be talked of: to be famous, or notorious. ~ मचाना, to create an uproar, &c.; to make a great to-do. — धूम-धड़क्का, m. = next. धूम-धाम, m. = ~, 2. धूम-धाम से, adv. grandly; ostentatiously (of a celebration, &c).

[2]**धूम** *dhūm* [S.], m. smoke, &c. (= धुआँ). — धूम-केतु, m. a comet; a falling star. धूम-पट, m. smoke-screen. धूम-पान, m. = धूम्र-पान. धूम-पोत, m. a steamer. धूमवाला, adj. smoky; smoked, dark (as glasses).

धूमक *dhūmak* [S.], m. a fumigator.

धूमक-धैया *dhūmak-dhaiyā* [H. [1]*dhūm*+H. *dhāvā*], f. **1.** turmoil. **2.** fig. display, ostentation.

धूमला *dhūmlā* [cf. *dhūmra-*], adj. = धूमिल.

धूमायित *dhūmāyit* [S.], adj. = धूमित.

धूमित *dhūmit* [S.], adj. made smoky, or obscure.

धूमिल *dhūmil* [cf. *dhūmra-*], adj. **1.** smoke-coloured; grey; purple. **2.** dim (of light). **3.** sooty, dirty.

धूमिलता *dhūmilatā* [cf. H. *dhūmil*], adj. dimness, indistinctness.

धूमी *dhūmī* [cf. H. *dhūm*], adj. boisterous, noisy.

धूम्र *dhūmra* [S.], adj. & m. **1.** adj. = धूमिल. **2.** m. a greyish or purplish colour. **3.** धूम्र-. smoke. **4.** incense. — धूम्र-पान, m. smoking. धूम्र-पान करना, to smoke. धूम्र-तापन, m. fumigation. धुम्रीकरण, m. fumigation.

धूम्रीकरण *dhūmrīkaraṇ* [S.], m. see s.v. धुम्र.

[1]**धूर** *dhūr*, f. dust (= धूल). — धूरधान, m. Brbh. a pile of dust. °ई, f. sthg. which contains powder: a musket, firelock (*Pl. HŚS*). धूर-सँझा, m. evening, dusk.

[2]**धूर** *dhūr*, f. **1.** *Pl. HŚS.* a kind of coarse grass. **2.** reg. (E.) the twentieth part of a *bisvā*.

धूरकट *dhūrkaṭ*, f.(?) m. *Pl. HŚS. hist.* advance of rent paid by villagers to the landlord in the months of Jeth and Asārh.

धूरकी *dhūrkī*, f. *Pl.* a small measure of land, the twentieth part of a *dhūr*.

[1]**धूरधानी** *dhūrdhānī*, m. reg. a person or creature of great bulk or size.

[2]**धूरधानी** *dhūrdhānī* [H. *dhūldhānī*], f. Brbh. a pile of dust; destruction.

धूरा *dhūrā* [*dhula-*], m. **1.** dust. **2.** powder. **3.** fig. trick, deception. — ~ देना (को), to deceive, to take in.

धूरि *dhūri*, f. Brbh. Av. = धूल.

धूरियाना *dhūriyānā* [cf. H. *dhūl*], v.t. **1.** to blow dust, &c., from. **2.** to winnow (grain).

धूरिया-बेला *dhūriyā-belā* [*dhūli-* + *velli-*], m. a species of large jasmine.

धूरिया-मल्लार *dhūriyā-mallār* [*dhūli-* + *mallārī-*], , m. (f., *Pl.*) name of a *rāgiṇī* (sung esp. at the beginning of the monsoon).

धूरी *dhūrī*, f. reg. strand of a rope.

धूर्त *dhūrt* [S.], adj. & m. **1.** adj. cunning, deceitful, sly. **2.** villainous; corrupt; licentious. **3.** m. a crafty or deceitful person. **4.** a villain.

धूर्तता *dhūrtătā* [S.], f. **1.** cunning, craft; deceit. **2.** villainy, &c.

धूर्तताई *dhūrtătāī* [cf. H. *dhūrtătā*], f. Brbh. crafty behaviour, &c. (= धूर्तता).

धूल *dhūl* [*dhūli-*], f. **1.** dust. **2.** fig. anything trivial, or useless. **3.** fig. shame, disgrace. — ~ उड़ना, dust to blow or to fly; a commotion to be raised; to be deserted, desolate (a place); to be reduced to poverty; to be disgraced. ~ उड़ाना, to stir up dust; to wander aimlessly; to stir up a commotion; to make fun (of, की); to defame. ~ की रस्सी बटना, 'to twist a rope of dust': to attempt the impossible. ~ चाटना, to lick dust: to abase oneself (before another: के सामने). ~ छानना, to wander about; to endure difficulties or distress. ~ झड़ना (की), colloq. to be given a beating. ~ झाड़ना (की, or से), to beat; to dust; pej. to minister obsequiously (to). ~ फाँकना, 'to eat dust': to wander aimlessly. ~ बरसना, = धूल उड़ना, 3. ~ समझना, to think of as worthless. ~ होना, to come to naught (hopes, &c). अपने सिर पर ~ डाहना, fig. to repent. — धूल-धक्कड़, m. a dust-storm; utter confusion. धूल-दूसर, adj. = next. धूल-दूसरित, adj. covered with dust; desolate. धूल-धानी, adj. & f. trampled underfoot, ruined; scattered (*Pl.*); destruction (*HŚS*). धूल-रोक, adj. dust-proof.

धूलक *dhūlak* [? conn. H. *dhūl*], m. *Pl. HŚS.* poison.

धूलि *dhūli* [S.], f. dust.

धूलिया *dhūliyā* [cf. H. धूल], adj. & f. **1.** adj. of dust, made of dust. **2.** f. = धूल, 1. — ~ पीर की क़सम खाना, joc. to swear an oath understood to have no significance.

धूसना *dhūsnā*, v.t. reg. **1.** to cram (= ठूँसना). **2.** *Pl.* to butt; to gore.

धूसर *dhūsar* [S.], adj. & m. **1.** adj. dust-coloured; grey, khaki. **2.** dusty. **3.** m. grey or grey-brown (colour).

धूसरित *dhūsarit* [S.], adj. made dusty (cf. धूसर).

धूहा *dhūhā*, m. a scarecrow.

धृत *dhṛt* [S.], adj. **1.** held; supported, sustained; held back, kept (as troops in reserve). **2.** seized. — धृतात्मा [°*ta* + *ā*°], adj. firm-minded; calm, collected.

धृति *dhṛti* [S.], f. **1.** holding; seizing. **2.** steadfastness, resolution. **3.** self-possession, calm; contentment. — धृतिमान, adj. steadfast; calm; content.

धृष्ट *dhṛṣṭ* [S.], adj. **1.** brash, presumptuous; shameless. **2.** insolent. **3.** daring.

धृष्टता *dhṛṣṭătā* [S.], f. **1.** brashness; shamelessness. **2.** insolence. **3.** daring.

धेड़ी *dheṛī* [?? cf. H. *daheṛ*], adj. *Pl. HŚS.* term descriptive of certain birds: — ~ कौवा, m. raven, crow; nutcracker; *Coracias*.

धेनु *dhenu* [S.], f. **1.** a milch cow. **2.** the earth. **3.** transf. a gift (to a brāhmaṇ: cf. H. *go-dān*).

धेनुका *dhenukā* [S.], f. = धेनु, 1., 3.

धेला *dhelā*, m. **1.** half a *paisā* (= अधेला). **2.** *Pl.* (brokers' jargon) fifty rupees.

धेली *dhelī*, f. = अधेली.

धेवता *dhevtā*, m. = दोहता.

धेवती *dhevtī*, f. = दोहती.

धैर्य *dhairyă* [S.], m. = धीर. — **धैर्य-धारण**, m. steadfastness; patience, perseverance; calm. °**-धारी**, adj. **धैर्यमान**, adj. possessing steadfastness, patience, &c. **धैर्यवान**, adj. id. **धैर्यशील**, adj. id. **धैर्य-सहन**, m. (?) steadfastness, resoluteness.

धैवत *dhaivat* [S.], m. the sixth note of the Indian musical scale.

धोंटी *dhomṭī*, f. *Pl.* a shepherd's crook; a tool having a hooked end.

[1]**धोंडा** *dhomḍā*, m. reg. (W.) a kind of grass which grows wild in rice-fields.

[2]**धोंडा** *dhomḍā*, m. *Pl.* stone, rock (? = *dhomdhā*).

धोंडी *dhomḍī*, f. *Pl.* = [1]*dhomḍā*.

धोंधा *dhomdhā* [*dhondha-], m. **1.** lump, clod. **2.** small mound of earth. **3.** a pot-belly. **4.** fig. an ignorant or foolish person. — **मिट्टी का ~**, = धोंधा, 1., 4.

धों-धों *dhom-dhom*, f. = धूँ. — **धों-धों-मार करना**, colloq. to make haste.

धोआ *dhoā*, m. *Pl.* a present of fruit, &c. on an auspicious occasion (= ढोआ).

धोई *dhoī* [*dhautikā-; or cf. H. *dhonā*], f. **1.** pulse, husked and soaked before boiling. **2.** drippings of poppy-juice.

धोक *dhok* [cf. H. *dhoknā*], f. (? m.) E.H. bowing, salutation.

धोकड़ *dhokaṛ*, adj. reg. robust, sturdy.

धोकना *dhoknā* [*dhaukyate], v.i. *Pl.* to bow (to an idol); to lean (against).

धोका *dhokā*, m. pronun. var. = धोखा.

धोखा *dhokhā* [*dhrokṣa-], m. **1.** deceit. **2.** false impression; sthg. seen indistinctly; mirage. **3.** mistake, blunder. **4.** disappointment. **5.** uncertainty, doubt; alarm. **धोखे का काम**, m. a risky matter. **6.** false appearance; trap, snare; camouflage; a scarecrow. — **~ उठाना**, to be taken advantage of (by another); to suffer unexpected loss. **~ खाना**, to be deceived (by, से), to be taken in. **~ देना** (को), to deceive; to mislead; to disappoint; to fail (a weapon, a stratagem, medicine). **~ दे जाना**, fig. to die prematurely. **~ न लगाना**, to allow no mistake or shortcoming (in, में. **~ पड़ना** (को), to be deceived, deluded, &c. (as by events). **धोखे की टट्टी**, f. a hunter's hide; camouflage (of an ambush, or hostile intention). **धोखे में आना**, = **~ खाना**. **धोखे में डालना**, or **रखना**, or **लाना**, to deceive; to fill with false hopes, &c., to mislead; to lure into a trap. **धोखा लगना**, to feel doubt or suspicion (about, में). **धोखे में**, or **से**, adv. in error; by accident. — **धोखाधड़ी**, f. cheating. **धोखेबाज़** [P. *-bāz*], adj. deceitful, fraudulent; m. a deceitful person; an impostor. °**ई**, f. deceit, &c. **धोखे-भरा**, adj. false, fraudulent.

धोड़ *dhoṛ* [*dhoḍa-*: ← Austro-as.], m. a kind of water-snake.

धोतर *dhotar* [cf. *dhotra-*, or **dhotta-*], f. *Pl.* *HŚS.* **1.** a kind of coarse cloth. 2. = धोती.

धोता *dhotā* [*dhaurtaka-*], adj. & m. *Pl.* **1.** adj. cunning. **2.** m. a rogue.

[1]**धोती** *dhotī* [**dhotta-*, or *dhotra-*], f. **1.** a dhotī, a piece of cloth worn round the lower body, one end of which passes between the legs and is tucked in behind. **2.** a cotton sari. — **~ बाँधना**, to put on a *dhotī*; to gird up the loins. **~ ढीला होना**, 'the dhotī to loosen': courage to falter. – **धोती-प्रसाद**, m. joc. = next. **धोतीबंद**, adj. wearing a *dhotī*; m. one who wears a *dhotī*.

[2]**धोती** *dhotī*, m. *Pl.* *HŚS.* a kind of falcon (the female of which is called *besrā*).

धोना *dhonā* [**dhauvati*: Pa. *dhovati*], v.t. **1.** to wash (one's person). **2.** to wash (clothes). **3.** to wash out, to efface (a stain; a sin, &c). — **धोना-धाना** [*dhāvati*[2]], to wash and cleanse thoroughly.

[1]**धोप** *dhop*, f. Brbh. **1.** a kind of sword (long and straight). **2.** *Pl.* fig. a broad leaf or blade.

[2]**धोप** *dhop*, m. *Pl.* running; a race; exertion.

धोब *dhob* [cf. **dhauvati*: MIA *dhovvaï* 'is washed'], m. washing; a wash. — **~ पड़ना** (पर), to be washed.

धोबिन *dhobin* [cf. H. *dhobī*], f. **1.** a washerman's wife. **2.** a washerwoman. **3.** a wagtail.

धोबी *dhobī* [cf. **dhauvati*: MIA *dhovvaï* 'is washed'], m. a washerman. — **~ का कुत्ता**, m. a washerman's dog: an idle or worthless person; one who turns his hand first to one thing, then to another; a jack-of-all-trades. **~ का कुत्ता न घर का न घाट का**, prov. the washerman's dog belongs neither to house nor to waterside. — **धोबी-ख़ाना**, m. a laundry. **धोबीगिरी**, [P. *-garī*] f. the washerman's trade. **धोबी-घर**, m. = **धोबी-ख़ाना**. **धोबी-पछाड़**, m. = next, 2. **धोबी-पाट**, m. a washerman's board or stone; (in wrestling) throwing one's opponent with both hands, across back or hip (as a *dhobī* beats clothes on a stone).

धोरा *dhorā*, m. *Pl.* a kind of medicine (cf. *dhatūrā*).

धोरी *dhorī* [*dhaureya-*], m. **1.** ox, bullock. **2.** leader. **3.** pl. cattle (= ढोर).

धोरे *dhore* [*dhaureya-*], adv. **1.** nearby, close. **2.** ppn. near, close (to). — **धोरे-धारे**, adv. about, approximately.

धोवत *dhovat*, f. *Pl.* washing.

धोवती *dhovtī*, f. Brbh. = **धोती**.

धोवन *dhovan* [cf. H. *dhonā*], m. **1.** water in which anything has been washed. **2.** washing (the action, process). — **पैर का ~ होना**, fig. (a person) to be much inferior (to another: **के**).

धोसा *dhosā* [**dhorśa-*], m. *Pl.* = **धुस्सा**.

धौं *dhaum̐* [*dhruva-*: Pk. *dhuvaṁ*], conj. Brbh. Av. **1.** indeed. **2.** whether.

धौंक *dhaum̐k* [cf. H. *dhaum̐knā*], f. **1.** blowing (a fire). **2.** puffing, panting. **3.** transf. asthma. **4.** heat, blast. — **~ लगना (को)**, = **लू लगना**.

धौंकना *dhaum̐knā* [cf. *dhamati*: ? × MIA *phukk-*, *phum̐k-*], v.t. & v.i. **1.** v.t. to blow (with bellows); colloq. to puff at (a cigarette). **2.** to breathe upon. **3.** to impose (a fine, a burden: upon, **पर**). **4.** v.i. to puff, to pant.

धौंकनी *dhaum̐knī* [cf. H. *dhaum̐knā*], f. **1.** bellows; tube used to blow on a fire. **2.** blow-lamp. **3.** panting, hard breathing. — **~ लगना (को)**, to suffer from shortness of breath; to puff, to pant.

धौंका *dhaum̐kā* [cf. H. *dhaum̐knā*], m. reg. = **लू**.

धौंकिया *dhaum̐kiyā* [cf. H. *dhaum̐knā*] m. one who works a bellows; solderer, tinsmith; blacksmith.

धौंकी *dhaum̐kī* [cf. H. *dhaum̐knā*], f. *Pl. HŚS.* = **धौंकनी**.

धौंज *dhaum̐j*, f. Brbh. **1.** trouble, effort. **2.** anxious thought.

धौंताल *dhaum̐tāl*, adj. *Pl. HŚS.* **1.** brisk, active; keen. **2.** Brbh. mischievous; wicked.

धौंस *dhaum̐s*, f. **1.** overbearing conduct, arrogance; bluster. **2.** threatening; exacting (a payment); blackmail. **3.** deception. — **~ की चलना**, = **~ देना**. **~ जताना**, or **जमाना**, to behave arrogantly, or intimidatingly (towards). **~ देना (को)**, to threaten; to deceive, to trick. **~ बाँधना (पर)**, to exact a payment due (from). **~ में आना**, to be intimidated (by, **की**); to be taken in (by). **~ में लेना**, to take by force or threat. — **धौंस-धड़ल्ला**, m. blustering; rush, attack (of an excited crowd). **धौंस-पट्टी**, f. = ~, 1.

धौंसा *dhaum̐sā*, m. **1.** a kettledrum. **2.** fig. ability; strength. **3.** attack, shock. — **~ खाना**, to suffer a shock or blow; to be ill-fated.

धौंसिया *dhaum̐siyā* [cf. H. *dhaum̐s*], m. **1.** a bold or overbearing person. **2.** an extortioner. **3.** a trickster, cheat. **4.** blackmailer.

[1]**धौ** *dhau* [*dhava-*], m. The tree *Grislea tomentosa* (used in dyeing), or *Lythrum fruticosum*, and its wood.

[2]**धौ** *dhau*, f. *Pl.* the iron band, or strake, of a wheel.

धौजन *dhaujan*, m. reg. *Pl.* worry, annoyance, bother.

धौत *dhaut* [S.], adj. **1.** washed, cleansed, purified. **2.** bright, white.

धौर *dhaur* [*dhavala-*], m. **1.** *Pl. HŚS.* a large species of dove. **2.** *Pl.* a kind of sugar-cane.

धौरहर *dhaurhar* [**dhavalaghara-*], m. Brbh. white house: splendid structure. — **धुएँ का ~**, m. a castle in the air.

धौरा *dhaurā* [*dhavala-*], adj. Brbh. Av. white.

धौरी *dhaurī* [cf. H. *dhaulā*], f. Brbh. Av. a white cow.

[1]**धौल** *dhaul*, m. **1.** a blow with the fist. **2.** a slap. **3.** fig. a blow; loss. — **~ खाना**, to suffer or to take a blow. **~ जमाना (पर)**, to strike or to land a blow. **~ पड़ना**, or **लगना (को)**, to be struck a blow; to receive a shock, to suffer loss. **~ मारना**, or **लगाना (को)**, to strike a blow. — **धौल-धक्कड़**, m. a fight, brawl. °**-धक्का**, m. a hefty blow, or slap. **धौल-धप्पड़**, m. a fight, brawl. °**-धप्पा**, m. id.

[2]**धौल** *dhaul* [*dhavala-*], adj. Brbh. **1.** white. **2.** egregious, arrant. **3.** m. *Pl. HŚS.* a species of sugar-cane; the stalk of the *jvār* plant.

धौला *dhaulā* [*dhavala-*], adj. white; dazzling. — **~ पड़ना**, to turn white or pale.

धौलाई *dhaulāī* [cf. H. *dhaulā*], f. whiteness; brightness; cleanness.

धौलाना *dhaulānā* [cf. H. [1]*dhaul*], v.t. reg. = **धौलियाना**.

धौलापन *dhaulāpan* [cf. H. *dhaulā*], m. = **धौलाई**.

धौलियाना *dhauliyānā*, v.t. to thump, to strike.

ध्यान *dhyān* [S.], m. **1.** meditation, contemplation; deep thought. **2.** consideration, reflection. ***3.** attention; the mind. **4.** keeping (sthg.) in mind; thought; memory. — **~ आना**,

to come to mind. ~ करना (का, or पर, or की ओर), to contemplate, to meditate (on); to give thought or attention (to); to notice. ~ दिलाना, to remind (one, को) of (का). ~ देना (को), to give attention or heed (to). ~ धरना (पर), = ~ करना. ~ पर चढ़ना, to engross the attention; to take the fancy. ~ बँटना, the attention to be distracted. ~ में आना, to come into the mind (a thought), to be understood. ~ में लाना, to understand, to absorb (mentally); to pay regard or heed to. ~ रखना, to keep the mind fixed (on, पर); to bear in mind, to pay attention (to, का); to think (about). ~ लगना, the attention to turn (to, पर or की ओर). ~ लगाना (पर), = ~ करना. ~ रहना, to remain in mind, not to be neglected (a matter). ~ से, adv. attentively. ~ से उतरना, to slip the mind, to be overlooked. — ध्यानपूर्वक, adv. attentively. ध्यान-योग, m. devout meditation, religious contemplation. ध्यानस्थ, adj. absorbed in meditation, or thought. ध्यानावस्थित [°*na*+*a*°], adj. id.

ध्यान- *dhyān-* [cf. H. *dhyān*: w. H. *dhyāv-*], v.t. Brbh. = ध्याव-.

ध्यानी *dhyānī* [S.], adj. & m. **1.** adj. contemplative; religious. **2.** absorbed in meditation. **3.** attentive, considerate. **4.** m. one who meditates, &c. — ध्यानी-ज्ञानी, m. person of contemplative turn of mind.

ध्यानीय *dhyānīyă* [S.], adj. & m. *Pl.* **1.** adj. to be meditated upon. **2.** m. an object suitable for or deserving meditation or consideration.

ध्याम *dhyām* [S.], m. *Pl. HŚS.* **1.** the plant *Artemisia indica*, wormwood (= [1]दौना). **2.** a fragrant grass.

ध्याव- *dhyāv-* [*dhiyāyati*], v.t. Brbh. = ध्यान करना, 1.; to adore.

ध्रुपद *dhrupad* [ad. *dhruvapada-*], m. **1.** a partic. style of singing short verses (*padas*); such verses, as sung. **2.** the introductory verse of a poem or song (repeated as a chorus).

ध्रुव *dhruv* [S.], adj. **1.** fixed, immovable; stable. **2.** constant, permanent. **3.** certain. **4.** the pole star. **5.** a pole (of the earth). **6.** terminal (of a battery); electrode. — ध्रुव-तारा, m. the pole star. ध्रुव-दर्शक, m. a compass; *astron.* the Great Bear. °-दर्शन, m. the rite of pointing out the pole star to a newly married husband. ध्रुव-पद, m. = ध्रुपद. ध्रुव-लोक, m. *mythol.* one of the divisions of paradise. ध्रुव-वृत्त, m. a meridian. ध्रुवीकरण, m. polarisation; strengthening, consolidation.

ध्रुवता *dhruvătā* [S.], f. **1.** fixity; stability. **2.** constancy, permanence.

ध्रुवा *dhruvā* [S.], f. *Pl. HŚS.* ? the bush *Sanseveria roxburghiana* (S. *mūrvā*), or 'bowstring hemp'.

ध्रुवीकरण *dhruvīkaraṇ* [S.], m. see s.v. ध्रुव.

ध्रुवीय *dhruvīyă* [S.], adj. of the pole, polar; fixed.

ध्वंस *dhvaṃs* [S.], m. **1.** destruction; demolition; ruin. **2.** harm. — ध्वंसकारी, adj. destructive. ध्वंसात्मक [°*sa*+*ā*°], adj. destructive; having to do with demolition.

ध्वंसक *dhvaṃsak* [S.], adj. **1.** destructive; dangerous. **2.** m. *naut.* destroyer.

ध्वंसन *dhvaṃsan* [S.], m. **1.** destroying (= ध्वंस). **2.** sabotage.

ध्वंसित *dhvaṃsit* [S.], adj. destroyed, &c.

ध्वंसी *dhvaṃsī* [S.], adj. **1.** suffering destruction, or decline. **2.** destroying, destructive.

ध्वज *dhvaj* [S.], m. **1.** flag, banner; standard. **2.** symbol, emblem. **3.** penis. — ध्वज-दंड, m. standard; staff. ध्वज-पात, m. = ध्वज-भंग. ध्वज-पोत, m. flagship. ध्वज-भंग, m. impotence.

ध्वजा *dhvajā* [S.], f. = ध्वज, 1., 2. ध्वजारोपण [°*jă*+*ā*°], m. the planting of a flag. ध्वजारोहण [*jă*+*ā*°], m. the raising or flying of a flag.

ध्वजी *dhvajī* [S.], adj. & m. **1.** adj. carrying a banner. **2.** bearing a symbol or emblem. **3.** m. standard-bearer.

ध्वनि *dhvani* [S.], f. **1.** sound; echo; tone; tune; noise. **2.** transf. implication (of a statement). **3.** *ling.* a phoneme. — ध्वनिगत, adj. phonetic. ध्वनि-ग्रहण, m. reception (radio); tuning in. ध्वनि-ग्राम, m. the sounds, or phonemes, of a language. ध्वनिप्रधान, adj. phonetic (a script). ध्वनिमय, adj. loud, resonant; sound, sonar. ध्वनिमात्र, m. sound-measure: phoneme. ध्वनि-विज्ञान, m. the science of phonetics, or of acoustics. ध्वनि-विपर्यय, m. *ling.* metathesis. ध्वनि-विस्तारक, adj. amplifying sound (as a loudspeaker). ध्वनि-वेधी, adj. sound-piercing: supersonic. ध्वनि-शास्त्र, m. = ध्वनि-विज्ञान. ध्वन्यंग [°*ni*+*a*°], m. sound segment: *ling.* allophone. ध्वन्यात्मक [°*ni*+*ā*°], adj. phonetic; of suggestive sound, onomatopoeic. °ता, f. onomatopoeic quality, sound symbolism. ध्वन्यार्थ [°*ni*+*a*°], m. = ~, 2.

ध्वनिक *dhvanik* [S.], adj. phonetic.

ध्वनित *dhvanit* [S.], adj. **1.** sounded, voiced; reverberating (as a drum). **2.** implied, suggested (of the further or non-literal sense of any utterance).

ध्वस्त *dhvast* [S.], adj. destroyed; ruined. (also transf.)

ध्वांत *dhvānt* [S.], m. covered: darkness.

ध्वान *dhvān* [S.], m. *HŚS.* sound; echo.

ध्वानिक *dhvānik* [S.], adj. acoustic.

ध्वानिकता *dhvānikătā* [S.], f. acoustic quality.

ध्वानिकी *dhvānikī* [S.], f. acoustics.

न

न *na*, the twentieth consonant of the Devanāgarī syllabary. — नकार, m. the sound /n/; the letter न; see s.v.

नंग *naṅg* [*nagna-*], adj. & m. /nə̃g/. = नंगा. — नंग-धड़ंग, adj. stark naked. नंग-पैरा, adj. barefoot.

नंगटा *naṅgṭā*, adj. naked.

नंगा *naṅgā* [*nagna-*], adj. & m. /nə̃ga/. 1 adj. naked; bare. **2.** shameless. **3.** m. a shameless person. **4.** a disgraced, or base person. — ~ करना, to strip (of clothes); to bare, to uncover; to despoil; to disgrace, to dishonour. ~ मादरज़ाद [P. *mādar-zād*], adj. naked as at birth. नंगी तलवार, f. a naked sword; fig. one who speaks his mind freely. नंगे पाँव, adv. barefoot. नंगे पैर, or पैरों, adv. id. नंगे सिर, adv. bare-headed. – नंगा-झोली, f. search of the person. नंगा-झोली देना, to order a search (of, को); नंगा-झोली लेना (की), to search (one). नंगा-धड़ंगा, adj. stark naked. नंगा-बुच्चा [*vr̥tya-*], adj. poverty-stricken. °-बूचा, adj. id. नंगा-मुंगा, adj. stark naked. नंगा-लुच्चा, adj. stark naked; shameless; base. नंगा-सिर, adj. bare-headed.

नंगाई *naṅgāī* [cf. H. *naṅgā*], adj. nakedness; bareness.

नंगापन *naṅgāpan* [cf. H. *naṅgā*], m. nakedness.

नँगियाना *naṁgiyānā* [cf. H. *naṅgā*], v.t. reg. to make naked.

नंद *nand* [S.], m. **1.** joy, delight. **2.** fig. son. **3.** *mythol.* name of the foster-father of Kr̥ṣṇa. 4. = ननद. — नंद-किशोर, m. son of Nand: a title of Kr̥ṣṇa. नंद-कुमार, m. id. नंद-दुलारो, m. Brbh. Nand's dear (son): a title of Kr̥ṣṇa. नंद-नंदन, m. the delight of Nand: a title of Kr̥ṣṇa. नंद-लाल, m. Nand's dear (son): a title of Kr̥ṣṇa.

नंदक *nandak* [S.], adj. & m. **1.** adj. making happy (esp. family, dependants). **2.** m. name of Kr̥ṣṇa's sword.

नंदन *nandan* [S.], adj. & m. **1.** adj. gladdening, delighting. **2.** m. a son. **3.** title of Viṣṇu, and of Śiva. **4.** *mythol.* name of a garden in paradise (= the heaven of Indra). — नंदन-वन, m. = ~, 4. नंदन-वाटिका, f. = ~, 4.

नंदा *nandā* [S.], f. **1.** joy. **2.** prosperity. **3.** title of Durgā.

नंदिक *nandik* [S.], m. the toon-tree or Indian mahogany, *Cedrela toona.*

नंदिनी *nandinī* [S.], f. **1.** daughter. **2.** *Pl. HŚS.* husband's sister (= ननद).

नंदी *nandī* [S.], adj. & m. **1.** adj. finally in comp. rejoicing. **2.** [? × *nandika-*] a name given to several trees (as the fig, banyan, toon-tree). **3.** m. name of the bull of Śiva.

नंदोई *nandoī* [*nanāndr̥pati-*], m. husband of a husband's sister, brother-in-law.

नंबर *nambar* [Engl. *number*], m. f. **1.** number; particular number (as of telephone, house, periodical). **2.** mark, position (as in examination). **3.** transf. rank (military, &c). **4.** turn. ~ आना (का), (one's) turn to come round, or up. — ~ देना (को), to number; to mark (an examination paper), to class. एक ~ का, adj. = नंबरी. – अच्छा ~ पाना, to get a good mark, or result. अच्छे ~ पाना, to get good marks. नंबरदार [P. *-dār*], m. the representative of a community of cultivators responsible for the payment of their revenue, village headman. नंबरवार [P. *-vār*], adv. numbered; in order, by number; by turns.

नंबरी *nambărī* [cf. H. *nambar*], adj. **1.** numbered; by number. **2.** of the first rank, prime, notorious. **3.** of high value (a bank-note).

न *na* [*na*], adv. **1.** not. **2.** no; rhetor. is it not so? **3.** (finally, rhetor.) why not, why don't you? अंदर जाओ न, just go in. **4.** (ellipt. for न … न.) (neither) … nor. — ~ करना, to refuse. ~ … ~, neither … nor. आप जानते हैं ~? you know, don't you? वहाँ जो गाड़ी खड़ी है ~, वह …, do you see the car over there? it ….

नक- *nak-*. the nose (cf. नाक).

नककटा *nakkaṭā*, adj. & m. **1.** adj. = नकटा. **2.** m. = नकटा. **3.** a type of indecent song (sung by women at marriages).

नककटी *nakkaṭī* [H. *nāk*+H. *kaṭnā*], f. having the nose cut off: disgrace, infamy.

नकघिसनी *nakghisnī* [H. *nāk*+H. *ghisnā*], f. rubbing the nose (on the ground, in prostration). — ~ करना, to entreat humbly.

नकचढ़ा *nakcaṛhā* [H. *nāk*+H. *caṛhnā*], adj. having the nose turned up: **1.** haughty. **2.** bad-tempered, irritable. **3.** angry.

नकटा *nakṭā* [H. *nāk*+H. *kaṭnā*], adj. & m. **1.** adj. having the nose cut off, noseless. **2.** fig. disgraced, dishonoured. **3.** shameless. **4.** m. a man whose nose has been cut off. **5.** a villain. **6.** a shameless person. **7.** the comb-duck, *Sarkidiornis melanotos* (the drake has a swelling at the base of the bill). **8.** pej. a man having a small flat nose. — नकटी का जना, m. son of a shameless woman; one of base birth.

नकड़ा *nakṛā* [cf. H. *nāk*], m. *Pl. HŚS.* inflammation of the nose (in cattle).

नकतोड़ा *naktoṛā* [H. *nāk*+H. *toṛnā*], m. turning up the nose: **1.** sneering; jeer, gibe. **2.** colloq. flirtatious behaviour. — ~ करना, to sneer (at), &c.

नक़द *naqad* [A. *naqd*], adj. & m. **1.** adj. cash (payment); liquid (funds). **2.** prompt, or ready (payment). **3.** colloq. good, choice (article or goods). **4.** adv. for cash (of a purchase). **5.** m. ready money, cash. **6.** colloq. a fine fellow. — ~, or ~ में, ख़रीदना, to buy for cash.

नक़दी *naqdī* [A. *naqdī*], adj. **1.** having to do with cash or ready money; cash (a payment, &c.); in cash; funded. **2.** possessing ready money. — ~ करना, to convert into cash.

नक़ब *naqab* [A. *naqb*], f. *Pl. HŚS.* digging through or under a wall, breaking in. — ~ देना, or लगाना (में), to break in (to a house). – नक़बज़न [P. *-zan*], m. a housebreaker, burglar.

नकबेसर *nakbesar* [H. *nāk*+H. *besar*], m. Brbh. a heavy nose ring (worn as an ornament by women).

नक़ल *naql* [A. *naql*], f. transporting: **1.** copying. **2.** a copy; an imitation. **3.** mimicking, mimicry. **4.** a duplicate. **5.** an anecdote, story. — ~ उतारना, or बनाना, to make a copy (of, की). ~ करना (की), = id.; to imitate, to mimic; to impersonate. ~ मारना (की), to copy fraudulently. – नक़लनवीस [P. *-navīs*], m. a copyist; clerk, recorder. नक़ल-बही, f. record-book. नक़लबाज़ [P. *-bāz*], m. an imitator. °ई, f.

नक़लची *naqlcī* [cf. A. *naql*], m. one who copies, or imitates.

नक़लिया *naqliyā* [cf. H. *naql*], m. reg. **1.** an actor, mime. **2.** a jester, joker, clown.

नक़ली *naqlī* [A. *naqlī*], adj. **1.** imitated; artificial; synthetic. **2.** copied fraudulently; counterfeit; forged. **3.** spurious.

नकवा *nakvā* [cf. H. *nāk*], m. reg. **1.** the nose. **2.** point, end. **3.** eye of a needle. **4.** point of supension (of beam of a pair of scales). **5.** *Pl.* a disease of the nose.

नकवासा *nakvāsā*, m. *Pl.* = नकवा, 5.

नकसीर *naksīr* [**nakkasirā-*: Pk. *ṇakkasirā-*], f. bleeding of the nose. — ~ फूटना, or चलना, or छूटना, the nose to bleed. ~ फोड़ना (की), to cause (one's) nose to bleed.

नक़ाब *naqāb* [A. *niqāb*], m. f. **1.** a veil; hood. **2.** the end of the sari, used to hide the face. **3.* mask. — नक़ाबदार [P. *-dār*], adj. = next. नक़ाबपोश [P. *-poś*], adj. veiled; masked.

नकार *nakār* [cf. H. *na*], m. denial; refusal. — नकारात्मक [°*a*+*ā*°], adj. denying, negative (a response); opposing (a motion). नकारवाद, m. nihilism.

नकारना *nakārnā* [cf. H. *nakār*], v.t. **1.** to deny. **2.** not to agree.

नकारा *nakārā* [P. *nakāra*], adj. worthless, useless.

नक़ीब *naqīb* [A. *naqīb*], m. *Pl. HŚS.* a servant or herald who has the duty of proclaiming the titles of his master; adjutant, aide.

नक़ीर *naqīr* [A. *naqīr*], adj. insignificant, unimportant.

नकुल *nakul* [S.], m. mongoose.

नकेल *nakel* [**nakkakīla-*], f. **1.** halter-pin (fixed in an animal's nose, esp. that of a camel). **2.** halter.

नक्का *nakkā* [cf. H. *nāk*], adj. & m. *Pl.* **1.** adj. nasal. **2.** m. one who speaks through the nose. **3.** a single item: the ace (at cards or dice). **4.** *HŚS.* the eye of a needle. — नक्का-मूठ, m. a game played with cowrie shells, &c., odds or evens.

नक़्क़ारख़ाना *naqqārkhānā* [P. *naqqārkhāna*], m. place where drums are beaten (as at the porch of a palace, the gate of a mansion).

नक़्क़ारची *naqqārcī* [cf. P. *naqqāra*], m. a drummer.

नक़्क़ारा *naqqārā* [P. *naqqāra*], m. a kettledrum. — नक़्क़ारे की चोट, adv. with fanfare, publicly; openly. ~ बजाकर, adv. id. ~ बजाते फिरना, to proclaim on all sides.

नक़्क़ाल *naqqāl* [A. *naqqāl*], m. **1.** a mimic; imitator. **2.** an actor.

नक़्क़ाली *naqqālī* [A. *naqqāl*+P. *-ī*], f. **1.** mimicry. **2.** acting.

नक़्क़ाश *naqqāś* [A. *naqqāś*], m. **1.** painter, designer. **2.* a carver (in stone, wood or metal); sculptor. **3.** an embroiderer. **4.** a gilder (of books).

नक़्क़ाशी *naqqāśī* [P. *naqqāśī*], f. **1.** carving. **2.** engraving. **3.** sculpture, sculpted work. **4.** embroidery. — नक़्क़ाशीदार [P. *-dār*], adj. decorated with carving, sculpture, &c.

नक्की *nakkī* [cf. H. *nakkā*], f. a single item (= नक्का, 3). — ~ पर रखना, or लगाना, to hazard, to stake.

नक्कू *nakkū* [cf. H. *nāk*], adj. **1.** having a big nose. **2.** pej. haughty. **3.** headstrong. **4.** fig. notorious (a person). **5.** attracting mockery, ridiculous (a person). — ~ बनाना, or करना, to make infamous, or an object of scorn.

नक्र *nakr* [S.], m. Brbh. Av. a crocodile.

नक़श *naqś* [A. *naqś*], m. **1.** a painting, drawing. **2.** a carving. **3.** an impression. **4.** a magic device, design; charm, amulet. — ~ करना, to imprint, to impress; to engrave; to adorn with designs. ~ बैठाना, to make a strong impression (on, पर); to establish influence or authority (over). नक़शे पा [P. *pā*], m. footstep, footprint. – नक़शबंद [P. *-band*], m. painter; embroiderer. °ई, f.

नक़शा *naqśā* [A. *naqśa*], m. **1.** a picture; portrait. **2.** map. **3.** plan; sketch, draft; diagram; model, pattern. **4.** features (facial). **5.** fig. state of affairs, situation; prospects; predicament. **6.** a problem (in chess). **7.** an image (in the mind's eye). — ~ उतारना, or खींचना, or बनाना, to make a sketch (of, का), to sketch; to draw a map, plan, &c.; to trace, to copy. ~ जमाना, to make a plan, &c. (of, का); to lay the foundation, or basis (of, or for); to acquire influence, or ascendancy (over, पर). ~ तेज़ होना (का), prospects to be bright: (one's) star to be rising. – नक़शाकश [P. *kaś*], m. a draughtsman; map-maker. °ई, f. drawing plans; cartography. नक़शानवीस [P. *-navīs*], m. a draughtsman.

नक्षत्र *nakṣatr* [S.], m. **1.** a star; a planet, a heavenly body. **2.** a lunar asterism. — नक्षत्र-चक्र, m. a diagram for astrological calculations; the sphere of the fixed stars; the ring of lunar asterisms along the ecliptic. नक्षत्र-नाथ, m. lord of the stars: the moon. नक्षत्र-माला, f. a group of stars; a table of the lunar asterisms; = नक्षत्र-चक्र, 3.; a necklace of twenty-seven pearls. °-मालिनी, adj. f. spangled with stars. नक्षत्र-राज, m. king of the stars: the moon.

नक्षत्री *nakṣatrī* [S.], adj. & m. **1.** adj. born under a lucky star. **2.** m. a fortunate person, &c.

नख *nakh* [S.], m. **1.** nail (of the finger or toe). **2.** claw. — ~ से सिख तक, adv. from toe-nails to top-knot: from head to toe. – नख-रेख, f. Brbh. the mark or scratch of a nail, or claw. °आ, f. id. नख-शिख, m. = next. नख-सिख, adj. & adv. toe-nail to top-knot: systematic, all-embracing (of a conventionalised type of description, esp. of heroines, in poetry); entirely. नाखा-नखी, f. clawing at each other, fighting tooth and nail.

नख- *nakh-* [*nakṣati*], v.i. Brbh. to cross, to go beyond.

नखत *nakhat*, m. Brbh. Av. = नक्षत्र.

नखर *nakhar* [S.], m. *Pl. HŚS.* finger-nail; claw.

नख़रा *nakhrā* [P. *nakhră*], m. **1.** flirtatious airs or mannerisms. **2.** airs (of pride, disdain); affectation. **3.** whimsical behaviour. **4.** sham, pretence. — ~ करना, or बघारना, or लाना, to flirt; to show affectation, &c.; to put on a sham or show. – नख़रा-तिल्ला, m. =, ~ 1.-3. नख़रेबाज़ [P. *-bāz*], adj. & m., f. flirtatious; affected, &c.; given to pretence; a flirtatious person, &c. °ई, f. flirtatiousness, &c.

नखरौट *nakhrauṭ*, f. reg. the mark or scratch of a finger-nail or of a claw.

नख़ल *nakhl* [A. *nakhl*], m. a date-palm. — नख़लिस्तान, m. palm-grove.

नखलौ *nakhlau*, m. metath. colloq. = लखनऊ.

नख़ास *nakhās* [A. *nakhkhās*], m. **1.** a market (for livestock). **2.** *hist.* tax levied in some states on the sale of horses and cattle. — ~ की घोड़ी, f. sl. prostitute. ~ पर भेजना, or चढ़ाना, to send (stock) to market, to offer for sale.

नखियाना *nakhiyānā* [cf. H. *nakh*], v.t. to scratch, to claw.

[1]नखी *nakhī* [S.], adj. & m. *Pl.* **1.** adj. having nails, or claws. **2.** m. a wild beast.

[2]नखी *nakhī* [cf. H. *nakh*], f. *Pl.* **1.** a kind of perfume (so called from the shape of its fragments: see नख). **2.** *mus.* reg. quill, or wire ring worn on the finger, plectrum.

नग *nag* [S.], m. sthg. motionless: **1.** a mountain, rock; tree. **2.** a precious stone; a stone set in a signet-ring (= नगीना). **3.** reg. (in enumeration) an item. — नगधर, m. mountain-holder; a title of Kr̥ṣṇa. नग-पति, m. chief of mountains: the Himālayas. नग-पेच, m. a turban decorated with a jewel.

नगचा- *nagcā-* [cf. H. *nagīc*, *nazdīk*], v.i. reg. to approach, to draw near.

नगद *nagad*, m. pronun. var. = नक़द.

नगनी *nagnī* [ad. *nagnă-*], f. Brbh. a young (pre-adolescent) girl.

नग़मा *nagmā* [A. *nagma*], m. **1.** melodious voice or sound. **2.** song.

नगर *nagar* [S.], m. a city, a town; municipality. — नगर-निगम, m. = नगरपालिका. नगर-निवासी, adj. & n. = नगरवासी. नगरपाल, m. member of a city council. °-पालिका, f. city corporation; town or borough council. नगर-प्रमुख, m. mayor. नगर-महापालिका, f. = नगरपालिका.

नगरवासी, adj. & m. town-dwelling, urban; townsman, citizen. नगराध्यक्ष [°ra+a°], m. mayor. नगरोपांत [°ra+u°], m. outer suburb.

¹**नगरी** *nagărī* [cf. H. *nagar*], f. a small town; a town; village.

²**नगरी** *nagărī* [cf. H. *nagar*], adj. & m. **1.** adj. having to do with a town or city; civic; urban. **2.** m. an inhabitant of a town or city, townsman.

नगरीय *nagărīyă* [S.], adj. = ²नगरी, 1.

नगरौथा *nagarauthā* [-*musta*-; ad. *nāgara*-], m. reg. a tuberous sedge of the genus *Cyperus*.

नगला *naglā* [cf. H. *nagar*], m. a village.

नगीच *nagīc*, adj. & ppn. corr. = नज़दीक.

नगीना *nagīnā* [P. *nagīna*], m. **1.** a precious stone (esp. as set in a ring). **2.** a signet-ring. — ~ जड़ना, to set a stone (in, में). ~ सा, adj. like a stone set in a ring: pretty, charming.

नग्न *nagnă* [S.], adj. naked.

नग्नता *nagnătā* [S.], f. nakedness.

नच- *nac-* [*nṛtyati*], v.i. Brbh. = नाचना.

नचनिया *nacniyā* [cf. H. *nācnā*], m. a dancer.

नचवाना *nacvānā* [cf. H. *nācnā*], v.t. **1.** to cause to be danced (by, से). 2. = नचाना.

नचाना *nacānā* [cf. H. *nācnā*], v.t. **1.** to cause to dance. **2.** fig. to make (one) jump (to commands, requests), to harass, to trouble; to lead (one) a dance. **3.** to spin (a top, &c).

नज़दीक *nazdīk* [P. *nazdīk*], adv. **1.** near; close. **2.** ppn. (w. के) near (to). **3.** approximately, almost. **4.** on the point (of). **5.** in the opinion (of).

¹**नज़दीकी** *nazdīkī* [P. *nazdīkī*], f. proximity, vicinity.

²**नज़दीकी** *nazdīkī* [P. *nazdīk*+-*ī*], adj. & m. **1.** adj. = नज़दीक. **2.** m. a near relative; close associate.

नज़म *nazm* [A *naẓm*], f. U. order, arrangement: **1.** poetry. **2.** a poem.

¹**नज़र** *nazar* [A. *naẓar*], f. **1.** sight. **2.** look, glance. **3.** observation; inspection; supervision. **4.** favour, regard. **5.** view, opinion. **6.** prospect, intention. **7.** point of view, regard. **8.** influence of the evil eye. — ~ आना, to come into view, to appear, to appear as. ~ उठाना, to raise the eyes (to, की ओर, पर). ~ उतारना, or झाड़ना, to remove the effect of the evil eye. ~ करना (पर), to observe; to supervise. ~ खाना, to be affected by the evil eye, to be bewitched. ~ चढ़ना, to take the eye or fancy (of, के). ~ चुराना, = आँख चुराना. ~ डालना, to throw a glance (at, पर); to fix the eyes (on). ~ दौड़ाना, to run the eyes (in a direction, की तरफ़). ~ पड़ना (को), to fall under (one's) notice, to chance to be seen (by). ~, or नज़रों, पर चढ़ना, to be much liked, or envied (by, की); to attract the attention of (as of police). ~ फेंकना, to cast a glance. ~ बचाना (से), = आँख बचाना. ~ भरकर देखना, = आँख भरकर देखना, 1. ~ मारना, = आँख मारना. ~ में, adv. in sight (of, की); in the opinion (of). ~ में आना, = ~ आना. ~ में ~ मिलाना, to look straight at, to meet the eyes (of, की). ~ में, or नज़रों में, रखना, to keep in sight; to keep under one's own control. ~ रखना (पर), to behold; to keep the eye (on), to supervise, to attend (to); to be intent (on); to have in view, to intend; to look wistfully (at). ~ लगना, to be influenced by the evil eye. ~ लगाना, to cast an evil eye (upon, पर). ~ से, or नज़रों से, गिरना, to fall in the eyes (of, की); to fall into disgrace. ~ से, or नज़रों से, गिरा देना, to look down on, to hold cheap; to disgrace (in the eyes of others). नज़रों में गिरना, = नज़रों से गिरना. नज़रों में जँचना, to be appraised (by, की); to be approved of (by). नज़रों में तौलना, = id., 1. नज़रों में समाना, to be always before the eyes, or in the mind (of, की). नज़रों में होना, to be in view, in prospect. अपनी नज़रों में भरना, fig. to devour with the eyes. – नज़रंदाज़ [P. -*andāz*], adj. cast from sight: disregarded, unnoticed; rejected. °ई, f. casting the eye (upon): valuation, appraisal. नज़रबंद [P. -*band*], adj. & m. under surveillance; under house arrest; detained on parole; confined; a prisoner, detainee. नज़रबंद रखना, or करना, to keep under surveillance, &c.; to detain (a suspect). °ई, f. surveillance; house arrest; detention; deluding the sight: juggling, conjuring. नज़रबाज़ [P. -*bāz*], m. one who plays with, or deceives, the eyes: an ogler; a juggler. नज़र-सानी [A. *s̱ānī*], f. U. second inspection; revision; review (as of a decision).

²**नज़र** *nazar* [A. *naẕr*], f. an offering, gift (to a superior). — ~ करना, or देना, or गुज़ारना, to make an offering or gift (to, को).

नज़राना *nazrānā* [P. *naẕrāna*], m. 1. = ²नज़र. **2.** a customary payment or fee. **3.** a bribe.

नज़रिया *nazriyā* [A. *naẓarīya*], m. a point of view.

नज़ला *nazlā* [A. *nazla*], m. U. descent (of bodily humours): a cold; catarrh. — ~ उतरना, or गिरना, fig. any of several bodily functions (as sight, or hearing) to be impaired; (one's) displeasure to fall (on, पर).

नज़ाकत *nazākat* [conn. P. *nāzuk*], f. **1.** softness (cf. नाज़ुक). **2.** delicacy. **3.** elegance; politeness.

नजात *najāt* [A. *najāt*], f. U. **1.** escape; deliverance. **2.** salvation.

नज़ारा *nazārā* [A.: cf. P. *naẓ(ẓ)āra*], m. **1.** look, glance. **2.** sight, view; scene. — ~ करना (से), or मारना, to ogle. ~ लड़ाना, to exchange flirtatious glances. – नज़ारेबाज़ी [P. *-bāzī*], f. flirtatious glances, ogling.

नजीक *najīk*, adj. = नज़दीक.

नजीब *najīb* [A.], adj. U. of noble birth; honourable.

नज़ीर *nazīr* [A. *naẓīr*], f. U. **1.** an example, instance. **2.** a precedent.

नजूमी *najūmī* [A. *nujūmī*], m. an astrologer.

नट *naṭ* [S.], m. **1.** an actor. **2.** a dancer. **3.** a member of the *naṭ* community; juggler, acrobat. — नटखट, adj. naughty, mischievous; playful, roguish. °ई, f. नट-नागर, m. courtly dancer: a title of Kṛṣṇa. नटराज, m. king of the dance: a title of Śiva, and of Kṛṣṇa. नटवर, m. chief actor or dancer; skilful actor, &c. नटसाल, f. Brbh. a thorn piercing the flesh; the barb of an arrow; a pang. नटेश [°*ṭa*+*ī*°], m. lord of dancers: a title of Śiva. नटेश्वर, m. id.

नटखट *naṭkhaṭ* [? *anartha*-+H. *khaṭ*, *khaṭkhaṭānā*], adj. & m. **1.** adj. naughty, mischievous; roguish. **2.** m. a naughty child.

नटखटी *naṭkhaṭī* [cf. H. *naṭkhaṭ*], f. naughtiness.

[1]**नटना** *naṭnā* [? conn. *naṣṭa*-], v.i. to say 'no': **1.** to deny. **2.** to refuse.

[2]**नटना** *naṭnā* [*nartayati*], v.i. **1.** to dance. **2.** to act; to strut.

नटनी *naṭnī* [cf. H. *naṭ*], f. **1.** wife of a *naṭ*. **2.** actress, dancer, &c.

नटवा *naṭvā*, m. E.H. = नट.

नटा *naṭā* [cf. H. [2]*naṭnā*], m. the fever-nut (a climbing shrub), *Caesalpinia bonducella*.

नटी *naṭī* [S.], f. = नटनी.

नटेरना *naṭernā*, v.t. *Pl.* to close (the eyes) or turn up the pupils, as in death.

नड़ *naṛ* [*naḍa*-], m. a type of reed.

नड़ड़ा *naṛṛā* [cf. *naḍa*-], m. sthg. tubular: *Pl.* reg. the hard inner part of a carrot.

नत *nat* [S.], adj. **1.** bowed, lowered (as the head). **2.** bent, crooked. — नतमस्तक, adj. having the head (sc. brow) lowered (in devotion, deference, or in defeat). नतमुख, adj. having the face, or eyes, lowered. नतशिर, adj. id.

नतरु *nataru*, adv. Brbh. Av. = नातरु. — नतरुक, adv. id.

नति *nati* [S.], f. **1.** bowing, bending. **2.** a deferential greeting, bow. **3.** deferential manner. **4.** curvature; crookedness.

नतीजा *natījā* [A. *natīja*], m. **1.** result; consequence; outcome. **2.** inference. **3.** corollary; moral (of a story, &c). **4.** sum, substance. — ~ निकालना, to infer (from), to conclude. इसके नतीजे में, adv. as a result of this.

नतैत *natait* [cf. H. *nātā*], m. Brbh. a relative.

नत्थी *natthī* [conn. *nastā*-], f. a file (of papers) threaded together. — ~ करना, to string (papers) together, to attach, to file.

नथ *nath* [*nastā*-, Pk. *ṇatthā*-; ? ← Panj.], f. **1.** a large nose ring of gold or silver wire (worn on the left nostril by married women). **2.** hymen. ~ उतरना (की), virginity to be lost. — ~ बढ़ाना, to take off the nose ring, to become a widow.

[1]**नथना** *nathnā* [cf. *nastā*-, Pk. *ṇatthā*-], m. **1.** septum of the nose; nostril. **2.** a large nose ring. — नथने फुलाना, or चढ़ाना, to distend the nostrils: to be angry, or displeased. नथनों में दम आना, = नाक में दम आना. प्राण नथनों तक आना, the vital breath to reach the nostrils: to be exhausted (by cares, or by physical effort).

[2]**नथना** *nathnā* [cf. H. *nāthnā*], v.i. **1.** to have the nose bored, and a string passed through it (a bullock). **2.** to be pierced. **3.** to be filed (papers). **4.** transf. to be constantly toiling (as a bullock).

नथनी *nathnī* [cf. H. [2]*nathnā*], f. **1.** a nose ring (see नथ). **2.** a jewel worn in the nose. **3.** cord attached to a bullock's nose.

नथली *nathlī*, f. reg. 1. = [1]नथना, 1. 2. = नथनी, 2., 3.

नथुना *nathunā*, m. = [1]नथना.

नद *nad* [S.], m. **1.** a river the name of which is masculine, e.g. the Brahmaputra, Son, Indus. ***2.** a large river.

नदना *nadnā* [cf. H. *nādh*-], v.i. to be tied; to be clenched (fist).

नदारद *nadārad* [P. *na dārad* 'it has not'], adj. **1.** absent, wanting. **2.** finished, consumed (as a lamp that has gone out). **3.** gone, lost; extinct.

नदी *nadī* [S.], f. a river.

नदीदा *na-dīdā* [P. *nadīda*], adj. **1.** unseen. **2.** who has not seen: greedy; eager, longing. — नदीदों की तरह ताकना, to stare greedily, or wistfully (at).

ननंद *nanand*, f. reg. = ननद.

ननका *nankā* [cf. H. *nanhā*], m. little child, son (an expression of endearment).

ननद *nanad* [*nanăndṛ-*], m. husband's sister, sister-in-law. — ~ के बीर, or भाई, sister-in-law's brother: husband (auspicious form of reference on a wife's part).

ननदिनी *nanadinī*, f. = ननद.

ननदी *nanădī*, f. = ननद.

ननसार *nansār*, f. Brbh. = ननिहाल.

ननिया *naniyā* [**nānna-*: Pk. *ṇaṇṇa-*], adj. inv. having to do with a maternal grandfather. — ~ ससुर, m. husband of mother-in-law's mother. ~ सास, f. mother-in-law's mother.

ननिहाल *nanihāl* [cf. **nānnī-*], m. /nənijal/. **1.** house and family of a maternal grandfather. **2.** maternal kindred.

नन्हाँ *nanhāṁ*, adj. see नन्हा.

नन्हा *nanhā* [*ślakṣṇa-*], adj. & m. **1.** adj. little, small; tiny; young. **2.** trivial, petty; of low status (as a community). **3.** m. a darling child.

नपना *napnā* [cf. H. *nāpnā*], v.i. **1.** to be measured; to be surveyed (land). **2.** to be measured (against, से). **3.** colloq. to square off against, to clash or to quarrel (with).

नपाई *napāī* [cf. H. *nāpnā*], f. *HŚS.* measuring; surveying.

नपुंसक *napuṃsak* [S.], adj. & m. not virile: **1.** adj. impotent; effeminate. **2.** sexless, neuter. **3.** unmanly, cowardly. **4.** *gram.* neuter. **5.** m. an impotent man, &c. **6.** a eunuch. **7.** an unmanly person. **8.** *gram.* neuter gender.

नपुंसकता *napuṃsakătā* [S.], f. **1.** impotence, &c. **2.** cowardice.

नफ़र *nafar* [A. *nafar*], m. U. **1.** a servant. ***2.** an individual.

नफ़रत *nafrat* [A. *nafra*: P. *nafrat*], m. aversion, abhorrence; hatred. — ~ करना, or खाना, to feel disgust or loathing (for, से).

नफ़री *nafrī* [P. *nafrī*], f. a day's work, or wage.

[1]**नफ़स** *nafs* [A. *nafs*], m. U. breath of life, soul; animating force.

[2]**नफ़स** *nafas* [A.], m. U. **1.** breath. **2.** a moment, an instant.

नफ़सानियत *nafsāniyat* [A. *nafsānīya*: P. *nafsāniyat*], f. U. carnal desire, lust.

नफ़सानी *nafsānī* [A. *nafsānī*], adj. U. carnal, lustful.

नफ़ा *nafā* [A. *naf'*], m. profit, gain, advantage. — ~ उठाना, or करना, or कमाना, to profit, to benefit (from, से). – नफ़ा-नुक़सान, m. profit and loss. नफ़ाबाज़ी [P. *-bāzī*], f. profiteering.

नफ़ासत *nafāsat* [A. *nafāsa*: P. *nafāsat*], f. **1.** exquisiteness, choiceness. **2.** refinement; elegance.

नफ़ीरी *nafīrī* [P. *nafīrī*], f. *Pl. HŚS.* **1.** a small trumpet. **2.** *mus.* a small pipe.

नफ़ीस *nafīs* [A. *nafīs*], adj. **1.** exquisite; choice. **2.** refined; elegant.

नफ़्स *nafs*, m. see [1]नफ़स.

नबज़ *nabz* [A. *nabẓ*], f. the pulse. ~ पहचानना, to have one's finger on the pulse (of, की). नबज़ें छूटना, the pulse to be absent.

नबी *nabī* [A. *nabī*], m. a prophet.

नब्बे *nabbe*, adj. see नव्वे.

नभ *nabh* [S.], m. **1.** the sky, the heavens. **2.** space. **3.** *chronol.* zero. **4.** *Pl. HŚS.* names of the months Sāvan or Bhādoṃ (July-September). — नभग, m. Av. a bird. °-नाथ, m. *mythol.* Garuṛ. नभचर, adj. & m. 19c. = next. नभश्चर, adj. & m. sky-going: flying, aerial; a bird; a cloud; a heavenly being, or body. नभ-स्थल, m. = ~, 1. °ई, f. id. नभस्थित, adj. living, or to be found, in the sky.

नम *nam* [P. *nam*], adj. & f.(?) **1.** adj. moist, damp; humid. **2.** f.(?) = नमी.

नम- *nam-*, v.i. Av. to bow down.

नमक *namak* [P. *namak*], m. **1.** salt. **2.** transf. savour, flavour. **3.** fig. means of subsistence. **4.** charm; grace. — ~ अदा करना, to be faithful to one's salt, to discharge obligations. ~ का तेज़ाब, m. hydrochloric acid. ~ का सहारा, m. fig. help in a trivial matter. ~ चखना (का), to taste or to try the savour (of food). ~ फूटकर निकलना, (one's) salt to break out in sores (on the body): to be ungrateful, disloyal. घाव पर, or कटे पर, ~ छिड़कना, or लगाना, to rub (to sprinkle) salt on a wound). सेंधा ~, m. rock salt. नमकख़्वार [P. *-khvār*], m. one eating (a person's) salt: servant; dependant. नमकदान, m. salt-cellar. °ई, f. id. नमक-मिर्च, f. salt and chilli: spicing. नमक-मिर्च लगाना, or मिलाना, to add spice; to add vividness, colour (to a description); to exaggerate. नमकसार [P. *-sār*], adj. salty; a salt-pit. नमक-हराम, adj. & m. untrue to one's salt: ungrateful; disloyal, disobedient; an ungrateful wretch, &c. °ई, f. ingratitude; disloyalty, &c. नमक-हलाल, adj. & m. grateful; loyal, true; dutiful; a loyal, or dutiful person. °ई, f. gratitude; loyalty.

नमकीन *namkīn* [P. *namkīn*], adj. & m. **1.** adj. salty; salted. **2.** saline, brackish. **3.** fig. racy. **4.** charming, attractive. **5.** m. salted food.

नमकीनी *namkīnī* [P. *namkīnī*], f. **1.** saltiness, &c. **2.** attractiveness of complexion.

नमदा *namdā* [P. *namda*], m. **1.** felt. **2.** rug, coarse carpet (to sit on, or to spread out wares on, &c). — ~ बँधना, (one's) carpet to be folded up: to have become bankrupt.

नमन *naman* [S.], m. & adj. **1.** m. bowing down. **2.** salutation, greeting. **3.** adj. bowed, bending; stooping.

नमस *namas* [S.], m. bowing; bow; salutation, greeting. — नमस्कार, m. and interj. uttering the word '*namas*': greeting; respectful salutation; greetings!; honour to! नमस्कार करना (को), to greet, &c. नमस्ते, m. & interj. greetings to you: = नमस्कार.

नमस्य *namasyă* [S.], adj. **1.** to be worshipped. **2.** to be respected; venerable.

नमस्यित *namasyit* [S.], adj. *Pl. HŚS.* reverenced; worshipped.

नमाज़ *namāz* [P. *namāz*], m. prayer (esp. the prayers prescribed by Islamic law, to be said five times daily). — ~ पढ़ना, or करना, to say (one's) prayers. – नमाज़-गाह, f. the place in a mosque where prayers are read.

नमाज़ी *namāzī* [P. *namāzī*], adj. & m. **1.** adj. having to do with prayers. **2.** devout; pure. **3.** m. a prayer-cloth. **4.** one who prays: a devout Muslim.

नमित *namit* [S.], adj. **1.** bowed, bent down. **2.** bowing in humble greeting.

नमी *namī* [P. *namī*], f. moistness; humidity.

नमूद *namūd* [P. *namūd*], f. **1.** appearance. **2.** prominence. **3.** show, pomp, display. **4.** honour. — नमूदार [P. *-ār*], adj. apparent, evident.

नमूदार *namūdār*, adj. see s.v. नमूद.

नमूदिया *namūdiyā* [cf. H. *namūd*], m. a boaster.

नमूना *namūnā* [P. *namūna*], m. **1.** a sample, specimen. **2.** pattern, model. **3.** example. **4.** type, form.

नमेरू *namerū* [ad. *nameru-*], m. a large tree, *Eleocarpus ganitrus* (of which the nuts are used in rosaries).

नम्मा *nammā* [*navaka-*²], m. a nine (as in multiplication, or cards).

नम्र *namr* [S.], adj. **1.** bent, bowed down. **2.** mild (of manner); affable, courteous. **3.** humble, reverential. **4.** submissive.

नम्रता *namrătā* [S.], f. bent or bowed state: . **1.** mildness. **2.** humility. **3.** submissiveness; obeisance. — ~ करना, to practise humility (towards, से); to be mild, or meek.

नय *nay* [S.], m. *Pl. HŚS.* **1.** guiding, leading. **2.** course or way of life (= नीति). **3.** prudence; policy. **4.** statesmanship. **5.** plan, design. **6.** principle. **7.** justness, fitness.

नय- *nay-* [*namati*], v.i. Brbh. = नव-.

¹**नयन** *nayan* [S.], m. leading, guiding.

²**नयन** *nayan* [S.], m. the eye. — नयन-पट, m. Av. eyelid.

नयनिमा *nayănimā* [S.], f. sight, vision.

नया *nayā* [*naviya-*], adj. **1.** new; novel. **2.** fresh; young, inexperienced. **3.** recent; modern. **4.** strange. — ~ करना, to renew; to renovate; to taste for the first time; to eat the first fruits (of); euph. to burn (old clothes). ~ फल, m. first fruits. नए सिरे से, adv. from the beginning, over again; anew. नए सिरे से जन्म लेना, to be born again; to obtain a new lease of life. – नया-पुराना होना, to cease to be new; to lose novelty; to continue as before (a practice).

नयापन *nayāpan* [cf. H. *nayā*], m. newness, novelty; modernity.

¹**नर** *nar* [*nara-*], m. **1.** a man, a male. **2.** man, mankind. — नर-केसरी, m. Av. man-lion: = नर-सिंह. नर-नारी, m. pl. men and women. नर-देह, m. the human body; fig. life or birth as a man. नर-तन, m. Av. id. °उ, m. id. नर-नाह, m. Brbh. Av. lord of men: = नरेश. नर-पति, m. lord of men: king, prince. नर-पाल, m. protector of men: king. नर-पुर, m. abode of men: the world. नर-भक्षी, m. a cannibal. नर-रूप, m. & adj. human form; having human form. °ई, adj. id. नर-लोक, m. the world of men, the earth. नरवई, m. Brbh. = नर-पति. नर-वध, m. homicide, murder. नर-सिंगा, m. = next. नर-सिंघा, m. a trumpet, horn (curved in shape). °-सिंघिया, m. trumpeter. नर-सिंह, m. the man-lion or fourth avatār of Viṣṇu (= नृसिंह). नर-हत्या, f. homicide, murder. नर-हरि, m. = नर-सिंह. नराकार [°*ra*+*ā*°], adj. having human form. नराधम [°*ra*+*a*°], m. a base man, villain. नरेंद्र [°*ra*+*i*°], m. id. नरेश [°*ra*+*ī*°], m. lord of men: king, prince. नरेतर [°*ra*+*i*°], m. one other than man: a god; a living creature (not human). नरोत्तम [°*ra*+*u*°], m. best of men: a title of Viṣṇu.

²**नर** *nar* [P. *nar*], m. & adj. **1.** m. a male: the male of an animal; a cock bird. **2.** adj. male. — नर-मादा, m. male and female (animals; or as in describing a screw-thread).

नरई *naraī* [cf. *naḍa-*], f. **1.** stalk (of wheat, &c). **2.** stubble.

नरक *narak* [S.], m. hell. — ~ भुगतना, or भोगना, to suffer the pangs of hell. ~ में पड़ना, to be cast into hell. – नरक-कुंड, m. *hind.* a pit in hell (one of many such, where the wicked are tormented). नरक-वास, m. abode in hell.

नरकट *narkaṭ* [*naḍa-*; and ad. *kaṭa-*[2]], m. = नरकुल.

नरकुल *narkul* [? *naḍa-*; +*kaṭa-*[2]], m. a kind of large reed.

नरकी *narǎkī* [cf. H. *narak*], adj. hellish; infernal.

नरगिस *nargis* [P. *nargis*: ← Gk.], f. the narcissus.

नरगिसी *nargisī* [P. *nargisī*], adj. & f. **1.** adj. having to do with or resembling the narcissus; lovely. **2.** f. a type of embroidered cloth, or garment.

नरजा *narjā* [? ad. *nārācī-*], m. a goldsmith's scales.

नरत- *nart-* [cf. *nṛtyati*], v.i. Brbh. to dance.

नरता *narǎtā* [S.], f. human state or condition.

नरम *narm* [P. *narm*], adj. **1.** soft; easily digestible. **2.** mild, gentle; moderate (in views). **3.** low, subdued (as a tone); indifferent (health). **4.** moderate (as a price). **5.** slack (as trade); depressed (a market). **6.** worn, defaced (a coin). — ~ **कोयला**, m. peat. ~ **दल**, m. *pol.* a moderate party; the moderates. – **नरम-गरम**, adj. & m. moderate (of heat); changeable (of temperament); varying (in quality, price); things good and bad, of varying quality. **नरम-गरम सहना**, to endure the vicissitudes (of, **के**). **नरमदली**, adj. moderate; liberal. **नरमदिल**, adj. tender-hearted.

नरमट *narmaṭ* [H. *narm*+H. *maṭṭī*], f. reg. soft clay soil.

नरमा *narmā* [cf. P. *narm*], m. reg. the silk-cotton plant, *Gossypium religiosum*.

नरमाई *narmāī* [cf. H. *narm*], f. = **नरमी**.

नरमाना *narmānā* [cf. H. *narm*], v.t. & v.i. **1.** v.t. to soften. **2.** to soothe, to pacify; to assuage. **3.** to reduce (as a price). **4.** v.i. to become soft. **5.** to grow gentle, or mild. **6.** to grow less.

नरमी *narmī* [P. *narmī*], f. **1.** softness; pliancy. **2.** mildness; easiness (of manner); want of firmness. **3.** moderateness (of price); reduction in prices. **4.** slackness (as of trade). — **नरमी-पसंद**, adj. *pol.* moderate.

नरसल *narsal* [cf. *naḍa-*], m. a kind of large reed.

नरसों *narsoṁ* [cf. H. *parsoṁ*], adv. three days previously, or ahead.

नराच *narāc* [ad. *nārāca-*], m. Brbh. an arrow.

नरिया *nariyā* [cf. *naḍa-*], f. reg. a roofing tile (of semi-circular section).

नरी *narī* [P. *narī*], f. sheepskin or kid leather; morocco leather.

नरूख *narūkh* [? H. *purukh* (ad. *puruṣa-*) × H. *nar*], adj. reg. male; masculine.

नरेट *nareṭ* [cf. *naḍa-*], m. reg. the throat, gullet.

नरेटी *nareṭī*, f. reg. = **नरेट**.

नर्तक *nartak* [S.], m. a dancer; a mime.

नर्तकी *nartǎkī* [S.], f. **1.** a female dancer. **2.** a dancing-girl.

नर्तन *nartan* [S.], m. dancing; miming.

नर्तित *nartit* [S.], adj. **1.** in motion, dancing. **2.** danced.

नर्द *nard* [P. *nard*], f. U. a counter, piece (in a board game).

नल *nal* [*naḍa-*], m. **1.** a species of reed; a hollow shaft of bamboo. **2.** a tube, pipe; spout. **3.** water-channel. **4.** sewer, drain. **5.** urethra. — ~ **की कोठरी**, f. bathroom, wash-room; lavatory.

नलका *nalkā* [Panj. **नलका**], m. = **नल**, 1., 2.

नलकी *nalkī* [cf. H. *nalkā*], f. **1.** a small reed, or pipe, &c. (see **नल**). **2.** a small drain.

नलद *nalad* [S.], m. **1.** a perennial herb, *Nardostachys jatamansi*, the source of a perfume: Indian spikenard (= **जटामासी**). **2.** the grass *Andropogon muraticus* (= **ख़स**).

नलवा *nalvā* [cf. H. *nal*], m. reg. **1.** a small tube or pipe. **2.** straw, stalk; stubble.

नला *nalā* [*naḍaka-*], m. **1.** a large pipe, water-pipe. **2.** urethra. **3.** sewer. **4.** *Pl. HŚS.* a long bone (as thigh, shin or arm).

नलिन *nalin* [S.], m. a lotus; a water-lily.

नलिनी *nalinī* [S.], f. **1.** a lotus. **2.** a bed of lotuses.

नलिया *naliyā* [cf. H. *nal*], m. reg. a bird-catcher (who uses a limed bamboo).

नली *nalī* [cf. H. *nalā*], f. **1.** a hollow reed. **2.** a tube, pipe; spout. **3.** barrel (of a firearm). **4.** shinbone. **5.** a vessel, esp. of the body; windpipe; urethra; capillary.

[1]**नव** *nav* [S.], adj. **1.** new; neo-. **2.** fresh, first; recent. **3.** young. — **नवजागरण**, m. reawakening; renaissance. **नवजात**, adj. new-born. **नवयुवक**, m. = **नौजवान** s.v. [1]**नौ-**. °-**युवती**, f. girl, young woman. **नवगौवन**, m. youth; prime of life. °**आ**, f. = **नवयुवती**. **नव-श्राद्ध**, m. the first series of sacrifices performed to the spirit of a deceased relative (on alternate days from the first to the eleventh after death). **नवागंतुक** [°*va*+*ā*°], adj. &

m. = next. नवागत [°va+ā°], adj. & m. newly arrived; a new arrival. नवागमन [°va+ā°], m. arrival, recent arrival, or appearance. नवान्न [°va+a°], m. *Pl. HŚS.* new rice, or grain; a ceremony observed on first eating new rice or grain; freshly cooked food. नवाभ्युत्थान [°va+a°], m. = नवोत्थान. नवीकरण, m. renewal; restoration; modernisation. innovator. °-ईकृत, adj. made new, renewed, &c. नवीभूत, adj. become new, renewed; revived. नवोदक [°va+u°], m. new water: first rains; the first water taken from a new well. नवोढ़ा [°va+o°], f. a newly married woman; *rhet.* a woman afraid or embarrassed to keep an assignation. नवोत्थान [°va+u°], m. revival, regeneration. नवोन्मेष [°va+u°], adj. emergence, new currency; mode, fashion. °ई, adj.

²**नव** *nav* [S.], adj. nine. — नवखंड, m. *mythol.* the nine divisions of *Jambudvīp*, the (known) world. नवग्रह, m. the 'nine planets' (viz. sun, moon, Mars, Mercury, Jupiter, Saturn, Venus, with Rāhu and Ketu). नवद्वार, m. & adj. the nine openings of the body; nine-doored; the body. नवधा, adj. inv. ninefold; nine times; of nine kinds (devotion, esp. as specified by the *Bhāgavata Purāṇa*). नव-निधि, f. *mythol.* the treasure of Kuvera (consisting of nine fabulous gems). नवरंग, m. the pitta (a small multicoloured bird). नवरत्न, m. the nine jewels (viz. pearl, ruby, topaz, diamond, emerald, lapis lazuli, coral, sapphire, and one called *gomeda*); nine paragons (of literature: esp. as at the court of Vikramāditya). नवरस, m. the nine savours or pleasures (of aesthetic emotion). नवरात्र, m. the first nine days of the light half of the month Āśvin (during which Durgā is worshipped). °-रात्रि, f. id.

नव- *nav-* [*namati*], v.i. Brbh. Av. **1.** to bow, to bend down; to stoop. **2.** fig. to submit.

नवंबर *navambar* [Engl. *November*], m. November.

नवनीत *navnīt* [S.], m. fresh butter.

नवम *navam* [S.], adj. ninth.

नवमी *navămī* [S.], adj. the ninth day of a lunar fortnight.

नवल *navăl* [S.; and *navala-*], adj. & m. **1.** adj. new; novel. **2.** fresh (as new season's growth). **3.** young. **4.** beautiful; bright, clear. **5.** m. a sapling.

नवली *navlī* [cf. H. *naval*], f. reg. **1.** freshness (as of youth). **2.** newness, youngness. **3.** clearness, brightness; bloom.

नवाँ *navāṁ* [*navama-*], adj. ninth.

¹**नवा** *navā* [*nava-*], adj. reg. = नया.

²**नवा** *navā* [P. *navā*], m. *Pl. HŚS.* **1.** voice, sound. **2.** song; tune.

³**नवा** *navā*, m. reg. = नाई.

नवा- *navā-* [cf. H. *nayā*, ¹*nava-*], v.t. Brbh. to make new, to renew.

नवाज- *navāj-* [cf. P. *navāz*], v.t. **1.** to show favour or mercy. **2.** to cherish. **3.** to caress, to coax.

-नवाज़ *-navāz* [P. *navāz*], adj. showing favour, or mercy, &c. (see नवाज-). — बंदानवाज़, m. cherisher of slaves or servants, kindly lord.

नवाज़िश *navāziś* [P. *navāziś*], f. **1.** kindness; favour. **2.** courtesy; courtliness.

नवाज़ी *navāzī* [P. *navāzī*], f. **1.** kindness. **2.** courtesy.

नवाड़ा *navāṛā*, m. 19c. a boat; barge.

नवाना *navānā* [cf. *namayati*], v.t. **1.** to bend, to bow. **2.** to cause to bow, or to stoop.

नवाब *navāb* [A. *navvāb*], m. **1.** *hist.* governor (of a town or region), nabob; lord, prince. **2.** fig. one who flaunts his wealth or power. — नवाबज़ादा [P. *-zāda*], m. son of a *navāb*; = ~, 2. °-ज़ादी, f.

नवाबी *navābī* [A. *navvāb*+P. *-ī*], adj. & f. **1.** adj. having to do with a *navāb*, or with the later Mughal period. **2.** f. position or status of *navāb*. **3.** the later Mughal period. **4.** anarchy, misrule. **5.** princely luxury. — ~ करना, to live like a prince.

नवारी *navārī*, f. *Pl. HŚS.* = नेवारी.

नवासा *navāsā* [P. *navāsa, nabīsa*], m. daughter's son, grandson.

¹**नवासी** *navāsī* [cf. H. *navāsā*], f. daughter's daughter, granddaughter.

²**नवासी** *navāsī* [*navāśīti-*], adj. eighty-nine.

नवीकरण *navīkaraṇ* [S.], m. see s.v. ¹नव.

नवीकृत *navīkr̥t* [S.], adj. see s.v. ¹नव-.

नवीन *navīn* [S.], adj. **1.** new; novel. **2.** fresh. **3.** recent; modern. **4.** young. — नवीनीकरण, m. making new, renewal.

नवीनता *navīnătā* [S.], f. **1.** newness; novelty. **2.** freshness. **3.** recentness; modernity.

नवीनीकरण *navīnīkaraṇ* [S.], m. see s.v. नवीन.

नवीभूत *navībhūt* [S.], adj. see s.v. ¹नव.

नवेला *navelā* [cf. *nava-*¹], adj. & m. **1.** adj. new; novel. **2.** young. **3.** rare, unusual; wonderful; beautiful. **4.** sprightly (of manner), smart (of dress) (= बाँका, 3). **5.** m. a handsome, or smartly dressed young man.

नवेली *navelī* [cf. H. *navelā*], f. a beautiful young woman.

नव्य *navyă* [S.], adj. **1.** new. **2.** recent, modern.

नव्यता *navyătā* [S.], f. **1.** newness; novelty. **2.** freshness. **3.** modernity.

नव्वे *navve* [*navati-*], adj. ninety.

नशा *naśā* [P. *naśa*], m. **1.** intoxication; stupor. **2.** intoxicant, alcohol. **3.** a narcotic. **4.** fig. pride; conceit; self-delusion. — ~ उतरना, to become sober, to return to one's senses. ~ करना, to intoxicate; to be in the habit of, or to be addicted to, alcohol or drugs. ~ किरकिरा हो जाना, intoxication to grate (on one): to be brought to one's senses. ~ चढ़ना, or जमना, drink to go to the head. ~ छाना, drink to cloud (the brain, the eyes). ~ टूटना, = ~ उतरना. ~ हिरन हो जाना, intoxication to flee (like a deer): to sober up in an instant. ~ होना (को), to be drunk, &c. नशे का उतार, or ख़ुमार, m. sobering up; hangover. नशे में, adv. in stupor, drunk. नशे में चूर, adv. dead drunk. – नशाख़ोर [P. *-khor*], a drunkard; one who takes drugs. °ई, f. नशा-पानी, m. alcohol; drugs; intoxication, stupor. नशा-पानी करना, to take alcohol, &c.; to drink heavily. नशाबंदी [P. *-bandī*], f. prohibition on alcohol. नशेदार [P. *-dār*], adj. intoxicating. नशेबाज़ [P. *-bāz*], m. = नशाख़ोर. °ई, f.

नशीला *naśīlā* [cf. H. *naśā*], adj. **1.** intoxicating (drink). **2.** intoxicated. **3.** drowsy, drooping (eyes).

नश्तर *naśtar* [P. *niśtar*], f. m. a lancet. — ~ देना, or लगाना (को), to lance; to bleed (v.t).

नश्वर *naśvar* [S.], adj. **1.** perishing; transitory. **2.** destructive, mischievous.

नश्वरता *naśvarătā* [S.], f. perishable nature, transitoriness.

नष्ट *naṣṭ* [S.], adj. **1.** destroyed; ruined. **2.** squandered. **3.** doomed (a life, to failure); base, immoral. **4.** lost, vanished. — ~ करना, to destroy, &c. – नष्टचित्त, adj. whose consciousness is destroyed: crazed; dead drunk; unconscious. नष्टचेष्ट, adj. apathetic. नष्ट-प्राय, adj. almost destroyed; about to be destroyed. नष्ट-भ्रष्ट, adj. utterly destroyed. नष्टार्थ [°*ṭa*+*a*°], adj. having lost (one's) property, wealth; changed in meaning (a word).

नष्टत्वा *naṣṭatvā* [S.], f. state of destruction or ruin.

नष्टि *naṣṭi* [S.], f. *HŚS.* destruction (= नाश).

नस *nas* [*snasā-*, Pk. *ṇasā-*], f. **1.** a vein. **2.** a sinew, tendon. **3.** a muscle. **4.** a nerve. **5.** transf. the genital organs. **6.** *bot.* vein, fibre. — ~ चढ़ना, a tendon or muscle to be strained or torn. ~, or नसें, ढीली होना, to be exhausted; to be dejected. ~ ~ में (की), adv. in every fibre (of one's body, or being). ~ भड़कना, = ~ चढ़ना; fig. to go out of one's mind. ~ पहचानना, to discern the real character (of, की). – नस-कटा, m. a eunuch. नसदार [P. *-dār*], adj. sinewy, veiny. नसबंदी [P. *-bandī*], f. ligature, vasectomy.

नस- *nas-* [*nasyati*], v.i. Brbh. **1.** to be destroyed. **2.** *Pl. HŚS.* to flee.

नसतालीक़ *nastālīq* [A. *nasta'līq*], m. a particular writing style of the Perso-Arabic script.

नसल *nasl* [A. *nasl*], f. **1.** offspring, descendants; family. ***2.** breed, stock; race. — ~ बढ़ाना (अपनी), to propagate (one's family line); to breed. – नसलकशी [P. *-kaśī*], f. breeding (animals). नसलवाद, m. racialism. °ई, m. racialist.

नसली *naslī* [A. *nasl*], adj. having to do with breed, stock, &c.; racial.

नसवार *nasvār*, f. snuff.

नसहा *nasăhā*, adj. veined, sinewy.

नसा- *nasā-*, v.t. & v.i. Brbh. Av. **1.** v.t. to destroy. **2.** v.i. to be destroyed.

नसावन *nasāvan* [cf. H. *nasā-*], adj. reg. destructive.

नसी *nasī* [conn. **nāsikā-*, H. *nāsī*], f. reg. (E.) ploughshare, or sole of a plough.

नसीब *nasīb* [A. *naṣīb*], m. **1.** (often pl.) destiny, fate, fortune. **2.** good fortune. क्या ~! what good luck! — ~ करना, to allot (to, को). ~ खुलना, or जागना (जगना), or चमकना (के), fortune to turn (one's) way. ~ फूटना, luck to change (for the worse); to have bad luck. ~ लड़ना, fortune to fight for or to favour (a person, का or के); one's luck to turn (for the better); to try one's luck. ~ होना, to fall to the lot (of, के or को), to have the good luck (to gain sthg.); to be destined (for). – नसीब-जला, adj. burnt, or doomed by fate: unlucky, wretched.

[1]**नसीला** *nasīlā* [cf. H. *nas*], adj. **1.** sinewy. **2.** veined.

[2]**नसीला** *nasīlā* [A. *nasl*+H. *-īlā*], adj. of good breed.

नसीहत *nasīhat* [A. *naṣīḥa*: P. *naṣīḥat*], f. **1.** advice, counsel; exhortation. **2.** reprimand. **3.** a chastening experience; punishment. **4.** will, testament. — ~ करना, = next. ~ देना (को), to advise.

नसीहा *nasīhā* [cf. *nasī*], m. reg. a plough having a light share (for soft soils).

नसेनी *nasenī*, f. = निसेनी.

नसैनी *nasainī*, f. = निसेनी.

नह *nah* [*nakha-*], m. nail (of the finger or toe).

नह- *nah-* [*nahati*], v.t. Brbh. to bind, to tie.

नहछू *nahchū*, m. (ceremonial) nail-paring.

नहन *nahan* [cf. H. *nah-*], m. a tie; rope, cord (as a well-rope).

नहनी *nahnī*, f. **1.** a nail-parer (= नहरनी). **2.** *Pl.* = [1]निहानी.

नहन्नी *nahannī*, f. reg. a nail-paper (= नहरनी).

नहर *nahr* [A. *nahr*], f. **1.** stream, flow. ***2.** a canal; an irrigation channel. — ~ काटना or खोदना, to cut a canal, &c.

नहरनी *naharnī* [**nakhakaraṇa-*], f. **1.** a nail-parer. **2.** [? cf. *nakhara-*] a shoemaker's awl.

नहरी *nahrī* [A. *nahrī*], adj. & f. **1.** adj. having to do with a canal, or an irrigation ditch. **2.** f. land irrigated by a canal.

नहरुआ *naharuā*, m. Av. see नहारवा.

नहलवाना *nahalvānā* [cf. H. *nahālnā*], v.t. to cause to be bathed, &c. (by से).

[1]**नहला** *nahlā*, adj. the nine (in cards). — नहले पर दहला रहना, to go one better, to repay in (one's) own coin.

[2]**नहला** *nahlā*, m. *Pl. HŚS.* a small trowel (as used by craftsmen).

नहलाई *nahlāī* [cf. H. *nahlānā*], f. **1.** bathing, washing (a person, an animal). **2.** payment for bathing, &c.

नहलाना *nahlānā* [cf. H. *nahānā*], v.t. to bathe, to wash (a person, an animal). — नहलाना-धुलाना, = नहलाना.

नहवाना *nahvānā*, v.t. = नहलाना.

नहान *nahān* [*snāna-*], m. bathing, washing; ritual bathing.

नहाना *nahānā* [*snāti*], v.i. **1.** to bathe, to wash. **2.** to be bathed, or drenched (as in sweat, blood). — ठंडे पानी से ~, to wash in cold water.

नहानी *nahānī* [cf. H. *nahānā*], adj. f. & f. reg. **1.** adj. impure, menstruating. **2.** f. menstruation.

[1]**नहार** *nahār* [P. *năhār*; ? cf. *anāhāra-*], m. not taking food, fasting. — ~ तोड़ना, to break fast, to take a light morning meal. – नहार-मुँह, adj. & adv. not having eaten; on an empty stomach.

[2]**नहार** *nahār*, m. *Pl.* = नहारवा.

नहारी *nahārī* [P. *nahārī*], f. a light breakfast.

नहारवा *nahārvā* [**snāru-*, Pa. *nhāru-*], m. *Pl. HŚS.* a thread-like insect; specif. the guinea-worm, *Filaria medinensis.*

नहिं *nahiṁ*, adv. Brbh. Av. = नहीं.

नहि *nahi*, adv. Brbh. Av. = नहीं.

नहिन *nahin*, adv. Brbh. = नहीं.

नहीं *nahīṁ* [cf. *nahi*, MIA *ṇāhi*], adv. **1.** no. **2.** not. **3.** (finally, rhetor.) is it not so? **4.** (initially in a clause) otherwise (= नहीं तो). **5.** f. saying 'no': denial; refusal. — ~ करना, to say no: to deny; to refuse; to disclaim; to reject. ~ के बराबर, adv. as if nothing: a very small amount, very little; very few; hardly at all. ~ तो, adv. & conj. no indeed; otherwise (= 'if not, then ...'). ~ सही, adv. no matter, never mind.

नहूसत *nahūsat* [A. *nuḥūsa*: P. *nuḥūsat*], f. misfortune, evil; a bad omen.

नहेरना *nahernā*, m. = नहरनी.

नहोत *na-hot* [cf. H. *honā*], f. reg. poverty, want.

नाँगल *nāṁgal* [*lāṅgala-* (? ← Austro-as.); Pa. *naṅgala-*], m. reg. a plough.

नाँघ- *nāṁgh-* [*laṅghayati*], v.t. Brbh. Av. to jump across; to cross over.

नांठ *nāṁṭh* [**naṭṭha-*], m. *Pl.* the estate or property of a deceased person who leaves no heir.

नांठा *nāṁṭhā* [**naṭṭha-*: ? = *naṣṭa-*], m. *Pl.* one who dies without heirs.

नांद *nāṁd* [**nānda-*: Pk.*ṇaṁda-*], f. **1.** a trough. **2.** an open-mouthed earthen jar (for water).

नांद- *nāṁd-* [*nandati*], v.i. Brbh. to live happily (with, at or in); to be settled, to stay.

नांदिया *nāṁdiyā* [cf. *nandin-*], m. the bull and vehicle of Śiva. — नांदिया-बैल, m. *Pl.* id.; a bull led from door to door, and taught to obey commands.

नांदी *nāndī* [S.], f. **1.** joy; prosperity. ***2.** invocatory verses (as recited at the opening of a play, or a ceremony); inauguration.

नाँव *nāṁv*, m. reg. = नाम. — नाँव-ठाँव, m. whereabouts, particulars (of a person).

ना *nā*, [cf. *na*], adv. **1.** no (= नहीं, न). **2.** not (= न). **3.** rhetor. why not? — ~ करना, to say no: to refuse; to deny. – ना-नुकुर, colloq. refusal, denial.

[1]ना- *nā-* [P. *nā*], pref. **1.** not; un-, in-, dis-, &c. **2.** without. — ना-इत्तिफ़ाक़ी, f. disharmony, discord. ना-इनसाफ़, adj. unjust. °ई, f. injustice. नाउम्मीद, adj. without hope; despairing. नाउम्मीद करना, to cause to despair (of, से); to disappoint. °ई, f. despair. नाउम्मेद, adj. = नाउम्मीद. नाकाफ़ी, adj. insufficient. नाक़ाबिल, adj. incapable; unfit (for a purpose). नाकाम [P. *-kām*], adj. disappointed; unsuccessful; unserviceable, useless. °ई, f. failure, &c. नाकामयाब [P. *-yāb*], adj. unsuccessful. नाकारा [P. *-kār(a)*], adj. inv. worthless. नाख़ुश, adj. displeased (with, से); unpleasant, disagreeable. °ई, f. displeasure; dissatisfaction. नागवार, unpalatable, unpleasant; unacceptable. °आ, inv. adj. id. नाचीज़, adj. & m. insignificant, worthless; an insignificant thing, or person. नाजायज़, adj. not permissible; unlawful; contraband (goods). नातमाम, adj. incomplete. नातवाँ, adj. = next. नातवान [P. *-tavān*], adj. weak, feeble. नादान [P. *-dān*], adj. ignorant; foolish; innocent; an ignorant person. °ई, f. ignorance; stupidity; infatuation. नादार [P. *-dār*], adj. & m. *Pl. HŚS.* having nothing: poor, impoverished (E.H.); blank; drawn (a game); a pauper. °ई, f. नादिहंदी [P. *-dihandī*], f. non-payment. नापसंद, adj. disapproved of, disliked; unacceptable; rejected. नापसंद करना, to disapprove of; to reject, to refuse. °ई, f. disapproval; displeasure; unwillingness; disagreeableness. °गी, f. id. नापाक, adj. impure, unclean; defiled; lewd. नापाक करना, to defile, to pollute. नापैद, adj. unborn. °आ, adj. inv. id. नाफ़रमानी, f. disobedience, non-compliance; contempt (of court). नाबालिग़ [A. *-bālig*], adj. & m. under age; a minor; ward. °पन, = next. °ई, f. minority, nonage. नाबूद [P. *-būd*], reduced to nothing: utterly destroyed; annulled; disappeared; non-existent. नाबूद करना, to annihilate. नामंज़ूर, adj. not accepted, or approved. °ई, f. non-acceptance, rejection. नामर्द, adj. & m. unmanly; cowardly; impotent; a coward; an impotent man. °ई, f. unmanliness; cowardice; impotence. नामाक़ूल, adj. irrational: improbable; absurd; improper. नामालूम, adj. unknown; uncertain. नामुनासिब, adj. not proper, inappropriate; unbecoming. नामुमकिन, adj. impossible. नामुराद [A. *-murād*], adj. having the desires unrealised: unsuccessful; dissatisfied; undesirable, pej. unlucky, wretched; adverse (times, fortune). °ई, f. lack of success; dissatisfaction; undesirability; an unwelcome thing. नामुलायम, adj. hard, rough, coarse; austere; severe; uncivil. नामुवाफ़िक़, adj. not suitable, or adapted (to); discordant, contrary; adverse. ना-मौजूदगी, f. absence. नायाब [P. *-yāb*], adj. unobtainable; rare, costly. नाराज़ [A. *-rāẓī*], adj. dissatisfied, displeased (with, से); angry. °गी, f. dissatisfaction, &c. °ई, f. id. नालायक़ [A. *-lāyiq*], adj. unworthy; incapable; unsuitable. °पन, m. unworthiness, &c. °ई, f. id. नावक़्त, adj. out of time: unseasonable; late; premature. नावाक़िफ़ [A. *vāqif*], adj. unacquainted (with, से); ignorant (of); inexperienced (in). नावाजिब [A. *-vājib*], adj. improper; inappropriate. नाशाद [P. *śād*], adj. & m. depressed, dejected; an unhappy or wretched person. नाशुक्र [A. *śukr*], adj. ungrateful; discontented. °आ, adj. id. °ई, f. unthankfulness; discontent. नाशुक्री करना, to be ungrateful, &c. नासमझ, adj. foolish; unintelligent. °ई, f. foolishness; lack of intelligence; misunderstanding. नासाज़ [P. *-sāz*], adj. out of tune; indifferent (health). नाहक़, adj. & adv. unjust, wrong; unjustly, improperly; without good cause, needlessly; to no purpose.

[2]ना- *nā-*, v.t. Brbh. Av. = नाव-.

-ना *-nā* [S. *-na-*]. suffix (forms infinitives: some esp. colloq. or poet. or reg., e.g. तलाशना, to look for, संकेतना, to indicate; निर्माना, = बनाना; independent f. nouns can be formed, e.g. कहनी, an utterance).

नाइन *nāin* [*nāpinī-*], f. **1.** a barber's wife. **2.** a woman of the barber caste.

नाइब *nāib*, m. see नायब.

नाईं *nāīṁ* [**jñāti-²*: Pk. *ṇāi-* or cf. *jñāpayati*], f. similarity: used as ppn. (with की) like, resembling; just as.

नाई *nāī* [*nāpita-*], m. a barber.

नाऊँ *nāūṁ*, m. Av. metr. = नाम.

नाऊ *nāū* [*snāpaka-*], m. reg. = नाई.

[1]नाक *nāk* [**nakka-*: Pk. *ṇakka-*], f. **1.** nose. **2.** transf. a prominent person or thing. **3.** fig. honour, prestige. — ~ आना, or बहना (की), the nose to run. ~ उतारना, or उड़ाना, to take off, or to lop off, the nose (of, की); to disgrace. ~ ऊँची रखना, = ~ रखना, 1. ~ कटना, the nose to be cut off; to be disgraced, or dishonoured. ~ का बाल, m. a hair of the nose: one respected or honoured; one having influence over another; a right-hand man. ~ काटना, to cut off the nose (of, की); to disgrace, to dishonour. ~ की सीध, f. & adv. the line of the nose; as straight as an arrow; as the crow flies. ~ की सीध में, id. ~ घिसना, to rub the nose (on the ground: before, के आगे, के सामने): to entreat abjectly. ~ चढ़ाना, to turn up the nose (in contempt, pride or fastidiousness); to look, or to be, displeased or angry (with, पर). ~, or नाकों, चने चबवाना, to cause (one, को) to chew gram with or in the nose: to plague, to harass. ~ छेदना, to bore the nose (of, की). ~ झाड़ना, to blow the nose. ~ तक खाना, to eat all one can and more. ~ पर उँगली रखकर बात, or बातें, करना, to act effeminately. ~ पर दिया बालकर आना, fig. to appear with head held high (in victory, or with honour). ~ पर गुस्सा होना, or रहना, fig. to have a

short temper. ~ पर टका रख देना, fig. to pay readily (for a thing). ~ पर पहिया फिर जाना, a wheel to pass over the nose (of, की): the nose to become flattened. ~ पर मक्खी न बैठने देना, fig. to be meticulous in habits, standards, or conduct. ~ बजना, to snore. ~ मलना, to rub the nose; to twist the nose (of, की). ~ में दम आ जाना, to be plagued, harassed (see next). ~ में दम करना, or लाना, fig. to plague, to harass. ~ में बोलना, to speak through the nose. ~ रखना (अपनी), to keep (one's) nose: to preserve (one's) honour; to have a good name. ~ रगड़ना, = ~ घिसना. ~ लगाकर बैठना, to shun others contemptuously. ~ साफ़ करना, or सिनकना, to blow the nose. ~ सिकोड़ना, = ~ चढ़ाना. नाकों, or नाकों में, दम करना, = ~ में दम करना. सुआ सी ~, or सुए की सी ~, f. a hooked nose. सुतवाँ ~, f. a long thin nose. — नाक-कान, m. the ears and nose. नाक-कान काटना, to cut off the ears and nose (of, के); to disgrace, to dishonour. नाक-चोटी काटना, fig. to punish cruelly. नाक-चोटी गिरफ़्तार होना, nose and top-knot to be entangled: to be in difficulties, distress. नाक-नक़्शा, m. (facial) features. नाकबंद [P. *-band*], m. nose-band (of a bridle). नाक-भौं, f. nose and brows: नाक-भौं चढ़ाना, or सिकोड़ना, = नाक चढ़ाना. नाकवाला, m. an honourable man; a proud man; a person of rank. नाकों-नक, adv. brimful, quite full.

²नाक *nāk* [S.], m. Av. heaven; paradise. — नाक-नटी, f. an *apsarā*.

नाकड़ा *nākṛā* [cf. H. *nāk*], m. an inflammation, or a tumour, of the nose.

¹नाका *nākā* [**nakka-*], m. **1.** end or beginning (of a road, &c.); entrance (as to a pass, a walled town); boundary. **2.** junction (of roads). **3.** passage; lane, alley; defile; waterway. **4.** toll or customs station. **5.** eye (of a needle); aperture. — ~ बाँधना, to close a passage-point, road, &c. – नाकाबंदी [P. *-bandī*], f. closing a road, or a frontier; collecting toll or customs; blockade. नाकेदार [P. *-dār*], adj. & m. having an opening ; a guard; a toll or customs officer.

²नाका *nākā* [*nakra-*¹: ← Drav.], m. *Pl. HŚS.* a crocodile.

नाक़िस *nāqis* [A. *nāqiṣ*], adj. **1.** defective, wanting. **2.** base; worthless.

¹नाकी *nākī* [cf. H. *nāk*], adj. having to do with the nose, nasal.

²नाकी *nākī* [S.], adj. E.H. heavenly.

नाकू *nākū* [*nakra-*¹ (← Drav.); × H. *nāk*], m. *Pl. HŚS.* a crocodile.

नाक्षत्र *nākṣatră* [S.], adj. **1.** lunar. **2.** sidereal.

नाख़ुन *nākhun* [P.], m. see नाख़ून.

नाख़ुना *nākhunā* [P. *nākhuna*], m. **1.** *mus.* a plectrum, or bow. **2.** haw, cataract (in the eye). **3.** a cloth woven of silk and cotton. **4.** a gouge.

नाख़ून *nākhūn* [P. *nākhun*], m. **1.** nail (of the finger or toe); horn of a hoof (horses, cattle). **2.** talon, claw. — ~ गड़ाना, fig. to get (one's) teeth into (a matter). ~ में पड़े रहना, to be in (one's) (immediate) possession. ~ लेना, to cut the nails; colloq. to stumble (a horse). ~ नीले होना, the nails to be blue: death to be near.

नाग *nāg* [S.], m. **1.** a snake; a cobra. **2.** *mythol.* a *nāga* (a demon having a human face and a snake-like lower body). **3.** an elephant. 4. = नागा, 3. — काला ~, m. a cobra; fig. a venomous or dangerous person, a viper. — ~ खिलाना, to nourish a serpent: to endanger one's life (see also next). ~ खेलाना (or खिलाना) to play with a snake: to play with fire. – नाग-केसर, m. a small evergreen tree having fragrant yellow flowers, rose-chestnut (*Mesua roxburghii* or *ferrea*). नाग-दौना, m. wormwood, *Artemisia vulgaris*. नाग-पचमी, f. a Hindu festival falling on the fifth day of the light half of the month Sāvan (when women worship snakes to obtain blessings on their children). नाग-पाश, m. a noose; lassoo. नाग-फाँस, m. id. नाग-फनी, f. the prickly pear. नाग-लोक, m. world of *nāgas*: = पाताल. नागेंद्र [°*ga* + *i*°], m. lord of snakes, or of elephants: *mythol.* a title of the snake Śeṣa; a large or noble elephant.

नागन *nāgan*, f. = नागिन.

नागर *nāgar* [S.], adj. & m. **1.** adj. = नागरिक. **2.** courtly, gallant. **3.** m. a citizen. **4.** a city-bred person. **5.** name of a brāhmaṇ community of Gujarat; a member of that community. — नागर-बेल, m. betel leaf. नागर-मोथा, m. = नगरौथा.

नागरिक *nāgărik* [S.], adj. & m. **1.** adj. urban; municipal. **2.** civic, civil (as duties, rights). **3.** city-bred; pej. knowing, cunning; urbane. **4.** m. a citizen; a townsman.

नागरिकता *nāgarikătā* [S.], f. **1.** citizenship. **2.** city-bred qualities: knowingness, cunning; urbanity.

नागरिका *nāgărikā* [S.], f. = नागरी, 1., 2.

नागरी *nāgărī* [S.], f. **1.** a female citizen. **2.** a knowing, or urbane woman. **3.** the Devanāgarī script.

नागल *nāgal* [*lāngala-*; Pa. *naṅgala-*], m. reg. **1.** a heavy plough. **2.** transf. cord used to tie oxen to a plough-yoke, trace. **3.** *Pl.* hooks on a plough-yoke to which the traces are tied.

नागा *nāgā* [*nagna-*], m. **1.** a naked ascetic. **2.** the Naga tribe (of Assam). **3.** a Naga tribesman.

नाग़ा *nāgā*, adj. & m. **1.** adj. vacant; blank. **2.** absent. **3.** m. adjournment, intermission; free day, or time; closure (of shops, &c). **4.** absence (esp. from work). — ~ **करना**, to adjourn, &c.; to be absent. ~ **देना**, to take a day, or time off, work; to play truant.

नागिन *nāgin* [cf. H. *nāg*], f. **1.** a female snake. **2.** *mythol.* a female *nāga*. **3.** fig. a venomous woman. **4.** a ringlet, or fringe of hair.

¹**नागी** *nāgī* [S.], adj. having snakes (sc. around the neck): a title of Śiva.

²**नागी** *nāgī* [S.; w. H. *nāg*], f. a female snake.

¹**नागेसरी** *nāgesărī* [H. *nāg-kesar* × *-īśvarī-*], f. Av. = नाग-केसर.

²**नागेसरी** *nāgesărī* [cf. H. *nāg-kesar*; × *-īśvara-*], adj. *Pl. HŚS.* of the colour of *nāg-kesar*, yellow.

नागौरी *nāgaurī*, adj. **1.** having to do with Nagaur (in Rajasthan). **2.** of good breed (bullocks).

नाच *nāc* [*nṛtya-*], m. **1.** dancing; a dance (performance). **2.** a dance (social occasion). — ~ **दिखाना** (**को**), to dance before (one). ~ **नचाना** (**को**), v.t. to make a person dance (to one's tune, &c.); to lead (one) a dance, to harass. ~ **न आवे**, or **जाने**, **आँगन टेढ़ा**, for an unskilled dancer the courtyard is uneven: a bad workman blames his tools. – **नाच-कूद**, f. dancing, fesitivity; fig. capering, fuss. **नाच-गान**, m. dancing and singing. **नाच-घर**, m. a ballroom; theatre. **नाच-महल**, m. = **नाच-घर**. **नाच-रंग**, m. music and dancing; joyful or festive mood.

नाचना *nācnā* [*nṛtyati*], v.i. **1.** to dance. **2.** to caper (frivolously, or pointlessly). — **सिर पर** ~ (**के**), to assail (one: as misfortunes); to be impending (death).

नाचनी *nācnī* [cf. H. *nāc*], f. *Pl.* a dancing-girl.

नाज *nāj*, m. grain, &c. = **अनाज**. — **नाजवाला**, m. a grain merchant.

नाज़ *nāz* [P. *nāz*], m. **1.** flirtatious behaviour. **2.** airs, affectations; conceit; self-indulgent pride. **3.** elegance, grace. **4.** delicacy, indulgence (as of upbringing). — ~ **उठाना**, to bear with the airs or whims (of, **का**). ~ **करना**, or **दिखाना**, to behave flirtatiously; to give oneself airs. — ~ **होना**, to allow oneself, or to affect, pride (in, **पर**). – **नाज़-अदा** [A. *-adā*], f. = next. **नाज़-नख़री**, f. = **नाज़**, 1., 2. **नाज़बरदार** [P. *-bardār*], m. indulging the conceit of: a flatterer. °**ई**, f. **नाज़ों-पला**, adj. brought up indulgently.

नाज़िम *nāzim* [A. *nāẓim*], m. U. an administrator (esp. the governor of a Mughal province).

नाज़िर *nāzir* [A. *nāẓir*], m. U. one who sees: a spectator; inspector, supervisor; a court officer; bailiff.

नाज़ुक *nāzuk* [P. *nāzuk*], adj. **1.** thin, slender. **2.** delicate, tender; fine; light; brittle. **3.** finely balanced, nice; subtle (as thought, wit); tricky, delicate (as a situation), critical. **4.** sensitive (as feelings, or temperament); irritable. **5.** elegant. **6.** facetious. — ~ **घड़ी**, f. critical hour or moment; a crisis. ~ **मौक़े पर**, adv. at a critical moment; in a delicate situation. — **नाज़ुक-मिज़ाज**, adj. of sensitive or finely balanced temperament; touchy, or irritable.

नाजो *nājo* [cf. P. *nāz*], f. **1.** a flirtatious woman. **2.** a term of endearment: darling.

¹**नाट** *nāṭ* [*nṛtta-*, or *nāṭya-*], m. *Pl. HŚS.* dancing; a dance; a play.

²**नाट** *nāṭ* [? conn. *yaṣṭi-*], f. *Pl.* reg. **1.** pillar; beam. **2.** log.

नाट- *nāṭ-*, v.i. Brbh. to deny, &c. (= ¹**नटना**).

नाटक *nāṭak* [S.], m. **1.** a drama. **2.** dramatic art, the drama; acting. **3.** an actor. — **नाटककार**, m. a dramatist. **नाटक-शाला**, f. a theatre.

नाटकत्व *nāṭakatvă* [S.], m. **1.** dramatic qualities; stageability (of a drama). **2.** theatrical qualities (of an event).

नाटकिया *nāṭakiyā* [cf. H. *nāṭak*], m. *HŚS.* an actor.

¹**नाटकी** *nāṭăkī* [cf. H. *nāṭak*], Brbh. an actor.

²**नाटकी** *nāṭakī* [S.], f. *Pl.* **1.** a dancing-girl. **2.** a type of drama.

नाटकीय *nāṭăkīyă* [S.], adj. **1.** dramatic. **2.** theatrical, striking.

नाटा *nāṭā* [**naṭṭa-*; × *naṣṭa-*], adj. & m. **1.** adj. short of stature. **2.** reg. bad; naughty. **3.** m. a dwarf. **4.** reg. a depraved person; a naughty boy. — ~ **बैल**, m. reg. (Bihar) a bullock used in a sugar-mill or oil-mill.

नाटापन *nāṭāpan* [cf. H. *nāṭā*], m. shortness of stature.

नाटिका *nāṭikā* [S.], f. **1.** a type of drama, in which most of the characters are female. **2.** *mus.* name of a *rāgiṇī*.

नाट्य *nāṭyă* [S.], m. **1.** the dramatic arts (acting, dancing, music); acting; miming; drama. **2.** dramatic representation. — **नाट्य-कला**, f. dramatic art, drama. **नाट्यकार**, m. = **नाटककार**. **नाट्य-मंच**, f. the stage. **नाट्य-रूपांतरण**, m. dramatisation. **नाट्य-शाला**, f. a theatre. नाट्य-शास्त्र, m. dramatic theory (with that of dancing and music); a work of that title by Bharata. नाट्योक्ति [°ya+u°], f. any conventional form of address used in dramas on traditional themes, e.g. *ārya* (to a brāhmaṇ), or *dev* (to a king).

नाठ *nāṭh* [*naṣṭa-*], m. *HŚS.* **1.** destruction. **2.** goods or property having no inheritor (see नांठ).

नाठा *nāṭhā*, m. *HŚS.* see नांठा.

नाड़ *nāṛ* [*nāḍī-*¹], f. **1.** the neck (cf. नाड़ी, 1). **2.** *Pl. HŚS.* = नाड़ी, 4., 5.

नाड़ा *nāṛā* [*nāḍī-*³: Pk. *ṇāḍī-*], m. **1.** tape, draw-string (of skirt, women's *dhotī*). **2.** knotted red or yellow thread (offered to gods).

नाड़ी *nāṛī* [*nāḍikā-*], f. **1.** a stalk. **2.** a tube, pipe (= नली). **3.** a blood-vessel. **4.** the pulse. **5.** a fistula, ulcer. — ~ की गति, f. the pulse-beat. ~ चलना, the pulse to beat. ~ छूटना, the pulse to stop; to have no pulse. ~ बोलना, the pulse to be perceptible.

नातरु *nātaru* [*na-+tarhi*], adv. Brbh. otherwise.

नाता *nātā* [**jñātra-*], m. **1.** relationship. **2.** connection; alliance. **3.** ppn. (w. के) by virtue of, because of; in connection with, *à propos* of; in the capacity of. — ~ जोड़ना, to form a connection, or alliance (with, से or के साथ). किस नाते? on what basis, or grounds? – नाता-गोता, m. a relative. नाता-रिश्ता, m. relationship; family alliance. नातेदार [P. *-dār*], adj. & m. related; a relative. °ई, f. relationship, &c.

नातिन *nātin* [cf. *naptṛ-*; Pk. *nattuṇiā-*, f.], f. daughter's daughter, granddaughter.

नाती *nātī* [*naptṛ-*], m. daughter's son, grandson.

¹**नाथ** *nāth* [S.], m. **1.** lord; protector; master. **2.** husband. **3.** *hist.* a title of followers of the Śaiva sect of Gorakhnāth. — नाथ-पंथ, m. Nāth community: the sect of Gorakhnāth. °ई, m. a member of the sect of Gorakhnāth.

²**नाथ** *nāth* [*nastā-*, Pk. *ṇatthā-*], f. nose-rope (of an ox).

नाथता *nāthătā* [S.], f. *Pl. HŚS.* office or status of a protector, &c.

नाथत्व *nāthatvă* [S.], f. *Pl. HŚS.* = नाथता.

नाथना *nāthnā* [cf. H. ²*nāth*], v.t. **1.** to bore the nose (as of a bullock) and thread it with a nose-rope. **2.** to bring under control. **3.** to thread or to string together.

नाद *nād* [S.], m. **1.** sounding, resonance; a loud sound, noise; cry. **2.** a roar. **3.** singing, a song.

नादान *nādān*, adj. see s.v. ¹ना-.

नादिम *nādim* [A. *nādim*], adj. U. **1.** penitent. **2.** ashamed, abashed.

नादिर *nādir* [A. *nādir*], adj. **1.** unusual. **2.** excellent, wonderful; choice.

नादिरशाही *nādirśāhī* [cf. H. *nādirśāh*], adj. & f. **1.** adj. having to do with or recalling the Persian king Nādirśāh; harsh, cruel. **2.** f. invasion of India by Nādirśāh. **3.** harsh rule, misrule; terror.

नादी *nādī* [S.], adj. sounding, resonant.

नाध- *nādh-* [cf. *naddha-*], v.t. Brbh. **1.** to yoke; to link, to attach. **2.** to begin, to turn to (as a task).

नान *nān* [P.], f. **1.** bread. **2.** a cake of bread. नानकार, m. *hist.* an assignment of part of the land or revenue of an estate, made to a tenant or landlord for his maintenance; a similar assignment to a tax or village officer. नान-खटाई, f. a sweet made from rice flour, with *ghī* and sugar. नान-बाई [P. *bā'ī*; ? f. A. *bā'i'*], m. a baker.

नानक *nānak*, m. name of the founder of the Sikh faith. — नानक-पंथ, m. the community, or the religion, of Nānak. °ई, m. a follower of Nānak, a Sikh. नानक-शाह, m. = ~. °ई, m. = नानकपंथी; *hist.* a *paisā* in use in Sikh territories (from five to seven went to one anna).

नानकिया *nānăkiyā* [cf. H. *nānak*], adj. having to do with Nānak.

नानकीन *nānkīn* [Engl. *nankeen*], m. Nankeen cotton cloth (= मारकीन).

नानस *nānas*, f. *Pl. HŚS.* mother-in-law's mother (= ननिया सास).

नानसरा *nānasrā*, m. *Pl. HŚS.* husband of a mother-in-law's mother (= ननिया ससुर).

¹**नाना** *nānā* [**nānna-*: Pk. *ṇanna-*], m. maternal grandfather.

²**नाना** *nānā* [S.], adj. inv. different, various. — ~ प्रकार से, adv. in various ways. – नानाकार [°nā+ā°], m. = नानारूप. नानार्थ [°nā+a°], adj. of different meanings; having a different aim or object. नानारूप, m. = of various forms, multiform. नानावर्ण, adj. variegated.

नानात्व *nānātvă* [S.], m. variety, diversity.

नानियाल *nāniyāl*, m. (f., *Pl.*). = ननिहाल.

नानिहाल *nānihāl*, m. (f., *Pl.*) = ननिहाल.

नानी *nānī* [**nānna-*: Pk. *ṇanna-*], f. maternal grandmother.

ना-नुकर *nā-nukar* [cf. H. *nāh-nūh*], m. denial, refusal.

नान्ह *nānh*, adj. Brbh. = नन्हा.

नान्ह- *nānh-*, adj. Brbh. = नन्हा.

नाप *nāp* [cf. H. *nāpnā*], f. m. **1.** measure; scale; proportion. **2.** measuring; survey. **3.** measurement. **4.** criterion. — ~ करना, or लेना (की, का), to measure. ~ का पूरा, adj. of full measure, or height, &c. – **नाप-काट**, f. cut, style (of a garment). **नाप-तौल**, or **नाप-जोख**, f. measuring, weighing; assessing; measure, weight.

नापना *nāpnā* [*jñāpyate*], v.t. to measure; to weigh; to measure out (as a liquid). — रास्ता ~, to wander about, to saunter. सिर ~ (का), to behead.

नापित *nāpit* [S.], m. = नाई.

नाफ़ *nāf* [P. *nāf*], f. **1.** the navel. **2.** middle, centre (of anything).

नाभि *nābhi* [S.], f. **1.** navel. **2.** hub (of a wheel). **3.** fig. centre, focus. — **नाभि-छेदन**, f. m. reg. cutting the umbilical cord. **नाभि-नाल**, f. m. umbilical cord. **नाभि-नाड़ी**, f. id.

नाभिक *nābhik* [S.], f. *phys.* nucleus.

नाभिकीय *nābhikīyă* [S.], adj. nuclear (energy, explosion, &c).

नाभ्य *nābhyă* [S.], adj. *Pl. HŚS.* umbilical.

नाम *nām* [*nāman-*], m. & adv. **1.** m. name; title; term. **2.** *gram.* a nominal form. **3.** good name, reputation. **4.** the divine name. **राम-नाम**, m. the name of Rām. **5.** adv. by name. — ~ उछलना (का), (one's) name to be bandied about, sullied. ~ उछालना (अपना, का), to bring notoriety or disgrace (upon). ~ उठ जाना, trace or memory (of, का), to vanish. ~ करना (का), to give a name (to); to perform (an action) for appearance's sake. ~ का, adj. named, by name; nominal. ~ का कुत्ता न पालना, colloq. not to be able to bear mentioning (a person's) name. ~ के लिए, adv. for one's reputation's sake. ~ को, adv. to a nominal degree: a very small amount. ~ को नहीं, nothing at all (of). ~ को, or पर, बट्टा लगाना (अपने, के), to disgrace (one's) name. ~ को मरना, to face death, or to endure the worst, for honour's sake. ~ गँवाना, to squander, to throw away one's good name. ~ चढ़ाना, to enter a name (on a list); to sign one's name. ~ चलना, the name (of, का) to be current, or remembered. ~ जगना (का), (one's) name to become famous, or current. ~ जगाना, to make one's name famous, &c. ~ जपना, to repeat the name (of a god); to contemplate the name (of Rām, &c). ~ डालना, to credit or to debit to the name (of, के); to ascribe (to). ~ डुबाना (का), to destroy one's good name or reputation. ~ देना, to give a name (to, को); to make conspicuous; to credit to the name (of, के). ~ धरना, to give a name (to, को), to call; to saddle with a name; to defame. ~ न(हीं) लेना, not to mention, to overlook; to refrain entirely (from का); to shirk; to be long in doing (sthg). ~ निकलना, one's name to become known; to become notorious. ~ पड़ना, a name to be given (to, के); to be debited (to, के); to be recorded against (के). ~ पर जान देना, or मरना, or मिटना, to be utterly devoted (to, के); to be infatuated (with). ~ पर बैठना, to rest on (one's) laurels. ~ पाना, to win a name. ~ बिगाड़ना, to ruin the name (of, का), to defame. ~ रखना, to name (one, को: as, का)); to preserve (one's) name, or honour. ~ रौशन होना, to become celebrated. ~ लगना, to be ascribed (to, के); to be charged (with). ~ लगाना, to give a bad name (to, को); to accuse (of, का); to ascribe a fault (to). ~ लिखना, to ascribe (to, के); to hold responsible (for); = ~ डालना. ~ लिखवाना (का), to enter (one's) name (on a list); to enrol (a person). ~ लेना, to refer (to, का), to mention; to name (a person); to single out by name; to scold, to curse; to praise; to invoke the name (of: esp. of a god); to raise (a question). ~ से, adv. by or under the name (of, के); in the name (of). ~ होना (का), to acquire a name: = ~ रौशन होना. अपना ~ करना, to make one's name. के ~, adv. addressed to, for (as a letter). के ~ पर, adv. in the name of (God, &c.); in memory of. ...तो मेरा ~ नहीं, fig. ...then I'm a Dutchman. – **नाम-करण**, m. the ceremony of naming a child after birth; giving a name (to, का). **नाम-कीर्तन**, m. glorifying the (divine) name by repeating it. **नाम-ग्रहण**, m. calling by name. **नामज़द** [P. *-zad*], adj. named, nominated; designated, appointed, elected; celebrated; engaged, spoken for (a girl). °गी, f. nomination, &c. **नामदार** [P. *-dār*], adj. famous, celebrated. **नाम-धराई**, f. giving a name (to); nicknaming; vilification. **नाम-धातु**, f. *gram.* a denominative verb. **नामधारी**, adj. & m. named; namesake. **नामधेय**, adj. & m. named; name, title. **नाम-निर्दिष्ट**, adj. nominated. °-**निर्देश**, m. nomination. °अन, m. id. **नाम-निवेश**, m. registration of a name. **नाम-निशान**, **नामो-निशान** (U.), m. sign, trace, vestige. **नाम-निशान मिटाना** (का), to eradicate utterly (from, से). **नाम-पट**, m. a signboard. **नाम-पत्र**, m. a label. **नाम-बोला**, m. one who repeats devoutly the divine name. **नाम-मात्र**, adj. & adv. nominal; trivial; nominally, &c. **नाम-रासी**, m. a namesake. **नाम-लेवा**, m. one to bear, or to invoke, the name (of, का), a son. **नामवर** [P. *-var*], adj. famous, celebrated. °ई, f. reputation, fame. **नाम-वाचक**, adj. expressive of a name: **नामवाचक संज्ञा**, f. *gram.* a proper noun.

नामशेष, adj. of whom or which the name only remains: vanished; dead. नाम-हंसाई, f. mockery. नामांकन [°*ma* + *a*°], m. registration; nomination. नामांकित, adj. नामात्मक [°*ma* + *ā*°], adj. having to do with a name, &c. नामात्मक क्रिया, f. a denominative verb.

नामक *nāmak* [S.], adj. predic., or finally in comp. (prop. m. only) named, called.

नामन *nāman* [S.], m. naming; nominating. — नामन-कर्ता, m. inv. nominator.

नामा *nāmā* [P. *nāma*], m. U.: H. esp. in comp. a letter, document. — निकाह-नामा, m. musl. marriage contract.

नामी *nāmī* [cf. H. *nām*], adj. **1.** well-known, famous. **2.** of good name. **3.** having a name. – नामी-धामी, adj. of good name and reputation. नामी-गिरामी, [P. *girām*], adj. = ~, 2.

नामे *nāme*, adv. colloq. in, or against, a name (as credit or debit).

नाम्नी *nāmnī* [S.], adj. f. named (see नामक).

नायक *nāyak* [S.], m. **1.** leader. **2.** chief, principal; overseer. **3.** *mil.* a junior non-commissioned officer. **4.** leading character, hero (as of a drama, novel). **5.** *poet.* a lover. **6.** a skilled musician; conductor (of band, &c).

नायकत्व *nāyakatvă* [S.], m. **1.** leadership; command, direction. **2.** leading role.

नायन *nāyan*, m = नाइन.

नायब *nāyab* [A. *nā'ib*], m. **1.** a deputy. **2.** an assistant, lieutenant. **3.** vicegerent.

नायबी *nāybī* [A. *nā'ib* + P. *-ī*], f. post, duties and status of a deputy, &c.

नायिका *nāyikā* [S.], f. **1.** wife of a *nāyak*. **2.** leading female character, heroine; leading lady (in a drama); *rhet.* mistress, beloved. **3.** leader, &c. (female).

नारंग *nāraṅg* [*nāraṅga-*], m. = नारंगी, 1.

नारंगी *nāraṅgī* [*nāraṅga-*], f. & adj. **1.** f. an orange (the tree, and its fruit). **2.** fig. a woman's breast. **3.** orange (colour). **4.** adj. orange.

¹नार *nār* [S.], adj. & m. *HŚS.* **1.** adj. having to do with men; male. **2.** m. *Pl.* a calf.

²नार *nār*, f. Brbh. = नारी.

³नार *nār* [*nāḍī-*¹], f. Brbh. = ¹नाल.

नारक *nārak* [S.], adj. & m. **1.** adj. having to do with hell; hellish, infernal. **2.** m. hell. **3.** one dwelling in hell.

नारकी *nārăkī* [S.], adj. & m. **1.** adj. = नारक. **2.** m. = नारक, 3.

नारकीय *nārăkīyă* [S.], adj. = नारक.

नारद *nārad* [S.], m. *mythol.* **1.** name of a sage (one of the four sons of Brahmā, and inventor of the *vīṇā*; a friend and devotee of Kṛṣṇa). **2.** transf. a tale-bearer, causer of quarrels. **3.** an argumentative person.

नारा *nārā* [A. *na'ra*], m. **1.** a shout, cry. **2.** slogan. — ~ बुलंद करना, to raise the slogan (of, का). नारे लगाना, to raise or to shout slogans; to deal in slogans. – नारेबाज़ [P. *bāz*], m. sloganeer. °ई, f.

नाराच *nārāc* [S.], m. *Pl. HŚS.* an iron arrow, an arrow.

नाराज़ *nārāz*, adj. see s.v. ²ना-.

नारायण *nārāyaṇ* [S.], m. var. /nərayən/. *hind.* a title of the primeval being; title of Viṣṇu/Kṛṣṇa. — सत ~, m. the true Nārāyaṇ, the true God.

नारायणी *nārāyaṇī* [S.], f. *hind.* **1.** a title of Lakṣmī, and of Durgā. **2.** a title of the river Ganges.

नारिकेल *nārikel* [S.], m. a coconut.

नारियल *nāriyal* [*nārikela-*: ← Drav.], m. **1.** the coconut tree. **2.** a coconut. **3.** a hookah made from a coconut. **4.** sl. head, skull. — ~ का तेल, m. coconut oil. ~ का पानी, m. milk of a coconut. ~ की खोपड़ी, f. a coconut shell.

नारियली *nāriyalī* [cf. H. *nāriyal*], f. **1.** a cup made from a coconut shell. 2. = नारियल, 3. **3.** reg. palm-wine, toddy.

नारी *nārī* [S.], f. a woman. — नारीगत, adj. particular to, or characteristic of, women.

नारीत्व *nārītvă* [S.], f. female nature, femininity; womanhood.

¹नाल *nāl* [*nāḍī-*¹, *nāla-*], f. m. **1.** stalk (esp. of the lotus); blade (of grass). **2.** tube, pipe; barrel (of a firearm); jeweller's blow-torch. **3.** reg. pipe (as container for a firework). **4.** umbilical cord. **5.** reg. artery, vein. **6.** reg. gullet. — ~ गड़ी (गड़ा) होना (की/का), (one's) umbilical cord to be buried (somewhere): to have ties of affection to, or a hereditary claim to (a place).

²नाल *nāl* [A. *na'l*], m. **1.** a horseshoe. **2.** transf. hoof. **3.** the bank (in cards); money put into the bank. — ~ बाँधना, or जड़ना (का), to shoe (a horse). — नालबंद [P. *-band*], m. a blacksmith; farrier. °ई, f. shoeing (a horse, &c.); *hist.* a partic. tax or tribute (as exacted under Muslim rule on pretext of keeping up the cavalry of the state or preventing it from devastating the country); (under the Marāṭhās) the equipment of field cavalry, or an advance made (sc. for equipment) to a troop of horse.

नालकी *nālkī*, f. reg. a kind of open palanquin (*pālkī*).

1 **नाला** *nālā* [*nāḍī-*[1], *nāla-*], m. **1.** a watercourse (natural). **2.** water-channel (man-made). **3.** drain; gutter.

2 **नाला** *nālā* [P. *nāla*], m. **1.** moaning; weeping. **2.** whining (as a dog).

नालिश *nāliś* [P. *nāliś*], f. *law.* complaint, accusation; suit, charge. — ~ करना, to complain (of, की), to bring an action (against, की, के ख़िलाफ़). ~ दाग़ना, or दायर करना, or पेश करना, to file a complaint, &c.

नाली *nālī* [*nāḍī-*[1], *nāla-*], f. **1.** a blood-vessel. **2.** stalk (esp. of the lotus). **3.** a slender tube or pipe. **4.** reg. artery, vein (= नाड़ी). **5.** reg. intestine. **6.** a small water-race or channel; drain, gutter. **7.** a hollow, groove (as along a sword-blade). — ~ बनाना (में), to make a drain; to drain. पटी ~, f. a covered drain.

नाव *nāv* [*nāvā-*], f. **1.** a boat; a ship. **2.** [× P. *nāb*] anything long and hollow: a pipe, tube. ~ चलाना, to sail. ~ पार लगा देना, to get (one's) boat to the far shore: to complete a task, or a duty, successfully. काग़ज़ की ~, f. a paper boat: any frail thing. दो नावों पर पैर चलाना, to embark on two incompatible, or contradictory, courses.

नाव- *nāv-* [*nāmayati*], v.t. Brbh. Av. **1.** to bend, to bow. **2.** to lower; to pour (in or out).

1 **नावक** *nāvak*, m. Brbh. = नाविक.

2 **नावक** *nāvak* [P. *nāvak*], m. Brbh. **1.** a small arrow. **2.** a blowpipe (for shooting); crossbow. **3.** a bee's sting.

नाविक *nāvik* [S.], m. **1.** helmsman. **2.** boatman, sailor.

नाश *nāś* [S.], m. **1.** destruction; ruin, devastation; loss. **2.** annihilation. — ~ करना, to destroy, &c.; to spoil, to mar. – नाशकारी, adj. = नाशक. नाशमान, adj. = नाशवान. नाशमूलक, adj. destructive, &c. नाशवाद, m. nihilism. °ई, adj. & m. नाशवान, adj. liable to perish, impermanent.

नाशक *nāśak* [S.], adj. **1.** destructive; ruinous; pernicious (an effect). **2.** (esp. finally in comp.) destroying, removing (an adverse influence or effect). तिमिर-नाशक, adj. removing darkness.

नाशन *nāśan* [S.], m. **1.** destructive action, &c. **2.** destructive effect: elimination, removal; ruin.

नाशपाती *nāśpātī* [P. *nāśpātī*], f. a pear.

नाशित *nāśit* [S.], adj. destroyed.

नाशी *nāśī* [S.], adj. & m. **1.** adj. destructive, &c. 2. = नाशवान. **3.** m. a destroyer, &c.

नाश्ता *nāśtā* [P. *nāśitā*], m. the first light meal of the day; light snack.– ~ करना, to breakfast (on, का).

नाश्य *nāśyă* [S.], adj. to be destroyed; subject to destruction.

नाष- *nāṣ-* [conn. *nakṣati*], v.t. Brbh. to cross.

1 **नास** *nās* [*nāśa-*], m. = नाश. — नास-पिटा, colloq. doomed, cursed. नास मिटा, m. pej. or joc. doomed to destruction: a rascal, ruffian.

2 **नास** *nās* [**nāsyā-*: Pk. *ṇassā-* 'nose'], f. snuff. — ~ लेना, to take snuff. — नासदान [P. *-dān*], m. snuff-box.

नास- *nās-*, v.i. & v.t. Av. **1.** v.i. [*naśyati*] to be destroyed; to vanish. **2.** v.t. [*nāśayati*] to destroy.

नासपाल *nāspāl* [P. *nāspāl*], m. pomegranate rind.

नासपाली *nāspālī* [P. *nāspālī*], adj. **1.** having to do with, or obtained from, pomegranate rind. **2.** light green in colour.

नासा *nāsā* [S.], f. the nose. — नासाग्र [°*sā*+*a*°], m. the tip of the nose. नासा-पुट, m. the nostril.

नासिका *nāsikā* [S.], f. **1.** the nose; a nostril (*Pl.*) **2.** an elephant's trunk.

नासी *nāsī* [*nāsikā-*], f. reg. (E.) sole (of a plough).

नासूर *nāsūr* [A. *nāsūr*], m. a running sore, an ulcer. — ~ पड़ना, an ulcer, &c. to form (in, or on, में).

नास्तिक *nāstik* [S.], adj. & m. **1.** adj. saying *nāsti* 'it is not': atheistic. **2.** m. an atheist; an unbeliever. — नास्तिकवाद, m. atheism. °ई, adj. & m. atheistic; an atheist.

नास्तिकता *nāstikātā* [S.], f. **1.** atheism; non-belief. **2.** heterodoxy (as in denial of the authority of the Vedas).

नास्तिक्य *nāstikyă* [S.], m. = नास्तिकता.

नास्तिवाद *nāstivād* [S.], m. = नास्तिकवाद.

नास्य *nāsyă* [S.], adj. & m. **1.** adj. having to do with the nose, nasal. **2.** m. = [2]नाथ.

नाह *nāh*, m. Brbh. Av. = [1]नाथ.

नाह-नूह *nāh-nūh* [cf. H. *nă*, *nāhīṁ*], adv. & f. (m., *Pl.*) reg. **1.** adv. no, no! **2.** f. denial, refusal; demurring.

नाहर *nāhar* [**nakhadara-*, or **nakharin-*], m. Brbh. Av. a tiger; a lion.

नाहिं *nāhiṁ*, adv. Brbh. Av. = नहीं.

नाहीं *nāhīṁ*, adv. = नहीं.

निंद- *niṁd-* [*nindati*], v.t. Brbh. Av. to blame, &c. (see निंदा).

निंदक *nindak* [S.], m. **1.** one who blames, or scorns. **2.** slanderer, &c. **3.** blasphemer (see s.v. निंदा).

निंदन *nindan* [S.], m. = निंदा.

निंदनीय *nindănīyă* [S.], adj. **1.** blameworthy; reprehensible. **2.** deserving of scorn; contemptible; base.

निंदनीयता *nindănīyătā* [S.], f. **1.** blameworthiness. **2.** contemptible nature.

निंदर- *niṁdar-* [**nirdarati × nindati*], v.t. reg. = निदर-.

निंदरिया *niṁdariyā* [cf. H. *nīṁd*], f. dimin. Brbh. sleep.

निंदा *nindā* [S.], f. **1.** blame; reproach; censure. **2.** scorn; abuse. **3.** defamation, slander. — ~ करना (की), to blame, to criticise harshly, or unjustly, &c. ईश्वर की ~, f. blasphemy. निंदा-स्तुति, f. ironical praise.

निंदाई *niṁdāī*, f. = निदाई.

निंदास *nindās* [cf. H. *nīṁd*], f. sleepiness; drowsiness.

निंदासा *nindāsā* [cf. H. *nīṁd*], adj. **1.** sleepy, drowsy. **2.** heavy (the eyes).

निंदित *nindit* [S.], adj. **1.** blamed; reproached; censured. **2.** scorned. **3.** slandered. **4.** worthy of blame, or scorn; odious; despicable (= निंदनीय).

निंदैल *nindail* [cf. H. *nīṁd*], adj. reg. sleepy; drowsy.

निंद्य *nindyă* [S.], adj. **1.** blameworthy; reprehensible. **2.** contemptible; vile.

निंद्रा *nindrā*, f. corr. 1. = निद्रा. 2. = निंदा.

निंब *nimb* [S.], m. the neem (*nīm*) tree. — निंब-तरु, m. the coral tree. निंब-कौड़ी, f. the berry of the neem tree.

निंबू *nimbū*, m. = नीबू.

निंबोली *nimbolī* [**nimbagulikā-*: Pk. *ṇiṁboliyā-*], f. the berry of the *nīm* tree.

निः- *niḥ-* [S.], pref. (for some compounds alternative forms exist based on निस्- or निश्-). **1.** out, away, forth; utterly, quite. **2.** not; not having, without; non-, in-, &c.

निःशंक *niḥ-śaṅk* [S.], adj. **1.** fearless. **2.** not apprehensive.

निःशक्त *niḥ-śakt* [S.], adj. powerless, weak.

निःशब्द *niḥ-śabd* [S.], adj. noiseless, silent.

निःशस्त्र *niḥ-śastră* [S.], adj. **1.** unarmed. **2.** disarmed. — ~ करना, to disarm. – निःशस्त्रीकरण, m. disarming; disarmament.

निःशील *niḥ-śīl* [S.], adj. of bad moral character.

निःशुल्क *niḥ-śulk* [S.], adj. not subject to charge, free.

निःशून्य *niḥ-śūnyă* [S.], adj. quite empty, vacant.

निःशेष *niḥ-śeṣ* [S.], adj. without remainder: **1.** vanished. **2.** entire, complete.

निःश्वास *niḥ-śvās* [S.], m. breathing out: the breath: a sigh.

निःसंकोच *niḥ-saṅkoc* [S.], adj. **1.** without constraint or reserve. **2.** without embarrassment, or shyness.

निःसंख्य *niḥ-saṅkhya* [S.], adj. innumerable.

निःसंग *niḥ-saṅg* [S.], adj. **1.** companionless; not attached. **2.** indifferent; disinterested.

निःसंदेह *niḥ-sandeh* [S.], adj. **1.** undoubted; certain. **2.** free from anxiety.

निःसंधि *niḥ-sandhi* [S.], adj. not having joins or intermediate weaknesses; solid, strong.

निःसंशय *niḥ-saṃśay* [S.], adj. **1.** undoubted; infallible, certain. **2.** not doubting, confident.

निःसत्य *niḥ-satyă* [S.], adj. untrue, false; insincere.

निःसरण *niḥ-saraṇ* [S.], m. **1.** exit; egress. **2.** fig. death.

निःसार *niḥ-sār* [S.], adj. **1.** without pith or sap. ***2.** without content or substance; insubstantial, worthless.

निःसीम *niḥ-sīm* [S.], adj. limitless; immeasurable.

निःसृत *niḥ-sṛt* [S.], adj. gone forth.

निःस्पृह *niḥ-spṛh* [S.], adj. without desire; indifferent (to).

निःस्पृहता *niḥ-spṛhătā* [S.], f. freedom from, or absence of, desire.

निःसृत *niḥ-sṛt* [S.], adj. gone forth; originated.

निःस्राव *niḥ-srāv* [S.], m. outflow.

निःस्व *niḥ-svă* [S.], m. without worth, valueless.

निःस्वार्थ *niḥ-svârth* [S.], adj. selfless, disinterested.

नि:स्वीकरण *niḥ-svīkaraṇ* [S.], m. expropriation, confiscation.

नि- *ni-* [S.], pref. **1.** down, back, into (e.g. निलंबित, adj. suspended). 2. = नि:-, निर्-, &c.

निकंद *nikand* [? ad. *niḥ-*, w. *kanda-*], adj. & m. **1.** *Pl.* rooted up; eradicated. **2.** Av. uprooting; destroying.

निकंदन *nikandan* [cf. H. *nikand*], m. Av. **1.** destruction. **2.** fig. destroyer.

निकट *ni-kaṭ* [S.], adj. & ppn. **1.** adj. near, close (of space, or time). **2.** close (of affinity, rapport). **3.** ppn. (w. के). near, close (to). **4.** in the opinion (of). — ~ माँगना, to ask (of, के), to address a request (to). – निकटकालीन, adj. impending. निकटवर्ती, adj. living or situated near: neighbouring; adjacent. निकटस्थ, adj. id.; = ~, 2.

निकटता *ni-kaṭătā* [S.], f. nearness; proximity.

निकटत्व *ni-kaṭatvă* [S.], m. = निकटता.

निकटपना *ni-kaṭpanā* [cf. H. *nikaṭ*], m. reg. = निकटता.

निकटी *ni-kaṭī* [cf. H. *nikaṭ*], f. = निकटता.

निकती *niktī*, f. *Pl. HŚS.* a small scale (as used by goldsmiths, bankers).

निकम्मा *nikammā* [*niṣkarman-*], adj. **1.** unemployed. **2.** worthless, good for nothing (a person); wretched. **3.** useless, unserviceable.

निकर *ni-kar* [S.], m. **1.** heap, pile; abundance. *__2.__ an assemblage, multitude; host. **3.** essence.

निकलना *nikalnā* [**niṣkalati*], v.i. **1.** to be taken out (of, से); to be pulled out. **2.** to be extracted (as minerals); to be pressed out (juice); to be distilled. **3.** to be removed, taken off. **4.** to come out, to emerge; to pour out, to leak out (a substance); to flow; to shoot (sprouts); to be shot forth. **5.** to turn out, to result (a matter); to prove to be; to be debited or credited as a balance (to, पर, or के नाम). बात ऐसी ही निकली, that was just how the matter turned out. **6.** to go out; to go on its way (a procession); to go away. **7.** to be lost (the character or quality of sthg.); to disappear. **8.** to pass by (as time, life); to be wasted. **9.** to go ahead, to advance; to go (beyond, से), to exceed, to excel. **10.** to project; to be prominent (also fig). **11.** to find expression or utterance (feelings, words). **12.** to get out, to escape; to slip or to slink away; to break loose; to secede; to be aloof, uninvolved. **13.** to be freed or extricated (from a difficulty). **14.** to go back (on or from, से: as on a promise). **15.** to be brought out, produced; to be issued or published; to be in force, or observed (law, custom). **16.** to be hatched. **17.** to get under way (as a discussion); to be held (a procession); to begin, to develop; to progress well (an enterprise); to be attended to (a matter). **18.** esp. w. चलना. to set aside inhibitions, to come out of (one's) shell. **19.** to be built out, to run (from, से: as a road or canal, from a starting-point). **20.** to slip (from its place), to be dislodged; to come undone (a fastening). **21.** to run out (a stock of goods).

निकलवाना *nikalvānā* [cf. H. *nikālnā*], v.t. to cause to be taken out, or ejected, &c. (by, से).

निकष *ni-kaṣ* [S.], m. touchstone.

निकषण *ni-kaṣaṇ* [S.], m. **1.** touchstone. **2.** rubbing: putting to the test (as on a touchstone).

निकस- *nikas-* [**niṣkasati*: Pk. *ṇikkasijjaï*], v.i. Brbh. Av. = निकलना.

[1]**निकाई** *nikāī* [cf. P. *nek*], f. Brbh. **1.** goodness, good quality. **2.** beauty.

[2]**निकाई** *nikāī* [cf. H. *nikānā*], f. reg. **1.** weeding. **2.** price paid for weeding.

निकाना *nikānā* [? cf. H. *nīkā*], v.t. reg. to weed, to clear (ground).

[1]**निकाम** *nikām* [*niṣkarma-*; × H. *kām*], adj. *Pl. HŚS.* = निकम्मा.

[2]**निकाम** *ni-kām* [ad. *nikāmam*], adv. *Pl. HŚS.* willingly; to one's satisfaction, or heart's content; very, exceedingly.

निकाय *ni-kāy* [S.], m. **1.** heap, collection. **2.** crowd, flock. **3.** group, body (of persons); an organisation.

निकाल *nikāl* [*niṣkāla-*], m. **1.** outlet, &c. (= निकास). **2.** expedient, contrivance. **3.** ejection, &c. (see निकालना).

निकालना *nikālnā* [*niṣkālayati*], v.t. **1.** to take out (of, से); to pull out; to extract. **2.** to extract (as minerals); to press out (juice); to distil. **3.** to take out, to deduct (as a sum from an account). **4.** to pick out, to select. **5.** to remove (from, से); to take out, or off; to discard. **6.** to extricate (from difficulties); to take away; to evacuate (from a place). **7.** to make off with, to abduct. **8.** to exclude, to except; to strike out (from a list). **9.** to drive out, to eject; to send out (from a room, &c.); to expel (from a caste, or group); to dismiss (from a post). **10.** to beat out; to thresh (corn); to dig out. **11.** to get rid of (sthg. unwanted). **12.** to bring out or forth, to produce; to issue (sthg.), to publish. **13.** to hatch. **14.** to set under way (as a conversation); to hold (a procession). **15.** to build out, to extend (as a house; or as a canal or road, across a region). **16.** to work out, to arrive at (a conclusion, &c.); to solve (a problem); to deduce (a motive or intention); to invent, to develop (a technique, &c.); to find, to strike (a balance). **17.** to achieve (an aim, or success). **18.** to make out, to ascertain (as a path). **19.** to express (as an intention); to give vent to (emotion). **20.** to break in, to train (a horse). **21.** to let out, to utter (words, a secret). — निकाल लाना, to bring away; to abduct. निकाल ले आना, id.

निकास *nikās* [*niṣkāsa-*], m. **1.** exit, issue. **2.** place of exit. **3.** Brbh. opening (from a herdsmen's enclosure). **4.** outlet; vent; discharge nozzle. **5.** drainage. **6.** source, origin. **7.** product, yield (as of an estate); income. **8.** sale, sales. **9.** export; transit duties. **10.** means of escape (from a difficulty; from rebirth). — निकास-पत्र, m. statement of outgoings: *Pl.* statement of adjusted accounts, or of gross produce of an estate receivable by the landlord.

निकास- *nikās-* [*niṣkāsayati*], v.t. reg. = निकालना.

निकासी *nikāsī* [*niṣkāsa-*], f. 1. = निकास, 1., 5. **2.** yield, output; income; profit. **3.** trade, profit. **4.** transit duties; clearance. **5.** extraction (of minerals). 6. = निकास-पत्र.

निकाह *nikāh* [A. *nikāḥ*], m. *musl.* marriage. — ~ करना, to marry. ~ कर देना (का), to give (a person) in marriage (to, से). ~ पढ़ाना, to perform the marriage ceremony (of, का), to marry. – निकाह-नामा, m. marriage contract.

निकिष्ट *ni-kiṣṭ*, adj. Brbh. = निकृष्ट.

निकुंज *ni-kuñj* [S.], m. **1.** an overgrown place, thicket. **2.** arbour, bower; specif. in the later Kr̥ṣṇa story, a partic. meeting-place of Rādhā and Kr̥ṣṇa in Vr̥ndāvan.

निकुंभला *nikumbhălā* [ad. *nikumbhilā-*], f. *mythol.* name of a sacrificial grove at Laṅkā.

निकृत *ni-kr̥t* [S.], adj. brought down: **1.** offended, injured. ***2.** base, wicked.

निकृति *ni-kr̥ti* [S.], f. **1.** baseness; dishonesty, fraud. **2.** insult.

निकृष्ट *ni-kr̥ṣṭ* [S.], adj. & m. drawn down: **1.** adj. debased, vile. **2.** wretched (as conditions, way of life). **3.** crude.

निकृष्टता *ni-kr̥ṣṭătā* [S.], f. debased state, &c.; outcaste state.

निकेत *ni-ket* [S.], m. **1.** mansion, abode. **2.** Brbh. fig. the body.

निकेतन *ni-ketan* [S.], m. 1. = निकेत. **2.** temple.

निकोटना *nikoṭnā*, v.t. to pinch or to pick (with the nails).

निकोसना *nikosnā* [**niṣkoṣati*], v.t. **1.** to bare (the teeth); to grin. **2.** to grind the teeth.

निकौड़िया *nikauṛiyā* [*niḥ-*, w. H. *kauṛī*], adj. & m. reg. **1.** adj. not having a cowrie, not having a farthing. **2.** m. a penniless person.

निक्षिप्त *ni-kṣipt* [S.], adj. **1.** thrown away, or down. **2.** rejected, abandoned. **3.** placed (in), deposited; staked (in a wager); pawned.

निक्षेप *ni-kṣep* [S.], m. **1.** throwing away, or down. **2.** abandoning. **3.** placing, depositing; a deposit.

निक्षेपक *ni-kṣepak* [S.], m. a depositor.

निक्षेपण *ni-kṣepaṇ* [S.], m. **1.** throwing away, &c. **2.** abandoning. **3.** placing, depositing.

निक्षेपता *ni-kṣepătā* [S.], m. *Pl.* depositor.

निक्षेपित *ni-kṣepit* [S.], adj. = निक्षिप्त.

निक्षोभ *ni-kṣobh* [S.], m. *Pl.* tranquillity, quiet.

निखंड *nikhaṇḍ*, adj. *Pl. HŚS.* exactly half. — ~ आधी रात, f. exactly midnight.

निखट्टू *nikhaṭṭū* [cf. H. *khaṭnā*], adj. & m. **1.** adj. idle; feckless. **2.** unemployed. **3.** useless, worthless. **4.** m. an idler, &c.

निखद *nikhad*, adj. reg. bad, worst, dire.

निखरना *nikharnā* [**niḥkṣarati*], v.i. **1.** to become clear, or clean (as a liquid, standing). **2.** to be strained. **3.** to become clear (the complexion; the sky); to become composed, serene. **4.** to be purified; to be refined, perfected.

निखरवाना *nikharvānā* [cf. H. *nikharnā*], v.t. to cause to be made clear or clean, &c. (by, से).

निखराना *nikhrānā*, v.t. = निखरवाना.

निखार *nikhār* [cf. H. *nikhārnā*], m.f. clearing: **1.** enhancement; beautifying. **2.** refinement, development.

निखारना *nikhārnā* [**niḥkṣārayati*], v.t. **1.** to make clear or clean; to allow to stand (liquid). **2.** to strain. **3.** to bleach. **4.** to wash out (clothes, or a stain). **5.** reg. to peel.

निखिल *ni-khil* [S.], adj. whole, entire; all.

निखुटना *nikhuṭnā* [**niṣkhuṭyate*], v.i. (*HŚS.*) to run out (as provisions, or time); to be exhausted.

निखेद *ni-khed* [ad. *niṣedha-*], adj. E.H. = निषेध.

निखेदित *ni-khedit* [S.], adj. *Pl.* ? whose suffering or sorrow has been removed.

निखोट *nikhoṭ* [**niṣkhoṭṭa-*], adj. Brbh. **1.** without defect or fault. **2.** straightforward, honest, open.

निखोड़ना *nikhoṛnā* [**niṣkhoṭayati*], v.t. *Pl. HŚS.* **1.** to tear off, or out. **2.** to flay.

निखोड़ा *nikhoṛā* [cf. H. *nikhoṛnā*], adj. & m. *Pl. HŚS.* **1.** adj. mercilessly cruel. **2.** m. one who flays: an inhuman wretch.

निगंदना *nigandnā* [cf. P. *nigandan*], v.t. *Pl. HŚS.* to quilt; to sew with long stitches.

निगंदा *nigandā* [cf. H. *nigandnā*], m. *Pl.* quilting; a long stitch.

निगंदाई *nigandāī*, f. *Pl.* = निगंदा.

निगड़ *nigaṛ* [ad. *nigaḍa-*], m. **1.** an iron chain for the feet (esp. of elephants). **2.** a fetter.

निगद *ni-gad* [S.], m. *Pl. HŚS.* reciting, recitation (esp. of prayers or charms).

निगम *ni-gam* [S.], m. **1.** the Vedic text; scripture. **2.** a particular passage or word cited from the Vedas. **3.** a sacred precept. **4.** a corporation; municipal council. **5.** a municipality. **6.** name of a sub-group of the Kāyasth community; a merchant, trader. — **निगम-कर**, m. corporation tax. **निगम-आगम**, m. the Vedas and *śāstras*.

निगमन *ni-gaman* [S.], m. **1.** insertion (as of the name of a deity into a liturgical formula). **2.** quotation (of words from the Vedas). **3.** conclusion, deduction. **4.** *admin.* incorporation.

निगमी *ni-gămī* [S.], m one versed in the Vedas.

निगर *nigar* [**nirguru-*[1]], adj. reg. dense, solid; heavy.

निगरा *nigrā* [cf. **nirgarati*; ? **nirgaḍati*], adj. squeezed out (thick sugar-cane juice).

निगरान *nigarān* [P. *nigarān*], adj. U. watching; guarding.

निगरानी *nigrānī* [P. *nigarānī*], f. **1.** watch, supervision; surveillance. **2.** inspection. — **~ करना**, or **रखना** (की), to watch, &c. **~ में**, adv. under surveillance, &c.

निगलना *nigalnā* [*nigalati*: w. MIA *-gg-*], v.t. **1.** to swallow; to gulp down. **2.** fig. to misappropriate (assets); to embezzle.

निगह- *nigah-* = निगाह: — **निगहबान** [P. *-bān*], m. watchman. **°ई**, f.

निगाल *nigāl* [**niṅgāla-*], f. a bamboo, *Arundinaria elegans.*

निगाली *nigālī* [**niṅgāla-*], f. **1.** a type of bamboo, cane or reed. **2.** hookah stem made of cane, &c.

निगाह *nigāh* [P. *nigāh*], f. **1.** look, glance. **2.** consideration, estimation; judgment. **3.** attention, care. — **~ उठाकर न देखना**, = आँख उठाकर न देखना. **~ करना**, to look (at, पर), to observe; to inspect. **~ फेरना**, = आँख फेरना. **~ बदलना**, to withdraw (one's, की) favour; to be changed (a person). **~ मिलाना** (से), to look (one) in the eye; to catch the eye (of, की). **~ में रखना**, to keep in sight, or in view; to watch over. **~ रखना**, to observe, to watch; to take care (of, की), to watch over; to attend (to, पर), to inspect; to have a discriminating eye (in a matter, में). **~ लड़ाना**, to look lovingly, or flirtatiously (at, से). **निगाहें दौड़ाना**, to run the eyes (over, पर), to glance (at, की तरफ़).

निगुन *nigun* [ad. *nirguṇa-*], adj. = निर्गुण.

निगुनी *nigunī* [cf. H. *nigun*], adj. & m. Brbh. **1.** adj. without good qualities (cf. निर्गुण). **2.** m. a man devoid of good qualities.

निगुरा *nigurā* [*nirguru-*[2]], adj. E.H. not having a teacher.

निगूढ़ *ni-gūṛh* [S.], adj. secret, mysterious; profound. — **निगूढ़ार्थ** [°*ṛha+a*°], adj. & m. having a hidden sense; hidden sense.

निगोड़ा *nigoṛā* [cf. H. *goṛ*], adj. & m. crippled (and hence also, having no heirs, or relatives): **1.** adj. pej. miserable, wretched. **2.** (as an endearment to a child) helpless, dependent, poor. **3.** colloq. wretched. **4.** m. a wretched person; rogue, villain.

निग्गर *niggar*, adj. reg. = निगर.

निग्रह *ni-grah* [S.], m. holding down or back: **1.** restraining, checking; subduing. **2.** restraint, control. **3.** punishment. **4.** aversion. — **~ करना** (का), to restrain, to control, &c.

निग्रह- *nigrah-* [ad. *nigṛhṇāti* or *nigraha-*; w. H. *gahnā*], v.t. Brbh. to restrain; to seize.

निग्रहण *ni-grahaṇ* [S.], m. **1.** subduing; suppression. **2.** confinement. **3.** defeat.

निग्रही *ni-grahī* [S.], adj. & m. **1.** adj. restraining, &c. (see निग्रह). **2.** m. one who restrains, &c.

निघंटु *ni-ghaṇṭu* [S.], m. a glossary (esp. of Vedic terms).

निघट- *nighaṭ-* [**nirghaṭṭati*], v.i. Brbh. to be greatly decreased.

निघरा *nigharā* [**nirghara-*], adj. & m. **1.** adj. homeless. **2.** pej. wretched. **3.** m. a homeless person; bachelor.

निघर्षण *ni-gharṣaṇ* [S.], m. rubbing, grinding.

निघात *ni-ghāt* [S.], m. a blow, downward blow.

निचड़ना *nicaṛnā*, v.i. = निचुड़ना.

निचय *ni-cay* [S.], m. **1.** heap, pile. **2.** collection. **3.** fund.

[1]**निचला** *niclā* [cf. H. *nīcā*], adj. lower, nether.

[2]**निचला** *niclā* [*niścala-*], adj. motionless; still, quiet.

निचाई *nicāī* [cf. H. *nīcā*], f. **1.** lowness. **2.** depth. **3.** bottom (of water, river). **4.** inferiority; baseness.

निचान *nicān* [cf. H. *nīcā*], f. m. 1. = निचाई, 1., 2. **2.** low ground; a hollow; valley. **3.** sloping ground.

निचास *nicās*, f. reg. = निचाई.

निचिंत *nicint*, adj. = निश्चिंत.

निचीतौ *nicītau*, adj. Brbh. = निश्चिंत.

निचुड़ना *nicuṛnā* [cf. H. *nicoṛnā*], v.i. **1.** to ooze out; to drip; to distil. **2.** to be squeezed, pressed or wrung out (liquid).

निचुड़वाना *nicuṛvānā* [cf. H. *nicoṛnā*], v.t. to cause (liquid) to be wrung out, or strained, &c. (from, से).

निचोड़ *nicoṛ* [cf. H. *nicoṛnā*], m. **1.** liquid pressed or wrung out; juice, extract. **2.** transf. essence; gist.

निचोड़ना *nicoṛnā* [**niścoṭayati*; ? infld. in meaning by **niścyoṭayati*], v.t. **1.** to press or to wring out (liquid); to strain. **2.** fig. to extort; to milk, to bleed.

निचोड़ू *nicoṛū* [cf. H. *nicoṛnā*], m. colloq. **1.** extortionist, blackmailer. **2.** skinflint, miser.

निचोल *ni-col* [S.], m. women's outer garment, wrap; skirt.

निचौह- *nicauh-*, adj. Brbh. lowered, low (as the eyes, glance).

निछत्र *nichatr*, adj. Brbh. devoid of kṣatriyas (the earth).

निछनियाँ *nichaniyāṁ*, adv. Brbh. truly, indeed.

निछावर *nichāvar*, f. m. **1.** an offering. **2.** money scattered at marriages and on other festive occasions. **3.** a sacrifice. — ~ करना, to offer up; to sacrifice.

निछावरि *nichāvari*, f. Brbh. Av. = निछावर.

निज *nij* [S.], adj. **1.** one's own. **2.** personal; private. **3.** particular, special. **4.** true, real (as the ultimate being). — ~ कर-, E.H. to ascertain. ~ करके, adv. *HŚS.* entirely; certainly. ~ का, adj. own; personal; special; private. ~ के लिए, adj. for (one's) private use. ~ जोत, m. land cultivated by the owner or tenant himself. ~ पुत्र, m. own son, legitimate son. — निज-तिज, or निज-तिझ, f. propriety, correctness; निज-तिज से, adv. properly, as requisite. निज-वाचक, adj. *gram.* reflexive. निजस्व, m. personal property; particular character or nature. °ता, f. individuality.

निज़ा *nizā* [A. *nizā'*], m. f. U. dispute.

निजात *nijāt*, f. see नजात.

निज़ाम *nizām* [A. *niẓām*], m. **1.** arrangement, organisation. **2.** structure, system. **3.** a governor, administrator.

निज़ामत *nizāmat* [A. *niẓāma*: P. *niẓāmat*], f. U. arrangement, government, administration: — ~ अदालत, f. *hist.* Supreme Court of Criminal Justice.

निज़ार *nizār* [P. *nizār*], adj. U. thin; emaciated.

निजी *nijī* [S.], adj. = निज, 1., 2. — ~ कालेज, m. a private college.

निझर *ni-jhar* [S.], m. **1.** waterfall, cascade. **2.** mountain stream. **3.** spring.

निझर- *nijhar-*, v.i. Brbh. to be found not at fault.

निझरना *nijharnā* [**nirjharati*], v.i. to fall (leaves, &c).

निझा- *nijhā-* [*nidhyāyati*], v.t. Brbh. to look at attentively, or fixedly.

निझोटना *nijhoṭnā*, v.t. **1.** to snatch. **2.** to twitch, to tug.

निठल्ला *niṭhallā*, adj. **1.** idle, indolent. **2.** without work; not having work, free. **3.** reg. = निठाला.

निठल्लापन *niṭhallāpan* [cf. H. *niṭhallā*], m. idleness.

निठल्लू *niṭhallū*, adj. = निठल्ला, 1.

निठाला *niṭhālā*, m. **1.** idleness. **2.** unemployment.

निठुर *niṭhur* [*niṣṭhura-*], adj. 1. = निष्ठुर. **2.** obdurate, relentless. **3.** wilful.

निठुरता *niṭhurtā*, f. = निठुराई.

निठुराई *niṭhurāī* [cf. H. *niṭhur*], f. 1. = निष्ठुरता. **2.** obduracy, relentlessness. **3.** wilfulness.

निठौर *niṭhaur* [H. *ni-*: ? via *niḥ-*, +H. *ṭhaur*], adj. Brbh. having no place, or support.

निडर *niḍar* [*nirdara-*], adj. **1.** fearless. **2.** brash.

निडरता *niḍartā* [cf. H. *niḍar*], f. reg. = निडरपन.

निडरपन *niḍarpan* [cf. H. *niḍar*], m. **1.** fearlessness. **2.** brashness.

निडरपना *niḍarpanā*, m. = निडरपन.

निढाल *niḍhāl* [H. *nir-*: ? via *niḥ-*, +H. [1]*ḍhāl*], adj. weak, faint; listless; inert.

निढालपन *niḍhālpan* [cf. H. *niḍhāl*], m. listlessness, inertia.

नित *nit* [cf. H. *nitya-*], adv. always, daily. नित-नया, adj. ever new; variable. नित-नव, adj. Brbh. Av. id. नित-नित, adv. = नित. नित-नेम, m. & adv. daily religious duty; regularly, daily.

नितंब *nitamb* [S.], m. buttocks (esp. of a woman).

नितंबिनी *nitambinī* [S.], f. a physically attractive woman.

नितांत *ni-tānt* [S.], adj. & adv. **1.** adj. extreme; excessive. **2.** adv. utterly, very; excessively.

नित्ता *nittā*, f. *Pl.* = नित्यता.

नित्य *nitya* [S.], adj. & adv. **1.** adj. perpetual, eternal. **2.** constant; daily. **3.** adv. for ever; always. — ~ कर्म, m. a daily act, rite or obligation. ~ क्रिया, f. id. — नित्य-प्रति, adv. = ~. नित्यशः, adv. = ~.

नित्यता *nityătā* [S.], f. perpetual, or constant nature.

निथरना *nitharnā* [*nistarati*], v.i. **1.** to stand (a liquid); to be purified. **2.** to be strained, or filtered.

निथार *nithār* [*nistāra-*], m. **1.** water or fluid from which material in suspension has settled. **2.** sediment, residue. **3.** ? f. reg. the action or process of drawing off liquid, filtering, &c.

निथारना *nithārnā* [*nistārayati*], v.t. **1.** to allow to stand (a liquid; to draw off (clear water, &c.); to decant. **2.** to strain, to filter (a liquid). **3.** *chem.* to precipitate (a substance from a solution).

निदर- *nidar-* [**nirdarati*], v.t. Brbh. Av. to treat with disrespect, or contempt.

निदर्शन *ni-darśan* [S.], m. **1.** showing, indicating. **2.** an indication; evidence; example. **3.** direction, leadership. — ~ में, adv. under the direction, or supervision (of, के).

निदर्शनी *ni-darśanī* [S.], f. a guide, manual.

निदर्शित *ni-darśit* [S.], adj. **1.** shown, indicated. **2.** adduced.

निदाई *nidāī* [cf. H. *nidānā*], f. reg. **1.** weeding. **2.** reaping.

निदाघ *ni-dāgh* [S.], m. **1.** heat; body heat. **2.** the hot season.

निदान *ni-dān* [S.], m. & adv. **1.** m. first or prime cause. **2.** cause of a disease; pathology; diagnosis. **3.** end, conclusion; outcome. **4.** point of death. **5.** adv. in the end, finally. **6.** altogether, all things considered. — ~ यह कि..., the fact (or conclusion) of the matter is that.... — निदान-गृह, m. clinic. निदान-शास्त्र, m. diagnostics.

निदाना *nidānā* [**nirdāti*: Pk. *ṇiṁdiṇī-*], v.t. reg. **1.** to weed, to clear. **2.** to cut, to reap.

निदिग्ध *ni-digdh* [S.], adj. **1.** smeared. **2.** piled up or upon.

निदिष्ट *ni-diṣṭ* [S.], adj. directed; advised.

निदेश *ni-deś* [S.], , m. **1.** order, command. **2.** provision, specification. **3.** direction; leadership; guidance. — निदेशालय [°*śa*+*ā*°], m. directorate.

निदेशक *ni-deśak* [S.], m. **1.** director (of an institution). **2.** guide, supervisor (of work, activity).

निदेशन *ni-deśan* [S.], m. direction, control; supervision.

निदेशिका *ni-deśikā* [S.], f. directory.

निद्रा *nidrā* [S.], f. sleep. — निद्राकर, adj. soporific; narcotic. निद्रालस [°*rā*+*ā*°], adj. somnolent, drowsy.

निद्रालु *nidrālu* [S.], adj. sleepy, drowsy.

निद्रालुता *nidrālutā* [S.], f. drowsiness.

निद्रित *nidrit* [S.], adj. asleep.

निधड़क *nidhaṛak* [H. *nir-*: ? via *niḥ-*, +H. *dhaṛak*], adj. & adv. **1.** adj. bold, fearless. **2.** adv. fearlessly. **3.** without hesitation; without reflection.

निधन *ni-dhan* [S.], m. end; death, decease. — निधन-सूचना, f. obituary.

निधनी *nidhanī* [*nirdhana-*], adj. Brbh. poor (without wealth).

निधान *ni-dhān* [S.], m. **1.** putting aside, storing; depositing. ***2.** a store, treasury; receptacle. **3.** the subject in which any quality inheres. **4.** sthg. stored up, a treasure.

निधि *nidhi* [S.], f. **1.** store, treasury. **2.** fig. a person endowed (with good qualities). **3.** a hoard, treasure. **4.** a layer, deposit (of valuable minerals). **5.** a fund. — निधिकरण, m. funding. निधि-नाथ, m. *mythol.* lord of treasure: a title of Kuvera. निधि-निधान, m. a storehouse of riches: sthg. infinitely precious.

निधुवन *ni-dhuvan* [S.], m. *Pl. HŚS.* shaking about: **1.** sexual intercourse. **2.** reg. amusement, diversion.

निधेय *ni-dhey* [S.], adj. to be instituted, or preserved.

निन- *nin-* [cf. *nirṇāmayati*, v.t.], v.i. Brbh. to be lowered (as the eyes).

निनाद *ni-nād* [S.], m. sound, noise; rumble, roar; buzz, hum; ringing sound.

निनादित *ni-nādit* [S.], adj. made to resound: ringing, &c.

निनादी *ni-nādī* [S.], adj. *Pl. HŚS.* **1.** resounding: ringing, &c. 2. = निनादित.

निनानवे *ninānve*, adj. = निन्यानवे.

निनावाँ *nināvāṁ* [**nirṇāmaka-*], adj. & m. **1.** adj. nameless; something which it is unlucky to name (as cholera, diphtheria). **2.** m. *med.* thrush.

निन्यानवे *ninyānve* [*navanavati*], adj. ninety-nine. — ~ के फेर, or चक्कर, में पड़ना, to be over-engrossed in acquiring wealth; to be involved in difficulties.

निपट *nipaṭ* [**nispraṣṭha-*: Pk. *ṇippaṭṭha-*; ? × H. *nibaṭnā, nipaṭnā*], adv. **1.** completely, quite. **2.** very, extremely; excessively.

निपटना *nipaṭnā* [cf. H. *nipṭānā*], v.i. = निबटना.

निपटान *nipṭān* [cf. H. *nipṭānā*], m. disposal.

निपटाना *nipṭānā* [cf. H. *nibṭānā*], v.t. = निबटाना.

निपटारा *nipṭārā* [cf. H. *nipaṭnā*], m. = निपटाव.

निपटारू *nipṭārū* [cf. H. *nipṭārā*], m. reg. one who settles, accomplishes, &c.

निपटाव *nipṭāv*, m. **1.** completion. **2.** settlement, conclusion (of a matter, &c).

निपटेरा *nipṭerā*, m. = निपटाव.

निपठ *nipaṭh*, adv. reg. = निपट.

निपतन *ni-patan* [S.], m. = [1]निपात, 1.

निपतित *ni-patit* [S.], adj. **1.** fallen down. **2.** overthrown.

[1]**निपात** *ni-pāt* [S.], m. **1.** falling down, or upon; attack, swoop. **2.** downfall; destruction; death. **3.** incidence, occurrence. **4.** *gram.* an unanalysable form, a particle (specif. in Sanskrit).

[2]**निपात** *nipāt* [*niṣpattra-*; ? via *niḥ-*], adj. Av. leafless.

निपात- *ni-pāt-* [cf. *nipāta-*], v.t. Brbh. Av. **1.** to cause to fall down, or upon. **2.** to cause the downfall (of, का); to kill.

निपातक *ni-pātak* [S.], m. sin.

निपातन *ni-pātan* [S.], m. **1.** causing to fall down, or upon. **2.** causing the downfall (of, का); killing. **3.** *gram.* classing as an exception to a rule.

निपातित *ni-pātit* [S.], adj. **1.** thrown down, felled, &c. **2.** laid low.

निपाती *ni-pātī* [S.], adj. & m. **1.** adj. throwing down, &c. **2.** m. an overthrower, destroyer.

निपुण *ni-puṇ* [S.], adj. **1.** clever, skilled; expert, accomplished. **2.** distinguished, eminent.

निपुणता *ni-puṇătā* [S.], f. **1.** skill; experience. **2.** distinction, eminence.

निपुणत्व *ni-puṇatvă* [S.], m. *Pl.* = निपुणता.

निपुनाई *nipunāī*, f. Av. = निपुणता.

निपूत *nipūt*, adj. = निपूता.

निपूता *nipūtā* [*niṣputra-*], adj. childless.

निपेटौ *nipeṭau* [*ni*+H. *peṭ*], adj. Brbh. greedy, gluttonous.

निपोड़ना *nipoṛnā* [cf. **niṣpuṭati*], v.t. to show (the teeth); to grin; to snarl; to gnash (the teeth).

निफ़ाक़ *nifāq* [A. *nifāq*], m. U. **1.** disagreement, dissension. **2.** rancour, malice.

निबंध *ni-bandh* [S.], m. **1.** binding, fastening; attachment. ***2.** a composition; an essay; article; dissertation, thesis. **3.** a report, memorandum. — निबंधकार, m. an essayist. निबंधावली [°*dha*+*ā*°], f. series of essays, &c.; collected essays (of a writer).

निबंधन *ni-bandhan* [S.], m. **1.** binding, fastening. **2.** restraining. **3.** a composition. **4.** registration (of a letter, &c). **5.** a term, expression.

निबंधनी *ni-bandhănī* [S.], f. *Pl. HŚS.* bond, fetter.

निबंधित *ni-bandhit* [S.], adj. **1.** bound, fastened. **2.** composed (as an essay). **3.** registered (as a letter).

निबंधी *ni-bandhī* [S.], adj. *Pl. HŚS.* **1.** binding. **2.** having a connection, connected. **3.** being a cause of, causing.

निबटना *nibaṭnā* [cf. *nirvartate*], v.i. **1.** to be completed. **2.** to be settled, adjusted (a matter, a dispute, a debt). **3.** to be consumed, exhausted. **4.** to be finished, or done (with, से); to deal (with). — **निबटी रक़म**, f. colloq. fig. a dispensable or useless person.

निबटाना *nibṭānā* [cf. *nirvartayati*], v.t. **1.** to complete; to get through (work). **2.** to settle, to adjust (as a matter, a debt).

निबटारा *nibṭārā*, m. = **निपटारा**.

निबटाव *nibṭāv* [cf. H. *nibṭānā*], m. settlement (as of a dispute, or a debt).

निबटेरा *nibṭerā*, m. *Pl. HŚS.* = **निपटारा**.

निबद्ध *ni-baddh* [S.], adj. **1.** bound. **2.** set in place (as a precious stone). **3.** composed (as a treatise).

निबल *nibal*, adj. reg. Brbh. = **निर्बल**.

निबहना *nibahnā*, v.i. = **निभना**.

निबाह *nibāh* [*nirvāha-*], m. **1.** carrying on or through (a task, &c.), coping; accomplishing, performance, fulfilment; completion. **2.** maintaining, maintenance. **3.** sufficiency; livelihood. **4.** spending, passing (time). **5.** making do; living in peace, getting on (with, से). **6.** steadfastness, perseverance. — **~ करना**, to carry through, to cope, to accomplish, &c.; to pass (time).

निबाहना *nibāhnā* [*nirvāhayati*], v.t. **1.** to carry on or through (as a task, a relationship); to complete, &c.; to fulfil. **2.** to support, to maintain. **ओर निबाह-**, Av. to carry (sthg.) through (to its end).

निबुक- *nibuk-* [**nirmukna-*: Pk. *ṇimmukka-*], v.i. Brbh. Av. to be loosened, or released.

निबेड़ना *nibeṛnā* [cf. *nirvṛta-*[1]; ? × *nirvartate*], v.t. **1.** to separate, to divide. **2.** to adjust, to decide. **3.** to accomplish, to manage; to fulfil; to complete. — **अपनी ~**, to mind one's own business.

निबेर- *niber-* [cf. *nirvṛta-*[1]], v.t. Brbh. Av. = **निबेड़ना**.

निबेरा *niberā* [cf. H. *niber-*], m. Brbh. Av. **1.** separation. **2.** settlement, decision. ***3.** passage, transit; getting through, deliverance.

निबौरी *nibaurī* [**nimbagulikā-*: Pk. *ṇimboliyā-*], f. Brbh. fruit of the *nīm* tree.

-निभ *-nibh*, adv. formant. like, resembling. — **हिमगिरि-निभ**, adv. like the Himalayas.

निभना *nibhnā* [*nirvahati*], v.i. **1.** to be carried on or through (a task, a relationship); to be accomplished, or completed; to be fulfilled (a promise). **2.** to last, to endure (as a situation). **3.** to come to an end (as a light when extinguished). **4.** to succeed. **5.** to serve, to be sufficient or satisfactory. **6.** to subsist, to live; to eke out a livelihood. — **दोनों में नहीं निभेगी**, the two will not (manage to) get on together.

निभाना *nibhānā* [*nirvāhayati*], v.t. = **निबाहना**. — **भूमिका ~**, to play, or to fill, a role.

निभाव *nibhāv* [cf. *nibhnā*], m. = **निबाह**.

निभृत *ni-bhṛt* [S.], adj. placed down: secret, secluded.

निमंत्रक *ni-mantrak* [S.], m. one who summons or invites.

निमंत्रण *ni-mantraṇ* [S.], m. **1.** call, summons. ***2.** invitation. — **~ करना**, to invite (a person, **का**). **~ देना (को)**, to summon, or to invite (a person: to, **का**).

निमंत्रित *ni-mantrit* [S.], adj. **1.** invited. **2.** summoned.

निमक *nimak*, m. = **नमक**.

निमकी *nimkī* [cf. H. *nimak*], f. salted savouries.

निमकौड़ी *nimkauṛī*, f. = **निंब-कौड़ी**.

निमछड़ा *nimchaṛā* [? P. *nīm*], adj. & m. reg. **1.** adj. not unduly crowded. **2.** m. a place or space that is not unduly crowded.

निमता *nimtā* [ad. **nirmatta-*], adj. Av. not intoxicated, sober.

निमाणी *nimāṇī*, adj. E.H. = **निमाना**, 1.

निमाना *nimānā* [*nirṇāmayati* × *nīpa-*[1] or H. *nimn*], adj. **1.** *Pl.* simple, artless. **2.** Brbh. low (of level).

निमित्त *nimitt* [S.], m. & ppn. **1.** m. cause; motive, reason. **2.** sign; omen. **3.** (? × *nimita-* 'measured') share, allotment; fortune. **4.** ppn. (w. **के**) for the sake (of); for the purpose (of).

निमित्तक *ni-mittak* [S.], adj. Av. caused by, springing from.

निमित्तता *ni-mittātā* [S.], f. causality, instrumentality.

निमित्ती *nimittī* [cf. H. *nimitt*], adj. reg. fortunate, possessing means.

निमिलिका *ni-milikā* [S.], f. = **निमीलन**.

निमिष *ni-miṣ* [S.], m. **1.** winking or blinking (of the eye). **2.** a twinkling of the eye, moment. — **निमिष-मात्र के लिए**, adv. for just a moment.

निमीलन *ni-mīlan* [S.], m. **1.** closing the eyes: dying, death. ***2.** blinking. **3.** conniving (at).

निमीली *ni-mīlī* [S.], adj. & m. *Pl.* **1.** adj. having the eyes shut. **2.** m. one who has the eyes shut.

निमुछिया *nimuchiyā* [cf **mucchā-*], adj. moustacheless; young (a man).

निमुहाँ *nimuhāṁ* [**nirmukha-*], adj. mouthless: **1.** speechless, struck dumb. **2.** silent (by temperament).

निमेष *ni-meṣ* [S.], m. = निमिष.

निमोना *nimonā*, m. Brbh. a preparation from gram or pea flour, fried with spices in *ghī*.

निमौनी *nimaunī* [? cf. *nirmāpayati*], f. reg. the first planting of sugar-cane; the day when this is done; ? the first cutting of sugar-cane.

निम्न *nimn* [S.], adj. & m. **1.** adj. low. **2.** low of rank, or of status (as community); lower, lowest; junior; petty. **3.** m. low ground or place; depth. — **निम्नलिखित**, adj. mentioned below; following. **निम्न-हस्ताक्षरकर्ता** [°*ta*+*a*°], m. inv. the undersigned. **निम्नांकित** [°*na*+*a*°], adj. = निम्नलिखित.

निम्नतम *nimnătam* [S.], adj. lowest.

निम्नता *nimnătā* [S.], f. lowness.

निम्मन *nimman* [*nirmala-*], adj. reg. good, nice.

नियंता *ni-yantā* [S.], m. inv. **1.** ruler, governor. **2.** master.

नियंत्रक *ni-yantrak* [S.], adj. & m. **1.** adj. controlling. **2.** m. controller; one who drives, or steers. **3.** *engin.* governor, regulator.

नियंत्रण *ni-yantraṇ* [S.], m. **1.** governing; guiding. **2.** control. **3.** restriction, limitation. **4.** repression. — ~ **में होना**, to be under (the) control (of, के).

नियंत्रित *ni-yantrit* [S.], adj. **1.** governed. **2.** controlled; restrained, checked. **3.** repressed.

¹**नियत** *ni-yat* [S.], adj. **1.** restrained; subdued. **2.** established, fixed; appointed. **3.** prescribed. — ~ **करना**, to establish (as a procedure); to fix (as a time); to appoint (to a post). – **नियतकालिक**, adj. fixed as to time: periodical; predetermined. **नियतांक** [°*ta*+*a*°], m. *math.* a constant. **नियतात्मा** [°*ta*+*ā*°], adj. inv. self-restrained, self-controlled. **नियताहार** [°*ta*+*ā*°], adj. moderate in eating habits; abstemious. **नियतेंद्रिय** [°*ta*+*i*°], adj. having the passions subdued or restrained.

²**नियत** *niyat*, f. = नीयत.

नियतन *ni-yatan* [S.], m. fixing, determining; allocating.

नियति *ni-yati* [S.], f. **1.** destiny, fate. **2.** injunction, obligation. **3.** control; self-control. — **नियतिवाद**, m. determinism.

नियम *ni-yam* [S.], m. **1.** restraint, restriction. **2.** fixed rule, law; principle; regulation. **3.** custom, normal practice. **4.** self-imposed restraint or religious observance (as fasting, prayer, pilgrimage); vow; penance; piety. **5.** moderation, temperateness. **6.** *gram.* mood. — **नियम-निर्धारक**, adj. & m. legislative; legislator. **नियम-पत्र**, m. written agreement. **नियमपूर्वक**, adv. according to rule or custom; officially, formally. **नियमबद्ध**, adj. = नियमित. **नियमानुकूल** [°*ma*+*a*°], in accordance with rule, or with the law. **नियमानुसार** [°*ma*+*a*°], adv. id.; regularly, habitually. **नियमावली** [°*ma*+*ā*°], m. body of rules (as of a society).

नियमन *ni-yaman* [S.], m. **1.** restraining; subduing. **2.** governing, control; establishing rules. **3.** restriction. **4.** fixed practice or rule.

नियमित *ni-yamit* [S.], adj. **1.** restricted, limited. **2.** fixed, regulated, prescribed. **3.** regular (of occurrence). **4.** in accordance with rule, or law. — ~ **रूप से**, adv. regularly. ~ **परिमाण में**, adv. in limited measure.

नियमी *ni-yamī* [S.], adj. **1.** regular, punctual. **2.** following rule, law or custom. **3.** observing restraint; pious. **4.** moderate, temperate (in thought, behaviour).

नियर *niyar* [*nikaṭam*], adv. Av. near, nearby.

नियरा- *niyarā-* [cf. H. *niyar*], v.i. Brbh. Av. to approach.

नियराई *niyarāī* [cf. H. *niyar*], f. Brbh. Av. nearness, closeness.

नियरे *niyare* [cf. *nikaṭam*], adv. Brbh. Av. = नियर.

नियाज़ *niyāz* [P. *niyāz*], f. **1.** petition; request. **2.** eager desire; respects (as paid to a revered person). **3.** offering; a thing dedicated. **4.** payment of respects, meeting (with). — **नियाज़मंद** [P. *-mand*], adj. supplicating, requesting humbly; dutiful.

नियादर *niyādar* [ad. *nirādara-*], m. reg. = अनादर.

नियामक *ni-yāmak* [S.], adj. & m. **1.** adj. restraining; controlling; regulating. **2.** restrictive. **3.** determining, defining. **4.** m. one who restrains or controls; coachman; steersman.

नियामकता *ni-yāmakătā* [S.], f. *Pl.* controlling power.

नियामत *niyāmat* [f. A. *niʿma*, P. *nĕʿmat*], f. = नेमत.

नियार *niyār* [*nigāra-*], m. reg. fodder. — नियार-फूँस करना, to put fodder out at set times (for cattle).

नियारा *niyārā*, adj. see न्यारा.

नियुक्त *ni-yukt* [S.], adj. **1.** appointed (to, से: as to a post). **2.** engaged (in, में: as in a task). — ~ करना, to appoint.

नियुक्ति *ni-yukti* [S.], f. appointment, post.

नियुद्ध *ni-yuddh* [S.], m. contest, combat; struggle (as of warriors, athletes).

नियोक्ता *ni-yoktā* [S.], m. inv. **1.** ruler; master. ***2.** employer.

नियोग *ni-yog* [S.], m. **1.** attachment, connection (with, से, के साथ). **2.** appointment; appointed task or duty; trust. **3.** employment, use (of). **4.** a directive. **5.** authority. **6.** effort, application. **7.** *Pl. gram.* imperative mood.

नियोगी *ni-yogī* [S.], adj. **1.** appointed; having authority. **2.** occupied, engaged (in, में). **3.** having a connection (with, से, के साथ). **4.** appointing, hiring (for work).

नियोजक *ni-yojak* [S.], m. **1.** employer. **2.** organiser.

नियोजन *ni-yojan* [S.], m. **1.** appointing (to, से), engaging; employing, employment. **2.** ordering, organising; applying (the mind, to a task). **3.** a directive. **4.** planning; calculating; limiting. — नियोजनालय [°*a*+*ā*°], m. employment bureau.

नियोजित *ni-yojit* [S.], adj. **1.** attached (to, से), connected (with). ***2.** appointed (to); engaged. **3.** established, organised. **4.** planned; calculated; limited.

नियोज्य *ni-yojyă* [S.], adj. **1.** to be appointed, or engaged; deserving appointment. **2.** to be planned.

नियोद्धा *ni-yoddhā* [S.], m. inv. **1.** warrior. **2.** contender; competitor.

निर्- *nir-* [S.], pref. **1.** out, away, forth; utterly, quite. **2.** not; not having, without; un-, in-, non-, &c.

निरंकार *nir-aṅkār*, adj. = निराकार.

निरंकुश *nir-aṅkuś* [S.], adj. **1.** unrestrained, unbridled, self-willed. **2.** absolute, autocratic (power, sway).

निरंकुशता *nir-aṅkuśătā* [S.], f. lack of restraint, self-will.

निरंजन *nir-añjan* [S.], adj. & m. without collyrium: **1.** untainted, pure. **2.** a title of the god Śiva. **3.** a title of the ultimate being.

निरंतर *nir-antar* [S.], adj. without gaps or intervals (esp. of time): **1.** continuous; uninterrupted. **2.** eternal. **3.** similar, identical. **4.** contiguous.

निरंध *nir-andh* [S.], adj. E.H. quite blind.

निरंबु *nir-ambu* [S.], adj. Av. **1.** abstaining from water (as during a fast). **2.** waterless.

निरंभ *nir-ambh* [S.], adj. Brbh. = निरंबु.

निरंस *nir-aṃs* [ad. *niraṃśa-*], adj. Brbh. without a share, having no share (of).

निरक्ष *nir-akṣ* [S.], adj. & m. having no latitude: **1.** adj. equatorial. **2.** m. the equator.

निरक्षर *nir-akṣar* [S.], adj. illiterate.

निरक्षरता *nir-akṣarătā* [S.], f. illiteracy.

निरख़ *nirkh* [P. *nirkh*], m. U. price, tariff; market price (as fixed by magistrates or police).

निरखना *nirakhna* [*nirikṣate*], v.t. to look with care at, to observe.

निरखी *nirkhī*, m. reg. = निरीक्षक.

निरचू *nircū*, adj. free of, finished (with, से).

निरजोस *nirjos*, m. Av. = निश्चय.

निरत *ni-rat* [S.], adj. **1.** engaged, engrossed (in, में). **2.** attached, devoted (to).

निरति *ni-rati* [S.], f. **1.** absorption, engrossment (in, में). **2.** passion (for).

निरदहनी *nir-dahănī* [S.], f. the bush *Sanseviera roxburghiana* (bow-string hemp).

निरधार *nir-dhār* [ad. *nirdhāra-*], adv. Brbh. assuredly, certainly.

निरधार- *nir-dhār-* [ad. *nirdhārayati*], v.t. Brbh. to imagine.

निरन्न *nir-ann* [S.], adj. without food, without eating.

निरन्ना *nirannā* [ad. *niranna-*], adj. who or which has no food: — निरन्ने मुँह, adv. without eating.

निरन्वय *nir-anv-ay* [S.], adj. disconnected; illogical.

निरपराध *nir-apă-rādh* [S.], adj. not at fault; innocent.

निरपराधी *nir-apă-rādhī* [S.], m. one who is innocent, &c.

निरपवाद *nir-apă-vād* [S.], adj. **1.** blameless. ***2.** not admitting exceptions (a rule, or practice).

निरपेक्ष *nir-ăpêkṣ* [S.], adj. **1.** not looking for, not desiring. ***2.** not having regard (to); indifferent, impartial.

निरपेक्षता *nir-ăpêkṣătā* [S.], f. = निरपेक्षा.

निरपेक्षा *nir-ăpêkṣā* [S.], f. **1.** indifference, disregard. **2.** impartiality.

निरपेक्षित *nir-ăpêkṣit* [S.], adj. not looked for, not expected or wished.

निरपेक्षी *nir-ăpêkṣī* [S.], adj. = निरपेक्ष.

निरबाह- *nirbāh-* [ad. *nirvāhayati*], v.t. Brbh. Av. = निबाहना.

निरबिसी *nirbisī* [ad. *nirviṣī-*: w. H. *bis*], f. a non-poisonous aconite; a grass called *jadvār*, of which the root is used as an antidote to poison.

निरबैना *nirbainā* [cf. *vacana-*], adj. *Pl.* speechless, silent.

निरभ्र *nir-abhră* [S.], adj. cloudless.

निरमा- *nir-mā-* [ad. *nirmāti*], Brbh. to make, to build; to create; to compose.

निरमोल *nir-mol* [cf. *maulya-*], adj. Brbh. priceless.

निरर्थक *nir-arthak* [S.], adj. **1.** senseless, pointless, vain. **2.** meaningless (as a word); pleonastic. **3.** negligent, careless.

निरवनीकरण *nir-vanīkaraṇ* [S.], m. deforestation.

निरवलंब *nir-avă-lamb* [S.], m. = निरालंब.

निरस *niras* [ad. *nīrasa-*], adj. **1.** without sap. **2.** without flavour, insipid; dull. **3.** unfeeling. **4.** disabused (of, से).

निरसन *nir-asan* [S.], m. throwing out: **1.** removing, rejecting. **2.** cancellation, repeal. **3.** extirpation.

निरसा *nirasā* [conn. *nīrasa-*], adj. reg. **1.** flavourless, insipid. inferior in quality; adulterated.

निरस्त *nir-ast* [S.], adj. thrown out: **1.** removed, rejected; cancelled, repealed. **3.** extirpated.

निरस्त्र *nir-astră* [S.], adj. unarmed. — निरस्त्रीकृत, adj. disarmed.

निरहंकार *nir-ahankār* [S.], adj. free from egoism, or pride.

निरा *nirā* [*nīraja-*: Pk. *ṇĭraya-*], adj. & adv. **1.** pure, unadulterated; real. **2.** absolute; sheer, downright (as nonsense). **3.** mere; only. निरी दाल के साथ रोटी खाना, to eat *roṭī* with nothing but *dāl*. **4.** adv. absolutely, entirely. **5.** merely, only. – वह ~ गाएँगे, बोलेंगे नहीं, he'll only sing, he won't speak.

निरा- *nirā-* [**nīḍāti*: Pa. *niḍḍāyati*], v.t. Av. to clear, to weed (ground).

निराई *nirāī* [cf. H. *nira-*], f. reg. weeding.

निराकरण *nir-ā-karaṇ* [S.], m. **1.** removal (as of error), refutation; extirpation (as of vice). **2.** annulment.

निराकांक्ष *nir-ā-kānkṣ* [S.], adj. without desire, expectation or ambition.

निराकांक्षा *nir-ā-kānkṣā* [S.], f. absence of desire, &c.

निराकांक्षी *nir-ā-kānkṣī* [S.], m. one free from desire, &c.

निराकार *nir-ā-kār* [S.], adj. & m. **1.** adj. formless; without form (as the ultimate being). **2.** malformed. **3.** m. the ultimate being.

निराकृत *nir-ā-kr̥t* [S.], adj. **1.** removed (as error), refuted; extirpated. **2.** annulled.

निराकृति *nir-ā-kr̥ti* [S.], adj. & f. *HŚS.* **1.** adj. not having form (= निराकार). **2.** f. = निराकरण.

निराघात *nir-ā-ghāt* [S.], adj. *ling.* unstressed.

निराचार *nir-ā-cār* [S.], adj. Av. of bad conduct, wicked.

निरादर *nir-ā-dar* [S.], adj. & m. **1.** adj. not respected. **2.** disrespectful ***3.** m. disrespect; scorn; insult. — ~ करना, to show disrespect, &c. (to, का)

निरादृत *nir-ā-dr̥t* [S.], adj. treated disrespectfully; insulted.

निरादेश *nir-ā-deś* [S.], m. payment of a debt.

निराधार *nir-ā-dhār* [S.], adj. **1.** without support, helpless. **2.** baseless, unfounded.

निरापद *nir-ā-pad* [S.], adj. & f. **1.** f. safe or prosperous state. ***2.** adj. free from misfortune or harm; safe (as a place). **3.** not causing misfortune or harm; safe (a medicine, or other substance). **4.** unobjectionable (cf. H. आपत्ति).

निरापदता *nir-ā-padătā* [S.], f. state of safety or immunity.

निरामय *nir-āmay* [S.], adj. Av. free from disease; untainted, pure.

निरामिष *nir-āmiṣ* [S.], adj. meatless: vegetarian.

निरामिषी *nir-āmiṣī* [cf. H. *nirāmiṣ*], adj. = निरामिष.

निरायास *nir-ā-yās* [S.], adj. not requiring trouble, or effort.

निरायुध *nir-ā-yudh* [S.], adj. unarmed.

निरालंब *nir-ā-lamb* [S.], adj. without support; destitute.

निरालस्य *nir-ālasyă* [S.], adj. **1.** adj. not idle, active; unwearied. **2.** m. energy.

निराला *nirālā* [**nirālaya-*: Pa. *nirālaya-*], adj. **1.** adj. separate, apart; lonely (a place); solitary (a person). **2.** distinct; strange, unusual; peculiar, odd. **3.** rare; extraordinary; unique. **4.** m. a lonely place. **5.** a private place.

निरालापन *nirālāpan* [cf. H. *nirālā*], m. **1.** strangeness, peculiarity. **2.** rareness, &c.

निरावरण *nir-ā-văraṇ* [S.], m. **1.** unveiling, revealing. **2.** unveiled or uncovered state.

निराश *nir-āś* [S.], adj. **1.** without hope, despairing. **2.** disappointed (in or with, **से**). **3.** hopeless (as a situation). — ~ **करना**, to deprive of hope, to cause to despair; to disappoint.

निराशा *nir-āśā* [S.], f. **1.** lack of hope, despair. **2.** disappointment. **3.** hopelessness. — **निराशावाद**, m. pessimistic outlook, pessimism. °**ई**, adj. & m. pessimistic; a pessimist.

निराशिष *nir-ā-śiṣ* [S.], adj. corr. without a blessing (cf. **आशिष**).

निराशी *nir-āśī* [S.], adj. hopeless, despairing.

निराश्रय *nir-ā-śray* [S.], adj. without support, shelter or refuge; destitute.

निराश्रित *nir-ā-śrit* [S.], adj. unsupported, &c. destitute.

निरास *nir-ās* [S.], m. throwing out, removing; destroying.

निरासी *nir-āsī* [cf. *nirāśa-*], f. reg. despair.

निराहार *nir-ā-hār* [S.], adj. & m. **1.** adj. without food. **2.** m. fasting, a fast; starvation.

निरीक्षक *nir-īkṣak* [S.], m. **1.** an observer. **2.** an inspector. **3.** a superintendent.

निरीक्षण *nir-īkṣaṇ* [S.], m. **1.** observing, regarding. **2.** inspection. **3.** investigation, study. **4.** supervision, control. **5.** *astron.* aspect. — **निरीक्षणकारी**, adv. observing; inspecting; supervisory.

निरीक्षा *nir-īkṣā* [S.], f. 1. = **निरीक्षण**. **2.** *Pl.* hope, expectation.

निरीक्षित *nir-īkṣit* [S.], adj. **1.** observed. **2.** inspected. **3.** investigated. **4.** supervised.

निरीक्ष्य *nir-īkṣyă* [S.], adj. to be inspected, investigated, &c.

निरीखना *nirīkhnā* [*nirīkṣate*], v.t. = **निरखना**.

निरीह *nir-īh* [S.], adj. **1.** inert. **2.** indifferent. **3.** meek, submissive.

निरीहता *nir-īhătā* [S.], f. **1.** inertness. **2.** indifference. **3.** submissiveness.

निरुक्त *nir-ukt* [S.], adj. & m. **1.** adj. uttered, expressed, defined. **2.** etymological interpretation of words (esp. as to do with Vedic compositions).

निरुक्ति *nir-ukti* [S.], f. = **निरुक्त**, 2.

निरुत्तर *nir-uttar* [S.], adj. **1.** without an answer: silenced, nonplussed. **2.** unanswerable (a question).

निरुत्साह *nir-ut-sāh* [S.], adj. & m. **1.** adj. without ardour or energy; with dampened ardour. **2.** m. lack of ardour or energy.

निरुत्साहित *nir-ut-sāhit* [S.], adj. discouraged; of lowered morale.

निरुद्देश्य *nir-ud-deśyă* [S.], adj. aimless (an activity); not having a purpose (a person).

निरुद्ध *ni-ruddh* [S.], adj. **1.** checked. **2.** blocked (as an account). **3.** choked (as the throat).

निरुद्यम *nir-ud-yam* [S.], adj. inactive, lazy; unoccupied.

निरुद्यमी *nir-ud-yamī* [S.], m. one who is inactive, &c.

निरुद्योग *nir-ud-yog* [S.], adj. without application, negligent, unindustrious.

निरुपद्रव *nir-upă-drav* [S.], adj. not turbulent, peaceful (a region, a mood).

निरुपम *nir-upa-m* [S.], adj. incomparable.

निरुपमित *nir-upă-mit* [S.], adj. uncompared: = **निरुपम**.

निरुपाधि *nir-upâdhi* [S.], adj. without attributes (the ultimate being).

निरुपाय *nir-upây* [S.], adj. **1.** without expedient or remedy; helpless (a person). **2.** irremediable (a situation).

निरुवर- *niruvar-* [cf. H. *niruvār-*], v.i. Av. to be disentangled, &c.

निरुवार *niruvār* [cf. H. *niruvār-*], m. Brbh. **1.** release. **2.** resolution (of a question).

निरुवार- *niruvār-* [*nir-+vārayate*: ad.], v.t. Brbh. Av. to undo, to disentangle.

निरूप *nirūp* [ad. *nīrūpa-*], adj. & m. **1.** adj. formless. **2.** misshapen. **3.** m. the formless one, the supreme being.

निरूपक *ni-rūpak* [S.], m. an investigator.

निरूपण *ni-rūpaṇ* [S.], m **1.** determining, defining; ascertaining. **2.** investigation, examination (of a subject). **3.** exposition (of a viewpoint). **4.** settling, arranging.

निरूपित *ni-rūpit* [S.], adj. **1.** determined, defined. **2.** investigated. **3.** set forth, expounded. **4.** fixed upon, settled; appointed.

निरूप्य *ni-rūpyă* [S.], adj. to be defined, investigated, &c.

निर्ऋति *nirṛti* [S.], f. dissolution: disaster, death.

निरेख- *nirekh-* [*nirīkṣate* × H. *dekhnā*], v.t. Brbh. = निरखना.

निरोग *nirog* [ad. *nīroga-*], adj. & m. **1.** adj. not ill, in good health (= नीरोग). **2.** m. good health.

निरोगी *nirogī* [cf. H. *nirog*], adj. & m. **1.** adj. = निरोग. **2.** m. a healthy person.

निरोगीपन *nirogīpan* [cf. H. *nirogī*], m. reg. good health.

निरोध *ni-rodh* [S.], m. **1.** stopping, checking; interference; prohibition. **2.** preventing, resistance; a preventative. **3.** besieging; siege. **4.** detention (of a criminal, &c).

निरोधक *ni-rodhak* [S.], adj. stopping, checking, &c.

निरोधन *ni-rodhan* [S.], m. = निरोध. — निरोधन-शिविर, m. concentration camp.

निरोधी *ni-rodhī* [S.], adj. = निरोधक.

निरौषध *nir-auṣadh* [S.], adj. *Pl. HŚS.* not having medicine, incurable.

निर्गंध *nir-gandh* [S.], adj. without smell or scent.

निर्गत *nir-gat* [S.], adj. gone out, or away; vanished.

निर्गम *nir-gam* [S.], m. **1.** going out, or away; exit. **2.** issue, publication; issue (of stock). **3.** divergence (of view). **4.** a matter at issue.

निर्गम- *nir-gam-* [ad. **nirgamati*], v.i. Av. to go out.

निर्गमन *nir-gaman* [S.], m. = निर्गम, 1., 2.

निर्गमित *nir-gamit* [S.], adj. gone out, &c.; issued (as stock).

निर्गुंडी *nirguṇḍī* [S.}, f. the shrub *Vitex negundo* (a source of potash).

निर्गुट *nir-guṭ* [S.], adj. not part of a group: non-aligned (nation).

निर्गुटता *nir-guṭătā* [S.], f. non-alignment (political).

निर्गुण *nir-guṇ* [S.], adj. & m. **1.** adj. without qualities or attributes, unqualified (as the ultimate being). **2.** without good qualities. **3.** transf. professing or inculcating devotion to the ultimate being viewed as unqualified (a person, a sect, a body of literature). **4.** m. the unqualified ultimate being. **5.** song on the theme of the bride's departure from her family home at marriage.

निर्गुणता *nir-guṇătā* [S.], f. **1.** *philos.* absence of qualities. **2.** absence of good qualities.

निर्गुणिया *nir-guṇiyā* [S.], m. a believer in an unqualified ultimate being.

निर्गुणी *nir-guṇī* [S.], adj. & m. **1.** adj. without good qualities, worthless; without skills, or gifts. 2. = निर्गुण, 3. **3.** m. a believer in an unqualified absolute being.

निर्घंट *nir-ghanṭ* [S.], m. a word-list; index.

निर्घृण *nir-ghṛṇ* [S.], adj. **1.** Brbh. merciless, cruel. **2.** without aversion, shameless; detestable.

निर्जन *nir-jan* [S.], adj. & m. **1.** adj. uninhabited; deserted, desolate. **2.** m. deserted place, &c.

निर्जल *nir-jal* [S.], adj. & m. **1.** adj. waterless, arid. **2.** not containing or involving water (a process, a fast). **3.** m. an arid region. **4.** a fast in which water is not drunk.

निर्जला *nir-jalā* [S.], m. *hind.* the fast kept on the eleventh day of the light half of the month Jeṭh.

निर्जलित *nir-jalit* [S.], adj. dehydrated.

निर्जीव *nir-jīv* [S.], adj. **1.** lifeless; inanimate. **2.** not lively, dull (as manner).

निर्जीवन *nir-jīvan* [S.], adj. without life, lifeless.

निर्झर *nir-jhar* [S.], m. a waterfall; cascade.

निर्णय *nir-ṇay* [S.], m. **1.** coming to a conclusion; decision (esp. as between alternatives); determination (of a matter). **2.** *law.* judgment, verdict. — ~ करना (का), to ascertain, to determine; to decide. ~ देना, to give a decision or judgment. — निर्णयकारी, adj. decisive. निर्णयात्मक, adj. id.

निर्णयन *nir-ṇayan* [S.], m. giving a decision, judgment, &c.

निर्णायक *nir-ṇāyak* [S.], adj. deciding, decisive; casting (vote).

निर्णीत *nir-ṇīt* [S.], adj. **1.** determined, settled. **2.** decreed.

निर्दय *nir-day* [S.], adj. merciless; cruel.

निर्दयता *nir-dayătā* [S.], f. mercilessness; cruelty (towards, **के साथ**).

निर्दयी *nir-dayī* [S.], adj. = **निर्दय**.

निर्दिष्ट *nir-diṣṭ* [S.], adj. **1.** pointed out, indicated. **2.** determined; designated, specified; given.

निर्दिष्टि *nir-diṣṭi* [S.], f. **1.** assignment, allotment. **2.** assigned portion or part.

निर्देश *nir-deś* [S.], m. **1.** pointing out. **2.** direction, instruction; guidance. **3.** command, order. **4.** designation; specification. **5.** reference, allusion (to, **की ओर**). — **निर्देश-ग्रंथ**, m. reference book, manual. **निर्देश-वाचक**, adj. *gram.* demonstrative. **निर्देशांक** [°*śa*+*a*°], m. *math.* coordinate. **निर्देशात्मक** [°*śa*+*ā*°], adj. id.

निर्देशक *nir-deśak* [S.], adj. & m. **1.** adj. giving instructions, or orders. **2.** providing instructions (for use). **3.** referring (to, **की ओर**). **4.** m. director (as of an institute). **5.** director (of a film, a drama). **6.** supervisor (as of research).

निर्देशन *nir-deśan* [S.], m. **1.** direction, control. **2.** supervision. **3.** reference (to a source, &c). — ~ **में**, adv. under the direction (of, **के**).

निर्देशिका *nir-deśikā* [S.], f. directory.

निर्देशित *nir-deśit* [S.], adj. **1.** directed, instructed; guided. **2.** determined, designated. **3.** pointed out.

निर्दोष *nir-doṣ* [S.], adj. without fault, or blemish; blameless; innocent. — ~ **ठहराना**, to ascertain to be innocent, to acquit; to exonerate.

निर्दोषिता *nir-doṣătā* [S.], f. faultlessness, blamelessness; innocence.

निर्दोषिता *nir-doṣitā* [S.], f. = **निर्दोषता**.

निर्दोषी *nir-doṣī* [S.], adj. = **निर्दोष**.

निर्द्वंद्व *nir-dvandvă* [S.], adj. **1.** indifferent to opposites: as to pleasure and pain). ***2.** not containing contradictions. **3.** even, calm (of temperament). **4.** not forming one of a pair, not dependent (on another). **5.** not disputed (a matter).

निर्धन *nir-dhan* [S.], adj. & m. **1.** adj. poor, needy. **2.** m. a poor man. — ~ **करना**, to reduce to poverty.

निर्धनता *nir-dhanătā* [S.], f. poverty.

निर्धारण *nir-dhāraṇ* [S.], m. **1.** determining, ascertaining. **2.** settling, assessing (as a price, a rate). **3.** an agreement, arrangement.

निर्धारित *nir-dhārit* [S.], adj. **1.** determined, ascertained; defined; laid down, prescribed. **2.** fixed, settled. — ~ **करना**, to determine, &c.

निर्धार्य *nir-dhāryă* [S.], adj. to be determined, &c.

निर्धूत *nir-dhūt* [S.], adj. Brbh. shaken off: washed away (as sins).

निर्निमेष *nir-ni-meṣ* [S.], adj. unblinking.

निर्पक्ष *nir-pakṣ* [S.], adj. corr. = **निष्पक्ष**.

निर्फल *nir-phal* [S.], adj. corr. = **निष्फल**.

निर्बंध *nir-bandh* [S.], m. **1.** restraint; inhibition. **2.** limitation. **3.** obstinacy, perseverance.

निर्बंधन *nir-bandhan* [S.], m. limitation, restriction.

निर्बल *nir-bal* [S.], adj. weak.

निर्बलता *nir-balătā* [S.], f. weakness.

निर्बाध *nir-bādh* [S.], adj. unrestricted; uninterrupted.

निर्बीज *nir-bīj* [S.], adj. & m. **1.** adj. seedless. **2.** infertile (a man); childless. **3.** having no descendants, extinct. **4.** baseless (a statement). **5.** reg. failure of seed or crops to germinate.

निर्बीजन *nir-bījan* [S.], m. sterilisation.

निर्बुद्धि *nir-buddhi* [S.], adj. = **निर्बोध**.

निर्बुद्धिता *nir-buddhitā* [S.], f. *Pl.* folly.

निर्बोध *nir-bodh* [S.], adj. ignorant; foolish.

निर्भय *nir-bhay* [S.], adj. fearless, not afraid (of, **से**); secure (from harm).

निर्भयता *nir-bhayătā* [S.], f. **1.** fearlessness. **2.** freedom from fear or concern; security.

निर्भर *nir-bhar* [S.], adj. & m. **1.** adj. extreme, abounding. ***2.** dependent (on, **पर**). **3.** dependence. — ~ **करना**, = ~ **होना**. ~ **रहना**, to rely (on). ~ **होना**, to depend (on a person, or a matter).

निर्भरता *nir-bharătā* [S.], f. dependence.

निर्भीक *nir-bhīk* [S.], adj. fearless.

निर्भ्रम *nir-bhram* [S.], adj. **1.** not erring or wandering. **2.** not wavering or hesitating, assured.

निर्भ्रांत *nir-bhrānt* [S.], adj. = **निर्भ्रम**.

निर्मम *nir-mam* [S.], adj. selfless: **1.** disinterested, indifferent. ***2.** without tenderness; cruel.

निर्ममता *nir-mamătā* [S.], f. harshness; cruelty.

निर्मल *nir-mal* [S.], adj. clear (as sky, water); pure.

निर्मांस *nir-māṃs* [S.], adj. emaciated, wasted.

निर्माण *nir-māṇ* [S.], m. **1.** building, construction; building works. **2.** manufacture. **3.** creation, development, nurture (as of views, attitudes). **4.** a structure, building; measuring. — **निर्माणकारी**, adj. having to do with construction; constructive. °-**कार्य**, m. construction; creation, development. **निर्माणमूलक**, adj. creative (as activity). **निर्माण-विद्या**, f. the science of architecture. **निर्माणात्मक** [°*ṇa*+*ā*°], adj. constructive.

निर्माता *nir-mātā* [S.], m. inv. **1.** founder. **2.** creator. **3.** maker; (film) producer.

निर्मायक *nir-māyak* [S.], adj. & m. **1.** adj. constructing, creating, &c. (see **निर्माण**). **2.** m. = **निर्माता**, 3.

निर्माल्य *nir-mālyă* [S.], m. **1.** purity. ***2.** the remains of an offering made to a deity.

निर्मित *nir-mit* [S.], adj. **1.** made, built, constructed. **2.** manufactured. **3.** formed, fashioned, developed; founded.

निर्मिति *nir-miti* [S.], f. manufacture, construction, &c. (see **निर्माण**).

निर्मुक्त *nir-mukt* [S.], adj. **1.** released. **2.** granted amnesty.

निर्मूल *nir-mūl* [S.], adj. **1.** rootless; baseless. **2.** eradicated.

निर्मूलन *nir-mūlan* [S.], m. **1.** uprooting, eradication. **2.** showing to be baseless, refutation.

निर्मेघ *nir-megh* [S.], adj. cloudless.

निर्मोह *nir-moh* [S.], adj. **1.** free from illusion. ***2.** not moved by affection or love; cold, harsh.

निर्मोहिया *nir-mohiyā* [cf. H. *nirmoh*], m. one lacking in warmth or affection.

निर्मोही *nir-mohī* [S.], m. = **निर्मोहिया**.

निर्यात *nir-yāt* [S.], m. export; exports. — ~ **करना**, to export. – **निर्यात-कर्ता**, m. inv. an exporter.

निर्यातक *nir-yātak* [S.], m. = **निर्यातकर्ता**.

निर्यान *nir-yān* [S.], m. **1.** going forth; departure (as of an army on campaign). **2.** take-off (of an aircraft); launch (as of a rocket).

निर्यूथ *nir-yūth* [S.], adj. who has left his detachment: deserted (a soldier).

निर्लज्ज *nir-lajj* [S.], adj. shameless, brazen; immodest.

निर्लज्जता *nir-lajjătā* [S.], f. shamelessness; immodesty.

निर्लिप्त *nir-lipt* [S.], adj. **1.** unsmeared, unanointed. **2.** uncontaminated. ***3.** detached (from the world).

निर्लेप *nir-lep* [S.], adj. not smeared (with) or tainted (by) (= **निर्लिप्त**).

निर्लोभ *nir-lobh* [S.], adj. free from desire; free from greed; contented.

निर्वंश *nir-vaṃś* [S.], adj. **1.** not having family, or children. **2.** extinct (race or family).

निर्वंशी *nir-vaṃśī* [cf. H. *nirvaṃś*], adj. esp. pej. = **निर्वंश**, 1.

निर्वनीकरण *nir-vanīkaraṇ* [S.], m. deforestation.

निर्वस्त्र *nir-vastră* [S.], adj. unclothed.

निर्वाक् *nir-vāk* [S.], adj. speechless.

निर्वाचक *nir-vācak* [S.], m. an elector, voter. — **निर्वाचक-सूची**, f. electoral roll.

निर्वाचकता *nir-vācakătā* [S.], f. suffrage. (= **मताधिकार**.)

निर्वाचन *nir-vācan* [S.], m. choice, selection; election, ballot. — ~ **करना**, to choose; to elect. ~ **क्षेत्र**, m. constituency. — **निर्वाचन-अधिकारी**, m. returning officer. **निर्वाचन-अफ़सर**, m. id. **निर्वाचन-जन्य**, adj. filled by election (a post).

निर्वाचित *nir-vācit* [S.], adj. elected.

निर्वाच्य *nir-vācyă* [S.], adj. **1.** not to be uttered. **2.** unobjectionable. ***3.** subject to election.

निर्वाण *nir-vāṇ* [S.], adj. & m. blown out: **1.** adj. dead. **2.** m. death, extinction; eternal bliss (in reunion with the ultimate being); annihilation (of the personality, at death). — **निर्वाण-काल**, m. date of decease.

निर्वात *nir-vāt* [S.], adj. & m. **1.** adj. sheltered from wind or storm. **2.** exhausted of air, made a vacuum. **3.** m. a vacuum.

निर्वाद *nir-vād* [S.], m. **1.** censure, reproach. **2.** negligence.

निर्वापित *nir-vāpit* [S.], adj. scattered, dispersed.

निर्वासन *nir-vāsan* [S.], m. banishment, expulsion; transportation.

निर्वासित *nir-vāsit* [S.], adj. banished, &c.

निर्वाह *nir-vāh* [S.], m. **1.** carrying on or through; accomplishing, fulfilling. **2.** continued existence; subsistence. **3.** conclusion. — ~ करना, to carry on, to manage (by, से); to accomplish, &c.; to bring to a conclusion. – निर्वाह-भत्ता, m. subsistence allowance. निर्वाह-व्यय, m. cost of living.

निर्वाहक *nir-vāhak* [S.], adj. & m. **1.** adj. conducting, carrying out. **2.** m. one who accomplishes, &c.; executor.

निर्वाहन *nir-vāhan* [S.], m. carrying on (an enterprise, &c.: = निर्वाह, 1).

निर्विकल्प *nir-vi-kalp* [S.], adj. not allowing for distinction or difference; changeless (as the ultimate being).

निर्विकार *nir-vi-kār* [S.], adj. unchanged; without defect; changeless (as the ultimate being).

निर्विघ्न *nir-vi-ghnă* [S.], adj. m. **1.** adj. unobstructed; untroubled, secure. **2.** m. lack of obstruction, smooth course.

निर्विघ्नता *nir-vi-ghnătā* [S.], f. = निर्विघ्न, 2.

निर्विधायन *nir-vi-dhāyan* [S.], m. annulment.

निर्विधायित *nir-vi-dhāyit* [S.], adj. annulled.

निर्विभाग *nir-vi-bhāg* [S.], adj. without portfolio (a minister of state).

निर्विवाद *nir-vi-vād* [S.], adj. indisputable.

निर्विवेक *nir-vi-vek* [S.], adj. lacking discretion or judgment.

निर्विवेकता *nir-vi-vekătā* [S.], f. want of discretion or judgment.

निर्विषी *nir-viṣī* [S.], f. = जदवार.

निर्वृत्त *nir-vṛtt* [S.], adj. accomplished, completed.

निर्वृत्ति *nir-vṛtti* [S.], f. **1.** completion, conclusion; result, fruit. **2.** (prop. निवृत्ति) final beatitude.

निर्वेद *nir-ved* [S.], m. disregard (of worldly things).

निर्वैर *nir-vair* [S.], adj. peaceable.

निर्वैरता *nir-vairătā* [S.], f. E.H. peaceableness.

निर्व्यलीक *nir-vy-alīk* [S.], adj. Brbh. without deceit.

निर्व्याज *nir-vy-āj* [S.], adj. without duplicity, sincere; open, candid.

निर्हेतु *nir-hetu* [S.], adj. causeless.

निलंबन *ni-lamban* [S.], m. **1.** suspension (from a function). **2.** suspension (as of a constitution).

निलंबित *ni-lambit* [S.], adj. suspended (see निलंबन).

निलज *nilaj*, adj. = निर्लज्ज.

निलजई *nilajaī*, f. Brbh. shamelessness.

निलजता *nilajătā*, f. E.H. = निर्लज्जता.

निलज्ज *nilajj*, adj. Av. = निर्लज्ज.

1 **निलज्जा** *nilajjā* [*nirlajja-*], adj. & f. (-ई) m. **1.** adj. shameless, &c. (= निर्लज्ज). **2.** f. reg. a shameless or immodest woman.

2 **निलज्जा** *nilajjā* [ad. *nirlajjā-*], f. a shameless or immodest woman.

निलय *ni-lay* [S.], m. resting-place; dwelling-place.

निलोह *niloh* [*nirlobha-*], adj. reg. **1.** without fault or flaw. **2.** unmixed, unadulterated. **3.** nett (profit).

निवर्तमान *ni-vartămān* [S.], adj. serving for the present, provisional (office-holder).

निवस- *ni-vas-* [cf. H. *nivās-*, or ad. *nivasati*], v.i. Brbh. to stay, to reside, to dwell.

1 **निवसन** *ni-vasan* [S.], m. *Pl. HŚS.* dwelling-place; village.

2 **निवसन** *ni-vasan* [S.], m. *Pl. HŚS.* putting on a garment; a garment.

निवह *ni-vah* [S.], m. E.H. multitude.

निवाई *nivāī* [*nivāta-*[1]], f. *Pl.* warmth, sultriness.

निवाड़ *nivāṛ*, f. = [1]निवार.

निवान *nivān* [cf. *nīpa-*[1]], adj. reg. **1.** low (as ground). **2.** level.

निवाना *nivānā* [cf. *namayati*; also *nipātayati*], v.t. = नवाना.

निवाया *nivāyā* [*nivāta-*[1]], adj. warm, sultry.

1 **निवार** *nivār* [P. *navār*], f. coarse, broad tape (as used to lace beds).

2 **निवार** *nivār* [**nemiyākāra-*], f. wooden ring or wheel at the bottom of a well (serving as a foundation for masonry walls).

3 **निवार** *ni-vār* [ad. *nivāra-*], m. **1.** warding off; prevention. **2.** impediment, obstacle.

निवार- *ni-vār-* [*nivārayati*], v.t. Brbh. Av. to ward off, &c. (cf. निवारण).

निवारक *ni-vārak* [S.], adj. & m. **1.** adj. hindering, &c.; preventive. **2.** forbidding. **3.** m. one who hinders, &c. (cf. निवारण).

निवारण *ni-vāraṇ* [S.], m. **1.** warding off, averting; checking; prevention. **2.** impediment, obstacle. **3.** prohibition. **4.** removal (of a fault, a weakness); cure (of an illness). **5.** exclusion. — ~ करना (का), to ward off, &c.

निवारित *ni-vārit* [S.], adj. **1.** warded off; hindered; checked; prevented. **2.** forbidden.

निवारी *nivārī*, f. *Pl. HŚS.* = [2नेवारी.

निवार्य *ni-vāryă* [S.], adj. **1.** able to be warded off, &c. **2.** needful to be warded off, &c.

निवाला *nivālā* [P. *navāla*], m. a mouthful, morsel. — निवाले करना, or मारना, to swallow or to gulp down greedily (food). सोने का ~, m. golden morsel: a lavish feast.

निवास *ni-vās* [S.], m. **1.** residing; residence. **2.** dwelling-place, residence. — ~ करना, to dwell. – निवास-बस्ती, f. residential quarter; a block of flats. निवास-स्थान, m. place of residence; ~, 2.

निवास- *ni-vās-*, v.i. *Pl.* = निवास करना.

निवासन *ni-vāsan* [S.], m. 1. = निवास. **2.** spending, passing (time).

निवासित *ni-vāsit* [S.], adj. settled, inhabited (a locality).

निवासिनी *ni-vāsinī*, f. a resident, &c. (see निवासी).

निवासी *ni-vāsī* [S.], adj. & m. **1.** adj. living (in), inhabiting. **2.** m. a resident. **3.** a native-born citizen, national (of, का).

निविड़ *ni-viṛ* [ad. *niviḍa-*], adj. **1.** not having spaces or gaps. ***2.** thick (as darkness, or as cloth); dense; intense (feeling). **3.** heavy (rain). **4.** sound (sleep). **5.** large, bulky.

निविदा *ni-vidā* [S.], f. tender (for work).

निवृत्त *ni-vṛtt* [S.], adj. turned back: **1.** free (from, से). **2.** detached (from); abstaining (from). **3.** discontinued; refrained, or abstained (from); retired. **4.** [= *nivṛta-*] checked, stopped, hindered. **5.** [= *nirvṛtta-*] finished, completed.

निवृत्ति *ni-vṛtti* [S.], f. returning, return: **1.** release (from, से); escape; release from rebirth. **2.** suspension, discontinuation. **3.** abstinence. **4.** retirement.

निवेदन *ni-vedan* [S.], m. **1.** making known; reporting; revealing. **2.** representing (a fact, a case, esp. to a superior); request; petition. **3.** presenting (as an offering); dedication. **4.** transmission, handing over. — ~ करना, to state, to represent (to, से); to request; to apply. पाठक से ~ है कि..., the reader is urged to....

निवेदित *ni-vedit* [S.], adj. **1.** made known. **2.** represented, &c. **3.** presented, offered.

निवेश *ni-veś* [S.], m. entering, settling: **1.** a dwelling-place (cf. निवास). **2.** settling down, marrying. ***3.** an investment.

निश्- *niś-* [S.], pref. (for some compounds alternative forms exist based on नि:-). **1.** out, away, forth; utterly, quite. **2.** not; not having, without; in-, non-, &c.

निशब्द *niśabd* [ad. *niḥśabda*], adj. = नि:शब्द.

निशांत *ni-śānt* [S.], adj. & m. **1.** adj. calm, tranquil. **2.** m. peaceful place: house, dwelling.

1**निशा** *niśā* [S.], f. night. — निशाचर, adj. & m. moving by night, noctural; a demon, evil spirit; a thief; a noctural animal. °ई, f. a demoness; a woman meeting her lover at night. निशा-काल, m. night-time. निशा-नाथ, m. lord of night: the moon.

2**निशा** *niśā* [P. *niśān*], m. assurance: — निशा-ख़ातिर, f. satisfaction of mind, assurance, content. निशा-ख़ातिर रखना, or रहना, to rest assured.

निशान *niśān* [P. *niśān*], m. **1.** m. sign, signal; marker. **2.** flag, standard; colours. **3.** mark; impression. **4.** scar. **5.** trace; trail; clue. **6.** vestige; monument. **7.** address. **8.** mark, target (= निशाना). — ~ करना, to make a sign or signal; to make a mark, &c. (on or in, में). ~ डालना, = ~ करना, 2. ~ पड़ना, a mark, &c. to be evident. – निशानदार [P. *-dār*], m. & adj. a standard-bearer; having markings, marked. निशानबरदार [P. *-bardār*], m. standard-bearer.

निशानची *niśāncī* [P. *niśān*+P. *-cī*], m. **1.** standard-bearer. **2.** marksman.

निशाना *niśānā* [P. *niśāna*], m. **1.** mark, sign; impression. **2.** a target, mark; bull's-eye. **3.** aim (as of a shot). **4.** butt (of jokes). — ~ करना, to practise shooting. ~ ठीक बैठना, one's aim to be true: = निशाने पर बैठना. ~ बाँधना, to take aim (at, पर). ~ मारना, or लगाना, to shoot (at, पर); to hit the mark. ~ सीधा बैठना, or लगना, (one's) aim to be straight. निशाने पर बैठना, or लगना, to hit the mark; to hit the bull's-eye (a bullet, &c). – निशानेबाज़ [P. *-bāz*], m. a marksman. °ई, f. marksmanship.

निशानी *niśānī* [P. *niśānī*], f. **1.** a distinctive mark; sign, evidence. **2.** a token, souvenir. **3.** a memorial (pillar, &c). **4.** a secret sign.

निशास्ता *niśāstā* [P. *niśāsta*], m. **1.** starch. **2.** a thick, floury gruel.

निशि- *niśi-* [S.: loc. of *niś*], Brbh. Av. night: — निशि-दिन, adv. by night and day. निशि-वासर, adv. id.

निशित *ni-śit* [S.], adj. & m. **1.** adj. whetted, ground. **2.** m. iron.

निशीथ *ni-śīth* [S.], m. midnight; night.

निश्चय *niś-cay* [S.], m. & adv. **1.** m. ascertainment; verification, proof. **2.** determination, decision; firm opinion. **3.** assurance, certainty. ***4.** decision, resolve. **5.** adv. certainly, definitely. — ~ करना, to ascertain, &c.; to determine, to come to a decision (about, पर); to be convinced (of); to decide, to resolve. ~ दिलाना (को), to assure, to reassure. ~ रहना (को), to feel assured or certain (of sthg., का). निश्चयकारी, adj. effecting a decision, decisive (step, action, moment). निश्चयवाचक, adj. expressing assurance, &c.; *gram.* definite. निश्चयात्मक [°*ya*+*ā*°], adj. definite, undoubted; resolute; decisive (a step). निश्चयार्थ [°*ya*+*a*°], adj. *gram.* indicative. °अक, adj. having a precise meaning (a word, a term).

निश्चयन *niś-cayan* [S.], m. ascertaining; determining, deciding.

निश्चयेन *niś-cayenă* [S.], adv. **1.** undoubtedly. **2.** decisively.

निश्चल *niś-cal* [S.], **1.** motionless; immovable, fixed. **2.** unwavering, unfluctuating. **3.** absolute (a majority).

निश्चला *niś-calā* [S.], f. fixed: the earth.

निश्चायक *niś-cāyak* [S.], adj. & m. **1.** adj. causing decision, &c.: decisive (step, development). **2.** one who determines, decides, &c.

निश्चिंत *niś-cint* [S.], adj. **1.** free from care, or anxiety. **2.** at peace, at leisure. **3.** thoughtless, inconsiderate; unconcerned (about, से).

निश्चिंतता *niś-cintătā* [S.], f. **1.** freedom from care or anxiety. **2.** thoughtlessness, &c.

निश्चित *niś-cit* [S.], adj. **1.** ascertained; not subject to doubt. यह बात ~ है कि..., it is certainly the case that.... **2.** determined, fixed, settled; definite, decided. — ~ करना, to ascertain; to make definite, &c., to agree upon.

निश्चिति *niś-citi* [S.], f. **1.** determination, settlement. **2.** ascertainment.

निश्चेतन *niś-cetan* [S.], adj. & m. **1.** adj. unconscious. **2.** m. unconsciousness.

निश्चेष्ट *niś-ceṣṭ* [S.], adj. **1.** without action or impulse: inert, motionless. **2.** unconscious.

निश्चेष्टता *niś-ceṣṭătā* [S.], f. **1.** inertness, motionlessness. **2.** unconsciousness.

निश्चेष्टा *niś-ceṣṭā* [S.], f. loss of consciousness.

निश्छल *niś-chal* [S.], adj. not deceitful.

निश्श्रेयस *ni-śreyas* [ad. **niḥśreyas-*], m. release from rebirth.

निश्वास *ni-śvās* [S.], m. breathing in; breathing, breath.

निष्- *niṣ-* [S.], pref. **1.** out, away, forth; utterly, quite. **2.** not; not having, without; non-, in-, &c.

निषंग *ni-ṣaṅg* [S.], m. a quiver.

निषंगी *ni-ṣaṅgī* [S.], m. a bowman.

निषध *niṣadh* [S.] m. *hist. mythol.* **1.** name of a mountain, or mountain range, to the north of the Himālayas. **2.** name of a region to the south of the Ganges plain, and of its inhabitants. **3.** the ruler of the Niṣadha people.

निषाद *ni-ṣād* [S.], m. **1.** *hist.* name of partic. non-Aryan tribes of hunters, fishermen, &c. **2.** a Niṣād man; a low-caste man, an outcaste. **3.** *mus.* a note of the heptatonic scale.

निषिद्ध *ni-ṣiddh* [S.], adj. prohibited, forbidden, banned.

निषिद्धता *ni-ṣiddhătā* [S.], f. state of being prohibited, banned, &c.

निषिद्धि *ni-ṣiddhi* [S.], f. prohibition, &c.

निषेचन *ni-ṣecan* [S.], m. watering (of plants); fertilisation.

निषेक *ni-ṣek* [S.], m. **1.** sprinkling. **2.** percolating; distilling; infusion. **3.** impregnation, fertilisation.

निषेध *ni-ṣedh* [S.], m. **1.** warding off, prevention: prohibition, ban; veto; embargo. **2.** dissuasion (from). **3.** refusal, denial. — ~ करना, to prohibit; to hinder, to prevent; to dissuade, &c. निषेधाज्ञा [°*dha*+*ā*°], f. prohibitory order, injunction (against). निषेधात्मक [°*dha*+*ā*°], adj. prohibiting, prohibitory. निषेधाधिकार [°*dha*+*a*°], m. right of veto.

निषेधक *ni-ṣedhak* [S.], adj. preventing: prohibiting, prohibitory.

निषेधन *ni-ṣedhan* [S.], m. prohibiting, &c. (= निषेध).

निषेधित *ni-ṣedhit* [S.], adj. = निषिद्ध.

निषेधी *ni-ṣedhī* [S.], adj. **1.** obstructing, prohibiting. **2.** *Pl.* inauspicious, evil.

निष्क *niṣk* [S.], m. *hist.* **1.** a gold coin, or ornament. **2.** *Pl.* a weight of gold of 108 *rattīs*.

निष्कंटक *niṣ-kaṇṭak* [S.], adj. **1.** free of thorns. **2.** free of trouble, or of obstacles (as a path, or progress).

निष्कपट *niṣ-kapaṭ* [S.], adj. not deceitful; honest, sincere.

निष्कपटता *niṣ-kapaṭătā* [S.], f. honesty, sincerity.

निष्कपटी *niṣ-kapăṭī* [S.], adj. honest, sincere.

निष्कर *niṣ-kar* [S.], adj. not taxable.

निष्कर्ष *niṣ-karṣ* [S.], m. **1.** deduction; conclusion. **2.** essence, gist. — ~ **करना**, or **निकलना**, to make a deduction, to draw a conclusion.

निष्कलंक *niṣ-kalaṅk* [S.], adj. without stain; without reproach; pure.

निष्कलंकित *niṣ-kalaṅkit* [cf. *niṣkalaṅka-*], adj. = **निष्कलंक**.

निष्कलंकी *niṣ-kalaṅkī*, adj. = **निष्कलंक**.

निष्काम *niṣ-kām* [S.], adj. **1.** without desires. **2.** disinterested.

निष्कारण *niṣ-kāraṇ* [S.], adj. **1.** not having cause or reason (a happening, or an attitude). **2.** not having point, unprofitable.

निष्कास *niṣ-kās* [S.], m. **1.** exit, egress. **2.** projection, projecting part (e.g. the verandah of a house).

निष्कासन *niṣ-kāsan* [S.], m. expulsion, ejection; exile.

निष्कासित *niṣ-kāsit* [S.], adj. expelled, ejected, &c.

निष्कीटक *niṣ-kīṭak* [S.], adj. & m. **1.** adj. sterile, disinfecting (as a solution). **2.** m. steriliser.

निष्कीटन *niṣ-kīṭan* [S.], m. sterilisation (see **निष्कीटक**).

निष्कीटित *niṣ-kīṭit* [S.], adj. sterilised (see **निष्कीटक**).

निष्कृत *niṣ-kr̥t* [S.], adj. freed, released; removed.

निष्कृति *niṣ-kr̥ti* [S.], f. freedom, discharge, release.

निष्कृष्ट *niṣ-kr̥ṣṭ* [S.], adj. extracted (as juice).

निष्क्रम *niṣ-kram* [S.], adj. & m. **1.** adj. not in sequence or order. **2.** m. = **निष्क्रमण**.

निष्क्रमण *niṣ-kramaṇ* [S.], m. going out: loss of caste, outcasting; *hind.* the ceremony of taking an infant out of the house for the first time to see the sun.

निष्क्रय *niṣ-kray* [S.], m. **1.** payment for sthg. **2.** ransom (= **छुड़ौती**). **3.** sale.

निष्क्रांत *niṣ-krānt* [S.], adj. **1.** gone out or forth. **2.** released, freed.

निष्क्रामित *niṣ-krāmit* [S.], adj, caused to go out (see **निष्क्रांत**).

निष्क्रिय *niṣ-kriy* [S.], adj. inactive; inert; passive.

निष्क्रियता *niṣ-kriyătā* [S.], f. inactivity, &c.

-निष्ठ *-ni-ṣṭh* [S]. adj. formant. characterised by (e.g. **संस्कृतनिष्ठ**, Sanskritised (vocabulary)).

निष्ठा *ni-ṣṭhā* [S.], f. firm position: **1.** certain knowledge: faith, belief. **2.** reverence; devotion (to, **के प्रति, की ओर**). — **निष्ठा-शपथ**, f. oath of allegiance. **निष्ठावान**, adj. believing, faithful; reverent, devout; fulfilling all religious duties.

निष्ठान *ni-ṣṭhān* [S.], m. *Pl. HŚS.* sauce; condiment.

निष्ठित *ni-ṣṭhit* [S.], adj. **1.** placed in or on. **2.** having implicit faith (in).

निष्ठुर *ni-ṣṭhur* [S.], adj. **1.** harsh; cruel; severe. **2.** rough, coarse (of speech, manner).

निष्ठुरता *ni-ṣṭhurătā* [S.], f. harshness, &c.

निष्णात *ni-ṣṇāt* [S.], adj. well-versed, or steeped (in a field), learned; skilled.

निष्पक्ष *niṣ-pakṣ* [S.], adj. impartial, objective; neutral.

निष्पक्षता *niṣ-pakṣătā* [S.], f. impartiality, &c.

निष्पत्ति *niṣ-patti* [S.], f. going forth: birth; production; completion, consummation.

निष्पन्न *niṣ-pann* [S.], adj. gone forth: **1.** born, produced; **2.** brought about; completed, accomplished.

निष्पलक *niṣ-palak* [S.], adj. = **अपलक**.

निष्पादक *niṣ-pādak* [S.], m. one who accomplishes or completes sthg.

निष्पादन *niṣ-pādan* [S.], m. producing, causing; carrying out, completing.

निष्पादित *niṣ-pādit* [S.], adj. produced, caused; carried out, &c.

निष्पाप *niṣ-pāp* [S.], adj. sinless, guiltless.

निष्पापता *niṣ-pāpătā* [S.], f. freedom from sin, or from guilt.

निष्पाव *niṣ-pāv* [S.], m. *Pl. HŚS.* a legume; pulse.

निष्पुत्र *niṣ-putr* [S.], adj. not having a son.

निष्पुरुष *niṣ-puruṣ* [S.], adj. unmanly, effeminate.

निष्प्रकारक *niṣ-pra-kārak* [S.], adj. of no particular kind, ordinary.

निष्प्रभ *niṣ-pra-bh* [S.], adj. not radiant: dull, lifeless.

निष्प्रभवता *niṣ-pra-bhavătā* [S.], f. absence of influence or force.

निष्प्रमाण *niṣ-pra-māṇ* [S.], adj. without authority, unauthorised, inauthentic.

निष्प्रयोजन *niṣ-pra-yojan* [S.], adj. **1.** without motive, disinterested. **2.** without reason, pointless; uncalled for.

निष्प्राण *niṣ-prāṇ* [S.], adj. lifeless; not animated, dull.

निष्फल *niṣ-phal* [S.], adj. **1.** not bearing fruit. **2.** unsuccessful; fruitless, useless. **3.** barren, unproductive.

निष्फलता *niṣ-phalătā* [S.], f. fruitlessness, unproductivity.

निष्फला *niṣ-phalā* [S.], f. reg. a woman who has reached the menopause.

निष्फली *niṣ-phalī* [S.], adj. reg. = निष्फला.

[1]**निस्-** *nis-* [S.], pref. (for some compounds alternative forms exist based on निः). **1.** out, away, forth; utterly, quite. **2.** not; not having, without; non-, in-, &c.

निसंठ *nisaṁṭh* [cf. *saṁsthā-*], Av. **1.** without capacity; without money. **2.** ill-omened, unlucky.

निस *nis* [*niśā-*], f. night (= निशा). — निसचर, adj. & m. = निशाचर. °ई, f. निस-दिन, adv. day and night.

निसक *nisak*, adj. & m. Brbh. weak, powerless.

निसबत *nisbat* [A. *nisba*: P. *nisbat*], f. & ppn. **1.** f. relation, connection. **2.** comparison. **3.** engagement, bethrothal. **4.** ppn. (w. की) with reference (to), in respect (of). **5.** in comparison (with). — ~ देना, to make a comparison (between, में), to compare. ~ रखना, to have reference (to, से), to have to do (with).

निसबतन *nisbatan* [A. *nisbatan*], adv. **1.** relatively. **2.** comparatively.

निसर्ग *ni-sarg* [S.], m. natural state, nature; creation.

निसाँस *nisāṁs* [cf. H. *sāṁs*], adj. Av. at the point of death.

निसाँसी *nisāṁsī*, adj. Av. = निसाँस.

निसार *nisār* [A. *niṣār*], m. **1.** offering, sacrifice. **2.** devotion. — ~ करना, to offer, &c.; to devote oneself (to, पर).

निसार- *nisār-* [*niḥsārayati*], v.t. reg. = निकालना.

निसावरा *nisāvrā*, m. *Pl. HŚS.* the carrier pigeon.

निसास *nisās*, m. Brbh. Av. = निःश्वास.

निसुख *nisukh* [ad. *niḥsukha-*], adj. joyless, unhappy.

निसेनी *nisenī* [*niśrayaṇi-*], f. Av. a ladder.

निसोता *nisotā*, adj. Brbh. Av. pure; unalloyed.

निसोथ *nisoth* [*niśotrā-*], f. (°सोत, *Pl.*) a purgative root, *Ipomœa turpethum*.

निस्तनद्र *nis-tandră* [S.], adj. sleepless, tireless.

निस्तब्ध *ni-stabdh* [S.], adj. **1.** motionless, still. **2.** numb.

निस्तब्धता *ni-stabdhătā* [S.], f. **1.** motionlessness, stillness. **2.** numbness.

निस्तर- *nis-tar* [cf. H. *nistārnā*; S. *nistarati*], v.i. Brbh. Av. to be released (as from rebirth).

निस्तल *nis-tal* [S.], adj. bottomless.

निस्तार *nis-tār* [S.], m. crossing over: release (as from rebirth); salvation.

निस्तारक *nis-tārak* [S.], m. saviour, deliverer.

निस्तारण *nis-tāraṇ* [S.], m. conveying across: rescuing, delivering.

निस्तारना *nis-tārnā* [ad. *nistārayati*], v.t. to save, to deliver (as from rebirth).

निस्तीर्ण *nis-tīrṇ* [S.], adj. conveyed across: released, &c.

निस्तेज *nis-tej* [S.], adj. without spirit, or energy; spiritless.

निस्तोख *nis-tokh* [ad. *toṣa-*], m. & adv. (*Pl.* °तोक). reg. **1.** m. full and final settlement (of a claim or case). **2.** adv. in full satisfaction (of), wholly.

निस्पंद *ni-spand* [ad. *niṣpanda-*], adj. motionless, without tremor; still; steady.

निस्पृह *nispṛh*, adj. = निःस्पृह.

निस्फ़ *nisf* [A. *nisf*], m. U. a half. — निस्फ़ानिस्फ़ [P. *-ā-*], adv. half and half; by halves; in halves, (divided) in two.

निस्फ़ी *nisfi* [A. *nisfi*], adj. & f. U. **1.** adj. a half. **2.** f. a half (share, &c).

निस्यंदन *ni-syandan* [S.], m. flowing down: filtration.

निस्वन *ni-svan* [S.], m. sound, voice.

निस्संक्रामक *nis-saṅ-krāmak* [S.], adj. not infectious; not contagious.

निस्संतान *nis-san-tān* [S.], adj. childless.

निस्सहाय *nis-sahây* [S.], adj. without helpers or assistance; helpless.

निस्सार *nis-sār* [S.], adj. without essential content; insubstantial; worthless.

निस्सारित *nis-sārit* [S.], adj. pressed out (fluid).

निहंग *nihaṅg*, adj. reg. **1.** naked. **2.** free from care; spoiled (a child). **3.** barefaced, shameless.

निहचय *nihcay* [ad. *niścaya-*: w. *niḥ-*], m. Brbh. = निश्चय.

निहत्ता *nihattā*, adj. = निहत्था.

निहत्था *nihatthā* [*nirhasta-*], adj. **1.** unarmed. **2.** empty-handed.

निहल *nihal*, m. *Pl. HŚS.* land recovered on the shifting of watercourses.

निहाई *nihāī* [*nighāti-*], f. Av. anvil.

निहाउ *nihāu*, m. Av. = निहाई.

निहाना *nihānā* [*nidāna-*¹], m. reg. rope used to tie a cow's legs when milking it. — **गाय को ~ देना**, to tie a cow's legs (when milking it).

¹**निहानी** *nihānī* [**nikhādana-*: Pa. *nikhādana-*], f. reg. (W.) a gouge; chisel.

²**निहानी** *nihānī*, f. reg. (W.) = निहाना.

³**निहानी** *nihānī* [cf. P. *nihān*], adj. E.H. hidden.

निहायत *nihāyat* [A. *nihāya*: P. *nihāyat*], adj. & adv. **1.** very much, extreme, exceeding. **2.** extremely, &c. — **~ दरजे का**, adj. (also pej.) first rate.

निहार *nihār*, m. Av. = नीहार.

निहारना *nihārnā* [*nibhālayati*, **nibhārayati*], v.t. to look at intently or expectantly; to gaze at.

निहारी *nihārī* [Panj. *nihārī*], f. reg. = नहारी.

¹**निहाल** *nihāl*, adj. **1.** prosperous; wealthy. **2.** gratified; content; happy. — **~ करना**, to make prosperous, or rich; to make happy or content.

²**निहाल** *nihāl* [P. *nihāl*], m. **1.** a sapling; shoot. **2.** a carpet. **3.** cushion. **4.** quilt, bedcloth.

निहालचा *nihālcā* [P. *nihālca*], m. reg. (W.) = ²निहाल, 4.

¹**निहाली** *nihālī* [**nighātana-*], f. reg. (W.) an anvil.

²**निहाली** *nihālī* [P. *nihālī*], f. = ²निहाल.

निहित *ni-hit* [S.], adj. placed: **1.** contained; latent. **2.** entrusted. — **~ स्वार्थ**, m. vested interest(s).

निहुड़- *nihuṛ-*, v.i. reg. = निहुर-.

निहुर- *nihur-* [*nipatati*; ? or *nibhṛta-*], v.i. Brbh. to bend, to stoop.

निहुराना *nihurānā* [cf. H. *nihur-*], v.t. reg. to bend to cause to bend; to hang (the head).

निहोर- *nihor-*, v.t. Brbh. Av. 1. = निहोरा करना, 1. 2. = निहोरा मानना.

निहोरा *nihorā*, m. **1.** entreaty. **2.** favour, kindness. **3.** Brbh. Av. cause, sake. — **~ करना** (का), to beseech; to place under an obligation; to reproach by alluding to past favours. **~ मानना** (का), to acknowledge a favour (on the part of), to be grateful (for).

नींद *nīṁd* [*nidrā-*], f. sleep. — **~ आना** (को), to feel sleepy. **~ उचटना**, sleep to vanish: (one's) sleep to be broken; to be unable to sleep. **~ का दुखिया**, m. a sleepy person; sleepy-head. **~ ख़राब करना**, to disturb the sleep (of, की). **~ पड़ना**, sleep to come (to one, को). **~ भर सोना**, to sleep soundly; to be easy in mind. **~ मारना**, to sleep soundly. **~ में पड़ना**, to fall asleep. **~ में होना**, to be sleepy. **~ लेना** (? = नींदना), to manage to sleep. **~ हराम करना**, to disturb the sleep (of, की). **अपनी ~ सोना**, fig. to be a law unto oneself.

नींदना *nīṁdnā* [*nidrāyati*], v.i. to fall asleep; to sleep.

नींदी *nīṁdī* [cf. H. *nīṁd*], adj. reg. sleepy (= निंदासा).

नींबू *nīṁbū*, m. = नीबू.

नींव *nīṁv* [*nemi-*], f. **1.** foundation. **2.** transf. basis. — **~ डालना**, or **जमाना**, or **देना**, to lay the foundation (of, की); to found; to provide the basis (for). **~ धरना**, = **~ डालना**, 1. **~ पड़ना**, a foundation to be laid; a basis to be established, or formed (for, की).

¹**-नी** *-nī* [*-nīya-*; × H. *-nā*], suffix (forms f. nouns often referrable to H. infinitives, e.g. कटनी, harvesting; बोनी, planting; करनी, deeds, acts; चटनी, chutney; छोलनी, f. a scraper).

²**-नी** *-nī* [ad. *-inī-*], suffix (forms feminines for m. nouns referring to animate beings, e.g. हथनी, she-elephant; मासटरनी, schoolmistress).

नीक *nīk* [*nikta-*], adj. Brbh. Av. **1.** good, fine. **2.** elegant, attractive.

नीका *nīkā* [*nikta-*], adj. Av. 1. = नीक. **2.** adv. well; rightly; easily. — **~ लग-**, to seem good, or pleasing.

नीकौ *nīkau*, adj. Brbh. = नीका.

नीच *nīc* [*nīca-*; infld. by *ucca-*], adj. & m. **1.** adj. low. **2.** base, mean. **3.** inferior. **4.** m. a base person. — ~ कमाई, f. ill-gotten gain. ~ कोटि का, adj. of inferior quality. ~ जात, f. low caste; the low castes; m. a low-caste man. – नीच-ऊँच, f. rise and fall: vicissitudes (of life); inequalities (of position); the bad and the good, loss and gain.

नीचता *nīcătā* [S.], f. = नीचपन.

नीचपन *nīcpan* [cf. H. *nīcā*], m. **1.** lowness. **2.** baseness.

नीचा *nīcā* [*nīca-*; infld. by *ucca-*], adj. **1.** low. **2.** base, mean; expressive of a low opinion (the glance). **3.** inferior. — ~ करना, to lower (an object, or the eyes; also fig). ~ खाना, to suffer humiliation; to suffer a reverse. ~ दिखाना, to bring about the disgrace (of, को); to get the better (of). ~ पड़ना, to fall low; to come below; to be subdued or humbled. नीची नज़रों से, adv. with downcast eyes. नीची निगाह, or निगाहों, से देखना, to think (one) of little worth. – नीचा-ऊँचा, adj. & m. high and low, uneven, unequal; fig. the various aspects (of a matter); = नीच ऊँच.

नीचाई *nīcāī*, f. = निचाई.

नीचान *nīcān*, f. = निचान.

नीचे *nīce* [cf. H. *nīcā*], adv. **1.** low; down; downwards. **2.** below; underneath. **3.** (ppn. w. के) below; under; underneath. — ~ आना, to come down; to dismount; to fall down; to come under (a horse's hoofs). ~ करना, = नीचा करना; to humiliate. ~ का, adj. lower; inferior. ~ गिरना, to fall (in conduct, or standing); to fall down. ~ गिराना, to throw or to knock down; to bring about the disgrace or humbling of. ~ जाना, to go down; to subside; to submit. ~ लाना, to bring down (an opponent, as in wrestling). ~ से, adv. from below. ~ से ऊपर तक, adv. from bottom to top; from head to foot. – नीचे-ऊपर, adv. upside down, in disorder.

नीठि *nīṭhi* [**aniṣṭi-*], f. & adv. Brbh. **1.** f. dislike. ***2.** adv. somehow or other; with difficulty; scarcely, hardly. — ~ ~, or ~ ~ करके, = ~, 2.

नीठौ *nīṭhau* [*aniṣṭa-*], adj. Brbh. displeasing.

नीड़ *nīṛ* [*nīḍa-*], m. **1.** nest. **2.** reg. den. — ~ का पंछी, m. a fledgling.

नीत *nīt* [S.], adj. **1.** led. **2.** Brbh. perceived.

नीति *nīti* [S.], f. **1.** manner of conducting oneself. **2.** right, or moral conduct; morality. **3.** ethics. **4.** prudent counsel, policy; polity (of a state). **5.** political wisdom; statesmanship. — नीति-कथा, f. any work on ethics or politics; a moral tale. नीति-कुशल, adj. politic; tactful. नीतिगत, adj. having to do with *nīti*: moral; ethical; political. नीतिज्ञ, adj. politic, prudent; a prudent person; a politician. नीतिपूर्ण, adj. virtuous; ethical, moral. नीति-भ्रष्ट, adj. immoral. नीतिमान, adj. moral; prudent; sagacious; virtuous. नीति-शास्त्र, m. ethics; political science; a work on ethics or politics. नीतिविद्या, = नीति-शास्त्र, 1., 2.

नीप *nīp* [S.], m. Brbh. the *kadamba* tree (*Nauclea cadamba*, or *orientalis*).

नीपूर *nīpūr*, m. penis.

नीबू *nībū* [*nimbū-*: ← Austro-as.], m. the lime tree and its fruit; the lemon. — नीबू-निचोड़, m. squeezer of limes: a self-invited guest; an idler.

नीम *nīm* [*nimba-*], m. the neem tree, *Melia azadirachta* (known for its bitter fruit, and for medicinal and antiseptic properties of its leaves). — ~ का घूँठ पीकर रह जाना, to have a bitter draught to drink: to be destitute. ~ की टहनी हिलाना, to apply the *nīm*-twig (in hope of cure): to suffer from syphilis.

नीम- *nīm-* [P. *nīm-*], adj. half: — नीमजोश [P. -*jos*], adj. half-boiled. नीमटर, adj. pej. half-educated. नीम-हकीम, m. half-doctor: a quack. नीम-सरकारी, adj. pej. quasi official: officious.

नीयत *nīyat* [A. *nīya*: P. *nīyat*], f. **1.** intention; object; design. **2.** resolve, will. **3.** desire. — ~ करना or बाँधना (की), to intend; to form a design (to); to resolve. ~ के साथ, adv. with intention, by design. ~ पूरी करना, an intention, &c. to be realised. ~ में फ़रक़ आना, to have bad or underhand intentions. ~ लगी रहना, to be intent (on, पर); to be desirous (of).

नीरंध्र *nī-randhră* [S.], adj. *Pl. HŚS.* without holes or gaps; without defects.

नीर *nīr* [S.], m. **1.** water. **2.** liquid. **3.** fig. tears. — नीर-छीर पारखी, adj. discriminating (as the goose which is supposed to be able to separate mixed milk and water). नीरज, m. water-born: a lotus; water-lily; a pearl. नीरद, m. water-giver: a cloud. नीरधि, m. Brbh. receptacle of water: the ocean.

नीरना *nīrnā* [cf. H. [1] [2]*nīr*], v.t. reg. **1.** to water (animals). **2.** to feed (animals).

नीरव *nī-rav* [S.], adj. silent.

नीरवता *nī-ravătā* [S.], f. silence.

नीरस *nī-ras* [S.], adj. & m. **1.** adj. without sap. **2.** without taste, or flavour. **3.** dry, arid (terrain). **4.** empty, uninteresting (remarks, writings). **5.** unfeeling, insensitive. **6.** m. [? **-rasya-*] dryness; dullness.

नीरसता *nī-rasătā* [S.], f. = नीरस, 6.

नीराँजनी *nī-rāṁjănī* [cf. H. *nīrājan*], f. candlestand used in worship (*ārtī*).

[1]**नीरा** *nīrā* [*nīra-*], m. palm juice.

[2]**नीरा** *nīrā* [*nigara-*], m. reg. (N., Raj.) fodder.

नीराजन *nī-rājan* [S.], m. **1.** Brbh. causing to shine (on) or to gleam: 1. = आरती. **2.** *hist.* ceremonial cleaning of weapons before a campaign.

नीरोग *nī-rog* [S.], adj. in good health.

नीरोगता *nī-rogătā* [S.], f. state of good health.

नीरोगी *nī-rogī* [S.], adj. = नीरोग.

[1]**नील** *nīl* [*nīla-*], adj. & m. **1.** adj. blue; dark blue or green; dark. **2.** m. the colour blue. **3.** blue mark or weal. **4.** indigo (plant and dye). **5.** copper sulphate. — ~, or ~ का माठ, बिगड़ना, the indigo(-vat) to be spoiled: to tell an exaggerated tale; to make a needless commotion (as a child); to suffer great loss or misfortune; to lose one's sanity. ~ की सलाई फिरवा देना, to blind (a person). ~ घोंटना, v.t. to press or to beat indigo; to quarrel, to wrangle. ~ दिखाई देना, the bluish-green of young cereal shoots to appear (in a field earlier sown). – नीलकंठ, m. blue-throat: the blue jay; the peacock; a title of Śiva. नील-गाय, m. a species of large antelope (iron-grey in colour). नील-मणि, f. sapphire. नीलवसन, m. clothed in dark blue: a title of Śiva (alluding to the colour of the god's throat). नीलवाला, m. maker or seller of indigo; a dyer; an indigo planter. नीलसर, m. a mallard duck. निलांजन [°*la*+*a*°], copper sulphate; antimony. नीलांबर [°*la*+*a*°], adj. & m. wearing a dark-blue garment; such a garment. नीलाभ [°*la*+*ā*°], m. a dark cloud; a blue lotus. नीलोत्पल [°*la*+*u*°], m. lapis lazuli. नीलोपल [°*la*+*u*°], m. id.

[2]**नील** *nīl* [A. *nīl*], m. the river Nile.

नीलक *nīlak* [S.], adj. *Pl.* blue; dyed blue.

नीलता *nīlătā* [S.], f. = नीलापन.

नीलम *nīlam* [conn. *nīlamaṇi-*], m. sapphire.

[1]**नीला** *nīlā* [*nīla-*], adj. blue, &c. (= [1]नील). — ~ करना, to dye blue; to beat (one) black and blue; pej. to disgrace. ~ पड़ना, to change colour (as the face: in fear, shock, anger). नीले पड़ना, blueness, or paleness to appear (as on the face); blue marks to appear. – नीला-काला, adj. fig. sad, difficult (a time). नीला-पीला, adj. black and yellow, all discoloured: pale (with anger); black and blue (from a beating).

[2]**नीला** *nīlā* [P. *nīla*], m. blue dye (from the indigo plant).

नीलाई *nīlāī* [cf. H. [1]*nīlā*], f. = नीलापन.

नीलापन *nīlāpan* [cf. H. [1]*nīlā*], m. blueness; dark blue or green colour; darkness.

नीलाम *nīlām* [Pt. *leilão*: ← A. (*al*) *a'lām*], m. & adv. **1.** m. an auction. **2.** adv. by auction; at auction. — ~ करना, or कराना, to sell by auction. ~ ख़रीदना, to buy at auction. ~ पर चढ़ना, to be put up for auction. ~ में रखना, to send for auction. ~ होना, to be sold by auction. – नीलाम-कर्ता, m. inv. auctioneer.

नीलामी *nīlāmī* [cf. H. *nīlām*], adj. & f. **1.** adj. for auction; auctionable. **2.** bought by auction. **3.** f. an auction. — नीलामीवाला, m. auctioneer.

नीलाहट *nīlāhaṭ* [cf. H. [1]*nīlā*], f. = नीलापन.

नीलिमा *nīlimā* [S.], f. m. = नीलापन.

नीलोपर *nīlopar* [P. *nīlopar*], m. = नीलोफ़र.

नीलोफ़र *nīlofar* [P. *nīlofar*], m. a blue lotus; blue water-lily.

नीवि *nīvi* [S.], f. **1.** part of a woman's *dhotī* (as drawn round the waist and loins). **2.** draw-string (for a woman's *dhotī*).

नीवी *nīvī*, f. = नीवि.

नीसान *nīsān* [? P. *niśān*], m. metr. Brbh. a kettledrum.

नीहार *nī-hār* [S.], m. **1.** mist; fog. **2.** hoar-frost. **3.** heavy dew.

नीहारिका *nī-hārikā* [S.], f. nebula.

नुकटा *nukṭā* [? H. *nakṭā*×H. *nok*], m. the comb-duck (= नकटा, 7).

नुकता *nuktā* [A. *nukta*], m. a (sharp) point: **1.** a pointed or witty expression. **2.** a nice or subtle point; point of criticism; a particular point, matter. — नुकता-चीन [P. *-cīn*], adj. & m. (wilfully) fault-finding; a captious critic. °ई, f. नुकताचीनी करना, to carp (at, की).

नुक़ता *nuqtā* [A. *nuqṭa*], m. **1.** a point; diacritical point, or dot. **2.** a dot, spot. **3.** a cipher, zero. **4.** transf. point, location (as on a map).

नुकती *nuktī*, f. a type of small sweet (made of *besan* flour, or ground pulse, cooked in *ghī*).

नुक़रा *nuqrā* [A. *nuqra*], m. & adj. *Pl. HŚS.* **1.** m. silver (esp. after it has been melted down). **2.** white or cream colour (of horses). **3.** adj. white or cream in colour (horses).

नुक़सान *nuqsān* [A. *nuqṣān*], m. **1.** loss. **2.** harm; damage. — ~ उठाना, to suffer a loss. ~ करना (का), to do harm, or damage (to); to destroy, to ruin. ~ पहुँचाना (को), to cause loss, or damage (to). ~ भरना, to make good loss (on the part of, का). – नुक़सानदेह [P. *-dih*], adj. harmful, injurious.

नुक़सानी *nuqsānī* [cf. A. *nuqṣān*], adj. & f. **1.** adj. harmful; detrimental. **2.** reg. spoiled, damaged. **3.** f. = नुक़सान. **4.** compensation.

नुकीला *nukīlā* [cf. H. *nok*], adj. **1.** pointed; tapering. **2.** fig. charming, attractive.

नुक्कड़ *nukkaṛ* [cf. H. *nok*], f. **1.** a projection; point, end. **2.** corner (of a street, &c). **3.** end (as of a cul-de-sac).

नुक्का *nukkā* [cf. H. *nok*], m. reg. a point; a pointed stick.

नुक़्ल *nuql* [A. *nuql*], f. (m., *Pl.*) a snack (with wine).

नुक़्स *nuqs* [A. *naqṣ*], m. fault, flaw.

नुचना *nucnā* [cf. H. *nocnā*], v.i. **1.** to be plucked or pulled out, or off. **2.** to be scratched, clawed. **3.** to be pinched.

नुचवाना *nucvānā* [cf. H. *nocnā*], v.t. to cause to be scratched, pinched, &c. (by, से).

-नुमा *-numā* [P. *numā*, present stem of *namūdan*], m. inv. & adj. formant. var. /numa~/. showing; appearing as (e.g. रहनुमा, m. a guide; गाँवनुमा, village-like).

नुमाइंदगी *numāindagī* [cf. P. *numāyanda*], f. U. representation.

नुमाइंदा *numāindā* [P. *numāyanda*], m. U. **1.** an exhibitor. **2.** a representative; delegate.

नुमाइश *numāiś* [P. *numā'iś*], f. **1.** show (of), display; semblance. ***2.** show, spectacle; exhibition. **3.** pomp. — नुमाइश-गाह, f. exhibition site.

नुमाइशी *numāiśī* [P. *numā'iśī*], adj. **1.** for show or display; beautiful, lovely. **2.** having to do with an exhibition. **3.** affected, ostentatious. **4.** specious.

नुमायान *numāyān* [P. *numāyān*], adj. U. **1.** apparent, evident. **2.** conspicuous, prominent. **3.** striking, bold (as a picture).

नुसखा *nuskhā* [A. P. *nuskha*], m. **1.** a prescription. **2.** a recipe. — ~ बाँधना, to dispense a prescription.

नुहट्टा *nuhaṭṭā* [**nakhaghṛṣṭa-*], m. *Pl.* a scratch (with nails or claws).

नूतन *nūtan* [S.], adj. **1.** new. **2.** fresh; recent. **3.** modern; fashionable, novel. **4.** young.

नूतनता *nūtanătā* [S.], f. **1.** newness. **2.** modernity; novelty.

नून *nūn*, m. = नोन.

नूनी *nūnī* [**nunna-*], f. penis of a pre-adolescent boy.

नूपुर *nūpur* [S.], m. f. a hollow anklet containing tiny bells or pieces of metal.

नूर *nūr* [A. *nūr*], m. **1.** light; brilliance, radiance. **2.** fig. something splendid or grand. — ~ का तड़का, m. first gleam of light, very early morning. ~ बरसना, beauty to rain down: (a person) to be radiant with beauty. ~ की बातें, f. = ~, 2. आँखों का ~, m. light of the eyes: someone loved deeply.

नूर- *nūr-* [cf. H. *nūr*], adj. Brbh. brilliant, radiant.

नूरानी *nūrānī* [A. *nūrānī*], adj. U. **1.** bright, resplendent. **2.** serene.

नूह *nūh* [A. *nūḥ*], m. Noah.

नृ- *nṛ-* [S.], m. man, human being: — नृवराह, m. the man-boar or third avatār of Viṣṇu. नृसिंह, m. the man-lion or fourth avatār of Viṣṇu.

नृत्य *nṛtyă* [S.], m. dancing (the art, or the activity); mime. — नृत्यकार, m. a dancer. नृत्य-शाला, f. a dance hall; theatre.

नृप *nṛp* [S.], m. Av. a king. — नृप-गृह, m. royal palace. नृप-तनय, m. son of a king, prince. नृप-नय, m. royal policy. नृप-सुत, m. = नृप-तनय.

नृपता *nṛpătā* [S.], f. **1.** royalty, kingly status. **2.** sovereignty, rule.

नृपति *nṛpati* [S.], m. lord of men: king.

नृशंस *nṛśaṃs* [S.], adj. cruel.

ने *ne*, ppn. used in ergative constrctions in the standard language: — उस्~ किताब पढ़ी, he read the book. उस ~ सोचा, he thought.

नेऊन *neūn* [*navanī-*], f. reg. butter.

[1]**नेक** *nek* [P. *nek*], adj. **1.** good, virtuous. **2.** excellent. **3.** adv. very, exceedingly. — ~ चलन, m. good conduct. – नेकचलन, adj. virtuous, upright. °ई, f. good conduct; integrity. नेकदिल, adj. sincere, cordial. °ई, f. नेकनाम, adj. of good repute; celebrated. °ई, f. good name, good character; reputation. नेकनीयत, adj. well-intentioned, well-disposed. °ई, f. नेकबख़्त, adj. & m., f. fortunate, blessed; of good disposition; faithful, true (as a wife); dutiful; a fortunate person, &c. °ई, f.

[2]**नेक** *nek* [? conn. *naika-*], adv. Brbh. **1.** a little, just (= ज़रा). **2.** for a short while.

नेकी *nekī* [P. *nīkī*], f. **1.** goodness, virtue. **2.** good or proper treatment (of another); kindness. **3.** good (as opposed to ill). — ~ करना, to do good (to, के साथ, के हक़ में); to act well. – नेकी-बदी, f. good and evil; weal or woe.

नेकु *neku* [? H. [2]*nek*+Brbh. Av. *-ku*], adv. Brbh. Av. = [2]नेक.

नेग *neg* [cf. H. *negī*], m. f. **1.** the custom of giving presents at marriages and other auspicious occasions. **2.** presents given at marriages, &c. — ~ करना, to begin (a work) at an auspicious moment [? infld. by [1]*nek*]. ~ देना (को), to give customary presents. ~ लगना, presents to be given. – नेग-जोग, m. = ~, 2. नेग-निछावार, m. customary presents.

नेगी *negī* [? ad. *niyogī*: × *niyogya-*], m. one who claims or expects a customary present or fee at a marriage or other auspicious occasion (as a servant, tenant, dependant).

नेज़ा *nezā* [P. *neza*], m. lance; javelin.

नेटा *neṭā*, adj. reg. left-handed.

नेड़- *neṛ-* [cf. *nikaṭa-*], v.t. reg. to keep near (one), to care for.

नेत *net* [*netra-*[3]], m. Brbh. cord used to turn a churning-stick.

[1]**नेता** *netā* [S.], m. inv. a leader. — नेतागीरी [P. *-gīrī*], f. pej. leadership; leader's position or status. नेताशाही [P. *-śāhī*], f. supreme position or status as leader.

[2]**नेता** *netā* [*netra-*[3]], m. reg. (W.) = नेती.

नेताई *netāī* [cf. H. *netā*], f. leadership.

नेती *netī* [*netra-*[3]], f. reg. (W.) cord used to turn a churning-stick.

नेतृत्व *netṛtvă* [S.], m. leadership; management, direction (of an institution, an activity). — ~ करना (का), to lead; to direct. – नेतृत्वकारी, adj. leading, principal.

नेत्र *netr* [S.], m. the eye. — नेत्र-जल, m. tears; a tear. नेत्रवान, adj. possessing eyes; clear-sighted. नेत्र-विज्ञान, m. ophthalmology. नेत्रहीन, adj. without eyes; blind. नेत्रौषध [°*ra*+*au*°], m. eye-medicine: ferrous sulphate; collyrium.

नेत्री *netrī* [S.], f. a leader.

नेत्र्य *netryă* [S.], adj. **1.** beneficial to the eyes. **2.** ophthalmic, ocular.

नेनुआ *nenuā*, m. reg. (Bihar) ? a plant resembling the *turaī*; or an aloe (= घीकुवाँर).

नेपथ्य *nepathyă* [S.], m. **1.** costume (of an actor); decoration. ***2.** the part of a stage out of view of the audience; back-stage; the wings.

नेपाल *nepāl* [S.], m. Nepal.

[1]**नेपाली** *nepālī* [S.], adj. & f. **1.** adj. Nepali. **2.** f. the Nepali language.

[2]**नेपाली** *nepālī* [cf. H. *nepāl*], m. a Nepali man.

नेफ़ा *nefā* [P. *nefă*], m. **1.** a doubled seam carrying the draw-string of cotton trousers. **2.** trouser-belt.

नेब *neb*, m. Av. = नायब.

नेम *nem* [ad. *niyama-*], m. **1.** rule; principle. **2.** custom, practice. **3.** religious observance; vow, &c. — ~ करना, or बाँधना (का, or कि ...), to make a strict rule, or a vow; to observe, to practise. – नेम-धर्म, m. a religious observance (as fasting, prayer) or rite; moderation, good conduct.

नेमत *nemat* [A. *niʿma*: P. *nĕʿmat*], f. **1.** affluence, wealth. ***2.** grace, beneficence; favour, boon. **3.** delight, joy. **4.** a delicacy. — नेमत-ख़ाना, m. affluent abode; palace; paradise.

नेमि *nemi* [S.], f. **1.** rim of a wheel. **2.** framework (for a well-rope); windlass. **3.** platform of a well.

नेमी *nemī* [cf. H. *nem*], adj. **1.** devout. **2.** principled.

-नेर *-ner* [*nagara-*]. m. noun formant. town, city (e.g. बीकानेर, Bikaner).

नेरा *nerā* [*nikaṭa-*], adj. Brbh. Av. near. — नेरे, adv. nearby.

नेरुआ *neruā*, m. reg. **1.** straw; millet-stalk; a woman's neck ornament made from pieces of straw. **2.** drain for a cane-pressing mill.

नेव *nev*, f. reg. = नींव.

नेवत *nevat* [**nimantra-*], m. Av. = न्योता.

नेवत- *nevat-* [*nimantrayate*], v.t. Brbh. Av. to invite (to a feast or entertainment).

नेवता *nevtā* [**nimantra-*], m. = न्योता.

नेवर *nevar* [*nūpura-*; MIA *ṇeura-*], m. **1.** m. pastern-joint of a horse. **2.** sore on the pastern-joint. **3.** *Pl. HŚS.* = नूपुर.

नेवला *nevlā* [*nakula-*], m. mongoose.

नेवार *nevār* [*nepāla-*], m. a Nevar (of Nepal).

[1]**नेवारी** *nevārī* [cf. H. *nevār*], f. the Nevari language.

[2]**नेवारी** *nevārī* [*naipālī-*], f. Arabian jasmine (*Jasminum zambac* or *elongatum*).

नेस्त *nest* [cf. P. *nīst*], v.i. it is not. — ~ करना, to annihilate; to destroy; to squander; to abolish. ~ नाबूद [P. *nābūd*], adj. annihilated, &c. ~ नाबूद होना, to be annihilated, &c.; to perish; to become extinct.

नेस्ती *nestī* [P. *nīstī*], f. **1.** non-existence. **2.** ruin, destruction. **3.** non-activity: idleness. **4.** transf. poverty. — ~ छाना, to be in ruins. – नेस्ती-भरा, adj. unfortunate; idle.

नेह *neh* [*sneha-*], m. **1.** oiliness; oil. *2. = स्नेह. — ~ लगना, to feel affection or love (for, का).

नेहा *nehā*, m. Av. = नेह.

नेही *nehī* [cf. H. *neh*], adj. & m. reg. **1.** adj. tender, loving. **2.** m. a lover, friend.

नै *nai* [*nadi-*], f. Brbh. river. — बै ~, f. the (onward-rushing) river of age.

नैक *naik* [S.], adj. *Pl. HŚS.* not one; several, various. — नैकधा, adv. in various ways.

नैकट्य *naikaṭyă* [S.], m. proximity.

नैगम *naigam* [S.], adj. **1.** having to do with the Vedas; an Upaniṣad. **2.** a way, means.

नैचक *naicak* [*nemi+cakra-*], reg. (W.) the wooden support for the masonry of a well.

नैचा *naicā* [P. *naica*], m. **1.** tube of a hookah. **2.** iron. a very thin man. **3.** a depraved man.

नैची *naicī* [? conn. **naicya-*], f. reg. (W.) the slope down which bullocks walk while working an irrigation system; specif. the bottom of the slope.

नैतिक *naitik* [S.], adj. **1.** moral. **2.** ethical.

नैतिकता *naitikătā* [S.], f. **1.** morality. **2.** ethical character, or standards.

नैदानिक *naidānik* [S.], adj. clinical.

नैन *nain* [ad. [2]*nayana-*], m. the eye (= [2]नयन). — नैनमुत्ती, f. sl. always crying (a woman). नैन-मूतना, m. a cry-baby. नैन-सुख, m. eyes' delight: a kind of thick muslin (plain or striped); euph. term of reference to a blind person.

नैना *nainā* [[2]*nayana-*], m. reg. the eye.

नैनू *nainū* [cf. H. *nain*; and *nain-sukh*], m. sprigged or ornamented muslin.

नैपाली *naipālī* [S.], adj. & m. = [1,2]नेपाली.

नैपुण्य *naipuṇya* [S.], m. = निपुणता.

नैमित्तिक *naimittik* [S.], adj. produced by some special cause: occasional; periodical.

नैमिष *naimiṣ* [S.], m. name of a forest and place of pilgrimage in north India. — नैमिषारण्य, m. id.

नैयमिक *naiyămik* [S.], adj. according to rule, or law; prescribed.

नैया *naiyā* [cf. *nāvā-*], f. Brbh. dimin. a boat.

नैरंग *nairaṅg* [P. *nairang*], m. **1.** deception, cunning. **2.** wonderful performance; sleight of hand (as of a magician or juggler).

नैरपेक्ष्य *nairapekṣyă* [S.], f. neglect; undifference.

नैरर्थ्य *nairarthyă* [S.], m. meaninglessness, senselessness.

नैराश्य *nairāśyă* [S.], m. = निराशा.

नैरुक्त *nairukt* [S.], adj. & m. **1.** adj. having to do with the Nirukta, or Vedic glossary. **2.** m. an etymologist, philologist.

नैर्ऋत्य *nairr̥tyă* [S.] m. the south-west.

नैर्गुण्य *nairguṇyă* [S.], m. **1.** absence of qualities. **2.** absence of virtues; lack of gifts.

नैर्मल्य *nairmalyă* [S.], m. purity, freedom from blemish.

नैवेद्य *naivedyă* [S.], m. food consecrated to a deity; offering. — ~ चढ़ाना, to make an offering (to a deity).

नैश *naiś* [S.], adj. having to do with night; nocturnal. — ~ गगन, m. the night sky, or heavens.

नैषध *naiṣadh* [S.], adj. & m. *Pl. HŚS.* **1.** adj. having to do with Niṣadh. **2.** m. a Niṣadh prince (esp. Nala). **3.** the Niṣadh people.

नैषाद *naiṣād* [S.], adj. & m. *Pl. HŚS.* **1.** adj. belonging to the Niṣādas. **2.** m. the Niṣāda people. **3.** a Niṣāda man.

नैसर्गिक *naisargik* [S.], adj. natural (esp. of processes or phenomena; also of a person's manner).

नैसर्गिकी *naisargikī* [S.], f. naturalism.

नैहर *naihar* [**jñātighara-*: Pa. *ñātighara-*], m. **1.** wife's paternal home. **2.** wife's family, relatives.

नोई *noī* [*niyoga-*], f. reg. rope used to tie a cow's legs when milking it.

नोक *nok* [P. *nūk*], f. **1.** point, tip, end. **2.** angle (as between walls). **3.** projecting land; headland. **4.** colloq. fine or tip-top attire. — नोक-झोंक, f. barbed remarks, sarcasm; innuendo; squabbling; ornaments, finery; splendid manner. नोकदार [P. *-dār*], adj. pointed; barbed (a remark); fine, splendid (of attire, manner). नोक-दुम, adv. with pointed tail: नोक-दुम भागना, to take to one's heels.

नोकीला *nokīlā* [cf. H. *nok*], adj. = नुकीला.

नोखा *nokhā*, adj. reg. = अनोखा.

नोच *noc* [cf. H. *nocnā*], f. (m., *Pl.*) **1.** scratching, clawing. **2.** pinching. **3.** plucking out. **4.** colloq. snatching away (esp. of money); filching. — नोच-खसोट, f. clawing and tearing (each other); = ~, 4.

नोचना *nocnā*, v.t. **1.** to scratch, to claw. **2.** to pinch, to grip. **3.** to pluck out. **4.** to snatch away (as money); to filch. — **नोचा-खसोटी**, f. = **नोच-खसोट**, 1. **नोचा-नाची**, f. id. **नोचा-नोची**, f. id.

नोचू *nocū* [cf. H. *nocnā*], m. one who scratches, or pinches, &c.

नोट *noṭ* [Engl. *note*], m. a note: **1.** sthg. noted down; an observation. **2.** a communication. **3.** a bank-note. — **~ करना**, to note (sthg. down); to notice (sthg).

नोन *non* [*lavaṇa-*], m. salt. — **घाव पर ~ छिड़कना**, = **घाव पर नमक छिड़कना**. – **नोनचय**, m. see s.v. **नोन-छार**, m. brine; a kind of salt. **नोन-तेल**, m. salt and oil: household essentials. **नोन-राई उतारना**, = **राई-नोन उतारना**.

नोनचय *noncay*, m. *Pl.* a factitious salt (made of the ashes of burnt straw previously steeped in brine, and used to adulterate cooking salt).

नोनचा *noncā*, m. **1.** saline soil. **2.** salty pickle.

[1]**नोना** *nonā* [*lavaṇa-*], adj. **1.** salty, saline; brackish. **2.** fig. attractive. — **~ पानी**, m. salt water, sea-water. **~ मिट्टी**, f. saline soil; earth impregnated with nitrates and phosphates (as found in walls: used as manure and in manufacturing saltpetre).

[2]**नोणा** *noṇā* [? *lavana-*], m. reg. a kind of custard-apple, *Anona reticulata*.

[1]**नोनिया** *noniyā* [*lāvaṇika-*], m. **1.** a maker of, or dealer in, salt. **2.** a manufacturer of saltpetre.

[2]**नोनिया** *noniyā*, m. reg. a green vegetable, purslain. — **नोनिए का साग**, m. id.

नोनियार *noniyār*, m. reg. = [1]**नोनिया**.

[1]**नोनी** *nonī* [*navanīta-*], f. fresh butter.

[2]**नोनी** *nonī* [cf. H. *non*], f. **1.** saline soil. **2.** efflorescence of salt (on a wall).

नोव- *nov-* [*niyojayati*], v.t. Brbh. to tie a cow's feet when milking it.

नोश *nos̈* [P. *nos̈*], m. a drink; something drunk. — **~ करना**, to drink; to sup; to eat. **~ फ़रमाना**, id.

नौ *nau* [*nava*[2]], adj. nine. — **~ तेरह बाईस बताना**, to say sthg. irrelevant: to prevaricate. **~ दो ग्यारह होना**, colloq. to slip quietly away; to take to one's heels. **~ नक़द न तेरह उधार**, fig. a bird in the hand is worth two in the bush. **~ निध बारह सिद्ध होना**, to have the nine treasures (of Kuvera) and twelve magical powers: to have all that the heart can desire. – **नौटंकी**, f. weighing nine *ṭaṅkās*: title of a legendary princess, and (hence) name of a type of folk-drama in Brajbhāṣā or Kharī Bolī on legendary themes, with music; iron. charade. **नौनगे** [H. *-nag*], m. pl. an ornament consisting of nine jewels, worn on the arm. **नौरात्र**, f. a period of nine days at the beginning of the light half of the month Āśvin when Durgā is worshipped. **नौलक्खा**, adj. worth nine lacs, precious (specif. a partic. legendary chain).

[1]**नौ-** *nau-* [*nava-*; and P. *nau*], adj. **1.** new. **2.** fresh; recent. **3.** young. — **नौ-गढ़ंत**, adj. newly formed; newly coined. **नौजवान**, adj. & m. youthful; young, in one's prime; a youth, young man. °**ई**, f. youth; prime of life. **नौतोड़**, adj. newly broken: newly brought under the plough (land). **नौबढ़**, adj. recently prosperous, or rich. **नौ-बनौ** [P. *-ba-*], adv. ever and again. **नौबहार**, f. early spring; the spring. **नौरोज़**, m. the first day of the Iranian New Year (on which the sun enters Aries). **नौशा** [P. *-śāh*], m. bridegroom, young husband. **नौसिखिया**, m. see s.v.

[2]**नौ-** *nau-* [S], a ship; a boat (= **नाव**). — **नौचालन**, m. navigation. **नौ-परिवहन**, m. navigation (the activity). **नौ-भार**, m. tonnage, tare. **नौसेना**, f. navy. °**पति**, m. commander of a fleet. **नौसैनिक**, adj. & m. naval; a (naval) sailor. **नौविज्ञान**, m. navigation (the art or science).

नौकर *naukar* [P. *naukar*], m. **1.** a servant, attendant, retainer. **2.** one serving in a post; a government or public servant. — **~ रखना (को)**, to employ as a servant. – **नौकर-चाकर**, m. pl. servants. **नौकरशाह** [cf. P. *-śāhī*], m. a bureaucrat. °**ई**, adj. & f. **नौकरशाहियत**, f. bureaucracy. **नौकरशाहीकरण**, m. bureaucratisation.

नौकरनी *naukarnī*, f. = **नौकरानी**.

नौकरशाहाना *naukarśāhānā* [H. *naukarśāh* + P. *-āna*], adj. inv. bureaucratic.

नौकरशाहीकरण *naukarśāhīkaraṇ*, m. see s.v. **नौकर**.

नौकरानी *naukrānī* [cf. H. *naukar*], f. a woman servant.

नौकरी *naukrī* [P. *naukrī*], f. **1.** service. **2.** employment (esp. in government or public service). **3.** a post, situation. — **~ करना**, to serve, to give service (to, **की**). **~ पर होना**, to be in service; to hold a position; to have work. **~ बजाना**, to attend diligently to the needs (of, **की**). **~ से लगना**, to obtain employment. – **नौकरी-चाकरी**, f. = **नौकरी**. **नौकरी-पेशा** [P. *-peśa*], m. a servant (public or private).

नौका *naukā* [S.], f. **1.** a boat; a ship. **2.** the castle (in chess). — **नौकाधिकरण** [°*kā* + *a*°], m. admiralty. **नौका-नयन**, m. traffic of ships, navigation (= जहाज़रानी). नौका-विहार, m. a pleasure-trip by boat; excursion.

नौग्रही *naugrahī* [S.], f. *Pl. HŚS.* a bracelet consisting of nine precious stones (see नवरत्न, s.v. नव) set in gold or silver.

नौछावर *nauchāvar*, f, m. = निछावर.

नौज *nauj* [A. *na'ūẕu*], interj. see नौज़.

नौज़ *nauz* [A. *na'ūẕu*], interj. U. we seek protection or preservation: **1.** God preserve us! **2.** God forbid!

नौतना *nautnā* [*nimantrayate*], v.t. to invite (to a feast or entertainment).

नौतपन *nautpan* [cf. H. [2]*nautā*], m. *Pl.* witchcraft, sorcery.

नौतहार *naut'hār*, f. reg. feast, festival; festivity.

नौतहारू *naut'hārū*, m. reg. one who has received an invitation; specif. wedding guest.

[1]**नौता** *nautā*, m. = न्योता.

[2]**नौता** *nautā* [*nimantraka-*], m. reg. wizard, magician.

नौध *naudh* [**navavṛddha-*], m. *Pl. HŚS.* a sapling; a fresh shoot of a tree or plant.

नौबत *naubat* [A. *nauba*: P. *naubat*], f. **1.** period, time, turn. **2.** fit (as of fever). **3.** occasion, opportunity. **4.** state of affairs; plight. **5.** moment of need. **6.** musical instruments, esp. kettledrums or pipes (as sounded on ceremonial occasions). — ~ आना, or पहुँचना, (की), matters to reach (such) a pass, the time for (certain actions or things) to come. ~ को पहुँचना, or होना (की), to reach (such) a pass (a matter). ~ बजना, or झड़ना, drums to be beaten (as an assertion of status, or to celebrate a birth, &c.); one's time, or nemesis, to come. ~ बजाकर, adv. with fanfare. ~ यहाँ तक पहुँचना कि ..., the situation (of, की) to reach such a pass that .... – नौबत-ख़ाना, m. upper porch or room where drums or other musical instruments are sounded (as of a palace, mansion, or temple). नौबतवाला, m. musician or drummer at ceremonial occasions.

नौबती *naubătī* [P. *naubatī*], adj. & m. occurring at, or having to do with, an occasion: **1.** adj. periodical; intermittent (as a fever). **2.** m. one who beats a kettledrum. **3.** door-keeper; watchman, guard. **4.** a tent.

नौमी *naumī*, adj. = नवमी.

नौरते *naurte*, m. corr. reg. = नौरात्र.

नौशाह *nauśāh*, m. = नौशा (see s.v. [1]नौ-).

नौशी *nauśī* [cf. H. *nauśā*], f. colloq. a bride (= दुलहन).

नौसादर *nausādar* [P. *nauśādur*], m. sal-ammoniac, ammonium chloride.

नौसिख *nausikh*, m. = नौसिखिया.

नौसिखिया *nausikhiyā*, m. a beginner.

नौहा *nauhā* [A. *nauḥa*], m. U. a lament.

नौहरा *nauhrā*, m. reg. (Raj. or N.) a barn.

न्यग्रोध *nyag-rodh* [S.], m. the banyan tree.

न्यर्बुद *ny-arbud* [S.], m. one hundred millions, ten crores.

न्यस्त *ny-ast* [S.], adj. **1.** put down, placed; deposited. **2.** entrusted, consigned; invested. **3.** accumulated.

न्याति *nyāti* [ad. *jñāti-*; Pk. *ṇāi-*], f. Brbh. species, kind; community, caste.

न्याय *ny-āy* [S.], m. **1.** right or fitting manner, or method. ***2.** justice. **3.** law; entitlement, right. **4.** just or proper act, or judgment. **5.** adjudication, decision (in a case). **6.** *philos.* the Nyāya system; logic. **7.** demonstration, fitting illustration (of a case). — ~ करना, to administer justice; to adjudicate; to act justly or rightly (towards, के साथ). ~ से, adv. justly; fittingly; lawfully. – न्याय-कर्ता, m. inv. an adjudicator, judge; one who acts justly. न्यायज्ञ, m. one versed in law, a jurist. न्याय-पंचायत, f. a partic. village panchāyat. न्याय-पत्र, m. decree of a court. न्याय-पालिका, f. judiciary. न्यायपूर्ण, adj. just (an action or a person); proper; lawful. न्याय-प्रिय, adj. righteous. न्यायवादी, m. attorney. न्यायवान, adj. acting rightly, or properly; in accordance with right, equitable. न्याय-शास्त्र, m. = ~, 6.; jurisprudence. °-शास्त्री, m. न्यायशील, adj. acting justly. न्याय-संगत, adj. just (an action); fitting; lawful. न्याय-सभा, f. law court. न्यायांग [°*ya*+*a*°], m. judiciary. न्यायाधिकरण [°*ya*+*a*°], m. tribunal. न्यायाधीश [°*ya*+*a*°], m. judge. न्यायालय [°*ya*+*ā*°], m. law court. न्यायासन [°*ya*+*ā*°], m. seat of justice: the Bench. न्यायोचित [°*ya*+*u*°], adj. just (an action); lawful.

न्यायता *ny-āyătā* [S.], f. *Pl. HŚS.* fitness, propriety.

न्यायिक *ny-āyik* [S.], adj. **1.** judicial. **2.** having to do with a court.

न्यायी *ny-āyī* [S.], adj. & m. **1.** adj. just (a person). **2.** right-thinking. **3.** m. a judge, arbitrator. **4.** a right-thinking person.

न्याय्य *ny-āyyă* [S.], adj. just, lawful; appropriate.

न्यारा *nyārā* [**anyakāra-*], adj. & m. **1.** adj. separate, distinct; different. **2.** unusual; rare. **3.** removed, distant. **4.** waste (from the refining of precious metals). — ~ करना, to separate; to detach; to place apart. न्यारे, adv.

separately, apart; aloof; individually; at a distance, far.

न्यारिया *nyāriyā* [cf. H. *nyārā*], m. & adj. **1.** m. a refiner of precious metals. **2.** panner for gold, prospector. **3.** adj. prudent; shrewd.

न्यास *ny-ās* [S.], m. **1.** putting down, placing; depositing; entrusting. ***2.** a deposit; investment. **3.** a trust; endowment. **4.** mark, sign, trace.

न्यासी *ny-āsī* [S.], m. a trustee.

न्यून *ny-ūn* [S.], adj. **1.** less; diminished; low. **2.** deficient, lacking. **3.** inferior; insignificant. — ~ **कोण**, m. an acute angle. **न्यूनाधिक** [°*na*+*a*°], adj. less or more, smaller or greater. **न्यूनाधिक मात्रा**, or **परिमाण, में**, adv. to a greater or less extent. **न्यूनाधिक्य**, m. smaller or greater amount, deficiency or excess; inequality, imbalance. **न्यूनोन्नत** [°*na*+*u*°], adj. under-developed; depressed (as an area).

न्यूनतम *ny-ūnătam* [S.], adj. minimal.

न्यूनता *ny-ūnătā* [S.], f. **1.** small amount or level; small size. **2.** deficiency, lack. **3.** inferiority. — **न्यूनता-बोधक**, adj. *gram.* diminutive.

न्यूनन *ny-ūnan* [S.], m. **1.** curtailment. **2.** diminution.

न्योछावर *nyochāvar*, f. = **निछावर**.

न्योता *nyotā* [**nimantra-*], m. **1.** invitation (esp. to a meal). **2.** feast; festive occasion. **3.** a present given with an invitation. **4.** *HŚS.* a present given by a guest. — ~ **खाना**, to partake as a guest in a meal, &c. ~ **देना (को)**, to invite.

न्यौतना *nyautnā* [*nimantrayate*], v.t. to invite.

न्हाठ *nhāṭh* [*naṣṭi-*], f. reg. (Raj.) fleeing, flight.

न्हाठ- *nhāṭh-* [cf. *naṣṭa-*], v.i. reg. (Raj.) to flee.

प

प *pa*, the twenty-first consonant of the Devanāgarī syllabary. — **पकार**, m. the sound /p/; the letter प.

पंक *paṅk* [S.], m. **1.** mud; mire; dirt. **2.** bog, swamp. **3.** trans. ointment, salve. — **पंकज**, m. mud-born: a lotus. °**-बन**, m. lotus-thicket; °**-राग**, m. Brbh. ruby; °**-आसन**, m. he who sits in the lotus posture: a title of Brahmā. **पंकरुह**, m. Av. = **पंकेरुह**. **पंकेज**, m. born in mud: a lotus. **पंकेरुह**, m. Brbh. growing in mud: id.

पंकचर *paṅkcar*, m. = पंचर.

पंका *paṅkā*, m. *Pl.* = पंक.

पंकार *paṅkār* [S.], m. *Pl.* **1.** name of certain water plants. **2.** dam, dike.

पंकिल *paṅkil* [S.], m. **1.** muddy. **2.** fig. impure, defiled.

पंकीला *paṅkīlā*, adj. *Pl.* = **पंकिल**, 1.

पंकेरुह *paṅkeruh* [S.], m. see s.v. **पंक**.

पंकेला *paṅkelā*, adj. rcg. = **पंकिल**, 1.

पंक्ति *paṅkti* [S.], f. **1.** a row, line; queue. **2.** rank; series; group. **3.** commensal group; row of persons sitting down at a meal. **4.** any caste, or sub-caste. — **पंक्ति-बद्ध**, adj. arranged in a line, or in lines, &c.

पंख *paṅkh* [*pakṣa-*], m. **1.** wing. **2.** fin. — **~ जमना**, or **निकलना (को)**, to be sprouting wings: to be about to leave (home, post, &c). **~ लगना (को)**, to be winged: to be fast, fleet. – **पंख-कटा**, adj. having the wings clipped.

पँखड़ी *paṁkhṛī* [cf. *pakṣa-*], f. a petal.

पंखा *paṅkhā* [*pakṣa-*], m. **1.** a fan (worked by hand, or electric). **2.** propeller. — **~ करना**, to fan. **हाथ का ~ करना**, to fan (the face) with the hand.

पंखिया *paṅkhiyā* [? cf. H. *paṅk*], adj. & m. corr. *Pl.* **1.** adj. impure; wicked. **2.** m. an immoral or wicked man.

[1]**पंखी** *paṅkhī* [cf. H. *paṅkhā*], f. **1.** wing (of an aircraft). **2.** a small fan. **3.** petal. **4.** mudguard, wing (of bicycle, car).

[2]**पंखी** *paṅkhī* [*pakṣin-*], m. a bird.

[3]**पंखी** *paṅkhī* [cf. H. *paṅkh*], f. *Pl.* a kind of (light or soft) woollen material.

पंग *paṅg* [ad. *paṅgu-*], adj. Brbh. **1.** lame. **2.** fig. immobilised: entranced (the eyes).

पंगत *paṅgat* [ad. *paṅkti-*], f. Brbh. = **पंक्ति**, 1.-4. — **~ से बाहर**, adj. out of caste.

[1]**पंगा** *paṅgā* [*paṅgu-*], m. **1.** lame. **2.** maimed; deformed.

[2]**पंगा** *paṅgā*, adj. **1.** watery, thin. **2.** delicate, tender.

पंगास *paṅgās* [ad. *piṅgāsya-*], m. tawny-faced: a kind of fish.

पंगु *paṅgu* [S.], adj. & m. **1.** adj. lame; crippled; deformed. **2.** m. a lame person.

पंगुता *paṅgutā* [S.], f. lameness; deformity.

पंगुल *paṅgul* [S.], adj. = **पंगु**.

पंगुला *paṅgulā*, adj. *Pl.* = **पंगु**.

पंच *pañc* [S.], adj. & m. **1.** adj. in comp. five. **2.** m. a council (originally of five men); a jury. **3.** an arbitrator; umpire. **4.** transf. Brbh. Av. people generally (as being of a partic. view or disposition). **5.** the headman of a caste or village community. — **~ मानना**, to appoint, or to accept, as an arbitrator. – **पंचकल्याणक**, m. name of a Jain festival celebrating five stages in the life of Jinendra. **पंचकोण**, m. pentagon. **पंचकोसी**, adj. living at five *kos'* distance (a person). **पंच-गव्य**, m. five products of the cow: milk, curds, *ghī*, urine, dung. **पंच-जन**, m. five classes of beings: gods, men, *gandharvas* and *apsaras*, snakes, spirits of ancestors. °**ई**, f. gathering of five persons. **पंचजन्य**, m. id.; (= **पांच-**°) name of Kṛṣṇa's conch shell (taken from the demon Pañcajana). **पंच-तत्त्व**, m. = **पंच-भूत**. **पंचतपा**, m. an ascetic who in the hot weather sits in the sun between four fires (see **पंचाग्नि**). **पंच-तीर्थ**, m. any five chief places of pilgrimage. **पंचदश**, adj. fifteenth. **पंच-देव**, m. five deities (worshipped as a group by *smārta* Hindus): Viṣṇu, Śiva, Gaṇeś, Sūrya, Durgā. °**ता**, m. id. **पंचनद**, m. the five rivers (of the Panjab); the Panjab. **पंच-परमेश्वर**, m. the five supreme gods: a village court or tribunal. **पंचपात्र**, m. a wide-mouthed glass (used in worship). **पंचपिरिया**, m. one who worships the five *pīrs* or Muslim saints. **पंच-पीर**, m. the five *pīrs* or Muslim saints. °**-पीरिया**, m. = **पंचपिरिया**. **पंच-फ़ैसला**, m. judgment by arbitration. **पंचबाण**, adj. having five arrows: a title of the god Kāmdev. **पंचभुज**, m. pentagon. **पंच-भूत**, m. the five elements: earth, air, fire, water, *ākāś*.

°-भूतात्मा, adj. & m. inv. composed of the five elements (as the body); a human being. पंचभौतिक, adj. (= पांच-°), id. पंचमुख, adj. five-faced: a title of Śiva. पंचरंगा, adj. of five colours; multicoloured. पंच-रत्न, m. a collection of five jewels, or precious things (e.g. gold, diamond, sapphire, ruby, pearl); a quintet of five splendid things. पंचरस, adj. composed of five fluids. पंच-रात्र, adj. & m. lasting five nights or days; a period of five nights; name of a sacrifice which lasts five days; general term for the sacred books of certain *śākta*-influenced Vaiṣṇava sects. पंच-लड़ा, adj. consisting of five strings, or rows. पंचवर्षीय, adj. five-year (as a plan); quinquennial. पंचवाँसा [-*māsya*-], m. ceremony in the fifth month of pregnancy. पंचवार्षिक, adj. quinquennial. पंचशर, m. = पंचबाण. पंच-शील, m. the five rules (Buddhist) of moral conduct; a set of five political principles (promoted by the Bandung Conference, 1954). पंचसाला [P. -*sāla*], adj. = पंचवर्षीय. पंचांग [°*ca*+*a*°], m. almanac treating five topics (solar and lunar days, asterisms, *yogas*, *karaṇas*). पंचाग्नि [°*ca*+*a*°], m. five fires: a penance in which the performer sits in the sun in the hot weather, between four fires placed one at each quarter around him. पंचाध्यायी [°*ca*+*a*°], f. a quintet of chapters (of the *Bhāgavata Purāṇa* or of other works) on the theme of Kṛṣṇa's relationships with the *gopīs*. पंचानन, m. having five faces: a title of Śiva. पंचामृत [°*ca*+*a*°], m. a mixture of milk, curds, *ghī*, sugar and honey. पंचोत्तर, m. *hist.* a duty of five per cent; deduction of five per cent from estimated gross revenue of a village; customs point for inland traffic.

पंचक *pañcak* [S.], adj. & m. **1.** adj. consisting of five parts. **2.** m. an aggregate of five; quintet, pentad. **3.** a payment, or charge, of five per cent.

पंचता *pañcătā* [S.], f. **1.** fivefold state or nature. 2. = पँचा. **3.** *Pl. HŚS.* dissolution (of the body) into its five constituents: death.

पंचत्व *pañcatvă* [S.], m. = पंचता.

पंचम *pañcam* [S.], adj. & m. **1.** adj. fifth. **2.** melodious (see 4). **3.** m. the fifth or the seventh note of the musical scale. **4.** *mus.* name of a *rāg*. **5.** *gram.* a nasal consonant. — पंचमांग [°*ma*+*a*°], m. fifth column. °ई, m. fifth columnist.

पंचमी *pañcămī* [S.], adj. the fifth day of a lunar half month.

पंचर *pañcar* [Engl. *puncture*], m. f. a puncture. — ~ ठीक करना, or लगाना, to repair a puncture. ~ होना, to be punctured.

पँचवाई *paṁcvāī*, f. a kind of rice wine (= पचवाई).

पँचा *paṁcā* [cf. H. *pāṁc*], m. any collection or aggregate of five.

पंचाट *pañcāṭ*, f. award of a court or tribunal.

पंचानवे *pañcānve*, adj. = पचानवे.

पंचानवे *pañcānve* [*pañcanavati-*], adj. ninety-five.

पंचायत *pañcāyat* [*pañca-*+H. v.n. in *āv-*], f. **1.** a village council (consisting of five, or more, members), a panchayat: village court or arbitrating body. **2.** a caste council (in a village); arbitrators in an intra-caste matter. **3.** meeting of any body (to discuss a particular question); village meeting. **4.** iron. chatter, talk. — ~ अदालत, f. village court or arbitrating body. ~ करना, or जोड़ना, to assemble a council; to form a village court. ~ बैठाना, id., 1. – पंचायत-नामा, m. written decision or award of a panchayat. पंचायत-समिति, f. district panchayat council.

पंचायती *pañcāyătī* [cf. H. *pañcāyat*], adj. **1.** having to do with a panchayat. **2.** decided, or authorised, by a panchayat; regarded as equitable. **3.** public, common (as a building, an area). — ~ राज, m. system of local self-government. ~ साला, m. pej. the whole council's (or, everyman's) brother-in-law: a term of abuse.

पंचाल *pañcāl* [S.], m. **1.** an ancient tribe, and their territory in north India. **2.** a member of the Pañcāla tribe.

पँचाल *paṁcāl* [? *pāñcāla-*], adj. clever; cunning, deceitful.

पंचालिका *pañcālikā* [S.], f. **1.** Brbh. a dancing-girl. **2.** *HŚS.* a doll.

पंचावन *pañcāvan*, adj. pronun. var. = पचपन.

पंचासी *pañcāsī*, adj. pronun. var. = पचासी.

पंछाला *pañchālā*, m. corr. = पन-छाला, see s.v. [1]पन-.

पंछी *pañchī* [ad. *pakṣin-*], m. a bird.

पंजर *pañjar* [S.], m. **1.** skeleton. **2.** the ribs, rib-cage. **3.** the human frame. **4.** a cage. — ~ होना, to waste away (the body). – अंजर-पंजर ढीला होना, the bones to become loose: to be impaired (by age, or injury); to be exhausted.

[1]**पंजरी** *pañjrī* [cf. H. *pañjar*], f. a rib.

[2]**पंजरी** *pañjrī* [P. *panj*+H.], f. the number five in the game of *causar*.

पंजा *pañjā* [P. *pañja*], m. **1.** an aggregate of five. **2.** a five (in cards, at dice). **3.** the hand with the fingers. **4.** paw, claw (of an animal). **5.** fig. clutch, grasp; power. **6.** the toe of a shoe. — ~ करना, = ~ लड़ाना. ~ फेरना, to twist an opponent's wrist (having one's fingers interlocked with his). ~ फैलाना, or बढ़ाना (पर), to stretch out the hand, &c., to seize; fig. to threaten or to attempt to invade (a country). ~ भर, m. a handful, fistful. ~ मारना, to claw at, to snap at; to snatch at. ~ लड़ाना (से), to try to twist over (a rival's) wrist or forearm: a trial of strength. ~ लेना, = ~ फेरना. पंजे में, or के नीचे, आना, to fall into the clutches (of, के). पंजे में करना, or लाना, to bring into, or to consign to, the power, or clutches (of, के). पंजों के बल चलना, to walk on tiptoe; to strut.

पंजाब *pañjāb* [P. *panjāb*], m. five rivers: the Panjab.

पंजाबिन *pañjābin* [cf. H. [1]*pañjābī*], f. a Panjabi woman.

[1]**पंजाबी** *pañjābī* [cf. H. *pañjāb*], m. a Panjabi.

[2]**पंजाबी** *pañjābī* [cf. H. *pañjāb*], adj. & f. **1.** adj. having to do with the Panjab. **2.** f. the Panjabi language.

पंजारा *pañjārā*, m. reg. = पिंजियारा.

पंजाला *pañjālā*, m. reg. (W). flat board forming driver's seat in a cart.

पंजाली *pañjālī*, f. reg. a door-frame.

पंजिका *pañjikā* [S.], f. a list, register, roll; calendar, almanac; account book; register of ancestry. — पंजिकाकार, m. keeper of any register, or account; almanac-maker; astronomer.

पंजी *pañjī* [S.], f. list, register, &c. (= पंजिका). — पंजीकार, m. keeper of any register or account. — पंजीकरण, m. entering (in a list or account); registration. पंजीकृत, adj. entered (details); registered.

पंजीकरण *pañjīkaraṇ* [S.], m. see s.v. पंजी.

पंजीकृत *pañjīkr̥t* [S.], adj. see s.v. पंजी.

पंजीरी *pañjīrī*, f. = पनजीरी, s.v. [2]पन-.

पंजेरा *pañjerā*, m. *Pl.* a coppersmith, tinsmith.

पंड *paṇḍ* [S.], m. a eunuch; an impotent man.

[1]**पंडा** *paṇḍā* [*paṇḍita*-], m. **1.** a brāhmaṇ superintending as a hereditary function a place of pilgrimage, *ghāṭ* or temple; a registrar of genealogies. **2.** a brāhmaṇ cook.

[2]**पंडा** *paṇḍā* [S.], f. *Pl. HŚS.* wisdom, intelligence, understanding.

पंडाल *paṇḍāl*, m. pavilion (site of a religious ceremony).

पंडित *paṇḍit* [S.], adj. & m. **1.** adj. learned, wise; clever. **2.** m. a scholar; a learned brāhmaṇ. **3.** title of respect to a brāhmaṇ (esp. if learned). **4.** a teacher. — पंडित-ख़ाना, m. (corr. of बंदी-ख़ाना) jail; gambling-house. पंडित-मानी, m. an ignorant would-be scholar.

पंडिताइन *paṇḍitāin* [H. *paṇḍit*+-*ānī*-, -*inī*-], f. = पंडितानी.

पंडिताई *paṇḍitāī* [cf. H. *paṇḍit*], f. **1.** learning, scholarship. **2.** the status or duties of a paṇḍit. — ~ करना, or छाँटना, to make a display of learning.

पंडिताऊ *paṇḍitāū* [cf. H. *paṇḍit*], adj. typical of a paṇḍit (esp. language or style); pedantic.

पंडितानी *paṇḍitānī* [H. *paṇḍit*+-*ānī*-], f. **1.** wife of a paṇḍit. **2.** teacher, schoolmistress. **3.** brāhmaṇ woman.

पँड़िया *paṁṛiyā* [cf. **pāḍḍa*-: ? ← Drav.], f. dimin. a buffalo calf (= [2]पाड़ा). — ~ का ताऊ, a calf's uncle: dolt, idiot.

पंडियायन *paṇḍiyāyan* [cf. H. *paṇḍitāin*], f. = पंडितानी.

पंडु *paṇḍu* [*pāṇḍu*-: ? ← Austro-as.], adj. & m. **1.** adj. yellow or tawny; white. **2.** Brbh. five (with reference to the five Pāṇḍavas). **3.** m. *hist. mythol.* name of a king of ancient Delhi.

पंडुक *paṇḍuk* [conn. *pāṇḍu*-], m. poet. a turtle-dove; dove.

पंडुनि *paṇḍuni* [cf. H. *paṇḍu*], adj. *Pl. hist. mythol.* relating to the Pāṇḍavas.

पंडुर *paṇḍur*, m. E.H. a water-snake.

पंडू *paṇḍū*, m. reg. ripe fruit; a berry (see पंडु, 1).

पंडूरी *paṇḍūrī*, f. *Pl.* a species of hawk or falcon (? the shāhīn falcon).

पंत *pant*, Brbh. (Raj.) way, road (= पंथ).

पंतवा *pantvā*, m. *Pl.* a kind of sweet.

पंथ *panth* [ad. *panthā*-], m. **1.** path, way; road; course. **2.** fig. moral course; conduct of life. **3.** sect. — ~ जोहना, or देखना, or निहारना, or सेना, to watch the path (of): to await the coming, or return (of, का). ~ लगना, to follow, or to dog the path (of, के); to harass. पंथवाद, m. sectarianism. °ई, adj. & m. sectarian.

पंथी *panthī* [cf. H. *panth*], m. **1.** a wayfarer. **2.** -पंथी. an adherent (to partic. views, customs). **3.** a sectarian.

पंद *pand* [P. *pand*], f. U. advice, counsel.

पंद्रह *pandrah* [*pañcadaśa*-], adj. fifteen.

पंद्रही *pandrahī* [cf. H. *pandrah*], f. a fortnight.

पंधरस *pandhras* [cf. H. *pandrah*], f. *Pl.* the fifteenth day of a month.

पँवाड़ा *paṁvāṛā* [*pravāda-*+MIA *-ḍa-*], m. an encomium; a long or boring tale.

पँवाड़िया *paṁvāṛiyā* [cf. H. *paṁvāṛā*], m. *Pl.* panegyrist, bard, story-teller.

[1]**पँवार** *paṁvār* [*pravāḍa-*], m. Brbh. coral.

[2]**पँवार** *paṁvār* [*prapunāḍa-*], m. the shrub *Cassia tora* (used in the treatment of ringworm).

पँवार- *paṁvār-* [*pravārayati*[1]], v.t. E.H. **1.** to drive off. **2.** to shun.

पंसारता *paṃsārtā* [cf. H. *paṃsārī*], f. *Pl.* the business of a *paṃsārī*; dealing in drugs, spices, &c.

पंसारी *paṃsārī* [*prasārin-*], m. a grocer; seller of spices, drugs.

-प *-pă* [S.], v. suffix (forms nouns). **1.** guarding, protecting, ruling (e.g. अवनिप, m. ruler of the earth). **2.** drinking (e.g. मधुप, m. bee).

पकड़ *pakaṛ* [cf. H. *pakaṛnā*], f. **1.** seizing; hold, clutch. **2.** seizure, capture. **3.** bout (as wrestling); set-to. **4.** colloq. gain, profit; haul. **5.** fig. alertness, intelligence; grasp (of a subject). **6.** occasion for criticism (in a work). — **~ में आना**, to fall into the hands, or power (of, की). – **पकड़-धकड़**, f. = ~, 3.

पकड़ना *pakaṛnā* [**pakkaḍ-*: cf. Pk. *paggaï*], v.t. **1.** to seize, to catch; to check. **2.** to capture; to arrest. **3.** to come up to; to overtake. **4.** to catch (a train). **5.** to detect (as a sound, or a fault); to discover; to object to (faults); to carp at. **6.** to acquire, to take on (a habit, or an attribute). **7.** to grasp mentally. **8.** to catch (fire). **9.** to afflict (one, को: a disease). — **आग ~**, to catch fire. **जड़ ~**, to take root. **रंग ~**, to take colour, to be dyed, or dyeable; to blush.

पकड़वाना *pakaṛvānā* [cf. H. *pakaṛnā*], v.t. = पकड़ाना, 1.

पकड़ाई *pakṛāī* [cf. H. *pakaṛnā, pakṛānā*], f. **1.** seizing. **2.** seizure, capture. — **~ देना**, to be seized; to be grasped, revealed (a situation, &c).

पकड़ाना *pakṛānā* [cf. H. *pakaṛnā*], v.t. **1.** to cause to be caught, seized (by, से). **2.** to deliver (to, को); to hand over (to).

पकना *paknā* [cf. *pakva-*: Ap. *pakāvaï*], v.i. **1.** to be cooked, to cook; to boil; to bake. **2.** to ripen; to mature. **3.** to be fixed, baked (bricks, earthenware). **4.** to come to a head (a boil). **5.** to turn grey or white (hair).

पकरिया *pakariyā*, f. dimin. reg. = पाकड़.

पकला *paklā*, m. *Pl. HŚS.* a sore; sore between the toes.

पकली *paklī* [conn. H. *pakaṛnā*], f. reg. (W.) net for holding straw, chaff, &c.

पकवाई *pakvāī* [cf. H. *pakvānā*], f. **1.** cooking. **2.** price paid for cooking.

पकवान *pakvān* [ad. *pakvānna-*], m. cooked food: bread-cake, pastry or sweet fried in *ghī*, e.g. *pūrī, kacaurī*.

पकवाना *pakvānā* [cf. H. *paknā*], v.t. **1.** to cause to be cooked, baked, &c. (by, से). **2.** to cause to ripen.

पकाई *pakāī* [cf. H. *paknā, pakānā*], f. **1.** cooking. **2.** ripeness; maturity, &c. (see पक्का). **3.** firmness, definiteness. **4.** payment for cooking.

पकाऊ *pakāū* [cf. H. *paknā, pakānā*], adj. ripening; coming to a head (a boil).

पकाना *pakānā* [cf. H. *paknā*], v.t. **1.** to cook; to bake; to boil. **2.** to ripen. **3.** to fire (bricks, earthenware). **4.** fig. to cause distress to (the heart). **5.** colloq. to arrange, to settle in full (a transaction). **चार रुपए का गुड़ पका दो**, give me four rupees' worth (or amount) of molasses. **6.** to get or to learn (sthg.) by heart. — **बाल ~**, to cause (one's) hair to grow grey; to spend one's life (in). – **पका-पकाया**, adj. ready-cooked.

पकाव *pakāv* [cf. H. *paknā*], m. **1.** ripening. **2.** coming to a head (a boil, &c).

पकोड़ा *pakoṛā* [**pakvavaṭa-*], m. a savoury consisting of vegetables cut up, coated in batter of gram flour, and deep-fried.

पकोड़ी *pakoṛī* [**pakvavaṭa-*], f. a small *pakoṛā*.

पकौड़ा *pakauṛā* [**pakvapūpaḍa-*], m. = पकोड़ा.

पकौड़ी *pakauṛī*, f. = पकोड़ी.

पक्का *pakkā* [*pakva-*], adj. **1.** cooked; boiled; baked; cooked in *ghī*. **2.** transf. ripe, mature; experienced, knowing; astute. **3.** processed; baked, fired (bricks, earthenware); refined (as sugar, oil); boiled (water); of high quality. **~ करना**, to process. **4.** complete, finished, well-made; made of bricks or stone with mortar (a building); metalled, or sealed (a road). **5.** grey or white (hair); dark (complexion). **6.** fast, firm (a colour). **7.** ripe (as a boil). **8.** genuine, real; thoroughgoing, solid (work); inveterate, incorrigible; reliable (advice, or calculations); fixed, standard (amount, price, weight, quality); nett (gain, profit); classical (music). **9.** undoubted, proved. **~ दावा**, m. sound title; a good case. **10.** fixed, determined, definite; firm (as a resolve); of binding force. **पक्की बात**, f. sthg. definite, assured; sthg. arranged.

11. finalised, revised (as accounts, work in preparation); audited. — ~ आम, m. ripe mango: colloq. an ancient man or woman. ~ करना, to establish (as a fact, a claim); to authenticate; to settle (a matter), to make sure; to complete (sthg. imperfectly or provisionally done); to enforce. ~ गाना, m. singing in classical style. ~ पान, ripe *pān* leaf; colloq. = ~ आम.

पक्कापन *pakkāpan* [cf. H. *pakkā*], m. **1.** ripeness; maturity, &c. **2.** firmness, definiteness. **3.** genuineness; quality.

पक्ति *pakti* [S.], f. (*Pl.*) *HŚS.* **1.** cooking, &c. **2.** digestion.

पक्व *pakvă* [S.], adj. **1.** cooked. **2.** ripe; mature. **3.** digested.

पक्वता *pakvātā*, [S.], f. ripeness; maturity.

पक्ष *pakṣ* [S.], m. **1.** side (of the body); flank. **2.** transf. side, party; wing. **3.** side (of an argument); case, thesis. **4.** aspect (of a question). **5.** direction, quarter. आपके ~ में, adv. from your point of view. **6.** wing (of a bird). **6.** either of the halves (light and dark) of a lunar month. — ~ करना, to take the side (of, का); to support, to favour. ~ में, adv. in support (of, के), favouring. ~ विपक्ष, m. thesis and counter-thesis, pro and con. – पक्षधर, m. supporter (of a side, an argument). पक्षपात, m. partiality, preference; favouritism. पक्षपात करना, to show partiality (towards, का); to favour. °ई, adj. & m. partial, biased; a supporter, partisan (of, का). पक्ष-मुक्त, adj. impartial; independent of either side (as a candidate). पक्ष-हत, adj. paralysed on one side. पक्षहीन, adj. wingless. पक्षांतर [°*kṣa*+*a*°], m. opposite side. पक्षाघात [°*kṣa*+*ā*°], m. *med.* a stroke.

पक्षि- *pakṣi-* [S]. birds': — पक्षिविज्ञान, m. = पक्षी-विज्ञान.

पक्षी *pakṣī* [S.], adj. & m. **1.** adj. winged. **2.** transf. siding (with, का). **3.** partial, biased. **4.** m. a bird. **5.** supporter, adherent. — पक्षी-विज्ञान, m. ornithology.

-पक्षीय *-pakṣīyă* [S.], adj. taking a side or viewpoint (e.g. बामपक्षीय, adj. left-wing).

पक्ष्मिल *pakṣmil* [ad. *pakṣmala-*], adj. poet. having long eyelashes, or hair.

पख *pakh* [cf. H. *pākh*], f. a cause of trouble or difficulty. — ~ निकालना, to find fault. ~ लगाना, to be obstructive (in, में).

पखड़ी *pakhṛī* [cf. *pakṣman-*], f. a petal (= पँखड़ी).

पखरवाना *pakharvānā* [cf. *prakṣālayati*], v.t. to cause to be washed.

पखरौटा *pakhrauṭā* [cf. **praskara-*, MIA *pakkhara-*], m. *Pl. HŚS.* gold or silver leaf covering a folded betel leaf.

¹पखवाड़ा *pakhvāṛā* [conn. **pakṣavāra-*], m. half of a lunar month; a fortnight.

²पखवाड़ा *pakhvāṛā* [**pakṣapāṭaka-*], m. *Pl. HŚS.* gable end (of a house).

पखवारा *pakhvārā* [**pakṣavāra-*], m. Av. = पखवाड़ा.

पखाटा *pakhāṭā* [cf. *pakṣa-*], m. **1.** *Pl. HŚS.* the horn tip at the two ends of a bow. **2.** Pl. root of a bird's wing (= *pakhauṭā*, 1).

पखानो *pakhāno* [*prakhyāna-*], m. Brbh. tale, story.

पखारना *pakhārnā* [*prakṣālayati*], v.t. to wash; to rinse clean.

¹पखाल *pakhāl* [**pakṣakhallā-*], f. reg. (W). **1.** a large leather water-bag (carried by bullocks). **2.** one side of a bellows.

²पखाल *pakhāl* [*prakṣāla-*], m. reg. **1.** mud, dirt; rubbish. **2.** dysentery.

पखाला *pakhālā*, m. *Pl.* = ¹पखाल.

पखाली *pakhālī* [cf. H. ¹*pakhāl*], m. reg. water-carrier.

पखावज *pakhāvaj* [**pakṣātodya-*: Pk. *pakkhāujja-*], m. a side-drum, small drum.

पखावजी *pakhāvjī* [cf. H. *pakhāvaj*], m. a drummer.

पखुड़ी *pakhuṛī* [cf. *pakṣman-*], f. **1.** a petal. **2.** reg. the shoulder-blade.

पखुवा *pakhuvā* [cf. *pakṣa-*], m. reg. 1. = पक्ष, 1. **2.** the upper arm. **3.** gable end (of a house).

पखेरू *pakherū* [**pakṣikarūpa-*], m. a bird.

पखेव *pakhev* [*prakṣepa-*], m. reg. (Bihar) food given to cows and buffaloes after calving.

पखेस *pakhes*, m. *Pl.* mark, stamp.

पखौटा *pakhauṭā* [**pakṣapaṭṭa-*], m. reg. **1.** bird's wing; root of a bird's wing. **2.** fin. 3. = पक्ष, 1.

पखौड़ा *pakhauṛā* [*pakṣapuṭa-*], m. the shoulder-blade.

पग *pag* [*padga-*], m. **1.** the foot. **2.** a step. — ~ उठाना, to stop running; to move off (in a given direction). ~ धरना, to step out, to proceed. ~ ~ पर, adv. at every step. ~ पट ताल बजाना, to beat time with the foot. ~ पर-, Av. to fall at the feet (of). ~ फूँककर धरना, to proceed cautiously (as if blowing away the dust, to avoid dirtying one's feet). ~ रखना, = ~ धरना. ~ से ~ मिलाकर, adv. in step. – पग-डंडी, f. straight line for the feet: path, track.

पगड़ी *pagṛī* [cf. **paggā-*], f. **1.** a turban. **2.** transf. head (in a count of persons). **3.** a mark of distinction; honour, dignity. **4.** key-money (paid over and above initial rent). — ~ **अटकना**, to be obstinate, to persist. ~ **उछालना (की)**, fig. to disgrace, to dishonour; to make fun (of). ~ **उतरना (की)**, to be disgraced, dishonoured; to be crestfallen. ~ **उतारना**, = **पगड़ी उछालना**, 1. ~ **ढीली होना**, the turban to loosen: to be or to become crestfallen. ~ **बँधना**, a turban to begin to be worn: honour, wealth or position to be achieved (by, **के सिर (पर)**). ~ **बदलना**, to exchange turbans: to be close friends (with, **के साथ**). ~ **बाँधना**, to put on a turban; to achieve honour, wealth or position.

पगना *pagnā*, v.i. **1.** to be dipped or soaked (in syrup, &c). **2.** to be infatuated (with, **के प्रेम में**).

पगला *paglā*, adj. = **पागल**.

पगहा *pag'hā*, m. see **पघा**.

[1]**पगार** *pagār* [**pragaḍḍa-* (? **pragāḍa-*), or *prakara-*, Pa. *pākāra-*], m. Brbh. enclosure (round a field, or a building); trench, mound, bank.

[2]**पगार** *pagār* [**pragāra-*], m. reg. (W.) **1.** wet earth or clay for plastering, or mortaring. **2.** [? = [1]*pagār*] a shallow piece of water (that can be crossed on foot).

[3]**पगार** *pagār*, m. f. wage, wages.

पगिया *pagiyā* [cf. **paggā-*], f. Brbh. = **पगरी**.

पगुराना *pagurānā*, v.i. to chew the cud (= **पागुराना**).

पघा *paghā* [*pragraha-*], m. **1.** tether. **2.** tail-rope (of bullock harness).

पघाल *paghāl*, m. *Pl. HŚS.* a kind of hard iron or steel; metal.

पघिलना *paghilnā* [**praghilati*], v.i. reg. = **पिघलना**.

पघैया *paghaiyā*, m. reg. a trader in cloth, iron, &c.

पच *pac*, m. *Pl.* support, prop.

पच- *pac-* [*pañca-*], adj. five: — **पचगुना**, adj. fivefold. **पचख़ाना**, adj. consisting of five parts (a house, &c). **पचगुटिया**, m. a game played by boys with five pebbles. **पचतोरिया** [? cf. H. *tolā*], m. Brbh. a kind of (? light) cloth. **पचधातु**, or **पचरस**, m. bell-metal (a kind of bronze). **पचपकवानी**, f. reg. five types of sweets (as served at a feast). **पचपहलू**, adj. pentagonal. **पचमहला**, adj. consisting of five storeys, rooms or apartments (a house). **पचमेल**, adj. & m. of five components: assorted; confused; a mixture, mess. **पचरंग**, adj. of five different colours; variegated. °**आ**, °**ई**, adj. id. **पचलड़ा**, adj. & m. of five rows or strings; a necklace of five strings. °**ई**, f. id. **पचलोना**, m. a digestive containing five kinds of salt. **पचहरा**, adj. of five folds, or layers; fivefold. **पचोतरा** [ad. *pañcottara-*], m. reg. duty or commission of five per cent.

पचड़ा *pacṛā* [cf. H. *pāc-*, ← *pacyate*], m. trouble, bother.

पचतोरिया *pactoriyā*, m. Brbh. see s.v. **पच-**.

पचन *pacan* [S.], m. **1.** digesting. **2.** cooking.

पचना *pacnā* [cf. H. *pāc-*, ← *pacyate*], v.i. **1.** to be digested. **2.** to be consumed. **3.** to be soaked up, absorbed. **4.** fig. to be assimilated. **5.** to be enjoyed or made use of improperly (goods or funds: by **को**). **6.** to be concealed (a matter). **7.** to toil vainly; to exhaust oneself. — **मर** ~, to give up (one's) life. – **पच मरना**, to be worked, to work oneself, to death. **पच हारना**, to toil in vain.

पचनीय *pacanīya* [S.], adj. digestible.

पच-पच *pac-pac*, f. a splashing or squelching sound.

पचपचा *pacpacā*, adj. **1.** soft, flabby. **2.** moist, clammy. **3.** watery, squelchy (soil).

पचपचाना *pacpacānā* [cf. H. *pacpacā*], v.i. **1.** to be damp, or wet. **2.** to sweat.

पचपन *pacpan* [*pañcapañcāśat-*], adj. fifty-five.

पचवाई *pacvāī*, f. *Pl. HŚS.* an intoxicating drink made from fermented rice or other grain.

पचहत्तर *pac'hattar* [*pañcasaptati-*], adj. seventy-five.

पचानवे *pacānve* [*pañcanavati-*], adj. ninety-five.

पचाना *pacānā* [cf. H. *pacnā*], v.t. **1.** to digest. **2.** to cause to rot, to ferment. **3.** to get rid of (unwanted weight, fat). **4.** to tax, to burden (body or mind). **5.** fig. to assimilate (knowledge, experience). **6.** to enjoy improperly the use of funds or goods; to embezzle. **7.** to soak up (liquid); to require (as rice does *ghī*).

पचाव *pacāv* [cf. H. *pacānā*], m. digestion, assimilation, &c.

पचावा *pacāvā* [cf. H. *pacānā*], m. reg. = **पचाव**.

पचास *pacās* [*pañcāśat-*], adj. fifty.

पचासा *pacāsā* [cf. H. *pacās*], m. **1.** a quantity or total of fifty (verses, rupees, &c). **2.** a weight of fifty *tolās* (*c.*50g).

पचासी *pacāsī* [*pañcāśīti-*], adj. eighty-five.

पचीस *pacīs*, adj. pronun. var. = पच्चीस.

पचूका *pacūkā*, m. reg. = पिचकारी.

पचौनी *pacaunī* [cf. H. *pacānā*], f. reg. **1.** the stomach; entrails. **2.** a digestive medicine.

पच्चर *paccar* [cf. H. *pac*], m. **1.** a wedge. **2.** fig. an obstacle. — ~ अड़ाना, to put in or to drive in a wedge; to obstruct (a matter); to thwart (a design). ~ ठोंकना, = prec. ~ मारना, or डालना, = ~ अड़ाना. ~ लगाना, = ~ अड़ाना, 1.

पच्ची *paccī* [? cf. H. *pāc-*, ← *pacyate*], adj. & f. **1.** adj. joined, sticking; flush (with sthg). **2.** fixed, firm. **3.** f. (-पच्ची.) troubling, tormenting (as in माथा-°). — ~ होना, to be joined; to be stuck together (as two surfaces); to be jammed, or wedged; to be intimate (with); to be hand in glove (with); to be lost in, invisible against (a background). पच्चीकारी, [P. *-kārī*], f. inlay work, mosaic; patching, darning.

पच्चीस *paccīs* [*pañcaviṁśati-*], adj. twenty-five.

पच्चीसी *paccīsī* [cf. H. *paccīs*], f. **1.** a group or collection of twenty-five units (e.g. short stories). **2.** the first twenty-five years of life (as preceding full maturity). **3.** pachisi (a board game somewhat like backgammon, but played on a different board, or cloth, in which the highest throw is twenty-five). **4.** a pachisi board.

पच्छम *paccham*, adj. & m. reg. = पच्छिम.

पच्छमी *pacchāmī* [cf. H. *pacchim*], adj. & m. **1.** adj. western. **2.** m. a westerner.

पच्छिम *pacchim* [ad. *paścima-*], adj. & m. **1.** adj. western. **2.** m. the west.

पछ *pach*, m. Brbh. Av. = पक्ष.

पछड़ना *pacharṇā* [cf. H. *pachāṛnā*], v.i. **1.** to fall; to be knocked down. **2.** fig. to suffer a defeat, or reverse.

पछताना *pachtānā* [**paścottāpa-*: Pk. *pacchuttāvia-*], v.t. to repent; to regret.

पछताव *pachtāv*, m. = पछतावा.

पछतावा *pachtāvā* [**paścottāpa-*: Pk. *pacchuttāvia-*], m. repentance; regret.

पछना *pachnā*, m. **1.** making incisions with a lancet, or knife; tattooing; blood-letting; lancing. **2.** a lancet, &c.

पछवाँ *pachvāṁ* [*paścima-*], adj. & f. reg. **1.** adj. westerly. **2.** the west wind.

पछाँह *pachāṁh* [*paścārdha-*], m. western region, the west.

पछाड़ *pachāṛ* [cf. H. *pachāṛnā*], f. falling on the back: **1.** a fainting fit. **2.** a fall, throw (in wrestling). — ~, or पछाड़ें, खाना, to fall on the back; to faint; to be beside oneself with grief, or agony; to be thrown on the back.

पछाड़ना *pachāṛnā* [**pracchaṭ-*: Pk. *pacchāḍida-*], v.t. **1.** to throw flat on the back. **2.** to dash down; to beat (clothes on a stone). **3.** fig. to overpower; to overcome.

पछाड़ी *pachāṛī*, f. *Pl. HŚS.* = पिछाड़ी.

पछिया *pachiyā*, f. = पछियाव.

पछियाना *pachiyānā*, v.t. reg. = पीछा करना, see s.v. पीछा.

पछियाव *pachiyāv* [**paścimavāta-*], m. a west wind.

पछीत *pachīt*, m. reg. rear part of a house.

पछुआ *pachuā*, f. = पछिया.

पछेरू *pacherū* [H. *pakherū*; ad. *pakṣa-*], adj. & m. reg. **1.** adj. winged. **2.** m. a bird.

पछेली *pachelī* [cf. *paśca-*], f. a bracelet (worn uppermost on the arm with bangles).

पछोड़न *pachoṛan* [cf. H. *pachoṛnā*], f. the chaff winnowed from grain.

पछोड़ना *pachoṛnā* [**prakṣoṭayati*: Pk. *pakkhoḍaï*], v.t. **1.** to winnow (with a basket). **2.** fig. to examine, to scrutinise.

पजर- *pajar-* [*prajvalati*], v.i. Brbh. **1.** to catch fire. **2.** to burn; to be burnt up.

पजौड़ा *pajauṛā* [cf. *padya-*], adj. *Pl. HŚS.* base, vile.

पजौड़ापन *pajauṛāpan*, m. baseness, vileness (= पाजीपन).

पटंतर *paṭantar* [? cf. H. [1]*paṭṭā*], m. E.H. equivalent, exchange.

[1]**पट** *paṭ* [? conn. H. [4]*paṭ*, m.], adj. **1.** lying flat, lying on the face, or prone; overturned. **2.** falling flat, ineffective (as the blow of a sword). **3.** flat; bare (terrain); uncultivated (land); deserted (a village). **4.** slack, inactive (as trade). **5.** ruined. — ~ पड़ना, to fall flat; to be flat, &c.; to be slack; to be desolate. ~ हो जाना, to be closed. पटपर, adj. reg. = ~, 3. पटपड़ा, m. reg. a flat surface; bare plain; flatness.

[2]**पट** *paṭ* [*paṭ-*[2]], m. & adv. **1.** m. = ~ ~. **2.** adv. at once. — ~ ~, m. & adv. sound of falling (as of rain), or of beating; a beating; continuously. — पटापट, f. & adv. = ~.

[3]**पट** *paṭ* [*paṭṭa-*[2]], m. **1.** cloth; garment; piece or fold of cloth; coarse cloth or canvas. **2.** covering, screen; veil. **3.** roof or canopy (as on boat, cart). **4.** chequered cloth (on which

chess, &c. is played). **5.** turban. — ~ खोलना (का), to open, or to remove (a screen, veil, &c). – पटच्चर, m. poet. old or ragged clothes. पटापटी, f. bright or variegated colours; a brightly coloured object. पटापटी का, adj. brightly coloured.

⁴पट *paṭ* [*paṭṭa-*¹], m. **1.** flat surface; board. **2.** slab; plate (for inscriptions, &c.); document. **3.** sheet of paper; a notice. **4.** chequered board (cf. ³पट, 4). **5.** chair, throne. **6.** leaf of a door. **7.** shutter. — ~ खोलना, to open a door. ~ उड़कना, or भिड़ाना, or भेड़ना, or लगाना, or मारना, to close a door. – पट-देवी, or पट-रानी [? × H. ¹*pāṭ*], f. the principal wife of a king. पट-बंधक, m. a mortgage.

पटक *paṭak* [S.], m. *Pl. HŚS.* **1.** cotton cloth. **2.** camp, encampment.

पटकन *paṭkan* [cf. H. *paṭaknā*], f. **1.** knocking-down, a fall. **2.** a sharp blow; stamping, dashing down. **3.** transf. weakness, after-effects (of a disease, &c). — ~ खाना, to be knocked down; to be thrown (as in wrestling).

पटकना *paṭaknā* [cf. *paṭ-*²], v.t. & v.i. **1.** v.t. to dash down (on, पर); to knock down, or over. **2.** to flail (the limbs). **3.** v.i. to subside (a swelling); to dry out (moist grain). **4.** [cf. *paṭ-*¹] to crack (an earthen vessel). — सिर ~, to load or to palm off (upon, के: as unwanted work).

पटकना *paṭkanā*, f. = पटकनी.

पटकनी *paṭkanī* [cf. H. *paṭaknā*], m. a knock-down; throw, fall (in wrestling). — ~ खाना, to be knocked down violently; to be thrown. ~ देना (को), to knock down, to dash down.

पटका *paṭkā* [cf. *paṭṭa-*²], m. **1.** sash, belt. **2.** decorative moulding; cornice. — ~ पकड़ना, to hinder, to restrain (one, का). ~ बाँधना, to prepare (for, पर or के लिए), to determine (to do sthg).

पटकाना *paṭkānā*, v.t. = पटकना.

पटकारना *paṭkārnā*, v.i. reg. = पटकना.

पटकी *paṭkī*, f. = पटकनी.

पटड़ा *paṭṛā*, m. = पटरा.

¹पटन *paṭan*, m. roofing, &c. (= ¹पाटन).

²पटन *paṭan*, m. Av. city, town (= पट्टन).

पटना *paṭnā* [**paṭyati*, and cf. *paṭṭa-*¹; or cf. H. *pāṭnā*], v.i. **1.** to be filled in, to be made level. **2.** to be boarded over (a floor, roof); to be thatched. **3.** to be irrigated (a field). **4.** to be glutted (a market). **5.** to be paid, or repaid (an account, a sum). **6.** to be settled (an arrangement, a bargain). **7.** to go well (affairs, a relationship). हमारी उनकी, or हम में, ख़ूब पटती है, we get on very well together.

पटनी *paṭnī* [cf. *paṭṭana-*], m. *Pl.* a boatman, ferryman.

पटपटाना *paṭpaṭānā*, v.i. to crackle; to beat (as rain).

पटबंधक *paṭbandhak* [cf. H. ¹*paṭṭā*, ⁴*paṭ*], m. see s.v. ⁴*paṭ*.

पटबीजना *paṭbījnā* [cf. H. *bījnā*], m. a firefly.

पटम *paṭam*, adj. reg. closed, shut (the eyes). — ~ होना, to be blind.

¹पटरा *paṭrā* [cf. *paṭṭa-*¹], m. **1.** a plank, board; washing-board; board for kneading flour, &c. **2.** bench. **3.** plank used as a harrow. — ~ कर देना, to level, to raze; to clear (ground); to lay low; to leave (one, को) without an answer (in argument). ~ फेरना (पर), to level, to raze; to harrow. ~ होना, to be laid low.

²पटरा *paṭrā*, m. reg. unripe grain.

पटरी *paṭrī* [cf. H. ¹*paṭrā*], f. **1.** strip of wood or metal. **2.** writing-board or slate. **3.** pavement, paved or flat surface; path. **4.** bank of a canal (with path or road). **5.** railway track(s). **6.** edge, border (of sari, &c). **7.** *Pl. HŚS.* a broad metal armlet or bracelet. — ~ जमना, to have a firm (even) seat (on a horse); to be firmly in the saddle. ~ न खाना, = next. ~ न बैठना, fig. not to get on well or easily (with, की: a person, की).

पटल *paṭal* [S.], m. **1.** roof, thatch. **2.** covering, screen; veil. **3.** a cataract (of the eye). **4.** *Pl. HŚS.* basket. **5.** *Pl. HŚS.* heap, mass, amount; (Bihar) gleanings. **6.** a sandalwood mark on the forehead.

¹पटवा *paṭvā* [*paṭṭa-*²], m. **1.** a shrub of the genus *Hibiscus*, red sorrel (a substitute for hemp and jute). **2.** jute. — ~ सन, m. jute substitute made from sorrel.

²पटवा *paṭvā* [**paṭṭavaya-*], m. a stringer of beads, pearls, &c.; a maker of braid, fringe, &c.

पटवाना *paṭvānā* [cf. H. *paṭānā*], v.t. **1.** to cause to be filled in, or levelled, &c. (see पटाना: by, से). **2.** to cause to be settled; to settle (an outstanding account, or transaction).

पटवार *paṭvār* [**paṭṭapāla-*], m. = पटवारी: — पटवारगिरी [P. *-garī*], f. the office or duties of a *paṭvārī*.

पटवारी *paṭvārī* [**paṭṭapālin-*], m. registrar of a village's land accounts.

पटसन *paṭsan* [*paṭṭa-*² + *śaṇa-*], m. jute (the plant, and its fibre).

पटहा *paṭăhā* [ad. *paṭaha-*], m. reg. drum, kettledrum.

पटा *paṭā*, m. **1.** (= [1]पट्टा, 1.) a board on which to sit to eat, or while taking part in religious ceremonies. **2.** a wooden sword; a cudgel. ~ बँधा-, Brbh. to take as queen (a king: see पट-रानी s.v. [4]पट).

पटाक *paṭāk* [? cf. *paṭ*[2]], m. a loud sound, crash, crack. — ~ से, adv. with a crash, loudly.

पटाका *paṭākā* [? cf. *paṭ-*[2]], m. 1. = पटाक. **2.** a cracker. **3.** colloq. a resounding slap.

पटाख *paṭākh*, m. = पटाका. — ~ से, adv. loudly, resoundingly.

पटाखा *paṭākhā*, m. = पटाका.

पटाना *paṭānā* [cf. H. *pă̄ṭnā*], v.t. **1.** to fill up, to make level (a ditch, &c.); to plaster flat (a cooking area). **2.** to cause to be boarded, roofed, or covered. **3.** to irrigate (a field). **4.** transf. to settle (an account, an arrangement, a deal); to obtain the agreement (of, को). **5.** to realise (a sum).

पटाव *paṭāv* [cf. H. *paṭānā*], m. **1.** filling in, levelling. **2.** boarding over; a roofing of beams and pressed mud. **3.** *Pl.* flooding (a field); watering (a crop); irrigation.

पटावन *paṭāvan* [cf. H. *paṭānā*], m. reg. irrigating (a field or crop).

पटिया *paṭiyā* [cf. H. [1] [3] [4]*paṭ*], f. **1.** writing-board, slate. **2.** stone slab. **3.** paved surface; footpath. 4. = [1]पट्टी, 1. 5. = [2]पट्टी, 3.

पटियाना *paṭiyānā* [cf. H. *paṭiyā*, 5.], v.t. to smoothe; to slick down (hair).

पटियाला *paṭiyālā* [cf. H. [1]*paṭṭī*], f. *Pl.* (in schools) the punishment of piling several writing-boards on a boy's back.

पटी *paṭī* [S.], f. **1.** curtain of a stage. **2.** [= *paṭṭa-*[2]] strip: ribbon; belt; turban.

पटीमा *paṭīmā* [cf. *paṭṭa-*[1]], m. *Pl. HŚS.* plank on which cloth is spread for printing.

पटीलना *paṭīlnā* [cf. H. *paṭel*], m. colloq. **1.** to win, to gain (agreement); to capture (a prize). **2.** to cheat. **3.** to cudgel, to beat.

पटु *paṭu* [S.], adj. **1.** clever; deft; expert. **2.** cunning. **3.** sharp-witted. **4.** diligent.

पटुता *paṭutā* [S.], f. cleverness; deftness; skill.

पटुवा *paṭuvā*, m. Av. = [2]पटवा.

पटेर *paṭer* [conn. *paṭṭeraka-*], f. Brbh. **1.** a sedge, reed (the leaves of which are used to make mats, &c).

[1]**पटेल** *paṭel* [*paṭṭakila-*], m. **1.** headman of a village; village elder. **2.** name of a Gujarati trading community.

[2]**पटेल** *paṭel*, m. reg. fencing with the *paṭā*; cudgelling. — ~ डालना, to put daunting obstacles (in the way of); to beat, to cudgel.

पटेला *paṭelā* [cf. *paṭṭa-*[1]], m. reg. a large flat-bottomed sailing boat of clinker construction.

पटैत *paṭait* [cf. H. [1]*paṭṭā*], m. lease-holder; village priest.

[1]**पटैला** *paṭailā*, m. reg. (Bihar) = पटेला.

[2]**पटैला** *paṭailā* [cf. *paṭṭa-*[1]], m. door-stop, or bar.

पटैली *paṭailī*, f. reg. = पटेला.

पटोतन *paṭotan*, m. reg. **1.** *Pl.* roofing with planks or boards. **2.** (Bihar) layer of loose grass spread beneath the tiles of a roof.

पटोना *paṭonā* [cf. *paṭṭa-*[1]], m. Brbh. a flat surface.

पटोरी *paṭorī*, f. Brbh. = पटोली.

पटोल *paṭol* [S.], m. a kind of cucumber eaten as a vegetable (= परवल).

पटोलिका *paṭolikā* [S.], f. *HŚS.* a small striped cucumber (= तरोई).

पटोली *paṭolī* [**paṭṭadukūla-*], f. E.H. a kind of cloth (? silken); a silk-embroidered sari or *dhotī*.

पटोहिया *paṭohiyā*, m. *Pl.* an owl.

पटौनी *paṭaunī* [cf. *paṭṭana-*], m. *Pl. HŚS.* a boatman (= पाटौनी, पटनी).

[1]**पट्ट** *paṭṭ* [ad. *paṭṭa-*[1]], m. = [4]पट, 1., 2., 4., 5.

[2]**पट्ट** *paṭṭ* [ad. *paṭṭa-*[2]], m. 1. = [3]पट. **2.** woven silk. **3.** bandage.

[3]**पट्ट** *paṭṭ* [conn. *paṭṭana-*], m. a town, or village.

पट्टक *paṭṭak* [S.], m. **1.** document. **2.** slate or board; metal plate. **3.** strip or ornamental band of cloth; bandage.

पट्टन *paṭṭan*, m. = पत्तन.

[1]**पट्टा** *paṭṭā* [*paṭṭa-*[1]], m. **1.** a board on which to sit (while eating, or participating in religious ceremonies). **2.** a deed; lease; contract. **3.** share; assessment (of dues). — ~ देनेवाला, m. lessor. – पट्टा-दाता, m. inv. lessor. पट्टा-धारी, m. lessee. पट्टा-फेर, m. exchange of seats by bride and groom at conclusion of marriage ceremony. पट्टेदार [P. *-dār*], m. lessee. पट्टेवार, adj. & adv. according to shares or assessments.

[2]**पट्टा** *paṭṭā* [cf. *paṭṭa-*[2]], m. **1.** strap; belt; girth (of harness). **2.** collar (of an animal). **3.** shoulder-strap and badge (of a servant, waiter, &c). **4.** strip; blaze (on a horse's forehead). **5.** a lock of hair. **6.** reg. pendant to an ear-ring. — ~ उतारना, to deprive of insignia of office, to dismiss from service. ~ तुड़ाना, or तोड़ना, to get loose, to run away (an animal).

पट्टिका *paṭṭikā* [S.], f. **1.** a strip of wood or metal. **2.** strip of cloth. **3.** ribbon.

[1]**पट्टी** *paṭṭī* [*paṭṭa-*[1]], f. **1.** a board, strip of board; side-piece of a frame; frame; lath; beam, rafter. **2.** writing-board; slate; transf. lesson, instruction. **3.** reg. a wooden sword (= पटा). **4.** blade (of a saw); working surface. **5.** document; specif. tax assessment. **6.** metal plate (worn on turban as a sign of authorised status or function). — ~ पढ़ाना (को), to teach (letters, &c., to a child) from a board; to explain sthg., to give a lesson (to); to put one up to (trickery, &c). ~ पूजना, to worship the slate: to initiate (a child) ceremonially into his school-days; to give a gift symbolising hopes for an infant's progress.

[2]**पट्टी** *paṭṭī* [*paṭṭa-*[2]], f. **1.** piece or strip of cloth; ribbon; bandage; puttee. **2.** headband. **3.** the hair brushed sideways from the parting; locks of hair at the temple or over the ear. **4.** a piece, portion; a division of a village; division of cultivable land of a village into strips; a major share in village land. **5.** strip of land (other than as under 4.); airstrip; cricket wicket; path, strip of grass. **6.** a kind of sweet. — ~, or पट्टियाँ, जमाना (पर), to paste or to comb the hair down (on the temples). ~ बाँधना, to apply a bandage (to, पर); to blindfold (the eyes). पट्टियाँ पाड़ना, id. – पट्टीदार [P. *-dār*], m. holder or proprietor of a share in a coparcenary tenure of land. °ई, f. coparcenary tenure, partnership; land cultivated by coparcenary tenants, or owned jointly.

पट्टू *paṭṭū* [*paṭṭa-*[2]], m. a kind of coarse woollen cloth.

[1]**पट्ठा** *paṭṭhā* [**pasṭha-*], m. **1.** a young, but full-grown animal. **2.** a vigorous young man.

[2]**पट्ठा** *paṭṭhā*, m. a sinew, tendon, ligament. — ~ चढ़ना, a ligament to be torn.

[3]**पट्ठा** *paṭṭhā*, m. a long pointed leaf (as of tobacco).

पठ *paṭh* [**pasṭha-*], m. reg. = [1]पट्ठा.

पठक *paṭhak* [S.], m. reader, reciter.

पठन *paṭhan* [S.], m. reading, reciting. — पठन-पाठन, m. reading and teaching.

पठनीय *paṭhănīyă* [S.], adj. requiring or deserving to be read.

पठवा- *paṭhvā-* [cf. H. *paṭhā-*], v.t. to cause to be sent (by, से); to send.

पठान *paṭhān* [**pasṭāna-*: ← Ir.], m. a Pathan.

[1]**पठानी** *paṭhānī* [cf. H. *paṭhān*], f. a Pathan woman.

[2]**पठानी** *paṭhānī* [cf. H. *paṭhān*], adj. & f. **1.** adj. Pathan. **2.** f. transf. bravery.

पठार *paṭhār* [**pr̥ṣṭhadhāra-*], m. a plateau.

पठा(व)- *paṭhā(v)-* [*prasthāpayati*], v.t. Brbh. Av. to send.

पठित *paṭhit* [S.], adj. **1.** read, recited. **2.** literate (cf. H. पढ़ा हुआ).

पठिया *paṭhiyā* [cf. H. [1]*paṭṭhā*], f. **1.** a young, full-grown female animal. **2.** a young, full-grown woman.

पठ्य *paṭhyă* [S.], adj. to be read.

पड़त *paṛat*, f. reg. = पड़ता.

पड़ता *paṛtā* [H. *paṛnā*], m. what falls to one: **1.** cost price (of sthg). **2.** rate (of charge, of wage); average rate; share, due quota (of an amount). — ~ फैलाना, to distribute an aggregate charge among those who must pay it; to calculate.

पड़ताल *paṛtāl*, f. **1.** testing, examining. **2.** review, check (of date); remeasuring (a field, &c.); reweighing; recounting. **3.** audit. **4.** colloq. correcting, punishment. — ~ करना (की), to test; to review, to check, &c.

पड़तालना *paṛtālnā*, v.t. = पड़ताल करना.

पड़ती *paṛtī* [cf. H. *paṛnā*], f. uncultivated or fallow land. — ~ उठाना, to work previously uncultivated or fallow land. ~ छोड़ना, to leave fallow (land).

पड़ना *paṛnā* [*patati*; Pk. *paḍaï*], v.i. **1.** to fall. **2.** lie; to lie idle or useless. पड़ा पाना, to find lying; to get easily, or for nothing. **3.** esp. w. जाना. to be laid, spread. **4.** to fall to the lot (of, को). **5.** w. infinitives. to have to. मुझे जाना पड़ेगा, I must go. **6.** to be met with, to be found. आपको स्टेशन बाएँ पड़ेगा, you'll find the station on the left. **7.** to have an abode (in, में); to stay (in a place). **8.** to halt, to camp. **9.** pej. to be dependent (on, पर); to sponge (on). **10.** to be, to become (by unassisted process); to prove to be. हवा धीमी पड़ गई, the wind dropped. मालूम पड़ना (को), to be borne in (on one), to seem. **11.** to occur; to take place; to come round (an event); to arise (a matter, an opportunity). ज़रूरत ~ (को), need to arise (of, की). **12.** to fall (on, पर), to befall (a calamity, a punishment);

to be struck (a blow). **13.** to affect (one: as a longing, a wish, a habit). **मुझे सिगरेट पीने का चस्का पड़ा**, I acquired the habit of smoking. **14.** to intervene, to interfere (in, **में**). **15.** to concern (one). **उसे अपनी पड़ी है**, he is concerned (only) about his own affairs. **16.** to amount to (a sum); to stand credited or debited (to, **को** or **पर**: an amount). **पचास रुपए फ़ीस पड़ेगी**, there will be fifty rupees fees. **17.** to suit, to agree (with, **को**). **18.** to resemble; to be the image (of, **पर**). **19.** to be digested. **20.** to follow intently (after, **के पीछे**): to plague (one). **21.** to copulate (a male animal: with, **पर**). — **पड़ रहना**, to remain lying; to be idle; to be prostrate; to be helpless, destitute. – **पड़ता**, m. an amount due, total sum or expense. **पड़ा**, adj. horizontal (plane, surface, line). **पड़ा चक्कर**, m. parallel of latitude.

पड़पड़ाना *parparānā* [cf. *paṭ-*²], v.i. **1.** to chatter. **2.** to sound noisy, to beat (as rain on a roof).

पड़यल *paryal* [cf. H. *parnā*], f. reg. rubbish, sweepings.

¹**पड़वा** *parvā*, m. = **परिवा**.

²**पड़वा** *parvā*, m. = ²**पाड़ा**.

पड़वाया *parvāyā* [**pratipādaka-*: Pa. *paṭipādaka-*], m. reg. wooden saucers placed under the feet of a bed.

पड़वी *parvī*, f. reg. a kind of sugar-cane (sown in autumn).

पडा *paḍā*, m. reg. boundary of a field.

पड़ाना *parānā* [cf. H. *parnā*], v.t. **1.** to lay down; to put to sleep. **2.** to knock down.

पड़ापड़ *parāpar*, adv. = **पटापट** (s.v. ²**पट**).

पड़ाव *parāv* [cf. H. *parnā*], m. **1.** halting-place; camping-ground. **2.** camp; asemblage; army. **3.** stage (as of a march). **4.** stopping-place (of a transport service). — **~ डालना**, to halt, to encamp.

पड़िया *pariyā* [cf. H. ²*pārā*], f. a buffalo calf (female).

पड़ोस *paros* [*prativeśa-*], m. neighbourhood, vicinity. — **~ करना**, to settle in the neighbourhood (of).

पड़ोसिन *parosin* [cf. H. *parosī*], f. female neighbour.

पड़ोसी *parosī* [**prativeśiya-*: Pk. *paḍivesia-*], m. neighbour.

पढ़ंत *parhant*, f. **1.** reading. **2.** a saying, maxim. **3.** a spell.

पढ़त *parhat*, f. reading, reading through (of a parliamentary bill).

पढ़न *parhan* [cf. H. *parhnā*], f. the act of reading.

पढ़ना *parhnā* [*paṭhati*: Pk. *paḍhaï*], v.t. **1.** to read; to read out (an announcement, a poem). **2.** to repeat aloud (as a text being learnt); to speak, to say (a talking bird). **3.** to study. **4.** to utter (a prayer); to cast a spell (on, **पर**). — **पढ़ना-लिखना**, m. to be literate; to study. – **पढ़ा**, adj. read; well-read. **पढ़ा-गुना**, adj. educated, experienced. **पढ़ा-लिखा**, adj. literate; educated.

पढ़वाना *parhvānā* [cf. H. *parhnā*], v.t. **1.** to cause (one) to read (sthg). **2.** to cause (one) to be taught (by, **से**). — **दो बोल ~**, to obtain verbal agreement (to a proposal).

पढ़ाई *parhāī* [cf. H. *parhnā*, *parhānā*], f. **1.** study. **2.** teaching. **3.** tuition fee. — **पढ़ाई-लिखाई**, f. schooling; teaching.

पढ़ाकू *parhākū* [cf. H. *parhnā*], adj. colloq. able, or keen, to read. — **~ तबक़ा**, m. those who read.

पढ़ाना *parhānā* [cf. H. *parhnā*], v.t. **1.** to cause to read. **2.** to teach. **3.** to teach (a bird) to talk. **4.** transf. to cause (one) to utter (a spell): to induce, to put one up (to doing sthg).

पण *paṇ* [S.], m. **1.** gambling; a throw (of dice). **2.** a bet; stake. **3.** an agreement, compact; wage, hire; reward; price; fee. **4.** promise, vow. — **~ लगाना (का)**, to wager; to risk (one's life, &c).

पणव *paṇav* [S.], m. a small drum.

पण्य *paṇyă* [S.], adj. & m. *Pl. HŚS.* **1.** adj. saleable. **2.** m. goods for sale; a commodity. **3.** trade. **4.** trading place; shop; bazaar. — **पण्य-वस्तु**, f. goods, merchandise; a commodity.

पतंग *pataṅg* [S.], m. sthg. that flies: **1.** a moth. **2.** a grasshopper. **3.** a paper kite. **4.** Av. a ball. **5.** *Pl. HŚS.* the sappan-wood tree (source of a red dye). — **~ उड़ाना**, to fly a kite. **~ काटना**, to cut the string of (another's) kite with that of one's own; to cut loose. – **पतंगबाज़** [P. *-bāz*], m. kite-flyer. **°ई**, f. kite-flying.

पतंगा *pataṅgā* [**pattaṅga-*], m. 1. = **पतंग**, 1., 2. **2.** a spark. **3.** a live coal. — **~ होना**, colloq. to go briskly about one's work. **जलकर ~ हो जाना**, to flare up (in anger) and then subside.

पतंगी *pataṅgī* [cf. H. *pataṅg(ā)*], adj. multicoloured; attractively coloured.

पत *pat*, f. good name, reputation; honour. — **~ उतारना**, or **लेना**, to destroy the reputation (of, **की**); to disgrace. **~ जाना**, one's reputation, &c. to be lost; to be disgraced. **~ रखना (अपनी)**, to preserve (one's) good name, &c.

पतई *pataī*, f. reg. straw or grass spread over a field to protect a freshly planted crop from the sun.

पतझड़ *patjhaṛ* [H. *pattā*+H. *jharnā*], m. & adj. **1.** m. fall of leaves, autumn. **2.** time of decline or decay. **3.** adj. leafless.

पतत्री *patătrī* [S.], f. Brbh. winged: **1.** a bird. **2.** an arrow.

पतन *patan* [S.], m. **1.** falling. **2.** settling, subsiding. **3.** decline. **4.** falling (in battle). — **पतनशील**, adj. tending to fall: in decline. **पतनोन्मुख** [°*na*+*u*°], adj. facing, or in, decline, &c.

पतना *patnā*, m. vulva.

पतपिती *patpitī*, f. *Pl.* a kind of small bird, the grass-warbler.

पतरिंगा *patriṅgā*, m. name of several birds: **1.** the green bee-eater, *Merops orientalis*. **2.** the drongo or king crow. **3.** the fork-tailed shrike. — **बड़ा** ~, m. the blue tailed bee-eater. **लालसिर** ~, m. the chestnut-headed bee-eater.

पतला *patlā* [*pattrala-*, Pk. *pattala-*], adj. **1.** thin; lean. **2.** weak, frail; delicate. **3.** fine, drawn out; slender; sharp, tapering. **4.** narrow, small (a river). **5.** reduced (circumstances). **6.** thin, watery (of consistency). **7.** subtle. — ~ **करना**, to make thin, &c.; to sharpen (as a pencil); to thin (liquid). ~ **हाल**, m. straitened circumstances. **पतले कान**, m. pl. credulous ears. – **पतला-दुबला**, adj. weak, frail.

पतलाई *patlāī* [cf. H. *patlā*], f. = **पतलापन**.

पतलापन *patlāpan* [cf. H. *patlā*], m. **1.** thinness. **2.** weakness. **3.** fineness (shape, texture), &c. **4.** narrowness. **5.** wateriness. **6.** subtlety.

पतलून *patlūn* [Engl. *pantaloon(s)*], m. trousers.

पतलो *patlo* [**pattralava-*], m. **1.** reeds, or leaves cut from reeds, used for thatching. **2.** *Pl.* dead leaves fallen from a tree.

पतवार *patvār*, f. a rudder; an oar used as a rudder. — ~ **चलाना**, to steer, to pilot (a boat, &c). ~ **सँभालना**, to take over the helm.

पतसर *patsar*, m. = **सरपत**.

पता *patā* [P. *pata*], m. **1.** trace, track, clue. **2.** information; particular mention. **3.** address; whereabouts. — ~ **चलना**, to become known (to, **को**: a matter, &c). ~ **देना** (**का**), to give the clue, or information (to sthg.); to give the address or whereabouts (of). ~ **पाना**, to obtain a clue (to, **का**), to trace; to learn sthg. secret, or confidential. ~ **लगना**, = ~ **चलना**. ~ **लगाना** (**का**), to trace, to discover (facts, information); to follow up a clue. **पते की**, or **पते की बात**, **कहना**, to disclose sthg. secret or confidential. – **पता-ठिकाना**, m. = ~, 3. **पता-निशान**, m. = ~, 1.

पताई *patāī* [cf. H. *pattā*], f. collection or bunch of fallen leaves. — ~ **झोंकना**, or **लगाना**, to kindle a fire with leaves.

पताक *patāk* [S.], m. Brbh. = **पताका**.

पताका *patākā* [S.], f. **1.** flag, banner. **2.** flagstaff or pole. **3.** emblem. **4.** *Pl. HŚS.* an episode in a drama.

पताकी *patākī* [S.], m. standard-bearer.

पतिंगा *patiṅgā*, m. = **पतंगा**.

[1]**पति** *pati* [S.], m. **1.** master, lord. **2.** husband. **3.** finally in comp. leader, chief; one who controls, of disposes (of). — **पति-भक्ति**, f. = next. **पति-व्रत**, m. loyalty or fidelity to a husband. °**आ**, f. a faithful and devoted wife. **पति-सेवा**, f. devotion of a wife to her husband. **लखपति**, m. a millionaire.

[2]**पति** *pati*, f. reg. honour (= **पत**): — **पति-पानी**, m. honour.

पतित *patit* [S.], adj. & m. **1.** adj. fallen. **2.** fig. degraded; abject. **3.** lapsed (from religion); sinful. **4.** outcast. **5.** m. a fallen person, &c. — **पतित-पावन**, adj. purifying the sinful: a title of the supreme being.

पतित्व *patitvă* [S.], m. marital state (of husband); matrimony.

पतिया- *patiyā-* [*pratyāyayati*], v.t. Brbh. Av. to believe, to have trust.

पतियार- *patiyār-* [cf. *pratyāyayati*], m. Brbh. belief, trust.

पतीरी *patīrī*, *Pl. HŚS.* a kind of mat.

[1]**पतील** *patīl* [A. *fatīl*: P. *patīl*], m. *Pl.* wick; linstock (for gun).

[2]**पतील** *patīl*, m. *Pl.* fallow land.

पतीला *patīlā* [cf. *pātra-*], m. a wide-mouthed copper pot or pan.

पतीली *patīlī* [cf. H. *patīlā*], f. dimin. a small pot or pan.

पतुकी *patukī*, f. Brbh. a small pot; earthen vessel.

पतुरिया *paturiyā* [cf. H. *pātur*], f. **1.** a prostitute. **2.** a dissolute woman.

पतूरिया *patūriyā*, f. reg. = **पातुरिया**.

पतोहू *patohū* [*putravadhū-*)], f. daughter-in-law.

पतौवा *patauvā*, m. Brbh. a leaf.

पत्तन *pattan* [S.], m. chiefly in comp. **1.** city, town; settlement. **2.** port.

पत्तनी *pattănī* [cf. H. *pattan*], adj. ordered, commissioned (sc. from a town).

पत्तर *pattar*, m. = पत्र.

पत्तल *pattal* [*pattrala-*; ? ← Panj.], f. m. **1.** a leaf-plate. **2.** a plateful of food. — ~ **खोलना,** colloq. to start a meal (after a delay). ~ **पड़ना,** leaf-plates to be set out (for a meal). ~ **बाँधना,** to delay a meal (until preliminaries are observed). **एक ~ में खानेवाले,** m. pl. fig. intimate friends. **जूठी पत्तल,** f. leavings of food.

पत्ता *pattā* [*pattraka-*], m. **1.** leaf. **2.** a leaf-shaped design. **3.** leaf-shaped ornament worn in the ear. **4.** a playing-card. **5.** a banknote. — ~ **खड़कना,** a leaf to crackle: trouble to be impending. ~ **तोड़कर भागना,** to run away with a leaf (as in a children's game): to take to one's heels. ~ **होना,** to run off, to flee.

पत्ती *pattī* [*pattrikā-*], f. **1.** leaf; leaves; hemp leaves (used to make *bhāṃg*). **2.** petal. **3.** a leaf or thin plate (of metal); blade (of knife, razor). **4.** share, portion; specif. share of land. — ~ **झड़ना,** leaves to be shed (from a tree). – **पत्तीदार** [P. *-dār*], m. = **पट्टीदार.**

पत्थर *patthar* [*prastara-*], m. **1.** stone. **2.** a precious stone. **3.** hailstone. **4.** fig. anything troublesome, trying, &c. **5.** sthg. useless, unserviceable. — ~ **का,** adj. of stone; hard, unfeeling; brave (the heart); lithographic (printing). ~ **की लकीर,** a line cut in stone: sthg. ineffaceable, unalterable. ~ **छाती पर रखना,** to suffer sthg. patiently. ~ **ढोना,** to carry stones: to toil. ~ **तले हाथ आना,** or **दबना,** (one's) hand to become caught under a stone: to have serious difficulties to deal with. ~ **निचोड़ना,** fig. to draw blood from a stone. ~ **पड़ना,** stones to fall (on, **पर**); to hail; to be overwhelmed with trouble; to be destroyed (as hopes). ~ **बरसना,** to hail. ~ **पसीजना,** or **पिघलना,** a stony heart to be melted; the improbable to occur. ~ **से सिर फोड़ना,** fig. to attempt sthg. which cannot succeed; to waste time teaching a fool. ~ **होना,** to petrify; to become hard, rigid; to be burdensome; to be unfeeling; to be or to become motionless; to freeze, to congeal; to be quite blind; to be useless. – **पत्थरकला** [H. *patthar*+H. [3]*kal*], m. a flint-lock gun. **पत्थर-कोयला,** m. coal. **पत्थर-चटा,** m. stone-licker: one who clings to and refuses to leave his house; a skinflint. **पत्थर-पानी,** m. rain and hail; destruction, chaos. **पत्थर-फूल,** m. moss. **पत्थर-फोड़,** m. stone-breaker. **पत्थरबाज़** [P. *-bāz*], m. thrower of stones; °**ई,** f. stone-throwing. **पत्थरवाह,** m. stoning (punishment). **पत्थर-सा खींच,** or **फेंक, मारना,** to answer abruptly, or bluntly, or without due thought.

पत्थरा *patthrā*, m. *Pl.* a kind of stone weight.

पत्नी *patnī* [S.], f. wife. — **पत्नीव्रत,** m. marital vow: fidelity to one's wife.

पत्र *patr* [ad. *pattra-*], m. **1.** wing, feather. **2.** leaf (of a tree, plant). **3.** sheet (of paper). ***4.** letter. **5.** document; diplomatic note. **6.** thin piece or plate of metal. **7.** page. **8.** journal, periodical. **9.** fledging (of an arrow). **10.** lines or designs painted on the face with musk, &c. — **पत्रकार,** m. journalist; correspondent. °**इता,** f. journalism. **पत्र-पाल,** m. postmaster. **पत्र-पुष्प,** m. red *tulsī* or basil, *Ocymum sanctum*; a gift of flowers, &c., bouquet. **पत्रवाह,** m. postman; courier. **पत्र-व्यवहार,** m. correspondence. **पत्रव्यवहार करना,** to correspond (with, **से**). **पत्रांक** [°*ra*+*a*°], m. page number; enfolding leaves (of foliage around a flower). **पत्रालय** [°*ra*+*ā*°], m. post office. **पत्रावलि** [°*ra*+*ā*°], f. Brbh. Av. leaf-platter; lines or designs painted on the face with musk, &c. by women on festive occasions.

पत्रक *patrak* [S.], m. **1.** a form; document. **2.** a note (brief letter). — **पत्रक-धन,** m. paper money.

पत्रा *patrā*, m. **1.** an almanac. **2.** a leaf; a page.

पत्रिका *patrikā* [S.], f. **1.** magazine, journal. **2.** letter. **3.** document.

[1]**पत्री** *patrī* [S.], f. **1.** letter; document; note. **2.** a leaf-bowl.

[2]**पत्री** *patrī* [S.], adj. **1.** winged, feathered (a bird, an arrow). **2.** Brbh. having leaves (a lotus).

[1]**पथ** *path* [S.], m. **1.** way, road; path. **2.** course. – **पथ-कर,** m. road-tax: toll. **पथ-दर्शक,** m. = next. **पथ-प्रदर्शक,** m. one showing the way: guide; leader; °-**प्रदर्शिका,** f. guide, &c.; guide-book. °-**प्रदर्शन,** m. guidance, direction. **पथ-भ्रष्ट,** adj. strayed from the path; fallen by the wayside.

[2]**पथ** *path* [ad. *pathya-*], m. Brbh. proper food or diet (for a patient).

पथना *pathnā* [cf. H. *pāthnā*], v.i. to be made into fuel cakes (cow-dung).

पथनौड़ा *pathnauṛā* [? H. *pāthnā*+H. *-auṛā* ← *vāṭa-*[1]], m. reg. place where cow-dung is made into fuel cakes.

पथरना *patharnā*, v.i. reg. to sharpen on a stone; to hone, to whet.

पथराना *pathrānā* [cf. H. *patthar*], v.i. & v.t. **1.** v.i. to petrify. **2.** to grow hard, stony. **3.** to grow glazed (the eyes). **4.** v.t. to stone (= **पथराव करना**).

पथराव *pathrāv* [cf. H. *pathrānā*], m. **1.** stoning. **2.** transf. stony look (of the eyes).

पथरी *pathrī* [cf. *prastara-*], f. **1.** grit, gravel. **2.** a flint; whetstone. **3.** stone in the bladder.

पथरीला *pathrīlā* [cf. H. *patthar*], adj. stony; rocky; gravelly; gritty.

पथरौटा *pathrauṭā* [**prastaravarta-*], m. a stone bowl (for grinding spices).

पथरौटी *pathrauṭī* [**prastaravarta-*], f. a small stone bowl.

पथवारी *pathvārī* [H. *pāthnā*+H. *vāṛī*, *vārī*], f. place where cow-dung is made into fuel cakes.

पथिक *pathik* [S.], m. a traveller; sojourner. — **पथिकाश्रय** [°*ka*+*ā*°], m. travellers' rest: inn.

पथेरा *patherā* [**prastaraharaka-*], m. a brickmaker.

पथ्य *pathyă* [S.], adj. & m. **1.** adj. belonging to the (right) road: proper, wholesome (esp. of diet); Av. beneficial. **2.** m. wholesome food, or diet. **3.** moderate way of life. — **पथ्यापथ्य** [°*ya*+*a*°], m. wholesome and unwholesome diet, or regime. **पथ्याशन** [°*ya*+*a*°], m. wholesome food.

पद *pad* [S.], m. **1.** foot; step, pace. **2.** footprint; trace; mark, sign. **3.** place, abode; position; square (of chess-board). **4.** position, rank; status. **5.** appointment, post; office. **6.** *gram.* a word; stem. **7.** *pros.* a quarter unit; a foot; line; couplet. **8.** a verse of devotional poetry (esp. intended to be sung). **9.** sthg. having properties of its own, an object. **9.** *law.* topic, matter, head. — **~ ~ पर**, adv. at every step. – **पद-कमल**, m. lotus foot: a conventional reference to the feet of a much-respected person, or of a deity. **पद-क्रम**, m. sequence of terms, order of words. **पदचर**, m. a person on foot. **पद-चाप**, f. foot-fall, footstep. **पद-चार**, m. poet. gait, movement. °**ई**, adj. Av. (going) on foot. **पद-चिह्न**, m. footprint. **पद-च्युत**, adj. fallen from office: removed or dismissed from a post or a function; degraded; deposed. °**इ**, f. dismissal, &c. **पदज**, Brbh. a toe. **पद-तल**, m. sole of the foot. **पद-त्याग**, m. resignation; retirement. **पद-त्रान**, m. Av. foot-protection: shoe, slipper. **पद-दलित**, adj. trodden under foot: oppressed. **पद्-धति**, f. see s.v. **पद-नामित**, adj. named to a post, designated. **पद-न्यस्त**, adj. relieved of a post, on leave. **पद-न्यास**, m. placing the feet: gait (Brbh.); leave of absence. **पद-पंकज**, m. = **पद-कमल**. **पद-भ्रष्ट**, adj. dismissed with dishonour. **पद-मुद्रा**, f. official seal. **पद-योजना**, f. verse composition. **पद-रचना**, f. *gram.* accidence, morphology; = **पद-योजना**. **पद-विन्यास**, m. order of words (in a sentence). **पद-व्याख्या**, f. parsing. **पदस्थ**, adj. holding a post, incumbent. **पदस्थ करना**, to appoint to a post. **पदांतर** [°*da*+*a*°], m. a second pace; distance of one pace, step; a different place, or post. **पदांत्य** [°*da*+*a*°], adj. found at the end of a verse; final in a word. **पदाक्रांत** [°*da*+*ā*°], adj. trampled underfoot. **पदाघात** [°*da*+*ā*°], m. blow with the foot: kick. **पदाचार**, m. movement, motion (? for °-**चार**). **पदाति** [°*da*+*ā*°], m. a foot-soldier. °**क**, adj. & m. foot (regiment, &c.); a pawn (in chess). **पदाधिकारी** [°*da*+*a*°], m. holder of a post or office. **पदान्वय** [°*da*+*a*°], m. paraphrase. **पदार्थ** [°*da*+*a*°], m. see s.v. **पदार्पण** [°*da*+*a*°], m. setting foot: arrival (of a respected or prominent person). **पदावधि** [°*da*+*a*°], f. tenure, term of post, &c. **पदावली** [°*da*+*ā*°], f. collection of verses; a poet's collected verse; a vocabulary, glossary. **पदासन** [°*da*+*ā*°], m. footstool. **पदासीन** [°*da*+*ā*°], adj. holding a post, incumbent (= **पदस्थ**). **पदोन्नति** [°*da*+*u*°], f. promotion.

पदक *padak* [S.], m. **1.** a decoration; medallion, medal. **2.** badge. — **पदकधारी**, adj. & m. decorated; the holder of a decoration.

पदक्कड़ *padakkaṛ* [cf. H. *pādnā*], adj. & m. **1.** adj. = **पदोड़ा**, 1. **2.** m. one who passes wind often.

पदना *padnā* [? cf. H. *pādnā*], adj. = **पदोड़ा**.

पदवी *padvī* [S.], f. **1.** rank, status; position. **2.** title. **3.** position, post. — **~ देना (को)**, to confer rank, &c. (on).

पदाना *padānā* [cf. H. *pādnā*], v.t. to cause to pass wind: **1.** fig. to harass. **2.** pej. to put to flight.

पदार्थ *padārth* [S.], m. **1.** meaning of a word. ***2.** an object. **3.** a substance, material; *phys.* matter. **4.** a product. **5.** aim, end. **चार ~**, m. the four goals of life (viz. *dharm, arth, kām, mokṣa*). — **पदार्थवाद**, m. materialism. °**ई**, adj. & m. materialistic; a materialist.

पदास *padās*, m. habit of passing wind.

पदासा *padāsā* [cf. H. *padās*], adj. inclined to pass wind.

पदिक *padik* [S.], Av. **1.** an ornament of gold and (?) jewels worn at the throat. **2.** a priceless gem; fig. a gem among women. — **पदिक-हार**, m. a costly necklace.

पदोड़ा *padoṛā* [cf. H. *pādnā*], adj. **1.** inclined to pass wind. **2.** colloq. easily frightened.

पद्दू *paddū* [cf. *parda-*], adj. = **पदोड़ा**.

पद्धति *paddhati* [S.], f. **1.** way, path. **2.** manner; method. ***3.** tradition, custom. ***4.** system (as of government, or philosophy; or of teaching, &c). **5.** manual, treatise; account (of a rite or ceremony).

पद्म *padmă* [S.], m. a lotus. — **पद्म-चय**, m. cluster of lotuses. **पद्म-भूषण**, m. third highest decoration awarded by the Indian state. पद्म-राग, m. lotus-coloured: a ruby. पद्म-विभूषण, m. second highest decoration awarded by the Indian state. पद्म-श्री, m. fourth ranking decoration awarded by the Indian state. पद्माकर [°*ma*+*ā*°], m. tank or pool containing many lotuses; cluster of lotuses. पद्मासन [°*ma*+*ā*°], m. lotus posture: a partic. cross- legged posture (esp. as adopted in meditition); lotus-shaped seat, or throne. °आ, f. a title of the goddess Lakṣmī.

पद्मकी *padmăkī* [S.], f. *Pl. HŚS.* the birch tree.

पद्मिनी *padminī* [S.], f. **1.** a lotus; a cluster of lotuses. **2.** fig. a woman of beauty and accomplishments (hence belonging in the first of four traditional classes of women).

पद्य *padyă* [S.], m. verse, poetry. — पद्य-बद्ध, adj. given verse form. पद्यमय, adj. poetic. पद्यात्मक [°*ya*+*ā*°], adj. poetic. पद्यावली [°*ya*+*ā*°], f. collection of verse.

पद्या *padyā* [S.], f. a path, pedestrian way.

पधराना *padhrānā* [cf. H. *padhārnā*], v.t. **1.** to give a seat to (one, को); to seat. **2.** to set up, to establish (an idol at a sacred site).

पधारना *padhārnā* [**paddhārayati*: Pk. *pādhāraï*], v.i. to proceed, to take one's way: **1.** to set out. **2.** to arrive. **3.** to take a seat.

-पन *-pan* [cf. *-tva*], suffix (forms m. nouns from nominal stems, e.g. बचपन, childhood; सीधापन, m. simplicity, directness).

[1]**पन-** *pan-* [cf. H. *pānī*]. water: – पनकपड़ा, m. a wet cloth; a compress. पनकाल, m. bad time for water: drought; famine caused by excess of rain. पन-कौवा, m. a cormorant, shag. पनगोटी, f. chicken-pox. पनघट, m. a well or tank, &c. from which water is drawn or taken. पनचक्की, f. a water-mill. पनछाला, m. a blister. पनडुब्बा, m. a diver; a diving bird; fig. the ghost of a drowned person. °ई, darter (a black diving bird); submarine. पनबिजली, f. hydro-electric power. पनसाल [×*parṇaśālā*-], m. a place where water is available to travellers. °-सल्ला, m. reg. id. पनमेला, m. a person who distributes water to beds of crops, or of flowers, as it flows from the irrigation point. पनसुही, f. reg. (E.) a small rowing-boat. °-सूही, f. id. °-सोई, f. id. पनहरा, m. a water-carrier; irrigater (of plots, fields). °-हारा, m. id. °-हारिन, f.

[2]**पन-** *pan-* [cf. H. *pāṁc*, and *pañca*-]. five: — पनजीर, m. a mixture of spices or other ingredients: cf. next. °ई, f. a mixture of spices, &c. offered as a *prasād*; a medicine of five ingredients (as sugar, *ghī*, flour, cumin, ginger) given to women after childbirth. पनसेरा, m. a quantity of sthg. weighing five seers; = next. °-सेरी, f. a weight of five seers.

[3]**पन-** *pan-* [cf. H. [1]*pān*]. betel: — पनबट्टा, m. betel-box. पनवाड़ी, m. betel-seller; f. betel plot or garden.

पनच *panac*, f. Brbh. bow-string.

पनचक *pancak*, f. *Pl.* = पनच.

पनपना *panapnā*, v.i. **1.** to be refreshed, revived. **2.** to recover (after illness). **3.** to grow luxuriantly (vegetation). **4.** to flourish.

पनपाना *panpānā* [cf. H. *panapnā*], v.t. **1.** to refresh, to revive. **2.** to cause to flourish (a style, fashion).

[1]**पनवाड़ी** *panvāṛī*, m. a betel-seller.

[2]**पनवाड़ी** *panvāṛī* [**parṇavāṭikā*-], f. *HŚS.* garden or area where betel is grown.

पनवार *panvār*, m. Av. = पनवारा.

पनवारा *panvārā* [**parṇapāṭaka*-], m. Brbh. Av. a leaf-platter.

पनस *panas* [S.], m. the jack-fruit tree (= कटहल).

पनसा *panăsā* [S.], f. pustular inflammation of the skin.

पनसारी *pansārī*, m. see पंसारी.

पनसोई *pansoī*, f. reg. see s.v. [1]पन-.

[1]**पनहा** *panhā* [cf. *paṇa*-][1]], m. Brbh. person to whom a fee is paid (as for investigating a theft).

[2]**पनहा** *panhā* [P. *pahna*], adj. **1.** breadth. **2.** fig. full import (of a hidden matter).

पनहाई *panhāī* [cf. H. [1]*panhā*], f. reg. (W.) money paid to thieves for the return of stolen goods (especially cattle).

पनहियाई *panhiyāī* [cf. H. *panihā*], adj. *Pl.* adj. suffering from leucorrhoea.

पनही *panhī* [*upānaḥ*-], f. reg. shoe; slipper.

पना *panā* [*pāna*-], m. reg. a drink made from the juice of fruits (as tamarind, mango) with certain spices.

-पना *-panā* [cf. *-tva*-], suffix. = -पन.

पनाना *panānā* [**prasnāvayati*], v.t. to cause to flow down (milk, into an animal's udder).

पनाला *panālā* [*praṇālī*-], m. **1.** water channel; gutter; drain. **2.** vertical drain-pipe. **3.** spout.

पनाली *panālī* [*praṇālikā*-], f. **1.** a small water-channel, &c. **2.** fig. the hollow along the backbone of animals when fat. — ~ पड़ना (पीठ में), to be fat, well fattened (an animal).

पनाह *panāh* [P. *panāh*], f. protection, shelter; refuge. — ~ देना (को), to protect; to give refuge (to). ~ पाना, to find protection, &c. ~ माँगना (से), to seek protection, or refuge (from, से); to ask for mercy, or quarter. ~ लेना, to seek the shelter (of, की).

पनाही *panāhī* [P. *panāhī*], f. in comp. protection.

पनिया *paniyā* [cf. H. *pānī*], adj. **1.** having to do with water; aquatic. **2.** watery; diluted; adulterated (as milk).

पनियाना *paniyānā* [cf. H. *pānī*], v.t. & v.i. **1.** v.t. to water, to irrigate. **2.** v.i. to yield water (as milk in coagulating); to become watery. **3.** to water (the mouth).

पनियार *paniyār* [? **pānīyadhāra-*], m. reg. **1.** place where water collects. **2.** direction of flow of water.

पनियारा *paniyārā* [**pānīyadhāraka-*], m. & adj. reg. **1.** m. flood. **2.** adj. flooded.

पनियाला *paniyālā* [conn. *pānīyāmalaka-*], m. *Pl. HŚS.* a kind of fruit, *Flacourtia cataphracta.*

पनिहा *panihā* [cf. H. *pānī*], adj. = पनिया.

पनिहार *panihār* [**pānīyahāra-*: c6p. Pa. *udahāraka-*], m. E.H. = पनहारा (see s.v. [1]पन-).

पनी *panī* [**paṇin-*], adj. Brbh. **1.** under a vow. **2.** resolute.

पनीर *panīr* [P. *panīr*], m. **1.** cheese. **2.** curds. — ~ चटाना, colloq. to flatter (for a purpose). – पनीर-मावा, m. *Pl.* rennet.

पनीरक *panīrak*, m. *Pl.* = [2]पनीरी.

[1]पनीरी *panīrī* [P. *panīrī*], adj. made of cheese.

[2]पनीरी *panīrī*, f. **1.** young plants grown for transplanting. **2.** a plot of young plants; seed-bed. — ~ जमाना, *Pl.* fig. to implant an idea (in another's mind).

पनीला *panīlā* [cf. H. *pānī*], adj. **1.** watery; adulterated (as milk). **2.** insipid.

पनेरी *panerī*, f. *Pl.* = [2]पनीरी, 1.

पनौला *panaulā*, m. reg. land watered after ploughing.

पन्नग *pannag* [S.], m. moving while low or fallen: **1.** a snake. **2.** [× H. [3]*pannā*] an emerald. — पन्नगारि [°*ga*+*a*°], f. Av. *mythol.* snake's enemy: the bird Garuḍa.

[1]पन्ना *pannā* [*parṇa-*], m. **1.** leaf (of a book). **2.** a page. **3.** gold or silver leaf, foil; thin sheet (of metal).

[2]पन्ना *pannā* [*upānah-*], m. reg. the upper part of a shoe.

[3]पन्ना *pannā*, m. an emerald.

पन्नी *pannī* [*parṇa-*], f. metal foil; tinsel.

पपड़ा *papṛā* [*parpaṭa-*[1], Pa. *pappaṭa-*], m. crust, scab; rough surface.

पपड़ियहा *papṛiyahā*, adj. = पपड़िया, 1.

पपड़िया *papṛiyā* [cf. H. *papṛā*], adj. **1.** encrusted. **2.** crystallised, sugared.

पपड़ियाना *papṛiyānā* [cf. H. *papṛā*], v.i. **1.** to form a crust, &c. **2.** to crack (as dry soil); to be chapped (lips). **3.** to crystallise.

पपड़ी *papṛī* [*parpaṭa-*[1], Pa. *pappaṭa-*], f. **1.** thin crust, scab; incrustation (as on a liquid); scale, scurf. **2.** cracked or chapped surface. **3.** a crystallised sweet. 4. = पापड़, 1. — ~ आना, to become rough or chapped (as the lips); to dry and crack (soil). ~ जमना, or पड़ना, to form a crust; to crystallise. ~ छोड़ना, to dry and crack (soil). – पपड़ीदार [P. *-dār*], adj. encrusted, scabby; flaky.

पपड़ीला *papṛīlā* [cf. *parpaṭa-*[1], Pa. *pappaṭa-*, adj. = पपड़ीदार.

पपनी *papnī* [*pakṣman-*], f. reg. the eyelash.

पपीता *papītā* [f. H. [1]*papaiyā*; ? w. *pā-*, *pepīyate*, H. *pīnā*], m. the papaya tree, and its fruit.

पपीहा *papīhā* [conn. Pk. *vappīa-*], m. **1.** the pied crested cuckoo, *Clamator jacobinus* (= चातक). **2.** the hawk-cuckoo, *Cuculus varius.* **3.** transf. a child's reed whistle.

[1]पपैया *papaiyā*, m. *Pl.* = पपीता.

[2]पपैया *papaiyā* [cf. H. *papīhā*], m. ? f. **1.** Brbh. = पपीहा. **2.** transf. a child's whistle (made from a mango stone).

पपोटन *papoṭan*, m. *Pl. HŚS.* **1.** a medicinal plant resembling the *makoy* or Cape gooseberry.

पपोटा *papoṭā* [**pakṣmapaṭṭa-*], m. eyelid.

पपोलना *papolnā*, v.i. **1.** to munch with toothless lips. **2.** to mumble.

पबार- *pabār-*, v.t. Av. to throw, to scatter (seed, &c).

पम्मन *pamman* , f. *Pl. HŚS.* a strain of wheat.

पम्ह *pamh* [*pakṣman-*], m. reg. (Bihar) (a youth's) first moustache.

पय *pay* [S.], m. anything to drink; milk; water. — पयद, adj. & m. Brbh. Av. giving water or milk; a cloud; the female breast. पय-निधि, f. Brbh. Av. store of milk, or of water: *mythol.* ocean of milk; ocean.

पयस *payas* [S.], m. **1.** water. **2.** milk. पयस्विनी, f. a milch cow; Av. name of a tributary of the river Jumna.

पयस्य *payasyă* [S.], adj. **1.** made from milk; a milk product. **2.** transf. nourishment. — **पयस्य-परिपूर्ण**, adj. full of nourishment.

पयस्या *payasyā* [S.], f. *Pl.* curds.

पयस्वी *payasvī* [S.], adj. milky; watery.

पयान *payān* [*prayāṇa-*], m. Brbh. **1.** departure. **2.** death.

पयानक *payānak* [ad. *prayāṇaka-*: w. H. *payān*], m. reg. a journey, march.

पयाम *payām* [P. *payām*], m. = पैग़ाम.

पयाल *payāl* [*palāla-*], m. = पुआल.

पयो- *payo-* [S.], m. **1.** water. **2.** milk: — **पयोज**, m. water-born: lotus. **पयोधर**, m. water-holder, &c.: cloud; woman's breast; udder. °**धि**, m. = next. **पयोनिधि**, m. store of water: ocean, cloud.

पयोर *payor* [S.], m. *Pl. HŚS.* the tree *Acacia catechu* (= ख़ैर).

परंतु *paran-tu* [S.], conj. but; however; nevertheless.

परंपर *param-par* [S.], m. & adv. **1.** m. a series, succession. **2.** adv. in succession.

परंपरा *param-parā* [S.], f. **1.** series, succession. ***2.** tradition. **3.** family line. — ~ **से**, adv. traditionally; in continuous succession. – **परंपरागत**, adj. traditional.

परंपरित *param-parit* [S.], adj. done in accordance with, or following the norm of, tradition.

परंपरीण *param-parīṇ* [S.], adj. *Pl. HŚS.* = परंपरित.

[1]**पर** *par* [**uppari-*: Pk. *upparim̐*], ppn. colloq. or reg. var. **पै**. **1.** on, upon; over. … ~ **का**, adj. the one, the thing, on… **2.** (esp. of a somewhat precise orientation in space or time) at, in; near to; by; to; on. **3.** for, at a cost of. **सौ पाँच** ~, a hundred (runs) for five (wickets). — **घर** ~, adv. at home. **छह बजकर तीन मिनट** ~, adv. at 6.30. **छुट्टी ~ जाना**, to go on holiday. **ठीक समय** ~, adv. punctually, on time. **तोप लगाना**, to point a gun (at, ~). **दरवाज़े** ~, adv. at, or by, the door. **दुकान ~ नहीं है**, (he's) not in the shop. **दुकान ~ लौटा**, (he) returned to the shop. **पहाड़ ~ जाना**, to go to the hills. **पार्टी ~ जाना**, reg. (N.) to go to a party. **बड़े दिन ~ तमाम करना**, to finish (sthg.) by Christmas. **वहाँ** ~, adv. at that place. **4.** fig. on; up to; upon; through; by; (with **भी**) notwithstanding. **अपने पैसे** ~, adv. on, or using, one's own money. **आपके कहने ~ अमल करूँगा**, I shall act as you say. **आपके कहने ~ ही जाऊँगा**, I shall go only if you say so. **आपको आने ~ मालूम होगा**, you'll find out when you come. **इस ~ फ़ीस देनी है**, there are the fees to pay as well. **इस ~ भी जाऊँगा**, despite this I shall go. **उसने इस ~ किताब लिखी**, he wrote a book about this. **चंदों की रक़म दो सौ ~ पहुँच गई है**, subscriptions now total two hundred rupees. **मेरी आशा सब आप ~ है**, all my hopes hang on you. **वह जाने ~ ही था कि…**, he was just about to go when….

[2]**पर** *par* [*para-*], conj. but; still.

[3]**पर** *par* [S.], pref. (chiefly **पर-**). **1.** distant, removed. **2.** previous, former; ancient. **3.** subsequent, future; next; latter. ***4.** other; different; foreign. **5.** belonging to another. **6.** pre-eminent, supreme. — **परजन्म**, m. a subsequent birth. **परतंत्र**, adj. dependent on another; subject (to, **का**). °**ता**, f. **परदुख**, m. another's distress. **परदेश**, m. & adv. a foreign country; abroad. °**ई**, adj. & m. foreign; a foreigner; one living abroad. **परदार**, f. Av. another's wife. **परद्रोही**, adj. Av. hostile to others. **परद्वेषी**, adj. Av. hating others. **परधर्म**, m. another's *dharma*; another's religion. °**-ग्रहण**, m. changing one's religion. **परनारी**, f. Av. = **परस्त्री**. **परनिंदा**, f. Av. abusing others; slander. **परपक्ष**, m. other, or opposite, side or opinion. **परपत्नी**, f. another's wife; °**-व्यभिचार**, m. adultery. **परपार**, m. Brbh. far bank. **परपीड़क**, m. Av. causer of pain or distress to others. **परपुरुष**, m. another's husband; a lover. **परमुखापेक्षिता**, f. looking to others (for guidance), lack of self-assurance. **परराष्ट्र**, m. foreign state, country. °**-नीति**, f. foreign policy. °**इक**, m. foreigner, alien. °**ईय**, adj. foreign. **परलोक**, m. the next world; paradise. **परलोक सिधारना**, euph. to depart for the next world, to die. °**-गत**, adj. deceased. °**-गमन**, m. decease. °**-गामी**, adj. dying; °**-वासी**, adj. deceased. **परवर्ती**, adj. subsequent; secondary (as development). **परवश**, adj. in another's power, subject, dependent. °**ता**, f. **परवश्य**, adj. = **परवश**. **परसर्ग**, m. *gram.* postposition. **परस्त्री**, f. another's wife. °**-गमन**, m. adultery. °**-गामी**, adulterer. **परस्वार्थ**, m. Av. another's welfare; beneficence. °**ई**, adj. & m. **परहित**, m. another's well-being. °**-कारी**, adj. beneficent; altruistic. °**-वाद**, m. altruism. **परात्पर** [°**आत**, abl.], adj. & m. better than the best: supreme; the supreme being. **पराधीन** [°*ra*+*ā*°], adj. subject, dependent (as a country). °**ता**, f. **परार्थ** [°*ra*+*a*°], m. & adj. another's interest or profit; (one's) highest interest; having another purpose; done for another; adv. for another's sake, or good. °**-वाद**, m. altruism. °**-वादी**, adj. & m. **परार्द्ध** [°*ra*+*a*°], m. second half. **परावर** [°*ra*+*a*°], adj. far and near, first and last; ancestors and descendants; whole extent, totality. **पराश्रय**, m. dependence on another. °**ई**, adj. dependent; subsisting on another, parasitic. **पराह्न** [°*a*+*a*°], m. afternoon. **परोपकार** [°*ra*+*u*°], m. assistance to others, beneficence.

°अक, adj. & m. = °ई. °इता, f. beneficence. °ई, adj. assisting others, beneficent; kind. परोपजीवी [°*ra+u*°], living on another, parasitic.

[4]**पर** *par* [P. *par*], m. **1.** feather. **2.** wing. — ~ कटना, the wings to be clipped: to be made powerless, helpless. ~ की/का क़लम, f. m. a quill pen. ~ जमना, the feathers to grow in; fig. to gain freedom of action (as at adolescence). ~ जलना, the feathers to be burnt: to be made powerless. ~ झड़ना, the feathers to fall, to be moulting. ~ झाड़ना, to shake the feathers (before flying); to flap the wings; to moult. ~ टूटना, = ~ कटना. ~ निकलना, feathers to grow in (of a bird); to begin to be a free agent (as an adolescent). ~ निकालना, to display one's new feathers, to show off; euph. to get up to one's pranks. ~ मारना, to flap the wings, to fly. – परकट, adj. = next. परकटा, adj. having clipped wings.

-परक *-parak* [S.], adj. formant. characterised by (e.g. चिंतापरक, thoughtful).

परक- *parak-* [cf. **prarakta-*: anal.], v.i. Brbh. = परचना.

परकटना *pra-kaṭnā*, v.i. reg. = प्रगट-.

परकान *parkān*, m. **1.** *HŚS.* touch-hole (of cannon). **2.** *Pl.* trunnion.

परकाना *parkānā* [cf. H. *parak-*], v.t. reg. = परचाना.

परकार *parkār* [P. *parkār*], m. a pair of compasses.

परकार- *parkār-* [cf. H. *parkār*], v.t. Brbh. to draw a circle (as with compasses).

परकारी *parkārī* [P. *parkārī*], adj. made or done with compasses.

[1]**परकाला** *parkālā*, m. reg. **1.** stair, steps. **2.** door-frame.

[2]**परकाला** *parkālā* [P. *parkāla*], m. **1.** a spark. **2.** a piece of glass; pane.

परकास- *prakās-* [ad. *prakāśayati*; and H. *prakāś*], v.i. Brbh. to be evident, or revealed (a matter).

परकीय *parakīyă* [S.], adj. belonging to another.

परकीया *parakīyā* [S.], f. the wife of another person (than her lover).

परकोटा *parkoṭā* [cf. *koṭṭa-*[1]], m. **1.** a wall round a town, or fortified place; an area so enclosed. **2.** dike.

परख *parakh* [*parīkṣā-*], f. **1.** inspection, test; assay. **2.** investigation. **3.** discrimination, judgment (concerning, की). — ~ में आना, to be scrutinised, tested or investigated (by, की).

[1]**परखना** *parakhnā* [*parīkṣate*], v.t. **1.** to inspect; to assay. **2.** to investigate. **3.** to judge, to assess (a matter).

[2]**परखना** *parakhnā* [*parirakṣati*, or *pra-*°], v.i. to obtain.

परखवाई *parakhvāī* [cf. H. *parakhvānā*], f. = परखाई.

परखवाना *parakhvānā* [cf. H. [1]*parakhnā*], v.t. = परखाना.

परखाई *parkhāī* [cf. H. *parkhānā*], f. **1.** inspecting, testing, assaying. **2.** price paid for testing, &c.

परखाना *parkhānā* [cf. H. [1]*parakhnā*], v.t. to cause to be inspected (by, से); to get (sthg.) tested, or assayed.

परखिया *parkhiyā* [cf. *parīkṣin-*], m. an assayer.

परखैया *parkhaiyā*, m. = परखिया.

परगना *parganā* [P. *pargana*], m. **1.** sub-division of a *zilā*; district. **2.** the country (as opposed to town). **3.** transf. any distant place, a place of distant employment.

परगनाती *parganātī* [cf. P. *parganāt* (w. A. pl. *-āt*)], adj. *Pl. hist.* having to do with a *pargana* or *parganas*. — ~ जमा [P. *jam'*], f. total amount of revenue assessed on a district. ~ ख़र्च, m. expenses and charges of a district (to be deducted from the gross revenue).

परगहनी *pargahnī*, f. reg. (Bihar) a goldsmith's ingot mould.

परघट *parghaṭ*, adj. E.H. = प्रगट.

परघटी *parghaṭī*, f. *Pl.* = परगहनी.

परचना *paracnā* [**prarajyate*: with MIA *-cc-*], v.i. **1.** to be made, or to become, acquainted (with, से). **2.** to be or to become accustomed; to be tamed (an animal); to become intimate or familiar.

परचम *parcam* [P. *parcam*], m. the tassel of a spear or lance, or of a standard; transf. standard.

[1]**परचा** *parcā* [P. *parca*], m. **1.** a piece of paper. **2.** a note; letter; prescription. **3.** pamphlet; handbill, advertisement. **4.** an examination paper. **5.** a paper (to be read). — ~ बाँचना, to read from a text.

[2]**परचा** *parcā* [? ad. *paricaya-*], m. **1.** test, trial; proof (as of sanctity). **2.** expert or extensive knowledge. — ~ लेना (का), to test, to examine.

परचा- *parcā-*, v.t. Av. to kindle, to light.

परचाना *parcānā* [cf. H. *paracnā*], v.t. **1.** to make acquainted (with, से). **2.** to make accustomed; to instil a habit (in); to tame (an animal); to treat in an intimate way. **3.** to fascinate, to charm.

परची *parcī*, f. dimin. = परचा.

परचून *parcūn* [ad. **pracūrṇa-*; cf. *cūrṇa-*], m. meal, flour; provisions, groceries.

परचूनिया *parcūniyā* [cf. H. *parcūn*], m. seller of flour, &c.; grocer.

परचूनी *parcūnī* [cf. H. *parcūn*], f. selling flour, meal, &c.; trading as a grocer.

परछ- *parach-* v.t. E.H. to sanctify a bridegroom by means of a ceremony of *ārtī* (a preliminary rite to marriage).

परछती *parchatī*, f. reg. = परछत्ती.

परछत्ती *parchattī* [**paricchatti-*], f. **1.** a projecting shelf. **2.** small projecting thatch (over walls, on roofs).

[1]**परछा** *parchā*, m. reg. **1.** an earthenware jug. **2.** a large earthen vessel, cauldron. **3.** catch-basin (to hold water for irrigation of fields).

[2]**परछा** *parchā*, m. *Pl.* = परेता.

[3]**परछा** *parchā* [conn. H. *pharchā*; ? w. *aparicchādita-*], adj. & m. reg. **1.** adj. cleared (as the sky of clouds). **2.** m. thinning, dispersal.

परछाईं *parchāīṁ* [*praticchāyā-*], f. **1.** [? × *pracchāya-*] shadow. **2.** reflection (as in a mirror). — ~ पड़ना (पर), the shadow (of an evil spirit, a strange man) to fall (upon an unborn child, causing it to take after or to resemble the person concerned). ~ से भागना, to run from (one's own, अपनी) shadow; to be afraid or unwilling to approach (another, की).

परछावाँ *parchāvāṁ*, m. pronun. var. = परछाईं.

परछाहीं *parchāhīṁ*, f. pronun. var. = परछाईं.

परछी *parchī*, f. *Pl.* a saddle-bag (double or single).

परज *parăj*, m. *Pl.* hilt (of a sword); handle (of a shield); *mus.* name of a *rāgiṇī*.

परजोत *parjot*, m. *Pl.* = परजौट.

परजौट *parjauṭ* [? conn. H. *prajā*, 2.], m. *Pl.* ground rent on a house.

परठ- *paraṭh-*, v.t. reg. (Raj.) to offer, to present, to consecrate (cf. प्रतिष्ठा).

परत *parăt*, f. m. **1.** fold, ply. **2.** layer; stratum. **3.** thin sheet (as paper, metal). — ~ लगाना, to add a layer (of, की); to make a fold (in, की or को). काग़ज़ की एक ~, f. a sheet of paper. – परतदार [P. *-dār*], adj. consisting of layers, &c. परतदार लकड़ी, f. plywood. परतबंदी [P. *-bandī*], f. flaking, splitting into layers.

परतंत्र *par-tantră* [S.], adj. see s.v. [3]पर.

परतल *partal*, m. f. baggage; pack, load (as of a horse). — ~ का टट्टू, m. pack-horse.

परतला *partalā*, m. sword-belt; bandolier.

परता *partā*, m. reg. a large reel for winding off thread on a spinning-wheel; drum.

परतोख *partokh* [ad. *paritoṣa-*], m. reg. (E.) satisfaction (on a matter): valid example.

परत्र *paratră* [S.], adv. Av. **1.** elsewhere. **2.** in another world, or life.

परदा *pardā* [P. *parda*], m. **1.** curtain, hanging; screen; partition; blind. **2.** veil. **3.** lid (of the eye). **4.** membrane, diaphragm. कान का ~, m. ear-drum. **5.** thin covering, layer, veneer; film. **6.** transf. the surface of the earth. दुनिया के परदे पर, on the face of the earth. **7.** seclusion (esp. of a Muslim woman); privacy. यहाँ ~ है, fig. this is the private part of the house. **8.** concealment (as of a secret); pretence, pretext. **9.** *Pl. HŚS.* frets (as of a guitar). — ~ उठना, to be unveiled; to be revealed. ~ उठाना (का), to raise the curtain (from); to unveil; to reveal, to expose. ~ करना, to be secretive, or furtive. ~ खोलना, = ~ उठाना, 2., 3. ~ छोड़ना, to drop a curtain, or veil; to come into public view. ~ डालना (पर), to draw a veil (over). ~ फ़ाश करना [P. *fāś*], to reveal the secrets or shortcomings (of, का), to expose. ~ रखना, to conceal sthg. (from, से); to allude to a matter obscurely. ~ होना, to be concealed; to be private (as women's quarters). परदे में, adv. in seclusion, in purdah. — परदानिशीन [P. *-niśīn*], adj. kept in purdah (a woman). परदापोशी [P. *-pośī*], f. drawing a veil (over, की), covering up (a secret, &c).

परदादा *pardādā* [cf. H. *dādā*; ad. *pra-*], m. inv. paternal great-grandfather; a forefather.

परदादी *pardādī* [cf. H. *dādī*; ad. *pra-*], f. paternal great-grandmother.

परन *paran*, m. *mus.* **1.** *Pl.* very quick time. **2.** interspersal of minor sections of speech or singing in a performance with drums.

परना- *parnā-* [*pariṇāpayati*], v.t. E.H. to cause to be led round the sacred fire: to give in marriage.

परनाना *parnānā* [cf. H. *nānā*; ad. *pra-*], m. maternal great-grandfather.

परनानी *parnānī* [cf. H. *nānī*; ad. *pra-*], f. maternal great-grandmother.

परनाला *parnālā*, m. = पनाला.

परनाली *parnālī*, f. = पनाली.

परनी *parnī* [*pariṇīta-*], f. reg. a bride; maiden.

परपर *parpar*, m. **1.** tingling sensation. **2.** throbbing.

परपराना *parparānā*, v.i. to sting, to burn (esp. the tongue); to taste bitter or acid.

परपराहट *parparāhaṭ* [cf. H. *parparānā*], f. **1.** tingling, stinging. **2.** fig. acrimony.

परपैंठ *parpaiṁṭh* [cf. *pratiṣṭhā-*], f. reg. (Bihar) duplicate of a bill of exchange.

परपोता *parpotā* [cf. H. *potā*; ad. *prapautra-*], m. great-grandson.

परपोती *parpotī* [cf. H. *potī*; ad. *prapautrī-*], f. great-granddaughter.

परब *parb*, m. *Pl. HŚS.* a gem, a flat diamond.

परम *param* [S.], adj. **1.** highest, chief, best; supreme; ultimate, perfect. **2.** extreme. — परम-गति, f. highest condition: merging of the soul with the ultimate. परम-तत्त्व, m. the highest reality; the ultimate *brāhmaṇ*. परम-धाम, m. heaven, the heaven of Viṣṇu. परम-पिता, m. the supreme being. परम-पुरुष, m. = परमात्मा. परम-वीरचक्र, m. name of an Indian military decoration, first grade. परम-हंस, m. supreme soul: an ascetic of utmost sanctity. परमाकांक्षा [°*ma*+*ā*°], f. supreme desire. परमाणु [°*ma* +*a*°], m. an atom. °-बम, m. atomic bomb. °-भार, or °-मान, m. *chem.* atomic weight. परमात्मा [°*ma*+*ā*°], m. the supreme spirit. परमानंद [°*ma*+*ā*°], m. supreme or ultimate bliss. परमायु [°*ma*+*ā*°], f. full age, greatest age. परमार्थ [°*ma*+*a*°], highest truth, or knowledge; greatest, or spiritual, good; important aim; virtue, merit; release from rebirth. परमार्थ सुधरना, to do good deeds tending to secure salvation. °ई, adj. & m. pursuing the highest aim, &c., a religious or virtuous person. परमावश्यक [°*ma*+*ā*°], adj. supremely necessary, indispensable. परमेश्वर [°*ma*+*ī*°], m. the supreme lord: a title of Viṣṇu, or Śiva. परमोप्योगी [°*ma*+*u*°], adj. extremely useful; vital.

परमट *parmaṭ* [Engl. *permit*], m. f. **1.** permit. **2.** *Pl.* customs post.

परमल *parmal*, m. grain first soaked, then parched for eating.

परमाणीकृत *pra-māṇīkṛt* [S.], adj. see s.v. प्रमाण.

परमाणु *paramâṇu* [S.], m. see s.v. परम.

परमाण्विक *paramâṇvik* [S.], adj. atomic.

परमाण्विकी *paramâṇvikī* [S.], f. atomic physics.

परमिलू *parmilū*, m. reg. a kind of dance.

परला *parlā* [*para-*+MIA *-illa-*], adj. **1.** at the far side, or end. **2.** next in order. **3.** extreme. — परले दरजे, or सिरे, का, extreme(ly), real(ly), of or in the highest degree. परले पार, adv. on the far side; far beyond; far off; through (to the far side).

परवरदिगार *parvardigār* [P. *parvardagār*], m. cherisher, provider: a title of the supreme being.

परवरिश *parvariś* [P. *parvariś*], f. **1.** fostering, rearing (a family, &c.); nurture. **2.** maintenance, support. — ~ करना (की), to foster, to rear; to support.

परवल *parval* [*paṭola-*: ← Drav.], m. a creeper, *Tricosanthes dioica*, and its cucumber-like fruit (eaten as a vegetable).

परवा *parvā*, f. = परवाह.

परवाज़ *parvāz* [P. *parvāz*], m. E.H. flight.

परवान *parvān*, m. Brbh. Av. = प्रमाण.

1**परवाना** *parvānā* [P. *parvāna*], m. **1.** warrant, written authority; order. **2.** licence, grant (of a right, privilege). **3.** pass; passport. — मौत का ~, m. sentence of death. तलाशी का ~, m. search warrant.

2**परवाना** *parvānā* [P. *parvāna*], m. **1.** a moth; butterfly. **2.** fig. one obsessed (as a moth by a flame): a lover. — ~ होना, to be infatuated (with, का, के पीछे ; to be an ardent lover (of).

परवाल *pravāl* [S.], m. **1.** shoot, sprout. **2.** coral.

परवाल *parvāl* [cf. *vāla-*], m. a complaint of the eyes in which the lashes fall off, and new, crooked hairs grow in.

परवाह *parvāh* [P. *parvā(h)*], f. care, concern. — ~ करना, to care (about, की). ~ रखना, to be attentive (to, की: as to a responsibility) ~ होना (को), to care (about, की), to be concerned.

परश *paraś*, m. = परस, 2.

परशु *parăśu* [S.], m. battle-axe. — परशुराम, m. name of the sixth avatār of Viṣṇu (destroyer of the kṣatriyas).

परस *paras* [ad. *sparśa-*], m. **1.** touch, touching. **2.** Av. touchstone.

1**परसना** *parasnā* [*sparśayate*], v.t. to touch.

2**परसना** *parasnā*, v.t. = परोसना.

परसर्ग *par-sarg* [S.], m. *gram.* a postposition.

परसाल *par-sāl*, adv. = पारसाल, s.v. 2पार.

परसिया *parsiyā* [cf. *paraśu-*], m. reg. a sickle.

परसों *parsoṁ* [*paraśvas*], adv. **1.** the day after tomorrow. **2.** the day before yesterday.

-परस्त *-parast* [P. *parast*], adj. **1.** worshipping. **2.** devoted to; subject to.

-परस्ती *-parastī* [P. *parastī*], f. worship (of); devotion (to).

परस्पर *paras-par* [S.], adj. **1.** mutual, reciprocal. **2.** interchanging. **3.** adv. mutually, &c.; between each other, among one another. — ~ का, adj. mutual, reciprocal. दोनों में ~ युद्ध होता था, the two used often to be at war with each other.

परस्मैपद *parasmai-pad* [S.], m. the Sanskrit active or transitive verb, and its endings.

परहेज़ *parhez* [P. *parhez*], m. abstention; moderation; temperance; continence. — ~ करना or रखना, to abstain (from, से), to avoid, &c.; to follow a diet. ~ से रहना, to live an abstemious life, &c. – परहेज़गार [P. *-gār*], adj. abstemious, &c.; an abstemious or temperate person; an ascetic. °ई, f.

परहेज़ी *parhezī* [P. *parhezī*], adj. **1.** = परहेज़गार. **2.** forming part of a diet (food).

पराँठा *parāṁṭhā*, m. pronun. var. = पराठा.

परा *parā* [P. *par(r)a*], m. Brbh. body or line (as of troops).

[1]**परा-** *parā-* [S.], pref. away; forward (e.g. पराक्राम, m. vigour, might; पराबैंगनी, adj. ultra-violet).

[2]**परा-** *parā-* [*palāyate*], v.i. Av. to run, to flee.

पराकाष्ठा *parā-kāṣṭhā* [S.], f. summit, peak; climax.

पराक्रम *parâkram* [S.], m. **1.** vigour; might. **2.** valour. **3.** valiant deed, exploit.

पराक्रमी *parâkramī* [S.], adj. **1.** vigorous, mighty. **2.** bold, valiant.

पराक्रांत *parâkrānt* [S.], adj. **1.** vigorous, powerful. **2.** attacked.

पराग *parāg* [S.], m. **1.** pollen. **2.** a fragrant powder used after bathing. **3.** *Pl. HŚS.* dust. **4.** *Pl. HŚS.* sandalwood.

पराङ्मुख *parāṅ-mukh* [S.], adj. **1.** having the face averted; turned away (from, से). **2.** averse (to); indifferent (to).

पराङ्मुखता *parāṅ-mukhātā* [S.], f. **1.** aversion; disgust. **2.** indifference.

पराजय *parā-jay* [S.], m. defeat; victory (over another), conquest. — ~ करना (का), to defeat, &c. – पराजयवाद, m. defeatism. °ई, adj. & m.

पराजयी *parā-jayī* [S.], adj. *Pl.* defeating; suffering defeat.

पराजित *parā-jit* [S.], adj. defeated; conquered; beaten (in a contest). — ~ करना, to defeat, &c.

पराजेता *parā-jetā* [S.], m. inv. conqueror.

पराठा *parāṭhā* [? *pallaṭṭ-*: Pk. *pal(l)aṭṭaï* (cf. H. *palṭā*, 6.) × *paryasta-*], m. a round cake of unleavened wheat flour fried in *ghī* or oil on a griddle.

परात *parāt*, f. a large circular metal dish having a raised edge.

पराभव *parā-bhav* [S.], m. **1.** defeat. **2.** humiliation, disgrace.

पराभूत *parā-bhūt* [S.], adj. **1.** defeated. **2.** disgraced.

परामर्श *parā-marś* [S.], m. **1.** reflection. ***2.** discussion, consultation. **3.** counsel, advice; recommendation. **4.** decision (as of a committee). — ~ करना, to discuss, to consult (with, से; about, पर). ~ देना, to advise. ~ लेना, = ~ करना. – परामर्शदाता, adj. & m. inv. advisory, consultative; adviser.

परामर्शन *parā-marśan* [S.], m. consulting, discussing; advising.

परामर्शी *parā-marśī* [S.], m. adviser, counsellor.

परायचा *parāycā* [P. *parā'ica*], m. *Pl. HŚS.* shreds, bits of cloth, &c.

-परायण *-parâyaṇ* [S.], adj. devoted to, engrossed in; characterised by (e.g. सेवापरायण, devoted in service).

पराया *parāyā* [*paragata-*; Pk. *parāya-*], adj. & m. **1.** adj. another's, others'. **2.** [? *parāgata-*] strange, foreign. **3.** m. a stranger. — ~ मुँह ताकना, to look outside one's family for help. अपना ~ समझना, to know relatives from strangers: to have good sense.

परार *parār*, adj. reg. = पराया.

पराल *parāl* [*palāla-*], m. straw (= पुआल).

परालब्ध *parālabdh*, m. reg. (W. E.) = प्रारब्ध.

परावर्तक *parā-vartak* [S.], m. a reflector.

परावर्तन *parā-vartan* [S.], m. **1.** turning back or round; reversion. **2.** return to (a matter). **3.** reflection (of light). **4.** exchange.

परावर्तित *parā-vartit* [S.], adj. **1.** turned back, &c.; reverted. **2.** reflected.

परावर्ती *parā-vartī* [S.], adj. turning back, &c.; reverting.

परावर्त्य *parā-vartyă* [S.], adj. under reconsideration (a matter); to be reconsidered.

परावृत्त *parā-vṛtt* [S.], adj. = परावर्तित.

परावृत्ति *parā-vṛtti* [S.], f. = परावर्तन.

परास *parâs* [S.], m. range (of trajectory, or operation).

परास्त *parâst* [S.], adj. thrown: defeated; beaten (in a contest).

परास्तता *parâstătā* [S.], f. defeat, &c.

पराह *parāh*, f. *Pl.* fleeing; flight, escape.

परिंद *parind* [P. *parind*], m. = परिंदा.

परिंदा *parindā* [P. *parinda*], m. winged: a bird. — ~ हो जाना, fig. to move very swiftly.

परि- *pari-* [S.], pref. **1.** around (e.g. परिधि, f. circle; परिप्रेक्ष्य, m. context). **2.** abundantly (e.g. परिपूर्ण, adj. replete). **3.** from, away from (e.g. परित्यक्त, adj. abandoned). **4.** according to (e.g. परिभाषा, f. definition).

परिकथा *pari-kathā* [S.], f. a tale, story; specif. a story incorporated in another.

परिकर *pari-kar* [S.], m. **1.** attendants, dependants. **2.** Av. sash, cloth worn round the hips. **3.** *Pl. HŚS.* a bed.

परिकलन *pari-kalan* [S.], m. calculation.

परिकल्पना *pari-kalpănā* [S.], f. **1.** imagination. **2.** a presumption; hypothesis.

परिकल्पित *pari-kalpit* [S.], adj. **1.** contrived, devised. **2.** imagined; presumed; hypothetical.

परिक्रमण *pari-kramaṇ* [S.], m. **1.** circumambulating. **2.** revolving, orbiting.

परिक्रमा *pari-kramā* [S.], f. **1.** circumambulation (= प्रदक्षिणा). **2.** revolution, orbit. **3.** covered path round a temple. — ~ करना, or देना, or लेना (की), to walk around in reverence, to circumambulate.

परिक्रय *pari-kray* [S.], m. *Pl. HŚS.* buying (sthg.) back; redemption (of).

परिक्लिष्ट *pari-kliṣṭ* [S.], adj. afflicted, harassed.

परिख्यात *pari-khyāt* [S.], adj. **1.** regarded as. **2.** called, named. 3. = प्रख्यात.

परिग्रह *pari-grah* [S.], m. **1.** taking; accepting; receiving. **2.** specif. taking a wife. **3.** property. **4.** dependants, family; household. **5.** favour.

परिघ *pari-gh* [S.], m. *Pl. HŚS.* **1.** an iron bar. **2.** an iron club.

परिचय *pari-cay* [S.], m. **1.** acquaintance (with, से). **2.** knowledge, experience (of, से). **3.** information; data. पात्र-परिचय, m. list of characters (in a play). — ~ कराना (से), to introduce (one, का) to; to acquaint (with). ~ देना (को), to make known (to), to demonstrate (as qualities, a skill). - परिचय-पत्र, m. letter of introduction; memorandum; visiting card. परिचयात्मक [°*a*+*ā*°], adj. providing information, or an introduction (as notes, a summary).

परिचर *pari-car* [S.], m. attendant, servant.

परिचर्या *pari-caryā* [S.], f. **1.** attendance, service. **2.** nursing. **3.** homage, worship. **4.** a symposium.

परिचायक *pari-cāyak* [S.], m. sthg. that gives knowledge (of, का): an indication, illustration.

परिचार *pari-cār* [S.], m. **1.** attending, serving. **2.** nurture. **3.** nursing. **4.** a servant. — परिचार-गाड़ी, f. an ambulance (= अस्पताल-गाड़ी).

परिचारक *pari-cārak* [S.], m. **1.** servant. **2.** nurse.

परिचारिका *pari-cārikā* [S.], f. **1.** attendant, servant; stewardess. **2.** nurse.

परिचारित *pari-cārit* [S.], adj. nursed.

परिचारी *pari-cārī* [S.], adj. & m. **1.** adj. attending, serving; paying homage to. **2.** m. servant. **3.** orderly.

परिचालक *pari-cālak* [S.], m. a conductor.

परिचालन *pari-cālan* [S.], m. conducting, guiding, or running (an activity).

परिचालित *pari-cālit* [S.], adj. conducted, operated.

परिचित *pari-cit* [S.], adj. & m. **1.** adj. acquainted (with, से: with a topic, or a person). **2.** m. an acquaintance. — ~ कराना, to acquaint (with); to introduce (to).

परिचिति *pari-citi* [S.], f. familiarity, acquaintance (with a thing, or a person).

[1]**परिचेय** *pari-ceyă* [S.], adj. worth (one's) becoming acquainted with.

[2]**परिचेय** *pari-ceyă* [S.], adj. worth collecting.

परिच्छद *pari-cchad* [S.], m. **1.** outer garment. **2.** household possessions, baggage. **3.** attendants; family.

परिच्छन्न *pari-cchann* [S.], adj. **1.** covered, enveloped. **2.** encompassed, attended.

परिच्छिन्न *pari-cchinn* [S.], adj. **1.** cut off. **2.** detached. **3.** defined, circumscribed.

परिच्छेद *pari-cched* [S.], m. **1.** separation. **2.** discrimination (of false from true); distinguishing (as between different cases). **3.** section (of a book, &c.); chapter.

परिजन *pari-jan* [S.], m. **1.** attendants; retinue. **2.** dependants, family.

परिणति *pari-ṇati* [S.], m. bowing: transformation; further development.

परिणय *pari-ṇay* [S.], m. leading (the bride round the sacred fire): marriage.

परिणयन *pari-ṇayan* [S.], m. solemnising a marriage.

परिणाम *pari-ṇām* [S.], m. **1.** change; transformation. ***2.** result, effect. **3.** final stage or state. **4.** conclusion, deduction. — परिणाम-दर्शी, adj. foreseeing, prudent. परिणाम-स्वरूप, adv. as a result (of, के).

परिणामी *pari-ṇāmī* [S.], adj. consequential, resultant.

परिणाह *pari-ṇāh* [S.], m. *Pl. HŚS.* extent, compass.

परिणीत *pari-ṇīt* [S.], adj. led round (the sacred fire): married.

परिताप *pari-tāp* [S.], m. **1.** glow, heat. **2.** suffering. **3.** remorse.

परितापित *pari-tapit* [S.], adj. suffering anguish.

परितापी *pari-tāpī* [S.], adj. & m. **1.** adj. suffering anguish. **2.** m. Av. one who causes suffering or distress.

परितुष्ट *pari-tuṣṭ* [S.], adj. quite satisfied; delighted.

परितुष्टि *pari-tuṣṭi* [S.], f. = परितोष.

परितोष *pari-toṣ* [S.], m. full satisfaction; contentedness; pleasure.

परितोषक *pari-toṣak* [S.], adj. satisfying, gratifying; giving pleasure.

परितोषण *pari-toṣaṇ* [S.], m. **1.** satisfying, satisfaction. **2.** person or thing giving satisfaction or pleasure. **3.** remunerating; remuneration.

परितोषी *pari-toṣī* [S.], adj. & m. **1.** adj. quite satisfied; contented. **2.** m. a contented person.

परित्यक्त *pari-tyakt* [S.], adj. **1.** abandoned, deserted. **2.** deprived (of). **3.** fired, or hurled (a weapon).

परित्यजन *pari-tyajan* [S.], m. = परित्याग.

परित्याग *pari-tyāg* [S.], m. **1.** abandonment; desertion. **2.** renunciation; abdication. **3.** loss, deprivation.

परित्याज्य *pari-tyājyă* [S.], adj. to be given up (a habit, &c).

परित्राण *pari-trāṇ* [S.], m. inv. **1.** protection; defence. **2.** deliverance.

परित्राता *pari-trātā* [S.], m. **1.** protector. **2.** deliverer.

परिदर्शन *pari-darśan* [S.], m. (tour of) inspection.

परिदाह *pari-dāh* [S.], m. **1.** fierce burning. **2.** anguish of mind.

परिदृश्य *pari-dṛśyă* [S.], m. **1.** perspective, wide view; spectacle. **2.** scenario.

परिधान *pari-dhān* [S.], m. **1.** wrapping round, putting on. **2.** a garment; attire.

परिधारण *pari-dhāraṇ* [S.], m. supporting; suffering, enduring.

परिधि *pari-dhi* [S.], f. **1.** circumference; circle, ring. **2.** enclosing wall, fence, &c. **3.** halo. **4.** transf. sphere (of action, responsibilities); scope (of a work).

परिधेय *pari-dheyă* [S.], adj. **1.** adj. wearable (a garment). **2.** m. a garment.

परिनिष्ठित *pari-ni-ṣṭhit* [S.], adj. standardised (language); standard.

परिपक्व *pari-pakvă* [S.], adj. **1.** fully cooked, or prepared; fully fired (a brick). **2.** fully digested. **3.** quite ripe; mature (as of skill, art); highly cultivated, or educated (a person).

परिपक्वता *pari-pakvătā* [S.], f. **1.** fully cooked, or prepared, state. **2.** ripeness; maturity. **3.** wide experience, shrewdness.

परिपाक *pari-pāk* [S.], m. **1.** fully cooked, or prepared, state. **2.** digestion; assimilation. **3.** ripening; maturity (as of an art, a skill). **4.** experience, shrewdness. **5.** Av. due outcome.

परिपाटी *pari-pāṭī* [S.], f. **1.** succession, order. **2.** method. ***3.** tradition.

परिपात्र *pari-pātr* [S.], m. a circular.

परिपालक *pari-pālak* [S.], adj. & m. **1.** adj. supporting, fostering. **2.** guarding. **3.** m. guardian, &c.

परिपालन *pari-pālan* [S.], m. **1.** bringing up, rearing; nurture. **2.** guarding, cherishing. **3.** observance (as of custom, rule). **4.** implementation (of a directive).

परिपालित *pari-pālit* [S.], adj. **1.** brought up, reared; nurtured. **2.** guarded, cherished.

परिपूजन *pari-pūjan* [S.], m. *Pl. HŚS.* honouring highly, worshipping devoutly.

परिपूजित *pari-pūjit* [S.], adj. *Pl. HŚS.* much honoured, or worshipped.

परिपूरक *pari-pūrak* [S.], adj. supplementary.

परिपूरित *pari-pūrit* [S.], adj. **1.** filled, brimful. **2.** quite satisfied, fulfilled (as wishes, hopes). **3.** lived through, completed (as time).

परिपूर्ण *pari-pūrṇ* [S.], adj. **1.** quite full, brimful; entire, complete; replete. **2.** quite satisfied, fulfilled.

परिपूर्णता *pari-pūrṇătā* [S.], f. **1.** completeness, entireness; fullness. **2.** full satisfaction.

परिपेल *pari-pel* [S.], m. a proliferating plant, *Cyperus rotundus*, having fragrant rhizomes (= मोथा).

परिप्रेक्ष्य *pari-prêkṣyă* [S.], m. perspective, viewpoint.

परिप्लावित *pari-plāvit* [S.], adj. = परिप्लुत.

परिप्लुत *pari-plut* [S.], adj. **1.** inundated. **2.** immersed.

परिभव *pari-bhav* [S.], m. *Pl. HŚS.* **1.** insult, degradation. **2.** disgrace.

परिभावना *pari-bhāvănā* [S.], f. thought, reflection (on a topic).

परिभावी *pari-bhāvī* [S.], adj. & m. *Pl. HŚS.* **1.** adj. slighting, down-grading. **2.** one who slights, or mocks.

परिभाषा *pari-bhāṣā* [S.], f. **1.** exact explanation, definition (of a word). **2.** words used in a special sense; technical language.

परिभाषित *pari-bhāṣit* [S.], adj. explained, defined. — ~ **करना**, to define.

परिभाषी *pari-bhāṣī* [S.], adj. *Pl. HŚS.* speaking; explaining.

परिभाष्य *pari-bhāṣyă* [S.], adj. **1.** definable. **2.** to be defined.

परिभोग *pari-bhog* [S.], m. **1.** enjoyment; sexual intercourse. **2.** obtaining the benefit of assets belonging to another.

परिभ्रमण *pari-bhramaṇ* [S.], m. **1.** revolving (around sthg). **2.** going about, wandering, travelling.

परिभ्रष्ट *pari-bhraṣṭ* [S.], adj. fallen; corrupted.

परिमंडल *pari-maṇḍal* [S.], adj. & m. **1.** adj. round. **2.** m. a circle. **3.** ball, globe, sphere.

परिमंडलता *pari-maṇḍalătā* [S.], f. roundness.

परिमल *pari-mal* [S.], m. **1.** fragrance, perfume. **2.** a fragrant substance.

परिमा *pari-mā* [S.], f. periphery, circumference.

परिमाण *pari-māṇ* [S.], m. **1.** measuring. **2.** measure; amount, quantity; size, dimensions; capacity. **3.** extent; scope. — **किस** ~ **में?** adv. to what extent? — **परिमाणगत**, adj. quantitative. **परिमाणवाचक**, adj. *gram.* quantitative.

परिमार्गन *pari-mārgan* [S.], m. *Pl. HŚS.* tracing, tracking (a lost person).

परिमार्जन *pari-mārjan* [S.], m. refining, purifying.

परिमार्जित *pari-mārjit* [S.], adj. refined, purified.

परिमित *pari-mit* [S.], adj. **1.** measured. **2.** limited; restricted; moderate (in scope or scale). — **परिमितव्यय**, m. economy, frugality. °**ई**, adj. **परिमिताहार** [°*ta*+*ā*°], adj. & m. abstemious (in food or drink); moderation.

परिमिति *pari-miti* [S.], f. **1.** measure. **2.** limitation; moderation; circumspection (in conduct).

परिमोहन *pari-mohan* [S.], m. infatuating, bewitching.

परिम्लान *pari-mlān* [S.], adj. *Pl. HŚS.* **1.** faded, withered. **2.** impaired. **3.** soiled, stained.

परिया *pariyā* [cf. H. *parī*], adj. reg. fairy-like.

परियोजना *pari-yojănā* [S.], f. a project.

परिरंभ *pari-rambh* [S.], m. poet. embrace.

परिरेखा *pari-rekhā* [S.], f. a contour line.

परिवर्जन *pari-varjan* [S.], m. avoidance (of liability to tax).

परिवर्त *pari-vart* [S.], m. **1.** revolution (of a planet, &c). **2.** period of time. **3.** end of an age. 4. = परिवर्तन, 1., 2.

परिवर्तक *pari-vartak* [S.], adj. **1.** causing to revolve. **2.** revolving. **3.** exchanging.

परिवर्तन *pari-vartan* [S.], m. **1.** change. **2.** exchange (of objects, goods); conversion (of funds, currency). **3.** transformation. — **परिवर्तनकारी**, adj. effecting change. **परिवर्तनशील**, adj. prone to change, variable.

परिवर्तनीय *pari-vartanīyă* [S.], adj. needing, or admitting of, change.

परिवर्तित *pari-vartit* [S.], adj. **1.** changed. **2.** exchanged. **3.** transformed.

परिवर्ती *pari-vartī* [S.], adj. **1.** revolving. **2.** changing, changeable. **3.** being exchanged.

परिवर्त्य *pari-vartyă* [S.], adj. exchangeable; convertible (as a currency).

परिवहन *pari-vahan* [S.], m. transport, transportation.

परिवा *parivā* [*pratipad-*], f. the first day of a lunar fortnight.

परिवाद *pari-vād* [S.], m. **1.** reproach, censure; abuse. ***2.** slander. **3.** complaint. **4.** instrument used in playing the *vīṇā*.

परिवादक *pari-vādak* [S.], adj. & m. **1.** adj. reproaching, &c. (see परिवाद). **2.** m. one who reproaches, &c. **3.** player on the *vīṇā*.

परिवादी *pari-vādī* [S.], adj. & m. **1.** adj. speaking ill of, reproaching, &c. **2.** m. one who reproaches, &c. (see *parivād*). **3.** plaintiff, complainant.

परिवार *pari-vār* [S.], m. **1.** family, dependants; relatives. **2.** attendants, retinue. — परिवार-नियोजन, m. family planning. – परिवारवाला, m. member of a family; a man having a family.

परिवारी *pari-vārī* [S.], m. & adj. **1.** m. family member, relative. **2.** adj. having a family (a man or woman).

परिवास *pari-vās* [S.], m. residence, stay.

परिविष्ट *pari-viṣṭ* [S.], adj. **1.** surrounded, enclosed. **2.** served (food).

परिवीक्षा *pari-vīkṣā* [S.], f. probation.

परिवृत्त *pari-vṛtt* [S.], adj. **1.** revolved. **2.** [× *parivṛta-*] surrounded; covered. **3.** exchanged; converted (as funds, a currency).

परिवृत्ति *pari-vṛtti* [S.], f. **1.** turning, revolution. 2. = परिवर्तन. **3.** [× *parivṛti-*] enclosure.

परिवेदन *pari-vedan* [S.], m. **1.** full or accurate knowledge. **2.** discussion; dispute. 3. = वेदना.

परिवेश *pari-veś* [S.], m. = परिवेष.

परिवेष *pari-veṣ* [S.], m. **1.** circle, circumference. **2.** transf. halo. **3.** fig. surroundings, environment; atmosphere.

परिवेषण *pari-veṣaṇ* [S.], m. **1.** surrounding; enclosing. 2. = परिवेष, 1., 2. **3.** attendance (on); serving food.

परिवेष्टन *pari-veṣṭan* [S.], m. 1. = परिवेषण, 1. 2. = परिवेष, 1.

परिवेष्टित *pari-veṣṭit* [S.], adj. **1.** surrounded, enclosed. **2.** covered, veiled.

परिव्यय *pari vyay* [S.], m. cost (as of implementation).

परिव्राजक *pari-vrājak* [S.], m. a wandering ascetic.

परिशंकनीय *pari-śaṅkănīyă* [S.], adj. *Pl.* to be distrusted or regarded with apprehension.

परिशाप *pari-śāp* [S.], m. cursing.

परिशिष्ट *pari-śiṣṭ* [S.], adj. & m. **1.** adj. left over, remaining. **2.** m. an appendix, or supplement. **3.** epilogue.

परिशुद्ध *pari-śuddh* [S.], adj. **1.** quite pure, quite cleansed. **2.** discharged (of obligation, or a debt). **3.** accurate, precise.

परिशुद्धि *pari-śuddhi* [S.], f. **1.** pure state. **2.** release, discharge. **3.** accuracy, precision.

परिशेष *pari-śeṣ* [S.], adj. & m. **1.** adj. left over, remaining. **2.** m. remnant, remainder. **3.** end, conclusion.

परिशोध *pari-śodh* [S.], m. = परिशोधन.

परिशोधन *pari-śodhan* [S.], m. **1.** cleansing, purifying. **2.** correcting, revising (as a text). **3.** justification (as against a charge). **4.** discharging (a debt).

परिशोधित *pari-śodhit* [S.], adj. **1.** cleansed, &c. (see परिशोधन). **2.** corrected, revised (as an edition). **3.** paid off (a debt).

परिशोष *pari-śoṣ* [S.], m. *Pl. HŚS.* complete dryness; evaporation.

परिश्रम *pari-śram* [S.], m. **1.** (hard) work. **2.** diligence; effort; pains. — ~ करना, to work hard, &c.

परिश्रमी *pari-śramī* [S.], adj. **1.** industrious, hard-working; energetic. **2.** painstaking.

परिश्रांत *pari-śrānt* [S.], adj. worn out, exhausted.

परिश्रांति *pari-śrānti* [S.], f. **1.** exhaustion. **2.** exhausting toil.

परिषद् *pari-ṣad* [S.], m. **1.** assembly. **2.** council. **3.** society.

परिष्करण *pari-ṣkaraṇ* [S.], m. = परिष्कार.

परिष्कार *pari-ṣkār* [S.], m. **1.** cleansing, purification. **2.** finishing; adorning, embellishing.

परिष्कृत *pari-ṣkṛt* [S.], adj. **1.** cleansed, purified. **2.** well-prepared, equipped. **3.** highly finished; refined (style, vocabulary); adorned, embellished.

परिष्कृति *pari-ṣkṛti* [S.], f. 1. = परिष्कार, 1. **2.** refinement (of style, &c).

परिसंख्या *pari-saṅ-khyā* [S.], f. full enumeration; reckoning.

परिसंख्यात *pari-saṅ-khyāt* [S.], adj. *Pl. HŚS.* counted up; enumerated.

परिसमापन *pari-sam-āpan* [S.], m. **1.** finishing completely. **2.** winding up (a firm's affairs); liquidating.

परिसमाप्त *pari-sam-āpt* [S.], adj. **1.** fully completed. **2.** wound up (affairs), liquidated.

परिसमाप्ति *pari-sam-āpti* [S.], f. **1.** full completion; conclusion. **2.** winding up (of affairs).

परिसर *pari-sar* [S.], m. **1.** proximity, neighbourhood; precinct. **2.** extent, dimension.

परिसरण *pari-saraṇ* [S.], m. *HŚS.* moving or going about.

परिसाधन *pari-sādhan* [S.], m. **1.** accomplishing, effecting. **2.** determining, ascertaining.

परिसीमन *pari-sīman* [S.], m. delimiting, demarcation.

परिसीमा *pari-sīmā* [S.], f. **1.** extreme limit. **2.** boundary; perimeter. **3.** fig. climax.

परिसीमित *pari-sīmit* [S.], adj. delimited, demarcated.

परिस्तान *paristān* [P. *parīstān*], m. fairyland.

परिस्थिति *pari-sthiti* [ad. *pariṣṭhiti-*; ? ← B., w. Engl. *circumstance*], f. circumstance, circumstances. — विशेष ~ में, adv. in a special case, or circumstances.

परिहर- *pari-har-* [*pariharati*], v.t. Brbh. Av. **1.** to abandon. **2.** to remove, to eliminate.

परिहरण *pari-haraṇ* [S.], m. = परिहार, 1.-4.

परिहार *pari-hār* [S.], m. **1.** repelling. **2.** seizing, holding. ***3.** removing, eliminating, annulling; avoidance (as of taxation). **4.** leaving, abandoning. **5.** booty, plunder. **6.** common pasture.

परिहारी *pari-hārī* [S.], adj. **1.** repelling. **2.** removing, eliminating.

परिहार्य *pari-hāryă* [S.], m. **1.** to be avoided, or removed; avoidable. **2.** esp. neg. liable to be defeated.

परिहास *pari-hās* [S.], m. (f.) **1.** laughter; banter. **2.** ridicule. — ~ करना, to joke, to banter.

परिहासक *pari-hāsak* [S.], adj. & m. **1.** adj. laughing at, joking. **2.** m. a joker, wit.

परिहास्य *pari-hāsyă* [S.], adj. laughable, ridiculous.

परिहीण *pari-hīṇ* [S.], adj. **1.** deprived (of), wanting (in). **2.** wasted, faded.

परी *parī* [P. *parī*], f. **1.** a fairy. **2.** fig. a beautiful woman. — ~ का साया, m. fairy's shadow: possession by an evil spirit. लाल ~, f. colloq. wine. – परीज़ाद, [P. *-zād*], adj. & m. fairy-born: beautiful; a fairy. परी-पैकर, adj. U. fairy-faced: beautiful. परीस्तान, m. fairyland.

परीक्षक *parîkṣak* [S.], m. **1.** investigator, &c. **2.** examiner.

परीक्षण *parîkṣaṇ* [S.], m. **1.** investigating, inspection. **2.** examination (of a witness). **3.** trial, test, experiment; probation.

परीक्षा *parîkṣā* [S.], f. **1.** inspection, investigation, examination. **2.** experiment; test, trial. ***3.** examination (of a student). **4.** trial by ordeal. — ~ करना (की), to test, to examine. ~ देना, to take an examination (as a candidate). ~ में उतरना, to pass a test; to survive an ordeal. ~ में उत्तीर्ण, or पास. होना, to pass an examination. ~ में बैठना, to sit an examination. ~ लेना, to examine (a candidate, से); to supervise an examination. परीक्षात्मक [°*ṣā* + *ā*°], adj. experimental. परीक्षार्थी [°*ṣā* + *a*°], m. candidate for examination.

परीक्षित *parîkṣit* [S.], adj. **1.** investigated, &c. **2.** examined. **3.** tried, proved.

परीक्ष्य *parîkṣyă* [S.], adj. to be investigated, &c.; worth examination.

परीवा *parīvā* [*pratipadā-*], f. reg. first day of the lunar fortnight.

परुष *paruṣ* [S.], adj. **1.** rough. **2.** keen (as wind). **3.** harsh; stern. **4.** coarse; abusive.

परे *pare* [pare], adv. **1.** beyond; further off, away. **2.** on the other side. **3.** beyond reach. **4.** afterwards; in the hereafter. **5.** ppn. (w. के, or से) beyond, on the far side (of); away (from). **6.** beyond the reach (of); beyond the capacity (of). **7.** apart (from). — ~ करना, to move (one) on, or away; to keep (one) away. ~ कहना, to tell (one) to move on, &c. ~ बैठाना, to keep (one) away; to outmanoeuvre. ~ भागना, to get out of the reach (of, से), to get away (from). ~ रहना, to stay far, or aloof (from, से); to abstain (from).

परेख- *parekh-* [*parekṣate*, or *parīkṣate* × H. *pekhnā*], v.t. Brbh. Av. to investigate, to examine.

परेखा *parekhā* , m. reg. = परेखो.

परेखो *parekho* [? conn. *prekṣā-*, f.], m. Brbh. **1.** faith. **2.** regret, remorse.

परेट *pareṭ*, m. = परेड.

परेड *pareḍ* [Engl. *parade*], f. m. **1.** a parade. **2.** parade-ground.

परेता *paretā* [*parivarta-*], m. a large reel, bobbin.

परेती *paretī* [cf. H. *paretā*], f. small reel or bobbin.

परेवा *parevā* [*pārāvata-*], m. a dove, pigeon.

परेशान *pareśān* [P. *pareśān*], m. **1.** disordered; dishevelled (as hair). *__2.__ troubled, distressed; worried; embarrassed; perplexed. — ~ करना, to cause trouble (to, को), to distress, &c.; to disarrange.

परेशानी *pareśānī* [P. *pareśānī*], f. **1.** disorder. *__2.__ trouble, distress; embarrassment; perplexity. — ~ में डालना, to cause trouble, &c. (to, को).

[1]**परेह** *pareh* [*praleha-*], m. reg. **1.** W. rice soup. **2.** Bihar. pea soup.

[2]**परेह** *pareh* [conn. *parivāha-*], m. reg. (W.) **1.** the irrigation of land; irrigation before ploughing. **2.** caking (in the sun) of sown soil after rain.

परेहा *parehā*, m. *Pl.* = [2]परेह.

परोक्ष *parokṣ* [S.], adj. & m. **1.** adj. not visible, not evident; hidden (as a meaning); implied. **2.** indirect (a process). **3.** absent. **4.** past (time); complete (an action). **5.** m. sthg. hidden; the occult.

[1]**परोता** *parotā* [**parapautra-*], m. great-grandson.

[2]**परोता** *parotā*, m. *Pl. HŚS.* **1.** a basket made of wheat straw. **2.** a present (as of flour, molasses, turmeric, betel) given at marriages to the barber, laundress, musician, &c.

परोसना *parosnā* [*pariveśati*], v.t. to serve food.

परोसा *parosā* [cf. H. *parosnā*], m. **1.** portion of food (esp. as served to a guest). **2.** dish of food (as sent to a neighbour or friend).

परोसिया *parosiyā* [cf. H. *parosnā*], m. one who serves food (waiter, or host).

परोसैया *parosaiyā*, m. reg. = परोसिया.

परोहन *parohan* [ad. *pravahaṇa-*: w. N. or Panj. *pohaṇ*], m. reg. **1.** W. a wheeled carriage, usu. covered. **2.** Bihar. an animal (as a donkey) to ride on.

परोहना *parohnā* [*parivahati*], v.i. to draw water with a leather bag; to irrigate.

परोहा *parohā* [*parivāha-*], m. large leather bag for drawing water in.

पर्जन्य *parjanyă* [S.], m. **1.** a rain-cloud. **2.** *mythol.* the god of rain, personified; Indra.

पर्ण *parṇ* [S.], m. **1.** wing, feather. *__2.__ a leaf. — पर्ण-कुटी, f. leaf-hut: arbour; hermitage. पर्ण-कुटीर, m. id. पर्ण-शाला, f. = पर्ण-कुटी.

पर्णी *parṇī* [S.], f. *Pl. HŚS.* **1.** a water plant, *Pistia stratiotes*. **2.** the *palāś* tree, *Butea frondosa*.

पर्पटी *parpaṭī* [S.], f. = गोपीचंदन.

पर्यंक *pary-aṅk* [S.], m. a bed.

पर्यंत *pary-ant* [S.], m. & ppn. **1.** m. boundary, limit. **2.** ppn. up to, until. मरण-पर्यंत, adv. until death.

पर्यटक *pary-aṭak* [S.], m. a wanderer; traveller; tourist.

पर्यटन *pary-aṭan* [S.], m. **1.** wandering about; travelling; touring. **2.** tourism.

पर्यवसान *pary-avă-sān* [S.], m. end, conclusion.

पर्यवसित *pary-avă-sit* [S.], adj. ended, terminated.

पर्यवेक्षक *pary-avêkṣak* [S.], m. monitor, supervisor (as of a truce); scrutineer.

पर्याप्त *pary-āpt* [S.], adj. obtained: enough, sufficient; considerable (amount).

पर्याय *pary-āy* [S.], m. **1.** recurrence, succession. **2.** regular order. *__3.__ an equivalent: a synonym. — पर्याय-क्रम, m. sequence, order. पर्यायवाचक, adj. = next. °-वाची, adj. synonymous.

पर्यायकी *paryāyăkī* [S.], f. synonymy.

पर्यावरण *pary-ā-varaṇ* [S.], m. the environment.

पर्व *parv* [S.], m. knot, joint: **1.** a particular period of the year (as equinox, solstice). **2.** a term (school, university). **3.** a recurring festival; holiday. **4.** part, section (of a book). **5.** a particular occasion, moment.

पर्वणिका *parvăṇikā* [S.], f. *Pl. HŚS.* a disease of the eye.

पर्वणी *parvaṇī* [S.], f. *Pl. HŚS.* partic. dates of the lunar month: **1.** the day of the full moon. **2.** the first day of the moon's waxing or waning.

पर्वत *parvat* [S.], m. a mountain; a hill. — पर्वत-माला, f. a mountain range. पर्वत-शृंखला, or °-श्रेणी, f. id. पर्वतारोहण [°*ta*+*ā*°], m. mountaineering. °रोही, m. mountaineer.

पर्वती *parvatī* [cf. H. *parvat*], adj. & m. **1.** adj. having to do with hills or mountains. **2.** hilly, &c. **3.** m. a hill-dweller.

पर्वतीय *parvatīyă* [S.], adj. = पर्वती.

पलंग *palaṅg* [*palyaṅka-*; ← NW], m. a bed. — ~ तीन चोर, m. reg. a bed and three thieves: the stars of the Great Bear. पलंग-तोड़, m. one who is fond of his bed; an aphrodisiac. पलंगपोश [P. *-poś*], m. coverlet.

पलंगड़ी *palaṅgṛī* [cf. H. *palaṅg*], f. small bed.

पल *pal* [*pala-*[1]], m. **1.** a partic. measure, esp. one of time: a moment, an instant. **2.** [× H. *palak*] the eyelid. — ~ के ~ में, adv. in (the space of) an instant. ~ ~, or ~ ~ में, or पर, at every moment. ~ भर (के लिए), adv. for just a moment. ~ भर में, adv. in (the space of) just a moment. ~ मारते, adv. in the twinkling of an eye. ~ मारना, to wink. एक ~ बाद, adv. a moment later. – पल-ओट, adv. for a twinkling of an eye: for an instant.

पलई *palaī* [*pallava-*[1]], f. reg. young branch, or shoots, of a tree.

पलक *palak* [P. *palak*], f. (m., poet.) **1.** the eyelid. **2.** an eyelash. **3.** the blinking of an eye: a moment, instant. — ~ झपकते, adv. in (the space of) a moment, in a trice. ~ पसीजना, tears to come to the eyes; to be moved. ~ पर लेना, to show all honour or love (to or for, को). ~ बिछना, the eyelids to be lowered (before one): all devotion to be felt (for one). ~ मार लेना, to take a nap. ~ मारना, to wink. ~ मारते, adv. = ~ झपकते. ~ लगना, the eyes to close; to doze, to sleep.

पलटन *palṭan* [Engl. *platoon*], f. **1.** a battalion, regiment. **2.** transf. troop, horde (as of children; or of insects).

पलटना *palaṭnā* [**pallaṭṭ-*: Pk. *pal(l)aṭṭaï*], v.i. & v.t. **1.** v.i. to turn over; to overturn. **2.** to turn back, to return; to retreat (from, से: as from an undertaking). **3.** to rebound; to ricochet (as a bullet). **4.** to be changed, transformed (a situation). दिन ~ (के), (one's) fortunes to change. **5.** v.t. to overturn, to capsize. **6.** to send back, to return (as goods); to transfer (a person). **7.** to change (one thing for another); to exchange, to barter (goods).

पलटनी *palṭanī* [cf. H. *palaṭnā*], f. turning over, or rolling.

पलटा *palṭā* [**pallaṭṭ-*: Pk. *pa(l)laṭṭaï*], m. **1.** turning over. **2.** turning back, return; retreat. **3.** change, transformation. **4.** return, retaliation. **5.** reg. a broad iron spoon having a long handle (used to turn cakes when cooking). **6.** reg. (W.) a type of bread or cake in which the dough is in three layers. — ~ खाना, to be turned upside down; to rebound; to be transformed (a situation); to suffer a reverse. ~ लेना, to exact retribution (from, से).

पलटाना *palṭānā* [cf. H. *palaṭnā*], v.t. **1.** to turn over. **2.** to turn back, to repel.

पलटाव *palṭāv* [cf. H. *palaṭnā*], m. **1.** return; rebound, reaction. **2.** exchange (as of goods).

पलड़ा *palṛā* [cf. H. [2]*pallā*, 3.], m. weighing-pan (of a scales).

पलड़ी *palṛī*, dimin. f. = पलड़ा.

पलथी *palthī*, f. = पालथी.

पलना *palnā* [cf. H. *pālnā*], v.i. **1.** to be reared, or brought up. **2.** to thrive; to grow fat, or sturdy. **3.** to become tender or soft (as ripening fruit).

पलम *palam*, m. reg. calumny, scandal. — ~ लगाना, to calumniate, &c.

पलल *palal* [S.], m. **1.** ground sesame. **2.** mud, clay.

पलवल *palval*, m. = परवल.

पलवाना *palvānā* [cf. H. [1]*pālnā*], v.t. to cause to be reared, or brought up (by, से).

पलवार *palvār* [cf. H. [2]*pāl*], m. *Pl. HŚS.* **1.** a large freight boat of clinker construction, with sails (= पटैला). **2.** Bihar. a small sailing boat, skiff.

पलवारी *palvārī* [cf. H. *palvār*], m. boatman; crewman of a *palvār*.

पलवैया *palvaiyā* [cf. *palnā*], m. rearer, fosterer.

पलस्तर *palastar* [Engl. *plaster*], m. **1.** plaster. **2.** stucco, roughcast. **3.** cement (floor.) — ~ ढीला करना, colloq. to give a sound beating (to, का). ~ लगाना, to apply plaster, &c. — पलस्तरकारी, f. plastering, stucco work.

पलहिंडी *palhiṇḍī*, f. = पलेहुंडी.

[1]**पला** *palā* [*pala-*[1]], m. **1.** a moment (= पल). **2.** a large ladle; Brbh. = पलड़ा.

[2]**पला** *palā* m. Brbh. Av. metr. = [2]पल्ला, 2., 3.

[1]**पला-** *palā-* [*palāyate*], v.i. reg. to flee; to escape.

[2]**पला-** *palā-* [**palāpayati*], v.t. Brbh. to put to flight.

[3]**पला-** *palā-* [cf. **prasnāvayati*], v.i. reg. to come down (milk, into the udder).

पलातक *palātak*, adj. fugitive; fleeting (as a light).

[1]**पलान** *palān* [*palyāṇa*: ← Ir.], m. a pack-saddle.

[2]**पलान** *palān* [*paryāṇa-*[1]], m. *Pl. hist.* space of ground left for future disposal between two occupied lots.

पलान- *palān-* [*palyāṇayati*], v.t. Brbh. Av. **1.** to saddle (a horse or bullock). **2.** fig. to prepare to attack.

पलाना *palānā* [cf. H. *palāv*], v.t. reg. to thatch.

पलानी *palānī* [cf. H. *palānā*], f. thatching.

पलायक *palāyak* [S.], m. **1.** a fugitive; deserter.

पलायन *palāyan* [S.], m. flight, escape; desertion. — पलायनवाद, m. escapism. °ई, adj. & m.

पलायमान *palāyămān* [S.], adj. fleeing, fugitive.

पलायित *palāyit* [S.], adj. fled, fugitive.

पलाल *palāl* [*palāla-*], m. straw.

पलाव *palāv* [*palāva-*], m. thatching.

पलाश *palāś* [S.], m. **1.** a leaf; foliage. ***2.** the *ḍhāk* tree, *Butea frondosa*. **3.** a species of *Curcuma* (= कचूर).

पलाशक *palāśak* [S.], m. = पलाश.

1**पलाशी** *pălāśī* [H. *palāś*], f. *Pl. HŚS.* lac.

2**पलाशी** *pălāśī* [S.], adj. & f. *Pl. HŚS.* **1.** adj. leafy. **2.** f. = पलाश.

पलित *palit* [S.], adj. & m. *Pl. HŚS.* **1.** adj. grey, grey-haired. **2.** m. greyness.

पली *palī* [*pala-*1], f. a ladle (for measuring oil, *ghī*, &c). — ~ ~ जोड़ना, to collect little by little.

1**पलीत** *palīt*, adj. = पलीद.

2**पलीत** *palīt*, m. reg. = प्रेत.

पलीता *palītā* [A. *fatīla*: P. *patīl(a)*, *palīta*], m. **1.** match (of a gun). **2.** fuse (to explosive). **3.** wick. **4.** a candle. **5.** roll of paper having *mantras*, &c. written on it (used as a wick, or smoked). – ~ चाट जाना, a match, &c. to catch alight, but no more: to make a flash in the pan. ~ लगाना, to touch off (a quarrel). – पलीतादानी, m. Brbh. ? match-holder.

पलीती *palītī* [cf. H. *palītā*], f. a small fuse, wick, &c.

पलीद *palīd* [P. *palīd*], adj. & m. **1.** adj. polluted, impure; foul. **2.** m. a foul or base person. — ~ करना, to pollute, to defile.

1**पलुआ** *paluā*, *Pl. HŚS.* a type of hemp, *Hibiscus cannabinus*.

2**पलुआ** *paluā* [cf. H. *palnā*], adj. & m. *Pl. HŚS.* **1.** adj. domesticated (an animal). **2.** m. one fostered, a protégé.

पलुह- *paluh-* [*pallavayati*], v.i. Av. to bud; to bloom.

पलुहा- *paluhā-* [cf. H. *paluh-*], v.i. & v.t. **1.** v.i. Av. to bud; to bloom. **2.** v.t. Brbh. to cause to bud, &c.

पलेथन *palethan* [*paryasta-*], m. **1.** flour spread under and over dough (to assist rolling). **2.** fig. an expense additional to what has been necessarily incurred. ~ निकालना (का), to beat to a pulp. ~ पकाना, to contrive or to hatch the ruin (of).

पलेना *palenā* [**plavayati*], v.t. reg. **1.** to irrigate land after ploughing. **2.** W. to irrigate land before ploughing.

1**पलेव** *palev* [*plāvita-*], adj. reg. **1.** land irrigated after ploughing. **2.** W. land irrigated before ploughing.

2**पलेव** *palev* [*praleha-*], m. *Pl. HŚS.* **1.** soup, broth. **2.** ground rice or flour (used as a thickening for soup).

पलेहंडी *palehṇḍī*, f. *Pl.* stand or shelf on which water-jars are placed; place where water is kept.

पलोट- *paloṭ-* [**pralortati*: Pk. *paloṭṭaï*, and *paloṭṭei*, v.t.], v.i. & v.t. Brbh. Av. **1.** v.i. to tread gently. **2.** to be restless (as in pain or grief). **3.** v.t. to massage (the feet).

पलोथन *palothan*, m. = पलेथन.

पल्लव *pallav* [S.], m. **1.** a shoot; spray of foliage; new foliage. **2.** a bud; flower. **3.** *HŚS.* a bracelet. — ~ लेना, to gain a superficial knowledge (of, का). – पल्लव-ग्राही, adj. seizing on straws, or trivialities; fastidious; superficial.

पल्लवक *pallăvak* [S.], m. *Pl. HŚS.* a species of fish, *Cyprinus denticulatus*.

पल्लवन *pallăvan* [S.], m. appearance of new shoots or foliage.

पल्लविक *pallăvik* [S.], adj. *HŚS.* licentious.

पल्लवित *pallăvit* [S.], adj. **1.** sprouting; in new leaf. **2.** in bud, young flower. **3.** flourishing, developing (see पुष्पित).

पल्लवी *pallăvī* [S.], adj. *Pl. HŚS.* sprouting, having young shoots.

1**पल्ला** *pallā* [*palya-*; × H. 2*pallā*], m. **1.** a sack for grain. **2.** a weight of three maunds; a burden. — ~ भारी होना, to be heavily laden; to have burdensome responsibilities; a scale to tip (in favour of); to prevail, to dominate (an argument). – पल्लेदार [P. *-dār*], m. a porter. °ई, f. the carrying of loads, a porter's work.

2**पल्ला** *pallā* [*palla-*3, *pallava-*2], m. **1.** sheet, shawl. **2.** side, border, edge (of a garment, &c). **3.** side; single part; the pan of a scales; single leaf (of a door, shutter); single blade (of shears, &c.); step of a ladder. — ~ करना, to draw the edge of the sari over (one's) face.

~ छुड़ाना, to shake off (the supervision or restraint of, का). ~ दबना, to be outweighed, to lose a dominant position. ~ पकड़ना (का), to cling or to turn to for support; to detain (one). ~ पसारना, or फैलाना, to spread the hem of (one's) garment (in entreaty before another: के आगे). ~ लेना, to condole (with, का). पल्ले पड़ना, to come into the keeping (of, के); to be married (to: used of a woman); to be familiar (as a word, a topic); to be understood (by). पल्ले पर, adv. at the side (of, के); enjoying the protection or help (of) (see also ³पल्ला). पल्ले बाँधना to tie to oneself: to marry; to cherish; to derive support or advantage from; to bear in mind, to take to heart; to assign, to entrust (to, के).

³**पल्ला** *pallā*, m. **1.** distance. **2.** reach, range (as of a voice, a gun). — पल्ले पर, adv. at a distance (see also ²पल्ला). — पल्लेदार [P. *-dār*], adj. carrying far (a voice); of long range (as a gun).

पल्ली *pallī* [S.], f. **1.** a small village, settlement. **2.** a house with other adjoining buildings. **3.** a house-lizard (= छिपकली).

पल्लू *pallū*, m. = ²पल्ला. — पल्लूदार [P. *-dār*], m. edged: a garment with a border of gold or silver lace.

पल्लेदार *palledār* [cf. H. ¹*pallā*], m. see s.v. ¹ ³पल्ला.

पल्लेदारी *palledārī* [cf. H. *palledār*], f. see s.v. ¹पल्ला.

पवन *pavăn* [S.], m. purifying, purifier: **1.** wind, air. **2.** winnowing. **3.** fig. the breath of life. **4.** reg. spell, charm. **5.** reg. evil spirits (called up by a magician). — ~ का भूसा, a straw in the wind: sthg. insubstantial. पवन-चक्की, f. windmill. पवन-तनय, m. = पवन-सुत. पवन-पूत, m. Brbh. = पवन-सुत. पवन-बान, m. an arrow which when shot makes the wind blow. पवन-सुत, m. Av. son of the wind: a title of Hanumān.

पवमान *pavămān* [S.], m. wind, air.

पवाई *pavāī*, f. *Pl. HŚS.* **1.** fetter, stocks. **2.** *HŚS.* millstone. **3.** an odd shoe or slipper.

पवाड़ा *pavāṛā*, m. = पँवाड़ा.

पवाना *pavānā* [cf. H. *ponā*], v.t. to cause to be baked (as bread: by, से).

पवि *pavi* [S.], m. poet. a thunderbolt.

पवित्र *pavitr* [S.], adj. **1.** pure (as the soul). **2.** holy, sacred. — ~ बनाना, to purify; to sanctify. पवित्रात्मा [°*ra*+*ā*°], m. inv. the holy spirit, supreme spirit. पवित्रीकरण, m. purification; sanctification.

पवित्रता *pavitrătā* [S.], f. purity; holiness; sanctity.

पवित्रताई *pavitrătāī* [cf. H. *pavitr*], f. = पवित्रता.

¹**पवित्रा** *pavitrā* [S.], f. *Pl. HŚS.* = तुलसी.

²**पवित्रा** *pavitrā* [ad. *pavitr̥-*], m. corr. *Pl. hind.* a purifying agent: **1.** sacred thread (= जनेऊ). **2.** a ring of *kuśa* grass.

पवित्री *pavitrī* [S.], f. *Pl. HŚS. hind.* a ring of *kuśa* grass, or (*Pl.*) of gold, silver or copper.

पवित्रीकरण *pavitrīkaraṇ* [S.], m. see s.v. पवित्र.

पवी *pavī* [*plava-*], f. *Pl.* channel (for letting water in or out).

पवेरा *paverā* [**pravapakara-*], m. reg. sowing seed by hand.

पव्वा *pavvā*, m. colloq. sthg. drunk, a quarter measure.

पशम *paśm* [P. *paśm*], m. **1.** wool. **2.** body hair. **3.** sthg. worthless. — ~ न उखड़ना, not a hair to be pulled out: to be quite unaffected (by another's criticism, or hostility).

पशमी *paśmī* [P. *paśmī*], adj. woollen.

पशमीना *paśmīnā* [P. *paśmīna*], m. woollen material; woollen shawl.

पशाना *paśānā*, v.i. reg. to smell very badly, to stink.

पशु *paśu* [S.], m. **1.** cattle. **2.** an animal (domesticated); a beast. **3.** pej. beast, brute. — पशु-चिकित्सक, m. veterinary surgeon. °-चिकित्सा, veterinary science. पशुजीवी, adj. pastoral. पशु-धन, m. livestock. पशु-धर्म, m. the characteristics of cattle, or of animals; animal behaviour. पशु-पति, m. lord of the animals: a title of Śiva. °नाथ, m. id. पशु-पलवल, m. a tuberous plant which grows at the edges of poools: *Cyperus rotundus* (= मोथ), or *Scirpus Kysoor*. पशु-पाल, m. a herdsman; cattle-breeder. °अक, adj. & m. having to do with the raising of animals; = prec. °अन, m. the tending, or rearing of cattle. पशुवत, adj. like an animal; irrational, brutal.

पशुता *paśutā* [S.], f. **1.** animal nature, brute nature. **2.** brutality; savagery.

पशुत्व *paśutvă* [S.], m. = पशुता.

पश्च *paścă* [S.], adj. hinder, rear, back; earlier; later; western. — ~ अंक, m. back number (of a publication). – पश्चगमन, m. a regression. पश्चार्ध [°*śca*+*a*°], m. rear part; later part.

पश्चात् *paścāt* [S.], adv. & ppn. **1.** afterwards. **2.** behind. **3.** ppn. (w. के) after. **4.** behind. — पश्चात्ताप, m. repentance, remorse. °ई, m.

one who repents, &c. पश्चाद्भावी, adj. arising later, subsequent. पश्चाद्वर्ती, adj. following, subsequent; derivative.

पश्चाद्वर्ती *paścādvartī* [S.], adj. see s.v. पशचात.

पश्चिम *paścim* [S.], adj. & m. **1.** adj. western. **2.** westerly. **3.** m. the west; specif. the western world. — पश्चिमांचल [°*ma*+*a*°], m. western region, district; the west. पश्चिमोत्तर [°*ma*+*u*°], adj. & m. north-west.

पश्चिमी *paścimī* [cf. H. *paścim*], adj. western.

पश्चिमीय *paścimīyă* [S.], adj. = पश्चिमी.

पश्तो *paśto* [P. *paśto*], m. the Pashtu language.

पश्म *paśm*, m. see पशम.

पषान *paṣān*, m. Brbh. Av. = पाषाण.

पसंगा *pasaṅgā*, m. reg. = पासंग.

पसंद *pasand* [P. *pasand*], adj. & f. **1.** adj. approved, liked. **2.** f. approval. **3.** choice; preference. — ~ आना, to be approved, liked (by, को); to please. ~ करना, to approve, to like; to choose, to prefer; to accept (a submission, &c). — अमनपसंद, adj. who approve(s) peace: peace-loving. दिलपसंद, adj. pleasing to the heart, or mind.

पसंदा *pasandā* [P. *pasanda*+H. *-ā*], m. chopped meat.

पसंदीदगी *pasandīdăgī* [P. *pasandīdagī*], f. agreeableness.

पसंदीदा *pasandīdā* [P. *pasandīda*], adj. inv. **1.** approved, liked; pleasing. **2.** chosen.

[1]**पस** *pas* [P. *pas*], adv. esp. in comp. **1.** after, behind. **2.** finally. — पसोपेश [P. *-o-peś*], m. behind and before: indecision, hesitation; prevarication.

[2]**पस** *pas* [*paśu-*], f. reg. a buffalo heifer.

[1]**पसर** *pasar* [*prasṛta-*; MIA **pasaṭa-*], m. **1.** the hollowed hand held out. **2.** a handful.

[2]**पसर** *pasar* [cf. H. *pasarnā*], m. f. grazing cattle at night (esp. on forbidden pasture). — ~ चराना, to graze cattle at night.

पसरना *pasarnā* [*prasarati*], v.i. **1.** to be spread out, stretched out. **2.** to stretch (oneself) out. **3.** to be set (on: as the heart).

पसला *paslā*, m. reg. a heavy shower of rain.

पसली *paslī* [**parśu-*[1]], f. rib. — ~ ढीली करना, colloq. to loosen the ribs (of, की); to thrash. ~ फड़कना, to feel a throbbing around the ribs (omen of a visit from an absent friend).

पसा *pasā* [*prasṛta-*], m. *Pl. HŚS.* as much as can be held in the cupped hands.

पसाई *pasāī* [*prasātikā-*], f. reg. (W.) a wild rice (that grows in ponds or tanks).

पसाउ *pasāu* [*prasāda-*], m. Av. = प्रसाद.

पसाना *pasānā* [**prasrāvayati*], v.t. **1.** to pour off cooking-water (from rice, &c). **2.** to skim.

पसार *pasār* [*prasāra-*], m. **1.** spreading, stretching out. **2.** expansion, extension; extent.

पसारना *pasārnā* [*prasārayati*], v.t. **1.** to spread out, to stretch out. **2.** to expand, to extend. — पाँव ~, to stretch out the legs; colloq. to die. हाथ ~, to stretch out the hand (as in begging).

पसारा *pasārā* m. reg. = पसार. — ~ करना, = पसारना.

पसावन *pasāvan* [cf. H. *pasānā*], m. cooking-water (of rice).

पसीज *pasīj* [P. *pasīj*], m. *Pl.* **1.** provision or preparation for a journey.

पसीजना *pasījnā* [**prasvidyati*], v.i. **1.** to sweat. **2.** transf. to exude. **3.** to melt, to dissolve. **4.** to feel sorrow or pity (for); to melt (the heart); to be damp (the eyes). **5.** to simmer.

पसीना *pasīnā* [**prasvidana-*, or *prasvinna-*], m. sweat. — ~ आना (को), to sweat; fig. to feel shame. ~ निकलना, to sweat. पसीने का काम, m. hard physical work. पसीने पसीने होना, to be covered in sweat; to feel utter shame; to be alarmed.

पसूज *pasūj* [cf. H. *pasūjnā*], f. **1.** basting (a garment). **2.** running stitch.

पसूजना *pasūjnā* [**prasyūyati*], v.t. to sew with a running stitch; to baste.

पसेउ *paseu* [*prasveda-*], m. reg. **1.** exudation. **2.** Av. sweat (= पसीना). **3.** effervescence. **4.** portion of food taken out of the pot to see if it is cooked.

पसेरी *paserī* [cf. H. *pāṁc*, H. [1]*ser*], f. a measure, or weight, of five seers.

पस्त *past* [P. *past*], adj. **1.** low, inferior; humble. **2.** base. **3.** weary; without spirit or energy. — ~ करना, to humiliate; to defeat. – पस्तक़द, m. a dwarf. पस्तहिम्मत, adj. discouraged, demoralised; faint-hearted; unambitious. °ई, f.

पस्ती *pastī* [P. *pastī*], f. weariness, lack of spirit or energy.

पहचान *pahcān* [cf. H. *pahcānnā*], f. **1.** recognition. **2.** distinction, discrimination (of or between, की); judgment. **3.** distinguishing mark or feature(s); characteristic; sign, token (of sthg.); identity. **4.** acquaintance (with, की: as with a person, or with a topic). — ~ करना (की), to recognise, to identify. वह मेरी ~ का है, I am acquainted with him.

पहचानना *pahcānnā* [*pratyabhijānāti*], v.t. **1.** to recognise; to identify. **2.** to perceive; to understand. **3.** to distinguish, to discriminate. **4.** to be acquainted (with a person, को); to know (one) well.

पहनना *pahannā* [**pinahati*], v.t. to put on (clothes); to wear. — उसने साड़ी पहन रखी है, she is wearing, has on, a sari. उसने साड़ी पहनी हुई है (N. and Panj.-infld. usage), id. वह साड़ी पहने हुए है, she is wearing a sari.

पहनवाना *pahanvānā* [cf. H. *pahannā*], v.t. to cause to be put on, or worn (by, से).

पहनाई *pahnāī* [cf. H. *pahnānā*], f. **1.** dress, clothing. **2.** payment for dressing, robing, &c.

पहनाना *pahnānā* [**pināhayati*; or cf. H. *pahannā*, *pahrānā*], v.t. **1.** to cause to put on; to clothe in (garments). उसे नए कपड़े पहना दिए गए, he was given new clothes to wear. **2.** colloq. to belabour with (blows), to beat.

पहनावन *pahnāvan*, m. *Pl.* = पहरावन.

पहनावा *pahnāvā* [cf. H. *pahannā*], m. **1.** clothing, dress. **2.** a garment. **3.** any partic. uniform or attire. — फ़ौजी ~, military uniform.

पहर *pahr* [*prahara-*], m. a watch of the day, a three hours' period. — ~ रात को, adv. आठों ~, adv. the entire twenty-four hours of a day.

पहरना *paharnā* [*paridadhāti*], v.t. = पहनना.

पहरा *pahrā* [*prahara-*: ? ← P. *pahra*], m. **1.** a turn of watch. **2.** a watch, guard. — ~ देना, to keep watch (over, का or पर); to mount guard. ~ बदलना, to change the watch or guard; a guard, &c. to be changed. ~ बैठाना, or लगाना, to place a guard (over or at, पर). पहरे में डालना, or बैठाना, to place under guard; to place in custody. पहरे में पड़ना, to be taken into custody. पहरे में रखना, to keep in custody. – पहरेदार [P. *-dār*], m. a watchman, guard; sentinel. °ई, f. watch, guard.

पहराना *pahrānā* [*paridhāpayati*], v.t. = पहनाना.

पहरावन *pahrāvan* [cf. H. *pahrānā*], m. reg. dress, attire.

पहरावनी *pahrāvnī* [cf. H. *pahrāvan*], f. **1.** Brbh. garments presented as a ceremonial gift. **2.** *Pl.* a woman who attires the guests at a wedding.

पहरावा *pahrāvā*, m. = पहनावा.

पहरिया *pahriyā* [cf. H. *pahrā*], m. a watchman (= पहरेदार).

पहरू *pahrū*, m. reg. a watchman (= पहरेदार).

[1]**पहल** *pahl*, m. side (of an object); facet. — पहलदार [P. *-dār*], adj. having sides or facets.

[2]**पहल** *pahl* [**prathilla-*: Pk. *pahill-*], m. beginning; initiative; aggressive action. — ~ करना, to start, to be responsible (for, में: as for ill-will in a matter). – पहलक़दमी, f. enterprise, initiative.

[3]**पहल** *pahl*, m. flock, piece (of cotton).

पहलवान *pahlvān* [P. *pahlvān*], m. **1.** a wrestler, athlete. **2.** a sturdily built man.

पहलवानी *pahlvānī* [P. *pahlvānī*], f. **1.** calling of a wrestler. **2.** athletic exercise. **3.** transf. bold demeanour.

पहलवी *pahlavī* [P. *pahlavī*], f. the Pahlavi language.

पहला *pahlā* [**prathilla-*: Pk. *pahill-*], adj. & adv. **1.** adj. first; former, previous; original, primary. **2.** leading, principal. **3.** adv. before; previously, earlier; already; at first. **4.** chiefly; rather (than, से). **5.** ppn. (w. के or से) before; previously; earlier (than); ahead (of). — पहले से, adv. from the first, from the beginning; at first, in the first place; previously; already. उसके पहले, adv. before that; before him, or her. उससे पहले, adv. id., 1. – पहले-पहल, adv. = पहले; at first, in the first place.

पहलू *pahlū* [P. *pahlū*], m. **1.** side (of the body, or of an object); flank; facet. **2.** flank, wing (as of an army). **3.** fig. side (of a question); aspect. **4.** vicinity. **5.** an indirect or hidden profit or advantage. — ~ गरम करना, colloq. to sit close (to a loved person, का). ~ पर होना, to be at, or on, the side (of, के), to have come to the assistance (of). ~ बचाना, to keep (oneself) clear of, to avoid (difficulties, entanglements). ~ बसाना (का), to settle near. ~ में रहना (के), to live near. – पहलूदार [P. *-dār*], adj. having sides, facets or aspects.

पहलौटा *pahlauṭā*, adj. & m. = पहलौठा.

पहलौठा *pahlauṭhā*, adj. & m. **1.** adj. first-born. **2.** m. first-born (son).

पहलौठी *pahlauṭhī*, f. **1.** a woman's first delivery of a child. **2.** first-born (daughter). — ~ का बच्चा, m. first-born child.

पहलौठेपन *pahlauṭhepan* [cf. H. *pahlauṭhā*], m. *Pl.* ? primogeniture.

पहाड़ *pahāṛ* [**pāhāḍa-*], m. **1.** mountain, hill. **2.** rock. **3.** fig. anything huge or overwhelming; sthg. burdensome or daunting; a very difficult problem. — ~ उठना, a weight to be lifted (from the mind). ~ होना, to be burdensome (a task, &c.: to, को). – पहाड़-सा, adj. mountain-like: burdensome, wearisome.

पहाड़ा *pahāṛā*, m. a multiplication table.

[1]**पहाड़ी** *pahāṛī* [cf. H. *pahāṛ*], adj. & m. **1.** adj. of or belonging to the hills; hill-dwelling; alpine (as climate, produce). **2.** hilly, mountainous. **3.** m. a hill-dweller.

[2]**पहाड़ी** *pahāṛī* [cf. H. *pahāṛ*], f. **1.** a low hill. **2.** hillock; mound.

पहिचान *pahicān*, f. = पहचान.

पहिचानना *pahicanna*, v.t. = पहचानना.

पहिनना *pahinnā*, v.t. = पहनना.

पहिया *pahiyā* [*pradhi-*], m. wheel.

पहिला *pahilā*, adj. = पहला.

पहुँच *pahuṁc* [cf. H. *pahuṁcnā*], f. **1.** arrival; acknowledgment (of arrival: of a letter, goods). **2.** access (to, के पास, तक). **3.** reach, scope (of intelligence or knowledge); capacity; capability. **4.** scope (of a work, &c).

पहुँचना *pahuṁcnā* [cf. *prabhūta-*, and the MIA alternation *mutta-: muṁcaï*], v.i. **1.** to arrive, to reach; to reach (as far as, तक, में, पर, को). दिल्ली ~, to reach Delhi. **2.** to make (one's) way (into, में, के अंदेर); to penetrate (into); to have access (to, के पास). **3.** to arrive at an understanding (of, तक), to fathom; to be well versed (in, में). **4.** to be obtained, had, felt (by, को). उन्हें इससे कोई लाभ नहीं पहुँचा, they had no benefit of this. **5.** to compare (with, को, के बराबर).

पहुँचवाना *pahuṁcvānā* [cf. H. *pahuṁcnā*], v.t. to cause to be delivered, or accompanied (= पहुँचाना).

पहुँचा *pahuṁcā* [**pahuñca-*], m. forearm; wrist. — ~ पकड़ना, to seize by the arm: to detain forcibly; colloq. to force (into an action).

पहुँचाई *pahuṁcāī* [cf. H. *pahuṁcnā*], f. cost of, or sum paid for, delivering or supplying.

पहुँचाना *pahuṁcānā* [cf. H. *pahuṁcnā*], v.t. **1.** to cause to arrive, or to reach; to convey (to a place); to forward, to deliver. **2.** to escort, to accompany; to see off (as at a station). **3.** to cause, to occasion (grief, loss, &c.: to, को); to inflict (on).

पहुँची *pahuṁcī* [cf. H. *pahuṁcā*], f. a wrist ornament; bracelet.

पहुनाई *pahunāī* [cf. H. *pāhun*], f. reception (of guests or visitors); hospitality. — ~ करना, to act hospitably (to, की), to receive as host.

पहेली *pahelī* [*prahelikā-*], f. **1.** a riddle; puzzle. **2.** a mystery; enigma.

पाँक *pāṁk* [*paṅka-*], m. reg. mud.

पाँखुड़ *pāṁkhuṛ* [cf. *pakṣa-*], m. reg. (Bihar) the upper arm.

पाँग *pāṁg* [? *prāṅga-*], m. *Pl.* weaver's woof-frame.

पाँगा *pāṁgā*, ? m. reg. salt obtained from sea sand. — ~ नोन, m. id.

पाँगुराना *pāṁgurānā*, v.i. = पगुराना.

पाँच *pāṁc* [*pañca-*], adj. & m. **1.** adj. five. **2.** fig. a few. **3.** colloq. shrewd (see 4). **4.** m. the five wise men, elders (of a community, or council). **5.** E.H. the five senses. — पाँच-सात, adj. half a dozen. पाँच-सात करना to quarrel. पाँच-सात में पड़ना, to be at sixes and sevens, to fall into confusion. पाँचों उँगलियाँ घी में होना, fig. (one) to flourish, everything to go swimmingly (for, की).

पाँचवाँ *pāṁcvāṁ* [*pañcama-*], adj. fifth. — ~ सवार होना, or बनना, to be the fifth horseman: to claim association with an established or dominant group, to tag along. – पाँचवें, adv. fifthly.

पाँचा *pāṁcā* [*pañcaka-*], m. reg. a five-pronged rake.

पांचाल *pāñcāl* [S.], adj. & m. **1.** adj. *hist.* having to do with the Pāñcālas. **2.** a Pāñcāla king or prince. **3.** a craft association of five guilds: the carpenters, weavers, barbers, washermen and potters.

पांचाली *pāñcālī* [S.], f. name of an ornate poetical style making use of long compound words.

पाँजना *pāṁjnā* [**prāñjati*], v.t. **1.** to solder. **2.** to fill in (a hole, esp. in metal).

पाँजर *pāṁjar* [*pañjara-*], m. **1.** the ribs, the side. **2.** colloq. vicinity.

पाँड़ *pāṁṛ* [*paṇḍa-*], f. reg. a woman who has no breasts, or no milk.

पांडर *pāṇḍar* [S.], adj. & m. **1.** adj. whitish, yellowish. **2.** m. whitish or pale colour. **3.** Brbh. a jasmine, *Jasminum elongatum*.

पाँडरा *pāṁḍrā* [*pāṇḍara-*], m. reg. **1.** W. land left fallow for sugar-cane. **2.** *Pl. HŚS.* a species of sugar-cane.

पाँडरी *pāṁḍrī* [*pāṇḍara-*], f. reg. **1.** *Pl.* whitish, chalky soil. **2.** W. = पाँडरा, 1.

पांडव *pāṇḍav* [S.], adj. & m. *hist. mythol.* **1.** adj. having to do with the Pāṇḍavas. **2.** m. a descendant (esp. one of the five sons) of Pāṇḍu.

पाँडवा *pāṁḍvā* [cf. *pāṇḍu-*: ? ← Austro-as.], m. reg. whitish, chalky soil.

पांडित्य *pāṇḍityă* [S.], m. learning, erudition. — पांडित्यपूर्ण, adj. erudite.

पांडु *pāṇḍu* [S.], adj. **1.** adj. yellowish-white; pale. **2.** m. yellowish or pale colour. **3.** light-coloured soil; a mixture of clay and sand. **4.** jaundice. — पांडु-लिपि, f. a manuscript; a hand-written draft. पांडु-लेख, m. id. पांडु-वर्ण, adj. = ~.

पांडुर *pāṇḍur* [S.], adj. & m. **1.** adj. yellowish-white. **2.** m. jaundice. **3.** white leprosy. **4.** chalk.

पाँड़े *pāṁṛe* [*paṇḍita-*], m. **1.** a sub-community of brāhmaṇs (= पांडेय). **2.** a member of the Pāṇḍey sub-community. 3. = पंडित.

पांडेय *pāṇḍey* [*paṇḍita-*], m. = पाँड़े, 1., 2.

पाँत *pāṁt* [*paṅkti-*], f. **1.** line, row; rank. **2.** *mil.* line, position (of troops, armies). **3.** *hind.* commensal group; sitting (of a meal). — ~ बनाना (की), to place in a row, line.

पाँतर *pāṁtar* [*prāntara-*], m. **1.** desert field or place. **2.** dangerous place.

पाँति *pāṁti*, f. Brbh. Av. = पाँत.

पांथ *pānth* [S.], m. traveller. — पांथशाला, m. = धर्मशाला.

पाँव *pāṁv* [*pāda-*], m. **1.** foot. **2.** leg. **3.** transf. footing, base. — ~ अड़ाना, to interfere or to meddle (in a matter). ~ उखड़ना, to lose one's footing; to take to flight. ~ उखाड़ना, to dislodge (from a position, or (fig.) a stance). ~ उठाना, to set out; to step out, to hasten. ~ उतरना, the ankle to be dislocated. ~ कट जाना, fig. not to go about, or to visit; to have no means of support; to leave this world, to die. ~ क़ब्र में, or (U.) गोर में, लटकाना, to have one foot in the grave. ~ का अँगूठा, m. the big toe. ~ की उँगली, f. a toe. ~ के भार बैठना, to squat. ~ खींचना, to withdraw (from a place, से); to give up (a bad habit). ~ घिसना, the feet to be worn: to go to and fro incessantly and to little avail. ~ छूटना, to menstruate; to have a flooding during menstruation; a woman's (के or का) menstrual period to continue a long time. ~ जमना, or ठहरना, to stand firmly; to keep a foothold. ~ ज़मीन पर न ठहरना, = ज़मीन पर ~ न रखना. ~ डालना, to set foot (on, पर or में); to enter (into); to begin. ~ तोड़ना, to wear out the legs in vain; to be exhausted. ~ तोड़कर बैठना, not to move (from a locality), to be always present. ~ धरना, to set foot (on, पर); to enter (into, में); to prepare (for), to begin (an understanding). ~ धो-धोकर पीना, to show exaggerated reverence or respect (for, के). ~ न होना, fig. to be terrified. ~ निकालना, to exceed one's proper limits; to get up to no good; to show one's true colours; to withdraw (from, से). ~ पकड़ना, to seize the feet (of, के); to beseech (one); to prevent (one) from going; to curl up (to sleep). ~ पड़ना, to fall at the feet (of, के), to entreat. ~ पर ~ रखना, to follow in the footsteps (of, के); to imitate; to sit cross-legged. ~ पर ~ रखकर बैठना, or सोना, to be idle; to be indifferent. ~ पसारना, to stretch out comfortably; to be relaxed, contented; euph. to die. ~ ~ adv. on foot. ~ ~ चलना, = next; to go on foot. ~ ~ फिरना, or डोलना, to toddle. ~ पीटना, to stamp the feet (in vexation or anger); to thresh the legs about (in pain, or at death); to struggle vainly against difficulties. ~ फटना, fig. to have chilblains. ~ पूजना, to worship (one's, के) feet; specif. to pay respect to a bridegroom (the bride's family). ~ फूँक-फूँककर रखना, to tread softly, or warily. ~ फूलना, the feet to swell; to be weary; to be at a loss (in embarrassment or puzzlement); to be paralysed (from fear). ~ फैलाना, = ~ पसारना, 1., 2.; to covet, to encroach (upon, पर); to be obstinate, or wayward (as a child). ~ फेरना, to turn the footsteps: (a woman) to visit her parents' house after marriage, or (esp.) childbirth. ~ बढ़ाना, to go ahead, to lengthen one's stride, to overstep bounds. ~ बीच में होना, to have a finger (in), to have a share (in); to be responsible (for). ~ भर जाना, the legs or feet to grow weary, or numb. ~ भारी होना, to be pregnant. ~ में चक्कर होना, to be always on the move. ~ में मेहंदी लगाना, to apply henna to the feet: to be reluctant to go anywhere, or to do anything. ~ रखना = ~ धरना. ~ रगड़ना, to rub the feet: = ~ घिसना. ~ लगना = ~ पड़ना. ~ समेटना, to withdraw (from, से), to give up. ~ से ~ बाँधना, to keep close (to one), not to let (another) out of one's sight. ~ से ~ भिड़ाना, to be close (to), to be cheek and jowl (with). ~ सो जाना, the foot to go to sleep. अपने ~ में कुल्हाड़ी मारना, fig. to injure or to ruin oneself, to cut one's own throat. एक ~ पर हाज़िर होना, to be ready on one foot: to be ready and eager. ज़मीन पर ~ न रखना, or पड़ना, to give oneself airs; to be beside oneself with delight. फटे में ~ देना, to stand in the breach; to risk one's life for another. – पाँव-चप्पी [cf. H. *cāṁpnā*], f. rubbing or pressing the feet. पाँव-तले, adv. underfoot. पाँव-प्यादा [P.-*pyāda*], adv. on foot.

पाँवड़ा *pāṁvṛā* [**pādapaṭa-*], m. cloth or carpet (as spread to receive a guest).

पाँवड़ी *pāṁvṛī* [**pādapaṭa-*], f. **1.** wooden shoes (= खड़ाऊँ). **2.** sandals.

पांशु *pāṃśu* [S.], f. m. = पाँस.

पांशुल *pāṃśul* [S.], adj. & m. *Pl. HŚS.* **1.** adj. dusty. **2.** fig. disgraced. **3.** m. a wicked or base man.

पाँस *pāṁs* [*pāṁśu-*; × (?) *pāṣi-*], f. m. **1.** dust; speck of dust. **2.** dung, manure.

3. sand. **4.** fermentation. — ~ डालना (में), to manure.

पाँसना *pāṁsnā* [cf. H. *pāṁs*], v.t. to manure.

पाँसा *pāṁsā*, m. 1. = पासा. 2. = पाँस. — ~ फेंकना, fig. to cover (one's) tracks.

पाँसी *pāṁsī* [*pāśa-*], f. a net.

पाँसुरी *pāṁsurī* [cf. *parśu-*], f. Brbh. rib; ribs, the side.

-पा *-pā* [cf. *-tva-*], m. suffix (forms m. nouns from nominal stems, e.g. बुढ़ापा, old age).

पा- *pā-* [P. *pā*], m. foot, leg: — पाख़ाना, m. lavatory; transf. faeces. पाख़ाना आना, or लगना (को), to need to defecate: पाखाना फिरना, to go to defecate. पाजामा [P. *-jāma*], loose cotton trousers; colloq. a fool. पाजामे से बाहर हो जाना, colloq. to get beside oneself in rage. पाज़ेब [P. *-zeb*], f. m. ornament for the feet or ankles (a chain with small bells). पापोश [P. *-poś*], m. cloth used for wiping the feet. पाबंद [P. *-band*], adj. & m. tied by, or a tie for, the foot or leg: restrained; encumbered (as with a family); dependent; a servant; a hobble. °ई, f. restriction; due observance, dependence; custom, rule; prohibition (on, पर). पाबंदी से, adv. customarily, regularly; lawfully, according to rule. पामाल [P. *-māl*], adj. trodden underfoot; destroyed. °ई, f.

पाईं *pāīṁ* [P. *pā'īn*], adj. lower, back: — ~ बाग़, m. garden at rear (of a palace, or house).

¹पाई *pāī* [*pādikā-*], f. **1.** a quarter part. **2.** a vertical line: sign representing a quarter of a number or sum (as in writing prices, accounts); or marking off a quarter of a verse; or marking the end of a sentence. **3.** a third of a *paisā*.

²पाई *pāī*, f. **1.** *Pl.* reg. (W.) canes on which thread is stretched before weaving. **2.** (Bihar) woof. **3.** reg. a light cane, switch. — ~ करना, to brush and clean the warp after it has been stretched for weaving.

¹पाक *pāk* [S.], m. **1.** cooking or preparing food. **2.** sthg. cooked. **3.** a medicine. **4.** digestion. — पाक-विज्ञान, m. the science or practical skill of cookery. पाकशाला, f. kitchen. पाक-शास्त्र, m. = पाक-विज्ञान.

²पाक *pāk* [P. *pāk*], adj. **1.** pure. **2.** clear, clean. — ~ करना, to purify (of, से); to clean; to clarify (*ghī*), to strain; to winnow; to wash; to settle (a difficult or unpleasant matter). – पाक-दामन, adj. pure, virtuous; innocent. पाक-साफ़, adj. pure, clean, undefiled.

पाक- *pāk-*, v.i. & v.t. **1.** v.i. Av. = पकना. **2.** v.t. reg. to boil in syrup (cf. पागना).

पाकड़ *pākaṛ* [*parkaṭī-*], m. a type of fig-tree, *Ficus infectoria.*

पाकी *pākī* [P. *pākī*], f. **1.** purity. **2.** euph. the genitals.

पाकीज़गी *pākīzăgī* [P. *pākīzagī*], f. **1.** purity; chasitity. **2.** cleanliness; neatness.

पाकीज़ा *pākīzā* [P. *pākīza*], adj. **1.** pure; chaste. **2.** delicate; lovely, pretty.

पाक्य *pākyă* [S.], adj. & m. **1.** adj. digestible. **2.** m. a medicinal salt, black salt.

पाक्ष *pākṣ* [S.], adj. belonging to a side or party.

पाक्षपातिक *pākṣăpātik* [S.], adj. biased, partial.

पाक्षिक *pākṣik* [S.], adj. **1.** fortnightly (an occurrence, a publication). **2.** taking one side: partial, biased.

पाखंड *pākhaṇḍ* [ad. *pāṣaṇḍa-*], m. **1.** dissimulation (esp. in religious matters); hypocrisy. **2.** heresy. **3.** trans. villainy. — ~ करना, or फैलाना, to act deceitfully, or hypocritically.

पाखंडी *pākhaṇḍī* [ad. *pāṣaṇḍin-*], adj. & m. **1.** adj. dissembling; hypocritical. **2.** heretical. **3.** m. an impostor; hypocrite. **4.** a heretic.

पाख *pākh* [*pakṣa-*], m. **1.** the bright or the dark half of a lunar month; a fortnight. **2.** m. f. wing. **3.** *Pl.* gable. **4.** bias. ~ निकालना, to find fault gratuitously (in, में).

पाखर *pākhar* [*prakṣara-*, Pa. *pakkhara-*], m. **1.** armour for a horse, or elephant. **2.** trans. tarpaulin or treated canvas covering.

पाखा *pākhā* [*pakṣaka-*], m. side: **1.** Brbh. region. **2.** reg. side-wall; built-on shed.

पाखी *pākhī* [*pakṣin-*], m. reg. a bird.

¹पाग *pāg* [cf. H. *pāgnā*], m. **1.** syrup, a syrup. **2.** fruit cooked in syrup.

²पाग *pāg*, m. **1.** reg. = पगड़ी. **2.** *hist.* a poll-tax levied in the Delhi region.

पागन *pāgan* [conn. *prāṅgana-*], m. *Pl.* a kind of drum.

पागना *pāgnā*, v.t. **1.** to dip in, or to cover with, syrup. **2.** Brbh. fig. to be engrossed (in love).

पागल *pāgal* [*paggala-], adj. & m. **1.** adj. insane, mad. **2.** crazed; rabid (a dog). **3.** foolish. **4.** m. a madman. **5.** a fool. — पागल-ख़ाना, m. a hospital for the insane.

पागलपन *pāgalpan* [cf. H. *pāgal*], m. **1.** insanity. **2.** folly. **3.** frenzy.

पागलपना *pāgalpanā*, m. = पागलपन.

पागुर *pāgur* [**pragura-*: w. MIA *-gg-*], m. chewing the cud.

पागुराना *pāgurānā* [**pragurati*: w. MIA *-gg-*], v.i. to chew the cud.

पाच- *pāc-* [*pacyate*], v.t. Brbh. to cook, or to heat.

पाचक *pācak* [S.], adj. & m. **1.** adj. digestive. **2.** m. a digestive; bile. **3.** a cook.

पाचन *pācan* [S.], m. **1.** digestion. **2.** a digestive, tonic. **3.** appropriate medicine (for a complaint). **4.** assimilation (as of new trends, words).

पाचनीय *pācănīyă* [S.], adj. digestible.

पाच्य *pācyă* [S.], adj. **1.** digestible. **2.** able to be cooked.

[1]**पाछ** *pāch* [cf. H. *pāch-*], m. reg. (W.) **1.** a cut. **2.** incision made in poppy heads to allow the juice to run out.

[2]**पाछ** *pāch* [**paśca-*; Pk. *paccha-*], m. kicking, or a (horse's) kick with the hind legs.

पाछ- *pāch-* [*pracchyati*], v.t. Av. to cut, to puncture.

पाछिल *pāchil* [cf. **paśca-*: Pk. *paccha-*], adj. Brbh. Av. = पिछला.

पाछें *pāchem̐* [**paśca-*: Pk. *paccha-*], adv. Brbh. Av. = पीछे.

पाजामा *pājāmā*, m. see s.v. पा-.

पाजी *pājī* [cf. *padya-*], adj. & m. **1.** adj. base. **2.** worthless. **3.** m. a scoundrel. **4.** Av. foot-soldier; guard.

पाजीपन *pājīpan* [S.], m. baseness, villainy.

पाजीपना *pājīpanā* [cf. H. *pājī*], m. = पाजीपन.

[1]**पाट** *pāṭ* [*paṭṭa-*[1]], m. a flat surface or object: **1.** slab, board, plank; leaf (of door); ledge; reg. wedge. **2.** flat stone (as a millstone, or washing surface). **3.** bed, plot (for cultivation); terrace. **4.** (in a sugar- or oil-mill) beam; driver's seat or position. **5.** throne; seat. **6.** (Bihar) cylindrical section of earthenware (as used in building a well). — पाट-रानी, f. = पट-रानी, s.v. [4]पट.

[2]**पाट** *pāṭ* [*paṭṭa-*[2]], m. **1.** cloth; surface or piece of cloth. **2.** silk cloth; [← B. *pāṭ*] reg. jute. **3.** turban.

[1]**पाटन** *pāṭan* [cf. H. *pāṭnā*], f. **1.** filling in (as a ditch). **2.** planking over; roofing. **3.** (also m.) a roof.

[2]**पाटन** *pāṭan* [*paṭṭana-*], m. *Pl.* a city, town.

पाटना *pāṭnā* [**paṭyati*; and cf. *paṭṭa-*[1]], v.t. **1.** to fill in, to fill up (a well, ditch, &c). **2.** to plank over; to board (a floor); to roof. **3.** to glut (a market). **4.** to settle (a debt, a purchase; a feud). **5.** to overstock, to amass (goods).

पाटल *pāṭal* [S.], adj. & m. Brbh. **1.** adj. pink, reddish. **2.** m. the trumpet flower, *Bignonia suaevolens*. **3.** a rose.

पाटव *pāṭav* [S.], m. cleverness; skill; cunning.

पाटविक *pāṭăvik* [S.], adj. *Pl. HŚS.* clever; cunning.

पाटा *pāṭā* [*paṭṭa-*[1]], m. = [1]पाट, 1., 2., 5. ~ फेरना, to change seats: *hind.* a ritual performed by bride and groom during the marriage ceremony.

[1]**पाटी** *pāṭī* [*paṭṭa-*[1 2]], f. **1.** childrens' writing-board; transf. the rudiments of education. **2.** side-pieces of a bedstead. **3.** parting of the hair. **4.** a kind of mat. — ~ पढ़ना, to receive elementary education. ~ पारना, or बैठाना, to part the hair; to comb the hair. ~ पूजना, to worship ceremonially the writing-board (of a child beginning school).

[2]**पाटी** *pāṭī* [S.], f. E.H. = परिपाटी.

पाटौनी *pāṭaunī* [*paṭṭana-*], m. reg. ferryman.

पाठ *pāṭh* [S.], m. **1.** reading; study (esp. of a sacred text). **2.** recitation (of a sacred text). **3.** text, version; textual reading (as in a manuscript). **4.** lesson; lecture. — ~ करना, or पढ़ना, to read, to study; to go over a lesson aloud; to recite. ~ पढ़ाना (को), euph. to teach a text (to, को): to corrupt; to deceive. ~ फेरना, to repeat the same (old) story. उलटा ~ पढ़ाना, to explain incorrectly, to mislead. – पाठशाला, m. a school (esp. a primary school); a Sanskrit school. पाठांतर [°*ṭha+a*°], m. textual variant.

पाठक *pāṭhak* [S.], m. **1.** a reader. **2.** a teacher. **3.** a brāhmaṇ who recites sacred texts in public. **4.** a custodian of Hindu law or custom. **5.** name of a brāhmaṇ sub-community. **6.** a member of the Pāṭhak community.

पाठन *pāṭhan* [S.], m. **1.** reading (esp. aloud). **2.** teaching.

पाठशालीय *pāṭhśālīyă* [S.], adj. having to do with a school.

पाठा *pāṭhā* [**paṣṭha-*], m. **1.** a young, full-grown animal. **2.** a sturdy young man.

पाठान *pāṭhān*, m. *Pl.* bdellium, gum-resin (*Balsamodendron*).

पाठिका *pāṭhikā* [S.], f. **1.** female student. **2.** female teacher.

पाठित *pāṭhit* [S.], adj. instructed.

पाठीन *pāṭhīn* [S.], m. Av. a kind of sheat-fish; cat-fish.

पाठ्य *pāṭhyă* [S.], adj. **1.** to be read; deserving, or prescribed for, study. **2.** legible. — **पाठ्य-क्रम**, m. syllabus. **पाठ्य-पुस्तक**, f. text-book; prescribed book.

[1]**पाड़** *pāṛ* [*pāṭa-*, Pa. *pāṭikā-*], m. **1.** scaffolding; platform. **2.** wooden frame over a well.

[2]**पाड़** *pāṛ* [**pāḍi-*: Pk. *pāli-*], m. edging, border (on *dhotī*, sari).

पाड़ना *pāṛnā* [*pātayati*: Pk. *pāḍei*], v.t. to cause to fall: **1.** to make, to collect (lampblack, on a plate, &c). **2.** Brbh. Av. see [2]पार-.

[1]**पाड़ा** *pāṛā* [*pāṭaka-*, or *padra-*: ? both ← Drav.], m. **1.** quarter of a town, district. **2.** cluster of huts separate from the village to which they belong.

[2]**पाड़ा** *pāṛā* [**pāḍḍa-*: ? ← Drav.], m. male buffalo-calf.

[3]**पाड़ा** *pāṛā*, m. = [1]पाड़.

पाड़ी *pāṛī* [cf. H. [2]*pāṛā*], f. female buffalo-calf.

पाढ़ *pāṛh*, m. *HŚS.* **1.** stool; platform. **2.** an engraving tool used by goldsmiths.

[1]**पाढ़ा** *pāṛhā*, m. reg. (Bihar) = [1]पाड़ा.

[2]**पाढ़ा** *pāṛhā* [**pāḍhaka-*], m. the spotted antelope; the hog-deer.

पाणि *pāṇi* [S.], m. f. the hand. — **पाणि-ग्रह**, m. = next. **पाणि-ग्रहण**, m. taking the hand: the wedding rite of the joining of the hands of bride and groom by the bride's father; marriage. **पाणि-गृहीत**, adj. married by due ritual.

पाणिनीय *pāṇinīyă* [S.], adj. having to do with the grammarian Pāṇini.

[1]**पात** *pāt* [*pattra-*], m. **1.** a leaf. **2.** leaf or sheet (of paper). **3.** [? × *paṭṭa-*[1]] a thin sheet of metal. — **पातों आ लगना**, the leaves to fall, autumn to come; to have one's power or endurance exhausted; to be reduced to want; to have one's patience tried or exhausted. – **पात-गोभी**, f. cabbage. **पातबंदी**, f. *hist.* assembling the papers: statement of the assets and liabilities of an estate.

[2]**पात** *pāt* [S.], m. esp. finally in comp. **1.** falling. **2.** fig. decline. **3.** downfall.

पातक *pātak* [S.], m. **1.** sin; offence. **2.** defilement.

पातकी *pātăkī* [S.], m. a sinner; offender.

पातन *pātan* [S.], m. throwing down; overthrowing.

[1]**पातर** *pātar* [*pattrala-*, Pk. *pattala-*], adj. Brbh. leaflike: thin; frail.

[2]**पातर** *pātar* [ad. *pātra-*; w. H. [1]*pāt*], m. Brbh. leaf-basket.

[3]**पातर** *pātar*, f. = पातुर.

[1]**पाता** *pātā* [*pattraka-*], m. = [1]पात.

[2]**पाता** *pātā* [S.], m. inv. *Pl. HŚS.* protector.

पाताल *pātāl* [S.], m. *mythol.* **1.** one of the seven subterranean regions; the underworld; hell. **2.** fig. chasm; deep hole.

पाताली *pātālī* [cf. H. *pātāl*], adj. having to do with the underworld.

पातित *pātit* [S.], adj. **1.** thrown down; overthrown. **2.** fig. downcast.

पातिली *pātilī* [S.], f. *Pl. HŚS.* a kind of small earthen pot used by ascetics.

पातिव्रत *pātivrat* [ad. *pātivratya-*], m. faithfulness to (one's) husband; marital fidelity. — **पातिव्रत-धर्म**, m. id.

पातिव्रत्य *pātivratyă* [S.], m. = पातिव्रत.

पाती *pātī* [*pattrikā-*], f. **1.** leaf. **2.** letter.

पातीर *pātīr* [S.], m. sandalwood.

पातीला *pātīlā*, m. = पतीला.

पातुर *pātur* [ad. *pātrā-*], f. a dancing-girl; prostitute. — **पातुरबाज़** [P. *-bāz*], m. one who frequents prostitutes.

पात्र *pātr* [S.], m. **1.** vessel; dish; goblet; bowl. **2.** finally in comp. fit vessel: recipient; proper object (of esteem, &c). **3.** character (in a literary work); actor (in a drama).

पात्रता *pātrătā* [S.], f. suitability, worthiness (as for a post, an honour); eligibility.

पात्री *pātrī* [S.], f. **1.** a small vessel. **2.** female character (in a literary work); actress (in a drama).

पाथ *pāth* [S.], m. *Pl. HŚS.* water. — **पाथोज** [°*thas*+*ja*°], m. Brbh. Av. water-born: a lotus; the deity Viṣṇu (who holds a lotus). **पाथोद** [°*thas*+*da*°], m. Av. water-giving: a cloud. **पाथोधि** [°*thas*+*dhi*°], m. Av. store of waters: the ocean.

पाथना *pāthnā* [f. H. *thāpnā*], v.t. to make (cow-dung) into cakes for fuel, and to set these out to dry.

पाथेय *pātheyă* [S.], adj. & m. **1.** adj. having to do with a journey: provisions. **2.** m. provisions for a journey.

[1]**पाद** *pād* [S.], m. **1.** foot. **2.** leg. **3.** a pace. **4.** fig. lower or lowest part; bottom; root (of a tree); foot (of a mountain); foothill. **5.** quarter; a quarter of a stanza, or of a verse; a line of verse. — पाद-ग्रहण, m. touching the feet of a brāhmaṇ, or of a superior, in respect. पादचारी, m. pedestrian. पाद-चिह्न, m. footprint. पाद-टिप्पणी [f. Engl.], f. footnote. पाद-तल, m. & adv. sole of the foot; as low as the feet; under the feet. पादप, drinking with the foot or root: m. a plant, a tree. पाद-प्रणाम, m. bowing to the feet: low bow. पाद-प्रहार, m. a kick. पाद-सेवन, m. massaging (another's) feet; touching another's feet in respect. °-सेवा, f. id. पादांगुली, [°*da*+*a*°], m. a toe. पादाक्रांत [°*da*+*ā*°], adj. trodden underfoot; downtrodden. पदाघात [°*da*+*ā*°], m. a kick. पादाहत [°*da*+*ā*°], adj. kicked; trodden; touched with the foot. पादोदक [°*da*+*u*°], m. water in which the feet of a revered person have been ceremonially washed.

[2]**पाद** *pād* [*parda-*], m. breaking wind. — ~ मारना, or छोड़ना, or उड़ाना, to fart. – पाद-पाबरा, adj. colloq. frightened at a puff of wind: timorous.

पादना *pādnā* [*pardate*], v.i. to fart.

पादरी *pādrī* [Pt. *padre*], m. **1.** Christian priest or minister; chaplain. **2.** missionary.

पादविक *pādăvik* [S.], m. *Pl. HŚS.* a wayfarer.

पादशाह *pādśāh* [P. *pādśāh*], m. protecting king: king, emperor (= बादशाह).

पादशाही *pādśāhī* [P. *pādśāhī*], adj. having to do with a king or an emperor; royal, imperial.

पादी *pādī* [S.], adj. & m. **1.** adj. having feet (as an animal, or an amphibious creature). **2.** entitled to a quarter share. **3.** m. an amphibious creature.

पादुका *pādukā* [S.], f. **1.** a wooden shoe. **2.** shoe, slipper, sandal.

[1]**पादू** *pādū* [ad. *pādukā-*], m. a wooden shoe.

[2]**पादू** *pādū* [cf. H. [2]*pād*], adj. & m. prone to break wind.

पाद्य *pādyă* [S.], m. water for washing the feet (of a revered person).

पाधा *pādhā* [? ad. *upādhyāya-*], m. **1.** tutor, teacher; pandit. 2. = पुरोहित. **3.** pej. henchman.

[1]**पान** *pān* [*parṇa-*], m. **1.** leaf. ***2.** betel leaf. **3.** embroidered work resembling a leaf. **4.** hearts (in cards). — ~ उठाना, = बीड़ा उठाना. ~ का बीड़ा, m. a rolled *pān* leaf; fig. a challenge. ~ खिलाना, to have *pān* eaten: a marriage to be symbolically agreed to by the families of the parties. ~ देना, to offer *pān* (to, को); to encourage or to induce a person to take up a challenge. ~ बनाना, or लगाना, to prepare betel leaf for eating by adding areca nut, vegetable extract, lime, &c. ~ लेना, to undertake sthg. difficult. – पान-खिलाई, f. celebration of an engagement. पानदान [P. *dān*], m. container for betel-leaf, &c.; पानदान का ख़र्च, m. minor personal expenditure (esp. that of women).

[2]**पान** *pān* [S.], m. **1.** drinking; inhaling. **2.** a drink. — ~ करना, to drink.

[3]**पान** *pān*, m. *Pl. HŚS.* the starch, or the unwoven threads, of new cloth.

पाना *pānā* [*prāpayati*], v.t. **1.** to get, to obtain; to receive; to accept. **2.** to win, to gain; to earn. **3.** to come upon, to find; to meet, to overtake. **4.** to feel, to perceive, to experience; to enjoy; to suffer. मैंने ऐसा पाया कि..., I had the impression that.... **5.** to find to be, to gauge as; to fathom (sthg. obscure). **6.** (as dep. auxil. or with obl. inf.) to manage (to); to result (in). **7.** to equal (one, को; at, में).

पानी *pānī* [*pānīya-*], m. **1.** water. **2.** rain; the rainy season; transf. year. **3.** fluid; a solution; a bodily secretion. **4.** sap, juice. **5.** colloq. alcohol. **6.** brightness, lustre; water (as of a jewel); temper (of a blade); edge (of a blade). **7.** reputation, honour; sense of modesty; sense of shame. **8.** vigour, manliness. **9.** breed, breeding. — ~ आना, water, rain, &c. to collect; rain to fall. ~ उतरना, to subside (a flood); a cataract to form (in the eye); to suffer from hydrocele. ~ उतारना (का), to insult; to shame. ~ करना, to melt; to simplify (a difficulty); to abash; to make water. ~ का बताशा, or बुलबुला, m. fig. sthg. insubstantial or short-lived. ~ का रहनेवाला, adj. & m. aquatic; an aquatic animal. ~ काटना, to turn off, or to deflect a flow of, water; to cleave (waves). ~ के मोल, adv. dirt cheap. ~ के रेले में बहाना, to consign to the flood: to squander; to sell dirt cheap, or at a loss. ~ चढ़ना, water to rise; water to flood (over, पर: fields). ~ चुराना, to absorb water (a wound); to be pregnant. ~ छूना, to touch water: to wash after defecation. ~ छोड़ना, to ooze water, sap, &c. ~ जाना, tears to be shed; reputation to go, to be disgraced. ~ तोड़ना, to draw water (a ship); to stir up the water (oars). ~ दिखाना (को), to water (an animal). ~ देना, to offer water (incl. to the spirit of a deceased relative); to irrigate; to whet; to give water (to plants, में); to gild or to veneer (over, पर). ~ न माँगना, to die instantly or suddenly (not having time to ask for water). ~ पड़ना, to rain; cold water to fall (on, पर), to be dashed (hopes). ~ ~ होना, to be consumed by shame. ~ पी-पीकर, adv. moistening the throat repeatedly: continuously, excessively (of praying, cursing). ~ फिरना (पर), water to inundate (a field, &c.); hopes, &c. to be destroyed. ~ फेरना, to gild, to coat; to polish. ~ बुझाना, to purify water by immersing a heated object in it. ~ भरना (में), to draw or to fetch water; fig. to feel inferiority (in the presence of, के सामने). ~ भर आना मुँह में, the mouth to water. ~ मरना, water to leak, or to be absorbed, or evaporated; disgrace to come (upon one: के सिर). ~ मारना, to draw water (a ship). ~ में आग लगाना, fig. to set irreconcilables together: to revive an old quarrel. ~ में होना, to be ashamed, embarrassed. ~ लगना, water, or climate (of a place) to be unwholesome; cold water to make (the teeth: को) ache. ~ से पतला, adj. thinner than water: watery; worthless. ~ होना, to melt away, to dissolve; to melt (the heart); to fail (courage); to become watery; to become loose; to grow cold as water; to be very easy. – उसकी आँखों का ~ मर गया है, fig. he has no shame. गरम ~, m. alcoholic drink. नरम ~, m. a mild climate. पानीदार [P. *-dār*], adj. bright, tempered (steel); respected; manly, vigorous. पानी-देवा, m. one who must offer a libation (to an ancestor's spirit): a son; a relative.

[1]**पानीय** *pānīyă* [S.], adj. & m. **1.** adj. drinkable. **2.** m. Brbh. drink, draught.

[2]**पानीय** *pānīyă* [S.], adj. Brbh. to be preserved.

पाप *pap* [S.], m. **1.** sin; evil; wickedness, wrong; moral guilt. **2.** transf. difficulty, suffering (seen as arising from sin). — ~ उदय होना, to reap the reward of sins committed in an earlier birth. ~ कमाना, or मोल लेना, to commit a sin; to incur guilt. ~ करना, to sin. ~ काटना, or दूर करना (का), to remove (one's) sin, to deliver from sin. ~ चढ़ना, or लगना (को), to be stained with sin, to commit sin. ~ बिसाना, to commit sin. ~ लगाना, to impute evil, &c. (to, को). – पाप-कर्म, m. sinful act. पाप-ग्रह, m. inauspicious planet, or conjunction; transf. calamity, fatal destiny. पाप-फल, m. & adj. the fruit of sin; having evil as its result, inauspicious. पापमय, adj. sinful, &c. (an action). पाप-मोचन, m. liberation from sin. पाप-रोग, m. a dire disease (seen as the penalty of sin in a former life). पापहर, adj. removing or destroying sin. पापाचरण [°*pa*+*ā*°], m. sinful ways. पापाचार [°*pa*+*ā*°], m. sinful conduct, &c. °ई, adj. & m. sinful; a sinner. पापात्मा [°*pa*+*ā*°], adj. & m. of a sinful or wicked nature; a sinner, &c.

पापड़ *pāpaṛ* [*parpaṭa-*[1], Pa. *pappaṭa-*], m. & adj. **1.** m. a thin crisp cake made of pulse. **2.** transf. crust, scab. **3.** adj. reg. light, fertile (of soil). — ~ बेलना, to roll out *pāpaṛ* cakes; to suffer hardship; to work hard and have little.

[1]**पापा** *pāpā* [P. *pāpā*], m. father.

[2]**पापा** *pāpā*, m. reg. (W.) **1.** a weevil. **2.** an insect which attacks millets and rice.

पापिनी *pāpinī* [S.], f. a sinful or wicked woman, &c.

पापिष्ठ *pāpiṣṭh* [S.], adj. most sinful.

पापी *pāpī* [S.], adj. & m. **1.** adj. sinful; wicked; guilty (of, का). **2.** cruel, hard-hearted. **3.** m. a sinner, &c.

पाबंद *pāband*, adj. & m. see s.v. पा-.

पामर *pāmar* [S.], adj. & m. suffering from a skin disease: **1.** adj. vile. **2.** base. **3.** m. a vile person, &c.

[1]**पामरी** *pāmrī* f. Brbh. = पाँवड़ी.

[2]**पामरी** *pāmrī*, f. **1.** Brbh. a kind of silken cloth; a shawl. **2.** *Pl.* a name of a sweet-smelling flower.

पामा *pāmā* [S.], f. a skin complaint, or complaints; prickly heat.

पायँचा *pāyaṁcā* [P. *pā'eca*], m. leg of trousers or shorts.

पायता *pāyătā* [*pādānta-*], m. the foot of a bed.

पायती *pāyătī*, f. = पायँता.

पाय *pāy* [*pāda*], m. Av. **1.** foot, leg.

पाय- *pāy-* [P. *pā'e*], m. foot, leg. (most cpds. in use in Hindi have more common variants showing the shortened form पा, q.v.) — पायजामा, m. = पाजामा. पायतख़्त, m. U. capital (city). पायदान, m. foot-rest; running-board; gangway. पायदार [P. *-dār*], adj. durable, strong. °ई, f.

पायताना *pāytānā*, m. = पायँता.

पायक *pāyak* [P. *paik*], m. **1.** footman; armed attendant. **2.** messenger.

पायठ *pāyaṭh* [**pādakāṣṭha-*], m. *Pl. HŚS.* scaffolding, scaffold.

पायल *pāyal* [**pādala-*], adj. & m. **1.** adj. sure-footed. ***2.** m. anklet with bells.

पायस *pāyas* [S.], m. **1.** rice boiled in milk with sugar. **2.** resin. **3.** *chem.* emulsion.

पाया *pāyā* [P. *pāya*], m. **1.** foot or leg (of an object). **2.** reg. piece of wood (tied to the neck and leg of vicious cattle). **3.** transf. foundation; base. **4.** rank, status.

[1]**पार** *pār* [*pāra-*[1]], m. & adv. **1.** m. the far bank, or side. **2.** reverse or opposite side (of an object). **3.** end, limit; furthest extent; depth. **4.** adv. on, or to the far bank or side; over, across; through, beyond. **5.** (ppn. w. के.) id. — ~ उतरना, to get across (e.g. the ocean of

existence); to be finished with (a task); to be free of (a burden); to succeed (in an aim). ~ उतारना, or लगाना, to convey across, to ferry over; to extricate (from difficulties); colloq. to despatch (from this life). ~ करना, = ~ उतारना; to get through (a difficult time, &c.); to pierce right through. ~ पड़ना, to come to an end, to be over; to be seen through, managed (by, से). ~ पहुँचना, = ~ उतरना. ~ पाना, to reach the end (of, का); to plumb the depth or scope (of); to get the better (of, से). ~ लगना, or होना, to reach the far bank; to be accomplished (by, से, or का); to pierce or to soak right through; to be successful; to escape; to survive. उस ~, adv. on the far bank, or shore; in the next life. तुम्हारा कैसे ~ लगेगा? how will you manage (it: a difficulty)? – पारंगत [S. *pāram-*], adj. having crossed over, or reached the end: well versed, expert (in, में), का). पार-गमन, m. crossing over, transit. पारदर्शक, adj. transparent. °-दर्शिता, f. long-sightedness; far-sightedness; transparency. °-दर्शी, adj. पार-पत्र, m. a passport. पारप्रेषण, m. forwarding, despatch. पारवहन, m. transportation. पार-वार, adv. on both sides, or banks; through and through, entirely. पारापार [°*ra*+*a*°], m. = पारावार. पारायण [°*ra*+*a*°], m. see s.v. पारावार [°*ra*+*a*°], m. & adv. the further and nearer banks of a river; the ocean; limit, bounds; = पार-वार.

[1]**पार-** *pār-* [*pārayati-*[1]], v.i. Av. **1.** to be finished with (a task); to accomplish. **2.** to be able. — पिंडा ~, *hind.* to offer *piṇḍā* to the spirits of dead relatives.

[2]**पार** *pār* [P. *pār*], adj. past, last; next. — पारसाल, m. & adv. last year; next year.

[2]**पार-** *pār-*, v.t. Brbh. Av. **1.** to cause to fall (= पाड़ना, q.v.); to throw down. **2.** to cause to lie, to place; to make (a hair-parting). **3.** to wear.

पारंपरिक *pāramparik* [S.], adj. traditional.

[1]**पारक** *pārak* [S.], adj. **1.** enabling to cross (a river); enabling to get through (the world). **2.** getting through, accomplishing.

[2]**पारक** *pārak*, adj. reg. versed (in), expert (= पारंगत).

पारखी *pārkhī* [cf. **pārīkṣya-*], adj. & m. **1.** adj. discerning; critical. **2.** m. tester, assayer. **3.** connoisseur.

[1]**पारचा** *pārcā* [P. *pārca*], m. **1.** piece, fragment; scrap. **2.** piece of cloth; rag.

[2]**पारचा** *pārcā*, m. reg. (W.) **1.** catch-basin (trough or reservoir into which water drawn at a well, or by a Persian wheel, is emptied). **2.** boiling-pan (at a sugar-mill). **3.** [cf. H. [1]*pāṛ*] *HŚS.* beam at well-mouth (from which the bucket is hung).

पारण *pāraṇ* [S.], m. **1.** crossing to the far bank. **2.** accomplishing (a task); success. **3.** concluding (a fast). **4.** approving (as a parliamentary bill).

पारतंत्र्य *pārtantryă* [S.], m. dependence.

पारद *pārad* [S.], m. mercury.

पारदर्शी *pārdarśī* [S.], adj. see s.v. [1]पार.

पारदिक *pārădik* [S.], adj. mercurous, mercuric.

पारदेश्य *pārdeśyă* [S.], adj. = पारदेशी.

पारधी *pārădhī*, m. Brbh. a fowler; a hunter.

पारमाण्विक *pārămāṇvik* [S.], adj. atomic.

पारमार्थिक *pārămārthik* [S.], adj. having to do with supreme truth, or reality; spiritual.

पारमार्थ्य *pārămārthyă* [S.], m. highest truth or reality.

पारमित *pārămit* [S.], adj. gone to the far shore: crossed over.

पारलौकिक *pārlaukik* [S.], adj. having to do with the next world.

[1]**पारस** *pāras* [conn. *sparśa-*], m. & adj. **1.** m. touchstone (for assaying metals, gems). **2.** philosopher's stone. **3.** transf. a valuable or useful object. **4.** adj. fig. sound, healthy (the body). – शरीर ~ हो जाना, (one's) health to be restored. – पारस-पत्थर, m. = पारस.

[2]**पारस** *pāras* [ad. *pārśva-*], m. & adv. Brbh. **1.** m. side. **2.** adv. nearby.

[3]**पारस** *pāras* [? conn. H. *parasnā*], m. **1.** a serving, helping of food. **2.** a leaf-plate.

[4]**पारस** *pāras*, m. the bird-cherry tree, *Prunus padus*.

पारसा *pārsā* [P. *pārsā*], adj. S.H. faithful (a wife).

पारसाई *pārsāī* [P.], f. U. purity, virtue.

पारसी *pārsī* [*pārasika-*: ← Middle P.], adj. & m. **1.** adj. Parsee. **2.** Persian; Iranian. **3.** m. a Parsee. **4.** an Iranian.

पारस्परिक *pārasparik* [S.], adj. mutual; reciprocal.

पारस्परिकता *pārasparikătā* [S.], m. mutuality; reciprocity.

[1]**पारा** *pārā* [*pāra-*[2]: ← Ir.], m. **1.** mercury. **2.** fig. anger. — ~ पिलाना, or भरना (में), to fill with mercury; to weigh down. पारे का काफ़ुर, m. *Pl.* mercurous chloride, calomel.

[2]**पारा** *pārā* [P. *pāra*], m. **1.** piece, fragment. **2.** *HŚS.* dry-stone wall.

पारायण *pārâyaṇ* [S.], m. **1.** crossing over: completing (an activity). **2.** reading through (esp. a Purāṇa). **3.** commissioning (an entire reading of a work).

पारायनिक *pārâyanik* [S.], m. a reader of the Purāṇas (see पारायण).

पारावत *pārāvat* [S.], m. pigeon.

पारिकांक्षी *pārikāṅkṣī* [S.], adj. contemplative, ascetic.

पारिजात *pārijāt* [S.], m. **1.** the coral tree. **2.** *mythol.* name of one of the five trees of paradise (produced at the churning of the ocean).

पारिणाय *pāriṇāy*, adj. & m. = पारिणाय्य.

पारिणाय्य *pāriṇāyyă* [S.], adj. & m. **1.** adj. pertaining to marriage. **2.** m. property received by a woman at the time of her marriage.

पारित *pārit* [S.], adj. passed (esp. a motion, a bill).

पारितोषिक *pāritoṣik* [S.], m. **1.** award, prize. **2.** remuneration.

पारिपार्श्विक *pāripārśvik* [S]. a personal servant, an aide.

पारिभाषिक *pāribhāṣik* [S.], adj. technical (a term).

पारिभाषिकी *pāribhāṣikī* [S.], f. terminology.

पारिवारिक *pārivārik* [S.], adj. having to do with family, or with a family.

पारिश्रमिक *pāriśramik* [S.], m. remuneration; fee.

पारिषद *pāriṣad* [S.], adj. & m. **1.** adj. having to do with an assembly, or council. **2.** m. member of, or person present at, an assembly, &c. **3.** spectator.

पारिस्थितिक *pāristhitik* [S.], adj. circumstantial.

पारी *pārī* [*pāḍi-: Pk. *pālī-*], f. **1.** time, turn (= बारी); shift (of work). **2.** *athl.* innings. — ~ **बाँधना**, to decide on an order of turns.

पारुष्य *pāruṣyă* [S.], m. **1.** roughness, harshness. **2.** transf. abusive language.

पार्थक्य *pārthakyă* [S.], m. **1.** separateness. **2.** individual nature. — **पार्थक्यवाद**, m. separatism.

पार्थिव *pārthiv* [S.], adj. & m. **1.** adj. earthly, terrestrial; mortal (remains). **2.** made of earth, earthen. **3.** belonging to a ruler of the earth: princely. **4.** m. a king, prince. **5.** earthen vessel. **6.** *hind.* earthen lingam.

पार्वण *pārvaṇ* [S.], m. *Pl. hind.* a sacrifice to ancestors performed at particular occasions, esp. at the new moon.

पार्वती *pārvatī* [S.], f. a title of Durgā (as daughter of Himavat, king of the Himālayas).

पार्वतीय *pārvatīyă* [S.], adj. **1.** living in the mountains. **2.** mountainous.

पार्वत्य *pārvatyă* [S.], adj. = पार्वतीय.

पार्श्व *pārśvă* [S.], m. **1.** side (of the body); ribs; flank. **2.** side; edge. **3.** adjacent position, vicinity. — **पार्श्वगत**, adj. close (to), nearly; attending. **पार्श्व-गायन**, m. play-back song (in cinema). **पार्शव-नायक**, m. *mil.* a commissioned rank (air force). **पार्श्व-भूमि**, f. = ~, 3. **पार्श्ववर्ती**, adj. attendant; adjacent. **पार्श्व-शूल**, m. an ache in the side. **पार्श्वस्थ**, adj. adjacent, near (a locality or person).

पार्श्विक *pārśvik* [S.], adj. having to do with the side; lateral.

पार्षद *pārṣad*, [S.], m. corr. = पारिषद, 2.

पालंक *pālaṅk*, m. reg. = [1]पालक.

[1]**पाल** *pāl* [*pālī-*], f. an embankment (to confine water for irrigation); dike.

[2]**पाल** *pāl* [*palla-[3]], m. **1.** sail. **2.** tent. **3.** hanging, curtain (on a vehicle). — ~ **चढ़ाना**, or **तानना**, to hoist sail. **पालदार** [P. *-dār*], adj. having sails (a boat).

[3]**पाल** *pāl* [*pākala-*], m. layers of straw, leaves, &c. in which fruit is placed to ripen. — ~ **का पका**, adj. or **पक्का**, ripened in straw.

-पाल *-pāl* [S.], m. **1.** protector; guardian. **2.** one who rears, or cherishes.

[1]**पालक** *pālak* [*pālaṅkī-*, Pk. *pālaṁka-*], m. a type of spinach.

[2]**पालक** *pālak* [S.], adj. & m. **1.** adj. protecting. **2.** supporting, rearing; cherishing. **3.** m. protector; guardian. **4.** groom (of animals).

[3]**पालक** *pālak* [*palyaṅka-*], m. Av. bedstead (= पलंग).

पालकड़ा *pālakṛā* [cf. H. [2]*pālak*], m. reg. an adopted son.

पालकी *pālkī* [*palyaṅka-*], f. a litter, conveyance carried on the shoulders.

पालट *pālaṭ* [cf. H. *pālnā*], m. a viper nursed in the bosom.

पालती *pāltī*, f. = पालथी.

पालतू *pāltū* [? H. *paltā* × H. *pālnā*], adj. domestic (an animal).

पालथी *pālthī* [*paryastikā-*], f. cross-legged posture. — ~ बाँधना, or लगाना, = next. ~ मारकर बैठना, to sit cross-legged.

पालन *pālan* [S.], m. **1.** protecting. **2.** fostering, rearing; keeping (as stock); cherishing. **3.** keeping, observing (as a promise, a command). **4.** protection. **5.** support, maintenance. — ~ करना, to protect, to rear, &c. – पालन-पोषण, m. rearing, upbringing.

1**पालना** *pālnā* [*pālayati*], v.t. **1.** to protect. **2.** to foster, to rear; to keep (as stock). **3.** to keep (a promise).

2**पालना** *pālnā* [*pālana-*], m. a cradle.

1**पाला** *pālā* [*prāleya-*], m. **1.** frost, hoar-frost. **2.** dew. **3.** snow. **4.** afterbirth (of an animal). — ~ पड़ना, or गिरना, to freeze; frost to fall (on, पर), to be blighted (as hopes). ~ मारना, frost to strike or to blight (plants).

2**पाला** *pālā* [? cf. H. *pālnā*], m. **1.** protection, shelter. ***2.** maintenance; charge, keeping. **3.** power, sway; grasp, clutches. **4.** connection. — ~ डालना, to protect (from, से). ~ पड़ना, to be in the keeping (of, का); to be supported (by). पाले पड़ना, to fall into the power, or clutches, (of, के); to be supported (by); to have to do (with); to be fascinated (by).

3**पाला** *pālā* [cf. *pālī-*, and H. 1*pāl*], m. heap of earth (serving as marker in the game *kabaḍḍī*); dividing line.

4**पाला** *pālā* [*palya-*], m. stack of corn.

5**पाला** *pālā* [*pallava-*], m. reg. (W.) **1.** a twig (having leaves). **2.** reg. leaves of the *jhaṛberī* (jujube) tree (used as fodder for milch cows and goats).

6**पाला** *pālā*, m. reg. = पारी.

पालागन *pālāgan* [H. *pāṁ(v)*+H. *lāg-*], f. **1.** bowing down to another's feet, reverential greeting. **2.** (as a term of address) greetings!

पालाश *pālāś* [S.], adj. having to do with the *palāś* tree.

पालि *pāli* [S.], f. Av. = 1पाली.

पालित *pālit* [S.], adj. **1.** protected; supported, reared. **2.** kept (as a promise).

1**पाली** *pālī* [S.], f. **1.** edge; boundary, limit. **2.** tip, point; tip of the ear. **3.** line, row. **4.** turn (cf. पारी); shift; innings. **5.** embankment; pond. **6.** lap, bosom. **7.** cock-pit; transf. cock-fight. **8.** the Pāli language. — ~ बदना, a line to be announced or agreed (as by teams playing the game *kabaḍḍī*).

2**पाली** *pālī* [S.], adj. **1.** protecting. **2.** fostering, rearing.

पालू *pālū*, adj. = पालतू.

पालो *pālo* [*pallava-*], m. foliage; shoot(s).

पाल्य *pālyă* [S.], adj. to be protected, &c.

पाव *pāv* [*pāda-*], m. **1.** a fourth part, quarter. **2.** an amount weighing a quarter seer (about half a pound). **3.** a weight of a quarter seer. — ~ भर, adj. weighing one *pāv*. ~ रोटी, a loaf (as opposed to flat cakes) of bread.

पाव- *pāv-*, v.t. Brbh. Av. = पाना.

पावक *pāvak* [S.], adj. & m. **1.** adj. purifying. **2.** pure. **3.** m. fire. **4.** fig. good conduct.

पावती *pāvtī* [cf. H. *pānā*], f. anything gained or received: **1.** gain, income. **2.** acceptance. **3.** receipt (as for payment). **4.** receipt (of a letter).

पावदान *pāvdān* [cf. *pāda-*], m. = पायदान, see s.v. पाय-.

पावन *pāvan* [S.], adj. & m. **1.** adj. purifying. **2.** pure; holy. **3.** m. the name of various purifying or cleansing things, esp. fire; water; cow-dung. **4.** the nuts of the tree *Elaeocarpus ganitrus* (from which rosaries and bracelets are made). **5.** fig. repentance; penance.

पावना *pāvnā* [= H. *pāv-*], m. **1.** a sum due; credit. **2.** a banker's credit.

पावमान *pāvămān* [S.], adj. purificatory (as fire).

पावला *pāvlā* [cf. H. *pāv*], m. a quarter rupee, a four-anna piece.

पावली *pāvlī*, f. = पावला.

पावस *pāvas* [*prāvṛṣ(a)-*], f. m. **1.** the rainy season. **2.** rain.

पावित *pāvit* [S.], adj. *Pl.* purified.

1**पाश** *pāś* [S.], m. **1.** noose. **2.** net; snare; clutches.

2**पाश** *pāś* [P. *pāśīdan*], adj. in comp. scattering: — ~ ~, adj. broken in pieces, shattered.

पाशविक *pāśvik* [S.], adj. pertaining to or characterising animals; bestial.

पाशा *pāśā* [P. *pāśā*: ← T. *paşa*], m. a pasha.

पाशित *pāśit* [S.], adj. **1.** noosed; caught. **2.** tied, bound.

पाश्चात्य *pāścātyă* [S.], adj. & m. **1.** adj. behind, rear. **2.** western; specif. having to do with the western world. **3.** m. rear part. — पाश्चात्यीकरण, m. westernisation.

पाश्चात्यीकरण *pāścātyīkaraṇ* [S.], m. see s.v. पाश्चात्य.

पाषंड *pāṣaṇḍ* [S.], m. = पाखंड, 1., 2.

पाषंडी *pāṣaṇḍī* [S.], adj. & m. = पाखंडी.

पाषाण *pāṣaṇ* [S.], m. a stone. — पाषाण-चतुर्दशी, f. *Pl. HŚS.* the fourteenth day of the light half of the month Māgh (sacred to Gaurī; stone-shaped rice-cakes are eaten by women on that day). पाषाणमय, adj. stony. पाषाण-हृदय, adj. stony-hearted.

पाषाणी *pāṣāṇī* [S.], f. **1.** a small stone used as a weight. **2.** stonemason's chisel. **3.** stonemason's hammer.

पाषाणीय *pāṣāṇīyă* [S.], adj. = पाषाणमय.

पासंग *pāsaṅg* [P. *pāsang*], m. a makeweight, counterweight (to balance a scales, a load). — ~ बराबर न होना, not to be the equivalent, or the equal (of, के), to be wanting. ~ भी न होना, nothing comparable to exist (to, का).

पासंघ *pāsaṅgh* [f. H. *pāsaṅg*], m. reg. (Bihar) = पासंग.

[1]**पास** *pās* [*pārśve*], adv. & m. **1.** adv. nearby. **2.** m. Av. side, direction. **3.** (ppn. w. के) beside, near. **4.** up to, towards, to (a person); towards (a partic. place). **5.** on the person of; with, on; owned by. **6.** (without के) Brbh. of, from (as of requests in audience). — ~ आना, to come near (to, के), to come up (to), to approach; to have a sexual liaison (with). ~ का, adj. nearby, neighbouring. ~, or ~ तक, न फटकना, to stay away, to keep clear. ~ बैठना, to consort (with, के). ~ रखना, to keep near, to retain; to appoint (to one's service); to lodge, to deposit (with, के). ~ रहना, to remain near; to attend (on, के); to live (with). आपके ~ कितने पैसे हैं? how much money have you? के ~ से, adv. from nearby, away from; from (one's) own pocket. वह गाड़ी के ~ गया, he went over to, or towards, the car. वह डाक्टर के ~ गया, he went to the doctor. — पास-पास, adv. side by side, quite near; round about, approximately. पास-पड़ोस, m. neighbourhood.

[2]**पास** *pās*, m. = पाश.

[3]**पास** *pās* [Engl. *pass*], m. a pass; ticket.

पासना *pāsnā* [*prasravati*], v.i. **1.** to descend to the udder (an animal's milk). **2.** colloq. to be consumed eagerly (food and drink after a fast).

पासबान *pāsbān* [P. *pāsbān*], m. a watchman; guard.

[1]**पासबानी** *pāsbānī* [P. *pāsbānī*], f. watch, guard.

[2]**पासबानी** *pāsbānī* [cf. H. *pāsbān*], m. name of a north Indian community (whose members have traditionally worked as watchmen, &c).

पासा *pāsā* [*pāśa-*[1]], m. **1.** die, dice. **2.** throw of dice. **3.** a dice game. **4.** *Pl.* lump, cube. — ~ खेलना, to gamble with dice. ~ पड़ना, dice to be thrown; to have a stroke of luck (in dice, or otherwise). ~ पलटना, the die to fall wrongly: things to turn out, or to go, wrong.

[1]**पासी** *pāsī* [cf. H. [2]*pās*], f. **1.** cord or rope for tying the feet of a horse, donkey, &c. **2.** net.

[2]**पासी** *pāsī* [*pāśin-*], m. **1.** a fowler. **2.** a toddy-extractor.

पाहन *pāhan* [*pāsāṇa-*], m. Brbh. Av. stone.

पाहिं *pāhiṁ* [*pakṣa-*], adv. & ppn. Av. = पास.

पाही *pāhī*, adj. & m. *hist.* **1.** adj. non-resident (a cultivator whose land and living-place are in different villages). **2.** non-resident (a cultivator of village land). **3.** m. a non-resident cultivator; temporary occupant of village land.

पाहुन *pāhun* [*prāhuna-*], m. reg. a guest.

पाहुना *pāhunā* [*prāhuṇa-*], m. **1.** guest. **2.** reg. (E.) son-in-law.

पाहुनाई *pāhunāī* [cf. H. *pāhun*], f. hospitality.

पाहुनी *pāhunī* [cf. H. *pāhun*], f. 1. = पाहुनाई. **2.** female guest. **3.** euph. concubine.

पिंग *piṅg* [S.], adj. reddish, yellowish, tawny.

पिंगल *piṅgal* [S.], adj. & m. **1.** adj. = पिंग. **2.** m. prosody. **3.** specif. Brajbhāṣā as used in Rajasthan for literary purposes, esp. during the Mughal period.

पिंगला *piṅgălā* [S.], f. (in yoga) the right of three vessels of the body running from the loins to the head.

पिंगलिका *piṅgălikā* [S.], adj. *Pl. HŚS.* a creature of tawny colour (as a bee, an owl, a crane).

पिंगूड़ा *piṅgūṛā*, m. *Pl.* = पिंघूरा.

पिंगूरा *piṅgūrā*, m. *Pl. HŚS.* = पिंघूरा.

पिंघूरा *piṅghūrā* [conn.*preṅkhola-*], m. E.H. child's hammock, cradle.

पिंजड़ा *piñjṛā*, m. = पिंजरा.

पिंजट *piñjaṭ* [S.: ← Drav.], m. *Pl. HŚS.* excretion from the eyes.

पिंजना *piṁjnā*, v.i. reg. to be joined, or soldered.

[1]**पिंजर** *piñjar* [*piñjara-*[2], *pañjara-*], m. **1.** a cage. 2. = पंजर, 1.-3.

[2]**पिंजर** *piñjar* [S.], adj. & m. **1.** adj. reddish-yellow, tawny. **2.** m. a reddish-yellow colour.

पिंजरा *piñjrā* [*piñjara-*², *pañjara-*], m. a cage.

पिंजरी *piñjrī* [cf. H. *piñjrā*], f. *Pl.* **1.** a small cage. **2.** reg. bier; coffin.

पिंजवाना *piṁjvānā*, v.t. reg. to join, to solder.

पिंजारा *piñjārā* [conn. **piñjākāra-*], m. reg. = पिंजियारा.

पिंजियारा *piñjiyārā* [**piñjākāra-*], m. a cotton-carder.

पिंड *piṇḍ* [S.], m. **1.** a lump; a ball. **2.** a mouthful of food. **3.** cake or ball of meal, flour or rice offered to spirits of ancestors; oblation to ancestors offered by nearest surviving relatives. **4.** lump, ingot (of metal). **5.** a body; the human body. — ~ छुड़ाना (अपना), to get free (of, से); to avoid (as an obligation). ~ छूटना (अपना), to escape (from, से), to be free (of). ~ छोड़ना (का), to leave (one) in peace. ~ पड़ना, to stick (to, के), to follow persistently; to be bent (on); to become pregnant. – पिंड-खजूर, m. the edible date (*Phoenix dactylifera*); the wild date (*P. sylvestris*). पिंडज, adj. *zool.* viviparous. पिंडद, m. the relation who offers *piṇḍ* (see above). °-दान, m. the offering of *piṇḍ* (see 3. above). पिंड-रोग, m. debility, wasting; leprosy. °ई, adj. & m. पिंडाधिकारी [°*ḍa*+*a*°], m. superintendent of funeral rites. पिंडालु [°*ḍa*+*ā*°], m. a round yam; sweet potato.

पिंडक *piṇḍak* [S.], m. 1. = पिंड, 1. **2.** *Pl.* incense.

पिंडली *piṇḍlī* [cf. *piṇḍa-*], f. calf of the leg. — ~ की नली, f. the shinbone.

पिंडा *piṇḍā* [*piṇḍaka-*], m. **1.** lump; ball. 2. = पिंड, 3. **3.** the body. **4.** the womb. **5.** a ball or hank of string. — ~ देना, to offer cakes of rice or flour, &c. to the spirits of ancestors (see पिंड). ~ दिखाना, to encourage adultery (a woman).

पिंडार *piṇḍār* [S.], m. **1.** a name of the ground-nut. **2.** name of the trees *Flacourtia sepida*, and *Trewia nudiflora*.

पिंडारा *piṇḍārā* [*piṇḍāra-*, Pk. *piṁḍāra-*], m. *Pl. HŚS.* freebooter (= पिंडारी).

पिंडारी *piṇḍārī* [cf. *piṇḍāra-*, Pk. *piṁḍāra-*], m. *hist.* a Marāṭhā freebooter.

पिंडी *piṇḍī* [S.], f. 1. = पिंड, 1. 2. = पिंडा, 5. **3.** nave of wheel. **4.** upper part of a Śiva *liṅgam*. **5.** small altar (for offerings to ancestors). **6.** name of an evergreen aromatic tree, *Myristica canarica*.

पिंडीर *piṇḍīr* [S.], m. *Pl. HŚS.* cuttle-fish bone.

पिंडोल *piṇḍol* [cf. *pāṇḍu-* (? ← Austro-as.): Pk. *paṁḍullaïya-*], f. a yellow or white soil used to smear or wash the walls of houses. — पिंडोल-मिट्टी, f. id.

पिंपियाना *piṁpiyānā*, v.i. to be shrill (a song, music).

पिंशन *piṁśan* [Engl. *pension*], m. a pension. — ~ देना (को), to grant a pension or retiring allowance (to). ~ पाना, colloq. to be pensioned off. ~ लेना, to retire on a pension.

[1]**पिउ** *piu* [*priya-*], adj. & m. Av. = पिया.

[2]**पिउ** *piu* [*pitā*], m. reg. father.

पिक *pik* [S.], m. the Indian cuckoo. — पिक-बयनी, adj. f. cuckoo-voiced: clear-voiced. °-बैनी, adj. f. Av. id.

पिकी *pikī* [S.], f. *Pl. HŚS.* female of the Indian cuckoo.

पिघलना *pighalnā* [**praghilati*], v.i. **1.** to melt. **2.** to dissolve. **3.** fig. to be softened, moved; to yield (to entreaties).

पिघलवाना *pighalvānā* [cf. H. *pighalnā*], v.t. to cause to be melted, &c. (by, से).

पिघलाऊ *pighlāū* [cf. H. *pighalnā, pighlānā*], adj. **1.** melting easily (as lead). **2.** used in smelting (a furnace). ~ भट्टा, m. blast furnace.

पिघलाना *pighlānā* [cf. H. *pighalnā*], v.t. **1.** to melt; to smelt or to cast (metal). **2.** to dissolve. **3.** to soften, to mollify (an angry or a hard person). — पिघलाकर जोड़ना, to weld.

पिघलाव *pighlāv* [cf. H. *pighalnā, pighlānā*], m. melting; liquid state.

पिचकना *picaknā* [cf. *piccayati*], v.i. **1.** to be pressed flat; to be squeezed; to be dented. **2.** to be sunken, or shrivelled (as cheeks). **3.** to be reduced (a swelling).

पिचकाना *pickānā* [cf. H. *picaknā*], v.t. **1.** to press flat; to squeeze. **2.** to reduce (a swelling); to burst.

पिचकारी *pickārī*, f. **1.** a syringe; a squirt (for water). **2.** syringing. **3.** a jet, squirt (of liquid). **4.** enema. — ~ छूटना, to shoot in a jet (as water from a pipe, blood from an artery). ~ छोड़ना (की), to squirt out; to spit out. ~ देना (को), to give an enema (to). ~ मारना, to squirt (water, &c). ~ लगाना, to prick. ~ लेना, to take an enema.

पिच-पिच *pic-pic*, f. a splashing or squelching sound.

पिचपिचा *picpicā*, adj. **1.** sticky; adhesive. 2. = पचपचा.

पिचपिचाना *picpicānā* [cf. H. *picpicā*], v.i. = पचपचाना.

पिचर-पिचर *picar-picar*, m. a splashing noise (= पच-पच).

पिच्च *picc* [conn. H. *pīc*], f. spittle. — ~ से थूकना, to spit (out).

पिच्चट *piccaṭ* [S.: ← Drav.], f. an eye complaint.

पिच्ची *piccī*, adj. reg. crushed, smashed.

पिच्छल *picchal* [S.], adj. slimy, slippery.

पिच्छिका *picchikā* [S.], f. *Pl. HŚS.* a bundle of peacock's tail-feathers.

पिछड़ना *picharnā* [cf. H. *piche, pichla*], v.i. **1.** to be backward; to be not developed (industry, &c). **2.** to fall behind, to lag; to be late.

पिछड़ापन *pichṛāpan* [cf. H. *picharnā*], m. **1.** backward state, &c. **2.** poor position (in a class).

पिछड़ेपान *pichṛepān*, m. = पिछड़ापन.

पिछल *pichal-*. = पिछला. — पिछलपाई, f. a female evil spirit having the feet turned backward; the ghost of a woman.

पिछलग *pichlag*, m. = पिछलगा.

पिछलगा *pichlagā* [H. *pīche*+H. *lagnā*], m. **1.** a hanger-on, attendant. **2.** a follower.

पिछलगुआपन *pichlaguāpan* [cf. H. *pichlaggū*], m. fawning, subservience.

पिछलग्गू *pichlaggū*, m. = पिछलगा.

पिछलना *pichalnā*, v.i. reg. = फिसलना.

पिछला *pichlā* [cf. **paśca-*; × *pṛṣṭha-*], adj. & m. **1.** adj. back, rear. **2.** last; late, past, old; previous. **3.** latest, recent. — ~ पहर, m. the last watch of the night; the afternoon. पिछली रात, f. last night; the previous night. पिछले पाँव फिरना, to return (from a place) the moment one has reached it. पिछले पाँव हटना, to retreat (from a place); to withdraw (from an agreement). – पिछली मत [ad. *mati-*], f. an afterthought; sthg. thought too late; a misconception.

पिछवाड़ा *pichvāṛā* [**paśca-*+*vāṭa-*[1]], m. **1.** rear part. **2.** back garden, yard. — पिछवाड़े, adv. at the back; astern.

पिछवाड़ी *pichvāṛī*, f. = पिछवाड़ा.

पिछाड़ी *pichāṛī* [*paścārdha-*; × *pṛṣṭha-*], f. & adv. **1.** f. rear part. **2.** hind quarter. **3.** ropes used to hobble a horse. **4.** one bringing up the rear, last man. **5.** adv. at the back (of, की), behind. — ~ मारना, to kick with the hind legs (a horse); to attack the rear (of, की).

पिछूत *pichūt* [**paścābhukta-*], m. & adv. reg. **1.** m. rear part of a house (= पिछवाड़ा). **2.** adv. behind.

पिछेलना *pichelnā* [conn. H. *pīchā*], v.t. to push back.

पिछैत *pichait* [cf. H. *pīchā*], adj. & f. reg. **1.** adj. last (= पिछला). **2.** f. late cultivation; late crop.

पिछौरा *pichaurā* [**paścapaṭa-*], m. Brbh. Av. a shawl (men's).

पिछौरी *pichaurī* [cf. **paścapaṭa-*], f. dimin. Brbh. a shawl (women's).

पिटना *piṭnā* [cf. H. *pīṭnā*], v.i. **1.** to be beaten; to be about to be taken (a piece, as at chess). **2.** to lose (at a game); to fail (a play, film). **3.** to be struck together (as clapped hands). **4.** fig. to suffer financial loss.

पिटपिटाना *piṭpiṭānā* [cf. H. *pīṭnā*], v.i. to flail, or to flap, helplessly.

पिटवाना *piṭvānā* [cf. H. *pīṭnā*], v.t. to cause to be beaten (by, से).

पिटारा *piṭārā* [**peṭṭāra-*], m. **1.** a large woven basket with a lid. **2.** a box.

[1]**पिटारी** *piṭārī* [cf. H. *piṭārā*], f. **1.** a small basket, or box; a woven basket with a lid. 2. = पानदान. — ~ का ख़र्च, m. pej. payment; pocket-money.

[2]**पिटारी** *piṭārī*, f. reg. a weevil.

पिटारू *piṭārū* [cf. H. *piṭārā*], m. hind. name of an order of ascetics (= अघोरी).

पिट्टक *piṭṭak* [S.], m. tartar (on teeth).

पिट्टस *piṭṭas* [cf. H. *pīṭnā*], f. weeping and wailing, beating the breast.

पिट्ठू *piṭṭhū* [cf. H. *pīṭh*], m. **1.** a follower. **2.** a backer, supporter. **3.** partner (in a game).

पिड़कुली *piṛkulī*, f. a partic. small bird.

पिढ़ुली *piṛhulī* [cf. H. *pīṭha-*], f. reg. a stool.

पितर *pitar* [S. (*pitaraḥ*)], m. pl. paternal ancestors.

पितराई *pitrāī* [cf. *pittala-*[2], Pk. *pittala-*], f. reg. **1.** verdigris, copper acetate. **2.** the taint of verdigris.

पितलाना *pitlānā* [cf. H. *pītal*], v.i. to be contaminated with verdigris (as acid food kept in brass or copper vessels); to be spoiled.

पिता *pitā* [S.], m. inv. father.

पितामह *pitāmah* [S.], m. paternal grandfather.

पितामही *pitāmahī* [S.], f. paternal grandmother.

पितिया *pitiyā* [*pitriya-*], m. *Pl. HŚS.* paternal uncle. — ~ **सास**, f. wife's aunt on father's side.

पितियानी *pitiyānī* [cf. H. *pitiyā*], f. *Pl. HŚS.* paternal aunt.

पितु *pitu* [ad. *pitā*], m. Av. = **पिता**.

पितृ *pitr̥* [S.], m. **1.** father. ***2.** paternal ancestor. **पितृओं को पानी देना**, to offer an oblation to the spirits of one's ancestors. **3.** *mythol.* the progenitor of mankind. — **पितृ-ऋण**, m. debt to (one's) fathers: the duty of fathering offspring. **पितृ-कर्म**, m. funerary rites in honour of deceased ancestors. **पितृ-क्रिया**, f. id. **पितृ-गृह**, m. paternal home; cremation-ground. **पितृ-घात**, m. the act of parricide. °**ई**, m. a parricide. **पितृ-तर्पण**, m. gifts, or oblation in honour of deceased ancestors. **पितृ-तिथि**, m. day of the full moon (when ancestors are honoured). **पितृ-तीर्थ**, m. pilgrimage-place in which to honour ancestors: a title of the city of Gaya. **पितृ-पक्ष**, m. the dark fortnight of the month Bhādoṁ (when rites are performed in honour of deceased ancestors). **पितृ-पैतामह**, adj. ancestral. **पितृ-भक्ति**, f. filial devotion. **पितृ-भोजन**, m. food offered to the spirits of deceased ancestors. **पितृ-लोक**, m. the world inhabited by the ancestors of men. **पितृ-लोग**, m. forefathers. **पितृवत्**, adv. paternally. **पितृ-सत्ताक**, adj. = next. °-**सत्तात्मक**, adj. patriarchal. **पितृ-हत्या**, f. the act of parricde.

पितृक *pitr̥k* [S.], adj. **1.** paternal. **2.** ancestral. **3.** having to do with obsequies, funerary.

पितृत्व *pitr̥tvă* [S.], m. **1.** fatherhood. **2.** state of a *pitr̥*, deified paternal ancestor.

पितृव्य *pitr̥vyă* [S.], m. **1.** a paternal uncle. **2.** an elderly male relative.

पित्त *pitt* [S.], m. = **पित्ता**. — **पित्त-कोष**, m. = **पित्ताशय**. **पित्त-ज्वर**, m. jaundice. **पित्ताशय**[°*a*+*ā*°], m. the gall-bladder.

[1]**पित्तल** *pittal* [S.], m. = **पीतल**.

[2]**पित्तल** *pittal* [S.], adj. *Pl. HŚS.* bilious.

पित्ता *pittā* [**pittaka-*], m. **1.** bile. ***2.** the gall-bladder. **3.** anger, passion. **4.** daring. — ~ **निकालना**, to vent spleen, &c., on; to harass. ~ **मरना**, anger to subside. ~ **मारना**, v.t. to control one's anger, or passions; to be able to take pains (in doing sthg). – **पित्ता-मारू**, adj. & m. restraining anger, &c.; painstaking.

पित्ती *pittī* [cf. H. *pitt(ā)*], f. **1.** bile. **2.** hives. — ~ **उछलना**, or **निकलना**, hives to break out.

पिदड़ी *pidr̥ī* [cf. H. *piddī*], f. **1.** any of several small migratory birds. **2.** fig. an insignificant creature.

पिद्दा *piddā*, m. the brown-backed Indian robin (cock). — **काला** ~, the pied bushchat (*Saxicola caprata*).

पिद्दी *piddī* [cf. H. *piddā*], f. a hen robin; a robin; a bushchat. — **क्या** ~, **क्या** ~ **का शोरवा** (**शोरबा**)! fig. how (very) insignificant, or worthless (a person).

पिधान *pidhān* [S.], m. **1.** *Pl. HŚS.* cover. **2.** Brbh. leaf of a door.

पिन *pin* [Engl. *pin*], f. **1.** a pin. **2.** a bolt, pin.

पिनक *pinak*, f. = **पीनक**.

पिनकी *pinkī* [cf. H. *pĭnak*], f. intoxication (as from taking opium); drugged or drowsy state.

पिनपिन *pinpin*, m. whining (of a child, a dog, &c.; or of a bullet).

पिनपिनहाँ *pinpinhāṁ* [cf. H. *pinpin*], adj. & m. reg. **1.** adj. whining; detestable. **2.** m a whining child.

पिनपिनाना *pinpinānā*, v.i. to whine.

पिनपिनाहट *pinpināhaṭ* [cf. H. *pinpinānā*], f. whining, &c.

पिनसी *pinsī* [*pīnas-*], f. inflammation or ulceration of the nose.

पिनाक *pinăk* [S.], m. **1.** bow (esp. *mythol.* the bow of Śiva). **2.** trident. **3.** Brbh. a single-stringed musical instrument. — **पिनाक-नयन**, adj. having hard eyes: unfeeling.

[1]**पिनाकी** *pinākī* [S.], adj. & m. **1.** adj. armed with a *pinăk*. **2.** m. a title of Śiva.

[2]**पिनाकी** *pinākī* [S.], f. = **पिनाक**, 3.

[1]**पिन्ना** *pinnā*, m. **1.** residue of seeds which have been ground for oil. **2.** oil-cake made from sesame or poppy-seeds.

[2]**पिन्ना** *pinnā* [*piṇḍa-*; ? ← Panj.], m. a lump; ball (of thread); reel.

पिन्नी *pinnī*, f. a type of sweet (made of flour and sugar).

पिन्हाना *pinhānā*, v.t. = **पहनाना**.

पिपासा *pipāsā* [S.], f. **1.** thirst. **2.** desire; greed. — **पिपासार्ति** [°*sā*+*ā*°], f. torment of thirst.

पिपासित *pipāsit* [S.], adj. = **पिपासु**.

पिपासु *pipāsu* [S.], adj. **1.** thirsty (= **प्यासा**). **2.** thirsting, desirous.

पिपीलक *pipīlak* [S.], m. a large black ant.

पिपीलिका *pipīlikā* [S.], f. the common small red ant.

पिपौली *pipaulī*, f. *Pl.* the fruit of the *pīpal* tree.

पिप्पल *pippal* [S.], m. = पीपल.

पिप्पलक *pippălak* [conn. *pippalaka-*], m. *Pl. HŚS.* a nipple.

पिप्पली *pippălī* [S.], f. long pepper.

पिबियाना *pibiyānā* [cf. H. *pīb*], v.i. to suppurate.

पिबियाहट *pibiyāhaṭ* [cf. H. *pibiyānā*], f. suppuration.

[1]**पिय** *piy*, adj. & m. Brbh. Av. = पिया.

[2]**पिय** *piy* [*pika-*], m. Av. a cuckoo.

पियक्कड़ *piyakkaṛ* [cf. H. *pīnā*], m. a drinker, drunkard.

पिया *piyā* [*priya-*], adj. & m. **1.** adj. dear, beloved. **2.** m. darling.

पियाना *piyānā*, v.t. reg. = पिलाना.

पियाबाँसा *piyābāṁsā*, m. *Pl.* **1.** a variety of the common bamboo. **2.** a plant from which a red dye is obtained.

पियाल *piyāl* [S.], f. the tree *Buchanania latifolia* (a source of gum and varnish) (= चिरोंजी).

पियाला *piyālā*, m. see प्याला.

पियासी *piyāsī*, f. *Pl. HŚS.* a kind of fish.

पिरकी *pirkī*, f. reg. a boil; a sore.

पिरवाना *pirvānā* [cf. H. *pernā*], v.t. to cause to be pressed (by, से); to crush; to squeeze.

पिरा- *pirā-* [cf. *pīḍā-*], v.i. Brbh. Av. to ache; to feel pain or distress.

पिराइन *pirāin* [cf. P. *pīr*], f. wife of a *pīr*.

पिरिंच *piriñc* [f. Engl. *press*, H. *peṁc*] m. *HŚS.* reg. a saucer (= पिरिच).

पिरिच *piric* [f. Engl. *press*], m. *Pl.* reg. a flat surface (as used in pressing out indigo); a saucer.

पिरीज *pirīj*, m. *Pl.* reg. = पिरिच.

पिरोजा *pirojā* [P. *fīroza*: S. *peroja-*], m. a turquoise.

पिरोना *pironā* [*parivayati*], v.t. **1.** to string (as pearls: on, में). **2.** to run a thread, or string (through, में); to thread (a needle).

पिलई *pilaī* [*plīhan-*], f. reg. **1.** the spleen. **2.** enlargement of the spleen.

पिलचना *pilacnā* [? H. *lipaṭnā* × H. *cipaṭnā*], v.i. reg. **1.** to cling, to stick (to). **2.** fig. to close together (in fight). **3.** to be engrossed (in work).

पिलड़ी *pilṛī*, f. reg. spiced, chopped meat (= क़ीमा).

पिलना *pilnā* [cf. H. *pelnā*], v.i. **1.** to rush. **2.** (w. पड़ना.) to rush (at, पर); to jostle; to attack. **3.** to be crushed, pressed (as sugar-cane). **4.** to toil, to drudge (at में).

पिलपिला *pilpilā* [*pilippila-*], adj. **1.** slippery; smooth. ***2.** soft; flabby. **3.** clammy. — पिलपिली ठिकरी, f. also sl. a smooth piece of tile. पिलपिले गट्टे, m. pl. soft fruit stones: an absurd idea, an impossibility.

पिलपिलाना *pilpilānā* [cf. H. *pilpilā*], v.i. & v.t. **1.** v.i. to become soft. **2.** to be enervated, feeble. **3.** v.t. to crush, to squash (as fruit).

पिलपिलाहट *pilpilāhaṭ* [cf. H. *pilpilānā*], f. softness, flabbiness.

[1]**पिलवाना** *pilvānā* [cf. H. *pīnā*], v.t. to cause drink to be given (to, को; by, से).

[2]**पिलवाना** *pilvānā* [cf. H. *pilnā*], v.t. **1.** to cause to be pushed (by, से). **2.** to cause (cane, &c.) to be crushed (by).

पिलाई *pilāī* [cf. H. *pilānā*], f. **1.** giving to drink. **2.** feeding at the breast. **3.** filling (cracks). — पानी-पिलाई, f. price or sum paid for drinking-water.

पिलाना *pilānā* [cf. H. *pīnā*], v.t. **1.** to cause to drink; to give (one, को) sthg. to drink. **2.** to water, to irrigate (land). **3.** to pour (as a liquid: into, में); to fill (a crack, &c.); to load (a gun). **4.** to insinuate (a notion into the mind: of, में).

पिलास *pilās* [cf. H. *pilānā*], f. a refreshing drink, draught.

पिल्ला *pillā* [**pilla-* (← Drav.): Pa. *pillaka-*], m. a puppy.

पिल्लू *pillū* [*pīlu-*[2]: ← Drav.], m. a worm; an insect.

पिव- *piv-* [*pibati*], v.t. Brbh. = पीना.

पिशंग *piśaṅg* [S.], adj. m. *Pl. HŚS.* **1.** adj. reddish brown; tawny. **2.** m. a reddish brown, or tawny colour.

पिशाच *piśāc* [S.], m. fiend, demon.

पिशाचक *piśācak* [S.], m. *Pl. HŚS.* = पिशाच.

पिशाचिनी *piśācinī* [S.], f. demoness.

पिशाची *piśācī* [S.], f. demoness.

पिशित *piśit* [S.], m. flesh, meat.

पिशुन *piśun* [S.], adj. & m. **1.** adj. treacherous; villainous. **2.** slandering; mischievous. **3.** m. an informer, a traitor; villain. **4.** tale-bearer. **5.** a crow.

पिशुनता *piśunătā* [S.], f. **1.** treachery; villainy, wickedness. **2.** slandering.

पिष्ट *piṣṭ* [S.], adj. finely ground, ground to powder. **पिष्ट-पेषण**, m. grinding what is ground: useless repetition, rehash. °-**पेषित**, adj.

पिसता *pistā* [P. *pista*], m. pistachio nut.

पिसनहारा *pisanhārā* [cf. H. *pīsnā*], m. a grinder (of corn), miller.

पिसनहारी *pisanhārī* [cf. H. *pisanhārā*], f. **1.** woman who grinds corn. **2.** miller's wife.

पिसना *pisnā* [cf. H. *pīsnā*], v.i. **1.** to be ground; to be crushed (to fragments, powder). **2.** to be injured. **3.** fig. to suffer; to be ruined. **4.** to be exhausted.

पिसलाना *pislānā* [cf. H. *pīsna*], v.t. to cause to be ground (by, **से**).

पिसवाई *pisvāī* [cf. H. *pisvānā*], f. price paid for grinding.

पिसवाना *pisvānā* [cf. H. *pīsnā*], v.t. to cause to be ground, or crushed (by, **से**).

पिसाई *pisāī* [cf. H. *pisānā*], f. **1.** grinding. **2.** price paid for grinding. **3.** hard, grinding work.

पिसान *pisān* [cf. H. *pīsnā*], m. flour, meal.

पिसाना *pisānā* [cf. H. *pīsnā*], v.t. = **पिसवाना**.

पिसोरा *pisorā*, m. the small mouse-deer or chevrotain.

पिस्तई *pistaī* [P. *pistaī*], adj. of the colour of pistachio, greenish.

पिस्तौल *pistaul* [Pt. *pistola*], f. a pistol; revolver.

पिस्सू *pissū* [**priṣu-*: Pk. *pisua-*], m. **1.** a flea. **2.** mosquito, gnat.

पिहकना *pihaknā*, v.i. to call (a bird).

पिहान *pihān* [*pidhāna-*], m. reg. cover (as for the mouth of a grain-store).

पिहाना *pihānā* [*pidhāna-*], m. reg. (W.) = **पिहान**.

पिहानी *pihānī* [*pidhāna-*], f. Brbh. lid, cover (of a jar, &c).

पिहुआ *pihuā* [cf. H. ²*piy*], m. *Pl. HŚS.* a bird (? a cuckoo).

पींग *pīṁg*, f. = **पेंग**.

पींजना *pīṁjnā* [**piñjati*: Pk. *piṁjaï*], v.t. reg. to card cotton.

पींड *pīṁḍ* [*piṇḍa-*], m. Brbh. Av. **1.** lump, piece. **2.** the body. **3.** tree-trunk. **4.** date (fruit). **5.** reg. (Bihar) embankment (round a tank).

पींडी *pīṁḍī* [cf. *piṇḍa-*], f. a lump of fried sweet (given to women after childbirth).

पी *pī* [*priya-*], adj. & m. = **पिया**.

पीक *pīk* [**pikkā-*], f. juice of chewed betel, spat out. — **पीकदान** [P. *-dān*], m. spittoon. °**ई**, f. id.

पीच *pīc* [*picchā-*], f. rice-water.

पीचना *pīcnā*, v.t. reg. to tread underfoot.

पीचू *pīcū*, m. *Pl. HŚS.* the red fruit of the shrub *Capparis aphylla* (= **करील**).

पीछा *pīchā* [**paśca-*: Pk. *paccha-* × *pr̥ṣṭa-*], m. **1.** rear or back part. **2.** fig. pursuit. **3.** persecution. — ~ **करना** (**का**), to pursue; to track (a criminal, &c.); to importune, to persecute. ~ **छुड़ाना** (**का**), to shake off (as pursuit). ~ **छोड़ना**, to give up the pursuit, &c. (of, **का**); to leave alone. ~ **दिखाना**, to show the back: to turn tail; to leave in the lurch. ~ **देना**, to turn the back (to, **को**): id., 2. ~ **पकड़ना**, to attach oneself (to, **का**: as to a patron's coat-tails). ~ **फेरना**, to turn away (from, **से**). ~ **भारी होना**, to have strong backing or support.

पीछू *pīchū*, adv. reg. = **पीछे**.

पीछे *pīche* [cf. H. *pīchā*], adv. & ppn. **1.** adv. behind, at the rear; astern. **2.** afterwards, later; then, next. **3.** back. ~ **हटना**, to withdraw. **4.** ago. **5.** ppn. (usu. w. **के**.) behind, &c.; behind the back (of); after; out of concern for, for the sake of; as a consequence of. — ~ **करना**, to put behind (one); to leave (one) behind; to keep back, to restrain. ~ **छूटना**, to fall or to lag behind; to be set to spy (on, **के**). ~ **छोड़ना**, to leave behind, to surpass; to set (a person) to spy (on, **के**), or to detain (another). ~ **डालना**, or **रखना**, = prec. ~ **पड़ना**, to fall behind (as in progress). ~ **पड़ना** (**के**), to dance attendance (on); to importune, to persecute; to pursue tenaciously (an object). ~ ~, adv. in succession; following. ~ ~ **चलना** (**के**), to walk along behind, to follow. ~ **लगना** (**के**), to follow, to track; to attend (on); importune; to plague, to dog (as illness, misfortune). ~ **लगाना**, to involve (one, **के**) in, to bring on (a misfortune, a difficulty); = ~ **छोड़ना**, 2. ~ **से**, adv. from behind, &c.; subsequently. ~ **हो लेना** (**के**), to follow behind; to come in behind (a person, an animal).

पीटना *pīṭnā* [*piṭṭayati*], v.t. **1.** to beat; to thump, to strike; to pound; to thresh (grain); to flatten. **2.** to thrash (in fight, or punishment). **3.** to beat (the breast, in lamentation). **4.** colloq. to finish (a difficult task); to work hard, to drudge. **5.** to manage to earn, to make (a wage, or profit). **6.** (in board games) to capture (a piece). — नाम ~, colloq. to take advantage of (another's, को) name or standing.

1**पीठ** *pīṭh* [*pṛṣṭha-*], m. **1.** the back. **2.** back part (of anything). **3.** fig. backing, support, aid. — ~ का, adj. next in order of birth (to, की); equal or comparable (to). ~ चारपाई से लग जाना, to be bedridden. ~ ठोंकना (की), to slap (one) on the back; to encourage. ~ दिखाना (को), to turn one's back (on); to turn tail. ~ देना (की ओर), = prec.; to lie down and rest. ~ पर का, adj. = ~ का. ~ पर हाथ फेरना, to stroke or to pat on the back; to encourage. ~ पर होना (की), to be behind, to support; to be next (to) in order of birth. ~ पीछे, adv. behind the back (of, के); in the absence (of). ~ फेरना, to depart, to withdraw; to turn one's back (on, की ओर: in displeasure, &c.); = ~ दिखाना. ~ लगना (की), the back (of an animal) to be galled; to be thrown on the back (as in wrestling). ~ लगाना (की, or अपनी), to rest the back (against, से); to throw down (on the ground, ज़मीन से), to overcome; to lie down to rest.

2**पीठ** *pīṭh* [S.], m. **1.** seat; bench; desk. **2.** *hind.* seat of a deity. **3.** altar. **4.** base, plinth (as of a statue). **5.** -पीठ. place, abode. विद्यापीठ, f. college of higher learning; university. — पीठासीन [°*ṭha*+*ā*°], adj. in the chair, presiding. न्याय-पीठ, f. *law.* bench.

पीठा *pīṭhā* [*piṣṭa-*], m. a kind of pastry containing pulse which has been soaked and ground.

पीठिका *pīṭhikā* [S.], f. **1.** small seat, stool. **2.** base, plinth; stand (as for an idol). **3.** esp. in comp. section (of a book). **4.** background.

पीठी *pīṭhī* [*piṣṭa-*], f. pulse, soaked and ground (for filling for pastries).

पीठौता *pīṭhautā* [? **pṛṣṭhapattra-*], m. *Pl.* ?? a page.

पीड़ *pīṛ* [*pīḍā-*], f. **1.** pain. **2.** suffering.

पीड़क *pīṛak* [S.], adj. & m. **1.** adj. causing pain, or suffering. **2.** m. oppressor; persecutor.

पीड़न *pīṛan* [S.], m. **1.** the causing of pain, or suffering. **2.** crushing.

पीड़ना *pīṛnā* [*pīḍayati*], v.i. reg. to ache.

पीड़ा *pīṛā* [S.], f. **1.** pain. **2.** suffering; affliction. **3.** transf. wrong; oppression. **4.** harm, loss. **5.** compassion. — ~ देना, to give pain (to, को); to ache; to cause suffering, &c. (to); to oppress; to injure. – पीड़ाकर, adj. causing pain, &c. पीड़ा-नाशक, adj. pain-killing.

पीड़ित *pīṛit* [S.], adj. **1.** suffering (from, से), afflicted (by). **2.** oppressed. **3.** squeezed, crushed.

पीढ़ा *pīṛhā* [*pīṭhaka-*], m. a stool, seat. — ऊँचा ~, m. seat of honour.

पीढ़ी *pīṛhī* [*pīṭhikā-*], f. **1.** a small stool, seat. **2.** a generation. **3.** genealogy, pedigree. — ~ दर ~, adv. from generation to generation.

1**पीत** *pīt* [S.], adj. & m. **1.** adj. yellow. **2.** m. yellow colour. — पीत-चंदन, m. yellow (inferior) sandalwood. पीत-तुंड, m. yellow-belly: ? a species of sunbird (= शकरख़ोरा). पीत-धातु, f. Brbh. a yellow mineral earth. पीत-पट, m. Brbh. = पीतांबर, 2. पीत-मणि, f. a yellow gem, topaz. पीत-मस्तक, m. yellow-head: a small bird, *Loxia philippensis*. पीत-रक्त, m. = पीत-मणि. पीताभ [°*ta*+*ā*°], adj. glowing yellow. पीतांबर [°*ta*+*a*°], adj. dressed in yellow clothes; a yellow silk garment; (hence) a title of Kṛṣṇa; a religious mendicant wearing yellow clothes.

2**पीत** *pīt*, f. Brbh. = प्रीति.

पीतक *pītak* [S.], adj. & m. **1.** adj. yellow. **2.** m. brass. **3.** saffron.

पीतता *pītătā* [S.], f. yellowness.

पीतम *pītam* [ad. *priyatama-*: w. H. 1*piy*], adj. & m. dearest (= प्रियतम).

पीतल *pītal* [*pittala-*2, Pk. *pittala-*], m. brass.

पीतस *pītas*, f. *Pl.* wife of a father-in-law's brother (= पितिया सास).

पीतसरा *pītasrā*, m. *Pl. HŚS.* father-in-law's brother (= पितिया ससुर).

पीन *pīn* [S.], adj. **1.** fat. **2.** large, gross; ample. — पातक-पीन, adj. Brbh. grossly sinful.

पीनक *pīnak* [f. P. *pīnakī*, *pīnagī*: ? × *pīnā*], f. stupor, drowsiness (esp. as caused by alcohol or drugs).

पीनना *pīnnā*, v.t. reg. = पींजना.

1**पीनस** *pīnas* [*pīnasa-*], m. **1.** a cold in the nose. **2.** inflammation of the nose.

2**पीनस** *pīnas*, f. reg. an ornamented palanquin.

1**पीना** *pīnā* [*pibati*], v.t. **1.** to drink; to absorb, to soak up (liquid). **2.** to smoke (a cigarette, &c). **3.** fig. to suppress (emotion). **4.** to bear patiently (an unwelcome situation); to refrain from answering; Av. to rely implicitly on (one's strength or situation). **5.** to swallow up (time or resources). — लज्जा घोलकर पी जाना, fig. to be without all sense of shame or modesty.

2**पीना** *pīnā* [*piṇyāka-*], m. oil-seed cake.

पीप *pīp*, m. = पीब.

पीपड़ा *pīpṛā* [**pippīḍa-*], m. *Pl.* a large black ant.

पीपड़ी *pīpṛī* [**pippīḍa-*], m. *Pl.* a small red ant.

[1]**पीपल** *pīpal* [*pippala-*], m. the pīpal or holy fig-tree, *Ficus religiosa*.

[2]**पीपल** *pīpal* [*pippalī-*], f. long pepper, *Piper longum*.

[1]**पीपला** *pīplā* [cf. H. [1] [2]*pīpal*], adj. reg. having to do with the pīpal tree, or the long pepper plant. — ~ मूँड़ [**mūḍa-*], m. = next. ~ मूल, m. root of long pepper.

[2]**पीपला** *pīplā* [*pippalaka-*], m. *Pl.* point of a sword with the part that is near the point; metallic point of a sheath.

पीपा *pīpā* [Pt. *pipa*], m. **1.** a cask, barrel. **2.** cylinder (of gas). **3.** *engin.* a pontoon.

पीब *pīb* [? **pīvra-*: Pk. *pivva-, pibba-*], m. pus. — ~ पड़ना (में), to suppurate.

पीयूष *pīyūṣ* [S.], m. **1.** the milk of a cow which has recently calved. **2.** *mythol.* the food of the gods, nectar.

[1]**पीर** *pīr* [P. *pīr*], m. **1.** a venerable old man, an elder (Muslim); a spiritual guide. **2.** a Muslim saint. **3.** a Muslim sectarian leader. — पीर-मर्द, m. U. an old man. पीर-ज़ादा [P. *-zāda*], m. son of a *pīr*.

[2]**पीर** *pīr* f. Brbh. Av. = पीड़.

पीरी *pīrī* [P. *pīrī*], f. **1.** old age. **2.** status or condition of a *pīr*. **3.** fig. power, influence.

पीरू *pīrū* [Port. *peru*], m. a turkey.

पील *pīl* [P. *fīl, pīl*], m. **1.** an elephant. **2.** (in chess) the bishop. — पील-निशीन [P. *-niśīn*], adj. & m. U. mounted on an elephant. पील-पाँव, m. elephantiasis. पील-पा [P. *-pā*], m. & adj. id.; suffering from elephantiasis. पील-बान [P. *-bān*], m. elephant keeper; elephant-driver. °-वान [P. -*vān*], m. id.

पीलक *pīlak* [cf. H. *pīlā*], m. **1.** the Indian oriole. 2. = पीत-मस्तक.

पीला *pīlā* [*pītala-*[1], Pk. *pīala-*], adj. **1.** yellow. **2.** pale. — ~ पड़ना, to turn pale.

पीलाई *pīlāī* [cf. H. *pīlā*], f. yellowness.

पीलापन *pīlāpan* [cf. H. *pīlā*], m. **1.** yellowness. **2.** paleness.

पीलाम *pīlām*, m. *Pl.* satin.

पीलिया *pīliyā* [cf. H. *pīlā*], m. **1.** jaundice. **2.** reg. yellow sheet worn by a woman from the sixth day after giving birth.

पीली *pīlī* [cf. H. *pīlā*], f. **1.** yellowish or orange sky at dawn. **2.** colloq. *Pl.* a gold coin.

[1]**पीलू** *pīlū*, m. *mus.* name of a classical *rāg*.

[2]**पीलू** *pīlū* [*pīlu-*], m. **1.** a thorny tree of which shoots are used in brushing the teeth. **2.** (? = 1.) *Pl.* the tree *Careya arborea*, or *Salvadora persica*.

[3]**पीलू** *pīlū* [*pīlu-*[2]: ← Drav.], m. a worm in fruit.

पीलो *pīlo*, m. a partic. bird.

पीवर *pīvar* [S.], adj. Brbh. **1.** fat. **2.** heavy (as the breasts).

पीवा *pīvā* [conn. H. *pīnā*], f. water, drink.

पीसन *pīsan* [cf. H. *pīsnā*], m. reg. (E.) flour.

पीसना *pīsnā* [*piṁśati*], v.t. **1.** to grind, to crush. **2.** to gnash (the teeth). **3.** fig. to oppress. **4.** colloq. to drudge, to slave.

पीसनी *pīsnī* [cf. H. *pīsnā*], f. reg. grain for grinding.

पीहर *pīhar* [**pitr̥ghara-*: Pk. *piuhara-*], m. wife's father's house, or family.

पीहू *pīhū* [**priṣu-*; ← NW], m. a flea (= पिस्सू).

पुं- *puṃ-* [S]. man, male: — पुंगव, adj. & m. chief, best; a bull; an eminent person, a hero. पुन्नाग, m. elephant among men: a distinguished man; the tree *Rottleria tinctoria* (source of a drug, and of a yellow dye). पुंलिंग, m. see hw.

पुंगरिया *puṅgriyā*, f. *Pl.* a kind of nose ornament.

पुँगरी *puṁgrī* [cf. H. *pūṁgī*], f. reg. a long pipe (wind instrument).

पुंगव *puṅgav*, m. see s.v. पुं-.

पुंगी *puṅgī*, f. **1.** betel nut (= पूग). 2. = पूँगी. — पुंगी-फल, m. = ~, 1.

पुंज *puñj* [S.], m. mass, accumulation; aggregate. — पुंजीभूत, adj. accumulated; hoarded.

पुंजित *puñjit* [S.], adj. accumulated.

पुँछल्ल *puṁchalla* [cf. H. *pūṁch*], m. an appendage.

पुंजीभूत *puñjībhūt* [S.], adj. see s.v. पुंज.

पुंडरिया *puṇḍariyā* [*puṇḍarin-*], m. reg. a medicinal plant (used to treat eye complaints).

पुंडरीक *puṇḍarīk* [S.], m. **1.** a lotus (esp. white). **2.** *HŚS.* silk-worm. — पुंडरीकाक्ष [°*ka*+*a*°], adj. & m. lotus-eyed; a title of Viṣṇu.

पुंड्र *puṇḍrā* [S.], m. **1.** a kind of sugar-cane. 2. = पुंडरीक. **3.** a sectarian mark or line drawn on the body.

पुंडेरिया *puṇḍeriyā* [conn. *puṇḍarīyaka-*], m. *Pl.* = पुंडरिया.

पुंलिंग *puṃliṅg* [S.], m. & adj. **1.** m. male organ. **2.** fig. virility. ***3.** *gram.* masculine gender. **4.** adj. *gram.* masculine.

पुंश्चली *puṃścalī*, f. see s.v. पुंस्.

पुंस् *puṃs* [S.], m. man, male. — पुंश्चली, f. a loose woman.

पुंसत्व *puṃsatvă* [S.], m. **1.** masculinity. **2.** semen. **3.** *gram.* masculine gender.

पुआ *puā* [*pūpa-*], m. a sweet cake made of flour and sugar or molasses, and fried in *ghī* or oil.

पुआल *puāl* [*palāla-*], m. straw. — ~ गाहना or झाड़ना, to tread out, or to sweep, straw: to spend (one's) time unprofitably.

पुकार *pukār* [cf. H. *pukārnā*], f. **1.** calling out; a shout; cry (as for help); call (to action). **2.** invocation. **3.** petition; suit, complaint. **4.** call, need (for, की); lack (of). **5.** fig. outcry, agitation; complaint (against).

पुकारना *pukārnā* [**pukkār-*: Pk. *pukkārei*, &c.], v.i. & v.t. **1.** v.i. to call out; to shout. **2.** to call (to, को); to summon. **3.** to make petition, or complaint; to call for. **4.** v.t. to invoke (a name). **5.** to call, to name as. — पुकारकर कहना, to speak aloud; to call out. कहकर ~, = ~, 5. हाज़िरी ~, to call a roll.

पुकारा *pukārā* [cf. H. *pukārnā*], m. a call, shout, &c. (= पुकार).

पुख *pukh* [ad. *puṣya-*], m. Av. *astron.* the eighth *nakṣatra* or lunar mansion.

पुखराज *pukhrāj* [ad. **puṣyarāja-*, for *puṣparāga-*, °*rāja-*], m. topaz.

पुख़्ता *pukhtā* [P. *pukhta*], adj. inv. **1.** baked, fired (as bricks). **2.** firm, strong (= पक्का); fixed, definite; confirmed (as a misgiving). **3.** U. mature; wise. — ~ करना, to make firm, strong, &c.

पुचकारना *puckārnā*, v.t. **1.** to coax; to stroke, to pat; to fondle. **2.** transf. to urge on (a horse).

पुचकारा *puckārā*, m. reg. = पुचारा.

¹**पुचकारी** *puckārī*, f. stroking, patting, &c.

²**पुचकारी** *puckārī*, f. Brbh. = पुचारा, पुचकारा.

पुचाड़ा *pucāṛā*, m. = पुचारा.

पुचारा *pucārā*, m. a rag for applying grease or ointment; a whitewashing brush: **1.** coating of clay, or grease, &c., or whitewash. **2.** wiping, rubbing; cleaning. **3.** gloss, polish. **4.** colloq. jejune flattery. — ~ देना (को), to wipe with a wet or greasy cloth, or brush; to apply a coating; to clean, to polish; to softsoap, to flatter. ~ फेरना (पर), = prec.

पुच्छ *pucch* [S.], f. m. **1.** tail. **2.** rear part.

पुच्छत्तर *pucchattar* [cf. H. *pūchnā*], m. colloq. one who is deferential or subservient (in speech).

पुच्छल *pucchal*, adj. having a tail. — ~ तारा, m. a comet.

पुच्छी *pucchī* [cf. H. *pūṁch*], f. *Pl.* a tax 'per tail' on cattle.

पुछना *puchnā* [cf. H. *poṁchnā*], v.i. to be wiped, or erased.

पुछल्ला *puchallā*, m. colloq. tail, sthg. attached: a hanger-on.

पुछवाना *puchvānā* [cf. H. *pūchnā*], v.t. to cause to be asked (by, से).

पुछवैया *puchvaiyā* [cf. H. *pūchnā*], m. one who asks or enquires; one who takes notice (of, का), or shows concern (for); one who looks up (to).

पुछार *puchar*, m. reg. **1.** asking, enquiring. **2.** enquiry.

¹**पुजना** *pujnā* [cf. H. *pūjnā*], v.i. to be worshipped.

²**पुजना** *pujnā* [cf. H. *pūj-*], v.i. *Pl.* to be filled, or completed.

¹**पुजवाना** *pujvānā* [cf. H. *pūjnā*], v.t. = पुजाना.

²**पुजवाना** *pujvānā* [cf. H. *pūj-*], v.t. reg. to cause to be filled, or completed.

पुजा- *pujā-* [cf. H. *pūj-*], v.t. Brbh. **1.** to cause to be filled, or completed; to fill; to complete, to accomplish. **2.** to make good (a lack). **3.** transf. to heal (a wound).

पुजाना *pujānā* [cf. H. *pūjnā*], v.t. to cause to be worshipped (as an idol: by, से); to cause homage to be paid (by).

पुजापा *pujāpā*, m. **1.** objects used in worship. **2.** offering; libation. — ~ फैलाना, colloq. to make great disorder, to make a mess.

पुजारी *pujārī*, m. **1.** the priest of a temple. **2.** a worshipper.

¹**पुट** *puṭ* [S.], m. **1.** cavity, hollow; the hollowed hands. **2.** rounded receptacle or vessel. **3.** covering.

²**पुट** *puṭ*, m. **1.** sprinkling, splashing. **2.** tinge; admixture (as of dialect).

पुटकी *puṭkī*, f. calamity; sudden death; divine wrath. — ~ पड़ना, calamity, &c. to befall (one, पर).

पुटपुटाना *puṭpuṭānā*, v.i. to interject.

पुटी *puṭī* [S.], f. Brbh. Av. **1.** a small bowl. **2.** hollow place; place of concealment.

पुट्ठा *puṭṭhā* [*pr̥ṣṭha-*], m. the rump; haunch. — पुट्ठे पर हाथ न रखने देना, to be hard to approach, inapproachable (a domestic animal, a person); not to be caught, to slip out of trouble; to be repulsive. कितने पुट्ठे घोड़े लाए? how many head of horses did you bring?

पुठवाल *puṭhvāl* [**pr̥ṣṭhapāla-*], m. *Pl. HŚS.* one who gives backing or support.

[1]**पुड़ा** *puṛā* [*puṭa-*], m. a large parcel or packet.

[2]**पुड़ा** *puṛā* [conn. *puṭa-*], m. *Pl.* rump. — पुड़े तोड़ना, to be about to calve (a cow).

पुड़िया *puṛiyā* [cf. *puṭa-*], f. **1.** a small packet. **2.** sthg. contained in a packet; a powder; a medicine. **3.** colloq. a quantity. आफ़त की ~, f. iron. bundle of trouble. **4.** money; belongings, things. **5.** offering (to a god, or at a saint's tomb). — ~ बाँधना, to make up a packet (of medicine). पुड़ियाँ उड़ाना, to make offerings of *abīr* (red powder) and vermilion to a saint.

पुड़ी *puṛī* [*puṭikā-*], f. reg. skin of a drum.

पुण्य *puṇyă* [S.], adj. & m. **1.** adj. auspicious. **2.** virtuous, meritorious (an act). **3.** holy, sacred (an observance, a duty, a place). **4.** pleasing (as a deity to devotees). **5.** m. moral or spiritual merit; virtue. **6.** virtuous act. **7.** welfare (of the individual); happiness. **8.** good fortune. — ~ कर्म, m. meritorious or auspicious act. ~ तिथि, f. auspicious date (as of a holy day); anniversary (of a death). ~ स्मृति, f. auspicious memory. – पुण्य-कर्ता, m. inv. performer of good or meritorious works, benefactor, philanthropist. पुण्य-प्रताप, m. efficacy, or splendidness, of virtue or merit: great merit, &c. पुण्य-फल, m. the fruit of meritorious actions. पुण्य-भूमि, f. the sacred territory of the *madhyadeśa* or Āryāvarta, i.e. north India. पुण्य-लोक, m. world of the holy: paradise. पुण्यवान, adj. virtuous, meritorious. पुण्य-शती, f. centenary anniversary. पुण्यात्मा [°*ya+ā*°], adj. virtuous, righteous, pious; charitable. पुण्यार्थ [°*ya+a*°], for a meritorious purpose: charitable (gift, fund).

पुण्याई *puṇyāī* [cf. H. *puṇya-*], f. *hind.* a virtuous act of which the reward is to be received in a future rebirth.

पुतना *putnā* [cf. H. *potnā*], v.i. to be smeared, &c.

पुतला *putlā* [**putrala-*: Pk. *puttalaya-*], m. **1.** a puppet; a doll. **2.** an idol; effigy. **3.** transf. embodiment. — ~ बनाकर जलाना, to burn in effigy. ~ बाँधना, to censure (one, का); to defame, to slander.

पुतली *putlī* [**putrala-*: Pk. *puttaliyā-*], f. **1.** a puppet; a doll. **2.** an image, effigy. **3.** the pupil of the eye. **4.** transf. a lovely woman. — ~ का तारा करना, to think of as the apple of (one's) eye. ~ का स्वाँग (साँग), or नाच, a puppet show. ~, or पुतलियाँ, फिरना, the eyes to turn up in dying.

पुतवाई *putvāī* [cf. H. *potnā*], f. = पुताई.

पुतवाना *putvānā* [cf. H. *potnā*], v.t. to cause to be smeared, &c. (by, से).

पुताई *putāī* [cf. H. *potnā*], f. **1.** whitewashing. **2.** plastering. **3.** price paid for whitewashing, &c.

पुत्तलिका *puttălikā* [S.], f. = पुतली.

पुत्र *putr* [S.], m. a son; a boy, child. — पुत्र-पौत्रीण, adj. descended from son to son, hereditary. पुत्रवत्, adj. like a son, filial. °ई, f. a woman who has a son. पुत्र-वधू, f. son's wife, daughter-in-law. पुत्रवान, adj. having a son. पुत्रेष्टि [°*tra+i*°], f. sacrifice performed to obtain a son, or when adopting a son.

पुत्रता *putrătā* [S.], f. state or condition of being a son; filial relationship.

पुत्रिका *putrikā* [S.], f. **1.** daughter (esp. one whose son is to perform the funeral obsequies of her father, and to become his heir). **2.** doll, puppet. **3.** pupil of the eye.

पुत्री *putrī* [S.], f. daughter.

पुदीना *pudīnā* [P. *pudīna*], m. mint. — पुदीने का सत, m. peppermint.

पुन *pun*, adv. Brbh. = पुनि.

पुनः *punaḥ* [S.], adv. & pref. **1.** again, anew; re-. **2.** thereafter. **3.** moreover. 4. = पुनश्च. — ~ ~, adv. again and again, ever anew. – पुनःसंगठन, m. reorganisation. °-संगठित, adj. पुनःस्थापना, f. re-establishment; restoration.

पुनना *punnā* [? cf. *puṇya-*], v.i. iron. to be abusive (towards).

पुनर्- *punar-* [S.], pref. again, anew, re-: — पुनरपि, adv. even so; ever anew. पुनरागमन, return; second coming. पुनरारंभ, m. beginning anew, renewal. पुनरावर्तन, m. recurrence; second coming. °-आवर्ती, adj. पुनरावृत्त, adj. recurred (an incident, &c.); repeated. °इ, f. पुनरीक्षण, m. review (of a case, a matter); revision. पुनरुक्त, adj. & m. repeated; tautology. °इ, f. repetition, &c. पुनरुत्थान, m. revival, renaissance; resurrection. पुनरुत्पादन, m. reproduction. पुनरुद्धार, m. revival; restoration. पुनर्गठन, m. reconstruction, reorganisation. पुनर्जन्म, m. rebirth, transmigration; revival, regeneration. पुनर्जागरण, m. renaissance. पुनर्जात, adj. reborn. पुनर्जीवन, m. new life, rebirth. °-जीवित, adj. given new life, revived; resuscitated. पुनर्नवा, f. hogweed. पुनर्निर्माण, m. reconstruction; restoration, renewal. °-निर्मित, adj. पुनर्मुद्रण, m. reprinting; a reprint. °-मुद्रित, adj. पुनर्मूल्यन, m. revaluation. पुनर्वार, adv. for a second time, anew. पुनर्वास, m. resettlement; rehabilitation. °अन, act of resettlement, &c. पुनर्विचार, m. reconsideration (of, पर: as of a view, or a decision). पुनर्विलोकन, m. review (of a matter, a case). पुनर्विवाह, m. remarriage. °इत, adj.

पुनश्- *punaś-* [S.], pref. again, &c. (= पुनर्-): — पुनश्च, adv. and further, P.S. (to a letter).

पुनाग *punāg*, m. reg. = पुन्नाग (see s.v. पुं-).

पुनि *puni* [cf. H. *punar*], adv. Brbh. Av. **1.** again. **2.** moreover.

पुनीत *punīt* [cf. *puṇya-*: ?? × *pavitra-*], adj. pure.

पुन्न *punn*, m. reg. = पुण्य.

पुरंजन *purañjan* [S.], m. Brbh. *hind.* the soul (as dwelling within the 'city' of the body).

पुरंदर *purandar* [S.], m. Brbh. Av. fortress-destroyer: a title of Indra, and of Viṣṇu/Kr̥ṣṇa.

[1]**पुर** *pur* [S.], m. **1.** a town; a fortified place. **2.** (esp. -पुर.) village; locality. — पुरवासी, m. townsman, citizen.

[2]**पुर** *pur* [? *puṭa-*], m. reg. (W. E.) a leather bag used in drawing water for irrigation.

पुर- *pur-* [P. *pur*], adj. chiefly U. full of; very: — पुर-अमन, adj. peaceful. पुर-असर, adj. effective. पुरज़ोर, adj. powerful. पुरजोश, adj. burning (as zeal); passionate. पुरतकल्लुफ़, adj. standing on ceremony, formal. पुरदर्द, adj. painful. पुर-नम, adj. moist (eyes). पुरमज़ाक़, adj. witty (anecdote, &c).

पुरइन *pura'in* [*puṭakinī-*], f. **1.** Brbh. Av. lotus; lotus leaf. **2.** *Pl.* euph. placenta.

पुरः- *puraḥ-* [S.], pref. **1.** before, in front, ahead. **2.** in the presence of: — पुरःसर, adj. & m. preceding, leading; accompanying; a precursor; leader; attendant.

पुरखा *purkhā* [ad. *puruṣa-*], m. **1.** ancestor. **2.** old man, elder. **3.** *Pl.* forefathers.

पुरचक *purcak*, f. *Pl. HŚS.* **1.** sign, hint. **2.** encouragement (to do sthg.), support. **3.** *Pl.* coaxing, trick.

पुरज़ा *purzā* [P. *purza*], m. **1.** part, component (of a mechanism). **2.** piece, bit; scrap. **3.** a note (written on a piece of paper). — पुरज़े उड़ाना, or करना (के), to cut to pieces, to make mincemeat (of). — चलता ~, m. colloq. a shrewd operator.

पुरट *puraṭ*, m. poet. gold.

पुरता *purtā*, adv. reg. fully, completely.

पुरनिया *puraniyā* [cf. H. *purānā*], adj. & m. reg. **1.** adj. old, ancient. **2.** m. an old man, an elder. **3.** colloq. patron.

पुरवट *purvaṭ* [cf. H. [2]*pur*], m. a large leather bag for drawing water from wells for irrigation.

[1]**पुरवा** *purvā* [cf. H. [1]*pur*], m. a village, small town.

[2]**पुरवा** *purvā* [**pūruvavāta-*], m. easterly wind.

पुरवाना *purvānā* [cf. H. *pūr-*], v.t. to cause to be filled (as a container: by, से).

पुरवैया *purvaiyā* [cf. H. *pūrv*], m. reg. the east wind.

पुरश्- *puraś-* [S.], pref. = पुरः: — पुरश्चरण, m. a preliminary rite; repetition of the name of a deity, with burnt offerings (to obtain a purpose).

पुरस्- *puras-* [S.], pref. = पुरः: — पुरस्कर्ता, m. one advancing, promoting (sthg). पुरस्कार, m. placing before, honouring: a reward, prize. पुरस्कृत, adj. rewarded; awarded a prize (a person, or an object, a work). पुरस्तात्, adv. previously. पुरस्सर, m. = पुरःसर.

पुरसा *pursā* [*puruṣa-*], adj. & m. *Pl. HŚS.* **1.** adj. of a man's height. **2.** m. measure of height or depth corresponding to the extent of a man's reach.

[1]**पुरा** *purā* [*pura-*], m. **1.** large village, town. **2.** ward, quarter (of a town).

[2]**पुरा** *purā* [S.], adv. & pref. Brbh. **1.** adv. of old, formerly. **2.** pref. existing of old, former (e.g. पुरातन, adj. ancient, old). — पुरावशेष [°*a*+*a*°], m. an ancient relic; *archaeol.* a find.

[3]**पुरा** *purā* [? *puṭa-*], m. skin of a drum. — दोनों पुरे बजाना, to beat both sides of a drum: to behave hypocritically.

पुरा- *purā-* [*pūrayati*], v.t. Brbh. **1.** to fill. **2.** to fulfil (a wish, a command). **3.** to complete; to form, to trace (decorative designs).

पुराण *purāṇ* [S.], adj. & m. **1.** adj. old; ancient; primeval. **2.** m. a *purāṇa* (a class of voluminous work in Sanskrit dealing with aspects of ancient Indian history, legend, mythology or theology). — ~ खोलना, to start up anew a long-standing or endless dispute.

पुरातत्त्व *purā-tattvă* [S.], m. archaeology. — पुरातत्त्वज्ञ, m. archaeologist.

पुरातन *purā-tan* [S.], adj. & m. **1.** adj. of the past, ancient; old. **2.** m. the past, antiquity. — पुरातनपंथी, adj. & m. conservative.

पुरातनता *purā-tanātā* [S.], f. age, antiquity.

पुरातात्त्विक *purā-tāttvik* [S.], adj. archaeological.

पुराना *purānā* [*purāṇa-*], adj. **1.** old; ancient; of long standing, recurring (as a complaint). **2.** old-fashioned; obsolete. **3.** worn out, useless. **4.** experienced, knowing (a person). — **पुराना-चिराना**, adj. = next. **पुराना-धुराना**, adj. thoroughly old, out of date, worn out, &c.

पुरानापन *purānāpan* [cf. H. *purānā*], m. **1.** age; antiquity. **2.** dated style or nature. **3.** worn-out state, uselessness.

पुरालिपि *purā-lipi* [S.], f. palaeography.

पुरालेख *purā-lekh*, [S.], m. epigraphy; an archive. — **पुरालेख-शास्त्र**, m. epigraphy.

पुरावशेष *purâvă-śeṣ* [S.], m. pl. antiquities, ancient monuments.

[1]**पुरी** *purī* [S.], f. **1.** a town, city. **2.** abode; palace. **3.** fig. the body.

[2]**पुरी** *purī* [cf. H. *pūrā*], f. reg. fullness; completeness.

पुरीष *purīṣ* [S.], m. *Pl. HŚS.* **1.** refuse, rubbish; remains (of food in a container). **2.** excrement.

पुरुष *puruṣ* [S.], m. **1.** a man, human being. ***2.** a male. **3.** a person, individual. **4.** pl. *Pl.* ancestors. **5.** *gram.* person. **उत्तम ~**, m. first person. **6.** the supreme being or soul of the universe. **7.** the primary being, source of the universe. **8.** the human soul. — **पुरुषोचित** [°*ṣa+u*°], adj. proper to a man, or to a male. **पुरुषोत्तम** [°*sa+u*°], adj. best of men; the supreme being, a title of Viṣṇu or Kṛṣṇa. **पुरुषोत्तम मास**, m. intercalary month (= **मल-मास**). **पुरुषगमन**, m. male homosexual intercourse. °**-गामी**, m. a male homosexual. **पुरुषबोधक**, adj. *gram.* masculine. **पुरुषवाचक**, adj. *gram.* personal (a pronoun); indicating or belonging to the masculine gender. **पुरुषानुक्रम** [°*ṣa+a*°], m. succession in the male line. °**इक**, adj. hereditary in the male line. **पुरुषार्थ** [°*ṣa+a*°], m. manliness; exertion, vigour; a goal of man, esp. any one of the *cār padārth* (see s.v. **पदार्थ**). °**ई**, adj. manly; vigorous.

पुरुषत्व *puruṣatvă* [S.], m. **1.** the state of being a man. ***2.** manhood, virility. **3.** manliness.

पुरो- *puro-* [S.], pref. = **पुरः**: — **पुरोगमन**, m. advance; progression. **पुरोगामी**, adj. going forward, pioneering; progressive. °**-गामिता**, f. progressive attitude. **पुरोडाश**, m. cake of ground rice offered as an oblation in fire. **पुरोधा**, m. corr. = next. **पुरोहित**, m. family priest; domestic chaplain. °**आई**, f. office or duties of a family priest; fees of an officiating priest. °**आनी**, f. wife of a family priest.

पुरोता *purotā* [**parapautra-*], m. = **परोता**.

पुरौती *purautī*, f. reg. full repayment (of a debt).

[1]**पुल** *pul* [P. *pul*], m. **1.** a bridge. **2.** an embankment, causeway. **~ बाँधना**, to build a bridge; to provide an abundance (of, **के**). **आशाओं का ~ बाँधना**, to have unlimited hopes. **तारीफ़ का ~ बाँधना**, to praise lavishly. **~ टूटना**, a bridge or embankment to break: (people, &c.) to surge forward, to crowd. **नाक का ~**, m. the bridge of the nose. **हवाई ~ बाँधना**, to build castles in the air. – **पुलबंदी** [P. *-bandī*], f. keeping bridges in repair; sl. male homosexual intercourse. **पुल-सरात** (for **सिरात** [A. *-ṣirāṭ*], m. Av. *musl.* a bridge over which the righteous will pass to paradise on judgment day, while the wicked fall from it into hell.

[2]**पुल** *pul* [S.], m. *Pl. HŚS.* = **पुलक**.

पुलंदा *pulandā* [? cf. *pūla-*], m. a bundle, package.

पुलक *pulak* [S.], m. **1.** erection of the hair on the body (considered as a sign of ecstasy); horripilation. ***2.** thrill of rapture, ecstasy; sudden feeling of terror. — **पुलकस्पंद**, adj. thrilling with ecstasy.

पुलकना *pulaknā* [cf. H. *pulak*], v.i. to feel a thrill of delight.

पुलकाना *pulkānā* [cf. H. *pulak*], v.t. to cause delight, or ecstasy (in).

पुलकित *pulăkit* [S.], adj. enraptured, ecstatic.

[1]**पुलकी** *pulăkī* [S.], m. a type of *kadamba* tree, *Nauclea cadamba.*

[2]**पुलकी** *pulăkī* [S.; or cf. H. *pulak*], adj. = **पुलकित**.

पुलटिस *pulṭis* [Engl. *poultice*], f. a poultice.

[1]**पुलपुलाना** *pulpulānā* [cf. *pilippila-*], v.t. reg. to soften by chewing, to suck at (food).

[2]**पुलपुलाना** *pulpulānā* [conn. H. *pulak*], v.i. reg. the hair on the body to stand up through fright: to be terror-stricken.

पुलपुलाहट *pulpulāhaṭ* [cf. H. *pulpulānā*], f. softness.

पुलस्ति *pulasti* [ad. *pulastya-*], m. Av. *mythol.* the sage Pulastya (one of the mind-born sons of Brahmā).

पुलहाना *pulhānā*, v.t. corr. metath. *Pl.* = **फुसलाना**.

पुलाव *pulāv* [conn. *pulāka-*[1]], m. a dish of fried or boiled rice and meat with spices.

पुलिंदा *pulindā*, m. = पुलंदा.

पुलिज *pulij*, m. reg. land which is never allowed to lie fallow.

पुलिन *pulin* [S.], m. **1.** alluvial land; sandy river-bank. **2.** island; sand-bank.

पुलिया *puliyā* [cf. H. *pul*], f. **1.** a small bridge. **2.** a culvert; drainage pipe.

पुलिस *pulis* [Engl. *police*], f.; m. **1.** police. **2.** m. policeman. — **पुलिस-फ़ौज** [× Engl. *force*], f. police force. **पुलिसवाला**, m. policeman. **पुलिस-सिपाही**, m. id.

पुलीद *pulīd*, adj. & m. = पलीद.

पुल्लिंग *pulliṅg*, m. & adj. = पुंलिंग.

पुश्त *puśt* [P. *puśt*], f. **1.** the back. ***2.** generation, descent, extraction. **3.** rearguard. **4.** back (of a chair). — **~ दर ~**, adv. from generation to generation. – **पुश्तनामा**, m. genealogy, genealogical tree. **पुश्त-बपुश्त** [P. -*ba*-], adv. id. **पुश्तहा-पुश्त** [P. *puśthā*, pl.], id.

पुश्तक *puśtak* [P. *puśtak*], m. kicking with the hind legs (a horse). — **~ झाड़ना**, or **मारना**, to kick out with the hind legs.

पुश्ता *puśtā* [P. *puśta*], m. **1.** buttress. **2.** bank, mound; embankment. **3.** back (as of a chair). **4.** quay. — **पुश्ताबंदी** [P. -*bandī*], f. building an embankment, &c.; buttressing.

पुश्ती *puśtī* [P. *puśtī*], f. U. **1.** support, prop; alliance, aid. **2.** cover of a book.

पुश्तैनी *puśtainī* [cf. H. *puśt*], adj. **1.** hereditary. **2.** ancestral; traditional.

पुषित *puṣit* [S.], adj. nourished, nurtured.

पुष्कर *puṣkar* [S.], m. **1.** a lotus. **2.** water. ***3.** a tank, pond.

पुष्करिणी *puṣkariṇī* [S.], f. **1.** a tank, pond (esp. one containing lotuses). **2.** *Pl. HŚS.* female elephant.

पुष्कल *puṣkal* [S.], adj. **1.** abundant; full, complete. **2.** excellent.

पुष्ट *puṣṭ* [S.], adj. **1.** nourished, fostered; well-fed; fat. **2.** sturdy, strong. **3.** confirmed (information). **4.** healthy, fortifying (as a food). — **पुष्टांग** [°*ta*+*a*°], adj. fat of body or limbs, well-fed. **पुष्टीकरण**, m. confirmation; ratification.

पुष्टई *puṣṭāī* [cf. H. *puṣṭ*], adj. & f. **1.** adj. nutritive; invigorating. **2.** f. nourishment. ***3.** *med.* a tonic.

पुष्टता *puṣṭātā* [S.], f. 1. = पुष्टि, 1. 3. **2.** restorative power (of a food, a medicine).

पुष्टि *puṣṭi* [S.], f. **1.** well-nourished condition; plumpness. **2.** sturdiness. **3.** growth, prosperity. **4.** confirmation (as of a statement, a view). **5.** fostering. — **पुष्टिकर**, adj. = पुष्ट, 4. °**-कारक**, adj. id. **पुष्टि-मार्ग**, m. path of fostering, or tending (the soul): the philosophico-devotional system of Vallabha.

पुष्टीकरण *puṣṭīkaraṇ* [S.], m. see s.v. पुष्ट.

पुष्प *puṣp* [S.], m. **1.** a flower. **2.** transf. menstruation. **3.** an eye complaint; specks on the eye. — **पुष्प-फल**, m. flowers and fruit. **पुष्प-माला**, f. garland of flowers. **पुष्प-रस**, m. nectar or honey. **पुष्प-राग**, flower-coloured: topaz. **पुष्प-रेणु** m. pollen. **पुष्पवती**, adj. f. flowering; flower-like; menstruating. **पुष्प-सार**, m. nectar or honey; perfume. **पुष्पांजलि** [°*pa*+*a*°], f. offering, tribute of flowers.

पुष्पक *puṣpak* [S.], m. **1.** a flower. **2.** *mythol.* the aerial vehicle of Kuvera. **3.** *Pl.* ferrous sulphate. **4.** *Pl. HŚS.* a disease of the eye, albugo.

पुष्पिका *puṣpikā* [S.], f. **1.** a scribe's colophon. **2.** chapter of a book. **3.** euph. incrustation of dirt (as tartar on teeth).

पुष्पित *puṣpit* [S.], adj. **1.** flowering. **2.** abundant in flowers. — **पुष्पित-पल्लवित**, adj. flourishing (an enterprise, or hopes).

पुष्पिता *puṣpitā* [S.], adj. f. *Pl. HŚS.* = पुष्पवती, 3.

पुष्पी *puṣpī* [S.], adj. flowering, blossoming.

पुष्य *puṣyă* [S.], m. *astron.* the eighth lunar asterism.

पुसपूत *puspūt* [ad. *poṣyaputra*-: w. H. *pūt*], m. reg. an adopted son.

पुस्त *pust* [S.], m. *Pl. HŚS.* **1.** working or modelling in clay, or in other materials. 2. = पुस्तक.

पुस्तक *pustak* [S.: ← Ir.], f. a book; a volume; manuscript. — **पुस्तककार**, m. writer or compiler of a book. **पुस्तकाकार** [°*ka*+*ā*°], adv. in book form, (appearing) as a book. **पुस्तकाध्यक्ष** [°*ka*+*a*°], m. librarian. **पुस्तकालय** [°*ka* +*ā*°], m. library. °**आध्यक्ष**, m. librarian.

पुस्तकीय *pustăkīyă* [S.], adj. having to do with books; bookish.

पुस्तिका *pustikā* [S.], f. a small book; booklet; brochure.

पुहना *puhnā* [cf. H. [1]*ponā*], v.i. to be strung, threaded.

पुहुप *puhup* [*puṣpa*-], m. a flower.

पुहुमि *puhumi* [ad. *bhūmi*-], f. Brbh. Av. = भूमि.

पूँगड़ा *pūṁgṛā* [**poṅga-²*], m. *Pl.* reg. a boy.

पूँगी *pūṁgī* [*poṅga-¹* × H. *phūṁknā*], f. reg. = पौंगी.

पूँछ *pūṁch* [cf. *puccha-*], f. **1.** tail. **2.** rear part (as of an aircraft). **3.** fig. a hanger-on. — ~ पकड़कर चलना, to follow blindly and in a dependent way. बड़ी ~ का, adj. colloq. prominent; ostentatious. पूँछदार [P. *-dār*], adj. having a tail. पूँछ-हिलौवल, m. reg. (E.) tail-wagging: abject or cringing flattery.

पूँछार *pūṁchār*, adj. & m. *Pl.* **1.** adj. having a tail. **2.** m. an animal having a long tail.

पूँजी *pūṁjī* [cf. *puñja-*], f. heap, quantity: **1.** funds, capital; assets; money. **2.** a fund. **3.** wealth, store. — पूँजीगत, adj. having to do with capital (as expenditure). पूँजी-पति, m. a wealthy man; a capitalist. पूँजी-प्रधान, adj. capitalist (a country, &c). पूँजीवाद, m. capitalism, theory of capitalism. °ई, adj. & m. capitalist. पूँजीवाला, adj. id. पूँजीशाही [P. *-śāhī*], adj. & f. capitalist; capitalism.

पूग *pūg* [S.: ← Drav.], m. **1.** betel (nut and plant). **2.** the jack-fruit. — पूग-फल, m. betel nut.

पूग- *pūg-* [*pūryate*, w. MIA anal. *-gg-*], v.i. **1.** to be completed. **2.** to elapse (a period of time). **3.** reg. (Raj.) to arrive.

पूगी *pūgī* [cf. H. *pūg*], f. = पूग, 1.

पूछ *pūch* [*pṛcchā-*, and H. *pūchnā*], f. **1.** enquiry (into, की). **2.** demand, request (for sthg. needed, की). **3.** attention, respect (for a person's wishes or opinion). — पूछ-गछ, f. = next. पूछ-ताछ, f. enquiry, investigation; interrogation. पूछ-ताछ करना, to enquire, &c. (into). पूछ-पाछ, f. = पूछ-ताछ.

पूछन *pūchan* [cf. H. *pūchnā*], m. reg. asking, enquiring.

पूछना *pūchnā* [*pṛcchati*], v.t. **1.** to ask, to enquire (of, से). **2.** (usu. neg., or in rhetor. contexts) to take notice (of, को); to show due care or regard (for). — बात ~, to ask a question. बात न ~, to take no notice (of, को). वह इतना अमीर है कि कुछ न पूछिए, don't ask about his wealth: he is incredibly rich. – पूछा-ताछी, f. = पूछ-ताछ. पूछा-पाछी, f. id.

पूछा *pūchā* [ad. *pṛcchā-*; cf. H. *pūch*], f. reg. enquiry (into the future: by a wizard).

पूज- *pūj-* [*pūryate*], v.i. reg. **1.** to be filled; to be healed (a wound). **2.** to be completed; to elapse (a full year, &c.); to be paid (a debt). **3.** Av. to be fulfilled (as a wish). **4.** Brbh. to be even (with), the equal (of).

पूजक *pūjak* [S.], adj. & m. **1.** adj. worshipping, &c. (see पूजा). **2.** venerating. **3.** m. a worshipper.

पूजत *pūjat* [cf. H. *pūjnā*], f. worshipping; venerating.

पूजन *pūjan* [S.], m. **1.** worshipping, &c. (see पूजा). 2. = पूजा. **3.** venerating; receiving with due respect (a visitor).

पूजना *pūjnā* [*pūjayati*: Pk. *pujjaï*], v.t. **1.** to worship; to adore. **2.** to venerate. **3.** iron. to bribe. **4.** colloq. to beat.

पूजनीय *pūjănīyă* [S.], adj. = पूज्य.

पूजयिता *pūjayitā* [S.], m. inv. a worshipper.

पूजा *pūjā* [S.], f. **1.** worship; adoration (of a deity, &c). **2.** veneration; homage. **3.** idolatry. **4.** iron. a bribe. **5.** colloq. a beating. — ~ करना (की), to worship, &c. — पूजा-पाठ, m. worship, with the reading of religious texts, = ~, 1.

पूजित *pūjit* [S.], adj. **1.** worshipped; adored. **2.** venerated.

पूजेरू *pūjerū*, m. reg. = पुजारी.

पूज्य *pūjyă* [S.], adj. **1.** to be worshipped (a deity). **2.** venerable; honoured. — पूज्यपाद, adj. whose feet are to be revered: = ~. पूज्यमान, adj. = ~. पूज्यवर, adj. greatly venerable, &c.

पूज्यत्व *pūjyatvă* [S.], m. *Pl.* worshipfulness; venerability.

पूट *pūṭ* [**puṭṭa-¹*], m. *Pl.* sacrum bone of a cow.

पूठ *pūṭh* [*pṛṣṭha-*], m. reg. = पुट्ठा.

पूठा *pūṭhā* [*pṛṣṭha-*], m. *Pl.* the cover of a book; pasteboard.

पूड़ा *pūṛā* [cf. *pūpa-*], m. *Pl. HŚS.* 1. = पुआ. 2. = पूड़ी.

पूड़ी *pūṛī* [cf. *pūpa-*], f. = पूरी.

¹पूत *pūt* [*putra-*], m. a son. — पूतों फलना, to bear fruit in sons: to be prolific; to prosper.

²पूत *pūt* [S.], adj. purified; pure. — पूत-फल, m. inv. pure-fruited: the jack-fruit. पूतात्मा [°*ta* + *ā*°], adj. & m. pure-souled; one whose soul is pure.

¹पूति *pūti* [S.], f. purification, purity, sanctity.

²पूति *pūti* [S.], f. Brbh. putrefaction; stench.

पूनम *pūnam* [*pūrṇimā-*], f. full moon (day, night).

पूनसलाई *pūn-salāī* [H. *pūnī* + H. *salāī*], f. *Pl. HŚS.* a thin roller on which cotton is prepared for spinning.

पूनी *pūnī* [**pūna-*: Pk. *pūṇī-*], f. a roll of cotton prepared for spinning, a skein. — **चरखा-पूनी**, f. (spinning-)wheel and skein: hard work at spinning.

पूनो *pūno* [*pūrṇamās-*], m. reg. = **पूनम**.

पूप *pūp* [S.], m. *Pl. HŚS.* = **पुआ**.

पूपला *pūplā*, m. reg. = **पुआ**.

पूय *pūyă* [S.], m. pus.

[1]**पूर** *pūr* [[1]*pūra-*], adj. full. — ~ **पड़ना**, to able to be perform (a task: **में**).

[2]**पूर** *pūr* [S.], m. **1.** filling; rising (of water). **2.** large expanse of water. **3.** filling (of a pastry, &c). — **पूरंपूर**, adv. full, brimful (= **पूरा**).

पूर- *pūr-* [*pūrayati*], v.t. Av. **1.** to fill, &c. (= **पूरा करना**). **2.** to trace, or to fill in, with flour or coloured powder, or stones (geometrical designs, on auspicious occasions). **3.** to weave (as a spider). **4.** to blow (a conch).

पूरक *pūrak* [S.], adj. & m. **1.** adj. filling, filling up. **2.** completing; complementary; supplementary. **3.** m. a complement, or supplement (to, **का**); sthg. the equal (of). **4.** *math.* a multiplier.

पूरण *pūraṇ* [S.], m. **1.** filling, filling up. **2.** completing. **3.** populating (a region). **4.** *med.* pouring drops (into, **में**: as into the ear). — ~ **करना**, to fill up, &c.

पूरन *pūrn* [ad. *pūrṇa-*], adj. Brbh. = **पूर्ण**.

पूरब *pūrab* [ad. *pūrva-*], adj. & m. = **पूर्व**.

[1]**पूरबी** *pūrbī* [cf. H. *pūrab*], adj. & m. = **पूर्वी**.

[2]**पूरबी** *pūrbī* [cf. H. *pūrab*], f. **1.** eastern language; eastern Hindi. **2.** an eastern product (as tobacco, or rice). **3.** *mus.* name of a *rāgiṇī*.

पूरबीपन *pūrbīpan* [cf. H. [2]*pūrbī*], m. eastern dialect characteristics or usage (in standard Hindi).

पूरा *pūrā* [*pūra-*[1]], adj. **1.** full, complete; satisfied (as desires). **पुरे का** ~, adj. quite complete, &c. **2.** entire, whole; made good (a deficiency). **3.** completed, accomplished (as a task); spent (a period of time). **4.** fulfilled, kept (as one's word); fulfilling. **बात का** ~, adj. keeping one's word. **5.** exact, precise; sufficient. ~ **सामान**, m. everything needed (for a purpose). **6.** complete, absolute; real (a friend, &c.); unqualified, unrestricted; arrant (as a villain). ~ **उस्ताद**, m. a real master; **पूरी बहार पर**, adv. in full bloom (as youth, vigour). — ~ **उतरना**, to come up to a mark or standard; to be satisfactory, to pass a test; to be proved correct (as an assertion). ~ **करना**, to fill, to fill up; to complete, to finish; to carry out, to keep (a promise, a condition); to act in accordance with (a prophecy); to make good (a deficiency); to satisfy (a desire); to spend, to complete (a period of time). ~ **पड़ना**, to be enough, to suffice. **पूरे दिन लगना**, to approach full term (of pregnancy). **दिन पूरे होना (के)**, (one's) time (in the world) to end; to come to full term (of pregnancy).

पूराई *pūrāī* f. reg. = **पूरापन**.

पूरापन *pūrāpan* [cf. H. *pūrā*], m. fullness, completeness, &c.

पूरित *pūrit* [S.], adj. **1.** filled. **2.** complete; accomplished.

पूरिया *pūriyā* m. f. *mus. Pl. HŚS.* name of a *rāg*, or of a *rāgiṇī*.

पूरी *pūrī* [*pūra-*[2]], f. a small round cake of unleavened wheat flour, deep-fried in *ghī* or oil.

पूर्ण *pūrṇ* [S.], adj. & m. **1.** adj. full, filled, &c. (= **पूरा**). **2.** *gram.* perfective. **3.** m. a whole (as opposed to a part). — **पूर्णकाम**, adj. of fulfilled desire(s). **पूर्णकालिक**, adj. full-time (work). **पूर्णतः**, adv. completely, entirely. °**-तया**, adv. id. **पूर्ण-प्रतापी**, m. one whose glory is complete or unqualified. **पूर्णमासी**, f. the day or night of full moon; a ceremony or sacrifice performed on the day of full moon. **पूर्णरूपेण**, adv. = **पूर्णतः**. **पूर्णवयस्क**, adj. of full age, adult. **पूर्ण-विराम**, m. full stop. **पूर्णांक** [°*ṇa*+*a*°], m. a whole number; **पूर्णांकों में**, adv. in round numbers. **पूर्णाकार** [°*ṇa*+*ā*°], m. full scale (as a model). **पूर्णाधिकार** [°*ṇa*+*a*°], m. full authority. °**प्राप्त**, adj. with full powers; plenipotentiary. **पूर्णायु** [°*ṇa*+*ā*°], f. full age, entire life; extreme age. **पूर्णाहुति** [°*ṇa*+*ā*°], f. *hind.*, complete oblation: the burnt offering which concludes a ceremony; fig. concluding act or rite.

पूर्णता *pūrṇătā* [S.], f. **1.** fullness. **2.** completeness, completion. **3.** perfect state, perfection.

पूर्णिमा *pūrṇimā* [S.], f. the night or day of full moon.

पूर्ति *pūrti* [S.], f. **1.** filling. **2.** accomplishment (of a purpose, an aim). ***3.** making good (a want); satisfying, meeting (a need, demand); supply (of a commodity). **4.** solving, solution (of a problem). **5.** fullness, completeness. **6.** *math.* multiplication.

पूर्व *pūrv* [S.], adj. & m. **1.** adj. forward, foremost. **2.** eastward; east, eastern; first (light). **3.** prior, preceding, former. **4.** initial; preliminary; pre-: e.g. **पूर्व-निश्चित**, adj. pre-determined. **5.** ancient. **6.** adv. before, previously, formerly. **7.** ppn. (w. **के, से**) in front (of); before, previous (to). **8.** m. the east. — पूर्व-कल्पना, f. preconceived idea; conjecture. °-कल्पित, adj. पूर्वकालिक, adj. of former times, ancient; *gram.* past (tense). °-कालीन, adj. id., 1. पूर्व-कृत, adj. done formerly; done in a prior existence. पूर्व-गत, adj. preceding, former. °-गामी, adj. & m. preceding; a predecessor. पूर्वज, adj. & m. born before: elder; ancestor; elder brother. पूर्व-ज्ञान, m. foreknowledge; prior knowledge (from an earlier birth). पूर्वदैहिक, adj. having to do with, or performed in, a former bodily existence. पूर्व-निर्धारित, adj. predetermined. पूर्व-पक्ष, m. first side (of an argument), assertion; plaintiff's statement or case; fortnight of the waxing moon. पूर्व-फलगुनी, f. = next. पूर्व-फालगुनी, f. *astron.* the eleventh lunar asterism. पूर्व-पीठिका, f. background; background or introductory information. पूर्व-प्रत्यय, m. *gram.* prefix. पूर्व-भाद्रपदा, f. *astron.* the twenty-sixth lunar asterism. पूर्ववत्, adv. as before. पूर्ववर्ती, adj. & m. previous, preceding; a predecessor. पूर्व-शर्त, f. precondition. पूर्वसर्ग, m. *gram.* preposition. पूर्वाग्रह [°*va* + *ā*°], m. prejudice, bias. पूर्वाधार [°*va* + *ā*°], m. premise (for action, of an argument). पूर्वाधिकारी [°*va* + *a*°], m. former proprietor; predecessor in office. पूर्वानुमान [°*va* + *a*°], , m. supposition; forecast (as of weather). पूर्वानुराग [°*va* + *a*°], m. love arising before the lovers have met. पूर्वापर [°*va* + *a*°], m. & adj. first and last, all aspects (of a matter); east and west; in front and rear, in all aspects. पूर्वाभास [°*va* + *ā*°], m. foreboding, premonition. पूर्वाभ्यास [°*va* + *a*°], m. prior practice, rehearsal. पूर्वार्द्ध [°*va* + *a*°], m. first half. पूर्वावस्था [°*va* + *a*°], f. previous condition, or situation. पूर्वाषाढ़ा [°*va* + *a*°], f. *astron.* the first of two constellations called Aṣāṛhā; the eighteenth or the twentieth lunar asterism. पूर्वाह्न [°*va* + *a*°], m. morning. पूर्वोक्त [°*va* + *u*°], adj. mentioned before, or above. पूर्वोत्तर [°*va* + *u*°], adj. & m. north-east. °ई, adj. id. पूर्वोपाय [°*va* + *u*°], m. precaution. °ई, adj.

-पूर्वक *-pūrvak* [S.], suffix (forms adverbs of manner from nouns, e.g. आदरपूर्वक, respectfully).

पूर्वता *pūrvătā* [S.], f. priority, precedence.

पूर्वी *pūrvī* [S.], adj. eastern.

पूर्वीय *pūrvīyă* [S.], adj. = पूर्वी.

पूला *pūlā* [*pūla-*], m. **1.** bundle, sheaf (of grass, straw). **2.** hank, skein (of thread).

पूली *pūlī* [*pūla-*], f. **1.** a small sheaf. **2.** small hank or skein.

[1]**पूष** *pūṣ*, m. *Pl.* = पुष्य.

[2]**पूष** *pūṣ* [S.], m. *Pl. HŚS.* the mulberry *Morus indica*.

पूषन *pūṣan* [S.], m. poet. the sun.

[3]**पूस** *pūs* [*puṣya-*[2]], m. the tenth lunar month of the Hindu year (December-January).

पृच्छा *pr̥cchā* [S.], f. asking, questioning; enquiry.

पृथक् *pr̥thak* [S.], adj. **1.** separate, distinct. **2.** aside, apart. **3.** individual. — ~ करना, to separate, to distinguish; to isolate.

पृथकता *pr̥thakătā* [S.], f. **1.** separateness; diversity. **2.** individuality. — पृथकतावाद, m. separatism; isolationism. °ई, adj. & m.

पृथिवी *pr̥thivī*, f. = पृथ्वी.

पृथु *pr̥thu* [S.], adj. broad; spacious.

पृथ्वी *pr̥thvī* [S.], f. **1.** the wide world, the earth. **2.** earth, ground, soil. — पृथ्वीतल, m. surface of the earth; ground, bare ground. पृथ्वीनाथ, m. lord of the earth: king. पृथ्वीपुत्र, m. son of earth: the planet Mars.

पृश्नि *pr̥śni* [S.], f. *Pl. HŚS.* **1.** dappled, spotted; variegated. **2.** small of stature.

पृष्ठ *pr̥ṣṭh* [S.], m. **1.** the back. **2.** hinder or rear part; back (of a document, &c.); spine, or cover (of book). **3.** upper surface. **4.** page. — पृष्ठ-पोषक, m. supporter, partisan. पृष्ठ-भूमि, f. background, rear; atmosphere, milieu; context (of events). पृष्ठभौमिक, adj. serving as background, underlying. पृष्ठांकन [°*ṭha* + *a*°], m. endorsement (of a document).

पें *peṁ* [onom.], m. **1.** singing; humming, buzzing. **2.** squeak, squeal. **3.** whimper, whine. — ~ निकाल देना, to knock the conceit out (of, का).

पेंग *peṁg* [cf. *prenkhā-*], f. m. swinging. — ~ बढ़ना, to rise, to increase (as intoxication, exultation). ~ मारना, or लेना, to swing high.

पेंच *peṁc*, m. = पेच.

पेंड- *peṁḍ-* [**peṇḍa-*[2]]. reg. a lump, &c. (= पिंड, पींड):— पेंड-खजूर, m. a date. पेंडालू, m. the round yam; sweet potato.

पेंदा *peṁdā* [**penda-*[1]], m. **1.** bottom (of a pot, box, or of a ship, &c). **2.** backside. **3.** transf. breech (of a cannon). — पेंदे के बल बैठना, to squat cross-legged; to have no answer, to be subdued.

पेंदी *peṁdī* [cf. H. *peṁdā*], f. **1.** bottom, base, &c. (= पेंदा, 1., 2). **2.** transf. breech (of a gun, musket). **3.** colloq. a root vegetable. — बे-पेंदी का लोटा, m. pot with a rounded bottom: a person of constantly varying views or conduct, an undependable person.

पेंशन *peṁśan* [Engl. *pension*], m. a pension. — पेंशन-याफ़्ता [P. *-yāfta*], adj. inv. having a pension, pensioned.

पेंसिल *pemsil* [Engl. *pencil*], f. pencil.

पेई *peī*, f. *Pl. HŚS.* a small box or chest.

पेख- *pekh-* [*prekṣate*], v.i. Brbh. Av. **1.** to see. **2.** to desire.

पेखनो *pekhno* [cf. H. *pekh-*], m. Brbh. puppet-show; spectacle; illusion.

पेच *pec* [P. *pec*], m. **1.** turn, twist; bend (as of a road). **2.** turn, revolution. **3.** coil (as of a turban); plait, fold. **4.** entanglement; contest (as between kite-flyers). **5.** complication, obstacle, difficulty. **6.** stratagem, device; trick (as in wrestling). **7.** guile. **8.** transf. a screw. **9.** a propeller (= पंखा). **10.** Brbh. an ornament (for the ear). — ~ करना, to trick, to deceive. ~ कसना, to bind on (a turban) tightly; to adjust (a turban). ~ का, adj. awkward, complicated. ~ काटना, to cut another's kite-string with one's own. ~ खाना, to be twisted; to bend (a river); to coil; to writhe; to fall into difficulties. ~ डालना, to throw obstacles in the way (of, में); to entangle (another's kite-string). ~ देना, to give a turn (to, को), to twist, to screw; to deceive. ~ पड़ना, a complication to arise (in, में); to be entangled (in). ~ बाँधना, to grapple (with, से). ~ लड़ाना, or लेना, to fight paper kites (with, से). ~ लगाना, to try a trick (as in wrestling). – पेचकश, [P. *-kaś*], m. screwdriver; corkscrew. पेच-ताब [P. *-tāb*], m. twisting and turning; anxiety; suppressed anger. पेचदार [P. *-dār*], adj. twisting, twisted; coiled; spiral; involved, tortuous; deceitful. पेच-पाच, m. entanglement, complication(s); guile. पेचवान [P. *-vān*], m. colloq. a large hookah.

पेचक *pecak* [P. *pecak*], f. ball, or skein (of thread).

पेचा *pecā* [ad. B. *pemcā*], m. *Pl.* an owl.

पेचिश *peciś* [P. *peciś*], f. **1.** bowel pain. ***2.** dysentery; diarrhoea.

पेचीदगी *pecīdagī* [P. *pecīdagī*], f. **1.** twisting, twistedness. **2.** complexity.

पेचीदा *pecīdā* [P. *pecīda*], adj. **1.** twisted. **2.** complex, involved, complicated.

पेचीला *pecīlā* [cf. H. *pec*], adj. **1.** twisted, coiled, &c. **2.** involved, complicated.

पेट *peṭ* [**peṭṭa-²*: Pk. *peṭṭa-*], m. **1.** the belly. **2.** the stomach. **3.** the womb. **4.** transf. pregnancy. ~ होना (को), to be pregnant. **5.** transf. inner or hidden part; cavity; capacity; bore (of a firearm). **6.** fig. inner thoughts, sthg. secret. **7.** appetite. **8.** livelihood. ~ काटना, to deprive (one) of the means of existence. — ~ आना (को), to have diarrhoea; to be pregnant. ~ का कुत्ता, m. a person dog-like in (his) appetites: a greedy or mercenary person. ~ का टूटा, adj. broken-bellied: starving. ~ का धंधा, m. the daily round of obtaining food; = ~, 7. ~ का पानी न पचना, fig. to be impatient. ~ का पानी न हिलना, iron. not be inconvenienced in the slightest degree. ~ की अँगार, m. craving for food; violent emotion. ~ की आग, f. the pangs of hunger. ~ की आग बुझाना, to satisfy hunger. ~ की बात, or बातें, f. close or intimate secret(s). ~ की मार, f. starvation, want of food. ~ के लिए, adv. for the stomach's sake, for food. ~ के हाथ बिकना, (one's conduct) to be at the mercy of one's stomach. पेट खला-, Brbh. to reveal one's inner thoughts, or one's misery. ~ गड़ना, the stomach to sink: to suffer indigestion. ~ गिरना (का), to miscarry. ~ गिराना (का), to cause an abortion. ~ चलना (का), to be purged; to have diarrhoea; food to be found (for). ~ छूटना, id., 1., 2. ~ जारी होना, = ~ आना. ~ दिखाना, to point at the stomach: to complain of hunger and poverty; to beg for food. ~ पानी होना, to have diarrhoea or dysentery; fig. to be fearful. ~ पालना (अपना), to manage to live decently; to live from hand to mouth; to be self-indulgent; to be selfish. ~ पीठ एक होना, belly and back to be one; to be no more than skin and bone. ~ फटना, the belly to burst; to be impatient; to burst with envy, &c. ~ फूलना, the belly to swell; to be pregnant; to be bursting (as with laughter; or with painful emotion). ~ बढ़ाना, to eat greedily; to take another's share, or rights. ~ बाँधना, to go short of, or without, food. ~ बोलना, the stomach to rumble. ~ भर, adv. to satiety; a bellyful. ~ भरना, v.i. the belly to be filled; to be satisfied, or surfeited (with, से). ~ मारना (अपना), to subdue hunger; to go short of food; to stab (oneself) in the belly; to take a punishment on oneself: to excuse a child's misdeed (out of maternal love). ~ मुँह चलना, to have cholera. ~ में घुसना, or पैठना, or बैठना, to worm oneself into the confidence, or favour (of, के); to become intimate (with). ~ में डालना, to swallow; to conceal (a secret). ~ में दाढ़ी होना, fig. to have an old head on young shoulders. ~ में पड़ना, to be conceived (a child). ~ में पाँव होना, fig. to be sly, or designing. ~ में बल पड़ना, the stomach to ache (from laughing, &c). ~ में बात पचना, sthg. to be kept to oneself. ~ में बात रखना, to keep sthg. to oneself. ~ रखाना, to cause to be pregnant; to get oneself pregnant. तू किससे ~ रखा आई है? who have you got yourself pregnant by? ~ रहना (को), to conceive, to be pregnant. ~ से, adj. pregnant. ~ से पट्टी बाँधना, to bind a tight bandage round the stomach (to dull hunger). ~ से पाँव निकालना, fig. to go beyond decent bounds (in conduct), to show (one's) teeth, or claws. न ~ में आँत न मुँह में दाँत, having neither innards nor teeth: a totally wretched or craven person. – पेट-चोट्टी, f. reg. a pregnant woman whose condition is not yet noticeable. पेट-पालू, adj. greedy, gluttonous. पेट-पोंछन, m. colloq. a woman's last child. पेट-भर, m. a full meal, a good feed. °आ, adj. iron. well-off. पेट-भराऊ, adj. & m. enough (food) to fill the stomach; a bellyful. पेट-मरानी, f. a prostitute. पेटवाली, adj. f. pregnant.

पेटक *peṭak* [S.], m. Brbh. **1.** a covered basket (for books, clothes, &c). **2.** fig. a multitude.

पेटल *peṭal* [cf. **peṭṭa*-[2]], adj. big-bellied.

पेटा *peṭā* [**peṭṭa*-[2]], m. **1.** middle part; belly. **2.** breadth, width; distance across. **3.** circumference, girth. **4.** slackness, sag (in a rope, string). **5.** a round or total sum. पेटे में, adv. for the round sum (of, के). — ~ भरना, to fill in details.

पेटारा *peṭārā*, m. Brbh. = पिटारा.

पेटारी *peṭārī*, f. Av. = [1]पिटारी.

पेटिका *peṭikā* [S.], f. a small box.

पेटिया *peṭiyā* [cf. H. *peṭ*], m. ? f. Brbh. a day's allowance of food; allowance.

[1]**पेटी** *peṭī* [cf. **peṭṭa*-[2]], f. **1.** belt; girth (of a horse). **2.** Brbh. belly (= पेट, 1). **3.** track (of caterpillar tractor, &c). — ~ उतरना, to take off one's belt: to be discharged; to be dismissed (from a uniformed service). ~ लड़ाना, to have sexual intercourse (with, से). – पेटीदार [P. *-dār*], adj. having tracks (a vehicle).

[2]**पेटी** *peṭī* [**peṭṭa*-[1]], f. box, case (of equipment, &c.); bundle.

पेटुनी *peṭunī* [cf. H. *peṭ*], f. colloq. reg. a pregnant woman.

पेटू *peṭū* [cf. H. *peṭ*], adj. & m. having a stomach: **1.** adj. gluttonous. **2.** m. a glutton.

पेटौखा *peṭaukhā*, m. *Pl.* looseness of the bowels.

पेठा *peṭhā*, m. **1.** the white gourd-melon, *Benincasa cerifera* = (कुम्हड़ा). **2.** sugared slices of *peṭhā*.

[1]**पेड़** *peṛ*, m. a tree; a shrub.

[2]**पेड़** *peṛ* [**peḍa*-: Pk. *peḍa*-], m. reg. a lump, round mass.

पेड़ना *peṛnā* [*prapīḍayati*], v.t. reg. = पेरना.

पेड़ा *peṛā* [**peḍa*-: Pk. *peḍa*-], m. **1.** reg. (W.) a lump (as of dough). **2.** a sweet made of milk, sugar and spices.

[1]**पेड़ी** *peṛī*, f. = पेड़ा, 2.

[2]**पेड़ी** *peṛī* [cf. H. *peṛ*], f. reg. **1.** Av. the trunk of a tree. **2.** a second crop which grows from the stubble of the original plants. **3.** E. a rate paid by cultivators to landlords for use of valuable trees (as palm, mango, *mahuā*).

पेड़ू *peṛū* [**peḍḍuka*-], m. **1.** the lower belly. **2.** the genital region.

पेन्हाई *penhāī* [? conn. *prekṣate*: Pk. *pehaï*], f. reg. maternal tenderness, fondness.

पेय *pey* [S.], adj. & m. **1.** adj. drinkable. **2.** m. any drink: water; milk.

पेयूष *peyūṣ* [S.], m. = पीयूष.

पेरना *pernā* [cf. *prapīḍayati*], v.t. **1.** to press, to crush (cane, &c.); to grind. **2.** fig. to afflict.

पेल *pel* [cf. H. *pelnā*], m., f. **1.** m. a shove, push. **2.** -पेल, f. crush, crowd (see रेल-पेल). — ~ मारना, to shove. – पेल-पाल, adj. shoving, pushing.

पेलड़ *pelaṛ* [*pela*-], m. a testicle.

पेलड़ा *pelṛā* [cf. *pela*-], m. = पेलड़.

पेलढ़ *pelaṛh*, m. = पेलड़.

पेलना *pelnā* [**prelayati*: Pk. *pellei*], v.t. **1.** to shove, to push, to thrust, to jostle. **2.** to push on, to impel. **3.** to push in or down (also pej). **4.** to squeeze out. **5.** Brbh. Av. to disregard; to reject, to abandon.

[1]**पेला** *pelā* [cf. H. *pelnā*], m. **1.** push, shove. **2.** fig. quarrel. **3.** attack.

[2]**पेला** *pelā* [*pela*-], m. = पेलड़.

पेलू *pelū* [cf. H. *pelnā*], m. pusher, shover.

पेवड़ी *pevṛī* [**pītamṛdikā*-], f. *Pl. HŚS.* **1.** yellow chalk. **2.** transf. a yellow dye of animal origin.

पेवस *pevas* [*peyūṣa*-, Pk. *peūsa*-], m. = पेवसी.

पेवसी *pevsī* [cf. *peyūṣa*-, Pk. *peūsa*-], f. = पीयूष, 1.

पेवस्त *pevast*, adj. = पैवस्ता.

पेश *peś* [P. *peś*], adv. **1.** forward, in front; present. **2.** previously. — ~ आना, to come forward; to present (itself: as a new topic, &c.); to occur, to happen; to behave (towards, से), to deal (with). ~ करना, to put forward, to submit (a proposal, &c.); to offer, to present (to, के सामने). ~ चलना, to go forward, to advance; to serve (its purpose), to be effective. ~ पाना (से), to overcome (an opponent). ~ होना, to be present. — पेशक़दमी, f. going ahead of, outstripping. पेश-क़ब्ज़, m. a dagger worn in front. पेशकश [P. *-kaś*], m. gift to a superior; a submission, request. पेशकार [P. *-kār*], m. agent, secretary; a junior court officer. °ई, f. office or duties of a *peśkār*. पेश-ख़ैमा, m. *Pl. HŚS.* advance baggage or party. पेशवाज़, [P. *-vāz*], m. open in front: skirt (as worn by dancing-girls). पेशोपस, m. = पसोपेश, see s.v. [1]पस.

पेशगी *peśgī* [P. *peśgī*], f. an advance (of money); transf. assurance (for the future).

पेशतर *peśtar* [P. *peśtar*], adv. & ppn. before, previously; earlier (than, से, or के).

पेशवा *peśvā* [P. *peśvā*], m. **1.** guide, leader. **2.** *hist.* leader of the Marāṭhās.

पेशवाई *peśvāī* [P. *peśvāī*], f. **1.** leadership. **2.** position and duties of a *peśvā*. — ~ करना, to receive, to welcome; to escort.

पेशा *peśā* [P. *peśa*], m. **1.** occupation; profession; trade; business. **2.** art, skill. **3.** caste, community. **4.** pej. the occupation of a prostitute. ~ कमाना or करना, to earn one's living as a prostitute. — पेशावर [P. *-var*], m. & adj. a professional person; craftsman; tradesman; professional.

पेशानी *peśānī* [P. *peśānī*], f. **1.** the brow. **2.** fig. destiny (as written on the brow).

पेशाब *peśāb* [P. *peśāb*], m. **1.** urine. **2.** sl. semen; transf. offspring. — ~ करना, to urinate. ~ बंद होना, to be unable to urinate. ~ लगना (को), to want to urinate. ~ लानेवाला, adj. diuretic. – पेशाब-ख़ाना, m. lavatory. पेशाब-घर, m. id. पेशाब-बंद, m. stoppage of urine.

पेशावरी *peśāvrī* [cf. H. *peśāvar*], adj. & f. **1.** adj. having to do with, belonging to or made in the city of Peshawar. **2.** a kind of slipper or shoe.

[1]**पेशी** *peśī* [P. *peśī*], f. **1.** hearing (of a case). **2.** appearance (in court). **3.** lead, precedence; superior rank. **4.** an advance (of money: = पेशगी). — ~ का मुहर्रिर, m. clerk of a court.

[2]**पेशी** *peśī* [S.], f. **1.** a piece of flesh, or meat. **2.** an opened flower-bud. **3.** a scabbard. — माँस-पेशी, f. a muscle.

पेशीन- *peśīn-* [P. *peśīn*]. U. former; anticipated:— पेशीनगोई [P. *-goī*], f. prediction.

पेषण *peṣaṇ* [S.], m. grinding, crushing.

पेषनी *peṣānī* [S.], f. a stone slab on which spices, &c. are ground.

पैंकड़ा *paiṁkṛā* [cf. *pada(ra)-*; ?+*kaṭa-*[1]], m. reg. a hobble (for cattle, camels, &c).

पैंच *paiṁc*, f. *Pl. HŚS.* **1.** a peacock's tail. **2.** reg. (W.) a small bundle of sugar-canes.

पैंचना *paiṁcnā* [? **pratiyācyate*], v.t. reg. **1.** to winnow. **2.** to sift.

पैंचा *paiṁcā* [**pratikṛtya-*], m. reg. **1.** a loan; repayment of a loan. **2.** exchange of labour among farmers.

पैंजन *paiṁjan*, f. = पैंजनी.

पैंजनी *paiṁjnī*, f. **1.** an anklet with small bells. **2.** housing for axle (of ox-cart, &c).

पैंठ *paiṁṭh* [*pratiṣṭhā-*], f. **1.** a fixed market; market day. **2.** shop, stall. **3.** duplicate of a bill (document).

पैंड़ *paiṁṛ* [**padaḍa-*: ? and **padadaṇḍa-*], f. Brbh. **1.** pace, step. **2.** path, way.

पैंड़ो *paiṁṛo* [**padadaṇḍa-*], m. Brbh. path, way. — ~ मारना, to stop (one) on the road; to rob on the highway; = मंज़िल मारना.

पैंतरा *paiṁtrā* [*pādāntara-*], m. changing a stance (as in wrestling, duelling); feint, dodge; squaring up (to an adversary). — पैंतरे बदलना, to change stance, &c. पैंतरेबाज़ [P. *-bāz*], m. one whose footwork is deft. °ई, f.

पैंता *paiṁtā*, m. reg. (W.) = पैड़ा, 3.

पैंताना *paiṁtānā*, m. = पायँता.

पैंतालीस *paiṁtālīs* [*pañcacatvāriṁśat-*], adj. forty-five.

पैंतीस *paiṁtīs* [*pañcatriṁśat-*], adj. thirty-five.

पैंथी *painthī*, f. *Pl.* the place where a man stands when raising water for irrigation (= पैड़ा, 3).

पैंसठ *paiṁsaṭh* [*pañcaṣaṣṭi-*], adj. sixty-five.

[1]**पै** *pai*, ppn. colloq.; also reg. = [1]पर.

[2]**पै** *pai*, conj. Brbh. Av. 1. = [2]पर. 2. = तो (non-initial).

पै- *pai-* [P. *pai*], m. **1.** the foot. **2.** footprint: — पैकार [P. *-kār*], m. Brbh. see s.v. पै-ख़ाना, m. = पा-ख़ाना.

पैकर *paikar* [P. *paikar*], f. U. face, form.

पैका *paikā* [cf. H. *pāī*; ? ad. *pādikā-*, f.], m. E.H. a small sum of money, a penny.

पैकाकार *paikākār*, m. corr. E.H. = पैकार.

पैकार *paikār* [P. *pā'ekār*], m. reg. **1.** a wholesaler; agent, dealer. **2.** a hawker.

पैग़ंबर *paigambar* [P. *paigambar*], m. message-bearer: prophet; apostle.

पैग़ंबरी *paigambarī* [P. *paigambarī*], adj. & f. **1.** adj. having to do with a prophet, or apostle. ***2.** f. mission (of a prophet, &c).

पैग़ाम *paigām* [P. *paigām*], m. **1.** message. **2.** news, information. **3.** proposal of a marriage arrangement (by the boy's family, to the girl's). — पैग़ामबर [P. *-bar*], m. = पैग़ंबर.

पैगू *paigū* [P. *pegū, paigū*], m. *Pl.* **1.** Pegu (the country). **2.** a sort of green-coloured stone (brought from Pegu).

पैज *paij* [*pratijñā-*], f. Brbh. Av. promise, vow. — ~ कर-, to promise.

पैजना *paijnā* [cf. H. *paij*], v.i. *Pl.* = पैज कर-.

पैजनी *paijnī*, f. = पैंजनी.

पैज़ार *paizār* [P. *paizār*], f. a slipper, shoe (cf. *jūtī*).

पैठ *paiṭh* [cf. H. *paiṭhnā*], f. **1.** entry, admission. **2.** penetration (into, में); infiltration. **3.** fig. understanding, command (of a topic).

पैठना *paiṭhnā* [cf. *praviṣṭa-*], v.i. **1.** to enter, to penetrate (into, में); to dive (into). **2.** to force an entry; to intrude; to infiltrate.

पैठाना *paiṭhānā* [cf. H. *paiṭhnā*], v.t. **1.** to cause to go in or to enter. **2.** to force (sthg.) in. **3.** to introduce (into, में); to insinuate (an idea).

पैठार *paiṭhār* [cf. H. *paiṭhālnā*], m. ? Av. entry, forced entry.

पैठालना *paiṭhālnā*, v.t. = पैठाना.

पैठाव *paiṭhāv* [cf. H. *paiṭhnā*, *paiṭhānā*], m. entrance, access; penetration.

पैड़ा *paiṛā* [**padaḍa-*], m. reg. **1.** wooden sandals (= खड़ाऊँ). **2.** circular or sloping path trodden by working oxen. **3.** W. post or station where a workman stands while drawing water.

पैड़ी *paiṛī* [*padaḍa-*], f. **1.** a ladder; flight of steps or stairs. **2.** Av. a step, rung. **3.** reg. path trodden by oxen in drawing water, &c. **4.** reg. (W.) a cut crop spread on the threshing-floor (= पैर, 3).

पैतरा *paitrā*, m. = पैंतरा.

पैताना *paitānā*, m. = पायँता.

पैतृक *paitṛk* [S.], adj. **1.** paternal, ancestral. **2.** inherited; hereditary.

पैत्तिक *paittik* [S.], adj. **1.** having to do with bile. **2.** bilious (of temperment).

पैथला *paithlā*, adj. reg. shallow.

पैदल *paidal* adj., adv. & m. **1.** adj., adv. walking, on foot. **2.** m. a foot-soldier, infantryman. **3.** (in chess) a pawn. — ~ का रास्ता, m. a path walked on foot, footpath. ~ चलनेवाला, adj. & m. going on foot; a pedestrian. ~ चाल, f. *athl.* walking race. ~ सिपाही, f. a foot-soldier.

पैदा *paidā* [P. *paidā*], adj. inv. & f. **1.** adj. born. **2.** produced. **3.** arisen; become evident. **4.** acquired; earned. **5.** f. earnings, income. — ~ करना, to create; to produce; to occasion; to raise, to breed (animals, &c.); to originate, to invent; to acquire. ~ होना, to be born; to be created; to be produced (as crops, manufactures); to be occasioned (as a dispute); to be acquired.

पैदाइश *paidāiś* [P. *paidā'iś*], f. **1.** birth; origin, rise. 2. = पैदावार, 1., 2. **3.** profits, earnings.

पैदाइशी *paidāiśī* [P. *paidā'iśī*], adj. inborn, innate; natural. — ~ हक़, m. birth-right.

पैदावार *paidāvār* [P. *paidāvār*], f. **1.** produce (as of land). **2.** production (as of an industry). **3.** profits, income.

पैदावारी *paidāvārī* [P. *paidāvārī*], f. = पैदावार.

पैन *pain*, m. **1.** reg. (E.) a water channel made for irrigation. **2.** *Pl.* a reservoir of water.

पैना *painā* [**pratīkṣṇa-*], adj. & m. **1.** adj. sharp. **2.** pointed. **3.** shrill. **4.** fig. acute (as vision, or insight). **5.** m. reg. goad (for oxen, &c). — ~ करना, to sharpen.

पैनाना *paināna* [cf. H. *painā*], v.t. **1.** to sharpen. **2.** to make pointed.

पैनापन *paināpan* [cf. H. *painā*], m. sharpness, &c. (see पैना).

पैनाला *painālā*, m. reg. **1.** water-channel (= पैन). **2.** spout.

पैनी *painī* [cf. H. *painā*], f. reg. a goad (= पैना, 5).

पैमक *paimak*, f. *Pl. HŚS.* gold or silver lace or brocade.

पैमाइश *paimāiś* [P. *paimā'iś*], f. **1.** measuring. **2.** surveying; survey.

पैमाना *paimānā* [P. *paimāna*], m. **1.** measure (of length or volume). **2.** a scale (of measurement); gauge. **3.** cup, measure (of wine, &c). **4.** fig. the cup of life, measure of (one's) days. — झूठा ~, m. short measure. बड़े पैमाने पर, adv. on a large scale; mass (production).

¹पैया *paiyā* [cf. H. *pā(y)-*], f. dimin. Brbh. little foot.

²पैया *paiyā* [cf. H. ¹*pāī*], m. *hist.* an allowance of half an anna on each rupee of revenue set apart for the *paṭvārī*.

पैर *pair* [**padara-*], m. **1.** the foot, footstep. (= पाँव, which see for many collocations of पैर also.) 2. footprint. **3.** transf. reg. a cut crop spread on the threshing-floor (to be trodden by oxen); a crop so trodden. **4.** reg. (W.) circular or sloping path trodden by working oxen. — ~ की जूती, f. & adj. a worthless or contemptible person or thing; worthless, &c. ~ न होना, to have no feet: to have no place of refuge (as a criminal). - पैरों, adv. on foot. पैरों-तले, adv. underfoot.

पैरना *pairnā* [*pratarati* or *pratirati*], v.i. to swim; to float.

पैरवी *pairăvī* [P. *-ravī*], f. following (a course of action); attachment, adherence; endeavour. — ~ करना (की), to follow, to pursue; to comply with (as regulations); to prosecute (a case). – पैरवीकार, m. follower, supporter; prosecutor.

¹पैरा *pairā* [*padara-*], m. reg. (E.) **1.** coming, arrival; place, position, territory. **2.** an anklet. **3.** a pathway made of timber poles.

²पैरा *pairā* [Engl. *paragraph*], m. a paragraph.

पैराई *pairāī* [cf. H. *pairnā*, *pairānā*], f. *Pl. HŚS.* the act, or the skill, of swimming.

पैराक *pairāk* [cf. H. *pairnā*], m. a swimmer.

पैराकी *pairākī* [cf. H. *pairāk*], f. the activity of swimming.

पैराना *pairānā* [cf. H. *pairnā*], v.t. to cause to swim or to float; to teach (one) to swim.

पैराव *pairāv* [cf. H. *pairānā*, *pairnā*], m. a depth of water requiring swimming (too great to be forded).

पैरी *pairī* [*padara-*], f. **1.** Av. a heavy metal anklet. **2.** reg. (W.) the grain obtained after a session of threshing.

पैरोकार *pairokār*, m. = पैरवीकार, see s.v. पैरवी.

पैला *pailā*, m. **1.** Brbh. an earthen vessel for measuring grain or oil. **2.** reg. a large wicker basket for winnowing or storing grain.

पैलार *pailār*, adv. reg. ~ का बरस, m. the year before last.

पैवंद *paivand* [P. *paivand*], m. **1.** a patch. **2.** a graft. — ~ करना, to join to, to make (a person or thing) one with. ज़मीन का ~ करना, to consign to the earth (in burial). ~ लगाना (में), v.t. to patch; to graft. – पैवंदकारी [P. *-kārī*], f. patching; cobbling.

पैवंदी *paivandī* [P. *paivandī*], f. **1.** patched. **2.** grafted. **3.** mixed (of breed). — ~ मूँछें, f. whiskers that join and are twisted in the form of a circle on the cheek.

पैवस्ता *paivastā* [P. *paivasta*], adj. inv. U. **1.** joined (to, से), closely attached (to); adorned (by, से). **2.** absorbed (in, में), soaked up (into).

पैशाच *paiśāc* [S.], adj. having to do with a *piśāca*; demonic, diabolical.

पैशाचिक *paiśācik* [S.], adj. = पैशाच.

पैशाची *paiśācī* [S.], adj. & f. **1.** adj. = पैशाच. **2.** f. *piśāca* language: a partic. form of Prakrit.

पैशुन्य *paiśunyă* [S.], m. = पिशुनता.

पैसना *paisnā* [*praviśati*], v.i. reg. to enter.

पैसा *paisā* [**padāṁśa-*], m. **1.** *hist.* a copper coin, a quarter anna. **2.** a coin equal in value to one hundredth of a rupee. **3.** esp. pl. money. — ~, or पैसे, उड़ाना, to squander money; to embezzle or to misappropriate money. ~, or पैसे, खाना, to squander money; to live by one's wages or work; to embezzle money; to take bribes. ~ डुबोना, to spend money without return. ~, or पैसे, लगाना, to lay out money (on, में). – टूटा ~, m. a broken coin; sthg. valueless, a farthing. नया ~, m. new *paisā*: = ~, 2. पैसा-धेला, m. a trivial sum, a farthing. पैसेवाला, adj. having money, well or comfortably off.

पैसार *paisār* [? **pratisāra-*; × *praviś-*], m. **1.** access; entrance. **2.** fig. reach, compass; ability.

पों *poṁ*, f. **1.** sound of a pipe or flute. **2.** sound of passing wind. **3.** sound of a motor. — ~ बजाना, to agree in a subservient way, to be a yes-man. ~ बोलना, to give in, to be defeated; to go bankrupt.

पोंकना *poṁknā* [**pramukna-*: Pk. *pamukka-*], v.i. **1.** to have diarrhoea. **2.** fig. to be fear-stricken.

पोंका *poṁkā*, m. **1.** *Pl.* = पोका. **2.** *HŚS.* a large flying insect found around plants (= *boṁkā*).

पोंगल *poṁgal* [Tam. *poṁgaḷ*], m. name of a south Indian festival held at *makar saṅkrānti*.

पोंगा *poṁgā* [*poṅga-*¹: ? ← Drav.], adj. & m. **1.** adj. empty, hollow. **2.** fig. stupid. **3.** m. a hollow piece or tube (bamboo, metal).

पोंछन *poṁchan* [*proñchana-* (? ← Drav.): and H. *poṁchnā*], f., m. **1.** f. wiping; dusting. **2.** m. *Pl.* a rag, &c. for wiping. **3.** m. refuse wiped away.

पोंछना *poṁchnā* [*proñchati*: ? ← Drav.], v.t. **1.** to wipe; to dust. **2.** to erase, to expunge.

पोंछियाहा *poṁchiyāhā*, adj. *Pl.* = पूँछार.

पोंटा *poṁṭā*, m. snot.

पोंटी *poṁṭī*, f. *Pl. HŚS.* a species of small carp, *Cyprinus pausius*, or *C. chrysopareius*.

पोंठी *poṁṭhī*, f. *Pl.* = पोंटी.

पोआ *poā*, m. reg. young of any animal (= पोई).

पोइया *poiyā* [cf. H. ³*poī*], f. reg. gallop. — हलकी ~, f. canter.

पोइस *pois*, adv. corr. Brbh. quickly, smartly (cf. ³पोई, पोइया).

¹**पोई** *poī* [*pūtīka-*], f. any of several creepers having edible leaves.

²**पोई** *poī* [*pota-¹*: ? ← Drav.], f. **1.** shoot, sprout. **2.** young plant; sprouting sugar-cane; young wheat.

³**पोई** *poī* [P. *pūy*], f. reg. gallop (of a horse).

पोका *pokā* [**pokka-²*], m. caterpillar, grub, worm.

पोखर *pokhar*, m. = पोखरा.

पोखरा *pokhrā* [*pauṣkara-*], m. pond, pool, tank.

पोच *poc* [P. *puc*], adj. Brbh. Av. **1.** worthless, useless; trivial. **2.** base; depraved.

पोची *pocī* [cf. H. *poc*], f. Brbh. Av. base thought, speech, or conduct.

पोट *poṭ* [**poṭṭa-¹*: Pk. *poṭṭa-*], f. **1.** bundle, bale; package. **2.** a load. **3.** heap, pile. **4.** reg. a cloth wrapping. **5.** the sewing of a book.

पोटला *poṭlā* [*poṭṭala-*, Pk. *poṭṭala-*], m. a large bundle.

पोटली *poṭlī* [*poṭṭala-*, Pk. *poṭṭala-*], f. a small bundle; a parcel; packet.

¹**पोटा** *poṭā* [**poṭṭa-³*: ? ← Drav.], m. reg. **1.** the young of an animal or bird. **2.** colloq. young children, small fry. **3.** colloq. household gods.

²**पोटा** *poṭā* [**poṭṭa-²*: Pk. *poṭṭa-*], m. reg. **1.** the crop (of a bird). **2.** stomach.

पोटिया *poṭiyā* [cf. H. *poṭ*], m. load-carrier, porter.

पोटी *poṭī*, f. reg. = ²पोटा, 1.

पोठी *poṭhī*, f. reg. a small fish (cf. पोंठी).

पोढ़ा *poṛhā* [*pravr̥ddha-*, or *prodha-*], adj. **1.** firm, strong; hard; stiff. **2.** dense, thick. **3.** wide. **4.** Brbh. ? refreshed.

पोढ़ी *poṛhī* f. *Pl.* = पौड़ी.

¹**पोत** *pot* [पोत-³, Pk. *poa-*], m. a vessel, ship. — पोत-भार, m. cargo.

²**पोत** *pot* [*pravr̥tti-*], f. **1.** Brbh. disposition, nature; habit. **2.** turn, time. — के ~, in the manner of.

³**पोत** *pot* [**pottī-*: Pk. *potti-*], f.; m. Brbh. glass bead.

⁴**पोत** *pot* [S.], m. **1.** the young of an animal, or bird. **2.** a young plant or tree; shoot.

⁵**पोत** *pot* [P. *pota-*: w. P. *fuvaṭ*, pl.], m. *hist.* **1.** assessment on cultivated fields. **2.** the collected monies of an assessment. — ~ पूरा करना, to make up a shortfall (as in a payment). पोतदार [P. *-dār*], m. a treasurer; °ई, f. office of treasurer.

⁶**पोत** *pot* [? cf. H. *potnā*], m. dung.

पोतक *potak* [S.], m. Av. young creature; child.

पोतड़ा *potṛā* [**potta-²*: Pk. *potta-*], m. baby's napkin, diaper. — पोतड़ों का अमीर, or रईस, m. fig. iron. a gentleman to the manner born.

पोतना *potnā*, v.t. & m. **1.** v.t. to smear or to wash over with mud, plaster or whitewash, &c. **2.** fig. to gloss over or to cover over (a shortcoming). **3.** m. a straw brush.

¹**पोता** *potā* [*pautra-*], m. son's son, grandson.

²**पोता** *potā* [**potta-²* (? ← Drav.): Pk. *potta-*], m. **1.** a cloth, brush or stick used to apply plaster, mud or whitewash. **2.** [× *pavitraka-*] a piece of cloth used, soaked in water, to cool distilling apparatus.

³**पोता** *potā* [P. *pota*], m. *Pl. HŚS.* = ⁵पोत. — पोतादार [P. *-dār*], m. a treasurer; °ई, f. office. पोतेदार, m. id.

⁴**पोता** *potā*, m. = फ़ोता.

¹**पोतिया** *potiyā* [cf. H. ²*potā*], f. dimin. cloth worn when bathing.

²**पोतिया** *potiyā* (? for पोथिया), m. *Pl. HŚS.* a kind of toy (see पोस्ती, 3).

³**पोतिया** *potiyā* [cf. H. ²*pot*], m. *Pl.* next in turn.

¹**पोती** *potī* [*pautrī-*], f. son's daughter, granddaughter.

²**पोती** *potī* [cf. H. ²*potā*; × *pavitra-*], f. *Pl. HŚS.* a piece of cloth or similar substance soaked in red dye (for staining, &c.) or in water (for cooling sthg.: as in distillation).

पोथ *poth*, m. *Pl.* = ³पोत.

पोथकी *pothkī* [S.], f. *Pl. HŚS.* an eye complaint: itching and running of the eyes, with pimples appearing.

पोथला *pothlā*, m. a large bundle or load (= पोटला).

पोथा *pothā* [**postaka-* (← Ir.): Pa. *potthaka-*], m. **1.** a large book, tome. **2.** a manuscript having its separate leaves tied together; a bundle of papers.

¹**पोथी** *pothī* [**postaka-* (← Ir.): Pa. *potthaka-*], f. a book, volume. — पोथी-ख़ाना, m. library, book-depository. पोथीपंडित, m. one whose learning is from books only.

[2]पोथी *pothī*, f. a clove of garlic.

पोदना *podnā*, m. **1.** a small bird (which builds a domed nest in grass). **2.** a dwarf, pigmy. **3.** *Pl.* an evil spirit.

पोदीना *podīnā* [P. *podīna*], m. = पुदीना.

पोद्दार *poddār* [cf. H. [5]*pot*], m. *hist.* **1.** an assayer of coin. **2.** a cashier.

[1]पोना *ponā* [*pravayati*], v.t. **1.** to string (pearls, &c). **2.** to thread (a needle).

[2]पोना *ponā* [*pratapati*], v.t. **1.** to bake (bread). **2.** to prepare (*capātī*, &c.) for baking.

[3]पोना *ponā* [*pavana-*[1]], m. see [2]पौना.

पोपटा *popṭā*, m. *Pl.* a species of the winter cherry, *Physalis angulata* (cf. पपोटन).

पोपनी *popnī* f. reg. **1.** a wind instrument. **2.** mouthpiece (consisting of a leaf) for certain wind instruments. **3.** a child's whistle made of a leaf or of a mango stone.

पोपला *poplā* [**poppa-*], adj. & m. **1.** adj. toothless. **2.** m. a toothless man.

पोपलाना *poplānā* [cf. H. *poplā*], v.i. Brbh. to be toothless (the mouth).

पोमचा *pomcā*, m. *Pl.* a showy kind of cloth or garment; wedding skirt.

पोर *por* [**pora-*[2]: Pk. *pora-*], f. **1.** a joint (of the body, or of bamboo, sugar-cane, &c). **2.** space between two joints. — ~ ~, adv. every joint; every inch, entirely.

पोरवा *porvā* [cf. H. *por*], m. a joint of the fingers. — पोरवे भर, a tiny bit (of). तीन पोरवे पानी, three or four inches' depth of water.

पोरवाल *porvāl* [cf. H. [1]*pol*], m. name of a trading community of Mālvā.

पोरा *porā* [**pora-*[2]], m. **1.** beam, log; block (of wood). **2.** fig. a heavily built man.

पोरी *porī* [cf. H. *por*], f. **1.** a joint (esp. a finger-joint). **2.** knot (as in sugar-cane); section of bamboo. — पोरियाँ करना, to cut into small pieces.

पोरुआ *poruā* [cf. H. *por*], m. a knuckle. — ~ तोड़ना, to crack the knuckle-joint(s).

[1]पोल *pol* [*pratolī-*], m. **1.** gate of town or fort. **2.** courtyard. **3.** town ward having its own gate.

[2]पोल *pol* [**polla-*: Pk. *polla-*], f. **1.** emptiness, hollowness. **2.** fig. superficiality; pretension(s). — ~ खुलना (की), (one's) pretensions, &c. to be revealed. ~ खोलना, to lay bare pretensions, &c. — पोलदार [P. *-dār*], adj. pretentious. पोल-पाल, f. id.

[3]पोल *pol* [Engl. *pole*], m. a pole (land measure).

[1]पोला *polā* [**polla-*: Pk. *polla-*], adj. & m. **1.** adj. hollow; empty. **2.** spongy, porous; friable (soil). **3.** flabby. **4.** fig. superficial; facile. **5.** m. a superficial person.

[2]पोला *polā*, m. reg. (Bihar) = पूला.

पोलापन *polāpan* [cf. H. [1]*polā*], m. hollowness, superficiality.

पोली *polī* [cf. H. [1]*polā*], f. *Pl.* **1.** a honeycomb, anything spongy. **2.** colloq. an empty-headed fellow.

पोशाक *pośāk* [P. *pośāk*], f. clothing, dress; costume, attire. — ~ बढ़ाना, to undress. फ़ौजी, or सैनिक ~, f. uniform.

पोशाकी *pośākī* [P. *pośākī*], adj. fit for making clothes from (material).

पोशीदगी *pośīdăgī* [P. *pośīdagī*], f. concealment, secrecy.

पोशीदा *pośīdā* [P. *pośīda*], adj. inv. hidden; secret.

पोष *poṣ* [S.], m. **1.** nurturing, bringing up. **2.** thriving, growth, welfare. — पोषाहार [°*ṣa* + *ā*°], m. nourishing food.

पोष- *poṣ-*, v.t. Brbh. Av. = पोसना.

पोषक *poṣak* [S.], adj. & m. **1.** adj. nurturing. **2.** nourishing. **3.** fostering, encouraging (as an attitude). **4.** m. one who nurtures, rears, &c. — ~ तत्त्व, m. nourishing substance; a vitamin.

पोषकत्व *poṣakatvă* [S.], m. nutriment, nourishment.

पोषण *poṣaṇ* [S.], m. **1.** nurturing, bringing up. **2.** encouraging (a hope, or an attitude). **3.** maintenance. — ~ करना (का), to bring up (a child); to encourage (a view, &c.); to maintain.

पोषणीय *poṣāṇīyă* [S.], adj. = पोष्य, 1.

पोषयिता *poṣayitā* [S.], m. inv. one who nurtures, &c.

पोषित *poṣit* [S.], adj. nurtured, &c.

पोष्य *poṣyă* [S.], adj. **1.** to be nurtured, or cherished, &c.; deserving to be cared for. **2.** adopted (a son).

पोस *pos* [*poṣa-*], m. **1.** care, raising (esp. of animals). **2.** upbringing, nurturing. — ~ मानना, to repay the care (of, का) with devotion; to respond to care or attention.

पोसना *posnā* [*poṣayati*], v.t. **1.** to nurture, to bring up (children); to cherish. **2.** to breed, to rear (animals). **3.** to tame. **4.** fig. to be prey to (a habit, a vice).

पोस्त *post* [P. *post*], m. **1.** outer skin, rind. **2.** poppy-head. **3.** opium.

पोस्ता *postā* [P. *posta*], m. **1.** the opium poppy; poppy seed. **2.** reg. oil-cake of poppy seeds.

पोस्ती *postī* [P. *postī*], m. **1.** an opium addict. **2.** fig. an indolent person. **3.** *Pl. HŚS.* a toy weighted at the bottom so that it comes to rest in a vertical position after rocking or wobbling about.

पोस्तीन *postīn* [P. *postīn*], m. U. a fur or leather coat.

पोह *poh*, f. = ¹पौ.

¹**पोहा** *pohā* [*pṛthuka-²*], m. **1.** any large domestic animal. **2.** specif. horned cattle.

²**पोहा** *pohā* [? **praguphita-*], m. *Pl.* a flock of cotton (= फाहा).

पौंगी *pauṁgī* [conn. H. *poṅgā*], f. reg. a pipe; snake-charmer's pipe or drone.

पौंचा *pauṁcā*, m. **1.** five and a half times. ***2.** the five and a half times multiplication table.

पौंड *pauṇḍ* [Engl. *pound*], m. a pound (weight, or sterling).

पौंडा *pauṁḍā* [*pauṇḍra-*], m. a red, or a straw-coloured, or a dark variety of sugar-cane.

¹**पौ** *pau* [*prabhā-*], f. dawn. — ~ फटना, dawn to break. ~ फटे, adv. at dawn.

²**पौ** *pau* [**padu-*], f. the one or ace on dice. — पौ-चक्का, m. gambling (as an obsession). पौ-बारह, f. ace and twelve: good luck, a win; success. पौ-बारह पड़ना (को), = next. पौ-बारह होना (के), to have good luck (as in dice); to succeed.

³**पौ** *pau* [*prapā-*], f. roadside watering-place.

पौगंड *paugaṇḍ* [S.], adj. & m. Brbh. **1.** adj. not fully grown. **2.** m. a boy (from his fifth to sixteenth year); a youth.

पौड़ी *pauṛī* [cf. H. *pauṛhā*], f. heavy soil.

पौढ़ना *pauṛhnā* [*pravardhate*], v.i. to lie down, to rest; to sleep.

पौढ़ा *pauṛhā*, adj. = पोढ़ा.

पौढ़ाना *pauṛhānā* [cf. H. *pauṛhnā*], v.t. to cause to lie down; to put to sleep; to lay flat.

पौत्तलिक *pauttalik* [S.], m. *Pl. HŚS.* an image-worshipper.

पौत्र *pautr* [S.], adj. & m. **1.** adj. filial. **2.** m. son's son, grandson.

पौत्रिक *pautrik* [S.], adj. having to do with a son or a grandson.

पौत्री *pautrī* [S.], f. son's daughter, granddaughter.

पौद *paud* [*pravṛddha-*], f. **1.** a young plant; seedling. **2.** young child; offspring, new generation.

पौदा *paudā*, m. U. = पौधा.

पौध *paudh*, f. = पौद. — पौधपालक, m. a nurseryman.

पौधा *paudhā* [*pravṛddha-*], m. **1.** a young plant; seedling; sapling. **2.** a shrub.

पौधेला *paudhelā*, m. *Pl.* nursery, seed-bed.

¹**पौन** *paun* [**padūna-*], adj. less by a quarter. — ~ बजा, m. a quarter to one. ~ सेर, m. three-quarters of a seer.

²**पौन** *paun*, m. = पवन. — ~ चलाना, or मारना, to practise magic; to cast spells (on, पर). ~ बैठाना, = id., 2.

¹**पौना** *paunā* [**padūna-*], adj. & m. **1.** adj. less by a quarter. **2.** m. the multiplication table of three-quarters. – पौने दो, adj. one and three-quarters. पौने दो सौ, adj. two hundred and seventy-five. पौने सोलह आना, m. fifteen and three-quarters annas: almost the whole (of). पौने सोलह आने, adv. almost entirely.

²**पौना** *paunā* [*prapavaṇa-* or *pavana-¹*], m. a perforated ladle; skimmer, strainer.

पौनी *paunī* [conn. H. *pāvnā*], f. reg. (E.) the recipients of gifts at marriages and other festivals (as barbers, shoemakers, washermen).

¹**पौर** *paur* [**pradura-*], f. **1.** threshold. **2.** gate, door.

²**पौर** *paur* [S.], adj. & m. **1.** adj. having to do with a town; urban, municipal. **2.** m. townsman, citizen. — महापौर, m. mayor.

पौरा *paurā*, m. arrival of a wife (at her husband's family home).

पौरव *paurav* [S.], adj. *mythol.* connected with or descended from Puru.

पौरा *paurā*, m. reg. (E.) a calf.

पौराणिक *paurāṇik* [S.], adj. & m. **1.** adj. having to do with the *purāṇas*; told in the *purāṇas*. **2.** ancient (as events, traditions); mythological; legendary. **3.** versed in ancient legends, &c. **4.** m. a brāhmaṇ versed in the *purāṇas*.

पौरिया *pauriyā* [**pratolika-*], m. door-keeper, gate-keeper.

¹**पौरी** *paurī* [*pratolī-*; or **pradura-*], f. = पौली.

²**पौरी** *paurī* [cf. *pādu-*, or *pāda-*], f. Av. **1.** step (of a ladder or stand). **2.** stool. **3.** wooden sandals (= खड़ाऊँ).

पौरुष *pauruṣ* [S.], adj. & m. **1.** adj. manly. **2.** human. **3.** m. manly strength or courage; vigour, virility. **4.** transf. exploit, effort.

पौरुषता *pauruṣătā* [S.], f. manliness, manly strength or spirit.

पौरुषीय *pauruṣīyă* [S.], adj. manly; masculine, male.

पौरुषेय *pauruṣeyă* [S.], adj. **1.** derived from or relating to a man; manly. **2.** spiritual.

पौरुष्य *pauruṣyă* [S.], m. = पौरुष.

पौरोहित्य *paurohityă* [S.], m. the office, character or duties of a *purohit*; priesthood.

पौर्णमासी *paurṇmāsī* [S.], f. = पूर्णमासी, see s.v. पूर्ण.

पौर्वात्य *paurvātyă* [S.], adj. eastern.

पौर्विक *paurvik* [S.], m. former, ancient.

पौल *paul*, m. = [1]पोल.

पौलिया *pauliyā*, m. = पौरिया.

पौली *paulī* [*pratolī-*], f. **1.** gate of town. **2.** threshold, entrance.

पौवा *pauvā* [*pāda-*], m. **1.** a weight, or an amount, of a quarter of a seer. **2.** a quarter-seer measure.

पौष्टिक *pauṣṭik* [S.], adj. nourishing, invigorating (a food, a tonic).

पौष्ण *pauṣṇă* [S.], m. *astron.* the twenty-eighth lunar mansion.

पौह *pauh*, m. (?) *Pl.* = [3]पौ.

प्याऊ *pyāū* [conn. *prapā-*], ? m. = [3]पौ.

प्याज़ *pyāz* [P. *piyāz*], f. (m.) an onion.

प्याज़ी *pyāzī* [P. *piyāzī*], adj. **1.** like an onion; reddish, pinkish (in colour).

प्यादा *pyādā* [P. *piyāda*], m. **1.** one on foot, a pedestrian. **2.** specif. a foot-soldier. **3.** a messenger, peon. **4.** (in chess) a pawn.

प्यार *pyār* [*priyakāra-*], m. **1.** love; affection. **2.** caress; kiss (from a child). — ~ करना, to love (a person: से, or को); to caress (a person: को). ~ रखना, to feel love or affection (for, से).

प्यारा *pyārā* [*priyakāra-*], adj. & m. **1.** adj. dear, beloved; precious. **2.** charming; agreeable. **3.** m. darling. — ~ लगना, to be dear, &c. (to, को); to seem dear (to).

प्याला *pyālā* [P. *piyāla*], m. **1.** drinking-vessel, cup; glass. **2.** priming-pan (of a musket). **3.** transf. alcohol. — ~ पीना, to drink the cup (of, का); to imbibe the teaching or to become a disciple (of); to take alcohol. ~ पूरा होना, or भरना, the cup (of life) to be full, one's days to be numbered; to be puffed up with pride; to go beyond tolerable limits (misdemeanours, &c). ~ बहना, sl. ? obs. a miscarriage or an abortion to occur. ~ लेना, to take alcohol. – प्याला-निवाला, m. food and drink.

प्याली *pyālī* [cf. H. *pyālā*], f. a small cup or glass; a cup. — एक ~ चाय, a cup of tea.

प्यास *pyās* [*pipāsā-*], f. **1.** thirst. **2.** desire, craving. — ~ मरना, thirst no longer to be felt. ~ मारना, to endure thirst. ~ लगना, thirst to be felt (by, को). मुझे ~ लगी है, I am thirsty. प्यासों मरना, to die of thirst.

प्यासा *pyāsā* [**pipāsaka-*: Pk. *pivāsaa-*], adj. **1.** thirsty (for, का). **2.** desirous. — ~, or प्यासे, मारना, to be dying of thirst; to be very thirsty.

प्यासी *pyāsī* [cf. H. *pyās*], adj. thirsty.

प्र- *pra-* [S.], pref. **1.** forward, forth (e.g. प्रभाव, m. influence; प्रपौत्र, m. great-grandson). **2.** very (e.g. प्रबल, adj. very strong).

प्रकंप *pra-kamp* [S.], m. trembling, shaking.

प्रकंपन *pra-kampan* [S.], m. **1.** trembling, shaking. **2.** a violent wind.

प्रकंपित *pra-kampit* [S.], adj. shaken; trembling.

प्रकंपी *pra-kampī* [S.], adj. trembling, shaking (as in a strong wind).

प्रकट *pra-kaṭ* [S.], adj. **1.** evident, clear; obvious. **2.** displayed, revealed; appeared; public. **3.** broken out (an epidemic). — ~ करना, to make evident; to express (as feelings); to reveal. ~ होना, to become clear; to appear, &c. – प्रकटतः, adv. evidently, &c. प्रकटीकरण, m. making evident; displaying.

प्रकटता *pra-kaṭătā* [S.], f. **1.** visibility. **2.** publicity. — ~ पाना, to become visible.

प्रकटित *pra-kaṭit* [S.], adj. **1.** made evident, &c. **2.** displayed, revealed; proclaimed.

प्रकटीकरण *pra-kaṭīkaraṇ* [S.], m. see s.v. प्रकट.

प्रकरण *pra-karaṇ* [S.], m. **1.** treatment, exposition. **2.** treatise. ***3.** topic. **4.** section (of a book, a study); part (of a whole). **5.** introduction, prelude. **6.** event, incident; affair.

प्रकरी *pra-karī* [S.], f. *Pl. HŚS.* **1.** episode in a play. **2.** a kind of song.

प्रकर्ष *pra-karṣ* [S.], m. pre-eminence.

प्रकांड *pra-kāṇḍ* [S.], adj. & m. **1.** adj. great, vast, mighty. **2.** superlative. **3.** m. *Pl. HŚS.*

trunk or branch of a tree. — ~ पंडित, m. a man of vast learning.

प्रकार *pra-kār* [S.], m. **1.** kind, sort, type. **2.** way, manner, method. **3.** special feature or features (of sthg). **4.** *gram.* mood. — एक ~ से, adv. to some extent, in a way. किस ~ (से)? in what way? how? जिस ~ ... उसी ~ ..., just as... so.... भले ~, adv. well, nicely. भले ~ का, adj. of good kind or type, fine, admirable; congenial. प्रकारांतर [°*ra* + *a*°], m. a different type, or means, &c.

प्रकाश *pra-kāś* [S.], m. & adj. **1.** m. brightness, light; splendour. **2.** daylight, sunshine. **3.** transf. display, pomp. **4.** appearance, disclosure. ~ में आना, to come to light. **5.** transf. vision, eyesight. **6.** a light. **7.** adj. clear, evident; public. **8.** renowned. **9.** bright, shining. — ~ पाना, to obtain publicity; to become notorious. ~ करना (को), to display; to make clear; to turn on a light; to provide light. ~ डालना, to throw light (on, पर). ~ में लाना, to illuminate (an area; or a topic). – प्रकाशमान, adj. bright, radiant; brilliant, splendid, famous. प्रकाशवान, adj. id. प्रकाश-वाह, m. light-bearer: the sun.

प्रकाशक *pra-kāśak* [S.], adj. & m. **1.** adj. illuminating. **2.** making clear or evident. **3.** m. light-giver: the sun. ***4.** publisher. **5.** discoverer.

प्रकाशकीय *pra-kāśăkīyă* [S.], m. publisher's preface or remarks.

प्रकाशता *pra-kāśătā* [S.], f. *Pl. HŚS.* **1.** brightness. **2.** visibility. **3.** transf. fame.

प्रकाशन *pra-kāśan* [S.], m. **1.** making known; pointing out. ***2.** publishing; publication. **3.** a published work.

प्रकाशिकी *pra-kāśikī* [S.], f. the study of light: optics.

प्रकाशित *pra-kāśit* [S.], adj. **1.** brought to light; evident. **2.** illuminated. **3.** displayed. **4.** published. — ~ करना, to publish, &c.

प्रकाश्य *pra-kāśyă* [S.], adj. **1.** to be brought to light. **2.** to be published, worth publishing. **3.** clear, open; audible.

प्रकीर्ण *pra-kīrṇ* [S.], adj. **1.** scattered, dispersed. **2.** made public. **3.** miscellaneous.

प्रकीर्णक *pra-kīrṇak* [S.], adj. & m. **1.** adj. = प्रकीर्ण. **2.** *Pl. HŚS.* fly-whisk; tuft of hair.

प्रकीर्तन *pra-kīrtan* [S.], m. **1.** proclaiming; declaring. **2.** praising.

प्रकीर्ति *pra-kīrti* [S.], f. **1.** proclaiming; formal declaration. **2.** celebration (of an event). **3.** great fame.

प्रकीर्तित *pra-kīrtit* [S.], adj. **1.** proclaimed; declared. **2.** celebrated.

प्रकुपित *pra-kupit* [S.], adj. enraged, incensed.

प्रकृत *pra-kr̥t* [S.], adj. **1.** original; genuine; real. **2.** natural. **3.** just, proper.

प्रकृतता *prakr̥tătā* [S.], f. **1.** natural state or condition. **2.** genuineness, realness.

प्रकृति *pra-kr̥ti* [S.], f. **1.** original form or state. **2.** nature, character; temperament. **3.** nature, the natural world. **4.** *philos.* a force or principle evolving the material world. **5.** *math.* a multiplier, factor. — प्रकृति-चित्र, m. a landscape painting. प्रकृति-भाव, m. natural state. प्रकृतिवाद, m. naturalism. प्रकृति-विज्ञान, m. natural science. प्रकृति-शास्त्र, m. id. °ई, m. natural scientist. प्रकृतिस्थ, adj. being in the original or natural state; inherent, innate; in good or normal health.

प्रकृष्ट *pra-kr̥ṣṭ* [S.], adj. pre-eminent; chief, best.

प्रकृष्टता *pra-kr̥ṣṭătā* [S.], f. pre-eminence, excellence.

प्रकोप *pra-kop* [S.], m. **1.** violent agitation; rage, wrath. **2.** violent outbreak (as of a disease). **3.** excess (of a bodily humour).

प्रकोपन *pra-kopan* [S.], m. exciting, agitating.

प्रकोपित *pra-kopit* [S.], adj. incensed, enraged.

प्रक्रम *pra-kram* [S.], m. step, pace: **1.** order, sequence. **2.** stage (of progress, or process). **3.** a sequential process.

प्रक्रिया *pra-kriyā* [S.], f. **1.** manner, method; technique. ***2.** process; processing (of, की). **3.** procedure. **4.** rite, observance.

प्रक्षालन *pra-kṣālan* [S.], m. **1.** washing off, cleansing. **2.** bathing. **3.** fig. purifying, expiating.

प्रक्षालित *pra-kṣālit* [S.], adj. **1.** washed, cleansed. **2.** expiated (a sin, a crime).

प्रक्षिप्त *pra-kṣipt* [S.], adj. **1.** thrown, flung. **2.** interpolated (in a text). **3.** *math. phys.* projected.

प्रक्षीण *pra-kṣīṇ* [S.], adj. **1.** wasting, waning. **2.** perished; vanished.

प्रक्षेप *pra-kṣep* [S.], m. 1. = प्रक्षेपण. **2.** flight, trajectory (of a projectile).

प्रक्षेपक *pra-kṣepak* [S.], m. projector.

प्रक्षेपण *pra-kṣepaṇ* [S.], m. **1.** throwing forth, projecting. **2.** launching, launch (of a missile). **3.** interpolation (in a text). — प्रक्षेपणास्त्र [°*na* + *a*°], m. rocket-borne missile.

प्रक्षेपित *pra-kṣepit* [S.], adj. thrown, hurled, launched, &c. (see प्रक्षेपण).

प्रक्षेप्य *pra-kṣepyă* [S.], adj. **1.** to be launched (as a missile). **2.** subject to insertion (interpolated material).

प्रक्षोभण *pra-kṣobhan* [S.], m. **1.** agitating, exciting. **2.** agitation.

प्रखर *pra-khar* [S.], adj. **1.** very hot; biting; acrid, pungent. **2.** very sharp; piercing (as a glance); cutting, barbed (a remark); keen (intelligence). **3.** very hard. **4.** fig. huge, vast.

प्रखरता *pra-kharătā* [S.], f. fierceness, keenness, etc.

प्रख्यात *pra-khyāt* [S.], adj. **1.** celebrated (= विख्यात). **2.** pej. notorious.

प्रख्याति *pra-khyāti* [S.], f. **1.** celebrity; renown. **2.** notoriety.

प्रख्यान *pra-khyān* [S.], m. publicity.

प्रख्यापन *pra-khyāpan* [S.], m. publicising; promulgation.

प्रख्यापित *pra-khyāpit* [S.], adj. made publicly known; promulgated.

प्रगट *pragaṭ* [ad. *prakaṭa-*] adj. = प्रकट.

प्रगट- *pra-gaṭ-* [cf. H. *pragaṭ*], v.i. & v.t. Brbh. Av. **1.** v.i. to be revealed. **2.** to reveal.

प्रगटाना *pragăṭānā* [cf. H. *pragaṭ*], v.t. arch. to make known.

प्रगटित *pragaṭit*, adj. Brbh. = प्रकटित.

प्रगति *pra-gati* [S.], f. progress. — प्रगतिशील, adj. progressive.

प्रगल्भ *pra-galbh* [S.], adj. **1.** bold, confident; skilful. **2.** arrogant, brash.

प्रगल्भता *pra-galbhătā* [S.], f. **1.** boldness, &c. (see प्रगल्भ). **2.** arrogance.

प्रगाढ़ *pra-gāṛh* [S.], adj. **1.** great, vast; excessive. **2.** hard, difficult. **3.** firm, steady; deep (sleep). **4.** very dense (material, colour). **5.** serious, profound.

प्रगाढ़ता *pra-gāṛhătā* [S.], f. **1.** abundance, &c. **2.** firmness, &c. **3.** seriousness.

प्रगामी *pra-gāmī* [S.], adj. & m. **1.** adj. setting out. **2.** m. one about to depart.

प्रगोपन *pra-gopan* [S.], m. *Pl.* protection; salvation.

प्रग्रहण *pra-grahaṇ* [S.], m. **1.** taking, seizing. **2.** holding.

प्रघण *pra-ghaṇ* [S.], m. *Pl. HŚS.* **1.** covered terrace, or porch. **2.** iron club or bar. **3.** copper pot.

प्रचंड *pra-caṇḍ* [S.], adj. **1.** vehement. **2.** raging; fearsome, terrible. **3.** burning. **4.** excessive, intolerable.

प्रचंडता *pra-caṇḍătā* [S.], f. vehemence, violence, &c.

प्रचलन *pra-calan* [S.], m. **1.** moving to and fro. **2.** currency, vogue; force.

प्रचलित *pra-calit* [S.], adj. **1.** current, in vogue, in force; in use (a word; speech). **2.** current, in progress (year, month).

प्रचार *pra-cār* [S.], m. **1.** spreading, spread; diffusion (as of beliefs, a language); publicity (for views, a cause), propaganda. **2.** currency, usage (as of a language). — ~ करना (का), to spread, to make current; to divulge; to make propaganda (for). – प्रचार-अधिकारी, m. press attaché. प्रचार-कर्ता, m. inv. promulgator, proclaimer; propagandist. प्रचार-प्रसार, m. = ~, 1. प्रचारात्मक [°*ra* + *ā*°], adj. = परचारक.

प्रचार- *pra-cār-* [ad. **pracārayati* or *pracāra-*], v.t. Brbh. Av. = प्रचार करना.

प्रचारक *pra-cārak* [S.], adj. & m. **1.** adj. spreading, publicising, &c. **2.** proclaiming. **3.** m. a promulgator, proclaimer. धर्म-परचारक, m. a missionary. **4.** propagandist.

प्रचारण *pra-cāraṇ* [S.], m. **1.** spreading, &c. **2.** promulgating, proclaiming.

प्रचारिणी *pra-cāriṇī*, adj. f. = प्रचारी.

प्रचारित *pra-cārit* [S.], adj. **1.** spread, made public; divulged. **2.** promulgated, proclaimed.

प्रचारी *pra-cārī* [S.], adj. 1. = प्रचारक. **2.** propagandist.

प्रचुर *pracur* [S.], adj. **1.** abundant, plentiful. **2.** full. **3.** ample (of build). — ~ मात्रा में, adv. in abundant measure.

प्रचुरता *pracurătā* [S.], f. abundant measure, abundance.

प्रचोदन *pra-codan* [S.], m. **1.** instigation, incitement; enjoining. **2.** sending.

प्रचोदित *pra-codit* [S.], adj. **1.** impelled; incited; enjoined. **2.** sent.

प्रच्छद *pra-cchad* [S.], m. a covering; blanket.

प्रच्छन्न *pra-cchann* [S.], adj. **1.** covered; clad. **2.** secret, hidden; obscure (as a motive).

प्रच्युत *pra-cyut* [S.], adj. **1.** fallen (from). **2.** deviated (from), strayed.

प्रच्युति *pra-cyuti* [S.], f. fall.

प्रजनन *pra-janan* [S.], m. **1.** procreation. **2.** giving birth. **3.** breeding (as livestock).

प्रजा *pra-jā* [S.], f. **1.** people (of a state); subjects (of a king). **2.** tenants (of a landlord). **3.** offspring; descendants. — **प्रजा-जन**, m. pl. = ~, 1., 2. **प्रजातंत्र**, m. democracy; republic. °**वाद**, m. belief in democracy; republicanism. °-**तंत्रात्मक** [°*ra*+*ā*°], adj. democratic; republican. °-**तंत्री**, adj. democratic; republican. **प्रजा-पति**; lord of creatures: the creator; a title of Brahmā, and of other creatures; a king. **प्रजा-पालक**, m. protector of his people: king; a title of Kr̥ṣṇa. °-**पालन**, m. protection of subjects, or dependants. **प्रजा-सत्ता**, f. democracy. °-**सत्तात्मक**, adj. °-**सत्तावाद**, m. = **प्रजातंत्रवाद**; °**ई**, adj. & m. **प्रजाहित**, m. & adj. a people's well-being; good or kind to subjects, or dependants.

प्रजात *pra-jāt* [S.], adj. given birth to.

प्रजायिनी *pra-jāyinī* [S.], f. *Pl. HŚS.* mother.

प्रजार- *pra-jār-*, v.t. Brbh. = **जलाना**.

प्रज्ञ *pra-jñă* [S.], adj. **1.** learned, wise. **2.** versed (in).

प्रज्ञता *pra-jñătā* [S.], f. **1.** learning; knowledge. **2.** judgment.

प्रज्ञा *pra-jñā* [S.], f. **1.** understanding, intelligence. **2.** wisdom, knowledge.

प्रज्ञात *pra-jñāt* [S.], adj. well-known; celebrated.

प्रज्ञान *pra-jñān* [S.], m. cognisance.

प्रज्ञापक *pra-jñāpak* [S.], m. placard, announcement.

प्रज्वलन *pra-jvalan* [S.], m. blazing up; burning.

प्रज्वलित *pra-jvalit* [S.], adj. **1.** flaming, blazing. **2.** bright, radiant.

प्रण *praṇ* [ad. *paṇa-*: ? ×*pratijñā-*], m. **1.** a promise. **2.** a vow. — ~ **करना**, to make a promise; to take a vow.

प्रणत *pra-ṇat* [S.], adj. **1.** bent forwards. **2.** bowed, bowing. **3.** fig. reverential; humble. — **प्रणत-पाल**, adj. Av. cherishing the humble.

प्रणति *pra-ṇati* [S.], f. bowing; respectful greeting.

प्रणना *praṇnā* [H. *praṇav-*]. v.i. *Pl.* to bow down before.

प्रणय *pra-ṇay* [S.], m. **1.** confidence, trust. ***2.** love; friendship. **3.** loving entreaty. — **प्रणयाकुल** [°*ya*+*ā*°], adj. suffering pangs of love. **प्रणयार्थी** [°*ya*+*a*°], m. f. one desiring the love (of, **का**).

प्रणयन *pra-ṇayan* [S.], m. bringing forth: inaugurating (as a literary tradition). **2.** composing (as a literary work).

प्रणयिनी *pra-ṇayinī* [S.], adj. f. & f. **1.** adj. = **प्रणयी**, f. **2.** f. mistress, wife.

प्रणयी *pra-ṇayī* [S.], adj. & m. **1.** adj. feeling love or attachment (for). **2.** m. lover, husband.

प्रणव *pra-ṇav* [S.], m. the mystical or sacred syllable *om*.

प्रणाद *pra-ṇād* [S.], m. **1.** loud sound; shout; roar or cry (of an animal). **2.** cry of delight.

प्रणाम *pra-ṇām* [S.], m. & interj. **1.** m. bow; respectful greeting. **2.** interj. respectful greetings! — ~ **करना** (**को**), to greet respectfully.

प्रणाल *pra-ṇāl* [S.], m. *Pl. HŚS.* = **प्रणाली**.

प्रणालिका *pra-ṇālikā* [S.], f. **1.** small water channel; small tube. **2.** any tubular vessel of the body.

प्रणाली *pra-ṇālī* [S.], f. **1.** particular method or way. **2.** system (as of government, &c). **3.** tradition. **4.** water-channel, drain.

प्रणिधान *pra-ṇi-dhān* [S.], m. **1.** attention, regard. ***2.** profound meditation. **3.** great effort.

प्रणिपात *pra-ṇi-pāt* [S.], m. falling down (in worship).

प्रणी *praṇī* [cf. H. *praṇ*], adj. under a vow; resolute.

प्रणीत *pra-ṇīt* [S.], adj. **1.** accomplished; made, constructed; composed. **2.** sent, despatched; thrown.

प्रणेता *pra-ṇetā* [S.], m. inv. **1.** maker; author, causer; composer, compiler. **2.** founder.

प्रणोदन *pra-ṇodan* [S.], m. driving, directing; uttering (words).

प्रताड़ना *pra-tāṛănā* [S.], f. an attack: scolding, chiding.

प्रतान *pra-tān* [S.], m. **1.** a shoot, tendril. **2.** a climbing plant. **3.** *Pl. HŚS.* epilepsy.

प्रताप *pra-tāp* [S.], m. **1.** ardour; vigour, energy; valour. **2.** brilliance; majesty, glory; prowess; possession of rank and power. **3.** transf. magnanimity; generosity. — **प्रतापवान**, adj. = **प्रतापी**.

प्रतापी *pra-tāpī* [S.], adj. **1.** ardent, &c. **2.** brilliant, glorious, &c. (see **प्रताप**.)

प्रतारक *pra-tārak* [S.], adj. & m. **1.** adj. deceitful. **2.** m. a deceiver; rogue.

प्रतारण *pra-tāraṇ* [S.], m. = **प्रतारणा**.

प्रतारणा *pra-tārăṇā* [S.], f. deceiving; cheating; deception.

प्रतारित *pra-tārit* [S.], adj. deceived.

प्रति *prati* [S.], f. & pref. & ppn. **1.** f. copy (of a book, &c). **2.** copy (of an original). **3.** section, group (of a larger whole). **4.** pref. again, back again, re- (e.g. **प्रतिभाषण**, m. answering speech). **5.** towards, against, anti-, counter- (e.g. **प्रतिकूल**, adj. contrary, adverse); pertaining (to). **6.** each, every; per (e.g. **प्रतिदिन**, adv. daily). **7.** similar to (e.g. **प्रतिलिपि**, f. a copy). **8.** for, in exchange, by proxy. **9.** ppn. w. **के**. against. **10.** towards, in regard to (of feelings, opinions). **भारत के ~ रुचि**, f. interest in India.

प्रतिकर *prati-kar* [S.], m. esp. *law.* making good, compensation.

प्रतिकरण *prati-karaṇ* [S.], m. counter-effect.

प्रतिकर्म *prati-karm* [S.], m. **1.** retaliation. **2.** counter-action. **3.** *Pl. HŚS.* dress, attire.

प्रतिकर्मक *prati-karmak* [S.], m. *chem.* a reagent.

प्रतिकार *prati-kār* [S.], m. **1.** making return; retaliation; retribution; revenge. **2.** making good; compensation. **3.** counter-action; warding off (an attack); effect (of a medicine).

प्रतिकारक *prati-kārak* [S.], adj. & m. **1.** adj. avenging, &c. **2.** counter-acting. **3.** m. avenger. **4.** transf. antidote.

प्रतिकारी *prati-kārī* [S.], adj. = **प्रतिकारक**.

प्रतिकार्य *prati-kāryă* [S.], adj. to be avenged, or made good, &c. (see **प्रतिकार**).

प्रतिकूल *prati-kūl* [S.], adj. **1.** contrary. **2.** adverse, unfavourable; untoward. **3.** opposed; hostile (as forces). **4.** (ppn. w. **के**) against, counter to. **5.** contrary to.

प्रतिकूलता *prati-kūlătā* [S.], f. **1.** contrary direction (as of wind). **2.** adverseness (as of circumstances). **3.** contrary behaviour.

प्रतिकृति *prati-kṛti* [S.], f. copy; facsimile.

प्रतिक्रम *prati-kram* [S.], m. reversed order or sequence. — **प्रतिक्रमात्**, adv. vice versa.

प्रतिक्रियक *prati-kriyak* [S.], adj. reacting.

प्रतिक्रिया *prati-kriyā* [S.], f. reaction; repercussion. — **प्रतिक्रियात्मक** [°*yā* + *ā*°], adj. reactive. **प्रतिक्रियावादी**, adj. & m. reactionary. **प्रतिक्रियाशील**, m. reactive; quick to react (a person).

प्रतिक्षण *prati-kṣaṇ* [S.], adv. at every moment, moment by moment.

प्रतिगामी *prati-gāmī* [S.], adj. regressive.

प्रतिगृहीत *prati-gṛhīt* [S.], adj. accepted, taken on.

प्रतिग्रह *prati-grah* [S.], m. **1.** receiving, accepting. **2.** gift (as to a brāhmaṇ).

प्रतिग्रहण *prati-grahaṇ* [S.], m. **1.** accepting (sthg. offered). **2.** receiving, welcoming (a guest, &c).

प्रतिग्राहक *prati-grāhak* [S.], m. receiver.

प्रतिघात *prati-ghāt* [S.], m. **1.** warding off a blow; repulsing. **2.** a return blow. **3.** reaction. **4.** hindrance, opposition.

प्रतिघाती *prati-ghātī* [S.], adj. & m. **1.** adj. warding off, repulsing. **2.** opposing, hostile. **3.** m. adversary.

प्रतिचिंतन *prati-cintan* [S.], m. reflection, consideration.

प्रतिच्छवि *prati-cchavi* [S.], f. = **प्रतिछाया**.

प्रतिच्छायित *prati-cchāyit* [S.], adj. reflected.

प्रतिछाया *prati-chāyā* [S.], f. **1.** reflected image. **2.** image; picture; statue; shadow.

प्रतिजीव *prati-jīv* [S.], adj. antibiotic.

प्रतिजीवन *prati-jīvan* [S.], m. new birth, rebirth.

प्रतिज्ञा *prati-jñā* [S.], f. **1.** assertion, declaration; assurance; vow. ***2.** promise. **3.** acknowledgement (of a fact, &c.); assent. — **~ करना (की)**, to promise. – **प्रतिज्ञा-पालन**, m. fulfilment of a promise, keeping of a vow.

प्रतिज्ञात *prati-jñāt* [S.], adj. **1.** promised. **2.** asserted; affirmed.

प्रतिदत्त *prati-datt* [S.], adj. given back; refunded.

प्रतिदान *prati-dān* [S.], m. **1.** giving back, returning (a deposit). **2.** restitution; compensation. **3.** a gift in return. **4.** exchange, barter.

प्रतिदिन *prati-din* [S.], adv. **1.** every day. **2.** always, continually. — **~ का**, adj. daily, everyday.

प्रतिद्वंद्व *prati-dvandvă* [S.], m. opposition, conflict; duel.

प्रतिद्वंद्विता *prati-dvandvitā* [S.], f. **1.** rivalry, conflict. **2.** conflict.

प्रतिद्वंद्वी *prati-dvandvī* [S.], m. rival; competitor.

प्रतिध्वनि *prati-dhvani* [S.], f. echo, reverberation; resonance.

प्रतिध्वनित *prati-dhvanit* [S.], adj. echoing; reverberating, ringing.

प्रतिनाद *prati-nād* [S.], m. = प्रतिध्वनि.

प्रतिनिधि *prati-ni-dhi* [S.], m. & adj. **1.** m. a representative; a delegate. **2.** a deputy. **3.** a substitute. **4.** adj. esp. प्रतिनिधि-. representative (as government). **5.** typical, characteristic (of). — प्रतिनिधि-मंडल, m. delegation. °ई, f. id.

प्रतिनिधिक *pratinidhik* [cf. H. *pratinidhi*; w. H. *-ik*], adj. representative.

प्रतिनिधित *prati-ni-dhit* [S.], adj. represented (a group, an interest).

प्रतिनिधित्व *prati-ni-dhitvă* [S.], m. **1.** representation (of a group). **2.** representative status. — ~ करना (का), to represent.

प्रतिनियुक्त *prati-ni-yukt* [S.], adj. deputed, delegated.

प्रतिनिर्देशन *prati-nir-deśan* [S.], m. **1.** renewed directive or request. **2.** a cross-reference.

प्रतिपक्ष *prati-pakṣ* [S.], m. opposite side, or opinion.

प्रतिपक्षता *prati-pakṣătā* [S.], f. **1.** opposition. **2.** antithesis.

प्रतिपक्षी *prati-pakṣī* [S.], adj. & m. **1.** adj. opposing. **2.** opposite (opinion, &c). **3.** m. opponent; rival.

प्रतिपत्ति *prati-patti* [S.], f. **1.** exposition. **2.** causing, effecting, accomplishing.

प्रतिपद *prati-pad* [S.], adv. at every step; at every moment; everywhere.

प्रतिपद् *prati-pad* [S.], m. = प्रतिपदा.

प्रतिपदा *prati-padā* [S.], f. the first day of a lunar fortnight.

प्रतिपन्न *prati-pann* [S.], adj. **1.** approached; obtained, gained. ***2.** ascertained, determined; demonstrated, proved. **3.** assented to, accepted.

प्रतिपादन *prati-pādan* [S.], m. **1.** affirming, representing (as a case), expounding. **2.** establishing, proving. **3.** giving, delivering. **4.** causing.

प्रतिपादित *prati-pādit* [S.], adj. *lit.* **1.** stated, represented (as a case); expounded. **2.** established, proved. **3.** given, delivered. **4.** caused, effected.

प्रतिपाद्य *prati-pādyă* [S.], adj. to be treated of, or expounded.

प्रतिपाल *prati-pāl* [S.], m. **1.** protecting, protection. **2.** fostering; rearing. 3. = प्रतिपालक.

प्रतिपाल- *pratipāl-* [ad. *pratipālayati*], v.t. Av. **1.** to protect. **2.** to foster; to cherish.

प्रतिपालक *prati-pālak* [S.], m. **1.** protector. **2.** fosterer; guardian.

प्रतिपालन *prati-pālan* [S.], m. **1.** protecting. **2.** fostering. **3.** following (a directive, &c).

प्रतिपालित *prati-pālit* [S.], adj. **1.** protected. **2.** fostered; maintained; cherished. **3.** practised, followed (an ordinance, &c).

प्रतिपाल्य *prati-pālyă* [S.], adj. to be protected, &c.

प्रतिपूजक *prati-pūjak* [S.], adj. & m. **1.** adj. honouring duly, venerating. **2.** m. one who venerates, or worships.

प्रतिपूजन *prati-pūjan* [S.], m. showing due honour (to).

प्रतिफल *prati-phal* [S.], m. **1.** return, reward; proper retribution. **2.** compensation (for loss, injury). **3.** result.

प्रतिफलित *prati-phalit* [S.], adj. poet. to be seen, in view.

प्रतिबंध *prati-bandh* [S.], m. **1.** restriction, limitation. **2.** obstacle, hindrance; interruption (of traffic, &c). **3.** prohibition, ban; embargo; blockade. — ~ लगाना, to place a restriction, &c. (on, पर). – प्रतिबंधात्मक [°*dha* + *ā*°], adj. restrictive; obstructive.

प्रतिबंधक *prati-bandhak* [S.], adj. **1.** restrictive. **2.** obstructive.

प्रतिबंधित *prati-bandhit* [S.], adj. **1.** restricted. **2.** obstructed.

प्रतिबंधी *prati-bandhī* [S.], adj. = प्रतिबंधक.

प्रतिबद्ध *prati-baddh* [S.], adj. restricted, &c. (see प्रतिबंध).

प्रतिबाधक *prati-bādhak* [S.], adj. opposing, preventing.

प्रतिबाधन *prati-bādhan* [S.], m. obstacle.

प्रतिबाधित *prati-bādhit* [S.], adj. opposed, prevented.

प्रतिबाधी *prati-bādhī* [S.], adj. & m. **1.** adj. opposing, preventing. **2.** m. an adversary.

प्रतिबिंब *prati-bimb* [S.], m. **1.** reflection (of an image). **2.** image, picture; shadow. **3.** mirror.

प्रतिबिंबक *prati-bimbak* [S.], adj. following inseparably like a shadow.

प्रतिबिंबित *prati-bimbit* [S.], adj. reflected (as an image).

प्रतिबोध *prati-bodh* [S.], m. **1.** awaking. **2.** knowledge; discernment.

प्रतिबोधक *prati-bodhak* [S.], adj. & m. **1.** adj. awakening. **2.** instructing, enlightening. **3.** m. teacher, preceptor.

प्रतिबोधन *prati-bodhan* [S.], m. **1.** awakening. **2.** instructing, instruction.

प्रतिबोधित *prati-bodhit* [S.], adj. **1.** awoken. **2.** instructed.

प्रतिबोधी *prati-bodhī* [S.], adj. quick (of intelligence), alert.

प्रतिभट *prati-bhaṭ* [S.], m. Av. rival, equal.

प्रतिभा *prati-bhā* [S.], f. **1.** light, splendour. **2.** fig. brilliance, talent; genius. **3.** brilliant conception; audacious act. **प्रतिभान्वित** [°*ā* + *a*°], adj. = प्रतिभाशाली. **प्रतिभावान**, adj. = next; shining, splendid. **प्रतिभाशाली**, adj. brilliant; talented.

प्रतिभाग *prati-bhāg* [S.], m. **1.** division, portion. **2.** excise duty.

प्रतिभाव *prati-bhāv* [S.], m. corresponding character or disposition.

प्रतिभाषा *prati-bhāṣā* [S.], f. answer, rejoinder.

प्रतिभास *prati-bhās* [S.], m. **1.** appearance, look. **2.** illusion.

प्रतिभासन *prati-bhāsan* [S.], m. **1.** appearing, appearance. **2.** illusion. **3.** brightness, radiance.

प्रतिभिन्न *prati-bhinn* [S.], adj. separated, divided.

प्रतिभू *prati-bhū* [S.], m. one standing surety (as for a loan).

प्रतिभूति *prati-bhūti* [S.], f. **1.** security, deposit. **2.** a bond (undertaking payment). **3.** bail.

प्रतिभेद *prati-bhed* [S.], m. **1.** division. **2.** distinction.

प्रतिभेदन *prati-bhedan* [S.], m. **1.** dividing. **2.** distinguishing. **3.** penetrating; divining (a mystery).

प्रतिमा *prati-mā* [S.], f. **1.** image, likeness; idol; representation (as of a deity). **2.** symbol. **3.** [? × *pratimān*] *HŚS.* a weight.

प्रतिमान *prati-mān* [S.], m. counterpart: **1.** model, pattern. **2.** a specimen. **3.** a standard; a weight. **4.** image, &c. (= प्रतिमा). — **प्रतिमानीकरण**, standardisation.

प्रतिमानित *prati-mānit* [S.], adj. standardised.

प्रतिमानीकरण *prati-mānīkaraṇ* [S.], adj. see s.v. प्रतिमान.

प्रतिमास *prati-mās* [S.], adv. per month; month by month.

प्रतिमासिक *prati-māsik* [S.], adj. monthly.

प्रतिमूर्ति *prati-mūrti* [S.], f. counterpart of any form: image, likeness; embodiment.

प्रतियोग *prati-yog* [S.], m. **1.** opposition, hostility. **2.** controversy. **3.** association, cooperation.

प्रतियोगिता *prati-yogitā* [S.], f. **1.** competition, rivalry. **2.** a contest, competition. **3.** hostility. — ~ **करना**, to compete (with, से); to be a rival (of). **प्रतियोगितात्मक** [°*tā* + *ā*°], adj. competitive (an examination).

प्रतियोगिनी *prati-yoginī* [S.], f. a female competitor, &c.

प्रतियोगी *prati-yogī* [S.], adj. & m. **1.** adj. competing, rivalling. **2.** hostile. **3.** m. competitor, rival. **4.** an equal, a match. **5.** ? associate, partner.

प्रतियोद्धा *prati-yoddhā* [S.], m. adversary.

प्रतिरक्षण *prati-rakṣaṇ* [S.], m. preserving, defending.

प्रतिरक्षा *prati-rakṣā* [S.], f. **1.** preservation, protection. **2.** defence (as of a country). — **प्रतिरक्षात्मक** [°*ā* + *ā*°], adj. defensive.

प्रतिरात्र *prati-rātr* [S.], adv. every night.

प्रतिरूप *prati-rūp* [S.], m. & adj. **1.** m. counterpart (of a real form), representation; image; likeness. **2.** fabrication, forgery. **3.** adj. counterfeit, forged. **4.** representative.

प्रतिरूपक *prati-rūpak* [S.], m. a forger.

प्रतिरूपी *prati-rūpī* [S.], adj. representative, typical.

प्रतिरोध *prati-rodh* [S.], m. **1.** opposition. **2.** obstruction. **3.** siege. **4.** blockade.

प्रतिरोधक *prati-rodhak* [S.], adj. & m. **1.** adj. opposing, resistant. **2.** m. an opponent. **3.** an obstacle.

प्रतिरोधन *prati-rodhan* [S.], m. opposing, resisting.

प्रतिरोधित *prati-rodhit* [S.], adj. **1.** checked, barred. **2.** beset, besieged.

प्रतिरोधी *prati-rodhī* [S.], adj. & m. = प्रतिरोधक. — ~ **आक्रमण**, m. counter-attack.

प्रतिलंभ *prati-lambh* [S.], m. **1.** obtaining. **2.** censure; abuse.

प्रतिलिपि *prati-lipi* [S.], f. a copy, duplicate.

प्रतिलोम *prati-lom* [S.], adj. against the hair: **1.** unnatural. **2.** contrary, inverted (as order).

3. disagreeable. **4.** *math.* inverse. **5.** base, depraved.

प्रतिवचन *prati-vacan* [S.], m. **1.** answer. **2.** echo.

प्रतिवर्ष *prati-varṣ* [S.], adv. every year; year by year.

प्रतिवाक्य *prati-vākyă* [S.], m. **1.** answer. **2.** echo.

प्रतिवाद *prati-vād* [S.], m. **1.** rejoinder. **2.** objection; protest. **3.** contradiction. **4.** argument, dispute.

प्रतिवादी *prati-vādī* [S.], adj. & m. **1.** adj. replying, objecting, &c. **2.** m. opponent (in a dispute). **3.** *law.* defendant.

प्रतिवासी *prati-vāsī* [S.], m. a neighbour.

प्रतिविधि *prati-vi-dhi* [S.], f. **1.** countermeasure. **2.** remedy.

प्रतिवेदन *prati-vedan* [S.], m. submission, representation, report.

प्रतिवेदित *prati-vedit* [S.], adj. submitted (as an argument).

प्रतिशंका *prati-śaṅkā* [S.], f. constant fear or doubt.

प्रतिशत *prati-śat* [S.], adv. (also m.) per cent; percentage.

प्रतिशतता *prati-śatătā* [S.], f. percentage.

प्रतिशब्द *prati-śabd* [S.], m. & adv. **1.** m. an equivalent term. ***2.** echo, reverberation; resonance. **3.** adv. in every word. — **उसके फटकार में ~ घृणा थी**, his aversion was evident in every word of his rebuke.

प्रतिशाखा *prati-śākhā* [S.], f. branch, offshoot.

प्रतिशोध *prati-śodh* [S.], m. retaliation; revenge.

प्रतिशोधन *prati-śodhan* [S.], m. retaliating, obtaining revenge.

प्रतिश्याय *prati-śyāy* [S.], m. a cold.

प्रतिश्रुत *prati-śrut* [S.], adj. & m. **1.** adj. promised. **2.** accepted. **3.** m. an echo.

प्रतिश्रुति *prati-śruti* [S.], f. sthg. heard in response: **1.** promise; guarantee. **2.** echo.

प्रतिषिद्ध *prati-ṣiddh* [S.], adj. **1.** forbidden. **2.** refused.

प्रतिषेध *prati-ṣedh* [S.], m. **1.** prohibition. **2.** refusal. **3.** rejection.

प्रतिष्ठ *prati-ṣṭh* [S.], adj. prominent, celebrated.

प्रतिष्ठा *prati-ṣṭhā* [S.], f. **1.** position, rank. **2.** honour. ***3.** prestige; reputation; fame. **4.** euph. notoriety. **5.** installation (as of an idol in a temple), inaugurating, consecration. **6.** endowment (of a temple). **7.** performance of rites, &c. (in accordance with a vow). — **~ करना**, to install; to inaugurate; to consecrate.

प्रतिष्ठान *prati-ṣṭhān* [S.], m. **1.** installation (as of an idol). **2.** appointment (to a post). ***3.** an establishment, foundation; institute.

प्रतिष्ठापन *prati-ṣṭhāpan* [S.], m. **1.** installation. **2.** establishing, establishment.

प्रतिष्ठापित *prati-ṣṭhāpit* [S.], adj. **1.** installed. **2.** established.

प्रतिष्ठित *prati-ṣṭhit* [S.], adj. **1.** situated. ***2.** transf. of position or rank; prominent, celebrated; famous; distinguished. **3.** installed (as an idol); inaugurated, consecrated (as a temple). **4.** established. **5.** standard, standardised (modern Hindi usage).

प्रतिसर्ग *prati-sarg* [S.], m. *hind.* **1.** creation of the world by Brahmā and other deities. **2.** dissolution of the world.

प्रतिस्पर्धा *prati-spardhā* [S.], f. rivalry, competition.

प्रतिस्पर्धी *prati-spardhī* [S.], adj. & m. **1.** adj. competing; competitive. **2.** m. a rival.

प्रतिहत *prati-hat* [S.], adj. struck a counter-blow: **1.** beaten back. **2.** obstructed; averted. **3.** fig. dejected; disappointed.

प्रतिहति *prati-hati* [S.], f. return blow.

प्रतिहार *prati-hār* [S.], m. = **प्रतिहारी**.

प्रतिहारी *prati-hārī* [S.], m. a door-keeper; chamberlain.

प्रतिहिंसक *prati-hiṃsak* [S.], adj. retaliating, retaliatory; vengeful.

प्रतिहिंसा *prati-hiṃsā* [S.], f. counter-violence, retaliation, revenge.

प्रतिहिंसित *prati-hiṃsit* [S.], adj. injured in return.

प्रतीक *pratīk* [S.], m. **1.** a symbol. **2.** a part; first words, or word, of a verse. — **प्रतीक-कथा**, f. symbolic tale, allegory. **प्रतीकवाद**, m. symbolism (as a theory). **°ई**, adj. & m. **प्रतीकात्मक** [°*ka* + *ā*°], adj. symbolic.

प्रतीकार *pratīkār* [S.], m. = **प्रतिकार**.

प्रतीक्षा *pratīkṣā* [S.], f. looking for: waiting for. — **~ करना (की)**, to wait for; to expect. **प्रतीक्षालय** [°*ṣā* + *ā*°], m. waiting-room (at a station, &c).

प्रतीक्षित *pratīkṣit* [S.], adj. **1.** awaited, looked forward to. **2.** respected, revered.

प्रतीक्षी *pratīkṣī* [S.], adj. waiting, or expecting.

प्रतीक्ष्य *pratīkṣyă* [S.], adj. = प्रतीक्षित, 1.

प्रतीची *pratīcī* [S.], f. the west.

प्रतीच्य *pratīcyă* [S.], adj. western.

प्रतीत *pratīt* [S.], adj. **1.** acknowledged, known; evident; apparent. **2.** well-known, celebrated. — ~ होना, to be evident (to, को); to seem (to).

प्रतीति *pratīti* [S.], f. **1.** clear knowledge; experience. **2.** conviction. **3.** faith, belief; trust (placed in someone or sthg). **4.** fame; notoriety. — ~ आना (को), to feel conviction (of, की); to feel trust. ~ करना, to form a clear conception (of, की); to believe (in), &c.

प्रतीप *pratīp* [S.], adj. against the stream: **1.** adverse, contrary. **2.** refractory, cross.

प्रतीयमान *pratīyamān* [S.], adj. being believed, or admitted; apparent; purported.

प्रतीर *pra-tīr* [S.], m. shore, bank.

प्रत्यंग *praty-aṅg* [S.], m. minor part or member; sub-division; section.

प्रत्यंचा *praty-añcā* [S.], f. bow-string.

प्रत्यक *pratyak* [ad. *pratyakṣa-*], adj. E.H. = प्रत्यक्ष.

प्रत्यक्ष *praty-akṣ* [S.], adj. & m. **1.** adj. visible, perceptible; clear, evident; vivid; real, actual. **2.** express, explicit. **3.** direct, immediate; personal (as acquaintance); direct (as a tax, election). **4.** m. visible reality; actuality. — ~ करना, to make evident, &c. ~ रूप से, adv. clearly, unmistakably, &c. – प्रत्यक्षवाद, positivism. °ई, adj. & m. प्रत्यक्ष-सिद्ध, adj. self-evident. प्रत्यक्षीकरण, m. making visible, or evident; representation.

प्रत्यक्षतया *praty-akṣătayā* [S.], adv. clearly, evidently.

प्रत्यक्षी *praty-akṣī* [S.], adj. & m. **1.** adj. seeing with one's own eyes. **2.** m. an eye-witness.

प्रत्यक्षीकरण *praty-akṣīkaraṇ* [S.], m. see s.v. प्रत्यक्ष.

प्रत्यनंतर *praty-an-antar* [S.], m. & adv. **1.** m. nearest heir, or successor. **2.** adv. next in succession; immediately following.

प्रत्यभिज्ञेय *praty-abhi-jñeyă* [S.], adj. distinctive.

प्रत्यभियोग *praty-abhi-yog* [S.]. m. counter-charge (at law).

प्रत्यय *praty-ay* [S.], m. going towards: **1.** implicit belief; trust. **2.** ascertainment, proof (as of identity). **3.** knowledge. **4.** *gram.* sthg. attached, an affix. **5.** *fin.* credit. — प्रत्यय-पत्र, m. letter of credit; written credentials. प्रत्ययवाद, m. idealism. °ई, adj. & m. प्रत्ययांत [°*ya*+*a*°], adj. suffixed (a word).

प्रत्ययित *praty-ayit* [S.], adj. **1.** confided in; trusted (a person). **2.** believed implicitly (a matter). **3.** suffixed (a word).

प्रत्ययी *praty-ayī* [S.], adj. & m. **1.** adj. believing in; trusting. **2.** m. a trustworthy person. **3.** a believer.

प्रत्यर्थी *praty-arthī* [S.], m. an adversary.

प्रत्यर्पण *praty-arpaṇ* [S.], m. extradition (cf. वापसी).

प्रत्यवाय *praty-avāy* [S.], m. *Pl. HŚS.* **1.** harm. **2.** offence, sin.

प्रत्यहं *praty-ahaṁ* [S.], adv. *Pl.* daily; in the morning.

प्रत्याक्रमण *praty-ā-kramaṇ* [S.], m. counter-attack.

प्रत्यागत *praty-ā-gat* [S.], adj. **1.** returned. **2.** arrived (at).

प्रत्यागमन *praty-ā-gaman* [S.], m. **1.** return. **2.** arrival.

प्रत्यादिष्ट *praty-ā-diṣṭ* [S.], adj. **1.** prescribed, recommended. **2.** informed. **3.** warned. **4.** rejected.

प्रत्यादेश *praty-ā-deś* [S.], m. **1.** order, command. **2.** information, declaration. **3.** warning. **4.** rejection, repudiation.

प्रत्याभूत *praty-ā-bhūt* [S.], adj. guaranteed (financially).

प्रत्यायोजित *praty-ā-yojit/* [S.], adj. delegated.

प्रत्यावर्तन *praty-ā-vartan* [S.], m. return.

प्रत्याशा *praty-āśā* [S.], f. confident hope, trust; expectation; anticipation.

प्रत्याशित *praty-āśit* [S.], adj. confidently hoped for; awaited (as an answer to a request).

प्रत्याशी *praty-āśī* [S.], adj. & m. **1.** adj. hoping, expecting; anticipating. **2.** m. a candidate.

प्रत्याहार *praty-ā-hār* [S.], m. **1.** withdrawal, retreat (military, &c). **2.** withdrawing (esp. the senses from external objects). **3.** *gram.* any group of letters or terms denoted for concision's sake by a single syllable.

प्रत्याहृत *praty-ā-hṛt* [S.], adj. **1.** withdrawn. **2.** depressed (the emotions).

प्रत्युक्त *praty-ukt* [S.], adj. **1.** said in answer. **2.** contradicted, refuted.

प्रत्युक्ति *praty-ukti* [S.], f. reply, rejoinder.

प्रत्युत *praty-ut* [S.], adv. but, but rather (= बल्कि).

प्रत्युत्तर *praty-uttar* [S.], m. rejoinder; retort.

प्रत्युत्थान *praty-ut-thān* [S.], m. rising as a mark of respect (to a visitor, or one entering a room).

प्रत्युत्पन्न *praty-ut-pann* [S.], adj. **1.** reproduced. **2.** ready, prompt (as wit).

प्रत्युपकार *praty-upă-kār* [S.], m. **1.** returning a service, or a favour. **2.** a favour returned.

प्रत्युपकारी *praty-upă-kārī* [S.], adj. & m. **1.** adj. returning a favour. **2.** m. a grateful person.

प्रत्युष *praty-uṣ* [S.], f. daybreak, dawn.

प्रत्यूष *praty-ūṣ*, f. = प्रत्युष.

प्रत्यूह *praty-ūh* [S.], m. obstacle, impediment.

प्रत्येक *praty-ek* [S.], adv. each, every.

प्रथम *pratham* [S.], adj. **1.** first. **2.** primary. **3.** prior, former. **4.** chief; best. **5.** adv. at first. **6.** previously, before. — प्रथमाक्षर [°*ma*+*a*°], m. first letter (of a word); pl. initials. प्रथमोपचार [°*ma*+*u*°], m. first aid.

प्रथमता *prathamătā* [S.], f. precedence.

प्रथमा *prathămā* [S.], f. *gram.* nominative.

प्रथा *prathā* [S.], f. sthg. which has spread, or arisen: **1.** custom; institution (social, procedural). **2.** particular system (as of government). — प्रथागत, adj. customary; institutionalised.

प्रथित *prathit* [S.], adj. made broad or wide, or known: widely known, acknowledged, famous.

-प्रद *-prad* [S.], suffix (forms adjectives from nouns). giving (e.g. शिक्षाप्रद, instructive).

प्रदक्षिण *pra-dakṣiṇ*, m. E.H. = प्रदक्षिणा.

प्रदक्षिणा *pra-dakṣiṇā* [S.], f. circumambulation to the right (as a mark of veneration for a person, or an object).

प्रदच्छिन *pra-dacchin* [ad. *pradakṣiṇa*-], m. Brbh. = प्रदक्षिणा.

प्रदर *pra-dar* [S.], m. **1.** splitting. **2.** discharge (from the vagina).

प्रदर्शक *pra-darśak* [S.], adj. & m. **1.** adj. showing, &c. **2.** m. expounder; demonstrator. **3.** *Pl. HŚS.* prophet.

प्रदर्शन *pra-darśan* [S.], m. **1.** showing; exhibiting. **2.** a demonstration. **3.** exhibition. — प्रदर्शनकारी, adj. & m. demonstrating; demonstrator; exhibitor.

प्रदर्शनी *pra-darśănī* [S.], f. **1.** an exhibition. **2.** *Pl.* fee (to an officiant at a ceremony).

प्रदर्शिका *pra-darśikā* [S.], f. **1.** a guide-book. **2.** guide.

प्रदर्शित *pra-darśit* [S.], adj. **1.** shown; exhibited; pointed out, declared. **2.** *Pl. HŚS.* prophesied.

प्रदाता *pra-dātā* [S.], m. inv. a donor, bestower.

प्रदान *pra-dān* [S.], m. **1.** giving, granting; bestowing. **2.** giving in marriage. **3.** gift. — प्रदान-पत्र, m. deed of gift.

प्रदाय *pra-dāy* [S.], m. supply, provision.

-प्रदायी *-pra-dāyī* [S.], adj. formant. giving, bestowing.

प्रदिशा *pra-diśā* [S.], f. *HŚS.* an intermediary (sub-cardinal) point of the compass.

प्रदीप *pra-dīp* [S.], m. **1.** a light; lantern **2.** light, radiance.

प्रदीपक *pra-dīpak* [S.], adj. & m. **1.** adj. illuminating. ***2.** a light; lantern.

प्रदीपन *pra-dīpan* [S.], m. **1.** kindling, igniting. **2.** exciting (the emotions). **3.** illuminating. **4.** a partic. mineral poison (red in colour, and caustic).

प्रदीपिका *pra-dīpikā* [S.], f. **1.** small light; lantern; candle. **2.** fig. commentary (on a text).

प्रदीप्त *pra-dīpt* [S.], adj. **1.** kindled. **2.** excited, inflamed (the emotions); awoken (appetite). **3.** illuminated.

प्रदीप्ति *pra-dīpti* [S.], f. = प्रदीप, 2.

प्रदूषण *pra-dūṣaṇ* [S.], m. damage, pollution (to or of the environment).

प्रदेश *pra-deś* [S.], adj. **1.** place, region. ***2.** province; state (of India). **3.** fig. realm (of thought, imagination). — देश-प्रदेश, m. the nation (sc. India) and the states. प्रदेशवाद, m. regionalism; provincialism.

प्रदेशन *pra-deśan* [S.], m. euph. gift; bribe.

प्रदेशनी *pra-deśănī* [ad. *pradeśinī*-], f. = प्रदेशिनी.

प्रदेशित *pra-deśit* [S.], adj. pointed out; indicated.

प्रदेशिनी *pra-deśinī* [S.], f. the forefinger (which directs, or points).

प्रदेशीय *pra-deśīyă* [S.], adj. **1.** regional. **2.** provincial; having to do with a state.

प्रदेह *pra-deh* [S.], m. *Pl. HŚS.* plaster; ointment.

प्रदोष *pra-doṣ* [S.], m. **1.** fault, sin (cf. दोष). **2.** the first part of the night, evening twilight.

प्रधान *pra-dhān* [S.], adj. & m. **1.** adj. chief, principal. **2.** -प्रधान. consisting predominantly (of). (e.g. घटनाप्रधान उपन्यास, m. novel of incident). **3.** m. chief, leader, head. **4.** minister, counsellor. **5.** headman (of a village). **6.** principal thing, prime object. — ~ मंत्री, m. f. prime minister; chief or general secretary. प्रधानतः, adv. chiefly, principally.

प्रधानता *pra-dhānătā* [S.], f. **1.** pre-eminence, leading status. **2.** leadership; guidance (of an enterprise).

प्रध्वंस *pra-dhvaṃs* [S.], m. **1.** utter destruction. **2.** loss.

प्रध्वंसी *pra-dhvaṃsī* [S.], adj. & m. **1.** adj. destructive. **2.** m. a destroyer.

प्रनव- *pranav-* [ad. *praṇamati*], v.t. Brbh. Av. to bow down to.

प्रनामी *pra-nāmī* [S.], adj. & f. **1.** adj. bowing to, greeting. **2.** f. sthg. given in greeting, visitor's gift.

प्रपंच *pra-pañc* [S.], m. **1.** development, expansion. ***2.** the visible world; the toils of the world, worldly affairs and entanglements. **3.** error, illusion. **4.** trick; deceit.

प्रपंचित *pra-pañcit* [S.], adj. **1.** amplified, expanded. ***2.** presented in a false light. **3.** mistaken, erring. **4.** deceived.

प्रपंची *pra-pañcī* [S.], adj. & m. **1.** adj. insidious, deceitful; scheming. **2.** m. a guileful person, &c.

प्रपितामह *pra-pitāmăh* [S.], m. great-grandfather (on father's side).

प्रपितामही *pra-pitāmăhī* [S.], f. great-grandmother (on father's side).

प्रपुनाट *prapunāṭ* [S.], m. a small shrub, *Cassia alata* (the leaves of which are used in treating ringworm).

प्रपुनाल *prapunāl* [S.], m. = प्रपुनाट.

प्रपूर्ण *pra-pūrṇ* [S.], adj. = परिपूर्ण.

प्रपौत्र *pra-pautr* [S.], m. = परपोता.

प्रपौत्री *pra-pautrī* [S.], f. = परपोती.

प्रफुला *pra-phulā* [ad. *praphulla-*], f. Brbh. 19c. white water-lily, or lotus.

प्रफुलित *pra-phulit*, adj. Brbh. = प्रफुल्लित.

प्रफुल्ल *pra-phull* [S.], adj. **1.** blossoming, wide open (a flower); covered with flowers (a tree). **2.** radiant (face, eyes); smiling; joyful.

प्रफुल्लता *pra-phullătā* [S.], f. brightness, cheerfulness.

प्रफुल्लित *pra-phullit* [S.], adj. = प्रफुल्ल.

प्रबंध *pra-bandh* [S.], m. **1.** connection, tie. ***2.** arrangement, organisation (of an activity); management (as of a company); administration. **3.** measure, step (to an end). **4.** a literary composition; specif. a long narrative poem. **5.** a dissertation. — प्रबंध-कार्ता, m. inv. manager, director, organiser. प्रबंधकार, m. author of a composition. °-कारी, adj. managing, organising; directing. °-कारिणी, f. प्रबंध-काव्य, m. = ~, 4., 2. प्रबंध-परिषद्, m. board of management, board of directors. प्रबंध-समिति, f. management committee. प्रबंधात्मक [°*dha*+*ā*°], adj. administrative, organisational, managerial; having to do with literary composition; narrative (style, genre). प्रबंधाधिकार [°*dha*+*a*°], m. grant of probate.

प्रबंधक *pra-bandhak* [S.], m. manager, organiser, arranger.

प्रबंधन *pra-bandhan* [S.], m. **1.** arranging, organising. **2.** manner of composition; style.

प्रबंधी *pra-bandhī* [S.], adj. **1.** administrative. **2.** being in charge, managing (as a director).

प्रबल *pra-bal* [S.], adj. **1.** very strong; mighty; dominant. **2.** violent (as a storm). **3.** weighty (as an argument). — प्रबलीकरण, m. reinforcing, reinforcement.

प्रबलता *pra-balătā* [S.], f. strength, &c.

प्रबलन *pra-balan* [S.], m. reinforcement.

प्रबलित *pra-balit* [S.], adj. **1.** strengthened. **2.** fortified, reinforced.

प्रबलीकरण *prabalīkaraṇ* [S.], m. see s.v. प्रबल.

प्रबुद्ध *pra-buddh* [S.], adj. **1.** wakened. ***2.** enlightened; wise; learned.

प्रबोध *pra-bodh* [S.], m. **1.** waking; arousal, vigilance. ***2.** enlightenment; persuasion (of a fact, a truth); consolation. **3.** understanding, intelligence.

प्रबोधक *pra-bodhak* [S.], adj. & m. **1.** adj. awakening, &c. **2.** enlightening, &c. **3.** m. one who wakens, arouses, &c. (see प्रबोध).

प्रबोधन *pra-bodhan* [S.], m. **1.** awakening, arousal. **2.** making aware, enlightening, &c.

प्रबोधना *pra-bodhnā* [ad. *prabodhayati*; w. H. *prabodh*], v.t. to encourage.

प्रबोधित *pra-bodhit* [S.], adj. **1.** awakened; aroused; vigilant. **2.** enlightened, aware; consoled.

प्रभंजन *pra-bhañjan* [S.], m. **1.** destruction. **2.** wind, storm; dust-storm.

प्रभव *pra-bhav* [S.], m. **1.** production, birth. **2.** origin, source.

प्रभा *pra-bhā* [S.], f. light; radiance; splendour. — **परभाकर**, m. light-maker: the sun; the moon. **प्रभा-मंडल**, m. ring of light: halo.

प्रभात *pra-bhāt* [S.], m. dawn. **परभातकालीन**, adj. characterising, or occurring at, dawn.

प्रभाती *pra-bhātī* [S.], adj. & f. **1.** adj. sung in a musical mode appropriate to dawn. **2.** f. a song sung at dawn.

प्रभान *pra-bhān* [S.], m. *Pl. HŚS.* light, radiance.

प्रभाव *pra-bhāv* [S.], m. **1.** power, might; majesty. ***2.** influence (upon, **पर**); effect; impression. — **~ डालना**, to exert or to have an influence (upon, **पर**). **~ में आना**, to be influenced (by, **के**). – **प्रभाववाद**, m. impressionism. **°ई**, adj. & m. impressionist. **प्रभावशाली**, adj. effective; influential; impressive. **प्रभावशील**, adj. = prec. **प्रभावहीन**, adj. ineffective; unimpressive.

प्रभावित *pra-bhāvit* [S.], adj. influenced (by, **से**); impressed (by).

प्रभावी *pra-bhāvī* [S.], adj. influential, &c. (see **प्रभाव**, 2).

प्रभु *pra-bhu* [S.], m. **1.** master, lord; ruler. **2.** God. — **प्रभु-भक्त**, adj. & m. devoted to one's master; devout; a devoted servant, &c. **°इ**, f. **प्रभु-सत्ता**, f. sovereignty. **°क**, adj. **°त्मक** [°*ā*+*ā*°], id. **°-संपन्न**, adj. vested with sovereignty, sovereign.

प्रभुता *pra-bhutā* [S.], f. = **प्रभुत्व**.

प्रभुताई *prabhutāī* [cf. H. *prabhutā*], f. Brbh. Av. = **प्रभुता**.

प्रभुत्व *pra-bhutvă* [S.], m. **1.** lordship. **2.** supremacy, power; sovereignty, rule. **3.** greatness, might; majesty. — **~ करना**, to win ascendancy (over, **पर**); to exercise sovereignty; to lord it. **~ जमाना (पर)**, = id., 1.

प्रभूत *pra-bhūt* [S.], adj. **1.** produced, generated. **2.** developed; abundant.

प्रभूतता *pra-bhūtătā* [S.], f. abundance; great number.

प्रभूति *pra-bhūti* [S.], f. *HŚS.* **1.** birth, origin. **2.** abundance.

प्रभृति *pra-bhṛti* [S.], adv. beginning with: et cetera.

प्रभेद *pra-bhed* [S.], m. **1.** distinction, difference; disparity. **2.** sub-division; variety.

प्रभेदक *pra-bhedak* [S.], adj. distinguishing, discriminating.

प्रभेदन *pra-bhedan* [S.], m. distinguishing, discriminating.

प्रभेदी *pra-bhedī* [S.], adj. distinctive.

प्रमत्त *pra-matt* [S.], adj. **1.** intoxicated. **2.** lustful. **3.** intoxicated with delight, enraptured.

प्रमत्तता *pra-mattătā* [S.], f. state of intoxication, &c.

प्रमद *pra-mad* [S.], m. & adj. **1.** m. intoxication. **2.** fig. joy, rapture. **3.** adj. intoxicated; frenzied. **4.** lustful. **5.** careless.

प्रमा *pra-mā* [S.], f. *Pl. HŚS.* true perception or knowledge.

प्रमाण *pra-māṇ* [S.], m. **1.** measure, standard; authority (as for a view); precedent. **2.** *philos.* means of knowledge. ***3.** proof, evidence; verification; warrant. **4.** evidence (as to a matter). — **~ करना**, to authenticate, to verify; to regard as authentic. **~ देना**, to give evidence, to witness. – **प्रमाण-पत्र**, m. certificate; diploma; credentials. **प्रमाण-स्वरूप**, adv. by way of proof, or confirmation. **प्रमाणीकरण**, m. authentication (of a document); witnessing (a signature); verification (of a matter). **°कृत**, adj.

प्रमाणक *pra-māṇak* [S.], m. certificate; voucher.

प्रमाणित *pra-māṇit* [S.], adj. **1.** proved. **2.** confirmed (as an assertion); certified.

प्रमाणीकरण *pra-māṇīkaraṇ* [S.], m. see s.v. **प्रमाण**.

प्रमातामह *pra-mātāmăh* [S.], f. maternal great-grandfather.

प्रमातामही *pra-mātāmăhī* [S.], f. maternal great-grandmother.

प्रमाद *pra-mād* [S.], m. **1.** intoxication. ***2.** frenzy; lust. **3.** negligence, oversight. **4.** error, mistake.

प्रमादी *pra-mādī* [S.], adj. & m. **1.** adj. intoxicated. ***2.** frenzied; lustful. **3.** negligent. **4.** m. a careless person, &c.

प्रमित *pra-mit* [S.], adj. **1.** measured out; limited, moderate; restricted. **2.** established, proved. **3.** authentic.

प्रमितता *pra-mitătā* [S.], f. limitation, moderation.

प्रमिति *pra-miti* [S.], f. **1.** measuring out. **2.** accepted fact or notion, established knowledge.

प्रमुख *pra-mukh* [S.], adj. & m. **1.** adj. chief, principal; prominent. **2.** dominant (as an attitude). **3.** m. chief person, leader; a leading official; a distinguished person.

प्रमुखता *pra-mukhătā* [S.], f. **1.** leading position or status, primacy. **2.** predominance.

प्रमुदित *pra-mudit* [S.], adj. delighted.

प्रमेय *pra-mey* [S.], m. a proposition (for discussion); theorem.

प्रमेह *pra-meh* [S.], m. urinary disease: **1.** diabetes (= मधुमेह). **2.** gonorrhoea.

प्रमोचक *pra-mocak* [S.], m. *Pl. HŚS.* liberator.

प्रमोचन *pra-mocan* [S.], m. *Pl. HŚS.* liberating, releasing.

प्रमोद *pra-mod* [S.], m. joy, delight; happiness. — **प्रमोद-वन**, m. pleasure-grove; specif. *mythol.* name of a grove at Ayodhyā, a meeting-place of Rām and Sītā.

प्रमोदक *pra-modak* [S.], adj. causing joy, &c., gladdening.

प्रमोदित *pra-modit* [S.], adj. delighted.

प्रमोदी *pra-modī* [S.], adj. = **प्रमोदक**.

प्रमोह *pra-moh* [S.], m. **1.** infatuation. **2.** fainting.

प्रयत्न *pra-yatn* [S.], m. **1.** attempt, endeavour. **2.** effort, exertion. — **~ करना**, to attempt, &c. (to, **का**). **प्रयत्नपूर्वक**, adv. energetically, &c. **प्रयत्नवान**, adj. = next. **प्रयत्नशील**, adj. energetic; industrious; zealous.

प्रयाग *prayāg* [S.], m. place of sacrifice: **1.** a pilgrimage-place, esp. that at the confluence of Ganges and Jamna at Allahabad. **2.** Allahabad. — **प्रयाग-राज**, m. a title of Prayāg (signifying its status as foremost of pilgrimage-places). **प्रयागवाल**, m. a *paṇḍā* (brāhmaṇ superintendent of pilgrims' observances) at Allahabad; a temple priest of Allahabad.

प्रयाण *pra-yāṇ* [S.], m. **1.** departure (on a journey). **2.** journey. **3.** a march; invasion; campaign. **4.** euph. death.

प्रयास *pra-yās* [S.], m. **1.** attempt, endeavour; eager pursuit (of an aim, &c). **2.** effort, exertion. — **~ करना**, to make an effort, &c. (to, **का**).

प्रयासी *pra-yāsī* [S.], adj. **1.** energetic, persevering; zealous. **2.** industrious.

प्रयुक्त *pra-yukt* [S.], adj. **1.** joined, yoked. ***2.** used, employed. **3.** compact.

प्रयुक्ति *pra-yukti* [S.], f. use.

प्रयोक्ता *pra-yoktā* [S.], m. inv. **1.** user. **2.** experimenter (= **प्रयोग-कर्ता**).

प्रयोग *pra-yog* [S.], m. **1.** use, application. **2.** practice, usage. **3.** a usage (of words or idiom). **4.** manner of action, procedure. **5.** an experiment. **6.** *gram.* a verb form (as used in subject or object concord, or impersonally). **7.** *fin.* capital (as bearing interest), principal. — **~ करना (का)**, to use, to employ. **प्रयोग-कर्ता**, m. inv., user; experimenter, investigator. **प्रयोगवाद**, m. experimentalism (in literature). **°ई**, adj. & m. experimentalist. **प्रयोग-शाला**, f. laboratory. **प्रयोगात्मक** [°*ga*+*ā*°], adj. practical; experimental. **प्रयोगालय** [°*ga*+*ā*°], m. = **प्रयोग-शाला**.

प्रयोगी *pra-yogī* [S.], adj. **1.** experimental. **2.** having a particular purpose, or object.

प्रयोजक *pra-yojak* [S.], adj. & m. **1.** adj. occasioning, causing. **2.** m. one who instigates or promotes (an act or an effect).

प्रयोजन *pra-yojan* [S.], m. **1.** need (of, **से**), use (for); concern (with). **2.** occasion, motive (for an action). **3.** purpose, object. **4.** advantage. — **~ सिद्ध होना**, a purpose to be achieved.

प्रयोजनिक *pra-yojănik* [S.], adj. = **प्रयोजनीय**.

प्रयोजनीय *pra-yojănīyă* [S.], adj. & m. **1.** adj. to the purpose, applicable, requisite. **2.** m. *Pl. fin.* capital, principal.

प्रयोजनीयता *pra-yojanīyătā* [S.], f. applicability, aptness.

प्रयोज्य *pra-yojyă* [S.], adj. = **प्रयोजनीय**.

प्रलंब *pra-lamb* [S.], adj. & m. **1.** adj. hanging down; Av. long (the arms). **2.** m. delay (= **विलंब**). **3.** Brbh. name of a demon killed by Balrām.

प्रलंबन *pra-lamban* [S.], m. **1.** hanging down. **2.** resting (upon). **3.** delay.

प्रलय *pra-lay* [S.], m. *hind.* **1.** dissolution of the world at the end of a *kalpa*. **2.** disaster, catastrophe. — **प्रलयकर**, adj. catastrophic. **°-कारक**, adj. id. **°-कारी**, adj. id.

प्रलयंकर *pra-layaṅkar* [S.], adj. catastrophic (as a war, a disaster).

प्रलाप *pra-lāp* [S.], m. **1.** conversation (esp. incoherent); chatter. **2.** raving, delirium. **3.** lamentation.

प्रलापक *pra-lāpak* [S.], m. = **प्रलापी**.

प्रलापी *pra-lāpī* [S.], adj. & m. **1.** adj. talkative, chattering. **2.** raving, delirious. **3.** m. an idle chatterer.

प्रलेख *pra-lekh* [S.], m. a document.

प्रलेप *pra-lep* [S.], m. ointment.

प्रलेपन *pra-lepan* [S.], m. smearing; dressing (a wound, &c).

प्रलोठन *pra-loṭhan* [S.], m. *Pl. HŚS.* **1.** rolling on the ground. **2.** tossing (of waves).

प्रलोठित *pra-loṭhit* [S.], m. made to toss, tossing (waves).

प्रलोभ *pra-lobh* [S.], m. **1.** desire, greed; lust. **2.** temptation.

प्रलोभन *pra-lobhan* [S.], m. **1.** tempting, alluring; seducing. **2.** a temptation. — ~ में आना (के), to be tempted, &c. (by); to yield to a temptation.

प्रलोभित *pra-lobhit* [S.], adj. tempted; seduced.

प्रलोभी *pra-lobhī* [S.], adj. **1.** tempting; seductive. **2.** desirous, covetous; lustful.

प्रवंचक *pra-vañcak* [S.], adj. & m. **1.** adj. deceitful, fraudulent; villainous. **2.** m. a cheat, &c.

प्रवंचना *pra-vañcănā* [S.], f. deceit, fraud; villainy.

प्रवंचित *pra-vañcit* [S.], adj. deceived, taken in.

प्रवक्ता *pra-vaktā* [S.], m. inv. **1.** a spokesman. **2.** one who expounds; a preacher; a skilful speaker.

प्रवचन *pra-vacan* [S.], m. **1.** declaring. **2.** expounding, interpreting; exposition (esp. of a religious text or topic); sermon. — प्रवचन-पटु, adj. skilled in exposition, or in using words.

प्रवचनीय *pra-vacănīyă* [S.], adj. requiring exposition, or interpretation.

प्रवणता *pra-vaṇătā* [S.], f. inclination (towards): — भाव-प्रवणता, f. sensibility.

प्रवर *pra-var* [S.], adj. & m. **1.** adj. most excellent; chief, best (in); eminent. **2.** m. *hind.* ancestor; family, lineage. **3.** an important personage.

प्रवर्तक *pra-vartak* [S.], m. initiator; founder.

प्रवर्तन *pra-vartan* [S.], m. initiation; founding; promotion.

प्रवर्तित *pra-vartit* [S.], adj. initiated, founded; promoted.

प्रवर्षण *pra-varṣaṇ* [S.], m. raining; the first rain.

प्रवसन *pra-vasan* [S.], m. **1.** setting out on a journey. **2.** living abroad. **3.** euph. death.

प्रवह *pra-vah* [S.], m. = प्रवाह, 1. — प्रवहमान, adj. flowing swiftly.

प्रवहण *pra-vahaṇ* [S.], m. *Pl. HŚS.* **1.** the act of flowing. **2.** a covered carriage; litter for women.

प्रवाचक *pra-vācak* [S.], adj. & m. **1.** adj. explanatory. **2.** m. one who explains, or discourses (esp. on religion). **3.** reader (in a university).

प्रवाद *pra-vād* [S.], m. **1.** discourse; a fable, tale. **2.** rumour. **3.** gossip. **4.** scandal-mongering.

[1]**प्रवारण** *pra-vāraṇ* [S.], m. prohibition.

[2]**प्रवारण** *pra-vāraṇ* [S.], m. *Pl. HŚS.* a desirable gift.

प्रवाल *pra-vāl* [S.], m. coral.

प्रवास *pra-vās* [S.], m. **1.** residence away from home (esp. abroad). **2.** a journey away from home. **3.** migration; exile. **4.** transf. foreign lands. — ~ में रहना दिलचस्प है, it is interesting to live abroad. – प्रवास-पत्र, m. visa.

प्रवासन *pra-vāsan* [S.], m. **1.** residence abroad. **2.** exile.

प्रवासित *pra-vāsit* [S.], adj. sent abroad; exiled.

प्रवासी *pra-vāsī* [S.], adj. & m. **1.** adj. residing abroad. **2.** migratory (a bird). **3.** m. one living abroad; emigrant; immigrant. **4.** a traveller abroad. **5.** an exile.

प्रवास्य *pra-vāsyă* [S.], adj. liable to be sent abroad; liable to be exiled.

प्रवाह *pra-vāh* [S.], m. **1.** current, flow; course. **2.** course or bed of a river. **3.** transf. current, course (of affairs, or time). **4.** electric current. **5.** *hind.* the disposal in a river of cremated ashes. — प्रवाहपूर्ण, m. flowing; fluent. प्रवाहमय, adj. flowing; fluent (as speech).

प्रवाहक *pra-vāhak* [S.], adj. carrying forwards; furthering (a matter).

प्रवाहिका *pra-vāhikā* [S.], f. river.

प्रवाहित *pra-vāhit* [S.], adj. **1.** disposed of in a river (as cremated ashes). **2.** let drift (as a boat). **3.** in flow, or in movement. **4.** carried forward; advanced, initiated (as a trend). — ~ करना, to dispose of (ashes); to let drift; to float (sthg.) down (a river).

प्रवाही *pra-vāhī* [S.], adj. **1.** causing to flow, or to float. **2.** furthering (a matter). **3.** flowing, liquid.

प्रविख्यात *pra-vi-khyāt* [S.], adj. very widely celebrated or famous.

प्रविख्याति *pra-vi-khyāti* [S.], f. wide fame.

प्रविधि *pra-vi-dhi* [S.], f. a technique.

प्रविष्ट *pra-viṣṭ* [S.], adj. **1.** entered (into, में). **2.** admitted (to a college, &c). — ~ होना, to enter (a room, or a class, &c).

प्रविष्टि *pra-viṣṭi* [S.], f. **1.** entry. **2.** admission. **3.** transf. an entry (item in a ledger, participant in a competition).

प्रवीण *pra-vīṇ* [S.], adj. skilled, proficient, expert; accomplished, able.

प्रवीणता *pra-vīṇătā*[S.], f. skill, proficiency, expert knowledge; ability.

प्रवीर *pra-vīr* [S.], adj. & m. **1.** adj. heroic, brave. **2.** most excellent. **3.** m. a hero; distinguished person.

प्रवृत्त *pra-vṛtt* [S.], adj. **1.** engaged, occupied (in, में); beginning, undertaking. **2.** inclined, having a tendency (towards, की ओर).

प्रवृत्ति *pra-vṛtti* [S.], f. **1.** tendency. **2.** inclination, disposition; taste (for, की, की ओर). **3.** application, use; currency (of a practice). **4.** *hind.* active life (as opposed to a life of contemplation). **5.** conduct, behaviour (esp. as characterising a group). **6.** applicability (of a rule).

प्रवेक्षण *pra-vekṣaṇ* [S.], m. foreseeing; foresight.

प्रवेक्षित *pra-vekṣit* [S.], adj. foreseen, anticipated.

प्रवेट *pra-veṭ* [S.], m. *Pl. HŚS.* barley.

प्रवेणी *pra-veṇī* [S.], f. *Pl. HŚS.* **1.** a braid of hair. **2.** plaited, unadorned hair (as worn by widows).

प्रवेश *pra-veś* [S.], m. **1.** entry. **2.** penetration; invasion. **3.** admission; access (to a person, a place). **4.** transf. proficiency (in a subject, an activity). **5.** interference (in, में). **6.** an inaugural ceremony (performed before entering a new house, &c). **7.** an entrance. — ~ करना (में), to enter. – प्रवेश-द्वार, m. main door, or entrance. प्रवेश-शुल्क, m. admission fee. प्रवेशार्थी [°*śa*+*a*°], m. one seeking admission; an applicant.

प्रवेशक *pra-veśak* [S.], adj. & m. **1.** adj. entering, penetrating. **2.** m. an interlude (in a drama).

प्रवेशन *pra-veśan* [S.], m. entering, penetrating.

प्रवेशिका *pra-veśikā* [S.], f. **1.** entrance examination. **2.** entry ticket. **3.** entry fee. **4.** *techn.* input.

प्रवेश्य *pra-veśyă* [S.], adj. permeable.

प्रव्रजित *pra-vrajit* [S.], m. gone forth: a wandering ascetic, or (Jain) monk.

प्रशंसक *pra-śaṃsak* [S.], adj. & m. **1.** adj. praising, speaking well of. **2.** m. = प्रशंसाकारी.

प्रशंसन *pra-śaṃsan* [S.], m. praising, &c.

प्रशंसनीय *pra-śaṃsănīyă* [S.], adj. praiseworthy; commendable.

प्रशंसा *pra-śaṃsā* [S.], f. **1.** praise; commendation; eulogy. **2.** fame, glory, — ~ करना (की), to praise, &c. – प्रशंसाकारी, adj. & m. praising, &c.; a eulogiser, flatterer. प्रशंसात्मक [°*sā*+*ā*°], adj. laudatory; commendatory. प्रशंसा-पत्र, m. letter of recommendation. प्रशंसापूर्ण, adj. laudatory, &c. (= प्रशंसात्मक). प्रशंसायुक्त, adj. id.

प्रशंसित *pra-śaṃsit* [S.], adj. praised, &c.

प्रशंसी *pra-śaṃsī* [S.], adj. & m. = प्रशंसक.

प्रशमन *pra-śaman* [S.], m. **1.** pacifying, calming (anger, or anxiety). **2.** *Pl. HŚS.* destroying, killing.

प्रशमित *pra-śamit* [S.], adj. calmed; calm, tranquil.

प्रशस्त *pra-śast* [S.], adj. **1.** praised, commended. **2.** laudable; excellent; best; right. **3.** transf. broad (as a good road, or highway).

प्रशस्तता *pra-śastătā* [S.], f. excellence, eminence.

प्रशस्ति *pra-śasti* [S.], f. **1.** praise, eulogy. **2.** expression of compliments (at the beginning of a letter). **3.** *hist.* royal edict. **4.** scribe's colophon.

प्रशांत *pra-śānt* [S.], adj. **1.** calm, quiet; peaceful. **2.** pacified. — ~ महासागर, m. the Pacific Ocean. प्रशांतचित्त, adj. whose mind is calm; calm; pacified.

प्रशांति *pra-śānti* [S.], f. **1.** tranquillity, calm. **2.** composure.

प्रशाखा *pra-śākhā* [S.], f. **1.** small branch, twig. **2.** sub-division.

प्रशासक *pra-śāsak* [S.], m. one who directs, or governs; administrator.

प्रशासकीय *pra-śāsăkīyă* [S.], adj. administrative.

प्रशासन *pra-śāsan* [S.], m. **1.** directing, governing. **2.** directing body; administration. — भारतीय प्रशासन-सेवा, f. Indian Administrative Service.

प्रशासनिक *pra-śāsănik* [S.], adj. administrative.

प्रशासित *pra-śāsit* [S.], adj. directed; administered.

प्रशास्ता *pra-śāstā* [S.], m. inv. *Pl. HŚS.* governor; administrator.

प्रशिक्षण *pra-śikṣaṇ* [S.], m. training; apprenticeship.

प्रशिक्षित *pra-śikṣit* [S.], adj. trained.

प्रशिक्षु *pra-śikṣu* [S.], m. a trainee; apprentice.

प्रशीतन *pra-śītan* [S.], m. refrigeration.

प्रश्न *praśn* [S.], m. **1.** question; enquiry. **2.** problem, matter. — ~ उठना, a question to arise. ~ उठाना, to raise a question. ~ करना, to ask a question (of, से), to enquire. – प्रश्न-कर्ता, m. inv. a questioner. प्रश्न-पत्र, m. a questionnaire, form; examination paper. प्रश्न-बोधक, adj. = next. प्रश्नवाचक, adj. *gram.* interrogative. प्रश्न-सूचक, adj. questioning; = prec. प्रश्नात्मक [°*na*+*ā*°], adj. = prec., 1. प्रश्नावली [°*na*+*ā*°], f. set of questions, or exercises; questionnaire. प्रश्नोत्तर [°*na*+*u*°], m. question(s) and answer(s): dialogue; interrogation, examination. °ई, f, dialogue; catechism.

प्रश्रय *pra-śray* [S.], m. support (as for a belief).

प्रष्ठ *pra-ṣṭh* [S.], adj. standing in front; prior.

प्रसंग *pra-saṅg* [S.], m. **1.** attachment; connection. **2.** subject, topic; section of a book (on a partic. topic); context. **3.** occasion, motivating cause; opportunity. **4.** *Pl.* sexual intercourse. — प्रसंगप्राप्त, adj. relevant (to a matter). प्रसंगयुक्त, adj. relevant; timely.

प्रसंगी *pra-saṅgī* [S.], adj. connected; relevant.

प्रसक्त *pra-sakt* [S.], adj. **1.** attached (to, से); devoted (to). **2.** engaged, or engrossed (in). **3.** *Pl. HŚS.* obtained, gained.

प्रसक्ति *pra-sakti* [S.], f. **1.** attachment (to). **2.** absorption (in: an activity).

प्रसन्न *pra-sann* [S.], adj. **1.** clear, bright; pure. ***2.** pleased (with, से); delighted. **3.** contented; cheerful; flourishing, well. **4.** propitiated (as a deity); gracious, well-disposed (to, पर). **5.** obs. = पसंद. — ~ करना (को), to give pleasure, &c. (to); obs. to be pleased (with). ~ रखना (को), to keep (one) pleased, to satisfy (one). ~ होना to be pleased, &c. (with, से); to approve (of: a person, or a thing); to show favour (to, पर). – प्रसन्नचित्त, adj. = ~, 2., 3. प्रसन्नमुख, adj. looking pleased, or contented. प्रसन्नात्मा [°*na*+*ā*°], adj. = ~, 2., 3.

प्रसन्नता *prasannătā* [S.], f. **1.** pleasure, &c. **2.** contentment. **3.** favour.

प्रसव *pra-sav* [S.], m. **1.** childbirth, labour. **2.** *Pl. HŚS.* offspring. **3.** *Pl. HŚS.* = प्रसून. — प्रसववेदना, f. labour pains. प्रसवोत्तर [°*va*+*u*°], adj. post-natal.

प्रसविनी *pra-savinī* [S.], f. = प्रसूता.

प्रसाद *pra-sād* [S.], m. **1.** propitiatory offering or gift; boon, blessing. **2.** food offered to an idol; the remnants of such food.

प्रसादन *pra-sādan* [S.], m. soothing, gratifying.

प्रसादी *pra-sādī* [S.], adj. & f. **1.** adj. offered to idols. **2.** f. = प्रसाद, 2.

प्रसाधक *pra-sādhak* [S.], adj. & m. **1.** adj. accomplishing. **2.** adorning. **3.** m. a valet.

प्रसाधन *pra-sādhan* [S.], m. **1.** accomplishing, effecting, completing. **2.** attiring, adorning. **3.** attire. — प्रसाधन-सामग्री, f. toilet items, cosmetics.

प्रसाधनी *pra-sādhănī* [S.], f. *Pl. HŚS.* a comb.

प्रसाधित *pra-sādhit* [S.], adj. **1.** accomplished, completed. **2.** dressed up, attired.

प्रसार *pra-sār* [S.], m. spread, extension; expansion (as of an activity); diffusion (as of a view).

प्रसारक *pra-sārak* [S.], adj. & m. **1.** adj. causing to spread, &c. (see प्रसार). **2.** m. carrier (of a disease, an infection).

प्रसारण *pra-sāraṇ* [S.], m. **1.** spreading, expanding, &c. (see प्रसार). **2.** broadcasting. — प्रसारण-गृह, m. broadcasting station.

प्रसारित *pra-sārit* [S.], adj. **1.** spread, extended; expanded; diffused. **2.** broadcast.

प्रसिद्ध *pra-siddh* [S.], adj. **1.** well-known. **2.** celebrated, famous. **3.** pej. notorious.

प्रसिद्धि *pra-siddhi* [S.], f. **1.** celebrity, fame. **2.** notoriety. **3.** sthg. well known or accepted.

प्रसू *pra-sū* [S.], f. *Pl. HŚS.* mother (= प्रसूता).

प्रसूत *pra-sūt* [S.], adj. & m. **1.** adj. begotten. **2.** given birth to, born; produced. **3.** m. *Pl. HŚS.* a sickness of women after childbirth.

प्रसूता *pra-sūtā* [S.], f. a woman who has recently given birth.

प्रसूति *pra-sūti* [S.], f. = प्रसव.

प्रसून *pra-sūn* [S.], adj. & m. **1.** adj. produced, born. **2.** m. flower.

प्रसौती *prasautī* [ad. *prasavatī-*], f. **1.** a woman in labour. **2.** a woman who has had a child. **3.** = प्रसूता.

प्रस्तर *pra-star* [S.], m. **1.** a scattering (of things), or a flat surface; strewn bedding.

*2. stone; rock. 3. transf. a precious stone. प्रस्तरीभूत, adj. *geol.* petrified.

प्रस्तार *pra-stār* [S.], m. **1.** spreading. **2.** extent. **3.** bed, layer.

प्रस्ताव *pra-stāv* [S.], m. **1.** introduction; commencement (of discussion, exposition). ***2.** proposal (for discussion); motion; suggestion. **3.** *Pl. HŚS.* occasion, time. — ~ उठाना, to raise a matter; to introduce a motion, or topic. – प्रस्ताव-कर्ता, m. inv. proposer (of a motion, &c). विषय-प्रस्ताव, m. introduction of, or to a topic.

प्रस्तावक *pra-stāvak* [S.], m. introducer, proposer (of a motion, &c.); mover.

प्रस्तावना *pra-stāvănā* [S.], f. **1.** introduction; preface. **2.** prologue.

प्रस्ताविक *pra-stāvik* [S.], adj. *Pl. HŚS.* **1.** suggested by previous mention. **2.** suited to the occasion.

प्रस्तावित *pra-stāvit* [S.], adj. suggested; proposed; moved.

प्रस्तुत *pra-stut* [S.], adj. **1.** praised. ***2.** proposed. **3.** mentioned; relevant (to a matter in hand); in question (a topic under discussion); submitted (documents, &c). **4.** present (time, or circumstance). **5.** ready (to do sthg., को, के लिए). **6.** prepared, made. — प्रस्तुत-कर्ता, m. inv. presenter (of a programme); producer (of a programme, or of goods). प्रस्तुतीकरण, m. presentation; submission.

प्रस्तुति *pra-stuti* [S.], f. **1.** praise; inauguration (of a function).

प्रस्तुतीकरण *pra-stutīkaraṇ* [S.], m. see s.v. प्रस्तुत.

प्रस्तोता *pra-stotā* [S.], m. inv. one who presents, or publishes; organiser (of an event).

प्रस्थ *pra-sth* [S.], adj. & m. **1.** adj. going to. **2.** m. level expanse; flat mountain-top.

प्रस्थान *pra-sthān* [S.], m. **1.** setting forth, departure. **2.** euph. death. **3.** transf. *hind.* method, system. — ~ करना, to set out, to depart; to go away; to march (as an army).

प्रस्थापन *pra-sthāpan* [S.], m. **1.** sending forth or away; despatching. **2.** establishing, installing (as equipment).

प्रस्थापना *pra-sthāpănā* [S.], m. 1. = प्रस्थापन. **2.** an offer; proposal.

प्रस्थापित *pra-sthāpit* [S.], adj. **1.** sent forth, or away; despatched. **2.** installed; set up (as equipment).

प्रस्थित *pra-sthit* [S.], adj. **1.** set out, departed. **2.** despatched. **3.** *HŚS.* established, installed.

प्रस्फुट *pra-sphuṭ* [S.], adj. **1.** burst open (as a flower). **2.** evident (a matter); become known.

प्रस्फुटन *pra-sphuṭan* [S.], m. **1.** bursting open; unfolding. **2.** becoming known.

प्रस्फुटित *pra-sphuṭit* [S.], adj. 1. = प्रस्फुट. **2.** exploded. — ~ करना, to explode (sthg).

प्रस्फोटन *pra-sphoṭan* [S.], m. **1.** explosion; eruption. **2.** bursting open (as a flower).

प्रस्मृत *pra-smr̥t* [S.], adj. forgotten.

प्रस्मृति *pra-smr̥ti* [S.], f. forgetting, forgetfulness.

प्रस्रव *pra-srav* [S.], m. **1.** flowing forth; gushing. **2.** a flow.

प्रस्रवण *pra-sravaṇ* [S.], m. flowing, flow.

प्रहर *pra-har* [S.], m. = पहर, 1.

प्रहरण *pra-haraṇ* [S.], m. **1.** striking. **2.** attacking. **3.** hurling. **4.** removing, seizing.

प्रहरी *pra-harī* [S.], adj. & m. **1.** adj. watching, guarding. **2.** m. a watchman, guard.

प्रहर्ष *pra-harṣ* [S.], m. great delight; rapture, ecstasy.

प्रहर्षित *pra-harṣit* [S.], adj. delighted, overjoyed.

प्रहसंती *pra-hasantī* [S.], f. Arabian jasmine.

प्रहसन *pra-hasan* [S.], m. **1.** loud laughter. **2.** ridicule; satire. **3.** a farce (drama).

प्रहसित *pra-hasit* [S.], adj. & m. **1.** adj. laughing, smiling (face, &c). **2.** laughed at, ridiculed. **3.** m. *HŚS.* a laugh, a smile.

प्रहार *pra-hār* [S.], m. **1.** a blow. **2.** an attack; *mil.* fire. — ~ करना (पर), to strike; to beat.

प्रहार- *prahār-* [ad. *prahārayati*, or H. *prahār*], v.t. Brbh. **1.** to strike. **2.** to strike with: to hurl (a weapon).

प्रहारक *pra-hārak* [S.], adj. **1.** striking. **2.** attacking, assaulting. **3.** destroying.

प्रहारित *pra-hārit* [S.], adj. **1.** struck. **2.** fired or hurled (a shot, projectile).

प्रहारी *pra-hārī* [S.], adj. = प्रहारक.

प्रहास *pra-hās* [S.], m. **1.** loud laughter. **2.** ridicule.

प्रहासी *pra-hāsī* [S.], adj. **1.** laughing loudly. **2.** causing laughter.

प्रहृष्ट *pra-hr̥ṣṭ* [S.], adj. = प्रहर्षित.

प्रहेलिका *pra-helikā* [S.], f. **1.** a riddle. **2.** a mystery.

प्रह्लाद *pra-hlād* [S.], m. **1.** joy. **2.** *mythol.* name of a famous devotee of Viṣṇu, son of Hiraṇyakaśipu.

प्रह्लादन *pra-hlādan* [S.], m. the causing of joy.

प्रह्लादित *pra-hlādit* [S.], adj. joyful.

प्रांगण *prâṅgaṇ* [S.], m. **1.** a courtyard. **2.** an enclave.

प्रांजल *prâñjal* [S.], adj. natural, simple (as speech, language).

प्रांजलि *prâñjali* [S.], f. **1.** holding out the hands, cupped together (esp. as making an offering). **2.** joining the palms of the hands (as a respectful greeting).

प्रांत *prânt* [S.], m. **1.** region; province; state. **2.** border, limit.

प्रांतर *prântar* [S.], m. lonely, or wild region; lonely road.

प्रांतीयता *prântīyătā* [S.], f. regionalism, provincialism.

प्राक्- *prāk-* [S]. **1.** preceding, former; pre-; ancient. **2.** eastern: — प्राक्कथन, m. foreword; introduction. प्राक्कलन, m. preliminary estimate. °-कलित, adj. प्राक्काल, m. former age, or time; °ईन, adj. former, ancient.

प्राकार *prâkār* [S.], m. **1.** enclosure, boundary. **2.** enclosing wall.

प्राकाश्य *prākāśyă* [S.], m. **1.** clearness, brightness. **2.** celebrity, fame.

प्राकृत *prākr̥t* [S.], adj. & m. (f.) **1.** adj. natural. **2.** uncultivated (as language). **3.** m. (f.) Prakrit: any form of Middle Indo-Aryan language. **4.** Av. a vernacular speech.

प्राकृतिक *prākr̥tik* [S.], adj. **1.** *philos.* having to do with *prakr̥ti.* ***2.** natural.

प्राग *prāg*, m. Brbh. = प्रयाग.

प्राग्- *prāg-* [S]. = प्राक्-: — प्रागभाव, m. *Pl. HSS.* previous existence; superiority, excellence. प्रागैतिहासिक, adj. prehistoric.

प्रागल्भ्य *prāgalbhyă* [S.], m. **1.** boldness. **2.** arrogance, effrontery. **3.** resolution, determination. **4.** transf. pomp, show.

प्राचार्य *prâcāryă* [S.], m. **1.** principal (as of a college). **2.** a scholar.

प्राची *prācī* [S.], f. the east.

प्राचीन *prācīn* [S.], adj. **1.** eastern. ***2.** ancient, old; primeval. **3.** long-standing, immemorial. — ~ काल, m. ancient times; the distant past. प्राचीनकालिक, adj. having to do with ancient times. °-कालीन, adj. id.

प्राचीनता *prācīnătā* [S.], f. **1.** age, antiquity. **2.** archaic character (as of language). — प्राचीनतावाद, m. conservatism (of approach).

प्राचीर *prācīr* [S.], m. enclosure; wall, rampart; hedge; fence.

प्राच्य *prācyă* [S.], adj. **1.** eastern; oriental. **2.** ancient. — ~ विद्या, f. Asian studies.

प्राज्ञ *prājñă* [S.], adj. & m. **1.** adj. wise; learned. **2.** m. a learned person.

प्राज्ञता *prājñătā* [S.], f. wisdom; learning.

प्राज्ञत्व *prājñatvă* [S.], m. = प्राज्ञता.

प्राज्ञा *prājñā* [S.], f. E.H. knowledge, understanding.

प्राज्ञी *prājñī* [S.], f. a wise, or learned woman.

प्राण *prâṇ* [S.], m. **1.** breath. **2.** (usu. pl.) vital breath, life. **3.** fig. one's (very) life: a beloved person, or thing. — ~ आँखों में आना, to be overtaxed, exhausted. ~ आना, to recover (from mortal fear or devastating shock). ~ उड़ जाना, to be terrified; to be aghast. ~ खाना, to plague or to harass (one, के) intolerably. ~ गले तक आना, to be at the point of death. ~ घुटना, life to be extinguished. ~ छुड़ाना, to save the life (of, के); to manage to escape alive; to release the soul (of), to kill. ~ छूटना, the breath to leave (the body), to die; to be exhausted. ~ छोड़ना, to give up life; to lose heart, or presence of mind. ~ जाना, life to depart. ~ डालना (में, to revive; to invigorate. ~ देना, to give up one's life; to end one's days; to love (another, पर) more than life. ~ निकलना, to expire; to be terrified. ~, or प्राणों, पर आ बनना, or पड़ना, to be a matter of life and death. प्राणों पर खेलना, to risk one's life. ~, or प्राणों. पर बीतना (के), to be in mortal danger; to die. ~ बचाना, to save the life (of, के); to free, or to extricate oneself (from, से). ~ मुँह तक आना, to be at the point of death; to be terrified, or aghast. ~ रखना, to save the life (of, के); to revive. ~ रहते (तक), adv. while life remains, &c. ~ लेना, or हरना, to kill; to torment, to harass. ~ सूखना, to be half-dead with fear. ~ हारना, to lose life, to die. प्रानों में ~ आना, to recover (from fear, shock). अपने ~ हथेली पर, or में, लेना, to take one's life in the palm of one's hand, to risk one's life. – प्राणकर, adj. encouraging or refreshing the soul. प्राणघात, m. killing, murder. °अक, adj. °ई, m. a killer, &c. प्राण-दाता, m. inv. life-giver: one who saves another's life. °त्री, f. प्राण-ध्वनि, f. *ling.* glottal, or pharyngeal. प्राण-त्याग, m. abandonment of life: death; suicide. प्राण-त्याग करना, to commit suicide. प्राण-दंड, m. capital punishment. प्राण-दंड देना, to pronounce the death sentence (on, को); to execute. प्राण-दान, m. the gift of life: saving anyone's life; giving one's life for another. प्राण-धारण, m. support or maintenance of life. °-धारी, adj. &

m. animate; a living creature. **प्राण-नाथ**, m. husband; lover. **प्राण-नाश**, m. loss of life. **°अक**, adj. **प्राण-पण**, m. wagering, risking life. **प्राण-पण से**, adv. desperately (of a mortal struggle). **प्राण-पति**, m. life-lord: the soul, heart; a husband. **प्राण-प्रतिष्ठा**, f. imparting life: the ceremony of consecration of an idol. **प्राणप्रद**, adj. life-giving. **प्राण-प्रिय**, adj. & m. dear as life, beloved; a husband, lover. **प्राणमय**, adj. living, breathing. **प्राणवान**, adj. id. **प्राणहर**, adj. mortal, deadly; destructive. **प्राणहारी**, adj. id. **प्राणहीन**, adj. without breath or life; lacklustre. **प्राणांत** [°*ṇa*+*ā*°], m. the end of life: death. **°इक**, adj. mortal, deadly; lasting as long as life. **प्राणाधार** [°*ṇa*+*ā*°], m. support of life: husband; beloved. **प्राणापहारकता** [°*ṇa*+*a*°], f. murderous nature. **प्राणायाम** [°*ṇa*+*ā*°], m. (in yoga) breath-exercise: restraining the breath. **प्राणाशय** [°*ṇa*+*ā*°], m. vital strength. **प्राणेश, प्राणेश्वर** [°*ṇa*+*ī*°], m. = **प्राण-नाथ**. **प्राणोद्बोधन** [°*ṇa*+*u*°], m. arousing the spirit: renaissance.

प्राणक *prâṇak* [S.], m. *Pl. HŚS.* = **प्राणी**.

प्राणि- *prâṇi-* [S.], having to do with living creatures; zoo-; bio-: — **प्राणि-शास्त्र**, m. next. **प्राणिवाचक**, adj. *gram.* referring to an animate being. **प्राणि-विज्ञान**, m. zoology; ? biology (= **जीव-विज्ञान**).

प्राणिक *prâṇik* [S.], adj. animate; animal.

प्राणी *prâṇī* [S.], adj. & m. **1.** adj. animate. **2.** m. a living creature; an animal. — **दोनों ~**, m. pl. husband and wife.

प्रात *prāt*, m. & adv. **1.** m. early morning (= **प्रातः**). **2.** adv. in the early morning. — **प्रात-कृत** (= °**-कृत्य**), m. Av. = next. **प्रात-क्रिया**, f. Av. an observance to be performed in the morning.

प्रातः *prātaḥ* [S.], m. early morning, dawn. — **प्रातःकाल**, m. & adv. = **प्रातः**; morning; in the early morning. **°ईन**, adj.

प्रातर्- *prātar-* [S]. = **प्रातः**. — **प्रातराश**, m. breakfast.

प्रातिपदिक *prātipadik* [S.], m. *gram.* a noun stem.

प्रातिभासिक *prātibhāsik* [S.], adj. illusory.

प्राथमिक *prāthamik* [S.], adj. **1.** having to do with what is first: primary, elementary (as schooling); initial. **2.** prior; preliminary (as a measure). **3.** prime (in importance). — **~ उपचार**, m. first aid.

प्राथमिकता *prāthamikătā* [S.], f. priority, precedence.

प्राथम्य *prāthamyă* [S.], m. priority, precedence.

प्रादुर्भाव *prādur-bhāv* [S.], m. manifestation, appearance; rise; genesis, origin.

प्रादुर्भूत *prādur-bhūt* [S.], adj. manifested, arisen, &c.

प्रादेश *prâdeś* [S.], m. a mandate. — **प्रादेशात्मक** [°*śa*+*ā*°], adj. mandatory.

प्रादेशिक *prādeśik* [S.], adj. **1.** regional; having to do with a state; provincial. **2.** territorial (as national rights).

प्रादेशिकता *prādeśikătā* [S.], f. regionalism.

प्राधान्य *prādhānyă* [S.], m. **1.** predominance. **2.** pre-eminence. **3.** supremacy.

प्राधिकार *prâdhi-kār* [S.], m. = **अधिकार**, 1., 3.

प्राधिकरण *prâdhi-karaṇ* [S.], m. an authority, (administrative) board.

प्राधिकृत *prâdhi-kr̥t* [S.], adj. authorised.

प्राध्यापक *prâdhy-āpak* [S.], m. a (university) teacher; lecturer.

प्रापक *prâpak* [S.], adj. & m. **1.** adj. causing to attain to. **2.** obtaining, &c. **3.** m. one who obtains.

प्रापण *prâpaṇ* [S.], m. = **प्राप्ति**, 1.

प्रापी *prâpī* [S.], adj. obtaining; attaining.

प्राप्त *prâpt* [S.], adj. **1.** obtained; acquired; incurred. **2.** come upon, found; arrived at (as a situation). **3.** befallen (as a misfortune); endured. — **~ करना**, to obtain, &c. – **प्राप्त-काल**, m. & adj. favourable moment, fit time; the present; timely; destined. **प्राप्तदोष**, adj. having incurred guilt, at fault. **प्राप्तयौवन**, adj. adolescent. **प्राप्तवर**, adj. having obtained a husband, or a boon. **प्राप्तार्थ** [°*ta*+*a*°], adj. & m. successful; an object attained. **प्राप्तावसर** [°*ta*+*a*°], adj. opportune, timely.

प्राप्तव्य *prâptavyă* [S.], adj. & m. **1.** adj. due (as a payment). **2.** m. dues, fee(s).

प्राप्ति *prâpti* [S.], f. **1.** obtaining, acquisition; attainment (to a goal, a level); fulfilment (of a request). **2.** gain, advantage; income. **3.** receipt (of a letter, &c.); reception (of guests). **4.** transf. perception.

प्राप्तिका *prâptikā* [S.], f. a receipt, acknowledgement of receipt.

प्राप्य *prâpyă* [S.], adj. & m. **1.** adj. obtainable, &c. **2.** due (to be paid). **3.** m. a sum due.

प्राप्यक *prâpyak* [S.], m. a bill due for payment.

प्राबल्य *prābalyă* [S.], m. power, predominance; ascendancy.

प्राभव *prābhav* [S.], m. *Pl. HŚS.* superiority, pre-eminence.

प्रामाणिक *prāmāṇik* [S.], adj. **1.** based on evidence or authority, authoritative (as a source); standard (as a work). **2.** authentic (as a document).

प्रामाणिकता *prāmāṇikătā* [S.], f. **1.** authority (of a source, &c). **2.** authenticity.

प्रामाण्य *prāmāṇyă* [S.], m. = प्रामाणिकता.

प्रामाद्य *prāmādyă* [S.], m. *Pl. HŚS.* **1.** frenzy. **2.** intoxication. **3.** a careless oversight.

-प्राय *-prây* [S.], suffix. near; like, resembling; almost (e.g. मृतप्राय, adj. almost or as if dead, close to death).

प्राय- *prây-* [S.], noun and adj. formant. resembling. — प्रायद्वीप, m. peninsula. °ईय, adj.

प्रायः *prâyaḥ* [S.], adv. **1.** for the most part, generally; often. **2.** approximately; nearly, almost.

प्रायण *prâyaṇ* [S.], m. **1.** departure; death; fasting to death. **2.** rebirth.

प्रायश्चित्त *prâyăś-citt* [S.], m. **1.** penance; atonement. **2.** penitence; remorse. — ~ करना, to atone (for, का), &c.

प्रायश्चित्तिक *prâyaś-cittik* [S.], adj. **1.** penitent. **2.** to be repented (as sin).

प्रारंभ *prârambh* [S.], m. beginning. — ~ करना, to begin. ~ में, adv. at first, first of all.

प्रारंभिक *prârambhik* [S.], adj. **1.** initial; elementary (as teaching). **2.** preliminary. **3.** basic (as rights, or conditions).

प्रारब्ध *prârabdh* [S.], adj. & m. **1.** adj. begun. **2.** caused by fate. **3.** m. deeds performed in an earlier birth. ***4.** fate, destiny.

प्रारब्धि *prârabdhi* [S.], f. **1.** beginning. **2.** destiny.

प्रारब्धी *prârabdhī* [S.], adj. of good destiny, fortunate.

प्रारूप *prârūp* [S.], m. version, or sketch; prototype.

प्रार्थक *prârthak* [S.], adj. & m. = प्रार्थी.

प्रार्थना *prârthănā* [S.], f. **1.** earnest request, prayer, entreaty; petition, suit. **2.** application (for a post). **3.** devout wish. — ~ करना, to entreat (one, से; to, की); to petition, &c. प्रार्थना-घर, m. a chapel. प्रार्थना-पत्र, m. a petition; application.

प्रार्थनीय *prârthănīyă* [S.], adj. to be earnestly requested, or devoutly wished.

प्रार्थित *prârthit* [S.], adj. earnestly requested.

प्रार्थी *prârthī* [S.], adj. & m. **1.** adj. entreating. **2.** m. one requesting earnestly; a petitioner; applicant.

प्रालंब *prâlamb* [S.], m. *Pl. HŚS.* a garland hanging down to the waist.

प्रालेय *prāley* [S.], adj. poet. *mythol.* having to do with the dissolution of the world (as flood).

प्राविट *prāviṭ* [ad. *prāvr̥ṭ-*], f. Av. the rainy season.

प्राविधिक *prāvidhik* [S.], adj. technical.

प्रावीण्य *prāvīṇyă* [S.], m. = प्रवीणता.

प्रावृट् *prāvr̥ṭ* [S.], m. the rainy season.

प्रावृत *prāvr̥t* [S.], m. *Pl. HŚS.* cloak.

प्रावृत्ति *prāvr̥tti* [ad. *prāvr̥ti-*: incorr.], f. *Pl.* enclosure; covering.

-प्राशन *-prâśan* [S.], m. **1.** eating; tasting. **2.** causing to eat, &c.

प्रासंगिक *prāsaṅgik* [S.], adj. **1.** connected, relevant. **2.** timely, appropriate. **3.** incidental; secondary (as a plot, a motif).

प्रासाद *prāsād* [S.], m. **1.** a palatial building; palace. **2.** a temple.

प्रिय *priyă* [S.], adj. & m. **1.** adj. dear, beloved. **2.** agreeable, kind (a person). **3.** (often -प्रिय.) valued, liked (a person, a thing); favourite. लोक-प्रिय, adj. popular. **4.** -प्रिय. approving of. अनुशासनप्रिय, adj. observant of rules, &c. **5.** attractive. **6.** m. dear one; husband; lover. — ~ वचन, m. kind or loving words; well-intentioned words; welcome words. - प्रियकर, adj. doing a kindness; giving pleasure. °-कारी, id. प्रिय-जन, m. a relative; a dear friend. प्रियतम, adj. & m. f. dearest; darling; lover, sweetheart. °आ, f. °ता, f. extreme dearness. प्रियदर्शन, adj. attractive; beautiful. प्रिय-पोषण, m. favouritism. प्रियभाषी, adj. & m. = प्रियवादी. प्रियमान, adj. & m. *Pl.* beloved, dear; affectionate. प्रियवर, adj. dearest, beloved (esp. in letters, as a term of address). प्रियवादी, adj. & m. speaking kindly, or agreeably; flattering; one who speaks kindly, &c. °इनी, f. प्रियसत्य, adj. *HŚS.* truth-loving.

प्रियतम *priyătam*, adj. & m. f. see s.v. प्रिय.

प्रियता *priyătā* [S.], f. **1.** dearness (of a person to another). **2.** -प्रियता. dearness (to); popularity (with). e.g. लोक-प्रियता, adj. popularity.

प्रिया *priyā* [S.], adj. & f. **1.** adj. = प्रिय. **2.** f. dear one; wife; mistress.

प्रीत *prīt* [S.], adj. & f. **1.** adj. pleased; happy. **2.** dear, beloved. **3.** kind, affectionate. **4.** f. = प्रीति.

प्रीतम *prītam*, m. = प्रियतम.

प्रीति *prīti* [S.], f. **1.** love, affection; regard. **2.** gladness; enjoyment. — ~ करना, to show affection (for, से); to love. ~ जोड़ना, to become friendly or affectionate (towards, से). ~ रखना, or लगाना, = ~ करना, ~ जोड़ना. – प्रीतिकर, adj. causing love, or pleasure: affectionate; agreeable, kind (as acts, remarks). °-कारक, °-कारी, adj. id. प्रीति-गोष्ठी, f. a party. प्रीति-भोज, m. a formal dinner; banquet.

प्रेक्षक *prêkṣak* [S.], m. **1.** an observer. **2.** spectator.

प्रेक्षण *prêkṣaṇ* [S.], m. **1.** observing, viewing; observation. **2.** the eye. **3.** public show, spectacle.

प्रेक्षा *prêkṣā* [S.], f. **1.** looking at, observing. **2.** a sight; public show, spectacle. **3.** *Pl. HŚS.* discrimination, judgment.

प्रेक्षित *prêkṣit* [S.], adj. looked at, observed.

प्रेक्ष्य *prêkṣyă* [S.], adj. to be looked at, observed; worth seeing.

प्रेत *prêt* [S.], m. **1.** the spirit of a dead person (esp. before funeral rites are performed). **2.** a ghost, evil spirit, demon. **3.** pej. villain. — प्रेत-कर्म, m. funerary ceremonies (= श्राद्ध). प्रेत-कार्य, m. id. प्रेत-क्रिया, f. = प्रेत-कर्म. प्रेत-गृह, m. cremation-place. प्रेत-पक्ष, m. the dark half of the month (favourable for worship of the spirits of ancestors). प्रेत-योनि, f. = next. प्रेत-लोक, m. the world of disembodied spirits (which await performance of funerary rites). प्रेतात्मक [°*ta*+*ā*°], adj. ghostly. °इका, f.

प्रेतनी *prêtnī* [cf. H. *pret*], f. **1.** a female spirit (see प्रेत). **2.** demoness.

प्रेम *prem* [S.], m. love; affection; kindliness. — ~ करना (से or पर), to love; to feel affection (for). ~ रखना, to be in love (with, के साथ); to be firm friends (with). – प्रेम-गाथा, f. poem dealing with love (real or allegorical); love-song. प्रेम-पात्र, m. object of (one's) love, loved one. प्रेम-भक्ति, f. loving devotion (esp. to Kṛṣṇa, or Rām). प्रेम-रस, m. the sweetness or savour of love. प्रेमाख्यान [°*ma*+*ā*°], m. = प्रेम-गाथा, 1. °अक, m. id. °ई, adj. romantic. प्रेमालाप [°*ma*+*ā*°], m. loving words, or utterance. प्रेमालिंगन [°*ma*+*ā*°], m. loving embrace. प्रेमास्पद [°*ma*+*ā*°], m. abode of love: lover. प्रेमोद्रेक [°*ma*+*u*°], m. transport of love.

प्रेमिका *premikā* [S.], f. **1.** a woman who loves. **2.** a woman who is loved.

प्रेमी *premī* [S.], adj. & m. **1.** adj. loving; affectionate. **2.** m. an affectionate person; lover. **3.** one attached (to, का: as to a partic. interest, cause); supporter; champion; (finally in comp.) -phile.

प्रेर- *prer-* [ad. *prerayati*], v.t. Brbh. Av. to urge; to send.

प्रेरक *prêrak* [S.], adj. & m. **1.** adj. urging, impelling, &c.; motive (force). **2.** m. one who incites, or stimulates, &c.; initiator.

प्रेरण *prêraṇ* [S.], m. = प्रेरणा.

प्रेरणा *prêrăṇā* [S.], f. **1.** urging; impetus. **2.** incitement. **3.** stimulus, encouragement. — प्रेरणात्मक [°*ṇā*+*ā*°], adj. stimulating, encouraging; inspiring. प्रेरणार्थक [°*ṇā*+*a*°], adj. *gram.* causative.

प्रेरयिता *prêrayitā* [S.], m. inv. one who urges, incites, &c.

प्रेरित *prêrit* [S.], adj. **1.** urged, impelled; moved, motivated (to an action). **2.** incited. **3.** stimulated, encouraged.

प्रेषक *prêṣak* [S.], m. sender, despatcher.

प्रेषण *prêṣaṇ* [S.], m. **1.** sending, despatch; delivery. **2.** a consignment, item (of mail). **3.** remittance.

प्रेषणीय *prêṣăṇīyă* [S.], adj. = प्रेष्य.

प्रेषणीयता *prêṣăṇīyătā* [S.], f. communicability, effectiveness (as of a work of art).

प्रेषादेश *prêṣâdeś* [S.], m. a money order.

प्रेषित *prêṣit* [S.], adj. & m. **1.** adj. sent away, despatched. **2.** m. *HŚS. mus.* a partic. sequence of notes, scale.

प्रेषितव्य *prêṣitavyă* [S.], adj. = प्रेष्य.

प्रेष्ठ *prêṣṭh* [S.], adj. most beloved, or desired.

प्रेष्य *prêṣyă* [S.], adj. to be sent; worthy, or able to be sent.

प्रेस *pres* [Engl. *press*], m. **1.** the press. **2.** a printing-press, or house. — ~ में, adv. in the press (a publication). – प्रेस-मुलाक़ात, f. press conference. प्रेस-सम्मेलन, m. id.

प्रेय *prey* [S.], adj. dearer. — ~ से श्रेय, from good to better.

प्रोक्त *prôkt* [S.], adj. declared, uttered.

प्रोक्षण *prôkṣaṇ* [S.], m. **1.** sprinkling (as a sacrifice, in consecration). **2.** euph. immolation.

प्रोक्षित *prôkṣit* [S.], adj. **1.** sprinkled (in consecration). **2.** immolated, slaughtered.

प्रोत्साह *prôtsāh* [S.], m. zeal, ardour.

प्रोत्साहक *prôtsāhak* [S.], m. one who exhorts, encourages, &c.

प्रोत्साहन *prôtsāhan* [S.], m. stimulus, encouragement.

प्रोत्साहित *prôtsāhit* [S.], m. stimulated, encouraged; emboldened.

प्रोनोट *pronoṭ* [Engl. *promissory note*], m. a deed of loan on security.

प्रोषित *prôṣit* [S.], adj. living abroad; being away from home. — **प्रोषितनायिका**, or °-**पतिका**, f. a woman whose husband is away from home.

प्रौढ़ *praûṛh* [ad. *prauḍha-*]], adj. grown up, adult; mature. — ~ **शिक्षा**, f. adult education.

प्रौढ़ता *praûṛhătā* [ad. *prauḍha-*]], f. full growth, adulthood; maturity.

प्रौद्योगिकी *praudyogikī* [S.], f. technology.

प्लक्ष *plakṣ* [S.], m. **1.** the fig-tree, *Ficus infectoria*. **2.** *mythol.* one of the seven continents.

प्लच्छ *placch* [ad. *plakṣa-*], m. Brbh. = **प्लक्ष**.

प्लव *plav* [S.], m. = **प्लवन**.

प्लवन *plavan* [S.], m. **1.** swimming; bathing. **2.** flood (= **प्लावन**).

प्लावन *plāvan* [S.], m. **1.** inundation, flood. **2.** bathing. **3.** floating, swimming.

प्लावित *plāvit* [S.], adj. **1.** inundated. **2.** immersed. **3.** drenched, bathed.

प्लीहा *plīhā* [S.], f. the spleen.

प्लुत *plut* [S.], adj. wet, drenched.

फ

फ *pha*, the twenty-second consonant of the Devanāgarī syllabary. — **फकार**, m. the sound /ph/; the letter **फ**.

फंका *phaṅkā* [cf. **phakk*-[1]], m. = **फाँक**, 1. — ~ **करना** (**का**), to destroy, to crush. ~ **मारना**, or **लगाना**, = **फाँक मारना**.

फँकाना *phaṁkanā*, v.t. = **फाँकना**.

फँकी *phaṁkī* [cf. **phakk*-[1]]. **1.** a mouthful, small piece. **2.** a small packet, dose (of a medicinal powder, &c).

फंगा *phaṅgā*, [conn. *pataṅga*-], m. corr. *Pl.* a grasshopper.

फंद *phand*, m. Brbh. Av. = **फंदा**.

फँदना *phaṁdnā* [cf. H. *phāṁd*-], v.i. esp. in comp. **1.** to be ensnared. **2.** to be entangled (in difficulties).

फंदा *phandā* [*spāśa*-; × *bandha*-], m. **1.** noose; snare, net; trap. **2.** fig. grasp, clutches. **3.** tangle, difficulty. **4.** trickery, deceit. — ~ **डालना**, or **देना**, or **लगाना**, to set a snare, &c. ~ **पड़ना** (**में**; **पर**), to become tangled (as a string); to be noosed. ~ **लगना** (**पर**), to be caught, trapped (by, **का**). **फंदे में आना**, or **पड़ना**, or **फँसना**, to fall into a snare, &c.; to be taken in, tricked; to fall into the clutches (of, **के**). **फंदे में डालना**, or **लाना**, to entrap, to ensnare, &c.

फँदा- *phaṁdā*- [cf. H. *phāṁd*-], v.t. Brbh. **1.** to snare. **2.** to entangle; to beguile.

फँदाना *phaṁdānā* [cf. H. *phāṁdnā*], v.t. **1.** to cause to leap. **2.** to cause to jump over.

फँसड़ी *phaṁsṛī*, f. reg. = **फाँसी**, 1.

फँसना *phaṁsnā* [**spāśyate*], v.i. **1.** to stick, to sink (in or into, **में**: as in mud). **2.** to be stuck (in: as in a crack, or a narrow place). **3.** to be caught, snared; to be tricked, cheated. **4.** fig. to be entangled (in difficulties); to be involved (as in a suit); to be implicated.

फँसवाना *phaṁsvānā* [cf. H. *phāṁsnā*], v.t. to cause to be snared, &c. (by, **से**).

फँसाऊ *phaṁsāū* [cf. H. *phaṁsnā, phaṁsānā*], adj. colloq. treacherous, tricky (a person).

फँसाना *phaṁsānā* [cf. H. *phāṁsnā*], v.t. **1.** to cause to stick or to sink (in or into, **में**: as into mud). **2.** to cause to be imprisoned. **3.** to catch, to snare; to trick, to cheat. **4.** to entangle (in difficulties); to involve (in, **में**: as in a liaison); to implicate. **5.** to catch, to crush.

फँसाव *phaṁsāv* [cf. H. *phaṁsnā, phaṁsānā*], m. **1.** sticking, sinking in. **2.** entanglement; entrapment. **3.** an entangling affair. **4.** *Pl.* a muddy place, bog.

फँसावट *phaṁsāvaṭ* [cf. H. *phaṁsānā*], f. = **फँसाव**, 1.

फँसियारा *phaṁsiyārā* [cf. H. *phāṁsī*], m. a strangler; a thug.

फँसिहारिन *phaṁsihārin* [? cf. H. *phāṁsī*], f. Brbh. a treacherous woman.

फक *phak*, adj. **1.** clear, clean; bright, white. **2.** pale (as the face, in consternation). **3.** faded, wan.

फकड़ी *phakṛī*, [cf. H. *phakkaṛ*], f. 1. = **फक्कड़**, 2. **2.** disgrace, dishonour; disparagement. **3.** a lampoon.

फ़क़त *faqat* [A. *faqaṭ*], adv. & m. U. **1.** adv. only, merely. **2.** m. end (word used at the end of a document).

फकना *phaknā* [cf. H. *phāṁknā*], v.i. to be tossed into the mouth from the palm of the hand (as grain, nuts).

फ़क़ीर *faqīr* [A. *faqīr*], m. & adj. **1.** m. a beggar. **2.** a ascetic (esp. Muslim) faqīr. **3.** adj. penniless. — ~ **करना**, to reduce (one) to beggary.

फ़क़ीरनी *faqīrnī* [cf. H. *faqīr*], f. a female beggar.

फ़क़ीराना *faqīrānā* [P. *faqīrāna*], adj. inv. **1.** of or having to do with a beggar, or a fakir. **2.** adv. in the manner of a beggar, &c. — ~ **रहन-सहन**, m. fig. a very simple way of life. ~ **सूरत**, f. a face like a beggar's, a pathetic face.

फ़क़ीरी *faqīrī* [P. *faqīrī*], adj. & f. **1.** adj. of or having to do with a beggar, or a fakir; beggarly. **2.** f. beggary. **3.** the life of a fakir.

फक्कड़ *phakkaṛ* [cf. **phakk*-[2]], adj. & m. **1.** adj. uninhibited, carefree, happy-go-lucky. **2.** m. uninhibited language, ostentatiously coarse or casual speech or joke. — **फक्कड़बाज़** [P. -*bāz*], m. an abusive, or a crude, person. °**ई**, f. abuse.

फक्कड़पन *phakkaṛpan* [cf. H. *phakkaṛ*], m. = **फकड़ी**, 1., 2.

फ़ख़्र *fakhr* [A. *fakhr*], m. **1.** glory. **2.** just pride. **3.** vainglory, boasting. — ~ **करना**, to be justly proud (of, **का**); to boast (of). ~ **होना** (**को**), to feel just pride (in, **का**).

फगुआ *phaguā* [*phalgu-*[1]], m. 1. = **फाग**. 2. *Pl.* presents given at the Holī festival.

फ़जर *fajr* [A. *fajr*], f. **1.** dawn, early morning. **2.** *musl.* dawn prayer. — **बड़ी** ~, f. & adv. early morning; early in the morning.

फ़ज़ल *fazl* [A. *faẓl*], m. **1.** bounty. **2.** grace, favour. — ~ **करना**, to show grace, or favour (to, **पर**). ~ **है**, all is well (by God's grace). **ख़ुदा का** ~ **रहे**! God's grace be with you!

फ़ज़ीलत *fazīlat* [A. *faẓīla*: P. *faẓīlat*], f. an excellence; a virtue; great learning. — ~ **रखना**, to excel; to surpass (one, **पर**). ~ **की पगड़ी**, f. turban of excellence (as awarded to a Muslim scholar in recognition of his learning).

फ़ज़ीहत *fazīhat* [A. *faẓīḥa*: P. *faẓīḥat*], f. var. /phəjīta/. **1.** disgrace, shame; exposure of the vices or faults (of, **की**). **2.** wrangling. — ~ **करना**, (**की**), to disgrace, to put (one) to shame, &c.; to quarrel. ~ **होना**, to be disgraced, &c.; to become infamous.

फ़ज़ीहती *fazīhatī* [P. *faẓīḥatī*], adj. & f. **1.** adj. shameful (a matter). **2.** shamed; infamous (a person). **3.** f. = **फ़ज़ीहत**.

फ़ज़ूल *fazūl* [A. *fuẓūl*], adj. & f. **1.** adj. excessive. **2.** needless, pointless. **3.** f. folly. — ~ **बातें**, f. pl. useless talk; nonsense. – **फ़ज़ूल-ख़र्च**, adj. & m. wasteful in expenditure; extravagant; a spendthrift. °**ई**, f. waste of money; extravagance.

फट *phaṭ* [conn. **phaṭṭ-*[1]], m. a sudden movement, or sharp sound. — **फटफटिया**, m. colloq. moped or light motorcycle. **फटाफत**, adv. quickly, &c.

फटकन *phaṭkan* [cf. H. *phaṭaknā*], f. **1.** winnowing. **2.** sifting, straining. **3.** chaff or husk (winnowed from grain). **4.** siftings.

[1]**फटकना** *phaṭaknā* [**phaṭṭ-*[1]], v.t. & v.i. **1.** v.t. to winnow. **2.** to sift, to strain. **3.** to clean (cotton). **4.** to dust off (as a tablecloth, clothes). **5.** to flail (the limbs). **हाथ-पैर** ~, to flail about. **6.** to flap or to shake (as wings). **7.** v.i. (usu. w. neg.) to make one's way, to have access (to, **के पास**). **पास नहीं** ~, to keep away, aloof. **8.** to pay a flying visit (to, **के पास**). **9.** fig. to be restless, agitated.

[2]**फटकना** *phaṭaknā* [cf. H. *phaṭaknā*], m. *Pl. HŚS.* the tape in a pellet bow (*gulel*) which strikes the pellet.

फटका *phaṭkā* [cf. H. *phaṭaknā*], m. **1.** a bow used in carding cotton. **2.** clapper (for scaring birds). **3.** fig. trembling, alarm. **4.** *HŚS.* colloq. a doggerel poem. — **फटके भर में**, adv. quickly, at once.

फटकार *phaṭkār* [cf. H. *phaṭkārnā*], f. **1.** sound of a whip, or of beating, thumping; sound of dashing wet clothes against a stone. **2.** severe scolding, cursing. — ~ **खाना**, to be scolded, &c. ~ **बताना**, or **सुनाना** (**को**), to scold, &c.

फटकारना *phaṭkārnā* [cf. **phaṭṭ-*[1]], v.t. **1.** to crack (a whip). **2.** to wield (a weapon). **3.** to beat (clothes) on a stone (in washing); to beat (a carpet). **4.** to shake about (as the beard). **5.** Brbh. to throw away. **6.** fig. to scold severely. **7.** to curse. **8.** colloq. to make a gain of, to rake in (money).

फटकी *phaṭkī* [cf. H. *phaṭaknā*], f. **1.** *Pl. HŚS.* a fowler's cage; net; bag. 2. = **फटका**, 2.

फटना *phaṭnā* [cf. **sphāṭyate*: Pk. *phaṭṭaï*], v.i. **1.** to be torn, to be torn open; to be dispersed (as clouds). **2.** to split, to crack. **3.** to feel pain. **सिर** ~, to head to be splitting. **4.** to feel grief, or vexation. **छाती** ~, to heart to be breaking. **मन फटा जाना**, to be bitterly angry. **5.** to burst (as a dam); to explode. **6.** to be separated, detached. **फटके चलना**, to keep separate or aloof (from, **से**). **7.** to separate out: to be clarified (as butter); to turn sour (milk); to clot (blood). **8.** to suffer strain: to be bloodshot (the eyes); to become hoarse, or to break (the voice). — **फट पड़ना**, to burst (upon, **पर**), to be over-abundant (as troubles); to be abundant (wealth); to burst in (upon), to arrive suddenly; colloq. to grow fat suddenly. – **फटा बचपन**, m. a ruined childhood.

फटफटाना *phaṭphaṭānā* [cf. **phaṭṭ-*[1]], v.t. & v.i. **1.** v.t. to shake or to flap (the wings). **2.** to crack (a whip). **3.** colloq. to babble, to gossip. **4.** v.i. to make a flapping, or a cracking sound. **5.** to squeak (shoes). **6.** fig. to flail about (ineffectually).

फटफटिया *phaṭphaṭiyā* [*onom.*], f. colloq. a moped, or light motorcycle.

फटाना *phaṭānā*, v.t. reg. = **फाड़ना**.

फटाव *phaṭāv* [cf. H. *phaṭnā*], m. **1.** splitting, &c. **2.** fig. splitting pain. **3.** crack; separation; break.

फटिक *phaṭik* [ad. *sphaṭika-*], m. crystal.

फटीचर *phaṭīcar*, adj. colloq. decrepit; disreputable.

फट्टा *phaṭṭā* [H. or Panj. *phaṭ(ṭ)ā*], m. a piece of sacking.

फट्ठा *phaṭṭhā* m. reg. (E.) a sliver of bamboo.

फड़ *phaṛ*, f. reg. **1.** a market-place, place of business; cloth on which traders' wares are set out. *__2.__ gambling-house. **3.** a stake, wager. — ~ पर रखना, or लगाना, to wager. फड़बाज़ [P. *-bāz*], m. a gambler. °ई, f. gambling.

फड़क *phaṛak* [cf. H. *phaṛaknā*], f. **1.** fluttering, flutter; quivering, twitching; throbbing, pulsation. **2.** fig. agitation.

फड़कन *phaṛkan* [cf. H. *phaṛaknā*], f. = फड़क.

फड़कना *phaṛaknā* [cf. *phaṭ-*[1]; and **spharati*[1]], v.i. **1.** to pulsate; to flutter; to quiver, to twitch (as the eyelids, or the side or arm: an omen); to throb. **2.** to welter (in blood: a wounded person). **3.** to be agitated, or passionate. **4.** to yearn (for, को or के लिए).

फड़काना *phaṛkānā* [cf. H. *phaṛaknā*], v.t. **1.** to cause to flutter, &c. **2.** to show off, to make a display of. **3.** to agitate.

फड़की *phaṛkī* [cf. H. *phāṛnā*], f. *Pl.* a rough screen, partition.

फड़फड़ *phaṛphaṛ* [cf. H. *phaṛphaṛānā*], f. **1.** flapping, fluttering (of wings, a flag). **2.** crackling (of stiff paper, or rifle fire). — ~ करना, to flap, to flutter, &c.

फड़फड़ाना *phaṛphaṛānā* [cf. **phaṭ-*[1]], v.i. **1.** to move convulsively with an accompanying sound; to flap (wings), to flutter. **2.** to patter down (as rain). **3.** to crackle (as stiff paper, or as rifle fire). **4.** fig. to struggle; to be agitated.

फड़फड़ाहट *phaṛphaṛāhaṭ* [cf. H. *phaṛphaṛānā*], f. **1.** flapping, fluttering, &c. **2.** fig. struggle; agitation (of mind).

फड़फड़िया *phaṛphaṛiyā* [cf. H. *phaṛphaṛānā*], adj. & m. **1.** adj. brisk, bustling. **2.** m. a person easily agitated.

फड़वाना *phaṛvānā* [cf. H. *phāṛnā*], v.t. to cause to be torn, split, &c. (by, से).

फड़ाना *phaṛānā*, v.t. = फड़वाना.

फड़ाफड़ी *phaṛāphaṛī* [? cf. *phaṭ-*[2]], f. *Pl.* wrangling, squabbling; squabble.

फड़िंगा *phaṛiṅgā* [**phaṭiṅga-*], m. *Pl. HŚS.* = फतिंगा.

फड़िया *phaṛiyā* [cf. H. *phaṛ*], m. *Pl. HŚS.* **1.** a retailer of corn and other goods. **2.** keeper of a gambling-house. **3.** a pedlar, hawker.

फड़ी *phaṛī*, f. **1.** *Pl.* a stone slab. **2.** *HŚS.* a pile of stones or bricks.

फड़ैत *phaṛait* [cf. H. *phaṛ*], m. reg. a gambler.

फण *phaṇ* [S.], m. a snake's expanded hood (esp. that of a cobra). — ~ उठाना, to expand the hood (a snake). ~ मारना, to strike (at, पर: a snake); to make strenuous efforts.

फणिक *phaṇik* [S.], m. a snake.

फणी *phaṇī* [S.], m. hooded: a snake.

फ़तवा *fatvā* [A. *fatvā*], m. notification of a decision of Muslim law; decree; verdict.

फ़तह *fatah* [A. *fatḥ*], f. victory; triumph. — ~ करना, to conquer. ~ पाना, to gain a victory (over, पर). ~ होना, to be conquered. – फ़तहमंद [P. *-mand*], adj. victorious; triumphant.

फतिंगा *phatiṅgā* [**phattiṅga-*], m. a flying insect; moth; grasshopper.

फ़तीला *fatīlā* [A. *fatīla*], m. = पलीता.

फ़तुही *fatuhī*, f. = फ़तूही.

फ़तूर *fatūr* [A. *futūr*], m. **1.** defect; unsoundness. **2.** discord. **3.** quarrel, row. — ~ उठाना, or खड़ा करना, to sow discord (between, में), to cause a row. ~ चढ़ना, an irrational or obsessive desire to possess (one, पर). दिमाग़ में ~, unsoundness of mind.

फ़तूरी *fatūrī* [P. *futūrī*], adj. & m. **1.** adj. contentious; litigious. **2.** m. a contentious person, &c.

फ़तूह *fatūh* [A. *futūḥ*], m. **1.** pl. U. victories. **2.** Brbh. victory (= फ़तह); spoils.

फ़तूही *fatūhī* [P. *fatūḥī*], f. a short quilted waistcoat.

फदफदाना *phadphadānā* [? conn. *spandate*], v.t. **1.** to break out, to erupt (as a rash); to be inflamed. **2.** to shoot luxuriantly (a plant). **3.** to bubble (as boiling water). **4.** to fizz, to splutter (as a firework).

फन *phan* [*phaṇa-*], m. = फण.

फ़न *fan* [A. *fann*], m. **1.** an art; an accomplishment. **2.** art. **3.** a crafty trick; wile. — फ़न्न-फ़ितूर, m. art and cunning, wiles.

फनफना *phanphanā*, m. reg. the hiss of a snake.

फनफनाना *phanphanānā*, v.i. **1.** to expand the hood (a snake). **2.** to become erect. **3.** to hiss (as a snake).

फनस *phanas*, m. the jack-fruit (= पनस).

फना *phanā* [*phaṇa-*], m. reg. **1.** a snake's hood. **2.** *naut. Pl.* forecastle.

फ़ना *fanā* [A. *fanā*], f. & adj. **1.** f. perishing, death. **2.** (in Sufism, &c.) extinction of the self in the universal being. **3.** adj. departed, expired, no more. — ~ करना, to destroy, to annihilate. ~ होना, to pass away, to perish.

फनिंग *phaniṅg* [ad. **phaṇika-*], m. Brbh. a snake.

फनिग *phanig* [ad. *phaṇika-], m. Brbh. a snake.

फनी *phanī* [ad. *phaṇin-*; or cf. H. *phan*], m. **1.** hooded: a snake. **2.** reg. a wedge (so named from its shape). — फनींद्र [°nī+i°], m. *hind.* Brbh. lord of snakes: a title of Śeṣa.

फन्नी *phannī* [*phaṇa-*], f. reg. **1.** a wedge. **2.** spike used to fasten sections of a wheel together.

फ़न्नी *fannī* [cf. A. *fann*], adj. esp. pej. skilled; cunning, manoeuvring.

फपकना *phapaknā*, v.i. reg. **1.** to grow, to swell (= फबकना). **2.** to flare, to blaze (= भभकना).

फपका *phapkā* [cf. H. *phapaknā*, and (?) *phapholā*], m. reg. a blister.

फपसा *phapsā*, m. *Pl.* layer of mud on a wooden roof.

फफकना *phaphaknā*, v.i. to burst into tears.

फप्फस *phapphas* [conn. *phupphusa-*], adj. **1.** swollen. ***2.** bloated; fat; flabby. **3.** *Pl.* insipid.

फफसा *phaphsā*, adj. **1.** swollen; hollow. 2. = फप्फस, 2., 3.

फफूँद *phaphūṁd*, f. = फफूँदी.

फफूँदना *phaphūṁdnā*, v.i. to be mildewed, or to be mouldy.

फफूँदी *phaphūṁdī*, f. **1.** mould; fungus. **2.** mildew. — ~ लगना, to be mouldy, or mildewed.

फफोला *phapholā* [*prasphoṭa-], m. **1.** a blister. **2.** bubble (of water). — फफोले फूटना (पर), to be blistered. दिल के फफोले फोड़ना, to work out ill-will or rancour; to give vent to one's anger.

फब *phab*, f. = फबन.

फबकना *phabaknā* [cf. H. *phabnā*], v.i. *Pl.* *HŚS.* to flourish: to shoot (plants); to spread (disease).

फबती *phabtī* [cf. H. *phabnā*], f. **1.** an apt remark; witticism. **2.** a joke; fun. — ~ उड़ाना, to make fun (of, पर); to joke. ~ कसना, = ~ उड़ाना, 1. ~ कहना, id., 2.; to make guesses from a person's dress about what sort of person he is, or to what community he belongs.

फबन *phaban* [cf. H. *phabnā*], f. elegance, charm, beauty.

फबना *phabnā* [*sparvati: Pk. *phavvīhaï*; also *phabb-, conn. *phalph-*], v.i. 1., to become, to befit; to be pertinent. **2.** to suit; to grace, to adorn. — फबता, adj. = फबीला.

फबाना *phabānā* [cf. H. *phabnā*], v.i. & v.t. **1.** v.i. = फबना. **2.** v.t. Brbh. to set off well, to adorn.

फबीला *phabīlā* [cf. H. *phabnā*], adj. **1.** becoming, fitting; pertinent. **2.** attractive.

फ़रंगी *faraṅgī* [P. *firangī*], adj. & m., f. Frankish: **1.** adj. European. **2.** m. a European. **3.** f. Brbh. specif. a sword of European make.

फरक *pharak* [ad. *phalaka-*], m. reg. a shield.

फ़रक़ *farq* [A. *farq*], m. & adj. separation, space: **1.** m. distinction (between, में); difference. उनमें ~ है, they are different. **2.** discrimination. **3.** defect; deterioration. **4.** a discrepancy (as between figures). **5.** adj. colloq. distinct, different. यह ~ है, this one is different. — ~ आना, a difference or misunderstanding to arise (between, में); deterioration to occur (in). ~ करना (में), to distinguish (between); to discriminate (between); to alter, to modify. ~ पड़ना (में), = ~ आना, 1.; a discrepancy to occur (in).

फरछा *pharchā*, adj. & m. reg. **1.** adj. clear (as sky; cf. [3]परछा). **2.** cleaned. **3.** honest, candid. **4.** m. clearness (of the sky). **5.** settlement (of a debt); decision (= फ़ैसला).

फरछा- *pharchā-*, v.t. reg. **1.** to clear away (as clouds). **2.** to clean. **3.** to settle (as debts); to decide (a case).

फ़रज़ंद *farzand* [P. *farzand*], m. Brbh. a son; a child.

[1]**फ़रज़ी** *farzī* [P. *farzī*], m. vizier, minister: the queen (chess). — ~ बनाना, to make (a pawn) into a queen.

[2]**फ़रज़ी** *farzī* [P. *farẓī*], adj. **1.** obligatory. **2.** hypothetical. **3.** assumed (as a name). **4.** false (identity).

फ़रद *fard* [A. *fard*], adj. & f., m. **1.** adj. single, sole; unequalled (among, में). **2.** f. m. U. a single person or thing; a single sheet or strip (of paper, cloth). **3.** ? f. Brbh. list (of items).

फरफंद *pharphand* [? H. *prapañc* × H. *phand*], m. **1.** guile. **2.** cunning arts, wiles.

फरफंदी *pharphandī* [cf. H. *pharphand*], adj. & m. **1.** adj. guileful; fraudulent. **2.** artful; flirtatious. **3.** m. a guileful or an artful person.

फरफर *pharphar*, m. flapping sound (= फड़फड़).

फ़र-फ़र *far-far* [cf. A. *farfara*; also H. *pharphar*], adv. **1.** quickly. **2.** fluently (of speaking, reading aloud).

फरफराना *pharpharānā* [cf. *spharati[1]: Pa. *pharati*], v.i. **1.** to flap (as a flag). 2. = फुरफुराना, 1.

फ़रमा *farmā* [Engl. *form*], m. **1.** a mould, form. **2.** printer's form. **3.** [× L. *pro forma*, ← Engl.] a form (document).

फ़रमाइश *farmāiś* [P. *farmā'iś*], f. **1.** order, request (as for goods). **2.** will, pleasure. — ~ करना, to give an order (for, की); to make a request. ~ देकर बनवाना, to have sthg. made to order.

फ़रमाइशी *farmāiśī* [P. *farmā'iśī*], adj. **1.** ordered (as goods); requested. **2.** made to order. — ~ कार्यक्रम, m. a request programme.

फ़रमान *farmān* [P. *farmān*], m. an edict, decree; a royal letter, charter.

फ़रमाना *farmānā* [cf. P. *farmūdan*, *farmā*-], v.t. **1.** to order, to command. **2.** hon. to be pleased to say (in reference to another's remarks or requests).

फर्रा- *pharrā-*, v.i. E.H. = फहराना.

फ़रलांग *farlāṅg* [Engl. *furlong*], m. a furlong.

फ़रवरी *farvarī* [Engl. *February*], f. February.

फ़रश *farś*, m. see फ़र्श.

फ़रशी *farśī*, adj. & f. see फ़र्शी.

फरसा *pharsā* [*pharaśu-: Pk. *pharasu*-], m. **1.** an axe, hatchet. **2.** a grubbing spade.

[1]**फरहरा** *pharahrā* [cf. H. *pharpharānā*], m. 19c. flag, banner.

[2]**फरहरा** *pharahrā*, adj. half-dried, half-dry.

फरहरी *pharahrī*, f. *Pl.* small flag (cf. [1]फरहरा).

फ़राख़ *farākh* [P. *farākh*], adj. E.H. open, generous (the heart, spirit).

फ़राग़त *farāgat* [A. *farāga*: P. *farāgat*], f. **1.** respite (from work); leisure. **2.** ease, comfort; freedom from care. **3.** obeying a call of nature. — ~ करना, to finish (with, से), to make an end (of). ~ जाना, or फिरना, to go to defecate. ~ पाना, to have done (with, से); to get leisure. ~ में, adv. at leisure, at ease. ~ लगना (को), to have a call of nature. ~ से, adv. leisurely, easily.

फ़रामोश *farāmoś* [P. *farāmoś*], adj. & f. **1.** adj. forgotten. **2.** forgetfulness. **3.** in comp. forgetting (e.g. एहसान-फ़रामोश, adj. forgetful of kindness, ungrateful). — ~ करना, to forget.

फ़रामोशी *farāmośī* [P. *farāmośī*], f. forgetfulness.

फ़रार *farār* [P. *firār*], m. fleeing, flight. — ~ होना, to flee.

फ़रारी *farārī* [P. *firārī*], adj. & m. U. **1.** adj. fugitive, escaped. **2.** m. an escaped person.

फ़रासीस *farāsīs* [? conn. H. *farāsīsī*], adj. & m. **1.** adj. French. **2.** m. a Frenchman. **3.** 19c. France.

फ़रासीसी *farāsīsī* [P. *farāsīsī*], adj. = [1]फ़्रांसीसी.

फ़राहम *farāham* [P. *farāham*], adj. U. brought together, collected; assembled.

फ़राहमी *farāhamī* [P. *farāhamī*], f. U. collecting, assembling.

[1]**फरिया** *phariyā* [conn. *sphāṭita*-], m. Brbh. a short skirt worn by girls.

[2]**फरिया** *phariyā* [cf. H. *phaṛ*], m. reg. **1.** *Pl.* a contract harvest-worker. **2.** a retailer (W. specif. of corn).

फ़रियाद *fariyād* [P. *faryād*], f. var. /firyad/. **1.** complaint. **2.** cry for help; appeal. — ~ करना, to complain; to cry for help. ~ को पहुँचना to come on the appeal (of, की): to hear the complaint (of).

फ़रियादी *fariyādī* [P. *faryādī*], m. a complainant.

फ़रिश्ता *fariśtā* [P. *firiśta*], m. **1.** an angel. **2.** a prophet.

[1]**फरी** *pharī* [cf. *phalaka*-], f. a small shield. — फरी-गदका, m. fighting with shield and club.

[2]**फरी** *pharī* [? conn. *phalakin*-], f. a kind of carp.

फ़रीक़ *farīq* [A. *farīq*], m. U. division, section; a party (esp. in a law-suit).

[1]**फरुवा** *pharuvā*, m. *Pl.* = फावड़ा.

[2]**फरुवा** *pharuvā*, m. reg. (W). a beggar's wooden bowl.

फरुहा *pharuhā*, m. reg. = फावड़ा.

[1]**फरुही** *pharuhī*, f. a mixture of parched rice and barley used as food.

[2]**फरुही** *pharuhī*, f. reg. (E.) a kind of rake, or shovel.

फ़रेब *fareb* [P. *fireb*], m. **1.** deceit; fraud. **2.** guile. **3.** -फ़रेब, adj. formant. alluring, captivating (the heart). — करना, to practise deceit, &c. ~ खाना, = ~ में आना. ~ देना (को), to deceive; to defraud; to beguile. ~ में आना, or फँसना, to be deceived (by, की), &c. ~ से, adv. fraudulently, dishonestly. – फ़रेबकार, adj. & m. deceiving, deceitful; a deceiver, cheat. फ़रेबदिही [P. *-dihī*], f. cheating, swindling.

फ़रेबी *farebī* [P. *farebī*], adj. & m. **1.** adj. deceitful; fraudulent, dishonest. **2.** m. a cheat; a guileful person.

-फ़रेबी *-farebī* [P. *farebī*], f. allurement, seduction (of the heart).

फ़रो *faro* [P. *faro*], prep. down: — फ़रो-गुज़ाश्त [P. *-guzāśt*], adj. 19c. overlooked, neglected.

फ़रोख़्त *farokht* [P. *farokht*], f. selling, sale. — ~ करना, to sell.

-फ़रोश *-faroś* [P. *faroś*], m. a seller (e.g. किताबफ़रोश, m. book-seller).

फ़र्क़ *farq*, m. see फ़रक़.

फ़र्ज़ *farz* [A. *farz*], m. **1.** *musl.* a religious obligation. **2.** a moral obligation; a duty; responsibility. **3.** supposition, assumption. — ~ अदा करना, to discharge a duty, &c. ~ करना, to impose a duty, &c. (on, पर); to regard (sthg.) as a duty; to assume, to take for granted. ~ करें ..., suppose that .... ~ होना, to be incumbent (on, पर).

फ़र्ज़ी *farzī*, m. see [1]फ़रज़ी.

फ़र्द *fard*, adj. & f. see फ़रद.

फर्रा *pharrā*, m. a sheet or slip of paper.

फर्राटा *pharrāṭā* [conn. H. *pharpharānā*], m. **1.** swiftness, speed; sudden quick movement or activity. **2.** *Pl.* flapping; fluttering. **3.** *athl.* sprint. — ~, or फर्राटे, भरना, or मारना, to take flight (as birds); to move swiftly, to rush. फर्राटे से, adv. quickly, in a rush (of movement, or other activity).

फर्राना *pharrānā* [H. *pharpharānā*], v.i. **1.** to move briskly; to come quickly. **2.** to flutter, to flap (as a flag, a bird). **3.** to snort (as a horse).

फ़र्राश *farrāś* [A. *farrāś*], m. U. spreader (of carpets): tent-pitcher, bed-maker, servant.

फ़र्राशी *farrāśī* [P. *farrāśī*], f. U. the work or duties of a *farrāś*.

फर्रास *pharrās* [cf. H. *pharrānā*], m. *Pl.* a species of fir (so called from the noise made by its branches in the wind).

फ़र्श *farś* [A. *farś*], m. f. spreading: **1.** carpeting, floor-cloth. मीरे-फ़र्श, m. 19c. lord of the carpet: a carpet-weight. ***2.** a floor. **3.** paving, pavement. **4.** the ground. — ~ करना, to spread a carpet; to fell (a person, with a blow).

फ़र्शी *farśī* [P. *farśī*], adj. & f. **1.** adj. of or having to do with a carpet or floor, &c. (see फ़र्श). **2.** reaching to the floor (as an elaborate bow). **3.** f. a large flat-bottomed hookah. — ~ जूते, m. pl. slippers. ~ हुक़्क़ा, m. = ~, 3.

फलंग *phalaṁg* f. ? m. Brbh. = फलाँग.

फलँग- *phalaṁg-*, v.i. reg. = फलाँगना.

[1]**फल** *phal* [*phala-*], m. **1.** fruit. **2.** produce; crop; yield. **3.** result. कारण और ~, m. cause and effect. **4.** gain, advantage; return, reward. Brbh. Av. चारि ~, m. pl. = चार पदार्थ. **5.** *math.* result (of a process), answer (to a problem); quotient. **6.** answer (to a riddle, &c). **7.** area (= क्षेत्रफल). **8.** *astrol.* outcome of a given disposition of heavenly bodies; fulfilment of an omen. — ~ आना, fruit to appear; to bear fruit. ~ देना, to yield fruit. ~ पाना, to obtain the fruits or results (of, का), to get one's deserts. ~ लाना, id.; to requite, to reward. – फलतः, adv. as a result. फलद, adj. yielding fruit; fertile; bringing a result, fruitful, effective; bringing gain or advantage. फल-दाता, adj. & m. inv. yielding fruit; one who rewards. °-दायक, adj. = फलद. फलदार [P. *-dār*], adj. fruit-bearing; fruitful. फल-परिणाम, m. Av. the ripeness of fruit; due consequence of (one's) actions. फल-बुझौवल, m. *Pl.* working out the result: a child's game with numbers. फलप्राप्त, adj. rewarded appropriately; punished. °इ, f. फल-फलार [*phalāhāra-*], m. fruit of various kinds. °ई, id. फल-फलैरी, f. id. फल-भर, m. Av. burden of fruit. फलभरता, f. fecundity. फल-भोग, m. enjoying or suffering the consequences of one's actions; enjoyment of rent or profit. °ई, adj. फलवती, adj. f. = next. फलवान, adj. bearing fruit; fertile; producing results, fruitful. फलस्वरूप, adv. & ppn. as a due consequence (of, के). फलहीन, adj. not having fruit; fruitless. फलाफल [°*la*+*a*°], m. good and ill consequences. फलाहार [°*la*+*ā*°], m. eating, or living on fruit; a meal of fruit. °ई, adj. & m. fruit-eating; consisting of fruit (a meal); one living on fruit. फलीभूत, adj. fruitful, rewarded by success.

[2]**फल** *phal* [*phala-*[2]], m. **1.** blade (as of sword, knife). **2.** head, point (as of arrow). **3.** ploughshare. — फलदार [P. *-dār*], adj. having a blade (a weapon).

फलई *phalaī* [*phalakin-*], f. *Pl.* a kind of fish (= फलकी).

फलक *phalak* [S.], m. **1.** a board; bench. **2.** layer, base. **3.** flat surface; blade. **4.** sheet of paper; canvas (of a work). **5.** scale (of an instrument). **6.** medallion.

फ़लक *falak* [A. *falak*], m. heaven; the sky. — ~ टूटना, the heavens to fall (on, पर), a disaster to occur. दिमाग़ चौथे ~ पर होना, fig. to be in fourth heaven (the mind): to be conceited.

फलकी *phalkī* [S.], m. ? f. a species of freshwater fish, *Mystus capirat.*

फलठा *phalṭhā*, m. *Pl.* a small shoot.

फलड़ा *phalṛā*, m. *Pl. HŚS.* = [2]फल, 1.

फलत *phalat* [cf. H. *phalnā*], f. **1.** fruitful state; luxuriant state (as of produce). **2.** crop; gross product.

फलन *phalan* [S.], m. **1.** the bearing of fruit. **2.** the production of results; fruition.

फलना *phalnā* [*phalati*], v.i. **1.** to bear fruit; to be in fruit (a tree, shrub). **2.** to have issue, heirs (a couple). **3.** to thrive (as an activity). **4.** to prove successful or advantageous (to, को). **5.** to break out in blisters, pimples (as the skin). — फलना-फूलना, to flourish; to be marked, pocked (the skin).

फलस *phalas*, m. corr. *Pl. HŚS.* = पनस.

फलसई *phalsaī*, f. *Pl.* a species of freshwater fish (= फलकी).

फ़लसफ़ा *falsafā* [A. *falsafa*], m. philosophy.

फ़लसफ़ी *falsafī* [A. *falsafī*], adj. & m. **1.** adj. philosophical. **2.** m. a philosopher.

फलसा *phalsā*, m. E.H. **1.** door, gate. **2.** quarter (of a town).

फ़लाँ *falāṁ* [A. *fulān*], adj. inv. & m. **1.** adj. such and such, any. **2.** a particular, a certain. **3.** m. a certain (man, &c). **4.** pron. so and so.

फलाँग *phalāṁg* [cf. H. *phalāṁgnā*], f. **1.** a long stride. **2.** a leap, spring, bound. — ~ मारना, or भरना, to stride; to leap, &c.

फलाँगना *phalāṁgnā* [*pralaṅghati*: Pk. *palaṁgha-*; × *sphāla-*], v.i. & v.t. **1.** v.i. to stride. **2.** to leap, to spring, to bound. **3.** v.t. to leap over.

फलाँस *phalāṁs*, m. *Pl.* = फलाँग.

-फला *-phalā* [*phala-*[2]], adj. formant. -bladed, -headed (as a knife, an arrow).

फलाना *phalānā* [cf. H. *phalnā*], v.t. to cause to bear fruit; to make fruitful.

फ़लाना *falānā* [P. *fulāna*], adj. = फ़लाँ. — फ़लाना-ढिमाका, adj. id.

फलार *phalār* [*phalāhāra-*], m. a light meal of fruit, &c.

फलारी *phalārī* [cf. H. *phalār*], f. dimin. = फलार.

फलालैन *phalālain* [Engl. *flannel*], m. flannel.

फलित *phalit* [S.], adj. **1.** having produced fruit; yielding fruit. **2.** fruitful; successful. — फलित-ज्योतिष, m. astrology.

फलियाना *phaliyānā* [cf. H. *phal*, and *phalita-*], v.i. reg. to bear fruit.

[1]**फली** *phalī* [cf. *phala-*], f. **1.** a pod; seed-pod. **2.** *Pl.* a loop. **3.** reg. (W.) a pulse used as fodder, *Cyamopsis psoralioides*.

[2]**फली** *phalī* [*phalin-*], adj. **1.** having fruit. **2.** fruitful, advantageous. **3.** [*phala-*[2]] having a blade (a knife, a weapon).

फ़लीता *falītā*, m. = फ़तीला, [1]पतील. — फ़लीतेदार [P. *-dār*], adj. having a wick, match or fuse.

फलुआ *phaluā* [cf. H. [1]*phal*], m. *Pl.* a knotted fringe or border; knotted tassel.

फल्गु *phalgu* [S.], adj. & m. **1.** adj. feeble, weak. **2.** insignificant, worthless. **3.** m. powder thrown at the Holī festival (= फाग). **4.** transf. spring.

फल्य *phalyá* [S.], m. *Pl. HŚS.* a bud; flower.

फ़व्वारा *favvārā* [A. *favvāra*], m. a fountain. — ~ छूटना, a fountain to play; a jet (as of blood) to gush.

फसकड़ा *phaskaṛā* [cf. H. *phasaknā*], m. **1.** squatting (= पालथी). **2.** sitting on the ground with the legs stretched out. — ~ मारना, to squat, &c.

फसकना *phasaknā*, v.i. reg. **1.** [**phass-*] to become loose or slack. **2.** to burst open. **3.** [cf. **spāśyate*] to sink (into mud, &c). **4.** colloq. to become pregnant.

फसकाना *phaskānā* [cf. H. *phasaknā*], v.t. reg. **1.** to loosen, to slacken. **2.** to split, to burst.

फसकी *phaskī* [cf. H. *phasaknā*, 2.], f. reg. **1.** *hist.* a handful (of grain): a toll taken from each load brought to market. **2.** an extra amount given with a purchase (= घलुआ).

फसक्कड़ा *phasakkaṛā*, m. = फसकड़ा.

फसड्डी *phasaḍḍī*, adj. reg. = फिसड्डी.

फसफसा *phasphasā* [cf. **phass-*], adj. loose, soft, &c. (= फुसफुसा).

फ़सल *fasl* [A. *faṣl*], f. division; season: **1.** harvest-time; harvest (either autumn (*kharīf*) or spring (*rabī*)). **2.** crop, crops (either standing, or when ready for harvesting). नक़दी ~, f. a cash crop.

फ़सली *faslī* [P. *faṣlī*], adj. **1.** seasonal. **2.** having to do with the harvest. — ~ कौवा, m. migratory crow: a fair-weather friend. ~ बुख़ार, m. a fever caused by change of season. ~ भड़ुआ, m. colloq. a person who acts irresponsibly according to his mood of the moment. ~ मेवा, m. seasonal produce. ~ साल, m. *hist.* the revenue or harvest year (a solar year: the *faṣlī* era was introduced by Akbar and began on 10 September 1555, when it corresponded with the hijra lunar year).

फ़साद *fasād* [A. *fasād*], m. corruptness: **1.** a disturbance, brawl; violence (as on the streets); riot. **2.** quarrelling, strife. **3.** intrigue. — ~ उठाना, or करना, or मचाना, to create a disturbance, &c.

फ़सादी *fasādī* [P. *fasādī*], adj. & m. **1.** adj. trouble-making, violent. **2.** rioting, riotous. **3.** quarrelsome. **4.** m. a trouble-maker, &c.

फ़साना *fasānā* [P. *fasāna*], m. **1.** a tale; a romance. **2.** U. a novel.

फ़साहत *fasāhat* [A. *faṣāha*: P. *faṣāḥat*], f. **1.** good or correct language. **2.** eloquence. — ~ से, or के साथ, adv. eloquently.

फ़सील *fasīl* [A. *faṣīl*], f. U. **1.** rampart; city wall. **2.** *mil.* entrenchment.

फ़स्द *fasd* [A. *faṣd*], f. 19c. bleeding (a vein). — ~ देना, to bleed (one). ~ लेना (की), id.

फ़स्साद *fassād* [A. *faṣṣād*], m. 19c. a phlebotomist; surgeon.

फ़हम *fahm* [A. *fahm*], f. understanding, comprehension (see s.v. [2]आम).

फहरना *phaharnā* [cf. H. *phahrānā*], v.i. to wave, to flap; to fly (a flag).

फहराना *phahrānā* [conn. H. *pharpharana*], v.t. & v.i. **1.** v.t. to cause to wave or to flap; to fly (a flag). **2.** v.i. = फहरना.

फाँक *phāṁk* [*phakk-[1]], f. **1.** a mouthful of food; a bit, piece, slice; lith (of orange), clove (of garlic). **2.** crack. — ~ मारना, to toss any dry food into the mouth (from the palm of the hand).

फाँकड़ा *phāṁkṛā* [cf. **phakk-*[2]], adj. & m. **1.** adj. flashy; brash, bold. **2.** m. a smart or dashing person.

फाँकना *phāṁknā* [**phakk-*[1]], v.t. **1.** to toss (any dry food) into the mouth from the palm of the hand. **2.** colloq. to gape: to talk incessantly. — धूल ~, to live on dust: to live in dire poverty.

फाँका *phāṁkā* [cf. H. *phāṁknā*], m. **1.** a mouthful. ***2.** the act of tossing sthg. into the mouth. — ~ मारना, = फाँक मारना.

फाँकी *phāṁkī* [*phakkikā-*], f. **1.** an objection (in logic). **2.** sophistry; trick, fraud. **3.** [cf. H. *phāṁkā*] reg. = फाँक.

फाँत *phāṁt* [? incorr. for H. *phāṭ*], m. *hist.* a village register (sc. apportioning assessment).

[1]**फाँद** *phāṁd* [*spanda-*], m. leap, jump.

[2]**फाँद** *phāṁd*, m. Av. noose, net, snare (= फंदा).

फाँद- *phāṁd-* [*spāśayati* × *bandhati*], v.t. Brbh. to ensnare.

फाँदना *phāṁdnā* [*spandate*], v.i. & v.t. **1.** v.i. to leap. **2.** v.t. to jump over. **3.** to cover, to copulate with (of animals).

फाँदा *phāṁdā*, m. reg. net (= फंदा).

फाँदी *phāṁdī* [cf. H. [2]*phāṁd*], f. **1.** cord, tie (for a bundle). **2.** a bundle or load of sugar-cane.

फाँपना *phāṁpnā* [**p(r)asphāyate*, and *phalph-*], v.i. to swell; to be bloated.

फाँफट *phāṁphaṭ*, m. Brbh. rubbish; falsehood.

फाँफर *phāṁphar*, m. reg. an opening, a hole.

[1]**फाँस** *phāṁs* [*sparśa-*], m. **1.** a splinter. **2.** anything lodging under the nails and causing pain. — ~ निकलना, a source of pain or distress to be removed.

[2]**फाँस** *phāṁs* [*spāśa-*], m. Brbh. a noose; net.

फाँसना *phāṁsnā* [*spāśayati*], v.t. = फँसाना.

फाँसा *phāṁsā*, m. = [2]फाँस.

फाँसी *phāṁsī* [cf. *spāśă-*], f. **1.** noose; halter. **2.** hanging, death by hanging. **3.** transf. gallows. — ~ का तख़्ता, m. scaffold. ~ चढ़ना, v.i. a noose to be put on the neck (of, को); to be hanged. ~ चढ़ाना, or देना, to strangle; to hang. ~ पड़ना (को), or पाना, to be hanged. — फाँसी-काठ, m. gibbet, gallows. फाँसीगर [P. *-gar*], m. strangler; executioner; *hist.* thug.

फाँसू *phāṁsū*, adj. reg. = फँसाऊ.

फ़ाक़ा *fāqā* [A. *fāqa*], m. going without food; starving, starvation. — ~ करना, to go without food (from want, or ill-health). ~ होना, food to be gone without: a meal to be missed. फ़ाक़ों का मारा, adj. & m. starving; a starving person. फ़ाक़ों मरना, to die of hunger, to starve. फ़ाक़ों से रहना, to go habitually short of food. – फ़ाक़ाकश [P. *-kaś*], adj. starving, hungry. °ई, f. going hungry. फ़ाक़ेमस्त, adj. cheerful though starving: indomitably cheerful. °ई, f.

फ़ाख़्तई *fākhtaī* [P. *fākhta'ī*], adj. fawnish (coloured).

फ़ाख़्ता *fākhtā* [P. *fākhta*: ← A.], m. a (wild) dove, pigeon; turtle-dove. — ~ उड़ जाना, : to faint. ~ उड़ाना, to fly pigeons: to have no cares, to lead a life of prosperity. होश ~ होना, consciousness to fly: to faint.

फाग *phāg* [*phalgu-*[1]], m. **1.** the red powder thrown over one another by participants in the Holī spring festival; powder of other colours used in the same way. **2.** transf. the Holī festival. **3.** celebration of Holī. **4.** a kind of song sung at Holī. — ~ उड़ाना, to throw *phāg* powder. ~ खेलना, to take part in the celebration of Holī.

फागुन *phāgun* [*phălguna-*], m. the twelfth lunar month of the Hindu calendar, Phālgun (February-March).

फागुनी *phāgunī* [cf. H. *phāgun*], adj. having to do with the month Phālgun.

फ़ाज़िल *fāzil* [A. *fāẓil*], adj. & m. esp. U. **1.** adj. exceeding, abundant. **2.** spare, surplus. **3.** learned; accomplished. **4.** m. a surplus; a credit balance. — **फ़ाज़िल-बाक़ी**, f. favourable balance (of account).

फाट *phāṭ* [cf. H. *phāṭnā*], m. *hist.* division of the revenue assessment among the sharers in a joint tenancy village.

फाटक *phāṭak* [**phāṭṭakka-*], m. **1.** gate; entrance. **2.** barrier; sluice-gate. **3.** booth (of sentry, &c). **4.** bar (of a court). **5.** colloq. pound (for cattle). — **~ में देना**, or **दाख़िल करना**, to impound. – **फाटकदार** [P. *-dār*], m. gatekeeper; pound-keeper. **फाटकबंदी** [P. *-bandī*], f. custody; impoundment.

फाटका *phāṭkā*, m. speculation. — **फाटकेबाज़** [P. *-bāz*], m. speculator. **°ई**, f. speculation.

फाटकी *phāṭakī* [ad. *sphăṭikī-*], f. *HŚS.* alum (= **फिटकिरी**).

फाटना *phāṭnā*, v.i. & v.t. **1.** v.i. 19c. = **फटना**. **2.** v.t. *Pl.* = **फटाना**.

फाड़ *phāṛ* [cf. H. *phāṛnā*], m. a split, crack.

फाड़ना *phāṛnā* [*sphāṭayati*], v.t. **1.** to tear; to tear open; to disperse (as the wind clouds); to lacerate. **2.** to split. **3.** to open wide (as the eyes, ears, mouth, throat). **4.** to coagulate (milk); to clot (blood). — **फाड़ खाना**, to rend (as a wild beast), to gnaw; to rage with anger. **फाड़ डालना**, to tear to pieces. **आँखें फाड़ फाड़कर देखना**, to stare (at, **की ओर**). **गला फाड़ फाड़कर चिल्लाना**, to shout at the top of one's voice. – **फाड़-खाऊ**, adj. ferociously angry.

फाणि *phāṇi* [S.], f. molasses.

फ़ातिहा *fātihā* [A. *fātiḥa*], f. opening: **1.** the first chapter of the Qur'ān (read for dying Muslims); prayers for the dead. **2.** *musl.* prayers in the name of, and offerings to, saints. — **~ पढ़ना**, to say prayers (for, **की**); fig. to give (sthg.) up as lost.

फाना *phānā* [? **phaṇya-*], m. *Pl.* a shoemaker's wedge.

फ़ानी *fānī* [A. *fānī*], adj. perishing, transitory.

फ़ानूस *fānūs* [A. *fānūs*], f. **1.** lighthouse; light, lamp. ***2.** glass shade (of a lamp); chandelier.

फाब- *phāb-*, v.i. 1. = **फबना**. **2.** Av. to flourish.

फ़ायदा *fāydā* [A. *fā'ida*], m. **1.** advantage, benefit. **2.** gain; profit. **3.** value, use. **4.** convalescence. — **~ करना (को** or **का)**, to prove beneficial (to); to avail, to serve; to cure. **~ उठाना**, to benefit, or to profit (from, **से**); to make good use (of). **~ होना**, benefit, &c. to be had (by, **को**). **फ़ायदे का**, adj. advantageous; useful. – **फ़ायदेमंद** [P. *-mand*], adj. advantageous, beneficial; efficacious.

फ़ायर *fāyr* [Engl. *fire*], f. firing (of a shot); fire. — **~ करना**, to fire, to shoot.

फाया *phāyā* [*sphāta-*], m. = **फाहा**.

फ़ारख़ती *fārkhatī*, f. see s.v. **फ़ारिग़**.

फ़ार्मुला *fārmulā* [Engl. *formula*], m. a formula; prescription.

फ़ारसी *fārsī* [P. *fārsī*], adj. & f. **1.** adj. Persian. **2.** f. the Persian language. — **~ की टाँग तोड़ना**, to speak broken Persian. – **(अपनी) ~ अलग बघारना**, to air (one's) Persian (to the mystification of others). – **फ़ारसीदाँ** [P. *-dān*], adj. & m. knowing, or affecting, Persian; one knowing Persian, &c.

फ़ारिख़ती *fārikhătī*, f. 19c. see s.v. **फ़ारिग़**.

फ़ारिग़ *fārig* [A. *fārig*], adj. free (of, **से**: as of a task or burden). — **~ करना**, to make free (from). – **फ़ारिग़-ख़ती** [A. *khaṭī*], f. deed of release (from debt or obligation).

[1]**फाल** *phāl* [*phāla-*[1]], m. a ploughshare.

[2]**फाल** *phāl* [**phāla-*[2]: Pk. *phāla-*], m. a piece, cut or split off; flake of betel nut.

[3]**फाल** *phāl* [*sphāla-*], m. Brbh. **1.** a step, pace. **2.** leap.

फाल- *phāl-* [**sphālayati*], v.t. reg. to leap (= **फाँदना**).

फालगुन *phālgun* [S.], m. 1. = **फागुन**. **2.** Brbh. *mythol.* a name of Arjuna.

फालगुनी *phālgunī* [S.], f. **1.** the day of full moon in the month Phālgun (when the Holī spring festival is celebrated). **2.** the eleventh and twelfth lunar asterisms (distinguished as *pūrva* and *uttara*).

फ़ालतू *fāltū*, adj. **1.** surplus, spare, extra (as time, resources); not needed. **2.** additional (amount, payment). **3.** dispensable with: useless, incapable (a person).

फालसई *phālsaī* [cf. H. *phālsā*], adj. & f. **1.** adj. purple. **2.** f. purple colour.

फालसा *phālsā* [*parūṣaka-*, Pa. *phārusaka-*], m. the shrub or tree *Grewia asiatica*, and its berry.

फ़ालसा *fālsā* [*parūṣaka-*, Pa. *phārusaka-*], m. the tree *Grewia asiatica*, and its fruit (used medicinally, and the source of a fibre).

फाला *phālā* [*phāla-*[1]], m. reg. a ploughshare.

फ़ालिज *fālij* [A. *fālij*], m. paralysis (esp. resulting from a stroke). — **~ गिरना**, or **होना**

(पर), to be or to become paralysed; to suffer a stroke.

फाली *phālī* [cf. H. [1]*phal*], f. reg. **1.** a ploughshare. **2.** a large hoe or spade.

फ़ालूदा *fālūdā* [P. *fālūda*], m. **1.** a kind of drink, or its main ingredient prepared from parched, ground wheat. **2.** a kind of vermicelli.

फाल्गुनिक *phālgunik* [S.], adj. & m. **1.** adj. having to do with the month Phālgun. **2.** m. the Holī festival.

फाव *phāv* [**sphāva-*], m. a small amount added by the seller to an amount purchased.

फावड़ा *phāvṛā* [? conn. **sphiya-*: Pa. *phiya-*], m. **1.** a spade, mattock. **2.** a kind of rake, or hoe having a curved neck. — ~ चलाना, to labour, to toil.

फावड़ी *phāvṛī* [cf. H. *phāvṛā*], f. **1.** a small grubbing-spade, mattock. **2.** a small rake or hoe. **3.** *Pl.* a staff having projections at each end (as used by a yogī in performing the exercise of *daṇḍ*).

फ़ाश *fāś* [P. *fāś*], adj. **1.** revealed (a secret), made known. **2.** evident (an error). **3.** (from 1.) drawn aside (as a curtain). परदा ~ होना, fig. a secret to be out. — ~ करना, to divulge, to expose. राज़ ~ होना, a secret to be out.

फ़ासला *fāslā* [A. *fāṣila*], m. intervening space; distance (= दूरी). — पाँच मील के फ़ासले पर, adv. at a distance of five miles, five miles away.

फ़ासिद *fāsid* [A. *fāsid*], adj. U. **1.** corrupt, wicked. **2.** criminal. **3.** harmful, dire.

फ़ाहशा *fāhăśā*, f. see फ़ाहिशा.

फाहा *phāhā* [conn. H. *phāyā*; ? w. H. [2]*pohā*], m. a wad of cotton (used as a dressing, swab, &c., or as an artificial teat for a young animal).

फ़ाहिशा *fāhiśā* [A. *fāḥiśa*], f. an unfaithful wife.

फिंकना *phiṁknā* [cf. H. *pheṁknā*], v.i. to be thrown; to be thrown away.

फिंकवाना *phiṁkvānā* [cf. H. *pheṁknā*], v.t. to cause to be thrown, or thrown away (by, से).

फिंकाना *phiṁkānā* [cf. H. *pheṁknā*], v.t. to cause to be thrown.

फिंगा *phiṁgā* [conn. *phiṅgaka-*], m. reg. the fork-tailed shrike.

फ़िकर *fikr* [A. *fikr*], f. **1.** thought, reflection. **2.** care, concern; anxiety; grief. — ~ करना, to reflect (upon, की); to plan (for or about), to provide (for); to feel care or concern (about); to grieve; to pine. ~ में रहना, to be constantly thinking (about, की); to harbour designs (against). कोई ~ नहीं! there's nothing to worry about! – फ़िकरमंद [P. *-mand*], adj. thoughtful; anxious. °ई, f.

फ़िक़रा *fiqrā* [A. *fiqra*], m. **1.** a sentence. **2.** plausible, or specious words; deception. — ~ चलाना, or देना, or बताना, to use plausible words, to dissemble. ~ बनाना, to make up a fine speech, or story. – फ़िक़रेबाज़ [P. *-bāz*], adj. & m. plausible (a person), deceptive; a plausible person. °ई, f. dealing in plausible words, deception; factionalism.

फिकारना *phikārnā*, reg. to uncover the head (a woman); to undo the hair.

फिकैत *phikait* [cf. H. *pheṁknā*], m. *Pl. HŚS.* a javelin-thrower; fencer, club-fighter.

फिकैती *phikaitī* [cf. H. *phikait*], f. *Pl. HŚS.* fighting with javelins, fencing foils or clubs.

फ़िक्र *fiqr*, f. see फ़िक़र.

फिचकुर *phickur*, m. foam from the mouth.

फ़िज़ूल *fizūl*, adj. = फ़ज़ूल.

[1]**फिट** *phiṭ*, interj. esp. 19c. an exclamation of contempt. — ~ ~ करना, to cry shame on. – फिटकार, m. a curse. फिटकार बरसना, curses to be showered on (one).

[2]**फिट** *phiṭ* [Engl. *fit*], adj. fitting, telling, suitable. — ~ होना, to fit (as clothing). बात ~ पड़ना, (sthg.) to be suitable, or telling (in context).

फिटकारना *phiṭkārnā* [cf. H. *phiṭ*], v.t. reg. **1.** to cry shame on; to revile, to curse. **2.** to drive away showing contempt.

फिटकिरी *phiṭkirī* [ad. *sphaṭikārī-*], f. alum.

फिटना *phiṭnā* [**sphiṭyati*: Pk. *phiṭṭaï*], v.i. **1.** to be beaten, mixed, whipped (as eggs). **2.** colloq. to be wiped off, cleared (a debt).

फिटाना *phiṭānā*, v.t. reg. to mix by beating, to beat into a froth (= फेंटना).

फ़ितना *fitnā* [A. *fitna*], m. **1.** misfortune, disaster; serious trouble. **2.** colloq. troublesome person; a pest. यह लड़का बड़ा ~ है, this boy is a great nuisance. **3.** U. sedition; revolt. — ~ उठाना, to foment sedition; to raise a revolt. – फ़ितनाअंगेज़ [P. *-angez*], adj. & m. seditious; insurgent; a disaffected person, &c. फ़ितनापरदाज़ [P. *-pardāz*], adj. & m. 19c. id.

फ़ितरत *fitrat* [A. *fiṭra*: P. *fiṭrat*], f. creation: **1.** nature; natural property. **2.** constitution, temperament. **3.** shrewdness; cunning. — ~ करना, to plan, to plot. ~ लड़ाना, to plot and counterplot, to use cunning.

फ़ितरती *fitratī* [P. *fiṭratī*], adj. **1.** natural, constitutional (a characteristic). **2.** shrewd; crafty.

फ़ितूर *fitūr*, m. = फ़तूर.

फ़िदा *fidā* [A. *fidā*], f. & adj. inv. ransom: **1.** f. devotion, self-sacrifice. **2.** adj. devoted (to); sacrificing self (for). — ~ करना, to devote (oneself, or sthg.: to, पर, के ऊपर, में); to sacrifice. ~ होना, to be devoted (to, पर).

फ़िरंग *firaṅg* [P. *firaṅg*], m. obs. the country of the Franks: Europe.

फ़िरंगी *firaṅgī* [P. *firaṅgī*], m. obs. a European.

फिरंट *phiranṭ* [? conn. H. *phirnā*]], adj. adverse: **1.** displeased, angry (with, से); hostile (to). ***2.** turning or going away. — ~ हो जाना, to make good one's departure, or escape.

फिर *phir* [cf. H. *phirnā*], adv. **1.** anew, again. **2.** thereafter, afterwards; next; then. **3.** furthermore; but. **4.** in that case. — ~ आना, to come back, to return. ~ क्या है? then what matter? what harm is done? ~ भी, adv. even so, nonetheless. ~ से, adv. = ~, 1.

फिरकनी *phirkanī*, f. = फिरकी, 1.

फ़िरक़ा *firqā* [A. *firqa*], m. any distinct group or community of people; sect; tribe. — फ़िरक़ापरस्त [P. *-parast*], adj. schismatic; sectarian; clannish. °ई, f.

फिरकी *phirkī* [cf. H. *phirnā*], f. **1.** a spinning top (or other spinning toy). **2.** a reel. **3.** a spindle.

फिरत *phirat* [cf. H. *phirnā*], m. **1.** returned (rejected) things. **2.** return hire; expenses of a return journey.

फ़िरदौस *firdaus* [P. *firdaus*], m. a garden; Paradise.

फिरना *phirnā* [**phirati*: Pk. *phiraï*], v.i. **1.** to turn, revolve; to move (as a shadow, &c). **2.** to turn in a circle; to whirl. **3.** to go or to move about; to walk to and fro; to wander; to travel. **4.** to circulate (as a call, or information). **5.** to turn away; to turn (to right or left). **6.** to be averted (from, से); to be deflected (the attention, or affections); to deviate (from: as from a policy). **7.** to turn (from or against, से); to abandon; to revolt (against). **8.** to go or to come back, to return; to be returned (as goods). **9.** to turn over, to roll. **10.** to be applied, spread on (as paint). **11.** to be out of shape or line; to be bent; to be warped. **12.** to change, to be transformed. दिन ~, times to change. **13.** to go out (to defecate). झाड़ा फिरना, id. — फिर पड़ना, to turn away (from, से: in dissatisfaction or displeasure). – फिरता, adj. & m. turning; returning; walking about; return (of goods).

फ़िरनी *firnī* [P. *firnī*], f. a dish made of ground rice, milk and sugar.

फिरवाना *phirvānā* [cf. H. *phirnā*], v.t. to cause to turn, &c. (by, से).

फिराऊ *phirāū* [cf. H. *phirānā*], adj. **1.** to be returned. **2.** taken conditionally, on approval (as a purchase). **3.** returning periodically; held periodically (as a festival); cyclical.

फ़िराक़ *firāq* [A. *firāq*], m. **1.** separation. **2.** anxiety, care; keen desire. — ~ में रहना, to suffer at being separated (from, के). वह किस ~ में है? colloq. what is he wanting? what is he after?

फिराना *phirānā* [cf. H. *phirnā*], v.t. **1.** to cause to be turned, to turn. **2.** to turn in a circle; to whirl; to wheel. **3.** to turn round; to wind; to screw; to twist; to spin (a top); to roll. **4.** to take around; to take for a walk; to show round; to walk (a horse, &c). फिरा लाना, to take for a walk, &c. **5.** to turn away, to avert (the face). **6.** to return (sthg. taken). **7.** to turn (one) back (as on a road).

फिराव *phirāv* [cf. H. *phirānā*, m. **1.** revolving, rotation. **2.** return, restitution.

फिरौती *phirautī* [cf. H. *phirānā*], f. a ransom.

फ़िर्क़ा *firqā*, m. see फ़िरक़ा.

फ़िलफ़ौर *filfaur* [A. *fi'l-faur*], adv. U. in haste: at once, instantly.

फ़िलमाना *filmānā* [cf. H. Engl. *film*], v.t. to make a film (of).

फ़िलहाल *filhāl* [A. *fi'l-ḥāl*], adv. at the present time; for the time being.

फिल्ली *phillī*, f. *Pl. HŚS.* = पिंडली.

फिश *phiś*, interj. expression of disgust, disapproval.

फिसकना *phisaknā*, reg. to hiss (as a snake).

फिसड्डी *phisaḍḍī*, adj. colloq. **1.** of no use, not to be relied on (a person). **2.** lagging, behindhand.

फिसफिसा- *phisphisā-*, v.i. E.H. to be slack, or inert (cf. फुसफुसा).

फिसफिसाना *phisphisānā* [conn. H. *phus*], v.i. to hiss (a cat); to spit.

फिसलन *phislan* [cf. H. *phisalnā*], f. m. **1.** slipping. **2.** a slippery spot.

फिसलना *phisalnā* [cf. **phiss-*], v.i. & adj. **1.** v.i. to slip (as the foot, the hand). **2.** to make a slip, or an error (as of conduct). **3.** adj. slippery.

फिसलहा *phisalhā*, adj. reg. slippery.

फिसलाऊ *phislāū* [cf. H. *phislānā*], adj. slippery.

फिसलाना *phislānā* [cf.H. *phisalnā*], v.t. to cause to slip, &c.

फिसलाव *phislāv* [cf. H. *phisalnā, phislānā*], m. **1.** slipping. **2.** slipperiness.

फिसलाहट *phislāhaṭ* [cf. H. *phisalnā, phislānā*], f. **1.** slipping. **2.** slipperiness.

फिसलौनिया *phislauniyā* [cf. H. *phislānā*], m. reg. one who coaxes or seduces.

फ़िहरिस्त *fihrist*, f. = फ़ेहरिस्त.

फींचना *phīmcnā* [*pīḍayati* × *khiñc-*], v.t. **1.** to wring out (as washed clothes). **2.** to rinse, to wash.

फ़ी *fī* [A. *fī*], prep. in, into: **1.** per. ~ कस, adv. U. per head. ~ मन, adv. per maund. ~ रुपया, adv. per rupee. ~ सदी, or सैकड़ा, adv. per cent. **2.** as for, as of. ~ ज़माना, adv. nowadays.

फीक *phīk*, f. *Pl.* the lash of a whip.

फीका *phīkā* [**phikka-*], adj. **1.** tasteless, insipid; unsalted (food); weak, watery (as tea, &c). **2.** faded; pale; wan. **3.** fig. dull, uninteresting; valueless. **4.** faint (a sound).

फ़ीता *fītā* [Pt. *fita*], m. **1.** lace (as of a shoe). **2.** tape. **3.** ribbon. — लाल ~, m. red tape.

फ़ीरोज़ा *fīrozā* [P. *fīroza*], m. a turquoise.

फ़ीरोज़ी *fīrozī* [P. *fīrozī*], adj. turquoise-coloured.

फ़ील *fīl* [P. *fīl*], m. **1.** an elephant. **2.** the castle, rook (chess). — फ़ील-ख़ाना, m. elephant house or stable. फ़ील-पाँव, m. elephantiasis. फ़ीलबान [P. *-vān*], m. mahout.

फ़ीस *fīs* [Engl. *fees*], f. **1.** a fee. **2.** fees.

[1]**फुँकना** *phuṁknā* [**phūtka-*: Pk. *phukkai*], v.i. **1.** to be blown up, inflated. **2.** to be blown (as a fire). **3.** to be set fire to; to be heated up (a liquid). **4.** to be consumed by fire (a building); to be cremated (a corpse). **5.** transf. to be squandered (money). **6.** fig. to be ravaged (the emotions).

[2]**फुँकना** *phuṁknā* [cf. H. *phuṁknā*], m. **1.** = फुँकनी, 1. **2.** [? × **phokka-*] colloq. a bladder; bag, purse; kidney. **3.** *Pl.* a kind of firework.

फुँकनी *phuṁknī* [cf. H. *phuṁknā*], f. **1.** a bamboo or metal blowing-tube (for a fire). **2.** a bellows. **3.** colloq. obs. a pistol.

फुँकवाना *phuṁkvānā* [cf. H. *phūṁknā*], v.t. **1.** to cause to be blown (by, से). **2.** to cause to be set alight.

फुँकाई *phuṁkāī* [cf. H. *phūṁknā*], f. blowing, &c.; sowing (broadcast).

फुँकार *phuṁkār* [cf. H. *phuṁkārnā*], f. hissing, hiss (of a snake). — ~ मारना, to hiss.

फुँकारना *phuṁkārnā* [cf. *phūtkāra-*], v.t. to hiss (as a snake).

फुँकारी *phuṁkārī*, f. = फुँकार.

फुँदना *phuṁdnā*, m. a decorative knot, tassel.

फुंसी *phuṃsī*, f. a pimple; a small boil.

फुआ *phuā* [**phupphu-*: Pk. *pupphā-*], f. paternal aunt.

फुकना *phuknā*, v.i. pronun. var. = [1]फुँकना.

फुगाँ *phugāṁ*, m. cry (of distress). — ~ करना, to utter a cry of distress.

फुचड़ा *phucṛā*, m. *HŚS.* threads hanging from a cloth; fringe.

फुच्ची *phuccī*, f. reg. (Bihar) a pot for measuring milk.

फ़ुट *fuṭ* [Engl. *foot*], m. a foot (measure of length).

[1]**फुट** *phuṭ* [cf. H. *phūṭnā*], adj. **1.** single, unmatched. **2.** detached, separate. — फुटकर, adj. & m. separate; miscellaneous; retail (price, purchase); supplementary (income); loose coin, change. फुटकल, adj. id.

[2]**फुट** *phuṭ* [Engl. *foot*], m. a foot (measure).

[1]**फुटकी** *phuṭkī* [cf. H. *phūṭnā*], f. **1.** blot, stain, spot; splash. **2.** clotted, or undissolved material in a liquid; sediment.

[2]**फुटकी** *phuṭkī*, f. a small bird (= फुदकी).

फुट्टैल *phuṭṭail* [cf. H. [1]*phuṭ*], adj. single; solitary, lone (esp. an animal).

फुड़वाना *phuṛvānā* [cf. H. *phoṛnā*], v.t. to cause to be burst, &c. (by, से).

फुड़िया *phuṛiyā* [cf. H. *phoṛā*], f. **1.** a small boil. **2.** a sore, ulcer.

फुतूर *futūr*, m. = फ़तुर.

फुतूरी *futūrī*, adj. & m. = फ़तूरी.

फुदकना *phudaknā*, v.i. **1.** to hop, to skip (as birds, frogs, calves). **2.** to jump or to dance for joy.

फुदका *phudkā*, m. *Pl.* = फुदकी.

फुदकी *phudkī* [cf. H. *phudaknā*], f. **1.** hop, skip. **2.** *ornith.* any of several warblers; the tailor bird.

फुनंग *phunaṅg*, f. *Pl. HŚS.* **1.** tip, top (as of a tree). **2.** end (of a branch, &c.); projection.

फुनगा *phungā*, m. chick.

फुनगी *phungī* [cf. H. *phunaṅg*], f. reg. **1.** shoot, sprout. **2.** tip, point (as of an ear of corn, or of a branch).

फुनिंग *phuniṅg*, m. E.H. (Raj.) a snake.

फुनि *phuni* [? H. *puni* × H. *phir*], adv. Brbh. = पुनि.

फुन्ना *phunnā*, m. reg. a tassel, tuft; bunch (of threads).

फुन्नी *phunnī*, f. colloq. a boy's penis.

फुन्नो *phunno*, m. colloq. = फुन्नी.

फुप्पा *phuppā*, m. = फूफा.

फुफकार *phuphkār* [S.], f. **1.** hissing (of a snake). **2.** puffing, panting; snorting.

फुफकारना *phuphkārnā* [cf. H. *phuphkār*], v.i. **1.** to hiss. **2.** to puff, to pant, &c.

फुफिया *phuphiyā* [cf. H. *phūphī*], adj. inv. having to do with a paternal aunt. — ~ ससुर, m. husband of a father-in-law's sister. ~ सास, f. father-in-law's sister.

फुफेरा *phupherā* [cf. **phupphu-*: Pk. *pupphā-*], adj. related through a paternal aunt. — ~ भाई, m. cousin. फुफेरी बहन, f. cousin.

फुर *phur* [*sphuṭa-*; or conn. *sphurati*], adj. Av. **1.** true, genuine. **2.** correct.

फुर- *phur-* [*sphurati*[1]], v.i. Brbh. **1.** to be brilliant, to flash (as lightning). **2.** to burst out: to be uttered (words). **3.** [× *pūra-*[1]] to be completed, or fulfilled; to have effect.

फुरती *phurtī* [cf. H. *phur-*], f. **1.** activity, briskness, speed; liveliness. **2.** promptness. — ~ करना, to be active, brisk, &c.; to make haste. ~ से, adv. briskly, &c.; quickly; instantly.

फुरतीला *phurtīlā* [cf. H. *phurtī*], adj. **1.** active, brisk; lively; energetic. **2.** prompt.

फुरफुराना *phurphurānā* [cf. *sphurati*], v.i. & v.t. **1.** v.i. to quiver, to flutter (in the wind). **2.** to flap (as a flag). **3.** v.t. to cause to quiver, &c.

फुरफुराहट *phurphurāhaṭ*, f. = फुरफुरी.

फुरफुरी *phurphurī* [cf. H. *phurphurānā*], f. quivering, fluttering; tremor, shiver. — ~ लेना, to tremble, &c.; the hair, or the feathers (of an animal or bird) to stand erect in fear.

फ़ुरसत *fursat* [A. *furṣa*: P. *furṣat*], f. **1.** leisure, free time. **2.** opportunity (to do sthg). **3.** respite, rest (from, से); recovery (from illness). **4.** reg. leave. — ~ देना (को), to give (one) time or opportunity; to give relief or respite. ~ पाना, to find time or leisure (for, की); to be at leisure; to find respite. ~ मिलना, leisure, &c. to be found (by, को). ~ में, adv. at one's leisure or convenience. ~ से, adv. in a leisurely or convenient way.

फुरहरी *phurahrī*, f. = [1]फुरेरी, and फुरफुरी. — ~ लेना, to shiver, to shudder; the hair, or feathers, to stand erect through fear (an animal, a bird, &c).

[1]**फुरेरी** *phurerī* [cf. *sphurati*[1], and H. *phurahrī*], f. **1.** tremor, shiver (of fear, cold, emotion). **2.** fluttering (as of a flag).

[2]**फुरेरी** *phurerī*, f. cotton wad soaked in scent, oil, &c. and tied to a stick (for application).

फुरेरू *phurerū*, f. Brbh. = [1]फुरेरी, 1.

फुर्ती *phurtī*, f. see फुरती.

फुर्र *phurr* [onom.], m. **1.** whirring sound (of wings). **2.** buzzing sound.

फ़ुर्सत *fursat*, f. see फ़ुरसत.

फुलका *phulkā*, adj. & m. **1.** adj. puffed up; risen (as bread). **2.** m. a light, puffed up bread-cake. **3.** colloq. a boiling-pan (= कड़ाहा). **4.** Brbh. a blister. **5.** transf. *Pl.* soft earth or ground; arena, ring (= अखाड़ा).

फुलकारना *phulkārnā*, v.t. *Pl.* to puff out, to inflate (as a snake its hood).

फुलकारी *phulkārī* [H. *phūl*+H. *-kārī*], adj. & f. **1.** adj. flowered, embroidered (cloth or paper). **2.** f. embroidery of flowers, &c.; *qasīdā* work.

फुलकी *phulkī*, f. reg. 1. = फुलका, 2. **2.** a cake made of ground peas fried in *ghī* or oil. 3. = फुलका, 5.

फुलझड़ी *phuljhaṛī* [cf. H. *phūl, H. jhaṛnā*], f. a firework which shoots out streams of sparks. — ~ छोड़ना, to set off a firework; to cause a dispute to erupt.

फुलवाई *phulvāī*, f. Brbh. Av. = फुलवाड़ी.

फुलवाड़ी *phulvāṛī* [**phullavāṭikā-*], f. flower garden.

फुलवारी *phulvārī*, f. Brbh. Av. = फुलवाड़ी.

फुलसावा *phulsāvā* [cf. H. *phuslānā*], m. = फुसलावा.

फुलसुँघी *phulsuṁghī* [cf. H. *phūl*, H. *sūṁghnā*], f. flower-smeller: a partic. small bird.

फुलहत्था *phulhatthā*, m. colloq. a beating (with flower-covered sticks: wedding custom).

फुलाई *phulāī* [cf. H. *phūlnā*], f. **1.** flowering state. **2.** swelling.

फुलाना *phulānā* [cf. H. *phūlnā*], v.t. **1.** to cause to swell; to inflate; to fluff up (feathers). **2.** to fatten. **3.** to cause to feel pride, or vain delight. **4.** Brbh. to cause to bloom (flowers).

फुलायल *phulāyal*, m. corr. reg. scented oil (= फुलेल).

फुलाव *phulāv* [cf. H. *phūlnā*], m. **1.** swelling; puffiness. **2.** a swelling.

फुलावट *phulāvaṭ* [cf. H. *phulānā*], f. 1. = फुलाव. **2.** flowering, state of flower.

फुलासरा *phulāsrā*, m. corr. *Pl.* = फुसलावा.

फुलिया *phuliyā*, f. reg. (W). = फुल्ली, 2.

फुलेल *phulel* [*phullataila-], m. scented oil.

फुलेली *phulelī* [cf. H. *phulel*], f. a container for scented oil.

फुलेहरा *phulehrā*, m. Brbh. a garland or festoon of flowers, &c.

फुलौरी *phulaurī* [*phullapūra-], f. a small puffed cake of pulse, rice or pea-meal (sometimes with fruit), fried in *ghī* or oil.

फुल्ल *phull* [S.], adj. in bloom; wide open (as the eyes, a flower); radiant (as the face).

फुल्ला *phullā* [conn. *phulla-*], m. **1.** a speck (defect) in the eye. **2.** roasted grain.

फुल्लित *phullit* [S.], adj. Brbh. **1.** swollen. **2.** fig. delighted.

फुल्ली *phullī* [H. *phullā*], f. **1.** a cataract in the eye. **2.** *Pl. HŚS.* a women's flower-shaped ornament of gold or silver. **3.** transf. star (mark of rank). — उसकी आँख में ~ पड़ गई, he has a cataract in his eye.

फुवारा *phuvārā*, m. = फुहारा.

फुस *phus* [*phuss-[2]], f. a soft or low sound; whisper; hiss. — ~ से, adv. in a whisper. – ~ ~, f. whispering. ~ ~ करना, to whisper. फुस-फुसर, m. whispering (= खुसर-फुसर).

फुसका *phuskā*, adj. reg. = फुसफुसा.

फुसकी *phuskī* [cf. H. *phus*], f. **1.** noiseless passing of wind. **2.** fig. whispered slander.

फुसफुसा *phusphusā* [cf. *phuss-[1]], adj. **1.** soft, yielding; spongy; crumbling (as tobacco); slack (as a rope); flimsy; rotting, mouldering. **2.** fig. without substance; worthless.

फुसफुसाना *phusphusānā* [cf. H. *phusphus*], v.i. to whisper.

फुसफुसावट *phusphusāvaṭ*, f. = फुसफुसाहट.

फुसफुसाहट *phusphusāhaṭ* [cf. H. *phusphusānā*], f. **1.** whispering. **2.** a buzzing sound in the ear.

फुसलाऊ *phuslāū* [cf. H. *phuslānā*], adj. & m. **1.** adj. enticing, &c. **2.** cajoling. **3.** m. a cajoler, &c.

फुसलाना *phuslānā* [cf. *phuss-[2]], v.i. **1.** to entice, to inveigle. **2.** to cajole, to coax; to seduce. **3.** to humour (as a child).

फुसलावा *phuslāvā* [cf. H. *phuslānā*], m. cajolery, inveiglement; seduction.

फुसलाहट *phuslāhaṭ* [cf. H. *phuslānā*], v.t. = फुसलावा.

फुसाहिंदा *phusāhindā* [*phuss-[1], *gandha-*], adj. *Pl.* rotting, having a bad smell or stench.

फुहार *phuhār*, f. fine rain, drizzle; mist (as of droplets of water from a fountain). — ~ पड़ना, fine rain to fall.

फुहारा *phuhārā* [? H. *favvārā*×H. *phuhār*], m. **1.** a fountain. **2.** a sprinkler, watering-can.

फुही *phuhī*, f. Brbh. = फूही.

फूँ *phūṁ* [conn. H. *phuṁkār*], f. **1.** hissing, hiss (of a snake). **2.** snorting, snort (of a horse). **3.** snuffing (of a dog). — ~ करना, to hiss, &c. ~~ करना, to snort; to sniff; to fret and fume.

फूँक *phūṁk* [cf. H. *phūṁknā*], f. **1.** blowing; blowing up (a fire). **2.** a breath, puff of air; breath of air accompanying an incantation. **3.** colloq. the breath. — ~ चलाना, to practise incantation; to perform an incantation. ~ निकल जाना, to expire. ~ मारते ही, colloq. in a jiffy. ~ लगाना, to puff (as at a cigarette). — फूँक-सा, adj. frail, insubstantial.

फूँकना *phūṁknā* [*phūtka-: Pk. *phuṁkā-*], v.t. **1.** to blow; to blow (a wind instrument); to blow up (a fire). **2.** to breathe; to infuse (as new life: into, में); to breathe (an incantation). **3.** to whisper (in the ear); to influence (one). **4.** to puff at (a cigarette). **5.** to set fire to. **6.** to squander (wealth, &c). **7.** to spread about (news, rumour). **8.** fig. to cause distress (to a person). — फूँक-फूँककर चलना, to tread carefully, to act with caution (as if blowing dust from one's path). फूँक-फूँककर पाँव (पैर) धरना, or रखना, id.

फूकर *phūkar*, m. *Pl.* a fine sensible young fellow.

[1]**फूट** *phūṭ* [cf. H. *phūṭnā*], f. **1.** bursting open; split, break. **2.** dissension; rift; feud; schism. — ~ डालना, to cause, or to sow discord (between or among, में). ~ पड़ना, dissension to arise (between or among). – फूट-वैर, m. dissension and hostility.

[2]**फूट** *phūṭ* [*sphuṭi-*, MIA *phuṭṭi-], f. a melon, musk-melon.

फूटन *phūṭan* [cf. H. *phūṭnā*], f. **1.** bursting, breaking. **2.** ? m. a fragment. **3.** racking pain in the bones or joints. **4.** fig. wrangling.

फूटना *phūṭnā* [**sphuṭyati*: Pk. *phuṭṭai*], v.i. **1.** to burst open; to break (as a pot); to crack (as a glass); to split. **2.** to burst out; to gush (water, or tears); to be uttered (words); to ring out (sound, voice); to erupt (a rash); to be radiant (as sunbeams). एक बार भी मुँह से नहीं फूटा कि... he didn't once say that.... फूटे मुँह से न बोलना, not to speak on any account (to, से). **3.** to sprout, to shoot. **4.** to fork (as a road, a river). **5.** to break (with, से). **6.** to explode. **7.** colloq. to boil (water). **8.** to appear; to transpire (a matter). **9.** to be dispersed, scattered; to spread (as a smell). **10.** to be distorted (as the face, in displeasure); to be torn, injured (a part of the body). — उँगलियाँ ~, the finger-joints to crack. भाग्य ~ (के), (one's) luck to have broken; to be ill-fated. – फूट जाओ! colloq. clear out! फूट पड़ना, to break to pieces, to shatter; to erupt (on the skin, में). फूट, or फूट फूटकर, रोना, to burst into tears, to shed floods of tears. फूटी आँख, or आँखों, का तारा, m. a last remaining child, or dear thing. फूटी आँखों न देख सकना, not to be able to stand the sight (of, को). फूटी आँखों न भानना, to be detestable (to, को: a person). – फूट-बिखेरा, adj. scattered, dispersed.

फूटला *phūṭlā*, adj. *Pl.* cracked, bad (coin).

फूटी *phūṭī*, f. reg. = ²फूट.

फूतकी *phūtkī*, f. corr. = फुदकी.

फूत्कार *phūtkār* [S.], f. hissing (of a snake).

फूपस *phūpas*, f. reg. aunt of a wife or husband (= फूफिया सास).

फूपसरा *phūpasrā*, m. reg. uncle of a wife or husband (= फूफिया ससुर).

फूफा *phūphā* [**phupphu-*: Pk. *pupphā-*, f.], m. husband of paternal aunt, uncle.

फूफी *phūphī* [**phupphu-*: Pk. *pupphī-*], f. paternal aunt.

फूल *phūl* [*phulla-*], m. **1.** a flower. **2.** a round, or flower-shaped, object or ornament: knob; boss, stud; rosette. **3.** sthg. white, or bright: bell-metal; a spark; a white patch (as of leprosy). **4.** the ashes of a cremated body. **5.** a dimple. **6.** menstrual discharge. — ~ आना, flowers to appear (on, में); menstruation to come on. ~ उठना, cremated ashes to be consigned to the Ganges, or scattered; the Muslim ceremony of *phūl* (on the third day after a death) to be performed. ~ चढ़ाना (पर), to offer or to strew flowers (at a shrine, on a tomb). ~ झड़ना, drops of burning oil to fall (from a lamp); sparks to shoot or to fall (as from flames); fig. to speak eloquently. ~ झाड़ना, to quench (a flame). ~ सूँघकर जीना, or रहना, to live on the scent of flowers: to have a soul above food. फूलों का गहना, m. a garland of flowers. फूलों में तुलना, to live in luxury. – फूल-गोभी, f. cauliflower. फूल-छड़ी, f. flower-stick (as used in a marriage ceremony, see छड़ी). फूल-डोल, m. flower-swing: ceremony in honour of Kr̥ṣṇa, held on the eleventh day of the bright half of the month Cait. फूल-दान [P. *-dān*], m. receptacle for flowers. फूलदार [P. *-dār*], adj. having flowers; flowered (as a pattern). फूल-पत्ती, f. flower-leaf: petal. फूल-पान, adj. fig. tender, soft. फूलवाला, adj. & m. flowering; flowered (as a design); a flower-seller; gardener. फूल-सा, adj. flower-like: delicate, frail. फूल-सुँघी, फूल-सुँघनी, f. = फुलसुँघी.

फूलना *phūlnā* [*phullati*], v.i. **1.** to flower. **2.** to swell; to be inflated; to become very fat or heavy. **3.** to flourish; to bloom, to be radiant. **4.** to swell (as with joy; or with vain pride, or anger). — फूल उठना, to bloom, to be radiant. ~, or फूले (adv.) न समाना, to be unable to contain oneself (for joy). – फूला, m. roasted (burst) grain; colloq. a wide boiling-pan. फूला-फला, adj. blooming, flourishing.

फूला *phūlā*, m. see s.v. *phūlnā*.

फूस *phūs* [**phussa-*], m. old dry straw (esp. as used for thatching); hay. — ~ का तापना, warming oneself before a fire of straw: a vain attempt; a vain hope. ~ में चिनगारी डालना, to throw a spark into straw: to excite contention or strife.

फूसड़ा *phūsṛā* [**phussa-*], m. *Pl.* a rag.

फूहड़ *phūhaṛ* [**phūha-*], adj. & f., m. **1.** adj. uncouth, awkward; stupid. **2.** slovenly. **3.** shameless, obscene (as language). **4.** f., m. an uncouth person, &c.

फूहड़पन *phūhaṛpan*, m. **1.** uncouthness, &c. **2.** slovenliness. **3.** shamelessness, obscenity.

फूहड़पना *phūhaṛpanā*, m. = फूहड़पन.

फूहड़ाई *phūhaṛāī*, f. reg. = फूहड़पन.

फूहा *phūhā*, m. = फाहा.

फूही *phūhī*, f. **1.** fine rain (= फुहार). **2.** mildew, mould (= फफूँदी).

फेंक *pheṁk* [cf. H. *pheṁknā*], f. a throw; a handful of small change (*Pl.*).

फेंकना *pheṁknā* [**pheṅk-*], v.t. **1.** to throw; to hurl, to cast. **2.** to throw down. **3.** to throw out or away; to discard. **4.** to launch, to fire (an arrow, a shot). **5.** to launch (at, पर: a hawk at game, a horse into a charge (at)). **6.** to cast off, to shed (a burden: on to, पर). **7.** to shed, to spill, to pour out. **8.** to squander. **9.** to flail with (the limbs); to brandish, to wield (a staff, &c). **10.** fig. to disregard, to make light of.

फेंकर- *pheṁkar-*, v.i. Brbh. to howl (a jackal).

फेंकाऊ *pheṁkāū* [cf. H. *pheṁknā*], adj. fit (only) to be thrown away.

फेंकैत *pheṁkait* [cf. H. *pheṁknā*], m. wielder: cudgel-player, fencer (with wooden sword).

फेंगा *pheṁgā* [conn. *phiṅgaka-*], m. reg. the fork-tailed shrike.

[1]**फेंट** *pheṁṭ* [**pheṭṭa-*[1]], f. strip of cloth: **1.** waistband. **2.** the part of a *dhotī* which is tucked in at the waist. **3.** turn (of string, &c., around sthg). — **~ कसना**, or **बाँधना**, to make preparation (for, **पर**). **~ पकड़ना**, to restrain (one).

[2]**फेंट** *pheṁṭ* [cf. H. *pheṁṭnā*], f. **1.** stirring, mixing. **2.** shuffling (cards).

फेंटना *pheṁṭnā*, v.t. **1.** to mix (with, **में**). **2.** to stir into froth; to beat (as eggs). **3.** to shuffle (cards).

फेंटा *pheṁṭā* [cf. **pheṭṭa-*[1]], m. 1. = [1]**फेंट**. **2.** a small turban; specif. a piece of cloth worn as a turban.

फेंटी *pheṁṭī* [cf. H. *pheṁṭā*], f. **1.** skein (of thread, &c). **2.** thread (wound on reel or bobbin).

फेंपना *pheṁpnā*, m. mucus of the nose.

फेट *pheṭ*, f. = [1]**फेंट**.

फेटना *pheṭnā*, v.t. = **फेंटना**.

फेटा *pheṭā*, m. = **फेंटा**.

फेन *phen* [*phena-*], m. **1.** froth, foam; scum. **2.** lather. **3.** mucus.

फेनल *phenal*, adj. = **फेनिल**.

फेनाना *phenānā* [cf. H. *phen*, and *phenāyate*], v.i. to foam, to froth.

फेनिल *phenil* [S.], adj. & m. **1.** adj. foaming, frothy. **2.** m. the soap-nut tree (= **रीठा**).

फेनी *phenī* [cf. H. *phen*], f. a kind of sweet pastry fried in *ghī*.

फेनुस *phenus* [*pīyūṣa-* × H. *phen*], m. reg. the thick milk given by a cow, &c. for some days after calving, beestings.

फेफड़ा *phephṛā* [conn. *phupphu(sa)-*], m. the lungs. — **फेफड़े की सूजन**, f. inflammation of the lungs, pneumonia.

फेफड़ी *phephṛī*, f. reg. dry, or chapped lips (= **पपड़ी**). — **~ बँधना**, the lips to be dry: to be nervous.

[1]**फेर** *pher* [**phera-*: cf. Pk. *pheraṇa-*], m. **1.** turn, revolution. **2.** round; circuit. **3.** return. **4.** bend, twist; detour (of road). **5.** change, variation; discrepancy; change for the worse, misfortune. **समय का ~**, m. changing times. **6.** entanglement; error, delusion. **~ की बात**, f. an involved matter. **हो किस ~ में?** how blind you are (to reality)! **7.** difficulty, dilemma; influence of an evil spirit. **8.** equivocation, ploy; Brbh. stratagem. **9.** loss, damage. **10.** circulation, turnover (of capital). **11.** Av. side, direction. **चहुँ ~**, adv. all around. — **~ करना**, to wind (as a river, a road); to make a detour; to suffer a reverse (of fortune). **~ पड़ना**, to be indirect, round about (as a road); a discrepancy to arise. **~ बँधना (का)**, to occur periodically. **~ में आना**, or **पड़ना**, to fall into difficulties; to be swept off one's feet, to be deceived (by, **के**); to suffer loss; to be uncertain (how to act, **कि...**). **~ में डालना**, to involve (one) in difficulties, a dilemma; to mislead, to deceive. **~ लगाना**, fig. to set a trap. – **फेर-फार**, m. constant change; alternation, fluctuation, – **~**, 8. **फेर-फार करना**, to alternate, &c. **फेर-बदल**, m. change, transformation (often pej).

[2]**फेर** *pher*, adv. Brbh. Av. = **फिर**.

फेरना *phernā* [**pherayati*: Pk. *pheraṇa-*], v.t. **1.** to turn (sthg.) round; to twist, to bend. **2.** to turn in its course (a car, &c). **3.** to move (sthg.) around. **माला ~**, to tell one's beads. **4.** to turn back or away; to reject; to avert (as a disaster). **5.** to avert (as the eyes). **6.** to send back (a person). **7.** to return (money, goods). **8.** to turn (a person) against or away (from, **से**, **की ओर से**). **9.** to bring over (to one's side, **की तरफ़**). **10.** to turn over, to reverse; to turn inside out; to unsettle (the mind). **सिर**, or **दिमाग़**, **फेर देना**, to turn the head (of, **का**). **11.** to pass round (*pān*, &c.: to, **के सामने**). **12.** to send round (as a proclamation). **13.** to pass or to move (as the hand, or a brush) over a surface. **रंग ~**, to apply paint (to, **पर**). **हाथ ~**, to run the hand (over, **पर**); to smoothe; to caress. **14.** to alter (a statement, &c.) **ज़बान ~**, to go back on one's word. **15.** to go over (a lesson). **16.** to walk (a child, an animal).

फेरा *pherā* [**phera-*: cf. Pk. *pheraṇa-*], m. **1.** turn, revolution. **2.** round; circuit. **बाज़ार का ~**, m. a round of a bazaar. **3.** perambulation (of the sacred fire, by bride and groom at marriage). **4.** return. **5.** visit, call (in the course of activities). **6.** going round (sthg.), encompassing. **7.** *techn.* a winding, wrapping; coil. **8.** a roll (of material). **9.** alternation, fluctuation (as in business). **10.** a wooden frame used in measuring quantities of lime, sand, &c. by passing it over them. — **~ डालना**, to make a turn, &c. (round, **का**). **~ देना (को)**, to turn (a wheel, &c). फेरे डालना, to lead (a bride and bridegroom) round (the sacred fire, के): to give in marriage. फेरे पड़ना, to be led round (the sacred fire, के): to be married. फेरे लगाना, to go around (on travels, business). – फेरा-फारी, f. = फेर-फार, 1., 2.; change, exchange; coming and going, visits. फेरा-फेरी, f. id.

फेरी *pherī* [cf. H. *pherā*], f. **1.** going round; circumambulation (= परिक्रमा). **2.** round, circuit (as of a hawker, beggar). **3.** hawking. **4.** begging. **5.** an instrument used in twisting rope, &c. **6.** reg. trick, ploy. — ~ करना, to work as, or to be, a hawker; to go about begging. ~ पड़ना, the marriage rite (of circumambulation) to be performed (by, की). – फेरीदार [P. *-dār*], m. a vagrant; a hawker. फेरीवाला, m. a hawker.

फेल *phel* [Engl. *fail*], adj. **1.** failed (in an examination). **2.** failed, out of order (as a machine, or a service or supply). **3.** ineffective (as a measure). — ~ होना, to fail (in, में).

²**फ़ेल** *fel* [A. *fe'l*], m. U. an act.

फ़ेहरिस्त *fehrist* [P. *fĕhrist*], f. a list, catalogue; inventory.

फ़ैज़ *faiz* [A. *faiẓ*], m. U. **1.** liberality. **2.** favour, grace. **3.** benefit, profit.

फ़ैयाज़ *faiyāz* [A. *faiyāẓ*], adv. generous.

फ़ैयाज़ी *faiyāzī* [P. *faiyāẓī*], f. generosity, liberality. — ~ करना, to act generously, &c.

फैलना *phailnā* [cf. *prathita-* Pk. *pahia-*], v.i. **1.** to spread, to stretch out; to be spread or extended. **2.** to be spread out (as objects); to be scattered, dispersed. **3.** to be opened wide (as the mouth, eyes). **4.** to increase (in size); to grow fat; to grow bloated. **5.** to expand (as a sphere of activity). **6.** to be spread, to become current (as a view, a rumour, or a disease, or a practice). **7.** to become pressing (requirements or demands: for, के लिए).

फ़ैलसूफ़ *failāsūf* [A. *failasūf*], m. U. **1.** a philosopher. **2.** a cunning rascal.

फैलाना *phailānā* [cf. H. *phailnā*], v.t. **1.** to stretch out (as the hand); to extend; to spread (as wings). **2.** to spread, to spread out (as objects); to scatter; to apply (a coating). **3.** to distribute (among, में). **4.** to open wide (as the mouth, eyes). **5.** to enlarge, to expand (as a sphere of activity). **6.** to spread (as a view, a rumour, or a practice); to make current.

फैलाव *phailāv* [cf. H. *phailānā*], m. **1.** spread, extent. **2.** enlargement, expansion. **3.** diffusion (of an attitude, or a technique). **4.** distribution (as of a species). **5.** abundance, profusion. **6.** display. **7.** long-windedness. — फैलावदार [P. *-dār*], adj. extensive; widely extended.

फैलावट *phailāvaṭ* [cf. H. *phailānā*], f. spreading, spread, &c.

फैलावा *phailāvā*, m. = फैलावट.

फ़ैसला *faislā* [A. *faiṣala*], m. **1.** adjudication (of a case); judgment. **2.** decision (as between alternatives). — ~ करना, to adjudicate; to judge; to settle (a matter, का). ~ देना, id., 1., 2. ~ सुनाना, to pronounce judgment. ~ होना, to be adjudicated; to be decided, settled.

फोंक *phoṁk* [**phoṅka-*: ? ← Drav.], adj. & f. *HŚS.* **1.** adj. hollow (cf. ¹फोक). **2.** f. Brbh. Av. notch (of an arrow).

¹**फोंका** *phoṁkā* [**phoṅka-*: ? ← Drav.], adj. = फोंक.

²**फोंका** *phoṅkā* [? = H. *phoṅk*] reg. (E). young shoots of peas, &c. nipped off to make the plant spread.

फोंफी *phoṁphī* [**phompha-*], f. a hollow reed; bamboo pipe.

¹**फोक** *phok* [**phokka-*: Pk. *phukkā*], m. & adj. **1.** sthg. worthless: dregs; rubbish. **2.** adj. hollow (as a stalk), empty; light; soft. **3.** simple, mere.

²**फोक** *phok*, adj. *Pl. HŚS.* four (in the language of brokers or dealers).

फोकट *phokaṭ* [cf. **phokka-*: Pk. *phukkā*], adj. **1.** worthless. **2.** costing nothing, and given free. — ~ का, adj. costing nothing. ~ में, adv. for nothing, gratis.

फोकला *phoklā* [cf. H. *phok*], adj. & m. reg. **1.** adj. hollow. **2.** m. skin (of fruit, &c).

फोकी *phokī* [cf. H. *phok*], f. reg. soft or porous soil.

फोग *phog*, m. reg. dregs, sediment (= ¹फोक).

फोड़ना *phoṛnā* [*sphoṭayati*], v.t. **1.** to burst open; to break; to crack; to split; to penetrate (as a bullet). **2.** to send off or out (as shoots, branches). शाखाएँ ~, to fork (a river, a tree). **3.** to separate (from a group, a stock); to win over (to one's side); to suborn. **4.** to disclose (a secret): e.g. बात ~ (की), भंडा ~ (का). **5.** to strain, to weary (as the eyes, to see sthg). अपना सिर ~, to go to endless trouble (to, के लिए). — उँगलियाँ ~, to crack the finger-joints. – फोड़ना-फाड़ना, = फोड़ना, 1.

फोड़नी *phoṛnī* [cf. H. *phoṛnā*], f. reg. a tool for splitting, cleaver.

फोड़ा *phoṛā* [*sphoṭa-*²], m. a boil, sore; ulcer; abscess; tumour. — फोड़ा-फुंसी, f. eruption (on the skin).

फ़ोता *fotā* [P. *foṯa*], m. bag: **1.** scrotum. **2.** Brbh. dues (as from land).

फोया *phoyā*, m. = फाहा.

फोला *pholā* [**pholla-*], adj. reg. a blister.

फोसका *phoskā* [**phoss-*], m. *Pl.* a blister; swelling.

फोहा *phohā*, m. = फाहा.

फ़ौज *fauj* [A. *fauj*], f. an army. — ~, or ~ में, भरती करना, to enlist in an army. – क़िले की ~, f. garrison. पुलिस ~, f. police force. पैदल ~, f. infantry army or corps. फ़ौजदार [P. *-dār*], m. a military commander of a district; *hist.* a criminal judge or magistrate (of the Muslim government of India); a partic. rank (commissioned) in the police. °ई, adj. & f. having to do with a *faujdār*; criminal (case, court); the office of a *faujdār*; a criminal court, offence. फ़ौजदारी करना, to commit a criminal offence; to commit an assault, or a breach of the peace.

फ़ौजी *faujī* [P. *faujī*], adj. **1.** of or having to do with an army, military. **2.** having to do with defence (as expenditure). — ~ भरती, f. conscription; mobilisation. ~ रंगरूट, m. a conscript (soldier). — ~ सलामी, f. salute. – फ़ौजीवाद, m. militarism. °ई, adj. & m. militarist. फ़ौजीशाह, m. a militarist. °ई, f. militarism.

फ़ौरन *fauran* [A. *fauran*], adv. at once, immediately.

फ़ौलाद *faulād* [P. *fūlād*], f. steel. — ~ की चद्दर, f. steel plate.

फ़ौलादी *faulādī* [P. *fūlādī*], adj. **1.** made of steel. **2.** having to do with steel. **3.** steely; strong, unyielding.

फ़ौवारा *fauvārā*, m. see फ़व्वारा.

[1]**फ़्रांसीसी** *frāṃsīsī* [H. *farāsīsī* × Engl. *France*], adj. & m. **1.** adj. French. **2.** m. a Frenchman.

[2]**फ़्रांसीसी** *frāṃsīsī* [H. *farāsīsī* × Engl. *France*], f. the French language.

ब

ब *ba*, the twenty-third consonant of the Devanāgarī syllabary. — बकार, m. the sound /b/; the letter ब.

बंक *baṅk* [ad. *vaṅka-*[1], Pa. *vaṅka-*], adj. & m. Brbh. **1.** adj. bent, curved. **2.** inaccessible; difficult of access. **3.** gallant, courtly. **4.** m. a lover. **5.** reg. bend, curve (as in a river). — ~ कहनि, f. Brbh. courtly words.

बँकाई *baṁkāī* [cf. H. *baṅk*], f. Brbh. bent or curved shape (as a bow, or eyebrows).

बँकारना *baṁkārnā*, v.i. reg. to shout, to yell.

बंकिम *baṅkim* [S.], adj. bent, curved; drawn (a bow).

[1]**बंग** *baṅg* [ad. *vaṅga-*[4], Pk. *baṅga-*], m. Bengal. — बंग-भंग, m. the partition of Bengal (1905).

[2]**बंग** *baṅg*, m. reg. = भाँग.

बँग *baṁg* [[*vaṅga-*[1], Pa. *vaṅka-*], m. *Pl.* oxide of tin (taken as an aphrodisiac).

बँगरी *baṁgrī* [? M. *bāṁgṛī*], f. Brbh. a bangle made of glass or lac.

बँगला *baṁglā* [cf. H. *baṅgāl(ā)* or *vaṅga-*[4]], adj. inv. & m., f. inv. **1.** adj. Bengali. **2.** m. a bungalow; a cottage. **3.** a type of betel leaf. **4.** f. the Bengali language.

बंगलादेशी *baṁglādeśī*, adj. belonging to or having to do with Bangladesh.

बँगलिया *baṁgăliyā* [cf. H. *baṁglā*], f. small bungalow, cottage.

बंगा *baṅgā*, m. reg. (W.) ? corr. a split piece of bamboo (as used in basket-making).

बँगा *baṁgā* [*vaṅga-*[1]], m. reg. (W.) **1.** well-water having a metallic or oily taste. **2.** *Pl.* a kind of soil.

बंगाल *baṅgāl* [? **vaṅgālaya-*; H. *baṅg*], m. Bengal.

बँगाला *baṁgālā* [**vaṅgālaya-*], m. = बंगाल.

बंगालिन *baṅgālin* [cf. H. *baṅgāl*], f. a Bengali woman.

[1]**बंगाली** *baṅgālī* [cf. H. *baṅgāl*], adj. & f. **1.** adj. Bengali. **2.** f. the Bengali language.

[2]**बंगाली** *baṅgālī* [cf. H. *baṅgāl*], m. a Bengali.

[1]**बंगी** *baṅgī*, f. reg. = बिंगी, 2.

[2]**बंगी** *baṅgī* [P. *bangī*], m. one who takes *bhāṁg*.

बँचना *baṁcnā* [cf. H. *bāṁcnā*], v.i. to be read, read through.

बँचवाना *baṁcvānā* [cf. H. *bāṁcnā*], v.t. to cause to be read (by, से); to make or to hear (one) read.

बँचाना *baṁcānā* [cf. H. *bāṁcnā*], v.t. = बँचवाना.

बंजर *bañjar*, adj. & m. **1.** adj. barren. **2.** waste (land). **3.** m. waste land; scrub, jungle. **4.** fallow land.

बंझोटी *bañjhoṭī* [cf. *vandhya-*], f. *Pl.* pill or medicine given to abort a foetus, or to suppress ovulation.

बँटना *baṁṭnā* [cf. H. *bāṁṭnā*], v.i. to be divided, &c. (cf. बाँटना).

बँटवाई *baṁṭvāī* [cf. H. *baṁṭvānā*], f. **1.** allocation, distribution. **2.** payment for distributing, &c.

बँटवाना *baṁṭvānā* [cf. H. *baṁṭnā*], v.t. to cause to be divided (by, से); to distribute (among, में).

बँटवारा *baṁṭvārā*, m. **1.** division, sharing (as of assets); partition (of land, territory). **2.** allocation, distribution. **3.** split, division, schism. — ~ करना, to divide, &c. (between, में).

बँटवैया *baṁṭvaiyā* [cf. H. *bāṁṭnā*], m. one who divides, or distributes.

[1]**बंटा** *baṇṭā*, adj. colloq. small of stature, little.

[2]**बंटा** *baṇṭā* [? = [1]*baṇṭā*], m. reg. **1.** a small box (round or rectangular). **2.** a large brass water-pot.

बँटाई *baṁṭāī* [cf. H. *baṁṭnā*], f. dividing, division.

बंटाढार *baṇṭāḍhār* [? *vaṇṭa-*[2] (Pa. *-vaṇṭa-*); w. H. *baṭṭā-ḍhāl*], adj. & m. colloq. orig. E. ruined, done for; ruined state. — (का) ~ करना, to ruin (as hopes, plans).

बँटाना *baṁṭānā* [cf. H. *bāṁṭnā*], v.t. to cause to be divided, to share. — हाथ ~, to share the work (of, का): to help (in, में).

बँटाव *bam̐ṭāv* [cf. H. *bām̐ṭnā, bam̐tānā*], m. divisibility.

बंड *banḍ* [S.], m. **1.** maimed (in hands or feet). **2.** tailless. **3.** circumcised. **4.** impotent.

बंडा *banḍā*, m. a variety of arum plant, and its tubers.

बंडी *banḍī*, f. light waistcoat, vest.

बँड़ेरा *bam̐ṛerā* m. reg. (Bihar) ridgepole (of a roof) (= बड़ेरी).

बंडोआ *banḍoā*, m. *Pl.* whirlwind.

बंडोहा *banḍohā*, m. *Pl.* whirlwind (= बगूला).

बंद *band* [P. *band*], adj. & m. **1.** adj. fastened, tied, bound. **2.** enclosed; confined. **3.** closed, shut. **4.** stopped (as a mechanism); turned off (an appliance, electricity, &c). **5.** come to an end; stopped (as rain); finished. **6.** brought to an end (as a process, a discussion, an arrangement); put a stop to, halted (a practice, an abuse); prohibited. **7.** closed (as a road); blocked (a channel). **8.** filled (a hole, a gap). **9.** heavy, oppressive (air, atmosphere). **10.** m. a fastening, or tie; belt; lace, draw-string; bandage; band, strip, ribbon (of any material), knot. **11.** joint (of the body); knuckle. **12.** dam; embankment. **13.** confinement, imprisonment. **14.** twist, trick (in wrestling). **15.** verse (of a song). — ~ करना, to close, to turn off, &c. ~ ~ पकड़ना (का), to seize all the joints (rheumatism). ~ में आना, to be captured, or imprisoned. घोड़े की टाँगें ~ हैं, the horse is knock-kneed. – बंद-गोभी, f. cauliflower. बंददार [P. *-dār*], adj. having fastenings. बंदोबस्त [P. *-bast*], m. organisation, management; arrangement; settlement (of revenue).

बंदगी *bandagī* [P. *bandagī*], f. & interj. servitude: **1.** f. devotion, worship. **2.** salutation. **3.** interj. U. greetings! — ~ करना, to pay one's respects. ~ बजाना, or बजा लाना, to fawn (upon, की).

बंदनमाल *bandanmāl* [ad. **vandanamālā*-], f. Brbh. = बंदनवार.

बंदनवार *bandanvār* {ad. *vandana*-; *māla*-], f. festoon of leaves and flowers (at a gateway); garland of flowers (at a door).

[1]**बंदर** *bandar* [conn. *vanar*-, *vānara*-], m. monkey. — ~ की दोस्ती, f. monkey's friendship: fickle friendship. ~ ने छू दिया है, colloq. she is not to be touched (being menstruating). बंदर-घुड़की, f. impotent scolding, empty threat. बंदर-भाँट, f. a distribution wrangled over, or wrongly made. बंदर-भबकी, f. = बंदर-घुड़की.

[2]**बंदर** *bandar* [P. *bandar*], m. harbour, port; docks. — बंदरगाह [P. *-gāh*], f. id. फ़ौजी बंदरगाह, f. naval base.

बंदरा *bandrā* [cf. H. *bām̐dā*], m. reg. mistletoe.

बंदरिया *bandăriyā* [cf. H. *bandar*], f. a female monkey.

[1]**बंदरी** *bandărī* [cf. H. *bandar*], f. a female monkey.

[2]**बंदरी** *bandărī* [cf. H. *bandar*], adj. having to do with a harbour or port: imported, foreign (goods).

[1]**बंदा** *bandā* [P. *banda*], m. **1.** servant; slave. **2.** your servant (self-deprecatory term used in addressing a superior). — बंदानिवाज़ [P. -*navāz*], m. cherisher of servants or dependants: patron; your honour. °ई, f. kindliness to servants. बंदापरवर [P. -*parvar*], m. = बंदानिवाज़. °ई, f. = बंदानिवाज़ी.

[2]**बंदा** *bandā*, m. reg. **1.** *Pl.* a grain-store. **2.** W. the roof of a grain-store.

बंदिश *bandiś* [P. *bandiś*], f. **1.** a tying, binding. ***2.** restriction, limitation; requirement. **3.** plan, precaution; plot. **4.** structure, pattern (of verse, music); words (of a song).

[1]**बंदी** *bandī* [ad. P. *bandī*; S. *bandī*-], m. **1.** a prisoner. **2.** a slave. — बंदी-ख़ाना, m. = next. बंदी-गृह, m. prison. बंदी-घर, m. id. बंदी-शिविर, m. concentration camp.

[2]**बंदी** *bandī* [ad. *vandin*-], m. a bard, panegyrist (= भाट). — बंदीजन, m. a bard; bardsfolk, bards.

[3]**बंदी** *bandī* [P. *bandī*], f. **1.** binding, tying; attaching (as a horseshoe). **2.** shutting, closing (as a shop); stopping, blocking (traffic, a road). **3.** construction. **4.** imprisonment. **5.** arrangement, settlement (as of revenue). **6.** -बंदी. charge, levy; binding, &c.

[4]**बंदी** *bandī*, f. reg. an ornament worn on the forehead.

बंदूक़ *bandūq* [P. *bundūq*; A. pl. *banādīq*], f. **1.** musket. ***2.** rifle. — ~ चलाना, or छोड़ना, or मारना, or लगाना, to fire a rifle (at, पर); to shoot. ~ भरना, to load a rifle.

बंदूक़ची *bandūqcī* [P. *bandūqcī*], m. rifleman.

बंदोड़ *bandoṛ* [cf. H. *bandā*], f. pej. base-born girl or woman.

बंध *bandh* [S.], m. **1.** tie, fastening; string; lace; bandage; knot. **2.** dam; embankment. **3.** confinement, imprisonment. **4.** witholding of labour, strike. **5.** composition, structure (as of a poem). **6.** pledge, deposit (= बंधक).

बंधक *bandhak* [S.], m. **1.** sthg. pawned, or pledged. **2.** a mortgage. **3.** a hostage. — ~ करना, or धरना, or रखना, to pawn, to mortgage (with, के पास). – बंधक-कर्ता, m. inv. mortgagor.

बंधकी *bandhăkī* [cf. H. *bandhak*], adj. mortgaged.

बंधन *bandhan* [S.], m. **1.** fastening, tying together. **2.** a tie, fastening; knot. **3.** joint (of the body). **4.** bond, fetter; transf. obligation. **5.** tie(s) (as of affection, duty). **6.** confinement, captivity. **8.** established rule or custom; daily practice, observance. — बंधनकारी, adj. binding (a clause, &c).

बँधना *baṁdhnā* [cf. H. *bāṁdhnā*], v.i. & m. **1.** v.i. to be fastened, bound, tied (to, से, के साथ). **2.** to be enclosed, confined; to be imprisoned. **3.** to be caught, ensnared. **4.** to be under obligation, to have no choice (in a matter). **5.** to be built, erected. **6.** to be continuous, uninterrupted (as thought); to be kept in mind (a memory); to be regular or constant. **7.** to be fixed (as a wage). **8.** to be customary. **9.** to be involved, entangled (with, से). **10.** m. cord, string, thread. **11.** wrapper; needlecase. – बँधा, adj. fastened, &c.; concealed. बँधा हुआ खर्च, m. regular expenses. बँधी आवाज़, f. a monotonous tone or voice. बँधी बात, f. established practice or rule. बँधी मुट्ठी, f. closed fist: sthg. kept secret; a close family. बँधा-बँधाया, adj. fixed, all arranged; regular, continuous (any arrangement).

बँधनी *baṁdhnī* [cf. *bandhana-*], f. reg. sthg. for tying or holding together: **1.** a cord, rope. **2.** a small cloth wrapper (as for needles, thread), hold-all.

बंधव *bandhav* [H. *bāndhav* ×H. *bandhu*], m. Brbh. = बांधव.

बँधवाई *baṁdhvāī* [cf. H. *baṁdhvānā*], f. *Pl.* imprisonment, captivity.

बँधवाना *baṁdhvānā* [cf. H. *bāṁdhnā*], v.t. **1.** to cause to be bound, &c. (by, से); to have (sthg.) bound. **2.** to cause to be imprisoned. **3.** to cause to be built, made (by). **4.** to cause to be fixed, determined. — हिम्मत ~, to strengthen (another's, की) courage or resolve.

बँधवास *baṁdhvās*, m. reg. land embanked all round so as to hold in water.

बँधाई *baṁdhāī* [cf. H. *bāṁdhnā, baṁdhānā*], f. **1.** the act of binding. **2.** the business of binding (books). **3.** bond, tie. **4.** binding (of a book). **5.** price paid for binding.

बँधान *baṁdhān* [cf. H. *baṁdhnā*], m. **1.** fixed allowance, or wage; *hist.* pension. **2.** *hist.* purchase of grain in advance of the harvest. **3.** reg. (Bihar) an agreement as to wages or terms. **4.** dam, embankment. **5.** Brbh. Av. *mus.* fixed measure, rhythm.

बँधाना *baṁdhānā* [cf. H. *bāṁdhnā*], v.t. **1.** to cause to be bound (by, से); to bind. **2.** to enjoin upon. **3.** to fix, to establish.

बँधानी *baṁdhānī* [cf. H. *baṁdhān*], m. *Pl.* **1.** porter. **2.** pensioner.

बँधावट *baṁdhāvaṭ* [cf. H. *bāṁdhnā*], f. **1.** binding. **2.** bond, tie.

बंधिनी *bandhinī* [S.], f. woman servant, or slave.

[1]**बंधी** *bandhī*, f. reg. a customary arrangement.

[2]**बंधी** *bandhī*, f. reg. an embankment, dam (= बंद, बंध).

बंधीवान *bandhīvān* [cf. H. [1]*bandī*], m. E.H. = [1]बंदी.

बंधु *bandhu* [S.], m. **1.** relative. **2.** brother. **3.** friend. — बंधु-जन, m. pl. relatives; friends. बंधु-जीव, m. Brbh. a plant and its flower (= दुपहरिया).

बँधुआ *baṁdhuā* [cf. H. *baṁdhnā*], m. reg. **1.** a prisoner, captive. **2.** a slave. **3.** W. an animal kept in a stall.

बंधुता *bandhutā* [S.], f. = बंधुत्व.

बंधुत्व *bandhutvă* [S.], m. **1.** close relationship. **2.** friendship.

बंधुर *bandhur* [S.], adj. rough, difficult (as a road).

बंधुरा *bandhurā* [S.], f. a prostitute.

बंधूक *bandhūk* [S.], m. a red-flowering shrub.

बंधेज *bandhej* [**bandheyya-*], m. **1.** stability, permanence. **2.** regular practice; gift (as to relatives, servants on partic. occasions). **3.** prohibition, restriction; embargo. **4.** temperance. **5.** parsimony.

बंध्य *bandhyă* [S.], adj. **1.** barren, unfruitful. **2.** requiring to be bound, &c. (cf. बँधना). — बंध्यकरण, m. sterilisation.

बंध्या *bandhyā* [S.], adj. f. & f. = बाँझ. — बंध्यकरण, m. sterilisation (to prevent the bearing of offspring).

[1]**बंब** *bamb*, m. **1.** Brbh. a shout; a drum (= [3]बम). 2. = [1]बम.

[2]**बंब** *bamb*, m. *hist.* a revenue defaulter.

बंबा *bambā* [Pt. *pompa*], m. **1.** a pump. **2.** reg. (W.) a water-channel.

बंबू *bambū* m. *Pl. HŚS.* opium-pipe made of reed.

बँवर *baṁvar* [? conn. *bhramara-*[1]], m. reg. **1.** creeper, vine (cf. बौंड़). **2.** tendril.

बंस *baṃs* [ad. *vaṁśa-*], m. **1.** बंस-. bamboo. **2.** family line, family; offspring, descendants. — बंस-फोड़, m. bamboo-splitter: worker in bamboo, cane, or reed. बंस-रोचन, m. = next. बंस-लोचन, m. manna of bamboo (a colloidal concretion found in the stems of most bamboos, and used medicinally). बंस-वाड़ी, f. bamboo plantation, or thicket.

बंसरी *baṃsrī*, f. Brbh. = बाँसरी.

बंसा *baṃsā*, m. *Pl.* a kind of grass which grows in rice-fields.

1**बंसी** *baṃsī* [ad. *vaṁśī-*], f. flute, pipe.

2**बंसी** *baṃsī*, f. **1.** a fish-hook. **2.** a fishing-line, or rod.

ब- *ba-* [P.], prep. with, by; in; upon: — बआसानी, adv. easily. बख़ुद, adv. to oneself. बख़ुद आना, to come to one's senses. बख़ुशी, adv. with pleasure, gladly. बख़ूबी, adv. well, excellently; thoroughly, completely. बख़ैर, adv. safely (of an arrival, &c.); successfully; for a good purpose. बग़ैर [A. *gair*], ppn. usu. inverted w. के. without. बज़रिआ [A. *-zarī'a*], adv. U. by means (of: as by post, air). बजा, adv. in place: appropriate; right, true. बजा लाना, to perform, to carry out in full (an order, &c.); to obey, to observe (instructions, proprieties). बजा है, just so, precisely. बजाय [P. *-e-*], prep. & ppn. instead (of, के, की). बज़ोर, adv. by force. बतारीख़, adv. U. on the day of (in citing dates). बतौर, ppn. usu. inverted. U. by way (of, के), as; in the manner (of), like. बदर, adv. out of doors, outside. बदर करना, to put out, to eject; to banish. बदस्तूर, adv. according to custom, or practice; as usual, as before. बदिक़्क़त, adv. U. with trouble or difficulty. बदिल, adv. heartily, cordially. बदिलो जान, adv. U. with heart and soul. बदौलत, adv. by the good fortune, or favour (of, की); thanks (to). बनाम, adv. in the name (of) (U.); addressed (to); versus, against. बनिस्बत, ppn. in respect (of, के); in comparison (with). बमुक़ाबला, ppn. being set before: compared with; against, opposed to. बमूजिब, ppn. (w. or without के) U. because of; in accordance with, as per. बराय [P. *barā'e*], prep. & ppn. for, for the sake (of, के). बराय ख़ुदा, interj. for God's sake. बराय नाम, adv. nominally, ostensibly. बवक़्त, adv. U. in the time (of), at the time (of). बशर्ते [A. *śarṭ*], conj. on condition (that, कि), provided (that). बसबब, adv. by reason (of), on account (of). बसर, adv. to a head, to an end. बसर करना, to accomplish (a task); to spend (time). बसरो-चश्म, adv. with head and eyes: most gladly; most carefully. बसूरत, adv. U. in the form, or capacity (of); by way of (gratitude, &c). बहर हाल, adv. at all events, in any case; by all means. बहाल [A. -*ḥāl*], adj. in the usual state, as previously; in good state or health (a person); established (a law, &c.); restored, reinstated (to health, or in office). बहाल करना, to establish (as a law); to reinstate (in, पर), to restore (to); to re-establish. बहाल रखना, to maintain in the previous state, to uphold. बहाल रहना, to remain unaltered, unimpaired, intact. °ई, f. being, or remaining, in an unchanged state; good state, prosperity; being in office or favour; establishment (of a law); restoration (as to health); reinstatement. बहुक्म, prep. by order, or authority (of, के). दिन बदिन, adv. day by day.

1**बक** *bak* [ad. (or conn.) *baka-*], m. heron. — बक-चाल, f. heron's walk: strut. बक-ध्यान, m. semblance of meditation: बकध्यान लगाना, to await (the moment to strike). बकासुर [°*ka+a*°], m. *mythol.* name of a demon who took the form of a crane or heron, and was killed by Kṛṣṇa.

2**बक** *bak* [cf. H. *baknā*], f. chatter; nonsense. — ~ लगना, to be talkative or garrulous. – बक-झक, f. = ~. बक-झक करना, to chatter, to talk nonsense. बक-बक, f. id. बकलगनी, f. reg. talkativeness; raving. बकवाद, f. idle talk. °ई, adj. & m. garrulous, chattering; idle talker.

बकटा *bakṭā*, adj. reg. astringent (= कसैला).

बकतर *baktar* [P. *baktar*], m. coat of mail, armour. — बकतरपोश [P. *-poś*], adj. mail-clad. बकतरबंद [P. *-band*], adj. id.; armoured (a vehicle).

बकना *baknā* [**bakk-*; Pk. *bakk-*], v.i. **1.** to chatter, to babble; to talk nonsense; to rave. **2.** to blurt out words incoherently (a statement, a confession).

बकबकाना *bakbakānā*, v.i. reg. to chatter, &c. (= बकना).

बकर-बकर *bakar-bakar* [? cf. H. *bakrā*], adv. blankly (of look).

बक़र *baqr* [A.], m. f. U. **1.** m. ox, bull. **2.** f. cow. — बक़र-ईद, f. a Muslim festival commemorating Abraham's readiness to sacrifice his son.

बकरा *bakrā* [*barkaraka-*], m. billy-goat. — बकरे की माँ कब तक ख़ैर मनाएगी? how long will the nanny-goat entreat for her kid?: (fated) evil must happen; evil will out.

बकरी *bakrī* [cf. H. *bakrī*], f. **1.** a nanny-goat; a goat. **2.** colloq. an avid eater: glutton. **3.** iron. an idler. **4.** a simpleton.

बकल *bakal*, m. = बक्कल.

बकलस *baklas* [f. Engl. *buckle*; cf. H. *baksuā*], m. **1.** a buckle. **2.** tongue of a buckle. — ~ लगाना, to do up a buckle.

बकला *baklā* [*valkala-*], m. = बक्कल.

बक़ला *baqlā* [A. *baqla*], m. reg. a kind of bean.

बकल्लम ख़ुद *bakallam khud*, adv. corr. in (one's) own words (see कलाम).

बकवाना *bakvānā* [cf. H. *baknā*], v.t. to cause to chatter, &c.

बकवास *bakvās* [cf. H. *bakvānā*], f. **1.** chatter, idle talk. **2.** talkativeness.

बकवासिन *bakvāsin* [cf. H. *bakvās*], f. garrulous woman.

बकवासी *bakvāsī* [cf. H. *bakvās*], m. chatterer, garrulous person.

बकवाहा *bakvāhā* [cf. H. [2]*bak*], m. colloq. a great talker.

बकस *baks* [Engl. *box*], m. box. — बकसवाला, m. itinerant salesman, box-wallah.

बकसा *baksā*, m. reg. astringent (= कसैला).

बकसाहट *baksāhaṭ*, f. reg. astringency.

बकसुआ *baksuā* [f. Engl. *buckle*: ? × H. *sūī*], m. **1.** a buckle. **2.** tongue of a buckle.

बक़ा *baqā* [A. *baqā*], f. continued existence, immortality; eternity.

बकायन *bakāyan*, m. the Persian lilac, *Melia azedarach* (a tree of which the fruit-stones are used in making beads).

बक़ाया *baqāyā* [A. *baqāyā*, pl.], m. & adj. inv. **1.** m. remainder, balance; arrears, dues. **2.** adj. remaining; outstanding, due (a sum).

बकार *bakār*, m. *hist.* value of a crop fixed by an appraiser by word of mouth.

बकारना *bakārnā*, v.t. *Pl. HŚS.* to answer.

बकुचा *bakucā* [cf. H. *buqcā*], m. a bundle; a washerman's bundle of clothes.

[1]**बकुची** *bakucī* [cf. H. *buqcī*], f. small bundle (= बुक़ची). — ~ बाँधना, to make up a small bundle.

[2]**बकुची** *bakucī*, f. *Pl. HŚS.* the plant *Vernonia anthelmitica* or *parvat jīrā* (the seeds of which are used medicinally as a substitute for black caraway, *kālī jīrī*).

बकुल *bakul* [ad. *vakula-*], m. the tree *Mimusops elengi* (= मौलसिरी).

बकुला *bakulā* [cf. *baka-*], m. = बगला.

बकेन *baken* [*baṣkayinī-*], f. reg. a cow or buffalo that is still giving milk (long after calving).

बकेल *bakel*, m. *Pl. HŚS.* twine made from the root of the *ḍhāk* tree.

बकैनी *bakainī* [cf. *baṣkayinī-*], f. reg. = बकेन.

बकोटना *bakoṭnā* [conn. H. *bukṭā*], v.t. **1.** to claw, to scratch. **2.** to tear (sthg.) out or away. **3.** colloq. to extort.

बकोटा *bakoṭā* [cf. H. *bakoṭnā*], m. a scratch, mark of claws or nails.

बकोली *bakolī*, f. reg. (W.) a green caterpillar, harmful to rice crops.

बक़्क़म *buqqam* [A. *baqqām*], m. the sappan-wood tree, *Caesalpinia sappan* (source of a red dye).

बक्कल *bakkal* [*valkala-*], m. **1.** bark; rind; skin. **2.** inner rind, bast.

बक़्क़ाल *baqqāl* [A. *baqqāl*], m. a grain-dealer; shopkeeper.

बक्की *bakkī* [cf. H. *baknā*], adj. & m. **1.** adj. garrulous. **2.** m. garrulous person, chatterer.

[1]**बक्खर** *bakkhar* [? **vyāskara-*: Pk. *vakkhala-*], m. house, &c. (= [1]बाखर).

[2]**बक्खर** *bakkhar*, m. reg. **1.** syrup. **2.** oil-seed. **3.** ferment; yeast.

बक्री *bakrī* [ad. *vakra-*], adj. *astron.* retrogressing (a planet, in its apparent orbit).

बक्स *baks*, m. = बकस.

बक्सा *baksa* [cf. H. *baks*], m. box; case; trunk.

बखर *bakhar*, m. reg. a kind of plough having a wide share (cf. [4]बाखर).

बख़रा *bakhrā* [P. *bakhra*], m. share (as in a village).

बखरिया *bakhriyā* [cf. H. [1]*bakkhar*], m. reg. householder.

बखरी *bakhrī* [cf. H. [1]*bakkhar*; and *vakṣaskāra-*, f. reg. **1.** house, cottage. **2.** grain-store (raised on piles).

बख़री *bakhrī* [cf. H. *bakhrā*], m. reg. shareholder.

बख़रैत *bakhrait* [cf. H. *bakhrā*], m. reg. a shareholder.

बखान *bakhān* [*vyākhyāna-*], m. **1.** exposition; description; account. **2.** comment, interpretation. **3.** praise. — ~ करना (का), to expound, &c.

बखानना *bakhānnā* [cf. H. *bakhān*], v.t. **1.** to expound, &c. **2.** to praise. **3.** iron. to vilify. — सात पुरखा ~ (के), to vilify (another's) ancestors to the seventh generation.

बखानी *bakhānī* [cf. H. *bakhān*], f. reg. = बखान.

बखार *bakhār* [*vakṣaskāra-*, Pk. *vakkhāra-*], m. storehouse, granary.

बखारी *bakhārī*, f. = बखार.

बख़िया *bakhiyā* [P. *bakhya*], m. **1.** stitching, back-stitch; basting; quilting. **2.** sl. money; strength, ability, reach. — ~ करना, to stitch, &c. ~ उधेड़ना, fig. to reveal a secret. बख़िए उखेड़ना, id. कुछ घर में ~ भी है? iron. I don't suppose you have any money in the house?

बख़ियाना *bakhiyānā* [cf. H. *bakhiyā*], v.t. to stitch, &c.

बखेड़ा *bakheṛā* [cf. *vyākṣepa-*], m. **1.** entanglement, difficulty, trouble; care, worry. **2.** obstacle, impediment. **3.** fig. possessions, furniture; lumber; rubbish. **4.** wrangle; quarrel. **5.** clever dodge, trick. — ~ करना, or खड़ा करना, or मचाना, to make difficulties (in a matter, में); to cause a wrangle, &c. ~ चुकाना, to finish a troublesome business; to settle a dispute.

बखेड़िया *bakheṛiyā* [cf. H. *bakheṛā*], adj. & m. **1.** adj. quarrelsome, trouble-making. **2.** m. quarrelsome person, trouble-maker.

बखेर *bakher* [cf. H. *bakhernā*], f. **1.** scattering (cf. बिखेरना). **2.** sthg. scattered; anything dropped.

बखेरना *bakhernā*, v.t. = बिखेरना.

बख़्त *bakht* [P. *bakht*], m. portion, lot; fate; good luck. — बख़्तों-जला, adj. unlucky.

बख़्तर *bakhtar*, m. corr. = बकतर.

-बख़्श *-bakhś* [P. *bakhś*], adj. giving (e.g. समरबख़्श, adj. 'fruit-giving').

बख़्शना *bakhśnā* [cf. H. *bakhś*], v.t. **1.** to bestow. **2.** to forgive. — जान बख़्शो! save my life (and go away)!

बख़्शवाना *bakhśvānā* [cf. H. *bakhśānā*], v.t. to cause to be forgiven (by, से); to obtain forgiveness (for oneself).

बख़्शाना *bakhśānā* [cf. H. *bakhśnā*], v.t. **1.** to cause to give. 2. = बख़्शवाना.

बख़्शिश *bakhśiś* [P. *bakhśis*], f. **1.** a gift. **2.** gratuity, tip. **3.** liberality. **4.** forgiveness.

बख़्शी *bakhśī*, m. paymaster (in Muslim armies).

बग *bag* [*baka-*], m. Av. **1.** heron. **2.** ? crane (= सारस). — बग-पाँति, f. a line, or flight of herons. बग-हंस, m. the grey goose; heron-goose: flamingo.

बग- *bag-* [*vrajati*: MIA anal. **vagga-*], v.i. Brbh. **1.** to move, to go. **2.** reg. to be in use (a road).

बगछुट *bagchuṭ* [H. *bāg*+H. *chūṭnā*], adv. with loose rein: at full gallop.

बगटुट *bagṭuṭ* [H. *bāg*+H. *ṭūṭnā*], adv. with broken rein: at full gallop.

[1]**बगड़** *bagaṛ* [**baggaḍa-*], m. *Pl.* **1.** rice roughly husked. **2.** rice or sesame seed.

[2]**बगड़** *bagaṛ*, m. reg. (Raj). = बगर.

[1]**बगड़ा** *bagṛā*, m. *Pl.* = [1]बगड़.

[2]**बगड़ा** *bagṛā*, m. *Pl.* evasion, cheating.

बगद- *bagad-*, v.i. Brbh. **1.** v.i. to return.

बगदा- *bagdā-*, v.t. E.H. **2.** v.t. to corrupt, to ruin.

बग़बग़ाना *bagbagānā*, v.i. to bray.

बग-मेल *bag-mel* [H. *bāg*+H. *melnā*], adv. Brbh. Av. with united rein: (charging or moving off) all together.

बगर *bagar*, m. reg. (W.) **1.** a house. **2.** enclosure for cattle (cf. [2]बागर, and [2]बगड़).

बगरना *bagarnā*, v.i. reg. to spread, to scatter.

बगराना *bagrānā*, v.t. reg. to be spread, to be scattered.

बगरेंडी *bagreṁḍī*, f. *Pl.* the physic nut, *Jatropha curcas* (an evergreen shrub, the source of an oil used medicinally: = *bag-bhereṇḍā*).

बग़ल *bagl* [P. *bagal*], f. m. & adv. **1.** f. m. side (of the body); flank; side (of an object, a place). **2.** armpit. **3.** gusset under the arm of a garment. **4.** adv. at one side; at the next counter. **5.** to one side, out of the way. — ~ का, adj. at one side; adjoining, nearby; side-on, profile (as a portrait); kept close, concealed. ~ की गोलाबारी, f. *mil.* flanking or enfilade fire. ~ गरम करना, fig. to sleep (with). ~ में, adv. = ~, 4., 5. ~ में ईमान दबाना, to put faith or conscience aside, to act faithlessly. ~ में गरदन झुकाना, to hang the head in shame. ~ में दबाना, or मारना, to conceal (sthg.) under the arm; to make away with (sthg.; fig. to silence (conscience). ~ में मुँह डालना, = ~ में गरदन झुकाना. ~ में लेना, to embrace. ~ में सिर नीचा करना, id. ~ सूँघना, to smell the armpit: colloq. = ~ में मुँह डालना. ~ हो जाना, to move out of the way. बग़लें झाँकना, to avert the eyes (in shame or embarrassment); to desire to slink or to slip away. ~, or बग़लें, बजाना, to make a sound by squeezing air with the arm from the hand held under the armpit; fig. to jump for joy. — बग़लगीर [P. *-gīr*], adj. clasping, embracing; sitting or standing very close (to).

बग़लगीर होना, to be embraced (by, से). °ई, f. a hug, embrace. बग़लबंदी [P. *-bandī*], f. a type of men's jacket.

बगला *baglā* [cf. *baka-*], m. **1.** heron. **2.** ? crane. — बगला-भगत, m. false devotee, hypocrite (one whose behaviour suggests that of the heron, which stands motionless, as if performing devotions, until its prey comes within reach).

बग़लाना *baglānā*, [cf. H. *bagl*], v.i. to move out of the way.

बग़लियाना *bagliyānā*, v.t. colloq. to shift (sthg.) out of the way.

बग़ली *baglī* [P. *baglī*], adj. & f. **1.** adj. at the side; side, lateral. **2.** f. a small bag (as carried at the side: by tailors, &c). **3.** hole made in a house wall (beside the door) by thieves. **4.** a trick in wrestling. — ~ घूँसा, m. a side-blow: a treacherous blow; a secret enemy. ~ देना, or काटना, to make a hole in a house wall to gain entry.

बगान *bagān*, m. pronun. var. = बगान.

बगार *bagār* [*vargacāra-], m. reg. (W.) **1.** pasture-ground. **2.** waste land.

बगार- *bagār-*, v.t. Brbh. to spread out; to deploy (skill).

बगारना *bagārnā*, v.t. = बघारना.

बग़ावत *bagāvat* [A. *bagāva*: P. *bagāvat*], f. **1.** revolt; rebellion. **2.** violence, lawbreaking. — ~ करना, to revolt, &c. (against, से).

बग़िया *bagiyā* [cf. H. *bāg*], f. a small garden.

बग़ीचा *bagīcā* [P. *bāgīca*], m. = बाग़ीचा.

बगुला *bagulā*, m. = बगला.

बगूला *bagūlā*, m. whirlwind.

बगेरी *bagerī*, f. a kind of yellowhammer, or other finch (= बरगेल).

बगेलना *bagelnā*, v.i. reg. to push, to shove (= ढकेलना).

बग़ैर *ba-gair*, ppn., usu. inverted. see s.v. ब-.

बग्गी *baggī*, f. = [1]बग्घी.

[1]**बग्घी** *bagghī* [Engl. *buggy*], f. buggy, trap.

[2]**बग्घी** *bagghī*, f. reg. a horsefly; a kind of gnat.

बघछाला *bagh-chālā* [cf. H. *bāgh*], m. tiger-skin.

बघनखा *bagh-nakhā* [cf. H. *bāgh*], m. **1.** a claw (weapon) resembling a tiger's claw. **2.** a necklace containing tigers' claws.

बघनहाँ *bagh-nahāṁ*, m. E.H. 1. = बघनखा, 2. **2.** *Pl.* name of a medicinal herb with a fragrant root; a kind of perfume.

बघार *baghār* [*vyāghāra-: anal. MIA *-ggh-*], m. seasoning (see बघारना).

बघारना *baghārnā* [*vyāghārayati*: anal. MIA *-ggh-*], v.t. **1.** to brown onions and spices in heated oil or *ghī*; to season. **2.** fig. to display (knowledge) in an elaborate way. बात ~, to speak elaborately. शेख़ी ~, to behave arrogantly.

बघेरा *bagherā* [*vyāghratara-], m. **1.** tiger cub. **2.** leopard. **3.** hyena.

बघेल *baghel* [*vyāghratara-], m. 1. = बघेरा. **2.** name of a Rājpūt community.

बच *bac* [ad. *vaca-*], f. sweet-flag, *Acorus calamus*, a semi-aquatic herb having medicinal properties, and used as a flavouring.

बचकाना *backānā* [P. *baccagāna*], adj. & m. **1.** adj. children's, juvenile (in size, style: as shoes). **2.** immature, child's (mind, nature). **3.** reg. m. a dancing-boy.

बचकानी *backānī* [cf. H. *backānā*], f. dimin. reg. a little girl.

बचत *bacat* [cf. H. *bacnā*], f. **1.** saving (as of time, effort; or of money); economy. **2.** amount saved, savings; gain, profit. **3.** remainder; surplus. **4.** state of safety; escape (from a predicament).

बचन *bacan*, m. = वचन.

बचना *bacnā* [*vacyate*], v.i. **1.** to be saved, to be safe; to escape (from, से); to survive; to be spared (by fate, illness); to recover. **2.** to be left over; to be saved (as money, food). **3.** to turn away (from); to avoid (as error, vice); to avoid (as an unwanted visitor); to keep clear (of: as of vehicles). — बचके रहना, to avoid, to keep clear (of, से). बचो! look out! वह मरते मरते बचा, he very nearly died. – बचा-खुचा, adj. left over, &c.

बचनाग *bacnāg* [f. *vatsanābha-*], m. the poisonous aconite *Aconitum spicatum*; the root of this plant.

बचपन *bacpan* [cf. H. *baccā*], m. **1.** childhood. **2.** childishness.

बचपना *bacpanā* [cf. H. *baccā*], m. = बचपन.

बचा *bacā*, m. reg. = बच्चा.

बचाना *bacānā* [cf. H. *bacnā*], v.t. **1.** to save, to preserve (from, से); to rescue; to set free. **2.** to keep safe (from); to guard; to defend. **3.** to save up, not to use (as money, food). **4.** to hold back (a part of anything, fraudulently). **5.** to avoid, to keep (oneself) clear (of, से); to shun (a vice, &c). **6.** to avert (the eyes: from, से).

बचाव *bacāv* [cf. H. *bacănā*], m. **1.** preservation, safety; escape (as from an accident). **2.** protection; defence. **3.** holding oneself back: reserve, reservation. **4.** evasion. **5.** defence (as in law). **6.** saving (as of money). — ~ करना, to save, to protect, &c.; to save or to guard oneself (from, से, में); to be reserved (by temperament). ~ में रहना, to live in safety, to find refuge. – बच-बचाव, m. keeping safe, &c.

बच्चल *baccal*, adj. Brbh. Av. = वत्सल.

बच्चा *baccā* [P. *bacca*], m. **1.** a child; a boy; infant. **2.** young (of any creature). **3.** usu. pej. a simple, thoughtless or inexperienced person; lad, fellow, son. **4.** pej. one who takes after his father. — ~ देना, to give birth. बच्चों का खेल, m. child's play. बच्चों का-सा, adj. child-like; childish. गोद का ~, m. a child at the breast, a baby. सूअर का ~, m. pej. a contemptible wretch. अरे डामू के बच्चे! hey there, you Ḍāmū! – बच्चाकश [P. *-kaś*], adj. f. prolific (in reproduction). बच्चे-कच्चे, m. pl. colloq. children, little ones. बच्चेदानी [P. *-dān-*], f. womb. – बच-कच, m. pl. colloq. = बच्चे-कच्चे.

बच्ची *baccī* [cf. H. *baccā*], f. child, girl; baby girl.

बछ *bach* [ad. *vatsa-*[1]; or H. *bachṛā*], m. Brbh. a calf (= बछड़ा).

बछड़ा *bachṛā* [cf. *vatsa-*[1]], m. **1.** calf. **2.** child, boy (a term of endearment). **3.** pej. fool.

बछरू *bachrū*, m. Brbh. = बछड़ा.

बछा *bachā*, m. reg. = बछड़ा.

बछिया *bachiyā* [cf. H. *bach(ṛā)*], f. **1.** a calf (female). **2.** colloq. girl, child (term of endearment). — ~, or पँड़िया, का ताऊ, calf's uncle: a dolt, idiot.

बछेड़ा *bacheṛā* [cf. *vatsatara-*], m. **1.** foal, colt. **2.** calf.

बछेड़ी *bacheṛī* [cf. *vatsatara-*], f. **1.** foal, filly. **2.** female calf.

बजंत्री *bajantrī* [cf. H. *bājā*; ad. *yantra-*], m. a musician.

बजना *bajnā* [cf. H. *bajānā*], v.t. to sound, to resound: **1.** to be played (a musical instrument). **2.** to be struck (a bell, gong, &c); to be clapped (the hands). **3.** to strike (a clock). **4.** to be fired, to go off (a gun, &c). **5.** to chatter (the teeth). **6.** to be wielded violently (as swords, staves; or shoes: against, पर). **7.** fig. to be known (as), to go under the name (of). – बजा, adj. struck; o'clock. एक बजा, m. one o'clock. एक बजा है, one o'clock has struck. एक बजे adv. at one o'clock.

बजनिया *bajaniyā* [cf. H. *bajānā*], m. Av. musician.

बजनी *bajnī* [cf. H. *bajnā*], f. reg. sounding, resounding: **1.** sound of bells. **2.** an uproar.

बजबजाना *bajbajānā*, v.i. reg. to swarm, to seethe; to ferment.

बजम *bajam*, adj. *Pl.* still, quiet; lying still.

बजमार्यो *bajmāryo* [ad. *vajra-*; H. *mārnā*], adj. Brbh. struck by lightning: wretched.

बजर *bajr* [ad. *vajra-*], adj. & m. **1.** adj. hard, dense. **2.** massive. **3.** heavy, slow. **4.** severe, difficult. **5.** m. *mythol.* (= वज्र) thunderbolt (the weapon of Indra). **6.** lightning. **7.** diamond. — ~ पड़े! a curse (upon, पर)! – बजरंग, adj. strong of frame; title of Hanumān. °ई, id. बजर-खपटा, m. hard-scaled: the pangolin. बजर-कीट, m. the hard reptile: id. बजर-बट्टू, m. the broad-leafed palm *Corypha umbraculifera*, and its black seeds (of which necklaces are said to avert the evil eye).

[1]**बजरा** *bajrā* [? cf. H. *bajr*], m. **1.** a keelless, round-bottomed passenger boat (used for river travel). **2.** a barge.

[2]**बजरा** *bajrā*, m. reg. (W.) millet (= बाजरा).

बज़रिआ *ba-zariā*, adv. see s.v. ब-.

[1]**बजरी** *bajrī* [cf. H. *bajr*], f. **1.** gravel. **2.** a small hailstone.

[2]**बजरी** *bajrī*, f. reg. (W.) small (reddish-grained) millet.

बजवाई *bajvāī* [cf. H. *bajvānā*], f. fee or charge for playing music.

बजवाना *bajvānā* [cf. H. *bajānā*], v.t. to cause to be sounded, played, or struck, &c. (by, से).

बजाक *bajāk* [? f. *vakrāṅga-*], m. *Pl.* a kind of snake.

बज़ाज़ *bazāz* [A. *bazzāz*], m. cloth-merchant, draper.

बज़ाज़ा *bazāzā* [A. *bazāza*], m. cloth-market.

बज़ाज़ी *bazāzī* [A. *bazzāz*+P. *-ī*], f. **1.** cloth-merchant's or draper's business, or occupation. **2.** drapery, haberdashery.

[1]**बजाना** *bajānā* [cf. H. *bājnā*], v.t. to cause to sound: **1.** to play (an instrument, a recording). **2.** to strike (a bell, gong); to beat (a drum); to clap (the hands). **3.** colloq. to shoot off, to fire (a gun, &c). **4.** trans. to test by its ring (a coin). **5.** to wield violently (swords, staves; or shoes). — बजाकर, adv. resoundingly: openly, publicly. ताली, or तालियाँ, ~, to clap the hands.

[2]बजाना *bajānā* [cf. H. *bajā*], v.t. = बजा लाना, see s.v. ब-.

बजाय *ba-jāy*, prep. & ppn. see s.v. ब-.

बजुल्ला *bajullā* [cf. H. *bāzū*], m. *Pl. HŚS.* a woman's armlet (worn on the upper arm).

बज़ोर *ba-zor*, adv. see s.v. ब-.

बज्जा *bajjā*, m. *Pl.* cutting open, lancing; piercing.

बज़्म *bazm* [P. *bazm*], f. U. assembly, company; banquet.

बझना *bajhnā* [cf. H. *bajhā-*], v.i. reg. **1.** to be entangled, ensnared. **2.** to be stuck, or mired.

बझवट *bajhvaṭ* [cf. H. *bāṁjh*], f. reg. (E.) stalk (of corn) without ear.

बझा *bajhā*, m. reg. (W.) marshy soil.

बझा- *bajhā-* [cf. H. *bājh-*], v.t. Brbh. to entangle; to ensnare (as game).

[1]बट *baṭ* [? *varta-*[1]], m. **1.** turn, twist, fold, ply. **2.** wrinkle, fold (as of fat).

[2]बट *baṭ*, m. esp. in comp. a road (= [1]बाट). — बटपाड़, m. = next. बटमार, m. highwayman, robber. °ई, f. highway robbery.

[3]बट *baṭ* [S.], f. a banyan tree.

बट- *baṭ-*. a weight (= [2]बाट): — बटखरा, m. a weight used in weighing goods.

बटखरा *baṭkharā*, m. see s.v. बट-.

[1]बटना *baṭnā* [conn. *vartayati*], v.t. & v.i. **1.** v.t. to twist (= बाटना), to make (as a rope); to plait, to weave. **2.** v.i. [cf. *bāṭnā*] to be twisted, &c. **3.** reg. to be pounded, ground.

[2]बटना *baṭnā*, v.i. = बँटना. — बटा, adj. divided; divided by. दो बटे पाँच, or दो बटे पाँचवाँ हिस्सा, m. two-fifths. नौ बटे बीस, (ward) 9, (no.) 20 (address).

[3]बटना *baṭnā*, m. reg. = उबटन.

बटनिया *baṭaniyā* [cf. H. [2]*baṭnā*], m. *Pl.* a shareholder.

बटमोगरा *baṭmogrā*, m. *Pl.* the twining or climbing jasmine; *Jasminum zambac.*

बटरी *baṭrī* [*varta-*[2], Pk. *vaṭṭa-*], f. reg. a small cup.

बटलोई *baṭloī* [*vartaloha-*, Pa. *vaṭṭaloha-*], f. brass cooking-pot.

बटवाई *baṭvāī* [cf. H. *baṭvānā*], f. **1.** twisting (ropes, &c). **2.** price paid for twisting.

बटवाना *baṭvānā* [cf. H. [1]*baṭnā*], v.t. to cause to be twisted, &c. (by, से); to have (rope, fibre, &c.) twisted.

बटवार *baṭvār* [**vartmapāla-*], m. *hist.* customs or police officer stationed on a road to collect transit duties.

बटवारा *baṭvara*, m. = बँटवारा.

[1]बटाई *baṭāī* [cf. H. *baṁṭnā*], f. **1.** division; partition. **2.** share; share of produce. **3.** *hist.* apportionment in kind. **4.** tenure of land by the cultivator against payment of a portion of the crop (rather than rent) to the landlord. — बटाईदार [P. *-dār*], m. a cultivator who shares the crop with the landlord.

[2]बटाई *baṭāī*, f. = बटवाई.

बटाऊ *baṭāū* [cf. H. [1]*bāṭ*], m. Brbh. Av. wayfarer.

[1]बटाना *baṭānā* [cf. H. [1]*baṭnā*], v.t. to cause to be twisted (by, से).

[2]बटाना *baṭānā*, v.t. to cause to be divided (= बँटाना).

बटाव *baṭāv*, m. = बँटाव.

[1]बटिया *baṭiyā* [cf. H. [1]*bāṭ*], f. reg. narrow path or passage.

[2]बटिया *baṭiyā* [cf. H. [2]*bāṭ*], f. **1.** a small weight. **2.** a small stone (as for grinding, weighing). **3.** a lump (as of clay, stone); idol.

बटुरना *baṭurnā* [cf. *vartula-*], v.i. to be collected.

[1]बटुवा *baṭuvā* [cf. H. [2]*baṭnā*], m. a small bag or wallet with inner divisions (for holding money, betel, &c.) and a draw-string.

[2]बटुवा *baṭuvā* [cf. *varta-*[2]], m. reg. = बटलोई.

बटेंठ *baṭeṁṭh*, m. reg. a shareholder.

बटेर *baṭer* [**vartakara-*], m. a quail.

बटेरा *baṭerā*, m. = बटेर.

बटेस *baṭes*, m. reg. a path, way, passage.

बटैड़ी *baṭairī*, f. *Pl.* = बटैरी.

बटैत *baṭait* [cf. H. *baṁṭānā*], m. reg. one who distributes or allots.

[1]बटैया *baṭaiyā* [cf. H. [1]*baṭānā*], m. maker of braid, &c. of gold and silver thread twisted together with silk (*kalā-baṭṭū*).

[2]बटैया *baṭaiyā* [cf. H. *baṁṭānā*], m. reg. (Bihar) division (of crops, between tenant and landlord).

बटैरा *baṭairā* [**vartatara-*], m. reg. (W.) weights and scales.

बटैरी *baṭairī*, f. *hind. Pl.* marriage ceremony at which the bride presents the bridegroom with a wedding garment and some money.

बटोई *baṭoī*, m. = बटोही.

बटोर *baṭor* [cf. H. *baṭornā*], m. **1.** a gathering, crowd. **2.** a collection; pile (of refuse).

बटोरन *baṭoran* [cf. H. *baṭornā*], f. m. **1.** gathering, collecting. **2.** sthg. collected: gleanings; sweepings.

बटोरना *baṭornā* [cf. H. *baṭurnā*], v.t. **1.** to gather, to collect; to amass. **2.** to gather together, to draw in (as a loose garment). **3.** to concentrate (as the mind).

बटोही *baṭohī* [**vartmapathika-*], m. wayfarer, traveller.

[1]**बट्टा** *baṭṭā* [conn. *varta-*[1]], m. **1.** discount, rebate. **बट्टे पर**, adv. at a discount. **2.** deduction (of a sum); commission (as on exchange of currency); discount rate. **3.** an allowance; supplementary allowance (to a salary); commission (on sales). **4.** loss. **5.** fault, offence. **6.** stigma, slur. — ~ **आना**, a slur to fall or to be cast (upon, में). ~ **देना**, to pay a discount, &c.; to suffer, or to make up, a loss. ~ **लगना**, a discount to be chargeable (on, को, में); = ~ आना. ~ **लगाना**, to charge a discount (on, को, में); to cast a slur (on, में). ~ **लेना**, = ~ लगाना, 1. – **बट्टा-खाता**, m. ledger of losses, bad debts. **बट्टे-खाते डालना**, or **लिखना**, to write off as a loss, &c.

[2]**बट्टा** *baṭṭā* [**varta-*[3]], m. wooden or stone roller (for spices, &c). — **बट्टा-ढाल**, adj. & m. level, even; fig. state of being razed, complete destruction.

[3]**बट्टा** *baṭṭā* [**varta-*[2]: Pk. *vaṭṭa-*], m. **1.** round box or casket (for betel, or jewellery). **2.** jugglers's cup or box.

बट्टी *baṭṭī*, f. reg. = [2]बटिया.

[1]**बड़** *baṛ* [*vaṭa-*[1]], m. the banyan tree. — **बड़-कौला**, m. fruit of the banyan tree. **बड़-बट्टा**, id.

[2]**बड़** *baṛ*, adj. & f. **1.** adj. (in comp., or Av.) = बड़ा. **2.** f. boasting; crazy talk. — ~ **मारना**, or **हाँकना**, to boast. – **बड़कन्ना**, adj. long-eared. **बड़दंता**, adj. having large teeth. **बड़नक्का**, adj. having a big nose. **बड़पेटा**, adj. & m. pot-bellied; gluttonous; a pot-bellied man, &c. **बड़पेटू**, m. a glutton. **बड़बोला**, adj. & m. garrulous; boastful; a garrulous person, &c. **बड़भकुआ**, m. reg. talker of nonsense: a fool. **बड़भागी**, adj. & m. f. very fortunate; a very fortunate person. **बड़होंटा**, adj. thick-lipped.

बड़ँगा *baṛaṁgā*, m. *Pl. HŚS.* ridgepole (= बरंगा, बड़ेंरी).

बड़का *baṛkā* [cf. H. *baṛā*], adj. & m. reg. **1.** adj. large, &c. **2.** m. big, or bigger one; senior or elder (brother, son).

बड़प्पन *baṛappan* [cf. H. [1]*baṛā*], m. **1.** largeness. **2.** greatness, &c.

बड़बड़ *baṛbaṛ* [cf. H. *baṛbaṛānā*], f. **1.** muttering; grumbling; babbling. **2.** talking in sleep; raving (as in delirium).

बड़बड़ाना *baṛbaṛānā* [**baḍabaḍa-*: Pk. *baḍabaḍaï*], v.i. **1.** to mutter; to grumble; to babble (nonsensically). **2.** to talk in sleep; to rave (deliriously).

बड़बड़ाहट *baṛbaṛāhaṭ* [cf. H. *baṛbaṛānā*], f. **1.** muttering, &c. **2.** talking in sleep, &c. — ~ **करना**, to mutter, &c.

बड़बड़िया *baṛbaṛiyā* [cf. H. *baṛbaṛ*], m. mutterer, babbler, &c.

बड़वाग्नि *baṛăvâgni*, f. = बड़वानल.

बड़वानल *baṛăvânal* [ad. *vaḍavā-*], m. *mythol.* mare-fire: fire beneath the sea (imagined as personified, with the head of a mare).

बड़हल *baṛ'hal* [**vaḍraphala-*], m. the trees *Artocarpus lakoocha* (source of a yellow dye), or *Cordia latifolia*, and their fruit.

[1]**बड़ा** *baṛā* [*vadra-*, Pk. *vaḍḍa-*], adj. **1.** big, large; great. **2.** great (in prestige, standing); noble, eminent; important; wealthy. **बड़े लोग**, m. pl. noble, or influential people; the upper or educated classes. **3.** senior (in years); elder; adult. **4.** chief, principal (in rank or standing); senior; upper, high (as a court). **बड़े लोग**, m. pl. superiors. **5.** important (a matter, an occasion); grave, serious. **6.** adv. very, exceedingly; excessively. ~ **ख़ुश हूँ**, I'm very happy. — ~ **असामी**, m. great or high-ranking man; f. high position, post. ~ **आना**, to assume an unjustified status; ~ **आया (घर में रहनेवाला)**! he thinks he's a great man (now he has, or when he is in, his house)! ~ **करना**, to enlarge; to increase; to lengthen; to promote (in position). ~ **घर**, m. large, or grand house; great house or family; sl. a lavatory; a prison. ~ **दिन**, m. Christmas Day. ~ **नाम**, m. great reputation, fame. ~ **बोल**, m. big talk, boasting. ~ **रोग**, m. colloq. tuberculosis; an infectious disease of cattle. **बड़ी बहू**, f. elder son's wife; colloq. a wife older than her husband. **बड़ी बात**, f. an important matter; a difficult matter. **बड़ी बात हुई**, interj. thank heavens (that sthg. is finished or over)! **बड़ी माता**, f. euph. smallpox. **बड़े अक्षर**, m. pl. capital letters. **बड़े मियाँ**, m. master of the household; voc. (to a Muslim) honoured sir! **बड़े लाट**, m. *hist.* great lord: viceroy. **बड़ों में मिलना**, to be grown up; to associate with one's seniors, or with the great.

[2]**बड़ा** *baṛā* [*vaṭa-*[3]], m. lump of spiced, ground pulse fried in ghī, butter or oil.

बड़ाई *baṛāī* [cf. H. [1]*baṛā*], f. **1.** largeness; bulk, size; volume; extent. **2.** prestige, standing. **3.** seniority; rank. **4.** praise, commendation; self-praise, boasting. — ~ करना (की, or अपनी), to praise; to vaunt superiority, to boast. ~ जताना, = ~ करना; to boast of superiority (over, पर). ~ देना (को), to show respect or deference (to), to honour. ~ मारना, = ~ करना, 2. – बड़ाई-छुटाई, f. difference, distinction (as between numbers, quantities).

बड़ाड़ *baṛāṛ*, m. *Pl.* a drove of laden bullocks.

बड़ापन *baṛāpan* [cf. H. *baṛā*], m. = बड़प्पन.

बड़ापा *baṛāpā* [cf. H. *baṛā*], adj. = बड़प्पन.

बड़ी *baṛī* [*vaṭikā-*], f. small lumps of spiced pulse, fried and dried in the sun (used as seasoning).

बड़ेंरी *baṛeṁrī* [**vaḍradaṇḍa-*, **vaḍratara-*], f. reg. (Bihar) ridgepole (of a roof).

बड़ेर- *baṛer-* [**vaḍratara-*: Pk. *vaḍḍayara-*], adj. Brbh. large; senior; great (= बड़ा).

बड़्ड़ाना *baṛṛānā*, v.i. = बड़बड़ाना.

बढ़ई *baṛhaī* [*vardhaki-*], m. **1.** carpenter. **2.** the carpenter caste. **3.** colloq. woodpecker.

बढ़कर *baṛhkar* [cf. H. *baṛhnā*], adj. & adv. going beyond: **1.** adj. greater, more (than, से); better (than). **2.** adv. apart (from).

बढ़त *baṛhat* [cf. H. *baṛhnā*], f. **1.** increase (= बढ़ती). **2.** lead (as in a game).

बढ़ती *baṛhtī* [cf. H. *baṛhnā*], f. **1.** increase, growth. **2.** rise (as in prices, or wages). **3.** advancement, progress; prosperity. **4.** surplus, excess. — ~ पर, or से, adv. at an excessive price.

बढ़ना *baṛhnā* [*vardhate*], v.i. **1.** to increase; to grow larger; to be extended; to be prolonged (a period). **2.** to grow (living creatures, plants). **3.** to rise; to swell; to rise in price. **4.** to be quickened (gait, pace). **5.** to be advanced; to develop (as an activity). **6.** to be extended (as influence). **7.** to prosper, to flourish. **8.** to go forward or ahead; to be let loose or free (as a kite). **9.** to be stretched out (a hand, &c). **10.** to surpass, to go beyond (से). **11.** to be acquired, gained (in or from, में; to be put aside (funds). **12.** to be stopped (as a supply); to be checked. दूध बढ़ जाना, to be weaned. **13.** to be taken off (bangles, by a widow). **14.** to be closed (a shop, a stall). **15.** to be extinguished (a lamp). — बढ़ चलना, to rise, to make progress; to become arrogant; to behave pretentiously. बढ़ बढ़कर बोलना, or बातें करना, to speak insolently, or boastfully. – बढ़कर बोलना, to raise one's bid (in an auction). बढ़ा-चढ़ा, adj. advanced, developed (an activity). बढ़ा-चढ़ी, f. excess, impropriety; rivalry.

[1]**बढ़नी** *baṛhnī* [cf. H. *baṛhnā*], f. reg. 1. = बढ़ती. **2.** *hist.* an advance of money on a contract for goods or grain.

[2]**बढ़नी** *baṛhnī* [*vardhanī-*, Pk. *vaḍḍhaṇī-*], f. a broom made of reeds.

बढ़वार *baṛhvār*, m. increase, advance, &c. (= बढ़ाव).

बढ़ाई *baṛhāī* [cf. H. *baṛhnā, baṛhānā*], f. increasing, increase, &c. (= बढ़ाव).

बढ़ाना *baṛhānā* [*vardhāpayati*[2]], v.t. **1.** to increase; to enlarge; to extend (in area or scope); to prolong (a period). **2.** to draw out (as wire); to beat out (metal). **3.** to advance, to promote; to develop (an activity); to sell (sthg.) cheaply. **4.** to magnify; to exaggerate. बात ~, to cause a matter to assume large proportions. बढ़ा-चढ़ाकर प्रशंसा करना, to praise extravagantly. **5.** to incite, to egg on. बढ़ा-चढ़ाकर लड़ा देना, to incite to fight (with, से, के साथ). **6.** to move forward. आगे ~, to urge (a horse, &c). क़दम ~, to go forward (a person). **7.** to allow to go forward; to set under way (a procession); to let fly free (a kite). **8.** to close (a shop, stall). **9.** to stop (as a supply); to check. दूध ~, to wean. **10.** to take off (bangles: a widow). **11.** to postpone, to delay. **12.** to extinguish (a lamp). — बढ़ा लाना, to bring forward, to lead on (an army, &c). – बढ़ाया-चढ़ाया, adj. exaggerated, inflated.

बढ़ार *baṛhār*, m. *hind.* marriage feast.

बढ़ाव *baṛhav* [cf. H. *baṛhnā, baṛhānā*], m. **1.** increase; enlargement; extension; prolongation. **2.** rise (of water). **3.** advance, development (as of an activity). **4.** advance, movement forward. **5.** excess.

बढ़ावन *baṛhāvan* [cf. H. *baṛhānā*], m. reg. a cake of cow-dung placed on a pile of grain to avert the evil eye or to discourage thieves.

बढ़ावा *baṛhāvā* [cf. H. *baṛhānā*], v.t. inducement to move forward: **1.** encouragement. **2.** stimulus, incentive. **3.** incitement. **4.** flattery. — ~ देना (को), to encourage, &c. बढ़ावे में आना, to be taken in by the encouragement, &c. (of a designing person: के).

बढ़ियल *baṛhiyal*, adj. colloq. = [1]बढ़िया.

[1]**बढ़िया** *baṛhiyā* [*vardhita-*], adj. inv. **1.** excellent, good (of quality), fine; nice. **2.** fertile (soil). **3.** high-priced.

[2]**बढ़िया** *baṛhiyā* [? = H. [1]*baṛhiyā*], m. reg. a kind of stone (obtained at Chunar).

[3]**बढ़िया** *baṛhiyā* [cf. H. *baṛhnā*], m. reg. (W.) a disease of cereal crops, sugar-cane, &c. which prevents the head from shooting.

बढ़ी *baṛhī* [cf. H. *baṛhnā*], f. reg. = बढ़ोतरी, 4.

बढ़ैया *baṛhaiyā*, m. Brbh. = बढ़ई.

बढ़ोतरी *baṛhotrī* [cf. H. *baṛhnā*; *uttara-*], f. **1.** increase; growth; increment. **2.** rise, advance; progress. **3.** gain, profit (as in trade). **4.** surplus. **5.** rise, or raising, of prices.

बणज *baṇaj*, m. = बनिज.

बत- *bat-* [cf. H. *bāt*]. = बात: — बत-उँगली, f. reg. see s.v. बत-कहा, adj. garrulous; a garrulous person. बत-कही, f. conversation, dialogue. बत-चल, adj. Brbh. talkative. बत-बना, m. a great talker; concocter of stories, romancer. बत-बढ़ाव, m. talkativeness; wrangling. बत-बाती, f. reg. claptrap, nonsense; conversation, discussion. बत-रस, m. Brbh. pleasure from conversation, delightful conversation.

बतक *batak* [cf. P. *baṯṯakh*], m. = बतख़.

बतक्कड़ *batakkaṛ* [cf. H. *bāt*], adj. & m. **1.** adj. garrulous. **2.** m. a great talker.

बतख़ *batakh* [P. *baṯṯakh*], f. a duck.

बतरा- *batrā-*, v.t. Brbh. = बतलाना.

बतलाना *batlānā* [cf. H. [1]*batānā*], v.t. = बताना.

[1]**बताना** *batānā* [cf. H. *bāt*], v.t. **1.** to inform; to state, to tell; to relate (to को); to describe. **2.** to point out, to explain; to show (as a road); to indicate by gestures. **3.** to indicate (as facts a conclusion). **4.** colloq. to teach (one) a lesson, to punish. — बहाना ~, to give a (lame) excuse.

[2]**बताना** *batānā* [?? conn. *varta-*[2]] m. *Pl. HŚS.* **1.** a metal bracelet or ring. **2.** an under-turban.

बतारीख़ *ba-tārīkh*, adv. see s.v. ब-.

बतावी *batāvī* [cf. Du. *Batavia*: ← L. *Batavus*], adj. *Pl.* Javanese. — ~ नीबू, m. shaddock (a citrus fruit: = चकोतरा).

बताशा *batāśā*, m. = बतासा.

बतास *batās* [**vātatrāsa-*], m. **1.** strong wind. **2.** flatulence. **3.** gout. — बतास-फेनी, f. = बतासा.

बतासा *batāsā* [cf. H. *batās*], m. **1.** a light, hollow sugar-cake. **2.** a kind of firework (a small *anār*). **3.** a bubble. — बतासा-सा घुलना, to melt away (sthg. insubstantial); to fade away. दूध-बतासा राजा खाए, the king eats the sugar-cake: refrain in a children's game resembling king of the castle.

बतिया *batiyā*, f. & adj. **1.** f. a variety of egg-plant. **2.** green or unripe fruit or vegetable(s). **3.** adj. unripe, green. **4.** soft, tender.

बतियाना *batiyānā* [cf. H. *bāt*], v.t. colloq. to talk, to converse.

बत-उँगली *bat-uṁglī* [cf. H. *bāt*], f. reg. the pointing finger, forefinger (= तर्जनी).

बतूरी *batūrī*, f. reg. (E.) a small variety of chick-pea (*canā*).

बतोला *batolā* [*vr̥tta-*; H. *bāt*], m. talking (one) into (sthg.); cajoling; duping. — बतोले में आना, to be hoodwinked (by, के).

बतोलिया *batoliyā*, adj. garrulous, loquacious; deceitful.

बतोली *batolī*, f. reg. empty or frivolous talk.

बतौर *ba-taur*, ppn., usu. inverted. see s.v. ब-.

बतौरी *batauri* [ad. *vāta-*], f. reg. **1.** a swelling caused by wind or liquids. ***2.** a tumour. **3.** a boil.

बत्तक *battak* [cf. P. *baṯṯakh*], f. = बतख़.

बत्तख़ *battakh* [P. *baṯṯakh*], m. = बतख़.

बत्ती *battī* [*vartikā-*], f. **1.** wick; fuse. **2.** light, candle; match; taper. **3.** lamp; light (on a vehicle). लाल ~, f. a red light (to stop). **4.** bundle (of thatching, &c.); faggot. **5.** stick (of sealing-wax). **6.** lint. **7.** twisted folds (of a turban, &c.) — ~ चढ़ाना to set a candle (in a candlestick); to turn up a wick. ~ दिखाना, to show a light; to put a match (to, को). ~ बढ़ाना, to put out a light.

बत्तीस *battīs* [*dvātriṁśat-*], adj. thirty-two.

बत्तीसी *battīsī* [cf. H. *battīs*], f. **1.** a collection of thirty-two things (as tales, fables). **2.** colloq. the teeth. — ~ दिखाना, to show the teeth, to grin (at one, को); to laugh. ~ बजना, the teeth to chatter (from cold).

बथान *bathān* [**vrajasthāna-*], m. reg. **1.** cattle enclosure; cattle yard. **2.** pasturage.

बथिया *bathiyā* [? conn. *vā̆stu-*], m. a pile of dried cow-dung cakes.

बथुआ *bathuā* [conn. *vāstu-*], m. **1.** a pot-herb, *Chenopodium album*: goose-foot. **2.** a weed; fat-hen. — ~ साग, m. = ~, 1.

[1]**बद** *bad* [P. *bad*], adj. **1.** bad. **2.** wicked. **3.** unlucky. — बद-अमनी, f. disturbance of the peace. बद-इंतज़ामी, f. bad management or organisation; maladministration; misrule, anarchy. बदकार, adj. & m. wicked; an evil-doer. °ई, f. wrongdoing. बदक़िस्मत, adj. unlucky, ill-starred. °ई, f. बदगुमान, adj. suspicious; disaffected (towards, से). बदगुमान करना, to make one suspicious (of), or disaffected (towards). °ई, f. बदचलन, adj. ill-behaved; depraved,

vicious. °ई, f. bad or wrong behaviour; depravity. बदज़बान, adj. bad-tongued, abusive. °ई, f. बदज़ात, adj. base-born; vicious. °ई, f. बदज़ायक़ा, adj. inv. bad-tasting. बदडौल, adj. misshapen. बदतमीज़, adj. not civil, discourteous. °ई, f. incivility. बदतर, adj. worse. °-तरीन, adj. worst. बददयानत, adj. dishonest, fraudulent. बददिमाग़, adj. discontented (by disposition). °ई, f. ill-will; discontent. बददुआ, f. a curse. बददुआ देना, to curse. बदनसीब, adj. = बदक़िस्मत. °ई, f. misfortune. बदनसल, adj. & m. of bad breed; a bastard. बदनज़र, adj. unpleasant-looking (a person, or animal). बदनाम, adj. infamous; disgraced. बदनाम करना, to destroy (one's) reputation; to vilify. °ई, f. bad reputation or character; disgrace; vilification. बदनामी उठाना, to endure disgrace, &c. बदनीयत, adj. of bad disposition or intention: malevolent; avaricious; lustful. °ई, f. बदपरहेज़, adj. uncontrolled, intemperate; gluttonous. °ई, f. बदबख़्त, adj. unlucky, wretched; accursed; evil. बदबू, f. bad smell, stench. °-दार, adj. stinking, smelling. बदमज़ा, adj. inv. of bad taste or flavour; tasteless; out of sorts; displeased. तबीयत बदमज़ा होना, not to be feeling well. बदमस्त, adj. drunk; lascivious. °ई, f. बदमाश [A. *ma'āś*], adj. & m. of bad ways, wicked, villainous; immoral; a villain, &c. °ई, f. villainy, &c. बदमाशी करना, to act wickedly or villainously. बदमिज़ाज, adj. bad-tempered. °ई, f. बदरंग, adj. discoloured; dull, faded; of a different colour (a card). बदराह, adj. on a wrong course; wicked, sinful. बदलगाम, adj. hard to rein in: hard to control (a horse); wilful, unrestrained in speech or manner (a person); uncontrollable. बदलिहाज़, adj. unmannerly, rude; immodest. बदशकल, adj. misshapen; ugly. बदशगून [P. *śugūn*], adj. ill-omened, unlucky. °ई, f. a bad omen. बदसलूकी [P. *-sulūkī*], f. bad behaviour, ill-treatment (of, से); discourtesy. बदसूरत, adj. ugly; misshapen. बदसूरत करना, to disfigure. °ई, f. बदहज़मी [A. *hazm*+P. *-ī*], f. indigestion. बदहवास [A. *ḥavās*], adj. unconscious; stupefied; bewildered; senseless, foolish. °ई, f. बदहाल, adj. in bad state (as through poverty, sickness). °ई, f.

²**बद** *bad*, m. f. Brbh. exchange. — ~ में, adv. in exchange for.

³**बद** *bad*, m. *Pl. HŚS.* a swelling of the glands (as from plague).

बदतर *badtar* [P. *badtar*], adj. see s.v. ¹बद.

¹**बदन** *badan* [A. *badan*], m. the body. — ~ टूटना, to suffer racking pains; fig. the body to be 'broken-in', exercised or trained. ~ फलना, the skin to be widely covered with a rash or eruption.

²**बदन** *badan* [ad. *vadana-*], m. = वदन.

बदना *badnā* [*vadati*], v.t. to speak: **1.** to settle, to arrange; to ordain. **2.** to name, to invoke (as a witness). **3.** to vow, to pledge (one's word); to affirm. **4.** to wager. शर्त ~, to bet. **5.** to be joined (as combat, rivalry). **6.** to acknowledge (as). — बदकर, or कह-बदकर, adv. holding to (one's) vow or word, resolutely. सधी-बदी बात, f. a matter not allowing of any doubt, foregone conclusion. - बदा-बदी, f. & adv. rivalry; in rivalry.

बदनी *badnī* [cf. H. *badnā*], f. *hist.* a contract by which a borrower gives a bond at high interest, assigning his crops as security to the lender at a rate far below the market value.

बदबदाना *badbadānā*, v.i. = बुदबुदाना.

बदर *badar* [S.], m. the Indian jujube (= ¹बेर).

¹**बदरा** *badrā* [*vārdala-*], m. Brbh. cloud(s); cloudiness.

²**बदरा** *badrā*, m. a gum-resin, *Ferula galbaniflua*, of Iranian origin.

बदरी *badrī* [S.], f. **1.** the Indian jujube, *Zizyphus jujuba* (= ¹बेर). **2.** the cotton plant. **3.** name of one of the sources of the Ganges (an important place of pilgrimage).

बदल *badal* [A. *badal*], m. **1.** change; exchange, substitution. **2.** return, retaliation. **3.** reg. = बदला, 5. — ~ करना, to exchange (with, or for, के साथ, or से); to substitute (for, से). – ज़िला-बदल, m. change of district, or residence.

बदलना *badalnā* [cf. H. *badal*], v.i. & v.t. **1.** v.i. to change, to be changed; to vary; to be transformed. **2.** to be exchanged (for sthg. else). **3.** to be removed; to be transferred; to be transplanted. **4.** to change for the worse; to look older; to fade. **5.** v.t. to change (sthg.), to alter; to transform; to disguise. **6.** to exchange (for, से); to barter. **7.** to remove; to transfer; to transplant. **8.** to misrepresent (a meaning, an intention). **9.** to shift (one's ground). बात ~, to prevaricate.

बदलवाई *badalvāī* [cf. H. *badalvānā*], f. = बदलाई.

बदलवाना *badalvānā* [cf. H. *badalnā*], v.t. to cause to be changed, &c. (by, से); to change.

बदला *badlā* [cf. A. *badal*], m. **1.** exchange. **2.** a substitute. **3.** recompense; compensation; restitution. **4.** return, retaliation; revenge; reprisal. **5.** ppn. (w. के). in exchange or return (for). — ~ करना (का), to exchange (for, से). ~ चुकाना, to exact a return (= ~ लेना). ~ देना (को), to give in return; to make recompense, &c.; to give back what one gets, to retaliate. ~ लेना, to take revenge (for, का, on, से); to get one's own back, to retaliate. बदले में, adv. in exchange, &c.

बदलाई *badlāī* [cf. H. *badlānā*], v.t. **1.** exchange; barter. **2.** sthg. given in exchange; a replacement. **3.** price of exchange.

बदलाना *badlānā* [cf. H. *badalnā*], v.t. = बदलवाना.

बदलाव *badlāv* [cf. H. *badalna*], v.t. exchange; replacement.

बदलाहट *badlāhaṭ* [cf. H. *badalnā*], f. change; a change.

1**बदली** *badlī* [cf. H. *badlā*], f. **1.** change; exchange; substitution. **2.** sthg. or someone exchanged; substitute; relief (of a watch). **3.** transfer. — ~ करना (की), to change; to exchange; to relieve; to transfer. ~ में, adv. in exchange.

2**बदली** *badlī* [*vārdalikā*-], f. **1.** cloudiness. **2.** a small cloud.

बदान *badān* [cf. H. *badnā*], f. a bet, wager.

1**बदी** *badī* [ad. *vadi*], f. the dark half of a lunar month (from full to new moon).

2**बदी** *badī* [P. *badī*], f. **1.** evil, mischief; misfortune. **2.** transf. defamation, slander. — ~ करना, to do wrong or harm (to, की); to malign. ~ चेतना, to think ill (of, की). ~ डालना, to sow evil or mischief (between, में). ~ पर आना, to be intent on causing mishcief, &c.

बद्ध *baddh* [S.], adj. **1.** bound. **2.** restrained, in check. **3.** fixed; joined together (as the cupped hands: see अंजलि); intent (as the mind). **4.** -बद्ध. settled, determined (e.g. क्रमबद्ध, placed in order or sequence; अनुशासनबद्ध, disciplined; वचनबद्ध, bound by one's word). — बद्ध-परिकर, adj. fig. having the loins girt: ready, alert. बद्ध-मूल, adj. firmly rooted.

बद्धी *baddhī*, f. **1.** cord, strap. **2.** rein. **3.** garland of flowers, strands of which are worn across the chest and back. **4.** streak, weal.

1**बध-** *badh-* [*vardhate*], v.i. to increase, to grow, &c. (= बढ़ना).

2**बध-** *badh-* [ad. **vadhati*: Pa. *vadhati*], v.t. Brbh. Av. to kill.

बधक *badhak* [ad. *vadhak*], m. = बधिक.

बधन *badhan* [ad. *vadhana*-], m. Brbh. killing.

बधना *badhnā* [cf. *vardhanī*-], f. reg. an earthen or copper pot with a spout.

1**बधा-** *badhā*- [*vardhāpayati*2], v.t. Av. to increase (= बढ़ाना).

2**बधा-** *badhā*- [*vardhāpayati*1], v.t. Brbh. to cause to be killed.

बधाई *badhāī* [cf. *vardhāpayati*2], f. **1.** congratulation(s). **2.** festivity, festivities. **3.** congratulatory gift. **4.** growth, increase. — ~ देना (को), to congratulate (one: on, पर, के लिए, की).

बधाव *badhāv*, m. Av. = बधावा.

बधावा *badhāvā* [cf. *vardhāpayati*2], m. **1.** congratulations; specif. congratulations on the birth of a child. **2.** presents given to a new mother following childbirth. **3.** growth, increase. **4.** Av. festivity. — ~ देना (को), to congratulate, &c.

बधिक *badhik* [conn. H. *badhak*], m. **1.** hunter; fowler. **2.** killer; executioner.

बधिया *badhiyā* [*vadhri*-], m. a castrated animal; bullock; gelding. — ~ करना, v.t. to castrate. ~ बैठना, fig. a crippling loss to be sustained (as in business).

बधिर *badhir* [S.], adj. deaf.

बधिरता *badhiratā* [S.], f. deafness.

बधिरिमा *badhirimā* [S.], f. deafness.

बध्य *badhyă*, adj. = वध्य.

1**बन** *ban* [*vana*-1], m. **1.** forest, jungle; scrub country; wood; grove, thicket. **2.** reg. cotton in the field, cotton crop. **3.** reg. payment in kind for field-work (as weeding, reaping). **4.** *Pl.* price paid for pasturage. — ~ झाड़ना, or मारना, to beat or to scour forest. – बन-कंडा, m. cow-dung found in scrub country (and used as fuel). बन-ककड़ी, f. a small herbaceous plant, *Podophyllum emodi*, the source of a gum used medicinally. बन-खंड, m. forest region, forest. °ई, m. forest-dweller; f. forest. बनचर, adj. & m. grazing or living in a forest, wild; a wild creature. बन-तुलसा, m. = next. बन-तुलसी, f. wild basil. बन-धातु, f. Brbh. a reddish mineral earth. बन-पाल, m. a forester. बन-बास, m. residence in a forest; exile. °ई, adj. & m. forest-dwelling; a forester; hermit. बन-बिलार, m. = next. बन-बिलाव, m. id. बन-बिल्ली, f. wild cat. बन-मानुस, m. ape; joc. wild man. बन-माल, f. = next. बन-माला, f. garland of forest flowers worn hanging to the feet (esp. as by Kṛṣṇa). °-माली, adj. & m. garlanded with forest flowers; a title of Kṛṣṇa. बन-रखा, m. reg. = बन-पाल; name of a community of hunters. बन-रीठा, m. the soap-nut tree, *Sapindus mukorossi*, and its fruit. बनवासी, adj. & m. = °-बासी.

2**बन** *ban* [P. *band*], m. reg. a hoop, band.

बनक *banak* [P. *banak*], f. Brbh. attire, decoration.

बनज- *banaj*- [cf. H. *banij*], v.t. E.H. to trade in (a commodity).

बनजरिया *banjariyā* [cf. H. *bañjar*], f. reg. waste land, or newly cleared land.

बनजारा *banjārā* [**vaṇijyākāra-*: Pk. *vaṇijjāraya-*], m. trader or carrier of grain, salt, &c.; merchant.

बनजारिन *banjārin* [cf. H. *banjārī*], f. Brbh. = ¹बनजारी.

¹**बनजारी** *banjārī* [cf. H. *banjārā*], f. wife of a *banjārā*.

²**बनजारी** *banjārī* [cf. H. *banjārā*], adj. having to do with *banjārās*; trading.

बनत *banat* [cf. H. *bannā*], f. **1.** style, make, cut. **2.** *Pl.* lace. **3.** *Pl. HŚS.* band or ribbon set with spangles, edging (of cloth or garment).

बनना *bannā* [*vanati*], v.i. **1.** to be made (from, से; of, का). यह किसका बना है? what is this made of? **2.** to be created, formed; to be composed; to be invented. **3.** to be constructed, built. **4.** to be established. **5.** to be prepared; to be cooked. **6.** to be finished, completed; to be managed, or achieved. **7.** to turn out right; to fit. **8.** to be possible, contrivable. जिस तरह बने, in whatever way possible. **9.** to be fixed, settled (a matter). **10.** to be set to rights; to be repaired (as a watch); to be operated on successfully (a part of the body); to be adjusted; to be improved, to improve; to be trimmed (hair, beard); to be decorated (a garment, &c.); to be dressed up. **11.** to become; to be appointed (to a post). बड़ा होकर वकील ~, to become a lawyer on growing up. **12.** to be assumed (an air; a disguise); to act (a part); वह सच्चा बनता है, he gives the appearance of truthfulness. वह राणा प्रताप बनेगा, he will act Rāṇā Pratāp. **13.** to be changed into (from, से). **14.** to be gained, made (as profit). **15.** to come about, to happen. **16.** to continue. बना रहना, to carry on (in present state); to remain unchanged; to be still alive, or in health. **17.** to be suitable or appropriate (for a purpose, an occasion). **18.** to prosper; to get on well or harmoniously (with). उनमें ख़ूब बनती है, they get on very well. **19.** to be healthy, robust. **20.** to make oneself look foolish; to be ridiculed. — बन आना, to have good fortune; to succeed (as a venture); to come to pass; to turn (on, पर). इज़्ज़त पर बन आना, to be a question of honour. उसकी बन आई है, he is in luck. बन आए की बात, f. a lucky chance. उनकी प्रशंसा करते बनती है, they are worthy of praise. – बनकर, adv. as, like. मित्र बनकर मिले जुले रहो, live together harmoniously as friends. बना, adj. made, formed, prepared, finished, &c.; well-arranged, in good order; healthy, robust; stout; counterfeit; artificial. बना-ठना, adj. dressed up; adorned. तैयार बने बैठना, to be in readiness, or awaiting. बने रहना, to remain (in a place or a condition). बना-बनाया, adj. ready-made; complete.

बनफ़शा *banafśā* [P. *banafśa*], m. f. a violet.

बनरा *banrā* [cf. **vanva-*; ← Panj.], m. reg. bridegroom.

बनरी *banrī*, f. reg. bride.

बनवाई *banvāī* [cf. H. *banvānā*], f. **1.** making, manufacture. **2.** price paid for making (sthg.), cost of manufacture.

बनवाना *banvānā* [cf. H. *banānā*], v.t. to cause to be made, &c. (by, से); to have (sthg.) made.

बनवैया *banvaiyā* [cf. H. *banvānā*], m. maker, manufacturer.

बनात *banāt*, f. broad-cloth.

बनाती *banātī* [cf. H. *banāt*], adj. made of broad-cloth; woollen.

बनाना *banānā* [cf. *vanati*; Pa. *vanāyati*], v.t. **1.** to cause to be or exist, to make; to create; to compose (as a literary work); to paint (a picture); to form (a group). **2.** to appoint (a person as). **3.** to construct, to build; to make (any object or product: from, से). **4.** to do, to perform; to complete (a task). **5.** to set right, to attend, to repair; to treat (an injured hand, &c.); to trim (beard, hair); to adjust; to decorate. **6.** to make into, to change; to misrepresent as. झूठ को सच ~, to present falsehood as truth. **7.** to cause to agree; to reconcile (with, से). **8.** to contrive, to invent. **9.** to prepare (as food); to pluck (a fowl). **10.** to assume (an air, a pretence). **11.** to make fun of; to hoax. — बनाकर, adv. thoroughly, exhaustively. बनाए न बनना, not to succeed, or to get done, despite all efforts. बनाए रखना, to preserve; to retain (sthg. in its existing state); to stay on good terms (with, से). उसने तसवीर बनाई, लेकिन वह नहीं बन पाई, he painted the picture, but it was a failure.

बनाम *ba-nām*, adv. see s.v. ब-.

बनारस *banāras* [*vārāṇasī-*], m. the city of Banaras.

बनारसी *banārsī* [cf. H. *banāras*], adj. & m. **1.** adj. belonging to or made in Banaras. **2.** a resident of Banaras.

बनाव *banāv* [cf. H. *banānā*], m. **1.** manner of formation; composition; nature. **2.** adornment, embellishment. **3.** harmony, concord. **4.** E.H. means, remedy. — ~ करना (का), to adorn, to decorate. – बनाव-चुनाव, m. = next. बनाव-सिंगार, m. fine attire, adornment.

बनावट *banāvaṭ* [cf. H. *banānā*], f. **1.** make, construction; structure. **2.** build (of body).

3. nature, character; composition (as of soil). 4. form, appearance. 5. show, display; affectation. 6. artifice, art. 7. a fiction, pretence; forgery; an imitation.

बनावटी *banāvṭī* [cf. H. *banānā*], adj. 1. artificial; synthetic; imitation, false (as jewels). 2. put on, forced (emotion). 3. contrived, factitious. 4. conventional (signs, symbols).

बनावरी *banāvărī*, f. reg. 1. preparation. 2. art, skill, dexterity.

बनासपती *banāspatī* f. Brbh. & 19c. = वनस्पति, 1., 2.

बनिज *banij* [*vaṇijyā-*, f.], m. 1. trade, commerce. 2. merchandise. — ~ करना, to trade.

बनिजार *banijār*, m. Av. = बनजारा.

बनिया *baniyā* [*vaṇija-*], m. 1. merchant. 2. shopkeeper; grocer. 3. pej. a petty-minded man, money-grubber; niggard. 4. a timid man.

[1]**बनियाइन** *baniyāin* [cf. H. *baniyā*], f. 1. wife of a *baniyā*. 2. shopkeeper (female).

[2]**बनियाइन** *baniyāin*, f. = बनियान.

बनियान *baniyān* [f. H. *baniyā*], f. singlet, vest.

बनियानी *baniyānī*, f. = [1]बनियाइन.

बनिस्बत *ba-nisbat*, ppn. see s.v. ब-.

बनिहार *banihār* [cf. H. [2]*bannī*], m. reg. ploughman or labourer paid in kind, or with daily wages.

बनी *banī* [cf. H. *ban*], f. small wood, grove.

बनेटी *baneṭī*, f. pronun. var. reg. = बनेठी.

बनेठी *baneṭhī* [**vahniyaṣṭi-*], f. *Pl. HŚS.* a staff or stick weighted at both ends (used in gymnastic exercises).

बनेरा *banerā* [? ← P. *banerā*], m. reg. (N.) parapet (of a house wall).

बनेला *banelā*, adj. = बनैला.

बनैला *banailā* [cf. *vana-*[1]], adj. forest, forest-dwelling; wild.

बनौट *banauṭ*, f. pronun. var. = बनावट.

बन्ना *bannā* [**vanva-*; ? ← Panj.], m. bridegroom.

[1]**बन्नी** *bannī* [cf. H. *bannā*], f. bride.

[2]**बन्नी** *bannī*, f. portion of grain given to a labourer as payment in kind.

बन्नू *bannū*, f. = बन्नो.

बन्नो *banno* [cf. **vanva-*], f. lady, darling.

बन्हियाँ *banhiyāṁ*, m. reg. (cf. बन्ना). bridegroom.

बपुरा *bapurā*, adj. Brbh. = बापुरा.

बपैती *bapaitī*, f. reg. = बपौती.

बपौती *bapautī* [**bāppavṛtti-*], adj. & f. 1. inherited from a father; hereditary, ancestral. 2. f. patrimony; inheritance. 3. hereditary right. — ~ अधिकार, m. hereditary right. ~ माल, m. patrimony.

बप्तिस्मा *baptismā* [Pt. *baptismo*: ← Gk.], m. baptism.

बफरना *bapharnā*, v.i. to talk boastfully; to shout; to roar.

बफारा *baphārā* [**bāṣpākāra-*], m. 1. vapour, steam. 2. vapour bath, a steaming (with balsam, &c).

बबई *babaī* [*barbā-*], f. *Pl.* a basil, *Ocimum pilosum*, and its seed.

बबर *babar* [P. *babar*], m. lion. — बबर-शेर, m. tiger.

बबरी *babrī* [cf. *barbarā-*[2]], f. *Pl.* 1. cropped hair (esp. of a horse). 2. fringe of hair.

बबरूता *babrūtā* [conn. *barbara-*[1]], m. reg. an uncouth person.

बबुआ *babuā* [cf. H. *bābū*], m. 1. toy, doll (in the shape of a boy). 2. colloq. little boy.

बबुआई *babuāī* [cf. H. *babuā*], adj. boy's, boyish.

बबूल *babūl* [*babbūla-*], m. f. the acacia tree. — ~ के पेड़ बोना, to plant acacias: to do sthg. which can produce no good result.

[1]**बबूला** *babūlā* [**bābbūlaka-*], adj. having to do with the *babūl* tree.

[2]**बबूला** *babūlā*, m. 1. whirlwind (= बगूला). 2. *HŚS.* a bubble (= बुलबुला).

बब्बी *babbī*, f. colloq. a kiss. — मुखड़े की ~ लेना, to take a kiss (from, के).

बभना *babhnā*, m. reg. (E.) a brāhmaṇ.

बभनी *babhnī*, colloq. obs. brahminical (script): the Devanāgarī script (cf. बाह्मनी).

बभ्रु *babhru* [S.], adj. 1. brown, greyish-brown. 2. bald through disease.

[1]**बम** *bam*, interj. term of greeting used by Śaiva devotees; term used in addressing Śiva (expresses the devotee's helplessness and devotion). — ~ बोलना, all strength, wealth or power to be lost; colloq. to be bankrupt. ~ महादेव! greetings in Śiva's name!

²**बम** *bam* [conn. H. *bambā*], m. **1.** a spring of water; fountain. **2.** a pump. — **बम-पुलिस** [Engl. *place*], m. a public lavatory.

³**बम** *bam* [P. *bam*], m. reg. a deep sound; a drum. — ~ **बजना**, a shout, or noise to ring out.

⁴**बम** *bam* [Engl. *bomb*], m. a bomb. — ~ **बरसाना**, to shower bombs, to bomb heavily. — **बम-कांड**, m. a bombing (incident). **बमबाज़** [P. *-bāz*], adj. delivering bombs (an aircraft). °**ई**, f. a bombing raid. **बमबारी** [P. *-bārī*], f. a bombing raid. **बममार**, m. a bomber (aircraft). °**ई**, f. bombing, a bombing raid. **बमवर्षक** (**विमान**), m. = **बममार**. **बमवर्षण**, m. = **बममारी**.

बमकना *bamaknā*, v.i. reg. **1.** to swell. **2.** to boast; to speak arrogantly. **3.** to be jumping, hopping (with rage).

बमना *bamnā* [ad. *vamati*], v.i. & v.t. reg. **1.** v.i. to vomit. **2.** v.t. to vomit forth.

बमय *bamay* [P. *ba-*+A. *ma'*], prep. together with, provided with.

बमला *bamlā* [cf. H. ²*bam*], m. reg. spring, source (of water).

बमीठा *bamīṭhā*, m. reg. **1.** an ant-hill (= **बाँबी**). **2.** a snake's hole.

बमुक़ाबला *ba-muqāblā*, ppn. see s.v. **ब-**.

बमूजिब *ba-mūjib*, ppn. U. see s.v. **ब-**.

बम्हनी *bamhănī*, f. colloq. reg. a light red soil.

बयँ-हत्था *bayaṁ-hatthā* [H. *bāyāṁ*+H. *hāth*], adj. left-handed.

¹**बया** *bayā* [*vaya-*¹], m. the weaver-bird.

²**बया** *bayā* [? conn. A. *bai'*], m. reg. (E.) a weigher of grain.

³**बया** *bayā* [f. H. *bainā*; *upāyana-* infld. by *upāya-*], m. presents (of sweets, or brass vessels, &c.) given by a bride to her mother-in-law at festival times.

बयाई *bayāī* [cf. H. ²*bayā*], f. *Pl.* weighman's fee, or perquisite.

बयाज़ा *bayāzā* [cf. A. *bayāẓ*], f. U. sthg. white: a notebook.

बयान *bayān* [A. *bayān*], m. **1.** description, exposition; account. **2.** declaration, assertion. **3.** circumstantial evidence. — ~ **करना**, to relate, to give an account (of, **का**); to declare; to make clear. ~ **देना**, to make a declaration, &c.

बयाना *bayānā* [A. *bai'*+P. *-āna*], m. deposit (on an intended purchase).

बयाबान *bayābān*, m. = **बियाबान**.

बयार *bayār* [**vātāra-*: Pk. *vāyāra-*], m. cool wind. — ~ **करना**, to fan (a person).

बयारा *bayārā* [**vātāra-*: Pk. *vāyāra-*], m. reg. wind, storm.

बयारी *bayārī* [cf. H. *bayār*], f. Brbh. Av. wind, storm.

बयाल- *bayāl-* [**vātālaya-*], m. Brbh. **1.** peep-hole (in a door). **2.** niche (in a wall). **3.** embrasure (in a wall).

बयालीस *bayālīs* [*dvācatvāriṁsat-*], adj. forty-two.

बयासी *bayāsī* [*dvyaśīti-*], adj. eighty-two.

बरंगा *baraṅgā*, m. **1.** the square corner beam of a house roof. **2.** roofing plank. **3.** Brbh. roofing slate, or shingle.

बरंडा *baraṇḍā* [H. *barāmdā* × Engl. *verandah*], m. a verandah (= **बरामदा**).

¹**बर** *bar* [*vara-*], m. & adj. **1.** m. a choice. **2.** a boon; blessing. **3.** bridegroom; husband. **4.** adj. choice, excellent. — ~ **का पानी**, m. water in which first a bridegroom, then his bride, wash before their marriage. – **बर-जोग**, adj. marriageable (a girl).

²**बर** *bar* [*varam*], adv. Brbh. Av. preferably, rather.

³**बर** *bar* [*vaṭa-*¹], f. Brbh. Av. banyan tree.

⁴**बर** *bar*, m. Brbh. Av. = **बल**.

⁵**बर** *bar* [P. *bar*], ppn. on, upon, up, above; at, in; forth, away, against. — ~ **आना**, to have a good outcome, to turn out very well; to be fulfilled (a wish). ~ **पाना**, id. – **बरक़रार रखना**, to establish, &c.; to uphold; to confirm, to ratify. **बरक़रार**, adj. fixed, established, settled, &c. (see **क़रार**); maintained. **बरख़ास्त** [P. *-khāst*], f. breaking up, closing: removal (from office), dismissal. **बरख़ास्त करना**, to dismiss. °**गी**, f. rising or breaking up (as of an assembly); dissolution; dismissal. **बरख़िलाफ़**, adv. & ppn. contrary, or opposite (to, **के**). **बरज़ोर**, adv. by force. °**ई**, f. coercion; rape. **बरतरफ़**, adj. aside, away, out of the way. **बरतरफ़ करना**, to dismiss (from office). **बरदाश्त** [P. *-dāśt*], f. endurance, bearing, tolerating. **बरदाश्त करना**, to endure, &c. **बरपा** [P. *-pā*], adj. inv. raised, set afoot (as a question, a quarrel). **बरपा करना**, to stir up. **बरबाद** adj. (cast) to the wind: laid waste, destroyed; ruined; plundered. **बरबाद करना**, to destroy, &c. °**ई**, f. destruction, &c. **बराबर**, adj. & adv. see s.v. **बरामद** [P. *-āmad*], m. coming up or forth: outgoings, expenditure, expenses; alluvial land; laying information (esp. about bribery). **बरामद होना**, to come forth; to accrue; to be recovered (as stolen property, or money due). **बरामदा**, m. see s.v.

⁶**बर** *bar* [P. *bar*], m. fruit: — **बरख़ुरदार** [P. *-khvurdār*], adj. & m. eating or enjoying the

fruit (of life), obtaining (one's) desires: prosperous; blessed with sons; male offspring.

-बर *-bar* [P. *bar*], adj. U. bearing, carrying off (e.g. दिलबर, adj. & m. captivating the heart; captor of (one's) heart).

बरइन *bara'in* [cf. H. *baraī*], f. **1.** wife of a betel seller, or grower. **2.** a woman who sells betel leaf.

बरई *baraī*, m. [? cf. *vāṭa-*¹]. **1.** betel-grower. **2.** seller of betel leaf.

बरक़ *barq* [A. *barq*], f. lightning: — बरक़ंदाज़ [P. *-andāz*], m. lightning-thrower: a guard; peon; bailiff. °ई, f. work of a guard, &c.

बरकत *barkat* [A. *baraka*: P. *barakat*], f. var. /bərəkkət/. **1.** blessing, benediction. *__2.__ increase, abundance. **3.** prosperity; success. **4.** good fortune. **5.** auspicious quality which produces abundance, &c.; the number one (esp. in counting, weighing). **6.** euph. nothing (at all). — ~ उठना, good days to end. ~ देना (को), to give increase, prosperity, &c.; to bless.

बरक़रार *bar-qarār*, adj. see s.v. ⁵बर.

बरकाव *barkāv*, m. reg. a flanking attack.

बरकौठा *barkauṭhā*, *Pl.* spear-grass.

बरख़ास्त *bar-khāst*, adj. see s.v. ⁵बर.

बरख़िलाफ़ *bar-khilāf*, adv. & ppn. see s.v. ⁵बर.

बरगद *bargad* [cf. *vaṭa-*¹], m. the banyan tree.

बरगा *bargā* [ad. *varga-*], adj. reg. of the same kind, like, similar (to).

बरगी *bargī* [conn. P. *bargī*], m. = बारगीर, 2.

बरगेल *bargel*, m. *Pl. HŚS.* a kind of yellowhammer, or other finch (= बगेरी).

बरछा *barchā*, m. spear, lance. — बरछाबरदार [P. *-bardār*], m. *Pl.* = बरछैत. बरछेबरदार, m. id.

बरछी *barchī* [cf. H. *barchā*], f. small spear or lance; javelin.

बरछैत *barchait* [cf. H. *barchā*], m. spearman, lancer.

बरजना *barăjnā* [ad. *varjita-*, *varjana-*], v.t. to stop, to check; to forbid.

बरजतिया *barjatiyā*, m. *Pl.* a harmless kind of snake.

बरजोर *barjor* [H. *bal*+H. *zor*], adj. doubly strong: overwhelming in strength; coercive.

बरजोरी *barjorī* [cf. H. *barjor*], f. overwhelmimg strength; coercion.

बरडा *barḍā* [? conn. *vālukā-*], m. reg. (W.) a kind of light sandy, or stony soil.

बरडी *barḍī*, f. reg. (W.) = बरडा.

¹बरत *barat* [*varatrā-*], f. **1.** thong, girth. **2.** Brbh. rope, well-rope; cord, string (as of puppets). **3.** fig. *Pl.* mark, streak, weal.

²बरत *barăt*, m. = व्रत.

³बरत *barat*, m. *Pl.* a disease of rice crops.

बरतन *bartan* [cf. H. *baratnā*], m. vessel, utensil; dish; plate; basin; bowl; pot. — बरतन-भाँड़ा, m. utensils, pots and pans.

बरतना *baratnā* [ad. *vartate*, *vartayati*], v.i. & v.t. **1.** v.i. to happen (to, पर), to take place. **2.** to deal (with, से or के साथ); to treat. **3.** to elapse (time). **4.** to be served (food). **5.** v.t. to make use of, to use; to employ or to practise (as care, discretion). **6.** to revolve, to think over (a matter).

बरतनी *bartanī* [cf. H. *baratnā*], f. **1.** a pen, writing implement. **2.** spelling (of a word).

बरतरफ़ *bar-taraf*, adj. U. see s.v. ⁵बर.

¹बरताना *bartānā* [cf. H. *baratnā*], v.t. **1.** to cause to use; to use, to apply. **2.** reg. to act, to have effect, to behave. **3.** *Pl.* to distribute.

²बरताना *bartānā* [cf. H. ¹*bartānā*], m. reg. **1.** usage, custom (= बरताव). **2.** old or second-hand clothing.

बरताव *bartāv* [cf. H. *baratnā, bartānā*], m. **1.** behaviour; treatment (of a person). **2.** usage, custom. **3.** reg. use, expenditure. — ~ करना, to act or to behave (towards, के साथ); to treat, to deal (with).

बरतुश *bartuś*, m. (?) reg. (W.) land sown with sugar-cane after a rice crop.

बरद *barăd* [*balivarda-*], m. Av. ox.

बरदाना *bardānā* [cf. H. *barad*], v.t. = बरधाना.

-बरदार *-bardār* [P. *bardār*]. bearing; bearer (e.g. हुक़्क़ाबरदार, m. servant responsible for a *hookah*).

-बरदारी *-bardārī* [P. *bardārī*], f. bearing, carrying (e.g. a load: बारबरदारी, f).

बरदाश्त *bar-dāśt*, f. see s.v. ⁵बर.

बरदी *bardī* [cf. H. *barad*], f. E.H. a drove of laden cattle.

बरदौर *bardaur* [**balivardavāṭī-*], f. reg. enclosure or shed for cattle.

बरध *barădh*, m. = बरद.

बरधना *baradhnā* [cf. H. *baradh(ā)*], v.i. reg. to be put to a bull (a cow).

बरधा *bardhā*, m. reg. = बरध, बरद.

बरधाना *bardhānā* [cf. H. *baradh(ā)*], v.t. to put (a cow) to a bull.

[1]**बरन** *baran*, conj. = [2]बर.

[2]**बरन** *baran* [*varaṇa-*[1]], m. a moderate-sized deciduous tree, *Crataeva religiosa*, of which the leaves and bark are used medicinally.

बरन- *baran-* [ad. *varṇayati*], v.t. Brbh. Av. to describe.

[1]**बरना** *barnā* [**varati*: Pa. *varati*], v.t. **1.** to marry (of groom or bride). **2.** to choose, to select.

[2]**बरना** *barnā*, v.i. reg. = [1]बलना.

[3]**बरना** *barnā*, v.t. reg. = [2]बलना.

[4]**बरना** *barnā*, m. *Pl. HŚS.* = [2]बरन.

बरनार *barnār*, m. *Pl.* ? corr. coloured. — ~ मट्टी, f. a soil of mixed (yellow and white) colouration (? = [2]बरवा).

बरपना *barapnā* [cf. H. *barpānā*], v.i. to be set afoot, to be stirred up.

बरपा *bar-pā*, adj. inv. see s.v. [5]बर.

बरपाना *barpānā* [cf. H. *barpā*], v.t. = बरपा करना.

[1]**बरबट** *barbaṭ* m. reg. a kind of bean, *Dolichos catjang.*

[2]**बरबट** *barabaṭ* [? *bala-*+*varta-*[1]], adv. Brbh. by force, irresistibly.

बरबटी *barbaṭī* [ad. *varvaṭa-*: ? ← Austro-as.], f. a kind of bean, *Dolichos lablab* (= लोबिया).

बरबत *barbat* [P. *barbaṭ*], f. *Pl. HŚS.* a musical instrument, the Persian lute.

बरबर *barbar* [S.], adj. stammering, non-Aryan: harsh; savage.

बरबरता *barbarătā* [S.}, f. harshness; savagery.

बरबरी *barbarī* [cf. A. *barbar*], f. a Barbary goat.

बरबस *barbas* [? H. *bal*+*vaś*], m. & adv. **1.** m. power, vigour; prowess. **2.** adv. by force. **3.** to no point. **4.** unexpectedly.

बरबाद *bar-bād*, m. see s.v. [5]बर.

बरभस *barbhas*, m. reg. = बुढ़भस.

बरभसिया *barbhasiyā*, adj. reg. affected (cf. बुढ़भस).

[1]**बरमा** *barmā*, m. **1.** a borer worked with a string; a drill. **2.** auger, gimlet.

[2]**बरमा** *barmā*, m. *Pl.* name of a plant used medicinally to treat ulcerations.

बरमाना *barmānā* [cf. H. *barmā*], v.t. to bore, to drill; to pierce.

बरमी *barmī*, adj. & m. f. see [1] [2]बर्मी.

बरवट *barvaṭ* [? cf. H. *baṛhnā*], m. reg. **1.** enlargement of the spleen. **2.** an abdominal tumour.

[1]**बरवा** *barvā*, m. f. **1.** m. = बरवै. **2.** f. *Pl. mus.* name of a *rāgiṇī.*

[2]**बरवा** *barvā* [*vālūka-*], m. reg. a sandy soil; a mixture of sand and clay.

बरवै *barvai* [? **varapādika-*], m. a Hindi metre of nineteen instants.

बरस *baras* [*varṣa-*], m. year. — ~ दिन, m. & adv. = ~ भर. ~ दिन का, adj. a (whole) year's, annual (festival, &c). ~ भर, m. & adv. the whole year; all the year round. वह दस ~ का है, he is ten. – बरस-गाँठ, f. ceremony of tying a knot on one's birthday; birthday; anniversary. बरस-बधावा, m. celebration of (the first) year: the taking away from the bride of the *god* (q.v.) given to her at marriage.

बरसता *barastā* [cf. H. *barasnā*], m. reg. rain, the rain.

बरसना *barasnā* [*varṣati*], v.i. **1.** to rain. **2.** to fall in showers. **3.** to be scattered. **4.** transf. to be winnowed. **5.** fig. (cf. 2.) to be strikingly evident; to be radiant. **6.** reg. to burst (a boil).

बरसवाँ *barasvāṁ* [cf. H. *baras*], adj. yearly, annual. — बरसवें दिन, adv. once a year.

बरसा *barsā* [*varṣa-*], m. reg. a year (= बरस).

बरसाऊ *barsāū* [cf. H. *barsānā*], adj. **1.** threatening rain (clouds). **2.** rainy (as climate).

बरसात *barsāt* [*varṣārātri-*; or (? ×) *varṣartu-*], f. the rainy season.

बरसाती *barsātī* [cf. H. *barsāt*], adj. & f. **1.** adj. having to do with rain; belonging to the rainy season. **2.** m. a raincoat. **3.** waterproof covering. **4.** porch; balcony. **5.** *Pl. HŚS.* name of several physical complaints associated with the rainy season. **6.** the lesser florican (a bustard, *Sypheotides indica*, which migrates locally during the rains).

बरसाना *barsānā* [cf. H. *barasnā*], v.t. to cause to rain: **1.** to pour down; to shower. **2.** to scatter. **3.** transf. to winnow.

बरसी *barsī* [cf. H. *baras*], f. a ceremony marking the completion of a year; specif. a commemorative ceremony held a year after the death of a relative.

बरसील- *barsīl-* [cf. *varṣa-*], adj. Brbh. rainy.

बरसोदिया *barsodiyā* [cf. H. *baras*], m. ? *Pl. HŚS.* a servant engaged by the year.

बरसौड़ी *barsauṛī* [cf. H. *baras*], adj. & f. *Pl. HŚS.* **1.** adj. annual. **2.** f. annual tax; the amount of an annual tax.

बरह *barh* [ad. *varha-*], m. Brbh. tail-feathers of a peacock.

बरहनगी *barahnagī* [P. *barahnagī*], f. nakedness.

बरहना *barahnā* [P. *barahna*], adj. naked. — बरहनापा, adv. inv. barefoot.

[1]**बरहा** *barhā* [*vaṭa-*[2]: ? ← Drav.], m. reg. a rope.

[2]**बरहा** *barhā* [? *vāha-*+MIA *-ḍ-*, w. metath.], m. reg. an irrigation channel.

[3]**बरहा** *barhā*, m. reg. the lands of a village most distant from it; grazing land.

[1]**बरही** *barhī* [ad. *varhin-*], m. Brbh. a peacock.

[2]**बरही** *barăhī* [cf. H. *bārah*], adj. *hind.* name of ceremonies (including naming) held on the twelfth day after a child's birth.

[1]**बरा-** *barā-* [conn. H. [1]*bār-*], v.t. Brbh. Av. **1.** to hold (oneself) aloof (from), to avoid. **2.** to abstain.

[2]**बरा-** *barā-* [cf. *varayati*], v.t. E.H. to cause to be chosen, to choose.

बरात *barāt* [*varayātrā-*], f. **1.** marriage procession or journey (of bridegroom to bride's house). **2.** transf. marriage party, wedding guests. **3.** troop, crowd. — ~ करना, to take part in a marriage procession. ~ में जाना, id.

बराती *barātī* [cf. H. *barāt*], m. member of a marriage procession or party.

बराना *barānā* [cf. *vāri-*], v.t. reg. to fill with water (an irrigation channel); to irrigate (fields).

बराबर *bar-ā-bar* [P. *barābar*], adj. & adv. **1.** adj. abreast, level (with, के); equal (as a score); even, quits (as rivals). **2.** adjacent (to); neighbouring; opposite (to). **3.** comparable, equal, exact; approximate. **4.** uniform, similar. **5.** smooth all over, level; filled in (a ditch); levelled, razed; finished (as work); brought to nothing, squandered (as a fortune). **6.** parallel. **7.** adv. leading directly, direct (a route). **8.** constantly, regularly; continuously; straight on without interruption. **9.** without delay. — ~ आना, to come level (with, के); to overtake. ~ करना, to make level or smooth; to raze; get through, to complete (a task); to run through. to spend (a fortune); to square, to settle (a debt); to make equal or comparable, to adjust, to match. ~ का, adj. equal, comparable (as in size, age, standing, quality); grown-up. ~ का चिह्न, m. *math.* sign of equality. ~ का जोड़, m. = next. ~ की टक्कर, or चोट, f. an equal (in abilities, rank, wealth, &c.: of, के); a good match, or partner. ~ जाइए, go straight on, continue as before. ~ ~, adv. breast to breast, side by side; in a row or line; equally, evenly. बाल ~, adv. & m. as much as a hair; hair's breadth, least bit. – बराबर-जोड़, m. *math.* an equation. – बराबरवाला, adj. & m. equal; adjacent; opposite; an equal.

बराबरी *barābărī* [P. *barābarī*], f. **1.** equality (between, में or की); comparability (between); agreement, correspondence; parallelism. **2.** aspiring to, or presuming, equality. — ~ करना (की), to equal; to copy, to imitate; to vie (with), to rival; to cope or to strive (with); to confront, to resist; to be presumptuous.

बरामद *bar-āmad*, m. see s.v. [5]बर.

बरामदा *barāmdā* [Pt. *varanda*; w. P. *bar āmada* 'come forth'], m. verandah; balcony.

बराय *ba-rāy*, prep. & ppn. see s.v. ब-.

बरारा *barārā* [*varāṭaka-*], m. *Pl.* a strong rope or line.

बरारी *barārī* [P. *barārī* 'one who brings up'], m. *hist.* a shareholder in village lands paying his portion of the assessment.

बराव *barāv* [cf. H. [1]*barā-*], m. Brbh. **1.** avoidance; watch or guard (against). **2.** abstinence.

बराह *barāh*, m. = वराह.

बराहिल *barāhil*, m. reg. (Bihar) a man who watches crops.

बरिया *bariyā*, [cf. H. *bāṛī*], f. reg. a garden; specif. a betel garden.

बरिया- *bariyā-*, v.i. Brbh. to be proud or arrogant.

बरियाई *bariyāī* [cf. H. *bariyā-*], f. boasting; arrogance.

बरियार *bariyār* [*balakāra-], adj. & m. **1.** Av. strong. **2.** m. the perennial shrub *Sida carpinifolia* (the hornbeam-leaved Sida).

बरिस *baris* [*varṣa-*, Pk. *varisa-*], m. Av. = बरस.

[1]**बरी** *barī* [cf. H. [1]*bar*], f. gifts sent from the bridegroom's house to the bride's before the wedding.

[2]**बरी** *barī* [A. *barī*], adj. **1.** free (from, से), exempt (from); absolved (from blame); acquitted (of a charge), innocent. — ~ करना, to free (from, से), &c.

बरीस *barīs*, m. Brbh. = बरस.

बरु *baru*, adv. Brbh. Av. = ²बर.

बरुक *baruk* [cf. *varam*; and P. *balki*], conj. but rather (= ²वर).

बरुन *barun* [*varuṇa-*], m. Brbh. **1.** name of the Vedic god Varuṇa. **2.** water.

बरुना *barunā* [*varaṇa-*¹], m. *HŚS.* = ²बरन.

बरुनी *barunī*, f. Brbh. = बरौनी.

बरूथ *barūth* [ad. *varūtha-*], m. Brbh. Av. host, army.

बरेंड़ा *bareṁṛā*, m. reg. ridgepole (of a roof) (= बड़ेरी).

¹**बरेखी** *barekhī* [H. *var*+H. *dekhī*], f. Brbh. Av. first meeting between a prospective bride and groom.

²**बरेखी** *barekhī*, f. reg. a women's arm ornament.

बरेज *barej*, m. reg. a betel garden.

बरेजा *barejā*, m. reg. = बरेज.

बरेठन *bareṭhan* [cf. H. *bareṭhā*], f. **1.** washerwoman. **2.** washerman's wife.

बरेठा *bareṭhā*, m. washerman.

बरेत *baret* [? *varāṭaka-* × *varatrā-*], m. reg. (? N.) a rope (as used at a well, or in irrigation).

बरेरा *barerā*, m. reg. a wasp (= बर्र).

बरोंथा *baroṁthā*, m. *Pl.* = बरौंथा.

बरोठा *baroṭhā* [*dvārakoṣṭhaka-*], m. Brbh. **1.** porchway. **2.** inner room, sitting-room.

बरोठी *baroṭhī* [cf. H. *baroṭhā*], f. reg. (W). ceremony of welcome of a bridegroom at the bride's house by the bride's female relatives.

बरोबर *barobar*, adj. & adv. corr. = बराबर.

बरौंखा *baraumkhā*, m. reg. (Bihar) = बरौखा.

बरौंथा *baraumthā*, m. reg. (W.) the part of a wall above a doorway; keystone (of an arch).

बरौंधा *baraundhā*, m. reg. (W.) land under cotton in the past season.

बरौखा *baraukhā* [f. **vadrapaṅkha-*], m. reg. (W.) a tall, reddish variety of sugar-cane having long, broad leaves.

बरौनी *baraunī* f. eyelash.

बर्खी *barkhī* [ad. *varṣa-*: H. *-ī*], f. anniversary (esp. of a death).

बर्ग *barg* [P. *barg*], m. a leaf.

बर्ताव *bartāv*, m. see बरताव.

बर्फ़ *barf* [P. *barf*], f. m. **1.** ice. **2.** snow; hail. **3.** an ice-cream (= कुलफ़ी). — ~ का तूफ़ान, m. snowstorm. ~ का पहाड़, m. iceberg. ~ की नदी, f. glacier. ~ गलना, to be intensely cold. ~ गिरना, = next, 2. ~ पड़ना, to freeze; to snow. – बरफ़-ख़ाना, m. ice-box. बर्फ़बारी [P. *-bārī*], f. a snowfall. बर्फ़ाच्छादित, adj. snow-covered.

बर्फ़ानी *barfānī* [cf. H. *barf*: w. H. *himānī*], adj. **1.** icy. **2.** snowy; snow-covered.

बर्फ़िस्तान *barfistān* [H. *barf*+P. *(i)stān*], m. snowy waste.

बर्फ़ी *barfī* [P. *barfī*], adj. & f. **1.** adj. icy, &c. (= बरफ़ानी). **2.** f. a sweet made in rectangular shapes from thickened milk and sugar (sometimes containing nuts, &c). **3.** transf. a section, square (as in embroidery).

बर्फ़ीला *barfīlā* [cf. H. *barf*], adj. = बर्फ़ानी.

बर्मा *barmā* [Engl. *Burma*], m. Burma.

¹**बर्मी** *barmī* [cf. H. *barmā*], adj. & f. **1.** adj. Burmese. **2.** f. the Burmese language.

²**बर्मी** *barmī* [cf. H. *barmā*], m., f. a Burmese.

बर्र *barr* [*varaṭa-*²], f. a wasp.

बर्रा *barrā* [*vaṭāraka-*], m. reg. **1.** a rope. **2.** (E.) a thick rope of grass as used in tug-of-war contests.

बर्राक़ *barrāq* [A. *barrāq*], adj. **1.** flashing, brilliant. **2.** snow-white; unblemished.

बर्राना *barrānā* [? **baḍabaḍa-*: Pk. *baḍabaḍaï*], v.t. to babble; to talk in one's sleep.

बर्राहट *barrāhaṭ* [cf. H. *barrānā*], f. babbling; muttering in sleep.

बर्रे *barre*, m. = बर्रै.

बर्रै *barrai* [*varaṭa-*¹], m. *Pl. HŚS.* seed of safflower.

¹**बल** *bal* [*bala-*], m. & adv. **1.** m. power, strength; might. **2.** force, vigour. **3.** stress, emphasis; weight, significance. **4.** a force (military, &c). **5.** support; reliance (on, पर); dependence (on). **6.** side, direction, way. आड़े ~, adv. slantwise; खड़े ~, adv. vertically. **7.** semen. **8.** *mythol.* Balrām, Kr̥ṣṇa's elder brother. **9.** name of a Daitya king (= बलि, 3). **10.** adv. by dint or strength (of, के), by virtue (of). **11.** supported (by, के); resting (on); on to. एड़ी के ~ घूमना, to turn on the heel. — ~ देना, to lay stress (on, पर). ~ मिलना, to be given weight or importance; to be seen in a new light. ~ लगाना, to exert strength, to make an effort. घुटनों के ~ चलना, to crawl. पीठ के ~, adv. on the back; backwards. मुँह के ~, adv. on the face, face downwards. सिर के ~, adv. headlong,

head-first. — बलदार [P. *-dār*], adj. strong, powerful. बलदेव, m. = ~, 8. बल-बूता, = ~, 1. बल-राम, m. = ~, 8. बलवंत, adj. Brbh. Av. = बलवान. बल-वर्द्धक, adj. fortifying, tonic (a medicine). बलवान, adj. strong, powerful; *ling.* bearing stress, or emphasis. बल-विज्ञान, m. mechanics. बलशाली, adj. = बलवान, 1. बलहीन, adj. weak, infirm. °ता, f. बलाघात [°*la*+*ā*°], m. *ling.* emphasis, stress. बलाधिकृत [°*la*+*a*°], m. *mil.* commander, leader. बलाधिक्य [°*la*+*ā*°], m. superiority in strength. बलान्वित [°*la*+*a*°], adj. possessing power, &c. बलाबल [°*la*+*a*°], m. strength and weakness.

[2]**बल** *bal* [*vali-*, f. (m.)], m. **1.** twist, hitch (as in a rope). **2.** turn (of rope, &c., round sthg.); coil. **3.** bend, meandering (of a river). **4.** fold of skin; wrinkle. **5.** wrinkle (as in cloth). **6.** ripple. **7.** colloq. hitch, malfunction. न जाने इस घड़ी में क्या ~ है, something or other is wrong with this watch. **8.** discrepancy (as in accounts). **9.** crookedness; a grudge. — ~ आना, a wrinkle to appear (as on the brow, में). ~ करना, to turn and twist, to wriggle; to strut. ~ खाना, to be twisted, wound, coiled; to wind (as a river); to bend; to move, to jerk (the body). ~ देना (को), to twist, to wind, to coil; to bend. ~ पड़ना, = ~ आना; a sudden pain to be felt. ~ निकलना, folds or twists to be removed, to become straight or smooth; fig. to be humbled, taught a lesson. – बलदार [P. *-dār*], adj. twisted, coiled; bent, curved; winding (as a river); folded, wrinkled.

[3]**बल** *bal* [*bali-*], m. = बलि.

बलक- *balak-* [**balakk-*], v.i. reg. **1.** to bubble up (as boiling milk). **2.** to speak indistinctly (through excitement, or intoxication).

बलकट *balkaṭ* [H. [2]*bālī*+H. *kāṭnā*], m. reg. **1.** cutting ears of corn without the stalk. **2.** cash rent of land fixed after estimating the value of the crop.

बलकटी *balkaṭī* [cf. H. *balkaṭ*], f. *hist.* a tax formerly paid at the beginning of reaping.

बलकल *balkal*, m. Brbh. Av. = वल्कल.

बलकावा *balkāvā* [cf. H. *balak-*], m. Av. **1.** bubbling up, surge (of youth). **2.** reg. indistinct speech (see बलक-).

बलकि *balki* adv. = बल्कि.

बलकौह- *balkauh-* [cf. H. **balak-*], adj. Brbh. agitated (speech).

बलग़म *balgam* [A. *balgam*], m. phlegm, mucus; running of the nose.

बलगर *balgar*, adj. reg. = बलवान, see s.v. [1]बल.

बलतोड़ *baltoṛ*, m. = बाल-तोड़ (see s.v. [3]बाल).

बलत्कार *balatkār*, m. = बलात्कार.

बलद *balad*, m. = बरद.

बलदाना *baldānā* [H. *balad*+P.*-āna*], m. *hist.* tax on laden oxen.

बलदिया *baldiyā* [cf. H. *balad*], m. **1.** bullock-driver. **2.** cowherd. **3.** ? grain merchant.

[1]**बलना** *balnā* [**dvalati*], v.i. to burn; to be lit (as a lamp).

[2]**बलना** *balnā* [*valati*], v.i. reg. **1.** to twist, to turn (cf. [2]बल). **2.** to braid, to weave.

बलबलाना *balbalānā*, v.i. **1.** to make a bubbling noise; to low (as a camel, esp. when in rut). **2.** to be in a violent rage. **3.** to babble, to talk nonsense. **4.** reg. to ferment (= बजबजाना).

बलबलाहट *balbalāhaṭ* [cf. H. *balbalānā*], f. lowing, &c.

बलभाना *balbhānā* [cf. *vallabha-*, ad.], v.t. reg. to allure, to tantalise.

बलम *balam*, m. = [1]बल्लम.

बलमा *balmā*, m. reg. = [1]बल्लम.

बलराँड़ *balrāṁṛ* [H. [1]*bāl*+H. *rāṁṛ*], f. a child widow; a very young widow.

बलवा *balvā*, m. **1.** riot, disturbance. **2.** revolt, rebellion. — ~ करना, to riot, &c.

बलवाई *balvāī* [cf. H. *balvā*], m. rioter, rebel.

बलसुंदर *balsundar* [H. *bālū*+H. *sundar*], m. reg. (E.) a rich clayey loam.

बला *balā* [A. *balā*], f. **1.** misfortune, calamity; affliction. **2.** evil spirit. **3.** an awful or terrible person or thing. **4.** colloq. a vast amount (of). — ~ का, adj. colloq. fearful, awful; a vast amount of. ~ का बोलनेवाला, m. a dreadfully talkative person. ~ की मिरचें, f. an awful lot of spices. ~ दूर! may the disaster be far off! (said to avert an evil omen). ~ पीछे लगा लेना, to bring trouble (upon, के). ~, or बलाएँ, लेना (की), to wish or to seek to take (another's) misfortunes on oneself; to sacrifice oneself for another. ~ से, adv. I, or we, don't care; let him, let them (do a partic. thing); तुम्हारी ~ से (काम है), it concerns your evil genius: it is no concern of yours. जाने मेरी ~ से! I'm damned if I know! तू क्या ~ है? what awful creature are you?: you do not deserve attention. हमारी ~ ऐसा करे, I would never do that. – बलानसीब, adj ill-fated.

बलाइ *balāi* [cf. H. *balā*], f. Brbh. = बला. ~ ले-, = बला लेना.

बलाका *balākā* [S.], f. a crane.

बलाग़त *balāgat* [A. *balāga*: P. *balāgat*], f. U. eloquence.

बलात् *balāt* [S.], adv. by force, forcibly. — बलात्कार, m. violence, coercion; rape (of a woman: पर or के साथ). बलात्कार से, adv. = ~. °ई, m. one who commits a violent assault. बलात्कृत, adj. done by force (an assault).

बलात्कार *balātkār* [S.: MIA *balakkāra-*], m. var. /bələtkar/. see s.v. बलात्.

बलाव *balāv*, adj. & m. reg. **1.** adj. cheaply bought. **2.** m. a great bargain.

बलाहर *balāhar*, m. reg. (W.) **1.** a low-caste village servant, messenger, or watchman. **2.** *Pl.* a community of fishermen and basket-makers.

बलाही *balāhī*, m. reg. a worker in hides and leather.

बलि *bali* [S.], m. **1.** offering. **2.** sacrifice; sacrificial beast. **3.** *mythol.* name of a Daitya king, whose pride was humbled by Kr̥ṣṇa. — ~ करना (का), to sacrifice. ~ चढ़ाना, to offer in sacrifice. ~ जाना (का), to serve as a sacrifice, to be sacrificed; to sacrifice or to devote oneself (for or to, पर); to implore devotedly. – बलिदान, m. making of an offering, or a sacrifice; an offering, &c. बलिदान करना (का), to sacrifice. °ई, adj. & m. बलि-पशु, m. sacrificial beast. बलिहारी, f. making of an offering, or a sacrifice. बलिहारी जाना, to sacrifice, or to devote oneself. बलिहारी लेना, = बलैयाँ लेना. बलिहारी है! I am delighted!

बलित *balit*, adj. = वलित.

बलिश्त *baliśt* [P. *biliśt*], m. a span of the hand.

बलिष्ठ *baliṣṭh* [S.], adj. strongest; very strong; sturdy.

[1]**बली** *balī* [S.], adj. & m. **1.** adj. powerful; mighty. **2.** m. a powerful or mighty being. — भाग्य का ~, adj. extremely fortunate.

[2]**बली** *balī* [cf. H. [2]*bal*], f. reg. a wrinkle.

बलुआ *baluā* [*vāluka-*], adj. sandy, gritty (soil).

बलुक *baluk*, conj. reg. = बलकि.

बलूत *balūt* [A. *ballūṭ*], m. an oak-tree.

बलेंड़ी *balem̐ṛī* [cf. **balidaṇḍa-*], f. reg. (W.) the ridgepole of a house.

बलैया *balaiyā* [cf. H. *balā*], f. = बला, 1. ~ लेना, = बला लेना.

बल्कि *balki* [A. *bal*+P. *ki*], adv. but rather; moreover.

बल्य *balyă* [S.], adj. **1.** powerful, strong. **2.** invigorating.

[1]**बल्लम** *ballam* [ad. *vallabha-*; H. *bālam*], m. lover; husband.

[2]**बल्लम** *ballam*, m. **1.** short spear. **2.** pike, lance. **3.** staff. **4.** mace.

बल्ला *ballā* [conn. *valaka-*], m. **1.** beam. **2.** pole; an unsquared rafter. **3.** bat, racquet. — बल्लेबाज़ [P. *-bāz*], m. batsman, batter. °ई, f. batting; batsmanship.

बल्लाई *ballāī*, m. *Pl.* a village workman (who cuts wood and maintains the village boundaries).

बल्ली *ballī* [conn. *vala-*], f. **1.** pole. **2.** rafter. — ~ मारना, to propel by punting (a flat-bottomed craft). बल्लियों उछालना, to be beside oneself with delight.

बवँड़- *bavam̐ṛ-*, v.i. Brbh. to wander aimlessly around.

बवंडर *bavaṇḍar* [*vātamaṇḍalī-*, Pa. *vātamaṇḍala-*; or *vāyu-*°], m. whirlwind; storm.

बवक़्त *ba-vaqt*, adv. U. see s.v. ब-.

बवादा *bavādā*, m. *Pl. HŚS.* a medicinal herb (of similar appearance to turmeric).

बवाल *bavāl* [A. *vabāl*: ? × H. *bāvelā*], m. corr. turmoil; furore.

बवासीर *bavāsīr* [A. *bavāsīr*, pl.], f. piles, haemorrhoids.

बशर्ते *ba-śarte*, conj. see s.v. ब-.

बसंत *basant* [ad. *vasanta-*], m. **1.** spring. **2.** *mus.* name of a *rāg.* **3.** a garland of yellow flowers. — ~ फूलना, yellow flowers to bloom (as of mustard); to turn pale, or yellow (the face). आँखों में ~ फूलना, the eyes to be dazzled. – बसंत-ऋतु, m. = ~, 1. बसंत-पंचमी, f. spring festival held on the fifth day of the light half of the month Māgh. बसंत-मालती, f. a powder supposed to contain gold leaf and crushed pearls, and said to cure or to check tuberculosis. उल्लू-बसंत, m. pej. a complete fool.

बसंता *basantā* [cf. H. *basant*], m. the barbet (a brightly coloured bird having several sub-species differing in size). — छोटा ~, m. the crimson-breasted barbet, or coppersmith. नीलकंठ ~, m. the blue-throated barbet. बड़ा ~, m. the large green barbet.

बसंती *basantī* [cf. H. *basant*], adj. **1.** yellow (as spring flowers). **2.** a yellow garment (esp. that worn by Kr̥ṣṇa).

बसंदर *basandar*, m. Av. title of Agni, the Vedic god of fire; fire.

[1]**बस** *bas* [P. *bas*], adj., adv. & interj. **1.** adj. enough. **2.** ample; very much; too much. **3.** adv. and so; in short, in a word. **4.** only, merely. ~ यही कहना चाहता हूँ ..., I just want to say.... **5.** interj. & fig. f. enough! stop! — ~ करना, to stop, to desist; to make an end to, or of (a task); to lay aside. ~ ठीक! very good! that's just right! agreed! ~ ~, adv. enough!; yes yes, quite right.

[2]**बस** *bas* [*vaśa-*], m. **1.** power. **2.** command, control; influence. — ~ की बात (के), f. sthg. in (one's) power to do. ~ चलना (का), to have power or ability to act in a matter. ~ में, adv. in the power, or authority, or discretion (of, के); in subjection (to). ~, or ~ में, आना, or पड़ना, to be obtained, got hold of (by, के); to come or to fall into the power (of); to be charmed, bewitched (by). ~, or ~ में, करना, or लाना (अपने), to make subject (to oneself), to subdue; to charm, to bewitch. ~ में रखना (अपने), to keep (one, को) under control, in subjection; to restrain. ~ में रहना, to be subject (to, के); to be controlled (by), to obey. – बसवर्ती, adj. obs. obedient (to, का, अपना), docile; obsequious.

[3]**बस** *bas* [Engl. *bus*], f. a bus.

बसगत *basgat*, f. reg. = बसगित.

बसगित *basgit*, f. reg. residence; site of a village.

बसत *basat* [cf. H. *basnā*], adj. inhabited, taken up (land).

[1]**बसना** *basnā* [*vasati*], v.i. **1.** to dwell, to reside. **2.** to be settled, populated. **3.** to be cultivated (land). **4.** to settle, to lodge; to camp; to roost. बसा हुआ, adj. situated (in or on, में or पर). **5.** to be set up (a household). उसका घर बस गया है, he is married, settled down. **6.** to prosper (as a household).

[2]**बसना** *basnā* [cf. *vāsayati*[3], H. *bāsnā*], v.i. to be perfumed, fragrant. — सुगंध ~, a fragrant smell to be perceptible.

[3]**बसना** *basnā* [*vasana-*[1]], m. **1.** a wrapper; cloth, sack-cloth. **2.** cloth on which a money-changer or money-lender places his scales and weights. **3.** *Pl. HŚS.* transf. a money-changing or money-lending firm.

बसनी *basnī* [cf. H. [3]*basnā*], f. reg. a small purse, or money-bag.

बसबब *ba-sabab*, adv. U. see s.v. ब-.

बस-बास *bas-bās* [cf. H. [1]*basnā*; H. *vās*], m. reg. dwelling, residence.

बसर *ba-sar*, adv. see s.v. ब-.

बसवारी *basvārī* [*vaṁśavāṭikā-*], f. a bamboo plantation; bamboo thicket.

बसह *basah* [*vṛṣabha-*], m. bull; ox.

[1]**बसा** *basā* [ad. *vasā-*], f. **1.** marrow (of bones). **2.** fat, suet.

[2]**बसा** *basā*, f. Av. a wasp.

[1]**बसाना** *basānā* [cf. H. [1]*basnā*], v.t. **1.** to cause to dwell; to settle (a country, a region). **2.** to bring into cultivation (land). **3.** to take into one's house to stay (a traveller, &c). **4.** to found (a town; a household or family). — (अपना) घर ~, fig. to take a wife. मन में, or हृदय में, ~, to take to heart (as advice).

[2]**बसाना** *basānā* [cf. *vāsayati*[3], Pa. *vāsāpeti*], v.t. & v.i. **1.** v.t. to perfume. **2.** v.i. to smell unpleasant.

बसाव *basāv* [cf. H. [1]*basnā*, [1]*basānā*], m. dwelling; living, life; residence (in a place).

बसावरी *basāvrī* [cf. H. [1]*basānā*], f. reg. ground rent from village houses (payable by those not cultivating village land).

बसियाना *basiyānā* [cf. H. *bāsī*], v.i. to grow stale, or mildewed.

बसीठ *basīṭh* [*vasiṣṭha*], m. **1.** headman of a village. **2.** responsible agent, or envoy. **3.** intermediary.

बसीठी *basīṭhī* [cf. H. *basīṭh*], f. **1.** business of a village headman. **2.** business or partic. task of an envoy, &c.

बसुला *basulā*, m. = बसूला.

बसूरत *basūrat*, adv. see s.v. ब-.

बसूला *basūlā* [cf. *vāśī-*], m. carpenter's axe, adze.

बसूली *basūlī* [cf. H. *basūlā*], f. mason's or builder's hatchet.

बसेंड़ा *basemṛā* [**vaṁśadaṇḍa-*], m. reg. a thin bamboo.

बसेरा *baserā* [**vāsakara-*], m. **1.** night's lodging; place of staying or halting. **2.** roosting; a roost. **3.** Av. refuge. — ~ करना, to stay, to halt; to settle (in a place); to roost. ~ देना (को), to give a night's lodging (to); to give shelter (to). ~ लेना, to roost (on, पर); to settle (in a place).

बसोबास *basobās*, m. Brbh. abode (= बसबास).

बस्ता *bastā* [P. *basta*], m. **1.** cloth wrapper. **2.** bundle (as of papers, books); schoolchild's books, &c. **3.** parcel. — ~ बाँधना, to tie up, or to put away papers (preparatory to leaving work).

बस्ती *bastī* [cf. H. *basat*], f. **1.** a settlement; a new settlement or suburb. **2.** a makeshift settlement of homeless people. **3.** inhabitants, population (= आबादी).

बहँगी *bahaṁgī* [cf. **vahaṅga-*], f. a pole with slings at the ends for carrying loads. — बहँगीबरदार [P. *-bardār*], m. porter equipped with a *bahaṁgī*.

बहक *bahak* [cf. H. *bahakna*], f. confusion, &c.; frantic speech, flood of words. — बाव-बहक, f. 19c. = ~, 2.

बहकना *bahakna* [cf. *vyathate*], v.i. **1.** to be misled, to be deluded; to be disappointed. **2.** to stray. **3.** to be lulled, or dispelled (as fears). **4.** to lose control of oneself, to become intoxicated; to be enraged. **5.** to miss its mark (a blow, a bullet). — बहकी बातें, f. pl. incoherent, or deluded words.

बहकाना *bahkānā* [cf. H. *bahaknā*], v.t. **1.** to mislead, to delude; to disappoint (as hopes), to decoy, to seduce. **3.** to lull (justified fears, doubts). **4.** to frighten (one) away; to dispel (unjustified fears). **5.** to set (a person) against (another). **6.** to cause (a person) to forget himself; to intoxicate (one). — बहका ले जाना, to lure away; to run away with (a misled person).

बहकावट *bahkāvaṭ* [cf. H. *bahkānā*], f. = बहकावा.

बहकावा *bahkāvā* [cf. H. *bahkānā*], m. misleading, &c.; deception; trick, ruse. बहकावे में आना, to be deceived or beguiled, or imposed on (by, के). बहकावे में डालना, to deceive, &c.

बहत्तर *bahattar* [cf. *dvāsaptati-*], adj. seventy-two. — ~ घाट का पानी पिए हुए होना, fig. to be experienced, wise or shrewd.

बहन *bahn* [*bhaginī-*], f. **1.** sister. **2.** female cousin. **3.** term of address to a woman.

बहना *bahnā* [*vahati*], v.i. **1.** to flow. **2.** to float; to drift; to glide. **3.** to overflow (as a tank). **4.** to run, or to ooze (as a wound). **5.** to melt, to run (as wax). **6.** to blow (a wind). **7.** Av. to carry. **8.** to be carried away; to be separated, dispersed; to fly (in the wind: a kite). **9.** to slip, to fall or to fly from place (a piece of clothing). **10.** Brbh. to wander, to stray. **11.** esp. w. चलना. to be ruined, depraved. **12.** to be squandered (money). **13.** to exist no more (an attitude). **14.** to become watery; to dissolve.

बहनापा *bahnāpā* [cf. H. *bahn*], m. sisterliness, sisterly affection.

बहनेऊ *bahneū* [*bhaginīpati-*], m. reg. = बहनोई.

बहनेला *bahnelā* [cf. H. *bahn*], m. = बहनापा. — ~ जोड़ना (से), to form a friendship (a woman, with another).

बहनेली *bahnelī* [cf. H. *bahn*], f. female friend (among women).

बहनोई *bahnoī* [*bhaginīpati-*], m. sister's husband, brother-in-law.

बहनोत *bahnot* [**bhaginīputra-*], m. *Pl.* sister's son.

बहनौता *bahnautā* [**bhaginīputra-*], m. sister's son, nephew.

बहबहा *bahbahā* [cf. H. *bahnā*], adj. reg. Brbh. flowing along; wandering.

बहबूदी *bahbūdī* [P. *bahbūdī*], f. U. benefit, advantage.

बहम *baham*, adv. see s.v. ब-.

बहर *bahr*, m., f. see बह्र.

बहर- *ba-har-*. see s.v. ब-.

बहरा *bahrā* [*badhira-*], adj. deaf.

बहरा- *bahrā-* [H. *bahlānā*], v.t. Brbh. **1.** to amuse, to divert. **2.** to trick, to deceive.

बहरापन *bahrāpan* [cf. H. *bahrā*], m. deafness.

बहरारू *bahrārū*, adj. *Pl.* outsider; upstart.

बहरिया *bahriyā* [cf. H. *bāhar*], m. reg. an outsider, stranger.

बहरियाना *bahriyānā* [cf. H. *bāhar*], v.i. & v.t. reg. **1.** v.i. to go out. **2.** v.t. to push out (a boat).

बहरी *bahrī* [cf. *vadhati*, and *vyādha-*], f. Brbh. female hunting hawk, falcon.

बहल *bahl* [*vahala-*], m. a two-wheeled covered cart pulled by oxen. — बहल-ख़ाना, m. place for carts. बहलवान, m. driver of an ox-cart.

बहलना *bahalnā* [cf. H. [1]*bihar-*, or **velya-*], v.i. **1.** to be amused, entertained. **2.** to be diverted, distracted.

बहला *bahlā* [cf. *vehat-*], adj. reg. barren, worn-out (esp. of a cow).

[1]**बहलाना** *bahlānā* [cf. H. *bahalnā*], v.t. **1.** to amuse; to entertain. **2.** to divert (the mind from cares); to distract. **3.** to distract (the attention). — जी ~, to amuse; to divert. मन ~, id.

[2]**बहलाना** *bahlānā* [cf. H. *bahānā*], v.t. reg. to flood for irrigation (a field).

बहलावा *bahlāvā* [cf. H. *bahlānā*], m. amusement, diversion. — ~ देना, to please (one, को).

बहवाना *bahvānā*, v.t. = बहाना.

बहस *bahs* [A. *bahs̤*], f. **1.** dispute, argument; controversy, debate. **2.** wrangle, quarrel. — ~ करना, to argue, to dispute, &c. (with, से). – बहसा-बहसी [cf. H. *bahsnā*], f. continuing argument, controversy.

बहसना *bahsnā* [cf. H. *bahs*], v.i. reg. to argue.

बहादुर *bahādur* [P. *bahādur*], adj. & m. **1.** adj. brave, bold. **2.** m. hero. **3.** (affixed to a name) a partic. honorific title.

बहादुरी *bahādurī* [P. *bahādurī*], f. bravery, courage.

[1]**बहाना** *bahānā* [cf. H. *bahnā*], v.t. **1.** to cause to flow; to pour forth or out; to shed (tears, blood); to express (liquid). **2.** to cause to float; to set adrift (a boat, &c.); to launch. **3.** to wash away (as dirt, or sin). **4.** to sweep away, to ruin (as a reputation). **5.** to drive away (clouds). **6.** to squander (money). **7.** to sell very cheaply.

[2]**बहाना** *bahānā* [P. *bahāna*], m. **1.** excuse, pretext. **2.** evasion, subterfuge. **3.** affectation. — ~ **करना**, to make an excuse; to sham; to prevaricate. ~ **बताना**, = id., 1. ~ **बनाना**, to make up an excuse. **बहाने**, adv. under the pretext, &c. (of, **के**).

बहार *bahār* [P. *bahār*], f. **1.** spring. **2.** flourishing state; youth; prime. **3.** beauty, splendour; elegance. **4.** delight. **5.** *mus.* name of a *rāgiṇī*. — ~ **उड़ाना**, or **लूटना**, to enjoy the delights (of, **की**), to revel (in). ~ **का तेल**, m. oil scented with orange blossom. ~ **देना**, to impart splendour (to, **पर**), to set off. ~ **पर आना**, to bloom; to be in full glory. ~ **पर होना**, to be in bloom, or in full glory.

बहारी *bahārī* [P. *bahārī*], adj. having to do with spring.

बहाल *ba-hāl*, adj. see **ब-**.

बहाली *ba-hālī*, f. see **ब-**.

बहाव *bahāv* [cf. H. *bahnā*, *bahānā*], m. **1.** flow; current (of water, or air). **2.** fluid state. **3.** flow, rhythm (of a verse).

बहिन *bahin*, f. see **बहन**.

बहियार *bahiyār*, m. reg. outlying lands of a village.

बहिर्- *bahir-* [S.], pref. out, outside: — **बहिरंग**, adj. & m. external; separate; superfluous; exterior. **बहिर्गमन**, m. going out; way out, exit. **बहिर्जगत**, m. the external world. **बहिर्मुख**, adj. looking out or away; extroverted; neglectful; pej. impious, immoral. **बहिर्वासी**, adj. living out or away (from a partic. place).

बहिश्त *bahiśt* [P. *bihiśt*], f. paradise. — ~ **का**, adj. fig. delightful, refreshing (as climate, &c.) – **समर-बहिश्त**, f. fruit of paradise: a type of mango.

बहिष्- *bahiṣ-* [S]. out, &c. (= **बहिर्-**): — **बहिष्करण**, m. outcasting, banning; exiling; boycotting. **बहिष्कार**, m. outcasting, ban; exile; boycott. °**-कृत**, adj.

बहिया *bahiyā* [cf. H. *bāhī*], m. reg. (E.) a servant; labourer.

बही *bahī* [*vahikā-*], f. account-book, ledger. — ~ **पर**, or **में**, **चढ़ाना**, to enter in an account-book. – **बही-खाता**, f. = **बही**.

बहीर *bahīr* [P. *bahīr*: ? ← H. *bhīṛ*], f. Brbh. the baggage, equipment and camp followers of an army.

बहु- *bahu-* [S.], adj. (rarely **बहु**). **1.** much, many; multi-; poly-. **2.** large, great. **3.** excessive; over- . — **बहुकरोड़ा**, adj. multi-million. **बहुकाल**, m. a great length of time. °**ईन**, adj. of long standing; ancient. **बहुगुण**, adj. of many strands; multiple, multifarious; having many virtues. **बहुचर्चित**, adj. much-discussed, well-known. **बहुजन**, m. a large group of people; the community. **बहुजातिक**, adj. multinational. °**-जातीय**, adj. id. **बहुज्ञ**, adj. knowing much; learned. °**ता**, f. erudition. **बहुदर्शिता**, f. wide experience (as of life). °**दर्शी**, adj. seeing much, or far; knowing. **बहुदेववाद**, m. polytheism. **बहुदेवोपासना** [°*va+u*°], f. id. **बहुधन**, adj. very rich. **बहुधा**, adv. see s.v. **बहुपतित्व**, m. polyandry. **बहुपत्नीक**, adj. polygamous. **बहुपुत्र**, m. having many sons. **बहुप्रकार**, adj. various, multiform. **बहुबाहु**, adj. & m. Av. *mythol.* many-armed; a title of Rāvaṇ. **बहुभाषी**, adj. polyglot, °**-भाषीय**, adj. multilingual. **बहुमंज़िला**, adj. multi-storeyed; of many or several stages. **बहुमत**, m. the opinion of a majority; majority (of votes or voices); variety of opinions. **बहु-मात्र**, m. large quantity, bulk, mass. **बहुमान**, m. great respect, reverence. °**-मान्य**, adj. much respected; generally accepted (as a view). **बहुमूल्य**, adj. high in price; precious, valuable. °**ता**, f. **बहुरंगा**, adj. multi-coloured; of changing colour(s); various; changeable, fickle. °**-रंगी**, adj. id. **बहुराष्ट्रीय**, adj. multinational. **बहुरूप**, adj. & m. multiform; variegated; diverse. °**ता**, f. **बहुरूपिया**, m. /-rup-/. actor, mimic; dissembler. **बहुवचन**, m. *gram.* plural number. **बहुविध**, adj. of many, or various kinds. **बहुविवाह**, m. polygamy; polyandry. **बहुव्रीहि**, m. *gram.* having much rice: a term used as the name of a class of adjectival compounds in which the last member is a noun (the word itself exemplifies the class). **बहुशः**, adv. many times; in many ways. **बहुश्रुत**, adj. much heard of; who has heard much: widely informed. **बहु-संख्यक**, adj. numerous; preponderant, or vast (in number). °**संख्या**, f. majority, preponderance in number. **बहुस्तरीय**, adj. multi-level, multi-stage.

बहुटनी *bahuṭanī*, f. Brbh. an ornament for the (? upper) arm.

बहुत *bahut* [*bahutva-*], adj. & adv. **1.** adj. many, much. **2.** abundant, ample; (esp. w. **ही**) too much. **3.** enough. **4.** adv. very. **5.** very much, considerably; extremely; (esp. w. **ही**) excessively. — ~ **अच्छा**, adv. very good! very well! ~ **अधिक**, or **ज़्यादा**, very many; very much.

~ करके, adv. for the most part; mostly, often; at most, at best; surely. ~ कुछ, m. & adv. a good deal, a lot; often; to a great extent. ~ ख़ूब, adv. splendid! ~ बड़े पेड़, m. very large trees. ~ ही, adj. & adv. very much indeed; too much. ~ हुआ तो पाँच रुपए दिए होंगे, at most he will have given five rupees. ~ है! enough! – बहुत-सा, adj. a lot of, much; pl. many. बहुत-से बड़े पेड़, many large trees.

बहुता *bahutā* [S.], f. plenty, abundance.

बहुताई *bahutāī*, f. = बहुतायत.

बहुतात *bahutāt*, f. pronun. var. = बहुतायत.

बहुतायत *bahutāyat* [cf. H. *bahut*], f. **1.** abundance, plenty. **2.** excess. **3.** majority.

बहुतेरा *bahuterā* [**bahutvatara-*], adj. & adv. **1.** adj. many. **2.** abundant. **3.** adv. very much. **4.** for the most part, mostly.

बहुत्व *bahutvă* [S.], m. = बहुतायत.

बहुधा *bahudhā* [S.], adv. **1.** in many ways. **2.** at many times; often; generally.

बहुर- *bahur-* [**vyāghuṭati*: Pk. *vāhuḍia-*], v.i. Brbh. Av. to go or to come back, to return.

बहुरा- *bahurā-* [cf. H. *bahurnā*], v.t. Brbh. to send off, to send back.

बहुरि *bahuri* [cf. **vyāghuṭati*: Pk. *vāhuḍia-*], adv. Brbh. Av. **1.** again, anew. **2.** then, next, further.

बहुरिया *bahuriyā* [*vadhūtikā-*], f. daughter-in-law.

बहुल *bahul* [S.], adj. **1.** ample, abundant. **2.** -बहुल. abounding (in). **3.** broad, spacious.

बहुलता *bahulătā* [S.], f. **1.** abundance. **2.** multiplicity.

बहुला *bahulā* [S.], f. Brbh. productive one: name given to a cow.

बहू *bahū* [*vadhū-*], f. **1.** daughter-in-law. **2.** young wife; bride. — बहू-बेटियाँ, f. pl. the younger women of an extended family.

बहूआर *bahūār* [*bahuvāra-*], m. *Pl.* the fruit *Cordia myxa* (= लसोड़ा).

बहेड़ा *baheṛā* [**vibhīṭaka-*: Pk. *baheḍaa-*], m. *Beleric myrobalan* (a large tree, the source of a gum, and of a fruit used medicinally and in dyeing and tanning).

बहेतू *bahetū* [cf. H. *bahtā*], adj. reg. (W.) lost, strayed (cattle).

बहेलिया *baheliyā* [cf. *vyādha-*], m. **1.** hunter, fowler. **2.** an armed attendant (esp. a bowman).

बहोंडा *bahoṇḍā*, m. *Pl.* land given rent-free to a village watchman.

बहोड़ा *bahoṛā* [cf. *vadhū-*], m. food sent by the bride's family for the bridegroom and his party (बरात).

बहोर *bahor* [cf. H. *bahor-*], m. (?) Av. return.

बहोर- *bahor-* [cf. H. *bahurnā*], v.t. Brbh. Av. to return.

बहोरि *bahori*, adv. Brbh. Av. = बहुरि.

बहोरो *bahoro* [? cf. *vāha-*], m. reg. (W.) the sloping pathway for bullocks drawing water from a well.

बहौंडा *bahauṇḍā*, m. *Pl.* = बहोंडा.

बह्या *bahyā*, m. *Pl.* flowing water: flood (= बहाव).

बह्र *bahr* [A. *baḥr*], m., f. U. **1.** m. the sea. **2.** f. a metre; verse.

बह्री *bahrī* [A. *baḥrī*], adj. **1.** having to do with the sea. **2.** naval.

बाँ *bām̐* [onom.], m. bellowing; lowing. — ~ ~ करना, to bellow; to low, to moo; colloq. to babble, to blurt out (a secret, &c).

बाँक *bām̐k* [*vaṅka-*[1], Pa. *vaṅka-*], adj. & m. f. **1.** adj. crooked, curved. **2.** Av. glancing (the eyes). **3.** m. crookedness; curvature. **4.** fig. duplicity. **5.** curve, bend (as of a river). **6.** hook (to cut cane, &c). **7.** a vice (implement). **8.** usu. f. curved dagger. **9.** an armlet, or anklet. — बाँक-पट्टा, m. fighting with wooden dagger and sword. बाँक-बनावट, f. the art of wielding a dagger.

बाँकपन *bām̐kpan* [cf. H. *bām̐k*], m. **1.** crookedness. **2.** showiness, modishness; elegance; swagger. **3.** flirtatiousness.

बाँका *bām̐kā* [*vaṅku-*], adj. & m. **1.** adj. crooked, bent; curved; awry. **2.** oblique. **3.** showy, smart (of manner, attire); flirtatious. **4.** disaffected (in mood). **5.** dissolute. **6.** m. hook (to cut cane, &c). **7.** a smart or modish person. **8.** a showily dressed youth (carried in a palanquin at festivities). **9.** reg. = बाँकी, 2. — ~ चोर, m. an expert thief, prince of thieves. बाल ~ न होने देना, not to allow the hair to be ruffled: not to allow to be in the slightest harmed. – बाँका-तिरछा, adj. crooked, curved, &c.; glancing, flirtatious (the eyes).

बाँकुरा *bām̐kurā* [cf. H. *bām̐k*], adj. bold or skilful (in love, or war).

बाँकी *bām̐kī* [cf. H. *bām̐kā*], f. reg. **1.** a curved knife (as used by *ḍoms* and by workers in bamboo). **2.** a water-beetle or caterpillar which attacks rice.

बाँकैत *bāṁkait*, m. reg. = **बाँका**, 7.

बाँग *bāṁg* [P. *bāng*], f. **1.** cry, shout. **2.** *musl.* muezzin's call to prayer (= **अज़ान**). **3.** crowing (of a cock). — ~ **देना**, to call (Muslims) to prayer; to crow (a cock). ~ **मारना**, to cry out, to call. ~ **लगाना**, to start to crow.

बाँगड़ *bāṁgaṛ*, m. **1.** hilly, or high ground; table-land. **2.** the Hariyāṇā area, or part of it. **3.** a field (for cattle-grazing).

बाँगड़ू *bāṁgṛū*, adj. & m. **1.** adj. upland. **2.** rough, crude, boorish. **3.** stupid. **4.** m. one from an upland region. **5.** Bāṁgṛū speech, a form of Hindi in use in Hariyāṇā.

बाँगर *bāṁgar*, m. = **बाँगड़**, 1., 3.

बाँगा *bāṁgā* [conn. *vaṅga-*²], m. reg. **1.** the cotton plant. **2.** raw cotton.

बाँच- *bāṁc-* [*vañcati*], v.i. & v.t. Av. **1.** v.i. = **बचना**. **2.** v.t. to disregard, to neglect.

बाँचना *bāṁcnā* [ad. *vācayati*], v.t. to read; to read through, to decipher.

बाँछ *bāṁch*, f. = ¹**बाछ**.

बाँछ- *bāṁch-* [*vāṁchati*], v.t. Brbh. to desire.

¹**बाँझ** *bāṁjh* [*vandhya-*], adj. **1.** barren (a woman; or a cow, &c). **2.** not bearing fruit (a tree). **3.** unproductive, barren (soil).

²**बाँझ** *bāṁjh* [**vañj(h)a-*], f. *Pl. HŚS.* the Himālayan grey oak, or green oak.

बाँझपन *bāṁjhpan* [cf. H. ¹*bāṁjh*], m. infertility.

¹**बाँट** *bāṁṭ* [[cf. H. ¹*bāṁṭnā*; and *vaṇṭa-*¹], f. m. **1.** dividing, division. **2.** partition (as of India, in 1947). **3.** distribution, apportionment. **4.** part, share; lot. **5.** deal, hand (at cards). — ~ **पड़ना**, to fall to the lot or share (of, **की**). – **बाँट-चूँट**, f. sharing out; share. **बाँट-फल**, m. *Pl. arith.* quotient. **बाँट-बूँट**, f. = **बाँट-चूँट**.

²**बाँट** *bāṁṭ*, m. reg. = ²**बाट**.

¹**बाँटना** *bāṁṭnā* [*vaṇṭati*], v.t. **1.** to divide (among, **में**); to partition. **2.** to distribute, to apportion (between or to, **में**). **3.** (esp. w. **लेना**) to participate, to go shares (in, **में**). **4.** to deal out (as cards). — **बाँटे पड़ना**, to fall to the share of.

²**बाँटना** *bāṁṭnā*, v.t. reg. to twist (a rope) (= ¹**बटना**).

बाँटा *bāṁṭā* [cf. H. *bāṁṭnā*], m. reg. **1.** dividing; distribution. **2.** a share, portion. **3.** *Pl.* tying up a crop into sheaves, &c.

बाँटू *bāṁṭū* [cf. H. ¹*bāṁṭnā*], m. **1.** divider, distributor. **2.** *Pl. arith.* divisor.

बाँड़ *bāṁṛ* [*baṇḍa-*]. reg. (Bihar) **1.** a broken-tailed animal. **2.** blighted ears of millet. **3.** the bed of a river from which water has receded.

बाँड़ा *bāṁṛā* [*baṇḍa-*], adj. & m. *Pl.* maimed: **1.** adj. tailless; docked; broken-tailed. **2.** fig. not having home or family. **3.** pej. a circumcised man.

बाँड़ी *bāṁṛī* [cf. H. *bāṁṛā*], f. *HŚS.* **1.** bent piece of wood: cudgel. **2.** Brbh. a tongue of land (often fertile) lying at the confluence of two rivers. — ~ **चलना**, or **चटकना**, clubs to be wielded, a fight with clubs to be going on. – **बाँड़ीबाज़** [P. *-bāz*], m. wielder of a cudgel.

बाँदर *bāṁdar*, m. Av. = ¹**बंदर**.

बाँदरा *bāṁdrā*, m. reg. = ¹**बंदर**.

बाँदरी *bāṁdrī*, f. reg. = ¹**बंदरी**.

बाँदा *bāṁdā* [*vandā-*, f.], m. *Pl. HŚS.* a parasitical plant, *Epidendrum tesselatum*, or *Cymbidium tessalloides*.

बाँदी *bāṁdī* [*bandī-*: ← Middle P.], f. **1.** female slave. **2.** servant girl (= **लौंडी**). — ~ **का बेटा**, m. fig. a person submissive to authority.

बाँध *bāṁdh* [*bandha-*], m. a binding, fastening: **1.** embankment; dam, barrage. **2.** barrier, barricade. **3.** transf. barrage (of fire). **4.** a fetter.

बाँधना *bāṁdhnā* [*bandhati*], v.t. **1.** to bind, to tie (to, **से**); to fasten; to tether; to tie in place (as hair); to set (a broken bone). **2.** to tie, to wrap (round or on, **पर**). **3.** to tighten (around, **में**). **कमर में पेटी** ~, to put a belt round the waist. **4.** to wrap, to tie up (in, **में**). **5.** to tie up (with, **में**); to confine, to imprison. **6.** to captivate (as the eyes, the sight); to bring under one's influence; to bind (as with an oath). **7.** to fix (the eyes, or aim; or the hopes, &c.: on, **पर**). **8.** to check, to confine (water in its course); to embark. **9.** to shut off (a supply: as water); to restrict. **10.** to tie or to bring together; to gather, to pack (luggage); to make up (a packet); to form into (lumps: as dough). **11.** to build, to construct (as a bridge, a dam; or a house). **12.** to form, to produce, to make; to form (a line, &c.); to devise (a plan); to form (an ambition, &c.); to compose (verses). **13.** to form (a relationship: as of friendship, enmity, with, **से**). **14.** to close together; to fold (the arms); to join (the hands); to clench (the fist). **15.** to unite (in marriage). **16.** to decide, to determine (a limit; or an amount, &c). **17.** to regard as, to compare (a person or thing: to, **को**).

बाँधनू *bāṁdhnū* [cf. H. *bāṁdhnā*], m. **1.** a course determined on: plan, plot; strategy;

approach. **2.** a fabrication; slander. **3.** a mode of dyeing (as used in preparing *cunrī* cloth) in which parts of the cloth are tied up so as not to receive the dye.

बांधव *bāndhav* [S.], m. **1.** kinsman. **2.** friend.

बाँब *bāṁb* [conn. *brāhmī-*], f. *Pl. HŚS.* an eel; snake.

बाँबी *bāṁbī* [*vamriya-*], f. **1.** ant-hill. **2.** snake's hole.

बाँभी *bāṁbhī*, f. reg. = बाँबी.

बाँस *bāṁs* [*vaṁśa-*], m. bamboo; a bamboo rod, or pole. — ~ चलाना, to fight with sticks, &c. ~ पर चढ़ना, to climb a bamboo: to be held up to ridicule, to be infamous. ~ पर चढ़ाना, or टँगना, to hold up to ridicule, or disgrace. बाँसों उछलना, or कूदना, to jump for joy (sc. as if on stilts); to leap, to pound (the heart). बाँसपूर, m. = next. बाँसपोर, m. Av. a type of fine (? silk) cloth. बाँसफोड़, m. a community of bamboo-workers; a man of that community. बाँस-वाड़ी, f. bamboo thicket, or plantation.

बाँसरी *bāṁsrī*, f. reg. (W.) a weed which springs up in the hot weather after the spring crop is cut.

बाँसा *bāṁsā* [*vaṁśaka-*], m. *Pl. HŚS.* **1.** reg. bamboo tube of a drill; drill-plough. **2.** a type of bamboo, *Dendrocalamus tulda*, which yields a red dye (= *piyā-bāṁsā*). **3.** reg. the bridge of the nose. **4.** the backbone.

¹बाँसी *bāṁsī* [*vaṁśīya-*], adj. & f. **1.** adj. having to do with, or made of, bamboo. **2.** f. reg. (Bihar) a plant which interferes with the growth of rice.

²बाँसी *bāṁsī* [cf. H. *bāṁs*, or *bāṁsī*, adj.], f. *Pl. HŚS.* **1.** a reed of which hookah tubes and mouthpieces are made (used also by weavers and makers of artificial flowers). **2.** a kind of dark-haired wheat. **3.** a kind of fragrant rice. **4.** a kind of whitish-yellow stone.

बाँसुरी *bāṁsurī* [cf. *vaṁśī-*], f. pipe, flute.

बाँह *bāṁh* [*bāhu-*], f. **1.** the upper arm. **2.** sleeve. आधी ~ की क़मीज़, f. short-sleeved shirt. **3.** support; protection; supporter. **4.** power, strength. — ~ की छाँह लेना, to seek or to accept the support, &c. (of). ~ गहना, or पकड़ना, to take the arm (of, की): to support, to aid, to protect; to marry. ~, or बहिं. चढ़ाना, to roll up the sleeves; to prepare (for, against, पर). ~ टूटना, fig. to be without friends or protectors. ~ देना (को), to support, to aid. ~ बुलंद होना, the arm to be raised: to be in a position of power, or to help (one) actively. – बाँह-मरोड़, m. arm-twister: a hold in wrestling (which throws the opponent off balance).

बाँहाजोरी *bāṁhājorī* [H. *bāṁh*+H. *joṛnā*, *joṛī*], adv. Brbh. arm in arm (a couple).

बाँहियाँ *bāṁhiyāṁ* [cf. H. *bāṁh*], m. *Pl.* supporter, ally, protector, patron.

बा- *bā-* [P. *bā*], prep. **1.** with, by. **2.** possessed of. — बाअसर, adj. effective. बाईमान, adj. acting according to conscience; faithful; religious. बा-क़ायदा, adj. according to rule or practice, regular, established. बाख़बर, adj. informed, intelligent. बाज़ाबता [P. *-ẓābiṭa*], adj. inv. according to rule, usual, normal; certified (a copy: = प्रमाणित). बामज़ा [P. *-maza*], adj. inv. tasty, delicious. बामुराद [P. *-murād*], adj. having achieved one's aim, successful. बामुहावरा [A. *muḥāvrā*], adj. expressive, idiomatic (language). बाशऊर [A. *śu'ūr*], adj. wise, understanding. बाशौक़, adv. with pleasure, willingly. बावजूद, ppn. see hw. बावफ़ा, adj. inv. keeping faith.

बाइस *bāis* [A. *bā'is̤*], m. f. (?). **1.** cause, reason. **2.** adv. because (of, के); by means (of).

¹बाई *bāī*, f. lady.

²बाई *bāī* [*vāta-*], f. **1.** wind. ***2.** flatulence. **3.** rheumatism. **4.** fig. frenzy. — ~ पचाना (की), fig. to take one down a peg. – बाई-बिरंग, m. a medicinal seed, *Embelia ribes*, used in treating flatulence or rheumatism.

बाईनी *bāīnī*, f. *Pl.* a basket in which snakes are carried about for show.

बाईस *bāīs* [*dvāviṁśati-*], adj. var. /bais/. twenty-two.

बाकंद *bakand*, m. *hist. Pl.* proportion of two-fifths of a crop, paid as rent to *zamīndārs* by cultivators.

बाकल *bākal* [*valkala-*], m. Brbh. = वल्कल.

बाक़ला *bāqlā* [A. *bāqla*, P. *bāqilā*], m. *Pl. HŚS.* a bean, *Vicia faba*; a pea.

बाक़ली *bāqlī* [cf. H. *bāqlā*], m. reg. boiled grain.

बाक़ी *bāqī* [A. *bāqī*], adj. & f. **1.** adj. remaining, enduring; extant. ***2.** left over. ~ उत्तर हिंदुस्तान, m. the rest of north India. **3.** still to happen. अब तो मरना ~ है, now (I) have just to die. **4.** f. remainder. **5.** surplus; credit balance. **6.** balance outstanding, arrears, sum due. **7.** adv. but yet, nonetheless. — ~ करना, to subtract. ~ निकालना (की), to find the remainder (of a subtraction); to calculate a balance(-sheet). ~ पड़ना, to fall into arrears. ~ रहना, to be left over; to be still due (a sum); to have a balance. - बाक़ी-साक़ी, f. remainder, surplus, balance.

बाख *bākh* [*vakṣas-*], m. *Pl.* udder.

बाखड़ी *bākhṛī* [cf. *baṣkaya-*], f. reg. (W.) **1.** a cow in milk long after calving. **2.** a cow gone about five months in calf.

[1]**बाखर** *bākhar* [? **vyāskara-*], m. **1.** collection of sheds or houses forming one farmyard enclosure; buildings and courtyard. **2.** Brbh. house. **3.** granary (= बखार).

[2]**बाखर** *bākhar* [*vakṣaskāra-*], m. *Pl.* bag (for tools: as a goldsmith's).

[3]**बाखर** *bākhar* [? B.], m. reg. a compound made from the leaves and roots of several plants and used as a ferment.

[4]**बाखर** *bākhar*, m. reg. (W.) a kind of bullock hoe or plough.

बाखरि *bākhari* [? **vyāskara-*], f. Brbh. cattle-shed, milking area, &c. (= [1]बाखर).

बाखरी *bākhrī* [cf. H. [1]*bākhar*], f. reg. (W.) inner part of a house (private to the family members).

बाग *bāg* [*valgā-*], f. **1.** rein. **2.** bridle. **3.** fig. curb, restraint; control. — ~ उठाना, to give free rein (to, की: a horse); to set at a gallop. ~ खींचना (की), to rein in (as a horse); to curb, to restrain. ~ छोड़ना or ढीली करना, to give a loose rein (to, की); to set at a gallop (a horse). ~ फेरना, = ~ मोड़ना. ~ मोड़ना, to turn a horse's head; to turn back or away. ~ हाथ से छूटना, to lose control or power (over, की); to lose an opportunity. ~ हाथ से छोड़ना, = ~ ढीली करना. – बाग-डोर, m. halter; fig. control. बाग-पकड़ाई, f. holding the reins (of the bridegroom's horse): = next. बाग-मुड़ाई, f. *hind.* leading the bridegroom's horse (by sons-in-law of his family: part of a marriage ceremony); present given to those who lead the bridegroom's horse.

बाग़ *bāġ* [P. *bāġ*], m. **1.** large garden; park. **2.** orchard. **3.** grove. **4.** plantation (as of tea bushes). — सब्ज़ ~ दिखाना, to lead up the garden path. – बाग़कारी [P. *-kārī*], f. gardening. बाग़दार [P. *-dār*], adj. & m. = बाग़वाला. बाग़-बाग़ होना, to be delighted, overjoyed. बाग़बान [P. -*bān*], m. gardener. °ई, f. gardening; supervision of parks and gardens. बाग़वाला, adj. & m. having a garden or gardens (house, suburb); owner of a garden; gardener.

[1]**बागर** *bāgar* [**vaggaḍa-*: Pk. *vagaḍā-*], m. Brbh. high river bank, dike.

[2]**बागर** *bāgar* [? conn. H. [1]*bākhar*], m. reg. (W.) a hedge or fence of thorns or twigs; an enclosure.

बागा *bāgā* [? *valgu-*], m. **1.** knee-length outer garment worn by men. **2.** wedding garment (of bridegroom; also of members of groom's party).

बाग़ाती *bāġātī* [cf. P. *bāġāt*: *-āt*, Ar. pl.], adj. *hist. Pl.* **1.** fit for, or used in, garden cultivation (land, &c). **2.** assessed or levied on gardens (tax).

बागान *bāgān* [? B. *bāgān*], m. plantation (of tea).

बाग़ी *bāġī* [A. *bāġī*], adj. & m. **1.** adj. rebellious. **2.** m. a rebel; insurgent. — ~ होना, to revolt, to rebel; to turn rebel; colloq. to be offended or displeased (with, से).

बाग़ीचा *bāġīcā* [P. *bāġīca*], m. **1.** a small garden; a flower or vegetable garden; orchard. **2.** plantation, garden.

बाघ *bāgh* [*vyāghra-*], m. tiger; lion. — बाघंबर, m. a tiger-skin; a hairy blanket resembling a tiger-skin. °ई, m. an ascetic. बाघ-गोटी, f. a children's game (throwing a stone to a line).

बाघनी *bāghnī* [cf. H. *bāgh*], f. tigress.

बाघिन *bāghin* [cf. H. *bāgh*], f. tigress.

बाचना *bācnā*, v.t. = बाँचना.

[1]**बाछ** *bāch*, f. corner of the mouth. — बाछें खिलना, to be delighted; to laugh loud and long.

[2]**बाछ** *bāch* [cf. H. *bāchnā*], f. m. *hist.* selection: proportionate rate, share (of land tax).

बाछना *bāchnā* [*vraścati*], v.t. reg. to pick out, to choose.

बाछा *bāchā* [*vatsa-*[1]], m. Brbh. 1. = बछड़ा. **2.** a child.

बाज *bāj* [ad. *vājin-*], m. Brbh. a horse.

[1]**बाज़** *bāz* [A. *bāz*], m.; f. hawk; falcon (properly female).

[2]**बाज़** *bāz* [P. *bāz*], adv. back, again. — ~ आना, to draw back (from, से); to desist or refrain (from), to give up; to decline, to refuse. ~ करना, to restrain (from, से). ~ रखना, id. ~ रहना, to hold aloof (from); to desist (from). — बाज़गश्त [P. *-gaśt*], f. U. a return; fig. echo.

[3]**बाज़** *bāz* [A. *ba'ẓ*], adj. U. some, certain, various. — ~ लोग, m. pl. certain people.

-बाज़ *-bāz* [P. *bāz*], noun formant. playing, player (e.g. ठट्ठेबाज़, m. joker).

बाजंतरी *bājantārī* [cf. H. *bājā*; ad. *yantra-*], f. Pl. **1.** a musician; band of musicians. **2.** *hist.* a tax (under Muslim rule) on professional singers, dancers and musicians.

बाजन *bājan* [? cf. H. *bājnā*], m. Brbh. Av. = बाजा.

बाजना *bājnā* [*vādyate*], v.i. **1.** to sound (as a musical instrument). **2.** to strike (a clock). **3.** Av. to resound: to be struck (a blow).

बाजरा *bājrā* [**bājjara-*], m. millet. — **बाजरा-सा बिखरना**, fig. to be restless, disturbed; to be weary.

बाजरी *bājrī* [*bājjara-*], f. a small millet.

बाजा *bājā* [*vādya-*], m. **1.** musical instrument. **2.** music. — **~ बजाना**, to play a musical instrument; to strike up (music). **फ़ौजी ~**, transf. a military band. — **बाजा-गाजा**, m. assortment of musical instruments; the sound of assorted instruments; fanfare. **बाजा-बजंतर** [ad. *yantra-*], m. reg. the various instruments (of a band): band of musicians.

बाज़ार *bāzār* [P. *bāzār*], m. **1.** market-place or area, bazaar; market. **2.** rate, price; demand (for sthg). — **~ उतरना (का)**, not to be in demand, to fall in price. **~ करना**, to do marketing, to go shopping. **~ का भाव**, m. market rate or price. **~ (के) भाव पीटना**, to beat (one, **को**) soundly. **~ गरम होना**, the market (in, **का**) to be brisk or active; to sell well, to be in demand; to be prevalent (an undesirable practice); to rage (an epidemic). **~ गिरना**, prices to drop. **~ चमकना**, or **चलना**, = **~ गरम होना**, 1., 2. **~ तेज़ होना (का)**, = **~ गरम होना**, 1., 2.; to rise in price. **~ दिखाना (का)**, to display for sale. **~ नापते फिरना**, to wander about in a bazaar; to roam. **~ मंदा होना (का)**, = **~ उतरना**. **~ लगाना**, to establish a market; to open shops; to display one's wares; to be about one's business or trade; colloq. to spread or to scatter things about in disorder; to make an uproar. **खुला ~**, m. an open market. **बाज़ार-बैठक**, f. fee or tax on market stall-holders or traders.

बाज़ारी *bāzārī* [P. *bāzārī*], adj. **1.** having to do with a market; commercial, business (activity, &c). **2.** ordinary, common. — **~ आदमी**, m. pl. ordinary people. **~ औरत**, f. a common woman, prostitute. **~ ख़बर**, or **गप**, or **बात**, f. bazaar talk, mere rumour.

बाज़ारू *bāzārū* [cf. H. *bāzār*], adj. **1.** vulgar, coarse (as temperament, speech). **2.** crude (in manufacture).

बाज़ी *bāzī* [P. *bāzī*], f. **1.** game, play; a game, contest. **2.** a game of chance; gambling. **3.** wager, bet. **4.** turn, play (in a game). — **~ आना**, to have been dealt a good hand (cards). **~ खाना**, to be beaten, to lose. **~ जीतना**, or **पाना**, or **लेना**, to win (a game, a bet, stakes). **~ देना (को)**, to beat (in a game); to checkmate; to trick; to make fun (of). **~ बदना**, or **लगाना**, to lay a bet (on, **की**); to stake. **~ बीस होना**, to have superiority over other players (in a game); to make a good profit. **~ मारना**, = **~ जीतना**. **~ ले जाना**, to achieve a win (over, **से**); to excel. **~ हारना**, to lose (a game, &c). – **बाज़ीगर** [P. *-gar*], m. juggler; conjurer. **°ई**, f. juggling, &c.

[1]**बाजी** *bājī* [ad. *vājin-*], m. *Pl. HŚS.* a horse.

[2]**बाजी** *bājī* [T. *bāci*], f. reg. elder sister.

बाज़ू *bāzū* [P. *bāzū*], m. **1.** arm; upper arm; shoulder. **2.** wing (of bird). **3.** flank (as of an army). **4.** side (of a framework: as a door). **5.** wing (of a door). **6.** sleeve (of a garment). — **~ देना (को)**, to support, to give a hand (to). – **बाज़ूबंद** [P. *-band*], m. armlet; bracelet.

बाझ- *bājh-* [*badhyate*], v.i. Brbh. Av. to be entangled, ensnared.

[1]**बाट** *bāṭ* [*vartman-*], f. way, road, path. — **~ करना**, to make a road or way. **~ काटना**, to get a road or journey behind one; to cut, to block a road. **~ चलना**, to travel, to journey. **~ जोहना**, or **देखना**, to watch for the coming (of, **की**). **~ दिखाना (को)**, to direct, to guide; to keep one waiting or in expectation. **~ पर-**, Av. to come upon on (one's) path or road. **~ बाट पार-**, Brbh. to waylay, to rob. **~ रोकना**, to close or to obstruct a road; to block (one's) way. – **बाट-दिखाऊ**, m. a guide. **बाट-सारू**, m. reg. a traveller.

[2]**बाट** *bāṭ* [**varṭa-*[3]], m. **1.** a weight, measure of weight. **2.** reg. a grindstone. — **बाट-घाट**, adv. corr. = **बाटी-घाटी**. **बाट-छपाई**, f. stamping weights (as genuine); fee for stamping weights. **बाट-तराज़ू**, m. weights and scales.

बाटना *bāṭnā* [*vartayati*], v.t. **1.** to twist, to twine. **2.** to pound, to grind.

[1]**बाटी** *bāṭī* [? **varta-*[3]], f. **1.** a lump. **2.** a thick bread-cake baked on cinders.

[2]**बाटी** *bāṭī* [**varta-*[2]], f. a deep open dish, tureen.

[3]**बाटी** *bāṭī* [*vāṭikā-*], f. **1.** site of a house; residence, home. **2.** reg. the groin. — **बाटी-घाटी**, adv. at home or at the river-bank: somewhere or other.

बाड़ *bāṛ* [*vāṭa-*[1]], f. **1.** enclosure; fence; hedge. **2.** line, margin, edge; edge of a blade. **3.** barricade; railing. — **~ बाँधना**, to enclose (in, **में**). **~ लगाना**, to put up a fence, &c. **काँटेदार तारों की ~**, f. barbed wire entanglement.

बाड़वानल *bāṛavânal* [S.], m. fire under water, submarine fire.

बाड़ा *bāṛā* [*vāṭa-*[1]], m. **1.** enclosed area; fold or pen (for animals). **2.** fence, hedge (= **बाड़**). **3.** *Pl.* cemetery.

बाड़िया *bāṛiyā* [cf. H. [2]*bāṛh*], m. *Pl.* knife-grinder.

बाड़ी *bāṛī* [*vāṭikā-*], f. **1.** enclosed ground; garden; vegetable garden; orchard. **2.** house and garden, establishment. — ~ करना, to do garden-work, &c. ~ चुगना, or बीनना, to gather the crop of a garden, or field.

¹**बाढ़** *bāṛh* [*vr̥ddhi-*²], f. **1.** increase (as of funds). **2.** growth (as of vegetation). **3.** rise (of a river); flood. **4.** fig. volley (of fire). — ~ आना (में), a river to rise, &c. ~ पर आना, to have begun to grow, &c. ~ मारी जाना, growth to be stunted. – बाढ़-ग्रस्त, adj. affected by flood (area, or residents); in flood (river). बाढ़-पीड़ित, adj. affected by flood (residents, area).

²**बाढ़** *bāṛh* [**varddhrī-*], f. **1.** edge (of a blade). **2.** reg. (Bihar) a book-binder's paper-cutter, guillotine. **3.** whetstone. — ~ पकड़ाना, to egg on, to incite. ~ पर चढ़ाना, to whet.

³**बाढ़** *bāṛh* [*vardha-*¹], f. *Pl.* stubble.

बाढ़- *bāṛh-*, v. Brbh. = बढ़ना.

बाढ़ना *bāṛhnā* [*vardhayati*¹], v.t. *Pl.* to cut, to cut off.

बाढ़ी *bāṛhī* [*vr̥ddhi-*²], f. *Pl. HŚS.* 1. = ¹बाढ़, 1. **2.** interest paid on grain; interest in kind paid on seed-grain.

बाण *bāṇ* [S.], m. arrow; barb.

बात *bāt* [*vārttā-*], f. **1.** sthg. said, a word, remark; speech, talk, words; conversation; discussion. ~, or बातें, करना, to talk, &c. **2.** a matter, topic, subject, concern; fact; thing. क्या ~ है? what is it? what's the matter? अच्छी ~, or अच्छी ~ है, very good, very well. ~ तो यही है की..., the fact of the matter is that.... **3.** news, account; report. — ~ आँचल में, or गाँठ में, बाँधना, to remember sthg. carefully. ~ आगे आना, sthg. to happen in due course. ~ आना, conversation or discussion to turn (to or on, पर). ~ उठाना, to raise a matter; to neglect to carry out (a duty, &c.); to endure hostile remarks (from, की). ~ उठा न रखना, to leave nothing undone. ~ उलटना (की), to contradict. ~ ऊँची रखना, to keep one's word. ~ करते में, or कहते, adv. in an instant, all at once. ~ का धनी, or पक्का, or पूरा, or सच्चा, adj. true to one's word. ~ का बतंगड़ करना, or बनाना, to exaggerate; to make a mountain out of a molehill. ~ काटना (की), to interrupt (another's words). ~ कान पड़ना, a matter to be learnt of (by, के). ~ की ~ में, adv. in an instant, forthwith. ~ खुलना, a matter to become known; to transpire. ~, or बातें, गढ़ना, to choose one's words carefully; to speak to the point, or with effect; to fabricate, to romance. ~ गाँठना, to remember carefully. ~ चबा चबाकर करना, to speak with suppressed anger; to speak off-handedly, or non-committally. ~ चलाना, to start a conversation (about, की), to broach (a subject). ~ चिकनाना, to speak unctuously. ~ छाँटना, to talk much; to be a great talker. ~ छेड़ना (की), to broach (a subject). ~ टालना, to put off; to make excuses; to prevaricate. ~ डालना, to ask in vain; to propose (sthg. unusual or unlikely). ~ ढालकर कहना, to speak allegorically, in a parable. ~ धराना, to make continued excuses; to evade (decision of a matter). ~ तोड़ना, = ~ काटना. ~ धराना, to cause sthg. to be delayed or deferred (by making excuses). ~ न करना, not to deign to converse (with, से), or to deal (with). ~ न पूछना, not to make enquiry (of, से); not to take due notice (of), not to show care or feeling (for). ~ पकड़ना (की), to carp or to cavil (at). ~ पर आना, to come as promised; to maintain or to insist upon a point. ~ पर जाना, to heed, or to accept the words (of, की). ~ पलटना, to go back on one's word; to prevaricate. ~ पाना, to get to the bottom of a matter; to understand (another's, की) purpose; to attain (one's, अपनी) purpose. ~ पीना, to swallow one's words, to bear in silence; to suppress one's feelings. ~ फूटना, = ~ खुलना. ~ फेंकना (पर), to taunt. ~ फेरना, = ~ पलटना. ~ बघारना, colloq. to be a great talker. ~ बढ़ना, a difference or a quarrel to grow more serious. ~ बढ़ाना, to make more serious, or to prolong, a quarrel, &c. ~ बदलना, to equivocate, to prevaricate. ~ बनना, sthg. to prove a success; to gain credit or honour, to prosper. ~ ~ में, adv. in every word, or case; at every point; throughout, altogether; for the least thing. ~ बनाना, to invent a story; to invent excuses; to boast. ~ बिगड़ना, a plan, &c. to be spoiled; to lose credit, to be disgraced. ~ बिगाड़ना, to spoil a plan, or a plot; to thwart; to bring disgrace (on). ~ बेबात पर, adv. at any occasion (at all). ~ मत करो, hold your tongue! ~ मन में उतरना, or बसना, words, &c., to be borne in mind, or taken to heart. ~ मानना, to heed what is said; to obey; to accept a matter. ~ मारना, to lead conversation away from a subject; to neglect (a person's) words; to make (a person) silent; to taunt. ~ में, adv. in a short time, in a moment. ~ में पड़ना, to interrupt. ~ में फ़रक़ आना, (one's, की) words to prove not to hold good: credit or repute to be lost (by). ~ में फ़ी, or पाख, निकालना, to find fault unnecessarily. ~ में ~ कहना, to interrupt while another is speaking. ~ में से ~ निकालना, to drag out an argument, or dispute; to carp, to cavil; to draw inferences. ~ में बोलना, to interrupt. ~ रखना, to assent (to, की), to comply (with); to act as one has said. ~ रहना, (one's) words to be fulfilled; to prevail in argument; a matter to be accepted. ~ लगाना, to speak (of or about, की); to impute (to), to lay to the charge (of). ~ लाना, to make a marriage proposal. ~, or बातें, हाँकना, to tell tall stories; to talk much. बातें मिलाना (में), to agree (readily) with what is said. बातें लगाना, = ~ लगाना, 2. बातें सुनना, to listen attentively; to bear (abuse, &c.) tolerantly. बातें सुनाना (को), to speak harshly (to), to censure; to abuse; to tell one's story (to). बातों का झाड़, or की झड़ी, बाँधना, to pour out a flood of words. बातों में आना, to be taken in, deceived. बातों में उड़ाना, to make light of (an unwelcome remark, &c.); to make excuses. बातों में गिरा देना, or धर लेना, to overcome in argument. बातों में पड़ना, to fall into conversation. बातों में फुसलाना, or बहलाना, to beguile by one's words; to delude. बातों में लगाना, to engage (one) in conversation. कोई ~ नहीं, it doesn't matter. जहाँ तक...की ~ है, as for... बस की ~ न होना, to be beyond the powers (of, के). सौ साल पहले की ~ है, this happened a hundred years ago (sthg. about to be related). बातों बातों, or बातों बातों में, adv. while talking; by the way. — बातचीत [*-citti-*[1]], f. conversation; discussion. बातचीत करना, to converse, &c. (with, से). बात-फ़रोश, [P. *-faroś*], m. seller of tales: romancer. बात-बनाऊ, m. one who makes excuses; one who speaks as he thinks is in his interest. लंबी-चौड़ी बातें, f. boastful, pretentious or exaggerated remarks.

बातचीत *bātcīt*, f. see s.v. बात.

बाती *bātī*, f. = बत्ती.

बातूनी *bātūnī*, adj. & m. **1.** adj. talkative, garrulous. **2.** m. a garrulous person.

[1]**बाद** *bād* [ad. *vāda-*], m. **1.** speech: discussion, dispute; argument. **2.** assertion. **3.** case, claim, plea. **4.** a negotiated sum; commission; rebate; (Av. बादि [×H. *bāzī*]) a bet; *hist.* remission of revenue or rent on account of a bad season. — बादि मेल-, Av. to make bets together.

[2]**बाद** *bād* [P. *bād*], m. f. wind. — बादबान [P. *-bān*], m. sail; °ई, f. sailing boat. बादनुमा [P. *-numā*], m. inv. weathercock, wind-indicator.

[3]**बाद** *bād* [A. *ba'd*], adv. **1.** afterwards. एक साल ~, a year later. **2.** ppn. w. के. after. एक साल के ~, after a year. — ~ को, adv. = next. ~ में, adv. later on, afterwards.

-बाद *-bād* [P. *-bād*, precative], suffix. may it be. — ज़िंदाबद! exclam. long live! मुरदाबाद! exclam. death to! down with!

बाद- *bād-* [ad. *vādayati*, or *vāda-*], v.i. Brbh. Av. **1.** to speak: to dispute. **2.** to utter a challenge.

[1]**बादर** *bādar*, adj. Brbh. happy (of expression, face).

[2]**बादर** *bādar* [S.], adj. & m. *Pl. HŚS.* **1.** adj. made of cotton. **2.** m. the cotton plant.

बादल *bādal* [*vārdala-*], m. cloud. — ~ गरजना, to thunder. ~ छँटना, or फटना, clouds to disperse. ~ छा गए हैं, it is overcast.

बादला *bādlā* [conn. *bādara-*], m. Av. gold or silver cloth; = कलाबत्तू.

बादली *bādlī*, f. *Pl. HŚS.* = बादला.

बादशाह *bādśāh* [P. *pādśāh*; ? ×H. [1]*bādī*], m. **1.** sovereign, monarch, king; emperor. **2.** (in chess) king. **3.** fig. one skilled (in, का).

बादशाहत *bādśāhat* [P. *bādśāhat*], f. **1.** sovereign rule, sway. **2.** empire, kingdom. — ~ करना, to rule (over, की), to reign.

बादशाहाना *bādśāhānā* [P. *pādśāhāna*], adj. inv. & adv. **1.** adj. regal, royal. **2.** adv. in a royal or regal way.

बादशाही *bādśāhī* [P. *bādśāhī*], adj. & f. **1.** adj. regal, royal; pertaining to the crown (as lands, court); imperial. **2.** f. = बादशाहत. — ~ करना, to rule, &c. (in or over, में).

बादाम *bādām* [P. *bādām*], m. /bədam/. **1.** almond (tree and nut). **2.** the Indian almond, *Terminalia catappa* (*janglī* ~). **3.** cashew-nut.

बादामी *bādāmī* [P. *bādāmī*], adj. **1.** made of or containing almonds. **2.** almond-coloured, light brown (as eyes, a horse). **3.** almond-shaped.

बादार *bādār*, m. *Pl.* a large house; granary raised on piles.

[1]**बादि** *bādi* [? = H. *bād-*], adv. Brbh. Av. **1.** in vain. **2.** in a challenging way: being without (sthg).

[2]**बादि** *bādi*, ? f. Av. see s.v. [1]बाद, 4.

[1]**बादी** *bādī* [cf. H. [1]*bād*; or ad. *vādin-*], m. speaking, affirming, claiming: one who speaks or argues; a plaintiff. — ~ का चोर, m. an inveterate thief.

[2]**बादी** *bādī* [P. *bādī*], adj. & f. **1.** adj. causing flatulence. **2.** f. flatulence. — ~ का बदन, m. bloated body.

बादुर *bādur* [**vālguḍa-*: ← Drav.], m. reg. flying fox; bat.

बाध *bādh* [S.], f. hindrance; difficulty.

बाध- *bādh-* [ad. *bādhate*, or *bādh(ă)-*], v.t. Brbh. Av. to obstruct; to check; to thwart.

[1]**बाध-** *bādh-*, v.t. Brbh. Av. = [1]बध-.

बाधक *bādhak* [S.], adj. & m. **1.** adj. obstructive, hindering; restrictive. **2.** Av. causing distress. **3.** m. one who obstructs, &c. **4.** obstacle.

बाधन *bādhan* [S.], m. **1.** opposing, hindering. **2.** obstruction; refutation. **3.** the causing of distress.

बाधना *bādhnā* [cf. H. *bādh-*], f. poet. = बाधा.

बाधवाई *bādhăvāī*, adj. wandering, vagrant.

बाधा *bādhā* [S.], f. **1.** obstacle. **2.** Brbh. Av. affliction, distress. — ~ करना, to cause difficulties, or distress. ~, or बाधाएँ, डालना, or पहुँचाना, to cause difficulties (in one's doing sthg., में). ~, or बाधाएँ, देना (को), to cause difficulties (to).

बाधित *bādhit* [S.], adj. **1.** obstructed. **2.** compelled.

बाध्य *bādhyă* [S.], adj. **1.** obstructed, hindered. **2.** compelled, obliged (to, के लिए, को).

[1]**बान** *bān* [*varṇa-*[1]], f. **1.** quality, nature; character. **2.** habit, custom (of a person). **3.** Brbh. aspect, appearance; dress, attire. **4.** E.H. glow, lustre. — ~ डालना, to lay foundations of (one's) character; to cultivate a habit; to accustom, to inure (to, की). ~ पड़ना, a habit to be acquired; to be trained; to be accustomed (to, की).

[2]**बान** *bān* [*bāṇa-*], m. **1.** arrow; projectile. **2.** reg. an implement used in scutching cotton.

[3]**बान** *bān* [*vanyā-*, *vāna-*], m. bore (on a river).

[4]**बान** *bān* [**vāṇa-*[2]], m. cord of twisted grass (as *mūṁj* or *ḍāb*: used for stringing bed-frames, &c).

बानक *bānak*, m. a favourable situation; an opening, chance. — ~ बनना, or बैठना, an opportunity to occur. ~ बनाना, to provide an opportunity.

[2]**बानक** *bānak* [cf. *varṇa-*[1]], cf. Brbh. mode of dress, attire.

बानगी *bāngī* [cf. H. [1]*bān*], f. specimen, sample; pattern.

बानर *bānar* [*vānara-*], m. monkey.

बानवे *bānve* [*dvinavati-*; Pa. *dvānavuti-*], adv. ninety-two.

[1]**बाना** *bānā* [*vāna-*[2]], m. **1.** weaving, weave. ***2.** woof. **3.** fine silk thread.

[2]**बाना** *bānā* [*varṇa-*[1]], m. **1.** nature, &c. (= [1]बान, 1). **2.** habit (= [1]बान, 2). **3.** garment; attire; disguise. **4.** reg. group, community. — ~ बदलना, to change (one's) clothing, to disguise oneself.

[3]**बाना** *bānā* [*vāṇa-*[1]], m. reg. ? a sword. — ~ बाँधना, to arm, gird (oneself).

[4]**बाना** *bānā* [*vyādadāti*], v.t. & v.i. **1.** v.t. to open wide. **2.** v.i. to be wide open, to gape; to burst open. — मुँह बाए, adv. agape (the mouth).

बानि *bāni*, f. Brbh. Av. = [2]बानी, 1.

[1]**बानी** *bānī* [ad. *vāṇī-*[1]], f. **1.** sound, voice. **2.** speech. **3.** verses, teachings (esp. of the *nirguṇī* sectarians or their followers).

[2]**बानी** *bānī* [*varṇa-*[1]], f. **1.** partic. property or character (of sthg.); colour. **2.** reg. (W.) a yellow clay with which potters sometimes ornament vessels. **3.** reg. (Bihar) ashes.

[3]**बानी** *bānī* [*vāna-*[1]], f. reg. **1.** weaving. **2.** thread. — बानी-बोनी, f. colloq. cost of weaving.

बानुवा *bānuvā*, m. *Pl.* a kind of water-bird.

बानू *bānū* [P. *bānū*], f. U. lady (term of address or reference).

बानैत *bānait* [cf. *bāṇa-*], m. Brbh. Av. an archer.

बाप *bāp* [**bāppa-*: Pk. *bappa-*], m. father. — ~ करना, to regard (one, को) as a father. ~ का होना, to be regarded as inherited from (one's, के) father: to be kept and not returned (borrowed property). ~ तक जाना, to go to the length of abusing one's father. ~ बनाना, = ~ करना; to flatter. ~ रे! or ~ रे ~! interj. good heavens! (expressing surprise, or grief). बाप-दादा, m. pl. forefathers. बाप-मारे का वैर, m. feud caused by a father's murder, family feud.

बापिका *bāpikā* [ad. *vāpikā-*], f. Av. = बावली.

बापुरा *bāpurā* [**bappuḍa-*: Pk. *bappuḍa-*], adj. **1.** wretched, destitute. **2.** Brbh. of no account.

बाप्तिस्मा *bāptismā* [Pt. *baptismo*; ← Gk.], m. baptism.

बाफ *bāph* [*vāṣpa-*], m. reg. = भाप.

बाफ़ता *bāftā* [P. *bāfta*], adj. & m. E.H. **1.** adj. woven. **2.** m. *HŚS.* a kind of silk cloth embroided with gold and silver brocade.

बाब *bāb* [A. *bāb*], m. U. **1.** door, gate. **2.** section, chapter (of a book). **3.** topic.

बाबत *bābat* [A. *bāba*: P. *bābat*], f. & adv. **1.** f. account, matter, business. **2.** adv. in respect (of, की), concerning.

बाबन *bāban* [Engl. *bobbin*], m. **1.** bobbin, spool. **2.** transf. electric coil. — बाबन-नेट, f. bobinet, cotton or silk lace.

बाबनी *bābnī*, f. reg. a snake's hole (= बाँबी).

[1]**बाबर** *bābar* [*barbarī-*], m. reg. (W.) a kind of long grass used for thatching, and for making bed-strings.

[2]**बाबर** *bābar* [*barbara-*], adj. reg. **1.** harsh; cruel. **2.** low, base (of origin).

बाबरी *bābrī* [*barbara-*[2]], f. long, uncut hair (of a man).

बाबा *bābā* [**bābba-*; and P. *bābā*], m. inv. **1.** father. **2.** grandfather. **3.** colloq. senior, or respected person (term of address). **4.** young child (affectionate term of address).

बाबी *bābī* [cf. H. *bābā*], f. reg. a female ascetic; voc. term of affectionate address (to a young girl).

बाबुल *bābul*, m. = बाबा, 1., 3., 4.

बाबू *bābū* [cf. **bābba-*], m. **1.** an educated or distinguished person. **2.** title of respectful address, father. **3.** a transf. clerk, government servant. 4. = बाबा, 4. — ~ जी, m. = ~, 2., 3. – बाबूगिरी [P. *-gīrī*], f. pej. pettiness of outlook or conduct. बाबूगिरी करना, to work as a clerk, to push a pen.

बाभन *bābhan*, m. reg. = ब्राह्मण.

[1]**बाम** *bām* [P. *bām*], m. terrace or roof of a house.

[2]**बाम** *bām* [conn. *brāhmī-*], f. **1.** *Pl. HŚS.* a spiny-backed eel. **2.** *Pl.* a snake.

[3]**बाम** *bām*, f. = [12]वाम.

[1]**बामन** *bāman*, m. = ब्राह्मण.

[2]**बामन** *bāman*, m. = वामन. — ~ होकर भी चाँद छूना, to touch the moon, though a dwarf: to do sthg. wildly impossible.

बामनहट्टी *bāman-haṭṭī*, f. *Pl.* the shrub *Clerodendrum siphonanthus*.

बाम्हन *bāmhan* [*brāhmaṇa-*], m. a brāhmaṇ.

बाम्हनी *bāmhnī* [*brāhmaṇī-*], f. *Pl.* 1. = ब्राह्मणी. 2. [f. *brāhmī-*] a kind of lizard.

बायना *bāynā*, m. = बैना.

[1]**बायब** *bāyăb*, adj. separate; quite different.

[2]**बायब** *bāyăb* [*vāyavya-*], m. the north-west.

बायबी *bāybī* [cf. H. *bāyab*], adj. strange.

बायस *bāyas*, m. f. (?). = बाइस.

बायाँ *bāyāṁ* [*vāmaka-*], adj. & m. **1.** adj. left, left hand. **2.** Av. contrary, adverse. **3.** *mus.* a bass drum (played with the left hand). — ~ दे-, Brbh. to turn the left side to: not to acknowledge, to avoid; to duck (a blow). ~ पाँव, or पैर, पूजना, to worship the left foot (of, का): to acknowledge the superiority (of). बाईं ओर, adv. & ppn. on the left; to the left (of, के). बाएँ, adv. on the left; to the left. बाएँ पड़ना, to be found on the left (as a place, a building). बाएँ हाथ का खेल, m. fig. sthg. very easily done, child's play.

बारंबार *bārambār* [*vāram vāram*], adv. = बार बार.

[1]**बार** *bār* [*vāra-*[2]], f. **1.** partic. time, occasion. **2.** delay. — ~ ~, adv. repeatedly; at every moment, constantly. अबकी ~, f. & adv. the present occasion, this time; on or for the present occasion. एक ~, adv. on, or for, one occasion; once upon a time. कितनी ~? adv. how many times? छप्पन में सात आठ ~, seven into fifty-six goes eight times. बार-नारी, f. a common woman, prostitute. बार-स्त्री, f. id.

[2]**बार** *bār* [*dvāra-*; ? with *vāraka-*], m. **1.** gate, door; doorway. **2.** fig. access. — ~ देना, to give access (to, को). – बारगाह [P. *-gāh*], f. place of audience, court. घरबार, m. see s.v. घर. दरबार, m. see s.v. बार-रुकाई, f. stopping (one) at the gate: exaction of money by the bridegroom's sister before allowing the bride and bridegroom to enter the latter's house.

[3]**बार** *bār* [cf. *vāraka-*], m. obstacle.

[4]**बार** *bār* [P. *bār*], m. **1.** load, burden. **2.** cargo, freight. **3.** weight. — ~ देना, to load (one, को); to cause trouble (to). – बारगीर [P. *-gīr*], m. *hist.* a Marāṭhā horseman whose horse is provided for him; *HŚS.* groom. बार-दाना [P. *-dāna*], m. supplies; containers (for goods); tools of trade. बारबरदार [P. *-bardār*], adj. & m. burden-bearing; a porter; a beast of burden. °ई, f. transport, freighting; means of transport; load, freight; freightage (dues). बरबरदारी का, adj. draught, freight-bearing (animal).

[5]**बार** *bār* [? = H. [1]*bār*], m. *Pl.* cowherd's payment in kind (as the milk of every eighth day).

[6]**बार** *bār* [*vāri-*], m. Brbh. water.

[1]**बार-** *bār-* [*vārayate*], v.t. Brbh. Av. to forbid, to prohibit.

[2]**बार-** *bār-*, v.t. Brbh. to burn (= जलाना).

बारंबा *bār-ambā*, m. *Pl.* fruit of mango trees; revenue derived from mango trees.

बारक *bārak*, adv. Brbh. = एक बार.

बारजा *bārjā* [P. *bārja*], m. an upper porch.

बारजात *bārjāt* [P. *bārjāt*], m. *hist. Pl.* a custom of forcing people to purchase goods at more than the market price.

बारजाय *bārjāy* [P. *bārjāy*], m. *hist. Pl.* **1.** grant of land rent-free by a *zamīndār* to one of his dependants. 2. = बारजात.

बारह *bārah* [*dvādaśa*], adj. var. /bara/. twelve. — ~ बाट, m. twelve roads: scattered; destroyed, ruined; in confusion. ~ बाट करना, to scatter, &c. ~ बाट होना, to be scattered, &c.; to be homeless. ~ महीने, adv. for twelve months; all the year round, always. – बारहखड़ी, f. see hw. बारहदरी [P. -*dar*-], twelve-doored: a summer-house. बारह-बानी [-*varṇa*-], adj. & m. reg. pure, genuine; sound, very well (in health); pure, unadulterated; pure state or quality. बारह-बानी का सोना, twenty-four-carat gold. बारहमासा, m. a poem or song describing each of the months of the year, esp. as symbolic of the emotions of separated lovers. °-मासी, adj. lasting twelve months, perpetual, perennial; flowering all year round. बारहसिंगा, m. twelve-tined: an antelope.

बारहखड़ी *bārahkhaṛī* [cf. H. *bārah*, H. *ākhar*], f. the sets of twelve syllables: the twelve vocalic sounds of the Devanāgarī syllabary (excluding *r̥* and including *aṁ* and *aḥ*) in combination with the consonants of the syllabary (as recited by schoolchildren).

[1]**बारा** *bārā*, m. reg. = [5]बार.

[2]**बारा** *bārā*, m. reg. = [1]बाहरा.

[3]**बारा** *bārā*, m. reg. the process of wire-drawing.

[4]**बारा** *bārā*, adj. pronun. var. = बारह.

बारात *bārāt*, f. pronun. var. = बरात.

बारानी *bārānī* [P. *bārān*+H. -*ī*], adj. & f. reg. (W.) **1.** adj. depending on rain. **2.** f. land depending on rain, unirrigated land. **3.** a waterproof outer garment.

बाराह *bārāh*, m. = वराह.

बाराही *bārāhī*, adj. **1.** having to do with a boar. **2.** specif. having to do with the boar incarnation of Viṣṇu.

बारिश *bāriś* [P. *bāriś*], f. rain. — ~ होना, rain to fall.

[1]**बारी** *bārī* [**vāpakārin*- ← *vāpa*-[3]], m. **1.** a community whose traditional work is to sew leaf-plates. **2.** a man of the *bārī* community; a seller of betel leaf.

[2]**बारी** *bārī* [**vāpakārin*-: Pk. *vāria*-], m. *Pl.* **1.** a community whose traditional work is to sell torches. **2.** a man of the *bārī* community; torch-bearer; barber.

[3]**बारी** *bārī* [*vāra*-[2]], f. **1.** time, turn (for duty, or to play, &c.) आपकी ~ आई, its your turn. **2.** shift, spell (of work). — ~ ~, or ~ ~ से, adv. in turn; by turns.

[4]**बारी** *bārī* [*dvāra*-], f. **1.** small door. **2.** small window.

बारीक *bārīk* [P. *bārīk*], adj. **1.** fine, thin, slender. **2.** delicate, fine (as of texture, form, or work). **3.** shrill, high (sound). **4.** nice (a point, a distinction); subtle; precise, exact (as understanding). — ~ काम, m. delicate work; a delicate matter.

बारीकी *bārīkī* [P. *bārīkī*], f. **1.** fineness. **2.** delicacy (as of texture). **3.** shrillness. **4.** subtlety (of discrimination); precision. **5.** nice point; a detail. — बारीकियाँ छाँटना, or निकालना, to deal in or to make subtle distinctions; to be hypercritical, or to make captious criticism. ~ से, adv. with exactitude; with care.

बारूद *bārūd* [P. *bārūd*], f. gunpowder. — बारूद-ख़ाना, m. magazine, arsenal. बारूद-गोला, m. powder and shot: ammunition.

बारूदी *bārūdī*, adj. having to do with gunpowder. — ~ हथियार, m. pl. firearms.

[1]**बारे** *bāre* [P. *bāra*], m. matter, respect: — के ~ में, or (esp. reg. (N.)) के ~, ppn. concerning, about.

[2]**बारे** *bāre* [P. *bāre*], adv. U. finally, at length.

[1]**बाल** *bāl* [*bāla*-], adj. & m. **1.** adj. young. **2.** m. a young person; child, boy; youth; infant. **3.** a minor, a juvenile. **4.** one yet immature. **5.** a young animal; a colt; young elephant. — बाल-कांड, m. section of the *Rāmāyaṇa, Rām-carit-mānas*, &c. dealing with the childhood of Rām. बाल-केलि, f. children's games; playing, trifling (with, के साथ); child's play. बाल-क्रीड़ा, f. id., 1.; the amusements, or exploits, of the infant and child Kr̥ṣṇa. बाल-गोपाल, m. the child Kr̥ṣṇa; children, (one's) family. बाल-घात, m. infanticide. बाल-चंद्र, m. the young, or new moon. बाल-चर, m. Boy Scout, or member of similar youth movement. बाल-चरित, m. the childhood exploits of Kr̥ṣṇa, or of Rām. बालचर्या, f. child care. बाल-दिन, m. Children's Day: 14 November (the birthday of Javāharlāl Nehrū). बाल-दिवस, m. id. बाल-बच्चे , m. pl. children; [× [2]*bāl*] wife and children, family. °-दार [P. -*dār*], adj. having children. बाल-बुद्धि, f. & adj. immature mind; having a childish mind. बाल-बोध, adj. & m. comprehensible to children; a name for the Devanāgarī script (esp. in Madhya Pradesh and in the Marathi-speaking region); name of any children's reader, manual, &c. बाल-भोग, m. an early morning offering to a deity, esp. to Kr̥ṣṇa. बाल-राँड़, f. a child widow. बाल-लीला, f. = बाल-चरित. बाल-विधवा, f. child widow, young widow. बाल-विवाह, m. child marriage. बाल-हत्या, f. infanticide. बालावस्था [°*la*+*a*°], f. childhood. बालेंदु [°*a*+*i*°], m. the new moon.

[2]**बाल** *bāl* [*bālā*-], f. girl.

[3]**बाल** *bāl* [*vāla*-], m. **1.** a hair. **2.** a crack, hair-line (in glass, porcelain; or in a pearl). **3.** pl. the hair of the head. — ~ आना, the hair to grow; hair to begin to grow on the face. ~ उतरना, to be shaved. ~ काटना, to cut the hair,

or the beard. ~ का कंबल, or की भेड़, बनाना, to make a blanket, or a ewe, out of a single hair: to exaggerate; to make a mountain out of a molehill. ~ की खाल खींचना, or निकालना, to split hairs. ~ खिचड़ी होना, the hair to be greying. ~ देना, *hind.* to give the hair: to be shaved before performing funerary rites. ~ नोचना, to pluck or to pull out hair. ~ पकना, the hair to ripen: to grow grey. बाल पकाना, to make (one's) hair grey (in, में), to spend one's adult years (in). ~ बनाना (के), to do the hair; to shave. ~ बराबर, adv. & m. as much as a hair, the least, or slightest (amount); hair's breadth, least bit. ~ बराबर फ़रक़ नहीं, not the slightest difference. ~ बढ़ाना, to allow the hair to grow. ~ ~, adv. hair by hair, altogether, thoroughly; by a hair's breadth. ~ ~ बचना, to escape by a hair. ~ बीका न होना, not a hair to be out of place, not to be harmed in the slightest. ~ भर, adv. = ~ बराबर. ~ रखना, to wear (one's) hair, not to have the head shaven. – बाल-कटवाई, f. getting the hair cut; payment for a haircut. बाल-कमानी, f. hair-spring. बाल-गृह, m. crèche. बाल-छड़, f. an aromatic herb used medicinally (= जटामासी); a perfume. बाल-ख़ोरा [P. [khora], m. a disease of horses that causes their hair to fall out. बाल-तोड़, m. pimple, boil or sore caused by the plucking or tearing out of a hair. बालदार [P. -*dār*], adj. hairy; shaggy; cracked (as china, &c). बाल-बाँधा, adj. precise, exact; skilful (*Pl.*). बाल-संध्या, f. first light, early dawn. बाल-सफ़ा, adj. inv. depilatory; hair-cleansing.

[4]**बाल** *bāl* [*valla-*: Pk. *vālā-*], f. ear or spike of corn. — बाल-रखा, m. reg. platform from which a watch can be kept on growing crops.

[5]**बाल** *bāl* [P. *bāl*], m. wing. — बाल-पर निकलना, to be fledged: pej. to show (one's) true nature; to mature, to mend (one's) ways; to flourish.

बालक *bālak* [S.], m. a child, a boy.

बालकता *bālakătā* [S.], f. Brbh. childhood.

बालकपन *bālakpan* [cf. H. *bālak*], m. childhood.

बालकपना *bālakpanā*, m. = बालकपन.

बालका *bālkā* [cf. H. *bālak*], m. **1.** a young follower of a yogī. **2.** Av. offspring, stock.

बालकीय *bālăkīyă* [S.], adj. **1.** adj. having to do with children. **2.** childish.

बालछड़ *bālchaṛ*, m. see s.v. [3]बाल.

बालटी *bālṭī* [Pt. *balde*], f. a bucket.

बालना *bālnā* [**dvālayati*], v.t. to light (a fire, candle).

बालपन *bālpan* [cf. H. [1]*bāl*], m. childhood (= बचपान).

बालम *bālam* [*vallabhatama-*], m. dearest one, lover; husband. — बालम-खीरा [*-kṣīra-*], m. a variety of white cucumber (in season in the rains).

बालहा *bālahā* [*vallabha-*], m. or adj. beloved, dear (one).

[1]**बाला** *bālā* [*bāla-*], adj. & m. **1.** adj. young; childlike. **2.** simple, innocent. **3.** m. a child; a childish person. — ~ चाँद, m. the new moon. बाली उमर, f. youth, early adulthood; childhood.

[2]**बाला** *bālā* [S.], f. a girl; a young woman.

[3]**बाला** *bala* [*valaka-*[1]], m. **1.** a large ear-ring. **2.** reg. (E.) a bracelet.

[4]**बाला** *bālā* [P. *bālā*], adj. inv. **1.** high; above. **2.** apart: concealed. — ~ ~, adv. apart: secretly, stealthily; outwardly. बालाए ताक़ रखना [P. *-e-*], to put on the shelf: to pass over, not to take notice of. – बालानिशीन [P. *-niśīn*], adj. seated on high: best, choice, finest.

[5]**बाला** *bālā*, m. reg. (E.) a grub which attacks young wheat and barley.

[1]**बालाई** *bālāī*, f. = [1]मलाई.

[2]**बालाई** *bālāī* [P. *bālā'ī*], adj. U. additional, extra; superficial.

बालापन *bālāpan* [cf. H. [1]*bālā*], m. childhood.

बालिका *bālikā* [S.], f. a girl.

बालिग़ *bālig* [A. *bālig*], adj. & m. **1.** adj. of mature age. **2.** m. an adult. — ~ हो जाना, to reach adulthood, to be grown up; to reach adolescence.

बालिश *bāliś* [P. *bāliś*], m. pillow, cushion.

बालिश्त *bāliśt* [P. *bāliśt*], f. a span of the extended hand.

बालिश्तिया *bāliśtiyā* [cf. H. *bāliśt*], m. a tiny dwarf.

बालीं *bālīṁ* [P. *bālīn*], f. U. **1.** pillow, cushion. **2.** transf. head of bed, bedside.

[1]**बाली** *bālī* [*vālaka-*[1]], f. an ear-ring with pendants worn from the centre of the ear.

[2]**बाली** *bālī* [*valla-*], f. ear or spike of corn (= [4]बाल).

बालुक *bāluk* [S.], m. *Pl. HŚS.* a kind of drug and perfume (= एलुआ).

बालुका *bālukā* [ad. *vālukā-*], f. = [1]बालू.

[1]**बालू** *bālū* [*vālukā-*], f. sand, gravel. — ~ की, adj. sandy (soil). ~ की दीवार, f. = next. ~ की भीत, f. a wall of sand: anything not to be relied on, frail. – बालूचर, m. land covered by a deposit of sand; sand-bank. °आ, m. id. बालूबुर्द [P. *-burd*], m. arable land covered by a deposit

of alluvial sand. बालूशाही, f. a sweet consisting of pastries fried in *ghī*, dipped in molasses or syrup and sprinkled with sugar.

²बालू *bālū*, m. ear or spike of corn (= ⁴बाल).

बालूचरी *bālūcarī*, adj. & f. *Pl.* **1.** adj. having to do with a place named Baluchar, near Murshidabad in Bengal. **2.** f. a kind of silk cloth manufactured at Baluchar.

बालेय *bāleyă* [S.], adj. *Pl. HŚS.* **1.** fit or proper for children. **2.** tender, soft.

बाल्टी *bālṭī*, f. see बालटी.

बाल्य *bālyă* [S.], adj. & m. **1.** adj. having to do with children. **2.** m. childhood; infancy. — बाल्यावस्था [°*lya+a*°], f. childhood stage or condition.

बाव *bāv* [*vāta-*, and *vāyu-*], m. f. **1.** wind (हवा). **2.** flatulence. **3.** rheumatism. **4.** reg. a syphilitic swelling. — ~ (के घोड़े) पर सवार होना, fig. to be as swift as the wind; to be puffed up, conceited, vain. ~ बाँधना, to use specious words (as flattery, or mockery) to gain a purpose. ~ सरना, to pass wind. – बाव-गोला, m. colic; flatulence with constipation. बावबंदी [P. -*bandī*], f. building castles in the air; a futile effort; exaggerated praise of an unworthy object. बाव-सूल, m. colic.

बावग *bāvag* [**vāpayogya-*], m. reg. **1.** the sowing season. **2.** broadcast sowing.

बावजूद *bāvājūd* [P. *bāvujūd*], ppn. in spite (of, के); notwithstanding.

¹**बावटा** *bāvṭā* [cf. *vāta-*], m. reg. **1.** a flag. **2.** *Pl.* rheumatism; cramp; convulsions.

²**बावटा** *bāvṭā* [? **bāhuvarta-*], m. *Pl.* an armlet (of gold or silver).

बावड़ी *bāvṛī*, f. reg. = बावली.

बावन *bāvan* [*dvāpañcāśat-*], adj. fifty-two. — ~ तोले पाव रत्ती, adj. & adv. fifty-two *tolās* and a ninety-sixth: to the last grain (of weight), absolutely exact(ly). ~ बीर, m. one man worth fifty-two: a hero indeed.

¹**बावनी** *bāvnī* [*vāpana-*; or *vāpanīya-*], f. reg. (W). sowing time; sowing.

²**बावनी** *bāvnī* [cf. H. *bāvan*], f. **1.** Brbh. a poem of fifty-two verses. **2.** *Pl.* a group of people, an informal society.

बावरचिनी *bāvarcinī* [cf. H. *bāvarcī*], f. a cook (female).

बावरची *bāvarcī* [P. *bāvar*+T. -*cī*], m. one who can be trusted: a cook. — बावरचीगरी [P. -*garī*], f. the art or skill of cooking.

बावला *bāvlā* [*vātula-*: ? w. *vyākula-*, or *vāyura-*], adj. **1.** mad, crazy. **2.** raging, furious.

बावलापन *bāvlāpan* [cf. H. *bāvlā*], m. **1.** madness, craziness. **2.** frenzy.

¹**बावली** *bāvlī* [cf. *vāpī-*], f. a large masonry well with steps down to the water; a small, deep tank with steps.

²**बावली** *bāvlī* [cf. P. *bāvar*], f. *Pl.* a lure (to train an animal or bird).

बावाँ *bāvāṁ*, adj. Brbh. Av. = बायाँ.

बावा *bāvā*, m. reg. = बाबा.

बावी *bāvī* [*vāpikā-*], f. reg. = ¹बावली.

बावेला *bāvelā* [P. *vā-vailāh*], m. reg. turmoil; creating turmoil; weeping and wailing.

बाशिंदा *bāśindā* [P. *bāśanda*], m. resident, inhabitant.

¹**बास** *bās* [*vāsa-*³], m. **1.** esp. in comp. perfume; fragrance. **2.** offensive smell, stench. **3.** trace, whiff (of, का). — बासमती, adj. & f. fragrant (a type of rice); *bāsmatī* rice.

²**बास** *bās* [²*vāsa-*], m. **1.** residence (at a place). **2.** dwelling-place; shelter; camp-site (of workmen). — ~ करना, to lodge, to stay (with); to reside; to nest, to roost (a bird).

³**बास** *bās* [*vāsas-*], m. Brbh. clothing.

बासठ *bāsaṭh* [*dvāṣaṣṭi-*], adj. sixty-two.

¹**बासन** *bāsan* [*vāsana-*²], m. vessel, dish, pot.

²**बासन** *bāsan* [cf. H. *bāsnā*], m. f. (?) *Pl.* perfume, &c. (= ¹बास).

बासना *bāsnā* [*vāsayati*³], v.t. to perfume, to scent.

बासर *bāsar*, m. = वासर.

¹**बासा** *bāsā* [²*vāsa-*], m. 1. = ²बास. **2.** eating-place; communal eating-place.

²**बासा** *bāsā* [*vāsaka-*], m. *Pl.* the shrub *Justicia ganderussa* (which has been used to make charcoal).

¹**बासी** *bāsī* [*vāsita-*], adj. & f. **1.** adj. stale (as food, water). **2.** faded (as flowers). **3.** left-over food. — ~ ईद, f. fig. the day after a festival. ~ करना, to allow to go stale. ~ बचे न कुत्ता खाए, fig. not a scrap being left (to be saved, or given to the dog). ~ मुँह, m. & adv. unwashed face or mouth; with unwashed face, on an empty stomach. — बासी-तिबासी, f. three days' stale food.

²**बासी** *bāsī*, m. esp. -बासी. = वासी.

बाहना *bāhnā* [*vāhayati*¹], v.t. **1.** to carry forward; to drive (as a horse, a vehicle). **2.** to load. **3.** to plough. **4.** fig. to toil. **5.** to shoot, to fire (a weapon). **6.** to copulate (a male animal). **7.** to open out; to show (the teeth); to comb out (the hair).

बाहर *bāhar* [**bāhira-*: Pa. *bāhira-*], adv. & ppn. **1.** adv. outside, out; outwards. **2.** away (from one's home district); abroad. **3.** interj. out with (a thing, a person)! get out! **4.** ppn. (w. के or से) outside. **5.** (w. से) beyond. **6.** (w. से) dissenting (from). — ~ करना, to put out, to eject; to leave out, to exclude. ~ का, adj. outer, outside, external; from another region; foreign. ~ जाना, to go out; to go away; to go abroad; to be sent abroad (exports). ~ निकलना, to come out (of, से), to emerge (from); to be out, away, abroad; to withdraw (from). ~ भेजना, to send away or abroad; to evacuate; to export. ~ से, adv. from away, or abroad; superficially. ~ होना, to be outside (of, के, से); to be excluded (from, से); to dissent (from), to disapprove (of). आपे से ~ होना, to be beside oneself (with joy, anger). – बाहर-भीतर, adv. outside and inside; away and at home, everywhere.

[1]**बाहरा** *bāhrā* [**vāhakara-*], m. *Pl.* one who works at pouring well-water from the bucket into an irrigation channel.

[2]**बाहरा** *bāhrā* [cf. H. *bāhar*], m. *Pl.* the far or off side, left side.

बाहरी *bāhrī* [cf. H. *bāhar*], adj. & m. **1.** adj. outer, external. **2.** from another region; foreign. **3.** outward, superficial. **4.** Brbh. dissenting. **5.** m. a stranger, a foreigner; an outsider.

बाहा *bāhā* [*vāha-*], m. **1.** outflow of, or exit for, water; water-channel. **2.** vessel into which the juice of sugar-cane flows from the press.

बाहिज *bāhij*, adj. Av. = बाह्य.

बाही *bāhī* [*vāhin-*], adj. freight-bearing (animal).

बाहु *bāhu* [S.], f. the upper arm. – बाहुज, m. poet. a kṣatriya. °ता, f. valour. बाहु-पाश, m. the joined arms, embrace. बाहु-बल, m. strength of arm, bodily strength or vigour. बाहु-मूल, m. shoulder-joint; armpit.

बाहुल्य *bāhulyă* [S.], m. **1.** abundance, plenty. **2.** variety. **3.** excess.

बाह्मनी *bāhmanī* [cf. H. *bāmhan*; ad. *brāhmaṇa-*], adj. having to do with a brāhmaṇ. — ~ चील, the Brahminy kite (a reddish bird having a white head and a rounded tail). ~ बतख, the Brahminy duck or ruddy sheldrake (= चकवा).

बाह्य *bāhyă* [S.], adj. **1.** outer; external. **2.** foreign. **3.** outward, apparent (as the external world). **4.** intended for show (conduct). — बाह्य-वासी, adj. living away from home; living abroad, emigrant. बह्यांचल [°*hya*+*a*°], m. outskirts.

बिंगी *biṅgī* [? conn. *bhṛṅga-*[1]], f. reg. **1.** S.H. a beetle. **2.** a humming top.

बिंजन *biñjan* [ad. *vyañjana-*], m. **1.** any seasoning or relish. **2.** vegetables.

बिंडा *biṇḍā* [cf. H. *bīṁṛ*], m. reg. **1.** a bundle, or heap (of sticks, or grass or straw). **2.** W. = ईंडुआ.

बिंदा *bindā* [conn. *bindu-*], m. a large round mark (sectarian or decorative) made on the forehead.

बिंदिया *bindiyā* [cf. H. *bindī*], f. an eye complaint (in which the cornea is affected).

बिंदी *bindī* [conn. *bindu-*], f. **1.** dot; mark. **2.** a nought, zero. **3.** dot, mark or spangle ornamenting the forehead.

बिंदु *bindu* [S.], f. m. **1.** a drop. **2.** a point, dot; the Devanāgarī script sign *anusvāra*. **3.** mark, point (as on a scale). **4.** semen; (in yoga) the seed of Śiva.

बिंधना *biṁdhnā* [cf. H. *bīṁdhnā*], v.i. & v.t. **1.** v.i. to be pierced; to be stung (as by sharp words). **2.** to be engrossed, caught (by a topic). **3.** v.t. = बींधना.

बिंधवाना *biṁdhvānā* [cf. H. *bīṁdhnā*], v.t. to cause to be pierced, &c. (by, से); to have pierced (as the ears).

बिंब *bimb* [S.], m. **1.** reflection (as in a mirror); image. **2.** shadow. **3.** disc of sun or moon. **4.** a plant, *Momordica monadelpha*, and its fruit, a red gourd. — बिंब-फल, m. Brbh. a red gourd. बिंब-योजना, imagery.

बिक *bik* [ad. *vṛka-*], m. reg. wolf.

बिकट *bikaṭ* [Engl. *picket*], m. reg. picket, guard, watch. — ~ का पहरा, m. = ~.

बिकना *biknā* [*vikrīyate*, also H. *bikānā*], v.i. **1.** to be sold. **2.** fig. to be dependent (on, के हाथ); to be the servant, or slave (of).

बिकवाना *bikvānā* [cf. H. *bikānā*], v.t. to cause to be sold (by, से).

बिकसना *bikasnā* [ad. *vikasati*], v.i. **1.** to open (a flower), to bloom. **2.** to become radiant with joy.

बिकाऊ *bikāū* [cf. H. *bikānā*], adj. **1.** for sale. **2.** saleable; sound (quality).

बिकाना *bikānā* [**vikrāpayati*: Pk. *vikkāyamāṇa-*], v.t. & v.i. **1.** v.t. to cause to be sold, to sell. **2.** v.i. to be sold, to sell (= बिकना).

बिकाल *bikāl* [ad. *vikāla-*], m. *Pl. HŚS.* afternoon.

बिकाव *bikāv* [cf. H. *biknā, bikānā*], m. reg. sale.

बिक्री *bikrī* [cf. H. *biknā*; ad. *vikraya-*], f. **1.** selling, sale; sales; trade; demand, market. **2.** proceeds of selling. — **बिक्री-कर**, m. sales tax. **बिक्री-ख़ाता**, m. sales ledger: account sales. **बिक्री-पत्र**, m. deed or bill of sale. **बिक्री-बट्टा**, m. = ~, 2.

बिखरना *bikharnā* [**viṣkarati*: Pk. *vikkharaï*], v.i. **1.** to be scattered (as seed); to be dispersed. **2.** to be disarranged; to be dishevelled (hair). **3.** to be wasted, spoiled. **4.** to become infatuated (with, **पर**). **5.** to become angry, enraged.

बिखराना *bikhrānā* [cf. H. *bikharnā*], v.t. = **बिखेरना**.

बिखा *bikhā*, f. reg. trouble, misfortune.

बिखेरना *bikhernā* [**viṣkerayati*], v.t. **1.** to scatter (as seed); to disperse. **2.** to dishevel (the hair).

बिगड़ना *bigaṛnā* [conn. *vighaṭate*; ? × *vigraha-*], v.i. **1.** to be spoiled, to deteriorate; to be spoiled in the making (as a garment). **2.** to fail, to go wrong (as a scheme); to be bungled. **3.** to be corrupted; to become depraved. **4.** to be damaged; to break down (a machine); to be destroyed (as a reputation). **5.** to be wasted (money). **6.** to grow angry; to become estranged (friends); to quarrel. **दोनों में बिगड़ी है**, they are now on bad terms. **7.** to be intractable; to be disaffected; to revolt. — **बिगड़ी ज़बान**, f. a foul tongue. – **बिगड़ खड़ा होना**, to become suddenly angry.

बिगड़ाव *bigṛāv* [cf. H. *bigaṛnā*] m. = **बिगाड़**.

बिगड़ी *bigṛī* [cf. H. *bigaṛnā*], f. **1.** damage, harm; wretched state. **2.** loss of rapport, misunderstanding. **3.** colloq. war, battle.

बिगड़ैल *bigṛail* [cf. H. *bigaṛnā*], adj. **1.** truculent. **2.** short-tempered.

बिगहटी *bigahṭī*, adj. *hist.* assessed, or divided, by *bīghās* (rents, lands).

बिगाड़ *bigāṛ* [cf. H. *bigāṛnā*], m. state of being spoiled: **1.** deterioration; corruption; disorder, disturbance. **2.** harm, injury, damage. **3.** defect. **4.** falling out; quarrel; defection, revolt. — **~ करना**, to do harm (to, **का**), to spoil; to quarrel (with, **से**). **~ पर आना**, to be on the point of quarrelling.

बिगाड़ना *bigāṛnā* [conn. **vighāṭayati*: Pa. *vighāṭita-*; ? × *vigraha-*], v.t. **1.** to spoil. **2.** to corrupt (a person). **3.** to cause loss; destroy, to ruin (as a reputation). **4.** to waste (money). **5.** to cause a misunderstanding (between friends). **6.** to foul (one's clothes). — **बात**, or **मामला**, **~**, to spoil matters; to bungle.

बिगाड़ू *bigāṛū* [cf. H. *bigāṛnā*], adj. & m. **1.** adj. harmful. **2.** m. one who spoils, or causes loss or harm, &c.

बिगाना *bigānā*, adj. = **बेगाना**.

[1]**बिगो-** *bigo-* [**vigopayati*: Pk *viggovaï*], v.t. Av. to hide.

[2]**बिगो-** *bigo-* [**vigrocati*, or **viglapayati*: cf. *viglāpayati*], v.t. Brbh. Av. **1.** to do harm to; to oppress; to destroy. **2.** to mislead. **3.** to speak ill of, to criticise. **4.** to pass (time) idly.

बिघड़ना *bighaṛnā*, v.i. reg. = **बिगड़ना**.

[1]**बिघन** *bighan* [ad. *vighana-*], m. reg. killing; slaughter.

[2]**बिघन** *bighan*, m. Brbh. Av. = **विघ्न**.

बिघनता *bighanātā* [cf. H. [2]*bighan*], f. Brbh. obstacle; difficulty.

बिघौटी *bighauṭī*, f. **1.** *Pl.* land measurement. **2.** reg. (W.) land assessed at a rate per *bīghā*.

बिच- *bic-*. middle (= **बीच**): – **बिचकन्ना**, m. reg. the middle finger.

बिचकना *bicaknā*, v.i. **1.** to be twisted awry (as the face, in displeasure). **2.** to be startled, alarmed. **3.** reg. = **बिचलना**.

बिचकन्ना *bickannā*, m. reg. **1.** the middle finger. **2.** *Pl.* an ear ornament.

बिचकाना *bickānā*, v.t. **1.** to distort, to twist awry. **मुँह ~**, to grimace. **2.** [H. *bijhukā-*] to startle, to alarm.

बिचरना *bicarnā* [ad. *vicarati*], v.i. **1.** to move about; to wander; to lose one's way; to be lost, missing. **2.** to shift; to slip.

बिचलना *bicalnā* [ad. *vicalati*], v.i. **1.** to shift; to slip. **2.** reg. to be spoiled or marred. **3.** reg. to withdraw (as from a promise). 4. = **बिचरना**, 1.; Av. to flee.

बिचला *biclā* [cf. **vīcya-*: Pk. *vicca-*], adj. **1.** intermediate, middle (of three things, persons). **2.** middling (of quality).

बिचला- *biclā-* [cf. H. *bicalnā*], v.t. Av. to cause to move, or to slip, &c. (see **बिचलना**).

बिचवई *bicvaī* [cf. H. *bīc*], m., f. reg. **1.** m. an intermediary, agent. **2.** f. mediation (in a dispute).

बिचवान *bicvān*, m. an intermediary.

बिचवानी *bicvānī*, f. mediation.

बिचार *bicār*, m. = विचार.

बिचारा *bicārā*, adj. = बेचारा.

बिचाली *bicālī* [? conn. H. *bichānā*], f. reg. straw or grass used as a bedding.

बिचूरना *bicūrnā*, v.t. reg. to pull to pieces; to break (sthg.) up.

बिचौलिया *bicauliyā*, m. a middleman, agent; broker.

बिच्छी *bicchī* [conn. *vṛścika-*], f. scorpion.

बिच्छू *bicchū* [conn. *vṛścika-*: Pk. *bicchua-*], m. **1.** scorpion. **2.** the sign Scorpio (of the zodiac). **3.** colloq. *HŚS.* a stinging-nettle. **4.** *Pl.* a kind of firework.

बिछड़ना *bichaṛnā* [**vikṣuṭati*: Pk. *vicchuḍia-*], v.i. **1.** to be separated (from, से); to be parted. **2.** to turn away, aside (from). **3.** transf. to be sprained (a joint).

बिछड़ाना *bichṛānā* [cf. H. *bichaṛnā*], v.t. to cause to be separated, to part; to divide.

बिछड़ाव *bichṛāv* [cf. H. *bichṛānā*], m. **1.** separation (from, से). **2.** alienation.

बिछड़ाहट *bichṛāhaṭ* [cf. H. *bichṛānā*], f. separating, separation (from, से).

बिछना *bichnā* [cf. H. *bichānā*], v.t. **1.** to be spread out; to be laid (as bedding, or as flooring). **2.** to be scattered; to be laid (as mines). **3.** colloq. to be laid low, felled; to be humbled; to be floored (as by a problem).

बिछलहर *bichalhar* [cf. H. *vichalnā*], adj. reg. slippery.

बिछवाना *bichvānā* [cf. H. *bichānā*], v.t. to cause to be spread or laid, &c. (by, से: as bedding, flooring).

बिछवैया *bichvaiyā* [cf. H. *bichvānā*], m. **1.** one who spreads (beds, &c). **2.** reg. sweeper.

बिछाई *bichāī* [cf. H. *bichānā*], f. **1.** spreading. **2.** payment for spreading.

बिछाना *bichānā* [**vicchādayati*], v.t. **1.** to spread out; to lay (on, पर); to unroll (bedding). **2.** to lay (a road, &c). **3.** to scatter; to lay (as mines). **4.** fig. (esp. w. देना.) to lay (one) low, to fell.

बिछावन *bichāvan*, m. = बिछौना.

बिछिया *bichiyā*, f. = बिछुआ, 4.

बिछुआ *bichuā* [conn. *vṛścika-*: Pk. *vicchua-*], m. **1.** scorpion. **2.** a curved dagger; stiletto. **3.** Brbh. an iron claw (weapon). **4.** a ring worn on the big toe by married women. **5.** colloq. a stinging-nettle.

बिछुई *bichuī*, f. reg. toe ornament (= बिछुआ, 4).

बिछुड़ना *bichuṛnā*, v.t. = बिछड़ना.

बिछो- *bicho-* [*vikṣobhayati-*], v.t. Av. **1.** to divide, to separate; to leave, to abandon. **2.** to empty (liquid from a container).

बिछोड़ना *bichoṛnā* [**vikṣoṭayati*: Pk. *vicchoḍaï*], v.t. **1.** to separate, to part; to card (cotton). **2.** to pull to pieces.

बिछोड़ा *bichoṛā* [**vikṣoṭa-*], m. separation (as of friends, lovers).

बिछोव *bichov*, m. Av. = बिछोह.

बिछोह *bichoh* [*vikṣobha-*], m. **1.** separation. **2.** grief at separation.

बिछोह- *bichoh-* [*vikṣobhayati*], v.t. Brbh. to divide, to separate (lovers).

बिछौना *bichaunā* [**vicchādana-*: Pa. *vicchādana-*], m. **1.** bedding; bed. **2.** floor-covering. — ~ करना, to make a bed; colloq. to lay (one) flat, to fell.

बिछौनी *bichaunī* [cf. H. *bichaunā*], f. dimin. = बिछौना.

बिजना *bijnā*, m. reg. a fan (= बीजना).

बिजया *bijayā* [ad. *vijayā-*], f. reg. hemp leaves; the hemp plant, *Cannabis sativa.*

[1]**बिजली** *bijlī* [*vidyullatā-*], f. **1.** lightning. **2.** electricity. — ~ कड़कड़ाना, or गरजना, thunder to rumble. ~ का, adj. electric. ~ की बत्ती, f. an electric lamp, light. ~ की कड़क, f. clap of thunder. ~ कौंधना, or चमकना, lightning to flash. ~ गिरना, or टूटना, or पड़ना, lighting to fall (on, पर), to be struck by lighting.

[2]**बिजली** *bijlī* [cf. H. *bīj*], f. **1.** kernel of a mango-seed. **2.** pendant (to necklace, or of ear-ring).

बिजाइ *bijāi* [ad. *bīja-*; cf. *bījavāpa-*], f. **1.** reg. (W.) sowings: surplus seed given to field-workers after sowing. **2.** wages for sowing. **3.** N. sowing of seed.

बिजायठ *bijāyaṭh*, m. an armlet consisting of several linked pieces.

बिजायठन *bijāyṭhan*, m. Brbh. = बिजायठ.

बिजार *bijār*, m. reg. (W.) **1.** a bull; a stallion. **2.** fig. a profligate man.

बिजाला *bijālā*, adj. *Pl.* **1.** having seed or grain. **2.** run to seed.

बिजूका *bijūkā* [cf. H. *bijhuk-*], m. E.H. a scarecrow.

बिज्जू *bijjū*, m. **1.** a kind of badger, (?) hog-badger. **2.** reg. hyena.

बिझरा *bijhrā*, m. reg. grain or seed (as peas, gram, barley, wheat) for mixed sowing.

बिझुक- *bijhuk-* [**vijhukkati*], v.i. Brbh. to be startled, to take fright.

बिझुका- *bijhukā-* [cf. H. *bijhuk-*], v.t. Brbh. to startle, to alarm.

बिटर-बिटर *biṭar-biṭar*, adv. steadily, fixedly.

बिटमास *biṭmās*, m. *Pl.* a coarse pulse (of the *māś* or *kalāī* kind).

बिटलवण *biṭlavaṇ*, m. black salt (obtained by heating salt with myrobalans and soda-ash: used medicinally).

बिटाना *biṭānā*, v.t. reg. to scatter.

बिटालना *biṭālnā* [**viṭṭāla-*: Pk. *viṭṭāla-*], v.t. to make impure: to put into the mouth, to taste (food). — मुँह ~, = ~.

बिटिया *biṭiyā* [cf. H. *beṭī*], f. little daughter, dear daughter; daughter.

बिटोना *biṭonā*, v.t. reg. = बिंटाना.

बिटौरा *biṭaurā* [conn. *viṣṭhā-*, **viṭṭa-*; ?+*puṭa-*], m. reg. a pile of dried cow-dung cakes plastered on the outside to protect them from rain.

बिटौरी *biṭaurī*, f. *hist.* a village tax on tradesmen and shopkeepers.

बिट्टी *biṭṭī*, f. *Pl.* a pair, couple, match.

बिठक *biṭhak*, m. reg. (W). a white-ant hill.

बिठलाना *biṭhlānā*, v.t. = बैठाना.

बिठाना *biṭhānā*, v.t. = बैठाना.

बिठालना *biṭhālnā*, v.t. reg. = बैठाना.

बिडर- *biḍar-* [cf. H. *biḍār-*], v.i. Brbh. Av. to be startled; to be frightened.

बिडार- *biḍār-* [conn. *vidārayati*], v.t. Brbh. Av. **1.** to drive away; to put to flight. **2.** fig. to be far superior (to).

बिड़ाल *biṛāl* [*biḍāla-*], m. a tom-cat.

बिढ़- *biṛh-* [*vivardhate*], v.i. Av. to be collected, acquired.

बित- *bit-*, v.i. Brbh. = बीतना.

बितर- *bitar-* [ad. *vitarati*, cf. H. *vitaraṇ*], v.t. Brbh. to bestow; to distribute.

बितराबंदी *bitrābandī*, f. *hist.* arrangements for payment of the revenue.

बितव- *bitav-*, v.t. reg. = बिताना.

बिताना *bitānā* [cf. H. *bītnā*], v.t. to cause to pass, to spend (time).

बित्तम-बित्तम *bittam-bittam*, adv. little by little; gradually.

बित्ता *bittā* [*vitasti-*], m. span (of the hand).

बित्तिया *bittiyā* [cf. H. *bittā*], f. a dwarf.

बित्ती *bittī*, f. reg. a small round potsherd; a boys' game played with a potsherd (which is held in the toes and thrown forward, then retrieved by another boy who must hold his breath all the while and keep saying *bittī*).

बिथक- *bithak-* [**visthakk-*: Pk. *vitthakk-*], v.i. Brbh. Av. **1.** to be tired. **2.** to be astonished; to be delighted, enchanted.

बिथकित *bithakit* [cf. H. *bithak-*], adj. Brbh. Av. astonished; delighted, enchanted.

बिथर- *bithar-* [*vistarati*], v.i. Brbh. Av. **1.** to be scattered; to be spread; to be sown; to be sprinkled. **2.** to become separate (things joined).

बिथरना *bitharnā* [*vistarati*], v.i. **1.** to be scattered, to be separate; to be sown. **2.** to be sprinkled, or splashed. **3.** to bloom.

बिथराना *bithrānā*, v.t. = बिथार-.

बिथार *bithār* [*vistāra-*], m. reg. (Bihar) a large dish.

बिथार- *bithār-* [*vistārayati*], v.t. Brbh. to scatter; to spread; to sprinkle.

बिथारी *bithārī* [cf. H. *bithārnā*], f. *Pl.* brushing or cleaning warp threads (in weaving).

बिथोरना *bithornā*, v.t. reg. = बिथराना.

बिदकना *bidaknā* [?? conn. H. *biḍar-*], v.i. **1.** to start; to be scared; to shy (a horse). **2.** to move, to stir; to move aside or back; to be dissuaded.

बिदका- *bidkā-*, v.t. Brbh. to tear (at flesh), to wound.

बिदकाना *bidkānā* [?? conn. H. *biḍār-*], v.t. **1.** to startle; to scare. **2.** to cause to draw back; to frighten off, to dissuade; to alienate.

बिदर *bidar*, m. **1.** a metallic alloy, esp. of copper and lead with zinc, or zinc and tin (= बिदरी). **2.** a vessel made of *bidar*, and silver-plated by beating. — बिदरसाज़ [P. *-sāz*], m. maker of *bidar* vessels, silver-plater.

बिदरी *bidrī* [cf. H. *bidar*], f. 1. = बिदर, 1., 2.

बिदा *bidā* [A. *vidā'*], f. **1.** permission to depart; taking leave. **2.** departure. **3.** specif. departure of a newly married wife to her husband's family's home. — ~ करना, to dismiss, to despatch (a person); to say goodbye (to, को); to see off. ~ देना, to allow to leave; = prec., 2., 3. ~ लेना, to take leave (of, से). ~ हो! goodbye! ~ होना, to depart; to depart life, to die.

बिदाई *bidāī* [cf. H. *bidā*], f. **1.** dismissal. 2. = बिदा, 1., 2. **3.** gift given to one departing.

बिदायगी *bidāygī* [H. *bidā*+P. *-gī*], f. *Pl.* **1.** sending off; departure. **2.** gift given to one departing.

बिदारना *bidārnā* [*vidārayati*, w. MIA anal. *-dd-*], v.t. **1.** to tear, to rend (as prey). **2.** to split. **3.** to break (as the heart).

बिदाह *bidāh* [cf. H. *bidāhnā*], ? f. reg. **1.** a light ploughing or harrowing after sowing rice (to cover the seed and remove weeds). **2.** a ploughing or harrowing of millets when they are about a foot high.

बिदाहना *bidāhnā* [**vidr̥mhati*], v.t. **1.** to plough lightly or to harrow after sowing rice. **2.** to plough or to harrow millets when they are about a foot high.

बिदेसिया *bidesiyā* [cf. H. *videś*], m. a partic. kind of dance-drama (Bihar).

बिदोर- *bidor-* [cf. **vidrohayati*], v.t. Brbh. **1.** to show (the teeth), to grin. **2.** to draw back (the lips, in a grin).

बिध *bidh* [ad. *vidhi-*], f. **1.** rule, precept; ordinance; sacred text. **2.** prescribed act or ceremony. **3.** method, way, means. **4.** *Pl.* balance of an account; adjustment of an account. **5.** fate, destiny. — ~ मिलाना, to consult sacred texts (in connection with performing a ceremony); to compare the horoscopes of bride and bridegroom before performing a marriage; to balance (accounts).

[1]**बिधना** *bidhnā* [cf. H. *bimdhnā*, also H. *bedhnā*], v.i. **1.** to be pierced or perforated. **2.** transf. to be wounded.

[2]**बिधना** *bidhănā* [ad. *vidhinā*, instr.], m. = विधाता.

बिधवपन *bidhavpan* [cf. H. *bidhvā*], m. Av. widowhood.

बिधवा *bidhvā*, f. = विधवा.

बिधावट *bidhāvaṭ* [cf. H. *bimdhānā*], f. piercing, perforation.

बिन *bin* [*vinā*], prep. without; not, un-. — ~ जाने, adv. unknowingly. ~ जुता, adj. unploughed. ~ दाने-पानी, adj. without food and drink. ~ धन, adj. without money, needy. ~ देखा, adj. unobserved, unseen. ~ बोया, adj. unplanted, growing wild. ~ ब्याहा, adj. unmarried. उससे ~ आए न बने, he must come.

बिनती *bintī* [*vijñapti-*], f. **1.** bowing down. **2.** humility. ***3.** entreaty; request; petition. — ~ करना, to make entreaty (of or to, से)

[1]**बिनना** *binnā* [**vināti*: Pa. *vināti*], v.t. = बुनना.

[2]**बिनना** *binnā* [cf. H. *bīnnā*], v.i. & v.t. **1.** v.i. to be picked, culled. **2.** to be cleaned. **3.** v.t. = बीनना.

बिनवट *binvaṭ* [? conn. **vahniyaṣṭi*], f. a staff or stick weighted at both ends (used in gymnastic exercises). — बिनवट-पटे, m. pl. cudgels and wooden swords.

बिनवाई *binvāī*, f. = बुनवाई.

[1]**बिनवाना** *binvānā*, v.t. = बुनवाना.

[2]**बिनवाना** *binvānā* [cf. H. [1]*bīnnā*], v.t. to cause to be picked, &c.

बिनसना *binasnā* [*vinaśyati*], v.i. **1.** to be destroyed. **2.** to spoil; to perish, to die.

[1]**बिना** *binā* [S.], prep. & ppn. **1.** prep. without. ~ काम किए, adv. without working; unless work is done. ~ पैसे के, adv. without money. **2.** prep. w. के. without. पैसे के ~, adv. without money, not having money.

[2]**बिना** *binā* [A. *binā*], f. **1.** foundation, base; basis. **2.** cause; reason, motive. — इस ~ पर कि... on the basis that....

बिनाई *bināī* [cf. H. *binnā*], f. = बुनाई.

बिनावट *bināvaṭ*, f. = बुनावट.

बिनासना *bināsnā* [*vināśayati*], v.t. reg. to destroy.

बिनोला *binolā*, m. = बिनौला.

बिनौना *binaunā* [*vinamati*], v.t. reg. to adore, to revere.

बिनौरिया *binauriyā*, m. reg. a grass which grows in autumn crops (used as fodder for cattle).

बिनौला *binaulā* [cf. **vīnopala-*], m. **1.** cotton-seed. **2.** fruit of the *nīm* tree. — ~ चाबना, to eat unpleasant food; to say unpleasant things.

बिनौली *binaulī* [cf. H. *binaulā*], f. cotton-seed.

बिपत *bipat* [ad. *vipatti-*], f. **1.** misfortune. **2.** suffering.

बिपता *biptā*, m. f. disaster, misfortune.

बिपति *bipati*, f. Brbh. = बिपत.

बिपल *bipal* [ad. *vipala-*], m. *astron.* a moment, an instant.

बिफरना *bipharnā* [**vispharati*, or *visphurati*], v.i. **1.** to become irritated or angry (with, से). **2.** to break out of control; to revolt.

बिबि *bibi* [conn. *dva-*], adj. Brbh. two.

बिबिया *bibiyā*, f. dimin. = बीबी.

बिबियाना *bibiyānā* [cf. P. *-āna*], adj. obs. having to do with women, women's.

बिमोचना *bimocnā* [ad. *vimocayati*], v.t. to free, to loose.

बिमोह- *bimoh-* [ad. *vimohayati*], v.t. & ? v.i. **1.** v.t. Av. to charm. **2.** ? v.i. Brbh. to be charmed.

बियाड़ *biyāṛ* [**bījavāṭī-*], f. reg. (W.) seed-bed, nursery bed (as for rice).

बियाबान *biyābān* [P. *biyābān*], m. wilderness.

बियाबानी *biyābānī* [P. *biyābānī*], adj. wild, desolate.

बियार *biyār*, f. reg. (Bihar) = बियाड़.

बियास *biyās* [**bījās(y)a-*], m. reg. **1.** land prepared for sowing the following year. **2.** W. land under rice. **3.** W. offshoots from rice or other plants.

बिरंचि *birañci* [ad. *virañci-*], m. Brbh. Av. a title of the god Brahmā.

बिरचन *bircan* [cf. H. *ber*], m. reg. flour or powder made from the fruit of the *ber* tree (jujube).

बिरछा *birchā* [ad. *vr̥kṣa-*], m. poet. a tree.

बिरत *birt* [ad. *vr̥tti-*], f. **1.** means of subsistence, &c. (= वृत्ति). **2.** specif. a grant, endowment (as of land: either free or at a fixed rate).

बिरता *birtā* [ad. *vr̥tta-*: cf. H. *būtā*], m. **1.** power, means; capacity. **2.** help, support. — बिरते पर उछलना, to rejoice, or to glory, in the power or support (of, के). किस बिरते पर ? on what basis ? with whose support, or authority?

बिरतिया *birtiyā* [cf. H. *birt*], m. *hist.* a tenant holding land at a fixed rate.

बिरद *birăd*, m. = विरद.

बिरदैत *birdait* [cf. H. *birad*], m. **1.** panegyrist, bard. **2.** *HŚS.* a renowned warrior (?).

बिरम- *biram-* [**viramyati*], v.i. Brbh. **1.** to cease, to stop; to rest. **2.** to dally (with a loved one).

बिरमा *birmā*, m. *Pl.* = [2]बरमा.

बिरमाना *birmānā* [cf. **viramyati*], v.t. & v.i. reg. to cause to stop, or to desist: **1.** v.t. to stop, to check. **2.** to subdue; to tame. **3.** to tantalise. **4.** v.i. to stop, to rest (= बिरम-).

बिरयानी *biryānī* [P. *biryān*+H. *-ī*], f. sthg. roasted or fried: a dish of meat and fried rice.

बिरला *birlā* [*virala-*], adj. **1.** few, little. **2.** scarce, rare. — बिरले ही, adv. scarcely, seldom.

बिरव *birav*, m. Av. = [1]बिरवा.

[1]**बिरवा** *birvā* [*viṭapa-*], m. **1.** a sapling; a tree. **2.** [*vīrudha-*] a plant.

[2]**बिरवा** *birvā* [? *vīra-*], m. reg. child, boy.

[3]**बिरवा** *birvā*, m. reg. a man who works the water-basket in irrigation (= [1]बाहरा).

बिरवाही *birvāhī* [cf. H. [1]*birvā*], m. reg. **1.** an orchard, garden. **2.** *Pl.* enclosure of a planted area.

बिरस- *biras-* [*vilasati*], v.i. Av. to take delight, to revel.

बिरसना *birasnā* [*virahayati*; ? × H. *basnā*], v.i. reg. to remain, to stay.

बिरहा *birhā* [*viraha-*], m. 1. = विरह. **2.** a song of separation, lament. **3.** name of a two-line metre used in Bhojpuri folk songs.

बिरहाना *birhānā* [**vīrudhādhāna-*], m. reg. (W.) land where vegetables are grown.

बिरही *birăhī* [ad. *virahī-*], adj. & m. = विरही.

बिरादर *birādar* [P. *birādar*], m. U. brother.

बिरादराना *birādarānā* [P. *birādarāna*], adj. inv. brotherly, fraternal.

बिरादरी *birādărī* [P. *birādarī*], f. **1.** brotherhood. **2.** kinship. **3.** community, fraternity; caste. — ~ से ख़ारिज, or बाहर, करना, to outcaste. ~ से निकालना, id.

[1]**बिराना** *birānā*, adj. another's (= पराया).

[2]**बिराना** *birānā* [*virādhayati*], v.t. **1.** to tease, to mock. **2.** to vex. मुँह ~, to tease (one, का), &c.

बिरियाँ *biriyāṁ* [cf. *velā-*: ? ← Drav.], f. **1.** time, space of time. **2.** hour; occasion. — एक ~, adv. once; once upon a time.

बिरिया *biriyā*, f. ear ornaments (of a woman).

बिर्रा *birrā*, m. reg. a mixed crop, or crops, sown in the same field.

[1]**बिलंगना** *bilaṅgnā* [*vilaṅghayati*], v.t. reg. to leap up to; to rise towards, to climb.

[2]**बिलंगना** *bilaṅgnā* [conn. **vilagyati*: Pa. *vilaggita-*], v.i. *Pl.* to hang on (by), to swing.

बिलंगनी *bilaṅgnī* [cf. H. [2]*bilaṅgnā*], f. reg. a clothes-line; rod for hanging clothes on.

[1]**बिल** *bil* [*bila-*[1]], m. hole (of a rodent, a snake); burrow. — ~ ढूँढ़ना, to look for a hole (to hide in).

[2]**बिल** *bil* [Engl. *bill*], m. **1.** bill, account. **2.** bill of exchange, draft. **3.** parliamentary bill.

बिलकना *bilaknā* [cf. *vilagati*], v.i. reg. **1.** to cling to, to grasp. **2.** to grasp at: to crave for.

बिलकुल *bilkul* [A. *bi'lkul*], adv. entirely, completely; quite. — ~ ठीक, adj. absolutely correct.

[1]**बिलखना** *bilakhnā* [*vilakṣayati*], v.t. & v.i. **1.** v.t. to behold, to perceive. **2.** v.i. to vanish.

[2]**बिलखना** *bilakhnā* [*vilakṣayati*], v.i. **1.** to sob. **2.** to be distressed; to be chagrined.

बिलखाना *bilkhānā* [cf. H. [2]*bilakhnā*], v.t. & v.i. **1.** v.t. to make (a person) sob. **2.** v.i. बिलखा-. Av. = [1]बिलखना.

बिलग *bilag* [**vilagna-*[2]], adj. & m. **1.** adj. separate, detached (from, से). **2.** m. Brbh. Av. separation; aversion. — ~ मान-, to be displeased, offended.

बिलगना *bilagnā* [cf. H. *bilag*], v.i. to be separated, to separate.

बिलगाना *bilgānā* [cf. H. *bilag*], v.t. & v.i. **1.** v.t. to separate, to divide; to distinguish. **2.** v.i. Brbh. Av. to be separate, or different; to separate.

बिलगाव *bilgāv* [cf. H. *bilgānā*], m. separation; parting.

बिलचना *bilacnā*, v.i. reg. to mark (a passage in a book); to select, to excerpt (a passage).

बिलटना *bilaṭnā* [cf. *vinaṣṭa-*], v.i. **1.** to be lost, destroyed. **2.** to become bad, or adverse (= बिगड़ना).

बिलटी *bilṭī* [cf. Engl. *bill*], f. bill of lading, receipt for goods to be transported.

बिलनी *bilnī*, f. a stye in the eye.

बिलप- *bilap-* [ad. *vilapati*: w. H. *vilāp*], v.i. Brbh. to wail, &c. (cf. s.v. विलाप).

बिलफ़र्ज़ *bilfarz* [A. *bi'lfarz̤*], adv. on the supposition (that), granted (that).

बिलबिलाना *bilbilānā* [cf. *vilapati*, *vilāpayati*[1]], v.i. **1.** to be restless; to feel pain. **2.** to complain, to whine (as from pain, hunger). **3.** to be rife (as infection in a wound).

बिलम- *bilam-* [*vilambate*], v.i. Brbh. to delay; to stay; to dally.

बिलमाना *bilmānā* [cf. H. *bilam-*], v.t. to keep (one) waiting, to delay (one).

बिलला- *billā-*, v.i. Brbh. = बिल्लाना.

बिलल्ला *bilallā*, adj. & m. **1.** adj. stupid, silly. **2.** feckless. **3.** m. a stupid, or feckless person.

बिलल्लापन *bilallāpan* [cf. H. *bilallā*], m. **1.** stupidity, &c. **2.** fecklessness.

बिलवा- *bilvā-* [cf. H. *bilam-*], v.t. Brbh. Av. **1.** to keep back; to delay; to restrain. **2.** to embrace.

बिलसना *bilasnā* [*vilasati*], v.i. **1.** to be delighted, to enjoy oneself. **2.** to take delight, to revel (in).

बिलस्त *bilast* [P. *bilist*, H. *balist*], m. a span.

बिलहरा *bilahrā*, m. *Pl. HŚS.* a long, narrow betel-box made of strips of bamboo, &c.

बिलाँद *bilāṁd*, m. a span.

[1]**बिला** *bilā*, m. reg. = [1]बिल.

[2]**बिला** *bila* [A. *bila*], prep. U. without. — ~ नाग़ा, adv. without interruption, regularly. ~ वजह, adv. without reason or motive. ~ शक, adv. without doubt.

बिला- *bila-* [cf. *vilīyate*; Pk. *vilāi*], v.i. **1.** to vanish. **2.** to be effaced, to be destroyed. **3.** to be depraved, degenerate.

बिलाई *bilāī* [*biḍālikā-*], f. a cat. — बिलाई-कंद, m. cat's root: a large climbing perennial, *Ipomoea digitata*, having tuberous roots which are eaten and used medicinally.

बिलाना *bilānā* [**vilābhayati*], v.t. reg. to bestow, to distribute.

बिलापना *bilāpnā* [ad. *vilāpayati*[1]], v.i. to weep.

बिलाबंदी *bilābandī*, f. *hist.* an inventory of the lands of a district, cultivators' names, rents, &c.

बिलार *bilār* [*biḍāla-*], m. a tom-cat (= [1]बिल्ला).

बिलाव *bilāv* [conn. *biḍāla-*], m. a tom-cat.

बिलावड़ *bilāvaṛ* [cf. *biḍāla-*], m. reg. a tom-cat.

बिलावल *bilāval*, m. *mus.* name of a *rāg*.

बिलुला *bilulā*, adj. **1.** slovenly. **2.** awkward.

बिलूखा *bilūkhā* [cf. H. [1]*bil*], m. *Pl.* opening, crack.

बिलोइया *biloiyā* [cf. H. *bilonā*], m. churner.

बिलोकना *biloknā* [ad. *vilokayati*], v.t. poet. **1.** to look at, to behold; to examine. **2.** to see, to perceive.

बिलोड़ना *bilornā* [*viloḍayati*], v.t. **1.** to stir, to shake about. **2.** to churn.

बिलोना *bilonā* [*vilobhayati*²], v.t. **1.** to stir, to shake. **2.** to churn. **3.** reg. to shed (tears).

बिलोनी *bilonī* [cf. H. *bilonā*], f. **1.** a churn. **2.** reg. (W.) milking-pail.

बिलौंगी *bilaungī*, f. *Pl.* a kind of grass.

¹**बिलौटा** *bilauṭā* [cf. **billa-*], m. kitten.

²**बिलौटा** *bilauṭā*, m. reg. a betel-basket.

बिलौर *bilaur*, m. = बिल्लौर.

बिल्कुल *bilkul*, adv. see बिलकुल.

¹**बिल्ला** *billā* [**billa-*; w. *biḍāla-*], m. tom-cat.

²**बिल्ला** *billā*, m. **1.** badge (as worn by *caprāsīs*, or policemen). **2.** any flat piece of metal. **3.** reg. string holding the hilt of a sword or dagger to the sheath.

बिल्लाना *billānā* [conn. *vilapati*, and *vilāpayati*¹], v.i. to wail, to lament; to sob.

¹**बिल्ली** *billī* [**billa-*; w. *biḍāla-*], f. cat; specif. female cat. — ~ उलाँघना, to come across a cat (a bad omen for a journey). ~ का रास्ता काटना, to cross a cat's path, id. ~ के भाग्य से छींका टूट पड़ना, fig. fortune to smile on one in need. मेरी ~ और मुझीको म्याऊ? colloq.: does he presume to question me? – बिल्ली-लोटन, m. valerian.

²**बिल्ली** *billī*, f. reg. bolt, bar (as on a door).

बिल्लूर *billūr*, m. = बिल्लौर.

बिल्लौर *billaur* [A. *billaur*], m. **1.** crystal. **2.** rock-crystal; quartz.

बिल्लौरी *billaurī* [A. *billaurī*], adj. **1.** made of crystal, or of glass. **2.** crystalline. **3.** quartz-bearing.

बिवाई *bivāī* [*vipādikā-*], f. **1.** crack or chap on heel. **2.** chilblain. — ~ फटना, to suffer from cracked heels, &c. जिसकी फटी न ~, वह क्या जाने पीड़ पराई? fig. only he can understand another's predicament who has himself been in it.

बिस *bis* [*viṣa-*], m. poison (= विष). — ~ उगलना, to vomit poison: to speak venomously (of); to unburden oneself of disagreeable or spiteful thoughts; to take revenge. ~ की पुड़िया, f. poison-packet: fig. a viper, trouble-maker. ~ खाना, to take poison. ~ देना (को), to poison. ~ बोना, to sow discord (between, में). ~ मिलाना, to mingle poison or gall (with, में), to poison, to embitter; to spoil (pleasure). – बिस-खपरा, m. name of several plants; a species of lizard, *Lacerta iguana* (generally regarded as poisonous). बिस-खोपरा, m. id. बिसधर, adj. poison-holding: poisonous (a snake).

बिसन *bisan*, m. = व्यसन.

बिसनी *bisnī* [ad. *vyasanī-*], adj. & m. addicted to vice: **1.** adj. vicious, depraved. **2.** ostentatious in dress. **3.** m. a dissolute person, &c.

बिसबिसाना *bisbisānā*, v.i. reg. **1.** to ferment (= बजबजाना). **2.** to smart, to tingle.

बिसमना *bisamnā* [**viśamyate*], v.i. reg. to be broken (cf. बिसमाना).

बिसमाना *bismānā* [cf. H. *bisamnā*], v.t. reg. to smash (as a widow the ornaments worn during her husband's lifetime).

बिसर *bisar* [cf. H. *bisarnā*], m. reg. **1.** forgetfulness. **2.** oversight, omission.

बिसरना *bisarnā* [*vismarati*], v.t. & v.i. **1.** v.t. to forget. **2.** v.i. [cf. H. *bisārnā*] to be forgotten.

बिसरा *bisrā* [cf. H. *bisar*], adj. reg. forgetful; neglectful.

बिसराना *bisrānā* [cf. H. *bisarnā*], v.t. **1.** = बिसारना. **2.** to distract, to beguile. **3.** to mislead.

बिसराहट *bisrāhaṭ* [cf. H. *bisarnā*], f. **1.** forgetfulness. **2.** oversight.

बिसवाँसी *bisvāṁsī* [**viṁśamāṁśa-*], f. the twentieth part of a *bisvā*.

बिसहर *bishar* [*viṣadhara-*], m. reg. a snake.

बिसहरी *bisahrī* [*viṣadhara-*], f. **1.** a snake. **2.** a boil on the hand.

बिसहरू *bisahrū*, m. reg. buyer.

बिसहा *bishā* [cf. H. *bis*], adj. poisonous (a snake, &c).

बिसाँइधि *bisāṁidhi*, f. Av. = बिसायँध.

बिसा- *bisā-* [cf. H. *baisnā*], v.t. Brbh. to place (a burden).

बिसाइत *bisāit* [cf. H. *bisāt*], f. corr. reg. miscellaneous small goods.

बिसात *bisāt* [A. *bisāṯ*], f. sthg. spread out: **1.** cloth on which goods are displayed. **2.** carpet; bedding. **3.** chess-cloth, chess-board. ***4.** goods, wares. **5.** capital, substance. **6.** means, power; capacity, ability. **7.** importance, standing, worth. — उसकी क्या ~ कि ...? how can he have the means, &c. to...? – बिसात-ख़ाना, m. small shop or stall selling haberdashery, trinkets.

बिसाती *bisātī* [cf. H. *bisāt*], m. seller of miscellaneous goods (as haberdashery, trinkets); pedlar.

बिसाना *bisānā* [cf. H. *bis*], v.t. reg. to become poisoned (a wound).

बिसायँध *bisāyaṁdh* [*visragandha-*], f. & adj. **1.** f. smell (as of meat, fish). **2.** adj. foul-smelling.

बिसार *bisār*, m. reg. loan of seed, to be repaid with increase after the harvest.

बिसारत *bisārat*, f. corr. reg. = बिसात.

बिसारना *bisārnā* [*vismārayati*], v.t. to cause to be forgotten; to efface from memory, to forget.

बिसारौ *bisārau* [cf. **viṣāgāra-*], adj. Brbh. poisoned (of an arrow).

बिसासी *bisāsī*, adj. = विश्वासी.

बिसाह *bisāh* [cf. H. *bisāhnā*], f. purchasing.

[1]**बिसाहना** *bisāhnā* [**viṣādhayati*: Pk. *visāhia-*], v.t. **1.** to acquire; to purchase. **2.** to bring on oneself (trouble, ill-will).

[2]**बिसाहना** *bisāhnā* [cf. H. [1]*bisāhnā*], m. E.H. ? purchasing, a purchase.

बिसाहनी *bisāhnī* [cf. H. [1]*bisāhnā*], f. Brbh. Av. ? a purchase.

बिसुखना *bisukhnā* [cf. **viśuṣka-*: Pa. *visukkha-*], v.i. reg. milk to run dry (of a cow).

बिसुरना *bisurnā*, v.i. = बिसूरना.

बिसूरना *bisūrnā* [**viśūrate*: Pk. *visūraï*], v.i. to be distressed; to grieve openly.

बिसैला *bisailā* [cf. *viṣa-*], adj. & m. **1.** adj. poisonous; venomous; poisoned (as a well). **2.** m. a snake. **3.** a boil on the hand.

बिस्ठी *bisṭhī*, f. reg. (Bihar) a boy's loin-cloth.

बिस्तर *bistar* [P. *bistar*], m. bedding, bed-roll. — ~ बाँधना, to roll up (one's) bedding. ~ लगाना, or बिछाना, to spread bedding, to prepare a bed. अपना ~ गोल करना, to roll up one's bedding: to clear out, bag and baggage. – बिस्तर-बंद [P. *-band*], m. container for rolled bedding; hold-all.

बिस्तरा *bistrā* [cf. H. *bistar*], m. bed, bedding.

बिस्तार- *bistār-* [ad. *vistārayati*], v.t. to spread, to extend.

बिस्तुइया *bistuiyā*, f. house-lizard (= छिपकली).

बिस्मिल्ला *bismillā* [A. *bi'smi'llāh*], **1.** in the name of Allah (formula in use among Muslims at the beginning of any activity). **2.** celebration (among Muslims) of a child's first beginning to learn to read. **3.** interj. God be with you!: very well! all right! — ~ करना, to begin, to set to; to slaughter (an animal).

[1]**बिस्वा** *bisvā* [**viṁśama-*], m. twentieth part; a measure of land, a twentieth of a *bīghā*. — बीस ~, m. twenty twentieths: without fail, undoubtedly; entirely. - बिस्वादार [P. *-dār*], m. *hist.* the holder of a share or shares in a village tenure. °ई, f. tenure of shares, shared (sub-proprietary) tenure.

[2]**बिस्वा** *bisvā*, f. pronun. var. = बेस्वा.

बिहँसना *bihaṁsnā*, v.i. = बिहसना.

बिहना *bihnā* [**vihanaka-*], m. reg. cotton-carder (= धुनिया).

बिहपै *bihpai* [*br̥haspati-*], m. reg. Thursday.

[1]**बिहर-** *bihar-* [*viharati*], v.i. Brbh. Av. to wander; to find pleasure or delight.

[2]**बिहर-** *bihar-* [*vighaṭate*], v.i. Av. to be torn apart, rent (as the heart).

बिहरना *biharnā* [*viharati*], v.i. **1.** to wander. **2.** to feel or to take pleasure; to revel.

बिहसना *bihasnā* [ad. *vihasati*], v.i. to laugh; to smile; to be pleased.

बिहाँड़ *bihāṁr̥* [**vikhaṇḍa* : Pk. *vihaṇḍa-*], m. reg. (W.) land cut up by ravines.

[1]**बिहा-** *bihā-* [*vijahāti*], v.t. to leave behind; to give up, to abandon.

[2]**बिहा-** *bihā-*, v.i. E.H. to be spent (time).

बिहाई *bihāī* [*vidhātr̥-*], m. reg. (W.) a spirit which is supposed to whisper alternately sad and pleasant things in children's ears when they are asleep (and is responsible for their laughing and crying when awake).

बिहाग *bihāg*, m. *mus.* name of a *rāg* (assigned to the period after midnight).

बिहान *bihān* [**vibhāna-*, or Pa. *vibhāyaṇa-*], m. dawn; period just before dawn. बिहाने, adv. Brbh. at dawn; early the next day.

बिहार *bihār* [ad. *vihāra-*], m. 1. = विहार. **2.** the state of Bihar.

बिहार- *bihār-* [cf. *vihāra-*], v.i. Brbh. to disport oneself, to revel.

[1]**बिहारी** *bihārī* [ad. *vihārin-*], adj. & m. **1.** adj. sportive (as Kr̥ṣṇa with the herdgirls). **2.** m. a Bihari.

[2]**बिहारी** *bihārī* [cf. H. *bihār*], adj. & f. **1.** adj. of Bihar, Bihari. **2.** f. Bihari speech; a Bihar dialect.

बिहिश्त *bihiśt*, f. = बहिश्त.

बिहिश्ती *bihiśtī* [P. *bihiśtī*], adj. & m. **1.** adj. heavenly. **2.** m. inhabitant of paradise. **3.** euph. see भिश्ती.

बिही *bihī* [P. *bihī*], f. **1.** a quince. **2.** a guava.

बिहून *bihūn* [**vidhūna-*: Pk. *vihūṇa-*], adj. Brbh. = विहीन.

बिहूना *bihūnā* [cf. H. *bihūn*], adj. E.H. **1.** deprived (of), not having, without. **2.** *Pl.* ? foreign, strange.

बिहूनी *bihūnī* [cf. H. *bihūn*], adj. reg. abandoned, destitute.

बींड़ *bīṁṛ* [*vr̥nda-*], m. **1.** bundle (as of straw, rushes). **2.** reg. woven material (as rushes, &c. used to face the wall of a well). **3.** reg. (W.) = ईंडुरी. **4.** reg. the leading bullock of a group of three or five yoked together.

बींड़ा *bīṁṛā*, m. reg. = बींड़.

बींड़ी *bīṁṛī* [cf. H. *bīṁṛ*], f. *Pl.* the hair plaited behind.

बींध *bīṁdh* [cf. H. *bīṁdhnā*], m. ? f. **1.** piercing, boring. **2.** perforation, hole.

बींधना *bīṁdhnā* [**vindhati*: Pk. *viṁdhaï*], v.t. **1.** to pierce; to bore through or into. **2.** to string (pearls, beads). **3.** to wound (with sharp words).

[1]**बी** *bī*, f. = बीबी.

[2]**बी** *bī*, interj. f. = [1]बे.

[1]**बीअड़** *bīaṛ*, f. *Pl.* = बियाड़. ?

[2]**बीअड़** *bīaṛ* [conn. *vikāla-*], f. *Pl.* evening.

बीअर *bīar* [*vivara-*], m. reg. hole of a snake or rat.

बीआ *bīā* [*bījaka-*], m. reg. (E.) seed (= बीज).

बीका *bīkā* [**vr̥kṇa-*[2]: *vr̥kta-*], adj. disordered, awry. — बाल तक ~ न होना, not a hair of the head to be harmed.

बीघा *bīghā* [*vigraha-*], m. a measure of land (the official or *sarkārī bīghā* equals about five-eighths of an acre; a *kaccā bīghā* varies from a quarter to a third of an acre).

बीच *bīc* [**vīcya-*: Pk. *vicca-*], m. & ppn. **1.** m. middle. **2.** intervening space, or time; distinction, difference, separation. **3.** average, mean. **4.** mediation. **5.** ppn. w. के. between, among. **6.** during. — ~ करना, to intervene (in a dispute); to patch up (a quarrel, rift). ~ का, adj. middle, intervening, &c. ~ की रास (का), adj. mediocre; passable. ~ खेत, adv. openly, for all to see. ~ बाज़ार में, adv. in the open market. ~ मानना, to call to witness; to accept as arbitrator, negotiator. ~ में, adv. meanwhile; in between. ~ में आना, or पड़ना, to intervene, to interfere; to negotiate (an arrangement); to be surety (for). ~ में बोलना, to interrupt (a conversation, discussion). — बीच-बचाव, m. corr. = बीच-बिचाव. बीच-बराबर, adj. parallel. बीच-बिचाव, m. intervention (in a dispute); mediation, arbitration. बीच-बिचाव करना, to intervene, &c. बीचों-बीच, m. & adv. the very middle; in the very middle, or midst (of, के).

बीचड़ा *bīcṛā* [cf. H. *bīc*], m. **1.** *Pl.* bed in which growing plants are transplanted. **2.** reg. (W.) a seedling.

बीचि *bīci* [ad. *vīci-*], f. a wave.

बीछी *bīchī* [*vr̥ścika-*], f. Av. **1.** a scorpion (= बिच्छू). **2.** a toe-ring.

बीछू *bīchū*, m. Brbh. = बिच्छू.

बीज *bīj* [*bīja-*], m. **1.** seed; kernel; grain. **2.** roe. **3.** foetus, embryo. **4.** source, primary cause. **5.** kernel, central motif (of plot). **6.** symbol, sign, token; a cryptic allusion. — ~ जमना, seed to germinate, or to sprout. ~ बोना, or जमाना, or डालना, to sow seed; to sow the seed (of, का), to give rise (to). ~ नाश करना (का), to extirpate, to annihilate. – बीज-खाद, m. *hist.* advance of seed and food to cultivators. बीज-गणित, adj. algebra. बीज-मंत्र, m. incantation consecrated to a partic. deity; an unfailing means or recourse. बीजांक [°*a*+*a*°], a secret code, cypher. बीजांकुर [°*ja*+*a*°], m. shoot, sprout. बीजाणु [°*ja*+*a*°], m. spore. बीजारोपण [°*ja*+*ā*°], m. sowing seed; planting.

बीज- *bīj-* [cf. *vījyate*], v.t. Brbh. to fan.

बीजक *bījak* [S.], m. **1.** ticket, tag (on goods). **2.** invoice, inventory. **3.** collection of verses (esp. sectarian).

[1]**बीजना** *bījnā* [? ad. *vījana-* or cf. *vījyate*], m. a fan (hand-operated). — ~ डुलाना, to fan.

[2]**बीजना** *bījnā*, v.t. to sow.

बीजार *bījār*, adj. *Pl.* **1.** full of seed (a fruit). **2.** sown, or to be sown (soil).

[1]**बीजी** *bījī* [cf. H. *bīj*], adj. & f. **1.** adj. *Pl.* having seed; produced from seed. **2.** f. reg. a kernel.

[2]**बीजी** *bījī*, f. *Pl.* weasel; mongoose (cf. बिज्जू).

बीजीसर *bījīsar* [H. *bīj*+H. *īśvar*], m. the sāl tree, *Shorea robusta* (the seeds of which have served as a food in times of famine).

[1]**बीजू** *bījū* [cf. H. *bīj*], m. a seedling (plant).

[2]**बीजू** *bījū*, adj. *HŚS.* = [1]बीजी.

बीझना *bījhnā*, v.t. & v.i. **1.** v.t. [*vidhyati*] *Pl.* to tear up earth with the horns or hooves (a bull). **2.** v.i. [**vibadhyate*], Brbh. to be entangled, or smeared; to mingle (among). **3.** *Pl.* to be worm-eaten.

[1]**बीट** *bīṭ*, [*viṣṭhā-*], f. excrement (esp. of birds).

[2]**बीट** *bīṭ*, f. *Pl.* = बीत.

बीठ *bīṭh* [*viṣṭhā-*], f. = [1]बीट.

बीठा *bīṭhā*, m. reg. circle or coil of material placed on the head for carrying water-pots, &c. (= ईंडुरी).

बीड़ *bīṛ* [*vīṭaka-*], m. reg. (E.) sthg. rolled.

बीड़ा *bīṛā* [*vīṭaka-*], m. **1.** a betel leaf with areca nut, lime, spices, &c., folded to be eaten. **2.** an earnest of a pledge; a token thrown down in challenge: gauntlet. **3.** reg. tie, fastening; thong holding a sword in its scabbard. — ~ उठाना, to accept the challenge (of, का); to take up a challenging task. ~ डालना, to challenge any of a group to volunteer to perform a daunting task. ~ देना (को), to entrust a challenging task (to); to engage (musicians) to attend a future occasion. ~ लेना, = ~ उठाना.

बीड़ी *bīṛī* [*vīṭikā-*], f. a twist of tobacco rolled in a tobacco leaf, to be smoked.

बीत *bīt* [*vṛtti-*], f. reg. (W.) **1.** grazing fee charged by herdsmen. **2.** *Pl.* land cultivated by unpaid labour.

बीतना *bītnā* [cf. *vṛtta-*], v.i. **1.** to pass, to elapse (time). **2.** to come to pass, to happen. **3.** to be experienced (as events). — आप-बीती कहानी, f. a tale of one's own experiences.

बीती *bītī* [cf. H. *bītnā*], f. past events or experiences; the past.

बीदर *bīdar* [*vidar-*: MIA anal. *-dd-*], m. reg. (W.) an ox-drawn harrow used in young rice crops.

बीध *bīdh*, f. *Pl. hind.* a marriage ceremony in which turmeric, salt, &c. are ground on the seventh or the third day before the wedding.

बीन *bīn* [*vīṇā-*], f. 1. = वीणा. **2.** [× *veṇu-*] snake-charmer's flute (made from a gourd). — बीनकार, m. a vīṇā-player.

[1]**बीनना** *bīnnā* [*vicinoti*], v.t. **1.** to pick, to gather. **2.** to select.

[2]**बीनना** *bīnnā*, v.t. reg. = बुनना.

बीबी *bībī* [P. *bībī*], f. **1.** lady; wife; elder sister; sister-in-law. **2.** a term of endearment: lady, &c.

बीम *bīm* [P. *bīm*], m. U. **1.** fear. **2.** danger, risk.

बीमा *bīmā* [P. *bīma*], m. **1.** insurance; insurance premium, or rate. **2.** colloq. sthg. insured (parcel, letter). — ~ उठानेवाला, m. reg. an insurer. ~ करना, to effect insurance (on, का), to insure. ~ कराना, to take out insurance (on, का). – बीमा-कराई, f. insurance premium. बीमाकर्ता, m. inv. an insurer. °-कृत, adj. insured. बीमादार [P. *-dār*], m. an insurance underwriter; an insured person.

बीमार *bīmār* [P. *bīmār*], adj. ill, unwell. — बीमारदार [P. *-dār*], m., f. nurse, attendant. °ई, f. nursing.

बीमारी *bīmārī* [P. *bīmārī*], f. illness. — ~ से उठना, to recover from illness.

बीर *bīr* [*vīra-*], adj. & m. **1.** brave, heroic, &c. (= वीर). **2.** friend, brother (esp. as term of address). **3.** magician. **4.** reg. harmful spirits in a magicians's service. **5.** ? f. an ear ornament. **6.** Brbh. a ornament of the wrist or forearm. — बीर-बहूटी, f. see s.v.

बीरण *bīraṇ*, m. *Pl.* a kind of coarse, tough grass found covering uncultivated land. — बीरण-आखर, m. id.

बीर-बहूटी *bīr-bahūṭī* [*vīra-*, *vadhūṭī-*], f. the red-velvet insect (appears during the monsoon).

बीरा *bīrā* [*vīra-*], m. brother (= वीर, 2).

बीरौ *bīrau* [*vīrudha-*], m. Brbh. a small tree.

बील *bīl* [*bila-*[1]: w. *-ll-*, or ← B.], m. reg. waterlogged or swampy land.

बीवी *bīvī* [P. *bībī*], f. = बीबी.

बीस *bīs* [*viṁśati-*], adj. **1.** twenty. **2.** fig. superior (to, से). — ~ पड़ना, to be superior (to). ~ बिसवे, m. pl. & adv. twenty twentieths: the whole amount; surely, absolutely.

बीसर *bīsar*, reg. (W). gleanings.

बीसा *bīsā* [cf. H. *bīs*], m. **1.** a score (= बीसी). **2.** an animal having twenty nails (esp. a dog).

बीसी *bīsī* [cf. H. *bīs*], f. **1.** a score. **2.** *hist.* a measure of weight (often five seers); a measure of land area.

बीहड़ *bīhaṛ*, adj. & m. f. **1.** adj. uncultivated, waste (land). **2.** rough (of terrain). **3.** wild (jungle, scrub). **4.** m. f. rough terrain.

बीहन *bīhan* [**bījadhānya-*], m. reg. (E.) seed-corn.

बुँदकी *buṁdkī* [cf. **bundu-*]. **1.** a small drop. **2.** small mark, speck, dot. — ~ की छींट, f. spotted chintz. – बुँदकीदार [P. *-dār*], adj. spotted, &c.

बुंदा *bundā* [cf. **bundu-*], m. **1.** an ear-ring. 2. = टिकली.

बुँदिया *buṁdiyā* [cf. H. *būṁd(ī)*], f. a kind of sweet; drops.

बुंदेला *bundelā*, m. **1.** name of the Rājpūts of Bundelkhand. **2.** an inhabitant of Bundelkhand. **बुंदेली**, f. name of the dialect of Bundelkhand.

बुक *buk*, f. *Pl. HŚS.* **1.** muslin. **2.** tinsel.

बुक़चा *buqcā* [P. *buqca*], m. a small bundle (as of clothes); satchel, bag.

बुक़ची *buqcī* [cf. H. *buqcā*], f. = **बुक़चा**.

बुकटा *bukṭā* [cf. **bukka-*[3]: Pk. *bukkā-*], m. **1.** clawing. **2.** claw, handful. — **~ भर**, m. a handful. **~ भरना**, to scratch, to claw; to fill the hand (with).

[1]**बुकना** *buknā* [cf. *bukka-*[5]: Pk. *bukka-*], v.t. to grind to powder.

बुकनी *buknī* [cf. **bukka-*[5]: Pk. *bukka-*], f. **1.** a powder. **2.** reg. a small piece, shred. — **~ कर डालना (की)**, to grind to powder.

बुकवाना *bukvānā* [cf. H. *būknā*], v.t. to cause to be ground, or pounded (by, **से**)

बुकारा *bukārā* [? conn. H. *buknā*], m. reg. (W.) land flooded by a river and made useless by a deposit of sand.

बुक्कट *bukkaṭ*, m. = **बुकटा**.

[1]**बुक्का** *bukkā* [conn. H. [1]*būknā*], m. Brbh. powdered mica (an ingredient of *gulāl*). — **~ फाड़कर रोना**, to weep bitterly.

[2]**बुक्का** *bukkā* [conn. **bukka-*[3]; Pk. *bukkā-*], m. Brbh. Av. a handful.

बुक्की *bukkī* [cf. H. [2]*bukkā*], f. dimin. a handful.

बुख़ार *bukhār* [A. *bukhār*], m. **1.** fever. **2.** fig. feverish passion, agitation; anger; animosity; grief; terror. — **~ आना**, or **चढ़ना**, **(को)**, to have a fever; to become feverishly agitated, &c. **~ निकालना**, to vent (one's) ire or spleen (on, **पर**).

बुख़ारी *bukhārī* [P. *bukhārī*], f. hole or pit (in corner of a house) used for storing grain.

बुगमार *bugmār* [P. *bugmār*], m. obs. *Pl.* conqueror: a kind of blunderbuss.

बुग़्ज़ *bugz* [A. *bugz*], m. U. malice; rancour.

बुछियाना *buchiyānā*, v.t. *Pl.* to lay back (the ears: an animal).

बुज़दिल *buzdil* [P. *buzdil*], adj. goat-hearted: cowardly.

बुज़दिलापन *buzdilāpan* [cf. H. *buzdil*], m. cowardice.

बुज़दिली *buzdilī* [P. *buzdil*+H. *-ī*], f. goat's courage: timidity, cowardice.

बुज़ुर्ग *buzurg* [P. *buzurg*], adj. & m. **1.** adj. great, venerable; aged. **2.** m. old man, elder. **3.** forefather. — **बुज़ुर्गों का**, adj. ancestral, inherited, passed down. – **बुज़ुर्गवार** [P. *-vār*], adj. & m. = ~.

बुज़ुर्गाना *buzurgānā* [P. *buzurgāna*], adj. great, fine; lordly.

बुज़ुर्गी *buzurgī* [P. *buzurgī*], f. greatness; dignity, venerability; high rank or birth.

बुज़्ज़ा *buzzā* [conn. P. *buzak*], m. ? the white or the black ibis.

बुझना *bujhnā* [**vijjhāyati*: Pa. *vijjhāyati*, × **avajjhāyati*], v.i. **1.** to be extinguished (a fire, light, &c). **2.** to be cooled, slaked (hot iron, lime); to be tempered (steel). **3.** to be relieved (hunger, thirst). **4.** to be calmed (agitated feelings). **5.** to be dampened (as ardour, morale). **6.** to be subdued (as the emotions; or the voice). — **बुझी तबीयत**, f. depressed state.

[1]**बुझाई** *bujhāī* [cf. H. [1]*bujhānā*], f. **1.** explaining. **2.** persuading, convincing.

[2]**बुझाई** *bujhāī* [cf. H. [2]*bujhānā*], f. **1.** extinguishing. **2.** cooling, slaking. **3.** quenching (hunger, thirst).

[1]**बुझाना** *bujhānā* [Pa. *bujjhāpeti*], v.t. to cause to know: **1.** to explain. **2.** to persuade, to convince.

[2]**बुझाना** *bujhānā* [**vijjhāpayati*: Pa. *vijjhāpeti*, × **avajjhāyati*], v.t. **1.** to put out (a fire, light, &c). **2.** transf. to cool, to slake (hot iron, lime); to temper (steel); to disinfect (water, by plunging a hot piece of iron into it: **में**); to soak (indigo plants). **3.** fig. to relieve (hunger, thirst). **4.** to calm, to allay (agitated feelings). **5.** to dampen (as ardour, morale). **6.** to repress, to smother (anger, &c).

बुझारत *bujhārat*, f. *hist.* audit or adjustment of accounts.

बुझावा *bujhāvā* [cf. H. *bujhānā*], m. **1.** extinguishing. **2.** tempering.

बुझोंता *bujhoṁtā* [conn. H. [1]*bujhānā*], m. *hist.* annual account of a village cooperative showing the profit on each share.

बुझौवल *bujhauval* [cf. [1]*bujhānā*], m. **1.** guessing. **2.** a riddle; puzzle.

बुड़ *buṛ* [? **buḍa-*], f. vulva. — **बुड़चोद**, m. vulg. villain.

बुड़क *buṛak* [cf. H. *būṛnā*], f. **1.** sound of sthg. splashing or sinking down into water. — **बुड़क-बुड़क**, f. gurgling sound.

बुड़का *buṛkā* [cf. **bukka-*[3]: Pk. *bukkā-*], m. snap, bite. — **~ मारना**, to snap, &c.

बुड़की *burkī* [cf. H. *būṛnā*], f. dive, plunge. — ~ मारना, to dive, &c.

बुड़ना *buṛnā*, v.i. = बूड़ना.

बुड़बकपन *buṛbakpan*, m. reg. (E.) stupidity.

बुड़बुड़ा *buṛbuṛā*, m. reg. = बुलबुला.

बुड़बुड़ाना *buṛbuṛānā*, v.i. to mutter (cf. बड़बड़ाना).

बुड़ाना *buṛānā* [cf. H. *būṛnā*], v.t. reg. to cause to sink (= डुबोना).

बुड्ढा *buḍḍhā*, adj. = बूढ़ा.

बुड्ढापन *buḍḍhāpan*, m. = बुढ़ापा.

बुड्ढी *buḍḍhī*, adj. & f. = बुढ़िया.

बुढ़ऊ *buṛhaū* [cf. H. *būṛhā*], m. & f. **1.** m. old man, aged man. **2.** f. usu. pej. old woman, old creature.

बुढ़भल *buṛhbhal*, m. reg. = बुढ़भस.

बुढ़भस *buṛhbhas* [f. H. *būṛhā*+? *bhṛṣyati*], f. trying to act the young man while old; state of dotage.

बुढ़भसिया *buṛhbhasiyā* [cf. H. *buṛhbhas*], m. a dotard.

बुढ़ाई *buṛhāī* [cf. H. *būṛhā*], f. = बुढ़ापा.

बुढ़ापना *buṛhāpanā* [cf. H. *būṛhā*], m. = बूढ़ापन.

बुढ़ापा *buṛhāpā* [cf. H. *būṛhā*], m. old age.

बुढ़िया *buṛhiyā* [cf. H. *būṛhā*], adj. & f. **1.** adj. old (a woman). **2.** f. old woman.

बुढ़ौती *buṛhautī*, f. old age.

[1]**बुत** *but* [P. *but*], m. & adj. **1.** m. idol; image; statue. **2.** a beloved or idolised person. **3.** adj. fig. stock-still; dumb. **4.** stupefied; dead drunk. — बुत-ख़ाना, m. temple. बुत-तराश [P. *-tarāś*], m. carver of images, sculptor. °ई, f. sculpture. बुतपरस्त [P. *-parast*], m. idol-worshipper. °ई, f. idolatry. बुत-शिकन [P. *-śikan*], m. iconoclast. °ई, f. idol-breaking.

[2]**बुत** *but*, m. reg. gambling-board (for rolling dice).

बुतना *butnā* [cf. *vṛtta-*], v.i. to go out (a lamp, fire, &c).

बुतात *butāt* [cf. *vṛtti-*], m. reg. (E.) expenditure.

बुताना *butānā* [cf. *vṛtta-*], v.t. & v.i. **1.** v.t. to extinguish (a fire, light). **2.** v.i. reg. to be extinguished.

बुताम *butām* [Engl. *button*], m. button.

बुतारद *butārad*, m. *hist.* a name given to an extra tax upon a cultivator.

[1]**बुत्ता** *buttā* [*vṛtta-*; ? ← Panj.], m. reg. pretext, evasion; deceit.

[2]**बुत्ता** *buttā*, m. reg. a blow with the fist.

बुत्ती *buttī* [*vṛtti-*], f. *Pl.* means of subsistence; provision for a journey.

बुदबुद *budbud*, m. = बुलबुला.

बुदबुदा *budbudā*, m. = बुलबुला.

बुदबुदाना *budbudānā* [cf. **budabuda-*], v.i. **1.** to bubble (a liquid). **2.** to mutter; to speak unclearly.

बुद्ध *buddh* [S.], adj. & m. **1.** adj. awakened; enlightened; wise. **2.** m. the Buddha.

बुद्धि *buddhi* [S.], f. **1.** intelligence, understanding; mind; sense; wisdom. **2.** thought, reflection. – सामान्य ~, f. common sense. बुद्धिगम्य, adj. knowable. बुद्धिजीवी, adj. living by the intelligence: rational; intellectual; educated, professional. बुद्धितत्त्व, m. intellect. बुद्धिबल, m. mental power, intellect. बुद्धिभ्रंश, m. mental decline, incapacity. बुद्धिभ्रम, m. mental aberration. बुद्धिमत्ता, f. intelligent or rational nature, good sense. बुद्धिमान, adj. intelligent; wise. °ई, f. wisdom; a wise thought or act. बुद्धिवाद, m. belief in reason. बुद्धिवान, adj. = बुद्धिमान. बुद्धिसंगत, adj. rational. बुद्धिहीन, adj. senseless, foolish; ignorant. °ता, f.

बुद्धू *buddhū* [cf. H. *buddh*], m. iron. blessed fellow: stupid fellow. — ~ कहकर उकसाना, to egg (one) on by calling one names. ~ बनाना, to fool, to hoodwink.

बुध *budh* [S.], adj. & m. **1.** adj. wise, enlightened. **2.** m. the planet Mercury. ***3.** Wednesday. — बुधवार, m. = ~, 3.

बुनना *bunnā* [**vunāti*: Pk. *vuṇiya-*], v.t. **1.** to weave; to plait. **2.** to knit. **3.** to intertwine.

बुनवाई *bunvāī* [cf. H. *bunvānā*], f. cost of weaving, &c.; price paid for weaving, &c.

बुनवाना *bunvānā* [cf. H. *bunnā*], v.t. to cause to be woven, &c. (by, से).

बुनाई *bunāī* [cf. H. *bunnā*], f. **1.** weaving. **2.** knitting; knit (of sinews, &c). **3.** price paid for weaving, &c.

बुनाला *bunālā*, m. *Pl.* the woof of lace.

बुनावट *bunāvaṭ* [cf. H. *bunnā*], f. **1.** weaving. **2.** knitting. **3.** texture. **4.** interlacing, mesh (as of cords on a bedstead).

बुनियाद *buniyād* [P. *buniyād*], f. **1.** foundation. **2.** basis, base. **3.** groundwork; beginning; rudiments (of knowledge). — ~

डालना, or रखना, to lay the foundation, &c. (of or for, की); to found; to make a beginning.

बुनियादी *buniyādī* [P. *buniyād*+H. *-ī*], adj. **1.** basic. **2.** elementary (as education).

बुभुक्षा *bubhukṣā* [S.], f. desire for food, hunger.

बुभुक्षित *bubhukṣit* [S.], adj. desirous of food, hungry.

बुर *bur* [*buri-*], f. vulva. — बुर-जली, f. slut.

बुरकना *buraknā* [cf. **būra-*], v.t. to sprinkle.

बुरक़ा *burqā* [A. *burqaʿ*], m. a long veil reaching nearly to the feet, as worn by Muslim women. — बुरक़ापोश [P. *-poś*], adj. f. wearing a *burqā*. बुरक़ेवाली, adj. f. id.

बुरकाना *burkānā* [cf. H. *buraknā*], v.t. to cause to be sprinkled; to sprinkle.

बुरकी *burkī* [cf. H. *buraknā*], f. **1.** a pinch (of salt, &c). **2.** pinch of dust or ashes (used as a charm); a charm.

बुरबक *burbak* [? H. *burā* or *būṛhā*+H. *baknā*], adj. & m. **1.** adj. stupid. **2.** senile. **3.** m. a stupid, or senile person.

बुरबोला *burbolā* [H. *bur*+H. *bolnā*], adj. foul-mouthed, abusive.

बुरला *burlā* [? *varola-*], m. reg. a small kind of wasp.

बुरसी *bursī*, f. = बोरसी.

बुरा *burā* [**bura-*], adj. & m. **1.** adj. bad; wicked, evil; disaffected (the heart); depraved; base. **2.** hurtful, injurious; disagreeable. **3.** ugly. **4.** m. evil, wrong. **5.** an evil person. — ~ करना, to do wrong, or harm, &c. (to, का). ~ कहना (को), to speak ill (of), to abuse. ~ काम, m. wrongful or unlawful act; malpractice; vice. ~ बनाना, to cause to lose credit or standing. ~ मानना, to take amiss; to be angered (at). ~ लगना, to be displeasing, &c. (to, को). ~ स्वप्न, m. bad dream, nightmare. ~ हाल, m. a bad, or sad state. ~ हाल करना (का), to reduce to a sad state; to mistreat; to ruin. बुरी गत, or गति, f. id. बुरी घड़ी, f. = बुरे दिन. बुरी तरह, adv. badly, &c.; severely. बुरी नज़र से देखना, to look malevolently at. बुरे दिन, m. pl. hard times. हँसते-हँसते ~ हाल होना, to die laughing. – बुरा-भला, adj. & m. tolerable, passable; a bad or wicked person; bad and good (words): बुरा-भाला कहना, or सुनाना (को), to reproach bitterly, to scold severely.

बुराई *burāī* [cf. H. *burā*], f. **1.** evil, wickedness; vice. **2.** defect. **3.** harm, mischief. **4.** speaking ill, slander. — बुराई-भलाई, f. evil and good; damage, mishap; reproach, blame, detraction.

बुरादा *burādā* [P. *burāda*], m. **1.** sawdust. **2.** filings. **3.** powder.

[1]**बुर्ज** *burj* [A. *burj*], m. **1.** bastion, turret. **2.** tower. **3.** dome.

[2]**बुर्ज** *burj*, m. reg. a heavy rope, cable.

बुर्जी *burjī* [cf. H. *burj*], f. **1.** small turret, or tower. **2.** gun-turret. **3.** cut-water (of bridge pier).

बुर्रा *burrā*, m. *Pl.* **1.** a cavity; anything hollow. **2.** pimple on the skin.

बुर्राक़ *burrāq*, adj. = बर्राक़.

बुर्री *burrī*, f. reg. (W.) sowing seed in the furrow by hand.

बुलंद *buland* [P. *buland*], adj. **1.** high, lofty. **2.** loud. — ~ करना, to raise up; to proclaim on high (as a slogan). – बुलंदहिम्मत, adj. of high intentions, ambitions. बुलंदहौसला, adj. of high spirit: id.

बुलंदी *bulandī* [P. *bulandī*], f. **1.** height, loftiness. **2.** volume (of sound); height (of ardour).

बुलबुल *bulbul* [A. *bulbul*], f. **1.** the nightingale; a song-bird. **2.** the forked-tailed shrike.

बुलबुला *bulbulā* [cf. *buḍabuḍa-*], m. **1.** bubble. **2.** anything frail or short-lived.

बुलवाना *bulvānā* [cf. H. *bulānā*], v.t. **1.** to cause to be called, summoned, &c. (by, से). **2.** to cause to speak. — ख़ुदा झूठ न बुलवाए! fig. I swear to God I am not lying! पहाड़े ~, to ask (a child) his tables. — बुलवा भेजना, = बुला भेजना.

बुलाक़ *bulāq* [T.], m. f. **1.** septum of the nose. ***2.** pendant worn from the septum of the nose.

बुलाना *bulānā* [cf. **boll-*: Pk. *bollāv-*], v.t. **1.** to call; to summon; to send for. **2.** to invite. **3.** to call (a meeting). **4.** to cause to bubble (a hookah). — बुला भेजना, or लाना, to send for (a person).

बुलावन *bulāvan*, m. = बुलावा, बुलाहट.

बुलावा *bulāvā* [cf. H. *bulānā*], m. **1.** call, summons. **2.** invitation. **3.** challenge. — ~ भेजना, to send an invitation, &c. (to, को).

बुलाहट *bulāhaṭ* [cf. H. *bulānā*], f. call, calling, &c. (= बुलावा).

बुल्ला *bullā*, m. reg. bubble (= बुलबुला).

बुवाना *buvānā* [cf. H. *bonā*], v.t. **1.** to cause to be sown (by, से); to have sown (a field). **2.** reg. to have (a cow or buffalo) put to a bull.

बुसना *busnā* [H. *ubasnā*×H. [2]*basnā*], v.i. **1.** to smell (as food gone bad). **2.** to go bad (food). **3.** to become sticky.

बुहारन *buhāran* [cf. H. *buhārnā*], f. **1.** sweepings. **2.** a duster.

बुहारना *buhārnā* [cf. *bahukāra-*], v.t. **1.** to sweep; to dust. **2.** to sweep away, to get rid of.

बुहारनी *buhārnī* [cf. H. *buhārnā*], f. a broom.

बुहारा *buhārā* [cf. H. *buhārī*], m. a heavy broom.

बुहारी *buhārī* [*bahukāra-*], f. a broom. — ~ देना, to sweep.

बुहारू *buhārū* [cf. H. *buhārī*], m. reg. a sweeper.

बूँट *būṁṭ* [**būṭṭa-*], m. the chick-pea or gram plant with its green pods; green chick-pea pods. — बूँट-पुलाव, a dish of rice and gram.

बूँद *būṁd* [**bundu-*], f. & adj. **1.** f. drop; rain-drop; speck, iota. **2.** semen. **3.** a kind of spotted silk. **4.** adj. colloq. the best of, very fine (steel, or wine). — ~ की ~, adj. double-distilled, strong (alcohol). ~ चुराना, to conceive (a woman).

बूँदा *būṁdā* [**bundu-*], m. **1.** a large drop. **2.** a jewel worn as a nose or ear ornament. — ~-~, adv. drop by drop; to the last drop. – बूँदा-बाँदी [H. *būṁd*], f. sprinkling of rain; drizzle.

बूँदी *būṁdī* [cf. H. *būṁdā*], f. **1.** a small drop. **2.** a sweet, drops.

बू *bū* [P. *bū*], f. **1.** smell; scent. **2.** bad smell, odour. **3.** whiff, tinge; suspicion; inkling. — ~ आना, a smell to be perceived. ~ उड़ना, or फैलना, a suspicion or adverse rumour (of or about, की) to spread. ~ पाना, to perceive a smell (of, की). बूदार [P. *-dār*], adj. & m. scented; scented leather.

बूआ *būā*, f. paternal aunt.

बूक *būk* [**bukka-*[3]: Pk. *bukkā-*], m. Av. a handful.

[1]**बूकना** *būknā* [cf. *bukka-*[5]], v.t. to pound, to crush. — अँग्रेज़ी ~, colloq. to show off one's English.

[2]**बूकना** *būknā* [cf. H. [1]*būknā*], m. a powder.

[3]**बूकना** *būknā* [cf. **bukka-*[3]: Pk. *bukkā-*], v.t. reg. to take in, to enjoy (as food, fresh air).

बूकनी *būknī* [cf. H. [1]*būknā*], f. = बुकनी.

बूका *būkā*, m. **1.** Brbh. = [1]बुक्का. **2.** [cf. H. [1]*būknā*] alluvial soil.

बूचा *būcā* [**bucca-*[1]], adj. **1.** earless. **2.** incomplete, wanting; leafless; lopped, maimed; without bangles (a woman's wrist).

बूज़ा *būzā* [P. *būza*], m. reg. an alcoholic drink made from rice, or from barley or millet. — बूज़े-ख़ाना, liquor-stall.

बूझ *bujh* [cf. H. *būjhnā*], f. **1.** understanding, perceiving. **2.** perception. **3.** guessing, guess. — बूझ-बुझक्कड़, adj. vain of knowledge or intelligence. बूझ-बुझौवल, m. = बुझौवल.

बूझना *būjhnā* [*budhyate*], v.i. **1.** to understand, to perceive. **2.** to consider, to think. **3.** to ascertain; to enquire (of, से). — बूझकर, adv. knowingly, intentionally. – बूझा-बूझी, f. guessing; a children's guessing game.

बूटा *būṭā* [**būṭṭa-*], m. **1.** bush, shrub. **2.** flower, sprig (esp. as embroidered, or painted). — ~ काढ़ना, to work flowers (on, पर), to embroider. – बूटे का-सा क़द, m. small stature. बूटेदार [P. *-dār*], adj. flowered (cloth).

बूटी *būṭī* [cf. H. *būṭā*], f. 1. = बूटा, 1.; any medicinal plant. 2. = बूटा, 2. **3.** dot, spot, mark (as suit symbols in cards). **4.** a narcotic (= भाँग).

बूड़ना *būṛnā* [**budyati*: Pk. *buḍḍaï*], v.i. **1.** to be immersed, sunk. **2.** to dive. **3.** to sink; to be drowned. **4.** to be immersed or swamped (in or by, में: as by cares, work).

बूड़िया *būṛiyā* [cf. H. *būṛnā*], m. f. a diver.

बूढ़ा *būṛhā* [**buḍḍha-*[2]: Pa. *buḍḍha-*], adj. **1.** adj. & m. old; aged. **2.** m. an old man. — ~ चोचला, m. affectation of youthfulness in old age. ~ होना, to grow old. बड़ा ~, m. respectable, or respected, old man; patron.

बूढ़ापन *būṛhāpan* [cf. H. *būṛhā*], m. old age.

बूढ़ी *būṛhī* [cf. H. *būṛhā*], f. old woman.

बूत *būt*, ? f. Av. = बूता.

बूता *būtā* [*vṛtta-*], m. **1.** strength, power. **2.** ability, capacity. — बूते का काम, m. work within the power (of, के) to do. बूते बाहर, or के बाहर, adv. beyond (one's, के) power, or strength.

बूबक *būbak*, m. reg. a fool, old fool (cf. बुरबक).

बूबू *būbū*, f. reg. **1.** elder sister. **2.** (term of address.) lady.

बूम *būm* [A. *būm*], m. E.H. an owl.

[1]**बूर** *būr* [**būra-*], f. **1.** chaff, husk. **2.** sawdust; filings. **3.** rubbish. — ~ का लड्डू, m. a sweet: balls made with husk; a person, or a prospect, outwardly promising which proves a disappointment.

[2]**बूर** *būr*, m. a sweet-scented grass, used medicinally and (while tender) as fodder (= खैर).

[3]बूर *būr* [**bora-*[2]], m. nap, pile (on material).

[1]बूरा *būrā* [**būra-*], m. **1.** powder. **2.** sawdust; filings. **3.** coarse sugar.

[2]बूरा *būrā*, m. *hist.* a redeemable mortgage.

बृहत् *bṛhat* [S.], adj. **1.** great, large; mighty. **2.** extensive (as a study). — बृहत्तर, adj. greater (= ~, 2).

बृहद्- *bṛhad-* [S.], adj. = बृहत्.

बृहस्पति *bṛhaspati* [S.], m. **1.** *astron.* the regent of the planet Jupiter. **2.** the planet Jupiter. **3.** Thursday. — बृहस्पतिवार, m. Thursday.

बेंग *beṁg* [**viyaṅga-*[2]], m. Brbh. frog.

बेंगत *beṅgat*, m. reg. (E.) an advance of seed, grain or money to tenants.

बेंच- *beṁc-*, v.t. Brbh. = बेचना.

बेंट *beṁṭ*, m. reg. = बेंटा.

बेंड़ा *beṁṛā* [cf. *viyama-*], adj. & m. **1.** adj. crooked. **2.** awkward, unmanageable. **3.** uncouth. **4.** m. reg. a wooden door-bar.

बेंड़ी *beṁṛī*, f. reg. a small swing-basket on ropes (used in irrigation: = [2]बेड़ी).

बेंत *beṁt* [*vetra-*], m. f. **1.** cane. **2.** a cane; a stick. **3.** a blow with a cane. — ~ मारना, or लगाना (को), to beat with a cane.

बेंदा *beṁdā*, m. = बेंदा.

बेंधना *beṁdhnā* [*veṣṭayati* × *bandhati*], v.t. reg. to plait.

[1]बे *be*, interj. pej. m., (f.) you! you wretch! — बे-तबे कहना, *Pl.* to speak to rudely. बे-ते करना, id.

[2]बे- *be-* [P. *be*], pref. without; in-, un-, im-, dis-, -less, &c. — बेअक़्ल, adj. stupid; senseless. °ई, f. बेअदब, adj. uncouth; unmannerly; insolent. °ई, f. बेअसर, adj. ineffective. बेआबरू, adj. dishonoured, disgraced; dishonourable. °ई, f. बेइंतहा, adj. inv. = बेहद. बेइंसाफ़, adj. unjust. °ई, f. बेइख़्तियार, adj. & adv. involuntary; forced, compelled; in spite of oneself. बेइज़्ज़त, adj. dishonoured, disgraced. °ई, f. बेइत्तफ़ाक़ी, f. want of agreement or harmony. बेईमान, adj. dishonest; untrustworthy, unscrupulous. °ई, f. बेएतबार, adj. untrustworthy; unbelieving. °ई, f. बेऔलाद, adj. childless. बेक़द्र, adj. without importance, worth or significance. °ई, f. बेक़रार, adj. uneasy; unsettled, inconstant. °ई, f. बेकल, adj. = बेचैन. °ई, f. बेकस [P. *-kas* 'who?'], adj. friendless, forlorn; destitute. °ई, f. बेक़सूर, adj. = बेक़ुसूर. बेकाज, adj. = बेकाम. बेक़ानूनी, adj. illegal. बेक़ाबू, adj. powerless; beyond one's power, or control; headstrong. बेकाम, adj. useless, ineffective; worthless; without work. बेक़ायदा, adj. not in order; irregular; improper. बेकार, adj. & m. = बेकाम; without force, invalid; unoccupied (time); an unemployed person. बेकार करना, to render useless, &c.; to invalidate; to thwart, to frustrate (as a plan). बेकार जाना, to go for nothing, to prove ineffective or vain. °ई, f. idleness; unemployment. बेक़ीमत, adj. priceless, invaluable; gratis. बेक़ुसूर, adj. faultless, innocent. बेखटक, adj. free from anxiety or apprehension. °-खटका, adj. id. °-खटके, adv. बेख़बर, adj. unknowing, uninformed (of, से); ignorant; incautious, heedless. °ई, f. बेख़ुद, adj. beside oneself (with emotion). बेग़म, adj. without care(s). बेग़रज़, adj. disinterested. °ई, f. बेगार, f. & m. unpaid labour (esp. as performed compulsorily for a landowner); one doing unpaid labour. °ई, f. & m. = बेगार. बेगुनाह, adj. guiltless, innocent. °ई, f. बेग़ैरत, adj. shameless. बेघर, adj. homeless. बेचारा, adj. & m. without means or recourse, helpless; poor, wretched; a wretched person. बेचैन, adj. uneasy, restless. °ई, f. बेज़बान, adj. dumb; meek. °ई, f. बेज़मीन, adj. landless. बेजला, adj. unlit (a lamp, cigarette). बेजा, adj. inv. misplaced, inappropriate; unjustifiable; irrelevant; inaccurate, wrong. बेजान, adj. lifeless; inanimate; weak, faint. बेज़ार, adj. displeased (with, से): sick, tired (of); bored. °ई, f. बेजुर्म, adj. faultless, innocent. बेजून, adj. untimely. बेजोड़, adj. incomparable; without joins. बेजोत, adj. & m. uncultivated (land); land left uncultivated. बेटिकट, adj. ticketless (travel). बेठिकाना, adj. having no resting-place; homeless; not to be depended on, uncertain; pointless, vain. बेठिकाने, adv. unfounded, out of place, &c. बेठीक, adj. unsatisfactory; wrong. बेठौर, adj. out of place, improper; = बेठिकाना, 3., 4. बेडौल, adj. misshapen, ugly; awkward; uncouth. बेढंग, adj. uncouth. °आ, adj. id.; disordered, chaotic; wrong-headed (approach). °ई, f. uncouthness. बेढब, adj. = बेडौल; difficult, troublesome; uncontrollable, reckless; harsh, cruel; strange. बेतकल्लुफ़, adj. unceremonious, informal; frank. °ई, f. बेतरतीब, adj. unsystematic, unmethodical. °ई, f. बेतरह, adj. uncivil, uncouth; excessive, unconscionable. बेतहाशा [A.: P. *-taḥāśā*], adj. inv. without care or check; rash, reckless; headlong, swiftly. बेताज, adj. uncrowned. बेताज का, adj. id. बेतान, adj. out of tune. बेताब, adj. agitated, impatient; faint, weak. °ई, f. बेतार, adj. & m. without wires; a wireless, radio. बेताल, adj. out of time (in music); out of time, rhythm. °आ, adj. id. बेतुका, adj. unrhyming, not assonating; without rhyme or reason, pointless; uncouth. °-तुकी, f. a senseless remark. बेतुकी उड़ाना, or हाँकना, to talk nonsense. °पन, m. बेतौर, adj. = बेतरह, 1. बेदख़ल, adj. dispossessed, evicted; expropriated (land). बेदख़ल करना, to evict, &c. °ई, f. बेदम, adj. breathless; lifeless. °ई, f. बेदर्द, adj. unfeeling, without pity. °ई, f. बेदाग़, adj. spotless; without fault, or reproach. बेदाढ़ी, adj. beardless. बेदाना, adj. inv. & m. seedless;

pomegranate. बेदाम, adj. free of charge. बेदिल, adj. dejected; discontented. °ई, f. बेधड़क, adj. fearless; unhesitant, confident; bold. बेनज़ीर, adj. U. incomparable, without parallel. बेनथा [cf. H. [2]*nathnā*], m. an ownerless bull or bullock. बेनसीब [*naṣīb*], adj. unfortunate, ill-fated. बेनाप, adj. unmeasured, unsurveyed. बेनाम, adj. nameless, anonymous; without fame or reputation. बेनियाज़, adj. not in want or need, independent (of, से). °ई, f. बेपढ़ा-लिखा, adj. illiterate. बेपता, adj. inv. = लापता; undeliverable (a letter). बेपर, adj. wingless. बेपर की उड़ाना, fig. to say impossible things, to talk nonsense. बेपर की बात, f. sthg. impossible, or absurd. बेपरदा, adj. unveiled, uncovered; immodest; open, unconcealed. बेपरवा, adj. = next. बेपरवाह, adj. heedless, thoughtless; indifferent; uninhibited, impulsive. °ई, f. बेपरहेज़, adj. incontinent. [1]बेपीर, adj. U. without a spiritual mentor. [2]बेपीर, [cf. H. *pīṛā*], adj. unfeeling, merciless. बेपेंदी, adj. without a base: wavering (in attitudes, opinions). बेपेंदी का लोटा, m. a round-bottomed vessel: a waverer. बेफ़ायदा, adj. useless; pointless. बेफ़िकर, adj. free from care(s); thoughtless, inconsiderate. °आ, m. a thoughtless person. °ई, thoughtlessness, &c. बेबस, adj. without power or authority; helpless, weak; subject. °ई, f. बेबाक, adj. fearless, bold; forthright. °ई, f. बेबाक़, adj. without remainder: paid in full (as a debt). °ई, f. बेबात, f. sthg. trivial, or nonsensical (a remark, pretext): बेबात की बात, f. id. बेबुनियाद, adj. groundless, unfounded. °ई, f. बेमज़ा, adj. insipid, tasteless; dull. बेमतलब, adj. senseless; pointless. बेमन, adj. & m. listless, apathetic; listlessness, &c. बेमाने [H. [4]*mānī*], adj. meaningless; senseless, absurd. बेमिसाल, adj. unexampled, incomparable. बेमुरौवत, adj. unkind, inconsiderate; uncivil. °ई, f. बेमेल, adj. inharmonious, incompatible, incongruous. बेमौक़ा, adj. untimely, inopportune. बेमौसम, adj. unseasonable. बेरंग, adj. colourless, dull. बेरहम, adj. merciless, cruel. °ई, f. बेरुख़ी, f. disfavour; displeasure. बेरोक, adj. unhindered, unrestrained. बे-रोकटोक, adj. id. बेरोज़गार, adj. & m. unemployed; an unemployed person. °ई, f. बेरौनक़, adj. dull; lacklustre. बेलगाम, adj. unbridled; unrestrained; licentious. बेलगाव, adj. unconnected, independent; inaccessible; candid; categorical (as an assurance). बेलाग, adj. unconnected: uninvolved, impartial; candid, frank (speech); without rancour. बेलिहाज़, adj. unmindful, indiscreet; unmannerly. बेवक़ूफ़ [*vuqūf*], adj. foolish; ignorant. °ई, f. बेवक़्त, adj. untimely. बेवजह, adj. without cause or reason. बेवफ़ा, adj. faithless; ungrateful; treacherous. °ई, f. बेशऊर, adj. ignorant, uninformed; uncouth. °ई, f. बेशक, adv. undoubtedly, certainly. बेशरम, adj. shameless, brazen. °ई, f. बेशुमार, adj. countless, innumerable. बेसबब, adj. causeless. बेसब्र, adj. impatient. °ई, f. बेसमझ, adj. unintelligent, stupid. °ई, f. बेसरा [H. *sarāy*] adj. inv. Brbh. having no place of rest or shelter. बेसाख़्ता [P. -*sāḵhta*], adv. unaffectedly; spontaneously. बेसिर-पैर, headless and footless: बेसिर-पैर का, adj. baseless, nonsensical (as remarks). बेसिलसिले, adv. disconnectedly. बेसुध, adj. unconscious; beside oneself (with joy or grief). °ई, f. बेसुर, adj. = next. बेसुरा, adj. out of tune; discordant. बेसोच, adj. thoughtlessness; heedlessness. बेसोचे [H. *socnā*], adv. बेहथ्यार, adj. disarmed. बेहद, adj. unbounded, limitless. बेहया, adj. inv. shameless, brazen. °ई, f. बेहाथ, adj. handless, armless; idle; helpless; beyond control. बेहाल, adj. in a bad state or plight, or wretched (a person); damaged, useless (a thing). °ई, f. बेहिकमत, adj. unskilful. बेहिम्मत, adj. without spirit or vigour. बेहिसाब, adj. countless, incalculable; excessive. बेहुनर, adj. unskilled; inadept. °ई, f. बेहूदा adj. see s.v. बेहोश, adj. unconscious. °ई, f.

[2]**बेकस** *bekas*, m. (?) *Pl.* a kind of grass that grows on low ground (used for fodder).

बेग *beg* [T. *beg*], m. lord, master (Mughal title).

बेगड़ *begaṛ*, m. **1.** *Pl.* gold tinsel. **2.** reg. (W.) tin-foil.

बेगड़ी *begṛī* [cf. H. *begaṛ*], f. reg. (W.) one who cuts and sets precious stones, a jeweller.

बेगम *begam* [T. *begam*], f. **1.** lady of rank. **2.** queen. **3.** (in cards, and chess) the queen.

बेगमा *begămā* [H. *begam*+A. -*a*], f. a young woman of rank.

बेगमी *begămī* [cf. H. *begam*], adj. having to do with a queen; queen's.

बेगानगी *begānăgī* [P. *begānagī*], f. strangeness, foreignness.

बेगाना *begānā* [P. *begāna*], adj. & m. **1.** adj. strange, foreign, alien. **2.** m. a stranger, foreigner; outsider.

बेगार *begār*, m. see s.v. [2]बे-.

बेचना *becnā* [**vetyayati*: Pk. *veccaï*], v.t. to sell (to, को, के हाथ; at a price, पर). — बेचा-बाची, f. buying and selling, trade.

बेचवाल *becvāl* [cf. H. *becnā*], m. a seller, trader.

बेजी *bejī*, f. *Pl.* = [2]बीजी.

बेझड़ *bejhaṛ*, m. a mixed crop (as wheat and barley, chick-pea and barley).

बेझरा *bejhrā*, m. reg. (Bihar) = बेझड़.

बेझा *bejhā* [*vedhya-*], m. mark (to shoot at).

बेटा *beṭā* [**beṭṭa-*: Pk. *biṭṭa-*], m. son. — ~ **कर लेना**, or **बनाना** (**को**), to adopt as a son. – **बेटेवाला**, m. father of the bridegroom.

बेटी *beṭī* [**beṭṭa-*: Pk. *biṭṭa-*], f. daughter. — ~ **देना**, to give one's daughter in marriage. – **बेटीवाला**, m. father of the bride.

बेठन *beṭhan* [*veṣṭana-*], m. wrapper (for a packet, parcel).

बेड़ *beṛ* [*veṣṭa-*], m. enclosure, fence (= **बेड़ा**). — **बेड़बंदी** [P. *-bandī*], f. fencing in, enclosing.

बेड़मीं *beṛmīṁ*, f. = **बेड़वीं**.

बेड़वीं *beṛvīṁ* [conn. *veḍhamikā-*], f. a bread-cake (*roṭī*) filled with pulse.

[1]**बेड़ा** *beṛā* [*veṣṭa-*], m. **1.** enclosure; yard; court. **2.** fence, hedge. **3.** siege. **4.** body of soldiers; party, band. — ~ **बाँधना**, to assemble an army, or a body, crowd, &c.

[2]**बेड़ा** *beṛā* [*beḍā-*, Pk. *beḍaya-*, m. **1.** a raft. **2.** a boat. **3.** a naval unit; fleet. **4.** a raft of timber (to be brought down a river). — ~ **डूबना**, the raft to sink: an enterprise to fail. ~ **पार करना**, or **लगाना** (**का**), to get a raft, &c., to the far bank: to see (one) through a difficulty.

[1]**बेड़ी** *beṛī* [*veṣṭa-*], f. **1.** fetter, fetters; bonds. **2.** ankle-ring. **3.** thread tied round children's ankles (as a charm). — ~, or **बेड़ियाँ**, **कटना** (**की**), fetters to be taken off, to be freed. ~, **बेड़ियाँ**, **डालना**, or **पहनाना**, to put fetters (on, **में**). ~, or **बेड़ियाँ**, **पड़ना** (**के पाँव में**), to be fettered, in irons.

[2]**बेड़ी** *beṛī* [H. [2]*beṛā*], f. **1.** a small boat. **2.** bamboo basket used to scoop water for irrigation.

बेढ़ *beṛh* [*veṣṭa-*], m. reg. **1.** enclosing, surrounding. **2.** the surrounding and driving off of cattle.

बेढ़ईं *beṛhaīṁ* [conn. *veḍhamikā-*], f. reg. = **बेड़वीं**.

बेढ़ना *beṛhnā* [*veṣṭayati-*], v.t. reg. to enclose, to surround.

[1]**बेढ़ा** *beṛhā* [*veṣṭa-*], m. = [1]**बेड़ा**.

[2]**बेढ़ा** *beṛhā* [H. *beṁṛā* × H. *ṭeṛhā*], adj. crooked, slanting; zigzag.

बेणी *beṇī* [*veṇi-*], f. **1.** braided hair. **2.** fig. streams meeting at a confluence (cf. **त्रिवेणी**).

बेत *bet*, m. f. = **बेंत**.

बेताल *betāl*, m. = **बैताल**.

बेद *bed* [P. *bed*], m. f. **1.** a willow tree. **2.** cane.

बेदी *bedī* [ad. *vedin-*], m. a learned brāhmaṇ; scholar, teacher.

बेध *bedh* [ad. *vedha-*], m. **1.** piercing, penetrating; breaking through. **2.** a hole (through or into sthg.); crack. — ~ **करना**, to pierce, &c.; to observe (the stars).

बेधक *bedhak* [ad. *vedhak*], adj. & m. **1.** adj. piercing; sharp. **2.** m. borer. **3.** stabber.

बेधना *bedhnā* [**vindhati*: Pk. *viṁdhaï*; cf. H. *biṁdhnā*, v.i.], v.t. **1.** to pierce, to penetrate; to bore through (= **बींधना**). **2.** to wound, to stab.

बेधी *bedhī* [ad. *vedhin-*], m. & adj. **1.** m. piercer, borer. **2.** adj. **-बेधी**. piercing.

बेन *ben* [*veṇu-*], f. **1.** pipe, flute. **2.** bamboo.

[1]**बेना** *benā* [*vyajana-*], m. E.H. a fan.

[2]**बेना** *benā* [*vīraṇa-*], m. reg. the grass *Andropogon muraticus* (= **ख़स**).

[3]**बेना** *benā*, m. an ornament worn on the forehead.

बेपार *bepār* [ad. *vyāpāra-*], m. **1.** trade. **2.** business. — ~ **करना**, to trade.

बेपारी *bepārī* [cf. H. *bepār*], m. trader, merchant.

बेब *beb*, m. *Pl.* name of a grass (used to make twine, and in thatching).

[1]**बेर** *ber* [*badara-*], m. the jujube tree, and its small plum-like fruit. **बेर-गुठली**, f. reg. colloq. plum and stone: the good and the bad together, hodge-podge. **बेर-जरी**, f. Brbh. = ~ (cf. H. **जड़ी**).

[2]**बेर** *ber* [*velā-*: ? ← Drav.], f. **1.** time, occasion. **2.** lapse of time; delay. — ~ ~, adv. repeatedly, often.

बेरा *berā*, m. = **बैरा**.

बेराना *berānā*, adj. reg. var. /birana/. another's, others' (= [1]**बिराना**).

[1]**बेरी** *berī* [*badarikā-*], f. = [1]**बेर**.

[2]**बेरी** *berī* [cf. H. *velā*], f. = [2]**बेर**, 1.

बेरीज़ *berīz*, m. *hist.* the account, or total amount, of a revenue settlement (= **जमा**).

[1]**बेल** *bel* [*bailva-*], m. the wood-apple tree and its fruit (= **श्रीफल**). — **बेल-गिरी** (**-गरी**) f. sun-dried slices, or pulp, of wood-apple (used in treating diarrhoea and dysentery). **बेल-पत्र**, m. = next. **बेल-पात**, m. leaf of the wood-apple tree (as offered to Śiva).

[2]**बेल** *bel* [*velli-*, Pk. *vellī-*], f. **1.** any climbing or creeping plant; a vine. **2.** festoons of leaves, flowers. **3.** embroidery; strips of decorative material. **4.** offspring; descendants. **5.** a small reward of money (as given to barbers, &c. at the time of a wedding). — ~ **फलना**, to have

offspring. ~ मँढ़े (मढ़े) चढ़ना, a creeper to reach the top (of); to reach completion (as a large task); to flourish. – बेलदार [P. *-dār*], adj. embroidered, flowered. बेल-बूटा, m. creepers and shrubs; embroidery; a flowered border. °-बूटेदार, adj. = बेलदार.

³बेल *bel*, m. a type of jasmine (= ¹बेला).

⁴बेल *bel* [P. *bel*], m. **1.** spade. **2.** mattock; hoe. **3.** reg. an oar, or punt-pole. **4.** line (as of a road) marked out with a spade. बेलदार [P. *-dār*], m. digger, labourer.

बेलकी *belkī* [cf. H. *bail*], m. reg. cattleman: **1.** cowherd. **2.** cattle-breeder.

बेलचा *belcā* [P. *belca*], m. **1.** small spade. **2.** hoe.

बेलन *belan* [*vellana-*], m. **1.** a roller. **2.** a rolling-pin.

¹बेलना *belnā*, m. = बेलन, 2.

²बेलना *belnā* [*vellayati*], v.t. **1.** to roll out, to roll flat. **2.** colloq. to flatten, to destroy.

बेलनी *belnī* [cf. H. *belnā*], f. **1.** a small rolling-pin. **2.** reg. (W.) spindle, shaft; treadle (of loom).

¹बेला *belā*, m. the jasmine, *Jasminum zambac.*

²बेला *belā*, m. *mus.* a stringed instrument.

³बेला *belā* [ad. *velā-*], f. limit, boundary: **1.** time, period; moment. **2.** occasion. **3.** Brbh. edge, shore. **4.** Brbh. wave. — साँझ की ~, f. evening.

¹बेली *belī* [*velli-*, Pk. *vellī-*], f. a creeper (= ²बेल, 1).

²बेली *belī*, m. Av. companion, supporter; preserver, protector.

बेलू *belū*, f. 1. = बेलन. 2. = ²बेल, 1.

बेवा *bevā* [P. *beva*], f. a widow.

बेवाई *bevāī*, f. reg. = बिवाई.

बेवान *bevān*, m. = विमान, 1.

बेवापन *bevāpan* [cf. H. *bevā*], m. widowhood.

बेवापा *bevāpā* [cf. H. *bevā*], m. widowhood.

बेश *beś* [P. *beś*], adj. **1.** more; greater. **2.** good, excellent.

बेशी *beśī* [P. *beśī*], f. **1.** excess, surplus. **2.** increase (as of rent assessment).

बेसन *besan* [*vesana-*], m. gram flour.

बेसनी *besnī* [cf. H. *besan*], adj. made of, or with, *besan* flour.

बेसनौटी *besnauṭī* [cf. **vesanăpūpa-*], f. reg. a cake of gram-flour or pulse flour.

¹बेसर *besar* [*vesara-*], m. a mule.

²बेसर *besar*, m. a small heavy nose-ring (ornament).

बेसरा *besrā*, m. a small falcon.

बेसा *besā* [ad. *veśyā-*], f. Av. a prostitute.

बेसवा *besvā*, f. reg. prostitute (= वेश्या).

बेह *beh* [*vedha-*], m. Brbh. Av. a hole.

बेहड़ *behaṛ*, adj. = बीहड़.

बेहतर *behtar* [P. *bĕhtar*], adj. **1.** better. **2.** good, very good. **3.** preferable; advisable. — ~ जानना, to consider better; to prefer.

बेहतरी *behtarī* [P. *bĕhtarī*], f. **1.** welfare. **2.** benefit, advantage.

बेहतरीन *behtarīn* [P. *bĕhtarīn*], adj. best, choice.

बेहना *behnā*, m. reg. (W.) a cotton-cleaner (= धुनिया).

बेहनौर *behnaur* [**bījadhānyavāṭa-*], m. reg. (E.) a nursery for rice plants.

बेहरा *behrā*, m. reg. (W.) grass kept for pasturage.

बेहरी *behrī*, f. reg. **1.** a contribution (as for expenses of village worship). **2.** *hist.* assessment on a share (of revenue). **3.** distribution, or collection, of a sum of money between, or from, individuals.

बेही *behī* [**vivāhikā-*], f. *Pl.* an earthen vessel presented to a newly married couple by the potters of a village.

बेहूदगी *behūdăgī* [P. *behūdagī*], f. **1.** uncouthness. **2.** coarseness, indecency. **3.** foolishness, crassness.

बेहूदा *behūdā* [P. *behūda*], adj. inv. **1.** uncouth. **2.** coarse; indecent. **3.** foolish, crass.

बैंगन *baiṁgan* [*vātiṅgaṇa-* (← Drav.), Pa. *vātiṅgaṇa-*], m. egg-plant, aubergine.

बैंगनी *baiṁgnī* [cf. H. *baiṁgan*], adj. & f. **1.** adj. purple. **2.** f. reg. pieces of egg-plant fried in *besan* flour.

बैंजनी *baiṁjnī* [**vātiñjana-*], adj. = बैंगनी.

बैंटा *baiṁṭā*, m. reg. handle (of a tool).

बैंदा *baiṁdā* [conn. *bindu-*], m. **1.** mark made on the forehead. 2. = टिकली.

बैंदी *baiṁdī*, f. 1. = टिकली. **2.** circular decorative mark made on the forehead. **3.** an ornament worn on the forehead by women.

बैंहत्था *baiṁ-hatthā* m. = बैन-हत्था.

बैगन *baigan*, m. pronun. var. = बैंगन.

बैगनी *baignī*, adj. pronun. var. = बैंगनी.

बैजंती *baijantī* [ad.*vaijayantī*-], f. **1.** banner; the standard of Viṣṇu. 2. = ~ माला. — ~ माला, f. a garland or necklace worn by Viṣṇu or Kṛṣṇa (see वैजयंती).

बैजीला *baijīlā*, m. reg. (W.) a species of black pulse.

बैठक *baiṭhak* [cf. H. *baiṭhnā*], f. **1.** a sitting-room. **2.** assembly-room. **3.** meeting; session. **4.** sitting-place, seat. **5.** bottom, base (= पेंदा). **6.** the act of sitting: a physical exercise involving the action of sitting or squatting. — ~ बुलाना, to call a meeting. – बैठक-ख़ाना, m. = ~, 1., 2. बैठकबाज़ [P. *-bāz*], a gossiper; intriguer. °ई, f.

बैठका *baiṭhkā* [cf. H. *baiṭhak*], m. = बैठक, 1., 2., 4.

बैठकी *baiṭhkī* [cf. H. *baiṭhak*], f. = बैठक, 4.-6.

बैठना *baiṭhnā* [*upaviśati*], v.i. **1.** to sit, to sit down. **2.** to board, to mount (on or in, पर or में: any conveyance); to mount (a horse). **3.** to brood (a hen). **4.** to sink; to decline, to be impaired; to grow hoarse (the voice); to founder (as a business). **5.** to subside (as a swelling); to settle (a precipitate). **6.** to collapse (a building). **7.** to grow lukewarm (in support). **8.** to take up, to assume occupancy. गद्दी पर ~, to mount a throne; to be seated (a shopkeeper, to receive custom); to assume leadership of a sect. **9.** to be expended (on, पर: money). **10.** to take part (in, में: a class); to sit (an examination). **11.** to take root, to grow (a crop). **12.** to alight, to settle; to take (as a graft); to take up residence. **13.** to sit idle, unemployed. **14.** to set (as the sun). **15.** to pair, to couple (with, के साथ: animals, birds). **16.** to lose quality, taste, flavour, &c. **17.** to weigh (on a scales, &c.); to amount to (in weight, value). **18.** to strike home, or true (a blow, a shot). **19.** to be placed, to sit (on, पर: as a hat). **20.** to have force. ठीक ~, to carry conviction (words, &c). **21.** to become practised (as the hand, in a skill). — बैठे-ठाले, adv. (while) sitting doing nothing.

बैठलाना *baiṭhlānā*, v.t. = बिठलाना.

बैठवाँ *baiṭhvāṁ* [cf. H. *baiṭhnā*], adj. flat; flat-soled; flat-bottomed.

बैठाई *baiṭhāī* [cf. H. *baiṭhānā*], f. reg. **1.** settling; allaying. **2.** seating, accommodating.

बैठाना *baiṭhānā* [cf. H. *baiṭhnā*], v.t. **1.** to cause to sit, to give a seat (to, को). **2.** to install (in a position); to place (in a school: a child); to keep (in a house: a concubine). **3.** to set (a guard, &c.: over, पर). **4.** to set up (as a monument). **5.** to set in place; to set (a stone); to set (a bone or joint); to plant (a tree); to sow (seed). **6.** to place (for the moment); to put in a cooking vessel (ingredients). **7.** to cause to coagulate (as rice in cooking); to cause to solidify. **8.** to cause to be convened (a session, &c). **9.** to cause to settle (a community, in an area). **10.** to establish (a fair rent, &c). **11.** to impose (a tax). **12.** to cause to settle (a precipitate; or dust). **13.** to cause to subside (as a swelling). **14.** to allay (feelings). **15.** to impress (an idea or feeling on the mind: में or पर); to win acceptance for a (view). **16.** to depress (the feelings). मन, or दिल ~, to cause the heart to sink. **17.** to expound (as the sense of an obscure verse). **18.** to perform (a calculation); to calculate (a sum). जोड़ ~, to add. **19.** to assign, to risk (money or a stake: on, में or पर). **20.** (esp. w. देना) to cause to subside (a building); to depress (a market). **21.** to demolish, to raze. **22.** to knock down (with a blow, में). **23.** (w. रखना) to keep seated; to detain; to keep (a marriageable daughter) at home.

बैठार- *baiṭhār-*, v.t. Brbh. Av. = बिठाना.

बैठालना *baiṭhālnā*, v.t. reg. = बिठाना.

बैत *bait* [A. *bait*], f. E.H. a verse couplet.

बैतरा *baitrā*, f. a kind of dry ginger.

बैताल *baitāl* [ad. *vaitāla-*, *vetāla-*], m. **1.** evil spirit, demon (esp. as said to haunt cemeteries and to animate corpses). **2.** a dead body animated by a demon.

बैतालिक *baitālik* [ad. *vaitālika-*], m. court bard, panegyrist.

बैद *baid* [ad. *vaidya-*], m. Brbh. Av. = वैद्य.

बैदई *baidaī* [cf. H. *baid*], f. Brbh. a doctor's work, or skill; treatment.

बैन *bain* [*vacana-*], m. word, speech.

बैनहत्था *bain-hatthā* [H. *bayāṁ*+H. *hāth*], m. f. a left-handed person.

बैना *bainā* [*upāyana-*, and *vāyana-*], m. **1.** a present of sweets (made at weddings and other festivals). **2.** offering of sweets to a god.

बैपार *baipār*, m. = बेपार.

बैपारी *baipārī*, m. = बेपारी.

बैयर *baiyar*, f. Brbh. a woman.

बैर *bair* [*vaira-*: and ad.], m. enmity; hostility, ill-will.

बैरंग *bairaṅg* [Engl. *bearing*], adj. bearing (postage due), unpaid (a letter or consignment). — ~ लौटाना, to reject or to return; to send back unwanted.

बैरा *bairā* [Engl. *bearer*], m. porter; room-servant; waiter.

बैराग *bairāg*, m. = वैराग्य.

बैरागन *bairāgan* [cf. H. *bairāgī*], f. **1.** wife of a वैरागी. **2.** a female ascetic.

बैरागा *bairāgā* [cf. H. *vairāgī*], m. *Pl.* a cross-shaped stick or prop used by an ascetic to lean on as he sits.

बैरागी *bairāgī*, adj. & m. an ascetic (= वैरागी).

बैरी *bairī* [*vairin-*: and ad.], m. an enemy.

बैल *bail* [**balilla-*: Pk. *baïlla-*], m. **1.** bullock, ox. **2.** the sign Taurus (of the zodiac). **3.** fool, dolt. — बैल-गाड़ी, f. an ox-cart.

बैला *bailā*, adj. reg. barren (a cow: = बहला).

[1]**बैस** *bais* [ad. *vayas-*], f. Brbh. **1.** age, time of life. **2.** young adulthood.

[2]**बैस** *bais* [ad. *vaiśya-*], m. 1. = वैश्य. **2.** name of a Rājpūt community. — बैसवाड़ा, m. a name for the western part of Avadh. बैसवाड़ी, f. western Avadhī speech.

बैसंदर *baisandar* [f. *vaiśvānara-*: ? × *purandara-*], m. E.H. *mythol.* a title of Agni; fire.

बैसना *baisnā* [*upaviśati*], v.i. reg. to sit (= बैठना).

बैसनी *baisnī* [cf. H. *bais*], f. a vaiśya woman.

बैसाख *baisākh* [ad. *vaiśākha-*], m. the second of the twelve lunar months of the Hindu calendar (April-May).

बैसाखी *baisākhī* [cf. H. *baisākh*], adj. & f. **1.** adj. having to do with the month Baisākh. **2.** f. the day of full moon in Baisākh. **3.** reg. a crutch (= बैरागा). — ~ नंदन, m. fig. a fool.

बो *bo* [cf. H. *bonā*], f. sowing. — बो-जोत, f. sowing and ploughing.

बोआई *boāī* [cf. H. *boānā*], f. **1.** sowing, seed-time. **2.** wages for sowing.

बोआना *boānā*, v.t. = बुवाना.

बोआरा *boārā*, m. reg. sowing; the sowing season.

बोई *boī* [cf. H. *bonā*], f. sowing, cultivation.

बोक *bok*, m. reg. = बोका.

बोकरा *bokrā*, m. reg. = बोका.

बोकरी *bokrī* [cf. H. *bokrā*], f. reg. nanny-goat.

बोकला *boklā* [? cf. H. *baklā*], m. reg. bark of a tree.

बोका *bokā* [**bokka-*[1]], m. reg. **1.** a billy-goat. **2.** W. bucket (of hide) used in irrigation.

बोज़ा *bozā* [P. *būza*], m. Brbh. = बूज़ा.

बोझ *bojh* [*vahya-*: Pk. *vojjha-*], m. **1.** load, burden; cargo; freight. **2.** weight (esp. weight to be carried). इसका बहुत ~ नहीं, it doesn't weigh much. **3.** responsibility; onus. — ~ उठाना, to lift, or to carry, a load, &c.; to assume a responsibility. ~ उतारना, to put down a load; to help (one) down with a load ; to relieve oneself of, or to discharge, a responsibility. ~ लादना, to place a load (on, पर), to load. बोझों मरना (के), to groan and sweat under a burden. एहसान का ~ दूसरे के सिर पर लादना, to make it seem that gratitude is owed by another (rather than by oneself).

[1]**बोझना** *bojhnā* [cf. *vahya-*: Pk. *vojjha-*], v.t. reg. to load.

[2]**बोझना** *bojhnā*, v.t. reg. to scald or to parch rice.

बोझा *bojhā*, m. = बोझ.

बोझाई *bojhāī* [cf. H. [1]*bojhnā*], f. *Pl. HŚS.* **1.** the act of loading. **2.** lading, cargo. **3.** payment for loading.

बोझिल *bojhil* [cf. H. *vahya-*: Pk. *vojjha-*], adj. **1.** ponderous, massive. **2.** burdensome. **3.** heavily laden.

बोझी *bojhī* [cf. H. *bojh*], m. porter (as on an expedition).

बोझैल *bojhail*, adj. reg. = बोझिल.

बोट *boṭ*, m. **1.** an earthen pot (as used for pickles). **2.** reg. (W.) a flat earthen flask.

बोटा *boṭā* [**boṭṭa-*[1]], m. reg. (W.) a lump or log of wood.

बोटी *boṭī* [cf. H. *boṭā*], f. **1.** a piece, or slice of meat or flesh. **2.** fig. the body. — ~ उतारना, to bite off a piece of flesh. बोटियाँ उड़ाना, or काटना (की), to cut to pieces, to make mincemeat (of). ~ चढ़ना, to grow fat. ~ ~ काटना, = बोटियाँ काटना. बोटियाँ काँपना, to be trembling, full of premonitions. गिनी ~ नपे शोरबा, let the soup be reckoned after counting the meat: spend according to your income.

बोड़ना *boṛnā* [**boḍayati*: Pk. *bolaï*], v.t. **1.** to immerse; to steep; to dye. **2.** to cause to dive, or to sink; to drown. **3.** to ruin (as a reputation).

[1]**बोड़ा** *boṛā* [conn. *vodra-*], m. *Pl. HŚS.* a constrictor, python.

[2]बोड़ा *boṛā* [conn. *varvaṭa-*: ? ← Austro-as.], m. ? a kind of bean, *Dolichos lablab*.

बोतल *botal* [Pt. *botelha*, Engl. *bottle*], f. bottle. — (उसने) ~ चढ़ाई है, he is drunk. — बोतल-ख़ाना, m. pantry.

बोतली *botlī* [cf. H. *botal*], f. dimin. a small bottle.

बोता *botā*, m. reg. a young camel.

बोतू *botū*, m. reg. (Bihar) a billy-goat.

बोदर *bodar* [? conn. *-tala-*], m. reg. point or place to which water is lifted to allow its use in irrigation.

बोदला *bodlā*, adj. simple, innocent; foolish.

बोदा *bodā* [**bodda-*], adj. **1.** weak, enfeebled; inert. **2.** soft, deficient (in character, spirit). **3.** mean, worthless.

बोदापन *bodāpan* [cf. H. *bodā*], m. inertness, &c.

बोद्दा *boddā*, adj. = बोदा.

बोध *bodh* [S.], m. **1.** understanding, intelligence. **2.** right understanding (of a question); good sense. **3.** perception, cognition. — बोधगम्य, adj. perceptible, knowable. °ता, f. intelligibility, comprehensibility.

बोध- *bodh-* [ad. *bodhayati*], v.t. Brbh. **1.** to give knowledge (to); to instruct, to explain. **2.** to console. **3.** to flatter.

बोधक *bodhak* [S.], adj. & m. **1.** adj. -बोधक. indicating, indicative of. **2.** m. one who imparts information; an informer.

बोधन *bodhan* [S.], m. **1.** giving knowledge (of, का). **2.** arousing, awaking. **3.** kindling.

बोधव्य *bodhavyă* [S.], adj. perceptible.

बोधि *bodhi* [S.], m. perfect knowledge or wisdom. — बोधि-वृक्ष, m. tree of wisdom (Buddhism), the sacred fig-tree.

बोधित *bodhit* [S.], adj. **1.** imparted (as knowledge). **2.** made perceptible, expressed.

बोधिसत्त्व *bodhisattvă* [S.], m. one whose essence is perfect knowledge: a Buddhist saint when he has only one birth to undergo before attaining to supreme Buddhahood.

बोना *bonā* [*vapati*], v.t. & m. **1.** v.t. to sow, to broadcast (seed); to plant. **2.** m. sowing, seed-time.

बोनी *bonī* [H. *bonā*], f. = बोना, 2.

बोब *bob* [cf. *vapati*], m. *Pl.* the sowing of grain with a drill.

बोबा *bobā*, m. Brbh. nipple, or breast.

बोबी *bobī*, f. Brbh. a bundle (as of washing).

बोय *boy*, f. Brbh. = बू.

बोयर *boyar*, m. reg. (W.) land constantly under cultivation.

बोयाम *boyām*, reg. a jar (for pickles, &c).

बोर *bor* [conn. *badara-*], m. the fruit of the jujube (= *ber*): **1.** small bells, esp. part of an ornament for the feet. **2.** ornamental studs of gold or silver.

बोर- *bor-*, v.t. Brbh. Av. = बोड़ना.

बोरसी *borsī*, f. a pot for holding fire; crucible (as of a goldsmith).

बोरा *borā* [**bora-*[2]], m. a sack.

बोरियत *boriyat* [cf. Engl. *boring*], f. colloq. boringness.

बोरिया *boriyā* [cf. H. *borā*], f. dimin. a small sack or bag. — बोरिया बँधन, m. household effects, goods and chattels. बोरिया-बिस्तर, m. esp. pej. bag and baggage.

बोरी *borī* [cf. H. *borā*], f. **1.** a sack, bag. **2.** a measure of three maunds.

बोरो *boro* [conn. *vorava-*], m. reg. (E.) a poor kind of rice sown in autumn on the banks of streams and tanks, and transplanted several times in the winter months.

[1]बोल *bol* [cf. H. *bolnā*], m. **1.** an utterance; word; cry; sound. **2.** speech, conversation. **3.** words (of a song). **4.** verse. **5.** assertion; promise. **5.** taunt, jeer. — ~ चबाना, colloq. to eat one's words. ~ मारना, to make fun (of, का); to disregard sthg. said (to one). दो ~ पढ़वाना, to get the agreement of a prospective bridegroom's family to a marriage. — बोल-चाल, f. talk, conversation; manner of speech; altercation. बोल-चाल होना (की), to be on speaking terms again (after a quarrel). बोल-बाला [P. *-bālā*], m. high repute, pre-eminence; prosperity, success.

[2]बोल *bol* [*vola-*], m. *Pl. HŚS.* gum-myrrh (used medicinally, and in a cement).

बोलना *bolnā* [**boll-*: Pk. *bollaï*], v.i. & v.t. **1.** v.i. to speak; to talk. **2.** to utter a sound (as any animal or bird); to bark, to chirp, &c. **3.** to make a sound; to strike (a clock); to crack, to shiver; to creak (a board, a shoe). **4.** v.t. to speak, to say; to tell. सच ~, to speak the truth. **5.** to declare, to announce (as a decision); to assign (work). **6.** Brbh. to call out. — बोल आना, to leave word; to order (as goods). बोल जाना, to leave word (with, or at); to be over, or finished; fig. to yield (as to wear, or age); to be bankrupt. – बोलना-चालना, to converse together, to have speech or dealings. – बोलता, adj. & m. speaking, &c.; power of speech; the soul. बोलता सिनेमा, m. a sound film, talkie. बोलती, f. = बोलता, 2. बोलती बंद कर देना, colloq. to shut (one) up. बोला-चाली, f. = बोल-चाल, 1., 3.

बोली *bolī* [cf. **boll-*: Pk. *bollā-*], f. **1.** speech, manner of speech; dialect; language; idiom. **2.** talk, conversation; words. **3.** bid (at auction). **4.** song or note (of birds). **5.** taunt; ridicule. — ~ करना, or कसना, or बोलना, or मारना (पर), to reproach; to make fun (of), to ridicule. ~ देनेवाला, m. bidder (at an auction). – बोली-ठोली, f. a sarcastic or derogatory remark. बोलीदार [P. *-dār*], m. a tenant holding land by verbal agreement only.

बोवैया *bovaiyā* [cf. H. *bonā*], m. reg. sower of seed.

बोसा *bosā* [P. *bosa*], m. a kiss. — ~ देना (को), to kiss. ~ लेना, to take a kiss (from, से), to kiss.

बोहनी *bohnī* [cf. *bodhana-*], f. **1.** first sale of the day (regarded as a good or bad omen). **2.** an auspicious start.

बोहरा *bohrā* [*vyavahāraka-*], m. **1.** a community of village bankers or traders in western India. **2.** a man of the Bohrā community.

बोहित *bohit* [*vahitra-*, Pk. *vohitta-*], , m. Brbh. Av. boat.

बोहित्थ *bohitth* [*vahitra-*, Pk. *vohitta-*, *bohittha-*; ad.], m. poet. boat.

[1]**बौंगा** *baum̐gā*, adj. reg. **1.** awkward, uncouth. **2.** stupid.

[2]**बौंगा** *baum̐gā*, m. reg. (W.) **1.** a stack or heap of straw, for chaff. **2.** *Pl.* a hollow bamboo.

बौंड़ *baum̐ṛ* [? **vātamaṇḍa(la)-*], m. ? f. Av. a twining, hairy creeper (= *Ipomoea hederacea*).

बौंड़- *baum̐ṛ-*, v.i. Brbh. to creep, to twine (as a vine); to extend.

[1]**बौंड़ा** *baum̐ṛā*, m. reg. (W.) pod, seed-vessel.

[2]**बौंड़ा** *baum̐ṛā*, f. reg. (W.) land given to village sweepers, &c. in exchange for their services.

[1]**बौंड़ी** *baum̐ṛī*, f. Brbh. pod (= [1]बौंड़ा).

[2]**बौंड़ी** *baum̐ṛī*, m. reg. (W.) = [2]बौंड़ा.

बौ *bau*, m. ? reg. landholder's fee when the daughter of one of his tenants is married.

बौखल *baukhal*, adj. furiously angry.

बौखला *baukhlā* [**vyavaskhalita-*], adj. very agitated, or angry.

बौखलाना *baukhlānā* [cf. **vyavaskhalita-*], v.i. to rage with anger.

बौखलाहट *baukhlāhaṭ* [cf. H. *baukhlānā*], f. raging anger.

बौछाड़ *bauchāṛ* [cf. *vāyu-*; ? conn. *chaṭā-*], f. **1.** heavy shower, squall. **2.** massive amount; hail (as of abuse, or of stones: against, पर); shower, flood (of money). — ~ करना, to shower, to pelt down (rain); to raise a spray; to shower (abuse, &c).

बौछार *bauchār*, f. = बौछाड़.

बौड़म *bauṛam*, adj. crazy, stupid.

बौतीज़मीन *bautīzamīn* [? cf. H. *bonā*], f. *hist.* land assigned to cultivators by the owner of a village (the crop to be shared with the latter).

बौद्ध *bauddh* [S.], adj. & m. Buddhist. — बौद्ध-धर्म, m. Buddhism. बौद्ध-गत, m. Buddhist viewpoint or doctrine, Buddhism.

बौद्धिक *bauddhik* [S.], adj. having to do with mind or intellect; intellectual.

बौना *baunā* [*vāmana-*], adj. & m. **1.** adj. dwarfish. **2.** m. dwarf. **3.** the fifth or dwarf avatār of Viṣṇu.

बौर *baur* [cf. **bakula-*[2]], m. blossom, esp. that of the mango tree.

बौर- *baur-* [conn. **mukurayati*], v.i. Brbh. to flower (the mango tree).

बौरहा *baurhā* [? con. H. *baurāh(ā)*], adj. reg. = [1]बौरा.

[1]**बौरा** *baurā*, adj. – बावला.

[2]**बौरा** *baurā*, m. = बेरा.

बौराना *baurānā* [cf. H. [1]*baurā*], v.i. & v.t. **1.** v.i. to go mad, or crazy, or rabid; to be mad, &c. **2.** to lose one's presence of mind. **3.** v.t. to drive mad, to make crazy.

बौरापन *baurāpan* [cf. H. [1]*baurā*], m. reg. madness.

बौराह *baurāh*, adj. E.H. = [1]बौरा.

बौराहट *baurāhaṭ* [cf. H. [1]*baurā*], f. madness, craziness.

बौराहा *baurāhā*, adj. reg. = [1]बौरा.

बौरी *baurī*, f. reg. parched barley.

ब्याज *byāj* [ad. *vyāja-*], m. **1.** deceit. **2.** interest (on money). — ~ पर ~, m. compound interest. ~ में देना, to lend at interest. – ब्याज-ख़ोर [P. *-khor*], m. interest-eater: a money-lender. °ई, f. usury.

ब्याजि *byāji* [cf. H. *byāj*], adj. interest-bearing.

ब्यान *byān* [cf. *vijāyate*; Pk. *vijāyana-*], m. giving birth (an animal).

ब्याना *byānā* [*vijāyate*], v.i. & v.t. **1.** v.i. to give birth (an animal). **2.** v.t. to produce (young).

ब्यानू *byānū*, m. *Pl.* the extent of one's reach with arms outspread.

ब्याप- *byāp-* [ad. *vyāpnoti*], v.i. Brbh. Av. **1.** to pervade, to spread through. **2.** to work, to have effect.

ब्यालू *byālū* [cf. *vikāla-*], m. the evening meal.

ब्याह *byāh* [*vivāha-*], m. marriage. — ~ **करना**, v.t. to make a marriage: to marry (to, **से** or **के साथ**); to take a wife; to celebrate a marriage. ~ **रचाना (का)**, to celebrate a marriage. – **ब्याह-कराई**, f. marriage fees paid to a brāhmaṇ.

1**ब्याहना** *byāhnā* [*vivāhayati*], v.t. **1.** to marry. **2.** to arrange the marriage (of, **को**: to, **से** or **के साथ**). — **ब्याह देना**, to give in marriage. **ब्याह लाना**, or **ले आना**, to take in marriage (a wife). **ब्याह लेना**, id. – **ब्याहता**, adj. & f., m. married; married woman, wife; husband.

2**ब्याहना** *byāhnā*, v.t. pronun. var. = **ब्याना**.

ब्याहला *byāhlā*, m. *Pl.* marriage song (of a god).

ब्याहली *byāhlī*, f. a bride.

ब्याहुला *byāhulā*, adj. *HŚS.* connubial (as a song).

ब्योंगा *byoṁgā*, m. reg. (W.) a wooden implement for scraping and cleaning tanned leather.

ब्योंड़ा *byoṁṛā*, m. = **बेंड़ा**.

ब्योंत *byoṁt* [cf. H. *byoṁtnā*], f. m. **1.** the cutting out of clothes. **2.** cut, style. **3.** plan, scheme; means, way. **4.** suitable time, opportunity. **5.** agreement, concurrence. **6.** retrenching, cutting back. — **कतर-ब्योंत**, f. ~, 6.

ब्योंतना *byoṁtnā* [**viyavakṛntati*], v.t. **1.** to cut out (clothes); to fit (clothes). **2.** colloq. to slash, to hack; to kill.

ब्योंतवाना *byoṁtvānā*, v.t. = **ब्योंताना**.

ब्योंताना *byoṁtānā* [cf. H. *byoṁtnā*], v.t. to cause to be cut out, or made up (clothes: by, **से**).

ब्योत *byot*, f. m. reg. = **ब्योंत**.

ब्योपार *byopār* [H. *bepār*; ad. *vyavahāra-*], m. = **बैपार**, **व्यापार**.

ब्योपारी *byopārī* [cf. H. *byopār*], m. = **बैपारी**.

ब्योर- *byor-* [**vivarati*: Pa. *vivarati*], v.t. Brbh. to disentangle (the hair).

ब्योरा *byorā* [cf. H. *byor-*], m. account, explanation, statement; details. — ~ **देना**, to relate, to describe; to inform. **ब्योरेवार** [P. *-vār*], adj. detailed, circumstantial.

ब्योहर *byohar* [? cf. H. *byohār*], m. reg. money-lending.

ब्योहरा *byohrā*, m [H. *bohrā*; ad. *vyavahāra-*], reg. **1.** a trader. **2.** a money-lender.

ब्योहार *byohār*, m. business, trade, &c. (= **व्यवहार**).

ब्योहारी *byohārī*, adj. & m. **1.** adj. commercial, mercantile. **2.** customary. **3.** m. a trader, merchant. **4.** party (to a matter). **5.** money-lender.

ब्रज *braj* [ad. *vraja-*], m. **1.** cattle-enclosure. ***2.** name of the Agra-Mathura district (the scene of Kṛṣṇa's childhoood adventures). — **ब्रज-नाथ**, m. lord of Braj: a title of Kṛṣṇa. **ब्रज-भाखा**, f. reg. (W.) = next. **ब्रज-भाषा**, f. the speech or dialect of Braj. **ब्रज-मंडल**, m. the area containing the major Kṛṣṇa shrines and sites around Brindavan, U.P.

ब्रह्म *brahm* [S.], m. **1.** the impersonal ultimate being called *brahma* or *brahman*, the all-pervading spirit of the universe. **2.** Brbh. Av. = **ब्रह्मा**. **3.** **ब्रह्म-**. = ~; = **ब्रह्मा**. 4. = **ब्राह्मण**. — **ब्रह्म-घात**, m. murder of a brāhmaṇ. °**क**, m. °**ई**, adj. **ब्रह्मचर्य**, m. religious studentship, the state of a brāhmaṇ or student in the first of the four stages of life; asceticism; chastity. **ब्रह्मचारिणी**, f. a chaste and virtuous woman. **ब्रह्मचारी**, m. a religious student; one practising *brahmacarya*. **ब्रह्म-जन्म**, m. birth in the spirit: investiture with the sacred thread. **ब्रह्म-ज्ञान**, m. knowledge of *brahma*, or of the Veda; spiritual wisdom. °**ई**, adj. & m. **ब्रह्म-तत्त्व**, v. the true knowledge of *brahma*. **ब्रह्मदेशीय**, adj. Burmese. **ब्रह्मद्रोही**, adj. hostile to brāhmaṇs. **ब्रह्म-द्वार**, m. Brbh. = **ब्रह्म-रंध्र**. **ब्रह्मपर**, adj. Av. one having true knowledge of *brahma*. **ब्रह्म-बान**, m. Av. Brahmā's arrow: a fabulous weapon supposed to deal infallible destruction. **ब्रह्म-भाव**, m. absorption into the ultimate (= *mokṣa*). **ब्रह्म-भोज**, m. the feeding of brāhmaṇs. **ब्रह्म-मुहूर्त**, m. the moments just before sunrise. **ब्रह्म-रंध्र**, m. (in yoga) the opening at the top of the skull through which the soul is said to escape to union with the absolute, or on death. **ब्रह्म-राक्षस**, m. the ghost of a brāhmaṇ. **ब्रह्म-रात्रि**, f. a night of Brahmā: an aeon of time. **ब्रह्म-रूप**, adj. of the nature of *brahma*. **ब्रह्म-रेखा**, f. line of destiny (written on the brow). **ब्रह्म-लोक**, m. the world or heaven of Brahmā. **ब्रह्मवाद**, m. the theory of *brahma*, Vedānta. °**ई**, adj. & m. vedantic; a vedantist. **ब्रह्म-विद्या**, f. knowledge of *brahma*:

sacred knowledge (of the Veda); theosophy. ब्रह्म-सर, m. Av. = ब्रह्म-बान. ब्रह्म-हत्या, f. killing a brāhmaṇ. ब्रह्महा, m. inv. Brbh. the killer of a brāhmaṇ. ब्रह्मांड [°*ma*+*a*°], m. the egg of Brahmā: the universe; outer space, cosmos; the crown of the head. ब्रह्माक्षर [°*ma*+*a*°], m. sacred syllable: the syllable *oṁ*. ब्रह्मावर्त [°*ma*+*ā*°], m. sacred land: a traditional title of the region to the north-west of Delhi. ब्रह्मासन [°*ma*+*ā*°], m. a posture considered conducive to religious meditation.

ब्रह्मण *brahmaṇ* [H. *brāhmaṇ*: ? w. H. *brahm*], m. = ब्राह्मण.

ब्रह्मणी *brahmaṇī*, f. = ब्राह्मणी.

ब्रह्मण्य *brahmaṇyă* [S.], adj. **1.** having to do with *brahma*, or with Brahmā. **2.** devout; well-disposed towards brāhmaṇs. — ब्रह्मन्य-देव, m. Av. a title of Viṣṇu.

ब्रह्मत्व *brahmatvă* [S.], m. **1.** state or condition of *brahma*. **2.** identification (of the *ātmā*) with *brahma*. **4.** transf. brahmanhood.

ब्रह्मा *brahmā* [S.], m. inv. the supreme being regarded as personal and esp. in his capacity as creator of the world.

ब्राह्म *brāhmă* [S.], adj. having to do with the ultimate *brahman*; holy. — ब्राह्म-मुहूर्त, m. the hour, or time, before dawn. ब्राह्म-समाज, m. the Brahma Samaj (a reform movement in religion, founded 1828). °ई, adj. & m.

ब्राह्मण *brāhmaṇ* [S.], m. **1.** a brāhmaṇ. **2.** a *brāhmaṇa* (Vedic treatise). — ब्राह्मणेतर [°*ṇa*+*i*°], adj. non-brahman.

ब्राह्मणत्व *brāhmaṇatvă* [S.], m. brahmanhood, brahminical status.

ब्राह्मणी *brāhmaṇī* [S.], f. **1.** a brāhmaṇ woman. **2.** wife of a brāhmaṇ.

ब्राह्मणेटा *brāhmaṇeṭā*, m. a young brāhmaṇ.

ब्राह्मण्य *brāhmaṇyă* [S.], m. **1.** status or business of a brāhmaṇ. **2.** the brāhmaṇs (collectively). **3.** *astron.* the planet Saturn.

ब्राह्मी *brāhmī* [S.], f. **1.** a title of Durgā. **2.** name of an ancient Indian script (from which all the modern scripts descend). **3.** penny-wort, *Hydrocotyle asiatica*: a small herbaceous plant used medicinally.

ब्राह्म्य *brāhmyă* [S.], m. *hind.* worship to brāhmaṇs.

ब्रितानी *britānī* [cf. P. *bar̤ṯānīya*], adj. British.

ब्लैक *blaik* [Engl. *black*], m. black market. — ~ में बेचना, to sell on the black market.

भ

भ *bha*, the twenty-fourth consonant of the Devanāgarī syllabary. — **भकार**, m. the sound /bh/; the letter **भ**.

[1]**भंग** *bhaṅg* [ad. *bhaṅga-*[2]], m. = **भाँग**. — **भंग-घोटना** [× H. *bhāṁg-*], m. stick used to rub down hemp leaves in preparing *bhāṁg*.

[2]**भंग** *bhaṅg* [S.], m. & adj. **1.** m. breaking; splitting. **2.** partition. **बंग-भंग**, m. the partition (1905) of Bengal. **3.** damage, destruction. **4.** defeat. **5.** disappointment; dejection. **6.** interruption (of a flow, current). **7.** infringement, breach. **8.** adjournment (of a parliament). **9.** dispersing (a crowd). **10.** bend, curve. **11.** adj. (?) broken, &c. — ~ **करना**, to break, &c.

भंग- *bhaṅg-* [ad. *bhaṅga-*[1]], v.i. Brbh. to be broken; to be found wanting (mind, ingenuity).

भंगड़ *bhaṅgaṛ* [cf. H. [1]*bhaṅg*], m. a drinker of *bhāṁg*.

भँगड़ा *bhaṁgṛā* [Panj. *bhaṁgṛā*], m. a Panjabi folk-dance.

भँगरा *bhaṁgrā* [*bhṛṅgarāja-*], m. **1.** the spreading shrub *Eclipta prostrata*. **2.** reg. (W.) a creeping plant, *Verbesina prostrata*, which is harmful to growing rice.

भंगराज *bhaṅgrāj*, m. the racket-tailed drongo.

भंगान *bhaṅgān*, m. *Pl. HŚS.* a kind of fish.

भंगिन *bhaṅgin* [cf. H. [1]*bhaṅgī*], f. **1.** a woman of the sweeper caste. **2.** wife of a *bhaṅgī*. **3.** female sweeper.

भंगिमा *bhaṅgimā* [S.], f. = [3]**भंगी**.

भँगियाना *bhaṁgiyānā* [cf. H. *bhāṁg*], v.i. to get intoxicated on *bhāṁg*.

[1]**भंगी** *bhaṅgī*, m. **1.** name of a community of sweepers. **2.** a man of the *bhaṅgī* community.

[2]**भंगी** *bhaṅgī*, m. = **भंगड़**.

[3]**भंगी** *bhaṅgī* [S.], f. **1.** breaking; angular position of the limbs (see **त्रिभंगी**); partic. facial expression. **2.** winding or tortuous course. **3.** fraud, trick, disguise. **4.** peculiar or idiosyncratic behaviour.

भँगेड़ा *bhaṁgeṛā*, adj. addicted to *bhāṁg* (= **गँजेरी**).

भँगेर- *bhaṁger-*, m. reg. *bhāṁg* prepared for drinking: — **भँगेर-ख़ाना**, m. a shop or place where *bhāṁg* is sold or drunk.

[1]**भँगेरा** *bhaṁgerā* [**bhaṅgakara-*], m. reg. a maker and seller of *bhāṁg*.

[2]**भँगेरा** *bhaṁgerā*, m. reg. = **भँगेला**.

भँगेला *bhaṁgelā*, m. reg. hempen cloth or sacking.

भँगोरिया *bhaṁgoriyā*, m. *Pl.* name of a community of thread-makers or rope-makers.

भंजक *bhañjak* [S.], adj. breaking, destroying.

भँजत *bhaṁjat* [cf. H. *bhaṁjnā*], f. **1.** breaking. **2.** reg. discount on changing money.

भंजन *bhañjan* [S.], m. **1.** breaking, destroying; destruction. **2.** destroyer (as of sin).

भँजना *bhaṁjnā* [**bhañjati*: Pa. *bhañjati*], v.i. & v.t. **1.** v.i. to be broken, or destroyed. **2.** to be divided; to be changed (money). **3.** to be folded or twisted (as paper). **4.** to be brandished (a sword, staff). **5.** v.t. to break, &c.

भँजाई *bhaṁjāī* [cf. H. *bhaṁjānā*], f. **1.** changing money. **2.** a sum of money to be changed. **3.** folding, twisting.

भँजाना *bhaṁjānā* [cf. H. *bhāṁj-*], v.t. to cause to be broken: **1.** to change (money). **2.** to cause to be folded or twisted.

भँटमास *bhaṁṭmās*, m. reg. the fruit of the water-lily (*koī*).

भँटवास *bhaṁṭvās*, m. reg. = **भँटमास**.

भंटा *bhaṇṭā* [conn. *bhaṇṭākī-*, Pa. *bhaṇḍākī-*], m. a round variety of egg-plant.

[1]**भंड** *bhaṇḍ* [S.], m. & adj. **1.** m. = [2]**भाँड़**. **2.** adj. making pretence (of virtue), bogus. **3.** indecent.

[2]**भंड** *bhaṇḍ*, m. reg. **1.** breaking. **2.** spoiling. **3.** confusion. — ~ **करना**, to break. – **भंड-ख़राबा**, m. = ~.

भंडन *bhaṇḍan* [S.], m. *Pl. HŚS.* **1.** deception; wickedness. **2.** Brbh. armour. **3.** war, battle.

भंडरिया *bhaṇḍriyā*, m. = **भंडेरी**.

भँड़सार *bhaṁṛsār* [? *bhāṇḍaśālā-* × *āgāra-*], m. E.H. storehouse, grain-store.

भंडसाल *bhaṇḍsāl*, f. = भँड़साल.

भँड़साल *bhaṁṛsāl* [*bhāṇḍaśālā-*], f. reg. domestic storehouse, grain-store.

भँड़साली *bhaṁṛsālī* [cf. H. *bhaṁṛsāl*], m. one having a storehouse; specif. colloq. a hoarder of grain.

भंडा *bhaṇḍā*, m. earthen pot, &c. (= भाँड़ा). — भंडा-फोड़, m. pot-breaker: discloser of a secret; disclosure of a secret. भंडा-फोड़ करना (का), to uncover (a plot, &c).

भंडार *bhaṇḍār* [*bhāṇḍāgāra-*], m. **1.** place of storage, store-room; warehouse. **2.** a reserve, store, or fund; field (of oil). **3.** *hist.* a reserved estate (farmed or managed by the owner or landholder himself, not by others). — भंडार-घर, m. = भंडार.

भंडारा *bhaṇḍārā*[*bhāṇḍāgāra-*], m. 1. = भंडार. **2.** the stomach. **3.** a meal provided for holy men.

भंडारित *bhaṇḍārit* [S.], adj. stored, in store.

भंडारी *bhaṇḍārī* [*bhāṇḍāgārika-*], m. **1.** supervisor of a storehouse, &c.; steward. **2.** treasurer. **3.** cook.

भंडारीपन *bhaṇḍārīpan* [cf. H. *bhaṇḍārī*], m. position or status of steward, &c.

भंडिल *bhaṇḍil* [S.], adj. *Pl. HŚS.* fortunate, auspicious.

भंडेरिया *bhaṇḍeriyā*, adj. & m. = भंडेरी.

भंडेरी *bhaṇḍerī* [cf. *bhaṇḍa-*[2]], adj. & m. **1.** adj. having to do with conjuring, fortune-telling, &c. **2.** m. conjuring, fortune-telling. **3.** a community of conjurers, &c. **4.** conjurer, &c.

भँड़ेरी *bhaṁṛerī*, m. = भंडेरी.

भंडेलन *bhaṇḍelan* [cf. H. *bhaṇḍelā*], f. wife of an actor, &c.

भंडेला *bhaṇḍelā* [cf. *bhaṇḍa-*[2]], m. = [2]भाँड़.

भँड़ैती *bhaṁṛaitī*[cf. H. *bhāṁṛaitī*], f. buffoonery.

भंडोली *bhaṇḍolī* [**bhāṇḍāvali-*], f. reg. a row, or a vertical pile of water-pots.

भँडौवा *bhaṁḍauvā*, m. = भँड़ौवा.

भँड़ौवा *bhaṁṛauvā* [**bhaṇḍapāda-*], m. a humorous or satirical verse.

भंबक *bhambak*, m. = भंबाका.

भंबाका *bhambākā*, m. large hole, or gap.

भंबो *bhambo*, f. colloq. a fat woman.

भँभीरी *bhaṁbhīrī* [cf. *bhambha-*], f. Brbh. Av. **1.** a dragon-fly. **2.** a butterfly. **3.** a child's top.

भँभोड़ना *bhaṁbhoṛnā*, v.t. reg. to gnaw; to tear at, to devour.

भँव- *bhaṁv-* [*bhramati*], v.i. Brbh. **1.** to revolve. **2.** to wander.

भँवर *bhaṁvar* [*bhramara-*], m. **1.** gyration, turn. **2.** whirlpool. **3.** a black bee. — ~ में पड़ना, to whirl round; to get into a state of turmoil. – भँवर-गीत, m. = भ्रमर-गीत. भँवर-जाल, m. the world and its snares.

भँवरा *bhaṁvrā*, m. = [1]भौंरा.

भँवरी *bhaṁvrī* [*bhramara-*], f. = भँवर.

भँसना *bhaṁsnā*, v.i. reg. = भसना.

भई *bhaī* [? *bhagin-*], m. & f. dimin. esp. voc. friend.

भक *bhak* [**bhakabhaka-*], f. onom. puff; flash (in the pan); flap, flop; explosion. — ~ से, adv. with a sudden puff, flap, whoosh, &c. ~ से उड़ जाना, to fly off with a flapping or flopping sound; to explode. - भक-भक, f. puffing (of an engine); roaring (of a fire). भक-भक होना, to puff, &c.

भकभकाना *bhakbhakānā* [cf. H. *bhak*], v.i. **1.** to blaze; to glow. **2.** to rage, to fume in anger.

भकसा *bhaksā*, adj. reg. astringent; spoiled in taste (food: = कसैला; cf. बकसा).

भकुआ *bhakuā*, adj. & m. **1.** adj. stupid. **2.** confused. **3.** m. a fool.

भकुआना *bhakuānā* [cf. H. *bhakuā*], v.i. to talk or to act in a confused or foolish way.

भकोसना *bhakosnā*, v.t. to eat (sthg.) greedily (cf. ढकोसना).

भकौवाँ *bhakauvāṁ*, m. reg. a bogy-man.

[1]**भक्त** *bhakt* [S.], adj. & m. **1.** adj. devoted, pious. **2.** m. a devotee; follower, sectarian. — भक्त-जन, m. a devotee. भक्त-वत्सल, adj. showing a parental kindliness to devotees (a deity).

[2]**भक्त** *bhakt* [S.], adj. divided.

भक्तता *bhaktătā* [S.], f. devotedness, faith.

[1]**भक्ति** *bhakti* [S.], f. religious devotion; adoration; loving faith, piety; devoted service. — भक्ति-काल, m. a period (as in Hindi literature) defined as especially characterised by religious devotion. भक्तिमान, adj. devoted; devout, pious. भक्तिमार्ग, m. the path of devotion. भक्तिवाद, m. adherence to *bhakti*; devotionalism. भक्ति-रस, m. savour of *bhakti*: the essential quality of *bhakti* as analysed by Caitanya and other theologians. भक्त्यानंद [°*ti*+*ā*°], m. Brbh. bliss of devotion.

[2]भक्ति *bhakti* [S.], f. esp. *-bhakti.* division; part.

भक्ष- *bhakṣ-* [ad. *bhakṣati*], v.t. Brbh. to eat.

भक्षक *bhakṣak* [S.], adj. & m. **1.** adj. -भक्षक. eating, devouring; feeding upon. **2.** m. eater, feeder. **3.** a glutton; a person of voracious appetites.

भक्षण *bhakṣaṇ* [S.], m. **1.** eating, devouring; feeding. **2.** food. — ~ करना, to eat, &c.

भक्षणीय *bhakṣăṇīyă* [S.], adj. **1.** proper to be eaten. **2.** fit to eat, edible.

भक्षित *bhakṣit* [S.], adj. eaten, devoured.

भक्षी *bhakṣī* [S.], adj. & m. = भक्षक.

भक्ष्य *bhakṣyă* [S.], adj. & m. **1.** adj. = भक्षणीय. **2.** m. food. — भक्ष्याभक्ष्य [°*ya*+*a*°], adj. edible and inedible.

भख- *bhakh-* [*bhakṣati*; ← Panj. Raj.; ? or ad.], v.t. Brbh. to eat.

भग *bhag* [S.], f. vulva.

भगत *bhagat* [ad. *bhakta-*], adj. & m. **1.** adj. = [1]भक्त. **2.** abstaining from meat and alcohol. **3.** m. = [1]भक्त. **4.** a Vaiṣṇava ascetic. **5.** a Rāmaite community of musicians and dancers (Rajasthan). **6.** colloq. = ओझा. **7.** a kind of dramatic farce put on at the time of the Holī festival. — ~ खेलना, to act (a play); to mimic.

भगता *bhagtā* [cf. H. *bhagat*], m. *Pl.* a tribe of *ahīrs*.

भगतानी *bhagtānī* [cf. H. *bhagat*], f. 1. = भगतिन, 2. **2.** iron. prostitute.

भगतिन *bhagtin* [cf. H. *bhagat*], f. **1.** a devout woman. **2.** wife of a *bhagat.* **3.** a female ascetic.

भगतिया *bhagtiyā* [cf. H. *bhagat*], m. **1.** a community of musicians and dancers. **2.** dancer, dancing boy; actor.

भगदड़ *bhagdaṛ*, f. a panic, stampede. — ~ मचना, panic to break out.

भगल *bhagal*, m. **1.** deceit, swindling. **2.** sham, disguise; acting a part. **3.** reg. (W.) grain which has rotted in store. — ~ बना रखना, to make a pretence.

भगलिया *bhagliyā* [cf. H. *bhagal*], m. pretender, cheat; charlatan.

भगली *bhaglī* [cf. H. *bhagal*], adj. **1.** deceitful, pretended, sham. **2.** mock (jewellery).

भगवंत *bhagvant* [S.], adj. & m. = भगवान.

भगवत् *bhagăvat* [S.], adj. & m. = भगवान.

भगवती *bhagăvatī* [S.], f. var. /bhəgəutī/. **1.** goddess. **2.** title of Lakṣmī, Durgā. **3.** a revered lady.

भगवद्- *bhagăvad-* [S.], adj. = भगवत्. — भगवद-गीता, f. name of an episode of the *Mahābhārata* inculcating devotion to Kṛṣṇa, along with Vedānta and some Sāṅkhya views.

भगवदीय *bhagvădīyă* [S.], adj. worshipping the supreme being; devout.

भगवन् *bhagvan* [S.], interj. worshipful Lord!

भगवा *bhagvā*, m. reg. **1.** a red ochre (= गेरू). **2.** cloth (as worn by ascetics) dyed with *bhagvā.* — ~ ध्वज, m. saffron banner (esp. of conservative Hindu factions).

भगवान *bhagvān* [S.], adj. & m. **1.** adj. glorious, divine, to be adored; worshipful. **2.** m. the supreme being (esp. as equated with Viṣṇu-Kṛṣṇa). **3.** title of a venerated deity (as the Buddha). **4.** any revered person (term of address).

भगवाना *bhagvānā* [cf. H. [1]*bhāgnā*], v.t. to cause to be chased away (by, से); to put to flight.

भगाना *bhagānā* [cf. H. [1]*bhāgnā*], v.t. & v.i. **1.** v.t. to cause to flee: to chase away; to put to flight. **2.** v.i. Brbh. Av. = [1]भागना. — भगा ले जाना, to abduct; to elope with.

भगाल *bhagāl*, m. reg. the human skull.

भगाली *bhagālī*, adj. reg. wearing a necklace of skulls: a title of Śiva.

भगिनी *bhaginī* [S.], f. **1.** sister. **2.** reg. niece.

भगीरथ *bhagīrath* [S.], m. *mythol.* name of a king who brought the Ganges down from heaven to earth by his austerities. — ~ परिश्रम, m. fig. Herculean labour.

भगेल *bhagel*, m. reg. **1.** defeat, rout. **2.** a fugitive.

भगोड़ा *bhagoṛā*, adj. & m. = भग्गू.

भगौना *bhagaunā*, m. reg. a cooking vessel.

भग्गी *bhaggī* [cf. H. *bhāgnā*], f. reg. flight; panic.

भग्गू *bhaggū* [cf. H. *bhāgnā*], adj. & m. **1.** adj. fugitive. **2.** cowardly. **3.** m. a fugitive; deserter.

भग्न *bhagn* [S.], adj. **1.** broken. **2.** defeated. **3.** wretched, dejected. — भग्न-दूत, m. an emissary disappointed in his object. भग्नावशेष [°*na*+*a*°], m. broken remains: ruins, debris. भग्नाश [°*na*+*ā*°], adj. disappointed in (one's) hopes, discouraged.

भचक *bhacak* [cf. H. *bhacaknā*], f. **1.** limping, a limp. **2.** astonishment, &c.

भचकना *bhacaknā*, v.i. **1.** to limp. **2.** to be astounded, amazed. — ~ रहना, to be astounded, &c.

भचकाना *bhackānā* [cf. H. *bhacaknā*], v.t. to astound, to amaze.

भचक्र *bhacakră* [S.], m. *Pl. HŚS.* the stars, or the major constellations, collectively; the zodiac.

भज- *bhaj-* [cf. H. *bhājnā*], Brbh. to flee.

भजन *bhajan* [S.], m. **1.** worship, adoration. **2.** devotional song, hymn. — ~ करना, to worship; to sing a hymn or hymns (to, का). – भजन-कीर्तन, m. singing and praising (a deity). भजन-पूजन, m. singing and worship.

भजना *bhajnā* [ad. *bhajati*[1], *bhajate*], v.t. **1.** to worship, &c. (= भजन करना); to serve. **2.** 19c. to receive, to endure.

भजनी *bhajnī* [cf. H. *bhajan*], m. Brbh. one much concerned with devotional songs, a singer, worshipper.

भजनीय *bhajănīyă* [S.], adj. deserving to be worshipped, &c.

भजाना *bhajānā*, v.t. reg. = भगाना.

[1]**भट** *bhaṭ* [cf. *bhraṣṭra-*], m. **1.** oven, kiln (= भट्ठा). **2.** pit. **3.** lair, den; hole (of animal). **4.** a misfortune, a curse.

[2]**भट** *bhaṭ* [S.], m. warrior; combatant, competitor.

[3]**भट** *bhaṭ*, m. the soy bean.

भटई *bhaṭaī* [cf. H. *bhāṭ*], f. **1.** the occupation, or the verse of a bard; eulogy. **2.** eloquent flattery.

भटकटैया *bhaṭkaṭaiyā* [cf. *kaṇṭakita-*], m. a prickly plant, *Solanum jacquini* (used medicinally in treating several complaints).

भटकना *bhaṭaknā* [cf. *bhraṣṭa-*], v.i. **1.** to stray, to wander. **2.** to lose the way. **3.** to err. **4.** to be restless, to pine (for, के लिए). — भटकता फिरना, to wander about (aimlessly, or lost).

भटकवाना *bhaṭakvānā* [cf. H. *bhaṭaknā*], v.t. = भटकाना.

भटकाना *bhaṭkānā* [cf. H. *bhaṭaknā*], v.t. **1.** to cause to stray or to wander; to lead astray. **2.** to mislead.

भटनास *bhaṭnās*, m. = [3]भट.

भटा *bhaṭā*, m. reg. the egg-plant.

भटिनी *bhaṭinī* [cf. H. *bhāṭ*], f. wife of a bard, &c.

भटिया *bhaṭiyā*, m. reg. poor quality land (? = भटुवा).

भटियारा *bhaṭiyārā*, m. pronun. var. = भठियारा.

भटुला *bhaṭulā*, m. *Pl.* bread or cakes made of flour of mixed pulses.

भटुवा *bhaṭuvā*, m. reg. (W.) a light, dry soil (yielding only an autumn crop).

भटू *bhaṭū*, f. **1.** Brbh. a woman. **2.** reg. interj. woman! lady!

भटूरा *bhaṭūrā*, m. a fried bread-cake.

भटोलर *bhaṭolar*, m. *hist.* land granted to brāhmaṇs (specif. to Bhaṭṭ brāhmaṇs).

भट्ट *bhaṭṭ* [S.], m. lord, learned man: title of several brāhmaṇ communities. — भट्टाचार्य [°*ṭa*+*ā*°], m. title of a Bengal brāhmaṇ community.

भट्टारक *bhaṭṭārak* [S.], adj. & m. **1.** adj. venerable. **2.** m. learned, or wise man.

भट्टी *bhaṭṭī*, f. pronun. var. = भट्ठी.

भट्ठा *bhaṭṭhā*, m. = भट्ठी.

भट्ठी *bhaṭṭhī* [*bhraṣṭra-*], m. **1.** oven. **2.** stove, furnace (as of goldsmith, distiller); kiln. **3.** boiler, copper (for washing clothes). **4.** forge. **5.** atomic reactor. — भट्ठीदार [P. *dār*], m. a distiller; keeper of a liquor-shop.

भठियाना *bhaṭhiyānā* [cf. H. *bhāṭ(h)ā*], v.i & v.t. reg. **1.** v.i. to ebb (the tide). **2.** to go downstream with the tide. **3.** v.t. to wash down or away; to ruin (one).

भठियारख़ाना *bhaṭhiyārkhānā* [cf. H. *bhaṭhiyārā*], m. also pej. inn; eating-house.

भठियारपन *bhaṭhiyārpan* [cf. H. *bhaṭhiyārā*], m. work or position of an innkeeper.

भठियारा *bhaṭhiyārā* [*bhr̥ṣṭakāra-*], m. innkeeper.

भठियारिन *bhaṭhiyārin* [cf. H. *bhaṭhiyārā*], f. **1.** female innkeeper. **2.** innkeeper's wife.

भठियारी *bhaṭhiyārī* [cf. H. *bhaṭhiyārā*], f. = भठियारिन.

भठियाल *bhaṭhiyāl* [**bhraṣṭakāla-*], m. *Pl. HŚS.* **1.** m. ebb tide. **2.** adv. *Pl.* with the current, downstream.

[1]**भड़** *bhaṛ*, m. *Pl.* a barge.

[2]**भड़** *bhaṛ* [**bhaṭ-*], m. = भड़भड़.

भड़क *bhaṛak* [cf. H. *bhaṛaknā*], f. **1.** splendour, blaze. **2.** pomp, show, pageantry. **3.** burst, explosion; flash, flame. **4.** outburst (of anger). **5.** starting, alarm; shying (of a horse). — भड़कदार [P. *-dār*], adj. splendid, glittering; inspiring awe or alarm.

भड़कना *bhaṛaknā* [cf. **bhaṭ-*: Pk. *bhaḍakka-*], v.i. **1.** to flare up (flame); to shoot up (prices). **2.** to burst out (in anger). **3.** to be startled, or alarmed; to shy (a horse). **4.** reg. = फड़कना.

भड़काऊ *bhaṛkāū* [cf. H. *bhaṛkānā*], adj. provocative.

भड़काना *bhaṛkānā* [cf. H. *bhaṛaknā*], v.t. **1.** to blow into flame. **2.** to inflame (the feelings); to incite. **3.** to startle, to scare.

भड़कीला *bhaṛkīlā* [cf. H. *bhaṛaknā*], adj. **1.** splendid, showy; flashy. **2.** shy, skittish; timid.

भड़कीलापन *bhaṛkīlāpan* [cf. H. *bhaṛkīlā*], m. showiness, &c.

भड़कैल *bhaṛkail*, adj. = भड़कीला.

भड़कौवल *bhaṛkauval* [cf. H. *bhaṛak*], adj. splendid, showy, &c. (= भड़कदार, भड़कीला).

भड़भड़ *bhaṛbhaṛ* [cf. H. *bhaṛbhaṛānā*], f. **1.** crashing or roaring sound; rattle (as of rifle fire); fierce crackling (of fire). **2.** rush, whir. — ~ करना, to crash, to rattle, &c. ~ मचाना, to create an uproar.

भड़भड़ाना *bhaṛbhaṛānā* [cf. *bhaṭabhaṭāyate*; Pk. *bhaḍakka-*], v.i. **1.** to crash, to roar; to rattle (as rifle fire); to crackle. **2.** [× *phaṭ-*[1]] to whir, to flutter (wings).

भड़भड़ाहट *bhaṛbhaṛāhaṭ* [cf. H. *bhaṛbhaṛānā*], f. crash, roar; rattle (as of rifle fire); fierce crackling (of fire).

भड़भड़िया *bhaṛbhaṛiyā* [cf. H. *bhaṛbhaṛ*], adj. & m. **1.** adj. impulsive in speech. **2.** chattering (esp. indiscreetly). **3.** m. chatterer, babbler.

भड़भाँड़ *bhaṛbhāṁṛ*, m. reg. (Bihar) = भरभंडा.

भड़भूँजन *bhaṛbhūṁjan* [cf. H. *bhaṛbhūṁjā*], f. **1.** woman of the *bhaṛbhūṁjā* community. **2.** wife of a *bhaṛbhūṁjā*. **3.** woman grain-parcher.

भड़भूँजा *bhaṛbhūṁjā* [H. [1]*bhāṛ*, H. *bhūṁjnā*], m. **1.** a community of grain-parchers. **2.** a grain-parcher.

भड़री *bhaṛarī*, m. conjurer, juggler, fortune-teller (= भंडेरी).

भड़वाई *bhaṛvāī* [cf. H. *bhaṛuā*], f. earnings of a pimp.

भड़वाना *bhaṛvānā* [cf. H. [2]*bhār*, *bhaṛuā*], v.i. to procure, to pimp.

भड़साईं *bhaṛsāīṁ*, f. (m., *Pl.*) reg. a grain-parcher's furnace.

भड़ास *bhaṛās* [? cf. **bhaṭ-*], f. anger, spleen. — ~ निकालना, to vent one's anger or spleen.

भड़िहाई *bhaṛihāī*, f. E.H. theft.

भड़ुआ *bhaṛuā* [cf. **bhārta-*: Pk. *bhāḍa-*], m. **1.** a pimp, procurer. **2.** accompanist to the singing of a dancing-girl. **3.** straw effigy (carried in a Holī procession).

भड़ैत *bhaṛait*, m. = भड़ैती.

भड़ैती *bhaṛaitī* [cf. H. *bhāṛā*], m. **1.** tenant. **2.** hired labourer.

भणित *bhaṇit* [S.], adj. & m. **1.** adj. uttered, spoken. **2.** m. utterance; speech, talk.

भणिता *bhaṇitā* [S.], m. inv. speaker: composer (of a verse).

भणिति *bhaṇiti* [S.], f. = भणित.

भतार *bhatār* [*bhartṛ-*: *bhartāram*, acc.], m. husband.

भतीजा *bhatījā* [*bhrātrīya-*], m. **1.** brother's son, nephew. **2.** wife's brother's son. — भाई-भतीजावाद, m. nepotism.

भतीजी *bhatījī* [*bhrātrīya-*], f. **1.** brother's daughter, niece. **2.** wife's brother's daughter.

भत्ता *bhattā* [**bhārta-*: MIA *bhatta-*], m. additional allowance; expenses (of subsistence or travel). — आवास ~, m. residential allowance.

भद *bhad*, m. thud, thump. — ~ से, adv. with a thud, &c. – भद-भद, m. & adj. repeated thuds, thudding; shapeless, fat.

भदई *bhadaī* [**bhādrapadīya-*], adj. & f. **1.** having to do with the month of, or with the harvest of, *Bhādoṁ*. **2.** the autumn crop.

भदभदाना *bhadbhadānā* [cf. H. *bhadbhad*], v.t. to knock (two objects) together with a thud; to knock fruit down from a tree.

भदभदाहट *bhadbhadāhaṭ* [cf. H. *bhadbhadanā*], f. a repeated thudding sound.

भदरंगा *bhadraṅgā* [H. *bhaddā* + *raṅg*], adj. faded (= बदरंग).

भदवार *bhadvār*, m. reg. (W.) land prepared during the rains for the sowings of sugar-cane.

भदाहर *bhadāhar*, m. reg. the cutting of grain when it is only half ripe.

भदेस *bhades*, adj. Av. = भद्दा.

भद्दा *bhaddā* [*bhadra-*[1]], adj. **1.** clumsy, awkward; unwieldy; fat. **2.** uncouth, coarse (as remarks). **3.** ill-made, ugly. **4.** dull, stupid. — भद्दे ढंग से बना, slipshodly made.

भद्र *bhadră* [S.], adj. & m. **1.** adj. good, excellent; auspicious, fortunate (an augury).

2. gracious, kindly. 3. worthy; of good family, or education; ritually pure. 4. m. an excellent person, &c. 5. prosperity. 6. iron. an impostor, hypocrite. — ~ होना, to be purified by shaving the head and beard after the death of a relative, or in a holy place. – भद्रपदा, f. name of the third and fourth lunar asterisms. भद्राक्ष [°a+a°], m. *Pl.* a partic. seed of which beads are made.

भद्रक *bhadrak* [S.], adj. Brbh. good, worthy.

भद्रा *bhadrā* [S.], f. 1. the second, seventh and twelfth days of a lunar fortnight. 2. *mythol.* the heavenly Ganges. 3. iron. an unlucky moment; misfortune.

भद्री *bhadrī* [cf. H. *bhadr*], adj. Brbh. fortunate, auspicious.

भनक *bhanak* [cf. H. *bhanbhanānā, bhinaknā*], f. 1. a low or distant sound; buzz, hum; ring, din. 2. rumour. — ~ पड़ना, a sound, or whisper (of, की) to be heard, or to be audible.

भनना *bhannā* [*bhanati, bhaṇati*], v.i. reg. to speak.

भनभन *bhanbhan* [cf. H. *bhanbhanānā*], v.i. buzzing, &c. (= भिनभिन).

भनभनाना *bhanbhanānā* [cf. **bhan*-[2]], v.i. 1. to buzz, to hum (as insects). 2. to ring (in the ear). 3. to speak nasally.

भनभनाहट *bhanbhanāhaṭ* [cf. H. *bhanbhanānā*], f. buzzing, &c. (= भिनभिन).

भनसाघर *bhansāghar* [? H. *bhansār*], m. reg. kitchen.

भनसार *bhansār* [-*āgāra*-], m. reg. oven, fireplace (= [1]भाँड़).

भनसाल *bhansāl* [*bhāṇḍaśālā*-], f. reg. storehouse, granary (= भँड़साल).

भनैजी *bhanaijī* [*bhāgineya*-; ? ← G. *bhā̆ṇejī*], f. Brbh. sister's daughter (= भानजी).

भन्नाना *bhannānā*, v.i. = भनभनाना.

भपाड़ा *bhapāṛā*, m. trickery, deception.

भपारा *bhapārā* [**bāṣpakāra*-], m. *Pl.* 1. steam, vapour. 2. steam bath, steaming. 3. fumigation.

भब्भड़ *bhabbhaṛ* [cf. **bhaṭ*-; ? × *bhram*-], f. m. 1. uproar, alarm; panic. 2. a turbulent crowd. — ~ पड़ना (में), to be alarmed, &c.; to take to flight. – भीड़-भब्भड़, f. turbulent crowd, turmoil.

भब्भल *bhabbhal*, adj. reg. fat.

भभक *bhabhak* [cf. H. *bhabhaknā*], f. 1. bursting or flaring out (as of flame, steam, water); exhaust. 2. suddenly or newly emitted smell; fumes.

भभकना *bhabhaknā* [cf. **bhabh*-], v.i. 1. to be heated up; to boil, to bubble. 2. to flare up. 3. to give off fumes. 4. to become angry or exasperated; to fume. 5. to be in full cry (a galloping horse, a raging tiger).

भभका *bhabhkā* [cf. H. *bhabhak*], m. 1. blast from a furnace. 2. a still.

भभकाना *bhabhkānā* [cf. H. *bhabhaknā*], v.t. 1. to cause to flare up, or to boil up. 2. to provoke. 3. to excite (as passions).

भभकी *bhabhkī* [cf. H. *bhabhaknā*], f. threat. — ~ में आना, to be influenced by a threat.

भभर- *bhabhar-* [cf. H. *bhabbhaṛ*], v.i. Brbh. Av. 1. to be anxious. 2. to be alarmed or frightened. 3. to be deluded.

भभूका *bhabhūkā*, adj. 1. blazing. 2. glowing (as a coal). 3. raging with anger. 4. shining; resplendent.

भभूत *bhabhūt* [ad. *vibhūti*], f. var. /bhəbrūt/. ashes of cow-dung (as rubbed on the body or the forehead by Śaiva devotees). — ~ मलना, or लगाना, or रमाना, to smear the body with ashes.

भयंकर *bhayaṅkar* [S.], adj. fearsome, terrible (= भयानक).

भय *bhay* [S.], m. fear; misgivings. ~ करना, to be afraid (of, से). ~ खाना (से), id. ~ दिखाना, or देना (को), to put in fear; to intimidate, to threaten. ~ लगना, fear to be felt. ~ होना, fear to be felt (by, को). – भयचक, adj. reg. astonished, alarmed (cf. भौचक). भय-भीत, adj. frightened, afraid. भयातुर [°ya+ā°], adj. fearful.

भयानक *bhayānak* [S.], adj. 1. fearsome, terrible; dangerous. 2. desolate (region).

भयावन *bhayāvan* [? f. H. डरावना], adj. Brbh. = भयानक.

भयावना *bhayāvănā*, adj. reg. = भयावन.

भयावह *bhayāvah* [S.], adj. = भयानक.

भयौ *bhayau* [cf. *bhavati*], v.i. perf. Brbh. = हुआ. — होत ~, was (= 'began and remained so': inceptive).

[1]**भर** *bhar* [cf. H. *bharnā*], adv. & pref. & m. 1. adv. the amount of; the whole of. 2. at most, just. 3. pref. (usu. w. verbal elements.) the amount of; the whole of. 4. m. load; bulk, size. — ~ पाना, to be paid in full; to be paid out, to get (one's) deserts. उमर ~, adv. all (one's) life, for the rest of (one's) life. क्षण ~ (के लिए), adv. for just a moment. दिन ~, adv. the whole day. पल ~, adv. = क्षण ~. पेट ~ खाना, to eat all that the stomach can hold. बाँस ~, adv. the height or length of a bamboo. – भरपाई, f.

receipt of, or for, payment in full. भरपूर, adj. quite full, filled up; completely finished; quite enough; high (tide); full (moon). °ई, f. भरपेट, m. & adv. eating one's fill; a stomachful, full meal; to the full. भरसक, adv. to the extent of one's ability; with all one's might.

²भर *bhar*, m. name of a *cāṇḍāl* community of U.P. and Bihar.

भरई *bharaī* [cf. H. *bharnā*], f. *hist.* an allowance made, or a tax levied, in the Banaras and Bareilly districts in connection with expenses of collecting revenue.

भरका *bharkā*, m. a light, arid soil.

भरण *bharaṇ* [S.], m. **1.** carrying. **2.** maintaining, nourishing; nurturing. **3.** filling, satisfying; payment, a wage. — भरण-पोषण, m. maintenance (of dependants).

भरणी *bharăṇī* [S.], f. *astron.* the second lunar mansion.

¹भरत *bharat* [S.], m. **1.** *mythol.* name of a younger brother of Rāma. **2.** *mythol.* name of several kings or princes. **3.** name of the supposed inaugurator of the theory of dramatic art. — भरत-खंड, m. *mythol.* the region of India (a division of the world).

²भरत *bharat* [ad. *bharadvāja-*], m. the small Indian skylark, *Alauda gulgula*.

³भरत *bharat* [cf. H. *bharnā*], ? f. m. reg. (W.) the full amount of revenue to be paid by a sharer in a coparcenary village.

⁴भरत *bharăt* [? cf. H. *bharnā*], m. an alloy of copper, zinc, and (?) tin or lead.

भरता *bhartā*, m. = भुरता.

भरतार *bhartār* [ad. *bhartāram*, acc.], m. = भर्ता.

भरतिया *bhartiyā* [cf. H. ⁴*bharat*], m. *Pl. HŚS.* a worker in copper-alloy (*bhart*).

भरती *bhartī* [cf. H. *bharnā*], f. **1.** a filling, stuffing, &c. **2.** cargo. **3.** store, stock. **4.** filling out (a form); entering, registering (in, में). **5.** admission (to any institution), enrolment; enlistment, recruiting; hiring (a servant). **6.** mobilisation. **7.** extra and irrelevant matter; embroidery (on facts). — ~ करना, to fill; to load; to store; to fill out, to enter; to enrol, to enlist, &c. ~ का, adj. everyday, average (in quality); nondescript.

भरन *bharan* [cf. H. *bharnā*], f. m. **1.** filling. **2.** a heavy shower.

¹भरना *bharnā* [*bharati*], v.i. & v.t. **1.** v.i. to be filled, to fill; to be full (of, से). **2.** to be finished, complete (as days, time). **3.** to abound (in, से); to be covered (with: as a table with books; or as the face with pock-marks). **4.** esp. with जाना. to be blocked up. **5.** to be loaded or charged (a firearm). **6.** to be loaded (a burden: on, पर). **7.** to be covered, clogged, coated (with, से). **8.** to be put or poured (into a container or space, so as to fill it wholly or partly: में); to be cast (in a mould). धान के खेत में पानी भरा हुआ है, the rice-field is full of water. बोतल में पानी भरा हुआ था the bottle had been filled with water. **9.** to be daubed, applied (as paint: to, में). **10.** to be paid, remitted (a full amount: as fees, tax); to be refunded, or made good (a loss). **11.** to fill, to ripen; to come to a head (as a boil). **12.** to fill out (the body). **13.** to heal (a wound). **14.** to swell (as the feet from walking). **15.** to be mated (a female animal); to conceive.**16.** to be satisfied. पेट ~, the stomach to be full. मन ~, to be satisfied (with, की तरफ़). **17.** (w. आना.) to be moved (by feelings, emotion). जी भर आना, the soul to be moved by compassion, or grief. आँखें भर आना, the eyes to well with tears. **18.** (w. जाना.) to be overcome. **19.** v.t. to fill (with, से). **20.** to perform. स्वाँग ~, to mimic. **21.** to complete, to live out (one's days). **22.** to bestow in abundance. **23.** to load (on to,पर, में). **24.** to coat liberally (with, से: as the feet with lac). **25.** to put or to pour (an object or substance into a container or space so as to fill it wholly or partly: में). गुब्बारे में हवा ~, to inflate a balloon; खिड़की में ईटें ~, to brick up a window; बाहों में ~, to embrace (one). **26.** to insert (into, में); to cram (in). लिफ़ाफ़े में चिट्ठी ~, to put a letter in an envelope. भूसा ~, to stuff with straw. **27.** to load (a firearm). **28.** to stow away (in, में); to hoard. **29.** to pay (a full amount: as fees, tax); to refund or to make good (a loss); to deposit (a pledge). **30.** Brbh. to steep, to soak (in, में). **31.** to daub, to apply (on or to, में); to paint; to paint a vivid or exaggerated picture (of). **32.** to wind, to twine (on, में). **33.** to give, to depose (evidence, &c). **34.** to pay (the penalty of); to suffer in full measure for. **35.** esp. w. लेना. to exact a payment (from, से). **36.** to satisfy. मन ~ (का), to give (one) pleasure or satisfaction. — भर लाना, to allow to well up (tears: to the eyes, में). गोद ~, the lap to be full: to have children (a mother).

²भरना *bharnā* [H. *bharnā*], m. a bribe.

भरनी *bharnī* [cf. H. *bharnā*], f. cross-threads, woof.

भरभंडा *bharbhaṇḍā*, m. reg. (E.) a kind of prickly plant having yellow cup-like flowers (= घमोय).

भरभराना *bharbharānā* [cf. H. *bharnā*], v.i. reg. to be puffy and inflamed (the skin, the eyes).

भरभराहट *bharbharāhaṭ* [cf. H. *bharbharānā*], f. swelling, inflammation.

भरम- *bhram-* [ad. *bhramati*], v.i. Brbh. **1.** to wander. **2.** to err.

भरमाना *bharmānā* [cf. H. *bhram*], v.t. & v.i. **1.** v.t. to cause to stray, to mislead; to deceive. **2.** to confuse; to tempt, to allure. **3.** to alarm. **4.** Brbh. v.i. to be confused, &c.

भरमार *bharmār* [H. *bharnā*+H. *mār(nā)*], f. abundance; bewildering variety.

भरमीला *bharmīlā*, adj. **1.** *Pl.* round; spherical. **2.** confusing; dubious (a matter).

भरवाई *bharvāī* [cf. H. *bharvānā*], f. **1.** act or process of having sthg. filled. **2.** cost of having filled. **1.** adj. filled, full, &c. **2.** m. fullness, filling: contents; load, cargo; charge (of firearm). — भरा-पूरा, adj. prosperous, thriving; happy (as a household); abounding (in); thriving (physically). लाज-भरा, adj. very modest or shy.

भराई *bharāī* [cf. H. *bharānā*], f. 1. = भरावट. **2.** price paid for filling, or stuffing.

भराना *bharānā* [cf. H. *bharnā*], v.t. **1.** to cause to be filled. **2.** to fill out (a form). **3.** to feed its young (a bird). **4.** to have made pregnant (a mare by a stallion).

भराव *bharāv* [cf. H. *bharnā, bharānā*], m. **1.** fullness. **2.** the act of filling; filling in spaces (as in embroidery). **3.** substance used in filling. **4.** reg. (W.) lintel.

भरावट *bharāvaṭ* [cf. H. *bharānā*], f. filling, stuffing (any substance so used).

भरित *bharit* [S.], adj. **1.** filled, full. **2.** nurtured.

[1]**भरिया** *bhariyā*, m. a porter.

[2]**भरिया** *bhariyā* [cf. H. *bharnā*], m. *Pl.* diked-in land watered by irrigation.

[1]**भरी** *bharī* f. the weight of a one-rupee coin.

[2]**भरी** *bharī*, f.*Pl.* a long grass (used for thatching).

भरुका *bharukā*, m. an earthen basin or pot.

भरोटा *bharoṭā*, m. *Pl. HŚS.* load (of grass, hay, &c).

भरोसा *bharosā* [**bharavaśya-*], m. **1.** reliance, confidence. **2.** faith; hope. — ~ करना, or रखना, to rely (on, पर); to have confidence. ~ दिलाना (को), to assure. ~ देना (को), to give hope; to reassure. भरोसे होना, to hope. वह किस भरोसे का है? what reliance can be placed on him? – भरोसेदार [P. *-dār*], adj. reliable, trustworthy. भरोसेमंद [P. *-mand*], adj. id.

भरौती *bharautī* [cf. H. *bharnā*], f. reg. = भरपाई, see s.v. [1]भर.

भर्जन *bharjan* [S.], m. roasting, frying.

भर्ता *bhartā* [S.], m. inv. **1.** lord, protector. ***2.** husband.

भर्तार *bhartār*, m. Brbh. = भतार.

भर्त्सना *bhartsănā* [S.], f. **1.** scolding; abuse. **2.** threat. — ~ करना (की), to scold, &c.

भर्त्सनीय *bhartsănīyă* [S.], adj. deserving censure or rebuke.

भर्रा *bharrā*, m. *Pl. HŚS.* alarm, panic; moment of fear.

भर्राटा *bharrāṭā*, m. a whirring, or rattling sound.

भर्राना *bharrānā*, v.i. to become hoarse or husky (the throat or voice).

भल *bhal*, m. reg. side, direction.

भल- *bhal-* [cf. H. *bhalā*], adj. good: – भलमनसत, f. = next. भलमनसाहत [?? × *sādhu-*] f. good or kindly nature; courteousness; honourableness. भलमनसाई, f. id. °-मनसी, f. = भलमनसाहत. भलमानुस, adj. = भलामानस.

भलका *bhalkā* [cf. *bhalla-*], m. E.H. an arrow-head (? crescent-shaped); pendant of a nose-ring.

भलभल *bhalbhal* [cf. H. *bhalbhalānā*], f. the sound of flowing or gushing water.

भलभलाना *bhalbhalānā*, v.i. to gush, to bubble.

भला *bhalā* [cf. *bhalla-*[1]], adj. & m. & interj. **1.** adj. good; excellent. **2.** honest, righteous. **3.** kind, kindly. **4.** in good health. **5.** m. welfare. **6.** advantage, benefit. **7.** interj. well! how lucky! **8.** indeed, in truth. — ~ करना, to do good (to, का); to act well; to prosper. ~ चाहना (का), to wish (one) well. ~ लगना, to appear or to look well; = अच्छा लगना. भली कही! well said! भले आइए! welcome! भले ही, adv. let it be the case: even if; it may well be (but). – भला-चंगा, adj. in good order or condition; = ~, 4. भला-बुरा, m. good and ill. भला-बुरा कहना, or सुनाना (को), to scold, to rail (at); to vilify. भलामानस, m. a good or kindly man; a courteous person; an honourable person; a person of rank; iron. a simpleton. भलामानुष, m. id.

भलाई *bhalāī* [cf. H. *bhalā*], f. **1.** goodness; excellence. **2.** kindness; humanity. **3.** benefit, profit. **4.** welfare. — ~ करना, to be good or kind (to, के साथ, से). — भलाई-बुराई, f. the good and the bad, pro and con.

भलापन *bhalāpan* [cf. H. *bhalā*], m. = भलाई.

भवंत *bhavant* [S.], m. Av. your honour, his honour, the lord (term of worshipful address or reference).

भव *bhav* [S.], m. **1.** existence, life. **2.** birth, origin. **3.** the world. **4.** a title of Śiva. — भव-चाप, m. Av. the bow of Śiva. भव-जाल, m. the snares of the world; worldly cares. भव-भामा, f. Av. title of Pārvatī. °-भामिनी, f. id. भव-भार, m. Brbh. wordly care(s). भव-भीर, m. Av. fear of rebirth in the world. भव-वारिधि, m. = भव-सागर. भव-विलास, m. worldly pleasures; illusory pleasures. भव-सागर, m. the ocean of life or of existence; the present life. भव-सिंधु, m. Av. id. भवांतर [°*va*+*a*°], m. Av. a preceding or following birth. भवांबु [°*va*+*a*°], m. Av. = भवसागर. °-नाथ, m. id.

भवन *bhavan* [S.], m. **1.** place of being or abode: building (esp. a public building); chamber (legislative); mansion; palace. **2.** coming to being, birth.

भवानी *bhavānī* [S.], f. a title of the goddess Pārvātī.

भवितव्य *bhavitavyă* [S.], adj. & m. **1.** adj. fated, destined. **2.** m. fate.

भवितव्यता *bhavitavyătā* [S.], f. Av. fate, destiny.

भविष्य *bhaviṣyă* [S.], adj. & m. **1.** adj. future. **2.** m. the future. **3.** *gram.* future tense. — भविष्य-काल, m. = भविष्य. भविष्य-निधि, f. provident fund. भविष्य-वक्ता, m. inv. foreteller of the future, prophet. भविष्य-वाणी, f. prophecy.

भविष्यत् *bhaviṣyat* [S.], adj. & m. = भविष्य.

भविष्यद्- *bhaviṣyad-* [S.], m. = भविष्य-. — भविष्यद्वक्ता, m. inv. = भविष्य-वक्ता. भविष्यद्वाणी, f. = भविष्य-वाणी.

भवैया *bhavaiyā* [? cf. H. *bhāv*], m. Brbh. dancer; story-teller.

भव्य *bhavyă* [S.], adj. **1.** likely or necessary to occur; proper, true. ***2.** splendid, magnificent. **3.** prosperous, happy,

भव्यता *bhavyătā* [S.], f. splendour, magnificence.

भसकना *bhasaknā* [? ad. *bhakṣayati*], v.t. to eat up, to devour.

भसक्कू *bhasakkū* [cf. H. *bhasaknā*], m. var. /bhəsəkko/. one who is always eating.

भसना *bhasnā* [*bhraśyati*], v.i. reg. **1.** to float, to be carried downstream. **2.** to be drowned.

भसभासा *bhasbhāsā*, adj. reg. loose, flabby.

भसाना *bhasānā* [cf. *bhraśyati*], v.t. reg. (E.) to cause to float; to launch.

भस्म *bhasm* [S.], m. ashes; cinders. — ~ करना, to reduce to ashes, to burn. ~ रमाना, to rub ashes on the body or forehead (a Śaiva ascetic). ~ होना, to be reduced to ashes; to be utterly destroyed. – भस्म-पत्ती, f. = भाँग. भस्मसात्, adj. reduced to ashes, consumed. भस्मावशेष [°*ma*+*ā*°], m. ashes remaining (after a fire or cremation). भस्मीकरण, m. burning to ashes; calcining. °ईकृत, adj. burned to ashes; calcined.

भस्मक *bhasmak* [S.], m. **1.** a chronically unsatisfied hunger. **2.** an eye complaint; unclear sight.

भस्मित *bhasmit* [S.], adj. reduced to ashes.

भस्मी *bhasmī* [S.: in comp.], f. corr. **1.** ashes; ashes of a corpse. **2.** *Pl.* cremation.

भस्मीकरण *bhasmīkaraṇ* [S.], m. see s.v. भस्म.

भस्मीकृत *bhasmīkr̥t* [S.], adj. see s.v. भस्म.

भहराना *bhahrānā*, v.i. **1.** Brbh. to totter, to stagger. **2.** to fall with a crash, to collapse.

भाँग *bhāṁg* [*bhaṅga-*[2]], m. **1.** hemp. **2.** a narcotic drink made from hemp leaves.

भाँज *bhāṁj* [cf. H. *bhāṁj-*], f. reg. **1.** twisting. **2.** a twist, turn, coil. **3.** a fold, wrinkle. **4.** small change.

भाँजना *bhāṁjnā* [*bhañjati*], v.t. **1.** to break; to destroy. **2.** to turn; to twist; to fold; to count (prayer-beads). **3.** to whirl, to brandish (as a sword).

भांजा *bhāṁjā*, m. = भानजा.

भाँजी *bhāṁjī* [**bhañjaka-*], f. **1.** interference, hindrance. **2.** malicious or slanderous remark. — ~ मारना, to interfere; to thwart; to make malicious remarks, &c.

भाँट *bhāṁṭ*, m. *Pl.* the medicinal plant *Clerodendron infortunatum*, or *Volkameria infortunata*.

भाँटा *bhāṁṭā* [conn. *bhaṇṭākī-*, Pa. *bhaṇḍākī-*], m. reg. the egg-plant.

[1]**भाँड़** *bhāṁṛ* [*bhāṇḍa-*[1]], m. **1.** earthenware vessel (= भाँड़ा). **2.** goods, wares. **3.** stock; capital.

[2]**भाँड़** *bhāṁṛ* [*bhāṇḍa-*[2]], m. **1.** jester, joker; buffoon. **2.** itinerant actor, mime.

भाँड़- *bhāṁṛ-* [*bhaṇḍate*], v.t. Brbh. **1.** to reproach. **2.** to abuse; to mock.

भाँड़ा *bhāṁṛā* [*bhāṇḍaka-*], m. earthenware vessel, pot. — ~ फूटना (का), to be revealed (a secret, a vice). ~ फोड़ना (का), to betray a secret. – भाँड़ा-फोड़, m. one who lets out a secret.

भांडार *bhāṇḍār*, m. = भंडार.

भांडारी *bhāṇḍārī*, m. = भंडारी.

भाँड़िन *bhāṁṛin* [cf. H. *bhāṁṛ*], f. actress, female mimic.

भांडीर *bhāṇḍīr* [S.], m. 19c. a fig-tree.

भाँड़ू *bhāṁṛū*, m. pej. = ²भाँड़, 2.

भाँड़ैत *bhāṁṛait* [cf. H. ²*bhāṁṛ*], m. an actor, mime.

भाँड़ैती *bhāṁṛaitī* [cf. H. *bhāṁṛait*], f. acting, miming.

भाँति *bhāṁti* [*bhakti-*¹ × *bhangī̆-* 'manner', &c.], f. **1.** way, manner. **2.** ppn. w. की. in the manner of, like. — ~ ~ के/की, adj. pl. various kinds (of). –भली-भाँति, adv. well, thoroughly, quite.

भाँपना *bhāṁpnā* [conn. *bhāpyate*], v.t. **1.** to conceive, to imagine; to understand. **2.** to guess; to see through (a disguise, &c).

भाँपू *bhāṁpū* [cf. H. *bhāṁpnā*], m. an astute or cunning person.

भाँव- *bhāṁv-* [*bhrāmayati*], v.t. Brbh. to turn (on a lathe); to form.

भाँवर *bhāṁvar* [*bhrāmarī-*], f. **1.** going or turning round. **2.** *hind.* circumambulation (of the sacred fire by bride and groom, five or seven times, at the conclusion of the marriage ceremony). — ~ पड़ना, or फिरना (कि)), a circuit, or circumambulation, to be made. ~ पाड़ना (की), to go round (an area, &c.); to circumambulate; to be married.

भाँवरि *bhāṁvări*, f. Brbh. Av. = भाँवर.

भाई *bhāī* [*bhrātṛ-*], m. **1.** brother. **2.** kinsman; cousin. चचेरा ~, m. cousin on father's side. ममेरा ~, m. cousin on mother's side. **3.** fellow-member of a group (as a class, or community); friend. **4.** friend (familiar term of address; may be applied to persons of either sex). — ~ सहाब, m. = बड़ा ~. बड़ा ~, m. elder brother. – भाईचारा, m. relationship; brotherly relationship or tie. °पन, id. °पूर्ण, adj. fraternal, friendly. भाईबंद [P. *-band*; ? × H. *bandhu*], m. relations; friends (see 3. above). °ई, f. = भाईचारा. भाई-बंधु, m. id.

भाईपन *bhāīpan* [cf. H. *bhāī*], m. brotherly relationship, brotherly terms or ties.

भाई-भिन्ना *bhāī-bhinnā*, m. reg. (W.) name of a festival held on the twelfth of the dark half of Bhādoṁ (= ओग-दुवास).

भाएँ-भाएँ *bhāeṁ-bhāeṁ*, f. ominous or fearsome sound; moaning of wind; mood of desolation. ~ ~ करना, to sound fearsome; to seem desolate.

भाकसी *bhāksī*, f. Brbh. oven, furnace.

भाकुर *bhākur* [conn. *bhākuṭa-*], m. reg. (Bihar) a kind of fish.

भाख- *bhākh-* [ad. *bhāṣate*], v.i. & v.t. Brbh. Av. = बोलना.

भाखा *bhākhā* [ad. *bhāṣā-*], f. = भाषा.

भागंभाग *bhāgambhāg*, m. = भागा-भाग (see s.v. ¹भागना).

भाग *bhāg* [S.], m. **1.** part; share; division; section. **2.** *math.* fraction. दो बटे पाँचवाँ ~, m. two-fifths. **3.** degree (of angle). **4.** *math.* division. ~ देना, to divide (into, में, by, का). **5.** fate, lot (= भाग्य). **6.** ? distribution, apportionment. — ~ करना, to divide (sthg., के) into parts or shares; to divide (sthg., को, by, से). ~ खुलना, or जागना, fortune to turn favourable. ~ फूटना (का), luck to break. ~ लगना, = ~ खुलना; *math.* to be divided. ~ लगाना, = ~ करना. ~ देना. ~ लेना, to take part (in, में), to be involved (in). – भागदार [P. *-dār*], m. a shareholder. भाग-फल, m. *arith.* quotient. भाग-बँटाई, f. allocation of shares, or portions.

भागड़ *bhāgaṛ*, m. reg. flight, escape; stampede.

भागनर *bhāgnar*, m. reg. (W). rich alluvial land on the banks of the Jumna in U.P.

¹**भागना** *bhāgnā* [cf. *bhagna-*¹], v.i. **1.** to run away, to flee. **2.** to run off, to vanish. **3.** to keep clear (of, से), to avoid (a task, &c). – भाग-दौड़, m. flight, stampede, panic. भागा-भाग, m. & adv. flight, stampede; helter-skelter.

²**भागना** *bhāgnā*, v.t. to be divided. — दस भागे दो बराबर पाँच, ten divided by two equals five.

भागलपुरी *bhāgalpurī* [cf. H. *bhāgalpur*], adj. & m. **1.** adj. having to do with or belonging to Bhagalpur. **2.** m. a kind of silk and cotton cloth, first made at Bhagalpur.

भागवत *bhāgăvat* [S.], m. & adj. **1.** adj. having to do with Bhagvat, or Viṣṇu. ***2.** m. the *Bhāgavata Purāṇa*. **3.** a devout Vaiṣṇava.

भागिनेय *bhāgineyă* [S.], m. sister's son, nephew.

भागी *bhāgī* [cf. H. *bhāg*], adj. & m. **1.** adj. sharing. **2.** participating. **3.** m. sharer; one having a share. **4.** partner. — भागीदार [P. *-dār*], m. = ~. °ई, f. participation, partnership.

भागीरथ *bhāgīrath* [S.], m. = भगीरथ.

भागीरथी *bhāgīrathī* [S.], f. *mythol.* a title of the river Ganges (supposed to have been brought down to earth by King Bhagīrath).

भागू *bhāgū*[cf. H. *bhāgnā*], m. deserter, absconder.

भाग्य *bhāgyă* [S.], m. **1.** fortune; fate; destiny. **2.** chance. — ~ का बली, m. one favoured by fortune. ~ में लिखा होना, to be written in (one's, के) fate. – भाग्यवाद, m. fatalism. भाग्यवान, adj. fortunate, lucky. भाग्यशाली, adj. id. भाग्य-संपन्न, adj. = भाग्यवान. भाग्यहीन, adj. unfortunate.

भाजक *bhājak* [S.], adj. & m. **1.** adj. dividing. **2.** m. *math.* divisor.

भाजन *bhājan* [S.], m. **1.** vessel, dish. **2.** worthy recipient (of favour, &c). **3.** *math.* division.

भाजना *bhājnā* [*bhajyate*], v.i. reg. = भागना.

भाजी *bhājī* [*bharjita-*], f. greens (esp. fried).

भाज्य *bhājyă* [S.], adj. & m. **1.** adj. to be divided. **2.** divisible. **3.** m. portion. **4.** *math.* dividend.

भाट *bhāṭ* [*bhaṭṭa-*[2]], m. **1.** name of a mixed caste of hereditary bards. **2.** bard; panegyrist. **3.** flatterer.

भाटन *bhāṭan* [cf. H. *bhāṭ*], f. **1.** woman of the *bhāṭ* caste. **2.** wife of a *bhāṭ*. **3.** female minstrel.

[1]**भाटा** *bhāṭā* [H. *bhāṭhā*], m. **1.** outward flow, ebb-tide. **2.** low tide.

[2]**भाटा** *bhāṭā*, m. the egg-plant.

भाठ *bhāṭh* [*bhraṣṭa-*], f. reg. soil deposited after a flood.

भाठा *bhāṭhā* [*bhraṣṭa-*], m. = [1]भाटा.

[1]**भाठी** *bhāṭhī* [cf. *bhraṣṭa-*], f. *Pl. HŚS.* current, stream; downstream.

[2]**भाठी** *bhāṭhī*, f. reg. = भाथी.

[1]**भाड़** *bhāṛ* [*bhrāṣṭra-*: Pk. *bhāḍa-*], m. oven for parching grain. — ~ झोंकना, to heat an oven, to feed the (oven) fire; to do menial work; to waste one's time. ~ में जाए, it (or he, she) can go to hell. ~ में झोंकना, or डालना, to throw into the oven, to burn up; to throw out or away; to consign to the devil. एक चने से ~ नहीं फूटता, fig. one swallow doesn't make a summer.

[2]**भाड़** *bhāṛ* [**bhārta-*: Pk. *bhāḍa-*], m. *Pl.* wages of prostitution. — ~ खाना, to live on the earnings of prostitution (the woman's dependants).

भाड़ा *bhāṛā* [**bhārta-*: Pk. *bhāḍaya-*], m. **1.** charge, levy; hire charge. ***2.** fare. **3.** freight charge. **4.** rental or lease charge. — ~ करना, to hire out; to take on hire. भाड़े का, adj. hired; rented, &c.; mercenary (a soldier). भाड़े का टट्टू, m. a hired pony; a hircling, hack. भाड़े पर देना, to hire out, &c. भाड़े पर रखना, or लेना, to hire; to rent, &c.

भाड़ू *bhāṛū* [**bhārta-*: MIA *bhāṭa-*], m. pej. **1.** a husband whose wife is unfaithful. **2.** a pimp, procurer.

भाड़ोती *bhāṛotī* [cf. **bhārtavṛtti-*], m. *Pl.* one who plies for hire.

भाण *bhāṇ* [S.], m. a Sanskrit literary form (taken over experimentally in Hindi in the 19th century) in which the events of a drama are narrated by a single speaker.

भात *bhāt* [*bhakta-*], m. **1.** boiled rice. **2.** a ceremony taking place on day of a marriage, in which the bridegroom's father is offered rice by family of the bride and presents are given to the bride.

भातई *bhātaī* [cf. H. *bhāt*], m. a giver of gifts, or of rice at the wedding ceremony called *bhāt*.

भाति *bhāti*, f. = भाँति.

भाथा *bhāthā* [*bhastrā-*], m. leather bag: **1.** quiver. **2.** bellows.

भाथी *bhāthī* [cf. *bhastrā-*], f. bellows.

भादवा *bhādvā* [*bhādrapada-*], m. = भादों.

भादों *bhādoṁ* [*bhādrapada-*], m. the sixth month of the Indian lunar calendar (mid-August to mid-September). — ~ की भरन, f. heavy August rains (which fill tanks, and flood fields).

भाद्र *bhādră* [S.], m. = भादों. — भाद्रपद, m. = भादों. °आ, f. *astron.* name shared by the third and fourth lunar asterisms.

भान *bhān* [*bhāna-*[1]], m. **1.** appearance. **2.** consciousness (of, का); recollection. 3. = भानु, 2.

भान- *bhān-* [cf. **bhanna-*, for *bhagna-*[1]], v.t. Brbh. Av. to break.

भानजा *bhānjā* [*bhāgineya-*], m. sister's son, nephew.

भानजी *bhānjī* [cf. H. *bhānjā*], f. sister's daughter, niece.

भानना *bhānnā* [conn. **bhṛgṇa-*], v.t. esp. in comp. = भूनना.

भानमती *bhānmatī* [? cf. H. *bhān*], f. **1.** sorceress. **2.** female juggler, conjuress. — ~ का कुनबा, m. witch's family: weird assortment. ~ की पिटारी, f. witch's box: id.

भाना *bhānā* [*bhāti*], v.i. **1.** to be approved of, or liked (by, को); to seem good (to). **2.** to suit, to fit (clothes). — भावै...भावै, Av. whether...or. फूटी आँखों नहीं ~, fig. to be thoroughly disliked (a person : by, को).

भा- *bhā-* [*bhāpayate*], v.t. **1.** Av. to cause to shine (as gold, or polished metal). **2.** to make (sthg.) beautiful.

भानु *bhānu* [S.], m. **1.** the sun. **2.** brightness, light; ray.

भाप *bhāp* [**bhāṣpa-*], m. steam; vapour; fumes.

भाफ *bhāph* [**bhāṣpa-*], m. = भाप.

भाबर *bhābar*, m. **1.** *Pl. HŚS.* a grass found in drier districts, from which rope is made. **2.** *Pl.* a nettle, *Girardinia zeylanica*, a source of fibre. **3.** *Pl.* a light black soil.

भाभी *bhābhī*, f. var. /bhabi/. elder brother's wife; sister-in-law.

भाम *bhām*, f. Brbh. = भामा.

भामा *bhāmā*[S.], f. a woman; a passionate or angry woman.

भामिनी *bhāminī* [S.], f. = भामा.

भामी *bhāmī* [S.], adj. *Pl. HŚS.* passionate; indignant.

भार *bhār* [*bhāra-*], m. **1.** load, burden. **2.** weight. **3.** charge, responsibility. — ~ उठाना, to lift a burden; to take up a responsibility. ~ उतारना (का), to set down a load; to throw off a responsibility; to deliver (from), to redeem. — भार-क्षम, adj. able to carry a burden; equal to a responsibility. भार-ग्रस्त, adj. burdened; oppressed. भार-भूत, adj. become a burden, burdensome. भारवाह, m. = next. भार-वाहक, adj. & m. carrying a load; a porter. °-वाहन, m. carrying a load; transportation, freightage. ° वाही, adj. = भारवाहक; bearing an (electric) charge. भारहीन, adj. weightless. °ता, f. भाराक्रांत [°*ra*+*ā*°], adj. burdened.

भारत *bhārat* [S.], m. belonging to or relating to the Bharatas: **1.** India. **2.** the *Mahābhārata*. — ~ सरकार, f. the Indian Government. – भारत-रत्न, m. Jewel of India: the highest decoration awarded by the Indian state. भारतवर्ष, m. region of Bharata: India. °ईय, adj. °ई, adj. corr. id. भारत-वासी, adj. & m. resident in India; a citizen of India.

भारती *bhārătī* [S.], f. **1.** a title of the goddess Sarasvatī. **2.** speech.

भारतीय *bhārătīyă* [S.], adj. & m. **1.** adj. Indian. **2.** m. an Indian. — ~ आर्य भाषा, f. an Indo-Aryan language. – भारतीयकरण, m. Indianisation.

भारतीयकरण *bhārătīyăkaraṇ* [S.], m. see s.v. भारतीय.

भारतीयता *bhārătīyătā* [S.], f. characteristically Indian quality or qualities, Indianness.

भारथ *bhārath* m. Brbh. Av. = भारत, 2.; war, battle.

[1]**भारा** *bhārā* [*bhāraka-*], m. reg. **1.** a load. **2.** scaffolding.

[2]**भारा** *bhārā* [*bhāra-*], adj. Brbh. Av. = भारी.

भारी *bhārī* [*bhārika-*[2]], adj. **1.** heavy. **2.** massive; vast; crowded (a gathering). **3.** great, grand, vast; high (as hopes); large, great (as an amount, an expense); momentous (as a topic). **4.** burdensome, difficult; grave (a responsibility, a problem); grievous (as a blow); dire (danger, disease); tiresome; oppressive (as climate). **5.** of weight or substance (as an authority, proof, evidence). **6.** precious, valuable. **7.** heavy, sluggish (as the head, the energies); slow (of pace). **8.** loud-sounding; deep (voice); hoarse. **9.** burdened, dejected. — ~ पड़ना, to outweigh; to be burdensome (to, को). ~ रहना, to remain quiet (as being burdened, or inhibited). ~ लगना, to weigh heavily (on, को), to be tedious. ~ होना, to be heavy, or burdensome, or a trial (to, पर); to be dejected; to weigh heavier (than, पर), to preponderate, or to be superior (to). पाँव, or पैर, ~ होना, to be pregnant. – भारी-भरकम, adj. massive, vast; grave, weighty; solemn; precious; long-suffering.

भारीपन *bhārīpan* [cf. H. *bhārī*], m. heaviness, weightiness, &c.

भारोपीय *bhāropīyă* [H. *bhāratīya*+H. *yūropī*], adj. neol. Indo-European.

भार्या *bhāryā* [S.], f. wife.

[1]**भाल** *bhāl* [*bhallī-*[1]], f. **1.** arrow-head. 2. = भाला. — भालदार [P. *-dār*], m. spearman; lancer.

[2]**भाल** *bhāl* [*bhāla-*[1]], m. **1.** the forehead. **2.** light, lustre.

भालना *bhālnā* [*bhālayate*], v.t. see s.v. देखना.

भाला *bhālā*[*bhalla-*[3]], m. **1.** spear, lance. **2.** reg. (W.) a heavy wooden rake. — ~ मारना, to spear. – भालाबरदार [P. *-bardār*], m. spearman; lancer.

भालू *bhālū*[*bhallūka-*[1]], m. bear.

भालैत *bhālait* [cf. H. *bhāl(ā)*], m. spearman.

भाव *bhāv* [S.], m. **1.** being, existence. **2.** natural state, character or quality; disposition, temperament. **3.** way, manner. गंभीर ~ से, adv. seriously. **4.** intention, purpose. **5.** meaning, purport. **6.** *astron.* aspect (of heavenly bodies). **7.** mind, heart, soul. **8.** emotion, feeling; instinctive good-will; implicit belief; inclination. **9.** notion, idea. **10.** outward indication of emotion or meaning;

expression; gesticulation. **11.** *gram.* mood. **12.** price; going rate, rate of exchange. — ~ चढ़ना, a price to rise. ~ बढ़ाना, to raise the price or value (of, का). ~ बताना, to display the feelings (in singing or dance); to gesticulate. - भाव-गति, f. intention, attitude. भाव-चेतना, f. sensibility; attitude; disposition. भावज्ञ, adj. perceptive of thoughts, feelings &c., sensitive. भाव-ताव, m. price; nature, quality. भाव-ताव करना, to bargain, to haggle. भाव-प्रवण, adj. inclined to be emotional, sentimental. °ता, f. sentimentality; sensibility. भाव-प्रधान, adj. & m. characterised by feeling or emotion; *gram.* impersonal (a verb). भाव-भंगी, f. = ~, 10.; partic. manner, mannerism. भावमय, adj. full of feeling, &c. भाववाचक, adj. & m. abstract; an abstract noun. °-वाची, id. °-वाच्य, m. *gram.* an impersonal form. भाववादी, adj. & m. expressionist. भाव-सत्ता, f. independent existence. भावहीन, adj. emotional, dispassionate. भावार्थ [°*va*+*a*°], m. implied meaning (as of a verse). भावावेश [°*va*+*ā*°], m. access of emotion, frenzy; emotionality. भावानुवाद [°*va*+*a*°], m. free translation. भावात्मक [°*va*+*a*°], adj. full of feeling; aware; free (a rendering). भावांतर [°*va*+*a*°], m. change of mood, emotion, &c. भावोद्गार [°*va*+*u*°], m. impulse of emotion. भावोद्रेक [°*va*+*u*°], m. = भावावेश. – भावे-प्रयोग, m. impersonal construction (of a verb).

भाव- *bhāv-* [*bhāpayate*], v.i. Brbh. Av. = [1]भाना, 1.

भावक *bhāvak* [S.], adj. Brbh. **1.** moved by feeling, devoted. **2.** adv. a little.

भावज *bhāvaj* [*bhrāturjāyā-*], f. elder brother's wife.

भावतो *bhāvato* [cf. H. *bhāv-*], adj. & m. Brbh. (Av.) **1.** adj. liked, loved. **2.** m. beloved.

भावन *bhāvan* [S.], m. *Pl. HŚS.* creator, cause; founder.

भावना *bhāvănā* [S.], f. causing to be: **1.** perception, consciousness. **2.** feeling; mood; spirit; morale. **3.** mental process; recollection; imagination; premonition. **4.** thought; meditation. **5.** desire. — भावनात्मक [°*nā*+*ā*°], adj. emotional; spiritual. भावनाहीन, adj. dispassionate.

भावली *bhāvlī* [cf. *bhāva-*], f. **1.** distribution of the crop between landlord and tenant in proportions previously agreed. **2.** rent paid in kind.

भाविक *bhāvik* [S.], adj. & m. **1.** natural, innate. **2.** having to do with feeling, sentimental. **3.** pertaining to the future.

भावित *bhāvit* [S.], adj. **1.** thought, reflected upon. **2.** animated, inspired (by). **3.** anxious, apprehensive.

भाविनी *bhāvinī* [S.], f. a distinguished-looking woman.

भावी *bhāvī* [S.], adj. & f. m. **1.** adj. future. **2.** predestined. **3.** f. m. the future; fate. — ~ बस, adv. Av. under the influence of (one's) fate, as fated.

भावुक *bhāvuk* [S.], adj. **1.** sentimental. **2.** sensitive, impressionable. **3.** reflective, thoughtful.

भावुकता *bhāvukătā* [S.], f. sentimentality, &c.

भाव्य *bhāvyă* [S.], adj. & m. **1.** adj. about to come to pass, future. **2.** possible; probable. **3.** m. the future.

भाषण *bhāṣaṇ* [S.], m. **1.** a speech; a lecture; talk. **2.** speaking, utterance, speech. — ~ करना, or देना, to make or to give a speech, &c. – भाषण-कर्ता, m. inv. speaker, &c.

भाषा *bhāṣā* [S.], f. **1.** language, speech. **2.** a language; a dialect. **3.** vernacular usage (as distinct from a classical or semi-classical standard). — भाषांतर [°*ṣā*+*a*°], m. translation. °-कार, m. translator. भाषाकृत, adj. determined linguistically (an area). भाषागत, adj. expressed in language; linguistic; oral. भाषात्मक [°*ṣā*+*ā*°], adj. linguistic in character. भाषापरक, adj. linguistic. भाषाबद्ध, adj. expressed in language, or in a vernacular; put down in writing. भाषावाद, m. adherence to a viewpoint about languages and their use. भाषावार [P. *-vār*], adj. linguistic. भाषा-विज्ञान, m. linguistics. °ई, m. linguist. भाषाविद्, m. one versed in a language or languages, a linguist. भाषा-वेत्ता, m. inv. id. भाषा-वैज्ञानिक, adj. & m. having to do with linguistics, linguistic; a linguist. भाषाशास्त्र, m. = भाषा-विज्ञान. °ई, m. भाषा-स्वातंत्र्य, m. freedom of speech.

भाषाई *bhāṣāī* [cf. H. *bhāṣā*], adj. having to do with language(s), linguistic.

भाषिक *bhāṣik* [S.], adj. having to do with language, linguistic.

भाषिकी *bhāṣikī* [S.], f. linguistics.

भाषित *bhāṣit* [S.], adj. **1.** uttered, voiced. **2.** spoken, colloquial (style).

-भाषी *-bhāṣī* [S.], adj. & m. f. speaking, a speaker (of a language).

भाष्य *bhāṣyă* [S.], m. exposition, commentary. — भाष्यकार, m. commentator.

भास *bhās* [S.], m. **1.** shining, radiance. **2.** gleam; gleam of thought, inkling.

भासना *bhāsnā* [*bhāsati*], v.i. to appear, to be known.

भासित *bhāsit* [S.], adj. **1.** resplendent. **2.** evident.

भासुर *bhāsur* [S.], adj. & m. **1.** adj. shining, splendid. **2.** m. crystal. **3.** a hero.

भास्कर *bhāskar* [S.], adj. & m. **1.** adj. shining, radiant. **2.** m. the sun; fire.

भास्वर *bhāsvar* [S.], adj. shining, radiant (= भास्कर).

भिंगाना *bhiṁgānā*, v.t. = भिगोना.

भिंचना *bhiṁcnā* [conn. H. *bhīcna*], v.i. **1.** to be broken, or split, into pieces; to crumble. **2.** to shrivel. **3.** to be contracted (as the mouth, the eyes). **4.** to be coerced, compelled.

भिंड *bhiṇḍ* [conn. **bhiṇḍa-*], m. reg. (E.) embanked ground round a tank.

भिंडा *bhiṇḍā*, m. *Pl.* lump, mass; block.

भिंडी *bhiṇḍī* [cf. *bhiṇḍā-*], f. the plant called lady's-fingers (*Hibiscus esculentus*: its fruit is eaten as a vegetable from about August to November).

भिंदिपाल *bhindipāl* [S.], m. poet. a weapon for throwing, or a sling.

भिक्षा *bhikṣā* [S.], f. **1.** begging. **2.** alms; begged food. — **भिक्षा-वृत्ति**, f. living by begging. **भिक्षाटन** [°*kṣā+a*°], m. going about begging.

भिक्षु *bhikṣu* [S.], m. a beggar; a holy man living by begging alms.

भिक्षुक *bhikṣuk* [S.], m. = भिक्षु.

भिक्षुकी *bhikṣukī* [S.], f. **1.** a female beggar. **2.** a Buddhist nun.

भिक्षुणी *bhikṣuṇī* [S.], f. = भिक्षुकी.

भिखमँगा *bhikhmaṁgā* [H. *bhīkh*+H. *māṁgnā*], m. beggar.

भिखारिन *bhikhārin* [cf. H. *bhikhārī*], f. a female beggar.

भिखारी *bhikhārī* [**bhikṣācārin-*; Ap. *bhiccāri-*], m. beggar.

भिगवाना *bhigvānā* [cf. H. *bhīgnā*], v.t. to cause to be soaked or moistened (by, से); to soak, &c.

भिगाना *bhigānā*, v.t. = भिगोना.

भिगोना *bhigonā* [cf. H. *bhīgnā*], v.t. to wet; to soak; to steep. — **भिगो-भिगोके मारना**, or **लगाना**, to pay mocking respects; to beat soundly.

भिचना *bhicnā*, v.i. = भिंचना.

भिजवाना *bhijvānā* [cf. H. *bhejnā*], v.t. to cause to be sent (by, से).

[1]**भिजाना** *bhijānā* [cf. H. *bhiṁjnā*], v.t. = भिगोना.

[2]**भिजाना** *bhijānā* [cf. H. *bhejnā*], v.t. to cause to be sent (= भिजवाना).

भिटना *bhiṭnā* [cf. H. *bheṁṭna*]. v.i. to come into contact (with, से).

भिटनी *bhiṭnī*, f. reg. nipple (of a woman's breast).

भिड़ंत *bhiṛant* [cf. H. *bhiṛnā*], f. a clash.

भिड़ *bhiṛ*, f. **1.** a wasp; hornet. — **~ के छत्ते में हाथ डालना**, to stir up dire trouble for oneself. **सोती भिड़ों को जगाना**, to rouse sleeping wasps: to stir up a hornets' nest.

भिड़ना *bhiṛnā* [**bhiṭ-*: Pk. *bhiḍaï*], v.i. **1.** to come close; to meet, to join. **2.** to slam (a door). **3.** to clash, to grapple (opponents); sl. to have sex (with, से). **4.** to collide (as vehicles).

भिड़ाई *bhiṛāī* [cf. H. *bhiṛānā*], f. **1.** contact. **2.** closing together. **3.** collision, shock.

भिड़ाना *bhiṛānā* [cf. H. *bhiṛnā*], v.t. **1.** to bring together, to join. **2.** to close (a door). **3.** to knock together; to cause to fight. **4.** transf. to use, to deploy. **जुगत ~**, to employ ingenuity.

भित्ति *bhitti* [S.], f. **1.** wall. **2.** fragment. **3.** foundation, base. — **भित्ति-चित्र**, m. wall-painting.

भिदना *bhidna* [cf. H. *bhednā*], v.i. to be pierced.

भिनकना *bhinaknā* [cf. **bhin-*], v.i. **1.** to buzz, to hum (as insects); to swarm (insects: over sthg., पर). **2.** to feel revulsion (the soul, spirit). **भिनका चेहरा**, m. a nasty expression of the face. **3.** to be dirty or filthy. **4.** to sit idle, to have nothing to do.

भिनभिन *bhinbhin* [cf. H. *bhinbhinānā*], f. **1.** buzzing, humming (as of insects). **2.** ringing (in the ears).

भिनभिनाना *bhinbhinānā* [cf. **bhin-*], v.i. 1. = भनभनाना. **2.** to swarm (= भिनकना). **3.** to feel nausea.

भिनभिनाहट *bhinbhināhaṭ* [cf. H. *bhinbhinānā*], f. buzzing, &c. (भिनभिन).

भिनसार *bhinsār*, m. dawn.

भिनसारा *bhinsārā*, m. = भिनसार.

भिन्न *bhinn* [S.], adj. & m. **1.** adj. divided, separated; separate. **2.** distinct, different; other. **3.** split, broken. **4.** open (a flower). **5.** m. a fraction. — **भिन्न-गोत्र**, adj. & m. f. not belonging to the same *gotra*; a person of different *gotra*. भिन्न-वर्ण, adj. & m. of different colour; of different community group, or caste; a man of different community, &c.

भिन्नता *bhinnătā* [S.], f. **1.** separateness; difference, distinction. **2.** dissimilarity.

भिन्नाना *bhinnānā* [cf. *bhin-], v.i. 1. = भनभनाना. **2.** to feel dizzy or faint (as at a bad smell). **3.** to be fearful (of).

भिलावाँ *bhilāvām̐* [*bhallāta-*], m. the marking-nut tree, *Semecarpus anacardium* (source of a black dye, and of a varnish).

भिल्लिनि *bhillini* [cf. *bhilla-*], f. Av. a Bhīl woman.

भिश्ती *bhiśtī* [P. *bihiśtī*], m. euph. a water-carrier.

भिषज *bhiṣaj* [S.], m. a doctor.

भिष्टा *bhiṣṭā* [ad. *viṣṭā-*], f. corr. excrement.

भिस *bhis* [*bhisa-: Pa. *bhisa-*], ? m. reg. the edible root of the lotus.

भिसलना *bhisalnā*, v.i. reg. to be dazzled (the sight).

भींगना *bhīṁgnā*, v.t. pronun. var. = भीगना.

भींच *bhīṁc* [cf. H. *bhīṁcnā*], f. **1.** squeezing, &c. **2.** miserliness. — ~ करना, to behave in a miserly way.

भींचना *bhīṁcnā* [cf. *bhicc-], v.t. **1.** to press, to squeeze; to wring; to hold tightly. **2.** to close tightly; to clench (the fists).

भींजना *bhīṁjnā* [*bhiyañjati: Pk. *bhiṁjā-*], v.i. = भीगना.

भी *bhī* [conn. *api*], adv. & conj. encl. **1.** also; too. आप ~? you too? **2.** as much as, even. अब ~, even now, still. एक ~ नहीं, not even one. **3.** besides, additionally; still. और~ बड़ा, still larger. **4.** furthermore. मैं यह ~ कह सकता हूँ कि … I can say further that…. **5.** of any quantity or identity. कुछ ~ हो, whatever it may be. **6.** by any means, by all means; at all events. चलिए ~! do come on, come on then! उसे रहने ~ दो, do leave that alone. — ~…~, conj. both…and. तो ~, adv. but even so.

भीख *bhīkh* [*bhikṣā-*], f. **1.** begging. **2.** alms. — ~ का ठीकरा, m. begging-bowl. ~ माँगना, to beg (from, से).

भीगना *bhīgnā* [cf. *bhiyagna-], v.i. to be wet; to be damp; to be soaked. — भीगी बिल्ली, f. a wet cat: a timid, wretched person; a quiet, crafty person. भीगी बिल्ली बनना, to behave abjectly. भीगी रात, f. the later, colder part of the night.

भीज- *bhīj-* [*bhiyajyate], v.i. Brbh. to be wet (= भीगना).

भीटा *bhīṭā* [*bhiṭṭa-], m. **1.** mound, hillock. **2.** embanked or sloping ground.

भीठा *bhīṭhā* [conn. *bhr̥ṣṭa-*[2], Pa. *bhaṭṭha-*]. reg. (Bihar) a light soil.

भीड़ *bhīṛ* [*bhīṭ-: Pk. *bhīḍaï*], f. **1.** a crowd, crush. **2.** transf. great quantity (of work, or troubles). — ~ पड़ना, to be overwhelmed with troubles, misfortunes. ~ लगना, a crowd to collect. ~ लगाना, or करना, to crowd, to throng. – भीड़-भड़क्का, m. = next. भीड़-भाड़, f. crowd, &c.

[1]**भीत** *bhīt* [*bhitti-*], f. **1.** a wall; partition. **2.** an embankment. — बालू की ~, f. wall of sand: ill-conceived basis (as for plans).

[2]**भीत** *bhīt* [S.], adj. frightened, afraid.

भीतर *bhītar* [*bhiyantara-: Pk. *bhittara-*], adv. & ppn. **1.** adv. inside, within. **2.** contained, included (in). **3.** in the mind, to oneself (of thought, emotions). **4.** ppn. w. के. inside, &c. — ~ आना, to come in. ~ का, adj. inner; internal. – भीतर-बाहर, adv. inside and outside; half in, half out.

भीतरिया *bhītariyā* [*bhiyantarika-: Pk. *abbhiṁtaria-*], m. f. one having access to within: **1.** a family member; member of a household. **2.** an inmate. **3.** guest (specif. at a wedding, where he or she eats with the bride's relatives). **4.** one privy to a secret; member of an inner group; reg. (Bihar) temple *pujārī*.

भीतरी *bhītrī* [cf. H. *bhītar*], adj. **1.** inner, internal; close (a friend); acute (an angle). **2.** hidden, secret. **3.** worn next to the body (an undergarment).

भीति *bhīti* [S.], f. fear; alarm.

भीतौरी *bhītaurī* [cf. *bhittivāṭa-], f. reg. ground rent paid for the site of a house (by resident tradesmen).

भीना *bhīnā* [cf. *bhiyagna-: MIA *bhinna-], adj. **1.** wet, moist. **2.** light (colour, smell, breeze).

भीनना *bhīnnā* [cf. H. *bhīnā*], v.i. = *bhīgnā*.

भीम *bhīm* [S.], adj. & m. **1.** adj. fearsome, terrible. **2.** vast. **3.** m. *mythol.* name of the second son of Paṇḍu. — भीम-राज, m. the racket-tailed drongo. भीम-सेनी, f. a Malaysian tree, *Dryobalanops aromatica*, which yields a coarse camphor.

भीमता *bhīmătā* [S.], f. Brbh. fearsomeness.

भीरु *bhīru* [S.], adj. **1.** timid. **2.** cowardly.

भीरुता *bhīrutā* [S.], f. **1.** timidity. **2.** cowardliness.

भील *bhīl* [*bhilla-*], m. **1.** name of a tribal people of central India. **2.** a man of that people.

भीलनी *bhīlnī* [cf. H. *bhīl*; Av. *bhillini*], f. reg. a Bhīl woman.

भीषण *bhīṣaṇ* [S.], adj. **1.** terrible, fearsome; awesome. **2.** desolate (as a forest).

भीषा *bhīṣā* [S.], f. *Pl. HŚS.* fear; intimidation.

भीष्म *bhīṣm* [S.], adj. & m. **1.** adj. terrible; fearsome. **2.** m. horror. **3.** a goblin, demon. **4.** *mythol.* name of the grand-uncle of the Pāṇḍavas, and son of the Ganges. — **भीष्माष्टमी** [°*ma+a*°], f. the eighth day of the light half of the month Māgh (when a festival honouring Bhīṣma is held).

भीस *bhīs* [conn. **bhisa-*: Pa. *bhisa-*], m. reg. (W.) edible root of the lotus (= भिस).

भुंगा *bhuṅgā* [? *bhujaṅga-*], m. *Pl.* the black drongo (cf. भुजंग, 2).

भुँजना *bhuṁjnā* [*bhuñjate*], v.t. to enjoy (= भुगतना).

भुंजा *bhuñjā*, m. parched grain (= भुजना).

भुंड- *bhuṇḍ-* [**bhuṇḍa-*[1]], adj. reg. inauspicious. — भुंडपैरा, adj. whose steps are unlucky (a person).

भुँडरी *bhuṁḍrī*, f. *hist.* = भूँदरी.

भुंडली *bhuṇḍlī*, f. *Pl. HŚS.* a partic. hairy caterpillar, the palmer-worm.

भुअंगिनि *bhuaṅgini*, f. Av. = भुजंग, 1.

भुआ *bhuā*, m. Av. = [2]भूआ, 1.

भुईं *bhuīṁ* [*bhūmi-*], f. land, &c. (= भूमि). — ~ आँवला, m. an annual plant, *Sesbania aculeata*, the source of a fibre. – भुईंहार, m. see s.v.

भुईंहार *bhuīṁhār* [**bhūmihāra-*], m. name of a community of cultivators (chiefly of Bihar).

भुकभुकाना *bhukbhukānā*, v.i. = भकभकाना.

भुक्त *bhukt* [S.], adj. **1.** enjoyed; eaten. **2.** possessed. **3.** experienced, suffered. **4.** paid, cashed (as a cheque).

भुक्ति *bhukti* [S.], f. **1.** enjoyment, eating. **2.** possession. **3.** payment, encashment.

भुखमरी *bhukhmarī* [H. *bhūkh*, *marnā*], f. starvation.

भुगतना *bhugatnā* [ad. *bhukta-*], v.t. **1.** to experience: to suffer, to endure; (esp. iron.) to enjoy. **2.** to pay for, to work out (as past sin). **3.** to bear (an expense).

भुगतमान *bhugatmān* [ad. *bhukta-*; ? × **bhuktavāna-*], adj. *Pl.* fit to enjoy; deserving punishment.

भुगतान *bhugtān* [cf. H. *bhugtānā*], m. **1.** full payment, paying off (a loan or charge); sum due. **2.** a fine. **3.** reg. (Bihar) a bill of exchange. — नक़द ~, m. payment by cash.

भुगताना *bhugtānā* [cf. H. *bhugatnā*], v.t. **1.** to cause to be carried out; to perform, to discharge (a function); to complete. **2.** to settle, to pay off (a debt, a loan). **3.** to spend, to take (time: in doing sthg., में). **4.** to cause to experience: to cause to suffer or to undergo; (esp. iron.) to cause to enjoy. **5.** to distribute, to apportion.

[1]**भुग्गा** *bhuggā*, adj. stupid.

[2]**भुग्गा** *bhuggā*, m. a sweet made from crushed sesame seeds.

भुच्च *bhucc* [**bhucca-*], adj. & m. **1.** adj. rough, uncouth. **2.** stupid. **3.** m. an uncouth, or stupid person.

भुच्चड़ *bhuccaṛ* [cf. H. *bhucc*], adj. = भुच्च.

भुजंग *bhujaṅg* [S.], m. & adj. moving by bending: **1.** m. a snake; specif. cobra. **2.** name of several birds: the black drongo or king crow; the white-bellied drongo; ? a shrike. **3.** adj. black, jet-black. — काला ~, adj. = ~.

भुजंगा *bhujaṅgā* [cf. H. *bhujaṅg*], m. = भुजंग. — भुजंगे उड़ाना, to be in dire poverty; to spread harmful stories.

भुजंगी *bhujaṅgī* [cf. H. *bhujaṅgā*], f. a female snake.

भुज *bhuj* [S.], m. **1.** the arm; the upper arm. **2.** *math.* side (of any figure). — भुज-दंड, m. arm-staff: muscular arm. भुज-पाश, m. the enfolding arms, embrace. भुज-बंद {P. *-band*], m. armlet. भुज-बल, m. strength of arm, bodily strength. भुज-मूल, m. upper arm near the shoulder.

भुजना *bhujnā* [cf. *bhṛjjati*], m. parched or roasted grain.

भुजिया *bhujiyā* [**bhṛjjita-*: Pk. *bhujjiya-*], f. **1.** roasted rice or grain. ***2.** roasted vegetables.

भुट्टा *bhuṭṭā* [*bhṛṣṭa-*[1]], m. **1.** an ear of corn; a roasted corn-cob. **2.** corn, maize. **3.** a cluster (as of gems). — भुट्टा-सा, adj. stumpy, smallish. भुट्टा-सा उड़ना, to fly off (when hit), to be cut clean off.

भुट्टू *bhuṭṭū*, m. reg. corn-head: blockhead, fool.

भुतना *bhutnā*, m. dimin. devil; goblin; ghost.

भुतनी *bhutnī*, f. demoness; hag (= भूतनी).

भुतरा *bhutrā* [**bhuttara-*], adj. blunt (= भोथरा).

भुतहा *bhutāhā* [cf. H. *bhūt*], adj. var. /bhutaha/. **1.** possessed or inhabited by an evil spirit, bewitched. **2.** fiendish; fierce. **3.** peevish.

भुतियाना *bhutiyānā* [cf. H. *bhūt*], v.i. to become like a devil, to rage.

भुनगा *bhungā* [*bhṛṅgaka-*], m. a kind of insect, or wasp.

भुनचट्टी *bhuncaṭṭī*, f. a partic. small river fish.

[1]**भुनना** *bhunnā* [cf. H. *bhūnnā*], v.i. **1.** to be roasted, parched. **2.** to be fried.

[2]**भुनना** *bhunnā* [cf. *bhagna-*[1]; Pk. *bhagga-*, repl. by **bhanna-*], v.i. to be changed (money).

भुनभुनाना *bhunbhunānā* [cf. H. [1]*bhunnā*], v.i. to rage; to fume.

[1]**भुनवाई** *bhunvāī* [cf. H. [1]*bhunvānā*], f. price paid for parching grain.

[2]**भुनवाई** *bhunvāī* [cf. H. [2]*bhunvānā*], f. discount on exchange (of money).

[1]**भुनवाना** *bhunvānā* [cf. H. *bhūnnā*], v.t. to cause to be fried, or parched (by, से).

[2]**भुनवाना** *bhunvānā* [cf. H. [2]*bhunnā*], v.t. to get changed (money: by, से); to change.

[1]**भुनाई** *bhunāī* [cf. H. [1]*bhunānā*], f. price paid for parching grain.

[2]**भुनाई** *bhunāī* [cf. H. [2]*bhunānā*], f. **1.** exchange of money. **2.** discount on exchange.

[1]**भुनाना** *bhunānā* [cf. H. *bhūnnā*], v.t. **1.** to cause to be fried, or parched (by, से). **2.** transf. to inflame (a mood, &c.)

[2]**भुनाना** *bhunānā* [cf. H. [2]*bhunnā*], v.t. to cause to be changed (money: by, से); to change.

भुन्नास *bhunnās*, m. **1.** strong post (to which an elephant is tied). **2.** sl. penis.

भुन्नासी *bhunnāsī* f. colloq. a heavy lock.

भुभुक्षित *bhubhukṣit* [S.], adj. corr. = बुभुक्षित.

भुरकस *bhurkas*, m. **1.** fragments, pieces. **2.** husk, chaff. — ~ निकालना (का), to smash to pieces, or to pulp; to thrash soundly.

[1]**भुरका** *bhurkā* [cf. **bhūra-*], m. reg. dust.

[2]**भुरका** *bhurkā* [cf. H. *bhor*], m. *Pl.* the morning star.

[3]**भुरका** *bhurkā*, m. a small jar (cf. भरुका).

भुरका- *bhurkā-*, v.t. Brbh. **1.** to sprinkle. **2.** to deceive.

[1]**भुरकी** *bhurkī* f. reg. **1.** hole, gap. **2.** hole or pit for water.

[2]**भुरकी** *bhurkī* [cf. H. [1]*bhurkā*], m. **1.** dust. **2.** *Pl.* (*bhurṣī*) spell (cast by an ascetic, by scattering ashes over the head and repeating a *mantra*).

भुरकुस *bhurkus*, m. = भुरकस.

भुरता *bhurtā*, m. a mash of boiled or fried vegetables. — ~ करना or निकालना, (का), to thrash soundly.

भुरभुरा *bhurbhurā* [cf. **bhūra-*], adj. **1.** powdery, crumbly (as sandy soil). **2.** mealy, short (as bread). **3.** crisp; roasted (grain).

भुरभुराना *bhurbhurānā* [cf. **bhūra-*], v.t. & v.i. **1.** v.t. to crumble (sthg). **2.** to sprinkle (on, पर). **3.** v.i. fig. reg. to hanker (for).

भुरभुराहट *bhurbhurāhaṭ* [cf. H. *bhurbhurānā*], f. **1.** powderiness. **2.** mealiness, shortness (of bread).

भुलक्कड़ *bhulakkaṛ* [cf. H. *bhūlnā*], adj. **1.** adj. forgetful; absent-minded. **2.** thoughtless; negligent. **3.** m. a forgetful person, &c.

भुलसना *bhulasnā* [H. *jhulasnā*; ? w. H. *balnā*], v.i. & v.t. **1.** v.i. to be burnt or scorched. **2.** v.t. = भुलसाना.

भुलसाना *bhulsānā*, v.t. to burn, to scorch.

भुलाऊ *bhulāū* [cf. H. *bhulānā*], adj. misleading, deceiving.

भुलाना *bhulānā* [cf. H. *bhūlnā*], v.t. & v.i. **1.** v.t. to cause to be forgotten, to erase from the mind; to forget. **2.** to deceive, to mislead. **3.** to bewilder; to fascinate. **4.** v.i. Brbh. Av. to be bewildered, or beguiled. **5.** to forget.

भुलावट *bhulāvaṭ* [S.], f. forgetfulness, obliviousness.

भुलावा *bhulāvā* [cf. H. *bhulānā*], m. deception, fraud; trick, hoax. — ~ देना (को), to deceive, &c. भुलावे में आना, or पड़ना, to be deceived or taken in (by, के).

भुवंग *bhuvaṅg* [*bhujaṅga-*], m. Brbh. = भुजंग.

भुव *bhuv* [S.], m. **1.** heaven, sky. **2.** earth.

भुवन *bhuvan* [S.], m. **1.** the world. **2.** a world, cosmological region. ~ चारिदस, m. pl. Av. the fourteen cosmological regions above, below and including the world. **3.** transf. mankind.

भुवाना *bhuvānā*, v. i. reg. to become sticky.

भुवाल *bhuvāl* [*bhūpāla-*], m. Brbh. king.

भुवि *bhuvi* [*bhūmi-*], f. Av. earth, ground.

भुस *bhus* [**bhusa-*: Pk. *bhusa-*], m. = भूसा.

भुसरा *bhusrā* [**bhussara-*], m. reg. an inferior wheat.

भुसावन *bhusāvan* [cf. H. *bhūsā*], m. *hist.* a tax on river-boats carrying grain.

भुसौरा *bhusaurā* [**bhusakuṭaka-*], m. reg. a storehouse for chaff or straw; barn.

भुसौरी *bhusaurī*, f. reg. = भुसौरा.

भूँकना *bhūṁknā* [*bhukkati*], v.i. = भौंकना.

भूँजना *bhūṁjnā* [**bhr̥ñjati*], v.t. to roast, to parch (grain).

भूँदरी *bhūṁdrī* [cf. H. *bhūīṁ*], f. *hist.* a piece of land let rent-free (as to village servants).

भूँयारा *bhūṁyārā* [**bhūmiyagāra-*], m. reg. = ²भौंरा.

भूँसना *bhūṁsnā*, v.i. reg. to bark (= भूँकना).

भूँहरा *bhūṁharā*, m. reg. = ²भौंरा.

भूँहार *bhūṁhār*, m. reg. = भुईहार.

भू *bhū* [S.], f. **1.** the earth, the world. **2.** land, ground. **3.** place; site. — भूकंप, m. earthquake. °विज्ञान, m. seismology. भू-खंड, m. region; area (of land, or of the earth). भू-गर्भ, m. womb of earth: the inner earth. °-गर्भित, adj. taking place underground (as atomic tests). भूगोल, m. the earth, the globe; geography. °-विज्ञान, or °-विद्या, or °-शास्त्र, m. geography. भू-चक्र, m. the equator. भू-चाल, m. motion or rotation of the earth; earthquake. भू-डोल, m. earthquake. भू-तल, m. surface of the earth. भूदान, m. grant of land, or of land revenue; the movement led by Vinoba Bhave to make agrarian land available by voluntary grants from landowners. भूधर, m. earth-supporter: a mountain. भूभाग, m. = भू-खंड. भूप, m. = भूपाल. भूपति, m. earth-lord: king. भूपाल, m. id. भूपुत्र, m. son of the earth: the planet Mars. भू-बंदी, adj. *hist.* pertaining to foot-soldiers: ~ लड़ाई, f. foot skirmish. भूभार, m. burden of the world (as sustained by Viṣṇu when incarnate). भूमंडल, m. = भूगोल, 1. भूमध्यरेखा, f. equator. °-रेखीय, adj. भूमध्यसागर, m. the Mediterranean Sea. °ईय, adj. भूमध्यस्थ, adj. surrounded by land; situated in the middle of the earth. भूलोक, m. the terrestrial world. भूविज्ञान, m. geology. °ई, m. geologist. °-वैज्ञानिक, adj. geological. भूसुर, m. Av. earth-god: a brāhmaṇ. भूस्वामी, m. landlord, landowner.

¹**भूआ** *bhūā*, f. = बूआ.

²**भूआ** *bhūā* [**bhūva-*], m. **1.** fine hair, down: cotton of the *semal* tree. **2.** reg. a hairy caterpillar (harmful to certain crops).

¹**भूई** *bhūī* [*bhūti-*], f. Av. ashes.

²**भूई** *bhūī*, m. reg. carrier of a palanquin.

¹**भूक** *bhūk*, f. pronun. var. = भूख.

²**भूक** *bhūk*, m. *Pl. HŚS.* **1.** hole; cleft (as in the earth). **2.** time.

भूकड़ *bhūkaṛ* [cf. H. *bhūkh*], adj. reg. hungry.

भूख *bhūkh* [*bubhukṣā-*], f. **1.** hunger; appetite. **2.** desire. — ~ मरना, hunger or appetite, &c. to subside. ~ लगना (को), hunger to be felt (by), to be hungry. भूखों मरना, to starve; to die of hunger. भूखों मार डालना, v.t. to starve (one) to death. – भूख-प्यास, f. hunger and thirst; appetite.

भूखा *bhūkhā* [**bubhukṣaka-* or **b(h)ukṣaka-*], adj. & m. **1.** adj. hungry. **2.** starving. **3.** desirous, hungry (of or for, का). **4.** m. a hungry, or starving person, &c. — ~, or भूखे. मरना, to starve; to die of hunger. भूखे पेट, adv. on an empty stomach. – भूखा-नंगा, adj. hungry and naked, destitute.

भूजी *bhūjī*, f. = भुजिया.

भूड़ *bhūṛ* [**bhuḍḍa-*], f. a sandy, porous soil.

भूड़ल *bhūṛal*, m. reg. **1.** soapstone, potstone. **2.** mica (= भोड़ल).

भूत *bhūt* [S.], adj. & m. **1.** adj. been, become; existent. **2.** happened, past. **3.** m. *philos.* one of the five elements: earth, water, fire, air, ether. **4.** the existent world or creation. **5.** a great devotee or ascetic. **6.** an evil spirit, fiend; ghost. **7.** an evil person. **8.** colloq. an ugly person. **9.** *gram.* past (tense), perfective (aspect). **10.** -भूत. become: serving as; taking on qualities or the nature of (e.g. आधारभूत, adj. basic). — ~ उतारना, to cast out an evil spirit (from, से). ~ चढ़ना, or सवार होना (पर), a fiend to possess (one): to rage; to be obsessed. ~ बनना, fig. to become drunk, to rage. ~ लगना, to be or to become possessed. ~ होना, to rage. – भूत-काल, m. the past; *gram.* past tense. °इक, adj. past (of time, or tense). भूत-ख़ाना, m. colloq. fiends' house: dirty or neglected living quarters. भूत-ग्रस्त, adj. possessed by an evil spirit. भूत-नाथ, m. lord of spirits: a title of Śiva. भूत-पूर्णिमा, m. the full moon of the month Āśvin. भूतपूर्व, adj. previous, former. भूत-प्रेत, m. ghosts and spirits; specif. spirits of the dead which are not yet reincarnated. भूत-यज्ञ, m. a sacrifice to be performed by a householder. भूतात्मा [°*ta*+*ā*°], m. composed of the (five) elements: the body; the soul; the supreme being. भूतारि [°*ta*+*a*°], m. enemy of evil beings: asafoetida.

भूतनी *bhūtănī* [cf. H. *bhūt*], f. demoness.

भूति *bhūti* [S.], f. **1.** state of being, existence. **2.** production, birth. **3.** power, dignity; superhuman or magical power (as attributed to yogīs). **4.** prosperous state. **5.** Av. ashes.

भूनना *bhūnnā* [cf. **bhr̥gna-*: MIA **bhunna-*], v.t. **1.** to roast; to parch (grain); to bake. **2.** to fry. **3.** to scorch, to burn; to cause suffering (to).

भूभल *bhūbhal* [**bhubbhala-*], f. m. hot embers.

भूभुरि *bhūbhuri*, f. Brbh. = भूभल.

भूमा *bhūmā* [S.], m. poet. the earth.

भूमि *bhūmi* [S.], f. **1.** earth, soil; land; agrarian land. **2.** region, country. **3.** place, site, area. **4.** the earth, world. — भूमि-क्षरण, m. erosion. भूमि-दान, m. = भूदान. भूमि-दाहा, adj. cremated (a corpse). भूमिसात्, adj. levelled to the ground; in ruins (a plan). भूमिहार, m. a community of cultivators in Bihar and U.P.; a man of that community. भूमिहीन, adj. landless. भूम्युच्च [°*i*+*u*°], m. apogee.

भूमिका *bhūmikā* [S.], f. **1.** introduction (to a book); preface. **2.** preamble. **3.** role. — ~ अदा करना, or निभाना, to play a role, or part. ~ बाँधना, to beat about the bush (verbally). ~ में आना, = ~ निभाना.

भूमिया *bhūmiyā* [cf. *bhūmya-*], m. reg. (W.) **1.** Brbh. landowner, landlord. **2.** original or prior inhabitant. **3.** local deity.

भूमियाल *bhūmiyāl* [cf. *ālaya-*], m. reg. home region.

भूमियावत *bhūmiyāvat*, f. *hist.* plundering, laying waste (by local chiefs).

भूमियावती *bhūmiyāvătī* [cf. H. *bhūmiyāvat*], m. *hist.* an insurgent or rebel chief.

भूयः *bhūyaḥ* [S.], adv. **1.** again; further. **2.** repeatedly. **3.** afterwards.

भूयन *bhūyan*, m. reg. the headman of a Gond village.

[1]**भूर** *bhūr* [**bhūra-*], m. Brbh. sand.

[2]**भूर** *bhūr* [? conn. H. [1]*bhurkī*], m. reg. a spring, fountain.

[3]**भूर** *bhūr*, m. reg. alms.

भूर्- *bhūr-* [S.], adv. *mythol.* the earth (the first of the seven upper worlds). — भूर-लोक, m. the earth, this world.

[1]**भूरा** *bhūrā* [**bhrūra-*], adj. & m. **1.** adj. light brown, brownish; greyish. **2.** m. brown colour, &c. **3.** raw sugar. **4.** pej. westerner, a westernised Indian.

[2]**भूरा** *bhūrā*, m. reg. section of village land lying furthest from the village itself.

भूरि *bhūri* [S.], adj. much, many; abundant. — ~ ~ प्रशंसा करना, to lavish praise (on, की).

भूरी *bhūrī* [cf. **bhūra-*], f. reg. a sandy soil (?? = भूड़).

भूर्ज *bhūrj* [S.], m. *Pl. HŚS.* a birch (= [2]भोज).

भूल *bhūl* [cf. H. *bhūlnā*], f. **1.** forgetfulness, oversight; omission. **2.** mistake, slip, error. — ~ करना, to make a mistake, &c. भूल-चूक, f. = ~, 1. भूल-भुलैयाँ, f. maze, labyrinth.

भूलना *bhūlnā* [**bhull-*: Pk. *bhulla-*], v.i. & v.t. **1.** v.i. to be forgotten. **2.** to go astray, to err. **3.** to be deceived. **4.** v.t. to forget. **5.** to omit, to overlook. — भूलकर भी, adv. on no account. यह भूलकर भी न सोचना, don't think this on any account. – भूला-चूका, adj. & m. = भूला-बिसरा. भूला चेता, m. a forgetful or bad memory. भूला-बिसरा, adj. & m. forgotten, quite forgotten; wandering, astray; a casual visitor. भूला-भटका, adj. wandering, astray.

भूषण *bhūṣaṇ* [S.], m. ornament, decoration; piece of jewellery; adornment.

भूषा *bhūṣā* [S.], f. esp. in comp. **1.** ornamentation (specif. of dress). **2.** fashionable style (of clothing). — वेष-भूषा, f. attire, manner or kind of dress.

भूषित *bhūṣit* [S.], adj. adorned.

भूस *bhūs*, m. = भूसा.

भूसा *bhūsā* [**bhussa-*[2]], m. **1.** husk. **2.** straw, chaff. **3.** bran. — भूसा उड़ाना (का), fig. to thrash; *musl.* (Shīas) to lament. ~ भरना (में), to stuff with straw, &c. ~ भराना, or भरवाना, to cause to be stuffed with straw; to flay (a person) and burn the stuffed skin. – भूसा-जिंस, m. the (various) varieties of unhusked grain.

भूसी *bhūsī* [**bhussa-*[2]], f. **1.** bran. **2.** chaff, husk.

भृकुटि *bhṛkuṭi* [S.], f. = भृकुटी.

भृकुटी *bhṛkuṭī* [S.], f. **1.** the eyebrow. **2.** a frown; scowl.

भृंग *bhṛṅg* [S.], m. **1.** a large black bee (cf. भ्रमर). **2.** a bird: ? racket-tailed drongo. 3. = भृंगी, 3.

भृंगी *bhṛṅgī* [S.], f. 1. = भृंग. **2.** a species of wasp. **3.** the ichneumon fly (which stings and immobilises, then lays its eggs in the body of, a caterpillar or grub: the supposed transformation of this into the fly serves, in Kṛṣṇa poetry, as a metaphor for the transforming effect of love of God, following the pain of love's sting).

भृगु *bhṛgu* [S.], m. *mythol.* name of a sage. — भृगु-नाथ, m. Av. a title of Paraśurām (the avatār of Viṣṇu). भृगु-पति, m. Brbh. Av. id. भृगु-रेखा, f. Brbh. mark on Kṛṣṇa's breast where he had been kicked by Bhṛgu.

भृत *bhṛt* [S.], m. & adj. **1.** m. hired servant. **2.** adj. Brbh. bearing, carrying.

भृति *bhṛti* [S.], f. **1.** wages or hire. **2.** maintenance; food.

भृत्य *bhṛtyă* [S.], m. dependant: servant.

भृत्यत्व *bhṛtyatvă* [S.], m. state of servitude.

भृत्या *bhṛtyā* [S.], f. **1.** maintenance; hire, wages. **2.** a female servant.

भें *bhem̐*, f. onom. bleating (as of sheep). — ~ ~ करना, to bleat.

भेंगा *bhem̐gā* [*bheṅga-], adj. squinting.

भेंट *bhem̐ṭ* [*bheṭṭ-: Pk. *bhiṭṭā*-], f. **1.** meeting (with, से); visit. **2.** an interview. **3.** present (as to a superior); an offering (to a deity). **4.** a votive hymn. — ~ करना, to make a present, or an offering (of, की); to meet; to give an interview (to, से). ~ चढ़ाना, to make an offering (of, की; to, को). – भेंट-मुलाक़ात, f. = ~, 1., 2. भेंट-वार्ता, f. = ~, 2.

भेंटना *bhem̐ṭnā* [cf. *bheṭṭ-: Pk. *bhiṭṭ*-], v.t. **1.** to meet (with, से). **2.** to embrace. **3.** to make a present (to a superior).

भेंड *bhem̐ḍ*, m. *Pl.* the water-plant *Aeschenomyne aspera* (= सोला), a source of pith.

भेक *bhek*, m. *Pl. HŚS.* a frog.

भेकी *bhekī*, f. reg. a frog.

भेज *bhej* [*bhedya*-], m. *hist.* a proportionate share in a village tenure. — भेज-बरार [P. -*barār*], a partic. adjustable tenure (Bundelkhand).

भेजना *bhejnā* [*bhejj-], v.t. to send.

भेजवाना *bhejvānā*, v.t. = भिजवाना.

भेजा *bhejā* [conn. *majjan*-], m. the brain. — ~ खाना, to eat the brain (of, का): to bore with chatter, to plague.

भेटू *bheṭū*, m. *Pl.* stalk, stem.

भेड़ *bheṛ* [*bhedra*-: ← Austro-as.], f. **1.** a sheep; ewe. **2.** colloq. a simple or stupid person. — भेड़-चाल, f. fig. unthinking imitation on the part of a group. भेड़-पालन, m. sheep-raising.

भेड़ना *bheṛnā* [*bheṭ-], v.t. **1.** to close, to shut up. **2.** to enclose.

भेड़नी *bheṛnī* [cf. H. [1]*bheṛiyā*], f. she-wolf.

भेड़ा *bheṛā* [*bhedra*-: ← Austro-as.], m. a ram.

[1]**भेड़िया** *bheṛiyā* [cf. H. *bheṛ*], m. a wolf.

[2]**भेड़िया** *bheṛiyā* [cf. H. *bheṛ*], adj. inv. sheep-like, sheep's. — ~ चाल, f. blind following, mass imitation. ~ धँसान, or धसान, f. flock crowded together: id.

भेड़ी *bheṛī* [? cf. H. *bheṛā*], f. reg. a sheep (= भेड़).

भेड़ू *bheṛū* [cf. *bhedṛā*], m. **1.** *HŚS.* a ram. **2.** reg. a truculent man.

भेद *bhed* [S.], m. splitting, separating: **1.** difference, distinction; peculiarity. **2.** kind, species. **3.** discrimination (between, में; against, के साथ). **4.** secret matter, mystery. **5.** division (as between allies); breach, rupture (in relations).**6.** fissure. — ~ करना, to distinguish (between, में). ~ खोलना (का), to reveal a secret; to unmask. ~ देना (को), to reveal a secret (to). ~ पाना, to discover a secret; to solve (as a mystery). ~ रखना (का), to keep (sthg.) secret. ~ लेना (का), to probe (as a motive, a secret); to sound (one). – भेदपूर्ण, adj. discriminatory. भेद-बुद्धि, f. spirit of dissension, disaffection. भेद-भाव, m. distinction, discrimination; inequality; sense of discord.

भेदक *bhedak* [S.], adj. **1.** dividing; severing. **2.** causing dissension. **3.** distinguishing, marking out.

भेदना *bhednā* [ad. *bhedayati*: w. H. *bhed*], v.t. to penetrate; to pierce.

भेदित *bhedit* [S.], adj. divided; severed.

भेदिया *bhediyā* [cf. H. *bhed*], m. **1.** a scout, spy; informer, a mole. **2.** a confidant.

भेदी *bhedī* [S.], adj. & m. dividing: **1.** adj. discriminating, discerning. **2.** m. = भेदिया.

भेदू *bhedū* [cf. H. *bhed*], m. reg. = भेदिया.

भेद्य *bhedyă* [S.], adj. **1.** to be divided, &c. **2.** to be kept secret. **3.** pierceable; vulnerable.

भेमड़ा *bhemṛā* , m. *Pl.* a wry face.

भेरि *bheri* [*bherī̆*-], f. E.H. **1.** a kettledrum. **2.** reg. a pipe or bugle of copper.

[1]**भेरी** *bherī* [cf. H. *bheri*], m. reg. bugler; piper.

[2]**भेरी** *bherī* [S.], f. bugle, &c. (= भेरि). — भेरीकार, m. bugler; piper.

भेल *bhel* [*bhel-], f. reg. a mixture; sthg. mixed in. — भेल-सेल, f. id.

भेला *bhelā* [*bhella-[2]], m. ball, lump.

भेली *bhelī* [cf. H. *bhelā*], f. lump (esp. of coarse sugar, or molasses).

भेव *bhev* [*bheda*-], m. Brbh. = भेद.

भेव- *bhev*-, v.t. Av. = भिगोना.

भेषज *bheṣaj* [S.], m. **1.** a medicine. **2.** medical treatment. — भेषज-संग्रह, m. pharmacopoeia.

भेस *bhes* [*veṣa*-[2] × *bheda*-], m. **1.** appearance. **2.** likeness, resemblance (to, का); air, manner. **3.** dress. **4.** disguise. — ~ बदलना, or बनाना, or भरना, to assume a disguise; to simulate (an attitude, &c).

भैंस *bhaiṁs* [*mahiṣī-*], f. buffalo cow. — ~ के आगे बीन बजाना, fig. to cast pearls before swine. ~ बराबर, adj. like a buffalo: difficult to deal with.

भैंसा *bhaiṁsā* [*mahiṣa-*], m. buffalo bull.

भैंसिया *bhaiṁsiyā* [cf. H. *bhaiṁs*], adj. inv. reg. having to do with buffaloes. — ~ दाद, m. ringworm (= ²दाद).

भैंसी *bhaiṁsī* [cf. H. *bhaiṁsā*], f. = भैंस.

भैंसोंदा *bhaiṁsoṁdā*, m. *Pl.* charge for the right to graze buffaloes.

भैक्ष *bhaikṣ* [S.], m. = भिक्षा.

भैया *bhaiyā* [cf. H. *bhāī*], m. **1.** dimin. brother. **2.** esp. voc. friend. — भैयाचारी, adj. coparcenary (estate). भैया-दूज, m. the second day of the bright half of the month Kārttik (when sisters pay symbolic respects to brothers).

भैयापन *bhaiyāpan* [cf. H. *bhaiyā*], m. brotherliness, brotherly feeling.

भैयापा *bhaiyāpā*, m. = भैयापन.

भैरव *bhairav* [S.], adj. & m. **1.** adj. fearsome, terrible. **2.** m. fearsomeness. **3.** *hind.* a manifestation of Śiva. **4.** *mus.* a *rāg* (sung at dawn).

भैरवी *bhairăvī* [S.], f. **1.** *hind.* a partic. form of Durgā. **2.** *mus.* a *rāgiṇī.*

भैरारी *bhairārī*, f. *Pl.* reg. *mus.* name of a *rāgiṇī* (? = भैरवी).

भैषज्य *bhaiṣajyă* [S.], m. = भेषज.

भैहू *bhaihū* [*bhrātṛvadhū-*], f. reg. younger brother's wife (= भावज).

भों *bhoṁ*, f. a deep, bass sound; sound of a wind instrument; lowing; deep bark. — ~ ~, f. = ~.

भोंकना *bhoṁknā* [cf. *bhoṅka-*²], v.t. to thrust in, to stab; to stick in clumsily (a needle, in material). — भोंका-भोंकी, f. thrusting and stabbing.

भोंकस *bhoṁkas*, m. reg. a wizard believed to have the power to cause death.

भोंगली *bhoṁglī*, f. **1.** Brbh. a bamboo tube. **2.** roll (of paper).

भोंटा *bhoṁṭā* [**bhonṭa-*], adj. blunt (= भोथरा); stupid.

भोंडा *bhoṇḍā* [**bhoṇḍa-*], adj. reg. **1.** ugly. **2.** uncouth.

भोंडापन *bhoṇḍāpan*, [cf. H. *bhoṇḍā*], m. ugliness; uncouthness.

भोंदू *bhoṁdū* [**bhonda-*], m. **1.** pej. simple (a person). **2.** stupid, silly.

भोंपा *bhoṁpā*, m. = भोंपू.

भोंपू *bhoṁpū* [cf. H. *bhoṁ*], m. **1.** a horn (= नरसिंघा); a car horn. **2.** colloq. loudspeaker.

भोई *bhoī* [*bhogin-*], m. a chair-porter, *pālkī* carrier; headman (of a Gond village).

भोक्तव्य *bhoktavyă* [S.], adj. to be enjoyed, consumed, or experienced.

भोक्ता *bhoktā* [S.], m. inv. enjoyer: **1.** consumer (of food); good liver; epicure. **2.** one who makes use of (goods, a service, &c). **3.** one who experiences (joy, sorrow, &c).

¹**भोग** *bhog* [S.], m. **1.** enjoyment; pleasure in food; eating. **2.** use; benefit (of funds, property). **3.** experiencing (an emotion); pleasure, gratification; suffering. **4.** sexual enjoyment, sexual intercourse. **5.** any object of enjoyment: food; food offered to an idol. **6.** *astron.* presence (of a planet in a partic. constellation). — ~ करना, to experience; to suffer; to suffer for (as for sins); to enjoy sexually. ~ लगाना, to partake of food; to place food before (one); to offer food to (an idol). — भोग-बंधक, m. mortgage with possession. भोग-लिप्सा, f. licentiousness. भोग-विलास, m. luxurious life; licentiousness. °ई, m. one who delights in luxury; a voluptuous person. भोगाधिकार [°*ga*+*a*°], m. right of benefit, or occupancy. °ई, m.

²**भोग** *bhog* [S.], m. *Pl. HŚS.* a snake's hood.

भोगना *bhognā* [cf. H. *bhog*], v.t. **1.** to enjoy. **2.** to suffer for (as for sins). **3.** to experience; to suffer; to endure.

भोगा *bhogā*, m. reg. deception.

भोगी *bhogī* [S.], adj. & m. **1.** adj. enjoying, using, experiencing, &c. (see ¹भोग). **2.** voluptuous. **3.** m. one who enjoys the pleasures of the senses. **4.** a voluptuous person.

भोगोत्र *bhogotră* [? ad. **bhogyottara-*], m. *hist.* grant of revenue for the benefit of an individual (esp. of a brāhmaṇ).

भोग्य *bhogyă* [S.], adj. & m. **1.** adj. to be enjoyed, used or experienced, &c. (see ¹भोग). **2.** m. anything that may be enjoyed or used; wealth.

¹**भोज** *bhoj* [*bhojya-*], m. **1.** food. ***2.** feast; banquet. **3.** reception.

²**भोज** *bhoj* [**bhaurja-*], m. a species of birch-tree. — भोज-पत्र, m. = ~.

भोजन *bhojan* [S.], m. **1.** eating; a meal. **2.** food. — ~ करना, to eat, to dine; to give food (to, का). भोजन-शाला, f. eating-place; kitchen. भोजन-सूची, f. menu. भोजनालय [°*na*+*ā*°], m. eating-place; restaurant (esp. vegetarian).

भोजनीय *bhojănīyă* [S.], adj. = भोज्य.

भोजपुरी *bhojpurī*, adj. & f. **1.** adj. having to do with the region of Bhojpur (Shahabad). **2.** f. the speech of the Bhojpur area.

भोज्य *bhojyă* [S.], adj. & m. **1.** adj. edible. **2.** m. sthg. edible, food.

भोटिया *bhoṭiyā* [ad. *bhoṭa-*], adj. & m., f. **1.** adj. Bhutanese. **2.** m., f. a Bhutanese. **3.** f. language of Bhutan.

भोड़ल *bhoṛal*, m. **1.** reg. mica. **2.** E.H. glint, gleam; ? a faint star, or firefly.

भोता *bhotā*, adj. reg. blunt (= भोथरा).

भोतीहार *bhotīhār*, m. reg. a labourer.

भोथरा *bhothrā* [cf. **bhottha-*], adj. blunt.

भोथराना *bhothrānā* [cf. H. *bhothrā*], v.i. to become blunt.

[1]**भोपा** *bhopā*, m. **1.** a kind of ascetic; a magician. **2.** an idiot.

[2]**भोपा** *bhopā*, m. = भोंपा.

भोमीरा *bhomīrā*, f. *Pl. HŚS.* coral.

[1]**भोर** *bhor* [**bhorā-*], f. m. daybreak, the period just before dawn. — ~ को, or ~ होते, adv. at daybreak.

[2]**भोर** *bhor* [**bhora-*], m. Brbh. Av. deceit.

[3]**भोर** *bhor*, adj. E.H. = भोला.

[4]**भोर** *bhor*, adj. Brbh. = विभोर.

भोला *bholā* [**bhola-*: Pk. *bhola-*], adj. **1.** simple; innocent. **2.** silly. — भोलानाथ, m. title of Śiva. भोला-भाला, adj. = भोला.

भोलापन *bholāpan* [cf. H. *bholā*], m. **1.** simplicity; innocence. **2.** silliness.

भोलेपन *bholepan*, m. = भोलापन.

भोसड़ा *bhosṛā* [**bhossa-*], m. vulg. vulva.

भोसड़ी *bhosṛī* [cf. **bhossa-*], f. vulg. 1. = भोसड़ा. **2.** slut. — भोसड़ीवाली, f. = ~, 2.

भौं *bhaum̐*, f. = भौंह.

भौंकना *bhaum̐knā* [*bhukkati*], v.i. **1.** to bark. **2.** to talk nonsensically or foolishly.

भौंघरा *bhaum̐ghrā* [H. [2]*bhaum̐rā*×H. *ghar*], m. reg. an underground vault or room.

भौंचक्का *bhaum̐cakkā*, adj. = भौचक्का.

भौंर *bhaum̐r*, m. Brbh. = [1]भौंरा.

[1]**भौंरा** *bhaum̐rā* [*bhramara-*[1 2]], m. **1.** a black beetle. **2.** a large black bee. **3.** a whirlpool. **4.** a spinning top. **5.** fig. dilemma.

[2]**भौंरा** *bhaum̐rā* [**bhaumaghara-*], m. **1.** an underground vault, or room. **2.** reg. (E.) a pit for storing grain.

भौंराला *bhaum̐rālā* [*bhramara-*[1]], adj. reg. curly (hair).

भौंरियाना *bhaum̐riyānā* [cf. *bhramara-*[1]], v.i. reg. to turn round, to revolve.

भौंरी *bhaum̐rī* [cf. *bhramara-*[1]], f. reg. a lock or curl of hair.

भौंह *bhaum̐h* [cf. **bhrumu-*: Pa. *bhamukha-*], f. the eyebrow. ~ चढ़ाना, to frown, to scowl. ~, or भौंहें, तानना, or टेढ़ी करना, id. ~ जोहना, or ताकना, to act with an eye to (another's, की) likely pleasure.

भौ *bhau* m. Brbh. = भय.

भौचक *bhaucak*, adj. = भौचक्का.

भौचक्का *bhaucakkā* [H. *bhaum̐h*+H. *cakk-*], adj. **1.** astonished, taken aback. **2.** alarmed.

भौजाई *bhaujāī* [*bhrāturjāyā-*], f. brother's wife.

भौजी *bhaujī*, f. = भौजाई.

भौतिक *bhautik* [S.], adj. **1.** existing; material, real; of this world. **2.** physical. — भौतिकवाद, m. materialism. °ई, adj. & m. materialistic; materialist. भौतिक-विज्ञान, m. physics. °ई, m. physicist.

भौतिकता *bhautikătā* [S.], f. material nature, real existence.

भौतिकी *bhautikī* [S.], f. physics. — भौतिकी-विज्ञ, m. physicist.

भौम *bhaum* [S.], adj. & m. **1.** adj. -भौम. having to do with the earth. **2.** m. the planet Mars. — भौमवार, m. Tuesday.

भौमिक *bhaumik* [S.], adj. & m. **1.** adj. having to do with the earth. **2.** m. name of a north Indian and Bengal community.

भौमिकी *bhaumikī* [S.], f. geology.

भौलिया *bhauliyā*, m. 19c. ? a small covered boat.

भ्रंश *bhraṃś* [S.], m. **1.** fall, decline. **2.** destruction, ruin.

भ्रम *bhram* [S.], m. wandering: **1.** perplexity, confusion; doubt, suspicion. **2.** error; misapprehension; aberration. — ~ करना, to doubt, to question; the head to be turned, to be vain; to labour under a misapprehension.

~ खुलना, to be disclosed (sthg. unknown); to be exposed (pretensions). ~ में डालना, to mislead; to cause perplexity, &c. (to, को). – भ्रमकारी, adj. misleading, deceptive; giving rise to doubt, &c. भ्रमवश, adv. by, or in, error. भ्रमात्मक [°*ma*+*ā*°], adj. erroneous.

भ्रमण *bhramaṇ* [S.], m. **1.** wandering. **2.** a tour; journey. — भ्रमणकारी, adj. wandering; itinerant; mobile. भ्रमणशील, adj. habitually wandering or travelling.

भ्रमता *bhramătā* [S.], f. state of error.

भ्रमर *bhramar* [S.], m. **1.** a large black bee. **2.** fig. a lover (esp. a faithless lover). — भ्रमर-गीत, m. bee's song: any poem dealing with the theme of Kr̥ṣṇa's abandoning the herdgirls of Braj, and the devotion of the latter to him.

भ्रमरी *bhramărī* [S.], f. **1.** a black bee. **2.** *Pl. HŚS.* a plant of the genus *Ferula*.

भ्रमित *bhramit* [S.], adj. **1.** set turning, revolving. ***2.** erring, misled.

भ्रमी *bhramī* [S.], adj. revolving, wandering: **1.** erring, mistaken. **2.** pej. sceptical.

भ्रष्ट *bhraṣṭ* [S.], adj. **1.** fallen. **2.** corrupted, corrupt. **3.** debased; polluted; violated. — ~ करना, to corrupt, &c.

भ्रष्टता *bhraṣṭătā* [S.], f. fallen or corrupt state. — भ्रष्टाचार [°*ṭa*+*ā*°], m. depraved or corrupt conduct or behaviour. °इता, f. id. °ई, m. a depraved person, &c.

भ्रष्टपन *bhraṣṭpan* [cf. H. *bhraṣṭ*], m. *Pl.* fallen or degraded state.

भ्रांत *bhrānt* [S.], adj. **1.** astray, lost. **2.** erring, mistaken.

भ्रांति *bhrānti* [S.], f. **1.** whirling round. **2.** wandering. **3.** error, delusion; aberration.

भ्राज- *bhrāj-* [ad. *bhrājate*], v.i. Brbh. Av. to shine, to gleam.

भ्राता *bhrātā* [S.], m. inv. brother.

भ्रातृ- *bhrātr̥-* [S.], m. brother-. भ्रातृ-भाव, m. = भाईपन.

भ्रात्रीय *bhrātrīyă* [S.], adj. fraternal.

भ्रामक *bhrāmak* [S.], adj. & m. **1.** adj. causing error; misleading; deceptive. **2.** perplexing. **3.** deceitful. **4.** m. a deceiver, cheat.

भ्रू *bhrū* [S.], f. m. **1.** f. the eyebrow. **2.** m. frown, scowl. — भ्रू-निक्षेप, m. sidelong glance. भ्रू-पात, m. = भ्रू, 2. भ्रू-भंग, m. = ~, 2. भ्रू-विलास, m. sidelong, flirtatious glance.

भ्रूण *bhrūṇ* [S.], m. foetus. — भ्रूण-विज्ञान, m. embryology. भ्रूण-हत्या, f. pej. an induced abortion.

म

म *ma*, the twenty-fifth consonant of the Devanāgarī syllabary. **मकार**, m. the sound /m/; the letter **म**.

मंग *maṅg* [*maṅga-*], m. *Pl. HŚS.* the head (of a boat).

मँग- *maṁg-* [conn. *mārgati*], v.t. Brbh. = **माँगना**.

मँगत *maṁgat*, m. Brbh. = **मँगता**.

मँगता *maṁgtā* [cf. H. *māṁgnā*], m. a beggar.

मँगती *maṁgtī* [cf. H. *māṁgnā*], f. reg. **1.** asking; request. **2.** begging, importuning.

मँगनी *maṁgnī* [cf. H. *māṁgnā*], f. **1.** asking. **2.** sthg. borrowed, or lent; sthg. obtained for the asking, or without payment. **3.** asking in marriage; engagement. — ~ **करना (की)**, to betroth. ~ **का**, adj. borrowed. ~ **देना**, to lend. ~ **माँग लेना**, to ask for on loan, to borrow.

मँगरा *maṁgrā* [cf. *maṅga-*], m. reg. (Bihar) ridging-tile(s) (on a roof).

मँगरी *maṁgrī* [cf. *maṅga-*], m. reg. (W.) ridge-pole (of a roof).

मँगरैला *maṁgrailā*, m. black cumin (= **कलौंजी**).

मंगल *maṅgal* [*maṅgala-*], adj. & m. **1.** adj. fortunate, prosperous. ***2.** auspicious. **3.** m. good fortune; prosperity. **4.** auspiciousness. **5.** well-being. **कुशल-मंगल है?** is everything going well (with you)? **6.** glad or auspicious event (as a marriage); festival; festivities. **7.** a good omen. **8.** an auspicious prayer; blessing. **9.** an auspicious song (as at a wedding). **10.** name of the planet Mars. **11.** Tuesday. **12.** (in chronograms) the number eight. — **मंगल-कलश**, m. a pitcher, as filled or set out for worship or as decoration on some auspicious occasion. **मंगल-कामना**, f. good wish(es); benevolence. **मंगलकारक**, adj. = next. **°कारी**, adj. causing well-being, or prosperity; beneficent, benevolent; auspicious. **°-कार्य**, m. a festive, or auspicious occasion; auspicious rite. **मंगल-ग्रह**, m. an auspicious planet (esp. Mars); a lucky star. **मंगल-चार**, m. = **मंगलाचरण**. **मंगल-जनक**, adj. = **मंगलकारी**. **मंगलदाय**, adj. conferring well-being, &c. **मंगलमय**, adj. auspicious. **°ई**, adj. id. **मंगलवाद**, m. blessing. **मंगलवार**, m. Tuesday. **मंगल-सूचक**, adj. Av. announcing a glad event. **मंगल-सूत्र**, m. lucky thread: a string tied by a bridegroom round his bride's neck (to be worn as long as the husband lives); an auspicious string tied round the waist. **मंगलाचरण** [°*la*+*ā*°], m. the pronouncing of a blessing; prayer for success (of any undertaking); auspicious ceremony or observance; festivity. **मंगलाचार** [°*la*+*ā*°], m. id. **मंगलाचार करना**, to revel; to wish joy (to, **का**); to sing a marriage song; to join (a couple) in marriage. **मंगल-समाचार**, m. good tidings; the Gospel.

मंगला *maṅgalā* [S.], f. a title of the goddess Pārvatī.

मंगली *maṅgalī* [cf. H. *maṅgal*], adj. born under the influence of the planet Mars.

मँगवाना *maṁgvānā* [cf. H. *māṁgnā*], v.t. to cause to be sent for or asked for (by, **से**); to obtain, to order (through).

मँगसिर *maṁgsir*, m. reg. = **मार्गशीर्ष**.

मँगाना *maṁgānā* [cf. H. *māṁgnā*], v.t. **1.** to send for. **2.** to ask for. **3.** to order, to obtain (as books, &c.); to take (as a newspaper).

मँगुरी *maṁgurī*, f. reg. (Bihar) name of a fish.

मँगेतर *maṁgetar* [**mārgayitṛ-*: Panj. *mãgetar*], m.; f. **1.** fiancé. **2.** fiancée.

मँगौरी *maṁgaurī* [**mudgavaṭikā-*], f. reg. a ball of pulse flour.

मंच *mañc* [S.], m. **1.** stage, platform; dais. **2.** watchman's platform (in fields). **3.** the stage. **4.** reg. bedstead; chair, stool.

मंचन *mañcan* [S.], m. staging (of a play).

मंचा *mañcā*, m. reg. = **मंच**. — **मंचातोड़**, adj. colloq. bed-breaking: hefty (of build).

मंचित *mañcit* [S.], adj. staged (a drama, &c).

मंचीय *mañcīyă* [S.], adj. having to do with the stage, or with a dramatic performance.

मंजन *mañjan* [cf. H. *maṁjnā*], m. **1.** Brbh. wiping or rubbing (the body) clean. **2.** a toothpaste.

मँजना *maṁjnā* [cf. H. *māṁjnā*], v.i. **1.** to rubbed, wiped, or scoured clean; to be smoothed. **2.** to become practised or trained (as the hand at a skill).

मंजर *mañjar* [S.], m. *Pl. HŚS.* = **मंजरी**.

मंज़र *maṁzar* [A. *manzṁar*], m. **1.** a sight, view. **2.** a landscape.

मंजरित *mañjarit* [S.], adj. covered with blossom.

मंजरी *mañjārī* [S.], f. **1.** cluster of buds and flowers. **2.** blossom. **3.** flower-bud. **4.** shoot, sprig, stalk.

मंजा *mañjā* [*mañca-*; ←Panj.], m. *Pl.* **1.** a bed. **2.** a raised seat.

मंजा *maṁjā* [S.], f. *Pl. HŚS.* **1.** cluster of flowers. **2.** a creeper.

मँजाई *maṁjāī* [cf. H. *māṁjnā*], f. **1.** cleaning, scouring; polishing. **2.** payment for cleaning, &c.

मँजाना *maṁjānā* [cf. H. *māṁjnā*], v.t. to cause to be rubbed, scoured, &c. (by, से).

मँजार *maṁjār* [*mārjāra-*¹], f. reg. a cat.

मंज़िल *maṃzil* [A. *manzil*], f. **1.** halting-place. **2.** inn. **3.** stage (of journey, or progress). **4.** destination, goal. **5.** storey, floor. — ~ करना, = next. ~ काटना, to complete a stage; to complete a journey. ~ पहुँचाना, to convey (one) to a destination; to convey (one) to one's last resting-place. ~ मारना, to get as far (as, की: with a journey, a task). – मंज़िले-मक़सूद, f. intended destination; goal.

-मंज़िला *-maṃzilā* [P. *manzila*], adj. formant, inv. -storeyed (e.g. दुमंज़िला, two-storeyed).

मंजिष्ठा *mañjiṣṭhā* [S.], f. madder (= मजीठ).

मंजीर *mañjīr* [S.], m. *Pl. HŚS.* **1.** anklet. **2.** post round which the string of a churning-stick passes.

मँजीरा *maṁjīrā*, m. = मजीरा.

मंजु *mañju* [S.], adj. **1.** lovely, charming; graceful. **2.** soft, melodious.

मंजुल *mañjul* [S.], adj. **1.** lovely, charming. **2.** soft, melodious.

मंजुलता *mañjulătā* [S.], f. loveliness, sweetness.

मंज़ूर *maṃzūr* [A. *manzmūr*], adj. **1.** approved of, accepted; agreeable (to, को). **2.** sanctioned, granted. — ~ करना, to approve, &c.

मंज़ूरी *maṃzūrī* [A. *manzmūr*+P. *-ī*], f. **1.** approval, acceptance. **2.** sanction, consent. — ~ देना, to give approval, &c.

मंजूषा *mañjūṣā* [S.], f. box, container.

मँझ *maṁjh* [*madhya-*], m. & adv. Av. **1.** m. middle. **2.** adv. in the middle. — मँझ-धार, f. midstream.

मँझला *maṁjhlā* [cf. *madhya-*], adj. middle.

मँझा *maṁjhā*, m. reg. a bed.

मँझार *maṁjhār* [**madhyāra-*], m. Brbh. the middle.

मँझुवा *maṁjhuvā* [cf. *madhya-*], adj. middle.

मँझोला *maṁjholā*, adj. = मझोला.

मंठा *maṇṭhā*, adj. reg. **1.** wiped out, effaced. **2.** ruined.

¹**मंड** *maṇḍ* [ad. *maṇḍa-*¹], m. reg. rice-water; starch; skimmings.

²**मंड** *maṇḍ* [*maṇḍa-*²; Pk. *maṁḍaya-*], m. f. reg. **1.** m. ornament, decoration. **2.** f. the raised rim and platform of a well.

मंड- *maṇḍ-* [*maṇḍayati-*], v.t. Brbh. to adorn.

मँड- *maṁḍ-* [cf. H. *māṁṛnā*], v.i. Brbh. to be trampled.

मंडन *maṇḍan* [S.], m. ornamenting, adorning; ornamentation.

मंडप *maṇḍap* [S.], m. **1.** a temporary building or shed (erected at times of festivals, or marriages, &c). **2.** a pavilion; arbour. **3.** building consecrated to a deity; temple.

मँडराना *maṁḍrānā* [cf. H. *maṇḍal*], v.i. **1.** to fly around; to flutter round or about; to hover around. **2.** to wander round or about; to float about (as clouds).

मंडल *maṇḍal* [*maṇḍala-*], m. **1.** disc, circle. **2.** ring; coil (as of a snake); band. **3.** circular course, revolution; orbit (of a heavenly body). **4.** halo. **5.** globe, sphere, orb. मुख-मंडल, m. a round face. **6.** the vault of the sky. **7.** the horizon. **8.** transf. region, district; zone. **9.** amphitheatre; circular stage (esp. that on which Kṛṣṇa's round-dance is performed). **10.** company, circle; society, association, body; sect; committee. **11.** a type of mystical diagram. — ~ बाँधना, to form a circle, or a ring; to overspread, to lower (clouds). सौर ~, m. the solar system. मंडलाकार [°*la*+*ā*°], adj. round; spherical.

मँडलाना *maṁḍlānā*, v.i. = मँडराना.

मंडलिया *maṇḍliyā* [? cf. H. *maṇḍal*], m. *Pl.* a tumbler pigeon.

मंडली *maṇḍlī* [*maṇḍalikā-*], f. **1.** a small circle, disc, ring, or coil. **2.** a circle, group, party; society; flock (of birds, animals).

मंडवा *maṇḍvā* [*maṇḍapa-*], m. a frame (for vines), arbour.

¹**मंडा** *maṇḍā* [*maṇḍaka-*], m. reg. (N.) a kind of thin bread-cake.

²**मंडा** *maṇḍā*, m. reg. (E.) a small measure of land (= two *bisve*).

मंडित *maṇḍit* [S.], adj. **1.** adorned; crowned (as with success). **2.** overlaid (as with gold). **3.** covered over.

मँड़ियाना *mamṛiyānā* [cf. H. *mamṛ*], v.t. reg. **1.** to starch. **2.** to dye.

मंडी *maṇḍī* [? conn. *maṇḍa-*[2] or *maṇḍa-*[6]], f. a market, esp. a wholesale market for a particular thing (as grain, vegetables, stock).

[1]**मँड़ुआ** *mamṛuā* [*maṇḍapa-*], m. = मंडप, 1., 2.

[2]**मँड़ुआ** *mamṛuā*, m. a millet (= मड़ुआ).

मंडुक *maṇḍuk*, m. Brbh. = मंडूक.

मंडूक *maṇḍūk* [S.], m. a frog.

मंढप *maṇḍhap*, m. pronun. var. = मंडप.

मंढा *maṇḍhā* [**maṇḍhaka-*], m. 1. = मंडप. **2.** light framework for a canopy. **3.** bower. — मंढे चढ़ना, to climb a trellis (a creeper); to ascend to the wedding hall or bower, to be married.

मंतर *mantar*, m. = मंत्र. — छू ~ हो जाना, to vanish. – मंतर-जंतर, m. = मंत्र-यंत्र.

मंत्र *mantră* [S.], m. **1.** a sacred verse or text, esp. of the Vedas. **2.** a formula sacred to a partic. deity. **3.** a magical formula; incantation, spell. **4.** spiritual instruction; counsel. — ~ चलाना, or पढ़ना, or फूँकना, or मारना, to cast or to recite or to breathe a spell (over, पर). ~ देना (को), to give spiritual advice; to make a disciple (of); to give counsel. – मंत्र-पूत, adj. sanctified by a mantra. मंत्र-बीज, m. opening syllable or line, essential part, of a mantra. मंत्र-मुग्ध, adj. enchanted, fascinated. मंत्र-यंत्र, m. sorcery; exorcism; a talisman. मंत्रालय [°*ra*+*ā*°], m. ministry; secretariat.

मंत्रण *mantraṇ* [S.], m. counselling, advising.

मंत्रणा *mantrăṇā* [S.], f. **1.** consultation, deliberation. **2.** counsel, advice. — मंत्रणाकार, m. a consultant.

मंत्रि- *mantri-* in comp. of a minister or ministers (cf. मंत्री, 1.): — मंत्रिमंडल, m. *govt.* cabinet.

मंत्रित *mantrit* [S.], adj. **1.** initiated or consecrated by recitation of a *mantra.* **2.** counselled.

मंत्रित्व *mantritvă* [S.], m. position, office or activity of a minister of state, or of a counsellor.

मंत्री *mantrī* [S.], m.; f. **1.** a minister of state. **2.** a king's counsellor; a counsellor. **3.** secretary (of an organisation). **4.** (in chess) the queen. — प्रधान ~, m. f. Prime Minister. – मंत्री-मंडल, m. see मंत्रिमंडल.

मंथ *manth*, m. *Pl. HŚS.* **1.** churning, stirring. **2.** shaking.

मंथन *manthan* [S.], m. **1.** churning, stirring. **2.** shaking, agitating (the feelings). **3.** delving into, sifting through (a matter).

मंथनी *manthănī* [S.], f. a churning-vessel, churn.

मंथर *manthar* [S.], adj. **1.** slow, sluggish; inert; idle. **2.** stupid. **3.** crooked; devious. **4.** base.

मंथिनी *manthinī*, f. = मंथनी.

मंद *mand* [S.], adj. & m. **1.** adj. slow, sluggish; inert; slack (as a market); cheap. **2.** faint, weak (as light, or sound; or a smile). **3.** low (as fire). **4.** low, deep (as sound, voice). **5.** mild, gentle (as a breeze). **6.** stupid. **7.** wicked, base. **8.** m. the planet Saturn. — ~ करना, to retard; to slacken (speed, gait); to abate. ~ पड़ना, to become slow, slack, reduced, &c.; to be allayed, or pacified. ~ गति, f. slow or soft gait or movement; slow progress. मंदतर, adv. more slowly; quite slowly. ~ ~, adv. slowly; softly; slightly, &c. – मंदबुद्धि, f. slow-witted. मंदभागी, adj. unfortunate, wretched. °-भाग्य, m. misfortune. मंदागिन, f. = next. मंदाग्नि [°*da*+*a*°], f. indigestion. मंदादर [°*da*+*ā*°], adj. disrespectful; inattentive, neglectful.

-मंद *-mand* [P. *-mand*], suffix (forms adjectives having the sense 'possessed of ...', e.g. एहसानमंद, grateful).

मंदता *mandătā* [S.], adj. slowness, &c. (see मंद).

मंदन *mandan* [S.], m. slackening, abatement.

मंदर *mandar* [S.], m. *mythol.* name of a mountain (used by the gods and *asuras* in the churning of the ocean).

मंदरा *mandrā*, m. Brbh. a drum or other musical instrument (cf. मंदल).

मँदरा *mamdrā* [cf. *manda-*], adj. reg. of low stature.

मंदल *mandal*, m. reg. a drum, kettledrum.

मंदना *mandnā* [H. *mamdānā*], v.i. = मँदाना.

मंदा *mandā* [*manda-*], adj. = मंद. —~ करना, = मंद करना; to mitigate. ~ बेचना, to sell cheap. ~ लगाना, to set a low price on, to sell cheap.

मंदाकिनी *mandākinī* [S.], f. **1.** *mythol.* the stream of the celestial Ganges. **2.** the Milky Way. **3.** a galaxy.

मँदाना *mamdānā* [cf. H. *mand(ā)*], v.i. **1.** to become slow, inert, &c. **2.** to abate.

मंदार *mandār* [S.], m. **1.** the coral tree. **2.** swallow-wort (= [1]मदार).

मंदिर *mandir* [ad. *mandira-*], m. **1.** a temple. **2.** a palace. **3.** an abode, dwelling. **4.** fig. the body.

मंदिरा *mandirā* [cf. H. *mandir*], m. *Pl. HŚS.* a stable.

मंदी *mandī* [cf. H. *mand*], f. **1.** fall in prices. **2.** slackness (of trade); depression.

मंद्र *mandră* [S.], adj. pleasant; low, deep (sound).

मंशा *maṃśā* [A. *manśā'*], f. m. **1.** desire. **2.** intention.

मंसब *maṃsab* [A. *manṣab*], m. **1.** post, office. **2.** *hist.* a Mughal military title and rank. — **मंसबदार** [P. *-dār*], m. an office-holder, official; *hist.* holder of a *mansab.* °**ई**, f. office, appointment; official position.

मंसूबा *maṃsūbā*, m. = **मनसूबा**.

मई *maī* [Engl. *May*], m. the month of May.

मकई *makaī* [conn. *markaka-*], f. maize, corn (= [1]**मक्का**).

[1]**मकड़ा** *makṛā* [*markaṭa-*[2], Pa. *makkaṭaka-*], m. **1.** a large spider. **2.** fig. a person of gangling build.

[2]**मकड़ा** *makṛā* [*markaṭaka-*], m. reg. a millet, *Eleusine coracana* and (?) *aegyptica* (= **मडुआ**).

मकड़ाना *makṛānā*, [cf. H. [1]*makṛā*], v.t. *Pl. HŚS.* **1.** to move crookedly or tortuously. **2.** to walk affectedly; to swagger (cf. **अकड़ना**).

मकड़ी *makṛī* [*markaṭa-*[2], Pa. *makkaṭaka-*], f. a spider. — ~ **का जाला**, m. a spider's web. ~ **मली जाना**, reg. = next. ~ **फलना**, to be touched by a spider and to have eruptions on the skin.

मकतब *maktab* [A. *maktab*], m. place of writing: **1.** a school. **2.** a ceremony, or feast, held when a boy is first sent to school. — ~ **का यार**, m. school-friend.

मकतूब *maktūb* [A. *maktūb*], adj. & m. U. **1.** adj. written. **2.** m. a letter.

मक़दूर *maqdūr* [A. *maqdūr*], m. U. **1.** capacity, power. **2.** means, resources. — ~ **न रखना**, not to have the capacity (to, **का**), to be unable (to).

मक़बरा *maqbarā* [A. *maqbara*], m. place of a grave: a tomb; mausoleum.

मक़बूल *maqbūl* [A. *maqbūl*], adj. U. **1.** accepted, approved. **2.** agreeable, pleasing.

मकरंद *makărand* [S.], m. **1.** nectar. **2.** pollen. **3.** a lotus filament.

[1]**मकर** *makar* [S.], m. **1.** a sea-monster. **2.** a crocodile. **3.** the sign Capricorn (of the zodiac). 4. = **मकर-संक्रांति**. — **मकर-ध्वज**, m. a title of the god of love, Kāmdev. **मकर-महीना**, the month Māgh (January-February). **मकर-रेखा**, f. the tropic of Capricorn. **मकर-संक्रांति**, f. *astron.* entry of the sun into Capricorn.

[2]**मकर** *makr* [A. *makr*], m. **1.** deceit; wile, trick. **2.** pretence. — **मकर-चाँदनी**, f. Brbh. faint (or deceptive) moonlight.

मकरी *makrī* [S.], f. Brbh. a female crocodile.

मक़रूज़ *maqrūz* [A.*maqrūz*], adj. in debt.

मकरेड़ा *makreṛā*, m. reg. (W.) a maize stalk, or stalks.

मक़सद *maqsad* [A. *maqṣad*], m. **1.** intention, purpose; aim; goal. **2.** desire.

मक़सूद *maqsūd* [A. *maqṣūd*], f. intended: intention, &c. (= **मक़सद**).

मक़सूम *maqsūm* [A. *maqsūm*], adj. & m. **1.** adj. divided. **2.** m. *arith.* dividend.

मकान *makān* [A. *makān*], m. a place, station: **1.** a house; dwelling. **2.** a flat, apartment. — ~ **किराए**, or **किराए पर**, **देना** (**को**), to let a house, &c. (to). ~ **किराए**, or **किराए पर**, **लेना**, to rent a house, &c. - **रिहायशी** ~, m. block of flats, or residential quarters. — **मकानदार** [P. *-dār*], m. the owner of a house. **मकान-मालिक**, m. id.; landlord. °**-मालकिन**, f.

मक़ाम *maqām* [P. *maqām*], m. = **मुक़ाम**.

मक़ामी *maqāmī*, adj. = **मुक़ामी**.

मकु *maku* [? *mā+khalu*], adv. Brbh. Av. but, moreover; indeed, even.

मको *mako*, m. = **मकोय**.

मकोड़ा *makoṛā* [*matkoṭaka-*], m. a large ant.

मकोय *makoy*, m. **1.** the Cape gooseberry, *Physalis peruviana.* **2.** a medicinal plant, *Solanum rubrum.*

मकोल *makol* [conn. *makkola-*], m. *Pl.* calcium sulphate, gypsum.

मक्कड़ *makkaṛ*, m. = **मकड़ा**.

[1]**मक्का** *makkā* [conn. *markaka-*], m. maize, corn.

[2]**मक्का** *makkā* [A. *makka*], m. Mecca.

मक्कार *makkār* [A. *makkār*], adj. & m. **1.** adj. deceitful, crafty. **2.** hypocritical. **3.** m. a deceiver. **4.** a hypocrite.

मक्कारपन *makkārpan* [cf. H. *makkār*], m. deceitfulness, &c.

मक्कारी *makkārī* [A. *makkār*+P. *-ī*], f. deceitfulness, &c.

मक्खन *makkhan* [*mrakṣaṇa-*; ← Panj.], m. butter. — ~ निकालना (से or का), to make butter, to churn.

मक्खा *makkhā* [*makṣa-*], m. a large fly.

मक्खी *makkhī* [*makṣikā-*], f. **1.** a fly. **2.** a bee (i.e. शहद की ~). **3.** foresight (of a rifle). — ~, or मक्खियाँ, उड़ाना, or झलना, to drive away flies (from off, पर से); to have little to do, to kill time. ~ की तरह निकालना, to remove (someone or sthg. unwanted, as a fly from milk). ~ मारना, = ~ उड़ाना, 2. मक्खियाँ भिनकना, flies to buzz (about), to settle (on, पर): to be filthy. – मक्खीचूस, m. fly-sucker: a miser. मक्खीमार, m. fly-killer; a filthy person; an idle person; a slavish copyist. जीती ~ निगलना, fig. to bring evil on oneself; to tell arrant lies; to turn a blind eye (to shortcomings). नाक पर ~ न बैठने देना, fig. to shrink from incurring an obligation; to wish to be not less than perfect.

मक्खीर *makkhīr*, m. reg. honey.

मक्खो *makkho*, f. reg. rumour, gossip.

मक्र *makr*, m. see [2]मकर.

मक्षिका *makṣikā* [S.], f. **1.** a fly. **2.** a bee.

मख *makh* [S.], m. a sacrifice, sacrificial offering.

मख़ज़न *makhzan* [A. *makhzan*], m. store-room, arsenal, magazine.

मखनिया *makhaniyā* [cf. H. *makkhan*], m. reg. a maker or seller of butter.

मख़मल *makhmal* [A. *mukhmal*: P. *makhmal*], m. velvet.

मख़मली *makhmalī* [A. *mukhmal*: +P. *-ī*], adj. **1.** of velvet. **2.** velvety.

मख़मसा *makhmasā* [A. *makhmasa*], m. U. wretchedness, hunger: a difficulty, dilemma.

मख़मूर *makhmūr* [A. *makhmūr*], adj. U. intoxicated.

मख़रूती *makhrūtī* [A. *makhrūṭī*], adj. U. turned, shaped: tapering.

मख़लूक़ *makhlūq* [A. *makhlūq*], adj. & m. U. **1.** adj. created. **2.** m. a created being or thing.

मख़सूस *makhsūs* [A. *makhṣūṣ*], adj. U. particularised: particular, special.

[1]**मखाना** *makhānā* [cf. *mrakṣati*], v.t. to smear, to apply (as oil, ointment).

[2]**मखाना** *makhānā*, m. seed of the water-lily.

मखौल *makhaul* [Panj. *makhaul*], m. a joke (= मज़ाक़).

मगंद *magand*, m. reg. (W.) = मगद.

मग *mag* [*mārga-*], m. Brbh. Av. way, road.

मग़ज़ *magz* [P. *magz*], m. **1.** brain. **2.** pith, pulp, marrow. **3.** essential substance (of anything). **4.** a pearl of the best quality. — ~ उड़ना, the head or brain to reel. ~ का, adj. having to do with the brain; cerebral. ~ खाना, or चाटना (का), to plague, to harass. ~ ख़ाली करना, to empty the brain: to tire (oneself) by talking too much; to harass, to worry. ~ चलना (का), (one's) head to be turned (in pride); to go off (one's) head, to go crazy. ~ पचाना, to rack the brain; to torment, to harass. ~ फिराना, id., 2. ~ भिन्नाना, the head to ring; the senses to reel. ~ मारना, m. to rack the brain. ~ से उतारना, or निकालना, to invent, to fabricate. – मग़ज़-चट्टी, f. reg. idle talk. मग़ज़दार [P. *-dār*], adj. Brbh. brainy, clever. मग़ज़-पच्ची, f. racking the brain. मग़ज़-पच्ची करना, to rack the brain.

मग़ज़ी *magzī* [P. *magzī*], f. edging, border; hem.

मगद *magad*, m. reg. a sweet made of *mūṁg* flour and *ghī*.

मगध *magadh* [S.], m. name of the region of south Bihar.

[1]**मगर** *magar* [P. *magar*], conj. if not: but, however. — अगर-मगर करना, to say if and but, to be reluctant to acquiesce.

[2]**मगर** *magar* [ad. *makara-*[1]], m. **1.** a crocodile. **2.** crocodile-shaped pendant to an ear-ring. — मगर-मच्छ, m. = ~, 1.

मगरा *magrā* [? conn. *maṅga-*], adj. reg. **1.** proud, haughty. **2.** shameless. **3.** stubborn, perverse; sullen.

मगराई *magrāī* [cf. H. *magrā*], f. reg. stubborness, &c.

मगराना *magrānā* [cf. H. *magrā*], v.i. reg. to be stubborn, &c.

मगरापन *magrāpan* [cf. H. *magrā*], m. reg. stubborn, &c.

मग़रिब *magrib* [A. *magrib*], m. U. **1.** the west. **2.** the western world.

मग़रिबी *magribī* [A. *magribī*], adj. & m. U. **1.** adj. western. **2.** m. a westerner.

मगरी *magrī* [conn. *maṅga-*], f. reg. (W.) upper or outer part: **1.** roof-ridge (of thatch); coping (of a wall). **2.** ridgepole. **3.** *Pl.* raised boundary (of a field). **4.** raised water channel (in a garden-bed).

मग़रूर *magrūr* [A. *magrūr*], adj. proud, haughty; presumptuous.

मग़रूरी *magrūrī* [A. *magrūr*+P. *-ī*], f. pride, haughtiness.

मगरेला *magrelā*, m. *Pl.* black cumin, *Nigella indica*.

मगरो *magro*, m. reg. (W.) river sand-banks made cultivable by a deposit of good soil.

मगस *magas* [P. *magas*], f. a fly.

मगही *mag'hī* [cf. *magadha-*], adj. & f. **1.** adj. having to do with the Magadh region. **2.** f. the speech of Magadh.

मगहैया *mag'haiyā* [cf. H. *mag'hī*], m. reg. **1.** a person from the Magadh region of Bihar. **2.** a community of Bihar cultivators.

मगुरी *magurī* [*madgura-*], f. a kind of fish, *Macropteronatus magur* or *Silurus pelorius*.

मग़ज़ *magz*, m. = मग़ज़.

मग्न *magn* [S.], adj. **1.** immersed, sunk or drowned (in, में). **2.** engrossed (in activity). **3.** absorbed (in joys, cares).

मग्नता *magnătā* [S.], f. absorption, &c. (see मग्न); delight.

मघ *magh* [S.], m. *Pl. HŚS.* **1.** reward, prize. **2.** riches.

मघवा *maghăvā* [S.], m. inv. Brbh. the god Indra.

मघा *maghā* [S.], f. *astrol.* name of the tenth lunar asterism.

मघावट *maghāvaṭ*, f. = महावट.

मघी *maghī*, f. reg. (E.) a mustard: Indian rape.

मचक *macak* [cf. H. *macaknā*], f. reg. **1.** a creaking, or pain (in the joints). **2.** Brbh. = मच-मच.

मचकना *macaknā* [**macc-*], v.i. reg. **1.** to creak (as a bed, a door). **2.** to have pains in the joints.

मचका *mackā* [cf. H. *macaknā*], m. reg. **1.** slackness (of a market). **2.** swinging to and fro (as a hammock).

[1]**मचकाना** *mackānā*, v.t. = मिचकाना.

[2]**मचकाना** *mackānā*, v.t. reg. to shake, to bend; to cause (a bed, &c.) to creak.

मचना *macnā* [**macyate*: Pk. *maccaï*], v.i. to be caused, produced: **1.** to be stirred up (as noise, strife). **2.** to break out (as rejoicing).

मच-मच *mac-mac* [**macc-*], m. creaking sound (as of a bed).

[1]**मचमचाना** *macmacānā* [cf. H. *mac-mac*], v.i. reg. to creak (under a weight).

[2]**मचमचाना** *macmacānā* [cf. H. *macnā*], v.i. reg. to become sexually excited. — मचमचाके लिपटना, to embrace passionately.

मचमचाहट *macmacāhaṭ* [cf. H. [1]*macmacānā*], f. reg. **1.** creaking. **2.** passion, lust; heat (of an animal).

मचलना *macalnā* [cf. *macyate*], v.i. **1.** to be headstrong, stubborn. **2.** to be restive, or fractious.

मचला *maclā* [cf. H. *macalnā*], adj. **1.** headstrong, stubborn. **2.** restive, fidgety; fractious.

मचलाई *maclāī*, f. Brbh. = मचलापन.

[1]**मचलाना** *maclānā* [cf. H. *macalnā*], v.i. = मचलना.

[2]**मचलाना** *maclānā* [? conn. *macyate*], v.i. reg. = मतलाना.

मचलापन *maclāpan* [cf. H. *maclā*], m. stubbornness; restiveness.

मचलाहट *maclāhaṭ* [cf. H. *macalnā*], f. reg. = मचलापन.

मचवा *macvā* [cf. H. *mācī*, *maciyā*], m. reg. **1.** a bed. **2.** leg of a bed or stool.

मचवाना *macvānā* [cf. H. *macānā*], v.t. to cause to be stirred up, &c. (by, से).

मचान *macān* [cf. *mañca-*], m. **1.** a platform (as for hunters, watchmen). **2.** stage. **3.** raised seat, or sleeping-place. **4.** raised place for a lamp.

मचाना *macānā* [cf. H. *macnā*], v.t. to cause, to produce; to stir up (as noise, strife).

मचामच *macāmac*, m. = मच-मच.

मचिया *maciyā* [cf. *mañcikā-*], f. a four-legged stool having a seat of woven cord or cane.

मचोड़ना *macoṛnā*, v.t. reg. **1.** to twist. **2.** ? to jolt.

मच्छ *macch* [ad. *matsya-*, or ← Panj. *macch*], m. **1.** a fish. **2.** name of the first avatār of Viṣṇu.

मच्छड़ *macchaṛ* [? H. *macchar*], m. a mosquito, &c. (= मच्छर).

मच्छर *macchar* [*matsara-*[2]], m. **1.** a mosquito. **2.** a gnat; midge. — मच्छरदानी [P. *-dān*], f. mosquito-net.

[1]**मच्छी** *macchī* [*matsya-*], f. a fish (= मछली). — मच्छीमार, m. a fisherman.

[2]**मच्छी** *macchī* [ad. *makṣikā-*: w. H. *makkhī*], f. a fly.

मछमारी *machmārī* [H. *macch*, or [1]*māchī*, +H. *mārnā*], f. reg. fishing.

मछरंगा *machraṅgā* [conn. *matsyaraṅga-*], m. a kingfisher.

मछराँद *machrāṁd* [conn. H. *machlī*, H. *gandh*], f. the smell of fish.

मछली *machlī* [cf. *matsya-*], f. **1.** a fish. **2.** a sign of the zodiac (Pisces). **3.** a silverfish. **4.** an ear-ring pendant shaped like a fish. **5.** a muscle or tendon of the arm or leg. — ~ की तरह तड़पना, to flounder like a fish (out of water); to be agitated or distressed; to jump about in pain. ~ पकड़ना, or मारना, to catch a fish; to fish. ~ पड़ना, muscle to develop (in, में). – मछलीमार, adj. & m. fishing; a fisherman.

मछुआ *machuā* [cf. *matsya-*], m. **1.** fisherman. **2.** fishmonger. — मच्छुआगिरी [P. *-garī, -girī*], fishing (the occupation).

मज *maj*, adj. reg. soft, ripe.

मज़कूर *mazkūr* [A. *mażkūr*], adj. S.H. mentioned; previously mentioned.

मजदा *majdā*, m. *Pl.* a mixed soil of clay and sand.

मज़दूर *mazdūr* [P. *muzdūr*], m. a labourer; a porter; workman. — मज़दूर-संघ, m. trade union. मज़दूर-सभा, f. id.

मज़दूरा *mazdūrā* [cf. H. *mazdūr*], m. reg. = मज़दूर.

मज़दूरिन *mazdūrin* [cf. H. *mazdūr*], f. a woman labourer, &c.

मज़दूरी *mazdūrī* [P. *muzdūrī*], f. **1.** bodily labour; work as a labourer. **2.** wages, day-wages. **3.** charge (for work done; or for a service). — ~ करना, to work as a labourer.

मजनूँ *majnūṁ* [A. *majnūn*], adj. & m. possessed by a jinn: **1.** adj. crazy; crazed with love. **2.** m. name of the lover of Lailā (in Persian poetry). **3.** fig. a wasted, frail person. — रोता ~, m. fig. the weeping willow.

मज़बूत *mazbūt* [A. *mażbūṭ*], adj. **1.** strong (esp. of things, but also of persons). **2.** fixed, firm; tight (as a tie); steady; immovable. **3.** firm (of market prices).

मज़बूती *mazbūtī* [A. *mażbūṭ*+P. *-ī*], f. strength, firmness, &c. — ~ पकड़ना, to grow in strength, to be strengthened.

मजबूर *majbūr* [A. *majbūr*], adj. **1.** compelled. **2.** helpless, having no option. **3.** oppressed. — ~ करना, to compel, &c. (to,पर, के लिए).

मजबूरन *majbūran* [A. *majbūran*], adv. = मजबूरी से.

मजबूरी *majbūrī* [A. *majbūr*+P. *ī*], f. **1.** compulsion. **2.** powerlessness, helplessness. — ~ से, adv. compulsorily; yielding to force; of necessity.

मजमा *majmā* [A. *majma'a*], m. place of assembly: an assembly of people.

मजमुआ *majmuā* [A. *majmū'a*], adj. & m. inv. U. **1.** adj. collected. **2.** m. a collection.

मज़मून *mazmūn* [A. *mażmūn*], m. U. **1.** contents (as of a letter, book); subject-matter. **2.** import, sense. **3.** an essay, an article. — मज़मून-निगार [P. *-nigār*], m. essayist; journalist; editor.

मज़म्मत *mazammat* [A. *mażamma*: P. *mażammat*], f. 19c. blame; censure.

मजरूह *majrūh* [A. *majrūḥ*], adj. U. wounded; love-sick.

मज़र्रत *mazarrat* [A. *mażarra*: P. *mażarrat*], f. harm, damage. — ~ पहुँचाना (को), to cause harm, &c.

मजलिस *majlis* [A. *majlis*], f. **1.** an assembly; meeting; conference. **2.** a society. **3.** session (of a committee, conference). **4.** social gathering. — ~ करना, to convene or to hold a meeting. – मजलिस-घर, m. place of meeting or assembly.

मजलिसी *majlisī* [A. *majlis*+P. *-ī*], m. participant in an assembly, &c.

मज़लूम *mazlūm* [A. *mażlūm*], adj. U. wrongfully treated; oppressed.

मज़हब *mazhab* [A. *mażhab*], m. U. way, manner of going: religion. — ~ में मिलाना, or लाना, to convert to a religion.

मज़हबी *mazhabī* [cf. A. *mażhab*], adj. having to do with a religion; religious. — ~ लड़ाई, f. religious war; crusade.

मज़ा *mazā* [P. *maza*], m. **1.** taste, relish. **2.** pleasure, enjoyment; contentment. **3.** amusement, fun; joke. — ~ आना (को), relish, or pleasure, &c. to be felt (by: at or in, में). ~ उड़ाना, to enjoy to the full, to revel (in, का). ~ चखाना, colloq. to give (one) a taste (of, का: as of a stick, in punishment); to give (one) pleasure, &c. ~ लूटना, = ~ उड़ाना. ~ लेना, to take pleasure, to enjoy oneself. मज़े करना, to enjoy oneself; to make fun (of). मज़े की बात, f. sthg. giving pleasure, or amusement; a joke. मज़े में, adv. contented. यहाँ मज़े में हूँ, things are fine with (me) here. मज़े से हैं? are (you) getting on all right? मज़े हैं, colloq. things are going nicely. – मज़ेदार [P. *-dār*], adj. tasty; pleasant; amusing, interesting. °ई, f.

मज़ाक़ *mazāq* [A. *mażāq*], m. **1.** taste, relish. ***2.** a joke. **3.** humour, wit. — ~ उड़ाना, to make fun (of, का). ~ करना, to joke. ~ का, adj. humorous, witty; liking to joke. ~ में, adv. = next, 1. ~ से, adv. as a joke, in fun; humorously, wittily. – मज़ाक़पसंद, [P. *-pasand*], adj. = ~ का, 2.

मज़ाक़न *mazāqan* [A. *mazāqan*], adv. = मज़ाक़ से.

मज़ाक़िया *mazāqiyā* [cf. H. *mazāq*], adj. usu. inv. humorous. — ~ तौर पर, adv. as a joke; humorously.

मजाज़ी *majāzī* [cf. A. *majāz*], adj. allowable, licit: **1.** figurative, allegorical (as love). **2.** not real; artificial, insincere.

मज़ार *mazār* [A. *mazār*], m. *musl.* **1.** place of pilgrimage; shrine. **2.** tomb; grave.

मजारा *majārā* [A. *muzārī'*], m. contracting: a tenant farmer.

मजाल *majāl* [A. *majāl*], f. U. **1.** strength, power; courage, nerve. **2.** right. — उसकी क्या ~ है कि..., what power, or right, has he to...?

मजिस्ट्रेट *majisṭreṭ* [Engl. *magistrate*], m. magistrate.

मजिस्ट्रेटी *majisṭreṭī* [cf. H. *majisṭreṭ*], f. magistracy.

मजीठ *majīṭh* [*mañjiṣṭhā-*], f. the madder plant, and its dye.

मजीठी *majīṭhī* [cf. H. *majīṭh*], adj. Av. madder-coloured: red.

मजीद *majīd* [A. *majīd*], adj. U. **1.** exalted, high. **2.** elaborate (as a superfluous proof).

मजीरा *majīrā* [*mañjīra-*], m. **1.** a tinkling ornament for the feet. ***2.** cymbals.

मजूर *majūr*, m. reg. = मज़दूर.

मज्ज- *majj-* [*majjati*], v.i. Brbh. to sink, to drown.

मज्जन *majjan* [S.], m. immersion; bathing.

मज्जा *majjā* [S.], f. marrow (of a bone); pith; sap.

मझ *majh*, m. & adv. Av. = मँझ.

मझला *majhlā*, adj. = मँझला.

मझार *majhār* [**madhyāra-*], adv. Brbh. **1.** adv. in the middle of, in.

[1]**मझेला** *majhelā*, adj. *Pl.* = मझोला.

[2]**मझेला** *majhelā*, m. *Pl.* a shoemaker's awl (cf. मझोली).

मझोतर *majhotar*, m. reg. (Bihar) rope or strap joining the yokes of a four-bullock team.

मझोला *majholā* [cf. *madhya-*], adj. **1.** middle. **2.** middling, average (as in size, age, position).

मझोली *majholī* [cf. H. *majholā*], f. reg. **1.** a light, two-wheeled ox-cart. **2.** a medium-sized chisel or awl. **3.** W. the fields of a village lying at a middling distance from it.

मटक *maṭak* [cf. H. *maṭaknā*], f. flirtatious glances or manner. — मटक-चटक, f. id.

मटकन *maṭkan* [cf. H. *maṭaknā*], f. flirtatious glances, gestures or gait.

[1]**मटकना** *maṭaknā* [cf. **maṭṭ-*], v.i. to make flirtatious glances or gestures.

[2]**मटकना** *maṭaknā* [cf. H. *maṭkā*], m. a small pot or mug (as used for taking water out of a large container).

मटकनि *maṭăkani* [cf. H. *maṭăknā*], f. Brbh. = मटकन.

मटका *maṭkā* [cf. **mārtta-*], m. a large earthen jar or pot.

मटकाना *maṭkānā* [cf. H. *maṭaknā*], v.t. to make flirtatious movements (with the eyes or body).

[1]**मटकी** *maṭkī* [cf. H. *maṭaknā*], f. a flirtatious gesture; a wink.

[2]**मटकी** *maṭkī* [cf. H. *maṭkā*], f. a small earthen jar or pot.

[3]**मटकी** *maṭkī*, f. *Pl.* a baby's teething-stick (= मुट्ठी, 6).

मटकैना *maṭkainā* [cf. H. *maṭkā*], m. reg. (E.) a drinking-vessel having a wide mouth and sloping sides.

मटकोठा *maṭkoṭhā* [H. *maṭṭī*+H. *koṭhā*], m. reg. a house made of earth or clay.

मटक्को *maṭakko* [cf. H. *maṭaknā*], f. colloq. a woman who walks so as to attract men's attention.

मटकौवल *maṭkauval*, m. (? & adj.) = मटक.

मटमैला *maṭmailā* [H. *maṭṭī*, H. *mailā*], adj. earth-coloured: dirtied, dusty; dull.

मटमैलापन *maṭmailāpan* [cf. H. *maṭmailā*], m. earthy, dusty or dull colour.

मटर *maṭar* [**maṭṭara-*[1]], m. a pea; peas. — मटर-सी आँखें, f. pl. tiny eyes. – मटरगश्त [P. *-gaśt*], f. m. strolling, wandering मटरगश्ती करना, to stroll; to wander about.

मटरगश्ती *maṭargaśtī*, f. see. s.v. मटर.

मटरा *maṭrā* [**maṭṭara-*[1]], m. reg. **1.** a large species of pea; a large pea. **2.** *Pl.* a kind of silk cloth.

मटराला *maṭrālā* [cf. H. *maṭar*], m. barley mixed with peas.

मटरी *maṭrī* [cf. H. *maṭar*], f. a small pea; a pea.

मटरीला *maṭrīlā* [cf. H. *maṭar*], adj. mixed with peas (as a crop).

मटिया *maṭiyā* [cf. H. *maṭṭī*], adj. inv. & m. **1.** adj. made of earth, earthen. **2.** earth-coloured; dirty. **3.** fig. frail; infirm. **4.** m. reg. a well not having a frame (and liable to fall in). — ~ तेल, m. kerosene. – मटिया-ठस, adj. & m. lazy; a lazy person. मटिया-फूँस, adj. reg. = ~, 3. °-फूस, adj. id. मटिया-मसान, adj. = ~, 3.; a waste or ruined place. मटिया-मेट, adj. razed, destroyed.

[1]**मटियाना** *maṭiyānā* [cf. H. *maṭṭī*], v.t. & v.i. reg. **1.** v.t. to scour, or to smear, with mud. **2.** v.i. to be reduced to dust; to be levelled, razed.

[2]**मटियाना** *maṭiyānā* [H. *maṭṭī*, and cf. [1]*maṭiyānā*], v.t. reg. to take no notice of; to turn a deaf ear to.

मटियार *maṭiyār*, f. m. a clay soil.

मटियाला *maṭiyālā* [cf. H. *maṭṭī*], adj. earth-coloured.

मटीला *maṭīlā* [cf. H. *maṭṭī*], adj. reg. 1. = मटिया, 1., 2. **2.** lazy (= मटिया-ठस).

मटुका *maṭukā*, m. = मटका.

मटुकी *maṭukī*, f. Brbh. = [2]मटकी.

मटोला *maṭolā* [cf. H. *maṭṭī*], m. *Pl.* heap of earth; boundary-marker; fixed survey point.

मट्टी *maṭṭī*, f. = मिट्टी.

मट्ठर *maṭṭhar*, adj. = [2]मट्ठा.

[1]**मट्ठा** *maṭṭhā* [? *mr̥ṣṭa-*[1]], m. buttermilk (milk remaining after the churning of butter).

[2]**मट्ठा** *maṭṭhā* [**maṭṭha-*[1]], adj. slow, sluggish; stolid.

मट्ठापन *maṭṭhāpan*, m. slowness, sluggishness; stolidity.

मट्ठी *maṭṭhī*, f. = मठरी.

मठ *maṭh* [S.], m. **1.** residence of a devotee and his disciples; religious establishment. **2.** a temple. — मठधारी, m. head of a residential religious community.

मठरी *maṭhrī* [cf. *mr̥ṣṭa-*[1]], f. **1.** a kind of crisp, salted savoury made from refined flour. **2.** a sweet cake.

मठारना *maṭhārnā* [cf. *mr̥ṣṭa-*[1]], v.t. **1.** to hammer (a metal vessel) into shape. **2.** fig. to talk over (a matter).

[1]**मठी** *maṭhī* [S.], f. a small religious house; cell, cloister.

[2]**मठी** *maṭhī* [S.], m. Brbh. resident, or (?) supervisor of a religious house.

मठोर *maṭhor* [? cf. **mr̥ṣṭa-*[1]], f. a tall earthen jar (as for buttermilk).

मठोल- *maṭhol-* [**mastaphulla-*], adj. Brbh. ? filled out or puffed out, ample (a turban).

मठौरा *maṭhaurā*, m. Brbh. a heavy plane (for preliminary work).

मड़ाड़ *maṛāṛ*, f. reg. hollow, indentation (of a pool or tank).

मड़ार *maṛār*, f. reg. the pit of a ruined well (= मड़ाड़).

मड़ी *maṛī*, f. reg. **1.** a border; a small field, or patch of sown ground. **2.** a bank.

मड़आ *maṛuā* [conn. *maḍaka-*], m. the millet *Eleusine coracana.*

[1]**मड़ैया** *maṛaiyā* [*mayaṭa-*, Pk. *mayaḍa-*], f. reg. small platform for watching crops from.

[2]**मड़ैया** *maṛaiyā*, m. = मढ़ैया.

मड्डी *maḍḍī*, f. m. reg. **1.** f. dregs. **2.** m. colloq. the pits, bottom of the barrel: a stupid person.

मड्डीपना *maḍḍīpanā* [cf. H. *maḍḍī*], m. reg. stupidity.

मढ़न *maṛhan* [cf. H. *maṛhnā*], f. covering; lining; membrane (of a drum).

मढ़ना *maṛhnā* [**maḍh-*: Pk. *maḍhia-*], v.t. **1.** to cover (as a book, a drum); to spread (as paper, lining: upon or over, पर); to fix, to set (as a frame to a picture, पर). **2.** to coat; to gild; to set (with jewels). **3.** to attribute wrongly (as blame: to, पर, के सिर). **4.** to charge or to saddle (with, के सिर: as with a task).

मढ़वाई *maṛhvāī* [cf. H. *maṛhvānā*], f. act of, or cost of, having (sthg.) covered, &c.

मढ़वाना *maṛhvānā* [cf. H. *maṛnā*], v.t. to cause to be covered, &c. (by, से).

मढ़ा *maṛhā* [*maṭha-*[1]], m. any open building, or marquee (as erected on festive occasions).

मढ़ाई *maṛhāī* [cf. H. *maṛhānā*], f. **1.** covering (as with a veneer). **2.** cost of covering.

मढ़ाना *maṛhānā*, v.t. = मढ़वाना.

मढ़ी *maṛhī* [*maṭhikā-*], f. **1.** a cottage, hut. **2.** small shed. **3.** small temple.

मढ़ैया *maṛhaiyā* [cf. *maṭha-*[1]], m. small shed, hut.

मणि *maṇi* [S.], f. m. **1.** a precious stone, jewel. **2.** a bead, or similar ornament. **3.** colloq. glans penis. — मणि-बंध, m. wrist; bracelet. मणिभ, m. crystal. मणिमय, adj. formed of or with jewels; bejewelled. मणि-माला, f. necklace of jewels. मणि-राजी, f. cluster of jewels: the stars.

मतंग *mataṅg* [S.], m. **1.** an elephant. **2.** fig. a looming cloud.

[1]**मत** *mat* [cf. *mā*: Pk. *maṁta*], adv. w. imp. (properly of 2nd pers). not, do not. — मत जाओ! don't go! जाओ मत! don't go! don't you go!

[2]**मत** *mat* [S.], m. **1.** opinion, view; feeling. **2.** system of opinions; doctrine; persuasion (religious, philosophical, political). **3.** fig. sect, party. **4.** thought, idea; intention. **5.** advice. **6.** vote. — ~ देना, to give one's opinion; to vote. ~ रखना, to hold an opinion (of or about, पर). ~ मारी जाना, one's senses to be lost. ~ में आना, to be converted to the view(s) (of, के). एक ~ से, adv. unanimously. मेरे ~ में, or से, adv. in my opinion. – मत-दान, m. voting. मातदान करना, or देना, to vote. °-दाता, m. inv. a voter. मत-भेद, m. difference of opinion, &c.; divergence of views. मत-मतांतर [°*ta*+*a*°], m. different opinions, variety of opinion. मतवाद, m. doctrinal dispute. मतांतर [°*ta*+*a*°], m. different opinion, &c. मतांतर से, adv. as others would have it. मताग्रह[°*ta*+*ā*°], m. insistence on a view, dogmatism. मताधिकार [°*ta*+*a*°], m. right to vote. °ई, m. ensuffraged person. मतानुयायी [°*ta*+*a*°], m. adherent of a view or doctrine. मतानुसार [°*ta*+*a*°], adv. according to the view, &c. (of, के). मतावलंबी [°*ta*+*a*°], m. = मतानुयायी. मतैक्य [°*ta*+*ai*°], m. unity of opinion, agreement in views.

[3]**मत** *mat* [ad. *mati-*], f. pronun. var. = मति.

मतना *matnā*, m. a type of sugar-cane having several sub-types.

मतबा *matbā* [A. *maṭbaʿ*], m. inv. printing-house, printing-press.

मतबूआ *matbūā* [A. *maṭbūʿa*], adj. inv. printed.

मतलब *matlab* [A. *maṭlab*], m. **1.** object, intention; purpose; desire. **2.** meaning. **3.** sense, point. इससे क्या ~? what is the sense, point, of that? — ~?, colloq. what is the meaning (of this)?: what do you think you're doing? ~ का यार, m. a time-serving, or self-interested, friend. ~ गाँठना, or निकालना, to achieve (one's, अपना) object. ~ रखना, to have a motive or interest (in, से). आपका इससे क्या ~ है? what is that to do with you?

मतलबिया *matlabiyā*, adj. = मतलबी.

मतलबी *matlabī* [cf. H. *matlab*], adj. & m. **1.** adj. self-seeking, self-interested. **2.** m. a self-seeking person.

मतलाई *matlāī* [cf. H. *matlānā*], f. nausea.

मतलाना *matlānā* [? cf. *matta-*; or conn. **makta-*: cf. H. *macalnā*, and *macyate*], v.i. to feel nausea. — जी ~, id.

मतली *matlī* [cf. H. *matlānā*], f. nausea. — ~ आना (को), to feel nausea.

मतवार *matvār*, adj. Brbh. = मतवाला.

मतवाला *matvālā* [**mattapāla-*: Pk. *mattavāla-*], adj. & m. **1.** intoxicated, &c. (see मत्त). **2.** a drunken man. **3.** *HŚS.* a heavy boulder (for throwing down from a fort on besiegers). **4.** a child's toy having a curved and weighted base (which always brings it to rest in a vertical position). **5.** transf. a free spirit.

मता *matā* [cf. H. [2]*mat*], m. reg. = [2]मत, 1., 5. — ~ करना, to consult (with, से); to conspire (with).

मतारी *matārī*, f. reg. = [1]माँ.

मति *mati* [S.], f. **1.** mind, understanding. **2.** thought, idea (= [2]मत, 4.); opinion. — मति-भ्रंश, m. mental breakdown. मति-भ्रम, m. perplexity; error; hallucination. मति-भ्रांति, f. id., 1., 2. मतिमंद, adj. slow-witted; devious, malign. मतिमान, adj. intelligent, discerning.

मतेई *mateī* [**mātreya-*: Pa. *matteyya-*], f. Av. a stepmother.

मतौना *mataunā*, m. reg. name of a sub-type of the millet *kodoṁ* of which the grain becomes intoxicating or poisonous during a damp season.

मत्त *matt* [S.], adj. **1.** intoxicated (as by alcohol, lust, pride). **2.** maddened, frenzied; enraged. **3.** exhilarated. **4.** pleased, happy.

मत्तता *mattātā* [S.], f. intoxication, &c. (see मत्त).

मत्ती *mattī* [A. *mattī*], m. **1.** the evangelist Matthew. **2.** the Gospel according to Matthew.

मत्सर *matsar* [S.], m. **1.** envy. **2.** jealousy. **3.** hostility. **4.** anger.

मत्सरी *matsarī* [S.], adj. envious, &c. (see मत्सर).

मत्स्य *matsyă* [S.], m. **1.** a fish. **2.** the first or fish avatār of Viṣṇu. — मत्स्यगंधा, f. a tree that grows near water. मत्स्य-न्याय, m. way of the fish: law of the jungle. मत्स्यावतार [°*ya*+*a*°], m. = ~, 2.

मथन *mathan* [S.], m. **1.** churning. **2.** stirring.

मथना *mathnā* [*mathnāti*], v.t. **1.** to churn. **2.** to stir, to mix; to knead, to work (to a soft consistency). **3.** to revolve (a question); to ponder; to discuss (a question). **4.** to agitate (the feelings). **5.** to search through with care.

मथनिया *mathniyā* [cf. *manthana-*], f. a churn.

मथनी *mathnī* [*manthana-*], f. a churning-stick.

मथानी *mathānī* [*manthāna-*], f. **1.** a churn. **2.** a milk-pan. **3.** a churning-stick. — ~ पड़ना, fig. excitement, or agitation, to arise.

मथित *mathit* [S.], adj. churned; stirred; shaken.

मथुरनी *mathurnī* [cf. H. *mathuriyā*], f. the wife of a Caube brāhmaṇ.

मथुरा *mathurā* [S.], f. name of a city and district in U. P.

मथुरिया *mathuriya* [ad. *mathura-*; or cf. H. *māthur*, 1., 3.], m. **1.** name of a brāhmaṇ community of Mathurā (cf. चौबे). **2.** a man of that community.

मथौट *mathauṭ* [**mastapaṭṭa-*], m. *hist.* a poll-tax (Bengal); a subsidiary tax.

1**मथौरा** *mathaurā*[**mastavaraka-*], m. reg. (W.) **1.** mat worn over the head and shoulders as a protection from rain. **2.** *Pl.* sunshade.

2**मथौरा** *mathaurā*, m. Brbh. ?? see *maṭhaurā*.

1**मद** *mad* [S.], m. **1.** any intoxicant. ***2.** intoxication. **3.** frenzy. **4.** lust, rut; liquid oozing from a rutting elephant's temples. **5.** passion, ardour. **6.** pride. **7.** joy. — मदकल, adj. sounding intoxicated (as wind); excited, frenzied. मदमता, adj. haughty; lustful; in youth's bloom. मदमत्त, adj. intoxicated; excited, frenzied. मदमस्त, adj. id. मदमाता, adj. = मदमता. मद-मोचन, adj. causing frenzy, &c. to subside. मदालस [°*da*+*ā*°], adj. drowsy (as from drink).

2**मद** *mad* [A. *madd*], f. extension, mark indicating an entry: item, heading (of accounts). — ~ में आना, to come under the head or heading (of, की).

3**मद** *mad*, adj. *Pl.* having an oily smell; rancid.

मदक *madak*, f. a narcotic: a mixture of hemp, or of opium with betel or acacia leaves for smoking or chewing. — मदकबाज़ [P. *-bāz*], m. one addicted to *madak*; drug addict.

मदकची *madakcī* [H. *madak*+P. *-cī*], m. = मदकबाज़.

मदकी *madăkī* [cf. H. *madak*], m. = मदकबाज़.

मदद *madad* [A. *madad*], f. **1.** help, aid. **2.** support; means of support; relief. — ~ करना (की), to provide help, &c. ~ देना (को), to help, &c. ~ बाँटना (को), to distribute relief; to pay wages (to labourers). ~ लेना, to receive help, &c. (from, से). – मदद-ख़र्च, m. financial assistance; an advance of money. मददगार [P. *-gār*], m. helper; assistant; supporter; ally. °ई, f. help or assistance given.

मदन *madan* [S.], m. the act of intoxicating or exhilarating: **1.** a title of Kāmdev, the love-god. **2.** passion, lust. **3.** name of several plants. **4.** spring. — मदन-गोपाल, m. a title of Kṛṣṇa. मदन-मस्त, m. tubers of the plant *Amorphophallus campanulatus*, peeled and dried. मदन-मोहन, m. infatuator of the god of love: a title of Kṛṣṇa. मदनोत्सव [°*na*+*u*°], m. *hind.* a festival held in the month of Cait in honour of Kāmdev.

मदरसा *madrasā* [P. *madrasa*], m. a school.

मदहोश *mad'hoś* [A. *madhūś*], adj. intoxicated; carried away (as by rapture); besotted.

मदहोशी *mad'hośī* [A. *madhūś*+P. *-ī*], f. intoxication, &c.

1**मदार** *madār* [*mandāra-*], m.; f. the giant swallow-wort (*Asclepias gigantea*).

2**मदार** *madār* [S.], m. *Pl. HŚS.* an elephant.

1**मदारिया** *madāriyā*, m. = मदारी.

2**मदारिया** *madāriyā* [cf. A. *madār*], m. *Pl. HŚS.* a follower of a Muslim saint called Śāh Madār.

1**मदारी** *madārī* [*mantrakāra-*; ← Panj.], m. **1.** a conjuror, juggler. **2.** one who trains and shows monkeys, or dancing bears.

2**मदारी** *madārī*, m. *Pl. HŚS.* = 2मदारिया.

मदिर *madir* [S.], adj. & m. **1.** adj. intoxicating; arousing passion. **2.** the red catechu plant (= खैर).

मदिरता *madirātā* [S.], f. entrancing sweetness (as of song).

मदिरा *madirā* [S.], f. intoxicating drink: wine; alcohol. — मदिरा-पान, m. the drinking of alcohol. मदिराभ [°*rā*+*ā*°], adj. flushed, or bloodshot (the eyes) with alcohol. मदिरालय [°*rā*+*ā*°], m. wine-hall, tavern.

मदीय *madīyă* [S.], adj. poet. my.

मद्दे *madde* [A. P. *madda-*], adv. on account (of, के).

मद्धम *maddham* [ad. *madhyama-*], adj. & m. pronun. var. = मध्यम.

मद्धिम *maddhim* [ad. *madhyama-*], adj. reg. = मध्यम. — ~ रफ़्तार से, adv. at a slow, or slack pace.

मद्धे *maddhe* [ad. *madhye*], ppn. = में.

मद्य *madyă* [S.], m. any intoxicating drink; wine; alcohol. — मद्य-पान, m. the drinking of alcohol.

मध *madh* [ad. *madhu-*], m. E.H. 1. = मधु. 2. = [1]मद.

मधि *madhi* [ad. *madhya-*], ppn. & m. Brbh. **1.** ppn. = में. **2.** m. middle.

मधु *madhu* [S.], m. & ? adj. **1.** m. honey. **2.** nectar. **3.** sweetness. **4.** an intoxicating drink; a drink made from flowers of the *mahuā* tree. **5.** the *mahuā* tree, *Bassia latifolia*. **6.** spring; the month of Cait. **7.** name of a demon killed by Viṣṇu. **8.** adj. Brbh. sweet; tasty. — मधुकर, m. honey-maker: a black bee; a voluptuous person. °ई, f. id.; [ad. *mādhukarī-*] iron. alms (consisting of cooked food) collected from door to door. °-कारी, f. Brbh. id. मधु-कोष, m. beehive. मधु-चक्र, m. id. मधुप, m. honey-drinker: bee. मधुपर्क, m. an offering to guests, or to a bridegroom, of curds, *ghī*, water, honey, milk and sugar. मधूपुर, m. Brbh. the city of Mathurā. °ई, f. id. मधु-बन, m. Brbh. Av. forest of Madhu: the Braj area around Mathurā; a forest near Kiṣkindhā. मधुबारा, f. Brbh. what is made use of at the time of drinking: = मदिरा. मधुबाला, f. a woman who drinks, or serves, alcohol; a bee attracted to honey: one drawn to any object. मधु-मक्खी, f. honey-bee. °-माखी, f. Brbh. id. मधुमय, adj. sweet; honeyed. °ता, f. मधु-मास, m. spring month: the month of Cait. मधु-मालती, f. jasmine. मधुमेह, m. diabetes. °ई, m. a diabetic. मधु-राका, f. spring full moon; moonlit spring night. मधु-राज, m. Brbh. a bee. मधुलिह, m. Brbh. honey-licker: bee मधुवात, m. spring breeze. मधुशाला, f. wine-hall, tavern (= मयख़ाना); liquor-stall. मधु-सूदन, m. destroyer of Madhu: a title of Viṣṇu or Kṛṣṇa.

मधुत्व *madhutvă* [S.], m. sweetness.

मधुर *madhur* [S.], adj. **1.** sweet. **2.** attractive, charming. **3.** melodious. **4.** soft, gentle (as gait, manner). — मधुर-सरण, adj. moving gently, softly.

मधुरता *madhurătā* [S.], f. sweetness, &c. (see मधुर).

मधुरत्व *madhuratvă* [S.], m. sweetness.

मधुरिका *madhurikā* [S.], f. aniseed (= सौंफ, 2).

मधुरित *madhurit* [S.], adj. sweetened.

मधुरिमा *madhurimā* [S.], f. = मधुरता.

मधूकरी *madhūkrī* [conn. *mādhukarī-*], f. reg. **1.** bread-cakes baked in ashes, or on coals. 2. = मधुकरी, 2. (s.v. मधु).

मध्य *madhyă* [S.], adj. & m. **1.** adj. middle; central. **2.** intervening. **3.** middling (of quality, position). **4.** m. middle, midst; centre. **5.** interval. **6.** waist. **7.** the inside of anything. **8.** ppn. w. के. in the middle, &c. (of); between. — मध्यकाल, m. the medieval period, middle ages. °इक, °ईन, adj. मध्यदेश, m. the middle region of north India: that part of the Ganges basin lying between the Panjab and Allahabad. मध्यपूर्व, m. the Middle East. मध्यमान, m. mean standard, average. मध्ययुग, m. = मध्यकाल. °ईन, °ईय, adj. medieval. मध्यरात्रि, f. midnight. मध्यवयस्क, adj. middle-aged. मध्यवर्ग, m. the middle class. °ई, °ईय, adj. मध्यवर्ती, adj. situated between, separating (regions, &c.); central, middle; internal. मध्यस्थ, adj. & m. standing between, intervening; arbitrating; neutral; a middle-man; mediator, arbitrator; umpire. °ता, f. mediation, &c.; neutrality. मध्यस्थित, adj. situated in the middle, middle. मध्यांतर [°*ya*+*a*°], m. interval. मध्यान, m. corr. = next. मध्याह्न [°*ya*+*a*°], m. midday; middle of the day. मध्याह्नरेखा, f. *astron.* meridian.

मध्यम *madhyam* [S.], adj. & m. **1.** adj. middle (= मध्य); medium, moderate; intermediate. **2.** mediocre. **3.** m. the middle (of anything). 4. = मध्यदेश. **5.** the fourth note of the Indian (heptatonic) musical scale. — ~ पुरुष, m. *gram.* second person. ~ वर्ग, m. the middle class.

मध्यमा *madhyamā* [S.], f. **1.** the middle finger. **2.** *rhet.* a girl who has reached adolescence.

[1]**मन** *man* [*manas-*], m. **1.** the mind (as seat of perception and feeling). **2.** the heart. **3.** the soul. **4.** wish, inclination; will; purpose. **5.** character, temperament. — ~ अटकना, or उलझना, the mind or heart to be captivated (by, से); to fall in love (with). ~ आना, the mind or heart to turn towards: to fall in love (with, पर). ~ उकटाना, the mind or heart to grow weary (of, से). ~ उचटना, the mind or heart to turn away (from, से: as in distaste, disgust). ~ उठना, the mind or heart to be withdrawn (from, से), to be tired (of); to be displeased, or disgusted (with). ~ उलझना, = ~ अटकना. ~ कच्चा करना, to lose heart; to discourage (another); to deter. ~ करना, to desire, or to long. ~ का, adj. pleasing, congenial. ~ का मारा, adj. dejected; troubled; ~ का मैला, adj. disingenuous, deceitful; disaffected. अपने ~ का होना, to be in a desired situation or condition. ~ की बात, f. sthg. in the mind = a secret thought; a dear wish. ~ की ~ में रहना, sthg. desired to remain unaccomplished. ~ की मौज, f. = मन-मौज. ~ के लड्डू खाना, or फोड़ना, fig. to build castles in the air. ~ के ~ में, adv. in the depths of the heart, or soul. ~ खट्टा होना (का), to feel displeasure or chagrin. ~ ख़राब होना (का), to feel displeasure: to feel unwell. ~ चलना, to wish, or to long or to crave (for, पर);

to become crazy. ~ छूना, to touch the heart. ~ टटोलना (का), to attempt to fathom (a person's) mind. ~ डोलना, the mind to waver; appetite or desire to be awakened. ~ तोड़ना, to discourage, to depress (hope, enthusiasm, &c). ~ देना, to give one's heart (to, को); to apply one's mind (to, में), to be intent; to be attentive (to). ~ पक्का करना, to take a firm resolve. ~ पर आना, to come into the mind (a thought, a resolve). ~ पर धरना, or लाना, to resolve. ~ फटना, the heart to be torn: dislike to be felt. ~ फिरना, affection or attention to be withdrawn; aversion to be felt. ~ बढ़ना (का), courage, or morale, to rise. ~ बढ़ाना (का), to encourage; to raise the morale (of). ~, or ~ में, बसना, to dwell in the heart (of, के). ~ बहलाना (का), to divert or to amuse (oneself). ~ बुरा करना, to take offence, to be displeased. ~ बूझना, = ~ लेना, 2. ~ भरना, the mind to be filled, to be satisfied, content; the mind to be sated or cloyed (with, से); to be fed up. ~ भाना, to be pleasing to the mind. ~ भारी करना, to burden the mind; to give way to grief; to take to heart. ~ मनाना, to cause (one, का) to agree, to persuade; to talk (one) round. ~ मानना, the heart to accept (sthg.): to be comforted (as by consolation); to agree (to sthg). ~ न माना, (he) could not bring himself (to do or to say sthg). ~ मारना (अपना), to repress or to restrain feelings or desires; to deny oneself (a pleasure, &c.); to be dejected, or troubled. ~ मिलना, hearts to meet (in love); temperaments to be congenial. ~ मिलाना, to adjust to (another's mood); to feel accord or sympathy (with, से). ~ में, adv. in one's heart, mind. ~ में आना, sthg. to occur (to, के); sthg. to win the approval or liking (of). ~ में कहना, to say to oneself. ~ में गाँठ पड़ना, displeasure, ill-will or disaffection to arise in the heart. ~ में ठानना, to resolve firmly. ~ में लाना, to conceive (an idea, a resolve). ~ रखना (का), to carry out a wish (of), to gratify. ~ लगना, the mind to be fixed (on, में); the affections to be given (to, से); pleasure to be felt. यहाँ ~ लगता है, I like it here, I feel at home here. ~ लगाना, to fix the mind, or the attention (on, में); to set the heart (on, से), to love. ~ लेना (का), to captivate, to charm; to fathom the mind (of). ~ से, adv. sincerely. अपने ~ से, adv. willingly, voluntarily. ~ से उतरना (के), to fall in the opinion (of); to be forgotten (by). ~ हरा होना, to be mentally or emotionally refreshed; to cheer up. ~ हलका होना, to feel a sense of relief. ~ होना, the heart to be inclined, to wish; to long; to crave. ~ ही ~, adv. in the heart, to oneself (of unspoken thoughts, words). - मन-कामना, f. Av. heart's desire, wish, objective. मन-गढ़ंत, adj. & f. fabricated; fanciful; a fabrication. मन-चला, adj. capricious, self-indulgent; flirtatious. °-चली, f. मन-चाहता, adj. wished for; dear. °-चाहा, adj. = id., 1. °-चाही, f. self-will; obstinacy. मन-चाही करना (अपनी), to act wilfully, &c. मन-चीता, adj. = मन-चाहता. मन-पसंद, adj. pleasing, agreeable. मन-बच-क्रम, m. Brbh. Av. thought, word and deed. मन-बहलाव, m. relaxation. मन-भाया, adj. pleasing, agreeable; amusing; charming. मनमति, adj. 19c. self-willed. मन-मानता, adj. = next. मन-माना, adj. & m. agreeable to heart or mind: soothing; charming; optional; arbitrary; sweetheart, darling. °माना करना, to act arbitrarily, or at will. °-माने, adv. arbitrarily; as one pleases, to the heart's content. °-मानी, f. heart's desire; self-will; arbitrary choice. मन-मुटाव, m. ill-will; aversion. मन-मोदक, m. an imaginary sweet: a castle in the air. मन-मोहन, adj. & m. enchanting heart or mind, captivating, charming; sweetheart, darling; a title of Kṛṣṇa. मन-मौज, f. a fancy; whim, caprice; delight, rapture. °ई, adj. °ईपन, m. मन-वांछित, adj. Brbh. desired by the heart. मन्मथ, m. heart-arouser: a title of Kāmdev.

[2]**मन** *man* [*maṇa-*: ← A. *mann*], m. a measure of weight, a maund (about 40kg). — *mankhap*, reg. (Bihar) a land tenure in which a fixed amount of the crop is paid to the landlord. मनहुंडा, reg. (Bihar) id.

मनई *manaī*, m. reg. a man; husband.

मन:- *manaḥ-* [S.], mind, heart, &c. (= [1]मन): — मन:प्रसाद, m. peace of heart. मन:शास्त्र, m. psychology. मन:स्थिति, f. state of mind; mood.

मनका *mankā* [cf. *maṇi-*[1]], m. **1.** a bead. **2.** a rosary. — (गरदन का)~ ढलना, or ढलकना, the vertebrae (of the neck) to bend down: to be at the point of death.

मनगट *mangaṭ* [**maṇigranthi-*], f. *Pl.* **1.** the wrist; the ankle. **2.** pastern (of a horse).

मनगटी *mangaṭī* [cf. **maṇigranthi-*], f. *Pl.* bracelet.

मनन *manan* [S.], m. **1.** thinking over (a matter); reflection. **2.** careful study (of a topic or subject). – मननशील, adj. reflective; studious.

मनवाना *manvānā* [cf. H. *manānā*], v.t. to cause to be accepted, agreed to, &c. (by, से).

[1]**मनस-** *manas-* [S.], mind, heart, &c. (= [1]मन): — मनस्तल, m. deepest or inmost heart or soul. मनस्ताप, m. sorrow, compassion; remorse.

[2]**मनस-** *manas-*, v.t. Brbh. Av. **1.** to wish. **2.** to resolve, to intend.

मनसब *mansab*, m. = मंसब.

[1]**मनसा** *manasā* [S.], f. **1.** mind, thought. **2.** wish. **3.** intention. **4.** *hind.* name of a snake-goddess.

[2]**मनसा** *manasā* [S.], adv. in the mind, &c. (cf. [1]मन). — मनसा वाचा कर्मणा, adv. in thought, word and deed.

मनसिज *manasij* [S.: *manasi*, loc.], m. born in the mind or heart: **1.** the god of love, Kāmdev. **2.** love, passion.

मनसिल *mansil* [*manaḥśilā-*], m. = मैनसिल.

मनसूख़ *mansūk͟h* [A. *mansūk͟h*], adj. cancelled, revoked. — ~ करना, to cancel, &c.

मनसूख़ी *mansūk͟hī* [A. *mansūk͟h*+P. *-ī*], adj. cancellation, annulment.

मनसूब *mansūb* [A. *manṣūb*], adj. appointed, named, destined (for, से).

मनसूबा *mansūbā* [A. *manṣūba*], m. **1.** intention; ambition; resolve. **2.** plan, scheme. — ~ करना, or ठानना, or बाँधना, to form an ambition, or a plan.

मनसेधू *mansedhū*, m. reg. a man, a male.

मनसेरू *manserū* [**manuṣyarūpa-*], m. reg. a man, a male.

मनस्विता *manasvitā* [S.], f. intelligence, &c. (see मनस्वी).

मनस्वी *manasvī* [S.], adj. **1.** intelligent; wise. **2.** intellectual. **3.** spiritual. **4.** having a mind of one's own, self-willed.

मनहुं *manahuṁ*, conj. Brbh. Av. = मानों.

मनहु *manahu*, conj. E.H. = मानों.

मनहूस *manhūs* [A. *manḥūs*], adj. **1.** unlucky, ill-omened; wretched (a person, or an object). **2.** forbidding, ominous (of aspect, atmosphere).

मना *manā* [A. *man'*], adj. inv. forbidden; prohibited. — ~ करना, to forbid, &c.

-मना *-manā* [S.], adj. inv. formant. having thoughts, or feelings (e.g. उदारमना, of generous or noble spirit).

मनाक *manāk* [S.], adv. Brbh. a little; slightly.

मनाग *manāg* [S.], adv. Av. = मनाक.

मनाना *manānā* [cf. H. *mānnā*], v.t. to make mindful: **1.** to cause to agree, to persuade; to reason with; to prevail on. **2.** to console. **3.** to conciliate (an opponent, one offended); to placate; to soothe. **4.** to invoke (a deity); to worship; to propitiate (a patron, &c). **5.** to cause to be kept, to celebrate (as a festival, a holiday). **6.** poet. to acknowledge (a fault). **7.** to meditate, to reflect on.

मनावन *manāvan* [cf. H. *manānā*], m. reg. **1.** talking round, persuasion. **2.** placation (of one offended).

मनाही *manāhī* [A. *manāhī*, pl.], f. prohibited things: prohibition (of, की).

मनिया *maniyā* [cf. H. *manī*], f. m. jewel, or pearl, or bead (of necklace, or rosary).

मनियार *maniyār* [**maṇikāra-*], adj. **1.** Brbh. possessing a jewel (a snake). **2.** E.H. bejewelled, glittering, brilliant.

मनिहार *manihār* [*maṇikāra-*], m. a maker and trader of bracelets, beads, &c.

मनिहारी *manihārī* [cf. H. *manihār*], f. the work, or trade, of a *manihār*.

मनी *manī*, f. reg. = मणि.

मनीषा *manīṣā* [S.], f. thought, wisdom; intelligence.

[1]**मनु** *manu* [S.], m. *mythol.* man: a progenitor of the world and its inhabitants, seen as a son of or personification of Brahmā (fourteen Manus preside in succession over the universe in each *kalpa*). — मनुज, m. Manu-born: a man. मन्वंतर, m. the age of a Manu, an aeon.

[2]**मनु** *manu*, conj. Brbh. = मानों.

मनुआ *manuā* [*manu-*], m. reg. **1.** a man. **2.** a monkey.

मनुष *manuṣ* [ad. *manuṣya-*], m. Brbh. **1.** a man. **2.** husband.

मनुष्य *manuṣyă* [S.], m. **1.** human being; a man, a person. **2.** mankind. — मनुष्य-जाति, f. = ~, 2. मनुष्य-तन, m. the human body; human existence. मनुष्य-तन पाना, or धारना, to be born as a man; to become incarnate.

मनुष्यता *manuṣyătā* [S.], f. state or condition of man; humanity.

मनुष्यत्व *manuṣyatvă* [S.], m. = मनुष्यता.

मनुसाई *manusāī* [cf. H. *manuṣ*], f. Av. **1.** human state or condition; humanity. **2.** manliness.

मनुहार *manuhār* [? cf. H. *manuhār-*], f. Brbh. Av. sthg. intended to please: entreaty, request; conciliation; consideration, respect.

मनुहार- *manuhār-*, v.i. & v.t. **1.** v.i. Av. to be or to become satisfied. **2.** v.t. Brbh. to conciliate; to show consideration.

मनों *manoṁ*, conj. Brbh. = मानों.

मनो- *mano-* [S]. mind, heart, &c. (= [1]मन): — मनोकामना, f. corr. heart's desire. मनोगत, adj. gone to or found in heart or mind: mental (a process); secret, hidden; desired. °इ, f. mental process; impulse of the heart; desire. मनोग्रंथि, f. *psychol.* a complex. मनोज, m. mind-born: a title of the god Kāmdev. मनोज्ञ, adj. delightful, lovely, charming. मनोजीवी, adj. living by the mind or intellect. मनोदाह, m. distress of mind or heart. मनोनयन, m. selection, choice.

मनोनियोग, m. concentration (of mind). मनोनिवेश, m. id. मनोनीत, adj. taken by the mind: selected, chosen; acceptable. मनोबल, m. strength of mind or spirit. मनोभव, m. Av. = मनोज. मनोभाव, m. disposition; mentality; mental process. मनोभावना, f. state of mind; mood; a feeling. मनोमय, adj. spiritual; mental. मनोमालिन्य, m. ill-will, disaffection; alienation. मनोमोही, adj. entrancing. मनोयोग, m. concentration, attention. मनोरंजक, adj. entertaining; interesting; recreational. °ता, f. मनोरंजन, m. entertainment, amusement; recreation. मनोरथ, m. mind's vehicle: heart-felt wish; cherished purpose or aim. मनोरम, adj. delightful, lovely, charming. मनोरोग, m. mental illness. मनोलीला, play of mind or fancy: illusion. मनोलौल्य, m. *Pl. HŚS.* whim, caprice. मनोल्लास [°*na*+*u*°], m. delight, rapture. मनोवांछित, adj. desired by the heart. मनोविकार, m. impulse of the mind, emotion. °-विकृति, f. mental derangement: a psychosis. मनोविज्ञान, m. psychology. °ई, m. psychologist. मनोविश्लेषण, m. psychoanalysis. मनोवृत्ति, f. state of mind; disposition, temperament. मनोवेग, m. impulse of the mind, emotion. मनोवैज्ञानिक, adj. & m. psychological; a psychologist. मनोहर, adj. heart-stealing : charming, delightful. °ता, f. मनोहारित्व, m. attractiveness, charm.

मनौती *manautī* [cf. H. *manānā*], f. **1.** talking round, persuasion; wheedling. **2.** vow to propitiate (a deity) by worship. **3.** security, surety; bail. — मनौतीदार [P. *-dār*], m. *hist.* one who becomes a surety, esp. for a revenue payment.

मनौवल *manauval*, m. = मनौती, 1., 2.

मन्नत *mannat* [cf. H. *mānnā*, or *manānā*], f. promise, vow. — ~ उतारना, or बढ़ाना, to fulfil a vow. ~ मानना, to make a vow.

मन्नू *mannū* [*manu-*], m. reg. a monkey.

मन्मथ *manmath* [S.], m. heart-stirrer (?): **1.** love, passion. **2.** the god of love, Kāmdev.

मन्मथी *manmathī* [S.], adj. *Pl. HŚS.* desirous, amorous.

मपत *mapat* [cf. H. *mapnā*], f. *Pl.* measuring: measure, extent.

मपना *mapnā* [cf. H. *māpnā*], v.i. to be measured.

मपवाना *mapvānā* [cf. H. *māpnā*], v.t. to cause to be measured (by, से).

मपाना *mapānā*, v.t. to cause to measure.

मफ़रूर *mafrūr* [A. *mafrūr*], adj. absconded, fugitive. — ~ होना, to abscond, to flee.

मम *mamă* [S.], adj. my, mine.

ममता *mamătā* [S.], f. interest or affection for persons or things connected with oneself: **1.** proprietary interest. **2.** affection, attachment; tenderness. **3.** pride, arrogance.

ममत्व *mamatvă* [S.], m. = ममता.

ममनून *mamnūn* [A. *mamnūn*], adj. U. obliged; grateful; appreciative.

ममाखी *mamākhī* [*madhu-*+*makṣikā-*], f. reg. (E.) a bee.

ममिया *mamiyā* [cf. H. *māmā*], adj. inv. having the standing of a maternal uncle. — ~ ससुर, m. husband's or wife's maternal uncle. ~ सास, f. husband's or wife's maternal aunt.

ममेरा *mamerā* [cf. *māma-*], adj. maternal uncle's. ~ भाई, m. first cousin on mother's side. ममेरी बहन, f. first cousin on mother's side.

ममोला *mamolā*, m. the large pied wagtail.

मयंक *mayaṅk* [*mṛga-*: ad. *mṛgāṅka-*], m. deer-marked: the moon.

[1]**मय** *may*, f. = [1]मै.

[2]**मय** *may* [A. *ma'(a)*], prep. (also inverted). together (with, के), in addition.

-मय *-may* [S.], suffix (forms adjectives having the sense 'consisting of ...', e.g. मधुमय, sweet, honied).

मयस्सर *mayassar*, adj. = मुयस्सर.

मयूख *mayūkh* [S.], m. **1.** the gnomon of a sundial. **2.** ray. **3.** brilliance, splendour.

मयूर *mayūr* [S.], m. a peacock.

मरंद *marand* [S.], m. = मकरंद.

मर *mar* [cf. H. *marnā*], m. dying, death.

[1]**मरक** *marak*, f. Brbh. a secret, or hidden emotion.

[2]**मरक** *marak* [cf. *mara-*; or S.], m. a deadly epidemic.

मरकचा *markacā*, m. *Pl.* ridge (of a house).

मरकज़ *markaz* [A. *markaz*], m. U. centre.

मरकज़ी *markazī* [A. *markazī*], adj. central.

मरकत *markat* [S.], m. an emerald.

मरकहा *markahā*, adj. = मरखना.

मरखना *markhanā*, adj. one who beats, or strikes; an animal that butts.

मरखन्ना *markhanna*, adj. reg. = मरखना.

मरखाह *markhāh*, adj. reg. = मरकहा.

मरगंग *margaṅg*, m. *Pl.* a dry river-bed.

मरगजा *margajā* [cf. H. *malnā*], adj. Brbh. Av. crushed; squeezed (as flowers, or the body in an embrace); rumpled (as clothing).

मरगल *margal*, m. *Pl.* fried fish.

मरग़ोलना *margolnā* [cf. P. *margūl*], v.i. S.H. to warble (birds).

मरग़ोला *margolā* [P. *margūl(a)*], m. a ring; sthg. ring-shaped.

मरघट *marghaṭ* [H. *marnā*+H. *ghāṭ*], f. place of cremation.

मरज़ *marz* [A. *marẓ*], m. **1.** a disease, complaint. **2.** bad habit, vice. — किस ~ की दवा है? iron. of what disease is it (or he) the medicine?: of what use is it, &c.?

मरजिआ *marajiā* [Pk. *marajīvaya-*], adj. & m. Av. **1.** adj. one on the point of death; a person who escapes with (his) life. **2.** [×*majjati*: Brbh. *majj-*], a diver.

मरज़ी *marzī* [A. *marẓī*], f. pleasure, wish; choice. — ~ के मुताबिक़, adv. in accordance with the wish or pleasure (of, की). ~ मिलना, or पटना (की), to be of one mind, to agree; to suit, to be compatible (persons). अपनी ~ से, adv. willingly, voluntarily. यह आपकी ~ है, this is at your discretion, it is up to you.

मरण *maraṇ* [S.], m. **1.** dying, death. **2.** fig. mortification, dying with shame. — मरण-पर्यंत, adv. until death. मरणशील, adj. whose nature is to die: mortal; fig. moribund, feeble. मरणासन्न [°*na*+*ā*°], adj. having reached death: near death. मरणोत्तर [°*na*+*u*°], adj. posthumous.

मरतबा *martabā* [A. *martaba*], m. step, degree: **1.** time, occasion. **2.** position, office. — एक ~, adv. on one occasion.

मरतबान *martabān* [P. *martabān*], m. a glazed earthenware jar (for keeping preserves, pickles, &c. in).

मरदनिया *mardaniyā* [cf. H. *mardan*], m. a masseur.

मरदानगी *mardānăgī* [P. *mardānagī*], f. manliness; bravery, valour.

मरदाना *mardānā*, adj. = मर्दाना.

मरदानी *mardānī* [cf. H. *mardānā*], f. a heroic woman.

मरदूद *mardūd* [A. *mardūd*], adj. rejected: a censurable person.

मरन *maran* [*maraṇa-*], m. = मरण.

मरना *marnā* [*marate*], v.i. **1.** to die. **2.** to fade, to wither. **3.** to cease, no longer to be felt (as hunger, or an emotion). **4.** to go out (a fire); to be settled (dust, by sprinkling). **5.** to be soaked up, to dry away (a liquid). **6.** to be captured (a piece in a game); to be out (a player, as in the game *kabaḍḍī*). **7.** esp. w. जाना. to be lost (a bet, a bad debt). **8.** to be ready to die (for); to set the heart (on, पर); to be wildly in love (with). **9.** to set store (by or on, पर: as on one's honour); to long (for, के लिए). **10.** fig. to endure toil or distress (for, पर, के लिए, or को). मर-मरकर रुपए इकट्ठे करना, to amass money by long or hard toil. — मरने की छुट्टी, or फ़ुरसत, न होना, to have no time to die: to be overwhelmed with work. – मर पचना, to work (oneself) to death; to suffer dire distress; to sacrifice one's life (for, के लिए). मर मिटना, to be killed; to be wiped out (as a defending force); to be ruined, or to sacrifice oneself (for, के लिए); to throw away one's life (for, के पीछे). – मरकर जीना, barely to excape death. मरता, m. a dying man. मरे जाना, to be infatuated (with, पर).

मरभुक्खा *marbhukkhā* [H. *marnā*, H. *bhūkhā*], adj. famished.

[1]**मरमर** *marmar* [P. *marmar*: ←Gk.], m. marble.

[2]**मरमर** *marmar* [onom.: *marmara-*], f. (m., *Pl.*) a rustling sound (as of leaves, or clothing); crackling; crunching.

[1]**मरमरा** *marmarā* [? cf. H. [2]*marmar*], adj. fragile, brittle.

[2]**मरमरा** *marmarā*, adj. reg. (W.) = मलमला, 1.

मरमराना *marmarānā*, v.i. = मुरमुराना.

मरम्मत *marammat* [A. *maramma*: P. *marammat*], f. repairing, repair. — ~ करना (की), to repair; to put right; fig. to give a sound beating (to).

मरम्मती *marammatī* [P. *marammatī*], adj. **1.** repaired. **2.** needing repair.

[1]**मरवट** *marvaṭ*, f. *hist.* rent-free land given to the families of soldiers killed in battle.

[2]**मरवट** *marvaṭ*, f. painting the face of the bride with *rolī*.

मरवाना *marvānā* [cf. H. *mārnā*], v.t. to cause to be killed, or beaten (by, से).

मरसा *marsā*, m. **1.** a green vegetable, *Amaranthus oleraceus* (= [2]माट, [3]माठ). **2.** a plant yielding a fine grain, *A. paniculatus*.

मरसिया *marsiyā* [A. *marṡiya*], m. *musl.* a dirge, lament (esp. as commemorating Ḥasan and Ḥusain). — ~ पढ़ना, to read or to chant a lament.

मरहटा *marhaṭā* [*mahārāṣṭra-*], m. pronun. var. = मराठा.

मरहटी *marhaṭī*, adj. & f. /mərɛhṭi/. **1.** adj. Maratha; Maharastrian. **2.** f. the Marathi language. **3.** plunder; maladministration, chaos.

मरहठ *marhaṭh* [*mahārāṣṭra-*], adj. Brbh. = मराठा.

मरहठा *marhaṭhā*, m. = मराठा.

मरहठी *marhaṭhī*, adj. = मरहटी.

मरहम *marham* [P. *marham*], m. **1.** plaster, dressing. **2.** ointment. — मरहम-पट्टी, f. dressing, binding (of a wound); applying ointment. मरहम-पट्टी करना, to dress and bandage (a wound).

मरहला *marhalā* [A. *marḥala*], m. U. **1.** a day's journey; stage. **2.** inn.

मरहूम *marhūm* [A. *marḥūm*], adj. U. on whom mercy is shown: deceased; the late.

मराठा *marāṭhā* [*mahārāṣṭraka-*], adj. inv. & m. **1.** adj. having to do with Mahārāṣṭra, or with the Marathas. **2.** m. a Maharastrian; a Maratha.

मरातिब *marātib* [A.*marātib*, pl.], m. Brbh. steps, grades: **1.** storeys. **2.** ? banner.

मराना *marānā* [cf. H. *mārnā*], v.t. pej. to cause to be struck (by, से).

मराल *marāl* [S.], m. a species of goose.

मरियम *mariyam* [A. *maryam*], f. Mary; the Virgin Mary.

मरियल *mariyal* [cf. H. *marnā*], adj. **1.** half-dead; inert; feeble. **2.** wasted (as by sickness).

मरी *marī* [cf. *mara-*], f. an outbreak of serious illness; epidemic; cholera.

मरीच *marīc* [**maricca-*: ← Austro-as.], m. (?) reg. = मिर्च.

मरीचि *marīci* [S.], f. ray, beam; light.

मरीचिका *marīcikā* [S.], f. **1.** mirage. 2. = मरीचि.

मरीची *marīcī* [S.], m. the sun.

मरीज़ *marīz* [A. *marīẓ*], adj. & m. **1.** adj. sick, ill. **2.** m. a sick person, patient.

मरु *maru* [S.], m. **1.** a desert; a dry region; dry ground. **2.** name of the region of Mārvāṛ. — मरु-भूमि, f. = ~, 1. मरु-स्थल, m. id.

[1]**मरुआ** *maruā* [*maruvaka-*], m. **1.** a variety of basil. **2.** sweet marjoram. **3.** Indian wormwood, *Artemisia vulgaris.*

[2]**मरुआ** *maruā*, m. **1.** Brbh. cross-beam (of a swing). **2.** *HŚS.* ridgepole.

मरुका *marukā*, m. reg. (Bihar) roofing (built over a watchman's platform, or a threshing-floor).

मरुत् *marut* [S.], m. **1.** *mythol.* a god of storm or wind. **2.** wind; air.

मरेठी *mareṭhī*, f. reg. (E.) hauling-ropes of a harrow.

मरैठा *maraiṭhā* [? conn. H. *aiṃṭhna*], adj. *Pl.* twisted; wound up; bound round (a handle with cord).

मरोड़ *maroṛ* [cf. H. *maroṛnā*], f. **1.** bending; bend, turn. **2.** twisting; twist; contortion; affectation. **3.** ache, pang; colic. **4.** fig. haughtiness. — ~ उठना, gripes or colic to come on. ~ खाना, v.t. to bend, to turn, to meander; to be perplexed. – मरोड़-फली, f. *Pl. HŚS.* the screw-tree, *Helicteres isora*, and its fruit (used medicinally for colic). मरोड़बाज़ [P. *-bāz*], m. an affected person.

मरोड़ना *maroṛnā* [**muroṭati*; Pk. *moḍaï*: ← Drav.], v.t. **1.** to bend; to fold. **2.** to twist; to wring. **3.** to gripe; to cause distress (to). **4.** to destroy; to gobble up (food). — अंग ~, to stretch the body.

मरोड़ा *maroṛā* [cf. H. *maroṛnā*], m. = मरोड़, 2., 3.

मरोड़ी *maroṛī* [cf. H. *maroṛnā*], f. 1. = मरोड़, 2., 3. **2.** anything twisted (as a screw). — ~ खाना, to be twisted; to turn; to coil; to be perplexed. ~ देना (को), to twist. – मरोड़ी-फली, f. = मरोड़-फली.

मरोह *maroh* [conn. *smaramoha-*], m. Av. **1.** love, tenderness. **2.** compassion.

मरोही *marohī* [cf. H. *maroh*], adj. reg. **1.** loving, tender. **2.** compassionate.

मर्क *mark* [S.], m. *Pl. HŚS.* the wind in the body, vital breath.

मर्कट *markaṭ* [S.], m. monkey.

मर्करा *markărā* [S.], f. *Pl. HŚS.* **1.** a hollow, hole. **2.** a pot. **3.** an infertile woman.

मर्ग *marg* [P. *marg*], m. death.

मर्ग़ *marġ* [P. *marġ*], m. meadow, valley-meadow.

मर्ज़ *marz*, m. see मरज़.

मर्ज़बान *marzbān* [P. *marzbān*], m. *hist.* a prince, noble, estate-holder.

मर्तबा *martabā*, m. = मरतबा.

मर्तव्य *martavyă* [S.], adj. doomed to die, mortal.

मर्त्य *martyă* [S.], adj. & m. **1.** adj. doomed to die, mortal. **2.** m. a mortal. **3.** the body. — **मर्त्य-लोक**, m. the world of mortals, this world.

मर्द *mard* [P. *mard*], m. **1.** a man. **2.** a male. **3.** a husband. **4.** a brave man; hero. — **मर्द-आदमी**, m. colloq. he-man, tough guy. **मर्द-बच्चा**, m. a dauntless or heroic young man. **मर्दबाज़** [P. *-bāz*], f. a promiscuous woman. °**ई**, f.

मर्द- *mard-* [ad. *mardati*], v.t. Brbh. Av. **1.** to rub; to anoint. **2.** crushing. **3.** destroying.

मर्दन *mardan* [S.], m. **1.** rubbing; anointing (with oil or cosmetic paste). **2.** crushing, grinding. **3.** trampling; destroying. — ~ **करना**, to rub, &c.

मर्दाना *mardānā* [P. *mardāna*], adj. often inv. **1.** manly, brave. **2.** having to do with, or typical of, men; male; men's (clothing, &c.); men's or public part (of a house).

मर्दित *mardit* [S.], adj. **1.** rubbed. **2.** squeezed. **3.** crushed, ground; broken. **4.** pulverised; destroyed.

मर्दी *mardī* [P. *mardī*], f. **1.** manhood; virility. **2.** manliness.

मरदुआ *marduā* [cf. H. *mard*], m. usu. pej. a man, fellow.

मर्दुम *mardum* [P. *mardum*], m. U. men, people. — **मर्दुमख़ोर** [P. *-khor*], m. a cannibal. **मर्दुमशुमारी** [P. *-śumārī*], f. census.

मर्दुमी *mardumī* [P. *mardumī*], f. **1.** manliness, bravery. **2.** humanity, humaneness. 3. = **मर्दी**, 1. **4.** courtesy.

मर्म *marm* [S.], m. **1.** vital, or vulnerable spot. *__2.__ core, heart, essential nature; inmost heart (of a person). **3.** sthg. to be kept secret (as a purpose, a meaning, a weakness). **4.** an essential truth, ultimate mystery. — **मर्मज्ञ**, adj. & m. knowing the essential nature (of, **का**); knowing secrets, vulnerable points, &c. (concerning); deeply versed (in: a subject); one having profound knowledge (of). **मर्मभेदी**, adj. piercing to the quick; making out a secret, or an inner mystery. **मर्म-वचन**, m. words cutting to the quick. **मर्मस्थल**, m. a vital spot, the vitals; inward part. **मर्मस्पर्शी**, adj. touching the inner heart, inward emotions. °**-स्पर्शिता**, f. **मर्मांतक** [°*ma*+*a*°], adj. inner, piercing (pain, distress). **मर्मांतिक** [°*ma*+*a*°], id. **मर्माघात** [°*ma*+*ā*°], m. blow to the vitals, dire blow. **मर्माहत** [°*ma*+*ā*°], adj. wounded to the quick.

मर्मी *marmī* [S.], m. = **मर्मज्ञ**.

मर्यादा *maryādā* [S.], f. **1.** limit, boundary. **2.** bounds (of law, usage); custom; convention. **3.** correct behaviour; decorum. **4.** station, dignity; honour. **5.** merit (cf. **धर्म**, 6).

मर्यादित *maryādit* [S.], adj. limited, restricted.

मर्यादी *maryādī* [S.], adj. **1.** falling within, or observing, due bounds (of propriety, &c).

मर्री *marrī* [cf. H. *marī*], f. = **मरी**.

मलंग *malaṅg* [P. *malang*; ? or *mālaṅga-*], m. **1.** Brbh. a Muslim ascetic (esp. as in a state of trance). **2.** a careless or inconsiderate person. **3.** a tall, robust man. **4.** *Pl. HŚS.* a large white bird.

मलंगा *malaṅgā*, m. = **मलंग**.

मल *mal* [*mala-*], m. **1.** dirt. **2.** excrement; other excretion, mucus. **3.** impurity; waste matter. — **मल-त्याग**, m. defecation. **मल-द्वार**, m. anus. **मल-मास**, m. see hw. **मल-मूत्र**, m. excrement and urine. **मलावरोध** [°*la*+*a*°], m. constipation. **मलाशय** [°*la*+*ā*°], m. rectum.

मलई *malaī*, f. *Pl.* rich alluvial soil on the banks of rivers.

मलक- *malak-* [cf. *maḍamaḍ-*; and **maṭ-*, H. *maṭaknā*], v.i. Brbh. to walk with, or to make, exaggerated movements; to flounce; to strut.

मलका *malkā* [A. *malika*], f. a queen.

मलकाना *malkānā*, v.t. reg. to move (the eyes, or limbs) to convey a mood or feeling. — **आँख मलका-**, to gaze haughtily.

मलखम *malkham*, [? H. *mall*+H. *khaṁbh*], m. **1.** an upright post (as used in gymnastic exercises). **2.** reg. (W.) the upright post in a sugar-mill.

मलता *maltā* [cf. H. *malnā*], adj. & m. **1.** adj. worn (a coin). **2.** m. *Pl.* a worn coin.

मलन *malan* [cf. H. *malnā*], m. crushing, crushed state.

मलना *malnā* [**malati*: Pk. *malaï*], v, t, **1.** to rub; to rub down (a horse). **2.** to scrub, to scour. **3.** to tread on: to tread out (corn); to grind, to crush. **4.** to wring (the hands). **5.** esp. w. **डालना**. to squeeze; to massage.

मलबा *malbā*, m. **1.** rubble (as of a fallen building, wall). **2.** rubbish, refuse.

मलमल *malmal*, f. muslin.

मलमला *malmalā*, adj. *Pl.* **1.** brackish. **2.** downcast, depressed.

मलमलाहट *malmalāhaṭ* [cf. H. *malmalānā*], f. **1.** sadness, depression. **2.** *Pl.* brackishness.

मलमास *malmās* [S.], m. impure month: an intercalary (thirteenth) month or short period in the Hindu lunar calendar (when no religious ceremonies should be performed).

मलय *malay* [S.], m. **1.** name of the southern end of the western Ghats, towards and in Kerala. **2.** the region of Malabar, or Kerala. **3.** white sandal. **4.** *mythol.* a *dvīpa* or division of the world. — मलय-गिरि, m. = ~, 1. मलया-गिरि, m. Av. id. मलयज, adj. & m. coming from the Malaya mountains, soft, fragrant (the wind); growing on the Malaya mountains (the sandal tree). मलयाचल [°*ya+a*°], m. = मलय-गिरि. मलयानिल [°*ya+a*°], m. the south or Malaya wind, fragrant breeze.

मलयालम *malayālam*, f. the Malayalam language.

[1]**मलयाली** *malayālī*, adj. & m. **1.** adj. having to do with Malabar, or Kerala. **2.** m. a Malayālī.

[2]**मलयाली** *malayālī*, f. the Malayalam language.

मलवाई *malvāī* [cf. H. *malvānā*], f. price paid for rubbing, scouring, &c.

मलवाना *malvānā* [cf. H. *malnā*], v.t. to cause to be rubbed, &c. (by, से).

मलवैया *malvaiyā* [cf. H. *malnā*], m. one who rubs, scours, &c.

मलसी *malsī* [cf. *malla*-[3]], f. reg. a container for oil.

[1]**मलाई** *malāī*, f. **1.** skimming (as from boiled milk). **2.** cream; clotted cream. — ~ पड़ना, cream to form (on, में). – मलाईदार [P. *-dār*], adj. creamy.

[2]**मलाई** *malāī* [cf. H. *malānā*], f. **1.** rubbing. **2.** scouring. **3.** rubbing down (a horse, &c). **4.** price paid for rubbing, &c.

मलाका *malākā* [S.], f. Brbh. a woman filled with desire.

मलाना *malānā* [cf. H. *malnā*], v.t. *Pl.* to cause to be rubbed, &c. (by, से).

मलामत *malāmat* [A. *malāma*: P. *malāmat*], f. **1.** rebuke; reproach, blame. **2.** [× H. *mal*] dross.

मलामती *malāmātī* [P. *malāmatī*], adj. *Pl.* *HŚS.* blameworthy.

मलार *malār* [cf. *mallārī*-], m. f. *mus.* **1.** name of a *rāg.* **2.** name of a *rāgiṇī* sung in the rains. — ~ गाना, to sing in the *malār* mode; to sing merrily, to be merry; to dwell (on a topic: का).

मलाल *malāl* [A. *malāl*], m. **1.** dejection; depression. **2.** grief. **3.** vexation. — ~ आना (को), dejection, &c. to come upon (one).

मलिक *malik* [A. *malik*], m. **1.** king. **2.** master, lord (an honorific title).

मलिका *malikā*, f. = मलका.

मलिन *malin* [S.], adj. **1.** dirty. **2.** base, foul. **3.** dull, tarnished, stained. **4.** wicked, vicious; disaffected (towards a person). **5.** disturbed (in mind); sad, dejected. — मलिन-मुख, m. dirty-faced: a ghost, spirit; a base or wicked person.

मलिनता *malinātā* [S.], f. dirt, &c. (see मलिन).

मलिया *maliyā* [cf. *malla*-[3]], m. reg. a vessel for holding oil, made of wood or coconut shell.

मलिया-मेट *maliyā-meṭ* [cf. H. *malnā, meṭnā*], adj. effaced or erased utterly, destroyed; razed; ruined; at an end (as a quarrel).

मलिष्ठ *maliṣṭh* [S.], adj. **1.** very dirty, filthy. **2.** most wicked or sinful.

मलीदा *malīdā* [P. *malīda*], m. **1.** a cake made of pounded meal with milk, butter and sugar. **2.** *Pl. HŚS.* a kind of fine woollen cloth woven from Kashmir lamb's wool. — ~ कर देना, to reduce (one) to a helpless state (as by harsh scolding).

मलीन *malīn*, adj. = मलिन.

मलूक *malūk*, adj. Brbh. beautiful, handsome.

मलूल *malul* [A. *malul*], adj. S.H. dejected, sad.

मलैया *malaiyā*, m. reg. (W.) = मलिया.

मलोलना *malolnā* [cf. H. *malolā*], v.i. to grieve; to regret.

मलोला *malolā* [? A. *malūla*], m. **1.** vexation. **2.** grief; melancholy. — मलोले आना, or खाना, to feel or to suffer vexation; to feel grief, &c.

मल्ल *mall* [ad. *malla*-], m. **1.** wrestler; prize-fighter; boxer. **2.** athlete: gymnast; acrobat. **3.** an athletic person. — मल्ल-भूमि, f. arena, ring; site of any conflict. मल्ल-युद्ध, m. wrestling, or other athletic contest.

मल्लार *mallār*, m. f. = मलार.

मल्लाह *mallāh* [A. *mallāḥ*], m. **1.** sailor. **2.** boatman.

मल्लाहिन *mallāhin* [cf. H. *mallāh*], f. **1.** a sailor's or boatman's wife. **2.** boatwoman.

मल्लाही *mallāhī* [A. *mallāḥ*+P. *-ī*], adj. & f. **1.** adj. sailors'. **2.** f. sailor's or boatman's work, trade or craft. **3.** reg. fare paid to a boatman. — ~ काँटा, m. a boathook.

मल्लिका *mallikā* [S.], f. jasmine.

मल्ली *mallī* [*mallikā*-], f. Arabian jasmine.

मल्लू *mallū* [cf. H. *mall*], m. reg. a monkey.

मल्हार *malhār*, m. f. = मलार.

मवाजिब *mavājib* [A. *mavājib*], m. pl. sums due (to one), dues; allowances; wages.

मवाद *mavād* [A. *mavādd*, pl.], m. pus.

मवाशी *mavāśī*, f. = मवेशी.

मवास *mavās*, m. Brbh. **1.** refuge, shelter; a fort. **2.** sheltering trees, or grove.

[1]**मवासी** *mavāsī* [cf. H. *mavās*], f. Brbh. small fort.

[2]**मवासी** *mavāsī* [cf. H. *mavās*], m. Brbh. commander of a fort.

मवेशी *maveśī* [A. *mavāšī*: P. *maveśī*], f. **1.** cattle. **2.** goats. **3.** sheep. — मवेशी-ख़ाना, m. pen for cattle, &c.; pound.

मश *maś* [S.], m. *Pl. HŚS.* a mosquito.

मशक *maśk* [P. *maśk*], f. var. /məśək/. a leather water-bag. — ~ छोड़ना, to empty a water-bag: to quench thirst; to appease (the goddess of smallpox); to remove the influence (of an evil spirit).

मशकूक *maśkūk* [A. *maśkūk*], adj. doubtful; ambiguous.

मशक़्क़त *maśaqqat* [A. *maśaqqa*: P. *maśaqqat*], f. U. **1.** labour, toil. **2.** hard labour (as of a prisoner). **3.** distress, suffering.

मशग़ूल *maśgūl* [A. *maśgul*], adj. occupied, engaged (in, में); busy.

मशरिक़ *maśriq* [A. *maśriq*], m. U. the east.

मशरिक़ी *maśriqī* [A. *maśriqī*], adj. U. eastern.

मशरू *maśrū* [A. *maśrū'*], m. a kind of striped cloth of silk and cotton.

मशवरा *maśvarā*, m. = मशविरा.

मशविरा *maśvirā* [A. *maśvara*], m. **1.** consultation, discussion. **2.** advice. — ~ करना, to consult (with, से). ~ लेना, to seek, or to take, advice (from, से).

मशहूर *maśhūr* [A. *maśhūr*], adj. **1.** well-known; public (as information). **2.** celebrated; famous. **3.** notorious. — ~ करना, to make well known.

मशाल *maśāl* [A. *maś'al*], f. **1.** a torch. **2.** *mil.* a flare. — ~ लेकर, or जलाकर, ढूँढ़ना, fig. to search with care.

मशालची *maśālcī* [A. *mas'al*+P. *-cī*], m. torch-bearer.

मशीन *maśīn* [Engl. *machine*], **1.** a machine. **2.** an apparatus.

मशीर *maśīr* [A. *muśīr*], m. counsellor.

मश्क़ *maśq* [A. *maśq*], m. U. **1.** practice. **2.** a copy.

मष्ट *maṣṭ* [S.], f. Brbh. Av. silence. — ~ कर- or धार-, to be silent. ~ मारना, 19c. id.

[1]**मस** *mas* [*śmaśru-*], f. down on the upper lip. — मसें भीगना or भींजना, (की), the moustache to begin to appear.

[2]**मस** *mas* [conn. *maśa-*], m. a mosquito.

मसक *masak* [cf. H. *masaknā*], f. **1.** a tear, rent. **2.** a pinch, a squeeze.

मसकना *masaknā* [cf. *maṣati*], v.t. & v.i. **1.** v.t. to press; rub, to stroke. **2.** v.i. [cf. H. *maskā-*] to be torn. **3.** to split apart. **4.** to be distressed (the heart). — उससे मसका तो जाता है नहीं, fig. he is too inert to lift a finger. – मसका-मसकी, f. pinching and squeezing.

मसका *maskā* [P. *maska*], m. **1.** butter. **2.** buttermilk. — ~ लगाना, colloq. to flatter, to butter (one) up.

मसका- *maskā-* [cf. *maṣati*], v.t. E.H. to tear, to split: to prepare for use (hemp).

मसकोड़ना *maskoṛnā*, v.t. to twist, to contort (the face). — मुँह ~, to make a wry face; to turn up the nose.

मसकोरा *maskorā*, m. reg. turning over in sleep: = करवट बदलना.

मसख़रा *maskharā* [A. *maskhara*], m. & adj. inv. **1.** m. a joker. **2.** a clown, buffoon. **3.** adj. facetious, amusing.

मसख़रापन *maskharāpan* [cf. H. *maskharā*], m. **1.** joking, jocularity. **2.** buffoonery.

मसख़री *maskharī* [P. *maskharagī*], f. joking, a joke. — ~ करना, to joke, to joke about. ~ में उड़ाना, to turn (a matter) aside with a joke.

मसजिद *masjid* [A. *masjid*], f. a mosque. — जामा ~ [A. *jāmi'*], f. congregational or principal mosque (of a town or city).

मसजिदी *masjidī* [A. *masjidī*], adj. having to do with a mosque.

मसनद *masnad* [A. *masnad*], f. **1.** large cushion (to sit or to lean against). **2.** couch. **3.** seat (of honour); throne.

मसनवी *masnavī* [A. *maṡnavī*], f. **1.** narrative or allegorical verse in rhyming couplets; heroic or epic verse. **2.** a narrative poem in couplets (esp. one on Persian subject-matter or one containing a Ṣūfī allegorical interpretation).

मसमसाना *masmasānā* [**muss-*], v.i. reg. **1.** to cry quietly. **2.** to mutter, to murmur. **3.** to hide one's feelings out of fear.

मसरफ़ *masraf* [A. *maṣraf*], m. use, purpose. — ~ में आना, to be of use. किसी ~ का न होना, to be useless.

मसरूफ़ *masrūf* [A. *maṣrūf*], adj. engaged, occupied (in, में); busy.

मसल *masal* [A. *maṡal*], f. **1.** saying, proverb. **2.** example, instance. **3.** comparison; simile; metaphor.

मसलन *maslan* [A. *maṡalan*], adv. for example.

मसलना *masalnā* [cf. *maṣati*], v.t. **1.** to rub to pieces; to crush between the palms. **2.** to crush, to pulverise.

मसलहत *maslahat* [A. *maṣlaha*: P. *maṣlaḥat*], f. sthg. good or advisable; advice, counsel.

[1]**मसला** *maslā* [A. *mas'ala*], m. a problem.

[2]**मसला** *maslā* [cf. H. *masalnā*], m. pressing, squeezing.

मसलो *maslo* [A. *mas'ala* × H. *masal*], m. corr. Brbh. a saying.

मसविदा *masvidā*, m. = मसौदा.

मसहरी *masahrī* [conn. *maśakaharī-*], f. **1.** a mosquito-net. **2.** bed with mosquito-net.

[1]**मसा** *masā* [*maśaka-*], m. a mosquito.

[2]**मसा** *masā*, m. = मस्सा.

मसान *masān* [*śmaśāna-*], m. **1.** a place of cremation. **2.** a cemetery. **3.** fig. desolate place. — ~ जगा-, Av. to recite incantations over a corpse.

मसानिया *masāniyā* [cf. H. *masān*], adj. & m. **1.** adj. having to do with a cremation-ground. **2.** m. attendant at a cremation-ground; one who removes the influence of evil spirits by tantric rites. **3.** an ascetic living at a cremation-ground.

मसानी *masānī* [cf. H. *masān*], f. **1.** a demoness (regarded as haunting a burning-ground). **2.** *Pl.* one of the goddesses of smallpox, measles, scarlet fever, whooping-cough, &c.

मसाला *masālā* [A. *maṣāliḥ*, pl.], m. **1.** raw material, materials. **2.** ingredients. **3.** spices, seasoning; a spice. — ~ देना, or डालना (में), to season. मसालेदार [P. *-dār*], adj. seasoned, spiced; trimmed, edged.

मसि *masi* [*maṣi-*, *masi-*: ← Drav.], f. **1.** ink. **2.** lampblack. 3. = [2]सुरमा. **4.** stain, blot; disgrace. — मसि-धान, m. *Pl. HŚS.* inkwell. मसि-पत्र, m. blotting paper. मसि-बुंदा, m. Brbh. Av. design drawn with lampblack on a child's face (to avert the evil eye).

मसीत *masīt*, f. corr. E.H. mosque (= मसजिद).

मसीद *masīd*, f. corr. Brbh. = मसजिद.

मसीना *masīnā* [conn. *masīnā-*], m. **1.** a vetch; pulse. **2.** m. f. linseed.

मसीह *masīh* [A. *masīḥ*], m. the Messiah, Christ.

मसीहा *masīhā* [A. : P. *masīḥā*], m. inv. 1. = मसीह. **2.** fig. (one who represents) a great hope (to others).

मसीहाई *masīhāī* [P. *masīḥāī*], f. reg. messianic power, or feat. — ~ करना, to perform a miracle.

मसीही *masīhī* [A. *masīḥī*], adj. & m. **1.** adj. Christian. **2.** m. a Christian.

मसूड़ा *masūṛā* [**māṁsapuṭaka-*], m. the gums (of the teeth).

मसूर *masūr* [*masūra-*], f. a small-grained pulse, *Lens esculenta*. — ~ की दाल, f. = ~.

मसूरिका *masūrikā* [S.], f. **1.** measles. **2.** chicken-pox.

मसृण *masṛṇ* [S.: ← Pk.], adj. delicate.

मसोसना *masosnā*, v.i. & v.t. **1.** v.i. to be twisted, wrung (esp. the heart: दिल, [1]मन); to feel a pang. **2.** v.t. to twist. **3.** to press; to repress (emotion). **4.** to grieve; to regret. — दिल मसोसकर रह जाना, the heart to feel a continued sense of frustration, or hurt. मसोस मसोसकर रोना, to weep bitterly.

मसोसा *masosā* [cf. H. *masosnā*], m. repressed emotion; sense of hurt or wrong; constant grief, or regret. — ~ दे दे रहना, to keep an emotion repressed.

मसौदा *masaudā* [A. *musavvada*], m. **1.** draft (as of a letter, report). **2.** a proposed scheme, project. **3.** copy (hand-written). — ~ करना, to make a draft (of, का); to write out a copy (of). ~ गाँठना, or बाँधना, to form or to develop a scheme or plan.

मस्त *mast* [P. *mast*], adj. **1.** intoxicated (with, में). **2.** passionate; lustful. **3.** exhilarated; enraptured; delighted. **4.** arrogant, proud. **5.** engrossed (in, में); indifferent (as to others); carefree. — ~ महीना, m. the month of passion, &c.: February. – मस्त-मौला, m. a drunkard; a carefree or easy-going person. मस्तराम, adj. carefree.

मस्तक *mastak* [S.], m. **1.** the forehead; the head. **2.** top, summit. — मस्तक-नत, adj. with bowed head.

[1]**मस्ताना** *mastānā* [cf. H. *mast*], v.i. **1.** to become drunk. **2.** to grow passionate or lustful. **3.** to grow vigorous, or hearty. **4.** to become puffed up with pride, conceit.

[2]**मस्ताना** *mastānā* [P. *mastāna*], adj. inv. **1.** drunken, drunk. **2.** like a drunkard (as in speech, gait). **3.** carefree, happy-go-lucky.

मस्तिष्क *mastiṣk* [S.], m. the brain.

मस्ती *mastī* [P. *mastī*], f. **1.** intoxication. **2.** passion; lust. **3.** delight, unrestrained joy. **4.** overweening pride. **5.** effusion in rut (as of an elephant). **6.** exudation (as from trees). — ~ आना (पर), to grow drunk; to feel passion, &c. ~ उतारना, or झाड़ना, or निकालना, to bring (a person) to his senses; to shock (a person) out of lust, or pride.

मस्तूल *mastūl* [Old Pt. *masto*], m. mast.

मस्सा *massā* [conn. *māṁsa-*], m. **1.** a wart. **2.** the ulcerations of piles. **3.** transf. *Pl.* a gun-sight. — मसेदार [P. *-dār*], adj. warty.

महँ *mahaṁ* [*madhya-*], ppn. Brbh. Av. = में.

महँकना *mahaṁknā* [? conn. H. *mahaknā*], v.t. reg. to smell.

महँग *mahaṁg*, adj. E.H. = महँगा.

महँगा *mahaṁgā* [*mahārgha-*], adj. expensive; dear in price. — ~ पड़ना (को), to cost much.

महँगाई *mahaṁgāī* [cf. H. *mahaṁgā*], f. **1.** high (level of) prices. **2.** rise in prices.

महँगापन *mahaṁgāpan* [cf. H. *mahaṁgā*], m. = महँगाई.

महँगी *mahaṁgī* [cf. **māhārghiya-*], f. reg. (E.) **1.** = महँगाई. **2.** time of scarcity; famine.

महंत *mahant* [S.], m. the superior of a monastery.

महंताई *mahantāī* [cf. H. *mahant*], f. = महंती.

महंती *mahantī* [cf. H. *mahant*], f. the position, duties and status of a *mahant*.

महक *mahak* [cf. *magha-*], f. **1.** fragrance, perfume, scent. **2.** aroma (as of spices). — महकदार [P. *-dār*], adj. fragrant.

महकना *mahaknā* [cf. H. *mahak*], v.i. to be fragrant.

महकमा *mahakmā* [A. *maḥkama*], m. any administrative department.

महकाना *mahkānā* [cf. H. *mahak*], v.t. **1.** to exhale (a fragrance). **2.** to perfume, to scent.

महकीला *mahkīlā* [cf. H. *mahak*], adj. **1.** fragrant. **2.** aromatic.

महकूम *mahkūm* [A. *maḥkūm*], adj. U. governed, subject.

महज़ *mahz* [A. *maḥẓ*], adj. & adv. pure, unmixed: only, merely; simply, nothing but (= निरा). — ~ क़ैद, f. ordinary imprisonment (without special conditions).

महज़र *mahzar* [A. *maḥẓar*], m. f. U. place of assembly. — महज़र-नामा, m. public petition.

महत् *mahat* [S.], adj. great, &c. (= महा-, 1., 2).

महता *mahtā*, m. = महतो.

महताब *mahtāb* [P. *mahtāb*], m. **1.** the moon. **2.** moonlight. 3. = महताबी.

महताबी *mahtābī* [P. *mahtābī*], f. **1.** a kind of firework, a rocket. **2.** a raised open terrace. — ~ लेंबो, f. reg. (Bihar) a shaddock.

महतारी *mahtārī*, f. Brbh. Av. mother.

महतिया *mahatiyā*, m. dimin. E.H. = महतो.

[1]**महती** *mahătī* [S.], adj. f. = महत्.

[2]**महती** *mahtī*, f. Brbh. (°द.) = महत्त्व.

महतो *mahto* [*mahānt-*], m. a village headman, leading tenant; the person responsible for the collection of rent from a village.

महत्ता *mahattā* [S.], f. = महत्त्व.

महत्त्व *mahattvă* [S.], m. **1.** greatness. **2.** high position or status, authority. ***3.** importance; significance. — ~ रखना, to be of importance, to matter. – महत्त्वपूर्ण, adj. important; significant. महत्त्व-संपन्न, adj. outstanding, significant (an achievement). महत्त्वकांक्षी [°*va*+*ā*°], adj. ambitious; vain. °क्षा, f. महत्त्वान्वित [°*va*+*a*°], adj. = महत्त्वपूर्ण.

महद् *mahad* [S.], adj. esp. in comp. = महत्.

महदूद *mahdūd* [A. *maḥdūd*], adj. U. limited, restricted.

महन *mahan* [*mathana-*], m. Brbh. churning.

महना *mahnā* [*mathati*], v.t. reg. to churn.

महनिया *mahniyā* [cf. *mathana-*], m. reg. a churner; a seller of butter.

महनीय *mahnīyă* [S.], adj. praiseworthy; illustrious.

महफा *mahphā*. reg. (Bihar) a kind of palanquin having a curved roof.

महफ़िल *mahfil* [A. *maḥfil*], f. **1.** assembly, gathering. **2.** an entertainment with dancing.

महफ़ूज़ *mahfūz* [A. *maḥfūẓ*], adj. U. guarded, protected; safe.

महबूब *mahbūb* [A. *maḥbūb*], adj. & m. **1.** adj. loved, beloved. **2.** m. loved one.

महबूबा *mahbūbā* [A. *maḥbūba*], adj. inv. & f. **1.** adj. beloved. **2.** f. sweetheart.

[1]**महर** *mahar* [? cf. H. [2]*mahrā*], m. Brbh. **1.** an honorific title: chief, headman; a title of Kṛṣṇa. **2.** ? Av. a bird (cf. महरि, 2).

[2]**महर** *mahar* [S.], m. Brbh. *mythol.* the fourth of the seven worlds above the earth. — महर-लोक, m. id.

[3]**महर** *mahr* [A. *mahr*], m. *musl.* a marriage-portion settled on the wife, or paid to her family before the marriage; dowry. — ~ **बाँधना**, to settle a dowry (on a wife).

महरम *mahram* [A. *maḥram*], m. f. U. Brbh. **1.** m. any close male relative of a woman. **2.** m. f. close friend, confidant(e). **3.** f. bodice.

[1]**महरा** *mahrā* [? *mahārāja-*], m. a domestic servant (= कहार, and मेहरा, 2).

[2]**महरा** *mahrā* [? *mahārāja-*], m. inv. **1.** Av. master, chief. **2.** Av. father-in-law.

महराई *mahrāī* [cf. H. [1] [2]*mahrā*], f. **1.** Av. status of master, or captain. **2.** reg. a domestic servant's work. **3.** reg. a type of cowherds' song.

महरि *mahri*, f. **1.** Brbh. lady (= मेहरी). **2.** Av. name of a bird (? = ग्वालिन, or दहिंगल).

महरी *mahrī* [cf. *mahilā-*], f. **1.** a servant woman. **2.** Brbh. woman, lady (= मेहरी).

महरूम *mahrūm* [A. *maḥrūm*], adj. deprived (of से), denied.

महर्षि *maharṣi* [S.], m. great *ṛṣi*, sage (= *mahā+ṛṣi*).

महल *mahl* [A. *maḥall*], m. place of alighting, or of abode: **1.** palace; mansion; imposing building. **2.** women's quarters of a house.

महशर *mahśar* [A. *maḥśar*], m. f. U. the day of judgment.

महसूल *mahsūl* [A. *maḥṣūl*], m. **1.** revenue (to government). **2.** tax. **3.** duty, excise, customs; toll; charge. — **डाक का ~**, m. postage charge(s). **~ चुकाना**, to pay duty, &c. **~ लगाना**, to levy a tax or duty (on, **पर**).

महसूस *mahsūs* [A. *maḥsūs*], adj. **1.** perceived, felt; experienced. **2.** perceptible. **3.** understood, appreciated. — **~ करना**, to feel, to suffer from; to be sensible of; to realise. **~ होना**, to be perceived, &c. (by, **को**); to seem (to). **आपको भारत कैसा ~ होता है?** how do you like India?

महसूसना *mahsūsnā* [cf. H. *mahsūs*], v.i. = **महसूस करना**.

महा- *mahā-* [S.], adj. **1.** great; mighty; large; chief; eminent; general (as a committee, an assembly). **2.** excessive; dire; heavy. **3.** (w. adjs.) very, extremely. — **महाकाल**, m. a title of Śiva in his character as destroyer (when he is represented as black; and through the word *kāl* also as a personification of time, seen as universal destroyer). **°ई**, a title of Durgā, or Kālī. **महाकाय**, m. vast of body or stature, huge. **महाकाव्य**, m. great poem: conventional designation of a single poetical work of large scope and formal style (such as, in Hindi, *Kāmāyanī*). **महाकुल**, adj. & m. high-born; a man of great or noble family. **°ईन**, adj. id. **महाजन**, m. an eminent personage: a money-lender, banker; merchant; **°ई**, adj. & f. mercantile, commercial; pertaining to a money-lender; money-lending; usury; name of a simplified form of the Devanāgarī script in which accounts, &c. are kept. **महातल**, m. *mythol.* Brbh. name of the sixth of the seven worlds below the earth. **महात्मन्**, voc. see next. **महात्मा** [°*ā+ā*°], adj. & m. inv. high-souled, of noble nature; a noble or venerable man. **महादान**, m. great gift: name given to various traditional gifts to brāhmaṇs; a gift made to leather-workers, cremation-workers, &c. at certain times. **महादेव**, m. great deity: a title of Śiva. **°ई**, f. a title of Durgā, or Pārvatī. **महाद्वीप**, m. a continent. **°ई**, **°ईय**, adj. **महाधन**, adj. & m. Brbh. very costly, precious; very rich; great wealth or treasure. **महाधमनी**, f. *med.* aorta. **महाधिवक्ता** [°*hā+a*°], m. inv. *law.* Advocate-General. **महाधिवेशन** [°*ā+a*°], m. plenary session. **महानगर**, m. a great city; conurbation. **महानवमी**, f. the ninth day of the light half of the month Āśvin; the festival honouring Durgā held on that day. **महानाटक**, m. a drama of ten acts. **महानुभाव**, m. [°*ā+a*°], m. one of great worth, dignity: a gentleman; an eminent person. **°ता**, f. **महान्यायालय**, m. Supreme Court. **°-न्यायवादी**, m. Attorney-General. **°-न्यायाभिकर्ता**, m. inv. Solicitor-General. **महापत्रपाल**, m. Postmaster-General. **महापातक**, m. a heinous sin, or offence. **°ई**, m. one guilty of heinous sin or offence. **महापात्र**, m. a brāhmaṇ who officiates at a *śrāddh* ceremony. **महापाप**, m. heinous sin, or offence. **महापालिका**, f. municipality, city corporation. **महापुरुष**, m. a great or eminent man; iron. consummate villain. **महापौर**, m. mayor. **महाप्रभु**, m. great master (esp. as a title of the philosopher Vallabhācārya); the supreme being (esp. as Viṣṇu, or as Śiva). **महा-प्रलय**, m. *mythol.* annihilation of the universe at the end of a *kalpa*. **महाप्रसाद**, m. food offered to a deity, and then distributed among those present; food so offered to Jagannāth; iron. sthg. inedible. **महाप्राण**, m. & adj. *ling.* an aspirated sound, or letter; aspirated. **°ईकरण**, m. aspiration (the process). **महाबल**, Brbh. very powerful. **°आधिकृत** [°*ā+a*°], m. commander-in-chief. **°ई**, adj. = **महाबल**. **महाबाहु**, adj. long-armed: a title of Viṣṇu-Kṛṣṇa. महाब्राह्मण, m. = महापात्र. महाभारत, m. the great war of the Bharatas; the Sanskrit epic poem describing that war; a great war, epic struggle; transf. vast tome. महाभारत मचाना, to stir up a fearful fight, or wrangle. महाभियोग [°*ā*+*a*°], m. impeachment. महामंत्री, m. Secretary-General. महामना, adj. inv. noble-minded, noble. महाभाग, adj. very fortunate, or prosperous; illustrious; °ई, adj. महामहिम, adj. very great: distinguished, illustrious. महामहोपाध्याय [°*ā*+*u*°], m. distinguished teacher, or scholar (esp. of Sanskrit). महामाई, f. Brbh. great mother: a title of Durgā. महामात्रोत्पादन, m. mass production. महामाया, f. the divine power of illusion (as to the reality of the material world); the illusory nature of worldly objects, personified; a title of Durgā. महामारी, f. plague, epidemic. महायान, m. great vehicle: one of the two early schools of Buddhism. महायुग, m. great age: an age of the gods, embracing the Satya, Tretā, Dvāpara and Kali ages. महारथी, m. one having a great chariot: a great warrior; prestigious person. महाराज [S.], m. great king: emperor; form of address to a brāhmaṇ (often as cook), or to a superior. °आधिराज [°*a*+*a*°], m. emperor. महाराजा, m. inv. = महाराज, 1. महाराणा, m. inv. title of the rajahs of Mevar, Cittor and Udaipur. महारात्रि, f. (in *mythol.*) the night of the destruction of the world; midnight; the time just after midnight. महारानी, f. great queen: empress; respectful form of address to a lady of rank. महाराष्ट्र, m. great kingdom: the state of Maharashtra. °ई, f. name of a Prakrit. °ईय, adj. & m. Maharashtrian. महार्घ [°*ā*+*a*°], adj. & m. very costly, or valuable; (time of) high prices. महार्ह [°*ā*+*a*°], adj. poet. very worthy or precious. महाविद्यालय, m. college (of higher education).महावीर, adj. & m. very brave; a great hero; name of the founder of the Jain faith; a title of Hanumān. °-चक्र, m. name of an Indian military decoration, 2nd grade. महा-शक्ति, f. great power: a title of Śiva, and of Durgā. महाशय [°*ā*+*ā*°], m. a gentleman; voc. sir! (term of respectful address). महाश्वास, m. last breaths (of life). महाष्टमी [°*ā*+*a*°], f. the eighth day of the light half of the month Āśvin; the worship of Durgā taking place on that day. महासभा, f. great council; senate; general assembly; *pol.* Hindū Mahāsabhā. °ई, adj. & m. महासागर, m. ocean. महोत्सव [°*hā*+*u*°], m. great festival; great rejoicing. महोदय [°*hā*+*u*°], m. eminence: gentleman; a term of honorific reference or address (e.g. मंत्री ~, m. the secretary, Mr Secretary); sir (at the beginning of formal letters). °आ, f. महौषध [°*hā*+*au*°], m. = next; title of certain pungent plant products, e.g. garlic, ginger, long pepper. महौषधि [°*hā*+*au*°], f. a very effective remedy; panacea.

महातम *mahātam*, m. Brbh. Av. = माहात्म्य.

महाताब *mahātāb*, m. Brbh. corr. = महताब.

महान *mahān* [S.], adj. great, &c. (= महा-, 1., 2).

महानतम *mahānătam* [S.], adj. greatest, &c. (see महान).

महानता *mahānătā* [S.], f. greatness.

महारत *mahārat* [A. *mahāra*: P. *mahārat*], f. U. skill, expertness; experience; practice. — ~ रखना, to be skilled, practised (in).

महाल *mahāl* [A. *maḥāll*, pl. of *maḥall*], m. places: **1.** 19c. = मुहल्ला. **2.** Brbh. a district.

महावट *mahāvaṭ* [**māghavr̥ṣṭi*-], f. m. winter rain, shower (esp. in the month of Māgh).

महावत *mahāvat* [*mahāmātra*-], m. a mahout, elephant-driver.

महावर *mahāvar*, m. lac (a scarlet dye: used esp. by married women to stain their feet).

महासिल *mahāsil* [A.*maḥāṣil*, pl.], m. U. proceeds, revenue; profits.

महिं *mahiṁ* [*madhya*-], ppn. Brbh. Av. = में.

महि *mahi* [*madhya*-], ppn. Brbh. = में.

महिउ *mahiu*, m. Av. = [1]मही.

महिमा *mahimā* [S.], f. **1.** greatness. ***2.** grandeur, glory. **3.** might, power. **4.** high rank. — महिमाधर, E.H. possessed of greatness, &c. महिमा-मंडित, adj. adorned with grandeur: glorious.

महियाउर *mahiyāur* [**mathitacāmala*-], m. reg. (Bihar) = महेर.

महिला *mahilā* [S.], f. a woman.

महिष *mahiṣ* [S.], m. a buffalo.

महिषी *mahiṣī* [S.], f. **1.** a buffalo cow. **2.** a high-ranking woman, esp. a queen-consort.

[1]**मही** *mahī* [*mathita*-], f. Brbh. buttermilk.

[2]**मही** *mahī* [S.], f. **1.** the earth, world. **2.** earth, soil, ground. — मही-तल, m. surface of the earth, ground. महीदेव, m. = महीसुर. महीधर, m. Brbh. earth-supporter: a mountain; (??) the serpent Śeṣnāg. महीप, m. earth-protector: king. महीपति, m. id. महीपाल, m. = महीप. महीरुह, m. earth-grower: a tree; the teak tree. महीसुर, m. a god on earth: a brāhmaṇ. महेश [°*hā*+*ī*°], m. great lord: a title of Śiva. °श्वर, m. id. °श्वरी, f. a title of Durgā or Pārvatī.

महीन *mahīn* [P. *mahīn*], adj. **1.** fine, delicate (of texture, quality). **2.** fine (of gauge: as a needle); thin. **3.** high (of pitch). **4.** thin, feeble (a voice). — ~ काम, m. delicate work (as inlaying, embroidery).

महीना *mahīnā* [P. *mahīna*], m. **1.** a month. **2.** monthly wage or salary. **3.** menstruation. — ~ **चढ़ना**, a month to be completed: a due monthly date (as for a payment, or for a woman's period) to pass. **उसका ~ है**, she has her period. — **महीने**, adv. per month. **महीने महीने**, adv. month by month. **महीने से होना**, (a woman) to have her period. **महीनेवार** [P. *-vār*], adj. pertaining to a month; taking place monthly. °**ई**, f. ~, 2. **महीनों**, adv. for months.

महुअर *mahuar* [*madhukara-*], m. musical instrument made from a hollow gourd (used by snake-charmers, &c).

महुअरि *mahuari*, f. Brbh. = **महुअर**.

महुअरी *mahuarī*, f. reg. a cake of flour or pulse made with *mahuā* alcohol or *mahuā* flowers, soaked and crushed.

महुआ *mahuā* [*madhūka-*], m. the tree *Bassia latifolia*, and its flower (from which an intoxicating drink is distilled; the nuts or seeds yield an oil). — **महुए का सुखावन**, m. *mahuā* seeds, &c. laid out to dry.

महुआरी *mahuārī* [**madhūkavāṭikā-*], f. a grove of *mahuā* trees.

महूक *mahūk*, m. pronun. var. reg. = **महूख**.

महूख *mahūkh* [*madhūka-* × *vr̥kṣa-*], m. Brbh. = **महुआ**.

महूरत *mahūrat*, m. 19c. = **मुहूर्त**.

महेर *maher* [cf. *mathita-*, and °*yavāgu-*], m. reg. rice boiled in buttermilk (*mahī*) or in sour milk.

महेरा *mahera*, m. 1. = **महेर**. **2.** reg. (E.) a preparation of pulse flour boiled in buttermilk. **3.** reg. (W.) a mash (of pulse, sugar, butter, &c.) fed to horses and cattle.

महेरि *maheri*, f. Brbh. = **महेर**.

महेला *mahelā*, m. *Pl. HŚS.* = **महेरा**, 3.

महेसरी *mahesrī* [ad. *maheśvarī-*], m. having to do with Śiva (*Maheśvara*): the name of a Śaiva sect.

महेसुर *mahesur*, m. Av. = **महेश्वर**: see s.v. **महा-**.

महोख *mahokh* [**madhukapakṣin-*], m. Av. ? a kind of cuckoo, *Cuculus castaneus* (cf. **महोखा**).

महोखा *mahokhā* [**madhukapakṣin-*], m. reg. the crow-pheasant (a bird resembling the black cuckoo, but having red wings).

महोदय *mahôday*, m. see s.v. **महा-**.

महोदया *mahôdayā*, f. see s.v. **महा-**.

महोपाध्याय *mahôpâdhy-āy*, m. see s.v. **महा-**.

महोर *mahor*, m. pronun. var. reg. = **मोर**.

महौषध *mahauṣadh*, m. see s.v. **महा-**.

महौषधि *mahauṣadhi* [S.], f. see s.v. **महा-**.

मह्यो *mahyo* [cf. H. *mahnā*], Brbh. buttermilk (= [1]**मही**).

[1]**माँ** *mām̐* [*mātr̥-*], f. **1.** mother. **2.** term of respectful address or reference to an older woman. **3.** a title of the goddess Lakṣmī. — **माँ-जाया**, adj. & m., f. born of the same mother; full brother (m.), sister (f). **माँ-बहन**, f. mother and sister. **माँ-बहन करना**, to abuse one's mother and sister. **माँ-बाप**, m. mother and father, parents.

[2]**माँ** *mām̐* [cf. *madhya-*], ppn. Av. = **में**.

[1]**माँग** *mām̐g* [*mārga-*], m. parting (of the hair). — ~ **उजड़ना**, or **सूना होना**, (**की**), the parting not to be decorated (with vermilion): to become a widow. ~ **खुलना**, an engagement, or a marriage, to be ended by the death of one of the partners. – ~ **निकालना** or **पारना**, to part the hair. ~ **भरना**, to decorate the parting with vermilion (or red lead, or pearls, &c.); to marry (a woman). ~ **सँवारना**, to do the hair. – **माँग-चोटी**, f. hair-do. **माँग-जली**, f. a widow. **माँग-पट्टी**, f. = **माँग-चोटी**. **माँग-टीका**, m. an ornament worn on the parting of the hair. **माँग-भरी**, f. a married woman.

[2]**माँग** *mām̐g* [cf. H. *mām̐gnā*], f. **1.** a request. **2.** demand (as for a product); popularity. **3.** a demand, requirement. **आखिरी ~**, f. an ultimatum. — ~ **करना**, to make a request, or a demand (to, **से**). – **माँग-ताँग करना**, colloq. to ask for; to borrow.

माँगना *mām̐gnā* [*mārgati*], v.t. **1.** to ask for, to request (from, **से**); to entreat; to beg (as alms). **2.** to demand. **3.** to borrow. — **माँगा**, adj. & m. asked for, &c.; borrowing, hire. **माँगे का**, adj. borrowed. **माँगे देना**, to lend.

मांगलिक *māṅgălik* [S.], adj. auspicious: propitious.

मांगलिकता *māṅgălikătā* [S.], f. = **मांगल्य**, 2.

मांगल्य *māṅgalyă* [S.], m. **1.** sthg. auspicious. **2.** good fortune, prosperity. **3.** festivity.

माँच- *mām̐c-* [**macyate*: Pk. *maccaï*], v.i. Brbh. to be produced, stirred up.

माँचा *mām̐cā*, m. reg. = **माचा**.

[1]**माँज** *mām̐j* [*majjan-*], m. reg. pus.

[2]**माँज** *mām̐j*, f. reg. **1.** marshy land. **2.** alluvial land.

माँज- *mām̐ja-* [*mārjya-*], m. Av. foam on water formed during the first rains (supposed to have an adverse effect on fish).

माँजना *mām̐jnā* [*mārjati*], v.t. **1.** to rub, to scour; to cleanse; to clean (the teeth). **2.** to practise (performance). **हाथ ~**, to improve one's hand (at writing); to improve one's skill (in, **में**). **3.** to smear (as a kite-string with paste, to harden it).

मांजिष्ठ *māñjiṣṭh* [S.], adj. & m. **1.** adj. madder-coloured, red. **2.** m. a red colour.

[1]**माँझ** *mām̐jh* [*madhya-*], ppn. & m. Brbh. Av. **1.** ppn. = **में**. **2.** m. Brbh. interval of time.

[2]**माँझ** *mām̐jh*, f. name of a partic. stanza (of four lines, or multiples of four lines) used in later Kṛṣṇa Brajbhāṣā poetry.

[1]**माँझा** *mām̐jhā* [*madhya-*], m. reg. **1.** ornament worn on a turban. **2.** (Bihar) a medial board or plank (as in a cart, a loom); medial bracket; connecting thong. **3.** fulcrum, axle. **4.** secluded state of bride and groom between completion and consummation of the marriage.

[2]**माँझा** *mām̐jhā* [*madhya-*], m. reg. tree-trunk.

[3]**माँझा** *mām̐jhā* [conn. H. *mām̐jnā*], m. a paste (as smeared on a kite-string to toughen it).

[1]**माँझी** *mām̐jhī* [**majjhika-*], m. boatman, sailor.

[2]**माँझी** *mām̐jhī* [cf. H. *mām̐jh*], m. Av. go-between, mediator.

माँट *mām̐ṭ*, m. Brbh. = [1]**माट**.

माँटी *mām̐ṭī*, f. Av. = **माटी**.

माँठ *mām̐ṭh*, f. Av. a kind of sweet (see [2]**माठ**).

माँड़ *mām̐ṛ* [*maṇḍa-*[1]], m. **1.** rice-water. **2.** starch made of rice flour.

माँड़- *mām̐ṛ-* [*maṇḍayati*], v.t. reg. **1.** to adorn; to besmear; to starch. **2.** to write down (sc. to put on paper).

माँड़ना *mām̐ṛnā* [*mardati*], v.t. **1.** to rub. **2.** to press, to flatten; to knead. **3.** to tread out (corn); to thresh corn (by beating it on the ground). **4.** Brbh. to stir up, to perpetrate (as hostilities); to be engaged in, to be active.

माँड़नी *mām̐ṛnī* [*maṇḍana-*], f. Brbh. border, edging.

माँड़ा *mām̐ṛā* [*maṇḍa-*[1]], m. **1.** *Pl. HŚS.* a pastry made with refined flour, and fried in *ghī*. **2.** a cataract (of the eye).

माँड़ी *mām̐ṛī* [*maṇḍa-*[1]], f. starch made of rice flour.

माँथ *mām̐th*, m. Av. = **माथा**.

[1]**माँद** *mām̐d* [*manda-*], adj. **1.** faded; dull. **2.** inferior.

[2]**माँद** *mām̐d* [? = [1]*mām̐d*], f. **1.** a heap of dung. ***2.** den, lair.

माँदगी *mām̐dăgī* [P. *māndagī*], f. **1.** illness. **2.** fatigue.

माँदा *mām̐dā* [P. *mānda*], adj. **1.** [? × *manda-*], unwell. **2.** [? × *manda-*], tired. **3.** U. left over, remaining.

माँदर *mām̐dar*, m. E.H. = **मादल**.

मांद्य *māndyă* [S.], m. **1.** sluggishness; inertness. **2.** languor. **3.** illness.

मांस *mām̐s* [*mām̐sa-*], m. meat; flesh. — **मांसख़ोर** [P. *-khor*], adj. meat-eating. **मांस-पेशी**, f. a muscle. **मांसभक्षी**, adj. meat-eating. **मांसाहार**, m. non-vegetarian food. **°ई**, adj. non-vegetarian; carnivorous.

मांसल *mām̐sal* [S.], adj. **1.** fleshy. **2.** muscular. **3.** well-nourished.

माँहिं *mām̐him̐* [*madhya-*], ppn. Brbh. Av. = **में**.

मा *mā*, f. see [1]**माँ**.

[1]**मा-** *mā-* [*māyate*], v.i. Brbh. to be contained in (= **समाना**).

[2]**मा-** *mā-* [*māpayati*], v.t. Brbh. to measure.

[1]**माईं** *māīm̐*, f. 1. = [1]**माई**, 2. 2. = [1]**माँ**, 2.

[2]**माईं** *māīm̐*, f. = [1]**मामी**.

[1]**माई** *māī* [*mātṛkā-*], f. 1. = **माँ**, 1., 2. **2.** a cake cooked and offered to maternal ancestors on the occasion of a marriage. — **~ का लाल**, m. a fine or bold young man.

[2]**माई** *māī* [cf. *māma-*], f. = [1]**मामी**.

माऊँ *māūm̐*, m. **म्याऊँ**.

माकड़ा *mākṛā* [*mārkaṭa-*], adj. reg. monkey-like: lean, thin; haggard.

माक़ूल *māqūl* [A. *ma'qūl*], adj. according with reason: proper, appropriate (to a purpose); reasonable; satisfactory; good.

माक़ूलियत *māqūliyat* [A. *ma'qūliya*: P. *ma'qūliyat*], f. U. appropriateness, reasonableness, &c.

माखन *mākhan*, m. butter (= **मक्खन**). — **माखन-चोर**, m. butter-thief: a title of Kṛṣṇa.

माखी *mākhī*, f. Brbh. Av. = **मक्खी**.

माखो *mākho*, f. *Pl. HŚS.* a rumour.

मागध *māgadh* [S.], adj. & m. **1.** adj. having to do with the region of Magadh. **2.** m. Brbh. minstrel, bard (= भाट).

मागधक *māgădhak* [S.], m. **1.** a bard. **2.** an inhabitant of Magadh.

मागधी *māgadhī* [S.], f. a partic. Prakrit (connected traditionally with the region of Magadh).

[1]माघ *māgh* [S.], m. the eleventh month of the Hindu lunar calendar (January-February). — माघ-मेला, m. name of a bathing festival held annually in Māgh at the confluence of the Ganges and Jumna rivers.

[2]माघ *māgh* [conn.*māghya-*], m. Brbh. jasmine.

माघी *māghī* [cf. H. *māgh*], f. the full moon of the month Māgh.

माच- *māc-*, v.i. Brbh. = मचना.

माचा *mācā* [*mañca-*], m. reg. **1.** a watchman's platform. 2. = माची, 1. **3.** large bedstead.

माची *mācī* [*mañcikā-*], f. reg. **1.** a four-legged stool (= मचिया). **2.** a small bed. **3.** yoke for oxen. **4.** *Pl.* a harrow. **5.** netting to carry luggage (as attached to a cart).

माछ *māch* [*matsya-*], m. Av. = [1]माछी.

माछर *māchar*, m. reg. = मच्छर.

[1]माछी *māchī* [*matsya-*], f. a fish.

[2]माछी *māchī* [*makṣikā-*], f. Brbh. a fly.

माजरा *mājrā* [A. *mājarā*], m. **1.** event, occurrence. **2.** state, condition.

माज़ी *māzī* [A. *māẓī*], m. S.H. the past.

माजू *mājū* [P. *māzū*], m. gall-nut. — माजू-फल, m. id.

माजून *mājūn* [A. *ma'jūn*], m. **1.** a sweet made with hemp (*bhāṁg*). **2.** a drink of hemp or (?) opium, spiced with aniseed, cardamoms, &c.

माजूम *mājūm*, m. reg. = माजून.

माज़ूर *māzūr* [A. *ma'zūr*], adj. **1.** excused. **2.** helpless, powerless.

माझ *mājh* [*madhya-*], adj. & m. **1.** adj. middle. **2.** m. the middle.

माझे *mājhe* [cf. *madhya-*], adv. reg. in the middle, or midst.

[1]माट *māṭ* [**mārtta-*], m. **1.** large earthen vessel or jar. **2.** a vat (as used by dyers).

[2]माट *māṭ*, m. *Pl. HŚS.* a pot-herb or vegetable, *Amaranthus oleraceus*, or *A. tristis*.

माटी *māṭī* [*mṛttikā-*], f. **1.** earth, soil; clay. **2.** dust. **3.** fig. the body. **4.** E.H. a dead body. — ~ में रुलना, to mingle with the dust: to die.

[1]माठ *māṭh*, m. = [1]माट.

[2]माठ *māṭh* [*mṛṣṭa-*[1]], m. Brbh. a kind of sweet.

[3]माठ *māṭh*, m. *Pl.* = [2]माट.

माड़- *māṛ-* [*maṇḍayati*], v.t. Brbh. **1.** to adorn; to deck out. **2.** to put on clothes.

माड़ना *māṛnā*, v.t. = माँड़ना.

माड़नी *māṛnī* [cf. H. *māṁṛ-*], f. reg. paste; starch.

माड़ा *māṛā*, adj. reg. **1.** lean, skinny. **2.** poor (of quality), worthless; little (of amount). **3.** mean, miserable (in attitude).

माड़ी *māṛī*, f. rice-water, &c. (= माँड़ी).

माढ़ा *māṛhā* [**maṇḍhaka-*; *maṇḍapa-*], m. var. /maṛa/. an upper room, or balcony.

माणिक *māṇik*, m. = माणिक्य.

माणिक्य *māṇikyă* [S.], m. a ruby; a jewel.

मातंग *mātaṅg* [S.], m. Brbh. **1.** an elephant. **2.** an outcaste (= चांडाल).

[1]मात *māt* [ad. *mātā-*], f. reg. mother.

[2]मात *māt* [A. *māt* 'he is dead': P. *māt*, adj.], adj. & f. **1.** adj. taken aback, astonished. **2.** defeated, outdone; checkmated. **3.** f. defeat; checkmate. — ~ करना, to beat (a record). ~ खाना, to suffer a defeat. ~ देना (को), to defeat; to checkmate; to outdo; to confound.

मात- *māt-* [cf. *matta-*], v.i. Brbh. Av. **1.** to be drunk. **2.** to be intoxicated with pride.

मातबर *mātbar* [A. *mu'tabar*], adj. U. regarded: trustworthy, reliable.

मातम *mātam* [A. *ma'tam*], m. mourning; grief. — ~ करना, or मनाना (का), to mourn, to lament; to sing a dirge. ~ रखना, to observe mourning. – मातम-ख़ाना, m. house where a death has occurred. मातमदार [P. *-dār*], adj. & m. *Pl.* mourning; a mourner. मातमपुरसी [P. *-pursī*], f. condolences (at a death). मातमपुरसी करना, to express condolences (to, की).

मातमी *mātamī* [A. *ma'tam*+P. *-ī*], adj. **1.** appropriate to mourning (as garments). **2.** grieving. **3.** wretched, of little account.

मातल *mātal*, adj. reg. drunk (= मत्त).

मातहत *māt'hat* [A. *mā taḥt*], adj. & m. what is under: **1.** adj. & adv. subordinate (to, के). **2.** m. a subordinate.

मातहती *māt'hatī* [cf. H. *māt'hat*], f. subordination, or subjection.

माता *mātā* [S.], f. **1.** mother. 2. = माँ, 2. **3.** the goddess Devī (esp. as supposed to inflict smallpox). **4.** transf. smallpox. — ~ निकलना, smallpox to erupt (on a person). ~ पूजना, to worship the goddess of smallpox. छोटी ~, f. measles. – माता-पिता, m. pl. mother and father, parents. मातामह, m. maternal grandfather. °-मही, f. maternal grandmother.

माता *mātā* [cf. H. *māt*], adj. E.H. = मत्त.

मातारी *mātārī*, f. reg. = महतारी.

मातुल *mātul* [S.], m. Brbh. **1.** maternal uncle. **2.** the thorn-apple (धतूरा).

मातुला *mātulā* [S.], f. *Pl. HŚS.* **1.** maternal aunt. 2. = भाँग.

मातुलानी *mātulānī* [S.], f. *Pl. HŚS.* = मातुला.

मातृ- *mātr̥-* [S]. mother's, maternal: — मातृतंत्र, m. matriarchy. मातृदेश, m. motherland. मातृनिष्ठ, adj. matriarchal. मातृपरंपरा, f. maternal line. मातृपूजा, f. worship of (maternal) ancestors prior to marriage. मातृभाषा, f. mother tongue. मातृभूमि, f. motherland. मातृमाता, f. grandmother. मातृवत, adv. maternally. मातृसत्ता, f. matriarchy. °त्मक, adj. matriarchal.

मातृका *mātr̥kā* [S.], f. *Pl. HŚS.* **1.** mother. **2.** wet-nurse; nurse. **3.** title of various tantric goddesses.

मातृत्व *mātr̥tvă* [S.], m. motherhood.

मात्र *mātr* [S.], adj. & adv. usu. in comp. of the amount of: **1.** adj. mere. **2.** sole. **3.** adv. merely, only; just; solely. — एक ~, adj. sole, single. – क्षण-मात्र के लिए, for just a moment. नाम-मात्र, adv. in name only.

मात्रक *mātrak* [S.], m. & adj. **1.** m. unit of measurement. **2.** adj. -मात्रक. *Pl.* of the amount of, as much as.

मात्रा *mātrā* [S.], f. **1.** measure; quantity. **2.** dose (of medicine). **3.** *rhet.* a metrical instant: the length of a short syllable. **4.** an intra-syllabic vowel symbol. **5.** a part, constituent. — किस ~ में? to what extent? how far? मात्रा-वृत्त, m. a metre analysable in terms of metrical instants (rather than syllables).

मात्रिक *mātrik* [S.], adj. *rhet.* analysable in terms of metrical instants (a metre).

मात्रिका *mātrikā* [S.], f. *Pl.* = मात्रा, 3.

मात्सर *mātsar* [S.], adj. **1.** envious. **2.** jealous.

मात्सर्य *mātsaryă* [S.], m. envy, &c. (cf. मात्सर).

माथ *māth*, m. Av. = माथा.

माथा *māthā* [*mastaka-*], f. **1.** the forehead; the head. **2.** upper part; summit. **3.** prow. — माथा खपाना, to rack the brains. ~ खाना, to plague, to harass. ~ गरम होना, to be or to become angry. ~ टिकाना, to rest the head (on the ground: to prostrate oneself). ~ टेकना, id. ~ ठनकना, the head to ring or to throb: to have a premonition. ~ धुनना, to beat the brow. ~ पीटना, to beat the brow; to make strenuous efforts. ~ मारना, to rack the brains; to beat the brow. ~ रगड़ना, to rub the forehead (on the ground): to prostrate oneself. माथे जाना, to fall (upon, के: as disgrace). माथे धर-, Brbh. = माथे पर चढ़ाना. माथे पर चढ़ना, = सिर पर चढ़ना. माथे पर चढ़ाना, to receive or to accept respectfully. माथे पड़ना, to be the responsibility (of, के: as cares, duties). माथे पर बल न पड़ने देना, fig. not to show displeasure, or unease. माथे भाग होना, to be fortunate. माथे मढ़ना, to attribute (a fault, &c.: to, के). – माथापच्ची, f. racking the brains. माथापच्ची करना, to rack the brains. माथापिट्टन, m. beating the brow; racking the brains.

माथुर *māthur* [S.], m. connected with Mathurā: **1.** name of a brāhmaṇ community. ***2.** name of a Kāyasth community. **3.** member of a Māthur community.

माद *mād* [S.], m. *Pl. HŚS.* **1.** intoxication. **2.** passion. **3.** rapture. **4.** pride.

मादक *mādak* [S.], adj. & m. **1.** adj. intoxicating; narcotic. **2.** exhilarating. **3.** m. an intoxicant, &c.

मादकता *mādakătā* [S.], f. intoxicating quality, &c.

मादर *mādar* [P. *mādar*], f. U. mother. — मादरज़ाद [P. *-zād*], adj. born of the same mother; adv. as when born (naked); congenitally (blind, &c).

मादरी *mādrī* [P. *mādarī*], adj. U. mother's, maternal. — ~ ज़बान, f. mother tongue.

मादल *mādal* [*mardala-*], m.f. a kind of drum.

मादा *mādā* [P. *māda*], adj. f. & f. **1.** adj. female (bird, animal, &c). **2.** f. a female.

माद्दा *māddā* [A. *mādda*], m. matter, material: **1.** capacity, ability. **2.** source, root. **3.** pus.

माधव *mādhav* [S.], m. **1.** descendant of Madhu: a title of Kr̥ṣṇa. **2.** Brbh. the month Baisākh; spring.

माधवी *mādhăvī* [S.], f. **1.** a large creeper bearing white fragrant flowers, *Gaertnera racemosa*. **2.** an alcohol distilled from *mahuā* flowers.

माधुर *mādhur* [S.], m. *HŚS.* jasmine.

माधुरी *mādhurī* [S.], f. **1.** a type of jasmine, *Jasminum zambac*. **2.** sweetness. **3.** charm. **4.** wine.

माधुर्य *mādhuryă* [S.], f. **1.** sweetness. **2.** charm.

माध्य *mādhyă* [S.], adj. *Pl. HŚS.* = **माध्यम.** — **माध्यस्थ**, m. = **मध्यस्थ.**

माध्यम *mādhyam* [S.], adj. & m. **1.** adj. middle, mid-. **2.** m. a means. **3.** specif. language of instruction or study.

माध्यमिक *mādhyamik* [S.], adj. middle; intermediate, secondary (as education); transitional (stage, &c).

माध्वी *mādhvī* [S.], f. = **माधवी.**

[1]**मान** *mān* [S.], m. **1.** good opinion of self; self-respect, honour. **2.** pride. **3.** honour, respect (to or for other persons or things), regard; heed, obedience; acceptance (as of a view). **4.** reputation, prestige; status. **5.** wounded honour or pride; anger; caprice (of an offended woman), sulkiness. — **~ करना**, to be proud or vain (of, **का**); to give oneself airs; to be offended (at, **से**), to sulk. **~ मथ-**, Brbh. to disconcert (and so to humble) the pride (of, **का**). **~ मनाना (का)**, to talk round, to placate (an offended person). **~ मोर-**, Brbh. to give up anger, &c. **~ रखना**, to show respect, &c. (to, **का**); to heed, to obey. **~ रहना**, to be dependent (on, **के**). – **मान-कंद**, m. dried orchid tuber(s), salep. **मान-गुमान**, m. honour, dignity. **मानद**, adj. honorary. °**-देय**, m. honorarium. **मान-पान**, m. honour, respect. **मान-पत्र**, m. honorary address. **मान-भंग**, m. disgrace; humbling, humiliation; disillusionment (of hopes); placation. **मान-मनौती**, = next. **मान-मनौवल**, m. persuasion, cajoling; placating. **मान-मर्यादा**, f. honour, prestige, dignity. **मान-मोचन**, m. *HŚS.* placation of offended dignity or pride. **मान-सम्मान**, m. honourable reception; welcome. **मान-हानि**, f. disrespect (suffered); slander; contempt (of court). **मानापमान** [°*na+a*°], m. honour and dishonour. **मानाभिषेक** [°*na+a*°], m. investiture. **मानार्थ** [°*na+a*°], adj. (given or done) by way of respect; complimentary (ticket, copy).

[2]**मान** *mān* [S.], m. **1.** measure, proportion; size; amount. **2.** scale (for comparison); standard; level (as of salary). **3.** unit of measurement. **4.** warrant, authority, grounds. **5.** capacity (to perform a task). **5.** resemblance, likeness. — **मान-चित्र**, m. a map. °**अण**, m. cartography. **मान-चित्रावली**, f. an atlas. **मान-दंड**, m. measuring-rod, or line; a standard; scale. **मानीकरण**, m. standardisation.

-मान् *-mān* [S.], suffix. = [1] [2]**-मान.**

[1]**-मान** *-mān* [S.], suffix (forms adjectives which are properly masculines, chiefly from nouns, having the sense 'possessed of … ', e.g. **दीप्तिमान**, illuminated, brilliant; **श्रीमान**, voc. auspicious one, sir: feminines properly in °**मती**).

[2]**-मान** *-mān* [S.], suffix (forms a few participles, historically middle voice, e.g. **पलायमान**, fleeing, seeking refuge).

[1]**मानक** *mānak* [S.], adj. & m. **1.** adj. standard. **2.** m. a standard.

[2]**मानक** *mānak* [ad. *mānaka-*[1]], m. the plant *Arum indicum* (the bulbous root of which is eaten).

[3]**मानक** *mānak* [*mānikya-*], m. = **माणिक्य.**

मानत *mānat*, f. reg. likeness, resemblance.

मानता *mānătā* [? ad. **mānyatā-*], f. **1.** belief; religious belief. **2.** a vow. **3.** acknowledgement, acquiescence.

मानना *mānnā* [*manyate*], v.t. **1.** to consider sthg. as such; to accept (as valid), to agree or to assent to; to accept (a situation); to admit. **2.** to acknowledge (the position, or a partic. quality, of: as of a regime, or a person). **3.** to suppose, to assume. **मान लीजिए कि…**, imagine that…. **4.** to believe, to credit (as true). **5.** to hold in respect or regard, or in favour; to observe, to obey (a request, a command). — **काली जी को बकरा ~**, to dedicate a goat (as a fit offering) to Kālī. **बुरा ~**, to take amiss. **मानी हुई बात**, f. an accepted fact or case, sthg. understood.

माननीय *mānănīyă* [S.], adj. deserving of honour or esteem.

मानव *mānav* [S.], m. **1.** a human being; a man. **2.** mankind. — **मानव-कृत**, adj. man-made. **मानवजाति-विज्ञान**, m. ethnography. **मानव-द्रोही**, adj. & m. misanthropical; misanthropist. **मानववाद**, m. humanism. °**ई**, adj. & m. **मानव-शत्रु**, m. = **मानव-द्रोही. मानव-शास्त्र**, m. anthropology. °**ई**, m. anthropologist. °**ईय**, adj. anthropological. **मानव-विज्ञान**, m. anthropology. **मानवाधिकार** [°*va+a*°], m. human rights. **मानवोचित** [°*va+u*°], adj. proper to man, human (as qualities).

मानवक *mānăvak* [ad. *māṇavaka-*], m. **1.** a youth. **2.** pej. little man.

मानवता *mānavătā* [S.], f. state of being a man; human attributes; humanity. — **मानवतावाद**, f. humanism (see also s.v. **मानव**); humanitarianism. °**ई**, adj. & m. humanist; humanitarian.

मानवी *mānăvī* [S.], f. *mythol. Pl. HŚS.* daughter of man or of Manu: a woman.

मानवीय *mānăvīyă* [S.], adj. **1.** having to do with man, human. **2.** humane.

मानवीयता *mānăvīyătā* [S.], f. **1.** human status, humanity. **2.** humanity (of conduct).

[1]मानस *mānas* [*mānuṣa-*], m. **1.** a human being, a man. **2.** a person.

[2]मानस *mānas* [S.], adj. & m. **1.** adj. having to do with the mind or spirit; mental; spiritual. **2.** m. mind (as the seat of thought and feeling); heart; soul. **3.** thought, wish. 4. = मानसरोवर. **5.** the *Rām-carit-mānas* of Tulsīdās. — मानसरोवर (corr. of मानस-सरोवर), m. name of a sacred lake and pilgrimage-place on mount Kailās in the Himālayas (Tibet). मानस-चिकित्सक, m. psychiatrist; psychotherapist. मानस-पटल, m. screen of the mind: memory. मानस-विज्ञान, m. psychology. मानस-शास्त्र, m. psychology. °ई, m. psychologist.

मानसरोवर *mānsarovar*, m. see s.v. मानस.

मानसिक *mānăsik* [S.], adj. **1.** mental. **2.** psychic. **3.** spiritual.

मानसिकता *mānăsikătā* [S.], f. mentality.

मानिंद *mānind* [P. *mānand*], ppn. w. की or के. like.

[1]मानिक *mānik* [*māṇikya-*], m. a ruby; a jewel. — मानिक-जोड़, m. (bird) having a necklace: the white-necked stork, *Ciconia episcopus*.

[2]मानिक *mānik* [S.], adj. quantitative.

मानित *mānit* [S.], adj. **1.** accepted. **2.** honoured.

मानिता *mānitā* [S.], f. **1.** respect, honour. **2.** sense of honour; pride. **3.** unworthy pride.

मानिनी *māninī* [S.], f. **1.** a haughty woman. **2.** a woman offended by her lover.

[1]मानी *mānī* [S.], adj. **1.** proud, haughty. **2.** resentful; sulky. **3.** [× *mānita-*] honoured.

[2]मानी *mānī*, f. reg. (W.) **1.** ring-fastening (of a spade-handle to its blade). **2.** bush (of an upper millstone).

[3]मानी *mānī* [cf. H. [1]*mān*], adj. **1.** honoured, respected. **2.** (rare) honouring, respecting.

[4]मानी *mānī* [P. *ma'nī*; ? and A. *ma'ānin*, pl. of *ma'nā*], f. meanings: meaning (= माने).

मानीकरण *mānīkaraṇ* [S.], m. see s.v. [2]मान.

मानुष *mānuṣ* [S.], adj. & m. **1.** adj. = मानुषिक. **2.** m. = मनुष्य.

मानुषिक *mānuṣik* [S.], adj. having to do with man; human.

[1]मानुषी *mānuṣī*, adj. Brbh. = मानुषीय.

[2]मानुषी *mānuṣī* [S.], f. *Pl. HŚS.* a woman.

मानुषीय *mānuṣīyă* [S.], adj. = मानुषिक.

मानुष्य *mānuṣyă* [S.], m. **1.** the human state or condition. **2.** humanity (in aggregate). **3.** humanity (of conduct); manliness.

मानुस *mānus*, m. = [1]मानस.

माने *māne* [A. *ma'nā*, P. *ma'nī* (? with form infld. by H. [4]*mānī*, a historical plural)], m. sg. & pl. & adv. **1.** m. meaning. **2.** adv. that is (= यानी). — ~ बयान करना, to explain the meaning (of, के). ~ रखना, to denote, to imply. इसका (or के) क्या ~ है (or हैं)? what does this mean? सही मानों में, truth to tell.

मानों *mānoṁ* [E.H. *mānahu*], conj. one might suppose: as if.

मानो *māno*, conj. = मानों.

मान्य *mānyă* [S.], adj. **1.** worthy of honour, honoured. **2.** deserving credence; accepted (as an opinion); authoritative. **3.** authenticated (a document). **4.** recognized (as a society, a sub-sect). — मान्यवर, adj. & m. highly respected; respected guest, &c. (term of formal address).

मान्यता *mānyătā* [S.], f. **1.** belief, opinion; pl. values. **2.** acceptance (as of a view); authority (of an opinion); validity; recognition (of a body). **3.** permission (to, की). — मान्यता-प्राप्त, adj. accepted, authoritative, &c.

माप *māp* [cf. H. *māpnā*; and *māpya-*], f. m. **1.** measuring; survey. **2.** a measure. **3.** size, scale. **4.** fig. placing (sthg.) lengthwise alongside (another object). व्यस्त ~, poet. close contact. — माप-जोख, f. = ~, 1. माप-तौल, f. mensuration; system of weights and measures. माप-दंड, m. scale (as of a map); standard.

मापक *māpak* [S.], adj. & m. **1.** adj. measuring, for measuring (an appliance). **2.** m. *HŚS.* a scale, measure. **3.** measuring appliance. **4.** a surveyor.

मापन *māpan* [S.], m. **1.** measuring. **2.** *Pl. HŚS.* a scale, balance.

मापना *māpnā* [**māpyate*], v.t. to measure.

मापनी *māpnī* [cf. H. *māpnā*], f. a scale.

माफ़ *māf* [A. *mu'āfā*: P. *mu'āf*], adj. **1.** forgiven, excused (as an offence). **2.** excused, spared (as an obligation); exempted (from); remitted (as fees, rent). — ~ करना, to forgive; to excuse, &c. ~ कीजिए! excuse me! I beg your pardon!

माफ़िक़ *māfiq*, adj. = मुआफ़िक़.

माफ़ी *māfī* [A. *mu'āfā* + P. *-ī*], f. **1.** forgiveness. **2.** exemption (from an obligation); remission (of fees, rent). **3.** rent-free land, or estate. **4.** amnesty. — माफ़ीदार [P. *-dār*], m. a holder of rent-free land, a grantee.

मामता *māmătā* [cf. S. *mama-*: ? **māmya-*], f. *Pl. HŚS.* affection, esp. maternal affection.

मामला *māmlā* [A. *mu'āmala*], m. **1.** an affair, matter, concern; dealings. **2.** case, suit (in law: against, पर, के ऊपर). **3.** colloq. sexual intercourse. — ~ पक्का करना, to settle a matter finally or definitely; to conclude a deal, a bargain. ~ बनना, a matter to be settled, or to succeed; a deal or a bargain to be concluded; an end to be gained. ~ करना, or लड़ाना, or लगाना, or बनाना, to have sexual intercourse.

मामा *māmā* [*māmaka-*], m. maternal uncle.

[1]**मामी** *māmī* [cf. H. *māmā*], f. wife of a maternal uncle, aunt.

[2]**मामी** *māmī* [cf. S. *mama-*: ? **māmya-*], f. Brbh. stubborn insistence (on one's view, or interests). — ~ पीना, to be insistent; *Pl.* to show partiality.

मामू *māmū*, m. = मामा.

मामूर *māmūr* [A. *ma'mūr*], adj. E.H. inhabited, peopled: flourishing.

मामूल *māmūl* [A. *ma'mūl*], m. **1.** practice, custom. **2.** fixed or customary allowance.

मामूली *māmūlī* [A. *ma'mūl*+P. *-ī*], adj. **1.** ordinary, customary. **2.** ordinary (of standard, quality, or rank); average. — ~ तौर पर, adv. in the usual way. भाव ~ नरम रहे, prices remained rather slack. वह ~ गाता है, he's (just) an average singer.

मायका *māykā* [cf. *mātṛ-*], m. mother's house, parental home (of a married woman).

मायने *māyne*, m. sg. & pl. = माने.

मायल *māyal* [A. *mā'il*], adj. **1.** inclined towards. **2.** -मायल. mixed with (of shades of colour). सफ़ेदी-~ भूरा रंग, m. a dappled brown.

[1]**माया** *māyā* [S.], f. **1.** supernatural power; magical or wonderful power. **2.** illusion; deceit, deception. **3.** sthg. illusory; conjuring; jugglery; magic. **4.** *philos.* the world as perceived by the senses (considered as illusory). **5.** [×H. [2]*māyā*] wealth. **6.** fig. a woman. **7.** feeling, affection (for, पर); compassion; mercy. — न ~ मिली न राम, fig. neither of two different objectives were attained. – माया-जाल, m. the snares of this illusory world. मायातीत [°*yā*+*a*°], adj. beyond the influence of *māyā*; without compassion, &c. माया-पति, m. Av. lord of *māyā*: a title of the supreme being. माया-पात्र, m. a wealthy person. मायामय, adj. Av. unreal; enchanted; wondrous. माया-मोह, m. illusion and infatuation (with what is unreal). मायारूप, adj. unreal, illusory. मायावर, m. lord of *māyā*: a title of the absolute being. माया-विद्या, f. magic. मायावाद, m. theory of the illusory nature of all things except the ultimate being, Vedānta theory. °ई, adj. & m. Vedantist. मायावान, adj. possessing powers of illusion; having magical powers; deceptive; magical. मायाशय [°*yā*+*ā*°], m. a vessel for *māyā*: one who is subject to illusion.

[2]**माया** *māyā* [P. *māya*], m. U. **1.** essence, substance. **2.** wealth; means. **3.** capital (in trade). **4.** ferment, leaven. **5.** capability. — ~ जोड़ना, to amass wealth. – मायादार [P. *-dār*], adj. strong, thick, solid; wealthy.

मायावी *māyāvī* [S.], adj. & m. **1.** adj. = मायावान. **2.** m. a magician; juggler. **3.** a deceiver.

मायिक *māyik* [S.], adj. Av. illusory; deceptive.

मायी *māyī* [S.], adj. illusory; deceptive.

मायूस *māyūs* [A. *māyūs*], adj. despondent. — ~ करना, to disappoint (hopes, &c).

मायूसी *māyūsī* [A. *māyūs*+P. *-ī*], f. despondency.

[1]**मार** *mār* [cf. H. *mārnā*], f. **1.** beating. **2.** a beating. **3.** a blow; stroke, shot (with a bat, racquet); kick (at goal). **4.** a fight, brawl. **5.** barrage (of fire). **6.** plunder; extortion. **7.** loss. **8.** cure (as for an itch, an ache). **9.** reg. (W.) a rich, black, friable soil found in Bundelkhand. — ~ खाना, to be given a beating. ~ खिलाना (को), to cause (another) to be beaten, or punished. ~ देना (को), to give a beating (to). ~ पड़ना, a beating to be the lot (of, पर). – मार-कटाई, or मार-काट, f. beating and wounding: fighting; assault and battery; carnage. मार-कुटाई, f. = मार-पीट. मार-धाड़, f. attack; fighting, violence. मार-पीट, f. beating; fighting; assault and battery. मार-पेच [P. *mār-*], m. snake's twisting (*Pl.*); deviousness, intrigue. मारात्मक [°*ra*+*ā*°], adj. murderous; destructive.

[2]**मार** *mār* [cf. H. *mārnā*], adv. colloq. very much.

[3]**मार** *mār* [S.], m. *hind.* a title of the god Kāmdev.

[4]**मार** *mār* [P. *mār*], m. S.H. a snake (see also मार-पेच s.v. [1]मार).

मारक *mārak* [S.], adj. & m. **1.** adj. killing. **2.** suppressing, combatting (a poison, &c). **3.** -मारक. anti-. **4.** m. antidote.

मारकत *mārkat* [S.], adj. *Pl.* emerald-like.

[1]**मारका** *mārkā* [A. *ma'raka*], m. U. **1.** field or scene of battle. **2.** fight, strife. — मारके का, adj. important, momentous.

[2]**मारका** *mārkā* [Engl. *mark*], m. a mark; trademark. — चोटी ~ ब्राह्मण, m. a brāhmaṇ marked out by his top-knot.

मारकीन *mārkīn* [? f. Engl. *Nankeen*], m. 19c. a durable, machine-woven cotton cloth.

मारण *māraṇ* [S.], m. *Pl. HŚS.* killing.

मारतौल *mārtaul* [f. Pt. *martelo*], m. obs. a heavy hammer.

मारना *mārnā* [*mārayati*], m. **1.** to beat; to hit, to strike. **2.** to kill. **3.** to strike with; to fire (a shot, missile). डंक ~, to sting. दाँत ~, to bite (as a dog). लात ~, to kick. गोली ~ (को), to shoot (a person); colloq. to have done with, to make an end of (sthg. trivial or wretched). बंदूक़ ~, to fire a rifle or gun. **4.** to shoot (game). **5.** to seize, to capture. मछली ~, to fish. **6.** to drive in, or home (as a nail). **7.** to throw, to dash (at or upon, को). **8.** to give (the hand, as a sign of good faith). **9.** to throw down (an opponent). **10.** to destroy; to ruin (as storm a crop). **11.** to attack (as a village, a house; or a traveller). **12.** to make, to mount (an attack: see s.v.छापा). **13.** to move (sthg.) about, to agitate; to flutter (wings). मुँह ~, to browse (among, में). हाथ पाँव ~, to struggle (in bonds). **14.** to obtain by fraud; to embezzle. **15.** esp. w. खाना. to earn, to rake in (great or excessive profits). **16.** to blunt (a blade, an edge); to round off (as a corner). **17.** to assail, to afflict (as hunger, emotion, or perplexity; or as a vice). सिर ~, to rack one's brains. **18.** to suppress, to mortify (feelings, passions). **19.** to allay (as a remedy, or antidote). **20.** to oxidise (a metal). **21.** to win (a contest, a bet). **22.** to perform an action with vigour or decisiveness; to close (a door); to turn (a key in a lock). ग़ोता ~, to dive; चक्कर ~, to go or to swing (around sthg). **23.** to assert aggressively. डींग ~, to boast. **24.** to cast (a spell). जादू ~, to bewitch. — मार गिराना, to knock down; to shoot down (a person, an aircraft).मार डालना, to kill. मार भगाना, to drive off by force; to put to flight. मार मरना, to commit suicide; to die fighting. मार रखना, to slay; to keep, to withhold (wrongfully or illegally). मार लेना, to overcome, to conquer. – मारा, adj. & m. beaten, killed, destroyed, &c.; overturned, or sunk (a boat) (*Pl.*); a beating; a blow; a beaten person; a victim; general destruction; great abundance. मारा पड़ना, to lie dead; to lie ruined (as a crop). मारा-कूटी, f. = मार-कुटाई. मारामार, f. scuffle, affray; bustle, rush; constant or dire struggle; great abundance. मारामार करना, to bustle; to hasten; to toil. मारा-मारा फिरना, or मारा फिरना, to wander about; to live wretchedly. मारामारी, f. = मारामार. मारे, ppn. see s.v.

मारफ़त *mārfat* [A. *ma'rifa*: P. *ma'rifat*], adv. knowledge: **1.** by means (of, की), through. **2.** care of (in a postal address).

मारवाड़ *mārvāṛ* [cf. *maru-*, **māru-*], m. the region of Mārvāṛ.

[1]**मारवाड़ी** *mārvāṛī* [cf. H. *mārvāṛ*], adj. & m. **1.** adj. having to do with Mārvāṛ. **2.** a man from Mārvāṛ.

[2]**मारवाड़ी** *mārvāṛī* [cf. H. *mārvāṛ*], f. the language or dialect of Mārvāṛ.

मारित *mārit* [S.], adj. **1.** killed. **2.** *ayur.* reduced to ash, calcined.

[1]**मारी** *mārī* [cf. H. *mārnā*], f. *Pl.* **1.** a beating. **2.** a blow.

[2]**मारी** *mārī* [*mārikā-*], f. **1.** any deadly disease (= महामारी); plague; cholera. **2.** epidemic.

मारुत *mārut* [S.], m. *mythol.* **1.** air, wind. **2.** a god of air or wind. — मारुत-सुत, adj. Brbh. Av. son of the wind: Hanumān; Bhīm.

मारुति *māruti* [S.], m. *mythol.* son of the Maruts, or of the wind: a title of Hanumān, and of Bhīm.

मारुती *mārutī* [S.], adj. & m. having to do with the wind: brand name of a partic. Hindustan car.

[1]**मारू** *mārū* [cf. H. *mārnā*], adj. **1.** adj. striking; ready or able to strike (a force); destructive, deadly. **2.** fatally charming (a heroine's eyes).

[2]**मारू** *mārū* [? *maru-*, **māru-*], m. Brbh. Av. **1.** *mus.* a martial *rāg*. **2.** 19c. a kettledrum. — **3.** Brbh. one who lives in a desert region. **4.** m. a type of egg-plant, *Solanum diffusum*. — मारू-बाजा, m. a kettledrum. मारू-बैंगन, m. = ~, 4.

मारूफ़ *mārūf* [A. *ma'rūf*], adj. U. **1.** well-known. **2.** celebrated; notorious.

मारे *māre* [cf. H. *mārnā*], ppn., often inverted. because (of, के); on account (of). — ~ भूख के तड़पता, adj. restless from hunger.

मार्का *mārkā*, m. see [2]मरका.

मार्ग *mārg* [S.], m.**1.** road, way; passage, channel; course, path; trajectory. **2.** way, method; means. **3.** fig. doctrine, belief. पुष्टि-मार्ग, m. path of fostering (the soul, by divine grace: doctrine of the sect of Vallabha). **4.** the lunar month Ag'han. — मार्गगीरी [P. *-gīrī*], f. obs. journeying. मार्गदर्शक, adj. & m. showing the way; pioneering (as a work); a guide. °-दर्शन, m. guiding, guidance. °-दर्शी, adj. & m. id. मार्ग-पाल, m. *Pl.* watch, patrol(man). मार्ग-प्रदर्शक, m. guide; leader. °-प्रदर्शन, m. guiding, guidance, &c. मार्ग-प्रवर्तक, m. one striking out a (new) way, a pioneer. मार्गशीर्ष, m. see s.v.

मार्गण *mārgaṇ* [S.], m. *Pl. HŚS.* **1.** investigation. **2.** request.

मार्गशीर्ष *mārgăśīrṣ* [S.], m. the ninth month of the Hindu lunar year (November-December: = अगहन).

मार्गी *mārgī* [S.], m. **1.** traveller, wayfarer; pilgrim. **2.** esp. -मार्गी. adherent, follower (of a belief).

मार्जन *mārjan* [S.], m. **1.** cleansing, scouring; cleaning. **2.** purification by sprinkling with water (before undertaking a religious ceremony).

मार्जना *mārjanā* [S.], f. **1.** cleansing. **2.** transf. pardon.

मार्जनी *mārjănī* [S.], f. a brush, broom.

मार्जार *mārjār* [S.], m. a cat; wild cat.

मार्जारी *mārjārī* [S.], f. *Pl. HŚS.* = मार्जार.

मार्जित *mārjit* [S.], adj. cleansed.

मार्तंड *mārtaṇḍ* [S.], m. the sun.

[1]**माल** *māl* [A. *māl*], m. **1.** wealth. *__2.__ property, possessions, goods, things; luggage. **3.** merchandise, goods; produce. **4.** material(s) (of or for manufacture). **5.** finance (esp. governmental). **6.** land revenue. **7.** a prize (of money). **8.** *math.* the square of a number. **9.** sthg. fine or splendid. **10.** colloq. an attractive girl. — ~ उड़ाना, to squander wealth, &c.; to feed on delicacies. ~ कटना, property to be cut off, or to be stolen; goods to be sold in large quantities. ~ चीरना, or मारना, to embezzle property. माल-असबाब, m. = ~, 2. माल-ख़ाना, m. treasury; warehouse. माल-गाड़ी, m. goods train; freight wagon. माल-गुज़ार [P. *-guzār*], m. one paying revenue to (or holding land under) government: tenant; landlord. °ई, f. land-revenue; state of a tenant; assessed land. माल-घर, m. warehouse. माल-जहाज़, m. merchant ship. माल-ज़ामिन, m. a person standing surety. माल-टाल, m. = माल-असबाब. मालदार [P. *-dār*], adj. & m. wealthy; a wealthy person. माल-न्यायालय [°*ya*+*ā*°], m. land tribunal. माल-पूआ, m. a kind of fritter containing *ciraumjī* nuts, pistachios, &c. माल-मंत्री, m. finance minister. माल-मसाला, m. materials, raw materials. माल-मस्त, adj. delighting in worldly possessions. °ई, f. माल-महकमा, m. revenue department. माल-मोटर, m. lorry, truck. माल-वाहक, adj. & m. freight-carrying; a freighter. °-वाही, id. – मालामाल, adj. heaped brimful, abundant. मालामाल करना, to fill full; to enrich (with, से).

[2]**माल** *māl* [*mālā-*: ← Drav.], f. **1.** a garland, &c. (= माला). **2.** string (of a spinning-wheel, or of a reel, &c). **3.** line, row. — माल-कँगनी, f. the staff-tree or black-oil plant, *Celastrus paniculata*: source of an oil used medicinally.

[3]**माल** *māl* [*malla-*[1]: ← Drav.], m. Brbh. Av. a wrestler; champion.

मालकोस *mālkos* [ad. *mālakauśa-*], m. *mus.* name of a *rāg*.

मालखम *mālkham*, m. reg. (E.) the upright post in a sugar-mill.

मालती *mālătī* [S.], f. **1.** name of several plants and flowers; jasmine. **2.** bud, blossom. **3.** a young woman. **4.** moonlight; night. — मालती-बसंत, m. = बसंत-मालती.

मालन *mālan*, f. = मालिन.

मालव *mālav* [S.], m. = मालवा.

मालवा *mālvā* [*mālava-*], m. the region of Mālvā.

मालश्री *mālăśrī* [S.], f. *mus.* name of a *rāgiṇī*.

माला *mālā* [S.], f. **1.** garland. **2.** a necklace; string of beads. **3.** a row, line. **4.** esp. -माला. collection (as of books in a series). — वर्ण-माला, f. syllabary, alphabet. — ~ जपना, or फेरना, to tell (one's) beads to perform devotions.

मालामाल *mālāmāl*, adj. see s.v. [1]माल.

मालिक *mālik* [A. *mālik*], m. possessor: **1.** master, owner; lord. **2.** God. **3.** husband. — मालिक-मकान, m. master of a house, householder.

मालिकपन *mālikpan* [cf. H. *mālik*], m. state of owning, ownership.

मालिका *mālikā* [S.], f. garland, &c. (= माला).

मालिकाना *mālikānā* [P. *mālikāna*], adj. & m. **1.** adj. owner's, proprietary. **2.** like an owner. **3.** m. rent or other allowance paid to a zamīndār.

मालिकी *mālikī* [A. *mālik*+P. *-ī*], f. **1.** status of master, &c. **2.** ownership (= मिल्कियत).

मालिकीयत *mālikīyat* [A. *mālikīya*: P. *mālikīyat*], f. = मिल्कियत.

मालिन *mālin* [cf. H. *mālī*], f. **1.** gardener's wife. **2.** woman gardener; flower-seller.

मालिनी *mālinī* [S.], f. *mus.* name of a *rāgiṇī*.

मालिन्य *mālinyă* [S.], m. **1.** foulness, filth. **2.** gloom. **3.** disaffection, dislike.

मालिश *māliś* [P. *māliś*], f. **1.** rubbing (as of oil on the body). **2.** massage.

मालियत *māliyat* [cf. H. [2]*mālī*], f. **1.** cost or charge. **2.** rent, or rate (of assessment).

[1]**माली** *mālī* [*mālin-*], m. a gardener.

[2]**माली** *mālī* [A. *mālī*], adj. **1.** financial; having to do with revenue. **2.** economic. **3.** wealthy.

मालीदा *mālīdā* [P. *mālīda*], adj. & m. U. **1.** adj. rubbed, crushed. **2.** m. a cake of bread, or pounded meal, with butter. **3.** a Kashmir woollen cloth.

मालूम *mālūm* [A. *ma'lūm*], adj. **1.** known. **2.** evident, apparent. — ~ करना, to discover, to ascertain. ~ देना, = next. ~ पड़ना, to seem, to appear. ~ होना (को), to be or to become known (to); to be supposed; to seem. मुझे ~ है, I know. मुझे ~ होता है, it seems to me, it appears.

माल्य *mālyă* [S.], m. 1. = माला, 1. **2.** a flower.

मावठ *māvaṭh* [**māghavṛṣṭi-*], f. winter rain, untimely rain.

मावस *māvas*, f. = अमावस.

मावा *māvā* [conn. H. ²*māyā*], m. f. **1.** substance (of anything). **2.** starch. **3.** yolk. **4.** curd. **5.** milk thickened by boiling. **6.** yeast. **7.** rice-water. **8.** sandal oil.

माश *māś* [P. *māś*], m. a pulse (*mūṁg* or *uṛad*). — ~ मारना, *Pl.* to throw *māś* at: to bind by a spell.

¹**माशा** *māśā* [*māṣaka-*²; P. *māśa*], m. a jeweller's weight (= one twelfth of a *tolā*).

²**माशा** *māśā*, m. *Pl.* a reel; reed (used by weavers to wind their thread on).

माशी *māśī* [cf. H. *māś*], adj. & m. **1.** adj. of the colour of *māś*: dark green. **2.** m. dark green colour.

माशूक़ *māśūq* [A. *ma'śūq*], adj. & m. **1.** adj. beloved. **2.** m. loved person.

माशूक़ा *māśūqā* [A. *ma'sūqa*], f. sweetheart; mistress.

माशूक़ाना *māśūqānā* [P. *ma'śūqāna*], adj. inv. charming. — माशूक़ाना-अंदाज़, adj. id.

माशूक़ियत *māśūqiyat* [A. *ma'śūq*: P. *ma'sūqiyat*], f. U. loveliness, charm.

माशूक़ी *māśūqī*, f. U. = माशूक़ियत.

माष *māṣ* [S.], m. 1. = माश. 2. = ¹माशा.

मास *mās* [S.], m. a month. — मासकालिक, adj. lasting a month; occurring monthly. मासांत [°*sa*+*a*°], m. end of a month. मासोत्सव [°*sa*+*u*°], m. month's celebration; month's campaign (for an official purpose).

मासिक *māsik* [S.], adj. & m. **1.** adj. having to do with a month; monthly; month-long. **2.** m. monthly wages, salary or hire. **3.** a monthly publication. **4.** a monthly event. — ~ धर्म, m. menstruation.

मासी *māsī*, f. = मौसी.

मासूम *māsūm* [A. *ma'ṣūm*], adj. protected: innocent, simple.

मासूमियत *māsūmiyat*, f. = मासूमी.

मासूमी *māsūmī* [A. *ma'ṣūm*+P. *-ī*], f. innocence, &c.

माह *māh* [P. *māh*], m. U. **1.** the moon. **2.** a month. — माहताब [P. *-tāb*], m. (f., *Pl.*) moonlight; the moon. °ई, f. a kind of firework; moonlit place (in a courtyard). माहवार [P. *-vār*], adj. & m. monthly; monthly wage; the revenue collected in a month. °आ, adj. & m. id., 1., 2. °ई, adj. & f. id.; menstruation.

माहात्मिक *māhātmik* [S.], adj. **1.** magnanimous, noble. **2.** glorious. **3.** sacred.

माहात्म्य *māhātmyă* [S.], m. **1.** greatness, majesty. **2.** the partic. virtue of any deity or shrine. **3.** a work celebrating any sacred place or object.

माहियाना *māhiyānā* [P. *māhiyāna-*], adj. & m. *Pl. HŚS.* **1.** adj. monthly. **2.** m. monthly wage.

माहिर *māhir* [A. *māhir*], adj. & m. **1.** adj. skilful, expert. **2.** m. an expert (in, से).

माहिरी *māhirī* [cf. H. *māhir*], f. expertness.

माहीं *māhīṁ* [*madhya-*], ppn. Av. = में.

माही *māhī* [P. *māhī*], f. a fish. — माहीगीरी [P. *-gīrī*], f. fishing.

माहुर *māhur* [*mādhurī-*], m. ? f. Av. poison.

माहौल *māhaul* [(A.) *mā ḥaul*], m. what changes: mood, atmosphere; environment (of one's upbringing).

मिंती *mintī*, f. pronun. var. = बिनती.

मिक़दार *miqdār* [A.], m. U. **1.** measure; amount, quantity. **2.** bulk, size. — ज़्यादा ~ में, adv. in large amounts, &c.

मिक़नातीस *miqnātīs* [A. *miqnāṭīs*: ← Gk.], m. *Pl. HŚS.* a magnet.

मिचकाना *mickānā* [cf. **micc-*: Pk. *miṁcana-*], v.t. to wink, to blink (= मीचना).

मिचकारना *mickārnā*, v.t. reg. to rinse.

मिचकी *mickī* [cf. H. *mickānā*], f. a wink, blink.

मिचना *micnā* [cf. H. *mīcnā*], v.i. **1.** to be closed (esp. the eyes). **2.** to blink.

¹**मिचराना** *micrānā* [? = H. ²*micrānā*], v.t. reg. to pick at (food) without appetite.

²**मिचराना** *micrānā*, v.i. reg. = ²मचलाना, and मतलाना.

मिचलाना *miclānā*, v.i. to feel nausea (= ²मचलाना).

मिचली *miclī*, f. nausea (= मतली).

मिचौनी *micaunī* [cf. H. *mīcnā*], f. **1.** closing, or covering the eyes; blindfolding. **2.** blind-man's buff. — आँख-मिचौनी, f. = ~, 2.

मिचौली *micaulī*, f. = मिचौनी.

मिचौह- *micauh-* [cf. H. *mīcnā*], adj. Brbh. half-closed (the eyes).

मिज़राब *mizrāb* [A. *mizrāb*], m. a plectrum.

मिज़ाज *mizāj* [A. *mizāj*], m. mixture: **1.** nature, temperament. **2.** mood, humour, temper. **3.** fastidiousness. **4.** haughtiness. **5.** esp. U. health. — ~ ख़राब होना, = ~ बिगड़ना. ~ पाना (का), to understand (a person's) nature, temperament. ~ पूछना, to ask for the health (of). ~ में आना, to appeal (to one, के), to be congenial; to stand on (one's) dignity. ~ बिगड़ना, to grow irritated, or angry. ~ मिलना, (one's) nature or temperament to be fathomed (by, को). ~ शरीफ़? U. how is your good health: how are you? मिज़ाजदार [P. *-dār*], adj. haughty; conceited. °ई, f.

मिज़ाजी *mizājī* [cf. A. *mizāj*], adj. **1.** haughty; conceited. **2.** fastidious.

मिटना *miṭnā* [conn. cf. *mr̥ṣṭa-*¹], v.i. **1.** to be erased, or obliterated; to be cancelled, abolished. **2.** to be destroyed, or ruined. **3.** to be reduced or eliminated (as an abuse). **4.** to be allayed (as pangs of hunger, or of distress). **5.** fig. to be infatuated (with, पर). **5.** to expire; to be reduced to extinction (a species).

मिटाना *miṭānā* [cf. H. *miṭnā*], v.t. **1.** erase; to obliterate; to cancel (as a decree). **2.** to destroy. **3.** to eliminate (as an abuse); to mitigate. **4.** to allay (as pangs of hunger, or of distress).

मिटारना *miṭārnā*, v.t. = मिटाना.

मिटिया *miṭiyā* [cf. H. *miṭṭī*], adj. inv. & f. **1.** adj. = मटिया. **2.** f. reg. a small earthen pot.

मिट्टी *miṭṭī* [*mr̥ttikā-*], f. **1.** earth, soil; clay. **2.** dust. **3.** fig. the body. **4.** a dead body. **5.** dirt, filth. — ~ उठना, a dead body to be disposed of. ~ करना, to destroy (one, की). ~ का तेल, m. kerosene. ~ का माधव, m. pej. an utter idiot. ~ की मूरत, f. a clay statue; the perishable body. ~ के मोल, adv. dirt cheap. ~ ख़राब करना, to ruin, to destroy; to corrupt (as a former custom); to beat severely. ~ ख़राब होना, (a person's) honour to be defiled; to live wretchedly; funeral rites to be marred. ~ ठिकाने लगना, a corpse to be carried to the place of cremation or burial; last rites to be performed. ~ डालना, to throw earth (on, पर); to conceal (a crime, or a fault). ~ देना (को), to throw a handful of earth (on a corpse at burial), to consign to the ground. ~ पलीद करना (की), to dishonour. ~ में, or से, ~ मिलना, to be laid in the grave. ~ में मिलना, to be razed; to be destroyed; to be ruined or disgraced. ~ में मिलाना, to raze; to destroy. ~ होना, to turn to clay or to dust, &c.; to die; to grow cold or insipid (food); to be spoiled, ruined. चीनी ~, f. porcelain. पांडु ~, f. a light red soil. पीली ~, f. a yellow earth. — मिट्टी-ख़राबी, total destruction; wretched state.

मिट्ठा *miṭṭhā* [*mr̥ṣṭa-*¹], m. a kiss.

मिट्ठी *miṭṭhī* [*mr̥ṣṭa-*¹], f. a kiss (esp. from a child). — ~ लेना, to take a kiss (from, की), to kiss.

मिट्ठू *miṭṭhū* [cf. *mr̥ṣṭa-*¹], m. sweet-voiced one: **1.** a child (term of endearment). **2.** a parrot. — मियाँ ~ बनना, to parrot sweet phrases: to speak flatteringly or unctuously (to another person). अपने मुँह मियाँ ~ बनना, to indulge in self-praise.

मिठ- *miṭh-*. sweet (= मीठा): — मिठबोला, adj. & m. of pleasant voice; smooth-tongued, hypocritical; a flatterer, hypocrite. मिठलोना sweet and salty: undersalted.

मिठाई *miṭhāī* [cf. H. *mīṭhā*], f. **1.** a sweet, sweet food or dish. **2.** sweetness. — मिठाईवाला, m. maker or seller of sweets.

मिठास *miṭhās* [cf. *mr̥ṣṭa-*¹], f. **1.** sweetness. **2.** pleasantness.

मित- *mit-* [S.], adj. measured out; limited; restricted: — मितव्यय, adj. & m. = °-व्ययी, °-व्ययिता. °-व्ययिता, f. economy, frugality. °-व्ययी, adj. economical, frugal. मिताशन [°*ta*+*a*°], m. = next. मिताहार, adj. & m. moderate in diet; moderation in diet.

मितली *mitlī*, f. = मतली.

मिताई *mitāī* [cf. H. *mīt*], f. Brbh. friendship.

मिति *miti* [S.], f. **1.** measuring. **2.** measurement, measure. **3.** Av. limit, end.

मिती *mitī* [? ad. *miti-*], f. **1.** a particular day of a lunar month, a date; date for payment (of a sum). **2.** a day (as reckoned in assessing interest or other charge). **3.** interest (on money). — ~ काटना, to deduct interest, to discount. ~ चढ़ाना (में), to date (a letter); to finish (a letter). ~ डालना, or रखना, id. – मिती-काटा, m. deduction made on early completion of a payment.

मित्र *mitr* [S.], m., f. **1.** a friend. **2.** an ally. **3.** मित्र-. friendly, allied (as states). — मित्रद्रोही, adj. treacherous or hurtful to a friend, false (a friend). मित्रवत्, adv. in a friendly manner.

मित्रता *mitrătā* [S.], f. **1.** friendship. **2.** friendliness. **3.** alliance. — **मित्रतापूर्ण**, adj. friendly (a relationship).

मिथक *mithak* [Engl. *myth*], m. a myth.

मिथिला *mithilā* [S.], f. **1.** the region of Mithilā, north Bihar. **2.** *hist.* the city of Tirhut. — **मिथिलेश** [°*lā*+*ī*°], m. lord of Mithilā: a title of king Janak.

मिथुन *mithun* [S.], m. **1.** a couple, pair; male and female. **2.** sexual intercourse. **3.** the sign Gemini (of the zodiac).

मिथ्यता *mithyătā* [S.], f. falsehood.

मिथ्या *mithyā* [S.], adj. inv. & f. **1.** adj. false, incorrect; untrue. **2.** vain, useless; deceptive (as hope, pride). **3.** feigned, sham, spurious. **4.** reg. f. (m., *Pl.*) falsehood, lie. — **मिथ्याचार** [°*yā*+*ā*°], m. deceitful behaviour. **मिथ्यापर**, adj. inclined to falsehood, or deceit. **मिथ्यावादी**, adj. & m. lying; a liar. **मिथ्याव्यय**, m. expense to no purpose, for show.

मिथ्यात *mithyat* [? ad. *mithyatva-*], m. E.H. falsehood.

मिथ्याती *mithyātī* [cf. H. *mithyāt*], m. reg. a believer in what is false.

मिथ्यात्व *mithyātvă* [S.], m. falsehood.

मिथ्यापन *mithyāpan* [cf. H. *mithyā*], m. falsehood.

मिनकना *minaknā*, v.i. to speak very softly; to murmur. — **मिनका तक नहीं**, (he) took no notice (did not react).

मिनमिन *minmin*, adv. indistinctly (of speaking); nasally; low, murmuring.

मिनमिना *minminā*, adj. speaking indistinctly, &c. (see **मिनमिन**).

मिन्नत *minnat* [A. *minna*: P. *minnat*], f. **1.** kindness, favour. ***2.** entreaty, supplication. — ~ **करना** (**से**), to beseech. – **मिन्नतगुज़ार** [P. -*guzār*], adj. grateful. **मिन्नत-समाजत**, f. entreaty and exhortation.

मिन्नू *minnū*, m. reg. a cat.

मिमियाना *mimiyānā* [cf. H. *memnā*], v.i. to bleat.

मियाँ *miyāṁ* [P. *miyān*], m. term of respectful, or affectionate reference or address: **1.** master; gentleman (esp. used of a Muslim). **2.** *musl.* husband. **3.** (esp. ~ **जी**). schoolmaster. **4.** joc. young master (used of a child). — **मियाँ-मिट्ठू**, adj. & m. sweet-speaking, unctuous; a parrot; one who parrots (information, &c). **मियाँ-मिट्ठू बनाना**, to flatter; to set (students) to rote-learning. **अपने मुँह मियाँ-मिट्ठू बनना**, to speak of or to regard oneself complacently.

मियाद *miyād* [A.*mī'ād*], f. m. **1.** fixed term, period. **2.** term of imprisonment. — ~ **काटना**, to pass the term (of); to remain in prison for the full term. ~ **पूरी होना**, a term to be complete, or to expire. ~ **बढ़ाना**, to extend a term.

मियादी *miyādī* [A. *mī'ād*+P. -*ī*], adj. **1.** lasting (or falling at) a fixed term. **2.** periodical. **3.** having served a term of imprisonment. — ~ **बुख़ार**, m. intermittent fever. ~ **हुंडी**, f. a bill after date.

मियान *miyān* [P. *miyān*], m. = **म्यान**.

मियाना *miyānā* [P. *miyāna*], adj. inv. & m. **1.** adj. medium, moderate. **2.** reg. (W.) the intermediate belt of fields surrounding a village.

मियानी *miyānī*, f. = **म्यानी**.

मिरग- *mirg-* Av. = **मृग**: — **मिरग-आरन**, m. wild region with animals.

मिरगिया *mirgiyā* [cf. H. *mirgī*], adj. & m., f. **1.** adj. epileptic. **2.** m., f. an epileptic.

मिरगिहा *mirgihā*, m. f. reg. = **मिरगिया**.

मिरगी *mirgī* [conn. *mr̥gī-*], f. epilepsy. — ~ **आना** (**को**), to be epileptic.

मिरचा *mircā*, m. = **मिर्च**.

मिरचाई *mircāī*, f. reg. = **मिर्च**.

मिरचानी *mircānī*, f. reg. = **मिर्च**.

मिरजई *mirjaī* [P. *mirzā'ī*], f. a short jacket of wool, cotton or muslin, usu. without sleeves.

मिरज़ा *mirzā* [P. *mirzā* (for *mīr-*)], m. a Persian and Mughal title: **1.** (following a name) prince. **2.** (esp. preceding a name) a gentleman, Mr.

मिरजाई *mirjāī*, f. = **मिरजई**.

मिरोना *mironā*, v.i. reg. to stroll, to wander.

मिर्च *mirc* [**maricca-*: ← Austro-as.], f. pepper, chilli. — **मिरचें(-सी) लगना**, to sting, to burn; to tingle; to cut (words); to be taken amiss. – **काली** ~, f. black pepper. **दक्खिनी** ~, f. white pepper. **लाल** ~, f. red pepper. **हरी** ~, f. green pepper.

मिर्ची *mircī*, f. = **मिर्च**.

मिर्ज़ा *mirzā*, m. see **मिरज़ा**.

मिलक *milak*, f. Brbh. see **मिल्क**.

मिलन *milan* [cf. H. *milnā*; and S.], m. **1.** meeting, joining (with, **से**); contact; union. **2.** mixing. **3.** agreement, harmony. — **मिलनसार**, adj. sociable; friendly; affable. °**पन**, m. id. °**ई**, f.

मिलना *milnā* [*milati*], v.i. **1.** to be mixed or mingled; to mix, &c. **2.** to be joined or united (persons, or things); to join, to adjoin; to meet (as roads, boundaries). **3.** to be or to become connected (with, से); to be adjacent. **4.** to be found; to be obtained, available (as an object or a commodity ; or as time, or an opportunity; or as any quality, e.g. strength, or rest, or peace: by, को). **5.** to be received; to accrue (to, को). आपका पत्र मिला, (I) received your letter. **6.** to be found (as an object or goal after search or striving). **7.** to be given (as a prize, a punishment). **8.** to meet (with a person, से: where intent is implied); to visit. मैं आपसे कल मिल लूँगा, I shall come to see you tomorrow. **9.** to be encountered (by, को); to meet, to encounter (by chance). वह मुझे कल मिला, I happened to meet him yesterday. **10.** to associate (with, से). मिल रहना, to live in harmony (with). **11.** to assemble. **12.** to be similar (to, से); to coincide; to correspond; to resemble (in respect of, से). दोनों भाई चेहरे से मिलते-जुलते हैं, the two brothers look very much alike. **13.** to be in harmony (as views, moods); to be in tune (musical instruments). **14.** to be reconciled. — मिलना-जुलना, = ~, 1.; to meet freely; to keep on good terms (with, से); to agree; to be similar. – मिलकर, adv. together, as a group; unitedly; on good terms (with).

मिलनी *milnī* [cf. H. *milnā*], f. **1.** a meeting. **2.** ceremonial meeting and embracing of the bride's relatives and the groom's on the occasion of a betrothal; a gift made by the bride's relatives on that occasion. **3.** a present made to a bride by her relatives. **4.** a present made by a visitor.

मिलवाई *milvāī* [cf. H. *milnā*], f. **1.** causing a meeting to take place; introducing, introduction (to, से). **2.** fee or money paid for an introduction.

मिलवाना *milvānā* [cf. H. *milnā*], v.t. to cause to be mixed, joined, &c. (by, से).

मिलाई *milāī* [cf. H. *milānā*], f. **1.** joining, uniting, &c. **2.** introducing. **3.** reuniting (an outcaste to his caste). 4. = मिलनी, 2.

मिलान *milān* [cf. H. *milnā*], m. **1.** bringing together; joining; mixing. **2.** comparing, comparison (of); check, verification (as of figures). **3.** adjustment (as of differences); reconciliation). **4.** [cf. **mell-*] Brbh. settlement or camp (for the night). — ~ मिलाना (का), to adjust accounts (as of land under cultivation).

मिलाना *milānā* [cf. H. *milnā*], v.t. **1.** to bring together, to join (to, से); to mix (with); to connect, to attach; to unite (with, से). **2.** to add (as material, or an ingredient; or a new factor in a situation: to, में). **3.** *math.* to add. **4.** to incorporate, to assimilate (in, में); to include (within a group). **5.** to cause to meet; to introduce (to, से). **6.** to adjust, to harmonise (differences, &c). **7.** to tune (musical instruments); to set (a watch). **8.** to bring together, to reconcile (opponents or factions: with each other, आपस में, or से); to win over (to one's side, अपनी तरफ़). **9.** to compare. — क़दम ~, to keep step. फ़ोन ~, to call (one, by phone: को). हाथ मिलाकर, adv. lending a hand, sharing in an effort or endeavour.

मिलानी *milānī* [cf. H. *milānā*], f. reg. mixing, mingling, &c.

मिलाप *milāp* [S.], m. **1.** meeting (with, से). **2.** mixing, mingling; junction. **3.** union, harmony (as of ideas). **4.** reconciliation. — ~ करना (से), to harmonise; to make friends (with), to make peace (with).

मिलापी *milāpī* [cf. H. *milāp*], adj. sociable, affable; convivial.

मिलाव *milāv* [cf. H. *milānā*], m. state of being mixed, joined, &c. (see मिलावट).

मिलावट *milāvaṭ* [cf. H. *milānā*], f. **1.** a mixture; sthg. mixed in, an admixture. **2.** act of mixing; adulteration. **3.** an alloy. **4.** state of concord, harmony. **5.** assimilation (in or to, में); annexation. **6.** adjustment, arbitration. **7.** reconciliation. **8.** comparison.

मिलावटी *milāvāṭī* [cf. H. *milāvaṭ*], adj. mixed, diluted, adulterated.

मिलिंद *milind* [S.], m. poet. a bee.

मिलित *milit* [S.], adj. **1.** united, connected. **2.** mixed, combined.

मिलीभगत *milībhagat* [? H. *milnā* + *bhagat* ad. *bhakti-*[1]], f. collusion.

मिलौनी *milaunī* [cf. H. *milānā*], f. reg. **1.** a liquid added (as water to milk, in adulterating it). **2.** a mixture.

मिल्क *milk* [A. *milk*], f. possession: **1.** landed property. **2.** reg. (W.) a kind of rent-free tenure.

मिल्कियत *milkiyat* [P. *milkiyat*], f. **1.** property, possessions (esp. real estate). **2.** possession, ownership.

[1]**मिल्लत** *millat* [conn. H. *milnā*], f. sociability, friendliness.

[2]**मिल्लत** *millat* [A. *milla*: P. *millat*], f. U. a religious community; a nation, a people.

मिश्र *miśră* [S.], adj. **1.** mixed. **2.** compound (as a ratio, or a sentence; or as a process); composite. **3.** name of a community of brāhmaṇs. — मिश्र-जाति, adj. of mixed kind, caste or parentage; hybrid. मिश्र-धातु, f. an alloy.

मिश्रण *miśraṇ* [S.], m. **1.** mixing. **2.** a mixture. **3.** *chem.* a compound. **4.** an alloy.

मिश्राइन *miśrāin* [cf. H. *miśra*], f. a woman of the Miśra community.

मिश्राणी *miśrāṇī*[S.], f. = मिश्राइन.

मिश्रित *miśrit* [S.], adj. **1.** mixed. **2.** joint, common (as funds). **3.** composite; based on a coalition (a government).

मिष *miṣ* [S.], m. **1.** deception; trickery. **2.** pretext; excuse; guise. **3.** envy.

मिष्ट *miṣṭ* [S.], adj. & m. **1.** adj. sweet; tasty. **2.** pleasant, agreeable (as words, behaviour). **3.** m. a sweet, sweet dish or food. — मिष्टान्न [°*ṭa*+*a*°], m. = ~, 3.

मिष्ठान्न *miṣṭhānn*, m. corr. = मिष्टान्न.

मिस *mis* [*mṛṣā*], m. **1.** pretext; excuse. **2.** sham; false appearance, disguised form. **3.** stratagem. **4.** ppn., usu. w. के. under the pretext of; in the guise of; as, as to.

मिसक़ाल *misqāl* [A. *miṡqāl*], m. a weight of one and three-sevenths drachmas.

मिसक़ाली *misqālī* [cf. A. *miṡqāl*], adj. weighing a *misqāl.*

मिसकीन *miskīn*, adj. see मिस्कीन.

मिसकीनता *miskīnătā* [cf. H. *miskīn*], f. Brbh. lowliness, &c.

मिसन *misan* [*miśraṇa-*], m. reg. (W). a loamy, manured soil.

मिसना *misnā* [cf. H. *mīsnā*, v.t.], v.i. reg. **1.** to be ground, crushed. **2.** to be rumpled, or crumpled.

मिसमार *mismār* [A. *mismār*], adj. U. razed, demolished.

मिसर *misr* [A. *miṣr*], m. Egypt.

मिसरा *misrā* [A. *miṣrā*ʻ], m. inv. U. a single line (of a poem), hemistich.

मिसरानी *misrānī* [ad. *miśrāṇī-*], f. a woman of the Miśra (brāhmaṇ) community; a cook.

मिसरी *misrī* [A. *miṣrī*], adj. & m. f. **1.** adj. Egyptian. **2.** m. an Egyptian. **3.** f. sugar candy. — ~ का कूज़ा, m. a cup-shaped lump of candy. ~ की डली, f. sugar-basket: sthg. very sweet. ~ खिलाना, to give (one, को) sugar candy (specif. in formalising an engagement).

मिसल *misl* [A. *miṡl*], adj. & f. U. **1.** adj. like, resembling. **2.** alike. **3.** f. likeness. **4.** the papers on a partic. case; a file. — ~ बैठाना (की), to sort out (an involved matter). – मिसले-लोथ, adj. like a corpse, inert.

मिसाल *misāl* [A. *miṡāl*], f. **1.** likeness. **2.** comparison; simile. ***3.** example, precedent. **4.** a saying, proverb. — ~ के लिए, or के तौर पर, adv. for example. ~ देना, to give an example; to compare (sthg., की; with, से).

मिसाली *misālī* [A. *miṡālī*], adj. U. like, resembling.

मिस्कीन *miskīn* [A. *miskīn*], adj. **1.** lowly, humble. **2.** meek. **3.** poor, needy; wretched.

मिस्कीनी *miskīnī* [A. *miskīn*+P. *-ī*], f. reg. **1.** lowliness. **2.** poverty.

मिस्तरी *mistrī* [Pt. *mestre*], m. a skilled tradesman; mechanic. — मिस्तरी-ख़ाना, m. workshop.

मिस्त्री *misrī*, adj. & m. f. = मिसरी.

मिस्सा *missā* [*miśra(ka)-*], adj. & m. **1.** adj. mixed. **2.** coarse, poor (as grain, food). **3.** m. coarse flour of mixed grain. — ~ आटा, m. = ~, 3. मिस्सी रोटी, f. bread-cake(s) made of *missā.*

मिस्सी *missī* [*miśrita* ; ? or *maṣi*], f. a powder (containing yellow myrobalan, gall-nut, iron filings, copper sulphate, &c.) used cosmetically to stain the teeth or lips black. — ~ लगाना, or मलना, to apply *missī* (to, में). – मिस्सी-काजल, m. *missī* and lampblack. मिस्सी-काजल करना, to make up one's face (a woman). मिस्सीदान [P. *-dān*], m. *missī*-box. °ई, f. id.

मिहाना *mihānā* [**mehayati*, or *meghāyate*], v.i. reg. to become damp.

मिहिर *mihir* [S.], m. the sun.

मींगी *mīṁgī*, f. **1.** marrow (of a bone). **2.** kernel. **3.** pith.

मींचना *mīṁcnā*, v.t. = मीचना.

मींजना *mīñjnā* [**mr̥ñjati*: Pa. *sammiñjati*], v.t. **1.** to rub with the hands. **2.** to crush; to knead. **3.** to scrub, to scour.

मींड़ *mīṁṛ* [cf. H. *mīṁṛ-*], f. *mus.* a grace note obtained by deflection (of a string).

मींड़- *mīṁṛ-* [**mr̥ndati*], v.t. Brbh. = मींजना.

मीआद *mīād*, f. m. = मियाद.

मीच *mīc* [*mr̥tyu-*], f. Brbh. Av. death.

मीचना *mīcnā* [**micc-*: cf. Pk. *miṁcaṇa-*], v.t. to shut (the eyes). — आँख, or आँखें, ~, to wink.

मीज़ान *mīzān* [A. *mīzān*], f. a balance, scales: total, sum. — ~ करना, देना, or लगाना, to add up, to total. ~ मिलना, a total to be obtained: amounts to add up correctly.

मीटरी *mīṭrī* [cf. H. *mīṭar*], adj. metric.

मीठा *mīṭhā* [*mr̥sta-*¹], adj. & m. **1.** adj. sweet. **2.** agreeable (to the taste); mild (as tobacco);

good, fresh, sweet (as water); soft (water). **3.** pleasant, agreeable (as speech, thoughts, manner); mild. **4.** gentle, soft (as breeze, rain). **5.** low, slight, slow (as pain, a complaint; or as a fire).**6.** tender, affectionate; not intended to wound (as a rebuke). **7.** iron. outwardly agreeable, but in fact hostile or harmful. **8.** m. sweet things generally (as sugar, molasses). **9.** the sweet lime (*santarā nībū*). — **~ ज़हर**, m. a small, black, poisonous root, *Aconitum chasmanthum*. **~ तेल**, m. sesame oil, or rape-seed oil. **~ तेलिया**, m. = ~ **ज़हर**. **~ मुँह कराना**, to make (one, **का**) a present, esp. of sweets. **मीठी चुटकी**, f. colloq. a joke, dig (at another's expense). **मीठी छुरी**, f. cold steel; a treacherous friend. **मीठी छुरी चलाना**, v.t. to strike a concealed blow (at, **में**); to damn with faint praise. **मीठी नींद**, f. untroubled sleep. **मीठी मार**, f. a blow, or wound, which shows no trace; a joking or sarcastic remark at someone's expense; slow torture.

मीत *mīt* [*mitra-*], m. Brbh. Av. **1.** friend. **2.** lover.

मीतन *mītan* [cf. H. [1]*mītā*], f. reg. **1.** friend, sweetheart. **2.** a female namesake.

[1]**मीता** *mītā* [*mitra-*], m. **1.** friend. **2.** lover.

[2]**मीता** *mītā* [conn. *mr̥tti-*], m. reg. **1.** an earthen pitcher. **2.** an earthen cup (cf. **मेटा**).

मीन *mīn* [S.], m. f. **1.** a fish. **2.** the sign Pisces (of the zodiac). **3.** the first or fish avatār of Viṣṇu. — **मीन-केतन**, m. fish-bannered: a title of Kāmdev. **मीन-मेख**, m. Brbh. Av. unwarranted hesitation. **मीन-मेख निकालना**, to make an (unwarranted) distinction between the last of Pisces and the first of Aries: to be hypercritical, or unsparing in criticism.

[1]**मीना** *mīnā* [P. *mīnā*], m. **1.** a stone resembling lapis lazuli (used to tinge silver). ***2.** enamel (esp. as applied to precious metals). **3.** transf. a goblet, glass. — **मीनाकार**, m. an enameller; °**ई**, f. enamelling. **मीना-बाज़ार**, m. a bazaar where enamelled ware, trinkets, &c. are sold. **मीनासाज़** [P. *-sāz*], m. = **मीनाकार**.

[2]**मीना** *mīnā*, m. *Pl. HŚS.* name of a martial community of Rajasthan.

मीनाई *mīnāī* [cf. H. *mīnā*], adj. & f. reg. **1.** adj. enamelled. **2.** f. enamel.

मीनार *mīnār* [A. *manār*: P. *mīnār*], f. m. minaret; tall tower.

मीमांसक *mīmāṃsak* [S.], m. **1.** investigator. **2.** *philos.* adherent of the *mīmāṃsā* system.

मीमांसा *mīmāṃsā* [S.], f. **1.** investigation, consideration. **2.** name of one, or of two of the Hindu philosophical systems.

मीमांसित *mīmāṃsit* [S.], adj. investigated, considered.

मीमांस्य *mīmāṃsyă* [S.], adj. *HŚS.* deserving investigation or consideration.

मीर *mīr* [P. *mīr*], m. **1.** leader, chief, head. **2.** *musl.* title of the Saiyyids (descendants of the family of Muḥammad). **3.** (in cards) the king. — **मीर-फ़र्श**, m. a stone or weight holding down the edge of a carpet, &c. **मीर-बख़्शी**, m. *hist.* paymaster-general. **मीर-मंज़िल** m. *hist.* quartermaster-general. **मीर-मजलिस**, m. U. master of ceremonies; president, chairman. **मीर-मुंशी**, m. chief clerk. **मीर-सामान**, m. *hist.* head steward.

मीरज़ा *mīrzā*, m. U. = **मिरज़ा**.

मीरास *mīrās* [A. *mīrāṡ*], m. U. **1.** inheritance. **2.** bequest.

मीरासी *mīrāsī* [A. *mīrāṡ*+P. *-ī*], m. a member of a Muslim community of professional folk-singers and dancers.

मील *mīl* [Engl. *mile*], m. a mile.

मीसना *mīsnā* [cf. **mr̥ṣyate*, v.i.], v.t. **1.** to grind. **2.** to rumple, to crumple.

मुँगौची *muṁgaucī* [? cf. **mudgapathya-*], f. Av. a dish made with *mūṁg* flour.

मुँगौरा *muṁgaurā*, f. Av. = **मुँगौरी**.

मुँगौरी *muṁgaurī* [**mudgavaṭikā-*], f. reg. a lump of pulse fried in *ghī*.

मुंज *muñj* [S.], m. a rush or grass, from which a type of cord is made (= **मूँज**).

मुंजा *muñjā*, m. *Pl.* eye-worm (of horses).

मुंजल *muñjal*, m. reg. the inner part of the nut of the Palmyra palm (*tāṛ*).

मुंड *muṇḍ* [S.], adj. & m. **1.** adj. having the head shaven. **2.** without top-leaves or branches (a tree). **3.** m. a shaven head; a bald head. **4.** head, poll; skull. **5.** a pollarded tree. — **मुंड-कर**, m. poll-tax. **मुंडकरी**, f. a curled-up posture of sitting or lying, with the knees drawn up to the head. **मुंड-चीरा**, m. a fakīr who extorts alms by threatening to wound himself; an extortionist; a brawler, trouble-maker. **मुंड-माल**, f. = next. °-**माला**, f. a necklace of heads, or skulls.

मुंडन *muṇḍan* [S.], m. **1.** shaving the head. **2.** the first, ceremonial, shaving of a child's head.

मुंड़ना *muṁṛnā* [cf. H. *mumṛna*], v.i. **1.** to be shaved. **2.** to be fleeced, swindled.

मुँड़वाना *muṁṛvānā* [cf. H. *mūṁṛnā*], v.t. to cause to be shaved (by, **से**).

[1]**मुंडा** *muṇḍā* [*muṇḍa-*[1]: ? ← Drav.], adj. & m. **1.** adj. having the head shaven. **2.** bald. **3.** without top-leaves or branches (a tree). **4.** without a pinnacle (as a mosque); open at the toe (a shoe). **5.** m. a man or boy having a shaved head. **6.** a disciple, attendant; boy, lad. **7.** colloq. the Kaithī script (a simplification of the Devanāgarī, written without headstrokes). **8.** reg. a hornless ox, ram, &c.

[2]**मुंडा** *muṇḍā*, m. inv. name of a tribe living in east central India.

मुँड़ाई *mum̐ṛāī* [cf. H. *mum̐ṛānā*], f. **1.** shaving. **2.** payment or charge for shaving.

मुँड़ाना *mum̐ṛānā* [cf. H. *mum̐ṛnā*], v.t. to shave.

मुँड़ासा *mum̐ṛāsā*, m. a kind of small, loose turban. **मुँड़ासे-पीटा**, m. pej. a wretched person, wretch.

मुंडित *muṇḍit* [S.], adj. **1.** shaven (the head). **2.** bald. **3.** lopped, pollarded.

मुँड़िया *mum̐ṛiyā* [cf. H. *mum̐ṛnā*], m. shaven: a disciple, an ascetic.

मुँडेर *mum̐ḍer* [? **mūrḍhatara-*], f. **1.** parapet, coping, (as of a wall). **2.** ridge (of a roof). **3.** *arch.* capital.

मुँडेरा *mum̐ḍerā*, m. = मुँडेर.

मुंडो *muṇḍo* [cf. H. *mūm̐ṛnā*], f. **1.** a woman with a shaved head. **2.** pej. a promiscuous woman.

मुंतज़िम *muntazim* [A. *muntaẓim*], adj. & m. U. **1.** adj. ordered, arranged. **2.** m. superintendent, administrator.

मुंतज़िर *muntazir* [A. *muntaẓir*], adj. expecting, awaiting. — ~ रखना, to keep (one) waiting. ~ रहना, or होना (का), to watch (for), to expect; to await.

मुंतही *muntahī* [A. *muntahin*: P. *muntahī*], adj. U. **1.** terminated, concluded (as studies). **2.** learned, proficient.

मुँदना *mum̐dnā* [cf. H. *mūm̐dnā*], v.i. **1.** to be closed (esp. the eyes). **2.** to end (day). **3.** to be filled (as a hole).

मुँदरा *mum̐drā* [cf. *mudrā-*: ? ← Ir.], m. **1.** an ear-ring (esp. as worn by yogīs). **2.** a ring.

मुँदरी *mum̐drī* [cf. *mudrā-*: ? ← Ir.], f. a ring; signet-ring.

मुंशियाना *muṃśiyānā* [P. *munśiyāna*], adj. inv. pertaining to, or characterising, a *munśī*; clerk-like.

मुंशी *muṃśī* [A. *munśī'*], m. **1.** a writer, clerk. **2.** a teacher, tutor (esp. of Urdu and Persian). **3.** title of respect to an educated man. — मुंशीगिरी [P. *-garī*], f. *munśī's* work; clerkship; tutorship.

मुंसरिम *muṃsarim* [A. *munṣarim*], m. **1.** manager, administrator. ***2.** head clerk (as of a court).

मुंसिफ़ *muṃsif* [A. *munṣif*], adj. & m. causing to be fairly adjusted: **1.** adj. U. just, fair. ***2.** m. a subordinate judge. **3.** an arbitrator.

मुंसिफ़ाना *muṃsifānā* [P. *munsifāna*], adj. inv. just, fair.

मुंसिफ़ी *muṃsifī* [A. *munṣif*+P. *-ī*], f. **1.** office or duty of a *munsif*. **2.** a *munsif's* court. — ~ करना, to follow the profession of a *munsif*; to preside over a court of justice.

मुँह *mum̐h* [*mukha-*], m. **1.** mouth; muzzle; beak. **2.** face. **3.** mouth, opening. **4.** fig. regard, consideration. **5.** standing, prestige; pretension. **6.** capacity. 7. boldness, face. — ~ अँधेरे, adv. before daybreak; at dawn. ~ आना, the mouth to become ulcerated; to utter taunts; to incur the censure (of, के). ~ उजला होना, not to be disgraced; to succeed with credit, or with flying colours. ~ उजाले, adv. = ~ अँधेरे. ~ उठाकर, or उठाए, adv. with the face upwards; without looking ahead, blindly; headlong, impetuously. ~ उठे, adv. on waking. ~ उतरना, the face to become drawn, or thin. ~ करना, to turn the face (towards, की ओर, की तरफ़); to confront; to direct the steps (towards). ~ काला करना (अपना, or का), to blacken (one's own or another's) face: to incur disgrace; to disgrace; to punish; to break off connection (with), to be finished with. ~ काला हो जाना, to incur disgrace. ~ की खाना, to suffer a severe reverse (as a rebuke, or a disgrace, or a blow, or an unexpected turn of events); to eat one's words; to be convicted out of one's own mouth. ~ की बात छीनना, = ~ से बात लेना. ~ कीलना (के), to gag; to silence; to tie the tongue (of: by enchantment); to exorcise. ~ के कौवे उड़ जाना, fig. the face to blanch. ~ के बल गिरना, to fall on the face, face downwards. ~ को लहू लगना, to get a taste for blood; vice to grow (on one, के). ~ खुलना, the mouth to open; to become abusive; to dare to speak. ~ खुलवाना, to make or to provoke to speak. ~ खुले का खुला रह जाना, to remain with mouth agape. ~ खोलना, to open the mouth; to speak; to be abusive; to uncover the face; to reveal. ~ चढ़ना, to become familiar or intimate (with, के); to attach oneself (to); to confront (with hostile intention). उसका ~ चढ़ गया, he was visibly offended. ~ चढ़ाना, to offend, to displease; to spoil (a child). ~ चलना, the mouth to move or to work; to babble pointlessly; to be foul-mouthed; to chew the cud. ~ चलाना, to bite, to snap (as a horse); to move or to work the mouth or jaws. ~ चाटना

(का), to curry favour (with); to caress. ~ चिढ़ाना (का), to make faces (at); to mock; to caricature. ~ चुराना, to hide the face (from, से); to be bashful; to skulk; to avoid, to shun. ~ छिपाना, = ~ चुराना; to keep *pardā*. ~ छूना, to touch the face (of, का); to give a formal invitation (to); to speak insincerely. ~ ज़रद होना, the face to turn yellow: to pale from fear. ~ जुठारना, = next. ~ जूठा करना, to take or to try (food). ~ जोड़कर बातें करना, to talk in whispers (to, से); to talk scandal (with). ~ टेढ़ा करना, to make a wry face; to put on airs. ~ डालना (में), to poke the nose (into); to thrust the muzzle or beak (into); to beg, to request. ~ ढाँककर लेट रहना, = ~ लपेटकर पड़ रहना. ~ ढाँकना, to cover the face (prior to sleeping); to mourn one dead. ~ तक आना, to be full to overflowing; to be on the tip of the tongue (a word). ~ ताकना, to gaze at the face (of, का: blankly, or in astonishment, or in expectation).~ तो देखो! just look at (his, &c.; or your) face!: what check, what a nerve!; what a poor creature you look! ~ थामना (का), to restrain from speaking. ~ दर ~, adv. face to face; to (one's) face. ~ दिखाना, to show one's face (to, को); to appear in public with self-confidence. ~ देखकर जीना, to live by the sight of, to idolise. ~ देखकर बात कहना, to speak with an eye to the reaction, to flatter; to fawn. ~ देखते रह जाना, to do nothing but gaze in astonishment (at). ~ देखना, to see one's face (in a mirror); to look about idly; to stare in astonishment or helplessness; to look to (one, का: as for help), to depend on; to have regard (for one). ~ देखते रह जाना, to do nothing but gaze in astonishment (at). ~ देखे का, adj. feigned, calculating (as friendliness, &c). ~ देना, to put the mouth or lips (into, or to, में); to favour, to countenance. ~ न देखना (का), to avoid, to shun; to dislike (a person). ~ न पड़ना, not to have the face (to). ~ निकलना, = ~ उतरना. ~ निपोड़ना, to look blank or foolish; to simper. ~ पकड़ना, to stop the mouth (of, का), to silence. ~ पड़ना (के), to be eaten (by); to behave boldly or brashly (before). ~ पर, adv. on, or at, or into the face or mouth; before the face, in the presence (of, के). ~ पर गरम होना, to become angry in the presence (of, के). ~ पर थूकना (के), to spit on the face (of); to insult, to dishonour. ~ पर दाना न रखना, to go without a crumb of food. ~ पर नाक न होना, the face to be noseless: to be without shame. ~ पर फ़ाख़्ता उड़ जाना, to blanch (the face); to look taken aback. ~ पर बात आना, to be on the tip of the tongue (words); to be uttered (words, remarks). ~ पर लाना, to utter (words). ~ पर हवाई, or हवाइयाँ, उड़ना, a firework to go off against the face: to change colour or expression; to look blank, or astonished. ~ फ़क़ हो जाना, to turn pale (esp. from fear). ~ फुलाना, to puff out the cheeks; to make a wry face; to be wilfully angry. ~ फेरना, to turn the face (from, से); to avoid, to shun; to be averse (to); to desist (from); to put to flight. ~ फैलाना, to gape; to be greedy (for); to ask a high or inflated price. ~ बंद करना, to hold one's tongue; to silence (a person); to bribe to secrecy. ~ बनना, displeasure or distaste to be shown (by, का). ~ बनाना, to assume an expression; to make faces (at), to mock; to show displeasure, distaste. ~ बाँधकर बैठना, to sit silent. ~ बाना, to gape, to yawn; to give a forced laugh; reg. to covet, to be greedy (for, पर). ~ बिचकाना, to grimace. ~ बिगड़ना, the face to be distorted, to be displeased; to have a foul mouth; to have a bad taste in the mouth. ~ बिगाड़ना, to frown, to scowl; to sulk; to make faces; to disconcert, to put (one) in one's place; to leave a bad taste in the mouth. ~ भर आना, the mouth to water; to feel nausea. ~ भर बोलना, to speak kindly, or affectionately (to, से). ~ भरकर, adv. filling the mouth: completely, thoroughly; roundly (of abuse). ~ भरना (का), to fill the mouth (of), to feed well; to buy the silence of. ~ मारना, to browse (in, में); to bribe (one, का). ~ मीठा करना, to give sweets (to, का); to gratify (as with a gift). ~ मीठा होना, to be gratified. ~ में ख़ून, or लहू, लगना, to acquire a thirst (for prey). ~ में तिनका लेना, to look meek or submissive (like a grazing cow). ~ में पड़ना, to be uttered (by, के). ~ में पढ़ना, to read to oneself, to mumble. ~ में पानी चुआना, to perform the last offices (for, के). ~ में पानी भर आना, the mouth to water; to feel desire or temptation. ~ में बोलना, to speak indistinctly or inaudibly. ~ में लगाम देना, to curb one's tongue. ~ मोड़ना, = ~ फेरना. ~ रखना, to keep on good terms (with). ~ लगना, to burn the mouth (of, के: as spices, &c.); to suit the palate, or tastes (of); to become intimate (with); to bandy words (with). ~ लगाना, to put the mouth or lips (to, में); to be familiar (with, के: as with an inferior); to spoil by kindness (a child); to fondle. ~ लटकाना, to hang the head; to be down in the mouth. ~ लपेटकर पड़, or लेट, रहना, to take to one's bed (in a sulk, or in grief). ~ लाल करना, to redden the mouth, or face (of, का: as by giving *pān*; or by slapping, or by making one angry). ~ सँभालना, to speak with regard for propriety; to hold (one's) tongue. ~ सीना, to sew up the mouth (of, का); to silence (a person). ~ सुजाना, to puff out the cheeks; to sulk; to cause (one's) face to swell (as by a slap).~ सूखना, the mouth to be dry (from thirst; or from fear); the face to become thin. ~ से दूध टपकना, milk to drip from the mouth (of, के); to be still a child. ~ से फूल झड़ना, flowers (of eloquence) to fall from the lips (of, के); iron. to berate. ~ से बात लेना (के), to take the words out of (one's) mouth; to stop (another) from speaking by speaking oneself. ~ से लार टपकना, saliva to flow from the mouth (of, के): to be insatiably eager or greedy. ~ हाथ टूटना, face and hands to be broken: to be badly injured. ~ ही ~ में, adv. inwardly, to oneself. अपना ~ लेकर रह जाना, to have the hand held to the mouth, or face: to be filled with admiration, or astonishment, or disappointment. अपना-सा ~ लेकर रह जाना, to remain with the expression unchanged; to be disconsolate (as at failure); to be utterly astonished. अपना-सा मुंह लेकर लौटना, to return disappointed, unsuccessful. काला ~! may he be disgraced! shame! किस ~ से ऐसा करे? how can he do this (and keep his self-respect or reputation)? कौन ~ लेकर, adv. = किस ~ से. सीधे ~ बोलना, to speak courteously (to). — मुँह-काला, m. disgrace. मुँह-चंग, m. Brbh. a Jew's harp. मुँह-चढ़ा, adj. familiar, intimate; having the ear (of), having an ascendancy (over). मुँहचोर, adj. bashful, timid. °ई, f. मुँह-छुआई, f. making conversation for politeness' sake only. मुँह-ज़बानी, adj. verbal; oral. मुँह-जला, adj. pej. burnt-mouthed: wretched, base. मुँहज़ोर, adj. restive; headstrong; outspoken; foul-mouthed. °ई, f. मुँह-झौंसा, adj. pej. scorched-mouthed: villainous. मुँहतोड़, adj. mouth-breaking: crushing, shattering (a retort). मुँह-दिखावा, m. the ceremony of unveiling a bride's face to her relatives-in-law after marriage, or on her first arrival at their home. मुँह-दिखाई, f. id.; a present given to the bride by her female relatives-in-law. मुँह-देखनी, f. = prec. मुँह-देखा, adj. feigned, calculating (friendliness, &c). मुँह-फट, adj. outspoken; abusive. मुँह-बंद, adj. & m. closed; corked (a bottle); a muzzle. मुँह-बोला, adj. so-called; adopted. मुँह-भराई, f. hush-money, a bribe. मुँह-माँगा, adj. & m. demanded or requested by word of mouth; something wished and asked for. मुँह-माँगा मोल, or दाम, m. asking price. मुँह-माँगी मुराद, f. object striven for; heart-felt wish. मुँह-लगा, adj. familiar (in manner); presumptuous. मुँह-सुँघाई, f. sniffing the face (of): a fleeting interview; fee paid for same. – मुँहामुँह, adv. face to face; brimful. °ई, f. squabble, wrangle.

मुँहासा *muṁhāsā*, m. pimples on the face (esp. those of adolescence).

मु- *mu-* [cf. *mṛta-*], v.i. Brbh. Av. to die.

मुअज़्ज़न *muazzan* [A. *mu'aẕẕin*], m. muezzin.

मुअज़्ज़िज़ *muazziz* [A. *mu'azzaz*], adj. corr. honoured, esteemed.

मुअत्तल *muattal* [A. *mu'aṭṭal*], adj. **1.** unemployed. **2.** suspended (from work); locked out. — ~ करना, to suspend; to put out of work.

मुअत्तली *muattalī* [A. *mu'aṭṭal*+P. *-ī*], adj. suspension (from work).

मुअम्मा *muammā* [A. *mu'ammā*], m. U. sthg. obscure, an enigma; riddle.

मुअल्ला *muallā* [A. *mu'allā*], adj. inv. U. high, exalted.

मुअल्लिम *muallim* [A. *mu'allim*], m. U. a teacher, instructor.

मुआ *muā* [*mṛtaka-*], adj. & m. **1.** adj. reg. dead. **2.** pej. wretched, cursed. **3.** m. a wretched creature. — ~ बादल, m. a sponge.

मुआफ़ *muāf*, adj. = माफ़.

मुआफ़िक़ *muāfiq* [A.*muvāfiq*], adj. **1.** agreeing, suitable. **2.** similar. **3.** favourable, propitious. — ~ आना (को), to agree, to suit; to prove favourable, &c.

मुआफ़िक़त *muāfiqat* [A. *muvāfiqa*: P. *muvāfiqat*], f. **1.** concord. **2.** affinity, sympathy, friendship.

मुआफ़ी *muāfī*, f. = माफ़ी.

मुआयना *muāynā* [A. *mu'āyana*], m. inspection, examination. — ~ करना, to inspect; to examine, to consider (a matter).

मुआवज़ा *muāvāzā* [A. *mu'āvaẓa*], m. **1.** compensation. **2.** exchange, barter. **3.** *Pl. HŚS.* retaliation.

मुआहिदा *muāhidā* [A. *mu'āhada*], m. U. compact, agreement; treaty.

मुक़त्तर *muqattar* [A. *muqaṭṭar*], adj. *Pl. HŚS.* distilled.

मुक़त्ता *muqattā* [A. *muqaṭṭa'*], adj. inv. cut into pieces: trimmed, shaped (as a beard).

मुक़दमा *muqadmā* [A. *muqaddama*], m. a law-suit; case; proceedings; prosecution. — ~ उठाना, = ~ बनाना. ~ खड़ा करना, to institute proceedings; to go to law (with, से or के ख़िलाफ़). ~ चलाना, id., 2. ~ बनाना, to fabricate a case. ~ लड़ाना, to fight a case (with, से). – मुक़दमा-पेशी [P. *-peśī*], f. the presentation, or hearing of a case; trial. मुक़दमेबाज़ [P. *-bāz*], m. one who goes to law. °ई, f. readiness to go to law.

मुक़द्दम *muqaddam* [A. *muqaddam*], adj. & m. U. **1.** adj. given precedence; superior, chief; more important. **2.** prior, former; ancient. **3.** m. chief, leader; village headman, chief revenue officer.

मुक़द्दमा *muqaddamā*, m. = मुक़दमा.

मुक़द्दर *muqaddar* [A. *muqaddar*], m. fate, destiny.

मुक़द्दस *muqaddas* [A. *muqaddas*], adj. U. sanctified; holy.

मुकम्मल *mukammal* [A. *mukammal*], adj. **1.** completed, complete, perfect. **2.** accomplished.

मुकरना *mukarnā* [?? cf. A. *munkar* 'denied'], v.i. **1.** to go back on one's word. **2.** to refuse to admit (sthg).

मुकरी *mukrī* [cf. H. *mukarnā*], f. a type of Brajbhāṣā poem: a quatrain in the last line of which it turns out that a woman who has seemed to be talking to her confidante about her lover has in fact been referring to something, or someone, else.

मुकर्रर *mukarrar* [A. *mukarrar*], adv. a second time, again. —~ करना, to repeat.

मुक़र्रर *muqarrar* [A. *muqarrar*], adj. **1.** adj. settled, fixed, determined; assigned (as a share); imposed. **2.** appointed (to a post). — ~ करना, to settle, &c.; to appoint (to, पर).

मुक़र्ररी *muqarrarī* [A. *muqarrar*+P. *-ī*], f. **1.** appointment. **2.** *hist.* fixed tenure, or lease. **3.** fixed rent. **4.** fixed wage.

मुकलावा *muklāvā* [cf. **mukna-*: Pk. *mukka-*], m. reg. the sending of a bride to her husband's home.

मुक़ाबला *muqābălā* [A. *muqābala*], m. & ppn. **1.** confrontation; challenge. **2.** opposition, resistance (as of enemy forces). **3.** competition, rivalry. **4.** comparison; contrast. **5.** ppn. w. के. in comparison (with, में). — ~ करना (का, or से), to confront, &c. – मुक़ाबलेबाज़ी [P. *-bāzī*], f. rivalry.

मुक़ाबिल *muqābil* [A. *muqābil*], adj. & adv. **1.** confronting. **2.** comparable. ***3.** adv. in confrontation, face to face.

मुक़ाबिला *muqābilā*, m. & ppn. corr. = मुक़ाबला.

मुक़ाम *muqām* [A. P. *muqām*], m. **1.** staying, stopping. **2.** stopping-place, halt; camping-place. **3.** place of residence; dwelling. **4.** position, situation. **5.** *mil.* an objective. — ~ बोलना, to order a halt.

मुक़ामी *muqāmī* [A. *maqām*+P. *-ī*], adj. resident (as an official); local.

मुकियाना *mukiyānā* [cf. H. *mukkī*], v.t. colloq. to pound, to thump with the fist.

मुक़िर *muqir* [A. *muqirr*], adj. & m. U. **1.** adj. asserting (as a fact). **2.** admitting (an offence). **3.** m. one who asserts, or admits, &c.

मुकुंद *mukund* [S.], m. a title of Viṣṇu, and of Kṛṣṇa.

मुकुट *mukuṭ* [S.], m. **1.** crown; diadem; tiara. **2.** crest.

मुकुर *mukur* [S.], m. Brbh. Av. mirror.

मुकुल *mukul* [S.], m. **1.** bud. **2.** blossom.

मुकुलित *mukulit* [S.], adj. **1.** opening, slightly opened (as buds, or the eye). **2.** covered with buds (a branch).

मुकेस *mukes*, m. Brbh. = मुक़्क़ैश.

मुक्का *mukkā* [**mukka-*[1]: ? ← Drav.], m. **1.** the fist. **2.** a blow with the fist. — ~ मारना (को), to strike (one) with the fist. ~ लगना (को), a blow to be received (by). – मुक्केबाज़ [P. *-bāz*], m. fist-fighter, boxer. °ई, f. boxing.

मुक्की *mukkī* [cf. H. *mukkā*], f. **1.** the fist. **2.** a light blow with the fist. — ~ चलाना, to use the fist; to strike with the fist; to box. ~ लगाना, or मारना (में), to strike with the fist; to knead (dough); to massage.

मुक़्क़ैश *muqqaiś* [? f. H. *keś*], m. **1.** brocade. **2.** gold or silver thread.

मुक्खी *mukkhī*, f. *Pl. HŚS.* a kind of pigeon.

मुक्त *mukt* [S.], adj. & m. **1.** adj. set free; emancipated. **2.** released from rebirth (the soul). **3.** free, unrestricted (as trade). **4.** unconstrained, uninhibited. **5.** fired, shot (as an arrow). **6.** m. Av. one set free. — ~ कंठ से, adv. openly, frankly; loudly. ~ छंद, m. free verse. मुक्तात्मा [°*ta*+*ā*°], adj. whose soul is released (sc. from rebirth).

मुक्तक *muktak* [S.], m. **1.** a lyrical poem. **2.** a verse or stanza unconnected by subject-matter to others.

मुक्ता *muktā* [S.], f. m. a pearl. – मुक्ता-फल, m. id.; camphor; fig. fine writing. मुक्तावली [°*tā*+*ā*°], f. a pearl necklace. मुक्ताहल, m. Av. = मुकताफल.

मुक्ति *mukti* [S.], f. **1.** release, deliverance. **2.** freedom, emancipation. **3.** release of the soul from the body and from further rebirth; salvation. — मुक्तिदाता, adj. & m. inv. giving freedom, or salvation; deliverer; saviour. °-दायक, adj. id. °-दायी, adj. = मुक्तिदाता.

मुखंड *mukhanḍ*, m. *Pl.* **1.** adj. leading, chief; having authority or power. **2.** m. a leader, &c.

मुछंदर *muchandar*, m. **1.** 19c. = Matsyendranāth (guru of the yogī Gorakhnāth). **2.** a keeper or trainer of monkeys. **3.** a buffoon, clown; fool.

मुछंदर *muchandar*, m. moustached, bewhiskered: *Pl. HŚS.* a rat (cf. छछूँदर).

[1]**मुख** *mukh* [S.], m. **1.** face. **2.** mouth; muzzle, snout; beak. **3.** fore-part, front; prow (of a boat); nose (of an aircraft). **4.** mouth, opening. **5.** fig. speech. — ~ करना, turning the face (towards, की ओर). – मुख-चित्र, m. frontispiece. मुख-पृष्ठ, m. title-page. मुख-मंडल, m. orb of the face: a lovely face; face showing a rapt, or

devout, or complacent expression. **मुख-मलीन**, adj. sad-faced. **मुखाकृति** [°*kha*+*ā*°], f. features (of a face). **मुखाग्नि** [°*kha*+*a*°], m. fire put into the mouth of a corpse when the funeral pyre is lit; a forest fire, all-destructive fire. **मुखारविंद** [°*kha*+*a*°], m. lotus face, lovely or handsome face.

[2]**मुख** *mukh*, adj. corr. = **मुख्य**. — **मुख-द्वार**, m. main entrance, or gate.

मुखड़ा *mukhṛā* [cf. H. *mukh*], m. dimin. face; delicate or lovely face; pinched, wan, or dejected face.

मुख़तलिफ़ *mukhtalif*, adj. see **मुख़्तलिफ़**.

मुख़तसर *mukhtasar* [A. *mukhtaṣar*], adj. U. **1.** abridged. **2.** concise.

मुख़तार *mukhtār* [A. *mukhtār*], m. one chosen: **1.** an agent, representative. **2.** an attorney, solicitor. — **मुख़तार-नामा**, m. written authority; power of attorney.

मुख़तारन *mukhtāran* [A. *mukhtāran*], adv. through (one's) representative.

मुख़तारी *mukhtārī* [A. *mukhtār*+P. *-ī*], f. **1.** duties or practice of an attorney. **2.** duties or position of an agent. — **~ करना**, to practise as an attorney.

मुखबरी *mukhbarī* [A. *mukhbirī*], f. secret information.

मुख़बिर *mukhbir* [A. *mukhbir*], m. U. causing news to be given: an informer; a spy.

मुखर *mukhar* [S.], adj. **1.** talkative. **2.** abusive. **3.** prominent (in a role).

मुखरित *mukharit* [S.], adj. **1.** ringing, resounding. **2.** uttered, voiced.

मुख़ातिब *mukhātib* [A. *mukhātib*], adj. conversing with, addressing. — **~ होना** (**की तरफ़**), to address; to turn (to) in speaking.

मुख़ालिफ़ *mukhālif* [A. *mukhālif*], adj. & m. U. **1.** adj. opposite, opposed. **2.** unfavourable. **3.** m. an opponent.

मुख़ालिफ़त *mukhālifat* [A. *mukhālifa*: P. *mukhālifat*], f. U. **1.** opposition. **2.** hostility.

मुखिया *mukhiyā* [ad. *mukhya-*], adj. & m. usu. inv. **1.** adj. chief. **2.** m. chief, leader, head. **3.** village headman.

मुखेरा *mukherā*, m. reg. muzzle (for an animal's mouth).

मुखौटा *mukhauṭā*, m. mask (as worn by an actor); disguise; outward aspect.

मुख़्तलिफ़ *mukhtalif* [A. *mukhtalif*], adj. U. **1.** different. **2.** various.

मुख़्तार *mukhtār*, m. see **मुख़तार**.

मुख्य *mukhyă* [S.], adj. & m. **1.** adj. chief, principal; leading; high, supreme; primary, original. **2.** m. principal, leader, head. — **~ द्वार**, m. main gateway or entrance. **~ मंत्री**, m. chief minister. **~ रूप से**, adv. chiefly. — **मुख्यतः**, adv. id. **°तया**, adv. id.

मुख्यता *mukhyătā* [S.], f. pre-eminent, or leader's, position or status.

मुगदर *mugdar* [ad. *mudgara-*[1]], m. **1.** a wooden mallet. **2.** a gymnast's club; dumb-bell. **3.** colloq. a mace. — **~ उठाना**, or **घुमाना**, or **फेरना**, or **हिलाना**, to exercise with dumb-bells.

मुग़ल *mugal* [P. *mugul*], adj. & m. **1.** adj. Mongol. ***2.** Mughal. **3.** m. a Mongol. ***4.** a Mughal. **5.** name of the third of four traditional sub-divisions of Indian Muslims.

मुग़लई *muglaī* [cf. H. *mugal*], adj. of Mughal style (as dress, art, ornamentation).

मुग़लानी *muglānī* [cf. H. *mugal*], f. **1.** a woman of the Mughal class (see **मुग़ल**, 5). **2.** the wife of a Mughal. **3.** female attendant (in women's apartments). **4.** sempstress.

मुग़लिया *mugliyā* [cf. H. *mugal*], adj. inv. having to do with the Mughals.

मुग़ली *muglī* [P. *mugulī*], adj. having to do with the Mughals.

मुग़ालता *mugālātā* [A. *mugālaṭa*], m. error, delusion.

मुग्ध *mugdh* [S.], adj. **1.** infatuated; fascinated; enchanted. **2.** simple, artless; erring. **3.** charming, enchanting. — **~ होना**, to be infatuated, &c. (with, **पर**). – **मुग्धकर**, adj. = ~, 3. **मुग्ध-चकित**, adj. fascinated, fond (eyes, or expression).

मुग्धता *mugdhătā* [S.], f. infatuated state, &c. (cf. **मुग्ध**).

मुग्धा *mugdhā* [S.], f. *rhet.* an artless and immature young girl.

मुचंग *mucaṅg* [? H.*mumh*+H. *caṅg*], f. *Pl.* a Jew's harp.

मुचलका *mucalkā* [T.], m. bond; recognisance, undertaking. — **~ देना**, or **लिखना**, to give a recognisance. **~ लिखवाना**, or **लेना**, to take a recognisance (from, **से**).

मुचा- *mucā-* [conn. **micc-*: Pk. *mimcana-*], v.t. Brbh. to cause to close; to close (the eyes).

मुच्चा *muccā*, m. *Pl. HŚS.* a large lump (as of meat).

मुछ- *much-*. = **मूँछ**: — **मुछ-मुँड़ा**, adj. having the moustache shaved, clean-shaven.

[1]मुछंदर *muchandar*, m. **1.** a keeper or trainer of monkeys. **2.** a buffoon, clown.

[2]मुछंदर *muchandar*, m. moustached, bewhiskered: *Pl. HŚS.* a rat (cf. छछूँदर).

मुछक्कड़ *muchakkaṛ*, adj. = मुछैल.

मुछरक *muchrak*, f. reg. down on the upper lip (cf. [1]मस).

मुछैल *muchail*, adj. having large or long moustaches.

मुज़म्मा *muzammā* [? corr. A. *muzammima*], m. reg. (W.) heel-rope (tied around a horse's hocks).

मुजरा *mujrā* [A. *mujrā*], m. caused to run or to flow: **1.** allowance, deduction (against a total due). **2.** deposit (against payment of balance). **3.** payment of respects; attendance. **4.** musical performance by a dancing-girl. — ~ करना, to allow, to deduct; to pay respects, &c. ~ देना, = ~ करना; to pay a deposit (as surety for the total).

मुजराई *mujrāī* [P. *mujrāī*], f. *hist.* **1.** allowance, deduction. **2.** remission or reduction of revenue (on account of expenses).

मुजरिम *mujrim* [A. *mujrim*], adj. & m. **1.** adj. offending, criminal. **2.** m. an offender, criminal. — ~ ठहराना, to find guilty; to convict; to sentence.

मुजरिमाना *mujrimānā* [P. *mujrimāna*], adj. inv. criminal.

मुजर्रब *mujarrab* [A. *mujarrab*], adj. U. tried, proved (as a medicine).

मुजल्लद *mujallad* [A. *mujallad*], adj. U. bound (a book).

मुजस्सिम *mujassim* [A. *mujassam*], adj. corr. having a body; bodily.

मुज़ायक़ा *muzāyqā* [A. *muẓāyaqa*], m. **1.** difficulty. ***2.** consequence, significance. — कोई ~ नहीं, it doesn't matter. क्या ~, what does it matter?

मुजावर *mujāvar* [A.*mujāvir*], m. *musl.* S.H. neighbour: one who is constantly at prayer or meditation in a mosque or shrine.

मुजाहिद *mujāhid* [A. *mujāhid*], m. vigorous warrior (for Islam, or for a cause).

मुजाहिदीन *mujāhidīn* [A. *mujāhidīn*], m. pl. vigorous warriors (for Islam).

मुज़ाहिम *muzāhim* [A. *muzāḥim*], adj. & m. **1.** adj. obstructing, preventing. **2.** m. one who obstructs. — ~ होना, to obstruct; to check.

मुझ *mujh* [*mahyam*], obl. base. see मैं.

मुझे *mujhe* [cf. *mahyam*], alt. obj. see मैं.

मुटकना *muṭaknā* [cf. H. *moṭā*], adj. **1.** plump. **2.** good-looking.

मुटमरदी *muṭmardī* [H. *moṭā*, P. *mard*], f. arrogance.

मुटर *muṭar* adv. redupl. sidelong: — ~ ~ ताकना, to glance sidelong (at, की तरफ़).

मुटरी *muṭrī* [conn. H. *muṭṭhā*], f. reg. a small bundle.

मुटल्ला *muṭallā*, adj. = मोटा.

मुटाई *muṭāī*, f. = मुटापा.

मुटाना *muṭānā* [cf. H. *moṭā*], v.i. **1.** to grow fat. **2.** fig. to grow proud.

मुटापा *muṭāpā*, m. fatness. — ~ छाना, to grow fat.

मुट्ठा *muṭṭhā* [cf. *muṣṭi-*], m. **1.** a handful. **2.** a bundle. **3.** handle (as of a plough); hilt. — ~ बाँधना (का), to make a bundle (of).

मुट्ठी *muṭṭhī* [*muṣṭi-*], f. **1.** the fist. **2.** clutch, grasp. **3.** a handful. **4.** fetlock (of a horse). **5.** a hand's width. **6.** a baby's teething-stick (cf. [3]मटकी). — ~ गरम करना, to give a bribe (to, की). ~ ढीली होना, to be open-handed, generous. ~ बाँधना, to close the fist. ~ भर, adv. a handful. ~ में, adv. in the fist or hand (of, की); in the clutches or power (of). बँधी ~, f. the closed fist; fistful, bundle (as of firewood). मुट्ठियाँ भरना, reg. to work the hands (in kneading or massaging). — मुट्ठी-चापी, f. massage.

मुठ- *muṭh-*. the fist (= मुट्ठी, मूठ). — मुठभेड़, f. hand-to-hand fight; encounter, clash. मुठमरद, m. *Pl.* a violent person. °ई, f.

मुठिया *muṭhiyā* [cf. H. *mūṭh*], f. m. **1.** handle of any tool or implement. **2.** stick with which a cotton-carder strikes the string of his bow.

मुड़ना *muṛnā* [*muṭati*: ← Drav.], v.i. **1.** to turn, be turned (back, down, or over); to be rolled up (sleeves). **2.** to turn (to right or left); to turn back. **3.** to be bent, or crooked; to be folded (the arms). **4.** to be twisted. **5.** to pucker up (as cloth, paper, leaves). **6.** to become blunted (a blade, a point). **7.** to be deflected.

मुड़ला *muṛlā* [cf. **muḍḍa-*], m. reg. **1.** shaved. **2.** reg. (Bihar) hornless (a bullock). **3.** beardless (wheat).

मुड़वाना *muṛvānā* [cf. H. *moṛnā*], v.t. to cause to be turned, &c. (by, से).

मुड़िया *muṛiyā* [**muḍḍa-*], m. f. **1.** m. a man with a shaven head (esp. an ascetic). **2.** f. the *kaithī* form of the Devanāgarī script (in which no headstrokes are used).

मुडेर *muḍer*, f. pronun. var. = मुँडेर.

मुड्ढा *muḍḍhā* [*muḍḍha-*²], m. shoulder.

मुढ़ियाना *muṛhiyānā*, v.i. reg. to be twisted, &c. (= मुड़ना).

मुतना *mutnā* [cf. H. *mūtnā*], m. an incontinent person.

मुतनी *mutnī* [cf. H. *mūtnā*], f. colloq. penis (a child's or mother's word).

मुतफ़न्नी *mutafannī* [A. *mutafannin*], adj. U. crafty.

मुतबन्ना *mutabannā* [A. *mutabannā*], adj. & m. inv. U. **1.** adj. adopted (as a son). **2.** m. an adopted son. — ~ करना, to adopt (a son: = गोद लेना).

मुतमइन *mutma'in* [A. *muṯma'inn*], adj. U. satisfied.

मुतलक़ *mutlaq* [A. *muṯlaq*], adv. freed, unrestricted: wholly, absolutely. — ~ नहीं, not at all.

मुतअल्लिक़ *mutaalliq* [A. *muta'alliq*], adj. & ppn. U. /mutalliq/. **1.** adj. connected (with). **2.** ppn. w. के. concerning.

मुतवज्जह *mutavajjah* [A. *mutavajjah*], adj. U. attentive.

मुतवल्ली *mutavallī* [A. *mutavallī*], m. U. guardian, or trustee (of a minor).

मुतवातिर *mutavātir* [A. *mutavātir*], adv. U. successively, continuously.

मुतसव्विर *mutasavvir* [A. *mutaṣavvar*], adj. corr. 19c. imagined. — ~ होना, to be imagined or regarded (as).

मुताना *mutānā* [cf. H. *mūtnā*], v.t. to cause to urinate. — मुतानेवाला, adj. diuretic.

मुताबिक़ *mutābiq* [A. *muṯābiq*], adj. & ppn. **1.** adj. conformable, corresponding (to,के). **2.** similar (to). **3.** ppn. w. के. in accordance (with), according (to). — ~ करना, to make comformable or similar (to, के); to reconcile; to compare.

मुतालबा *mutālăbā* [A. *muṯālaba*], m. U. **1.** demand. **2.** a sum demanded, or in arrear. **3.** claim; suit. — ~ करना, to demand, to claim; to sue.

मुताली *mutālī*, f. **1.** urine-hole (in a stable). **2.** urinal.

मुतास *mutās* [cf. H. *mūtnā*], f. urge to urinate. — ~ लगना (को), to want to urinate.

मुत्तफ़िक़ *muttafiq* [A. *muttafiq*], adj. agreeing, in agreement (about, पर).

मुथरा *muthrā* [**mutthara-*¹], adj. reg. blunt; stupid.

मुथरा- *muthrā-*, v.t. Brbh. to blunt.

मुद *mud* [S.], m. Av. joy.

मुदर्रिस *mudarris* [A. *mudarris*], m. a schoolteacher.

मुदर्रिसी *mudarrisī* [cf. A. *mudarris*], f. schoolmaster's post.

मुदाख़लत *mudākhalat* [A. *mudākhala*: P. *mudākhalat*], f. intrusion, interference (in, में).

मुदा *mudā*, m. & esp. adv. = मुद्दा.

मुदाम *mudām* [A. *mudām*], adv. Brbh. caused to continue: continuously; always.

मुदामी *mudāmī* [A. *mudām*+P. *-ī*], adj. Brbh. continuous, everlasting.

मुदित *mudit* [S.], adj. delighted, happy.

मुदिता *muditā* [S.], f. *rhet.* Brbh. joyful: a category of heroine.

मुद्गर *mudgar*, m. = मुगदर.

मुद्दआ *muddaā* [A. *mudda'ā*], m. /mudda/. sthg. asserted, claimed: **1.** object, intention; wish. **2.** meaning. **3.** issue, matter (of discussion). — ~ यह है, the point, or question, is this.

मुद्दई *muddaī* [A. *mudda'ī*], m. **1.** claimant. **2.** plaintiff.

मुद्दत *muddat* [A. *mudda*: P. *muddat*], f. **1.** a period of time. **2.** a lengthy period. — ~ का, adj. of long standing, ancient. ~ तक, adv. for some time, or for a long time (into the future). ~ से, adv. for some time, or for a long time (up to the present). ~ हुई, adv. a long time ago. एक ~, f. a long time, an age.

मुद्दती *muddatī* [A. *mudda*+P. *-ī*], adj. **1.** of fixed duration (as a bond). **2.** ancient (jewellery, &c).

मुद्दा *muddā*, m. see मुद्दआ. — मुद्देनज़र, adv. from the viewpoint (of, के).

मुद्र *mudră* [S.], m. type (for printing).

मुद्रक *mudrak* [S.], m. printer; typesetter.

मुद्रण *mudraṇ* [S.], m. **1.** printing. **2.** typesetting. — मुद्रणालय [°*na*+*ā*°], m. a printing-house, press.

मुद्रा *mudrā* [S.], f. **1.** a seal, stamp. **2.** a signet-ring. **3.** stamp, impression; a piece of type. **4.** a coin. **5.** currency. **6.** facial expression. **7.** bodily posture; aspect. **8.** position, esp. a stylised position (as of the hands, in dance; or in meditation). — अंतर्राष्ट्रीय मुद्रा-कोष, m. International

Monetary Fund. – मुद्रांक [°*rā*+*a*°], m. the relief on a seal, &c.; stamp, mark (as on paper, envelope, or document). °अण, m. stamping; printing. °इत, adj. sealed, stamped; printed. मुद्रा-शास्त्र, m. numismatics. मुद्रा-स्फीति, f. inflation of a currency.

मुद्रिका *mudrikā* [S.], f. 1. = मुद्रा, 2., 4. **2.** Brbh. a ring of *kuśa* grass (worn on the fourth finger while sacrificing to ancestors).

मुद्रित *mudrit* [S.], adj. **1.** sealed; closed (as eyes, flowers). **2.** struck, stamped (as coin). **3.** printed (as a book).

मुधा *mudhā* [S.], adv. & adj. inv. & m. Brbh. Av. **1.** adv in vain. **2.** adj. vain, useless. **3.** m. what is vain or false: untruth.

मुनगा *mungā* [*muraṅgī-*: ← Drav.], m. the horse-radish tree (= सहिजन).

मुनक़्क़ा *munaqqā* [A. *munaqqā*)], m. cleaned, cleared: a large raisin.

मुनब्बत *munabbat* [A. *munabba*: P. *munabbat*], *Pl. HŚS.* made raised: embossing, ornamentation in relief.

मुन-मुन *mun-mun*, interj. puss-puss!.

मुनमुना *munmunā*, m. *Pl. HŚS.* a black-grained, bitter grass that grows with wheat.

मुनहसिर *munhasir* [A. *munḥaṣir*], adj. U. dependent (on, पर).

मुनादी *munādī* [A. *munadan*: P. *munādī*], f. U. proclamation, by drum. — ~ करना, or फेरना, to proclaim by beat of drum.

मुनाफ़ा *munāfā* [A. *manāfi'*, pl.], m. **1.** profits, gains; income (as from an estate). **2.** benefits, benefit. — ~ उठाना, to realise a profit, to gain an income. मुनाफ़ाख़ोर [P. *khor*], m. a profiteer. °ई, f. profiteering.

मुनाल *munāl* [**munāla-*], m. reg. the Himālayan pheasant.

मुनासिब *munāsib* [A. *munāsib*], adj. **1.** suitable, proper; appropriate. **2.** fitting, right (as a step, a measure).

मुनासिबत *munāsibat* [A. *munāsiba*: P. *munāsibat*], f. U. **1.** appropriateness. **2.** rightness.

मुनाह *munāh* [**mukhanātha-*], adj. *Pl.* reg. chief, leading. — ~ के लोग, m. pl. leading people.

मुनि *muni* [S.], m. a saint, a sage; seer; ascetic. — मुनि-वर्ज [°-*varya*], m. Av. chief of sages or ascetics. मुनि-व्रत, m. vow of asceticism. मुनीश [°*ni*+*ī*°], m. chief of sages.

मुनिता *munitā* [S.], f. sainthood, &c. (see मुनि).

मुनिया *muniyā* [cf. **munna-*], f. any of several varieties of finch.

मुनीम *munīm* [A.*munīb*], m. factor, agent; accountant, book-keeper.

मुन्ना *munnā* [**munna-*], m. dear, darling (in reference or address to a boy).

मुन्नी *munnī* [**munna-*], f. dear, darling (in reference or address to a girl).

मुन्नू *munnū* [cf. **munna-*], adj. reg. little, small.

मुफ़लिस *muflis* [A. *muflis*], adj. **1.** insolvent. ***2.** in want, poor. — ~ करना, or बनाना, to impoverish.

मुफ़लिसी *muflisī* [A. *muflis*+P. *-ī*], f. **1.** insolvency. ***2.** poverty. — ~ छाना, poverty to overshadow (one), to be sunk in poverty. ~ में आटा गीला, = ग़रीबी में आटा गीला.

मुफ़स्सल *mufassal* [A. *mufaṣṣal*], adj. & m. **1.** adj. separated. **2.** detailed. **3.** m. particular mention. ***4.** the subordinate and outlying divisions of a district. **5.** the country (as distinguished from the town).

मुफ़स्सिल *mufassil*, adj. & m. corr. = मुफ़स्सल.

मुफ़ीद *mufīd* [A. *mufīd*], adj. profitable, beneficial.

मुफ़्त *muft* [P. *muft*], adj. & adv. **1.** adj. free, not paid for. **2.** adv. free, gratis. **3.** in vain, uselessly. — ~ का, adj. free; having no point. ~ का माल, m. sthg. obtained for nothing. ~ में, adv. at no cost, for nothing. – मुफ़्तख़ोर [P. *-khor*], m. one who eats for nothing, a sponger, parasite. °ई, f.

[1]**मुफ़्ती** *muftī* [*muftī*], m. an official expounder of Muslim law, a mufti.

[2]**मुफ़्ती** *muftī*, f. mufti, plain clothes (as opposed to uniform of soldiers, police, &c).

[3]**मुफ़्ती** *muftī* [cf. H. *muft*], adj. = मुफ़्त.

मुबादला *mubādlā* [A. *mubādala*], m. exchange, barter.

मुबारक *mubārak* [A.*mubārak*], adj. & interj. **1.** adj. blessed. **2.** fortunate. **3.** interj. blessings! congratulations! — ईद ~! good wishes on the occasion of *īd*! – मुबारकबाद [P. *-bād*], m. blessing(s); congratulation(s); good wishes. मुबारकबाद कहना (से), or देना (को), to bless, to congratulate, &c. °ई, f. = मुबारकबाद.

मुबारकी *mubārākī* [A. *mubārak*+P. *-ī*], f. **1.** blessings; congratulations. **2.** good fortune.

मुबाह *mubāh* [A. *mubāḥ*], adj. U. allowable, lawful.

मुबाहिसा *mubāhisā* [A. *mubāḥaṣa*], U. **1.** argument. **2.** debate.

मुब्तला *mubtalā* [A. *mubtalā*], adj. inv. **1.** tried, afflicted, suffering (from, में). **2.** entangled (in, में: as in difficulties). **3.** fascinated, captivated.

मुब्तिला *mubtilā*, adj. corr. = मुब्तला.

मुमकिन *mumkin* [A. *mumkin*], adj. possible; feasible.

मुमतहिन *mumtahin* [Ar. *mumtaḥin*], m. U. an examiner.

मुमताज़ *mumtāz* [A. *mumtāz*], adj. U. distinguished, select; eminent.

मुमाखी *mumākhī*, f. = ममाखी. a bee.

मुमानियत *mumāniyat* [A. *mumāna'a*: P. *mumāna'at*], f. opposition: prohibition; restriction.

मुमानी *mumānī*, f. reg. (E.) maternal aunt.

मुमुक्षा *mumukṣā* [S.], f. desire for release (from rebirth in this world).

मुमुक्षु *mumukṣu* [S.], adj. & m. **1.** adj. desiring release (from rebirth in this world). **2.** one desiring release, &c.

मुमूर्षु *mumūrṣu* [S.], adj. & m. **1.** adj. wishing to die. **2.** about to die, dying. **3.** m. a dying man.

मुयस्सर *muyassar* [A. *muyassar*], adj. U. **1.** obtainable, available. **2.** obtained. — ~ होना (को), to be obtainable, &c. (by).

मुरंडा *muraṇḍā*, adj. inv. & m. reg. **1.** adj. doubled over, folded; curled (as a leaf). **2.** m. Av. a medicinal sweet (roasted wheat soaked in molasses); a preparation of curds. **3.** a bitter wild vegetable. — ~ करना, to double up, or over; to tie up; to roast (wheat); to captivate; to thrash.

मुरक- *murak-* [cf. *muṭati*], v.i. Brbh. **1.** to twist, to bend. **2.** to turn away (from). **3.** to be broken, snapped.

मुरकाना *murkānā* [cf. H. *murak-*], v.t. & v.i. reg. **1.** v.t. to cause to twist, or to turn. **2.** v.i. to twist, to writhe.

मुरकी *murkī* [cf. H. *murak-*], f. Brbh. an ear-ring, or nose-ring (a stone set in wire).

मुरकूँडी *murkūṁḍī*, f. *Pl.* **1.** sitting with the head on the knees, and the arms folded round them. (see s.v. मुरग़ा). **2.** a partic. posture of ascetics.

मुरग़ा *murgā* [cf. P. H. *murg*], m. a cock. — ~ बनाना, to punish (a child) by making him sit with his arms round his knees, holding his ears. ~ लड़ाना, to fight cocks.

मुरग़ी *murgī* [cf. H. *murg*], f. a hen; fowl. — ~ का बच्चा, m. a chicken. – अंडे-मुरग़ी की बहस, f. circular reasoning. मुरग़ीवाला, m. a poultry-farmer.

मुरचंग *murcaṅg* [cf. P. *cang*], m. *Pl. HŚS.* a Jew's harp.

मुरछा- *murchā-*, v.i. Brbh. = मुरझाना, 3.

मुरज *muraj* [S.], m. poet. a drum.

मुरझ- *murjh-*, v.i. Brbh. = मुरझाना, 3.

मुरझाना *murjhānā* [? ad. *mūrchā-*], v.i. **1.** to wither; to fade. **2.** to become dispirited; to pine. **3.** to feel faint; to swoon.

मुरट *muraṭ*, adj. *Pl.* headstrong, stubborn.

मुरदनी *murdanī* [P. *murdanī*], f. **1.** deathly stillness; deathly pallor. **2.** funeral rites. — ~ छाना, a deathly pallor to come (upon, पर). ~ में जाना, to go to the funeral (of, की).

मुरदा *murdā* [P. *murda*], adj. & m. **1.** adj. dead. **2.** m. a dead body. — ~ उठाना, to lift a corpse, or bier (for the funeral procession). ~ करना, to do to death; to beat to within an inch of (one's) life. उसका ~ उठे! to the devil with him! मुरदे का माल, m. a dead man's things: goods for sale at a knock-down price. – मुरदा-घर, m. mortuary. मुरदादिल, adj. lifeless; unfeeling, stony-hearted; dejected. °ई, f. मुरदाबाद [P. *-bād*], interj. down with! damnation to! मुरदा-संग, m. lead oxide, litharge.

मुरदार *murdār* [P. *murdār*], m. & adj. **1.** m. a corpse. **2.** a carcass; carrion. **3.** adj. dead. **4.** unfeeling (as diseased skin). **5.** polluted. **6.** reg. (W.) useless (land).

मुरदारी *murdārī* [cf. H. *murdār*], f. reg. **1.** the hide of an animal that has died a natural death. 2. = मुरदार, 6.

[1]**मुरब्बा** *murabbā* [A. *murabba'*], adj. & m. made four: **1.** adj. square. **2.** *math.* squared. **3.** m. a square; a plot (of land).

[2]**मुरब्बा** *murabbā* [A. *murabbā*], m. preserved: preserved fruit; jam. — ~ डालना, to preserve (fruit: in, में).

मुरमुर *murmur*, f. = [2]मरमर.

मुरमुरा *murmurā* [onom.: cf. Pa. *murumurā-*], adj. & m. **1.** adj. crackling, crisp. **2.** swollen; burst, puffed (rice). **3.** m. puffed rice; popcorn. — मुरमुरों का थैला, m. colloq. an abnormally fat person.

मुरमुराना *murmurānā* [onom.: Pa. *muramurāpeti*], v.i. & v.t. **1.** v.i. to rustle. **2.** to murmur. **3.** to creak, to grate. **4.** to crackle; to crack, to snap. **5.** v.t. to crunch (food).

मुरल *mural* [S.], m. *Pl. HŚS.* a kind of freshwater fish.

मुरली *murălī* [S.], f. a flute. — मुरलीधर, m. flute-bearer: a title of Kṛṣṇa.

मुरवा *murvā* [? cf. H. *muṛnā*], m. Brbh. the ankle-joint.

मुरव्वत *muravvat* [A. *muruvva*: P. *muruvat*], f. humanity, kindness; courtesy. — ~ करना, to behave kindly, generously, &c. (towards, से).

मुरव्वती *muravvătī* [P. *muravvatī*], adj. kindly; considerate.

मुरशिद *murśid* [A. *murśid*], m. **1.** *musl.* a spiritual guide. **2.** head of an Islamic religious order. **3.** iron. a rascal.

मुरहा *murhā* [conn. *mūla-*; or *mūḍha-*], m. & adj. reg. **1.** m. an orphan. **2.** a rascal. **3.** [*mūḍha-*] m. & adj. a stupid person; stupid.

मुराई *murāī*, m. *Pl.* a grower and seller of vegetables.

मुराऊ *murāū*, m. *Pl.* = मुराई.

मुराद *murād* [A. *murād*], f. **1.** sthg. desired; cherished wish; a boon. **2.** intention, object. **3.** purport, sense, drift. **4.** a vow. — ~ पाना (अपनी), or मिलना (को), or हासिल होना, to obtain (one's) wish; to gain (one's) end. ~ मानना, to make a vow. ~ रखना, to have a desire, or an intention. मुरादों के दिन, m. pl. fig. the prime of life. इस ~ से, adv. with this intention or object.

मुराना *murānā* [*murati-[1]: Pk. *muraï*], v.t. reg. to chew.

मुरायठ *murāyăṭh*, m. reg. a turban (= मुरेठा).

मुरार *murar* [*mṛṇala-*], m. Brbh. lotus root, or stalk.

मुरारि *murâri* [S.], m. *mythol.* enemy of (the demon) Mura: a title of Kṛṣṇa.

मुरीद *murīd* [A.*murīd*], f. U. a follower, disciple.

मुरेठा *mureṭhā*, m. reg. a turban.

मुरेरा *murerā* [conn. *mūḍha-*], adj. reg. stupid.

मुरौवत *murauvat*, f. = मुरव्वत.

मुर्ग़ *murg* [P. *murg*], m. a cock; fowl. — मुर्ग़-केश, m. the cockscomb, *Celosia cristata*. मुर्ग़बाज़ [P. -*bāz*], m. cock-fancier; cock-fighter. °ई, f. cock-fighting. मुर्ग़-मुसल्लम [A. -*musallam*], m. a whole roasted chicken. मुर्ग़ाबी [P. -*ābī*], f. a water-fowl; a wild duck.

मुर्ग़ा *murgā*, m. see मुरग़ा.

मुर्ग़ी *murgī*, f. see मुरग़ी.

मुर्रम *murram*, m. reg. a crumbling trap-stone.

मुर्री *murrī* [cf. H. *muṛnā*], f. reg. (W). the fold of a dhotī through which the waist-string runs.

मुल *mul*, adv. *Pl. HŚS.* reg. **1.** at last, after all. **2.** but. **3.** in short, in sum.

मुलक *mulk*, m. see मुल्क.

मुलतवी *multavī* [A. *multavin*: P. *multavī*], adj. U. delayed; postponed; deferred.

[1]**मुलतानी** *multānī* [cf. H. *multān*], adj. & m. **1.** adj. having to do with Multan. **2.** m. a man from Multan.

[2]**मुलतानी** *multānī* [cf. H. *multān*], f. **1.** *mus.* name of a *rāgiṇī*. **2.** yellow ochre.

मुलम्मा *mulammā* [A. *mulamma'*], adj. inv. & m. made to glitter: **1.** adj. gilded; plated. **2.** m. gilding; plating. **3.** specious glitter. — ~ चढ़ाना (पर), to gild; to plate; to gloss over; to give plausibility (to: as to wrong figures). – मुलम्मासाज़ [P. -*sāz*], m. a gilder; a plater; a plausible rascal.

मुलहठी *mulahṭhī*, f. = मुलेठी.

मुलाक़ात *mulāqāt* [A. *mulāqāt*], f. **1.** meeting. **2.** a meeting; interview; visit. **3.** introduction, acquaintanceship. — ~ करना, to encounter, to meet (with, से). ~ करवाना (में), to bring about a meeting (between). ~ रखना, to be on friendly terms (with, से). पुरानी ~, f. an old acquaintance.

मुलाक़ाती *mulāqātī* [cf. H. *mulāqāt*], adj. & m. **1.** adj. seen much of, met often. **2.** having to do with visiting. **3.** m. an acquaintance. **4.** a visitor. — ~ कार्ड, m. visiting card.

मुलाज़मत *mulāzămat* [A. *mulāzama*: P. *mulāzamat*], f. **1.** service (esp. government service). **2.** attendance (as on a superior). — ~ करना, to work in government service.

मुलाज़मी *mulāzmī*, f. = मुलाज़मत.

मुलाज़िम *mulāzim* [A. *mulāzim*], m. **1.** a servant. **2.** a government or public servant.

मुलाज़िमत *mulāzimat*, f. corr. = मुलाज़मत.

मुलायम *mulāyam* [A.*mulā'im*], adj. **1.** soft. **2.** tender, delicate. **3.** mild (of nature); affable. **4.** pliable, weak (of character). **5.** weak, yielding (as market prices). — ~ चारा, m. pej. soft recourse: one easy to deal with.

मुलायमत *mulāyămat* [*mulā'ima*: P. *mulāyamat*], f. softness, &c. (cf. मुलायम, 1.-4).

मुलायमियत *mulāyămiyat* [cf. H. *mulāyam*], f. softness, &c. (cf. मुलायम).

मुलायमी *mulāyămī* [A. *mulā'im*+P. *-ī*], f. softness, &c. (cf. मुलायम).

मुलाहज़ा *mulāhazā* [A. *mulāḥaẓa*: P. *mulaḥāẓat*], m. **1.** inspection, examination. **2.** attention, regard (to or for a person); favour. — ~ करना, to examine closely; to pay regard or heed, &c. (to, का). मुलाहज़े में आना, to come under consideration or notice.

मुलेठी *mulethī* [**madhulaṣṭi-*: Pa. *madhulaṭṭhikā-*; or **mūlayaṣṭi-*], f. liquorice.

मुल्क *mulk* [A. *mulk*], m. **1.** country. **2.** region; home territory.

मुल्की *mulkī* [A. *mulkī*], adj. **1.** having to do with government; civil; national; internal. ***2.** having to do with a country (esp. one's own country).

मुल्ला *mullā* [T. *mollà*: ← A.], m. inv. **1.** a Muslim priest. **2.** a Muslim jurist.

मुल्लाई *mullāī* [cf. H. *mullā*], f. office or profession of *mullā*.

मुल्लानी *mullānī* [cf. H. *mullā*], f. **1.** the wife of a *mullā*. **2.** a learned Muslim woman; schoolmistress.

मुवक्कल *muvakkal* [A. *muvakkal*], m. *Pl. HŚS.* one appointed, or having a trust or charge.

मुवक्किल *muvakkil* [A. *muvakkil*], m. one who appoints an agent: client (esp. of a lawyer).

मुवाफ़िक़ *muvāfiq*, adj. = मुआफ़िक़.

मुशज्जर *muśajjar* [A. *muśajjar*], m. U. material worked or printed with forms of trees, shrubs or leaves.

मुशफ़िक़ *muśfiq* [A. *muśfiq*], adj. U. **1.** kind, affectionate. **2.** tender, compassionate. **3.** dear (a friend).

मुशायरा *muśāyrā* [*muśā'ara*], m. a gathering at which poets recite their poems.

[1]**मुश्क** *muśk* [P. *muśk*], m. musk. — मुश्क-नाफ़ा [P. *-nāfa*], m. *Pl. HŚS.* musk-bag. मुश्क बिलाई, f. musk-rat.

[2]**मुश्क** *muśk*, f. the upper arm. — मुश्कें बाँधना, or चढ़ाना, to tie the arms behind the back.

मुश्किल *muśkil* [A. *muśkil*], adj. & f. **1.** adj. difficult. **2.** distressing (as circumstances). **3.** doubtful (a matter). **4.** f. difficulty; trouble. **5.** hardship. **6.** perplexity. — ~ आ पड़ना, a difficulty to arise (for, पर). ~ आसान, or दूर, करना (की), to remove or to alleviate a difficulty. ~ करना, to make difficult. ~ में पड़ना, to get into a difficulty; to be at a loss. ~ से, adv. with difficulty; hardly, scarcely.

मुश्की *muśkī* [P. *muśkī*], adj. & m. musk-coloured: **1.** dark bay. **2.** very dark, black. **3.** m. a dark bay, or black, horse.

मुश्त *muśt* [P. *muśt*], m. f. **1.** the fist. **2.** a fistful, handful. — एक ~, adv. in a lump; as a lump sum, all at once.

मुश्तरका *muśtarkā* [A. *muśtaraka*], adj. inv. U. shared, participated (in); held in common.

मुश्तरी *muśtarī* [A. *muśtarin*: P. *muśtarī*], f. U. the planet Jupiter.

मुश्ताक़ *muśtāq* [A. *muśtāq*], adj. U. desirous, longing (for, का).

मुष्टंडा *muṣṭaṇḍā*, m. = मुस्टंडा.

मुष्टि *muṣṭi* [S.], f. **1.** the fist. **2.** a fistful, handful. **3.** handle, hilt.

मुसकराई *muskarai*, f. reg. = मुसकराहट.

मुसकराना *muskarānā* [cf. **muss-*], v.i. to smile; to grin.

मुसकराहट *muskarāhaṭ* [cf. H. *muskarānā*], f. a smile; a grin; a smirk.

मुसकान *muskān* [cf. H. *muskānā*], f. a smile.

मुसकाना *muskānā*, v.i. = मुसकराना.

मुसकुराना *muskurānā*, v.i. see मुसकराना.

मुसकुराहट *muskurāhaṭ*, f. see मुसकराहट.

मुसक्याई *musăkyāī* [cf. H. *muskānā*], f. Brbh. = मुसकराहट.

मुसक्यान *muskyān* [cf. H. *muskānā*], f. reg. = मुसकराहट.

मुसद्दस *musaddas* [A. *musaddas*], adj. & m. U. **1.** adj. composed of six; hexagonal. **2.** m. a hexagon. **3.** a verse of six lines.

मुसन्निफ़ *musannif* [A. *muṣannif*], m. U. author, writer.

मुसब्बर *musabbar* [? conn. A. *ṣabir*, or *ṣibr*], f. aloes (= घीकुवाँर): dried and thickened juice of aloes (used medicinally).

मुसमुसा *musmusā*, m. *Pl.* rough bryony, *Bryonia scabra*.

मुसम्मात *musammāt* [A. *musammāt*, pl.], f. *musl.* named: title prefixed to a lady's name.

मुसल *musal*, m. reg. = मूसल.

मुसलमान *musalmān* [P. *musulmān*], m. a Muslim. — ~ बनाना, to convert to Islam.

मुसलमानी *musalmānī* [P. *musulmānī*], adj. & f. **1.** adj. having to do with a Muslim, or with Muslims. **2.** f. the Muslim religion. **3.** circumcision. — ~ करना, to circumcise.

मुसलिम *muslim* [A. *muslim*], adj. & m. **1.** adj. causing to be safe: Muslim. **2.** m. a Muslim.

मुसल्लम *musallam* [A. *musallam*], adj. caused to be safe: whole, entire. — मुर्ग़ ~, m. a roasted whole fowl.

मुसल्लह *musallah* [A. *musallaḥ*], adj. armed (with, से).

मुसल्ला *musalla* [A. *muṣalla*], m. a prayer-mat.

मुसव्विर *musavvir* [A. *muṣavvir*], m. U. an artist, painter; sculptor.

मुसहर *mushar*, m. reg. **1.** a person who lives by selling medicinal herbs collected from the forests.

मुसाफ़िर *musāfir* [A. *musāfir*], m. **1.** a traveller. **2.** a passenger. — मुसाफ़िर-ख़ाना, m. an inn.

मुसाफ़िराना *musāfirānā* [P. *musāfirāna*], adv. U. like a traveller.

मुसाहब *musāhab* [A. *muṣāhib*], m. consorting with: **1.** companion; associate. **2.** favourite (of a prince).

मुसाहबी *musāhăbī* [cf. H. *musāhab*; or P. *muṣāhibī*], f. **1.** companionship. **2.** pej. consorting, hob-nobbing (with).

मुसीबत *musībat* [A. *muṣība*: P. *muṣībat*], f. **1.** a misfortune; a disaster. **2.** trouble, adversity. — ~ का मारा, adj. & m. unfortunate, &c. (a person). ~ पड़ना, a misfortune, &c. to befall (one). ~ में पड़ना, or होना, to fall into, or to be in, misfortune, &c. कोई ~ नहीं! colloq. no problem!

मुसुका- *musukā-*, v.i. Brbh. = मुसकाना.

मुस्कराना *muskarānā*, v.i. see मुसकराना.

मुस्टंडा *musṭaṇḍā*, adj. & m. **1.** adj. sturdy, stalwart. **2.** m. a depraved person. **3.** a lout.

मुस्तक़िल *mustaqil* [A. *mustaqill*], adj. **1.** fixed, firm (as an intention). **2.** permanent (as a tenure, a right).

मुस्तक़ीम *mustaqīm* [A. *mustaqīm*], adj. erect: upright; resolute.

मुस्तनद *mustanad* [A. *mustanad*], adj. U. supported: **1.** to be relied on. **2.** authenticated.

मुस्तहकिम *mustahkim* [A. *mustaḥkam*], adj. corr. stable, fixed (as an opinion).

मुस्तैद *mustaid* [A. *musta'idd*], adj. ready; prompt; alert.

मुस्तैदी *mustaidī* [A. *musta'idd*+P. *-ī*], f. **1.** readiness, &c. **2.** vigour, enthusiasm. — ~ से, adv. at the ready; readily, &c.

मुस्तौफ़ी *mustaufī* [A. *mustaufī(n)*], m. Brbh. examiner of accounts, auditor.

मुहँकना *muhaṁknā*, v.t. reg. = महँकना.

मुहकम *muhkam* [A. *muḥkam*], adj. Brbh. U. strong, firm; solid, stout (as doors).

मुहतरम *muhtaram* [A. *muḥtaram*], adj. U. /muhtərim/. respected, honoured.

मुहताज *muhtāj* [A. *muḥtāj*], adj. & m. **1.** adj. in want, needy. **2.** m. a pauper. **3.** a beggar. **4.** a handicapped person; a cripple. — ~ करना (को), to reduce to poverty, or want (of, को). ~ होना, in extreme need (of, का or को). दाने-दाने को ~, hard put to it to find even crumbs (to eat).

मुहताजी *muhtājī* [A. *muḥtāj*+P. *-ī*], f. want, poverty.

मुहब्बत *muhabbat* [A. *maḥabba*: P. *maḥabbat*; ? ×A. *muḥabb* 'beloved'], f. **1.** love, affection. **2.** warm friendship. — ~ करना, or रखना, to feel love, &c. (for, से or की). ~ का दम भरना, to declare (one's) love. मुँह देखे की ~, f. pretended love or affection.

मुहब्बती *muhabbatī* [cf. H. *muhabbat*], adj. loving, affectionate.

मुहम्मद *muhammad* [A. *muḥammad*], m. much praised: name of the prophet and founder of Islam.

मुहम्मदी *muhammadī* [A. *muḥammadī*], adj. & m. **1.** adj. believing in Muḥammad; Muslim. **2.** m. a Muslim.

मुहर *muhar* [P. *muhr*], m. **1.** a seal; impression, stamp. **2.** signet-ring. **3.** a locket. **4.** a gold coin. — ~ लगाना (में, or पर), to seal; to set the seal (of, की, on, पर). – मुहरबंद [P. *-band*], adj. sealed.

मुहरा *muhrā*, m. 1. = ² ¹मोहरा. **2.** a stamp (cf. मुहर, 1).

मुहरी *muhrī*, f. = मोहरी.

मुहर्रम *muharram* [A. *muḥarram*], m. forbidden; sacred: **1.** name of the first month of the Muslim year (when the killing of Ḥusain is mourned). **2.** mourning, lamentation. — ~ की पैदाइश, f. fig. a creature of gloom.

मुहर्रमी *muharramī* [A. *muḥarram*+P. *-ī*], adj. **1.** having to do with the month Muḥarram. **2.** mournful, sad.

मुहर्रिर *muharrir* [A. *muḥarrir*], m. a clerk, writer.

मुहर्रिरी *muharrirī* [A. *muḥarrir*+P. *-ī*], f. clerk's duties or post.

मुहलत *muhlat*, f. pronun. var. = मोहलत.

मुहल्ला *muhallā* [A. *maḥalla*], m. suburb; quarter (of a town); ward. — मुहल्लेदार [P. *-dār*], m. person in administrative charge of a suburb, or ward; neighbour.

मुहसिन *muhsin* [A. *muḥsin*], adj. & m. U. **1.** adj. obliging, beneficent. **2.** m. helper, benefactor.

मुहाना *muhānā* [**mukhāyana-*], m. **1.** mouth (as of a river); confluence. **2.** estuary.

मुहाफ़िज़ *muhāfiz* [A. *muḥāfiẓ*], adj. & m. **1.** adj. defending, keeping. **2.** m. custodian. — मुहाफ़िज़-ख़ाना, m. record-room. मुहाफ़िज़-दफ़्तर, m. record-keeper.

मुहार *muhār* [P. *mahār*], m. reg. a camel's nose-pin, with attached rope.

मुहाल *muhāl* [A. *muḥāl*], adj. **1.** absurd, impossible. ***2.** very difficult.

मुहावरा *muhāvrā* [A. *muḥāvara*], m. **1.** an idiom; a current expression. **2.** usage. **3.** practice, habit. — मुहावरेदार [P. *-dār*], adj. idiomatic; expressive (language).

मुहासबा *muhāsabā* [A. *muḥāsaba*], m. E.H. account, accounts.

मुहासा *muhāsā*, m. see मुँहासा.

मुहासिब *muhāsib* [A. *muḥāsib*], m. Brbh. keeper of an account, or of accounts.

मुहिम *muhim* [A. *muhimm*], f. U. **1.** an important matter; an enterprise. **2.** an expedition; campaign. **3.** an exploit.

मुहुर्मुहुः *muhurmuhuḥ* [S.], adv. poet. suddenly; momentarily; constantly.

मुहूर्त *muhūrt* [S.], m. var. /muhūrət/. a moment (specif. astrologically ausicious). — ~ करना, to begin (a task) at an auspicious moment. ~ देखना, or विचारना, to ascertain an auspicious moment.

मुहैया *muhaiyā* [A. *muhaiyā*], adj. inv. U. **1.** prepared, ready. **2.** procured, available. — ~ कराना, to offer (services).

मूँग *mūṁg* [*mudga-*], m. any variety of the pulse *Phaseolus radiatus*: green gram. ~ की दाल, id. ~ की दाल खानेवाला, a weak or timorous person. छाती पर ~ दलना, fig. to give (one, की) a hard time. – मूँग-फली, f. peanut.

[1]मूँगा *mūṁgā*, m. coral.

[2]मूँगा *mūṁgā*, m. a variety of sugar-cane.

[3]मूँगा *mūṁgā* [*muraṅgī-*: ← Drav.], m. *Pl.* a shrub, *Moringa pterygosperma*, yielding a gum: a hog-gum.

[1]मूँगिया *mūṁgiyā* [cf. H. *mūṁg*], adj. of the colour of *mūṁg*: dark green.

[2]मूँगिया *mūṁgiyā* [cf. H. [1]*mūṁgā*], adj. coral-coloured.

मूँगी *mūṁgī*, f. = मूँग.

मूँछ *mūṁch*, f. **1.** moustache. **2.** *zool.* antennae. — ~ का बाल, a hair of the moustache (of, की): one close (to), an intimate (of). मूँछें उखाड़ना, to pluck the moustaches (of): to teach (one) a painful lesson, to humble (one). मूँछेंचढ़ाना, to twist the moustaches upwards: = मूँछों पर ताव देना. मूँछें तानकर, adv. fig. (speaking, or behaving) arrogantly. मूँछें नीची होना, to be shamed, or disgraced. मूँछों पर ताव देना, to twist or to twirl the moustaches: to act in an affected, haughty or vain way; to boast. मूँछों पर हाथ फेरना, to preen the moustaches: id. – मूँछ-मरोड़ा रोटी-तोड़ा, one who preens his moustache and breaks bread: one delighted to live at others' expense.

मूँज *mūṁj* [*muñja-*], f. a type of tall rush or grass (of the fibres of which ropes or cords are made).

मूँठ *mūṁṭh*, f. reg. = मूठ.

मूँड़ *mūṁṛ* [*muṇḍa-*[1]; (?) or *mūrdhan-*], m. the head. — ~ पाना, reg. to get a person's ear, attention, or favour. ~ मारना, to beat the brow; to rack the brains; to make strenuous efforts; fig. to throw (sthg.) at the head (of, के).~ मुड़ाना, to get the head shaved; to become an ascetic. – मूँड़कटा, m. *HŚS.* a cut-throat, murderer.

मूँड़न *mūṁṛan* [cf. H. *mūṁṛnā*], m. = मुंडन. — मूँड़न-छेदन, m. the first ceremonial shaving of a child's head, and the piercing of his ears.

मूँड़ना *mūṁṛnā* [*muṇḍayati*], v.t. **1.** to shave (esp. the head). **2.** fig. to make a disciple of. **3.** to shear (a fleece). **4.** to cheat, to fleece (of, से). —उलटे छुरे, or उस्तुरे, से ~, to cheat flagrantly.

मूँडला *mūṁḍlā* [cf. *muṇḍa-*[1]], adj. reg. shaven.

मूँड़ा *mūṁṛā*, m. reg. pretence; hypocrisy.

मूँड़िया *mūṁṛiyā*, f. dimin. the head (= मूँड़).

मूँड़ी *mūṁṛī* [*muṇḍa-*[1]; or *mūrdhan-*], f. **1.** the head. **2.** head, top (of sthg). — ~ मरोड़ना (की), to strangle; to cheat, to fleece.

मूँद *mūṁd* [cf. H. *mūṁdnā*], f. shutting, fastening, &c.

मूँदना *mūṁdnā* [*mudrayati*], v.t. to seal: **1.** to close, to shut. **2.** to fasten. **3.** to imprison.

मू *mū*, m. reg. = मुँह.

मूक *mūk* [S.], adj.**1.** dumb. **2.** silent, mute. — मूक-बधिर, adj. deaf and dumb.

मूकता *mūkătā* [S.], f. dumbness; muteness.

मूका *mūkā*, m. Brbh. = मोखा.

मूचकाना *mūckānā* [conn. *mucyate*], v.t. reg. to sprain, to twist.

मूछाकड़ा *mūchākṛā* [cf. H. *mūṁch*], m. reg. a large or heavy moustache.

मूज़ी *mūzī* [A. *mu'zin*: P. *mūzī*], m. U. **1.** tormentor; oppressor. **2.** villain. **3.** miser.

मूठ *mūṭh* [*muṣṭi-*], f. **1.** the fist. **2.** handle; hilt. **3.** handful; first sowing (for good luck). **4.** a spell; witchcraft. — ~ चलाना, to cast a spell (over, पर); to practise witchcraft. ~ मारना, colloq. to masturbate.

मूठा *mūṭhā* [*muṣṭi-*], m. reg. **1.** a sheaf, bundle (as of straw). **2.** a handle.

मूठी *mūṭhī*, f. reg. = मुट्ठी.

मूढ़ *mūṛh* [*mūḍha-*], adj. & m. stupefied: = मूर्ख.

मूढ़ता *mūṛhătā* [S.], f. = मूर्खता.

मूढ़त्व *mūṛhatvă* [S.], f. *Pl. HŚS.* = मूर्खता.

मूढ़ा *mūṛhā*, m. = मोंढ़ा.

मूढ़ी *mūṛhī*, f. reg. (Bihar) = लाई.

मूत *mūt* [*mūtra-*], m. urine. — ~ अटकना, to be unable to pass urine. ~ निकल पड़ना, urine to be passed (through fear). ~ मारना, to urinate (through fear). ~ से निकलकर गू में गिरना, fig. to fall out of the frying pan into the fire.

मूतना *mūtnā* [*mūtrayati*], v.i. to urinate.

मूत्र *mūtră* [S.], m. urine. — मूत्र-मार्ग, m. urethra. मूत्रालय [°*tra*+*ā*°], m. urinal. मूत्राशय [°*tra*+*ā*°], m. the bladder.

मूदरी *mūdrī*, f. a finger-ring (= मुँदरी).

1**मूनना** *mūnnā* [cf. **mūna-*: Pk. *mūṇa-*], v.i. reg. **1.** to be silent. **2.** to forget.

2**मूनना** *mūnnā*, v.t. reg. = मुँदना.

मूना *mūnā* [cf. *mṛta-*], v.i. reg. to die.

मूरख *mūrakh*, adj. & m. = मूर्ख.

मूरत *mūrat*, f. Brbh. = मूर्ति.

मूरति *mūrati*, f. Av. = मूर्ति.

मूरा-मेट *mūrā-meṭ* [? cf. H. *murānā, meṭnā*], adj. reg. **1.** crushed, ground down. **2.** destroyed utterly.

मूरिस *mūris* [A. *mūriṣ*], m. U. making an heir: legator, testator.

मूर्ख *mūrkh* [S.], adj. & m. **1.** adj. stupid, foolish; ignorant. **2.** m. a fool; an ignorant person.

मूर्खता *mūrkhătā* [S.], f. stupidity, foolishness; ignorance.

मूर्खताई *mūrkhtāī*, f. Brbh. Av. = मूर्खता.

मूर्खत्व *mūrkhatvă* [S.], m. = मूर्खता.

मूर्खपन *mūrkhpan* [cf. H. *mūrkh*], m. = मूर्खता.

मूर्खपना *mūrkhpanā* [cf. H. *mūrkh*], m. = मूर्खपन.

मूर्च्छा *mūrcchā*, f. = मूर्छा.

मूर्छन *mūrchan* [S.], m. **1.** causing to faint; a spell. **2.** fainting, swooning.

मूर्छना *mūrchănā* [S.], m. *mus.* modulation of sounds in a scale; melody.

मूर्छा *mūrchā* [S.], f. a faint, swoon. — ~ आना (को), = next. ~ खाना, to faint; to lose consciousness.

मूर्छित *mūrchit* [S.], adj. fainted: unconscious. — ~ होना, to faint.

मूर्त *mūrt* [S.], adj. having material form: tangible, perceptible; incarnate.

मूर्ति *mūrti* [S.], f. **1.** any body having material form; figure; form. ***2.** idol; statue; image. **3.** embodiment, manifestation; personification. — मूर्ति-कला, f. the art of sculpture. मूर्तिधर, adj. having, or assuming, form or body. मूर्ति-पूजन, m. = next. मूर्ति-पूजा, f. image-worship. मूर्ति-भंजक, m. iconoclast. °-भंजन, m. iconoclasm. मूर्तिमत्तता, f. possession of material, bodily or incarnate form. °-मान, adj. possessing material, bodily or incarnate form; personified.

मूर्तित *mūrtit* [S.], adj. embodied, incarnate.

मूर्धन्य *mūrdhanyă* [S.], adj. **1.** leading, head, chief. ***2.** *ling.* cerebral, retroflex (as the Sk. and H. consonants *ṭ, ḍ*, &c). —मूर्धन्यीकरण, m. retroflexion (the process).

मूर्धा *mūrdhā* [S.], m. inv. *Pl. HŚS.* the head.

मूल *mūl* [*mūla-*: ? ← Drav.], m. & adj. **1.** m. root. **2.** source, origin; cause. **3.** basis, foundation. **4.** *fin.* capital, principal. **5.** original (text, or language). **6.** *math.* root. **7.** a lunar asterism (considered unlucky): the stars in the tail of Scorpio. अभुक्त ~, m. the concluding minutes of the moon's period in *mūl.* **8.** adj. radical, basic, fundamental; essential (as cause, substance, development, contribution); real. **9.** ancient, of long standing (as a home, a people). **10.** principal, chief, main; primary (as a source); dominant. ~ लागत, f. prime cost. — **मूलगत**, adj. = ~, 8. **मूल-ग्रंथ**, m. original text (of a work). **मूलतः**, adv. basically, fundamentally. **मूल-तत्त्व**, m. fundamental nature; fundamental assumption or principle; *chem.* element. **मूलतया**, adv. = मूलतः. **मूल-द्रव्य**, m. = ~, 4. **मूल-धन**, m. id. **मूलभूत**, adj. = ~, 8. **मूल-मंत्र**, m. fig. a primary recourse (to some end). **मूलोच्छेदन** [°*la*+*u*°], m. extirpation.

मूलक *mūlak* [S.], adj. & m. **1.** adj. -मूलक. rooted in; giving rise to (e.g. समस्यामूलक, problematical). **2.** m. Av. a radish (= मूली).

मूलन *mūlan*, adv. reg. entirely, wholly; surely, indeed.

मूला *mūlā* [*mūla*-: ? ← Drav.], m. *Pl.* angle, corner (as of a wall or building).

मूलिका *mūlikā* [S.], f. Brbh. a medicinal root.

मूलिया *mūliyā* [cf. H. *mūl*], adj. born under the asterism *mūl* (in Scorpio); unlucky.

मूली *mūlī* [*mūlikā*-: ? ← Drav.], f. **1.** a radish. **2.** colloq. anything worthless or insignificant.

मूल्य *mūlyă* [S.], m. price, &c. (= मोल). — **मूल्यवान**, adj. valuable; precious. **मूल्य-ह्रास**, m. depreciation. **मूल्यांकन** [°*ya*+*a*°], m. evaluation, assessment (of worth or price). **मूल्यांकित** [°*ya*+*a*°], adj. valued, assessed. **मूल्यादेय** [°*a*+*ā*°], adj. having postage due (a letter).

मूल्यन *mūlyan* [S.], m. valuation.

मूश *mūś* [P. *mūś*], m. a rat; a mouse.

मूष *mūṣ* [S.], m. = ¹मूस.

मूषक *mūṣak* [S.], m. Av. a rat; a mouse.

मूषा *mūṣā* [S.], f. a rat; a mouse.

मूषिका *mūṣikā* [S.], f. a rat; a mouse.

मूषी *mūṣī* [S.], f. *Pl. HŚS.* a rat; a mouse.

¹मूस *mūs* [*mūṣa*-], m. a rat; a mouse.

²मूस *mūs* [*mūṣā*-], f. *Pl.* reg. a crucible.

मूसना *mūsnā* [*mūṣati*], v.t. **1.** to steal, to rob (of); to pilfer. **2.** to cheat, to swindle (of).

मूसल *mūsal* [*musala*-; Pk. *mūsala*-], m. **1.** a pestle. **2.** a club. — **मूसलचंद**, m. pej. an uncouth person; an able-bodied but idle person. **दालभात में मूसलचंद**, fig. mouse in the food-store: an unwelcome presence. **मूसलधार**, m. pelting rain. **मूसलधार बरसना**, to rain in torrents.

मूसला *mūslā* [*musala*-; Pk. *mūsala*-], m. **1.** a club. **2.** a tap-root. **3.** an upright beam, post. — **मूसलाधार**, m. = मूसलधार.

मूसली *mūslī* [*musala*-; Pk. *mūsala*-], f. **1.** a small pestle. **2.** a small club. **3.** *Asparagus racemosa* (= वरी).

¹मूसा *mūsā* [*mūṣaka*-], m. a rat; a mouse. — ~ **हरिन**, f. the mouse-deer (= पिसोरा). – **मूसा-कानी**, f. mouse-ear: a creeper used medicinally, *Salvinia cucullata*.

²मूसा *mūsā* [A. *mūsā*], m. inv. Moses.

मूसाई *mūsāī* [A. *mūsā*+P. -*ī*], f. & m. **1.** f. the religion of Moses, Judaism. **2.** m. an Israelite, a Hebrew.

मूसीक़ार *mūsīqār* [P. *mūṣīqār*], m. one who brings forth music: a musician.

मूसीक़ी *mūsīqī* [A. *mūsīqī*: ← Gk.], f. music.

मृग *mr̥g* [S.], m. **1.** a deer, antelope. **2.** Brbh. an animal, creature. **3.** a name of the ninth month of the Hindu lunar calendar (= अगहन). — **मृग-छाल**, a deer-skin. **मृगछौना**, m. young of a deer, &c., a fawn. **मृग-जल**, m. Av. deer-water: a mirage. **मृग-तृषा**, f. = next. **मृग-तृष्णा**, f. deer-thirst: mirage. **मृगनयनी**, adj. deer-eyed: having soft or lovely eyes. **मृग-पति**, m. Brbh. lord of deer, &c.: lion. **मृग-मद**, m. musk. **मृग-शावक**, m. a fawn. **मृग-शिरा**, f. *astrol.* a lunar mansion: the constellation Orion.

मृगया *mr̥gayā* [S.], f. hunting.

मृगिनी *mr̥ginī* [S.], f. Brbh. a doe.

मृणाल *mr̥ṇāl* [S.], m. a lotus-stalk.

मृणालिनी *mr̥ṇālinī* [S.], f. a clump or bed of lotuses.

मृणाली *mr̥ṇālī* [S.], f. **1.** (m., *Pl.*) a lotus. **2.** clump or bed of lotuses.

मृन्पात्र *mr̥npātr* [S.], m. earthenware vessel: pottery.

मृत *mr̥t* [S.], adj. dead. — **मृतकल्प**, adj. = मृतप्राय. **मृतप्राय**, adj. almost dead; half-dead; seemingly dead. **मृतवत्**, adj. deathlike; dead. **मृत-संजीवनी**, f. *mythol.* Brbh. name of a herb supposed to revive the dead if eaten. **मृत-स्नान**, m. *hind.* bathing after a death or funeral; bathing a corpse. **मृताशौच** [°*ta*+*a*°], m. *hind.* state of ritual impurity of the relatives of a deceased person.

मृत्- *mr̥t*- [S]. earth, clay: — **मृत्कला**, f. the art of pottery, ceramics.

मृतक *mr̥tak* [S.], m. a corpse. — **मृत-कर्म**, m. pl. Av. funeral rites. **मृत-धूम**, m. Brbh. the ashes of a cremated body.

मृति *mr̥ti*, f. *Pl. HŚS.* = मृत्यु.

मृत्तिका *mr̥ttikā* [S.], f. earth, soil; clay. — **मृत्तिका-शिल्प**, m. ceramics.

मृत्यु *mr̥tyu* [S.], f.; m. **1.** f. death. **2.** m. *mythol.* death personified: the god of death, Yama. — ~ होना (की), to die. – मृत्यु-कर, m. death duty. मृत्युप्राय, adj. = मृतप्राय. मृत्यु-लोक, m. the world of the dead. मृत्यु-शोक, m. mourning. मृत्यु-संख्या, f. death-toll. मृत्यु-समाचार, m. an obituary.

मृदंग *mr̥daṅg* [S.], m. a double drum, tapering from the middle towards the ends.

मृदंगी *mr̥daṅgī* [cf. H. *mr̥daṅg*], m. a *mr̥daṅg*-player, drummer.

मृदु *mr̥du* [S.], adj. **1.** soft, gentle. **2.** tender (of the emotions); mild, gentle (of voice, temperament). **3.** moderate, gentle (as pace, gait).

मृदुता *mr̥dutā* [S.], f. softness, &c. (see मृदु).

मृदुल *mr̥dul* [S.], adj. soft, &c. (see मृदु).

मृषा *mr̥ṣā* [S.], adj. & adv. **1.** adj. false. **2.** useless, vain. **3.** adv. falsely, &c.

1**में** *meṁ* [conn. *madhya-*], ppn. **1.** in (of place). **2.** into; to. कमरे ~ जा रहे हो? are you going to your room? पौधों ~ पानी देना, to water plants. **3.** in the midst of, within; among, of. आपस ~, adv. among themselves, &c. भाषाओं ~ सबसे सुंदर, the most beautiful of languages. **4.** on, to. कमर ~ पेटी बाँधना, to tie a belt round (one's) waist. बकसे ~ ढक्कन लगाओ, fix a top on the box. पेड़ ~ फल लगना, fruit to form on a tree. **5.** in (of time). सितंबर ~, adv. in September. इतने ~, adv. with this, with that. **6.** in the course of, in. एक साल ~ हिंदी सीख लेंगे, you'll learn Hindi within one year. **7.** after the period of, in. एक घंटे ~ तैयार रहूँगा, I'll be ready in an hour. **8.** for, at (of cost). कितने ~ बेचोगे? How much will you sell (it) for? **9.** between (of distance, or distinction). दिल्ली और इलाहाबाद ~ 500 मील का फ़ासिला है, there is a distance of 500 miles between Delhi and Allahabad. उनमें फ़रक़ क्या है? what is the difference between them? **10.** in, under (of situation). उसके निर्देशन ~, adv. under his direction. **11.** to serve as, as. भेंत ~, adv. as a gift. **12.** in respect of (a matter). — ~ से, adv. from inside; from among; out of. उनमें से आप दो-तीन चुन लें, please pick out two or three of these.

2**में** *meṁ* [onom.], f. bleating, bleat. — ~ ~ करना, to bleat.

मेंकना *meṁknā*, v.i. *Pl.* to bleat (as a goat or a sheep).

मेंगनी *meṁgnī* [*meṅgana-], f. small round droppings (as of goats, sheep, deer, rats).

मेंड़ *meṁṛ* [?? conn. H. 1*maiṛā*], f. limit: **1.** dike, embankment. **2.** boundary-mound (of a field); hedge; fence. — मेंड़बंदी [P. *-bandī*], f. the fixing, or making, of boundaries; a record of boundaries.

मेंडक *meṁḍak* [*maṇḍukka-; Pk. *maṁḍukka-*], m. = मेंढक.

1**मेंड़ा** *meṁṛā* [cf. H. *meṁṛ*], m. reg. edge or parapet of a well.

2**मेंड़ा** *meṁṛā*, m. reg. = मेंढ़ा, 2.

मेंड़ियाना *meṁṛiyānā* [cf. H. *meṁṛ*], v.t. to skirt, or to enclose (a field, &c.), with a bank or ridge of ground.

मेंड़ी *meṁṛī*, f. reg. = मेंढ़ी.

मेंढक *meṁḍhak* [conn. *maṇḍūka-* and H. *meṁḍak*], m. a frog.

मेंढकी *meṁḍhkī* [cf. H. *meṁḍhak*], f. a frog.

मेंढ़ल *meṁṛhal*, m. *Pl.* **1.** the fever-nut, *Caesalpinia bonducella* (= कटकरंज). **2.** a firework made out of the fever-nut.

मेंढ़ा *meṁṛhā* [*meṇḍhaka-*, Pk. *meṁḍha-*], m. **1.** a ram. **2.** reg. a billy-goat.

मेंढ़ी *meṁṛhī* [cf. H. *meṁṛhā*], f. reg. a nanny-goat with curling horns.

मेंढुक *meṁḍhuk*, m. reg. = मेंढक.

मेंबरी *membārī* [cf. Engl. *member* (→ H.)], f. membership.

1**मेंह** *meṁh* [*megha-*], m. rain. — ~ आना, rain to come, or to threaten. ~ छूटना, to rain (hard). ~ बरसना, or पड़ना, rain to fall.

2**मेंह** *meṁh* [*methī̆-*]. reg. (Bihar) post to which oxen are tied while treading out grain.

मेंहदी *meṁhdī*, f. = मेहँदी.

मेख़ *mekh* [P. *mekh*], f. **1.** a peg, pin; nail. **2.** stake. — ~ ठोंकना, to drive a nail, &c. (into, में); to impale, to crucify; to spike (a gun). ~ मारना (में), = prec., 1.; to block, to thwart, to spoil (a plan).

मेखला *mekhălā* [S.], f. **1.** belt, girdle. **2.** sword-belt. **2.** *hind.* sacred thread (= जनेऊ). **3.** fig. slope of a mountain.

1**मेखली** *mekhălī* [S.], adj. & m. *Pl. HŚS.* **1.** adj. wearing a belt, &c. **2.** m. *hist.* an unmarried brāhmaṇ student.

2**मेखली** *mekhlī*, f. **1.** sack-cloth. **2.** a cape-like covering which leaves the arms free.

3**मेखली** *mekhălī*, f. a belt (cf. मेखला).

मेगज़ीन *megzīn* [Engl. *magazine*], m. **1.** magazine, arsenal. **2.** magazine (of a firearm). *3. magazine, journal.

मेघ *megh* [S.], m. **1.** a cloud. **2.** *mus.* name of a *rāg* (associated with the rainy season and the hours before dawn). — **मेघ-डंबर**, m. thunder; mass, or shadow of clouds; canopy; the umbrella of Indra; a large, high tent; palanquin. **मेघ-नाद**, m. cloud-noise: thunder; *mythol.* name of a son of Rāvaṇ. **मेघ-माल**, f. Brbh. = next. **मेघ-माला**, f. a mass of clouds. **मेघ-राग**, m. *mus.* name of a *rāg.* **मेघ-राज**, m. cloud-king: Indra (causer of thunder). **मेघ-वर्तक**, m. *mythol.* name of a cloud supposed to appear when the dissolution of the world is impending. **मेघ-श्याम**, adj. cloud-dark (esp. the body of Kṛṣṇa). **मेघाच्छन्न** [°*gha*+*ā*°], adj. overspread with clouds. °**-आच्छादित**, adj. id. **मेघाडंबर** [°*gha*+*ā*°], m. = **मेघ-डंबर**. **मेघावरि** [°*gh*+*ā*°], f. Av. mass of clouds.

मेचक *mecak* [S.], adj. & m. **1.** adj. dark blue, dark, black. **2.** m. darkness, &c.

मेचकताई *mecakātāī* [cf. H. *mecak*], f. Av. darkness, &c. (= **मेचक**).

मेज़ *mez* [P. *mez*], f. a table. — **मेज़-कुरसी**, f. table and chairs. **मेज़पोश** [P. *-poś*], m. tablecloth. **मेज़बान** [P. *-bān*], m. master of a house, or feast; host. °**ई**, f. entertainment (of guests), hospitality.

मेझुकी *mejhukī*, f. reg. (Bihar) an inflammation between the teeth (in animals).

[1]**मेट** *meṭ* [cf. *mārttika-*], m. reg. (? E.) = [2]**मीता**.

[2]**मेट** *meṭ* [Engl. *mate*], m. **1.** mate (of a ship's crew). **2.** foreman.

मेटना *meṭnā* [cf. H. *miṭnā*], v.t. **1.** to erase, to efface. **2.** to destroy utterly. **3.** to annul, to cancel.

मेटा *meṭā* [cf. *mārttika-*], m. reg. (Bihar) an earthen pitcher.

मेटी *meṭī* [cf. H. *meṭā*], f. reg. a small earthen pot or pitcher.

मेटुला *meṭulā* [S.], f. *Pl. HŚS.* the myrobalan tree (= **आमलक**).

मेड़ *meṛ*, f. see **मेंड़**.

मेढ *meḍh*, m. *Pl.* gleanings of corn left on the field.

मेढक *meḍhak*, m. = **मेंढक**.

मेढ़ा *meṛhā* [*meṇḍhaka-*, Pk. *meṁḍha-*], m. a ram.

मेढी *meḍhī* [*meṭhī-*], f. reg. (W). post to which oxen are tied while treading out grain.

मेढ़ी *meṛhī*, f. E.H. a woman's hair braided in three strands.

मेथी *methī* [**metthī-*, *methī-*: ← Drav.], f. fenugreek.

[1]**मेद** *med* [S.], m. Brbh. **1.** fat; fatness. **2.** secretion: musk.

[2]**मेद** *med* [ad. *medā-*], m. Av. = [2]**मैदा**.

मेदस्वी *medasvī* [S.], adj. fat.

मेदा *medā* [*mi'dā*], m. the stomach. — ~ **कड़ा होना**, to be constipated.

मेदिनी *medinī* [S.], f. what is fat, or fertile: **1.** Brbh. Av. the earth, the world. **2.** a body of pilgrims going to visit the tomb of a saint; reg. (W.) a village festival.

मेदुर *medur*, f. a grass.

[1]**मेध** *medh* [S.], m. sacrificial offering, sacrifice.

[2]**मेध** *medh* [ad. *medhī-*: w. H. [2]*meṁh*], f. *Pl.* = **मेढी**.

[3]**मेध** *medh*, m. reg. (W). rinderpest (a complaint of cattle).

मेधा *medhā* [S.], f. mental power, intelligence; wisdom; judgment.

मेधावी *medhāvī* [S.], adj. **1.** intelligent. **2.** wise; judicious. **3.** learned.

मेम *mem* [Engl. *ma(da)m*], f. madam: **1.** a European woman. **2.** (in cards) the queen. — **मेम-साहब**, f. = ~, 1. °**आ**, f. voc. hon. good lady.

मेमना *memnā* [onom.], m. **1.** a kid. **2.** a lamb.

मेरा *merā* [cf. *ma-*, and Pk. *maeṁ*], adj. my; mine.

मेराज *merāj* [A. *mi'rāj*], f. *Theol.* E.H. **1.** a ladder. **2.** ascent to heaven.

मेरु *meru* [S.], m. **1.** *mythol.* mount Meru (said to form the central point of *Jambudvīpa*). **2.** transf. the largest bead in a rosary (with which telling starts and ends). — **मेरु-दंड**, m. backbone; bulwark, support; axis (of the earth). °**ई**, adj. vertebrate.

मेमार *memār* [A. *mi'mār*], *Pl. HŚS.* a stonemason.

मेल *mel* [cf. H. *melnā*: or *mela-*], m. **1.** meeting; assembly. **2.** mixture, mixing. **3.** connection; association (with, **से**), combination. **4.** concord, harmony. **5.** reconciliation. **6.** consistency, balance, proportion (between parts); similarity. **7.** counterpart; kind, sort. **8.** balance (as of an account); tally. **9.** band, company; union, alliance. — ~ **करना**, to unite or to combine (with, **से** or **के साथ**); to mix or to associate (with).~ **का**, adj. of matching kind or type; congenial; sociable. ~ **खाना**, to unite or to mix (with, से); to pair (with), to match; to accord, or to be in harmony (with); to find congenial. ~ बैठना, harmony or congruence, &c. to exist (between, में). ~ बैठाना (में), to concert in common (as interests). ~ रहना, similarity, &c. to exist (between, में). मेल-जोल, m. familiarity, friendly terms. मेल-मिलाप, m. combination, unison; conciliation; reconcilation; = मेल-जोल. मेल-मुलाहज़ा, m. a compromise. मेल-मुलाक़ात, f. = मेल-जोल.

मेल- *mel-* [*melayati*], v.t. Brbh. Av. to cause to come together: **1.** to put (in), to mix (with). **2.** to put (on). **3.** to send.

मेलन *melan* [S.], m. usu. in comp. **1.** meeting, assembling, associating (with). **2.** a gathering.

मेला *melā* [*melaka-*], m. **1.** a large crowd of people. ***2.** a fair (religious, or secular), festival. **3.** a market held regularly at a fixed place. — ~ करना, to hold a fair; to convene a large gathering. ~ जुड़ना, or लगना, a large crowd to assemble; a fair to be held. – मेला-ठेला, m. jostling and pushing; a jostling, or festive, crowd. मेला-तमाशा, m. = ~, 1., 2.

मेलान *melān* [cf. H. *mel-*], m. **1.** reg. (Bihar) irrigation of land direct from a canal (by cutting the bank). **2.** *Pl.* the herding and feeding of cattle at night.

मेलानी *melānī* [cf. H. *melān*], f. reg. (Bihar) land irrigated from a tank or pond.

मेल्हना *melhnā* v.i. to be idle; to toss and turn (= करवट लेना).

मेली *melī* [cf. H. *mel*], adj. & m. **1.** adj. friendly, sociable. **2.** congenial. **3.** similar (as in type, interests). **4.** m. a friendly or sociable person; friend, acquaintance. — मेली-मुलाक़ाती, m.pl. acquaintances, friends.

मेवड़ी *mevṛī*, f. the plant *Vitex*: the chaste-tree (= निर्गुंडी, सँभालू).

मेवा *mevā* [P. *meva*], m. fruit, esp. dried fruit. — मेवादार [P. *-dār*], adj. fruit-bearing; laden with fruit; made with or containing fruit.

[1]**मेवाती** *mevātī*, adj. & f. **1.** adj. of or belonging to Mevāt (in Rajasthan). **2.** the speech of Mevāt.

[2]**मेवाती** *mevātī*, m. **1.** a man of Mevāt. **2.** obs. a Mevātī robber tribesman.

मेष *meṣ* [S.], m. **1.** a ram. **2.** the sign Aries (of the zodiac). — ~ कर-, Brbh. to hesitate (see s.v. मीन. – मेषग, adj. *astron.* having entered Aries (the sun).

मेषा *meṣā* [cf. H. *meṣ*], m. *Pl. HŚS.* skin of a sheep or goat; kid leather.

[1]**मेह** *meh* [S.], m. **1.** urine. **2.** diabetes.

मेह *meh* [conn. *meṣa-*[2]], m. *Pl. HŚS.* a ram (= मेष).

मेहँदी *mehaṁdī* [conn. *mendhikā-*], f. **1.** the henna plant (powdered leaves of which are made into a paste with catechu and used esp. by women to dye their hands and feet). **2.** transf. the marriage feast when the bride's hands and feet are dyed with henna. — ~ रचाना, or लगाना, to apply henna (to).

मेहतर *mehtar* [P. *mihtar*; ? × *mahattara-*], m. euph. a sweeper.

मेहतराई *mehtrāī* [cf. H. *mehtar*], f. reg. earnings or perquisites of a sweeper.

मेहतरानी *mehtrānī* [cf. H. *mehtar*], f. **1.** a sweeper's wife. **2.** a woman sweeper.

मेहनत *mehnat* [A. *miḥna*: P. *mĕḥnat*], f. **1.** labour, work; toil. **2.** industry, application. — ~ उठाना, to exert oneself, to take pains. ~ करना, to work hard (for or after, के पीछे). ~ ठिकाने लगना, hard work to bring its reward. – मेहनतकश [P. *-kaś*], adj. labouring, drudging. मेहनत-मज़दूरी, f. work and wages; day-labour.

मेहनताना *mehntānā* [P. *mĕḥnatāna*], m. **1.** wages. **2.** fee, fees (for services).

मेहनती *mehntī* [A. *miḥnat*+P. *-ī*], adj. hardworking, industrious.

मेहना *mehnā* [*methana-*], m. poking fun, taunting. — ~ फेंकना, to taunt.

मेहमान *mehmān* [P. *mĕhmān*], m. **1.** a guest. **2.** a son-in-law. — चार दिन का, or थोड़ी देर का, ~, m. a fleeting guest (in this world: man). – मेहमान-ख़ाना, m. guests' quarter; inn; reception-room. मेहमानदार [P. *-dār*], adj. hospitable. °ई, f. मेहमानदारी करना (की), to entertain guests. मेहमाननवाज़ [P. *-navāz*], adj. = मेहमानदार. °ई, f. मेहमानबाज़ी [P. *-bāzī*], f. giving hospitality.

मेहमानी *mehmānī* [P. *mĕhmānī*], f. entertainment of guests; hospitality. — ~ करना, to entertain (guests), to treat hospitably.

मेहरबान *mehrbān* [P. *mĕhrbān*], adj. **1.** kind, benevolent. **2.** compassionate, merciful. — ~ होना, to be kind, &c.; to favour (as with a visit, &c).

मेहरबानी *mehrbānī* [P. *mĕhrbānī*], f. kindness, favour. — ~ करके, adv. by (your) kindness. ~ से पेश आना, to show kindness. आपकी ~ (है), it is very kind of you.

मेहरा *mehrā* [*mahilā-*], m. **1.** [? ad. *mahilā-*], an effeminate man. **2.** a servant having access to women's quarters (= [1]महरा).

मेहराब *mehrāb* [A. *mihrāb*], f. an arch. — **मेहराबदार** [P. *-dār*], adj. having an arch, or arches, arched; bowed (as a window, or a drill).

मेहराबी *mehrābī* [*mihrāb*+P. *-ī*], adj. = मेहराबदार.

मेहरारू *mehrārū* [**mahilārūpa-*], f. reg. = मेहरी.

मेहरी *mehrī* [cf. *mahilā-*], f. reg. (E.) **1.** woman (= महरी). **2.** wife.

मैं *maiṁ* [cf. *mayā*: Pk. *maïṁ*], pron. I. — ~ ~ **करना**, to be egotistical, full of oneself.

मैंढ़ *maiṁṛh*, m. *Pl.* reg. gleanings of corn left on a field.

मैंढ़ल *maiṁṛhal*, m. *Pl.* = मेंढ़ल.

[1]**मै** *mai* [P. *mai*], f. wine. — **मैकश** [P. *-kaś*], m. a drinker, drunkard. °ई, f. drinking; carousal; drunkenness. **मै-ख़ाना**, m. tavern; liquor-shop. **मैपरस्त** [P. *-parast*], adj. & m. very fond of, or addicted to, alcohol. °ई, f. fondness of alcohol, &c.

[2]**मै** *mai*, m. reg. (W.) **1.** a plank-harrow, clod-crusher. **2.** *Pl.* a ladder.

मैका *maikā*, m. = मायका.

[1]**मैड़ा** *maiṛā* [*mayaṭa-*, Pk. *mayaḍa-*], m. a platform for watching crops from.

[2]**मैड़ा** *maiṛā* [cf. H. [2]*mai*], m. reg. (W.) a plank-harrow, clod-crusher.

मैत्र *maitr* [S.], adj. & m. **1.** adj. of or belonging to a friend. **2.** amicable.

मैत्री *maitrī* [S.], f. friendship, friendliness. — **मैत्रीपूर्ण**, adj. friendly, amicable.

मैथिल *maithil* [S.], adj. of or belonging to Mithilā (N.E. Bihar).

मैथिली *maithilī* [S.], f. **1.** the speech or language of Mithilā (N.E. Bihar). **2.** *mythol.* a title of Sītā.

मैथुन *maithun* [S.], m. coupled: sexual intercourse.

मैथुनिक *maithunik* [S.], adj. having to do with sexual intercourse; sexual.

मैथुनी *maithunī* [S.], adj. having sexual intercourse.

[1]**मैदा** *maidā* [P. *maida*], m. fine flour. — ~ **करना**, to grind very fine.

[2]**मैदा** *maidā* [ad. *medā-*], m. *Pl.* a root resembling ginger and used in a drug (esp. against fever and tuberculosis).

मैदान *maidān* [P. *maidān*], m. **1.** flat, open field, open area; large lawn; race-ground; playing-field. **2.** plain. **3.** transf. & fig. field of battle; field of conflict, or activity. **4.** a parade. — ~ **करना**, to convert into a plain, to level (an area); to raze (a building). ~ **छोड़ना**, to leave the field; to take flight. ~ **जाना**, euph. to go to defecate. ~ **जीतना**, or **मारना**, to win a field, to win the day. ~ **देना (को)**, to give ample space (to); to give a wide berth (to). ~ **में**, adv. in the plain; in the open. ~ **में आना**, to come into the field, &c. (esp. to fight). ~ **में उतरना**, to enter a fight, a quarrel, or a war. **खुले** ~ **(में)**, adv. in the open, out in the open. — **मैदाने-जंग**, m. = ~, 3., 1.

मैदानी *maidānī* [P. *maidānī*], adj. having to do with, or used in, a field or area (esp. of battle: as a field hospital, field gun).

मैन *main* [*madana-*[1]], m. Brbh. **1.** a title of Kāmdev, the god of love (= मदन). **2.** wax; a mixture of wax and gum-resin (used in making moulds). — **मैन-फल**, m. the fruit of the plant *Vangueria spinosa* (used as an emetic); seed of *Strychnos nux vomica.*

मैनसिल *mainsil* [f. H. *mansil*; ? × H. *main*], m. red orpiment (mineral sulphide of arsenic).

मैना *mainā* [*madana-*[2]], m. **1.** a mynah (a kind of starling). **2.** colloq. darling (term of endearment used to children). — **अबलग (अबलक़)** ~, m. the pied starling, *Sturnus contra.* **आगा** ~, m. superior mynah: a talking mynah. **गंगा** ~, m. the bank mynah, *Acridotheres ginginianus.* **गुलाबी** ~, m. the rose-coloured starling, *Sturnus roseus.* **पहाड़ी** ~, m. the black hill mynah, *Gracula religiosa.* **बाह्मनी** ~, m. the black-headed mynah, *Sturnus pagodarum.* **तेलिया** ~, m. the common starling.

मैनाक *maināk* [S.], m. Brbh. *mythol.* name of a mountain (son of Himavat by Menā).

मैभा *maibhā*, f. reg. stepmother.

मैया *maiyā* [cf. H. [1]*māṁ*], f. dim. mother.

मैयत *maiyat* [A. *maiyit*], f. U. a corpse.

मैल *mail* [cf. **malin-*: Pk. *mali-*, and *maïla-*], f. **1.** dirt; filth; scum, refuse. **2.** baseness, pollution; rust. **3.** fig. ill-will. **4.** fig. sadness. — ~ **काटना (की)**, to refine, to purify (a substance); to wash (clothes). ~ **छाँटना (की)**, to refine (a substance); to strain; to purify; to wash (clothes). **मन में** ~ **रखना**, to nurse ill-will, or a grudge. **मन में** ~ **लाना**, to be sad, or sorry. – **मैलख़ोरा** [P. *-khora*], adj. & m. dark or dull-coloured; an overall; undergarment; saddle-pad.

मैला *mailā* [**malin-*: cf. Pk. *mali-*, and *maïla-*], adj. & m. **1.** adj. dirty; foul; offensive.

2. defiled, polluted; faded (as flowers); rusty. 3. fig. clouded (the heart); sad. 4. m. dirt; filth. — ~ करना, to dirty (sthg.); to defecate. मैले सिर से होना, to be with the head unwashed: to be menstruating. – मैला-कुचैला, adj. dirty and ragged; very dirty.

मैलापन *mailāpan* [cf. H. *mailā*], m. 1. dirtiness. 2. foulness.

मों *mom* [H. *maham*], ppn. Brbh. Av. = में.

मोंढ़ा *momṛhā* [**moṭha-*[2]], m. a seat, or stool, esp. three-legged (made of cane, or reeds, and cord).

मो *mo*, obl. base. 1. = मुझ. 2. Brbh. = मेरा.

मोइया *moiyā*, m. *Pl.* a skein of thread.

[1]**मोई** *moī* [? cf. *modaka-*; and P. *māya*, H. *māvā*], m. flour soaked in *ghī* and then dyed, for use in making chintz patterns.

[2]**मोई** *moī* [? cf. *modaka-*], f. reg. (Raj). a medicinal powder made from poppy-heads or from hemp, with other ingredients.

मोकला *moklā* [cf. **mukna*: Pa. *mukka-*; ? × *mokṣa-*], adj. opened, extended; unrestricted.

मोक्ष *mokṣ* [S.], m. 1. release from rebirth in the world. 2. deliverance, emancipation; release. — मोक्षदायक, adj. & m. giving or causing release, &c.; deliverer, saviour.

मोक्षक *mokṣak* [S.], m. deliverer, saviour.

मोक्षण *mokṣaṇ* [S.], m. releasing, delivering; release, deliverance.

मोक्षित *mokṣit* [S.], adj. released, liberated.

मोक्ष्य *mokṣyă* [S.], adj. deserving of release, &c.

मोख *mokh* [*mokṣa-*], m. Brbh. Av. = मोक्ष.

मोखा *mokhā* [? *mokṣa-*], m. 1. an air-hole, ventilator (in a wall or roof). 2. a peep-hole. 3. drainage hole (in wall).

मोगरा *mogrā* [**modgara-*: Pk. *moggara-*], m. 1. a mallet. 2. a partic. jasmine, the double jasmine.

मोगरी *mogrī* [cf. H. *mogrā*], f. a small mallet.

मोघ *mogh* [S.], adj. vain, useless; unprofitable.

मोघा *moghā* [S.], f. (?) m. *Pl. HŚS.* the trumpet-flower, *Bignonia suaevolens.*

[1]**मोच** *moc* [cf. H. *mocnā*], f. a sprain, strain; twist. — ~ आना (को), to be sprained, &c.

[2]**मोच** *moc* [S.], m. name of several trees and plants. — मोच-रस, m. resin of the *semal* tree (used medicinally).

मोच- *moc-* [cf. *mucyate*], v.t. Brbh. 1. to release. 2. reg. to extinguish.

मोचक *mocak* [S.], adj. & m. 1. adj. liberating. 2. m. *Pl. HŚS.* an ascetic, a devotee.

[1]**मोचन** *mocan* [cf. H. *mocī*], f. a shoemakers's wife.

[2]**मोचन** *mocan* [S.], m. 1. releasing, liberating. 2. release, freedom. 3. redemption (as of a bond).

[1]**मोचना** *mocnā* [**mocc-*], v.t. reg. to pinch, to nip.

[2]**मोचना** *mocnā* [cf. H. [1]*mocnā*], m. reg. 1. a pair of forceps, pincers. 2. (W.) a pair of tweezers.

मोचनी *mocnī* [cf. H. [2]*mocnā*], f. *Pl.* a pair of tweezers.

मोचयिता *mocayitā* [S.], m. inv. deliverer.

मोचा *mocā* [S.], f. *Pl. HŚS.* 1. the banana, *Musa sapientum*. 2. the silk-cotton (*semal*) tree.

मोचिनि *mocini*, f. E.H. = [1]मोचन.

मोची *mocī* [*mocika-*: ← Ir.], m. 1. a leather worker, a shoemaker. 2. obs. saddler.

मोज़ा *mozā* [P. *moza*], m. stocking, sock.

मोजिज़ा *mojizā* [A. *mu'jiza*], m. U. a miracle (performed by a prophet: cf. करामत). — ~ करना, or दिखाना, to perform or to show a miracle. मोजिज़े का, adj. miraculous.

मोट *moṭ* [**moṭṭa-*[2]: ← Drav.], f. m. 1. bundle, load. 2. reg. a leather bucket used in irrigation. — ~ का ~ बेचना, to sell the entire bundle or load; to sell wholesale.

मोटकी *moṭkī*, f. reg. heavy tool: a mattock, a pickaxe.

मोटमरदी *moṭmardī*, f. = गुटमरदी.

मोटला *moṭlā* [cf. H. *moṭā*], adj. reg. = मोटा.

मोटा *moṭā* [**moṭṭa-*[1]], adj. 1. fat. 2. large, bulky; heavy (a coat); thick; stout, heavy (a stick). 3. coarse (grain, texture, consistency); rough. 4. approximate. मोटे तौर पर, adv. roughly; in general. 5. inferior (in quality); dull (of mind), stupid. 6. massive (in quantity). 7. important; self-important. 8. plain, evident (a matter); gross, glaring (an error). 9. bold (lettering, hand); capital (a letter). — ~ आसामी, m. a wealthy or well-to-do person. ~ दिखाई देना (को), to have bad sight. मोटी चिड़िया, f. colloq. an important person; a wealthy client. मोटी नज़र, f. a casual or inattentive look. — मोटा-झोटा, adj. coarse, rough, poor (of food, clothing). मोटा-ताज़ा, adj. plump, well-fed, sleek. – मोटा-मोटी, adv. approximately, roughly.

मोटाई *moṭāī* [cf. H. *moṭā*], f. = मुटापा, मोटापन.

मोटाना *moṭānā* [cf. H. *moṭā*], v.i. to grow fat; to grow rich, or important.

मोटापन *moṭāpan* [cf. H. *moṭā*], m. **1.** fatness. **2.** bulk, &c. **3.** self-importance.

मोटापा *moṭāpā* [cf. H. *moṭā*], m. = मुटापा, मोटापन.

मोटिया *moṭiyā* [cf. H. *moṭ*], m. a porter (= कुली).

मोठ *moṭh* [conn. *makuṣṭa-*], m. a kidney-bean, *Phaseolus aconitifolius*.

मोठड़ा *moṭhṛā* [cf. H. *moṭh*], m. *Pl.* **1.** a kind of printing consisting of *moṭh*-like spots on cloth, leather, &c. **2.** a kind of mixed cotton and silk cloth.

मोड़ *moṛ* [cf. H. *moṛnā*], m. **1.** turn, bend (as of a road, or river); corner (of a street). **2.** a twist, coil. **3.** twist, sprain. **4.** a turning away, or aside. **5.** turning-point (as of a struggle, a process, a life; or of a year); new departure, direction (as in research). **6.** turning back, or over; folding, creasing (as of a page). — **मोड़-तोड़**, m. twists, turns (in a road); fig. deviousness, guile.

मोड़का *moṛkā*, m. *Pl.* sprout, shoot.

मोड़ना *moṛnā* [*moṭati*: ← Drav.], v.t. **1.** to turn, to bend. **2.** to twist; to sprain. **3.** to turn away, or aside; to deflect. **4.** to fold (as the arms). **5.** to fold, to crease (as a page). **6.** to roll up (sleeves). **7.** to twist (meaning or words). **8.** to give back, to return; to take back.

मोड़ा *moṛā* [? **moḍḍa-* or **moṇḍa-*], m. reg. **1.** a person having a shaved head. ***2.** a young boy.

मोढ़ा *moṛhā*, m. = मोंढ़ा.

मोतदिल *motădil* [A. *mu'tadil*], adj. U. **1.** moderate, temperate (of climate). **2.** mild (in effect: as a medicine).

मोतबर *motbar* [A. *mu'tabar*], adj. U. **1.** reliable, trustworthy. **2.** authentic (as information).

मोतबिर *motbir*, adj. corr. = मोतबर.

मोतिया *motiyā* [cf. H. *motī*], adj. **1.** adj. like a pearl, or pearls (in colour, shape); pearly. **2.** m. name of a kind of jasmine. — **मोतिया-बिंद**, f. cataract (of the eye).

मोती *motī* [*mauktika-*], m. **1.** a pearl. **2.** fig. a tear. **3.** a pearl of speech or eloquence. — **~ की-सी आब उतरना**, lustre to be lost: to be disgraced. **~ की सीपी**, pearl-shell: mother-of-pearl. **~ छेदना**, = **~ बींधना**. **~ पिरोना**, to string pearls; to speak eloquently; to shed tears. **~ बींधना**, to pierce a pearl; to have sexual intercourse with a virgin. **~ रोलना**, fig. to coin money. **मोतियों से माँग भरना**, to set the parting of the hair with pearls; to shower wealth (on a woman). – **मोती-चूर**, m. a kind of sweet: droplets coated with crystallised sugar. **मोती-चूर आँख**, f. a bright or shining eye. **मोती-पाक**, m. = next. **मोती-पाग**, m. a sweet made of flour, curds and sugar. **मोती-बेल**, f. jasmine. **मोती-सिरी**, f. Brbh. a pearl necklace.

मोथरा *mothrā* [**motthara-*[2]], m. reg. (W). spavin (in a horse's leg).

मोथा *mothā* [**mosta-*: Pk. *motthā-*, f.], m. a kind of grass, *Cyperus rotundus*, and its tuberous root.

मोथी *mothī* [**mosta-*: Pk. *motthā-*], f. **1.** reg. (Bihar) a grass. **2.** *Pl.* a kind of sweet, yellow, leguminous seed.

मोद *mod* [S.], m. **1.** pleasure, delight. **2.** transf. Av. songs of joy. **3.** Brbh. fragrance.

मोदक *modak* [S.], adj. & m. **1.** adj. gladdening, delighting. **2.** m. one who causes joy or delight. **3.** a kind of small, round sweet. **4.** reg. molasses. **5.** a medication, pill.

मोदन *modan* [S.], m. **1.** causing delight. **2.** Brbh. making fragrant, perfuming.

मोदित *modit* [S.], adj. = मुदित.

मोदी *modī*, m. a grocer, merchant. — **मोदी-ख़ाना**, m. grocer's or merchant's shop, store.

मोधू *modhū* [cf. **moddha-*], reg. simple, stupid.

मोनी *monī*, f. *Pl.* reg. point, tip, end.

मोम *mom* [P. *mūm*], m. wax. — **~ करना**, to make into wax: to make soft or pliable; fig. to melt, to move. – **~ की नाक**, f. wax-nose: one whose opinions or viewpoint are easily changed. **~ की मरियम**, f. a tender-hearted woman. — **मोम-जामा**, m. waxed cloth; oil-skin. **मोमदिल**, adj. tender-hearted, compassionate. **मोम-बत्ती**, f. wax candle. **मोम-रोग़न**, m. wax and oil (mixed): furniture polish.

मोमिन *momin* [A. *mu'min*], adj. & m. U. **1.** adj. believing, orthodox (a Muslim). **2.** m. *musl.* a believer. **3.** a Muslim weaver.

मोमिया *momiyā* [P. *mūmiyā*], m. **1.** a mummy. **2.** a preservative used in embalming.

मोमियाई *momiyāī* [P. *mūmiyāī*], f. a mineral tar salve used in treating wounds. — **~ निकालना**, to beat (one, **की**) to a jelly.

मोमी *momī* [P. *mūmī*], adj. **1.** waxen; soft as wax; wax-coloured. **2.** easily melted (a substance); made with wax (imitation pearls).

3. sized (chintz). — ~ काग़ज़, m. wax paper; tracing paper.

¹**मोर** *mor* [**mora-*: Pa. *mora-*], m. a peacock. — मोर-चंदा, m. Brbh. the moon or eye in a peacock's tail-feather; a peacock's tail-feather (as worn by Kṛṣṇa). °-चंद्रिका, f. id. मोर-चाल, f. walking on the hands, with the feet in the air. मोर-छल, m. whisk or fan of peacock feathers. मोर-पंख, m. a peacock's wing, or feather. °-पंखी, adj. deep blue; m. a deep blue colour; f. a fan (sc. of peacock feathers); *Pl. HŚS.* a pleasure-boat, barge (having a peacock figure-head). मोर-मुकुट, m. peacock's crest; crest or crown of one or more peacock feathers (as worn by Kṛṣṇa).

²**मोर** *mor*, adj. Av. (Brbh.) = मेरा.

¹**मोरचा** *morcā* [P. *morca*], m. **1.** entrenchment; fortification; emplacement. **2.** front (line); place of battle. **3.** transf. (political) front. — ~ जमना, fig. a contentious issue to emerge. ~ जीतना, m. to capture an entrenchment, redoubt, &c. ~ मारना, id.; to wrangle, to bandy words (with, से). ~ लेना (का), = ~ जीतना; to oppose; to make headway (against), to gain ground. मोरचे पर, adv. on, or in, the trenches, &c. संगठित, or संयुक्त, ~, m. a united front. – मोरचाबंद [P. *-band*], adj. entrenched, fortified. °ई, f.

²**मोरचा** *morcā* [P. *morca*], m. rust. — ~ खाना, to suffer rusting. ~ लगना (पर or को), to rust.

मोरछली *morchalī*, f. reg. = मौलसिरी.

मोरनी *mornī* [cf. **mora-*: Pa. *morinī-*], f. **1.** a peahen. **2.** pendant (of a nose-ring).

¹**मोरा** *morā*, m. reg. = ¹मोर.

²**मोरा** *morā*, adj. E.H. = मेरा.

मोरी *morī* [H. *mohrī*], f. **1.** a drain, open drain; a sewer. **2.** an outlet, opening. **3.** hole. — ~ छूटना, f. colloq. to have diarrhoea. ~ पर जाना, colloq. to go to relieve oneself.

मोर्चा *morcā*, m. see मोरचा.

मोल *mol* [*maulya-*], m. price; value, worth. — ~ करना, to bargain; to settle a price, or value (of, का). ~ चढ़ाना (का), to raise a price; to bid (against, as at auction); to outbid. ~ देना (को), to give for a price: to sell (to). ~ तोड़ना (का), to beat down a price; to cut a price. ~ लगाना (का), to fix a price, or value. ~ लेना, to take for a price: to buy; to take on, to incur. – मोल-तोल, m. bargaining, haggling; deal, transaction. मोल-तोल करना, = ~ करना.

मोलना *molnā* [cf. *maulya-*], v.t. reg. to buy (=मोल लेना).

मोस- *mos-* [conn. H. *masosnā*], v.t. **1.** E.H. to twist, to wring (as the neck). **2.** Brbh. = मसोसना.

मोह *moh* [*moha-*], m. **1.** bewilderment. ***2.** delusion (esp. as to the supposed reality of the world); ignorance; folly; error; infatuation; attachment, love. **3.** allurement, charm. — ~ करना, to feel love, affection, or compassion (for, का). ~ में फँसना, to be ensnared by delusion, &c. ~ होना (पर), = ~ करना. – मोह-रात्रि, f. night of bewilderment: *mythol.* dissolution of the world; title given to the night of Kṛṣṇa's birth (the eighth night of the dark half of the month Bhādoṁ). मोहरूपी, adj. delusive; illusory; infatuating; charming. आत्ममोह, m. narcissism.

मोहक *mohak* [S.], adj. enchanting.

मोहताज *mohtāj*, adj. pronun. var. = मुहताज.

मोहन *mohan* [S.], adj. & m. **1.** adj. infatuating, charming. **2.** Brbh. deceiving. **3.** m. enchanter; specif. a title of Kṛṣṇa. **4.** enchanting, enchantment. — मोहन-भोग, m. a kind of sweet (*halvā*) made with sugar, butter and fine flour; a variety of mango. मोहन माला, f. Brbh. a necklace of gold beads; (?) a necklace of gold beads, corals, pearls and *rudrākṣa* seeds.

मोहना *mohnā* [*mohayati*], v.t. & v.i. **1.** v.t. to beguile. **2.** to make infatuated, to charm. **3.** v.i. Brbh..Av. to be deluded; to be charmed; to faint.

¹**मोहनी** *mohnī* [*mohanīya-*; or S.], f. **1.** incantation, spell; magic. **2.** fascination. — ~ डालना, to cast a spell. ~ लगना (को), to be under or to come under a spell.

²**मोहनी** *mohănī* [ad. *mohinī-*], adj. f. & f. **1.** adj. = मोहन, 1. **2.** f. a charming woman. — ~ मूरत, f. enchanting form (specif. of Kṛṣṇa).

मोहर *mohar*, m. = मुहर.

¹**मोहरा** *mohrā*, m. **1.** [cf. *mukha-*] mouth, opening (as of a pot, or a pipe). **2.** [*mukhara-*], front part; van (of an army). — मोहरे पर, adv. in the front, in the van.

²**मोहरा** *mohrā* [P. *muhra*], m. **1.** a piece (in a board game); pawn. **2.** a clay mould. **3.** a vertebra. — मोहरेदार [P. *-dār*], adj. polished, glossy, smooth.

मोहरी *mohrī* [cf. H. ¹*mohrā*], f. **1.** opening, mouth; an outlet pipe (to drain off water); bore (of a rifle barrel). **2.** end, cuff (of trousers). **3.** *Pl.* headstall, bridle.

मोहरो *mohro* [cf. *mukha-*], m. Brbh. bridle, or headstall (cf. ¹मोहरा).

मोहलत *mohlat* [A. *muhla*: P. *mŏhlat*], f. **1.** a delay, deferment granted for an appointed period; extension (as of time to pay). **2.** time, leisure. — ~ देना (को), to allow time (for, की). ~ मिलना (को), to be allowed time.

मोहल्ला *mohallā*, m. pronun. var. = मुहल्ला.

मोहित *mohit* [S.], adj. **1.** infatuated; charmed (by, पर or से). **2.** deluded.

मोहिनी *mohinī* [S.], f. 1. = ²मोहनी. 2. = ¹मोहनी.

मोही *mohī* [S.], adj. **1.** bewildering. **2.** beguiling, deluding. **3.** charming. **4.** infatuated (as the heart).

मौंजी *mauñjī* [S.], f. the brahmanical sacred thread (= जनेऊ). — मौंजी-बंधन, m. investiture with the sacred thread.

मौंड़ा *mauṁṛā*, m. Brbh. = मोड़ा, 2.

मौक़ा *mauqā* [A. *mauqa'*], m. **1.** site of any occurrence, or incident; an incident, accident. ★**2.** fit place, or time: opportunity, occasion; chance. — ~ देखना, or ताकना, to watch for an opportunity (to, का). ~ निकल जाना, an opportunity to be lost. ~ मिलना, or लगना (को), an opportunity or chance to arise. ~ हाथ लगना (के), = ~ मिलना. मौक़े का, adj. opportune, advantageous; proper, fit. मौक़े को हाथ से देना, to let slip an opportunity. मौक़े पर, adv. in the right place; at the right time; on occasion. मौक़े पर आना, to come to or to reach the scene (of an accident, &c). मौक़े से, adv. opportunely; timely. –मौक़ापरस्त [P. *-parast*], adj. & m. opportunist. °ई, f. opportunism. मौक़ाबाज़ [P. *-bāz*], m. an opportunist. मौक़े-बेमौक़े, adv. appropriately or not, regardless of circumstances.

मौक़ूफ़ *mauqūf* [A.*mauqūf*], adj. **1.** stopped, abolished (a practice). **2.** suspended (from a post); dismissed. **3.** postponed. **4.** dependent (on, पर).

मौक़ूफ़ी *mauqūfī* [A. *mauqūf*+P. *-ī*], f. abolition, &c. (see मौक़ूफ़).

मौखिक *maukhik* [S.], adj. **1.** given by word of mouth, spoken; oral (an examination). **2.** vocal (as opposed to instrumental).

मौख्य *maukhyă* [S.], m. = मुख्यता.

मौज *mauj* [A. *mauj*], f. **1.** a wave. **2.** surge (of emotion); ecstasy; delight. **3.** whim. — ~ आना (को), an idea or whim to come into the mind; to be moved, or thrilled. ~ करना, to surge (the sea); to be capricious; to enjoy oneself without restraint. ~ मारना, id., 2., 3. ~ में आना, to become excited, or ecstatic. मन की ~, f. a whim, an impulse.

मौज़ा *mauzā* [A. *mauẓa'*], m. place, site: village.

मौजी *maujī* [A. *mauj*+P. *-ī*], adj. **1.** whimsical; capricious. **2.** emotional, temperamental. **3.** happy, good-tempered.

मौज़ूँ *maujūṁ* [A. *mauẓū'*], adj. placed: fitting, suitable.

मौजूद *maujūd* [A. *maujūd*], adj. **1.** present; at hand, ready; available. **2.** existent. — ~ करना, to bring before, to produce; to provide, to supply. ~ रहना, to be present; to remain in attendance; to continue; to exist.

मौजूदगी *maujūdăgī* [P. *maujūdagī*], f. **1.** presence. **2.** existence. — ~ में, adv. in the presence (of, की); during the existence (of).

मौजूदा *maujūdā* [A. *maujūda*], adj. inv. U. present, present-day. existing. — ~ हालत, f. pl. present circumstances.

मौड़ *mauṛ* [*makuṭa-*: ← Drav.], m. **1.** a crown or high-crowned hat worn by a bridegroom at marriage. **2.** a crest; tuft.

मौड़ा *mauṛā*, m. reg. = मोड़ा.

मौत *maut* [A. *maut*], f. **1.** death. **2.** mortality. — ~ का, m. mortal (as a blow); presaging or accompanying death. ~ के घाट उतारना, to despatch from life, to put to death. ~ के मुँह में, staring death in the face. ~ लगना, death to be risked or courted (by, को). ~ सिर पर खेलना, death to be near; death or disaster to be likely. अपनी ~ मरना, to die a natural death.

मौता *mautā* [A. *mauta*], m. reg. **1.** death, a death; the pallor of death. **2.** funeral rites.

मौद्रिक *maudrik* [S.], adj. monetary, fiscal, financial.

मौन *maun* [S.], adj. & m. **1.** adj. silent. **2.** m. silence. **3.** a vow of silence. — ~ बाँधना, or साधना, to remain silent, not to reply. मौनावलंबन [°*na*+*a*°], m. recourse to silence, keeping silent.

मौना *maunā* [cf. ★*madhukuṇḍikā-*], m. *Pl. HŚS.* a beehive: **1.** a large jar, or basket. **2.** [°*kuṇḍaka-*, or °*varṇa-*] reg. (N.) a bee.

मौनी *maunī* [cf. H. *maunā*], m. *Pl. HŚS.* a small round jar, or basket (usu. woven of *mūṁj* or other grass).

मौनी *maunī* [S.], adj. & m. **1.** adj. silent; having vowed silence. **2.** m. an ascetic who has taken a vow of silence. — ~ अमावस्या, f. the new moon of the month of Māgh.

¹मौर *maur* [*mukura-*: ← Drav.], m. Brbh. **1.** bud. **2.** blossom.

[2]**मौर** *maur*, m. = मौड़.

[3]**मौर** *maur* [ad. *mauli-*], m. **1.** Brbh. the head; (?) nape of the neck. **2.** *Pl.* (?) the shoulder.

मौराना *maurānā* [cf. *mukulāyate*], v.i. reg. to blossom; to flourish.

मौरूसी *maurūsī* [A. *maurūṣ*+P. *-ī*], adj. inherited: hereditary; ancestral.

मौल *maul* [S.], adj. radical, &c. (= मूल, 8).

मौलना *maulnā*, v.i. & v.t. reg. **1.** v.i. [*mukulāyate*], to blossom. **2.** v.t. [*mukulayati*] to intoxicate (of *bhāṁg*).

मौलवी *maulvī* [cf. A. *maulā*: P. *maulavī*], m. **1.** one learned in Muslim law. ***2.** a learned man; a teacher (esp. of Arabic or Persian).

मौलसरा *maulasrā* [**mātulaśvaśura-*], m. *Pl.* the maternal uncles of a husband and wife (as related to each other).

मौलसरी *maulsarī*, f. = मौलसिरी.

मौलसिरी *maulsirī* [conn. *bakula-*, Pk. *baülasirī-*], f. a large evergreen tree, *Mimusops elengi*, and its fruit (its flowers are used in making perfumes).

मौला *maulā* [A. *maulā*], m. inv. **1.** lord, master. **2.** the Lord, God. — मस्त ~, m. a carefree, happy-go-lucky man. — मौलाना [A. *-nā*], our lord: a title given to learned Muslims. मौला-दौला [A. *daula*], m. a benefactor; a man of liberality.

[1]**मौलाना** *maulānā* [*mukalāyate*], v.i. to bloom, to flower.

[2]**मौलाना** *maulānā*, m. see s.v. मौला.

मौलि *mauli* [S.], m. f. **1.** the head. ***2.** a crown; crest. **3.** a red thread (= कलावा).

मौलिक *maulik* [S.], adj. 1. = मूल, 5., 8. **2.** original (in conception, execution).

मौलिकता *maulikātā* [S.], f. original nature, originality.

मौली *maulī* [ad. *mauli-*], f. 1. = मौलि, 1., 2. **2.** a red thread (= कलावा).

मौलूद *maulūd* [A. *maulūd*], adj. & m. U. **1.** adj. born. **2.** m. birth (esp. of the prophet Muḥammad).

मौलेरा *maulerā* [*mātuleya-* × *-tara-*], adj. *Pl.* = मौसेरा.

मौसम *mausam* [A. *mausim*], m. **1.** time, season (of the year). **2.** the weather. **3.** appropriate time, season (for sthg).

मौसमी *mausămī* [A. *mausim*+P. *-ī*], adj. **1.** of, or happening at, a partic. season. **2.** appropriate to a season, seasonable. **3.** in season (as fruit).

मौसा *mausā* [*mātuḥṣvasṛ-*], m. maternal uncle.

मौसिम *mausim*, m. = मौसम.

मौसी *mausī* [*mātuḥṣvasṛ-*], f. maternal aunt.

मौसूम *mausūm* [A. *mausūm*], adj. U. named, called.

मौसेरा *mauserā* [**mātuḥṣvasṛghara-*], adj. pertaining to, or related to, a maternal aunt. — ~ भाई, मौसेरी बहन, f., m. maternal cousin.

म्याँव *myāṁv*, m. = म्याऊँ.

म्याऊँ *myāūṁ* [onom.], f. mewing (of a cat). — ~ का ठौर, m. cat's muzzle: a dangerous or inaccessible place (for mice). ~ का मुँह, m. id. मेरी बिल्ली और मुझीको ~, see s.v. बिल्ली.

म्यान *myān* [P. *miyān*], m. scabbard, sheath. — ~ में करना, to sheathe (a weapon). ~ से खींचना, to draw (a weapon). ~ से निकलना, or बाहर होना, to be unsheathed; to go beyond bounds; to be beside oneself with anger. – म्यानदार [P. *-dār*], adj. having a sheath, sheathed.

म्यानी *myānī* [P. *miyanı*], f. **1.** an insert (of cloth), gusset. **2.** a mezzanine floor, or flat.

म्यों *myoṁ*, f. = म्याँव.

म्रियमान *mriyămān* [S.], adj. dying.

म्लान *mlān* [S.], adj. **1.** withered, faded. **2.** wearied; languid. **3.** weak, wan (a smile). **4.** dejected, sad. **5.** dirtied, dirty.

म्लानि *mlāni* [S.], f. **1.** withering, fading. **2.** weariness. **3.** dejection. **4.** dirt, filth. **5.** dark areas (of the moon's surface).

म्लेच्छ *mlecch* [S.], adj. & m. **1.** adj. barbarian; non-Aryan; non-Indian. **2.** base; sinful; non-believing. **3.** m. a barbarian, &c. **4.** a base person, &c. — म्लेच्छाक्रांत [°*ccha*+*ā*°], adj. attacked by barbarians.

य

य *ya*, the twenty-sixth consonant of the Devanāgarī syllabary. — **यकार**, m. the sound /y/; the letter **य**.

यंत्र *yantră* [S.], m. **1.** an instrument, appliance. **2.** a machine. **3.** a musical instrument. **4.** an astrological diagram, magic square. **5.** an amulet, charm. — **यंत्रकार**, m. a mechanic. **यंत्र-मंत्र**, m. magic. **यंत्र-मानव**, m. a robot. **यंत्रवत्**, adv. mechanically. **यंत्र-संचालित**, adj. mechanically operated. **यंत्रालय** [°*tra*+*ā*°], m. machine-shop; printing press. **यंत्रीकरण**, m. mechanisation. **°कृत**, adj. mechanised.

यंत्रक *yantrak* [S.], m. a mechanic.

यंत्रणा *yantrăṇā* [S.], f. **1.** torment, suffering. **2.** torture.

यंत्रिका *yantrikā* [S.], f. a small or delicate instrument; gadget.

यंत्रित *yantrit* [S.], adj. **1.** restrained. **2.** fastened, confined. **3.** locked. **4.** mechanised.

यंत्री *yantrī* [S.], m. Brbh. a musician.

यंत्रीकरण *yantrīkaraṇ* [S.], m. see s.v. **यंत्र**.

यंत्रीकृत *yantrīkr̥t* [S.], adj. see s.v. **यंत्र**.

-य *-yă* [S.], suffix (forms adjectives expressing potentiality from verb roots; also m. abstract nouns from nouns or adjectives, with *vr̥ddhi* of root or initial vowel, e.g. **प्राप्य**, obtainable, accessible; **पांडित्य**, learning; **धैर्य**, steadfastness).

यक *yak* [P. *yak*], adj. U. one (= **एक**, q.v. for some cpds). — **यक-अंगी**, m. f. Brbh. having one spouse. **यकजा** [P. *-jā*], adv. in one place, together. **यकक़लम**, adv. entirely; at one stroke, at once, suddenly. **यकायक**, adv. suddenly.

यक़ीन *yaqīn* [A. *yaqīn*], m. & adv. **1.** m. certainty, confidence; conviction. **2.** truth, certain fact. **3.** adv. with certainty, truly. — ~ **आना** (**को**), to be assured, convinced (of, **का**). ~ **करना**, to ascertain; to believe for sure. ~ **कराना**, = ~ **दिलाना**. ~ **जानना**, to know for certain. ~ **दिलाना** (**को**), to cause (one) to believe; to assure (one). ~ **मानना**, to believe for sure. ~ **रखना**, id. ~ **लाना**, to have faith in (**पर**), to give credence (to).

यक़ीनन *yaqīnan* [A. *yaqīnan*], adv. certainly, assuredly.

यक़ीनी *yaqīnī* [A. *yaqīnī*], adj. certain, reliable; trustworthy (as a source).

यक्ष *yakṣ* [S.], m. *mythol.* **1.** a kind of demigod attending Kuvera and guarding his garden and treasures. **2.** a title of Kuvera. — **यक्ष-पति**, m. Brbh. lord of the *yakṣas*: a title of Kuvera.

यक्षन *yakṣan* [cf. H. *yakṣ*], f. Brbh. = [1]**यक्षी**, 1.

यक्षिणी *yakṣiṇī* [S.], f. = [1]**यक्षी**, 1.

[1]**यक्षी** *yakṣī* [S.], f. *mythol.* **1.** a female *yakṣa*. **2.** name of Kuvera's wife.

[2]**यक्षी** *yakṣī* [cf. H. *yakṣ*], Brbh. m. ? worshipper of *yakṣas*.

यक्ष्मा *yakṣmā* [S.], m. inv. tuberculosis. — **यक्ष्मा-ग्रस्त**, adj. attacked by tuberculosis, consumptive.

यक्ष्मी *yakṣmī* [S.], adj. & m. **1.** adj. consumptive. **2.** m. one suffering from tuberculosis.

यख़नी *yakhnī* [P. *yakhnī*], f. **1.** a meat stew. **2.** gravy, sauce (for *pulāv*). — **यख़नी-पुलाव**, m. a *pulāv* with gravy.

यजन *yajan* [S.], m. the act of sacrificing.

यजमान *yajămān* [S.], m. = **जजमान**.

यजमानी *yajămānī* [S.], f. = **जजमानी**.

यजुर्- *yajur-* [S.], m. a sacrificial prayer or formula: — **यजुर्वेद**, m. the Yajur or second of the four Vedas, dealing with sacrificial rites. **°ई**, m. one versed in, or believing in, the Yajurveda.

यज्ञ *yajñă* [S.], m. a sacrificial act; sacrifice, offering. — **यज्ञ-कर्म**, m. sacrificial act, or rite. **यज्ञ-कुंड**, m. fire-pit, altar. **यज्ञ-पशु**, m. sacrificial animal. **यज्ञ-भूमि**, site of, or for, a sacrifice. **यज्ञ-शाला**, f. hall of sacrifice: place for keeping the sacrificial fire; temple. **यज्ञशील**, adj. & m. habitually performing sacrifice; a brāhmaṇ. **यज्ञ-सिद्धि**, f. completion or due performance of a sacrifice, or sacrificial ceremony. **यज्ञ-सूत्र**, m. = **यज्ञोपवीत**. **यज्ञ-स्थान**, m. place of sacrifice, altar. **यज्ञोपवीत** [°*jña*+*u*°], m. the brahmanical sacred thread; investiture of a youth with the sacred thread.

यज्ञीय *yajñīyă* [S.], adj. fit for sacrifice, sacrificial.

यत *yat* [S.], adj. restrained; moderate, temperate.

यतनीय *yatănīyă* [S.], adj. to be striven for.

[1]**यति** *yati* [S.], f. **1.** restraint, check. ***2.** *pros.* caesura.

[2]**यति** *yati* [S.], m. an ascetic. — **यति-धर्म**, m. asceticism, ascetic life.

यतिनी *yatinī* [S.], f. **1.** female ascetic. **2.** a widow.

यती *yatī* [S.], m. = [2]यति.

यतीम *yatīm* [A. *yatīm*], m. an orphan. — **यतीम-ख़ाना**, m. an orphanage.

यतीमी *yatīmī* [A. *yatīm*+P. *-ī*], f. & adj. **1.** f. orphanhood. **2.** adj. orphan-like; sad (expression).

यत्किंचित् *yatkiñcit* [S.], adv. a little (of); to a small extent.

यत्न *yatn* [S.], m. **1.** effort, attempt. **2.** exertion; assiduity, pains. — **यत्नवान**, adj. strenuous, energetic (as an effort); laborious; painstaking. **यत्नशील**, adj. id.

यत्र *yatr* [S.], adv. in the place where; wherever; when; whereas. — **यत्र-तत्र**, adv. in whatsoever place, there: here and there; everywhere.

यथा *yathā* [S.], adv. in the manner which, just as; like; according to. — **~ तथा**, adv. in a suitable way; in any way. – **~ ~**, adv. in whatever manner, however; according as; to whatever extent. – **यथाकथित**, adv. as aforesaid. **यथाकर्तव्य**, adv. as (is) proper to be done. **यथाकाम**, adj. according to (one's) wish. **°ई**, adj. & m. self-willed; a wilful or wayward person. **यथाकाल**, adv. according to time: at the right time, opportunely. **यथाक्रम**, adv. in proper order or sequence; systematically. **यथात्मक** [°*thā*+*ā*°], adj. natural. **यथानियम**, adv. according to rule or practice. **यथापूर्व**, adj. as previously, previous. **यथापूर्व स्थिति**, f. the status quo. **यथाभाग**, adj. *HŚS.* proportional; appropriate. **यथामूल्य**, adj. in relation to value. **यथायोग्य**, adj. according with what is proper: suitable; deserved. **यथार्थ** [°*thā*+*a*°], m. see s.v. **यथालाभ**, adj. Brbh. as much as may be obtained or occur. **यथावत्**, adv. as previously; properly. **यथावश्यकता** [°*thā*+*ā*°], f. as necessary. **यथावस्थित** [°*thā*+*a*°], adj. restored to its previous state. **यथाविधि**, adv. according to precept or rule; properly. **यथाशक्ति**, adv. as far as strength allows: as far as possible. **यथाशीघ्र**, adv. as quickly as possible. **यथासंभव**, adv. as far as possible; as...as possible. **यथासमय**, adv. timely; as far as time, or the time, allows. **यथासाध्य**, adv. as far as practicable, or possible. **यथास्थान**, adv. each in (his, &c.) proper place. **यथास्थिति**, f. status quo. **यथेष्ट** [°*thā*+*i*°], adj. as wished: enough, sufficient. **यथोचित** [°*thā*+*u*°], adj. suitable, fitting, proper.

यथार्थ *yathârth* [S.], adj. & m. **1.** adj. in accordance with reality: real, actual, genuine; true (as sthg. said); realistic (as an account, a portrayal). **2.** objective; dispassionate. **3.** m. reality; objectivity. — **~ में**, adv. in reality; in effect. – **यथार्थतः**, adv. in reality. **यथार्थदर्शिता**, f. realism of view. **यथार्थवाद**, m. realism (of attitude). **°ई**, adj. & m. realistic; down-to-earth; dispassionate; a realist. **°-वादिता**, f. adherence to reality, realism (as in argument); objectivity. **यथार्थोन्मुख** [°*tha*+*u*°], adj. characterised by realism, realistic (a viewpoint).

यथार्थता *yathârthătā* [S.], f. **1.** accordance with reality: real or factual nature; genuineness; truth; fact. **2.** reality. **3.** objectivity; dispassionateness.

यथेष्ट *yathêṣṭ* [S.], adj. see s.v. **यथा**.

यदपि *yadăpi* [S.], conj. = **यद्यपि**.

यदा *yadā* [S.], adv. at the time when; whenever. — **यदा-कदा**, adv. from time to time.

यदावधि *yadâvădhi* [S.], adv. *Pl.* **1.** at the time of completion of a given period. **2.** from a given time onward.

यदि *yadi* [S.], conj. if; whether.

यदु *yadu* [S.], m. *mythol.* **1.** name of a legendary king, eldest son of Yayāti, and ancestor of Kr̥ṣṇa. **2.** the people or descendants of Yadu. — **यदु-कुल**, m. the family of Yadu. **यदु-नाथ**, **यदु-पति**, or **यदु-राज**, m. lord of the Yadus: a title of Kr̥ṣṇa. **यदु-वंश**, m. the line or family of Yadu. **°ई**, adj. & m. = **यादव**.

यद्यपि *yadyăpi* [S.], conj. although; even if.

यद्वा-तद्वा *yadvā-tadvā* [S.], adv. somehow or other, as best may be.

[1]**यम** *yam* [ad. *yama-*[2]], m. *mythol.* name of the god of who judges and punishes the dead. — **यम-घंट**, m. any of several astrologically determined inauspicious periods of the day (falling differently for each day of the week); the day following the Dīvālī festival. **यम-दिया**, Yama's lamp: a lamp lit on the thirteenth day of the dark half of the month Kārttik (i.e. three days before Dīvālī). **यमदूत**, m. Yama's messenger (who brings the souls of the dead to judgment, and thence to their final destination). **यम-द्वितीया**, f. the second day of the light half of the month Kārttik (when brothers and sisters exchange gifts). **यम-धार**, m. a kind of two-edged sword or dagger. **यम-पुर**, m. the city or abode of Yama, hell. **यमराज**, m. King

Yama: = ~. यम-लोक, m. the world of Yama, hell. यम-व्रत, m. the meting out of impartial justice (a duty of kings).

[2]यम *yam* [S.], m. one of a pair; a twin. — यमज, adj. twin-born. यमजात, adj. id.

[3]यम *yam* [S.], m. esp. -यम. restraint; self-control.

यमक *yamak* [S.], m. *rhet.* repetition (in the same stanza) of words or syllables of similar sound but different meaning.

[1]यमन *yaman* [ad. *yavana-*], m. 1. = यवन. 2. *mus.* name of a *rāg*.

[2]यमन *yaman* [A. *yaman*], m. *geog.* the Yemen.

यमनी *yamnī* [A. *yamanīya*], adj. & m. **1.** adj. having to do with the Yemen. **2.** m. a Yemeni. **3.** *min.* carnelian.

यमल *yamal* [S.], m. a pair, couple. — यमलार्जुन, m. *mythol.* a pair of *arjuna* trees which were uprooted by the child Kr̥ṣṇa.

यमली *yamālī* [S.], f. *Pl. HŚS.* two objects making up a pair (as skirt and blouse).

[1]यमानी *yamānī* [ad. *yavānī-*], f. = अजवायन.

[2]यमानी *yamānī* [S.], f. *mythol. Pl.* Yama's wife.

यमी *yamī* [S.], f. *mythol.* name of the twin-sister of Yama (identified with the river-goddess Yamunā).

यमुना *yamunā* [S.], f. the river Jumna.

यरक़ान *yarqān* [A. *yarqān*], m. jaundice.

यव *yav* [S.], m. barley. — यव-दोष, m. a flaw in a precious stone.

यवन *yavan* [S.], m. **1.** a Greek, an Ionian. **2.** usu. pej. a foreigner (by origin); a Muslim; a European; a barbarian.

यवनिका *yavănikā* [S.], f. curtain, stage-curtain.

यवनी *yavănī* [S.], f. **1.** a female *yavan*. **2.** the wife of a *yavan*.

यवानी *yavānī* [S.], f. = अजवायन.

यश *yaś* [S.], m. **1.** glory, honour; fame, reputation. **2.** praise, praises (of a person). — ~ कमाना, to win fame; to earn a reputation. ~ गाना, to sing the praises (of, का); to glorify. ~ पाना, or लूटना, = ~ कमाना. ~ मानना, to acknowledge the fame or excellence (of).

यशवी *yaśvī*, adj. corr. = यशस्वी.

यशस्- *yaśas-* [S]. = यश: — यशस्कर, adj. shedding glory, &c. (on). यशस्वान, adj. = next. यशस्वी, adj. glorious, honoured; famous, celebrated.

यशो- *yaśo-* [S]. = यश: — यशोदा, f. glory-giving: name of the foster-mother of Kr̥ṣṇa and wife of Nand. यसोमति, adj. glorious: = यशोदा.

यष्टि *yaṣṭi* [S.], f. staff, stick; pole; club.

यष्टिका *yaṣṭikā* [S.], f. 1. = यष्टि. **2.** *Pl. HŚS.* a kind of necklace.

यह *yah* [*eṣa-*[1]], pron. & adj. & adv. /jīh/, /jəh/. **1.** pron. & adj. this; pl. these. **2.** pron. he, she, it. **3.** adv. as to this, to this degree. अरे आप ~ क्या कर बैठे हैं! oh, what have you gone and done (here)?

यहाँ *yahāṁ* [cf. *iha*], adv. **1.** here. **2.** hither. **3.** at, or to, the house (of, के). — ~ कहीं, adv. somewhere here, hereabouts. ~ का, adj. of this place (or region, or country). ~ का यहीं, adv. right here. ~ तक, adv. as far as this, up to here; until now; to this degree or extent. ~ पर, adv. at this place, here. ~ ... वहाँ, adv. on the one hand ... on the other. मेरे ~, adv. at, or to, my house. — यहाँ-यहाँ, adv. here and there. यहाँ वहाँ की बात, f. desultory remarks; evasive remarks.

यहीं *yahīṁ*, adv. right here (= यहाँ+ही). — ~ से, adv. from this very place; for this very reason, hence.

यही *yahī*, pron. this very, &c. (= यह+ही).

यहूद *yahūd* [A. *yahūd*], m. a Jew.

यहूदिन *yahūdin* [cf. H. *yahūd*], f. a Jewess.

[1]यहूदी *yahūdī* [A. *yahūdī*], adj. & m. **1.** adj. Jewish. **2.** m. a Jew.

[2]यहूदी *yahūdī* [A. *yahūdīya*], f. the Hebrew language.

यांत्रिक *yāntrik* [S.], adj. mechanical.

यांत्रिकी *yāntrikī* [S.], f. mechanics.

[1]या *yā* [P. *yā*], conj. or; either. — ~ कि, conj. = ~. ~ (तो)...~, conj. either...or.

[2]या *yā* [A. *yā*], interj. oh! — ~ अल्लाह! oh God! ~ इलाही! id. ~ नसीब! oh (my) fate!

[3]या *yā*, sg. obl. base. Brbh. this (see यह).

याक़ूत *yāqūt* [A. *yāqūt*], m. a ruby; a garnet.

याक़ूती *yāqūtī* [A. *yāqūt*+P. *-ī*], adj. having to do with, or like, a ruby or rubies.

याग *yāg* [S.], m. poet. an offering, sacrifice.

याचक *yācak* [S.], adj. & m. **1.** adj. -याचक. entreating. **2.** m. petitioner. **3.** a beggar.

याचन *yācan* [S.], m. entreating, begging.

याचना *yācănā* [S.], f. **1.** entreaty, begging. **2.** petition.

याचना *yācnā* [H. *jācnā*: w. S. *yācyate*], v.t. to entreat.

याचिका *yācikā* [S.], f. request, petition.

याचित *yācit* [S.], adj. begged for, prayed for.

याचिता *yācitā* [S.], m. inv. *Pl. HŚS.* one who begs, or beseeches.

याच्य *yācyă* [S.], adj. to be asked for, entreated.

याजक *yājak* [S.], m. a sacrificing priest.

याजन *yājan* [S.], m. causing, or assisting in, performance of a sacrifice; sacrificing.

याज्ञ *yājñă* [S.], adj. sacrificial.

याज्ञिक *yājñik* [S.], adj. & m. **1.** adj. sacrificial. **2.** m. a priest officiating at a sacrifice. **3.** institutor of a sacrifice. **4.** name of a brāhmaṇ community.

याज्य *yājyă* [S.], adj. to be sacrificed, sacrificial.

यातना *yātănā* [S.], f. **1.** torment; *mythol.* the torments of hell (meted out by Yama). **2.** dire suffering.

यातायात *yātâyāt* [S.], m. going and coming: **1.** movement (as of traffic, freight). **2.** transport. ***3.** traffic (esp. between destinations); local travel.

यातु *yātu* [S.], m. *mythol.* one who goes, or wanders: a demon. — यातु-धान, m. Brbh. id.

यात्रा *yātrā* [S.], f. **1.** going, proceeding. ***2.** journey; expedition; pilgrimage. **3.** travel. **4.** a group of pilgrims. **5.** a procession of idols. **6.** (in Bengal) a popular dramatic entertainment featuring dance and song. — ~ करना, to make a journey.

यात्रिक *yātrik* [S.], adj. & m. **1.** adj. having do with a journey, &c. (see यात्रा). **2.** making a journey, &c. **3.** customary, usual. **4.** m. a traveller; pilgrim.

यात्री *yātrī* [S.], m. **1.** a traveller; a pilgrim. **2.** a passenger. **3.** a tourist. — यात्री-गाड़ी, f. passenger train. यात्री-निवास, m. a hotel; inn. यात्री-सेवक, adj. assisting tourists: यात्री-सेवक मंडल, m. tourist bureau.

याथार्थ्य *yāthârthyă* [S.], *Pl. HŚS.* = यथार्थता.

याद *yād* [P. *yād*], f. **1.** memory. **2.** a memory, recollection. — ~ आना, or पड़ना (को), to come to mind. ~ करना, to learn by heart; to think of, to call to mind; to send for, to require the presence of (a subordinate). यह घटना अभी तक ~ की जाती है, people still hark back to this incident. ~ दिलाना (को), to remind (of, की); to remember (one, की: to another person). ~ रखना, to bear in mind, not to forget (sthg). ~ फ़रमाना, to send (for: as for an assistant). ~ रहना, to remain in mind, not to be forgotten. ~ होना (को), to be in mind, to be remembered (by); to be learned by heart (by). आपको यह मामला ~ ही होगा, you must remember this matter, case. ज़बानी ~ होना, to be learned by heart. – यादगार, [P. *-gār*], m. a present or token for memory's sake, souvenir; a monument; anything memorable. याददाश्त [P. -*dāśt*], f. a memorandum; memory.

यादव *yādav* [S.], adj. & m. *mythol.* **1.** adj. having to do with, or descended from, Yadu. **2.** m. a descendant of Yadu. **3.** name of an *ahīr* community.

यान *yān* [S.], m. **1.** going; going against, attacking. ***2.** a vehicle of any kind (incl. ships, aircraft, &c). — यान-यात्रा, f. journey, trip (in a car, cart, &c).

यानी *yānī* [A. *ya'nī*], conj. it meant: that is, i.e.

यापन *yāpan* [S.], m. **1.** causing to go; driving away. **2.** spending (time, or life); wasting (time).

यापित *yāpit* [S.], adj. spent (time).

-याफ़्ता *-yāftā* [P. *yāfta*], adj. inv. U. received, obtained (e.g. तालीम-याफ़्ता, educated).

याबू *yābū* [P. *yābū*], m. *Pl. HŚS.* a pony.

¹याम *yām* [S.], m. & f. **1.** m. a watch of the day or night, period of three hours. **2.** [× *yāminī-*] f. Brbh. night.

²याम *yām* [S.], adj. *mythol.* having to do with Yama.

यामनी *yāmnī* [cf. H. *yāvan*], adj. = यावन. — ~ भाषा, f. Persian; Arabic.

यामल *yāmal* [S.], m. a twin (= यमल).

यामवती *yāmavătī* [S.], f. = ¹यम, 2.

यामाता *yāmātā* [S.], m. inv. = जमाई.

यामिका *yāmikā* [S.], f. night (= यामिनी).

यामिनी *yāminī* [S.], f. night.

यामुन *yāmun* [S.], adj. & m. **1.** adj. having to do with the river Yamunā. **2.** m. antimony, collyrium.

याम्य *yāmyă* [S.], adj. & m. **1.** adj. southern. **2.** m. the right hand; the south. — याम्योत्तर, m. (running from) south to north: a meridian. याम्योत्तर रेखा, f. id.

यायावर *yāyāvar* [S.], m. frequently going: a wanderer.

यार *yār* [P. *yār*], m., f. **1.** friend. **2.** lover. — ~ करना (को), to make friends (with); to take as lover or mistress. ~ बनना (का), to become, or to be, friendly (with). ~ बनाना (को), = ~ करना. यारों का ~, m. a sociable person. — यारबाज़ [P. *-bāz*], adj. sociable; pej. having many men friends (a woman).

यारनी *yārnī* [cf. H. *yār*], f. **1.** female friend (of a girl). **2.** mistress.

याराना *yārānā* [P. *yārāna*], adj. & m. **1.** adj. friendly. **2.** m. friendliness. — याराने में, adv. in a friendly way.

यारी *yārī* [P. *yārī*], f. **1.** friendship. **2.** love outside marriage. **3.** liaison, affair. **4.** friendly assistance. — ~ करना, to form a friendship, or a liaison (with, से); to assist, to befriend (one, की); to side (with, की). ~ गाँठना, or जोड़ना, = prec., 1. ~ देना (को), = करना (की).

यावत *yāvat* [S.], adv. & conj. **1.** adv. as much as, as many as; as often as. **2.** conj. while, as long as, until. **3.** in order that.

यावन *yāvan* [S.], adj. & m. *hist.* **1.** having to do with the Yavanas: Greek, Ionian; Muslim; barbarian. **2.** m. a Yavana.

यासमन *yāsman*, f. m. = यासमीन.

यासमीन *yāsmīn* [P. *yāsmīn*], f. m. jasmine.

यीसु *yīsu*, m. = ईसा.

युक्त *yukt* [S.], adj. **1.** joined (to, से); connected, attached; united; combined. **2.** fit, right, proper. **3.** appointed (to a post). **4.** -युक्त. endowed (with), possessed (of).

युक्तता *yuktătā* [S.], f. **1.** application, use. **2.** suitability, appropriateness.

युक्ति *yukti* [S.], f. **1.** joining; connection; union; combination. **2.** application, use; practice, usage. **3.** appliance, means, device. **4.** expedient; trick; stratagem. **5.** fitness, suitability. **6.** dexterity, ingenuity; skill. **7.** policy. **8.** reasoning, argument; inference. — युक्ति-पूर्ण, adj. reasonable, rational; logical. युक्ति-युक्त, adj. = prec.; appropriate. युक्ति-विरुद्ध, adj. irrational. युक्ति-संगत, adj. = युक्ति-पूर्ण. °ता, f.

युग *yug* [S.], m. **1.** a yoke. **2.** a pair. **3.** an age, era. **4.** *mythol.* one of the four ages of the world (viz. *satya*, *tretā*, *dvāpara*, and *kali*, the present age), an aeon. — ~ ~, adv. through successive ages. युग-प्रवर्तक, adj. initiating a new age; epoch-making. युग-युगांतर, m. successive ages; a very long time, a period of centuries. युगांत [°*ga*+*a*°], m. end of an age; *mythol.* the end of the world. युगांतर [°*ga*+*a*°], m. another age, a new age. °कारी, adj. epoch-making, revolutionary.

युगल *yugal* [S.], m. **1.** a pair, couple. **2.** a twin. — युगल-जोड़ी, f, union, wedlock. युगल-मैच, m. *athl.* a doubles match.

युग्म *yugmă* [S.], m. a pair, couple. — युग्मज, m. a twin.

युग्मक *yugmak* [S.], m. a pair, couple; dyad.

-युत *-yut* [*yukta-*], adj. formant. = युक्त (e.g. श्रीयुत, adj. s.v. श्री).

युद्ध *yuddh* [S.], m. **1.** war. **2.** battle; fight. **3.** युद्ध-. military; war. — युद्धकारी, adj. & m. belligerent (a party to war). युद्ध-क्षेत्र, m. theatre of war. युद्ध-कौशल, m. military tactics. युद्ध-नीति, f. military strategy. युद्धबंदी [P. *-bandī*], m. a prisoner of war. युद्ध-विराम, m. cessation of hostilities. युद्ध-स्थित, adj. engaged in hostilities. युद्धाभ्यास [°*dha*+*a*°], m. military manoeuvres. युद्धोत्तर [°*dha*+*u*°], adj. post-war.

युयुत्सा *yuyutsā* [S.], f. desire to fight: pugnacity.

युयुत्सु *yuyutsu* [S.], adj. wishing to fight: pugnacious.

युव *yuv* [S.], adj. young: — युव-राज, m. Av. heir apparent, crown prince. °ई, f. Brbh. status of crown prince.

युवक *yuvak* [S.], m. a youth, young man.

युवता *yuvătā* [S.], f. *Pl.* youthfulness, period of youth.

युवती *yuvătī* [S.], adj. f. & f. **1.** adj. f. young, &c. (cf. युवा). **2.** f. a girl, young woman.

युवा *yuvā* [S.], adj. m. inv. (incorr. f.) **1.** young. **2.** being in early manhood. — युवाकाल, m. time or years of youth. युवावस्था [°*va*+*a*°], f. id.

युवापन *yuvāpan* [cf. H. *yuvā*], m. youth, young manhood.

यूँ *yūṁ*, adv. = यों.

यूथ *yūth* [S.], m. **1.** flock, herd, troop (of animals, birds). **2.** band, troop (as of soldiers). — यूथ-नाथ, m. leader of a group, or band, &c.

यूथी *yūthī* [ad. *yūthikā-*, cf. H. *jūhī*], f. Brbh. = जूही.

यूनान *yūnān* [A. *yūnān*], m. Ionia: ancient Greece.

[1]यूनानी *yūnānī* [A. *yūnānī*], adj. & m. **1.** adj. Ionian, Greek. **2.** m. a Greek.

[2]यूनानी *yūnānī* [A. *yūnānīya*], f. **1.** the Greek language. **2.** the Greek system of medicine.

यूप *yūp* [S.], m. **1.** post or stake to which a sacrificial animal is tied. **2.** victory column.

यूरोप *yūrop* [Engl. *Europe*], m. Europe.

यूरोपी *yūropī* [cf. H. *yūrop*], adj. European.

यूरोपीय *yūropīyă*, adj. = यूरोपी.

यूह *yūh* [H. ²*jūh*, ad. *yūtha-*], m. *Pl. HŚS.* flock, troop, band.

ये *ye* [cf. H. *yah*], pron. & adj. **1.** pron. they (near reference). **2.** pron. hon. he, she (near reference). **3.** adj. these.

यों *yoṁ*, adv. **1.** thus. **2.** well, in fact, actually. — **~ तो**, adv. = ~, 2.; in the first place; in this case; generally speaking. **~ तो मैं इलाहाबाद का हूँ, फिर...**, first of all I'm from Allahabad; then.... **~ भी**, adv. as normal, usually. **~ ही**, adv. just in this way; casually, simply; cursorily; by chance. **~ ही सही**, be it so, as you please. **मैं यह किताब ~ ही देख रहा था**, I was just looking at this book. – **यों-त्यों करना**, fig. to berate, to curse.

योग *yog* [S.], m. **1.** connection, union. **2.** combination; conjuncture (as of heavenly bodies); agreement, similarity. **3.** application, use. **4.** means; occasion, opportunity. **5.** yoga, a theory or practice of abstract meditation undertaken to bring the soul towards or into union with the supreme spirit; bodily exercises or disciplines, as conducive to the above. **6.** sum, total. **7.** contribution. — **योग-क्षेम**, m. acquisition and keeping (of property): prosperity, well-being; property, assets; profit. **योग-दान**, m. esp. fig. contribution (to, **में**). **योग-निद्रा**, f. the sleep of a deity, or of a devotee; enchanted sleep (specif. *mythol.*, of the palace guards at the birth of Kṛṣṇa); light sleep. **योग-फल**, m. = ~, 6. **योग-बल**, m. the power of yoga; magical or supernatural power. **योग-माया**, f. the creative power of the supreme spirit personified (as in the daughter born to Yaśodā at the time of Kṛṣṇa's birth); the magical power said to be possessed by yogīs. **योग-शक्ति**, f. supernatural power (as that of a yogī). **योग-सिद्ध**, m. & adj. one who has successfully attained the goal of yoga; perfected by yoga. **योगात्मक** [°*ga*+*ā*°], adj. combinatory: *ling.* agglutinative. **योगारूढ़** [°*ga*+*ā*°], adj. & m. absorbed in abstract meditation; a yogī. **योगासन** [°*ga*+*ā*°], m. a posture furthering meditation, yogic posture. **योगेश्वर** [°*ga*+*ī*°], m. a great yogī, or sage; master magician; a deity, esp. Śiva.

योगिनिद्रा *yogi-nidrā* [S.], f. = योग-निद्रा.

योगिनी *yoginī* [S.], f. a female ascetic.

योगी *yogī* [S.], m. **1.** an ascetic; specif. a Nāth Śaiva ascetic. **2.** name of a mixed community of weavers.

योग्य *yogyă* [S.], adj. **1.** suitable, suited (for, **के**). **2.** capable (of, **के**); able; gifted. **3.** worthy (of, **के**, &c). **देखने ~**, worth seeing.

योग्यता *yogyătā* [S.], f. **1.** suitability. **2.** ability, capacity; gifts. **3.** worth, merit. **4.** qualification(s).

योजन *yojan* [S.], m. **1.** joining. **2.** union, connection. **3.** a traditional measure of distance, reckoned variously as between about four and eighteen miles. **4.** the supreme spirit.

योजना *yojănā* [S.], f. **1.** joining: forming, establishing (a group, a committee). **2.** employment, use. **3.** combination, conjunction (as of circumstances). **4.** step, measure. ***5.** plan; planning. **पंचवर्षीय ~**, five-year plan. — **योजनापूर्ण**, adj. planned (as an economy). **योजनाबद्ध**, adj. planned, determined by plan.

योजनीय *yojănīyă* [S.], adj. = योज्य.

योजित *yojit* [S.], adj. **1.** joined. **2.** formed, established. ***3.** planned.

योज्य *yojyă* [S.], adj. & m. **1.** adj. to be joined, or added. **2.** to be implemented; advantageous. **3.** m. a quantity (for addition).

योद्धव्य *yoddhavyă* [S.], adj. worth fighting, to be fought (a battle, a struggle).

योद्धा *yoddhā* [S.], m. inv. **1.** a warrior, soldier. **2.** contender, champion (for, of).

योद्धापन *yoddhāpan* [cf. H. *yoddhā*], m. **1.** soldiering. **2.** bravery, valour.

योधन *yodhan* [S.], m. *Pl. HŚS.* **1.** fighting, battle. **2.** military materials, weapons.

योधापन *yodhāpan*, m. = योद्धापन.

योध्य *yodhyă* [S.], adj. deserving or requiring to be fought (as a war).

योनि *yoni* [S.], f. **1.** the womb. **2.** the female genital organs. **3.** birth; rebirth, reincarnation. **4.** source, origin. — **योनिज**, adj. mammalian.

योषिता *yoṣitā* [S.], f. a woman.

यौगिक *yaugik* [S.], adj. *gram.* having a meaning conformable to its etymology (a word). **2.** formed by composition, compound (a word). **3.** having an application: remedial. **4.** having to do with yoga.

यौतुक *yautuk* [S.], m. 19c. wedding gifts, dowry.

यौन *yaun* [S.], adj. **1.** having to do with the womb, uterine. **2.** uterine (a sibling). **4.** sexual. **5.** venereal (disease). **यौनाकर्षण** [°*na*+*ā*°], m. sex appeal.

यौम *yaum* [A. *yaum*], m. U. a day, esp. a partic. day or date.

यौवन *yauvan* [S.], m. **1.** youth. **2.** young adulthood; adolescence. **3.** young people (of a community, a nation, &c). **4.** transf. breasts of a young woman. — **यौवन-काल,** m. the years of youth. **यौवनावस्था** [°*na*+*a*°], f. state of youth; years of youth.

र

र *ra*, the twenty-seventh consonant of the Devanāgarī syllabary. — **रकार**, m. the sound /r/; the letter र.

रंक *raṅk* [S.], adj. & m. **1.** adj. poor. **2.** miserly. **3.** m. a pauper.

रंकता *raṅkătā* [S.], f. poverty.

रंकिणी *raṅkiṇī* [S.], f. a poor, or deprived, woman.

[1]**रंग** *raṅg* [conn. *raṅga*-[1], and P. *rang*], m. **1.** colour. **2.** paint, dye; pigment. **3.** complexion; beauty. आज तो उसपर ~ है, she's looking beautiful today. **4.** aspect, appearance; expression (facial); atmosphere, mood. **5.** condition. बाज़ार का ~, m. state of the market. **6.** manner, style; influence (exercised upon another, पर). किसी पर ~ डालना, to impress another (as with one's manner, importance). **7.** character, nature; kind, type. **8.** (in cards) suit. **9.** place of entertainment, stage. **10.** the dramatic arts: acting; dancing; singing. **11.** entertainment, enjoyment, merry-making; mood or time of youth. **12.** sthg. splendid, a spectacle. **13.** battle; battle-field. — ~ उड़ना, to fade; to grow pale (as from emotion, fear). ~ उतरना (का), to fade; to grow pale; to be grieved; to sober up. ~ करना, to colour; to paint. ~ खेलना, to throw colour or red powder, &c. (on one another: at the Holī festival); fig. to enjoy oneself very much. ~ चढ़ना (में), to be coloured, dyed; to be flushed. ~ चढ़ाना (पर), to colour; to paint. काले कंबल पर ~ चढ़ाना, to dye a black blanket: to waste one's time. ~ चूना, = ~ टपकना. ~ जमाना, to make an impression (on, पर); to influence. ~ टपकना, colour to drip: to be very bright. ~ डालना, = ~ खेलना, 1.; to apply colour (to, में); to exercise an influence (on, पर). ~ देखना, to examine the condition or effectiveness (of, का); to remain uncommitted. ~ देना, to apply colour (to, में); to feel strong love (for, पर). ~ निकालना, to be bright, or showy; to succeed with flying colours. ~ पीला, or फीका, पड़ना, colour to fade; to become pale. ~ बदलना, = ~ उड़ना. ~ बिगड़ना, colour to fade, to be discoloured; to be changed (for the worse), to be spoiled. ~ भरना (में), to colour; to paint. ~ मचा-, Brbh. to fight boldly or mightily. ~ मारना, to hit the winning colour (in the game of *caupar*): to win (a game). ~ में (or पर) आना, to be in the mood (to, के). ~ में भंग, m. sthg. spoiling happiness or contentment. ~ में रँगना, to dye (sthg.) the colour (of, के); fig. to fall in love (with). ~ लगाना, to colour, to paint (= ~ भरना); to stir up a quarrel. ~ लाना, to flush, to blush; to bloom, to look splendid; to find resources; to accomplish wonders; to bring about a change. ~ है! interj. splendid! bravo! – रंग-ढंग, m. manner, air (of a person); appearance; kind, sort. रंग-ढंग से मालूम होता है, पानी बरसेगा, it looks as though it will rain. रंगदार [P. *-dār*], adj. coloured; bright, showy. रंग-पाशी [P. *-pāśī*], f. sprinkling colour (esp. during, or shortly before the Holī festival). रंग-बिरंगा [P. *rang-ba-rang*], adj. multicoloured; motley; diverse. रंग-भरिया, m. reg. a painter. रंग-भूमि, f. stage, theatre; arena (of conflict), battle-ground. रंग-भेद, m. discrimination by colour, colour bar. रंग-मंच, m. the stage, the theatre. °ईय, adj. dramatic, theatrical. रंग-महल, m. apartment (of a palace, or large house) used for festivities or for love-making. रंग-रलियाँ, f. pl. merriment; music and dancing, a lover's dalliance. रंग-रस, m. pleasure; merriment; melody. °इया, m. a voluptuous or lascivious person. रंग-रूप, m. colour; beauty and form, attractive appearance; character, nature. रंगरेज़ [P. *-rez*], m. a dyer. °ई, f. dyeing. रंग-रोग़न, m. polish. रंग-शाला, f. = रंग-भूमि, 1. रंगसाज़ [P. *-sāz*], m. a painter; colour-manufacturer. °ई, f. painting, &c.. रंग-आमेज़ी [P. *āmezī*], f. *Pl.* colouring, painting. रंगारंग, adj. multicoloured; of various sorts (as an entertainment, a programme)

[2]**रंग** *raṅg*, m. = राँगा.

रंगत *raṅgat* [cf. H. *raṁgnā*], f. **1.** colouring; tint, shade; complexion. **2.** good mood, pleasure. **3.** reg. cloth for dyeing. **4.** *Pl.* plan, design. — ~ आना (में), to acquire a colour.

रँगना *raṁgnā* [cf. H. *raṁgānā*], v.i. & v.t. **1.** v.i. to be coloured, dyed, painted. **2.** v.t. to colour, &c. **3.** to make (another) of the same complexion, or character, or tastes, &c. as oneself. — रँगा, adj. coloured; flushed (as with wine); excited. रँगे हाथ, or हाथों, पकड़ा जाना, to be caught red-handed.

रंगरूट *raṅgrūṭ* [Engl. *recruit*], m. a recruit.

रँगवाई *raṁgvāī* [cf. H. *raṁgvānā*], f. price paid for dyeing or painting.

रँगवाना *raṁgvānā* [cf. H. *raṁgnā*], v.t. to cause to be coloured, dyed, painted (by, से).

रँगाई *raṁgāī* [cf. H. *raṁgnā*], f. **1.** dyeing, colouring. **2.** price paid for dyeing, &c.

रँगाना *raṁgānā* [**raṅgayati*: Pk. *raṁgaï*], v.t. = रँगवाना.

रँगारा *raṁgārā* [*raṅgakāra-*], m. reg. a dyer.

रँगावट *raṁgāvaṭ* [cf. H. *raṁgnā*], f. **1.** dyeing, colouring. **2.** colour. **3.** the business of dyeing, &c.

1**रंगी** *raṅgī* [S.], adj. & m. **1.** adj. impassioned. **2.** devoted (to). **3.** m. *Pl. HŚS.* an actor. **4.** *Pl. HŚS.* a dyer.

2**रंगी** *raṅgī* [cf. H. *raṅg*], f. *Pl.* chintz; a chintz of which the colour washes out.

रंगीत *raṅgīt* [? H. *raṅg*+H. *gidh*], m. the white yellow-headed vulture 'Pharaoh's chicken' (= सफ़ेद गिध).

रंगीन *raṅgīn* [P. *rangīn*], adj. **1.** coloured, painted. **2.** multicoloured. **3.** showy, gaudy; adorned. **4.** ornate (as language, style). **5.** lively (a person); interesting (as a conversation). **6.** pleasure-loving. **7.** picturesque (a scene).

रंगीनी *raṅgīnī* [cf. H. *raṅgīn*], f. **1.** state of being coloured. **2.** bright colouring. **3.** showiness (of dress); elegance. **4.** liveliness, &c. (see रंगीन, 4.-7).

रँगीला *raṁgīlā* [cf. *raṅgita-*], adj. **1.** bright, showy, gaudy. **2.** lively, merry. **3.** pleasure-loving; flirtatious.

रंगोली *raṅgolī* [*raṅgāvalĭ̄-*], f. reg. (W.) painted decoration (on a house wall).

रंच *rañc*, adv. Brbh. a little, somewhat. — रंच...न, adv. not at all.

रंचक *rañcak*, adj. Brbh. a little.

1**रंज** *rañj* [P. *ranj*], m. **1.** grief. **2.** suffering, distress. **3.** displeasure; annoyance; anger; disgust. — ~ उठाना, to suffer sorrow, or distress; to feel displeasure, &c. ~ करना (को), to cause grief, distress, or displeasure (to).

2**रंज** *rañj* [ad. *araṇya-*], m. reg. = रन.

1**रंजक** *rañjak* [S.], adj. & m. **1.** adj. colouring, dyeing. **2.** -रंजक. moving, exciting (emotion, or the heart: e.g. मनोरंजक, entertaining). **3.** m. a dyer. **4.** a dye (as henna, red sandalwood or vermilion).

2**रंजक** *rañjak* [P. *ranjak*], f. **1.** priming-powder; powder-fuse. **2.** priming-pan; touch-hole. **3.** match (of a musket, or a firework). — ~ उड़ना, priming to flash in the pan. ~ उड़ाना, to touch off priming. ~ चाट जाना, = ~ उड़ना; fig. anger to flare, but to no effect. ~ पिलाना (को), to prime. – रंजकदान [P. *-dān*], m. priming-pan; powder-flask, or powder-horn. °ई, f. id.

रंजन *rañjan* [S.], m. **1.** colouring, dyeing. **2.** esp. -रंजन. causing emotion, delighting (the heart, &c). **3.** red sandalwood. — रंजनकारी, adj. colouring, &c.; decorating, decorative; attractive. रंजनकारी साहित्य, m. belles lettres.

रंजित *rañjit* [S.], adj. **1.** coloured, stained. **2.** moved, delighted.

रंजिश *rañjiś* [P. *ranjiś*], f. 1. = 1रंज. **2.** coolness (of attitude).

रंजीदगी *rañjīdăgī* [P. *ranjīdagī*], f. = रंजिश, 1.

रंजीदा *rañjīdā* [P. *rañjīda*], adj. inv. **1.** sad. **2.** displeased; chagrined. — ~ करना, to make sad; to displease, &c.

रँझना *raṁjhnā*, v.i. **1.** to flower; to flourish. **2.** reg. to become deeply rooted or chronic (as a disease).

रंट *ranṭ*, adj. colloq. reg. quarrelsome.

1**रंड** *ranḍ* [conn. *eraṇḍa-*], m. the castor-oil plant.

2**रंड** *ranḍ* [S.], adj. & m. *Pl. HŚS.* **1.** adj. faithless; barren. **2.** m. one who dies without sons.

रंडा *ranḍā* [S.], f. **1.** a widow. **2.** pej. term of abuse.

रंडापन *ranḍāpan* [**ranḍātvana-*: cf. H. *ranḍā*], m. widowhood.

रंडापना *ranḍāpanā*, m. = रंडापन.

रंडापा *ranḍāpā* [cf. H. *ranḍā*], m. widowhood.

रंडी *ranḍī* [*ranḍā-*; ← Panj.], f. a prostitute. — रंडी-ख़ाना, m. a brothel. रंडी-घर, m. id. रंडीबाज़ [P. *-bāz*], m. a whoremonger. °ई, f. fornication. रंडी-मुंडी, f. pej. harlot.

रँडुआ *raṁḍuā* [cf. *ranḍā-*, and H. *ranḍā*], m. a widower. — रँडुआ-भँडुआ, m. pej. riff-raff.

रंथी *ranthī*, f. reg. pronun. var. = अरथी.

रंद *rand* [?? ad. *randhra-*], m. opening; air-hole, loop-hole.

रंदा *randā* [P. *randa*], m. a plane; a rasp; grater. — ~ करना, or फेरना (पर), to plane, &c.

रंधन *randhan* [S.], m. *Pl. HŚS.* the act of cooking.

रँधना *raṁdhnā* [cf. H. *rāṁdhnā*], v.i. to be cooked.

रंध्र *randhră* [S.], m. **1.** a crack, hole, opening. **2.** fig. a defect.

रंबा *rambā* [cf. H. 1*rambhā*], m. reg. **1.** a mortice chisel. **2.** *Pl.* a kind of hoe.

रँभा *ramͫbhā* [cf. H. *ramͫbhānā*], f. bellowing; lowing (of cattle).

[1]**रंभा** *rambhā* [? conn. **rambhati*[2], Pk. *ramͫbhaï*], m. reg. **1.** a grubber, hoe. **2.** a crowbar.

[2]**रंभा** *rambhā* [S.], f. *mythol.* **1.** name of Gaurī or Pārvatī. **2.** name of one of a class of female deities (*apsarā*) of Indra's paradise.

रँभाना *ramͫbhānā* [cf. *rambhate*], v.i. to bellow, to low (as cattle).

[1]**रई** *raī* [cf. **rapaka-*: Pk. *ravaya-*], f. churning-staff. — ~ चलाना, to churn.

[2]**रई** *raī* [cf. **rava-*[2]], f. Brbh. crushed or ground material; coarse flour; bran.

रईस *raīs* [A. *ra'īs*], m. a person of rank or status: **1.** a substantial landowner. **2.** a nobleman; gentleman. **3.** a person of substance (as a banker, merchant). — रईसज़ादा [P. -*zāda*], m. son of a gentleman, &c.

रईसा *raīsā* [A. *ra'īsa*], f. a woman of rank or status.

रईसी *raīsī* [cf. H. *raīs*], f. status of a *raīs*; rank, substance.

रक़बा *raqbā* [A. *raqba*], m. **1.** enclosed space, or area. **2.** area, extent.

रक़म *raqm* [A. *raqm*], f. **1.** mark (as of price); notation of numerals in Perso-Arabic script. ***2.** an amount, sum; total. **3.** entry, item (in an account or list). **4.** a valuable possession, or article. **5.** kind, type. — ~ करना, to note (as a price or sum due), to record. ~ मारना, to take money due (to another, की). – चलती ~, f. colloq. fig. a dubious quantity: a clever operator.

रक़मी *raqmī* [P. *raqmī*], adj. marked down, recorded (an amount, a tally).

रकाब *rakāb* [A. *rikāb*], f. **1.** a stirrup. 2. = रकाबी.

रकाबी *rakābī* [P. *rakābī*], f. a dish, plate; bowl.

रक़ीब *raqīb* [A. *raqīb*], m. a watcher: rival, competitor.

रक़्क़ासा *raqqāsā* [A. *raqqāṣa*], f. a dancer.

रक्खना *rakkhnā*, v.t. pronun. var. or obs. = रखना.

[1]**रक्त** *rakt* [S.], adj. & m. **1.** adj. coloured, dyed, tinged. **2.** m. red colour. ***3.** blood. **4.** *hind.* fig. degree of consanguinity. — रक्तक्षीणता, f. anaemia. रक्त-चंदन, m. either of two varieties of red sandalwood; the red-wood, *Adenanthera pavonina*. रक्त-दिग्ध, adj. blood-stained. रक्त-पाणि, adj. whose hands are blood-stained: murderous. रक्त-पित्त, m. blood and bile: bleeding from the mouth, nose, &c. accompanied by symptoms of illness. रक्त-पात, m. bloodshed; bleeding (from a wound). रक्त-रंजित, adj. blood-stained. रक्तश्वेतानुमेयता [°*ta*+*a*°], m. leukaemia. रक्त-संचार, m. circulation of the blood; the pulse; fig. vigour. रक्त-स्राव, m. haemorrhage. रक्तहीन, adj. bloodless; anaemic; without natural warmth or vigour. रक्ताभ [°*ta*+*ā*°], adj. glowing red, coloured red.

[2]**रक्त** *rakt* [S.], adj. attached (to, से), fond (of).

रक्तता *raktātā* [S.], f. redness.

रक्तिम *raktim* [S.], adj. red-coloured; blood-coloured.

रक्तिमा *raktimā* [S.], f. redness, red colour.

रक्ष *rakṣ* [S.], m. **1.** guard, protector (= रक्षक). **2.** protecting, protection. **3.** Brbh. = राक्षस.

रक्षक *rakṣak* [S.], adj. & m. **1.** adj. protecting, &c. (see रक्षा). **2.** m. protector; guardian. **3.** defender.

रक्षण *rakṣaṇ* [S.], m. the act of protecting, &c. (see रक्षा). — क्षेत्र-रक्षण [Engl.], m. fielding (cricket).

रक्षणीय *rakṣăṇīyă* [S.], adj. needing or deserving to be protected, &c.

रक्षस *rakṣas*, [S.], m. *Pl. HŚS.* = राक्षस.

रक्षा *rakṣā* [S.], f. **1.** protection; preservation; protection against spirits. **2.** custody, care. **3.** defence. **4.** ash. — ~ करना (की), to protect, &c. (from, से); to defend (against). – रक्षा-कवच, m. protective armour; fig. a safeguard, amulet, charm. रक्षाबंधन, m. *hind.* the festival of *rakṣābandhan* held on the full moon of the month Sāvan, when sisters tie a talisman (*rākhī*, q.v.) on the arm of their brothers and receive small gifts of money from them. रक्षात्मक [°*ṣā*+*ā*°], adj. protective; defensive.

रक्षित *rakṣit* [S.], adj. **1.** protected; kept safe, looked after (as a child; or an object). **2.** defended. **3.** held in reserve (as a fund). — ~ जंगल, or वन, m. a wild life reserve. ~ राज्य, m. a protectorate.

[1]**रक्षी** *rakṣī*, m. Brbh. ? a worshipper of spirits or demons.

[2]**रक्षी** *rakṣī* [S.], m. a protector; watchman.

रक्ष्य *rakṣyă* [S.], adj. = रक्षणीय.

रक्ष्यमाण *rakṣyamāṇ* [S.], adj. having protection or defence, defended (as a position).

रख *rakh* [? cf. H. *rakhnā*], f. (m., *Pl.*) reg. land kept free for grazing.

रखना *rakhnā* [*rakṣati*], v.t. **1.** to put, to place; to leave (in the keeping of, के पास); to pledge, to pawn (an article); to deposit (money). गिरवी ~, to pawn. **2.** to submit, to depose (as proof, an argument, a charge: to, के सामने). **3.** to keep (in a place); to keep (as a tradesman his stock); to keep (animals); to collect (partic. articles). **4.** to keep (in a partic. state). बंद करके ~, to keep closed. **5.** to keep (a concubine). **6.** to keep or to hold back (as facts, information; or money, goods); to put aside (money). मन में ~, not to reveal (sthg). **7.** to protect; to preserve; to care for; to put up (guests). **8.** to possess, to have (in one's possession); to have (as of right); to feel, to harbour (emotions). कार ~, to have a car. छड़ी ~, to have a stick (with one). अधिकार ~, to have the right (to, का), to exercise a right; to dare (to, का); आशा ~, to cherish the hope (of, की). **9.** esp. w. देना. to engage, to appoint. **10.** w. देना. to assign (to a sphere of duties). **11.** to apply (a reference: to, पर). मैंने यह बात उसपर रखकर कही, I said that with him in mind. **12.** to ascribe, to impute (a fault, &c.: to, पर). **13.** to assign, to give (a name). उसका नाम कृष्णकुमार रखा गया. he was named Kr̥ṣṇakumār. **14.** to stipulate (a condition). **15.** to observe, to keep (a rule). **16.** to maintain a relationship (with, से). उसे सबसे संबंध ~ पड़ता है, he has to keep on good terms with everyone. **17.** to defer (until a fixed time, पर). अब इसका निश्चय कल पर रखें, let's put off deciding this until tomorrow. **18.** to lay (eggs). **19.** sl. to have sexual intercourse with (a woman). — रखकर कहना, to speak with reservation; to speak in innuendoes. बनाए ~, to maintain in force (a situation, a practice or usage).

रखनी *rakhnī* [cf. H. *rakhnā*], f. a mistress.

रख-रखाव *rakh-rakhāv* [cf. H. *rakhnā*, and *rakhānā*], m. **1.** maintenance, upkeep (of an object). **2.** maintenance, support (of a person).

रखवाई *rakhvāī* [cf. H. *rakhvānā*], f. **1.** arranging watch or guard (over fields). **2.** price paid for keeping, watching, guarding, &c.

रखवाना *rakhvānā* [cf. H. *rakhnā*], v.t. to cause to be placed, kept, protected, &c. (by, से).

रखवाल *rakhvāl* [*rakṣapāla-*], m. **1.** protector, guardian. **2.** herdsman. **3.** watchman, guard.

रखवाला *rakhvālā*, m. = रखवाल.

[1]**रखवाली** *rakhvālī* [cf. H. *rakhvālā*], f. a protectress, &c. (see रखवाल).

[2]**रखवाली** *rakhvālī* [cf. H. *rakhvāl*], f. **1.** guard, watch, care; supervision; tending (animals). **2.** wages of a guard, watchman, or supervisor. **3.** money paid to a chief for protection of property. — ~ करना (की), to guard; to look after.

रखवैया *rakhvaiyā* [cf. H. *rakhvānā*], m. one who protects, guards, &c.

रखाई *rakhāī* [cf. H. *rakhnā*], f. **1.** protecting, guarding (= रक्षण). **2.** price paid for guarding, &c. (= रखवाई).

रखाना *rakhānā* [cf. H. *rakhnā*], v.t. **1.** to cause to be kept, &c. (by, से). **2.** to watch (fields).

[1]**रखिया** *rakhiyā* [*rakṣita-*], m. reg. (W). a grove of trees near a village, maintained for religious purposes.

[2]**रखिया** *rakhiyā* [ad. *rakṣā-*[1]], f. *Pl.* protection, keeping, care.

रखियाना *rakhiyānā* [cf. H. *rākh*], v.t. reg. to scour (dishes) with ash.

रखी *rakhī* [ad. *rakṣin-*], m. reg. a protector, &c. (= रक्षक).

रखैया *rakhaiyā* [cf. H. *rakhnā*], m. = रखवैया.

रखैली *rakhailī* [cf. *rakhnā*], f. a concubine.

रख़्श *rakhś* [P. *rakhś*], m. U. light, or reflection of light; name of Rustam's horse.

रग *rag* [P. *rag*], f. **1.** a blood vessel: artery; vein. **2.** sinew, tendon; fibre (of the body). **3.** vein (in a leaf). **4.** fig. inner nature, character. **5.** fig. obstinacy. — ~ उतरना, *Pl. HŚS.* to recover from a fit of obstinacy. ~ खड़ी होना, a vein to stand out or to swell. ~ चढ़ना, to pull a muscle or tendon; to show mulish obstinacy. ~ चढ़ रहना, id.; to have a confirmed weakness or vice. ~ दबना, a vital point to be hurt: a weak point (in a person) to be found. ~ ~ पहचानना, to know (a person's, की) inner nature. ~ मरना, to lose virility, to become impotent. दुखती ~, f. a weak point; Achilles' heel. – रग-पट्ठा, m. = next. रग-रग से, adv. to the core (of one's being), utterly. रग-रेशा, m. sinews and fibres; entire or essential nature (of a living being); (one's) entire being.

रगड़ *ragaṛ* [cf. H. *ragaṛnā*], f. **1.** rubbing against; friction, wearing. **2.** state of being worn; abrasion. — ~ खाना, to be rubbed, worn. – रगड़-झगड़, f. friction, wrangling.

रगड़ना *ragaṛnā* [cf. *ragg-], v.t. **1.** to rub; to grind; to scour; to polish. **2.** to push against (persons in a crowded space). **3.** to wear away; to wear out. **4.** colloq. to work hard, to work away (at sthg). **5.** colloq. to finish, to 'polish off' (sthg).

रगड़ा *ragṛā* [cf. H. *ragaṛnā*], m. **1.** rubbing; grinding; scouring. **2.** wrangling. — रगड़ा-झगड़ा, m. dissension, dispute; strife.

रगड़ान *ragṛān* [cf. H. *ragaṛnā*], f. reg. rubbing, friction (= रगड़).

रगड़ी *ragṛī* [cf. H. *ragaṛ*], adj. reg. abrasive, truculent.

रगना *ragnā* [cf. *rakta-*²: anal.], v.i. reg. to be attached (to), to be in love (with).

रग़बत *ragbat* [A. *ragba*: P. *ragbat*], f. U. **1.** desire. **2.** inclination.

रगी *ragī* [cf. H. *rag*], adj. & m. **1.** adj. self-willed, obstinate; intractable. **2.** m. a self-willed person, &c.

रगेद *raged* [cf. H. *ragednā*], f. *Pl. HŚS.* **1.** chase, hunt. **2.** mating (birds).

रगेदना *ragednā*, v.t. reg. to chase, to hunt.

रघु *raghu* [S.], m. *mythol.* **1.** name of a king of Avadh, the great-grandfather of Rāmcandra. **2.** the lineage of Raghu (= रघु-वंश). — रघु-कुल, m. = रघु-वंश. रघु-नाथ, m. lord of the race of Raghu: a title of Rām's father Daśrath, and of Rām. रघु-पति, m. id. रघु-वंश, m. the race or line of Raghu. °ई, adj.

रच *rac* [cf. H. ¹*racnā*], m. reg. **1.** make, form. **2.** workmanship. — रच-बनाव, m. composition (as of a literary work).

रचक *racak* [S.], m. Brbh. = रचयिता.

¹**रचना** *racnā* [**racyate*], v.i. & v.t. **1.** v.i. to be created, made, or formed. **2.** to be composed (as a book). **3.** to be set afoot, initiated (as acts, or a scheme). **4.** v.t. [= H. ¹*racānā*] to create, to make, to form. **5.** to compose (as a book). **6.** to initiate (an action, a scheme); to prepare; to plan. **7.** to celebrate (as a marriage). **8.** reg. to arrange in order; to string together.

²**रचना** *racnā* [cf. *rakta-*¹: anal.], v.i. & v.t. **1.** v.i. to be dyed; to be stained (the hands, feet: with henna). **2.** to make a stain (as betel on the mouth: में). **3.** v.t. [= H. ²*racānā*] to dye, to stain. **4.** [? = ¹*racnā*] to work, to carve. **5.** to decorate, to adorn.

³**रचना** *racnā* [cf. *rakta-*²: anal.], v.i. **1.** to be attracted, to draw close (to, से). **2.** to fall in love (with, से). **3.** reg. to be tamed (an animal).

⁴**रचना** *racănā* [S.], f. **1.** creating, forming. **2.** sthg. created or formed; a creation; a literary or artistic work. **3.** establishment, arrangement. **4.** structure (as of a literary work). — ~ करना (की), to form, to create; to produce (as a literary work). – रचनात्मक [°*nā*+*ā*°], adj. creative (art, genius); constructive (as a suggestion); *gram.* formative. रचनावली [°*nā*+*ā*°], f. collected works.

रचयिता *racayitā* [S.], m. inv. **1.** creator, maker. **2.** composer, author (of a work).

रचयित्री *racayitrī* [S.], f. authoress, &c. (see रचयिता).

¹**रचाना** *racānā* [cf. H. ¹*racnā*], v.t. **1.** to cause to be made; to arrange, to set in train. **2.** to celebrate (an occasion).

²**रचाना** *racānā* [cf. H. ²*racnā*, or H. ¹*rāc-*], v.t. to stain (the hands, feet: with henna).

रचावट *racāvaṭ* [cf. H. ²*racānā*], f. staining (the hands or feet) with henna.

¹**रचित** *racit* [S.], adj. **1.** made, formed; created. **2.** composed (a work).

²**रचित** *racit* [S.], adj. made coloured or bright, adorned. — मणि-रचित, adj. adorned with jewels (a garland).

¹**रज** *raj* [ad. *rajas*, neut.], f. & m. **1.** f. dust. **2.** pollen. **3.** m. menstrual discharge. **4.** = रजस्. — रज-कण, m. speck of dust; grain of pollen. रजवती, adj. f. menstruating.

²**रज** *raj* [conn. H. *rajat*], m. Brbh. silver.

³**रज** *raj* [conn. H. *rajak*], m. Brbh. a washerman.

रजक *rajak* [S.], m. *Pl. HŚS.* a washerman.

रजकी *rajăkī* [S.], f. *Pl. HŚS.* a washerman's wife; a washerwoman.

रजत *rajat* [S.], adj. & m. **1.** adj. white, silvery. **2.** m. the colour white. ***3.** silver. **4.** ivory. — रजत-जयंती, f. silver jubilee. रजताभ [°*ta*+*ā*°], m. silvery lustre.

रजधानी *rajdhānī*, f. Brbh. Av. = राजधानी.

¹**रजना** *rajnā* [*rajyate*¹; ← Panj.], v.i. reg. to be brightly coloured or brilliant.

²**रजना** *rajnā* [*rajyate*²; ← Panj.], v.i. reg. to be satisfied.

¹**रजनी** *rajănī* [S.], f. night. — रजनीकर, m. Brbh. night-maker: the moon. रजनीगंध, m. a plant having fragrant flowers that open at night. °आ, m. id. रजनीचर, m. night-wanderer: a demon; the moon. रजनी-पति, m. lord of night: the moon. रजनी-मुख, m. nightfall. रजनीश [°*nī*+*ī*°], m. = रजनी-पति. रजनीहासा, m. a plant having flowers that open at night (? = रजनीगंध).

²**रजनी** *rajnī* [ad. *rañjinī-*], f. *Pl. HŚS.* **1.** lac. **2.** indigo.

रजपूत *rajpūt*, m. Brbh. = राजपूत.

रजपूतनी *rajpūtnī* [cf. H. *răjpūt*], f. reg. a Rājpūt woman.

रजपूती *rajpūtī* [cf. H. *rājpūt*], f. Brbh. Rājpūt rank or status; bravery.

रजबहा *rajbahā* [H. *rāj*+H. *bāhā*], m. *Pl. HŚS.* main channel, or main branch, of a canal.

रजवाड़ा *rajvāṛā* [H. *rāj*+H. *-vāṛā*], m. rajah's territory; princely state.

रजस् *rajas* [S.], m. **1.** *philos.* the quality of *rajas*: activity, or passion (the second of the three inherent qualities or *guṇas* of living beings). **2.** [cf. [1]*raj*] रजस-. menstrual discharge. — रजस्वला, adj. f. menstruating; of marriageable age (a girl).

रज़ा *razā* [A. *riẓā*], f. **1.** pleasure; (one's) pleasure, or will. **2.** contentment. **3.** approval, assent; *mil.* leave. — रज़ाकार, m. volunteer (esp. a member of a Muslim volunteer organisation in pre-1947 India). रसामंद [P. *-mand*], adj. willing, consenting; permitting. °ई, f.

रजाई *rajāī* [cf. H. *rajānā*], f. **1.** enjoyment of sovereignty; rule. **2.** royal decree.

रज़ाई *razāī* [P. *razāī, razāī*], f. a quilted blanket.

रजाना *rajānā* [cf. H. [2]*rāj*], v.t. to cause to rule; to put, or to keep, on the throne. — राज ~, id.

रजिस्टर *rajisṭar* [Engl. *register*], m. a register. — ~ करना, to enter (in a register).

रजिस्टरी *rajistrī* [cf. H. *rajisṭar*], f. **1.** registration (of mail). **2.** registration (of a document). — ~ करना (की), to register. – रजिस्टरीवाला, (or °-कृत), adj. registered (document).

रजिस्ट्री *rajisṭrī*, f. see रजिस्टरी.

रजो- *rajo-* [S]. = रजस्: — रजोगुण, m. *philos.* the quality of *rajas*. °ई, adj. & m.

रज़्ज़ाक़ *razzāq* [A. *razzāq*], m. S.H. provider of subsistence: Providence, God.

रज्जु *rajju* [S.], f. m. **1.** f. string, cord. **2.** m. f. *Pl. HŚS.* reins. **3.** m. f. *Pl. HŚS.* braided hair.

[1]**रझना** *rajhnā* [cf. H. *rajhānā*], v.i. reg. to be cooked, boiled.

[2]**रझना** *rajhnā* [conn. *rañjana-*[2]: H. [1]*rāṁjhan*], m. reg. pot in which a dyer strains his dyes.

रझनी *rajhnī* [H. [2] [1]*rajhnā*], f. reg. (W). pot for boiling milk.

रझाना *rajhānā* [cf. **radhyate*], v.t. reg. to cook, to boil.

रझाव *rajhāv* [cf. H. *rajh(ā)nā*], m. reg. cooking, boiling.

रट *raṭ* [cf. H. *raṭnā*], f. **1.** repeating, repetition; rote-learning. **2.** a worn-out slogan, or a familiar claim. — ~ लगाना, colloq. to repeat the same old things.

रटंत *raṭant* [cf. H. [1]*raṭnā*], f. continued repeating, rote-learning; parrotting (sthg).

रटन *raṭan* [cf. H. *raṭnā*], f. repeating, &c.

[1]**रटना** *raṭnā* [**raṭyati*], v.i. **1.** to repeat; to learn by rote. **2.** to importune. **3.** Brbh. to make a repeated sound.

[2]**रटना** *raṭnā*, f. **1.** repetition. **2.** persistent demand; importunity. — ~ लगना (को), (a person) to repeat, or to request continuously.

रड़क *raṛak* [cf. H. *raraknā*], f. *Pl.* pricking; pain.

रड़कना *raṛaknā*, v.i. *Pl.* to prick, to pain (as in the eye).

रड़का *raṛkā* [cf. H. *raṛkānā*], m. reg. (W). a coarse broom made of cotton twigs.

रड़काना *raṛkānā* [cf. **raḍḍ-*: Pk. *raḍḍa-*], v.t. *Pl.* to shove, to push.

रण *raṇ* [S.], m. **1.** battle; conflict; battle-field. **2.** war. — रण-कौशल, m. military tactics. रण-छोड़, who flees from battle: a title of Kṛṣṇa. रणधीर, adj. steady in battle, brave. रण-भूमि, f. battle-field. रण-रंग, m. warlike, or martial, mood. रण-विधि, m. military strategy. रण-सिंघा, m. = next. रण-सिंहा, m. war-trumpet. रण-स्तंभ, m. monument to a battle or war.

रणित *raṇit* [S.], adj. sounded: ringing.

[1]**रत** *rat* [S.], adj. **1.** attracted to, enjoying; in love (with, से). **2.** intent (on, में), engrossed (in).

[2]**रत** *rat*, ? m. f. Brbh. = रति.

[1]**रत-** *rat-*. = रात: — रत-जगा, m. watching all night, vigil (on religious or on festive occasions). - रतावा [? H. *-ā(v)-* 'come'], m. *Pl.* night attack.

[2]**रत-** *rat-* [cf. H. [2]*rāt-*], v.i. *Pl.* to be dyed red.

रतन *ratan* [ad. *ratna-*], m. = रत्न. — रतन-जोत, m. *Pl.* the plant *Lithospermum vestitum*; a kind of medicine (said to be good for the eyes). रतन-पुरुष, m. *Pl. HŚS.* a plant, *Ionidium suffruticosum*, widely found all across the Ganges plain and in Bundelkhand.

रतना *ratnā* [cf. *rakta-*[2]], v.i. to be moved by desire or passion.

रतनार *ratnār*, adj. & m. **1.** adj. red; bright; glowing. **2.** m. red colour.

रतनारा *ratnārā*, adj. reg. red, &c. (= रतनार).

रतनिया *ratniyā* [?? conn. **rakta*-[1]], *Pl.* a kind of rice: wild, red-husked rice.

रतल *ratl* [A. *ratl*], m. reg. (W.) **1.** a weight equally an amount somewhat less than one pound (453g). **2.** one *ratl's* amount (of anything).

रतवाही *ratvāhī*, f. *Pl.* a night attack.

रता- *ratā-* [cf. *rakta*-[2], and H. [1]*rat*], v.i. Brbh. to feel sexual desire.

रतालू *ratālū* [*raktālu*-], m. a variety of yam (*Dioscorea purpurea*, or *pulchella*).

रतावा *ratāvā*, m. *Pl.* see s.v. [1]रत-.

रति *rati* [S.], f. **1.** enjoyment. **2.** passion; love. ***3.** sexual intercourse. **4.** *mythol.* name of the wife of the god of love Kāmdev. **5.** intentness, absorption (in, में). — रति-केलि, f. = ~, 3. रति-क्रिया, f. id. रतिजन्य, adj. sexually produced, or transmitted (disease); venereal. रति-नाथ, m. = next. रति-पति, Rati's lord: title of Kāmdev.

रतुआ *ratuā* [cf. *rakta*-[1]], m. reg. (W.) **1.** rust (a fungus appearing on plants during periods of unbroken rainy weather). **2.** *Pl.* a kind of red stone hung round the neck of a child as a charm against fever and other diseases. **3.** *Pl.* a red insect which destroys a wheat crop.

रतौंधा *rataumdhā* [conn. **rātryāndha*-], m. night-blindness.

रतौंधिया *rataumdhiyā* [cf. H. *rataumdhā*], adj. night-blind.

रतौंधी *rataumdhī* [conn. **rātryāndhiya*-], f. night-blindness.

रत्ती *rattī* [*raktikā*-], f. **1.** the seed of the climbing shrub crab's eye (*Abrus precatorius*), used as a weight. **2.** a jewellers' weight, equal to eight barley-corns. **3.** transf. a very small object or quantity. — ~ भर, adj. & adv. a *rattī's* weight; a tiny amount, very little. ~ भर भी नहीं, adv. not even a drop, not a shred. ~ ~, adv. minutely; inch by inch (of a careful search).

रत्थी *ratthī*, f. pronun. var. = [2]रथी.

रत्न *ratn* [S.], m. **1.** jewel, precious stone; treasure. **2.** -रत्न. fig. sthg. precious or excellent. — रत्नकार, m. a jeweller. रत्न-जटित, adj. set with jewels. रत्नमय, adj. made of or consisting of jewels; bejewelled. रत्न-माला, f. necklace of jewels. रत्न-शाला, f. treasure-room; bejewelled, lavishly decorated hall. रत्नसिंहासन, m. bejewelled throne. रत्नाकर [°*na*+*ā*°], m. mine for precious stones; the sea. रत्नावली [°*na*+*ā*°], f. = रत्न-माला.

रथ *rath* [S.], m. **1.** chariot. **2.** vehicle (as of the gods; see रथ-यात्रा). — रथ-यात्रा, f. chariot-procession: the procession of a Vaiṣṇava idol on a vehicle (esp. that of Jagannāth at Puri). रथवाह, m. charioteer; chariot-horse. रथांग [°*tha*+*a*°], m. Brbh. wheel; Av. = चकवा.

[1]**रथी** *rathī* [S.], m. **1.** charioteer. **2.** warrior who fights from a chariot.

[2]**रथी** *rathī*, f. = अरथी.

रथ्या *rathyā* [S.], f. Brbh. water-channel.

[1]**रद** *rad* [S.], m. **1.** tooth. **2.** tusk. — रद-छद, m. Brbh. tooth-covering: the lip. रद-दान, m. Brbh. tooth-gift: love-bite. रद-पट, m. E.H. = रद-छद.

[2]**रद** *rad*, adj. pronun. var. = रद्द.

रदन *radan* [S.], m. = [1]रद.

रदवा-खदवा *radvā-khadvā*, m. colloq. reg. **1.** a wanderer. **2.** a good-for-nothing person.

रदीफ़ *radīf* [A. *radīf*], m. U. a word following the rhyming word at the end of a line of verse.

रद्द *radd* [A. *radd*], m. & adj. returning, rejecting: **1.** m. rejection, &c. (see adj. senses). ***2.** adj. rejected; refused. **3.** cancelled (an arrangement); annulled; rescinded. **4.** disproved. — ~ करना, to reject, &c.; to refute; to cancel, &c.; to write off (stock, a debt) – रद्द-बदल, m. = next. रद्दो-बदल [P.-*o*-], m. constant change, turmoil; changing hands (as property).

[1]**रद्दा** *raddā* [P. *rada*], m. **1.** layer; course (of bricks); single stratum (in the building up of an earthen wall). **2.** a series of rows or layers of objects, forming a pile.

[2]**रद्दा** *raddā*, m. pushing (one's way), warding off. — वह भीड़ में ~ लगाते आगे बढ़ा, he elbowed his way through the crowd.

रद्दी *raddī* [H. *radd*+-*ī*], adj. & f. **1.** adj. unwanted, waste (as paper, scrap). **2.** worthless; bad, harmful. **3.** f. waste (as paper); scrap (material). — ~, interj. rubbish! nonsense! ~ करना (की), to waste (sthg. serviceable); to throw away. – रद्दी-ख़ाना, a scrap-yard.

रन *ran* [*araṇya*-; × H. *ban*], m. wilderness; forest. — रन-बन, m. id.

रनवास *ranvās* [**rājñīvāsa*-], m. **1.** women's quarters (of a palace); harem. **2.** inner rooms (of a private house).

रनिवास *ranivās*, m. = रनवास.

[1]**रपट** *rapaṭ* [Engl. *report*], f. = रिपोर्ट. — ~ करना, to make a report (of, की), to report.

[2]रपट *rapaṭ* [cf. H. *rapaṭnā*], v.i. **1.** slip, slipping. **2.** slipperiness.

[3]रपट *rapăṭ*, m. f. pronun. var. = रब्त, 3.

रपटना *rapaṭnā*, v.i. **1.** to slip, to slide. **2.** Brbh. to rush. — रपटा-रपटी, scurry, bustle, bother.

रपटाना *rapṭānā* [cf. H. *rapaṭnā*], v.t. **1.** to cause to slip or to slide. **2.** to cause to rush; to urge on; to expedite (a matter). — रपटाकर, adv. with all speed.

रपटीला *rapṭīlā* [cf. H. *rapaṭ*], adj. slippery.

रपट्टा *rapaṭṭā* [conn. H. *rapaṭnā*], m. reg. **1.** slipping (= [2]रपट, 1). **2.** scurrying, bustle (= [1]रबड़). **3.** [? × H. *jhapaṭnā*], colloq. grasp, clutches. — ~ मारना, or लगाना, colloq. to rush, to dash.

रप-रप *rap-rap* [onom.], f. the sound of a horse's feet (trotting, or galloping).

रपरपाना *raprapānā* [cf. H. *rap-rap*], v.i. to trot, or to gallop, fast (a horse).

रपेट *rapeṭ* [cf. H. *rapeṭnā*], f. reg. hunting, chasing.

रपेटना *rapeṭnā* [? conn. H. *rapaṭnā*], v.t. reg. to hunt, to chase; to hunt down.

रपोट *rapoṭ*, m. = रिपोर्ट.

[1]रफ़ल *rafl* [Engl. *rifle*], f. a rifle.

[2]रफ़ल *rafl* [? A. *rifl*, P. *rafl*], f. a woollen shawl, wrapper.

रफ़ा *rafā* [A. *raf'*], m. inv. removing, ending (a difficulty, a need; or a quarrel, &c). — ~ करना, to remove, to end; to settle (a dispute). – रफ़ा-दफ़ा, m. = ~.

रफ़ू *rafū* [P. *rafū*], m. darning, mending; a darn. — ~ करना, to darn, to mend. – रफ़ूगर [P. *-gar*], m. a darner. °ई, f. darning. रफ़ू-चक्कर, m. colloq. making off, slipping away. रफ़ू-चक्कर में आना, to be enmeshed (as by guile: of, के); रफ़ू-चक्कर होना, to slip away.

रफ़्ता- *raftā-* [P. *rafta*]. gone: — रफ़्ता-रफ़्ता, adv. U. gradually, step by step; quietly, gently.

रफ़्तार *raftār* [P. *raftār*], f. **1.** going, motion; gait. ***2.** pace, speed. **3.** manner of proceeding, behaviour.

रफ़्ते *rafte* [P. *rafta*]. gone: — रफ़्ते-रफ़्ते, adv. Brbh. = रफ़्ता-रफ़्ता.

रब *rab* [A. *rabb*], m. *isl.* the Lord, God.

[1]रबड़ *rabaṛ* [cf. H. *rabaṛnā*], f. *Pl. HŚS.* **1.** scurrying, bustle. **2.** drudgery. **3.** strain, exertion.

[2]रबड़ *rabaṛ* [Engl. *rubber*], m. rubber.

रबड़ना *rabaṛnā* [? ←Panj.], v.i. **1.** to scurry, to bustle. **2.** to toil; to toil to little purpose.

रबड़ी *rabṛī* [**rabbā-*: Pk. *rabbā-*], f. thickened and sweetened milk.

रबर *rabar* [Engl. *rubber*], m. = [2]रबड़.

रबाब *rabāb* [A. *rabāb*], m. a stringed musical instrument (resembling the *sāraṅgī*).

रबाबिया *rabābiyā* [cf. H. *rabāb*], m. = रबाबी.

रबाबी *rabābī* [A. *rabābī*], m. a player on the *rabāb*.

रबी *rabī* [A. *rabī'*], f. **1.** spring. **2.** the spring crop, or harvest (March-April).

रब्त *rabt* [A. *rabṭ*], m. **1.** connection. ***2.** contact, association; friendship. **3.** familiarity, practice, habit. — रब्त-ज़ब्त [A. *ẓabṭ*], m. = ~, 2.

रमक *ramak* [cf. H. *ramnā*], f. Brbh. swaying (as of gait), rocking (as of a swing); impulse.

रमक़ *ramaq* [A. *ramaq*], f. **1.** last breath (of life). ***2.** tiny bit or quantity, spark.

रमचेरा *ramcerā* [cf. H. *rām*, H. *cerā*], m. a servant.

रमज़ान *ramzān* [A. *ramaẓān*], m. **1.** the ninth month of the Muslim calendar. **2.** the fast observed by Muslims during the month of Ramaẓān.

रमज़ानी *ramzānī* [A. *ramaẓānī*], adj. having to do with the month, or the fast, of Ramaẓān; born in the month of Ramaẓān.

रमझोल *ramjhol*, m. (f., *Pl.*), reg. an anklet.

रमझोला *ramjholā*, m. reg. an anklet.

रमण *ramaṇ* [S.], adj. & m. **1.** adj. delighting. ***2.** m. a lover; husband. **3.** delight, dalliance. **4.** sexual intercourse.

रमणी *ramăṇī* [S.], f. a beautiful woman; a young woman.

रमणीक *ramăṇīk* [S.], adj. = रमणीय.

रमणीय *ramăṇīyă* [S.], adj. lovely, charming.

रमणीयता *ramăṇīyătā* [S.], f. **1.** loveliness, charm (of a young woman). **2.** charm (of nature).

रमत *ramat* [cf. H. *ramnā*], f. wandering about, stroll.

[1]रमना *ramnā* [**ramyati*], v.i. **1.** to wander happily, to roam; to stroll; to go (one's) way. **2.** to take pleasure or delight (in); to be attracted (to), or engrossed (in). — मन ~, to

take delight (in); to be distracted (the thoughts).

[2]**रमना** *ramnā* [? cf. H. [1]*ramnā*], m. Brbh. a park, pasture.

रमल *raml* [A. *raml*], m. *Pl. HŚS.* sand: fortune-telling by lines or figures drawn in the sand, or on the ground.

रमा *ramā* [S.], f. beloved: **1.** a wife. ***2.** *mythol.* a title of Lakṣmī. — रमा-पति, m. lord of Ramā (a title of Viṣṇu).

रमाना *ramānā* [cf. H. [1]*ramnā*], v.t. **1.** to delight (a person). **2.** to attract; to take possession of (the heart, &c.); to distract (from grief: the heart). **3.** to enact (a symbolic observance: as the *rās* dance, or the lighting of a *dhūnī* or penance-fire). — भभूत ~, to smear ash on the forehead.

रमास *ramās*, m. pronun. var. = रवाँस.

रम्य *ramyă* [S.], adj. = रमणीय.

रय *ray* [*rajas-*], f. (? m.) Brbh. dust.

रलना *ralnā*, v.i. **1.** to be pounded, to be ground. **2.** to be mixed, mingled; to be lost in a mass. **3.** Brbh. to be held (in the hand). **4.** to be in league or collusion (with). — रलना-मिलना, to be or to become close (friends).

रलाना *ralānā* [cf. H. *ralnā*], v.t. **1.** to pound together, to grind; to mix.

रव *rav* [S.], m. **1.** cry (of living creatures); voice. **2.** sound, noise; din. **3.** fig. reputation, fame.

रव- *rav-* [P. *rav*]. going: रवा-रवी [P. *-ā-*], f. haste, scurry.

रवथ *ravath* [S.], m. *Pl. HŚS.* the cuckoo (= कोयल).

रवन *ravan*, m. Brbh. = रमण.

रवनि *ravani* [ad. *ramaṇī-*; × H. *ravan*], f. Brbh. wife, lady.

रवन्ना *ravannā* [H. *ravānā*], m. pronun. var. reg. **1.** a pass, permit. **2.** an invoice.

रवाँस *ravāṁs*, m. a kind of bean, *Dolichos sinensis*.

[1]**रवा** *ravā* [**rava-*[2]], m. **1.** a grain (as of sand, gunpowder); a speck. **2.** a bit, piece; *chem.* crystal. **3.** reg. (W.) crushed or ground material (as husk of wheat, or metal filings). — रवेदार [P. *dār*], adj. granular.

[2]**रवा** *ravā* [P. *ravā*], adj. inv. **1.** current. **2.** proper, right; suitable. — रवादार [P. *-dār*], adj. considering proper, &c., approving; proper, &c. (= ~). रवादार होना (का), to consider proper.

रवाटा *ravāṭā* [cf. H. *roṭī*], m. pronun. var. reg. bread made from the millets *kodoṁ* or *sāṁvāṁ*.

रवानगी *ravānăgī* [P. *ravānagī*], f. **1.** departure. **2.** despatch (of a parcel, &c.); forwarding.

रवाना *ravānā* [P. *ravāna*], adj. inv. **1.** departed. **2.** despatched, sent. — ~ करना, to send off, to see off; to despatch. ~ होना, to depart, to set off or out; to be despatched.

रवानी *ravānī* [P. *ravānī*], f. going: **1.** flow (of a liquid). **2.** fluidity. **3.** fluency (of speech, reading).

रवाल *ravāl* [cf. **rava-*[2]], adj. *Pl.* granulous.

रवि *ravi* [S.], m. the sun. — रवि-कुल, m. *mythol.* the solar race. रवि-तनया, Brbh. f. daughter of the sun: a title of the river Jumna. रवि-नंदन, m. Brbh. title of the monkey Sugrīva. °-नंदिनी, f. Brbh. = रवि-तनया. रविवार, m. Sunday, °ईय, adj. रविवासर, m. = रविवार.

रविश *raviś* [P. *raviś*], f. **1.** motion, gait. **2.** practice, custom. **3.** conduct. **4.** means, method. **5.** path (in a garden).

रवैया *ravaiyā* [cf. P. *rav*], m. **1.** behaviour, conduct; manner, attitude. **2.** rule, law, institution.

रशना *raśănā* [S.], f. *Pl. HŚS.* a woman's belt of woven strands.

रश्क *raśk* [P. *raśk*], f. envy; jealousy.

रश्की *raśkī* [P. *raśkī*], adj. envious; jealous.

रश्ती *raśtī*, f. *Pl.* sum paid by a cultivator in return for being allowed to reclaim waste land.

रश्मि *raśmi* [S.], m. a ray of light.

रस *ras* [*rasa-*], m. **1.** juice, sap; liquid; liquor. **2.** gravy, broth. **3.** essence, essential part (of anything). **4.** a bodily secretion. **5.** exudation; gum. **6.** taste, flavour (of which six kinds were traditionally distinguished). **7.** savour, relish. **8.** pleasure; joy; elegance, charm; wit. **9.** *rhet.* any of several tastes or sentiments characterising a literary work (from eight to ten such *rasas* are usually distinguished). **10.** mercury. — ~ आना (को), to relish, to enjoy. – ~ टपकना, juice to drop or to trickle; to be in full bloom or vigour; to be sexually stirred. ~ पड़ना (में), juice or sap to fill or to well (into); delight to be had (from). ~ भीगना, fig. adolescence to be under way. ~ लेना, to extract the essence (of, का); to savour, to enjoy. रस-खान, m. *ras*-mine: a title of Kṛṣṇa. रस-खीर, m. rice boiled in milk, or in sugar and water; sugar-cane juice. रस-गुल्ला, m. a sweet: balls of soft milk-cheese soaked in syrup. रसज्ञ, adj. &

m. discriminating (of taste; or in art or culture); knowing the essence, or the spirit (of); a discriminating person, connoisseur; one versed in the *rasas* (see 9. above); an alchemist. °ता, discrimination, taste, &c. रसद, adj. Brbh. giving delight, &c. रसदार [P. *-dār*], adj. juicy; tasty. रस-पानी, m. a light snack, light breakfast. रस-प्रिया, f. ? name of a song current among Vidyāpati singers (Bihar). रस-भरा, adj. flavour-filled, luscious. °-भरी, f. a type of small plum. रस-भस्म, m. mercuric oxide. रसमय, adj. savorous; charming. रस-रस, adv. Av. slowly, gently. रस-राज, m. Brbh. king of *ras*: mercury; the amatory (*śr̥ṅgār*) *rasa* (see 9. above). रसवत्ता, f. juiciness, &c. °-वान, adj. juicy; tasty; charming; elegant; witty. °-वती, °-वंती, f. रसवाद, m. amorous conversation; savorous or quarrelsome conversation. रस-सिद्ध, adj. successful in the evocation of a *ras*. रस-सिंदूर, m. a mercuric salt used in homeopathy. रसहीन, adj. dry (of manner). रसाकर्षण [°*sa*+*ā*°], m. *chem.* osmosis. रसात्मक [°*sa*+*ā*°], adj. juicy; artistic (as imagination, or a literary style). °ता, f. रसायन [°*sa*+*a*°], m. chemistry; alchemy; a draught, elixir. °ज्ञ, m. chemist. °-विज्ञान, m. chemistry. °-विद्या, f., °-शास्त्र, m. id. °ई, m. Brbh. an alchemist, chemist. रसास्वादन [°*sa*+*ā*°], m. savouring, enjoying. °-आस्वादी, adj.

रसद *rasad* [P. *rasad*], f. incoming: **1.** provisions, supplies (esp. of grain). **2.** allowance, ration. **3.** a share, portion. — रसद-विभाग, m. commissariat.

रसना *rasănā* [S.], f. **1.** the tongue (properly as the organ of taste). **2.** transf. taste. — रसनावली [°*na*+*ā*°], f. *Pl.* language, speech.

रसना *rasnā* [*rasati*[2], and H. *ras*], v.i. **1.** [× H. [1]*risnā*] to drip. **2.** Brbh. to feel delight, or ecstasy (see रस).

रसबटा *rasbaṭā* [H. *rassā, rassī*+H. [2]*bāṁṭnā*], m. a rope-maker.

रसमसा *rasmasā*, adj. **1.** wet; wet with perfume, or with sweat. **2.** Brbh. ecstatic.

रसमसाना *rasmasānā* [cf. H. *rasmăsā*], v.i. reg. **1.** to be wet (with perfume, or sweat). **2.** to be in ecstasy.

रसरा *rasrā* [*raśmi-*], m. Brbh. Av. = रस्सा.

रसरी *rasrī* [cf. *raśmi-*], f. = रस्सी.

रसवाई *rasvāī*, f. reg. (W). **1.** the ceremony of distributing sugar-cane juice on the first day of pressing the cane. **2.** *Pl.* the cane-pressing season.

[1]**रसा** *rasā* [*rasaka-*], m. **1.** gravy, broth. **2.** sauce. — रसादार [P. *-dār*], adj. = next. रसेदार, adj. served with sauce (a curry).

[2]**रसा** *rasā* [S.], f. **1.** the earth. **2.** *mythol.* the nether world. — रसा-तल, m. name of the lowest of the seven hells, = ~, 2.

रसाई *rasāī* [P. *rasā'ī*], f. U. **1.** access, entrance. **2.** reach, compass (of ability, mind, knowledge).

[1]**रसाना** *rasānā* [cf. *rasati*[2]], v.t. reg. **1.** to solder. **2.** Brbh. to dissipate (anger).

[2]**रसाना** *rasānā* [? cf. H. *ras*], v.i. reg. to be delighted.

रसानिया *rasāniyā*, m. *Pl.* = रसायनी.

रसायन *rasāyan*, m. see s.v. रस.

रसाल *rasāl* [*rasāla-*], adj. & m. **1.** adj. juicy. **2.** tasty, &c. (= रसीला). **3.** m. a mango tree. **4.** *Pl. HŚS.* sugar-cane. — रसाल-शर्करा, f. cane-sugar.

रसाला *rasālā* [S.], f. curds mixed with sugar and spices.

रसाव *rasāv* [? cf. H. *rasānā*], m. reg. (W). preparing for rain: preparing and sowing, then ploughing or harrowing land before the first rain (while the soil is still too dry to allow germination).

रसावल *rasāval*, m. reg. (W). rice cooked in sugar and water.

रसि रसि *rasi rasi*, adv. E.H. = रसे रसे.

रसिक *rasik* [S.], adj. & m. **1.** adj. full of feeling or passion; sentimental; witty; elegant. **2.** taking pleasure; fanciful; voluptuous. **3.** m. a discriminating person (as in literature, art); a connoisseur. **4.** *hind.* a person moved by passionate religious devotion (esp. for Kr̥ṣṇa). **5.** a man of feeling, passion, &c. **6.** a voluptuary.

रसिकता *rasikătā* [S.], f. **1.** artistic discrimination or sense. **2.** feeling, passion, &c. (see रसिक). **3.** voluptuousness.

रसिका *rasikā* [S.], f. the tongue.

[1]**रसिया** *rasiyā* [*rasika-*], m. **1.** a man of feeling or passion, &c. (see रसिक). **2.** a pleasure-seeker; a dissolute man.

[2]**रसिया** *rasiyā* [cf. H. *ras*], m. reg. (W). a type of Holī song (Braj and Bundelkhand).

रसियाना *rasiyānā* [cf. H. *ras*], v.i. **1.** to be juicy, or moist; to run with juice. **2.** to ripen.

[1]**रसियावल** *rasiyāval*, m. reg. (W). = रसवाई, 1.

[2]**रसियावल** *rasiyāval* [**rasikācāmala-*], m. reg. (W). sugar-cane juice and rice.

रसी *rasī* [S.], adj. reg. = रसिक.

रसीद *rasīd* [P. *rasīd*], f. **1.** receipt (of sthg). **2.** acknowledgement of receipt; a receipt. — ~ करना, colloq. to strike, to land (a blow: on को). ~ देना (को), to give an acknowledgement or receipt (of or for, की).

रसीला *rasīlā* [cf. *rasin-*], adj. **1.** juicy; underdone (meat). **2.** tasty. **3.** savorous, spicy (speech, language). **4.** voluptuous. **5.** attractive, charming.

रसूख़ *rasūkh* [A. *rusūkh*], m. **1.** friendship (with, से). **2.** weight, influence.

रसूम *rasūm* [A. *rusūm*], m. f. pl. U. **1.** customs, &c. (see रस्म). **2.** fees, dues. **3.** customary gifts of money made by tenants to a landlord.

रसूल *rasūl* [A. *rasūl*], m. U. a prophet.

रसे *rase* [H. *rasnā*], adv. reg. slowly, softly. — ~ ~, adv. id.

रसोई *rasoī* [*rasavatī-*], f. **1.** kitchen. **2.** food, a dish; a meal. — ~ करना, or पकाना, or बनाना, to cook or to prepare food. कच्ची ~, f. cooked food which is not fried; uncooked food. पक्की ~, f. fried food. — रसोई-घर, m. kitchen. रसोईदार [P. *-dār*], m. cook. °ई, f. cooking; cookery.

रसोइया *rasoiya* [cf. H. *rasoī*], m. a cook.

रसोईपन *rasoīpan* [cf. H. *rasoī*], m. the skill or art of cookery.

रसौंत *rasaumt* [**rasavantī-*], f. *Pl. HŚS.* = रसौत.

रसौत *rasaut* [**rasavantī-*], f. and adj. **1.** *Pl. HŚS.* a watery extract prepared from the stem and root of the barberry, *Berberis* (used in treating ophthalmia). ***2.** fig. reg. anything bitter or disagreeable.

रसौता *rasautā*, m. reg. = रसौती.

रसौती *rasautī*, f. reg. 1. = रसाव. **2.** sowing rice early in the rainy season.

रसौली *rasaulī* [**rasapūlikā-*], f. **1.** a swelling, or growth; tumour. **2.** a boil.

रस्ता *rastā*, m. = रास्ता.

रस्म *rasm* [A. *rasm*], f. marking out: **1.** manner, custom; tradition. **2.** a customary practice, usage. **3.** a ceremony. — ~ पर चलना, or जाना, to follow custom. – रस्म-रिवाज, m. = ~, 2.

रस्मी *rasmī* [A. *rasmī*], adj. usual, customary; traditional.

रस्य *rasyă* [S.], adj. tasty, savorous.

रस्सा *rassā* [*raśmi-*], m. a heavy rope. — रस्साकशी [P. *-kaśī*], f. tug-of-war.

रस्सी *rassī* [*raśmi-*], f. **1.** rope. **2.** cord; string. **3.** reins. **4.** fig. control. **5.** fig. a tie, bond.

रह- *rah-* chiefly U. a road, way (= राह): — रहगीर [P. *-gīr*], m. a wayfarer. रहनुमा [P. *-numā*], m. inv. a guide. °ई, f. guidance. रहगुज़र, m. a wayfarer. °ई, m. f. id.; f. highway; a passage. रहगुज़ार, m. road; pass; a wayfarer. रहबर [P. *-bar*], m. a guide.

रहँकला *rahamklā*, m. Brbh. = रहकला.

रहँट *rahamṭ* [*araghaṭṭa-*], m. a Persian wheel (for drawing water). — ~ लगाना, fig. to come and go repeatedly, in an unbroken cycle.

रहँटा *rahamṭā* [cf. H. *rahamṭ*], m. reg. a spinning-wheel.

रहँटी *rahamṭī* [cf. H. *rahamṭā*], f. **1.** a small water-wheel. **2.** reg. a spinning-wheel.

रहकल *rahkal* [cf. *ratha-*; +H. [3]*kal*], m. reg. (W.) = रहकला.

रहकला *rahaklā* [cf. *ratha-*; +H. [3]*kal*], m. var. /rɔhkəla/. reg. (W). a light two-wheeled cart.

रहट *rahaṭ*, m. = रहँट.

रहटा *rahṭā*, m. **1.** a small water-wheel. 2. = रहँटा.

रहड़ू *rahṛū* [cf. *ratha-*], m. reg. a light open cart.

रहत *rahat* [cf. H. *rahna*], m. *Pl.* staying, remaining; abode.

[1]**रहन** *rahn* [cf. H. *rahnā*], f. manner of life. — रहन-सहन, f. m. id.; age-old way of life.

[2]**रहन** *rahn*, m. = रेहन.

रहना *rahnā* [**rahati*: Pk. *rahaï*], v.i. **1.** to remain; to stay (in a place); to reside, to live. **2.** to be left (over, or behind); to be omitted. **3.** to be, to exist, to be found. बहुत अच्छा रहेगा, that will be very good (an arrangement, &c). **4.** to last, to endure. **5.** to hold back; to remain (without, से); to be deprived (of); to be inert, helpless (the body, from exhaustion or cold); to be helpless (to act). — जाता ~, to keep diminishing (to zero): to vanish, to evaporate (as joy, zeal). – रहना-सहना, to live (one's life), to live (in or at). – रह-रहकर, adv. stopping repeatedly; at intervals; again and again. – रहते, adv. in the presence (of, के); in the lifetime (of); despite the fact (that). रहा-सहा, adj. remained, left over; indifferent, wanting (as in energy, zeal); slack. रही-सही आशा, f. a forlorn hope.

रहम *rahm* [A. *raḥm*], m. pity, compassion; tenderness. — ~ करना, to take pity (on, पर); to show kindness (to). ~ खाना, to feel pity, &c. (for, पर). – रहमदिल, adj. tender-hearted, compassionate; kind-hearted. रहमोकरम [A. *karam*], m. grace and favour.

रहमत *rahmat* [A. *raḥma*: P. *raḥmat*], f. **1.** = रहम. **2.** divine mercy. **3.** a gift or blessing from Allāh.

रहमान *rahmān* [A. *raḥmān*], adj. & m. **1.** adj. merciful. **2.** m. *isl.* the merciful one: a title of Allah.

रहला *rahlā* [**rahala-*], m. reg. the chick-pea, gram.

रहवा *rahvā* [cf. *rahita-*], m. dimin. reg. (E.) a destitute person (taken into a family).

रहवाई *rahvāī* [cf. H. *rahnā*], f. reg. house-rent.

रहवारी *rahvārī*, m. *Pl.* a community of camel-traders.

रहवास *rahvās* [cf. H. *rahnā+vāsa-*], m. **1.** residence. **2.** a resident.

रहवैया *rahvaiyā* [cf. H. *rahnā*], m. reg. a resident.

रहस *rahs* [A. *raḥs*], m. *Pl.* trampling.

¹**रहस** *rahas* [*rabhasa-*], m. **1.** merriment; delight. **2.** m. f. = रास; a partic. dance form evolved at the court of Vājid Alī Śāh of Lucknow. — ~ ~, adv. merrily, gaily. – रहस-बधाव, m. = मुँह-दिखावा. रहस-बधावा, m. id.

²**रहस्** *rahas* [S.], m. *Pl. HŚS.* a lonely place, solitude.

रहस- *rahas-* [cf. H. ¹*rahas*; ? and *rabhasa-*], v.i. Brbh. Av. to rejoice.

रहस्य *rahasyă* [S.], adj. & m. **1.** adj. secret, mysterious. **2.** m. a secret; a mystery; secret, or mystical doctrine. – रहस्य-भरा, adj. mysterious. रहस्यमय, adj. = ~; mystical. रहस्यवाद, m. mysticism. °ई, adj. & m. रहस्यात्मक [°*sya+ā*°], adj. = रहस्यमय.

रहाइश *rahāiś*, f. see रिहाइश.

रहाई *rahāī* [cf. H. *rahnā*], f. Brbh. rest, ease, comfort.

रहाऊ *rahāū* [cf. H. *rahnā*], adj. reg. (N.) lasting; durable, firm.

रहाना *rahānā* [cf. H. *rāhnā*], v.t. to cause to be roughened, notched, &c. (a millstone).

रहाव *rahāv* [cf. H. *rahnā*], m. reg. (N.) **1.** stay, rest, pause. **2.** E.H. a repeated verse.

रहित *rahit* [S.], adj. also -रहित. **1.** deprived (of, से). **2.** devoid (of), free (from); without. — ~ करना, to deprive (of); to free (from).

रहीम *rahīm* [A. *raḥīm*], m. = रहमान.

¹**राँग** *rāṁg* [*raṅga-*¹], m. reg. dye, juice of plants used in dyeing.

²**राँग** *rāṁg* [*raṅga-*³, Pk. *raṁga-*], m. = राँगा. — ~ होना, to be melted; to fall in value. – राँगभरा, m. *Pl.* pewter-worker: a maker of pewter toys.

राँगा *rāṁgā* [*raṅga-*³, Pk. *raṁga-*], m. pewter; tin.

¹**राँच-** *rāṁc-* [*rajyate*¹; × *rañj-*], v.i. Av. to be dyed.

²**राँच-** *rāṁc-* [*rajyate*²; × *rañj-*], v.i. Brbh. **1.** to be affected (by); to be attracted (to).

राँजना *rāṁjnā* [*rañjayati*¹], v.t. reg. **1.** to dye; to mark. **2.** [× H. *rāṁgā*], to solder.

¹**राँझन** *rāṁjhan* [conn. *rañjana-*²], m. (? f.) reg. a large (earthen) water-jar.

²**राँझन** *rāṁjhan* [conn. *rañjana-*²; ? ← Panj. *ramjhaṇ*], m. reg. lover, sweetheart.

राँझना *rāṁjhnā*, m. reg. = ²राँझन.

राँझरा *rāṁjhrā*, m. reg. a maker or seller of coloured or painted toys.

राँझा *rāṁjhā* [Panj. *rāṁjhā*], m. reg. (? N.) fig. lover, sweetheart.

राँड़ *rāṁṛ* [*raṇḍā-*], f. **1.** a widow. **2.** a promiscuous woman; prostitute. — ~ का साँड़, m. colloq. a womaniser. बाल ~, f. a young widow; a child widow.

राँड़का *rāṁṛkā* [cf. *raṇḍa-*], m. reg. a blockhead, stupid person.

राँड़ा *rāṁṛā* [*raṇḍa-*], adj. & m. reg. **1.** adj. barren, unproductive. **2.** m. a widower.

राँड़ापा *rāṁṛāpā* [cf. H. *rāṁṛ*], m. = रंडापा.

¹**राँद** *rāṁd*, adv. pronun. var. reg. = ¹राँध.

²**राँद** *rāṁd*, f. reg. quarrel.

राँदना *rāṁdnā* [P. *rāndan*], v.t. reg. to drive out, or away.

¹**राँध** *rāṁdh*, adv. Av. near. — राँध-पड़ोस, m. neighbourhood.

²**राँध** *rāṁdh*, f. reg. = ²राँद.

राँधना *rāṁdhnā* [*randhayati*], v.t. to prepare food, to cook.

राँपी *rāṁpī* [**rampa-*: Pk. *raṁpa-*], f. a scraper (as used by workers in leather).

राँभना *rāṁbhnā* [*rambhate*], v.i. to bellow, to roar (animals).

रांँवा *rāṁvā* [*ārāma-*], m. reg. **1.** wooded or waste land (esp. near a town or village). **2.** *Pl.* a tax on cattle grazing on waste land.

राई *rāī* [*rājikā-*], f. **1.** a mustard seed. **2.** transf. a tiny particle, grain. **3.** a type of mustard, *Sinapis racemosa*, having small seeds. — ~ **को पर्वत गिनना**, fig. to make a mountain out of a molehill. ~ **भर**, adv. a grain, a tiny amount. ~ **से पर्वत करना**, fig. to make a mountain out of a molehill. **काली** ~, f. black mustard. **सफ़ेद** ~, f. white mustard. – **राई-काई**, broken to pieces, smashed, pulped. **राई-नोन उतारना**, to avert the effect of the evil eye from a child by passing a quantity of mustard and salt ceremonially around the child and then burning it. **राई-रत्ती**, f. mustard and crab's eye seed(s). **राई-रत्ती करके**, adv. little by little, minutely, painstakingly.

राउर *rāur* [*rājakula-*], adj. & m. Brbh. Av. **1.** adj. your, yours. **2.** m. royal palace, or court; royal apartment.

राउल *rāul* [*rājakula-*], m. 1. = **राव**. **2.** warrior, knight. 3. = **राउर**, 2. **4.** Panj. a yogi; a beggar.

राकड़ *rākaṛ* [cf. *raṅka-*], f. (?) reg. (W). stony, sandy soil; uneven ground.

राका *rākā* [S.], f. **1.** the day of full moon; full moon. 2. *Pl. HŚS.* itch, scab. — **राका-पति**, m. husband of *rākā*; full moon. **राकेश** [°*ka*+*ī*°], m. lord of rākā: full moon; a title of Śiva.

राक्षस *rākṣas* [S.], m. **1.** an evil spirit, demon. **2.** fig. a fiendishly wicked person. **3.** fig. a glutton. — **राक्षस-पति**, m. *mythol.* lord of demons: a title of Rāvaṇ. **राक्षस-विवाह**, m. a marriage which has entailed violent abduction of the bride. **राक्षस-वेला**, f. the time when evil spirits are about, evening twilight.

¹**राक्षसी** *rākṣasī* [S.], f. a demoness.

²**राक्षसी** *rākṣasī* [cf. H. *rākṣas*], adj. demoniacal, fiendish.

राख *rākh* [*rakṣā-*²], f. ashes. — **राखदानी** [P. -*dānī*], ash-tray.

राख- *rākh-*, v.t. Brbh. Av. = **रखना**.

राखड़ी *rākhṛī* [? cf. *rakṣā-*¹], f. *Pl. HŚS.* a women's head ornament.

राखस *rākhas* [*rākṣasa-*], m. = **राक्षस**. — **राखस-पत्ता**, m. *Pl.* the aloe plant.

राखात *rākhāt*, m. (?) reg. grazing lands.

¹**राखी** *rākhī* [cf. *rakṣā-*¹], f. **1.** protective talisman: a piece of thread, &c., with a rosette, tied ceremonially round a protector's or patron's wrist on the full moon of the month Śrāvaṇ: esp. by a sister round a brother's wrist, when the brother gives a small gift of money. **2.** the festival of *rakṣābandhan*. **3.** euph. protection money.

²**राखी** *rākhī*, f. = **राख**.

³**राखी** *rākhī* [cf. *rakṣin-*], m. reg. guard, watchman (over a ripening crop).

राग *rāg* [S.], m. **1.** colour (esp. red). **2.** passion; desire; love. **3.** a musical mode or sequence. harmony; melody; a musical note (as falling within a partic. *rāg*). — ~ **अलापना**, or **गाना**, to sing a song. ~ **पूरना**, v.t. fig. to tell a long story. **अपना** ~ **अलापना**, or **गाना**, to sing (only) one's own song: to talk only of oneself. – **रागदारी** [P. -*dārī*], f. having, or following, *rāga*: the Indian classical style of singing. **राग-द्वेष**, m. love and hatred. **राग-रंग**, m. music and merriment: fun, enjoyment. **राग-रंग में रहना**, to have fun, a good time. **राग-रलियाँ**, f. pl. = **राग-रंग**. **रागात्मक** [°*ga*+*ā*°], adj. emotional, passionate. **रागान्वित** [°*ga*+*a*°], adj. moved by passion, &c.

राग- *rāg-* [cf. H. *rāg*], v.t. Brbh. to sing.

रागिणी *rāgiṇī* [S.], f. = **रागिनी**.

रागिनी *rāginī* [ad. *rāgiṇī-*], f. a modification (thought of as a feminine personification) of a main musical mode or *rāg*.

¹**रागी** *rāgī* [S.], adj. **1.** coloured; red. **2.** imbued (with). **3.** passionate.

²**रागी** *rāgī* [ad. *rāgī-*], f. a millet, *Eleusine coracana*.

राघव *rāghav* [S.], m. *mythol.* of the family of Raghu: a patronymic of Rāmcandra.

¹**राच-** *rāc-* [*rajyate*¹, *rakta-*¹: anal.], v.i. Brbh. to be dyed.

²**राच-** *rāc-* [*rajyate*², *rakta-*²: anal.], v.i. Brbh. Av. **1.** to be affected or imbued (with love, passion; or by concern). **2.** to be attached (to).

राछ *rāch* [*rathya-*], m. reg. *Pl.* **1.** a toothed instrument. **2.** reg. (W.) the heddles of a loom. **3.** pivot (of a hand-mill).

राछ- *rāch-*. E.H. see hww. in **राक्ष-**.

राछसनी *rāchasănī*, f. = ¹**राक्षसी**.

राज़ *rāz* [P. *rāz*], m. a secret; a mystery. — ~ **देना**, to let out a secret. ~ **फ़ाश करना**, id. – **राज़दान** [P. -*dān*], adj. & m. knowing secrets, &c. **राज़दार** [P. -*dār*], adj. & m. keeping a secret, trusty; a confidant; accessory (to a fact). °**ई**, f. secrecy; concealing what should be made known.

¹**राज** *rāj* [ad. *rājan-*], m. **1.** king; prince; lord, master, ruler. **2.** sthg. royal; anything the best or chief of its kind. **3.** a mason, builder (= **राजगीर**). — (in cpds. ¹**राज** often falls

together with ²राज.) राज-कन्या, f. princess; = केवड़ा. राज-काज, m. = next. राज-कार्य, m. royal duties; state affairs; public administration. राज-कुमार, m. prince. °ई, f. राज-कुल, m. royal family, or dynasty. राज-कोष, m. exchequer; king's treasury. राज-क्षमा, f. an amnesty. राज-गद्दी, f. royal cushion or seat, throne. राज-गद्दी का दिन, m. coronation day. राजगामी, adj. *law.* subject to escheat, or reversion to the state (land). राजगामी होना, to revert to the state; to be confiscated. राजगीर [P. *-gīr*], m. a mason, builder (properly a master-mason, &c.) °ई, f. mason's or builder's work or occupation; masonry. राज-गृह, m. palace. राज-तंत्र, m. monarchy. °ईय, adj. monarchical °वादी, adj. adhering to monarchism. राज-तिलक, m. a *tilak* serving as a sign of investiture or coronation; transf. coronation. राज-दंत, m. an incisor tooth. राज-दंड, m. sceptre; punishment at a king's order. राज-दूत, m. an ambassador. °आवास, m. embassy. °ईय, adj. राज-द्रोह, m. treason; rebellion. °ई, adj. & m. traitorous; rebellious; a traitor, &c. राजधानी, f. capital (city). राज-नय, m. = राज-नीति; diplomacy. °इक, adj. diplomatic. राज-नीति, f. royal policy or polity: politics. °क, adj. political; diplomatic. °ज्ञ, m. a politician; a diplomat. राजप, m. regent. राज-पति, m. emperor. °-पत्नी, f. empress. राजपत्रित, adj. gazetted (officially). राज-पथ, m. main road or street; highway. राज-पद, m. kingly rank or office; the throne; a government post. राज-पाट, m. throne (see also s.v. ²राज). राज-पुत्र, m. prince. °इका, f., °ई, f. princess. राजपूत, m. member of a loose grouping of Hindu communities equated ritually with the ancient *kṣatriyas*, a Rājpūt. °ई, adj. & f. Rājpūt; martial prowess. °आना, m. U. = राजस्थान. राज-बहा, m. = next. राज-बाहा, m. main branch or channel (as of a canal). राज-भक्त, adj. loyal. °इ, f. loyalty (as to a king). राज-भवन, m. royal palace; governor's residence; state guest-house. राज-भोग, m. name of a sweet; *hind.* a major (noon-time) daily offering of food to an idol; the endowment of a temple. राज-माता, f. king's mother. राज-मार्ग, m. = राज-पथ. राज-मिस्तरी, m. = राजगीर. राज-योग, m. royal yoga: an interior yoga; unity of consciousness. राज-राजेश्वर, m. great king of kings: emperor. °ई, f. राज-रोग, m. tuberculosis; a mortal illness; any dire affliction; a mania. राजर्षि [°*ja*+*r̥*°], m. royal seer or sage. राज-लक्ष्मी, f. royal majesty or power. राज-वंश, m. royal family, or dynasty. राजवाद, m. monarchism. °ई, adj. & m. monarchist. राजशाही [P. *-śāhī*], f. royal status, royalty. राज-श्री, f. = राज-लक्ष्मी. राज-सत्ता, f. kingly power or authority; power or authority of a state; a monarchy; a state, a power. °त्मक, adj. monarchic. °-सत्तावादी, adj. & m. monarchist. राज-सभा, f. royal assembly; royal council. राज-सूय, m. *hist.* a sacrifice performed at a coronation (by the king and his tributary princes). राजस्थान, m. the Indian state of Rajasthan. °ई, adj. & m., f. of or from Rajasthan; a man from Rajasthan; a dialect, or the dialects collectively, of Rajasthan. राजस्व, m. king's property; a state's revenue. °ई, adj. राज-हंस, m. a goose with red legs and bill; a flamingo. राजाधिदेय [°*ja*+*a*°], m. *govt.* privy purse. राजाधिराज [°*ja*+*a*°], m. king of kings: emperor. राजाधिकार [°*ja*+*a*°], m. paramount power; royal prerogative. राजाज्ञा, [°*ja*+*ā*°], f. royal edict, command. राजाश्रय [°*ja*+*ā*°], m. royal patronage. राजेंद्र [°*ja*+*i*°], m. an Indra among kings: high king, emperor.

²**राज** *rāj* [*rājya-*], m. **1.** royalty, kingly state. **2.** kingdom, realm, state; empire. **3.** rule, sway; government. (cf. with these senses also cpds. of ¹राज, which in comp. often falls together with ²राज-; see also राज्य-). — राज-पाट, m. kingdom and throne: dominion; administration or policy of a state. राज-भाषा, f. administrative or state language.

राज- *rāj-* [ad. *rājati*, *rājate*], v.i. Brbh. to be resplendent; to shine.

राजकीय *rājǎkīyǎ* [S.], adj. **1.** royal. **2.** concerning a state or nation (as a language, function, &c). **3.** concerning a government; official (as an announcement).

राजगीर *rājgīr*, m. see s.v. ¹राज.

राजता *rājǎtā* [S.], f. = राजत्व.

राजत्व *rājatvǎ* [S.], m. **1.** kingship. **2.** rule, reign.

राजमा *rājmā* [Panj. *rājmāṁ*], m. kidney beans.

राजस *rājas* [S.], adj. concerning, characterised by or arising from passion (रजस्).

राजसी *rājǎsī* [S.], adj. royal, regal.

राजस्व *rājasvǎ* [S.], m. see s.v. ¹राज.

राजा *rājā* [S.], m. inv. **1.** a rajah, king. **2.** lord, master; governor. **3.** *hist.* title awarded during the period of British rule in India. **4.** colloq. an extravagant and careless person.

राजाऊ *rājāū* [cf. H. *rājā*], adj. kingly, royal.

राजापन *rājāpan* [cf. H. *rājā*], m. kingship, royalty.

राजि *rāji* [S.], f. streak, line; line parting the hair.

राज़िक़ *rāziq* [A. *rāziq*], m. E.H. fosterer; the supreme being.

¹**राज़ी** *rāzī* [A. *rāẓī*], adj. **1.** pleased, content. **2.** regarding with favour, approving. **3.** coll. in good health, well. — ~ करना, to gratify, to satisfy; to persuade, to prevail (on, को; to, पर);

to conciliate (opponents). ~ होना, to be pleased (with, से); to approve (of); to be satisfied (with, से or पर); to consent (to, पर); to deign (to). – राज़ी-ख़ुशी, adj. & f. contented and happy; well and happy; willing consent. राज़ी-ख़ुशी से, adv. gladly.

²राज़ी *rāzī* [P. *rāz*+-*ī*], adj. secret.

राजीव *rājīv* [S.], m. striped, or streaked: **1.** a striped or spotted deer. ***2.** the blue lotus.

राज्ञी *rājñī* [S.], f. = रानी.

राज्य *rājyă* [S.], m. (for some cpds. see equivalent forms s.v. ¹राज; see also ²राज). **1.** royalty, kingly state, or status; sovereignty. ***2.** kingdom; state. **3.** state (of the Indian Union). **4.** rule, sway; government. — ~ करना, to rule. – राज्य-च्युत, adj. deposed, dethroned. °इ, f. राज्य-तंत्र, m. type of governmental system, polity. राज्य-त्याग, m. abdication of rule, or of a throne. राज्य-निष्ठा, f. allegiance to a state. राज्यपाल, m. governor of an (Indian) state. राज्य-भाषा, f. state language. राज्य-संघ, m. union of kingdoms or states, federation. राज्य-सभा, f. Council of States (upper house of the Indian Parliament). राज्याधिकार [°*ya*+*a*°], m. authority over a kingdom; right or title to sovereignty. °ई, adj. & m. having the authority of a king, or of a state; having a right or title to sovereignty; king, ruler, governor. राज्याभिषिक्त [°*ya*+*a*°], adj. anointed king: enthroned. राज्याभिषेक [°*ya*+*a*°], m. coronation. राज्यारोहण [°*ya*+*ā*°], m. ascent of a throne.

राज्यीय *rājyīyă* [S.], adj. = राजकीय, 2.

राठौर *rāṭhaur* [*rāṣṭrakūṭa*-], m. & adj. **1.** m. name of a community of Rājpūts. **2.** adj. reg. strong, tough, hardy.

¹राड़ *rāṛ* [*rāṭi*-, Pk. *rāḍi*-], f. fight; quarrel; dispute, strife. — ~ करना, to fight, &c. ~ मचाना, to create a disturbance; to stir up strife.

²राड़ *rāṛ* [**raḍḍa*-], adj. base; cowardly.

¹राड़ी *rāṛī* [cf. H. ¹*rāṛ*], adj. & m. **1.** adj. quarrelsome. **2.** m. a quarrelsome person.

²राड़ी *rāṛī*, f. reg. (E.) a coarse, hard grass found on poor soils.

³राड़ी *rāṛī*, f. reg. the sharp point of an arrow, or of a pen.

राढ़ *rāṛh* [conn. *raṭhati*], f. = ¹राड़.

राढ़ी *rāṛhī*, f. reg. = ²राड़ी.

राणा *rāṇā* [*rajana*-], m. usu. inv. **1.** title of a prince or king (esp. among Rājpūts). **2.** form of address to a Rājpūt. **3.** name of a Rājpūt communtiy.

रात *rāt* [*rātri*-], f. night. — ~, adv. (colloq.) = ~ को. ~ की ~, adv. the whole night (long); for one night, for the night. ~ की रानी, f. queen of night: name of a flower opening at night. ~ को, adv. at night; during the night. ~ भीगना, night to be advanced, dew to (have) fall(en). ~ में, adv. in the night (= ~ को). आधी ~, f. midnight. कुछ ~ रहे, adv. shortly before morning. गई ~ तक, adv. until late at night. बड़ी ~, adv. late at night. भारी ~, a long, wearisome or bad night. रात-दिन, adv. night and day. रात-राजा, m. inv. king of night: the owl. रातों-रात, adv. in the middle of the night; the night long; night by night.

¹रात- *rāt*- [cf. *rakta*-²], v.i. Brbh. Av. to be strongly attracted (to), to be in love (with).

²रात- *rāt*- [cf. *rakta*-¹], v.t. Brbh. to dye.

राता *rātā* [*raktaka*-], adj. Brbh. Av. red; dyed or stained red.

रातिब *rātib* [A. *rātib*], m. an allowance, or set amount (esp. of food for animals).

राती *rātī* [*rātrī*-], f. night.

रात्रि *rātri* [S.], f. night. — रात्रिचर, adj. & m. prowling or roaming at night; a thief; night-watchman; demon.

राद *rād*, f. reg. pus.

राध *rādh*, f. reg. pus.

राधा *rādhā* [S.], f. name (in popular and in later tradition generally) of the chief herdgirl or *gopī* of Braj, the favourite mistress (or the wife) of Kr̥ṣṇa. — राधा-कुंड, m. Rādhā's pool or well: name of a sacred site and place of pilgrimage at Mathurā. राधा-कृष्ण, Rādhā and Kr̥ṣṇa: a slogan of devotees of Kr̥ṣṇa and Rādhā. राधानगरी, m. ? f. *Pl.* a kind of silk cloth formerly made at Radhanagar. राधा-रमन, m. Brbh. lover of Rādhā: a title of Kr̥ṣṇa. राधा-वल्लभ, m. dear to Rādhā: a title of Kr̥ṣṇa. °ई, adj. & m. having to do with the Rādhāvallabhan sect; a member of that sect.

राधिका *rādhikā* [S.], f. dimin. = राधा.

रान *rān* [P. *rān*], f. the thigh. — ~ तले दबाना to press under the thigh: to keep in subjection or under control; to mount, to ride (a horse).

¹राना *rānā*, m. = राणा.

²राना *rānā* [*araṇyaka*-], adj. *Pl.* wild, growing untended (plants).

रानी *rānī* [*rājñī*-], f. **1.** queen. **2.** (in elaborately formal address) lady. **3.** (in cards) the queen.

राब *rāb* [**rabbā*-: Pk. *rabbā*-], m. thickened sugar-cane juice, molasses.

राबड़ी *rābṛī*, f. = रबड़ी.

राम *rām* [S.], m. *mythol.* **1.** name of Rāmcandra (the seventh avatār of Viṣṇu). **2.** name of Paraśurām (the sixth avatār of Viṣṇu). **3.** name of Balrām (the elder brother of Kṛṣṇa). ***4.** title of the supreme spirit (esp. used by Rāmaite Vaiṣṇavas); God. — ~ जी, m. good Rām: euph. a simple person. ~ दुहाई! I swear by Rām! ~ ~, interj. & m. a form of greeting: goodday; God forbid!; colloq. greeting. ~ ~ करना, or कहना, to say 'Rām Rām' (to, से): to greet; to invoke Rām; to express horror or concern at an unwelcome remark or disclosure. अकेले ~, adv. a single soul, on (one's) own, without relatives or friends. - राम-कथा, f. = next, 1. राम-कली, f. *mus.* name of a *rāgiṇī* associated with dawn. राम-कहानी, f. the story of Rām; a long story; tale of mishaps. राम-काँटा, the cylindrical acacia (= बबूल). राम-चंद्र, m. see 1. above. राम-चरितमानस, m. the Mānasa, or holy lake, of the acts of Rām: the version of the Rām story composed in Avadhī by Tulsīdās. राम-चगी, f. Brbh. a heavy gun. राम-तुरई, f. the vegetable called lady's fingers or okra, *Hibiscus esculentus*. राम-जनी, f. of unknown father (a girl or woman); euph. a prostitute. राम-जौ, m. reg. (W.) Rām's barley: oats. राम-झोल, m. reg. an anklet (see s.v. रम-°). राम-तिल, m. sesame. राम-तुलसी, f. a large basil, *Ocymum gratissimum*. राम-दाना, m. a partic. cereal, *Amarantus caudatus* ('love-lies-bleeding'). राम-द्वारा, m. inv. Rām's gate, means of access to Rām; a monastery. राम-धनुष, m. a rainbow. राम-नाम, m. the name of Rām, the (unknowable) name of God. राम-नाम सत्य है, *hind.* God's name is truth (words chanted by mourners in a funeral procession). राम-नवमी, f. the ninth day of the light half of the month Cait, and the festival held on that day. राम-नामी, adj. & f. having the name of Rām on it; a garment, &c. printed with the name of Rām. राम-फल, the sugar-apple, *Anona reticulata* (a fruit resembling the *sītā-phal* or custard-apple, but having a smooth skin). राम-बान, m. Rām's arrow: an immediately effective, or a reliable, medicine. राम-भक्त, m. & adj. a devotee of Rām; devoted to Rām. राम-भरोसे छोड़ना, to consign (one) to God's mercy. राम-रज, m. Rām's dust: name given to a yellow ochre used in making Vaiṣṇava sectarian marks. राम-रस, m. savour of Rām: salt. राम-राज्य, m. *mythol.* the kingdom of Rām: a perfect world (achievable only with the coming of Rām in a future avatār). राम-राम भजना, to invoke Rām; fig. to greet (one); to express pious horror. राम-राम होना, euph. to die. राम-रौला, m. colloq. an almighty commotion. राम-लीला, f. the deeds of Rām: a dramatic presentation of the deeds of Rām (staged during the Daśahrā festival of the first ten days of the month Āśvin). राम-सिंगा, m. *Pl.* a kind of horn or wind instrument having a deep bass sound. रामायण [°*ma*+*a*°], m. the goings, or deeds, of Rāma: name of an epic poem composed in Sanskrit by Vālmīki; name of various other poems in Sanskrit and in modern Indian languages on the theme of Rāma; iron. a long yarn or tale. °ई, m. one versed in the *Rāmāyaṇa*; one who sings or tells the story of Rāma.

रामा *rāmā* [S.], f. a beautiful or charming woman.

रामावत *rāmāvat*, m. follower(s) of Rām: name of a Vaiṣṇava ascetic community.

[1]**राय** *rāy* [*rājan-*], m. = राजा. – ~ बहादुर, m. *hist.* a high-ranking title (of the period of British rule in India). ~ साहब, m. *hist.* a title (of the period of British rule in India). - राय-जामन, m. a variety of *jāman* (a small evergreen tree yielding edible fruit and timber). राय-ज़ादा [P. - *zāda*], m. a king's son, young prince. राय-बेल, f. a species of jasmine. राय-भोग, m. Av. a kind of rice. राय-मुनी, m. f. the red muniya or wax-bill (a small finch: *Estrilda amandava*).

[2]**राय** *rāy* [P. *rā'ī*], f. **1.** opinion, judgment. **2.** advice. **3.** an individual vote (in an election). — ~ करना, to deliberate. ~ देना, to give an opinion, or (one's) advice; to vote. ~ लगाना, to pronounce judgment (in a case). ~ लेना, to take the opinion (of, की), to consult. मेरी ~ में, adv. in my opinion.

रायज *rāyj* [A. *rā'ij*], adj. U. current, customary.

रायता *rāytā* [**rājikātiktaka-*], m. cucumbers, or other vegetables (or bananas), sliced or chopped and pickled in curds. — ~ करना, fig. to beat (one, का) to a pulp.

[1]**राया** *rāyā* [cf. H. [1]*rāy*, and H. *rājā*], m. reg. = राजा.

[2]**राया** *rāyā* [cf. H. *rāī*], m. reg. **1.** a variety of mustard having large seeds (? = सरसों). **2.** chaff, bran.

रार *rār*, f. Brbh. = [1]राड़.

[1]**राल** *rāl* [S.], f. m. resin of the *sāl* tree *Shorea robusta*; pitch.

[2]**राल** *rāl* [*lālā-*[1]], f. **1.** spittle (= [1]लार). **2.** saliva; slaver (of an animal).

रालना *rālnā* [**rall-*], v.t. reg. **1.** to mix. **2.** to pour in, to throw down. **3.** to pound, to bruise (grain).

राला *rālā* [cf. H. *ralnā*], m. *Pl.* a millet, *Setaria italica*.

राली *rālī* [cf. H. *rālā*], f. a kind of small-grained millet, *Panicum miliaceum* (= चेना).

राव *rāv* [*rājan-*], m. = [1]राय.

राव-चाव *rāv-cāv* [cf. *rāga-*[2]; H. *cāv*], m. **1.** flirtation, dalliance; love. **2.** merriment.

रावटी *rāvṭī*, f. **1.** a small ridge tent. **2.** Brbh. a small room; pent-house room; summer-house.

रावण *rāvaṇ* [S.], m. *mythol.* name of a chief of the *rākṣasas* and ruler of Laṅkā (who was defeated and killed by Rām (Rāmcandra) in the battle for Laṅkā brought on by his kidnapping of Rām's wife Sītā). — ~ **होना**, to be notorious for cruelty.

रावत *rāvat* [*rājaputra-*], m. **1.** prince; chief. **2.** hero, warrior. **3.** master (of a household). **4.** euph. reg. a high caste of sweepers; E. a herding community. **5.** *Pl.* a land-bailiff. **6.** reg. a horse-soldier, trooper.

रावर *rāvar* [*rajakula-*], adj. Brbh. Av. your.

रावलिया *rāvliyā* [cf. H. *rāul*], adj. **1.** royal, princely. **2.** knightly.

राशन *rāśan* [Engl. *ration*], m. ration; a ration.

राशि *rāśi* [S.], f. **1.** heap, mass. **2.** sum, total. **3.** fund (of money). **4.** a sign of the zodiac. — **राशिकरण**, m. heaping up, accumulating. **राशिकृत**, adj. heaped up, collected, accumulated. **राशिचक्र**, m. the zodiac.

राष्ट्र *rāṣṭră* [S.], m. state, nation. — **राष्ट्रगत**, adj. having to do with a nation, national (as a policy, or a characteristic). **राष्ट्रपति**, m. lord or chief of the nation; president. °**-पतीय**, adj. **राष्ट्रभाषा**, m. national language. **राष्ट्रमंडल**, m. Commonwealth of Nations. °**ई**, °**ईय**, adj. **राष्ट्रवाद**, m. nationalism. °**ई**, adj. & m. nationalist. **राष्ट्रविरोधी**, adj. subversive. **राष्ट्रव्यापी**, adj. nation-wide. **राष्ट्र-संघ**, m. League of Nations; **संयुक्त राष्ट्र-संघ**, m. United Nations Organisation. **राष्ट्रीकरण**, m. nationalisation. **राष्ट्रीकृत**, adj. nationalised.

राष्ट्रिक *rāṣṭrik* [S.], adj. & m. **1.** adj. national. **2.** m. a national, a citizen.

राष्ट्रिकता *rāṣṭrikătā* [S.], f. **1.** nationality. **2.** sense of national identity or status.

राष्ट्रीकरण *rāṣṭrīkaraṇ* [S.], m. see s.v. **राष्ट्र**.

राष्ट्रीकृत *rāṣṭrīkr̥t* [S.], adj. see s.v. **राष्ट्र**.

राष्ट्रीय *rāṣṭrīyă* [S.], adj. pertaining to a state; national.

राष्ट्रीयता *rāṣṭrīyătā* [S.], f. **1.** nationality. **2.** status or identity as a nation; national quality. — **राष्ट्रीयतावाद**, m. nationalism.

[1]**रास** *rās* [*raśmi-*], f. reins. — ~ **कड़ी करना (पर)**, to rein in; to check. ~ **ढीली छोड़ना**, to give a free head (to, **पर**). ~ **में लाना**, to bring under rein, or control.

[2]**रास** *rās* [*rāśi-*], f. **1.** heap, pile, stock (= **राशि**). ***2.** a sign of the zodiac (= **राशि**). **3.** interest (on money). **4.** adoption (of a son). — ~ **आना (को)**, to agree (with), to suit (as climate, &c.); to be auspicious; to be cured (? corr. of **रास्त**). ~ **बैठाना**, or **लेना**, to adopt (a son). ~ **मिलना**, the constellations or stars (of, **की**) to agree; to be in harmony or agreement (as horoscopes). **बीच की ~ (का)**, adj. middling, mediocre. – **रास-चक्कर**, m. the zodiac; the ecliptic. **रास-निशीन** [P. *-niśīn*], adj. adopted (a son).

[3]**रास** *rās* [S.], m. **1.** noise, din. **2.** a dance of cowherds. **3.** specif. the round-dance of Kr̥ṣṇa with the herdgirls of Braj. **4.** a Kr̥ṣṇa festival including enactment of the round-dance, celebrated in the month Kārttik. **5.** a type of popular drama dealing with exploits of Kr̥ṣṇa. — **रास-क्रीड़ा**, f. Kr̥ṣṇa's dalliance and dance with the herdgirls of Braj. **रास मंडल**, m. the round-dance of Kr̥ṣṇa; a site of its enactment (see 4. above). **रास-यात्रा**, f. = ~, 4. **रास-रंग**, m. = **रास-क्रीड़ा**. **रास-लीला**, f. = **रास-क्रीड़ा**; = ~, 3.

[4]**रास** *rās* [A. *ra's*], m. U. head (as of cattle). — **कलानरास**, adj. long-headed: having a pedigree (a horse).

रासभ *rāsabh* [S.], m. Brbh. Av. an ass.

रासा *rāsā*, m. reg. 1. = [3]**रास**, 1. 2. = **रासो**.

रासायनिक *rāsāyanik* [S.], adj. & m. **1.** adj. chemical. **2.** m. a chemist.

रासो *rāso* [*rāsaka-*], m. a genre of lyrical or narrative verse exemplified in Apabhraṃśa and in early Hindi, Gujarati and Rājasthānī, sung originally to an accompaniment of music and acting, and later largely recited.

रासौ *rāsau*, m. E.H. = **रासो**.

रास्त *rāst* [P. *rāst*], adj. U. **1.** right, true. **2.** upright, honest. **3.** right (as opp. to left). **4.** straight, even, level.

रास्ता *rāstā* [P. *rāsta*], m. **1.** road. **2.** street, lane. **3.** way, manner. — ~ **कतराना**, to slink away; to turn aside from (one's) road. ~ **चलाना**, to make or to lay a road; to start or to set up a mode or tradition. ~ **देखना (का)**, to await; to be expecting, looking out (for). ~ **पकड़ना**, to take (one's) road, to set out. ~ **पकड़ो!** be on your way! be off! ~ **बताना (को)**, to show (one) the way (to, **का**). ~ **भूलना**, to lose (one's) way. **रास्ते में**, adv. on a road; in a road; on the way. **वह रास्ते में चला जा रहा था**, he was going along the road. – **रास्ता-चलता**, m. a wayfarer; a passer-by.

रास्ती *rāstī* [P. *rāstī*], f. rectitude.

राह *rāh* [P. *rāh*], f. **1.** road, way. **2.** transf. journey, progress. **3.** means of access, or of exit. **4.** manner, method; custom. — ~ करना, = ~ पैदा करना. ~ दिखाना (को), to show (one) a road; to open a prospect, to make one wait (for, की). ~ देना, to open a way, to give access; to admit. ~ नापना, to measure the road: to wander about idly, to waste (one's) time. ~ पड़ना, mutual confidence to be established. ~ पर आना, to find a (lost) road; to mend one's ways. ~ पर लाना, to guide on to the (right) road; to cause (one) to reform. ~ पैदा करना, to make a way or path; to gain ground (in a journey or task). ~ बताना (को), to show (one) the way (to, की), to guide; to show (one) the door; to dismiss, to fire. ~ बाँधना, to bar the way (of, की); to block access or exit. ~ मारना, to rob on the road, to waylay. ~ ~ चलना, to continue in (one's) usual way or practice; to behave in an unfailingly proper way. ~ लेना, to depart (for, की); अपनी ~ लो! be off! ~ से चलना, = ~ ~ चलना, 2. ~ से बेराह होना, to lose the way, to go astray; to exceed all bounds. – राह-ख़र्च, m. travel expenses. राहगीर [P. *-gīr*], m. a traveller, wayfarer. राह-चलता, m. id.; a passer-by; a person chosen at random, or out of a crowd. राह-चलतों का पल्ला पकड़ना, to catch at the hem of a passer-by's garment: to pick a quarrel. राहज़न [P. *-zan*], m. a highwayman, robber. °ई, f. highway robbery. राहदार [P. *-dār*], m. toll collector. °ई, f. toll(s), duty. राहनुमा [P. *-numā*], m. inv. guide; leader. °ई, f. guidance. राह-रीत, f. practice, usage, custom. राह-सिर, adj. just, right, proper.

राहक *rāhak* [Panj. *rāhak*], m. a farm worker, or tenant.

राहत *rāhat* [A. *rāḥat*], f. repose, ease; relief; peace of mind.

राहना *rāhnā* [*rādhati*], v.t. reg. to roughen a surface (as of a millstone, or a file).

राहित्य *rāhityă* [S.], m. non-possession, want (of anything); freedom (from anything).

राहिन *rāhin* [A. *rāhin*], m. U. mortgagor.

राही *rāhī* [P. *rāhī*], m. traveller, wayfarer. — ~ होना, to set off, to set out.

राहु *rāhu* [S.], m. *mythol.* name of a demon supposed (with *Ketu*) to seize the sun and moon in his mouth and so to cause eclipses. – राहु-ग्रास, m. eclipse. राहु-ग्राह, m. *Pl. HŚS.* id.

रिंगरिंगाना *riṃgriṃgānā*, v.i. reg. to be constantly whining or whimpering (a child).

रिंद *rind* [P. *rind*], m. a dissolute person.

रिंदगी *rindagī* [P. *rindagī*], f. E.H. dissoluteness.

रिआयत *riāyat* [A. *ri'āya*: P. *ri'āyat*], f. tending: **1.** favour, partiality; kindness; care, regard. **2.** leniency. **3.** remission, rebate (of a sum due); concession. **4.** abatement (of a sickness). — ~ करना, to show favour, &c. (to, की, or के साथ); to make a reduction (in, में).

रिआयती *riāyătī* [P. *ri'āyatī*], adj. **1.** granted as a favour, &c. **2.** reduced (as a price); concessionary (ticket, rate).

रिआया *riāyā* [A. *ra'āyā*, pl. of *ra'īya*], f. **1.** subjects; the people, the whole community. **2.** agricultural tenants, cultivators.

रिकशा *rikśā*, m. see रिक्शा.

रिकाब *rikāb*, f. = रकाब.

रिकाबी *rikābī*, f. = रकाबी.

रिक्त *rikt* [S.], adj. **1.** emptied, empty; vacant. **2.** void, destitute (of, से). — रिक्तहस्त, adj. empty-handed.

रिक्तता *riktătā* [S.], f. emptiness; void.

रिक्शा *rikśā*, m. a rickshaw.

रिझवार *rijhvār* [cf. H. *rījhnā*], adj. Brbh. feeling delight.

रिझवैया *rijhvaiyā* [cf. H. *rījhnā*], adj. dimin. = रिझवार.

रिझाना *rijhānā* [cf. H. *rījhnā*], v.t. to delight, to please; to charm.

रिड़कना *riṛaknā*, v.i. *Pl.* = रिरियाना.

रित- *rit-* [cf. H. *ritānā*], v.i. Brbh. to be empty, or emptied.

रितना *ritnā* [cf. H. *retnā*], v.i. reg. to be filed, or smoothed.

रितवाना *ritvānā* [cf. H. *ritānā*], v.t. to cause to be emptied.

रिता *ritā* [cf. H. *rit-*], adj. = रीता.

रिताना *ritānā* [cf. *rikta-*, and H. *rītā*], v.t. to empty.

रितु *ritu* [ad. *ṛtu-*], f. Brbh. Av. = ऋतु.

रिपु *ripu* [S.], m. enemy, foe.

रिपुता *riputā* [S.], f. enmity, hostility.

रिपोर्ट *riporṭ* [Engl. *report*], f. report. — ~ देना, to give or to make a report.

रिम-झिम *rim-jhim*, adv. & f. **1.** adv. pitter-patter (as rain). **2.** f. pattering sound (of rain). — ~ करना, to patter.

रियाज़ *riyāz* [A. *riyāẓ*], f. **1.** training, practice. **2.** toil. — ~ करना (का), to practise diligently. ~ का, adj. skilled; painstaking (as work).

रियायत *riyāyat*, f. = रिआयत.

रियायती *riyāyătī*, adj. = रिआयती.

रियासत *riyāsat* [A. *riyāsa*: P. *riyāsat*], f. **1.** *pol.* a state; an Indian princely state. **2.** rule, sway.

रियासती *riyāsătī* [H. *riyāsat*], adj. pertaining to a state.

रिरियाना *riri yānā*, v.i. **1.** to whine; to whimper. **2.** to beg, to beseech.

रिवाज *rivāj* [A. *ravāj*], m. being in demand: **1.** currency, usual occurrence. इस उत्सव का यहाँ ~ है, this festival is customary here. **2.** custom, practice. — ~ देना, to give currency (to, को). ~ पकड़ना, to become current. ~ होना, to become, or to be, current or customary.

रिवाजी *rivājī* [cf. H. *rivāj*], adj. customary, usual.

रिश्ता *riśtā* [P. *riśta*], m. string, line: **1.** connection, relationship (with, से). **2.** relationship (of blood or marriage). — ~ करना, to form a connection, or alliance (with, से). ~ रखना, to have a connection, to be connected (with, से). – रिश्तेदार [P. *-dār*], m. a relative. °ई, f. = ~, 2. रिश्तेदारी में जाना, to marry into the family (of, के). रिश्तेमंद [P. *-mand*], m. = रिश्तेदार.

रिश्तेदार *riśtedār*, m. see s.v. रिश्ता.

रिश्वत *riśvat* [A. *riśva*: P. *riśvat*], f. a bribe. — ~ खाना, or लेना, to take a bribe. ~ देना (को), to bribe. – रिश्वतख़ोर [P. *-khor*], m. one who takes bribes. °ई, f. acceptance of bribes. रिश्वतसितानी, f. = रिश्वतख़ोरी.

रिश्वती *riśvatī* [P. *riśvatī*], m. one who takes bribes.

[1]**रिष्ट** *riṣṭ* [S.], m. *Pl. HŚS.* **1.** happiness, prosperity. **2.** misfortune. 3. = रीठा.

[2]**रिष्ट** *riṣṭ*, adj. Av. = हृष्ट.

रिस *ris* [*riṣ-*; × *īrṣyā-*], f. anger; offence. — ~ आना (को), to be angry; to take offence. ~ होना (को), to be angry.

[1]**रिसना** *risnā* [? **riśyate*], v.i. **1.** to drip, to leak; to trickle. **2.** to exude, to ooze (as a container liquid, or as a wound).

[2]**रिसना** *risnā* [*riṣyati*], v.i. to be angry; to take offence.

रिसहा *rishā* [cf. H. *ris*], adj. Brbh. angry, offended.

रिसहायौ *rishāyau* [cf. H. *ris*], adj. Brbh. angered, offended (= रिसहा).

रिसाना *risānā* [cf. H. *ris*], v.i. to be or to grow angry.

रिसानी *risānī* [cf. H. *risānā*], f. Av. anger.

रिसालदार *risāldār* [H. *risālā* + P. *-dār*], m. commander of a troop of horse.

रिसालदारी *risāldārī* [cf. H. *risāldār*], f. command of a troop of horse.

रिसाला *risālā* [A. *risāla*], m. **1.** U. a periodical. **2.** U. a tract, short treatise. ***3.** [P.], a troop of horse; cavalry. — रिसालेदार, m. = रिसालदार. °ई, f. = रिसालदारी.

रिसियाना *risiyānā* [cf. H. *ris*], v.i. = रिसाना.

रिहा *rihā* [P. *rahā*], adj. inv. released, set free. — ~ करना, to release, &c.

रिहाइश *rihāiś* [cf. H. *rahā*], f. stay, residence.

रिहाई *rihāī* [P. *rahā'ī*], f. **1.** release (from, से); deliverance; discharge. 2. freedom (from). — ~ देना (को), to set free, &c.

रिहायशी *rihāyśī* [cf. H. *rihāiś*], adj. residential. — ~ मकान, m. building divided into residential apartments, flats.

रींगना *rīṁgnā*, v.i. reg. = रेंगना.

रींछ *rīṁch*, m. pronun. var. = रीछ.

रींधना *rīṁdhnā* [**r̥ndhati*], v.t. = राँधना.

री *rī* [H. *arī*], interj. used to females or with nouns of f. gender. see रे.

रीछ *rīch* [*r̥kṣa-*], m. a bear.

रीझ *rījh* [cf. H. *rījhnā*], f. **1.** pleasure, satisfaction. **2.** delight (in, से), enchantment. **3.** desire, inclination, liking.

रीझना *rījhnā* [*r̥dhyati*], v.t. **1.** to be pleased. **2.** to be delighted, enchanted.

रीठा *rīṭhā* [*ariṣṭa-*[2]], m. the soap-nut tree, *Sapindus detergens*, and its berry.

रीठी *rīṭhī* [cf. *ariṣṭa-*[2]], f. a small soap-nut (रीठा).

[1]**रीढ़** *rīṛh* [conn. *riḍhaka-*], f. the spine. — ~ की हड्डी, f. id.; a vertebra. – रीढ़दार [P. *-dār*], adj. vertebrate.

[2]**रीढ़** *rīṛh*, f. reg. emulation. — ~ पीटना, to follow old customs, to keep in the beaten track.

रीत *rīt*, f. = रीति.

रीतना *rītnā* [cf. *rikta-*], v.i. to be empty.

रीता *rītā* [*riktaka-*], adj. **1.** empty; free (as a seat). **2.** deprived (of).

रीति *rīti* [S.], f. going, course: **1.** manner, way: fashion, style. इस ~ से, adv. in this manner; accordingly. **2.** mannerism (the attitudes and style dominant in Hindi verse on poetics in the

16th-19th centuries). **3.** usage, custom; rite. **4.** rule, regulation. — ~ से, adv. according to custom. – रीति-काल, m. the period dominated by mannerism in Hindi literature (see 2. above). रीति-बद्ध, adj. mannered (style). रीति-मुक्त, adj. natural (style). रीति-रस्म, f. manners and customs, ways; observances. रीति-रिवाज, m. id. रीति-वाद, m. = ~, 2.; formalism (in art, literature).

रीस *rīs* [*riṣ-*: ? × *īrṣyā-*], f. **1.** envy. **2.** rivalry. — ~ आना (को), to be envious (of, की). ~ करना (की), to be envious (of); to vie (with).

रुंड *ruṇḍ* [S.], m. a headless body, trunk. — रुंड-मुंड, m. trunk and (severed) head.

रुँदवा- *ruṁdvā-*, v.t. Brbh. to cause to be trampled upon.

रुँधना *ruṁdhnā* [cf. H. *rūṁdhnā*], v.i. **1.** to be checked; to be confined; to be surrounded. **2.** to be fenced or hedged off (as a road, a field). **3.** to be constricted (as the throat).

रुआँसा *ruāṁsā*, adj. tearful.

रुआई *ruāī* [cf. H. *ronā*], f. reg. weeping.

रुआब *ruāb*, m. = रोब.

रुआस *ruās*, f. tearfulness.

रुकना *ruknā* [cf. H. *roknā*], v.i. **1.** to stop, to halt; to come to an end (as rain, flood). **2.** to falter, to hesitate. **3.** to be hindered, stopped or prohibited (an event). — रुकना-रुकाना, to linger, to delay. – रुक-रुककर बोलना, to speak hesitatingly; to speak (a language) imperfectly.

रुकवाना *rukvānā* [cf. H. *roknā*], v.t. to cause to be stopped, &c. (by, से).

रुकवैया *rukvaiyā* [cf. H. *roknā*], m. one who stops or hinders.

रुकाना *rukānā* [cf. H. *roknā*], v.t. **1.** to cause to be enclosed, to surround. **2.** to hinder, to stop (= रोकना).

रुकाव *rukāv* [cf. H. *ruknā*], m. **1.** state of being blocked, &c. (see रुकावट). **2.** an obstacle, hindrance. **3.** constipation.

रुकावट *rukāvaṭ* [cf. H. *rukānā*], f. **1.** obstruction, obstacle. **2.** hitch, difficulty. **3.** backwardness, hesitation.

रुक़्क़ा *ruqqā* [A. *ruq'a*], m. piece, scrap (as of paper); a note; written undertaking; receipt; an invitation.

रुक्म *rukmă* [S.], m. **1.** *mythol.* name of the eldest son of Bhīṣmak and brother-in-law of Kṛṣṇa. **2.** gold.

रुक्मिणी *rukmiṇī* [S.], f. *mythol.* name of a daughter of Bhīṣmak (and sister of Rukma or Rukmī) who was carried off and married by Kṛṣṇa.

रुक्ष *rukṣ* [S.], adj. **1.** rough, dry. **2.** harsh.

रुख़ *rukh* [P. *rukh*], m. **1.** face; cheek. ***2.** facial expression; favour, countenance; attitude. ***3.** side, face, aspect; front. **4.** quarter, direction (as of wind). **5.** situation, aspect (of affairs). **6.** (in chess) the rook, castle. — ~ करना, or देना, to turn the face (towards, की तरफ़); to proceed (towards); to incline (to); to countenance, to favour; to attend (to). ~ बदलना, to change (one's) expression, or attitude; to turn away (from, से); to be inattentive; to change the aspect or direction (of, का: as of a discussion). ~ रखना, to keep the face (towards, की तरफ़), to show continuing favour (to). कुरसी का ~ इधर रखो, put the chair facing this way.

रुखचढ़वा *rukhcaṛhvā* [H. *rūkh*+*caṛhnā*], m. reg. (W). name given to a ghost supposed to live in trees (esp. the *pīpal* and the date tree).

रुख़सत *rukhsat* [A. *rukhṣa*: P. *rukhṣat*], f. **1.** permission to leave; departure; discharge. **2.** leave (of absence). — ~ करना, to allow to go; to see off; to send off or away. ~ देना (को), to give leave to go; to dismiss; to grant leave. ~ होना, to depart.

रुख़सताना *rukhsatānā* [P. *rukhṣatāna*], m. a gift to one departing.

रुख़सती *rukhsatī* [P. *rukhṣatī*], f. **1.** departure. **2.** departure of a bride to her husband's home. **3.** a parting gift.

रुखाई *rukhāī* [cf. H. *rūkhā*], f. **1.** dryness (as of bread); staleness. **2.** roughness (as of the skin). **3.** fig. harshness, coldness (of manner); indifference; unfriendliness.

रुखाना *rukhānā* [cf. H. *rūkhā*], adj. reg. **1.** dry, rough. **2.** insipid, jejune. **3.** curt, brusque (of manner).

रुखानी *rukhānī*, f. **1.** an auger, borer. **2.** a chisel; gouge. **3.** a cold chisel.

रुखावट *rukhāvaṭ* [cf. H. *rūkhā*], f. = रुखाई.

रुग्ण *rugṇ* [S.], adj. broken: ill, infirm. — रुग्णावस्था [°*ṇa*+*a*°], f. infirm state.

रुग्णता *rugṇătā* [S.], f. illness; infirmity.

रुचत *rucat* [cf. H. *rucnā*], f. reg. desire, appetite.

रुचना *rucnā* [*rucyate*], v.i. **1.** to be pleasant, agreeable (an experience, an activity). **2.** to be tasty; to be longed for. — रुचता-पचता, adj. well-liked, easily digested (food).

रुचि *ruci* [S.], f. light, beauty: **1.** liking (for, से or में); interest (in); inclination (towards, की ओर). **2.** taste, relish; appetite. **3.** desire. **4.** light; beauty. — ~ करना, to have a taste or fancy (for, की). ~ रखना, to have an interest or liking (in or for, में). – रुचिकर, adj. interesting; appetising; stimulating appetite. °-कारक, adj. awakening interest, or relish, &c. °-कारी, adj. id. रुचिमान, adj. bright, radiant. रुचिवर्धक, adj. increasing interest, &c.

रुचिर *rucir* [S.], adj. **1.** radiant, beautiful. **2.** attractive, agreeable. **3.** digestive (a medicine).

रुजू *rujū* [A. *rujū'*], f. ? m. Brbh. inclination (of mind). — ~ रह-, an inclination to be felt.

रुझना *rujhnā* [*rudhyate*], v.i. **1.** reg. to be blocked, or stopped; to be blocked up. ***2.** to heal (a wound).

रुझान *rujhān* [A. *rujḥān*], m. inclination (for). — ~ हो जाना, to acquire a taste (for, की तरफ़).

रुठाना *ruṭhānā* [cf. H. *rūṭhnā*], v.t. to anger, to displease.

[1]**रुत** *rut* [ad. *ṛtu-*], f. = ऋतु.

[2]**रुत** *rut* [S.], m. song, cry (of birds).

रुतबा *rutbā* [A. *rutba*], m. standing; rank, station; distinction. — रुतबेवाला, adj. of high rank, &c.; distinguished.

रुदन *rudan* [S.], m. weeping.

रुद्ध *ruddh* [S.], adj. **1.** stopped, checked (motion, progress). **2.** blocked, barred (as a road). **3.** enclosed; surrounded. **4.** choked (the voice).

रुद्र *rudră* [S.], adj. & m. **1.** adj. fearsome. **2.** m. *mythol.* a title of a Vedic storm-god. **3.** a title of Śiva. – रुद्र-पति, m. Brbh. = रुद्र, 2. रुद्र-भूमि, f. Śiva's ground: a cremation site. रुद्राक्ष [°*ra*+*a*°], m. Rudra-eyed: the tree *Elaeocarpus ganitrus*, and its berries (used for rosaries).

रुद्रक *rudrak* [S.], m. Brbh. = रुद्राक्ष.

रुद्राणी *rudrāṇī* [S.], f. *mythol.* Rudra's wife: a title of Pārvatī.

रुद्री *rudrī* [S.], f. *Pl. HŚS.* a kind of *vīṇā* or guitar.

रुधिर *rudhir* [S.], m. blood. — रुधिर-स्राव, m. haemorrhage.

रुनी *runī* [**aruṇikā-*], f. reg. (Bihar) a guava.

रुप- *rup-* [cf. H. *ropnā*], v.i. reg. **1.** to be planted. **2.** to be fixed. **3.** to be stopped, checked, held. **4.** Brbh. to stand fast (in battle), to fight boldly.

रुपया *rupayā* [cf. H. [2]*rūp*: ? and ad. *rūpaka-*, Pk. *rūaya-*], m. **1.** a rupee. **2.** esp. pl. money. — ~ उड़ाना, to waste or to squander money. ~ तुड़वाना, to change paper money for coin. – रुपया-पैसा, m. money; wealth.

रुपहला *rupahlā* [**rūpadhara-*], adj. of silver; silver-coloured.

रुबाई *rubāī* [A. *rubā'ī*], f. a quatrain.

रुमाल *rumāl*, m. = रूमाल.

रुलना *rulnā* [cf. H. *rolnā*], v.i. **1.** to be rolled or planed, to be smoothed, worn. **2.** E.H. to wander. **3.** to be dispersed. **4.** to be crushed.

रुलाई *rulāī* [cf. H. *ronā*, [1]*rulāna*], f. crying, tearfulness.

[1]**रुलाना** *rulānā* [cf. H. [1]*ronā*], v.t. to make (one) cry.

[2]**रुलाना** *rulānā* [cf. H. *rulnā*], v.t. reg. **1.** to cause to be rolled, or planed, &c. **2.** to cause to wander.

रुल्ल *rull*, m. reg. (E). = रुल्ला.

रुल्ला *rullā* [**rulla-*], m. reg. (E). worn-out land needing to be left fallow.

रुल्ली *rullī* f. reg. (Bihar) = रुल्ला.

रुवाना *ruvānā*, v.t. = [1]रुलाना.

रुश्द *ruśd* [A. *ruśd*], m. U. rectitude.

रुष्ट *ruṣṭ* [S.], adj. angered; offended; enraged.

रुसना *rusnā* [*ruṣyati*], v.i. to be angry, &c. (= [2]रिसना).

रुसवा *rusvā* [P. *rusvā*], adj. U. dishonoured, disgraced.

रुसवाई *rusvāī* [P. *rusvāī*], f. U. dishonour, disgrace.

रुसित *rusit* [ad. *ruṣita-*], adj. Brbh. angered; offended.

रुसियल *rusiyal* [cf. H. *rusnā*], adj. & m. **1.** adj. irritable. **2.** m. an irritable person.

रुसियाना *rusiyānā* [H. *risiyānā*×H. *rusnā*], v.i. = रिसियाना.

रुसीला *rusīlā* [cf. H. *rūsī*], adj. *Pl.* full of scurf or dandruff (the hair).

रुसूख़ *rusūkh* [A. *rusūkh*], m. firmness: weight, influence.

रुस्तम *rustam* [P. *rustam*], m. name of the Persian hero, son of Zāl. — छिपा ~, fig. one who hides his light under a bushel; an ace in the pack.

रूँघट *rūṃghaṭ*, f. reg. dirt, filth.

रूँथना *rūṁthnā*, v.t. to trample (= रौंदना).

रूँदना *rūṁdnā* [*rundhati* × **kṣundati*], v.t. = रौंदना, and रूँधना.

रूँध *rūṁdh* [cf. H. *rūṁdhnā*], f. & adj. **1.** f. enclosure. **2.** fence, hedge. **3.** adj. Brbh. restrained, checked.

रूँधना *rūṁdhnā* [*rundhati*], v.t. **1.** to enclose; to surround. **2.** to fence or to hedge in. **3.** to restrain. **4.** to block (as a road). **5.** reg. = रौंदना.

रू *rū* [P. *rū*], m. **1.** face. **2.** aspect; face (of the earth, &c). **3.** U. countenance, favour. — ~ गरदान करना [P. *gardān*], U. to turn the face (from, से); to abandon; euph. to beat; to turn inside out (as material). रूनुमाई [P. -*numāī*], f. = मुँह-दिखावा. रूबकार [P. -*ba*-], m. *law. Pl. HŚS.* face to the matter (in hand): a proceeding; an order. °ई, f. record (of a case); a warrant, order. रूबरू, [P. -*ba*-], adv. face to face; in the presence (of, के). रूबरू करना, or लाना, to bring (one, को) face to face (with, के); to confront (with). रूमाल, m. a handkerchief.

रूइया *rūiyā* [cf. H. *rūī*], m. a cotton-merchant.

रूइहा *rūihā*, m. ? pronun. var. = रूइया.

रूई *rūī* [cf. **rū-a-*: Pk. *rūa*-], f. **1.** cotton (carded or cleaned). **2.** cotton-wool. — रूईदार [P. -*dār*], adj. padded, quilted with cotton.

रूख *rūkh* [*vr̥kṣa*-], m. Brbh. Av. a tree.

रूखन *rūkhan*, f. ? m. a quantity extra to what is purchased, given free (= घलुआ).

रूखा *rūkhā* [*rūkṣa*-], adj. **1.** dry, plain (as bread, food). **2.** insipid, unseasoned. **3.** flat, stale, tame (as manner, style). **4.** rough. **5.** harsh; blunt (manner, words). **6.** indifferent, cold (manner, words). — रूखा-फीका, adj. = ~, 1., 2. रूखा-सूखा, adj. & m. = ~; plain or simple food.

रूखापन *rūkhāpan* [cf. H. *rūkhā*], m. **1.** dryness, &c. (see रूखा). **2.** roughness, &c.

रूझ- *rūjh-* [*rudhyate*], v.i. Brbh. to be harassed, worried.

रूठन *rūṭhan* [cf. H. *rūṭhnā*], f. anger, offence; sulking.

रूठना *rūṭhnā* [cf. *ruṣṭa*-[1]], v.i. **1.** to be offended; to sulk. **2.** to quarrel (with a friend). — रूठा-रूठी, f. mutual coolness, misunderstanding, tiff.

रूठनी *rūṭhnī* [cf. H. *rūṭhnā*], adj. f. & f. *Pl.* **1.** adj. irritable, touchy. **2.** f. a species of sensitive plant, *Mimosa natans*.

[1]**रूढ़** *rūṛh* [S.], adj. **1.** mounted, risen. **2.** arisen; born, produced. **3.** received, accepted (as the meaning of a word). **4.** prime (a number).

[2]**रूढ़** *rūṛh* [conn. **rūṣṭa*-], adj. **1.** hard, stiff, rough. **2.** surly, rude.

रूढ़ापन *rūṛhāpan* [cf. H. [2]*rūṛh*], m. **1.** hardness, roughness. **2.** surliness, rudeness.

रूढ़ि *rūṛhi* [S.], f. **1.** rise, ascent. **2.** increase. **3.** birth, origin. ***4.** tradition, custom; convention. **5.** accepted meaning (of a word: as opposed to its etymological meaning). — रूढ़िगत, adv. conventional. रूढ़िग्रस्त, adj. influenced by convention: traditional, conventional; conservative. रूढ़िबद्ध, adj. bound by convention: id. रूढ़िवाद, m. traditionality; conservatism. °इता, f. adherence to tradition, &c. °ई, adj.

रूत *rūt*, m. reg. cry, noise; song (of birds); hum (of bees).

[1]**रूप** *rūp* [S.], m. **1.** form, shape; appearance; aspect. **2.** face, features. **3.** beauty, handsomeness. **4.** manner, mode. ~ में, adv. in the form or capacity (of, के). ~ से, adv. formant (e.g. पूर्ण ~ से, fully, completely). **5.** character, nature; species; type. **6.** *gram.* a form. **7.** esp. -रूप, adj. formant. having the form of; consisting of (e.g. नररूप हर, m. Hara (Śiva) in human form). — ~ ग्रहण, or धारण, करना, to assume the form (of, का). ~ धरना, = ~ बनाना. ~ बनाना, to assume the form or character of (का), to impersonate. ~ बिगाड़ना (का), to mar the beauty (of), to disfigure; to sully. ~ भरना, = ~ बनाना. ~ लाना, to assume an attitude (towards, से), to threaten. – रूप-प्रक्रिया, f. *ling.* morphology. रूपमय, adj. beautiful. रूप-रंग, m. form and colour: appearance, aspect; beauty. रूप-राशि, f. an abundance of beauty: great beauty; a beautiful woman. रूप-रेखा, f. sketch, outline (of a topic). रूपवंत, adj. Brbh. = next. रूपवान्, adj. having form, or shape; beautiful; handsome. °-वती, f. id. रूपात्मक [°*pa*+*ā*°], adj. *ling.* formal (a classification, &c). रूपांकक [°*a*+*a*°], m. designer. रूपांकन [°*a*+*a*°], m. designing, design. रूपांतर [°*pa*+*a*°], m. changed or new form, transformation; version, rendering, adaptation (of a tale, a work). रूपांतर करना (का), to transform, &c. °अण, m. transforming; rendering. °इत, adj. रूपायन [°*pa*+*a*°], m. forming, creating. रूपायित, adj. रूपावली [°*pa*+*ā*°], f. *ling.* paradigm.

[2]**रूप** *rūp* [*rūpya*-], m. Av. silver. — रूप-जस्त, m. *Pl.* an alloy containing tin and lead with mercury; pewter. रूप-रस, m. *Pl.* oxidised silver.

रूपक *rūpak* [S.], m. **1.** a dramatic composition. **2.** a figure of speech; a metaphor. **3.** an allegory.

रूपसी *rūpsī* [conn. **rūpas-, rūpasvin-*], adj. f. shapely, beautiful (a woman).

रूपा *rūpā* [*rūpya-*], m. silver.

-रूपी *-rūpī* [S.], adj. having the form, appearance, or nature (of); like (e.g. विद्या-रूपी सागर, m. ocean of knowledge).

रूप्य *rūpyă* [S.], m. **1.** silver. **2.** stamped silver or gold coin (= रुपया).

रूम *rūm* [A. *rūm*], m. Asia Minor; *hist.* the Turkish empire.

रूमानियत *rūmāniyat*, f. romantic or sentimental feeling.

रूमानी *rūmānī*, adj. romantic, sentimental.

रूमाल *rūmāl*, m. see s.v. रु.

रूमाली *rūmālī* [cf. H. *rūmāl*], f. **1.** a head-covering made by knotting a handkerchief round the head. **2.** a loin-cloth of minimal size; children's underwear. **3.** a strenuous physical exercise with clubs (in which the clubs are lowered from the vertical to a point as far as possible behind the head).

रूमी *rūmī* [A. *rūmī*], adj. & m. Av. **1.** adj. belonging to Rūm (see s.v. रूम). **2.** m. a native of Rūm.

रूर- *rūra-* [*rūpa-*], adj. Brbh. beautiful; good, fine.

रूल *rūl* [Engl. *rule*], m. f. **1.** a ruler. **2.** rule.

¹**रूस** *rus* [P. *rūs*], m. Russia; the Soviet Union.

²**रूस** *rūs* [ad. *aṭarūṣaka-*], m. *Pl.* a shrub, *Adhatoda vasica.*

³**रूस** *rus*, m. a perennial grass, *Cymbopogon martini*, which yields an oil by distillation. — ~ का तेल, m. oil of *Cymbopogon martini.*

रूसना *rūsnā* [*ruṣyati*], v.i. = रूठना.

रूसा *rūsā*, m. = ² ³ रूस and ¹रौंस.

¹**रूसी** *rūsī* [P. *rūsī*], adj. & m. f. **1.** adj. Russian. **2.** m.; f. a Russian. **3.** f. the Russian language.

²**रूसी** *rūsī*, f. scurf, dandruff.

रूह *rūh* [A. *rūḥ*], f. the soul, spirit. — ~ किसी की प्यासी थी, someone's soul was thirsty (a phrase used when a water-vessel breaks of itself). ~ निकलना (की), the soul to depart, to die; to be frightened to death.

रूहत *rūhat* [P. *rū*; or P. *rūyat*], f. *Pl.* **1.** brightness, beauty. **2.** regard, attention to the wishes (of).

रूहा *rūhā*, m. reg. used, old (as crockery, or material).

रूहानी *rūhānī* [A. *rūḥānī*], adj. **1.** having a soul or spirit. **2.** spiritual.

रेंक *reṁk* [cf. H. *reṁknā*], f. braying (of an ass).

रेंकना *reṁknā* [**reṁk-*], v.i. **1.** to bray. **2.** to bellow (a buffalo, &c).

रेंगटा *reṁgṭā* [cf. H. *reṁknā*], m. reg. the foal of an ass.

रेंगना *reṁgnā* [conn. *riṅgati*], v.i. **1.** creep, to crawl. **2.** fig. to move slowly, to plod.

रेंगनी *reṁgnī* [cf. H. *reṁgnā*], f. *Pl. HŚS.* **1.** the shrub *Solanum jacquinī* (= भटकटैया: a small thorny plant with purple flowers). **2.** colloq. sciatica.

रेंगाई *reṁgāī* [cf. H. *reṁgnā*], f. reg. creeping, crawling.

रेंगाना *reṁgānā* [cf. H. *reṁgnā*], v.t. to cause to creep or to crawl, &c.

¹**रेंट** *reṁṭ*, f. mucus (of the nose).

²**रेंट** *reṁṭ*, f. pronun. var. = रहँट.

¹**रेंटा** *reṁṭā*, m. = ¹रेंट.

²**रेंटा** *reṁṭā*, m. *Pl. HŚS.* fruit of the *lisoṛā* tree (source of a pulp used medicinally).

रेंड़ *reṁṛ* [conn. *eraṇḍa-*], f. = रेंड़ी, 1. — रेंड़वार, f. reg. (E.) a plantation of castor-oil trees. °आ, m. id. °ई, f. id.

रेंड़ा *reṁṛā*, m. reg. (Bihar) a shoot (of wheat); a shooting ear (of millet).

रेंड़ी *reṁṛī* [cf. *eraṇḍa-*], f. **1.** the castor-oil plant, *Ricinus communis.* **2.** the berry or seed of the castor-oil plant. — ~ का तेल, m. castor oil.

रेंड़ु *reṁṛu*, m. pronun. var. = रेणु.

रें-रें *reṁ-reṁ*, f. **1.** constant crying or whimpering (of a child). **2.** discordant sounds (of a stringed instrument).

रे *re* [*are*], interj. used to males, or with nouns of m. gender. oh! why! alas! (expressing intimacy or contempt, or astonishment, or sorrow). — ~ मन! oh, heart (of mine...).

रेख *rekh* [ad. *rekhā-*: w. H. ²*reh*], f. **1.** a line. **2.** an astrologer's drawing, calculation. **3.** fig. the moustache (newly appeared in adolescence). — ~ भीगना, the moustache to begin to appear. – रेख-उठान, adj. Brbh. an emerging outline.

रेख़ता *rekhtā* [P. *rekhta*], m. scattered, mixed: **1.** mixed language: Persianised Urdu (esp. earlier literary Urdu, with reference to its numerous Persian and Arabic loanwords). **2.** a type of Urdu verse.

रेख़ती *rekhtī* [cf. H. *rekhtā*], f. a type of Urdu verse expressing the emotions and using the colloquial vocabulary of women, composed in an un-Persianised style (i.e. not in *rekhtā*).

रेखा *rekhā* [S.], f. **1.** a line; streak, stripe; row; mark, sign. **2.** an outline; contour. **3.** line (as on the palm); fig. fate. **4.** Av. numbering, inclusion (in a group). — रेखा-गणित, m. geometry. रेखा-चित्र, m. sketch, outline. रेखा-शास्त्र, m. palmistry. रेखांकित [°*khā* + *a*°], marked with a line, or lines; underlined; stressed; demarcated. °अन, m. demarcation. रेखांश [°*khā* + *a*°], m. *astron.* meridian.

रेखान *rekhān* [? cf. H. *rekhā*], f. *Pl.* land beyond the reach of river water.

रेग *reg* [P. *reg*], f. sand. — रेगमाल, m. sandpaper. रेगिस्तान, m. desert. °ई, adj.

रेगर *regar*, ? f. reg. (W). a black soil.

रेघारी *reghārī* [ad. *rekhā*-], f. *Pl.* a furrow.

-रेज़ *-rez* [P. *rez*]. scattering, dropping, shedding (e.g. रंगरेज़, m. a dyer).

रेज़गारी *rezgārī* [f. H. *rezagī*], f. a small coin; change (for, की).

रेज़गी *rezăgī* [P. *rezagī*], f. = रेज़गारी.

रेज़ा *rezā* [P. *reza*], m. a small piece, bit, scrap. — ~ ~ करना, to break into tiny pieces, to smash.

रेणु *reṇu* [S.], f. m. **1.** dust. **2.** particle, grain; sand, grit; pollen.

रेणुका *reṇukā* [S.], f. *mythol.* name of the wife of Jamadagni and mother of Paraśurām.

रेत *ret* [*retra*-], f. **1.** sand. **2.** sandy area at the bank of a river; sand-bank. **3.** Brbh. sandy or waste region. **4.** reg. (Bihar) a file.

रेतना *retnā* [cf. *retra*-], v.t. **1.** to file, to rasp; to cut into or through (wood, &c). **2.** to polish. — गला ~, to cut the throat (of, का).

रेतनी *retnī*, f. reg. a file (= रेती, 3).

रेतल *retal*, adj. & m. **1.** *Pl.* = रेतीला, रेतला. **2.** *Pl. HŚS.* m. the rufous-tailed finch-lark, *Ammomanes phoenicurus* (which frequents stony land).

रेतला *retlā* [cf. H. *ret*], adj. & ? m. **1.** adj. *Pl. HŚS.* = रेतीला. **2.** ? m. reg. a type of sandy or gravelly soil.

रेतली *retlī*, f. = रेतला, 2.

रेतस् *retas* [S.], m. **1.** seminal fluid. **2.** mercury.

रेता *retā* [*retra*-], m. **1.** sand; sandy soil.

रेताई *retāī* [cf. H. *retnā*], f. price paid for filing.

रेतियाना *retiyānā* [cf. H. *retī*], v.t. **1.** to file, to rasp. **2.** to polish.

रेती *retī* [cf. *retra*-], f. **1.** sandy area at the bank of a river. **2.** sand-bank. **3.** transf. a file.

रेतीला *retīlā* [cf. H. *ret*], adj. sandy; gravelly.

रेफ *reph* [S.], m. the superscript form of the letter र (written when this precedes a consonant).

[1]**रेल** *rel* [cf. H. *relnā*], f. a crowd (= रेल-पेल, the commoner form). — रेल-पेल, f. crowd, throng; abundance, profusion; glut (in a market). रेल-पेल करना, to crowd, to throng; to jostle.

[2]**रेल** *rel* [Engl. *rail*], f. **1.** a rail. **2.** railway. **3.** a train. — ~ का, adj. railway (station, line, bridge, &c). ~ की पटरी, or सड़क, f. railway track, line. ~ से जाना, to go by train. – रेल-गाड़ी, f. a railway train; a railway carriage.

रेलना *relnā* [cf. *raya*-], v.t. & v.t. **1.** v.i. Brbh. to be abundant. **2.** v.t. to push, to shove; to cram (into, में). **3.** to wash or to carry away (as a stream).

रेलवे *relve* [Engl. *railway*], f. a railway (company, network).

रेला *relā* [cf. H. [1]*rel*], m. **1.** a rushing stream. ***2.** a rush, shoving, crowding; attack. **3.** line or string of animals. — ~ देना, to give a push (to, को).

[1]**रेव** *rev* [**reva*-; Pk. *reva*-], m. *Pl.* **1.** sand; grit. **2.** a grain (as of sand, sugar). **3.** a shoal, shallows.

[2]**रेव** *rev* [P. *rev*], f. trick, fraud, guile.

रेवंती *revantī* [ad. *revatī*-], f. *Pl.* name of a jasmine.

रेवंद *revand* [P. *revand*], m. *Pl. HŚS.* rhubarb.

रेवड़ *revaṛ*, f. a string or file (of animals); a herd, flock (of goats, sheep).

रेवड़ी *revṛī* [**revaḍa*-], f. a small cake of sugar or molasses covered with sesame seeds. - ~ के फेर में आना, fig. to meet unexpected difficulties after rashly undertaking a task or challenge.

रेवती *revătī* [S.], f. **1.** *mythol.* name of the wife of Balrām. **2.** *astron.* name of the twenty-seventh, or fifth, lunar asterism.

रेशम *reśam* [P. *reśam*], m. silk.

रेशमी *reśmī* [P. *reśmī*], adj. **1.** made of silk. **2.** silky.

रेशा *reśā* [P. *reśa*], m. **1.** a fibre; filament; vein (of a leaf). **2.** fig. nerve. **3.** stringiness (as of a mango). — रेशेदार [P. *-dār*], adj. fibrous; stringy.

रेस्टरंट *resṭăranṭ* [Engl. *restaurant*], m. a restaurant.

रेस्टरेंट *resṭăreṁṭ* [Engl. *restaurant*], m. a restaurant.

रेस्तराँ *restărāṁ* [? P. *restūrān*: ← F.], m. a restaurant.

[1]**रेह** *reh* [**rehā-*], f. **1.** fossil alkali (consisting chiefly of sodium salts). **2.** alkaline soil. **3.** saline soil.

[2]**रेह** *reh* [*rekhā-*], f. reg. (Bihar) a furrow.

रेहकला *rehăklā*, m. pronun. var. Brbh. = रहकला.

रेहड़ *rehaṛ*, m. reg. = [1]रेह, 2., 3.

[1]**रेहड़ी** *rehṛī*, f. = रहकला.

[2]**रेहड़ी** *rehṛī* [cf. H. *reh*], f. *Pl.* sandy or saline soil; brackish land.

रेहन *rehn* [A. *rahn*], m. **1.** a pledge, pawn. **2.** a mortgage (esp. on land). — ~ करना, or रखना, to pledge, to pawn; to mortgage. ~ से छुड़ाना, to redeem from pawn, or mortgage. ~ होना, to be mortgaged. रेहनदार [P. *-dār*], m. mortgagee. रेहन-नामा, m. mortgage deed.

रेहना *rehnā* [cf. *rekhā-*], v.t. reg. to mark with lines.

रेहू *rehū* [conn. *rohita-*[1]], f. a fish (= रोहू).

रैंस *raiṁs*, m. pronun. var. = रहस.

रैदासी *raidāsī*, adj. of or belonging to a sect associated with the *sant* poet Raidās, of Banaras.

रैन *rain* [*rajanī-*], f. night. — रैन-चैन, m. reg. merry-making at night; perfect ease or comfort. रैन-बसेरा, m. reg. night's halt or lodging. दिन-रैन, adv. day and night.

रैनी *rainī* [*rajana-*], f. *Pl.* **1.** colouring, dyeing. **2.** extracting colour (from plants or flowers).

रैयत *raiyat* [A. *ra'īya*: P. *ra'īyat*], f. **1.** a subject. ***2.** a tenant, cultivator. **3.** a dependant. — रैयतवारी [P. *-vārī*], adj. *hist.* made by or with individual cultivators (a revenue settlement).

रैया *raiyā* [cf. H. *rāy*], m. dimin. **1.** dear king, dear chief. **2.** a petty king or chief. — रैया-राव, m. pl. cf. ~, 2.

रोंआर *roṁār* [cf. *roman-*], adj. reg. = रोआँसा.

रोंगटा *roṁgṭā*, m. = रोयाँ. — रोंगटे खड़े होना, the hairs (of the body) to stand on end (from cold, or from a thrill of fear or delight).

रोंगटी *roṅgṭī*, f. ? corr. Brbh. = रौंट, रौंटि.

रोंघटा *roṅghṭā*, m. *Pl.* = रौंट, रोंगटी.

रोंटगी *roṁṭgī*, f. ? corr. *Pl.* = रौंट.

रोंथना *roṁthnā* [*romanthăyate*], v.i. reg. to chew the cud.

रोंपना *roṁpnā*, v.t. pronun. var. = रोपना.

रोआँ *roāṁ*, m. = रोयाँ.

रोआँसा *roāṁsā* [*romaśa-* × H. *roāṁ*], adj. hairy, &c.

रोआब *roāb*, m. = रोब.

रोक *rok* [cf. H. *roknā*], f. **1.** coming, or bringing to a stop. ~ के लिए ब्रेक, brakes to stop with. **2.** stopping, restraint; restriction. **3.** obstacle; a barrier. **4.** probibition. **5.** interruption, stoppage. **6.** a prop, stay, support (against falling). **7.** screen, shelter. — ~ लगाना, to place a prohibition (on, पर); to ban. – रोक-टोक, f. obstruction; prohibition; interference; challenge (of a sentry). रोक-टोक करना, to obstruct, &c. रोक-थाम, f. stopping, check, restraint; support, prop; temporary remedy, patching up (a quarrel, a situation).

रोकड़ *rokaṛ* [cf. **rokka-*], m. **1.** (also pl.) cash, ready money. **2.** valuables; convertible assets. **3.** payment in cash. — ~ मिलाना, to draw up a cash balance. रोकड़-जमा, m. opening balance. रोकड़-बही, f. cash-book. रोकड़-बाक़ी, f. cash balance. रोकड़-बिकरी, f. cash sale.

रोकड़िया *rokṛiyā* [cf. H. *rokaṛ*], m. **1.** cashier; banker. **2.** reg. (Bihar) tester of coin.

रोकन *rokan* [cf. H. *roknā*], f. *Pl.* obstacle (= रोक).

रोकना *roknā* [**rokk-*], v.t. **1.** to stop; to check; to halt (a vehicle); to block (a road); to challenge (as a sentry). **2.** to restrain, to prevent (from, से); to obstruct. **3.** to prohibit (from, से). **4.** to detain; to arrest. **5.** to withhold, to keep back (as funds). **6.** esp. w. रखना, and w. देना. to reserve (a seat, berth); to engage (a person) contractually. **7.** to ward off, to avert (by means of, से, or पर). **8.** to block up (a hole, a gap); to close. **9.** *Pl.* to surround, to besiege. **10.** to revoke (an order, &c). **11.** to suppress, to repress (emotions). — पत्तल पर हाथ से रोके हुए होना, to hold the hand over (one's) plate (to prevent it being refilled).

रोकू *rokū* [cf. H. *roknā*], m. one who prevents, obstructs, &c.

रोग *rog* [S.], m. **1.** illness; disease; an illness. **2.** fig. an evil, worry, plague. **3.** a bad habit. — ~ देना (को), to infect (a person, with disease). ~ पालना, to have a disease, &c.; to incubate a disease; to acquire a bad habit. ~

लगा लेना, to fall ill; to acquire a bad habit. ~ से उठना, to recover from illness, to be convalescent. – रोग-ग्रस्त, adj. in the grip of disease, ill; ailing. रोग-नाशक, adj. curative, remedial, medical, medicinal. रोग-निरोधक, adj. prophylactic. रोग-निवारक, m. = रोग-नाशक. रोग-विज्ञान, m. pathology. रोगाणुनाशक [°*ga*+*a*°], adj. & m. disinfectant.

रोग़न *rogan* [P. *raugan*], m. **1.** fat, grease. **2.** clarified butter, *ghī*. **3.** varnish. **4.** polish. — रोग़न-जोश, m. a meat curry in hot sauce. रोग़नदार [P. *-dār*], adj. varnished; polished.

रोग़नी *rognī* [P. *rauganī*], adj. **1.** greasy, oily. **2.** fried in *ghī* or oil. **3.** varnished; polished.

रोगिणी *rogiṇī* [S.], f. an invalid; a patient.

रोगी *rogī* [cf. H. *rog*; & S.], adj. & m. **1.** adj. ill; ailing, unwell; diseased (plant, seed). **2.** an invalid; patient.

रोगीला *rogīlā* [cf. H. *rog*], adj. & m. = रोगी.

रोचक *rocak* [S.], adj. **1.** agreeable. **2.** interesting.

रोचन *rocan* [S.], adj. & m. **1.** adj. bright, beautiful; exciting desire, charming. **2.** m. name or title given to certain plants (regarded as sharpening taste or aiding digestion); onion; turmeric; pomegranate.

रोज *roj* [**rodya-*], m. Brbh. Av. weeping.

रोज़ *roz* [P. *roz*], m. & adj. **1.** m. a day; a day of twenty-four hours. **2.** adv. daily. — ~ का, adj. daily (work, bread); everyday, ordinary (as an event). ~ उठते बैठते, adv. from rising until resting, constantly, all day. ~ ~, adv. day by day, every day. चंद ~, adv. for a few days, a short space of time. हर ~, adv. every day. – रोज़-नामा, m. a daily newspaper; a diary; a daily account-book. °-नामचा, m. dimin. id., 2., 3. रोज़-बरोज़ [P. *-ba-*], adv. day by day, daily. रोज़-मर्रा [P. *marra*], adv. & m. daily; the daily round; everyday language.

रोज़गार *rozgār* [P. *rozgār*], m. employment, daily work; livelihood; work, trade. — ~ करना, to work for, to earn, a living; to set up in business. ~ छूटना, to lose (one's) livelihood; to be out of work. ~ जाता रहना, to go out of business. ~ लगना (को), to obtain a position. ~ से होना, to have a position, or work.

रोज़गारी *rozgārī* [P. *rozgārī*], adj. & m. **1.** adj. working, earning. **2.** m. one having work, a worker; tradesman; businessman. — ~ औरत, f. a working woman.

रोज़ा *rozā* [P. *roza*], m. **1.** a fast. **2.** *musl.* fasting during the month of Ramaẓān. — ~ खोलना, to break a fast. ~ तोड़ना, to break off a fast. ~ रखना, to keep a fast.

रोज़ाना *rozānā* [P. *rozāna*], adj. & m. **1.** adj. daily. **2.** m. daily pay or allowance.

रोज़ी *rozī* [P. *rozī*], f. **1.** daily food, daily bread. **2.** daily work, or wages. — रोज़ीदार [P. -*dār*], adj. having work, employed.

रोज़ीना *rozīnā* [P. *rozīna*], adj. & m. U. = रोज़ाना.

रोझ *rojh* [**rohya-*: Pk. *rojjha-*], m. the *nīlgāy* (a large dark-coated antelope).

रोट *roṭ* [**roṭṭa-*[1]: Pk. *roṭṭa-*], m. **1.** a large thick bread-cake. **2.** a sweet cake (offered to a deity); sweets (offered to Hanumān).

रोटा *roṭā*, m. Av. ground meal, flour (cf. रोट).

रोटिया *roṭiyā* [cf. H. *roṭī*], m. *Pl.* a servant who receives food in lieu of wages.

रोटी *roṭī* [**roṭṭa-*[1], *roṭikā-*], f. **1.** a bread-cake. **2.** food; fig. livelihood. — ~ करना, to provide food (for, की), to feed. ~ कमाना (अपनी), to earn (one's) bread. ~ का व्यवहार होना, to have commensal ties (with, से). ~ को रोना, to cry for bread, to be starving. ~ खाना, to eat bread; to live (by). रोटियाँ तोड़ना, to break bread (of or at the house of, की, के यहाँ): to live as a dependant (of). रोटियाँ लगना (को), to be well-nourished; to look prosperous. रोटियों का मारा, adj. starved; famine-stricken. हाथ की रोटी, f. the food one obtains, one's daily bread. – रोटी-कपड़ा, food and clothing, maintenance. रोटी-दाल, f. bread and lentils, simple food. रोटी-दाल चलाना, to make ends meet. रोटी-दाल से ख़ुश, having enough to live on. रोटी-बेटी का संबंध, m. commensal and matrimonial ties (between families).

रोड़ा *roṛā* [**roḍa-*[2]], m. **1.** a piece of stone or brick; a brickbat. **2.** fig. a stumbling-block, obstacle. **3.** colloq. an old inhabitant (of a place). — बाट का ~, m. = ~, 2.; a worthless or useless thing; a wretch, pauper.

रोड़ी *roṛī* [cf. H. *roṛā*], f. **1.** a small piece of broken stone or brick. **2.** gravel. — ~ कूटना, to pound or to break stones.

रोदा *rodā* [P. *-roda*], Brbh. gut: a sinew used as a bow-string.

रोदन *rodan* [S.], m. weeping.

रोध *rodh* [S.], m. **1.** an obstacle, obstruction. **2.** a blockade. **3.** a veto.

रोधक *rodhak* [S.], adj. obstructing, checking.

रोधन *rodhan* [S.], m. **1.** obstructing, checking; blockading. **2.** hindering.

[1]**रोना** *ronā* [*rodati*], v.i. & v.t. & adj. **1.** v.i. to cry, to weep. **2.** to lament, to be sad; to complain. **3.** to be displeased. **4.** v.t. to bewail

(one's fate, or troubles). **5.** adj. tearful, dejected. **रोनी सूरत**, f. a tearful face. — **~ धोना!** colloq. cry baby, cry! – **रोना-कलपना**, or **रोना-धोना**, to weep and wail. – **रो उठना**, to sob bitterly. **रो देना**, to give way to tears, to burst into tears. **रो पड़ना**, to burst into tears. **रो बैठना**, to have done with tears; to become resigned (to, **से**); to wash (one's) hands (of hope).

[2]**रोना** *ronā* [H. [1]*ronā*], m. **1.** crying, tears; sorrow. **2.** regret. — **अपना ~ रोना**, to bewail one's sad lot. **इसी का तो ~ है**, that is a matter for sorrow (or for regret).

रोनी-धोनी *ronī-dhonī* [cf. H. *ronā, dhonā*], f. tearfulness; sadness.

रोप *rop* [*ropya-*], m. **1.** *Pl.* a stalk of grass or growing corn. **2.** reg. (Bihar) a young plant intended for transplantation; seedling of rice. **3.** reg. (Bihar) shoot, sprout.

रोपक *ropak* [S.], m. one who plants, grows, or sets up or in place (see **रोपित**).

रोपण *ropaṇ* [S.], m. **1.** planting, sowing. **2.** laying, setting in place; erecting (as a wall). **3.** healing (a wound).

[1]**रोपना** *ropnā* [cf. *ropyate*], v.t. **1.** to plant, to sow; to transplant. **2.** to set, to lay; to erect. **3.** to take upon oneself, to undertake. **4.** to put out the hand (to receive sthg., or to ward sthg. off). — **पाँव ~**, to set foot, to plant (one's) foot.

[2]**रोपना** *ropnā*, m. *Pl.* **1.** marriage procession. **2.** bride's vehicle. **3.** betrothal.

रोपर *ropar*, m. reg. **1.** transplanted rice. **2.** *hist.* a rate in a lease for crops of transplanted rice.

रोपित *ropit* [S.], adj. made to grow: **1.** planted, sown; transplanted. **2.** set, laid (as tiles, bricks); erected (a building).

रोब *rob* [A. *roʻb*], m. causing fear: **1.** commanding or awe-inspiring presence; dignity, prestige. **2.** domineering manner. — **~ जमाना**, or **गाँठना**, or **बिठाना**, to inspire awe (in, **में**); to establish an ascendancy (over, **पर**). **~ दिखाना**, to seek to intimidate by (one's) manner. **~ मानना**, to be awed or intimidated (by, **का**). **~ में आना**, to be awed or intimidated (by, **के**). – **रोब-दाब**, m. = ~. **रोबदार** [P. *-dār*], adj. awe-inspiring; of commanding presence.

रोबीला *robīlā* [cf. H. *rob*], adj. imposing; domineering.

रोम *rom* [S.], m. = **रोयाँ**. — **~ ~ से**, adv. with, or in or from, every fibre or pore of (one's) body or being. – **रोम-हर्ष**, m. = next. **रोमांच** [°*ma*+*a*°], m. curl or thrill of the body hairs: thrill (of ecstasy or of horror). °**-कारी**, adj. thrilling; horrifying, dread. °**इत**, adj. ecstatic. **रोमावली** [°*ma*+*ā*°], f. a line of hair (above the navel).

रोमश *romaś* [S.], adj. hairy, woolly, bristly, &c. (= **रोआँसा**).

रोयाँ *royāṁ* [*roman-*], m. **1.** body hair. **2.** animal hair; wool; fur; bristle; down (of birds); coat. **3.** hair, fur (on leaves). **4.** nap, pile. — **~ खड़ा होना**, to feel a thrill (of ecstasy, or of fear); to have gooseflesh (with cold). **~ तक न उखड़ना**, fig. not a hair of the head to be harmed. **~ पसीजना**, fig. the heart to be melted. **रोयें रोयें से आशीर्वाद देना**, to bless (another) with every fibre of (one's) being. **रोयेंदार** [P. *-dār*], adj. hairy, woolly, furred, &c.

रोयाराट *royārāṭ* [H. *ronā*, H. [1]*raṭnā* (← **raṭyati*)], f. weeping and wailing.

रोर *ror* [cf. *rava-*[1]], f. **1.** outcry. **2.** *Pl.* fame, notoriety. — **मधु ~**, f. sweet voice (of a poet), sweet words.

रोरी *rorī* [H. *roṛī*], f. reg. a red clay, used to mark a *tilak*.

[1]**रोल** *rol*, f. Brbh. = **रोर**.

[2]**रोल** *rol* [Engl. *roll*], m. f. a roll, register; revenue roll. — **रोलदार** [P. *-dār*], adj. entered on a roll, &c.

[3]**रोल** *rol* [Engl. *role*], m. role.

रोलन *rolan* [cf. H. *rolnā*], f. *Pl.* anything picked out, the pick (of anything).

रोलना *rolnā* [*loḍayati*], v.t. **1.** to roll. **2.** to plane, to smoothe; to rub. **3.** to sift, to winnow; to select. **4.** colloq. to rake in (money). — **रोटी ~**, to roll out bread-cakes. (**जानवर को**) **रोलने देना**, to allow (an animal) to wallow (on dry earth, and so damage its hide).

रोला *rolā* [? **loḍa-*], f. a rhyming couplet of twenty-four instants in each line, having a pause at the eleventh, twelfth or thirteenth instant, and the last syllable (or last two syllables) long.

रोली *rolī*, f. **1.** a red powder made principally from turmeric and lime (used to make sectarian, or decorative, marks on the forehead). **2.** *Pl.* a red insect which attacks wheat crops.

रोव- *rov-*, v.i. Brbh. Av. = **रोना**.

रोशन *rośan* [P. *rauśan*], adj. **1.** light, bright; lighted (as a lamp). **2.** illuminated. **3.** evident. — **~ करना**, to light (as a lamp, candle); to illuminate; to bring (a fact, &c.) to light. **~ होना**, to be lighted; to become bright, or illuminated; to be or to become clear (to, **पर**). – **रोशन-चौकी**, f. *Pl. HŚS.* an illuminated square, or place: a performance of singing with flute, drum and cymbal accompaniment. रोशनदान [P. *-dān*], m. a skylight. भाई रोशनदान, m. colloq. he who gives light: a splendid fellow. रोशनदिल, m. enlightened, intelligent.

रोशनाई *rośnāī* [P. *rosnā'ī*], f. ink.

रोशनी *rośnī* [P. *rauśanī*], f. **1.** light; brightness; illumination (as of a building). **2.** brightness (of the eye); clearness of sight. **3.** a light, lamp; electric light bulb. **4.** enlightenment. नई ~, f. the new light: modern attitudes. — ~ करना (की), to light (a lamp); to illuminate. ~ देना, to illuminate. ~ डालना, to throw light (on, पर). बिजली की ~, f. electric light, or lighting.

रोष *roṣ* [S.], m. **1.** anger, rage; indignation. **2.** enmity, hostility. — ~ करना, to be angry, &c. (with, से).

रोषण *roṣaṇ* [S.], adj. *Pl. HŚS.* angry.

रोषित *roṣit* [S.], adj. angered, &c. (see रोष).

रोषी *roṣī* [S.], adj. Av. angry, &c. (see रोष).

रोस- *ros-* [*roṣati*], v.i. reg. to be angry (= रूसना).

रोहट *rohaṭ* [cf. H. [1]*ronā*], f. *Pl.* crying; tears.

रोहण *rohaṇ* [S.], m. **1.** rising; mounting. **2.** climbing, developing (as a plant).

रोहिण *rohiṇ* [S.], m. an astrologically determined period of time (comprising most of the last hour up to midday).

रोहिणी *rohiṇī* [S.], f. **1.** name of a lunar asterism (the ninth, or the fourth): Aldebaran and four other stars in Taurus. **2.** *mythol.* name of a wife of Vasudeva, and mother of Balrām.

रोहित *rohit* [S.], adj. & m. **1.** adj. red. **2.** m. the colour red. **3.** a species of fish, *Cyprinus rohita*, or *C. denticulatus* (= रोही, रोहू).

रोही *rohī* [*rohita-*[1]], adj. & m. **1.** adj. Brbh. red. **2.** m. = रोहू.

रोहू *rohū* [cf. *rohita-*[1]], m. f. a species of fish, *Cyprinus rohita*.

रौंट *rauṁṭ*, f. reg. quarrelling, wrangling (as when playing); cheating.

रौंटना *rauṁṭnā*, v.i. *Pl.* to shirk; to cheat.

रौंटि *rauṁṭi*, f. Brbh. = रौंट.

रौंटी *rauṁṭī* [cf. H. *rauṁṭ*], adj. & m. reg. **1.** adj. shirking, behaving unfairly. **2.** m. a shirker; rogue.

रौंदन *rauṁdan* [cf. H. *rauṁdnā*], f. *Pl. HŚS.* trampling, treading or crushing down.

रौंदना *rauṁdnā*, v.t. **1.** to trample on. **2.** to tread out (corn). **3.** to ride over (ground). **4.** to crush; to lay waste.

[1]**रौंस** *rauṁs*, m. *Pl.* ? a shrub (? *Streblus asper*) having irregularly shaped white flowers and used in making well-linings, &c.

[2]**रौंस** *rauṁs*, m. = [2] [3]रूस.

रौ *rau* [*raya-*], m. **1.** current, stream; torrent. **2.** impetuosity.

रौग़न *raugan*, m. = रोग़न.

रौज़ा *rauzā* [A. *rauẓa*], m. **1.** tomb (of a saint, &c.); mausoleum. **2.** a garden, Mughal garden.

रौताई *rautāī* [cf. H. *rāvat*], f. Brbh. Av. chiefly rank or status.

रौद्र *raudr* [S.], adj. & m. **1.** adj. violent, raging; fearsome; terrible. **2.** m. rage, passion. **3.** heat of the sun. **3.** *rhet.* one of the *rasas*: see रस, 9.

रौद्रता *raudrătā* [S.], f. fearsomeness, &c. (see रौद्र).

रौनक़ *raunaq* [A. *raunaq*], f. **1.** brightness, radiance; radiant expression. **2.** elegance, grace. **3.** lustre; water (of a sword). **4.** atmosphere of excitement (as in a drinking-house). **5.** flourishing state. — ~ पर होना, to be in full bloom or splendour; to be in (its) prime, at (its) best. – रौनक़-अफ़रोज़ [P. *-afroz*], adj. U. gracing or honouring (by one's arrival). रौनक़-अफ़रोज़ होना, to arrive. रौनक़दार [P. *-dār*], adj. bright, brilliant, splendid.

[1]**रौना** *raunā* [*ravati*], v.i. Brbh. to make a sound, to cry out.

[2]**रौना** *raunā* [H. [1]*raunā*], m. *Pl.* a rattle.

[3]**रौना** *raunā* [P. *ravāna*, H. *ravānā*; ? × H. *gaunā*], m. reg. a bride's departure for the bridegroom's home.

[1]**रौर** *raur*, f. Brbh. = रोर.

[2]**रौर** *raur* [*rājakula-*], pron. hon. Av. you.

रौरव *raurav* [S.], adj. & m. **1.** adj. fearsome, terrible. **2.** m. *mythol.* a hell; transf. hellishness.

रौरा- *raurā-* [cf. H. [1]*raur*], v.i. Brbh. to shout or cry aloud.

रौराट *raurāṭ*, f. reg. **1.** a tingling or smarting sensation. **2.** fig. compunction, remorse.

रौल *raul*, f. 1. = रोर. 2. = रौला, 2. — ~ पड़ना, a commotion to take place; to be excited, roused (a crowd).

रौला *raulā*, m. 1. = रोर. **2.** a disturbance. — ~ मचाना, to cause an uproar, a disturbance.

रौवार *rauvār*, m. *Pl.* cloth spread on a bed, &c. (for a person to lie on).

रौशन *rauśan*, adj. = **रोशन**.

रौस *raus*, f. Brbh. = **रविश**, 5.

रौसती *raustī*, f. *Pl.* ? = **रौसली**.

रौसली *rauslī*, f. reg. (W.) a light soil.

रौहिण *rauhiṇ* [S.], m. born under the asterism Rohiṇī.

ल

ल *la*, the twenty-eighth consonant of the Devanāgarī syllabary. **लकार**, m. the sound /l/; the letter ल.

लंक *laṅk* [conn. **lakka*-[3]], f. Brbh. the waist, lower back.

लंका *laṅkā* [S.], m. **1.** *mythol.* the region of Laṅkā. **2.** Sri Lanka, Ceylon. — **लंकापति**, m. Brbh. Av. lord of Laṅkā: *mythol.* a title esp. of Rāvaṇ. **लंकेश** [°*kā* + *ī*°], m. Brbh. Av. id.; a title of Vibhīṣaṇ. °**वर**, m. id. **लंकेसर**, m. see s.v.

लंकाई *laṅkāī* [cf. H. *(śrī) laṅkā*], adj. Singhalese.

लंकायिका *laṅkāyikā* [S.], f. a pot-herb resembling spinach, *Trigonella corniculata*.

लंकिलाट *laṅkilāṭ* [Engl. *long-cloth*], m. 19c. a partic. cotton cloth.

लंकेसर *laṅkesar* [ad. *laṅkeśvara*-], m. reg. (E.) a species of flowering plant.

लंग *laṅg* [P. *lang*], adj. & m. *Pl. HŚS.* **1.** adj. lame. **2.** m. lameness.

लंगड़ *laṅgaṛ*, m. reg. (Bihar) = **लंगर**.

लँगड़ *laṁgaṛ*, adj. reg. (Bihar) = **लँगड़ा**.

[1]**लँगड़ा** *laṁgṛā* [cf. *laṅga*-[1]], adj. & m. **1.** adj. lame. **2.** having a leg broken (as a chair). **3.** [Engl. *lame*] fig. lame, defective (an excuse). **4.** m. a cripple. — **लँगड़ा-लूला**, adj. halt and maimed, crippled.

[2]**लँगड़ा** *laṁgṛā*. name of a variety of mango.

लँगड़ाई *laṁgṛāī*, f. reg. = **लँगड़ाहट**.

लँगड़ाना *laṁgṛānā* [cf. H. *laṁgṛā*], v.i. to limp. — **लँगड़ाकर चलना**, id.

लँगड़ापन *laṁgṛāpan* [cf. H. *laṁgṛā*], m. lameness.

लँगड़ाहट *laṁgṛāhaṭ* [cf. H. *laṁgṛā*], f. lameness, limping.

लंगर *laṅgar* [P. *langar*], m. **1.** an anchor. **2.** a heavy block of wood attached to the neck of cattle to prevent them from straying. **3.** a heavy chain; fetters. **4.** an anchor-shaped object; pendulum. **5.** transf. a heavy rope; hawser. **6.** strip of cloth: a loin-cloth as worn by wrestlers. **7.** a public kitchen, alms-house; food distributed to the needy. **8.** tacking, basting. — ~ **उठाना**, to weigh anchor. ~ **छोड़ना**, or **डालना**, to drop anchor. ~ **पर होना**, to be at anchor. ~ **बाँधना**, to gird the loins (to wrestle); fig. to become a student (a brāhmaṇ, in the traditional way). – **लंगर-गाह**, f. an anchorage.

लँगरई *laṁgraī*, f. Brbh. metr. see **लँगराई**.

लंगरवा *laṅgarvā* [cf. H. *laṅgar*], m. dimin. reg. a dissolute person.

लँगराई *laṁgrāī* [cf. H. *laṅgar*], f. Brbh. sthg. burdensome, or oppressive: naughtiness, tricks.

लंगरी *laṅgrī* [f. P. *lagan*], f. *Pl.* a shallow pan of copper or brass to knead dough in.

लँगरैया *laṁgraiyā*, f. Brbh. = **लँगराई**.

[1]**लंगी** *laṅgī*, f. reg. urine.

[2]**लंगी** *laṅgī* [conn. H. *lāṁg*], f. a leg throw (wrestling).

लंगूर *laṅgūr* [*lāṅgūla*-], m. the long-tailed, black-faced monkey of north India. — **लंगूर-फल**, m. Brbh. coconut.

लंगूरी *laṅgūrī* [cf. H. *laṅgūr*], f. **1.** fig. Brbh. bounding action (of a horse). **2.** (?) *HŚS.* a reward given to one who traces stolen cattle; reg. (W.) money paid to a thief for the restoration of stolen cattle.

लँगोचा *laṁgocā*, m. *Pl. HŚS.* a sausage.

लँगोट *laṁgoṭ* [**laṅgapaṭṭa*-], m. loin-cloth. — ~ **कसना**, or **बाँधना**, to tie on a loin-cloth; to gird the loins (for, **पर**). ~ **का कच्चा**, adj. = next. ~ **का ढीला**, adj. loose, dissolute (sexually). ~ **का सच्चा**, adj. (an ascetic) who practises true renunciation. ~ **खोलना**, to unfasten the loin-cloth; to have sexual intercourse (with). - **लँगोट-बंद**, m. strip of cloth to which the loin-cloth is fastened; one whose loin-cloth is fastened, a confirmed bachelor. **लाल लँगोटवाला**, m. colloq. a monkey.

लँगोटा *laṁgoṭā*, m. = **लँगोट**.

लँगोटिया *laṁgoṭiyā* [cf. H. *laṁgoṭ*], adj. having to do with the loin-cloth: — ~ **यार**, m. a childhood friend; close friend.

लँगोटी *laṁgoṭī*, f. = **लँगोट**. — ~ **बँधवाना**, to leave (a man) with only his loin-cloth (thieves): to reduce (one) to poverty.

लंघन *laṅghan* [S.], m. **1.** leaping over; crossing over or beyond. **2.** overstepping (bounds); transgression. **3.** fasting, fast.

लँघना *laṁghnā* [*laṅghayati*: ? as v.t. ← Panj.], v.t. & v.i. **1.** v.t. to jump over; to cross over. **2.** to bestride, to mount. **3.** [cf. H. *lāṁghnā*] v.i. to be jumped over, or crossed. **4.** to elapse (time).

लँघनी *laṁghnī* [cf. H. *laṁghnā*], f. fasting, fast.

लँघाना *laṁghānā* [cf. H. *laṁghnā*], v.t. to cause to jump over.

लंघित *laṅghit* [S.], adj. **1.** leapt over; crossed over or beyond. **2.** overstepped, transgressed.

लंघ्य *laṅghyă* [S.], adj. crossable; traversible.

लंठ *lanṭh* [**lanṭha*-[1]], adj. & m. **1.** adj. stupid; boorish. **2.** m. a blockhead.

लंठई *lanṭhaī* [cf. H. *lanṭh*], f. boorishness.

लंड *lanḍ* [conn. **lanḍa*-[1]], m. penis.

लंडी *lanḍī*, m. pej. *Pl.* a contemptible man; an effeminate man.

लँडूरा *laṁḍura* [cf. **lanḍa*-[1]; × **lunḍa*-], adj. reg. tailless: **1.** friendless, forlorn. **2.** reg. (N.) a bachelor.

लंद-फंद *land-phand* [? cf. H. *phand(ā)*], m. reg. deceit.

लंपट *lampaṭ* [S.], adj. & m. **1.** adj. licentious; depraved. **2.** m. a licentious person.

लंपटता *lampaṭătā* [S.], f. licentiousness, lustfulness.

लंब *lamb* [S.], adj. & m. **1.** adj. long, tall, large, &c. (= लंबा). **2.** m. a perpendicular. — लंब-तड़ंग, adj. very tall. लंबोदर [°*ba*+*u*°], adj. & m. pot-bellied; a title of the deity Gaṇeś.

[1]लंबर *lambar* [Engl. *number*], m. reg. **1.** number. **2.** mark (in an examination); place. **3.** turn. — लंबरदार [P. -*dār*], m. village headman (responsible for the government revenue). °ई, f. office of headman. लंबरवार [P. -*vār*], adv. in order; by turns.

[2]लंबर *lambar*, m. reg. a fox (= लोमड़ी).

लंबरी *lambarī* [cf. H. [1]*lambar*], adj. reg. = नंबरी.

लंबा *lambā* [*lamba*-[1]], adj. **1.** long. **2.** tall. **3.** extensive; great, large (as expenditure). **4.** long-lasting; prolonged. — ~ करना, to lengthen, to extend; to stretch out (as the feet); colloq. to knock (one) down, or flat; to send off, send packing. ~ बनना, or होना, to make off, to make oneself scarce. लंबी ज़बान होना, (one) to be a great talker. ~ तनख़्वाह, f. colloq. a very good salary. लंबी तानना, to stretch oneself out full length (on the ground, or a bed). लंबी साँस भरना, to heave a deep sigh; to regret, to repent; to breathe hard (as a dying man). लंबे पाँव पसारना, to stretch out the legs; to die. लंबे मुँह से खाना, to eat with appetite or zest. – लंबा-खिंचा, adj. drawn-out, lengthy. लंबा-चौड़ा, adj. long and wide; extensive (account); spacious; vast. लंबा-तगड़ा, adj. tall and strong, sturdily built. लंबी-चौड़ी करना, or हाँकना, to tell a long story; to talk boastfully.

लंबाई *lambāī* [cf. H. *lambā*], f. **1.** length. **2.** tallness. — लंबाई-चौड़ाई, f. length and breadth, extent, area: capacity; size (as of clothes), fit.

लँबाड़ा *laṁbāṛā*, m. *Pl.* **1.** a community of carriers of grain, salt, &c. (= बनजारा). **2.** a man of the *laṁbāṛā* community.

लंबान *lambān* [conn. *lamba*-[1]], m. f. = लंबाई.

लंबाना *lambānā* [cf. *lambayati*], v.t. to lengthen; to prolong.

लंबायमान *lambāyămān*, adj. lying flat.

लंबाव *lambāv*, m. reg. = लंबाई.

लंबित *lambit* [S.], adj. **1.** hanging down; suspended. **2.** made long: extended.

लंबी *lambī* [cf. H. *lambā*], f. a prancing step (of a horse). — लंबियाँ करना, to prance; to caper.

लंबू *lambū* [cf. *lamba*-[1]], adj. & m. colloq. **1.** adj. tall, lanky. **2.** m. a tall or lanky person.

लंबोतरा *lambotrā* [ad. **lambottara*-], adj. elongated; oval.

लकड़- *lakaṛ*-. wood: — लकड़कोट, m. *Pl.* a stockade, barricade. लकड़तोड़, adj. as hard (on the feet) as wood: stiff (of shoes). लकड़दादा, m. inv. colloq. any distant ancestor. लकड़फोड़, m. woodpecker. °आ, m. id. लकड़बग्घा, m. hyena. लकड़हारा, m. wood-cutter; wood-seller. °-हारिन, f.

लकड़ा *lakṛā* [**lakkuṭa*-: Pk. *lakkuḍa*-], m. **1.** a beam. **2.** a log.

लकड़ी *lakṛī* [**lakkuṭa*-: Pk. *lakkuḍa*-], f. **1.** a stick; staff. **2.** wood, a piece of wood; pl. firewood. **3.** *mech.* a block. — ~ चलना, fighting to go on (between, में). ~, or लकड़ियाँ, देना (को), to build the funeral fire (of). ~ होना, colloq. to grow lean or thin; to grow hard (of bread). – लकड़ी-सा, adj. stick-like, thin. एक ~ सब को हाँकना, to drive everyone with the same stick: to treat all alike; to fail to show individual consideration.

लक़दक़ *luqdaq* [P. *laq o daq*], adj. **1.** desolate, bleak. **2.** gleaming, spick and span.

लक़लक़ *laqlaq* [A. *laqlaq*], m. a stork (= लगलग).

लक़वा *laqvā* [A. *laqva*], m. paralysis; a stroke. — ~ मारना (को), paralysis to strike (one).

लकीर *lakīr*, f. **1.** a line; a groove; rut. **2.** a streak; stripe. **3.** line (of writing, print). **4.** fig. line of movement, track. — ~ खींचना (पर), to draw a line; to mark a boundary; to cross out. ~ पीटना, to follow in the track (of ancestors, or convention). – ~ का फ़क़ीर, m. pej. one who follows a line: one of set, or conservative, outlook.

लकीरना *lakīrnā* [cf. H. *lakīr*], v.t. *Pl.* to mark with a line; to mark off; to outline.

लकुट *lakuṭ* [S.], m. a staff, club.

लकुटिया *lakuṭiyā* [cf. H. *lakuṭ*], f. a small club (esp. that held by Kr̥ṣṇa).

लकोरा *lakorā*, m. reg. (W.) a bundle of cut grass or fodder.

लक्कड़ *lakkaṛ* [**lakkuṭa-*: Pk. *lakkuḍa-*], m. = लकड़ा.

[1]**लक्का** *lakkā* [P. *laqā*], m. **1.** the Indian fantail (a pigeon). **2.** *Pl.* the Brahminy kite.

[2]**लक्का** *lakkā* [**lakka-*[2]], m. *Pl.* a lump, piece.

[1]**लक्खी** *lakkhī* [cf. H. *lākh*], adj. *Pl. HŚS.* **1.** possessing a lakh (of rupees), very wealthy. **2.** immensely valuable.

[2]**लक्खी** *lakkhī*, f. = लक्ष्मी.

लक्ष *lakṣ* [S.], m. **1.** one hundred thousand. **2.** a mark, object of aim. — लक्षाधिपति [°*kṣa*+*a*°], m. fig. a millionaire.

लक्षण *lakṣaṇ* [S.], m. **1.** a sign, indication; mark or spot (on the body). ***2.** a characteristic; distinguishing feature. **3.** a symptom. — लक्षण-ग्रंथ, m. a book dealing with characteristics of poetry, a work on literary criticism. [1]लक्षणात्मक [°*ṇa*+*ā*°], adj. symptomatic.

लक्षणा *lakṣaṇā* [S.], f. figurative sense (of a word). — [2]लक्षणात्मक [°*ṇā*+*ā*°], adj. figurative.

लक्षणीय *lakṣăṇīyă* [S.], adj. noteworthy.

लक्षित *lakṣit* [S.], adj. **1.** noted, observed. **2.** indicated. **3.** marked out, designated. — लक्षितार्थ [°*ta*+*a*°], m. a transferred or figurative sense.

लक्ष्मण *lakṣmaṇ* [S.], m. *mythol.* name of a son of Daśrath by his wife Sumitrā (the younger half- brother and faithful companion of Rāmcandra during his exile).

लक्ष्मी *lakṣmī* [S.], f. *mythol.* **1.** the goddess Lakṣmī (wife of Viṣṇu and goddess of good fortune and wealth). **2.** good fortune, prosperity; wealth. **3.** beauty. — ~ घर में आना, or उतरना, fortune to come to the house (of): to prosper; to have a run of good luck. – लक्ष्मीपति, m. husband or lord of Lakṣmī: a title of Viṣṇu; a wealthy man. लक्ष्मी-पूजा, f. name of a festival held on the fifteenth day of the dark half of the month Kārttik, at the end of the Dīvālī festival; worship of Lakṣmī by the bridegroom and bride after the bride has been brought to her father-in-law's house. लक्ष्मी-नारायण करना, reg. to make an offering to Lakṣmī and Nārāyaṇ before eating; to begin to eat.

लक्ष्य *lakṣyă* [S.], adj. & m. **1.** adj. observable. **2.** noteworthy. **3.** m. aim, object of aim; target. **4.** goal, purpose; plan. **5.** indirect or secondary meaning (of a word). — ~ करना (को), to aim (at); to allude (to). ~ लगाना (पर), to aim (at). – लक्ष्यहीन, adj. aimless.

लख *lakh*, chiefly लख-. one hundred thousand (= [1]लाख); fig. a vast number. — लखपति, m. one possessing vast wealth: a millionaire. नौलख, adj. costing, or worth, nine lacs.

लखना *lakhnā* [*lakṣati*], v.t. & v.i. **1.** v.t. [*lakṣati*] Brbh. Av. to see, to look at. **2.** to understand, to fathom. **3.** v.i. poet. [*lakṣyate*] to seem.

लखनऊ *lakhnaū*, m. the city of Lucknow.

लख़लख़ा *lakhlakhā* [P. *lakhlakha*], m. **1.** an aromatic preparation. **2.** smelling salts, strong perfume.

लखलखाना *lakhlakhānā* [onom.], v.i. reg. to pant (with heat: a dog); to suffer from thirst.

लखा- *lakhā-* [cf. H. *lakh-*], v.i. & v.t. Brbh. **1.** v.i. to be visible. **2.** v.t. to show. — लखाइ पर-, = ~, 1. (see also s.v. लखाई, f).

लखाई *lakhāī*, f. Brbh. **1.** appearing, appearance, look (= दिखाई). **2.** seeing. — ~ पर-, to be visible, to appear.

लखाउ *lakhāu* [cf. H. *lakhā-*], Brbh. Av. sthg. visible: a sign; a token.

लखिया *lakhiyā* [cf. H. *lakh-*], m. reg. **1.** an onlooker. **2.** *Pl.* a gadabout.

लखेरन *lakheran* [H. *lakherā*], f. *Pl.* **1.** wife of a bangle-maker. **2.** a woman who sells things made of lac.

लखेरा *lakherā* [**lākṣakara-*], m. **1.** one who lacquers or varnishes; a maker of lacquered bangles. **2.** name of a community of workers in lac.

लखौट *lakhauṭ* [**lākṣāvarta-*], m. Brbh. a lacquered bangle.

लखौटा *lakhauṭā* [**lākṣāvarta-*], m. *(Pl.) HŚS.* a lacquered container, usu. of brass (for toilet articles).

लख़्त *lakht* [P. *lakht*], m. chiefly U. piece: लख़्ते-दिल, m. piece of (one's) heart: darling.

लग *lag* [*lagna-*], ppn. **1.** up to, as far as; until. **2.** near; along with. **3.** while, during, as long as. **4.** Brbh. = के लिए. — लगभग, adv., & ppn. w. के. about, approximately; nearby, near; almost.

लगड़- *lagaṛ-*. = लकड़-: — लगड़बग्घा, m. a hyena.

लगड़ा *lagṛā*, m. *Pl.* a hyena (= लगड़बग्घा, लकड़बग्घा).

लगत *lagat* [cf. H. *lagnā*], adv. *Pl.* reg. connectedly, continuously; at the very time (of).

लगती *lagtī* [cf. H. *lagnā*], f. reg. attachment, affection, love.

[1]**लगन** *lagan* [cf. H. *lagnā*], f. **1.** attachment, affection. **2.** desire, longing. **3.** intentness; a craze (for, की). **4.** being attached: contact. — ~ लगना, to feel an intense interest in (to, की); to be in love (with).

[2]**लगन** *lagan*, m. = लग्न.

लगना *lagnā* [cf. *lagyati*], v.i. **1.** to be attached or applied (to, से or में); to be joined (to); to be fastened (to); to be added (to: an appendix, &c). **2.** to be or become fixed (in or on); to take root. **3.** to be found, to occur (as in a partic. habitat). **4.** to be applied (to: as paint). **5.** to be outlaid or expended (money, time, effort). आपको कुछ न लगेगा, it will cost you nothing. जाने में दो घंटे लगते हैं, it takes two hours to get there. **6.** to be staked, wagered (on, पर); to be invested. **7.** to be imposed (as a tax). **8.** to be accounted for, disposed of. **9.** to be put (in or into, में); to be inserted; to be planted (trees, &c). **10.** to be put in order, set out (as wares). **11.** to be occupied, engaged (in, में); to occupy oneself (in). घात में लगना, to lie in wait. लगे हाथ चर आम भी लाओ, while you're at it bring four mangoes too. **12.** to be intent or set (on). उन्हें घर जाने की लग रही है, they're intent on getting home. **13.** to be engaged, involved (as the heart). यहाँ मन लगता है, I like it here. **14.** (w. obl. inf.) to begin. **15.** to be or to come close (to); to adjoin; to touch; to wear, to rub (as clothing against the skin); to put down anchor (a ship); to arrive (as at a wharf). **16.** to stick, to adhere. **17.** to catch (on to; में, as fire). **18.** to catch (in, में); to falter (the tongue). **19.** to attach oneself (to, के पीछे: as to a patron or leader). **20.** to close (as a door, or eyelids). **21.** to contract (as the stomach, in hunger). **22.** to hit or to strike (against, को, के, or में); to chafe, to rub. छुरी लग जाना (को), to be cut by a knife. जूती लगना (को), to suffer a shoe-beating. **23.** to be felt (physical sensations: by, को). उसे भूख लगी है, he is hungry. उसे ठंड लगी है, he is cold. पेशाब ~, to want to urinate. **24.** to be felt (emotions, as fear, grief: by, को). **25.** to seem (to, को), to appear as. बच्चा माँ-जैसा लगता है, the child looks like its mother. आपको यह किताब कैसी लगती है? how do you like this book? मुझे लगता है (कि...), it seems to me (that..). **26.** to be felt (a want, a lack: by, को). **27.** to come to light (a trace, a clue). अब पता लगा कि..., it now became known that.... **28.** to have an effect (upon one); to strike home, to tell (as a remark). दवा ~, medicine to take effect. दिल में ~, to move the heart. **29.** to affect, to attack (as disease, or blight on crops). **30.** to be adversely affected, spoiled; to be unwholesome (food, water); to be tainted; to rot (fruit); to be burnt (a dish). **31.** to be successful, to come off well. **32.** to come into fashion, or use. **33.** to be imputed (to, के or को: an offence, a fault). **34.** to be involved emotionally (with one, से); to have sexual intercourse (with). **35.** to happen, to occur. सिर ~ (के), to be experienced (an event, an emotion). **36.** to be obtained (by, को: as employment). **37.** to form, to shoot (fruit, sprouts: on a tree, में). **38.** to set in (as rain, heat, cold); to strike (flood). **39.** to be established, to get under way; to be in full swing (as a market). **40.** to suit, to agree (with, को). **41.** to pertain (to, को); to concern. – लगा-लगी, f. attachment, intimacy; rivalry.

लगभग *lagbhag*, adv. see s.v. लग.

लगलग *laglag* [A. *laqlaq*: P. *laglag*], m. **1.** the white stork, *Ciconia ciconia*. **2.** the white-necked, black-bodied stork, *Ciconia episcopus*.

लगवा *lagvā* [cf. H. *lagnā*], m. reg. a lover.

लगवाना *lagvānā* [cf. H. *lagnā*], v.t. to cause to be attached, applied, put, &c. (by, से).

लगसी *lagsī*, f. *Pl.* a long hooked stick (for gathering fruit).

लगाई *lagaī* [cf. H. *lagānā*], f. attaching, applying, application, &c. (see लगाना). — लगाई-लुतरी, f. making false insinuations (cf. लावा-लुतरा s.v. [4]लावा).

लगातार *lagātār* [H. *lagnā*+H. *tār*], adv. in uninterrupted succession: continuously, constantly.

लगान *lagān* [cf. H. *lagānā*], f. (m., *Pl.*) **1.** rent payable or accruing on land; assessment (on land). **2.** mooring-place, landing-place. **3.** stopping-place, halt (for porters). **4.** tracking, tracing; search. — ~ पर देना, to rent or to lease (land, to a tenant).

लगाना *lagānā* [cf. H. *lagnā*], v.t. **1.** to attach; to join, to connect (to, से); to add on (as an appendix to a book). **2.** to fix (in place); to put, to set (in or on, में or पर); to fasten (to);

to install (an appliance); to stick on (a stamp). **3.** to moor (a boat: at or in, पर or में). **4.** to close (a door, a lid). **5.** to do up (a garment). **6.** to apply (a coating). रंग ~ (पर), to paint. **7.** to set (fire: to, में). **8.** to spread (carpet, bedding). दुकान ~, to spread one's goods (a shopkeeper). **9.** to wear (glasses, distinctive clothes). **10.** to apply (an instrument). क़ैंची ~ (में), to cut. **11.** to strike with (a stick, or the hand, &c.) थप्पड़ ~ (को), to slap (one). नाखुन ~, to scratch. **12.** to put in, to plant. **13.** to form, to build (a heap, a pile); to establish (a bond, or relationship). **14.** to arrange, to adjust; to mend (a puncture); to sharpen (a blade); to tune in (a radio). **15.** to direct (an aim or shot: at, पर). **16.** to make, to stake (as a bet). **17.** to set (the hand: to, में. (काम में) हाथ ~, to become practised (at). **18.** to apply (the mind: to, में). मन ~, to apply the mind (to); to have or to foster a liking (for: as for a person, or an activity). **19.** to apply (resources); to invest. **20.** to expend (money or time: in or on, में). देर ~, to take a long time (in). **21.** to impose (a fine, &c). **22.** to appoint, to fix (a time). **23.** to establish. पहरा ~, to mount a watch. **24.** to put or to set (to work); to employ (at or in, पर); to take on (workmen). **25.** to form (a thought, a conjecture; e.g. अनुमान ~). **26.** to calculate, to assess. हिसाब ~ (का), to total up. **27.** to lay (a charge, &c.: against, पर); to impute (sthg. discreditable: to, को); to call in question (the name or reputation of, का). **28.** to report, to expose (a scandal, &c). **29.** to set (persons) at odds. **30.** to set (a spy, &c.: after, के पीछे). **31.** to initiate (a quarrel: between, में). **32.** to cause to be held (a fair); to cause to assemble (a crowd). **33.** to cause to reach. पार ~, to get (one) over (a river, a difficulty, the sea of life). **34.** to set store by. वह अपने को बड़ा लगाता है, he thinks a lot of himself. **35.** to present (oneself, अपने को) as. **36.** (w. रखना) to put by, to save; to hoard. **37.** (w. लेना) to conciliate; to attract (a following). **38.** (w. लेना) to embrace. उसने उसे गले से लगा लिया, he embraced her. मुँह ~, to be over-considerate (to, के). – लगाना-बुझाना, to cause and to resolve discord: (a person) to be a continuing cause of trouble.

लगाम *lagām* [P. *lagām*], f. m. **1.** bridle. **2.** bit; bit and reins. — ~ कड़ी करना, to keep a tight rein (on, की). ~ चढ़ाना (पर), to bridle (a horse); to check, to control. ~ देना, or लगाना (को), to put a bridle (on); to rein in. ~ लिए फिरना (के पीछे), to chase intending to bring under restraint.

लगाव *lagāv* [cf. H. *lagānā*], m. **1.** attachment, connection; contact. **2.** fellow-feeling; affection. — ~ रखना, to be in contact (with, से); to have fellow-feeling, &c. (for).

लगावट *lagāvaṭ* [cf. H. *lagānā*], f. *Pl. HŚS.* attachment, &c. (= लगाव).

लगावन *lagāvan* [cf. H. *lagānā*], m. **1.** a relish (= ¹लावन). **2.** Brbh. = लगाव, 1.

लगि *lagi*, ppn. Brbh. Av. 1. = लग. 2. = लगकर.

लगी *lagī* [cf. H. *lagnā*], f. **1.** desire; craving. **2.** affection, love. — ~ बुझना, a desire, &c. to be satisfied. – लगी-लिपटी, f. assiduous attention; partiality, bias. °-लिपटी कहना, or रखना, to speak with bias, or obscurely, or with reservation.

लगुड़ *lagur̥* [ad. *laguḍa-*], m. *Pl. HŚS.* **1.** stick, staff; club. **2.** iron bar.

लगेज *lagej* [Engl. *luggage*], m. luggage; luggage compartment, &c.

लगौंह- *lagaum̐h-* [cf. H. *lagnā, lagā(v)nā*], adj. *Pl.* **1.** set close together. **2.** pleasing, attractive.

लगौना *lagaunā* [cf. H. *lagāvan*: H. *lagnā*], m. reg. a woman's lover.

लग्गा *laggā* [*lagna-*], m. reg. **1.** a long pole. **2.** catch, hold; first step, beginning. **3.** arrangement, plan. **4.** attachment, affection. **5.** similarity, resemblance. **6.** competition, rivalry. — ~ खाना, to be compatible (with); to rival. ~ लगना, to be begun; to become attached (to, से); to resemble. ~ लगाना, to form an attachment (to or with, से); to make preliminary arrangements (for, का); to begin. लग्गे से पानी पिलाना, fig. to keep (one) at arm's length. – लग्गा-सग्गा, m. intimacy, attachment (= ~, 4).

लग्गी *laggī* [cf. H. *laggā*], f. reg. **1.** a pole. **2.** a fishing-rod.

लग्न *lagn* [S.], adj. & m. **1.** adj. attached (-लग्न). **2.** m. *astron.* point of contact of two lines, one being usu. the ecliptic; moment of entry of the sun into a sign of the zodiac. **3.** diagram of the signs of the zodiac (used as a horoscope). ***4.** m. *hind.* an auspicious moment or period (for a ceremony). **5.** marriage. — लग्न-कुंडली, f. horoscope. लग्न-पत्र, m. list of *lagnas* involved in a wedding. °-पत्रिका, f. id. लग्नेश [°*na* + *ī*°], m. the dominant heavenly body of a particular *lagna*.

लघु *laghu* [S.], adj. & m. **1.** adj. light; easily digestible. **2.** nimble, active, swift. **3.** short (of length or elevation). **4.** *pros.* short (a vowel, a syllable). **5.** slight, small; small (of format); miniature; minor (a power). **6.** weak (a voice, a sound). **7.** young; junior. **8.** trivial, insignificant; unworthy. **9.** m. a short vowel or syllable. — लघु-उपन्यास, m. a novella. लघुगणक, m. a logarithm. °ईय, adj. लघु-तरंग, m. *phys. techn.* short wave. लघु-शंका, f. urination.

लघुता *laghutā* [S.], f. **1.** lightness. **2.** slightness, smallness. **3.** fig. insignificance; inferiority. — लघुताबोधक, adj. *gram.* diminutive. लघुतावाचक, adj. id.

लचक *lacak* [cf. H. *lacaknā*], f. **1.** bending; twisting (as of neck or shoulder). **2.** flexibility; suppleness, elasticity. **3.** fig. softness, mildness (of manner). — लचकदार [P. *-dār*], adj. flexible, yielding; elastic.

लचकना *lacaknā* [cf. **lacc-*], v.i. **1.** to bend, to yield, to give; to sag. **2.** to be supple, elastic. **3.** to be strained or sprained.

लचका *lackā* [cf. H. *lacaknā*], m. **1.** a strain, a sprain. **2.** *Pl. HŚS.* patterned gold or silver lace (used as an edging for turbans and garments).

लचकाना *lackānā* [cf. H. *lacaknā*], v.t. **1.** to bend. **2.** to strain, to sprain.

[1]**लचना** *lacnā*, v.i. reg. = लचकना. — लचदार [P. *-dār*], adj. (W.) springy (of bamboos, &c).

[2]**लचना** *lacnā*, m. *Pl.* a kind of grain, *Cynosurus coracanus.*

लचर *lacar* [cf. **lacc-*: H. *lacaknā*], adj. **1.** yielding, pliant. **2.** compliant, weak (a person). **3.** wanting force, weak (an argument); poor (in quality).

लचलच *laclac* [cf. H. *lac(ak)nā*], f. the swishing sound made by a slender or flexible object, when swung.

लचलचा *laclacā* [cf. H. *laclacānā*], adj. bending, flexible, elastic.

लचलचाना *laclacānā* [cf. **lacc-*], v.i. **1.** to bend; to be supple, &c. (= लचकना). **2.** to be sticky, &c. (= लिजलिजा, लसलसा).

लचाना *lacānā* [cf. H. *lac(ak)nā*], v.t. to cause to bend (= लचकाना).

लचाव *lacāv* [cf. H. *lac(ak)nā*], m. *Pl.* flexibility; elasticity.

लचीला *lacīlā* [cf. H. *lacaknā*], adj. flexible; supple, elastic.

लच्छा *lacchā* [? conn. *lapsuda-*], m. **1.** bundle (of threads); hank, skein. **2.** bracelet (or anklet) of two or more rows of chain-work. **3.** a tassel. **4.** shred, slice (as of ginger, or onion); strip. **5.** reg. (W.) a lump of thickened milk; a partic. sweet. — लच्छेदार [P. *-dār*], adj. made of, or having strips, or shreds (as the sweet *rabṛī*); tangled, confused, convoluted; consecutive, unbroken (flow of speech); entertaining (remarks).

लच्छी *lacchī* [cf. H. *lacchā*], f. a bundle, skein, bunch.

लछमन *lachman* [ad. *lakṣmaṇa-*], m. = लक्ष्मण.

लछियाना *lachiyānā* [cf. H. *lacchā*], v.t. *Pl.* to make skeins or reels (as of thread).

लजलजा *lajlajā*, adj. = लिजलिजा.

लजलजाना *lajlajānā*, v.i. reg. to become soft (as fruit); to become flabby.

लजवाना *lajvānā* [cf. H. *lajānā*], v.t. to cause to feel shame, &c.

लजाऊ *lajāū* [cf. H. *lajānā*], adj. **1.** ashamed, &c. (= लज्जालु). **2.** shaming, shameful, disgraceful.

लजाधुर *lajādhur* [cf. H. *lajjā*], adj. & m. = लज्जालु.

लजाना *lajānā* [*lajjāpayati*], v.i. & v.t. **1.** v.i. to be ashamed (of, से). **2.** to feel a sense of modesty or constraint; to be shy; to blush. **3.** v.t. to make ashamed; to shame (one).

लजालू *lajālū* [*lajjālu-*], adj. = लज्जालु.

लज़ीज़ *lazīz* [A. *laẕīẕ*], adj. delicious; delightful.

लजीला *lajīlā* [cf. H. *lāj*], adj. **1.** ashamed. **2.** bashful, shy; modest.

लज़्ज़त *lazzat* [A. *laẕẕa*: P. *laẕẕat*], f. pleasure, delight; agreeable taste, relish.

लज्जा *lajjā* [S.], f. **1.** shame; sense of decency or modesty. **2.** bashfulness, shyness. **3.** sense of honour. — ~ आना (को), to feel shame, &c. ~ करना, to be mindful of the honour (of, की). ~ रखना, to preserve the honour (of, की). ~ लगना, to be moved by a sense of shame, or modesty. – लज्जाकुल [°*jā*+*ā*°], adj. moved by shame, &c. लज्जाजनक, adj. shameful (an act, attitude, situation). लज्जारुण [°*jā*+*a*°], adj. flushed in embarrassment. लज्जावंत adj. filled with shame; modest, &c. लज्जावान, adj. id. लज्जाशील, adj. modest, shy. लज्जास्पद [°*jā*+*ā*°], adj. place of shame: = लज्जाजनक. लज्जाहीन, adj. shameless, &c.

लज्जालु *lajjālu* [S.], adj. & m. **1.** adj. modest; bashful, shy; ashamed. **2.** m. the sensitive plant, *Mimosa pudica* (= छुई-मुई).

लज्जित *lajjit* [S.], adj. **1.** ashamed. **2.** modest, &c. (see लज्जा). — ~ करना, to make ashamed, to shame.

[1]**लट** *laṭ* [conn. *laṭṭa-*[2]], f. **1.** a lock of hair; locks, hair. **2.** tangled hair. **3.** [× H. *lapaṭ*] Brbh. a tongue of flame. — ~ पड़ना, to be tangled or matted (the hair). – लटपट, adj. = next. लटपटा, adj. tangled; not properly folded or wound, hanging loose (as a turban); thick (a liquid dish); stumbling (gait); stammering; lively, or showy (manner). °-पटी, f. staggering, stumbling; showiness, &c.

[2]**लट** *laṭ*, f. reg. an insect that infests stored grain.

लटक *laṭak* [H. *laṭaknā*], f. **1.** hanging, dangling. **2.** affected walk. **3.** air, style (as of walking, speaking). **4.** a sudden impulse.

लटकन *laṭkan* [cf. H. *laṭaknā*], f. **1.** hanging; swinging. **2.** anything that hangs (pendant, bell-clapper, plummet). **3.** reg. = लटका, 2. **4.** the fruit *Bixa orellana (anatta)*, source of an orange-red dye. **5.** the lorikeet, *Loriculus vernalis* (a bird that roosts hanging head downwards).

लटकना *laṭaknā* [cf. **laṭṭa-*[2]], v.i. **1.** to hang, to be hanging; to dangle; to swing. **2.** to lean (out of the vertical). **3.** fig. to be kept waiting or in suspense. **4.** to be or to be kept pending (a matter). **5.** to delay, to linger.

लटका *laṭkā* [cf. H. *laṭaknā*], m. **1.** a device or remedy ready to hand; a magic spell. **2.** affected walk, or manner. **3.** an ostentatious habit. **4.** reg. a magician's rod or wand. **5.** sl. scrotum.

लटकाना *laṭkānā* [cf. H. *laṭāknā*], v.t. **1.** to cause to hang, to suspend, to hang (an object); to swing. **2.** to hang (sthg.) from, to attach (to, पर, or पर से: as a lock to a door). **3.** to hang (a person). **4.** fig. to keep (a person) in suspense. **5.** to keep pending, to defer (a matter).

लटकाव *laṭkāv* [cf. H. *laṭkānā*], m. state of suspension, hanging.

लटकौवा *laṭkauvā*, m. reg. a pendant (see लटकन, 2).

लटन *laṭan* [cf. H. *laṭnā*], f. *Pl.* an unsatisfactory crop: one sown too early in the spring (? and which 'hangs fire').

लटना *laṭnā* [**laṭṭa-*[2]], v.i. to be entangled: **1.** to be weakened (by sickness); to waste away. **2.** to grow weak or exhausted. — लटा-पटा, m. colloq. baggage, things, goods. लटाधारी [cf. H. *laṭ*] m. = जटाधारी.

लटपट *laṭpaṭ*, adj. see s.v. लट.

लटपटाना *laṭpaṭānā* [cf. H. *laṭpaṭ*], v.i. **1.** to rock, to shake; to stagger; to stumble, to trip. **2.** to walk affectedly. **3.** to stammer, to hesitate (in speech).

लटपटिया *laṭpaṭiyā* [cf. H. *laṭpaṭ(ī)*], adj. reg. **1.** lively, showy (in manner). **2.** double-dealing, devious. **3.** mischief-making.

लटाई *laṭāī*, f. reg. a small reel (as for a kite-string).

लटी *laṭī* [cf. H. *laṭ*], f. reg. a loose woman; prostitute.

लटू *laṭū*, m. Brbh. = लट्टू.

लटूरिया *laṭūriyā* [cf. H. *laṭūrī*], adj. & m. & f. **1.** adj. having tangled, or curly hair. **2.** m. & f. a person having tangled hair, &c.

लटूरी *laṭūrī*, f. Brbh. tangled hair.

लटोरा *laṭorā*, m. a shrike: the grey shrike or butcher-bird, *Lanius excubitor*; the rufous-backed shrike, *Lanius schach*.

लट्टू *laṭṭū* [cf. H. *laṭnā*], m. **1.** a top (toy). **2.** a knob; door-knob; plummet. **3.** colloq. an electric light bulb. — ~ नचाना, or फिराना, to spin a top. ~ होना, fig. to be or to become infatuated (with, पर).

लट्ठ *laṭṭh* [**laṣṭi-*: Pa. *laṭṭhi-*], f. m. **1.** a staff. **2.** a club. **3.** an (unsawn) log, trunk. — ~ मारना, to strike or to beat (one, पर or को) with a club; fig. to speak harshly (to); to treat harshly. अक़्ल के पीछे ~ लिए फिरना, fig. to act against all good sense. किसी के पीछे ~ लिए फिरना, colloq. to have it in for one. – लट्ठ-गँवार, m. a yokel. लट्ठबंद [P. *-band*], adj. armed with sticks or clubs. लट्ठबाज़, [P. *-bāz*], m. one who wields a staff or club. °ई, f. fighting with sticks or clubs. लट्ठमार, adj. crude, violent (as language).

लट्ठम-लट्ठा *laṭṭham-laṭṭhā* [cf. H. *laṭṭh*], m. cudgel-play, a fight with sticks or clubs.

लट्ठर *laṭṭhar* [**laṭṭhara-*], adj. reg. slack, slow, lazy.

लट्ठा *laṭṭhā* [**laṣṭi-*, Pa. *laṭṭhi-*], m. **1.** a beam; rafter. **2.** pole, marker (as of a boundary). **3.** a measure of length (usu. five and a half yards). **4.** sleeper, tie (under rail track). **5.** a coarse cotton cloth, long-cloth.

लठ-पठ *laṭh-paṭh*, adj. = लथ-पथ.

लठिया *laṭhiyā* [cf. H. *lāṭhī*, *laṭṭh*], f. a small *lāṭhī*: a stick, or cane.

लठैत *laṭhait* [cf. H. *laṭṭh*], adj. & m. **1.** adj. carrying (or armed with) a stick or club. **2.** obstinate, incorrigible. **3.** m. a person carrying a club, &c. **4.** an incorrigible person.

लड़ंगो *laṛaṅgo* [cf. H. *laṛnā*], m. Brbh. ? a warrior.

लड़ंत *laṛant* [cf. **laḍ-*[2]: H. *laṛnā*], f. *Pl. HŚS.* fighting; wrestling.

लड़ंतिया *laṛantiyā* [cf. H. *laṛant*], m. reg. a fighter, wrestler.

लड़ *laṛ* [**laḍa-*], f. **1.** a string (as of pearls); a strand (of a rope or cord). **2.** row, line, series. **3.** a chain. — ~ मिलाना, to become friendly (with, से). ~ में रहना, to be in the party or side (of, की), to be joined (with).

लड़क- *laṛak-* [cf. H. *laṛkā, laṛkī*]. boy's, girl's, child's: — लड़क-बुद्धि, f. a child's understanding; childishness.

लड़कपन *laṛakpan* [cf. H. *laṛkā*], m. boyhood; childhood.

लड़का *laṛkā* [**laḍ(ḍ)ikka-*], m. **1.** a boy; child. **2.** a son. — राह-बाट का ~, m. a foundling child. – लड़के-लड़कियाँ, m. pl. boys and girls, children. लड़केवाला, m. father of a boy; father of the bridegroom.

लड़काई *laṛkāī* [cf. H. *laṛkā*], f. = लड़कपन.

लड़की *laṛkī* [cf. **laḍ(ḍ)ikka-*], f. a girl; a daughter. — लड़कीवाला, m. father of a girl; father of the bride.

लड़कोरी *laṛkorī*, adj. & f. = लड़कौरी.

लड़कौरा *laṛkaurā*, adj. & m. **1.** adj. having a child, or children. **2.** m. a father.

लड़कौरी *laṛkaurī*, adj. & f. **1.** adj. having a child, or children. **2.** f. a woman having a young child.

लड़खड़ाना *laṛkhaṛānā* [conn. *laṭati*], v.i. **1.** to stagger, to totter; to wobble (as a bicycle). **2.** to stumble (the feet). **3.** to sway, to roll (of gait). **4.** to stutter, to stammer. **5.** to shake (the limbs).

लड़खड़ाहट *laṛkhaṛāhaṭ* [cf. H. *laṛkhaṛānā*], f. staggering, &c.

लड़खड़ी *laṛkhaṛī* [cf. H. *laṛkhaṛānā*], f. reg. = लड़खड़ाहट.

लड़ना *laṛnā* [**laḍ-*[2]], v.i. & v.t. **1.** to fight (with, से); to quarrel; to struggle (with). **2.** to strike (against, से); to collide (with: a vehicle). **3.** to rub, or to wear (against). **4.** to tally, to correspond (as an account). बात ही तो है, लड़ गई, that's right, it's correct. **5.** to be set in contention, or at risk. उसकी जान लड़ रही है, his life is at risk, or at stake. **6.** to be set or measured (against, से). आँखें ~ (से), to look (one) in the eyes; to exchange loving looks (with). मुक़द्दमा ~, to fight a law-suit. गप्प, or गप्पें, ~, gossip to be exchanged.

लड़बड़ा *laṛbaṛā*, adj. reg. **1.** soft, mellow (= लिजलिजा). **2.** sticky, viscous. **3.** flabby, limp. **4.** tottering, shaky. **5.** stammering (in speech).

लड़बड़ाना *laṛbaṛānā* [conn. *laṭati*], v.t. **1.** reg. to stagger, to totter. ***2.** to stammer. **3.** reg. to stick, to adhere.

लड़-बावर- *laṛ-bāvr-* [H. *laṛkā*+H. *bāvlā*], adj. Brbh. youthful, inexperienced; foolish.

लड़वाना *laṛvānā* [cf. H. *laṛnā*], v.t. to cause to collide (as vehicles).

-लड़ा *-laṛā* [cf. H. *laṛ*], adj. formant. of (one or more) strings, strands, &c. (e.g. पचलड़ा, of five strings).

लड़ाई *laṛāī* [cf. H. *laṛnā*], f. **1.** fighting; quarrelling; a fight, &c.; disturbance; struggle. **2.** a war; battle. **3.** enmity, hostility. — ~ करना, to fight, &c. (with, से); to make war. ~ का, adj. having to do with war, warlike, martial. ~ का घर, m. fig. cause of strife or quarrel; a firebrand; an arsonist. ~ डालना, to sow strife (between, में). ~ पल्ले बाँधना, to involve oneself in a quarrel, &c. ~ मोल लेना, to bring a quarrel, &c. upon oneself. ~ लड़ना, to fight (with, से), to wage war; to contend (as at law). ~ लेना, to join battle (with, से). – लड़ाई-झगड़ा, m. fighting and quarrelling. लड़ाईबंदी [P. *-bandī*], f. truce, armistice. लड़ाई-भिड़ाई, f. = ~, 1.

लड़ाका *laṛākā* [cf. H. *laṛnā*], adj. & m. **1.** adj. warlike. **2.** waging war, belligerent (a power). **3.** quarrelsome. **4.** m. a warrior, fighter; brawler. — लड़ाके देश, m. pl. belligerent countries.

लड़ाकू *laṛākū* [cf. H. *laṛnā*], adj. & m. **1.** adj. used in war, military. 2. = लड़ाका, 1., 3. — ~ जहाज़, m. a naval vessel. ~ दल, m. pl. hostile factions. ~ हवाई जहाज़, m. a fighter (aircraft).

लड़ाना *laṛānā* [cf. H. *laṛnā*], v.t. **1.** to cause to fight, or to clash together; to cause a clash or a fight between (persons, animals). **2.** to set against, to cause to vie with. **3.** to cause to meet. आँखें ~, to look fondly or lovingly (at, से). **4.** to direct the movements or campaign (of an army). — लाड़ ~, to caress. पंजा ~, to fight with wrists and forearms.

लड़ामनी *laṛāmnī* [cf. H. *laṛā(v)nā*], f. reg. *Pl.* **1.** pasture-ground. **2.** W. a cattle-manger.

लड़ी *laṛī* [**laḍa-*], f. **1.** a string (as of pearls, or flowers). **2.** row, line, series; chain (of hills).

लड़ैत *laṛait* [cf. H. *laṛnā*], m. **1.** a fighter; warrior. **2.** colloq. hooligan.

लड़ैत- *laṛait-* [cf. H. *laṛnā*], adj. & m. Brbh. **1.** [× *laḍ-*[1]] adj. dear (= लाड़ला). **2.** spoiled (a child). **3.** m. fighter, warrior.

लड़ोकरा *laṛokrā*, adj. colloq. truculent, &c. (= लड़ाका).

लड़ौरी *laṛaurī*, f. reg. (W). = लड़ामनी.

लड्डू *laḍḍū* [*laḍḍuka-*[1]], m. **1.** a sweet consisting of balls of gram-flour, or of thickened milk, with sugar, saffron and other ingredients. **2.** fig. benefit, gain. — ~ खिलाना (को), to feast (one). ~ बँटना, *laḍḍūs* to be distributed; to be advantaged. ~ बनाना, or

बाँधना, to make *laḍḍūs* (of, का). ~ बाँटना, to distribute *laḍḍūs* (among, में); to celebrate a piece of good luck. ~ मिलना, fig. to be well treated; = ~ बँटना, 2. ठग के ~ खा बैठना, fig. to eat drugged *laḍḍūs*: to be taken in or deceived (with serious consequences). मन के ~ खाना, or फोड़ना, fig. to build castles in the air.

लढ़ा *laṛhā*, m. reg. (W.) **1.** a light country cart. **2.** *Pl.* a sledge.

लढ़ी *laṛhī*, f. reg. (W.) = लढ़ा.

लत *lat*, f. **1.** a bad habit; vice. **2.** addiction. — ~ पड़ना (को), a habit to be contracted. ~ लगना (को), id.

लत- *lat-*. a kick (= लात): — लतख़ोर [P. *-khor*], adj. kicked; fig. contemptible; a contemptible person; mat (for the feet). °आ, adj. & m. id. लत-मर्दन, m. trampling; kicking. लत-मर्दन करना, to trample on; to kick. लत-मर्दन में पड़ना, to be trampled underfoot; to be treated insultingly.

लतर *latar*, f. reg. = लता.

[1]**लतरी** *latrī* [*lattara-], f. reg. a kind of sandal.

[2]**लतरी** *latrī*, f. reg. the chickling vetch, *Laythyrus sativus.*

लता *latā* [S.], f. **1.** a creeper, vine. **2.** tendril. — लता-कुंज, m. an overgrown place in a grove; an arbour overgrown with creepers. लता-गुल्म, m. an overgrown thicket. लता-पता, m. creepers and leaves: greenery; medicinal herbs. लता-भवन, m. Av. bower, arbour.

लताड़ *latāṛ* [cf. H. *latāṛnā*], f. **1.** spurning, rejecting with contempt. **2.** reviling, insulting. **3.** fig. burdensome pressure (as of work). **4.** colloq. a kick.

लताड़ना *latāṛnā* [cf. **lattā-*: Pk. *lattā-*], v.t. **1.** to spurn, to treat with contempt. **2.** to revile, to insult.

लताफ़त *latāfat* [A. *laṭāfa*: P. *laṭāfat*], f. U. **1.** slenderness, delicateness. **2.** elegance, grace; beauty. **3.** wit.

लतिका *latikā* [S.], f. a creeper, vine (= लता).

लतियल *latiyal* [cf.H. *lāt*], adj. liable to kick (an animal).

लतियाना *latiyānā* [cf. H. *lāt*], v.t. to kick.

लती *latī* [cf. H. *lat*], adj. vicious, depraved.

लतीफ़ *latīf* [A. *laṭīf*], adj. U. **1.** delicate, &c. (see लताफ़त). **2.** tasty, savoury. **3.** kind, courteous; agreeable.

लतीफ़ा *latīfā* [A. *laṭīfa*], m. an amusing or witty remark; a joke. लतीफ़ेबाज़ [P. *-bāz*], adj. & m. amusing, witty; a witty person.

लतेड़ना *lateṛnā*, v.t. *Pl.* = लथेड़ना. ?

लतैत *latait* [cf. H. *lāt*], m. an animal that kicks.

लत्तम-जुत्ता *lattam-juttā*, m. colloq. a fight, brawl.

लत्तर *lattar*, f. *Pl.* = लता.

लत्ता *lattā* [*latta-[1]], m. **1.** a tattered piece of cloth, rag. **2.** pej. esp. -लत्ता. clothes. — लत्ते उड़ाना (के), to tear to shreds. लत्ते लेना, colloq. to scold: to tear a strip (off).

[1]**लत्ती** *lattī* [cf. **lattā-*: Pk. *lattā-*], f. kicking, kick. – ~ मारना, to kick.

[2]**लत्ती** *lattī* [cf. H. *lattā*], f. reg. **1.** rag, scrap of cloth. **2.** tail of a paper kite. **3.** strip: string of a top.

लत्तू *lattū* [cf. H. *lāt*], adj. reg. kicking; vicious (a horse).

लथड़ना *latharnā* [conn. **lasta-*], v.i. reg. = लिथड़ना.

लथ-पथ *lath-path* [cf. H. *latharnā*], adj. **1.** soaked, drenched. **2.** smeared (with, से).

लथाड़ना *lathāṛnā*, v.t. = लताड़ना, 2.

लथेड़ना *latheṛnā*, v.t. **1.** to besmear (with, में), to soil; to make bedraggled. **2.** to soak, to drench. **3.** fig. to insult.

लदना *ladnā* [cf. H. *lādnā*], v.i. **1.** to be loaded (goods: on, पर); to be piled (on). **2.** to be laden (a vehicle, a vessel: with, से); to be piled or covered (as a table with books, a tree with fruit). **3.** to be burdensome (as time). **4.** to be burdened (as by debt). **5.** colloq. to be sent, carted off, to jail. **6.** sl. to be over (days, time); to die. — लद-लद गिरना, to fall in numbers (as a fruit) and lie (on the ground). – लदा-फँदा, adj. loaded, laden (with cargo).

लदनिया *ladniyā* [cf. H. *ladnā*], m. *Pl.* a carrier.

लदनी *ladnī* [cf. H. *ladnā*], f. reg. **1.** load, burden. **2.** reg. (Bihar) a pack-horse.

लद-फँदा *lad-phamdā*, m. reg. **1.** loading and packing. **2.** a sailor's knot.

लदवाना *ladvānā* [cf. H. *lādnā*], v.t. to cause to be loaded (by, से).

लदाई *ladāī* [cf. H. *ladānā*], f. **1.** load, freight. **2.** payment or charge for loading.

लदाऊ *ladāū*, adj. reg. = लद्दू.

लदाव *ladāv* [cf. H. *ladānā*], m. **1.** a load, burden. **2.** cargo. **3.** reg. (W.) a counterpoise weight. **4.** vaulted masonry, vaulting. **5.** reg. (W.) thatch protecting the top of a wall.

लड्डू *laddū* [cf. H. *ladnā*], adj. **1.** load-carrying (a pack-horse, &c). **2.** freight-carrying (vehicle, vessel).

लद्धर *laddhar* [**laddhara*], adj. *Pl.* **1.** heavily or clumsily patched. ***2.** [?] slow, lethargic.

लनतरानी *lantărānī* [A. *lan tarā nī* 'you will not see me'], f. vain boasting.

[1]**लप** *lap*, m. f. **1.** a handful. **2.** as much as can be held in the cupped palms. — ~ भर, m. a handful.

[2]**लप** *lap* [**lappa-*[1]], f. **1.** movement, flexibility. **2.** swishing sound (as of a cane); flashing (of a sword when swung). **3.** [? onom.] lapping sound. — ~ करना, to lap. ~ खाना, to eat quickly. ~ से, adv. at once. – लप-लप, adj. & m. nimble, quick; = ~, 3.; throbbing, palpitation (of the heart, as in fear).

लपक *lapak* [cf. H. *lapaknā*], f. **1.** spring, leap; bounce. **2.** springiness, elasticity. **3.** nimbleness. **4.** = लपका, 1. **5.** a bad habit; craze (for, की). **6.** flash (of flame, lightning). **7.** throb, pulsation. — लपक-झपक से, adv. with a leap, &c.; nimbly, briskly.

लपकना *lapaknā* [cf. **lappa-*[1]], v.i. **1.** to spring, to leap (upon, पर; at, की ओर); to rush (at); to snatch (at). **2.** to rush (after); to make haste. **3.** to flash, to dart (as lightning). **4.** to throb (as a wound); to beat (the heart, in agitation). — लपक लेना, to spring forward and snatch; to snap up (a ball); to anticipate (a remark). लपककर, adv. with a bound; with a rush.

लपका *lapkā* [cf. H. *lapaknā*], m. **1.** a bound forward (to snatch sthg). **2.** a bad habit; a vice; perversion. **3.** a snatcher, pilferer. — ~ पड़ना (को), a bad habit to be contracted (by).

लपकाना *lapkānā* [cf. H. *lapaknā*], v.t. **1.** to stretch or to dart out (the hand, to snatch sthg). **2.** to send (a person) swiftly (as on some errand).

लपकी *lapkī*, [cf. H. *lapaknā*], f. *Pl. HŚS.* a long stitch, a basting stitch.

लपची *lapcī*, f. reg. a skate-fish.

लप-झप *lap-jhap* [**lappa-*[1], **jhapp-*[1]], adj. **1.** lively (of gait). **2.** active, nimble.

लपट *lapaṭ* [cf. *lappa-*[2]], f. **1.** hot blast (of flame, or wind); tongue of flame. **2.** heat, glow. **3.** fig. wafted fragrance, or odour.

लपटना *lapaṭnā*, v.i. = लिपटना.

लपटा *lapṭā* [cf. H. *lapaṭnā*], m. reg. **1.** any sticky or glutinous food; a thin molasses. **2.** paste. **3.** *Pl. HŚS.* a kind of grass having burrs.

लपटाना *lapṭānā*, v.t. = लिपटाना.

लपटी *lapṭī*, f. reg. = लपटा, 1.

लपटीला *lapṭīlā*, adj. sticky, clinging.

लपड़-शपड़ *lapaṛ-śapaṛ*, f. **1.** confused speech; jargon. **2.** involved speech or account; equivocation, prevarication, distortion of the truth.

लपलपाना *laplapānā* [cf. H. [2]*lap*], v.i. & v.t. **1.** v.i. to be switched, or brandished (a cane, a sword). **2.** to flash (as a sword). **3.** to flicker back and forth (as a snake's tongue). **4.** v.t. to swing, to brandish; to cause (a sword) to flash.

लपलपाहट *laplapāhaṭ* [cf. H. *laplapānā*], f. **1.** a swishing sound. **2.** flashing (as of a sword). **3.** a flickering back and forth.

लपसी *lapsī* [**lappasikā-*: Pk. *lappasiyā-*], f. a glutinous food made of flour, milk and sugar or salt; a sticky mess (of food), gruel.

लपाटी *lapāṭī*, f. reg. telling tales (= लबाड़ी).

लपानक *lapānak* [? cf. H. *lapānā*], adj. reg. slender, delicate.

लपाना *lapānā*, v.t. *HŚS.* to cause (sthg. yielding or flexible) to bend, or to move.

लपेट *lapeṭ* [cf. H. *lapeṭnā*], f. **1.** covering; wrapping; coating (around sthg). **2.** winding, coil; bandage; fold, crease (in material). **3.** *electr.* coil. **4.** girth, circumference (as of a pillar). **5.** fig. enfolding, onset (as of a storm, or of some crisis); attack. **6.** entanglement; unwelcome consequence; seeking to mislead. **7.** consternation, anxiety. — ~ में आना, to become entangled (in a difficulty; or by another's guile). - लपेट-झपेट, f. confusion, disorder; evasion, subterfuge.

लपेटन *lapeṭan* [cf. H. *lapeṭnā*], f. & m. **1.** f. wrapping, winding. **2.** f. = लपेट, 1., 2. **3.** m. roller (of a loom, on which the cloth is wound as it is made). **4.** *Pl.* button.

लपेटना *lapeṭnā* [**lappeṭṭ-*], v.t. **1.** to wrap (as a parcel); to pack, to parcel (objects: in or with, से). **2.** to wrap or to roll (round sthg., में or पर: as wire, or paper). **3.** to twist, to make (rope). **4.** to smear, to spread (over, पर). **5.** to involve, to implicate (in, में). **6.** to enfold (in a clutch or grasp); to seize. — तागा लपेटकर गोली बनाना, to roll thread into a ball.

लपेटवाँ *lapeṭvāṁ* [cf. H. *lapeṭ*], adj. & m. **1.** adj. wrapped up. **2.** rolled, coiled. **3.** twisted. **4.** involved, ambiguous (speech); having a hidden meaning. **5.** *Pl.* = लपेटा, 2.

लपेटा *lapeṭā* [cf. H. *lapeṭ*], m. 1. = लपेट. **2.** *Pl.* a glass bracelet having gold or silver thread wound round it.

लप्पड़ *lappaṛ* [cf. *lappa-*[2]], m. a slap.

[1]**लप्पा** *lappā*, m. *Pl. HŚS.* a brocade; ornamental work with gold and silver thread.

[2]**लप्पा** *lappā*, m. reg. (Bihar) bamboo pole or runner (in a cart).

लफ़ंगा *lafaṅgā* [cf. P. *lāf*], m. **1.** a braggart; an empty talker; a loud-mouthed person. **2.** a depraved person. ***3.** an undesirable character (in general). — लौंडे-लफ़ंगे, pl. id.

लफड़ा *laphṛā*, m. sthg. tiresome or bothering.

लफ़्ज़ी *lafzī* [A. *lafẓī*], adj. U. **1.** having to do with a word, or words; verbal. **2.** literal. — ~ माने, m. literal sense.

लफ़्ज़ *lafz* [A. *lafẓ*], m. U. a word. — लफ़्ज़ बलफ़्ज़ [P. *ba-*], adv. word by word; word for word.

लफ़्टन *lafṭan* [Engl. *lieutenant*], m. lieutenant.

लफ़्टेंट *lafṭeṁṭ* [Engl. *lieutenant*], m. lieutenant.

लफ़्फ़ाज़ *laffāz* [A. *laffāẓ*], adj. U. wordy, verbose.

लफ़्फ़ाज़ी *laffāzī* [A. *laffāẓ*+P. *-ī*], f. U. verbosity.

लब *lab* [P. *lab*], m. (also f., *Pl.*). **1.** lip. **2.** brim. — ~ खोलना, or हिलना, to open (or to move) the lips, to speak. ~ बंद होना, the lips to be (or to remain) closed; to be silent; to relish a taste. जान लबों पर होना, to be about to expire. – लबरेज़ [P. *-rez*], adj. overflowing. लबालब [P. *-ā-*], adj. lip to lip; brimful.

लबड़- *labaṛ-*. = लबाड़: — लबड़-चटाई, f. reg. giving a dry breast to a child. लबड़-धौंधौं, f. colloq. senseless turmoil, confusion, mess; cheating, trickery. लबड़-सबड़, f. aimless gossip.

लबड़ना *labaṛnā*, v.i. reg. to babble; to lie.

लबड़ा *labṛā* [cf. **labba-*], adj. reg. awkward; left-handed.

लबदार *labdār*, m. *Pl.* mud; alluvial deposit on heavy clay.

लबना *labnā*, m. reg. (W). = लबनी.

लबनी *labnī*, f. a deep earthenware pot having a narrow neck (designed for easy carrying up palm trees to collect their juice).

लबरा *labrā* [cf. **labba-*], adj. E. H. 1. = लबाड़. **2.** reg. = लबड़ा.

लबलबाना *lablabānā* [conn. H. *labālab*], v.i. to be brimful; to overflow.

लबलबी *lablabī*, f. *Pl. HŚS.* = लिबलिबी.

लबाड़ *labāṛ* [cf. **labba-*], adj. & m. reg. **1.** adj. babbling, telling tales; lying. **2.** m. babbler, boaster; liar (= [2]लबाड़ी).

लबाड़िया *labāṛiyā* [cf. H. *labāṛ*], adj. & m. = लबाड़.

[1]**लबाड़ी** *labāṛī* [cf. **labba-*], f. a lie; fabrication, talking nonsense.

[2]**लबाड़ी** *labāṛī* [cf. **labba-*], m. a talker, babbler; liar.

लबादा *labādā* [A. *lubāda*], m. a quilted cloak, overcoat.

लबाब *labāb* [A. *lubāb*], m. essence; gist.

लबार *labār* [cf. **labba-*], adj. & m. Brbh. Av. = लबाड़.

लबारी *labārī*, adj. & f. Brbh. **1.** adj. = लबार. **2.** f. *HŚS.* = [1]लबाड़ी.

लबी *labī*, f. *Pl. HŚS.* boiled sugar-cane juice (= राब).

लबेड़ा *labeṛā*, m. the fruit *lisoṛā*.

लबेदा *labedā*, m. reg. **1.** E. a short stick; a rake used on the threshing-floor. **2.** a cudgel.

लबेल *label* [cf. H. *lab*], adj. *Pl.* having a lip, rim or edge.

लब्ध *labdh* [S.], adj. **1.** obtained, received. **2.** gained, won, earned. — लब्धप्रतिष्ठ, adj. celebrated, distinguished (an authority, &c). लब्धांक, m. *arith.* resultant figure, result.

लब्धि *labdhi* [S.], f. **1.** obtaining. **2.** attainment. **3.** gain, advantage, profit. **4.** *Pl. HŚS. arith.* quotient.

लभ्य *labhyă* [S.], adj. obtainable, available; accessible.

लम- *lam-*. long, &c. (= लंबा): — लमकना, adj. & m. long-eared; a hare, rabbit. लमछड़ा, adj. like a long stick: lanky. लमटंगा, m. *Pl. HŚS.* long-legged: a stork; a crane. लमडोर, f. *Pl.* long string: a fishing-line; a long-tailed bird. लमढेक, m. *Pl.* long-legged: a stork; a lanky person. लमतड़ंगा, adj. tall and strong (of build). लमतड़ाँग, adj. id.

लमकना *lamaknā* [cf. *lambate*], v.i. reg. to be stretched out (the legs): to stride, to hasten.

लमकाना *lamkānā* [cf. H. *lamaknā*], v.t. reg. to stretch out (the hands or legs).

लमहा *lamhā* [A. *lamḥa*], m. a moment, an instant.

लमेरा *lamerā*, m. reg. (Bihar) self-sown seed (seed fallen from crops, which shoots the following season: cf. लम्हर).

लम्हर *lamhar*, m. *Pl.* a tree which is self-seeded (cf. लमेरा).

[1]**लय** *lay* [S.], m. **1.** absorption (in); devotion (to). **2.** immersion. **3.** merging, coalescence. **4.** destruction (esp. that of the world). — ~ लगना, reg. = लौ लगना, see s.v. [2]लौ.

[2]**लय** *lay* [S.], f. **1.** time, rhythm (in music and dancing). **2.** singing in tune. **3.** tune, melody. — ~ देखना, to keep proper time; to keep in tune. – लय-बद्ध, m. rhythmical, melodious.

लयन *layan* [S.], m. state of being absorbed, or merged, &c. (see [1]लय).

लयारी *layārī*, m. reg. a wolf.

लर *lar*, m. *hist.* a measuring rod for land measure, varying from between about seven to thirteen feet.

लरज़- *larz-* [P. *larzīdan*], v.i. Brbh. **1.** to shake. **2.** to tremble (in fear).

लरज़ान *larzān* [P. *larzān*], adj. U. trembling.

लरज़ाना *larzānā* [cf. H. *larz-*], v.t. reg. to cause to shake, or to tremble.

लरिकाई *larikāī* [cf. **laḍikka-*], f. Brbh. = लड़कपन.

ललक *lalak* [cf. H. *lalaknā*], f. **1.** eager desire. **2.** whim, caprice. **3.** zeal, enthusiasm. **4.** colloq. sudden gush (of any liquid).

ललकना *lalaknā* [cf. *lalati*], v.i. to long for, to crave; to covet.

ललकाना *lalkānā* [cf. H. *lalaknā*], v.t. to arouse desire; to excite, to urge on.

ललकार *lalkār* [cf. **lallakka-*: Pk. *lallakka-*], f. **1.** a challenge. **2.** shout, call (as of encouragement).

ललकारना *lalkārnā* [cf. H. *lalkār*], v.t. **1.** to challenge. **2.** to shout, to whoop, &c.

ललचना *lalacnā* [cf. H. *lalcānā*], v.i. to feel desire; to covet; to lust for.

ललचाना *lalcānā* [cf. H. *lālac*], v.t. & v.i. **1.** v.t. to awaken desire in; to tantalise. **2.** v.i. Brbh. to feel desire or longing (for) (= ललचना).

ललचिटा *lalciṭā*, m. *Pl.* = ललचित्रा.

ललचित्रा *lalcitrā* [? H. *lāl*+H. *citr*], m. *Pl. min. Plumbago rosea.*

ललचौह- *lalcauh-* [cf. H. *lalcā(v)nā*], adj. Brbh. eagerly desirous.

ललछौंह- *lalchaumh-*, adj. reddish.

ललदंबु *laldambu*, m. **1.** *Pl.* the plant *Nerium odorum* (source of pearl-ash, and of a dye). **2.** *HŚS.* the lime tree.

ललन *lalan* [S.], m. Brbh. dear one (child, or husband).

[1]**ललना** *lalănā* [S.], f. a woman, an attractive woman.

[2]**ललना** *lalnā*, m. reg. a boy (= लला).

ललसाना *lalsānā* [cf. *lālasa-*], v.i. reg. to desire (= ललचाना).

लला *lalā* [*lala-*], m. **1.** boy; dear, son (term of address). **2.** dear, beloved (term of address to a lover or husband). **3.** euph. fool, blockhead. — बदाऊँ का ~, pej. a good fellow of Budaon: a blockhead, ass.

[1]**ललाई** *lalāī* [cf. H. [1]*lāl*], f. **1.** flush. **2.** a red mark (on the skin).

[2]**ललाई** *lalāī* [cf. H. *lalānā*], f. Brbh. = लालच.

ललाट *lalāṭ* [S.], m. **1.** the brow. **2.** fig. fate (conceived of as being written on one's brow). — ~ की रेखा, line on the brow: an augury of (one's) destiny; a wrinkle on the forehead; a sectarian mark made on the forehead.

ललाटिका *lalāṭikā* [S.], f. **1.** a red decorative mark made on the forehead. **2.** *Pl. HŚS.* an ornament worn on the forehead.

ललाना *lalānā*, v.i. poet. to feel desire or longing.

ललाम *lalām* [S.], adj. & m. **1.** adj. beautiful. **2.** Brbh. red. **3.** m. Brbh. an adornment; a jewel.

ललामक *lalāmak* [S.], m. *Pl. HŚS.* a garland of flowers worn on the forehead.

ललार *lalār*, m. reg. = ललाट.

ललित *lalit* [S.], adj. **1.** beautiful, lovely; graceful. **2.** wished for: attractive. — ~ कला, fine art, the fine arts. ~ साहित्य, m. artistic literature, belles lettres.

ललिता *lalitā* [S.], f. **1.** a beautiful woman; a woman. **2.** *mus.* name of a *rāgiṇī.*

[1]**ललियाना** *laliyānā* [cf. H. [1]*lāl*], v.i. reg. to grow red.

[2]**ललियाना** *laliyānā*, v.i. *Pl.* to long for (= ललकना).

लली *lalī* [*lala-*], f. a girl.

लल्ला *lallā*, m. = लला.

लल्लू *lallū*, m. a boy (= लला).

लल्लो *lallo*, f. colloq. the tongue. — लल्लो-चप्पो, f. flattery; wheedling. लल्लो-पत्तो, f. id.

लवंग *lavaṅg* [S.], m. **1.** the clove-tree. **2.** a clove. — लवंग-लता, f. name of a sweet made with refined flour and thickened milk.

लव *lav* [S.], m. **1.** a fragment, particle. **2.** Av. an instant, moment. **3.** *mythol.* name of a son of Rāmcandra and Sītā. — **लव-लेश**, m. a tiny particle (of, का), slightest trace.

लव- *lav-* [**lavati*: Pa. *lava-*], v.t. Brbh. to reap.

लवण *lavaṇ* [S.], m. **1.** salt. **2.** *chem.* a salt.

लवणता *lavaṇătā* [S.], f. salinity (= खारापन, 2).

लवन *lavan* [S.], m. reaping, harvesting.

लवनि *lavni*, f. Brbh. = लौनी.

लवनित *lavănit* [ad. *lavaṇita-*], adj. salted.

लवलीन *lavălīn*, adj. Brbh. see s.v. [2]लौ.

लवा *lavā* [*laba-*], m. name of one or more varieties of quail.

[1]**लवाई** *lavāī* [*navajāta-*], adj. f. Av. newly calved (a cow).

[2]**लवाई** *lavāī*, f. *Pl.* fondness, affection (cf. [2]लौ).

लवाक *lavāk* [S.], m. *Pl. HŚS.* a sickle.

लवाज़मा *lavāzmā* [A. *lavāzima*], m. pl. **1.** necessary things (for a purpose). **2.** baggage.

लवारा *lavārā*, m. reg. (E.) a calf (cf. लेरू).

लशकर *laśkar* [P. *laśkar*], m. **1.** army. **2.** military camp, encampment. **3.** crew (of a ship).

[1]**लशकरी** *laśkarī* [P. *laśkarī*], adj. & f. **1.** adj. of or belonging to an army; military. **2.** sailors'. **3.** f. soldiers' or sailors' slang.

[2]**लशकरी** *laśkarī* [cf. P. *laśkar*], m. **1.** a soldier. **2.** a sailor.

लश्टम-पश्टम *laśṭam-paśṭam*, adv. = लस्टम-पस्टम.

लस *las* [**lasa-*: Pa. *lasa-*], m. **1.** stickiness; viscosity. **2.** glue. **3.** *med.* serum. **4.** fig. attraction. — **लसदार** [P. *-dār*], adj. sticky, &c.

लस- *las-* [*lasati*[1]], v.i. Brbh. to shine; to be radiant or beautiful.

लसना *lasnā* [**lasati*[2]: Pk. *lasaï*], v.i. **1.** to stick (to); to be sticky or damp. **2.** to be or to become viscous. **3.** *Pl.* to be smeared or plastered (with).

लसनिया *lasaniyā*, m. = लहसुनिया.

लसलसा *laslasā* [cf. H. *las*], adj. sticky; viscous.

लसलसाना *laslasānā* [cf. H. *laslasā, lasnā*], v.i. to be sticky; to be viscous.

लसलसापन *laslasāpan* [cf. H. *laslasānā*], m. stickiness, &c.

लसलसाहट *laslasāhaṭ* [cf. H. *laslasā*], f. stickiness, &c.

लसी *lasī* [*lasīkā-*], f. **1.** stickiness. **2.** fig. attraction. *3. = लस्सी.

लसुन *lasun* [*laśuna-*], m. garlic (= लहसुन).

लसोड़ा *lasoṛā*, m. a tree, *Cordia myxa*, and its glutinous fruit.

लस्टम-पस्टम *lasṭam-pasṭam*, adv. colloq. **1.** somehow or another, with difficulty; carelessly, anyhow. **2.** with might and main. — **बाक्स में चीज़ें ~ रखना**, to put, or to cram, things into a box (just) anyhow.

लस्सा *lassā* [**lasya-*], m. *Pl.* = लस.

लस्सी *lassī* [*lasīkā-, *lasya-*], f. a drink of sweetened, diluted yoghurt. — **कच्ची ~**, f. euph. milk blatantly adulterated with water.

लहँगा *lahaṁgā*, m. a voluminous skirt.

लहंडा *lahaṇḍā*, m. reg. (W.) a herd (of buffaloes).

लह- *lah-* [*labhate*], v.t. Brbh. Av. to find, to get; to experience.

लहक *lahak* [cf. H. *lahaknā*], f. glow, glitter; blaze; flush, wave (of emotion: as of patriotism).

लहक *lahak* [cf. H. *lahaknā*], f. blaze; glare.

लहकना *lahaknā* [*lasati*[1]], v.i. **1.** to glitter, to flash. **2.** to blaze (a fire, the sun). **3.** to rise (wind). **4.** [× H. *lahrānā*] to wave (as crops, or a flag, in wind). **5.** to arise (strong desire). — **लहककर बोलना**, to speak loudly or confidently.

लहकाना *lahkānā* [cf. H. *lahaknā*], v.t. **1.** to cause to shine or to flash. **2.** to cause to blaze; to blow up or to fan (a fire). **3.** to urge, to incite. **4.** [× H. *lahrānā*], to cause to flap, or to fly (a flag).

लहकारना *lahkārnā*, v.t. reg. **1.** to stir up, to incite (= भड़काना). **2.** to set (a dog) on (one, पर).

लहकावट *lahkāvaṭ* [cf. H. *lahaknā*], f. reg. glittering, flashing; flash; blaze.

लहकीला *lahkīlā* [cf. H. *lahaknā*], adj. *Pl.* shining, glittering.

लहकौर *lahkaur* [H. *lah-* + H. *kaur*], f. m. **1.** a marriage rite in which the groom and bride put food in each other's mouths. **2.** songs sung at the performance of *lahkaur*.

लहकौरि *lahkauri*, f. Brbh. = लहकौर.

लहजा *lahjā* [A. *lahja*], m. **1.** intonation, accent. **2.** modulation of voice. — अच्छे लहजे में गाना, to sing well.

लहज़ा *lahzā* [A. *lahza*], m. U. a look, glance: moment, instant. — ~ भर, adv. for a moment.

लहनदार *lahndār* [*labhana-*: +P. *-dār*], m. creditor; money-lender.

लहना *lahnā* [cf. H. *lah-*], m. **1.** *Pl.* profit, gain. **2.** *Pl. HŚS.* an outstanding debt. **3.** lot, portion, fate.

लहबर *lahbar*, m. *Pl. HŚS.* **1.** a long loose garment. **2.** a kind of parakeet.

लहर *lahr* [*lahari-*], f. **1.** a wave; surge. **2.** loose fold (as of a hanging). **3.** waving line (as in a pattern). **4.** access of emotion; excitement; delight, rapture; frenzy. **5.** seizure, attack (of illness or pain); fit, convulsion. **6.** breath (of soft wind); wafted fragrance. **7.** fig. prosperity, heyday. — ~ आना, a wave to come; delight, &c. to be felt; to prosper; to suffer a fit or convulsion. ~ उठना, a wave to rise; emotion to surge (within, में). ~ चढ़ना (को), a seizure to take (one). ~ मारना, to be rough (the sea); to crawl (a snake). ~ लेना, to enjoy oneself to the full. लहरें मारना, to crawl (a snake). – लहरदार [P. *-dar*], adj. wavy (water, a line, a pattern; or hair); whimsical; crotchety; flashing, fine. लहर-पटोर, m. Av. a type of striped silk. लहर-बहर, f. prosperity, heyday; flush, glow (of delight).

लहर- *lahr-*, v.i. Brbh. = लहराना.

[1]**लहरा** *lahrā* [cf. *lahari-*, or H. *lahr*], m. **1.** *mus. Pl. HŚS.* a trill. **2.** a trilling or lively tune (introducing singing or dancing). **3.** *HŚS.* = लहर, 1., 4.

[2]**लहरा** *lahrā* [cf. H. *lahr*], m. a tall millet, the bulrush millet, *Pennisetum typhoideum.*

लहराना *lahrānā* [cf. H. *lahr*], v.i. & v.t. **1.** v.i. to rise in waves (water), to ripple. **2.** to wave (as foliage, crops). **3.** to wave, to flap (a flag). **4.** to wind (as a stream). **5.** to undulate in movement (a snake). **6.** to gust (as heat). **7.** to be moved suddenly (the heart, by emotion). **8.** to be wafted (fragrance). **9.** to be radiant (the beauty of nature). **10.** v.t. to cause to flutter, or to wave; to put out (a flag); to raise (a flag, standard). **11.** to raise delusive hopes in (a person); to excite, to tantalise. **12.** Brbh. to dandle (a child).

लहरिया *lahriyā* [cf. H. *lahr*], adj. & m. **1.** adj. wavy; waved, watered (a pattern); striped. **2.** cloth, or a garment, of waved pattern. **3.** embroidery or edging of waved pattern.

[1]**लहरी** *lahrī* [cf. H. *lahr*], adj. **1.** whimsical, wayward. **2.** inconsiderate, thoughtless. **3.** emotional; jovial.

[2]**लहरी** *lahrī* [S.], f. a wave; ripple. — शीत ~, f. *meteorol.* cold wave.

लहलहा *lahlahā* [cf. H. *lahr-*, *lahaknā*], adj. **1.** waving, bending (as ripening corn in the wind). **2.** flourishing, blooming; thriving.

लहलहाना *lahlahānā* [cf. H. *lahalahā*], v.i. **1.** to wave, to bend (as ripening corn in the wind). **2.** to thrive, to grow green, to bloom. **3.** to flourish (a person); to become radiant.

लहलहाहट *lahlahāhaṭ* [cf. H. *lahlahānā*], f. waving of corn (in the wind); luxuriant growth (of fields).

लहलही *lahlahī* [? cf. H. *lahlahā*: iron.], f. reg. mud left where the water of a tank, &c. dries up.

लहलोट *lahloṭ* [H. *lah-*+H. *loṭnā*], adj. & m. reg. **1.** adj. borrowing and never returning. **2.** m. one who borrows and never returns.

लहसुन *lahsun* [*laśuna-*; Pk. *lhasuṇa-*], m. **1.** garlic. **2.** a freckle. **3.** a blotch.

लहसुनिया *lahsuniyā* [cf. H. *lahsun*], m. the quartz stone called cat's-eye.

लहसुनी *lahsunī* [cf. H. *lahsun*], adj. *Pl. HŚS.* having to do with garlic. — ~ हींग, m. a kind of asafoetida.

लहसोड़ा *lahsoṛā*, m. pronun. var. = लसोड़ा.

[1]**लहास** *lahās*, f. reg. = लहासी.

[2]**लहास** *lahās*, f. colloq. = लाश.

लहासी *lahāsī*, f. reg. a ship's hawser or cable.

लहू *lahū* [H. *lohū*], m. blood. — ~ आना, blood to be passed from the bowels. ~ उतरना (में), blood to descend: to become bloodshot (the eyes). ~ का घूँट पीना, to drink a draught of blood: to repress anger or extreme frustration. ~ का प्यासा, adj. thirsting for the blood (of, का); bloodthirsty. ~ टपकना, blood to drop or to trickle (from); to be bloodshot (the eyes). ~ डालना, to spit or to vomit blood. ~ देना, to bleed. ~ पी पीकर रह जाना, = ~ का घूँट पीना. ~ पीना, to drink the blood (of, का); to worry or to plague to death. ~ फटना, the blood to be poisoned; to have leprosy. ~ बैठना, = ~ आना. ~ में हाथ रँगना, to dye (one's) hand in the blood (of, के), to kill. ~ लगाकर शहीदों में मिलना, to pass oneself off as a martyr, or a hero, by smearing oneself with blood. ~ रोना, to weep tears of blood. ~ सफ़ेद होना, fig. to grow cold or indifferent (to natural ties). – लहू-पसीना एक करना, to sweat blood, = next. लहू-पानी एक करना, to toil hard, to sweat. लहू-लुहान, adj. smeared with blood.

लहेरा *laherā* [**lākṣakara-*], m. reg. (Bihar) a lac bangle-maker.

[1]**लाँक** *lāṁk* [conn. *laṅkā-*[2]], f. reg. the chickling vetch, *Lathyrus sativus.*

[2]**लाँक** *lāṁk* [**laṅka-*[2]], f. *Pl. HŚS.* quantity, amount: fresh-cut crops.

[3]**लाँक** *lāṁk* [conn. **lakka-*[3]], f. Brbh. the loins (cf. लाँग).

लाँग *lāṁg* [**laṅga-*[3]], f. **1.** the end of a *dhotī* (passed between the thighs and fastened behind). **2.** colloq. leg. — ~ खुलना, euph. to be agitated. ~ मारना, to kick, to kick out (a horse). ~ में चोट, f. a blow on the leg.

लाँगल *lāṁgal* [*lāṅgala-*: ? ← Austro-as.], m. reg. (E). a plough.

लाँगूल *lāṁgūl* [*lāṅgūla-*], m. **1.** tail. **2.** penis.

लाँघन *lāṁghan* [*laṅghana-*], m. *Pl.* stepping across; bestriding.

लाँघना *lāṁghnā* [*laṅghayati*], v.t. **1.** to jump over; to step over; to cross; to straddle (a horse). **2.** to overstep (bounds); to violate (a frontier); to break (a regulation).

लाँच *lāṁc* [*lañcā-*], f. reg. a bribe.

लांछन *lāñchan* [S.], m. **1.** a disfiguring mark; a brand. **2.** pl. specif. the dark marks visible on the surface of the moon. **3.** stigma. — ~ लगाना (को or पर), to cast aspersions (on).

लांछना *lāñchănā* [S.], f. = लांछन, 1., 3.

लांछित *lāñchit* [S.], adj. **1.** marked, branded; stigmatised. **2.** insulted.

लाँड़ *lāṁṛ* [**laṇḍa-*[1]], m. penis.

लाँड़ा *lāṁṛā* [**laṇḍa-*[1]], adj. reg. **1.** docked (an animal). **2.** circumcised.

ला- *lā-* [A. *lā*], pref. **1.** not; there is not. **2.** without. — लाइलाज, adj. incurable. °ई, f. लाचार, adj. without recourse, helpless; disabled; destitute; having no alternative. लाचार करना, to render helpless, &c.; to compel. °ई, f. आँखों से लाचार होना, to have bad eyesight. लाजवाब, adj. without an answer: speechless, disconcerted; beyond question; beyond compare. लादावा [A. *-da'vā*], adj. inv. *law.* not having, or renouncing, a claim. लापता, adj. inv. of unknown whereabouts: missing (a person); lost (a thing). लापरवा, adj. careless, thoughtless; indifferent. लापरवाह, adj. id. °ई, f. thoughtlessness; indifference. लासानी [A. *-ṣānī*], adj. without a second: unequalled, incomparable. लावारिस, adj. leaving no heir; unclaimed as inheritance (property); stray (an animal). °ई, adj. id.; f. property unclaimed as inheritance. लाहाल, adj. insoluble. लाहौल बिला क़ूबत [A. *lā ḥaul va lā quvvat illa bi'l-lāhi*], interj. corr. there is no strength nor power but in God: how horrible! how disgusting!

लाइन *lāin* [Engl. *line*], f. **1.** line. **2.** railway line. **3.** row, rank. **4.** lines (of housing, &c.: civil, military, police); barracks; cantonment. — ~ बाँधना, to form a line or row. – लैन-डोरी, f. obs. lines and ropes: an advance party and its equipment to set up camp.

[1]**लाई** *lāī* [*lāja-*], f. **1.** parched grain (as rice, millet). **2.** a sweet made with parched rice.

[2]**लाई** *lāī* [conn. H. *lānā*, [1] [2]*lāv-*], f. reg. aspersion, tale-bearing. — ~ लगाना, to cast aspersions. – लाइ-लुतरी, f. = ~.

[3]**लाई** *lāī*, f. reg. = राई.

लाक्षणिक *lākṣaṇik* [S.], adj. characteristic.

लाक्षा *lākṣā* [S.], f. lac (= [1]लाख). — लाक्षा-गृह, m. house of lac (made by Duryodhana for the purpose of burning the Pāṇḍavas).

[1]**लाख** *lākh* [*lakṣa-*], adj. & m. **1.** adj. a hundred thousand, a lakh. **2.** m. a hundred thousand (of). **3.** a vast number (of). — ~ का घर ख़ाक होना, to be reduced from wealth to poverty. ~ टके (or रुपए) की बात, f. an invaluable remark. ~ मन का होना, to be immensely heavy; colloq. to be a person of great weight or importance. ~ सिर का होना, to have a hundred thousand heads: to be doggedly persistent; to turn a deaf ear. एक ~ आदमी, a hundred thousand men. तुम ~ काहो, मैं एक न मानूँगा, you may say it as often as you like but I shall not agree with one bit of it. मैंने उन्हें ~ समझाया, I counselled him over and over again. लाखों, adj. hundreds of thousands of; vast numbers of; in vast numbers. लाखों में, adv. in the presence (or face) of everybody, in public.

[2]**लाख** *lākh* [*lākṣā-*], f. (m., *Pl.*). **1.** lac; shellac. **2.** sealing-wax. **3.** reg. (W). a rust on wheat.

लाख- *lākh-* [cf. H. [2]*lākh*], v.t. Brbh. to seal (as with sealing-wax).

लाखा *lākhā* [*lākṣā-*], m. *Pl. HŚS.* **1.** lac-dye. **2.** a kind of rust on wheat.

लाखी *lākhī* [cf. H. [2]*lākh*], adj. & f. **1.** adj. made of lac. **2.** coloured or varnished with lac; dark-reddish. **3.** f. a red dye extracted from lac.

लाग *lāg* [cf. H. *lāg-, lagnā*], f. **1.** relation, connection; correspondence (of appearance and reality, or of means and end); suitability (of time, place); access (to a place). **2.** attachment, affection. **3.** aim, endeavour. **4.** touching, reaching; basis, ground (as for a conjecture). **5.** due expenditure, cost; Brbh. (?

m.) ground-rent. **6.** striking; stroke of ill-fortune. **7.** fault, reproach. **8.** hostility; spite, grudge; rivalry. **9.** intrigue, plot; a secret. **10.** trick, sleight of hand (as of a conjurer); a charm, spell. — ~ बाँधना, to bear enmity (against, से); to show hostility (to). ~ रखना, to have to do (with, से); to have an interest; to harbour ill-feeling (against). ~ लगना, to fall, or to be, in love (with, की). — लाग-डाँट, f. = ~, 8. लाग-लपेट, f. emotional involvement (cf. ~, 2.; hidden meaning, implication; wordiness (of style).

लाग- *lāg-* [*lagyati*], v.i. Brbh. Av. = लगना.

लागड़ *lāgaṛ* [cf. H. *lāg-*], m. *Pl.* a seedling transplanted (= लावड़).

लागत *lāgat* [cf. H. *lāg-, lagnā*], f. sthg. applied: **1.** outlay; expenditure; investment. **2.** cost price, production price. — ~ आना (पर), or बैठना (की), or लगना, (sthg.) to cost (a given amount). तुम्हारा यह कोट कितनी ~ का है? what did you spend on this coat?

लागि *lāgi* [cf. *lagna-*], ppn. Brbh. Av. **1.** because of, for the sake of. **2.** by means of. **3.** up to; as far as; as long as.

लागी *lāgī* [**lagni-*], f. reg. attachment, affection, love.

लागू *lāgū* [cf. H. *lāg-, lagnā*], adj. & m. **1.** adj. in force, applying (as a regulation); chargeable (as tax). **2.** valid (a document, a currency). **3.** applying (as a remark: to, पर). **4.** following, pursuing (as an animal its prey). **5.** intent (on), desirous (of, का). **6.** m. a supporter, partisan (of a person or cause). **7.** one who is intent on or in love (with, का/की); a pursuer. — ~ करना, to give effect to, to bring into force.

लाघव *lāghav* [S.], m. **1.** smallness, minuteness; insignificance. **2.** lightness, delicacy. **3.** swiftness; dexterity. **4.** frivolity. **5.** *pros.* shortness (of a vowel or syllable).

लाचार *lācār*, adj. see s.v. ला-.

लाची *lācī*, f. Brbh. = इलायची.

लाज *lāj* [*lajjā-*], f. **1.** shame; sense of decency or modesty. **2.** bashfulness. **3.** transf. honour, good name. — ~ आना, or लगना (को), to feel shame, or a sense of modesty. ~ करना, to show a sense of shame or modesty; to be bashful; to be mindful of the honour (of, की). ~ रखना, to protect the honour (of, की); to hide the shame (of); to have a sense of shame. ~ से मरना, to die of shame. लाजों मरना, = ~ से मरना. – लाजवंत, adj. Av. ashamed; modest; bashful. °ई, adj. & f. ashamed, &c.; the sensitive plant, *Mimosa pudica* (= छुई-मुई).

लाज- *lāj-* [*lajjate*], v.i. Brbh. Av. **1.** to feel ashamed. **2.** to feel shy. **3.** to blush.

लाजवर्त *lājvart* [P. *lājavard*], adj. Brbh. lapis lazuli.

लाजा *lājā* [ad. *lāja-*, Pa. *lājā-*], f. fried or parched grain (= [1]लावा). — लाजा-हवन, m. *hind.* offering of fried or parched grain during the marriage ceremony.

लाज़िम *lāzim* [A. *lāzim*], adj. **1.** necessary; indispensable; obligatory, incumbent (on one, को); inevitable (as a consequence). **2.** urgent (as a task). **3.** suitable, proper.

लाज़िमी *lāzimī* [A. *lāzim*+P. *-ī*], adj. = लाज़िम. — ~ तौर पर, adv. necessarily, &c.

लाजी *lājī* [cf. H. *lājā*], f. reg. (W.) corn or rice dampened and parched.

लाझा *lājhā*, m. *Pl.* **1.** stickiness; clamminess; sweltering state. **2.** semen.

[1]**लाट** *lāṭ* [Engl. *lord*], m. **1.** a lord. **2.** *hist.* governor (in British India). छोटा ~, *hist.* governor of a particular province. फ़ौजी ~, m. commander in chief. बड़े ~, m. *hist.* Viceroy; Governor-General; Lord Bishop; Chief Justice.

[2]**लाट** *lāṭ* [Engl. *lot*], m. lot (in a sale). — लाटबंदी [P. *-bandī*], f. division into lots.

[3]**लाट** *lāṭ* [cf. H. *lāṭh*], f. pronun. var. = लाठ.

[4]**लाट** *lāṭ* [*laṭṭa-*[1]], adj. & m. reg. **1.** adj. old, worn (clothes). **2.** m. old or worn-out clothes, or ornaments.

लाटा *lāṭā*, m. reg. **1.** a mixture of pounded *mahuā* nuts or dried flowers with rice or other grain. **2.** a sweet made with dried *mahuā* flowers.

लाटी *lāṭī*, f. pronun. var. reg. = लाठी.

लाठ *lāṭh* [**laṣṭi-*: Pa. *laṭṭhi-*], f. reg. **1.** pillar, column, monument; minaret, spire. **2.** vertical post, (as in a mill). **3.** axle (as in a spinning-wheel). **4.** beam, lever (as in a well, or a press). **5.** (E.) a long embankment (serving to retain water for rice-growing).

लाठा *lāṭhā*, m. *Pl.* **1.** a large club or staff (cf. लाठी). **2.** a pillar, &c. (= लाठ, 1).

लाठी *lāṭhī* [**laṣṭi-*, Pa. *laṭṭhi-*], f. **1.** a staff. **2.** a club. **3.** fig. prop, support. — ~ चलना, lāṭhīs to be wielded, an affray to take place. ~ टेककर चलना, or जाना, to walk with the help of a stick. एक ~ हाँकना, to treat everybody in the same unceremonious way. जिसकी ~, उसकी भैंस, he who has the stick gets the buffalo: might is right. – लाठी-चार्ज, m. lāṭhī charge (of police). लाठी-पाठी, f. reg. beating with a staff or club; a fight with staves. लाठी-पोंगा, m. reg.: ~ करना, to fight with staves. लाठीवाला, m. one having a staff, &c.; a henchman.

लाड़ *lāṛ* [**lāḍya-*: Pk. *laḍḍia-*], f. **1.** affection. **2.** caressing, caress; endearment. **3.** playfulness (of a child). — ~ करना, or लड़ाना (से), to caress. – लाड़-प्यार, m. = ~, 1., 2.; flirtation, dalliance. लाड़-लड़ैतो, Brbh. dear, darling. – लाड़ों-पला, adj. lovingly brought up; well treated (a domestic animal).

लाड़ला *lāṛlā* [cf. **lāḍya-*: Pk. *laḍḍia-*], adj. & m. **1.** adj. dear, darling. **2.** brought up affectionately. **3.** pampered (a child). **4.** m. darling. **5.** one brought up affectionately, &c.

¹लाड़ा *lāṛā* [cf. H. *lāṛ*], adj. & m. **1.** adj. dear, beloved. **2.** m. dear one. — लाड़ा-लाड़ी, m. f. bridegroom and bride.

²लाड़ा *lāṛā*, m. *Pl.* raw indigo.

लाड़ो *lāṛo* [cf. H. *lāṛ*], adj. & f. **1.** adj. dear (wife, or daughter). **2.** f. dear wife, dear daughter.

लाढ़िया *lāṛhiyā* [conn. H. *lāṛ*], m. *Pl. HŚS.* one who coaxes a hesitant buyer (being in league with the seller); one who bids up a price.

लाढ़ियापन *lāṛhiyāpan* [cf. H. *laṛhiyā*], m. *Pl. HŚS.* coaxing a buyer; bidding up a price.

लात *lāt* [**lattā-*: Pk. *lattā-*], f. a kick. — ~ खाना, to be kicked; fig. to be spurned. ~ चलाना (पर), to kick; to spurn. ~ मारना (पर, में, or को), id. लज्जा को ~ मारना, fig. to take no thought for shame or modesty, to do sthg. shameless; to have done with (sthg). – लात-मुक्की, f. reg. kicking and punching, beating.

लाद *lād* [cf. H. *lādnā*], f. **1.** load, burden. **2.** reg. the stomach; innards.

लादना *lādnā* [*lardayati*], v.t. **1.** to load (an animal, vehicle, or vessel). **2.** to pile, to heap (on, पर). **3.** to burden (one: with tasks, duties). **4.** to foist (an attitude or opinion: upon, पर). एहसान का बोझ ~ (पर), to insinuate that (another) should feel a sense of gratitude towards one. **5.** to lay (sthg.) on thickly. **6.** (in wrestling) to cross-throw (over the hip).

लादिया *lādiyā* [cf. H. *lādnā*], m. a loader; porter.

लादी *lādī* [? cf. H. *lādā*, part. adj.], f. small load (as a dhobī's load of clothes).

लादू *lādū* [cf. H. *lādnā*], adj. reg. bearing a load, or freight (an animal, a ship).

लानत *lānat* [A. *laʿna*: P. *laʿnat*], f. a curse. — ~ करना, (पर or को), to curse; to forswear; fig. to shun (as alcohol, &c). ~ भेजना, to call down a curse (on, पर): = ~ करना. ~ है! a curse (on, पर)! – लानत-मलामत, f. curses and reproaches.

लानती *lānătī* [P. *laʿnat+-ī*], adj. accursed; execrable.

लाना *lānā* [*lāti*], v.t. used without *ne* in perf. forms. **1.** to bring, to fetch. **2.** to bring forward or in; to bring about; to introduce (an innovation, &c.); to bring (a case: against, पर). **3.** to produce. फूल ~, to bear fruit (a tree). **4.** to purchase (and bring away).

लापसी *lāpsī* [**lappasikā-*: Pk. *lappasiyā-*], f. Brbh. = लपसी.

लाफना *lāphnā* [**lappha-*¹; ? < B.], v.i. reg. to jump.

¹लाभ *lābh* [S.], m. **1.** obtaining, acquiring; gain. **2.** profit, advantage; use; benefit. **3.** financial profit; interest. **4.** well-being. **5.** *astron.* name of the eleventh lunar mansion. — ~ उठाना, to profit (from, से), to take advantage (of); to make a profit (of, का). ~ करना, to acquire, to gain; to attain. ~ के साथ बेचना, to sell at a profit. – लाभकारक, adj. profitable, advantageous, &c. °-कारी, adj. id. लाभजनक, adj. = next. लाभदायक, adj. profitable, advantageous. लाभप्रद, adj. id. लाभान्वित [°*bha+a*°], adj. advantaged (by, से), benefiting (from); having, or having made, a profit. लाभांश [°*bha+a*°], m. *fin.* a dividend. लाभार्थ [°*bha+a*°], adv. for the benefit or advantage (of, के). लाभालाभ [°*bha+a*°], m. profit and loss; advantage and disadvantage.

²लाभ *lābh* [H. ¹*phāla-*], m. reg. (W.) the curved part of the blade of a spade.

¹लाम *lām*, f. *mil.* **1.** a line; line of battle; front. **2.** a brigade, army. — ~ पर भेजना, to send (troops) to the front. ~ बाँधना, to form up (troops) or units in line. – लाम-बंद [P. *-band*], adj. mobilised. °ई, f. mobilisation.

²लाम *lām* [A. *lām*], m. the name of the letter *l* of the Arabic script: — लाम-काफ़, m. l's and k's: abusive language.

लायक़ *lāyaq* [A. *lā'iq*], adj. **1.** fit, suitable (for, के). **2.** capable, able (a person). **3.** deserving, worthy. — पढ़ने ~, adj. worth reading.

लायक़ी *lāyaqī* [P. *lā'iqī*], f. **1.** fitness, suitability. **2.** capability. **3.** worthiness.

¹लार *lār* [*lālā-*¹], f. saliva; dribbling (of an infant) (= ²राल); slaver (of an animal). — ~ आना (को), to salivate, &c.

²लार *lār* [**lārā-*], f. Brbh. continuous line, row; string, succession. — ~, adv. in the company (of, की); following. ~ लगा-, to set a snare.

[1]**लाल** *lāl* [P. *lāl*], adj. & m. **1.** red. **2.** reddish; brownish. **3.** m. the male red munia or waxbill, *Estrilda amandava.* — ~ अँगारा, m. a red coal: sthg. red-hot; one flushed with anger. ~ आँखें दिखाना, to glare in anger. ~ गोला, m. reg. (W.) a light reddish sandy soil. ~ चंदन, m. red sandalwood. ~ तिकोन, m. red triangle: symbol indicating a family planning centre. ~ पड़ना, to flush; to grow angry; to become red-hot. ~ परी, f. ruby fairy (one of the fairies represented in the *Indar Sabhā* of Amānat (*c.*1850) as attending Indra's court); joc. = wine. ~ पानी, m. colloq. blood. ~ फ़ीता, m. red tape. ~ बत्ती, f. red light (danger signal). ~ मिर्च, f. red pepper, red chilli. ~ रग, colloq. an artery. ~ रहना, fig. to flourish, to prosper. ~ शक्कर, f. partly refined sugar. ~ साग, m. the red amaranth (*A. gangeticus*), used as a vegetable. ~ होना, to flush; to grow angry; to become red-hot; fig. to be getting warm (in a game); to be on the point of winning. – लाल-पगड़ी, m. red-turban: a policeman. लाल-पीली आँखें निकालना, to glare fiercely; to fly into a rage. लाल-सिर, m. red-head: the chestnut-headed bee-eater, *Merops leschenaulti*; the red-crested pochard, *Netta rufina.*

[2]**लाल** *lāl* [*lālya-*], adj. & m. **1.** adj. dear, darling. **2.** m. an infant boy; dear son. **3.** specif. a designation of Kṛṣṇa. — धरती के ~, m. sons of the soil. – लाल-बीबी, f. euph. dear lady: a prostitute. लाल-बुझक्कड़, m. one having pretensions to knowledge, a wiseacre. लालों का ~, adj. & m. dearest (of the dear).

[3]**लाल** *lāl* [P. *laʻl* (for *lāl*)], m. a ruby. — ~ परी, f. see s.v. [1]लाल.

लालच *lālac* [*lālitya-*], m. **1.** greed, covetousness. **2.** bait, lure. — ~ करना, to be greedy (for, का); to covet. ~ देना (को), to tempt; to decoy. ~ में आना, to yield to desire (for, के), to take a bait.

लालची *lālcī* [cf. H. *lālac*], adj. greedy, covetous.

लालन *lālan* [S.], m. & f. **1.** m. caressing, fondling. **2.** m. [× H. [2]*lāl*] Brbh. dear son; dear youth. **3.** f. *Pl.* sweetheart. — लालन-पालन, m. caressing and cherishing; bringing up (a child) with love.

लालसा *lālăsā* [S.], f. **1.** longing, desire; craving (for, की). **2.** covetousness.

लालसित *lālăsit* [S.], adj. eagerly desiring or wishful.

[1]**लाला** *lālā* [P. *lālā*], m. inv. **1.** a respectful designation (esp. of members of Vaiṣya or Kāyasth communities: as bankers, merchants, tradesmen, schoolmasters, clerks). **2.** a term of respectful address to a father, or father-in-law, or brother-in-law. **3.** Brbh. a term of affectionate address to a child. — लाला-भैया करना, to address (one) with some formality.

[2]**लाला** *lālā* [S.], f. *Pl. HŚS.* saliva (= [1]लार).

[3]**लाला** *lālā* [P. *lāla*], m. U. a tulip; a red poppy.

लालायित *lālāyit* [S.], adj. **1.** wishing eagerly (for) (cf. [2]लाला). **2.** [× H. [2]*lāl*] treated kindly (as a child).

लालित *lālit* [S.], adj. **1.** caressed, cherished. **2.** indulged.

लालित्य *lālityă* [S.], m. **1.** loveliness, grace; sweetness, charm; gentleness. **2.** gaiety.

लालिमा *lālimā* [H. [2]*lālī* × *-imā-*], f. poet. = [2]लाली, 1., 2.

[1]**लाली** *lālī* [cf. H. *lāṛlā*], f. **1.** a beloved, sweetheart. **2.** specif. a designation of Rādhā.

[2]**लाली** *lālī* [P. *lālī*], f. **1.** redness; red glow; red patch, mark. **2.** flush. **3.** fig. honour, good name.

लाले *lāle* [? conn. H. *lālac*], m. pl. strong desire (for, के). — ~ पड़ना, intense, or hopeless, longing to be felt (for, के); to be or to become unattainable; to be scarce or scanty.

[1]**लाव** *lāv*, m. **1.** Brbh. a rope; a well-rope. **2.** reg. the amount of land irrigated per day by working one well-rope.

[2]**लाव** *lāv* [A. *livā*; × H. *lāvā*, part. adj. ← [2]*lāv-*], m. banner, standard: — लाव-लशकर, m. an army with its equipment and camp-followers.

[3]**लाव** *lāv* [cf. H. [1] [2] *lāv-*], m. reg. a bringing or placing ; sthg. brought, or placed. ~ उठाना, to accept a pledge, to lend (money or goods) against security. ~ लगाना, to take over (another's property) in satisfaction of a debt.

[4]**लाव** *lāv* [*lāva-*], m. *Pl.* cutting, reaping.

[1]**लाव-** *lāv- labhate* × *dadāti*], v.i. reg. to bring (= लाना, ले आना).

[2]**लाव-** *lāv-* [*lāgayati*], v.t. reg. to place, to put down, &c.; to plant (= लगाना).

[3]**लाव-** *lāv-* [*lābha-*]. *Pl.* = लाभ: — लाव-साव [°*sāti-*[1]], m. profit, advantage.

[1]**लावक** *lāvak* [ad. *lābaka-*], m. Av. the quail *Perdix chinensis.*

[2]**लावक** *lāvak* [conn. H. [4]*lāv*], m. reg. (E.) the winter rice crop.

लावड़ *lāvaṛ* [cf. H. [2]*lāv-*], m. reg. (E). = लागड़.

लावणिक *lāvănik* [S.], adj. & m. **1.** adj. having to do with salt. **2.** salty. **3.** salted, savoury. **4.** fig. charming, lovely (a woman). **5.** m. *Pl. HŚS.* a salt-merchant. **6.** *Pl. HŚS.* a salt-cellar.

लावण्य *lāvaṇyă* [S.], m. **1.** saltiness; savour. **2.** charm.

[1]**लावन** *lāvan* [cf. H. [3]*lāv*], f. *Pl.* sthg. added: a relish added to food.

[2]**लावन** *lāvan* [conn. H. *dāman*], m. reg. lower edge; fringe, hem.

[1]**लावनी** *lāvnī* [**lāvana-*], f. **1.** reaping. **2.** reapers' wages in kind. — ~ करना, to reap.

[2]**लावनी** *lāvnī* [? *lāvaṇika-*; and M. *lāvṇī*], f. a type of popular song.

[1]**लावा** *lāvā* [*lāja-*], m. rice, corn or millet parched on hot sand.

[2]**लावा** *lāvā* [*lābaka-*], m. Av. the quail *Perdix chinensis.*

[3]**लावा** *lāvā* [*lāvaka-*], m. *Pl.* a reaper, harvest-hand.

[4]**लावा** *lāvā* [cf. H. [1] [2]*lāv-*], m. a bringer. — लावा-लुतरा, m. *Pl.* tale-bearer; slanderer.

लाश *lāś* [P. *lāś*], f. **1.** a corpse. **2.** a carcass. — ~ उठना, a body to be taken for cremation; a body to be consumed by fire. ~ पड़ना, to fall down dead.

लास *lās* [S.], m. **1.** jumping, skipping; dancing. **2.** Brbh. dalliance of lovers. — लहरों में ~, m. the dancing of waves.

लासक *lāsak* [S.], m. *Pl. HŚS.* **1.** a dancer; an actor. **2.** a peacock.

[1]**लासना** *lāsnā* [*lāsayati*[1], or **lāsyate*], v.i. reg. to shine.

[2]**लासना** *lāsnā* [**lasyati*], v.i. reg. to be sticky or glutinous.

लासा *lāsā* [**lasya-*], m. **1.** anything clammy or sticky (as the viscous juice of plants); size, starch. **2.** gum, glue, adhesive. **3.** bird-lime. — ~ लगाना, to set a snare.

लासानी *lā-sānī* [A. *lā*+A. *s̱ānī*], adj. without a second; unequalled.

लासिका *lāsikā* [S.], f. reg. a dancing-girl; a dissolute woman.

लास्य *lāsyă* [S.], m. a women's dance (often but not always accompanied by instrumental music and singing); a dance illustrating the emotions of love. — ~ रूपक, m. a drama with dancing.

[1]**लाह** *lāh* [*lākṣā-*: ← E.], f. (m., *Pl.*) lac (= [2]लाख).

[2]**लाह** *lāh* [*lābha-*], m. Av. = लाभ.

[3]**लाह** *lāh* [P. *lāh*], m. *Pl.* a kind of fine silk cloth.

लाहन *lāhan* [? cf. H. [2]*lāh*], m. reg. **1.** a yeast or leaven obtained from bark. **2.** dregs of *mahuā* distillation. **3.** [? × H. [1]*lāv-*, *lah-*] payment for carrying grain.

लाहाल *lāhāl*, adj. see s.v. ला-.

[1]**लाही** *lāhī*, f. reg. **1.** parched grain (= [1]लावा, [1]>लाई). **2.** wild rice.

[2]**लाही** *lāhī*, f. *Pl.* a kind of fine silk cloth resembling gauze (= [3]लाह).

[3]**लाही** *lāhī* [conn. H. *rāī*], f. reg. **1.** a mustard, *Brassica juncea* (= राई). **2.** rape seed, *Sinapis dichotoma* (= [1]तोड़ी).

[4]**लाही** *lāhī* [cf. H. [1]*lāh*], adj. & m. **1.** adj. Brbh. dark red. **2.** m. reg. (Bihar) the lac insect (that swarms on plants and trees).

लाहे *lāhe*, f. reg. dregs, sediment (of wine).

लाहौर *lāhaur*, m. the city of Lahore.

लाहौरी *lāhaurī* [cf. H. *lāhaur*], adj. & m. **1.** adj. of or having to do with Lahore (as by birth or residence, or by manufacture). **2.** m. a resident of Lahore. — ~ नामक, m. rock salt from Lahore.

लिंग *liṅg* [S.], m. **1.** sign, distinguishing mark. **2.** sex. **3.** penis. **4.** *hind.* a phallus, lingam (in which form Śiva is worshipped); an idol; phallic image. **5.** *gram.* gender. **6.** *philos.* nature (as the active power in creation); the subtle body which is not destroyed by death. — लिंग-भेद, m. difference of sex; *gram.* gender. लिंगवाचक, adj. & m. indicating gender; gender-marker. लिंगेंद्रिय [°*nga*+*i*°], m. organ of sex.

लिंगन *liṅgan* [S.], m. embracing, embrace.

लिंगायत *liṅgāyat*, m. *hind.* a member of the Liṅgāyat sect of lingam worshippers.

लिंगिता *liṅgitā* [S.], f. sexuality.

लिंगी *liṅgī* [S.], adj. & m. **1.** adj. distinguished by a mark or sign. **2.** m. = लिंगायत. **3.** name of the Lingāyat sect. **4.** an ascetic.

लिए *lie* [cf. H. *lenā*], perf. adv. & ppn. **1.** perf. adv. holding; taking with one. लाठी ~ खड़ा है, he stands (there) with, or holding, a stick. वह किताब हाथ में ~ बाहर गया, he went out with the book in his hand. **2.** ppn. because of. इसलिए, adv. for this reason, therefore, and so; for the reason (that, कि). किसलिए? why? **3.** ppn. w. के. for, on account of. मैंने आपके ~ ही यह किया, I did this just for you. **4.** in order to. हिंदी सीखने के ~ हिंदुस्तान जाऊँगा, I shall go to India to learn Hindi. **5.** for the period of. एक हफ़्ते के ~, adv. for a week. **6.** for, towards (a destination). दिल्ली के ~ चला जाना, to leave for Delhi.

लिक्खाड़ *likkhāṛ* [cf. H. *likhnā*], m. esp. iron. a writer.

लिखंत *likhant* [cf. *likhati*: H. *likhnā*], m. **1.** a writing, document. **2.** fig. fate, destiny.

लिखत *likhat* [cf. H. *likhnā*], f. **1.** writing. **2.** sthg. written; a letter; document. — लिखत-पढ़त होना, to be put in writing (an agreement, &c).

लिखन *likhan* [cf. H. *likhnā*], f. reg. **1.** the act of writing. **2.** ? m. sthg. written, a document.

लिखना *likhnā* [conn. S. *likhati*], v.t. **1.** to write; to enter, to note; to copy. **2.** to draw, to paint. **3.** to prescribe (a medicine). **4.** fig. to ordain (fate, by writing on the brow). — लिखना-पढ़ना v.t. & m., to read and write, to study; reading and writing, education. – लिखा-पढ़ा, adj. literate; educated. °-पढ़ी, f. reading and writing; correspondence; putting sthg. in writing; a written communication, advice by letter. °-पढ़ी करना, to correspond (with, से).

लिखनी *likhnī* [ad. *lekhanī-*; ×H. *likhnā*], f. *Pl.* reg. a pen.

लिखवाना *likhvānā* [cf. H. *likhnā*], v.t. to cause to be written, &c. (by, से).

लिखाई *likhāī* [cf. H. *likhnā*], f. **1.** writing. **2.** payment for writing or copying. — लिखाई-पढ़ाई, f. writing and reading, elementary schooling.

लिखाना *likhānā* [cf. H. *likhnā*], v.t. **1.** to cause (one, को) to write; to dictate (a letter: to). **2.** to cause to be written (by, से). — बोलकर ~, to dictate (as a letter). – लिखाना-पढ़ाना, to teach to write and read.

लिखावट *likhāvaṭ* [cf. H. *likhnā*], f. writing; handwriting.

लिखौटी *likhauṭī*, f. 19c. a written agreement.

लिखौती *likhautī*, f. a written agreement.

लिखित *likhit* [S.], adj. & m. **1.** adj. written; having a written form (a language). **2.** documentary (as evidence). **3.** m. sthg. written; a letter, document. **4.** penmanship, good handwriting.

लिखिया *likhiyā* [cf. H. *likhiyā*], m. a scribe.

लिजलिजा *lijlijā*, adj. **1.** sticky, viscous (cf. लचलचाना, लसलसा). **2.** soft, flaccid.

लिझड़ी *lijhṛī* [cf. H. *jhillī*], f. reg. (Bihar) afterbirth, placenta.

लिटवाना *liṭvānā* [cf. H. *leṭnā*], v.t. to cause to be laid down (by, से: a child or a sick person, in bed).

लिटाना *liṭānā*, v.t. = लेटाना.

लिट्ट *liṭṭ*, m. reg. = लिट्टी.

लिट्टी *liṭṭī* [*liṭṭa-*[3]], f. reg. (Bihar) **1.** a bread-cake or lump of flour baked on hot ashes. **2.** a ball or lump of tobacco.

लिड़बिड़ा *liṛbiṛā*, adj. *Pl.* = लड़बड़ा.

लिथड़ना *lithaṛnā* [cf. H. *latheṛnā*], v.i. **1.** to be smeared or daubed; to be dirty.

लिपटंत *lipṭant*, m. reg. bodily contact: **1.** embrace, hug. **2.** wrestling.

लिपटना *lipaṭnā* [*lipyate*], v.i. **1.** to stick (to, में or से). **2.** to cling (to, से). **3.** to wrap or to wind (around, में). **4.** fig. to stick (at, के पीछे: as at a task). **5.** to join (in bodily contact); to wrestle (with, से). **6.** to unite (with, से). **7.** to be enfolded (by, से); to be embraced (by). **8.** to be rolled into a ball; to be entangled, matted, or unravelled. **9.** to be involved, engrossed (in, में). **10.** to be implicated (in, में). **11.** to be smeared (= लिपना).

लिपटाना *lipṭānā* [cf. H. *lipaṭnā*], v.t. **1.** to cause to adhere (to, से), to stick (to). **2.** to unite, to involve together (two groups as allies, &c). **3.** to wrap or to fold (round, में); to wind or to tie (round). **4.** fig. to embrace.

लिपटाव *lipṭāv* [cf. H. *lipaṭnā*], m. stickiness; adhesion.

लिपड़ी *lipṛī* [cf. H. *lipnā*], f. *Pl.* (*HŚS.*) an old ragged turban, or garment.

लिपना *lipnā* [cf. H. *līpnā*], v.i. to be smeared (with, से); to be plastered; to be whitewashed. — लिपा-पुता, adj. smeared, dirtied (as paper); whitewashed (a wall).

लिपवाना *lipvānā* [cf. H. *līpnā*], v.t. to cause to be smeared, &c. (by, से).

लिपाई *lipāī* [cf. H. *līpnā*], f. **1.** smearing; plastering; whitewashing. **2.** cost of or payment for plastering, &c. **3.** fig. *Pl.* close handwriting.

लिपाना *lipānā* [cf. H. *līpnā*], v.t. **1.** to cause to be smeared; to cause to be plastered or whitewashed (by, से).

लिपि *lipi* [S.], f. **1.** writing, handwriting. **2.** a script, alphabet. **3.** sthg. written or inscribed. — लिपिकार, m. a copyist, writer. लिपि-बद्ध, adj. put in writing, not oral (a composition); written (a manuscript, a document).

लिपिक *lipik* [S.], m. a clerk, writer.

लिप्त *lipt* [S.], adj. **1.** smeared, spread over; plastered. **2.** stained, sullied (by, से). **3.** attached (to, से: as to the world of apparent reality); engrossed (in).

लिफ़ाफ़ा *lifāfā* [A. *lifāfa*], m. **1.** a cover, wrapper. ***2.** an envelope. **3.** outward show; ostentation. **4.** *Pl.* veneer; gilding, gloss. — लिफ़ाफ़ा खुलना, an envelope, or cover, to be opened or removed; an appearance to be removed (and reality exposed).

लिफ़ाफ़िया *lifāfiyā* [cf. H. *lifāfā*], adj. showy, ostentatious.

लिबड़ना *libaṛnā*, v.i. to be smeared (= लिपटना).

लिबलिबा *liblibā*, adj. & m. **1.** adj. sticky; slimy, viscous. **2.** pliable; delicate (to the touch). **3.** m. the pancreas.

लिबलिबी *liblibī* [cf. H. *liblibā*], f. **1.** sear spring (of a firing mechanism). **2.** trigger.

लिबास *libās* [A. *libās*], m. clothes, attire. — सादे ~ में होना, to be simply clad.

लियाक़त *liyāqat* [A. *liyāqa*: P. *liyāqat*], f. **1.** suitability, fitness. **2.** worth, merit. ***3.** ability, capacity. **4.** prudence, judgment. **5.** courtesy of manner.

लिरुआ *liruā*, m. reg. rice straw.

लिलाड़ *lilāṛ*, m. pronun. var. = ललाट.

लिलाना *lilānā* [cf. H. *līlnā*], v.i. colloq. reg. to feel eager desire, or longing, for.

लिवाना *livānā* [cf. H. *lenā*], v.t. to cause to be taken. — लिवा लाना, to cause to be taken and brought: to have brought, or fetched (esp. a person); to escort.

लिवाली *livālī* [cf. H. *livānā*], f. ? buying in, stockpiling.

लिवैया *livaiyā* [cf. H. *lenā, livānā*], m. **1.** one who takes. **2.** reg. one who brings.

लिसना *lisnā* [*śliṣyati*], v.i. to stick (to): = लसना.

लिसलिसा *lislisā* [cf. H. *lisnā*], adj. sticky (= लसलसा).

लिहाई *lihāī* [cf. H. *le(h)ī*], f. *Pl.* a glue used by book-binders.

लिहाज़ *lihāz* [A. *liḥāẓ*], m. **1.** attention, notice; account (taken of sthg.), regard. **2.** consideration, deference. **3.** sense of shame. **4.** respect, viewpoint. इस ~ से, adv. in this respect; from this point of view. — ~ उठना, or टूटना, all sense of shame to be lost. ~ करना (का), to notice, to observe; to have regard (to); to show respect or deference (to). ~ रखना, to show respect or deference (to, का).

लिहाज़ा *lihāzā* [A. *lihāẕā*], adv. U. for this: therefore, hence.

लिहाड़ा *lihāṛā*, adj. reg. base, contemptible.

लिहाड़ी *lihāṛī*, f. reg. making fun (of) unjustifiably or unfairly. — ~ लेना, to ridicule.

लिहाफ़ *lihāf* [A. *liḥāf*], m. **1.** a quilt. **2.** a quilted jacket.

लिहैंडी *lihaiṇḍī*, f. *Pl.* irrigation of land by throwing up water from a lower level (in a basket worked by two persons).

लीआ *līā* [cf. H. *lenā*], m. *Pl.* land that is flooded every year.

लीक *līk* [**likkā*-[2]], f. Brbh. Av. **1.** line, track. **2.** path; rut. **3.** established practice, custom; usage. **4.** Brbh. stain, disgrace. — ~, or ~ ~, चलना, to move in a well-worn path or in a rut; to follow established practice. ~ पीटना, = to follow the beaten path. ~ से बेलीक होना, to deviate from the path (of normal practice).

लीख *līkh* [*likṣā*-], f. a nit. — लीखें पड़ना (सिर में), to have nits or lice (in the hair).

लीचड़ *līcaṛ* [cf. *licca*-], adj. **1.** stingy. **2.** sluggish, slack. — ~ असामी, m. a bad payer (of debts).

लीचड़पन *līcaṛpan* [cf. H. *līcaṛ*], m. stinginess.

लीची *līcī* [← Chinese], f. the litchi (lychee).

लीझी *lījhī* [cf. H. *līјho*], f. reg. **1.** dregs, sediment. **2.** refuse, remains (as of plaster, or of ointment, after use).

लीझो *līјho* [**lijjha*-], adj. Brbh. without taste or substance; useless.

लीतड़ा *lītṛā* [cf. **litta*-], m. reg. an old shoe.

लीद *līd* [**lidda*-[3]], f. dung. — ~ करना, to make dung.

[1]**लीन** *līn* [*labhate* × MIA *deti* and *diṇṇa*-], perf. Brbh. taken (= लिया).

[2]**लीन** *līn* [S.], adj. **1.** immersed (in, में); dissolved; vanished (into). **2.** engrossed (in). **3.** closely connected (with). **4.** lapsed, extinguished (as a right).

लीन्ह *līnh* [*labhate* × MIA *deti* and *diṇṇa*-], perf. Brbh. Av.

लीन्हौ *līnhau*, perf. Brbh. = [1]लीन.

लीपन *līpan* [cf. H. *līpnā*], f. **1.** smearing, anointing; plastering. **2.** mortar; plaster. **3.** the refuse of mud plaster.

लीपना *līpnā* [*lipyate*], v.t. **1.** to smear. **2.** to plaster (as with mud). **3.** to whitewash. **4.** fig.

to gloss over (a shortcoming); to fudge (an account). **5.** to ruin, to destroy, to efface. — **लीप-पोतकर बराबर करना**, to raze, to level, to destroy. — **लीपा**, m. plastering, &c. **लीपा-पोती**, f. id.

लीबड़ *lībaṛ* [? H. *pīb, pīp* × *lep*], m. *Pl.* running eyes, rheum.

लीमू *līmū*, m. reg. = **नीबू**.

लीर *līr* [**līra-*; ← Panj.], f. *Pl. HŚS.* a strip of cloth (= **धज्जी**).

लील *līl*, adj. reg. blue, &c. (= [1]**नील**).

लीलना *līlnā* [**nigilati*: Pa. *niggilati*], v.t. to swallow, to bolt (food); to devour.

[1]**लीला** *līlā*, adj. = [1]**नीला**.

[2]**लीला** *līlā* [S.], f. **1.** play, sport. ***2.** the acts of a deity as performed at pleasure (esp. those of the avatārs Rām and Kr̥ṣṇa); the ways of God in the world. **3.** a wonder, an exploit. **4.** a dramatic representation, esp. of the acts of a deity. **5.** *rhet.* symbolic gestures or actions on the part of a heroine. — **~ करना**, to play, to sport; to play a part (in a drama). – **लीला गान**, m. singing the acts of a deity. **लीलाधारी**, m. one who plays a part (disguising himself); an actor, player. **लीलामय**, adj. sportive; performed by an avatār at will.

लीलावती *līlāvătī* [S.], adj. f. **1.** playful, sportive. ***2.** beautiful, charming.

लुँगाड़ा *luṁgāṛā* [cf. **luṅga-*], adj. dissolute, lewd.

लुंगी *luṅgī* [P. *lungī*], f. **1.** a rectangular cloth worn wrapped round the waist and falling to the ankles, by men. **2.** (*HŚS.*) a kind of red cloth used for the above purpose. **3.** sheet spread by barbers over their customers' legs (to catch hair).

लुंचन *luñcan* [S.], m. plucking out (hair, feathers).

लुंज *luṁj* [**luñja-*], adj. & m. **1.** adj. crippled (in hands or feet). **2.** mutilated. **3.** Brbh. leafless (a tree). **4.** m. a cripple. — **लुंज-पुंज**, adv. crippled; paralysed.

लुंठित *luṇṭhit* [S.], adj. rolled, rolling.

लुंड-मुंड *luṇḍ-muṇḍ* [cf. H. *luṇḍā* and H. *muṇḍ*], adj. reg. tailless and head(less): **1.** a mutilated torso. **2.** stripped, bare (a tree of leaves).

लुंडा *luṇḍā* [**luṇḍa-*], adj. **1.** tailless. **2.** docked (an animal).

लुंडी *luṇḍī* [conn. *luṇḍikā-*], f. a ball (of rolled thread, &c).

लुआठी *luāṭhī* [**lokakāṣṭha-*], f. *HŚS.* = **लुकाठी**.

लुआब *luāb* [A. *lu'āb*], m. **1.** spittle. **2.** mucus. — **लुआबदार** [P. *-dār*], adj. snotty, slimy.

[1]**लुक** *luk* [? *ulkā-*: MIA *ukkā-* reformed w. *l-* < *loka-*[2]], m. (f., *Pl.*) a meteor, falling star.

[2]**लुक** *luk* [A. *lukk*], m. **1.** varnish, glaze. **2.** a coating of varnish.

लुकटी *lukṭī* [? cf. H. *lakuṭ*; also H. *lukāṭhī*], f. reg. a stake burnt at one end; a firebrand.

लुकना *luknā* [cf. *lupta-*, and MIA *lukkaï*], v.i. **1.** to be hidden, to hide. **2.** to disappear. — **लुक-छिपना**, v.i. id. °-**छिपकर**, adv. secretly, furtively. – **लुका-छिपी**, f. hide-and-seek.

लुक़मा *luqmā* [A. *luqma*], m. a mouthful, morsel. — **~ देना (को)**, to give a morsel (to); to interrupt (one speaking).

लुक़मान *luqmān* [A. *luqmān*], m. name of a legendary story-teller; a wise man. — **इसका इलाज ~ से भी परे है**, he is past cure, or incorrigible.

लुकांजन *lukāñjan* [H. *lukānā*+H. *añjan*], m. *Pl.* a kind of ointment said to make one invisible when applied to the eyes.

लुकाठी *lukāṭhī* [H. *luāṭhī*; × H. *lakuṭ* w. vowel metath., or H. *kāṭh*], f. reg. a burning piece of wood.

लुकाना *lukānā* [cf. H. *luknā*], v.t. to hide, to conceal.

लुकाव *lukāv* [cf. H. *luknā*], m. *Pl.* hiding, concealment.

लुख *lukh*, m. reg. reed mace (used for matting, thatching, &c).

लुगड़ा *lugṛā* [cf. **lugga-*] m. reg. ragged cloth; old clothes, or garment.

लुगड़ी *lugṛī*, f. reg. tale-telling, slander.

लुग़त *lugat* [A. *luga*: P. *lugat*], f. U. **1.** a word. **2.** a language, dialect. **3.** a dictionary.

लुगदी *lugdī*, f. **1.** a soft, or clammy mass, or lump (as of dough, soil). **2.** papier mâché.

लुगवा *lugvā* [cf. H. *log*], m. reg. a man.

लुगाई *lugāī*, f. sometimes pej. **1.** a woman. **2.** wife. — **लुगाईवाला**, m. a married man.

लुच *luc* [**lucca-*], adj. reg. **1.** naked, bare. **2.** pure, sheer (= **निरा**) — **लुच्चा-गुंडा**, m. = **लुच्चा**.

लुचपन *lucpan*, m. reg. = **लुच्चापन**.

लुचरा *lucrā*, m. *Pl.* a spider.

लुचुई *lucuī* [cf. *-pūpa-*], f. Av. a soft, thin bread-cake of *maidā* flour, deep-fried in *ghī*.

लुच्चई *luccaī*, f. = लुच्चापन.

लुच्चा *luccā* [cf. **lucca-*], adj. & m. **1.** adj. low, base. **2.** corrupt, depraved; licentious. **3.** shameless. **4.** m. a depraved man; scoundrel.

लुच्चाई *luccāī*, f. reg. = लुच्चापन.

लुच्चापन *luccāpan* [cf. H. *luccā*], m. depravity.

लुजगुजा *lujgujā*, adj. colloq. = लिजलिजा, लुजलुजा.

लुजलुजा *lujlujā*, adj. = लिजलिजा.

लुटना *luṭnā* [cf. H. *lūṭnā*], v.i. **1.** to be plundered or looted; to be robbed. **2.** to be cheated. **3.** transf. to be squandered.

लुटवाना *luṭvānā* [cf. H. *lūṭnā*], v.t. **1.** to cause to be plundered or looted (by, से); to cause to be robbed. **2.** to cause to be cheated. **3.** to cause to be squandered.

लुटवैया *luṭvaiyā* [cf. H. *lūṭnā*], m. reg. **1.** a robber. **2.** a spendthrift.

लुटाई *luṭāī* [cf. H. *lūṭnā*], f. plunder, booty.

लुटाना *luṭānā* [cf. H. *loṭnā*], v.t. **1.** to cause to roll, or to wallow. **2.** to knock down, to bring down.

[1]**लुटाना** *luṭānā* [cf. H. *lūṭnā*], v.t. **1.** to cause to be looted, robbed; to give (a city, &c.) up to plunder. **2.** to squander (money). **3.** transf. to give (sthg.) away having no regard to its value.

[2]**लुटाना** *luṭānā* [cf. H. *loṭnā*], v.t. *Pl.* **1.** to allow (an animal) to roll or to wallow (on the ground). **2.** to bring down (quarry, with a shot).

लुटिया *luṭiyā* [cf. H. *loṭā*], f. a small metal pot. — ~ डुबोना, to sink the *loṭā*: to bring disgrace (on, अपनी/की). ~ डूबना (की), to be disgraced, ruined.

लुटेरा *luṭerā* [cf. **luṭṭati*: Pk. *luṭṭaï*], m. **1.** a plunderer, robber. **2.** swindler. **3.** fig. a waster (of money).

लुट्टस *luṭṭas* [cf. H. *lūṭ*], f. colloq. **1.** plundering, looting. **2.** devastation, ruin. — ~ मचाना, to plunder.

लुड़कना *luṛaknā*, v.i. pronun. var. = लुढ़कना.

लुड़का *luṛkā* [cf. H. *luṛhaknā*], m. reg. an ear-ring consisting of a stone set on a wire.

लुड़खुड़ी *luṛkhuṛī* [cf. H. *luṛhaknā*], f. *Pl.* falling or rolling (at the feet of): coaxing, fawning.

लुढ़कना *luṛhaknā* [cf. *luṭhati*[1]], v.i. **1.** to roll over; to topple over; to capsize. **2.** to slip or to tumble down; to fall down. **3.** to be spilt; to splash (from a container). **4.** colloq. to lie down (to rest). **5.** to drop down dead.

लुढ़कनी *luṛhkanī* [cf. H. *luṛhaknā*], f. *Pl.* the act of rolling, &c. — लुढ़कनियाँ खाना, to tumble head over heels.

लुढ़काना *luṛhkānā* [cf. H. *luṛhaknā*], v.t. **1.** to cause to roll over. **2.** to cause to slip or to slide. **3.** to spill.

लुढ़ना *luṛhnā* [*luṭhati*[1]], v.i. reg. to roll, &c. (= लुढ़कना).

लुढ़ियाना *luṛhiyānā*, v.i. *Pl. HŚS.* to hem (a garment); to seam.

लुढ़ियावन *luṛhiyāvan* [cf. H. *luṛhiyā(v)nā*], f. *Pl.* hemming; seaming.

-लुतरा *-lutrā* [**luttara-*], m. *Pl.* a tell-tale, babbler (see s.v. [2]लाई).

लुत्फ़ *lutf* [A. *lutf*], m. pleasure, enjoyment. — ~ उठाना, to take pleasure.

लुनना *lunnā* [*lunāti*], v.t. **1.** to reap. **2.** to choose, to cull. **3.** Brbh. to remove, to destroy.

लुनाई *lunāī* [cf. H. *lonā*], f. **1.** saltiness; savour. **2.** fig. charm.

लुपड़ी *lupṛī* [cf. **loppa-*], f. *Pl.* a moist lump (as of dough); a poultice.

लुप्त *lupt* [S.], adj. **1.** vanished; missing (a word from a text); lost. **2.** obsolete (a usage).

लुप्तता *luptătā* [S.], f. **1.** disappearance, absence. **2.** non-existence.

लुब्ध *lubdh* [S.], adj. eagerly desirous, covetous; lustful.

लुब्धक *lubdhak* [S.], m. **1.** a hunter. **2.** the star Sirius.

लुभाना *lubhānā* [cf. *lubhyati*], v.t. & v.i. **1.** v.t. to arouse desire in (for, पर); to entice; to charm. **2.** v.i. to feel desire (for, पर); to be tempted.

लुभाव *lubhāv* [cf. H. *lubhānā*], m. **1.** attraction. **2.** temptation. **3.** lure, bait. **4.** sthg. given additional to a purchase.

लुभावना *lubhāvnā* [cf. H. *lubhānā*], adj. tempting, seductive; charming.

लुवारा *luvārā* [? **lūṣākāra-*], m. Av. = लू.

लुहँगी *luhaṁgī*, f. reg. = लोहाँगी.

लुहंडा *luhaṇḍā*, m. reg. = लोहड़ा.

लुहार *luhār*, m. pronun. var. = लोहार.

लुहारिन *luhārin*, f. pronun. var. = लोहारिन.

लू *lū* [? conn. *lūṣā*-], f. **1.** the hot wind which blows in May and June on the north Indian plains. **2.** extreme heat. — ~ चलना, the *lū* wind to blow. ~ लगना (को), or मारना, (one) to suffer sunstroke.

[1]**लूक** *lūk* [? *ulkā*-: MIA *ukkā*- reformed with *l*- ← *loka*-[2]], m. (f.) **1.** Av. a meteor, shooting-star (= उल्का). **2.** Brbh. = लूका, 2.

[2]**लूक** *lūk* [?? ad. **lūṣā*-], f. **1.** fiery heat; blast. **2.** the hot wind of May-June (= लू).

लूकट *lūkaṭ*, m. & adj. **1.** m. a burnt stick (= लुआठी); wooden poker. **2.** adj. pej. jet-black (of complexion).

[1]**लूकना** *lūknā*, v.i. *Pl.* to be scorched by heat, or by a hot wind.

[2]**लूकना** *lūknā* [cf. H. *lūk(ā)*], v.t. reg. to set alight.

[3]**लूकना** *lūknā*, v.t. reg. to look at, to see.

लूका *lūkā* [cf. H. [1]*lūk*] m. **1.** Av. a shooting-star **2.** reg. burning stick, firebrand (cf. लुकाठी). **3.** reg. a piece of burning wood, or grass, thrown out from a fire. — ~ देना, or लगाना (में), to set alight.

लूकी *lūkī* [cf. H. *lūkā*], f. Av. a spark.

लूगा *lūgā* [**lugga*-] m. Brbh. cloth, wrapper (= लुगड़ा).

लूची *lūcī*, f. a thin, deep-fried bread-cake.

लूट *lūṭ* [cf. H. *lūṭnā*], f. **1.** plundering, looting. **2.** plunder. **3.** fig. exorbitant profit. — ~ का माल, m. ~, 2.; exorbitantly priced goods. ~ पड़ना, plundering to occur. ~ मचाना, or मारना, v.t. to plunder, to ravage. – लूट-खसोट, f. plundering, pillage; havoc; fig. exploitation. लूट-पाट, f. plundering and pillaging. लूट-मार, f. plundering and killing, looting and violence.

लूटना *lūṭnā* [**luṭṭati*: Pk. *luṭṭaï*], v.t. **1.** to plunder, to loot. **2.** to rob. **3.** to extort (money, &c.) from. **4.** to overcharge (customers). **5.** to misappropriate (funds). **6.** to revel, to delight in. — बहार ~ (की), मज़ा ~ (का), = ~, 6. लूटा-लाटी, f. = लूट-पाट s.v. लूट.

लूटी *lūṭī* [cf. H. *lūṭ*], m. reg. plunderer, looter, &c. (see लूटना).

लूत *lūt* [ad. *lūtā*-], f. Brbh. a spider.

लून *lūn* [S.], adj. **1.** cut, reaped. **2.** plucked (as flowers, fruit).

लूना *lūnā* [cf. *lavaṇa*-], m. the fruit *Anona squamosa* (= सीता-फल), or *A. reticulata*.

लूनी *lūnī* [*navanīta*-], f. reg. butter.

लूमना *lūmnā*, v.i. reg. to hang low; to lower (clouds).

लूला *lūlā* [**lulla*-], adj. & m. **1.** adj. maimed (esp. in the hands); crippled. **2.** withered, misshapen (a limb). **3.** m. a maimed or crippled person.

लूलुआ *lūluā*, m. reg. a paw.

लूलू *lūlū* [P. *lūlū*], m. reg. **1.** a goblin (or figure dressed up) to frighten children. **2.** a crazy person, fool.

लूह *lūh*, f. reg. (W). = लू.

लेंड *lemḍ* [*leṇḍa*-[2]], m. reg. a round lump of dung (as of camels, goats).

लेंड़ *lemṛ*, m. reg. = लेंड.

लेंडरा *lemḍrā* [cf. *leṇḍa*-[1]], m. reg. = [1]लेंड़ी.

[1]**लेंड़ी** *lemṛī* [cf. *leṇḍa*-[1]], adj. & m. **1.** adj. impotent. **2.** cowardly. **3.** m. an impotent man, &c.

[2]**लेंड़ी** *lemṛī* [*leṇḍa*-[2]], f. dung (as of sheep, goats).

[1]**लेंढ़ा** *lemṛhā* [**leṇḍha*-], m. reg. (W.) **1.** an empty corn-cob. **2.** smut, mildew (in wheat or barley).

[2]**लेंढ़ा** *lemṛhā*, m. reg. a small flock (of goats or sheep); a pack (of dogs).

लेंहड़ *lemhaṛ*, reg. (Bihar) a small flock (of goats or sheep).

लेंहड़ा *lemhṛā*, m. reg. a flock, pack (= [2]लेंढ़ा).

लेई *leī* [cf. *lepa*-], f. **1.** paste. **2.** mortar. — लेई-पूँजी, f. total assets (in real estate, and otherwise).

लेकिन *lekin* [A. *lākin*: P. *lekin*], conj. but; however.

लेख *lekh* [S.], m. **1.** sthg. written: an article; document; piece of writing; inscription. **2.** writing, handwriting. — लेख-पाल, m. a record-keeper. लेखबद्ध, adj. put down in writing.

लेख- *lekh*- [? cf. H. *lekhā*], v.t. Brbh. Av. **1.** to scratch; to engrave. ***2.** to consider, to estimate (as). — लेख-जोख-, to calculate; to assess.

लेखक *lekhak* [S.], m. **1.** a writer; an author. **2.** a scribe.

लेखकी *lekhăkī* [cf. H. *lekhak*], f. a writer's, or scribe's work or business; pen-pushing.

लेखन *lekhan* [S.], m. **1.** scratching (as on a writing surface). ***2.** writing. **3.** drawing, painting. **4.** calculating.

लेखनी *lekhănī* [S.], f. writing instrument; pen; artist's brush.

लेखनीय *lekhănīyă* [S.], adj. worthy of description, or record.

लेखा *lekhā* [*lekhya-*], m. **1.** an account (financial). **2.** reckoning, calculation. **3.** estimation, assessment. **उसके लेखे**, adv. in his judgment. — **~ करना (का)**, to calculate. **~ पूरा करना**, to settle an account; to close an account. **किसी लेखे नहीं**, adv. on no calculation, or account. – **लेखाकार**, m. an accountant. **लेखा-चित्र**, m. a graph. **लेखा-जोखा**, an account; a reckoning; report, account, assessment. **लेखा-पत्र**, m. correspondence, papers (on a matter). **लेखा-परीक्षक**, m. an auditor. **°-परीक्षण**, m. auditing. **लेखाबही**, f. ledger.

लेखिका *lekhikā* [S.], f. writer; authoress.

लेख्य *lekhyă* [S.], adj. & m. **1.** adj. to be written. **2.** having written form, documentary. **3.** m. a document, writing. **4.** a sketch. — **~ साक्ष्य**, m. documentary evidence.

लेज *lej* [*rajju-*], m. reg. a well-rope.

लेजुर *lejur* [*rajju-*], m. reg. = **लेज**.

लेजुरि *lejuri* [cf. H. *lejur*], f. Av. = **लेज**.

लेटना *leṭnā* [*leṭyati*], v.i. **1.** to lie down; to fall (at the feet of). **2.** to rest. **3.** to sink, to subside; to be beaten down (crops).

लेटाना *leṭānā* [cf. H. *leṭnā*], v.t. to cause (a person) to lie down; to lay (one) down.

लेत *let* [**leptra-*], m. *Pl.* plaster; paste.

लेन *len* [cf. H. *lenā*], m. **1.** taking, receiving. **2.** a sum due. — **लेनदार** [P. *-dār*], m. a creditor, a money-lender. **लेन-देन**, m. taking and giving: trade; business; dealings, intercourse (with, **से**). **लेन-देन करना**, to trade (in, **का**); to do business (with, **से**). **लेन-देन का लेखा**, m. current account.

लेना *lenā* [*labhate* × MIA *deti, neti*], v.t. **1.** to take; to receive; to accept; **मदद ~**, to receive help, to be helped. **2.** to grasp, to hold. **लाठी लिए चलना**, to walk with a stick. **3.** to obtain; to buy; to rent, or to lease; to borrow. **किराए पर ~**, to rent; to lease. **4.** to receive (arriving guests). **5.** to require, to demand (time, effort, money). **6.** to obtain, to get done (as work: by, **से**). **7.** to invoke (a name). **8.** esp. w. **लेना**. to take possession of; to capture; to conquer. **9.** to win (a game). **10.** to adopt, to take on (a manner: towards, **से**); to rebuke. **आड़े हाथों ~**, to take severely to task. **11.** to take (food or drink: esp. medicinally). **12.** to engage (an employee). **13.** to assume (a burden, a status). **व्रत ~**, to take a vow. **14.** to cut, to trim (hair, nails). **15.** to make fun of. **16.** to give or to supervise (an examination). — **~ एक न देना दो**, not to have one to receive nor two to give: to have nothing to gain or lose. **लेने के देने पड़ना**, to have to pay instead of receiving: to be drawn into an unexpected difficulty, to find the tables turned (on one); to be at death's door, past all hope. **साथ ~**, to take along (with one). – **लेना-देना**, m. = **लेन-देन**; connection, relationship, concern. – **लिए**, perf. adv. & ppn. see hw. **ले आना**, to come with, to bring (a person or thing); to produce; to import. **ले उड़ना**, to fly or to whisk away with; to abduct; to take off, to mimic. **ले चलना**, to take and go: to take away (a person or thing); to lead away. **ले जाना**, = id., 1.; to export. **ले डूबना**, to drag (another) down (with one). **ले देना (को)**, to procure (for). **ले पड़ना (को)**, to have sexual intercourse (with). **ले बीतना**, *Pl.* = **ले डूबना**. **ले बैठना**, to sit down (with); to go down with (its cargo: a ship) ; = **ले डूबना**; = ~, 5. **ले भागना**, to abduct, to kidnap (= **भगा ले जाना**). **ले मरना**, to die with. **ले रखना**, to put by; to save up. **ले रहना**, to manage to earn; to filch away. **ले-दे करना**, to exert oneself; to become involved in recriminations. **ले-दे करके**, adv. with much difficulty, somehow or other. **लेकर**, adv. having taken, &c.; taking along (with one). **से लेकर**, adv. beginning from (in space or time). **उत्तर से लेकर दक्षिण तक**, (all the way) from the north to the south. **लेते आना**, to bring, not to leave behind. **लो!** imp. & interj. take this! (in giving sthg.); take that! (a blow, &c.); behold!

लेप *lep* [*lepya-*], m. **1.** smearing. **2.** an ointment; a medicinal plaster; embrocation. **3.** plaster. **4.** whitewash.

लेपक *lepak* [S.], m. *Pl. HŚS.* a plasterer.

लेपन *lepan* [S.], m. **1.** smearing; plastering; veneering (= **लीपन**). **2.** an ointment. **3.** plaster.

लेपना *lepnā* [*lipyate* × *lepya-*], v.t. = **लीपना**, 1., 2.

लेप्य *lepyă* [S.], m. sthg. to be smeared: an ointment, plaster, &c.

लेमू *lemū*, m. reg. = **नीबू**.

लेरुआ *leruā*, m. reg. (E.) a calf.

लेरू *lerū*, m. reg. (Bihar) a calf (cf. **लवारा**).

लेला *lelā* [**lella-*[2]], m. reg. a lamb.

लेलियाना *leliyānā* [cf. H. *lelā*], v.i. reg. to bleat (a lamb).

लेव *lev* [*lepa-*], m. reg. plaster.

[1]**लेवा** *levā* [cf. H. *lenā*], m. a taker, receiver; buyer. — **नाम ~**, m. one who 'takes the name' or enquires (about, **का**).

²लेवा *levā* [*lepa-*], m. reg. **1.** plaster; ashes plastered on a new cooking-pot to protect it from fire. **2.** (Bihar) ploughing a flooded rice-field (to kill weeds); sowing in a wet field. **3.** the planks forming the bottom of a boat.

लेवार *levār*, m. reg. plaster (= ²लेवा); mud (for plastering).

लेश *leś* [S.], m. **1.** fragment. **2.** bit, whit, trace. — ~ मात्र भी नहीं, not the slightest trace (of, का).

लेस *les* [*śleṣman-*], m. **1.** stickiness. **2.** paste. — लेसदार [P. *-dār*], adj. sticky; adhesive.

¹लेसना *lesnā* [*śleṣayati*], v.t. reg. (W). **1.** to plaster (a wall or floor) with dung and mud; to daub over. **2.** fig. to foment (a quarrel).

²लेसना *lesnā* [? conn. *lasati*¹], v.t. Av. to light (a lamp).

लेसाई *lesāī*, f. *Pl.* plastering, daubing.

लेहन *lehan* [S.], m. Brbh. **1.** licking; lapping. **2.** tasting, trying.

लेहना *lehnā* [*lehana-*], m. reg. **1.** E. green chopped millet fodder. **2.** W. a portion of cut crops (payment in kind to harvesters). **3.** *Pl.* pasture.

लेही *lehī*, f. pronun. var. = लेई.

लेह्य *lehyă* [S.], adj. to be licked, or sipped.

लैंगिक *laiṅgik* [S.], adj. sexual.

लैन *lain* [Engl. *line*], f. = लाइन.

¹लैस *lais*, m. Brbh. an arrow having an elongated head.

²लैस *lais* [?? Eng. *dress*], adj. **1.** ready, prepared (as a soldier with uniform and weapon). **2.** equipped, or endowed (with, से). — ~ करना, to equip. ~ होना, to be equipped.

³लैस *lais* [Engl. *lace*], m. f. **1.** lace (embroidered). **2.** a lace (for shoes).

लों *loṁ*, ppn. Brbh. = लौं.

लोंहड़ा *loṁhṛā* [*lauhabhāṇḍa-*], m. reg. (E). = लोहड़ा.

¹लोई *loī* [*loga-*], f. a lump of dough.

²लोई *loī* [? **lomiya-*], f. a large blanket of fine wool.

³लोई *loī* [*loka-*¹], m. Brbh. Av. = लोग.

लोक *lok* [S.], m. **1.** the world; the universe. **2.** a world, cosmological region (supra- or subterranean). **3.** people, folk; the ordinary people, public; society. **4.** mankind. — लोक-कथा, f. folk-tale. लोक-गीत, m. folk-song. लोक-तंत्र, m. a democracy; democratic system. °वादी, adj. professing democracy; a democrat. °आत्मक, adj. democratic. °ई, लोक-तत्त्व, m. pl. popular features or traits (as in a work of art). लोकतांत्रिक, adj. democratic. लोक-त्रय, m. the three worlds (the heavens, earth, and nether regions), the entire universe. लोक-नाथ, m. lord of the world, &c.: a title of Brahmā, of Viṣṇu/Kr̥ṣṇa and of Śiva. लोक-निर्माण, m. *govt.* public works. लोकप, m. Av. = next. लोक-पाल, m. world-guardian: any deity presiding over a region of the universe (as Indra, Yama, Kuvera); king; *govt.* speaker of the Lok Sabhā; ombudsman. लोक-प्रिय, adj. popular. °ता, f. लोक-मत, m. popular opinion. °-मान्य, adj. widely popular or respected. लोक-लाज, f. the honour or credit of a people; regard for public opinion. लोक-सत्ता, f. a democracy. °त्मक, adj. °वादी, adj. professing democracy, democratic. लोक-सदन, m. = लोक-सभा. लोक-सभा, f. name of the lower house of the Indian Parliament. °सद, m. member of the Lok Sabhā. लोक-साहित्य, m. folk literature. लोक-सेवा, f. public or social service; national (military) service. लोक-हित, m. public or general well-being. °-हितैषी, m. & adj. altruist; altruistic. लोकांतरित [°*a*+*a*°], adj. late, deceased (= स्वर्गीय). लोकाचार [°*ka*+*ā*°], m. common usage or practice; the way of the world. °ई, adj. following usage or practice; shrewd, wise. लोकातीत [°*ka*+*a*°], adj. = लोकोत्तर. लोकापवाद [°*ka*+*a*°], m. public censure or accusation; public scandal. लोकायत [°*ka*+*ā*°], m. & adj. *philos.* a materialist; an atheist; materialism, &c. °इक, adj. & m. materialistic. लोकायतन [°*ka*+*ā*°], m. abode of man: the world. लोकोक्ति [°*ka*+*u*°], f. popular saying; proverb. लोकोत्तर [°*ka*+*u*°], adj. supernatural; transcendental. लोकोपकार [°*ka*+*u*°], m. beneficence; public well-being or interest. °ई, adj. लोकोपयोगी [°*ka*+*u*°], adj. generally useful, socially useful.

लोक- *lok-*, v.t. Brbh. to catch (sthg. falling); to snatch up.

लोकनी *loknī* [? cf. H. *lok*], f. reg. a servant-girl.

लोकाट *lokāṭ* [Engl. *loquat*: ← Chinese], m. the loquat tree, *Eriobotrya japonica*, and its fruit.

लोखंड *lokhaṇḍ* [**lohopaskara-* × *lauhabhāṇḍa-*; Pa. *lohabhaṇḍa-*], m. reg. (W). = लोखर.

लोखड़ी *lokhṛī*, f. a fox (= लोमड़ी).

लोखर *lokhar* [**lohopaskara-*], m. reg. (W). **1.** iron tools, implements. **2.** hardware; pots and pans.

लोग *log* [*loka-*¹; Pk. *loga-*], m. f. pl. **1.** people, folk. **2.** members of any group of people. — आप ~, pl. hon. you. – पुरुष ~, m. pl. men, menfolk; the menfolk (of a partic. group). बड़े

~, m. pl. grown-ups; important people. साधु ~, m. pl. holy men (as a class). – लोग-बाग [*-varga-*], m. people, ordinary people. लोग-लुगाई, f. men and women. लोग-हँसाई, f. cause for popular mockery; general ridicule.

लोगाई *logāī*, f. = लुगाई.

लोच *loc*, m. **1.** suppleness; flexibility, plasticity (as of dough). **2.** softness, tenderness (of a glance). — लोचदार [P. *-dār*], adj. supple, flexible, elastic.

लोचन *locan* [S.], m. **1.** the eye. **2.** sight. — लोचन-गोचर, adj. Av. = दृष्टिगोचर. लोचन-मग, m. Av. path of sight: the glance.

लोचना *locnā* [*locyate*], v.t. to desire, to long.

1**लोट** *loṭ* [cf. H. *loṭnā*], f. **1.** rolling or tossing about. **2.** wallowing. **3.** a roll. — ~ मारना, = next; fig. to be infatuated (by, one, पर). ~ लगाना, to lie down. – लोट-पुटिया, m. reg. watercresses. लोट-पोट, f. = ~, 1., 2.; helpless (as with laughter); restless, agitated. लोट-पोट करना, to roll about, &c. जी लोट-पोट हो जाना, to be delighted, thrilled.

2**लोट** *loṭ* [Engl. *note*], m. corr. a note; bank-note.

लोटन *loṭan* [cf. H. *loṭnā*], m. **1.** rolling. **2.** tumbling. **3.** a kind of pigeon, a tumbling pigeon.

लोटना *loṭnā* [**lortati*: Pk. *loṭṭaï*], v.t. **1.** to roll about, to toss about. **2.** to wallow. **3.** to flounce. **4.** to sprawl. **5.** to be turned or blunted, to yield (an iron blade). **6.** fig. Brbh. to be strongly attracted (to). — लोट जाना, to roll, &c.; to lie or to throw oneself down and roll over (as when sulking); to have been beaten down (as corn by rain); to fall (at, में: as at one's feet); to die (for, पर); to be ruined, or bankrupt.

लोटनी *loṭnī* [cf. H. *loṭnā*], f. reg. **1.** rolling or tossing (on a bed, or on the ground). **2.** wallowing; floundering. — लोटनियाँ खाना, to be restless (from pain, or anxiety).

लोटा *loṭā* [**loṭṭa-*[3]], m. a small round pot (usu. of brass or copper). — ~ उठाना, to perform menial services (for, का).

लोटा-सज्जी *loṭā-sajjī* [cf. *sarjikā-*], f. *Pl.* a kind of soil containing fossil alkali.

लोढ़ना *loṛhnā* [*loṭhayati*], v.t. **1.** to beat; to scutch (cotton). **2.** to glean. **3.** to hem (a garment).

लोढ़ा *loṛhā* [*loṭha-*], m. a stone pestle.

लोढ़िया *loṛhiyā*, f. reg. 1. = लोढ़ा. 2. = लोढ़ी. **3.** a hem; seam.

लोढ़ी *loṛhī* [cf. H. *loṛhnā*], f. reg. **1.** a stone for grinding spices. **2.** *Pl.* a machine for cleaning cotton. **3.** W. the horizontal part of a plough. **4.** Bihar. gleanings.

लोथ *loth* [**lottha-*[2]], f. a corpse. — ~ गिरना, to fall in battle. ~ डालना, to strike (one) dead. ~ पड़ना, to fall down dead. मिसले ~, adv. like a corpse: inertly. – लोथ-पोथ होना, colloq. to be exhausted.

लोथड़ा *lothṛā* [**lottha-*[2]], m. a lump of flesh (= बोटी).

लोथा *lothā* [*lottha-*[3]], m. *Pl.* a bag, sack.

लोथी *lothī* [**lottha-*[2]], f. a knotted staff or club.

लोदी *lodī*, m. = लोधी.

लोध *lodh* [*lodhra-*], m. a small tree, *Symplocos racemosa*, the bark of which yields a yellow dye; it is also used as a mordant with other dyes, as well as in medicine.

लोधी *lodhī*, m. name of a farming community of north-west India.

लोन *lon* [*lavaṇa-*], m. salt. — ~ खाना, to eat the salt (of, का): to be a dependant (of). ~ न मानना, fig. to be ungrateful to a benefactor. — लोन-मिर्च लगाना to apply salt and chilli (to, में): to spice (food); to use savorous language. लोन-हरामी, f. faithlessness to one's salt, ingratitude to a benefactor.

लोन- *lon-* [H. *lunnā* × H. *lav-*], v.t. Brbh. to reap.

लोना *lonā* [*lavaṇa-*], adj. & m. reg. **1.** adj. salty; savorous. **2.** saline (land). **3.** fig. attractive, charming. **4.** m. efflorescent salt (as found on walls, &c).

लोनी *lonī*, f. Av. = लुनाई.

लोनार *lonār*, m. reg. (W). **1.** a salt-pit. **2.** *Pl.* saline land or soil.

लोनिया *loniyā* [*lavaṇita-*], adj. & m. reg. **1.** adj. salty; saline. **2.** an acid pot-herb, purslain, *Portulaca oleracea*. **3.** a salt-maker, or trader in salt.

1**लोनी** *lonī* [*lavaṇa-*], f. reg. = लोना, 4.

2**लोनी** *lonī* [*navanīta-*], f. reg. butter.

लोप *lop* [S.], m. **1.** disappearance; dropping out, omission. 2. *ling.* elision. — ~ तारा, m. the disappearing star: the planet Neptune (= अंधा तारा).

लोपन *lopan* [S.], m. **1.** concealing, concealment. **2.** destroying, destruction.

लोबान *lobān* [A. *lubān*], m. a gum-resin, used as incense and medicinally.

लोबिया *lobiyā* [P. *lobiyǎ*], m. **1.** a pulse. **2.** specif. the cow-pea, *Vigna catjang*. **3.** (?) the bean *Dolichos lablab*.

लोभ *lobh* [S.], m. **1.** intense desire, covetousness, greed. **2.** avarice. **3.** temptation. — ~ करना, to be greedy (for, का), &c.

लोभ- *lobh-* [*lobhyate*], v.i. Brbh. Av. to feel desire or greed for.

लोभनीय *lobhǎnīyǎ* [S.], adj. tempting, inviting.

लोभा- *lobhā-*], v.i. Brbh. Av. = लोभ-.

लोभित *lobhit* [S.], adj. Brbh. Av. desirous, longing.

लोभी *lobhī* [S.], adj. & m. **1.** adj. desirous (of, का), covetous, greedy. **2.** avaricious. **3.** m. a covetous, or avaricious man.

लोम *lom* [S.], m. = रोम.

लोमड़ी *lomṛī* [**lompaṭa-*], f. a fox.

लोमश *lomaś* [S.], adj. & m. **1.** adj. hairy, shaggy; woolly; bristly; downy. **2.** m. *mythol.* name of a sage.

लोयन *loyan* [*locana-*], m. Av. the eye.

लोर *lor* [**loḍa-*, *lola-*], adj. & m. Brbh. **1.** adj. moving, unsteady. **2.** m. a tear.

लोर- *lor-* [conn. *loṭati*], v.i. Brbh. to bow down; to bend (branches).

[1]**लोरी** *lorī* [**loḍa-*, *lola-*], f. a lullaby.

[2]**लोरी** *lorī*, f. reg. the large Indian parakeet.

लोल *lol* [S.], adj. & m. **1.** adj. shaking, trembling; tremulous. **2.** rippling, dancing (waves). **3.** rolling (the eyes). **4.** fickle, changeable. **5.** eager. **6.** m. an ear pendant.

लोल- *lol-* [*loḍayati*], v.t. Brbh. **1.** to cause to shake. **2.** to move, to roll (the eyes).

लोलक *lolak* [S.], m. **1.** a pendant (from the ear, or nose). **2.** a pendulum.

लोलकी *lolkī*, f. **1.** *Pl.* a small ear pendant. **2.** the lobe of the ear.

[1]**लोला** *lolā* [**loḍa-*, *lola-*], m. **1.** pendant (of an ear-ring). **2.** a bell-clapper. **3.** penis (of a boy).

[2]**लोला** *lolā* [S.], f. **1.** *Pl. HŚS.* the tongue. **2.** *Pl.* the uvula.

लोलुप *lolup* [S.], adj. **1.** desirous, eager. **2.** greedy, covetous.

लोलुपता *lolupǎtā* [S.], f. eager desire, &c. (see लोलुप).

लोवा *lovā* [**lomaka-*], m. Av. a fox (= लोमड़ी).

लोह *loh* [S.], m. **1.** iron; steel. **2.** fig. Brbh. a weapon. — लोहकार, m. a blacksmith. लोह-चून, m. iron filings. °-चूर्ण, m. id. लोहमय, adj. made of iron; rich in iron.

लोहड़ा *lohaṛā* [**lohaghaṭa-*], m. an iron pot.

लोहाँगी *lohāṁgī* [**lauhāṅgika-*], f. *Pl. HŚS.* a staff tipped with iron; an iron bar, crowbar.

लोहा *lohā* [*loha-*], m. **1.** iron; steel. पक्का ~, m. steel. **2.** fig. a weapon, blade; arms. **3.** an iron (for clothes: = इस्तरी). — ~ करना, to iron. ~ बजना, weapons to clash, a fight to be joined. ~ मानना, to acknowledge the calibre (of, का); to acknowledge the strength or superiority (of). ~ लेना (का), to size up (an adversary); to measure up (to), to be the equal (of). लोहे का, adj. made of iron; hard; firm; strong; adamant. लोहे का चना iron gram: a hard nut (to crack). कच्चा ~, m. iron ore.

लोहागी *lohāgī*, f. *HŚS.* = लोहाँगी.

लोहाना *lohānā* [cf. H. *lohā*], v.i. to be tainted by metal (food).

लोहार *lohār* [*lohakāra-*], m. a blacksmith. — ~ की भट्ठी, f. a forge; furnace. – लोहार-ख़ाना, m. a smithy. लोहार-ख़ाने में सुइयाँ बेचना, to sell needles at a blacksmith's: to carry coals to Newcastle.

लोहारिन *lohārin* [cf. H. *lohār*], f. a blacksmith's wife.

लोहित *lohit* [S.], adj. & m. **1.** adj. red. **2.** m. red (colour); Av. the planet Mars. **3.** blood.

लोहिया *lohiyā* [? cf. H. *lohā*], adj. & m. **1.** adj. made of iron. **2.** m. an iron-worker, or trader of iron goods. **3.** specif. name of a trading community.

लोही *lohī* [*lohita-*], f. **1.** redness, flush (of the sky before dawn); dawn. **2.** flash (as of lightning); light (of flames). **3.** splendour (of face or expression). **4.** *Pl.* (? = [2]लोई) a kind of silk cloth.

लोहू *lohū* [*lohita-*], m. = लहू.

लौं *lauṁ*, ppn. Brbh. = लग.

लौंग *lauṁg* [*lavaṅga-*], f. **1.** the clove-tree. **2.** a clove. **3.** transf. a nose or ear ornament.

लौंगरा *lauṁgrā*, m. reg. name of a grass that grows during the rains.

लौंजी *lauṁjī*, f. sliced mango pieces for pickling; pickle.

लौंडपन *lauṁḍpan* [cf. H. *lauṁḍā*], m. boyishness, childishness.

लौंडा *laumḍā* [**lavaṇḍa-*], m. **1.** a boy, lad; brat. **2.** servant-boy. — **लौंडबाज़** [P. *-bāz*], m. = next. °**ई**, f. see next. **लौंडेबाज़** [P. *-bāz*], m. a homosexual man. °**ई**, f. homosexuality.

लौंडापन *laumḍāpan* [cf. H. *laumḍā*], m. = **लड़कपन**.

लौंडिया *laumḍiyā*, f. 1. = **लौंडी**, 1., 2. **2.** pej. = **लौंडी**, 3.

लौंडी *laumḍī* [**lavaṇḍa-*], f. **1.** a girl; daughter. **2.** a servant-girl. **3.** pej. a promiscuous woman.

लौंद *laumd*, m. an intercalary month (= **मलमास**). — ~ **का महीना**, m., id.

लौंदरा *laumdrā*, m. reg. (W.) a shower towards the end of the hot weather.

लौंदा *laumdā* [**londa-*], m. a lump (as of earth, or of butter); clod.

[1]**लौ** *lau*, f. a flame, tongue of flame. — ~ **उठना**, or **निकलना**, to blaze.

[2]**लौ** *lau* [*laya-*], m. **1.** absorption of mind; deep meditation. **2.** inclination. **3.** attachment; desire, longing; devotion. **4.** frequent and continued repetition (as of the name of God by a dying man, or by a devotee, or of a beloved's name by her lover). — ~ **लगना** (**को**), to be absorbed or intent (in or on, **की**); to desire passionately; to repeat with feeling (words of devotion). ~ **लगाना**, to fix the mind (on, **से**), to be intent (on). — **लौ-लीन**, adj. engrossed, absorbed utterly.

[3]**लौ** *lau*, f. lobe (of the ear).

लौआ *lauā* [*alābu-*: ← Austro-as.], m. a gourd.

लौकड़ा *laukṛā* [? H. *laumḍā*×H. *laṛkā*], m. *Pl.* boy, lad (esp. as an attendant on a goddess).

लौकना *lauknā*, v.i. reg. to flash, to shine.

[1]**लौका** *laukā*, m. the bottle-gourd (= **लौकी**).

[2]**लौका** *laukā*, m. *Pl.* lighting, flash.

लौकिक *laukik* [S.], adj. **1.** of this world; worldly (knowledge, power, pomp); secular, temporal. **2.** ordinary, mundane; customary.

लौकिकता *laukikătā* [S.], f. **1.** worldliness. **2.** worldly currency or custom.

लौकी *laukī* [cf. *alābu-*: ← Austro-as.], f. the bottle-gourd, *Lagenaria vulgaris*.

लौट *lauṭ* [cf. H. *lauṭnā*], f. (m., *Pl.*) **1.** return. **2.** turning over. — **लौट-पौट**, f. & adv. turning (sthg.) over; (printing cloth) on both sides; confusion, disorder. **लौट-फेर**, f. = **लौट-पौट**, 3.

लौटना *lauṭnā* [conn. H. *ulaṭnā* (cf. H. *lauṭ*, 2.)], v.i. **1.** to return, to go back. **2.** to go back (from or on, **से**: as on a promise). **3.** to turn over. — **पीछे** ~, = ~, 1.

लौटाना *lauṭānā* [cf. H. *lauṭnā*], v.t. **1.** to cause to return; to bring back; to give or to send back, to return (to, **को**). **2.** to turn over. **3.** to send away (as a petitioner, empty-handed); to reject.

लौठा *lauṭhā*, m. reg. a boor; lout.

लौड़ा *lauṛā* [*lakuṭa-*], m. colloq. penis.

लौदरा *laudrā*, m. reg. (W.) stalks (as of pulse, cotton) used for thatching, or basketmaking.

लौनी *launī* [cf. *lavana-*], f. reg. **1.** the harvest. **2.** wages for harvesting. **3.** payment in kind for harvesting.

लौस *laus* [A. *laus̱*], m. poet. contamination, impurity.

लौह *lauh* [S.], adj. & m. **1.** adj. made of iron. **2.** m. iron. **3.** metal. — **लौहावरण** [°*ha* + *ā*°], m. *mil.* armour-plating.

लौहड़ा *lauhṛā* [cf. *laghu-*], adj. & m. reg. **1.** adj. younger, junior. **2.** a younger son.

ल्हेसना *lhesnā*, v.t. pronun. var. = [1]**लेसना**, 1.

व

व *va*, the twenty-ninth consonant of the Devanāgarī syllabary. वकार, m. the sound /v/; the letter व.

वंका *vaṅkā* [S.], f. *Pl. HŚS.* curved: the pommel of a saddle.

वंकिम *vaṅkim* [S.], adj. **1.** curved, bent. **2.** attractive (the eyes).

वंग *vaṅg* [S.], m. Bengal. — वंग-भंग, m. the partition of Bengal.

वंगीय *vaṅgīyă* [S.], adj. having to do with Bengal (a society, &c).

वंचक *vañcak* [S.], m. a deceiver, cheat; villain.

वंचन *vañcan* [S.], m. = वंचना. — कर-वंचन, m. tax evasion.

वंचना *vañcănā* [S.], f. deceiving, cheating; deception.

वंचित *vañcit* [S.], adj. **1.** deceived, tricked (by man, or fate). **2.** deprived (of, से).

वंट *vaṇṭ* [S.], m. part, share.

वंटक *vaṇṭak* [S.], m. one who distributes or apportions.

वंटन *vaṇṭan* [S.], m. apportionment, distribution (as of land).

-वंत *-vant* [S.], suffix. = -वान.

वंदन *vandan* [S.], m. **1.** praising. **2.** praise; adoration. **3.** homage; reverential greeting (as by touching the feet). — ~ कर-, Brbh. to adore, to pay homage (to). – वंदन-माला, f. = next. वंदनवार [°*-mālā*], f. festoon of leaves and flowers (hung across gateways or in pavilions on festive occasions: = बंदनवार).

वंदना *vandănā* [S.], f. = वंदन, 2., 3.; prayer.

वंदनीय *vandănīyă* [S.], adj. **1.** praiseworthy, &c. (see वंदन). **2.** worthy of honour.

वंदित *vandit* [S.], adj. **1.** praised; adored. **2.** shown honour.

वंदी *vandī* [S.], m. a panegyrist; bard.

वंद्य *vandyă* [S.], adj. = वंदनीय.

वंश *vaṃś* [S.], m. **1.** a bamboo. **2.** a pipe, flute. **3.** family line or succession, family; offspring; dynasty. **4.** fig. breed, pedigree. — वंश-क्रम, m. family succession; genealogy. °आगत, adj. obtained by inheritance, hereditary. वंशगत, adj. = वंशागत. वंशज, m. descendant. वंशधर, m. id. वंश-परंपरा, f. family succession; heredity; °गत, adj. वंशागत [°*śa*+*ā*°], adj. obtained by right of birth: ancestral, hereditary. वंशावली [°*śa*+*ā*°], f. family line, genealogy.

वंशिक *vaṃśik* [S.], adj. **1.** pertaining to a family. **2.** lineal; genealogical.

वंशी *vaṃśī* [S.], f. pipe, flute. — वंशीधर, m. flute-holder: a title of Kr̥ṣṇa. °-धारी, m. id.

-वंशी *-vaṃśī* [ad. *vaṁśin-*, or cf. H. *vaṃś*], adj. formant. pertaining to, or belonging to a family. e.g. रघुवंशी, of the family of Raghu.

व *va* [A. *va*], conj. and. — दिन में ~ रात में, adv. by day and by night. नाम ~ पता, m. name and address.

वक *vak* [S.], m. a heron, or crane (= [1]बक). — वकाली (for वकावली: [°*ka*+*ā*°]), f. a line of flying cranes. वकासुर [°*ka*+*a*°], m. crane-demon: a demon killed by Kr̥ṣṇa.

वक़अत *vaqa'at* [cf. A. *vaq'a*], f. U. **1.** weight, force. **2.** regard, consideration, esteem. — ~ की निगाह से देखना, to regard with esteem, to set value on. ~ रखना, to carry weight; to command attention or consideration.

वकालत *vakālat* [A. *vakāla*: P. *vakālat*], f. **1.** the profession of a lawyer, practice at the bar. **2.** pleading or arguing (any case), advocacy. — ~ करना, to plead a case (on behalf of, की तरफ़ से); to advocate (any case or cause, की). – वकालत-नामा, m. power of attorney.

वकील *vakīl* [A. *vakīl*], m. one entrusted: **1.** a lawyer; barrister; solicitor. **2.** agent, representative. — ~ करना, to appoint (one) a *vakīl*; to declare one to be a representative (of).

वकीली *vakīlī* [A. *vakīl*+P. *-ī*], f. = वकालत.

वक़ूफ़ *vaqūf* [A. *vuqūf*], m. U. **1.** knowledge. **2.** sense, intelligence. **3.** experience.

वक़्त *vaqt* [A. *vaqt*], m. **1.** time; period of time. **2.** fixed or proper time, season (for); apppointed hour (of death). **3.** occasion, opportunity. **4.** fig. adversity, distress. — ~ आना, or आ पहुँचना, an appointed time to arrive; (one's) days to be numbered. ~ का, adj. belonging to a time; fashionable, the rage, a hit (as a song); occurring in season. ~ का पाबंद, adj. bound by or observant of time: punctual.

~ काटना, or गुज़ारना, to spend time; to kill time. ~ खोना, to waste time. ~ पड़ना, occasion or need to arise; misfortune to befall (one, पर). ~ पर, adv. on time, punctually; just at the right time, in the nick of time; in due time. ~ बराबर आ जाना, (one's) days to be numbered. ~ बवक़्त [P. *ba-*], adv. from time to time. ~ बेवक़्त [P. *be-*], adv. in and out of season, at all times, constantly. ~ हाथ से देना, to lose an opportunity. ~ हाथ से न देना, not to lose an opportunity; not to let time slip by. इस ~, adv. at this time, now; for or on this occasion. किस ~? at what time? when? ऐन ~ पर, adv. in the nick of time.

वक्तव्य *vaktavyă* [S.], m. to be spoken: **1.** speech, utterance. **2.** an utterance, remarks, statement (on a topic); communiqué. — वक्तव्य-शास्त्र, m. the science of rhetoric.

वक्ता *vaktā* [S.], m. inv. **1.** a speaker. **2.** an eloquent person.

वक्तृता *vaktṛtā* [S.], f. **1.** a speech; lecture. **2.** eloquence.

वक्त्र *vaktră* [S.], m. **1.** mouth. **2.** muzzle. — वक्त्र-ताल, m. musical time as indicated by spoken syllables, &c. (as opposed to beats).

वक़्फ़ *vaqf* [A. *vaqf*], m. U. **1.** an endowment (religious or charitable). **2.** making a bequest or donation (for religious or charitable purposes).

वक़्फ़ा *vaqfā* [A. *vaqfa*], m. pause; respite; interval.

वक्र *vakr* [S.], adj. & m. **1.** adj. crooked; winding, meandering. **2.** curved, bent; crescent (moon). **3.** devious. **4.** oblique (as a glance); malevolent. **5.** m. winding course (of a river); bend. **6.** *math.* a curve. — ~ गति, f. crooked or zigzag movement, &c.; retrogression (of a planet); modish airs or ways. — वक्रगामी, adj. moving crookedly, &c.; devious. वक्रोक्ति [°*ra*+*u*°], f. indirect speech or expression: *double entendre*; pun; insinuation.

वक्रता *vakrătā* [S.], f. crookedness, &c. (see वक्र).

वक्रिम *vakrim* [S.], adj. **1.** crooked. **2.** devious.

वक्री *vakrī* [S.], adj. 1. = वक्र, 1.-3. **2.** retrogressing (a planet).

वक्ष *vakṣ* [S.], m. **1.** the breast, chest, bosom. **2.** *med.* thorax. — वक्ष-स्थल, m. region of the breast: id. वक्षस्थल पर आघात, m. a mortal blow. वक्षोज [°*as*+-*ja*], m. poet. woman's breast.

वक्षः- *vakṣaḥ-* [S]. see वक्षः — वक्षःस्थल, m. the breast.

वखत *vakhat*, m. pronun. var. reg. = वक़्त.

वग़ैरह *vagairah* [A. *va gairu hu*: P. *va gaira*], adv. and the rest, and so on. — ~ ~, adv. and so on and so forth.

वग़ैरा *vagairā*, adv. pronun. var. = वग़ैरह.

वच *vac* [S.], m. the sweet-flag, *Acorus calamus*; orris-root (= बच). — बाल-वच, m. rhizome(s) of sweet-flag (used medicinally).

वचन *vacan* [S.], m. **1.** speech. **2.** word. **3.** declaration, affirmation. **4.** promise. **5.** *gram.* number. — ~ देना, to give (one's) word. ~ तोड़ना, to break (one's) word. ~ निभाना, to keep (one's) word. ~ पूरा करना, to fulfil a promise. ~ लेना, to obtain a promise (from, से). – वचनदत्त, adj. whose word is given: engaged; married.

वचवचाना *vacvacānā*, v.t. reg. = वटवटाना.

वचा *vacā*, f. *Pl. HŚS.* = वच, बच.

वजड़ी *vajṛī*, f. reg. the intestines: — वजड़ी-बोटी, f. tripe.

वज़न *vazn* [A. *vazn*], m. **1.** weight; displacement (of a ship). **2.** weighing. **3.** a measure of weight. **4.** fig. authority, standing, influence. **5.** significance (as of a contribution). — ~ करना (का), to weigh. ~ रखना, to be weighty, heavy; to carry weight. – वज़नदार [P. -*dār*], adj. weighty, heavy; of full weight; authoritative; significant.

वज़नी *vaznī* [A. *vaznī*], adj. **1.** weighty. **2.** important.

वजह *vajah* [A. *vajh*], f. face, aspect: cause; reason. — इस ~ से, adv. because of this, for this reason. किस ~? adv. why?

वज़ा *vazā* [A. *vaẓ'*], m. inv. U. **1.** nature. **2.** state. **3.** appearance. ***4.** mode, manner, way. — वज़ादारी [P. -*dārī*], f. style, elegance.

वज़ारत *vazārat* [A. *vazāra*: P. *vazārat*], f. **1.** the office, duties or status of a vizier, or (U.) of a government minister. **2.** U. *govt.* ministry.

वज़ीफ़ा *vazīfā* [A. *vaẓīfa*], m. **1.** a scholarship, bursary. **2.** stipend, allowance (to a dependant). **3.** *musl.* sthg. stipulated: daily worship. — ~ पढ़ना, to read or to repeat (one's) daily prayers. – वज़ीफ़ादार [P. -*dār*], m. one holding an allowance, &c.

वज़ीर *vazīr* [A. *vazīr*], m. **1.** vizier. **2.** U. *govt.* minister. **3.** (in chess) the queen. **3.** (at cards) the jack. — वज़ीरे-आज़म [P. -*e*-, A. *a'ẓam*], m. U. Prime Minister.

वज़ीरी *vazīrī* [P. *vazīrī*], f. **1.** status or office of vizier, or of minister of state. **2.** *Pl.* ministry (= वज़ारत).

वज़ू *vazū* [A. *vaẓū'*: P. *vuẓū*], m. ritual ablution of hands, face, arms and feet, in that order, performed by Muslims before prayer.

वजूद *vajūd* [A. *vujūd*], m. **1.** E.H. existence; body, birth. **2.** transf. personal integrity.

वज्र *vajră* [S.], m. & adj. **1.** m. a thunderbolt. **2.** *mythol.* the thunderbolt of Indra (which becomes also an emblem of Kr̥ṣṇa). **3.** lightning. **4.** diamond. **5.** adj. very hard, adamantine. **6.** dire, fearsome; arrant (a fool). — **वज्रधर**, m. holder of the thunderbolt: a title of Indra. **वज्र-पात**, m. fall of a thunderbolt; a stroke of lightning; a sudden disaster. **वज्रसार**, adj. having the essence of a diamond: very hard. **वज्राग्नि**, f. E.H. lightning and thunder. **वज्राभ्र** [°*ra*+*a*°], m. black mica. **वज्रावर्त** [°*ra*+*ā*°], m. Brbh. a swirling and fearsome cloud.

वज्रता *vajrătā* [S.], f. hardness; severity.

वज्री *vajrī* [S.], f. a small tree found in dry regions, *Euphorbia antiquorum* (often used as a hedge plant).

वट *vaṭ* [S.], m. a banyan tree.

वटका *vaṭkā* [? **varta-*²: Pk. *vaṭṭa-*], m. reg. a piece.

वटवट *vaṭvaṭ* [cf. H. *vaṭvaṭanā*], f. reg. nonsense, drivel.

वटवटाना *vaṭvaṭānā*, v.i. reg. to talk nonsense.

वटिका *vaṭikā* [S.], f. a (round) tablet, pill.

वटी *vaṭī* [ad. *vaṭikā-*], f. a globule, lump; (round) tablet, pill; a bead.

वटु *vaṭu* [S.], m. = **वटुक**.

वटुक *vaṭuk* [S.], m. a youth, esp. a brāhmaṇ student (of traditional learning).

वड़िस *vaṛis* [ad. *vaḍiśa-*], m. reg. a fish-hook.

वणिक *vaṇik* [S.], m. merchant, trader.

-वत *-vat*, suffix. = **-वत्**.

-वत् *-vat* [S.], suffix (forms a few adverbs, and compounding forms of nouns and adjectives in -**वान**, e.g. **विद्वत्-समाज**, m. a learned assembly).

वतन *vatan* [A. *vaṭan*], m. U. native country, country. — **वतन-परस्त** [P. *-parast*], m. worshipper of one's country: a patriot. °**ई**, f. patriotism.

वतनी *vatănī* [A. *vaṭanī*], adj. belonging to or having to do with one's native country. — **हमवतनी** [P. *ham-*], m. fellow-countryman.

वत्स *vats* [S.], m. **1.** a calf. **2.** (as an endearment) dear child.

वत्सर *vatsar* [S.], m. a year.

वत्सल *vatsal* [S.], adj. **1.** fond of children (esp. one's own); loving, tender. **2.** indulgent to a child. — **भक्त-वत्सल**, m. loving towards devotees (a god: esp. Kr̥ṣṇa).

वत्सलता *vatsalătā* [S.], f. = **वात्सल्य**.

वदन *vadan* [S.], m. **1.** the face. **2.** mouth. **3.** front part (of sthg).

वदि *vadi* [S.], f. = ¹**बदी**.

वदान्य *vadānyă* [S.], adj. generous.

वध *vadh* [S.], m. **1.** killing, slaying. **2.** slaughter. — **जन-वध**, m. genocide.

वधक *vadhak* [S.], m. **1.** a killer. **2.** a hunter.

वधू *vadhū* [S.], f. bride, young wife; son's wife (in a joint family).

वधूटी *vadhūṭī* [S.], f. = **वधू**.

वध्य *vadhyă* [S.], adj. to be killed.

वन *van* [S.], m. **1.** forest, jungle; scrub-land; thicket. — **वनचर**, adj. & m. roaming or living in a forest; a wild animal; = **वन-मानुष**. **वनेचर**, m. obs. id. **वनजीवी**, m. forest-dwelling: a forester, wood-cutter, &c. **वनपाल**, m. a forester. **वन-मानुष**, m. jungle-man: a wild man of the woods. **वन-माला**, f. garland of forest flowers. °-**माली**, adj. & m. wearing a garland; a title of Kr̥ṣṇa. **वन-यात्रा**, f. circumambulation of the region of Braj around Vrindaban via its eighty-four sacred localities. **वनरोपण**, m. afforestation. **वन-वसना**, whose robe is the forest: the earth. **वन-वास**, m. residence in, or banishment to, a forest region (also transf). °**ई**, adj. & m. **वनांत** [°*na*+*a*°], m. edge, or neighbourhood, of a forest. **वनाश्रम** [°*na*+*ā*°] m. forest abode: the forest stage, (traditional third stage) of a brāhmaṇ's life. **वनस्पति**, m. see s.v.

वनस्पति *vanaspati* [S.], m. lord of the forest, large tree: **1.** vegetation. **2.** flora. 3. = ~ **घी**. — ~ **घी**, m. *ghī* made from vegetable fats. ~ **तेल**, m. vegetable oil. – **वनस्पतिजन्य**, adj. *bot.* vegetable (a substance). **वनस्पतिज्ञ**, m. a botanist. **वनस्पति-विज्ञान**, m. botany.

वनानी *vanānī* [? *vanāni*, pl.], f. poet. forests, forest region.

वनिता *vanitā* [S.], f. loved one: **1.** wife; mistress. **2.** woman, lady.

वन्य *vanyă* [S.], adj. **1.** having to do with a forest; found or living in a forest; wild (beasts). **2.** forested, wooded (a region). — **वन्यचर**, m. = **वनचर**, see. s.v. **वन**.

वपन *vapan* [S.], m. sowing.

वपु *vapu* [S.], m. the body.

वफ़ा *vafā* [A. *vafā*], f. keeping faith, faithfulness (to a commitment or obligation). — ~ करना, to keep faith (with, से), to be loyal or true; to perform a promise, &c. – वफ़ादार [P. *-dār*], adj. faithful, trusty, loyal. °ई, f. fidelity, &c.

वफ़ाई *vafāī* [A. *vafā*+P. *-ī*], f. esp. in comp. = वफ़ा.

वफ़ात *vafāt* [A. *vafāt*], f. U. death. — ~ पाना, to die.

वबा *vabā* [A. *vabā*], f. U. an epidemic; specif. plague; cholera.

वबाल *vabāl* [A. *vabāl*], m. U. sthg. painful or distressing: turmoil, furore.

वमन *vaman* [S.], m. **1.** vomiting; nausea. **2.** an emetic. — ~ करना, to vomit. – वमनकारी, adj. emetic.

वमि *vami* [S.], f. *Pl. HŚS.* vomiting.

वय *vay* [S.], m. age (= वयस्).

वयन *vayan* [S.], m. weaving; weave, texture.

वयस् *vayas* [S.], m. f. age; age reached, time of life.

वयस्क *vayask* [S.], adj. **1.** adult. **2.** -वयस्क. of a partic. age (e.g. अल्पवयस्क, of tender years).

वयस्कता *vayaskătā* [S.], f. adult status, majority.

वयस्य *vayasyă* [S.], m. **1.** a contemporary. **2.** a companion.

वयस्या *vayasyā* [S.], f. **1.** a contemporary. **2.** a companion (= सखी).

वयो- *vayo-* [S]. = वयस्: — वयोवृद्ध, adj. elderly, aged.

वरंडा *varaṇḍā* [Engl. *verandah*], m. verandah (= बरामदा).

वरंच *varaṁ-că* [S.], adv. but rather, but (cf. -वर).

वर *var* [S.], adj. & m. **1.** adj. best, choice; excellent, fine. **2.** m. also fig. -वर. boon, blessing; best (of); gift (chosen by recipient). प्रियवर, m. dear one, dear friend. **3.** bridegroom; husband. — ~ देना (को), to grant a boon; to donate (to). ~ होना (को), to have received as a boon. – वरदान, m. the granting of a boon or request; benefaction. वर-दिखावा, m. arranging a daughter's meeting with her prospective bridegroom. वर-पक्ष, m. bridegroom's relatives (at a wedding and its preliminaries). वर-यात्रा, f. = बरात. वरासन [°*ra*+*ā*°], m. seat of honour; throne; bridegroom's seat (at a wedding). वरोरु [°*ra*+*ū*°], adj. Av. having shapely thighs.

-वर *-var* [P. *-var*], suffix (forms adjectives, chiefly, having the sense 'characterised by ...', e.g. नामवर, adj. having a name, famous; जानवर, m. animal.

वरक़ *varăq* [A. *varaq*], m. **1.** U. leaf (of a tree); petal (of a flower). **2.** leaf (of a book, or of metal, esp. silver or gold). **3.** a thin slice. — ~ उतारना, to cut off a slice (of or from, का); to page and line (a book). ~ कूटना, to beat out metal leaf. ~ तराशना, = ~ उतारना, 1. ~ मोड़ना, to fold over a page, or a corner of a page. सोने का ~, m. gold leaf. – वरक़दाग़ी [P. *-dāgī*], f. paging (of a book). वरक़साज़ [P. *-sāz*], m. maker of gold or silver leaf.

वरक़ा *varqā* [A. *varqa*], m. **1.** a leaf; a page. **2.** a sheet, letter.

वरग़लाना *vargalānā* [P. *vargalānīdan*], v.t. **1.** to inveigle, to entice. **2.** to incite, to provoke.

वरज़िश *varziś* [P. *varziś*], f. **1.** physical training, gymnastics. **2.** bodily exercise. — ~ करना, to undertake physical training, &c. (in, की: a partic. skill).

वरण *varaṇ* [S.], m. **1.** choosing, choice; selection. **2.** choice of a bride, or of a bridegroom; arrangement of marriage. — ~ करना (का), to choose. – वरण-माला, f. a garland given to the bridegroom by the bride during the marriage ceremony. वरणात्मक [°*ṇa*+*ā*°], adj. selective.

वरणीय *varăṇīyă* [S.], adj. worthy of being chosen, fine, splendid.

वरदी *vardī* [? cf. H. *urdū*, and H. *virad*, *virud*; ? w. A. *vardī(ya)*], f. **1.** uniform. **2.** badge of office (as of a peon, or porter). — ~ बजाना, *Pl.* to sound the bugle for a dress parade.

वरना *varnā* [P. *varna* (for *va agar na*)], conj. and if not: otherwise, or else.

वरम *varam* [A. *varam*], m. & adj. **1.** m. a swelling. **2.** inflammation. **3.** adj. swollen.

वरला *varlā* [cf. *apāra-*], adj. *Pl. HŚS.* belonging to, or situated on, this side (cf. वरा).

वरा *varā* [conn. *apāra-*], adj. reg. **1.** situated on this side (as of a river). **2.** near, close by. — वरे आना, to approach.

वराक *varāk* [S.], adj. wretched; base.

वराटक *varāṭak* [S.], m. *Pl. HŚS.* **1.** a cowrie shell. **2.** the seed-vessel of a lotus flower.

वराणसी *varāṇasī*, f. pronun. var. (also with /n/). = वाराणसी, बनारस.

वरासत *varāsat*, f. = विरासत.

वराह *varāh* [S.], m. **1.** a boar. **2.** name of the third or boar incarnation of Viṣṇu.

वरिष्ठ *variṣṭh* [S.], adj. **1.** best, choice. **2.** senior (in status).

1**वरी** *varī* [cf. H. *var*, 2.], f. presents to a bride from her parents.

2**वरी** *varī* [S.], f. **1.** ? *Asparagus racemosa* (= मूसली). **2.** ? = सतावर. **3.** millet, *Panicum miliaceum*.

वरीयता *varīyătā* [S.], f. **1.** seniority. **2.** higher ranking, precedence.

वरुण *varuṇ* [S.], m. *mythol.* the Vedic deity Varuṇa (often regarded as supreme deity, and later as god of the waters or ocean).

वर्ग *varg* [S.], m. **1.** m. class, group (of similar things or persons). **2.** social group, class. **3.** section, chapter (of a book). **4.** *math.* square (of a quantity). **5.** *geom.* a square (figure). **6.** *gram.* any of several classes of consonants sharing a point or area of articulation (esp. guttural, palatal, retroflex, dental, and palatal) and arranged as separate groups in the Devanāgarī syllabary; a syllable. **7.** वर्ग-. square. एक वर्ग-मील, m. a square mile. — वर्गगत, adj. pertaining to group or class. वर्ग-पद, m. *math.* square root. वर्ग-पहेली, f. a crossword puzzle. वर्ग-फल, m. the square (of a number). वर्ग-मूल, m. square root. वर्गहीन, adj. classless. वर्गाकार [°*ga* + *ā*°], adj. square in shape. वर्गीकरण, m. classification. °कृत, adj. classified.

वर्ग़लाना *vargalānā*, v.t. see वरग़लाना.

वर्गित *vargit* [S.], adj. **1.** *math.* squared (a number). 2. = वर्गीकृत.

वर्गीकरण *vargīkaraṇ* [S.], m. see s.v. वर्ग.

वर्गीकृत *vargīkr̥t* [S.], adj. see s.v. वर्ग.

वर्गीय *vargīyă* [S.], adj. **1.** falling into any class. **2.** *math.* existing as a square (= वर्गित, 1).

वर्चस्वी *varcasvī* [S.], adj. vigorous, energetic; vital.

वर्जन *varjan* [S.], m. **1.** forbidding; prohibition. **2.** abandoning. **3.** excluding, rejecting.

वर्जना *varjănā* [S.], f. = वर्जन, 1.

वर्जनीय *varjănīyă* [S.], adj. to be prohibited, &c. (see वर्जन); wrong, wicked.

वर्जित *varjit* [S.], adj. **1.** forbidden, unlawful, banned. **2.** -वर्जित. deprived, devoid (of). **3.** abandoned. **4.** excluded, rejected.

वर्ण *varṇ* [S.], m. **1.** colour; quality (of gold, as shown by its mark on a touchstone). **2.** class, type, kind; race. **3.** any of the four classes into which Indo-Aryan society was early divided, viz. brāhmaṇ, kṣatriya, vaiśya and śūdra; (in comp.) caste. **4.** form, aspect; manner of dress; theatrical costume. **5.** letter (of an alphabet, a syllabary). **6.** *ling.* a sound. **7.** a syllable. — वर्ण-क्रम, m. *phys.* spectrum; = वर्णानुक्रम. °-विज्ञान, m. spectroscopy. वर्ण-धर्म, m. ancestral or caste occupation. °ई, adj. following an ancestral occupation. वर्ण-माला, f. syllabary, alphabet. वर्ण-विन्यास, m. arrangement of letters: spelling (of a word). वर्ण-विपर्यय, m. *ling.* metathesis of sounds or syllables. वर्ण-वृत्त, m. *pros.* syllabic metre. वर्ण-व्यवस्था, f. arrangement (of society) in classes. वर्ण-संकर, m. a person of mixed varṇa, caste or blood. वर्णात्मक [°*ṇa* + *ā*°], adj. having to do with varṇa, or with caste; literal. वर्णानुक्रम [°*ṇa* + *a*°], m. syllabic or alphabetical order. वर्णांध [°*ṇa* + *a*°], adj. colour-blind. °ता, f. वर्णावली [°*ṇa* + *ā*°], f. syllabary or alphabet. वर्णाश्रम [°*ṇa* + *ā*°], m. class and stage (of life). °-धर्म, m. the particular socio-religious duty of members of each of the four varṇas in the four stages of life. °ई, adj. following *varṇāśram dharma*.

वर्णन *varṇan* [S.], m. description, account. — ~ करना (का), to describe. वर्णनातीत [°*na* + *a*°], adj. beyond description. वर्णनात्मक [°*na* + *ā*°], adj. descriptive. °ता, f. vividness, graphic nature.

वर्णनीय *varṇănīyă* [S.], adj. worthy of description.

वर्णित *varṇit* [S.], adj. **1.** described, expounded. **2.** praised. **3.** painted, drawn.

वर्ण्य *varṇyă* [S.], adj. **1.** to be described. **2.** worthy of description. — वर्ण्य-विषय, m. subject-matter.

वर्तक *vartak* [S.], m. *Pl. HŚS.* a kind of quail, *Perdix olivacea*; a cock quail.

वर्तन *vartan* [S.], m. **1.** turning, revolving. **2.** use, application. **3.** dealings. **4.** livelihood.

वर्तनी *vartănī* [S.], f. **1.** way, manner, esp. of writing; spelling. **2.** a pen.

वर्तमान *vartămān* [S.], adj. & m. **1.** adj. existing, present (time, situation); of the present day. **2.** current (month, year). **3.** present, confronting (one): a situation. **4.** m. the present (time). — वर्तमान-काल, m. *gram.* present tense. °इक, adj. having to do with the present; having to do with the present tense (a usage, a form).

वर्ति *varti* [S.], f. sthg. rolled, twisted or coiled: **1.** wick, &c. (= वर्तिका); candle, taper. **2.** ointment, collyrium. — वर्ति-लेख, m. a scroll.

वर्तिका *vartikā* [S.], f. **1.** wick of a lamp (= बत्ती). **2.** paint-brush (artist's).

-वर्ती *-vartī* [S.], adj. found, situated (at, in, &c.: e.g. तटवर्ती, found or lying along a bank or shore (as districts, population, fauna); निकटवर्ती, lying close at hand).

वर्तुल *vartul* [S.], adj. **1.** round; curling (wave). **2.** spherical. — वर्तुलाकार, adj. = ~.

-वर्धक *-vardhak* [S.], adj. formant. increasing. e.g. स्वास्थ्य-वर्धक, adj. furthering health: salubrious (air, climate); tonic (medicine).

वर्धन *vardhan* [S.], m. **1.** increase, growth. **2.** prosperity, success. **3.** rearing (children, young). — वर्धनशील, adj. increasing, growing.

वर्धनी *vardhănī* [S.], f. *Pl. HŚS.* **1.** a broom, brush. **2.** earthen or copper water-pot with a spout (cf. बधना).

वर्धमान *vardhămān* [S.], adj. & m. **1.** adj. increasing. **2.** m. name of a mountain and district (Burdwan in Bengal).

वर्धित *vardhit* [S.], adj. **1.** increased; fostered, furthered. **2.** grown, developed.

वर्म *varm* [S.], m. armour.

वर्मा *varmā* [S.], m. inv. protection: a title or last name in use in Kāyasth communities or (esp. in Madhya Pradesh) in communities affiliated to the kṣatriya group.

वर्य *varyă* [S.], adj. *Pl. HŚS.* **1.** fit to be chosen, eligible. **2.** worthy, excellent, best.

वर्वर *varvar* [S.], m. & adj. **1.** m. a barbarian. **2.** adj.. uncouth, barbaric.

वर्ष *varṣ* [S.], m. a year. — आगामी ~, adv. next year. गत ~, adv. last year. – वर्ष-गाँठ, f. year-knot: birthday; anniversary. वर्ष-फल, m. a horoscope made for a single year. वर्षारंभ [°*ṣa*+*ā*°], m. beginning of the year, new year.

वर्षण *varṣaṇ* [S.], m. raining; downpour.

वर्षा *varṣā* [S.], f. **1.** the rainy season. **2.** rain. **3.** rainfall, amount of rain. **4.** fig. rain (of flowers from heaven); hail (of bullets). — वर्षा-ऋतु, f. = ~, 1. वर्षाकाल, m. id. °ईन, adj. वर्षागम [°*ṣā*+*ā*°], m. beginning of the rains.

वर्षाना *varṣānā* [cf. H. *varṣā*], v.t. **1.** to cause to rain down (as the gods flowers). **2.** to cause to fall in great numbers (bombs, shells).

वर्ही *varhī* [S.], m. *Pl. HŚS.* a peacock.

वलय *valay* [S.], m. ring-shaped object: **1.** bracelet; armlet. **2.** a finger ring.

वलयित *valayit* [S.], adj. encircled, enclosed.

वलवला *valvalā* [A. *valvala*], m. **1.** howling, wailing. **2.** fit, access (of emotion). **3.** uproar.

वलवलाना *valvalānā*, v.i. = बलबलाना.

वलवलाहट *valvalāhaṭ* [cf. H. *valvalānā*], f. howling, wailing.

वला *valā*, adv. pronun. var. *Pl.* ? = वरला.

वलाक *valāk* [S.], m. a crane (cf. बलाका).

वलाका *valākā* [S.], f. a crane (= बलाका).

वलि *vali* [S.], m. 1. = [2]बल. 2. = बलि.

वलित *valit* [S.], adj. **1.** bent round, turned, curling (hair); curved; folded (rocks). **2.** Brbh. surrounded or accompanied by (as the eye with tears). **3.** covered by; set with (as the sky with stars).

[1]**वली** *valī* [S.], f. fold, wrinkle, &c. (= [2]बल); row, line.

[2]**वली** *valī* [A. *valī*], m. U. **1.** master, lord; governor. **2.** *isl.* saint.

वल्कल *valkal* [S.], m. **1.** bark (of a tree). **2.** bark garment (as of ascetics).

वल्गा *valgā* [S.], f. bridle.

वल्द *vald* [A. *valad*], m. U. son.

वल्दियत *valdiyat* [A. *valdīya*: P. *valdīyat*], f. U. family, parentage; paternity.

वल्लभ *vallabh* [S.], adj. & m. **1.** adj. beloved, dear. **2.** m. esp. -वल्लभ. lover; husband. **3.** overseer, master; chief herdsman.

वल्लभा *vallăbhā* [S.], f. mistress; wife.

वल्लाह *vallāh* [A. *va 'llāh*], interj. by Allah.

वश *vaś* [S.], m. **1.** power (= [2]बस). **2.** state of subjection. **3.** in comp. because of, out of. अभ्यासवश, adv. out of habit. — ~, or ~ में, होना, to be in the power or control (of, के). – वश-क्रिया, f. the act of overpowering (by drugs or magic); enchanting. वशवर्ती, adj. subject to, dominated by (as by a passion); amenable to authority. वशीकरण, m. overpowering, subjugating; enchanting. वशीकृत, adj. made subject: overpowered; enchanted. वशीभूत, adj. become subject: helpless; enchanted.

वशी *vaśī* [S.], adj. **1.** in subjection, under control. **2.** keeping (one's) passions under control.

वशीकरण *vaśīkaraṇ* [S.], m. see s.v. वश.

वशीकृत *vaśīkr̥t* [S.], adj. see s.v. वश.

वशीभूत *vaśībhūt* [S.], adj. see s.v. वश.

वश्य *vaśyă* [S.], adj. & m. **1.** adj. subject (to, का); in the power (of). **2.** m. Brbh. one subject (to another).

वसंत *vasant* [S.], m. 1. = बसंत. **2.** *Pl. HŚS.* dysentery. **3.** *Pl. HŚS.* smallpox. — बसंतोत्सव [°*ta*+*u*°], m. spring festival: the festival of Holī.

वसंती *vasantī* [S.], adj. & m. = बसंती.

वसती *vasătī* [S.], f. **1.** dwelling-place. 2. = बस्ती. **3.** *Pl. HŚS.* night.

[1]**वसन** *vasan* [S.], m. clothing.

[2]**वसन** *vasan* [S.], m. dwelling-place.

वसफ़ *vasf* [A. *vasf*], m. U. **1.** praise. **2.** quality, property.

वसली *vaslī* [P. *vaṣlī*], f. cardboard.

वसवास *vasvās* [A. *vasvās*: ? w. H. *aviśvās*], m. Av. a doubt (as suggested to the mind); distraction; temptation.

वसवासी *vasvāsī* [A. *vasvās*+-*ī*], adj. doubting, apprehensive, suspicious.

वसा *vasā* [S.], f. Brbh. **1.** marrow (of bone). **2.** fat.

वसित *vasit* [S.], adj. settled (as territory).

वसीक़ा *vasīqā* [A. *vaṣīqa*], m. U. trust, reliance: **1.** stock, bond (esp. issued by Government). **2.** dividend. — वसीक़ेदार [P. -*dār*], m. stock-holder.

वसीयत *vasīyat* [A. *vaṣīya*: P. *vaṣīyat*], f. **1.** will. **2.** bequest. — ~ में देना (को), to leave (to); to leave as a bequest. – वसीयत-नामा, m. will.

वसीला *vasīlā* [A. *vasīla*], m. U. **1.** means, cause. **2.** support, prop, help.

वसुंधरा *vasundharā* [S.], f. = वसुधा.

वसु *vasu* [S.], m. name of a partic. class of Vedic gods; wealth: — वसुधा, f. wealth-holder: the earth. वसुमती, f. having riches: the earth.

वसुक *vasuk* [S.], m. *Pl. HŚS.* rock salt (from Sambhar Lake, Rajasthan).

वसुधा *vasudhā* f. see s.v. वसु.

वसूल *vasūl* [A. *vuṣūl*], adj. **1.** acquired. ***2.** collected, levied, raised (rent, &c). — ~ करना, to receive; to collect, &c. ~ पाना, to receive (as rent, &c). ~ होना, to be received, or collected; to accrue. – वसूलयाबी [P. -*yābī*], f. U. = वसूली, 2.

वसूलना *vasūlnā* [cf. H. *vasūl*], v.t. to levy, to exact.

वसूली *vasūlī* [A. *vuṣūl*+P. -*ī*], adj. & f. **1.** adj. collectable (as rent, dues); recoverable (as a debt). **2.** f. collecting, levying (as of rent). **3.** recoverable amount.

वस्त *vast* [A. *vasaṭ*], m. U. middle, centre.

वस्ति *vasti* [S.], f. *Pl. HŚS.* = वसती.

वस्तु *vastu* [S.], f. **1.** anything real or existent; essence, substance. **2.** a thing, object, article; pl. goods; possessions. **3.** a commodity. **4.** -वस्तु. subject-matter (of a story, a drama). — वस्तुगत, adj. material, existent, real; objective. वस्तुतः, adv. because of the nature of a thing, as a consequence; in fact, really. वस्तु-निष्ठ, adj. objective. °ता, f. वस्तु-रचना, f. arrangement, structure (of a narrative, a work). वस्तुवाद, m. materialism. °ई, adj. & m. materialist(ic). वस्तु-संकलन, m. linking or organisation of subject-matter. वस्तु-स्थिति, f. real state of affairs.

वस्तुता *vastutā* [S.], f. real existence, reality.

वस्त्र *vastră* [S.], m. **1.** cloth; material. ***2.** clothes. — भोजन और ~, m. food and clothing, the necessaries of life. – वस्त्राभूषण [°*ra*+*ā*°], m. = वेष-भूषा. वस्त्रोद्योग [°*ra*+*u*°], m. the textile industry.

वस्ल *vasl* [A. *vaṣl*], m. union.

वह *vah* [cf. *asau*; ? anal. *cṣa* [1], or w. P. *o*], pron. & adj. & adv. /vŏh/, /vəh/. **1.** pron. he; she; it; pl. they. **2.** specif. he (term of reference used by a wife of her husband so as to avoid mentioning his name). **3.** adj. that; pl. those. **4.** adv. colloq. as to that; there. — देखिए, ~ रहा मंदिर! look, there's a temple over there!

-वह -*vah* [S.], noun and adj. formant. carrying (e.g. गंधवह, m. poet. the wind; दुर्वह, adj. hard to bear).

वहती *vahătī* [S.], f. *Pl. HŚS.* a river, stream.

वहन *vahan* [S.], m. **1.** carrying, conveying, bearing. **2.** transport. **3.** a vehicle. **4.** flowing (as a stream). **5.** *phys.* convection. — ~ करना, to transport, &c.; to meet (expenditure).

वहम *vahm* [A. *vahm*], m. **1.** an idea (esp. false); imagination, fancy; fantasy; delusion. **2.** suspicion; distrust. — ~ करना, to imagine; to suspect, &c. ~ का पुलाव पकाना, fig. to build up fantasies or delusions. ~ समाना, a notion or a fantasy to come into the mind.

वहमी *vahmī* [A. *vahmī*], adj. **1.** imaginary, fanciful (a thought or attitude). **2.** prone to delusions; suspicious, distrustful.

वहला *vahlā*, m. *Pl.* onset, attack.

वहशत *vahśat* [A. *vaḥśa*: P. *vaḥśat*], f. **1.** a deserted or desolate place. ***2.** wildness, savageness (of manner); barbarity. **3.** dejection. **4.** frenzy. — वहशत-ज़दा [P. -*zada*], adj. terror-struck, terrified.

वहशियाना *vahśiyānā* [P. *vaḥśīyāna*], adj. inv. = वहशी.

वहशी *vahśī* [A. *vaḥśī*], adj. & m. **1.** adj. wild, savage; uncouth. **2.** ferocious. **3.** m. a wild person, a savage. **4.** a wild animal.

वहशीपन *vahśīpan* [cf. H. *vahśī*], m. **1.** wildness, savageness. **2.** ferocity.

वहशीपना *vahśīpanā*, m. = वहशीपन.

वहाँ *vahāṁ* [H. *yahāṁ*× H. *vah*], adv. **1.** there. **2.** thither. — ~ का, adj. of that place; local (a resident, a product). ~ का ~, or वहीं, adv. in that very place. ~ पर, adv. in that (particular) place, = ~. के ~, adv. at the home (of).

वहाबी *vahābī* [A. *vahhābī*], adj. & m. *isl.* **1.** adj. having to do with Vahhāb, or his sect. **2.** m. a follower of Vahhāb.

वहीं *vahīṁ* [H. *vahāṁ*+H. *hī*], adv. **1.** in that very place, right there. **2.** at that very moment, then and there.

वही *vahī* [H. *vah*+H. *hī*], pron. & adj. that very, the very (thing or person).

वह्नि *vahni* [S.], m. fire.

-वाँ *-vāṁ* [*-ama-*], suffix (forms ordinal numerals, e.g. पाँचवाँ, fifth).

वांछनीय *vāñchănīyă* [S.], adj. desirable.

वांछनीयता *vāñchănīyătā* [S.], f. desirability.

वांछा *vāñchā* [S.], f. desire, longing.

वांछित *vāñchit* [S.], adj. desired, longed for.

वांछी *vāñchī* [S.], adj. desirous.

वांशिक *vāṃśik* [S.], adj. & m. **1.** adj. having to do with a family, familial (as a name). **2.** m. last name, family name.

¹वा *vā* [S. *vā*], conj. or.

²वा *vā*, sg. obl. base. Brbh. that, &c. (see वह).

³वा *vā* [P. *vā*], prefix and adv. U. back (see वापस); again; open: — दिन के ~, adv. at dawn.

-वा *-vā* [*-uka-*], suffix (forms diminutives: chiefly reg. (E.)). = -इया, 1., 2.

वाक *vāk* [S.], m. the night-heron, *Nycticorax nycticorax*.

वाक् *vāk* [S.], m. **1.** speech. **2.** a word. — वाक्-चतुर, adj. skilled in speech: eloquent; persuasive. वाक्-छल, m. deceit in speech: prevarication. वाक्-पटु, adj. skilled in speech, eloquent. °ता, f.

वाक़ई *vāqaī* [A. *vāqi'ī*], adj. & adv. **1.** adj. real, actual, true. **2.** adv. really, truly.

वाक़फ़ियत *vāqfiyat*, f. = वाक़िफ़ियत.

वाक़या *vāqayā* [A. *vāqi'a*], m. U. **1.** event, incident. **2.** news, information.

वाक़यात *vāqayāt* [A. *vāqi'āt*], f. pl. U. events, incidents.

वाक़िफ़ *vāqif* [A. *vāqif*], adj. **1.** having information (about, as to, से). **2.** knowledgeable; expert. **3.** acquainted (with a person, से).

वाक़फ़ियत *vāqfiyat* [A. *vāqifīya*: P. *vāqifīyat*], f. information; acquaintance (with), knowledge (of); experience.

वाक़ै *vāqai*, adj. 19c. = वाक़या.

वाक्य *vākyă* [S.], m. **1.** an utterance. ***2.** a sentence; a clause. — वाक्य-रचना, f. syntax. °गत, adj. वाक्य-विज्ञान, m. study of syntax. वाक्य-विन्यास, m. syntax. वाक्यांश [°*ya*+*a*°], m. sentence constituent: a phrase.

वाग- *vāg-* [S]. = वाक्: — वागाडंबर, m. inflated language. वाग्जाल, m. net of words: confused, or elaborate language; deceitful language. वाग्दत्ता, f. given by spoken word: an engaged girl. वाग्देवी, f. the goddess of speech or eloquence: a title of Sarasvatī. वाग्धारा, f. flow of speech. वाग्बाहुल्य, m. prolixity. वाग्युद्ध, m. word-war: controversy, dispute; a war of words. वाग्विदग्ध, adj. skilful or winning in speech; eloquent. वाग्विलास, m. grace or elegance of speech. वागीश, m. master of language; an eloquent man; a learned man; *mythol.* a title of Bṛhaspati, the teacher of the gods.

वागुरिक *vāgurik* [S.], m. hunter.

वाग्मिता *vāgmitā* [S.], f. eloquence.

वाग्मी *vāgmī* [S.], adj. loquacious; eloquent.

वाङ्- *vāṅ-* [S]. = वाक्: — वाङ्मय, adj. & m. consisting of words, or speech; literature. °ई, f. see s.v.

वाङ्मयी *vāṅmayī* [S.], f. *Pl. HŚS.* a title of Sarasvatī (the goddess of speech and eloquence).

वाच् *vāc* [S.], f. = वाक्.

वाचक *vācak* [S.], adj. & m. **1.** adj. speaking. **2.** -वाचक. *gram.* signifying. कर्तृ-वाचक, adj. indicating a subject or agent. **3.** m. a word, term. **4.** *gram.* a noun. **5.** a speaker.

वाचन *vācan* [S.], m. **1.** reading out, reciting. **2.** *govt.* reading (of a bill).

वाचनक *vācănak* [S.], m. a riddle.

वाचनिक *vācănik* [S.], adj. *Pl. HŚS.* expressed in words, verbal; oral.

वाचा *vācā* [S.], adv. by word (see **वाक्**). — **मनसा ~ कर्मना**, adv. Brbh. by, or in, thought, word and deed. – **वाचा-बंध**, m. verbal undertaking: promise.

वाचाल *vācāl* [S.], adj. **1.** garrulous. **2.** chattering idly. **3.** boastful, wordy.

वाचालता *vācālătā* [S.], f. garrulousness, &c.

वाचिक *vācik* [S.], adj. verbal, oral (communication). — **~ पत्र**, m. an agreement put down in writing.

-वाची *-vācī* [S.], adj. formant. = **वाचक**, 2.

वाच्य *vācyă* [S.], adj. & m. **1.** adj. to be spoken or said. **2.** expressible. **3.** m. an utterance; a sentence.

वाजपेयी *vājăpeyī* [S.], m. **1.** one who has performed a *vājapeya (soma)* sacrifice. **2.** name of a brāhmaṇ community. **3.** a member of the Vājpeyī community.

वाजिब *vājib* [A. *vājib*], adj. **1.** necessary. **2.** right, proper. **3.** fitting, appropriate. — **~ होना**, to be incumbent (on, **पर**); to be necessary, &c.

वाजिबी *vājibī* [A. *vājib*+P. *-ī*], adj. & f. **1.** adj. = **वाजिब**; due (as a payment). **2.** m. whatever is necessary, right, &c. — **~ दावा**, m. a just claim. **~ से**, adv. deservedly, rightly; fittingly.

वाजी *vājī* [S.], adj. & m. **1.** adj. swift; strong. **2.** m. a horse. — **वाजीकरण**, m. strengthener: an aphrodisiac.

वाटिका *vāṭikā* [S.], f. **1.** a small garden. **2.** a flower-bed.

-वाड़ा *-vāṛā* [*pāṭa(ka)-* × *vāṭa-*¹], m. **1.** place, dwelling-place. **2.** quarter, ward (of a town). **तेलीवाड़ा**, m. oilmen's quarter. **3.** region, territory.

-वाड़ी *-vāṛī*, f. a garden, &c. (= **बाड़ी**). **फूलवाड़ी**, f. a flower garden.

वाण *vāṇ* [S.], m. an arrow.

वाणिज्य *vāṇijyă* [S.], m. trade; commerce. — **वाणिज्य-दूत**, m. *govt.* consul. **वाणिज्य-दूताभिकर्ता** [°*ta*+*a*°], m. inv. consular official.

वाणी *vāṇī* [S.], f. **1.** speech, language; the faculty of speech. **2.** word. **3.** voice. **4.** a title of the goddess Sarasvatī. — **वाणी-दोष**, m. a speech defect. **वाणीमय**, adj. poet. endowed with a voice.

वात *vāt* [S.], m. **1.** wind; air. **2.** wind as a bodily humour. **3.** rheumatism; gout. — **वात-जात**, adj. Brbh. wind-born: a title of Hanumān. **वात-पित्त**, m. wind-bile: rheumatism with fever. **वात-रोग**, m. = ~, 3. **वातानुकूलन** [°*ta*+*a*°], m. air-conditioning. **वातानुकूलित**, adj. **वात-वसन**, m. wind-cloth: a sail. **वातायन**, m. wind-passage: window; ventilator. °**ई**, f. dim. **वातावरण** [°*ta*+*ā*°], m. air-covering: atmosphere (also fig.) °**इक**, adj. **वाताहत** [°*ta*+*ā*°], m. storm-beaten.

वातास *vātās* [H. *batās*: ? ← B.], f. wind; fresh breeze.

वातुल *vātul* [S.], adj. & m. **1.** adj. rheumatic. **2.** crazed, frenzied. **3.** chattering, babbling. **4.** m. whirlwind, gale.

वातूल *vātūl*, m. = **वातुल**, 4.

वात्या *vātyā* [S.], f. poet. a storm of wind.

वात्सल्य *vātsalyă* [S.], m. **1.** parental affection. **2.** affection, fondness.

वाद *vād* [S.], m. speaking, speech: **1.** dispute, controversy. **2.** an assertion, proposition. **3.** -**वाद**. a point of view, theory (specif. as propounded). e.g. **समाजवाद**, m. socialism. **4.** an allegation; a law-suit. **5.** explanation, elucidation (as of a scripture); dialogue, debate. — **वाद-प्रतिवाद**, m. assertion and rejoinder; controversy. **वाद विवाद**, m. discussion, argument; debate. **वादानुवाद** [°*da*+*a*°], m. assertion and rejoinder; controversy.

वादक *vādak* [S.], m. a player of a musical instrument. — **वादक-दल**, m. an orchestra.

वादन *vādan* [S.], m. playing (a musical instrument).

वादा *vādā* [A. *va'da*], m. **1.** a promise. **2.** an agreement; contract. **3.** stated period (for discharge of a debt or payment of a sum of money). — **~ आना**, a fixed period to elapse, a due time to arrive. **~ करना (का)**, to promise (to a person, **से**); to agree (with, **से**). **~ टालना**, to evade a promise or agreement. **वादे का सच्चा**, to be true to one's promise. **ज़बानी ~**, m. verbal promise; parole. – **वादा-ख़िलाफ़ी** [P. *khilāfī*], f. breach of promise. **वादा-फ़रामोश** [P. *-farāmōś*], adj. forgetful of one's promise.

वादित *vādit* [S.], adj. caused to sound: struck, resounding (a musical instrument).

वादित्र *vāditr* [S.], m. Brbh. = **वाद्य**, 1.

¹**वादी** *vādī* [A. *vādin*: P. *vādī*], f. **1.** a valley. **2.** low-lying ground. **3.** river channel.

²**वादी** *vādī* [S.], m. **1.** a speaker. **2.** a plaintiff.

-वादी *-vādī* [S.], adj. & m. formant. supporting a partic. viewpoint or cause (see **वाद**, 3).

वाद्य *vādyă* [S.], m. **1.** a musical instrument. **2.** instrumental music. — **वाद्यकर**, m. a musician. **वाद्यकार**, m. id. **वाद्य-मंडली**, f. an orchestra. **वाद्य-वृंद**, m. id.

वान *vān* [S.], m. **1.** *Pl. HŚS.* a mat of straw. **2.** *Pl.* a hole in the wall of a house.

[1]**-वान** *-vān* [S.], suffix (forms adjectives and nouns which are properly masculines, chiefly from nouns, having the sense 'possessed of ...', e.g. कलावान, artistic; विद्वान, knowing, learned, a scholar: feminines of forms derived from nouns are properly in °वती).

-वान् *-vān* [S.], suffix. see [1]-वान.

[2]**वान** *vān* [P. *-vān*], suffix (forms agent nouns, e.g. दरवान, door-keeper, &c.)

वानप्रस्थ *vānăprasth* [S.], m. a brāhmaṇ in the third of four traditional stages of life (who has left his house and family to live in the forest); a hermit.

वानर *vānar* [S.], m. a monkey.

वानरी *vānărī* [S.], f. **1.** a female monkey. **2.** *Pl. HŚS.* = केवाँच.

-वाना *-vānā* [conn. *-āpayati*], suffix (forms transitive verbs of specif. causative force, e.g. छपवाना, to have (sthg.) printed).

वानेय *vāneyă* [S.], adj. & m. *Pl. HŚS.* **1.** adj. having to do with forest or scrub country, or with water. **2.** m. a grass that grows in water (? = मोथा).

वापस *vāpas* [P. *vā-pas*], adv. back, back again. — ~ आना, to return, to come back. ~ करना, to give back; to send back; to remand. ~ जाना, to go back; to retire, to recede. ~ देना, = ~ करना. ~ मिलना, to be got back (sthg. lost, borrowed; or a right withdrawn). ~ रखना, to keep back; to detain. ~ लेना, to take back; to withdraw (as a right, an accusation).

वापसी *vāpsī* [cf. H. *vāpas*], adj. & f. **1.** adj. return (as fare, ticket, journey, post). **2.** f. returning, return. **3.** giving back; refund. **4.** sending back, or home. **5.** remand. **6.** a return ticket.

वापिका *vāpikā* [S.], f. = वापी.

वापिस *vāpis*, adv. pronun. var. = वापस.

वापी *vāpī* [S.], f. a large well, or tank (esp. one having steps down to the water).

[1]**वाम** *vām* [S.], adj. **1.** left (hand). **2.** Brbh. Av. adverse (as fate). **3.** *Pl. HŚS.* crooked; base. — वाम-देव, m. a title of Śiva. वाम-पक्ष, m. left side; *pol.* left wing. °ई, adj. & m. वाम-पंथ, m. = वामाचार. वाम-मार्ग, m. the left-hand way: = वामाचार. वामांगी [°*a*+*a*°], f. who sits at (her) husband's left: a wife. वामाचार [°*ma*+*ā*°], m. left-hand, i.e. tantric, or *śākta*, ritual or doctrine. °ई, adj. & m. following, or a follower of, tantras.

[2]**वाम** *vām* [ad. *vāmā-*], f. Brbh. lovely: a woman. — वामदार, f. beautiful woman.

वामता *vāmătā* [S.], f. contrariety, adverseness (as of fate).

वामन *vāman* [S.], adj. & m. **1.** adj. dwarfish. **2.** m. *mythol.* name of the fifth or dwarf incarnation of Viṣṇu.

वामा *vāmā* [S], f. **1.** a woman. **2.** title used of goddesses, esp. of Durgā.

वायक *vāyak* [S.], m. Brbh. a weaver.

वायदा *vāydā*, m. = वादा. — ~ बाज़ार, m. *fin.* futures market.

वायन *vāyan* [S.], m. presents sent to friends and relatives on festive occasions (= बैना).

वायविक *vāyăvik* [S.], adj. aerial (= वायवीय).

वायवीय *vāyăvīyă* [S.], adj. **1.** having to do with wind or air; aerial. **2.** fig. intangible.

वायव्य *vāyavyă* [S.], m. *Pl. HŚS.* the north-west.

वायस *vāyas* [S.], m. a crow.

वायु *vāyu* [S.], f. m. **1.** air. **2.** wind. **3.** one of the traditional airs or humours of the body. — वायुगतिकी, f. aerodynamics. वायुदाबमापी, m. a barometer. वायु-मंडल, m. the atmosphere. °ईय, adj. वायु-यान, m. an aircraft. °वेधी, adj. anti-aircraft (gun). वायु-शूल, m. flatulence; colic. वायु-सेना, f. air force.

वारंट *vāranṭ* [Engl. *warrant*], m. a warrant (as for arrest, or search). — ~ जारी करना, to issue a warrant.

[1]**वार** *vār*, m. **1.** a blow. **2.** an attack. **3.** a ruse. — ~ करना (पर), to strike; to make an attack (on). ~ ख़ाली जाना, a blow to miss; a ruse to fail. ~ ख़ाली करना, to dodge a blow, &c. ~ चलाना, to strike a blow (against, पर). ~ बचाना, to ward off a blow; to repulse an attack.

[2]**वार** *vār* [S.], m. **1.** particular time; turn; chance. **2.** esp. -वार. day of the week. सोमवार, m. Monday.

-वार *-vār* [P. *-vār*], suffix (forms adjectives having the senses 'in the manner of, according to, after': these deriving from the senses 'like' and 'fit for, characterised by', e.g. महीनेवार, adv. by the month, per month).

वार- *vār-* [*apāra-*], m. the near side: — वार-पार, adv. = next; वार-पार होना, to be settled (a dispute). वारापार, adv. & m. on both sides; right across; right through; furthest bounds, limit. कोई वारापार नहीं, there is no limit (to, की).

वारक *vārak* [S.], adj. obstructing; restraining; warding off.

वारण *vāraṇ* [S.], m. **1.** obstructing; restraining; warding off. **2.** prohibition, banning. **3.** obstacle. **4.** armour. — ~ करना, to prohibit, &c.

वारदात *vārdāt* [A. *vāridāt*, pl.], f. an event; incident (as an accident, or affray); a disaster.

¹**वारन** *vāran* [ad. *vāraṇa-*], m. Brbh. = वारण.

²**वारन** *vāran* [cf. H. *vārnā*], f. Brbh. sacrifice, offering.

वारना *vārnā* [cf. *vārayate*], v.t. **1.** to surround. **2.** to ward off, to avert (from, से). **3.** to pass (an object) round or over a person (as a means of averting evil, or as an offering); to offer (in sacrifice, or devotion); to devote oneself (to, पर). — वारा-फेरी, f. = वारी-फेरी.

वार-फेर *vār-pher*, f. Brbh. = वारा-फेरी (see s.v. वारना).

¹**वारा** *vārā* [cf. H. *vārnā*, and *vārayate*], m. esp. pl. **1.** goods. **2.** gain, benefit. **3.** thrift. — वारे-न्यारे, m. pl. possessions, wealth; gains, earning. वारे-न्यारे करना, to make money; to earn. वारे-न्यारे होना (के), to become well off, to prosper.

²**वारा** *vārā* [? conn. H. ¹*vārā*, 2., 3.], adj. reg. cheap.

वाराणसी *vārāṇasī* [S.], f. the city of Banaras.

वाराणसेय *vārāṇăseyă* [S.], adj. having to do with Banaras.

वारा-न्यारा *vārā-nyārā* [cf. H. *vār-*; w. H. *nyārā*], m. decision, resolution (of a matter, a dispute).

वाराफेरी *vārā-pherī*, f. see s.v. वारना.

वाराह *vārāh* [S.], adj. & m. **1.** adj. having to do with boars, or a boar. **2.** m. a boar (= वराह).

वारि *vāri* [S.], m. water. — वारि-चक्र, m. whirlpool. वारिज, m. water-born: a lotus. वारिद, m. water-giving: a cloud. वारिधि, m. water-holder: the ocean.

वारित *vārit* [S.], adj. **1.** checked, restrained; warded off. **2.** forbidden (of access).

वारिद *vārid* [A. *vārid*], adj. & m. U. present, appearing; happening; coming.

वारिदात *vāridāt*, f. = वारदात.

वारिस *vāris* [A. *vāriṣ*], m. **1.** heir. **2.** owner, master, lord. **3.** protector. — ~ होना, to become heir (to, का).

वारी *vārī* [cf. H. *vārnā*], f. & interj. **1.** f. a devoted one. **2.** interj. my life! dear one! — ~ जाना, or होना, to sacrifice or to devote oneself (for or to, पर); to be devoted (to). वारियाँ जाना, id. – वारी-फेरी, f. passing (an offering) round the head of a person (see वारना, 3).

वारुणी *vāruṇī* [S.], f. **1.** an alcoholic preparation; alcohol (generally); wine. **2.** *astron.* name of the twenty-fifth lunar asterism.

वार्ता *vārtā*, f. = वार्त्ता.

वार्त्ता *vārttā* [S.], f. **1.** conversation. **2.** discussion; negotiation. **3.** report, information; rumour. **4.** a written hagiography (esp. those of the Vallabhan sect). — वार्ताकार, m. participant in a discussion; a hagiographer; commentator. वार्तालाप, m. conversation; discussion; interview. वार्तालाप करना, to converse, &c. (with, से).

वार्तिक *vārtik* [S.], adj. & m. **1.** adj. having to do with a hagiography. **2.** m. commentary (on a text).

वार्धक्य *vārdhakyă* [S.], m. **1.** old age. **2.** growth, increase.

वार्षिक *vārṣik* [S.], adj. **1.** relating to a year, yearly (as income, tax). **2.** occurring once a year, annual.

वार्षिकी *vārṣikī* [S.], f. **1.** an annual payment received, annuity. **2.** an annual publication. **3.** annual commemoration.

-वाल *-vāl*, adj. & n. formant. = -वाला.

वाला *vālā* [P. *bālā*], adj. inv. U. pronun. var. high, lofty: — हुज़ूरे वाला [P. *-e-*], m. your highness.

-वाला *-vālā* [*pāla-*], suffix. **1.** w. nouns and adverbs (these compounds stand in a general adjectival relationship to a following noun, expressed or understood). **2.** w. verbs (these compounds have agentive force). — ऊपरवाला कमरा, m. the room upstairs. गाँववाला, m. a villager. घरवाला, m. master or owner of a (or the) house; घरवाली, f. wife. टोपीवाला लड़का, m. the boy wearing a hat. दिल्लीवाला, adj. & m. belonging to Delhi; a Delhi man. बाक्सवाला, m. box-man: a peddler. पचास पैसेवाला टिकट, m. a fifty pice stamp. – मैं जानेवाला हूँ, I am about to go; I am going, on my way. रहनेवाला, m. a resident; a citizen. हिंदी सीखनेवाले विद्यार्थी, m. pl. the students learning Hindi.

वालिद *vālid* [A. *vālid*], m. U. father.

वालिदा *vālidā* [A. *vālida*], f. /valda/. U. mother.

वालिदैन *vālidain* [A. *vālidain*, dual], m. pl. U. parents.

वावदूक *vāvădūk* [S.], adj. *Pl. HŚS.* **1.** talking much, chattering. **2.** eloquent.

वावदूकता *vāvădūkătā* [S.], f. *Pl. HŚS.* talkativeness; eloquence.

वाष्प *vāṣp* [S.], m. **1.** vapour; mist. **2.** steam. **3.** fig. a tear. **4.** a minute quantity, trace. — **वाष्प-पिंड**, m. body of vapour. **वाष्प-पुंज**, m. *astron.* nebula. **वाष्प-यंत्र**, m. steam-engine. **वाष्प-यान**, m. steam-driven vehicle, railway train. **वाष्पशील**, m. readily vaporising or evaporating, volatile. **वाष्पीकरण**, m. = **वाष्पन**.

वाष्पन *vāṣpan* [S.], m. **1.** evaporation. **2.** vaporisation.

वाष्पित *vāṣpit* [S.], adj. **1.** evaporated. **2.** vaporised.

वाष्पीकरण *vāṣpīkaraṇ* [S.], m. see s.v. **वाष्प**.

वाष्पीय *vāṣpīyă* [S.], adj. of the nature of, or produced by, steam.

वासंत *vāsant* [S.], adj. & m. **1.** adj. having to do with spring. **2.** m. the south or west wind.

वासंतिक *vāsantik* [S.], adj. *HŚS.* = **वासंत**.

वासंती *vāsantī* [S.], f. **1.** name of several species of jasmine. **2.** a festival held in the month Cait and honouring Kāmdev, or in some localities Durgā.

¹**वास** *vās* [S.], m. **1.** residing, residence. **2.** place of residence. — ~ **करना**, to reside. – **वास-स्थान**, m. place of residence.

²**वास** *vās* [S.], m. fragrance.

³**वास** *vās* [S.], m. clothes, dress.

¹**वासन** *vāsan* [S.], m. **1.** clothing. **2.** a garment.

²**वासन** *vāsan* [S.], m. perfuming with incense.

वासना *vāsănā* [S.: cf. H. ¹*vās*], f. an impression 'remaining' in the mind: **1.** fancy, imagination. ***2.** desire, passion. — **वासनात्मक** [°*nā*+*ā*°], adj. passionate.

वासर *vāsar* [S.], m. **1.** a day. **2.** [×H. ¹*vās*] first night of cohabitation (of bride and groom). **3.** bridal chamber.

¹**वासित** *vāsit* [S.], adj. settled, peopled (a region).

²**वासित** *vāsit* [S.], adj. **1.** made fragrant; perfumed, scented. **2.** spiced, seasoned.

वासिल *vāsil* [A. *vāṣil*], adj. & m. Brbh. U. joining together: **1.** adj. arrived. **2.** collected. **3.** m. an amount collected (of revenue). — **वासिल-बाक़ी**, f. receipt(s) and balances(s), account of payments.

वासी *vāsī* [S.], m. & adj. usu. **-वासी**. **1.** m. a resident. **2.** a citizen. **3.** adj. **-वासी**. residing (in). — **भारतवासी**, m. a resident or citizen of India.

वासुकि *vāsuki* [S.], m. *mythol.* name of a snake supposed to support the universe, and to have been used as a churning-rope at the gods' churning of the ocean.

वासुदेव *vāsudev* [S.], m. son of Vasudeva: a title of Kṛṣṇa.

वासोख़्त *vā-sokht* [P. *vāsokht*], f. U. a type of Urdu verse based on the theme of scorned love.

वास्तव *vāstav* [S.], adj. & m. **1.** adj. real, essential; actual; genuine. **2.** m. reality. — ~ **में**, adv. in reality, actually.

वास्तविक *vāstăvik* [S.], adj. real, &c. (= **वास्तव**). — ~ **बनाना**, to realise (an objective, a dream).

वास्तविकता *vāstăvikătā* [S.], f. **1.** reality. **2.** substance, essential nature.

वास्तव्य *vāstavyă* [S.], adj. & m. **1.** adj. fit to be lived in or at, habitable. **2.** m. a settled place.

वास्ता *vāstā* [A. *vāsiṭa*], m. sthg. intermediate or between: **1.** connection, business, concern, dealing(s). **2.** motive, reason, occasion. — ~ **पड़ना (को)**, a connection, &c. to exist (with, **से**). ~ **रखना**, to have to do (with, **से**), to concern. – **वास्ते**, ppn. w. **के**. on account of, because of, for; in order to.

वास्तु *vāstu* [S.], m. **1.** site (for a building). **2.** a building; a structure. — **वास्तु-कला**, f. architecture (as art). **वास्तुकार**, m. an architect. **वास्तु-विज्ञान**, m. = **वास्तु-शास्त्र**. **वास्तु-विद्या**, f. = next. **वास्तु-शास्त्र**, m. architecture (as a science). **वास्तु-शिल्प**, m. = **वास्तु-कला**. °**ई**, m. architect.

वास्ते *vāste*, ppn. see s.v. **वास्ता**.

वाह *vāh* [A. *vāh*], interj. **1.** splendid! wonderful! **2.** goodness! (expressing astonishment, displeasure, or regret). — ~ **रे**! = ~. ~ ~! id. ~ ~ **करना**, to applaud.

वाहक *vāhak* [S.], adj. & m. **1.** adj. & m. esp. **-वाहक**. transporting, carrying; carrier, &c. **2.** m. a carrier, haulier. **3.** porter. — **पत्र-वाहक**, m. bearer of a letter.

वाहन *vāhan* [S.], m. **1.** transporting, conveying. **2.** a vehicle. **3.** any animal used in riding or in freighting goods.

वाहवाही *vāhvāhī* [cf. H. *vāh vāh*], f. **1.** praise. **2.** applause; ovation. — ~ **करना**, to praise; to applaud. ~ लूटना, to revel in praise, or applause. ~ लेना, to receive praise, &c.

वाहिनी *vāhinī* [S.], f. **1.** an army. **2.** *mil.* a division. **3.** a vessel of the body.

वाहियात *vāhiyāt* [A. *vāhiyāt*, pl.], f. & adj. **1.** f. nonsense. **2.** vulgar behaviour. **3.** adj. vulgar; scurrilous.

वाही *vāhī* [A. *vāhin*: P. *vāhī*], adj. & f. & m. broken: **1.** adj. crazy, foolish. **2.** wandering; disreputable. **3.** f. nonsense. **4.** m. a vagrant. — वाही-तबाही [A. *-tabāh*], adj. & f. homeless, wandering; disreputable; nonsensical; nonsense; foul language. वाही-तबाही बकना, to talk nonsense; to use foul language.

¹**वाह्य** *vāhyă* [S.], adj. & m. **1.** adj. freight-drawing, draught (an animal). **2.** portable (a load). **3.** m. a means of transportation.

²**वाह्य** *vāhyă*, adj. = बाह्य.

विंदु *vindu* [H. *bindu-*], m. = बिंदु.

विंध्य *vindhyă* [S.], m. the Vindhya Hills (which divide the Ganges plain from the Deccan). — विंध्याचल [°*ya*+*a*°], m. id. विंध्य पर्वत, m. = विंध्य. विंध्य-वासिनी f. dwelling in the Vindhyas: a title of Durgā; a village and temple sacred to Durgā, situated near Mirzapur on the Ganges. विंध्यावासिनी [°*a*+*ā*°], f. id., 1.

विंशति *viṁśati* [S.], adj. twenty (in chapter-headings, &c).

वि- *vi-* [S.], pref. **1.** apart; away, off (e.g. विलग, adj. disconnected; विस्तार, m. extent). **2.** different, opposite (e.g. विक्रय, m. selling, sale; विविध, adj. of different kinds; विदेश, m. foreign lands). **3.** division, distinction (e.g. विभाषा, f. dialect; विश्लेषण, m. analysis). **4.** without; negation (e.g. विजन, adj. deserted; विमल, adj. without stain, pure). **5.** intensity; particular (e.g. विख्यात, adj. renowned; विजय, f. victory; विशुद्ध, adj. purified, quite pure).

विकंपित *vi-kampit* [S.], adj. trembling (as the hand); agitated (as the voice).

विकच *vi-kac* [S.], adj. opened (a flower); radiant.

विकट *vi-kaṭ* [S.], adj. **1.** vast. **2.** fearsome, dire. **3.** drawn, frowning (the brows); forbidding (tone, words). **4.** forbidding (as a problem).

विकराल *vi-kărāl* [S.], adj. **1.** hideous. **2.** most fearsome, dreadful.

विकर्ण *vi-karṇ* [S.], m. *math.* a diagonal.

विकल *vi-kal* [S.], adj. **1.** deprived of a part, esp. a limb; maimed; disabled; defective. **2.** restless, uneasy; distressed. **3.** disconcerted. — विकलांग [°*la*+*a*°], adj. maimed; crippled; disabled.

विकलता *vi-kalătā* [S.], f. **1.** impaired or disabled state. ***2.** distress.

विकलांगता *vi-kalāṅgătā*, [S.], f. state of physical disability.

विकला- *vi-kalā-* [cf. H. *vikal*], v.i. Brbh. to be distressed, sorrowful.

विकलाई *vikălāī* [cf. H. *vikal*], f. distress, sorrow.

विकलित *vi-kalit* [S.], adj. = विकल, 2.

विकल्प *vi-kalp* [S.], m. **1.** alternative, option. **2.** uncertainty, ambiguity; doubt. **3.** error. — ~ से, adv. optionally.

विकल्पित *vi-kalpit* [S.], adj. subject to doubt, ambiguous; indefinite.

विकसना *vi-kasnā* [ad. *vikasati*; w. H. *vikasit*], v.i. = विकसित करना.

विकसित *vi-kăsit* [S.], adj. **1.** opened, budding (as a flower). ***2.** developed (an enterprise, activity, &c).

विकार *vi-kār* [S.], m. **1.** change. ***2.** specif. change for the worse, deterioration (esp. of health). **3.** damage, harm (as to health). **4.** disorder, sickness; an abnormality. **5.** Av. agitation of mind. **6.** an altered form; *gram.* a declined or conjugated form. — विकारमय, adj. harmful, destructive.

विकारी *vi-kārī* [S.], adj. **1.** undergoing change, changed. **2.** harmful (as to health). **3.** Brbh. perturbed, agitated. **4.** *gram.* oblique (case). **5.** *gram.* declinable (form).

विकाल *vi-kāl* [ad. *vikāla-*], m. Av. twilight, dusk.

विकालत *vikālat*, f. = वकालत.

विकाश *vi-kāś* [S.], m. **1.** radiance. **2.** incorr. = विकास.

विकाशित *vi-kāśit* [S.], adj. made radiant: **1.** displayed. 2. = विकासित.

विकास *vi-kās* [S.], m. **1.** opening, expanding. **2.** budding, blooming (as a flower, or the heart); beauty, grace. ***3.** development; evolution. — ~ करना, to develop, &c. – विकास-क्रम, m. sequence of development, progress. विकासमान, adj. developing (as a country). विकासमूलक, adj. evolutionary in character. विकासशील, adj. developing (as a country).

विकासित *vi-kāsit* [S.], adj. made to open, to bloom, or to develop (cf. विकास).

विकिरण *vi-kiraṇ* [S.], m. radiation. — **विकिरणशील**, adj. radioactive; °ता, f.

विकीर्ण *vi-kīrṇ* [S.], adj. scattered; diffused.

विकृत *vi-kr̥t* [S.], adj. **1.** changed. ***2.** specif. changed for the worse: damaged, impaired (as health). **3.** mutilated, maimed. **4.** deformed. **5.** disordered (health, or mind). **6.** imperfect, incomplete. **7.** *gram.* oblique (case).

विकृति *vi-kr̥ti* [S.], f. **1.** change. **2.** impairment (as of health); defect. **3.** mutilation, maiming. **4.** disorder (of health, mind). **5.** agitation of mind. **6.** distortion; caricature. — **विकृति-विज्ञान**, m. *med.* pathology.

विकेंद्रीकरण *vi-kendrīkaraṇ*, m. decentralisation.

विक्रम *vi-kram* [S.], m. **1.** valour. **2.** power, might. 3. = **विक्रमादित्य**. — **विक्रमाजीत**, m. = next. **विक्रमादित्य** [°*ma*+*ā*°], m. name of a king of Ujjain and supposed founder of the Vikrama, Vikramāditya or *saṃvat* era, the first year of which ends in 57 B.C. **विक्रमाब्द** [°*ma*+*a*°], m. the Vikrama era.

विक्रमी *vi-kramī* [S.], adj. **1.** valiant, heroic. **2.** mighty. **3.** having to do with the Vikrama era.

विक्रय *vi-kray* [S.], m. sale. — **विक्रय-कर**, m. sales tax. **विक्रय-कर्ता**, m. inv. vendor.

विक्रयक *vi-krayak* [S.], m. vendor (= **विक्रेता**).

विक्रयण *vi-krayaṇ* [S.], m. selling.

विक्रयी *vi-krayī* [S.], m. vendor (= **विक्रेता**).

विक्रांत *vi-krānt* [S.], adj. **1.** victorious. **2.** courageous, valiant. **3.** mighty.

विक्रांति *vi-krānti* [S.], f. **1.** valour. **2.** power, might.

विक्रीत *vi-krīt* [S.], adj. sold.

विक्रेता *vi-kretā* [S.], m. inv. **1.** vendor. **2.** salesman, trader.

विक्रेय *vi-kreyă* [S.], adj. for sale.

विक्षिप्त *vi-kṣipt* [S.], adj. **1.** thrown about, or away; hurled, scattered. **2.** crazed, mad. **3.** agitated.

विक्षिप्तता *vi-kṣiptătā* [S.], f. insanity.

विक्षिप्ति *vi-kṣipti* [S.], f. insanity.

विक्षेप *vi-kṣep* [S.], m. **1.** throwing about or away; hurling; scattering. **2.** launching (of a missile, &c). **3.** madness, frenzy.

विक्षेपण *vi-kṣepaṇ* [S.], m. *Pl. HŚS.* = **विक्षेप**.

विख्यात *vi-khyāt* [S.], adj. **1.** famous, celebrated; well known as, named (as). **2.** notorious.

विख्याति *vi-khyāti* [S.], f. **1.** fame. **2.** notoriety.

विख्यापन *vi-khyāpan* [S.], m. **1.** making known, announcing; proclaiming. **2.** advertising, advertisement.

विख्यापित *vi-khyāpit* [S.], adj. made known, &c. (see **विख्यापन**).

विगंध *vi-gandh* [S.], m. Brbh. an unpleasant smell.

विगत *vi-gat* [S.], adj. **1.** gone, departed. **2.** last, previous (occasion); preceding (period). **3.** last but one. ~ **वर्ष**, m. the year before last. **4.** esp. **विगत-**. devoid or deprived (of). **विगतयौवना**, f. *rhet.* (a heroine) no longer young.

विगति *vi-gati* [S.], f. **1.** departure. **2.** state of separation, or deprivation. **3.** bad course, or conduct.

विगलित *vi-galit* [S.], adj. **1.** melted. **2.** drained (of, **से**).

विगुण *vi-guṇ* [S.], adj. = **निर्गुण**.

विगूढ़ *vi-gūṛh* [S.], adj. *Pl. HŚS.* **1.** concealed, hidden. **2.** obscure, esoteric (a doctrine).

विग्रह *vi-grah* [S.], m. **1.** separation. **2.** quarrel, strife. **3.** *gram.* resolution of a compound word into its parts. ***4.** a stretching out: control (of persons, or forces). **5.** a division, part. **6.** individual form or shape (as of a god): an idol. — ~ **होना**, control or discipline to be exercised (over, **का**); &c.

विग्रही *vi-grahī* [S.], adj. hostile, quarrelling.

विघटन *vi-ghaṭan* [S.], m. **1.** breaking up; destruction, ruin. **2.** disintegration (of a structure); decomposition (of a substance). **3.** dissolution (of any group or entity). — **विघटनशील**, adj. radioactive, °ता, f.

विघटित *vi-ghaṭit* [S.], adj. broken up, &c. (see **विघटन**).

विघात *vi-ghāt* [S.], m. *Pl. HŚS.* **1.** destructive or deadly blow. **2.** obstacle, hindrance.

विघातक *vi-ghātak* [S.], adj. *Pl. HŚS.* destructive, &c. (see **विघात**).

विघ्न *vi-ghnă* [S.], m. obstacle, impediment (to sthg., **में**); a difficulty. — ~ **डालना**, to place an obstacle, to interfere (with some activity, **में**). – **विघ्नकारी**, adj. causing any obstacle, hindrance or difficulty. **विघ्ननाशक**, m. *hind.* remover of obstacles: a title of the god Gaṇeś (who is traditionally invoked at the beginning of any undertaking). **विघ्नेश** [°*na*+*ī*°], m. lord of obstacles: id.

विघ्नित *vi-ghnit* [S.], adj. hindered, interfered with; prevented.

विचक्षण *vi-cakṣaṇ* [S.], adj. conspicuous: discerning, clear-seeing; sagacious; skilled.

विचरण *vi-caraṇ* [S.], m. **1.** wandering, roaming (cf. बिचरना). **2.** acting, behaving.

विचरना *vi-carnā*, v.i. to wander, to roam (= बिचरना).

विचल *vi-cal* [S.], adj. **1.** moving, unfixed, mobile. **2.** inconstant, fickle.

विचलन *vi-calan* [S.], m. moving, mobility; shifting.

विचलना *vi-calnā* [ad. *vicalati*: w. H. *vical*], v.i. **1.** to move, to shift; to be displaced, or unsteady. **2.** to be inconstant; to quail (in fear). **3.** to deviate, to go astray (from, से); to infringe (a norm); to break (a promise).

विचलित *vi-calit* [S.], adj. **1.** moved, shifted, &c. (see विचलना). **2.** inconstant. **3.** deviated (from, से); strayed.

विचार *vi-cār* [S.], m. **1.** thought, reflection. **2.** a thought, idea. **3.** opinion (concerning, के बारे में). **4.** usu. pl. cast or trend of thought, viewpoint. **5.** consideration (of a matter). — ~ आना (को), a thought to occur (to). ~ करना, to think, to reflect; to give consideration (to, पर, का). – विचार-कर्ता, m. = विचारक. विचार-गोष्ठी, f. seminar, symposium. विचार-दृष्टि, f. point of view. विचार-धारा, f. = ~, 4.; persuasion (religious, political, &c). °आत्मक, adj. doctrinal; ideological. विचारपूर्ण, adj. thoughtful (a remark, a work). विचारपूर्वक, adv. thoughtfully. विचारमूलक, adj. characterised by thought, thoughtful (= विचारपूर्ण). विचारवान, adj. thoughtful (a person); sensible; wise. विचार-वितर्क, m. discussion (= ~, 5). विचार-विनिमय, m. exchange of ideas. विचार-विमर्श, m. id. विचार-शक्ति, m. intellect. विचारशील, adj. = विचारवान. विचार-स्वतंत्रवाद, m. belief in freedom of thought. °ई, adj. & m. विचार-स्वातंत्र्य, m. freedom of thought; independence of thought. विचारात्मक [°*ra* + *ā*°], adj. thoughtful. विचाराधीन [°*ra* + *ā*°], adj. under consideration; *sub judice*. विचारार्थ [°*ra* + *a*°], adv. for discussion (a matter). विचारोत्तेजक [°*ra* + *u*°], adj. prompting or stimulating thought.

विचारक *vi-cārak* [S.], adj. & m. **1.** adj. thoughtful. **2.** m. *a thinker. **3.** one who deliberates; a judge.

विचारण *vi-cāraṇ* [S.], m. = विचार, 5.

विचारणा *vi-cārăṇā* [S.], f. consideration, reasoning; enquiry (into).

विचारणीय *vi-cārăṇīyă* [S.], adj. **1.** deserving thought or consideration; serious (a matter). **2.** questionable, doubtful.

विचारना *vi-cārnā* [ad. *vicārayati*: w. H. *vicār*], v.t. = विचार करना.

विचारित *vi-cārit* [S.], adj. **1.** considered (a matter), examined. **2.** decided, determined.

विचारी *vi-cārī* [S.], m. a thinker.

विचार्य *vi-căryă* [S.], adj. = विचारणीय.

विचिकित्सा *vi-cikitsā* [S.], f. doubt.

विचित्र *vi-citr* [S.], adj. **1.** variegated. ***2.** strange, unusual; peculiar. **3.** wonderful, surprising. — ~ नेत्रों से देखना, to look at with an odd expression.

विचित्रता *vi-citrătā* [S.], f. **1.** varied colouring. **2.** strange or unusual nature.

विचित्रित *vi-citrit* [S.], adj. decorated.

विच्छंदक *vi cchandak* [S.], m. *Pl. HŚS.* a building of several stories: a palace; temple.

विच्छिन्न *vi-cchinn* [S.], adj. **1.** severed, broken, &c. (cf. विच्छेदन). **2.** dissolved (a marriage).

विच्छुर *vi-cchur*, adj. poet. covered, strewn (= विच्छुरित).

विच्छुरित *vi-cchurit* [S.], adj. scattered or covered (with).

विच्छेद *vi-cched* [S.], m. **1.** severing; break, discontinuity. **2.** separating; separation (conjugal). **3.** section, part (as of a book). **4.** elimination, removal.

विच्छेदक *vi-cchedak* [S.], m. one who severs, or separates.

विच्छेदन *vi-cchedan* [S.], m. **1.** severing, separating; dissolution (of chemical compounds). **2.** amputating; amputation. **3.** removal, destruction.

विच्छेदित *vi-cchedit* [S.], adj. severed, &c. (cf. विच्छेदन).

विछलना *vi-chalnā* [H. *uchalnā* × H. *vicalnā*], v.i. to slip.

विछोह *vi-choh* [*vikṣobha-*], m. separation (of lovers); grieving, longing.

विजन *vi-jan* [S.], adj. & m. **1.** adj. uninhabited. **2.** desolate, lonely. **3.** m. desolate place, solitude.

विजनता *vi-janătā* [S.], f. uninhabited state, loneliness, desolateness.

विजनन *vi-janan* [S.], m. parturition, giving birth (= जनन).

विजन्मा *vi-janmā* [S.], m. inv. **1.** an illegitimate child. **2.** *HŚS.* one made an outcaste.

विजय *vi-jay* [S.], f. (m., *Pl.*). **1.** victory; conquest; capture. **2.** triumph. ~ का, adj. triumphant (a smile, &c). **3.** fig. progression: coming (as from a sitting-room) to eat. — ~ करना (पर), to conquer, to capture; to defeat. ~ पाना (पर, के ऊपर), to defeat, &c. – विजय-दशमी, f. = विजया-दशमी. विजय-लक्ष्मी, f. = next. विजय-श्री, f. the goddess of victory. विजय-स्तंभ, m. victory pillar, triumphal column.

विजया *vi-jayā* [S.], f. **1.** a title of the goddess Durgā. **2.** hemp. — विजया-दशमी, f. *hind.* the tenth day of the light half of the month Āśvin, and the festival celebrating the victory of Rām over Rāvaṇ held on that day.

विजयी *vi-jayī* [S.], adj. & m. **1.** adj. victorious, &c. (see विजय). **2.** m. a conqueror.

विजाति *vi-jāti* [S.], m. = विजातीय.

विजातीय *vi-jātīyă* [S.], adj. & m. **1.** adj. of or belonging to a different community, tribe, nationality or kind. **2.** of mixed origin. **3.** m. a person of different community, &c.

विजित *vi-jit* [S.], adj. **1.** conquered; defeated; won, gained. **2.** subdued (as the passions).

विजेता *vi-jetā* [S.], m. inv. victor, conqueror.

विजेय *vi-jey* [S.], adj. conquerable.

विज्ञ *vi-jñă* [S.], adj. & m. **1.** adj. knowing, knowledgeable; well-versed, adept. **2.** wise; prudent. **3.** learned. **4.** m. a knowledgeable person, &c.

विज्ञता *vi-jñătā* [S.], f. **1.** knowledgeableness; skill, experience. **2.** wisdom; prudence. **3.** learning.

विज्ञप्ति *vi-jñapti* [S.], f. **1.** announcement, report; communiqué. **2.** an advertisement (= विज्ञापन, 4.); a leaflet.

विज्ञात *vi-jñāt* [S.], adj. **1.** known well, understood. **2.** celebrated; notorious (= विख्यात).

विज्ञाता *vi-jñātā* [S.], m. inv. a knowledgeable or well-versed person; an expert.

विज्ञान *vi-jñān* [S.], m. **1.** *philos.* acquired knowledge of the world (as distinct from knowledge of *brahman* acquired by meditation and study). ***2.** science.

विज्ञानता *vi-jñānătā* [S.], f. *Pl. HŚS.* learnedness, learning; scientific attitude.

विज्ञानी *vi-jñānī* [S.], m. a scientist.

विज्ञापक *vi-jñāpak* [S.], adj. & m. **1.** adj. making known, announcing. **2.** m. one who informs or announces; an advertiser.

विज्ञापन *vi-jñāpan* [S.], m. **1.** making known (a matter or information); publicising. **2.** representing, urging (a matter). **3.** announcement, information. ***4.** an advertisement.

विज्ञापना *vi-jñāpănā* [S.], f. *Pl.* = विज्ञापन, 3., 4.

विज्ञापनीय *vi-jñāpănīyă* [S.], adj. deserving announcement or publicity.

विज्ञापित *vi-jñāpit* [S.], adj. announced, publicised, advertised.

विटप *viṭap* [S.], m. **1.** young branch or stem; shoot, sprout. **2.** bush. **3.** tree.

विटपी *viṭăpī* [S.], f. a tree.

विडंबन *vi-ḍamban* [S.], m. **1.** imitation; disguise (esp. of a god appearing in human form, or of a magician). ***2.** pretence, imposture, fraud. **3.** ridiculing.

विडंबना *vi-ḍambănā* [S.], f. 1. = विडंबन. **2.** frustration, vexation, distress; sthg. ironical, an irony.

विडंबित *vi-ḍambit* [S.], adj. **1.** imitated. **2.** ridiculed. **3.** frustrated, mortified.

वितंडा *vi-taṇḍā* [S.], f. **1.** captious or perverse criticism. **2.** pointless or frivolous controversy. — वितंडावाद, m. readiness to make captious criticisms, &c.

वितत *vi-tat* [S.], adj. stretched out; spread out.

वितति *vi-tati* [S.], f. **1.** spreading, extension. **2.** a quantity, mass; clump, cluster.

वितथ *vi-tath* [S.], adj. *Pl. HŚS.* **1.** at variance with fact or reality. **2.** vain, futile.

वितनु *vi-tanu* [S.], adj. & m. Brbh. **1.** adj. without body, bodiless. **2.** m. *mythol.* title of Kāmdev, the god of love. — ~ वितान, m. a canopy (of rays of light) for Kāmdev.

वितरक *vi-tarak* [S.], adj. & m. **1.** adj. distributing. **2.** *gram.* distributive. **3.** m. a distributor.

वितरण *vi-taraṇ* [S.], m. crossing over: distributing, distribution. — ~ करना, to distribute. – वितरणात्मक [°*ṇa*+*ā*°], adj. distributing; distributive.

वितरित *vi-tarit* [S.], adj. distributed.

वितर्क *vi-tark* [S.], m. **1.** consideration, argument (in a case). ***2.** consideration (of a case). — ~ करना (पर), to consider (a case). –

तर्क-वितर्क, m. discussion (of a matter); arguments pro and con.

वितर्क्य *vi-tarkyă* [S.], adj. requiring consideration (a matter); questionable, doubtful.

वितल *vi-tal* [S.], m. *mythol.* Brbh. the second, or the third of the seven regions below the earth.

वितस्ति *vi-tasti* [S.], f. Brbh. span of the hand.

वितान *vi-tān* [S.], m. sthg. stretched out; a canopy.

वितृष्णा *vi-tṛṣṇā* [S.], f. **1.** freedom from desire; indifference. **2.** aversion. **3.** strong desire.

वित्त *vitt* [S.], m. **1.** wealth. ***2.** finance; funds. — वित्त-पोषण, m. financing (a project, &c.) वित्त-मंत्री, m. *govt.* Finance Minister; treasurer (of a large institution).

वित्तीय *vittīyă* [S.], adj. financial, fiscal.

-विद् *-vid* [S.], n. formant. knower (of); scholar (of). e.g. भाषाविद्, m. knower of languages; linguist.

विदग्ध *vi-dagdh* [S.], adj. **1.** burnt up, consumed. **2.** inflamed. **3.** clever; skilled, versed; witty; cunning.

विदग्धता *vi-dagdhătā* [S.], f. cleverness, shrewdness, wit, &c. (see विदग्ध).

विदर *vidar*, m. reg. (Raj.) a child of mixed parentage.

विदर- *vi-dar-* [cf. H. *vidār-*], v.i. Brbh. to be torn or rent; to break (the heart).

विदा *vidā*, f. = बिदा.

विदाई *vidāī* [cf. H. *vidā*], f. farewelling, farewell.

विदाय *vidāy* [A. *vidā'*], m. = बिदा.

विदार- *vi-dār-* [ad. *vidārayati*], v.t. Brbh. Av. to tear; to split.

विदारण *vi-dāraṇ* [S.], m. **1.** tearing, rending; splitting. **2.** fig. killing, slaughter.

विदारित *vi-dārit* [S.], adj. torn; split, rent.

विदित *vidit* [S.], adj. known, perceived. — मुझे ~ होता है, it seems, or appears, to me.

विदीर्ण *vi-dīrṇ* [S.], adj. **1.** torn apart; broken open, split. **2.** killed.

विदुर *vidur* [S.], adj. & m. **1.** adj. knowing; learned; skilful. **2.** m. a knowledgeable man, &c.

विदुषी *viduṣī* [S.], adj. f. & f. **1.** adj. f. learned. **2.** f. a learned woman.

विदूर *vi-dūr* [S.], adj. & m. **1.** adj. very far off. **2.** [for *vidūraja-* or *vaidūrya-*] cat's-eye, or lapis lazuli.

विदूष- *vi-dūṣ-* [ad. *vidūṣayati*], v.t. & v.i. Brbh. Av. **1.** v.t. to slander. **2.** to torment. **3.** [? anal. f. *doṣa-*], v.i. to suffer distress.

विदूषक *vi-dūṣak* [S.], m. corrupting: a clown, jester.

विदूषण *vi-dūṣaṇ* [S.], m. attributing fault or blame, slandering.

विदेश *vi-deś* [S.], m. another country, a foreign country. — ~ जाना, to go abroad. ~ मंत्री, m. *govt.* Foreign Minister. ~ में, adv. abroad. – विदेशस्थ, adj. resident abroad.

विदेशी *vi-deśī* [S.], adj. & m. **1.** adj. foreign; external, overseas (as affairs, trade). **2.** m. a foreigner.

विदेशीपन *vi-deśīpan* [cf. H. *videśī*], m. **1.** foreign character. **2.** cultivation of foreign ways.

विदेशीय *vi-deśīyă* [S.], adj. = विदेशी.

विदेह *vi-deh* [S.], adj. **1.** without body, bodiless. **2.** Brbh. Av. unconscious. **3.** Av. a title of King Janaka of Videha (Tirhut).

विद्ध *viddh* [S.], adj. pierced.

विद्यमान *vidyamān* [S.], adj. existent, actual; presently existing or alive.

विद्यमानता *vidyamānătā* [S.], f. existence, presence.

विद्या *vidyā* [S.], f. **1.** knowledge, learning; study. **2.** a field of knowledge; science. **3.** a particular skill or art; a spell. ठग-विद्या, f. deceit. **4.** a title of the goddess Durgā. — ~ पढ़ना, to study, to acquire education. विद्याधर, *hind.* possessed of learning, or of spells: a kind of supernatural being attendant on Śiva and other deities, demigod. विद्या-दाता, m. inv. teacher, preceptor. विद्या-दान, m. teaching, instruction. विद्याध्ययन [°*yā*+*a*°], m. study, education. विद्यापीठ, f. a college of university status. विद्याभ्यास [°*yā*+*a*°], m. study, application to learning. विद्यारंभ [°*yā*+*ā*°], m. beginning of study: a ceremony performed when a child's schooling begins (see पट्टी पूजना). विद्यार्थिनी [°*yā*+*a*°], f. a pupil; a student. (= छात्रा). विद्यार्थी [°*yā*+*a*°], m. seeking knowledge: a pupil; a student. विद्यालय [°*yā*+*ā*°], m. place of learning: school; college; institute. °ईय, adj. विद्यावान, adj. learned. विद्याव्यसन, m. eager desire for learning.

विद्युज्- *vidyuj-*. = विद्युत्: — विद्युज्ज्वाला, f. flash of lightning.

विद्युत् *vi-dyut* [S.], f. **1.** lightning. **2.** electricity. **3.** electric charge. — विद्युत्-कण, m. a charged particle; an electron. विद्युत्-चुंबक, m. electromagnet. °ईय, adj. विद्युत्-दाब, m. electrical pressure: voltage. विद्युत्धारी, adj. carrying an electric current, charged. विद्युत्-विश्लेषण, m. electrolysis.

विद्युद्- *vidyud-* [S]. = विद्युत्: — विद्युदग्र, m. an electrode.

विद्युल्- *vidyul-*. = विद्युत्: — विद्युल्लता, f. flash of lightning.

विद्रुम *vi-drum* [S.], m. particular, or special, tree: **1.** coral. **2.** the coral-tree, *Erythrina*.

विद्रूप *vidrūp* [? ← B. (n.); cf. *virūpa-*], adj. distorted; ugly (features, glance).

विद्रोह *vi-droh* [S.], m. revolt, rebellion.

विद्रोही *vi-drohī* [S.], adj. rebellious.

विद्वत् *vidvat-*. = विद्वान: — विद्वत्-समाज, m. learned audience; the academic world.

विद्वत्ता *vidvattā* [S.], f. scholarship, erudition. — विद्वत्तापूर्ण, adj. scholarly, erudite.

विद्वन्- *vidvan-*. = विद्वान: — विद्वन्मंडली, f. group of scholars, scholars in a partic. field.

विद्वान *vidvān* [S.], adj. & m. **1.** adj. learned. **2.** m. a scholar.

विद्वेष *vi-dveṣ* [S.], m. **1.** enmity. **2.** ill-will, malice; rancour.

विद्वेषी *vi-dveṣī* [S.], adj. & m. **1.** adj. bearing enmity, hostile. **2.** malicious. **3.** m. an enemy.

विध- *vidha-* [cf. H. *bimdhnā*], v.t. Brbh. to pierce (= बींधना).

विधन *vi-dhan* [S.], adj. not having wealth, needy; poor.

विधना *vidhanā*, m. = विधिना.

विधर्म *vi-dharm* [S.], m. a different religion (from one's own).

विधर्मी *vi-dharmī* [S.], adj. & m. **1.** adj. irreligious, infidel. **2.** m. an infidel; a heretic.

विधवा *vidhăvā* [S.], f. a widow. — ~ रह जाना, to become widowed. – विधवा-विवाह, m. marriage to a widow, widow-remarriage. विधवाश्रम [°*vā* + *ā*°], m. home for widows.

विधवापन *vidhăvāpan* [cf. H. *vidhvā*], m. widowhood.

विधा *vi-dhā* [S.], f. **1.** form, type; genre. **2.** means, method. **3.** division, portion.

विधाता *vi-dhātā* [S.], m. inv. **1.** ordainer, arranger. **2.** Brahmā (as Creator and Ordainer).

विधात्री *vi-dhātrī* [S.], f. **1.** ordainer, arranger. **2.** a title of Sarasvatī (regarded as the wife of Brahmā).

विधान *vi-dhān* [S.], m. **1.** anything ordained. **2.** act, action; creation. **3.** arrangement (of any matter by proper means); legislation. **4.** rite. **5.** method, manner; means. **6.** rule, law. **7.** constitution (= संविधान). — विधान-परिषद्, f. Legislative Council. विधान-मंडल, m. legislature. विधानवाद, m. faith in, or adherence to, a constitution. °ई, adj. & m. constitutionalist. विधान-सभा, f. Legislative Assembly. °ई, adj. विधानांग [°*na* + *a*°], m. legislative branch.

विधायक *vi-dhāyak* [S.], adj. & m. **1.** adj. formative, creative. **2.** legislative. **3.** m. one who establishes or arranges. **4.** legislator, member of a legislature.

विधायन *vi-dhāyan* [S.], m. enactment (of laws).

विधायिका *vi-dhāyikā* [S.], f. legislature.

विधायी *vi-dhāyī* [S.], adj. = विधायक.

विधि *vi-dhi* [S.], f. (m., *Pl.*). **1.** rule, form, ordinance. **2.** law, statute. **3.** a rite, ceremony. **4.** method, manner. **5.** a title of Brahmā; fate, destiny. **6.** fig. what is ordained (for one, in life); horoscope. — ~ मिलना, (one's) horoscope to be confirmed (by events in life). – विधिकरण, m. legislation. °कर्ता, m. inv. legislator. विधितः, adv. by law, lawfully; *de jure*. विधिपूर्वक, adv. according to rule, &c. विधि-वक्ता, m. inv. law-speaker: barrister. विधिवत्, adv. according to rule, or to law, or to due form. विधि-विधान, m. ordainment of rule or law; established rules and ordinances; due or proper manner; the ordinance of fate. विधि-वेत्ता, m. inv. a jurist. विधि-शास्त्र, m. jurisprudence. विधि-संगत, adj. in conformity with ordinance, or law. विधि-सम्मत, adj. in accordance with law.

विधिक *vi-dhik* [S.], adj. legal.

विधिना *vi-dhinā* [S. (instr.)], m. by ordinance: = विधि, 5.

विधु *vidhu* [S.], m. the moon.

विधुर *vidhur* [S.], adj. & m. **1.** adj. separated (from a mistress or lover). **2.** bereaved. **3.** m. one separated, or pining. ***4.** a widower.

विधेय *vi-dhey* [S.], adj. & m. **1.** adj. to be arranged, performed or done; obligatory. **2.** tractable, compliant. **3.** *gram.* predicate. — विधेयात्मक [°*ya* + *ā*°], adj. predicative.

विधेयक *vi-dheyak* [S.], m. a parliamentary bill.

विधेयता *vi-dheyătā* [S.], f. **1.** fitness for enactment (as a rule or law). **2.** dependence, subjection.

विध्वंस *vi-dhvaṃs* [S.], m. **1.** ruin, destruction. **2.** demolition. — ~ करना (का), to destroy. विध्वंसात्मक [°*sa*+*ā*°], adj. harmful, ruinous, pernicious (as a creed, a theory).

विध्वंसक *vi-dhvaṃsak* [S.], adj. & m. **1.** adj. destructive. **2.** m. a destroyer, enemy. **3.** *naut.* destroyer.

विध्वंसी *vi-dhvaṃsī* [S.], adj. & m. **1.** adj. destructive. **2.** m. a destroyer, enemy.

विध्वस्त *vi-dhvast* [S.], adj. utterly destroyed.

विनत *vi-nat* [S.], adj. **1.** bent, bowed down. **2.** meek, humble. — विनतानन [°*ta*+*ā*°], adj. having the face or head lowered.

विनति *vi-nati* [S.], f. = बिनती.

विनय *vi-nay* [S.], m. **1.** courtesy, or refinement, or mildness of manner. **2.** modesty. **3.** meekness, humility. **4.** courteous, or humble request; petition. **5.** courteous act; a favour. — **विनयपूर्ण**, adj. courteous, &c. (remarks, conduct). **विनयवान**, adj. courteous, &c. (a person). **विनयशील**, adj. id.

विनयी *vi-nayī* [S.], adj. courteous, &c. (a person: see विनय).

विनशन *vi-naśan* [S.], m. perishing, loss; destruction.

विनशाना *vi-naśānā* [cf. H. *binasnā*], v.t. *Pl. HŚS.* **1.** to cause to deteriorate. **2.** to destroy.

विनष्ट *vi-naṣṭ* [S.], adj. **1.** utterly destroyed, or lost. **2.** corrupted (as values, morals).

विनष्टि *vi-naṣṭi* [S.], f. = विनाश.

विनस- *vinas-* [*vinaśyati*], v.i. Brbh. Av. = बिनसना.

विनाथ *vi-nāth* [S.], adj. Brbh. without a lord, or protector.

विनायक *vi-nāyak* [S.], m. **1.** remover (of obstacles). **2.** a title of the god Gaṇeś.

विनाश *vi-nāś* [S.], m. **1.** utter destruction; annihilation; laying waste. **2.** dire state. **3.** death. — **विनाशकारी**, adj. destructive.

विनाशक *vi-nāśak* [S.], adj. & m. **1.** adj. destroying, destructive. **2.** m. one who destroys.

विनाशन *vi-nāśan* [S.], m. 1. = विनाश, 1. **2.** E.H. = विनाशक.

विनाशित *vi-nāśit* [S.], adj. utterly destroyed, &c. (see विनाश).

विनाशी *vi-nāśī* [S.], adj. 1. = विनाशक. **2.** being destroyed, perishing.

विनाश्य *vi-nāśyă* [S.], adj. deserving, or liable, to be destroyed.

विनिंदित *vi-nindit* [S.], adj. severely criticised, or reproached.

विनिपात *vi-ni-pāt* [S.], m. great fall, ruin; calamity.

विनिमय *vi-ni-may* [S.], m. **1.** exchange. **2.** foreign funds, exchange. — ~ की दर, f. rate of exchange.

विनिमेय *vi-ni-meyă* [S.], adj. exchangeable.

विनियंत्रण *vi-ni-yantraṇ*, [S.], m. *govt.* decontrol.

विनियम *vi-ni-yam* [S.], m. a regulation.

विनियमन *vi-ni-yăman* [S.], m. subjecting to regulation or process, regulating.

विनियुक्त *vi-ni-yukt* [S.], adj. appropriated, applied, &c. (see विनियोग).

विनियोग *vi-ni-yog* [S.], m. **1.** appropriation (for a purpose); application, assignment (as of funds). **2.** conversion (funds).

विनिर्देश *vi-nir-deś* [S.], m. specification.

विनीत *vi-nīt* [S.], adj. **1.** courteous of manner, &c. (see विनय). **2.** modest; demure. **3.** meek, humble.

विनीतता *vi-nītătā* [S.], f. = विनय, 1.-3.

विनीति *vi-nīti* [S.], f. = विनय, 1.-3.

विनोद *vi-nod* [S.], m. **1.** pleasure, amusement. **2.** pastime. **3.** merriment; joke. **4.** enjoyable event; spectacle. **5.** delight. — **विनोदपूर्ण**, adj. amusing, humorous; cheerful; joking (remarks). **विनोदप्रिय**, adj. fond of joking, or fun. **विनोदशील**, adj. id.

विनोदी *vi-nodī* [S.], adj. taking pleasure or delight; cheerful (of temperament).

विन्यास *vi-ny-ās* [S.], m. **1.** orderly arrangement; adjustment. **2.** connection (as of words in a sentence). **वाक्य-विन्यास**, m. *ling.* syntax. — **केश-विन्यास**, m. hair-do, hair style.

विपंची *vi-pañcī* [S.], f. poet. lute, vīṇā.

विपक्ष *vi-pakṣ* [S.], adj. & m. **1.** adj. being on a different side, opposed; hostile. **2.** m. the opposite side (of a case); opposite party. **3.** a contrary instance. **4.** *gram.* an exception. — ~ में मत देना, to vote against (someone or sthg., के).

विपक्षता *vi-pakṣătā* [S.], f. opposition; hostility.

विपक्षी *vi-pakṣī* [S.], adj. & m. **1.** adj. = विपक्ष. **2.** m. an opponent, adversary.

विपण *vi-paṇ* [S.], m. a market.

विपणन *vi-paṇan* [S.], m. marketing.

विपत्ति *vi-patti* [S.], f. **1.** distress, adversity; a misfortune. **2.** disaster. — ~ उठाना, to suffer misfortune, &c. ~ झेलना, to endure misfortune. ~ भोगना, to suffer misfortune as one's lot. बड़ी ~ में होना, to be in dire distress. – विपत्ति-ग्रस्त, adj. overwhelmed by misfortune, or disaster; in distress (a ship).

विपथ *vi-path* [S.], m. **1.** wrong road. **2.** evil path, or conduct. – विपथगा, f. a river; one launched on an ill course. विपथगामी, m. id., 2.

विपद् *vi-pad* [S.], f. esp. विपद्-. = विपत्ति.

विपदा *vi-pădā* [S.], f. = विपत्ति.

विपन्न *vi-pann* [S.], adj. distressed; without means.

विपन्नता *vi-pannătā* [S.], f. misfortune: poverty.

विपरीत *vi-părît* [S.], adj. & ppn. **1.** adj. contrary, opposite; inverse. **2.** unfavourable, inauspicious. **3.** contrary (of disposition). **4.** ppn. w. के. contrary (to), otherwise (than). — ~ समझना, to misunderstand, to draw a wrong conclusion.

विपरीतता *vi-părîtătā* [S.], f. **1.** reverse or opposite state. **2.** contrariety, perverseness.

विपर्यय *vi-pary-ay* [S.], m. **1.** reversal, change; interchange, transference; inverted order. **2.** reverse, misfortune. **3.** misapprehension. **4.** *ling.* metathesis.

विपर्यस्त *vi-pary-ast* [S.], adj. reversed, changed, &c. (see विपर्यय).

विपर्याय *vi-pary-āy* [S.], m. = विपर्यय.

विपर्यास *vi-pary-ās* [S.], m. = विपर्यय.

विपल *vi-pal* [S.], m. a brief moment, instant of time.

विपाक *vi-pāk* [S.], m. **1.** ripening, maturing. **2.** consequence (of *karma* earlier acquired).

विपिन *vipin* [S.], m. trembling (in the wind): a forest grove.

विपुल *vi-pul* [S.], adj. **1.** ample, broad, extensive; vast. ***2.** abundant. **3.** deep, profound.

विपुलता *vi-pulătā* [S.], f. amplitude, abundance, &c. (see विपुल).

विपुला *vi-pulā* [S.], f. the extensive one: the earth in its abundance.

विपुलाई *vi-pulāī* [cf. H. *vipul*], f. Av. = विपुलता.

विप्र *vipr* [S.], m. **1.** a brāhmaṇ. **2.** a family priest (= पुरोहित).

विप्रतिपत्ति *vi-prati-patti* [S.], f. **1.** discrepancy, conflict (as of evidence). **2.** misconception.

विप्रयुक्त *vi-pra-yukt* [S.], adj. separated.

विप्रलंभ *vi-pra-lambh* [S.], m. deception: **1.** separation (of lovers). **2.** quarrel.

विप्रलब्ध *vi-pra-labdh* [S.], adj. deceived (a lover).

विप्लव *vi-plav* [S.], m. floating apart, dispersion: **1.** uprising, revolt. **2.** revolution. — विप्लवकारी, adj. rebellious; causing or encouraging revolution.

विप्लवी *vi-plavī* [S.], adj. having to do with revolt, or revolution.

विफल *vi-phal* [S.], adj. **1.** not bearing fruit (as a plant). **2.** unprofitable; ineffective; unsuccessful.

विफलता *vi-phalătā* [S.], f. fruitlessness, &c. (see विफल).

विबुद्ध *vi-buddh* [S.], adj. **1.** awakened; aroused. **2.** expanded; blossomed. ***3.** clever, experienced; wise.

विभक्त *vi-bhakt* [S.], adj. **1.** divided; separated. **2.** distributed (as a patrimony). **3.** partitioned (as a territory).

विभक्ति *vi-bhakti* [S.], f. **1.** a division. **2.** a part, share. **3.** *gram.* an inflexion, or inflexional affix. — विभक्तिपरक, adj. susceptible of inflexion, inflected (a language; a word); declinable.

विभव *vi-bhav* [S.], m. **1.** might, power. **2.** supreme power. **3.** wealth, abundance. — विभवशाली, adj. mighty; very wealthy.

विभा *vi-bhā* [S.], f. radiance, lustre. — विभाकर, m. Brbh. light-maker: the sun.

विभा- *vi-bhā-* [ad. *vibhāti*: w. H. *bhā(nā)*], v.i. Brbh. **1.** to shine. **2.** *Pl.* to appear.

विभाग *vi-bhāg* [S.], m. **1.** a division, section; part (as of a book). **2.** a department; section; unit. **3.** a fraction.

विभागीय *vi-bhāgīyă* [S.], adj. departmental.

विभाजक *vi-bhājak* [S.], adj. & m. **1.** adj. dividing. **2.** distinguishing, demarcating. **3.** m. *math.* a denominator.

विभाजन *vi-bhājan* [S.], m. **1.** division. **2.** distribution, apportionment. **3.** partition (of a territory).

विभाजित *vi-bhājit* [S.], adj. divided, &c. (see विभाजन).

विभाज्य *vi-bhājyă* [S.], adj. to be divided, &c. (see विभाजन).

विभाती *vi-bhātī* [ad. *vibhāta-*; H. *-ī*], f. Brbh. lustre.

विभाव *vi-bhāv* [S.], m. *rhet.* any cause of a particular emotion (e.g. as felt by the spectators of a classical drama).

विभावन *vi-bhāvan* [S.], m. *rhet.* suggestion (of the full significance of a particular event, motif, &c).

विभावना *vi-bhāvănā* [S.], f. imagination.

विभावरी *vi-bhāvărī* [S.], f. night, starry night.

विभाव्य *vi-bhāvyă* [S.], adj. **1.** conceivable, imaginable. **2.** to be experienced, or thought over.

विभाषा *vi-bhāṣā* [S.], f. a dialect.

विभास *vi-bhas* [S.], m. **1.** lustre, splendour. **2.** *mus.* name of a *rāg.*

विभिन्न *vi-bhinn* [S.], adj. **1.** separated. **2.** various, different, distinct; contradictory.

विभिन्नता *vi-bhinnătā* [S.], f. distinctness, variety, diversity; contradictoriness.

विभीषण *vi-bhīṣaṇ* [S.], m. *mythol.* terrifying: name of a brother of Rāvaṇ.

विभीषिका *vi-bhīṣikā* [S.], f. a frightening display; a threat.

विभु *vi-bhu* [S.], adj. & m. **1.** adj. all-pervasive (as the ultimate being). **2.** eternal. **3.** mighty. **4.** m. a title of the supreme being.

विभुता *vi-bhutā* [S.], f. **1.** might, power. **2.** sovereignty, supremacy.

विभूति *vi-bhūti* [S.], f. **1.** might, power. **2.** dominion, supremacy. **3.** *philos.* superhuman power. **4.** glory, grandeur. **5.** wealth; prosperity. **6.** transf. cow-dung ash (with which Śaivas smear their bodies in the way ascribed to Śiva).

विभूषण *vi-bhūṣaṇ* [S.], m. adornment, decoration; embellishment.

विभूषित *vi-bhūṣit* [S.], adj. adorned, decorated.

विभेद *vi-bhed* [S.], m. **1.** division; split (as in a party). **2.** distinction, difference. **3.** discrimination (adverse). **4.** a variant (form, category).

विभेदक *vi-bhedak* [S.], adj. & m. dividing, &c. (cf. विभेद, 1.-3).

विभेदन *vi-bhedan* [S.], m. **1.** dividing. **2.** making a distinction. **3.** discriminating (adversely).

विभोर *vibhor* [B. *vibhor*], adj. inspired, carried away.

विभ्रम *vi-bhram* [S.], m. **1.** wandering, &c. (see विभ्रांत). **2.** confusion, error. **3.** agitation. **4.** flirtatious glances, or gestures.

विभ्रांत *vi-bhrānt* [S.], adj. **1.** wandering, roving. **2.** whirling round. **3.** confused, in error. **4.** agitated.

विभ्रांति *vi-bhrānti* [S.], f. **1.** whirling or going round. **2.** confusion, error. **3.** agitation, alarm.

विभ्राट *vi-bhrāṭ* [S.], m. brightness, blaze.

विमत *vi-mat* [S.], adj. & m. **1.** adj. disagreeing, at variance. **2.** m. differing opinion. 3. = विमति.

विमति *vi-mati* [S.], f. disagreement.

विमर्श *vi-marś* [S.], m. **1.** consideration, deliberation; discussion, debate. **2.** investigation; study, critique. **3.** consultation.

विमर्षित *vi-marṣit* [S.], adj. poet. displeased, distressed.

विमल *vi-mal* [S.], m. **1.** free of dirt or stain, pure. **2.** lovely. **3.** without fault or sin.

विमलता *vi-malătā* [S.], f. purity, &c. (see विमल).

विमाता *vi-mātā* [S.], f. stepmother.

विमान *vi-mān* [S.], m. measurer, traverser: **1.** *hind.* an aerial vehicle (of the gods). ***2.** an aircraft. — ~ से, adv. by air. विमान-चालक, m. pilot of an aircraft. °-चालन, m. aviation. विमान-पट्टन, m. airport. विमान-परिचारिका, f. stewardess (in an aircraft). विमान-वाहक, m. aircraft carrier. विमानापहरण [°*a*+*a*°], m. hijacking of an aircraft.

विमानन *vi-mānan* [S.: f. Engl.], m. aviation.

विमार्ग *vi-mārg* [S.], m. wrong road, wrong course.

विमुक्त *vi-mukt* [S.], adj. **1.** released, set free; liberated. **2.** released from rebirth in the world. **3.** dismissed; isolated (life); abandoned. **4.** exempt. **5.** launched, shot (as an arrow).

विमुक्ति *vi-mukti* [S.], f. **1.** release, &c. (see विमुक्त). **2.** release from rebirth in the world.

विमुख *vi-mukh* [S.], adj. with face averted: **1.** displeased (with, से: as a god with men, &c.); opposed (to). **2.** indifferent (to), not interested (in). **3.** turning from hope, disappointed (as a rejected beggar).

विमुखता *vi-mukhătā* [S.], f. state of displeasure, &c. (see **विमुख**).

विमुग्ध *vi-mugdh* [S.], adj. **1.** charmed, delighted. **2.** fascinated, infatuated. **3.** bewildered. — **विमुग्धकर**, adj. fascinating (a topic). °-**कारी**, adj. fascinating, charming (a person).

विमूढ़ *vi-mūṛh* [S.], adj. **1.** bewildered. **किंकर्तव्य-विमूढ़**, adj. uncertain what to do. **2.** beguiled; infatuated. **3.** foolish, stupid.

विमोक्ष *vi-mokṣ* [S.], m. **1.** releasing; liberation. **2.** release from rebirth in the world.

विमोचन *vi-mocan* [S.], m. **1.** release (as of an issue, or item). **2.** redemption (as of a bond).

विमोचित *vi-mocit* [S.], adj. **1.** loosed, released. **2.** forgiven, pardoned.

विमोह *vi-moh* [S.], m. **1.** bewilderment, confusion. **2.** infatuation.

विमोह- *vi-moh-* [? cf. H. *vimoh*], v.i. Brbh. Av. to be enchanted, charmed.

विमोहन *vi-mohan* [S.], m. the act of confusing and charming (one); alluring; temptation. — **विमोहनशील**, adj. Av. charming, delighting.

विमोहनी *vimohănī* [cf. H. *vimohan*], adj. alluring, seductive.

विमोहित *vi-mohit* [S.], adj. **1.** charmed. **2.** unconscious.

विमोही *vi-mohī* [S.], adj. Av. confused, &c. (see **विमोहित**).

वियत् *viyat* [S.], m. *Pl. HŚS.* the sky.

वियुक्त *vi-yukt* [S.], adj. separated (cf. **वियोग**).

वियोग *vi-yog* [S.], m. separation (esp. of lovers). — **वियोगांत** [°*ga+a*°], adj. ending in separation, tragic (a story, a drama).

वियोगी *vi-yogī* [S.], adj. & m. **1.** adj. separated. **2.** distressed by separation (from a beloved one). **3.** m. a lover suffering the pangs of separation.

वियोजन *vi-yojan* [S.], m. **1.** separation. **2.** demobilisation. **3.** *arith.* subtraction.

वियोजित *vi-yojit* [S.], adj. **1.** separated; *mil.* discharged. **2.** subtracted.

विरंग *vi-raṅg* [S.], adj. **1.** faded, scorched, withered (as flowers). **2.** of different colours. **3.** adv. in different ways.

विरंच *vi-rañc* [S.], m. Av. = **विरंचि**.

विरंचि *vi-rañci* [S.], m. Brbh. Av. a name of Brahmā.

विरंजक *vi-rañjak* [S.], adj. & m. **1.** adj. bleaching. **2.** m. a bleach, bleaching agent.

विरंजन *vi-rañjan* [S.], m. bleaching (the process).

विरंजित *vi-rañjit* [S.], adj. bleached.

विरक्त *vi-rakt* [S.], adj. **1.** not feeling desire or passion; unattached to worldly objects. **2.** alienated (from, **से**); averse (to); weary (of).

विरक्तता *vi-raktătā* [S.], f. = **विरक्ति**.

विरक्ति *vi-rakti* [S.], f. **1.** absence of desire, &c. (cf. **विरक्त**). **2.** alienation, &c.

विरचन *vi-racan* [S.], m. **1.** composition (of a literary work). **2.** constructing, making (with art or skill).

विरचयिता *vi-racăyitā* [S.], m. inv. composer, author.

विरचित *vi-racit* [S.], adj. **1.** composed (a literary work). **2.** inlaid, set. **3.** ornamented.

विरज *vi-raj* [S.], adj. **1.** free of passion. **2.** pure, undefiled.

विरत *vi-rat* [S.], adj. ceased, stopped: **1.** indifferent (to, **से**); displeased with, disliking. **2.** desisted (from, **से**). **3.** detached (the mind, or heart: as that of an ascetic).

विरति *vi-rati* [S.], f. cessation: indifference, &c. (cf. **विरत**).

विरद *virad* [S.], m. Brbh. = **विरुद**.

विरल *viral* [S.], adj. **1.** having gaps; of open weave (cloth); open, not dense (as a wood). ***2.** rarely met with (as an unusual or odd person).

विरला *virlā* [*virala-*], adj. strange, unusual (= **बिरला**).

विरस *vi-ras* [S.], adj. **1.** tasteless, insipid. **2.** dull, jejune. **3.** ill-tasting.

विरसता *vi-rasătā* [S.], f. tastelessness, insipidity.

विरसा *virsā* [A. *virṣa*], m. 1. = **विरासत**, 1. **2.** a bequest.

विरह *vi-rah* [S.], m. **1.** separation. **2.** the anguish of separation. **3.** loneliness. — **~ में होना**, to suffer the anguish of separation. – **विरह-विधुर**, adj. bereft by separation: = **विरही**. **विरहाग्नि** [°*ha+a*°], m. fire of separation: = ~, 2.

विरहिणी *vi-rahiṇī* [S.], f. a woman suffering the pangs of separation.

विरहित *vi-răhit* [S.], adj. Brbh. **1.** *Pl. HŚS.* deserted, forsaken. ***2.** bereft (of).

विरहिया *virahiyā* [cf. H. *virahī*], adj. & m., f. **1.** adj. love-sick, suffering the distress of separation. **2.** m., f. a love-sick person.

विरही *vi-răhī* [S.], adj. & m. **1.** adj. separated (from: as from a loved one); love-sick. **2.** lonely. **3.** m. a lover suffering pangs of separation.

विराग *vi-rāg* [S.], m. **1.** absence of desire. **2.** indifference. **3.** aversion.

विरागी *vi-rāgī* [S.], adj. & m. **1.** adj. free of desire, &c. (see विराग). **2.** m. an ascetic.

विराजना *vi-rājnā* [ad. *virājati*], v.i. **1.** to shine, to be splendid. **2.** to be ensconced; to rule. **3.** hon. to take a seat.

विराजमान *vi-rājămān* [S.], adj. **1.** splendid, radiant. **2.** ensconced (as on a throne), ruling. — ~ होना, to ascend a throne; to reign.

विराजित *vi-rājit* [S.], adj. **1.** made splendid, radiant. **2.** assuming an air of splendour (as when occupying a seat of honour).

विराट् *vi-rāṭ* [S.], m. & adj. **1.** m. the ruler, or splendid one. **2.** adj. vast; imposing, splendid. — विराट्रूप, adj. having the form of Virāṭ: a title of the supreme being as able to assume a universal form in which the entire creation is manifest.

विराम *vi-rām* [S.], m. **1.** leaving off, stopping, pause. **2.** rest; respite. **3.** a rest, pause (in any activity). **4.** *gram.* the Devanāgarī script sign *virāma* (marking absence of the sound /ə/ after a consonant). — विराम-चिह्न, m. = ~, 4. विराम-संधि, f. truce; armistice.

विरासत *virāsat* [A. *virāṣa*: P. *virāṣat*], f. **1.** inheritance; heritage. **2.** hereditary right. **3.** a bequest. — ~ में पाना, to inherit. ~ से, adv. by inheritance; as an heirloom.

विरासतन *virāsatan* [A. *virāṣatan*], adv. U. = विरासत से.

विरुद *virud* [S.], m. fame, glory. — विरुदावली [°*da*+*ā*°], f. encomium, panegyric.

[1]**विरुदैत** *virudait* [cf. H. *virud*], m. a panegyrist, bard.

[2]**विरुदैत** *virudait*, m. *Pl.* a soldier in uniform.

विरुद्ध *vi-ruddh* [S.], adj. & ppn. **1.** adj. opposed, opposing; hostile. **2.** unfavourable, unpropitious. **3.** contrary, inconsistent (to or with, से: as actions, views). **4.** ppn. w. के. against, opposed, hostile (to).

विरुद्धता *vi-ruddhătā* [S.], f. **1.** opposition. **2.** inconsistency, incongruity (as of views).

विरूप *vi-rūp* [S.], adj. **1.** misshapen, deformed; ugly. **2.** of varied form, multiform.

विरूपण *vi-rūpaṇ* [S.], m. **1.** deformation. **2.** disfigurement; mutilation.

विरूपता *vi-rūpătā* [S.], f. a deformity.

विरूपित *vi-rūpit* [S.], adj. **1.** deformed (cf. विरूप). **2.** disfigured, mutilated.

विरूपी *vi-rūpī* [S.], adj. = विरूप.

विरेचक *vi-recak* [S.], adj. purgative, laxative.

विरेचन *vi-recan* [S.], m. **1.** a laxative. **2.** purging (the bowels).

विरोध *vi-rodh* [S.], m. **1.** opposition; resistance. **2.** conflict (as of opinions); inconsistency. **3.** hostility, enmity. — ~ करना (का), to oppose, to resist. – विरोध-पत्र, m. *dipl.* note of protest. विरोधाभास [°*dha*+*ā*°], m. appearance of contradiction; contradiction, paradox; contrast.

विरोधिता *vi-rodhitā* [S.], f. **1.** attitude or condition of being opposed, &c. (see विरोधी). **2.** contradictoriness (of signs).

विरोधी *vi-rodhī* [S.], adj. & m. **1.** adj. opposed, opposing; rebellious (as the heart or emotions). **2.** -विरोधी. anti-, &c. e.g. धर्म-विरोधी, adj. irreligious. **3.** conflicting, inconsistent. **4.** hostile. **5.** contentious (a person, or faction). **6.** m. an opponent; an enemy. — ~ पक्ष, m. the opposite side, opposition. परस्पर ~, adj. mutually inconsistent, contradictory.

विलंब *vi-lamb* [S.], m. slowness, delay. — ~ करना, to delay; to procrastinate.

विलंबन *vi-lamban* [S.], m. delaying, delay.

विलंबित *vi-lambit* [S.], adj. **1.** delayed; late; put off or back, deferred. **2.** *mus.* slow (time). **3.** Brbh. hanging down (as hair).

विलंभ *vi-lambh* [S.], m. *Pl. HŚS.* **1.** giving; liberality. **2.** gift, donation.

विलक्ष *vi-lakṣ* [S.], adj. **1.** strange, extraordinary. **2.** astonished. **3.** embarrassed, abashed.

विलक्षण *vi-lakṣaṇ* [S.], adj. **1.** having different, or distinguishing characteristics: strange, extraordinary. **2.** astonishing.

विलक्षणता *vi-lakṣaṇătā* [S.], f. **1.** strange aspect or feature(s), peculiarity. **2.** remarkability.

विलग *vi-lag* [S.], adj. separate, detached.

विलज्ज *vi-lajj* [S.], adj. **1.** shameless. **2.** immodest; impudent.

विलय *vi-lay* [S.], m. **1.** dissolving; dissolution. **2.** merging. **3.** destruction (esp. of the world).

विलयन *vi-layan* [S.], m. **1.** the act of dissolving, &c. **2.** merging, merger. **3.** *chem.* a solution.

विलसन *vi-lasan* [S.], m. **1.** flashing, gleaming. **2.** amusement, pleasure (see विलास).

विलाप *vi-lāp* [S.], m. weeping, lamentation. — ~ करना, to weep, to wail.

विलापी *vi-lāpī* [S.], adj. & m. **1.** adj. weeping. **2.** m. one who weeps or laments.

विलायत *vilāyat* [A. *vilāya*: P. *vilāyat*], f. a province, realm: **1.** *hist.* the Mughal province of Afghanistan. **2.** a realm beyond India; England, Britain; Europe; the west.

विलायती *vilāyătī* [A. *vilāyatī*], adj. & m. **1.** adj. foreign; English, British; European; western. **2.** foreign-made. **3.** m. a foreigner. **4.** a foreign-made article.

विलायतीपन *vilāyătīpan* [cf. H. *vilāyatī*], m. obsession with non-Indian (esp. western) things.

विलास *vi-lās* [S.], m. **1.** sensuous pleasure; luxurious life. **2.** pleasure with the opposite sex, flirting; flirtatious gesture. **3.** sensuousness (of movement, deportment). — ~ करना, to enjoy oneself; to give oneself up to pleasure.

विलास- *vi-lās-* [cf. H. *vilās-*], v.i. Brbh. to revel in.

विलासिता *vi-lāsitā* [S.], f. **1.** love of sensuous pleasure or of luxury. **2.** fondness for the opposite sex; flirtatiousness. **3.** sensuality. — विलासितामय, adj. consisting in luxury, luxurious.

विलासी *vi-lāsī* [S.], adj. & m. **1.** pleasure-loving. **2.** flirtatious. **3.** sensual. **4.** m. a pleasure-loving person, &c.

विलुलित *vi-lulit* [S.], adj. shaken, stirred.

विलोकन *vi-lokan* [S.], m. **1.** looking, seeing; gazing. **2.** contemplating (a matter). — ~ करना, to look at, &c.

विलोकनीय *vi-lokănīyă* [S.], adj. worthy of being looked at; beautiful.

विलोकित *vi-lokit* [S.], adj. **1.** looked at, observed. **2.** examined, considered.

विलोचन *vi-locan* [S.], m. **1.** the eye. **2.** fig. sight.

विलोड़न *vi-loṛan* [S.], m. **1.** shaking, stirring up (water, ocean). **2.** whirling round. **3.** churning. **4.** fig. thorough study (of a subject).

विलोड़ित *vi-loṛit* [S.], adj. shaken, stirred up, &c. (see विलोड़न).

विलोभ *vi-lobh* [S.], m. attraction, seduction.

विलोभन *vi-lobhan* [S.], m. **1.** beguiling, tempting; seducing. **2.** praise, flattery.

विलोम *vi-lom* [S.], adj. going against the hair: **1.** against the grain, improper, inauspicious; morganatic (a marriage). **2.** reverse, inverse, opposite. — ~ शब्द, m. an antonym.

विल्व *vilvă* [S.], m. the wood-apple tree (= [1]बेल).

विवक्षा *vi-vakṣā* [S.], f. **1.** desire to speak. **2.** meaning, sense, implication (as of a word).

विवक्षित *vi-vakṣit* [S.], adj. meant to be said: **1.** meant, intended. **2.** implied.

विवक्षिता *vi-vakṣitā* [S.], f. intention, meaning.

विवर *vi-var* [S.], m. **1.** an opening; crack; hole. **2.** a hole, burrow. **3.** cavity (as of the mouth, or abdomen).

विवरण *vi-varaṇ* [S.], m. **1.** exposition, detailed account; explanation. **2.** report (of proceedings). **3.** specification (of work to be done). — ~ करना, to give an account (of, का). – विवरणात्मक [°*ṇa* + *ā*°], adj. descriptive; detailed.

विवरणिका *vi-varăṇikā* [S.], f. a prospectus.

विवरणी *vi-varăṇī* [S.], f. detailed account or report of a partic. topic; return (of tax).

विवर्जन *vi-varjan* [S.], m. **1.** leaving, abandoning. **2.** shunning.

विवर्ण *vi-varṇ* [S.], adj. **1.** colourless, pale. **2.** bad-coloured: of low origin.

विवर्त *vi-vart* [S.], m. turning, revolving; changing: — विवर्तमान, m. changing, variable.

विवर्तन *vi-vartan* [S.], m. turning, revolving; change (as in times, attitudes).

विवर्धन *vi-vardhan* [S.], m. increase, growth; development, advance.

विवर्धित *vi-vardhit* [S.], adj. increased, grown; developed, advanced.

विवश *vi-vaś* [S.], adj. **1.** powerless, helpless. **2.** involuntary. **3.** [× *vaśya-*] not to be averted or deferred (a time). — ~ होकर, adv. having no power, or choice (in a matter).

विवशता *vi-vaśătā* [S.], f. powerlessness, helplessness.

विवसन *vi-vasan* [S.], adj. without clothing, naked.

विवस्त्र *vi-vastră* [S.], adj. without clothing, naked.

विवस्वत् *vi-vasvat* [S.], m. *Pl. HŚS.* the brilliant one: **1.** the sun. **2.** *mythol.* a title of the seventh or present (*vaivasvat*) Manu.

विवाक *vi-vāk* [S.], *Pl. HŚS.* judge (as in a debate).

विवाकी *vi-vākī* [cf. H. *vivāk*], f. *Pl.* judge's decision (as in a debate).

विवाचक *vi-vācak* [S.], m. arbitrator.

विवाचन *vi-vācan* [S.], m. arbitration.

विवाद *vi-vād* [S.], m. **1.** argument; debate. **2.** dispute; controversy; quarrel. **3.** a debate. — ~ उठाना, to raise a controversy; to raise a counter-argument or objection. ~ करना, to argue, to debate, &c. – विवाद-ग्रस्त, m. disputed (as a matter, or a title). विवादपूर्ण, adj. disputed (a matter). विवादशील, adj. argumentative. विवादास्पद [°*da*+*ā*°], adj. (which is) a subject of dispute: = विवाद ग्रस्त.

विवादित *vi-vādit* [S], m. disputed (a matter).

विवादी *vi-vādī* [S.], adj. & m. **1.** adj. involved in an argument, or dispute (see विवाद). **2.** m. one involved in an argument, or dispute.

विवाह *vi-vāh* [S.], m. marriage. — ~ करना, to arrange the marriage (of, का; to, से); to marry. — विवाह-बंधन, m. marriage tie(s). विवाह-भंग, m. break-up of marriage; divorce. विवाह-विच्छेद, m. = विवाह-भंग; separation. विवाह-विषयक, adj. matrimonial. विवाह-संबंध, m. marriage tie(s) or relationship. विवाहोचित [°*ha*+*u*°], adj. marriageable (age).

विवाहना *vi-vāhnā* [ad. *vivāhayati*; or cf. H. *vivāh*], v.t. = ब्याहना.

विवाहित *vi-vāhit* [S.], adj. married.

विवाह्य *vi-vāhyă* [S.], adj. *Pl. HŚS.* ready, or fit, to be married.

विविक्त *vi-vikt* [S.], adj. separated, distinguished (from each other); isolated.

विविक्ति *vi-vikti* [S.], f. state of separation, or isolation.

विविध *vi-vidh* [S.], adj. of different sorts, various; miscellaneous.

विविधता *vi-vidhătā* [S.], adj. variety (of things). — विविधता-भरा, adj. filled or piled with different things (as a table).

विवेक *vi-vek* [S.], m. **1.** discrimination, discernment; judgment. **2.** prudence. **3.** conscience. — ~ पर छोड़ना, to leave (a matter) to the good sense (of, के). – विवेकशील, adj. discerning, judicious. विवेक-शून्य, adj. undiscriminating, thoughtless. विवेक-संगत, adj. sensible, rational (as a procedure). विवेकाधीन [°*ka*+*a*°], adj. discretionary.

विवेकी *vi-vekī* [S.], adj. & m. **1.** adj. discriminating, discerning; judicious. **2.** m. a discerning person, &c.

विवेचक *vi-vecak* [S.], adj. & m. **1.** adj. discriminating; examining, investigating. **2.** m. a discriminating or judicious person; one wise or versed in (a topic, &c).

विवेचन *vi-vecan* [S.], m. **1.** the act of discrimination, discernment; judgment. **2.** investigation, enquiry (into, का); deliberation. **3.** an appraisal, evaluation. — ~ करना (का), to enquire (into); to weigh, to assess (a matter). विवेचनात्मक [°*nă*+*ā*°], adj. inquiring, critical.

विवेचना *vi-vecănā* [S.], f. = विवेचन.

विवेचनीय *vi-vecănīyă* [S.], adj. needing or deserving investigation, &c. (see विवेचन).

विवेचित *vi-vecit* [S.], adj. appraised, discussed.

विवेच्य *vi-vecyă* [S.], adj. = विवेचनीय.

विशद *vi-śad* [S.], adj. **1.** pure. **2.** clean, clear (as water). **3.** clear, lucid. **4.** evident. **5.** beautiful (as speech, voice).

विशाखा *vi-śākhā* [S.], f. *astron.* name of the sixteenth lunar asterism.

विशारद *vi-śārad* [S.], adj. well-versed, skilled, learned. — साहित्य-विशारद, adj. well-versed in literature: designation of one passing a partic. grade of examination in Hindi literature.

विशाल *viśāl* [S.], adj. **1.** broad, extensive. ***2.** vast, huge. **3.** grand, great. — विशालकाय, m. huge of body or frame.

विशालता *viśālătā* [S.], f. vastness, greatness, &c. (cf. विशाल).

विशिख *vi-śikh* [S.], m. an arrow.

विशिष्ट *vi-śiṣṭ* [S.], adj. **1.** distinctive, particular, special. **2.** unusual. **3.** pre-eminent, excellent. — विशिष्टाद्वैत [°*ṭa*+*a*°], m. *philos.* qualified non-duality (the doctrine of Rāmānuja).

विशिष्टता *vi-śiṣṭătā* [S.], f. **1.** special characteristic(s), individuality. **2.** excellence.

विशृंखल *vi-śr̥ṅkhal* [S.], adj. disorganised.

विशेष *vi-śeṣ* [S.], adj. & m. **1.** adj. particular, special, distinctive; unusual, exceptional. **2.** choice, excellent. **3.** esp. adv. extreme(ly). **4.** m. characteristic difference or feature, special quality. **5.** -विशेष. particular kind or type. e.g. व्यक्ति-विशेष, m. particular type of person. — विशेषकर, adv. especially, particularly, chiefly. विशेषज्ञ, m. a specialist. °ता, f. possession, cultivation, or field of specialised knowledge. विशेषत:, adv. = विशेषकर. विशेषतया, adv. = विशेषकर. विशेषांक [°*ṣa* + *a*°], m. special number (of a journal). विशेषाधिकार [°*ṣa* + *a*°], m. particular right: privilege. विशेषीकृत, adj. specialised. °-ईकरण, m. making particular or special.

विशेषक *vi-śeṣak* [S.], adj. & m. **1.** adj. distinguishing. **2.** diacritical (sign). **3.** m. a special sign, diacritic; a mark (esp. sectarian) on the forehead.

विशेषण *vi-śeṣaṇ* [S.], m. marking out, distinguishing: **1.** an adjective. **2.** a title, epithet.

विशेषता *vi-śeṣătā* [S.], f. particular feature, distinguishing property; characteristic.

विशेषित *vi-śeṣit* [S.], adj. distinguished, marked out.

विशेषीकरण *vi-śeṣīkaraṇ* [S.], m. see s.v. विशेष.

विशेषीकृत *vi-śeṣīkr̥t* [S.], adj. see s.v. विशेष.

विशेष्य *vi-śeṣyă* [S.], m. *gram.* a noun (as particularised or defined by an adjective).

विश्रंभ *vi-śrambh* [S.], m. confidence: intimacy. — विश्रंभ-कथा, f. lovers' quarrel.

विश्रब्ध *vi-śrabdh* [S.], adj. confident, fearless; calm.

विश्रांत *vi-śrānt* [S.], adj. **1.** resting; weary. **2.** ceased (from). **3.** finished. **4.** composed, calm; relaxed.

विश्रांति *vi-śrānti* [S.], f. 1. = विश्राम. **2.** break (as in work); relaxation.

विश्राम *vi-śrām* [S.], m. **1.** rest. **2.** calm, tranquillity (after toil).

विश्लिष्ट *vi-śliṣṭ* [S.], adj. **1.** made separate. **2.** analysed.

विश्लेष *vi-śleṣ* [S.], m. analysis (= विश्लेषण).

विश्लेषक *vi-śleṣak* [S.], m. an analyst.

विश्लेषण *vi-śleṣaṇ* [S.], m. analysis. — विश्लेषणात्मक [°*ṇa* + *ā*°], adj. analytical.

विश्लेषित *vi-śleṣit* [S.], adj. = विश्लिष्ट.

विश्लेष्य *vi-śleṣyă* [S.], adj. to be analysed.

विश्वंभर *viśvambhar* [S.], f. see s.v. विश्व.

विश्व *viśvă* [S.], adj. & m. **1.** adj. entire, whole, universal. **2.** m. the universe. **3.** freq. विश्व-. the world. — विश्वंभर, adj. all-supporting: the supreme being; the earth. °आ, f. the earth. विश्व-कर्ता, m. inv. creator of the world. विश्व-कर्मा, m. inv. *mythol.* all-maker: title of the creative architect and artist of the gods. विश्वकाया, f. a title of Durgā. विश्व-कोश, m. encyclopedia. °ईय, adj. विश्वगाथ, m. whose song is the universe: the supreme being. विश्व-नाथ, m. lord of the universe: a title of Śiva. विश्वचर, adj. = विश्वव्यापी. विश्वजित्, adj. all-conquering. विश्व-भरन, Av. supporting the universe, or world. विश्वभारतीय, adj. all-Indian. विश्व-युद्ध, m. world war; a world war. विश्वमय, adj. containing the universe: the supreme being. विश्वरूप, adj. & m. taking, or existing in, all forms; universal; universal form (specif. of Kr̥ṣṇa); Brbh. name of a comet. °-रूपिणी, f. having various forms, or a universal form: title of a śākta goddess. विश्व-वयन, m. world-weaving: the created universe. विश्ववाद, m. theory of or belief in the importance of the world as a unit (cultural, or otherwise). °ई, adj. & m. विश्व-विख्यात, adj. world-famed. विश्व-विदित, adj. known throughout the world. विश्वविद्यालय, m. abode of universal knowledge: a university. °ईय, adj. विश्वव्यापी, adj. pervading the universe or world: universal, general. विश्व-शब्दकोश, m. encyclopedic dictionary. विश्व-समुद्र, m. the oceans of the world. विश्वात्मवाद [°*va* + *ā*°], m. theory of or belief in the universal soul or spirit.

विश्वसनीय *vi-śvasănīyă* [S.], adj. **1.** trustworthy (a person). **2.** credible (a report, &c).

विश्वसित *vi-śvasit* [S.], adj. = विश्वस्त, 1.

विश्वस्त *vi-śvast* [S.], adj. **1.** trustworthy, reliable (a person); faithful. **2.** trustworthy (an authority, or a source). **3.** full of confidence, bold. **4.** unsuspecting.

विश्वस्तता *vi-śvastătā* [S.], f. reliability, dependability.

विश्वास *vi-śvās* [S.], m. **1.** trust, confidence, reliance. **2.** faith; belief. — ~ करना, to have confidence (about sthg., का), to believe. ~ करना (पर), = ~ रखना. ~ जमाना, to instil, or to strengthen, confidence or faith (in, में). ~ दिलाना, to give confidence or faith (to, को), to (re)assure. ~ धरना (में), = next. ~ रखना, to put trust, faith, &c. (in, पर or में); to believe (in). ~ होना (को), to believe, or to be sure (that, कि). – विश्वास-घात, m. treachery. °अक, adj. °ई, adj. & m. treacherous; a traitor. विश्वास-स्थित, adj. feeling a settled confidence, or faith.

विश्वासी *vi-śvāsī* [S.], adj. **1.** trusting, confident. **2.** inspired by faith, or belief. **3.** trustworthy; honest.

विश्वास्य *vi-śvāsyă* [S.], adj. *Pl. HŚS.* to be trusted (= विश्वसनीय).

विष *viṣ* [S.], m. poison. — ~ **की गाँठ**, (m.) knot or bundle of poison: an ill-intentioned and unwelcome person. **मज़े में ~ घोलना**, to poison the pleasure or happiness (of, **के**). **विषखोपरा**, m. colloq. a partic. lizard. **विषधर**, adj. & m. poison-holding: venomous; a snake. **विष-पान**, m. the taking of poison. **विष-पान करना**, to take poison. **विष-भरा**, adj. poisonous; venomous. **विषमंत्र**, m. a charm for curing snake-bites. **विषमार**, m. an antidote. **विष-वृक्ष**, m. poison-tree: a tree yielding poisonous fruit. **विषहर**, poison-remover: an antidote; Brbh. poison-carrier: a snake. **विषाक्त** [°*ṣa*+*a*°], adj. smeared with poison: poisonous (a substance, a remark); toxic; poisoned. °**ता**, f. toxicity. **विषाणु** [°*ṣa*+*a*°], m. a virus.

विषण्ण *vi-ṣaṇṇ* [S.], adj. dejected, &c. (see **विषाद**).

विषत्व *viṣatvă* [S.], m. toxicity.

विषम *vi-ṣam* [S.], adj. **1.** uneven, rough (road, terrain). **2.** disproportionate, unbalanced; irregular (in shape). **3.** odd (a number). **4.** difficult (to grasp: a topic). **5.** disagreeable (of temperament). **6.** dire (disaster). **7.** harsh, burdensome (suffering). **8.** unsatisfactory (a situation); unfair. **9.** odd, strange, unparalleled. — **विषमांग** [°*ma*+*a*°], m. heterogeneous. **विषमीकरण**, m. *ling.* dissimilation.

विषमता *vi-ṣamătā* [S.], f. **1.** unevenness, &c. (see **विषम**). **2.** discord.

विषमीकरण *viṣamīkaraṇ* [S.], m. see s.v. **विषम**.

विषय *vi-ṣay* [S.], m. **1.** subject, matter, topic; particular subject (as of study). **2.** object of concern; affair, matter. **3.** worldly or sensual enjoyment; sensuality. **4.** *philos.* any of the five objects of sense (as sound, form, taste, &c., each of which is referred to one of the five organs of sense). — **विषय-ज्ञान**, m. knowledge of a (particular) subject. **विषय-भोग**, m. enjoyment of objects of sense: sensuous or (esp.) sensual enjoyment. **विषय-लोलुप**, adj. eager for sensual pleasure. **विषय-वस्तु**, m. subject-matter, topic. **विषय-वासना**, f. sensual enjoyment. **विषय-सूची**, m. list or table of contents; index. **विषयांतर** [°*ya*+*a*°], m. change of subject, changing the subject. **विषयात्मक** [°*ya*+*ā*°], adj. having to do with a subject; sensual. **विषयासक्त** [°*ya*+*ā*°], adj. attracted to worldly or (esp.) sensual pleasures. °**इ**, f.

-विषयक *-vi-ṣayak* [S.], adj. formant. concerning (= **संबंधी**).

विषयी *vi-ṣayī* [S.], adj. & m. **1.** adj. sensual. **2.** m. one living for, or by, worldly or sensual enjoyment; a materialist. **3.** one knowledgeable or expert (in a field or fields).

विषाण *viṣāṇ* [S.], m. **1.** horn (of animal). **2.** tusk (of elephant, boar).

विषाणी *viṣāṇī* [S.], adj. & m. *Pl. HŚS.* **1.** adj. horned. **2.** having tusks. **3.** m. an animal having horns or tusks.

विषाद *vi-ṣād* [S.], m. **1.** sadness; dejection, despair. **2.** languor. — **विषादपूर्ण**, adj. melancholy, depressed.

विषादी *vi-ṣādī* [S.], adj. sorrowful, &c. (see **विषाद**).

विषालु *viṣālu* [S.], adj. poisonous.

विषुव *viṣuv* [S.], m. equinox.

विषुवद् *viṣuvad* [S.], adj. equatorial. — ~ **रेखा**, f. the equator. ~ **वृत्त**, m. id.

विषूचिका *vi-ṣūcikā* [S.], f. a disease identified in Ayurvedic medicine: cholera, or its first stage.

विषैला *viṣailā* [cf. H. *viṣ, bis*], adj. **1.** poisonous (a snake). **2.** poisonous (a substance). **3.** poisoned (as an arrow).

विषैलापन *viṣailāpan* [cf. H. *viṣailā*], m. poisonousness.

विष्कंभ *vi-ṣkambh* [S.], m. interlude between the acts of a drama.

विष्टंभ *vi-ṣṭambh* [S.], m. *Pl. HŚS.* obstruction, impediment.

विष्टा *viṣṭā*, f. = **विष्ठा**.

विष्ठा *viṣṭhā* [S.], f. excrement.

विष्णु *viṣṇu* [S.], m. the god Viṣṇu (who is regarded as the preserver of the world during each period of its existence, and who becomes manifest in the world in each period in successive avatārs). — **विष्णु-पद**, m. the place, or step, of Viṣṇu; a representation of the footprints of Viṣṇu; a devotional stanza of Vaiṣṇava emphasis, in Brajbhāṣā (properly consisting of four, six or eight lines).

विष्फारित *vi-ṣphārit* [S.], adj. poet. opened wide (eyes).

विस *vis* [S.], m. poet. stalk of lotus or water-lily.

विसंक्रमण *vi-saṅ-kramaṇ* [S.], m. disinfection.

विसंगति *vi-saṅ-gati* [S.], f. incoherence; disruption.

विसर्ग *vi-sarg* [S.], m. **1.** giving up, renouncing. **2.** release (specif. from the cycle of rebirth). **3.** a donation, gift. ***4.** *ling.* voiceless aspiration (of Sanskrit); the graph used to denote *visarga*. — **विसर्गांत** [°*ga*+*a*°], adj. *ling.* ending with *visarga*.

विसर्जन *vi-sarjan* [S.], m. **1.** relinquishing; renunciation (as of the body, or of desires). **2.** sending (a person) away, dismissing. **3.** departing. **4.** consigning (to water: as an image at the end of a festival; or as cremated remains). **5.** formal conclusion (of a ceremony, or a function).

विसर्जित *vi-sarjit* [S.], adj. **1.** left, given up, &c. (see विसर्जन). **2.** consigned (to water: an image; ashes). **3.** concluded.

विस्तर *vi-star* [S.], adj. & m. *HŚS.* **1.** adj. large, extensive. **2.** m. = विस्तार.

विस्तरण *vi-staraṇ* [S.], m. **1.** expansion, extension. **2.** diffusion (of ideas).

विस्थापित *vi-sthāpit* [S.: Engl. *displaced*], adj. displaced (a person).

विस्तार *vi-stār* [S.], m. **1.** spreading, spread; expansion. **2.** extent. **3.** expansion, development (of an organisation, an activity). **4.** amplitude; detail. ~ से, adv. in detail, fully. — ~ करना (का), to spread; to expand (as territory, frontiers); to develop (an activity). – विस्तारपूर्ण, adj. extensive, detailed. विस्तारपूर्वक, adv. in detail. spreading: e.g. ध्वनिविस्तारक (यंत्र), m. loudspeaker.

विस्तारित *vi-stārit* [S.], adj. **1.** expanded, extended. **2.** fully stated, detailed.

विस्तीर्ण *vi-stīrṇ* [S.], adj. 1. = विस्तारित. 2. = विस्तृत, 1.

विस्तृत *vi-stṛt* [S.], adj. **1.** adj. extensive; ample (in size, scope). **2.** enlarged. **3.** detailed, full (information).

विस्तृति *vi-stṛti* [S.], f. **1.** extent, extensiveness. **2.** prevalence.

विस्पष्ट *vi-spaṣṭ* [S.], adj. fully clear, evident.

विस्फारित *vi-sphārit* [S.], adj. wide-opened, staring (eyes).

विस्फोट *vi-sphoṭ* [S.], m. **1.** explosion. **2.** eruption (of a volcano). **3.** a badly inflamed boil. — ~ होना, an explosion, &c. to occur.

विस्फोटक *vi-sphoṭak* [S.], adj. & m. **1.** adj. liable to explode (as a chemical). **2.** explosive (as a weapon). **3.** m. an explosive. **4.** an eruption: smallpox.

विस्फोटन *vi-sphoṭan* [S.], m. explosion.

विस्फोटित *vi-sphoṭit* [S.], adj. exploded. — ~ करना, to explode (sthg.), to blow (sthg.) up.

विस्मय *vi-smay* [S.], m. **1.** astonishment, amazement. 2. dismay. — विस्मयकारी, adj. causing astonishment or wonder; striking. विस्मयजनक, adj. id. विस्मयबोधक, adj. denoting astonishment: विस्मयबोधक चिह्न, m. exclamation mark. विस्मयाहत [°*ya*+*ā*°], adj. struck by dismay: = विस्मित, 2.

विस्मयी *vi-smayī* [S.], adj. astonished, surprised.

विस्मरण *vi-smaraṇ* [S.], m. forgetting.

विस्मित *vi-smit* [S.], adj. **1.** astonished, amazed. **2.** taken aback.

विस्मृत *vi-smṛt* [S.], adj. passed into oblivion, forgotten.

विस्मृति *vi-smṛti* [S.], f. **1.** oblivion. 2. forgetfulness.

विस्वर *vi-svar* [S.], adj. discordant, inharmonious.

विस्वाद *vi-svād* [S.], adj. tasteless, flavourless.

विहंग *vi-haṅg* [S.], m. sky-goer: a bird.

विहंगम *vi-haṅgam* [S.], m. = विहंग.

विहग *vi-hag* [S.], m. = विहंग.

विहर- *vi-har-* [*viharati*], v.i. Brbh. **1.** to wander, to roam. **2.** to take pleasure, to delight.

विहरण *vi-haraṇ* [S.], m. *Pl. HŚS.* a taking away: **1.** taking a walk, strolling. **2.** relaxation, pleasure.

विहस- *vi-has-* [*vihasati*], v.i. Brbh. to smile, to laugh gently.

विहसन *vi-hasan* [S.], m. a smile; a gentle laugh.

विहसित *vi-hasit* [S.], adj. Brbh. smiling; gently laughing.

विहाग *vihāg* [f. H. *suhāg*], adj. & m. expressing separation: **1.** adj. sad. **2.** m. sthg. sad; *mus.* name of a rāga.

विहायस *vi-hāyas* [S.], m. the air, sky.

विहायसी *vi-hāyăsī* [S.], f. = विहायस.

विहार *vi-hār* [S.], m. **1.** walking for pleasure; wandering. **2.** recreation, pleasure. जल-विहार, m. water-sport: boating. **3.** a Buddhist or Jain temple. — ~ करना, to roam; to enjoy oneself; to disport oneself.

विहारी *vi-hārī* [S.], adj. **1.** wandering, roaming. **2.** enjoying oneself. **3.** sportive (esp. as Kṛṣṇa).

विहित *vi-hit* [S.], adj. **1.** ordained, prescribed; determined. 2. fit, proper.

विहीन *vi-hīn* [S.], adj. deprived of, without.

विह्वल *vi-hval* [S.], adj. shaking: **1.** agitated, perturbed. **2.** beside oneself (with strong emotion); frenzied; delirious. **3.** distressed, suffering (from, से).

विह्वलता *vi-hvalătā* [S.], f. agitation, &c. (see विह्वल).

वीक्षण *vîkṣaṇ* [S.], m. glance, gaze.

वीचि *vīci* [S.], f. Av. a wave.

वीज *vīj*, m. see बीज.

वीजन *vījan* [S.], m. **1.** fanning; being fanned. **2.** a fan.

वीटिका *vīṭikā* [S.], f. *Pl. HŚS.* the betel plant, *Areca catechu* (= बीड़ी).

वीणा *vīṇā* [S.], f. vina (a large instrument of the type of the lute). — वीणा-वादिनी, f. lute-player: a title of the goddess Sarasvatī as patron of the arts.

वीत *vît* [S.], adj. departed; free (from). — वीतराग, adj. free of passions, or of desire.

वीथि *vīthi* [S.], f. = वीथी.

वीथी *vīthī* [S.], f. **1.** row, line. ***2.** road, path, lane. **3.** terrace (in front of a house). **4.** gallery.

वीर *vīr* [S.], adj. & m. **1.** adj. brave, heroic; mighty. **2.** -वीर. eminent, excellent in. e.g. धर्मवीर, m. a most righteous man. **3.** m. a hero; warrior. — वीर-काव्य, m. heroic poetry: the early medieval bardic poetry of north India. वीर-गति, f. hero's departure: death in battle. वीर-गति पाना, to die in battle. वीर-गाथा, f. heroic song or ballad. वीर-चक्र, m. *mil.* a partic. decoration for bravery. वीर-रस, m. *rhet.* the heroic sentiment (see s.v. रस). वीरांगना [°*ra*+*ā*°], f. heroic woman, heroine. वीर-सू, f. poet. mother of heroes.

वीरता *vīrătā* [S.], f. heroism, courage; fortitude. — वीरतापूर्ण, adj. heroic (= वीर).

वीरान *vīrān* [P. *vīrān*], adj. **1.** laid waste; ruined (as a building). **2.** depopulated. **3.** desolate (a region). **4.** dreary, dismal. — ~ करना, to lay waste, &c.

वीराना *vīrānā* [P. *vīrāna*], m. a desolate place.

वीरानी *vīrānī* [P. *vīrānī*], f. **1.** desolation; ruin. **2.** depopulation.

वीरुध *vīrudh* [S.], m. a plant, or bush.

वीर्य *vīryă* [S.], m. **1.** courage; strength, vigour; virility. **2.** seminal fluid. **3.** seed (of plants). — वीर्यवत्ता, f. fertility (of a man). वीर्यवान, adj. courageous; vigorous; sexually virile.

वृंत *vr̥nt* [S.], m. stalk (of plant, flower, leaf).

वृक *vr̥k* [S.], m. **1.** a wolf. **2.** a jackal.

वृक्ष *vr̥kṣ* [S.], m. a tree. — वृक्षाच्छादित [°*ṣa*+*ā*°], adj. tree-covered, wooded. वृक्षारोपण [°*sa*+*ā*°], m. tree-planting.

वृज- *vr̥j-* [S]. = ब्रज.

वृत *vr̥t* [S.], adj. **1.** surrounded. **2.** covered.

वृति *vr̥ti* [S.], f. **1.** an enclosing hedge, or fence. **2.** enclosed piece of ground.

वृत्त *vr̥tt* [S.], m. **1.** circle. **2.** circumference. **3.** event, occurrence. **4.** course of action; behaviour, conduct; character. **5.** account, &c. (= वृत्तांत); pl. transactions (of a society). **6.** *pros.* a syllabic metre (as opposed to one determined by individual metrical instants). **7.** वृत्त-. documentary (as a film). — वृत्तांत [°*ta*+*a*°], m. the end of a course of action: event, occurrence; a tale, narrative; account (of a matter).

वृत्ति *vr̥tti* [S.], f. a turning: **1.** state, condition. **2.** behaviour, conduct; mode or habit of life. **3.** natural tendency; instinct. **4.** business, employment; profession. **5.** means of subsistence; allowance; pension. **6.** commentary (on a text). **7.** partic. usage (of a term or expression). — वृत्ति-कर, m. employment tax. वृत्ति-चक्र, m. a system (of attitudes, values). वृत्ति-साम्य, m. similar state (to, से). आकाश-वृत्ति, f. support from heaven: feckless or improvident life. छात्र-वृत्ति, f. a scholarship, bursary.

-वृत्ती *-vr̥ttī* [cf. H. *vr̥tti*], adj. & m. formant. having a partic. mode of life or conduct (e.g. स्वधर्मवृत्ती, adj. living in accordance with *dharma*, righteous).

वृथा *vr̥thā* [S.], adj. & adv. **1.** adj. in comp. vain, pointless. **2.** adv. in vain, to no effect.

वृंद *vr̥nd* [S.], m. **1.** a group, assemblage (of persons or things). **2.** -वृंद. marker of collective use of nouns, esp. nouns of animate reference, e.g. बाल-वृंद, m. children; वाद्य-वृंद, m. an orchestra. — वृंद-गीत, m. a chorus (song). वृंद-वादन, m. orchestration.

वृंदा *vr̥ndā* [S.], f. **1.** *mythol.* name of the forest area near Gokul in which Kr̥ṣṇa spent his childhood. 2. = तुलसी. — वृंदावन, m. = ~, 1.; the town of Vrindaban.

वृद्ध *vr̥ddh* [S.], adj. & m. increased: **1.** adj. advanced in years, old. **2.** grown up, full-grown. **3.** m. an old man. — वृद्धतम, adj. oldest, senior. वृद्धावस्था [°*dha*+*a*°], f. old age. वृद्धाश्रम [°*dha*+*ā*°], m. old people's home.

वृद्धता *vr̥ddhătā* [S.], f. old age, advanced age.

वृद्धापन *vr̥ddhāpan* [cf. H. *vr̥ddh*], m. old age.

वृद्धि *vr̥ddhi* [S.], f. **1.** growth, increase; development. **2.** prosperity, success. **3.** *fin.* interest. **4.** *gram.* a Sanskrit derivational process of lengthening or change of vowels whereby related words based on a single root are formed. — ~ पर होना, to be on the increase. – वृद्धिकर, adj. °ई, f. causing increase.

वृश्चिक *vr̥ścik* [S.], m. **1.** a scorpion. **2.** the sign Scorpio (of the zodiac).

वृष *vr̥ṣ* [S.], m. **1.** a bull. **2.** the sign Taurus (of the zodiac). **3.** *mythol.* name of a demon. **4.** *mythol.* a rat. — **वृषकेतु**, m. *mythol.* whose emblem or banner is the bull: a title of Śiva. **वृषध्वज**, m. *mythol.* whose banner or emblem is the bull: id.; a title of Gaṇeś. **वृषभानु**, m. *hind.* name of the father of Rādhā. **वृषासुर** [°*ṣa*+*a*°], m. = ~, 3.

वृषभ *vr̥ṣabh* [S.], m. **1.** a bull, &c. (= **वृष**, 1., 2). **2.** -**वृषभ**. mightiest, or best (of).

वृषल *vr̥ṣal* [S.], m. *Pl. HŚS.* a low-caste or outcaste man.

वृषली *vr̥ṣalī* [S.], f. E.H. a low-caste or outcaste woman.

वृषा *vr̥ṣā* [S.], f. name of several plants: **1.** *Pl.* = **केवाँच**. **2.** ? name of a bush, *Adhatoda vasica* (a source of pearl-ash).

वृष्टि *vr̥ṣṭi* [S.], f. rain.

वृहत् *vr̥hat* [S.], adj. great, large; extensive (a treatise, volume); important (service, duty, matter).

वृहस्पति *vr̥haspati* [S.], m. see **बृहस्पति**.

वे *ve* [cf. H. *vah*], pron. & adj. **1.** pron. they. **2.** hon. he; she. **3.** adj. those.

वेग *veg* [S.], m. **1.** movement (esp. swift, in a partic. course); speed, velocity; impetuosity. **2.** flow, current (of water). **3.** haste; impulsiveness. **4.** inner impulse (to an action). — ~ **से**, adv. swiftly, &c. – **वेगवान**, adj. swift, &c.

वेगि *vegi* [conn. *vegena*], adv. Brbh. Av. swiftly, quickly; soon.

वेगिनी *veginī* [S.], f. *Pl. HŚS.* a river.

वेगी *vegī* [S.], adj. & m. **1.** adj. swift, &c. (see **वेग**). **2.** m. a messenger.

वेणी *veṇī* [S.], f. **1.** braided hair. **2.** fig. confluence of two or more rivers. **3.** chain (of flowers).

वेणु *veṇu* [S.], m. **1.** a bamboo. **2.** a pipe, flute.

वेतन *vetan* [S.], m. **1.** salary; wage. **2.** regular allowance of money. — **वेतन-कर**, m. income tax. **वेतन-वृद्धि**, f. increase in salary, &c.

वेतसी *vetăsī* [S.], f. a rattan cane, or reed.

वेताल *vetāl* [S.], m. a demon (cf. **बैताल**.

वेत्ता *vettā* [S.], m. inv. esp. -**वेत्ता**. knower: an expert.

वेत्र *vetr* [S.], m. **1.** cane, rattan; a cane. **2.** a reed. — **वेत्रवती**, f. (river) having reeds: the river Betwa.

वेद *ved* [S.], m. knowledge: **1.** a Veda, any of the three (later four) early Indian sacred scriptures. **2.** Vedic literature generally (incl. the Upaniṣads, and various types of interpretative or auxiliary texts). — **वेद-पाठ**, m. study or recital of the Vedas. **वेद-वाक्य**, m. Vedic utterance; sthg. to be implicitly believed or trusted in. **वेद-व्यास**, m. Veda-arranger: a title of the sage Vyās, q.v. **वेद-सम्मत**, adj. conformable to the Vedas, scriptural; orthodox. **वेदांग** [°*da*+*a*°], m. limb or member of the Veda: any of various works or classes of work regarded as auxiliary to the Veda proper. **वेदांत** [°*da*+*a*°], m. end of the Veda: the Upaniṣads collectively (regarded as teaching an essentially monistic doctrine); a monistic philosophy and theology based on the Upaniṣads; = ~, 2. °ई, m. a follower of Vedānta. **वेदाभ्यास** [°*da*+*a*°], m. study of the Vedas; repetition of the myṣtic syllable *oṁ*.

वेदना *vedănā* [S.], f. **1.** pain; anguish. **2.** suffering.

वेदिका *vedikā* [S.], f. **1.** a small, or a makeshift, sacrificial altar. **2.** a platform.

¹वेदी *vedī* [S.], f. place prepared for a sacrifice; an altar.

²वेदी *vedī* [S.], m. a brāhmaṇ versed in the Vedas.

वेध *vedh* [S.], m. **1.** piercing, penetration. **2.** *Pl.* wounding. **3.** distinguishing; observing (heavenly bodies). — ~ **करना**, to pierce; to observe (as a planet). – **वेधशाला**, f. observatory.

वेधक *vedhak* [S.], adj. & m. **1.** adj. -**वेधक**. piercing; perforating. **2.** m. one who pierces (as jewels, or ears).

वेधन *vedhan* [S.], m. **1.** piercing, penetrating; perforating. **2.** striking (a mark). **3.** *Pl.* wounding.

वेधनी *vedhnī* [conn. *vedhanikā*-; cf. H. *bedhnā*], f. *Pl. HŚS.* a borer; auger, gimlet.

वेधनीय *vedhănīyă* [S.], adj. pierceable, penetrable.

वेधित *vedhit* [S.], adj. **1.** pierced, penetrated. **2.** observed with care (a heavenly body).

-वेधी *-vedhī* [S.], adj. piercing; perforating. e.g. **शब्द-वेधी**, adj. sound-piercing (as an arrow an unseen target).

वेला *velā* [S.], f. limit, boundary: **1.** boundary of sea and land, shore. ***2.** partic. time or moment; a time of day. **3.** period, season. **4.** opportunity.

¹**वेश** *veś*, m. dress, apparel, &c. (= वेष).

²**वेश** *veś* [S.], m. *Pl. HŚS.* house, dwelling.

वेश्या *veśyā* [S.], f. a prostitute. — **वेश्या-गमन**, m. frequenting prostitutes. **वेश्यागामी**, m. a frequenter of prostitutes. **वेश्या-घर**, m. brothel. **वेश्या-वृत्ति**, f. prostitution.

वेश्यापन *veśyāpan* [cf. H. *veśyā*], m. prostitution.

वेष *veṣ* [S.], m. **1.** dress (= ¹वेश). **2.** outward form; disguise. — **~ रखना**, or **धरना**, or **धारण करना**, to assume the clothing or aspect (of, **का**), to play the part (of). – **वेष-भूषा**, f. clothing and adornment: dress, attire.

वेष्टन *veṣṭan* [S.], m. **1.** anything which surrounds or encloses; a wall. **2.** wrapper. **3.** piece of cloth worn as a turban.

वेष्टित *veṣṭit* [S.], adj. **1.** surrounded; enclosed. **2.** wrapped (in).

वेंचना *vaiṁcnā*, v.t. reg. to tear off, to flay (skin).

वै *vai* [S.], emphat. encl. Brbh. indeed, truly.

वैकल्य *vaikalyă* [S.], m. **1.** impairment, deficiency. ***2.** unease, restlessness.

वैकाल *vaikal* [S.], m. *Pl. HŚS.* the afternoon or evening.

वैकालिक *vaikālik* [S.], adj. *Pl. HŚS.* having to do with, or occurring in, the afternoon or evening.

वैकुंठ *vaikuṇṭh* [S.], m. *hind.* the heaven of Viṣṇu, paradise.

वैखरी *vaikhărī* [S.], f. **1.** an articulate sound. **2.** power of speech; fig. the goddess of speech.

वैचारिक *vaicārik* [S.], adj. **1.** having to do with thought, or attitudes. **2.** ideological.

वैजयंती *vaijăyantī* [S.], f. **1.** a banner. **2.** *mythol.* the long necklace (of five gems, viz. pearl, ruby, emerald, sapphire and diamond) or multicoloured garland of Viṣṇu or Kṛṣṇa. — **वैजयंती-माला**, f. id., 2.

वैतनिक *vaitanik* [S.], adj. salaried, paid (a post).

वैतरणी *vaitarăṇī* [S.], f. *mythol.* name of the river dividing earth from the lower regions ruled over by Yama.

वैताल *vaitāl* [S.], m. = **बैताल**.

वैतालिक *vaitālik* [S.], m. **1.** a bard, panegyrist of a king. **2.** one possessed by a *vetāl* or demon. **3.** worshipper of a demon; magician.

वैदिक *vaidik* [S.], adj. & m. **1.** adj. relating to or connected with the Vedas, Vedic. **2.** scriptural; orthodox. **3.** m. a brāhmaṇ versed in the Vedas; an orthodox (*sanātan*) Hindu.

वैदिकी *vaidikī* [S.], adj. relating to or conformable to the Vedas: characterising the orthodox (as conduct).

वैदूर्य *vaidūrya* [S.], m. lapis lazuli.

वैदेशिक *vaideśik* [S.], adj. & m. **1.** adj. having to do with a foreign country or countries, foreign (as trade, policy). **2.** m. a foreigner.

वैदेही *vaidehī* [S.], f. Brbh. Av. daughter of Videha (king Janaka): title of Sītā.

वैद्य *vaidyă* [S.], adj. & m. **1.** adj. having to do with Ayurvedic medicine. **2.** m. an Ayurvedic doctor. — **वैद्य-नाथ**, m. *mythol.* lord of doctors: a title of Dhanvantari.

वैद्यक *vaidyak* [S.], adj. & m. **1.** adj. having to do with Ayurvedic medicine. **2.** m. medical (esp. Ayurvedic) knowledge or system.

वैध *vaidh* [S.], adj. **1.** conforming to rule or to law. **2.** orthodox (a practice); legal (a right); legally constituted.

वैधता *vaidhătā* [S.], f. **1.** legality. **2.** legitimacy (as of procedure). **3.** validity (as of a document).

वैधर्मिक *vaidharmik* [S.], adj. irreligious.

वैधव्य *vaidhavyă* [S.], m. widowhood.

वैधानिक *vaidhānik* [S.], adj. having to do with a constitution, constitutional.

वैधृत *vaidhṛt* [S.], m. *Pl. HŚS. astron.* name of an inauspicious position of the sun and moon (when they are on the same side of either solstice and of equal declination but of opposite direction).

वैपरीत्य *vaipărītyă* [S.], m. *Pl. HŚS.* contrariety, adverseness (cf. **विपरीत**).

वैभव *vaibhav* [S.], m. **1.** superhuman power or might. **2.** grandeur, majesty. **3.** power. **4.** wealth. — **वैभवशाली**, adj. mighty, powerful; wealthy.

वैभागिक *vaibhāgik* [S.], adj. departmental.

वैभाषिक *vaibhāṣik* [S.], adj. dialectal.

वैभिन्न्य *vaibhinnyă* [S.], f. variety, diversity.

वैमत्य *vaimatyă* [S.], m. **1.** difference of opinion. **2.** displeasure.

वैमनस्य *vaimanasyă* [S.], m. **1.** hostility; friction. **2.** indifference.

वैमात्र *vaimātr* [S.], m. born of a different mother: a half-brother.

वैमात्री *vaimātrī* [S.], f. half-sister (see वैमात्र).

वैमात्रेय *vaimātreyă* [S.], m. = वैमात्र.

वैमानिक *vaimānik* [S.], adj. **1.** adj. having to do with aircraft; aeronautical. **2.** m. a pilot; aircrew member.

वैमानिकी *vaimānikī* [S.], f. the science of flight, aeronautics.

वैयक्तिक *vaiyaktik* [S.], adj. individual, personal.

वैयक्तिकता *vaiyaktikătā* [S.], f. individuality.

वैयाकरण *vaiyākaraṇ* [S.], m. a grammarian.

वैर *vair* [S.], m. enmity; hostility (= बैर).

[1]**वैरना** *vairnā* [*avakirati*], v.t. reg. to pour (as rice, or seed) into a container or on to the ground; to sow by drill; to grind (seed).

[2]**वैरना** *vairnā* [*avakiraṇa-*], m. *Pl.* hopper (of a mill); drill (for sowing seed).

वैरा *vairā* [cf. H. *vairnā*], m. *Pl.* anything forced upon a person; sthg. which one is forced to purchase.

वैरागी *vairāgī* [S.], m. one free from worldly desire, an ascetic; specif. a Vaiṣṇava ascetic.

वैराग्य *vairāgyă* [S.], m. freedom from worldly desires, asceticism.

वैरिन *vairin* [ad. *vairiṇī-*: w. H. *bairī*], f. Brbh. Av. a female enemy, hostile woman.

वैरी *vairī* [S.], m. an enemy, antagonist.

वैरूप्य *vairūpyă* [S.], m. **1.** diversity of form. **2.** malformation; ugliness.

वैलक्षण्य *vailakṣaṇyă* [S.], m. **1.** distinctiveness. **2.** distinctive feature.

वैला *vailā* [? conn. H. *varlā*], adj. E.H. on this side.

वैवर्त *vaivart* [S.], m. revolving, turn (as of a wheel).

वैवस्वत *vaivasvat* [S.], m. *mythol.* title of the Manu (q.v.) of the present period.

वैवाहिक *vaivāhik* [S.], adj. matrimonial, married (life, ties, relationship).

वैशाख *vaiśākh*, m. = बैसाख.

वैशिष्ठ्य *vaiśiṣṭhyă* [S.], m. **1.** distinguishing feature or trait. **2.** particular virtue.

वैशेषिक *vaiśeṣik* [S.], adj. & m. *philos.* characteristic: **1.** adj. having to do with Vaiśeṣika doctrine. **2.** m. name of a division of the Nyāya school of philosophy. **3.** a follower of Vaiśeṣika doctrine.

वैश्य *vaiśyă* [S.], m. a member of the *vaiśya* or third *varṇa* (q.v.) of Indo-Aryan society, or of communities later assigned thereto.

वैषम्य *vaiṣamyă* [S.], m. **1.** inequality, unevenness. **2.** disproportion; disharmony; difference. **3.** harshness of treatment; injustice. **4.** difficulty, distress.

वैषयिक *vaiṣayik* [S.], adj. sensual, carnal.

वैष्णव *vaiṣṇav* [S.], adj. & m. **1.** adj. having to do with Viṣṇu (as a sect, a tradition). **2.** worshipping Viṣṇu. **3.** m. a devotee of Viṣṇu.

वैष्णवी *vaiṣṇavī* [S.], f. **1.** the *śakti* or personified energy of Viṣṇu; specif. a title of Durgā.

वैसा *vaisā* [conn. *tādr̥śa-*], pron. adj. & adv. **1.** adj. of that sort. ~ **ही**, adj. of just that sort. **जैसा आप कहेंगे, मैं ~ ही करूँगा**, I shall do just as you tell me. **2.** adv. **वैसे**. in that manner; in fact; casually, for no special reason (= वैसे ही). **वैसे मैं बोलने आनेवाला नहीं था, लेकिन ...**, well, I didn't come to speak, but.... **वैसे तो**, adv. on the whole, altogether; in fact (= वैसे); in other respects, otherwise. **वैसे तो वह सच्चा बनता है, लेकिन...**, it's like this: he acts like a trustworthy person, but.... **वैसे ही**, adv. just like this: merely, simply; casually. **मैंने यह बात वैसे ही कह दी थी**, I said this without thinking.

वों *voṁ*, adv. in that way, thus, like that (cf. यों 'like this').

वो *vo*, pron. & adj. corr. (infld. by norm of U. pronunciation.) = वह.

[1]**वोट** *voṭ* [Engl. *vote*], m. a vote. — ~ **देना** (को), to vote (for). ~ **लेना**, to take a vote (on, पर). – **वोट-दाता**, m. inv. voter. **वोट-दान**, m. voting. **वोटाधिकार**, m. the right to vote.

[2]**वोट** *voṭ*, f. Brbh. = ओट.

वोड्र *voḍră* [S.], m. *Pl. HŚS.* = [1]बोड़ा.

वोढा *voḍhā* [S.], m. inv. *Pl. HŚS.* a porter, bearer.

वोत-प्रोत *vot-prot*, adj. E.H. = ओत-प्रोत.

वोदाल *vodāl* [S.], m. *Pl. HŚS.* the sheat-fish, *Silurus boalis.*

व्यंग *vy-aṅg* [S.], adj. & m. *Pl. HŚS.* **1.** adj. deprived of a limb or member: maimed; deformed. **2.** m. = व्यंग्य.

व्यंग्य *vy-aṅgyă* [S.], m. **1.** suggestion, innuendo. **2.** irony, sarcasm. **3.** satire. — व्यंग्य-चित्र, m. a cartoon. व्यंग्यपूर्ण, adj. ironical, sarcastic; satirical (remarks, a work). व्यंग्यात्मक [°*ya*+*ā*°], adj. ironical, &c. (wit, outlook).

व्यंजक *vy-añjak* [S.], adj. indicating, expressing.

व्यंजन *vy-añjan* [S.], m. the act of indicating: **1.** mark, sign, symbol. **2.** a consonant. **3.** vegetables (as eaten with rice, lentils, &c). **4.** seasoning, relish. — व्यंजनांत [°*na*+*a*°], adj. ending in a consonant (a word).

व्यंजना *vy-añjănā* [S.], f. expression (esp. figurative, or suggestion of an idea). — व्यंजनात्मक [°*na*+*ā*°], adj. expressive; suggestive. व्यंजनापूर्ण, adj. id. व्यंजना-शक्ति, f. power of expression; expressiveness (of words or speech).

व्यंजित *vy-añjit* [S.], adj. expressed.

व्यक्त *vy-akt* [S.], adj. manifested: **1.** revealed. **2.** evident, clear. **3.** expressed, voiced. — ~ करना, to express, &c. व्यक्ताव्यक्त [°*ta*+*a*°], adj. clear and unclear. व्यक्तीकरण, m. making clear, expression (as of wishes, emotions).

व्यक्ति *vy-akti* [S.], m.; f. a person; a particular person. — व्यक्तिगत, adj. personal; private (as property); individual (as opposed to collective). व्यक्तिगत रूप से, adv. personally; individually. – व्यक्ति-निष्ठ, adj. subjective. व्यक्तिपरक, adj. individualistic. व्यक्तिमुखी, adj. personal in character (as a reaction). व्यक्तिवाचक, adj. denoting a person. व्यक्तिवाचक संज्ञा, f. *gram.* a proper noun.

व्यक्तित्व *vy-aktitvă* [S.], m. **1.** personality. **2.** individuality. — व्यक्तित्वप्रधान, adj. individualistic.

व्यक्तीकरण *vyaktīkaraṇ* [S.], m. see s.v. व्यक्त.

व्यग्र *vy-agră* [S.], adj. not intent on one point: **1.** distracted, bewildered. **2.** agitated; fearful. **3.** eager; eagerly engaged (in).

व्यग्रता *vy-agrătā* [S.], f. bewilderment, &c. (see व्यग्र).

व्यजन *vy-ajan* [S.], m. **1.** a fan. **2.** *Pl.* ventilator.

व्यतिक्रम *vy-ati-kram* [S.], m. going beyond: **1.** transgression, violation. **2.** excess, wrong-doing.

व्यतिक्रमण *vy-ati-kramaṇ* [S.], m. the committing of any transgression or excess.

व्यतिक्रांत *vy-ati-krānt* [S.], adj. transgressed (a rule).

व्यतिपात *vy-ati-pāt* [S.], m. *Pl. HŚS. astron.* name of an inauspicious position of the sun and moon (when they are on opposite sides of either solstice, and of equal declination).

व्यतिरिक्त *vy-ati-rikt* [S.], adj. = अतिरिक्त.

व्यतिरेक *vy-ati-rek* [S.], m. reaching beyond: **1.** distinction, difference; separateness; contrast, distinction. **2.** increase; excess.

व्यतीत *vy-atīt* [S.], adj. **1.** passed by, elapsed; spent (as time). **2.** preceding (year, &c). — ~ करना, to spend (time).

व्यत्यय *vy-aty-ay* [S.], m. inverse order; transposition.

व्यथा *vyathā* [S.], f. **1.** pain; ache; anguish. **2.** distress. **3.** alarm, fear.

व्यथित *vyathit* [S.], adj. suffering, distressed; tormented.

व्यभिचार *vy-abhi-cār* [S.], m. deviation, transgression: vice, specif. adultery.

व्यभिचारी *vy-abhi-cārī* [S.], adj. & m. going apart or away: **1.** adj. dissolute; vicious. ***2.** adulterous. **3.** *rhet.* short-lived (feeling or state). **4.** m. an adulterer, &c.

व्यभिचारीपन *vyabhicārīpan* [cf. H. *vyabhicārī*], m. dissolute behaviour, adulterous conduct.

व्यय *vy-ay* [S.], m. **1.** expenditure, expense. **2.** extravagance, waste. — ~ करना, to spend (on, में, पर, or के लिए); to expend (strength, resources). — व्ययशील, adj. wasteful, spendthrift.

व्ययी *vy-ayī* [S.], adj. extravagant, spendthrift.

व्यर्थ *vy-arth* [S.], adj. useless, vain (an attempt, &c.); pointless, senseless.

व्यर्थता *vy-arthătā* [S.], f. uselessness; pointlessness.

व्यलीक *vy-alīk* [S.], m. Brbh. anything disagreeable or displeasing: **1.** fault, sin. **2.** distress.

व्यवकलन *vy-avă-kalan* [S.], m. subtraction; deduction.

व्यवकलित *vy-avă-kalit* [S.], adj. subtracted; deducted.

व्यवच्छेद *vy-avă-cched* [S.], m. **1.** separation. **2.** distinction, discrimination; analysis. **3.** division, section (as of a book).

व्यवधान *vy-avă-dhān* [S.], m. placing apart or between: **1.** interval, gap, space. **2.** distinction (as between objects). **3.** intervening object; obstruction.

व्यवधायक *vy-avă-dhāyak* [S.], adj. & m. interposing, separating; screening.

व्यवसाय *vy-avă-sāy* [S.], m. activity: occupation; business, trade, profession; industry (= उद्योग).

व्यवसायी *vy-avă-sāyī* [S.], adj. & m. **1.** adv. active, enterprising; engaged in business, trade or profession, or in industry. **2.** pertaining to a partic. occupation. **3.** m. a businessman, &c.; merchant.

व्यवस्था *vy-avă-sthā* [S.], f. **1.** situation, state (of affairs). **2.** arrangement, organisation (of any entity or activity); system. **3.** statute, law; code of law. **4.** opinion or interpretation (of a matter involving law, or orthodox practice). **5.** order, method (as in work). **6.** arrangement (made for a purpose); step, measure. **7.** order, discipline.

व्यवस्थापक *vy-avă-sthāpak* [S.], adj. & m. **1.** adj. legislative (a body). **2.** m. organiser; director. **3.** one who settles or adjusts, adjudicator.

व्यवस्थापन *vy-avă-sthāpan* [S.], m. organising, organisation; management.

व्यवस्थापित *vy-avă-sthāpit* [S.], adj. arranged, organised; set up, formed (as a body); introduced (a rule, a law).

व्यवस्थित *vy-avă-sthit* [S.], adj. **1.** arranged, organised. **2.** well-organised, orderly, systematic (procedure, &c).

व्यवस्थिति *vy-avă-sthiti* [S.], f. orderliness, good arrangement, system.

व्यवहार *vy-avă-hār* [S.], m. **1.** action, act. **2.** customary practice, or usage. ***3.** conduct, behaviour; manner, bearing (towards a person); treatment (of). **4.** relationship, dealings (as in business, trade). **5.** use. 6 a case, action (in law). — **~ करना**, to perform an act; to conduct oneself (towards, **से**); to deal (with); to use, to make use of. **~ में आना**, to be of use; to come into use. **~ में लाना**, to bring into use.

व्यवहारिक *vy-avă-hārik*, m. corr. see व्यावहारिक.

व्यवहारित *vy-avă-hārit* [S.], adj. in use, &c. (= व्यवहृत).

व्यवहारी *vy-avă-hārī* [S.], adj. = व्यावहारिक, 1., 3.

व्यवहार्य *vy-avă-hāryă* [S.], adj. to be performed, practised or used: **1.** practicable, feasible. **2.** customary. **3.** usable.

व्यवहित *vy-avă-hit* [S.], adj. **1.** placed apart, separated. **2.** shut out; set aside.

व्यवहृत *vy-avă-hr̥t* [S.], adj. in use, customary, practised.

व्यष्टि *vy-aṣṭi* [S.], f. individuality: an individual.

व्यसन *vy-asan* [S.], m. **1.** addiction, passion (for an activity). **उसे केवल लिखने-पढ़ने का ~ है**, all he wants to do is study. **2.** a bad habit, vice. **3.** misfortune. — **व्यसनार्त** [°*na*+*ā*°], adj. suffering misfortune, wretched.

व्यसनी *vy-asănī* [S.], adj. **1.** having a passion (for an activity). **2.** having a vice, or vices; depraved.

व्यस्त *vy-ast* [S.], adj. thrown apart: **1.** scattered in pieces, shattered; dispersed. **2.** disordered (clothing). **3.** perturbed, distressed. ***4.** occupied, busy (with, **में**); preoccupied.

व्यस्तता *vy-astătā* [S.], f. **1.** state of being busy, &c. (see **व्यस्त**). **2.** agitation, confusion; preoccupation.

व्याकरण *vy-ā-kăraṇ* [S.], m. grammar.

व्याकरणिक *vy-ā-karăṇik* [S.], adj. grammatical (a form, category).

व्याकरणी *vy-ā-karăṇī* [cf. H. *vyākāraṇ*], m. a grammarian.

व्याकुल *vy-ākul* [S.], adj. **1.** confused, bewildered. **2.** agitated, distressed; troubled. **3.** anxious, longing (for or to, **के लिए**).

व्याकुलता *vy-ākulătā* [S.], f. agitation, distress, &c. (see **व्याकुल**).

व्याकुलित *vy-ākulit* [S.], adj. agitated, distressed, &c. (see **व्याकुल**).

व्याख्या *vy-ā-khyā* [S.], f. **1.** explanation, exposition. **2.** commenting, commentary; interpretation. 3. = **व्याख्यान**, 1. — **~ करना** (**की**), to explain, &c. – **व्याख्यात्मक** [°*yā*+*ā*°], adj. explanatory.

व्याख्यान *vy-ā-khyān* [S.], m. exposition, account: **1.** lecture. 2. = **व्याख्या**, 1., 2. — **~ देना**, to give a lecture. – **व्याख्यान-दाता**, m. inv. speaker, lecturer.

व्याख्यायित *vy-ā-khyāyit*, [S.], adj. interpreted, or understood (as).

व्याघात *vy-ā-ghāt* [S.], m. **1.** striking against; forceful impact. **2.** forceful or dire blow (often fig., as struck against beliefs, rights, &c.: **पर**). **3.** obstacle, hindrance.

व्याघाती *vy-ā-ghātī* [S.], adj. striking against; opposing; obstructing.

व्याघ्र *vyāghră* [S.], m. a tiger.

व्याज *vy-āj* [S.], m. deceit, &c. (see ब्याज). — व्याज-स्तुति, f. ironical or dissembling praise.

व्याजी *vy-ājī* [S.], m. = ब्याजी.

व्याध *vy-ādh* [S.], m. piercer: a hunter; fowler.

व्याधि *vy-ādhi* [S.], f. **1.** disease, illness. **2.** affliction; anguish.

व्यापक *vy-āpak* [S.], m. **1.** pervasive, extensive, diffused. सर्व-व्यापक, adj. all-pervasive: generally applicable (as a principle). **2.** comprehensive (as a view, a policy). **3.** broad, general. शब्द के ~ अर्थ में, in the broad sense of the word.

व्यापकता *vy-āpakătā* [S.], f. **1.** extensiveness. **2.** comprehensiveness.

व्यापन *vy-āpan* [S.], m. extension (as of a procedure, a policy).

व्यापना *vy-āpnā* [ad. *vyāpnoti*], v.i. **1.** to be pervasive (throughout, में); to spread (through). **2.** to have an effect, to work (on, को); to affect. तुम्हें यह मोह व्याप्त है, you are preyed on by this delusion.

व्यापार *vy-ā-pār* [S.], m. **1.** occupation, business; trade; profession. **2.** activity, act, action. मस्तिष्क का ~, m. mental activity. **3.** undertaking, enterprise; transaction. **4.** trade, commerce, business. ~ करना, to trade, &c. (in, का). — व्यापार-चिह्न, m. trade-mark. व्यापार-छाप, f. id.

व्यापारिक *vy-ā-pārik* [S.], adj. = व्यापारी.

व्यापारी *vy-ā-pārī* [S.], adj. & m. **1.** adj. having to do with business, commerce or trade (as an association; or as prices, or discussions); commercial; mercantile. **2.** m. a merchant; a trader.

व्यापी *vy-āpī* [S.], adj. pervasive, all-pervasive; general. विश्व-व्यापी, adj. found throughout the world (an attitude, &c).

व्याप्त *vy-āpt* [S.], adj. **1.** spread through, diffused (in or among, में). सारे देश में यह चेतना ~ है, this mood pervades the country. **2.** encompassed, surrounded.

व्याप्ति *vy-āpti* [S.], f. pervasion, diffusion (in or among, में).

व्याप्य *vy-āpyă* [S.], adj. able to be pervaded, permeable.

व्याप्यता *vy-āpyătā* [S.], f. permeability.

व्यामोह *vy-ā-moh* [S.], m. **1.** confusion, embarrassment. **2.** infatuation; state of unmindful happiness. — व्यामोहावस्था [°*ha*+*a*°], f. carefree, or delighted state.

व्यायाम *vy-ā-yām* [S.], m. **1.** physical exercise. **2.** gymnastics. — व्यायाम-शाला, f. gymnasium.

व्यायामिक *vy-ā-yāmik* [S.], adj. gymnastic.

व्यायामी *vy-ā-yāmī* [S.], m. & adj. **1.** m. one who takes exercise: a gymnast; sportsman. **2.** adj. well-developed (the body).

व्यारे *vyāre* [? conn. *vikāla-*], adv. *Pl.* reg. yesterday.

व्याल *vyāl* [S.], adj. & m. **1.** adj. wicked; cruel. **2.** m. a snake.

व्यालिनी *vyālinī* [S.], f. = व्याली.

व्याली *vyālī* [S.], f. a female snake.

व्यावसायिक *vyāvăsāyik* [S.], adj. having to do with business or occupation: **1.** occupational. **2.** professional.

व्यावसायिकता *vyāvăsāyikătā* [S.], f. **1.** business-like attitude: enterprise; acumen.

व्यावहारिक *vyāvăhārik* [S.], adj. having to do with practice, action or usage: **1.** practical (an attitude, a skill); applied. **2.** practicable. **3.** customary, current. **4.** colloquial (speech, language).

व्यावहारिकता *vyāvăhārikătā* [S.], f. **1.** practicability. **2.** current, or colloquial character (of speech, language).

व्यास *vy-ās* [S.], m. **1.** divider: diameter. **2.** arranger: *mythol.* name of a divine sage regarded as the compiler of the Vedas; title of any great compiler (as of the *Mahābhārata*, or *Bhāgavata Purāṇa*); reciter or singer (of a long traditional tale).

व्युत्क्रम *vy-ut-kram* [S.], m. going beyond, or astray: **1.** transgression. **2.** inverse order; disorder, confusion.

व्युत्थान *vy-ut-thān* [S.], m. rising, revolt.

व्युत्पत्ति *vy-ut-patti* [S.], f. **1.** origin, descent (from a source). **2.** derivation (of a word); etymology.

व्युत्पन्न *vy-ut-pann* [S.], adj. **1.** arising, produced (from, से); descended (from). **2.** derived (a word); formed (a derivative word).

व्युत्पादन *vy-ut-pādan* [S.], m. **1.** production from a source. **2.** deriving, etymologising (a word, &c).

व्यूह *vy-ūh* [S.], m. **1.** arrangement, disposition (esp. of an army drawn up to fight). **2.** army; army unit. **3.** formation, structure.

व्योम *vyom* [S.], m. **1.** the sky. **2.** space. — **व्योम-गंगा**, f. the Milky Way. **व्योम-यात्रा**, f. space travel. °-**यात्री**, m. astronaut. **व्योम-यान**, m. spacecraft; aircraft.

व्रज *vraj* [S.], m. = **ब्रज**.

व्रज्या *vrajyā* [S.], f. poet. sthg. travelled (on): a path.

व्रण *vraṇ* [S.], m. **1.** a wound. **2.** a sore, ulcer.

व्रत *vrat* [S.], m. **1.** vow. **2.** religious rite or observance (as enjoined by the gods or undertaken in devotion); a fast. — **~ करना**, to make a vow. **~ रखना**, to keep a vow, or any observance. **~ लेना**, to take a vow. — **व्रत-बंध**, m. Av. *hind.* sacred thread.

व्रतति *vratati* [S.], f. a creeper.

व्रती *vratī* [S.], adj. engaged in carrying out vows or religious observances (see **व्रत**); pious.

व्रात *vrāt* [S.], m. *Pl. HŚS.* a multitude, group, troop.

व्रात्य *vrātyă* [S.], m. **1.** an outcaste from the first three caste groups. **2.** a person having parents of mixed low caste.

व्रीड़ा *vrīṛā* [S.], f. **1.** shame. **2.** bashfulness, modesty.

व्रीड़ित *vrīṛit* [S.], adj. *Pl. HŚS.* ashamed, abashed; modest, bashful.

श

श *śa*, the thirtieth consonant of the Devanāgarī syllabary. — **शकार**, m. the sound /ś/; the letter श.

शंकर *śaṅkar* [S.], m. causing happiness: **1.** a title of Śiva. **2.** name of a Vedānta monist philosopher. **3.** *mus.* name of a *rāg*.

शंकरा *śaṅkarā* [S.], f. *mus. Pl. HŚS.* name of a *rāgiṇī*.

शंका *śaṅkā* [S.], f. **1.** doubt; misgiving, unease; suspicion. **2.** hesitation, scruple (about or to, से). **3.** fear; awe. — **~ करना**, to doubt, &c. **~ निवारण करना**, to set a doubt, &c. at rest. **शंकाकुल** [°*kā*+*ā*°], adj. perturbed by fear.

शंकित *śaṅkit* [S.], adj. **1.** filled with doubt, &c. (see **शंका**). **2.** fearful. **3.** anticipated with misgiving (an event). **4.** suspected (of an offence).

शंकु *śaṅku* [S.], m. **1.** stake, spike. **2.** spear. **3.** needle, gnomon, indicator. **4.** Brbh. ? a low dais or raised area of ground, the site of performance of a *rās* dance. **5.** *math.* a cone. — **शंकुरूप**, adj. conical.

शंख *śaṅkh* [S.], m. **1.** a conch shell (trad. used to pour libations). **2.** *mus.* horn made from a conch shell. **3.** a notional high number: ten, or a hundred, billions. — **शंखचूड़**, m. name of a demon killed by Kr̥ṣṇa. **शंखासुर** [°*kha*+*a*°], name of a demon (*daitya*) killed by Viṣṇu in his fish avatār.

शंखिनी *śaṅkhinī* [S.], f. one of four traditionally enumerated classes of women.

शंड *śaṇḍ* [S.], m. **1.** a bull. **2.** a eunuch. **3.** an impotent man.

शंबुक *śambuk* [ad. *śambukka-*, Pk. *saṁbukka-*], m. = **शंबूक**.

शंबूक *śambūk* [S.], m. a shell: **1.** a conch shell. **2.** a snail.

शंभु *śam-bhu* [S.], m. beneficent, benevolent: **1.** a title of Śiva. **2.** a title of Brahmā.

शऊर *śaūr* [A. *śu'ūr*], m. **1.** knowledge, wisdom; good sense. **2.** good manners or behaviour. — **शऊरदार** [P. *-dār*], adj. intelligent, sensible; having good manners.

-शः *-śaḥ* [S.], suffix (forms distributive and some other adverbs, e.g. **एकशः**, one by one, singly; **क्रमशः**, in sequence).

[1]**शक** *śak* [A. *śakk*], m. **1.** doubt; scepticism. **2.** suspicion. — **~ करना**, to doubt, &c. (sthg., का); to be suspicious (of a person, पर). **~ डालना**, to cast a doubt (upon, में), to call in question. **~ पड़ना**, or **होना**, doubt to be felt (by, को). **इस में क्या ~ है?** there is no doubt of this. – **शक-शुबहा**, m. = ~.

[2]**शक** *śak* [S.], m. **1.** a Scythian. **2.** name of the era of Śaka or Śālivāhana (beginning in A.D. 78).

शकट *śakaṭ* [S.], m. Brbh. a cart. — **शकटासुर** [°*ṭa*+*a*°], m. name of a demon killed by the infant Kr̥ṣṇa.

शकर *śakar*, f. = **शक्कर**. — **शकर-कंद**, m. sweet-root: the sweet potato. **°ई**, f. id. **शकरख़ोरा** [P. *khora*], m. a person fond of sweets; the purple sun-bird; the yellow-backed sun-bird. **शकर-पारा**, m. sugar cube: name of a partic. sweet; name of a partic. citrus fruit (less acidic than the lemon).

शकरी *śakrī* [P. *śakarī*: cf. H. *sak(k)ar*], adj. sugary; white: — **~ मुनिया**, m. the white-backed munia, *Lonchura striata*.

शकल *śakl* [A. *śakl*], f. **1.** likeness; appearance; features. **2.** shape, form. **3.** means, manner. — **~ देना (को)**, to give form or shape (to). **~ निकालना**, to find some means (of, की). **~ बनाना**, to make a likeness (of, की); to assume an outward form or character; to make a face. **~ बिगाड़ना**, to disfigure; fig. to thrash. – **शकल-सूरत**, f. = ~, 1.

शकुंत *śakunt* [S.], m. **1.** a bird; vulture. **2.** *Pl. HŚS.* blue jay.

शकुन *śakun* [S.], m. **1.** *Pl. HŚS.* a large bird. ***2.** an omen (esp. auspicious).

शकुनि *śakuni* [S.], f. *Pl. HŚS.* a bird; vulture; *Pl.* a kite.

शकुनी *śakunī* [S.], m. one who understands omens.

शक्कर *śakkar* [P. *śakkar*], f. **1.** sugar (= **शकर**). **2.** fig. sweet words. — **शक्करकंद**, m. = **शकरकंद**. **शक्करख़ोरा** [P. *-khora*], m. = **शकरख़ोरा**.

शक्की *śakkı* [P. *śakkı*], adj. **1.** doubtful (a matter, a person); sceptical. **2.** suspicious. **3.** wavering, hesitating. — **~ मिज़ाज का**, adj. of sceptical temperament.

शक्त *śakt* [S.], adj. **1.** able, capable. **2.** strong. **3.** hard, firm.

शक्ति *śakti* [S.], f. **1.** power, strength (physical, or otherwise); energy; transf. electric power. **2.** ability, capacity. **3.** *phys.* a force. **4.** *pol.* a power, nation. **5.** the energy of a deity personified as his wife (as Durgā or Gaurī of Śiva, Lakṣmī of Viṣṇu). **6.** the female genitalia (as counterpart of the phallic representation of Śiva; worshipped by *śāktas*). — ~ लगाना, to exert (one's) strength, to make efforts. शक्तिमतता, f. state or position of being powerful (शक्तिमान). शक्तिमान, adj. powerful; able, capable. शक्तिशाली, adj. powerful, strong. शक्ति-संतुलन, m. balance of forces. शक्तिहीन, adj. without strength or vigour; inert.

शक्य *śakyă* [S.], adj. possible, practicable.

शक्र *śakr* [S.], m. powerful one: a title of the god Indra.

शक्ल *śakl*, f. see शकल.

शख़स *śakhs*, m. see शख़्स.

शख़्स *śakhs* [A. *śakhs*], m. U. a man's self or person, a man; an individual.

शख़्सियत *śakhsiyat* [A. *śakhsīya*: P. *śakhsiyat*], f. U. individuality, identity.

शख़्सी *śakhsī* [A. *śakhsī*], adj. U. personal, individual.

शग़ल *śagl* [A. *śagl*], m. **1.** any activity: pastime, amusement. **2.** occupation. — आजकल क्या ~ है? what's going on nowadays?

शग़ला *śaglā* [cf. P. *śagl*], m. 19c. = शग़ल.

शगुन *śagun* [ad. *śakuna-*], m. **1.** an omen, augury (esp. favourable). **2.** a present (as money, sweets) given at an engagement by the fiancée's relatives to those of the fiancé. — ~ करना, to begin an activity, &c. at an auspicious moment; to consult omens (when beginning an enterprise). ~ लेना, to take an omen (from, से). ~ विचारना, to look for a good omen (when beginning an enterprise); to look for an auspicious conjunction of planets; to practise augury or astrology.

शगुनिया *śaguniyā* [P. *śagūniyā*], m. an augurer; astrologer.

शगून *śagūn* [P. *śugūn*] m. = शगुन.

शगूफ़ा *śagūfā* [P. *śigūfa*], m. **1.** a bud. **2.** fig. a minor cause of astonishment, consternation or quarrel. — ~ खिलना, a bud to blossom; a cause of astonishment, &c. to arise. ~ छोड़ना, colloq. to cause a minor row.

शचि *śaci* [S.], f. *mythol.* name of the wife of Indra.

शची *śacī* [S.], f. **1.** power, strength. **2.** *mythol.* = शचि.

शठ *śaṭh* [S.], adj. & m. **1.** adj. wicked, vicious. **2.** crafty, deceitful, unprincipled. **3.** m. Brbh. a false lover or husband. **4.** a rogue.

शठता *śaṭhătā* [S.], f. **1.** wickedness, &c. **2.** deceitfulness, &c. (see शठ).

शत *śat* [S.], adj. a hundred. — शतदल, m. having a hundred petals: a lotus. शतधा, adv. a hundredfold; in a hundred, or in countless, ways. शतपदी, f. a centipede. शतमुख, adv. in a hundred ways or directions. शत-वर्ष, m. a hundred years, a century. शत-वार्षिक, adj. centenary. °ई, f. a centenary. शतविध, adj. of a hundred, or of untold, kinds. शतशः, adv. in hundreds, a hundredfold. शत-शत, adj. a hundred hundreds, countless. शतांश [°*ta*+*a*°], m. a hundredth part; a degree centigrade. शताब्दी [°*ta*+*a*°], f. a century. प्रतिशत, adv. per cent.

शतक *śatak* [S.], m. collection of a hundred items; a century (of verses).

शतरंज *śatrañj* [P. *śatrañj*], m. chess. — शतरंजबाज़ [P. *-bāz*], m. chess-player. °ई, f. playing at chess.

[1]**शतरंजी** *śatrañjī* [P. *śatrañjī*], f. a thick floor-covering of chequered cotton.

[2]**शतरंजी** *śatrañjī* [cf. H. *śatrañj*], m. one who plays chess, a keen chess-player.

शती *śatī* [S.], f. **1.** a century. **2.** centenary anniversary.

शत्रु *śatru* [S.], m. an enemy; an opponent. — शत्रुघ्न, m. *mythol.* foe-slaying: name of one of the brothers of Rām. शत्रुहन, m. Av. id.

शत्रुता *śatrutā* [S.], f. enmity, hostility; ill-will.

शनाख़्त *śanākht* [P. *śanākht*], f. **1.** recognition; identification. **2.** knowledge, acquaintance, experience (of or with, की). — ~ करना (की), to recognise; to identify.

शनि *śani* [S.], m. slow-moving: **1.** the planet Saturn. **2.** misfortune. 3. = शनिवार. — ~ आना, or चढ़ना, hard times to arrive. – शनिश्चर, m. = शनि, 1., 3. शनिवार, m. Saturday.

शनिवार *śanivār* [S.], m. see s.v. शनि.

शनिश्चर *śaniścar*, m. see s.v. शनि.

शनैः *śanaiḥ* [S.], adv. **1.** slowly, softly. **2.** gradually. — ~ ~, adv. = ~.

शनैश्चर *śanaiścar* [S.], m. moving slowly: the planet Saturn (= शनि).

शप *śap* [P. *śap*], f. **1.** swishing or whizzing sound (as of a whip, or a weapon).

2. splashing sound; sound of lapping. — शपाशप, f. noise or splashing or slurping.

शपथ *śapath* [S.], f. (m., *Pl.*). an oath, a vow. — ~ खाना, to swear an oath (to, or by, की). ~ लेकर खाना, to say on oath, to swear (that, कि). — शपथ-ग्रहण, m. the taking of an oath. शपथ पत्र, m. sworn deposition, affidavit.

शपन *śapan* [S.], m. *Pl. HŚS.* cursing; abuse.

शप्त *śapt* [S.], adj. cursed; accursed.

शप्पा *śappā*, m. *Pl.* butt or mark for archers.

शफ़क़ *śafaq* [A. *śafaq*], f. m. **1.** U. = शफ़क़त. **2.** redness of the sky at evening or dawn. — ~ फूलना, the sky to grow red at dusk or dawn.

शफ़क़त *śafqat* [A. *śafaqa*: P. *śafaqat*], f. **1.** kindness, compassion. **2.** affection.

शफ़तालू *śaftālū* [P. *śaft-ālū*], m. a kind of peach.

शफर *śaphar* [S.], m. a small gold-coloured sea fish of the Bay of Bengal, the mango-fish. — शफर-वारि, m. calm water suddenly disturbed by the darting of small fish.

शफरी *śaphărī* [S.: w. H. *saphrī*], f. = शफर.

शफ़ा *śafā* [A. *śifā*], f. recovery (from sickness). — ~ देना (को), to cure. ~ पाना, to recover (from, से), to be cured (of). – शफ़ा-ख़ाना, m. a hospital.

शब *śab* [P. *śab*], f. U. night. — ~ बख़ैर [P. *ba-*], goodnight. – शब-बरात, f. *musl.* the eve of the fourteenth day of the month Śa'bān (when a vigil is kept and offerings are made to ancestors). शबनम, f. night-moisture: dew. °ई, adj. dewy; moist (eyes).

शबाब *śabāb* [A. *śabāb*], m. youth, youthfulness.

शबीह *śabīh* [A. *śabīh*], f. U. resemblance; a likeness.

शब्द *śabd* [S.], m. **1.** sound, noise (esp. as produced by any action). ***2.** a word (spoken or written). **3.** the word of God; the divine being as revealed through the Word. **4.** a song, hymn (esp. among Sikhs: = सबद). **5.** fig. the power of speech. **6.** *gram.* a word, a term. — ~ करना, to make a noise or sound (with, से), to sound, to blow. दो ~, m. two words: a few words (of conversation); a preface. – शब्दकार, m. composer of the words of a song. शब्द-कोश, m. word-store: dictionary. शब्दगत, adj. put into words, given verbal form. सब्द-चोर, m. word-thief: plagiarist. °ई, f. plagiarism. शब्द-ब्रह्म, m. the revealed Word, identified with the ultimate being; a Veda. शब्द-भंडार, m. word-stock, lexicon (of a language). शब्द-भेद, m. a part of speech. °-भेदी, adj. sound-piercing: = शब्दवेधी. शब्द-योनि, f. the source or origin of a word; *gram.* a root. शब्दरचना, f. *ling.* morphology. °त्मक, adj. शब्द-विधान, m. a partic. form or style of words or speech. शब्द-विन्यास, m. word-arrangement: turn of speech, phraseology. शब्दवेधी, adj. & m. piercing a target detected only by its sound (an arrow, or an archer). शब्दशः, adv. word for word. शब्द-संग्रह, m. a vocabulary. शाब्दांत [°*da*+*a*°], m. *gram.* ending of a word. शब्दाडंबर [°*da*+*ā*°], m. high-flown language; bombast. शब्दात्मक [°*da*+*ā*°], adj. concerning words, lexical. शब्दातीत [°*da*+*a*°], adj. beyond the reach of sound: the supreme being; beyond the power of words (to express). शब्दानुशासन [°*da*+*a*°], m. instruction in the use of words: a grammar; a guide to language usage. शब्दार्थ [°*da*+*a*°], m. meaning of a word, or words; literal sense. शब्दार्थ-विज्ञान, m. *ling.* semantics. शब्दालंकार [°*da*+*a*°], m. *rhet.* an adornment or figure of speech depending for its effect on sounds (as alliteration, assonance) rather than on meanings. शब्दावली [°*da*+*ā*°], f. terminology (of a partic. field); vocabulary (of a writer, or a partic. group). – शब्दाशब्द [P. -*ā*-], adv. word for word, verbatim.

शब्दायमान *śabdāyamān* [S.], adj. ringing out, resounding.

शंपा *śampā* [S.], f. lightning.

शम *śam* [S.], m. **1.** quiet, rest. **2.** peace of mind. **3.** restraint (of the senses); absence of passion. **4.** alleviation (of pain); cure (of disease).

शमन *śaman* [S.], m. **1.** quieting, calming. **2.** relieving (pain, disease). **3.** end, destruction; killing (sacrificial animals). **4.** cursing.

शमशाद *śamśād* [P. *śamśād*], m. S.H. **1.** the box tree, *Buxus sempervirens*. **2.** a tall, straight tree.

शमशेर *śamśer* [P. *śamśer*], f. a sword; scimitar. — शमशेरज़न [P. -*zan*], m. U. = next. शमशेरबाज़ [P. *bāz*], m. a swordsman. °ई, f. sword-play.

शमा *śamā* [A. *śam'*], m. **1.** a wax candle. **2.** fig. a lamp (= बत्ती). — शमादान, m. candlestick, candle-stand.

शमित *śamit* [S.], adj. **1.** calmed; calm. **2.** alleviated, relieved.

शमी *śamī* [S.], f. **1.** the tree *Acacia suma*. **2.** a legume, pod.

शय *śay* [ad. *śayyā-*], f. a bed.

शयन *śayan* [S.], m. **1.** lying down, resting, sleeping; sleep. **2.** -शयन. resting-place (*mythol.* as of Śeṣa), bed. — शयन-कक्ष, m. bedroom. शयन-गाड़ी, f. sleeping carriage, sleeper. शयनशाला, f. 19c. bedroom.

शय्या *śayyā* [S.], f. a bed.

शर *śar* [S.], m. **1.** a reed. ***2.** an arrow, shaft. **3.** *Pl.* name of a small bird, *Turdus gosalica* (considered as a variety of mynah). — शरास [°*a*+*ā*°], m. a bow.

शरई *śaraī* [A. *śar'ī*], adj. enjoined by Muslim religion or law (*śarī'at*). — ~ दाढ़ी, or मूँछें, f. a beard or moustache of orthodox cut.

शरच्- *śarac-* [S]. autumn: — शरच्चंद्र, m. the autumn moon (esp. of the month Kārttik).

शरण *śaraṇ* [S.], f. m. **1.** protection. **2.** shelter, refuge. — ~ आना, to come (to, की) for protection. ~ लेना, to take or to find protection (from or with, की). – शरणागत, adj. & m. come for protection: fleeing, displaced; a refugee. शरणापन्न [°*ṇa*+*ā*°], adj. having obtained protection: id. शरणार्थी [°*ṇa*+*a*°], adj. & m. seeking protection: a refugee.

शरण्य *śaraṇyă* [S.], m. Brbh. providing shelter: a protector.

शरत् *śarat* [S.], f. the autumn. — शरत्काल, m. id. °ईन, adj.

शरद् *śarad* [S.], f. autumn (= शरत्). — शरद्-ऋतु, f. id.

शरप्पा *śarappā*, m. colloq. noisy eating: a slurping or gulping sound.

शरबत *śarbat* [A. *śarba*: P. *śarbat*], f. **1.** any sweet drink, sherbet. **2.** a sweet medicine, syrup. — ~ पिलाना, to seal a marriage engagement by giving a drink of sherbet (to the barber who has arranged it: को). – शरबत-ख़ाना, m. colloq. a dispensary (= दवा-ख़ाना). शरबत-पिलाई, f. gift made to a barber who has acted as go-between in arranging a marriage.

शरबती *śarbatī* [P. *śarbatī*], adj. & f. **1.** having to do with sherbet. **2.** of orange-yellow colour. **3.** f. orange or pale yellow colour.

शरम *śarm*, f. see शर्म.

शरमाना *śarmānā* [cf. H. *śarm*], v.i. & v.t. **1.** v.i. to feel shame. **2.** to be bashful; to be embarrassed. **3.** v.t. to make (one) ashamed.

शरमिंदगी *śarmindăgī* [P. *śarmandagī*], f. **1.** shamefacedness. **2.** sense of embarrassment. **3.** feelings of modesty. — ~ उठाना, to suffer shame, &c.

शरमिंदा *śarmindā* [P. *śarmanda*], adj. inv. **1.** ashamed. **2.** abashed; embarrassed. **3.** modest. — ~ करना, to put to shame; to embarrass.

शरमीला *śarmīlā* [cf. H. *śarm*], adj. **1.** bashful, shy. **2.** modest. **3.** ? ashamed.

शरह *śarh* [A. *śarḥ*], f. U. exposition, commentary.

शराकत *śarākat* [A. *śarāka*: P. *śirākat*], f. **1.** sharing, participation. **2.** partnership; company, firm. — ~ करना, to participate (in); to form a partnership, &c. (with).

शराटि *śarāṭi* [S.], f. *Pl.* a bird; ? sandpiper.

शराफ़त *śarāfat* [A. *śarāfa*: P. *śarāfat*], f. **1.** nobility. **2.** courtly or well-born manner.

शराब *śarāb* [P. *śarāb*], f. wine, alcohol. — शराब-कबाब, m. alcohol and meat. °ई, m. one who drinks alcohol and eats meat. शराब-कबाब करना, to drink alcohol and eat meat. शराब-ख़ाना, m. a liquor-stall or shop. शराबख़ोर [P. *-khor*], m. a heavy drinker. °ई, f. drunkenness. शराबज़दा [P. *-zada*], adj. wine-struck: drunk. शराबबंदी [P. *-bandī*], f. prohibition of alcohol. – शराबुनतहूरा [A. *-ul-ṯahūra*], m. 19c. purifying, or pure draught: the water of Paradise, nectar.

शराबी *śarābī* [P. *śarābī*], adj. & m. **1.** adj. drunk. **2.** m. a heavy drinker. — शराबी-कबाबी, m. one who drinks alcohol and eats meat.

शराबीपन *śarābīpan* [cf. H. *śarāb*], m. addiction to alcohol.

शराबोर *śarābor*, adj. wet through, soaked.

शरारत *śarārat* [A. *śarāra*: P. *śarārat*], f. **1.** wickedness. **2.** mischievousness; naughtiness. — शरारत-भरा, adj. mischievous, &c. (an act, a prank; or a look).

शरारतन *śarārătan* [A. *śarāratan*], adv. wickedly; mischievously.

शरारती *śarārătī* [A. *śarāra*+P. *-ī*], adj. **1.** wicked. **2.** mischievous; naughty.

शराव *śarāv* [S.], m. *Pl. HŚS.* **1.** an earthenware cup (= कुल्हड़). **2.** a homeopathic measure of weight (= 64 *tolās*). **3.** a lid, cover.

शरीअत *śarīat* [A. *śarī'a*: P. *sarī'at*], f. the religious law of Islam.

शरीक *śarīk* [A. *śarīk*], adj. & m. **1.** adj. participating. **2.** m. a participant. **3.** a partner. — ~ करना, to make (one) a participant (in, में), to include (in). ~ होना, to take part (in, में); to be a partner; to have or to possess things in common.

शरीफ़ *śarīf* [A. *śarīf*], adj. noble, high-born.

शरीफ़ा *śarīfā* [P. *śarīfa*], m. the custard-apple, *Anona squamosa*.

[1]**शरीर** *śarīr* [S.], m. the body. — उसके ~ में दर्द है, he feels a pain. – शरीरक्रिया-विज्ञान, m. physiology. शरीर-त्याग, m. giving up the body: death. शरीर-विज्ञान, m. physiology; anatomy. शरीर-संस्कार, m. purification of the body (by

various ceremonies after conception and at birth, initiation and death). **शरीरांत** [°*ra*+*a*°], m. end of the body: death.

²**शरीर** *śarīr* [A. *śarır*], adj. **1.** wicked, depraved. **2.** mischievous (cf. **शरारत**).

शरीरी *śarīrī* [S.], adj. & m. **1.** adj. having to do with the body, bodily. **2.** embodied, living. **3.** m. a living creature; a man.

¹**शर्करा** *śarkarā* [S.], f. sugar.

²**शर्करा** *śarkarā* [S.], f. **1.** gravel, grit; gravelly soil. **2.** gravel, stone (in the bladder, &c).

शर्क़ी *śarqī* [A. *śarqī*], adj. U. eastern.

शर्त *śart* [A. *śarṭ*], f. **1.** a condition; a provision; terms. **2.** an agreement, bargain. **3.** a wager, bet. — ~ **करना**, or **बदना**, or **बाँधना**, or **लगाना**, to make a condition, to stipulate; to negotiate an agreement (with, **के साथ**; about, **की**); to bet (with). ~ **जीतना**, to win a bet. ~ **हारना**, to lose a bet. **इस** ~ **पर**, adv. on this condition. **विला** ~, adv. U. unconditionally. **बिला** ~ **का**, adj. – **शर्त-नामा**, m. a contract. **शर्ताशर्ती** [P. *-ā-*], f. mutual obligations.

शर्तिया *śartiyā* [A. *śarṭiya*], adj. **1.** reliable (as a medicine, &c). **2.** adv. definitely, certainly.

शर्म *śarm* [P. *śarm*], f. **1.** shame. **2.** bashfulness; embarrassment. **3.** modesty. — ~ **आना** (**को**), shame, &c. to be felt (by). ~ **करना**, or **खाना**, to feel ashamed, &c. (at or about, **की**). ~ **की बात है**, it is shameful; it is a shame (= **अफ़सोस की बात है**). ~ **दिलाना** (**को**), to make (one) ashamed, to put to shame. ~ **रखना** (**की**), to save (one) from shame or dishonour. ~ **लगना** (**को**), = ~ **आना**. – **शर्मज़दा** [P. *-zada*], adj. ashamed; bashful. **शर्मनाक** [P. *-nāk*], adj. id.; modest; shameful; causing embarrassment. **शर्म-गाह**, f. *Pl.* the genitals. **शर्मसार** [P. *-sār*], adj. ashamed; bashful, &c. **शर्म-हुज़ूरी**, f. embarrassment or confusion in confronting a person of rank. **शर्माशर्मी**, adv. & f. out of embarrassment; modestly; = ~, 2.

शर्मा *śarmā* [S.], m. inv. happy, prosperous: a title often taken by brāhmaṇs.

शर्माना *śarmānā*, v.i. & v.t. see **शरमाना**.

शर्मालु *śarmālu* [cf. H. *śarm*], adj. reg. = **शरमीला**.

शर्मिंदगी *śarmindāgī*, f. see **शरमिंदगी**.

शर्मिंदा *śarmindā*, adj. see **शरमिंदा**.

शर्मीला *śarmīlā*, adj. see **शरमीला**.

शर्राटा *śarrāṭā*, m. a sound, noise; ringing sound, echo.

शर्वरी *śarvārī* [S.], f. **1.** evening, night. **2.** a woman.

¹**शल** *śal* [S.], m. a porcupine's quill.

²**शल** *śal* [A. *śall*], adj. **1.** paralysed (a limb). **2.** withered (a limb). **3.** languid, inert.

शलग़म *śalgam* [P. *śalgam*], m. = **शलजम**.

शलजम *śaljam* [A. *śaljam*], m. a turnip.

शलभ *śalabh* [S.], m. **1.** a grasshopper; locust. **2.** a moth.

शलवार *śalvār* [P. *śalvār*], m. loose cotton trousers worn by women.

शलाका *śalākā* [S.], f. **1.** a thin bar, rod, or shaft of wood or metal. **2.** a shaft, arrow. **3.** sliver, piece (as of wood; cf. **सलाई**, **दिया-सलाई**). **4.** *med.* a probe. **5.** oblong piece of bone or ivory (used in partic. games), a domino. **6.** vote (as given by straws).

शलूका *śalūkā*, m. a women's garment for the upper part of the body, having long or half sleeves.

शल्य *śalyă* [S.], m. **1.** a spike, stake. **2.** splinter; thorn. **3.** transf. extraction of splinters or extraneous substances from the body; surgery. **4.** a porcupine. — **शल्य-क्रिया**, f. *med.* operation. **शल्य-चिकित्सक**, m. a surgeon. °-**चिकित्सा**, f. surgery. °-**विज्ञान**, m. surgery (as an art or science).

शल्लकी *śallakī* [S.], f. *Pl. HŚS.* a porcupine.

शव *śav* [S.], m. a corpse. — **शव-दाह**, m. cremation of a body. **शव-परीक्षा**, f. post mortem examination. **शव-यात्रा**, f. funeral procession.

शवता *śavătā* [S.], f. inert and lifeless state.

शवरी *śavărī* [S.], f. Brbh. a woman of the Śavara tribe, a tribal woman.

शश *śaś* [S.], m. **1.** a hare; a rabbit. **2.** the markings on the moon. — **शशधर**, m. carrying (marks like) a hare: the moon. **शशांक** [°*śa*+*a*°], m. hare-marked: the moon.

शश- *śaś-* [P. *śaś*], adj. U. six: — **शशदर**, m. six doors (a point in a board game where one's piece cannot move): astonished, perplexed.

शशक *śaśak* [S.], m. a hare; a rabbit.

शशि *śaśi* [S.], m. hare-marked: the moon. — **शशि-मंडल**, m. the moon's disc. **शशिमुख**, adj. moon-faced, lovely. **शशिवदन**, m. id. **शशिशेखर**, m. moon-crested: a title of Śiva.

शशी *śaśī* [S.], m. E.H. the moon (= **शशि**).

शस्त्र *śastra* [S.], m. **1.** a weapon, esp. for striking or cutting with; arms. **2.** any cutting implement. — ~ **चलाना**, to wield weapons, to fight. ~ **बाँधना**, to gird on arms, to arm (oneself). – **शस्त्रकार**, m. an armourer. **शस्त्र-गृह**, m. = **शस्त्र-शाला**. **शस्त्र-जीवी**, m. living by weapons:

a professional soldier. शस्त्रधारी, adj. & m. holding or taking weapons, armed; an armed person. शस्त्र-बल, m. armed strength. शस्त्र-बल से, adv. by force of arms. शस्त्र-शाला, f. armoury, arsenal. शस्त्रास्त्र [°ra + a°], m. weapons for striking with and throwing: arms. शस्त्रीकरण, m. taking up arms; arming; armament(s).

शस्य *śasyă* [S.], m. sthg. to be cut: **1.** harvest, crop. **2.** grain. **3.** grass. — शस्य-श्यामल, adj. dark with crops, abundant (land).

शहंशाह *śahaṃśāh* [P. *s̆āhanśāh*], m. king of kings, emperor.

शहंशाही *śahaṃśāhī* [cf. H. *śahaṃśāh*], adj. & f. **1.** adj. royal; imperial. **2.** f. fig. overweening arrogance.

शह *śah* [P. *śah*], f. m. (? f. fr. H. ²*māt*). **1.** (in chess) check. **2.** semblance of status or importance. **3.** [? × H. ¹*śai*] urging, incitement. — ~ खाना, to be checked (the king in chess). ~ देना (को), to check (the king, in chess), to seem to give importance (to); to incite, to instigate; to flatter; to loosen, to relax (as a kite-string). ~ पाना, (a person) to be given importance or countenance (by, की); to be allowed rope (by). ~ बचाना, to get out of check. ~ में मात, check and checkmate. ~ लगाना, = ~ देना. – शह-चाल, f. (in chess) king's move: a move out of check by the king.

शह- *śah-* [P. *śah*]. king; chief, best, large (see also s.v. शाह). — शहतीर, m. a heavy beam; the main roof-beam of a house. शहतूत [P. *-tūt*], m. mulberry. शहबाला, m. *musl.* a boy who accompanies the bridegroom in his marriage party. शहसवार, m. a good rider, fine horseman.

शहद *śahd* [A. *śahd*], m. **1.** honey. **2.** fig. anything very sweet. — ~ की मक्खी, f. a honey bee. ~ की छुरी, or ~ की मीठी छुरी, f. a honeyed knife: a secret enemy. ~ लगाकर चाटना, colloq. to put honey on sthg. (ill-tasting) and lick: to treasure sthg. useless.

शहना *śahnā* [A. *siḥna*], m. rent collector; a rent collector's peon, bailiff.

शहनाई *śahnāī* [P. *śahnāī*], f. great pipe: a large pipe, flute.

शहर *śahr* [P. *śahr*], m. a city; a town. — शहरख़बरा, m. *Pl. HŚS.* newsmonger, gossip-monger. शहर-गश्त [P. *-gaśt*], m. a city patrol or procession through a city; patrolling a city. शहर-पनाह, f. city wall, or fortifications. शहरवाला, m. a townsman; resident of a partic. city or town.

शहराती *śahrātī* [cf. H. *śahr* + P. *-ātī* (as in *qaṣbātī*)], adj. & m. **1.** adj. city-dwelling, town-dwelling. **2.** urbane. **3.** m. a townsman.

शहरियत *śahriyat* [P. *śahriyat*], f. **1.** population of a city or town. **2.** a township. ***3.** urbanity.

शहरी *śahrī* [P. *śahrī*], adj. & m. **1.** adj. urban; municipal. **2.** m. a townsman, city resident.

शहादत *śahādat* [A. *śahāda*: P. *śahādat*], f. **1.** evidence, testimony, witness. **2.** martyrdom. **3.** transf. valour. — ~ देना, to give evidence.

शहाब *śahāb* [P. *śahāb*], m. a dark red colour or dye.

शहीद *śahīd* [A. *śahīd*], m. a martyr (religious or political: properly, one martyred in the name of Islam). — ~ होना, to be killed in battle against unbelievers; fig. to become a patriotic hero; to fall desperately in love (with).

शांत *śānt* [S.], adj. **1.** quieted, pacified (turmoil, anger, uprising). **2.** assuaged (pain, thirst). **3.** extinguished (fire, flame). — ~ करना, to make quiet, to pacify, &c. ~ होना, to be quiet; calm, &c.

शांतता *śāntătā* [S.], f. **1.** state of quiet or calm, &c. (see शांत). **2.** quality of calmness, &c.; quietude.

शांति *śānti* [S.], f. **1.** calmness, quiet; stillness; peace (of mood). **2.** rest, repose. **3.** peace (between factions, powers). — ~ देना (को), to calm; to give rest; to bring peace (to). – शांति-दाता, m. inv. bringer of calm, peace, &c. °-दायक, adj. bringing calm, peace, &c. °-दायी, adj. id. शांतिपूर्ण, adj. peaceful. शांतिप्रद, adj. = शांतिदायी. शांतिप्रिय, adj. peace-loving, peaceful. शांति-प्रेमी, adj. peace-loving. शांति-भंग, m. breach of the peace. शांतिमय, adj. peaceful, calm. शांतिवाद, m. pacifism. °ई, adj. & m.

शांबरी *śāmbărī* [S.], f. **1.** jugglery. **2.** sorcery; illusion. **3.** a witch.

शांबुक *śāmbuk* [conn. *śāmbuka-*], m. *Pl. HŚS.* **1.** a bi-valve shell. **2.** a kind of snail.

शाकंभरीय *śākambharīyă* [S.], adj. having to do with Sambhar in Rajasthan: fossil salt from Sambhar Lake.

¹**शाक** *śāk* [S.], m. **1.** a vegetable; greens. **2.** a herb, herbs. — शाक-भक्षी, adj. herbivorous. शाकाहार [°ka + ā°], m. vegetarianism. °ई, adj. & m. vegetarian; herbivorous.

²**शाक** *śāk* [S.], adj. **1.** Scythian. **2.** having to do with the *śaka* era.

साकल *sākal* [ad. *śākalya-*], m. 19c. a mixture of sesame, barley, ghī, sugar and fruit (used in offerings).

शाकिनी *śākinī* [S.], f. *hind.* a kind of female demon attendant on Durgā, and on Śiva.

शाकिर *śākir* [A. *śākir*], adj. U. thankful, grateful; content.

शाकी *śākī* [A. *śākī*], adj. U. complaining.

शाक्त *śākt* [S.], m. *hind.* a worshipper of the *śakti* or divine power of Śiva personified as a woman (as Devī, Durgā, &c).

शाक्य *śākyă* [S.], m. descended from the Śakas: name of the family of the Buddha.

शाख़ *śākh* [P. *śākh*], f. **1.** branch; twig. **2.** slip, cutting. **3.** horn (of a deer). **4.** branch, section (as of a firm). **5.** tributary (river). — ~ लगाना, to plant a cutting; to graft (on to, में). – शाख़दार [P. *-dār*], adj. having branches; horned.

शाखा *śākhā* [S.], f. **1.** branch. **2.** division, section (esp. of an organisation); sect, school. **3.** branch (of a subject). **4.** tributary. — शाखा-मृग, m. Brbh. Av. creature of the branches: a monkey. शाखोच्चार [°*khā*+*u*°], m. reciting the family genealogies of bride and groom at a wedding.

शाखी *śākhī* [S.], adj. **1.** having branches, divisions, or ramifications. **2.** belonging to any branch, school, sect, &c.

शागिर्द *śāgird* [P. *śāgird*], m. **1.** pupil; disciple. **2.** apprentice. — ~ करना (को), to take (one) as a pupil, &c. – शागिर्द-पेशा, m. one whose work is as a pupil, &c. (of); a dependant, servant.

शागिर्दी *śāgirdī* [P. *śāgirdī*], f. pupilhood, &c. (see शागिर्द). — ~ करना, to learn or to study (from or with, की).

शाटिका *śāṭikā* [S.], f. *Pl. HŚS.* a piece of cloth, garment.

शाठ्य *śāṭhyă* [S.], m. wickedness, villainy.

[1]**शाण** *śāṇ* [S.], m. a grindstone.

[2]**शाण** *śāṇ* [S.], m. cloth made of hemp or of flax.

शातिर *śātir* [P. *śāṭir*], adj. & m. leaving one's family: **1.** adj. cunning, rascally. **2.** m. a rascal. **3.** pej. a chess-player.

शाद *śād* [P. *śād*], adj. U. delighted, rejoicing.

शादियाना *śādiyānā* [P. *śādiyāna*], adj. & m. **1.** adj. having to do with marriage, or with festivities. ***2.** m. music and singing at marriages or on other festive occasions. **3.** a band. — ~ बजाना, or देना, to play festive music, to rejoice.

शादी *śādī* [P. *śādī*], f. delight, glad occasion: marriage; a wedding. — ~ करना, to have (a person) married (to, से), to arrange a marriage. ~ होना, (one's) marriage to take place (to, से). राम की सीता से ~ हुई, Rām married Sītā. – शादी-ब्याह, m. = ~. शादीशुदा [P. *śuda*], adj. inv. U. married.

[1]**शान** *śān* [*śāna-*, *śāṇa-*], m. **1.** a grindstone, whetstone. **2.** touchstone.

[2]**शान** *śān* [A. *śa'n*], f. thing, affair: **1.** dignity, state; pomp, grandeur. **2.** majesty, glory. — ~ जमाना, to assume an air of importance (at the expense of another); to lord it (over). ~ जाना, pride to be humbled; pomp to be deflated. ~ झाड़ना, = ~ मारना. ~ दिखाना, to make a great display. ~ मारना, to deflate, to humble the pride or pomp (of, की). ~ में, adv. in the matter (of, की): concerning, about. ~ से, adv. with state or ceremony; pompously. – शानदार [P. -*dār*], adj. imposing; splendid, magnificent; pretentious. शान-शौक़त, f. fine or splendid material state. शान-शौक़त से होना, to be prospering greatly.

शाना *śānā* [P. *śāna*], m. U. **1.** comb. **2.** crest (of a bird).

शाप *śāp* [S.], m. a curse. — ~ देना (को), to curse. — शाप-ग्रस्त, adj. affected by a curse: cursed.

शापना *śāpnā* [ad. *śāpayati*: w. H. *śāp*], v.t. to curse.

शापित *śāpit* [S.], adj. cursed; accursed.

शाबाश *śābāś* [P. *śābāś*], interj. well done! splendid!

शाबाशी *śābāśī* [P. *śābāśī*], f. applause; praise. — ~ देना (को), to applaud, &c.

शाब्दिक *śābdik* [S.], adj. word for word, literal (sense, translation).

[1]**शाम** *śām* [P. *śām*], f. evening; late afternoon. — ~ के पाँच बजे, adv. at five p.m. ~ को, adv. in the evening, &c. ~ फूलना, evening twilight to come on. — शाम-सवेरे, adv. morning and/or evening: all the time; occasionally.

[2]**शाम** *śām* [A. *śām*], m. Syria.

[3]**शाम** *śām* [*śamba-*], m. reg. a metal ring, ferrule (as on the end of a wooden implement); bush (of a wheel); socket. — शामदान [P. *-dān*], m. reg. (W.) a small jewellers' anvil.

शामत *śāmat* [A. *śāma*: P. *śāmat*], f. **1.** misfortune; disaster. **2.** disgrace. — ~ आना (पर), misfortune to befall (one). ~ का मारा, adj. & m. unfortunate, wretched; disgraced, infamous; cursed; an unfortunate person, &c. ~ सिर पर खेलना (के), = ~ आना (पर). – शामतज़दा [P. *-zada*], adj. = ~ का मारा.

शामती *śāmătī* [P. *śāmatī*], adj. unfortunate; wretched.

शामन *śāman* [S.], m. **1.** calming, allaying; quieting. **2.** killing.

शामियाना *śāmiyānā* [P. *śāmiyāna*], m. **1.** a large tent, marquee; pavilion. **2.** canopy, awning.

शामिल *śāmil* [A. *śāmil*], adj. **1.** included (in, में). **2.** involved (in), participating. — ~ करना, to include, to incorporate (in); to attach (as papers to a file); to include (one in a group); to involve (in an activity).

शामिलात *śāmilāt* [A. *śāmilāt*, pl.], m. pl. (?) reg. (W). common lands (held in partnership) in a village.

शामी *śāmī* [A. *śāmī*], adj. & m. **1.** adj. Syrian. **2.** m. a Syrian. — ~ कबाब, m. fried, spiced minced meat in batter.

शायक *śāyak* [S.], m. **1.** an arrow. **2.** *Pl. HŚS.* a sword.

शायद *śāyad* [P. *śāyad*], adv. **1.** w. subj. perhaps. **2.** (not w. subj.) probably. — ~ ही, adv. hardly ever; scarcely, improbably.

शायर *śāyr* [A. *śā'ir*], m. a poet.

शायरनी *śāyrnī* [cf. H. *śāyr*], f. a poetess.

शायरा *śāyrā* [A. *sā'ira*], f. U. a poetess.

शायराना *śāyrānā* [P. *śā'irāna*], adj. poetic.

शायरी *śāyrī* [A. *sā'ir*+P. *-ī*], f. the art or practice of poetry; poetry.

शाया *śāyā* [A. *śā'i'*], adj. inv. U. published. — ~ करना, to publish.

¹शार *śār* [S.], adj. *Pl. HŚS.* speckled, mottled.

²शार *śār* [P. *śār*], m. *Pl.* a starling.

शारंगी *śārangī*, f. = सारंगी.

शारद *śārad* [S.], adj. **1.** having to do with autumn (as a festival, a crop). **2.** fresh, cool.

शारदा *śārădā* [S.], f. **1.** *mythol.* a title of Sarasvatī. **2.** *mythol.* a title of Durgā. **3.** name of a script used formerly in Kashmir.

शारदीय *śārădīyă* [S.], adj. autumnal.

शारी *śārī* [ad. *śāri*-¹], f. a mynah.

शारीर *śārīr* [S.], adj. having to do with the body. — ~ विज्ञान, m. *med.* anatomy.

शारीरक *śārīrak* [S.], adj. & m. **1.** adj. embodied. **2.** m. the soul.

शारीरिक *śārīrik* [S.], adj. having to do with the body; bodily; physical (as strength, fitness, pain).

शार्दूल *śārdūl* [S.], m. **1.** tiger. **2.** leopard.

¹शाल *śāl* [P. *śāl*], f. a shawl.

²शाल *śāl* [S.], m. **1.** the *sāl* tree (q.v). **2.** a kind of fish, *Ophiocephalus wrahl.* — शाल-ग्राम, m. *hind.* Śālagrām stone: a kind of black stone containing one or more ammonites which is supposed to be pervaded by the substance of Viṣṇu, and is sacred to Vaiṣṇavas. शाल-भंजी, f. a wooden puppet or doll.

शाला *śālā* [S.], f. esp. in comp. house, place, hall (esp. as devoted to a partic. purpose). — धर्म-शाला, f. rest-house, hostel.

शालि- *śāli-* [S.], m. a type of rice: — शालिहोत्र, m. receiving oblations of rice or corn: a horse; a partic. treatise by Śālihotra on veterinary science. °-होत्री, m. a veterinary surgeon.

-शालिनी *-śālinī* [S.], adj. formant, specif. f. = -शाली.

-शाली *-śālī* [S.], adj. formant. belonging to a house, &c. (see शाला): **1.** endowed with (an attribute). e.g. प्रतिभाशाली, adj. brilliant. **2.** inclined to.

शालीन *śālīn* [S.], adj. having a house or fixed abode: **1.** serene, mild; modest. **2.** noble.

शालीनता *śālīnătā* [S.], f. serenity, nobility, &c. (see शालीन).

शालेय *śāleyă* [S.], m. sown with rice: fennel.

शाल्मली *śālmalī* [S.], f. the silk-cotton tree (= सेमल).

शावक *śāvak* [S.], m. **1.** young of an animal. **2.** fledgling.

शाश्वत *śāśvat* [S.], adj. **1.** eternal. **2.** immortal. **3.** all.

शाश्वतता *śāśvatătā* [S.], f. eternity.

शासक *śāsak* [S.], adj. & m. **1.** adj. ruling, governing. **2.** m. ruler, governor.

शासकीय *śāsăkīyă* [S.], adj. governmental; official.

शासन *śāsan* [S.], m. instructing; command: **1.** governing, ruling. **2.** rule (of a government, a king); command (of a leader). **3.** control (as over the emotions); discipline. **4.** a government. **5.** a command, edict. **6.** deed, grant (as of land or privileges). — शासन-कर्ता, m. inv. ruler, governor.

शासनिक *śāsănik* [S.], adj. governmental.

शासनी *śāsănī* [S.], f. *HŚS.* instructress: a woman preacher.

शासनीय *śāsănīyă* [S.], adj. **1.** to be governed, controlled; requiring control. **2.** deserving punishment.

शासित *śāsit* [S.], adj. **1.** governed, controlled. **2.** punished.

शासी *śāsī* [S.], adj. ruling, governing.

शास्ति *śāsti* [S.], f. **1.** governing; rule. **2.** edict. **3.** punishment (esp. by royal command).

शास्त्र *śāstrā* [S.], m. **1.** a work or book dealing with religion, or with any branch of knowledge, which is regarded as of age-old or divine authority; treatise; a scripture; pl. the scriptures; ancient Indian learning. **2.** -शास्त्र. a body of knowledge, a science (e.g. अर्थ-शास्त्र, m. economics). — शास्त्रकार, m. compiler of a *śāstra*. शास्त्रज्ञ, m. knowing or versed in the *śāstras*. शास्त्र-मीमांसा, f. learning, knowledge. शास्त्राज्ञा [°*ra*+*ā*°], f. injunction of the *śāstras*. शास्त्रार्थ [°*ra*+*a*°], m. meaning or interpretation of a *śāstra*; a doctrinal debate, discussion; specif. debate between an Ārya Samājī and a sanātan Hindu or a Vaiṣṇava. °ई, m. participant in a *śāstrārth*. शास्त्रालोचन [°*ra*+*ā*°], m. = prec., 2. शास्त्रोक्त [°*ra*+*u*°], adj. declared or enjoined by the *śāstras*.

शास्त्री *śāstrī* [S.], adj. & m. **1.** adj. versed in the *śāstras*. **2.** m. one versed in the *śāstras*; a paṇḍit. **3.** specif. holder of a graduate qualification from certain academic institutions. — शास्त्री-फ़ास्त्री [f. H. *fārsī*], adj. & m. joc. bookish, owlish; a bookworm.

शास्त्रीय *śāstrīyă* [S.], adj. **1.** conformable to scripture or precept. **2.** classical (as music). **3.** academic. **4.** scientific.

शाह *śāh* [P. *śāh*], m. **1.** king. **2.** (in chess, cards) the king. **3.** a title taken by *faqīrs*. **4.** शाह-, शह-. royal; excellent; best, or largest (of its kind). शहसवार, m. a fine horseman. — शाहख़र्च, adj. extravagant, prodigal (in largesse or expenditure); °ई, f. extravagance, &c. शाहज़ादा [P. *-zāda*], m. king's son: a prince. °ई, f. a princess. शाह-दरा, m. a village near a palace; the highway. शाह-बाज़, m. the crested hawk-eagle. शाह-बुलबुल, m. the paradise fly-catcher, *Terpsiphone paradisi*. शाह-रुख़ी, f. *hist.* a coin stamped with a king's head.

शाहाना *śāhānā* [P. *śāhāna*], adj. **1.** royal, kingly; princely. **2.** splendid, magnificent.

शाही *śāhī* [P. *śāhī*], adj. & f. **1.** adj. royal, kingly. **2.** chief, principal (as a road). **3.** monarchic (as a government, or an age). **4.** f. esp. -शाही. dominion, rule. — तानाशाही, f. despotism, dictatorship. लालफ़ीताशाही, f. colloq. the rule of red tape: bureaucracy.

शाहीन *śāhīn* [P. *sāhīn*], f., m. the shahin falcon, *Falco peregrinator* (specif. the female).

शिकंजा *śikañjā* [P. *śikanja*], m. **1.** a press; clamp, vice. **2.** instrument of torture: stocks; rack. **3.** transf. clutch, grasp. — शिकंजे में कसना, to put on the rack. शिकंजे में खींचना, to put in a press; to put on the rack.

शिकन *śikan* [P. *śikan*], f. breaking: **1.** a fold. **2.** furrow, wrinkle (as on the face or brow). — ~ डालना (में), to fold; to crease, to crumple (a garment). ~ पड़ना (में), to be creased, &c.; to be wrinkled (by age, or in anxiety).

शिकमी *śikmī* [P. *śikamī*], adj. & m. *hist.* having to do with the belly: **1.** adj. own, private; dependent. ***2.** sub-tenanted (a farmer); cultivating land belonging to another person. **3.** m. a sub-tenant. — ~ काश्तकार, m. farmer holding a sub-tenancy (as of village lands).

शिकरा *śikrā* [P. *śikara*], m. U. a hawk.

शिकवा *śikvā* [A. *śikva*], m. **1.** complaint. **2.** reproach. — शिकवा-शिकायत, f. = ~.

शिकस्त *śikast* [P.], f. U. a breaking: a defeat. — ~ खाना, to suffer a defeat. ~ देना (को), to defeat. ~ होना, to be defeated.

शिकस्ता *śikastā* [P. *śikasta*], adj. & m. inv. **1.** broken; decrepit. ***2.** m. the running form of the Persian script.

शिकाकाई *śikākāī*, f. = सीकाकाई.

शिकायत *śikāyat* [A. *śikāya*: P. *śikāyat*], f. **1.** a complaint; request for improvement or redress. **2.** a reproach. **3.** an ailment, complaint. उसे दस्त की ~ है, he's suffering from dysentery. — ~ करना, to complain, &c. (of, की; to, से). ~ दूर करना, to remove a cause of complaint. उससे मुझे कोई ~ नहीं है, I have no complaint about him.

शिकायती *śikāyătī* [P. *śikāyatī*], adj. complaining, querulous.

शिकार *śikār* [P. *śikār*], m. **1.** hunting. **2.** game; prey. **3.** transf. victim. — ~ करना (का), to hunt; to prey (upon); fig. to pursue as prey. ~ खेलना (का), to hunt; to catch or to take (animals, birds or fish). ~ मारना, to kill game, to hunt. ~ माही [P. *śikār e māhī*], m. fishing rights. ~ होना, to be hunted; to fall prey (to, का). बहुत लोग हैज़े के ~ हुए, many fell victim to cholera. – शिकारपेशा, m. inv. one whose occupation is hunting.

शिकारा *śikārā* [cf. H. [2]*śikārī*], m. **1.** a houseboat (Kashmir). **2.** a light boat (Kashmir).

[1]**शिकारी** *śikārī* [P. *śikārī*], adj. & m. **1.** adj. having to do with hunting (as a dog, a shelter). **2.** taking prey. ~ चिड़िया, f. a bird of prey. **3.** m. a hunter; fowler; fisherman.

[2]**शिकारी** *śikārī* [P. *śikārī*], f. a light flat-bottomed boat (Kashmir).

शिक्षक *śikṣak* [S.], m. a teacher; an instructor.

शिक्षण *śikṣaṇ* [S.], m. teaching, instruction.

शिक्षणीय *śikṣăṇīyă* [S.], adj. teachable, educable; tractable.

शिक्षा *śikṣā* [S.], f. **1.** teaching, instruction. **2.** learning, study. **3.** education. **4.** doctrine (as of a sect). **5.** precept; advice. **6.** an instructive lesson (for the future). — ~ करना, to teach (a student, की). ~ देना, to teach (a subject, की; to a pupil, को). – शिक्षात्मक [°*ṣā+ā*°], adj. instructive, educational. शिक्षा-दीक्षा, f. initiation into learning: education. शिक्षाप्रद, adj. instructive; didactic. शिक्षाप्राप्त, adj. educated. शिक्षालय [°*ṣā+ā*°], m. place of teaching or study: educational institution; school. शिक्षा-शक्ति, f. ability to learn. शिक्षा-संबंधी, adj. educational.

शिक्षित *śikṣit* [S.], adj. **1.** instructed. **2.** educated. — ~ बनाना, to instruct; to educate.

शिक्षु *śikṣu* [S.], m. an apprentice.

शिखंड *śikhaṇḍ* [S.], m. **1.** top-knot; lock of unshaved hair at the side of the head. **2.** crest. **3.** Brbh. a peacock's tail.

शिखंडिका *śikhaṇḍikā* [S.], f. = शिखंड.

[1]**शिखंडी** *śikhaṇḍī* [S.], adj. & m. **1.** adj. wearing a lock of unshaved hair. **2.** crested. **3.** m. name of a *ṛṣi* or sage (one of the seven stars of the Great Bear). **4.** name of a son of Drupada; an effeminate man.

[2]**शिखंडी** *śikhaṇḍī* [S.], f. a peacock's tail (as worn by Kṛṣṇa).

शिखर *śikhar* [S.], m. **1.** peak; summit. **2.** tapering tower (as of a temple); pinnacle. **3.** dome. **4.** Brbh. a bright red (? or red and white) gem. — शिखर-सम्मेलन, m. *pol.* summit meeting.

शिखरी *śikhărī* [S.], adj. & m. **1.** adj. peaked, pointed. **2.** m. a peak, mountain.

शिखा *śikhā* [S.], f. **1.** point, tip; summit. **2.** top-knot, lock of unshaved hair. **3.** crest (as of a bird). **4.** tongue (of flame).

शिखी *śikhī* [S.], adj. & m. **1.** adj. having a top-knot. **2.** crested (a bird). **3.** Brbh. peacock.

शिगाफ़ *śigāf* [P. *śigāf*], m. U. **1.** split, crack. **2.** cutting, lancing (as of a boil).

शिग़ाल *śiġāl* [P. *śagāl*], m. a jackal. — शिग़ालख़ोर [P. *-khor*], m. pl. pej. *hist.* jackal-eaters: name used of a robber band active to the south of Avadh in the early nineteenth century.

शिगूफ़ा *śigūfā*, m. see शगूफ़ा.

शिंजिन *śiñjin* [S.], m. tinkling, sounding.

शिति *śiti* [S.], adj. **1.** white (= सित). **2.** dark blue, or black.

शिथिल *śithil* [S.], adj. **1.** loose, slack; loosened. **2.** weak (muscles, the grasp); relaxed; tired. **3.** lax (of manners or attitude); indolent. **4.** laxly performed or observed (as work, or a regulation). — ~ करना, to relax (as the body; or a regulation). ~ होना, to be or to become relaxed. – शिथिलीकरण, m. making loose, &c. °ईकृत, adj.

शिथिलता *śithilătā* [S.], f. looseness, weakness, laxity &c. (see सिथिल).

शिथिला- *śithilā-* [ad. *śithilāyate*: w. H. *śithil*], v.i. Brbh. to grow tired.

शिथिलित *śithilit* [S.], adj. made loose or slack: weakened, exhausted.

शिद्दत *śiddat* [A. *śidda*: P. *śiddat*], f. severity, rigour (as of climate).

शिनाख़्त *śinākht*, f. pronun. var. see शनाख़्त.

शिफ़ा *śifā*, f. pronun. var. see शफ़ा.

शिया *śiyā* [A. *śī'a*], m. a Shia Muslim (follower of 'Alī).

शियाई *śiyāī* [A. *śī'ī*], adj. & m. **1.** adj. Shiite. **2.** m. an adherent of the Shia Muslim sect.

शिर *śir* [S.], m. the head; upper or foremost part (= सिर).

शिरकत *śirkat* [A. *śirka*], f. partnership (= शराकत).

शिरस्- *śiras-* [S]. the head: — शिरस्त्राण, m. head-protection: a soldier's helmet.

शिरा *śirā* [S.], f. **1.** a blood-vessel: vein, artery. **2.** fig. nerve, fibre (of the body), tendon.

शिराल *śirāl* [S.], adj. veiny; sinewy.

शिरीष *śirīṣ* [S.], m. the tree *Acacia* (or *Mimosa*) *sirisa*, and its flower.

शिरो- *śiro-* [S]. the head: — शिरोधार्य, adj. to be placed on the head: to be carried out implicitly (as a command). शिरोबिंदु, m. uppermost point: apex; zenith. शिरोभूषण, m. = next. शिरोमणि, m. a jewel worn on the head, or in a head-ornament; one who is supreme, a paragon. शिरोरुह, m. growing on the head: hair.

शिला *śilā* [S.], f. **1.** a large stone (esp. flat). **2.** a rock. — शिलान्यास, m. the laying of a foundation-stone. शिला-मुद्रण, m. stone-printing: lithography. °-मुद्रित, adj. शिला-रस, m. rock-exudation: gum-resin of the tree *Altingia excelsa*. **शिला-रोपन**, m. = **शिलान्यास**. **शिला-लेख**, m. a rock inscription. °**ई**, adj. epigraphical. – **शिलीभूत**, adj. turned to stone; rocky.

शिली *śilī* [S.], f. Brbh. an arrow. — **शिलीमुख**, m. Brbh. a bee.

शिलीभूत *śilībhūt* [S.], adj. see s.v. **शिला**.

शिल्प *śilp* [S.], m. **1.** a craft; an art. **2.** art, skill. — **शिल्पकार**, m. a craftsman, skilled worker. °**ई**, m. id. **शिल्प-गृह**, m. (artist's) studio. **शिल्प-विज्ञान**, m. technology. **शिल्पविद्या**, f. skill in a craft or art; technology; architecture. °**-विद्यालय**, m. technical college. **शिल्प-विधान**, m. technological or artistic means; a partic. skill or technology. °**-विधि**, f. id. **शिल्प-शास्त्र**, m. = **शिल्प-विद्या**.

शिल्पिक *śilpik* [S.], adj. & m. = **शिल्पी**.

शिल्पिता *śilpitā* [S.], f. artistry.

शिल्पी *śilpī* [S.], adj. & m. **1.** adj. having to do with a craft or skill: technical. **2.** m. a craftsman, skilled worker.

शिव *śiv* [S.], adj. & m. **1.** adj. auspicious. **2.** m. name of the third god, with Brahmā and Viṣṇu, of the Hindu triad (Śiva's most distinctive function is to preside over the dissolution of the world at the end of each aeon in order that it may be created anew). **3.** the phallic emblem of Śiva. — **शिव-तांडव**, m. *mythol.* the dance of Śiva (at the time of the dissolution of the world). **शिव-धाम**, m. abode of Śiva: a name of Banaras, and of Kailash. **शिव-नंदन**, m. Brbh. dear son of Śiva: a title of Gaṇeś. **शिवनामी**, f. a garment marked all over with the name of Śiva. **शिव-पुर**, m. Śiva's city: Banaras. **शिव-प्रिय**, m. dear to Śiva: the nuts of the *rudrākṣa* tree (used in rosaries and bracelets). **शिवमौलिस्रुता**, f. flowing from Śiva's head, or crown: a title of the Ganges. **शिव-रात्रि**, f. Siva's night: name of a festival in honour of Śiva (kept, with a fast during the day and night and sometimes with observations extending over a longer period, on the fourteenth of the dark half of the month Phālgun). **शिव-लिंग**, m. = ~, 3. **शिव-वृषभ**, m. Śiva's bull, Nandī. **शिव-सेना**, f. Śiva's army: name of a right-wing organisation active in Bombay and Mahārāṣtra. **शिवालय** [°*va*+*ā*°], m. Śiva's abode: a temple or shrine dedicated to Śiva. **शिवाँसा** [*aṃśa*-], m. reg. (W.) harvest perquisite given to a Śaiva ascetic.

शिवता *śivătā* [S.], f. Brbh. the quality of Śiva; auspiciousness, perfection.

शिवा *śivā* [S.], f. the wife of Siva: **1.** title of Durgā. **2.** title of Pārvatī.

शिवानी *śivānī* [conn. *śivānī*-], f. Śiva's wife: title of Durgā or Pārvatī.

शिवाला *śivālā* [ad. *śivālaya*-], m. **1.** a temple or shrine dedicated to Śiva. **2.** colloq. ? obs. a charcoal kiln.

शिविका *śivikā* [S.], f. a palanquin.

शिविर *śivir* [S.], m. a camp, encampment.

शिशिर *śiśir* [S.], m. **1.** coolness, cold. **2.** frost; dew. ***3.** the cold season. — **शिशिर-काल**, m. id., 3. °**ईन**, adj. **शिशिरांत** [°*ra*+*a*°], m. end of winter: spring.

शिशु *śiśu* [S.], m. **1.** an infant; a young child. **2.** the young of any animal. — **शिशु-शाला**, f. nursery; crèche.

शिशुक *śiśuk* [S.], m. **1.** a child. **2.** the young of any animal.

शिशुता *śiśutā* [S.], f. early childhood.

शिशुत्व *śiśutvă* [S.], m. = **शिशुता**.

शिशुपन *śiśupan* [cf. H. *śiśu*], m. early childhood.

शिश्न *śiśn* [S.], m. penis. — **शिस्नोदर** [°*na*+*u*°], m. Av. fig. lust and gluttony.

शिष्ट *śiṣṭ* [S.], adj. **1.** well-ordered or regulated. ***2.** educated, cultivated; urbane. ***3.** well-behaved: polite; refined; obedient, good. — **~ समाज**, m. cultivated people, polite society. – **शिष्ट-मंडल**, m. delegation; deputation. **शिष्टाचार** [°*ṭa*+*ā*°], m. & adj. good or proper conduct; courtesy, civility; urbanity; courteous, &c. °**ई**, m. **शिष्टाचार करना**, to behave courteously, &c. (to, **का**).

शिष्टता *śiṣṭătā* [S.], f. **1.** cultivation (of mind). **2.** good behaviour: politeness, &c. (see **शिष्ट**).

शिष्य *śiṣyă* [S.], m. **1.** a pupil. **2.** disciple (= **चेला**).

शिष्यता *śiṣyătā* [S.], f. pupil's, or disciple's, state or condition.

शिस्त *śist* [P. *śast*, *śist*], m. *Pl. HŚS.* **1.** a gun-sight; theodolite sight. **2.** a large fish-hook.

शीआ *śīā*, m. see **शिया**.

शीकर *śīkar* [S.], m. **1.** fine rain. **2.** mist. **3.** spray.

शीघ्र *śīghră* [S.], adj. **1.** quick, swift. **2.** adv. quickly. **3.** adv. soon. — **~ करना** [f. H. *jaldī karnā*], to make haste. – **शीघ्रगामी**, adj. going quickly: quick; prompt; fleet. **शीघ्र-लिपि**, f. shorthand. **शीघ्रातिशीघ्र** [°*ra*+*a*°], adv. extremely quickly, as quickly as possible.

शीघ्रता *śīghrătā* [S.], f. **1.** quickness, speed; promptness. **2.** rush, hurry. — **~ करना**, to deal quickly (with, **की**), to expedite; to make haste.

शीत *śīt* [S.], adj. & m. **1.** adj. cold. **2.** m. cold, coldness. **3.** the cold season. **4.** numbness; torpor. — शीत-ऋतु, m. = शीत-काल. शीत-काल, m. = ~, 3. °ईन, adj. शीतप्रधान, adj. prevailingly cold (climate). शीत-युद्ध, m. cold war. शीतागार [°*ta*+*ā*°], m. cold store, or storage. शीताग्र [°*ta*+*a*°], m. *meteorol.* a cold front. शीतोष्ण [°*ta*+*u*°], adj. cold and hot (as weather); temperate (climate).

शीतता *śītătā* [S.], f. coldness, cold.

शीतल *śītal* [S.], adj. **1.** cool; refreshing. **2.** cold. — शीतल-पाटी, f. a straw mat (to sit on).

शीतलता *śītalătā* [S.], f. **1.** coolness. **2.** coldness.

शीतलताई *śītalătāī* [S.], f. Brbh. = शीतलता.

शीतला *śītălā* [S.], f. **1.** smallpox. **2.** name of the goddess supposed to inflict smallpox. — शीतलाष्टमी [°*lā*+*a*°], f. an observance in honour of the goddess Śītalā, taking place on the eighth day of the dark half of the month Cait.

शीर- *śīr-* [P. *śīr*], m. milk: — सीर-शक्कर, m. milk and sugar: close friendship, intimacy.

शीरा *śīrā* [P. *śīra*], m. **1.** juice (of fruit). **2.** sap. **3.** syrup.

शीराज़ा *śīrāzā* [P. *śīrāza*], m. U. the stitching or binding of the back of a book. — ~ खुलना, or टूटना, a binding, &c. to loosen or to come undone. ~ बिखरना, fig. id.

शीरनी *śīrnī*, f. = शीरीनी.

शीरीन *śīrīn* [P. *śīrīn*], adj. U. sweet; pleasant.

शीरीनी *śīrīnī* [P. *śīrīnī*], f. *Pl. HŚS.* **1.** a sweet. **2.** an offering of sweets.

शीर्ण *śīrṇ* [S.], adj. **1.** withered, shrivelled. **2.** wasted (the body). **3.** broken, shattered; ruined. **4.** esp. -शीर्ण. tattered (clothes); old.

शीर्णता *śīrṇătā* [S.], f. withered or wasted state, &c. (see शीर्ण).

शीर्ष *śīrṣ* [S.], m. **1.** the head. **2.** top part; tip; vertex (of a triangle). — शीर्ष-बिंदु, f. uppermost point; apex; vertex; crown (of the head). शीर्षस्थ, adj. standing at the head: in a leading position.

शीर्षक *śīrṣak* [S.], m. **1.** head. ***2.** heading; headline (in a newspaper); title (as of a book). — ~ देना (को), to give a headline (to); to entitle. ~ रखना (का), id.

शील *śīl* [S.], m. **1.** character, nature. **2.** virtuous nature; virtuous, moral or decent conduct. **3.** morality. **4.** moral quality or principle. पंच ~, m. the five moral principles (enunciated at the Bandung Conference of unaligned nations). **5.** -शील. tending naturally to, disposed to (e.g. प्रगतिशील, adj. progressive; सहनशील, adj. tolerant). — शील-स्वभाव, m. character, moral character. शीलवती, adj. f. = next. शीलवान, adj. of good or virtuous nature, or conduct.

शीलता *śīlătā* [S.], f. **1.** character, disposition. **2.** virtuousness of character. **3.** familiarity, expertise, practice.

1**शीश-** *śīś-*. glass: — शीश-महल, m. a room or building having walls inlaid with pieces of glass, or hung with mirrors.

2**शीश-** *śīś-* [ad. *śīrṣa-*: w. H. *sīs*]. head: — शीश-फूल, m. a women's head ornament.

शीशम *śīśam* [P. *śīśam, sīsam*: OIA *śiṁśapā-*], m. the tree *Dalbergia sisu*, and its wood.

शीशा *śīśā* [P. *śīśa*], m. **1.** glass; glass-ware; a glass bottle. **2.** a mirror. — ~ दिखाना, to show a mirror: to advertise one's services (a street barber). शीशे में उतारना, to bring down and confine (an evil spirit) in a bottle: to bring into one's power; to charm (a recalcitrant personality); to soothe (an over-excited person). – शीशा-दिखाई, f. tip to a barber. शीशा-बाशा, adj. fragile; delicate, tender.

शीशी *śīśī* [cf. H. *śīśā*], f. a small glass bottle; flask, phial. — ~ सुँघाना, to administer (chloroform, &c.) from a flask.

शीशों *śīśoṁ*, m. pronun. var. = शीशम.

शीशो *śīśo*, m. pronun. var. = शीशम.

शुंठ *śuṇṭh* [ad. *śuṇṭhi-*: w. H. *soṁṭh*], f. dry ginger.

शुंठी *śuṇṭhī* [S.], f. dry ginger (= सोंठ).

शुंड *śuṇḍ* [S.], m. an elephant's trunk (= सूँड़).

शुंभ *śumbhă* [S.], m. *mythol.* name of a demon who with his brother Niśumbha was killed by Durgā.

शुक *śuk* [S.], m. **1.** a parrot. **2.** name of several plants. **3.** *mythol.* name of the son of Vyās (narrator of the *Bhāgavata Purāṇa* to Parīkṣit). — शुक-देव, m. = ~, 3.

शुक्ति *śukti* [S.], f. a shellfish; an oyster.

1**शुक्र** *śukr* [S.], adj. & m. **1.** adj. resplendent. **2.** m. the planet Venus. **3.** Friday. **4.** semen. — शुक्रवार, m. Friday. शुक्राचार्य [°*ra*+*ā*°], m. *mythol.* name of a sage (regent of the planet Venus, and teacher of the *daityas*).

2**शुक्र** *śukr* [A. *śukr*], m. **1.** gratitude. **2.** thanksgiving. — ~ अदा करना, = next. ~ करना, to give thanks (for, का); to praise Allah (for). – शुक्रगुज़ार, adj. grateful. °ई, f. gratitude.

शुक्रिया *śukriyā* [A. *śukrīya*], m. & interj. **1.** m. = ²शुक्र. **2.** interj. thank you.

शुक्ल *śuklă* [S.], adj. & m. **1.** adj. bright; white. **2.** pure. **3.** m. white colour. **4.** the light half of the month (from new to full moon). **5.** name of a brahmaṇ community. **6.** silver. — शुक्ल-पक्ष, m. = ~, 4. °ई, adj.

शुक्लता *śuklătā* [S.], f. brightness, whiteness, &c. (see शुक्ल).

शुगन *śugan*, m. pronun. var. = शगुन.

शुग़ल *śuġl*, m. see शग़ल.

शुगून *śugūn* [P. *śugūn*], m. = शगुन.

शुचि *śuci* [S.], adj. & f. **1.** adj. bright, clean. **2.** pure; virtuous, pious; faultless. **3.** title of heavenly bodies: the sun; the moon; Venus. **4.** title of Śiva, and of Agni. **5.** name applied to the hot season. ***6.** f. purity; virtue. **7.** purification (by bathing).

शुचित *śucit* [S.], adj. purified, pure.

शुचिता *śucitā* [S.], f. purity, &c. (see शुचि).

शुतुर *śutur* [P. *śutur*], m. camel: — शुतुरदिल, adj. camel-hearted: timid. शुतुर-मुर्ग़, m. camel-fowl: ostrich.

शुदकार *śudkār* [P. *śudkār*], m. *hist.* reg. (E.) ground tilled and sown: **1.** crop estimate or valuation by inspection. **2.** field rent assessed on the area actually sown.

-शुदा *-śudā* [P. *śuda*], adj. formant, inv. become: e.g. शादीशुदा, adj. married.

शुद्ध *śuddh* [S.], adj. **1.** pure; uncontaminated (a substance, or a tradition, or speech, &c). **2.** sinless; virtuous. **3.** not ill-intentioned, honest, sincere (conduct). **4.** free from errors, correct (as a draft, a proof). **5.** nett (profit, return). **6.** simple, mere. **7.** very, unequalled. — ~ साहित्य, m. belles lettres. – शुद्धाद्वैत [°*dha*+*a*°], m. *philos.* pure monism. शुद्धीकरण, m. purification.

शुद्धता *śuddhătā* [S.], f. purity, &c. (see शुद्ध).

शुद्धि *śuddhi* [S.], f. **1.** purity. **2.** purification; expiation. **3.** removal (of faults). **4.** correctness, accuracy (of work). **5.** requital. – शुद्धिकरण, m. poet. one who purifies. °-कारक, adj. & m. purifying, correcting; corrector. °-कारी, adj. & m. id. शुद्धि-पत्र, m. list of errata. शुद्धिबोध, adj. being conscious of purity (the heart). शुद्धिवादी, m. a purist.

शुद्धीकरण *śuddhīkaraṇ* [S.], m. see s.v. शुद्ध.

सुबहा *sub'hā* [A. *śubha*], m. doubt, suspicion.

शुभ *śubh* [S.], adj. & m. **1.** adj. auspicious, lucky; good (as news, &c). **2.** Brbh. Av. handsome, beautiful. **3.** m. -शुभ. auspicious; good fortune, welfare. — शुभंकर, adj. = next. शुभकर, adj. causing well-being; auspicious; lucky. शुभकामना, f. good wish. शुभ-चिंतक, m. well-wisher. शुभद, adj. giving good fortune, auspicious (= ~, 1). °-दायक, adj. id. शुभ-फल, m. auspicious result or outcome. °प्रद, adj. of auspicious effect. शुभागमन [°*bha*+*ā*°], m. & interj. auspicious arrival; welcome! शुभारंभ [°*bha*+*ā*°], m. auspicious beginning. शुभाशुभ [°*bha*+*a*°], adj. & m. auspicious and inauspicious, good and bad; weal and woe. शुभेच्छा [°*bha*+*i*°], f. good wish. शुभेच्छु, adj. & m. well-wishing; well-wisher. शुभेच्छुक, m. id. शुभैषी [°*bha*+*e*°], adj. & m. well-wishing; well-wisher.

शुभ्र *śubhră* [S.], adj. **1.** radiant, bright. **2.** white.

शुभ्रता *śubhrătā* [S.], f. **1.** radiance. **2.** gleaming whiteness.

शुमार *śumār* [P. *śumār*], f. m. **1.** counting. **2.** number, amount. **3.** regard, account, estimation. — ~ करना, to count, to reckon, to calculate; to include (in, में). ~ बाँधना, to estimate. उसकी विशेषज्ञों में ~ होने लगी है, he has begun to be regarded as a specialist.

शुमारी *śumārī* [P.], f. esp. -शुमारी. **1.** counting. मर्दुम-शुमारी, f. counting the people: a census. **2.** colloq. exercises done to numbers.

शुमाल *śumāl* [A. *śamāl, śimāl*], m. U. the north.

शुरवाल *śurvāl*, m. pronun. var. = शलवार.

शुरुआत *śuruāt* [A. *śurū'āt*, pl.], f. beginning, beginning stage.

शुरुआती *śuruātī* [cf. H. *śuruāt*], adj. having to do with the beginning: initial.

शुरू *śurū* [A. *śurū'*], m. beginning. — ~ करना, v.t. to begin, to start. उसने काम ~ किया, he started work. ~ में, adv. at the beginning (of, के); at first. ~ ~ में, adv. at the very beginning (of, के). ~ से, adv. from the beginning. ~ से आख़िर तक, adv. from beginning to end. ~ होना, v.i. to begin, to start.

शुल्क *śulk* [S.], m. **1.** fee (as for entrance). **2.** a subscription. **3.** a due, payment; tariff.

शुश *śuś* [onom.; cf. **śuṣ(y)ati*²], m. noise made in setting on a dog. — ~ करना, to urge or to set on a dog.

शुशकारना *śuśkārnā*, v.t. = ~ करना.

शुष्क *śuṣk* [S.], adj. **1.** dried up; withered, shrivelled. **2.** dry; arid (as terrain). **3.** dry (of manner); unemotional. **4.** dry, dull (a topic).

शुष्कता *śuṣkătā* [S.], f. dryness, &c. (see **शुष्क**).

शूक *śūk* [S.], m. *Pl. HŚS.* **1.** awn, beard (of grain). **2.** bristle; sharp hair (of insects).

शूकर *śūkar* [S.], m. a hog; a wild boar.

शूकरी *śūkărī* [S.], f. a sow (= **सूअरनी**).

शूद्र *śūdră* [S.], m. a member of the fourth and lowest division of early Indo-Aryan society.

शूद्रता *śūdrătā* [S.], f. nature or condition of a śūdra (see **शूद्र**).

शूद्राणी *śūdrāṇī* [S.], f. = **शूद्रा**.

शून्य *śūnyă* [S.], adj. & m. **1.** adj. empty, void. **2.** -**शून्य**. devoid of. e.g. **विचार-शून्य**, adj. unthinking, mindless. **3.** m. nothingness; void; a vacuum. **4.** *math.* zero. **5.** outer space. — **सून्यवाद**, m. the (Buddhist) doctrine of the non-existence of any spirit, supreme or human. °**ई**, m. an atheist; a nihilist; a Buddhist.

शून्यता *śūnyătā* [S.], f. **1.** emptiness. **2.** non-existence; unreality, illusory nature (of existence).

शून्यत्व *śūnyatvă* [S.], m. emptiness, &c. (= **शून्यता**).

शूर *śūr* [S.], m. a hero; a warrior, champion. — **शूर-वीर**, adj. & m. valiant; a hero, &c. °**ई**, ***ता**, f. valour. **आरंभ-शूर**, m. a great one for beginnings: one who never finishes any task.

शूरण *śūraṇ* [S.], m. = **सूरन**.

शूरता *śūrătā* [S.], f. bravery, valour. — **शूरताधारी**, adj. & m. *Pl.* heroic; a hero.

शूर्प *śūrp* [S.], m. a winnowing-basket. — **शूर्पनखा** [for -*ṇākhā*], f. *mythol.* Brbh. having nails like winnowing-baskets: name of a demoness, the sister of Rāvaṇ.

शूर्पी *śūrpī* [S.], f. *Pl. HŚS.* **1.** a small winnowing-basket. **2.** a children's toy.

शूल *śūl* [S.], m. **1.** a stake, spike. **2.** any sharp or pointed weapon; the trident of Śiva. **3.** an iron rod. **4.** Brbh. pangs, distress. — **~ उठना**, or **पड़ना**, a sharp pain to be felt (by, **को**). – **शूलधारी**, m. trident-holder: a title of Śiva. **शूलपाणि**, m. Brbh. having a trident in the hand: a title of Śiva.

शूली *śūlī* [S.], adj. & f. see **सूली**.

शृंखल *śr̥ṅkhal* [S.], m. **1.** a chain; chain belt. **2.** a fetter.

शृंखला *śr̥ṅkhălā* [S.], f. **1.** a chain; chain belt. **2.** a mountain range. **3.** a connected series or sequence (as of events, or items). — **शृंखलाबद्ध**, adj. chained, or linked: uninterrupted, consecutive.

शृंखलित *śr̥ṅkhălit* [S.], adj. linked (as in a chain).

शृंग *śr̥ṅg* [S.], m. **1.** horn. **2.** summit, peak. **3.** *mus.* horn.

शृंगार *śr̥ṅgār* [S.], m. **1.** sexual passion, love. **2.** adornment (esp. of a woman); dress, finery; make-up, toilet; array. **3.** *rhet.* the amatory or erotic sentiment. **4.** *Pl. HŚS.* red lead (as used in ornamental markings on an elephant's head and trunk). **5.** *Pl. HŚS.* cloves. — **~ करना**, to dress or to adorn oneself (a woman); to make love. – **शृंगार-रस**, m. = ~, 3.

शृंगारिक *śr̥ṅgārik* [S.], adj. **1.** erotic (cf. **शृंगार**, 3). **2.** decked, arrayed.

शृंगारिकता *śr̥ṅgārikătā* [S.], f. eroticism (cf. **शृंगार**, 3).

शृंगारी *śr̥ṅgārī* [S.], adj. **1.** having to do with passionate love; erotic. **2.** feeling love; amorous. **3.** expressing the mood of *śr̥ṅgār* (a poet).

शृगाल *śr̥gāl* [S.], m. **1.** jackal. **2.** fig. coward; villain.

शृंगी *śr̥ṅgī* [S.], adj. & m. **1.** adj. horned; crested; peaked. **2.** m. *mythol.* name of a *r̥ṣi*, son of Gautama. **3.** *mus.* a musical instrument. **4.** a title of Śiva. **5.** *Pl. HŚS.* a kind of sheat-fish (= **सिंगी**).

शेख़ *śekh* [A. *śaikh*], m. **1.** an elder (of a Muslim community). **2.** head of a Muslim religious community. **3.** a reputed saint. **4.** a title taken by descendants of the prophet Muḥammad. **5.** the first of four classes into which South Asian Muslims have been traditionally divided; a member of that class. **6.** *Pl.* title given to converts to Islam. — **शेख़-चिल्ली**, a legendary fool or clown, jester; a crazy person. **शेख़-सद्दो**, m. a malevolent deity worshipped by Muslim women.

शेखर *śekhar* [S.], m. **1.** crest, garland; crown. **2.** summit (of a mountain: = **शिखर**).

शेख़ी *śekhī* [P. *śaikhī*], f. **1.** boasting; arrogance; bravado. **2.** boast. — **~ जताना**, or **बघारना**, or **मारना**, or **हाँकना**, to boast, to brag (about, **पर**). **~ झड़ना**, or **निकलना** (**की**), (one's) pride to be humbled. **~ में आना**, to grow boastful, to brag. – **शेख़ीबाज़** [P. -*bāz*], m. a boaster, braggart. °**ई**, f. boastfulness.

शेफाली *śephālī* [S. *śephālikā*-], f. the shrub *Vitex negundo* (= **निर्गुंडी**); the plant *Nyctanthes tristis*.

[1]**शेर** *śer* [P. *śer*], m. **1.** a tiger; a lion. **2.** fig. a brave man. — **~ का बच्चा**, m. tiger cub, lion

cub; a courageous person. ~ रहना, to be the tiger: to be superior or stronger, to get the better (of). ~ होना, id.; to be brave. – शेरगढ़ी, f. a pillar-capital in the shape of a four-headed lion (of the emperor Aśoka; now the symbol of the Indian state). शेरदिल, adj. lion-hearted. शेर-बबर, m. a lion. शेर-मर्द, adj. & m. lion-man: brave; a brave man. °ई, f. bravery.

²**शेर** *śer* [A. *śi'r*], m. **1.** poetry. **2.** a verse, a couplet. — ~ कहना, or सुनाना, to recite poetry. ~ बनाना, to compose poetry.

शेरनी *śernī* [cf. H. *śer*], f. a tigress; a lioness.

शेराना *śerānā* [P. *śerāna*], adj. inv. like a tiger; like a lion; fierce.

शेरी *śerī* [P. *śe'rī*], adj. having to do with poetry, poetic, poetical.

शेवाल *śevāl* [S.], m. = शैवाल.

शेष *śeṣ* [S.], adj. & m. **1.** adj. remaining, left over. **2.** last, final. **3.** m. remainder, the rest; balance (of an account); arrears (of payments). **4.** conclusion, end; outcome. **5.** *mythol.* name of a thousand-headed snake, regarded as the symbol of eternity, on which Viṣṇu sleeps throughout periods of dissolution of the world. — ~ कर-, Brbh. to finish, to complete. ~ कुशल है, everything else is fine (used in closing a letter). ~ रहना, to be left over, to be unfinished. – शेष-नाग, m. = ~, 5. शेषशयन, m. having Śeṣa as couch: a title of Viṣṇu. शेषशायी, m. reclining on Śeṣa: id.

¹**शै** *śai* [A. *śai*], f. U. a thing; a matter.

²**शै** *śai*, f. pronun. var. = शह, 3.

शैक्षणिक *śaikṣăṇik* [S.], adj. having to do with teaching or learning: instructional; educative; academic.

शैक्षिक *śaikṣik* [S.], adj. educational.

शैक्ष्य *śaikṣyă* [S.], m. *Pl. HŚS.* learning, skill.

शैतान *śaitān* [A. *śaiṭān*], m. **1.** the devil, Satan; a devil. **2.** fig. an evil person; a mischievous imp. — ~ उठाना, or मचाना, to raise the devil, to make a fiendish noise; to quarrel. ~ का बच्चा, in m. devil's imp or child: a rascal, villain. ~ की आँत, f. devil's gut: anything long and winding (as a lane); a fiendishly involved or tedious story. ~ की ख़ाला, f. the devil's aunt: a mischief-making woman. ~ की डोर, f. devil's thread: a spider's web. ~ छूटना, the devil to get or to be let loose: bad or wrongful impulses to be allowed free play. ~ लगना (को), = next. ~ सिर पर चढ़ना, the devil to get into (one's) head: to be possessed; to be hell-bent (on doing sthg). – शैतान-चौकड़ी, f. four fiends together: a group of naughty children.

शैतानी *śaitānī* [A. *śaiṭānī*], adj. & f. **1.** adj. devilish, fiendish. **2.** f. wicked or fiendish behaviour; naughtiness.

शैत्य *śaityă* [S.], m. coldness, &c. (see शीत).

शैथिल्य *śaithilyă* [S.], m. = शिथिलता.

शैदा *śaidā* [P. *śaidā*], adj. inv. possessed (as by love), distraught.

शैदाई *śaidāī* [P. *śaidā*+H. -*ī*], m. one who is infatuated.

शैल *śail* [S.], adj. & m. **1.** adj. stony, rocky. **2.** mountainous. **3.** m. a mountain. **4.** a rock, crag. — शैल-कुमारी, f. daughter of the mountain: a title of Pārvatī. शैलजा, f. mountain-born: a title of Durgā or Pārvatī. शैलेंद्र [°*la*+*i*°], m. lord of mountains: the Himālayas.

शैली *śailī* [S.], f. **1.** partic. means, method. **2.** style, manner; specif. literary style. **3.** *lit.* genre. — शैलीकार, m. a stylist. शैलीगत, adj. stylistic.

शैलेय *śailey* [S.], adj. having to do with mountains (cf. शैल).

शैव *śaiv* [S.], adj. & m. **1.** adj. having to do with the god Śiva. **2.** having to do with Śaivas (devotees of Śiva). **3.** m. a devotee of Śiva.

शैवाल *śaivāl* [S.], m. a kind of water-weed, *Vallisneria octandra* (= सिवार).

शैशव *śaiśav* [S.], m. infancy, young childhood.

शोआ *śoā* [**śatatama-*[2]], m. dill (*Anethum graveolens*), or anise.

शोक *śok* [S.], m. **1.** sorrow. **2.** regret; condolence. **3.** mourning. — ~ करना, to grieve. ~ मनाना, to express grief, to mourn. ~ होना (को), grief, &c. to be felt (by). – शोक-ग्रस्त, adj. consumed by sorrow. शोकजनक, adj. producing grief, being a matter for grief. शोक-प्रस्ताव, m. motion or expression of condolence. शोक-सारण, m. dispelling of grief; fig. means of dispelling grief. शोकाकुल [°*ka*+*ā*°], adj. distressed by grief: greatly distressed. शोकातुर [°*ka*+*ā*°], adj. id.

शोकी *śokī* [S.], adj. grieving; mourning.

शोख़ *śok͟h* [P. *śok͟h*], adj. **1.** cheerful, sprightly; pert, brash. **2.** capricious; mischievous. **3.** flirtatious. **4.** bright (as colour); garish.

शोख़ी *śok͟hī* [P. *śok͟hī*], f. **1.** playfulness, fun, mischief. **2.** brightness (of colour); garishness. **3.** impertinence, cheek. — ~ से, adv. playfully, &c.

शोच *śoc* [S.], m. **1.** sorrow. **2.** distress, care.

शोचन *śocan* [S.], adj. & m. **1.** adj. *Pl. HŚS.* sorrowing, grieving. **2.** m. sorrow, grief; distress.

शोचनीय *śocănīyă* [S.], adj. **1.** lamentable, dire (state, plight). **2.** causing concern.

शोचित *śocit* [S.], adj. saddened, grieved.

शोणित *śoṇit* [S.], m. red: blood.

शोथ *śoth* [S.], m. **1.** a tumour. **2.** a swelling; inflammation.

शोध *śodh* [S.], m. **1.** purification; refining. **2.** correction (of errors, faults). **3.** investigation; research; ascertainment (of facts, or auspicious dates). — **शोध-कर्ता**, m. inv. an investigator, &c. **शोध-कार्य**, m. investigative or research work. **शोधक्षमता**, f. solvency. **शोध-प्रबंध**, m. a research thesis, dissertation.

शोधक *śodhak* [S.], adj. & m. **1.** adj. purificatory, purifying; refining. **2.** cleansing; purgative. **3.** investigating. **4.** m. a purifier, &c. **5.** an investigator; researcher.

शोधन *śodhan* [S.], m. purifying, &c. (see **शोध**). — **शोधनाक्षम** [°*na*+*a*°], adj. insolvent.

शोधना *śodhnā*, v.t. = **सोधना**.

शोधनी *śodhănī* [S.], f. a broom.

शोधनीय *śodhănīyă* [S.], adj. to be corrected, &c. (see **शोध**).

शोभन *śobhan* [S.], adj. & m. **1.** adj. radiant, splendid. **2.** beautiful, handsome. **3.** auspicious. **4.** m. = **शोभा**.

शोभना *śobhnā* [ad. *śobhāyate*: w. H. *śobhā*], v.i. **1.** to be becoming (to); to grace. **2.** to befit, to beseem.

शोभनीय *śobhănīyă* [S.], adj. to be adorned: beautiful, splendid.

शोभा *śobhā* [S.], f. **1.** radiance, splendour. **2.** beauty; grace. **3.** transf. attractive dress or attire. — ~ **देना** (**को**), to befit, to beseem (one). **शोभान्वित** [°*bhā*+*a*°], adj. beautiful, ornamented; distinguished.

शोभायमान *śobhāyămān* [S.], adj. **1.** radiant, splendid. **2.** beautiful, handsome. **3.** adorning (as attire, ornaments).

शोभित *śobhit* [S.], adj. **1.** made splendid. **2.** beautified; adorned. **3.** beautiful.

शोर *śor* [P. *śor*], m. **1.** noise; outcry; din. **2.** uproar, tumult. **3.** transf. fame, renown. — ~ **करना**, or **मचाना**, to make a noise, din, &c. – **शोर-गुल**, m., **शोर-शराबा**, m. = ~, 1., 2. **शोर-शार**, m. id. **ज़ोर-शोर**, m. zest, enthusiasm; excitement.

शोरबा *śorbā* [P. *śorbā*], m. soup; broth. — **गिनी बोटी, नपा** ~, m. counted meat (pieces) and measured soup: careful economy. — **शोरबेदार** [P. *-dār*], adj. (served: a dish) with gravy, &c.

शोरा *śorā* [P. *śora*], m. saltpetre; potassium nitrate. — **शोरे का तेज़ाब**, m. nitric acid.

[1]**शोला** *śolā* [A. *śu'la*], m. **1.** a flame. **2.** blaze, flash (as of the eyes, in anger). — **शोले भड़कना**, flames to burst forth.

[2]**शोला** *śolā*, m. = **सोला**.

शोशा *śośā* [P. *śa'śa'a*], m. mixing, diluting: **1.** tail (of an Arabic letter). **2.** a false report; hoax. — ~ **छोड़ना**, to spread a false story.

शोष *śoṣ* [S.], m. **1.** drying up. **2.** dryness. **3.** emaciation, wasting. **4.** *Pl. HŚS.* tuberculosis.

शोषक *śoṣak* [S.], adj. & m. **1.** adj. drying. **2.** absorbing, absorbent. ***3.** exploiting; rapacious. **4.** m. an exploiter, &c.

शोषण *śoṣaṇ* [S.], m. **1.** drying up. **2.** drainage. **3.** sucking, suction; absorption. ***4.** exploitation. — **शोषण-दोहन**, m. sucking and milking: gross exploitation.

शोषित *śoṣit* [S.], m. **1.** made dry. **2.** absorbed. ***3.** exploited.

शोहदा *śohdā* [A. *śuhadā*, pl. of *śahīd*], m. pej. **1.** a scoundrel, rogue; a depraved person. **2.** a hooligan.

शोहदापन *śohdāpan* [cf. H. *śohdā*], m. **1.** villainy; depravity. **2.** hooliganism.

शोहरत *śohrat* [A. *śuhra*: P. *śõhrat*], f. fame, reputation; notoriety. — ~ **पैदा करना**, to acquire a reputation, &c. (for, **की**). ~ **देना** (**को**), to give publicity (to), to make notorious.

शौक़ *śauq* [A. *śauq*], m. **1.** desire, yearning. ***2.** predilection, taste (for, **का**); fancy (for). **3.** eagerness, pleasure (in doing sthg). **4.** a hobby. — ~ **चर्राना**, a keen desire or itch to arise. ~ **फ़रमाइए!** help yourself! take all you want! ~ **मिटाना**, to satisfy a desire, &c. (to, **का**). ~ **से**, adv. gladly, with pleasure; according to (one's) wish. ~ **होना** (**को**), to be fond (of some activity, **का**).

शौकत *śaukat* [A. *śauka*: P. *śaukat*], f. a piercing: impressive or splendid state. — **शान-शौकत**, f. id.

शौक़िया *śauqiyā* [P. *śauqiya*], adj. inv. **1.** loving, amorous. ***2.** keen, enthusiastic; amateur (a sportsman). — **वह डाक-टिकट** ~ **जमा करता है**, he collects stamps as a hobby.

शौक़ीन *śauqīn* [P. *śauqīn*], adj. & m. **1.** adj. desirous; amorous. ***2.** fond (of, **का**: as of a hobby, an activity), fancying, keen. **3.** specif. enjoying western things and ways. **4.** m. an enthusiast (for some activity). **5.** a connoisseur (of, **का**).

शौक़ीनी *śauqīnī* [H. *śauqīn*], f. **1.** enthusiasm (for a pursuit). **2.** modish tastes, or behaviour.

शौच *śauc* [S.], m. **1.** purification; purificatory act. **2.** defecation. **3.** purity. — **शौच-गृह**, m. = next. **शौच-स्थान**, m. a lavatory, public lavatory. **शौचालय** [°*a* + *ā*°], m. public lavatory.

शौनिक *śaunik* [S.], m. *Pl. HŚS.* **1.** a seller of meat or poultry; a butcher. **2.** hunting.

शौर्य *śauryă* [S.], m. heroism, valour.

शौहर *śauhar* [P. *śauhar*], m. a husband.

शौहरी *śauhărī* [P.], adj. of or belonging to a husband.

श्मशान *śmaśān* [S.], m. **1.** a cremation-ground. **2.** burial-ground. **3.** crematorium.

श्मशानक *śmaśānak* [S.], adj. having to do with a cremation-ground or burial-ground.

श्मशानी *śmaśānī* [S.], adj. var. /śəmśanī/. haunting cremation-grounds or burial-grounds (a spirit); fearsome.

श्मश्रु *śmaśru* [S.], m. f. beard and moustache.

श्याम *śyām* [S.], adj. & m. **1.** adj. dark, black; dark blue; dark brown; dark green. **2.** m. a name or title of Kr̥ṣṇa. — ~ **टीका**, m. Brbh. dark mark: specif. as made on children's foreheads to protect them from the evil eye. – **श्याम-चिड़ैया**, f. = **श्यामा**, 4. **श्याम-रंग**, adj. & m. dark, &c.; black colour, &c. **श्याम-वर्ण**, adj. & m. id. **श्याम-सुंदर**, m. dark and beautiful: a title of Kr̥ṣṇa. **श्यामांग** [°*ma* + *a*°], adj. of dark body, dark skin.

श्यामता *śyāmătā* [S.], f. **1.** blackness, &c. (see **श्याम**). **2.** dejection.

श्यामल *śyāmal* [S.], adj. dark, blackish, &c. (see **श्याम**); verdant (as trees, ripening crops).

श्यामला *śyāmălā* [S.], f. a name of Pārvatī, and of Durgā.

श्यामली *śyāmălī* [cf. H. *śyāmal*], adj. f. = **श्यामल**.

श्यामा *śyāmā* [S.], f. **1.** Brbh. wife or mistress of Śyām: a title of Rādhā. **2.** (in tantric worship) a partic. form of Durgā. **3.** dark woman: an attractive woman. **4.** a small song-bird, *Turdus macrourus* or *Copsychus malabaricus*, the head and upper body of which are black in the male.

श्यामायमान *śyāmāyămān* [S.], adj. dark (as with crops), verdant (a region).

[1]**श्याल** *śyāl* [S.], m. Brbh. wife's brother (= **साला**).

[2]**श्याल** *śyāl* [*sr̥gāla-*: *ś-* ad.], m. Brbh. a jackal.

श्यालक *śyālak* [S.], m. *Pl. HŚS.* wife's brother (= **साला**).

श्येन *śyen* [S.], m. reddish-white, white: a hawk or falcon; the shahin falcon.

श्रद्धा *śraddhā* [S.], f. **1.** faith, reverential belief (as in a deity); implicit confidence. **2.** reverence, veneration. — **श्रद्धांजलि** [°*dha* + *ā*°], f. respectful or reverential offering; homage. **श्रद्धादेही**, adj. f. embodying faith, &c. **श्रद्धावान**, adj. = **श्रद्धालु**. **श्रद्धास्पद** [°*dhā* + *ā*°], m. & adj. place of honour: revered person; much respected, revered.

श्रद्धालु *śraddhālu* [S.], adj. **1.** having faith, believing; devout. **2.** reverential; respectful.

श्रद्धालुता *śraddhālutā* [S.], f. quality or mood of devotion, &c. (see **श्रद्धालु**).

श्रद्धेय *śraddheyă* [S.], adj. **1.** worthy of faith, &c. (see **श्रद्धा**). **2.** worthy of reverence, &c.

श्रप *śrap*, corr. 1. = **सर्प**. **2.** *Pl.* = **शाप**.

श्रम *śram* [S.], m. **1.** exertion, effort; hard work; labour. **2.** fatigue. **3.** *econ.* labour. — ~ **करना**, to labour, to toil. – **श्रम-कण**, m. a drop of sweat. **श्रमजीवी**, adj. & m. living by work; a worker. **श्रम-दान**, m. gift of labour: voluntary work. °**ई**, m. voluntary worker. **श्रम-विवाद**, m. a labour dispute. **श्रम-संघ**, m. trade union. **श्रम-साध्य**, adj. achievable with hard work; laborious to complete (a task).

श्रमण *śramaṇ* [S.], m. an ascetic; specif. a Buddhist monk.

श्रमिक *śramik* [S.], m. & adj. **1.** m. a labourer, worker (= **श्रमजीवी**). **2.** adj. *econ.* having to do with labour.

श्रमित *śramit* [S.], adj. Brbh. tired.

श्रमी *śramī* [S.], adj. **1.** industrious. **2.** labouring, toiling.

श्रवण *śravaṇ* [S.], m. **1.** the act of hearing; specif. one of several (usu. nine) traditionally recognised avenues or procedures for cultivating devotion. **2.** sense of hearing. **3.** the ear. **4.** *astron.* the twenty-third lunar asterism. — **श्रवणामृत** [°*ṇa* + *a*°], adj. ear-nectar: a sweet voice or sound. **श्रवणेंद्रिय** [°*ṇa* + *i*°], m. organ of hearing: the ear.

श्रवणा *śravăṇā* [S.], f. *astron.* = **श्रवण**, 4.

श्रविष्ठा *śraviṣṭhā* [S.], f. *astron.* the twenty-fourth lunar asterism (also called *dhaniṣṭhā*).

श्रव्य *śravyă* [S.], adj. **1.** to be heard; to be read; oral (as poetry). **2.** worth hearing. **3.** audible.

श्रव्यता *śravyătā* [S.], f. audibility.

श्रांत *śrānt* [S.], adj. fatigued; exhausted.

श्रांति *śrānti* [S.], f. fatigue; exhaustion.

श्राद्ध *śrāddh* [S.], m. *hind.* a ceremony in honour and for the benefit of deceased relatives, observed at fixed periods and on occasions of rejoicing as well as of mourning (libations and offerings of *piṇḍas* (q.v.) are made to the spirits of the deceased and of food and gifts to brāhmaṇ officiants and to relatives). — ~ करना, to carry out a *śrāddh* ceremony (for, का).

श्राप *śrāp*, m. corr. Brbh. = शाप.

श्रावक *śrāvak* [S.], m. hearing, hearer: **1.** pupil, disciple. **2.** a class of Buddhist saints or ascetics; a Buddhist; a Jain.

श्रावण *śrāvaṇ* [S.], m. name of the fifth lunar month of the Hindu calendar (July-August).

श्रावणी *śrāvăṇī* [S.], f. the day of full moon in the month Śrāvaṇ (when the *rakṣābandhan* festival is celebrated).

श्री *śrī* [S.], f. **1.** prosperity, success; happiness. **2.** wealth. **3.** beauty; lustre, splendour. **4.** a title of the goddess Lakṣmī. **5.** a title of the goddess Sarasvatī. **6.** the *trivarga* or three objects of life (*kām, arth, dharm*). **7.** (from श्रीयुत) honorific prefix to a name (of a male deity, a man, a sacred place). ~ कृष्ण, m. Lord Krishna. श्री प्रसाद, m. Mr Prasad. श्री वृंदावन, m. Holy Vṛndāvan. — ~ करना, *hind.* to begin (an enterprise) in the name of (Śrī) Gaṇeś, or of Lakṣmī. – श्री-खंड, m. sandalwood; a sweet (curd and cheese with sugar, almonds, saffron and cardamom). श्री-गणेश, m. the revered Gaṇeś: fig. a beginning (of some activity). श्री-गणेश करना (का), to invoke Gaṇeś (in starting an activity): to begin. श्रीपति, m. lord of Śrī: a title of Viṣṇu. श्रीफल, m. the wood-apple tree and its fruit; a coconut. श्रीमंत, adj. & m. = श्रीमान; Brbh. a head ornament. श्रीमत्, adj. = श्रीमान. श्रीमती, f. an illustrious or beautiful woman: wife; hon. Mrs. श्रीमद, m. Brbh. Av. pride arising from prosperity or wealth. श्रीमन्, voc. = श्रीमान. श्रीमान, adj. & m. prosperous; wealthy; illustrious; voc. hon. sir. श्रीमुख, m. fair face; Brbh. face or mouth of Viṣṇu: the Vedas; the word *śrī* used in correspondence as an auspicious token. श्रीयुत, or -युक्त, adj. & m. = श्रीमान. श्री-वत्स, Brbh. a partic. mark or curl of hair on the breast of Viṣṇu or Kṛṣṇa. श्री-संपन्न, adj. prosperous; happy. श्रीहत, adj. = next. श्रीहीन, adj. not prospering; unhappy; wretched. °ता, f.

श्रुत *śrut* [S.], adj. **1.** heard. **2.** reported, rumoured. **3.** called. — श्रुतपूर्व, adv. heard or known before.

श्रुति *śruti* [S.], f. **1.** hearing; sense of hearing, the ear. ***2.** sthg. heard: report, rumour. **3.** revelation; specif. the Veda. **4.** *mus.* tone, note (of a scale). — श्रुति-गोचर, adj. perceptible by ear: audible. श्रुतिधर, m. a listener. श्रुति-पथ, m. range of hearing: hearing, the ear(s). श्रुति-परंपरा, f. aural transmission (as of poetry). श्रुति-मधुर, adj. soft or pleasing to the ear. श्रुति-सार, m. Brbh. essence of the Vedas. श्रुति-सेतु, m. Av. that bridge which is the Veda: the Vedas as an institution, accepted revelation.

श्रेणी *śreṇī* [S.], f. **1.** line, row; series; range (of mountains). **2.** a class, group (of people). **3.** troop, band. **4.** type, kind. **5.** class, grade, rank (as in examinations). — प्रथम ~ में आना, to come in the first class, to get a first class (mark). – श्रेणीबद्ध, adj. arranged in a line or row; grouped together. श्रेणी-हित, m. class or group interest, or advantage.

श्रेय *śrey* [S.], m. **1.** good fortune, auspiciousness. ***2.** merit, virtue; credit (for, का). उसमें यह ~ है कि..., he has the merit that....

श्रेयस्- *śreyas-* [S]. = श्रेय: — श्रेयस्कर, adj. auspicious; meritorious.

श्रेष्ठ *śreṣṭh* [S.], adj. **1.** best; most excellent, choice. **2.** most eminent, high. **3.** respected, honoured. **4.** senior (in age). — श्रेष्ठतम, adj. best of all, most excellent, &c. (= ~).

श्रेष्ठता *śreṣṭhătā* [S.], f. excellence, superiority, eminence, &c. (see श्रेष्ठ).

श्रेष्ठी *śreṣṭhī* [S.], m. *hist.* person of rank or authority: a prominent merchant, businessman, banker.

श्रोणी *śroṇī* [S.], f. hips or loins.

श्रोत *śrot* [ad. *śrotra-*], m. the ear.

श्रोतव्य *śrotavyă* [S.], adj. **1.** audible. **2.** E.H. deserving to be heard.

श्रोता *śrotā* [S.], m. inv. a listener. — श्रोतागण, m. pl. hearers, audience.

श्रोत्र *śrotră* [S.], m. **1.** the ear. **2.** E.H. revelation, the Veda (= श्रुति, 3).

श्लथ *ślath* [S.], adj. loose, slack; languid.

श्लाघन *ślāghan* [S.], m. praising; flattering.

श्लाघनीय *ślāghănīyă* [S.], adj. praiseworthy.

श्लाघा *ślāghā* [S.], f. praise; flattery.

श्लाघ्य *ślāghyă* [S.], adj. praiseworthy.

श्लील *ślīl* [S.], adj. poet. fortunate; happy.

श्लेष *śleṣ* [S.], m. **1.** connection, union. **2.** an embrace. **3.** double meaning (of words or expressions); pun. — **श्लेषोपमा**, [°*a*+*u*°], f. a comparison containing double meanings.

श्लेष्मा *śleṣmā* [S.], f. phlegm, mucus.

श्लोक *ślok* [S.], m. **1.** a verse; specif. a Sanskrit couplet consisting of lines of sixteen syllables. 2. = **सलोक**.

श्वपच *śvapac* [S.], m. Brbh. dog-cooker: an outcaste.

श्वशुर *śvaśur*, m. father-in-law.

श्वश्रू *śvaśrū* [S.], f. mother-in-law.

श्वान *śvān* [S.], m. a dog. — **श्वान-निद्रा**, f. a light sleep (= **कुत्ते की नींद**).

श्वानी *śvānī* [S.], f. a bitch.

श्वापद *śvāpad* [S.], m. a beast of prey.

श्वास *śvās* [S.], m. **1.** breathing. **2.** the breath. **3.** a sigh. **4.** transf. asthma. — **~ खींचना**, or **लेना**, to breathe in. **~ छोड़ना**, to breathe out. – **श्वास-नली**, f. the trachea.

श्वेत *śvet* [S.], adj. white. — **श्वेत-द्वीप**, m. *mythol.* white island: name of an imaginary region, the abode of the blessed; obs. iron. Europe. **श्वेतांग** [°*ta*+*a*°], adj. white-bodied: Caucasian, white. **श्वेतांबर** [°*ta*+*a*°], m. clothed in white: name of one of the two main Jain sects.

श्वेतता *śvetătā* [S.], f. whiteness.

श्वेती *śvetī* [cf. H. *śvet*; and H. *safedī*], f. *Pl.* white colour, whiteness.

ष

ष *ṣa*, the thirty-first consonant of the Devanāgārī syllabary. — **षकार**, m. the sound /ṣ/; the letter **ष**.

षट्- *ṣaṭ-* [S]. six, hex- : — **षट्-ऋतु**, m. the six seasons of the year (viz. spring, the hot season, the rains, autumn, winter, the cool season). **षट्कर्म**, m. the six acts or duties enjoined on a brāhmaṇ; the six means of subsistence allowed to a brāhmaṇ. **षट्कोण**, m. a hexagon. **षट्कोना**, m. id. **षट्पद**, adj. & m. six-footed; Brbh. a bee. **षट्मुख** (for **षण्**-), m. Brbh. = **षदानन**, see s.v. **षद्**-. **षट्राग**, m. six *rāgas*; discord; turmoil, confusion. **षट्वदन**, m. Av. = **षडानन**. **षट्शास्त्र**, m. = **षड्-दर्शन**.

षड्- *ṣaḍ-* [S]. six, hex-: — **षड्दर्शन**, m. the six systems of Indian philosophy. °**ई**, m. Brbh. one versed in the six systems. **षड्भुज**, adj. & m. hexagonal; a hexagon. **षड्यंत्र**, m. a plot, conspiracy. **षड्यंत्र रचना**, to lay a plot. **षड्यंत्रकारी**, m. a conspirator. **षड्रस**, m. the six flavours or tastes. **षडानन**, m. *hind.* six-faced: a title of the god Kārtikeya.

षन- *ṣan-* [ad. *ṣaṇ-*]. six: — **षनमुख**, m. Av. = **षडानन**.

षष्ट *ṣaṣṭ* [S.], adj. sixtieth.

षष्टि *ṣaṣṭi* [S.], adj. sixty. — **षष्टि-पूर्ति**, f. sixtieth anniversary.

षष्ठ *ṣaṣṭh* [S.], adj. sixth.

षष्ठी *ṣaṣṭhī* [S.], f. **1.** the sixth day of a lunar fortnight. **2.** *hind.* a ceremony performed on the sixth day after a child's birth. **3.** a title of the goddess Durgā. **4.** *gram.* genitive case.

स

स *sa*, the thirty-second consonant of the Devanāgarī syllabary. — **सकार**, m. the sound /s/; the letter **स**.

शंक- *śaṅk-* [ad. *śaṅkate*; ? w. E.H. *śaṅkā*], v.i. Brbh. to be afraid.

संकट *saṅ-kaṭ* [S.], m. **1.** a dire difficulty, strait; dire misfortune. **2.** danger; an emergency, crisis. **3.** hard place: a pass (in mountains). — **~ आना (पर)**, misfortune, &c. to befall (one). **~ चौथ**, m. name of a festival in honour of Gaṇeś, held on the fourth day of the dark half of the month Māgh. – **संकट-काल**, m. a time of dire difficulty; emergency. °**-ईन**, adj. having to do with an emergency. **संकटकालीन द्वार**, m. emergency door. **संकटापन्न** [°*ṭa*+*ā*°], adj. suffering distress or misfortune; E.H. dangerous (a position or situation).

सँकड़ा *saṁkṛā* [*saṁkaṭa-*], adj. **1.** narrow (as an alleyway). **2.** tight-fitting (a garment).

सँकड़ाना *saṁkṛānā* [cf. H. *saṁkṛā*], v.t. to make narrow or constricted.

संकर *saṅ-kar* [S.], m. & adj. **1.** m. mixing; specif. crossing (breeds). **2.** a mixed caste or race. **3.** a half-breed; one born of parents of different caste; a hybrid. **4.** adj. cross-breed; hybrid.

संकर्षण *saṅ-karṣaṇ* [S.], m. **1.** drawing together; drawing. **2.** ploughing. **3.** *mythol.* a title of Baldev, or Balrām (the brother of Kṛṣṇa).

[1]**संकल** *saṅkal* [*śṛṅkhalā-*], f. chain (as of a door).

[2]**संकल** *saṅ-kal* [S.], m. **1.** accumulation, quantity. **2.** *math.* addition.

संकलन *saṅ-kalan* [S.], m. **1.** collecting together; compilation. **2.** arranging; selection. **3.** *arith.* addition. — **~ करना (का)**, to compile, &c.

संकलप- *saṅ-kalp-* [ad. *saṁkalpate*, *saṁkalpa-*], v.t. 19c. to vow (= **संकल्प करना**); to make a grant, or to give alms in fulfilment of a vow; to bequeath.

संकलित *saṅ-kalit* [S.], adj. **1.** collected together; compiled. **2.** arranged; selected (as works of an author). **3.** *math.* added.

सँकली *saṁklī* [cf. *śṛṅkhalā-*], f. **1.** a small chain. **2.** an ankle-chain (women's ornament).

संकल्प *saṅ-kalp* [S.], m. **1.** definite intention, will; resolve. **2.** vow. **3.** a (formal) resolution. — **~ करना**, to resolve, &c.; to vow. – **संकल्प-विकल्प**, m. hesitation, uncertainty.

संकल्प- *saṅ-kalp-*, Brbh. see **संकलप-**.

संकल्पना *saṅ-kalpănā* [S.], f. concept, notion.

संकल्पित *saṅ-kalpit* [S.], adj. **1.** conceived, imagined (a notion). **2.** intended; desired; resolved on.

संकाय *saṅ-kāy* [S.], m. faculty (of a university, &c).

[1]**संकार** *saṅ-kār* [cf. H. *saṅkārnā*], f. reg. a sign; nod, wink; call (to).

[2]**संकार** *saṅ-kār* [S.], m. *Pl. HŚS.* sweepings, rubbish.

संकारना *saṅkārnā*, v.t. reg. **1.** to make a sign (to); to nod; to call out (to). **2.** to inveigle.

संकास *saṅ-kās* [ad. *saṁkāśa-*], adj. E.H. looking like, resembling.

संकीर्ण *saṅ-kīrṇ* [S.], adj. **1.** mixed together; crowded. ***2.** contracted, narrow; low (as the forehead). ***3.** restricted, narrow (as a view); parochial.

संकीर्णता *saṅ-kīrṇătā* [S.], f. narrowness, &c. (see **संकीर्ण**).

संकीर्तन *saṅ-kīrtan* [S] m. celebrating, glorifying (esp. a deity, with devotional songs).

संकुचित *saṅ-kucit* [S.], adj. **1.** contracted, narrow. **2.** shrivelled, shrunk. **3.** closed (a bud). **4.** embarrassed; diffident. **5.** restricted, limited (as a perspective); ungenerous (attitude).

संकुल *saṅ-kul* [S.], adj. **1.** adj. crowded together, dense (a throng); confused, disordered. **2.** filled, full (with or of).

संकुलता *saṅ-kulătā* [S.], f. congestion.

संकुलित *saṅ-kulit* [S.], adj. = **संकुल**.

संकुश *saṅkuś*, m. the ray (fish), *Trygon uarnak*.

संकेत *saṅ-ket* [S.], m. **1.** a sign; a gesture. **2.** indication; hint; clue; innuendo. **3.** a symbol. **4.** a signal. **5.** appointed meeting-place. — **~ देना (को)**, to give a sign, &c. – **संकेतपूर्ण**, adj. meaningful (remark, glance). **संकेतवाचक**, adj. & m. *gram.* demonstrative; a demonstrative pronoun or adjective. °-वाची, adj. id. संकेतात्मक [°*ta*+*ā*°], adj. symbolic; conventional. संकेतार्थ [°*ta*+*a*°], m. *gram.* conditional mood. °अक, adj.

संकेतन *saṅ-ketan* [S.], m. **1.** indicating. **2.** notation.

संकेतित *saṅ-ketit* [S.], adj. indicated, appointed, fixed (a place, time).

संकोच *saṅ-koc* [S.], m. contracting, contraction: **1.** embarrassment, bashfulness; diffidence; shyness. **2.** fear. — संकोचशील, adj. embarrassed, &c.

संकोचन *saṅ-kocan* [S.], m. contracting, contraction.

संकोचित *saṅ-kocit* [S.], adj. contracted: embarrassed, &c. (see संकोच).

संकोची *saṅ-kocī* [S.], adj. filled with embarrassment, or shame, &c. (see संकोच).

संक्रम *saṅ-kram* [S.], m. passage (= संक्रमण).

संक्रमण *saṅ-kramaṇ* [S.], m. **1.** moving, passage (as of the sun from one sign of the zodiac to another); transition. **2.** infection. — संक्रमणकालीन, adj. transitional (period, or arrangement).

संक्रांत *saṅ-krānt* [S.], adj. **1.** passed, transferred. **2.** entered (into a new sign of the zodiac).

संक्रांति *saṅ-krānti* [S.], f. **1.** proceeding, passage (from one point, or state, to another); transition. **2.** entry (of a sun or a planet) into a new sign of the zodiac. **3.** specif. = मकर-संक्रांति. — संक्रांतिकालीन, adj. transitional.

संक्रामक *saṅ-krāmak* [S.], m. infectious.

संक्रिया *saṅ-kriyā* [S.], f. a process; operation, activity.

संक्षय *saṅ-kṣay* [S.], m. complete ruin, destruction; destruction of the world.

संक्षिप्त *saṅ-kṣipt* [S.], adj. abridged, abbreviated; concise (as a dictionary), condensed. — ~ रूप से, or में, adv. concisely, succinctly. – संक्षिप्तीकरण, m. abridging; summarising.

संक्षिप्ति *saṅ-kṣipti* [S.], f. abridgment.

संक्षेप *saṅ-kṣep* [S.], m. **1.** abridgment; summary, abstract. **2.** concision. — ~ करना (का or को), to abridge, to condense, &c. ~ में, adv. in short; concisely.

संक्षेपक *saṅ-kṣepak* [S.], adj. & m. **1.** adj. abridging, &c. (see संक्षेप). **2.** m. an abridger, &c.

संक्षेपण *saṅ-kṣepaṇ* [S.], m. abridging; abridgment, &c. (see संक्षेप).

संक्षोभ *saṅ-kṣobh* [S.], m. **1.** agitation. **2.** pride, arrogance.

संखा *saṅkhā* [*śaṅku-*[1] × *śākhā-*], m. *HŚS.* **1.** the wooden handle of a flour-grinding machine (attached to the upper stone). **2.** reg. (W.) = ²साँखा, 2.

संखिया *saṅkhiyā* [conn. *śṛṅgika-*], m. (f., *Pl.*) a poison (= सींगिया); (?) arsenic.

संख्या *saṅ-khyā* [S.], f. **1.** reckoning, counting. **2.** a number. **3.** a figure; amount. **4.** *gram.* number. **5.** number (of an issue). — ~ तो कोई चीज़ है, numbers do count for something. – संख्यांकित [°*ā*+*a*°], adj. numbered. संख्यात्मक [°*khyā*+*ā*°], adj. numerical. संख्यावाचक, adj. & m. *gram.* numerical; a numeral.

संख्येय *saṅ-khyeyă* [S.], adj. reckonable, calculable.

¹संग *saṅg* [*saṅga-*; ? × *saṃgha-*], m. & adv. **1.** m. coming together, joining, meeting. **2.** association, connection; company, society (of a person or group); attachment, intimacy. **3.** a group; a sectarian body. 4. = संगम, 2. **5.** adv. together (with, के), along (with). — ~ करना, to associate (with, का). ~ चलना (के), to accompany. ~ छोड़ना, to give up friendship or connection (for or with, का). ~ जाना (के), to accompany. ~ लगना, to attach oneself (to, के), to follow. ~ लेना, to take (one, को; with or along with, अपने). – संगरोध, m. blocking of association: quarantine. संग-साथ, m. company, companionship.

²संग *saṅg* [P. *sang*], m. **1.** a stone; stone (material). **2.** a precious stone. — संग-तराश [P. *-tarāś*], m. a stone-cutter; stone-mason; jeweller. संगदिल, adj. stony-hearted. संगयशब [P. *-yaśb* 'jasper': w. P. *-yaśm*], m. jade; jadeite.

संगठन *saṅ-gaṭhan* [cf. H. *gaṭhnā*], m. **1.** organised state or condition. **2.** an organisation.

संगठित *saṅ-gaṭhit* [cf. H. *gaṭhnā*], adj. organised; integrated.

संगत *saṅ-gat* [S.], adj. & f. **1.** adj. come together. **2.** assembled, collected; ready. **3.** esp. -संगत. consonant (with), appropriate (to). न्याय-संगत, adj. just, fitting; condign. **4.** f. = संगति, 2.-5., 7.

संगतरा *saṅgtarā*, m. = संतरा.

संगति *saṅ-gati* [S.], f. **1.** meeting, joining; a chance, coincidence. **2.** consonance; compatibility. **3.** company, society (of a person or group); friendship. **4.** a group, society, band. **5.** visiting, frequenting (a place). **6.** a monastery. **7.** instrumental accompaniment. **8.** admixture (as of colours). **9.** sexual intercourse. — ~ करना, to keep company (with, की), to associate (with); to provide a musical accompaniment.

संगतिया *saṅ-gatiyā* [cf. H. *saṅgat*], m. **1.** an associate, friend. **2.** an accompanist.

संगम *saṅ-gam* [S.], m. **1.** meeting, joining. **2.** confluence; specif. that of the rivers Ganges and Jumna at Allahabad. **3.** junction (as of roads). **4.** association, contact (with); company, society (of). **5.** sexual intercourse.

संगमन *saṅ-gaman* [S.], m. coming together.

संगर *saṅ-gar* [S.], m. war, battle; misfortune.

सँगवाना *saṁgvānā* [cf. *saṅga-*], v.t. **1.** to collect. **2.** to put in order, to arrange. **3.** to attain.

संगाती *saṅgātī* [H. *saṅghātī*], m. = [1]संगी.

[1]**संगी** *saṅgī* [*saṅgin-*], m. & adj. one who is attached, or devoted (to): **1.** m. an associate, friend. **2.** an accomplice. **3.** a desirous, or a lascivious person. **4.** adj. devoted (to), fond (of). **5.** [? × *gacchati*] accompanying; allied (to), connected (with). — संगी-साथी, m. pl. friends, companions.

[2]**संगी** *saṅgī*, f. *Pl. HŚS.* a kind of striped silk cloth.

संगीत *saṅ-gīt* [S.], m. **1.** music. **2.** singing with music. **3.** a dramatic performance with song, music and dancing. — संगीतकार, m. a musician. संगीतज्ञ, m. one knowledgeable or skilled in music. संगीत-नाटिका, f. an opera. संगीत-शाला, f. concert hall. संगीत-सम्मेलन, m. concert. संगीतात्मक [°*ta*+*ā*°], adj. musical (as tone, rhythm). °ता, f. musical quality.

संगीन *saṅgīn* [P. *sangīn*], adj. & f. **1.** adj. stony; of stone. **2.** thick, close-woven (cloth, braid). **3.** grave, serious (offence). **4.** severe (punishment). **5.** f. bayonet. — ~ चढ़ाना, or लगाना, to fix bayonets, or a bayonet.

संगीनी *saṅgīnī* [P. *sangīnī*], f. hardness, severity.

संगोपन *saṅ-gopan* [S.], m. hiding or concealing (sthg.) completely.

संगोष्ठि *saṅ-goṣṭhi* [S.], f. a meeting together: seminar, symposium.

संग्रह *saṅ-grah* [S.], m. **1.** taking: collecting. **2.** a collection; compilation; anthology. **3.** store, provision; stockpile. **4.** taking on, accepting. — ~ करना, to collect, &c. संग्रह-कर्ता, m. inv. collector, &c. संग्रहालय [°*ha*+*ā*°], m. museum.

संग्रहण *saṅ-grahaṇ* [S.], m. **1.** taking; accepting; making use (of). **2.** collecting, &c. (see संग्रह). **3.** *Pl. HŚS.* inlaying (stones, mosaic).

संग्रहणी *saṅ-grahăṇī* [S.], f. **1.** irregularity of the bowels, diarrhoea and constipation. **2.** stomach cramp (as in cholera).

संग्रहणीय *saṅ-grahăṇīyă* [S.], adj. to be collected, worth collecting.

संग्रही *saṅ-grahī* [S.], m. = संग्रह-कर्ता.

संग्रहीत *saṅ-grahīt* [S.], adj. collected, &c. (see संग्रह).

संग्रह्य *saṅ-grahyă* [S.], adj. = संग्रहणीय.

संग्राम *saṅ-grām* [S.], m. battle, fight; struggle. — स्वतंत्रता-संग्राम, m. struggle for independence.

संग्राहक *saṅ-grāhak* [S.], m. = संग्रहकर्ता.

संघ *saṅ-gh* [S.], m. group: **1.** society, association, body; party; federation, union. **2.** sect, persuasion; community (of Buddhist or Jain monks). — संयुक्त-राष्ट्र ~, m. United Nations Organisation. – संघाराम [°*gha*+*ā*°], m. a Buddhist monastery or convent.

संघट *saṅ-ghaṭ* [ad. *saṅghaṭṭa-*; × *saṅghaṭa-*], m. **1.** meeting, joining together, union (= संघटन). **2.** multitude, mass.

संघटन *saṅ-ghaṭan* [S.], m. 1. = संघट, 1. **2.** structure, composition.

[1]**संघटित** *saṅ-ghaṭit* [S.], adj. collected.

[2]**संघटित** *saṅ-ghaṭit* [ad. *saṅghaṭṭita-*], adj. Brbh. struck, collided.

संघर्ष *saṅ-gharṣ* [S.], m. **1.** rubbing; friction; grinding. ***2.** clash, conflict; hostility; struggle. — संघर्षमय, adj. bitter (a struggle). संघर्षशील, adj. truculent, combative.

संघर्षी *saṅ-gharṣī* [S.], adj. & m. **1.** adj. clashing, quarrelling; truculent. **2.** rivalling. **3.** adj. *ling.* fricative. **4.** m. *ling.* a fricative sound.

संघात *saṅ-ghāt* [S.], m. **1.** a heavy blow. **2.** striking, impact; striking down. ***3.** collection, quantity, mass. ***4.** a group, body (= संघ).

संघाती *saṅ-ghātī* [cf. H. *saṅghāt*], m. **1.** associate, companion. **2.** accessory (to a crime). **3.** murderer, destroyer.

संघार *saṅghār* [*saṁhāra-*], m. = संहार.

संघीय *saṅghīyă* [S.], adj. federal.

संचन *saṁcan*, m. (?) collecting, amassing.

संचना *saṁcnā* [**saṁcayayati*; ? and ad. *sañcaya-*], v.t. to collect, to amass.

संचय *sañ-cay* [S.], m. **1.** collection; accumulation; hoard. **2.** *fin.* capital. **3.** *math.* a combination. — ~ करना (का), to collect, &c.

संचयन *sañ-cayan* [S.], m. collecting, &c. (see संचय).

संचयी *sañ-cayī* [S.], adj. & m. **1.** adj. collecting, amassing; cumulative. **2.** m. one who collects, or hoards.

सँचर- *saṁcar-* [*saṁcarati*], v.i. Brbh. **1.** to move; to blow (wind). **2.** to spread (as moonlight).

संचरण *sañ-caraṇ* [S.], m. **1.** motion, movement. **2.** transmission. — संचरणशील, adj. transmissible. °ता, f.

संचलन *sañ-calan* [S.], m. movement, running (of trains).

संचार *sañ-cār* [S.], m. passing through: **1.** circulation (as of the blood, or of traffic). **2.** setting in motion (as of ideas); impelling, inciting; an impulse (of emotion). **3.** communication, communications; transmission (as of ideas; or of a disease). **4.** *electr.* current. **5.** passage, progress; passage of a heavenly body into a new sign of the zodiac. — ~ मंत्रालय, m. *govt.* Ministry of Communication.

संचारण *sañ-cāraṇ* [S.], m. **1.** communicating, communication. **2.** *phys.* conductivity.

संचारिका *sañ-cārikā* [S.], f. a female go-between; a bawd.

संचारित *sañ-cārit* [S.], adj. **1.** set in motion. **2.** communicated, transmitted. (see संचार).

संचारी *sañ-cārī* [S.], adj. **1.** setting in motion; specif. *poet.* suggesting a mood or idea. **2.** communicable (a disease).

संचालन *sañ-cālan* [S.], m. managing, directing; disposing (as of funds).

संचित *sañ-cit* [S.], adj. collected together; amassed; hoarded. — ~ करना, to collect together, &c.

संचेत *sañ-cet* [S.], adj. mindful, conscious (of); alive (to).

संजात *sañ-jāt* [S.], adj. **1.** begotten; born. **2.** produced.

संजीदा *sañjīdā* [P. *sanjīda*], adj. weighed: grave, serious; solemn.

संजीवन *sañ-jīvan* [S.], m. **1.** making alive, giving life. **2.** re-animating. **3.** living together.

संजीवनी *sañ-jīvānī* [S.], f. a life-giving herb.

संजीवी *sañ-jīvī* [S.], adj. making alive; restoring to life.

सँजोना *saṁjonā* [*saṁyojayati*], v.t. **1.** to arrange, to make ready; to lay out (as things on a tray). **2.** to decorate.

संज्ञा *sañ-jñā* [S.], f. **1.** sense, consciousness. **2.** knowledge; mind, intellect. ***3.** name (of an object); title. ***4.** *gram.* a noun. — संज्ञावान, adj. having consciousssness, conscious; revived, recovered; having a name. संज्ञाहीन, adj. unconscious. °ता, f.

संज्ञात *sañ-jñāt* [S.], adj. well-known, understood.

संज्ञापन *sañ-jñāpan* [S.], m. informing, advising; advice.

संज्ञित *sañ-jñit* [S.], adj. *Pl. HŚS.* named, designated.

सँझना *saṁjhnā*, m. *Pl.* the horse-radish tree, *Moringa pterygosperma* (= सहजना).

[1]**सँझला** *saṁjhlā* [Pk. *sajjhila-*: ← *ślakṣṇa-* × *madhya-*], adj. & m. **1.** adj. third eldest (a brother) **2.** m. a third eldest brother.

[2]**सँझला** *saṁjhlā* [cf. *sandhyā-*], adj. having to do with twilight or evening.

सँझा *saṁjhā*, f. reg. = साँझ, संध्या.

सँटिया *saṁṭiyā*, f. Brbh. a thin stick, a cane.

संठ *saṇṭh* [conn. *śaṇṭha-*[1], Pk. *saṁṭha-*], adj. reg. = शठ.

संड-मुसंड *saṇḍ-musaṇḍ*, adj. = संडा-मुस्टंडा.

सँड़सी *saṁṛsī* [*saṁdaṁśikā-*], f. a pair of pincers or tongs.

संडा *saṇḍā* [*ṣaṇḍa-*[2] × *ṣaṇḍha-*], adj. & m. **1.** adj. big, burly, sturdy. **2.** m. a big or fat ox. — संडा-मुस्टंडा, adj. stout; burly.

संडास *saṇḍās*, m. latrine.

सँड़ासा *saṁṛāsā* [*saṁdaṁśa-*], m. a large pair of pincers or tongs.

सँड़ासी *saṁṛāsī* [*saṁdaṁśa-*], f. a pair of pincers or tongs.

सँड़ियाना *saṁṛiyānā* [cf. H. *saṇḍā*], v.i. to grow stout; to grow burly.

संत *sant* [S.], adj. & m. existent: **1.** adj. good, virtuous; pious. **2.** m. an ascetic (= साधु). ***3.** a member of one of the *sant* communities of northern India (who believe in an unqualified and non-incarnated ultimate being); a poet or singer of *sant* persuasion. **4.** a member of the Vārakarī devotional sect of Mahārāṣṭra.

संतत *san-tat* [S.], adj. continued, continuous; lasting, eternal.

संतति *san-tati* [S.], f. continued succession: **1.** offspring, descendants. **2.** a son or daughter. — संतति-निग्रह, m. birth control. संतति-निरोध, m. id.

संतना *santănā* [ad. *sāntvanā*-], f. reg. consolation.

संतनु *san-tanu* [S.], adj. Brbh. possessing a body.

संतप्त *san-tapt* [S.], adj. = संतापित, esp. senses 2., 3.

संतरण *san-taraṇ* [S.], m. crossing over.

संतरा *santrā* [P. *Cintra*], m. any of several varieties of *Citrus aurantium*, an orange having an easily removable peel. — ~ नीबू, m. the sweet lime.

संतरी *santrī* [Engl. *sentry*], m. a sentry.

संतान *san-tān* [S.], f.; m.f. **1.** f. offspring, children; descendants. **2.** m. f. a son or daughter. — संतानहीन, adj. childless.

संताप *san-tāp* [S.], m. **1.** burning heat. **2.** suffering, anguish; grief. **3.** remorse. — ~ देना (को), to inflict suffering, &c. (on).

संतापित *san-tāpit* [S.], adj. **1.** heated very hot. **2.** suffering, anguished. **3.** remorseful.

संतापी *san-tāpī* [S.], adj. feeling suffering, &c. (= संतापित, 2., 3).

संती *santī*, ppn. 19c. instead (of, की).

संतुलन *san-tulan* [S.], m. weighing against: balance, equilibrium.

संतुलित *san-tulit* [S.], adj. weighed: **1.** balanced. **2.** equable.

संतुष्ट *san-tuṣṭ* [S.], adj. **1.** satisfied (with, से); pleased. **2.** contented (with); not opposed, in agreement. **3.** resigned (to); consoled. — ~ करना (को), to satisfy; to get the agreement (of); to console.

संतुष्टता *san-tuṣṭătā* [S.], f. = संतोष.

संतुष्टि *san-tuṣṭi* [S.], f. = संतोष.

संतै *santai* [cf. *sant*-], adv. Brbh. by being, while being. — पोषै ~, adv. by, or while, fostering.

संतोष *san-toṣ* [S.], m. **1.** satisfaction; pleasure. **2.** contentment. **3.** patience, resignation. — ~ करना, to be content; to practise patience, to be resigned. ~ कराना (का), to satisfy, to gratify. ~ होना (को), to be satisfied, &c. – संतोषजनक, adj. satisfactory. संतोषप्रद, adj. id. संतोषमय, adj. satisfied, contented (disposition, life). संतोष-वृत्ति, f. contentedness (of disposition).

संतोषी *san-toṣī* [S.], adj. & m. **1.** feeling satisfaction, &c. (see संतुष्ट). **2.** m. a satisfied or contented person.

संथा *santhā*, f. reading, a lesson.

संद *sand* [ad. *sandhi*-: ? × H. *ched*, cf. H. *sem̐dh*], m. reg. a join: gap, crack.

संदर्भ *san-darbh* [S.], m. **1.** a context. **2.** contextual reference. — संदर्भ-ग्रंथ, m. reference book.

संदर्शन *san-darśan* [S.], m. gazing, beholding; sight, vision.

संदर्शिका *san-darśikā* [S.], f. a guide-book.

संदल *sandal* [A. *ṣandal*], m. sandalwood.

संदली *sandălī* [A. *ṣandalī*], adj. & m. **1.** adj. of the colour of sandalwood, light yellow. **2.** made of sandalwood. **3.** m. a light yellow colour.

संदा *sandā* [P. *sanda*], m. **1.** an anvil. **2.** a broad stone.

[1]**संदान** *sandān* [P. *sandān*], m. f. an anvil.

[2]**संदान** *san-dān* [S.], m. *Pl. HŚS.* a rope, cord (esp. for tying cattle).

संदिग्ध *san-digdh* [S.], adj. smeared over: **1.** doubtful, questionable (a matter); ambiguous (evidence, &c). **2.** unclear, obscure (a sense, a sentence). **3.** *gram.* expressing supposition, presumptive (a conjugational pattern). **4.** suspect, suspicious (as behaviour). **5.** despondent (the heart). — संदिग्धार्थ [°*dha* + *a*°], = ~, 3.

संदिग्धता *san-digdhătā* [S.], f. doubtfulness, &c. (see संदिग्ध).

संदीपन *san-dīpan* [S.], m. **1.** lighting, kindling. **2.** kindling (an emotion).

संदीप्त *san-dīpt* [S.], adj. well-lit, or illuminated.

संदूक़ *sandūq* [A. *ṣandūq*], m. **1.** box. **2.** chest, coffer.

संदूक़चा *sandūqcā* [P. *ṣandūqca*], m. small box; casket.

संदूक़ची *sandūqcī* [cf. H. *sanduqcā*], f. = संदूक़चा.

संदूरिया *sandūriyā*, adj. & m. pronun. var. = सिंदूरिया.

संदूषण *san-dūṣaṇ* [S.], m. the act of corrupting, or defiling.

संदूषित *san-dūṣit* [S.], adj. corrupted, defiled.

संदेश *san-deś* [S.], m. **1.** information, news. **2.** direction, behest. ***3.** message. **4.** name of a

Bengali sweet made of milk-cheese, nuts and sugar. — संदेश-वाहक, m. message-bearer, messenger.

संदेशी *san-deśī* [cf. H. *sandeś*], m. messenger, envoy.

सँदेसा *saṁdesā* [*saṁdeśa-*], m.

संदेह *san-deh* [S.], m. **1.** doubt; suspicion, mistrust. **2.** *Pl. HŚS.* doubtful or dangerous situation. — ~ होना (को), doubt, &c. to be felt (by). इसका उसे क्या ~ है, he has no doubt whatever of this. इसमें ~ नहीं है, there is no doubt of this. – संदेहजनक, adj. doubtful; arousing mistrust. संदेहात्मक [°*ha*+*ā*°], adj. = संदिग्ध 1., 2. संदेहार्थ [°*ha*+*a*°], adj. = संदिग्धार्थ.

संदेही *san-dehī* [S.], adj. & m. **1.** adj. doubting, doubtful; suspicious, mistrustful. **2.** m. a doubter, &c.

संदोह *san-doh* [S.], m. Av. **1.** store; exemplar (of virtue or vice). **2.** multitude.

संधव *sandhav* [conn. *saindhava-*], m. saltpetre, potassium nitrate.

संधा *san-dhā* [S.], f. **1.** union, agreement. **2.** a mixture, preparation. — ~ भाषा, f. name given to a figurative and obscure style of exposition of religious truths (as used by early *nirguṇī* sectarians) in which paradox is prominent.

संधान *san-dhān* [S.], m. **1.** the act of placing or joining together. **2.** fitting an arrow to a bow. **3.** aim. **4.** search, enquiry. **5.** association, alliance. **6.** preparing, treating, processing.

संधाना *sandhānā* [*saṁdhāna-*], m. pickle (= अचार).

संधानी *sandhānī* [*saṁdhāna-*], f. *Pl. HŚS.* **1.** pickle (= संधाना). **2.** a foundry. **3.** distilling, distillation.

संधि *san-dhi* [S.], f. **1.** union, junction; transition. **2.** reconciliation; a treaty. **3.** *gram.* combination or coalescence of the final sound of a word with the initial sound of a following word. **4.** a joint (of the body, &c). **5.** juncture: pause, rest (from action); interval. **6.** division, gap. **7.** breach (in a wall, as made by thieves). — संधि-विराम, cessation (of warfare) by agreement: armistice. संधि-शोथ, m. inflammation of the joints, arthritis.

संधित *san-dhit* [S.], adj. *Pl. HŚS.* **1.** joined together. **2.** fixed (as an arrow to a bow); strung (a bow).

संध्या *san-dhyā* [S.], f. juncture: **1.** twilight; evening; late afternoon. **2.** morning, midday and evening religious rites; evening prayer. **3.** intermission (between the end of one age, *yug*, and the beginning of the next). — ~ करना, to pray at sunrise, noon or sunset. – संध्या-काल, m. = ~, 1. °-ईन, adj. संध्या-समय, m. = संध्या-काल.

संन्यस्त *saṃ-ny-ast* [S.], adj. abandoned, renounced; laid down (life).

संन्यास *saṃ-ny-ās* [S.], m. /sən(n)yas/. **1.** laying down, abandonment; specif. renunciation of the world, becoming an ascetic. **2.** the fourth stage (*āśram*) of life, life as a wandering ascetic. **3.** *HŚS.* complete exhaustion; coma. — ~ ग्रहण करना, to renounce the world, &c. ~ लेना (से), to renounce; to renounce the world.

संन्यासिन *saṃ-ny-āsin* [cf. H. *saṃnyāsī*], f. a female renunciant or ascetic.

संन्यासी *saṃ-ny-āsī* [S.], m. /sən(n)yasī/. one who has renounced the world, an ascetic.

संपत्ति *sam-patti* [S.], f. **1.** wealth, riches; property, possessions; resources. **2.** success, prosperity. **3.** completion, accomplishment. — संपत्ति-दान, m. donation of property: specif. donation of land during the *bhūdān* movement of Vinobā Bhāve. संपत्तिवान, adj. wealthy, &c. संपत्तिशाली, adj. rich; prosperous. संपत्तिहीन, adj. poor, impoverished.

संपद *sam-pad* [S.], f. 1. = संपत्ति. **2.** abundance, excess. **3.** fate, luck.

संपदा *sam-padā* [S.], f. = संपद.

संपन्न *sam-pann* [S.], adj. **1.** prosperous, thriving; rich. **2.** accomplished, effected, completed. **3.** esp. -संपन्न. abundantly endowed (with), possessed (of: as of wealth, learning). — ~ करना, to bring to a successful conclusion; to endow abundantly (with).

संपन्नता *sam-pannătā* [S.], f. prosperity, affluence, &c. (see संपन्न).

संपर्क *sam-park* [S.], m. mixing together: **1.** contact; liaison. **2.** relationship, connection. — ~ में आना, to come into contact (with, के). ~ बनाए रखना, to keep in contact (with, से, के साथ). ~ जोड़ना, or स्थापित करना, to establish contact(s) (with). – संपर्क-भाषा, f. contact language: a language serving as a means of communication between those whose mother tongue it is and speakers of other languages to whom it is known, or between the latter among themselves.

संपात *sam-pāt* [S.], m. **1.** falling together, concurrence; coincidence. **2.** falling against or on; dire blow (as struck by a thunderbolt).

संपाति *sam-pāti* [S.], m. *mythol.* name of a bird (son of Garuṛ, brother of Jaṭāyu).

संपातिक *sam-pātik* [S.], adj. coincidental.

संपादक *sam-pādak* [S.], m. **1.** one who accomplishes, effects. ***2.** editor. — संपादक-मंडल, m. editorial board.

संपादकत्व *sam-pādăkatvă* [S.], m. editorship. — ~ में, adv. under the editorship (of, के).

संपादन *sam-pādan* [S.], m. **1.** accomplishing, effecting. ***2.** editing. — ~ करना (का), to edit.

संपादित *sam-pādit* [S.], adj. **1.** accomplished, effected. ***2.** edited.

सँपारना *sampārnā* [*sampātayati*; ? × *sampādayati*], v.t. reg. to bring (a task) to completion).

सँपारा *sampārā* [*sarpadhāraka-*], m. reg. *Pl.* = सँपेरा.

संपुट *sam-puṭ* [S.], m. **1.** a cavity. **2.** a box with a lid, casket. **3.** a small brass cup (such as offerings of flowers, &c. are put in).

संपुटी *sam-puṭī* [S.], f. dimin. = संपुट.

संपूर्ण *sam-pūrṇ* [S.], adj. & m. **1.** adj. complete; unlimited. **2.** entire, whole, all. **3.** full (the moon). **4.** completed (as a task, an activity). **5.** *mus.* any scale or melody in which all the notes of the partic. *rāg* or *rāgiṇī* are used. — ~ करना, to complete. ~ रूप से, adv. completely, entirely. – संपूर्णतया, adv. wholly, entirely.

संपूर्णता *sam-pūrṇătā* [S.], f. completeness, &c. (see संपूर्ण).

संपृक्त *sam-pṛkt* [S.], adj. mixed: connected, in contact (with, से).

सँपेरा *samperā* [**sarpaharaka-*], m. snake-catcher; snake-charmer.

सँपोला *sampolā* [**sarpapotala-*; Pa. *sappapotaka-*], m. a young snake.

सँपोलिया *sampoliyā* [cf. H. *sampolā*], m. a snake-catcher.

सँपोली *sampolī*, f. reg. basket in which a snake is kept.

संप्रति *sam-prati* [S.], adv. at the present time, now; for the present.

संप्रदान *sam-pra-dān* [S.], m. **1.** giving, bestowing. **2.** gift, donation. **3.** *gram.* dative case. **4.** recipient (of a gift).

संप्रदाय *sam-pra-dāy* [S.], m. **1.** an established doctrine, persuasion or system of teaching. ***2.** a religious sect; school (of thought). **3.** a religious community. — संप्रदायवाद, m. belief in or assertion of communal entities, values or purposes. °ई, m.

संप्रदायी *sam-pra-dāyī* [S.], m. member of a religious sect.

संप्राप्त *sam-prâpt* [S.], adj. **1.** attained; met with. **2.** obtained. **3.** eventuated, happened.

संप्राप्ति *sam-prâpti* [S.], f. attainment, &c. (see संप्राप्त).

संप्रीति *sam-prīti* [S.], f. attachment, affection; friendliness.

संप्रेषण *sam-prêṣaṇ* [S.], m. **1.** transmission, communication. **2.** effect (as of a work of art).

संप्रेषणीयता *sam-prêṣăṇīyătā* [S.], f. communicability, effectiveness.

संबंध *sam-bandh* [S.], m. **1.** connection; relationship (with, से). **2.** relationship (of blood or marriage). **3.** a connection (mail, air, telephone). **4.** *gram.* possessive case. — ~ करना (का), to join, to connect; to arrange the engagement (of). ~ में, adv. in connection (with, के), concerning. ~ रखना, to be connected (with, से: as one matter with another), to have to do (with); to be in contact (with: as with a colleague). इस ~ में, adv. in this connection. – संबंध-कारक, m. = ~, 4. संबंधवाचक, adj. & m. *gram.* relative; a relative word. संबंध-सूत्र, m. contact (with a person).

संबंधता *sam-bandhătā* [S.], f. = संबद्धता.

संबंधित *sam-bandhit* [S.], adj. **1.** connected. **2.** concerned (with), involved (in). — ~ करना, to connect (with, से or के साथ).

संबंधी *sam-bandhī* [S.], adj. & m. **1.** adj. -संबंधी. connected with, concerning (e.g. तत्-संबंधी, concerning that: concerning a partic. topic). **2.** m. a relative (by marriage).

संबद्ध *sam-baddh* [S.], adj. **1.** bound or tied together. **2.** connected; related; affiliated.

संबद्धता *sam-baddhătā* [S.], f. connectedness; relatedness; affiliation.

संबल *sam-bal* [S.], m. provisions (for a journey); support.

संबुद्ध *sam-buddh* [S.], adj. **1.** enlightened. **2.** alerted, awakened.

संबोधन *sam-bodhan* [S.], m. **1.** causing (one) to understand, explaining. **2.** calling out (to, को); form of address. **3.** *gram.* vocative case. **4.** consoling; consolation. — संबोधन-कारक, m. = ~, 3.

संबोधित *sam-bodhit* [S.], adj. **1.** given understanding, enlightened. ***2.** called out (to); addressed. — धरती को ~ करके, adv. addressing the ground: speaking with the head lowered or hanging.

संभरण *sam-bharaṇ* [S.], m. supply (as of a commodity).

सँभलना *saṁbhalnā* [cf. H. *saṁbhālnā*], v.i. **1.** to be supported, or propped up (by, से); to be borne (expenses). **2.** to manage, to get by (despite difficulties). **3.** to recover (from a stumble or fall; or from a reverse, or an illness). **4.** to be watchful, attentive. **5.** to be curbed, checked (the feelings). — सँभल जाओ! watch your step! सँभलकर बात करो! mind what you say!

सँभला *saṁbhlā* [cf. H. *saṁbhalnā*], m. *Pl. HŚS.* a crop which recovers after suffering a check.

संभलाना *sambhlānā* [cf. H. *saṁbhālnā*], v.t. to cause to be supported; to stop (one) from falling.

संभव *sam-bhav* [S.], m. & adj. **1.** m. birth, origin. ***2.** adj. possible; probable. ~ है कि वह फ़ेल हो गया है, he's probably failed. ~ है कि वह फ़ेल हो गया हो, he may have failed. — संभवत:, adv. possibly; probably. संभवतया, id.

संभाग *sam-bhāg* [S.], m. (constituent) district, region.

संभार *sam-bhār* [S.], m. collection, assemblage.

सँभार- *saṁbhār-*, v.t. Brbh. Av. to collect one's thoughts, to recollect.

सँभारना *saṁbhārnā*, v.t. pronun. var. = संभालना.

सँभाल *saṁbhāl* [cf. H. *saṁbhālnā*], f. **1.** care, attention (to, की). **2.** maintenance (as of family, relatives); upkeep.

सँभालना *saṁbhālnā* [*saṁbhārayati*], v.t. **1.** to support; to sustain (as expenditure, or an attack); to hold up. **2.** to adjust (clothing). **3.** to hold, not to let go. **4.** to take care of, to look after. **5.** to maintain (as family, relatives). **6.** to assist (one). **7.** to see to, to settle (a matter). **8.** to superintend. **9.** to regulate (as expenses, revenues). **10.** to curb (the feelings, the tongue). **11.** to correct (a child); to punish. — सँभालकर देखना, to look after with care. ज़बान सँभाल! hold your tongue!

सँभाला *saṁbhālā* [cf. H. *saṁbhālnā*], m. last rally (of one dying). — ~ लेना, to rally before death; life to flicker.

सँभालू *saṁbhālū* [cf. H. *saṁbhālnā*], m. *Pl. HŚS.* the plant *Vitex*: the chaste-tree (of which the leaves are used medicinally, and the twigs in making baskets).

संभावना *sam-bhāvănā* [S.], f. **1.** respect, regard, esteem; honour. **2.** imagination, assumption. **3.** fitness, capacity. ***4.** possibility. ***5.** probability. — ~ करना (की), to envisage. संभावनार्थ [°*nā*+*a*°], m. *gram.* subjective mood; optative.

संभावनीय *sam-bhāvănīyă* [S.], adj. **1.** imaginable; possible. **2.** probable.

संभावित *sam-bhāvit* [S.], adj. **1.** esteemed, well-regarded. **2.** well-conceived (for a purpose): suited, fitted. ***3.** conjectured; possible; probable.

संभाव्य *sam-bhāvyă* [S.], adj. **1.** well-regarded, esteemed; honoured. **2.** *gram.* subjunctive; optative. *3. = संभावनीय.

संभाषण *sam-bhāṣaṇ* [S.], m. conversation, talk; dialogue.

संभाषी *sam-bhāṣī* [S.], m. one spoken with; interlocutor.

संभूत *sam-bhūt* [S.], adj. born from; originated from.

संभूति *sam-bhūti* [S.], f. birth, origin.

संभोग *sam-bhog* [S.], m. **1.** sensual enjoyment. **2.** sexual intercourse.

संभोगी *sam-bhogī* [S.], adj. & m. **1.** adj. addicted to the pleasures of the senses; sensual. **2.** m. a sensual person.

संभोग्य *sam-bhogyă* [S.], adj. able to be enjoyed (an object of pleasure).

संभोजन *sam-bhojan* [S.], m. **1.** a meal eaten together, a meal with guests. **2.** food.

संभ्रम *sam-bhram* [S.], m. **1.** moving about or around; whirling round, revolving. ***2.** confusion, agitation. **3.** respect; awe.

संभ्रांत *sam-bhrānt* [S.], adj. **1.** confused, agitated. **2.** honoured, respected.

संभ्रांति *sam-bhrānti* [S.], f. **1.** confusion, agitation (= संभ्रम). **2.** respect.

संयंत्र *saṃ-yantră* [S.], m. *techn.* equipment, plant.

संयत *saṃ-yat* [S.], adj. restrained, controlled.

संयत *saṃ-yat* [S.], adj. **1.** restrained, controlled; suppressed (as emotions). **2.** confined (as in prison). **3.** repressed (as emotions).

संयम *saṃ-yam* [S.], m. **1.** restraint, control; self-control. **2.** abstinence (from partic. foods, &c.), moderation.

संयमी *saṃ-yamī* [S.], adj. **1.** practising restraint, discipline (of the senses, passions). **2.** abstemious, moderate.

संयुक्त *saṃ-yukt* [S.], adj. **1.** connected together; joined, compound (as a verb, a noun); conjunct (as consonant graphs). **2.** joined, united; joint (a family; an activity). ~ **प्रांत**, m. the United Provinces (*hist.*); Uttar Pradesh. — ~ **परिवार**, m. a joint family. ~ **राज्य**, m. United Kingdom. ~ **राष्ट्र**, m. the United Nations. ~ **राष्ट्र-संघ**, United Nations Organisation. °**ईय**, adj. ~ **सरकार**, f. a coalition government. — **संयुक्ताक्षर** [°*ta*+*a*°], a compound consonant graph.

संयुग *saṃ-yug* [S.], m. **1.** union; harmony. **2.** Brbh. conflict; battle.

संयुत *saṃ-yut* [S.], adj. = **संयुक्त**.

संयुति *saṃ-yuti* [S.], f. *astron.* conjunction (of planets).

संयोग *saṃ-yog* [S.], m. **1.** joining together; sthg. joined, a compound; combination. **2.** an event; a coincidence, chance. **3.** agreement (as of views). **4.** union (of a couple). — ~ **की बात**, f. sthg. occurring by chance, a chance. ~ **से**, adv. by chance. – **संयोगवश**, adv. id.

संयोजक *saṃ-yojak* [S.], adj. & m. **1.** adj. joining, linking. **2.** arranging, contriving. **3.** m. *gram.* a conjunction. **4.** an organiser; convener.

संयोजकता *saṃ-yojakătā* [S.], f. *chem.* valency.

संयोजन *saṃ-yojan* [S.], m. **1.** joining, linking, combining; link. **2.** organising, organisation. **3.** assembling (sthg. from its parts).

संयोजना *saṃ-yojănā* [S.], f. sthg. organised, or contrived; a gathering, a function.

संयोजित *saṃ-yojit* [S.], adj. joined, linked, &c. (see **संयोजन**).

संरक्षक *saṃ-rakṣak* [S.], m. **1.** protector. **2.** defender. **3.** guardian. **4.** patron.

संरक्षण *saṃ-rakṣaṇ* [S.], m. **1.** protecting; protection. **2.** defence. **3.** ward, charge; custody. — **संरक्षणात्मक** [°*ṇa*+*ā*°], adj. protective (as a function). **संरक्षणार्थक** [°*ṇa*+*a*°], adj. defensive (as a measure).

संरक्षा *saṃ-rakṣā* [S.], f. state of safety.

संरक्षित *saṃ-rakṣit* [S.], adj. **1.** protected. **2.** defended. **3.** under guardianship or ward. **4.** mandated, protected (a territory).

संरचना *saṃ-racănā* [S.], f. structure.

संलग्न *saṃ-lagn* [S.], adj. **1.** closely attached; associated, united (with, **से**). **2.** sticking, adhering. **3.** enclosed (with a letter). **4.** adjacent. **5.** absorbed, engrossed (in, **में**).

संलग्नक *saṃ-lagnak* [S.], m. enclosure (with a letter).

संलाप *saṃ-lāp* [S.], m. conversation.

संलेख *saṃ-lekh* [S.], m. a document.

संवत् *saṃ-vat* [S. *saṁvat(sara)-*], m. **1.** a year. **2.** an era, esp. that of Vikramāditya (beginning shortly after 57 B.C). — ~ **बाँधना**, to establish an era; to mark or to fix an epoch.

संवत्सर *saṃ-vatsar* [S.], m. = **संवत्**.

[1]**संवरण** *saṃ-varaṇ* [S.], m. choosing.

[2]**संवरण** *saṃ-varaṇ* [S.], m. **1.** covering over, concealing. **2.** checking.

सँवरना *saṁvarnā* [cf. H. *saṁvārnā*], v.i. **1.** to be prepared, fashioned. **2.** to be arranged; to be improved, or corrected. **3.** to be adorned; to be combed (hair).

संवर्धन *saṃ-vardhan* [S.], m. rearing, fostering; breeding. — **संवर्धन-गृह**, m. nursery (for plants).

संवलित *saṃ-valit* [S.], adj. associated with; suffused by (as knowledge by feeling).

संवात *saṁ-vāt* [S.], m. ventilation.

संवातित *saṃ-vātit* [S.], adj. ventilated.

संवाद *saṃ-vād* [S.], m. **1.** discussion together, debate; dialogue. **2.** information, news; report; rumour. — **संवाददाता**, m. inv. reporter, journalist. °-**सम्मेलन**, m. press conference.

संवादक *saṃ-vādak* [S.], m. a correspondent; spokesman.

संवादी *saṃ-vādī* [S.], adj. **1.** corresponding, similar. **2.** concordant; harmonious.

सँवार *saṁvār* [cf. H. *saṁvārnā*], f. preparation, arrangement, &c. (see **सँवारना**).

सँवारना *saṁvārnā* [*saṁvārayati*], v.t. **1.** to prepare, to fashion. **2.** to arrange; to adjust, to improve; to make good. **3.** to adorn. — **बाल** ~, to comb the hair; to do the hair.

संविधान *saṃ-vidhān* [S.], m. a constitution. — ~ **सभा**, f. Constituent Assembly (of India).

संविधानिक *saṃ-vidhānik* [cf. H. *saṁvidhān*], adj. constitutional.

संवेदन *saṃ-vedan* [S.], m. perception; sensation. — **संवेदनशील**, adj. sensitive. °**ता**, f.

संवेदना *saṃ-vedănā* [S.], f. sympathy.

संवेदी *saṃ-vedī* [S.], adj. able to sense, perceptive.

संशय *saṃ-śay* [S.], m. **1.** uncertainty, doubt; hesitation; mistrust. **2.** apprehension (of). **3.** anxiety; fear. — **संशयवाद**, m. scepticism. °**ई**, adj. **संशयात्मक** [°*ya*+*ā*°], adj. doubting, doubtful (a person; also a matter).

संशयालु *saṃ-śayālu* [S.], adj. doubting; irresolute; sceptical.

संशयित *saṃ-śayit* [S.], adj. **1.** doubted, &c. (see संशय). **2.** anticipated with misgiving or fear.

संशयी *saṃ-śayī* [S.], adj. & m. **1.** adj. doubtful, hestitant, &c. **2.** m. a doubter, &c.; a sceptic (see संशय).

संशोधक *saṃ-śodhak* [S.], adj. correcting, &c. (see संशोधन).

संशोधन *saṃ-śodhan* [S.], m. purifying: **1.** correcting, correction; improvement; amendment. **2.** revision.

संशोधित *saṃ-śodhit* [S.], adj. **1.** corrected. **2.** revised.

संश्रय *saṃ-śray* [S.], m. connection, association: **1.** refuge, resting-place. **2.** patronage. **3.** alliance.

संश्रित *saṃ-śrit* [S.], adj. finding refuge, &c. (see संश्रय).

संश्लिष्ट *saṃ-śliṣṭ* [S.], adj. **1.** synthesised; synthetic. 2., complex.

संश्लेषण *saṃ-śleṣaṇ* [S.], m. synthesis.

संसक्त *saṃ-sakt* [S.], adj. **1.** stuck together; connected; cohesive. **2.** absorbed, intent (in or on); attached (to). **3.** endowed (with: as with qualities, virtues).

संसक्ति *saṃ-sakti* [S.], f. close connection, cohesion (see संसक्त).

संसद *saṃ-sad* [S.], m. sitting together: parliament; specif. the Indian Parliament.

संसदीय *saṃsadīyă* [S.], adj. parliamentary.

संसर्ग *saṃ-sarg* [S.], m. mixture, union: **1.** contact, touch. **2.** association, dealings. **3.** cohabitation. — संसर्गज, adj. contagious (= छूत का).

संसर्गी *saṃ-sargī* [S.], adj. & m. **1.** adj. associated (with). **2.** m. an associate; friend.

संसा *saṃsā* [*saṁśaya-*], m. = संशय.

संसाधन *saṃ-sādhan* [S.], m. pl. resources.

संसार *saṃ-sār* [*saṁsāra-*], m. **1.** cycle of births or states, transmigration. **2.** transf. the world; the universe. **3.** life in this world; worldly concerns; illusion as to worldly reality. — संसार-गमन, m. passing from one birth or state to another, transmigration. संसार-चक्र, m. the cycle of transmigration. संसाररूपी, adj. of this world, secular. संसार-व्यापी, adj. diffused, or extending, or in force throughout the world.

संसारा *saṃsārā*, m. reg. = संसार.

संसारी *saṃ-sārī* [S.], adj. **1.** of the world; worldly (interests, gain). **2.** living in (not renouncing) the world. **3.** ephemeral (not eternal). **4.** subject to transmigration (living beings).

संसी *saṃsī* [*saṁdaṁśikā-*], f. reg. pincers, tongs (= सँड़सी).

संसृति *saṃ-sr̥ti* [S.], f. = संसार, 1., 2.

संस्करण *saṃ-skaraṇ* [S.], m. putting together: an edition.

संस्कार *saṃ-skār* [S.], m. **1.** perfecting, finishing; refining; adorning. ***2.** an inborn power or faculty; instinct. **3.** influence, impress (of nurture). **4.** a concept, idea. ***5.** *hind.* any of various essential sanctifying or purificatory rites (as the first taking of solid food, investiture with the sacred thread, marriage and funeral rites).

संस्कृत *saṃ-skr̥t* [S.], adj. & f. **1.** adj. well-formed, perfected; refined, cultivated (esp. language). **2.** *Pl. HŚS.* made the object of a ceremony or rite (*saṃskār*). **3.** f. the Sanskrit language.

संस्कृति *saṃ-skr̥ti* [S.], f. culture.

संस्था *saṃ-sthā* [S.], f. **1.** an institutional body; institute (of learning, &c). **2.** an organisation; an association, society. सहकारी ~, f. a cooperative organisation. **3.** an institutionalised rite or custom. धार्मिक ~, f. a religious rite.

संस्थान *saṃ-sthān* [S.], m. = संस्था, 1.

संस्थापक *saṃ-sthāpak* [S.], m. founder.

संस्थापन *saṃ-sthāpan* [S.], m. founding, establishing; foundation, establishment.

संस्थापित *saṃ-sthāpit* [S.], adj. founded, established.

संस्पर्श *saṃ-sparś* [S.], m. **1.** contact, touch. **2.** being touched, affected (by).

संस्पृष्ट *saṃ-spr̥ṣṭ* [S.], adj. **1.** touched together: in contact. **2.** touched, moved (by).

संहत *saṃ-hat* [S.], adj. stuck together: **1.** closely joined, or connected. **2.** made firm, or compact; consolidated. **3.** assembled, accumulated. **4.** hurt, wounded; killed.

संहति *saṃ-hati* [S.], f. **1.** close contact, connection, union, &c. **2.** compactness; consolidated state. **3.** bulk, mass. (see संहत.)

संहार *saṁhār* [S.], m. /sə̃har/, /sənhar/, /sənghar/. drawing together: **1.** total destruction, or ruin. **2.** killing; slaughter, carnage. **3.** *mythol.* final destruction of the world (= प्रलय). — ~ करना (का), to destroy, &c. – संहारकारी, adj. destructive.

सँहार- *saṁhār-* [*saṁhārayati*], v.t. Brbh. Av. **1.** to kill. **2.** to destroy.

संहारक *saṃ-hārak* [S.], adj. & m. **1.** adj. destructive, &c. **2.** m. destroyer, &c. (see संहार).

संहारित *saṃ-hārit* [S.], adj. destroyed, killed.

संहित *saṃ-hit* [S.], adj. **1.** collected, accumulated. **2.** codified.

संहिता *saṃ-hitā* [S.], f. /sənhita/. **1.** collection; specif. a collection of the hymns or other subject matter of a Veda. **2.** a code of law. दंड-संहिता, f. penal code. **3.** *ling.* = संधि.

स- *sa-* [S.], prefix. **1.** together with, along with (e.g. सपरिवार, adv. along with (one's) family; सहर्ष, adv. gladly, with joy). **2.** having, possessing (e.g. सहृदय, m. & adj. (one) who has a heart, a sensitive, or kindly person). **3.** equal, same (e.g. सवय, adj. of the same age; सवया, adj. & f. id).

सआदत *saadat* [A. *sa'adat*], f. U. prosperity, well-being; good fortune.

सकंटक *sa-kaṇṭak* [S.], adj. **1.** thorny. **2.** troublesome.

सकट *sakaṭ* [ad. *saṁkaṭa-*], m. *hind.* the festival of the birthday of Gaṇeś (= गणेश-चतुर्थी). — सकट-चौथ, f. id.

सकट *sa-kaṭ* [S.], adj. *Pl. HŚS.* bad, vile.

सकड़-दादा *sakaṛ-dādā*, m. *Pl.* paternal great-grandfather or great-great-grandfather.

सकड़-नाना *sakaṛ-nānā*, m. *Pl.* maternal great-grandfather or great-great-grandfather.

सकत *sakat* [ad. *śakti-*], f. 19c. = शक्ति.

¹**सकता** *saktā* [A. *sakta*], m. **1.** an apoplectic fit. **2.** fainting fit. **3.** fig. state of helplessness. — सकते में आना, colloq. to be astounded, stunned.

²**सकता** *saktā*, f. corr. 19c. ability, capacity (= शक्ति).

सकना *saknā* [*śaknoti*], v.i. **1.** to be able. **2.** to be in a position (to do sthg). — वह पढ़ सकता है, he can read. आप जा सकते हैं, you may go. मैं जा सकता हूँ, I can go; I may (perhaps) go. मैं भारत जा सकता था, I could have gone to India; I used to be able to go to India.

सकपकाना *sakpakānā*, v.i. to be taken aback; to be disconcerted.

¹**सकरा** *sakrā*, adj. reg. narrow, &c. (= सँकड़ा).

²**सकरा** *sakrā*, adj. *hind.* polluted (food); unfried (= सखरा).

¹**सकराई** *sakrāī*, f. narrowness, &c. (cf. सँकड़ा).

²**सकराई** *sakrāī* [cf. H. *sakārnā*], f. fee charged for accepting a bill of exchange.

सकरुण *sa-karuṇ* [S.], adj. compassionate.

सकर्मक *sa-karmak* [S.], adj. **1.** *gram.* having an object, transitive. **2.** active (as the forces of nature).

सकल *sakal* [S.], adj. **1.** all. **2.** entire, the whole; gross (amount).

सका *sakā* [cf. H. *saknā*], m. reg. might, power.

सका- *sakā-* [cf. *śaṅkā-*, *śaṅkate*], v.i. Brbh. Av. **1.** to fear, to be apprehensive. **2.** to grieve.

सकाम *sa-kām* [S.], adj. **1.** desirous. **2.** whose desire is fulfilled: contented. **3.** sensual, lascivious.

सकारण *sa-kāraṇ* [S.], adj. having some cause.

सकारना *sakārnā* [ad. *svīkāra-*], v.t. to accept; to endorse as accepted (a bill, immediately before it falls due for payment).

सकारा *sakārā* [cf. H. *sakārnā*], m. *Pl. HŚS.* charge for accepting or renewing (a bill of exchange).

सकारात्मक *sakārātmak* [S.], adj. compelling, effective; positive.

सकारे *sakāre* [cf. H. *sakāl*, and *savere*], adv. Brbh. Av. early in the morning.

सकाल *sa-kāl* [cf. H. *kāl*, and *saver(ā)*; also S. *sakāla-*], m. early morning.

सकाली *sakālī* [? cf. H. *sakāl(e)*], f. & adv. **1.** f. early morning. **2.** adv. early in the morning.

सकाले *sakāle* [cf. H. *sakāl*, and *savere*], adv. early in the morning.

सकिल- *sakil-* [*saṁkirati*], v.i. Brbh. Av. = सिकुड़ना, 1., 3.

सकुच *sakuc* [cf. H. *sakucnā*], f. **1.** shrinking, contraction. **2.** shrinking, shyness. **3.** shame.

सकुचना *sakucnā* [*saṁkucyate*], v.i. **1.** to shrink, &c. (= सकुचाना, 2.)

सकुचाना *sakucānā* [cf. H. *sakucnā*], v.t. & v.i. **1.** v.t. to cause to feel embarrassment, or shame. **2.** [× H. *sakuc*] v.i. to shrink (from); to be shy, or bashful; to hesitate.

सकुचाई *sakucāī* [cf. H. *sakucnā, sakucānā*, 2.], f. **1.** shrinking, shyness. **2.** apprehension. **3.** shame.

सकुचीला *sakucīlā* [cf. H. *sakucnā*], adj. shrinking, shy; embarrassed.

सकुचौंह्- *sakucaumh-*, adj. Brbh. = सकुचीला.

सकुल *sa-kul* [S.], adj. **1.** adj. of noble or good family. **2.** belonging to the same family. ***3.** adv. together with (one's) family.

सकुल्य *sa-kulyă* [S.], m. **1.** one of the same family and name (= सगोत्र). **2.** a relative.

सकृत् *sakṛt* [S.], adv. *Pl. HŚS.* **1.** once. **2.** at once, together. **3.** always.

सकेड़ना *sakeṛnā* [? **saṁkoṭayati* × *saṁkaṭa-*], v.t. *Pl.* = सिकोड़ना, सकेरना, सकेलना.

सकेत *saket*, m. (f., *Pl.*) Av. constraint, distress.

सकेतना *saketnā*, v.i. **1.** reg. to draw together, to narrow. **2.** Av. to close (a flower).

सकेती *saketī*, f. *Pl. HŚS.* = सकेत.

सकेरना *sakernā*, v.t. reg. to gather together, to collect.

सकेलना *sakelnā*, v.t. reg. to gather together, to collect (= सकेरना).

सकेला *sakelā*, m. *Pl. HŚS.* a partic. kind of iron; an iron implement; a sword.

सकोप *sa-kop* [S.], adj. Av. angered, angry.

सकोप- *sa-kop-* [cf. H. *sakop*], v.i. Brbh. to grow angry.

सकोरा *sakorā* [P. *sukūra*], m. a small earthen cup.

सकोरी *sakorī* [cf. H. *sakorā*], f. dimin. = सकोरा.

सकोह *sa-koh* [H. *sa* + *krodha-*], adj. Av. enraged, angry.

सक्कस *sakkas*, adj. Brbh. = सरकश (see s.v. ²सर).

सक़्क़ा *saqqā* [A. *saqqā*], m. inv. a water-carrier; waterer (of plants).

सक्खड़ई *sakkhaṛaī*, f. *Pl. mus.* name of a *rāgiṇī*; a kind of tune or music.

सक्ति *sakti*, f. Brbh. Av. power (= शक्ति). — सक्तिवान [*-māna-*], adj. Brbh. strong, powerful.

सक्थि *sakthi* [S.], f. *Pl. HŚS.* **1.** the thigh; thigh-bone. **2.** pole or shafts of a cart.

सक्रिय *sa-kriyă* [S.], active; effective.

सक्षम *sa-kṣam* [S.], adj. capable, competent.

सक्षमता *sa-kṣamătā* [S.], f. capability, competence.

सख *sakh* [? ad. *sakhā*], m. Av. friend, companion.

सखरा *sakhrā*, adj. *hind.* not cooked in *ghī*, impure (food): = ²सकरा.

सखरी *sakhrī*, f. *hind.* food not cooked in *ghī*, impure food.

सखा *sakhā* [S.], m. inv. friend, companion.

सखि *sakhi*, voc. = सखी, 1.

सखी *sakhī* [S.], f. **1.** a woman's or girl's female friend; specif. a confidante or female attendant. **2.** a sectarian, or beggar, who dresses like a woman. — ~ भाव, m. an attitude of religious devotion in which the devotee seeks to regard himself as a *sakhī* of Rādhā or of Sītā. ~ संप्रदाय, m. title of the Rām *rasik* community (who adopt the devotional attitude of *sakhī-bhav*).

सख़्त *sakht* [P. *sakht*], f. **1.** hard; stiff; strong, solid; tight. **2.** obdurate, obstinate. **3.** severe, intense, violent; oppressive (as weather). **4.** harsh, stern (words, attitude). **5.** difficult, hard (as a question); burdensome (as times). **6.** dire, (as necessity); grievous. **7.** gross, extreme (incompetence, &c). — सख़्तदिल, adj. hard-hearted. °ई, f.

सख़्ती *sakhtī* [P. *sakhtī*], f. **1.** hardness, &c. (see सख़्त). **2.** severity; violence; cruelty. **3.** harshness. **4.** distress, hard times; calamity. — ~ करना (पर, से), to treat with severity or harshness, &c. ~ से, adv. severely, harshly, &c.

सख्य *sakhyă* [S.], m. **1.** friendship, intimacy. **2.** specif. a partic. attitude of devotion to Kṛṣṇa in which the devotee imagines himself as a companion (सखा) of the deity. — ~ भाव, m. = ~, 2.

सगंध *sa-gandh* [S.], adj. having a smell, fragrant.

सगड़ी *sagṛī* [cf. H. *saggaṛ*], f. small cart, or trolley.

सगण *sa-gaṇ* [S.], m. *pros.* a unit of two short syllables followed by one long, an anapæst.

सगरा *sagrā* [ad. *sakala-*], adj. reg. = सकल.

सगर्भ *sa-garbh* [S.], adj. **1.** pregnant. **2.** uterine (brother, sister). **3.** Av. pregnant with meaning (words).

सगर्भ्य *sa-garbhyă* [S.], adj. *Pl. HŚS.* = सगर्भ.

सगर्व *sa-garv* [S.], adj. **1.** proud (in a good sense). **2.** haughty.

सगा *sagā* [**svagya-*: Ap. *sagga-*], adj. & m. **1.** adj. born of the same parents. ~ भाई, m. full brother. **2.** related by blood (as an uncle, &c). **3.** m. a blood relation. — सगा-सहोदरा [ad.

sahodara-], m. & adj. own brother; blood relation; = सगा. सगे-संबंधी, m. pl. relatives.

सगाई *sagāī* [cf. H. *sagā*], f. **1.** relationship of blood. **2.** engagement; marriage arrangement. **3.** remarriage. — ~ करना (की), to betroth; to arrange a marriage.

सगुण *sa-guṇ* [S.], adj. **1.** having attributes or qualities; qualified. **2.** having good qualities, virtuous. — ~ भक्ति, f. religious devotion directed towards the supreme being seen as positively qualified or personal. ~ साहित्य, m. literature expressing the attitude of *saguṇ bhakti*.

सगुणी *sa-guṇī* [S.], adj. & m. **1.** adj. = सगुण. **2.** m. a believer in the *saguṇ* deity, or in its worship.

सगुनिया *saguniyā* [cf. H. *sagun*], m. a fortune-teller, astrologer.

सगुनौती *sagunautī*, f. an omen, a good omen. — ~ कर-, Brbh. to see, or to consult omens. ~ निकालना, id.

सगोत्र *sa-gotră* [S.], adj. & m. **1.** adj. of the same *gotra*, related. **2.** m. one of the same family name and of common origin; a kinsman.

सगोत्रता *sa-gotrătā* [S.], f. kinship by *gotra*.

सग्गड़ *saggaṛ* [**śaggaṭa-*], m. cart; long trolley.

सघन *sa-ghan* [S.], adj. **1.** thick, dense (as vegetation, or clouds). **2.** dense, solid (a substance). **3.** dense, crowded (as population, or an assembly).

सघनता *sa-ghanătā* [S.], f. **1.** denseness. **2.** intensity.

संघार *saṅghār* [*saṁhārayati*], v.t. Brbh. to destroy, to kill.

सच *sac* [*satya-*], adj. & m. **1.** adj. true, &c. (= सच्चा). **2.** m. truth; the truth. — ~ पूछिए तो.... if the truth is asked, then: if the truth is told.... ~ बोलना, to speak the truth. ~ में, adv. truly, indeed, really. यह ~ है कि...., it is true that.... – सच-मुच, adv. in very truth (= ~ में).

सच्- *sac-* [S]. = सत्: — सच्चरित्र, adj. of good or virtuous character. सच्चिदानंद, m. being, thought, and bliss: a title of the ultimate being; a title of Viṣṇu as identified with the ultimate being.

सचराचर *sa-carâcar* [S.], adj. & m. **1.** adj. including all moving and motionless things: universal (as the world, the universe). **2.** m. all animate and inanimate things; the whole world.

सचल *sa-cal* [S.], adj. movable; mobile (= चल).

सचाई *sacāī* [cf. H. *saccā*], f. **1.** truth; the truth. **2.** authenticity. **3.** truthfulness. **4.** honesty, sincerity (as of intentions). **5.** faithfulness (to an original).

सचान *sacān* [*sañcāna-*], m. Brbh. Av. a falcon, hawk.

सचावट *sacāvaṭ*, f. reg. = सचाई.

सचाहट *sacāhaṭ*, f. reg. = सचाई.

सचिंत *sa-cint* [S.], adj. filled with anxious thought; attentive, considerate.

सचि *saci* m. *Pl. HŚS.* associate, friend.

सचित्र *sa-citr* [S.], adj. having pictures, illustrated; pictorial.

सचिव *saciv* [S.], m. **1.** secretary (of any organisation). **2.** minister (of a government). — सचिवालय [°*va*+*ā*°], m. secretariat.

सचु *sacu*, m. Brbh. joy, delight, happiness.

सचेत *sa-cet* [S.], adj. **1.** having consciousness, conscious; animate. **2.** thinking, intelligent; rational. **3.** mindful; alert. **4.** recovering consciousness. — ~ करना, to arouse (to consciousness); to bring (one) to (one's) senses. ~ रहना, to be watchful or wary (of, से). ~ होना, to recover consciousness; to be awake; to come to (one's) senses; to be alert, &c.

सचेतक *sa-cetak* [S.], m. *govt.* rouser: whip. — मुख्य ~, m. chief whip.

सचेतन *sa-cetan* [S.], adj. & m. **1.** adj. = सचेत. **2.** m. a conscious or rational being. — ~ अवस्था, f. state of consciousness.

सचेतनता *sa-cetanătā* [S.], f. consciousness.

सचेष्ट *sa-ceṣṭ* [S.], adj. making effort: energetic, active; zealous, intent.

सचौटी *sacauṭī*, f. *Pl.* truthfulness, &c. (see सच्चा).

सच्च *sacc*, m. see सच.

सच्चा *saccā* [*satya-*], adj. **1.** true. **2.** genuine, real (as craftsmanship, &c), pure (as a metal). **3.** truthful (as to one's word, का). **4.** honest, sincere (a friend); faithful; trustworthy, trusty. **5.** just, fair. —सच्चे अर्थ, or अर्थों में, in the real sense (of the word). हाथ का ~, adj. honest in (one's) dealing.

सच्चाई *saccāī*, f. = सचाई.

सच्चापन *saccāpan* [cf. H. *saccā*], m. = सचाई.

सच्चिदानंद *sac-cid-ānand* [S.], m. see s.v. सच-.

सज *saj* [cf. H. *sajnā*], f. **1.** decoration, ornamentation. **2.** attire. **3.** appearance, shape, style; build. – **सजदार** [P. *-dār*], adj. handsome; elegant. **सज-धज**, f. array, fine attire; elegance; splendour.

सज्- *saj-* [S]. = **सत्**: — **सज्जन**, m. see s.v.

सजंजल *sajañjal* [A. *sajanjal, sijanjal*], m. & adj. *Pl.* ? **1.** m. a mirror. **2.** spectacles. **3.** adj. pure, clear.

सजग *sa-jag* [S.], adj. **1.** vigilant. **2.** quick of mind. — **~ करना**, to alert (one, **को**; to, **से**).

सजगता *sa-jagătā* [S]. alertness, vigilance.

सजना *sajnā* [cf. H. *sajjānā*], v.i. & v.t. **1.** v.i. to be arranged, prepared; to be set in place. **2.** to be adorned; to be arrayed (in finery, &c). **3.** to look attractive (an object, a décor). **4.** to befit (one, **को**). **5.** v.t. = **सजाना**.

सजनी *sajănī* [cf. H. *sajjan*], f. mistress, sweetheart; lady.

सजमन *sajman*. reg. (Bihar) a bottle-gourd (= **कद्दू**).

सजल *sa-jal* [S.], adj. having or containing water: **1.** moist, damp. **2.** tearful.

सजवाना *sajvānā* [cf. H. *sajānā*], v.t. **1.** to cause to be arranged, &c. **2.** to cause to be decorated, &c.

सज़ा *sazā* [P. *sazā*], f. worthy, deserving: **1.** punishment. **2.** retribution. — **~ करना** (**की**), = next. **~ देना** (**को**), to punish, &c.; to sentence to punishment. **~ पाना**, to receive punishment, to be punished; (in law) to receive a sentence. **~ मिलना** (**को**), id. – **सज़ायाफ़्ता** [P. *yāfta*], adj. & m. imv. who has received punishment; a previous offender. **सज़ावार** [P. -*vār*], adj. *HŚS.* receiving punishment; worthy of punishment.

सजाई *sajāī* [cf. H. *sajānā*], f. **1.** arranging, &c. **2.** adorning, &c. **3.** price paid for adorning, &c.

सजात *sa-jāt* [S.], adj. **1.** of common origin; of the same sort or type. **2.** of the same community or race.

सजाति *sa-jāti* [S.], adj. & m. **1.** adj. = **सजात**. **2.** m. a person of the same community or race (as, **का**).

सजातीय *sa-jātīyă* [S.], adj. = **सजाति**.

सजातीयता *sa-jātīyătā* [S.], f. similarity of type, or (esp.) shared community or race.

सजाना *sajānā* [cf. *sajjayati*; Pa. *sajjāpeti*], v.t. **1.** to arrange, to prepare; to set in place. **2.** to furnish (as a room). **3.** to decorate, to adorn; to array (as in finery).

सजाव *sajāv* [? conn. *sadya-*; and *sajya-*, H. *sajānā*], m. reg. a yoghurt made from boiled or curdled milk. — **~ दही**, m. id.

सजावट *sajāvaṭ* [cf. H. *sajānā*], f. **1.** arrangement, &c. **2.** decoration, &c.; splendour.

सजावटी *sajāvăṭī* [cf. H. *sajāvaṭ*], adj. decorative, ornamental. — **~ कपड़े**, m. pl. (one's) best clothes.

सज़ावल *sazāval*, m. *Pl. HŚS.* a government land-rent collector; bailiff.

सज़ावली *sazāvălī* [P. *sazāvalī*], f. the work, or position of a rent collector or bailiff.

सजीला *sajīlā* [cf. *sajya-*], adj. **1.** shapely, graceful; handsome. **2.** elegant; modish. **3.** decorated.

सजीलापन *sajīlāpan* [cf. H. *sajīlā*], m. gracefulness, elegance, &c.

सजीव *sa-jīv* [S.], adj. & m. **1.** having life, animate. **2.** living (a language). **3.** filled with life, lively, spirited (as an attitude, a style). **4.** animated (a cartoon).

सजीवता *sa-jīvătā* [S.], f. liveliness.

सजीवन *sajīvan*, m. = **संजीवन**.

सजोना *sajonā*, v.t. reg. = **सजाना**.

सज्जन *sajjan* [S.], m. **1.** a good or virtuous man. **2.** a man of good family. **3.** a man, gentleman (term of courteous reference, or address). **4.** Brbh. lover; husband.

सज्जनता *sajjanătā* [S.], f. goodness, kindliness; honesty.

सज्जना *sajjănā* [S.], f. *Pl. HŚS.* ornamenting or caparisoning (an elephant).

सज्जा *sajjā* [S.], f. **1.** array; decoration, ornamentation; attire. **2.** equipment, outfitting; *mil.* supplies.

सज्जाद *sajjād* [A. *sajjād*], m. one who prostrates himself or bows in adoration (to Allāh).

सज्जादा *sajjādā* [A. *sajjāda*], m. a prayer-mat (as used by Muslims).

सज्जित *sajjit* [S.], adj. **1.** equipped (with). **2.** decorated, adorned.

सज्जी *sajjī* [*sarjikā-*], f. mineral or factitious carbonate of soda. — **सज्जी-खार**, m. id.

सज्ञात *sa-jñāt* [S.], adj. known, perceived.

सज्ञान *sa-jñān* [S.], adj. **1.** adj. knowing, wise. **2.** of good sense. **3.** m. = **सज्ञानी**.

सज्ञानता *sa-jñānătā* [S.], f. knowingness, wisdom.

सज्ञानी *sa-jñānī* [S.], m. a discerning or wise man.

सट *saṭ* [cf. H. *saṭnā*], f. attachment, liaison, league.

[1]**सटक** *saṭak* [cf. H. [1]*saṭaknā*], f. slipping away, disappearing.

[2]**सटक** *saṭak* [cf. H. [2]*saṭaknā*], f. Brbh. **1.** a switch, thin cane. **2.** a small snake. **3.** reg. a hookah tube.

[1]**सटकना** *saṭaknā* [cf. *saṭṭ-*[2]], v.i. to vanish, to disappear; to slip away.

[2]**सटकना** *saṭaknā* [cf. *saṭṭ-*[1]], v.t. to make a brisk movement or movements: to lash (a horse), to beat; to thresh (grain).

[1]**सटकाना** *saṭkānā* [cf. H. [1]*saṭaknā*], v.t. to cause to vanish or to disappear.

[2]**सटकाना** *saṭkānā* [cf. H. [2]*saṭaknā*], v.t. to cause a brisk movement (? or sudden sound); to strike (as with a cane or whip); to smoke (a hookah) briskly.

सटकार- *saṭkār-* [conn. *saṭā-*], adj. Brbh. long, lank (hair).

सटकारी *saṭkārī* [? cf. *saṭṭ-*[1]], f. *HŚS.* a cane, switch (= [2]सटक).

सटना *saṭnā* [cf. H. *sāṁṭnā*], v.i. **1.** to join together, to unite (with, से). **2.** to stick, to be stuck (together, on, or down). **3.** to be placed together, or against; to lean (against, के साथ, से). **4.** to nestle or to cling together.

सटपट *saṭpaṭ*, f. **1.** [cf. H. *saṭpaṭānā*] confusion; distraction. **2.** [cf. H. *saṭnā*] collusion, plot.

सटपटाना *saṭpaṭānā*, v.i. = सिटपिटाना.

सटर-पटर *saṭar-paṭar*, f. & adj. **1.** f. odd jobs; pottering about. **2.** adj. trivial (as a task, a job). — दिन ~ में बीत गया, the day was spent on this and that.

सटल्लो *saṭallo*, f. colloq. pej. *Pl.* a woman who chatters or gossips.

सटाना *saṭānā* [cf. H. *saṭnā*], v.t. to bring together (two objects): **1.** to join, to unite. **2.** to stick together; to stick on (as a stamp); to stick down. **3.** to place together or against; to lean (as a bicycle: against, के साथ, से). **4.** to engraft (on to, में). **5.** to put to stud (with, में).

सटाव *saṭāv* [cf. H. *saṭānā*], m. **1.** adhesion. **2.** attachment, connection.

[1]**सटासट** *saṭāsaṭ* [cf. H. *saṭnā*], f. sticking, or joining together.

[2]**सटासट** *saṭāsaṭ* [cf. **saṭṭ-*[1]], f. & adv. **1.** f. succession of blows or lashes. **2.** adv. in succession (as of blows).

सटिया *saṭiyā*, m. reg. a cane, switch (= [2]सटक).

सटी *saṭī* [S.], f. an aromatic root, zedoary (from the tubers of which the red powder *abīr* was formerly made).

[1]**सटीक** *sa-ṭīk* [S.], adj. accompanied by a commentary (a text).

[2]**सटीक** *saṭīk*, adj. colloq. correct, appropriate.

सटोरिया *saṭoriyā* [cf. H. *saṭṭā*], m. a speculator.

सट्टा *saṭṭā* [**saṭṭa-*[1]: Pk. *saṭṭa-*], m. **1.** a commercial transaction. **2.** a written agreement. **3.** a market. **4.** speculation. — सट्टे में कमाना, to make a financial profit in a market. सट्टे में लगाना, to invest. – सट्टा-बट्टा, m. exchange, barter; = ~, 2.; union, cabal; intrigue; liaison. सट्टा-बही, f. deed of exchange or transfer. सट्टेबाज़ [P. *-bāz*], m. a speculator. °ई, f. speculation.

सट्टी *saṭṭī* [cf. H. *saṭṭā*], f. a market, esp. one in a partic. item. — ~ चलाना, to hold a market; to make a din. ~ मचाना, id., 2.

सठियाना *saṭhiyānā* [cf. H. *sāṭh*], v.i. to reach sixty years of age; to grow old.

सठोरा *saṭhorā*, m. reg. a sweet made of meal, ginger, sugar and spices (given to women after childbirth).

सड़क *saṛak* [cf. *sṛti-*], f. **1.** road, highway; a main street. **2.** fig. means, way (to an objective). — ~ काटना or निकालना, to lay out a road; to make or to run a road. ~ पर, or में, adv. on the road or street; in the street. ~ पर जाना, to go out into the road; to go or to be going along a road. ~ से जाना, to go by road. कच्ची ~, f. an unmetalled road, dirt road. पक्की ~, f. a tar-sealed or a metalled road.

सड़क्का *saṛakkā*, m. *Pl.* a light shower.

सड़न *saṛan* [cf. H. *saṛnā*], f. **1.** decay, rotting. **2.** ferment.

सड़ना *saṛnā* [*śaṭati*[1], Pk. *saḍaï*], v.i. **1.** to decay, to rot; to go bad. **2.** to be poisoned, septic (as a finger). **3.** to ferment. — सड़ा-गला, adj. rotted: decayed, rotten; musty; foul-smelling; fig. disreputable (as opinions). सड़ी गरमी, f. stifling (humid) heat.

सड़पना *saṛapnā*, v.t. & v.i. = सुड़पना.

सड़प्पा *saṛappā*, m. noisy eating: a slurping or gulping sound.

सड़म *saṛam*, m. *Pl.* reg. tow from the Indian hemp plant, *Crotalaria juncea* (= [1]सन).

सड़ाँध *saṛāṁdh*, f. pronun. var. = सड़ायँध.

सड़ान *saṛān* [cf. H. *saṛnā*], f. reg. = सड़न.

सड़ाना *saṛānā* [cf. H. *saṛnā*], v.t. **1.** to cause to rot, to allow to rot. **2.** to allow to ferment. **3.** colloq. to allow to fall into disrepair, decay, or ruin.

सड़ायँध *saṛāyaṁdh* [conn. *śaṭati*[1], Pk. *saḍaï*: w. *gandha-*], f. **1.** stench. **2.** fig. foulness, filth. — ~ मारना, to stink.

सड़ासड़ *saṛāsaṛ* [cf. **saṭṭ-*[1]], f. & adv. **1.** f. whizz or whistle (as of a projectile). **2.* adv. following smartly, or sharply (as blows of a whip).

सड़ाहँद *saṛāhaṁd*, f. = सड़ायँध.

सड़ियल *saṛiyal* [cf. H. *saṛnā*], adj. decayed, rotten; musty; foul-smelling.

[1]**सत्** *sat* [S.], adj. & m. **1.** adj. existent. **2.** real, true, right. ***3.** good; virtuous; worthy. **4.** divine. **5.** m. that which is existent; the ultimate being. **6.** reality, truth (= सत्य). — सत्कर्म, m. = सत्कार्य; virtuous demeanour, piety. सत्कार, m. doing good or right: hospitable treatment or reception, hospitality; due reverence or respect; a pious act or observance. सत्कार करना (का), to receive hospitably; to entertain; to treat respectfully. अपने सत्कार के लिए धन्यवाद देना (को), to give thanks (to) for hospitality shown one. °ई, m. one who acts virtuously; a kindly, or hospitable man. °-कार्य, m. a good or virtuous act; an act of piety. सत्कीर्ति, f. good name or fame. सत्कृत, adj. done well; respectfully or kindly treated; welcomed. सत्-नाम, m. the true Name: (esp. in Sikh belief) title of the supreme being. सत्पात्र, m. a good or deserving person. सत्पुरुष, m. a good or worthy man; an honest man. सत्संग, m. association with the virtuous or the good; good people or company; a congregation gathered to worship and sing *bhajans*. सत्संग रखना, to keep good or virtuous company. °ई, m. one who keeps good company, &c. सत्संगति, f. = सत्संग, 1.

[2]**सत** *sat* [ad. *satya-*], m. & adv. **1.** m. honour, virtue. 2. = सत्य. **3.** adv. or interj. true, very true. — ~ डिगना, or डोलन), to be shaken in faith, or in (one's) virtue. ~ पर चढ़ना, to stand on (one's) dignity; to be unshaken in righteousness, or in faith. ~ पर रहना, to be or to remain true to one's word; to continue in virtue, or in chastity, to live honourably.

[3]**सत** *sat*, m. see सत्त.

[4]**सत** *sat*, adj. pronun. var. see शत.

सत- *sat-* [cf. H. *sāt*], seven. — सतकोना, adj. & m. seven-cornered; a heptagon. सतकंडा, adj. seven-storeyed. सतखाना, adj. having seven sections; seven-storied. सतगुना, adj. sevenfold. सतख़समी, f. colloq. pej. having seven husbands: a loose woman. सतनजा [H. *nāj*, for *anāj*], m. & adj. a mixture of seven sorts of grain; a mixture, hodge-podge; fig. mixed; heterogeneous. सतमासा, m. a child born in the seventh month of pregnancy; celebration held to mark the seventh month of pregnancy. सतलड़ा, adj. & m. consisting of seven strings or rows (as a chain or necklace); a necklace of seven strings. °-लड़ी, f. id. सतसई, f. a total of seven hundred: title of any collection of (nominally) seven hundred verses.

सतत *satat* [S.], adj. & adv. **1.** adj. constant, continual; uninterrupted. **2.** perpetual; eternal. **3.** adv. constantly, &c.

[1]**सतर** *satr* [? ad. *śatru-*], m. & adv. Brbh. (as) an enemy: angry; angrily.

[2]**सतर** *satr* [A. *saṭr*], m. a line, row.

सतरा- *satrā-* [? ad. *śatru-*], v.i. Brbh. to show or to feel anger (against, पर).

सतर्क *sa-tark* [S.], adj. **1.** provided with arguments (a case). ***2.** cautious; alert (as for danger). **3.** attentive, considerate.

सतर्कता *sa-tarkătā* [S.], f. **1.** logicality. **2.** caution; alertness.

सतवंती *satvantī* [ad. *satyavant-*; H. [1]*sat*], adj. virtuous, faithful (a wife).

सतवाँसा *satvāṁsā* [*saptamāsya-*], m. **1.** a child of seven months. **2.** a celebration held in the seventh month of a woman's pregnancy.

सतह *satah* [A. *saṭh*], f. **1.** surface. **2.** a flat surface. **3.** level (as of achievement, or activity).

सतहत्तर *sat'hattar* [*saptasaptati-*], adj. seventy-seven.

सतही *sat'hī* [A. *saṭhī*], adj. **1.** pertaining to a surface. **2.** apparent. **3.** superficial. — ~ तौर पर, adv. superficially.

सताऊ *satāū* [cf. H. *satānā*], adj. & m. **1.** adj. tormenting; troubling; teasing. **2.** m. a tormentor, &c.

सताना *satānā* [*saṁtāpayati*], v.t. **1.** to cause suffering or distress; to oppress, to persecute. **2.** to torment, to torture. **3.** to trouble, to annoy; to interrupt, to plague (one who is busy, &c). **4.** to tease.

सतालू *satālū* [P. *śaftālū*], m. a kind of peach.

सतावर *satāvar*, m. a thorny plant which yields a tonic drug from its roots or tubers.

सती *satī* [S.], adj. f. & f. **1.** adj. virtuous, faithful (a wife). **2.** f. a virtuous or faithful wife. **3.** *hist.* a widow who burns herself along with her husband's body. **4.** a title of Durgā or Pārvatī. — ~ **होना**, to be a faithful wife: to burn oneself along with one's dead husband's body, to commit suttee; fig. (a wife) to slave (for husband or child). – **सती-चौरा**, m. monument to a woman burnt with her dead husband. **सती-साध्वी**, adj. f. faithful and devoted (a wife). **सतीव्रता**, f. a woman who has vowed faithfulness: = ~, 1., 2. **सती-वाड़** [*vāṭī-*], f. *Pl.* = **सती-चौरा**.

सतीत्व *satītvă* [S.], m. virtue, faithfulness (of a wife). — ~ **बिगाड़ना**, or **नष्ट करना**, to violate (a married woman, **का**).

सतील *satīl* [cf. *śakti-*], adj. *Pl.* strong.

सतुआ *satuā* [cf. H. *sattū*], m. & adj. inv. dimin. **1.** m. = **सत्तू**. **2.** adj. non-fibrous: ~ **सोंठ**, f. non-fibrous ginger. — ~ **झाड़ना**, colloq. to beat (a person) to a pulp. — **सतुआ-संक्रांति**, f. transit of the sun into the sign Aries (on which day *sattū* meal is traditionally given to brāhmaṇs).

सतून *satūn* [P. *sutūn*], m. *Pl. HŚS.* a pillar.

सतूना *satūnā* [P. *sitūna*], m. Brbh. attack, stoop (of a bird of prey).

सतोगुण *satoguṇ*, m. corr. = **सत्त्व**, 7.

सतोड़ा *satoṛā* [? H. [3]*sat*+H. *toṛā*], adj. & m. *Pl.* **1.** adj. destroyed, annihilated (cf. **सत्यानाश** s.v. **सत्या-**). **2.** m. utter destruction.

सत्त *satt* [ad. *sattva-*], m. **1.** heart, essence, cream (as of an edible product); sap, pith. **2.** vigour, energy. **3.** spirit, courage. 4. = **सत्त्व**, 7. — ~ **छोड़ना**, or **हारना**, to lose heart. ~ **निकलना**, to lose strength or vigour, to become exhausted.

सत्तमी *sattămī* [ad. *saptamī-*], f. the seventh day of a lunar fortnight.

सत्तर *sattar* [cf. *saptati-*; Pa. *sattari-*], adj. seventy.

सत्तरवाँ *sattarvāṁ*, adj. **1.** [cf. H. *sattar*] seventieth. **2.** pronun. var. seventeenth (= **सत्रहवाँ**).

सत्तरह *sattrah*, adj. pronun. var. see **सत्रह**.

सत्तरा-बहत्तरा *sattrā-bahattrā* [cf. H. *sattar*, H. *bahattar*], adj. & m. colloq. **1.** adj. old, ancient (a man); old man's (talk). **2.** m. a dotard.

[1]**सत्ता** *sattā* [S.], f. **1.** existence, being. **2.** power, authority (political or administrative). **3.** sovereignty. **4.** *pol.* a power, a state. — ~ **चलाना** (**पर**), to control with effective authority, to hold sway (over). – **सत्ता-ग्रहण**, seizing or seizure of power; coup. **सत्ताधारी**, adj. holding power, having authority. **सत्तानशीन** [P. *-niśīn*], adj. established in power. **सत्तारूढ़** [°*tā*+*ā*°], adj. risen to power; come to power (a government or party). **सत्तावादी**, adj. & m. authoritarian, autocratic; an autocrat.

[2]**सत्ता** *sattā* [*saptaka-*], m. **1.** an aggregate of seven. **2.** a seven (at cards, dice).

सत्ताईस *sattāīs* [*saptaviṁśati-*], adj. twenty-seven.

सत्तानवे *sattānăve* [*saptanavati-*], adj. ninety-seven.

सत्तावन *sattāvan* [cf. *saptapañcāśat-*], adj. fifty-seven.

सत्तासी *sattāsī* [*saptāśīti-*, Pk. *sattāsīiṁ*], adj. eighty-seven.

सत्तू *sattū* [*saktu-*], m. coarse flour made from parched grain (barley, gram, &c). — ~ **बाँधकर पीछे पड़ना**, fig. to pursue (a person, or a goal) obsessively at much cost.

सत्त्व *sattvă* [S.], m. **1.** existence, being; essence, life. **2.** natural property or properties, character. **3.** thing, substance. **4.** living being, creature. **5.** a phantasmal being: demon, monster. **6.** vital energy, vigour; courage; self-possession. **7.** purity, goodness; specif. *philos.* the quality (*guṇa*) of purity or goodness (one of the three constituents of nature (*prakṛti*)).

सत्त्वता *sattvătā* [S.], f. purity, goodness, the property of *sattva* (q.v., 7).

सत्यं *satyaṁ* [S.], adv. truly, in truth, yes.

सत्य *satyă* [S.], adj. & m. **1.** adj. true. **2.** real, genuine; sincere, faithful (a friend). **3.** pure, virtuous, good. **4.** fulfilled, realised (as hopes). **5.** m. truth. **6.** reality; ultimate reality. **7.** goodness, virtue; sincerity. **8.** a true fact or conclusion. **9.** a statement under oath. **10.** *mythol.* name of the first of the four ages (*yuga*) constituting a recurrent cycle of time (*mahāyuga*); the golden age. — **सत्यकाम**, adj. & m. truth-loving; a lover of truth; one whose deeds are good. **सत्य-निष्ठ**, adj. truthful; just. °**आ**, f. **सत्य-युग**, m. see ~, 10. °**ई**, adj. having to do with the *satya-yug*; immemorially ancient; uncorrupted, of pristine virtue. **सत्य-लोक**, m. *mythol.* world of truth: name of the uppermost of the seven superior worlds, the heaven of Brahmā (from which the souls of men are not reborn). **सत्यवाद**, m. truthfulness. °**ई**, adj. & m. truthful; true (to one's word); a truthful person, &c. **सत्यवान**, adj. & m. true (in deed); truthful (in speech); name (in legend) of the husband of Sāvitrī. **सत्यव्रत**, adj. & m. devoted to a vow of truthfulness: truthful; honest, sincere; a vow of truthfulness. **सत्यशील**, adj. of truthful, faithful or loyal nature. °**ता**, f.

सत्यसंकल्प, adj. & m. true to one's resolve or promise; one who is true to his word. सत्याग्रह [°ya+ā], m. insistence on, or zeal for, truth: organised, non-violent protest having a political aim; non-violent resistance; civil disobedience. °ई, m. a non-violent protester, &c. सत्यात्मा [°ya+ā], adj. & m. inv. whose soul is true: upright, virtuous; an upright person, &c. सत्यार्थ [°ya+a], m. true goal or purpose: truth. °ई, adj. & m. whose goal is truth; one seeking truth.

सत्यता *satyătā* [S.], f. the quality of being true, &c. (see सत्य).

सत्या- *satyā-* [? ad. S. *satya-*; × *sattva-*]. truth, reality (= सत्य): — सत्यानाश, m. total destruction, ruin (of character, or prosperity, or hopes). सत्यानाश करना, to cause the utter ruin (of, का); to ruin the reputation (of). सत्यानाश जाना, or होना (का), to be ruined, &c. सत्यानाशी, adj. & m. ruined: wicked, depraved; destructive; wretched; a ruined man, &c.; one who brings ruin.

सत्यापन *satyāpan* [S.], m. verification, ratification.

सत्यापित *satyāpit* [S.], m. verified, ratified.

सत्र *satr* [ad. *sattra-*], m. **1.** session (as of courts, parliament). **2.** term (academic). **3.** place where food is distributed, an alms-house. — ~ न्यायालय, m. sessions court.

सत्रह *satrah* [cf. *saptadaśa*; Pa. *sattarasa*], adj. seventeen.

सत्व *satva*, m. pronun. var. see सत्त्व.

सत्वर *sa-tvar* [S.], adj. & adv. swift; swiftly; suddenly.

सत्वरता *sa-tvarătā* [S.], f. swiftness; suddenness.

सथराना *sathrānā* [cf. *saṁstarati*], v.t. reg. to strew, to scatter.

सथराव *sathrāv* [cf. H. *sathrānā*], m. reg. scattering; a heap, pile.

[1]**सथिया** *sathiyā* [*svastika-*], m. an auspicious sign, swastika mark.

[2]**सथिया** *sathiyā* [*śastr̥-*], m. *Pl. HŚS.* a surgeon.

[1]**सद** *sad* [? ad. *sadya-*], adj. E.H. fresh (of produce).

[2]**सद** *sad* [ad. *sadā*], adv. Brbh. always.

[3]**सद** *sad*, f. Brbh. predilection, weakness (? or = [2]सद).

सद्- *sad-* [S]. = सत्: — सद्गुरु, m. a true or virtuous guru; the only true guru, God. सद्गति, f. good state or condition; good behaviour; good fortune; beatitude. सद्गुण adj. & m. having good qualities, virtuous; a good quality, &c. सद्ग्रंथ, m. a good or holy book. सद्भाव, m. good or virtuous disposition; good feeling. सद्भाव सहित, adv. with compliments. °भावना, f. good feeling, good will. सदाचार, m. righteous or moral conduct; courteous demeanour; approved usage; transf. traditional observance, immemorial custom. °इता, f. righteousness, morality. °ई, adj. & m. righteous, moral, &c.; a virtuous man, &c.

सदक़ा *sadqā* [A. *ṣadqa*], m. **1.** alms. ***2.** an offering (to avert misfortune). — सदक़े, interj. my life is yours! – सदक़े उतारना, to exorcise (an evil spirit) by making an offering. सदक़े जाना, *musl.* = बलि जाना. – सदक़े-वारी, interj. = सदक़े.

सदन *sadan* [S.], m. a seat: **1.** residence; mansion; palace. **2.** house, chamber (of a parliament). **3.** shelter, hospice.

सदना *sadnā* [conn. *syandate*], v.i. *Pl. HŚS.* reg. to leak (as a ship), to sink.

सदमा *sadmā* [A. *ṣadma*], m. **1.** shock; blow. **2.** fig. a misfortune. — ~ उठाना, to suffer a shock or blow. ~ पहुँचाना, to cause (one) to receive a shock or blow. सदमे में, adv, in a state of shock. सदमे से, adv. with a shock, violently.

सदय *sa-day* [S.], adj. compassionate; kind, gentle.

सदर *sadr* [A. *ṣadr*], m. & adj. **1.** m. chief, head (of an organisation or body); chairman. **2.** headquarters. **3.** military cantonment. ***4.** adj. chief, principal, main (gate, market, magistrate, &c). — ~ अदालत, f. Supreme Court. ~ मक़ाम, m. headquarters (as of a district). ~ मालगुज़ार, m. *hist.* headman of a village of *mālguzārī* tenure.

सदरी *sadrī* [P. *ṣadrī*], f. a waistcoat, or jacket.

सदस् *sadas* [S.], m. *Pl. HŚS.* seat: assembly, meeting.

सदस्य *sadasyă* [S.], m. member (of a society or group); participant (in a meeting, a movement).

सदस्यता *sadasyătā* [S.], f. membership.

[1]**सदा** *sadā* [S.], adv. always; continually. — ~ के लिए, adv. for ever. ~ से, adv. for a long time down to the present; from the first. ~ का, adj. perpetual; constant, regular. – सदा-काल, adv. at all times. (= ~). सदा-क्वाँरी, f. a woman long unmarried; also iron. सदा-गति, f. the supreme spirit; release from the world. सदागुलाब, m. the China rose. सदानंद [°dā+ā°], adj. always, or eternally, happy. सदाफल, m. always bearing fruit: a name given to the shaddock (a citrus

fruit) and several other fruits. सदा-बहार, adj. evergreen; always flowering; perennial. सदावर्त [*vrata-*], m. the observance or act of distributing alms or food daily to the poor; alms or food so distributed. °ई, adj. one who has taken a vow to distribute alms, &c., daily; generous, munificent. सदाशिव, adv. always happy or prosperous; a title of Mahādev. सदा-सुहागिन, f. a woman whose husband is alive (also iron.); ? name of a white flower, *Hibiscus phoeniceus*. सदा-हज़ूरगनी, f. name of a small plant, *Phyllanthus Niruri* (?? = भुई आँवला). सदैव [°*dā*+*e*°], adv. emphat. always (= ~ ही).

²**सदा** *sadā* [A. *ṣadā*], f. **1.** sound; voice; echo. **2.** [× *śabda-*: /sədda/] invitation (as to a marriage).

सदाई *sadāī* [cf. H. *sadā*], f. (esp. as adv.) the continuing future; perpetuity.

सदाक़त *sadāqat* [A. *ṣadāqa*: P. *ṣadāqat*], f. **1.** sincerity; candour. **2.** loyalty (as of a friend).

सदानंद *sadānand*, adj. see s.v. सदा.

सदारत *sadārat* [A. *ṣadāra*: P. *ṣadārat*], f. esp. U. premiership; chief office. — ~ करना, to preside (as over a meeting, की).

सदिया *sadiyā*. **1.** f. the waxbill or red munia, *Estrilda amandava*. **2.** (?) m. [cf. *śabda-*; ← Panj. *sadd*], reg. a kind of ascetic.

सदी *sadī* [P. *ṣadī*], f. a century. — फ़ी ~ [A. *fī*], adv. per cent.

सदृश *sa-dṛś* [S.], adj. **1.** like, similar. **2.** fit, proper, suitable; worthy. **3.** ppn. w. के. similar (to); after the manner (of).

सदृशता *sa-dṛśătā* [S.], f. similarity.

सदेशी *sadeśī*, adj. & f. pronun. var. = स्वदेशी.

सदेह *sa-deh* [S.], adj. **1.** having a body; embodied, living. **2.** Brbh. personified; incarnate.

सदेही *sadehī* [cf. H. *sadeh*], adj. = सदेह.

सदैव *sadaiv* [S.], adv. see s.v. सदा.

सदोष *sa-doṣ* [S.], adj. **1.** having faults, defective. **2.** sinful. **3.** guilty.

सदोषी *sa-doṣī* [S.], adj. = सदोष.

सद्यः *sadyaḥ* [S.], adv. esp. in comp. on the same day: at, or of, the same time; just before, or after.

सधन *sa-dhan* [S.], adj. wealthy.

सधना *sadhnā* [cf. H. *sādhnā*], v.i. **1.** to be made; to be completed, perfected. **2.** to be trained (an animal). **3.** to be practised (as the hand). **4.** to be won over (= अपनाना). — सधा-सधाया, adj. tried and proved (as a remedy); reliable. सधी-बदी बात, f. a matter arranged and settled: a foregone conclusion.

सधर्म *sa-dharm* [S.], adj. = सधर्मी.

सधर्मिणी *sa-dharmiṇī* [S.], f. a wife married according to proper ritual; a lawful or virtuous wife.

सधर्मी *sa-dharmī* [S.], adj. & m. **1.** adj. having similar natures, or ritual and religious duties, &c. (see धर्म). **2.** m. one of the same community (as another). **3.** a co-religionist.

सधवा *sadhăvā* [S.], f. a wife whose husband is alive.

सधवाना *sadhvānā* [cf. H. *sādhnā*], v.t. to cause to be trained, &c. (by, से). (see सधाना).

सधाऊ *sadhāū* [cf. H. *sadhānā*], adj. trainable; tractable, docile.

सधाना *sadhānā* [cf. H. *sadhnā*], v.t. **1.** to bring to perfection, to perfect. **2.** to teach, to train (an animal). **3.** to train (the hand, &c).

सधाव *sadhāv* [cf. H. *sadhānā*], m. **1.** training; management. **2.** subjecting to discipline or control.

सधौर *sadhaur* [? **siddhapūra-*], f. reg. (W). craving of a pregnant woman.

¹**सन** *san* [*śaṇa-*], m. **1.** the plant *Crotalaria juncea* 'Indian hemp' (source of fibre). **2.** the plant *Cannabis sativa* (source of fibre, oil and a narcotic: *bhāṁg*, *caras*, *gañjā*).

²**सन** *san* [*svana-*], f. **1.** a vibrant and insistent sound: whizzing, whistling; swishing; singing (of a kettle); singing (in the ears); jingling; rustling. **2.** fig. [? × H. *sann*] thrill (of delight, &c). **3.** fig. [? × H. *sann*] darting pain (as of a boil). — ~ से, adv. with a whiz, &c.; quickly, all at once. – सन-सन करना, = सनसनाना.

³**सन** *san* [conn. *saṅga-*], ppn. Brbh. Av. **1.** with, together with. **2.** to, towards (of expression of feeling for, or of speech to, a person). **3.** away from, from. **4.** by (of agency).

⁴**सन्** *san* [A. *sana*], m. f. **1.** year (of a calendar). **2.** era. — ~ 1974 में, adv. in the year 1974. इस ~ में, adv. in this year. ईस्वी ~ में, adv. in the Christian era.

सनक *sanak* [cf. H. *sanaknā*], f. **1.** a whim; eccentricity. **2.** an obsession, or craze (with or for an activity); frenzy. — ~ चढ़ना (को), = next. ~ सवार होना (पर), a craze or passion (for, की) to obsess (one).

सनकना *sanaknā* [cf. *svanati*], v.i. **1.** to make a subdued noise or sound: to ring (the head);

to whizz (an arrow); to sing (a kettle). **2.** to become slightly drunk. **3.** to go crazy; to act crazily.

सनकी *sankī* [cf. H. *sanaknā*], adj. **1.** eccentric. **2.** crazy.

सनकीपन *sankīpan* [cf. H. *sankī*], m. **1.** eccentricity. **2.** crazy behaviour.

सनद *sanad* [A. *sanad*], f. anything rested or leant upon: **1.** an authoritative document; a deed, &c. **2.** certificate, diploma. — इसकी ~ कहाँ है? where is the authority, or precedent, for this (act, view)? – सनदयाफ़्ता [P. *-yāfta*], adj. holding a deed, or a certificate; accredited.

सनदी *sanadī* [A. *sanad*+P. *-ī*], adj. **1.** authentic. **2.** certificated, accredited.

सनना *sannā* [cf. H. *sānnā*], v.i. **1.** to be mixed (into, में: as water into flour). **2.** to be dirtied, soaked (as a garment in mud). **3.** to be mixed, or kneaded (as dough, earth). **4.** to be smeared (with, से). **5.** to be imbued or pregnant (with emotion: words, &c).

सनम *sanam* [A. *ṣanam*], m. **1.** idol. **2.* sweetheart.

सनमान *sanmān* [ad. *sammmāna-*: × *sanmāna-*], m. Brbh. Av. = सम्मान.

सनमान- *sanmān-* [ad. *sammmānayati*: × H. *sanmān*], v.t. Av. = सम्मान करना.

सनमानी *sanmānī* [cf. H. *sanmān*], adj. reg. respectful.

सनमुख *sanmukh*, adj. Av. = सम्मुख.

सनसन *sansan* [cf. H. *sansanānā*], f. **1.** a whizzing, or whistling sound, &c. **2.** a tingling feeling, &c.

सनसनाना *sansanānā* [cf. H. ²*san*], v.i. **1.** to make a whizzing or whistling sound; to sing, to simmer (a kettle); to hiss; to rustle. **2.** to tingle; to thrill (as with delight, or fear); to be beside oneself (with delight, or anger).

सनसनाहट *sansanāhaṭ* [cf. H. *sansanānā*], f. **1.** a whistling or whizzing sound, &c. **2.** a tingling sensation (see सनसनाना).

सनसनी *sansanī* [cf. H. *san*], f. a tingling sensation; thrill (of delight, or apprehension). — सनसनीख़ेज़ [P. *-khez*], adj. causing a thrill, exciting; sensational. सनसनीदार [P. *-dār*], adj. id.

सनाका *sanākā*, m. sound of movement. — ~ मारना, to make a rushing sound.

सनातन *sanātan* [S.], adj. existing from of old, immemorial; continuing, eternal. — ~ धर्म, m. immemorial *dharma*: Hinduism as involving acceptance of *śruti* and *smṛti*, orthodox belief and practice. – सनातन-धर्मी, m. one who accepts the *sanātan dharm*.

सनातनी *sanātanī* [cf. H. *sanātan*], adj. & m. **1.** adj. = सनातन. **2.** accepting the *sanātan dharm*. **3.** m. = सनातन-धरमी.

सनाथ *sa-nāth* [S.], adj. **1.** having a master or protector. **2.** having a husband.

सनापत *sanāpat* [? ad. *saṁnipāta-*], f. reg. a massacre.

सनाह *sanāh* [*saṁnāha-*], m. Av. armour, arms.

सनी *sanī* [*śaṇa-*], f. fine hemp.

सनीचर *sanīcar* [conn. *śanaiścara-*: Pk. *saṇiccara-*], m. slow-going: **1.** the planet Saturn. **2.** Saturday. **3.** fig. ill-luck. **4.** fig. euph. a strong drive, or energy. — ~ आना, Saturn's influence to come (upon, के सिर); misfortune to befall (one). पाँव में ~ होना, to be constantly on the move, to be restless by temperament. सिर पर ~ सवार होना, to be driven or possessed. – सनीचरवार, m. = ~, 2.

सनीचरा *sanīcārā* [cf. H. *sanīcar*], adj. & m. **1.** adj. having to do with Saturn, or with Saturday. **2.** fig. unlucky. **3.** m. an unlucky person.

सनीचरी *sanīcārī* [cf. H. *sanīcar*], f. *astrol.* Brbh. association with Saturn. मीन की ~, f. presence of Saturn in Pisces.

सनोढ़िया *sanoṛhiyā*, m. **1.** name of a brāhmaṇ community. **2.** a member of the Sanoṛhiyā community.

सनोबर *sanobar* [A. *ṣanaubar*], m. a conifer; a pine tree.

सन्न *sann* [? cf. H. *sannānā*], adj. **1.** numbed, paralysed (with fear, consternation). **2.** silent, speechless.

सन्नति *san-nati* [ad. *saṁnati-*], f. bowing down.

सन्नद्ध *san-naddh* [ad. *saṁnaddha-*], adj. bound together: **1.** armed, equipped; fig. ready. **2.** adjacent, contiguous.

सन्नाटा *sannāṭā* [? *saṁnaṣṭa-*; also H. *sannānā*], m. **1.** dead silence; stillness. **2.** a numbing blow; shock. **3.** state of fear, or consternation; stunned amazement. **4.** a penetrating sound (having a numbing, or stunning effect: as of wind, or rain). — ~ खींचना, to fall, or to become, quite silent. ~ आना (को), to receive a shock; to be utterly amazed; to be numb with fear; to faint. ~ छाना, dead silence to reign. ~ गुज़रना (पर), = next. ~ बीतना (पर), a shock to be felt (by). सन्नाटे का, adv. violent, terrible; shocking; fearsome; desolate; still. सन्नाटे में आना, to fall silent; = ~ आना, 1.-3.

सन्नाना *sannānā* [cf. *saṁnādayati*], v.i. to resound, &c. (= सनसनाना).

सन्नासी *sannāsī*, m. pronun. var. = सन्यासी.

सन्नाह *san-nāh*, adj. Brbh. = सनाह.

सन्निकट *san-ni-kaṭ* [ad. *saṁnikaṭa-*], adj. very close (to, के), adjacent.

सन्निकर्ष *san-ni-karṣ* [S.], m. drawing near: **1.** close contact, connection. **2.** near vicinity; presence.

सन्निध *san-ni-dh* [ad. *saṁnidha-*], m. proximity, vicinity.

सन्निधान *san-ni-dhān* [ad. *saṁnidhāna-*], m. **1.** being placed together: nearness, vicinity. **2.** receptacle.

सन्निपात *san-ni-pāt* [ad. *saṁnipāta-*], m. **1.** a collapse, collision; conjunction (of events, planets, influences). **2.** *ayur.* disorder of bodily humours.

सन्निविष्ट *san-ni-viṣṭ* [ad. *saṁniviṣṭa-*], adj. seated together: **1.** assembled; encamped. **2.** near, neighbouring. **3.** inserted.

सन्निवेश *san-ni-veś* [ad. *saṁniveśa-*], m. sitting together: **1.** assembly, assembling. **2.** situation, position. **3.** insertion; inclusion.

सन्निहित *san-ni-hit* [ad. *saṁnihita-*], adj. **1.** placed near together; near, adjacent. **2.** prepared, made ready. **3.** included, contained; involved.

सन्मार्ग *sanmārg* [ad. *saṁmārga-*], m. right road or path.

सन्यास *sanyās*, m. = संन्यास.

सन्यासी *sanyāsī*, m. = संन्यासी.

सपंग *sapaṅg* [cf. H. *apaṅg*], adj. complete, entire.

सपक्ष *sa-pakṣ* [S.], adj. & m. **1.** adj. having wings, winged. **2.** m. belonging to the same party (as); an adherent, ally.

सपड़ना *sapaṛnā* [*saṁpatati*], v.i. reg. = सपरना.

सपड़-सपड़ *sapaṛ-sapaṛ* [onom.], f. lapping. — ~ ~ करके खाना, to lap up.

सपड़ाना *sapṛānā*, v.t. reg. = सपराना.

सपत्नीक *sa-patnīk* [S.], adj. together with (one's) wife.

सपदि *sa-padi* [S.], adv. Av. at the same moment; at once.

सपना *sapnā* [? ad. *svapna-*], m. **1.** a dream. **2.** fig. a vision, longing. — ~ दिखाई देना (को), to have a dream.

सपरदाई *sapardāī* [ad. *sampradāyī-*], m. *Pl.* member of a troupe: musical accompanist (of women singers or dancing-girls).

सपरना *saparnā* [*sampatati*], v.i. **1.** to be caught, or involved (in). ***2.** [← H. *saprānā*], to be finished, concluded (work, a task).

सपराना *saprānā* [*sampātayati*; ? × *sampādayati*], v.t. *HŚS.* to finish, to conclude (work, a task).

सपरिवार *sa-pari-vār* [S.], adj. along with, or accompanied by, (one's) family. — आशा है, आप ~ कुशल हैं, (I) hope you and your family are well.

सपर्दा *sapardā*, m. *Pl.* = सपरदाई.

सपलाई *saplāī* [Engl. *supply*], f. supply (of a commodity).

सपल्लव *sa-pallav* [S.], adj. **1.** having foliage. **2.** together with (its) foliage.

सपाट *sapāṭ* [? cf. H. [1]*pāṭ*], adj. & m. **1.** adj. flat; level; smooth. **2.** levelled, smoothed. **3.** horizontal. **4.** m. level ground.

सपाटा *sapāṭā*, m. **1.** a leap, spring, bound; speed of motion. **2.** a quick or forced march. — ~ भरना, or मारना, or लगाना, to spring, to bound; to rush. सपाटे का, adj. quick (of motion, musical time). सपाटे से, or के साथ, दौड़ना, to run swiftly, to rush.

सपाद *sapād* [S.], adj. = सवा.

सपिंड *sa-piṇḍ* [S.], adj. & m. **1.** adj. *hind.* having the same *piṇḍa*, connected by the same funeral offering: related in direct line of ascent or descent. **2.** m. one entitled to *piṇḍa* (from others of the same group): any man in a direct line of ascent or descent extending over seven generations.

सपिंडी *sa-piṇḍī* [cf. H. *sapiṇḍ*], adj. & m. = सपिंड. — ~ रिश्ता, m. id.

सपीना *sapīnā* [Engl. *subpoena*], m. subpoena.

सपुत्र *sa-putr* [S.], adj. **1.** having a son. **2.** accompanied by a son.

सपूत *sapūt* [? **satputra-*], adj. & m. **1.** adj. good, dutiful (a son). **2.** m. a good son.

सपूती *sapūtī* [cf. H. *sapūt*], f. **1.** goodness or virtue in a son. **2.** a mother who has a good son.

सपेला *sapelā* [? **sarpatara-*], m. reg. a young snake (= सपोला).

सपोला *sapolā*, m. pronun. var. = सँपोला.

सप्त- *sapt-* [S.], adj. seven: — सप्त-ऋषि, m. = next. सप्तर्षि [°a+ṛ°], m. pl. the seven stars (supposed to represent seven great sages) of the Great Bear. सप्तदश, adj. seventeenth. सप्त-दीप, m. Brbh. *mythol.* the seven divisions of the world, the whole world. सप्तपदी, f. the seven steps (round the sacred fire) at marriage; the seven perambulations (of the sacred fire) which conclude the Hindu marriage ceremony. सप्तशती, f. a group or total of seven hundred (esp. verses). सप्ताह [°ta+a°], m. see s.v.

सप्तक *saptak* [S.], m. **1.** a group of seven, heptad. **2.** *mus.* an octave.

सप्तदश *saptadaś* [S.], adj. see s.v. सप्त.

सप्तम् *saptam* [S.], adj. seventh.

सप्तमी *saptămī* [S.], f. **1.** the seventh day of a lunar fortnight. **2.** *gram.* locative case.

सप्ताह *saptâh* [S.], m. seven days: a week. सप्ताह-पारायण, m. the ceremony of reading through the *Bhāgavata Purāṇa* in seven days. सप्ताह-यज्ञन, m. id. सप्ताहांत [°ha+a°], m. weekend.

सप्रमाण *sa-pra-māṇ* [S.], adj. accompanied by proof: convincing (an account); proven, demonstrated.

सप्राण *sa-prāṇ* [S.], adj. having life, animate.

सप्रीति *sa-prīti* [S.], adj. having affection, affectionate.

सप्लाई *saplāī* [Engl. *supply*], f. supply.

सफ़ *saf* [A. *ṣaff*], f. **1.** row, line. **2.** reg. a long mat; bedding.

सफ़र *safar* [A. *safar*], m. **1.** travelling. **2.** a journey. — ~ करना, to make a journey; to travel. ~ तय करना, to complete a journey.

सफर *saphra* [ad. *śapharī-*: dimin.], f. a small gold-coloured fish (see शफर).

[1]**सफ़री** *safărī* [P. *safarī*], adj. & f. **1.** adj. pertaining to a journey (as expenses, equipment, experiences). **2.** movable, mobile (as a field hospital or similar unit); expeditionary (force). **3.** f. provisions for a journey.

[2]**सफ़री** *safărī* [P. *safarī*], m. a traveller.

सफल *sa-phal* [S.], adj. **1.** fruitful; profitable. **2.** successful. **3.** fulfilled (in this life). — ~ होना, or हो जाना, to succeed. सफलीभूत, adj. realised, concluded successfully (as an arrangement); having achieved (one's) purpose, successful.

सफलता *sa-phalătā* [S.], f. **1.** fruitfulness. **2.** successfulness, success.

सफलीभूत *saphalībhūt* [S.], adj. see s.v. सफल.

सफ़हा *safhā* [A. *ṣafha*], m. U. a page, leaf (of a book).

सफ़ा *safā* [A. *ṣafā*], adj. inv. **1.** clean, pure (= साफ़). **2.** colloq. cleaned out, empty (the pocket). **3.** सफ़ा-. cleansing. — सफ़ाचट, adj. licked clean: bare (a plate); eaten up (food); shaved clean (head, beard); made smooth (any surface); run through (money). सफ़ाचट करना, to clean up, to make a clean sweep.

सफ़ाया *safāyā*, m. sweeping clear, removing.

सफ़ाई *safāī* [P. *ṣafāī*], f. **1.** clearness. **2.** cleanness. **3.** cleanliness. **4.** cleaning; tidying. **5.** openness, sincerity. **6.** freedom from guilt or fault; defence (at law). **7.** settlement (of an account); adjustment (of a difference). **8.** laying waste; destruction. **9.** dexterity. — ~ करना (की), to clean; to make a clean sweep (of: as in plundering, or razing); to settle, to adjust; colloq. to clean up (food); to offer a defence (at law). ~ जताना, to demonstrate one's blamelessness. ~ देना, to put forward a defence (to an accusation). ~ से, adv. candidly; dextrously. ~ होना (की), to be cleaned, &c. (see ~ करना); to be exonerated; colloq. to be shaved clean.

सफ़ाया *safāyā* [f. H. *safā*, or H. *safāī*], m. a clean sweep (of, का).

सफ़ीर *safīr* [A. *safīr*], m. U. ambassador; envoy; consul.

सफ़ेद *safed* [P. *safed*], adj. **1.** white; grey (the hair). **2.** pale-coloured (as dawn light, or chalky soil). **3.** clean (as light-coloured clothing); blank (paper). — ~ कद्दू, m. the sweet pumpkin (= कुम्हड़ा, पेठा). ~ करनाे, to whiten. ~ झूठ, f. an arrant lie. ~ दाग़, m. white leprosy. ~ पड़ जाना or होना, to turn pale or wan (the face, through illness or fear); to grow grey (hair). ~ मिट्टी, f. chalky soil; chalk. ~ संबुल [A. *sumbul*], m. white oxide of arsenic. लहू ~ होना, the blood to turn white: to grow cold or indifferent. – सफ़ेदपोश [P. *-poś*], adj. dressed in white; well-to-do. °ई, f.

सफ़ेदा *safedā* [P. *safeda*], m. **1.** a white mineral substance, esp. white lead (a compound of lead carbonate); chalk. **2.** a white discharge. **3.** a variety of mango; a variety of water-melon. **4.** white leprosy.

सफ़ेदी *safedī* [P. *safedī*], f. **1.** whiteness; greyness; pallor. **2.** whitewash. **3.** the white of an egg. **4.** reg. white leprosy. **5.** dawn light. — ~ करना (की), or फेरना (पर), to whitewash (also fig).

सब *sab* [*sarva-*], adj. & pron. **1.** pl. all (of a set or group); everybody. ~ जानते हैं, everyone knows. ~ से पहले, adv. first of all, first. **2.** entire (amount: = सारा). ~ खाना, all the food. **3.** every, each. ~ प्रकार से, adv. in every way. — ~ कहीं, adv. everywhere. ~ का, adj. general, common, public (as a duty, an opinion, &c). ~ का ~, m. & adv. the whole (of sthg.); altogether, entirely. ~ कुछ, pron. everything, all. ~ के ~, m. pl. & adv. all without exception, the lot (of sthg.); entirely, completely. ~ कोई, pron. everyone. ~ जगह, adv. everywhere. ~ मिलाकर, adv. taking all together, altogether. ~ ही, adj. & pron. every single (one), absolutely all.

सबक़ *sabaq* [A. *sabq*: P. *sabaq*], m. lesson. — ~ देना, or पढ़ाना (को), to give a lesson (to), to instruct. ~ लेना, to take a lesson (from, से), to be taught (by); fig. to learn a lesson (from: as from an experience).

सबतिया *sabatiyā*, adj. reg. = सौतिया.

सबद *sabad* [Panj. *sabad*], m. = शब्द, 4.

सबदरा *sabdarā*, m. *Pl.* bowsprit.

सबब *sabab* [P. *sabab*], m. a means of reaching or obtaining: **1.** m. cause. **2.** reason, motive. **3.** (ppn. with के) because, on account (of).

सबर्त *sabart*, m. *Pl.* a hare; rabbit.

सबल *sa-bal* [S.], adj. **1.** strong, powerful. **2.** *ling.* bearing a stress.

सबलता *sa-balătā* [S.], f. strength, &c. (see सबल).

सबलाई *sa-balāī* [cf. H. *sabal*], f. *Pl.* strength, power.

सबसबाना *sabsabānā* [? conn. *sarpati*], v.i. reg. to creep (like a snake).

सबा *sabā* [A. *ṣabā*], f. U. east wind: pleasant breeze.

सबील *sabīl* [A. *sabīl*], m. **1.** U. way, road; manner. **2.** *musl.* water or other drink given to passers-by during the month of Muḥarram.

सबूत *sabūt* [A. *ṣubūt*], m. proof, testimony. — ~ देना, to give testimony or evidence; to provide proof.

सबेर *saber*, adv. pronun. var. = सवेर.

सबेरा *saberā*, m. pronun. var. = सवेरा.

सबोतर *sabotar*, adv. *Pl.* everywhere.

सब्ज़ *sabz* [P. *sabz*], adj. **1.** green. **2.** fresh (as produce); flourishing. **3.** unripe. **4.** auspicious, lucky. **5.** dark (complexion, or coat: an animal). — ~ परी, f. the emerald fairy: one of four fairies represented in the *Indar Sabhā* of Amānat (c. 1850.) as attending Indra's court; lucky fairy; joc. *HŚS.* = लाल परी. ~ बाग़ दिखाना (को), to show a green or flourishing garden (to): to hold out deceptive hopes or promises.

सब्ज़ा *sabzā* [P. *sabza*], m. *Pl. HŚS.* **1.** greenery (= सब्ज़ी). **2.** term applied to several green or dark-coloured objects. 3. = भाँग.

सब्ज़ी *sabzī* [P. *sabzī*], f. **1.** greenery, foliage. ***2.** a vegetable. **3.** a vegetable dish, or curry. — सब्ज़ी-फ़रोश [P. *-faroś*], m. = सब्ज़ीवाला. सब्ज़ी-मंडी, f. vegetable market. सब्ज़ीवाला, m. a seller of vegetables; greengrocer.

सब्बल *sabbal*, m. (?) reg. a crowbar (= साबल).

सब्र *sabr* [A. *ṣabr*], m. patience; endurance. — ~ करना, to have patience; to bear up (under, में; to content oneself (with).

सभय *sa-bhay* [S.], adj. fearful, afraid.

सभा *sabhā* [S.], f. **1.** assembly, meeting, gathering. **2.** a society, association. **3.** a deliberative body: council; house, assembly (of parliament); राज्य ~, f. Council of States. विधान ~, f. Legislative Assembly. **4.** place of assembly, &c.: council, hall; levée. **5.** fig. deliberation. — ~ करना, to convene or to hold a meeting. भरी ~ में, adv. in a crowded meeting: in public. – सभाध्यक्ष [°*bhā+a*°], m. presiding officer of a meeting, or of a society, &c.; chairman. सभापति, m. id. °त्व, f. presidency, chairmanship. सभासद, m. member of a society, council, &c. °ई, f.

सभी *sabhī*, adj. = सब ही.

सभीत *sa-bhīt* [S.], adj. fearful, afraid; timid.

सभों *sabhoṁ*, pron. obl. pl. = सबों (see सब).

सभ्य *sabhyă* [S.], adj. **1.** cultivated, or educated in manner; polite. **2.** civilised.

सभ्यता *sabhyătā* [S.], f. **1.** cultivated, or educated manner; politeness. **2.** civilised state, civilisation.

समंजस *sam-añjas* [S.], adj. & m. *Pl. HŚS.* **1.** adj. proper, right, fit (for a purpose). **2.** correct, accurate, consistent. **3.** practised, skilled. ***4.** m. propriety, fitness. ***5.** consistency, agreement.

[1]**समंदर** *samandar*, m. = समुंदर, समुद्र.

[2]**समंदर** *samandar* [P. *samandar*], m. a salamander.

समंदरी *samandrī* [cf. H. [1]*samandar*], adj. = समुद्री.

सम्- *sam-* [S.], pref. **1.** with, together with (e.g. संयोग, m. chance; संस्था, f. organisation). **2.** (intensive) very, much; wholly; perfectly (e.g. संपूर्ण, adj. complete; समुन्नत, adj. fully developed; समीक्षा, f. review, assessment).

सम *sam* [S.], adj. & m. **1.** adj. even, level, flat. **2.** (often -सम). same, similar. तृणसम, adj. Av. like a blade of grass; of little account. **3.** all, whole, entire. **4.** *math.* even. **5.** m. adjustment, equilibrium. **6.** *mus.* the point where separate rhythms (of singer and instrumentalist) coincide. — समकक्ष, adj. of the same class, or category. °ता, f. समकालिक, adj. concerning the same time: contemporary. °ता, f. °-कालीन, adj. = समकालिक. °ता, f. समकोण, m. & adj. *geom.* a right angle; right-angled (a triangle); a rectangle. समचतुर्भुज, m. a quadrilateral having equal sides. समजातीय, adj. of the same kind or type; homogeneous. °ता, f. समतल, adj. level, even; plane (a surface). समदर्शी, adj. viewing equally: impartial, objective. समदृष्टि, f. even or equal view, impartial view. समदेशीय, adj. belonging to the same place, or country. समद्विबाहु, adj. having two equal arms: isosceles (a triangle). समनाम, adj. having the same name (as). समबाहु, adj. having equal arms: equilateral (triangle). समभाव, m. of similar nature: similarity, equality. समभुज, adj. having equal arms: equilateral (a triangle). समरस, adj. even, equable; harmonious. समरूप, adj. having the same form or shape (as); identical. समवयस्क, adj. & m. of the same age; a contemporary. समवर्ण, adj. of the same colour; of the same Hindu community. समवर्ती, adj. adjoining; contiguous. समवृत्त, m. *pros.* a type of metre having four similar feet. समवेदना, f. condolence, condolences. समसामयिक, adj. contemporary. समांग [°*ma*+*a*°], adj. having similar parts or constituents: homogeneous. समांतर [°*ma*+*a*°], adj. parallel (= समानांतर). समाधिकारी [°*ma*+*a*°], m. one having equal right or status; a co-heir. समीकरण, m. levelling, equalisation, adjustment; assimilation; *math.* an equation; *arith.* reducing fractions to a common denominator. °-ईकृत, adj. equalised, &c. समीचीन, adj. see s.v.

समई *samaī*, f. reg. (W.) the tube of a drill-plough.

समकक्ष *sam-kakṣ* [S.], m. see s.v. सम.

समकालिक *sam-kālik* [S.], adj. see s.v. सम.

समकालीन *sam-kālīn* [S.], adj. see s.v. सम.

समकोण *sam-koṇ* [S.], m. see s.v. सम.

समक्ष *sam-akṣ* [S.], adj. before the eyes (of, के); in the presence (of); visible.

समग्र *sam-agră* [S.], adj. all, entire; complete; total. — ~ रूप से, adv. in (its) entirety.

समग्रता *sam-agrătā*, f. entirety.

समचतुर्भुज *sam-caturbhuj* [S.], adj. see s.v. सम.

समजातीय *sam-jātīyă* [S.], adj. see s.v. सम.

समझ *samajh* [cf. H. *samajhnā*], f. **1.** understanding; mental grasp, intelligence; sense, judgment. **2.** mind; opinion, view. — ~ आना (को), to reach years of understanding or discretion; to recover (one's) senses. ~ पर पत्थर पड़ना, a stone to fall on the mind: to go out of (one's) mind. ~ में आना, to come into the understanding (of): to be understood, or perceived (by, की). मेरी ~ में, adv. to my mind, in my opinion. – समझदार [P. -*dār*], adj. discerning; intelligent; prudent. -ई, f. discernment, &c. समझ-बूझ, f. = ~, 1.

समझना *samajhnā* [*saṁbudhyate*], v.i. & v.t. **1.** v.i. to perceive, to understand; to think. **2.** v.t. to grasp, to understand (a matter, &c). **3.** to consider (a thing) to be the case, to consider (a person) as such. **4.** esp. w. लेना. to come to an understanding (with, से). **5.** esp. w. लेना. to settle accounts (with, से). — अच्छा ~, to think good: to prefer. आप समझे? do you understand? उलटा ~, to misunderstand. मैंने उसे अपना भाई समझा, I thought of him as my own brother. मैं समझता हूँ (कि) वह आ जाएगा, I think he'll come. समझकर, adv. = next. समझ-बूझकर, adv. in full knowledge; discreetly, with due caution; on purpose, intentionally.

समझाना *samjhānā* [cf. H. *samajhnā*], v.t. **1.** to cause to understand, to explain (to, को). **2.** to give (one) to know, to impress on the mind (of); to convince. **3.** to advise; to console. **4.** to admonish. **5.** to correct; to punish. — समझाना-बुझाना, = ~.

समझावा *samjhāvā* [cf. H. *samjhānā*], m. reg. **1.** explaining, instructing, &c. (see समझाना, 1.-3). **2.** an agreement.

समझौता *samjhautā*, m. **1.** an agreement, understanding. **2.** a compromise. **3.** conciliation. **4.** a pact, treaty. — ~ करना, to conclude an agreement (with, के साथ). — समझौताहीन, adj. uncompromising.

समझौती *samjhautī*, f. *Pl.* = समझौता, 1., 2.

समतल *sam-tal* [S.], adj. see s.v. सम.

समता *samătā* [S.], f. **1.** similarity; comparability. **2.** equality. **3.** harmony, compatibility (as of views, temperaments). **4.** equanimity.

समदर्शी *sam-darśī*, adj. see s.v. सम.

समदृष्टि *sam-dr̥ṣṭi* [S.], f. see s.v. सम.

समदेशीय *sam-deśīyă* [S.], adj. see s.v. सम.

समद्विबाहु *sam-dvibāhu* [S.], adj. see s.v. सम.

समधिन *samdhin* [*saṁbandhinī*-], f. mother of a son- or daughter-in-law.

समधियाना *samdhiyānā* [cf. H. *samdhī*], m. **1.** the relationship between two persons whose children are married to each other. **2.** the home or family of a child's father-in-law.

समधी *samdhī* [*sambandhin-*], m. father of a son- or daughter-in-law.

समन *saman* [Engl. *summons*], m. a summons (legal). — ~ जारी करना, to issue a summons.

समन्वय *sam-anv-ay* [S.], m. **1.** connection, succession, sequence. **2.** conjunction, union; coordination. **3.** falling together, coincidence, agreement (as of interests). — समन्वयकारी, adj. coordinating (as a committee).

समन्वयन *sam-anv-ayan* [S.], m. bringing together, coordinating; linking.

समन्वयी *sam-anv-ayī* [S.], adj. & m. **1.** adj. coordinating; integrating. **2.** m. coordinator, &c.

समन्वित *sam-anv-it* [S.], adj. **1.** connected, associated (with, से). **2.** combined (with), coordinated. **3.** fully endowed (with: as with a quality).

समपादकीय *sam-pādăkīyă* [S.], adj. & m. **1.** adj. editor's, editorial. **2.** m. an editorial, leading article.

समबाहु *sam-bāhu* [S.], adj. see s.v. सम.

समभाव *sam-bhāv* [S.], m. see s.v. सम.

समभुज *sam-bhuj* [S.], adj. see s.v. सम.

सममित *sam-mit* [S.], adj. measured out, of the same measure: **1.** like, similar (= समान). **2.** corresponding (as in size, shape); conformable. **3.** symmetrical.

समय *sam-ay* [S.], m. **1.** time. **2.** proper time; opportunity; due time, term. **3.** period, season; age; times (in general). **4.** date, dates (as of a writer's birth and death). **5.** leisure. **6.** obs. chapter, canto (of a narrative poem). — ~ पड़ने से, adv. on occasion arising. ~ पर, adv. on time, punctually. ~ पाकर, adv. on obtaining an opportunity. ~ ~, adv. from time to time. ~ ~ पर, adv. id.; at certain times; according to the times. ~ से पहले, adv. prematurely. इस ~, adv. at this time, now. इस ~ में, adv. id. किस ~? at what time? when? किसी ~, adv. at some time; once upon a time. कुछ ~ के लिए, adv. for some time. ठीक ~ पर, adv. = ~ पर. बहुत ~ से, adv. for, since, a long time; long ago. – समय-तालिका, f. timetable. समय-सारिणी, f. timetable. समयानुकूल [°*ya*+*a*°], adj. timely. समयोचित [°*ya*+*u*°], adj. suited to the time: timely, expedient. समयोपरि, m. overtime (work).

समयौ *samayau*, m. Brbh. = समय.

समयौन *sam-yaun* [S.], adj. lesbian.

[1]**समर** *sam-ar* [S.], m. clash: war; battle. — समर-भूमि, f. battle-field.

[2]**समर** *samar* [A. *samar*], m. U. fruit: — समर-बहिश्त, m. fruit of paradise: a type of mango.

समरस *sam-ras* [S.], adj. see s.v. सम.

समराट् *sam-rāṭ* [S.], m. emperor.

समरूप *sam-rūp*, adj. see s.v. सम.

समर्थ *sam-arth* [S.], adj. **1.** capable, competent. **2.** suitable (for a purpose). **3.** powerful. — कहने में ~, adj. capable of speaking, or pronouncing (as a child).

समर्थक *sam-arthak* [S.], adj. & m. **1.** adj. lending strength, supporting; favouring. **2.** m. supporter (of a policy, a cause, a team); seconder (of a motion).

समर्थता *sam-arthătā* [S.], f. = सामर्थ्य.

समर्थन *sam-arthan* [S.], m. **1.** support (in, में: as in an effort, an endeavour). **2.** confirmation. — ~ करना, to confirm (a statement, &c.); to give support (to, का). ~ देना, to support (one, को: as in an argument).

समर्थनीय *sam-arthănīyă* [S.], adj. deserving support.

समर्थित *sam-arthit* [S.], adj. supported, &c. (see समर्थन).

समर्पण *sam-arpaṇ* [S.], m. **1.** entrusting. **2.** handing over, &c. (see समर्पित); dedicating, dedication. **3.** *law.* assignment, transfer.

समर्पना *sam-arpnā* [ad. *samarpayati*; cf. H. *samarpaṇ*], v.t. reg. to entrust, to deliver, &c.

समर्पित *sam-arpit* [S.], adj. **1.** entrusted, committed (to, को). **2.** handed over, presented; surrendered; dedicated (to). **3.** *law.* made over, assigned (to). **4.** consigned, despatched. — ~ करना, to entrust, &c.

समर्पै *sam-arpai* [ad. *samarpita-*; cf. H. *saumpnā*], adj. reg. = समर्पित.

समल *sa-mal* [S.], adj. **1.** dirty. **2.** filthy, foul.

समलिंगी *sam-liṅgī* [S.], adj. & m. = समलैंगिक.

समलैंगिक *sam-laiṅgik* [S.], adj. & m. **1.** adj. homosexual. **2.** m. a homosexual man.

समलैंगिकता *sam-laiṅgikătā* [S.], f. homosexuality.

समवयस्क *sam-vayask* [S.], adj. see s.v. सम.

समवर्ण *sam-varṇ* [S.], adj. see s.v. सम.

समवर्ती *sam-vartī* [S.], adj. see s.v. सम.

समवाय *sam-ăvāy* [S.], m. a coming together: **1.** a collection, assemblage. **2.** a limited company.

समवृत्त *sam-vr̥tt* [S.], adj. see s.v. **सम**.

समवेत *sam-ăvêt* [S.], adj. come together: united, collective. –. ~ **गान**, m. chorus.

समवेदना *sam-vedănā* [S.], f. see s.v. **सम**.

समष्टि *sam-aṣṭi* [S.], f. **1.** an entire group (as distinct from its members); collectivity. **2.** *hind.* a meal provided for the ascetics of a locality. — **समष्टिवाचक**, adj. *gram.* collective. **समष्टिवाद**, m. collectivism. °**ई**, adj.

समसान *samsān*, m. pronun. var. = **श्मशान**.

समसामयिक *sam-sāmăyik* [S.], adj. see s.v. **सम**.

समस्त *sam-ast* [S.], adj. thrown or put together: **1.** all, whole, entire. **2.** joined into a single unit (as a compound word); contracted, abbreviated.

समस्या *sam-asyā* [S.], f. junction, union: **1.** the latter half of a verse (provision of a first part for which forms a test of poetic skill). ***2.** a problem. — ~ **उठाना**, to raise or to pose a problem. – **समस्या-पूर्ति**, f. completing a verse, meeting a test (see 1. above). **समस्यामूलक**, adj. problematic.

समाँ *samāṁ* [*samaya-*], m. **1.** time; season; times, period (of time, history). **2.** opportunity. **3.** (also f.) scene, view. — **समाँ बँधना**, time to be stopped: a mood to be created (as by music, drama, song).

समांग *samâṅg* [S.], adj. see s.v. **सम**.

समांतर *samântar* [S.], adj. see s.v. **सम**.

समा *samā* [A. *samā*], m. f. the sky.

समाई *samāī* [cf. H. *samānā*], f. **1.** the act of containing or holding. **2.** room, space; capacity (of a hall). **3.** volume (of a container). **4.** capability.

समाऊ *samāū* [cf. H. *samānā*], adj. able to contain: **1.** capacious (a container). **2.** spacious (as a room).

समाख्या *sam-ā-khyā* [S.], f. *Pl. HŚS.* fame; notoriety.

समागत *sam-ā-gat* [S.], adj. **1.** come together, met, united; assembled. ***2.** arrived (a visitor). **3.** come forward, present. ~ **प्रसंग**, m. the present matter.

समागति *sam-ā-gati* [S.], f. = **समागम**, 1.-4.

समागम *sam-ā-gam* [S.], m. **1.** coming together, meeting; union. **2.** association together. ***3.** arrival, approach. **4.** an assembly, meeting. **5.** sexual congress. — ~ **करना**, to associate (with, **के साथ**).

समाघात *sam-ā-ghāt* [S.], m. striking together: percussion.

समाचार *sam-ā-cār* [S.], m. proceeding, practice or behaviour; state, condition: **1.** an occurrence. ***2.** (often pl.) news, information. — **क्या ~ है?** what's new? **नए ~**, m. news, the news. – **समाचार-चित्र**, m. a newsreel. **समाचार-दाता**, m. inv. a journalist. **समाचार-पत्र**, m. newspaper.

समाज *sam-āj* [S.], m. **1.** a society, association. **2.** a meeting, gathering. **विद्वत-समाज**, m. learned gathering, gathering of scholars. **3.** society; a partic. community. **4.** Av. things pertaining (to an event), preparation(s). — **समाज-द्रोही**, adj. traitorous. **समाजवाद**, m. socialism. °**ई**, adj. & m. socialist. **समाजविरोधी**, adj. antisocial. **समाज-शास्त्र**, m. sociology; °-**शास्त्री**, m. sociologist. **समाजीकरण**, m. socialisation.

समाजत *samājat* [A. *samāja*: P. *samājat*], f. esp. -**समाजत**. **1.** entreaty. **2.** flattery.

समाजी *samājī* [cf. H. *samāj*], m. **1.** member of a society; specif. a member of the Ārya Samāj. **2.** a musician accompanying dancers.

समाजीकरण *samājīkaraṇ* [S.], m. see s.v. **समाज**.

समादर *sam-ā-dar* [S.], m. great respect, veneration.

समादरणीय *sam-ā-darăṇīyă* [S.], adj. worthy of deep respect, or veneration.

समादृत *sam-ā-dr̥t* [S.], adj. deeply respected, venerated.

समाधान *sam-ā-dhān* [S.], m. putting together: **1.** solution (of a problem); resolving, resolution (of a doubtful matter); decision, determination. **2.** the act of satisfying, propitiating. **3.** deep meditation, contemplation. — **समाधानकारक**, adj. decisive (step, argument); definite (an answer).

समाधि *sam-ā-dhi* [S.], f. (m., *Pl.*). **1.** profound meditation (esp. with the mind successfully fixed upon the ultimate being, and with the senses completely restrained in the final stage of yoga; state of trance, or absorption, or release. **2.** self-immolation (esp. by entombment) of an ascetic. **3.** place of cremation, burial or entombment (esp. of a saintly personage; also of one who has died heroically). — ~ **लगाना**, or **लेना**, to enter a state of *samādhi*. ~ **देना**, to attend to the last rites (of, **को**). **समाधि-लेख**, m. epitaph. **समाधिस्थ**, adj. absorbed in meditation. °-**स्थान**, m. place of cremation, or entombment.

समाधिकारी *samâdhikārī* [S.], m. see s.v. सम.

समान *samān* [S.], adj. & ppn. **1.** like, similar; equal. **2.** even, level. **3.** common, general. **4.** ppn. w. के. similar (to), equal (to); just as. — ~ करना, to make equal, comparable, level, &c. ~ रूप से, adv. in the same way; to the same extent. एक ~, adv. all in the same way. – समान-उत्तराधिकार, m. equal right of inheritance, or succession. °ई, m. co-heir. समानवयस्क, adj. of equal or similar age. समानाधिकरण [°*na*+*a*°], m. & adj. *ling.* common case, or syntactic relation: coordinate status (of clauses or sentences); coordinate. समानाधिकार [°*na*+*a*°], m. (pl.) m. equal right(s). समानांतर [°*na*+*a*°], adj. parallel. समानांतर चतुर्भुज, m. parallelogram. समानांतर रेखा, f. a parallel of latitude. °ता, f. parallelism. समानार्थ [°*na*+*a*°], adj. & m. = next. समानार्थक [°*na*+*a*°], adj. & m. synonymous; a synonym. °ता, f. समानार्थी, adj. id. समानीकरण, m. equalisation, making comparable.

समानता *samānătā* [S.], f. **1.** likeness, similarity (to, से). **2.** parity; equality.

समाना *samānā* [*saṁmāti*], v.i. & v.t. **1.** v.i. to be contained or held (in, में); to fit (into). **2.** to take up the available room or space (in); to fill; to pervade. **3.** fig. to sink (into: as into the earth, in shame). **4.** v.t. to place or to pour (objects or liquid into a container: के अंदर, or में). — फूले न समाना, not to be able to contain (oneself) for joy, &c.

समानीकरण *samānīkaraṇ* [S.], m. see s.v. समान.

समापन *sam-āpan* [S.], m. **1.** completing, perfecting; bringing to an end, winding up. **2.** putting an end to, killing. **3.** *Pl. HŚS.* section, chapter, division. — समापन-समारोह, m. concluding ceremony.

समापन्न *sam-ā-pann* [S.], adj. **1.** attained, obtained. **2.** occurred, arrived, come. 3. = समाप्त. **4.** *Pl. HŚS.* skilled, proficient (in).

समापित *sam-āpit* [S.], adj. caused to be completed: = समाप्त.

समाप्त *sam-āpt* [S.], adj. completed, perfected; finished, ended. — ~ करना, to complete, to finish, &c.

समाप्ति *sam-āpti* [S.], f. **1.** completion, perfection; conclusion, end. **2.** expiry (of a period). **3.** extinction (of a species).

समाप्य *sam-āpyă* [S.], adj. to be finished; worth finishing.

समायोजन *sam-ā-yojan* [S.], m. an arrangement; adjustment (legal, financial).

समार *samār*, m. reg. (Bihar) **1.** a second ploughing. **2.** cross-ploughing (of a field: as opposed to ploughing by circuits). **3.** covering seed sown in a furrow by ploughing a second furrow beside it.

समारोह *sam-a-roh* [S.], m. ascending: **1.** pomp, splendour. ***2.** a celebratory function; festival (secular or religious); ceremony.

समारोही *sam-ā-rohī* [cf. H. *samāroh*], adj. *Pl.* magnificent, grand, festal.

समालना *samālnā*, v.t. pronun. var. = सँभालना.

समाली *sa-mālī* [S.], f. *Pl. HŚS.* bunch or garland of flowers.

समालोचक *sam-ā-locak* [S.], m. = समीक्षक.

समालोचन *sam-ā-locan* [S.], m. = समीक्षण.

समालोचना *sam-ā-locănā* [S.], f. = समीक्षा. — समालोचनात्मक [°*nā*+*ā*°], adj. critical (appraising).

समाव *samāv* [cf. H. *samānā*], m. room, space (= समाई).

समाविष्ट *sam-ā-viṣṭ* [S.], adj. **1.** included, incorporated. **2.** engrossed (in thought).

समावेश *sam-ā-veś* [S.], m. entering, penetration: **1.** inclusion, incorporation. **2.** *Pl. HŚS.* possession (by evil spirits). — ~ करना (का), to include, to incorporate (in, में).

समावेशन *sam-ā-veśan* [S.], m. inclusion; incorporation.

समास *sam-ās* [S.], m. **1.** combination; specif. compounding, composition (of words). **2.** a compound word. समास चिह्न, m. a hyphen. समास-बहुल, adj. abounding in compound words (language).

समाहित *sam-ā-hit* [S.], adj. contained; collected.

समिति *sam-iti* [S.], f. **1.** committee. **2.** society, association.

समिध *sam-idh* [S.], f. firewood, or kindling materials (specif. for an oblation).

समिधा *sam-idhā* [S.], f. = समिध.

समिर *samir*, m. pronun. var. = समीर.

समीकरण *samīkaraṇ* [S.], m. see s.v. सम.

समीकृत *samīkṛt* [S.], m. see s.v. सम.

समीक्षक *sam-īkṣak* [S.], m. **1.** critic (as of a work). **2.** reviewer.

समीक्षण *sam-īkṣaṇ* [S.], m. commenting, reviewing.

समीक्षा *sam-īkṣā* [S.], f. **1.** close inspection or examination. **2.** close consideration; investigation; critical study (of a field, or topic); survey. **3.** a review (of a work). — **समीक्षात्मक** [°*ā*+*a*°], adj. critical (as a study or examination).

समीक्षित *sam-īkṣit* [S.], adj. reviewed (a work).

समीक्ष्य *sam-īkṣyă* [S.], adj. **1.** worth reviewing. **2.** to be reviewed, under review.

समीचीन *samīcīn* [S.], adj. concordant, consistent: proper, just, right (as a view); appropriate.

समीचीनता *samīcīnătā* [S.], f. fitness, propriety.

समीप *samīp* [S.], adj. & m. **1.** adj. near, adjacent (to, के); close. **2.** *Pl.* in the opinion (of). **3.** m. vicinity. — **समीपवर्ती**, adj. lying nearby, adjacent; later, latter-day.

समीपता *samīpătā* [S.], f. nearness, proximity (= सामीप्य).

समीपी *samīpī* [cf. H. *samīp*], m. *Pl.* a neighbour.

समीर *sam-īr* [S.], m. **1.** breeze; wind. **2.** Brbh. the breath (as controlled in yoga).

समुंद *samund* [ad. *samudra-*: × P. *samandar*], m. Av. = समुद्र.

समुंदर *samundar* [ad. *samudra-*], m. = समुद्र.

समुंदरी *samundrī* [cf. H. *samundar*], adj. = समुद्री.

समुचित *sam-ucit* [S.], adj. **1.** appropriate, suitable. **2.** condign (punishment).

समुच्चय *sam-uc-cay* [S.], m. **1.** assemblage, aggregate, mass. **2.** collection; anthology. **3.** *gram.* an assemblage of words or sentences. — **समुच्चयबोधक**, m. *gram.* a conjunction. **समुच्चयार्थक** [°*ya*+*a*°], adj. collective.

समुच्चित *sam-uc-cit* [S.], adj. collected, amassed.

समुच्छेद *sam-uc-ched* [S.], m. extirpation.

समुत्पत्ति *sam-ut-patti* [S.], f. = उत्पत्ति.

समुदय *sam-ud-ay* [S.], m. rise, ascent (as of the sun).

समुदाय *sam-ud-āy* [S.], m. **1.** collection, multitude; community; section, group (of a community); mass (of population). **2.** an association. **3.** quantity, large number. **4.** flock, herd (of animals, birds).

समुद्र *sam-udră* [S.], m. sea; ocean. — **समुद्रगामी**, adj. & m. sea-faring; ocean-going (a ship); a seafarer. **समुद्र-तट**, m. sea-shore; coast. °**-तटीय**, adj. id. **समुद्र-तल**, m. sea-level; surface of the sea; sea-bed (= ~ अधस्तल). **समुद्रपार**, m. & adv. overseas region(s). **समुद्रपार के देश**, m. pl. countries overseas. **समुद्र-फेन**, m. sea-foam: cuttle-fish bone. °**-वर्ती**, adj. maritime (region, province).

समुद्री *sam-udrī* [cf. H. *samudr*], adj. having to do with the sea; marine, maritime; naval (as a battle, manoeuvres). — **~ डाकू**, m. a pirate. **~ तार**, m. an undersea cable.

समुद्रीय *sam-udrīyă* [S.], adj. = समुद्री.

[1]**समुह-** *samuh-* [cf. *sammukha-*], v.i. Brbh. to face; to be in the presence of.

[2]**समुह-** *samuh-* [cf. *sammukha-*], adj. Brbh. facing; visible.

समूचा *samūcā* [*samuccaya-*], adj. all, entire, whole; complete. — **समूचे**, adv. in its entirety, as a whole.

समूल *sa-mūl* [S.], adj. **1.** having a root; having a cause. **2.** radical (as a reform); total. **3.** adv. with the root, by the roots; root and branch, utterly.

समूह *sam-ūh* [S.], m. **1.** a collection, aggregate. **2.** multitude, mass (of people). **3.** flock, herd (of animals, birds). — **द्वीप-समूह**, m. group of islands; archipelago. **समूहोत्पादन** [°*a*+*u*°], m. mass production.

समूहन *sam-ūhan* [S.], m. a grouping; aggregate.

समृद्ध *sam-ṛddh* [S.], adj. **1.** prosperous, thriving. **2.** wealthy. **3.** enriched (as a language, a literature). — **~ बनाना**, to enrich.

समृद्धि *sam-ṛddhi* [S.], f. prosperity, &c. (see समृद्ध).

समेट *sameṭ* [cf. H. *sameṭnā*], f. gathering together, rolling up.

समेटना *sameṭnā* [*saṁveṣṭayati*, and *saṁvṛtta-*], v.t. **1.** to gather up or together; to scrape together. **2.** to roll up or together; to wrap up. **3.** to finish, to dispose of; to wind up (a business).

समेत *sam-êt* [S.], adj. & ppn. **1.** assembled, united. ***2.** adv. together (with, के); collected together. **3.** ppn. together with.

समोना *samonā* [*saṁvapati*], v.t. to cool (warm water) by mixing cold water with it; to mix closely.

समोसा *samosā* [P. *samosa*], m. **1.** a triangular-shaped savoury fried in *ghī* or oil, containing spiced vegetables or meat. **2.** fig. anything triangular.

समौ *samau* [*samaya-*], m. Brbh. = समय.

सम्मत *sam-mat* [S.], adj. of one mind: **1.** agreeing. **2.** agreed to, approved (a proposal, &c). **3.** conformable (to rule, precedent); sanctioned (by). **4.** *HŚS.* ? like, resembling.

सम्मति *sam-mati* [S.], f. **1.** assent, agreement, approval. **2.** opinion; advice. **3.** *Pl. HŚS.* self-knowledge. — ~ लेना, to take advice, to consult (with, की or से).

सम्मान *sam-mān* [S.], m. **1.** honour, esteem; veneration, homage. **2.** an honour; a decoration. — ~ करना, to honour, to show esteem, &c. (for, का). – सम्मानजनक, adj. honorary (post). सम्मानपूर्वक, adv. with honour, &c. सम्मानसूचक, adj. & m. honorific; ling. an honorific (expression or usage). सम्मानार्थ [°*na*+*a*°], adv. in honour (of, के).

सम्मानन *sam-mānan* [S.], m. honouring, showing honour (to, का).

सम्माननीय *sam-mānănīyă* [S.], adj. = सम्मान्य.

सम्मानित *sam-mānit* [S.], adj. **1.** honoured, &c. (see सम्मान). **2.** honorary (a post, a membership).

सम्मानी *sam-mānī* [S.], adj. respectful.

सम्मान्य *sam-mānyă* [S.], adj. deserving of honour, &c. (see सम्मान); honourable.

सम्मिलन *sam-milan* [S.], m. joining, combining.

सम्मिलित *sam-milit* [S.], adj. **1.** met together, assembled, gathered. **2.** joined, joint, united; combined (forces).

सम्मिश्रण *sam-miśraṇ* [S.], m. **1.** mixing together. **2.** a mixture.

सम्मुख *sam-mukh* [S.], adv. facing, in front (of, के); face to face; opposite.

सम्मेलन *sam-melan* [S.], m. meeting together: **1.** a society. **2.** a conference; a gathering, meeting.

सम्मोद *sam-mod* [S.], m. great delight; pleasure.

सम्मोह *sam-moh* [S.], m. **1.** bewilderment, confusion. ***2.** fascination; infatuation. **3.** a fainting fit (as of ecstasy).

सम्मोहक *sam-mohak* [S.], adj. fascinating, charming, &c. (see सम्मोह).

सम्मोहन *sam-mohan* [S.], m. **1.** the act of charming, fascinating. **2.** hypnotism, hypnotic effect.

सम्मोहित *sam-mohit* [S.], adj. charmed, &c. (see सम्मोह).

सम्यक् *samyak* [S.], adj. **1.** whole, entire. **2.** correct, accurate; proper.

सम्राज्ञी *samrājñī* [S.], f. empress.

सम्राट *samrāṭ* [S.], m. emperor.

सम्हलना *samhalnā*, v.i. pronun. var. = सँभलना.

सम्हार *samhār* [H. *sammvār*+H. *sammbhālnā*], f. = सँवार.

सम्हार- *samhār-*, v.t. Brbh. = सँभालना.

सम्हालना *samhālnā*, v.t. pronun. var. = सँभालना.

सयान *sayān* [**sajāna-*: Pk. *sajāṇa-*], adj. & m. **1.** adj. = सयाना. **2.** m. cleverness, cunning. **3.** maturity.

सयानप *sayānap*, m. Brbh. = सयानापन.

सयानपन *sayānpan*, m. = सयानापन.

सयाना *sayānā* [**sajāna-*: Pk. *sajāṇa-*], adj. & m. **1.** adj. having reached years of discretion: adolescent; adult. **2.** knowing, wise. **3.** shrewd; cunning. **4.** m. a knowing, or a shrewd person, &c. **5.** an exorcist.

सयानापन *sayānāpan* [cf. H. *sayānā*], m. **1.** maturity: adolescence; adulthood. **2.** cleverness. **3.** cunning.

[1]**सर** *sar* [*saras-*], m. **1.** a lake; pool. **2.** tank. — सरवर, m. Brbh. a large, or fine lake (= सरोवर).

सरंजाम *sarañjām* [P. *sar-anjām*], m. **1.** bringing to completion; arrangement, organisation. **2.** issue, result. **3.** necessary equipment. — ~ करना (का), to complete, to accomplish; to organise (as an event).

[2]**सर** *sar* [P. *sar*], m. syn. सिर, q.v. for various expressions and cpds. **1.** head. **2.** top, tip; point; end. **3.** सर-, head, chief. — ~ करना, to fire (a gun, &c.); to overpower, to subdue; to take (a fort, &c). ~ होना, to come or to fall at the head or top, to win (a card, in a game). – सरंजाम, m. see s.v. सरकश [P. *-kaś*], adj. U. refractory, rebellious. सर-ख़त, m. Brbh. a rental agreement, or statement. सरग़ना [P. *-gana*], m. arch. leader, chief. सरगर्म, adj. U. enthusiastic, ardent, zealous; inflamed with love. °ई, f. enthusiasm, &c. सरगोशी [P. *-gośī*], f. U. whispering. सरजा [P. *-jāh*], m. Brbh. leader. सरज़ोर, adj. headstrong; rebellious. °ई, f. सरताज, m. best (one) of all. सर-दर्द, m. a headache. सरनाम, adj. of famous name, celebrated; notorious. सरनाम करना, to make famous, &c.; to make public. °-नामा, m. U. honorific formula (at the head of a letter); letterhead, address. सरपंच, m. head of a pancāyat. सर-परस्त, [P. *-parast*], m. guardian; patron. °ई, f.

patronage, protection. °-परस्ताना, adj. inv. solicitous (of attitude); condescending. सर-पोश [P. *-poś*], m. cover, lid. सर-पेच, m. an ornament of gold, silver or jewels worn on the turban; a broad band of silk or brocade worn round the turban. सरबाज़ी [P. *-bāzī*], f. risking one's head: great courage; rashness. सरबुलंद, adj. U. holding the head high: eminent, excellent. सर-मस्त, adj. very drunk. °ई, f. सर-रफ़्ता [P. *rafta*], adj. gone in the head: crazy. °-रफ़्तगी, f. craziness. सरशार, adj. see s.v. सरहद, f. see s.v. °ई, adj. see s.v. सरापा [P. *-pā*], adj. U. from head to foot: throughout, totally; up and down, comprehensive (scrutiny, or description , of a person). सरासर, adv. see s.v. °ई, adj. & f. see s.v. सरे आम, adv. openly, publicly. सरे बाज़ार, adv. in the open market: in public. सरे राह, f. & adv. a main road; the head of a street; on the main road. सरे शाम, adv. U. at the onset of evening. सरोकार, m. see s.v. सरोसामान, m. see s.v.

³**सर** *sar* [*śara-*], m. an arrow.

¹**सरक** *sarak* [cf. H. *saraknā*], f. moving, slipping.

²**सरक** *sarak* [S.], f. Brbh. **1.** liquor. **2.** intoxication; languor.

सरकंडा *sarkaṇḍā* [ad. *śarakāṇḍa-*], m. a reed, reed-stalk.

सरकना *saraknā* [cf. *sarati*], v.i. **1.** to be moved, displaced; to shift, to slip. **2.** to move along; to progress (work). **3.** to creep, to glide (as a snake). **4.** to draw back; to give way. **5.** to be put off, postponed.

सरकवाना *sarakvānā* [cf. H. *saraknā*], v.t. to cause to be moved away, &c. (by, से).

सरकाना *sarkānā* [cf. H. *saraknā*], v.t. **1.** to move to one side, or out of the way. **2.** to pass or to hand (to). **3.** to relegate. **4.** to put off, to postpone.

सरकार *sarkār* [P. *sar-kār*], m. **1.** m. master, lord; (as term of address) sir, your Honour. ⋆**2.** f. government, ruling authority; court (of a king).

सरकारी *sarkārī* [P. *sarkārī*], adj. **1.** of or pertaining to government, or to the state; governmental; official. **2.** pertaining to any public authority. ~ बाग़, m. public park. — ~ ऋण, m. government loan. ~ काग़ज़, m. government stock. ~ नौकरी, or मुलाज़मत, f. government service. ~ यात्रा, f. a state visit, official visit. ~ वकील, m. prosecuting counsel.

सरग़ना *sarganā* [P. *sargana*], m. a leader; chief.

सरगम *sargam* [? H. *sā, re, ga, ma* (or ad. *grāma-*)], m. *mus.* a scale.

सरगुन *sargun* [H. *saguṇ* × H. *nirguṇ*, (?) *sarvaguṇ*], adj. Brbh. qualified (= सगुण).

सरजीवन *sarjīvan* [conn. *saṁjīvana-*], adj. **1.** imperishable, immortal; evergreen. **2.** life-prolonging, life-giving.

सरजू *sarjū* [*sarayū-*], m. name of the river Sarayu.

सरटा *sarṭā*, m. reg. a lizard.

सरणी *saraṇī* [S.], f. **1.** road; street; path; way. **2.** Brbh. way, manner.

सरतान *sartān* [A. *sarṭān*], m. U. **1.** a crab. **2.** the sign Cancer (of the zodiac). **3.** cancer. **4.** a disease that attacks the feet of cattle.

सरदार *sardār* [P. *sardār*], m. having or being at the head: **1.** leader, head, chief; representative (of a group). **2.** chieftain. **3.** honorific title of a Sikh. ~ जी, m. term of address or reference to a Sikh.

सरदारनी *sardārnī* [cf. H. *sardār*], f. **1.** leader's wife. **2.** wife of a Sikh (term of address or reference); a Sikh woman.

सरदारिन *sardārin*, f. = सरदारनी.

सरदारी *sardārī* [P. *sardārī*], f. **1.** leadership, &c. (see सरदार). **2.** the rank or position of a *sardār*.

¹**सरन** *saran* [cf. H. *sarnā*], f. *Pl.* a blast (?) of wind.

²**सरन** *saran*, f. pronun. var. = शरण.

सरना *sarnā* [*sarati*], v.i. **1.** to move ahead, to proceed; to go ahead smoothly (a task, &c.); to be accomplished. **2.** to be passed, or lived (time, life); to be finished.

सरनाम *sarnām* [P. *sar-nām*], adj. see s.v. ²सर.

सरपट *sarpaṭ*, f. & adj. **1.** f. galloping hard. **2.** adj. level, even. **3.** adv. at a gallop. **4.** transf. glibly, smoothly. — ~ दौड़ना, to gallop.

सरपत *sarpat* [cf. *śara-*¹], m. a species of reed-grass, *Saccharum procerum* (different parts of which are used in thatching and in making mats, baskets, chairs, &c).

सरब- *sarab-*. Brbh. Av. see सर्व-.

सरबर *sarbar*, f. Brbh. = सरबरि.

सरबरि *sarbari* [P. *sar-varī-*); Pk. *saribharī*], f. Brbh. equality, rivalry, emulation.

सरबरी *sarbarī* [cf. H. *sarbar(i)*; P. *sar-varī*], adj. & m. Brbh. equal; an equal.

सरबस *sarbas*, m. Brbh. Av. = **सर्वस्व**.

सरभंग *sarbhaṅg*, m. *Pl.* a community of ascetics who do not believe in the Hindu ideas of caste and pollution, &c.

सरभंगी *sarbhaṅgī*, m. *Pl.* an ascetic of the *sarbhaṅg* community.

सरमाया *sarmāyā* [P. *sar-māya*], m. U. *fin.* **1.** principal; capital. **2.** assets. — **सरमायेदार** [P. *-dār*], m. a capitalist. °**ई**, f. capitalism.

सरल *saral* [S.], adj. **1.** straight, direct. ***2.** simple, straightforward (of character); honest. **3.** unaffected, unfeigned. **4.** not difficult, simple; easy. ~ **भाषा**, f. simple language. ~ **संगीत**, m. light music. — **सरलचित्त**, adj. of straightforward nature or disposition. **सरलीकरण**, m. simplification.

सरलता *saralătā* [S.], f. **1.** simplicity, straightforwardness (as of manner). **2.** simplicity, ease, &c. (see **सरल**).

सरलीकरण *saralīkaraṇ* [S.], m. see s.v. **सरल**.

सरवर *sarvar*, m. Brbh. a large, or fine lake (= **सरोवर**).

सरवैया *sarvaiyā* [cf. H. *sārnā*], m. reg. mender, repairer.

सरशार *sarśār* [P. *sar-śār*], adj. U. **1.** brimful. **2.** soaked; intoxicated.

सरस *sa-ras* [S.], adj. **1.** juicy, &c. (see **रस**). **2.** fresh (as fruit). **3.** tasty. **4.** charming, elegant. **5.** lively; engaging attention, interesting. **6.** full of feeling, sentimental (as verse, style, heart).

सरस्- *saras-* [S]. lake, pool; tank. — **सरस्वती**, f. see s.v. **सरसिज**, m. born in a lake: a lotus.

सरस- *saras-* [cf. H. *saras*], v.i. Brbh. **1.** to be fresh, or luxuriant (vegetation). **2.** to be charming, beautiful.

सरसठ *sarsaṭh* [*saptaṣaṣṭi-*], adj. sixty-seven.

सरसता *sarasătā* [S.], f. juiciness, freshness, &c. (see **सरस**).

सरसब्ज़ी *sarsabzī* [P. *sar-sabzī*], f. flourishing state.

सरसर *sarsar* [cf. H. *sarsarānā*], f. **1.** rustling sound (as of leaves, wind); sound of a snake crawling. **2.** creeping or tingling sensation. (= **सुरसुर**). — ~ **चलना**, to rustle; to move with a rustling sound.

सरसराना *sarsarānā* [*sarasarāyate*], v.i. **1.** to make a rustling sound; to glide, to crawl along (as a snake). **2.** to wave (as crops in the wind); to be flourishing. **3.** to creep, to tingle (the skin, flesh); to shiver suddenly (with cold). **4.** to hiss (as a firework); to make a whizzing sound.

सरसराहट *sarsarāhaṭ* [cf. H. *sarsarānā*], f. **1.** rustling sound (as of leaves, wind). **2.** a sudden shiver; a tingling sensation (= **सुरसुराहट**, 2). **3.** a hissing or whizzing sound.

सरसरी *sarsarī* [P. *sarsarī*], adj. **1.** cursory, casual (glance, manner); hasty; perfunctory, careless. **2.** summary (as of legal proceedings). — ~ **तौर पर**, or **से**, adv. perfunctorily, &c.; summarily, forthwith.

सरसाई *sarsāī* [cf. H. *saras*], f. reg. **1.** juiciness, freshness, &c. (see **सरस**). **2.** watered or fertile state: abundance.

सरसाम *sarsām* [P. *sarsām*], m. delirium.

सरसिज *sarasij* [S.], m. see s.v. **सरस्-**.

सरसी *sarăsī* [S.], f. a lake, &c. (= **सरस्**). — **सरसीरुह**, m. pond-growing: a lotus; a water-lily.

सरसुती *sarsutī*, f. pronun. var. = **सरस्वती**.

सरसों *sarsoṁ* [*sarṣapa-*], f. a type of mustard seed and plant, *Sinapis glauca*. — ~ **का तेल**, m. mustard oil.

सरसो *sarso*, f. pronun. var. = **सरसों**.

सरस्वती *sarasvatī* [S.], f. *mythol.* **1.** name of the goddess of speech and learning and patroness of the arts (often considered as the wife of Brahmā). **2.** name of a river running south-westwards from near Delhi into the Rajasthan desert; *mythol.* name of a river supposed to join the Ganges and Jumna at Allahabad.

सरहज *sarhaj*, f. reg. = **सलहज**.

सरहद *sarhad* [P. *sarḥad*: A. *ḥadd*], f. frontier, border; frontier region.

सरहदी *sarhadī* [P. *sarḥadī*], adj. having to do with a frontier, &c. (see **सरहद**).

सरहना *sarhnā*, m. *Pl. HŚS.* a fish-scale.

सरा *sarā* [A. *śar'*], m. E.H. a road: the teaching of Muḥammad; Muslim law (= **शरीअत**).

[1]**सरा** *sarā* [*śara-*[1]], m. **1.** *Pl.* a long straight bamboo. **2.** Av. a pyre (of grass, reeds).

[2]**सरा** *sarā* [*śarāva-*], m. reg. an earthen cover or lid (of a pot).

सराई *sarāī* [cf. H. *sarāvā*], f. *Pl. HŚS.* a small, shallow earthen dish (= **सराव**).

सराप *sarāp*, m. Brbh. Av. a curse (= **शाप**).

सराप- *sarāp-* [ad. H. *sarāp*; S. *śāpayati*], v.t. Brbh. to curse (cf. शाप).

सराफ़ *sarāf*, m. = सर्राफ़.

सराफ़ा *sarāfā* [P. *ṣarrāfa*], m. **1.** money-market; exchange. **2.** a bank. 3. = सराफ़ी, 1. — सराफ़े की कोठी, f. a banking firm.

सराफ़ी *sarāfī* [P. *ṣarrāfī*], f. **1.** money-changing; banking. **2.** banker's discount. 3. = महाजानी, 3. ~ करना, to carry on a banker's business. ~ हुंडी, f. a bill, draft on a bank.

सराबोर *sarābor* [cf. H. *bor-*], adj. soaked, drenched (cf. तराबोर).

सराय *sarāy* [P. *sarā'e*], m. **1.** house, abode. **2.** temporary lodging-place; inn. **3.** fig. the world. — ~ का कुत्ता, m. pej. hostelry dog: a shameless opportunist.

सराली *sarālī*, f. *HŚS.* a bird; ? sandpiper.

सराव *sarāv* [*śarāva-*], m. Brbh. shallow cup or dish, a lamp-holder (for oil and wick).

सरावग *srāvag* [ad. *śrāvaka-*], m. Brbh. a Jain (see श्रवक).

सरावगी *srāvgī* [cf. H. *srāvag*], m. *Pl. HŚS.* a Jain, member of the Jain community.

सरावा *sarāvā* [*śarāvaka-*], m. reg. = सराव.

सरासन *sarāsan* [*śarāsana-*], m. Av. seat of an arrow: a bow.

सरासर *sarāsar* [P. *sar-ā-sar*], adv. from end to end; throughout, totally; continuously. — ~ झूठ, m. an arrant lie.

सरासरी *sarāsărī* [P. *sarāsarī*], f. & adj. **1.** f. an average. **2.** a quick, or rough estimate. **3.** reg. (W.) *hist.* a system of leasing village land at a rate fixed by the area of the land irrespective of the crop. ***4.** adj. superficial, casual (= सरसरी). **5.** adv. hastily. — ~ देखना, to look over cursorily.

सराह *sarāh* [cf. H. *sarāhnā*], f. reg. praise (= सराहना).

सराहना *sarāhnā* [*ślāghate*], v. t. & f. **1.** v.t. to praise; to approve, to admire. **2.** f. [? × H. *sarāh*, f.] praise; admiration.

सरि *sari* [? conn. *sadṛśa-*], adj. & f. Brbh. Av. **1.** adj. equal, similar. **2.** f. equality, similarity.

सरि *sari* [S.], f. = सरिता.

सरित् *sarit* [S.], f. = सरिता.

सरिता *saritā* [S.], f. a river.

[1]**सरिया** *sariyā* [cf. *śara-*[1]], f. (m. ?). **1.** a piece of reed; a sliver of bamboo. **2.** a thin iron rod.

[2]**सरिया** *sariyā* [cf. **sarā-*[2]: Pk. *sarā-*], f. *Pl.* a chain of gold or silver wire.

सरियाना *sariyānā*, v.t. to put in place, or in order.

सरिश्ता *sariśtā* [P. *sar-riśta*], m. **1.** an administrative department. **2.** record-office, office. **3.** court. — सरिश्तेदार [P. *-dār*], m. superintendent of a department, or of an office; record-keeper; court recorder; specif. *hist.* superintendent of the Indian language department of an office. °ई, f. the post and duties, or the work, of a *sariśtedār*.

सरिस *saris*, adj. Brbh. Av. like, resembling (= सदृश).

सरी *sarī* [S.], f. *Pl. HŚS.* a waterfall; lake, pond; stream (flowing through a garden, &c).

सरीखा *sarīkhā* [*sadṛkṣa-*], adj. like, similar (to, के; but the obl. stem is often used). — हम सरीखे ग़रीब आदमी, poor men like us.

सरीर *sarīr*, m. *Pl. HŚS.* a grating or scratching sound.

सरीसृप *sarīsṛp* [S.], m. poet. crawling: a reptile.

सरुष *sa-ruṣ* [S.], adj. Av. angry, fierce.

[1]**सरूप** *sa-rūp* [S.], adj. **1.** having form or shape. **2.** of the same form, &c.: resembling, similar (to, के). **3.** [× *surūpa-*] attractive.

[2]**सरूप** *sarūp*, m. Brbh. Av. proper form, own form (= स्वरूप).

सरूपता *sa-rūpătā* [S.], f. similarity, resemblance.

सरूपी *sa-rūpī* [S.], adj. having the same form as: similar.

सरूर *sarūr* [A. *surūr*], m. exhilaration (caused by alcohol, &c.) — ~ गठना, or जमना, = next. ~ होना, to be slightly drunk. हल्का ~, m. tipsiness.

सरेख *sarekh*, adj. Av. = सरेखा.

सरेखा *sa-rekhā*, adj. Av. cunning, clever.

सरेश *sareś*, m. = सरेस.

सरेस *sares* [P. *śireś*], m. **1.** glue. **2.** starch. **3.** gelatine.

सरोंट *saroṁṭ* [? conn. *varta-*[1]], f. Brbh. fold, crease (in a garment: = सिलवट and [3]सल).

सरो *saro* [A. *sarv*], m. a cypress.

सरो- *saro-* [S]. lake, pool; tank: — सरोज, m. lake-born: a lotus; water-lily. सरोजिनी, f. a pond, &c. abounding in lotuses; a large cluster of lotuses; a lotus. सरोरुह, m. lake-growing: a lotus. सरोवर, m. large or fine lake, &c.

सरोकार *sarokār* [P. *sar o kār*], m. affair, concern, business (with, से); interest, involvement. — ~ रखना, to have dealings (with, से). इससे तुम्हारा कोई ~ नहीं है, this has nothing to do with you. यहाँ तुम्हारा कोई ~ नहीं है, you have no business to be here.

सरोता *sarotā* [? *sārapattra-*], m. a kind of scissors for cutting betel nut.

सरोद *sarod* [P. *sarod*], m. **1.** a kind of guitar. **2.** transf. singing, singing and dancing.

सरोरुह *saroruh* [S.], m. see s.v. सरो-.

सरोला *sarolā* [? conn. **surāvaṭa-*], m. *Pl. HŚS.* a sweet made from fine flour, poppy-seed, dates and almonds cooked in *ghī* and sugar.

सरोवर *sarovar* [S.], m. see s.v. सरो-.

सरोष *sa-roṣ* [S.], adj. angry; fierce.

सरोसामान *sarosāmān* [P. *sar o sāmān*], m. **1.** effects, goods, things. **2.** equipment.

सरौंची *saraum̐cī*, f. reg. (Bihar) a grass or fodder-plant of the genus *Achyranthes*.

सरौंज *saraum̐j*, m. *Pl.* a kind of seed.

सर्जन *sarjan* [S.], m. creating, &c. (cf. सृजन).

सर्टिफ़िकेट *sarṭifikeṭ* [Engl. *certificate*], m. **1.** certificate (= प्रमाण-पत्र). **2.** recommendation, testimonial.

सर्द *sard* [P. *sard*], adj. **1.** cold; cool. **2.** damp, moist. **3.** lukewarm (of emotion, attitude); indifferent. **4.** joyless, sad (a sigh); cold (of temperament, manner). — ~ हो जाना, to be or to become cold or cool, &c.; to become numbed or paralysed (as through fear); to die. – सर्द-ख़ाना, m. a (cool) basement room. सर्द-गरम, adj. & m. cold and hot; changeable, fickle; volatile (of temperament); fig. vicissitudes (of life). सर्द-मिज़ाज, adj. of cold temperament; cold-blooded; apathetic.

सर्दई *sardaī* [P. *sarda*], adj. & f. **1.** adj. greenish-yellow (the colour of the melon called *sardā*). **2.** m. a greenish-yellow colour.

सर्दा *sardā* [P. *sarda*], m. a kind of melon (native to Afghanistan).

सर्दी *sardī* [P. *sardī*], f. **1.** cold; coolness. **2.** esp. pl. the cold season, winter. **3.** a cold. — ~ का मौसम, m. = ~, 2. ~ पड़ना, cold to be felt or to strike, to be cold (climate, weather). ~ लगना (को), cold to be felt (by one); a cold to be caught (by). मुझे ~ लग रही है, I'm getting cold; I'm cold. मुझे ~ लगी है, I've got a cold. ~ होना (को), = ~ लगना, 2. – सर्दी-ज़ुकाम, m. a cold (in throat and chest as well as head).

सर्प *sarp* [S.], m. a snake. — सर्प-छत्र, m. snake's umbrella: a mushroom, toadstool. सर्प-दंश, m. snake-bite. सर्प-मणि, snake-gem: the jewel supposed to be found in a snake's head and to have the power of expelling poison. सर्प-राज, m. *mythol.* snake-king: a title of Śeṣa.

सर्पिल *sarpil*, adj. snake-like: sinuous; spiral.

सर्फ़ *sarf* [A. *ṣarf*], m. U. expenditure. — ~ करना, to outlay, to expend.

सर्राटा *sarrāṭā* [H. *pharrāṭā* × H. *sapāṭā*], m. swift movement, rush.

सर्राफ़ *sarrāf* [A. *ṣarrāf*], m. **1.** a money-changer; banker. ***2.** dealer in precious metal and stones, jeweller.

सर्राफ़ा *sarrāfā*, m. see सराफ़ा.

सर्राफ़ी *sarrāfī*, f. see सराफ़ी.

सर्व- *sarv-* [S.], adj. **1.** all. **2.** whole; entire; total. **3.** universal, general; omni-, pan-. **4.** adv. most of all, extremely. — सर्वकाल, adv. at all times; for all seasons; °ईन, adj. of all times, perpetual. सर्वक्षमा, f. an amnesty. सर्वगत, adj. all-pervading, omnipresent. सर्वग्रहण, m. a total eclipse. सर्वजन, m. all people: the general public. °ईन, adj. सर्वजयी, adj. all-conquering. सर्वजित्, adj. id. सर्वजेता, m. inv. conqueror of all: champion. सर्वज्ञ, adj. omniscient. °-ज्ञता, f. omniscience. °-ज्ञानी, adj. = सर्वज्ञ. सर्वतः, adv. from every direction; in every direction; on all sides, everywhere; wholly. सर्वतोमुख, adj. = next. सर्वतोमुखी [*as*+*mu*°], adj. facing in all directions; many-sided, versatile. सर्वथा, adv. see s.v. सर्वदर्शी, adj. all-seeing, omniscient. सर्वदली(य), adj. all-party. सर्वदा, adv. see s.v. सर्वधन, m. all (one's) wealth or property; *arith.* sum total. सर्वनाम, m. *gram.* a pronoun. सर्वनाश, m. complete destruction or ruin. °ई, adj. all-destroying. सर्वप्रथम, adj. the very first. सर्वप्रधान, chief of all; a title of the supreme being. सर्वप्रभुता, f. supremacy over all; unrestricted sovereignty. सर्वप्रिय, adj. dear to all, universally popular; friendly towards all. °ता, f. सर्वभक्षी, adj. omnivorous. सर्वभाव, m. & adv. whole being or nature; in every way, fully. सर्वभूत, m. all beings, all created things; all the elements. सर्वमय, adj. all-containing, comprehending all (as the ultimate being). sovereignty. सर्वमान्य, adj. universally honoured; generally accepted. सर्वलोक, m. all worlds, the universe. सर्वव्यापक, adj. all-pervading; found, or applying, everywhere, general as (a view). °-व्यापी, adj. id. सर्वशक्तिमत्ता, f. omnipotence. सर्वशक्तिमान, adj. almighty, omnipotent. सर्वश्री, m. (in addresses, letter-openings) Messrs. सर्वश्रेष्ठ, adj. best of all; choice; foremost. सर्वसत्ता, f. full power or sovereignty. °धारी, adj. absolute (as a monarchy, or a despotic rule); sovereign (a state). सर्वसत्तावाद, m. exercise of unrestricted governmental power: totalitarianism. °ई, adj. totalitarian. **सर्वसम्मत**, adj. approved or accepted unanimously. °ई, f. unanimous approval, &c. **सर्वसाधारण**, adj. & m. generally found, or the case; the common or ordinary people. **सर्वस्व**, m. the whole of (one's) possessions; whole substance or essence (of anything). **सर्वहार**, m. confiscation of a whole property. **सर्वहारा**, m. proletariat. **सर्वांग** [°*va*+*a*°], m. the whole body, or the trunk. °**पूर्ण**, adj. complete in all parts; comprehensive. **सर्वांगीण**, adj. pertaining to all members, or the whole body: complete, thorough-going, unlimited. **सर्वात्मवाद** [°*va*+*ā*°], m. belief in an all-pervading spirit; animism. °ई, adj. & m. **सर्वात्मा** [°*va*+*ā*°], m. f. the universal soul, the all-pervading spirit. **सर्वाधिक** [°*va*+*a*°], adj. most of all, most of; preponderant; predominant. **सर्वाधिकार** [°*va*+*a*°], m. all rights; full power; general superintendence or control. °ई, m. one having full rights, &c. **सर्वार्थ** [°*va*+*a*°], m. all purposes; the common good. **सर्वेक्षक** [°*a*+*ī*°], m. a surveyor. **सर्वेक्षण** [°*va*+*ī*°], m. general survey (of a topic); a general study. **सर्वेश** [°*va*+*ī*°], m. = next. **सर्वेश्वर**, m. lord of all: the supreme being; a universal monarch. °**वाद**, m. pantheism. **सर्वे-सर्वा**, adj. & m. inv. all-in-all, supreme; chief of all. **सर्वोच्छ** [°*va*+*u*°], adj. highest of all, chief, supreme (as rank, position). **सर्वोत्तम** [°*va*+*u*°], adj. best of all. **सर्वोदय** [°*va*+*u*°], m. general rise or progress (to well-being): name of a Gandhian movement aiming at the amelioration of life in all fields. **सर्वोपरि** [°*va*+*u*°], adv. & adj. above all; placed above all, chief, paramount.

सर्वतोमुखी *sarvătomukhī* [S.], adj. see s.v. **सर्व**.

सर्वत्र *sarvatr* [S.], adv. **1.** everywhere. **2.** in all cases, always.

सर्वथा *sarvăthā* [S.], adv. in every way, in every respect; entirely, completely; exceedingly.

सर्वदा *sarvădā* [S.], adv. always.

सर्वस्व *sarvasvă*, [S.], m. see s.v. **सर्व-**.

¹**सल** *sal* [*śalabha-*²], m. reg. a large green grasshopper; mantis.

²**सल** *sal* [*śalya-*¹; ← Raj. or Panj.], m. reg. **1.** a thorn; spike. **2.** fig. a difficulty. — ~ **से बैठना**, to be clear or free of difficulties; to be settled, composed.

³**सल** *sal*, f. reg. = **सिलवट**.

सलकी *salkī*, f. *Pl.* root of the lotus or water-lily.

सलग *salag* [*saṁlagna-*], adj. Brbh. joined together: continuous.

सलज्ज *sa-lajj* [S.], adj. **1.** feeling embarrassment or modesty. **2.** feeling shame.

सलतनत *saltanat* [A. *salṭana*: P. *salṭanat*], f. **1.** sovereign power, dominion, rule. **2.** a sultanate, kingdom.

सलना *salnā* [cf. H. *sālnā*], v.i. to be pierced; to feel a pang.

सलमा *salmā* [P. *salma*], m. **1.** a type of thread made with fine gold or silver wire and used in embroidery. — **सलमा-सितारा**, m. a kind of embroidery consisting of small stars between embroidered bands.

सलवट *salvaṭ*, f. = **सिलवट**.

सलवार *salvār*, m. pronun. var. = **शलवार**.

सलसलाना *salsalānā*, v.i. & v.t. **1.** v.i. to glide, to rustle (= **सरसराना**). **2.** to itch, to feel uncomfortable (= **सुरसुराना**). **3.** to feel an uneasiness, or doubt. **4.** v.t. to rub lightly.

सलसलाहट *salsalāhaṭ* [cf. H. *salsalānā*], f. an itching, &c.

सलहज *salhaj* [**syālabhāryā-*], f. brother-in-law's wife.

सलाई *salāī* [*śalākikā-*], f. **1.** a thin rod, or wire: a needle; surgical probe. **2.** a match. — ~ **फेरना**, to blind (one's eyes, **पर**) with a red-hot wire or needle.

सलाख़ *salākh* [? ad. *śalākā-*], f. **1.** an iron bar (window-bar, &c). **2.** any thin metal rod.

सलाद *salād* [? P. *salād*; Fr. *salade*], m. a salad.

सलाम *salām* [A. *salām*], m. (f.) safety, peace: **1.** salutation, greeting; a bow; salutation on departure. **2.** complimentary acknowledgement of another's superior position: specif. *mil.* a salute. — ~! may God protect you! greetings! ~ **है**! id. ~ **अलैकुम** [A. *alai-kum*], *musl.* peace be with you! ~ **करना** (**को**), to greet; to bid goodbye (to); to acknowledge the superiority (of); to salute; fig. to give up, to desist (from). ~ **देना** (**को**), id., 1.-4. ~ **फेरना**, to make a final obeisance (at prayer: *musl.*); not to acknowledge a greeting. ~ **लेना**, to acknowledge and return the greeting, &c. (of, **का**). **दूर से** ~ **करना**, to greet from far off: to keep (someone) at a distance. **फ़ौजी** ~, f. *mil.* a salute.

सलामत *salāmat* [A. *salāma*: P. *salāmat*], f. & adj. predic. **1.** f. safety, salvation; peace. **2.** safe, well. — ~ **भर की दोस्ती**, f. knowing a person (well enough) to say hallo to. ~ **रहना**, to be or to remain safe or well; to live long, to prosper.

सलामती *salāmătī* [P. *salāmatī*], f. **1.** state of safety, well-being; peace. **2.** health. — ~ **का जाम पीना**, to drink to the health (of, **की**). ~ **से**, adv. *musl.* by God's grace.

सलामी *salāmī* [P. *salāmī*], f. **1.** act of salutation (see सलाम). **2.** *mil.* ceremonial salute (as by a guard of honour, or by cannon). **3.** a complimentary present to one holding some favour in his gift. — ~ लेना, *mil.* to take a salute.

सलाह *salāh* [A. *ṣalāḥ*], f. **1.** advice. **2.** consultation. — ~ करना, to consult (with, से). ~ ठहरना (की), a matter to be settled (after discussion). ~ देना (को), to advise. ~ पर चलना, to act on the advice (of, की). ~ लेना, to take the advice (of, की); = ~ करना. – सलाहकार, m. adviser; consultant. °ई, adj. advisory, consultative.

सलिल *salil* [S.], m. water.

सलीक़ा *salīqā* [A. *salīqa*], m. **1.** taste, refinement. **2.** good disposition; courtesy. **3.** method, knack, way. **4.** skill, gift; address. — सलीक़ामंद [P. *-mand*], adj. U. = next. सलीक़ेदार [P. *-dār*], adj. possessing taste, manners, discernment; gifted.

सलीता *salītā*, m. *Pl. HŚS.* a coarse, heavy material (used in packing baggage).

सलीब *salīb* [A. *ṣalīb*], f. a cross. — ~ पर चढ़ाना, to crucify. ~ देना (को), to crucify.

सलील *sa-līl* [S.], adj. **1.** playful; sportive. **2.** flirtatious.

सलूक *salūk* [A. *sulūk*], m. **1.** behaviour, conduct (to or towards, के साथ), treatment. **2.** good behaviour: courtesy; amiability. **3.** good terms or relationship (with, के साथ). — ~ करना (के साथ), to treat well, kindly or courteously. ~ से रहना, to live on good terms.

सलैज *salaij*, f. pronun. var. = सलहज.

सलोक *slok* [ad. *śloka-*], m. E.H. a *dohā* couplet.

सलोकता *sa-lokătā* [S.], f. = सालोक्य.

सलोतर *salotar* [ad. *śālihotra-*], m. veterinary science.

सलोतरी *salotrī* [ad. *śālihotrī-*], m. a veterinary practitioner.

सलोन *salon*, adj. reg. = सलोना.

सलोना *salonā* [*salavaṇa-*], adj. **1.** salted; savoury. ***2.** attractive (esp. of a darkish complexion). **3.** savorous (as gossip, rumour).

सलोनापन *salonāpan* [cf. H. *salonā*], m. attractiveness, charm (see सलोना).

सलोनी *salonī*, adj. = सलोना.

सलोनो *salono*, m. (f., *Pl.*) *hind.* the day of full moon in the month Sāvan, the festival *rakṣā-bandhan*.

सल्मा *salmā* [P. *salma*], m. a band of embroidery. — सल्मा-सितारा, m. bands of embroidery with small stars.

[1]**सल्लू** *sallū* [conn. *śaṭha-*], adj. & f. **1.** adj. foolish, silly (a woman). **2.** f. a silly woman.

[2]**सल्लू** *sallū* [? cf. H. [1]*salnā*], m. *Pl. HŚS.* a thin strip of leather, an insert (in leatherwork).

सवर्ण *sa-varṇ* [S.], adj. **1.** of the same colour; of a single colour. **2.** of similar appearance, resembling. **3.** of the same *varṇa* (see वर्ण, 3). **4.** *ling.* of similar articulation (consonants). **5.** similarly spelt (different words).

सवा *savā* [*sapāda-*], adj. inv. **1.** plus a quarter. ~ दो, adj. two and a quarter; ~ बजे, adv. at a quarter past one. **2.** (w. सौ, हज़ार, लाख, करोड़) one and a quarter times. ~ हज़ार, twelve hundred and fifty.

सवाई *savāī* [cf. H. *sapāda-*], adj. & f. **1.** adj. one and a quarter times larger, or greater. **2.** f. increase or excess by a fourth; interest in kind on seed-grain at twenty-five per cent: payable at harvest time (when grain is cheap).

सवाब *savāb* [A. *ṣavāb*], m. U. **1.** what is right (in speech, thought or action). ***2.** reward (as of faith, good works).

सवामित्व *svamitvă* [S.], m. **1.** ownership. **2.** lordship, sovereignty.

सवायंभू *svāyaṁbhū* [S.], m. Av. *mythol.* relating to the self-existent: name of the first Manu.

[1]**सवाया** *savāyā* [*sapāda-*], adj. **1.** one and a quarter times larger, or greater. **2.** much larger, greater or better; great.

[2]**सवाया** *savāyā*, m. *Pl.* = सवैया.

सवार *savār* [P. *savār*], adj. & m. **1.** adj. mounted (on, पर); riding. **2.** aboard (passengers); embarked. **3.** colloq. drunk, tipsy, 'well away'. **4.** m. a rider; a trooper. **5.** a passenger. — ~ करना (पर or में), to cause to ride: to put (one) on a horse or in a vehicle. ~ होना, to ride (on, पर); to mount, to embark (on), to board; fig. to obsess (one: a craze, or a fear).

सवारी *savārī* [P. *savārī*], f. **1.** riding; horsemanship. **2.** a vehicle, conveyance. **3.** cavalcade, train (of animals or vehicles). **4.** a passenger. **5.** fare (for a journey). — ~ देना (को), to give (one) a ride, or a horse, &c.

सवाल *savāl* [A. *su'āl*], m. **1.** asking, questioning. **2.** a question. **3.** a problem. **4.** interrogation. **5.** request, entreaty; complaint (to a court). — ~ उठना, a question or matter to arise. ~ करना (से), to question; to examine (a student, or a witness); to ask for (alms). ~ देना (को), to set (one) a question or problem; to make a request, petition or complaint. – सवाल-जवाब, m. dialogue; discussion, debate; cross-examination; argument, quarrel. सवाल-जवाब करना, to debate (with, से), &c.

सवालात *savālāt* [A. *su'ālāt*, pl.], m. pl. questions, &c. (see सवाल).

सवालिया *savāliyā* [cf. H. *savāl*], adj. questioning, interrogative.

सविकार *sa-vi-kār* [S.], adj. changed (esp. for the worse).

सविता *savitā* [S.], m. inv. the sun.

सविलास *sa-vi-lās* [S.], adj. flirtatious, &c. (see विलास).

सवेर *saver* [**savela-*], adv. **1.** early. **2.** soon.

सवेरा *saverā* [**savela-*], m. early morning; morning. बड़े, or बहुत सवेरे, adv. very early in the morning; at or soon after dawn. सवेरे, adv. in the early morning; in the morning; early, soon. – सवेरे-सवेरे, adv. very early in the morning.

सवैया *savaiyā* [cf. H. *savā*], m. larger by a quarter: **1.** a weight of one and a quarter *ser*. **2.** *arith.* the one and a quarter times table. **3.** a Hindi quatrain of dactylic structure: each line includes seven feet, together with one or more prefixed or suffixed syllables (the number and arrangement of these being the same throughout the verse). **4.** a song consisting of *savaiyās*. **5.** [? H. [2]*savāyā*] a singer of *savaiyās*.

सव्य *savyă* [S.], adj. **1.** left-hand. **2.** reverse, contrary; inauspicious.

सशंक *sa-śaṅk* [S.], adj. **1.** fearful, alarmed (see शंका). **2.** suspicious, &c.

सशंकित *sa-śaṅkit* [S.], adj. made fearful, alarmed (= सशंक).

सशक्त *sa-śakt* [S.], adj. powerful, endowed with strength.

सशक्तता *sa-śaktatā* [S.], f. state of being powerful.

सशरीर *sa-śarīr* [S.], adj. **1.** embodied, incarnate. **2.** adv. bodily.

सशस्त्र *sa-śastră* [S.], adj. **1.** armed (a person, or a force). **2.** armoured (a vehicle).

सशुल्क *sa-śulk* [S.], adj. paying a fee or charge (and hence having membership or entitlement); paid-up (a current member).

सशोक *sa-śok* [S.], adj. sorrowful.

सश्रम *sa-śram* [S.], adj. characterised by industry or hard work (as a period of time). — ~ कारावास, m. imprisonment with hard labour.

ससिअर *sasiar* [*śaśadhara-*; ? × *-kara-* ← *dinakara-*], m. Av. hare-marked: the moon.

ससुर *sasur* [*śvaśura-*], m. **1.** father-in-law (of husband or wife). **2.** pej. a wretch, wretched old man.

ससुराल *sasurāl* [**śvaśuraśālā-*], f. **1.** father-in-law's house, or family. **2.** sl. prison.

ससुरी *sasurī* [cf. H. *sasur*], f. **1.** mother-in-law. **2.** pej. wretched woman.

सस्ता *sastā* adj. **1.** cheap. **2.** cheap, inferior; unworthy. — ~ करना, to bargain, to haggle over a price. ~ पड़ना, to fall in price; to cost little. ~ लगना, to be available cheaply. सस्ते दाम, or (usu.) दामों, पर, adv. at a cheap price, cheaply. सस्ते (में), adv. id.

सस्ताई *sastāī* [cf. H. *sastā*], f. cheapness.

सस्तापन *sastāpan* [cf. H. *sastā*], m. cheapness, low price.

सस्ती *sastī* [cf. H. *sastā*], f. reg. **1.** cheapness, low price. **2.** a time of low prices.

सह- *sah-* [S.], pref. **1.** with, along with, together with (e.g. सहगामी, adj. & m. accompanying; companion on a journey. **2.** united; common; co- (e.g. सहकार्य, m. cooperation).

सहकार *sah-kār* [S.], m. **1.** one who acts with: a colleague; assistant. **2.** acting together; cooperation.

सहकारिता *sah-kāritā* [S.], f. working together; cooperation.

सहकारी *sah-kārī* [S.], adj. & m. **1.** adj. cooperating, cooperative. **2.** m. a fellow-worker, colleague; assistant.

सहकार्य *sah-kāryă* [S.], m. cooperation.

सहगमन *sah-gaman* [S.], m. **1.** accompanying. **2.** Brbh. self-immolation of a widow on her husband's cremation fire.

सहगामिनी *sah-gāminī* [S.], f. see s.v. सहगामी.

सहगामी *sah-gāmī* [S.], adj. & m. **1.** adj. going with, accompanying. **2.** m. associate, companion. **3.** attendant; follower.

सहचर *sah-car* [S.], adj. & m. **1.** adj. going, or associating, with. **2.** m. associate, companion. **3.** attendant; follower.

सहचरी *sah-carī* [S.], f. see s.v. सहचर.

सहचारिणी *sah-cāriṇī* [S.], f. 1. = सहचरी. **2.** a wife.

सहचारी *sah-cārī* [S.], m. = सहचर.

सहज *saha-j* [S.], adj. & m. born together: **1.** adj. innate; natural, instinctive. **2.** unforced, unaffected (manner). **3.** easy, simple (as a task). **4.** m. a full brother. **5.** natural state or disposition. **6.** E.H. the unqualified absolute (as perceivable intuitively in the heart); Brbh. the supreme being. — ~ **ज्ञान**, m. instinctive knowledge, instinct. ~ **बुद्धि**, f. id. ~ **भाव से**, adv. in an unforced, easy manner. ~ **में**, easily; by degrees, slowly; softly, in a low tone. ~ **से**, adv. id. ~ **स्वभाव ही**, adv. = ~ **भाव से**. – **सहजानुभूति** [°*ja* + *a*°], f. instinctive sympathy.

सहजन *sahjan* [*śobhāñjana(ka)-*], m. the horse-radish or 'drum-stick' tree, *Moringa pterygosperma* or *oleifera*.

सहजन्मा *sah-janmā* [S.], adj. inv. born together (as twins).

सहजात *sah-jāt* [S.], adj. **1.** innate. **2.** twin-born.

सहता *sahta* [cf. H. *sahnā*], adj. **1.** bearing, &c. **2.** bearable. — ~ **पानी**, m. warm, hot (as opposed to very hot or boiling) water. ~ ~, adj. = ~, 2. **सहते सहते**, adv. patiently.

[1]**सहन** *sahn* [S.], m. **1.** patience; tolerance; forbearance. **2.** endurance. — ~ **करना**, to endure, to tolerate, &c. – **सहन-शक्ति**, f. power of endurance, or of tolerance. **सहनशील**, adj. of patient disposition; patient; tolerant; forbearing. °**ता**, f.

[2]**सहन** *sahn* [A. *ṣaḥn*], m. **1.** inner courtyard. **2.** open area adjoining a house: court, drive. **3.** *Pl. HŚS.* a kind of silk cloth.

[3]**सहन** *sahn* [cf. H. *sahnā*], f. see s.v. [1]**रहन**.

सहनक *sahnak* [P. *ṣaḥnak*], m. reg. a small dish or plate.

[1]**सहना** *sahnā* [*sahate*], v.t. & v.i. **1.** v.t. to endure; to tolerate; (w. **रहना**) to live out (one's days). **2.** to suffer (as grief, loss). **3.** to bear (a weight, strain). **4.** v.i. to be borne, or tolerated, &c. **5.** to be digested (as food). — **सहता पानी**, m. see s.v. **सहता**.

[2]**सहना** *sahnā*, m. = **शहना**.

सहनीय *sahnīyǎ* [S.], adj. endurable, tolerable.

सहपाठिनी *sah-pāṭhinī* [S.], f. fellow-student; class-fellow.

सहपाठी *sah-pāṭhī* [S.], m. fellow-student; class-fellow.

सहभागिता *sah-bhāgitā*, f. collaboration, &c. (= **सहयोग**).

सहभागी *sah-bhāgī* [S.], adj. & m. **1.** adj. sharing. **2.** m. partner; shareholder.

सहम *sahm* [P. *sahm*], m. fear. — **सहमनाक** [P. *-nāk*], adj. frightful, to be feared.

सहमत *sah-mat* [S.], adj. agreeing (with, **से**; about, **में**).

सहमति *sah-mati* [S.], f. agreement.

सहमना *sahamnā* [cf. P. *sahm*], v.i. to feel fear (of, **से**).

सहमरण *sah-maraṇ* [S.], m. dying together; a widow's burning herself with the corpse of her husband.

सहमाना *sahmānā* [cf. H. *sahamnā*], v.t. to frighten, to terrify.

सहयोग *sah-yog* [S.], m. cooperation; collaboration.

सहयोगी *sah-yogī* [S.], adj. cooperating; associated; cooperative (residence),

सहयोजित *sah-yojit* [S.], adj. co-opted.

सहर *sahr* [A. *saḥar*], m. f. the time just before dawn; dawn.

सहरना *saharnā*, v.t. **1.** Brbh. = [1]**सहना**. **2.** *Pl.* = **सँवारना**.

सहरा *sahrā* [A. *ṣaḥrā*], m. desert; wilderness.

सहराई *sahrāī* [P. *ṣaḥrāī*], adj. desert; wild.

सहरावन *sahrāvan* [cf. H. *sahlānā*], m. reg. = **सहलाहट**, 2.

[1]**सहरी** *sahrī* [P. *saḥrī*], f. *musl.* food eaten before dawn (prior to a day's fast during the month of Ramaẓān).

[2]**सहरी** *sahrī* [*śaphara-*], f. Brbh. a small gold-coloured fish (see **शफर**).

सहरोस *sah-ros* [*saroṣa-* × H. *saha-*], adj. angry.

सहल *sahl* [A. *sahl*], adj. **1.** easy, simple. **2.** facile. — ~ **करना**, to make easy, to simplify.

सहलाना *sahlānā* [H. *sihrānā*], v.t. **1.** to stroke, to caress. **2.** to tickle: to titillate. **3.** to harass, to tease.

सहलाहट *sahlāhaṭ* [cf. H. *sahlānā*], f. **1.** stroking, caressing. **2.** tickling; titillation.

सहवास *sah-vās* [S.], m. **1.** co-residence. **2.** sexual intercourse.

सहवासी *sah-vāsī* [S.], adj. & m. **1.** adj. co-resident. **2.** m. a co-resident; fellow-lodger.

सहवैया *sahvaiyā* [cf. H. *sahnā*], m. an endurer, or sufferer.

सहस- *sahas-* [*sahasra-*]. thousand: — सहसकर, m. Av. thousand-rayed: the sun. सहस-नयन, m. Av. thousand-eyed: title of the god Indra. सहसफनी, m. Brbh. *mythol.* thousand-hooded: title of the snake Śeṣa. सहसबाहु, m. Brbh. *mythol.* thousand-armed: title of Arjuna, a prince of the Haihayas; title of Śiva, and of Viṣṇu. सहसानन [°*sa*+*ā*°], m. Brbh. *mythol.* thousand-headed: title of the snake Śeṣa; title of Viṣṇu.

सहस् *sahas* [S.] m. strength, force, power.

सहसा *sahăsā* [S.] adv. **1.** suddenly. **2.** rashly, hastily.

सहस्र *sahasră* [S.], adj. & m. **1.** adj. a thousand. **2.** m. the amount of a thousand. e.g. एक ~ गाँव, m. pl. a thousand villages. — सहस्राक्ष [°*ra*+*ă*], adj. thousand-eyed: a title of Indra. सहस्रानन [°*ra*+*ā*°], adj. thousand-faced or -mouthed: a title of Viṣṇu, and of Śeṣnāg. सहस्रबाहु, adj. thousand-armed: a title of Śiva, Viṣṇu and the Haihaya prince, Arjun. सहस्रसीस, m. *mythol.* thousand-headed: a title of the snake Śeṣnāg. सहस्राब्दी [°*ra*+*a*°], f. a millenium. सहस्रार [°*ra*+*ā*°], m. thousand-spoked: = ब्रह्मरंध्र.

सहस्री *sahasrī* [S.] adj. & m. **1.** adj. having a thousand, or thousands; amounting to a thousand. **2.** m. a body of a thousand men. **3.** the commander or governor of a thousand.

सहाऊ *sahāū* [cf. H. *sahānā*], adj. bearable, endurable.

सहाना *sahānā* [cf. H. *sahnā*], v.t. to cause to bear or to endure, &c.

सहानुभूति *sahânu-bhūti* [S.], f. sympathy.

सहाय *sahây* [S.], m., f. **1.** m. helper; rescuer; patron. **2.** usu. f. help, assistance; protection. — ~ करना (की), to help, &c.

सहायक *sahâyak* [S.], adj. & m. going with: **1.** adj. assisting, assistant. ~ संपादक, m. assistant editor. **2.** auxiliary (force, service); gram. auxiliary (verb); secondary (industry); supplementary (list, table; benefits). **3.** tributary (a river). **4.** m. an assistant; companion.

सहायता *sahâyătā* [S.], f. help, assistance; aid. — ~ करना (की), to help, &c. ~ देना (को), to give help, to lend aid (in, में).

सहायिका *sahâyikā* [S.], f. assistant.

सहायी *sahâyī* [? cf. H. *sahāy*], adj. = सहायक.

सहार *sahār* [cf. H. *sahār-*], f. reg. bearing, suffering; endurance. — ~ करना, to bear patiently.

सहार- *sahār-* [conn. *sahakāra-*[1]], v.t. Brbh. **1.** to bear, to endure. **2.** reg. to trail, to drag.

सहारा *sahārā* [*sahakāra-*[1]], m. **1.** support. **2.** dependence, reliance. **3.** encouragement. **4.** assistance, aid. — ~ देना (को), to support; to encourage; to give aid (to). ~ लगाना (का), id.; to support oneself (on or against); to rely (on). ~ लेना, to rely for support or help, &c. (on, का). सहारे से, adv. with the support (of, के); gently, softly.

सहालग *sahālag* [H. *sāhā*+H. *lagnā*], m. **1.** auspicious date for a marriage, a wedding day. **2.** auspicious period for marriages.

सहावट *sahāvaṭ* [cf. H. *sahnā*], f. reg. power of passive endurance.

सहावटी *sahāvṭī*, f. *Pl.* a door-lintel; door-frame (= *caukhaṭ*).

सहावल *sahāval*, m. *Pl. HŚS.* a plummet, or plumb-line (= *sāhul*).

सहिँजन *sahiñjan*, m. = सहिजन.

सहिजन *sahijan* [*śobhāñjana-*], m. the horse-radish tree, *Moringa pterygosperma*.

सहित *sahit* [S.], ppn. with or without के. **1.** accompanied (by); attended (by). **2.** along (with), together (with). — सद्भाव ~, adv. with greetings (inscription, or closing formula in a letter).

सहियारना *sahiyārnā*, v.t. *Pl.* = सँवारना.

सहिष्णु *sahiṣṇu* [S.], adj. patient, tolerant; forbearing.

सहिष्णुता *sahiṣṇutā* [S.], f. patience, tolerance; forbearance.

सही *sahī* [A. *ṣaḥīḥ*], adj. & f. **1.** adj. sound, right, correct; real, actual. **2.** *arith.* whole (a number w. following fraction). **3.** adv. (it is) quite right, or correct; really; exactly. **4.** very well, all right. **5.** f. colloq. confirmation, corroboration; signature. — ~ अर्थों, or मानों, में, adv. in the real sense (of a word), properly. ~ करना, to make right, to correct; to adjust; to cure; to determine; to verify; to sign, to attest (a document). ~ पड़ना, to prove to be correct. अब उसकी वही मरज़ी है तो यही ~, if he (God) now desires that (for us), we must accept it. आओ तो ~, come on then: come if you wish, or dare. खोलो तो ~, do open (the door: expressing either impatience, or reassurance). यह न ~ तो वह दूसरा आपको ख़ूब लगता है, if this one doesn't suit you the other does. वह बात ~ है, that is correct. – सही-सलामत, adj. safe and sound.

सहुआइन *sahuāin* [H. [1]*sāh*+-*ānī*-, -*inī*-], f. a merchant's or shopkeeper's wife.

सहूलत *sahūlat* [A. *suhūla*: P. *suhulat*], f. = सहूलियत.

सहूलियत *sahūliyat* [cf. H. *sahūlat*], f. smoothness: **1.** convenience, ease. **2.** good manners, ease of manner. — ~ **सीखना**, to learn how to behave. ~ **से**, adv. conveniently, without difficulty.

सहृदय *sa-hṛday* [S.], adj. having feelings, sensitive; kindly.

सहेजना *sahejnā*, v.t. **1.** to examine, to check (as belongings, or money). **2.** to hand over (sthg.) with instructions for its use or care. — **आवाज़ ~**, to choose (one's) words with care.

सहेजा *sahejā*, m. reg. rennet.

सहेट *saheṭ* [conn. *saṅketa-*: ? w. E.H. *-bheṁṭ*], m. Brbh. a meeting-place.

सहेत *sahet* [conn. H. *sahit*; ? × H. *samet*], adv. pronun. var. = **सहित**.

सहेतु *sa-hetu* [S.], adj. = **सहेतुक**.

सहेतुक *sa-hetuk* [S.], adj. **1.** having a cause or reason. **2.** having an object or purpose.

सहेली *sahelī* [cf. *sakhī-*], f. a woman's female friend.

सहोढ़ *sahoṛh* [**sahoḍha-*], m. *Pl. HŚS.* brought with (a wife): the son of a woman pregnant at the time of her marriage.

सहोदर *sahôdar* [S.], adj. & m. **1.** adj. uterine; born of the same parents. **2.** m. a full brother.

सह्य *sahyǎ* [S.], adj. **1.** to be endured, &c. (see **सहना**). **2.** endurable; tolerable.

[1]**साँक** *sāṁk* [*śaṅkā-*], f. *Pl.* fear, apprehension.

[2]**साँक** *sāṁk*, f. pronun. var. = **शाख़**.

[1]**साँकर** *sāṁkar*, f. = **साँकल**.

[2]**साँकर** *saṁkar* [*saṁkaṭa-*], adj. & f. **1.** adj. narrow, confining. **2.** oppressive. **3.** f. distress, trouble, straits. **4.** a narrow lane or passage.

साँकरी *sāṁkrī* [*śṛṅkhalā-*], f. **1.** a small chain. **2.** Brbh. restriction of vision (by dust).

साँकल *sāṁkal* [*śṛṅkhalā-*], f. **1.** a chain; specif. a door-chain. **2.** staple (of a lock on a door). **3.** reg. a women's ornament, necklet. **4.** a fetter; handcuff.

साँका *sāṁkā* [conn. *sāmagrya-*], m. reg. (W.) network of string or cord (as the stringing of a *cārpāī*).

सांकेतिक *sāṅketik* [S.], adj. **1.** symbolic, allusive. **2.** coded.

[1]**साँखा** *sāṁkhā* [conn. *saṁkṣobha-*], m. Brbh. distress.

[2]**साँखा** *sāṁkhā* [*śaṅku-*[1] × *śākhā-*], m. reg. wooden axle (for a grindstone); wooden bushing for an axle.

सांखू *sāṅkhū* [**sākkhu-*], m. *Pl.* the *sāl* tree, *Shorea robusta*.

साँखौ *sāṁkhau* [*saṁkṣobha-*], m. Av. distress (cf. [1]**साँखा**).

सांख्य *sāṅkhyǎ* [S.], m. having to do with number or calculation: name of an Indian philosophical system.

सांख्यिकी *sāṅkhyikī* [S.], f. statistics.

सांख्यिकीय *sāṅkhyikīyǎ* [S.], adj. statistical.

सांग *sāṅg* [S.], adj. having all its members or parts: complete, entire. — **सांगोपांग** [°*ga*+*u*°], adj. having its major and minor members: complete, entire.

[1]**साँग** *sāṁg* [H. *svāṁg*], m. **1.** imitation, disguise, &c. (= **स्वाँग**). **2.** a type of popular drama featuring singing, and dealing predominantly with legendary or fabulous subject-matter (as well as with some modern subjects).

[2]**साँग** *sāṁg* [? conn. *śaṅku-*[1] or *śārṅga-*], f. **1.** a short spear. **2.** reg. (W.) rod, pole; lever. **3.** *Pl. HŚS.* a borer for wells.

[3]**साँग** *sāṁg*, m. = **साँगह**.

साँगर *sāṁgar* [conn. *saṁgara-*] m. *Pl.* **1.** a pod of fruit of the *śamī* (acacia). **2.** a kind of bean.

साँगह *sāṁgah* [*saṁgraha-*], m. reg. (Bihar) **1.** a plough and its accessory equipment. **2.** building material.

[1]**साँगी** *sāṁgī* [cf. H. [2]*sāṁg*], f. Av. **1.** a spear, &c. **2.** *Pl.* prop for the shaft of a cart.

[2]**साँगी** *sāṁgī* [cf. H. [1]*sāṁg*], m. *Pl.* mimic, actor, player.

[3]**साँगी** *sāṁgī* [H. *sāṁvgī*], f. reg. netting fixed underneath the seat of a cart (see **साँवगी**).

सांगीत *sāṅgīt* [H. [1]*sāṁg* × H. *saṅgīt*], m. = [1]**साँग**, 2.

साँगुस *sāṁgus*, f. a skate-fish or ray.

साँघर *sāṁghar* [**saṁghara-*: Pa. *saṁghara-*], m. *Pl.* a wife's son by a former husband, stepson.

साँघरा- *sāṁgharā-* [cf. *saṁghaṭayati*], v.t. reg. (E.) to reconcile a cow to its newly born calf (by plastering it with sugar).

साँच *sāṁc*, m. truth (= **सच**). — ~ **को आँच नहीं**, truth does not feel fire: truth has nothing to fear.

[1]**साँचा** *sāṁcā* [*sañcaka-*], m. **1.** a mould. **2.** form, outline. **3.** last (shoemaker's). **4.** a model, artist's or craftsman's mock-up. **5.** *Pl.* a cone (= शंकु). — **साँचे में ढला**, adj. the (very) image (of, के); perfectly made, shapely, beautiful. **साँचे में ढालना**, to cast in a mould, to form, to shape. **एक ही साँचे में ढले**, cast from one mould: identical, as like as two peas.

[2]**साँचा** *sāṁcā*, adj. = सच्चा.

साँची *sāṁcī* [cf. H. *sāṁcā*], m. page-size, format.

साँज *sāṁj*, f. pronun. var. = साँझ.

साँझ *sāṁjh* [*saṁdhyā-*], f. evening, twilight. — **साँझ-सवेरे**, adv. morning and evening.

साँझलो *sāṁjhlo* [cf. *saṁdhyā-*], m. reg. (W.) as much land as a pair of oxen can plough in one day.

साँझी *sāṁjhī*, f. **1.** designs traced out by women and girls on the floors of temples and houses (esp. in the dark half of the month Āśvin) with coloured powder, grain, flowers and leaves). **2.** songs sung by girls in praise of Rādhā. — ~ **खेल-**, Brbh. to trace *sāṁjhī* designs.

[1]**साँट** *sāṁṭ* [cf. H. *sāṁ}ṭnā*], f. **1.** joining, sticking. **2.** contact. **3.** a liaison (with, से). **4.** plot. — **साँट-गाँठ**, f. combining, plotting: = ~, 4. **साँट-बाँट**, f. id.

[2]**साँट** *sāṁṭ* [conn. **saṭṭ-*[1]], f. a weal.

साँटना *sāṁṭnā* [conn. **saṁsthāti*: Pk. *saṁṭhāi*], v.t. **1.** to stick together, to join. **2.** to unite. **3.** to join, to splice (as rope). **4.** to attach (a person) to oneself, to win (one) over or away (from). — **साँटा**, m. reg. (Bihar) a graft.

साँट-मारी *sāṁṭ-mārī* [H. [2]*sāṁṭā*+H. *mārnā*], f. reg. goading.

[1]**साँटा** *sāṁṭā*, m. reg. (Bihar) see s.v. **साँटना**.

[2]**साँटा** *sāṁṭā* [conn. *saṭṭ-*[1]], m. **1.** whip; stick, goad. **2.** a sugar-cane.

साँटि *sāṁṭi*, f. Brbh. = [1]**साँट**, 2.

साँठ *sāṁṭh*, f. = [1]**साँट**. — **साँठ-गाँठ**, f. = **साँट-गाँठ**.

साँठना *sāṁṭhnā* [**saṁsthāti*: Pk. *saṁṭhāi*], v.t. = **साँटना**.

साँठि *sāṁṭhi*, f. Av. = **साँठी**.

साँठी *sāṁṭhī* [*saṁstha-*], f. assets, capital.

साँड़ *sāṁṛ* [*sāṇḍa-*], m. **1.** a bull; specif. a wandering bull. **2.** a stallion. **3.** reg. a camel. **4.** colloq. a wild, independent fellow. — ~ **की तरह घूमना**, to wander at will.

साँड़नी *sāṁṛnī* [cf. H. *sāṁṛ*], f. reg. a female camel (for riding).

साँड़ा *sāṁṛā*, m. a species of sand-lizard (the fat of which yields a medicinal oil).

साँड़िया *sāṁṛiyā* [cf. H. *sāṁṛ*], m. reg. **1.** a young camel. **2.** *HŚS.* rider on a camel. **3.** *Pl.* a wheel used in lace-making.

सांत *sânt* [S.], adj. having an end: finite, limited.

सांत्वन *sāntvan* [S.], m. *Pl. HŚS.* **1.** conciliation, reconcilement. **2.** mild manner; appeasing.

सांत्वना *sāntvănā* [S.], f. consolation. — ~ **देना** (को), to console.

साँथरी *sāṁthrī* [*saṁstara-*], f. Av. a mat (= साथरी).

साँथल *sāṁthal* [cf. *sakthan-*], f. *Pl.* thigh.

साँद *sāṁd*, m. reg. (E.) = **साँदा**.

साँदा *sāṁdā* [*saṁdāya-*], m. reg. a hobble (used on a cow's legs at milking).

साँध *sāṁdh* [*saṁdhi-*], f. crack, crevice.

सांध्य *sāndhyă* [S.], adj. having to do with twilight or evening.

साँप *sāṁp* [*sarpa-*], m. **1.** a snake. **2.** fig. a malevolent person. — ~ **उतारना**, to treat a snake-bite successfully. ~ **कलेजे**, or **छाती**, **पर लोटना**, a snake to writhe in (one's) vitals: to be gnawed by jealousy or envy. ~ **कीलना**, to charm a snake. ~ **का काटा रस्सी से डारता है** (or **डरे**), one bitten by a snake fears a piece of rope: a burnt child dreads (even a thought of) the fire. ~ **सूँघ जाना** (को), euph. a snake to bite (one). **काला** ~, m. black snake: a villain. **दो-मुहाँ** ~, m. two-headed snake: a very dangerous person; an arrant villain.

साँपन *sāṁpan*, f. **1.** a female snake (= **साँपिन**). **2.** reg. (W.) blemish in a horse's coat (a downward-turning twist of hair, thought of as inauspicious). **3.** *Pl.* name of a complaint in which the hair falls out.

साँपा *sāṁpā*, m. pronun. var. = **स्यापा**.

साँपिन *sāṁpin* [cf. H. *sāṁp*], f. a female snake.

सांप्रतिक *sāmpratik* [S.], adj. & m. **1.** adj. of the present, current. **2.** contemporary. **3.** timely. **4.** m. a contemporary.

सांप्रदायिक *sāmpradāyik* [S.], adj. **1.** sectarian. **2.** communal.

सांप्रदायिकता *sāmpradāyikătā* [S.], f. **1.** sectarianism; bigotry. **2.** communalism.

सांबर *sāmbar* [*śambara-*], m. = [1]साँभर.

साँबर *sāṁbar* [*śambala-*, Pk. *sambala-*], m. Av. provisions for a journey.

[1]**साँभर** *sāṁbhar* [conn. *śambara-*], m. a type of large antelope.

[2]**साँभर** *sāṁbhar* [*śākambharī-*], m. a type of rock salt obtained from Sambhar Lake in Rajasthan.

[3]**साँभर** *sāṁbhar*, m. a spiced (south Indian) lentil and vegetable curry.

साँय *sāṁy*, f. esp. redupl. **1.** sighing, whistling (of the wind). **2.** whizzing. **3.** rustling, rustle. **4.** creeping or tingling sensation. — ~ ~, f. id.

साँव *sāṁv* [*sāman-*], m. *Pl.* calm, tranquillity. — साँव-चीत [*citta-*], adj. with a calm mind.

साँवगी *sāṁvgī* [*sāmagrya-*], m. reg. (Bihar) the body-work (esp. seat and canopy) of a two-wheeled cart. — ~ गाड़ी, f. a two-wheeled cart.

साँवटा *sāṁvṭā*, adj. *Pl.* = साँवठा.

साँवठा *sāṁvṭhā* [? conn. *saṁstha-*], adj. *Pl.* **1.** collected. **2.** ready, finished; ready (to, को).

साँवला *sāṁvlā* [*śyāmalaka-*], adj. **1.** dark-complexioned. **2.** title of a lover or husband; specif. title of Kṛṣṇa. — साँवला-सलोना, adj. dark and savorous: attractive (a dark complexion).

साँवलापन *sāṁvlāpan* [cf. H. *sāṁvlā*], m. darkness of complexion. — उसके चेहरे का रंग कुछ ~ लिए हुए था, his complexion was quite dark.

साँवलिया *sāṁvăliyā* [cf. H. *sāṁvlā*], adj. & m. dimin. **1.** adj. = साँवला. **2.** m. a title of Kṛṣṇa.

साँवाँ *sāṁvāṁ* [*śyāmaka-*], m. a quick-growing millet, *Panicum frumentaceum*.

साँस *sāṁs* [*śvāsa-*], f. **1.** breathing; breath. **2.** a sigh. — ~ उखड़ना, to breathe convulsively, to struggle for breath. ~ का रोग, m. asthma. ~ खींचना, to draw a deep breath; to hold the breath; to feign death. ~ चढ़ना, to be short of breath; to gasp, to pant. ~ छोड़ना, to breathe out. ~ टूटना, = ~ उखड़ना. ~ फूँकना (मुँह में), to revive, to resuscitate. ~ फूलना, to be breathless. ~ भरना, to draw a deep breath; to heave a sigh; to gasp, to pant. ~ रहते, adv. until one's last breath. ~ रुकना, the breath to be stopped: to feel suffocated, choked; to be smothered. ~ रोककर, adv. with bated breath. ~ लेना, to draw breath, to take a rest or spell; to sigh. उलटी ~ लेना, to draw in the breath urgently, to gasp (as at death). ठंडी ~ भरना, or लेना, to heave a sad sigh. जब तक ~, तब तक आस, while there's life there's hope.

साँसत *sāṁsat* [ad. *śāsti-*: w. H. *sāṁsnā*], f. **1.** punishment; specif. bodily punishment; hard labour. **2.** pain; torment. **3.** suffering. — जान ~ में डालना, to cause dire distress or suffering (to, की). – साँसत-घर, m. segregated cell (in a prison).

सांसद *sāṁsad* [S.], m. a member of parliament (cf. संसद).

साँसना *sāṁsnā* [*śāsati*], v.t. *Pl. HŚS.* **1.** to rebuke. **2.** to punish. **3.** to cause distress (to).

सांसर्गिक *sāṃsargik* [S.], adj. contagious.

साँसा *sāṁsā* [*saṁśaya-*], m. **1.** doubt, anxiety; apprehension. **2.** fear.

सांसारिक *sāṃsārik* [S.], adj. having to do with this world: worldly; secular.

साँसिया *sāṁsiyā*, m. **1.** a tribe of Indian gypsies. **2.** a member of that tribe.

सांस्कृतिक *sāṁskṛtik* [S.], adj. cultural.

-सा *-sā*, adj. resembling, like: **1.** (w. most adjs.) rather, quite, -ish (moderate degree of a quality). एक अच्छी-सी किताब, a rather good book. एक बहुत अच्छी-सी किताब, a very good book. एक-से, adj. pl. much the same (as each other, or one another). नीला-सा पानी, bluish water. **2.** (chiefly w. adjs. of quantity, to indicate that an exact or particular amount is not intended.) उसने मुझे बहुत-सा रुपया दिया था, he gave me a lot of money. उसे थोड़ी-सी हिंदी आती है, he knows a little Hindi. एक छोटी-सी दुकान, a little shop. एक बड़ा-सा शेर, a big tiger. ज़रा-सा पानी, m. a little water. ज़रा-सी लड़की, f. a slip of a girl. बहुत-से बड़े पेड़, many big trees. **3.** (indicating a restricted number of possibilities or choices.) कोई-से तीन विषय, any three subjects (as of a syllabus). कौन-सा दिन है? what day is today? (of the week, month). **4.** (expressing likeness: w. nouns and pronouns, functioning then as a ppn.; also w. verbal forms.) बंदर दीवार पर नाच(-सा) उठा, the monkey started a kind of dance on the wall. मुझ-सा ग़रीब आदमी, a poor man like me. शेर का-सा दिल, a heart like a lion('s). शेर-सा दिल, a heart like a lion('s).

साइका *sāikā* [cf. *sāyaka-*: ad.], f. (?) *Pl.* a small arrow, dart; lightning; thunderbolt.

साइत *sāit* [A. *sā'at*], f. **1.** an hour. **2.** a moment; an auspicious or inauspicious moment. — साइत-सगुन, m. omens, auguries.

साइर *sāir*, m. see [1] [2] सायर.

साईं *sāīṁ* [*svāmin-*], m. **1.** master, lord. **2.** the lord: God. **3.** husband. **4.** (esp. voc.) a Muslim ascetic.

[1]साई *sāī* [*sāti-*[1]], f. winning, gaining: earnest-money, pledge. — ~ देना, to give an advance (on a contract). ~ बजाना, to perform (as singers) by previous arrangement.

[2]साई *sāī* [**sahāyikā-*], f. reg. (W.) a cross-timber or brace (in carpentry).

साईस *sāīs* [A. *sāʾis*], m. **1.** a groom. **2.** one who hires out pack-horses.

साईसी *sāīsī* [P. *sāʾisī*], f. the work or duties of a groom or horse-keeper.

साउज *sāuj* [**śvāpadya-*], adj. & m. Av. **1.** adj. wild, savage. **2.** m. a wild animal.

[1]साऊ *sāū* [Ind. *sāgū*], m. the sago palm; sago.

[2]साऊ *sāū* [*sādhu-*], adj. & m. E.H. **1.** adj. good, virtuous. **2.** m. one who is good or beneficent (cf. [1]साह).

[1]साक *sāk* [ad. *śāka-*], m. = [1]शाक, साग.

[2]साक *sāk*, f. Brbh. = [1]साख.

साकल्य *sākalyă* [S.], m. totality, entirety.

साका *sākā* [*śākya-*], m. **1.** era, epoch. **2.** Av. the Śaka era. **3.** Av. time, moment (of death). **4.** poet. a heroic or epoch-making exploit. — ~ कर-, Brbh. Av. to perform an epoch-making exploit.

साकार *sâkār* [S.], adj. **1.** having form or shape; real, visible (not imaginary). **2.** incarnate.

साकिन *sākin* [A. *sākin*], adj. & m. U. at rest: **1.** adj. inhabiting, residing at. **2.** m. inhabitant, resident.

साक़ी *sāqī* [A. *sāqī*], m. **1.** cup-bearer. **2.** fig. loved one.

साक्ष *sâkṣ* [S.], adj. *Pl. HŚS.* having eyes. — साक्षीकरण, m. obtaining or providing an attestation (of sthg).

साक्षर *sâkṣar* [S.], adj. **1.** literate. **2.** formed of syllables or letters.

साक्षरता *sâkṣarătā* [S.], f. literacy.

साक्षात् *sâkṣāt* [S.], adv. & adj. & m. before the eyes: **1.** adv. in the sight or presence (of). **2.** visibly, manifestly. **3.** adj. visible, evident, veritable; incarnate. **4.** m. a (face-to-face) meeting. — साक्षात्कार, m. a meeting, interview. °ई, m. interviewee.

[1]साक्षी *sâkṣī* [S.], adj. & m. **1.** adj. observing, witnessing. **2.** testifying. **3.** m. an eye-witness. **4.** witness (in law). **5.** a spectator. — ~ करना, or बनाना, to make (one) a witness; to try (one) by ordeal.

[2]साक्षी *sâkṣī* [S. (**sākṣī-*)], f. witness's testimony, evidence. — ~ देना, to give evidence.

साक्षीकरण *sâkṣīkaraṇ* [S.], m. see s.v. साक्ष्य.

साक्ष्य *sâkṣyă* [S.], m. testimony, evidence. — साक्ष्यांकन [°*kṣya+a*°], m. attesting, attestation.

[1]साख *sākh* [**sākṣī-, sākṣya-*], f. m. **1.** credit, trust; credibility; standing. **2.** good name, reputation. **3.** *Pl. HŚS.* evidence (of a witness). **4.** Av. usefulness (for a partic. purpose). — ~ बनना (की), (a person) to be of good credit, &c.

[2]साख *sākh* [P. *śākh*; ? and ad. *śākhā-*], f. a branch, &c. (= शाखा, शाख़).

[1]साखा *sākhā* [cf. H. [2]*sākh*], m. reg. (W.) mill-post, shaft (for millstones).

[2]साखा *sākhā*, m. *Pl.* fight, quarrel.

[1]साखि *sākhi*, m. Brbh. Av. a witness (= [1]साखी).

[2]साखि *sākhi* [ad. *śākhya-*], m. Brbh. a tree.

[1]साखी *sākhī* [*sākṣin-*], m. a witness.

[2]साखी *sākhī* [**sākṣī-*], f. **1.** testimony, evidence. **2.** a rhyming verse (usu. a *dohā*) attesting to some aspect of ultimate truth as perceived by a *nirguṇī* (q.v.) devotee.

[3]साखी *sākhī* [? ad. *śākhin-*], m. ? f. Av. a tree (= [2]साखि).

साखू *sākhū* [**sākkhu-*], m. the teak tree.

साग *sāg* [ad. *śaka-*], m. greens, vegetable(s). — साग-पात, m. greens, different vegetables; fig. sthg. trivial or insignificant. साग-भाजी, f. = prec., 1. साग-सब्ज़ी, f. id. सागवाला, m. & adj. a greengrocer; seller of herbs; esp. adj. vegetarian.

साग-भत्ता *sāg-bhattā* [H. *sāg*+H. *bhāt*], m. *Pl. HŚS.* a stew of vegetables and rice.

सागर *sāgar* [S.], m. ocean, sea.

साग़र *sāgar* [P. *sāgar*], m. a cup (for wine), goblet.

सागू *sāgū* [Ind. *sagu*], m. the sago palm; sago.

सागून *sāgūn* [**sāgguvanya-*], m. = सागौन.

सागौती *sāgautī*, f. *Pl.* meat, butcher's meat.

सागौन *sāgaun* [**sāgguvanya-*], m. the teak tree; teak wood.

साज़ *sāz* [P. *sāz*], m. **1.** equipment; implements; apparatus (cf. [1]साज). **2.** arms. **3.** trimmings, decoration. **4.** harness. **5.** any musical instrument. **6.** -साज़. making, effecting: a maker; counterfeiter. — ~ छेड़ना, to strike up a tune. – साज़-बाज़ [P. *-bāz*], m. = ~, 1.; preparation. साज़-संगीत, m. instrumental music. साज़-समारोह, m. music and festivity. साज़ो-सामान, m. = ~, 1.

[1]**साज** *sāj* [*sajya-, sajjā-*], f. **1.** preparation. **2.** [× P. *sāz*] equipment, wherewithal, &c. (see साज़). — साज-सजावट, f. = next. साज-सज्जा, f. array, decoration; outward form or aspect (as of a book); outfitting, equipment (= ~, 2). साज-सामान, m. = ~, 2.; supplies, provisions. साज-सिंगार, m. dress, attire (of women).

[2]**साज** *sāj* [P. *sāj*], m. the teak tree.

साज- *sāj-*, v.t. & v.i. **1.** v.t. Brbh. Av. = सजाना. **2.** v.i. Av. = सजना.

साजन *sājan* [*sajjana-*[2]], m. **1.** lover. **2.** husband. **3.** lord: God. **4.** a good, kindly or noble man.

साज़िंदा *sāzindā* [P. *sāzanda*], m. a musician, instrumentalist; accompanist (of a dancer).

साज़िश *sāziś* [P. *sāziś*], f. a plot; conspiracy. — ~ करना, to conspire, &c.

साज़िशी *sāziśī* [P. *sāziśī*], adj. conspiring, colluding; fraudulent (as dealings, appearances).

साझा *sājhā* [*sāhāyya-*], m. & adj. **1.** m. partnership; association; sharing (in an activity). **2.** share (in produce; or in a company). **3.** adj. joint. — ~ करना, to enter into partnership; to form a company. ~ बाज़ार, m. the (European) Common Market. साझी मंडी, f. id. साझे में, adv. in partnership, jointly. – साझेदार [P. *-dār*], m. a partner, associate; a shareholder. °ई, f. partnership.

साझी *sājhī*, m. **1.** a partner, associate. **2.** a shareholder.

साट *sāṭ*, f. = [1]साँट.

साटक *sāṭak*, m. Brbh. sthg. worthless; husk; peel, rind.

साटन *sāṭan* [Engl. *satin*], f. satin.

साटना *sāṭnā*, v.t. = साँटना, सटाना.

[1]**साटा** *sāṭā* [**saṭṭa-*[1]: Pk. *saṭṭa-*], m. E.H. exchange; dealings.

[2]**साटा** *sāṭā* [cf. *saṭṭ-*[1]], m. reg. (Bihar) a whip having several lashes (used for driving cattle).

साठ *sāṭh* [*ṣaṣṭi-*], adj. sixty.

साठा *sāṭhā* [cf. H. *sāṭh*], m. **1.** a man of sixty years. **2.** reg. (W.) term applied to a large field. — साठे पर पाठा, m. a young man of sixty: an old man acting the part of a young one. – साठा-पाठा, m. id.

साठी *sāṭhī* [*ṣaṣṭikā-*], f. name of a short-stemmed, red- or dark-coloured rice (ripens in some sixty days from sowing).

साड़ी *sāṛī* [*śāṭī-*], f. a sari.

साढ़साती *sāṛhsātī*, f. see s.v. साढ़े.

[1]**साढ़ी** *sāṛhī* [**āṣāḍhīya-*], f. reg. grain sown in the month of Asāṛh, the spring crop or harvest.

[2]**साढ़ी** *sāṛhī*, f. reg. = साड़ी.

[3]**साढ़ी** *sāṛhī*, f. Brbh. clotted cream (= मलाई).

साढ़ू *sāṛhū* [**syā(līvo)ḍhṛ-*], m. wife's sister's husband.

साढ़े *sāṛhe* [*sārdha-*], adj. pl. (preceding numbers from three to ninety-nine) plus a half. — ~ तीन, adj. three and a half. ~ तीन सौ, adj. three hundred and fifty. ~ तीन हज़ार, adj. three thousand five hundred. ~ साती, f. a period of seven and a half years; malign influence of Saturn (extending through periods of seven and a half years, months or days); calamity; misfortune. – साढ़साती, f. Av. the planet Saturn; misfortune.

-सात् *-sāt*, suffix (forms adjectives expressing the result of transformation, e.g. धूलिसात्, turned to dust; आत्मसात्, assimilated completely to (one)self).

सात *sāt* [*sapta-*], adj. **1.** seven. **2.** fig. the total number (of any group). — ~ की नाक कटना, fig. a whole family or group to be disgraced (by one member's action). ~ परदों में रखना, to hide (a person) away completely. ~ भाई, m. pl. *Pl.* seven brothers: name of certain gregarious birds, specif. the jungle babbler, *Turdoides striatus*. ~ समुंदर पार, adv. beyond the seven seas, far across the world. – सात-पाँच, adj. & m., f. five or seven: several, a few; a number of persons; tricks, trickery. सात-पाँच करना (से, के साथ), to wrangle (with); to practise deceit (on); to make lame excuses (that do not tally); to be uncertain what to do. – सातों वचन, m. pl. the seven utterances: the marriage vows.

सातवीं *sātvīṁ* [cf. H. *sātvāṁ*], f. the seventh day of a lunar fortnight.

सातू *sātū*, m. = सत्तू.

सातूर *sātūr*, m. *Pl.* a large knife; a cleaver.

सात्तविक *sāttvik* [S.], adj. endowed with the quality *sattva*: **1.** true, genuine. **2.** honest, sincere. **3.** virtuous, excellent.

सात्त्विकता *sāttvikātā* [S.], f. genuineness, honesty, &c. (see सात्त्विक).

सात्विक *sātvik*, adj. corr. = सात्त्विक.

साथ *sāth* [*sārtha-*] m. & adv. **1.** m. company, society; sthg. accompanying. **2.** assistance.

3. adv. [*sārthena*], in the company (of, के), with, along (with). मेरे ~, adv. with me. ~ ~, adv. together. 4. additional (to, के). 5. adjoining. ~ ही, adv. along (with, के); at the same time; into the bargain; adjoining (as houses). 6. ppn. w. के. together with, along with (= से). ख़ुशी के ~, gladly. 7. ppn. w. के. together with, against (= से, which is more common). सब के ~ लड़ना ठीक नहीं, it is wrong to quarrel with everyone. साइकिल दीवार के ~ टिकाना, to rest (one's) bicycle against a wall. 8. Brbh. with, by means of (= से). — ~ का खेला, m. a playmate. ~ का पढ़ा, m. a classmate. ~ छूटना (का), (one) to part (from, से). ~ देना (का), to give (one) company or assistance (in, में); to take part (in an activity); to take the part or side (of), to support. ~ में, adv. together, in company. ~ लग लेना, = ~ हो लेना. ~ लगा रहना, = next. ~ लगे फिरना (के), to be always following (one) about. ~ रहना, to keep or to stay together, to be close associates. ~ लेना, to take (a person or thing) with one. ~ होना, to be one of a group, to be associates; to take part (in). ~ हो लेना, to attach oneself (to a group or person), to accompany. ~ ही ~, adv. = ~ ही. एक ~, adv. in one group or company, all together.

साथर *sāthar*, m. = साथरौ.

साथरी *sāthrī*, f. *Pl.* a small mat of *kuśa* grass (cf. साथरौ).

साथरौ *sāthrau* [*srastara-, saṁstara-*], m. ? Brbh. a mat (as of *kuśa* grass); bedding.

साथिन *sāthin* [**sārthinī-*], f. 1. female companion, or associate, or accomplice. 2. female attendant.

साथी *sāthī* [**sārthin-*], m. 1. companion; associate; ally; accomplice. 2. attendant, follower.

साद *sād*, m. 1. pronun. var. wish, longing, craving (= [1]साध). 2. reg. (Raj.) sound (= शब्द).

सादगी *sādăgī* [P. *sādagī*], f. 1. plainness, unadorned character. 2. simplicity (of manner), unpretentiousness. 3. frankness, sincerity.

सादर *sâdar* [S.], adj. paying respect, respectful.

सादरा *sādrā* [? cf. *śabda-*], m. *Pl.* a kind of song.

सादा *sādā* [P. *sāda*], adj. 1. plain, unadorned. सादे लिबास में होना, to be simply dressed. 2. white; blank (paper); unstamped (paper). 3. smooth; even, regular. 4. pure, unmixed; unseasoned. 5. simple (of manner); not special; unpretentious. 6. open, frank. — सादे रंग का, adj. of a single colour (as cloth). सादे सुभाव [H. *svabhāv*], adv. through artlessness of nature: unintentionally. – सादादिल, adj. simple-hearted: simple, unaffected. °ई, f.

सादापन *sādāpan* [cf. H. *sādā*], m. simplicity, &c.

सादृश्य *sādr̥śyă* [S.], m. resemblance, similarity; analogy.

सादृश्यता *sādr̥śyătā* [S.], f. similarity, comparability.

[1]**साध** *sādh* [*śraddhā-*], f. eager desire, longing; craving.

[2]**साध** *sādh* [cf. H. *sādhnā*], f. 1. earnest effort. 2. accomplishing, performing. 3. [× *śraddhā-*] present sent by parents to a daughter towards the end of her pregnancy.

[3]**साध** *sādh* [ad. *sādhu-*], adj. & m. 1. adj. Brbh. good, virtuous, excellent. 2. m. a member of the Sādh community; an ascetic.

साधक *sādhak* [S.], adj. & m. effective, accomplishing: 1. adj. adept, skilful. 2. holy. 3. m. a practiser, an adept. 4. a devotee; an ascetic. 5. a magician (= ओझा).

साधन *sādhan* [S.], m. 1. the act of accomplishing, or achieving. 2. an accomplishment, achievement. 3. means; expedient. ~ और साध्य, m. means and end. 4. appliance; pl. appliances, equipment. 5. resource; pl. resources.

[1]**साधना** *sādhănā* [S.], f. 1. accomplishment, achievement. 2. means. 3. devoted labour or striving (towards any end); adoration; entreaty; object of devotion.

[2]**साधना** *sādhnā* [*sādhnoti*], v.t. 1. to accomplish; to achieve by work or devotion; to study, to learn (as an esoteric skill). हाथ ~, to acquire a skill of hand, or knack. 2. to practise, to carry out. चुप ~, to keep silent. योग ~, to practise yoga. 3. to gain the good will, compliance or obedience of; to win over, to conciliate (an opponent); to break in (a horse). 4. to put in order or to rights: to adjust (as scales); to trim (a kite). 5. to substantiate: to show, to prove; to settle, to fix, to determine (an intention, a meaning). 6. to balance, to poise. शरीर ~, to balance (on, पर). 7. to point, to aim (a firearm). 8. to regulate. दम ~, to hold the breath. 9. to show deep or long-standing devotion (to).

साधनी *sādhnī* [cf. H. [2]*sādhnā*], f. 1. *Pl. HŚS.* a carpenter's level. 2. reg. (Bihar) a square. 3. *Pl.* a plumb-line. 4. *Pl.* edging, border (as the setting for a stone in a ring).

साधनीय *sādhănīyă* [S.], adj. 1. to be accomplished, or achieved, &c. (see [2]साधना). 2. to be proved.

साधारण *sādhāraṇ* [S.], adj. **1.** having the same basis: common, general; public. **2.** ordinary, usual, normal; average (of quality); plain (of features); common-place (as an event); trite (a remark). **3.** simple, plain (language). **4.** *gram.* simple (a form, a sentence); common (a noun). **5.** rudimentary (as education). — ~ बुद्धि, f. common sense. – साधारणतः, adv. usually; generally, on the whole. साधारणीकरण, m. giving general applicability (to): a generalisation.

साधारणतया *sādhāraṇtayā* [S.], adv. see s.v. साधारणता.

साधारणता *sādhāraṇătā* [S.], f. common or usual nature or quality: — साधारणतया, adv. usually; generally.

साधारणीकरण *sādhāraṇīkaraṇ* [S.], m. see s.v. साधारण.

साधित *sādhit* [S.], adj. **1.** achieved, accomplished. **2.** settled; paid off (a debt). **3.** substantiated, demonstrated. **4.** [×H. [2]*sādhnā*] fined, punished by fine.

साधु *sādhu* [S.], adj. & m. **1.** adj. righteous, virtuous; benevolent, good. **2.** pious, holy. **3.** ingenuous, guileless. **4.** Sanskritic, non-colloquial (language). **5.** m. a holy man, an ascetic. — साधुवाद, m. a voicing or expressing of approval; applause. साधु-संत, m. pl. holy men (see संत).

साधुता *sādhutā* [S.], f. **1.** righteousness, virtue; benevolence; honesty. **2.** piety, holiness.

साध्य *sādhyă* [S.], adj. & m. **1.** adj. feasible, attainable; easy. **2.** to be proved (as a theorem). **3.** curable (a disease). **4.** m. sthg. to be achieved: an end, goal. **5.** name of a class of minor deities.

-साध्य *-sādhyă* [S.], adj. achievable by means (of), involving (e.g. कष्टसाध्य, adj. involving effort for completion).

साध्वी *sādhvī* [S.], adj. f. & f. **1.** adj. f. = साधु. **2.** f. a virtuous woman or wife.

[1]**सान** *sān* [*śāṇa-*[2]], f. m. **1.** a grindstone. **2.** touchstone (= कसौटी). — ~ चढ़ाना, or धरना, or लगाना, to grind, to whet (a blade). ~ पर रखना, id.

[2]**सान** *sān* [*sañjñā-*], f. **1.** sign; trace. **2.** hint. — सान-गुमान, m. = ~; notion, idea. सान-गुमान होना (को), (a person) to have the notion (that, कि).

[1]**सानना** *sānnā* [*saṁdadhāti*, and *saṁnayati*], v.t. **1.** to mix in (with, में: as a substance with a liquid). **2.** to mix, to knead (as dough, earth, mash). **3.** to smear (with, में); to soil. **4.** to implicate (in).

[2]**सानना** *sānnā* [**śānayati*; *sānita-*], v.t. reg. to sharpen (a blade, on a stone).

[1]**सानी** *sānī* [cf. H. *sānnā*], f. water-soaked chaff mixed with grain, as fodder; mash. सानी-पानी, m. id.

[2]**सानी** *sānī* [A. *ṣānī*], adj. & m. second: a match, an equal.

सानु *sānu* [S.], m. a mountain; crest, summit.

सानुकूल *sânukūl* [S.], adj. attended by favourable circumstances: favourable (a wind, a person).

सानुज *sânuj* [S.], adv. Av. along with (one's) younger brother.

सानुनासिक *sânunāsik* [S.], adj. pronounced with a nasal sound, nasal (a vowel or consonant); nasalised.

सान्निध्य *sānnidhyă* [ad. *sāṃnidhya-*], m. **1.** vicinity, proximity. **2.** presence, attendance. **3.** *philos.* beatific state in which the soul attends on God.

सापराध *sâpărādh* [S.], adj. offending, at fault; guilty.

सापा *sāpā*, m. = साँपा, स्यापा.

सापेक्ष *sâpekṣ* [S.], adj. **1.** relative; comparative, qualified. **2.** corr. = सापेक्ष्य. — सापेक्षवाद, m. relativity.

सापेक्षता *sâpekṣătā* [S.], f. relativity.

सापेक्षिक *sâpekṣik* [S.], adj. = सापेक्ष.

सापेक्ष्य *sâpekṣyă* [S.], adj. to be kept in view: necessary, desirable.

साप्ताहिक *sāptâhik* [S.], adj. weekly.

साफ़ *sāf* [A. *ṣāf*], adj. **1.** clear, fair (as sky); bright (light). **2.** clean. **3.** unadulterated. **4.** unobstructed (way). **5.** clear (voice). **6.** sincere, open (of manner); simple, innocent; clean (game). **7.** plain, clear (any matter); lucid (language, ideas); express, flat (a refusal); peremptory. **8.** correct, true (a statement, account); exact (a calculation); fair (a likeness). **9.** legible. **10.** blank (paper). **11.** flat, level. **12.** practised (hand). **13.** adv. clearly. **14.** completely. **15.** safely, unharmed; lightly. — ~ करना, to clean; to wash (clothes, a floor); to clear away (obstacles); to finish up or off, to dispose of (as of resources); to clean out (of funds), to beggar; to clear (a debt); to make a fair copy of, to practise (the hand); (esp. ~ कर जाना) to get away with, to steal; to make a clean sweep, to rifle (belongings). ~ छूटना, or निकल आना, to escape unscathed; to get clean off (a charge). ~ निकल जाना, to get clean away; to get off scot-free. ~ रहना, to be clean, or clear, &c.; to go without food. ~ होना, to be clean, or cleaned, &c. (see ~ करना); fig. to be swept bare; to be devastated (as by epidemic). – साफ़दिल, adj. open-hearted; frank; guileless. साफ़-सफ़ेद, adj. clear and bright. साफ़-सुथरा, adj. clean, immaculate; neat (clothes); unblemished (character); untroubled (future).

साफल्य *sāphalyă* [S.], m. **1.** success. **2.** fruitfulness (as of an idea).

साफ़ा *sāfā*, m. a turban.

साफ़ा-पानी *sāfā-pānī* [H. *sāf*+H. *pānī*], f. colloq. cleaning or washing with water and soap, &c. — ~ करना, colloq. to clean or to wash (clothes, or one's person).

साफ़ी *sāfī* [P. *ṣāfī*], f, **1.** cloth, rag (used to strain liquids, esp. *bhāṁg*). **2.** kitchen cloth, or rag.

¹साबर *sābar* [*śāmbara-*], m. leather of deer-hide, chamois leather.

²साबर *sābar* [*śambara-*], m. *Pl. HŚS.* a deer (= ¹साँभर).

³साबर *sābar* [ad. *śābara-*], m. Brbh. barbarous: a barbarian; ? an incantantion of Śaiva yogīs in Prākṛt or Apabhraṃśa.

साबल *sābal* [*sarvalā-*, Pk. *sabbala-*], m. (?) Brbh. **1.** an iron crowbar or lever. **2.** *Pl.* a small anvil.

साबिक़ *sābiq* [A. *sābiq*], adj. Brbh. preceding, former (age, period). — साबिक़-दस्तूर, adj. U. according to custom, as usual (as a patient's condition).

साबक़ा *sābăqā* [A. *sābiqa*], m. long acquaintance: — ~ पड़ना, to become well acquainted (with, से); to have business or dealings (with).

साबित *sābit* [A. *ṣābit*], adj. **1.** established, confirmed; proved. **2.** sound, valid. — ~ करना, to establish, &c.; to prove; to substantiate.

साबुन *sābun* [A. *ṣābun*], m. soap. — ~ देना, or लगाना, to apply soap (to, में). – साबुनदानी [P. *-dānī*], f. soap-dish.

साबुत *sābut* [conn. H. *sābit*, *sabūt*], adj. corr. sound, undamaged; whole.

साबुनी *sābunī* [A. *ṣābunī*], adj. & f. **1.** adj. having to do with soap. **2.** f. *Pl. HŚS.* a kind of sweet (a mixture of almonds, honey and sesame oil).

सामंजस्य *sāmañjasyă* [S.], m. coordination, harmony.

सामंत *sāmant* [S.], m. **1.** feudatory prince, noble, leader, general. **2.** warrior, hero. — सामंत-काल, m. the feudal period. °ईन, adj. सामंतवाद, m. adherence to feudal atitudes, feudalism. सामंतशाही, f. rule through feudatories: the feudal system.

सामंती *sāmantī* [S.], adj. feudal.

सामंतीय *sāmantīyă* [S.], adj. feudal.

¹साम *sām* [S.], m. a hymn: a partic. kind of sacred text or verse, intended to be chanted. — साम-वेद, m. name of one of the three principal Vedas (the verses of which are chanted). साम-दाम-दंड-भेद, m. incantation, bribery, threat and guile: the traditional means for a king to attain his purposes.

²साम *sām* [*śamba-*], m. **1.** a ferrule (on an axle, or a handle); bushing, bush. **2.** fig. E.H. a weapon.

सामक *sāmak* [ad. *śyāmaka-*], m. *Pl. HŚS.* a millet, *Panicum miliaceum* (= साँवाँ).

सामग्री *sāmagrī* [S.], f. collected materials, stock, implements, &c. (cf. सामान): 1. = सामान, 1.-3. 2. = सामान, 4.; specif. data, information (on a topic). **3.** Brbh. = माल, 10.

सामन *sāman*, m. pronun. var. = सावन.

सामना *sāmnā* [cf. *saṁmukha-*], m. **1.** confronting, encountering; meeting face to face. **2.** opposition, resistance. **3.** competition, rivalry. **4.** match, comparison. **5.** front, front part; frontage (of a house). — ~ करना (का), to confront; to oppose; to compete (with); to be compared (to); to show insolence or overbearingness (to).

सामने *sāmne* [cf. H. *sāmnā*], adv. **1.** before, facing, in front (of, के). **2.** opposite, facing. **3.** fig. matched (with), in comparison (with). – ~ आना, to appear (before one). ~ करना, to put, to place or to lay in front (of, के). ~ का, adj. confronting; frontal, direct (as an attack); opposite; having to do with one's presence or lifetime or age. ~ का मकान, m. the house opposite. ~ की बात, f. sthg. with which (one) is faced: sthg. done or said in (one's) presence, or during (one's) lifetime. ~ पड़ना, to appear; to transpire (knowledge of an event). ~ होना (के), to come or to stand forward: (a woman) to show her face (to a strange man); to confront, to defy. – आमने-सामने, adv. = ~, 1., 2.

सामयिक *sāmăyik* [S.], adj. **1.** having to do with time, or with a partic. time. **2.** timely, opportune. **3.** periodical. **4.** contemporary (= संसामयिक).

सामयिकता *sāmayikătā* [S.], f. timeliness.

सामरिक *sāmarik* [S.], adj. concerning battle: military.

सामर्थ *sāmarth*, m. f. = सामर्थ्य.

सामर्थी *sāmarthī* [cf. H. *sāmarth*], adj. *Pl. HŚS.* able, capable; strong.

सामर्थ्य *sāmarthyă* [S.], f. (m). adequacy: **1.** capacity, ability; competence. **2.** power, strength. **3.** fig. wealth, money. **4.** *gram.* the force or sense of a word. — उसकी यह ~ कहाँ थी ? by no means did he have the ability to do so.

सामाँ *sāmām̐*, m. = सामान.

सामा *sāmā*, m. Brbh. = सामान.

सामाजिक *sāmājik* [S.], adj. **1.** having to do with society, social. **2.** (being) a member of an audience. — ~ सुरक्षा, f. social security.

सामान *sāmān* [P. *sāmān*], m. **1.** goods, things. **2.** possessions; luggage; a piece of luggage; furniture. **3.** equipment; utensils; tools. **4.** materials. **5.** *mil.* supplies. **6.** provisions, food. **7.** provision (for an occasion), necessary preparations. — ~ करना, to make provision (for, का), to arrange (for or to).

सामान्य *sāmānyă* [S.], adj. **1.** alike, equal (cf. समान). ***2.** shared by others: general, universal. ~ शिक्षा, f. general education. **3.** ordinary; normal, usual. **4.** commonplace; inferior, insignificant. **5.** *gram.* general, non-specific as to mode or time, simple (a conjugational pattern). ~ भूत-काल, m. the perfective (forms of a verb); ~ वर्तमान-काल, m. general present. — ~ तौर पर, adv. in the general way (of things). ~ लक्षण, m. a general feature or characteristic. – सामान्यीकरण, m. generalisation; a generalisation.

सामान्यीकरण *sāmānyīkaraṇ* [S.], m. see s.v. सामान्य.

सामान्यता *sāmānyătā* [S.], f. ordinary or normal state.

सामिष *sâmiṣ* [S.], adj. with meat: non-vegetarian.

[1]सामी *sāmī* [*śamba-*], f. a ferrule, &c. (= [2]साम).

[2]सामी *sāmī*, f. reg. (Bihar) a grass.

[3]सामी *sāmī*, m. pronun. var. reg. = स्वामी.

सामीप्य *sāmīpyă* [S.], m. **1.** vicinity, proximity. **2.** *philos.* beatific state of proximity of the soul to God.

सामुदायिक *samudāyik* [S.], adj. pertaining to a community.

सामुद्र *sāmudr* [S.], adj. & m. **1.** adj. having to do with the ocean: marine; maritime. **2.** m. *Pl. HŚS.* a seafarer; maritime trader. **3.** *Pl. HŚS.* sea salt. **4.** *Pl. HŚS.* cuttle-fish bone (= समुद्र-फेन).

[1]सामुद्रिक *sāmudrik* [S.], adj. = सामुद्र.

[2]सामुद्रिक *sāmudrik* [S.], m. the art of interpreting the marks (*mudrā*) of the body: palmistry, fortune-telling.

सामुद्रिकी *sāmudrikī* [cf. H. [2]*sāmudrik*], m. a fortune-teller.

सामुहें *sāmuhem̐* [cf. *sammukha-*], adv. reg. = सामने.

साम्य *sāmyă* [S.], m. **1.** sameness, similarity. **2.** equality, parity. **3.** harmony, concord. **4.** evenness, equability (of temperament). **5.** impartiality, indifference. — साम्यवाद, m. communism. °ई, adj. & m. communist. साम्यावस्था [°*mya*+*a*°], f. state of equilibrium.

साम्राज्य *sāmrājyă* [S.], m. empire. — साम्राज्यशाही, = next. साम्राज्यवाद, m. imperialism. °ई, adj. & m. imperialist.

साम्हना *sāmhnā*, adj. pronun. var. = सामना.

साम्हने *sāmhne*, adv. pronun. var. = सामने.

सायं *sāyaṃ* [S.], m. usu. सायं-. evening (= साय): — सायंकाल, m. evening; °ईन, adj. सायं-संध्या, f. evening; evening worship.

साय *sāy* [S.], m. end, close: close of day, evening (see सायं).

सायक *sāyak* [S.], m. an arrow.

[1]सायत *sāyat*, f. = साइत.

[2]सायत *sāyat*, adv. = शायद.

[1]सायर *sāyr* [*sāgara-*], m. Brbh. sea, ocean.

[2]सायर *sāyr* [A. *sā'ir*], adj. & m. *hist.* going: **1.** adj. contingent (expenditure). **2.** additional, supplementary (sources of income. **3.** m. *HŚS.* land the produce or profit of which is not taxed.

[1]साया *sāyā* [P. *sāya*], m. (f.) **1.** shade; shadow. **2.** shelter, protection. **3.** an apparition. **4.** influence (of an evil spirit: also fig.) — ~ डालना, to cast a shadow (on, पर); to take (one) under protection; to show favour (to); to influence (one). ~ पड़ना (पर), the shadow (of, का) to fall (upon); to come under the influence (of). ~ होना the influence (of, का) to be felt. साये में आना, to come under the shelter or protection (of, के); to come under the influence (of an evil spirit). साये से भागना, to flee the shadow (of, के), to shun. साये-तले आना (के), = साये में आना. – सायादार [P. *-dār*], adj. & m. shady; protective; a protector. सायाबान [P. *-bān*], m. canopy; sunshade; shed.

[2]**साया** *sāyā* [Pt. *saia*], m. petticoat, undershirt.

सायास *sāyās* [S.], adv. with effort, painstakingly.

सायुज्य *sāyujyă* [S.], m. *philos.* beatific state of communion of the soul with the divine being.

सारंग *sāraṅg* [S.], adj. & m. **1.** dappled, spotted; coloured; gaudy. **2.** Brbh. attractive, charming (as speech, or eyes). **3.** m. a deer; specif. the spotted deer. **4.** *mus.* name of a *rāg.* **5.** designation of several birds and other creatures: the *cātak* bird; the koel (cuckoo); the peacock; a lion; a bee; a snake. **6.** Brbh. designation of several objects: a conch shell; a lotus; gold; a tank; camphor; a bow. **7.** a title of Śiva.

सारंगिया *sāraṅgiyā* [cf. H. *sāraṅg*], m. a player on the *sāraṅgī.*

सारंगी *sāraṅgī* [S.], f. a kind of violin.

[1]**सार** *sār* [*sāra-*[2]], m. f. **1.** m. essence, substance, best or essential part; heart; core, marrow. **2.** sap. **3.** gist, sense; content. **4.** essential worth or value. **5.** name of a Hindi (Brajbhāṣā) metre containing twenty-eight mātrās to the line. — **6.** m. f. [f., H. *sār-* or ← G. or Panj.] Brbh. firmness, strength: help. – सार-गर्भित, adj. full of substance, substantial (a piece of writing, &c.); significant. सार-ग्राही, adj. extracting or understanding the essence or the best of sthg. °-ग्राहिणी, f. सार-भाटा, m. low water, low tide. सारभूत, adj. forming the essential, chief or best (thing or part). सारवान, substantial, significant (as an article, a contribution). सार-संग्रह, m. a digest. सारहीन, adj. insubstantial. सारांश [°*ra*+*a*°], m. essential part, or sense; an abstract, synopsis; summary. सारांश यह कि... the gist of the matter is....

[2]**सार** *sār* [*śālā-*], f. reg. a cowshed.

[3]**सार** *sār*, adj. formant. Brbh. = -सा.

[4]**सार** *sār* [*śāli-*], m. reg. (Bihar) a variety of transplanted rice.

सारक *sārak* [S.], adj. *Pl. HŚS.* laxative, purgative.

सारण *sāraṇ* [S.], m. purging.

सारणी *sārăṇī* [S.], f. a table, tabulation. — समय-सारणी, f. timetable.

सारथी *sārăthī* [S.], m. **1.** charioteer. **2.** leader of a caravan or convoy of vehicles. **3.** name of a partic. Hindu community.

सारना *sārnā* [*sārayati*], v.t. **1.** to make an end of, to consume, to exhaust. **2.** to make, to achieve, to accomplish; complete, to perfect. **3.** सार-. Av. to set, to apply (as a *tilak*, or a saw).

सारबान *sārbān* [P. *sārbān*], m. a camel-driver. — मलिक और ~ अंतर, fig. a world of difference.

सारल्य *sāralyă* [S.], m. = सरलता.

सारस *sāras* [*sārasa-*], m. having to do with a lake or pond: **1.** the Sarus crane, *Grus antigone.* **2.** [? ad. *sārasa-*] Brbh. Av. a lotus.

सारस्वत *sārasvat* [S.], adj. **1.** adj. having to do with the goddess Sarasvatī, or with the legendary river Sarasvatī. **2.** belonging to the Sārasvat country (as a partic. class of brāhmaṇs). **3.** m. name of the region around the Sarasvatī river to the north-west of Delhi.

[1]**सारा** *sārā* [*sāra-*[2]], adj. all, whole, entire. — ~ दिन, or सारे दिन, adv. all day long. सारे का ~, adj. the whole (of). बहुत ~, adj. = बहुत-सा.

[2]**सारा** *sārā* [? conn. *sārayati*], f. *Pl.* custom, usage.

[3]**सारा** *sārā*, m. **1.** reg. (Bihar) an axle. **2.** E.H. an arrow, shaft. **3.** [? *sāra-*[2]] reg. (Bihar) a funeral pile.

सारि *sāri* [*sāri-*[2]], f. Brbh. a piece (in chess, *causar*, &c.); Av. dice.

सारिका *sārikā* [S.], f. Brbh. **1.** a starling; mynah.

सारिखना *sārikhnā* [cf. H. *sārikhā*], v.t. & v.i. *Pl.* **1.** v.t. to see likeness, to compare (with), to liken. **2.** v.i. to resemble.

सारिखा *sārikhā* [conn. *sadṛkṣa-*], adj. & ppn. Brbh. Av. = सरीखा.

[1]**सारी** *sari* [*śārikā-*], f. a mynah.

[2]**सारी** *sari*, f. reg. = साड़ी.

सारो *sāro* [*śāri-*[2], *śāra-*[1]], m. Brbh. a starling; a mynah.

सार्थ *sārth* [S.], m. **1.** group of travellers. **2.** herd, flock.

सार्थक *sārthak* [S.], adj. **1.** having meaning, purpose; significant. **2.** effectual. **3.** profitable; fully realised (life in this world).

सार्थकता *sārthakătā* [S.], f. **1.** significance. **2.** use, purpose.

सार्वकालिक *sārvăkālik* [S.], adj. belonging to all times: everlasting; perennial.

सार्वजनिक *sārvăjanik* [S.], adj. pertaining to all people: **1.** public (as a meeting, an institution, a facility). **2.** general, widespread (as an opinion, an attitude); popular.

सार्वजनिकता *sārvăjanikătā* [S.], f. **1.** public character, openness (of procedure or attitude).

सार्वजनीन *sārvjanīn* [S.], adj. 1. = सार्वजनिक. **2.** universal.

सार्वत्रिक *sārvatrik* [S.], adj. found, or valid, everywhere; general, universal.

सार्वदेशिक *sārvădeśik* [S.], adj. applying to all countries; world-wide.

सार्वभौम *sārvăbhaum* [S.], adj. **1.** having to do with the whole world: universal, world-wide (as sway, power). **2.** *pol.* having to do with an entire territory; sovereign (a state); paramount (a power). — ~ सत्ता, m. sovereign power or right; paramountcy.

सार्वभौमिक *sārvăbhaumik* [S.], adj. 1. = सार्वभौम, 1. **2.** sovereign, unrestricted (as a right).

सार्वभौमिकता *sārvăbhaumikătā* [S.], f. universality, universal currency or validity.

[1]**साल** *sāl* [P. *sāl*], m. a year. — ~ बसाल [P. *ba-*], adv. year by year, annually. ~ भर, adv. (for) a whole year; all the year round. दो ~ बाद, adv. two years later. दो ~ हुए, adv. two years ago. हर ~, adv. every year. – साल-गिरह, f. year-knot: anniversary, birthday. सालों-साल, adv. year by year, year after year.

[2]**साल** *sāl* [*śāla-*], m. **1.** the *sāl* tree, *Shorea robusta*, and its wood. **2.** the plane tree. **3.** a fish, *Ophiocephalus wrahl.*

[3]**साल** *sāl* [*śalya-*[1]], m. **1.** a thorn. **2.** fig. pain, affliction. **3.** transf. a hole; a mortice. — ~ पड़ना, a shooting pain to be felt.

[4]**साल** *sāl*, f. E.H. = शाला.

सालक *sālak* [cf. H. [3]*sāl*], adj. Brbh. Av. causing suffering or distress.

सालन *sālan* [**samlepana-* or **samlāpāna-*]. **1.** a meat curry. **2.** a seasoning, sauce.

सालना *sālnā* [*śalyayati*], v.t. & v.i. **1.** v.t. to pierce, to prick; to bore. **2.** to cause pain or suffering. **3.** v.i. to be pierced. **4.** to feel pain.

सालरा *sālrā*, m. *Pl.* green barley (used as fodder).

सालस *sâlas* [S.], adj. languid.

सालसा *sālsā* [Pt. *salsaparrilha*], m. Indian sarsparilla, *Hemidesmus indicus* (= अनंत-मूल).

साला *sālā* [*syālaka-*], m. **1.** wife's brother, brother-in-law. **2.** transf. a term of abuse.

-साला *-sālā* [P. *sāla*], adj. formant, inv. ... years old (e.g. दुसाला, adj. inv of two years, biennial).

सालाना *sālānā* [P. *sālāna*], adj. inv. & m. **1.** adj. pertaining to a year, annual (as expenses, &c). **2.** occurring yearly, annual (a festival, &c.); made yearly (as a payment). **3.** m. a yearly payment; annuity (= वार्षिकी).

सालार *sālār* [P. *sālār*], m. advanced in years: leader, commander. — सालार-जंग, m. leader in war: general or commander-in-chief.

सालिग्राम *sāligrām*, m. = शालग्राम (s.v. [2]शाल).

सालियाना *sāliyānā*, adj. inv. = सालाना (the correct form).

सालिस *sālis* [A. *s̤ālis̤*], m. E.H. third: a third (person), mediator, arbitrator.

[1]**साली** *sālī* [P. *sālī*], adj. annual.

[2]**साली** *sālī* [*syāla-*], f. wife's sister, sister-in-law.

सालू *sālū* [**sālu-*], m. a kind of fine red cloth.

सालोक्य *sālokyă* [S.], m. residence (of the liberated soul) in the same world or heaven as Kr̥ṣṇa: the first stage of beatitude.

सालोतरी *sālotrī* [ad. *śālihotra-*], m. a veterinary practitioner; farrier.

सावंत *sāvant* [*sāmanta-*], m. = सामंत.

सावंती *sāvantī* [cf. H. *sāvant*], f. bravery, valour.

सावकरन *sāvkarn* [cf. *śyāma* ; ad. *karṇa-*], adj. & m. reg. **1.** adj. having black ears. **2.** m. a black-eared animal; Av. a kind of horse.

सावकाश *sâvăkāś* [S.], adj. & m. **1.** adj. having leisure. **2.** adv. at (one's) leisure, or convenience. **3.** m. leisure. **4.** occasion, opportunity.

सावड़ *sāvaṛ* [**sāvakuṭī-*], f. *Pl.* room used for a birth, delivery-room.

सावधान *sâvădhān* [S.], adj. **1.** attentive. **2.** careful, cautious; prudent. — ~! interj. watch out! look out! ~ करना, to warn; to alert (one) (to); to take care, to be careful. ~ रहना, to be careful or mindful (of or about, से or के लिए); to beware (of, से).

सावधानता *sâvădhānătā* [S.], f. *Pl. HŚS.* = सावधानी.

सावधानी *sâvădhānī* [S.], f. **1.** attention. **2.** care, caution; prudence. — ~ से, adv. attentively; carefully, &c.

सावधि *sâvădhi* [S.], adj. having a fixed term or time (as a loan, a deposit).

सावन *sāvan* [*śrāvaṇa-*], m. **1.** name of the fifth month of the Hindu lunar calendar (July-August). **2.** a type of song sung in the month Sāvan (= कजली). — ~ का फोड़ा, m. a boil developing in Sāvan: sthg. that causes continuing distress. ~ की झड़ी, f. the constant showers of Sāvan. ~ हरे न भादों सूखे, neither green in Sāvan nor dry in Bhādom̐: continuing unaffected by external changes. – सावन-भादों, m.

Sāvan and Bhādoṁ: the main part of the rainy season; sunshine and showers.

सावनी *sāvănī* [cf. H. *sāvan*], adj. & f. **1.** adj. having to do with or typical of the month of Sāvan. **2.** f. the day of full moon in the month Sāvan. 3. = सावन, 2. **4.** presents given by the relatives of a bridegroom-to-be to those of the fiancée in Sāvan; a ceremony called *sindhārā*; the ceremony of presenting a fiancée with the poles, ropes, &c. of a swing, in the month Sāvan; the parts of a swing as then presented. **5.** rice planted in Sāvan. **6.** tobacco sown in Sāvan.

सावयव *sâvăyav* [S.], adj. **1.** composed of parts or members. **2.** having all its parts, &c. (= सांग).

सावर *sāvar* [*śambara-* (via NIA *sāmar*)], m. Brbh. a deer.

सावर्ण्य *sāvarṇyă* [S.], m. **1.** identity of *varṇa* (q.v). **2.** identity or similarity of colour.

सावित्री *sāvitrī* [S.], f. **1.** name of a Vedic verse addressed to Savitṛ, the sun (= गायत्री, 2). **2.** *mythol.* a title or name of several figures: as of Umā the wife of Śiva; and of the wife of Satyavān.

साष्टांग *sāṣṭāṅg* [S.], adj. made with eight parts (of the body, viz. forehead, breast, shoulders, hands and feet: prostration of the body in greeting, or supplication). — ~ दंडवत्, m. id.

सास *sās* [*śvaśrū-*], f. mother-in-law.

सासत *sāsat*, f. reg. = साँसत.

सासरा *sāsrā* [*śvāśura-*], m. father-in-law's house.

सासु *sāsu*, f. = सास.

सास्ना *sāsnā*, m. *Pl. HŚS.* dewlap (of an ox).

[1]**साह** *sāh* [*sādhu-*], m. **1.** a merchant; shopkeeper. **2.** a banker. **3.** title of respect given to merchants, bankers, &c. **4.** an upright or honest man. ~ जी, m. id. — साह-ख़र्ची, f. extravagant expenditure.

[2]**साह** *sāh* [? *śākhā-*], m. *HŚS.* **1.** the side posts of a door. **2.** Bihar. an ornamental door-frame.

साहचर्य *sāhăcaryă* [S.], m. association, company (with another or others); companionship.

साहड़ *sāhaṛ* m. reg. (Bihar) a kind of plant.

साहपन *sāhpan* [cf. H. *sāh*], m. = साहूपन.

साहब *sāhab* [A. *ṣāḥib*], m. companion, associate: **1.** possessor, owner, master. **2.** a prominent person; esp. *hist.* a European; officer, official (as of a company). **3.** (hon. added to a name, or to a title) Mr; Sir. डाक्टर ~, m. doctor! (voc.); the doctor. **4.** voc. sir! **5.** (E.H.) God, the Lord. — ~ लोग, m. pl. the rulers: esp. *hist.* the British (in India); European people; (also) the Indian governing class. – ग्रंथ ~, m. The Book (sacred scripture of the Sikhs). साहबज़ादा [P. *-zāda*], m. sāhab's son, young gentleman. °-ज़ादी, f. young lady. साहब-बहादुर, m. *hist.* title or form of reference to a European official, or to an Indian receiving British patronage; a partic. rank conferred by the British. साहब-सलामत, f. formal salutation (on meeting).

साहबा *sāhabā* [A. *ṣāḥiba*], f. **1.** lady, dame. **2.** (hon. esp. voc., added to a name, or to a title.) Lady. – रानी ~, f. Your Highness, your Ladyship, good lady.

साहबाना *sāhabānā* [P. *ṣāḥibāna*], adj. inv. characterising prominent people (esp. *hist.* British people or Europeans).– ~ लिबास, m. European dress.

[1]**साहबी** *sāhabī* [P. *ṣāḥabī*], f. **1.** rule, dominance; influence. **2.** lordliness. — साहबी करना, to exercise dominance (over, पर); to lord it (over).

[2]**साहबी** *sāhabī* [cf. H. *sāhab*], adj. of or characterising prominent people; European (as manner, ways).

साहस *sāhas* [S.], m. **1.** boldness, courage; spirit, vigour. **2.** resoluteness. — ~ करना, to act bravely, &c. ~ करके, adv. bravely, &c. ~ छोड़ना, to lose courage, to grow faint-hearted. ~ दिलाना (को), to encourage. ~ बटोरना, to take one's courage in both hands, to muster one's courage. उसे ~ कहाँ था कि..., how could he dare to....

साहसिक *sāhăsik* [S.], adj. = साहसी.

साहसी *sāhăsī* [S.], adj. **1.** bold, brave; spirited. **2.** resolute.

साहा *sāhā* [? MIA or NIA *sāh-*, v.t. ← *sādhayati*], m. *hind.* astrologically auspicious time or date for a marriage.

साहाय्य *sāhāyyă* [S.], m. help, assistance.

साहि *sāhi*, m. Brbh. a king (= शाह).

साहित्य *sāhityă* [S.], m. association, combination: literary composition, literature. — साहित्यकार, m. writer, author. साहित्यज्ञ, m. one versed in literature. साहित्य-रत्न jewel of letters: title awarded to those passing the uppermost grade of a partic. examination in Hindi literature. साहित्यांग [°*ya*+*a*°], m. branch of literature, literary genre. साहित्यालोचन [°*ya*+*ā*°], m. literary criticism. साहित्येतर

[°ya+i°], adj. other than literature: non-literary (as a style, a genre).

साहित्यिक *sāhityik* [S.], adj. literary.

साहित्यिकता *sāhityikătā* [S.], f. literary quality.

साहिबा *sāhibā*, f. pronun. var. = साहबा.

[1]**साहिल** *sāhil* [A. *sāḥil*], m. shore, sea-shore; coast.

[2]**साहिल** *sāhil*, reg. (Bihar) a kind of rice, sown broadcast.

साहिली *sāhilī* [A. *sāḥilī*], adj. & f. **1.** adj. coastal. **2.** f. a heron (? = काला बगला, the reef heron: *Egretta gularis*).

साही *sāhī* [*śvāvidh-*], m. a porcupine.

साहुल *sāhul* [A. *śāqūl*: P. *śāqul*], m. *Pl. HŚS.* a plummet, or plumb-line.

साहू *sāhū* [*sādhu-*]. = [1]साह. — साहूकार, m. id., 1.-3. °आ, m. colloq. banking; money-lending; the money-market, exchange. °ई, f. banking; business, commerce; money-lending; brokerage.

साहूपन *sāhūpan* [cf. H. *sāhū*], m. **1.** state or position of a banker or merchant. **2.** mercantile or commercial credit.

सिंकना *siṁknā* [cf. H. *seṁknā*], v.i. **1.** to be warmed or heated. **2.** to be roasted (as an ear of corn); to be cooked (as *capātī*). **3.** to be fomented (as a boil).

सिंगड़ा *siṁgṛā*, m. E.H. = सींगा, 2.

सिंगरौर *siṅgraur* [*śṛṅgaverapura-*], m. Av. name of a town on the bank of the Ganges, the site of a ferry.

सिंगा *siṅgā* [*śṛṅga-*], m. *mus.* a horn.

सिंगार *siṅgār* [*śṛṅgāra-*], m. **1.** dress, array; adornment. **2.** sexual love; sexual intercourse. — ~ करना, to dress or to adorn oneself (a woman); to dress up, to deck (a child, an idol). – सिंगारदान [P. *-dān*], toilet-case. सिंगार-पटार, m. adornment, toilet (of a woman). सिंगार-पटार करना, = ~ करना, 1. सिंगार-मेज़, f. dressing-table. सिंगार-हाट, f. red-light district. सिंगार-हार, m. Av. the weeping Nyctanthes (a partic. flower).

सिंगार- *siṁgār-* [cf. H. *siṅgār*], v.t. Brbh. = सिंगार करना.

सिंगारिया *siṅgāriyā* [cf. H. *siṅgār*], m. temple priest or sectarian responsible for dressing an idol.

सिंगारी *siṅgārī*, m. Brbh. = सिंगारिया.

सिंगाला *siṅgālā* [cf. H. *sīṁg*], adj. horned (cattle).

सिंगिया *siṅgiyā*, m. reg. pronun. var. a vegetable poison; (?) = संखिया.

सिंगी *siṅgī* [ad. *śṛṅgī-*], f. reg. a sheat-fish.

सिंगौटा *siṅgauṭā* [**śṛṅgapaṭṭa-*], m. ? a polishing tool made of horn (cf. सिंघौटा).

[1]**सिंगौटी** *siṅgauṭī* [**śṛṅgavarta-*], f. reg. **1.** a small receptacle of horn. **2.** ? horns of dead cattle.

[2]**सिंगौटी** *siṅgauṭī* [**śṛṅgapaṭṭa-*], f. reg. a metal ornament for the horns of a bullock.

सिंघ *siṅgh* [ad. *siṃha-*], m. a lion, &c. (= सिंह).

सिंघल *siṅghal* [ad. *siṃhala-*], m. Av. the island of Ceylon, Sri Lanka. — सिंघल-दीप, m. id. °ई, adj.

सिंघाड़ा *siṁghāṛā* [*śṛṅgāṭaka-*, Pa. *sighāṭaka-*], m. **1.** the water-chestnut, *Trapa bispinosa*. **2.** a variety of *samosā*. **3.** fig. anything triangular (as a plot of land).

सिंघौटा *siṅghauṭā*, m. reg. Bihar. corr. see सिंगौटा.

सिंचन *siñcan* [S.], m. watering; irrigating.

सिंचना *siṁcnā* [cf. H. *sīṁcnā*], v.i. to be watered; to be irrigated.

सिंचाई *siṁcāī* [cf. H. *siṁcānā*], f. **1.** watering; irrigation. **2.** payment for irrigation, &c.

सिंचाना *siṁcānā* [cf. H. *sīṁcnā*], v.t. to cause to be watered, or irrigated (by, से).

सिंचित *siñcit* [S.], adj. watered; irrigated.

सिंदूर *sindūr* [*sindūra-*[1]], m. red lead, vermilion (applied by married women to the hair-parting). ~ पहनना, to apply vermilion. ~ पोंछना, v.t. fig. to become a widow. माँग में ~ डालना, or देना, or भरना, fig. to marry (a woman, की). – सिंदूर-दान, m. ceremonial application of vermilion to the bride's parting by the bridegroom at marriage. °ई, f. vermilion-box. सिंदुर-बंदन, m. Brbh. = सिंदूरदान.

सिंदूरा *sindūrā* [*sindūra-*[1]], m. a container for vermilion.

सिंदूरिया *sindūriyā* [cf. H. *sindūr*], adj. & m. **1.** adj. vermilion-coloured. **2.** m. a small, sweet-smelling, red-streaked mango.

[1]**सिंदूरी** *sindūrī* [cf. H. *sindūr*], adj. vermilion-coloured.

[2]**सिंदूरी** *sindūrī* [S.], f. the tree *Mallotus philippinensis* (source of a dye, and of a drug).

सिंधारा *sindhārā*, m. *hind.* a present (of pastries, &c.) given by a bridegroom to his bride on the third day of both halves of the month Sāvan (cf. सावनी).

सिंध *sindh* [ad. *sindhu-*], m. Sind.

सिंधिया *siṁdhiyā* [conn. *saindhava-*], m. *hist.* name of a Marāṭhā tribe based in the 18th century in Gwalior and Madhya Pradesh.

सिंधी *sindhī* [cf. H. *sindh*], adj. of Sindh.

सिंधु *sindhu* [S.], m. **1.** sea, ocean. **2.** the river Indus. **3.** Sindh. — सिंधुज, adj. & m. ocean-born: of ocean, &c.; Brbh. rock-salt. °आ, f. Brbh. a title of Lakṣmī. सिंधुवार, m. = सँभालू.

सिंधुर *sindhur* [S.], m. Brbh. an elephant.

सिंह *siṃh* [S.], m. **1.** a lion. **2.** -सिंह. a hero; an eminent person. **3.** a title taken by Sikh men, and frequently by Rājpūt men. **4.** the sign Leo (of the zodiac). — सिंह-द्वार, m. lion-gate: chief entrace (as to a palace). सिंह-ध्वनि, f. = next. सिंह-नाद, m. lion's roar; battle-cry. सिंह-पौर, Brbh. m. = सिंह-द्वार. सिंहमुखी, adj. fig. wide at the front, tapering at the rear. सिंह-वाहिनी, f. who rides a lion: a title of Durgā. सिंहावलोकन [°*ha*+*a*°], m. lion's look, a look to the rear, and hence, around: a survey, review. सिंहासन [°*ha*+*ā*°], lion's seat: throne. °आरूढ़ [°*ha*+*ā*°], adj. ascended the throne: crowned; ruling. °आरोहण [°*na*+*ā*°], m. accession to the throne. °आसीन [°*na*+*ā*°], adj. seated on the throne: ruling. सिंहोदरी [°*ha*+*u*°], adj. Brbh. lion-waisted: a title of Durgā.

सिंहल *siṃhal* [S.], m. /siṅghəl/. Sri Lanka.

[1]**सिंहली** *siṃhălī* [cf. H. *siṃhal*], m. a Sinhalese.

[2]**सिंहली** *siṃhălī* [cf. H. *siṃhal*], f. the Sinhalese language.

सिंहिका *siṃhikā* [S.], f. Brbh. a demoness, daughter of Hiraṇyakaśipu and mother of Rāhu.

सिंहिनी *siṃhinī* [S.], f. /siṅghnī/. **1.** a lioness. **2.** title of, or form of reference to, a Sikh woman.

सिंही *siṃhī* [S.], f. /siṅhī/, /siṅghī/. lioness.

सि- *si-* [P. *sih*]. three: — सिहद्दा, m. meeting-point of three boundaries.

सिकंदर *sikandar* [P. *sikandar*], m. Alexander the Great. — तक़दीर का ~, a man favoured by fate, or by destiny.

सिकंदरिया *sikandariyā* [A. *sikandarīya*], m. the city of Alexandria.

सिकटा *sikṭā*, m. reg. a broken piece of earthenware, potsherd.

सिकड़ना *sikaṛnā*, v.i. pronun. var. = सिकुड़ना.

सिकड़ी *sikṛī* [*śr̥ṅkhala-*], f. chain (as for a lock, or ornamental).

सिकता *siktā* [S.], f. **1.** sand; gravel. **2.** gall-stone.

सिकरी *sikrī*, f. reg. = सिकली, 1., and सिकड़ी.

[1]**सिकली** *siklī* [*śr̥ṅkhala-*], f. **1.** a chain (ornamental, or as used with a padlock). **2.** the staple used in padlocking a door.

[2]**सिकली** *siklī* [cf. A. *ṣaiqal*], f. Brbh. Av. polishing, grinding (of arms, or a mirror). — सिकलीगढ़, m. corr. = next. सिकलीगर [P. *-gar*], m. polisher, cleaner, grinder.

सिकहर *sik'har* [**śikyadhara-*], m. three or more cords tied together to form a network (for hanging pots, &c.); a rope-sling.

सिकुड़ण *sikuṛaṇ* [cf. H. *sikuṛnā*], f. **1.** drawing together, contraction; shrinking (of cloth). **2.** shrivelling; wrinkling. **3.** a wrinkle; gather, pucker.

सिकुड़ना *sikuṛnā* [cf. H. *sikoṛnā*], v.i. **1.** to draw in or together, to become of smaller size; to shrink (cloth). **2.** [× **sikka-*] to shrivel; to wrinkle. **3.** to be gathered or swept up together; to be squeezed in together (as passengers, &c.); to be bunched up. **4.** to suffer encroachment (as moonlight from cloud).

सिकोड़ *sikoṛ* [cf. H. *sikoṛnā*], f. drawing in or together, &c. (see सिकोड़ना).

सिकोड़ना *sikoṛnā* [**saṁkoṭayati*: Pk. *saṁkoḍiyā-*; ? × **sikka-*], v.t. **1.** to draw in or together; to contract. **2.** to squeeze or press in or together; to purse or to twist (the lips). **3.** to draw tight (as a brace). **4.** to wrinkle up (as the face or brow); to crumple up (paper, &c).

सिक्का *sikkā* [P. *sikka*], m. & adj. **1.** m. a stamp; a coining-die. **2.** impression on a coin. **3.** a coin; a rupee; currency. **4.** adj. minted: current (coin). — ~ चलाना, to introduce a new coin, or currency; = ~ बिठाना. ~ जमाना, id. ~ बनाना, or मारना, to mint coin, money. ~ बिठाना (अपना), to introduce (one's) coin: to establish (one's) rule, or authority. काग़ज़ी ~, m. paper money.

सिक्ख *sikkh* = सिख.

सिक्त *sikt* [S.], adj. watered; irrigated.

सिक्थ *sikthă* [S.], m. *Pl. HŚS.* boiled rice.

सिख *sikh* [ad. *śiṣya-*; ← Panj. *sikkh*], m. disciple, pupil; specif. a follower of Gurū Nānak, a Sikh.

सिखनी *sikhnī* [cf. H. *sikh*], f. a Sikh woman; wife of a Sikh.

सिखनौतु *sikhnautu*, m. reg. (?) a learner, novice.

सिखरन *sikharan*, f. Brbh. Av. a dish made of yoghurt and sugar with coconut, spices, &c.

सिखलाना *sikhlānā*, v.t. = सिखाना.

सिखव- *sikhav-*, v.t. Brbh. = सिखाना.

सिखवाना *sikhvānā* [cf. H. *sīkhnā*], v.t. to cause to be taught (by, से); to have instruction given (to, को).

सिखाई *sikhāī* [cf. H. *sikhānā*], f. instruction; advice.

सिखाना *sikhānā* [cf. H. *sīkhnā*], v.t. **1.** to teach; to instruct. **2.** to advise, prompt, to suggest (to, को). **3.** to teach (one) a lesson, to correct (one). — उसने उसे मोटर चलाना (or चलानी) सिखाया, he taught him to drive a car. उसने उसे सिखाया, he taught him. उसने उसे हिंदी सिखाई, he taught him Hindi. – सिखाना-पढ़ाना, to teach, to train.

सिखापन *sikhāpan* [cf. H. *sīkhnā*], m. reg. teaching, instruction; admonition.

सिखावन *sikhāvan* [cf. H. *sikhānā*], f. instruction; advice.

सिगड़ी *sigṛī*, f. a small stove.

सिगौता *sigautā* [**sṛṅgayukta-*], m. reg. a hide with horns attached.

सिजदा *sijdā* [A. *sijda*], m. bowing the forehead to the ground (in prayer to Allah). — सिजदा-गाह [P. *-gāh*], f. place of worship, mosque.

सिजल *sijal*, adj. colloq. = सजीला.

सिझाना *sijhānā* [cf. H. *sījhnā*], v.t. **1.** to boil; to cook (food). **2.** to tan (hides). **3.** fig. to cause suffering (to). **4.** colloq. to acquire (as money by sharp practice).

सिटकारी *siṭkārī*, adj. *Pl.* ? tapering: cf. सटकार-.

सिटकिनी *siṭkinī* [conn. *saṭṭa-*[2] or H. [2]*saṭaknā*], f. *HŚS.* an iron rod, bolt (for closing a door).

सिटपिटाना *siṭpiṭānā* [? H. *siṭṭī*+H. *piṭnā*], v.i. **1.** to be taken aback, disconcerted. **2.** to be restless, distracted.

सिट्टा *siṭṭā* [**siṭṭ-*; ← Panj.], m. *Pl.* an ear of corn.

सिट्टी *siṭṭī* [*sṛṣṭi-*], f. wits, senses. — ~ गुम होना, or बँधना, to lose one's senses, to act stupidly; = सिटपिटाना, 1. ~ भूलना, id.

[1]**सिट्ठी** *siṭṭhī*, f. *Pl. HŚS.* see सिट्टी.

[2]**सिट्ठी** *siṭṭhī*, f. *Pl. HŚS.* dregs, lees (= [1]सीठी).

सिठाई *siṭhāī*, f. 19c. tastelessness, insipidity (cf. [1]सीठी).

सिठानी *siṭhānī*, f. the wife of a merchant or banker (*seṭh*).

सियासी *siyāsī* [A. *siyāsa*, P. *siyāsat*+H. *-ī*], adj. corr. political.

सिड़ *siṛ*, f. **1.** madness, craziness. **2.** raving; drivel. — सिड़-बिल्ला, adj. & m. colloq. mad, crazy; a madman. सिड़-बिलिल्ला, adj. & m. id.

सिड़पन *siṛpan* [cf. H. *siṛ*], m. = सिड़.

सिड़पना *siṛpanā* [cf. H. *siṛ*], m. = सिड़.

सिड़ा *siṛā*, adj. reg. mad, crazy.

सिड़ी *siṛī* [cf. H. *siṛ*], adj. & m. **1.** adj. mad, crazy. **2.** m. a mad or crazy person.

सितंबर *sitambar* [Pt. *setembro*: w. Engl. *September*], m. September.

सित *sit* [S.], adj. & m. Brbh. Av. **1.** adj. white. **2.** bright. **3.** m. *Pl. HŚS.* the light half of the month. **4.** the planet Venus (= शुक्र). — सित-मेचक, adj. Brbh. white and black. सितवराह-तिय, f. Brbh. *mythol.* she who (was rescued by) the white boar: the earth. सित-सागर, m. Brbh. *mythol.* the ocean of milk. सिताभोज [°*ta*+*a*°], m. Brbh. a white lotus. सितासित [°*ta*+*a*°], adj. Brbh. white and black. सितोपल [°*ta*+*u*° in *utpala-*], m. *Pl. HŚS.* white stone: crystal; chalk, chalk-stone.

सितम *sitam* [P. *sitam*], m. **1.** tyranny, injustice. **2.** violence; outrageous behaviour; atrocity. **3.** fig. the indifference of a beloved one. — ~ करना (पर), to tyrannise, to oppress, &c.; fig. to do wonders, to perform prodigies. ~ टूटना, an outrage, &c. to be committed (against, पर). ~ ढाना, or तोड़ना, to commit an outrage, &c. (against, पर); colloq. to be devastating, charming (a woman). — सितमगर [P. *-gar*], adj. & m. U. tyrannical, oppressive; oppressor. °-गरी, [P. *-garī*], f. tyranny, &c.

सिता *sitā* [S.], f. Brbh. sthg. white: **1.** white or candied sugar. **2.** moonlight.

सिताब *sitāb* [P. *śitāb*], m. & adv. Brbh. **1.** speed, haste. **2.** adv. quickly.

सितार *sitār* [P. *sitār* 'three strings'], m. a musical instrument of, usually, three to seven strings, with a resonator. — सितारवादक, m. a sitār player.

[1]**सितारा** *sitārā* [P. *sitāra*], m. **1.** a star. **2.** fortune, fate. **3.** a kind of firework. **4.** a gold or silver spangle. — ~ चमकना (का), (one's) star to shine, to be prosperous or successful. ~ बुलंद

होना (का), one's star to be in the ascendant. सितारे-हिंद [P. *sitāra e hind*], m. *hist.* Star of India (the decoration).

²**सितारा** *sitārā* [P. *sitāra*], m. = सितार.

सिथल *sithal*, adj. pronun. var. reg. = शीतल.

सिथिल *sithil*, adj. pronun. var. = शिथिल.

सिदौस *sidaus* [? *sa-+divasa-*: cf. H. *saverā*], m. early morning, dawn.

सिदौसी *sidausī* [cf. H. *sidaus*], adv. E.H. **1.** early in the morning. **2.** quickly.

सिद्ध *siddh* [S.], adj. & m. **1.** adj. accomplished, brought about; realised (an objective, a wish); completed; perfected. **2.** obtained, acquired. जन्म-सिद्ध अधिकार, m. a right arising with birth. **3.** demonstrated, proved (a fact, a case); substantiated. **4.** sound, valid (as usage); mature (as judgment). **5.** decided, adjudicated (as a law-suit). **6.** accepted (as), famous (as). **7.** cooked (food); prepared, concocted (as a dye). **8.** thoroughly versed (in a field of knowledge; or in magic). **9.** endowed with supernatural powers; perfected or sanctified (as by penance). **10.** sacred, holy. **11.** m. a semi-divine being of great perfection, said to possess eight supernatural faculties or *siddhis*. **12.** an ascetic of great powers and saintliness. **13.** a magician who has acquired superhuman powers. — ~ करना, to accomplish, &c.; to demonstrate, to prove; to win to (one's) side (esp. by guile); to suborn; to bring under subjection by magic; to settle (a debt). ~ कर लाना, to carry into effect. – सिद्धहस्त, adj. of perfected hand: very skilled or experienced. °ता, f. great skill or craftsmanship. सिद्धांजन [°*dha+a*°], m. a magical ointment (which when applied to the eyes is believed to allow buried treasure, &c. to be seen underground). सिद्धांत [°*dha+a*°], m. final end or aim, demonstrated conclusion: a reliable doctrine, a principle (moral, philosphical, scientific, &c.); theory; doctrine. सिद्धांत रूप में, adv. in principle. °ई, adj. & m. (one) working in accordance with, or standing on, principles. सिद्धांत-निष्ठा, f. devotion to principle, moral scruple. सिद्धार्थ [°*dha+a*°], adj. & m. having attained one's aim, successful; name of Gautama the founder of Buddhism. स्वयं-सिद्ध, adj. self-evident.

सिद्धता *siddhătā* [S.], f. accomplishment, completion, &c. (see सिद्ध).

सिद्धि *siddhi* [S.], f. **1.** accomplishment, fulfilment; attainment, (of any object). **2.** success, prosperity. **3.** demonstration, proof (as of a case); substantiation (of a remark). **4.** correctness (of any contention). **5.** decision (of a law-suit). **6.** solution (of a problem); settlement (of a debt). **7.** complete knowledge or understanding. **8.** acquisition of supernatural powers by magical means; any supernatural skill or capability (e.g. the art of making oneself invisible, as practised by an *aiyyār*, q.v.) **9.** good effect or result, advantage. — सिद्धि-गोटिका, f. Av. a magic pill supposed to confer some supernatural power (such as the ability to fly).

सिधवाई *sidhvāī*, f. reg. (Bihar) prop (as placed at the rear of a cart, to hold it horizontal); block (used when removing a wheel).

सिधवाना *sidhvānā* [cf. H. *sīdhā*], v.t. reg. to put or to keep (sthg.) straight.

सिधाई *sidhāī* [cf. H. *sīdhā*], f. = सीधापन.

सिधाना *sidhānā* [cf. H. *sīdhā*], v.i. reg. = सिधारना.

सिधारना *sidhārnā* [cf. *siddha-*¹], v.i. **1.** to set out, to depart. **2.** to depart this life. — सिधारो! get going! go away! परलोक ~, to depart for the other world: = ~, 2.

सिधावट *sidhāvaṭ*, f. = सीधापन.

सिधौड़ *sidhauṛ*, f. *Pl.* = सधौर.

सिनक *sinak* [cf. H. *sinaknā*], f. **1.** blowing the nose. **2.** snot.

सिनकना *sinaknā*, v.i. to blow (the nose).

सिपर *sipar* [P. *sipar*], f. Brbh. shield.

सिपह- *sipah-*. army (= सिपाह): — सिपह-सालार, m. commander of an army.

सिपाह *sipāh* [P. *sipāh*], f. soldiery, troops; army. — सिपाह-सालार [P. *sālār*], m. commander of an army.

सिपाहियाना *sipāhiyānā* [P. *sipāhiyāna*], adj. like a soldier; military (as bearing).

सिपाही *sipāhī* [P. *sipāhī*], f. **1.** soldier; specif. an Indian soldier; *hist.* sepoy. **2.** police constable; warder. **3.** peon, messenger. **4.** (in chess) pawn.

सिप्पा *sippā*, m. **1.** a well-aimed or well-ranged blow. ***2.** an effective means; a plan. — ~ जमाना, to take steps or measures, to lay the ground (for). ~ भिड़ाना, or लड़ाना, to deploy all means (to an end). ~ मारना, to hit a mark, to achieve a goal.

सिफ़त *sifat* [A. *ṣifa*: P. *ṣifat*], f. quality, attribute.

सिफ़र *sifr* [A. *ṣifr*], m. a cipher: **1.** nought, zero; a zero. **2.** fig. a nonentity.

सिफ़ारत *sifārat* [A. *sifāra*: P. *sifārat*], f. U. making peace: an embassy; legation; mission.

सिफ़ारिश *sifāriś* [P. *sifāriś*], f. **1.** recommendation; introduction (to a person). **2.** intercession. **3.** recommendation (addressed to a prospective employer). — ~ करना (की), to recommend, to commend (to, को); to intercede (for); to recommend (a step, procedure).

सिफ़ारिशी *sifāriśī* [P. *sifāriśī*], adj. **1.** containing a recommendation or introduction (a letter). **2.** obtaining a post undeservedly through another's influence (an appointee). — ~ टट्टू, m. pej. one who obtains a post undeservedly through influence.

सिमई *simaī*, f. pronun. var. = सिवैयाँ.

सिमट *simaṭ* [cf. H. *simaṭnā*], f. the act of contracting, shrinking, &c.

सिमटन *simṭan* [cf. H. *simaṭnā*], f. crease, wrinkle (= सिलवट).

सिमटना *simaṭnā* [cf. *saṁveṣṭayati*, and *saṁvr̥tta-*], v.i. **1.** to be drawn together, to contract. **2.** to be collected, concentrated. **3.** to shrink, to shrivel; to shrink in shame. **4.** to be crumpled, or creased. **5.** to be accomplished, disposed of (as work); to be set right or straight.

सिमटी *simṭī* [? cf. H. *simaṭnā*], f. *Pl. HŚS.* a twill cloth.

सिमल *simal*, f. reg. peg, or notch, of a bullock-yoke.

सिमसिम *simsim* [cf. *simasimāyate*], f. **1.** the hissing of damp wood when burning. **2.** simmering.

सिमसिमाना *simsimānā* [*simasimāyate*], v.i. reg. to be damp (as firewood); to hiss (as wood) while burning.

सिमिटना *simiṭnā*, v.i. pronun. var. = सिमटना.

सिम्त *simt* [A. *samt*], f. U. side, direction.

सिय *siy* [*sītā-*], f. Av. = सीता.

सियह *siyah* [P. *siyah*], adj. U. = स्याह.

सियाऊ *siyāū* [**sītādevī-*], f. **1.** a deity presiding over agriculture or its fruits. **2.** tutelary goddess of a village.

सियार *siyār* [*sr̥gāla-*], m. a jackal. — ~ (की) लाठी, f. *Pl. HŚS.* a laburnum, *Cassia fistula*.

सियारनी *siyārnī*, f. = सियारिन.

सियारा *siyārā* [**sītādhārā*], m. reg. a piece of wood with handle attached, used to level furrows after ploughing.

सियारिन *siyārin* [**sr̥gālinī-*], f. a female jackal.

सियाल *siyāl*, m. Brbh. = सियार. — सियाल-काँटा, m. *Pl.* a kind of poppy; a kind of jujube (Zizyphus).

सियाला *siyālā* [*śītakāla-*], m. reg. (W.) Av. the cold season.

सियाली *siyālī* [cf. H. *siyālā*], f. reg. the autumn (*kharīf*) harvest.

[1]**सियावड़ी** *siyāvaṛī* [cf. *sītā-*], f. reg. a share of grain (given to priests or beggars).

[2]**सियावड़ी** *siyāvaṛī* [cf. H. *syāh*], f. reg. (W.) a black pot (used as a scarecrow, and to avert the evil eye).

सियावढ़ *siyāvaṛh*, f. reg. = [1]सियावड़ी.

सियासत *siyāsat* [A. *siyāsa*; P. *siyāsat*], f. U. management; politics.

सियाह *siyāh*, adj. see स्याह.

सियाहा *siyāhā*, m. see स्याहा.

सिर *sir* [*śiras-*], m. **1.** head. **2.** crown; top, summit. **3.** beginning. — ~ आँखों पर बिठाना, or रखना, to receive (a guest) with all honour. ~ आँखों पर होना, to be cherished; to be performed willingly (as a command). ~ आँखों से, adv. with all one's heart, willingly. ~ आना, to get into the head (of, के), to possess (one: an evil spirit). ~ उठाकर चलना, to walk with the head held high; to walk on tiptoe; to strut. ~ उठाना, to raise the head; to grow prominent; to look up; to hold up (one's) head (being unashamed, or feeling pride); to rebel; to be refractory or truculent; to turn aside (from pressing tasks). ~ ऊँचा करना, = ~ उठाना, 1.-5. ~ करना, to lay on the shoulders (of, के), to hold (one) responsible (for); to do the hair. ~ का बोझ उतारना, to free (oneself) of a burden; to shuffle off (a duty). ~ का बोझ हल्का होना, a burden to be removed from (one's) shoulders. ~ की आफ़त, f. an impending or threatening disaster. ~ की क़सम! I swear by my (or your) life! ~ के ज़ोर, adv. with all (one's) might; impetuously; head first, headlong. ~ के बल, adv. on the head, head first; head downwards. ~ खपाना, to destroy, or to exhaust, the head: to rack the brains; to bother (one's) head; to put one's head or life at stake. ~ खाना, to pester, to plague (one, का). (अपना) ~ खाओ! go to the devil! ~ खुजाना, to make the head itch: to scratch the head; fig. to court punishment. ~ गूँथना, to plait the hair; to adorn the hair (as with flowers). ~ घुठनों में देना, to place the head on the knees: to hang the head (in dejection, shame or embarrassment). ~ घूमना, or चकराना, to feel giddy, or faint; the head to be turned. ~ चढ़कर बोलना, to talk under the influence (of an evil spirit, &c). ~ चढ़कर मरना, to die laying the guilt for one's death at the door (of another, के). ~ चढ़ना, to mount on (one's) head: to take advantage (of,

के), to take liberties; to be insolent; to tyrannise (over); to be laid, or debited, to the account (of); to be attributed or imputed (to). ~ चढ़ाना, to place on the head: to make much of; to allow to obsess one, to spoil (a child); to honour, to revere; to offer oneself as a sacrifice, to devote oneself; to hold (one's, अपना) head high, to act arrogantly. ~ चीरना, to split the skull (of, का); to insist on having one's own way. ~ जाना, to be left to the responsibility (of, के: a matter). ~ चला जाना, to die. ~ जोड़कर बैठना, to put heads together; to plot; to deliberate. ~ झाड़ना, to comb out the hair. ~ झुकाना, to bow the head (as in greeting; or as in sorrow); to be submissive; to be shamed, humiliated. ~ टकराना, fig. to go to great pains (esp. pointlessly; to rack the brains). ~ टूटना, fig. to have a splitting headache. ~ डालना, to lay (upon, के: as a task); to foist (upon). ~ तोड़कर लेना, to take (sthg.) by force; to extort (money) by threatening to mutilate oneself. ~ तोड़ना, to crack the skull, to knock out the brains (of, का); to subdue. ~ ढाँकना, to cover the head (with the end of her sari, in respect: a married woman). ~ थामना, to hold, or to clutch, the head (as in grief). ~ थोपना, = ~ डालना. ~ धरना, to place (one's) head (low): to be submissive or obedient; to place the responsibility for sthg. (on, के). ~ दे मारना, to beat the head or brow (as in despair). ~ देना (का), to lay down (one's) life (for, के लिए). ~ धुनना, to beat the head or brow; to mourn. ~ न पाँव का, adj. without head or foot: nonsensical (words, a matter). ~ नवाना, = ~ झुकाना. ~ नीचा करना, to lower the head, = ~ नवाना. ~ पटकना, to dash the head (against the ground); = ~ मारना. ~ पड़ना (के), to come upon, to befall (as a misfortune); to devolve (upon). ~ पर, adv. on the head (of, के); close at hand (to protect one); burdening or besetting (one: as a misfortune, or a responsibility). ~ पर आना, to be impending. ~ पर आसमान उठाना, fig. to raise a great clamour or hullabaloo. ~ पर उठाना, to turn on (its) head: to reduce to a state of confusion (as a household). ~ पर काल चढ़ना, death to be close at hand. ~ पर काली हाँड़ी उठाना, colloq. to place a black pot on (one's) head: to be disgraced; to be shameless. ~ पर खड़ा होना, to be impending (sthg. unpleasant). ~ पर ख़ाक उड़ाना, or डालना (के), to throw dust on the head (of): to mourn, to lament. ~ पर चढ़ना, to impose oneself (on, के), to plague, to harass; to behave rudely or insultingly; to possess (one: an evil spirit); to be spoilt by (a child). ~ पर चढ़ाना, = ~ चढ़ाना, 1.-3. ~ पर जिन, or भूत, or शैतान, सवार होना, a fiend to ride one's head: to be possessed by a demon; to be hell-bent (on some purpose). ~ पर पड़ना, = ~ पड़ना. ~ पर पत्थर रखना, to place a stone on one's head: to be burdened or to suffer constantly. ~ पर पाँव रखकर भागना, to take to one's heels. ~ पर बीतना, to be experienced, to befall (one, के). ~ पर रखना, to place on the head; to honour, to revere. ~ पर लेना, to take responsibility (for); to risk one's life (for). ~ पर सवार होना, fig. to obsess (one, के). ~ पर हाथ धरना, or रखना, to put the hand on the head: to take under one's protection or care; to swear by (one's, अपने) head or life. ~ पर हाथ फेरना, fig. to comfort, to caress; = ~ पर हाथ धरना, 1. ~ पीटना, to beat the head, to lament. ~ फिरना, = सिर घूमना, 1.; to go off one's head. ~ फेरना, to turn the head (from, से), to look away; to be refractory, to rebel; to turn the head (of, का); to take in, to deceive. ~ फोड़ना, to break or to crack the head (of, का); to wrangle; to rack the brains vainly. ~ बाँधना, to tie up the hair; to plait the hair. ~ भारी होना, the head to be heavy: to have a headache; to feel giddy. ~ माथे चढ़ाना, to place the forehead: to indicate compliance or acceptance. ~ मारना, to beat the head or brow: to rack the brains; to make great efforts; to take pains (as in searching); colloq. to strike on the head (with), to hand (sthg.) over (to). ~ मूँड़ना, to shave the head (of); to cheat, to fleece. ~ में ख़ाक डालना, = ~ पर ख़ाक डालना. ~ रँगना, to bloody the head (of, का), to beat. ~ रहना, (one) to remain alive; to apply (oneself) steadily (to, के), to persevere; to pursue doggedly, to plague (one, के). ~ लगना, to be imputed (to, के), levelled (at: a charge, &c.); to be suffered (hardship). ~ लगाना, = ~ डालना; to impute, &c. ~ से कफ़न बाँधना, to wrap the shroud round the head: to take one's life in one's hands. ~ से टलना, to pass, to be escaped from (a threatened misfortune, &c). ~ से बोझ उतारना, to get free (of a burden, a care or a responsibility). ~ से बोझ बाँधना, to take a burden, &c. upon oneself. ~ सेहरा बँधना, or रहना, to have the badge of honour or distinction, to be the head or leader (of). ~ सूँघना (का), to sniff the head: to bless (a child). ~ हिलाना, to nod the head (in agreement); to shake the head (in disagreement). ~ होना, to pester, to harass, to be at (one, के); to pursue; to keep (one, के) at work, &c.; fig. to be laid at the door (of, के: a misfortune or misdeed). न ~ का न पैर का, adj. = ~ न पाँव का. – सिर-ठठौवल, m. a displeased greeting. सिर-ताज, m. the crown of the head; chief, leader. सिर-दर्द, m. a headache (= सर-दर्द). सिर-धरा, m. head (as of a family); patron, master. °-धरू, m. id. सिर-नाई [cf. H. *navānā*], f. bowing the head, obeisance. सिर-नामा, m. caption, heading. सिर-फिरा, adj. giddy, crazy. सिर-फुटौवल, m. wrangling. सिर-मुँड़ा, adj. having the head shaved. सिर-मौर, m. Brbh. crown, crest, diadem; fig. a paragon.

सिरका *sirkā* [P. *sirka*], m. vinegar.

सिरकी *sirkī*, f. **1.** reed-grass, the upper joint of *Saccharum procerum*. **2.** a mat made of reed-grass (used to make sheltered living-quarters or on carts, &c).

सिरज- *siraj-* [ad. *sarjayati*], v.t. Brbh. Av. to create; to form, to make. — सिरजनहार, m. creator.

सिरजनहार *sirjanhār*, m. Brbh. Av. see सिरज-.

सिरजना *sirajnā* [ad. *sṛjati*], v.t & v.i. **1.** v.t. to create, to form, to make. **2.** [cf. H. *sirjānā*] v.i. to be created.

सिरजाना *sirjānā* [cf. H. *sirajnā*], v.t. to cause to be created, to create.

सिरदार *sirdār*, m. Brbh. = सरदार.

सिरवाली *sirvālī*, f. *Pl.* name of a small black shiny seed (used medicinally).

सिरस *siras*, m. = शिरीष.

सिरसा *sirsā*, m. *Pl. HŚS.* = शिरीष.

सिरहाना *sirhānā* [**śiraādhāna-*], m. **1.** head of a bed. **2.** head of a tomb. — सिरहाने, adv. at the head of (a bed).

सिरांचा *sirāñcā* [P. *sarāca*], m. reg. (W.) a bamboo used in making chairs.

[1]**सिरा** *sirā* [*śiras-*], m. extremity, head: **1.** end (as of a piece of cloth); edge (of any area); tip. **2.** outset, beginning. — सिरे का, adj. excellent, first class; extreme, excessive. सिरे का बातूनी, adj. garrulous in the extreme. सिरे चढ़ना, to approach completion (a task, a project). सिरे से, adv. from the outset; first and foremost; from the end. नए सिरे से, adv. anew.

[2]**सिरा** *sirā* [S.], f. **1.** a blood-vessel. **2.** *Pl. HŚS.* an irrigation channel. **3.** *Pl.* a bucket, baling vessel. **4.** reg. (Bihar) = शीरा.

सिरा- *sirā-* [cf. *śītalayati*], Brbh. Av. v.i. & v.t. **1.** v.i. to become cold. **2.** to be cooled, assuaged (as eyes, sorrow). **3.** v.t. to cool. **4.** to assuage. **5.** fig. to set afloat.

सिराज *sirāj* [A. *sirāj*], m. U. **1.** a lamp; candle. **2.** the sun.

सिरावन *sirāvan*, m. reg. (W.) a harrow; a log, &c. used for levelling ground (= पाटा).

सिरिस *siris*, m. Av. = शिरीष.

सिरी *sirī* [cf. *śiras-*], f. the head (esp. of a sacrificial animal).

सिरीसाफ़ *sirīsāf* [U. *-ṣāf*] f. (?) *Pl.* a kind of muslin.

सिरेश *sireś*, m. = सरेस.

सिरेस *sires*, m. = सरेस.

सिरोही *sirohī*, f. m. **1.** f. a type of two-edged sword (made at Siroh in S.W. Rajasthan). **2.** m. f. a surname.

सिर्फ़ *sirf* [A. *ṣirf*], adv. only, merely (often used in conjunction with and supplementing ही).

सिल *sil* [*śilā-*], f. **1.** a stone, piece of stone; specif. a flat stone on which spices, &c. are ground; lump (of ice). **2.** a flagstone; threshold. — ~ का पत्थर, m. reg. stone for use in grinding spices. – सिलखड़ी, f. chalk-stone; soapstone, steatite. सिल-पट, adj. smooth, even, level; worn (a coin). सिल-बट्टा, m. stone slab and grinder. सिल-लोढ़ा, m. id.

सिलगना *silagnā*, v.i. = सुलगना.

सिलगाना *silgānā*, v.t. = सुलगाना.

सिलना *silnā* [cf. H. *silānā*], v.i. to be sewn. — सिला-सिलाया, adj. ready-sewn, ready-made (clothing).

[1]**सिल-पट** *sil-paṭ*, adj. see s.v. सिल.

[2]**सिलपट** *silpaṭ* [Engl. *slipper*], f. slipper: a shoe open at the heel.

सिलवट *silvaṭ* [? conn. H. *silnā*], f. **1.** a fold, seam (as in cloth). **2.** a crease; wrinkle, furrow (on the brow).

सिलवाई *silvāī* [cf. H. *silvānā*], f. cost of, or price paid for, sewing.

सिलवाना *silvānā* [cf. H. *sīnā*], v.t. to cause to be sewn or stitched (by, से); to have (sthg.) sewn.

सिलसिला *silsilā* [A. *silsila*], m. **1.** chain. ***2.** series; sequence; train (of thought). **3.** arrangement, order (of objects in series). **4.** fig. range (of mountains). **5.** connection; context. इस सिलसिले में, adv. in this connection. **6.** *musl.* a sect, persuasion (of Ṣūfīs). — ~ बैठना, a sequence to be established; arrangements to be completed (for an event, or occasion: का). – सिलसिलेवार [P. *-vār*], adj. linked; sequential, serial; consecutive; systematic; lineal.

सिलह *silah*, f. = सिलाह.

[1]**सिला** *silā* [*śila-*], m. gleanings of corn. — ~ चुगना, चुनना or बीनना, to glean. – सिलाहार, m. gleaner.

[2]**सिला** *silā* [A. *ṣila*], m. **1.** present, gift. **2.** remuneration; repayment.

[1]**सिलाई** *silāī* [cf. H. *silānā*], f. **1.** sewing; needlework. **2.** a seam. **3.** price paid for sewing. — ~ की मशीन, f. sewing machine. – सिलाई-मशीन, f. id.

[2]**सिलाई** *silāī* [? H. *salāī*], f. reg. a caterpillar, red and brown in colour, which burrows in the stalks and leaf sheaths of corn and sugar-cane.

सिलाजीत *silājīt* [conn. *śilājatu-*, *śilājit-*], m. **1.** a gum-resin, storax. **2.** red chalk, red ochre (= गेरू).

[1]**सिलाना** *silānā* [cf. H. *sīnā*], v.t. to cause to be sewn or stitched (by, से); to have made (a garment).

[2]**सिलाना** *silānā* [*śītalayati*], v.t. **1.** to pour out (the remains of holy water used in worship). **2.** reg. = सिरा-.

सिलाबाक *silābāk* [H. *silā-*+H. **bāk*: OIA *valka-*], m. *Pl. HŚS.* rock-bark: a moss or lichen (esp. one used medicinally).

सिलरास *silarās* [conn. *śilārasa-*], m. *Pl. HŚS.* a gum-resin, storax (= सिलाजीत).

सिला-सिलाया *silā-silāyā*, adj. see s.v. सिलना.

सिलाह *silāh* [A. *silāḥ*], f. Brbh. weapons; armour.

[1]**सिली** *silī*, f. reg. = [2]सिल्ली.

[2]**सिली** *silī*, f. *Pl.* = [3]सिल्ली.

सिलौट *silauṭ* [*śilāpaṭṭa-*], f. reg. a small stone (for grinding spices on with a roller).

सिलौटा *silauṭā*, m. reg. = सिलौट.

सिलौटी *silauṭī*, f. reg. = सिलौट.

सिल्ला *sillā* [**śilla-*], m. = [1]सिला.

[1]**सिल्ली** *sillī* [cf. **śillā-*], f. **1.** a block or slab of stone; block of ice. **2.** transf. colloq. bullion. **3.** whetstone; hone (of a jeweller). **4.** a shingle or slate (for roofing). **5.** reg. (W.) a plank.

[2]**सिल्ली** *sillī* [**śilla-*], f. reg. **1.** straw and threshed grain ready for winnowing. **2.** a heap of grain; refuse grain or straw on the threshing floor.

[3]**सिल्ली** *sillī*, f. *Pl. HŚS.* a wild duck, the whistling teal.

सिवई *sivaīṁ* [*śamitā-*], f. = सिवैयाँ.

सिवा *sivā* [A. *sivā*], ppn., often inverted. except (for, के), apart (from). — ~ आपके, or आपके ~, adv. apart from you. ~ तकलीफ़ उठाए और क्या चारा है? what can be done except to go to this trouble? तकलीफ़ उठाने के ~ और क्या चारा है? id.

सिवाई *sivāī*, f. reg. a light loam.

सिवाना *sivānā* [*sīmānam*], m. reg. (W.) boundary line (of a field or village).

सिवाय *sivāy* [P. *sivā-e*], adv. & ppn. = सिवा.

सिवार *sivār* [*śīpāla-*], m. (? f.) **1.** the water-plant *Vallisneria octandra.* **2.** a green scum forming on stagnant water. **3.** reg. river grass used as a filter in refining sugar.

सिवैयाँ *sivaiyāṁ* [*śamitā-*], f. pl. noodles, vermicelli. — ~ तोड़ना, or पूरना, or बटना, or बनाना, to make noodles.

सिसक *sisak* [cf. H. *sisaknā*], f. = सिसकी.

सिसकना *sisaknā* [conn. **śuṣati*[2]], v.i. **1.** to sob. **2.** to draw in the breath suddenly, to gasp (as from a shock, or in fear). — सिसकती-भिनकती, adj. f. colloq. (a woman) who grumbles or complains.

सिसकारना *siskārnā* [conn. **śuṣati*[2]], v.i. & v.t. **1.** v.i. to whistle. **2.** to hiss; to draw in the breath. **3.** v.t. to urge on (a dog).

सिसकारी *siskārī* [cf. H. *siskārnā*], f. **1.** a whistling, whistle. **2.** a hiss; drawing in the breath with a hissing sound; urging on a dog. 3. = सिसकी. — ~ भरना, to suck in the breath with a hissing sound; to sob.

सिसकी *siskī* [cf. H. *sisaknā*], f. **1.** sobbing; a sob. **2.** a gasp. **3.** a sigh. — ~, or सिसकियाँ, भरना or लेना, to sob; to gasp.

सिसियाँद *sisiyāṁd*, f. a fishy smell.

सिसियायँद *sisiyāyaṁd* [? conn. H. *bisāyaṁdh*], f. = सिसियाँद.

सिहरन *sihran* [cf. H. *siharnā*], f. a thrill: a creepy feeling; shiver, shudder.

सिहरना *siharnā* [cf. *śikhara-*], v.i. to thrill; to feel creepy; to shiver (as with cold); to shudder (with fear).

सिहरा *sihrā*, m. = सेहरा.

सिहराना *sihrānā* [cf. H. *siharnā*], v.t. to cause to thrill, or to shiver, &c. (see सिहरना).

सिहरी *sihrī* [cf. H. *siharnā*], f. *Pl. HŚS.* = सिहरन.

सिहा- *sihā-* [? cf. *śikhā-*], v.i. Brbh. to feel a thrill of emotion (= सिहरना); to desire.

सिहिरना *sihirnā* [**śṛthilayati*], v.t. reg. to liquefy; to dissolve.

सिहुड़ *sihūṛ* [*sehuṇḍa-*]. m. the milk-hedge or milk-bush, *Euphorbia tirucalli*: a spurgewort.

सींक *sīṁk* [**siṅkā-* (← Drav.): Pk. *siṁkā-*], f. **1.** the jointed stalk of the grasses *Andropogon muricatus*, or *Saccharum arundinaceum* (*mūṁj*). **2.** a rod, stick; sliver; toothpick. **3.** a line; streak, stripe (as on cloth). **4.** Brbh. a nose ornament.

सींका *sīṁkā* [cf. H. *sīṁk*], m. reg. = सींक, 1.-3.

सींकिया *sīṁkiyā* [cf. H. *sīṁk*], adj. & m. **1.** adj. thin, skinny. **2.** lined, streaked, striped (cloth). **3.** m. a fine-striped cloth — ~ पहलवान, m. iron. a frail or scrawny person.

सींकुर *sīṁkur* [cf. **siṅkā-* (← Drav.): Pk. *siṁkā-*], m. awn (of barley).

सींकौ *sīṁkau* [*śikya-*], m. Brbh. net for hanging up household pots (= छींका).

सींग *sīṁg* [*śṛṅga-*], m. **1.** a horn. **2.** *mus.* a horn. — ~ **कटाकर बछड़ों से मिलना**, to get rid of the horns and mix with the calves: to ape the young (an old man). ~ **निकलना**, v.i. horns to grow (on an animal); (a man) to become foolish, or truculent. ~ **मारना**, to butt, to gore. ~ **समाना**, to find room for (its) horns: to find or to take refuge.

सींगना *sīṁgnā* [cf. H. *sīṁg*], v.t. reg. (W.) to identify stolen cattle.

सींगा *sīṁgā* [*śṛṅga-*], m. reg. **1.** *mus.* a horn; a trumpet. **2.** *Pl.* a powder-horn.

सींगीया *sīṁgīyā* [conn. *śṛṅgika-*], m. the aconite *A. spicatum* (source of a poison).

सींगी *sīṁgī* [*śṛṅga-*], f. **1.** a horn or cup used letting blood. **2.** *mus.* a small horn. — ~ **लगाना** (**को**), to let blood.

सींच *sīṁc* [cf. H. *sīṁcnā*], f. watering, irrigation.

सींचना *sīṁcnā* [*siñcati*], v.t. **1.** to water; to irrigate. **2.** to moisten, to sprinkle.

सींची *sīṁcī* [cf. H. *sīṁcnā*], f. reg. the season for irrigation.

सींथ *sīṁth* [conn. *sīmanta-*], f. a woman's hair-parting. — ~ **भरना** (**की**), to fill the parting (of, **की**: with vermilion): to marry.

[1]**सीकर** *sīkar* [*śṛṅkhalā-*], f. a small chain.

[2]**सीकर** *sīkar*, m. Brbh. = **शीकर**.

सीकरा *sīkrā* [P. *śikara*], m. E.H. a hawk.

[1]**सीकरी** *sīkrī*, f. reg. = [1]**सीकर**.

[2]**सीकरी** *sīkrī* [ad. *śīkara-*: dimin.], f. dandruff.

सीकाकाई *sīkākāī*, f. a prickly bush, *Acacia concinna*.

सीकुर *sīkur*, m. Brbh. awn (of barley: = **सींकुर**).

सीख *sīkh* [*śikṣā-*], f. **1.** instruction. **2.** sthg. learned, a lesson. **3.** advice; fig. a sound talking-to. — ~ **देना** (**को**), to give advice, &c. (to). ~ **मानना**, to heed the advice (of, **की**). ~ **लेना**, to ask advice (of, **की**); to take the advice (of); to draw a lesson (from, **से**). ~ **सुहाना** (**की**), advice to commend itself (to, **को**).

सीख़ *sīkh* [P. *sīkh*], f. **1.** a long, thin metal rod. **2.** a skewer, spit. — ~ **का कबाब**, m. pieces of meat roasted on a skewer. ~ **पर लगाना**, to skewer; to roast; fig. to burn, to inflame. – **सीख़पर**, m. spit-feathered: the pintail duck, *Anas acuta*.

सीख़चा *sīkhcā* [P. *sīkhca*], m. 1. = **सीख़**, 1.; specif. a window-bar. 2. = **सीख़**, 2.

सीखना *sīkhnā* [*śikṣate*], v.t. **1.** to learn; to acquire (knowledge, or a skill). **बोलना** ~, to learn to speak. **2.** to acquire (experience). — **आपने हिंदी कहाँ सीख ली?** where did you learn Hindi? – **सीखा-पढ़ा**, adj. = next; literate. **सीखा-सिखाया**, adj. versed, experienced (in, **में**; trained (in).

सीख़िया *sīkhiyā* [cf. H. *sīkh*], adj. cooked on a spit (meat). — ~ **कबाब**, m. = **सीख का कबाब**.

सीज *sīj* [**sīhyu-*], m. **1.** *Euphorbia antiquorum* (a spurgewort). **2.** *Pl. HŚS.* the milk-hedge or milk-bush plant (= **सेहुँड़**).

सीजना *sījnā* [*svidyati*; w. H. *sījhnā*], v.i. **1.** to sweat, to be exuded. 2. = **सीझना**, 1.-3.

सीझ *sījh* [cf. H. *sījhnā*], f. boiling, softening, &c. (see **सीझना**).

सीझ- *sījh-* [*sidhyati*[1]], v.i. Brbh. to go to, or towards.

सीझना *sījhnā* [*sidhyati*[2] and (senses 1.-5.) *svidyati*], v.i. **1.** to boil, to be cooked (food). **2.** to soften (as in cooking); to be tanned (hides). **3.** to dissolve, to melt away; to be settled, or liquidated (a debt). **4.** to sweat, to be exuded (= **सीजना**, 1.); to be seasoned (timber). **5.** to filter, to percolate. **6.** to be received (as money).

सीटना *sīṭnā*, v.t. to boast.

सीटी *sīṭī* [**siṭṭa-*], f. **1.** whistling, whistle. **2.** a whistle (the object). — ~ **देना**, to whistle (with the mouth, or as a train, &c). ~ **बजाना**, to blow a whistle. ~ **मारना**, to whistle (with the mouth, or with an instrument). – **सीटीबाज़** [P. *-bāz*], m. a whistler.

सीठ *sīṭh* [**śiṣṭi-*[1]; or cf. *śiṣṭa-*[1]], f. *Pl. HŚS.* 1. = [1]**सीठी**. **2.** reg. (Bihar) dregs of indigo (used as manure).

सीठना *sīṭhnā* [? conn. *aśiṣṭa-*], f. *Pl. HŚS.* obscene or abusive songs (sung by women at weddings).

सीठा *sīṭhā* [*śiṣṭa-*[1]], adj. left over: **1.** without juice (as remains of fruit). **2.** insipid, stale; tasteless. **3.** pale, faded; sickly (plants).

सीठापन *sīṭhāpan* [cf. H. *sīṭhā*], m. saplessness, insipidity, &c. (see **सीठा**).

[1]**सीठी** *sīṭhī* [cf. H. *sīṭhā*], f. dregs, leavings.

[2]**सीठी** *sīṭhī*, f. pronun. var. = **सीटी**.

सीड़ *sīṛ*, m. reg. **1.** an irrigation channel leading into fields. **2.** [? cf. [1]*sīta-*[1]: w. H. *sīlā*] wet land; an irrigated field.

सीड़ा *sīṛā*, m. reg. = **सीड़**.

सीढ़ी *sīṛhī* [**śrīdhi-*: Pk. *siḍḍhi-*], f. **1.** a step (as of a stair). **2.** a ladder. **3.** a stage (of upward progress). — **~ का डंडा**, m. rung of a ladder. **~ चढ़ना**, to go up, or forward, a step. **~ पर चढ़ना**, id. **~ लगाकर चढ़ना**, to climb up by ladder. **~ ~ चढ़ना**, to rise, or to climb, step by step. **सीढ़ियाँ**, f. pl. a flight of steps; stairway. **चलती ~**, f. an escalator. – **सीढ़ीनुमा** [P. *-numā*], adj. inv. formed like a flight of steps, terraced.

सीत्कार *sītkār* [S.], m. a drawing in of the breath (in ecstasy, or in pain).

सीतल *sītal* [ad. *śītala-*], adj. cool, &c. (= **शीतल**). — **सीतल-चीनी**, f. allspice, *Myrtus pimenta*. **सीतल-पट्टी**, f. a kind of cool sleeping-mat; a kind of striped cloth. **सीतल-पाटी**, f. id.

सीतलता *sītalătā* (cf. H. *sītal*], f. coolness, &c. (see **शीतल**).

सीतलताई *sītalătāī*, f. Brbh. Av. = **शीतलता**.

सीतला *sītlā*, f. smallpox, &c. (= **शीतला**). — **~ की फूटी आँख**, f. an eye lost from smallpox. **मोतिया ~**, f. chicken-pox. — **सीतला-खाया**, adj. colloq. = next. **सीतला-मुँह**, or **सितला-मुँह-दाग़**, adj. having the face pitted by smallpox.

सीता *sītā* [S.], f. **1.** name of the daughter of king Janak and wife of Rāmcandra. **2.** a furrow. **3.** name of a deity presiding over agriculture and its fruits (see **सियाऊ**). — **सीता-नाथ**, m. next. **सीता-पति**, m. Sītā's lord: a title of Rāmcandra. **सीता-फल**, m. the custard-apple tree, *Anona squamosa*, and its fruit; the sweet pumpkin or musk-melon, *Cucurbita moschata*. **सीता-राम**, interj. Sītā-Rām!

सीथ *sīth* [*siktha-*[1]], m. Brbh. rice-water.

सीद- *sīd-*, v.i. Brbh. to suffer distress or affliction.

सीध *sīdh* [*siddhi-*], f. **1.** straightness. **2.** direct line, aim. — **~ बाँधना**, to lay a straight line (as for digging); to take aim (at, **की**); to make a bee-line (for). **~ में**, adv. in a straight line (with, **की**); in the direction (of). **नाक की ~ में चला जाना**, to follow one's nose.

सीधा *sīdhā* [*siddha-*[2]], adj. & m. **1.** adj. straight, direct. **2.** even, smooth, level. **3.** erect, upright. **4.** correct, right. **5.** close, literal (a translation). **6.** direct (of manner), straightforward; plain, simple; honest, candid. **7.** easy, simple (a matter, a task). **8.** easy, tractable (of manner); tamed; punished. **9.** favourable, kind. **10.** right (hand). **11.** auspicious; suitable (moment, opportunity). **12.** m. uncooked grain (as given to brāhmaṇs, or to wandering ascetics); a quantity of uncooked grain. — **~ करना**, to straighten; to smooth; to adjust, to correct; to punish, to set to rights; to tame, to train; to level (a firearm), to take aim. **~ जाना**, to go straight (ahead); to go directly. **~ बनाना**, = **~ करना**, 1.-5. **सीधी कहना**, or **सुनाना** (**को**), to speak plainly (to), to take to task; to berate, to abuse. **सीधी तरह**, adv. in a direct or straightforward manner; smoothly, gently; courteously. **सीधी बात कहना**, or **सुनाना**, id. **सीधे जाना**, = **~ जाना**. **सीधे स्वभाव**, adv. straightforwardly, unaffectedly; guilelessly. **सीधे मुँह बात न करना**, = next. **सीधे मुँह नहीं बोलना**, not to speak directly (to, **से**), to behave condescendingly (towards). – **सीधा-सादा** [P. *sāda*], adj. simple, ingenuous; plain (as dress, manner). °**पन**, m. **सीधा-साधा**, adj. = **सीधा-सादा**.

सीधाई *sīdhāī* [cf. H. *sīdhā*], f. = **सीधापन**.

सीधापन *sīdhāpan* [cf. H. *sīdhā*], m. straightness, directness, correctness, &c. (see **सीधा**).

[1]**सीना** *sīnā* [*sīvayati*], v.t. to sew; to stitch together, to darn. — **सी देना**, to sew up. – **सीना-पिरोना**, m. sewing, needlework.

[2]**सीना** *sīnā* [P. *sīna*], m. **1.** the chest. **2.** breast, bosom (for some collocations see similar expressions under **छाती**). — **~ उभारकर चलना**, to walk with the chest stuck out; to behave pretentiously. **~ तानकर**, or **ताने**, **चलना**, id. **~ दुगुना होना**, the chest to swell (with pride). **सीने पर पत्थर रखना**, fig. to repress sorrow. **सीने से लगाना**, to embrace. – **सीनाचाक**, adj. having the breast torn: grieving, afflicted. **सीनाज़ोर** [P. *-zor*], adj. robust; proud of strength; obstinate; overbearing, arrogant. °**ई**, f. **सीनाबंद** [P. *-band*], m. a padded *kurtā*.

सीप *sīp* [**sippī-* (← Drav.): Pa. *sippī-*], f. **1.** a shell. **2.** mother-of-pearl. — **सीपज**, m. Brbh. = next. **सीप-सुत**, m. Brbh. shell-born: a pearl.

सीपर *sīpar* [P. *sipar*], m. metr. Brbh. a shield.

सीपल *sīpal*, m. *Pl.* a broken piece of pottery.

सीपला *sīplā*, m. *Pl.* a patch or lock of curly hair in any part of a horse's coat (regarded as auspicious).

सीपी *sīpī*, f. = **सीप**.

सीमंत *sīmant* [S.], m. **1.** the parting of a woman's hair (= **सींथ**). **2.** *hind.* the ceremony of colouring or decorating the parting of a pregnant woman's hair. — **सीमंत-पूजा**, f. *hind.* ceremonial reception of the bridegroom at the outskirts of the bride's village.

सीमा *sīmā* [S.], f. **1.** limit, boundary; frontier. **2.** bounds, limit (of morality or convention). — ~ **के**, or **से**, **बाहर जाना**, to go beyond set limits. ~ **में रहना**, to remain within limits. – **सीमांकन** [°*mā* + *a*°], m. demarcation of a boundary, or frontier. **सीमांकित**, adj. **सीमांत** [°*mā* + *a*°], m. border, frontier; boundary area. °**वर्ती**, adj. situated, or living, or occurring at a frontier, &c. **सीमा-बंध**, m. the meeting of two boundaries. **सीमाबद्ध**, adj. limited, restricted; delimited. **सीमा-शुल्क**, m. customs duty. **सीमाहीन**, adj. limitless. **सीमोल्लंघन** [°*mā* + *u*°], m. crossing (esp. violating) a frontier.

सीमित *sīmit* [S.], adj. limited, restricted.

सीमिया *sīmiyā* [P. *sīmiyā*], m. *Pl. HŚS.* alchemy; magic.

सीमुर्ग़ *sīmurg* [P. *sīmurg*], m. *mythol.* a fabulous bird, the roc.

सीय *sīy*, f. Av. = **सीता**.

सीयन *sīyan* [cf. H. *sīnā*], m. reg. sewing.

सीर *sīr* [*sīra-*], m. f. **1.** land cultivated from year to year by the owner. **2.** *hist.* land recognised by village custom as the special holding of a co-sharer, or treated as such in the distribution of profits and charges.

सीरक *sīrak* [cf. H. *sīl*; and H. (*ṭhaṇḍh*)*ak*], f. Brbh. coolness.

सीरत *sīrat* [A. *sīra*: P. *sīrat*], f. U. way of life: nature, disposition; virtue, morals; qualities.

सीरौ *sīrau* [*śītala-*], adj. Brbh. **1.** cool, cold. **2.** unemotional (of temperament).

सील *sīl* [*śītala-*], f. dampness; rawness (of weather).

सीलन *sīlan* [cf. H. *sīlnā*], f. dampness (= **सील**).

सीलना *sīlnā* [*śītalayati*], v.i. to become damp.

[1]**सीला** *sīlā* [*śītala-*], adj. **1.** damp. **2.** marshy.

[2]**सीला** *sīlā* [**śilla-*], m. reg. gleanings (= **सिला**).

सीवन *sīvan* [*sīvana-*], m. f. **1.** sewing, stitching. **2.** seam, join.

सीवनी *sīvănī* [S.], f. suture: **1.** *HŚS.* perineum. **2.** *Pl.* frenum.

सीस *sīs* [*śīrṣa-*], m. **1.** the head; the skull. **2.** transf. reg. head or ear of crop. — ~ **चढ़ाना** (**को**), to place on the head; to show respect or honour (to); to behave arrogantly or presumptuously. ~ **नवाना**, to bow the head. – **सीस-ताज**, m. Brbh. hood (of hunting bird). **सीस-फूल**, m. woman's head ornament.

सीसा *sīsā* [*sīsaka-*], m. lead.

सीह *sīh* [*siṃha-*], m. Brbh. a lion, &c. (= **सिंह**).

सीहगोस *sīhgos* [H. *syăh* + P. *gos*], m. Brbh. black-eared: a lynx (= **स्याहगोसर**).

सीहों *sīhoṁ*, m. *Pl.* a kind of black grain that grows in wheat-fields.

सुंघन *sunghan* [H. *sūnghan*], f. scent: — ~ **लेना**, fig. to obtain, to sniff out (secrets).

सुँघनी *suṁghnī* [cf. H. *sūṁghnā*], f. snuff.

सुँघाई *suṁghāī* [cf. H. *sūṁghnā*], f. *Pl. HŚS.* sweet smell, fragrance.

सुँघाना *suṁghānā* [cf. H. *sūṁghnā*], v.t. to cause to be smelt (by, **से**); to get (one) to smell.

सुँघावट *suṁghāvaṭ* [cf. H. *sūṁghnā*], f. *Pl. HŚS.* sweet smell, fragrance.

सुंड *suṇḍ*, ? f. pronun. var. reg. = **सूँड़**.

सुंदर *sundar* [S.], adj. **1.** beautiful; handsome; charming. **2.** attractive, beautiful (as a scene); fine, splendid. **3.** auspicious (moment).

सुंदरता *sundarătā* [S.], f. beauty, &c. (see **सुंदर**).

सुंदराई *sundrāī* [cf. H. *sundar*], f. reg. = **सुंदरता**.

सुंदरापा *sundrāpā* [cf. H. *sundar*], m. colloq. = **सुंदरता**.

सुंदरी *sundărī* [S.], f. a beautiful woman.

सुँधावट *suṁdhāvaṭ* [cf. *sugandha-*, and H. *sauṁdhnā*], f. reg. **1.** smell; scent. **2.** an earthy smell.

सुंबा *sumbā*, m. reg. **1.** a ramrod, rammer. **2.** a metal punch, or borer. **3.** *Pl.* an iron tool used in splitting blocks of stone. — ~ **ठोकना** (**में**), to spike (a gun).

सुंबुल *sumbul* [A. *sumbal*], m. **1.** a hyacinth. **2.** = **जटामाँसी**.

सुंभ *sumbh*, m. *Pl.* a hole made in a wall (= **सेंध**).

सुंभा *sumbhā*, m. reg. (Bihar) = **सुंबा**.

सु- *su-* [*su-*; also S.], pref. **1.** good; well. e.g. **सुधार**, m. improvement, reform; **सुडौल**, adj. well-built. **2.** attractive, beautiful (persons or things). e.g. **सुदल**, adj. having fine petals. **3.** fine, imposing; worthy of respect. e.g. **सुवासिनी**, f. term of courtesy for a respectable married woman. **4.** very, very much; excessive. e.g. **सुप्रतिष्ठित**, adj. very famous, celebrated; **सुदूर**, adj. very far off; **सुविकसित**, adj. intensively developed (as agriculture, &c). **5.** readily, easily. e.g. **सुलभ**, adj. easily obtainable.

सुअवसर *su-avă-sar* [S.], m. convenient moment or opportunity.

सुआँसा *suāṁsā*, m. *Pl.* an alloy of gold and copper.

[1]**सुआ** *suā*, m. = [1]सुवा.

[2]**सुआ** *suā*, m. = [2]सुवा.

[3]**सुआ** *suā* [*śūka-*], m. reg. (Bihar) (?) a newly germinated shoot of wheat.

सुआर *suār* [*sūpakāra-*], m. Av. a cook.

सुक *suk*, m. pronun. var. = **सुख**.

सुकंठ *su-kanṭh* [S.], adj. & Brbh. Av. **1.** adj. graceful-necked. **2.** having a sweet voice. **3.** *mythol.* title of the monkey-king Sugrīva.

सुकटा *sukṭā* [cf. *śuṣka-*], adj. dried up; emaciated.

सुकड़ना *sukaṛnā*, v.i. = **सिकुड़ना**.

सुकड़ा *sukṛa*, adj. = **सिकुड़ा** (see **सिकुड़ना**).

सुकड़ाना *sukṛānā* [cf. H. *sikuṛnā*], v.t. reg. to draw together, &c.

सुकड़ाव *sukṛāv* [cf. H. *sukaṛnā, sukṛānā*], v. reg. contraction, &c. (cf. **सिकुड़ना**).

सुकर *su-kar* [S.], adj. **1.** easily done; practicable. **2.** beneficent.

सुक़रात *suqrāt* [A. *suqrāṭ*], m. Socrates.

सुकर्म *su-karm* [S.], m. a good act; meritorious act.

सुकर्मी *su-karmī* [S.], adj. & m. **1.** adj. beneficent. **2.** m. one who performs good acts, or works.

सुकवि *su-kavi* [S.], m. Brbh. Av. a good or excellent poet.

सुकीर्ति *su-kīrti* [S.], f. good fame, repute.

सुकुमार *su-kumār* [S.], adj. & m. **1.** adj. soft, tender (esp. hands, feet, limbs); delicate. **2.** youthful. **3.** m. a handsome or beautiful youth.

सुकुमारता *su-kumārătā* [S.], f. softness, tenderness, &c. (see **सुकुमार**).

सुकुमारी *su-kumārī* [S.], f. a beautiful young girl.

सुकुल *su-kul* [S.], adj. & m. **1.** adj. of good family. **2.** m. a good or virtuous family. **3.** Brbh. ? the Vaiṣṇava community. **4.** pronun. var. = **शुक्ल**.

सुकून *sukūn* [A. *sukūn*], m. quiet, rest, peace.

सुकृत *su-kṛt* [S.], adj. & m. **1.** adj. well done. **2.** easily done. **3.** *Pl. HŚS.* virtuous; auspicious. **4.** m. a meritorious act; a kindness. **5.** moral or religious merit.

सुकृति *su-kṛti* [S.], f. a good act or deed (= **सुकृत**).

सुकृती *su-kṛtī* [S.], adj. & m. Brbh. Av. **1.** adj. acting well or kindly. **2.** meritorious; virtuous. **3.** m. a benevolent person, &c. **4.** the supreme being.

सुकृत्य *su-kṛtyă* [S.], m. a good act or deed (= **सुकृत**).

सुक्का *sukkā*, adj. reg. (N.) dry (= **सूखा**).

सुखंडी *sukhanḍī* [? cf. *śuṣka-*], f. rickets.

सुख *sukh* [S.], m. **1.** happiness; pleasure; joy. **2.** ease, comfort; convenience. **3.** prosperity. **4.** rest, relief; peace. — **~ की नींद सोना**, to sleep an untroubled sleep: to have peace of mind, to live a life of contentment or ease. **~ मानना**, to be content (with one's situation or lot); to flourish (a plant). **~ से रहना**), to live happily, or comfortably. – **सुख-कंद**, m. Brbh. root or source of joy. **°अन**, m. id. **सुखकर**, adj. causing happiness or pleasure; beneficent, benevolent; beneficial. **°अण**, adj. Brbh. id. **सुखकारक**, adj. id. **°-कारी**, adj. id. **सुख-चैन**, m. ease, comfort; peace. **सुख-चैन से रहना**, to live peacefully, &c. **सुख-थर** [*sthala-*], m. Brbh. place or source of joy. **सुखद**, adj. giving happiness, &c.; giving ease; pleasant, glad; comforting. **सुखदायक**, adj. id. **°-दायी**, adj. id. **°-दायिनी**, adj. f. **सुखदेनी**, adj. Brbh. = **सुखदायिनी**. **सुखदैन**, Brbh. = **सुखदायक**. **सुख-धाम**, m. Av. home of happiness: paradise. **सुख-दुख**, adj. joy and sorrow. **सुखनिधान**, m. Brbh. store of joy: a title of Kṛṣṇa. **सुख-पाल**, m. Brbh. 19c. fig. a kind of elaborate palanquin or litter. **सुखपूर्वक**, adv. with ease, without difficulty. **सुख-भोग**, m. the enjoyment of pleasure. **°ई**, adj. & m. pleasure- loving; a lover of pleasure. **सुखमय**, adj. happy, joyous. **सुख-रास** [*rāśi-*], f. Brbh. store of joy: a happy or blessed person. **सुखवारी**, adj. f. 19c. = **सुखी**. **सुख-विलास**, m. enjoyment, pleasure. **°ई**, m. a pleasure-seeker. **सुख-वास**, m. pleasant or comfortable abode; paradise. **सुख-संदोह**, m. Av. = **सुख-रास**: a title of Rām. **सुख-संपत्ति**, f. happiness and prosperity. **सुख-सुभीता**, m. = next. **सुख-सुविधा**, f. = ~, 2. **सुख-स्थान**, m. place of happiness: paradise. **सुखांत** [°*kha* + *a*°], adj. & m. having a happy outcome; having a happy ending (a drama); a comedy. **°इकी**, id. **सुखार्थ** [°*kha* + *a*°], adv. for the sake of happiness, &c. **°ई**, adj. seeking happiness, &c. **सुखासन** [°*kha* + *ā*°], m. Av. comfortable seat: a litter, palanquin.

सुख़न *sukhan* [P. *sukhan*], m. U. **1.** speech, language. **2.** word; words.

सुखलाना *sukhlānā*, v.t. reg. = सुखाना.

सुखवाना *sukhvānā* [cf. H. *sūkhnā*], v.t. to cause to be dried, &c. (by, से).

सुखाना *sukhānā* [cf. H. *sūkhnā*], v.t. to make dry: **1.** to dry (as clothes); to dry up (as water). **2.** to drain (as a swamp). **3.** to cause to pine, or to waste (as from grief).

सुखारना *sukhārnā*, v.t. *Pl.* to make (one) happy.

सुखारा *sukhārā*, adj. Brbh. Av. **1.** happy. **2.** [MIA *sukkha-*+*ālaya-*] = सुखद.

सुखारी *sukhārī*, adj. Brbh. Av. happy.

सुखाल- *sukhāl-*, adj. **1.** Brbh. = सुखारा. **2.** *Pl.* easy.

सुखावन *sukhāvan* [cf. H. *sikhānā*], m. dryings, produce to be dried. — ~ डालना (का), to spread out (produce) to dry.

सुखित *sukhit* [S.], adj. Brbh. = सुखी.

सुखिया *sukhiyā* [dim. or MIA *sukkha-*], adj. inv. = सुखी.

सुखी *sukhī* [S.], adj. **1.** happy, &c. **2.** at ease, contented. (see सुख).

सुखेन *sukhen* [S.], adv. Av. gladly, happily.

सुख्यात *su-khyāt* [S.], adj. = विख्यात.

सुख्याति *su-khyāti* [S.], f. = विख्याति.

सुगंध *su-gandh* [S.], adj. & m. **1.** adj. sweet-smelling, fragrant; aromatic. **2.** m. fragrance; aroma.

सुगंधि *su-gandhi* [S.], f. = सुगंध.

सुगंधित *su-gandhit* [S.], adj. **1.** perfumed; aromatic. **2.** fragrant.

सुगंधिता *su-gandhitā* [S.], f. a fragrance, perfume, scent.

सुगंधी *su-gandhī* [cf. H. *sugandh*], adj. fragrant: — ~ पाला [? *-pallava-*], m. sarsparilla (= अनंत-मूल).

सुगड़ *su-gaṛ*, adj. pron. var. = सुगढ़, and सुघड़.

सुगढ़ *su-gaṛh* [cf. H. *gaṛhnā*], adj. well-made, well-formed (= सुघड़).

सुगत *su-gat* [S.], m. **1.** a Buddha. **2.** a Buddhist.

सुगति *su-gati* [S.], f. Av. good going: good state or condition; specif. release from rebirth in the world.

सुगना *sugnā* [cf. H. *suggā*], m. reg. dimin. a parrot.

सुगबुगाना *sugbugānā*, v.i. colloq. to quiver, to flicker; to show a trace of life.

सुगम *su-gam* [S.], adj. **1.** easily traversible. ***2.** easily accessible. **3.** attainable (a goal); easy. **4.** intelligible (a topic, a style of language).

सुगमता *su-gamătā* [S.], f. **1.** accessibility. **2.** ease, facility (as of speech in a foreign language). **3.** intelligibility (see सुगम).

सुगम्य *su-gamyă* [S.], adj. = सुगम.

सुगा- *sugā-* [cf. H. *sog* ad. *śoka-*], v.i. Brbh. (?) to be vexing (to).

सुग्गा *suggā* [ad. *śuka-*, Pk. *suga-*], m. a parrot.

सुग्रीव *su-grīv* [S.], m. *mythol.* having a graceful neck: name of a monkey-king who assisted Rām in his conquest of Laṅkā and defeat of Rāvaṇ.

सुघटित *su-ghaṭit* [S.], adj. **1.** well-formed, well-made. **2.** well-contrived or arranged.

सुघड़ *su-ghaṛ* [cf. H. *ghaṛnā*], adj. **1.** well-formed, well-made. **2.** of attractive or graceful build; beautiful. **3.** accomplished, skilful. — सुघड़-भलाई, f. skilful flattery, currying favour, wheedling.

सुघड़ई *su-ghṛaī*, f. = सुघड़ाई.

सुघड़पन *su-gharpan* [cf. H. *sughaṛ*], m. accomplishment, skill (= सुघड़ाई).

सुघड़ाई *su-ghṛāī* [cf. H. *sughaṛ*], f. **1.** attractiveness of form or build; beauty. **2.** skill, accomplishment (as of a craftsman).

सुघड़ी *su-ghaṛī* [cf. H. *ghaṛī*], f. auspicious, or opportune moment.

सुघराई *su-ghrāī*, f. reg. = सुघड़ाई.

सुचकना *sucaknā* [? conn. H. *socnā*], v.i. *Pl.* **1.** to be thoughtful, anxious. **2.** to be astonished. **3.** to shrink, to hesitate.

सुचरित *su-carit* [S.], adj. & m. **1.** adj. of good or right conduct. **2.** m. good conduct or behaviour.

सुचरित्र *su-caritr* [S.], adj. & m. = सुचरित.

सुचा *sucā* [? conn. H. *socnā*], f. Av. knowledge, consciousness (of).

सुचारु *su-cāru* [S.], adj. **1.** lovely, delightful. **2.** agreeable, satisfactory. ~ रूप से, adv. satisfactorily (referring to work, progress, &c.); conveniently.

सुचाल *su-cāl* [cf. H. *su*+H. *cāl*], f. & adj. **1.** f. graceful gait. **2.** good behaviour. **3.** adj. walking or moving gracefully (a woman). **4.** Brbh. good, proper, virtuous.

सुचिंतित *su-cintit* [S.], adj. Av. **1.** well thought about, or pondered (a matter). ***2.** concerned, feeling concern (a person).

सुचित *su-cit* [H. *sucitt*], adj. **1.** unoccupied; at leisure. **2.** untroubled in mind.

सुचितई *su-citaī* [cf. H. *sucit*], f. Brbh. ease of mind.

सुचिताई *su-citāī*, f. ease of mind.

सुचिती *su-citī* [cf. H. *sucit*], adj. & m. Brbh. **1.** adj. untroubled in mind. **2.** m. an untroubled person.

सुचित्त *su-citt* [S.], adj, see सुचित.

सुचेत *su-cet* [H. *su*+H. *cet*], adj. **1.** mindful, watchful, wary. **2.** conscious, aware.

सुचेती *su-cetī* [cf. H. *sucet*], f. **1.** mindfulness, watchfulness. **2.** attentiveness. **3.** discreetness, discretion.

[1]**सुजन** *su-jan* [S.], adj. & m. a good person: **1.** adj. good-natured, kindly. **2.** virtuous; honest. **3.** m. = सज्जन (see s.v).

[2]**सुजन** *sujan* [ad. *svajana-*], m. Brbh. members of (one's) family, dependants.

सुजनता *su-janătā* [S.], f. *Pl. HŚS.* **1.** kindliness, benevolence. **2.** virtue, honesty.

सुजाक *sujāk*, m. = सूज़ाक.

सुजात *su-jāt* [S.], adj. **1.** well-born; of high caste. **2.** legitimate (by birth).

सुजाति *su-jāti* [S.], adj. & f. **1.** adj. = सुजात. **2.** f. high caste.

सुजान *su-jān* [H. *su*+H. *jān*], adj. & m. **1.** adj. discerning, wise; intelligent. **2.** profiting from experience. **3.** m. a wise, or experienced person. **4.** Brbh. husband; lover. **5.** Brbh. the supreme being.

सुजानपन *su-jānpan* [cf. H. *sujān*], m. wisdom, &c. (see सुजान).

सुजाना *sujānā* [cf. H. *sūjnā*], v.t. to cause to swell.

सुज्ञान *su-jñān* [S.], m. & adj. **1.** m. discernment; wisdom. **2.** adj. discerning, &c. (= सुजान).

सुझा- *sujhā-*, v.i. Brbh. = सूझना.

[1]**सुझाई** *sujhāī* [cf. *sūjhnā*], f. perception. — ~ देना, to be perceived; to come to mind.

[2]**सुझाई** *sujhāī* [cf. H. *sujhānā*], f. reg. pointing out, explaining.

सुझाना *sujhānā* [cf. H. *sūjhnā*], v.t. to cause to perceive: **1.** to point out; to explain. **2.** to suggest. **3.** to indicate, to point out (as a road).

सुझाव *sujhāv* [cf. H. *sujhānā*], m. **1.** suggestion. **2.** pointing out (a matter, for consideration); explanation. — ~ करना (का), to suggest.

[1]**सुटकना** *suṭaknā*, v.i. = [1]सटकना.

[2]**सुटकना** *suṭaknā* [**suṭṭ-*], v.t. **1.** to gulp down. **2.** = [2]सटकना.

सुटुक- *suṭuk-*, v.t. Av. = [2]सुटकना, 2.

सुठान *su-ṭhān* [cf. H. *ṭhāṁv*: w. H. *sthān*, or ad. *susthāna-*], m. Brbh. proper place.

सुठार *su-ṭhār*, adj. Brbh. lovely, attractive.

सुठि *suṭhi* [*susthita-*], ? adj. & adv. **1.** adj. Brbh. Av. ? attractive, fine. **2.** adv. Av. [*susṭhu*]. extremely.

सुड़क *suṛak* [cf. H. [1]*suṛaknā*], f. **1.** sniffing. **2.** gulping.

[1]**सुड़कना** *suṛaknā*, v.t. **1.** to sniff up or in. **2.** to gulp (cf. सुड़पना).

[2]**सुड़कना** *suṛaknā* [? conn. H. [2]*suṭaknā*; or **suḍh-*: Pk. *suḍhia-*], v.t. *Pl.* to draw (a sword).

सुड़की *suṛkī* [? conn. H. [2]*suṭaknā*], f. *Pl.* a brisk movement: the act of letting a line or string run out suddenly, the sudden slackening of a kite-string.

सुड़ड़-सुड़ड़ *suṛaṛ-suṛaṛ*, f. colloq. **1.** a continued hissing sound (as of a kettle boiling dry). **2.** a prolonged whizzing, or whistling sound.

सुड़ना *suṛnā*, v.i. *Pl.* to shiver with cold.

सुड़प *suṛap* [cf. H. *suṛapnā*], f. slurping; gulping noisily.

सुड़पना *suṛapnā*, v.t. & v.i. **1.** v.t. to slurp; to gulp noisily. **2.** v.i. id.

सुड़सुड़ाना *suṛsuṛānā*, v.t. reg. = [1]सुड़कना.

सुडौल *su-ḍaul* [H. *su*+H. *ḍaul*], adj. well-built; shapely, graceful; handsome; strong.

सुडौलपन *su-ḍaulpan* [cf. H. *suḍaul*], m. good (bodily) build.

सुढंग *su-ḍhaṅg* [H. *su*+H. *ḍhaṅg*], adj. & m. **1.** adj. attractive, agreeable. **2.** fitting, appropriate. **3.** m. good or agreeable manner, or way.

सुढब *su-ḍhab* [H. *su*+H. *ḍhab*], adj. 1. = सुडौल. **2.** adv. in a good or fitting way.

सुढर *su-ḍhar* [H. *su*+H. *ḍhalnā*], adj. handsome; beautiful.

सुतंत्र *sutantra*, adj. pronun. var. = स्वतंत्र.

सुत *sut* [S.], m. begotten, brought forth: a son.

[1]**सुतना** *sutnā* [cf. *sūtra-*], v.i. to grow thin or drawn (as the cheeks).

[2]**सुतना** *sutnā* [cf. *supta-*], v.i. **1.** to be asleep, to sleep. **2.** to have lain down, to lie down, to rest.

सुतल *su-tal* [S.], m. Brbh. *mythol.* one of the seven subterranean regions.

सुतली *sutlī* [cf. *sūtra-*], f. twine.

[1]**सुतवाना** *sutvānā* [cf. H. [2]*sutnā*], v.t. = सुलवाना.

[2]**सुतवाना** *sutvānā* [cf. H. *sūṁtnā, sūtnā*], v.t. to cause to be stripped off (leaves of a branch, or of vegetables); to cause to be unsheathed.

सुता *sutā* [S.], f. daughter.

[1]**सुतार** *sutār* [*sūtradhāra-*], m. **1.** *Pl. HŚS.* a carpenter. **2.** reg. (Bihar) a head workman, craftsman; a thatcher.

[2]**सुतार** *su-tār*, m. *Pl. HŚS.* good occasion, opportunity.

[1]**सुतारी** *sutārī* [**sūtrārā-*], f. reg. a heavy needle, an awl (as used by shoemakers).

[2]**सुतारी** *sutārī* [cf. H. [1]*sutār*], f. reg. craftsmanship, craft, trade.

सुतीक्ष्ण *su-tīkṣṇă* [S.], adj. **1.** very sharp, or pungent. **2.** very subtle. **3.** very painful.

सुतुही *sutuhī* [cf. *śukti-*], f. reg. **1.** a shellfish, a pearl oyster. **2.** a shell (used to hold liquid, or as a scraper).

सुथनिया *suthniyā* f. reg. (W.) = सूथन, [1]सुथनी.

[1]**सुथनी** *suthnī* [cf. **sutthanā-*], f. reg. women's loose trousers.

[2]**सुथनी** *suthnī*, f. reg. (Bihar) a yam, *Dioscorea fasciculata*.

सुथन्ना *suthannā*, m. poet. = [1]सुथनी, सूथन.

सुथरा *suthrā* [*susthira-*], adj. **1.** neat, tidy; clean. **2.** elegant, adorned. — साफ़-सुथरा, adj. = ~.

सुथराई *suthrāī* [cf. H. *suthrā*], f. neatness, &c.

सुथरापन *suthrāpan* [cf. H. *suthrā*], m. neatness, &c. (see सुथरा).

सुदंत *su-dant* [S.], adj. having good teeth.

सुदर्शन *su-darśan* [S.], adj. & m. **1.** adj. good-looking: beautiful; handsome. **2.** m. *mythol.* name of the circular weapon or discus of Viṣṇu-Kr̥ṣṇa. **3.** a title of Śiva. **4.** a name given to the *jāmun* tree, or (esp.) to the rose-apple (*gulāb-jāmun*) tree. — सुदर्शन-चक्र, m. = ~, 2.

सुदशा *su-daśā* [S.], f. good condition or circumstances; happy state, prosperity.

सुदाय *su-dāy* [S.], m. *Pl. HŚS. hind.* a gift given on partic. special occasions (as on assumption of the sacred thread, or at marriage).

सुदि *sudi* [S.], f. = सुदी.

सुदिन *su-din* [S.], m. **1.** a clear or bright day (esp. morning). **2.** auspicious or happy day. **3.** pl. good or happy times.

सुदी *sudī* [ad. *sudi-*], f. the light half of the lunar month.

सुदुर्लभ *su-dur-labh* [S.], adj. **1.** very difficult of attainment (as birth as a human being, &c). **2.** very scarce, rare (as a virtuous man).

सुदृढ़ *su-dr̥ṛh* [S.], adj. **1.** very hard, very firm. **2.** firm, lasting (as ties, relationships). **3.** hard, fixed (a smile). **4.** steadfast.

सुदृश्य *su-dr̥śyă* [S.], adj. clearly visible.

सुदेश *su-deś* [S.], m. **1.** a good or fine country. **2.** Brbh. Av. attractive spot, or area; lovely body; proper place.

सुद्दा *suddā* [A. *sudda*], m. obstruction: compacted faeces.

सुद्दी *suddī* [cf. H. *suddā*], f. reg. = सुद्दा.

सुद्धाँ *suddhāṁ*, adv. reg. **1.** forming a (? homogeneous) group (with), together (with, के). **2.** [conn. *śuddha-*], only, simply, just.

सुधंग *sudhaṅg*, m. Brbh. a type or style of dance.

सुध *sudh* [ad. *śuddhi-*], f. **1.** consciousness. **2.** recollection, memory. **3.** attention, notice; care. **4.** intelligence. — ~ आना (को), consciousness to return, to come to one's senses (also fig). ~ करना (की), to remember, not to forget. ~ दिलाना (को), to remind (one: of, की). ~ बिसारना, or भूलना, to lose consciousness; to forget, to be forgetful. ~ रखना, to remember (= याद रखना). ~ लेना, to take thought (of or for, की); to take care (of) ; to enquire (into). उसे ~ ही न रही, he had completely forgotten. – सुध-बुध, f. consciousness and understanding: = ~, 1.; good sense; self-possession; sanity.

सुधकना *sudhaknā* [? cf. H. *dahaknā*], v.i. reg. to be kindled, lit; to blaze.

सुधकाना *sudhkānā* [cf. H. *sudhaknā*], v.t. reg. to kindle, to light; to inflame.

सुधड़न *sudhaṛan*, adj. reg. **1.** right, proper, correct. **2.** well-behaved.

सुधड़ना *sudhaṛnā*, v.i. reg. = सुधरना.

सुधना *sudhnā*, v.i. reg. to be cleaned, or put right; to be purified (metal).

सुधरना *sudharnā* [cf. H. *sudhārnā*], v.i. to be set right: **1.** to be improved; to be corrected; to improve, to come right (a situation). **2.** to be repaired; to be serviceable. **3.** to be reformed. **4.** to be or to seem right or good.

सुधराई *sudhrāī* [cf. H. *sudhārnā*], f. removing defects: improving, improvement; repair.

सुधर्मी *su-dharmī* [S.], adj. of good *dharma*: dutiful; devout.

[1]**सुधवाना** *sudhvānā* [cf. H. *sudhānā*], v.t. to cause to be reminded (by, से).

[2]**सुधवाना** *sudhvānā* [cf. H. *sudhnā*], v.t. reg. to cause to be cleaned, put right or purified.

सुधा *su-dhā* [S.], f. **1.** *mythol.* the nectar of the gods, ambrosia. **2.** nectar. — सुधांशु [°*dhā*+*a*°], m. nectar-rayed: the moon. सुधाकर [°*dhā*+*ā*°], m. nectar-store: the moon; moonlight. सुधा-घट, m. Brbh. nectar-vessel: id. सुधा-निधि, f. Brbh. nectar-store: id. सुधा-रस, m. nectar (as of lips). सुधा-सदन, m. Brbh. abode of nectar: id.

सुधा- *sudhā-* [cf. H. *sodhnā*], v.t. Brbh. to cause to be fixed: to fix, or to determine (an auspicious day).

सुधाई *sudhāī* [cf. H. *sūdhā*], f. Brbh. = सीधापन.

सुधाना *sudhānā* [cf. H. *sudh*], v.t. to cause (one, को) to remember, to remind.

सुधार *su-dhār* [cf. H. *sudhārnā*], m. **1.** an improvement; adjustment, repair. **2.** a reform. — सुधारवादी, adj. & m. reformist; a believer in reform. सुधारालय [°*a*+*ā*°], m. reformatory, correction centre.

सुधारक *su-dhārak* [S.], adj. & m. **1.** adj. reforming, reformist. **2.** m. a reformer.

सुधारना *sudhārnā* [cf. **śuddhakāra-*], v.t. to set right: **1.** to improve; to correct. **2.** to reform. **3.** Av. to clean, to polish. **4.** Av. to adjust, to arrange (clothing).

सुधारू *sudhārū* [cf. H. *sudhārnā*], m. an improver, reformer.

सुधि *sudhi* [ad. *śuddhi-*; H. *sudh*], f. = सुध.

सुधी *su-dhī* [S.], adj. & m. **1.** adj. intelligent; wise. **2.** learned. **3.** m. an intelligent or learned man.

सुधीर *su-dhīr* [S.], adj. **1.** steadfast, enduring. **2.** patient. **3.** having sthg. to endure: considerate.

सुनंद *su-nand* [S.], adj. giving pleasure, delighting.

सुनकाटर *sunkāṭar*, m. *Pl.* a kind of snake.

सुनकार *sunkār* [cf. H. *sunnā*], m. ? a discriminating judge of music and singing.

सुनट्टा *sunaṭṭā*, m. a goldsmith's son.

सुनन *sunan* [cf. H. *sunnā*], f. reg. hearing, listening.

सुनना *sunnā* [*śṛṇoti*], v.t. **1.** to hear. **2.** to listen (to). **3.** to hear abuse, to be abused; to receive a talking-to. — सुनने में आना, to be heard, to come to notice (a report, a rumour). – सुनना-गुनना, to hear and to take due account of (sthg). सुननेवाला, adj. & m. listening, &c.; a member of an audience. – सुन पड़ना, to be audible (= सुनाई देना). सुन पाना, v.t. to get to hear, to come to know; to overhear. सुना-सुनाया, adj. hearsay (as evidence). सुनी-अनसुनी कर देना, to turn a deaf ear. सुनी-सुनाई बात, f. hearsay. सुनिए! excuse me! (in attracting attention). उसने उसकी एक न सुनी, he paid not the slightest attention to anything he said.

सुनबहरी *sunbahrī* [cf. H. *sunn*], f. *Pl.* *HŚS.* **1.** a disease in which the sense of touch is lost. **2.** elephantiasis.

सुनवाई *sunvāī* [cf. H. *sunvānā*], f. **1.** causing or allowing to be heard. **2.** a (court) hearing.

सुनवैया *sunvaiyā* [cf. H. *sunvānā*], m. a listener, hearer.

सुन-सान *sun-sān* [cf. H. *sunn*], adj. & m. = सुन्न, 1., 2.

सुनसार *sunsār*, m. *Pl.* a kind of ornament (? सुनसर).

सुनसुन *sunsun*, f. = सनसन.

सुनसुना *sunsunā*, adj. having a cold in the nose, snuffling.

सुनहरा *sunahrā* [**suvarṇadhara-*], adj. **1.** made of gold; gilded. **2.** gold-coloured. **3.** fig. of the highest quality or value. — ~ पानी, m. wash or coating of gold, gilding.

सुनहरापन *sunahrāpan* [cf. H. *sunahrā*], adj. golden colour.

सुनहला *sunahlā*, adj. = सुनहरा.

सुनाई *sunāī* [cf. H. *sunānā*], f. **1.** hearing. **2.** reg. a hearing; notice, attention (to a matter). — ~ देना (को), to come within (one's) hearing, to be audible (to).

सुनाना *sunānā* [cf. H. *sunnā*], v.t. to cause to hear: **1.** to tell (a story, &c.; to, को). **2.** to give to know, to inform; to broadcast (by radio); to announce (a decision, a verdict). **3.** to play (music, an instrument, a radio: to, को). **4.** to say aloud (to), to repeat (a lesson). **5.** to rebuke, to scold. उसने उसे ख़ूब सुनाई, or सुनाया, he berated him severely. — कह ~, to inform by word of mouth; to say aloud (as a lesson); to berate (one, को). पढ़कर ~, to read aloud. – सुनी-सुनाई बात, f. hearsay.

सुनापट *sunāpaṭ* [conn. H. *sunn*], f. reg. stillness; desolateness.

सुनाम *su-nām* [S.], m. good name, or reputation.

सुनामी *su-nāmī* [cf. H. *sunām*], adj. of good reputation.

सुनार *sunār* [*suvarṇakāra-*], m. a goldsmith; jeweller.

सुनारनी *sunārnī* [cf. H. *sunār*], f. = सुनारिन.

सुनारिन *sunārin* [cf. H. *sunār*], f. a goldsmith's wife; jeweller's wife.

सुनारी *sunārī* [cf. H. *sunār*], f. **1.** a goldsmith's work; jeweller's work. **2.** cost of employment of a goldsmith. 3. = सुनारिन.

सुनावनी *sunāvnī* [cf. H. *sunā(v)nā*], f. *Pl. HŚS. hist.* news of the death of a relative in a foreign country; a ceremony performed on hearing such news.

सुनीति *su-nīti* [S.], f. **1.** good conduct or behaviour. **2.** good policy; prudence.

सुन्न *sunn* [*śūnya-*; ? ← Panj.], adj. & m. empty: **1.** adj. desolate, dreary. **2.** quiet, still (a place). **3.** [? × H. *sann*] silent, speechless (a person). **4.** [? × H. *sann*] numb; paralysed (as with fear). **5.** m. desolateness, &c. **6.** stillness. **7.** [? × H. *sann*] fainting-fit. **8.** zero, nought. — ~ करना, to benumb, &c.

सुन्नत *sunnat* [A. *sunna*: P. *sunnat*], f. rite: circumcision. — बेसुन्नत [P. *be-*], adj. uncircumcised.

सुन्नती *sunnatī* [cf. H. *sunnat*], m. a man or boy who has been circumcised.

सुन्ना *sunnā* [*śūnya-*], m. a blank; a zero.

सुन्नी *sunnī* [A. *sunnī*], adj. & m. lawful: **1.** adj. pertaining to the *sunnī* persuasion of Islam. **2.** m. a *sunnī* Muslim.

सुपच *su-pac* [? cf. H. *pacnā*], adj. easily digestible, wholesome.

सुपथ *su-path* [S.], m. **1.** a good road. **2.** proper course, right conduct. **3.** orthodoxy.

सुपथी *su-pathī* [S.], adj. **1.** of good conduct. **2.** orthodox.

सुपथ्य *su-pathyă* [S.], m. easily digestible, or wholesome, food.

सुपन *supn*, m. pronun. var. = सपना.

सुपनखा *supănakhā*, f. Av. = शूर्पणखा.

सुपना *supnā*, m. pronun. var. = सपना.

सुपना- *supnā-* [cf. H. *sapnā*], v.t. Brbh. to dream of.

सुपली *suplī* [cf. *śūrpa-*], f. *Pl.* a small winnowing basket or fan.

सुपात्र *su-pātr* [S.], m. good vessel: a worthy or deserving person; one suitable (for a task or purpose).

सुपात्रता *su-pātrătā* [S.], f. worthiness (for a task or purpose), deservingness.

सुपारी *supārī* [**suppāra-*], f. **1.** betel nut (*Areca catechu*). **2.** sl. glans penis.

सुपास *su-pās*, m. well-being, convenience.

सुपासी *su-pāsī*, adj. Brbh. **1.** gladdening, delighting (one). **2.** glad, happy.

सुपुत्र *su-putr* [S.], m. good son.

सुपुर्द *supurd* [P. *supurd*], f. charge, care, trust. — ~ करना (को), to entrust, to consign (to); to commit (for trial). – सुपुर्द-नामा, m. deed of trust or assignment.

सुपुर्दगी *supurdăgī* [P. *supurdagī*], f. **1.** entrusting, consigning; delivery, surrender. **2.** committal (by a magistrate). — ~ करना, to hand (a person or thing) over (to). ~ में लाना, to bring (one, को) under the trust or care (of, की).

सुपूत *su-pūt* [H. *su* + H. *pūt*], m. = सपूत.

सुपेती *supetī* [cf. H. *safed*], f. Av. white fabric: a sheet.

सुपेली *supelī* [cf. *śūrpa-*], f. reg. (W.) a small winnowing basket.

सुप्त *supt* [S.], adj. **1.** asleep, sleeping. **2.** inert. **3.** numbed, insensible. — सुप्तावस्था [°*ta* + *a*°], f. state of sleep.

सुप्ति *supti* [S.], f. **1.** sleep. **2.** sleepiness, drowsiness. **3.** numbness.

सुप्रतिष्ठ *su-prati-ṣṭh* [S.], adj. = सुप्रतिष्ठित.

सुप्रतिष्ठा *su-prati-ṣṭhā* [S.], f. **1.** high, or wide reputation, celebrity. **2.** establishment, or erection (as of a temple, or of an idol); consecration.

सुप्रतिष्ठित *su-prati-ṣṭhit* [S.], adj. of high, or wide reputation, celebrated.

सुप्रसन्न *su-pra-sann* [S.], adj. very pleased.

सुफल *su-phal* [S.], adj. **1.** very fruitful; fertile. **2.** having good results; very profitable; advantageous.

सुबंधु *su-bandhu* [S.], m. Av. a good friend.

सुबकना *subaknā*, v.i. to cry quietly.

सुबकाई *subkāī*, f. = सुबकी.

सुबकी *subkī* [cf. H. *subaknā*], f. sobbing; a sob.

सुबह *subah* [A. *ṣubḥ*], f. **1.** early morning; morning. **2.** adv. = ~ को. — ~ करना, to pass the night. ~ को, adv. in the early morning. ~ (ही) ~, adv. at dawn, very early. ~ होना, dawn to break. बहुत ~, adv. very early (in the day). – सुबह-शाम करना, fig. to put off (doing sthg.) from day to day.

सुबहा *sub'hā* [A. *śubha*], m. **1.** doubt. **2.** hesitation, suspicion. — ~ करना, to have doubt (about, का); to distrust, to suspect. शक-शुबहा, m. = ~.

सुबहान *sub'hān* [A. *subḥān*], m. U. glorifying, praising (God). — सुबहान-अल्लाह, interj. *musl.* God be praised! wonderful are God's ways!

सुबास *subās* [ad. *suvāsa-*; or H. [1]*bās*], adj. & m. **1.** adj. fragrant. **2.** m. fragrance. **3.** *HŚS.* a kind of rice that is cut in the month of Ag'han.

सुबासना *subāsănā* [ad. *vāsanā-*], f. Brbh. a fragrance (= सुबास).

सुबासिक *subāsik* [ad. *vāsaka-*], adj. Av. fragrant.

सुबाहु *su-bāhu* [S.], adj. **1.** having graceful arms. **2.** strong-armed, mighty.

सुबिस्ता *subistā*, m. pronun. var. reg. = सुभीता.

सुबीता *subītā*, m. pronun. var. = सुभीता.

सुबुक *subuk* [P. *sabuk*], adj. light; soft, delicate.

सुबुकना *subuknā* [cf. H. *subuk*], v.i. to be light, or gentle (touch, heart).

सुबुद्धि *su-buddhi* [S.], adj. & f. **1.** adj. of good understanding: intelligent; wise, shrewd. **2.** f. good sense.

सुबोध *su-bodh* [S.], adj. easily understood.

सुभग *su-bhag* [S.], adj. **1.** fortunate; blessed, auspicious. ***2.** beautiful; handsome; charming (a woman). **3.** agreeable; beautiful (a scene). **4.** *Pl. HŚS.* beloved (as a wife).

सुभगता *su-bhagătā* [S.], f. Av. auspicious nature; beauty, loveliness.

सुभट *su-bhaṭ* [ad. *subhaṭa-*], m. Brbh. warrior, champion.

सुभद्र *su-bhadră* [S.], adj. & m. **1.** adj. auspicious. **2.** well-mannered. **3.** *Pl. HŚS.* m. the auspicious one: a title of Viṣṇu.

सुभागी *su-bhāgī* [S.], adj. fortunate, lucky.

सुभान *subhān*. see सुबहान.

सुभाना *subhānā*, v.t. & v.i. **1.** v.t. *Pl.* to make beautiful; to give pleasure (to). **2.** v.i. Brbh. (?) to seem beautiful or attractive.

[1]**सुभाव** *subhāv* [ad. *svabhāva-*], m. Brbh. Av. = स्वभाव.

[2]**सुभाव** *su-bhāv* [S.], m. good disposition or nature.

सुभाषित *su-bhāṣit* [S.], adj. & m. **1.** adj. well-spoken; eloquently spoken. **2.** m. elegant speech or style. **3.** an aphorism.

सुभाषी *su-bhāṣī* [S.], adj. speaking elegantly, or eloquently.

सुभीता *subhītā*, m. **1.** convenient opportunity or occasion. **2.** convenience. **3.** satisfactory or comfortable circumstances. — सुभीते का, adj. convenient. सुभीते के अनुसार, adv. to suit (one's) convenience. सुभीते से, adv. conveniently.

सुभुज *su-bhuj* [S.], adj. Av. strong-armed (= सुबाहु).

सुमंगल *su-maṅgal* [S.], adj. very auspicious.

सुमंगली *su-maṅgălī* [S.], f. most auspicious: a newly married wife.

सुमंत्रणा *su-mantrăṇā* [S.], f. good advice or counsel.

सुम *sum* [P. *sum*], m. a hoof.

-सुम *-sum* [A. *ṣumm*], adj. deaf (see गुमसुम, s.v. गुम).

सुमत *su-mat* [S.], adj. well or kindly disposed, friendly.

सुमति *su-mati* [S.], f. & adj. **1.** f. good understanding, or judgment. **2.** good disposition, friendliness. **3.** adj. perceptive; wise; of good judgment. **4.** of good disposition. — ~ यथा, adv. Brbh. to the best of (one's) understanding.

सुमन *su-man* [S.], adj. & m. **1.** adj. beautiful, handsome. ***2.** well-disposed; benevolent. **3.** happy. ***4.** m. a flower; *Pl. HŚS.* specif. a jasmine. **5.** a deity. — सुमन-माल, f. Av. garland of flowers.

सुमनस *su-manas* [S.], adj. & m. Brbh. = सुमन, 2.

सुमनसी *sumanăsī* [cf. *sumanas*], f. *Pl.* a jasmine.

सुमनस्क *su-manask* [S.], adj. pleased; happy.

सुमर *sumar* [ad. *smara-*], m. remembrance, recollection.

सुमरना *sumarnā* [ad. *smarati*], v.i. to call to mind the supreme being (specif. by meditating on, or repeating, God's name: cf. **स्मरण**, 2).

सुमलिंद *sumalind*, m. reg. a black bee.

सुमसुम *sumsum*, f. pronun. var. = **सिमसिम**.

सुमिर *sumir* [ad. *smara-*], m. remembrance, recollection.

सुमिरत *sumirat* [cf. H. *sumarnā*], adj. remembered; made mention of.

सुमिरन *sumiran*, m. = **स्मरण**.

सुमिलंद *sumiland*, m. reg. a black bee.

सुमुख *su-mukh* [S.], m. & adj. **1.** m. good or beautiful mouth, or face. **2.** adj. lovely, beautiful; handsome.

सुमुखी *su-mukhī* [S.], f. a beautiful woman.

सुमेर *su-mer* [ad. *sumeru-*], m. 1. = **सुमेरु**, 1. **2.** an *ojhā*'s garland.

सुमेरु *su-meru* [S.], m. *mythol.* **1.** the sacred mountain Meru (see s.v). **2.** the North Pole.

सुमेल *su-mel* [S.], adj. sociable (= **मिलनसार**).

सुयश *su-yaś* [S.], m. & adj. **1.** m. fame, renown. **2.** adj. celebrated.

सुयोग *su-yog* [S.], m. favourable moment, or opportunity.

सुयोग्य *su-yogyă* [S.}, adj. very, or fully, capable.

[1]**सुरंग** *suraṅg* [*suraṅgā-*], f. **1.** a tunnel; underground passage; a built-over passage. **2.** hole made through a wall (= **सेंध**). **3.** a charge of explosive (for blasting). **4.** *mil., naut.* a mine. — ~ **उड़ाना**, to detonate a charge of explosive. ~ **काटना**, or **बनाना**, to dig a tunnel (underneath), to mine. **सुरंगें बतोड़ना**, to sweep mines. **सुरंगें बिछानेवाला जहाज़**, m. a mine-layer. – **सुरंग-बुहार**, m. a mine-sweeper.

[2]**सुरंग** *su-raṅg* [S.], adj. Brbh. **1.** bright-coloured. **2.** red; reddish. **3.** showy, fine, splendid.

[1]**सुर** *sur* [*svara-*], m. **1.** sound (of the voice, or of a musical instrument); tone. **2.** harmony. **3.** a melody, tune. **4.** *mus.* a note. **5.** *mus.* accompaniment (to the *śahnāī*); drone. — ~ **देना**, *mus.* to accompany. ~ **भरना**, to add (one's) voice, &c.: to join in (a song, or with an accompaniment). ~ **मिलाना (का)**, to tune an instrument (to another). ~ **में** ~ **मिलाना**, to say (just) what another says, to be a yes-man. **ऊँचा** ~, m. a soprano voice; a major key. **धीमा** ~, m. a low or soft sound; a tenor, or a contralto voice. **नीचा** ~, m. a bass voice; a minor key. **मध्यम** ~, m. a voice in the medium range (of strength or pitch): = **धीमा** ~.

[2]**सुर** *sur* [S.], m. a god. — **सुर-काज**, m. Av. a purpose or plan of the gods. **सुरगण**, m. gods, or the gods. **सुर-गुरु**, m. Brbh. Av. *mythol.* teacher of the gods: a title of Bṛhaspati. **सुर-तरंगिनी** [S.], f. river of the gods: the Ganges. **सुर-तरु**, m. Brbh. Av. tree of the gods (= **कल्पतरु**). **सुर-तात**, m. Brbh. *mythol.* father of the Ādityas (the sage Kaśyapa). **सुर-धाम**, m. Av. = **सुर-पुर**. **सुर-धुनि**, f. river of the gods: the Ganges. **सुर-धेनु**, f. Brbh. Av. = **काम-धेनु**. **सुर-नारी**, f. consort of a god. **सुर-पति**, m. Av. lord of the gods: Indra. **सुर-पुर**, m. *mythol.* the city of the gods, Amarāvatī; heaven. **सुर-बानी**, f. Brbh. speech of the gods: Sanskrit. **सुर-भानु**, m. Brbh. sun among the gods: a title of Indra. **सुर-मनि**, m. Brbh. = **चिंता-मणि**; ? = **कौस्तुभ**. **सुर-लोक**, m. the world of the gods, the heaven of Indra. **सुर-सरि**, f. = next. **सुर-सरिता**, f. divine river: a title of the Ganges. **सुर-साहिब**, m. Brbh. = **सुर-पति**. **सुर-सुंदरी**, f. Av. *mythol.* an *apsarā*, q.v. **सुरासुर** [°*ra*+*a*°], m. Brbh. gods and demons. **सुरेश** [°*ra*+*ī*°], m. lord of the gods: a title of Indra, Viṣṇu-Kṛṣṇa, or Śiva.

सुरक्षा *su-rakṣā* [S.], f. security, safety. — ~ **परिषद**, m. Security Council. – **सुरक्षाकर्मी**, m. a defender. **सुरक्षात्मक** [°*ā*+*ā*°], adj. defensive.

सुरक्षित *su-rakṣit* [S.], adj. well-protected; well-defended.

सुरखा *surkhā* [**surukṣa-*], m. reg. **1.** a tall, tapering tree. **2.** a tall, lank plant.

सुर्ख़ाब *surkhāb* [P. *surkhāb*], m. the ruddy sheldrake, *Anas casarca* (= **चकवा**). — ~ **का पर लगना**, to wear a sheldrake's feather (in the turban): to receive honour or distinction (as a nobleman at the Mughal court), to be marked out in some way. ~ **का पर होना (सिर पर)**, fig. to be proud, to hold the head in the air.

सुरजन *surjan* [cf. H. *sur*], m. Brbh. **1.** pl. the gods. 2. = **सज्जन**.

[1]**सुरत** *surat* [ad. *smṛti-*], f. **1.** remembrance, recollection, memory. **2.** thinking (of or about), reflection. — ~ **आना**, to come into the mind (of, **की**), to be remembered. ~ **करना**, to keep in mind, not to forget; to think (of, **की**). ~ **न रहना (की)**, to escape the memory, to be forgotten; thought not to be given (to); consciousness to be lost. ~ **बिसारना**, or **भुला देना**, to lose the recollection (of, **की**), to forget. ~ **में**

आना, to come to the mind (of, की), to occur (to); to come to one's senses.

²सुरत *su-rat* [ad. *surati-*], f. lovers' pleasure; sexual intercourse.

सुरता *surtā* [? cf. *suratiyā*], adj. *Pl. HŚS.* mindful, attentive.

सुरताई *surtāī* [cf. H. ¹*surat*], f. *Pl.* mindfulness, attention.

¹सुरति *surati* [ad. *smṛti-*], f. Brbh. = ¹सुरत.

²सुरति *su-rati* [S.], f. Brbh. = ²सुरत.

सुरतिया *suratiyā* [cf. H. ¹*surat*], adj. *Pl.* mindful, attentive.

सुरती *surtī* [cf. *sūrat* 'Surat'], f. Surat tobacco: tobacco for chewing.

सुरपुन *surpun*, m. the poon tree, *Calophyllum inophyllum.*

सुरभि *su-rabhi* [S.], adj. & f. **1.** adj. fragrant. **2.** f. (m., *Pl.*) fragrance; perfume. **3.** the earth. **4.** a cow; specif. *mythol.* the cow of plenty (see काम-धेनु).

सुरमई *surmaī* [P. *surma'ī*], adj. & f. **1.** adj. of the colour of *surmā*: dark grey, blackish. **2.** f. a dark shade of grey.

सुरमा *surmā* [P. *surma*], m. **1.** powdered sulphide of antimony, or of lead. **2.** specif. a cosmetic of antimony or lead sulphide applied to the eyes. — ~ करना, to apply *surmā*. सुरमे की क़लम, f. a lead pencil. ~ डालना, or लगाना, to apply *surmā* (to, में). – सुरमेदानी, f. container for *surmā*.

सुरवा *survā* [ad. *sruvā-*], m. reg. (W.) a wooden ladle (= स्रुवा).

सुरवाली *survālī*, f. *Pl.* = सिरवाली.

सुविधा *su-vi-dhā* [S.], f. **1.** convenience. **2.** pl. facilities.

सुरस *su-ras* [S.], adj. = सरस, 4.

सुरसा *su-răsā* [S.], f. juicy, savorous: **1.** name of several plants. **2.** a title of Durgā. **3.** *mythol.* name of a daughter of Kaśyapa and mother of the snakes, or *nāgas* (she opposed Hanumān's crossing to Laṅkā).

सुरसुर *sursur* [cf. H. *sursurānā*], f. = सरसर.

सुरसुराना *sursurānā* [cf. **sur-*], v.i. = सरसराना.

सुरसुराहट *sursurāhaṭ* [cf. H. *sursurānā*], f. **1.** rustling sound (as of leaves, wind = सरसराहट). **2.** creeping or tingling sensation; a sudden shiver.

सुरसुरी *sursurī* [cf. H. *sursurānā*], f. **1.** = सुरसुराहट. **2.** reg. (W.) a weevil (attacks stored grain).

सुरहर- *surahr-* [? conn. H. *sursurānā*], adj. Brbh. rustling: wheezing (breath).

¹सुरही *surhī* [cf. *surabhi-*], f. *Pl. HŚS.* a grass that grows on waste or uncultivated land.

²सुरही *surhī* [cf. H. *solah*], f. *Pl. HŚS.* a game of chance played with speckled cowrie shells (the number of the speckles being regarded nominally as sixteen).

सुरा *surā* [S.], f. liquor, alcohol; wine. — सुरा-पान, m. the drinking of alcohol. सुरा-पान करना, to drink alcohol (habitually). सुरामय, adj. consisting of alcohol.

सुराई *surāī* [cf. H. *śūr*], f. Av. bravery; show of prowess.

सुराख़ *surākh*, m. pronun. var. = सूराख़.

सुराग *su-rāg* [S.], m. Brbh. **1.** deep love. **2.** a fine *rāga*, sweet music.

सुराग़ *surāg* [P. *surāg*], m. **1.** sign, trace; clue. **2.** search, enquiry. **3.** spying. — ~ लगाना, or लेना, to search out; to seek. ~ मिलना, to be on the track (of, का), to obtain a clue; to get an inkling (of).

सुरा-गाय *surā-gāy*, f. the yak.

सुराग़ी *surāgī* [P. *surāgī*], m. searcher; detective, secret agent.

सुराज *surāj*, m. pronun. var. = स्वराज्य.

सुरावती *surāvătī* [S.], f. Brbh. *mythol.* Aditi (the mother by Kaśyapa of the Ādityas).

सुराही *surāhī* [P. *surāhī*], f. a jar (usu. earthen) with a long narrow neck. — सुराहीदार [P. *-dār*], adj. shaped like a *surāhī*; colloq. long and graceful (the neck).

सुरीति *su-rīti* [S.], f. good conduct or behaviour; good practice.

सुरीला *surīlā* [cf. H. ¹*sur*], adj. melodious, sweet (voice, sound, music).

सुरुंग *suruṅg* [*suruṅgā-*], f. = ¹सुरंग.

सुरुचि *su-ruci* [S.], adj. & f. **1.** adj. having a good taste, &c. (see रुचि). **2.** f. a good taste. **3.** lively interest. **4.** good or discriminating appetite; good taste. — आदर्श ~, f. a taste for the ideal (title of a 19c. essay). – सुरुचिपूर्ण, adj. tasteful; interesting.

सुरूप *su-rūp* [S.], adj. well-formed; handsome, beautiful; elegant.

सुरूर *surūr*, m. see सरूर.

सुरेतना *suretnā*, v.t. reg. (W.) to separate good grain from bad.

सुरेथ *sureth*, m. Brbh. the Ganges dolphin.

सुरैत *surait* [? conn. *surata-*], f. reg. a mistress; concubine (= रखेली).

सुरैतिन *suraitin*, f. reg. = सुरैत.

[1]**सुरैरी** *surairī* [H. *surahr-*], f. reg. whitewashing; whitewash. — ~ फेरना (पर), to whitewash (also fig).

[2]**सुरैरी** *surairī*, f. reg. a rustling sound, &c. (= सुरसुरी, 1).

सुर्ख़ *surkh* [P. *surkh*], adj. red. — ~ होना, to be red; to be ripe (as fruit); to flush (with anger, shame); to be or to become bloodshot. – सुर्ख़रू, adj. bright of face: honourable; enjoying prestige or success. °ई, f. honour, character; success. सुर्ख़-सफ़ेद, adj. red and white: reddish, red (as lips); fair (as complexion).

सुर्ख़ी *surkhī* [P. *surkhī*], f. **1.** redness. **2.** colloq. attraction. ~ आना, demand to arise (for, में). **3.** red ink. **4.** title, headline (as of a manuscript, picked out in red). **5.** reg. (Bihar) pounded brick (as used in making mortar). — सुर्ख़ी-मायल, adj. reddish (as the lips).

सुर्ती *surtī*, f. see सुरती.

सुलक्षण *su-lakṣaṇ* [S.], m. & adj. **1.** m. a good or auspicious sign, or trait; a good omen. **2.** adj. auspicious; of good omen.

सुलगन *sulgan* [cf. H. *sulagnā*], f. kindling, &c.

सुलगना *sulagnā* [cf. *saṁlagna-*; ? **samullagyati*], v.i. **1.** to be kindled (a fire); to be lit (a lamp, a cigarette). **2.** to smoulder. **3.** to be inflamed (passions).

सुलगाना *sulgānā* [cf. H. *sulagnā*], v.t. **1.** to kindle (a fire); to light (a lamp, or a cigarette). **2.** to set alight, to set fire to (as to a house). **3.** to inflame (passions). — बत्ती ~, to light a lamp; to switch on a light.

सुलझन *suljhan* [cf. H. *sulajhnā*], f. **1.** unravelling. **2.** disentanglement. **3.** solution (of a difficulty).

सुलझना *sulajhnā* [H. *su-*+H. *ulajhnā*], v.i. **1.** to unravel. **2.** to become disentangled. **3.** to be solved (a difficulty, a problem); to be set right again. — सुलझा दिमाग़, m. a clear mind. सुलझी भाषा, f. clear language.

सुलझाना *suljhānā* [cf. H. *sulajhnā*], v.t. **1.** to unravel (strands). **2.** to disentangle; to comb out (hair). **3.** to solve, to sort out (a difficulty, a problem); to set right again. **4.** to conciliate (parties).

सुलझाव *suljhāv* [cf. H. *suljhānā*], m. **1.** disentanglement. **2.** solution (of a difficulty, a problem); settlement.

सुलटना *sulaṭnā* [H. *su*+H. *ulaṭnā*], v.t. to deal with, to settle (a matter in hand). — सुलटा, adj. direct, straight.

सुलटा *sulṭā*, adj. see s.v. सुलटना.

सुलतान *sultān* [A. *sulṭān*], m. sultan, king, emperor.

सुलताना *sultānā* [A. *sulṭāna*], f. queen, empress. — ~ चंपा, f. the *surpun* or poon tree, *Calophyllum inophyllum* (source of a heavy timber, and of an oil).

सुलतानी *sultānī* [A. *sulṭānī*], adj. & f. **1.** adj. having to do with a sultan; royal. **2.** Brbh. red (material). **3.** f. = सलतनत, 1. **4.** dignity or office of sultan.

सुलफ़ा *sulfā*, m. a wad of tobacco smoked in a *hookah*, or in a *cilam*. — ~ हो जाना, colloq. to have gone up in smoke (money, assets). – सुलफ़ेबाज़ [P. *-bāz*], m. one addicted to smoking. °ई, f. the smoking habit.

सुलभ *su-labh* [S.], adj. **1.** easily obtained. **2.** easily attained or realised (an objective); natural (to). **3.** convenient, moderate (in price). — सुलभेतर [°*a*+*i*°], adj. other than easily obtained: hard to come by.

सुलभता *su-labhătā* [S.], f. ease of acquisition or attainment; feasibility.

सुलभ्य *su-labhyă* [S.], adj. easily obtainable, &c. (= सुलभ).

सुलवाना *sulvānā* [cf. H. [2]*sonā*], v.t. to cause to be put to sleep, &c. (by, से) (see सुलाना).

सुलह *sulh* [A. *ṣulḥ*], f. U. **1.** peace. **2.** peace agreement; truce; treaty. — ~ करना, to make peace (with, से); to make a peace agreement (with). – सुलह-नामा, m. peace agreement or treaty.

सुलाना *sulānā* [cf. H. [2]*sonā*], v.t. **1.** to cause to sleep: to put to bed; to lull to sleep. **2.** to allay (fears, doubts). **3.** sl. to kill, to murder.

सुलेमानी *sulemānī* [P. *sulaimānī*], adj. & f. *Pl. HŚS.* **1.** adj. having to do with Solomon. **2.** f. onyx. **3.** a white-eyed horse. — ~ मुरग़ी, f. the Malabar pied hornbill.

सुलूक *sulūk*, m. = सलूक.

सुवक्ता *su-vaktā* [S.], m. inv. a good speaker.

सुवचन *su-vacan* [S.], m. Av. fine speaking, eloquence.

सुवर्ण *su-varṇ* [S.], adj. & m. **1.** adj. of a good colour; bright, brilliant; golden. **2.** of good *varṇa* (see वर्ण, 3). **3.** m. a good colour. **4.** gold. **5.** a kind of red chalk or ochre. **6.** *hist.* a gold coin. **7.** *hist.* a weight of gold equal to sixteen *māśās*.

[1]**सुवा** *suvā* [*śuka-*], m. a parrot.

[2]**सुवा** *suvā* [cf. *sūcī-*, H. *sūī*], m. a large needle, packing-needle; an awl.

सुवाना *suvānā* [cf. H. [2]*sonā*], v.t. reg. = सुलाना.

[1]**सुवास** *su-vās* [S.], m. pleasant dwelling; good home.

[2]**सुवास** *su-vās* [S.], m. & adj. **1.** m. fragrance, scent. **2.** adj. = सुवासित.

[3]**सुवास** *su-vās* [S.], adj. well or elegantly dressed.

सुवासित *su-vāsit* [S.], adj. made fragrant, scented.

सुवासिनी *su-vāsinī* [ad. *svavāsinī-*], f. **1.** a woman (married or single) living in her father's house. **2.** term of courtesy for a respectable married woman.

सुवासी *su-vāsī* [S.], adj. **1.** [[1]*suvās*] living in a good house. **2.** [[2]*suvās*] perfumed.

सुविख्यात *su-vi-khyāt* [S.], adj. very famous, renowned.

सुविचार *su-vi-cār* [S.], m. good thought; well-thought-out decision.

सुविचारित *su-vi-cārit* [S.], adj. well-thought-out.

सुविज्ञ *su-vi-jñă* [S.], adj. **1.** very knowledgeable; very wise. **2.** expert.

सुविहित *su-vi-hit* [S.], adj. **1.** well-arranged; well-appointed. **2.** well-performed.

सुवेश *su-veś* [S.], adj. & m. **1.** adj. well-dressed; attractive in dress or outward appearance. **2.** m. attractive attire.

सुवेशी *su-veśī* [S.], adj. = सुवेश.

सुवैया *suvaiyā* [cf. H. [2]*sonā*], m. one who sleeps (= सोनेवाला).

सुशिक्षित *su-śikṣit* [S.], f. **1.** well-educated. **2.** well-trained.

सुशीतल *su-śītal* [S.], adj. very cool, &c. (see शीतल).

सुशील *su-śīl* [S.], adj. of good character or disposition, &c. (see शील).

सुशीलता *su-śīlătā* [S.], f. goodness of character, &c. (see शील).

सुशोभित *su-śobhit* [S.], adj. well-adorned; decorated, embellished. — ~ करना, to adorn, to grace (a post).

सुश्राव्य *su-śrāvyă* [S.], adj. **1.** clearly audible. **2.** pleasing to the ear.

सुश्री *su-śrī* [S.], adj. very splendid: (hon. title of address or reference) Miss.

सुषम *su-ṣam* [S.], adj. lovely, beautiful.

सुषमा *su-ṣămā* [S.], f. exquisite beauty, splendour.

सुषुप्त *su-ṣupt* [S.], adj. sound asleep.

सुषुप्ति *su-ṣupti* [S.], f. **1.** deep sleep. **2.** *philos.* state of complete unconsciousness.

सुषुम्णा *su-ṣumṇā* [S.], f. (in yoga) the channel of the spinal cord (opening to the *brahmarandhra*).

सुष्ट *suṣṭ* [ad. *suṣṭhu-*], adj. good, virtuous.

सुष्ठुता *su-ṣṭhutā* [S.], f. **1.** well-being; good fortune. **2.** aptness (as of words).

सुसंग *su-saṅg* [S.], m. good company: the company or fellowship of the good.

सुसंगति *su-saṅ-gati* [S.], f. = सुसंग.

सुसकारना *suskārnā* [conn. **śuṣati*[2]], v.i. & v.t. pronun. var. = सिसकारना.

सुसताना *sustānā* [cf. H. *sust*], v.i. to rest; to stop (work, &c.), to take a rest or break.

सुसमय *su-sam-ay* [S.], m. good time, or season.

सुसमाचार *su-sam-ā-cār* [S.], m. good news: the Gospel; a Gospel.

सुसर *susar*, m. pronun. var. = ससुर.

सुसरा *susrā* [*śvaśura-*], m. = ससुर.

सुसरालिया *susrāliyā* [cf. H. *sasurāl*], adj. having to do with the father-in-law's family.

सुसरी *susrī*, f. = ससुरी.

सुसार *susār* [**sūpaśālā-*], f. Av. foodstuffs (specif. prepared for cooking); cooked food.

सुसुम *susum* [ad. *suṣama-*], adj. **1.** equable: lukewarm (water). **2.** lovely, beautiful.

सुस्त *sust* [P. *sust*], adj. **1.** languid, inert. **2.** downcast. **3.** sluggish; slow (as a train). मेरी घड़ी ~ है, my watch is slow. **4.** depressed (as a market). **5.** lazy: negligent; remiss. उसका हाथ ~ है, he is slow at getting things done. **6.** slow, dull (of wit). — ~ करना, to slow, to retard; fig. to throw cold water on (as on hopes). गवाह चुस्त, मुद्दई ~, the witness is eager, the plaintiff indifferent (describes a situation where energy is being expended, but not at the proper time).

सुस्ताई *sustāī* [cf. H. *sustānā*], f. Av. resting, rest.

सुस्ती *sustī* [P. *sustī*], f. **1.** languor. **2.** sluggishness, &c. (see सुस्त). **3.** depression (of a market). **4.** laziness, &c. **5.** dullness. ~ उतारना, to shake off tiredness (as by stretching oneself). ~ करना, to be idle; to be slow, to delay (as with work).

सुस्थ *su-sth* [S.], adj. in a state of well-being: **1.** prosperous; happy, content. **2.** healthy.

सुस्थित *su-sthit* [S.], adj. placed in a state of well-being: = सुस्थ, 1.

सुस्थिर *su-sthir* [S.], adj. **1.** very firm, steady. 2. resolute; calm, cool.

सुस्थिरता *su-sthirătā* [S.], f. **1.** firmness, steadiness. **2.** resoluteness; calmness.

सुस्पष्ट *su-spaṣṭ* [S.], adj. very clear, distinct, or intelligible.

सुस्वाद *su-svād* [S.], m. & adj. **1.** m. delicious taste or flavour. **2.** adj. = सुस्वादु.

सुस्वादित *su-svādit* [S.], adj. made tasty or delicious.

सुस्वादु *su-svādu* [S.], adj. very tasty, delicious.

सुहाऊ *suhaū*, adj. reg. = सुहावना.

सुहाग *suhāg* [*saubhāgyā*-¹], m. **1.** the auspicious state of wifehood (as opposed to widowhood); married happiness. 2. = ~ की निशानी. **3.** a kind of marriage song sung by the female relatives of the bride, or of the bridegroom. **4.** a wedding garment. — ~ उतरना, fig. to become a widow (see ~, 1., 2). ~ की निशानी, f. sign of wifehood: ornaments such as bangles, and the vermilion in the hair-parting (which are discarded on a husband's death). ~ छिनना, to become a widow. ~ मनाना (की), to pray or to hope for a bride's married happiness. माँग में ~ भरना, to apply vermilion to the hair-parting. – सुहाग-पिटारा, m. trinket-box (presented to the bride by the groom, or by his party). सुहाग-पुड़िया, m. id. सुहाग-रात, f. wedding night.

सुहागवती *suhāgvatī* [cf. H. *suhāg*], f. = सुहागिन.

सुहागा *suhāgā* [*saubhāgya*-²: ? f. *sovāka*-], m. borax. — सोने में ~, borax (added to) gold: sthg. of heightened splendour or excellence (as gold or silver when cleaned, or as other metals transmuted by alchemy).

सुहागिन *suhāgin* [cf. H. *suhāg*], f. a woman whose husband is alive; a happily married woman.

सुहागिनी *suhāginī*, f. = सुहागिन.

¹**सुहाना** *suhānā* [*śubhāna*-], adj. = सुहावना.

²**सुहाना** *suhānā* [*śubhāyate*], v.i. **1.** to be or to seem attractive. **2.** to commend itself (to, को), to be liked (by). **3.** to be an adornment (to, को), to grace.

सुहाया *suhāyā* [cf. H. ²*suhānā*], adj. = सुहावना.

सुहाल *suhāl* [? conn. *āhāra*-], m. a savoury made with thin puff pastry, usu. triangular.

सुहाली *suhālī*, f. = सुहाल.

सुहावन *suhāvan*, adj. agreeable, &c. (= सुहावना). — ~ करना, reg. to decorate, to adorn.

सुहावना *suhāvnā* [cf. H. ¹ ²*suhānā*], adj. pleasant, agreeable; charming; attractive of aspect.

सुहावनी *suhāvnī* [cf. **suhāva*-: × H. *suhāvnā*], f. an attractive or charming woman.

सुहावा *suhāvā* [cf. H. ²*suhānā*], adj. = सुहावना.

सुहृद *su-hṛd* [S.], adj. & m. good-hearted: **1.** adj. affectionate; well-disposed. **2.** m. a friend.

सुहेल *suhel* [A. *suhail*], m. Av. the star Canopus.

सुहेलौ *suhelau* [? **suvelā*-], adj. Brbh. agreeable (season, time); auspicious.

सुहैया *suhaiyā* [? cf. *subhāga*-; and H. ²*suhānā*], m. *Pl.* a birth song (sung by women on the birth of a son).

¹**सूँ** *sūṁ*, ppn. Brbh. Raj. = से.

²**सूँ** *sūṁ* [? onom.], f. sound of sniffing: — ~ ~ करना, to sniff, to snuffle.

सूँघ *sūṁgh* [cf. H. *sūṁghnā*], f. **1.** the act of smelling; the sense of smell. **2.** smell; scent.

सूँघन *sūṁghan* [cf. H. *sūṁghnā*], f. reg. **1.** the act of smelling; smelling (sthg.) out. **2.** anything to smell (as snuff).

सूँघना *sūṁghnā* [**śṛṅkhati*: Pk. *suṁghaï*], v.t. **1.** to smell. **2.** to sniff; to inhale. **3.** fig. to sniff at, to pick at (food). **4.** to bite (a snake). — सिर ~, fig. reg. to bless (a child, का). सूँघता फिरना, to go sniffing about; to prowl about.

सूँघनी *sūṁghnī* [cf. H. *sūṁghnā*], f. sthg. to be smelt or sniffed: **1.** snuff. **2.** smelling salts. **3.** snuff-box. — ~ लेना, to sniff (at, की); to get scent (of).

सूँजा *sūṁjā*, m. pronun. var. = सूजा.

सूँट *sūṁṭ*, f. colloq. silence. — ~ मारे जाना, to go away in silence.

सूँड़ *sūṁṛ* [*śuṇḍā*-¹], f. **1.** an elephant's trunk. **2.** reg. (Bihar) = ³सूआ, 1. (?)

सूँड़का *sūm̐ṛkā*, m. *Pl.* saddle-pad; pack-saddle.

[1]**सूँड़ी** *sūm̐ṛī* [? cf. *śuṇḍā-*[1]], m. reg. (Bihar) a small insect, or weevil, which attacks crops, stored grain and wood.

[2]**सूँड़ी** *sūm̐ṛī* [*śuṇḍin-*], m. reg. **1.** a maker and seller of alcohol. **2.** *Pl.* a dealer in rice, a grocer.

सूँतना *sūm̐tnā*, v.t. reg. (W.) **1.** to rub down. **2.** to strip leaves (from a branch, a plant). **3.** to draw (a sword). **4.** to straighten out (a bent wire, &c). **5.** to bale out (water). **6.** to drain, to exhaust.

सूँथना *sūm̐thnā*, v.t. = सूँतना.

सूँस *sūm̐s*, m. the Ganges porpoise (= सूस).

सूअर *sūar* [*sūkara-*], m. **1.** a pig; a boar. **2.** pej. term of abuse. — ~ का गोश्त, m. pork. ~ की चरबी, f. pig's fat. ~ के बाल, m. pl. pig's bristles. जंगली ~, m. a wild boar. – सूअर-ख़ाना, m. a pigsty. सूअरबियान [H. *-byānā*], f. colloq. pej. a woman who produces a child every year.

सूअरनी *sūarnī* [cf. H. *sūar*], f. a sow.

सूअरी *sūarī*, f. = सूअरनी.

[1]**सूआ** *sūā*, m. pronun. var. = [1]सुवा.

[2]**सूआ** *sūā*, m. pronun. var. = [2]सुवा.

[3]**सूआ** *sūā* [*śūka-*], m. *Pl.* awn (as of barley); bristle.

सूई *sūī* [*śūcī-*], f. **1.** a needle; a pin. **2.** needle (of an instrument); hand (of a watch). **3.** needle of a syringe; injection. **4.** a prickle, thorn; fig. sthg. troublesome. — ~ का काम, m. needlework. ~ का फावड़ा, or भाला, बनाना, to make a needle into a spade, or spear: to attempt sthg. vain. ~ के नाके में से ऊँट निकालना, to make a camel pass through the eye of a needle. ~ पिरोना, m. to thread a needle. ~ लगाना, to give an injection (to, को). घड़ी की ~ देखके आना, to come on the dot (of an appointed time). – सूईकार, m. a needleworker. °ई, f. needlework. सूई-तागा, m. needle and thread.

सूक *sūk* [*śukra-*], m. Av. = शुक्र.

सूक- *sūk-*, v.i. Brbh. = सूखना.

सूकर *sūkar* [S.], m. a hog, boar.

सूकरी *sūkărī* [S.], f. a sow.

सूकवा *sūkvā*, m. *Pl.* a kind of vetch.

[1]**सूका** *sūkā* [*sūkṣma-*], m. *Pl. HŚS.* a four-anna piece (quarter-rupee).

[2]**सूका** *sūkā*, adj. pronun. var. = सूखा.

सूक्त *sûkt* [S.], m. a Vedic hymn; invocation, prayer.

सूक्ति *sûkti* [S.], f. good speech or word: wise or apt saying.

सूक्ष्म *sūkṣmă* [S.], adj. & m. **1.** adj. minute. **2.** slender, thin, fine. **3.** subtle (thought, distinction, analysis); searching (investigation). **4.** delicate; refined. **5.** shrill (voice). **6.** subtle, crafty. **7.** precise, exact. **8.** m. sthg. subtle, refined, &c. — स्थूल और ~, m. the gross and the subtle, outward appearance and inner reality. – सूक्ष्मजीवविज्ञान, m. microbiology. सूक्ष्मदर्शी, adj. *Pl.* keen of sight; acute of mind. सूक्ष्मदर्शी यंत्र, m. microscope. सूक्ष्म-बुद्धि, f. acute mind.

सूक्ष्मता *sūkṣmătā* [S.], f. minuteness, subtleness, fineness, &c. (see सूक्ष्म).

सूखना *sūkhnā* [**śuṣkati*: Pa. *sukkhati*], v.i. **1.** to dry; to dry up; to wither; to be lost from drought (a harvest). **2.** to grow dejected (the expression); to long, to pine. **3.** to waste away. — सूखकर काँटा होना, = ~, 3.

सूखा *sūkhā* [*śuṣkaka-*], adj. & m. **1.** adj. dry; dried up; withered (vegetation). **2.** emaciated. **3.** dry (manner); terse (remarks). **4.** lifeless, dejected (expression); uninteresting. **5.** without advantage or profit; without perquisites (a wage). **6.** m. dry land. **7.** drought. **8.** dry leaf (of tobacco or hemp). **9.** lung disease: croup; tuberculosis. — ~ जवाब, m. a dry answer; a flat refusal. ~ टकराना, or टालना, to rebuff (one making a request). ~ पड़ना, drought to occur. ~ लगना (को), to waste away, to become emaciated. सूखी धुलाई, f. dry cleaning. सूखी राह से, adv. = सूखे सूखे. सूखी सुनाना (को), to give a terse answer; to rebuke. सूखे खेत लहलहाना, dry fields to flourish: happy days to come. सूखे धानों पानी पड़ना, rain to fall on dry paddy: rain to fall when much needed; fig. to be revived. सूखे पर लगना, to come to shore. सूखे सूखे, adv. by land (as opposed to water). – सूखा-ग्रस्त, adj. drought-stricken. सूखा-पीड़ित, adj. id.

सूगा *sūgā*, m. reg. = सुग्गा.

सूचक *sūcak* [S.], adj. & m. **1.** adj. -सूचक. indicating (e.g. प्रश्नसूचक, enquiring (as a glance). **2.** meaningful (as words, a remark). **3.** m. an indicator. **4.** narrator of traditional tales. **5.** an informer, a spy.

सूचित *sūcit* [S.], adj. **1.** pointed out, indicated (to, को); made known. **2.** ascertained, learned. — ~ करना, to point out; to inform.

सूची *sūcī* [S.], f. **1.** needle. ***2.** a list; table, index; register. **3.** catalogue. — सूची-पत्र, m. = ~, 2., 3. सूच्यग्र, m. the point of a needle; a minute amount.

सूज *sūj* [cf. H. *sūjnā*], f. = सूजन.

सूजन *sūjan* [cf. H. *sūjnā*], f. **1.** swelling. **2.** inflammation.

सूजना *sūjnā* [*śūyate*], v.i. **1.** to swell. **2.** to become inflamed. **3.** to look sulky (the face).

सूजा *sūjā* [cf. H. [2]*sūjī*], m. **1.** a packing-needle. **2.** a gimlet, borer.

सूज़ाक *sūzāk* [P. *sūzāk*], m. gonorrhoea.

[1]**सूजी** *sūjī* [**sūjjī-*], f. a coarse wheat flour; semolina.

[2]**सूजी** *sūjī* [ad. *sūcī-*; cf. H. *sūī*], f. reg. **1.** a needle. **2.** a gimlet, borer.

[3]**सूजी** *sūjī* [ad. *sūci-*], m. 19c. a tailor.

सूझ *sūjh* [cf. H. *sūjhnā*], f. **1.** perception, understanding. **2.** fig. vision. **3.** a thought, notion. — सूझ-बूझ, f. = ~, 1.; reason, common sense.

सूझना *sūjhnā* [*śudhyati*], v.i. **1.** to be perceptible (to, को). **2.** to appear (to), to seem. **3.** to occur (to). — उसे यह बात सूझ आई, he thought of this (in a crisis, &c). उसे एक बात सूझ पड़ी, he thought (involuntarily) of sthg. आपको यह कैसा सूझता है? what do you think of this? how do you like this?

सूड़ी *sūṛī* [*śuṇḍin-*], m. a maker of alcohol.

[1]**सूत** *sūt* [*sūtra-*], m. **1.** thread; yarn. **2.** string, cord, line. **3.** a waist-string. **4.** a thread tied (as a charm) round a child's neck or arm. — ~ बाँधना, to tie a string (to, में or पर); to stretch a cord (for a straight line: as in building). ~ पटकना, to measure out (a distance) with a cord or line.

[2]**सूत** *sūt* [S.], m. **1.** charioteer, driver. **2.** bard. **3.** carpenter.

[3]**सूत** *sūt* [S.], adj. & ? m. **1.** adj. born, produced. **2.** m. (? for सुत) E.H. a son.

सूत- *sūt-* [cf. *supta-*], v.i. E.H. to sleep.

सूतक *sūtak* [S.], m. *hind.* state of ritual impurity existing after a birth, or in a household after a death of one of its members. — सूतकाशौच [°*ka* + *a*°], m. id.

सूतकी *sūtākī* [S.], adj. ritually impure, as a result of a birth or a death in one's household.

सूतना *sūtnā*, v.t. *Pl.* = सूँतना.

[1]**सूता** *sūtā* [*sūtra-*], m. = [1]सूत, 1., 2.

[2]**सूता** *sūtā* [S.], f. a woman who has recently given birth.

सूति *sūti* [S.], f. birth; giving birth.

सूतिका *sūtikā* [S.], f. a woman who has recently given birth. — सूतिका-गृह, m. delivery room; lying-in room.

[1]**सूती** *sūtī* [cf. H. [1]*sūt*; or *sūtrita-*: Pk. *suttia-*], adj. made of thread: made of cotton.

[2]**सूती** *sūtī* [*śukti-*], f. Brbh. = सीपी.

[3]**सूती** *sūtī* [ad. *sūti-*], f. birth; giving birth. — ~ लगना (को), to become ritually impure following a birth.

सूत्र *sūtr* [S.], m. **1.** thread, &c. (= [1]सूत). **2.** string, cord. **3.** a short rule or aphorism (as used in Sanskrit manuals of instruction). **4.** origin; source (of information). विश्वस्त सूत्रों से ज्ञात होता है, it is learned from reliable sources. सरकारी ~, m. pl. government sources of information. **5.** a clue. **6.** a formulation, partic. point (within a more complex topic). **7.** a formula. — सूत्रकार, m. a composer of *sūtras*. सूत्रधार, m. thread-holder: stage-manager (or principal actor) who traditionally superintends a dramatic performance and takes a leading part in the prelude; a puppet-master. सूत्रपात, m. beginning. सूत्रपात करना (का), to commence. सूत्रबद्ध, adj. organised in the form of *sūtras*.

-सूत्री *-sūtrī* [S.], adj. consisting of formulations (e.g. चार-सूत्री प्रस्ताव, m. four-point proposal).

सूथन *sūthan* [**sutthanā-*], f. Brbh. women's loose trousers.

सूद *sūd* [P. *sūd*], m. interest (on money); profit. — ~ खाना, to profit unjustifiably from interest received. ~ पर देना, to lend at interest. ~ पर लेना, to borrow at interest. ~ लगाना, to charge interest (on, में). – सूदख़ोर [P. *-khor*], m. interest-eater: a money-lender, usurer. °ई, f. usury. सूद-दर-सूद, m. interest on interest: compound interest.

सूध *sūdh* [cf. H. *sūdhā*], f. reg. direction, direct line.

सूधा *sūdhā* [*śuddha-*], adj. reg. = सीधा. — सूधे, adv. in a straightforward manner; unaffectedly.

सूधौ *sūdhau* [*śuddha-* × *siddha-*[2]], adj. Brbh. **1.** simple, direct; unaffected, natural. **2.** straight, not angular (posture).

सून *sūn*, adj. & m. = शून्य. — ~ खींचना or साधना, to keep silent. – सूनसान, adj. & m. = सुनसान.

सूना *sūnā* [*śūnya-*], adj. void: **1.** deserted, desolate; ruined; empty, unoccupied. **2.** desolate; blank (a glance). **3.** unadorned. — ~ करना, to lay waste, to destroy; to make empty. ~ ~ गला, m. a neck always without a necklace, locket, etc.

सूनापन *sūnāpan* [cf. H. *sunā*], m. **1.** desolate, ruined or deserted state. **2.** unadorned state.

[1]**सूप** *sūp* [*śūrpa-*], m. a winnowing basket. — सूपनखा, f. Brbh. Av. = शूर्पनखा s.v. शूर्प.

[2]**सूप** *sūp* [S.], m. **1.** lentil soup, broth. **2.** a sauce. — सूपकार, m. Brbh. a cook. °-कारी, m. Av. id.

सूपक *sūpak* [cf. H. *sūp*], m. Brbh. a cook.

सूपाबीना *sūpābīnā* [H. *sūpābenā* × H. [2]*bīnnā*], m. *Pl.* a swallow.

सूपाबेना *sūpābenā* [*śūrpa-* + *vayana-*], m. *Pl.* a swallow.

सूफ़ी *sūfī* [A. *ṣūfī*], m. & adj. wearing wool: **1.** m. a member of any of several Muslim mystical orders, a Ṣūfī. **2.** adj. having to do with the Ṣūfīs.

सूबड़ा *sūbṛā* [conn. *śulva-*], m. reg. silver alloyed with copper or tin.

सूबा *sūbā* [A. *ṣūba*], m. province. — सुबेदार, m. *mil.* captain; *hist.* governor of a province. °ई, f. captaincy; governorship; the government of a province.

सूम *sūm* [? conn. Ar. *śu'm*], m. reg. a miser.

सूमड़ा *sūmṛā* [cf. H. *sūm*], adj. **1.** ugly. **2.** miserly, stingy.

सूमपन *sūmpan* [cf. H. *sūm*], m. reg. miserliness.

सूमपना *sūmpanā*, m. reg. = सूमपन.

[1]**सूर** *sūr* [*śūra-*[1]], m. & adj. **1.** m. a hero; warrior; champion. **2.** adj. heroic; valiant, bold. — सूर-बीर, m. & adj. = ~.

[2]**सूर** *sūr* [*sūra-*], m. **1.** the sun. **2.** a wise or learned man. 3. = सूरदास. — सूरदास, m. name of a 16th-century north Indian devotional poet, believed to have been blind; (hence) a blind man.

सूरज *sūraj* [ad. *sūrya-*], m. the sun. — ~ को चिराग़ दिखाना, to show a lamp to the sun: to do sthg. pointless. ~ डूबना, or ढलना, the sun to sink, or to set. ~ डूबते, adv. at sunset. – सूरज-गहन, m. eclipse of the sun. सूरजबंसी, adj. *mythol.* belonging to the solar race. सूरजतनी, f. Brbh. daughter of the sun: the river Jumna. सूरज-नारायन, m. 19c. the sun as Nārāyaṇ, the sun deified. सूरजमुखी, f. sunflower; a kind of firework. सूरज-संसार, m. the solar system.

[1]**सूरत** *sūrat* [A. *ṣūra*: P. *ṣūrat*], f. form, appearance: **1.** face; features. **2.** outward aspect, appearance. **3.** likeness. **4.** fig. prospect, likelihood. उसके आने की कोई ~ नहीं है, there is no likelihood of his coming. **5.** state, condition, situation. इस ~ में, adv. in these circumstances. **6.** means. इस ~ से, adv. in this way. — ~ करना, to form a plan (for, की), to devise means. ~ दिखाना (की or अपनी), to show the face, to appear; to bring to pass (a situation, an event); to confront (one, को) with (a probable situation, or event); to make a show (of). ~ पकड़ना, to take form and shape; to assume the form (of, की), to look like; to grow, to become. ~ बनाना, to give shape or form (to, की); to take on a form: to impersonate, or to feign; to give a misleading impression, to pretend; to make faces (at). ~ बाँधना (की), to represent, to depict. ~ यह है, the fact or situation, is. किस ~ से? with what show of honour or decency? रोनी ~, f. a tearful face. – सूरत-शकल, f. form and likeness: outward aspect. सूरत-हराम, adj. good outwardly only, specious, plausible.

[2]**सूरत** *sūrat*, f. 19c. corr. = [1]सुरत.

सूरताई *sūrătāī* [cf. H. *śūrtā*], f. Brbh. bravery, valour.

सूरन *sūran* [*śūraṇa-*], m. an edible tuber, *Amorphophallus campanulatus* (cf. मदन-मस्त).

सूरमा *sūrmā*, m. a hero; warrior; valiant person.

सूरमापन *sūrmāpan* [cf. H. *sūrmā*], m. heroism, courage.

सूरा *sūrā* [*sūra-*], m. reg. a hero, &c. (= [1]सूर).

सूराख़ *sūrākh* [P. *sūrākh*], m. hole, opening. — ~ करना, to make a hole (in, में); to bore, to pierce. – सूराख़दार [P. *-dār*], adj. having holes; perforated; porous.

सूराख़ी *sūrākhī* [P. *sūrākhī*], adj. perforated, bored.

सूरातन *sūrātan* m. E.H. bravery, valour.

सुरावट *surāvaṭ* [? ad. **svarāvarta-*], m. poet. strains of song.

सूरि *sūri* [S.], m. the sun; a wise or learned man.

सूरी *sūrī* [S.], adj. & m. **1.** adj. wise, learned. **2.** m. a wise or learned man; a sage.

सूरीसीर *sūrīsīr*, f. *Pl.* a cattle-plague.

सूर्य *sūryă* [S.], m. **1.** the sun. **2.** *mythol.* the god Sūrya. — सूर्यकांत, m. sun-loved: the sunstone, a kind of crystal (supposed to give off heat when exposed to the sun). सूर्य-ग्रहण, m. eclipse of the sun. सूर्य-देव, m. the sun personified as a deity. °ता, m. id. सूर्य-भगवान, m. the sun personified as Bhagvat or Viṣṇu. सूर्यमुखी, f. sunflower. सूर्यवंश, m. *mythol.* the solar race or dynasty (descending from Ikṣvāku to Rāmacandra). °ई, adj. & m. belonging to the solar race; name of a community of kṣatriyas. सूर्य-संक्रांति, f. *astron.* the sun's entry into a new sign. सूर्यातप [°*ya* + *ā*°], m. heat of the sun.

सूर्यास्त [°*ya+a*°], m. sunset. सूर्योदय [°*ya+u*°], m. sunrise. सूर्योपासना [°*ya+u*°], m. sun-worship.

सूर्या *sūryā* [S.], f. *mythol.* **1.** the wife of Sūrya. **2.** the daughter of Sūrya.

सूल *sūl* [*śūla-*], m.; f. (Brbh.) **1.** a sharp pain. **2.** colic; indigestion. **3.** a thorn; prickle. **4.** Brbh. any pointed weapon.

सूल- *sūl-* [*śūlate*], v.i. Brbh. to suffer a pang (the heart).

सूली *sūlī* [*śūlikā-*], f. **1.** an impaling stake. **2.** gallows. **3.** fig. pang; anguish. — ~ चढ़ाना, to impale; to hang; to put to death; to torture. ~ देना (को), id. ~ पर चढ़ाना, id. जान ~ पर होना, to suffer mortal agonies.

सूस *sūs* [conn. *śiṁśuka-*; *śuṁśumāra-*], m. the Ganges porpoise (= सूँस). — सूसमार, m. *Pl. HŚS.* id.

सूसी *sūsī* [P. *sūsī*], f. *Pl. HŚS.* a kind of striped, or checked, cloth.

सूसूम *sūsūm*, adj. pronun. var. = सुसुम, 2.

सूहा *sūhā* [conn. *śubha-*], adj. & m. **1.** adj. bright red; saffron-coloured. **2.** m. *mus. Pl. HŚS.* name of a *rāg*.

सृजन *sṛjan* [S.], m. creating, forming; creation. — सृजनधर्मी, adj. whose *dharma* is to create: creative. सृजन-शक्ति, f. creativity. सृजनशील, adj. creative. सृजनात्मक [°*na+ā*°], adj. creative.

सृजना *sṛjnā*, v.t. = सिरज-.

सृष्ट *sṛṣṭ* [S.], adj. created, formed, produced.

सृष्टि *sṛṣṭi* [S.], f. **1.** creating. **2.** creation, production; invention. **3.** the creation, the world; nature. — ~ करना (की), to create, &c. – सृष्टिकर्ता, m. inv. the creator of the universe.

सेंक *seṁk* [cf. H. *seṁknā*], f. **1.** warming, heating; toasting. **2.** basking (in the sun). **3.** fomenting (a boil, &c). — ~ करना, to warm, &c. – सेंक-साँक करना, id.

सेंकना *seṁknā* [**sekk-*], v.t. **1.** to warm, to heat; to toast, to parch (grain), to bake. **2.** to foment (a boil, &c). **3.** to air by warming. **4.** to dry before a fire. **5.** to incubate (as birds their eggs). — आँखें ~, to assuage the eyes (with the sight of a beautiful woman). धूप ~, to bask in the winter sun.

सेंगर *seṁgar*, m. *Pl. HŚS.* = सेंगरी.

सेंगरी *seṁgrī*, m. a pod, seed-vessel.

सेंठा *seṁṭhā*, m. the lower part of the flowering stem of *mūṁj* grass, used in making chairs and stools (= सरकंडा).

सेंठी *seṁṭhī*, f. dimin. = सेंठा.

सेंत *seṁt*, f. & adv. **1.** sthg. obtained at no cost. **2.** sthg. unwanted. **3.** adv. for nothing. **4.** gratuitously, to no purpose. **5.** E.H. vainly. — ~ का, adj. costing nothing; unwanted. ~ में, adv. = ~. – सेंत-मेंत (में), adv. id.

सेंतना *seṁtnā*, v.t. = सैंत-.

सेंती *seṁtī*, ppn. Brbh. Av. = से.

[1]सेंद *send*, f. a melon, esp. *Cucumis momordica* (= [2]फूट).

[2]सेंद *send*, f. pronun. var. = सेंध.

सेंदुर *seṁdur* [H. *seṁdūr*, *seṁduriyā*], m. = सिंदूर.

सेंदुरिया *seṁduriyā* [cf. H. *seṁdūr*], adj. & m. **1.** adj. bright red. **2.** a partic. red fruit.

सेंदूर *seṁdūr* [*saindūra-*], m. vermilion (= सिंदूर).

सेंध *seṁdh* [*saṁdhi-*; × *cheda-*], f. **1.** a hole made in a wall by housebreakers. **2.** a tunnel (as of sappers). — ~ खोलना, or देना, or मारना, or लगाना, to make a hole (in a house wall, में); to commit a burglary. – सेंध-चोर, m. a housebreaker, burglar. सेंधमार, m. id.

सेंधना *seṁdhnā* [cf. H. *sendh*], v.t. reg. **1.** to bore for water. **2.** to draw water; to irrigate.

सेंधा *seṁdhā* [*saindhava-*], m. a white rock-salt found in regions near the river Indus. — सेंधा-लोन, m. id.

सेंधि *seṁdhi*, f. Av. = सेंध.

[1]सेंधिया *seṁdhiyā* [cf. H. *seṁdh*], m. a housebreaker, burglar.

[2]सेंधिया *seṁdhiyā* [cf. *saindhava-*], m. *hist.* = सिंधिया.

[1]सेंधी *seṁdhī* [cf. H. *sendh*], m. = [1]सेंधिया.

[2]सेंधी *sendhī*, f. *Pl. HŚS.* the wild date or date-sugar palm, and its juice (which yields molasses and an alcoholic drink (*tāṛī*)).

[1]सेंधुर *seṁdhur* [? ad. *samudra-* w. P. *samandar*, × *saindhava-*], m. E.H. the sea.

[2]सेंधुर *seṁdhur*, m. reg. = सिंदूर.

सेंबल *sembal*, m. pronun. var. = सेमल.

सेंभा *seṁbhā* [** śreṣman-*], m. **1.** *Pl.* rheum, phlegm. **2.** *HŚS.* a disease of horses.

से *se* [*sahita-*; ? *samena*], ppn. **1.** by means of: by; with. क़लम ~ लिखना, to write with a pen. गाड़ी ~ आना, to come by car, &c. डाक ~ भेजना, to send by post. **2.** because of: of, from, for. इस वजह ~, for this reason. दुख ~ मरना, to die of grief. **3.** (in expressions of manner formed on nouns) with; by, in; -ly. आसानी ~, adv. easily. इस तरह ~, adv. in this way. जल्दी ~, adv.

quickly. मुश्किल ~, adv. with difficulty. किस ~ काम है? who do you want to see? तुम्हारा इस ~ क्या मतलब है? what has that to do with you? (see also 6). **4.** (denoting literal or fig. connection.) to, with. आप किस ~ कहेंगे? who will you speak to? उस ~ बोलिए, please speak to him. उस ~ पूछिए, please ask him. किश्ती बल्ली ~ बँधी है, the boat is tied to the pole. **5.** (in comparisons.) आप उन ~ बड़े हैं, you are bigger than he. एक ~ एक बढ़िया, pl. each nicer than the one before. **6.** in respect of. अधिकार ~ वंचित, deprived of (one's) right(s). तुम्हारा इस ~ क्या मतलब है? what do you mean by that? (see also 3). दुख ~ रहित, adv. free of sorrow. **7.** (denoting separation.) from, away from. भारत ~ दूर, adv. far from India. **8.** (referring to passage of past time). since, for. कब ~? adv. since when? बहुत दिनों ~ आप दिखे नहीं, (I) haven't seen you for a long time. **9.** [? f. Engl. *with*] colloq. with, accompanied by. सामान ~ आना, to come with (one's) luggage.

सेगौन *segaun*, m. reg. a red-coloured soil, a mixture of sand and clay (found in eroded country in Bundelkhand).

सेचन *secan* [S.], m. = सिंचन.

सेचनी *secănī* [S.], f. reg. ? a bucket (as used for irrigation).

सेचित *secit* [S.], adj. watered; irrigated; moistened.

सेज *sej* [*śayyā-*], f. **1.** a bed. **2.** bedding. — ~ चढ़ना, to go to bed. ~ बिछाना, or लगाना, or सँवारना, to make a bed. –सेज-सुहाग, f. = next. सुहाग-सेज, f. the marriage bed.

सेठ *seṭh* [*śreṣṭha-*], m. **1.** a prosperous merchant. **2.** a banker; money-lender. **3.** title of respect given to merchants, bankers, &c.

सेठन *seṭhan* [cf. H. *seṭh*], f. the wife of a *seṭh*.

सेठानी *seṭhānī* [cf. H. *seṭh*], f. = सेठन.

[1]**सेत** *set* [ad. *setu-*], m. Brbh. = सेतु.

[2]**सेत** *set*, adj. Brbh. Av. = श्वेत.

सेती *setī*, ppn. Brbh. = से.

सेतु *setu* [S.], m. **1.** a ridge of earth: causeway; dam. **2.** raised strip of ground dividing fields; boundary. **3.** a bridge. **4.** Av. convention, observance. — सेतु-बंध, m. the ridge of rocks extending from India to Śrī Laṅkā, Adam's Bridge (supposed to have been formed by Hanumān to allow the passage of Rām's forces).

[1]**सेन** *sen* [*śyena-*], m. Brbh. a hawk, falcon.

[2]**सेन** *sen*, f. Av. = सेना.

[1]**सेना** *senā* [S.], f. an army; a force. — सेनाग्र [°*nā*+*a*°], m. vanguard of an army. सेनादार [P. *-dār*], m. 19c. commander, general. सेनाधिपति [°*nā*+*a*°], m. commander-in-chief. सेनाध्यक्ष [°*nā*+*a*°], m. id. सेनापति, m. army chief: divisional or other high-ranking commander, general. °त्व, m. command of an army. प्रधान सेनापति, m. commander-in-chief.

[2]**सेना** *senā* [*sainya-*], m. **1.** commander of a body of troops. **2.** *hist.* a village revenue-collector.

[3]**सेना** *senā* [*sevate*], v.t. **1.** to serve, to attend on; Brbh. to worship (a deity). **2.** to protect, to guard. ***3.** to brood, to hatch (eggs); Av. to languish (as in jail). **4.** to resort to, to take (a medicine, alcohol, a drug). **5.** ? to live constantly in or at (a place).

सेनानी *senānī* [*saināṇika-*], m. leader of an army, commander.

सेनी *senī* [*śreṇi-*], f. reg. line (cf. [2]सैनी): a flat, shallow metal tray or a flat metal plate (one of a set or series).

सेब *seb* [P. *seb*], m. an apple; apple tree.

सेम *sem* [*śaimbya-*], m. the bean *Dolichos lablab* (a twining plant); a bean of the genus *Phaseolus*.

सेमल *semal* [**śaimbala-*], m. the silk-cotton tree, and the cotton it yields (proverbial in poetry as a disappointment to birds attracted by the tree's large red flowers). — ~ की रुई, f. silk-cotton.

[1]**सेर** *ser* [**satera-*[1]], m. a measure of weight of about one kilogram (one fortieth of a *man*). — ~ का सवा ~ मिलना, fig. to be repaid with interest; to meet more than (one's) match; to catch a Tartar.

[2]**सेर** *ser* [P. *ser*], adj. Brbh. full, sated.

सेरवा *servā* [**śairapāda-*], m. reg. (W.) the head and foot of a bed.

सेरा- *serā-* [cf. *śaitala-*], v.i. **1.** v.i. Brbh. Av. to be cold, cool. **2.** to be finished or at an end. **3.** v.t. reg. to make cool or cold. **4.** to put into water, to set afloat.

सेल *sel* [S.], m. Brbh. Av. spear, javelin.

सेल- *sel-* [*śaila-*], f. stone, rock: — सेलखड़ी, f. soap-stone (= सिलखड़ी).

[1]**सेला** *selā*, m. **1.** *Pl. HŚS.* a kind of scarf or shawl of muslin or silk. **2.** Brbh. a silk turban.

[2]**सेला** *selā*, m. roasted, husked rice.

सेली *selī* [cf. **selli-*: Pk. *selli-*], f. Brbh. **1.** a necklace (of threads, silk, hair, &c.) worn by yogīs and faqīrs. **2.** a neck ornament.

सेव *sev*, f. = सिवैयाँ.

सेव- *sev-*, v.t. Brbh. = सेना.

सेवईं *sevaīṁ*, f. = सिवैयाँ.

सेवक *sevak* [S.], adj. & m. **1.** adj. serving. **2.** m. a servant. **3.** one attending (on). **4.** a worshipper, devotee; follower. **5.** one resorting or addicted (as to a medicine, or a drug).

सेवकाई *sevăkāī* [cf. H. *sevak*], f. Brbh. Av. = सेवा.

सेवकिन *sevăkin* [cf. H. *sevak*], f. 19c. = सेविका.

सेवकिनी *sevăkinī*, f. Brbh. = सेवकिन.

सेवकी *sevăkī* [cf. H. *sevak*], f. Brbh. = सेविका.

[1]**सेवड़ा** *sevṛā* [*śākhoṭaka-*], m. the small tree *Trophis aspera*.

[2]**सेवड़ा** *sevṛā*, m. a salted savoury made of fine wheat flour soaked in *ghī*.

[3]**सेवड़ा** *sevṛā*, m. reg. half-baked bricks or earthenware.

सेवती *sevtı* [conn. *semanti-*], f. Brbh. Av. a white rose.

सेवन *sevan* [S.], m. **1.** serving, service. **2.** devotion (to); fig. living constantly in a partic. place. **3.** implicit reliance (on): following, taking (a course of medicine). **4.** addiction (to).

सेवनीय *sevănīyă* [S.], adj. to be served, &c. (see सेवा); deserving service.

सेवड़ा *sevṛā* [*śvetapaṭa-*], m. Av. a (white-clothed) Jain ascetic; a conjurer.

सेवल *seval*, m. reg. a marriage ceremony in which the bridegroom is given a brass vessel, with a lamp, by a female relative.

सेवा *sevā* [S.], f. **1.** service. **2.** attendance (on); care (of or for a person or an animal); tending. **3.** employment, post. **4.** worship (as of the feet of a deity); homage. **5.** care (of an object: as plants, or the hair). **6.** a church service. **7.** an administrative or similar service. **8.** resort (to): following or taking (a course of medicine, or a drug). — ~ करना (की), to serve; to attend (on); to worship; to look after. ~ बजाना [P. *ba-jā-*], to perform a service (properly). ~ में, adv. for the attention (of, की: as a letter: also used as an inscription on a letter); in the serice (of); ~ में उपस्थित, adj. present, or ready. – सेवा-टहल, f. = ~, 1., 2. सेवा-निवृत्त, adj. retired; dismissed from (one's) post. °इ, f. सेवा-परायण, adj. devoted to or conscientious in (one's) work. सेवा-सुश्रूषा, f. = ~, 2.

सेवार *sevār* [*śevāla-*], m. = सिवार.

सेवाल *sevāl* [*śevāla-*], m. Brbh. = सिवार.

सेविका *sevikā* [S.], f. a female servant, &c. (see सेवक).

सेवित *sevit* [S.], adj. **1.** served. **2.** attended, waited on. **3.** honoured, worshipped. **4.** made use of.

सेवी *sevī* [S.], adj. & m. esp. -सेवी. **1.** adj. serving, &c. **2.** m. a servant, &c. (see सेवा, सेवक).

सेव्य *sevyă* [S.], adj. & m. **1.** adj. to be served, &c. (see सेवा); deserving service. **2.** honourable, worshipful (as a guru, a father). **3.** m. lord, master. **4.** the pīpal tree.

सेस *ses* [*śeṣa-*], m. & adj. = शेष.

सेसर *sesar*, m. *Pl. HŚS.* a card game.

सेह *seh* [*sedhā-*], m. a porcupine.

सेहत *sehat* [A. *ṣĕḥḥa*: P. *ṣĕḥḥat*], f. health. — ~ गँवाना, to ruin one's health. ~ पाना, to recover one's health. ~ होना (को), id. – सेहत-बख़्श [P. *-bakhś*], adj. health-giving, salubrious. सेहतमंद [P. *-mand*], adj. healthy.

सेहरा *sehrā* [*śekhara-*], m. **1.** garland of flowers or other materials worn by the bridegroom during a marriage ceremony. **2.** marriage song (sung by bride's or groom's relatives as the groom is garlanded). — ~ बँधना (के सिर), to be married; fig. to be distinguished or pre-eminent (for). सिर से ~ बँधना, id., 2. – सेहराबंदी [P. *-bandī*], f. the act of garlanding a bridegroom. सेहरा-बँधाई, f. present made to a brother-in-law, or to the bridegroom, after the former has garlanded the latter at a wedding ceremony. सेहरे-जलवे की, adj. *musl.* lawfully married (a woman).

सेही *sehī* [*sedhā-*: prob. ← Drav.], f. a porcupine.

सेहुँड़ *sehuṁṛ* [*sehuṇḍa-*], m. the milk-hedge or milk-bush (= सिहूड़).

सेहुआँ *sehuāṁ*, m. reg. a skin disease (in which the skin becomes flecked with grey).

सैंत- *saiṁt-*, v.t. **1.** Brbh. Av. to collect. **2.** to keep carefully, to put away. — सैंत रखना, = ~, 2.

सैंतालीस *saiṁtālīs* [*saptacatvāriṁśat-*], adj. forty-seven.

सैंतीस *saiṁtīs* [*saptatriṁśat-*], adj. thirty-seven.

सैंधव *saindhav* [S.], adj. & m. **1.** adj. having to do with Sindh, or with the river Indus. **2.** m. = सेंधा. **3.** a horse (esp. one bred in Sindh). **4.** one living in Sindh, or in the Indus region.

[1]सै *sai* [*śata-*], adj. Av. = [1]सौ.

[2]सै *sai* [? *sa(ṁ)pad-*], f. Brbh. success, prosperity.

सैकड़ा *saikṛā* [cf. *śata-*], m. & adv. **1.** m. an amount of a hundred. **2.** the hundreds' position (in a series). **3.** adv. per cent. — सैकड़े, adv. per cent. सैकड़ों, adv. hundreds of; in hundreds. सैकड़ों आदमी, m. pl. hundreds of men.

सैक़ल *saiqal* [A. *ṣaiqal*], m. polishing, cleaning (arms, tools). — सैक़लगर [P. *-gar*], m. polisher; armourer.

सैद *said* [A. *ṣaid*], f. U. hunting.

सैन *sain* [*saṁjñā-*], f. **1.** a sign, signal. **2.** nod, wink; hint. **3.** [×Engl. *sign*] mark, signature. — ~ चलाना, to make a sign; to beckon; to wink, to ogle.

सैनिक *sainik* [S.], adj. & m. **1.** adj. having to do with an army or soldiers, military. **2.** m. a soldier. — ~ पोशाक, f. military uniform.

[1]**सैनी** *sainī* [*śayan-*], f. Brbh. a bed.

[2]**सैनी** *sainī* [*śreṇī-*, **śrayaṇī-*], f. Brbh. a line.

सैन्य *sainyă* [S.}, adj. & m. **1.** adj. military. **2.** m. a soldier. **3.** an army. — सैन्य-दल, m. = ~, 3. सैन्यवाद, m. militarism. सैन्यीकरण, m. militarisation.

सैन्यीकरण *sainyīkaraṇ* [S.], m. see s.v. सैन्य.

सैयद *saiyad* [A. *saiyid*], m. **1.** a descendant of Muḥammad; specif. a descendant of Ḥusain, the grandson of Muḥammad. **2.** the second of the four classes into which Muslims have been (in India) traditionally divided; a man of that class.

सैयदानी *saiyădānī* [cf. H. *saiyad*], f. a *saiyad* woman.

सैयाद *saiyād* [A. *ṣaiyād*], m. **1.** a hunter, fowler, fisher. **2.** fig. one who captivates hearts.

सैर *sair* [A. *sair*], f. going: **1.** a walk, stroll. **2.** outing; trip, tour. **3.** recreation, amusement. **4.** Brbh. scene, view. — ~ करना, to walk, stroll (in or through, की); to make an outing, &c. (to); to browse (in, में), to enjoy (a book). – सैर-गाह [P. *-gāh*], f. place for walking, garden, park. सैर-सपाटा, m. = ~, 1., 2.

सैल *sail* [A. *sail*], f. esp. सैल-. flowing; torrent. — सैलाब, m. flood. °ज़दा [P. *-zada*], adj. inv. flood-stricken.

सैला *sailā* [*śalya-*], m. reg. (W., E.) pin in a plough-yoke.

सैलान *sailān* [ad. A. *sairān*], m. obs. = सैर, 1.-3.

सैलानी *sailānī* [cf. H. *sailān*], adj. & m. **1.** adj. strolling, wandering. **2.** fond of strolling, &c.; carefree. ~ लोग, m. walkers, sightseers, tourists. **3.** m. a sightseer, tourist.

सैलाब *sailāb* [P. *sailāb*], m. see s.v. सैल.

सैलाबी *sailābī* [P. *sailābī*], adj. **1.** pertaining to a flood. **2.** liable to be flooded (land). — ~ पानी, m. flood-water.

[1]**सों** *soṁ* [*sama-*[1]], ppn. Brbh. = से.

[2]**सों** *soṁ*, f. Brbh. = [1]सौं.

[3]**सों** *soṁ*, adj. particle. Brbh. = सा.

सोंटा *soṁṭā* [**śoṭṭha-*[2]], m. **1.** a club. **2.** a staff. **3.** a pestle. — ~ चलाना, to wield a club; to beat. ~ जमाना (पर), to beat. सोंटे पड़ना, sticks to fall (on, पर): to be soundly beaten. — सोंटा-राय, m. king of clubs: a burly man.

सोंठ *soṁṭh* [**soṇṭhi-*], f. **1.** dry ginger. **2.** fig. a miser, niggard. — ~ हो जाना, colloq. to dry up, to remain silent. – सोंठ-पनजीरी, f. a drink made with dry ginger (given to women after childbirth). सोंठ-पानी, m. *Pl.* a mixture of dried ginger, cumin, &c. (used as a digestive). सोंठ-राय, m. = सोंठू-राय.

सोंठू *soṁṭhū* [cf. H. *soṁṭh*], m. a miserly person. — सोंठू-राय, m. a prince of misers, skinflint.

सोंठोड़ा *soṁṭhoṛā* [**śoṇṭhī-*+*vaṭa-*[3]], m. balls of molasses and flour with ginger (eaten by women after childbirth).

सोंठौरा *soṁṭhaurā* [**śoṇṭhi-*+*pūra-*], m. a preparation of semolina flour with ginger (given to women after childbirth: = पनजीरी).

सोंधी *sondhī* [*sugandhi-*], f. reg. a good-quality fragrant rice grown in swampy ground.

[1]**सो** *so* [*sa*], pron. & adv. **1.** pron. chiefly obs. or reg. = वह. जो हो, ~ हो, what is to be must be. **2.** adv. thus, therefore, hence. **3.** conj. then, next. **4.** (introducing a remark) now, well.

[2]**सो** *so*, ppn. Brbh. = सौं.

सोअर *soar*, m. = [2]सोहर.

सोआ *soā* [*śatatama-*[2]], m. **1.** dill. **2.** fennel.

सोइ *soi*, pron. & adj. Brh. = वही (वह+ही).

सोक *sok*, m. reg. (W.) hole(s) made in a bedframe (for the stringing); gap(s) between the strings.

सोकना *soknā*, v.t. 19c. = सोखना.

सोखना *sokhnā* [ad. *śoṣayati*], v.t. **1.** to soak up. **2.** to drink or to suck up. **3.** to dry out, to drain (wet land).

सोख़्ता *sokhtā* [P. *sokhta*], adj. & m. chiefly U. **1.** burnt, scorched. **2.** suffering pangs (esp. of love); grieving. **3.** m. tinder. ***4.** blotting paper.

सोग *sog* [ad. *śoka-*], m. = शोक.

सोगी *sogī* [cf. H. *sog*], adj. & m. **1.** adj. sad; distressed. **2.** m. one who is distressed.

सोच *soc* [cf. H. *socnā*], m. **1.** thought, reflection. 2. concern. **3.** Av. sorrow, grief; regret. — ~ करना, to feel concern, or grief, &c. ~ में पड़ना, to fall into thought. ~ में रहना, to be absorbed in thought. यह ~ की बात है कि..., it is a matter for reflection, or concern, that .... – सोच-विचार, m. reflection, consideration (of a matter); discretion: caution, care. सोच-विचार करना, to take thought, or care, &c. सोच-विचार लेना, to take thought.

सोचना *socnā* [*śocyate*], v.t. **1.** to think, to reflect. **2.** to think out, to devise. **3.** to think anxiously, to feel concern. **4.** Av. to grieve. — उसने सोचा कि ..., he thought that .... उसने एक तजवीज़ सोची है, he thought out a scheme. – सोचना-विचारना, = सोचना, 1. सोचना-समझना, to think with due care. सोच-समझकर बात करना, to speak prudently, to mind one's words.

सोज़ *soz* [P. *soz*], m. U. **1.** burning. **2.** ardour. **3.** stanza of a *marsiyā* or elegy. — सोज़े वतन, m. patriotic lament for one's country (India): title of a collection of short stories by Premcand.

सोज़न *sozan* [P. *sozan*], m. **1.** needle. **2.** fig. Brbh. a stabbing pain. **3.** 19c. an embroidered coverlet: covering, shelter. — सोज़नकारी, f. needlework.

सोज़िश *soziś* [P. *soziś*], f. burning: inflammation.

सोझा *sojhā* [*śodhya-*], adj. E.H. **1.** straight, direct. **2.** straightforward (in nature). **3.** reg. right, true, accurate.

सोझाई *sojhāī* [cf. H. *sojhā*], f. reg. straightness, directness, &c.

[1]**सोटा** *soṭā*, m. = सोंटा.

[2]**सोटा** *soṭā* [H. *sūā*+H. *-ṭā*], m. Av. a (partic.) parrot.

सोत *sot*, m. = सोता.

सोता *sotā* [**srotra-*: Pk. *sotta-*], m. **1.** a spring. **2.** a stream. **3.** branch of a river.

[1]**सोती** *sotī* [cf. H. *sotā*], f. **1.** small spring, or stream. **2.** Av. stream, flow (of a river).

[2]**सोती** *sotī*, f. Brbh. = स्वाति.

सोधना *sodhnā* [ad. *śodhayati*: w. H. *śodh*], v.t. **1.** to cleanse, to purify. **2.** to refine. **3.** to clear of error, to correct. **4.** to investigate, to scrutinise. **5.** Brbh. Av. to search (for); to determine (an auspicious date). **6.** to pay off (a debt).

सोधी *sodhī* [cf. H. *śodh*], m. E.H. a searcher; God (as seeking out his devotees).

सोन *son*, m. a kind of water-bird (? bar-headed goose).

सोन- *son-*. gold: — सोन-केला, m. a partic. type of banana. सोन-जूही, f. a yellow jasmine.

सोनहरा *sonahrā*, adj. = सुनहरा.

सोनहला *sonahlā*, adj. = सुनहला.

[1]**सोना** *sonā* [*suvarṇa-*, or *sauvarṇa-*], m. **1.** gold. **2.** fig. sthg. precious. — सोने का, adj. of gold; golden; precious. सोने का कौर, m. a tasty morsel; delicate food. सोने का घर मिट्टी करना, fig. to squander one's wealth. सोने का निवाला, m. = सोने का कौर; fig. a costly banquet. सोने का पानी, m. gilding. सोने की चिड़िया, f. golden bird: a rich person; a fat prize. सोने में सुगंध, m. fragrance along with gold: an extra virtue. – सोना-चाँदी, f. gold and silver; riches. सोना-मक्खी, f. (*Pl.*) *HŚS*. = next. सोना-माखी, f. *HŚS*. iron or copper pyrites.

[2]**सोना** *sonā* [*svapati*, and **supati*: Pa. *supati*], v.i. **1.** to sleep; to lie down. **2.** to die. **3.** to cohabit (with, के साथ). **4.** to lose feeling, to go to sleep (a limb). — सोने का कमरा, m. bedroom. सोने चलें, let's go to bed. सो जाने से पहले, adv. before going to sleep; before going to bed. वह सो गया, he fell asleep; = next. वह सोने गया, he went to bed (intending to sleep). – सो-सोकर उठना, to keep waking from sleep; to doze intermittently.

सोनार *sonār*, m. = सुनार.

सोनारिन *sonārin*, f. = सुनारिन.

[1]**सोनी** *sonī*, f. pronun. var. a broom (= सोहनी).

[2]**सोनी** *sonī* [? cf. H. [1]*sonā*], m. Brbh. a goldsmith.

सोपान *sopān* [S.], m. **1.** stairs, steps; stairway. **2.** fig. pathway, ascent.

सोफ़ता *softā* [conn. H. *subhītā*], m. **1.** opportune moment; leisure. **2.** recovery (from sickness). — सोफ़ते में, adv. at a suitable moment.

सोभ- *sobh-* [ad. *śobhate*], v.i. Brbh. – [1]सोहना.

सोम *som* [S.], m. **1.** a partic. plant, the fermented juice of which was drunk at Vedic sacrifices, and offered to the gods. **2.** *mythol.* a beverage of the gods. **3.** a Vedic deity (= ~, 1. personified). **4.** the moon. **5.** Monday. — **सोम-जाजी** [*-yājñika-*], m. Brbh. officiant at a soma-offering. **सोमनाथ**, m. soma's lord: name of a particularly venerated liṅga of Śiva; name of the temple in Kāṭhiāwāṛ where this was set up. **सोम-यज्ञ**, m. a soma-offering. **सोमवती**, f. a Monday coinciding with the last day of a dark fortnight (celebrated as a festival and bathing-day). **सोम-वल्ली**, f. *Pl. HŚS.* name of several plants incl. a creeper called *giloy*, and a form of caraway. **सोमवार**, m. Monday. **°ई**, adj. & f. held on a Monday (as a bazaar); falling on a Monday; = **सोमवती**.

सोयन *soyan* [**sūtinī-*], f. *Pl.* a brood-mare.

सोया *soyā*, m. = **सोआ**.

सोरठ *soraṭh* [*saurāṣṭra-*], m. f. *mus.* name of a *rāg*; name of a *rāgiṇī*.

सोरठा *sorṭhā* [*saurāṣṭra-*], m. name of a Hindi metre (a couplet in which the first half-lines contain eleven *mātrās* or metrical instants, and rhyme, and the second half-lines thirteen *mātrās*).

सोरनी *sornī* [conn. **śodhakara-*], f. **1.** a broom. **2.** a rite performed on the third day after a death, when the ashes of the deceased person are collected and thrown into a river, or other water.

सोरही *sorhī* [cf. H. *solah*], f. *Pl. HŚS.* **1.** reg. Bihar. a measure of grain equalling sixteen head-loads. **2.** a gambling game played with sixteen cowrie shells.

सोरी *sorī*, f. *Pl.* a small hole (in a vessel); an eyelet, a vent.

सोलह *solah* [*ṣoḍaśa-*], adj. sixteen. — **~ ~ गंडे सुनाना**, to abuse (one, **को**) roundly. **~ सिंगार**, m. all sixteen (traditional) adornments: elaborate make-up (of a woman). **~**, or **सोलहों**, **आने**, adv. all sixteen annas (of a rupee): wholly, completely. **~ आने ठीक**, or **सही**, completely correct.

सोलही *solāhī* [cf. H. *solah*], f. *Pl. HŚS.* **1.** having sixteen parts or units (as a game played with cowries). **2.** funeral feast held on the sixteenth day after a death.

सोला *solā*, m. a bush, *Aeschynomene aspera*, found in watery places (source of a pith).

सोवत *sovat* [cf. H. [2]*sonā*], f. reg. the state of sleeping.

सोसन *sosan* [P. *sosan*], f. U. the lily; the iris. — **गुल ~**, f. pansy.

सोसनी *sosnī* [cf. H. *sosan*], adj. Brbh. iris-coloured, purple.

सोह *soh* [*śobhā-*], f. **1.** *Pl.* beauty, elegance. **2.** decoration, fine attire.

[1]**सोहन** *sohan* [*śobhana-*], adj. & m. **1.** adj. beautiful; handsome; charming. **2.** m. a lover. **3.** a kind of *halvā*, q.v.

[2]**सोहन** *sohan* [*śodhana-*, Pk. *sohaṇī-*], m. reg. (Bihar) **1.** a file. **2.** a paring implement.

[1]**सोहना** *sohnā* [*śobhate*], v.i. **1.** to shine; to be splendid; to look well or beautiful. **2.** to set off, to enhance the beauty, &c. (of, **को**). **3.** to be seen, to do credit (to, **को**).

[2]**सोहना** *sohnā* [*śodhayati*], v.t. reg. to clear, to weed.

सोहनी *sohnī* [*śodhanī-*; or cf. H. [2]*sohnā*], f. **1.** a broom. **2.** reg. Bihar. weeding, clearing.

सोहबत *sohbat* [A. *ṣuḥba*: P. *ṣŏḥbat*], f. **1.** companionship, company; association. **2.** cohabitation. — **~ उठाना**, to keep (good) company. **~ करना**, to keep company (with); to cohabit with.

[1]**सोहर** *sohar* [cf. *śobhā-*] m. **1.** auspicious song sung by the women of a household on the birth of a son. **2.** song of praise or welcome, auspicious song. **3.** Av. marriage song.

[2]**सोहर** *sohar* [**sūtighara-* or **sūtakāghara-*], m. delivery-room (= [1]**सौरी**).

सोहरा *sohrā* [*śobhā-*], adj. E.H. good, auspicious.

सोहला *sohlā*, m. = [1]**सोहर**.

सोहाग *sohāg*, m. 1. = **सुहाग**. **2.** Brbh. a marriage song. 3. = **सुहागा**.

[1]**सोहागा** *sohāgā*, m. = **सुहागा**.

[2]**सोहागा** *sohāgā* [? cf. *śodha-*], m. reg. (W.) a plank-harrow.

सोहागिन *sohāgin*, f. = **सुहागिन**.

सोहाना *sohānā* [H. [2]*suhānā*; × *śobhā-*], v.i. reg. **1.** to be pleasing. **2.** to be beautiful.

सोहारी *sohārī* [**śobhāhāra-*], f. Brbh. Av. a partic. kind of bread-cake fried in *ghī*.

सोहावन *sohāvan*, adj. = **सुहावना**.

सोहावना *sohāvnā*, adj. = **सुहावना**.

सोदर *sôdar* [S.], adj. & m. **1.** adj. uterine. **2.** m. a full brother.

सोदरा *sôdrā* [S.], f. a full sister (see **सोदर**).

[1]**सौं** *sauṁ* [*sama-*[1]], ppn. Brbh. = **से**.

[2]**सौं** *sauṁ*, f. Brbh. = [1]**सौंह**.

[3]**सौं** *sauṁ*, adj. encl. = **-सा**.

सौंदन *saum̐dan* [cf. H. *saum̐dnā*], f. soaking (washing) in an alkali.

सौंदना *saum̐dnā*, v.t. pronun. var. = ²सौंधना.

सौंदर्य *saundaryă* [S.], m. beauty.

सौंध *saum̐dh* [*sugandha-*], f. = सौंधाहट.

¹**सौंधना** *saum̐dhnā* [cf. H. *saum̐dh*], v.i. to be fragrant.

²**सौंधना** *saum̐dhnā* [**samuddadhāti*], v.i. **1.** to rub, to smear; to rub (cloth) with an alkali, or with mud, before washing it; to soak in alkali (washing). **2.** to be tainted, affected (by, से: as by greed). **3.** to mash, to mix; to knead.

सौंधापन *saum̐dhāpan* [cf. H. ¹*saum̐dhnā*], m. = सौंधाहट.

सौंधाहट *saum̐dhāhaṭ* [cf. H. ¹*saum̐dhnā*], f. **1.** fragrance. **2.** specif. the smell of dry earth, or fresh earthenware. **3.** the smell of parched gram, or fried potatoes, &c.

सौंधी *saundhī* [cf. H. ²*saum̐dhnā*], f. *Pl.* an alkali in which clothes are steeped before washing them (= रेह).

सौंप *saum̐p* [cf. H. *saum̐pnā*], f. charge, keeping; custody.

सौंपना *saum̐pnā* [*samarpayati*], v.t. **1.** to hand over, to entrust. **2.** to deposit (with, को). **3.** to hand over (as to police). **4.** to hand over, to give up (sthg).

सौंफ *saum̐ph* [*śatapuṣpa-*], f. **1.** fennel. **2.** aniseed. — ~ का अरक़, m. fennel water.

सौंरा *saum̐rā* [*śyāmala-*], m. *Pl. HŚS.* anything black; soot.

¹**सौंह** *saum̐h* [*śapatha-*], f. an oath. — ~ कहना, or खाना, to swear an oath (by, की). ~ खिलाना (को), to administer an oath (to); to adjure. ~ देना (को), to administer an oath (to). तुमहि ~, adv. Brbh. I swear to you.

²**सौंह** *saum̐h* [*sam̐mukha-*], adv. Brbh. Av. = सामने.

¹**सौ** *sau* [*śata-*], adj. **1.** a hundred. **2.** fig. a large number (of), much, many. — ~ की एक कहना, to say something succinctly, or trenchantly. ~ की सीधी बात कहना, id. ~ के सवाए, m. pl. twenty-five per cent. ~ जान से, adv. with a hundred lives: with all one's heart, intensely, utterly. ~ पर ~, adv. a hundred per cent: entirely. ~ बात, f. euph. cursing. ~ में एक, adv. one in a hundred (i.e. rare, or unique); very little. ~ सिर का, adj. having a hundred heads (and hence able to lose one or more): persistent in a risky enterprise; obstinate. ~ ~ घड़े पानी पड़ना, fig. to be highly embarrassed. ~ हाथ का कलेजा होना, the vital (spirit) to be vast, or abundant: to be radiant (with joy); to be vastly generous. ~ हाथ की ज़बान होना, to have a long tongue, to be garrulous. एक ~ एक, adj. a hundred and one. एक ~ एकवाँ, adj. hundred and first. एक ~ दोवाँ, adj. hundred and second.

²**सौ** *sau*, ppn. Brbh. = ¹ ³सौं.

सौकन *saukan* [cf. *sapatnī-*; Pk. *savakkī-*], f. a co-wife.

सौकर्य *saukaryă* [S.], m. ease (of accomplishment).

सौकुमार्य *saukumāryă* [S.], m. tenderness, delicateness.

सौख्य *saukhyă* [S.], m. state of happiness, or comfort.

सौगंद *saugand* [P. *saugand*], f. an oath, solemn oath. — ~ खाना, or धरना, to swear an oath. ~ देना (को), to administer an oath (to). ~ से कहना, to declare on oath. सच तुमको ~, (I) swear to you.

¹**सौगंध** *saugandh* [S.], adj. & m. **1.** adj. fragrant, scented. **2.** m. fragrance, perfume.

²**सौगंध** *saugandh*, f. corr. = सौगंद.

सौगंधिक *saugandhik* [S.], adj. fragrant.

सौगंध्य *saugandhyă* [S.], m. = ¹सौगंध, 2.

सौग़ात *saugāt* [P. *saugāt*], f. a present given on returning from a journey, a special gift.

सौग़ाती *saugātī* [P. *saugātī*], adj. **1.** suitable as a present. **2.** given as a present.

सौचेती *saucetī* [cf. H. *sucet*], f. *Pl.* alertness; guarding.

सौजन्य *saujanyă* [S.], m. **1.** goodness, kindness; generosity. **2.** magnanimity. **3.** urbanity; courtesy.

सौजा *saujā* [**śvāpadya-*], m. Brbh. Av. game (to be hunted).

सौत *saut* [*sapatnī-*], f. a co-wife; a rival.

सौतन *sautan* [cf. *sapatnī-*], f. Brbh. = सौत.

सौतनि *sautani* [cf. *sapatnī-*], f. Brbh. = सौत.

सौतपन *sautpan* [cf. H. *saut*], m. **1.** state or position of a co-wife. **2.** rivalry or jealousy of co-wives.

सौतापा *sautāpā*, m. = सौतपन.

सौति *sauti*, f. Brbh. = सौत.

सौतिया *sautiyā* [cf. H. *saut*], adj. having to do with a co-wife. — ~ झाल, f. = next. ~ डाह, f. jealousy or malice of a co-wife.

सौतेला *sautelā* [cf. H. *saut*], adj. **1.** having to do with a co-wife. **2.** half-, step-. — **~ बाप**, m. stepfather. **सौतेली बहन**, f. half-sister. **सौतेली माँ**, f. stepmother.

सौदा *saudā* [P. *saudā*], m. **1.** goods, wares. **2.** trade; marketing; shopping. **3.** a transaction, deal. **4.** a purchase; day-to-day purchase. **4.** fruits, sweets. — **~ करना**, to trade (with, **से**); to strike a bargain, to agree a price; to purchase. **~ करने जाना**, to go shopping. **~ चुकना**, **पटना**, or **बनना**, a bargain to be struck, a deal to be settled. **~ बनाना**, to strike a bargain. – **सौदाकारी**, f. trading; bargaining. **सौदा-सुलुफ़** [A. -*salaf*], m. trade; goods; purchases. **सौदेबाज़** [P. -*bāz*], m. a haggler, &c. (see next). **सौदेबाज़ी** [P. -*bāzī*], f. haggling; playing a market, speculation.

सौदागर *saudāgar* [P. *saudāgar*], m. a trader; a merchant.

सौदागरी *saudāgărī* [P. *saudāgarī*], adj. & f. **1.** adj. commercial, mercantile. ***2.** f. trade, commerce; the business of a merchant. — **~ करना**, to trade (in, **की**).

सौदामिनी *saudāminī* [S.], f. lightning.

सौध *saudh* [S.], m. stuccoed, whitewashed: a palace.

सौन *saun* [*śakuna-*], m. Brbh. a good omen; an omen. — **~ अपसौन**, or **कुसौन**, **हो-**, an omen to prove a bad one: to meet with an unlucky omen.

सौनक *saunak* [ad. *śaunika-*], m. Brbh. a hunter; butcher.

सौभागिनी *saubhāginī* [ad. *saubhāgyinī-*], adj. f. Brbh. Av. fortunate, &c. (see **सौभाग्य**).

सौभागी *saubhāgī* [cf. H. *saubhāgya*, *saubhāginī*], adj. fortunate.

सौभाग्य *saubhāgyă* [S.], m. **1.** good fortune. **2.** fortunate or blessed state. **3.** specif. happy state of a married woman. — **सौभाग्यवती**, adj. f. & f. = °**वान**; a woman whose husband is alive (esp. if she has children). **सौभाग्यवश**, adv. by good fortune. **सौभाग्यवान**, adj. fortunate; blessed. **सौभाग्यशाली**, adj. id.

सौमनस *saumanas* [S.], adj. & m. **1.** adj. made of flowers. **2.** agreeable, pleasing. **3.** m. Brbh. happiness, comfort.

सौमित्र *saumitr* [S.], m. Av. friendship: a title of Lakṣmaṇ (the son of Sumitrā).

सौम्य *saumyă* [S.], adj. having to do with *soma*, or with the moon: placid, mild.

¹सौर *saur* [S.], adj. & m. **1.** adj. solar. **2.** sacred to the sun. **3.** m. *mythol.* the planet Saturn (regarded as a son of the sun). — **~ मास**, m. a solar month.

²सौर *saur* [**sūtighara-* or **sūtakāghara-*], m. delivery room; lying-in room (= **¹सौरी**).

³सौर *saur* [**svāpapaṭa-*], f. a coverlet or quilt.

⁴सौर *saur* [*śakula-*], m. *Pl.* a kind of fish.

सौरभ *saurabh* [ad. *saurabh(y)a-*], m. **1.** fragrance. **2.** saffron. — **सौरभवाह**, m. fragrance-wafter: the wind.

सौराती *saurātī*, adj. pronun. var. = **सौराथी**.

सौराथ *saurāth* [? ad. *svārtha-*], m. reg. **1.** selfishness; greed. **2.** ambition.

सौराथी *saurāthī* [cf. H. *saurāth*], adj. reg. selfish, &c.

¹सौरी *saurī* [**sūtighara-*, or **sūtakāghara-*], f. labour room, lying-in room. — **~ कमाना**, to attend to a woman in childbirth.

²सौरी *saurī* [*śakula-*], f. Brbh. 19c. a species of carp.

सौर्य *sauryă* [S.], adj. solar.

सौवर्ण *sauvarṇ* [S.], adj. & m. **1.** adj. golden. **2.** m. gold.

सौष्ठव *sauṣṭhav* [S.], m. excellence; aptness; effectiveness (of language).

सौहरा *sauhrā* [*śvaśura-*], m. **1.** father-in-law. **2.** a term of abuse.

सौहार्द *sauhārd* [S.], m. affection, friendliness; friendship.

सौहार्द्य *sauhārdyă* [S.], m. = **सौहार्द**.

सौहृद *sauhṛd* [S.], m. 1. = **सौहार्द**. **2.** a friend.

स्कंद *skand* [S.], m. *mythol.* a name of Kārttikeya (a son of Śiva and Pārvatī, regarded as the god of war).

स्कंदित *skandit* [S.], adj. Brbh. fallen to the ground, ejaculated.

स्कंध *skandh* [S.], m. **1.** the shoulder. **2.** trunk (of a tree); large branch. **3.** branch, division; section, part (of a book); canto. **4.** *philos.* an object of sense.

स्कूली *skūlī* [cf. H. *skūl* 'school'], adj. having to do with school.

स्खलन *skhalan* [S.], m. stumbling: a fall, etc. (see **स्खलित**).

स्खलित *skhalit* [S.], adj. stumbling: **1.** marred, defective; corrupt (as a manuscript reading). **2.** erring (from the right course). **3.** discharged (semen).

स्टेशन *sṭeśan* [Engl. *station*], m. **1.** railway station. **2.** station, base (any civil or military facility). **3.** a hill station. **4.** a broadcasting station. — ~ पर, adv. at the station. – स्टेशन-मास्टर, stationmaster.

स्तंभ *stambh* [S.], m. **1.** a pillar, column; post. **2.** fig. prop, support. **3.** column (of or in a newspaper). **4.** paralysis, transfixation (as from fear); numbness.

स्तंभक *stambhak* [S.], adj. **1.** checking, restraining. **2.** invigorating; astringent.

स्तंभन *stambhan* [S.], m. **1.** propping, supporting. **2.** bringing to a stop, checking. **3.** paralysing (as with fear); numbing.

स्तंभित *stambhit* [S.], adj. **1.** propped, supported. **2.** standing stock-still (as in fear); benumbed, paralysed; astounded.

स्तन *stan* [S.], m. **1.** breast (of a woman). **2.** nipple; teat. — ~ पिलाना, to feed (a baby: को) from the breast. ~ पीना, to suck the breast. – स्तनधारी, adj. & m. mammalian; mammal. स्तनपायी, adj. & m. milk-drinking, = prec.

स्तब्ध *stabdh* [S.], adj. fixed, firm: **1.** brought to a standstill, motionless; inert. **2.** numb, insensible; dumbfounded. **3.** dull, oppressive (as a silence, a mood).

स्तर *star* [S.], m. a level, or grade.

स्तरीय *starīyă* [S.], adj. pertaining to a partic. level or grade.

स्तव *stav* [S.], m. **1.** praising, hymning. **2.** hymn; eulogy.

स्तवक *stavak* [S.], adj. & m. **1.** adj. praising; eulogistic. **2.** a bunch of flowers. **3.** fig. section (of a book).

स्तवन *stavan* [S.], m. praising; praise.

-स्तान *-stān* [P. *-stān*], noun formant (prefixed by *-i-* when following a consonant). chiefly U. place: — अफ़ग़ानिस्तान, m. Afghanistan. इंग्लिस्तान, m. England. हिंदुस्तान [P. *hindū-*], m. India.

स्तावक *stāvak* [S.], adj. & m. *Pl. HŚS.* **1.** adj. praising. **2.** m. a eulogist; flatterer.

स्तिमित *stimit* [S.], adj. poet. calm, tranquil (glance).

स्तुत *stut* [S.], adj. praised, celebrated, eulogised.

स्तुति *stuti* [S.], f. **1.** praise (devout, or lavish); celebration, eulogy. **2.** a song or hymn of praise. — ~ करना, to lavish praises (on, की). ~ गाना, to sing the praises (of, की). – स्तुति-गान, m. = ~, 2. स्तुतिवादक, m. panegyrist.

स्तेन *sten* [S.], m. *Pl. HŚS.* a thief, robber.

स्तेय *stey* [S.], m. *Pl. HŚS.* **1.** theft. **2.** anything stolen.

स्तोता *stotā* [S.], m. inv. praiser; panegyrist.

स्तोम *stom* [S.], m. quantity, mass.

स्त्री *strī* [S.], f. **1.** a woman. **2.** a wife. — स्त्रीगमन, m. going to a woman: sexual intercourse of a man with a woman. स्त्रीजाति, f. womankind, the female sex. स्त्रीजित, adj. Brbh. dominated or captivated by a woman. स्त्रीधन, m. a wife's personal property (esp. that given to her on her marriage). स्त्रीधर्म, m. the duties or obligations of a woman, or a wife. स्त्री-धर्म से होना, euph. to be menstruating. स्त्री-पुरुष, m. pl. men and women, people. स्त्रीप्रसंग, m. sexual intercourse of a man with a woman. स्त्रिरोग-विज्ञान, m. gynaecology. स्त्री-व्रत, m. vow (of faithfulness) to (one's) wife. स्त्रीलिंग, m. the female genitalia; *gram.* feminine gender. स्त्री-वर्ग, m. = स्त्री-जाति. स्त्री-संभोग, m. enjoyment of a woman: = स्त्रीगमन. स्त्रीसमागम, m. = स्त्री-गमन.

स्त्रीत्व *strītvă* [S.], m. **1.** womanhood. **2.** womanliness. **3.** *gram.* feminine gender.

स्त्रैण *strain* [S.], adj. **1.** having to do with or characteristic of women; female; feminine. **2.** dominated by (one's) wife, or by women.

स्थगन *sthagan* [S.], m. postponement, deferment; adjournment.

स्थगित *sthagit* [S.], adj. postponed, deferred; adjourned. — ~ करना, to postpone.

स्थल *sthal* [S.], m. **1.** firm ground; dry land; terrain. **2.** place; site; place of residence. **3.** region. **4.** place, or passage (in a book). **5.** point, topic (from within a body of material). **6.** occasion. — स्थल-फ़ौज, f. = स्थल-सेना. स्थल-मार्ग से, adv. by land, overland. स्थल-सेना, f. army, land force (as opposed to navy, air force).

स्थली *sthalī* [S.], f. place, locality; secluded spot.

स्थलीय *sthalīyă* [S.], adj. having to do with dry land; fought on land (a battle).

स्थान *sthān* [S.], m. **1.** place. **2.** particular place: locality; situation; site; house, place. **3.** position, post, appointment, place. **4.** station, position, rank. उनमें उनका ~ ऊँचा है, he is of high standing among them. — ~ पर रखना, to substitute (for, के), to replace with. – स्थानस्थ, adj. remaining in one place; local. स्थानांतर [°*na*+*a*°], m. another place. °अण [°*na*+*a*°], m. shifting to another place; a move (to a new locality); a transfer; evacuation. °आंतरित [°*na*+*a*°], adj. shifted, &c. स्थानापन्न [°*na*+*ā*°], adj. & m. substituting (in another's position); temporary; officiating; one serving as a substitute.

स्थानिक *sthānik* [S.], adj. & m. **1.** adj. = स्थानीय. **2.** m. *HŚS.* local incumbent (post-holder).

स्थानी *sthānī* [S.], adj. **1.** having a position or post. **2.** abiding, permanent; resident.

स्थानीय *sthānīyă* [S.], adj. pertaining to a partic. place, local.

स्थानीयता *sthānīyătā* [S.], f. local character or identity.

स्थापत्य *sthāpatyă* [S.], m. architecture; architectural style.

स्थापन *sthāpan* [S.], m. the act of establishing, &c. (see स्थापित).

स्थापना *sthāpănā* [S.], f. **1.** erection. ***2.** establishment, &c. (see स्थापित). **3.** establishing (of a fact, a case). **4.** presentation (of a drama). — ~ करना, to establish, &c.

स्थापना *sthāpnā* [ad. *sthāpayati*: w. H. [2]*thāpnā*], v.t. to place, to set up, to erect; to establish.

स्थापनीय *sthāpănīyă* [S.], adj. worth establishing, &c. (see स्थापित).

स्थापित *sthāpit* [S.], adj. **1.** fixed, placed; erected (as a monument). **2.** established, founded (as an institution); instituted (procedure); formed, set up (a group). **3.** established (a fact, a proposition). — ~ करना, to erect; to establish, &c.

स्थाप्य *sthāpyă* [S.], adj. to be established, &c. (see स्थापित).

स्थायित्व *sthāyitvă* [S.], m. permanence, stability, &c. (see स्थायी).

स्थायी *sthāyī* [S.], adj. **1.** continuing, permanent (as a post, or any situation); standing (committee). **2.** lasting, enduring (as a culture, &c). **3.** constant, regular (in attendance). **4.** firm, secure, well-based, stable. **5.** *rhet.* permanent, inherent (a quality). — ~ रूप से, adv. permanently. – स्थायीकरण, m. confirmation (as in a post); making (sthg.) permanent; stabilisation.

स्थायीकरण *sthāyīkaraṇ* [S.], m. see s.v. स्थायी.

स्थावर *sthāvar* [S.], adj. & m. **1.** adj. fixed, immovable (esp. real estate). **2.** m. real estate.

स्थित *sthit* [S.], adj. **1.** (also -स्थित.) situated (in, at, में, पर). **2.** placed, fixed. **3.** resting, remaining. **4.** immovable; fig. insistent (on, पर). — स्थितप्रज्ञ, adj. calm, unperturbed.

स्थिति *sthiti* [S.], f. **1.** state, situation (as of affairs); circumstances. **2.** state, condition (of a partic. thing or person). **3.** position. **4.** place of residence. — विशेष ~ में, adv. in special circumstances. – स्थितिशील [? f. H. *gatiśīl*], adj. static.

स्थिर *sthir* [S.], adj. **1.** fixed, firm; unmoving; stable; at rest (water). **2.** immovable. ~ संपत्ति, f. real assets or estate. **3.** lasting, enduring (fame, &c). **4.** unchanging, constant; steadfast. **5.** decided, determined (a matter). **6.** calm, equable (of temperament). — ~ करना, to decide, to determine. ~ जानना, to know for certain, to be assured (of). – स्थिरचित्त, adj. having a resolute mind; steady; calm, sedate (of temperament). स्थिरात्मा [°*ra*+*ā*°], adj. inv. = prec., 1., 2.

स्थिरता *sthirătā* [S.], f. **1.** fixity, immobility; stability. **2.** constancy, &c. (see स्थिर). **3.** calmness, equability. **4.** rest, inertia.

स्थूणा *sthūṇā* [S.], f. *Pl. HŚS.* a pillar.

स्थूल *sthūl* [S.], adj. **1.** bulky, fat. **2.** gross, coarse; undifferentiated; outward, apparent. **3.** crude, rough (of an estimate). **4.** gross (of amount). **5.** dense, stupid. **6.** *philos.* tangible, material (as opposed to *sūkṣma*, subtle). — स्थूलकाय, adj. bulky of build; fat. स्थूलबुद्धि, adj. dull-witted.

स्थूलता *sthūlătā* [S.], f. stoutness, &c. (see स्थूल).

स्थैर्य *sthairyă* [S.], m. = स्थिरता.

स्नात *snāt* [S.], adj. bathed.

स्नातक *snātak* [S.], m. **1.** a brāhmaṇ student who has completed and been ceremonially discharged from a traditional course of study under a guru. **2.** a graduate. — स्नातकोत्तर [°*ka*+*u*°], adj. & m. postgraduate; a postgraduate student. पूर्व-स्नातक, m. an undergraduate.

स्नातकीय *snātăkīyă* [S.], adj. characteristic of, or proper to, a graduate.

स्नातिका *snātikā* [S.], f. a woman graduate.

स्नान *snān* [S.], m. bathing, washing. — ~ करना, to bathe.

स्नानीय *snānīyă* [S.], adj. **1.** to be bathed. **2.** *Pl. HŚS.* for use in bathing.

स्नायविक *snāyăvik* [S.], adj. having to do with the nerves.

स्नायु *snāyu* [S.], f. (m. *Pl.*) **1.** sinew, tendon. **2.** muscle. **3.** nerve.

स्निग्ध *snigdh* [S.], adj. affectionate; dear.

स्नेह *sneh* [S.], m. **1.** oiliness; oily substance; grease, fat. ***2.** love; affection; kindness. — ~ **जोड़ना,** to form an attachment (with, **से**); to fall mutually in love. – **स्नेहमय,** adj. loving, affectionate; tender. **स्नेहालिंगन** [°*ha*+*ā*°], m. loving embrace.

स्नेहालु *snehālu* [S.], adj. loving.

स्नेहिल *snehil* [S.], adj. affectionate.

स्नेही *snehī* [S.], adj. & m. **1.** adj. loving, affectionate; kind. **2.** unctuous. **3.** m. a devoted friend; a lover.

स्नेह्य *snehyă* [S.], adj. lovable.

स्पंदन *spandan* [S.], m. **1.** trembling; quivering. **2.** throbbing, beating. **3.** vibrating, pulsating.

स्पंदित *spandit* [S.], adj. trembling, a-tremble, &c. (see **स्पंदन**).

स्पर्धा *spardhā* [S.], f. sense of rivalry, competition; envy. ~ **करना,** to compete, to contend (with, **से**).

स्पर्धी *spardhī* [S.], adj. rivalrous, competitive.

स्पर्श *sparś* [S.], m. **1.** touching; a touch. **2.** touch, feel (the sense). **3.** *ling.* contact: descriptive title of the four series (*varga*) of Indian plosive consonants together with the single series of nasal consonants, as analysed originally in Sanskrit. **4.** contact; *astron.* contact of planetary shadow with sphere of sun or moon at onset of an eclipse. **5.** touchability, non-defiling quality. — ~ **करना (का),** to touch. – **स्पर्श-जन्य,** adj. contagious. **स्पर्श-मणि,** f. touchstone (= **कसौटी**). **स्पर्श-रेखा,** f. *math.* tangent. **स्पर्श-रोग,** m. a contagious disease. **स्पर्श-संघर्षी,** adj. *ling.* affricate. **स्पर्शेंद्रिय** [°*śa*+*i*°], m. the sense of touch; the organ of touch, skin.

स्पर्शन *sparśan* [S.], m. **1.** touching, feeling. **2.** touch (the sense).

स्पर्शनीय *sparśănīyă* [S.], adj. **1.** tangible. **2.** perceptible.

-स्पर्शी *-sparśī* [S.], adj. touching; fig. reaching to, moving. e.g. **मर्मस्पर्शी,** adj. touching the vitals, causing a pang.

स्पष्ट *spaṣṭ* [S.], adj. **1.** clear; distinct. **2.** intelligible (as language, wording, thought). — ~ **करना,** to make clear, to explain. ~ **रूप से,** adv. clearly; distinctly. – **स्पष्टतः,** adv. = prec. **स्पष्टतया,** adv. id. **स्पष्टवादिता,** f. clear speaking, frankness in speech. °**-वादी,** adj. **स्पष्टीकरण** m. clarification, explanation. °**-कृत,** adj. clarified, &c.

स्पष्टता *spaṣṭătā* [S.], f. **1.** clearness, clarity; distinctness. **2.** intelligibility (as of language).

स्पष्टीकरण *spaṣṭīkaraṇ* [S.], m. see s.v. **स्पष्ट**.

स्पष्टीकृत *spaṣṭīkr̥t* [S.], adj. see s.v. **स्पष्ट**.

स्पृश्य *spr̥śyă* [S.], adj. = **स्पर्शनीय**.

स्पृष्ट *spr̥ṣṭ* [S.], adj. & m. **1.** adj. touched. **2.** *ling.* the plosive and nasal consonants (see **स्पर्श**, 3).

स्पृहणीय *spr̥hăṇīyă* [S.], adj. desirable.

स्पृहा *spr̥hā* [S.], f. eager desire, ambition.

स्पृही *spr̥hī* [S.], adj. eagerly desirous (for).

स्पृह्य *spr̥hyă* [S.], adj. eagerly desired; desirable.

स्फटिक *sphaṭik* [S.], m. **1.** quartz; rock-crystal. **2.** crystal.

स्फटी *sphaṭī* [S.], f. *Pl. HŚS.* alum (= **फिटकिरी**).

स्फाटक *sphāṭak* [S.], m. = **स्फटिक**.

स्फाटिक *sphāṭik* [S.], adj. & m. **1.** adj. made of crystal. **2.** m. crystal.

स्फाटित *sphāṭit* [S.], adj. torn open or apart.

स्फार *sphār* [S.], adj. poet. extensive; dense, thick (spray).

स्फीत *sphīt* [S.], adj. swollen, enlarged.

स्फुट *sphuṭ* [S.], adj. **1.** burst open (as buds). **2.** evident; known, understood. ***3.** miscellaneous. — **स्फुटीकरण,** m. clarification.

स्फुटन *sphuṭan* [S.], m. **1.** bursting, blossoming. **2.** appearing, becoming evident.

स्फुटिका *sphuṭikā* [S.], f. corr. alum (= **स्फटी**, **फिटकिरी**).

स्फुटित *sphuṭit* [S.], adj. burst open (buds), blooming.

स्फुटीकरण *sphuṭīkaraṇ* [S.], m. *HŚS.* see s.v. **स्फुट**.

स्फुरण *sphuraṇ* [S.], m. **1.** trembling, &c. (see **स्फुरित**). **2.** springing forth; energy, verve.

स्फुरित *sphurit* [S.], adj. **1.** trembling; throbbing. **2.** agitated.

स्फूर्त *sphūrt* [S.], adj. arisen, flashing (into the mind: a thought).

स्फूर्ति *sphūrti* [S.], f. **1.** throbbing. ***2.** vigour, energy; fig. enthusiasm; alacrity. **3.** flash (of thought).

स्फूर्तिमान् *sphūrtimān*, adj. vigorous, energetic, &c.

स्फोट *sphoṭ* [S.], m. **1.** bursting (sthg.) open. **2.** eruption, explosion. **3.** *philos.* sound (conceived of as eternal); the sound *om*; the concept that there exists an essential inherent element in sounds and words. **4.** a tumour, swelling.

स्फोटक *sphoṭak* [S.], adj. **1.** explosive. **2.** *ling.* plosive (certain consonants).

स्फोटन *sphoṭan* [S.], m. **1.** the act of bursting or splitting (sthg.) open. **2.** detonation, exploding (sthg).

स्मयमान *smayămān* [S.], adj. poet. smiling.

स्मरण *smaraṇ* [S.], m. **1.** remembering, recollecting; memory. **2.** calling to mind, or meditating upon, the supreme being. **3.** counting (one's) beads. **4.** mentioning, adverting (to). — ~ **आना (को)**, to come to mind. ~ **करना**, to recollect; to learn by heart. ~ **कराना**, or **दिलाना**, to remind (of, **का**); to remember (one, **का**; to, **को**). ~ **रखना**, to bear in mind, to remember. ~ **रहना**, to be remembered, not to be forgotten. ~ **होना**, to be in mind, to be remembered. – **स्मरण-पत्र**, m. a written reminder, memorandum. **स्मरण-शक्ति**, f. power of memory; the memory.

स्मरणी *smarăṇī* [S.], f. a rosary.

स्मरणीय *smarăṇīyă* [S.], adj. memorable.

स्मर्ता *smartā* [S.], adj. & m. inv. **1.** adj. mindful, attentive. **2.** m. one who remembers.

स्मशान *smaśān*, m. pronun. var. = **श्मशान**.

स्मारक *smārak* [S.], adj. & m. **1.** adj. commemorative, memorial (as an edition, a souvenir). **2.** m. a memorial. **3.** a souvenir.

स्मारिका *smārikā* [S.], f. a commemorative volume.

स्मार्त *smārt* [S.], adj. & m. *hind.* **1.** adj. mentioned or prescribed in the *smṛti* texts (a doctrine, a practice); orthodox. **2.** following *smṛti* in doctrine and practice; orthodox. **3.** m. one who follow *smṛti*, an orthodox Hindu.

स्मित *smit* [S.], adj. & m. **1.** adj. smiling. **2.** a smile.

स्मिति *smiti* [S.], f. a smile.

स्मृति *smṛti* [S.], f. **1.** recollection, memory; a memory. **2.** the body of sacred and profane brahmanical tradition as 'remembered' by men (as distinct from the 'revealed' knowledge of the Vedas). — **स्मृति-चिह्न**, m. remembrance token: a souvenir or memento. **स्मृति-पट**, m. canvas of memory: the mind, the memory. °**अल**, m. id. **स्मृति-शास्त्र**, m. = **स्मृति**, 2.

स्यंदन *syandan* [S.], m. **1.** a flowing, or rushing. **2.** trickling, or oozing. **3.** Brbh. a chariot.

स्यापा *syāpā* [cf. P. *siyā(h)*], m. mourning, lamentation; a lament. — ~ **करना**, to mourn (for, **का**). ~ **छाना**, a death-like atmosphere to prevail.

स्यार *syār*, m. see **सियार**.

स्यारी *syārī* [*śṛgālikā-*], f. a female jackal.

स्याह *syāh* [P. *siyāh*], adj. black. — ~ **करना**, to paint or to make black; to fill (a page) with writing; to blacken, to ruin (a reputation). ~ **और सफ़ेद का मालिक**, fig. undisputed master. — **स्याह-क़लम**, f. m. line-drawing. **स्याहगोसर** [P. -*gos*], m. Brbh. black-eared: a lynx. **स्याह-चश्म**, adj. black-eyed; unkind, cruel. **स्याहपोश** [P. -*poś*], adj. dressed in black, in mourning.

स्याहा *syāhā* [P. *siyāha*], m. Brbh. an account-book; rent-book; inventory.

स्याही *syāhī* [P. *siyāhī*], f. **1.** blackness; darkness. **2.** ink. **3.** blacking. **4.** stain, stigma. — ~ **जाना**, E.H. blackness (of hair) to leave (one): youth to depart). – **स्याहीचट**, m. blotter, blotting paper. **स्याहीचूस**, m. id. **स्याहीदान** [P. -*dān*], m. inkwell. **स्याही-सोख़**, [P. -*sokh*], m. = **स्याहीचट**.

स्रक *srak* [S.], f. Brbh. a garland (= **स्रज**).

स्रग *srag* [S.], m. Av. a garland.

स्रज *sraj* [S.], m. Brbh. a garland.

स्रवना *sravnā* [ad. *sravati*], v.i. to flow; to trickle; to ooze.

स्रष्टा *sraṣṭā* [S.], m. inv. a creator.

स्रस्त *srast* [S.], adj. poet. fallen down.

स्राप *srāp* [ad. *śāpa-*], m. corr. a curse (= **शाप**).

स्रापित *srāpit* [ad. *śāpita-*], adj. corr. cursed.

स्राव *srāv* [S.], m. flow; discharge.

स्रुवा *sruvā* [S.], f. Av. wooden ladle used to pour *ghī* on to the sacrificial fire.

स्रोत *srot* [S.], m. **1.** current (of water). **2.** stream, torrent. **3.** spring. **4.** fig. source.

स्रोतस्विनी *srotasvinī* [S.], f. poet. a river.

[1]**स्लीपर** *slīpar* [Engl. *slipper*], m. a slipper: light footwear.

[2]**स्लीपर** *slīpar* [Engl. *sleeper*], m. a sleeper, sleeping-car.

स्लेट *sleṭ* [Engl. *slate*], m. **1.** slate. **2.** a slate (for writing on).

स्लेटी *sleṭī* [cf. H. *sleṭ*], adj. & f. **1.** adj. slate-coloured. **2.** f. slate-pencil.

स्व- *sva-* [S.], pref. **1.** one's own; proper (to one). **2.** innate, natural. **3.** self-, auto- (e.g. स्वचालित, adj. automatic; worked by remote control).

स्वकर्म *sva-karm* [S.], m. own duty, function, or work.

स्वकर्मी *sva-karmī* [S.], adj. **1.** attending to one's own duty, &c. (see स्वकर्म). **2.** concerned only about one's own work, &c.

स्वकार्य *sva-kāryă* [S.], m. own duty, function, or work.

स्वकीय *svakīyă* [S.], adj. **1.** one's own. **2.** belonging to one's own family.

स्वकीया *svakīyā* [S.], f. *rhet.* a woman who is faithful to her husband.

स्वकुल *sva-kul* [S.], m. own family, or line.

स्वकृत *sva-kr̥t* [S.], adj. done or made by oneself.

स्वगत *sva-gat* [S.], adj. going on in one's own mind: **1.** said to oneself. **2.** adv. spoken aside, or as a soliloquy.

स्वच्छ *svacch* [S.], adj. **1.** fresh, clear (as air); healthy. **2.** clean. **3.** pure (as the heart); sincere.

स्वच्छंद *sva-cchand* [S.], adj. **1.** following one's own will. **2.** unrestrained: free, independent; spontaneous; wild (as emotions). **3.** self-willed; capricious. **4.** free (verse). **5.** romantic (as opposed to traditional, classical). — स्वच्छंदचारी, adj. & m. going about at will: ~, 1.-3.; a wandering ascetic.

स्वच्छंदता *sva-cchandătā* [S.], f. **1.** wilfulness, caprice. **2.** freedom from restraint; spontaneity.

स्वच्छता *svacchătā* [S.], f. clearness, purity, &c. (see स्वच्छ).

स्वजन *sva-jan* [S.], m. own people: **1.** own family, or household. **2.** a relative.

स्वजनी *sva-janī* [S.], f. **1.** female relative. **2.** female friend (= सखी).

स्वजाति *sva-jāti* [S.], f. **1.** own community, tribe or nation. **2.** own kind.

स्वजातीय *sva-jātīyă* [S.], adj. & m. **1.** adj. of or belonging to one's own community, &c. (see स्वजाति). **2.** of one's own kind. **3.** m. a member of one's own community.

स्वतंत्र *sva-tantră* [S.], adj. **1.** independent, free (from or of, से: as a nation, or an individual). **2.** unrestrained; acting as a free agent. **3.** self-willed, refractory. **4.** separate, individual. — ~ करना, to set free. ~ रूप से, adv. independently, on (one's) own account.

स्वतंत्रता *sva-tantrătā* [S.], f. independence, freedom. — स्वतंत्रता-संग्राम, m. struggle for independence.

स्वतः *svataḥ* [S.], adv. **1.** by oneself, on one's own (of performance of an action). **2.** of one's own accord or volition. **3.** involuntarily; automatically. **4.** by nature, naturally. — स्वतःप्रमाण, adj. its own proof, not needing proof. स्वतःसिद्ध, adj. self-accomplished: self-evident.

स्वतो- *svato-* [S.] = स्वतः: — स्वतोविरोधी, adj. inherently contradictory.

स्वत्व *svatvă* [S.], m. **1.** own, or personal right; proprietary right, ownership. **2.** personal identity. — स्वत्व-शुल्क, m. a royalty payment. स्वत्वाधिकारी [°*va*+*a*°], m. one having proprietary rights, copyright, royalty rights.

स्वदेश *sva-deś* [S.], m. own country, native land. — स्वदेश-प्रेम, m. patriotism. °ई, m. a patriot. स्वदेश-भक्ति, f. patriotism. स्वदेशाभिमान [°*śa*+*a*°], m. pride in country, patriotic pride.

स्वदेशी *sva-deśī* [S.], adj. & m. **1.** adj. of or belonging to one's own country; specif. manufactured in one's own country, not imported. **2.** m. a fellow-countryman. **3.** *hist.* the *svadeśī* movement to ban importation of foreign goods to India. — ~ कपड़ा, m. local cloth, Indian cloth.

स्वदेशीय *sva-deśīyă* [S.], adj. = स्वदेशी.

स्वधर्म *sva-dharm*, m. **1.** own or personal duty (as an individual, or a caste member, or as man or woman, &c.: see धर्म). **2.** own religion. — स्वधर्म-त्याग, m. apostasy; dereliction or neglect of duty. °ई, m. Av. apostate, &c.

स्वधर्मी *sva-dharmī* [S.], m. **1.** a dutiful person. ***2.** a supporter of one's own religion; a religious fanatic.

स्वन *svan* [S.], m. a sound.

स्वनाश *sva-nāś* [S.], m. self-destruction, suicide.

स्वपच *svapac* [S.], m. *Pl. HŚS.* dog-cooker, or dog-feeder: an outcaste.

स्वप्न *svapn* [S.], m. sleep: **1.** a dream, dreaming. **2.** reverie, fantasy. — स्वप्नदर्शी, adj. dreaming; visionary; day-dreaming; a dreamer. स्वप्न-दोष, m. nocturnal emission. स्वप्नद्रष्टा, m. inv. a dreamer. स्वप्नमय, adj. illusory (as a vision). स्वप्नवत्, adj. like a dream, insubstantial; dreamy. स्वप्न-विचार, m. interpretation of dreams. स्वप्नाविष्ट [°*na*+*ā*°], adj. lightly sleeping, dozing.

स्वप्नालु *svapnālu* [S.], adj. sleeping.

स्वप्निल *svapnil* [S.], adj. **1.** dreamy; drowsy. **2.** illusory, insubstantial (as a vision).

स्वभाव *sva-bhāv* [S.], m. own state: **1.** nature, character (of a person); temperament. **2.** nature, property, properties (of a thing). **3.** habit, way; custom, practice. — ~ पड़ना, a habit or attitude, &c. to be acquired (by, को). ~ से, adv. by nature, naturally. – स्वभावगत, adj. characteristic of nature or temperament. स्वभावतः, adv. naturally; in accordance with nature or character. स्वभाव-सिद्ध, adj. innate, instinctive.

स्वभावी *sva-bhāvī* [S.], adj. **1.** self-willed, temperamental. ***2.** -स्वभावी. having a partic. nature. e.g. नम्रस्वभावी, adj. meek.

स्वभूमि *sva-bhūmi* [S.], f. own country, native land.

स्वमत *sva-mat* [S.], m. own opinion or views.

स्वयं *svayaṁ* [S.], pron. & adv. /svəyəm/. **1.** pron. self, oneself. **2.** adv. by oneself, on one's own. **3.** of one's accord. **4.** स्वयं-. self-, auto-, of own accord. — ~ ही, adv. entirely by oneself; quite of one's own accord. तब वह ~ परलोक सिधारे, then he himself passed away. उसने यह काम ~ किया था, he did this work himself; he did this work unprompted. – स्वयंप्रकाश, adj. self-revealed, self-evident. स्वयंभू, m. the self-existent; title of Brahmā, Viṣṇu, Śiva; Brbh. title of the first Manu. स्वयंवर, m. (in ancient tradition) public choice of a bridegroom by the bride from among her assembled suitors. -आ, f. a bride who chooses her husband according to the custom of *svayaṁvar*. स्वयं-सिद्ध, adj. self-proved, self-evident. °इ, f. an axiom. स्वयंसेवक, m. a volunteer. °-सेविका, f. °-सेवा, f. voluntary service. °-सेवी, m. a volunteer. स्वयमेव, adv. = स्वयं ही.

स्वयमेव *svayamevă* [S.], adv. see s.v. स्वयं.

स्वर *svar* [S.], m. **1.** sound; noise. **2.** voice. **3.** *mus.* tone, key. **4.** *mus.* note. **5.** *ling.* a vowel. **6.** pronunciation, accent. — ~ उतारना, to lower the voice. ~ ऊँचा करना, to raise the voice. ~ मिलाना, to join in (singing); to accompany (with an instrument). एक ~ से, adv. with a single voice; unanimously. – स्वर-ग्राम, m. *mus.* scale. स्वर-तंत्रियाँ, f. pl. the vocal chords. स्वर-परिवर्तन, m. *ling.* vowel-change, umlaut. स्वर-पात, m. manner of pronunciation, accent (of speech). स्वरभक्ति, f. *ling.* vowel-separation: an epenthetic vowel. स्वर-यंत्र, m. the larynx. स्वर-विज्ञान, m. phonetics. स्वर-संगति, f. harmony. स्वर-सप्तक, m. *mus.* scale. स्वर-सूत्र, m. the vocal chords. स्वरांत [°*ra*+*a*°], adj. ending in a vowel (a word, a syllable). स्वराघात [°*ra*+*ā*°], m. accent, stress (in speech or music). °हीन, adj. unstressed (as a syllable). °इत, adj. stressed.

स्वर् *svar* [S.], m. **1.** the sun; heaven; the heavenly regions. **2.** one of three introductory words spoken after uttering the syllable *om*, before the Gāyatrī prayer. — स्वर्ग, m. see s.v. स्वर्गंगा, f. heavenly Ganges: the Milky Way. स्वर्लोक, m. heaven, paradise.

स्वराज्य *sva-rājyă* [S.], m. own rule, independence.

स्वराष्ट्र *sva-rāṣṭră* [S.], m. own state: *pol.* home (ministry, &c.: = गृह).

स्वरूप *sva-rūp* [S.], m. & adj. **1.** m. own form or shape. **2.** essential properties; character, nature. **3.** kind, type. **4.** appearance. **5.** identity. **6.** *hind.* form assumed by a deity, or by the ultimate being; image, idol. **7.** adj. of the same nature or character; similar. **8.** -स्वरूप, adj. & adv. formant. having the nature or character (of), by way of, as, amounting to. परिणाम-स्वरूप, adv. as the result (of, के); फलस्वरूप, adv. id. — स्वरूपज्ञ, m. 19c. one knowing the essential nature (of sthg). स्वरूपवान, adj. 19c. handsome, beautiful.

स्वरूपता *sva-rūpătā* [S.], f. identity of form or nature.

स्वरूपी *sva-rūpī* [S.], adj. esp. in comp. = स्वरूप, 7.

स्वर्ग *svarg* [S.], m. **1.** heaven; *mythol.* the heaven of Indra. **2.** the sky, heavens. **3.** symbol (in poetry) for the number 21. — ~ छूना, to touch heaven: to experience perfect bliss. ~ सिधारना, to depart this life. – स्वर्ग-गंगा, f. heavenly Ganges: the Milky Way. स्वर्गगत, adj. gone to heaven: deceased. °-गति, f. °-गमन, m. id., 1. स्वर्ग-धाम, m. paradise; heavenly life or state. स्वर्ग-नदी, f. the Milky Way. स्वर्ग-पति, m. *mythol.* lord of heaven: Indra. स्वर्ग-पुरी, f. *mythol.* city of heaven: Indra's city of Amarāvatī. स्वर्गस्थ, adj. deceased. स्वर्ग-वास, m. residence in heaven: decease. स्वर्गवास हो जाना (का), to depart this life. °ई, adj. deceased, the late...; celestial (as a being). स्वर्गारोहण [°*ga*+*ā*°], m. ascent to heaven.

स्वर्गिक *svargik* [cf. H. *svarg*], adj. **1.** celestial, divine. **2.** deceased (= स्वर्गीय).

स्वर्गी *svargī* [S.], adj. = स्वर्गीय.

स्वर्गीय *svargīyă* [S.], adj. of heaven: deceased; the late...

स्वर्ण *svarṇ* [S.], m. gold. — स्वर्णकार, m. a goldsmith. स्वर्ण-जयंती, f. golden jubilee. स्वर्णमय, adj. made of gold; golden.

स्वर्णिम *svarṇim* [S.], adj. golden; radiant.

स्वल्प *sv-alp* [S.], adj. **1.** very small or little. **2.** trifling, insignificant. — स्वल्पायु [°*pa*+*ā*°], m. of young age; of short life span; of recent standing. स्वल्पाहार [°pa+ā°], m. light refreshment.

स्वस्ति *sv-asti* [S.], f. & interj. **1.** m. blessing, benediction. **2.** interj. blessings (on)! **3.** (expressing sanction or approval) so be it! — ~ श्री, f. an opening formula in a letter. – स्वस्तिमान, adj. blessed, auspicious. °-मती, f.

स्वस्तिक *sv-astik* [S.], m. an auspicious mark or sign, swastika.

स्वस्थ *sv-asth* [S.], adj. **1.** healthy. **2.** settled (in mind), composed. — स्वस्थ-चित्त, adj. of sound mind.

स्वस्थता *sv-asthātā* [S.], f. health, &c. (see स्वस्थ).

स्वाँग *svāṁg* [*samāṅga-], m. **1.** imitation, mimicry. **2.** disguise. **3.** a sham, farce; pretence. **4.** a drama, folk-drama. **5.** a part in a play, a character, role. **6.** clowning. — ~ करना, to act, to play a part; to play the fool. ~ दिखाना, to represent a character; to sham, to pretend. ~ बनाना, to put on a play or entertainment. ~ भरना, or रचना, or लाना, to imitate, to play the part (of, का); to ape; = ~ दिखाना. ~ मचाना, = ~ करना, 2. ~ सजाना, to take up a role, to act a part.

स्वाँग- *svāṁg-* [cf. H. *svāṁg*], v.t. Brbh. to act out (a part).

स्वाँगी *svāṁgī* [cf. H. *svāṁg*], m. **1.** a mimic; an actor; satirist. **2.** a pretender, dissembler.

स्वांतःसुखाय *svāntaḥsukhāyă* [S.], adv. for personal pleasure, or satisfaction.

स्वाक्षर *svâkṣar* [S.], m. **1.** own handwriting. **2.** signature.

स्वागत *svâgat* [S.], m. **1.** welcoming; receiving (as guests, or delegates). **2.** a welcome; reception. — ~ करना (का), to welcome. – स्वागतकारी, adj. welcoming, receiving (guests, delegates). स्वागतपतिका, f. *rhet.* a wife who welcomes her husband home from a distant place.

स्वागतक *svâgatak* [S.], m. receptionist.

स्वागतिका *svâgatikā* [S.], f. receptionist, hostess, stewardess.

स्वातंत्र्य *svātantryă* [S.], m. = स्वतंत्रता.

स्वात *svāt* [ad. *svāti*], f. Av. = स्वाति.

स्वाति *svāti* [S.], f. **1.** the star Arcturus (as forming the fifteenth lunar asterism). **2.** the period when the moon is in *svāti* (during which alone the *cātak* bird is said to drink raindrops, and when raindrops falling into a shell are said to become pearls): October. — स्वाति-पंथ, m. Brbh. the Milky Way. स्वाति-बूँद, f. a raindrop falling in *svāti*, see above. स्वाति-सुत, m. Brbh. offering of *svāti*: a pearl. स्वाति-सुवन, m. Brbh. id.

स्वाद *svād* [S.], m. **1.** taste; flavour. **2.** enjoyment; appreciation; relish. — ~ चखना, to try the flavour (of, का), to taste. ~ चखाना, fig. to pay (one, को) back, to requite (for, का). ~ पड़ना, a taste to be acquired (by, को; for, का); to be addicted (to); to take interest (in). ~ लगना (को), the taste (of, का) to be perceived; to enjoy the taste (of). ~ लेना, to try the taste (of, का); to enjoy the taste (of); to appreciate (sthg).

स्वादक *svādak* [cf. H. *svād*], adj. & m. **1.** adj. tasty. **2.** m. taster (as of a king's food).

स्वादल *svādal* [cf. H. *svād*], adj. *Pl.* tasty.

स्वादित *svādit* [S.], adj. **1.** tasted. **2.** tasty; seasoned. **3.** enjoyed.

स्वादिष्ट *svādiṣṭ* [ad. *svādiṣṭha-*], adj. very tasty: tasty, sweet, &c. (see स्वाद, 1).

स्वादिष्ठ *svādiṣṭh* [S.], adj. = स्वादिष्ट.

स्वादी *svādī* [S.], adj. & m. **1.** adj. tasting. **2.** enjoying. **3.** m. a taster; one who relishes. **4.** a person of cultivated taste.

स्वादीला *svādīlā* [cf. H. *svād*], adj. 19c. = स्वादिष्ट.

स्वादु *svādu* [S.], adj. & m. **1.** adj. tasty. **2.** m. sweet taste; pleasant taste. **3.** molasses.

स्वाद्य *svādyă* [S.], adj. worth tasting, appetising.

स्वाधिकार *svâdhikār* [S.], m. own right or authority.

स्वाधिकारी *svâdhikārī* [S.], adj. subject to one's own authority: having freedom of action or initiative.

स्वाधिपत्य *svâdhipatyă* [S.], m. own supremacy: **1.** sovereignty. **2.** supreme authority.

स्वाधीन *svâdhīn* [S.], adj. self-dependent: **1.** having freedom of action or initiative (a person). **2.** independent (as a nation); free. — स्वाधीनपतिका, f. *rhet.* a woman whose husband acts according to her wishes.

स्वाधीनता *svâdhīnātā* [S.], f. **1.** independence (of action or initiative). **2.** independence (political); freedom.

स्वाधीनी *svâdhīnī* [cf. H. *svādhīn*], f. 19c. = स्वाधीनता.

स्वान *svān* [S.], m. a dog. — सिड़ी ~, m. a mad dog.

स्वाभाविक *svābhāvik* [S.], adj. belonging to, or proper to, one's own nature: **1.** natural. **2.** innate. **3.** peculiar (as to a species). **4.** true to life or nature (as a description). — यह ~, or ~ बात, है कि वह ऐसा करना चाहेगा, it is natural that he should want to do this.

स्वाभाविकता *svābhāvikătā* [S.], f. naturalness, accordance with nature.

स्वाभाविकी *svābhāvikī* [cf. H. *svābhāvik*], adj. obs. natural, according with nature.

स्वामित्व *svāmitvă* [S.], m. ownership, proprietorship; status of owner, &c. (see स्वामी).

स्वामिनी *svāminī* [S.], f. **1.** mistress, lady. **2.** the lady of a house (cf. स्वामी, 6).

स्वामी *svāmī* [S.], m. **1.** owner, proprietor. **2.** master, lord; king. **3.** title of the supreme being (esp. as Viṣṇu or Śiva). **4.** head of a religious order. **5.** title given to a renowned sage or devotee (as ~ Śaṅkarācārya, ~ Nanddās). **6.** husband; lover. — स्वामी द्रोह, m. *Pl.* hostility to one's master. treachery. °ई, m. a traitor.

स्वायत्त *svâyatt* [S.], adj. autonomous.

स्वायत्तता *svâyattătā* [S.], f. autonomy.

स्वाराज्य *svārājyă* [S.], m. **1.** own rule, sovereignty (= स्वराज्य); an independent state. **2.** *mythol.* the heaven of Indra.

स्वार्थ *svârth* [S.], m. & adj. **1.** m. one's own object or aim; own advantage, self-interest. **2.** selfishness. **3.** adj. self-interested, selfish. **4.** having a meaning. **5.** having the same meaning; pleonastic. — ~ कर-, 19c. to make useful, successful, or meaningful (as life). ~ लगना, to prove useful (to, को or के). ~ लेना, to have an interest (in, में). – स्वार्थपर, adj. seeking one's own advantage, self-interested. °ता, f. स्वार्थपरायण, adj. id. °ता, f. स्वार्थ-साधन, m. realisation of a selfish objective. स्वार्थ-सिद्धि, f. id.

स्वार्थता *svârthătā* [S.], f. selfishness.

स्वार्थिक *svârthik* [S.], adj. **1.** having one's own object, or interest. **2.** having a meaning. **3.** pleonastic. **4.** effective, successful; advantageous.

स्वार्थी *svârthī* [S.], adj. & m. **1.** adj. seeking one's own object or interest; selfish; oblivious to all but self. **2.** m. a selfish person.

स्वास *svās*, f. Av. = साँस.

स्वास्थ्य *svāsthyă* [S.], m. health.

स्वाहा *svāhā* [S.], interj. exclamation used when making a burnt offering to a Vedic deity. — ~ करना, to consume, to squander (an inheritance, &c).

स्वीकरण *svīkaraṇ* [S.], m. acceptance, &c. (see स्वीकार); acceptance of a bride in marriage.

स्वीकार *svīkār* [S.], m. making one's own: **1.** accepting, acceptance. **2.** assent, approval. **3.** acknowledgement. **4.** admission. — ~ करना, to accept; to assent to; to acquiesce in; to acknowledge; to admit, to grant; to bear patiently (as troubles). - स्वीकारात्मक [°*ra*+*ā*], adj. accepting, affirmative. स्वीकारार्थ [°*ra*+*a*°], adv. for acceptance, for approval. स्वीकारोक्ति [°*ra*+*u*°], f. a confession.

स्वीकारना *svīkārnā* [cf. H. *svīkar*], v.t. to accept.

स्वीकारी *svīkārī* [S.], adj. accepting, &c. (see स्वीकार).

स्वीकार्य *svīkāryă* [S.], adj. deserving or requiring acceptance, &c. (see स्वीकार).

स्वीकृत *svīkr̥t* [S.], adj. accepted, &c. (see स्वीकार).

स्वीकृति *svīkr̥ti* [S.], f. acceptance, &c. (see स्वीकार); ratification. — ~ देना, to accept, to give acceptance (to).

स्वीय *svīyă* [S.], adj. one's own.

स्वेद *sved* [S.], m. **1.** sweat. **2.** steam. — स्वेद-कण, m. a drop of sweat. स्वेदज, adj. sweat-born: a term referring to insects as a category of living things.

स्वेदन *svedan* [S.], m. sweating.

स्वेदित *svedit* [S.], adj. steamed; made dim from sweat or steam (the sight).

स्वेच्छा *svêcchā* [S.], f. one's own wish, or will. — ~ से, adv. willingly; voluntarily. स्वेच्छाचार [°*chā*+*ā*°], m. acting as one wishes; acting wilfully, or arbitrarily. °इता, f. = prec. °ई, adj.

स्वैच्छिक *svaicchik* [S.], adj. self-willed.

स्वैराचार *svairâ-cār* [S.], m. sthg. done of (one's) own volition.

ह

ह *ha*, the thirty-third consonant of the Devanāgarī syllabary. — **हकार**, m. the sound /h/; the letter ह.

हँकड़ना *hamkaṛnā*, v.i. to bellow; to low (cattle).

हँकवा *hamkvā*, m. dimin. = हाँका.

हँकवाना *hamkvānā* [cf. H. *hāmknā*], v.t. **1.** to cause to be shouted (to: by, से). **2.** to cause (animals) to be driven (by).

हँकाना *hamkānā*, v.t. 1. = हँकवाना. 2. = हाँकना.

हँकार *hamkār* [*hakkāra-*, Pk. *hakkāra-*; or H. *hamkārnā*], f. m. **1.** loud shout. **2.** driving off or away (by shouting).

हँकारना *hamkārnā* [**hakkārayati*: Pk. *hakkārei*], v.t. **1.** to shout out loudly (to). **2.** to drive (animals, by shouting). **3.** to set in motion (a vehicle, or boat).

हँकारा *hamkārā* [*hakkāra-*, Pk. *hakkāra-*], m. = हँकार.

हंगामा *hangāmā* [P. *hangāma*], m. **1.** tumultuous crowd; commotion, disturbance; din. **2.** affray; riot. — ~ **करना**, to create a commotion, &c.

हंटर *hanṭar* [Engl. *hunter*], m. a whip; blow with a whip.

हंड- *hanḍ-* [**hanḍ-*], v.i. Brbh. to move, to wander.

हंडा *hanḍā* [? conn. *hanḍikā-*], m. a large pot (earthenware or of metal), cauldron. — ~ **फोड़ना**, = भाँड़ा फोड़ना.

हँड़ाना *hamṛānā* [cf. H. *hāmrnā*], v.t. reg. **1.** to cause to wander to to go about; to send away. **2.** to disgrace by publicly parading (one).

हँड़िया *hamṛiyā* [cf. *hanḍikā-*], f. **1.** a small earthenware cooking-pot. **2.** a glass bowl containing a candle, a lamp. **3.** transf. an alcoholic drink made from grain. — ~ **गरम होना** the pot to be hot, to boil: money to be earned, or to roll in; bribes to be taken. ~ **चढ़ना**, the pot to be put on (the fire): money to come in, &c. (see above). ~ **पकना** the pot to boil: food to be cooked; a scheme to be concocted.

हंडी *hanḍī*, f. = हँड़िया.

हंत *hant* [S.], interj. alas!

हंतव्य *hantavyă* [S.}, adj. to be struck (down), or killed; deserving death.

हंता *hantā* [S.], m. inv. one who strikes: a killer, murderer.

हँफनी *hamphnī* [cf. H. *hāmphnā*], f. puffing, panting; shortness of breath.

हँफाना *hamphānā* [cf. H. *hāmphnā*], v.t. to cause to pant; to get (one) out of breath.

हँफैल *hamphail* [cf. H. *hāmphnā*], adj. reg. liable to pant: short of wind, or endurance.

हँभाना *hambhānā* [cf. *hambhā-*], v.i. = रँभाना.

हंस *hams* [S.], m. **1.** goose, gander; (by poetic licence) swan. **2.** flamingo (= राज-हंस). **3.** fig. the soul, migratory spirit. — **हंस-गति**, f. graceful gait. **हंस-गवनि** [*gamanī-*], f. Av. = next. **हंस-गामिनी**, f. a woman who moves gracefully. **हंस-राज**, m. *Pl. HŚS.* name of several plants: a grass found on walls or rocks; a kind of fern; a kind of rice.

हँस- *hams-*. laughing, laughter: — **हंसमुख**, adj. of cheerful face: cheerful, jovial; fond of joking. **हंसलोना**, adj. see s.v.

हँसना *hamsnā* [*hasati*], v.i. **1.** to laugh; to smile. **2.** to joke. **3.** to laugh (at, पर); to make fun (of, पर). **4.** fig. to be attractive (a scene). **5.** to be unhealed (a wound). — **हँसना-खेलना**, to laugh, to joke. **हँसना-बोलना**, id. – **हँस उठना**, to laugh loudly; = next. **हँस पड़ना**, to burst out laughing. **बात हँसकर उड़ाना**, to dismiss (a matter, words) as unimportant. **हम उनकी बातें सुनकर हँस दिए**, we laughed at what he said. – **भभाकर** ~, to roar with laughter. **हँसते-हँसते**, adv. in laughing, while laughing; with a smile, or a laugh. **हँसते-हँसते बुरा हाल हो जाना**, fig. to kill oneself with laughing. **हँसा जाना**, to be laughed at.

हँसनुआ *hamsanuā*, m. reg. a laughing-stock.

हँसली *hamslī*, f. = हँसुली.

हँसलोना *hamslonā* [? H. *hamsnā*+H. *lonā*], adj. reg. humorous, joky (a person).

हँसा *hamsā* [cf. H. *hamsnā*, and *hamsī*], m. laugh; laughter (= हँसी).

हँसाई *hamsāī* [cf. H. *hamsnā*, *hamsānā*], f. **1.** laughing, laughter; fun. **2.** cause or object of laughter. **3.** ridicule, derision.

हँसाऊ *hamsāū* [cf. H. *hamsānā*], adj. laughable, ridiculous.

हँसाना *haṁsānā* [cf. H. *haṁsnā*], v.t. to cause to laugh.

हंसिका *haṃsikā* [S.], f. a goose.

हँसिया *haṁsiyā* [*aṁs(i)ya-*: ? *h-* ← *haḍḍa-*], f. **1.** a sickle; pruning-hook. **2.** a type of large knife having the blade curving upward. from the handle (used by potters, and butchers).

हंसी *haṃsī* [S.], f. a goose; a female swan (see हंस).

हँसी *haṁsī* [*hasita-*], f. **1.** laughter; a smile. **2.** fun, joking; a joke. **3.** ridicule. — ~ आना (को), to be moved to laughter, to laugh. ~ उड़ाना, to make fun (of, की). ~ में, adv. in fun, as a joke. ~ में उड़ाना, to pass (sthg.) off with a joke. ~ में खाँसी होना, laughing to give way to coughing: to go from words to blows. ~ में टालना, or ले जाना, to take as a joke. ~ समझना, id. – हँसी-ख़ुशी, f. merriment; adv. gladly, with pleasure. हँसी-खेल, m. laughing and joking; a laughing matter, simple matter. हँसी-ठट्ठा, m. joking; fooling, horseplay; sthg. laughably easy, child's play. हँसी-दिल्लगी, f. id., 1., 2.; flirting.

हँसुआ *haṁsuā*, m. = हँसिया.

हँसुली *haṁsulī* [cf. *aṁsa-*: ? *h-* ← *haḍḍa-*], f. **1.** collar-bone. **2.** necklace. **3.** ornamental collar (of precious metal). **4.** reg. (Bihar) = हँसिया.

हँसोकर *haṁsokar* [cf. H. *haṁsnā*], adj. reg. = हँसोड़.

हँसोड़ *haṁsoṛ* [cf. H. *haṁsnā*], adj. & m. **1.** adj. always laughing, jovial. **2.** fond of joking. **3.** m. a jovial person; a joker.

हँसोड़पन *haṁsoṛpan* [cf. H. *haṁsoṛ*], m. fondness for joking; facetiousness.

हँसोड़पना *haṁsoṛpanā*, m. = हँसोड़पन.

हँसौहौं *haṁsauhauṁ*, adj. Brbh. **1.** cheerful. 2. = हँसोड़.

हई *haī*, 19c. = है ही.

हक़ *haq* [A. *ḥaqq*], adj. & m. **1.** adj. just, proper, right; true. ~ जानना, to consider as right, just; to approve. **2.** m. justness, right; equity. ~ तो यह है कि ..., it is right that .... **3.** justice. उसे इसका ~ मिलना ही चाहिए, he ought to be given justice in this (matter). **4.** a right; a claim; privilege; franchise. **5.** due share; due fee. **6.** duty, obligation. **7.** behalf, benefit; concern, advantage. ~ में दुआ करना, to pray (for one, के). तुम्हारे ~ में यह अच्छा न होगा, this will not be to your advantage. **8.** *isl.* truth; God. — ~ अदा करना, to do one's duty. ~ दबाना (का), to usurp a right; to deprive of a right; to dispossess wrongfully. ~ देना, to concede a right; to administer justice. ~ पर लड़ना, to fight for (one's) rights. ~ बात, f. a just remark, or viewpoint. ~ मारना, or लेना, = ~ दबाना. ~ से, adv. justly, fairly; deservedly. अपने ~ में काँटे बोना, fig. to make serious trouble for oneself. – हक़-तलफ़ी [P. *talafī*], f. deprivation of a right; discrimination. हक़दार [P. *-dār*], adj. & m. having a right, or claim; rightful, lawful; one having a right, or claim; proprietor. °ई, f. the holding of any right; entitlement. हक़-नाहक़, adv. without regard to (another's) rights; without cause or reason.

हकबकाना *hakbakānā* [cf. H. *hakkā-bakkā*], v.i. to be taken aback; to become confused; to be aghast.

हकला *haklā*, adj. & m. **1.** adj. stuttering, stammering. **2.** m. stutterer, &c.

हकलाना *haklānā* [cf. H. *haklā*], v.i. to stutter, to stammer. — हकलाकर बोलना, id.

हकलापन *haklāpan* [cf. H. *haklā*], m. stutter, stammer.

हकलाहट *haklāhaṭ* [cf. H. *haklā*], f. stuttering, stammering.

हकारना *hakārnā*, v.t. reg. = हँकारना.

हक़ीक़त *haqīqat* [A. *ḥaqīqa*: P. *ḥaqīqat*], f. truth, fact, reality. — ~ खुलना, the truth, or facts, to emerge. ~ में, adv. in fact, in reality. ~ यों है ..., the truth is (that ..).

हक़ीक़तन *haqīqatan* [A. *ḥaqīqatan*], adv. = हक़ीक़त में.

हक़ीक़ी *haqīqī* [A. *ḥaqīqī*], adj. U. **1.** essential, genuine. **2.** real, actual. **3.** own, full-blood (brother, &c). — इश्क़ ~, m. love of God (as opposed to worldly love).

हकीम *hakīm* [A. *ḥakīm*], m. **1.** a wise man; philosopher. **2.** a doctor. — नीम-हकीम, m. pej. half-doctor: a quack.

हकीमी *hakīmī* [P. *ḥakīmī*], adj. & m. **1.** adj. medical. **2.** f. the practice or profession of medicine. — ~ करना, to practise medicine.

हक़ीर *haqīr* [A. *ḥaqīr*], adj. **1.** contemptible; vile. **2.** U. insignificant.

हक्का-बक्का *hakkā-bakkā*, adj. taken aback; shocked, confused; aghast. — ~ रह, or हो, जाना, to be taken aback, &c.

हगना *hagnā* [*haḍati*; Pa. *hanna-*: anal.], v.i. to defecate.

हगाना *hagānā* [cf. H. *hagnā*], v.t. **1.** to cause to defecate; to get (a child) to relieve itself. **2.** to act as a purgative.

हगास *hagās* [cf. H. *hagnā*], f. wish to defecate. — ~ लगना (को), to wish to defecate.

हगासा *hagāsā* [cf. H. *hagās*], adj. **1.** wanting to defecate often. **2.** m. one who wants to defecate often.

हगोड़ा *hagoṛā* [cf. H. *hagnā*], m. **1.** one who is always defecating. **2.** pej. a coward.

हग्गू *haggū* [cf. H. *hagnā*], m. = हगोड़ा.

हचकोला *hackolā*, m. a jolt; shock. — हचकोले खाना, to be jolted, to suffer shocks.

हज़म *hazm* [A. *hazm*], m. **1.** digesting; digestion. **2.** fig. misappropriation, embezzlement. — ~ करना, to digest; to embezzle. ~ होना, to be digested, &c. (by, से). – हज़मवार [P. *-vār*], adj. = next. हज़मावर [P. *-āvar*], adj. aiding digestion, digestive.

हज़रत *hazrat* [A. *ḥazra*: P. *ḥazrat*], f. **1.** excellence, highness (a title; when used instead of a name, it takes the gender of the person referred to). ~ मुहम्मद, m. the prophet Muḥammad. ~ ईसा, m. inv. Jesus. **2.** iron. a rascal. — बड़े ~, m. a superior; an out-and-out villain.

हजामत *hajāmat* [A. *ḥajāma*: P. *ḥajāmat*], f. shaving; a shave. — ~ बनाना (की), to shave; fig. to rob, to fleece. ~ होना (की), to be robbed, fleeced.

हजामती *hajāmătī* [cf. H. *hajāmat*], adj. having to do with barbering or shaving: as utensils.

हज़ार *hazār* [P. *hazār*], adj. & m. **1.** adj. a thousand. **2.** fig. numerous; much. **3.** m. a thousand. एक ~ आदमी, m. pl. a thousand men. — ~ जान से, adv. fig. with all one's heart. ~ रंग बदलना, to vary or to change greatly; to be very fickle. हज़ारों में, adv. in the presence of thousands; in public, openly. हज़ारों में एक, adj. one in thousands, in a thousand. – हज़ार-दास्तान, m. U. (bird of) a thousand tales: the nightingale.

हज़ारहा *hazārhā* [P. *hazārhā*, pl.], adv. U. thousands (of).

हज़ारा *hazārā* [P. *hazāra*], adj. & m. consisting of innumerable parts: **1.** adj. many-petalled, double (a flower). **2.** m. a watering-rose; a fountain. **3.** name of an anthology of early Hindi poetry. **4.** a kind of firework. — ~ गेंदा, m. a marigold.

हज़ारी *hazārī* [P. *hazārī*], adj. & m. **1.** adj. pertaining to a thousand; abundant. **2.** m. *hist.* commander of a thousand men. **3.** f. force of a thousand men. — ~ उमर, f. fig. a long life. – हज़ारी-बाज़ारी, m. pl. soldiers and tradesmen; military and civil; high and low; one and all.

हज्ज *hajj* [A. *ḥajj*], m. pilgrimage to Mecca.

हज्जाम *hajjām* [A. *ḥajjām*], m. blood-letter: a barber.

हटकना *haṭaknā* [cf. H. *haṭānā*], v.t. reg. **1.** to drive (animals) back, or away. **2.** to check, to hinder; to forbid. — हटका-हटकी, f. driving back and being driven back: struggling for the upper hand.

हटका *haṭkā* [cf. H. *haṭaknā*], m. reg. (Bihar) a diagonal brace (in roof construction).

हटताल *haṭtāl*, f. pronun. var. = हड़ताल.

हटना *haṭnā* [**haṭṭ-*], v.i. **1.** to move away, or aside (from, से); to turn aside; to withdraw, to retire. **2.** to be driven back (as an enemy). **3.** to be removed (from a post). **4.** to desist (from). **5.** to shrink (from). **6.** to go back (on, से: as on a promise). **7.** to be postponed. — हट! हटो! out of the way! हटके! adv. watch out! get out of the way! (= हटके चलो). – हट-हटके, adv. persistently, (returning) again and again.

हटरी *haṭrī*, f. E.H. = हाट.

हटवा *haṭvā* [cf. H. *hāṭ*], m. reg. a shopkeeper; weigher of grain (in a market, or at threshing).

हटवाई *haṭvāī*, f. reg. **1.** shopkeeping. **2.** a shopkeeper's or weigher's work, or wages.

हटवाड़ा *haṭvāṛā* [**haṭṭavāṭa-*], m. E.H. market-place.

हटाऊ *haṭāū* [cf. H. *haṭṭā*], adj. marketable.

हटाना *haṭānā* [cf. H. *haṭnā*], v.t. **1.** to remove; to move away, or aside. **2.** to drive back or off, to repel. **3.** to remove (from a post). **4.** to postpone.

हटाव *haṭāv* [cf. H. *haṭnā*, *haṭānā*], m. **1.** falling back, retreating. **2.** shrinking (from, से), aversion (to). **3.** removal, &c. (see हटाना). **4.** dismissal. **5.** repulse (of attackers, an army).

हट्टा *haṭṭā* [*haṭṭa-*], m. reg. **1.** a market, market-place (= हाट). 2. = हट्टी, 2.

हट्टा-कट्टा *haṭṭā-kaṭṭā*, adj. sturdy, robust.

हट्टी *haṭṭī* [*haṭṭā*], f. **1.** a small market. **2.** shop, stall. **3.** group of houses in a village (esp. of people of the same community).

हट्ठर *haṭṭhar*, m. reg. hurry; impatience.

हठ *haṭh* [S.], m. **1.** stubbornness, insistence (esp. unreasonable insistence). **2.** crossness, sulks (of a child). **3.** firm promise, or resolve. **4.** force, violence. — ~ करना, to be stubborn, to insist (on, पर, के लिए); to be cross; to make a firm promise. ~ ठानना, id., 3. ~ पकड़ना, = ~ करना, 1., 2. ~ रखना, to act as another (का) has insisted, &c. – हठ-धर्म, adj. stubborn; bigoted, fanatical; unjust, ungrateful. °ई, f. stubbornness, &c.; m. a stubborn person,

&c. हठधर्मी करना, to be obstinate, &c. हठ-योग, m. the form of yoga in which emphasis is laid on physical disciplines and exercises (including breath-control) to achieve withdrawal of the mind from external objects.

हठ- *haṭh-* [cf. H. *haṭh*], v.i. Brbh. = ~ करना.

हठरना *haṭharnā*, v.i. reg. to hurry; to be impatient.

हठात् *haṭhāt* [S.], adv. **1.** by force, violently; under compulsion. **2.** suddenly. **3.** immediately. **4.** by chance.

हठी *haṭhī* [cf. H. *haṭh*], adj. & m. **1.** adj. stubborn, &c. (see हठ); importunate. **2.** bigoted, fanatical. **3.** m. a stubborn person, &c. **4.** a bigot.

हठीला *haṭhīlā* [cf H. *haṭh*], adj. 1. = हठी, 1. **2.** name of a partic. sub-community of Nāth Śaivas.

हठीलापन *haṭhīlāpan* [cf. H. *haṭhīlā*], m. stubbornness, tenacity; obstinacy.

हड़ *haṛ* [*harītaka-*; Pa. *harīṭaka-*], f. **1.** the yellow or 'black' myrobalan (= हरड़ा, हर्रा). **2.** an ornament, or ornamentation, resembling the myrobalan fruit. — ~ लगे न फिटकरी और रंग चोखा होय, a good (yellow) colour to be achieved without use of myrobalan or alum: a desirable result to be gained without expense.

हड़- *haṛ-* [cf. H. *haḍḍī-*]. bone: — हड़कंप, fig. turmoil, furore. हड़-फूटन, f. m. aching in the bones (as from fatigue). हड़-बैर, m. a deep-seated hostility. हड़-आवरि [ad. *-āvalī̆-*], f. Brbh. Av. skeleton.

हड़क *haṛak* [cf. H. *haṛaknā*], f. **1.** hankering, craving; fretting. **2.** hydrophobia. — ~ लगना (को), a craving to be felt (by).

हड़कना *haṛaknā* [cf. **haṭ-*], v.i. = हुड़कना. — एक हड़का हुआ कुत्ता, m. a mad dog.

हड़का *haṛkā* [cf. H. *haṛaknā*], m. reg. peevishness; hankering, fretting.

हड़काना *haṛkānā* [cf. H. *haṛaknā*], v.t. reg. **1.** to cause to long for: to tantalise; to stir up. **2.** reg. to drive away; to deter.

हड़किया *haṛkiyā* [cf. H. *haṛak*], adj. **1.** bad-tempered. **2.** fretful; pining. **3.** reg. mad (a dog).

हड़गिल्ल *haṛgill*, m. Brbh. = हड़गीला.

हड़गीला *haṛgīlā* [H. *haṛ-*; w. H. *gilnā*], m. bone-swallower: the adjutant stork, *Ardea argala* (a scavenging bird).

हड़ताल *haṛtāl* [H. *haṭṭ(ā)*, *hāṭ*+H. *tālā*], f. **1.** passive resistance (specif. shutting the shops of a market). ***2.** a strike. — ~ करना, to strike. ~ रखना, to be on strike.

हड़ताली *haṛtālī* [cf. H. *haṛtāl*], adj. & m. **1.** adj. having to do with a strike. **2.** striking. **3.** m. a striker.

हड़ना *haṛnā*, v.i. *Pl. HŚS.* to be tested (the accuracy of a weight).

हड़प *haṛap* [? cf. **happ-*], f. m. bolting (food); gobbling. — ~ करना, to bolt; to gobble; to embezzle.

हड़पना *haṛapnā* [cf. **happ-*, or H. *haṛap*], v.i. **1.** to bolt (food); to gobble. **2.** to appropriate (as land, &c.); to embezzle.

हड़प्पा *haṛappā* [cf. H. *harapnā*], m. **1.** a chunk of food; morsel. **2.** term of abuse (used by men about women).

हड़बड़ *haṛbaṛ* [cf. H. *haṛbaṛānā*], f. = हड़बड़ी.

हड़बड़ाना *haṛbaṛānā* [**haḍabaḍa-*], v.i. & v.t. **1.** v.i. to be confused, flurried. ***2.** to be in a hurry, to rush; to break out, to burst out (as an epidemic, or flood-water). **3.** to fidget; to rumble (the bowels). **4.** v.t. to confuse (one). **5.** to hurry (one) up.

हड़बड़िया *haṛbaṛiyā* [cf. H. *haṛbaṛī*], adj. & m. **1.** adj. easily agitated, &c. (see हड़बड़ाना). **2.** m. one who is easily agitated. **3.** one always in a hurry.

हड़बड़ी *haṛbaṛī* [cf. H. *haṛbaṛānā*], f. **1.** confusion, flurry; alarm. ***2.** haste, rush; rashness. — ~ करना, to make haste. ~ पड़ना, or लगना (को), to be alarmed, agitated; to clear out helter-skelter. ~ मचाना, to create a commotion. ~ में, adv. in confusion, or haste.

हड़हड़- *haṛ'haṛ-*, v.i. E.H. to crash, to rattle; to twang.

हड़हड़ाना *haṛ'haṛānā*, v.i. reg. **1.** to shiver; to tremble (as from excitement). 2. = हड़हड़-. **3.** v.t. *HŚS.* to urge on, to hurry (one).

हड़ावरि *haṛāvari*, f. Brbh. Av. see s.v. हड़-.

हड़ावल *haṛāval*, f. reg. collection of bones: a skeleton (see s.v. हड़-).

हड़ीला *haṛīlā* [cf. H. *hāṛ*], adj. bony; wasted in body.

¹हड्डा *haḍḍā* [*haḍḍa-*, Pk. *haḍḍa-*], m. **1.** bone (= हड्डी). **2.** a spavin.

²हड्डा *haḍḍā*, m. a wasp.

हड्डी *haḍḍī* [cf. H. *haḍḍa-*], f. **1.** a bone. **2.** a spavin. **3.** hard core (of a carrot or similar root). **4.** family; stock. — ~ उखड़ना, or उतरना, a joint to be dislocated. ~ काँपना, (one's) whole body to tremble. ~ बोलना, a bone to crack. पुरानी ~, f. colloq. a tough old fellow. हड्डियाँ

तोड़ना, or नरम करना, to break the bones (of, की); to beat severely. हड्डियाँ निकलना, fig. to be reduced to a skeleton. हड्डियों का ढाँचा, m. colloq. a very skinny man, a bag of bones. हड्डी-गुड्डी तोड़ना (की), to thrash (one). हड्डीचूस, adj. & m. miserly; a miser. हड्डी-तोड़, adj. bone-breaking: exhausting (work). हड्डी-पसली एक कर देना, to make backbone and ribs one: to thrash soundly, or unmercifully. हड्डी-सी हो जाना, to ossify.

हड्डीला *haḍḍīlā* [cf. H. *haḍḍī*], adj. bony.

हत *hat* [S.], adj. **1.** struck. **2.** struck down, killed. **3.** हत-. deprived of, having lost. **4.** damaged; destroyed. — हतचेत, adj. unconscious. हतप्रभ, adj. without (former or proper) splendour, beauty. हतबुद्धि, adj. without (one's) wits: at a loss; dejected. हतभागी, adj. unfortunate. °-भाग्य, m. misfortune. हतवीर्य, adj. without virility or manliness. हताश [°*ta*+*ā*°], adj. dejected; despairing; desperate (a situation). °आ, f. despair, &c. हताहत [°*ta*+*ā*], adj. & m. pl. killed and wounded. हतोत्साह [°*ta*+*u*°], adj. dejected. °इत, adj.

हत- *hat-* [ad. *hata-*], v.t. Brbh. to kill.

[1]**हतक** *hatak* [A. *hatk*], m. tearing (a veil, curtain): **1.** dishonouring. **2.** disrespect; affront. — हतक-इज़्ज़ती, f. defamation of character.

[2]**हतक** *hatak* [S.], adj. Brbh. murderous, wicked.

हत्ता *hattā*, m. pronun. var. = हत्था.

हत्था *hattha* [*hastaka-*], m. **1.** a handle; tap, cock; shuttle (of a loom); arm-rest. **2.** a long-handled wooden shovel used for throwing water into fields from irrigation ditches. **3.** a palm-print made (as an auspicious mark) on a house wall. **4.** a scoop, ladle. **5.** reg. a handful. **6.** fig. clutch, grasp, possession. — हत्थे से उखड़ना, to be cut loose (a kite, from its string). हत्थे चढ़ना, to come into the power, or clutches (of, के). हत्थे मारना, colloq. to pilfer, to get down on; to haul down quickly (a flag, a kite). हत्थे लगना, to fall into the clutches (of, के). – हत्था-हत्थी [H. *hāth*], adv. reg. hand-to-hand (of fighting).

हत्थी *hatthī* [cf. H. *hatthā*], f. a small handle.

हत्या *hatyā* [S.], f. **1.** killing; murder. **2.** destruction. **3.** a mortal sin. **4.** a wretched creature. **5.** fig. dire trouble; quarrel. — ~ करना (की), to kill; to murder; to commit a sin. ~ पल्ले बँधना, infamy, or dire suffering, to be incurred. ~ मोल लेना, or सिर लेना, to incur mortal sin, or infamy. ~ लगना, = ~ पल्ले बँधना. ~ सिर चढ़ना, a killing, or an infamous deed, to be imputed (to, के). — हत्या-कांड, m. an act or accident of murder; slaughter, carnage.

हत्यारा *hatyārā* [**hatyākāraka-*: ad.], adj. & m. **1.** adj. murderous; cruel; sinful. **2.** m. a murderer; assassin; sinner; villain.

हथ- *hath-*. the hand: — हथ-उधार, m. a loan into the hand: an informal loan of sthg. for immediate use. हथकंडा, m. often pl. skill, or sleight of hand; cunning, wiles; secret investigation. हथकड़ा, m. = next; sthg. to hold on to; a means. हथकड़ी, f. handcuff. हथकड़ी डालना, or पहनाना, or लगाना (को), to handcuff. हथकल, m. hand-tool or appliance (as a spanner, or a vice). हथगोला, m. hand grenade. हथफूल, m. an ornament worn on the outer side of the hand (being attached to the fingers and wrist). हथफेर, m. colloq. passing the hand over (sthg.): trickery, fraud; pilfering; borrowing sthg. informally for a short time; caressing. हथरस, m. masturbation. हथलपका, m. a light-fingered person, confirmed thief. °-लपकी, f. thieving, theft. हथलेवा, hand-taking: ceremonial joining of the bride's and groom's hands at marriage. हथसाल, f. Brbh. an elephant-house.

हथनी *hathnī* [H. *hāthī*: ad. *hastinī-*], f. a female elephant.

हथरा *hathrā*, m. reg. (Bihar) = हत्था.

हथवाँस- *hathvāṁs-* [cf. **hastapāśa-*], v.t. Av. to rope (boats) together (preventing their use).

हथा *hathā*, m. pronun. var. = हत्था.

हथिया *hathiyā* [cf. H. *hāth*, *hatthī*], f. *astron.* name of the thirteenth lunar mansion (represented by a hand; prob. part of the constellation Corvus). — ~ की राह, f. the Milky Way.

हथियाना *hathiyānā* [cf. H. *hāth*], v.t. **1.** to lay hands on; to seize. **2.** to get one's hands on: to appropriate; to pocket; to obtain by fraud.

हथियार *hathiyār* [**hastakāra-*: Pk. *hatthiyāra-*], m. **1.** an implement. **2.** a weapon; arms. **3.** sl. penis. — ~ उठाना or सँभालना, to take up arms. ~ करना, to wage an armed struggle. ~ चलाना, to use a weapon (against, पर). ~ बाँधना, or लगाना (में), to arm. – हथियार-घर, m. armoury; arsenal. हथियारबंद [P. *-band*], adj. armed, equipped. °ई, f. arming.

हथेली *hathelī* [cf. *hastatala-*], f. **1.** palm (of the hand). **2.** impression made by the palm. — ~ का फफोला, a blister on the palm: sthg. fragile. ~ खुजलाना, the palm to itch (a sign that money will be received); the desire to strike a blow to be felt. ~ देना (को), to give a helping hand (to). ~ पर दही जमना, = next, 2. ~ पर सरसों जमाना, to make mustard seed sprout on the palm: to perform wonders; not to let grass grow under one's feet. ~ बजाना, or पीटना, to clap the hands. ~ में आना, to be obtained, got hold of. ~ लगाना (को), = ~ देना. जान ~ पर रखना, or लेना, to take one's life in one's hands. सिर ~ पर रखना, or लेना, = जान ~ पर रखना.

हथोरी *hathorī* [**hastapuṭikā-*], f. Av. palm of the hand.

हथौटी *hathauṭī* [**hastavṛtti-*], f. skill, dexterity. — ~ जमना, or मँजना, or सधना, the hand to grow skilled.

हथौड़ा *hathauṛā* [**hastakūṭa-*], m. **1.** a heavy hammer; sledgehammer. 2. = हथौड़ी.

हथौड़ी *hathauṛī* [cf. H. *hathauṛā*], f. a hammer.

हथौना *hathaunā* [**hastopāyana-*], m. gift of sweets made to bride and groom.

हद *had* [A. *ḥadd*], f. **1.** boundary. **2.** limit, bounds; extent. **3.** bar, obstruction. **4.** adv. extremely, very. ~ बुरा मालूम होता है, (it) looks extremely bad. **5.** adv. at most; at least. — ~ करना, to do sthg. excessive, to go as far as (to, की). ~ दरजे का, adj. colloq. of the very best kind: superb. ~ पहुँचना, to reach a limit. ~ बाँधना, to fix boundaries, or limits (of or to, की). ~ में रखना, to keep within limits. ~ से ज़्यादा, adj. & adv. unlimited, very numerous; too many; extremely. ~ से बढ़ना, to go beyond limits. ~ से बाहर, adv. beyond bounds, extremely. किस ~ तक? to what extent? बहुत ~ तक, adv. to a great extent, largely. – हदबंदी [P. -*bandī*], f. fixing limits or boundaries (of); demarcation.

हदराना *hadrānā*, v.t. reg. to shake, to jolt; to agitate.

हदस *hadas* [A. *ḥad(a)ṣ*], m. sthg. becoming known: fear; constant fear of what may happen.

हदसना *hadasnā* [cf. H. *hadas*], v.i. to be fearful of what may happen.

हदीस *hadīs* [A. *ḥadīṣ*], f. U. *isl.* any tradition or narrative about a saying or an action of Muḥammad.

हद्द *hadd*, f. see हद.

हनन *hanan* [S.], m. **1.** striking; wounding; injuring. **2.** killing. **3.** destruction. — ~ करना, to wound; to kill; to destroy.

हनना *hannā* [*hanati*], v.t. **1.** to strike; to wound. **2.** to kill.

हननीय *hananīyă* [S.], adj. deserving death.

हनुमंत *hanumant* [S.], m. Av. = हनुमान.

हनुमान *hanumān* [S.], m. *mythol.* having (large) jaws: name of the monkey chief or deity who was Rāmcandra's ally in his invasion of Laṅkā.

हनू *hanū* [*hanūmant-*], m. Av. = हनुमान. — हनूमान, m. id.

हनोज़ *hanoz* [P. *hanoz*], adv. U. still. — ~ दिल्ली दूर है, Delhi is still far off: there is still much to be done.

हप *hap* [**happ-*], m. the sound of gulping in, or gobbling. — ~ कर जाना, to eat up, to gobble up. ~ से खाना, id. – हप-झप, adv. greedily, quickly (of eating). हप-हप, id.

हपकना *hapaknā* [cf. **happ-*], v.t. reg. **1.** to gulp in; to gobble; to bolt. **2.** to gape (in wonderment).

हप्पा *happā* [cf. H. *hap*], m. **1.** a mouthful. **2.** pap, mush (for children). **3.** a bribe, sop. — ~ देना (को), colloq. to feed; to bribe.

हप्पू *happū* [cf. H. *hap*], adj. & m. **1.** adj. gluttonous. **2.** m. a glutton. **3.** colloq. opium.

हफहफाना *haphhaphānā* [cf. H. *hāṁphnā*], v.i. to pant, to gasp.

हफ़्ता *haftā* [P. *hafta*], m. a week. — अगले हफ़्ते, adv. next week. अगले हफ़्ते में, adv. during next week. – हफ़्तेवार [P. -*vār*], adj. weekly. °ई, adj. & f. id.; a weekly (publication).

हबकना *habaknā*, v.i. = हपकना.

हबड़-दबड़ *habaṛ-dabaṛ*, adv. in haste, helter-skelter. — ~ करने से काम नहीं होता, more haste, less speed.

हबड़ा *habṛā* [**habba-*], adj. reg. **1.** clumsy; ill-shaped. **2.** forbidding; having large teeth.

हबन्नक़ *habannaq* [A. *habannaq*], adj. & m. **1.** adj. foolish, silly. **2.** m. a weak or foolish person.

हबशिन *habśin* [cf. H. *habśī*], f. an Ethiopian woman: a black African woman.

हबशी *habśī*, m. see हब्शी.

हबूब *habūb* [A. *ḥubūb*, pl.], m. **1.** E.H. grains: sthg. trivial. **2.** Brbh. [for *habāb*: A. *ḥabāb*] a bubble.

हब्बा-डब्बा *habbā-ḍabbā* [? cf. *hambhā-* 'lowing'], m. bronchial illness (in children).

हब्शी *habśī* [A. *ḥabśī*], m. an Ethiopian: a black African.

हम *ham* [*asmade*: Pa. *amhe*], pron. pl. **1.** we (by women often used in m. pl. verb concord: e.g. ~ जाते हैं). **2.** I (this usage can, but does not necessarily, imply assumption of superior status on a speaker's part).

हम- *ham-* [P. *ham*], pref. **1.** similar, equal. **2.** together, with; each other; co-. — हमउम्र, adj. of the same age. हमक़ौम, adj. & m. of the same tribe, or nation; a fellow-tribesman, fellow-countryman. हमख़ियाल, adj. & m. like-minded; one of like mind. हमचश्म, m. U. an equal, peer; °ई, f. equality, rivalry. हमज़बान, adj. sharing a language; conversing together; expressing the same opinion; unanimous. हमज़ाद [P. -*zād*], m. a twin; a spirit supposed to be produced at the birth of every child and to accompany him through life. हमजमात [A. *jamā'a(t)*], m. class-fellow. हमज़ात, adj. of the same species, nature or kind. हम-ज़ुल्फ़, f. a wife's sister's husband. हमदम, m. breath(ing) together: a bosom friend; spouse. हमजोली, m. f. an equal, peer; a contemporary; playmate. हमदर्द, adj. & m. sympathetic; tender-hearted; a person who shows sympathy, &c. °ई, f. sympathy, fellow-feeling. हमनसल, adj. of the same breed. हमनाम, adj. of the same name (persons). हमपेशा, adj. inv. of the same occupation (as another). हमबिस्तर, adj. & m. f. sleeping together; lover, mistress. °ई, f. liaison, cohabitation. हममज़हब, adj. & m. of the same religion; a co-religionist. हममानी, adj. synonymous. हमरकाब [A. *rikāb*], m. stirrup-fellow, fellow-rider. हमराज़, adj. & m. knowing each other's secrets; an intimate friend. हमराह, m. companion on the road. °ई, f. companionship, company; m. = हमराह. हमशहरी, m. fellow-townsman. हमवतन, adj. & m. of the same country; fellow-countryman. हमवार [P. -*vār*], adj. even, level (as ground); well-proportioned, well-made. हमवार करना, to make level. हमशकल, adj. of the same appearance, resembling. हमशीरा, f. of the same milk: a full sister. हमसफ़र, m. fellow-traveller. हमसाया P. *sāya*], m. under the same shade: a neighbour.

हमता *hamtā* [cf. H. *aham*], f. Brbh. selfishness.

हमरा *hamārā*, adj. metr. var. or reg. = हमारा.

हमल *haml* [A. *ḥaml*], m. carrying: gestation, pregnancy; foetus. — ~ गिरना, a miscarriage to occur. ~ गिराना, to cause an abortion. ~ रहना (को), to be pregnant.

हमला *hamlā* [A. *ḥamla*], m. **1.** an attack. **2.** assault (on a person). **3.** aggression. — ~ करना (पर), to attack, &c. ~ बोलना (पर), to launch an attack (on). – हमलाबाज़ी [P. -*bāzī*], f. aggressiveness. हमलावर [P. -*āvar*], adj. attacking; aggressive.

हमहस्ती *hamhastī*, f. coexistence.

हमाम *hamām*, m. Brbh. = हम्माम.

[1]**हमाम** *hamām*, m. = हम्माम.

[2]**हमाम** *hamām*, m. a mortar (= हिमाम).

हमायल *hamāyal* [A. *ḥamā'il*], f. a necklace of flowers, or of rupees.

हमार *hamār*, adj. Brbh. Av. = हमारा.

हमारा *hamārā* [cf. *asmāka*-: Ap. *amhāra*-], adj. **1.** our; ours. **2.** my; mine (see हम).

हमाल *hamāl*, m. Brbh. **1.** one who lifts, or uplifts (= हम्माल). **2.** a porter.

हमें *hamem̐* [*asmad*-: Pk. *amhehim̐*], pron. **1.** us. **2.** to us; concerning us (= हमको).

हमेल *hamel* [A. *ḥamā'il*], f. a necklace (usu. made of gold or silver coins, and having a pendant).

हमेव *hamev* [*aham̐* (? or H. *ham*)+*eva*], m. egoism.

हमेशा *hameśā* [P. *hameśa*], adv. always, constantly. — ~ का, adj. existing always; eternal. ~ के लिए, adv. for ever.

हमेस *hames*, adv. Brbh. = हमेशा.

हम्माम *hammām* [A. *ḥammām*], m. a bathroom or bathing-place with provision for hot water. — ~ करना, to bathe, to wash. ~ की लुँगी, f. bath-sheet; sthg. common to all, free.

हम्मामी *hammāmī* [A. *ḥammāmī*], m. owner of, or attendant at, a bathing-place (*hammām*).

हम्माल *hammāl* [A. *ḥammāl*], m. U. a porter.

हय *hay* [S.], m. a horse. — हय-साला, f. Av. stable. – हय-गय [*gaja*-], Brbh. Av. m. pl. horses and elephants.

हया *hayā* [A. *ḥayā*], f. **1.** shame; sense of shame, modesty. **2.** bashfulness. — ~ होना, shame, &c. to be felt (by, को). – हयादार [P. -*dār*], adj. modest; retiring. °ई, f.

हयात *hayāt* [A. *ḥayāt*], f. U. life.

हयो *hayo* [*hata*-], adj. Brbh. **1.** struck down, killed. **2.** fig. destroyed, doomed.

[1]**हर** *har* [P. *har*], adj. each, every. — ~ आन, adv. at every moment, constantly. ~ एक, adj. & pron. each one, each, every; everybody. ~ कहीं, adv. everywhere. ~ कोई, adj. & pron. = ~ एक. ~ घड़ी का, adj. of every moment, constant, perpetual. ~ जिंस, f. every sort or species; reg. (W.) cereals collectively (grain and pulse) excluding rice. ~ तरह, adv. in every direction. ~ तरह, or ~ तरह से, adv. in every way or respect; however possible, anyhow. ~ तरह का, adj. every kind of. ~ दम, adv. with each breath: at every moment, constantly. ~ दिन, adv. every day, daily. ~ बार, adv. at every time or occasion, always. ~ रोज़, adv. = ~ दिन. ~ वक़्त, adv. all the time, constantly. ~ हाल में, adv. = next, 1., 2. ~ हालत में, adv. in every case; in every respect; in any case, at least. – हरकारा [P. -*kāra*], m. doing all work: an errand-runner, messenger; डाक का हरकारा, m. 19c. postman. हरगुनी, adj.

having all qualities: skilful, clever. हर-चंद, conj. U. although; however much; as often as. हरजाई [P. *-jā*], adj. & m. f. belonging to every place: (a husband or wife) who has numerous affairs. हर-फ़न-मौला, m. master of every skill: jack-of-all-trades. हर-हमेश, adv. = next. हर-हमेशा, adv. always and ever.

[2]**हर** *har* [S.], adj. & m. **1.** adj. -हर. taking; conveying; captivating; removing; destroying. पापहर, removing sin; मनोहर, captivating the heart. **2.** m. destroyer: a name of Śiva. **3.** *arith.* divisor; denominator. — ~ जैसे को तैसा, Śiva helps, or gives, to each kind of person according to his needs. ~ ~, or ~ ~ महादेव, interj. & adv. shout of eagerness (for fight); with a loud shout, loudly. ~ ~ हँसना, to laugh loudly. – हरबोला, m. obs. whose war-cry is to Śiva: a (Hindu) soldier.

[3]**हर** *har*, m. reg. a plough (= [1]हल). — हर-पूजा, f. reg. (W.) plough-worship (performed at the end of a sowing season). °-पूजी, f. id. हरसज्जा [cf. H. *sājhā*], m. mutual assistance with ploughing. हर-सोत, f. reg. (W.) the first furrow ploughed, first ploughing of the season.

हरऔ *haraau*, adj. Brbh. = हलका. — हरऐं, adv. slowly, softly.

हरक *harak* [S.], adj. & m. **1.** adj. taking; stealing. **2.** m. a thief.

हर-कट *har-kaṭ* [H. *harā*+H. *kăṭnā*], ? m. reg. (W.) crops cut while unripe.

हरकत *harkat* [A. *ḥaraka*: P. *ḥarakat*], f. **1.** motion, movement. **2.** act; bad action, misdemeanour. **3.** a vocalisation mark (in Perso-Arabic script). — ~ करना, to move, to act, to work; to act wrongly or badly; to interrupt, to disturb (in, में).

हरकती *harkatī* [A. *ḥarakatī*], adj. & m. **1.** adj. interrupting, obstructive. **2.** m. an interrupter, &c.

हरकारा *harkārā*, m. see s.v. [1]हर.

हरकाह *harkāh* [? conn. H. *haraknā*], m. reg. (Bihar) a shying bullock.

हरगिज़ *hargiz* [P. *hargiz*], adv. used w. neg. **1.** at any time. **2.** on any account. — ~ नहीं, adv. never at all; on no account, absolutely not.

हरज *harj*, m. see हर्ज.

हरजाई *harjāī*, adj. & m. f. see s.v. [1]हर.

हरटिया *haraṭiyā* [conn. H. *rahaṭ*], m. reg. bullock-driver at a water-wheel (Persian wheel).

हरट्ट *haraṭṭ*, m. Brbh. strong, sturdy.

हरठिया *haraṭhiyā*, m. reg. = हरटिया.

हरड़ा *harṛā*, m. yellow or 'black' myrobalan (= हर्रा, हड़).

हरण *haraṇ* [S.], m. **1.** taking, seizing; carrying off; stealing. **2.** taking away; removing (a difficulty); curing (a disease); confiscation (of assets). **3.** destroying (sin). **4.** captivating (the heart). — ~ करना, to confiscate, &c.

हरणीय *haraṇīyă* [S.], adj. liable to confiscation.

हरता *hartā* [S.], m. inv. one who takes or seizes: robber, thief; plunderer, destroyer. — हरता-धरता, m. inv. one having power both to destroy and to preserve: करता-धरता, 2.

हरताल *hartāl* [ad. *haritāla-*], f. yellow orpiment, arsenic sulphide. — ~ फेरना, or लगाना (पर), fig. to destroy, to ruin (an endeavour, &c).

हरद *harad*, f. Brbh. Av. turmeric (= हल्दी).

हरदा *hardā* [cf. H. *harad*], m. reg. mildew; smut (in cereals); a disease of cereals in which the plant withers and turns yellow.

हरद्वार *hardvār*, m. = हरिद्वार, s.v. हरि.

हरना *harnā* [*harati*], v.t. & v.i. **1.** v.t. to take, to seize. **2.** to take away; to remove (difficulty, distress). **3.** to carry off; to steal; to kidnap. **4.** to plunder; to destroy. **5.** to captivate (the heart). **6.** [cf. H. *harānā*] v.i. reg. to be defeated, or beaten.

[1]**हरना** *harnā* [*hariṇaka-*], m. = हिरन.

[2]**हरना** *harnā*, m. *Pl.* pommel (of a saddle).

-हरनी *-harnī* [ad. *haraṇī-*], adj. f. **1.** removing, alleviating (grief, &c). **2.** captivating (the heart).

हरफ़ *harf* [A. *ḥarf*], m. changing, altering: **1.** a letter (esp. of the Perso-Arabic script). **2.** U. a word. ~ आना, a blot to fall (on, पर: name or reputation). ~ उठाना, to make out letters (of handwriting or lithographed script). ~ बनाकर लिखना, to write by syllables: to write clearly or well. ~ बहरफ़ [P. *ba-*], word for word, literally. ~ बिठाना, to compose (for printing). ~ ~, adv. word for word. ~ ~ बयान, m. a full account.

हरफ़नमौला *harfanmaulā*, m. see s.v. [1]हर.

हरफरौरी *harpharaurī*, f. *Pl.* = हरफारेवड़ी.

हरफारेवड़ी *harphārevṛī*, f. *Pl. HŚS.* a tree or bush resembling the *kamrakh*, *Averrhoa bilimbi* (it has small, bitter-sweet fruit).

हरबोंग *harboṁg*, m. **1.** utter confusion. **2.** uproar. — ~ मचना, confusion to arise or to reign; uproar to break out.

हरभरा *harbharā* [? H. *har(i)*+H. *bharā*], m. reg. a name given to the chick-pea (gram).

हरम *haram* [A. *ḥaram*], m. forbidden (place): harem. — हरम-खाना, m. = ~. ~ का जना, m. harem-born: a bastard.

हरवाहा *harvāhā* [**halavāha-*: Pk. *halavāhaga-*], m. reg. a ploughman; farm labourer.

हरवाही *harvāhī* [cf. H. *harvāhā*], f. reg. **1.** ploughman's work, ploughing. **2.** payment for ploughing; money (or grain) advanced to a ploughman.

हरवैया *harvaiyā* [cf. H. *hārnā*, *harānā*], m. reg. one who loses or is defeated, a loser.

हरसना *harasnā* [ad. *harṣate*], v.i. to be pleased, to rejoice.

हरसिंगार *harsiṅgār* [H. [2]*hār*+H. *siṅgār*], m. the tree *Nyctanthes arbor tristis* and its flower. — ~ की डंडी, f. the orange tube of the corolla of *Nyctanthes* (used for dyeing).

हरहराना *harharānā*, v.i. **1.** to make a rushing sound (wind, water). **2.** to reverberate (voice, laughter).

हरहा *harhā* [? conn. **haṭ-*], adj. & f. **1.** adj. wild or ill-trained (cattle). **2.** f. Brbh. a wild or ill-trained cow.

हरहाई *harhāī* [cf. H. *harhā*], adj. & f. **1.** adj. Brbh. wild, unbroken (an animal). **2.** f. E.H. wildness (of an unbroken animal).

हरा *harā* [*harita-*], adj. & m. **1.** adj. green. **2.** fresh, refreshed; happy, carefree. **3.** flourishing (as crops). **4.** young. **5.** unripe. **6.** half-cooked. **7.** unhealed (a wound). **8.** m. green colour. **9.** green food (for cattle). — ~ बाग़, m. a green garden or park; fig. delusive hopes. ~ बाग़ दिखाई पड़ना, or सूझना, delusive hopes to be nourished (by, को). ~ बाग़ दिखलाना (को), to raise delusive hopes (in). हरी फ़सल, f. greens, garden produce. हरी हरी सूझना (को), to look always on the bright side. मन ~ होना, to feel refreshed (physically and mentally); to become happy (as after anxiety). – हरा-भरा, adj. luxuriant; overgrown; fruitful; prosperous, happy; radiant (a face). हरे-भरे रहो, may you prosper and be happy.

[1]**हराई** *harāī* [cf. H. *harānā*], f. **1.** defeat. **2.** worsting; foiling. **3.** tiring, taxing; bothering.

[2]**हराई** *harāī* [cf. H. [3]*har*], f. reg. ploughing: **1.** W. first ploughing of the season. **2.** Bihar. the ploughing of a landlord's fields by a tenant. **3.** W. portion of land cultivated by one plough.

हरातर *harātar* [cf. H. [3]हर], m. reg. (W.) place where ploughing is being done.

हराती *harātī* [cf. H. [1]*hal*], adj. & m. reg. having to do with a plough, or ploughing: a ploughman.

हराना *harānā* [cf. *hārayati*: Pa. *hāreti*, *harāpeti*], v.t. to cause to be taken: **1.** v.t. to defeat (in, में); to beat (as at a game). **2.** to worst; to foil, to outwit. **3.** to hunt down. **4.** to tire out. **5.** to lose. — एक ज़ीरो से हरा देना, to beat (an opposing team) one-nil. जी हरानेवली एक बात, f. a tiring, or taxing business.

हरापन *harāpan* [cf. H. हरा], m. greenness, freshness, &c. (see हरा).

हराम *harām* [A. *ḥarām*], adj. & m. **1.** adj. forbidden (by Islamic law). **2.** unlawfully begotten. **3.** m. an unlawful or immoral act, wrong-doing. **4.** adultery. **5.** a wrong-doer. — ~ करना, to regard or to determine as unlawful; to do what is unlawful; to make (sthg. good or worthy, का) difficult or impossible, to put an end to. ~ का, adj. unlawful (as a pregnancy); ill-gotten (as wealth); illegitimate (a child); obtained without due effort (as food). खाना ~ होना, fig. not to want to touch (one's) food. हराम-ख़ोर [P. *-khor*], m. one who lives on money wrongfully earned or obtained; a good-for-nothing. °ई, f. living on wrongful earnings; dishonesty; baseness. हरामज़ादगी [P. *-zādagī*], f. illegitimacy (of birth); wickedness, villainy. हरामज़ादगी करना (की), to ill-treat; to abuse. °-ज़ादा [P. *-zādā*], adj. & m. (f. °ई). illegitimate (a child); a bastard; fig. a scoundrel.

हरामी *harāmī* [A. *ḥarāmī*], adj. & m. **1.** adj. = हराम, 1., 2. **2.** wicked, base. **3.** m. = हरमज़ादा. — ~ (का) पिल्ला, m. pej. son of a dog: = हरामज़ादा. ~ का बच्चा, m. id. ~ तिक्का, m. reg. base flesh, or offspring: id.

हरारत *harārat* [A. *ḥarāra*: P. *ḥarārat*], f. **1.** heat. ***2.** feverishness; a temperature. **3.** frenzy; enthusiasm.

हरावल *harāval* [P. *harāval*], m. E.H. vanguard (of an army).

हरि *hari* [S.], adj. & m. **1.** adj. yellowish; greenish; tawny. ***2.** m. a name of Viṣṇu-Kṛṣṇa; and of other deities: Śiva, Brahmā, Indra. — हरि-कथा, f. the story of the incarnations of Viṣṇu. हरि-चरित, m. the exploits of Kṛṣṇa, or of Viṣṇu in any other incarnation; name of several early Hindi works. हरि-जन, m. a devotee or servant of Hari; a Harijan, outcaste. हरि-देव, m. the asterism Śravaṇa. हरि-द्वार, Hari's gate: name of the town and pilgrimage-place where the Ganges enters the north Indian plain. हरि-पद, m. the feet of

Viṣṇu; transf. salvation in the heaven of Viṣṇu (*vaikuṇṭha*). हरि-भक्त, m. a devotee of Hari; a devout man. °-भक्ति, f. devotion to Hari. हरि-भजन, m. worshipping Hari with devotional songs. हरि-लीला, f. = हरि-चरित, 1. हरि-लोक, m. the world or heaven of Viṣṇu (= वैकुंठ). हरि-हर, m. Viṣṇu and Śiva.

हरिअर *hariar* [**haritara-*], adj. Av. greenish, green.

हरिण *hariṇ* [S.], m. = हिरन.

हरिणी *hariṇī* [S.], f. **1.** a doe (= हिरनी). **2.** *rhet.* one of the four kinds of women (= चित्रिणी).

हरित *harit* [S.], adj. green, &c. (see हरि). — हरित-मणि, m. green gem: emerald. हरिताभ [°*ta* + *ā*°], adj. green, greenish.

हरिताल *haritāl*, m. हरताल.

हरिताली *haritālī*, f. the black-oil plant (= माल-कँगनी).

हरिद्रा *haridra* [S.], f. turmeric.

हरिन *harin* [*hariṇa-*], m. = हिरन. — हरिनाच्छ [°*ṇa* + *a*°], adj. 19c. having eyes like a doe (a woman).

हरिना *harinā* [*hariṇaka-*], m. = हिरन.

हरिनी *harinī* [ad. *hariṇī-*], f. = हिरनी.

हरियर *hariyar* [**haritara-*], adj. poet. = हरा.

हरियल *hariyal* [**haritara-*], m. **1.** the green pigeon, *Treron phoenicoptera* (it has a yellow breast and yellow wing flashes). **2.** the green bee-eater, *Merops orientalis*.

हरिया *hariyā*, adj. E.H. = हरा.

हरियाई *hariyāī* [cf. H. *hariyā*], f. 19c. = हरियाली.

हरियाणा *hariyāṇā*, m. name of the state of the Indian union lying to the north-west of Delhi.

[1]**हरियाना** *hariyānā*, v.i. reg. to grow green, or luxuriant.

[2]**हरियाना** *hariyānā*, m. = हरियाणा.

हरियाल *hariyāl* [*haritāla-*], m. reg. **1.** the green pigeon (= हरियल). **2.** adj. E.H. green.

हरियाला *hariyālā* [*haritāla-*], adj. green, &c. (= हरा, 1., 3).

हरियाली *hariyālī* [cf. H. *hariyāl(ā)*], f. **1.** greenery, vegetation. **2.** green fodder. **3.** fig. happiness, delight. — ~ छाना, or होना, everything to be green (in the rainy season). ~ सूझना (को), fig. everything to appear in a rosy light (to).

हरिश्चंद्र *hari-ścandra* [S.], m. of golden splendour: **1.** *mythol.* name of a king of the solar race, proverbially true to his word. **2.** name of Hariścandra 'Bhāratendu', the first major writer of modern Hindi.

हरिस *haris* [*halīṣā-*], f. reg. a ploughshaft.

हरी *harī* [cf. H. [1]*hal*, [3]*har*], f. reg. (E.) ploughing: help with the ploughing of landlords' fields (exacted from tenants).

हरीतिमा *harītimā*, f. poet. greenery, vegetation.

हरीफ़ *harīf* [A. *ḥarīf*], m. E.H. a rival; an opponent.

[1]**हरीरा** *harīrā* [**haritara-*], adj. & m. reg. **1.** adj. green. **2.** radiant, happy. **3.** m. = हरियाली.

[2]**हरीरा** *harīrā* [A. *ḥarīra*], m. a preparation of semolina, milk, sugar and spices (as taken by women after childbirth).

हरुआ *haruā*, adj. Brbh. Av. = हलका. — हरुए, adv. slowly, softly.

हरुआई *haruāī*, [cf. H. *haruā*], f. Av. = हलकापन.

हरे *hare* [S.], voc. oh Hari!

हरेवा *harevā* [*harita-*: × H. *parevā*], m. *Pl. HŚS.* the green bulbul, *Chloropsis aurifrons*.

हरौती *harautī* [**laghuvetra-*], f. reg. a cane, light stick.

हरौरी *haraurī*, f. reg. 1. = हरवाही. **2.** a place where ploughing is being done.

हरौल *haraul*, m. Brbh. = हरावल.

हर्ज *harj* [A. *harj*], m. **1.** trouble, loss, harm; inconvenience. **2.** obstacle. — ~ करना, to cause loss or damage (to, का); (w. में) to put an obstacle (in the way of). इससे आपका क्या ~ है? what harm, or inconvenience, is this to you? कोई, or कुछ, ~ नहीं, it doesn't matter (said in denying loss or inconvenience).

हर्जा *harjā* [P. *harja*], m. damages, compensation.

हर्जाना *harjānā* [P. *harjāna*], m. compensation (= हर्जा).

हर्फ़ *harf* [A. *ḥarf*], m. see हरफ़.

हर्ब *harb* [A. *ḥarb*], f. U. war.

हर्म्य *harmya* [S.], m. mansion, palace.

हर्रा *harrā*, m. yellow or 'black' myrobalan (= हरड़ा, हड़).

हर्राफ़ *harrāf* [A. *ḥarrāf*], adj. U. clever, sharp, astute.

हर्ष *harṣ* [S.], m. joy, delight; rapture. — ~ करना, to be delighted, to rejoice. यात्रा के ~ में, adv. in eager anticipation of the journey. – हर्षकारक, adj. & m. causing joy, delighting; delighter. हर्ष-ध्वनि, f. sound of delighted applause. हर्षातिरेक [°*ṣa*+*a*°], m. an extreme of delight, ecstasy. हर्षोन्माद [°*ṣa*+*u*°], m. wild delight, rapture. हर्षोल्लास [°*ṣa*+*u*°], m., ecstasy.

हर्षण *harṣaṇ* [S.], m. state of ecstasy.

हर्षना *harṣnā* [ad. *harṣate*; cf. H. *harṣ*], v.i. reg. to be delighted; to rejoice; to be happy.

हर्षाना *harṣānā* [cf. H. *harṣnā*], v.t. & v.i. **1.** v.t. to delight. **2.** v.i. = हर्षना.

हर्षित *harṣit* [S.], adj. delighted, joyful; cheerful.

हलंत *halant* [S.], m. & adj. *ling.* ending in *hal* (a plough): **1.** m. a consonant together with the subscript sign *virāma*, indicating that it is not followed by the sound /ə/. **2.** adj. ending in a consonant (a word).

[1]**हल** *hal* [*hala-*[1]], m. **1.** a plough. **2.** fig. an amount of land requiring only one plough for upkeep: a small plot of farm or market garden land. **3.** हल-. see हलंत, s.v. — ~ चलना (में), to be ploughed (land). ~ चलाना, to plough. – हल-घसीट, f. reg. (W.) the cultivated lands of a village. हलदार [P. *-dār*], adj. owning a plough (a farmer). हलधर, m. plough-holder: a title of Balrām (Kr̥ṣṇa's elder brother). हलबंदी [P. -*bandī*], f. assessment for revenue according to the number of ploughs; the amount of land under cultivation by an individual. हलबाहा [H. -*bāhnā*], m. reg. a ploughman. हलवाहा, m. id.: see s.v. हलायता [? conn. *halayati*] m. reg. (W.) the first ploughing of the season (cf. [3]हर). हलायुध [°*la*+*ā*°], m. armed with a plough: = हलधर.

[2]**हल** *hal* [A. *ḥall*], m. solution (of a problem). — ~ करना, to solve (a problem). ~ होना, to be solved; to be overcome (as difficulties).

हलक़ *halaq* [A. *ḥalaq*], m. the throat; gullet; windpipe. — ~ के नीचे उतरना, to be swallowed; to be accepted, or digested (an idea, &c). ~ दबाना (का), to strangle (one); to make (one) disgorge (as ill-gotten gains). ~ बंद करना, to silence (a person, का).

हलकना *halaknā* [cf. **halati*], v.i. reg. to move, to stir; to swirl (liquid).

हलका *halkā* [cf. *laghu-*], adj. **1.** light (in weight, texture). **2.** of reduced or small quality, quantity or effect; pale (colour), mild, soft, slight (as wind, heat, cold, rain); shallow; neap (tide); soft (water); poor-quality (material); low (price); weak (tea, &c.); poor, light (soil); depressed (trade); light (sleep); light (blow); slight (smile, pain, error). **3.** easily digestible (food). **4.** manageable, easy (a task). **5.** refreshed (body, spirits); relieved (as of anxiety). **6.** unimportant (a matter); disregarded (a person); superficial, silly (words, argument); slight (a work). **7.** lowered, demeaned; base. — ~ करना, to lighten (as a burden); to ease; to mitigate; to exonerate; to abate (as a price); to lower (one), to disgrace (in another's esteem). – हलका-फुलका, adj. as light as a feather; mild (as tobacco); superficial. हलके-हलके, adv. slowly, gently.

हलक़ा *halqā* [A. *ḥalqa*], m. **1.** a circle. **2.** company, group (of people). **3.** Brbh. troop, herd. **4.** an area delimited by a boundary line; zone, region, area. — ~ बाँधना, to form a circle or ring; to surround; to besiege. – हलक़ाबंदी [P. *-bandī*], f. & adj. *hist.* arrangement of villages in circles or zones (for administrative purposes).

हलकाई *halkāī* [cf. H. *halkā*], f. reg. = हलकापन.

हलकान *halkān* [A. *halkān*], adj. **1.** harassed; wearied. **2.** confused. — जी ~ करना, to harass, to vex (oneself or another).

[1]**हलकाना** *halkānā* [cf. H. *halkā*], v.i. & v.t. reg. **1.** v.i. reg. to become light, &c. **2.** v.t. to lighten (= हलका करना).

[2]**हलकाना** *halkānā* [cf. H. *halaknā*], v.t. reg. **1.** to cause to move, or to stir. **2.** to set on, to incite (as a dog, a fighting cock).

हलकापन *halkāpan* [cf. H. *halkā*], m. lightness, &c.

हलकोरौ *halkorau*, m. Brbh. – हिलकोरा.

हलगी *halgī*, f. *Pl.* a kind of tambourine or small drum.

हलगे *halge* [? conn. H. *halkā*], adv. reg. softly, gently.

हलचल *halcal* [cf. **hallati*: Pk. *hallaï*; +H. *calnā*], f. **1.** stir, bustle; activity; commotion. **2.** confusion; anarchy. **3.** alarm, fright; panic. **4.** wavering. — ~ डालना, to strike confusion or terror (in, में). ~ पड़ना or मचना, a commotion, or panic, to break out (in, में). ~ होना, bustle, activity, &c. to go on or to arise (in).

हलद- *hald-*. = हल्द-.

हलफ़नामा *halfnāmā* [A. *ḥalf*+P. *nāma*], m. a sworn statement.

हलबल *halbal* [cf. **halla-*, **hala-*[2]], f. bustle, scurry (= हड़बड़ी).

हलबलाना *halbalānā* [cf. **hallati*: Pk. *hallaï*], v.i. & v.t. **1.** v.i. to bustle, to scurry. **2.** v.t. to impair.

हलबलाहट *halbalāhaṭ* [cf. H. *halbalānā*], f. = हलबल.

हलबली *halbalī* [cf. H. *halbalānā*], f. 19c. = हलबल. — ~ का, adj. hastily done, skimped (work).

हलभलिया *halbhaliyā* [cf. H. *halbhalī*], m. reg. a bustling, busy person; a busybody.

हलभली *halbhalī*, f. reg. = हलबली, हलबल.

हलरा- *halrā-* [cf. **hallati*], v.t. Brbh. Av. **1.** to rock (a baby, a cradle). **2.** to dandle, to play with (a baby).

हलवा *halvā* [A. *ḥalva*], m. **1.** a sweet made of flour, *ghī* and sugar, or of semolina, *ghī*, syrup, coconut and spices. **2.** fig. anything soft and sweet. — ~ करना, or निकालना (का), to beat to a pulp: to thrash soundly. ~ समझना, to think (sthg.) an easy or trifling matter. – हलवा-मच्छी, f. the pomfret (a sea fish), *Stromateus cinereus*, or *niger*. हलवे-माँड़े से काम होना, to be concerned with delicacies (for oneself: को), i.e. with one's own selfish interests.

हलवाइन *halvāin* [cf. H. *halvāī*], f. wife of a sweet-maker, &c.

हलवाई *halvāī* [P. *ḥalvāī*], m. a *halvā*-maker: sweet-maker, sweet-seller.

हलवाहा *halvāhā* [**halavāha-*: Pk. *halavāhaga-*], m. a ploughman.

हलवाही *halvāhī* [cf. H. *halvāh(ā)*], f. ploughing, cultivation.

हलहलाना *halhalānā* [cf. **hallati*: Pk. *hallaï*], v.i. & v.t. reg. **1.** v.i. to shake, &c. (= [1]हिलना); to shiver. **2.** v.t. to shake (sthg). **3.** fig. to curse.

हला *halā* [S.], voc. poet. obs. term of address used between women (as in Sanskrit drama).

हलाक *halāk* [A. *halāk*], adj. U. destroyed: killed. — ~ करना, to kill; to murder.

हलाकत *halākat* [A. *halāka*: P. *halākat*], f. U. destruction, killing; death.

हलाकान *halākān*, adj. 19c. = हलकान.

हलाकी *halākī* [P. *halākī*], f. Brbh. **1.** destruction, ruin. **2.** pang (as of separation).

हलाकू *halākū* [cf. H. *halāk*], adj. & m. **1.** adj. destructive; murderous. **2.** m. Hŭlāgū, name of the founder (13c.) of a large Mongol kingdom having its centre in Iran.

हलाल *halāl* [A. *ḥalāl*], adj. *musl.* lawful, allowable (to, को); lawful as food; lawfully acquired or earned. — ~ करना, to make lawful: to slaughter (an animal) in accordance with Islamic law; to kill, to murder; euph. to mistreat (a person) with the aim of obtaining money from him; to make an honest woman of (a mistress). ~ का, adj. lawful, legitimate. हलालख़ोर [P. *-khor*], m. one who eats lawful food; a sweeper. °ई, f.

हलाहली *halāhalī* [S.], f. *Pl.* = [1]हाला.

हलियाग *haliyāg* [**halibhāga-*: ad. *bhāga-*[2]], m. *hist.* the wages of a ploughman, esp. when paid in kind.

हलियाना *haliyānā*, v.i. reg. to feel nausea.

हल्का *halkā*, adj. = हलका.

हल्द- *hald-*. turmeric (= हल्दी): — हल्द-हाथ, f. *hind.* the ceremony of rubbing turmeric and oil on a bride and groom some days before their marriage.

हल्दिया *haldiyā* [cf. H. *haldī*], adj. inv. turmeric-coloured, yellow.

हल्दी *haldī* [cf. *haridra-*], f. turmeric (used as a spice, and as a dye). — ~ उठना, or चढ़ना, turmeric, &c. to be rubbed ceremonially on a bride and groom before marriage (see हल्द-हाथ). ~ चढ़ाना, m. = हलद-हाथ. ~ लगना, fig. a marriage to be about to take place. ~ लगाकर बैठना to sit down having applied *haldī*: sit and do nothing; to act grandly, or proudly; to presume. ~ लगी न फिटकरी, f. nothing was spent on turmeric or alum: the necessary arrangement (for a satisfactory outcome) was not made. आँबी ~, f. = next. आमा ~, f. yellow zedoary, *Curcuma aromatica* (a plant native to Bengal). उसके ~ के हाथ हुए, fig. she was married.

हल्ला *hallā* [**halla-*], m. **1.** noise, din; shout, outcry; uproar. **2.** assault. — ~ करना, to make a din; to make an outcry. ~ बोल देना, to sound the attack; to shout a war-cry. ~ मचाना, to raise a din, or outcry. – हल्ला-कल्ला, m. reg. = next. हल्ला-गुल्ला, m. = ~.

हव *hav* [S.], m. oblation, sacrifice.

हवन *havan* [S.], m. 1. = होम. **2.** sacrificial ladle. — हवन-कुंड, m. fire-pit: the vessel in which a brahmanical fire sacrifice is performed.

हवनीय *havănīyă* [S.], adj. to be sacrificed, used in sacrifice (as *ghī*).

हवलदार *havaldār* [cf. P. *ḥavāla*], m. **1.** *hist.* steward or agent (supervisor of crops, or collector of taxes). ***2.** sergeant (army, police).

हवस *havăs* [A. *havas*], f. intense desire: lust; ambition. — ~ करना, to long (for, की); to aspire (to).

हवसी *havăsī* [P. *havasī*], adj. lustful, lascivious.

हवा *havā* [A. *havā*], f. **1.** air. **2.** wind. **3.** a gas. **4.** a spirit, demon. **5.** fig. credit, good name. **6.** whim, fancy. **7.** state of the wind or climate: a general situation or prospect or mood. — ~ **आना**, wind or air to come (into, **में**); to be ventilated, aired. ~ **उड़ना**, news to spread; a thing to be got wind (of, **की**). ~ **उड़ाना**, to pass wind. ~ **करना**, to fan; to ventilate. ~ **का रुख़**, direction of the wind; the nature of a situation. ~ **के रुख़ जाना**, to sail with the wind; to move with the times. ~ **के घोड़े पर सवार होना**, to ride on a wind-horse: to be going like the wind; to make great haste; to be in the seventh heaven (of delight). ~ **को गाँठ**, or **गिरह. में बाँधना**, fig. to attempt the impossible. ~ **खाना**, to breathe the air (of, **की**: a place); to languish (in a prison); to take a walk, to stroll; colloq. to be off, to clear out. ~ **चलना**, the wind to blow. **अब तो ~ ही ऐसी चली है कि ...**, times are now such that .... ~ **छोड़ना**, or **छुड़ाना**, to pass wind. ~ **देखा करना**, to keep an eye on the wind, or fig. on a situation. ~ **देना (को)**, to give air (to); to let in air, to inflate (sthg.); to air (clothes); to blow (a fire); to encourage (an unfortunate development). ~ **बताना**, to make an unsatisfying answer or response (to, **को**: as to one having a claim). ~ **बदलना**, the wind to change; fig. a situation to change. ~ **बाँधकर चलना**, to sail against the wind. ~ **बाँधना**, to make a name; to boast; to fabricate, to romance. ~ **बिगड़ना**, the air to be polluted; standing or credit to be lost; a situation to worsen. ~ **भर जाना**, air to be blown, or pumped (into, **में**); to be puffed up, vain. ~ **में मिलना**, to evaporate. ~ **लगना (को)** air, &c. to reach, or to affect (one): to be struck by a wind, or blast; to catch cold; to be struck by rheumatism, or paralysis; fig. to lose one's head. ~ **से बात**, or **बातें, करना**, to talk to the air, &c.: to talk to oneself; to be very tall or high (as a building); to be fleet, swift. ~ **से लड़ना**, to quarrel with the wind: to be quarrelsome by nature; to find an occasion for quarrel. ~ **हो जाना**, to run (off) like the wind; to disappear, to vanish; to be lost (consciousness, the wits). — **हवा-ख़ोरी** [P. -*khorī*], f. taking the air, taking a walk. **हवादार** [P. -*dār*], open, airy (room, site); flighty, capricious. °**ई**, f. ventilation. **हवा-निकास**, m. a ventilator. **हवा-पानी**, m. climate. **हवाबंद** [P. -*band*], adj. air-tight, sealed. **हवाबंदी करना**, to build castles in the air; to spread false reports (about a person). **हवा-बदली**, f. change of air. **हवाबाज़** [P. -*bāz*], m. a pilot; an aircraft. °**ई**, f. piloting, flying (an aircraft). **हवारोक**, adj. airtight (a seal, &c).

हवाई *havāī* [P. *havāī*], adj. & m. **1.** adj. pertaining to the air, aerial. **2.** pertaining to flying, or to aircraft. **3.** pneumatic (a drill, &c). **4.** fig. imaginary, unreal; whimsical. **5.** obs. exc. fig. a rocket. — ~ **अड्डा**, m. an airfield, air base; airport. ~ **आतिशबाज़ी**, f. a rocket (firework). ~ **ख़बर**, f. a rumour. ~ **छतरी**, f. parachute. ~ **जहाज़**, m. an aircraft. ~ **डाक**, f. air mail. ~ **पट्टी**, f. airstrip. ~ **बेड़ा**, m. air fleet, air force. ~ **स्थिति**, f. hypothetical nature (of, **की**). **मुँह पर हवाइयाँ उड़ना**, or **छूटना**, rockets to fly across the face (of, **के**): to flush, then to turn pale. – **हवा-हवाई**, adj. colloq. vanished completely.

हवाना *havānā* [? cf. H. *hauā*], v.i. reg. to scream, to screech.

-हवाना *-havānā* [cf. H. *honā*], v.i. see s.v. **होना**.

हवाल *havāl* [conn. A. *aḥvāl*, pl.], m. E.H. state, condition.

हवालदार *havāldār*, m. = **हवलदार**.

हवाला *havālā* [A. *ḥavāla*], m. **1.** charge, keeping. **2.** reference, allusion. — ~ **देना**, to make a reference (to, **का**); to quote. **हवाले**, adv. in the charge, care or keeping (of, **के**). **हवाले करना**, to hand over (to, **के**); to entrust; to deposit.

हवालात *havālāt* [A. *ḥavāla*: P. *ḥavalāt*], f. **1.** custody, detention. **2.** cell(s) (as of a jail). — ~ **करना**, colloq. = next. ~ **में देना**, to place in custody. ~ **में रखना**, to detain (a suspect); to place in custody.

हवाली *havālī* [A. *ḥavālā*: P. *ḥavālī*], f. environs, outskirts. — **हवाली-मवाली**, m. pl. pej. associates, cronies.

हवास *havās* [A. *ḥavāss*, pl.], m. the senses; consciousness. — ~ **गुम होना**, to be unconscious; colloq. to be nonplussed. ~ **ठिकाने आना**, to come to one's senses. ~ **ठिकाने होना**, to be in one's right mind. ~ **पकड़ना**, to come to one's senses.

हविष्य *haviṣyă* [S.], m. & adj. **1.** m. sthg. to be offered in a brahmanical fire sacrifice. **2.** sacrificed; consumed.

हविस *havis*, f. pronun. var. = **हवस**.

हवेली *havelī* [A. *ḥavelī*], f. a house of brick or stone: **1.** an imposing house, or building. **2.** a temple building of the Vallabhan sect.

हव्य *havyă* [S.], m. **1.** m. = **हवन**, 1. 2. = **घी**.

हव्वा *havvā* [A. *ḥavvā*], f. Eve, the first woman.

हशमत *haśmat* [A. *ḥaśma*: P. *ḥaśmat*], f. U. retinue: **1.** pomp, state. **2.** riches.

हश्र *haśr* [A. *ḥaśr*], m. U. gathering, the resurrection: wailing; fig. dire result or effect. — ~ **बरपा करना**, to raise a commotion; to weep and wail.

हसरत *hasrat* [A. *ḥasra*: P. *ḥasrat*], f. **1.** grief; regret. ***2.** longing, desire. — ~ **करना**, to long (for, **की**); to desire. – **हसरतनाक** [P. *-nāk*], adj. sorrowful (a task, a fate).

हसली *haslī*, f. pronun. var. = **हँसली**.

हसाना *hasānā*, v.t. pronun. var. = **हँसाना**.

हसीन *hasīn* [A. *ḥasīn*], adj. beautiful (a woman); handsome (a man); elegant.

हस्त *hast* [S.], m. **1.** the hand. **2.** the forearm. **3.** *astron.* the thirteenth lunar asterism. — **हस्त-कला**, f. hand-art, handicraft. **हस्त-क्षेप**, m. interference; intervention. **हस्त-क्षेप करना**, to interfere, &c. (in, **में**). **हस्तगत**, adj. come into the hand(s) or possession of, acquired, obtained. **हस्त-मैथुन**, m. masturbation. **हस्त-रेखा**, f. a line on the palm of the hand. **हस्त-लिखित**, adj. hand-written. **हस्त-लिखित ग्रंथ**, m. manuscript. **हस्त-लिपि**, f. id.; handwriting. **हस्त-लेख**, m. manuscript. **हस्त-शिल्प**, m. handicraft. **हस्तांकित** [°*ta*+*a*°], m. hand-written. **हस्तांतरक** [°*ta*+*a*°], m. one who transfers, makes over (property, &c). **हस्तांतरण** [°*ta*+*a*°], m. transfer of possession. **हस्तांतरित** [°*ta*+*a*°], adj. transferred, &c. **हस्ताक्षर** [°*ta*+*a*°], m. signature. **हस्ताक्षर करना** (**पर**), to sign (a document), °**इत**, adj. signed.

हस्तक *hastak* [S.], m. Brbh. a musical (? stringed) instrument, or a partic. *mudrā* (cf. **मुद्रा**, 8).

हस्ता *hastā* [S.], f. *astron.* = **हस्त**, 3.

हस्ति- *hasti-* [S.], m. an elephant. — **हस्तिदंत**, m. elephant's tusk; ivory. **हस्ति-मद**, m. elephant's rut.

हस्तिनी *hastinī* [S.], f. **1.** a female elephant. **2.** the lowest of four traditionally enumerated classes of women.

हस्ती *hastī* [P. *hastī*], f. **1.** existence; the world; life. **2.** wealth. **3.** worth, merit. **4.** transf. an important person.

हस्ब *hasb* [A. *ḥasb*], m. counting: — **हस्ब-मामूल**, adv. & adj. (as) customary, or normal (of enquiries).

हहराना *haharānā* [? *hahā*, w. **hallati*: Pk. *hallaï*], v.i. to tremble.

[1]**हाँ** *hāṁ* [conn. *ām*], interj. & f. **1.** interj. yes. **2.** adv. (qualifying a prec. negative statement) but of course, but certainly. **3.** f. a 'yes', assent. — ~ **करना**, to say yes, to agree. ~ **जी**, interj. = ~. ~ **जी** ~ **जी करना**, to say 'yes' to everything, to agree eagerly or obsequiously. ~ **में** ~ **मिलाना**, id. **जी** ~, interj. = ~. – **हाँ-हाँ**, interj. yes, yes. **हाँ-हाँ करना**, to say 'yes, yes'; to hum and haw. **हाँ-हुज़ूरी**, f. submissiveness (to orders); obsequiousness. **हाँ-हूँ** (or **हूँ-हाँ**), adv. = **हाँ-हाँ**.

[2]**हाँ** *hāṁ*, adv. colloq. at the place or house (of, **के**): see **यहाँ**.

हाँक *hāṁk* [*hakka-*, Pk. *hakkā-*: w. H. *hāṁknā*], f. **1.** calling, shouting; shout, cry (as for help, to battle). **2.** urging on (animals). **3.** driving away (by shouting). **4.** colloq. topicality; notoriety. — ~ **चलाना**, or **देना**, or **मारना**, or **लगाना**, to shout, to call (to, **को**). – **हाँक-पुकार**, f. uproar, hullabaloo.

हाँकना *hāṁknā* [*hakkayati*], v.t. **1.** to shout, to call out (see **हाँक**, 1). **2.** to drive, to work (animals, as by shouting). **3.** to drive away (animals). **4.** to drive off (insects, with a fan); to fan (a person). **5.** to utter, to pour out (as boasts). — **झक** ~, to rave. **झूठी-सच्ची** ~, to utter or to deal in lies. **डींग**, or **दून की**, ~, to boast. **शेख़ी** ~, id. – **हाँक-पुकारकर कहना**, to announce (sthg.) to all and sundry, to proclaim. **हाँका-हाँकी**, f. loud or confused shouting, outcry; driving (animals).

हाँका *hāṁkā* [cf. H. *hāṁknā*], m. driving (of animals); a hunt with beaters.

हाँगर *hāṁgar*, m. *Pl. HŚS.* **1.** a shark. **2.** *Pl.* a crocodile.

हाँगा *hāṁgā*, m. reg. **1.** force; violence. **2.** bodily strength. — ~ **करना**, to employ violence, or coercion. ~ **छूटना**, (one's) strength, or nerve, to fail.

हाँगी *hāṁgī*, f. reg. (Bihar) a cloth-bottomed sieve (for sifting flour).

हाँड़ *hāṁṛ* [**hāṇḍa-*: ? conn. *bhāṇḍa-*[1]], m. a large cooking-pot, cauldron.

हाँड़ना *hāṁṛnā* [**haṇḍ-*], v.i. & adj. **1.** v.i. to wander about; to gad about. **2.** adj. gadding about (esp. a woman).

हाँडी *hāṁḍī*, f. pronun. var. = **हाँड़ी**.

हाँड़ी *hāṁṛī* [**hāṇḍa-*: ? conn. *bhāṇḍa-*[1]], f. an earthen pot (esp. for cooking). — ~ **उबलना**, a pot to boil; fig. to behave in an excited or exaggerated way. ~ **गरम होना**, the pot to grow warm: to pocket (an improper gain, a bribe). ~ **चढ़ना**, a pot to be placed (on, **पर**: the fire). ~ **पकना**, the pot to boil; to gossip; a plan to be concocted. ~ **फूटना**, a pot to be broken; an unknown matter to be revealed. ~ **फोड़ना**, to break a pot (over the name of, **के नाम पर**): to be glad at an unpleasant person's departure; to reveal an unknown matter (cf. **भाँड़ा-फोड़**). **दीवानी** ~, f. a crazy pot(-ful): a hodge-podge. **बावली** ~, f. id.

हाँफना *hāṁphnā* [**hamph-*], v.i. to puff, to pant.

हाँस *hāṁs* [*haṁsa-*], m. E.H. = **हंस**.

हाँसना *hāṁsnā*, v.i. reg. = हँसना.

हाँसी *hāṁsī*, f. Brbh. = हँसी.

[1]**हा** *hā* [*hā*[1]], interj. oh! alas! — ~ ~, interj. & m. = ~; sound of distress, or of lamenting; uproar (as of battle); tumult (as of storm waves). ~ ~ करना, to implore, to entreat. ~ ~ खाना, to entreat cringingly, to whine. – हाहाकार, m. sound of distress or of lamenting; uproar, tumult.

[2]**हा** *hā* [onom.], interj. oh! good! excellent! — ~ ~, interj. laughter. – हाहा-ठीठी, f. = next. हाहा-हीही, f. laughter, joking; giggling. हाहा-हूहू, f. id.

हाऊ *hāū* [*hāhābhūta-*], m. a bogy, hobgoblin.

हाकिम *hākim* [A. *ḥākim*], m. **1.** ruler, governor. **2.** an official of status; judge, magistrate. **3.** master, lord. — हाकिमे आला [P. -*e*], m. U. *hist.* highest authority, paramount power.

हाकिमाना *hākimānā* [P. *ḥākimāna*], adj. official (status, capacity).

हाकिमी *hākimī* [A. *ḥākimī*], adj. & f. **1.** adj. governmental. **2.** f. rule, government. **3.** authority, power.

हाजत *hājat* [A. *ḥāja*: P. *ḥājat*], f. **1.** U. want, need. **2.** a place of detention (for prisoners pending trial). **3.** a call of nature. — ~ में रखना, to keep or to place (a prisoner) in detention. – हाजतमंद [P. -*mand*], adj. needy.

हाज़मा *hāzmā* [A. *hāẓima*], m. the digestion; digestion (of food; of facts, &c).

हाज़िम *hāzim* [A. *hāẓim*], adj. U. digesting, digestive.

हाज़िर *hāzir* [A. *ḥāẓir*], adj. **1.** present. **2.** ready, prepared, willing (to, को, के लिए). — ~ करना, to cause to appear, to present (a person); to hand over; to make ready. ~ होना, to be present, or in attendance; to be ready, willing. – हाज़िरजवाब, adj. ready with an answer, quick-witted; pert. °ई, f. readiness with an answer, &c.; repartee.

हाज़िरी *hāzirī* [A. *ḥāẓirī*], f. **1.** presence, attendance (as at a class). **2.** audience (as at a royal court). **3.** appearance (in a court of law). **4.** obs. breakfast (of Europeans). — ~ देना, to indicate (one's) presence, to answer a roll-call; to be constantly present, or in attendance. ~ बजाना, = prec., 2. ~ में खड़ा रहना, to be in constant attendance. ~ लेना, to call a roll. – हाज़िरी-बही, f. attendance register.

हाजी *hājī* [A. *ḥāj(j)ī*], m. *musl.* a pilgrim (to Mecca); one who has been to Mecca.

हाट *hāṭ* [*haṭṭa-*], f. **1.** a market. **2.** a shop, stall. **3.** market day. — ~ करना, to go to market, to shop; to open a shop, &c.; to keep a shop. ~ लगाना, to prepare a shop for trading (by laying out goods). – हाट-बाज़ार करना, = ~ करना.

हाटक *hāṭak* [S.}, m. Brbh. Av. gold. — हाटकपुर, m. Av. city of gold: a name of Rāvaṇ's capital, Laṅkā.

[1]**हाड़** *hāṛ* [*haḍḍa-*, Pk. *haḍḍa-*], , m. **1.** a bone. **2.** a skeleton. **3.** fig. family, community. — हाड़-मांस, m. fig. one's body, or life.

[2]**हाड़** *hāṛ*, m. the month of Asāṛh.

[3]**हाड़** *hāṛ*, m. *Pl. HŚS.* a partic. plant, *Cissus quadrangularis.*

हाड़ी *hāṛī* [conn. *haḍḍika-*], m. a sweeper, scavenger.

हाड़ौती *hāṛautī*, f. **1.** the territories controlled by Hāṛā Rajputs: the Kotah-Bundi region of Rajasthan. **2.** the speech of that region.

हात *hāt*, m. corr. = अहाता.

हाता *hata*, m. reg. = अहाता.

हाथ *hāth* [*hasta-*], m. **1.** the hand; the wrist; the pulse. **2.** the arm; fig. the reach. **3.** paw. ~ अजमाना, to try (one's) hand (at, पर). **4.** a forearm's measure of length. **5.** hand, member (of a work team). **6.** a hand (at cards). **7.** hand, contribution (in some activity). **8.** handle; arm (of a chair). **9.** a blow with hand or fist; slap; sword-stroke. **10.** fig. possession; power; power of gift, patronage. **11.** adv. into the hands or keeping (of, के); by the hand (of), through. — ~ आना, to come to hand; to come into the possession, or power (of, के); to be gained. ~ उठाओ! hands off! ~ उठाना, to raise the hand; to give a greeting (to, को); to pray (for); to be generous (in giving); to raise the hand (against, पर), to strike; to withdraw the hands (from, से); to desist (from); to abandon (as hope, or a claim). ~ उतरना, the wrist to be dislocated. ~ ऊँचा रहना, or होना, the hand (of, का) to be raised: to be lavish in expenditure; to be well-off. ~ कट जाना, fig. to be helpless, or powerless; to be committed (to act in a partic. way). ~ कटाना, fig. to deprive oneself totally of freedom of action. ~ कमर पर रखना, fig. to be weak, feeble. ~ का काम, m. hand-work, handicraft. ~ का दिया, m. a gift, donation. ~ काटना, to cut off the hand (of, का): to render helpless, powerless; to commit oneself (to). ~ का मैल, m. what dirties the hand: lucre; trash. ~ का सच्चा, adj. trustworthy in dealings; true of hand or aim. ~ कानों पर रखना, to place the hands on the ears: to deny, to protest; to express astonishment. ~ की लकीर, f. line(s) on the hand; (one's) fate. ~ के नीचे आना, to come under the control, or into the clutches (of, के). ~ ख़ाली, adj. empty-handed, penniless; idle; free, at leisure. ~ ख़ाली जाना, a hand (at cards) to be without a picture card; a blow to miss; a plan to fail. ~ खींचना, to desist (from, से), to refrain; to abstain; to be sparing (in the use of). ~ खुजलाना, the palm to itch: to anticipate receiving some money; to feel like striking (one). ~ खुलना, the hand to be open: to be generous (as with money); to spend lavishly; to be ready to fight or to strike. ~ गरम होना, to make money from a bribe. ~ चढ़ना, = ~ आना. ~ चलना, the hand to grow skilled; a blow to be struck (on a pretext, or provocation); pl. fists to fly. ~ चलाना, to stretch out the hand (towards); to use the fist(s), to strike (at, पर); = ~ फेरना. ~ छोड़ना, = ~ चलाना, 2. ~ जमना, = ~ बैठना. ~ जूठा करना, to make the hand impure (by touching food), to taste (food). ~ जोड़ना (को), to fold the hands (in greeting, or in supplication, to). ~ झाड़ना, to strike out (at, पर; with, का: as with a weapon); to beat; to empty the hand (as of money), to spend all one has. ~ झुलाते आना, to come 'swinging the arms', empty-handed. ~ डालना, to thrust or to put the hand (in, into, on, में, पर); to interfere (in); to molest; to encroach (on); to plunder; to turn the hand (to). ~ तंग होना, to be in straitened circumstances; to have no time to spare. ~ तकना, to look (to, का) for support. ~ तले, adv. under the hand (of, के), in the power, or clutches (of). ~ तले आना, = ~ के नीचे आना. ~ दबाकर ख़र्च करना, to spend carefully, or frugally. ~ दिखाना, to show the hand or palm (to the palmist); to let (one's) pulse be taken; to show one's skill or prowess. ~ देना (को), to give the hand (to); to give help, a hand; to give one's hand (in settling any bargain); to lend one's support (to a cause); to turn one's hand (to); to interfere (in, में); to put the hand (on or over, पर): as in putting out a light, or in declining food. ~ देते ही पहुँचा पकड़ लेगा, fig. give him an inch and he'll take an ell. ~ धरना, to take (one, का) by the hand; to support, to maintain (one). ~ धोकर पीछे पड़ना (के), to pursue (an object) obsessively; to persecute unreasoningly. ~ धोना, to wash the hands; to despair (of, से); to give up (as hope, life, &c.); to be without. हाथ न धरने, or रखने, देना, not to allow a hand (on one: as a horse); not to yield or to agree to anything. ~ पकड़ना, to take or to seize the hand (of, का); to protect, to look after; to take to wife. ~ पत्थर तले आना, or दबना, fig. to be helpless, unable to act. ~ पड़ना, to fall or to come into the hands, or possession (of, के); to be caught (an elusive person: by another); looting, &c. to occur. ~ पर गंगाजली रखना, to place Ganges water on the hand: to administer a sacred oath; to swear a sacred oath. ~ पर धरा रहना, to be ready (as goods for collection); fig. to be on the tip of the tongue (words). ~ पर नाग, or साँप, खिलाना, to feed a snake on the hand: to place life in jeopardy. ~ पर ~ धरे, or रखे, adv. with arms folded. ~ पर ~ धरे बैठे रहना, to sit doing nothing. ~ पर ~ मारना, to strike the hands together; to wring the hands; to shake hands (on a promise or bargain). ~ पसारना, to stretch out the hand; to beg (from, के आगे, के सामने). ~ पसारे जाना, to depart life empty-handed. ~ पीले करना, to stain (a girl's) hands with turmeric: to get a girl married; to have a quiet or inexpensive wedding. ~ फेरना, to pass the hand (over, पर); to feel; to stroke, to caress; to retouch; to rob, to relieve (of). ~ फैलाना, = ~ पसारना; to encroach (on, पर). ~ बँटाना, to take a share (in, में: as in work). ~ बंद होना, = ~ तंग होना. ~ बढ़ाना, to stretch out the hand (towards, for, की ओर); to hand, to pass (sthg.); to gain improper possession (of, पर), to encroach (upon). ~ बाँधना, to fold the hands in supplication; to fold the arms. ~ बाँधे खड़ा रहना, to wait upon as a petitioner. ~ बैठना, the hand to grow practised, skill or knack to be acquired. ~ बैठाना, to practise a skill of hand. ~ भर का कलेजा होना, to have an indomitable heart, or courage; to be wildly delighted. ~ मँजना, skill (in, में) to be improved. ~ माँजना = ~ बैठाना. ~ मलकर रह जाना, to be left wringing the hands. ~ मारना, to strike (at, पर); to strike down; to get the hand on, to purloin; to embezzle; to plunder; to eat ravenously; = ~ देना, 4. ~ मिलाना, to shake hands) with, से); = ~ देना, 4.; to claim equality (with). ~ में (के), adv. in or into the hand (of); in the keeping, possession or power (of); at the mercy (of). ~ में करना, to get into (one's) hands, or power. ~ में ठीकरा देना, to put a beggar's bowl into the hands (of, के): to reduce to beggary, to ruin. ~ में दिल रखना, to put one's heart in the hand (of, के): to have a strong regard (for). ~ में मेंहदी लगा होना, iron. to have henna on (one's) hands: to be inert or incapable of necessary action (a man). ~ में पड़ा होना, to be under good control. ~ में ~ देना, to join hands (with, के); to join the hands (of), to give (a daughter) in marriage. ~ में हुनर होना, the hand to be skilled. ~ रँगना, to dye the hands (as with henna); to take bribes; to incur disgrace. ~ रवाँ होना [P. *ravān*], U. the hand to grow practised or used (to, पर); to acquire a knack. ~ रोकना, to check the hand (of, का); to withhold the hand, to refrain (from); to be sparing (in the use of). ~ लगना, = ~ आना; hands, or the hand, to be turned, or applied (to a task); the hand to touch (sthg., में); fig. one (का) to be concerned with or intent on obtaining (sthg., में); *arith.* to be carried on (as a figure in addition). ~ लगाना, to touch (sthg., को); (w. पर) to strike, to beat; = ~ डालना, 2.; to set about (a task, में); to lend a hand. ~ समेटना, or सिकोड़ना, to withold the hand (from, से), to refrain (from); to retrench. ~ साधना, to try (one's) hand; to form a hand, to practise handwriting; to practise (a skill). ~ साफ़ करना, id., 2., 3.; (w. पर) to beat, to trounce; to get away with, to purloin; to eat one's fill (of, से). ~ सिर पर रखना, to put the hand on (one's) head; to swear by (one's) life; to take (one) under protection. ~ से, adv. by, or from the hand(s) (of, के); by means of; through or out of the hands (of). हाथ से जाना, to get out of hand or control. हाथ से बेहाथ हो जाना [P. *be-*], id. हाथों के तोते उड़ जाना, fig. to lose sthg. precious; to become utterly confused, or dumbfounded. हाथों लगे, adv. while engaged (in some other task), while at it; at the same time. हाथों ~, adv. from hand to hand; briskly, swiftly (as of the progress of sales); violently (of the agitation of feelings). हाथों ~ ले जाना, to carry away quickly; to snatch away. हाथों ~ ले लेना, to receive (one) with all respect. उलटा ~ मारना, to strike a back-handed blow. पीठ पर ~ फेरना (की), fig. to soothe, to pacify; to satisfy, to assure. रँगे ~, हाथों, पकड़ा जाना, to be caught red-handed. हाथ-कंगन, m. bracelet. हाथ-कंगन को आरसी क्या? why use a mirror to look at a bracelet? (said when sthg. is, or should be, self-evident). हाथ-गाड़ी, f. hand-cart. हाथ-चालाक, adj. light-fingered. हाथ-पाँव, m. hand and foot, hands and feet, &c. हाथ-पाँव चलना, the limbs to move, to be able-bodied. हाथ-पाँव टूटना, the limbs to be broken; to suffer pains in the limbs (as in the onset of fever). हाथ-पाँव ठंडे हो जाना, the limbs to grow cold (as death approaches). हाथ-पाँव तोड़ना. to cripple; fig. to slave, to toil. हाथ-पाँव धोना, to wash hands and feet; euph. to go to defecate. हाथ-पाँव निकालना, to display (one's) arms and legs; the limbs (or body) to become well-developed; to begin to show off, or to make trouble; the old Adam to come out, to follow bad ways. हाथ-पाँव पटकना, to thrash about with the limbs (as in pain). हाथ-पाँव फूलना, the limbs to swell; to become distressed, or confused; fig. to get cold feet. हाथ-पाँव फैलाना, to extend one's activities or influence; (w. पर) to obtain (sthg.) dishonestly; to take bribes. हाथ-पाँव बचाना, to protect oneself, to watch out. हाथ-पाँव मारना, to sprawl; to flounder; to strike out (in swimming); to strive, to struggle; to flail about (as in pain); to be agitated. हाथ-पाँव हारना, to lose heart. हाथ-पाँव हिलाना, = हाथ-पाँव मारना. हाथ-पैर, m. = हाथ-पाँव. – हाथा-छाँटी [P. *-ā-*], f. sharp practice; embezzlement. हाथा-पाई, f. hitting and kicking, scuffle, brawl. हाथा-बाँही, f. hitting, &c. हाथा-हाथी, adv. = हाथों हाथ.

हाथा *hāthā* [*hastaka-*], m. **1.** handle. **2.** hand-print (as made on walls at festivals or in worship). **3.** a wooden inplement used in field irrigation.

हाथी *hāthī* [*hastin-*], m. **1.** an elephant. **2.** (in chess) the castle, rook. **3.** *astron.* name of the thirteenth lunar mansion. — ~ का खाया कैथ, m. a wood-apple eaten by an elephant: sthg. only outwardly good. ~ बाँधना, to tether an elephant (at one's gate): to acquire great wealth, or reputation. निशान का ~, m. the elephant which leads a procession. – हाथी-ख़ाना, m. elephant-house. हाथी-दाँत, m. elephant's tusk; ivory. हाथी-पाँव, m. elephantiasis. हाथी-पीच [f. Engl. *artichoke*], m. *Pl. HŚS.* the Jerusalem artichoke (used medicinally). हाथीवान, m. elephant-driver.

हादसा *hādāsā* [A. *ḥādiṣa*], m. an incident, an accident.

हानि *hāni* [S.], f. **1.** loss. **2.** damage, harm. **3.** destruction. — ~ उठाना, or सहना, to suffer loss, &c. ~ करना, to bring about harm, &c. (to, की). ~ पहुँचाना (को), to cause loss, damage, &c. (to). – हानिकर, adj. harmful, injurious. हानिकारक, adj. id. हानि-पूरण, m. compensation. हानि-लाभ, m. loss and gain.

हापना *hāpnā*, v.i. pronun. var. = हाँपना.

हापर *hāpar*, m. reg. (W.) a nursery for sugar-cane. ~ ~ खाना, to munch.

हाफ़िज़ *hāfiz* [A. *ḥāfiẓ*], m. **1.** guardian, protector. **2.** a title of Allah. **3.** E.H. one who knows the Qur'ān by heart.

हाबुस *hābus*, m. reg. **1.** green barley (roasted as food). **2.** (Bihar) a millet.

हाबूड़ा *hābūṛā*, m. **1.** a robber; highwayman. **2.** a bogyman.

हामिला *hāmilā* [A. *ḥāmila*], adj. f. U. carrying: pregnant (a woman).

[1]**हामी** *hāmī* [cf. H. *hām*; ? × A. *ḥāmī*], f. **1.** confirmation, assurance. **2.** assent. — ~ भरना (की), to confirm; to pledge oneself (to); to assent.

[2]**हामी** *hamī* [A. *ḥāmī*], m. a supporter; advocate (of).

हाय *hāy* [*hāyi*], interj. & f. **1.** interj. alas! **2.** f. distress, suffering. **3.** envy. — ~ करना, to sigh; to lament. ~ मरा! interj. I am done for! मेरी ~ तुझको लग जाएगी! interj. my suffering will be a curse on you! – हाय-तोबा [A. *tauba*], f. sighing (over a calamity). हाय-हाय, interj. & f. = ~. हाय-हाय मचना, sounds of grief or distress to be heard.

[1]**हार** *hār* [*hāri-*, Pk. *hāri-*; and cf. H. *hārnā*], f. **1.** a losing, defeat. **2.** loss (as of money). **3.** tiredness. **4.** dejection. — ~ खाना, to suffer a defeat, or a loss. ~ देना (को), to defeat. ~ मारना, to accept defeat. – हार-जीत, f. defeat and victory; losing and winning; loss and gain; gambling. हार-जीत करना, to gamble.

[2]**हार** *hār* [*hāra-*[2]], m. **1.** a necklace. **2.** a garland. — गले का ~ होना, to hang round the neck (of, के). गले में ~ डालना, to garland the neck (of, के).

[3]**हार** *hār* [*hāla-*; ? × *hāra-*[2]], m. reg. **1.** a field; grazing ground. **2.** the outer circle of the fields surrounding a village.

[4]**हार** *hār* [S.], m. necklace, &c. (= [2]हार). — हारावलि [°*ra* + *ā*°], f. Brbh. a string of pearls.

-हार *-hār*, adj. & n. formant. reg. = -हारा.

हारक *hārak* [S.}, adj. & m. **1.** adj. taking, seizing. **2.** captivating. **3.** m. plunderer, thief. **4.** *Pl. HŚS. arith.* divisor. **5.** *Pl. HŚS.* = [1]सेवड़ा.

हारना *hārnā* [*hārayati*], v.i. & v.t. to cause or to allow to be taken: **1.** v.i. to be defeated, beaten (in, में). **2.** to suffer loss (in). **3.** to become tired, tired out (the limbs). **4.** to become dejected. **5.** to become old or feeble. **6.** v.t. to lose (as a battle, a match, a bet). **7.** to lose (heart, courage). **8.** to give (one's word). — हार देना, to lose; to squander; to gamble away. हारकर, adv. being beaten, &c.; of necessity, perforce; reluctantly. आख़िर वह हारकर चला गया, finally he gave up and left. हारे दर्जे, adv. as one beaten, &c. (= हारकर).

हारसिंगार *hārsiṅgār*, m. = हरसिंगार.

-हारा *-hārā* [*dhāra-*[1]], adj. & n. formant (reg. in the former case, and often in the latter). = -वाला.

हारिल *hāril* [**hāritāla-*], m. Brbh. Av. the green pigeon (= हरियल).

-हारी *-hārī* [S.], adj. **1.** taking, seizing; plundering. **2.** destroying; alleviating.

हारीत *hārīt* [S.], m. the green pigeon (= हारिल).

हारू *hārū* [cf. H. *hārnā*], m. a loser; one who often or always loses.

हार्दिक *hārdik* [S.], adj. having to do with the heart: cordial, hearty (as greetings, congratulations); heart-felt.

हार्दिकता *hārdikātā* [S.], f. cordiality.

हार्य *hāryă* [S.], adj. to be taken; to be taken away.

[1]**हाल** *hāl* [A. *ḥāl*], m. **1.** state, condition. **2.** circumstances, situation. **3.** present and immediately preceding time. **4.** account, story; news. — ~ आना, to be inspired, to be thrown into ecstasies. ~ का, adj. present-time, present, of today; recent (event, development). ~ पतला होना, to be in bad or indifferent circumstances. ~ लाना, to get into a state of ecstasy or frenzy. ~ मिलना, news to be had (of, का). ~ में, adj. at, or for, the present (time); at once; recently. क्या ~ है (आपका)? how are things? how are you? बहर ~ [P. *ba-har*], adv. in any case. हर ~ में, adv. id. बुरे हालों होना, to be in a bad way. — हाल-चाल, m. state, routine condition (of a person). क्या हाल-चाल है? how are (you) getting on? हाल-बेहाल होना, to deteriorate (as health, or physical condition).

[2]**हाल** *hāl* [cf. H. *hālnā*], f. **1.** shaking; a shake, jerk; jolt. **2.** iron band (round a wheel). **3.** rudder (of a boat).

[3]**हाल** *hāl* [conn. *hāla-*], m. a plough.

हालत *hālat* [A. *ḥāla*: P. *ḥālat*], f. particular state, condition (sometimes = [1]हाल, 1.); state of affairs. — इस ~ में, adv. in this situation, these circumstances. नशे की ~ में, adv. in an intoxicated state, while drunk. बाज़ार की ~, f. state of market. बीमारी की ~, f. (present) state of a patient. मौजूदा ~, f. U. present circumstances. हर ~ में, adv. whatever the case.

हालना *hālna* [**hallati*: Pk. *hallaï*], v.i. **1.** to shake; to sway (in wind). **2.** to tremble, to vibrate. **3.** to be agitated (as water). — हाला-डोला, m. shaking: an earthquake.

हालाँकि *hālāṁki* [P. *hāl ān ki*], conj. that being the case: **1.** although. **2.** however, nonetheless.

[1]**हाला** *hālā* [S.], f. wine; alcohol.

[2]**हाला** *hālā* [A. *hāla*], m. halo (round the moon, &c). — चाँद में ~ पड़ना, the moon to have a halo.

[3]**हाला** *hālā* [conn. *hāla-*], m. *hist.* **1.** a plough-tax. **2.** an instalment of revenue.

हाला-डोला *hālā-ḍolā*, m. see s.v. हालना.

हालात *hālāt* [A. *ḥālāt*, pl.], f. pl. U. **1.** circumstances. **2.** facts, particulars (as of a case). — मौजूदा ~, f. pl. see s.v. हालत.

हालाहल *hālāhal* [S.], m. a deadly poison; *mythol.* the poison produced at the churning of the ocean by the gods and demons.

हालि *hāli* [conn. *hāla-*], f. reg. rudder.

हालिम *hālim*, m. cress, *Lepidium sativum.*

हाली *hālī* [*hālika-*], m. E.H. a ploughman; farm worker.

हाली-हाली *hālī-hālī* [cf. H. [1]*hāl*], adv. reg. presently, quickly.

हाव *hāv* [S.], m. *rhet.* call, cry: any flirtatious gesture (of a heroine). — हाव-भाव, m. blandishments; mannerisms, mammer.

हावन *hāvan* [P. *hāvan*], m. a mortar (for grinding in). — हावन-दस्ता [P. *-dasta*], m. mortar and pestle.

हावी *hāvī* [A. *ḥāvī*], adj. **1.** comprising, including. ***2.** getting within one's grasp: dominating, prominent. — ~ **होना**, to include; to dominate or to be prominent (at the expense of, पर). उसपर उम्र ~ है, age is taking its toll of him.

हाशिया *hāśiyā* [A. *ḥāśiya*], m. **1.** edge, border. **2.** hem. **3.** margin (of a page). **3.** marginal annotation. — ~ **चढ़ाना**, or **लगाना**, to write a marginal note; to make a marginal (joking or ironic) comment. ~ **छोड़ना**, to leave a margin (on a page, में). – **हाशियेदार** [P. *-dār*], adj. having a border, hem, or margin.

हास *hās* [S.], m. **1.** laughter; merriment. **2.** ridicule. — **हासकर**, adj. laughing, merry; laughable, ridiculous.

हासक *hāsak* [S.], m. a laugher, joker.

हासकर *hāskar*, adj. laughable, ridiculous.

हासिका *hāsikā* [S.], f. merriment, laughter.

हासिल *hāsil* [A. *ḥāṣil*], m. **1.** product, outcome, result. **2.** acquisition, gain. **3.** *math.* result, total. ***4.** obtained, gained; resulting. ~ **करना**, to acquire, to obtain; to gain; to collect. ~ **होना**, to be acquired, &c.

[1]**हासी** *hāsī* [S.], adj. laughing, smiling; happy.

[2]**हासी** *hāsī*, f. 19c. = हँसी.

हास्य *hāsyă* [S.], adj. & m. **1.** adj. comical. **2.** laughable, ridiculous. **3.** m. laughter; joking; facetiousness. **4.** *rhet.* the comic sentiment, comedy. (see रस, 9). — **हास्य-चित्र**, m. a cartoon. **हास्य-विनोद**, m. = ~, 3. – **हास्यास्पद** [°*ya*+*ā*°], adj. laughable, ridiculous.

हास्यक *hāsyak* [S.], adj. comical, humorous. — ~ **चित्र**, m. a caricature. – **हास्यकप्रिय**, adj. cheerful, happy (by nature). °**ता**, f.

हिंग *hiṅg* [P. *hing*], m. = हींग.

हिंगन *hiṅgan*, m. **1.** *Pl.* a thorny plant; a firework made from the fruit of this plant. **2.** *HŚS.* = हिंगोट.

हिंगु *hiṅgu* [S.], m. = हींग.

हिंगोट *hiṁgoṭ* [conn. *iṅguda-*], m. *Pl. HŚS.* the Indian almond, *Terminalia catappa.*

हिंडोल *hiṇḍol*, m. = हिंडोला.

हिंडोला *hiṇḍolā* [*hiṇḍolaka-*; Pk. *hiṁḍola-*], m. **1.** a swing. **2.** a cradle. **3.** *mus.* name of a *rāg.*

हिंताल *hintāl* [S.], m. 19c. the marshy date-tree, *Phoenix* or *Elate paludosa.*

हिंद *hind* [P. *hind*], m. north India; India (= हिंदुस्तान). — **जय** ~! long live India! — **हिंद-यूरोपी**, adj. Indo-European.

हिंदवाना *hindvānā* [P. *hindūvāna*], m. **1.** Indian fruit: water-melon; *Pl.* pumpkin. **2.** Brbh. India.

[1]**हिंदी** *hindī* [P. *hindī*], f. & adj. **1.** f. the Hindi language. **2.** adj. having to do with Hindi (as literature, dialect). — **हिंदीतर** [*-itara-*], adj. non-Hindi(-speaking).

[2]**हिंदी** *hindī* [P. *hindī*], adj. & m. chiefly obs. **1.** adj. Indian. **2.** m. an Indian.

[1]**हिंदुई** *hinduī* [P. *hindūī*], adj. & m. reg. **1.** adj. Indian; Hindu. **2.** m. an Indian; a Hindu.

[2]**हिंदुई** *hinduī* [P. *hindūī*], f. chiefly obs. = हिंदी.

हिंदुत्व *hindutvă* [cf. *hindu-*: ← P.], m. **1.** Hindu qualities; Hindu identity. **2.** Hinduism.

हिंदुस्तान *hindustān* [P. *hindūstān*], m. the region of hind: **1.** *hist.* north India (as opposed to the Deccan); specif., the area between Banaras and the river Sutlaj. **2.** India.

[1]**हिंदुस्तानी** *hindustānī* [P. *hindūstānī*], adj. & m. **1.** adj. Indian. **2.** m. an Indian.

[2]**हिंदुस्तानी** *hindustānī* [P. *hindūstānī*], f. Hindustani (a mixed Hindi dialect of the Delhi region which came to be used as a lingua franca widely throughout India and what is now Pakistan).

हिंदुस्थान *hindusthān* [H. *hindustān* × *sthāna-*], m. = हिंदुस्तान.

हिंदू *hindū* [P. *hindū*], m. **1.** *hist.* an Indian. ***2.** a Hindu. — ~ **धर्म**, m. the Hindu religion, or socio-religious system. ~ **मत**, m. Hindu belief.

हिंदूपन *hindūpan* [cf. H. *hindū*], m. **1.** state of being a Hindu; Hindu qualities. **2.** Hinduism.

हिंदोरना *hiṁdornā* [*hindolayati*], v.t. reg. to puddle, to stir.

हिंदोल *hindol* [S.], m. a swing (= हिंडोला).

हिंदोस्तान *hindostān* [P. *hindostān*], m. 19c. = हिंदुस्तान.

हिंसक *hiṁsak* [S.], adj. & m. **1.** adj. violent, dangerous; murderous. **2.** savage, cruel. **3.** prey-taking. **4.** m. a violent person, &c. **5.** a beast of prey. — ~ **पशु**, m. id.

हिंसन *hiṁsan* [S.], m. doing violence, &c. (see हिंसा).

हिंसा *hiṁsā* [S.], f. **1.** violence directed against living creatures; killing, slaughter; injury, hurt, harm. **2.** ill-will. — **हिंसात्मक** [°*sā*+*ā*°], adj.

violent. हिंसा-रत, Brbh. adj. delighting in doing harm, &c., malevolent.

हिंसालु *hiṃsālu* [S.], adj. **1.** inclined to violence; murderous; hurtful. **2.** prey-taking (an animal). **3.** malevolent.

हिंस्र *hiṃsră* [S.}, adj. = हिंसक.

हिंस्रक *hiṃsrak* [S.], adj. & m. **1.** adj. = हिंस्र. **2.** m. a beast of prey.

हिकमत *hikmat* [A. *ḥikma*: P. *ḥikmat*], f. **1.** wisdom; knowledge; mystery, miracle. *__2.__ cleverness, ingenuity; specif. the work or function of an Ayurvedic doctor. **3.** clever means, device. — ~ करना, to practise Ayurvedic medicine. ~ से, adv. cleverly; judiciously.

हिकायत *hikāyat* [A. *ḥikāya*: P. *ḥikāyat*], f. U. narrative, story, tale.

हिक़ारत *hiqārat* [A. *ḥiqāra*: P. *ḥiqārat*], f. contempt, scorn. — ~ करना (की), to treat with contempt; to despise. ~ की नज़र से देखना, to look down upon.

हिक्का *hikkā*, m. colloq. a hiccup (= हिचकी).

हिचक *hicak* [cf. H. *hicaknā*], f. drawing back (from, से or में); hesitation; reluctance; faltering.

हिचकना *hicaknā* [cf. **hicc-*], v.i. **1.** to draw back (from, से); to hesitate. **2.** to be reluctant or averse (to). **3.** to hiccup. **4.** to sob.

हिचकाना *hickānā* [cf. H. *hicaknā*], v.t. reg. to snatch away (from).

हिचकिचाना *hickicānā* [cf. H. *hicaknā*; ?+H. *khiṁcnā*], v.i. = हिचकना.

हिचकिचाहट *hickicāhaṭ* [cf. H. *hickicānā*], f. = हिचक.

[1]**हिचकिची** *hickicī* [cf. H. *hickicānā*], f. hesitation, &c. (= हिचक). — ~ बाँधना, to take to hesitating, to waver.

[2]**हिचकिची** *hickicī*, f. grinding the teeth (= किचकिची).

हिचकियाना *hickiyānā* [cf. H. *hickī*], v.i. reg. to hiccup.

हिचकी *hickī* [cf. H. *hicaknā*], f. **1.** hiccup. **2.** convulsive sobbing; choking (in crying). — हिचकियाँ आना (को), to have hiccups. हिचकियाँ बँधना (को), to hiccup uncontrollably; to sob bitterly. हिचकियाँ लगना (को), to breathe spasmodically (as at death). हिचकियाँ, or ~ लेना, to hiccup; to sob bitterly.

हिचकोला *hickolā*, m. = हचकोला.

हिचर-मिचर *hicar-micar*, m. reg. **1.** hesitation, wavering. **2.** excuse, pretext. **3.** dispute, cavil.

हिजड़ा *hijṛā* [**hijja-*[2]], m. **1.** a eunuch. **2.** an impotent man. **3.** pej. a masculine-looking woman.

हिजर *hijr* [A. *hajr*], m. U. separation.

हिजरत *hijrat* [A. *hijra*: P. *hijrat*], f. **1.** E.H. departure (from one's country and friends). **2.** emigration (to Mecca, or to a Muslim country). **3.** *musl.* the hegira, or flight of Muḥammad from Mecca to Medina (from which the beginning of the Muslim era is dated: 16th July 622).

हिजरी *hijrī* [A. *hijrī*], adj. & f. **1.** pertaining to the hijra or Muslim era. **2.** according to the hijra (a date). **3.** f. the Muslim era. — ~ सन सन छह सौ बाईस में शुरू हुआ था, the Muslim era began in 622. यह वारदात ~ एक हज़ार में हुई, this incident occurred in the year 1000 of the Muslim era.

हिज्जे *hijje* [A. *hijā*], m. syllabification, spelling. — ~ करना, to spell, &c.; to probe (a matter); to wrangle (over a matter). ~ निकालना, to find fault (with). ~ पकड़ना, to find mistakes (of detail: in).

हिडिंब *hiḍimb* [S.], m. *mythol.* name of a demon killed by Bhīm.

हिडिंबा *hiḍimbā* [S.], f. *mythol.* **1.** name of the sister of Hiḍimb (who changed herself into a woman and married Bhīm). **2.** name of the wife of Hanumān.

हित *hit* [S.], adj. & m. **1.** adj. good, beneficial. **2.** kind, affectionate. **3.** suitable, proper. *__4.__ m. well-being, welfare. **5.** advantage, interest. **6.** benevolence, favour. **7.** friendliness; affection, love. **8.** adv. for the sake (of, के). — ~ करना, to show kindness (to, को), to do (one) a service. – हितकर, adj. doing a service or kindness; benevolent; useful. °-कारी, adj. & f. = prec.; = ~, 7. हित-चिंतक, adj. well-wisher. हितार्थ [°*ta*+*a*°], adv. = ~, 8. °ई, adj. & m. benevolent; a well-wisher. हिताहित [°*ta*+*a*°], m. advantage and disadvantage; welfare and misfortune. हितेच्छा [°*ta*+*i*°], f. good will or wishes. °-एच्छुक, adj. हितैषिता [°*ta*+*e*°], f. well-wishing, good will. हितैषी [°*ta*+*e*°], adj. & m. well-wishing; a well-wisher. हितोपदेश [°*ta*+*u*°], m. profitable advice; name of a collection of Sanskrit fables interspersed with didactic comment.

हितू *hitū* [cf. H. *hit*], m. well-wisher, benefactor, friend.

हिदायत *hidāyat* [A. *hidāya*: P. *hidāyat*], f. guidance (esp. in conduct, or religion); instruction. — ~ करना, to guide, to direct. – हिदायत-नामा, m. book of precepts or instructions.

हिनकना *hinaknā* v.i. = हिनहिनाना.

हिनहिनाना *hinhinānā* [**hin-*], v.i. to neigh; to whinny.

हिनहिनाहट *hinhināhaṭ* [cf. H. *hinhinānā*], f. neighing; a neigh; whinny.

हिना *hinā* [A. *ḥinnā*], f. U. the henna plant (used as a dye for the hands and feet, and also the hair: = मेहंदी).

हिनाई *hināī* [A. *ḥinnā*+P. *-ī*], adj. of the colour of henna (dye), orange or reddish; stained with henna.

हिनौती *hinautī* [*hīnavr̥tti-*], f. *Pl.* humility, entreaty.

हिफ़ाज़त *hifāzat* [A. *ḥifāẓa*: P. *ḥifāẓat*], f. **1.** guarding, protection; preservation, care; defence. **2.** security, safety. — ~ करना (की), to guard, to defend, &c. (against, से); to take care (of sthg.); to be careful, on one's guard. ~ में रखना, to put in a safe place, to keep safe. ~ से, adv. carefully; in safety.

हिफ़ाज़ती *hifāzătī* [P. *ḥifāẓatī*], adj. **1.** protective (as measures); defensive. **2.** providing security.

हिब्बा *hibbā* [A. *hiba*], m. gift; bequest; grant. — ~ करना, to give; to make over (as land); to bequeath. – ~ हिब्बा-नामा, m. deed of gift.

हिम *him* [S.], m. **1.** cold. **2.** frost; snow; ice. **3.** the cold season. — हिम-कण, m. frost-crystal; snowflake. हिमकर, m. Av. causing cold: the moon. हिम-गिरि, m. snowy mountains: the Himālayas. हिम-नदी, f. a glacier. हिम-भूधर, m. Av. = हिम-गिरि. हिमवत्, adj. snowy, frosty, icy; snow-clad. हिमवंत, adj. & m. Av. id.; the Himālayas; the Himālayas personified. हिमवान, adj. & m. = हिमवत्; Av. the Himālayas; Brbh. the moon. हिमांशु [°*ma*+*a*°], m. having cool beams: the moon. हिमाचल [°*ma*+*a*°], m. snowy mountain: the Himālayas; name of a state of the Indian union. हिमाच्छादित [°*ma*+*ā*°], adj. covered with snow, &c. हिमाद्रि [°*ma*+*a*°], m. = हिमाचल, 1. हिमालय [°*ma*+*ā*°], m. abode of snow: the Himālaya mountains.

हिमा *himā* [S.], f. the cold season.

हिमाक़त *himāqat* [A. *ḥimāqa*: P. *ḥimāqat*], f. stupidity, fatuousness.

हिमानी *himānī* [S.], f. **1.** a mass of snow; ice; a glacier. — **2.** Brbh. a title of the goddess Pārvatī.

हिमाम *himām* [P. *hāvan*], m. corr. a mortar. — हिमाम-दस्ता [P. *-dasta*], m. mortar and pestle.

हिमायत *himāyat* [A. *ḥimāya*: P. *ḥimāyat*], f. **1.** protection, defence. **2.** support; guardianship; patronage. — ~ करना (की), to protect, &c.; to take up the cause (of), to give support (to). ~ का टट्टू, m. one who presumes on another's protection or support. ~ में आना, to come to be the protégé, &c. (of, की).

हिमायती *himāyătī* [cf. H. *himāyat*], m. **1.** protector. **2.** supporter; guardian; patron. **3.** fig. advocate (of a cause, a view).

हिम्मत *himmat* [A. *himma*: P. *himmat*], f. spirit, resolve; courage. ~ करना, to muster courage (to do sthg., की); to make bold, to dare; to attempt, or to perform, a feat or exploit. — ~ टूटना, = ~ हारना. ~ बाँधना (पर), = ~ करना. ~ हारना, to lose heart, to become dispirited. — हिम्मत-अफ़ज़ाई [P. *-afzāī*], f. display of courage.

हिम्मती *himmatī* [P. *himmatī*], adj. **1.** energetic, resolute. **2.** brave, bold.

हिय *hiy*, m. = हृदय.

हिया *hiyā* [*hr̥daya-*], m. the heart. — ~ फटना, the heart to break. हिये का अंधा, adj. blind of heart: senseless, crazy. हिये की फूटना, to go out of one's mind (to act senselessly).

हियाव *hiyāv* [**hr̥dayabhāva-*], m. heart, spirit, courage. — ~ पड़ना, to have the heart or courage (to); to dare. ~ खुलना, courage to be found, or mustered; inhibitions to be cast off.

हिरकना *hiraknā* , v.i. reg. **1.** to approach close (to). **2.** to scamper.

हिरण *hiraṇ* [S.], m. gold.

हिरण्य *hiraṇyă* [S.], m. gold. — हिरण्य-कशिपु, m. *mythol.* clothed in gold: name of a Daitya king, son of Kaśyap and father of the devotee Prahlād, who because of his persecution of the latter was killed by Viṣṇu. हिरण्य-गर्भ, m. *mythol.* golden foetus: a title of Brahmā, recalling his birth from a golden egg formed from the seed of the self-existent being.

हिरदा *hirdā* [ad. *hr̥daya-*; H. *hiyā*], m. E.H. the heart.

हिरदावल *hirdāval* [conn. *hr̥dāvarta-*], m. *Pl.* *HŚS.* a curl of hair (considered inauspicious) on the neck or chest, or behind the forelegs, of a horse).

हिरन *hiran* [*hariṇa-*], m. yellow or tawny one: **1.** a deer; an antelope. **2.** a stag. — ~ हो जाना, fig. to take to flight; to vanish.

हिरना *hirnā* [*hariṇaka-*], m. = हिरन.

हिरनी *hirnī* [*hariṇī-*[1]], f. **1.** a doe, hind.

हिरनौटा *hirnauṭā*, m. *Pl.* *HŚS.* a fawn.

हिराना *hirānā*, v.t. & v.i. pronun. var. **1.** v.t. = हराना. **2.** v.i. = हेराना.

हिरासत *hirāsat* [A. *ḥirāsa*: P. *ḥirāsat*], f. **1.** custody, detention. **2.** guard, escort. — ~ **में**, adv. in custody. ~ **में करना**, or **लेना**, to take into custody.

हिरासती *hirāsătī* [cf. H. *hirāsat*], adj. & m. **1.** adj. used for detention (a cell). **2.** m. a detainee.

हिर्स *hirs* [A. *ḥirṣ*], f. **1.** eager desire. *__2.__ aspiration, emulation. — ~ **पड़ना** (**को**), (a person) to imitate (someone or sthg., **की**) eagerly. ~ **में**, adv. in imitation, emulation (of, **की**).

हिलकना *hilaknā* [cf. **hillati*], v.i. **1.** 19c. to writhe (as in pain). **2.** *Pl.* = **हिलगना**.

हिलकोर *hilkor* [cf. H. *hilkornā*], f. *Pl. HŚS.* = **हिलकोरा**.

हिलकोरना *hilkornā* [H. *hilaknā* × H. *hilornā*], v.t. & v.i. **1.** v.t. to agitate (water, into waves or ripples). **2.** v.i. to surge; to ripple.

हिलकोरा *hilkorā* [cf. H. *hilkornā*], m. a wave. — ~, or **हिलकोरे**, **मारना**, or **लेना**, to surge; to ripple.

हिलग *hilag* [cf. H. *hilagnā*; and *hilati*[1]], f. Brbh. attachment, connection; love.

हिलगना *hilagnā* [**abhilagyati*; × **hilati*[2]], v.i. **1.** to be attached; to hang (from, **से**). **2.** to be entangled, involved. **3.** to stick, to adhere. **4.** to become acquainted. **5.** to become trained, or accustomed.

हिलगाना *hilgānā* [cf. H. *hilagnā*], v.t. reg. **1.** to attach (to, **से**); to suspend; to keep dangling. **2.** to make acquainted (one person with another). **3.** to train (a child); to tame (an animal).

हिल-डोल *hil-ḍol* [cf. H.[1]*hilnā*, H. *ḍolnā*], m. swaying, swinging.

हिलन *hilan* [cf. H. [1] [2]*hilnā*], f. **1.** *Pl.* shaking, &c. **2.** *HŚS.* acquaintanceship, familiarity.

[1]**हिलना** *hilnā* [conn. **hillati*], v.i. **1.** to shake. **2.** to swing, to sway. **3.** to stir, to move. **4.** to tremble. **5.** to be moved, agitated (as the heart). — **हिलना-डोलना**, = ~, 1.-3.; to wander. – **हिल-मिलकर**, adv. to be jumbled together; see s.v. [2]**हिलना**. **हिल-मिलना**, to be mixed, jumbled; see [2]**हिलना**.

[2]**हिलना** *hilnā* [**hilati*[2]], v.i. **1.** to become acquainted, familiar (with, **से**). **2.** to be tamed, trained. — **हिल-मिलकर रहना**, to live together on good terms, peaceably. **हिलना-मिलना**, to come together, to unite; colloq. to become intimate (with).

हिलसा *hilsā* [*illiśa-*], m. the hilsa fish of eastern India (a sea fish found in many rivers).

हिला *hilā* [**hilla-*[2]], m. reg. boggy ground.

[1]**हिलाना** *hilānā* [cf. H. [1]*hilnā*], v.t. **1.** to shake. **2.** to swing (legs, stick, &c.); to wave (hand); to wag (tail). **3.** to nod (the head, in agreement or disagreement). **4.** to shrug (the shoulders). **5.** to move, to dislodge. **6.** to rouse (from sleep; or to action). — **हिला-मिला देना**, to insinuate (an idea).

[2]**हिलाना** *hilānā* [cf. H. [2]*hilnā*], v.t. **1.** to familiarise (with), to inure (to). **2.** to tame (an animal).

हिलार *hilār* [cf. H. *hilārnā*], f. reg. shaking; swinging, rocking.

हिलारना *hilārnā*, v.t. reg. **1.** to shake (= [1]**हिलाना**). **2.** to swing, to rock (= **हिलोरना**).

हिलाव *hilāv* [cf. H. [1]*hilnā*, [1]*hilānā*], m. shaking, swinging, &c. — **हिलाव-दुलाव**, m. id.

हिलावा *hilāvā* [cf. H. [2]*hilānā*], m. **1.** reg. (W.) a draught animal not yet broken in and yoked to another to accustom him to work. **2.** *Pl.* a tamer, trainer.

हिलोर *hilor* [cf. *hillola-*], f. **1.** a wave; a ripple. **2.** agitation (of mind). — **हिलोरें मारना**, or **लेना**, to heave, to surge.

हिलोरना *hilornā* [*hillolayati*], v.i. & v.t. to shake: **1.** v.i. to surge with waves (water); to ripple. **2.** to be agitated (the mind). **3.** v.t. to shake together, to gather up.

हिलोरा *hilorā* [cf. *hillola-*], m. **1.** a wave; an eddy, surge. **2.** agitation (of mind); transport (of joy).

हिल्लोल *hillol* [S.], m. a wave, &c. (= **हिलोर**).

हिसका *hiskā*, m. *Pl. HŚS.* rivalry, vying (with).

हिसाब *hisāb* [A. *ḥisāb*], m. **1.** counting, calculation; a calculation. **2.** an account (business); accounts. **3.** arithmetic. **4.** a bill (of charges). **5.** rate, price, charge. **रोटी किस ~ से ख़रीदी है?** what did (you) pay for the bread? **6.** measure; proportion. **जिस ~ से ... उसी ~ से ...**, in proportion as ... so. **7.** calculation; rule, standard. **तुम्हारे आने जाने का कोई ~ भी है?** is there any rhyme or reason to your comings and goings? **8.** estimate, judgment. **मेरे ~ से तो दोनों बराबर हैं**, as far as I'm concerned they're both the same. **9.** calculated manner, manner of thought or action. **तुम्हें ऐसे ~ से चलना चाहिए कि ...**, you ought to act in such a way that .... **बहुत ~ से रहना**, to live carefully. **10.** condition, situation. **उसका ~ न पूछो**, don't ask (anything) on his account, don't talk (to me) about *him*.

— ~ करना, to calculate; to make up, or to settle, an account. ~ चुकाना, to settle an account. ~ जाँचना, or देखना, to examine, or to audit accounts. ~ जोड़ना, to add up an account, or a total. ~ देना, to render an account. ~ बराबार करना (अपना), to square accounts; fig. to bring a task to a finish. ~ बेबाक करना, to settle an account. ~ बैठना, a favourable opportunity to present itself. ~ में फ़रक़ आना, an account not to agree, money to be unaccounted for. ~ में लेना, to take into account, to consider. ~ रखना, to keep account (of, का); to keep accounts. ~ लगाना (का), to calculate, to reckon; to come to terms (with, से), to collude, to plot (with); to serve, to be employed. ~ समझाना, to render an account; to account (for). चलता ~, m. current account. – हिसाब-किताब, f. accounts; book-keeping; account, responsibility; = ~, 9. हिसाब-किताब होना, account to be given (for, का).

हिसाबिया *hisābiyā* [cf. H. *hisāb*], adj. & m. **1.** adj. calculating (a person). **2.** m. reg. one who works with accounts, or figures: accountant; mathematician.

हिसाबी *hisābī* [A. *ḥisābī*], adj. & m. **1.** adj. having to do with accounts. **2.** accountable, prudent. **3.** m. accountant (= लेखाकार).

हिसार *hisār* [A. *ḥiṣār*], m. U. encompassing: **1.** a fortress. **2.** enclosing wall. **3.** enclosure.

हिस्पानी *hispānī*, adj. Spanish.

हिस्सा *hissā* [A. *ḥiṣṣa*], m. **1.** part; section, division. **2.** portion, share. **3.** *fin.* a share. **4.** dividend. **5.** fig. sympathy. — ~ लेना, to take a share. हिस्से आना, to fall to the share (of, के). हिस्से करना (के), to divide; to share, to distribute. हिस्से लगाना, to divide (sthg., के) into parts. हिस्सों में आना, to be divisible, or divided. हिस्सों में बाँटना, to divide into parts. – हिस्सा-बाँट, f. division, sharing. हिस्सेदार [P. *-dār*], m. shareholder; sharer; partner. °ई, f. sharing; partnership.

हिहिनाना *hihinānā*, v.i. pronun. var. = हिनहिनाना.

हींकारना *hīṁkārnā* [cf. *hiṅkāra-*], v.t. to low (cattle).

हींग *hīṁg* [*hiṅgu-*], f. (Pl., m.) asafoetida (used in cookery and medicinally). — ~ लगे न फिटकरी, cf. s.v. हल्दी. ~ हगना, v.i. fig. to have dysentery or diarrhoea; to waste under a disease, or a curse); to pine. – हींगाष्टक [°*g(a)+a*°], m. *Pl.* a medicinal preparation of about eight ingredients, asafoetida being the chief.

हींस *hīṁs* [cf. H. *hīṁsnā*], f. neighing; braying.

हींसना *hīṁsnā* [*heṣati*; Pk. *hīs-*, *hiṁs-*], v.i. to neigh; to bray.

हीं-हाँ *hīṁ-hāṁ*, f. saying 'yes, yes'. — ~ भरना, to say 'yes, yes'; to make a concession.

हीं-हीं *hīṁ-hīṁ* [onom.], f. giggling; sniggering.

[1]ही *hī* [*hi+vai, eva*], encl. **1.** precisely; particularly (stressing a preceding word); one thing rather than another. जब वह दूर ~ था, तब ..., while he was still far off .... बनारस के लोग हिंदी ~ बोलते हैं, the people of Banaras speak Hindi. **2.** just, merely. मैं एक ~ बार वहाँ गया हूँ, I've been there just once. वह आते ~ काम करने लगा, he started work as soon as he arrived.

[2]ही *hī* m. Brbh. = हृदय.

हीक *hīk* [*hikkā-*], f. **1.** a hiccup. **2.** a bad smell. **3.** a bad taste or flavour. — ~ आना (से), to smell or to taste unpleasant. ~ मारना, id.

हीज *hīj* [**hijja-*[2]], adj. E.H. craven, cowardly.

हीन *hīn* [*hīna-*; and ad.], adj. **1.** -हीन, हीन-. without, deprived of (e.g. धनहीन, penniless; हीनमति, stupid). **2.** abandoned, destitute; deprived. **3.** deficient, wanting; inferior; low, base (a person, an action). **4.** Av. submissive. — हीन-भावना, f. inferiority complex. हीन-यान, m. lesser vehicle: the Hīnayāna school of Buddhism. हीनावस्था [°*na+a*°], f. abandoned or wretched state; state of decline.

हीनता *hīnătā* [S.], f. **1.** want, deprivation (of). **2.** destitution. **3.** deficiency, inferiority; baseness. — हीनता ग्रंथि, f. inferiority complex.

हीनत्व *hīnatvă*, m. = हीनता.

[1]हीर *hīr* [*hīra-*, Pa. *hīra-*], m. **1.** a diamond. **2.** thunderbolt; specif. Indra's thunderbolt.

[2]हीर *hīr* [conn. *hīra-*], m. **1.** essence, pith. **2.** energy, vigour. **3.** the part of a tree lying immediately under the bark.

हीरक *hīrak* [S.], m. a diamond. — ~ जयंती, f. diamond jubilee.

हीरा *hīrā* [*hīraka-*], m. **1.** a diamond. **2.** *Pl. HŚS.* a tulsī bead (as worn by ascetics). **3.** adj. invaluable. ~ आदमी, m. a treasure of a man. — ~ कसीस, m. iron sulphate. ~ खाना, to swallow (chippings of) diamond (and so to commit suicide). – हीरा-कट, adj. diamond-cut.

हीरामन *hīrāman*, m. an imaginary, gold-coloured type of parrot. — ~ तोता, m. the large Indian parakeet (= राय तोता).

हील *hīl* [**hilla-*[2]], m. reg. mud.

हीलना *hīlnā*, v.i. & v.t. reg. **1.** v.i. = [1]हिलना. **2.** v.t. = हिलाना.

हीला *hīlā* [A. *ḥīla*], m. **1.** evasion, deception. **2.** trick, trickery. — ~ करना, to practise deceit; to pretend; to try tricks. – हीलाबाज़ [P. *-bāz*], m. a trickster, impostor. °ई, f. fraud. हीला-हवाला, m. trickery, guile.

ही-ही *hī-hī* [onom.], interj. & f. **1.** interj. hee hee! **2.** f. giggling; giggle. — ~ ठी-ठी करना, to giggle.

[1]**हुँ** *huṁ*, adv. = [2]हूँ.

[2]**हुँ** *huṁ*, encl. Brbh. = [3]हूँ.

हुंकार *huṁkār* [S.], m. **1.** threatening shout, cry. **2.** challenge. **3.** a roar; bellow; grunt (of a boar). **4.** grunt (of assent).

हुँकारना *huṁkārnā* [cf. H. *huṁkār*], v.i. to shout aloud; to shout a challenge.

हुँकारा *huṁkārā* [*huṁkāra-*], m. a grunt of assent.

हुँकारी *huṁkārī* [cf. H. *huṁkārā*], f. **1.** a grunt of assent. **2.** Brbh. agreement, assent. — ~ दे-, or भर-, to agree, to assent.

हुंडा *huṇḍā* [cf. *huṇḍikā-*], m. reg. **1.** an inclusive agreement or contract. **2.** (Bihar) field-rent in kind. — हुंडा-भाड़ा, m. a contract for delivery of goods free of charge, or for insurance.

हुँड़ार *huṁṛār* [**huṇḍahāra-*], m. reg. a wolf.

हुंडावन *huṇḍāvan* [cf. H. *huṇḍī*], m. *Pl. HŚS.* commission paid on a bill of exchange; discount.

हुँड़ियावन *huṁṛiyāvan* [cf. H. *huṇḍī*], m. *Pl.* = हुंडावन.

हुंडी *huṇḍī* [*huṇḍikā-*], f. **1.** a bill of exchange; a draft. **2.** promissory note. — ~ करना, to remit money by a bill of exchange, &c.; to draw a bill (on, पर). ~ पटना, a bill to be cashed, or honoured. ~ पर बेची लिखना, to write 'sold' on a bill: to endorse a bill. दर्शनी ~, f. an open bank draft (payable on presentation). मीआदी ~, f. a bill payable at a stated term; a bill payable after date. – हुंडी-पत्री, f. reg. = ~. हुंडीवाल, m. a banker; exchange-dealer.

हुंडैत *huṇḍait* [cf. H. *huṇḍā*], m. *Pl.* a contractor for transportation, or for insurance.

हु *hu*, *encl.* Brbh. Av. = [1]हू.

हुआ *huā* [cf. H. *honā*], v.i. **1.** became; came about; was (see also s.v. होना). **2.** adv. ago. एक साल ~, a year ago.

हुकमी *hukmī* [A. *ḥukm*+P. *-ī*], adj. acting to order or direction: effective (a medicine); infallible.

हुकूमत *hukūmat* [A. *ḥukūma*: P. *ḥukūmat*], f. authority, rule; government. — ~ करना, to rule, to govern (over, पर). ~ जताना, to show off one's authority.

हुक्क-हुक्क *hukk-hukk*, f. snorting sound (of a pig).

हुक़्क़ा *huqqā* [A. *ḥuqqa*], m. a hookah (for smoking tobacco through water). — ~ ताज़ा करना, to change the water of a hookah. ~ पीना, to smoke a hookah. ~ लगाए बैठना, to sit at, drawing on, a hookah. हुक़्क़े का धतिया, m. = हुक़्क़ेबाज़. – हुक़्क़ाबरदार [P. *-bardār*], m. servant who tends a hookah. हुक़्क़ा-पानी, m. smoking and drinking: social intercourse. हुक़्क़ा-पानी बंद करना, to deprive (one, का) of social intercourse, to outcaste (one). हुक़्क़ेबाज़ [P. *-bāz*], m. a keen hookah-smoker.

हुक्काम *hukkām* [A. *ḥukkām*, pl.], m. pl. rulers, &c. (see हाकिम).

हुक्म *hukm* [A. *ḥukm*], m. **1.** order, command; instruction. **2.** judgment, finding (of a court); order, decree. **3.** jurisdiction, authority; rule. **4.** leave, permission, sanction. **5.** (in cards) spade. — ~ करना, to give an order, &c.; to exercise authority; to rule. ~ उठाना, to execute an order; to countermand an order. ~ चलाना, = ~ करना, 2., 3. ~ तोड़ना, to disobey an order. ~ देना (को, and के लिए), to give an order, &c.; to authorise, to empower; to sanction. ~ में रहना, or होना, to be under or subject to the authority (of, के). जो ~! as you command! – हुक्म-नामा, m. a written order; writ, warrant; decree; injunction. हुकम-रानी [P. *-rānī*], f. U. government, rule; administration.

हुचकी *huckī* [H. *hickī*, P. *hukca*], f. = हिचकी.

हुजूम *hujūm* [A. *hujūm*], m. a crowd.

हुज़ूर *huzūr* [A. *ḥuẓūr*], m. **1.** presence (of a person of high authority). **2.** Your Highness (mode of address usable to a person of high standing; sometimes used quizzically or jokingly). — ~ में, adv. in the presence (of, के), before.

हुज़ूरी *huzūrī* [P. *ḥuẓūrī*], f., m. **1.** f. attendance, audience (as upon a *rājā*). **2.** m. a courtier; attendant. **3.** pej. flattery.

हुज्जत *hujjat* [A. *ḥujja*: P. *ḥujjat*], f. U. **1.** an argument (esp. a foolish one). **2.** objection (esp. frivolous). **3.** dispute. — ~ करना, to raise arguments or pretexts.

हुज्जती *hujjatī* [A. *ḥujjatī*], adj. argumentative; truculent.

हुड़क *huṛak* [cf. H. *huṛaknā*], f. longing, fretting, pining; heart-ache.

हुड़कना *huṛaknā* [**haṭukk-*], v.i. **1.** to long (for, के लिए), to crave; to fret, to pine. **2.** reg. to be driven away.

हुड़दंग *huṛdaṅg* [H. *hūṛ*+H. *daṅgā*], m. **1.** noise, fracas; uproar. **2.** quarrel, row.

हुड़दंगा *huṛdaṅgā* [cf. H. *huṛdaṅg*], adj. & m. **1.** adj. noisy, riotous; quarrelsome. **2.** m. a trouble-maker; an idler.

हुड़दंगी *huṛdaṅgī* [cf. H. *huṛdaṅg*], adj. & f. **1.** adj. stirring up trouble. **2.** f. a trouble-making woman. **3.** trouble, commotion.

हुड़बुड़ाना *huṛbuṛānā*, v.i. & v.t. reg. = हड़बड़ाना.

हुड़क *huṛuk*, m. reg. **1.** [conn. *huḍukka-*] a kind of small drum (of the shape of an hour-glass). **2.** growl (of a tiger).

हुत *hut* [S.], adj. & m. **1.** adj. offered in sacrifice. **2.** m. oblation, sacrifice. — हुतात्मा [°*ta*+*ā*°], m. inv. whose soul is a sacrifice: a martyr. हुताशन [°*ta*+*a*], m. sacrifice-eater: a title of the god Agni; fire.

हुतो *huto*, v.i. Brbh. was (= था).

हुतौ *hutau*, v.i. Brbh = हुतो.

हुदहुद *hud'hud* [A. *hudhud*], m. the hoopoe.

हुन *hun* [conn. *hūna-*], m. a gold coin. — ~ बरसना, wealth to be showered down.

हुन- *hun-* [*hunati*], v.t. Av. to offer up, to sacrifice.

हुनकना *hunaknā*, v.i. reg. to sob, to weep (= सिसकना).

हुनर *hunar* [P. *hunar*], m. **1.** art, skill; accomplishment. **2.** good quality, merit (of a person); talent. — हुनरमंद [P. *-mand*], adj. U. skilful; &c. °ई, f. skill, &c.

हुनरी *hunarī* [P. *hunar*+*-ī*], adj. reg. skilful, &c.

हुमकना *humaknā*, v.i. **1.** to make an energetic physical effort. **2.** to rush, to leap (upon, पर). **3.** to try desperately to walk (a child). — हुमककर चलना, to totter (a child).

हुमचना *humacnā*, v.i. = हुमकना.

हुमसना *humasnā* [conn. H. *umahnā*], v.i. to feel excitement; to awake to new ideas (cf. उमहना).

हुमा *humā* [P. *humā*], m. 19c. name of a fabulous and auspicious bird (the head on which its shadow falls was supposed to be destined to wear a crown); phoenix.

हुमास *humās* [cf. H. *humasnā*], f. energy, excitement.

हुर *hur*, f. = हुर्र.

हुरमत *hurmat* [A. *ḥurma*: P. *ḥurmat*], f. U. **1.** respect, honour. **2.** reputation.

हुरमति *hurmati*, f. E.H. = हुरमत.

हुरसा *hursā*, m. reg. = होरसा.

हुरहुर *hurhur*, m. *Pl. HŚS.* = हुलहुल.

हुरहुराना *hurhurānā* [? conn. *ghurati*[1]], v.i. reg. to growl (an animal); to purr (a cat).

हुरूफ़ *hurūf* [A. *ḥurūf*, pl.], m. pl. U. letters (see हरफ़).

हुर्र *hurr* [?? conn. *phurr*], f. reg. sudden flight (of a bird); whirr (of wings). — ~ हो जाना, to vanish suddenly.

हुर्रा *hurrā* [cf H. *hurr*], m. reg. a rush; terrified flight.

हुलक *hulak* [cf. H. *hulaknā*], f. Brbh. rush, impetus.

हुलकना *hulaknā* [cf. **hūl-*], v.t. *Pl.* to rush (at or upon).

हुलक-बुलक *hulak-bulak*, f. reg. peeping. — ~ मारना, to peep.

हुलसना *hulasnā* [*ullasati*], v.i. to rejoice; to be cheered, encouraged.

हुलसाना *hulsānā* [cf. H. *hulasnā*], v.t. to gladden, to cheer.

हुलसित *hulasit* [ad. *ullasita-*: w. H. *hulasnā*], adj. gladdened, rejoicing; happy.

हुलहुल *hulhul*, m. *Pl. HŚS.* name of several plants that spring up in the rainy season (used as pot-herbs, or medicinally).

हुलारना *hulārnā* [cf. Panj. *hulārā*], m. reg. = हिलारना.

हुलास *hulās* [conn. *ullāsa-*], m. & f. **1.** m. joy. **2.** f. transf. snuff. — ~ लेना, or सूँघना, to take snuff. – हुलास-दानी [P. *dānī*], f. snuff-box.

हुलासी *hulāsī* [cf. H. *hulās*], adh. Brbh. delighted, rejoicing.

हुलिया *huliyā* [A. *ḥilya*], m. **1.** appearance, features (of the face). ***2.** description (as of a wanted person). — ~ तंग होना, to be clearly agitated or distressed. ~ बताना, or बयान करना, to give a description (of). ~ बिगड़ना, the face to lose composure. – हुलिया-नवीसी [P. *-navīsī*], f. U. description (of a wanted person).

[1]**हुलियाना** *huliyānā* [cf. **hūl-*], v.t. reg. to butt; to gore.

[2]**हुलियाना** *huliyānā*, v.i. reg. = हलियाना.

हुल्लड़ *hullaṛ* [cf. **hulla-*[1]], m. **1.** a noisy crowd. **2.** disturbance, uproar; row.

हुश *huś* [P. *huš*], interj. **1.** sound made in scaring away or in calling to birds or animals. **2.** sound indicating disapproval of sthg. said: be quiet!

हुसैन *husain* [A. *ḥusain*], adj. dimin. *musl.* good: name of the younger son of Muḥammad's son-in-law 'Alī.

हुस्न *husn* [A. *ḥusn*], m. U. **1.** beauty (of women). **2.** goodness, excellence. — **हुस्न-परस्त**, an admirer of beauty in a woman.

[1]**हूँ** *hūṁ* [*hŭṁ*], interj. & f. **1.** expression of assent, or of comprehension: yes; I see, carry on (as spoken to a narrator). **2.** expression of qualified agreement. **3.** expression of disapproval, or of astonishment. — ~ **करना**, to say 'yes', &c. – **हूँ-हाँ**, f. humming and hawing; uninvolved agreement (with whatever is said); babble (of a young child). **हूँ-हाँ करना**, to hum and haw, &c.

[2]**हूँ** *hūṁ*, encl. Brbh. = [1]**हू**.

[3]**हूँ** *hūṁ*, v.i. (I) am.

हूँठा *hūṁṭhā* [*ardhacaturtha-*], adj. E.H. three and a half; three and a half times.

हूँत *hūṁt*, ppn. 19c. reg. = **से**. — **फिर** ~ adv. again; anew.

हूँस *hūṁs*, [? conn. H. *havas, hauṁs*; ?? ×H. *khuns*], f. reg. **1.** envy; covetousness. **2.** the evil eye. — ~ **लगना**, the evil eye to fall (on one, **को**).

हूँसना *hūṁsnā* [cf. H. *hūṁs*], v.t. & v.i. reg. **1.** v.t. to look enviously or malignly at or upon. **2.** v.i. to feel envy or ill-will.

हूँसी *hūṁsī* [cf. H. *hūṁs*], adj. reg. **1.** envious; covetous. **2.** lustful.

[1]**हू** *hū* [conn. *khalu*], encl. Brbh. 1. = **भी**. 2. = **ही**.

[2]**हू** *hū* [A. *huva* 'he']. he, he is: — **हूबहू**, adv. exactly the same as, or similar to. **उनकी शकल हूबहू अहमद की तरह की है**, he looks exactly like Ahmad.

हूक *hūk* [**hūkkā-*], f. **1.** a shooting pain; stitch. **2.** an ache. **3.** Brbh. pang (of remorse). **4.** cry of pain. **5.** a sob.

हूक-चूक *hūk-cūk* [H. *ūk*: w. *hūrchati*; and H. *cūk(nā)*], f. reg. mistakes and blunders.

[1]**हूकना** *hūknā*, v.i. **1.** to be felt (an ache; or a pang). **2.** to cry out in pain. **3.** to sob. **4.** to fret, to pine. — ~ **उठना**, an ache, or pang, to be felt.

[2]**हूकना** *hūknā* [H. [1]*hūknā*], m. the Indian bustard.

हूजिए *hūjie* [cf. H. *honā*], imp. obs. please be, kindly be.

हूड़ *hūṛ* [**huḍḍa-*], adj. rash; foolish, ignorant.

हूड़पना *hūṛpanā* [cf. H. *hūṛ*], m. impetuosity, rashness; foolishness.

हूण *hūṇ* [S.], m. name of a barbarian people, the Huns.

हून *hūn*, m. Brbh. = **हुन**.

हूबहू *hū-ba-hū* [A. *huva* with P. *ba*], adv. see s.v. [2]**हू**.

हूर *hūr* [A. *ḥūr*], f. *musl.* a virgin of paradise.

हूरव *hūrav* [S.], m. making the sound *hū*: a jackal.

[1]**हूल** *hūl* [cf. H. *hūlnā*], f. **1.** a thrust; sharp pain. **2.** reg. a stick used in catching birds (with bird-lime). **3.** 19c. attack. **4.** Brbh. pang.

[2]**हूल** *hūl* [?. **hulla-*[1]], f. a noise, shout, cry.

[3]**हूल** *hūl* [conn. **hūl-*]. the butt-end of a stick, or haft.

हूलना *hūlnā* [**hūl-*], v.t. **1.** Brbh. to drive or to urge (an animal) forward. **2.** to thrust, to stab. **3.** v.i. reg. to rush (upon).

हूश *hūś*, m. reg. a wild, uncouth person (see **हूस**).

हूस *hūs* [**hussa-*], m. 19c. = **हूश**.

हूह *hūh*, f. Av. shout, (war-)whoop.

हूहा *hūhā* [onom.], m. **1.** uproar, commotion. **2.** show, pomp. **3.** hooting (of an owl). — ~ **करना**, to make an uproar, &c.; to hoot.

हृत्- *hr̥t-* [S]. the heart: — **हृत्कंप**, m. heart-beat; palpitation of the heart. **हृत्तल**, m. depth of the heart, innermost heart. **हृत्पिंड**, m. the heart. **हृत्स्थल**, m. region of the heart.

हृद् *hr̥d* [S.], m. the heart. — **हृद्गत**, adj. felt in the heart: secret, private (emotion); cordial; tender.

हृदय *hr̥day* [S.], m. (for some collocations see similar expressions s.vv. **दिल, मन**). **1.** the heart. **2.** the soul; mind. **3.** breast, bosom. **4.** heart, core. **5.** affection. — ~ **में घर करना**, to make a home in, to win (one's) heart : another's virtues, &c). ~ **से लगाना**, to clasp to (one's) heart, breast. – **हृदयनिकेत**, m. Av. who dwells in the heart: a title of Kāmdev. **हृदय-पट**, m. the heart, soul. **हृदय-मंथन**, m. heart-stirring: emotionalism. **हृदयवान**, adj. warm-hearted; compassionate; humane. **हृदय-विदारक**, adj. heart-rending. **हृदय-वेधी**, adj. heart-piercing. **हृदय-संपन्न**, adj. having a heart: = **हृदयवान**. **हृदयस्थ**, adj. close to the heart, heart-felt. **हृदय-स्पर्शी**, adj. touching, moving the heart; impressive. **हृदयहारी**, adj. captivating the heart. **हृदयहीन**, adj. heartless, soulless. **हृदयासन** [°*ya*+*ā*°], m. seat or throne of the heart. **हृदयेश** [°*ya*+*ī*°], m. heart's lord: husband, beloved. °**वर**, m. id. °**वरी**, f. **हृदयोद्गार** [°*ya*+*u*°], m. an impulse of the heart.

हृदयता *hṛdayătā* [S.], f. kindliness, warm-heartedness.

हृदयालु *hṛdayālu* [S.], adj. kind-hearted, affectionate; compassionate; friendly, sympathetic.

हृदयी *hṛdayī* [S.], adj. kind-hearted; affectionate, friendly.

हृदि *hṛdi* [S.: loc.], adv. Av. in (one's) heart.

हृषीकेश *hṛṣīkêś* [S.], m. lord of the organs of sense: **1.** a title of Viṣṇu or of Kṛṣṇa. ***2.** name of a pilgrimage-place near Hardwar.

हृष्ट *hṛṣṭ* [S.], adj. 1. = हर्षित. ***2.** हृष्ट-. delighted; hard, strong. — हृष्ट-चित्त, adj. = हर्षित. हृष्ट-पुष्ट, adj. strong and well-nourished: sturdy, robust.

हृष्टि *hṛṣṭi* [S.], f. delight.

हेंकड़ *heṁkaṛ*, adj. pronun. var. = हेकड़.

हेंगा *heṁgā*, m. a plank-harrow. — ~ चलाना, or फेरना (पर), to harrow.

हें-हें *heṁ-heṁ*, interj. expression of abject entreaty: — ~ करना, to implore abjectly.

हे *he* [*he*], interj. oh!

हेकड़ *hekaṛ*, adj. **1.** burly, bulky; robust. **2.** overbearing.

हेकड़ी *hekṛī* [cf. H. *hekaṛ*], f. **1.** force. **2.** overbearing or threatening manner; bravado. — ~ करना, or जताना, or दिखाना, or मारना, to behave in an overbearing way; to threaten. ~ से, adv. by force; by overbearingness of manner.

हेच *hec* [P. *hec*], adj. U. Brbh. anything: worthless; shallow, superficial. — हेच-पोच [P. -*poc*], adj. reg. worthless.

हेठ *heṭh* [**adhiṣṭāt*: Pa. *heṭṭhā*], adv. **1.** adv. below; down. **2.** ppn. w. के. beneath; at the bottom (of). **3.** adj. lowered, bowed; submissive.

हेठा *heṭhā* [cf. H. *heṭh*], adj. **1.** low, inferior. **2.** base; contemptible.

हेठापन *heṭhāpan* [cf. H. *heṭhā*], m. lowness, baseness, &c. (see हेठा).

हेठी *heṭhī* [cf. H. *heṭh*], f. disgrace, dishonour; humiliation. — ~ करना, to bring disgrace (on, की).

हेड़ *heṛ* [**heḍā*-: Pk. *heḍa*-], ? f. reg. (Bihar) a flock.

[1]**हेड़ी** *heṛī* [conn. *ākheṭika*-, or H. *heṛ*], m. **1.** a hunter. **2.** *Pl.* beast of prey.

[2]**हेड़ी** *heṛī* [**heḍā*-: Pk. *heḍā*-], f. reg. a flock, herd (of animals being driven).

हेत *het*, m. Brbh. = हेतु.

हेति *heti* [S.], f. Brbh. brightness, splendour.

हेतु *hetu* [S.], m. **1.** motive, purpose; object; vested interest. **2.** cause, reason; reason for an inference. **3.** meaning, purport; deduction (from facts). **4.** fig. Av. attachment, love. **5.** ppn. w. के. for the sake (of, के), because (of). — किस ~ से? adv. with what motive? for what reason? – हेतु-रहित, adj. Av. disinterested. हेतुवाद, Brbh. m. the viewpoint, or arguments, of an interested person: sophistry. हेत्वाभास [°*tu*+*ā*°], m. an apparent but unreal reason; a fallacy; sthg. unreal.

हेमंत *hemant* [S.], m. the cold season (comprising the months Ag'han and Pūs, about mid-November to mid-January).

हेमंती *hemantī* [cf. H. *hemant*], adj. having to do with the cold season.

हेम *hem* [S.], m. **1.** gold. **2.** Brbh. = हिम, 2. **3.** Av. = हिमालय. — हेम-तरु, m. golden tree: the thorn-apple (*dhatūrā*). हेम-फरद [P. -*fard*], m. Brbh. gold veneer or leaf. हेमवती, adj. f. golden. हेमवर्ण, adj. gold-coloured. हेमाभा [°*ma*+*ā*], f. golden light or glow.

हेम-खेम *hem-khem*, m. see s.v. खेम.

हेय *hey* [S.], adj. **1.** to be left, not to be taken. **2.** bad, base.

हेरंब *heramb* [S.], m. a name of Gaṇeś.

हेरना *hernā* [**herati* (← Drav.): Pk. *heraï*], v.t. **1.** to look (at), to gaze. **2.** to investigate. **3.** Brbh. to detect (a fault). **4.** to search for; to hunt, to chase. — हेरना-फेरना, to interchange, to exchange. हेर-फेरके तोलना, to weigh (sthg.) in each scale alternately (so as to test the accuracy of the scales). – हेरा-फेरी, f. change of order or position; rearrangement, adjustment (as of a frontier); fudging, obscuring (a matter); manipulation (of a market).

हेर-फेर *her-pher* [cf. H. *phernā*], m. **1.** turning, winding; confusion. **2.** maze, labyrinth; duplicity. **3.** [? × H. *hernā*] exchange, interchange; barter. **4.** wandering, roaming. — ~ करना, to exchange, to interchange (objects). — हेर-फेर की बातें, f. pl. confusing or involved language; equivocation.

हेराना *herānā* [cf. H. *hernā*], v.i. reg. (a thing) to require searching for: (sthg.) to be lost or mislaid; to stray (an animal).

हेरा-फेरी *herā-pherī*, f. esp. pej. altering, alteration (cf. हेर-फेर, 1.-3).

[1]हेलना *helnā* [*abhitarate*], v.i. reg. to swim; to float.

[2]हेलना *helnā* [*helate*[2]], v.i. reg. to flirt, to dally; to rush (esp. into water).

हेल-मेल *hel-mel* [**hella-*; H. *mel*], m. **1.** close friendship; intimacy. **2.** close contact (between, में). — ~ करना, to form a close friendship, &c. (with, से or के साथ).

[1]हेला *helā*, m. reg. a call, shout. — ~ मारना, to call out.

[2]हेला *helā* [cf. **hillati*], m. reg. a jolt, shock; onset, attack. — ~ मारना, to push, to shove; to rush into or through water.

[3]हेला *helā* [S.], f. **1.** disregard, disrespect. ***2.** dalliance, flirtation; specif. poet. a partic. gesture or aspect of a heroine's manner.

[4]हेला *helā* [cf. *heḍate*], m. pl. Av. a member of an outcaste community (? scavengers, or sweepers).

[1]हेली *helī* [cf. H.[2]*helnā*; and *heli-*], f. Brbh. flirtatious behaviour.

[2]हेली *helī*, f. Brbh. = सहेली.

हेली-मेली *helī-melī* [cf. H. *hel-mel*], m. close friend, mate.

हेलुआ *heluā* [cf. H. [2]*helnā*], m. Brbh. sporting in the water (as Kr̥ṣṇa with the herdgirls).

हेवँ *hevaṁ* [*haima-*], m. Av. **1.** ? snow, ice. **2.** ? mountain, mountains.

हेवंत *hevant*, m. Av. = हेमंत.

[1]हैं *haiṁ* [*ākṣeti*, w. *bhavati*], v.i. **1.** (they, we) are. **2.** hon. (you) are.

[2]हैं *haiṁ*, interj. **1.** hey! stop that! **2.** expression of astonishment. — ~ ~, id.

हैंगे *haiṁge* [H. *haiṁ*, w. *gata-*], v.i. colloq. are indeed; will be, must be.

है *hai* [*ākṣeti*, w. *bhavati*], v.i. **1.** (he, she, it) is. **2.** (zero hon. grade) (you) are.

हैकल *haikal* [Panj. *haiṅkal*], f. *Pl. HŚS.* a necklace; a charm inscribed with magic figures.

हैगा *haigā* [H. *hai*, w. *gata-*], v.i. 19c. is indeed; must be.

हैज़ा *haizā* [A. *haiẓa*], m. cholera. — ~ होना (को), to have cholera. हैज़े से मरना, to die of cholera.

हैदर *haidar* [A. *ḥaidar*], m. U. a lion.

हैफ़ *haif* [A. *ḥaif*], m. & interj. U. **1.** m. sorrow, regret. **2.** alas!

हैमावत *haimāvat* [S.], adj. having to do with the Himālayas.

हैरत *hairat* [A. *ḥaira*: P. *ḥairat*], f. **1.** amazement, wonder. **2.** consternation. — ~ की बात, f. a matter for amazement, or for concern. – हैरतंगेज़ [P. *-angez*], adj. U. giving rise to wonder, or to consternation. हैरतज़दा [P. *-zada*], adj. inv. U. struck with astonishment.

हैरान *hairān* [A. *ḥairān*], adj. **1.** harassed, plagued; worried; distressed. **2.** perplexed, confused. **3.** amazed. — ~ करना, to plague; to perplex; to amaze. ~ कर देनेवाला, adj. amazing. पता पाते हुए हम ~ हो गए, we had trouble finding the address.

हैरानी *hairānī* [A. *ḥairān*+P. *-ī*], f. **1.** worry, distraction; distress. **2.** perplexity. **3.** amazement.

हैवान *haivān* [A. *ḥaivān*], m. **1.** an animal. **2.** pej. beast, brute; monster.

हैवानियत *haivāniyat* [A. *ḥaivānīya*: P. *ḥaivāniyat*], f. **1.** animal nature. **2.** bestiality, brutality.

हैवानी *haivānī* [A. *ḥaivānī*], adj. **1.** animal. **2.** bestial, brutal.

हैस-बैस *hais-bais* [A. *ḥaiṣ*, *baiṣ*; × H. *bahs*], f. **1.** arguing. **2.** perplexity; dilemma.

हैसियत *haisiyat* [A. *ḥaiṣīya*: P. *ḥaiṣiyat*], f. **1.** capacity, ability. **2.** means, resources. **3.** condition of life, status; outward appearance. **4.** nature, character. — ~ ख़राब करना (की), to deface. ~ रखना, to have the capacity (to, की); to hold, to contain; to have means, property. ~ से, adv. in the capacity (of, की). अपनी अच्छी ~ बनाना, to establish oneself satisfactorily (in life).

हों *hoṁ* [cf. H. *honā*], v.i. (we, you, they) may be.

होंट *hoṁṭ*, m. pronun. var. = होंठ.

होंठ *hoṁṭh* [(*adha-*)*oṣṭha*], m. the lip. — ~ काटना, or चबाना, to bite the lips; to feel or to show remorse, or vexation, or astonishment. दाँत ~ तले, or से, दबाना, = ~ चबाना; to feel or to show satisfaction. ~ बिचकाना, to pout. ~ हिलाना, to move the lips; to speak. होंठों में कहना, to say in a low voice. होंठों में मुसकराना, to smile. होंठों पर होना, or नचाना, to be on the tip of the tongue. – होंठ-कटा, adj. having a split lip; hare-lipped.

होंठल *hoṇṭhal* [cf. H. *hoṇṭh*], adj. *Pl. HŚS.* thick-lipped.

[1]हो *ho* [cf. H. *honā*], v.i. **1.** 2 pl. (you) are. **2.** 2. 3. sg. subj. (you, he, &c.) may be; let (it) be. — जो ~ सो ~, what is to be will be.

[2]हो *ho* [*ho*], interj. hallo! I say! (in attracting attention).

होइ *hoi* [*bhavati*], v.i. Brbh. Av. 1. = है. 2. = [1]हो, 2.

होई *hoī* [? cf. *āhava-* 'sacrifice'], f. *Pl. HŚS.* = अहोई.

होगा *hogā* [cf. H. *honā*; +*gata-*], v.i. 2. 3. sg. will be.

होटल *hoṭal* [Engl. *hotel*], m. a hotel; eating-place.

होठ *hoṭh*, m. 19c. = होंठ.

होड़ *hoṛ* [**hoḍḍa-* (← Drav.): Pk. *hoḍḍa-*], f. **1.** a wager, bet. **2.** rivalry, spirit of competition. **3.** a contest. — ~ करना, to compete (with, से). ~ बदना, or बाँधना, to wager, to bet; to compete. ~ लगाना, = prec.; to be positive (as in a view); to be obstinate.

होड़ा-होड़ी *hoṛā-hoṛī* [cf. H. *hoṛ*], f. = होड़, 2.

होड़ी *hoṛī* [*hoḍa-*: ← Drav.], f. reg. a boat made of a hollowed tree; a small flat-bottomed boat.

होतव्य *hotavyă* [cf. H. *honā*; ad. *bhavitavya-*], adj. destined to happen.

होतव्यता *hotavyătā* [cf. H. *hotavya*], f. what is destined: destiny, fate.

होता *hotā* [S.], m. inv. a brāhmaṇ officiant at a fire sacrifice.

होत्र *hotr* [S.], m. an offering (as *ghī*) at a fire sacrifice.

[1]होत्री *hotrī* [S.], f. **1.** wife of priest officiating at a fire sacrifice. **2.** a priestess.

[2]होत्री *hotrī* [ad. *hotṛ-*], m. 19c. = होता.

होनहार *honhār* [cf. H. *honā*, *-hār*], adj. & m. f. **1.** adj. yet to be, future. **2.** expected to result, likely. **3.** impending. **4.** promising (as a young person). **5.** m. f. the future; destiny, fate.

होनहारी *honhārī* [cf. H. *honhār*], f. **1.** likelihood. **2.** feasability. **3.** promise.

होना *honā* [*bhavati*], v.i. **1.** to be; to exist; to be present. **2.** to become. वह ज़ख़मी हुआ, he suffered a wound, was wounded. **3.** esp. हो जाना. to be accomplished, effected, done. उसका जनेऊ हो गया, he was invested with the sacred thread. काम हो गया है, the job is finished. **4.** to be committed (as error &c.; by, से). **5.** to result. उसने ऐसा किया तो क्या हुआ? what does it matter if he did this? **6.** to happen. उसे क्या हो गया? what's happened to him? दुर्घटना हुई है, there's been an accident. यह क्या हो रहा है? what's going on here? **7.** to be born (a child; to, को or का/की). **8.** to serve (a purpose). होगा, that will do (nicely). **9.** to be felt, experienced (an emotion: by, को); to be suffered (as hunger: by, को). **10.** to elapse (time). उसे पढ़ते दो साल हुए हैं, he has been studying for two years. **11.** esp. हो जाना. to come to an end. हो गया? is (the meal, &c.) over? are you finished? — हो आना, to become all at once; to spring up, to arise; to appear, to drop in (on, के यहाँ); to have returned from, to have been in or to (a country, &c). हो गुज़रना, to come to pass (an event); to be past, over (a time). हो चलना, to progress (an action, a state); to reach a certain stage. अँधेरा हो चला था, darkness was drawing on. हो निकलना, to pass by, or near; to turn up; to slip away (by a partic. route: = होकर निकलना). हो बैठना, (a woman) to get her period suddenly. हो रहना, to remain or to continue as; to come into the permanent possession (of, का). हो लेना, to betake oneself, to go (in company with, के साथ; following, trailing, के पीछे); to be completed; to be born; to arise (as a quarrel). होने का, to be, future; likely. यह नहीं होने का, that's impossible. – हो-हवा जाना (i.e. हो with -हवाना), to happen (to, को). हुआ, adj. & adv. become, &c.; ago. एक बरस हुआ, a year ago. होकर, adv. having been, or become; passing by way of, via; despite being; in the capacity of. अमीर होकर भी मेहनती है, even though he is rich he works hard. होकर रहना, to remain permanently or as a fixture, or as an effect. होता, adj. being, becoming, &c. होता चला आना, to come down (from the past: a custom). होता रहेगा! it will fall on you! (of a curse which has just been uttered against one). होते, adv. passing near (by, से); via; during the existence (of, के); in the presence (of, के); in the possession of (के); notwithstanding (an admitted fact, के). होते होते, adv. in the course of change, gradually. होते हुए, adv. or ppn. (w. के, से) via.

होनी *honī* [cf. H. *honā*], f. **1.** being, existence. **2.** birth, origin. 3. = होनहार, 5.

होम *hom* [S.], m. a fire offering, sacrifice; an oblation of *ghī*. — ~ करना, to perform a *hom* sacrifice; to sacrifice (generally); fig. to consume, to destroy. ~ करते हाथ जलना, to suffer loss or harm in performing some meritorious act.

होमना *homnā* [cf. H. *hom*], v.t. **1.** to make an oblation of (*ghī*). **2.** to make a sacrifice of; to devote (as one's life: to, में).

होय *hoy*, v.i. Brbh. = होइ.

होरसा *horsā*, m. reg. a board or stone on which bread is made, or sandalwood ground.

होरा *horā* [S.: ← Gk.], f. *astron.* **1.** *Pl. HŚS.* an hour. **2.** *Pl.* the rising of a sign of the zodiac. — **होरा-फल**, m. the (astrological) effect of the rising of a sign.

होलड़ *holaṛ*, m. reg. a kind of song sung on the birth of a child.

¹**होला** *holā* [*holaka-*], m. gram or peas half-roasted in the pod.

²**होला** *holā* [*hoḍa-*: ← Drav.], m. *Pl.* a boat made from a hollowed tree; a large flat-bottomed boat; a raft (cf. होड़ी).

होलिका *holikā* [S.], f. *hind.* 1. = होली, 1., 2. **2.** name of a demoness worshipped at the Holī festival. — **होलिका-दहन**, m. lighting the Holī fire. **होलिकानल** [°*kā*+*a*°], m. the Holī fire.

होली *holī* [*holā-*, Pk. *holiyā-*], f. **1.** the Hindu spring festival, held on the day of the full moon of the month Phālgun. **2.** the pile of wood, &c. prepared for burning during the Holī festival; bonfire. **3.** a type of indecent song sung before and during the Holī festival. — **~ खेलना**, to 'play holī': to sprinkle coloured powder (*abīr* or *gulāl*) or to squirt coloured water on friends or passers-by at Holī. **~ जलाना** (**की**), to burn up; to rejoice at the destruction or end (of); to consume utterly; to squander. **~ होना** (**की**), to be consumed utterly; to be squandered.

होश *hoś* [P. *hoś*], m. **1.** consciousness, the senses. **2.** mind, understanding; the wits. **3.** sense, discretion. — **~ आना** (**को**), consciousness to return (to); to come to one's senses (as after rage); to become sober. **~ उड़ना**, to lose consciousness; to lose one's wits, or presence of mind. **~ करना**, to act with discretion. **~ की दवा करो!** colloq. get your mind seen to: get your head examined! **~ की बात**, f. sthg. sensible or prudent; good sense. **~ ठिकाने आना**, or **होना**, good sense to return: to recover one's senses. **~ दंग होना**, = **~ उड़ना**, 2. **~ दिलाना**, to make (one) conscious, or to remind (one, **को**: of sthg). **~ न रहना**, to lose consciousness; not to be conscious (of, **का**). **~ पकड़ना**, to attain to sense: to reach years of discretion; to mend one's ways. **~ में आना**, to recover consciousness; to recover one's senses. **~ में होना**, to be conscious (as after an accident). **~ सँभालना**, = **~ पकड़ना**. **~ हवा होना**, consciousness, or the wits, to be lost. **~ हिरन होना**, id. **उसके ~ फ़ाख़्ता हो गए**, he lost consciousness; he lost his wits (cf. **~ उड़ना**). – **होशमंद** [P. *-mand*], adj. intelligent, prudent, sensible. °**ई**, f. **होश-हवास**, m. = ~, 1., 2.

होशयार *hośyār*, adj. = होशियार.

होशियार *hośiyār* [P. *hośyār*], adj. **1.** intelligent. **2.** knowledgeable. **3.** skilful (at or in, **में**). **4.** careful, alert. **5.** sensible; sober. **6.** knowing, shrewd. — **~!** interj. watch out! be careful! **~ करना**, to apprise; to forewarn. **~ रहना**, to be on one's guard (against, **से**); to keep watch. **~ हो जाना**, to reach the age of discretion, to leave childhood behind (one).

होशियारी *hośiyārī* [P. *hośyārī*], f. **1.** intelligence. **2.** skill. **3.** watchfulness, care. **4.** sense, discretion.

हौं *hauṁ* [*aham*], pron. Brbh. I.

हौंकना *hauṁknā*, v.i. **1.** to pant. **2.** to roar.

हौंस *hauṁs*, m. pronun. var. (E.) = हवस.

हौंसी *hauṁsī* [cf. H. *hauṁs*], adj. reg. **1.** envious, covetous. **2.** lustful.

हौआ *hauā* [*hāhābhūta-*], m. a bogyman.

हौका *haukā*, m. **1.** greed. **2.** covetousness. **3.** frustrated desire, despair. — **~ करना**, to be greedy. **~ खाए जाना**, to suffer pangs of greed.

हौज़ *hauz* [A. *ḥauẓ*], m. **1.** a reservoir, tank; basin of fountain. **2.** trough (for food or water).

हौद *haud*, m. हौज़, 2.

हौदा *haudā* [P. *hauda*; cf. A. *haudaj*], m. howdah.

हौर *haur* [*apara-*; ← Panj.], conj. S.H. = और.

हौरा *haurā*, m. reg. noise, din.

¹**हौल** *haul* [A. *haul*], m. **1.** fright, terror. **2.** alarm. — **~ पैठना**, or **बैठना**, fear to seize (one: **के जी में**). – **हौलदिल**, adj. & m. frightened; alarmed. °**आ**, adj. id.

²**हौल** *haul* [A. *ḥaul*], m. U. strength, power. — **लाहौल बिला क़ूबत**, corr. see s.v. **ला**.

हौली *haulī*, f. a liquor-shop.

हौले *haule* [cf. *laghu-*], adv. **1.** softly, slowly; quietly. **2.** esp. redupl. little by little. — **~**, or **~ से**, **भागना**, to slip away inconspicuously.

हौस *haus*, f. = हवस.

हौसला *hauslā* [A. *ḥauṣala*], m. **1.** stomach: capacity; desire; ambition. ***2.** spirit, courage; energy, resolve. **3.** morale. — **~ निकालना** (**अपना**), to satisfy (one's) ambition or desire; to do (one's) best. **~ बाँधना**, to summon up courage or energies. – **हौसलाअफ़ज़ाई** [P. *-afzāī*], f. U. encouragement. **हौसलामंद** [P. *-mand*], adj. aspiring, ambitious; bold.

ह्याँ *hyāṁ*, adv. Brbh. = यहाँ.

ह्रद *hrad* [S.], m. poet. a lake.

ह्रस्व *hrasvă* [S.], adj. & m. **1.** adj. short; small. **2.** *ling.* short (a vowel). **3.** m. *ling.* a short vowel.

ह्रस्वता *hrasvătā* [S.], f. shortness, &c. (see ह्रस्व).

ह्रादिनी *hrādinī* [S.], f. *Pl. HŚS.* noisy: **1.** *mythol.* Indra's thunderbolt. **2.** lightning. **3.** (= ह्लादिनी) a river.

ह्रास *hrās* [S.], m. lessening; decrease; de‹ — ह्रासोन्मुख [°*sa*+*u*°], adj. facing decline, declining. -ई, adj. id.

ह्री *hrī* [S.], f. poet. shame, modesty.

ह्वाँ *hvāṁ*, adv. Brbh. = वहाँ.

ह्वै *hvai* [cf. H. *honā*], abs. Brbh. 1. = होकर. 2. = हुआ, 2.